ENCYCLOPAEDIA
JUDAICA

ENCYCLOPAEDIA JUDAICA

SECOND EDITION

VOLUME 3
Ba–Blo

Fred Skolnik, *Editor in Chief*
Michael Berenbaum, *Executive Editor*

MACMILLAN REFERENCE USA
An imprint of Thomson Gale, a part of The Thomson Corporation

IN ASSOCIATION WITH
KETER PUBLISHING HOUSE LTD., JERUSALEM

GALE

Detroit • New York • San Francisco • New Haven, Conn. • Waterville, Maine • London

THOMSON ★ GALE™

ENCYCLOPAEDIA JUDAICA, Second Edition

For more information, contact
Macmillan Reference USA
An imprint of Thomson Gale
27500 Drake Rd.
Farmington Hills, MI 48331-3535
Or you can visit our internet site at
http://www.gale.com

LIBRARY OF CONGRESS CATALOGING-IN-PUBLICATION DATA

Encyclopaedia Judaica / Fred Skolnik, editor-in-chief ; Michael Berenbaum, executive editor. -- 2nd ed.
v. cm.
Includes bibliographical references and index.
Contents: v.1. Aa-Alp.
ISBN 0-02-865928-7 (set hardcover : alk. paper) -- ISBN 0-02-865929-5 (vol. 1 hardcover : alk. paper) -- ISBN 0-02-865930-9 (vol. 2 hardcover : alk. paper) -- ISBN 0-02-865931-7 (vol. 3 hardcover : alk. paper) -- ISBN 0-02-865932-5 (vol. 4 hardcover : alk. paper) -- ISBN 0-02-865933-3 (vol. 5 hardcover : alk. paper) -- ISBN 0-02-865934-1 (vol. 6 hardcover : alk. paper) -- ISBN 0-02-865935-X (vol. 7 hardcover : alk. paper) -- ISBN 0-02-865936-8 (vol. 8 hardcover : alk. paper) -- ISBN 0-02-865937-6 (vol. 9 hardcover : alk. paper) -- ISBN 0-02-865938-4 (vol. 10 hardcover : alk. paper) -- ISBN 0-02-865939-2 (vol. 11 hardcover : alk. paper) -- ISBN 0-02-865940-6 (vol. 12 hardcover : alk. paper) -- ISBN 0-02-865941-4 (vol. 13 hardcover : alk. paper) -- ISBN 0-02-865942-2 (vol. 14 hardcover : alk. paper) -- ISBN 0-02-865943-0 (vol. 15: alk. paper) -- ISBN 0-02-865944-9 (vol. 16: alk. paper) -- ISBN 0-02-865945-7 (vol. 17: alk. paper) -- ISBN 0-02-865946-5 (vol. 18: alk. paper) -- ISBN 0-02-865947-3 (vol. 19: alk. paper) -- ISBN 0-02-865948-1 (vol. 20: alk. paper) -- ISBN 0-02-865949-X (vol. 21: alk. paper) -- ISBN 0-02-865950-3 (vol. 22: alk. paper)
1. Jews -- Encyclopedias. I. Skolnik, Fred. II. Berenbaum, Michael, 1945-
DS102.8.E496 2007
909'.04924 -- dc22

2006020426

ISBN-13:

978-0-02-865928-2 (set)
978-0-02-865929-9 (vol. 1)
978-0-02-865930-5 (vol. 2)
978-0-02-865931-2 (vol. 3)
978-0-02-865932-9 (vol. 4)
978-0-02-865933-6 (vol. 5)
978-0-02-865934-3 (vol. 6)
978-0-02-865935-0 (vol. 7)
978-0-02-865936-7 (vol. 8)
978-0-02-865937-4 (vol. 9)
978-0-02-865938-1 (vol. 10)
978-0-02-865939-8 (vol. 11)
978-0-02-865940-4 (vol. 12)
978-0-02-865941-1 (vol. 13)
978-0-02-865942-8 (vol. 14)
978-0-02-865943-5 (vol. 15)
978-0-02-865944-2 (vol. 16)
978-0-02-865945-9 (vol. 17)
978-0-02-865946-6 (vol. 18)
978-0-02-865947-3 (vol. 19)
978-0-02-865948-0 (vol. 20)
978-0-02-865949-7 (vol. 21)
978-0-02-865950-3 (vol. 22)

This title is also available as an e-book
ISBN-10: 0-02-866097-8
ISBN-13: 978-0-02-866097-4
Contact your Thomson Gale representative for ordering information.
Printed in the United States of America
10 9 8 7 6 5 4 3 2 1

TABLE OF CONTENTS

The illuminated letter "B" at the beginning of the Psalms in Extracts from Gregory the Great *shows King David playing his harp and the young David killing Goliath. N. France, 12th century, Douai, Bibliothèque Municipale, Ms. 315A, Vol. 1, fol. 5.*

BA–BLO

BAALAH (Heb. בַּעֲלָה), name of several biblical localities, evidently associated with the worship of Baal. (1) Mount Baalah is mentioned as one of the demarcation points on the northwestern boundary of the territory of Judah, between Shikkeron and Jabneel in the vicinity of Ekron (Josh. 15:11). Its location is dependent on the identification of *Ekron, but the prevailing opinion is the ridge of Mughār, near Wadi Qaṭra. (2) A city of Baalah is listed in the Negev district of Judah (Josh. 15:29). It is also among the settlements of Simeon as Balah (Josh. 19:3) or Bilhah (I Chron. 4:29). Its identification is unknown. (3) Baalah is mentioned as another name for *Kiriath-Jearim (Josh. 15:9–10); in I Chronicles 13:6 it is called Baalath (Heb. version). (4) A city of Baalath appears in the list of Danite settlements (Josh. 19:44) after Eltekeh and Gibbethon; this is perhaps identical with the Baalath fortified by Solomon (I Kings 9:18). It has been identified with the mound Mughār or of Qatra; in this case it would be identical with (1).

BIBLIOGRAPHY: (1) Kallai, in: BIES, 17 (1952), 63; Aharoni, in: PEQ, 90 (1958), 28–30; Mazar, in: IEJ, 10 (1960), 70; (2) Abel, Geog, 2 (1938), 258; (3) Mazar, in: *Sefer Dinaburg* (1949), 317; EM, s.v.; Aharoni, Land, index.

[Michael Avi-Yonah]

BAAL-BERITH (Heb. בַּעַל בְּרִית; "Lord of Covenant"), the name of the deity worshiped in the earliest Israelite period at the Temple of Shechem (Judg. 9:4). That temple was destroyed in the 12th century B.C.E. by *Abimelech, the half-Shechemite son of the great judge Gideon (Jerubbaal), after his suppression of a counter-revolt. Abimelech himself had come to power as "king" with the aid of funds from the Baal-Berith temple. As Abimelech's revenge moved apace, the terrified populace sought refuge in the "stronghold of El-Berith" (9:46), where they died en masse. The polemic of the narrative is directed against Abimelech and the conspirators who had profaned the great Shechem temple; it was never again rebuilt, except as a granary, as archaeological work has shown. Critics have suggested that the narrative of Abimelech seems to be an old pre-Deuteronomic account later inserted into the historical work because it explicated a brief Deuteronomic reference to an early particularist tendency in 8:33–35. In that place it is asserted that Israel's whoring after the Baalim consisted of making Baal-Berith their god and forgetting YHWH when they betrayed the family of YHWH's charismatic deliverer. In later circles the original significance of the "house of Baal-Berith" had long been lost, and the element "baal" in such a combination could only smack of the repudiated fertility cult. Something of its earliest significance can be glimpsed, however, in patriarchal stories connecting Abraham, Jacob, and Joseph with the site in various ways and in the archaeology of Shechem. The Baal-Berith temple was preceded on the same site by a Middle Bronze Age fortress-temple, which in turn perpetuated a piece of ground considered holy since the first half of the 18th century B.C.E. Genesis 34:2 personifies Shechem as one of the sons of Hamor ("ass"), reminiscent of Amorite treaty terminology at Mari, where "killing an ass" is a technical term for concluding a covenant. That Joshua-Judges contains no developed conquest tradition for the Shechem area is largely due, according to some scholars, to the influence of the Baal-Berith sanctuary (Josh. 24). According to tradition, such a situation had been anticipated by the strategists (Deut. 27; Josh. 8:30–35).

The Hebrew term Baal-Berit is also applied to the father of the child at a *circumcision (*berit*) ceremony, and in modern Hebrew the term means "ally" based on the plural form in Genesis 14:13.

BIBLIOGRAPHY: G.E. Wright, *Shechem: Biography of a Biblical City* (1965), 80–138. **ADD. BIBLIOGRAPHY:** T.J. Lewis, in: JBL, 115 (1996), 401–23; M. Mulder, in: DDD, 141–44.

[Robert G. Boling]

BA'ALEI TESHUVAH (pl. of *ba'al teshuvah*; literally "penitent ones"). Beginning with the Bible (see Deut. 30), Jewish tradition has always encouraged those who stray from the path of mitzvah observance to return, to do "teshuvah" and readopt a traditional life style. The talmudic sages speak about repentance, "teshuvah," on numerous occasions, their most famous statement being, "where *ba'alei teshuvah* stand, a complete *ẓaddik* cannot stand" (*Yalkut Shimoni*, Gen. 20). In the post-talmudic period, innumerable scholars wrote about "*teshuvah*," encouraging even the observant Jew to become a *ba'al teshuvah* and improve his fulfillment of God's commandments. Maimonides codified the laws of "*teshuvah*" in his *Mishneh Torah*; Jonah ben Abraham *Gerondi wrote the classic, *Gates of Repentance*; and in modern times, Abraham Isaac *Kook wrote *The Lights of Repentance*. Unfortunately, we have no statistical record of the number of *ba'alei teshuvah* throughout history, just as we have no record of the number of Jews who abandoned their Judaism and its observance.

In the second half of the 20th century, the words *ba'alei teshuvah* took on new significance. Beginning in the 1960s in the U.S., the rise of the counterculture in general American society together with the search for new meaning and spirituality led an increasing number of college-age Jews to explore Jewish observance, many for the first time. For most of these young Jews, the exploration led them to Orthodoxy, of one form or another.

The essential factor that turned individual searching into a full-fledged movement was the internal state of Orthodoxy itself. Orthodoxy was enjoying a resurgence, following the semi-moribund state which largely characterized it during the first half of the century. The first to take advantage of the new interest in Judaism was the *Chabad-Lubavitch ḥasidic movement. By the mid-1960s, the Lubavitcher Rebbe, Menaḥem Mendel *Schneersohn, had "emissaries" in place on most of the large college campuses with high concentration of Jews. Trained to reach out to other Jews, Chabad was most instrumental in assisting numerous young people to become *ba'alei teshuvah*, even if they did not become Chabad ḥasidim per se. At the same time, the first generation of "baby-boomers" graduated the Orthodox day schools and went to college. Through their involvement in Hillel, Yavneh (the religious Jewish students' organization), and NCSY (see below) they became a potent force in creating the *Ba'al Teshuvah* movement.

The *Ba'al Teshuvah* movement was further bolstered by the organized and institutionalized Orthodox community. A number of institutions that were in place began to have an increasing effect on the movement. The *Union of Orthodox Jewish Congregations of America, commonly known as the OU, established the National Conference of Synagogue Youth (NCSY) that effectively used Orthodox college students as counselors for the burgeoning number of non-Orthodox high school students who were interested in Judaism and in Jewish observance. To this day, NCSY continues to teach Orthodoxy to non-Orthodox high school children. Yeshiva University offered beginners-level Jewish studies for *ba'alei teshuvah* in its James Strier School. Many of those who graduated from this program went on to become Jewish educators and rabbis. Numerous other, more "right-wing" yeshivot opened their doors to *ba'alei teshuvah*. They include She'ar Yashuv, Far Rockaway, N.Y.; Hadar Ha Torah (Lubavitcher), Brooklyn, N.Y.; Maḥzikei Torah (Bostoner Rebbe), Brookline, Mass.; Or Yosef, Strasbourg, France. This helps explain one of the more interesting phenomena of the *Ba'al Teshuvah* movement. Throughout the 1970s, 1980s, and 1990s, increasing numbers of *ba'alei teshuvah* opted for stricter norms and uncompromising observance of "right-wing," "yeshivish" Orthodoxy.

In the wake of the Six-Day War, the nascent *Ba'al Teshuvah* movement in the former U.S.S.R. went public with demonstrations and an open call for more observance as well as permission to immigrate to Israel. As a result the KGB hounded those who wished to fulfill the Zionist dream and renew their Jewish observance. Hundreds of *refuseniks* were jailed. Ultimately, the Soviet Union opened its gates and the mass *aliyah* to Israel began. Two prominent *refuseniks*, Joseph Mendelevich and Eliyahu Essas, currently reside in Israel and continue to teach Judaism to the Russian immigrant community.

Eventually, the *Ba'al Teshuvah* movement spread to Israel. On the one hand, numerous institutions and organizations were created to teach and influence English-speaking students who arrived in Israel to continue their studies and enhance their Jewish observance. The most prominent are: Kefar Ḥabad (Lubavitcher), Kefar Ḥabad; Magen Avraham, Bene Berak; Diaspora Yeshiva (Har Ẓion), Jerusalem; Or Sameaḥ, Jerusalem; Kollel Or Sameaḥ, Zikhron Ya'akov; Or Sameaḥ Work and Study Program, Givat Ada; D'var Yerushalayim, Jerusalem; Aish HaTorah, Jerusalem; Kehillat Yaakov, Jerusalem; Hamivtar, Efrat; Shapell College, Jerusalem; Neve Yerushalayim, Jerusalem; Isralight, Jerusalem; Machon Pardes (co-ed), Jerusalem. These institutions, in many cases, function not only as schools, but as the centers of living communities. Many of their students marry, set up homes within the community, continue their studies and, even after the end of formal studies, continue to maintain strong ties with the yeshivah or school. Thus these yeshivot may be seen as the vital center of the entire *Ba'alei Teshuvah* movement. On the other hand, the native, Israeli society has also witnessed a growing, Hebrew-speaking *Ba'al Teshuvah* movement. Here, the movers and shakers are primarily Sephardi rabbis, many of whom preach to large crowds, exhorting them to return to their religious roots. On the whole, the Israeli *Ba'al Teshuvah* movement can be characterized as "right-wing" or ultra-Orthodox.

In the U.S., in 1987 an organization called National Jewish Outreach Program (NJOP) was created to provide support and in-service training for those engaged in outreach to potential *ba'alei teshuvah*. Founded by a leading outreach rabbi, Ephraim Buchwald, NJOP has guided thousands of volunteer teachers and tens of thousands of Jewish adults. They participated in programs advertised via the mass media and taught at Reform, Conservative, and Orthodox synagogues, as well as Jewish non-religious organizations, such as Jewish community centers. There is also a complementary organization called Association for Jewish Outreach Professionals & Programs (AJOP), which was founded in 1988.

The *Ba'al Teshuvah* movement, both in Israel and throughout the Diaspora, can certainly claim great success. Though no accurate records exist, literally thousands of Jews have returned to Jewish observance over the past 45 years of the movement's history. The movement has generated a whole library of books aimed at *ba'alei teshuvah*, strengthened existing and built new communities in Israel and abroad, and experienced its own unique set of problems, such as the growing difficulties in educating and maintaining the observance of the second generation, i.e., the children, of *ba'alei teshuvah*. Nevertheless, the movement has been an integral element in the resurgence of Orthodoxy throughout the Jewish world over the last half century.

BIBLIOGRAPHY: M.H. Danzger, *Returning to Tradition: The Contemporary Revival of Orthodox Judaism* (2005); D. Klinghoffer, *The Lord Will Gather Me In: My Journey to Jewish Orthodoxy* (1998).

[Jonathan Chipman / David Derovan (2nd ed.)]

BAAL-GAD (Heb. בַּעַל גָּד), biblical locality below Mount Hermon that was apparently sacred to *Gad, the god of fortune. Perhaps the name of the locale means "Baal is fortune." Baal-Gad is described as the northernmost point conquered by Joshua (Josh. 11:17; 12:7) and, accordingly, the "land that yet remaineth" (i.e., that the tribes did not conquer), extends "… from Baal-Gad under Mount Hermon unto the entrance of Hamath" (Josh. 13:5) or, as in a parallel passage "… from Mount Baal-Hermon unto Lebo-Hamath" (Judg. 3:3). The exact location of Baal-Gad is not known, but the sources clearly indicate that it must be situated in the southern part of the Lebanon Valley, at the foot of Mount Hermon, not far from Dan. It has been proposed to identify it with Ḥaṣbayyā on the Ḥasbani River.

BIBLIOGRAPHY: Maisler (Mazar), in: BJPES, 12 (1946), 91ff.; Abel, Geog, 2 (1938), 258ff.; Aharoni, Land, index. **ADD. BIBLIOGRAPHY:** N.S. Ahituv, *Joshua* (1995), 214; Na'aman, in: DDD, 144.

[Yohanan Aharoni]

BA'AL HA-BAYIT (Heb. בַּעַל הַבַּיִת, pl. *Ba'alei Battim*, "Head of the household"; in Yid., pronounced "*Balebos*"), head of a family. The term is often also associated with the notion of wealth and is used to describe a man of wealth and secure economic position, e.g., a landlord. The Yiddish adjective *balebatish*, in the sense of bourgeois, is derived from this term. *Ba'al ha-bayit* was also applied to married and tax-paying members of the congregation, as opposed to *baḥur ("young man"). In the learning sense *ba'al bayit* means a man whose Torah learning is basic but superficial, as against *baḥur yeshivah* (Yid. *yeshiveh bucher*) whose learning is intensive and deep. The feminine form is *ba'alat bayit*, in Yiddish *baleboste*, denoting a housewife, often in the sense of a good housekeeper.

BAAL-HAZOR (Heb. בַּעַל חָצוֹר), biblical locality "which is beside Ephraim" (II Sam. 13:23; a Greek version reads Tophraim, i.e., Ophrah?) where *Absalom had *Amnon killed to avenge his sister Tamar at the feast of sheepshearing. It may be identical with the *Hazor mentioned in the territory of Benjamin in the post-Exilic period (Neh. 11:33). The identification of Baal-Hazor with the highest point in the central range of Mount Ephraim, Jebel al-ʿAṣūr, a mountain 3,293 ft. (1,003 m.) high, north of Beth-El and near Ophrah (al-Ṭayba), has been strengthened by the mention of Ramath-Hazor as a high observation point in the *Genesis Apocryphon* found among the Dead Sea Scrolls. Baal-Hazor is possibly the "mountain of Azor," a proposed emendation of Azotus, which is found in I Maccabees 9:15 in the account of the battle of Eleasa, but the version is doubtful.

BIBLIOGRAPHY: EM, s.v.; N. Avigad and Y. Yadin, *Genesis Apocryphon* (1956), 28; Alt, in: PJB, 24 (1928), 12ff.; 25 (1929), 11ff.; Abel, in: RB, 23, p. 386–7.

[Michael Avi-Yonah]

BAALIS (Heb. בַּעֲלִיס), king of Ammon during the first half of the sixth century B.C.E. The name appears to be composed of the theophoric root "Baal" and a suffix of unclear meaning; it is ancient and appears in *Ugaritic documents in alphabetic writing as *Bʿls* and in syllabic writing as *Baʿala-si*. Although a connection has been made between the biblical Baalis and a stamp impression c. 600 B.C.E. from Ammonite territory reading *lmlkmr ʿbd bʿlyšʿ* this last, Baal-Yasha, is etymologicaly distinct from Baalis. The Bible mentions Baalis only once (Jer. 40:14), in connection with the murder of *Gedaliah, who had been appointed by the Babylonian king as governor of the Judean cities after the conquest of Jerusalem in 586 B.C.E. Johanan son of Kareah and some army officers warned Gedaliah that Baalis had dispatched Ishmael son of Nethaniah to murder him. For his motives, see *Ammonites and *Ishmael.

BIBLIOGRAPHY: Bright, Hist, 310; Ginsberg, in: *A. Marx Jubilee Volume* (1950), 366ff.; Yeivin, in: *Tarbiz*, 12 (1940/41), 261–2, 265–6; W. Rudolph, *Jeremia* (Ger., 1947), 685ff. **ADD. BIBLIOGRAPHY:** S. Ahituv, *Handbook of Ancient Hebrew Inscriptions* (1992), 241.

[Bustanay Oded]

BAAL-MAKHSHOVES (pen name of **Israel Isidor Elyashev**; 1873–1924), Yiddish literary critic, pioneer, and creator of Yiddish literary criticism as an art form. Born in Kovno, Baal-Makhshoves was educated at a Courland yeshivah which combined the moral severity of the *Musar movement with a modern curriculum, including mathematics, geography, and German. The influence of the Musar movement intensified his skepticism, melancholy, and analytic sagacity. After completing his studies at a Swiss high school, he studied medicine at Heidelberg and Berlin. Although he practiced medicine in Kovno, Vilna, Riga, Warsaw, and St. Petersburg, and also translated a few popular works of science into Yiddish, his main interest was in belles lettres. In 1896 he began to write in German and Russian and in 1901 published his first Yiddish critical reviews in *Der Yud*. Influenced by the writer I.L. *Peretz, Baal-Makhshoves continued to write in Yiddish. In a brilliant essay, "Tsvey Shprakhn – Eyneyntsike Literatur" ("Two Languages – One Literature"), he stressed the unity of Jewish literature despite its linguistic duality. In another famous essay, "Dray Shtetlakh" ("Three Towns") he called attention to the three different interpretations of *shtetl* culture in the works of Peretz, Sholem Asch, and I.M. Vaisenberg. An early admirer of Theodor Herzl, he translated *Altneuland* into Yiddish (1902) and participated in the Fifth and Twelfth Zionist Congresses. His war years were spent as a medical officer in the Russian Army. Another burst of literary activity as Yiddish editor of *Klal-verlag* (Berlin, 1922–23), was cut short by his illness and subsequent death. Baal-Makhshoves introduced European aesthetic standards and norms into his interpretation of Yiddish literature. He discovered new talents and encouraged H. *Leivick, David *Bergelson, and the postrevolutionary Kiev Group. He held that both Hebrew and Yiddish should be recognized as Jewish national languages, the former because it linked the Jewish people with its historic past and the latter because it united Jews in the Diaspora. He saw himself fulfilling a role in Yiddish literature similar to that of critics like Byelinski and Lessing in Russian and German literature, respectively, and as heralding a Jewish literary renaissance whose pioneers were Sholem Yankev *Abramovitsh (Mendele Mokher Seforim), *Sholem Aleichem, I.L. *Peretz, Sholem *Asch, and Ḥ.N. *Bialik, to each of whom he devoted a penetrating essay. He accepted Taine's theory that historical, geographical, and ethnic environment determined the character of literary creativity, and formulated the view that true creativity led from regionalism to national culture, illustrating it in his essay on the impact of South Russian Jewish life on Yiddish literature. He translated authors like Turgenev (*Foters un Kinder*, "Fathers and Children," 1922) and Tolstoy (*Kozakn*, "Cossacks," c. 1920) into Yiddish.

Less well-known but no less valuable are his *Ironishe Mayselekh* ("Ironic Tales," after 1910), in which he expressed his increasing pessimism and disillusionment. His selected works appeared in five volumes (1915, 1923², 1929³) and in a single volume in 1953.

BIBLIOGRAPHY: Rejzen, Leksikon, 2 (1927), 744–66; S. Niger, *Lezer, Dikhter un Kritiker* (1928), 495–565; Eliashev, in: *Lite*, 1 (1951), 1313–72; N.B. Minkoff, *Zeks Yidishe Kritiker* (1954), 227–90; LNYL, 1 (1956), 359–66; S. Niger, *Kritik un Kritiker* (1959), 360–82. **ADD. BIBLIOGRAPHY:** M. Krutikov, in: *Polin*, 17 (2004), 243–58.

[Simha Katz and Shlomo Bickel / Shifra Kuperman (2nd ed.)]

BAAL-MEON (Heb. בַּעַל מְעוֹן), city in Transjordan also called Beth-Baal-Meon (Josh. 13:17), Beth-Meon (Jer. 48:23), and apparently Beon (Num. 32:3). It was allotted to the tribe of Reuben (Num. 32:37–38; Josh. 13:17) and remained in Israelite hands until the revolt of Mesha, king of Moab (mid-ninth century B.C.E.). According to Mesha's stele (1.9), he captured the city from Israel and rebuilt it, constructing a pool or water channel there (*ashuʾaḥ*). Baal-Meon is listed among the cities of Moab by Jeremiah (48:23) and Ezekiel (25:9). Its identification with the modern village of Maīn, 4½ mi. (7 km.) southwest of Madeba, coincides with Eusebius (Onom. 44:21; 46:2), who identified Beelmaus with a large village nine miles from Heshbon near the hot springs of Baʿaru. The village is built on ancient remains, and the most important find there has been the mosaic pavement of a church on which a number of churches of the Holy Land are depicted. The Tosefta (Shev. 7:11) contains a reference to Baal-Meon in the Shephelah of Transjordan.

BIBLIOGRAPHY: Conder, Survey, 176–7; A. Musil, *Arabia Petraea*, 1 (1907), 397–9; Abel, Geog, 2 (1938), 259; Press, Ereẓ, s.v.

[Michael Avi-Yonah]

BAAL-PERAZIM (Heb. בַּעַל פְּרָצִים), locality (perhaps an old Canaanite sanctuary) near Jerusalem, where David defeated the Philistines in their attempt to conquer Jerusalem from the Israelites (II Sam. 5:20 and I Chron. 14:11, where the name is explained etiologically; called Mount Perazim in Isa. 28:21, where the same victory is referred to). Proposals for the identification of the site include the mountain of Sharafāt, the mountain of Ramat Raḥel, and Deir Abu Tor; the latter two are supported by the mention of the valley of Rephaim in the same context.

BIBLIOGRAPHY: EM, s.v.; Noth, Hist Isr, 187–8; Abel, Geog, 2 (1938), 259.

[Michael Avi-Yo\nah]

BA'AL SHEM (Heb. בַּעַל שֵׁם, "Master of the Divine Name"; lit. "Possessor of the Name"), title given in popular usage and in Jewish literature, especially kabbalistic and ḥasidic works, from the Middle Ages onward, to one who possessed the secret knowledge of the Tetragrammaton and the other "Holy Names," and who knew how to work miracles by the power of these names. The designation *ba'al shem* did not originate with the kabbalists, for it was already known to the last Babylonian *geonim*. In a responsum, Hai Gaon stated: "They testified that they saw a certain man, one of the well-known *ba'alei shem*, on the eve of the Sabbath in one place, and that at the same time he was seen in another place, several days' journey distant." It was in this sense that Judah *Halevi criticized the activities of the *ba'alei shem* (*Kuzari*, 3:53). In medieval German ḥasidic tradition this title was accorded to several liturgical poets, e.g., Shephatiah and his son Amittai of southern Italy (in *Abraham b. Azriel, *Arugat ha-Bosem*, 2 (1947), 181). The Spanish kabbalists used the expression *ba'alei shemot* from the middle of the 13th century onward. Some even said that there were different methods used by the *ba'alei sefirot*, the theoretical kabbalists, and the *ba'alei shemot*, the magicians, in their kabbalistic teachings. Isaac b. Jacob *ha-Kohen, Todros ha-Levi Abulafia, and *Moses de Leon all mentioned this tendency among the kabbalists without disapproval, whereas Abraham *Abulafia wrote disparagingly of the *ba'alei shem*. From the end of the 13th century, the term *ba'al shem* was also used for writers of amulets based on Holy Names (*Oẓar Neḥmad*, vol. 2, p. 133). There were large numbers of *ba'alei shem*, particularly in Germany and Poland, from the 16th century onward. Some were important rabbis and talmudic scholars, such as Elijah *Loans of Frankfurt and Worms, Elijah Ba'al Shem of Chelm, and Sekel Isaac Loeb *Wormser (the *ba'al shem* of Michelstadt). Others were scholars who devoted themselves entirely to the study of Kabbalah, such as Joel Ba'al Shem of Zamosc and Elhanan "Ba'al ha-Kabbalah" of Vienna (both 17th century), Benjamin Beinisch ha-Kohen of Krotoszyn (beginning of the 18th century), and Samuel Essingen. In the 17th and 18th centuries the number of *ba'alei shem* who were not at all talmudic scholars increased. But they attracted a following by their real or imaginary powers of healing the sick. Such a *ba'al shem* was often a combination of practical kabbalist, who performed his cures by means of prayers, amulets, and incantations, and a popular healer familiar with *segullot* ("remedies") concocted from animal, vegetable, and mineral matter. The literature of that period teems with stories and testimonies about *ba'alei shem* of this kind, some of which, however, were written in criticism of their characters and deeds. It was generally thought that the *ba'alei shem* were at their most efficacious in the treatment of mental disorders and in the exorcism of evil spirits (see *Dibbuk). There is a variation to the title *ba'al shem*, known as "*ba'al shem tov.*" The founder of modern *Ḥasidism, *Israel b. Eliezer Ba'al Shem Tov, usually referred to by the initials "BeShT," is the most famous and practically unique bearer of this title. The title "*ba'al shem tov*" existed before the Ḥasid, but it did not designate a special quality or a distinction between bearers of this title and *ba'alei shem*. For example, Elhanan Ba'al Shem Tov, who died in 1651; Benjamin Krotoschin, who so styled himself in his book *Shem Tov Katan* (Sulzbach, 1706); and Joel Ba'al Shem I, who actually signed himself "*BeShT,*" in common with the founder of Ḥasidism. In the 18th century, Samuel Jacob Ḥayyim *Falk, the "*ba'al shem* of London," achieved considerable prominence. He was called "Doctor Falk" by Christians. The theory propounded by several scholars that these wandering *ba'alei shem* were responsible for spreading Shabbateanism has not been proved. Several books by these *ba'alei shem* have been published concerning practical Kabbalah, *segullot* ("remedies"), and *refu'ot* ("healing"). These include: *Toledot Adam* (1720) and *Mifalot Elohim* (1727), edited by Joel Ba'al Shem and based on the works of his grandfather Joel Ba'al Shem I, *Shem Tov Katan* (1706) and *Amtaḥat Binyamin* (1716). The deeds of the *ba'alei shem* became legendary. Fictitious characters of the same type were sometimes invented, such as Adam Ba'al Shem of Binger, the hero of a series of miraculous stories in Yiddish which were printed as early as the 17th century. Ḥasidic legend subsequently created an imaginary connection between this character and Israel Ba'al Shem Tov. The leaders of the Haskalah generally regarded the *ba'alei shem* as charlatans and adventurers.

BIBLIOGRAPHY: N. Prilutski, *Zamelbikher far Yidischen Folklor*, 2 (1917), 40–42; J. Guenzig, *Die "Wundermaenner" im juedischen Volke* (1921); B. Segel, in: *Globus*, 62 (1892); Adler, in: JHSET, 5 (1908), 148–73; G. Scholem, in: *Zion*, 20 (1955), 80. **ADD. BIBLIOGRAPHY:** G. Nigal, in: *Sinai*, vol. 118 (1996), 88–95; M. Oron, *Samuel Falk, The Ba'al Shem of London* (Heb., 2002).

[Gershom Scholem]

BAAL WORSHIP

Name and Etymology

The word *ba'l*, common Semitic for "owner, master, husband," became the usual designation of the great weather-god of the Western Semites. In spite of the fact that the word is used as the theophorous element in personal names, such as Eshbaal, Merib-Baal, Jerub Baal, it was long believed that the term remained an appellation and did not become a proper name, except in the case of the Mesopotamian Bel and in late theological speculation. The basis for this view was the fact that in biblical usage the plural of the term, with the article, "the

Baalim," appears to designate minor local gods (Judg. 2:11; 3:7; 8:33), while the singular of the word in combination with other terms apparently designated minor or local gods, such as Baal-Berith, Baal-Gad, Baal-Hamon, Baal-Hazor, Baal-Hermon, or, in the feminine form, a goddess, Baalat-Beer, Baalat-Gebal. Further, in biblical usage when applied to the great weather-god, the singular regularly has the article, "the Baal," which suggests that the word was not regarded as a proper name. Nevertheless, despite the biblical tendency to avoid the use of the word as a proper name, it is now quite clear that by pre-Israelite times the term had become the usual name of the weather-god of Syria-Palestine. In the El-Amarna letters the logogram for the weather-god is conventionally read *Addu*, but that it is sometimes to be read *Baʿlu* is indicated by the addition of the phonetic complement-*lu*, as well as by the names like *Mut* ^{d}*Im* written syllabically as *mu-ut-ba-aḫ-lum*. In the El-Amarna letters Canaanite clients addressed the Egyptian king as "My Baal, my Addu." In the Ugaritic mythological texts Baʿlu (*bʿl*) is the name of the god which is used more than twice as often as his next most frequent name, Haddu (*hd*). The latter name (Amarna, Addu) is to be related to Arabic *hadda* ("break," "crash") with reference to thunder. The variant form Hadad (*hdd*) is attested to only once in Ugaritic.

That there were minor Baalim also at Ugarit is indicated by a god list in Akkadian (see *Ugaritica*, 5, p. 44 ll. 4–10; reconstructed text) which after the great "Weather-god, Lord of Mount Ḫazi" presents six other "weather-gods," numbered two through seven. In the parallel Ugaritic list, which is unfortunately very fragmentary, the "Weather-god, Lord of Mount Ḫazi" apparently corresponds to Baal Ṣapān, while those following are termed simply Baalim (*bʿlm*). It may be, however, that these extra Baalim are Baal's attendants, mentioned as the seven or eight lads whom Baal is ordered to take with him in his descent into the netherworld.

Other Titles and Epithets

Besides the names Baal and Haddu, the Ugaritic texts furnish a variety of other titles, such as "Mighty Baal" (*ʾaliyn bʿl*) and "Prince, Lord of Earth" (*zbl bʿl arṣ*). The latter title has a biblical echo in the corrupted form Baal-Zebub (II Kings 1:2ff.), from an original Baal-Zebul, which is preserved in this form in the New Testament (Matt. 10:25, 12:24; Mark 3:22; Luke 11:15, 18). A frequent epithet is "Cloud Rider" (*rkb ʿrpt*) which has an almost identical parallel in Psalms 68:5. A vivid description of theophany in a thunderstorm is found in Psalms 18:7–15 (= II Sam. 22:8–16). Of special interest is the designation *ʿAliy*(*ʿly*) which is twice applied to Baal in the Krt Epic:

To the earth Baal rained,
To the field rained ʿAliy.
Sweet to the earth was Baal's rain
To the field the rain of ʿAliy.

Before the discovery and recognition of this name in Ugaritic, H.S. Nyberg had restored it in Deuteronomy 33:12; I Samuel 2:10; II Samuel 23:1; Isaiah 59:18, 63:7; and Hosea 7:16. Since the Ugaritic verified the antiquity and authenticity of this divine name, additional instances have been alleged in the Psalter and in Job.

A common designation of Baal in the Ugaritic myths is *bn-dgn* "son of Dagān"; but Baal is also considered the son of El who is called "Bull El his [i.e., Baal's] father; El King who begot him [Baal]" (*tr il abh; il mlk dyknnh*). Since El and Dagān are distinct deities, this seeming confusion over Baal's paternity needs explanation. A solution has been supplied by a tradition ascribed to the ancient Phoenician priest Sakkunyaton (Greek Sanchuniathōn) that when El-Kronos defeated Ouranos, he captured in the battle Ouranos' pregnant concubine and gave her to Dagān. The divine child was named Demarous, one of the cognomens of Zeus-Baal-Hadad. The Semitic original of this name has been recognized in one of Baal's names in Ugaritic:

Then said Mighty Baal:
Foes of Hadd why haste ye?
Why haste ye opponents of Dmrn?

(The name is to be connected with the root ‡*dmr*, "be strong, brave," and is probably the same as that of Abraham's son Zimrān (‡*damarān*), the *-n* afformative being preserved in the genitive case of the Greek form Demarountos). Thus, according to Sakkunyaton, Baal's natural father was Ouranos and Dagān became his foster-father, while El-Kronos effected the transfer. That Baal appears to be a relative newcomer in the Ugaritic pantheon has been generally recognized, and it may be that Sakkhunyaton's story about Baal's paternity reflects a mythologizing of the process by which Baal was integrated into the family of El.

Baal's Residence

Baal's abode was Mount Ṣapān, identified as Jebel el-Aqraʿ ("Mount Baldy") some 30 mi. north of Ugarit. A god Baal Ṣapān was known from Egyptian and Akkadian sources before the discovery of the Ugaritic documents. In an Akkadian catalogue of Ugaritic deities Baal Ṣapān is listed as ^{d}*IM be-el ḫuršān ḫa-zi*, "Storm-God, Lord of Mount Ḫazi" (see above; Ḫaz [z] i being the Hurrian name of Mount Ṣapān which survives in the Greek and Latin Kasios/Casius as the name of the storied mountain of the gods). Isaiah 14:13 alludes to this divine abode as "the Mount of Assembly in the recesses of *ẓafon*" (*har moʿed be-yarkete ẓafon*), the latter phrase being the equivalent of Ugaritic *mrym ṣpn* or *ṣrrt ṣpn*, the height or fastness of Ṣapān. The cosmic character of *ẓafon* leads to its use as a synonym for "sky" in Job 26:7: "who stretched out *ẓafon* on emptiness who suspended earth on naught." That *ẓafon* designated the "north" in Hebrew is presumably due to the fact that Mount Casius lies directly north of Palestine. In Psalms 89:13 *ẓafon* and *yamin*, in parellelism with Tabor and Hermon, hardly designate the directions north and south; *yamin* is almost certainly a corruption of Amana, the southern portion of the Taurus mountains, the alteration of *ʾamanah* to *yamin* being occasioned by the misunderstanding of *ẓafon* as the direction rather than the name of the holy mountain. In Psalms 48:2–3, Mount Zion is equated with "the recesses of *ẓafon*" (the phrase quoted above from Isa. 14:13). The association of the name Baal-Zephon with Israel's exit from Egypt (Ex. 14:2, 9; Num. 33:7) has been made the basis of intriguing speculation by Eissfeldt.

Baal in the Ugaritic Myths

The bulk of the Ugaritic mythological texts is concerned with the activities of Baal. In correlating the sequence of events, Baal's victory over the sea-god, Yamm, is probably to be placed near the beginning of the action, since it was presumably this exploit which gained him the dominant position among the gods, just as *Marduk achieved preeminence by defeating the sea-monster Tiamat. With the help of wonder weapons supplied and blessed by the versatile Koshar (the craftsman god), Baal was able to defeat and rout the sea-god. It has been suggested that this clash was indirectly a conflict between Baal and El, with Yamm serving as champion for the venerable El, as the Titans fought on behalf of Kronos in the Greek version of the myth and the stone colossus Ulikummi for Kumarbi in the Hurrian-Hittite version which is roughly contemporary with the Ugaritic texts.

The biblical allusions to YHWH's victory over the sea preserve echoes of the older exploit of Baal (cf. Isa. 27:1, 30:7, 51:9–10; Ezek. 29:3–5, 32:2–6; Nah. 1:4; Hab. 3:8; Ps. 74:13–14, 89:9–10, 93:1ff.; Job 3:8, 7:12, 9:13, 26:12–13, 38:8–11, 40:25). YHWH's victory over the waters is connected either with the rescue of Israel at the Exodus (Ps. 114) or with eschatological victory (Isa. 27:1). The eschatological traits were taken over with the Canaanite myths. The triumph of Baal recounted in the myths and perhaps reenacted in ritual drama gave assurance of help in the present and the future as in the past. The prize of the victory was kingship over the gods and the enthronement ritual guaranteed the natural order of life and the welfare of the society. The motifs of these myths were adopted and adapted in Jewish and Christian eschatology.

The longest of the texts deals with the construction of Baal's house on top of Mount Ṣapān. A complaint is made to Bull El, father of the gods, that Baal has no house like other gods. Apparently in anticipation of developments the artisan god Koshar had cast furnishings of gold and silver. Asherah, mother of the gods, was prevailed upon to intercede with El to gain permission for the building. El is praised for his wisdom in granting the request since now it is insured that Baal will give his rain in season. The building materials, gold, silver, and lapis lazuli, were procured and the architect-builder Koshar was invited to dinner and consultation. Koshar twice recommended that a window be installed and Baal twice vetoed the suggestion, although Koshar insisted that Baal would have to reconsider. Baal's objection to the window somehow concerned his three daughters and the sea-god (Yamm), but the text is broken at this point. (The suggestion that Jer. 9:20 presents a parallel is mistaken since the Ugaritic text mentions the sea-god and not Death (Mot) in connection with the window.) Baal's house was constructed in an extraordinary fashion. For seven days a fire burned inside the building, and when it subsided, the house was plated with gold, silver, and lapis lazuli. Baal rejoiced and celebrated with a banquet. After a sortie against the sea-god, Baal returned to his house and ordered Koshar to install a window; Koshar laughed, reminded Baal of the debate, and complied. Through the window, a cleft in the clouds, Baal gave forth his holy voice which convulsed the earth and sent his enemies scurrying to the hills and woods. Issuing a challenge to his enemy Mot (death), who presumed to rule gods and men, Baal dispatched his messengers to Mot's infernal, filthy abode, warning them not to get close to Mot's rapacious jaws.

The sequel to this action is furnished by the group of texts which recount Baal's confrontations with Mot. In the first encounter, Baal is invited to a banquet at which he is to be both guest and main course. Baal's response to Mot's invitation to come and be devoured is abject surrender: "Thy slave am I, thine eternal." Before descending to the realm of death, Baal copulates with a heifer and begets a male offspring. After a textual gap, there is a report that Baal's corpse has been found. El and Anath mourn violently, mutilating their faces and bodies. With the help of the sun-goddess Shapsh, Anath locates the dead Baal, carries him to the height of Ṣapān, and weeping buries him with funerary sacrifices. Ashtar the Awful (*ʿṯtrʿrẓ*) was then nominated to replace Baal, but when he ascended the throne, his feet did not reach the footstool nor his head the top and so he declined to reign on the heights of Ṣapān and descended from Baal's throne, but ruled over all El's earth. Since the root *ʿtr* in Arabic is connected with artificial irrigation, it is apparent that Ashtar's failure to measure up to Baal represents the inadequacy of irrigation as a substitute for natural rainfall.

Baal's sister-consort Anath demanded that Mot release her brother. Mot refused and boasted how he had mangled Baal. Anath then dismembered Mot, scattered and burned the pieces, and gave them to the birds. Baal's resurrection followed Mot's demise, the good news being transmitted through a dream of El:

In a dream of Beneficent El Benign,
A vision of the Creator of Creatures,
The skies rained oil,
The wadies flowed honey.
So I knew that Mighty Baal lives,
The Prince, Lord of Earth, exists.

The fields were still parched from the drought and again Anath and Shapsh set out to find Baal. Next both Mot and Baal appear reconstituted and reactivated and again in conflict. They clash violently until both are prostrate and the Sun-goddess warns Mot not to fight with Baal lest El hear and overthrow him. This time, Baal puts up a fight and holds Mot off in battle. Thus it is clear that Baal, representing the life-giving rains, fluctuates in his ability to withstand the power of Mot, who represents drought, sterility, and death.

YHWH Versus Baal

The worship of Baal in Syria-Palestine was inextricably bound to the economy of the land which depends on the regularity and adequacy of the rains. Unlike Egypt and Mesopotamia, which depend on irrigation, the Promised Land drinks water from the rain of heaven (Deut. 11:10–11). During the summer months the rains cease, but the temporary drought is no threat unless it is abnormally prolonged. Figs and grapes ripen during the dry season and the grain harvest also takes place before the rains resume. In a normal good year, when the rains come in due season, there is no hiatus in productivity, for the land yields its increase, the trees produce their fruit, the threshing overlaps, the vintage overlaps the sowing, and there is food aplenty, prosperity, and peace (Lev. 26:4–6). But not all years are good, and in a bad year, or a series of bad years, when the rains fail, the skies become like iron, the land like brass, and man's toil is futile for the earth will not yield its increase (Lev. 26:19–20). A series of bad years, which were apparently believed to come in seven-year cycles (cf. Gen. 41; II Sam. 1:21), would be catastrophic. Thus in any year anxiety about the rainfall would be a continuing concern of the inhabitants which would suffice to give rise to rites to ensure the coming of the rains. Thus the basis of the Baal cult was the utter dependence of life on the rains which were regarded as Baal's bounty.

Biblical narrative incorporates tales of Baal worship into the traditions of the wilderness wandering, thus tracing Baal worship to the earliest period of Israel's existence. At Shittim they attached themselves to Baal-Peor, ate sacrifices for the dead, and indulged in sacred sexual orgies (Num. 25:1–11; Ps. 106:28). Life in a land dependent on rainfall enhanced the appeal of the Baal cult and its pervasive influence persisted through the centuries, as the unrelenting protests of the prophets and the sporadic efforts at reform attest. Horrendous and repulsive aspects of the worship – sexual excesses and perversions (Isa. 57:3–10), perhaps including copulation with animals (Hos. 13:2) such as Baal himself performed in the Ugaritic myth – are depicted in the prophetic tirades. Virtually all reference to Baal's consort, the violent "Virgin Anath" – with whom Baal copulates by the thousand in one of the Ugaritic mythological fragments – has been excluded from the Bible, but the goddesses Ashtart (Judg. 2:13) and *Asherah (Judg. 6:30; II Kings 16:32–33) are associated with him.

The conflict of Yahwism and Baalism reached a crisis with Elijah's challenge to Baal's prophets to settle the question whether it was Baal or YHWH who really supplied the rain (I Kings 18). The spectacular victory for Yahwism did not have a lasting effect. Extra-biblical evidence for the flourishing Baal cult at Samaria in the ninth and eighth centuries B.C.E. was furnished by Harvard University excavations in the form of personal names containing Baal as the theophorous element, such as *bʾybʿl*, "Baal is my father," *bʿl zmr*, "Baal sings" or "Baal is strong," *bʿl zkr*, "Baal remembers," *bʿl mʿny*, "Baal is my answer," etc. Jehu's massacre of the Baal worshipers (II Kings 10:18–28) did not eradicate bull worship (II Kings 10:31). In Judah the murder of the queen mother, *Athaliah, and of Mattan, priest of Baal, and the smashing of the altars and cult images in the Baal temple (II Kings 11:18) did not wipe out the cult (II Kings 12:3–4). Ahaz fostered Baal worship (II Chron. 28:2); Hezekiah attempted to eliminate it; Manasseh his son again gave it royal support (II Kings 21:3); and Josiah in his turn purged the Temple of YHWH of the utensils made for Baal and Asherah (II Kings 23:4).

The contest on Mount Carmel was reported as demonstrating that Baal was an impotent non-entity and that the rain came only from YHWH. This viewpoint was developed as the basic and final argument against Baalism. With Baal's functions accredited to YHWH, it was natural and fitting that some of Baal's titles would also be taken over. Portions of ancient Baal liturgy were adapted to the praise of Israel's God, as the Ugaritic poems have shown. To accommodate Baal ideology to Yahwism required some radical transformations. The summer drought did not mean that YHWH had died (like Baal), nor did the return of the rains signal the resurrection. The rains were fully controlled by YHWH who called them from the sea and poured them out on the surface of the earth (Amos 5:8b; 9:6b). He could, and did, withhold the rain from one city and lavish it on another (Amos 4:7). None of the foolish practices of the heathen could bring the rains; only YHWH could and did (Jer. 10:11–13; 14:22). If the rains failed and drought and death came upon the land and people, it was not because Mot had mangled Baal and made the glowing sun-goddess destructive; it was rather YHWH's way of meting out merited punishment to a faithless and sinful people (Deut. 11:17; I Kings 8:35–36; Jer. 3:2–3). The continued worship of Baal was given as one of the causes for the destruction of Judah (Jer. 19:5ff.). Payment of the full tithe to the food stores of the Temple, some thought, would guarantee that YHWH would open the windows of heaven and pour down overflowing blessings (Mal. 3:10; cf. Avot 5:11 on the connection between tithing and rain). The prophet Haggai attributed the drought and scarcity in his day to the failure to rebuild the Temple (Hag. 1:7–11).

When the rain failed, it was inevitable that some would question YHWH's power and resort to Baal. In distress some would naturally revert to the old ways of reviving or reactivating the rain-god – prayer, mourning, self-laceration, dancing, and water-pouring (I Kings 18:26–28; Hos. 7:14–16). The right remedy, according to Israel's prophets, was to repudiate Baal completely and to seek and return to Israel's true God (Isa. 55:6–13; Jer. 4:1–2; Hos. 14:2).

BIBLIOGRAPHY: O. Eissfeldt, *Beitraege zur Religionsgeschichte des Altertums I* (1932); H.L. Ginsberg, *Kitvei Ugarit* (1936); J. Oberman, *Ugaritic Mythology* (1948); A.S. Kapelrud, *Baal in the Ras Shamra Texts* (1952); M. Dahood, in: *Studi Semitici*, 1 (1958), 75–78; N. Habel, *Yahweh Versus Baal: A Conflict of Religious Cultures* (1964); J. Gray, *The Legacy of Canaan* (rev. ed., 1965); H.B. Huffmon, *Amorite Personal Names in the Mari Texts* (1965), 174; W.F. Albright, *Yahweh and the Gods of Canaan* (1968); Albright, Arch Rel; S.M. Paul, in: *Biblica*, 49 (1968), 343–6; U. Oldenburg, *The Conflict Between El and Baʿl in*

Canaanite Religion (1969). **ADD. BIBLIOGRAPHY:** W. Hermann, in: DDD, 132–38; M.S. Smith, *The Ugaritic Baal Cycle* (1994).

[Marvin H. Pope]

BAAL-ZEPHON (Heb. בַּעַל צְפֹן), a location, perhaps a sanctuary, in Egypt which, according to the Bible, the Israelites passed during the *Exodus from Egypt (Ex. 14:2, 9; Num. 33:7). Presumably the toponym takes its name from the god Baal Zephon known from texts beginning in the early second millennium B.C.E. and continuing well into the first. Scholars disagree as to the site of Baal-Zephon and locate it according to their view of the route that the Bible claims was followed by the Israelites when they departed from Egypt. Those who assume that a southern passage was meant suggest Jebel Abu Ḥasan, 8 mi. (13 km.) N. of Suez, which is identified with a Migdal Baal-Zephon mentioned in a papyrus from the Hellenistic period (Cairo papyrus 31169). Others who prefer a northern route identify Baal-Zephon with the sanctuary of Zeus Casius, which is known of from the fifth century B.C.E. onward in the vicinity of the Serbonic Lake (Baḥr al-Bardawīl, the "Reed Sea," according to this theory). Since another mountain called Mons Casius (Jebel Aqra on the Syrian coast) was known in earlier times as Baal-Zephon, it is consequently assumed that the southern Baal-Zephon was also called Casius. The site is identified with a hillock on the western extremity of the lake called *Maḥmūdiyya*. W.F. Albright has identified Baal-Zephon with the Egyptian port Taḥpanḥes (Daphne). A survey in 1967 directed by M. Dothan has identified Baal-Zephon with Ras Kasrun near the Serbonic Lake; the survey also identified it as the site of the Hellenistic-Roman city of Casius.

BIBLIOGRAPHY: O. Eissfeldt, *Baal Zaphon…* (Ger., 1932); Bourdon, in: RB, 41 (1932), 541ff.; Albright, in: BASOR, 118 (1950), 17; EM, 2 (1965), 291–2; Aharoni, Land, 179; M. Dothan, in: *Eretz-Israel*, 9 (1969), 48–59. **ADD. BIBLIOGRAPHY:** H. Niehr, DDD, 152–54.

[Michael Avi-Yonah]

BAAR, EMIL N. (1891–1985), U.S. Reform lay leader. Born in Vienna, Austria, Baar immigrated to the United States with his parents at the age of two. He received his J.D. degree from Columbia University in 1915 and practiced law until 1951, when he became a justice of the Supreme Court of the State of New York. He served as chairman of the board of the *Union of American Hebrew Congregations from 1959 to 1963, becoming lifetime honorary chairman in 1964. He was also a vice president of the *World Union for Progressive Judaism.

Baar presided over the UAHC during the stormiest period of Rabbi Maurice *Eisendrath's controversial social action leadership. Although a moderate Republican in his personal politics, Baar gave strong support to the Union's bold positions in support of civil rights, opposition to the war in Vietnam, and admission of a gay congregation into the UAHC. He will be remembered especially for leading the Union through the deeply emotional and potentially divisive battle that culminated in the establishment of the Religious Action Center in Washington, D.C., in 1961.

BIBLIOGRAPHY: K.M. Olitzky, L.J. Sussman, and M.H. Stern, *Reform Judaism in America: A Biographical Dictionary and Sourcebook* (1993).

[Bezalel Gordon (2nd ed.)]

BAAR, HERMAN (1826–1904), U.S. rabbi and educator. Born in Stadthagen, near Hanover, Germany, Baar received his early education at the gymnasium of Hanover and after graduation took a course in philology and theology at the University of Goettingen. On the completion of his studies he took a position as teacher at the school at Seesen, Germany, which he held eight years. In 1857 he was named rabbi in Liverpool, England, where he received what was then called the ministerial appointment in the Seel Street synagogue, where he spent a decade. When he lost his voice, he left the congregation and opened a school in Brussels. In 1870 he came to Washington, D.C., but believing a change of climate advisable he went to New Orleans, La., where he directed a school. From there he went to New York, where in 1876 he was appointed superintendent of the Hebrew Orphan Asylum, New York City – a position he filled with great success until his resignation in 1899. He earned his national reputation as an educator with his addresses to students that were published in *The American Hebrew*. They were collected in a two-volume study called *Homely and Religious Topics*. He retired in 1900 and wrote for Jewish periodicals and published Bible stories for use by children.

[Michael Berenbaum (2nd ed.)]

BAASHA (or **Baasa**; Heb. בַּעְשָׁא), son of Ahijah of the tribe of Issachar, king of Israel (906–883 B.C.E.). (A ninth century Aramean king bears the same name.) Baasha, perhaps an officer under King *Nadab, who was besieging *Gibbethon, then held by the Philistines, assassinated him there and proclaimed himself king. He massacred all the members of the House of Jeroboam I, which he had supported. By this act he overthrew the hegemony of Ephraim over the other tribes. Like his predecessor, he resided at Tirzah (I Kings 15:27ff.). After ensuring by alliance the friendship and neutrality of his northern neighbors – the Arameans of Damascus – he turned to the south. According to I Kings 15:16, 32, he was at war with King *Asa of Judah throughout his reign. He succeeded in occupying Ramah, a dominating height north of Jerusalem, and began to fortify it, threatening the Davidic capital. Asa, in turn, bribed Ben-Hadad, king of *Aram, to break his alliance with Baasha and invade Israel (*ibid.* 17–21; II Chron. 16:1–5), and Baasha was forced to withdraw from Ramah. It has been suggested that he fell in battle while fighting the Arameans, but the biblical report suggests a peaceful death at home (I Kings 16:16). Like Jeroboam before him, Baasha seems to have been sponsored by the prophet Jehu son of Hanani, who gave him the charismatic title *nagid*, and like Jeroboam he disappointed his sponsor (*ibid.* 16:1–4, 7).

According to rabbinic legend (Mid. Ag. to Num. 30:15), it was Baasha who murdered the prophet *Shemaiah.

BIBLIOGRAPHY: Noth, Hist Isr, 228, 230, 233, 239; Bright, Hist, index; EM, 2 (1965), 303–4 (incl. bibl.). **ADD. BIBLIOGRAPHY:** M. Cogan, *1 Kings* (AB; 2000), 408–12.

[Hanoch Reviv]

BAAZOV, HERZL (1904–1945), Georgian writer. Born several weeks after Theodor *Herzl's death and named after him, Baazov grew up in Kutaisi in the house of his father, David Baazov, which was the first Zionist, Hebrew-speaking home in Georgia. Baazov became a well-known Georgian playwright and poet, and most of his writings were dedicated to Georgian Jewish life. At the age of 19, he translated the Song of Songs into Georgian. His first play, about the life and death of Itzko (Abraham Isaac) Rizhinashvili – a young Jewish revolutionary who was killed during the upheaval of 1905 in a fight with Czarist gendarmes – was staged at the Tbilisi (Tiflis) State Theater. Another of his plays, *The Dumb Opened Their Mouths*, dealt with the social changes in the life of the Tat-speaking *Mountain Jews after the Russian Revolution. He also wrote poetry, including the well-known poem "Cain." In the 1930s he began to write a trilogy about the changes in Jewish life in Georgia after the revolution. In spite of his positive attitude to the revolution as a social phenomenon, he was suddenly arrested and deported in 1937, after the publication of the first part of the trilogy. No indictment against him was ever published, but it is assumed that he was accused of "Jewish bourgeois nationalism." In 1945 he died in exile, somewhere in the Soviet far north. An indirect rehabilitation of his name occurred in 1964, when the official Georgian Writers' Union celebrated his 60th birthday. Several of his writings were republished, but were not translated into Russian. The Georgian writer G. Tsitsishvili published a book on Baazov's life and work (1964) that, inter alia, mentions his close relations with S. *Mikhoels, P. *Markish, and other Soviet Jewish writers and artists.

His younger brother, MEIR BAAZOV (1915–1970), an engineer, was also a Hebrew scholar and served in the 1940s as director of the Hebrew section of the Georgian National Library in Tbilisi.

[Mordkhai Neishtat]

BAB, JULIUS (1880–1955), German drama critic and literary historian. Born in Berlin, where he studied literature and philosophy, Bab was a critic of the Berlin theater for more than three decades. He was also lecturer and adviser to the Berlin people's theater, the *Volksbuehne*. In June 1933, in an attempt to maintain cultural life among the Jews after the rise of Nazism, Bab founded the *Juedischer Kulturbund*, which had its own theater. In 1940 he fled to the U.S., where he became the dramatic critic of the *New York Staatszeitung*. Bab's collected reviews of the Berlin theater, *Die Chronik des deutschen Dramas* (1921–22), are an important source for the history of modern German drama. His other works include monographs on Shakespeare, Shaw, Dehmel, and Albert Bassermann and a volume of essays, *Am Rande der Zeit* (1915). A book of verse, *Ausgewaehlte Gedichte…* (1930), includes the poem "Der Jude."

BIBLIOGRAPHY: L. Rauschenbusch, in: *Quarterly Journal of Speech*, 2 (1946), 33–40; H. Bergholz, in: *Books Abroad*, 25 (1951), 26f. **ADD. BIBLIOGRAPHY:** H. Ricarda, "Geothe im Ghetto – Zum Selbstverständnis des Kulturbundes deutscher Juden (1933–1935)," in: *Tribüne*, 167 (2003), 138–47; M.H. Gelber, "Internationalismus in der deutsch-jüdischen Literatur – Glueckel von Hameln, Georg Hermann, Julius Bab und das 'Yale-Buch,'" in: *Die deutsch-jüdische Erfahrung* (2003), 69–84; E. Albanis, *German-Jewish Cultural Identity from 1900 to the Aftermath of the First World War* (2002); S. Rogge-Gau, *Die doppelte Wurzel des Daseins – Julius Bab und der juedische Kulturbund Berlin* (1999).

[Rudolf Kayser / Bjoern Siegel (2nd ed.)]

BABAD, a family of rabbis. The founder of the family was Isaac of Cracow, son of Issachar Berish, a *parnas* of the Council of Four Lands, and grandson of Heschel, *av bet din* of Cracow. He served as rabbi of Brzezany and then of Brody, where he died in 1704. His children added the word Babad (an acronym of **B**enei **A**v **B**et **D**in, "children of the *av bet din*") to their signatures, and it eventually became their surname. Among members of the family were the following:

JOSHUA HESCHEL B. ISAAC BABAD (1754–1838). Joshua Heschel b. Isaac Babad grandson of the communal leader, Jacob Jekel Babad of Brody, who served as rabbi of Budzanow and, from 1801, of Tarnopol. He was one of the opponents, in 1813, of the teaching system in the school founded by Joseph *Perl, where secular studies were also taught. After a short stay in Lublin (1828), he was compelled to leave the city because of his dispute with the *Mitnaggedim* there, and he returned to Tarnapol, where he died. Joshua's responsa on the four parts of the Shulḥan Arukh, *Sefer Yehoshu'a* (Zolkiew, 1829), was considered a basic halakhic work, upon which contemporary rabbis relied for their rulings.

MENACHEM MUNISH B. JOSHUA HESCHEL BABAD (1865–1938). Menachem Munish b. Joshua Heschel Babad a well-known personality in Galician Jewry and a halakhic authority of note. He was born in Brody where he was educated by his father and afterward by his father-in-law. He succeeded his father as *av bet din* of Strzyzow in 1892, and in 1894, after the death of his father-in-law, he accepted a call to serve as rabbi of Jaworow, a post which he occupied until 1911. The rest of his life was spent in Tarnopol. Menahem participated in rabbinical conferences of 1925 and 1927 in Cracow and Lvov. His method of study, resembling that of the Lithuanian yeshivot, was characterized by a logical analysis of the words of the sages, a comprehensive review of every aspect of the subject under discussion, and a summation of all the relevant views. His many responsa were collected in *Ḥavaẓẓelet ha-Sharon* (1931–38), covering all four parts of the Shulḥan Arukh.

BIBLIOGRAPHY: I.J. Eisenstadt and S. Wiener, *Da'at Kedoshim* (1898), 104, 128 (first pagination); Cohen-Zedek, in: *Dor Yesharim*, 30 – supplement to: *Ha-Goren*, 1 (1898); S.B. Nissenbaum, *Le-Korot ha-Yehudim be-Lublin* (1899), 96–97; Z. Horowitz, *Kitvei ha-Ge'onim* (1928), 35, 39; A. Polisiuk, *Tehillah le-David* (1937); Halpern, Pinkas, index; Friedmann, in: YIVO *Bleter*, 31–32 (1948), 170 n91; EG, 3 (1955), 262–6.

[Josef Horovitz]

BABAD, JOSEPH BEN MOSES (1800–1874/5), Polish rabbi and author. Little is known about him. His father was *av bet din* at Przeworsk. Babad served as rabbi at Bohorodezany, Zabariz, Sniatyn, and Tarnopol. Babad's best-known work is his *Minḥat Ḥinnukh*, consisting of expositions of the *Sefer* *ha-Ḥinnukh* ("The Book of Education") ascribed to Aaron ha-Levi of Barcelona (1869, frequently republished; the 1952 edition containing 26 addenda (commentaries, novellae, notes, and emendations) to *Sefer ha-Ḥinnukh* and *Minḥat Ḥinnukh* by various authors). The publisher, Reuben Kohen Rappaport, stated in the introduction that he had long tried to persuade the author to publish it, but in his modesty he had refused and finally agreed only after the theft of a manuscript containing his novellae on the Torah. As Babad himself states, the arrangement of his work is based on that of *Sefer ha-Ḥinnukh*. On each *halakhah* he quotes commentators and halakhic authorities. *Minḥat Ḥinnukh* together with *Sefer ha-Ḥinnukh* covers all the principles, laws, and customs concerning the commandments, from talmudic times to the *aḥaronim*. In his novellae and legal statements, Babad arrives at no final conclusion, but instead poses questions and problems, stimulating the reader to new ideas and further research. The many supplementary comments and novellae on *Minḥat Ḥinnukh* have created an entire literature around these two works.

There are extant two responsa addressed to Babad by his grandfather Joshua Hoeschel Babad, two from Joseph Joel Deutsch to Babad when he was *av bet din* at Zabariz and Sniatyn, and one responsum of Babad, dated 1850 (*Kovez Teshuvot*, Supplement to *Minḥat Ḥinnukh* (1952), 120ff.). His son Simeon Babad, who served as rabbi at Tarnopol until 1909, wrote glosses to *Minḥat Ḥinnukh*. He was succeeded in turn by his son Joshua Hoeschel who occupied the position until his death in 1919.

BIBLIOGRAPHY: Z. Horowitz, *Kitvei ha-Ge'onim* (1928), 39; H. Tchernowitz, *Toledot ha-Posekim*, 2 (1947), 98, 105; J. Lewinstein, *Dor va-Dor ve-Doreshav* (1949^2), 77, no. 1544; B. Wachstein, *Zur Bibliographie der Gedaechtnis- und Trauervortraege in der hebraeischen Literatur*, 1 (1922), 24; 2 (1927), 20; EG, 3 (1955), 262–3; *Sefer ha-Hashlamah le-Minḥat Ḥinnukh ha-Shalem*, 2 (1952), end.

[Yehoshua Horowitz]

BABAI BEN FARHAD (18th century), author of a versified short history of the Jews mainly of *Kashan and *Isfahan. His chronicle is called *Ketāb-e sargozasht-e Kāshān* and comprises approximately 1,300 verses written in Judeo-Persian (Persian using Hebrew script). The chronicle deals with the persecutions of the Jews in the above cities in the years 1729–30, when they were forced to convert to Islam for a period of seven months. The chronicle also notes some interesting details about the Afghan invasion of Isfahan and Kashan, as well as Naderqoli Khan's (later Nader Shah) wars against them. The author mentions Mahmud and Ashraf, the leaders of the Afghans (especially the latter), favorably while he criticizes Naderqoli for his harsh measures against the Jews. We know from other historical sources that the Zoroastrians also mention the Afghan conquests favorably and even assisted them (as in the occupation of Kerman). The Jews and Zoroastrians were accorded by the Afghan conquerors superior status to Shi'ites in the socio-political structure of Iran. According to the chronicle, the Jewish community of Kashan was wealthy, mostly involved in the silk trade. According to the author, there were 13 synagogues in Kashan; nevertheless, he mentions with disapproval the lack of religious observance among most of the Jews of his town. Another Jew from Kashan named Mashi'aḥ ben Raphael appended approximately 80 verses to Babai ben Farhad's narrative in which he mentions favorably Mollā Ebrāhim, the leader of the Jews of Kashan, who together with a number of supporters was instrumental in getting the Jews who had been forced to accept Islam to return to Judaism.

BIBLIOGRAPHY: W. Bacher, "Les Juifs de Perse aux xviie et xviiie siècles d'après les chroniques poétiques de Babai b. Loutf et de Babai b. Farhad," in: REJ 53 (1907), 85–110; A. Netzer, *Kronika shel Babai ben Farhad* (1978), 1–38 (photoprint of ms no. 917 of the Ben-Zvi Institute of Jerusalem); V.B. Moreen, *Iranian Jewry during the Afghan Invasion* (1990).

[Amnon Netzer (2nd ed.)]

BABAI BEN LUṬF (17th century), historian of Kashan who left the first and only written history of his time, covering a period from about 1613 until the beginning of the year 1662. His history, which contains about 5,300 lines of poetry in Judeo-Persian (Persian language written in Hebrew script), is called *Ketāb-e Anusi*. The work still remains in manuscript form, of which six copies are known to us in the major libraries of the U.S., Europe, and Israel. The author depicts the savage persecution of the Jews all over Iran by the two Safavid kings, *Abbas I (1588–29) and *Abbas II (1642–66). He mentions 19 cities by name whose Jewish population were killed, tortured, and forced to embrace Islam. The veracity of Babai's account is supported by the Iranian historians of the period, by the travelogue of Pietro della Valle, and by Arakel, the Armenian priest of Tabriz. The author speaks favorably of two Shi'ite priests with a strong Sufi orientation who interceded on behalf of the Jews: Shaikh Bahā al-Dīn Ameli (d. 1621), and Mollā Moḥsen Feiz of Kashan (d. 1680). Babai also mentions with respect Shah Safi (1629–42) who reigned after Abbas I. *Ketāb-e Anusi* is a valuable historical document also containing important information regarding Jewish demography and communal organization as well as historical events concerning Iran. We also know of a short Judeo-Persian poem, *Monājāt-Nāmeh*, composed by Babai ben Luṭf in praise of the prophet Elijah.

BIBLIOGRAPHY: A. Netzer, "*Redifot u-Shmadot be-Toledot Yehudei Iran be-Me'ah ha-17*," in: *Pe'amim* 6 (1980), 32–56; V.B. Moreen,

Iranian Jewry's Hour of Peril and Heroism (1987); H. Levy, *Comprehensive History of the Jews of Iran* (1999), 302ff.

[Amnon Netzer (2nd ed.)]

BĀB AL-ABWĀB ("Gate of the Gates"; Persian **Darband**; modern *__Derbent__), a pass and town at the eastern end of the Caucasus range, where the road narrows between the mountains and the Caspian Sea. Bāb al-Abwāb is mentioned in both the "Letter of Ḥasdai" and the "Reply of King Joseph" (see *Khazars), in the latter specifically as marking the southern limit of the Khazar domain. This agrees in general with the accounts of the Arabic geographers and historians. The latter described Bāb al-Abwāb as guarding one of the two main passes of the Caucasus through which the Khazars invaded the lands of Islam. Extensive arrangements for the defense of Bāb al-Abwāb are reported by the geographer al-Iṣṭakhrī (tenth century). Previously, the town had more than once been overrun from the north, though the successful Khazar attack against Ardabil (apparently in 730), referred to in the "Reply of King Joseph," was made via Dariel (now Daryal).

BIBLIOGRAPHY: Dunlop, Khazars, index; Dunlop, in: EIS² (incl. bibl.); al-Iṣṭakhrī, *Kitāb al-Masālik wa-al-Mamālik* (1961), 109–10; M. Artamonov, *Istoriya Khazar* (1962), index.

[Douglas Morton Dunlop]

BABA RABBAH (or **Baba ha-Gadol,** "the Great Baba," 4th cent. C.E.), Samaritan high priest, eldest son of the high priest Nethanel (300–332 C.E.). According to the dating of the Samaritan chronicles, Baba Rabbah lived in the middle of the fourth century C.E. He is regarded as the most outstanding Samaritan political leader and reformer. His epithet "the Great" distinguishes him from other high priests called Baba, before and after his time. All information about Baba Rabbah is derived solely from the Samaritan chronicles: the *Tolidah*, the Samaritan *Book of Joshua*, the *Kitāb al-Ta'rīkh* of *Abu al-Fat, and the *New Chronicle* (see *Samaritans, Literature). The last three embellish their narrative with much legendary material. Of special interest is the legend of the Roman agent Jarman or Jarmūn related in the Samaritan *Book of Joshua*. By the emperor's decree, the Roman had been posted at the high priest Nethanel's door to prevent him from circumcising his eldest son Baba Rabbah; but Jarman was a God-fearing man who preferred to obey the law of the Eternal King rather than the earthly ruler. In gratitude, the Samaritans continue to bless his name at every circumcision ceremony at the conclusion of a poem composed by Markah in glorification of this act. According to the other two chronicles, however, the high priest in this story is Akbon, Baba's brother, who succeeded him in office.

Baba Rabbah lived in an age of great political and religious upheaval; pagan Rome had been succeeded by the Byzantine Empire. This turning point, when the foreign rulers were preoccupied with their own affairs, provided a brief respite for the oppressed Samaritan community. Baba Rabbah achieved numerous victories over the Romans and some neighboring states and time and again succeeded in driving the enemy out of Samaritan territory. To secure the safety of his country, he maintained an army of 3,000 men on constant alert. After he led his people for 40 years, the Byzantine emperor invited him to Constantinople to conclude a peace treaty. On his arrival he was received with princely honors but was held as a prisoner until his death.

During his rule, Baba Rabbah divided the country into 12 administrative districts, each under the leadership of a layman and a priest. The list of these districts indicates that at this time Samaritan communities existed in all parts of the Holy Land. Baba founded a legislative council of three priests and four laymen and conferred upon each member the title *ḥakham*. They constituted, after Baba Rabbah himself, the highest authority in the community. One of their tasks was to tour the country at regular intervals to ensure that people were instructed in the laws of the Torah and to decide on difficult halakhic matters. In conjunction with his administrative reforms, Baba Rabbah made efforts to promote a revival of religion and literature. He reopened all the synagogues and schools that the Romans had closed and founded many new ones, building one of the nine new synagogues at the foot of Mt. Gerizim. He had a cistern installed at this holy place for the purification of the people who came to pray there. Many old manuscripts of the law were then collected and preserved. It was probably also at this time that the foundations of the *Defter*, the Samaritan common prayer book, were laid by *Amram Darah and his son Markah, who composed liturgical and midrashic poems in Aramaic.

BIBLIOGRAPHY: J.A. Montgomery, *The Samaritans* (1907, repr. 1968), 101–4; J. Macdonald, *Theology of the Samaritans* (1964), index; A.E. Cowley, *Samaritan Liturgy*, 2 (1909), xx–xxii; M. Gaster, *Samaritans* (1925), 39; I. Ben-Zvi, *Sefer ha-Shomeronim* (1935), 24; M. Avi-Yonah, in: *Eretz Israel*, 4 (1956), 127–32; R. Tsadaqa, *Aggadot Am Shomeroniyyot* (1965), 22–35; H.G. Kippenberg, *Garizim und Synagoge* (1971, index), TEXTS: E. Vilmar (ed.) *Abulfathi, Annales Samaritani* (1865), 125–47 (Arabic with Latin notes and introduction); T.G.J. Juynboll (ed.), *Chronicon Samaritanum, Liber Josuae* (1848), lii–lv (Arabic text); J. Bowman, *Transcript of the Original Text of the Samaritan Chronicle Tolidah* (1957), 16a–17b (Heb. with Eng. notes); E.N. Adler and M. Seligsohn (eds.), *Une Nouvelle Chronique Samaritaine* (1903), 51–61.

[Ayala Loewenstamm]

BABBITT, MILTON (1916–), U.S. composer and theorist. Born in Philadelphia, Babbitt started playing violin at the age of four and played in jazz performances and composed popular songs in high school. His father's involvement in mathematics stimulated Babbitt's interest in the subject. In 1931 he began studying mathematics at the University of Pennsylvania, but soon he transferred to the study of music at New York University. In 1935 he was a student of Roger Sessions in composition at Princeton University and in 1938–42 became a staff member there. During World War II Babbitt was active as a mathematician both in research (Washington) and teaching (Princeton University). In 1948 he rejoined the Department of Music at Princeton University, where in 1960 he became Conant Professor of Music. From 1973 he was a member of the composition faculty of the Juilliard School, and taught as a guest lecturer in the U.S. and Europe. His 1983 Madison lectures were published as *Words about Music*. Babbitt received several honors, including membership in the American Academy of Science and Letters (1986) and its Gold Medal in Music (1988).

Together with Roger Sessions, Elliot Carter, and George Perle, Babbitt represents the stratum of the American avant-garde which was devoted to the rational methods in composition. He wrote the first formal and systematic research paper on Schoenberg's compositional method (1946). In his articles of the 1950s and 1960s Babbitt was a pioneer in his thinking on music, involving terms from mathematics, such as "source set," "secondary set," "derived set," "combinatoriality." In his innovative compositions of that time Babbitt sought to use and sometimes to combine Schoenberg's and Webern's technique of composition. From the 1970s and on the composer continued his intellectual search in 12-tone sound combinatoriality. During the 1960s and 1970s he also worked with the synthesizer, experimenting with electronic sounds.

BIBLIOGRAPHY: NG²; MGG²; A. Mead, *An Introduction to the Music of Milton Babbitt* (1994).

[Yulia Krenin (2nd ed.)]

BABEL, ISAAC EMMANUILOVICH (1894–1940), Russian writer. He was born in Odessa, then the center of Yiddish as well as Hebrew literature (both Mendele and Bialik lived there), of Jewish communal and political life (Odessa was, simultaneously, the center of Zionist and Socialist movements), a cosmopolitan port with a strong Western European orientation. Although Russian was not, strictly speaking, Babel's native or even second language (he grew up in a Yiddish-speaking milieu, and his first literary efforts were written in French), he is now generally acknowledged as one of the truly great Russian stylists, and probably the most sophisticated Russian prose writer to emerge by mid-20th century. At the same time Babel is a profoundly Jewish writer not only in his choice of settings and of subject matter, but also in a more profound sense. His imagination is nourished primarily by the tension between his Jewish ethos and the non-Jewish environment and by his inability to conquer within himself traces of residual Jewishness, particularly those of a moral character.

Babel was not a prolific writer. His renown rests chiefly on two collections of short stories, *Red Cavalry* (*Konarmiya*, 1926) and *Odessa Tales* (1927). Together with two plays, *The Sunset* (1928) and *Maria* (1935), several tales and a few film scripts, these constitute his entire literary legacy.

The incongruities and paradoxes that are so characteristic of Babel's work are also, by a strange coincidence, to be found in Babel's biography. He fought for the Communist cause in the ranks of Cossack horsemen, those traditional archenemies of Jewish shopkeepers, whose role in the antisemitic pogroms Babel knew from personal experience and had, in fact, described in sharp outline in "The History of My Dovecote." A peaceful intellectual, he sought acceptance by fierce warriors. Only recently emancipated from a religious orthodoxy, he desperately tried to embrace a secular faith that was even more rigid. The author of a book that made an army immortal, he was denounced by that army's commander, Semyon Budyonnyi, as a slanderer. A fighter for the Soviet regime, he was executed by it..

A disciple of Flaubert and Maupassant, Babel excelled in the highly polished *conte*, often an extended anecdote related by the protagonist in his own language – be it a peasant dialect, soldier slang, or the strongly Yiddish-accented Russian of Odessa slums. Few writers could equal Babel in the ability to portray a character by means of a few malapropisms, a partiality for a single "fancy" foreign word, or a slightly irregular syntactical construction.

In the neo-Romantic Babel the traditional motif of infatuation with a "noble savage" is found often and in many different forms. Babel, however, posits the problem somewhat differently. Where other writers – from Rousseau to Tolstoy – saw a confrontation between an intellectual and the natural man, Babel sees a Jew aspiring to the status of a pagan, yet destined to remain frustrated in his desire by the restraints of the Jewish ethic. Try as he may, he will never learn the ways of violence and will, therefore, never gain acceptance into the gentile world: in one of his tales the narrator vainly implores Providence to grant him "the simplest of all proficiencies, the ability to kill fellow men." He loses his best friend, Afonka Bida (to an ear attuned to Yiddish, "the Russian Misfortune") because he would not shoot a wounded comrade. To be admitted into a circle of Cossacks, he must first hideously kill a goose – but then, that night, he must wrestle with his Jewish conscience which abhors murder. Babel's Jewish narrator envies his non-Jewish protagonists' ability to kill one's own father, trample to death a former master, or shoot a black marketeer masquerading as a helpless mother. His Jewishness and hence his alienations have numerous attributes – he wears glasses, he cannot learn to swim, he is a poor horseman, he carries with him books.

It is this envy of what he saw as gentile physical strength and absence of moral restraints that caused Babel to create a gallery of Jewish protagonists who bore little resemblance to pathetic Jews described in certain Yiddish literature or to the Zionist dreamers and visionaries in certain modern Hebrew novels. Babel's Odessa Jews who "bubble like cheap red wine" include an imposing amazon, who presides over a den of thieves and a brothel, dignified beggars with patriarchal beards who oversee Jewish cemeteries and discourse on the vanity of human existence, and the legendary Benya Krik ("Bennie the Howl"), a colorful gangster, the terror of Odessa's merchants and policemen. Babel's scenes of resplendent Jewish wedding feasts and magnificent funeral processions are reminiscent of the lush canvases of a Breughel.

The picturesque world of Polish Ḥasidim and Odessa cart drivers, of waterfront philosophers and ritual slaughterers was disappearing before Babel's eyes, a victim of secularism, pogroms, and the Revolution. Its death was recorded in some of Babel's best tales. A few of these relate only an amusing or a paradoxical incident – e.g., an old-age home receives a new lease on life as a funeral cooperative, but only for as long as it continues the swindle of not burying the corpse together with the only coffin it owns; the first honest funeral arranged by it will also spell its doom. Other stories have moral overtones of varying degrees of significance. An infant is named Karl by its Communist atheist parents in honor of Marx; but the grandparents conspire to have it secretly circumcised and the infant emerges with the hybrid name Karl-Yankel (i.e., Jacob). A rabbi's son joins the Communist Party but, for the time being, continues to live with his parents because he does not want to leave his mother. Just as Babel, long after ceasing to believe in God, could not shed the commandment "thou shalt not kill," so the rabbi's son remains faithful to another commandment which makes it incumbent upon us to honor our parents. In another story, the rabbi's son ultimately leaves his parental home to fight and then to die for the Revolution, but the break with his past is tortured and incomplete: among the killed soldier's belongings his comrades find a portrait of Lenin and another of Maimonides, Communist Party resolutions with Hebrew verse written in their margins, the text of the *Song of Songs*, and some empty cartridges.

The inability to shift one's allegiances completely was most poignantly illustrated in the short story "Gedali." The protagonist, an old Jew, the owner of a Dickensian curiosity shop, is puzzled because murder and looting are his town's lot no matter whether its current masters are Communist or anti-Communist: how then, he asks, can one tell which is the Revolution and which the counter-revolution? Old Gedali cannot agree to the proposition that ends justify means. He is troubled because the Revolution demands that all of the old values, the good as well as the bad, be discarded: "To the Revolution we say 'yes,' but can we say 'no' to the Sabbath?" And he tells his Communist visitor that what the world really needs is not more politics, but an International of Good Men, in which all men could live in peace and harmony, and in which "every soul would get first category rations."

After some twenty years of disgrace, Babel – or, more precisely, his memory – was cleared by the Soviet authorities of the false charges which caused his arrest and death. His best known works were reprinted in the 1950s and in 1966 but subsequently he was again ignored in the Soviet Union.

[Maurice Friedberg]

His Life

Until the age of 16, Babel was provided, by private tutors, with a thorough Jewish education, including Hebrew, Bible, and Talmud. At the same time he attended a Russian commercial school in Odessa. During his student years he seems to have been active in Zionist youth circles. In 1915, after graduating from the Kiev Institute of Financial and Business Studies, he went to Petrograd, where he had to avoid the police because as a Jew he had no residence permit. It was in prerevolutionary Petrograd that his first two stories were published in Maxim Gorki's *Letopris* (November 1916; in English in *The Lonely Years*, 1964). After the revolution, he served on the Romanian front in 1918 and contracted malaria. According to his autobiographical note, the details of which are sometimes contested, he subsequently served the new regime in various functions, e.g., in the Cheka (security police), the Commissariat of Education, in "expeditions for provisions" (i.e., confiscating agricultural products in the villages), in the northern army against the White counterrevolutionaries, etc. During his service on the Polish front in Budyonny's 1st Cavalry Army, he developed asthma, and while convalescing in Odessa and the Caucasus, between 1921 and 1924, he wrote and published most of his Jewish *Odessa Tales*.

In 1931, while reporting on the collectivization in the Ukraine, Babel conceived a full novel or a cycle of stories on the collectivization. One chapter appeared in *Novy Mir* (October 1931), but it did not meet ideological requirements and the publication was stopped. Only one other chapter was found and published posthumously (both are in *The Lonely Years*). A fragmentary story called "The Jewess" (published for the first time in the New York Russian magazine *Novy Zhurnal*, June 1968, and in English in *You Must Know Everything*) also seems to have originated in the same period as the beginning of a full-fledged novel. In 1928 and 1932 he was allowed to visit his wife and daughter, who had emigrated to Paris. Babel was sent abroad for the last time as a member of the Soviet writers' delegation to a left-wing congress in Paris in 1935, but in the meantime he had virtually stopped publishing. The literary authoritarianism inaugurated in 1934 with the establishment of the Soviet Writers Union induced him to become "a master of silence." He continued writing incessantly but evaded publishing by finding various excuses. "With the death of Gorki" (1936), says his daughter, Natalie, "Babel lost not only a friend but a powerful protector. The ground crumbled under him." Babel was arrested and disappeared in 1939, and all his manuscripts, except those which were deposited with personal friends, were probably destroyed by the secret police. The reason for his arrest is unknown, though Ilya *Ehrenburg indicated in a speech in 1964 that it was somehow connected with his frequent visits to the house of the head of the secret police (NKVD), Nikolai Yezhov, whose wife Babel had known for a long time. Since Yezhov was deposed and executed in 1938, there might be something to this theory. Officially the date of his death was subsequently given as 1941, but after his arrest he was never seen in a camp or in exile, and apparently he was executed in January 1940.

Babel's ties with Judaism never ceased. Six of his stories appeared in 1926 in Hebrew translation, "edited by the author," in the only issue of *Bereshit*, a Hebrew literary almanac in the U.S.S.R. In 1937 he was given the task of preparing the jubilee edition of *Sholem Aleichem's works. He reported for a newspaper on the new Jewish agricultural settlements established in 1928. Though not religious, he went to synagogue on the Day of Atonement, celebrated with his friends the Passover *seder*, and in his letters always reminded his family of approaching festivals. Jewish themes were constantly on his mind as a writer, from the folkloric "Shabbos Nahamu" (intended as the first story in a cycle centered on the figure of Hershele Ostropoler) to the Judaic concept of a "revolution of good people" in the *Red Cavalry* story "Gedali."

The first English edition of *Red Cavalry* appeared in 1929 and the *Collected Stories* (with introduction by Lionel Trilling) in 1955. His other writings became known in the West only in the 1960s, when his daughter, Nathalie, edited and published in English *The Lonely Years*, 1925–1939 (1964) containing unpublished stories and private correspondence and *You Must Know Everything* (1969), which also includes a biographical introduction and speeches and reminiscences by I. Ehrenburg, Konstantin Paustovsky, and others. Since that time his stories have appeared in various English editions along with his 1920 diary (1995) depicting the cruelty of the Polish and Russian armies toward the Jews. A definitive edition of his collected works, edited by his daughter, was published in 2001.

BIBLIOGRAPHY: J. Stova-Sander, *Isaac Babel', 1894–1941: l'homme et l'oeuvre* (1968); A.B. Murphy, in: *Slavonic and East European Review*, 44 (1966), 361–80; I. Ehrenburg, *Memoirs, 1921–1941* (1963), 108–18 and index; R. Rosenthal, in: *Commentary*, 3 (1947), 126–31; *Russkiye Sovetskiye Pisateli: Prosaiki*, 1 (1959), 103–18 (incl. bibl.). **ADD. BIBLIOGRAPHY:** H. Bloom, *Isaac Babel* (Modern Critical Views Series, 1987); A.N. Pirozhkova, *At His Side: The Last Years of Isaac Babel* (1996).

BABEL, TOWER OF, the edifice whose building is portrayed in Genesis 11:1–9 as the direct cause of the diversity of languages in the world and the dispersion of mankind over all the earth. According to the preceding narrative, mankind after the flood was descended from one common ancestor, *Noah. The story of Babel thus explains how the descendants of this one man came to be so widely scattered and divided into separate nations speaking so many different languages.

The story relates how, at the time when all men still spoke one language, there was a migration from the East to the plain of *Shinar (Babylonia). At this site it was decided to build a "city and a tower with its top in the sky," so that the builders would be able to make a name for themselves and avoid being scattered over the entire world. However, their building project was frustrated by the Lord who confounded their language. As a result, mankind was distributed over the face of the earth. The unfinished tower was called Babel, a name which was explained by its resemblance to the Hebrew verb *bll* ("to confuse"), since here the Lord "confounded the speech of the whole earth."

Scholars agree that the edifice referred to in Genesis 11 is clearly a *ziqqurat*, or Mesopotamian temple tower. The *ziqqurat* (from Akk. *zaqāru*, "to raise up," "elevate") was the central feature of the great temples which were built in all important Mesopotamian cities. Rising in progressively smaller, steplike levels from a massive base, these towers ranged from three or four stories to as many as seven and were ordinarily constructed of crude sun-dried bricks covered with kiln-fired bricks. Clearly, the writer of the account in Genesis 11 was familiar with the building techniques of Mesopotamia, since he is at pains to point out that bricks and bitumen were used in the construction; that is in contrast to the stone and clay which were the common building materials in Canaan.

The particular *ziqqurat* described here was formerly identified with the tower of Ezida, the temple of the god Nebo (Nabû) in Borsippa, a city southwest of Babylon. However, the discovery at the end of the 19th century of Esagila, the great temple of *Marduk in *Babylon, has led most scholars to agree that it is the tower of this temple which inspired the writer of Genesis 11. This *ziqqurat*, which was called E-temen-an-ki, "house of the foundations of heaven and earth," rose to a height of about 300 feet, and contained two sanctuaries: one at its base, which was 300 feet square, and one at its summit. The tower was probably constructed at the time of *Hammurapi, but was damaged or destroyed several times and repaired by Esarhaddon (seventh century B.C.E.) and Nebuchadnezzar II (sixth century B.C.E.), among others. It is interesting to note that the Babylonians believed that Esagila was built by the gods, thus making the statement in Genesis 11:5 "… which the sons of men had built," particularly meaningful, since it may be understood as a polemic against this belief. This tower, which was the object of such pride among the Babylonians, was the product of strictly human endeavor which can be quickly and easily destroyed in accordance with the Divine Will. In fact, it is quite likely that it was the sight of the ruins of Esagila (which was destroyed in the mid-16th century B.C.E with the destruction of Babylon by the Hittites) which inspired the creator of the Tower of Babel narrative.

Although it is clear from the story that the work on the city and tower displeased the Lord, the specific sin of the builders is nowhere mentioned. Many scholars believe that it was the presumption of these men in thinking that they could build a tower with "its top in the sky," and their conceit in wanting "to make a name" for themselves, which incurred the wrath of the Lord. Others believe that their goal was to storm the heavens and that it was for this sin that mankind was punished.

Modern scholars (already anticipated by R. *Samuel ben Meir) have pointed out that the desire to remain together in one place was in direct conflict with the divine purpose as is expressed to Noah and his sons after the flood: "Be fertile and increase and fill up the earth" (Gen. 9:7) and was, therefore, an affront to God and so necessarily doomed to failure. It is hardly likely that the expressed wish to "make a name for ourselves" could be construed as sinful, since a similar phrase is used in connection with the divine promises to Abraham (Gen. 12:2). Further, Babylonian temple inscriptions frequently refer to the "making great" of the name of the king under whom the particular temple was built or repaired, thereby demonstrating that this formula was commonly used in such instances and need not be understood as expressing an inordinate desire for fame. As for the phrase "with its top in the sky," it has been noted that there are several examples of Babylonian temple inscriptions which describe buildings as reaching to heaven so that the phrase should be understood not as an expression of the presumption of these people or of their desire to ascend to heaven, but rather as a borrowing by the biblical writer from the technical terminology of Mesopotamian temple inscriptions with which he was evidently familiar. According to this interpretation the sin of these people was, therefore, not presumption or a desire to reach heaven and gain fame, but rather an attempt to change the divinely ordained plan for mankind.

A new link to an ultimate cuneiform background of the Tower of Babel narrative has been provided by a Sumerian literary work, no doubt composed during the third Dynasty of Ur, which states that originally mankind spoke the same language, until Enki, the Sumerian god of wisdom, confounded their speech. Though the reason for the confusion of tongues is not stated, Kramer has suggested that it may have been inspired by Enki's jealousy of another god, Enlil. Hence, in the Sumerian version it was a case of the rivalry between two gods, whereas in the Bible the rivalry was between God and man (see below, "The Meaning of the Story").

The etymology of the name Babel given in this narrative is a contrived one, used ironically. The Babylonians understood it to mean "the gate of the god" (*bāb-ilim*), thereby endowing the city with additional honor and importance. By a play on words, the Bible has given it a pejorative sense, making the pride in this city seem almost ludicrous.

The Tower of Babel narrative is a turning point in history, as understood by the Bible, in that it signals the end of the era of universal monotheism which had existed since the beginning of time. Since the divine election of Abraham and his descendants immediately follows, it must be tacitly assumed that the incident led to the introduction of idolatry into the world.

[Myra J. Siff]

The Meaning of the Story

The bridge which some modern writers have constructed between the single short clause "and fill the earth" in Genesis 1:28 (or 9:7) and the account of the vain attempt of an early generation of men to avoid dispersal in Genesis 11:1–9, is superior homiletics but (quite apart from the finding of source analysis that the one belongs to document P and the other to document J) unsound exegesis. Genesis 1:28 reads as follows: "God blessed them [namely, the human beings, male and female, whose creation has just been narrated in the preceding verse] and God said to them, 'Be fertile and increase, fill the earth and master it; and rule the fish of the sea, the birds of the sky, and all the living things that move about on earth.'" This purports to be, and is, not a command but a blessing; moreover "and fill the earth" is preceded by "be fertile and increase." It is absurd to read into it a wish of God that the human species shall spread over the earth otherwise than as, with increasing numbers, its own interests may dictate. And in 11:1–9 there is nothing to suggest that the human population has already attained such a figure that there is a need for a migration of colonists to realms beyond the confines of the plain of Shinar; and neither is there a word in 11:1–9 about that being the Deity's motive in bringing about the dispersal. Instead, there is an explicit declaration of an entirely different motive by no less an authority than the Lord himself, who explains to the divine beings, verses 6–7; "If this is what, as one people with one language common to all, they have been able to do as a beginning, nothing they may propose to do will be beyond their reach. Come, let us go down, etc." It takes a willful shutting of the mind to avoid hearing the same anxiety lest man should wrest complete equality with the divine beings (or worse) in these words as in the Lord's earlier explanation to the same audience, in 3:22, of his motive in driving man out of the Garden of Eden: "Now that man has become like one of us in knowing good and bad [i.e., in being intellectually mature, the first evidence of which was his newfound modesty], what if he should stretch out his hand and take also from the tree of life and eat, and live forever!" Once, to obviate the danger of further baleful results from cooperation between man and snake, the Lord set up a barrier of enmity between them (3:15); now, in order to eliminate the threat of disastrous consequences from the cooperation of men with each other, he is erecting among them barriers of language and distance.

[Harold Louis Ginsberg]

In the Aggadah

The biblical account of the Tower of Babel is singularly brief and vague (Gen. R. 38). The prevailing opinion of the rabbis is that it was designed to serve the purposes of idolatry and constituted an act of rebellion against God (Sanh. 109a; Gen. R. 38:6; et al.), for which reason they also associated Nimrod ("the rebel") with its building (Ḥul. 89a). Many additional reasons are also suggested, among them the fear of a recurrence of the flood and the need to guard against such a recurrence by supporting the heavens or by splitting them so that waters would drain away slowly from the earth's surface (*Ma'asim al Aseret ha-Dibberot*; cf. Sanh. 109a). According to Josephus they were trying to dwell higher than the water level of the flood (Ant., I, IV). In this way the builders thought they would be spared, believing as they did that God had power over water alone (PdRE 24). At the same time the rabbis laud the unity and love of peace that prevailed among them (Gen. R. 38), as a result of which they were given an opportunity to repent, but they failed, however, to seize it (*ibid.*). Various opinions are expressed as to the punishment which the builders incurred (Tanḥ. B., 23). According to the Mishnah (Sanh. 10:3), they were excluded from a share in the world to come. In the view of one *amora*, their punishment varied with the differing aims that inspired them; those who thought to dwell in heaven being dispersed throughout the world, those who sought to wage war against God being transformed into apes and demons, and those bent on idol worship being caught up in a confusion of tongues (Sanh. 109a). One-third of the tower was destroyed by fire, one-third subsided into the earth, and one-third is still standing. It is so high that to anyone ascending and looking down from the top, palm trees look like locusts (*ibid.*). This *aggadah* testifies to the existence of ruins at that time, which were popularly believed as being of the Tower of Babel. *Aggadot* about the tower are also to be found in Josephus and in the apocrypha (cf. Jub. 10:18–28), while several of its motifs are much discussed in Hellenistic Jewish literature.

[Israel Moses Ta-Shma]

In the Arts

The biblical story of the tower of Babel appears repeatedly in medieval and Renaissance literature, treated as an historical incident with strong moral overtones. Some examples are the *Chronicon* of Isidore of Seville (c. 560–636 C.E.), the *Weltchronik* of Rudolf von Ems (1200–1254), and the *Speculum humanae salvationis* (c. 1324), a Dominican manual of devotion which was frequently copied. Giovanni *Boccaccio wrote on the subject in his *De casibus virorum illustrium* (1355–60), as did an anonymous poet of Lyons in *Le Triumphe de Haulte Folie* (c. 1550). Two 17th-century Spanish works were entitled *Torre de Babilonia*: one was an *auto sacramentale* by the eminent dramatist Pedro Calderón de la Barca, the other by the Marrano author Antonio Enríquez *Gómez. Modern treatments include *Tower of Babel* (1874) by the English poet Alfred Austin and *Babel* (1952), an apocalyptic work by the French poet Pierre Emmanuel (1916–1984).

The subject appealed to medieval artists, appearing in 12th-century mosaics at Palermo and Monreale in Sicily and in the 13th-century Cathedral of St. Mark, Venice. There are representations in illuminated manuscripts from the 12th to the 14th centuries, including the German *Hortus Deliciarum* (Garden of Delights) and the Sarajevo *Haggadah*. Two 15th-century painters who used the theme were the Frenchman Jean Fouquet and the Italian Benozzo Gozzoli, who painted the fresco of Campo Santo, Pisa, now destroyed. With its landscape setting and the opportunities it offered for fantasy and close observation of the daily scene, the Tower was of considerable interest to the early Flemish painters. It was generally depicted either as a multistory structure, diminishing in size as it rose or, more often, as a square or circular building surrounded by a ramp. Some artists illustrated contemporary building methods, a fine example occurring in the Book of Hours of the Duke of Bedford (Paris, c. 1423), where the construction of the Tower proceeds at night under the stars. In Pieter Brueghel's *Tower of Babel* (1563), the building – leaning slightly – is shown in a vast landscape near the banks of a river, with a king arriving to inspect the progress of the work.

Although the Babel story might appear to be a temptation to composers, since the confusion of tongues can be expressed most effectively in music, very few works have in fact been written on the theme. These are mainly oratorios including César Franck's *La Tour de Babel* (1865) and Anton Rubinstein's markedly unsuccessful *Der Turm zu Babel* (1858; revised as an opera, 1872). Two 20th-century works are *La Tour de Babel* (1932) by René Barbier and Igor Stravinsky's *Babel*, a cantata for narrator, men's chorus, and orchestra (1944, published in 1952).

BIBLIOGRAPHY: IN THE BIBLE: Abraham Ibn Ezra, Commentary to Gen. 11:1–9; M.D. Cassuto, *Mi-No'aḥ ad Avraham* (1959^3), 154–69; S.R. Driver, *The Book of Genesis* (1904^2), 132–7; Kaufmann Y., Toledot, 2 (1960), 412–5; N.M. Sarna, *Understanding Genesis* (1967), 63–80 (incl. bibl.); J. Skinner, *The Book of Genesis* (ICC, 1930), 223–31; S.N. Kramer, in: JAOS, 88 (1968), 108–11. IN THE AGGADAH: Ginzberg, Legends, index; U. Cassuto, *Commentary on the Book of Genesis*, 2 (1964), 225–49; J. Gutmann, in: *Oz le-David [Ben Gurion]* (1964), 584–94. IN THE ARTS: H. Minkowski, *Aus dem Nebel der Vergangenheit steigt der Turm zu Babel: Bilder aus 1000 Jahren* (1960); LL. Réau, *Iconographie de l'art chrétien*, 2 pt. 1 (1957), 120–3, incl. bibl.; T. Ehrenstein, *Das Alte Testament im Bilde* (1923), 125–32; H. Gressmann, *Tower of Babel* (1928), 1–19.

BABILÉE (Gutmann), JEAN (1923–), French dancer and choreographer. Babilée studied at the Paris Opera's ballet school and as a child showed astonishing technical facility and natural grace. His career began in Cannes during the German occupation, where he distinguished himself in *Le spectre de la rose* and the Bluebird pas de deux from *The Sleeping Beauty*. In 1945 he became the star of Roland Petit's Le Ballets des Champs Elysées (1945–50) in the role of *Jeune Homme et la Mort* (1946). His own choreography includes *L'Amour et son Amour* (1948) and *Til Eulenspiegel* (1940), as well as one of his best for the Monte Carlo opera – *Balance à trois* (1955). During the 1950s and 1960s he acted in French films and stage productions. In 1967 he earned the Gold Star for best dancer at the International Festival Dance in Paris. In 1979, at the age of 56, he danced in *Life*, created for him by Béjart. In 1995 a film, *Babilée '95*, was shown in France.

BIBLIOGRAPHY: *International Enyclopedia of Dance*, vol. 1, p. 251.

[Amnon Shiloah (2nd ed.)]

BABIN, VICTOR (1908–1972), pianist and composer. Babin was born in Moscow. He graduated from the Riga Conservatory in 1928, and then studied composition with Franz Schreker and piano with *Schnabel in the Berlin Hochschule fuer Musik (1928–31). He married the Russian pianist Victoria (Vitya) Vronsky in 1933 and with her formed a two-piano team, which soon became the most celebrated in the world. They immigrated to the United States in 1937; from 1951 to 1955, Babin was director of the Aspen Institute, Colorado, and director of the Cleveland Institute of Music from 1961 until his death. Babin composed mostly for Vronsky/Babin performances. Among his works are two concertos for two pianos and orchestra and other compositions for one and two pianos, chamber music and songs.

[Max Loppert and Marina Rizarev (2nd ed.)]

BABI YAR, ravine on the outskirts of *Kiev which has come to symbolize the murder of Jews by the *Einsatzgruppen* (mobile killing units) in the German-occupied Soviet Union and the persistent failure to acknowledge Jewish memory.

On September 19, 1941, the advancing German army captured Kiev, the capital of the Ukraine. Within a week, a number of buildings occupied by German military and civilian authorities were blown up by the NKVD, the Soviet secret police. In retaliation, the Germans proceeded to kill all the Jews of Kiev. An order was posted throughout the city in both Russian and Ukrainian:

> Kikes of the city of Kiev and vicinity! On Monday, September 29, you are to appear by 7:00 A.M. with your possessions, money, documents, valuables and warm clothing at Dorogozhitshaya Street, next to the Jewish cemetery. Failure to appear is punishable by death.

From the cemetery, the Jews were marched to Babi Yar, a ravine only two miles from the center of the city. A truck driver at the scene described what he saw:

> I watched what happened when the Jews – men, women and children – arrived. The Ukrainians led them past a number of different places where one after another they had to remove their luggage, then their coats, shoes, and overgarments and also underwear. They had to leave their valuables in a designated place. There was a special pile for each article of clothing. It all happened very quickly … I don't think it was even a minute from the time each Jew took off his coat before he was standing there completely naked….
>
> Once undressed, the Jews were led into the ravine which was about 150 meters long and 30 meters wide and a good 15 meters deep…When they reached the bottom of the ravine they were seized by members of the Schultpolizei and made to lie down on top of Jews who had already been shot. That all happened very quickly. The corpses were literally in layers. A police marksman came along and shot each Jew in the neck with a submachine gun … I saw these marksman stand on layers of corpses and shoot one after the other … The marksman would walk across the bodies of the executed Jews to the next Jew who had meanwhile lain down and shoot him.

In the days between Rosh Hashanah and Yom Kippur, the Jewish New Year and the Day of Atonement, 33,771 Jews were murdered at Babi Yar. In the following months, Babi Yar remained in use as an execution site for "gypsies" (Roma and Sinta) and Soviet prisoners of war. Soviet accounts after the war speak of 100,000 dead. Research does not substantiate such a number. The true number may never be known.

In August 1943, in the face of the Red Army advance against German troops, the mass graves of Babi Yar were dug up and the bodies burned in an attempt to remove the evidence of mass murder. Paul Blobel, the commander of *Sonderkommando* 4a, whose troops had slaughtered the Jews of Kiev, returned to Babi Yar. For more then a month, his men and workers conscripted from the ranks of concentration camp inmates dug up the bodies. Bulldozers were required to reopen the mounds. Massive bone-crushing machinery was brought to the scene. The bodies were piled on wooden logs, doused with gas, and ignited.

When the work was done, the workers from the concentration camp were killed. Under cover of darkness on September 29, 1943, 25 of them escaped. Fifteen survived to tell what they had seen.

Despite efforts to suppress the memory of Babi Yar, after the war the Soviet public at large learned of the murders through newspaper accounts, official reports, and belles lettres. In 1947 I. Ehrenburg in his novel *Burya* ("The Storm") described dramatically the mass killing of the Jews of Kiev in Babi Yar. Preparations were made for a monument at Babi Yar as a memorial to the victims of Nazi genocide. The architect A.V. Vlasov had designed a memorial and the artist B. Ovchinnikov had produced the necessary sketches.

But since the Soviet antisemitic campaign of 1948–49, an effort was made to eliminate all references to Babi Yar. This policy had as an objective the removal from Jewish consciousness of those historical elements that might sustain it. Even after the death of Stalin, Babi Yar remained lost in the "memory hole" of history. Intellectuals, however, refused to be silent. On Oct. 10, 1959, the novelist Viktor Nekrasov cried out in the pages of *Literaturnaya Gazeta* for a memorial at Babi Yar, and against the official intention to transform the ravine into a sports stadium. Far more impressive was the poem *Babi Yar* written by Yevgeni *Yevtushenko published in the same journal on Sept. 19, 1961.

> No gravestone stands on Babi Yar;
> Only coarse earth heaped roughly on the gash:
> Such dread comes over me.

With its open attack upon antisemitism and its implied denunciation of those who rejected Jewish martyrdom, the poem exerted a profound impact on Soviet youth as well as upon world public opinion. Dmitri Shostakovich set the lines to music in his 13th Symphony, performed for the first time in December 1962.

Russian ultranationalism struck back almost immediately. Yevtushenko was sharply criticized by a number of literary apologists of the regime and then publicly denounced by Premier Nikita Khrushchev in *Pravda* on March 8, 1963. The theme of a specific Jewish martyrdom was condemned. But Babi Yar would not remain suppressed. It again surfaced during the summer of 1966 in a documentary novel written by Anatoly Kuznetsov published in *Yunost* (Eng. tr. 1967). Earlier that year the Ukrainian Architects Club in Kiev held a public exhibit of more than 200 projects and some 30 large-scale detailed plans for a memorial to Babi Yar. None of the inscriptions in the proposed plans mentioned Jewish martyrdom. Only after the collapse of the Soviet Union did the new Ukrainian government acknowledge the specific

Jewish nature of the site and an appropriate rededication was held.

By the 2000s plans were underway for the creation of a Jewish Community Center and an appropriate Jewish memorial on the site. No stranger to controversy, the new use of the site has been challenged by some as being too close to the massacre site and being built therefore on sacred soil.

BIBLIOGRAPHY: Y. Yevtushenko, *A Precocious Autobiography* (London, 1963); W. Korey, in: *New Republic* (Jan. 8, 1962); idem, in: *Saturday Review* (Feb. 3, 1968); S.M. Schwarz, *Yevrei v Sovetskom Soyuze 1939–1965* (1966), 359–71. **ADD. BIBLIOGRAPHY:** E. Klee, W. Dressen, and V. Riess, *The Good Old Days: The Holocaust As Seen by Its Perpetrators and Bystanders* (1988); I. Ehrenburg and V. Grossman, *The Black Book* (1981).

[William Korey / Michael Berenbaum (2nd ed.)]

BABOVICH, SIMḤAH BEN SOLOMON BEN NAHAMU (1790–1855), Karaite *ḥakham* in the Crimea, living in Eupatoria (Yevpatoriya). Babovich mainly devoted himself to obtaining more rights for the Karaites in Russia. In 1827, in conjunction with the Karaite scholar Joseph Solomon *Luzki, he obtained exemption of the Karaites from the law pertaining to military service for Jews. The Karaites in Eupatoria commemorated this event in an annual prayer. In 1829/30 M. Jost asked Babovich to send him some Karaite books and to give him some information about these books. In 1830 Babovich made a pilgrimage to the Land of Israel together with A. *Firkovich, who at that time was a tutor of his children and his secretary. They visited Jerusalem, Hebron, Cairo, and Constantinople. In 1839 the Karaite Spiritual Council was founded through his support and he was appointed its head and remained so until his death, although he was not distinguished as a scholar. At the same year Babovich was instructed by the government to provide exact information on the origin, nature, and history of the Karaites. Babovich turned to A. *Firkovich, who then proceeded to produce a series of documents, some partly falsified.

He financially supported the Karaite community, donating the income from his mill to the community and after his demise bequeathed to it the village he had received from the government.

BIBLIOGRAPHY: O.B. Beliy, in: MAIET, 10 (2003), 664–66; A. Harkavy, *Altjuedische Denkmaeler aus der Krim* (1876), 206, 270 ff.; R. Fahn, *Sefer ha-Keraim* (1929), 94ff; J.M. Jost, *Geschichte des Judentums und seiner Sekten*, 2 (1858), 374; Isaac b. Solomon, *Pinnat Yikrat* (1834, with letters from Jost and their Tatar translation); Fuerst, Karaeertum, 3 (1869), 137; A. Firkovich, *Avnei Zikkaron* (1872), 2, 5, 18ff.; E. Deinard, *Massa Krim* (1878), 20–40.

[Golda Akhiezer (2nd ed.)]

BABYLON (Heb. *Bavel*, בָּבֶל, Gk. Βαβυλὼν), ancient city on the eastern bank of the Euphrates River in what is now Iraq. (In contemporary convention, "Babylon" is used for the city name and "Babylonia" for the country. In biblical Hebrew בבל is used for both.) Its ruins lie within the suburbs of the modern city of Baghdad. No satisfactory etymology for the city's name has been proposed. Akkadian scribes derived the name from the words *bāb-ili* ("gate of god"), but in Genesis 11:9 the name is explained derogatorily as a derivation from the root *bll* ("to confuse"). The English word follows the Greek spelling.

Biblical tradition lists the city with Erech and Akkad in the land of Shinar (Gen. 10:10), as one of the earliest cities in Babylonia. This view of the antiquity of Babylon was also current in Babylon itself in the period after *Hammurapi, but in fact before 2050 B.C.E. the city was only a small provincial town.

The first certain mention of Babylon in cuneiform texts is from the time of the Third Dynasty of Ur (2112–2004 B.C.E.), when it served as a provincial capital and seat of a governor. During the Isin-Larsa period (2017–1794) it became the capital of a small independent kingdom under an Amorite dynasty. Its kings enjoyed unusually long reigns, and this may symbolize the stability which allowed them eventually to take a dominant role in Mesopotamian politics. The city gained fame during the time of Hammurapi (1792–1750 B.C.E.), when it extended its influence over most of southern Mesopotamia through diplomacy and then military conquest. The kings of Babylon saw themselves as heirs of the Old Akkadian rulers who had first unified Mesopotamia 400 years before. Under Hammurapi's son Samsu-iluna, however, the southern part of the kingdom was lost.

During the subsequent Middle Babylonian period Babylon continued as a capital city in southern Mesopotamia. Assyria in northern Iraq tinkered in Babylon's politics. Under the Assyrian king Tukulti-Ninurta I (1244–1208), Babylon was partially destroyed. When Tiglath-Pileser III (745–727) took Babylon, he gave it the status of an independent kingdom united to Assyria. In Babylon he reigned under another name, Pulu, which is found in the Bible (II Kings 15:19). Shalmaneser V (726–722) continued the practice of employing another name in Babylon, Ululayu, an adjective meaning "of the sixth month," commemorating the month of his birth. The Chaldean Marduk-apla-iddina (biblical *Merodach-Baladan (Akk. Marduk-apla-iddina)) proclaimed an independent kingdom upon Shalmaneser's death, but *Sargon II (722–705) overthrew him in 710; and, though he did not adopt a different throne name in Babylon, he made it his residence for a time and added "the king of Akkad, governor of Babylon" to his titles.

Following Sargon's death Merodach-Baladan Marduk-apla-iddina returned, and this may be the time of his correspondence with *Hezekiah of Judah (2 Kgs. 20:12–19, II Chr. 32:31). Babylon again became a center of resistance to Assyria, inspiring the Assyrian king Sennacherib to destroy the city in 689, an act widely viewed as sacrilegious. His son Esarhaddon (680–669) rebuilt the city and expressed piety toward its gods. At the end of his life he divided his kingdom between his two sons, making Shamash-shum-ukin his heir in Babylon and Assurbanipal in Assyria. But Shamash-shum-ukin thwarted his father's plans by trying to make southern Mesopotamia completely independent of Assyria. Assurbanipal besieged

Babylon and recovered it from his brother, but at considerable cost to the strength of the empire.

As Assyria was collapsing, in 626 Nabopolassar, a Chaldean, made himself king of Akkad at Babylon. He and his successor, *Nebuchadnezzar II, proceeded to build the Neo-Babylonian empire at the expense of the Assyrians.

As the capital of the Neo-Babylonian empire, to which Judah was forcibly annexed in 586, Babylon underwent a vast program of public building and fortification. After the fall of the empire to the Persians, Babylon still maintained its dominant position. With the fall of the Persian Empire to Alexander the Great, Babylon offered no resistance and was made the capital of his new empire. But Seleucus I Nicator (312–281), Alexander's successor, founded Seleucia not far away on the Tigris, and the inhabitants of Babylon slowly moved to Seleucia, deserting Babylon, which may have been uninhabited in the first centuries of our era.

As early as the 1780s visitors observed that the site had been looted. Major excavations were conducted by the German architect R. Koldewey (1855–1925) from 1899 to 1917. These excavations revealed data for all levels of occupation from Old Babylonian (1894–1595 B.C.E.) to Parthian times (250 B.C.E.–224 C.E.), but their main importance lay in the extensive evidence for the Neo-Babylonian period (625–539 B.C.E.). Old Babylonian levels were rarely reached, and the high water table impeded excavation of early periods. The excavations are important also in the history of archaeology because Koldewey was the first European systematically to try to trace mud brick architecture and to distinguish between buildings and later pits, leading to what we call stratigraphy.

Koldewey uncovered two palaces of Nebuchadnezzar and an ancient fortress that adjoined the interior wall of the city. The façade of one palace was made of enamel-covered bricks, decorated with pillars and capitals in various colors on a blue background. The royal throne was located in an alcove in the wall opposite the entrance. The hanging gardens referred to by Greek authors including Diodorus Siculus (60–30 B.C.E.) (2, 10:1, "the garden called hung") and considered one of the wonders of the world have never been identified archaeologically. In the palace were discovered clay tablets upon which were inscribed allocations of food for those who ate at the king's table, including *Jehoiachin, the last legitimate king of Judah.

To the east of the palaces passed the main road, which was used for processions of the Babylonian New Year celebration. At the road's northern end the processions passed into the inner city by way of the Ishtar Gate, which was decorated with reliefs of fanciful animals with lion's feet. This gate has been partly reconstructed in Berlin and features in all histories of Mesopotamian art.

South of Nebuchadnezzar's palace, at the end of the parade road, was a large temple of Marduk, Esagila ("The house lifting [its] head [proudly]") whose walls were made of trees decorated with gold, marble, and precious stones. North of it stood the *ziqqurat*, a pyramid-shaped structure built in stepped stages on a square base. Each of its sides was 295 ft. (91 m.) long. The highest tower had a great temple according to Herodotus (1:181), who, however, may never have visited the city. The city and its suburbs, which extended to the west of the Euphrates, were connected by a bridge. Herodotus said that the city had many three- and four-story buildings (1:180).

The greatness of Babylon left its mark in biblical sources. Isaiah 13:19 called Babylon "the glory of kingdoms, the splendor and pride of the Chaldeans" while praying for its fall. Jeremiah was deeply concerned about Babylon, and his book has more than half of the references to the city in the Bible; in his day how one was to relate to Babylon was a major issue, and the prophet himself may have been seen by the Babylonians as a collaborator since he counseled not resisting Babylonian power.

Babylon's city-god, Marduk, became the dominant state god perhaps when Nebuchadnezzar I (1125–1104) recovered Marduk's statue from *Elam; the god was represented in the Creation Epic as having supremacy over the entire pantheon conferred on him by the other gods. Later the god was called Bel, "lord." Both names are known in the Bible, in Jeremiah 50:2 ("Bel is put to shame, Merodach is dismayed") and 51:44 ("and I will punish Bel in Babylon") and in Isaiah 46:1 ("Bel bows down, Nebo [another Babylonian god] stoops").

Babylon became synonymous in apocalyptic thought with decadence and evil and was sometimes equated with Rome and its empire. (For the figure in Christian apocalyptic see Rev. 17). But for most Jews it remained a real place where members of a thriving Jewish community made their homes. The Babylonian Talmud, for example, recalls that Babylon's Jewish community was healthy in terms of its orthodox practice in contrast to others in Media and Elam (Kid. 71b).

BIBLIOGRAPHY: R. Koldewey, *The Excavations at Babylon* (1914); E. Unger, *Babylon, die heilige Stadt* (1931); S.A. Pallis, *Early Exploration in Mesopotamia* (1954) 11–15; A. Parrot, *Babylon and the Old Testament* (1958); S.N. Kramer, in: EM, 2 (1965), 10–27; C.J. Gadd, in: CAH, 1 (1965), ch. 22; H.W.F. Saggs, in: D.W. Thomas (ed.), *Archaeology and Old Testament Study* (1967), 39–56; idem, *The Greatness That Was Babylon* (1962); J. Oates, *Babylon* (1979); R. Zadok, in: ZA, 74 (1984), 240–44; J.-C. Margueron, in: ABD, 1:563–65; H.W.F. Saggs, *Babylonians* (1995); E. Klengel-Brandt in: E. Meyers (ed.), *The Oxford Encyclopedia of Archaeology in the Near East*, 1 (1997), 251–56; J. Baer, in: *Brill's New Pauly* 5 (2004), 1125; M. Van de Mieroop, *King Hammurabi of Babylon* (2005).

[Daniel C. Snell (2nd ed.)]

BABYLONIA, ancient country in Mesopotamia between the Tigris and the Euphrates Rivers; corresponding approximately to modern *Iraq. Babylonia is the Greek form of the name *babili* – sometimes translated as "gate of God" – known from cuneiform texts.

Introduction

The area was settled by the Sumerians in the third millennium B.C.E. Sargon I (24th century B.C.E.) founded the Akkadian dynasty, which dominated the area for 200 years. At a later period (c. 1850 B.C.E.) the *Amorites (*mar-tu*, "people of the west") ruled over northern Babylonia. The city gained greater strength during the time of *Hammurabi (1792–1750 B.C.E.) when it extended its influence over most of southern Mesopotamia, as well as over parts of northern Mesopotamia. Later rulers of the area were the *Hittites, Kassites and the Assyrians. The Assyrian kingdom was overthrown in 612 B.C.E. and succeeded by the neo-Chaldean kingdom of which the outstanding figure was *Nebuchadnezzar II (604–562 B.C.E.). However, 25 years after his death, the country was captured by *Cyrus, king of Persia, and ceased to exist as an independent kingdom.

For a full description of this period up to Cyrus see *Mesopotamia.

Achaemenid Period

A turning point in Near Eastern history was heralded by the Medes' conquest of the Assyrian capital, Nineveh, in 612 B.C.E., and arrived when Babylon fell to the Achaemenid Persians in 539. After two millennia of Semitic rule in the ancient Near East, an age was beginning in which Iranians and then others would dominate; but the new masters of the area would continue to draw heavily on the older cultural heritage.

The first important Achaemenid, Cyrus, conquered Media in 549, Lydia in 546, and Babylon in 539; next, Cambyses took Egypt in 525; then *Darius extended the empire into northern India by some time before 513. This conquest ranks in its speed and its scale with the later exploits of Alexander (for whom it may have served as a model) and with the initial spread of Islam. While Persepolis, in an upland valley of what is today southwestern Iran, remained the Achaemenids' ceremonial capital, much of the business of the extended empire was handled from Susa, at the edge of the Mesopotamian plain. Babylon, further to the west, became a more local administrative center.

Organized into a score of satrapies or provinces and held together by an effective system of roads, communications, and standardized coinage, the empire introduced a largely new conception of legitimacy or imperial ideology to the area. The ancient Near Eastern empires had often ruled by the forcible displacement of local institutions or had placed them in subservient vassal relationships by treaty. The Achaemenids, though still relying on the universal language of force, sought to exercise it by posing as heirs of local dynastic traditions and by following wherever expedient the local idiom. Thus in Egypt the Persian kings ruled as pharaohs, and in Babylon as kings of Babylon; and Isaiah 45 provides evidence that Jews in Babylonia on the eve of the Persian conquest expected Cyrus to be the anointed of the Lord. On taking Babylon, Cyrus did not in fact promulgate the Judean cult but restored a variety of local cults. He relates in a cylinder inscription (Pritchard, Texts, 315) that he restored to their localities the divine images which Nabonidus, the last Babylonian king, had carried off to Babylon. Later, Darius reprimanded his satrap Gadatas in Asia Minor for abuse of local shrine property (text in A.T. Olmstead, *History of the Persian Empire*, 156). The policy seems to have been one of religious tolerance provided that subject populations were politically docile (Ezra 1 and 4–7); Xerxes' inscription in which he tells of suppressing the worship of *daevas*, gods false by Zoroastrian standards (text *ibid.*, 232) could be interpreted either as a case of political rebellion or of heresy in the Iranian heartland, to which the lenient policy of more westerly regions was inapplicable. In any event, diversity of religion under imperial patronage appears to have replaced the Near East's earlier close association of palace and temple wherever Jews were concerned.

Exiled from Judea by the Babylonians in 597 and 586 B.C.E., a small community of leading Judeans whose experience was to be adopted as the spiritual heritage of all Israel had been settled along the canals of Babylon (Ps. 137:1), such as the Chebar (Ezek. 1:1) and in ruined sites, such as Tel-Abib (Ezek. 3:15), Tel-Melah, and Tel-Harsha (Ezra 2:59; Neh. 7:61), which they were apparently expected to rebuild and cultivate (cf. Jer. 29:4–5). The initial feeling in this "foreign land" was one of intense yearning for Jerusalem (Ps. 137). Some not clearly datable biblical materials may describe this experience, such as the Tower of Babel account (Gen. 11, commonly regarded as much earlier), which associates the problem of linguistic diversity with the locality of Babylon; but Ezekiel provides the clearest contemporary evidence for conditions at the start of the Exile.

Following the Achaemenids' permission to return to Palestine and restore the Judean cult, there is virtually no specific evidence concerning the status of the Jewish community of Babylon. That such a community remained there is evident from its mention, for example, as the home of Ezra, and from its existence in post-Achaemenid times. Later tradition emphasizes the continuity of the Babylonian community; the *Seder Olam Zuta* sets forth a line of exilarchs back to the deported Jehoiachin (Jeconiah), the next to last of the kings of Judah – evidence at least that the idea of exiles who did not return was credible later on. Scholars have sought to document Jewish business success in Babylonia on the basis of personal names in cuneiform texts of the family of Murashu in Nippur from the reign of Artaxerxes I, an attempt which while plausible puts severe strain on the linguistic evidence. That, in the course of time, Jews attained positions of privilege and responsibility is inferred from Nehemiah's service as cupbearer at the Achaemenid court. Some may not have been trusted; Eusebius (*Eusebius Werke*, ed. by R. Helm 7 (1956), 112–3) relates Artaxerxes III's deportation of Jews to Hyrcania, on the Caspian Sea, as the result of a revolt around 350 B.C.E.

Seleucid Period

Alexander led a Macedonian army in the conquest of Babylon in 331 B.C.E. and died there after his Bactrian and Indian campaigns in 323. His generals thereupon dismembered his empire in a struggle for control of it. The dynasty of Seleucus, which was to rule Mesopotamia for two centuries, was heir to a domain without a stable ethnic base or heartland.

Whereas Persians had been rulers of "Iran and non-Iran," as later usage put it, the Macedonian Seleucids were rulers only of non-Macedonia. Seleucid imperial policy, therefore, began as a colonial policy throughout all the realm: it called for the founding of new cities, populated by immigrant Macedonian and Greek garrisons, administrators, and merchants, strategically situated and fortified along the principal roads and rivers. Seleucia on the Tigris, founded by Seleucus I, was one of these, and it tended to flourish at Babylon's expense. Antiochus I transferred a considerable Semitic population to Seleucia from Babylon in 275 B.C.E., a policy of centralization causing a decline in Babylon's material fortunes which is documented in cuneiform literature.

The initial Hellenization of Babylonia was followed in time by a more complex interaction between Seleucid institutions and those of the indigenous populations. In the name of royal if not divine prerogative, Antiochus III began to tap temple treasuries to pay the indemnity he owed after losing to the Romans, but encountered stiff resistance and was killed during one such attempt at a temple in Elam in 187. Antiochus IV sought to strengthen a shaky empire by extending Greek communities and institutions in the older centers of the empire, including a refurbishing of Babylon. But it was a desperate and futile attempt to stem the tide of history, and amounted to a Greek veneer on Semitic Babylon; the old local institutions survived, and individuals bore double, Greek-Babylonian, names. The Babylonia which came under Parthian rule in 129 B.C.E. was still ethnically and culturally heterogeneous.

With the Greeks as a ruling minority in Babylonia, the Jews as a subject minority appear to have prospered by trusting and being trusted. Josephus reports that Alexander reaffirmed the privileges which the Persians had accorded them (Ant., 11:338). Jews served in the Greek armies: Josephus (Apion, 1:192) mentions Alexander's excusing Jewish soldiers on grounds of religious scruples from the army's work on the temple of Bel in Babylon; and a Jewish contingent (in c. 220 B.C.E.) aided in the defense of Babylonia against a Galatian invasion (II Macc. 8:20). Antiochus III sent 2,000 Jewish families, about 210 B.C.E., as settlers to assist in an effort to control Asia Minor (Jos., Ant., 12:147–53).

The extent to which during the second century B.C.E. the declining fortunes of the Seleucids undermined any common interest between the Jews of the Babylonian Diaspora and the imperial government is difficult to judge, again owing to the scarcity of sources; but Babylonian silence during the Maccabean uprising in Palestine suggests that, to the end of Seleucid rule, loyalties were determined with reference primarily to local rather than distant conditions. A mark of Seleucid times which lasted when others passed was the Babylonian Jews' use of the Seleucid era (counting the years from 312 B.C.E.) as the basis of dating under Parthian and Sassanian rule down to the time of the *geonim*.

[Willard Gurdon Oxtoby]

Parthian Period

The Parthians, an Iranian people, were originally a nomadic tribe called the Parni. They had settled in the region east and north of the Caspian, called Parthia, and so came to be called by the name of that territory. The Arsacid dynasty was founded about 240 B.C.E. by Arsaces, and all subsequent rulers bore that name. The expansion of the Parthian territory began with the annexation of Hyrcania, but moved slowly until the Seleucid Empire had been weakened elsewhere. Then the Parthians rapidly inherited the portions of the empire east of the Euphrates. Mithridates I, the real founder of the Parthian Empire, ascended the throne in 171, reached Media in 155, and Seleucia on the Tigris in 141. For the next 20 years, Babylonia was contested by Parthians, Seleucids, and the Hellenistic state of Characene. By 120, however, Mithridates II had permanently established his rule on the Euphrates' frontier. Since the Parthians were fundamentally a military aristocracy, they were concerned with fostering local support among indigenous populations. They made little effort to win over the conquered peoples to their culture and religion. They preserved Greek legal forms and allowed the Jews to continue their usual way of life. The Greek colonies in the region accepted Parthian rule, which promised free access to, and preserved the security of, the trade routes of Central Asia. The Seleucids' attitude to the Jews was favorable, and the Jews allied themselves with their regime.

From around 120 B.C.E. to their fall in 224 C.E., the Parthians treated the Jewish settlements well. Palestinian Jewry under the Hasmoneans and Arsacid Parthia had a common interest in the destruction of Seleucid power. In 140/39, a circular from Rome informed the various countries of the civilized world, including Parthia, of Roman friendship for the Jews (I Macc. 15:16–24; Jos., Ant., 14:145–7). In 129 B.C.E. Hyrcanus was forced to accompany the Seleucid Antiochus VII in a Parthian campaign. As soon as he could, he returned to Palestine and reestablished his independence of the Seleucids. According to tannaitic tradition (TJ, Ber. 7:2, 11b; Naz. 5:5, 54b; Eccles. R. 7:12) a Parthian embassy was sent to the court of Alexander Yannai (104–78 B.C.E.). It may be that the embassy was intended to arrange joint opposition to the rise of the Armenian Tigranes, who invaded both Palestine and Parthian Babylonia around 87 B.C.E., and exiled Palestinian Jews to his empire. After their great victory over Rome at Carrhae, in 53 B.C.E., the Parthians for more than a decade became the dominant power in the Middle East, and attempted to contest Roman rule in Palestine. In 40–39 B.C.E., they deposed Herod, the ally of Rome, and put in his place as ruler of Judea Antigonus, nephew of Hyrcanus the Hasmonean. Elsewhere in the Middle East they replaced pro-Roman with pro-Parthian dynasties. The Parthian general, Pacorus, was killed in a brief engagement in 38 B.C.E., whereupon the Parthians withdrew across the Euphrates. Rome quickly reestablished her hegemony, which was never again seriously threatened by the Parthians. For the next century, domestic instability paralyzed the Parthian government.

Information on Babylonian Jewry under Parthian rule is not abundant. There is information on a Babylonian Jew, *Zamaris (Zimri), who emigrated to Palestine during Herod's reign. He went with his feudal retinue (Jos., Ant., 17:23ff.). All the information about him points to him as a Babylonian Jewish noble, who had fully mastered the arts of war as practiced by the Parthians. In later times, we hear of Babylonian Jews called Arda, Arta, and Pyl-y Barish; Arda/Arta would be the equivalent of the Hebrew Barukh, justified or blessed. Pyl-y Barish, meaning elephant rider, is also an Iranian name. These Jews (referred to in Git. 14b; TJ, Kid. 3:4, 64a) were dressed like Parthian nobles, in the tall *bashlyk* ("high hat") characteristic of the nobility. They were, moreover, well acquainted with the common law, for they insisted that rabbinical collectors of funds for the Palestinian schools supply them with a quit-claim for a silver cup being transported to Palestine. The Palestinians reported that the nobles had great power: "If they give an order to arrest you, you are arrested; to kill you, you are killed." They enjoyed the usual retinue of horses and mules. It may therefore be inferred that among the Jews in Babylonia was an upper class of "assimilated" nobility, familiar with Parthian culture and possessing considerable legal learning, as well as authority in the Jewish community. About the traditions and culture of the mass of Jews, who were farmers and tradesmen, nothing is known. It may be supposed that they revered the Scriptures, Jerusalem, and the Temple cult. There are many references to Babylonian pilgrimage before 70 C.E. The Babylonian Jews accepted the Jewish calendar from the Jerusalem authorities. Traditions on Hillel and Nahum "the Median" are confused, enigmatic, and in no way probative. What sects or groups existed is not known. About 40 C.E., the royal family of *Adiabene, situated between two tributaries of the Tigris, converted to Judaism. Josephus reports (Ant., 18:314ff.) that two Jewish brothers, *Anilaeus and Asinaeus (Ḥanilai, Ḥasinai) established a "Jewish state" in Babylonia, which lasted from about 20 to about 35 C.E.

Babylonian Jewry did little, if anything, to support the war against Rome. Its chief interest lay in the Temple cult. When the Temple was destroyed, the Romans quickly employed Josephus to absolve them of war-guilt, and he addressed himself specifically to "our brethren across the Euphrates." Similarly, the Bar Kokhba Revolt of 132–135 attracted no perceptible support from the Babylonian Jews. By contrast, when *Trajan invaded the Parthian Empire, in around 114 to 117, a great rebellion broke out behind his lines in the Jewish-occupied territories he had taken. The Jews in Cyprus, Egypt, and Cyrenaica also revolted. The chronology of Trajan's campaign is difficult to establish. It is not known for sure when the Jewish rebellions took place, or whether they were coordinated. The Babylonian one, however, seems clearly related to the Parthian cause.

The Jews normally profited from their position on both sides of the contested frontier between Rome and Parthia. The exilarch and patriarch, moreover, cooperated in the silk trade, one of the chief commodities of international commerce. Silk was imported to Babylonia from the Far East, transshipped for reweaving according to Roman taste from the coarse, thick fabric of China to the preferable sheer weave desired in Rome, and then manufactured into garments. The textile factories of Syria and Palestine thus depended upon a steady supply of silk. Ḥiyya, Simeon the son of Judah ha-Nasi, and Rabban Simeon b. Gamaliel together traded in silks at Tyre (Gen. R. 77:2) and Judah b. Bathyra of Nisibis and Abba b. Abba, father of Samuel, similarly were in the silk trade (Mid., Sam I. 10:3). Other evidences of Jewish participation in the silk trade are found in Christian Syriac sources (W. Cureton, *Ancient Syriac Documents*, 14). Silk merchants were, indeed, among the chief transmitters of Pharisaic Judaism and Christianity in the Orient. The earliest Christian apostles to Edessa and elsewhere in the Parthian Empire were originally Jewish silk merchants. Any effort to rearrange the trading routes of the Middle East thus would adversely affect the Jewish merchants of Babylonia and Palestine. Jewish opposition to Trajan may well have been motivated by considerations of international trade. But even without that the memory of the Roman destruction of the Temple would certainly have supplied a sufficient cause for opposition. Whether a messianic impulse motivated still others is not proved one way or the other. Further unrest in Palestine in the time of Parthian-Roman struggles, specifically in 161–165 and 193–197, suggests that some Jews regarded Parthian success as the harbinger of the Messiah. This is made quite explicit by Simeon b. Yoḥai, who said that if a man saw a Persian (Parthian) horse tethered to a gravestone in Palestine, he should listen for the footsteps of the Messiah.

Pharisaic Judaism exercised little influence in Babylonian Jewry before the destruction of the Temple. Only two Pharisaic authorities resident in the Parthian empire are known. One was Judah b. Bathyra, who was stationed at Nisibis, and was in charge of collecting and transmitting the contributions of the Jews of Mesopotamia to the Temple in Jerusalem. The other collection center was at Nehardea, in Babylonia, where lived Nehemiah of Bet Deli, about whom little more is known than that he lived in Babylonia before 70 C.E. and was originally a Palestinian Pharisee (Yev. 16:7). The first rabbinical academies were established in Parthian territory as a direct consequence of the Bar Kokhba Revolt. During the war and the consequent repressions, the students of Ishmael fled from Palestine to Huzal, in central Babylonia, and some of those of Akiva went to Nisibis. The latter, however, soon returned while those of Ishmael remained. There they educated the first native-born and -bred rabbis of Babylonia, in particular Aḥai the son of Josiah, and Issi b. Judah; other Babylonian *tannaim* included the group from Kifri, Ḥiyya, Rav, Rabbah b. Ḥana; and among the later figures were Ḥanina b. Ḥama, and the Nehardeans Abba b. Abba, father of Samuel, and Levi b. Sisi.

Nathan, son of the exilarch, was sent by his father to Palestine for studies with Akiva. The exilarch probably extended a warm welcome to Palestinian refugees, and certainly made use of the graduates of their academies in his courts and administration. Among Babylonian Jewry was a class of native-born aristocrats, who probably acted, like other Parthian nobles, as local strongmen. In attempting to create a central administration for the Jewish community, the exilarch found useful the well-trained lawyers coming out of the Pharisaic-rabbinic schools, who were eager to enforce "the Torah" as they had learned it in Pharisaic traditions, and, unlike the Jewish nobility, were dependent solely upon the exilarch for whatever power they might exercise. For his part, the exilarch made use of the rabbinical bureaucrats to circumvent the power of the local Jewish nobility. Their claim to exposit "the whole Torah" as revealed to Moses at Sinai would have won for themselves and their patron considerable popular attention and support. The Palestinian schools after 140 were anxious to retain control of the new academies in Babylonia. When, therefore, in about 145 C.E. Hananiah, a nephew of R. Joshua b. Hananiah, presumed to proclaim the Jewish calendar in Babylonia, the Palestinians sent two sages, one of them the grandson of the last high priest in Jerusalem, to rebuke him (Ber. 63a; TJ, Sanh. 1:2, 19a; Ned. 6:13, 40a).

Sasanian Period

The change of dynasty from Arsacids to Sasanians represented more than the mere exchange of one Iranian royal family for another. The Parthians had, as stated, few, if any, cultural pretensions. They bore no special fealty to a particular divinity or cult. They ruled their vast empire mostly through local satraps or (as in the Jewish instance) ethnic-religious figures, dependent upon them for legitimation, but bound mainly by ties of feudal loyalty. Throughout the whole period of their rule, they made extensive use of the Jews, in particular, as allies in international politics and trade. When Artapan V fell, Rav lamented, "The bond is parted" (Av. Zar. 10b–11a), and rightly so, for the ancient alliance between Iran and Israel in Babylonia had come to an end.

The Sasanians on the other hand sought not merely to reign but to rule. They originated as a priestly family in a temple in Staxr, in Fārs (Persia), and never neglected the divinities who, they believed, had favored them with a royal throne and empire. They moreover determined to rule directly, not merely through feudal powers, and so established great bureaus of administration in the capital Ctesiphon. They claimed the Achaemenids as their ancestors, and intended to recreate the glorious empire of their alleged forebears, including its religion. Unlike the Arsacids, they had had no experience in ruling a heterogeneous population. While the Arsacid Empire had gradually expanded from northeastern Iran so that it slowly gained experience in governing Hellenes, Jews, Syrians, Babylonians, and other Semites, not to mention other Iranian peoples, the Sasanians came to power suddenly. They emerged in a few years from the obscurity of a provincial temple to the authority of the whole Iranian Empire. They supposed, therefore, that they might quickly convert everyone to the worship of Ohrmazd, Anahita, and other divinities held sacred in Persia proper, and they founded a "state-church," hierarchically organized just like the secular bureaucracy, to achieve just that end. As a result the situation for Jewry suddenly deteriorated.

The Sasanian administration used the Mazdean religion to strengthen its hold on Iran proper, including Babylonia, as well as on Armenia, Georgia, Adiabene, and other regions. The Jews probably suffered, but certainly not alone. The times of Ardashir (224–41) proved difficult. There are, however, few unequivocal accounts of "persecutions of the Jews" or of Judaism. Two important talmudic stories show that the status of the Jewish community had changed radically. First, the Babylonian Talmud, *Bava Kamma* 117a contains the story of the execution of capital punishment in a Babylonian Jewish court by R. Kahana. Rav thereupon said, "Until now, the Greeks [= Parthians], who did not punish bloodshed, were here, but now the Persians, who do punish bloodshed, are here." R. Kahana was advised to flee to Palestine. Second, R. Shila administered lashes to a man who had intercourse with a gentile woman. The man informed against the Jewish judge, who successfuly hoodwinked the Persian agent (*frestak*) who had come to investigate the execution of judgment without proper government authorization (*hermana*). These stories prove that the status of the Jewish government required renegotiation. Apparently at the outset the Jews supposed they could continue as before. The Sasanian regime quickly made it clear that they could not. There are, moreover, some references to "decrees against Judaism." The Babylonian Talmud, *Yevamot* 63b, records that the Mazdean Mobads "decreed concerning meat… the baths… and they exhumed the dead." Use of fire on Mazdean festivals was restricted; Rav was asked whether one may move a Ḥanukkah lamp "on account of the Magi" on the Sabbath (Shab. 45a). An equivocal reference suggests that "the Persians destroyed synagogues" (Yoma 10a). In any event, Jews clearly at this time preferred the rule of Rome, as is clear from Rav's statement (Shab. 11a).

When *Shapur I came to power in 242, however, he extended freedom of religious and cultural life to all the disparate peoples of the Iranian Empire, hoping eventually to unify the disparate empire, possibly through the syncretistic teaching of Mani, who included in his pantheon Jesus, Zoroaster, and Buddha (though not Moses). Further, since the Persians planned to renew war with the West, it was to Shapur's advantage to reconcile the peoples of the Tigris-Euphrates Valley, whose brethren lived on the other side of the frontier. Shapur's success with Babylonian Jewry was complete. During his raid into Asia Minor in 260, he besieged Caesarea-Mazaca, the greatest city in Cappadocia. The Talmud (MK 26a) reports that when the amora Samuel heard Shapur had slain 12,000 Jews there, "he did not rend his clothes." The same account reports that Shapur told Samuel he had never killed a Jew in his life, "but the Jews of Caesarea-Mazaca had brought it on themselves." In the west, however, Shapur's armies pillaged, burned, and killed; they were out not to build a new empire in the Roman Orient, but to destroy an old one. So the Jews, among other peoples behind the Roman lines, fought for their lives and for Rome. A far greater threat to Babylonian Jewry came from the transient Palmyrene Empire, created by Odenathus (Papa b. Nezar of talmudic sources), who in 262–263 conducted a quick invasion of central Babylonia and devastated Jewish settlements there. Since Jewish and Palmyrene merchants competed with one another, an economic motivation may have played some part in the attacks on the Jews. The Palmyrene siege of Ctesiphon was raised by Shapur, but not before Nehardea was destroyed. The Jews of both Palestine and Babylonia applauded the fall of Odenathus' wife and successor, Zenobia.

Since the chief threat to Jewry lay in the cessation of the right to self-government, it was important to Samuel and to the exilarch whom he served to regain autonomous government. The early Sasanian regime, as noted, insisted upon supervising the Jewish court system. The best way to end that supervision was to agree at the outset that "the law of the land is law." This Samuel decreed (see *Dina de-Malkhuta Dina). The saying specifically applied to rules of land acquisition and tenure, collection of taxes, and similar matters of interest to the state. It was a strictly temporary and narrowly political agreement, which did not affect the religious or cultural policies of the Persians. The rabbis continued to work through prayer and study of Torah to hasten the coming of the Messiah, who would end the rule of all pagan kings and put into power the King of the king of kings.

Shapur I was succeeded by Hormizd I (272–73), Bahram I (273–76), Bahram II (276–92), and Bahram III (292). In the time of the Bahrams, Kartir, a leading Mazdean religious official, became a powerful influence in state policy. Calling himself "Soul-savior of Bahram," Kartir first saw to the martydom of Mani and the banishment of Manichaeans. He then turned to the extirpation of other non-Mazdean religions; in his famous inscription, he refers to his "opposition" to Jews, Brahmans, Nazoreans, Christians, and Manichaeans, among others. Shapur's policy of religious toleration, not to mention syncretism, was thus effectively reversed. There is little evidence in rabbinical sources to verify Kartir's claim to have given the Jews much trouble. The Babylonian Talmud, Gittin 16b–17a, tells the story that a Magus came and removed a lamp from the room of the ailing master, Rabbah b. Bar Ḥana, who thereupon exclaimed, "Merciful Lord! Either in your shadow or in the shadow of the son of Esau!" *Judah b. Ezekiel further refers to the exclusion of Jews from the offices of canal supervisor and chiliarch (Ta'an. 20a). But the Jews seem to have suffered less than did the Manichaeans, who were martyred and banished, and the Christians, whose churches were destroyed. No rabbi is known to have enjoyed the attentions of the king of kings, but possibly the rabbis simply did not preserve stories of what contacts did take place, presumably because exilarchic agents and not they were involved in the negotiations. In the time of Narseh (293–301), whatever persecutions earlier took place were brought to an end. Narseh renewed the tolerant policy of his father, Shapur. The reference of *Seder Olam Zuta* to a persecution of Jews in 313 is unverified by any earlier, more reliable source. Shapur II (309–79), crowned king at his birth, was then four years old. The Sasanian government was weak, and the empire was in a state of disorder. Perhaps a local Mobad or government authority somewhere made trouble for the Jews. In 331, Rabbah b. Naḥamani, head of the academy of Pumbedita, was arrested because he was accused of assisting Jews to evade taxes. According to a legendary account the heavenly court required Rabbah's traditions on a matter of ritual cleanness, so he was called to heaven (BM 86a), but one can hardly base upon that a general persecution of the Jews. The Talmud contains stories about the friendship for the Jews of Shapur's mother, Ifra Hormizd, who is otherwise unknown (BB 8a, 10b; Ta'an. 24b; Nid. 20b, Zev. 116b). In any event, during the reign of Shapur II, the Jewish community was unmolested. That is an important fact, for in the same period, particularly after Shapur II unsuccessfully besieged Nisibis in 339, the Christian community was devastated. Priests and bishops were put to death and monks and nuns tortured and forced to violate their vows. Ordinary Christians were pressured to apostatize. In 363, *Julian "the Apostate" invaded the Iranian Empire and besieged Ctesiphon. Among the many towns and villages he destroyed was one Jewish town, Birta, specifically referred to by Ammianus Marcellinus and Sozomen (3,20). Piruz Shapur, with its large Jewish population, and probably Maḥoza, the Jewish suburb of Ctesiphon, were also destroyed. After Julian had proclaimed his intention of rebuilding a Jewish temple in Jerusalem, a local Babylonian pseudo-messiah called upon Maḥozan Jewry to follow him to Palestine. The Persian government massacred those who did so. The fortunes of war, rather than a specific Jewish policy, thus caused considerable hardship between 360 and 370. In his Armenian campaigns after 363, Shapur II deported from Armenia to Isfahan and other parts of the Persian Empire large numbers of Armenian Jews and Christians, with the intention of strengthening the economy of the territories sheltered from Rome by the Zagros mountains, including Fārs proper.

The Babylonian Talmud contains references to Yezdegerd I (397–417), who supposedly had some contacts with leading rabbis as well as with the exilarch. The persecution of Christians, renewed in 414, was not marked by similar treatment of the Jewish communities. Bahram V (420–38) is not referred to in Jewish sources. Yezdegerd II (438–57) in 456 decreed that the Jews might not observe the Sabbath. He was, according to Jewish sources, shortly thereafter swallowed by a serpent, in answer to the prayer of the heads of the academies Mar b. R. Ashi and R. Zoma. Firuz (459–86) persisted in his father's anti-Jewish policy. The Jews of Isfahan were accused of having flayed alive two Magi. Half of the Jewish population was slaughtered and their children given to Mazdeans. Firuz "the Wicked" also killed the exilarch Huna Mari, son of Mar Zutra I. The year 468 is called in the Talmud "the year of the destruction of the world," and, from that date to 474, synagogues were destroyed, study of Torah was prohibited, children were forcibly delivered to the Mazdean priesthood, and, possibly, Sura was destroyed. The next significant trouble took place in the time of Kovad I (488–531), when Mazdak arose as a prophet of the doctrine of community of property and women. Kovad accepted the doctrine and, among other groups, the Jews were persecuted when they rejected Mazdakism. The exilarch Mar Zutra II gathered an armed force and defended the Jewish community for seven years. He was captured and killed in 520, in Maḥoza. Nevertheless, a number of Jews then served in the Persian armies fighting the Byzantines. Information on the century between Kovad's death and the Arab conquest (640) is slight. Chosroes (531–78) was well liked by Iranian and Arab historians. The Jews were apparently well treated. The Christian Nestorians in his day found refuge in Persia from Christian Byzantine persecution. Apparently some persecutions of Jews recurred under Hormizd IV (579–80), and Pumbeditan rabbis took shelter in Firuz Shapur, near Nehardea, then under Arab rule. Under Chosroes Parwez (590–628) Jewish life returned to normal. When the Persians invaded Palestine and took Jerusalem in 614, they were enthusiastically welcomed by local Jewry.

For the continuation of Jewish history in this area see *Iraq. See also *Academies; *Exilarch; Babylonian *Talmud.

[Jacob Neusner]

BIBLIOGRAPHY: ACHAEMENID AND SELEUCID PERIODS: A. Berliner, *Beitraege zur Geographie und Ethnographie Babyloniens im Talmud und Midrasch* (1883); S. Daiches, *The Jews in Babylonia in the Time of Ezra and Nehemiah according to Babylonian Inscriptions* (1910); Juster, *Juifs*, 1 (1914); A.T. Olmstead, *History of the Persian Empire* (1948); Taubenschlag, in: *Journal of Juristic Papyrology*, 7–8 (1953–54), 169–85; S.K. Eddy, *The King is Dead, Studies in the Near Eastern Resistance to Hellenism* (1961). J. Oates, *Babylon* (1986); H. Sancisi-Weerdenburg and A. Kurht (eds.), *Achaemenid History*, vol. 2 (1987); M. Roaf, *Cultural Atlas of Mespotamia and the Ancient Near East* (1990); S. Dalley, "Babylon and the Hanging Gardens: Cuneiform and Classical Sources Reconciled," in: *Iraq*, 56 (1994), 45ff. PARTHIAN AND SASANIAN PERIODS: Neusner, Babylonia, 4 vols. (1965–69); S. Funk, *Die Juden in Babylonien*, 2 vols. (1902–08); J. Obermeyer, *Die Landschaft Babylonien im Zeitalter des Talmuds und des Gaonats* (1929); A. Christensen, *L'Iran sous les Sassanides* (1944^2); M. Beer, *Ma'amadam ha-Kalkali ve-ha-Ḥevrati shel Amoraei Bavel* (1962); R.N. Frye, *The Heritage of Persia* (1962).

BACALL, LAUREN (**Betty Joan Perske**; 1924–), U.S. actress. Born in New York, Bacall studied at the American Academy of Dramatic Arts and then turned to modeling. She was featured on the cover of *Harper's Bazaar* and within one month had a Hollywood contract. At the age of 19, Bacall co-starred in her first film with Humphrey Bogart, whom she married one year later (1945). Bacall made four of her first films with Bogart – *To Have And Have Not* (1944), *The Big Sleep* (1946), *Dark Passage* (1947), and *Key Largo* (1948). She also appeared in *How to Marry a Millionaire* (1953), *Woman's World* (1954), *The Cobweb* (1955), *Blood Alley* (1955), and *Designing Woman* (1957). After Bogart died in 1957, Bacall continued her career in films, which spanned more than half a century and included performances in *Written on the Wind* (1956), *Sex and the Single Girl* (1964), *Harper* (1966), *Murder on the Orient Express* (1974), *The Shootist* (1976), *The Fan* (1981), *Health* (1982), *Appointment with Death* (1988), *Mr. North* (1988), *Tree of Hands* (1989), *Misery* (1990), *A Star for Two* (1991), *Ready to Wear (Pret a Porter)* (1995), *The Mirror Has Two Faces* (1996), *My Fellow Americans* (1996), *Diamonds* (1999), *The Venice Project* (1999), *Presence of Mind* (1999), *The Limit* (2003), *Dogville* (2003), and *Birth* (2004).

In 1961 Bacall married actor Jason Robards, Jr. They divorced in 1969. Their son, Sam Robards, is a film and TV actor.

Bacall won a Tony Award for her performance in the Broadway musical *Applause* (1970). In 1997 she was nominated for an Academy Award as best supporting actress in *The Mirror Has Two Faces.* That same year *People* magazine chose her as one of the 50 Most Beautiful People in the World.

Her autobiography, *Lauren Bacall by Myself*, won a National Book Award in 1980.

In 1994 she wrote a book entitled *Now*, which is described as "part career memoir and part meditation on what it's like to be a single woman of lingering glamour, enduring vitality, and advancing age."

[Jonathan Licht / Ruth Beloff (2nd ed.)]

BACAU (Rom. **Bacău**), city in Moldavia, Romania. A Jewish community is attested there in the 18th century. A *ḥevra kaddisha* was established in 1774. In 1820 there were 55 Jewish taxpaying heads of families in Bacau. The Jewish population numbered 3,810 in 1859 and 7,902 (48.3% of the total) in 1899. From 1803 to 1858 Isaac of Botosani ("Botoshaner"), who acquired renown as a miracle worker (*ba'al mofet*) was rabbi there. A *talmud torah* was founded in 1828, the Po'alei Ẓedek Tailors' Association in 1832, a Ḥevrat Gomelei Ḥasadim (mutual aid society; their minute books are in the YIVO Archives) in 1836, and a Ḥevrat Mishnayot in 1851. When the Jewish autonomous organization lost its official status in Romania in 1862, communal activity in Bacau also disintegrated. After 1866 Bacau became one of the centers of anti-Jewish agitation in Romania, and the community suffered frequent persecution. During the last quarter of the 19th-century secular education began to spread among the Jews of Bacau and at the end of the 1870s and beginning of the 1880s one-third of the pupils in general schools in Bacau were Jewish. The first Jewish elementary school was founded in 1863. The main occupations of the Jews in Bacau were commerce and crafts: of the commercial enterprises in the town in 1899, 563 (85.6%) were Jewish, and there were 573 (66.6%) Jewish artisans in 1901. Bacau was also a center of Hebrew printing.

The Jewish population numbered 9,593 (30.8% of the total) in 1930, of whom 50.8% declared Yiddish as their mother tongue. By this time the community had a well-organized communal framework. It maintained a kindergarten, two primary schools (for boys and girls), a hospital, an old age home, an orphanage, and a *mikveh*, as well as 25 synagogues. Bacau was also a center of the Zionist movement. Among the rabbis of Bacau was Bezalel Ze'ev *Safran (1866–1930), who officiated there from 1905 until his death. A ḥasidic center operated in the Leca Street synagogue.

[Eliyahu Feldman / Lucian-Zeev Herscovici (2nd ed.)]

Holocaust Period

With *Antonescu's rise to power, the Jews of Bacau were subjected to repression; their property and shops were confiscated, and a part of the Jewish cemetery was adapted for agriculture. When war against the Soviet Union broke out (June 22, 1941), the Jews from towns and villages in the district were driven from their homes and sent to Bacau, whose Jewish community did its best to help as the city's Jewish population rose to 12,000. The community kitchen dispensed 1,000 meals a day and 1,000 families received financial aid. The men were sent to Transylvania and Bessarabia on forced labor. In the spring of 1944, when the front was drawing near, the Jews were forced to dig defense trenches. Under Soviet occupation in the summer of 1944, all the local officials fled and the Jewish community took over municipal affairs, keeping law and order, burying the non-Jewish dead, running the municipal hospital, and paying the salaries of the municipal employees. The postwar Jewish population reached a peak of 18,000 but most subsequently emigrated to Israel. In 2004 there were 359 Jews in Bacau.

[Theodor Lavi]

BIBLIOGRAPHY: Edmond (E. Schwarzfeld), *Radu Porumbaru si ispravile lui la fabrica de hartie din Bacau* (1885); A.D. Birnberg, "Comunitatea Bacau" (1888; mss. In YIVO Archives, New York); A. Lachower, in YIVOA, 10 (1955), 300–13; E. Feldman, in: *Papers of the Fourth World Congress of Jewish Studies*, 2 (1968), 219–22 (Heb.); PK Romanyah, I, 10–17; M. Carp, *Cartea Neagra* 1 (1946), 66, 118; C. Cristian, *Patru ani de urgie* (1945), index; W. Filderman, in *Sliha*, 3 (1956). **ADD. BIBLIOGRAPHY:** I. Voledi-Vardi, *Kehillat Bacau, Historiyah Yehudit Mefu'eret: Sefer R. Mayer Eibschuetz z.l.* (1990); I. Kara, *Obstea evreiasca din Bacau* (1995); I. Iancu, *Noi copiii strazii Leca*, 4 vols. (1999–2004); M. Mircu, *La noi, la Bacau* (2000); S. Costachie: *Evreii din Romania: aspecte geografice* (2003), 45–65.

°**BACCHIDES** (second century B.C.E.), Syrian general and governor of Seleucid territories west of the Euphrates. A friend of Demetrius I, Bacchides was given the task of installing Alcimus as high priest. To this end he was assigned a large body of troops, for it was evident that opposition would be forthcoming from Judah Maccabee and the other leaders of the Hasmonean uprising. The pious *ḥasidim, rejoicing at the sight of a priest from the tribe of Aaron assuming the office of high priest, were inclined to accept the peaceful overtures of Bacchides. However, he disregarded his oath and immediately slew 60 of the *Ḥasidim*, thus reuniting the bulk of the Jewish population behind Judah. Leaving an army with Alcimus, Bacchides handed the country over to him and returned to Syria. Meanwhile, Judah decisively defeated another Syrian general, Nicanor (13 Adar, 161 B.C.E.). Within two months Bacchides returned to Judea, accompanied by a force of 20,000 foot soldiers and 2,000 horsemen. Judah's army, camped near Elasa, dwindled from 3,000 to 800, and in the fierce battle that ensued Judah was killed. Bacchides again entrusted the administration of Judea to the Hellenists, while the rebels, led by Jonathan and Simeon, dispersed and fled south and beyond the Jordan. Bacchides succeeded in tracking Jonathan down, but waited until the Sabbath to attack the Jewish army, thinking that they would not fight. However, Jonathan fought back and the Syrian general suffered many casualties in an indecisive battle. Bacchides retreated to Jerusalem and fortified the citadel there. He also fortified many places around Jerusalem in order to strengthen the Seleucid hold on the city. Believing that the royalist rule was secure, Bacchides returned to Syria and remained there for two years (until 158). His last expedition to Judea, at the request of the Hellenists, was virtually a disaster. By that time Bacchides had become dissatisfied with those Jews who repeatedly urged him to attack the Hasmonean brothers. Sensing this, Jonathan proposed peace and a release of prisoners. Bacchides agreed, considering this the most dignified way of withdrawing, and returned for the last time to Syria.

BIBLIOGRAPHY: I Macc., 7:8–20; 9; Jos., Ant., 12:393–7, 420–34; 13:4–33; Schuerer, Gesch, 1 (1901[4]), 216ff.; Klausner, Bayit Sheni, 3 (1959[2]), 40–41, 46–53.

[Isaiah Gafni]

BACHARACH (**Bacherach**), town in the Rhine Valley, Germany. Jews were living in Bacharach in the first part of the 12th century and were engaged in moneylending. While the troops were assembling there in preparation for the Second *Crusade, several families left the town and took refuge in the nearby castle of Stahleck. Three householders who went on royal orders to collect their debts were martyred by the crusaders on the eve of Pentecost, 1147. In 1283, 26 Jews were massacred as the result of a *blood libel. Heinrich Heine's incomplete epic, *Der Rabbi von Bacherach*, was based on a massacre in 1287 following a blood libel in Oberwesel. The Jews in Bacharach were attacked by the *Armleder in 1338–39, and others lost their lives in the *Black Death persecutions, 1348–49. A document dated 1510 shows that the Jewish community had by then been reestablished. In the early modern era a synagogue and a ritual bath, probably used by the Jews of Bacharach, existed in nearby Steeg. There were 34 Jews living in the town in 1924 and 200 in the area in 1932. The five Jews who remained in Bacharach were deported by July 26, 1942 by the Nazis. A number of noted Jewish families derived their name from Bacharach (see next entry).

BIBLIOGRAPHY: Germ Jud, 1 (1963), 17; 2 (1968), 44; AWJD (June 9, 1967), 17; Kahlenberg, in: *Zwischen Rhein und Mosel*…, 17 (1967), 643ff. **ADD. BIBLIOGRAPHY:** H. Kuenzl, in: G. Heuberger (ed.), *Mikwe* (Ger., 1992), 23–88; K.H. Debus, in: *Bacharach und die Geschichte der Viertaelerorte* (1996), 319–26.

[Zvi Avneri]

BACHARACH (**Bachrach**; also spelled **Bacherach, Bachrich**), name of several families originally from *Bacharach on the Rhine. GOTTSCHALK OF BACHARACH is mentioned in Frankfurt in 1391 and EPHRAIM GUMBRECHT BACHARACH in 1457. MENAHEM (Man) BACHARACH was rabbi in Worms from 1506 to 1520. Two *dayyanim* named Bacharach are mentioned in 15th-century Mainz. There were two branches of the family living in Frankfurt in the 16th and 17th centuries. ISRAEL and TOBIAS BEN JOSEPH SOLOMON were martyred in *Ruzhany on Sept. 19, 1659, following a *blood libel. Tobias' descendants lived at Tiktin and include the talmudist *Judah b. Joshua Ezekiel Bachrach and Jacob b. Moses *Bachrach, author of a history of the Hebrew script. The first Bacharach known in Vienna is JUDAH LOEB BEN AARON (d. 1657). His grandson JACOB found refuge in Třebíč, Moravia, in 1670 and became a leader of the community there. His descendants are found in Konice and Třešt (both in Moravia). Two Bacharachs are mentioned in a list of Nikolsburg (Mikulov) Jews of 1765. The best-known line, founded in Bohemia, is represented first by ABRAHAM SAMUEL BEN ISAAC BACHARACH (1575–1615), who was rabbi in Worms. His wife Eva (Ḥavvah; 1580–1651) had a wide knowledge of Hebrew and rabbinical literature rarely found among women in her day. She died in Sofia on her way to Ereẓ Israel. Their son was Moses Samson *Bacharach and their grandson was Jair Ḥayyim *Bacharach. Common in Bohemia was the abbreviation Bacher. Others of the family in Hungary include the Hebrew poet Simon *Bacher and his son the scholar Wilhelm *Bacher.

BIBLIOGRAPHY: I.T. Eisenstadt and S. Wiener, *Da'at Kedoshim* (1897–98), 32–41, 213–4 (first pagination); Flesch, in: *Zeitschrift fuer die Geschichte der Juden in der Tschechoslowakei*, 2 (1931), 229–35.

BACHARACH, family of business, political, and communal leaders in Atlantic City, New Jersey. BENJAMIN (1865–1936) was a local merchant and banker. Born in Philadelphia, he and his brothers Isaac and Harry were brought to Atlantic City in 1881 by their parents. Benjamin served as president of the Beth Israel Synagogue of Atlantic City, in which the entire family was active. ISAAC (1870–1956) was a businessman and banker who pursued a political career. After serving on the Atlantic City Council (1907–13), Isaac, a Republican, was elected to the State Assembly in 1911 and in 1915 to Congress, where he represented the Second District of New Jersey until 1936. A member of the House Ways and Means Committee, Bacharach wrote the 1931 act providing for emergency loans based on the value of insurance policies. HARRY (1873–1947), a Republican, was appointed postmaster by President McKinley (1901) and was reappointed by President Roosevelt in 1905 and 1909. He won elections as mayor of Atlantic City in 1911, 1916, and 1932. He served for many years as member and chairman of the New Jersey Public Utilities Commission and as a member of the Water Policy Commission. He was also active in local banking, real estate, and civic affairs, and was a founder of the Jewish Community Center of Atlantic City (1924–25). The Betty Bacharach Home for Afflicted Children (Longport, New Jersey) was founded by the Bacharach brothers and two sisters in 1924 in memory of their mother.

BIBLIOGRAPHY: *Biographical Directory of the American Congress* (1961); Philip R. Goldstein, *Centers in My Life* (1964), 76, 159.

[Joseph Brandes]

BACHARACH, ALFRED LOUIS (1891–1966), British chemist and writer on musical subjects. Bacharach was an innovator in the fortification of baby milks with vitamin D, which brought about the almost complete eradication of rickets in the northern cities of Britain. He was born in London, and graduated from Cambridge. After five years in the Wellcome Research Laboratory, he joined the Glaxo Laboratories in 1920. He pioneered the development of biological assay methods for vitamins and also in microbiological assay procedures. He wrote *Science and Nutrition* (1938), and edited *The Nation's Food* (1946), *Evaluation of Drug Activities: Pharmacometrics* (in two volumes, with D.R. Laurence, 1964), *Exploration Medicine* (with O.G. Edholm, 1965), and *The Physiology of Human Survival* (1965). Bacharach, an accomplished pianist, edited *The Musical Companion* (1934; new edition, 1957), *Lives of the Great Composers* (1935), *British Music of Our Time* (1946), and *The Music Masters* (1957).

BIBLIOGRAPHY: *Chemistry in Britain*, 3 (1967), 395.

[Samuel Aaron Miller]

BACHARACH, BURT (1928–), composer and pianist. Born in Kansas City, Missouri, Bacharach studied cello, drums, and piano from an early age. He studied music at the Mannes College of Music in New York, at the New School of Social Research, and at McGill University in Montreal. Among his composition teachers were Darius *Milhaud, Bohuslav Martinů, and Henry Cowell. He subsequently worked as an accompanist for several popular singers such as Polly *Bergen, Steve *Lawrence, Paula Stewart, and Marlene Dietrich from 1958 to 1961. He began composing popular songs in the mid-1950s, collaborating with the lyricist Hal David and later writing hit songs for Dionne Warwick. Bacharach's style includes heterogenous elements such as variable meter, pandiatonic and jazz harmonies, rhythmic ostinatos, and effects from black American styles. He won two Academy Awards for *Butch Cassidy and the Sundance Kid* (1969) with the well-known song "Raindrops Keep Failing on my Head." In the 1990s he collaborated with Elvis Costello. His compositions include the musicals *Promises, Promises* (1968) and *Lost Horizon* (1973), the film score for *Alfie*, and many popular songs

BIBLIOGRAPHY: Grove online; B.A. Lohof, "The Bacharach Phenomenon: a Study of Popular Heroism," in: *Popular Music and Society*, 1 (1972), 73–82.

[Israela Stein (2nd ed.)]

BACHARACH, EVA (**Ḥavvah**; 1580–1651), a rare example of a learned woman, credited with writing commentary on midrash and targum, although these writings are no longer extant. Born into an illustrious and scholarly family, Eva was the maternal granddaughter of the famous Rabbi *Judah Loew ben Bezalel (the Maharal) of Prague. Her father was Rabbi Isaac ha-Kohen (Katz), also a learned rabbi, and her mother was Vogele Kohen. Eva's two brothers, Ḥayyim and Naphtali, were respected rabbis in Poland. Eva married Rabbi Abraham Samuel Bacharach (see *Bacharach family), a student of both her grandfather and her father, and was the mother of two daughters and a son. Left a widow at 30, Eva spent most of the rest of her life in Prague. Her son Moses Samson *Bacharach became the rabbi of Worms and his son, Rabbi Yair Ḥayyim, is the main source on Eva Bacharach's life and learning. In the introduction to his book of responsa, Rabbi Yair Ḥayyim explains that the title, *Ḥavvat Yair*, evokes his famous and erudite grandmother Ḥavvah, whom he calls "my elder, the pious woman, Marat Ḥavvah, the mother of my father … who helped me to develop…." His grandmother, he continues, "was unique of her kind in her generation in Torah. She had an original explanation of *Midrash Rabbah*. She taught … through her comprehension and knowledge … and she explained in such a manner that all who heard her understood that she was correct…. She explained the festival and petitionary prayers and Rashi's commentary on the Torah, and the whole Bible, and the Targum and Apochrypha…. Her writing was superlative and her speech was clear and polished." Rabbi Yair Bacharach relates that Eva never remarried, although she had the opportunity to do so. At the age of 66, she died in Sofia en route to the Land of Israel; there she was honored, as she had been throughout her travels, "because her name was known."

BIBLIOGRAPHY: I. Eisenstadt, *Da'at Kedoshim* (1897–1898), 214–21; E. Taitz, S. Henry, and C. Tallan, *The JPS Guide to Jewish Women: 600 B.C.E.–1900 C.E.* (2003),134.

[Emily Taitz (2nd ed.)]

BACHARACH, ISAAC (1870–1956), U.S. congressman, philanthropist, and civic leader. Born in Philadelphia, Bacharach and his two brothers were brought to Atlantic City by their parents in 1881, thereby being among the very first Jews to live in that seaside resort community. Their father helped found Atlantic City's first synagogue, the Reform Beth Israel. Isaac's brother BENJAMIN (1865–1936) would serve as the synagogue's president for more than 20 years.

Starting with a single clothing store, Isaac Bacharach and his brothers expanded their interests into banking, real estate, and lumber. The brothers put together a syndicate that developed Brigantine, a resort community on nearby Absecon Island, and built the seaside resort's first hotel. Brother HARRY (1873–1947) was the first to enter politics, winning a seat on the Atlantic City City Council in 1900. In 1911, he was elected mayor, an office he would hold on-and-off until the mid-1930s. Together, the three brothers founded and helped underwrite the Jewish Community Center of Atlantic City.

Although limited to a high school education, Isaac excelled in business. Before he turned 30, he had become president of the Second National Bank of Atlantic City and a director of the city's Safe Deposit Company. Isaac joined brother Harry on the Atlantic City City Council in 1907. In 1912, he was elected as a conservative Republican to the New Jersey State Assembly. In November 1914, he was elected to the first of 11 terms in the U.S. Congress. Following the overwhelming victory of the national Republican Party in 1920, Bacharach, now a member of the majority, was appointed to the powerful House Ways and Means Committee. During his tenure in Congress, Bacharach was appointed, along with former House Speaker Nicholas Longworth of Ohio and future speaker (and vice president) John Nance Garner of Texas, to oversee the construction of a new House office building. Today the building is known as the "Longworth Building." In 1924, the three brothers, along with their two sisters, built and dedicated a Home for Afflicted Children in Longport, New Jersey. More than 80 years later, there is still a Betty Bacharach Rehabilitation Center in Pomona, New Jersey, and a Betty Bacharach Hospital in Longport, New Jersey.

Following his defeat in the 1936 elections, Bacharach returned to Atlantic City to oversee his many business interests.

BIBLIOGRAPHY: K.F. Stone, *The Congressional Minyan: The Jews of Capitol Hill* (2000), 10–11.

[Kurt Stone (2nd ed.)]

BACHARACH, JAIR ḤAYYIM BEN MOSES SAMSON (1638–1702), German talmudic scholar, with an extensive knowledge in the general sciences. Bacharach was the son of R. Moses Samson b. Abraham Samuel *Bacharach. Born in Leipnik, where his father officiated as rabbi, Bacharach, in his childhood, accompanied his father to Prague where the latter functioned as preacher, and then to Worms, where his father assumed the position of rabbi of the community. In 1653 Bacharach married Sarlan, the daughter of R. Sussmann Brilin of Fulda. He spent six years at the house of R. Sussmann, acquiring a profound knowledge of the Talmud and its commentaries, with special emphasis on Alfasi and Asher b. Jehiel. Deeply immersed in kabbalistic studies, he, like his father, became very much interested in the Shabbatean movement. He accumulated an impressive library of writings connected with Shabbetai Ẓevi's messianic pretensions. Moreover, a group of 13 talmudic scholars obligated themselves to meet daily under his leadership for purposes of study and self-sanctification in preparation of the impending redemption. Even decades later, after he recognized Shabbetai Ẓevi as a pseudo-Messiah, he always referred to him as "Rabbenu Shabbatai Ẓevi." His stepbrother, Tobias b. Moses *Cohn, in his *Ma'aseh Tuviyyah*, wrote apparently alluding to him: "Even many of the sages of the land and the great renowned rabbis, whom I would not want to mention publicly, accepted him as master and king over them."

In 1666, Jair was appointed rabbi and *rosh bet din* ("head of rabbinic court") at Coblenz. This was a position that carried prestige and comfort with it. Suddenly, in 1669, he was compelled to leave his office. This must have been the result of partisan intrigue. His character is shown by the fact that he did not record the names of the offenders. The same year he again settled at Worms. When his father died in 1670, Bacharach temporarily functioned in his place as rabbi of Worms. However, he was disappointed in his hope of assuming the rabbinate of Worms, the pretext being that it was against the rule to appoint a resident of the city as rabbi. His resentment at being passed over in favor of R. Aaron Teomim, whom he deemed far inferior in scholarship, appears to have found a measure of satisfaction in his work *Matteh Aharon*, left in manuscript, in which he severely criticized the scholarly methods of the elected rabbi who had just published a commentary on the Passover *Haggadah* under the same title. After the latter had suffered a violent death, Bacharach placed parentheses around the sharper expressions, solemnly instructing any future publisher to soften the more offending passages. The work was finally published by Jellinek in *Bikkurim* (1865), 4–26; and again in *Ha-Misderonah* (1887), 348–64.

In 1689 when Worms was occupied by the French armies of Louis XIV, Bacharach fled to Metz with his family. In March 1690 he left for Frankfurt by himself in an unsuccessful attempt to collect some debts, and at this time his family was in such dire straits that his wife, with his consent, sold his extensive library for 250 Reichsthaler. During the next few years he was often forced to change his domicile, residing in various cities in the Rhineland. At Frankfurt in 1699 he published his monumental collection of 238 responsa under the name *Ḥavvat Yair.* The title comes from Numbers 32:41, and means "The Tent-Villages of Jair," implying that his decisions were but modest expressions of his opinions in contrast to former respondents whose works were like fortified towns. In the German pronunciation the title becomes "Ḥaves Yoir," meaning also "the Jair of Ḥavvah," and thus constituting a tribute to his erudite grandmother, Ḥavvah or Eva, the granddaughter of *Judah Loew b. Bezalel and the female founder of the Bacharach house. This epoch-making work, which has gone through many editions, demonstrates not only Bacharach's exhaustive knowledge of all branches of traditional rabbinic learning, but also the whole extent of his knowledge of the general sciences, such as mathematics, astronomy, and music, and shows also his opposition to the distorted type of *pilpul* current in his day. It contains some writings of his father and his grandfather.

Other printed works of Bacharach include *Ḥut ha-Shani* ("Scarlet Thread," 1679) containing responsa of his father and grandfather, as well as 17 refutations of R. Samuel ben David's *Naḥalat Shivah* (1677) and notes on Alfasi published in the Vilna edition. Altogether he is said to have left 46 volumes of manuscripts (some of these being excerpts or collections of the works of others). The more important of these are *Ez Ḥayyim*, a compendium on the Jewish religion; glosses to Maimonides' *Guide*; a commentary on the *Shulḥan Arukh*; chronological tables and genealogical lists.

In 1699, the reestablished Jewish community of Worms finally chose Bacharach, now deaf, old, and sick, as their rabbi. He had been granted his dearest wish: the satisfaction of being elected by this historic congregation to succeed his father and grandfather. He lived three more years. Bacharach's method was one of strict logic. He manifested his independence vis-à-vis his father, citing the precedent of Maimonides. Thus, he says in one passage, vindicating his right to disagree with earlier authorities: "The spirit of God has made me, as it has made them" (Responsum no. 155). He was strict with respect to the obligatory nature of established religious custom. While he was a believer in the Kabbalah and busied himself with *gematria*, he warned against giving oneself over to the study of Kabbalah or philosophy – placing great value on simple faith.

BIBLIOGRAPHY: D. Kaufmann, *R. Jair Chajjim Bacharach* (Ger., 1894); idem, in: JQR 3 (1891), 292–313, 485–536 (earlier English outline of previous work); Marx, in: *Essays… J.H. Hertz* (1942), 307–11; S. Freehof, *Responsa Literature* (1955), 84–87; idem, *Treasury of Responsa* (1963), 171–5.

[Jacob Haberman]

BACHARACH, MOSES SAMSON BEN ABRAHAM SAMUEL (1607–1670), rabbi and author. Bacharach was born in Pohořelice, Moravia, where his father Abraham Samuel (a prominent scholar in rabbinics and in other fields) was then rabbi. His mother Ḥavvah, the daughter of Isaac Katz, son-in-law of R. Judah Loew ben Bezalel of Prague, was also distinguished for her learning and even wrote comments on Midrash and Targum. At the age of eight, upon the death of his father, Bacharach was taken to Prague, where he was educated under the tutelage of his two uncles, R. Ḥayyim and R. Naphtali ha-Kohen, both distinguished scholars. In 1627 he married a daughter of R. Isaac b. Phoebus, chief rabbi of Moravia. His father-in-law was taken prisoner, and the payment of a 10,000 gulden ransom left Moses impoverished, forcing him to accept the rabbinate of Hodonin (Moravian Slovakia) in 1629. In 1632 he became rabbi and head of the yeshivah at Leipnik. He experienced the travails of the Jews in the Thirty-Years' War, to which he gave expression in a *seliḥah* which the Jewish community of Leipnik recited annually on the 17th of Tammuz. Subsequently, on the foundation of a charitable religious association (the *Barukh she-Amar* society), he composed a joyous song of thanks for deliverance from danger during the war, which was recited every year on Simḥat Torah. In 1650 he was chosen rabbi of the community of Worms – perhaps the most influential position in German Jewry. He was in that office 20 years until his death. Some of his writings were included in the published works of his son, the famed R. Jair Ḥayyim *Bacharach.

BIBLIOGRAPHY: D. Kaufmann, *R. Jair Chajjim Bacharach…* (Ger., 1894), 23–28, 45, 53–54, 129 30; F. Hillel, *Leipniker Rabbiner* (1928), 16–43; A.E. Franklin, *Records of Franklin Family* (1935^2) 4, 45.

[Jacob Haberman]

BACHARACH, NAPHTALI BEN JACOB ELHANAN, kabbalist who lived in the first half of the 17th century. The dates of his birth and death are unknown. Bacharach was born in Frankfurt, but also spent some years in Poland with the kabbalists before he returned to his home town, and in 1648 he published his comprehensive book *Emek ha-Melekh* ("The King's Valley"), one of the most important kabbalistic works. The book contains a wide and systematic presentation of theology according to the Lurianic Kabbalah. It was based on many authorities, but relied mainly on Israel *Sarug's version presented in his book *Limmudei Aẓilut* (1897), which Bacharach included almost in its entirety into his own book with hardly an acknowledgment of the fact. Bacharach's claims that he brought back the sources of Luria's Kabbalah with him from Ereẓ Israel, where he supposedly lived for some time, do not deserve credit. He also accused Joseph Solomon *Delmedigo who he claimed had been his pupil, of transcribing kabbalistic manuscripts which were in Bacharach's possession, and then publishing them, with noticeable distortions, in his books *Ta'alumot Ḥokhmah* (1629) and *Novelot Ḥokhmah* (1631). However, the contrary seems much more likely; that it was Bacharach who culled from Delmedigo's work as well as from many other sources without acknowledging them. While Delmedigo's interest lay in the abstract philosophical aspect of Kabbalah, which he attempted to explain to himself, Bacharach appears as an enthusiastic and fanatical kabbalist, with a special flair for the mystical and non-philosophical traits of Kabbalah – in Isaac Luria's Kabbalah as well as in the Kabbalah of the early kabbalists. This accounts for the strong emphasis given to such elements as the doctrine of the *Sitra Aḥra* ("Other Side" – the Evil) and demonology. He wove the old kabbalistic themes together with the later ones in an elaborately detailed style. Without referring to Sarug, who is his most important source, Bacharach claims to derive his teachings from the books of Ḥayyim *Vital, although important chapters of his doctrine, such as his version of the doctrine of *Ẓimẓum* ("Withdrawal") and all it entails, are completely foreign to Vital's writings. The merger of both these traditions characterizes this book, written with talent and clarity. Bacharach also borrowed liberally from certain parts of the book *Shefa Tal* by R. Shabbetai Sheftel *Horowitz (1612). His style is pervaded by messianic tension. The book *Emek ha-Melekh* had a great impact on the development of the late Kabbalah. It was widely recognized as an authoritative source on the doctrine of Isaac Luria and kabbalists from many countries, especially Ashkenazim, the great Ḥabad Ḥasidim, and the school of the Gaon *Elijah b. Solomon Zalman of Vilna, quoted him extensively. His influence is also noticeable in Shabbatean literature, in Moses Ḥayyim *Luzzatto's system of Kabbalah, and in the book *Kelaḥ* [138] *Pitḥei Ḥokhmah*. On the other hand, strong criticism of the book was soon expressed. Already in 1655, Ḥayyim ha-Kohen of Aleppo, a disciple of Ḥayyim Vital, in the introduction to his book *Mekor Ḥayyim* (1655), protested against Bacharach's claim of being the true interpreter of Luria's doctrine. The protests of Benjamin ha-Levi in his approbation to *Zot Ḥukkat ha-Torah* by Abraham *Ḥazkuni (1659), and of the preacher Berechiah Berach, in his introduction to *Zera Berakh* (2nd part, 1662), against misrepresentations of Luria's Kabbalah were also intended for Bacharach. Moses *Ḥagiz says in *Shever Poshe'im* (1714) that *Emek ha-Melekh* is called *Emek ha-Bakha* ("Valley of Weeping"). Isaiah Bassan complains to M.Ḥ. Luzzatto about the numerous translations of chapters from *Emek ha-Melekh* in Latin referring to the *Kabbalah Denudata* by *Knorr von Rosenroth "which were among the important causes of prolonging our exile" (*Iggerot Shadal*, 29). Ḥ.J.D. *Azulai also wrote: "I have heard that no genuine writings got into his (Bacharach's) hands… therefore the initiated refrain from reading either it or the *Novelot Ḥokhmah*." In *Emek ha-Melekh* there is a reference to many other books by Bacharach concerning aspects of the kabbalist doctrine. Of these only a part of the *Gan ha-Melekh* on the Zohar is extant in an Oxford manuscript.

BIBLIOGRAPHY: Azulai, 2 (1852), 114 no. 406; G. Scholem, in: KS, 30 (1954/55), 413; Scholem, Shabbetai Ẓevi, 54–56; M. Horovitz, *Frankfurter Rabbinen*, 2 (1883), 41–45.

[Gershom Scholem]

BACHAUER, GINA (1913–1976), Greek born pianist of Austrian and Italian parentage. Bachauer studied at the Athens Conservatory under Woldemar Freeman. She then went to Paris, where she took lessons with Cortot. Between 1933 and 1935 she received lessons from Rachmaninoff in France and Switzerland. Her French solo début took place in the Salle Chopin, Paris, in 1929, and she first played in England in 1932. In 1933 she won the medal of honor at an international piano competition in Vienna, and in the 1930s played concertos with the Paris Symphony Orchestra conducted by Monteux and the Athens Symphony Orchestra under Mitropoulos. During World War II she lived in Alexandria and played numerous concerts for the Allied forces in the Middle East. In 1946 she made her début at the Albert Hall, playing Grieg's Piano Concerto with the New London Orchestra under Alec Sherman, who became her second husband in 1951. After her New York début in 1950 she received unanimous acclaim from the critics and her career was assured. She toured in the U.S. and Israel. Her unusually wide repertoire ranges from Mozart to Stravinsky. In both standard and modern works, she displayed impeccable taste. Her flair, grand style, big line, and exciting vigor are put to best use in big virtuoso works. Among her recordings are concertos by Beethoven, Brahms, Chopin, and Grieg, as well as solo works by Debussy. After her death in Athens, a Gina Bachauer International Piano Competition was founded. The Bachauer Archive at Brigham Young University preserves diaries, scores, and recordings from her distinguished career.

BIBLIOGRAPHY: Grove online; MGG^2; *Baker's Biographical Dictionary* (1997); W. Graham. *Gina Bachauer: A Pianist's Odyssey* (1999).

[Naama Ramot (2nd ed.)]

BACHE, U.S. family of investment bankers and art collectors. BACHE, JULES SEMON (1862–1944) was born in New York. After some years with his father's trading firm he became a cashier in 1880 for Leopold Cahn and Co., investment bankers. Twelve years later he became head of the firm, which he renamed J.S. Bache and Co. Under his leadership the company became prominent in investment banking and securities trading, with interests in railroads, mining, manufacturing, trading, and insurance. Bache's philanthropy included donations to hospitals and scientific research, civic institutions, and the arts. He gave his outstanding collection of paintings, sculptures, tapestries, enamels, furniture, and porcelains to the State of New York for the Metropolitan Museum of Art.

[Joachim O. Ronall]

BACHER, EDUARD (1846–1908), Austrian lawyer and journalist. Bacher was born in Postelberg (Postoloprty), Bohemia. While studying law in Prague and Vienna, he became interested in parliamentary affairs and soon was appointed stenographer of the Bohemian Parliament (c. 1861). After completing his studies, he became chief stenographer of the Vienna *Reichsrat* and practiced as a successful lawyer. In 1872, he joined the staff of the leading liberal Vienna daily *Neue Freie Presse* (est. 1864 by Max Friedländer and Michael Etienne) as parliamentary reporter. The same year, on Friedländer's death, he was appointed editor of the domestic politics section and on May 1, 1879, after Etienne died, became editor-in-chief (later also publisher and part owner). In 1881, Bacher was joined by Moritz *Benedikt as co-editor. For almost three decades the *Neue Freie Presse* was closely linked to Bacher's personality and political orientation, serving as an organ of the German Liberal Party in Austria. His editorials had considerable influence on Austro-Hungarian domestic politics, promoting a centrist structure set against anti-liberal, national, or federal aspirations, and therefore opposing the conservative Austrian government of Count Taaffe (until 1893) and later Count Badeni (1897). Bacher was a corresponding member of the Society for Promoting Science, Arts and Literature in Bohemia and served as literary adviser of the Austrian prince royal, Archduke Rudolf, who committed suicide in 1889. From 1896/97, Bacher's political creed also led him to reject the new Zionist movement of Theodor *Herzl, who had joined the *Neue Freie Presse* as Paris correspondent in 1891. As frequently deplored in Herzl's diaries, Bacher would not let him publish any reports on the Zionist movement or the Zionist Congresses in the paper. After Bacher's death, the *Neue Freie Presse* was continued by Benedikt until 1920.

BIBLIOGRAPHY: *Neue Freie Presse* (Jan. 1908); *Allgemeine Zeitung des Judentums* (Jan. 24, 1908), supplement *Der Gemeindebote*, 4; E. Dovifat, in: *Neue Deutsche Biographie*, 1 (1953), 496; A. Wandruszka, *Geschichte einer Zeitung. Das Schicksal der „Presse" und der „Neuen Freien Presse" von 1848 zur Zweiten Republik* (1958). **ADD. BIBLIOGRAPHY:** Th. Herzl, *Briefe und Tagebuecher* (ed. A. Bein et al.), 7 vols. (1983–96), index; H. Schmuck (ed.), *Jewish Biographical Archive*, (1995), F. 46, 41/109, 344–356; Series II (2003), F. II/35, 422–425; S. Blumesberger et al. (eds.), *Handbuch oesterreichischer Autorinnen und Autoren juedischer Herkunft*, 1 (2002), 55 (No. 422).

[Johannes Valentin Schwarz (2nd ed.)]

BACHER, ROBERT FOX (1905–2004), U.S. physicist. Born in Loudonville, Ohio, Bacher joined the staff of the Massachusetts Institute of Technology in 1932. After teaching at Cornell University for a time, he returned to MIT as a research associate in the radiation laboratory. During World War II he worked on the bomb project at the Los Alamos laboratory, and he became head of the bomb physics division. He was a member of the Atomic Energy Commission from 1946 to 1949. He was then appointed professor of physics at the California Institute of Technology, heading the Mathematics, Physics, and Astronomy Division. He retired in 1976.

BACHER, SIMON (1823–1891), poet and Hebrew translator. Bacher was born in Szent Miklos, Hungary, and was the father of the Orientalist Wilhelm *Bacher and a descendant of Jair Ḥayyim *Bacharach. When writing in Hebrew, he used the latter's surname. In 1867 he moved to Budapest, where he was employed as a bookkeeper. From 1874 until his death he served as the treasurer of the Jewish community. Bacher wrote poetry in the flowery style of the Haskalah and also translated German and Hungarian poetry into Hebrew. He was a regular contributor to the Hebrew periodicals *Ha-Ḥavaẓẓelet* and *Kokhevei Yiẓḥak*. In 1865 his Hebrew translation of Lessing's *Nathan der Weise* appeared in Vienna, and in 1868 he published *Zemirot ha-Areẓ* ("Songs of the Land"), an anthology of translations from Hungarian poetry. His selected works, *Sha'ar Shimon* (3 vols., 1894), were published posthumously by his son.

BIBLIOGRAPHY: W. Bacher, in: *Sha'ar Shimon*, 1 (1894), 9–36; J. Patai, *Mi-Sefunei ha-Shirah* (1939), 31–35.

[Gedalyah Elkoshi]

BACHER, WILHELM (1850–1913), Hungarian Semitic scholar. Bacher was born in Liptó-Szent-Miklós (now Liptovsky Svätý Mikuláš, Slovakia), the son of the Hebrew poet Simon *Bacher. In 1876 he was ordained and appointed rabbi of Szeged, Hungary, and the following year professor at the newly founded rabbinical seminary in Budapest, where he taught biblical exegesis, Midrash, homiletics, and Hebrew poetry and grammar. From 1907 until the end of his life he was head of the seminary. In 1884 with Joseph Banoczi he founded the Hungarian Jewish monthly *Magyar Zsidó Szemle*. In 1894 he helped found a Jewish-Hungarian literary society, Izraelita Magyar Irodalmi Társulat, and was the editor of its yearbook until 1899; this society instituted the publication of a Hungarian translation of the Bible (1898–1907). At the same time Bacher served as a consulting editor for the *Jewish Encyclopedia* (1901–06) and wrote a number of monographs for it. Bacher's fields of study included biblical exegesis, Hebrew philology, *aggadah* and Midrash, and Judeo-Persian literature. Many of his works were translated into Hebrew by A.Z. *Rabinovitz. In his works on *aggadah* he classified aggadic sayings by author determining the contribution of each *tanna* and *amora*. These works include *Die Agada der Babylonischen*

Amoräer (1878, also in Hg., 1913[2]); *Die Agada der Tannaiten* (2 vols., 1884–90); *Die Agada der Palaestinischen Amoräer* (3 vols., 1892–99; repr. 1965; *Die Prooemien der Alten juedischen Homilie* (1913); *Rabbanan, Beitrag zur Geschichte der anonymen Agada* (1914); and *Tradition und Tradenten in den Schulen Palaestinas und Babyloniens* (1914). In the last work Bacher discusses the manner in which the *amoraim* in Babylonia and Palestine transmitted the teachings of the early scholars, especially the *tannaim* of the *beraitot*. Of particular significance from the standpoint of content and style is Bacher's *Exegetische Terminologie der juedischen Traditionsliteratur* (2 parts, 1899, 1905, repr. 1965). In the first part of this work Bacher arranged the Hebrew and Aramaic terms used by the *tannaim* in their exegesis in alphabetical order and in the second part, those of the Palestinian and Babylonian *amoraim*. He also dealt with the terms used by the *amoraim* to explain the terminology of the *tannaim*. Bacher dealt extensively with medieval Jewish biblical exegesis. In addition to *Die Juedische Bibelexegese vom Anfange des Zehnten bis zum Ende des Fuenfzehnten Jahrhunderts* (1892), he wrote detailed studies on Abraham ibn Ezra's works, Saadiah's Arabic translation of the Book of Job (in: Derenbourg, *Oeuvres Complètes de R. Saadiah*, 1899), Moses ha-Kohen ibn *Gikatilla's work on the same book, and on *Samuel b. Hophni. He published a study in German and Hungarian on the biblical exegesis of Jewish religious philosophers before Maimonides, *Die Bibelexegese der Juedischen Religionsphilosophen des Mittelalters vor Maimûnis* (1892), and on the exegetical methods of Maimonides, *Die Bibelexeges Moses Maimünis* (1896). He wrote two works on the biblical commentaries of Ibn Janaḥ, *Leben und Werke des Abulwaîd Merwân ibn Ganâh* (1885), and a detailed study of the biblical exegesis of the Zohar. Bacher dealt extensively with the development of Hebrew during the Middle Ages, including the masorah, the beginning of the study of Hebrew grammar (*Die Anfaenge der hebraeischen Grammatik*, 1895), and the pioneering work of Judah ibn *Ḥayyuj in the field of Hebrew grammar (*Die Grammatische Terminologie des Jehuda b. Dawid Hajjug*, 1882). Bacher was the only Jewish scholar of his generation to deal with Judeo-Persian literature. His continuous flow of publications, based on the collection of Judeo-Persian manuscripts of Elkan Nathan *Adler, made him the undisputed authority in this field. Among his many works on Judeo-Persian literature are *Hebraeisch-Persisches Woerterbuch aus dem vierzehnten Jahrhundert* (1900) by Solomon b. Samuel of Turkestan; "Ein persischer Kommentar zum Buche Samuel" (in ZDMG, 51 (1897), 329–425); *Zwei juedisch-persische Dichter, Schahin und Imrani* (1907–08); and "Juedisch-Persisches aus Buchârâ" (in ZDMG, 55 (1901), 244–57; 56 (1902), 729–59). Bacher helped lay the foundations for the study of Hebrew grammar from the talmudic period to the end of the Middle Ages; he was the first scholar to deal with the Hebrew and Arabic poetry of Yemen. Above all, he was one of the first scholars to engage in the scientific study of *aggadah* and Midrash.

BIBLIOGRAPHY: S. Kraus, in: *Ha-Shilo'aḥ*, 30 (1914), 168–78, 384 92, 487–97; *Magyar Zsidó Szemle*, 27 (1910), 1–81, articles honoring Bacher, including bibliography of his works; L. Blau, *Bibliographie der Schriften Wilhelm Bachers* (1910), completed by D. Friedmann, *Nachtrag zu L. Blau's Bibliographie der Schriften Wilhelm Bachers* (1928); M. Liber, in: REJ, 67 (1914), 161–9; B. Heller, in: *Zsidó Plutarchos* (1928), 9–38 (Hg.); W.J. Fischel, in: L. Finkelstein (ed.), *The Jews, Their History, Culture and Religion*, 2 (1960), 1149–1190 (with bibliography); J.I. Dienstag, in: *Sinai*, 55 (1964), 65–82.

[Moshe Nahum Zobel]

BACHI, ARMANDO (1883–1943), Italian soldier. Born in Verona, Bachi went into the artillery where he was commissioned in 1902 and remained in this branch of the army for most of his career. In World War I he became deputy chief of staff of the 48th and 30th divisions, and was awarded the Military Cross. After the war he was a lecturer in artillery at the Turin Military Academy and in 1934 was given command of an artillery corps. By 1938 he had become a lieutenant general in command of a motorized army corps, but when the racial laws were enacted that year, he was forced to resign his commission. In 1943 he and his family were arrested in Parma and died in Auschwitz.

ADD. BIBLIOGRAPHY: A. Rovighi, *I Militari di Origine Ebraica nel Primo Secolo di Vita dello Stato Italiano* (1999), 96.

[Massimo Longo Adorno]

BACHI, RAPHAEL (1717–1767), French miniature painter. Born in Turin, he moved to Paris where he set up as tobacconist and snuff merchant. He learned the art of miniature painting through the decoration of snuff-boxes. His work was recognized when the French court employed him to paint miniature portraits on snuff-boxes presented to foreign notables. His clientele included many members of the nobility such as the Duke of Modena and the Prince de Condé. In an official list of the Jews residing in Paris during the years 1755–1759, he is mentioned as "peintre en miniature, de beaucoup de talent."

BACHI, RICCARDO (1875–1951), Italian economist and statistician. Bachi was born in Turin and studied in Venice. He laid the foundations for the scientific study of price fluctuations and wrote on the economic history of the Risorgimento. From 1904 to 1908 Bachi edited the Italian Labor Department bulletin on employment, and from 1909 to 1921 he issued *L'Italia Economica*, an annual publication which he founded. From 1915 Bacchi taught statistics and economics at the universities of Macerata, Parma, and Genoa, and in 1926 he was appointed to the chair of political economy at the Royal Institute of Economic Sciences in Rome. After the enactment of the anti-Jewish laws in Italy in 1938, he went to Palestine, where from 1940 to 1946, he lectured at the Tel Aviv branch of the Hebrew University. In 1946 he returned to the University of Rome. Interested in Zionism from the 1920s, he investigated the economic history of Jews, in particular the economic relations between Jews and non-Jews in the Diaspora. Noteworthy among Bachi's writings are his *Principi di scienza economica*, 2 vols. (1937–40), *Israele disperso e ricostruito* (1952), and his introduction to the Hebrew translation of Simḥah Luzzatto's "On the Jews of Venice" (*Ma'amar al Yehudei Veneẓyah,* 1950).

BIBLIOGRAPHY: L. Einaudi, *Riforma Sociale* (1931), 416ff.; RMI, 16 (1950), 14–216; A.M. Ratti, *Vita e opere di Riccardo Bachi* (1961), 69–100 (bibliography).

[Joseph Baruch Sermoneta]

BACHI, ROBERTO (1909–1995), statistician and demographer. Bachi was born in Rome and completed his studies in law and statistics at the University of Rome. He taught statistics in various universities in Italy and was appointed full professor in 1937. In 1938 he emigrated to Palestine soon after the decree of the Racial Laws by Fascist Italy. He worked as a statistician in the Hadassah Medical Organization, and during 1945–47 in the Department of Statistics of the Mandatory Government. From the early 1940s he taught statistics at the Hebrew University and was appointed full professor in 1947.

With the foundation of the State of Israel Bachi was appointed government statistician. He founded Israel's Central Bureau of Statistics, which he directed until 1971, and was responsible for its independent status and academic integrity. He was among the founders of the Faculty of Social Sciences of the Hebrew University and served as its first dean (1953–56). During the 1950s he headed the Department of Statistics and Demography and in 1959–60 he was pro-rector of the Hebrew University. In 1960 Bachi founded the Department of Demography and Statistics at the Institute of Contemporary Jewry of the Hebrew University, which became an international center. He devoted much attention to the practical implications of demographic studies, which are of vital importance to the Jewish people throughout the world. Under Prime Ministers Ben Gurion and Eshkol he chaired a committee on Israel's demographic policy. Bachi taught generations of students, many of whom have long occupied prominent positions in academic institutions. After his retirement in 1977 he concentrated on the two fields of methodological research, which occupied him throughout his life – geostatistics and graphical representation of statistical data. He developed innovative methods for reducing vast quantities of geographical-statistical data and their graphic representation in computerized maps. His most important work, summarizing these methods, was published posthumously: *New Methods of Geostatistical Analysis and Graphical Presentation: Distribution of Populations over Territories* (1999). Bachi published a large number of works, including: *La Mobilità della Popolazione all'interno delle grandi Città Europee* (Rome, 1933), *Graphical Rational Patterns* (Jerusalem, 1968), *Population Trends of World Jewry* (Jerusalem, 1976), and *The Population of Israel* (Jerusalem, 1977). He was member of the Israel Academy of Sciences and honorary member of the American Statistical Society.

BIBLIOGRAPHY: *Scritti in onore di Roberto Bachi* (1950); U.O. Schmelz and G. Nathan, *Studies in the Population of Israel in Honor of Roberto Bachi* (1986); "Roberto Bachi: A Selected Bibliography," in: *Scripta Hierosolymitana*, 30 (1986), 417–24; S. Della Pergola and N. Gad, "Le-Zekher Roberto Bachi," in: *Ma'adei ha-Yahadut*, 36 (1996), 187–89.

[Margalit Bejarano (2nd ed.)]

BACHMANN, JACOB (1846–1905), Russian *ḥazzan* and composer of synagogue music. Bachmann served as a boy-singer with the *ḥazzan* of his native town of Berdichev. He developed a phenomenal voice and was admitted to the Petrograd Conservatoire in 1864. Anton *Rubinstein became his teacher and later took him on his concert tours as a solo singer. Bachmann, nevertheless, decided to be a *ḥazzan* and established his reputation at the synagogues of Berdichev, Rostov, and Constantinople. During his stay at Lemberg until 1884, Bachmann founded a mixed choir and took up composition. As successor to Osias *Abrass at Odessa (1884–85), he was acclaimed by the public. He later settled in Budapest. Bachmann's voice is said to have covered the entire range from dramatic tenor to powerful bass, highlighted by an extraordinary echo-falsetto. His compositions are influenced by Rubinstein, the "Westerner" in Russian music. Bachmann was eager to show command of contemporary musical devices (*Schirath Jacob*, pp. 54, 79, 89, 95, 96), including reminiscences of Bach (*ibid.*, p. 188) or Meyerbeer (*ibid.*, p. 89), and was able to write striking, though rather conventional, choral settings (*ibid.*, pp. 18–19). However, Bachmann has to be judged by his improvisations in traditional *ḥazzanut*, a small part of which is included in his printed works. Bachmann's cantorial recitative was at its best at the sublime moments of the High Holy Days' liturgy (*ibid.*, 159–64). Works: *Cantata* (Ps. 45) for the silver jubilee of Francis I (1879); *Schirath Jacob* (1884); *Uwaschofor godol* (1889); and *Attah Zokher* (after 1905). Unpublished works exist in manuscript form in the David Putterman Library, N.Y.

See also G. Ephros, *Cantorial Anthology*, 2 (1929), 117–119.

BIBLIOGRAPHY: Wininger, Biog, 1 (1925), 214–5; E. Zaludkowski, *Kultur-Treger fun der Yidisher Liturgye…* (1930), 191–2; Sendrey, Music, indexes; Minkowski, in: *Reshumot*, 5 (1927), 145–60.

[Hanoch Avenary]

BACHRACH, JACOB BEN MOSES (also called **Ba'al ha-Ma'amarim** or **Jacob ha-Bachri**; 1824–1896), rabbi and grammarian. Bachrach, a descendant of Jair *Bacharach, was born in Sejny in the district of Suwalki; he studied with his grandfather Judah *Bachrach. In addition to being an accomplished talmudist he was versed in secular knowledge. For many years he was superintendent of the Hebrew department of a printing establishment in Koenigsberg. In 1858 he published in that press his *Maẓref ha-Avodah*, which deals with the controversy over Ḥasidism between Benjamin Wolf of Slonim, a disciple of *Elijah b. Solomon Zalman the Gaon of Vilna, and Joseph of Nemirov, a disciple of *Levi Isaac of Berdichev. Later editions of this book carry the title *Vikkuḥa Rabbah* ("Great Debate"). In 1858 he also published the *Sefer Yuḥasin* of Abraham *Zacuto with corrections and comments. Between 1861 and 1864 he published Jacob b. Asher's *Turim* with his own annotations. From Koenigsberg he moved to Sebastopol. There, while managing a refinery, he began to take an interest in the literature of the *Karaites and engage in polemics with them. In 1893 his book *Me-ha-Ibbur u-Minyan ha-Shanim* ("Concerning Intercalation and the Calendar") appeared in Warsaw. In it he attempted to prove the antiquity of the Hebrew *calendar, in opposition to the Karaite theory on one side and to the opinion of Ḥ.Z. Slonimsky on the other side. From there he moved to Bialystok, where he played an important role in founding the Ḥovevei Zion movement and was sent to Ereẓ Israel in 1882. His findings during his visit there are contained in his *Sefer ha-Massa le-Ereẓ Yisrael* (Warsaw, 1884), one of the earliest propaganda books of the Ḥovevei Zion. For a short time, he was also private secretary to Samuel *Mohilever. Bachrach also engaged in scientific study of the Hebrew language. Among other things, he tried to prove the antiquity of the Hebrew vowels and accents, in opposition to the opinion of Elijah *Levita who had held that these were not introduced until after the conclusion of the Talmud. These studies appeared in *Sefer ha-Yaḥas li-Khetav Ashuri ve-Toledot ha-Nekuddot ve-ha-Te'amim* ("History of the Assyrian Script, Vowels, and Accents," Warsaw, 1854) and *Hishtaddelut im Shadal* ("Engagement with Samuel David Luzzatto," Warsaw, 1897), a kind of extension to his earlier work. Despite the great acumen shown in his works, they did not meet with the general approval of the scholars of his time.

BIBLIOGRAPHY: E. Atlas, in: *Ha-Asif*, 1 (1884), 246ff.; S. Wiener, *Kohelet Moshe* (1893–1918), nos. 3311, 4521, 4723; *Lu'aḥ Aḥi'asaf*, 5 (1898), 326; EZD, 1 (1958), 291–3; Kressel, Leksikon, 1 (1965), 241–2.

BACHRACH, JUDAH BEN JOSHUA EZEKIEL (1775–1846), Lithuanian rabbi and author. Judah succeeded Isaac Avigdor as *av bet din* of Sejny (near Suwalki in Poland) where he remained until his death. After his death, his novellae and glosses to the Talmud and to Alfasi were published in the Vilna (Romm) edition under the title *Nimmukei ha-Grib* (= **Ha**-**G**aon **R**abbi **J**udah **B**achrach). His glosses to Maimonides' *Mishneh Torah* are also known. Bachrach is particularly important because of his ties with *Elijah b. Solomon Zalman Gaon of Vilna, who was a relative of his father-in-law, Israel Burlioner. Bachrach possessed a number of tractates of the Talmud which had been used by Elijah Gaon and which contained manuscript glosses by him, differing from those published in the Vienna edition of the Talmud of 1826–31. These volumes were purchased by the Romm publishers from Bachrach's children and the glosses were published in the Vilna edition of 1880–86.

BIBLIOGRAPHY: I.T. Eisenstadt and S. Wiener, *Da'at Kedoshim* (1897–98), 68; R.N.N. Rabinowicz, *Ma'amar al Hadpasat ha-Talmud*, ed. by A.M. Habermann (1952), 129, 176.

[Yehoshua Horowitz]

BACHRACH, MOSES BEN ISAIAH MENAHEM (also known as **Moses Mendels**; 1574–1641), talmudic scholar. Bachrach was *av bet din* in Szydlow, Wlodzimierz, Cracow, and Frankfurt from before 1605 until after 1614. Apparently he then went to serve in a similar capacity in the district of Cracow since Meir b. Gedaliah *Lublin mentions him in one of his responsa of that period as being there. He carried on a halakhic correspondence with Benjamin Aaron *Slonik in 1619, at which time he was in Vladimir. In 1636 he was succeeded by R. Yom Tov Lipmann *Heller as *av bet din* in Prague, moving from there to Posen, where he succeeded Simeon Wolf b. David Auerbach as *av bet din*, and where he remained for the rest of his life. He participated in the sessions of the Council of the Four Lands in Yaroslav (1614) and in Lublin (1639). Jacob *Reischer in his *Shevut Ya'akov* refers to him as an outstanding talmudic scholar. *Moshel ba-Elyonim Attah Yadata*, a *seliḥah* he wrote during an epidemic, is still extant. It is included in the *Seliḥot* of Posen, Cracow, Prague, Worms, and Alsace. One of his responsa is included in the responsa *Ḥinnukh Beit Yehudah* of Judah Leib b. Ḥanokh (Amsterdam, 1708, no. 76). His son ISRAEL wrote *Sefer Marot ha-Ẓedek* and an index to the *Shelah* of Isaiah *Horowitz (Amsterdam, 1682). His daughter, Edel, translated an abridged version of *Josippon into Yiddish (Cracow, 1770).

BIBLIOGRAPHY: M. Horovitz, *Frankfurter Rabbinen* (1969²), 38, 47, 62, 280–1; Dembitzer, in: *Oẓar ha-Sifrut*, 4 (1892), 230–1; Wettsein, in: *Ha-Eshkol*, 5 (1905), 253; Halpern, Pinkas, 61, 490; Davidson, Oẓar, 3 (1930), 107 no. 834; D. Avron (ed.), *Pinkas ha-Kesherim shel Kehillat Pozna* (1966), 72, 120.

BACK, SAMUEL (1841–1899), rabbi and scholar. Back, who was born in Galgocz (now Hlohovec, Slovakia), served as rabbi in Prague-Smichov from 1872. He wrote on philosophical, historical, and talmudical subjects. His published works include *Josef Albos Bedeutung in der Geschichte der juedischen Religionsphilosophie* (1869), *Das Synhedrion unter Napoleon I* (1879), *R. Meir ben Baruch aus Rothenburg* (1895), *Entstehungsgeschichte der portugiesischen Gemeinde in Amsterdam und Rabbi Menasse ben Israel* (1883), *Elischa ben Abuja-Acher* (1891), and "Die Fabel in Talmud und Midrash" (in MGWJ, vols. 25, 29, 30, 33). Back also published sermons and eulogies as well as articles in learned periodicals.

BACKER, GEORGE (1902–1974), U.S. publisher, politician, and communal leader. Backer was born in New York. He worked briefly in the family's real estate firm, but devoted himself mainly to politics and the arts. In 1937 and 1938 Backer ran unsuccessfully for Congress as an American Labor Party candidate, and served on the New York City Council. From World War II he was a leader of the reform wing of New York

Democrats, and was closely associated, as friend and political adviser, with W. Averell Harriman. In 1939 Backer purchased the *New York Post*, became its publisher and editor, and imbued it with a strong liberal outlook. His former wife, Dorothy *Schiff, assumed control of the newspaper after their divorce in 1942. Backer had a deep interest in music and drama, sponsoring theatrical productions and writing plays. His novel *Appearance of a Man* was published in 1966. Backer's Jewish activities date from the early 1930s when he became alarmed at the rise of Nazism. He visited Germany and Poland in 1933, 1934, and 1936, urging Jews to emigrate, and was active in American organizations aiding refugees. Among the Jewish groups with which he was affiliated are the American Jewish Joint Distribution Committee, American ORT, Jewish Telegraphic Agency, and American Jewish Committee.

BIBLIOGRAPHY: *New York Times* (July 20, 1966).

[Morton Rosenstock]

BACKMAN, JULES (1910–1982), U.S. Reform lay leader. Backman was born in New York and received his D.C.S. from New York University in 1935. He became an economic advisor to federal and state governments, a professor at NYU, and an editorial writer for the *New York Times*. Backman served as national chairman of the Reform Jewish Appeal (1965–69) and was a member of the executive committee of the Union of American Hebrew Congregations. He was elected to the Board of Governors at Hebrew Union College-Jewish Institute of Religion in 1963, rising to become its chairman from 1976 until his death. Backman, who was instrumental in relocating the New York school of HUC-JIR to its present home near Washington Square and the NYU campus, received the seminary's American Judaism Award in 1970.

[Bezalel Gordon (2nd ed.)]

BACON, HIRSCH LEIB (1875–1928), *ḥazzan*. Hirsch Leib Bacon was born in Kolbuszow into the Bacon family of cantors. He studied in the yeshivah in Tarnow and during the period of his studies sang with Cantor Eliyahu Brandsdorfer. He moved to Nowy Sacz and established a choir that performed ḥasidic melodies and Psalms. In 1905 he was appointed cantor in the great synagogue of Chryzanow. He composed music for the Sabbath and holiday prayers, and for other occasions. He wrote hundreds of compositions. His son, Prof. Yitzhak Bacon, chairman of the department of Yiddish at Ben-Gurion University in Beersheba, is now publishing his father's compositions, which he wrote down from memory. In 1919 Hirsch Leib Bacon moved to Berlin and served as cantor in the *bet midrash* at Grenadierstrasse 37 until 1924, when he returned to Chryzanow.

[Akiva Zimmerman]

BACON, ISRAEL (1910–1943), *ḥazzan*. Bacon was born in Chryzanow, to a family of cantors, originating from Kolbuszow in Galicia. He was the son of Hirsch Leib Bacon. At the age of nine he went with his parents to Berlin and sang in his father's choir. At the age of eleven he was asked by the Jewish theater in Berlin to sing at a performance. His father did not approve and as a result he returned to Chryzanow with his son. Israel Bacon studied in the yeshivot of Tschebin and Bobov. At the age of 21 he appeared in various cities of Europe. He served as a cantor in Czechoslovakia and sang in concerts in London, Hamburg, Antwerp, and Berlin, where he also participated in activities of the Kulturbund. In Berlin he produced several records, including selections of Psalms and songs in Yiddish and Hebrew. Among his piano accompanists on these records was the musician Arno *Nadel. In 1939 he was appointed cantor at the *bet midrash* "Ahavat Re'im" in Cracow, but when he arrived there, the war broke out. He was transferred to the Tarnow ghetto where he encouraged the Jews with his singing. In 1943 he was taken to the extermination camp in Belzec where he was killed.

[Akiva Zimmerman]

°**BACON, ROGER** (c. 1214–1294), English philosopher and Hebraist. Bacon studied at Oxford (probably) and – from 1236 at the latest – Paris. He learned Hebrew, and his transliterations, reflecting Sephardi pronunciation, imply Jewish assistance. Bacon's advanced criticisms of scientific and theological methodology led Bonaventura, general of the Franciscans, to stop his teaching at Paris; after Stephen Tempier's Paris condemnation (1277) of the 219 propositions and of magical instruction, he was allegedly imprisoned for 14 years by Jerome de Ascoli, later Pope Nicholas IV. Meanwhile, in 1266, Clement IV (Guy du Foulques) had directed him to disregard his order's instructions and to write up, *in extenso*, his scholarship and views on ecclesiastical abuses. Bacon's resultant writings contain frequent references to Hebrew as the fountainhead of all philosophical knowledge and as indispensable for Bible study, all Latin versions being corrupt. While criticizing *Andrew of Saint Victor for his addiction to Jewish exegesis and deprecating contemporary acknowledgment of Andrew as authoritative, Bacon commended the former's resort to the original Hebrew text. He extolled Robert Grosseteste's endeavors to promote Hebrew studies, and a certain "*homo sapientissimus*" (probably William of Mara) for pursuing them.

Besides substantial competence in biblical Hebrew, Bacon evinced interest in the Jewish calendar and a grasp of linguistic science; he appreciated the affinity of Hebrew, Aramaic, and Arabic as comparable to that of the Romance languages. He contemplated writing a Hebrew grammar, and a fragment – the earliest known Hebrew grammar by a named gentile scholar in the West – survives (Cambridge Ms. Ff. 6. 13; appended to Bacon's *Greek Grammar*, ed. E. Nolan, 1902). Hirsch, who assembled and translated the relevant passages in Bacon's works, tentatively connected some correspondence (Ms. Toulouse 402) regarding Hebrew grammar and the calendar with Bacon (S. Berger, *Quam Notitiam*... (1893), 37–38).

BIBLIOGRAPHY: S.A. Hirsch, in: JQR, 12 (1899/1900), 34 35; B. Smalley, *The Study of the Bible in the Middle Ages* (1952²), index; A.G. Little, *Roger Bacon* (1928). **ADD. BIBLIOGRAPHY:** B. Clegg, *The First Scientist: A Life of Roger Bacon* (2004); ODNB online.

[Raphael Loewe]

BACON, SHLOMO REUVEN (1899–1986), *ḥazzan*. Shlomo Reuven Bacon was born in Tchekova near Chryzanow into the Bacon family of cantors originating from Kolbuszow in Galicia. From childhood he had a beautiful voice and sang in the choir of father cantor Haim Bacon, who served as *ḥazzan* in the cities of Des, Berlin, and Klausenberg, and was killed in the Holocaust. Shlomo Reuven Bacon also sang in the opera in Klausenberg and won great acclaim, but his father's opposition caused him to leave the opera. He was appointed as a cantor in London and from there moved to South Africa, serving for many years as a cantor in the Yovel Synagogue in Johannesburg. He was the secretary of the Cantorial Association in South Africa.

[Akiva Zimmerman]

BACON, YEHUDA (1929–), Israel painter. Born in Moravska Ostrava, Czechoslovakia, Bacon spent the years 1942–45 in concentration camps and was later sent on the "death march" to *Mauthausen, where he was liberated. In 1946 he was taken to Israel by *Youth Aliyah and studied at the *Bezalel School of Art, Jerusalem, and then continued his studies in Italy, London (1956–57 at the Central School of Art), New York, and Paris (1957–58, Beaux Arts). He was the head of the department of etching and lithography at the Bezalel School of Art and taught at Haifa University. Bacon concentrated on graphic work, but turned to a variety of media including oils, watercolors, and inks. The horror of the Holocaust was present in his work, tempered by faith in humanity. His later work, however, had a gentle, romantic quality. He was a witness at the Eichmann Trial in Jerusalem, and the Auschwitz Trial in Frankfurt. He won the Gold Medal of the Academie International in 1972, the Moshe Kol Prize in 1984, and the Sussman Prize for Artists from Yad Vashem for using the Holocaust as a subject. His drawing *In Memory of the Czech Transport to the Gas Chambers* depicting his father's murder is displayed at the Yad Vashem Museum.

BACON, YIDEL (1886–1954), *ḥazzan*. Yidel Bacon was born in Kolbuszow and belonged to the Bacon family of cantors. He studied cantorial singing with Cantor Baruch Shorr in Lvov. He sang in the choir of Cantor Eliezer Goldberg in Cracow, where he studied at the conservatory. He served as a cantor in Lancut in Galicia and from there moved to Leipzig. Later he moved to the United States and served as cantor at the Attorney Synagogue in New York City. He composed music for many sections of the prayer service and assisted in the training of cantors. Some of his compositions for the prayers of the High Holy Days have been published by the Cantorial Council of America.

[Akiva Zimmerman]

BACRI, Algerian family prominent near the end of Ottoman rule, with special status within the community and at the dey's court. The family had an important role in diplomatic relations between the Ottomans and several European states as well as in ransoming Jewish captives and arming neutral fleets in the Mediterranean. It had two branches, one in the capital, *Algiers, which had relations with France in Napoleon's time, the other near the western borders, in *Oran, which had connections with Spain. Relations with France, however, were not smooth, as in 1795 when the authorities impounded their merchandise in retaliation for the family's arming a pirate ship. After the Napoleonic era the Bacris did increased business with Spain.

[Shalom Bar-Asher (2nd ed.)]

JOSEPH COEN BACRI (1740–1817), banker, trader, and communal leader, was born in Algiers. He founded the Bacri Frères firm which played a significant role in Algerian politics for fifty years. The firm was an important wheat supplier to France during the Napoleonic period. In 1811, after the execution on a charge of treason of his son David, who had been active manager of the firm for several years, Joseph reassumed the management of the firm's affairs and was appointed leader of the Algerian Jewish community by the dey. However, in 1816, the dey confiscated his possessions and banished him from Algiers. According to other sources, he fled because of the anti-Jewish atmosphere. Bacri died in poverty in Leghorn.

DAVID COEN BACRI (1770–1811), son of Joseph, was a financier and communal leader. David had widespread shipping and trading interests and served as the financial agent for many European firms and governments. In 1797 he married Aziza, a niece of Naphtali *Busnach. Busnach, a statesman who was able to manipulate the Algerian Regency for his own purposes, became a partner in the firm. Under David's management, the firm of Bacri Busnach became so powerful and its operations so extensive that it was able to defy the British government and buy captured allied vessels from French privateers.

Acting on the advice of Bacri Busnach, the dey authorized a five-million franc loan to the French Directory. The credit for the loan was later transferred to the firm. The subsequent 30-year-long dispute over the settlement of the loan was one of the factors which exacerbated relations between Algiers and France, and led eventually to the French occupation of Algeria in 1830. After Naphtali's assassination by a soldier of the dey's palace guard in June 1805, Bacri Busnach became insolvent. David was imprisoned for allegedly owing the government five million francs. The European governments, however, which had profited by David's business activities, put pressure on the Algerian Regency and secured his release. These same governments then helped David set up the Bacri firm in payment for his past services to them. In 1806 the dey named him head of the Jewish community. Subsequently, his enemy, David Duran, who wanted the leadership for himself, denounced Bacri to the authorities and he was executed for treason.

JACOB COEN BACRI (1763–1836), a financier, served as French consul in Algiers under the restored Bourbon monarchy. In 1827, he represented Charles X in negotiations with Dey Hassan in regard to a French claim. Hassan, angered by Bacri's impassioned defense of French interests, insulted him. The French government regarded the dey's action as a national insult and as an immediate excuse to declare war. The war resulted in the French conquest of Algiers in 1830 and the banishment of the dey.

Bacri, who had left Algiers at the outbreak of the war, settled in Paris. During the last years of his life, he was continually importuned by creditors because of his inability to collect a 35-million-franc debt from the Spanish government.

[Joachim O. Ronall]

BIBLIOGRAPHY: M. Eisenbeth, in: *Revue Africaine*, 96 (1952), 372–83; M. Rosenstock, "Economic and Social Condition among the Jews in Algeria," in: H.J. 18 (1956), 3–26; Hirschberg, Afrikah, index (includes bibliographies); R. Ayoun and B. Cohen, *Les Juifs d'Algérie*, (1982), 102–13. **ADD. BIBLIOGRAPHY:** M. Hoexter, "Ha-Edah ha-Yehudit be-Aljir ve-Mekoma …" in: *Sefunot*, 17 (1983), 133–63.

BACRI, JEAN-PIERRE (1951–), French actor, playwright, and screenwriter. Bacri was born in Castiglione (French Algeria), where his father was a mailman and part-time worker at the local movie theater. The family moved to Cannes at the end of Algeria's war of independence war and Bacri began to write copy for an advertising company in Paris in 1976 while studying theater at the prestigious Cours Simon and writing his first comedies, including the 1980 *Le grain de sable*, which was awarded the Tristan Bernard Prize. He began to make a name for himself as an actor in Alexandre Arcady's feature film *Le Grand Pardon*, dealing with the Jewish-Algerian mafia, and in Luc Besson's *Subway* (1985), where he established his trademark character, taciturn and grouchy but sensitive. After collaborating regularly with satiric playwright Jean-Michel Ribes, Bacri went on to create several witty, ironic, and biting but humanistic comedies, co-written with his wife, Agnes Jaoui, which became tremendous popular successes that were adapted for the screen: *Cuisines et dépendances* (1993) and *Un air de famille* (1995). The couple also adapted two plays by Alan Ayckbourn for the screen, *Smoking* and *No Smoking*, for renowned avant-garde film director Alain Resnais (1993). The collaboration with Resnais later gave birth to the musical comedy *On connait la chanson* (1997), a witty exploration of French popular culture. Actor and co-screenwriter in Agnes Jaoui's first movies, *Le goût des autres* (2002) and *Comme une image* (2005), Bacri was also worked in films by Sam Karmann, Alain Chabat, Nicole Garcia, and Claude Berry, establishing himself as one of France's most popular actors.

[Dror Franck Sullaper (2nd ed.)]

BADAJOZ, city in Castile, western Spain, near the Portuguese frontier. Jewish settlement evidently began to develop in the 11th century, when Jewish artisans and merchants engaged in international trade are mentioned. After the Christian reconquest, the Jews of Badajoz were ordered to pay the *oncena* in addition to other taxes for which they were liable (1258). In the 15th century the Badajoz community claimed that it had been exempted from all taxes and imposts and was required to produce evidence at the synod of *Valladolid. The tax assessment for Castilian Jewry of 1474 required the Badajoz and Almendral communities to pay the sum of 7,500 *maravedis*. The enactment ordering the segregation of Jews from Christians was implemented in Badajoz during the 1480s, and many Jews were turned out of their homes. After the edict of expulsion of the Jews from Spain in 1492, large numbers of the exiles passed through Badajoz on their way to Portugal. Badajoz remained an important Converso center. Between 1493 and 1499 the local inquisitional tribunal punished no fewer than 231 New Christians. David *Reuveni was burned at an auto-da-fé in Badajoz in 1535 after a long imprisonment there. The temporary union of Portugal and Spain in 1580 facilitated the return of some descendants of the Castilian refugees to Castile. In 1635 a large group of Portuguese Marranos was discovered in Badajoz and was relentlessly pursued by the Inquisition. In 1639 some members of the Acosta family, one of the most important families in the city – two sisters and their sister-in-law – were accused by the Inquisition in nearby Llerena of remaining loyal to Judaism. The family's Jewish origin was well known in the city. The family had arrived from Portugal at the end of the 16th century. The scandal that the trial of members of a very wealthy and influential family caused was devastating. The three women, Isabel, Beatriz, and Clara, belonged to a family that had originally left Castile for Portugal in 1492 because they wanted to remain Jewish but soon found themselves trapped in Portugal and forcibly converted in 1497. The three were thrown into prison. The trial was the consequence of a love affair between a female member of the family and an employee of the family business who was of Morisco origin. During the trial the differences between the members of the same New Christian family became clear: Some were Crypto-Jews, others wished to integrate within Christian society, while a few wished to maintain the family link at all costs.

BIBLIOGRAPHY: M. Ramón Martínez, *Historia del reino de Badajoz durante la dominación española* (1905), 80–81; J. Lucio d'Azevedo, *Evolução do Sebastianismo* (1918), 194ff.; H.C. Lea, *History of the Inquisition of Spain* (1922), index; Suárez Fernández, Documentos, index; Rodríguez- Moñino, in: REJ, 115 (1956), 73–86; Baer, Urkunden, index; A.Z. Aescoly, *Ha-Tenu'ot ha-Meshiḥiyyot be-Yisrael* (1956), 372; Ashtor, Korot, 2 (1966), 128–366. **ADD. BIBLIOGRAPHY:** P. Huerga Criado, in *Sefarad*, 49 (1989), 97–121

[Haim Beinart / Yom Tov Assis (2nd ed.)]

°**BADÈ, WILLIAM FREDERIC** (1871–1936), biblical archaeologist. Born in Carver, Minnesota, Badè taught Old Testament literature at Moravian Theological Seminary, Bethlehem, Pennsylvania, from 1898 to 1902; from 1902 to 1936 he was professor of Old Testament literature and Semitic languages at the Pacific School of Religion, Berkeley, California. He excavated Tell al-Naṣba (Mizpah?), north of Jerusalem, in five campaigns between 1926 and 1935, clearing the mound almost completely. Badè published *Old Testament in the Light of Today* (1915), *A Manual of Excavations in the Near East* (1934), and *Excavations at Tell al-Naṣba, 1926 and 1927: A Preliminary Report* (1928).

BIBLIOGRAPHY: Albright, in: BASOR, 62 (1936), 4–5; idem, in: JAOS, 52 (1932), 52–53.

[Michael Avi-Yonah]

BADEN, part of the *Land* of Baden-Wuerttemberg, Germany. The former grand duchy was created in 1806 from parts of various territories (including the Palatinate), where until then the Jews had formed no united community or shared a common history. The earliest records of the presence of Jews in these territories relate to Gruensfeld (1218), Ueberlingen (1226), *Freiburg (c. 1230), Lauda and *Tauberbischofsheim (1235), *Constance (1241), and Sinsheim (early 13th century). The Jews had been expelled from several of these areas at various times: the Palatinate in 1391, the margravate of Baden in 1470, Austrian Breisgau in 1573, and the diocese of Basle in 1581. Until 1806 the history of the Jews in the margravate of Baden, which subsequently formed the nucleus of the state of Baden, may be summarized briefly. After the *Black Death, 1348–49, few Jews lived there but even these were expelled in 1470, as a result of the blood libel of *Endingen (South Baden). Jews were allowed to return to Baden at the beginning of the 16th century. In 1535 the margravate of Baden was divided into Baden-Baden and Baden-Durlach, to be united again in 1771. The Jews were expelled from Baden-Baden in 1614, but readmitted during the Thirty Years' War (1618–48). According to the first legislation concerning the status of the Jews in Baden-Baden in 1714, the territorial organization of the Jewry was headed by two lay officers (*Schultheisse*) and a rabbi. In Baden-Durlach Jews were first tolerated officially in 1537, but were expelled during the Thirty Years' War and readmitted in 1666. The Jewish population numbered 24 families in 1709, increasing to 160 families by 1738.

After the grand duchy of Baden was created, the position of its *Schutzjuden* ("protected Jews") improved. In the first constitutional edict of May 14, 1807, Judaism was recognized as a tolerated religion; a year later, the sixth edict afforded the Jews irrevocable civil rights and abolished the marriage restrictions imposed on them (see *Familiants' Laws). Local civil rights, however, remained severely restricted. The ninth edict (the so-called "*Judenedikt*" of Jan. 13, 1809) granted the Jews an officially recognized state organization, required them to adopt permanent family names, and determined their as yet very curtailed civil status. The constitution of 1818 implicitly confirmed the civil rights granted to the Jews by the edicts but denied them equal political rights. The struggle for emancipation focused on local civil rights and met with fierce and sometimes violent resistance in many villages and towns. Baden's liberal movement failed to endorse the idea of Jewish emancipation, most of its leading figures echoing public sentiment on the matter instead. Anti-Jewish outrages, often connected with the issue of emancipation, occurred in Baden in 1819 (*Hep-Hep), 1830, 1848, and 1862. Severe and widespread anti-Jewish rioting accompanied the revolution of 1848, especially in Northern Baden, and as a consequence the Diet pulled back from granting full emancipation to the Jews once more. In 1862 local civil rights were eventually granted, and the last of Baden's cities to exclude Jews (Baden-Baden, Freiburg, Constance, and Offenburg), allowed them to settle there. Nevertheless, animosity toward the Jews continued to be expressed in Baden, where Adolph *Stoecker's antisemitic Christian Social Party found numbers of adherents. After the Baden Army Corps was incorporated into the Prussian army, no Jew was promoted to the position of reserve officer or medical officer. Professorships too were granted almost exclusively to baptized Jews.

In 1868 Grand Duke Frederick I appointed the Durlach lawyer, Moritz *Ellstaetter, his minister of finance, making

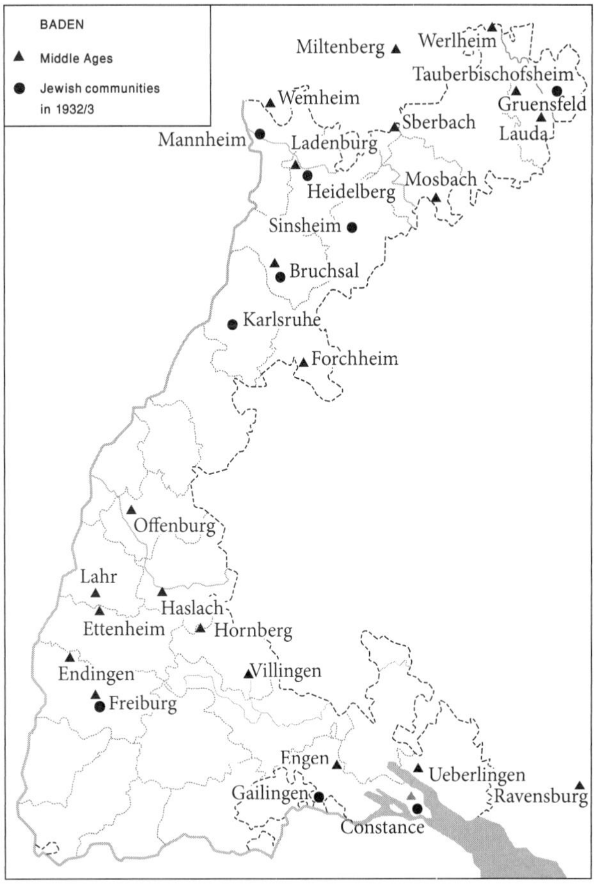

Jewish centers of population in Baden, Germany.

him the first German Jew to hold a ministerial position. Theodor *Herzl tried to interest the German emperor in Zionism through the intervention of the grand duke. The Jews of Baden also participated in its political life. In 1862 the lawyer R. Kusel was elected to represent Karlsruhe in the second chamber, and Ludwig Frank of Mannheim was elected to the Landtag and later to the Reichstag as Social Democratic member. He was among the 589 Baden Jews who fell in World War I. Two Jews were in the first postwar cabinet of Baden, L. Marum (minister of justice, murdered by the Nazis in 1933) and Ludwig *Haas (minister of the interior), who was also active in Jewish affairs.

In the Middle Ages Baden Jewry engaged in commerce and moneylending, later in livestock-dealing (which was the main source of income for the Jews in the countryside) and retail trading. In the 19th century occupational difficulties, the lack of progress in the struggle for emancipation, and anti-Jewish riots resulted in Jewish immigration to America. Baden Jewry was one of the earliest German Jewish Territorial Organizations to establish a state-recognized central organization (1809) – the Oberrat ("supreme council") – which in conjunction with the Synod (established in 1895) represented and directed the affairs of the community. Until its reorganization on May 14, 1923, the Oberrat was under state control. Religious controversy between the Orthodox and *Reform factions began in the early 19th century, the Reform later tending to predominate with the decline of the rural communities. When the *Karlsruhe community included an organ in its new synagogue (1868) and introduced reforms into the services, the Orthodox Jews, led by B.H. Wormser, established a separatist congregation there, the only one in Baden, which was given state recognition.

In 1806 Baden had a Jewish population of about 12,000, which had risen to 24,099 by 1862. As the result of emigration after the rise of Nazism, it decreased from 20,617 in 1933 to 8,725 by 1939. The Jews of Baden were among the first to be deported from Germany. On Oct. 22, 1940, some 5,600 Baden Jews, along with others from the Palatinate and the Saar, were transported to *Gurs concentration camp (southern France), from where they were further deported to Poland from 1942 onward. Approximately 500 Jews from Baden survived in France. The Oberrat was reestablished after the war. In 1962 the cemetery in Gurs was leased to the Baden Oberrat for 99 years. In 1969 there were 1,096 Jews in six communities (66 Jews in Baden-Baden, 248 in Freiburg, 135 in *Heidelberg, 260 in Karlsruhe, 387 in *Mannheim and Constance), with N.P. Levinson as chief rabbi. After 1989 new communities were founded in Emmendingen, Loerrach, *Pforzheim, and Rottweil-Villingen. As a result of the emigration of Jews from the former Soviet Union, the number of community members rose to 4,485 in 2003.

BIBLIOGRAPHY: B. Rosenthal, *Heimatgeschichte der badischen Juden* (1927), includes bibl.; *Gedenkbuch zum 125-jaehrigen Bestehen des Oberrats der Israeliten Badens* (1934); A. Lewin, *Geschichte der badischen Juden 1738–1909* (1909); R. Ruerup, in: *Zeitschrift fuer die Geschichte des Oberrheins*, 114 (1966), 241–300; N. Stein, in: YLBI, 1 (1956), 177–90; P. Sauer, *Dokumente ueber die Verfolgung der juedischen Buerger in Baden-Wuerttemberg…*, 2 pts. (1966); H. Schnee, *Die Hoffinanz und der moderne Staat*, 2 (1963), 43–86; idem, *Die Schicksale der juedischen Buerger Baden-Wuerttembergs 1933–45* (1969); F. Hundsnurscher and G. Taddey, *Die juedischen Gemeinden in Baden* (1968); Germ Jud, 2 (1968), 45–47; *Die Opfer der Nationalsozialistischen Judenverfolgung in Baden-Wuerttemberg* (1969). **ADD. BIBLIOGRAPHY:** M.A. Riff, in: YLBI, 21 (1976), 27–40; J.B. Paulus, *Juden in Baden 1809–1984* (1984); H.W. Smith, in: *Zeitschrift fuer die Geschichte des Oberrheins*, 141 (1993), 304–36; S. Rohrbacher, *Gewalt im Biedermeier* (1993), 186–201; U. Baumann, in: *Protestants, Catholics and Jews in Germany* (2001), 297–315; G.J. Teschner, *Die Deportation der badischen und saarpfaelzischen Juden …* (2002).

[Bernhard Brilling / Stefan Rohrbacher (2nd ed.)]

BADEN BEI WIEN, spa in N.E. Austria. During the later Middle Ages Jews doing business there lived in nearby Tribuswinkel. In 1805 Isaac Schischa of Mattersdorf was granted permission to settle in the town, opened a Jewish restaurant, and established a prayer room. From around 1800 there was a *Judenbad*, a bath frequented by Jews in Baden, but Jews were not granted the right of residence in the city until 1861. A synagogue for 500 was built in 1873, and the community of 80 members was officially recognized in 1878. The first rabbi, W. Reich, installed in 1880, brought about a compromise between Orthodox and Liberal elements and was active in the foundation of the Agudat Israel orphan home. The community increased mainly by settlers from Hungary. By 1928 it numbered 1,500 (6.7% of the total population), and was the third largest in Austria, but in 1934 there were only 1,108 Jewish inhabitants. On Nov. 10, 1938, the synagogue and all community buildings were blown up, and the Jewish population was arrested to "make room" for Aryans. In 1946 the congregation was reconstituted, with a prayer room; it had 30 members. There were about 80 Jews in Baden in 2004. A synagogue was built in 2004/5.

BIBLIOGRAPHY: W. Reich (ed.), *Festschrift zum 40-jaehrigen Jubileum der Chewra Kadische zu Baden bei Wien* (1914); *Juedisches Jahrbuch fuer Oesterreich* (1932); L. Moses, *Die Juden in Niederoesterreich* (1935), 203; Rosenkranz, in: *Yad Vashem Bulletin*, no. 14 (1964), 35–41. **ADD. BIBLIOGRAPHY:** H. Meissner, *Die Juden von Baden und ihr Friedhof* (2002).

[Henry Wasserman]

BADER, GERSHOM (Gustav; 1868–1953), Hebrew and Yiddish journalist and writer. Bader, who was born in Cracow, taught there after attending rabbinical seminaries outside Galicia. From 1893 until 1912 he lived in Lvov, where in 1904 he founded the first Yiddish daily in Galicia, the *Togblat* (from 1906, *Nayes Lemberger Togblat*), and contributed regularly to *Ha-Maggid* and other Hebrew papers. From 1896 to 1912 he published and edited the *Yidisher Folkskalender*, a popular Galician literary almanac. He translated Genesis into Polish and published Hebrew language textbooks. His anthologies,

Leket Peraḥim and *Zer Peraḥim* (1895–96), helped to popularize Hebrew literature and in 1896 he edited the fifth volume of the literary miscellany *Oẓar ha-Sifrut*. From 1896 to 1912 he produced the *Lukhes* annuals in Yiddish, and from 1903–04 a parallel Hebrew annual miscellany, *Ḥermon*. In 1912 Bader settled in New York, where he contributed to the *Togblat* and the *Jewish Morning Journal*. Of his Yiddish plays, the most successful was *Dem Rebens Nign* ("The Rabbi's Melody"), produced in 1919. His writings include: *Ḥelkat Meḥokek*, a life of Jesus (1889); *Medinah va-Ḥakhameha*, a lexicon of Galician Jewish cultural figures (1934); and *Mafte'aḥ le-Rashei Tevot...*, a dictionary of talmudic abbreviations (1951); *Jewish Spiritual Heroes* (3 vols., in English 1940); and his memoirs, *Mayne Zikhroynes* (1953).

BIBLIOGRAPHY: G. Bader, *Medinah va-Ḥakhameha* (1934), autobiographical preface; idem, in: *Genazim*, 1 (1960), 82–90 (autobiography); Rabbi Binyamin, *Mishpeḥot Soferim* (1959), 134–5.

[Getzel Kressel]

BADGE, JEWISH, distinctive sign compulsorily worn by Jews.

Muslim World

The introduction of a mark to distinguish persons not belonging to the religious faith of the majority did not originate in Christendom, where it was later radically imposed, but in Islam. It seems that Caliph Omar II (717–20), not Omar I, as is sometimes stated, was the first ruler to order that every non-Muslim, the *dhimmī*, should wear vestimentary distinctions (called *giyār*, i.e., distinguishing marks) of a different color for each minority group. The ordinance was unequally observed, but it was reissued and reinforced by Caliph al-Mutawakkil (847–61). Subsequently it remained in force over the centuries, with a few variations. Thus, in Sicily the Saracen governor in 887/8 compelled the Christians to wear on their garments and put on their doors a piece of cloth in the form of a swine, and the Jews to affix a similar sign in the form of a donkey. In addition, the Jews were compelled to wear yellow belts and special hats.

Christendom

Although written documentary testimony concerning distinctive signs worn by Jews from the 12th century is still lacking, pictorial representations of this period, especially in the Germanic countries, introduce the pointed hat. This is subsequently referred to as the "Jewish hat," worn by Jews or depicted in allegorical representations of Judaism ("Synagoga"). It would seem, however, that this distinction was instituted by the Jews themselves. There are some ambiguous references to the compulsory imposition of distinctive Jewish clothing in documents from the beginning of the 13th century (Charter of Alais, 1200: Synodal rules of Odo, bishop of Paris, c. 1200). The consistent record, however, can be traced back only to canon 68 of the Fourth *Lateran Council (1215): "In several provinces, a difference in vestment distinguishes the Jews or the Saracens from the Christians; but in others, the confusion has reached such proportions that a difference can no longer be perceived. Hence, at times it has occurred that Christians have had sexual intercourse in error with Jewish or Saracen women and Jews or Saracens with Christian women. That the crime of such a sinful mixture shall no longer find evasion or cover under the pretext of error, we order that they [Jews and Saracens] of both sexes, in all Christian lands and at all times, shall be publicly differentiated from the rest of the population by the quality of their garment, especially since that this is ordained by Moses...." Both the allusion to biblical law (Lev. 19), and the inclusion of the canon among a series of others regulating the Jewish position indicate that the decree was directed especially against the Jews.

Implementation of the council's decision varied in the countries of the West in both the form of the distinctive sign and the date of its application.

ENGLAND. In England papal influence was at this time particularly strong. The recommendations of the Lateran Council were repeated in an order of March 30, 1218. However, before long the wealthier Jews, and later on entire communities, paid to be exempted, notwithstanding the reiteration of the order by the diocesan council of Oxford in 1222. In 1253, however, the obligation to wear the badge was renewed in the period of general reaction, by Henry III, who ordered the *tabula* to be worn in a prominent position. In the *statutum de Judeismo* of 1275, Edward I stipulated the color of the badge and increased the size. A piece of yellow taffeta, six fingers long and three broad, was to be worn above the heart by every Jew over the age of seven years. In England the badge took the form of the Tablets of the Law, considered to symbolize the Old Testament, in which form it is to be seen in various caricatures and portraits of medieval English Jews.

FRANCE. In 1217 the papal legate in southern France ordered that the Jews should wear a *rota* ("wheel") on their outer garment but shortly afterward the order was rescinded. However, in 1219 King Philip Augustus ordered the Jews to wear the badge, apparently in the same form. Discussions regarding the permissibility of wearing the badge on the Sabbath when not attached to the garment are reported by *Isaac b. Moses of Vienna, author of the *Or Zaru'a*, who was in France about 1217–18. Numerous church councils (Narbonne 1227, Rouen 1231, Arles 1234, Béziers 1246, Albi 1254, etc.) reiterated the instructions for wearing the badge, and a general edict for the whole of France was issued by Louis IX (Saint Louis) on June 19, 1269. This edict was endorsed by Philip the Bold, Philip the Fair, Louis X, Philip V, and others, and by the councils of Pont-Audemer (1279), Nîmes (1284), etc. The circular badge was normally to be worn on the breast; some regulations also required that a second sign should be worn on the back. At times it was placed on the bonnet or at the level of the belt. The badge was yellow in color, or of two shades, white and red. Wearing it was compulsory from the age of either seven or thirteen years. Any Jew found without the badge forfeited his garment to his denunciator. In cases of a second offense a severe fine was imposed. When traveling, the Jew was exempted from wearing the badge. Philip the Fair extracted fiscal benefits from the compulsory wearing of the badge, by annual distribution of the badges by the royal tax collectors at a fixed price.

SPAIN. The obligation to wear the Badge of Shame was reenacted by the secular authorities in Spain shortly after the promulgation of the decrees of the Lateran Council, and in 1218 Pope Honorius III instructed the archbishop of Toledo to see that it was rigorously enforced. The Spanish Jews did not submit to this passively, and some of them threatened to leave the country for the area under Muslim rule. In consequence, the pope authorized the enforcement of the regulation to be suspended. The obligation was indeed reenacted sporadically (e.g., in Aragon 1228, Navarre 1234, Portugal 1325). However, it was not consistently enforced, and Jews who had influence at court would often secure special exemption. Alfonso X the Wise of Castile in his *Siete Partidas* (1263) imposed a fine or lashing as the penalty for a Jew who neglected the order. In 1268 James I of Aragon exempted the Jews from wearing the badge, requiring them on the other hand to wear a round cape (*capa rotunda*). In Castile, Henry III (1390–1406) yielded in 1405 to the demand of the Cortes and required even his Jewish courtiers to wear the badge. As a result of Vicente *Ferrer's agitation, the Jews were ordered in 1412 to wear distinctive clothing and a red badge, and they were further required to let their hair and beards grow long. The successors of Henry III renewed the decrees concerning the badge. In Aragon, John I, in 1393, prescribed special clothing for the Jews. In 1397 Queen Maria (the consort of King Martin) ordered all the Jews in Barcelona, both residents and visitors, to wear on their chests a circular patch of yellow cloth, a span in diameter, with a red "bull's eye" in the center. They were to dress only in clothing of pale green color – as a sign of mourning for the ruin of their Temple, which they suffered because they had turned their backs upon Jesus – and their hats were to be high and wide with a short, wide *cuculla*. Violators were to be fined ten *libras* and stripped of their clothes wherever caught. When in 1400 King Martin granted the Jews of Lérida a charter of privileges, he required them, nevertheless, to wear the customary badge. In 1474 the burghers of Cervera sought to impose upon the local Jews a round badge of other than the customary form. In the period before the expulsion of the Jews from Spain in 1492, the wearing of the Jewish badge was almost universally enforced, and some persons demanded that it should be extended also to Conversos.

ITALY. Presumably the order of the Lateran Council was reenacted in Rome very soon after its promulgation in 1215, but it was certainly not consistently enforced. In 1221–22 the "enlightened" emperor Frederick II Hohenstaufen ordered all the Jews of the Kingdom of Sicily to wear a distinguishing badge of bluish color in the shape of the Greek letter τ and also to grow beards in order to be more easily distinguishable from non-Jews. In the same year the badge was imposed in Pisa and probably elsewhere. In the Papal States the obligation was first specifically imposed so far as is known by Alexander IV in 1257: there is extant a moving penitential poem written on this occasion by Benjamin b. Abraham *Anav expressing the passionate indignation of the Roman Jews on this occasion. The badge here took the form of a circular yellow patch a handspan in diameter to be worn by men on a prominent place on the outer garment, while women had to wear two blue stripes on their veil. In 1360 an ordinance of the city of Rome required all male Jews, with the exception of physicians, to wear a coarse red cape, and all women to wear a red apron. Inspectors were appointed to enforce the regulation. Noncompliance was punished by a fine of 11 scudi; informers who pointed out offenders were entitled to half the fine. The ordinance was revised in 1402, eliminating the reward for informing and exempting the Jews from wearing the special garb inside the ghetto. In Sicily there was from an early period a *custos rotulae* whose function it was to ensure that the obligation was not neglected. Elsewhere in Italy, however, the enforcement was sporadic, although it was constantly being demanded by fanatical preachers and sometimes temporarily enacted. The turning point came with the bull *Cum nimis absurdum* of Pope Paul *IV in 1555, which inaugurated the ghetto system. This enforced the wearing of the badge (called by the Italian Jews *scimanno*, from Heb. *siman*) for the Papal States, later to be imitated throughout Italy (except in Leghorn), and enforced until the period of the French Revolution. In Rome, as well as in the Papal States in the south of France, it took the form of a yellow hat for men, a yellow kerchief for women. In the Venetian dominions the color was red. In Candia (Crete), then under Venetian rule, Jewish shops had to be distinguished by the badge. David d'Ascoli, who published in 1559 a Latin protest against the degrading regulation, was severely punished and his work was destroyed.

GERMANY. In Germany and the other lands of the Holy Roman Empire, the pointed hat was first in use as a distinctive sign. It was not officially imposed until the second half of the 13th century (*Schwabenspiegel*, art. 214, c. 1275; *Weichbild-Vulgata*, art. 139, second half of 13th century; cf. Council of Breslau, 1267; Vienna, 1267; Olmuetz, 1342; Prague, 1355, etc.). The church councils of Breslau and Vienna, both held in 1267, required the Jews of Silesia, Poland, and Austria to wear not a badge but the pointed hat characteristic of Jewish garb (the *pileum cornutum*). A church council held in Ofen (Budapest) in 1279 decreed that the Jews were to wear on the chest a round patch in the form of a wheel. The badge was imposed for the first time in Augsburg in 1434, and its general enforcement was demanded by Nicolaus of *Cusa and John of *Capistrano. In 1530 the ordinance was applied to the whole of Germany (*Reichspolizeiordnung*, art. 22). In the course of the

15th century, a Jewish badge, in addition to the Jewish hat, was introduced in various forms into Germany. A church council which met in Salzburg in 1418 ordered Jewish women to attach bells to their dresses so that their approach might be heard from a distance. In Augsburg in 1434 the Jewish men were ordered to attach yellow circles to their clothes, in front, and the women were ordered to wear yellow pointed veils. Jews on a visit to Nuremberg were required to wear a type of long, wide hood falling over the back, by which they would be distinguished from the local Jews. The obligation to wear the yellow badge was imposed upon all the Jews in Germany in 1530 and in Austria in 1551. As late as in the reign of Maria Theresa (1740–80) the Jews of Prague were required to wear yellow collars over their coats.

Discontinuance

In the new communities which became established in Western Europe (and later America) from the close of the 16th century under somewhat freer conditions the wearing of the Jewish badge was never imposed, though sometimes suggested by fanatics. In Poland, partly probably because the Jews constituted a distinct ethnic element, it was likewise virtually unknown except in some major cities under German influence. Similarly the Court Jews of Germany were unable to perform their function unless dressed like other people. In the course of the 18th century, although there was no official modification of the established policy, the wearing of the Jewish badge came to be neglected in a good part of Europe. In Venice the red hat continued to be worn by elderly persons and rabbis through sheer conservatism.

From the 17th century, there were some regional suspensions of the distinctive sign in Germany, as also for the Jews of Vienna in 1624, and for those of Mannheim in 1691. It was abrogated at the end of the 18th century with Jewish emancipation. Thus, on Sept. 7, 1781, the yellow "wheel" was abolished by Emperor Joseph II in all the territories of the Austrian crown. In the Papal States in France the yellow hat was abolished in 1791 after the French Revolution reached the area, although some persons retained it until forbidden to do so by official proclamation. In the Papal States in Italy, on the other hand, the obligation was reimposed as late as 1793. When in 1796–97 the armies of the French Revolution entered Italy and the ghettos were abolished, the obligation to wear the Jewish badge disappeared. Its reimposition was threatened but not carried out during the reactionary period after the fall of Napoleon, and it then seemed that the Badge of Shame was only an evil memory of the past.

It was to commemorate the yellow badge or hat that Theodor Herzl chose this color for the cover of the first Zionist periodical *Die Welt*. It was in the same spirit that the *Juedische Rundschau*, the organ of the Zionist Organization in Germany, wrote on the morrow of the Nazi rise to power: "Wear it with pride, this yellow badge" (no. 27, April 4, 1933).

[Bernhard Blumenkranz]

Yellow Badge in the Nazi Period

In 1938 the Nazis compelled Jewish shopkeepers to display the words "Jewish business" in their windows but did not introduce distinctive signs to be worn by Jews until after the occupation of Poland. The first to issue an order on his own initiative, without awaiting instructions from the central authority, was the town Kommandant of Wloclawek, s.s. Oberfuehrer Cramer, who, on Oct. 24, 1939, ordered that every Jew in Wloclawek was to wear a distinctive sign on the back in the form of a yellow triangle at least 15 cm. in size. The order was published in the *Leslauer Bote* (Oct. 25, 1939). The order applied to all Jews, without distinction of age or sex. This device was rapidly adopted by other commanders in the occupied regions in the East and received official approval, in consideration of the antisemitic sentiments prevailing among the local Polish public, which received the new German measure with enthusiasm. The dates of application of the measure varied. There were regions where the instructions were applied even before they were issued in the General-Government, such as in Cracow, where the Jews were compelled to wear the sign from Nov. 18, 1939, whereas the date throughout the General-Gouvernment was Dec. 1, 1939. In Lvov the order was applied as from July 15, 1941, and in eastern Galicia from Sept. 15, 1941. On the other hand, in certain places the instruction is known to have been applied only after publication of the general order, as for example in Warsaw on Dec. 12, 1939, and not on Dec. 1, 1939, even though Warsaw was included in the General-Government. In the smaller communities, the official German instructions were replaced by an announcement of the *Judenrat.

In the West, the situation was totally different. In the *Reichsgebiet* (the territory of the Reich proper, as opposed to the occupied territories), the order was issued on Sept. 1, 1941. It was published in the *Reichsgesetzblatt* and was applied as from Sept. 19, 1941. This date was also valid for the Jews of Bohemia, Moravia, and Slovakia. The age from which the wearing of the sign was compulsory was six years for Germany and Western Europe and ten years for Eastern Europe. In certain places the age differed. In Holland the order was applied as from May 1942, while in Belgium and France the Jews were compelled to wear the distinctive sign from June 1942. A meeting had been held in Paris in March 1942 to coordinate the application of the order in these three countries. In Bulgaria the order was applied from September 1942, in Greece from February 1943, and in Hungary from April 1944. The type of distinctive sign varied, the following being the principal forms: a yellow Shield (Star) of David inscribed with *J* or *Jude*, etc.; a white armband with a blue Shield of David on it; a Shield of David, with or without inscription and in various colors; a yellow armband with or without inscription; a yellow button in the form of a Shield of David; a metal tag inscribed with the letter *J*; a yellow triangle; a yellow circle. This general use of the Shield of David as the Jewish badge was unknown in the Middle Ages. The inscriptions appearing on the badges were specially chosen to resemble Hebrew characters. After the Jews were compelled to reside in ghettos, they were also forced to wear the distinctive sign in conformity with the order applying to the region in which the ghetto was located. In the concentration camps they wore the sign which designated political prisoners on which was sewn a triangle or a yellow stripe to distinguish them from non-Jewish prisoners. In the *Reichsgebiet*, as well as in several of the occupied countries, the Germans introduced distinctive signs on Jewish business premises, passports, and ration cards, where the letter *J* was overprinted in a most conspicuous manner.

REACTIONS. Jews reacted with dignity to the order and wore the sign as if it were a decoration. However, they did not realize the danger which lay in wearing a distinctive sign. Non-Jews, especially in Eastern Europe, generally accepted this anti-Jewish measure with enthusiasm and saw in it an opportunity to remove the Jews from commercial, economic, and public life. In the West, reactions varied. The Jews could often rely on the hatred of the Germans by the public, and this even brought active support to the Jews. The Dutch wore the badge out of solidarity with the Jewish citizens. Three-hundred thousand replicas of the badge were produced and distributed throughout Holland bearing the inscription: "Jews and non-Jews stand united in their struggle!" In Denmark the badge was never introduced as a result of the courageous resistance of King Christian X, who was said to have threatened to wear it himself.

CONSEQUENCES. The principal objective in introducing distinctive signs for the Jews was to erect a barrier between them and non-Jews and to restrict their movements. The Germans achieved this objective to a large extent, despite the various reactions which rendered application of the order difficult. The Jews increasingly concentrated in closed districts, even before the establishment of the ghettos by the Nazis, for fear of being arrested and deported to concentration camps. A Jew had the choice of concealing the sign and thus becoming an offender liable to a deportation sentence to the concentration camps, or of wearing the sign and becoming an easy prey to his enemies. The distinctive signs were thus an effective means in the hands of the Germans to facilitate their plan to exterminate the Jews.

For special articles of clothing worn compulsorily or voluntarily by Jews, see *Dress.

[B. Mordechai Ansbacher]

BIBLIOGRAPHY: G. Rezasco, *Segno degli ebrei* (1889); U. Robert, *Signes d'Infamie…* (1891); F. Singermann, *Kennzeichnung der Judea im Mittelalter* (1915); Kisch, in: HJ, 19 (1957), 89ff.; Lichtenstadter, *ibid.*, 5 (1943), 35ff.; Strauss, in: JSOS, 4 (1942), 59; A. Cohen, *Anglo-Jewish Scrapbook* (1943), 249–59; Aronstein, in: *Zion*, 13–14 (1948–49) 33ff.; B. Blumenkranz, *Le Juif médiéval au miroir de l'art chrétien* (1966); S. Grayzel, *Church and the Jews in the XIIIth Century* (1966), index; Baron, Social^2, II (1967), 96–106; A. Rubens, *History of Jewish Costume* (1967), index. NAZI PERIOD: L. Poliakov, *L'Etoile jaune* (1949); G. Reitlinger, *The Final Solution* (1953), index s.v. *Judenstern*.

BADḤAN (Heb. בַּדְחָן; "entertainer"), merrymaker, rhymester who entertained guests, especially at weddings. The Talmud mentions professional jesters who cheered the melancholy (Ta'an. 22a) or who amused bride and groom (Ket. 17a; Ber. 30b–31a). Jewish itinerant singers, called *badḥanim* or *leiẓanim* ("jesters") are mentioned in medieval rabbinical literature (e.g., R. Elijah b. Isaac of Carcassonne's *Asufot*); they seem to have appeared as professional entertainers at weddings and at Ḥanukkah and Purim celebrations, much after the pattern of the troubadours and ballad singers. The merrymaking of these *badḥanim*, who were also the forerunners of Jewish theatrical art, consisted not only of folksongs and comic stories but also of skillful puns on scriptural verses and talmudical passages, which required a certain amount of Jewish learning. As a result, the rabbinical authorities protested against the *badḥanim* who parodied the *Kaddish* at wedding festivities or who committed the near-blasphemy of "amusing the guests with jests on scriptural verses and holy words. Happy the man who abstains from such" (R. David ha-Levi, in *Turei Zahav* to Sh. Ar., OH 560:5).

In Eastern Europe the *badḥan* (or *marshalik*, from Ger. *marschalc*, in the sense of "master of ceremonies," and not from Heb. *mashal*, "proverb"), acted as the professional wedding jester. The *Chmielnicki persecutions (1648–49), and the rabbinical opposition to unbridled merrymaking, even at weddings (based upon Sot. 9:14), led the *badḥanim* to introduce a new style of entertainment – the *forshpil* – in which the *badḥan* addressed the bride with a rhymed penitential exhortation while the women performed the ceremony of *bedeken*, i.e., covering the bride with the veil before proceeding to the *ḥuppah* (see *Marriage Customs). In the case of orphans, the *badḥan's* rhymes invoked the memory of the departed parents and injected a sorrowful note. Later, at the wedding feast, the *badḥan* entertained the guests with music and with jests that contained personal allusions to the important guests and participants. In the course of time the literary style of the *badḥan* developed into a sort of Hebrew and Yiddish folk-poetry, the most renowned exponent of which was Eliakum *Zunser of Vilna, who composed over 600 songs of this kind. A fine portrayal of the *badḥan* is the character of Breckeloff in I. *Zangwill's *Children of the Ghetto*. In recent times the institution of the *badḥan* has been replaced by more modern forms of entertainment.

BIBLIOGRAPHY: A. Berliner, *Aus dem Leben der deutschen Juden im Mittelalter* (1900), 57, 58; I. Abrahams, *Jewish Life in the Middle Ages* (19322), 213–4; Hirsch, in: JQR, 13 (1901), 601–2; Lifschitz, in: *Arkhiv far di Geshikhte fun Yidishen Teater un Drame*, 1 (1930), 38–74; Eisenstein, Yisrael, 2 (1908), 302–3.

[Meir Ydit]

BADHAV, ISAAC BEN MICHAEL (1859–1947), Jerusalem rabbi and scholar. Badhav was born in Jerusalem and was the maternal grandson of Isaac *Covo. In his youth he studied in the *bet ha-midrash* Doresh Zion and in the yeshivah Shevet Aḥim. He engaged to a considerable extent in communal matters, and in 1886 was one of the founders of the Jerusalem Ḥevrat Shomerei Mitzvah u-Malbishei Arumim. In 1887 he was sent on a mission to Tripoli by the Beth El congregation, returning in 1889. In 1901 he was appointed teacher in the *bet ha-midrash* of Ḥayyim Hezekiah *Medini, Sedei Ḥemed in Hebron, but he remained there for a short time only, returning to Jerusalem. He lived in poverty all his life. Badhav devoted himself to collecting old Hebrew books and manuscripts and assembled a large library containing exceptionally important documentary archives which included ancient and valuable documents and records. These he obtained from members of the old Jerusalem families by persuading them to furnish him with their personal accounts of Israel and Jerusalem. They are a valuable source for research, particularly into Jerusalem.

In 1900 he published a catalog of his manuscripts entitled *Ginzei Ẓiyyon vi-Yrushalayim*. A second catalog, *Pardes ha-Torah ve-ha-Ḥokhmah*, was published in 1910. These manuscripts which contain materials dealing with the fields of *halakhah, aggadah*, philosophy, grammar, Kabbalah, geonica, medieval literature, history, poetry, and folklore are of great importance, because some of them are unique. Badhav also published many pamphlets containing laws and customs, poems and parables, amulets, prayers, petitions and memoirs, as well as responsa of early authorities, including some of the responsa of Maimonides. He translated into Ladino various historical studies. Because of his lack of means the pamphlets were issued in an irregular and haphazard manner. His two most important books are still in manuscript form: *Sefer ha-Gittin*, containing formulae of bills of divorce of the different communities, particularly those from Oriental countries – a book of importance not only for practical purposes but also for the purposes of research into Jewish history and folklore; and *Shem ha-Gedolim ha-Kelali*, an encyclopedia of great Jewish scholars and their works, both those which have been published and those which are extant in manuscript form.

BIBLIOGRAPHY: M.D. Gaon, *Yehudei ha-Mizraḥ be-Ereẓ Yisrael*, 2 (1937), 128–30; Benayahu, in: *Hed ha-Mizraḥ* (March 29, 1946), 6–7; idem, in: *Yerushalayim*, 1 (1948), 58–60. **ADD. BIBLIOGRAPHY:** J. Levi (ed.), *R. Isaac Badhav, Mifalo, Ḥayyav u-Shekhunato* (1977).

[Abraham David]

BADIḤI, YAḤYA BEN JUDAH (c. 1810–1887), Yemenite author of works on the Pentateuch and *halakhah*. Badiḥi belonged to one of the distinguished wealthy families of San'a, members of which were skilled goldsmiths by trade and served as minters to the Imams. This was a responsible but dangerous task for Jews since false accusations were frequently brought against them by the authorities. This was the case when Badiḥi and his father were imprisoned by the reigning Imam El-Mahdi (1815–1835). The father regained his freedom by paying a high ransom, but Badiḥi, faced with the choice between death or apostasy, succeeded in escaping to Karokaban, where the ruler treated the Jews with greater tolerance. Here he served as head of the local *bet din*. When Jacob *Saphir visited Yemen in 1859, he met Badiḥi, whom he described as one of the leading and most God-fearing scholars of Yemen Jewry. Badiḥi wrote three works which are still in manuscript: *Ḥen Tov*, a collection of rabbinic commentaries on the Pentateuch to which he added his original explanations with an appendix of 52 of his own responsa; *Zivḥei Shelamim*; and *Leḥem Todah* (based on the *Zevaḥ Todah* of Yaḥya Ṣalaḥ) both on the laws of *sheḥitah* and *terefot*. This latter work, a resume of the laws of *sheḥitah* and *terefot* according to Yemenite customs, was written both to supply exact information for *shoḥetim* in the villages and to stimulate Torah study, which had declined considerably.

BIBLIOGRAPHY: J. Saphir, *Massa Teiman*, ed. by A. Yaari (1951), 137–8, 186; Y. Ratzaby, in: KS, 28 (1952/53), 265, 270, and suppl. 34 (1958/59), 110–1.

[Yehuda Ratzaby]

BADINTER, ELIZABETH (1944–), French philosopher. Elizabeth Badinter is the daughter of Marcel Bleustein-Blanchet, founder of the Publicis advertising group, and remains its principal shareholder. Holding an "*agrégation*" degree in philosophy, she taught at the prestigious École Polytechnique for science and engineering. Married to the left-wing lawyer Robert Badinter, she was part of his successful fight against the death penalty during the 1970s, which led to its abolition by newly elected president Francois Mitterrand in 1981. Strongly influenced by the Enlightment movement, as an academic specialist in 18th-century philosophers, Badinter dealt mainly with questions related to secularism, separation of religion and state, and, under the influence of Simone de Beauvoir's works, the position of women in society. Herself an "intellectual" in the French, Sartrian sense of the term, meaning a thinker involved in the evolutions of society, "*engagée*" (politically committed), she took a deep interest in the intellectual history of France and its connection to politics, which she depicted in her major book *Les passions intellectuelles*, and which is central to her biography of Condorcet (*Condorcet, un intellectuel en politique*, co-written with Robert Badinter, 1988). The history of feminism since its inception in the 18th century (*Émile, Émilie: l'ambition feminine au XVIIIe siècle*) is also a major theme of hers. Reflections on the masculine and the feminine, on sexual identity, which she first developed in her book about the history of maternal love from the 17th to 20th century (*L'amour en plus*) and then in her essay *XY, le syndrome de l'identité masculine*, ultimately led her to take a sharp turn towards sharp criticism of the evolution of the feminist movement, which she developed in polemically in *Fausse route* (2003). She advocated a "moderate" feminism against what she viewed as the excessive claims of the feminists. Her provocative views were the subject of much controversy.

[Dror Franck Sullaper (2nd ed.)]

BADINTER, ROBERT (1928–), French lawyer and minister of justice. Born in Paris, Badinter studied law there and at

Columbia University. A lawyer and a professor of law, Badinter was a well-known opponent of the death penalty and fighter for civil rights. After taking office as minister of justice in 1981 he promoted and had passed – sometimes in the face of considerable opposition – legislation towards the abrogation of the death penalty, abrogation of the special tribunal for security offenses ("Cour de sécurité de l'Etat"), and curtailment of the powers of the police. His militant stand on these and related issues made him the target of virulent attacks, sometimes of an antisemitic nature. Prior to his joining the government he had been active in Jewish organizations.

Before the change in the political majority in 1986, Badinter was appointed president of the Constitutional Council, which is the highest authority in France for interpreting the constitution. He remained in this position till 1995. The same year, he was elected senator from the Hauts-de-Seine district and was reelected nine years later.

Badinter published *L'Execution* (1973); *Liberté* (1976); *L'abolition* (2000, about his fight against the death penalty); and two historical studies: *Libres et égaux, l'émancipation des Juifs sous la Révolution française* (1989), on the emancipation of Jews by the French Revolution, and *Un antisémitisme ordinaire, Vichy et les avocats juifs* (1997), on the treatment of Jewish lawyers by the Vichy regime.

[Gideon Kouts / Dror Franck Sullaper (2nd ed.)]

BADT, HERMANN (1887–1946), German civil servant and constitutional lawyer, active in the Zionist movement. He was the son of the classical scholar Benno Badt. Born in Breslau, he maintained Orthodox traditions and joined the *Mizrachi Party. From 1905 to 1908 he studied law in Breslau and Munich. During World War I Badt served as Feldkriegsgerichtsrat. In 1919, he was the first Jew in Prussia to be admitted to the civil service after the revolution of 1918, first as *Regierungsassessor*, then as a *Regierungsrat* in the German foreign office. From 1922 to 1926 he was a Social Democratic member of the Prussian Diet and then became the Ministerialdirektor in the Prussian Ministry of the Interior in charge of constitutional affairs. In 1932 he represented Prussia before the Staatsgerichtshof (State Court) of the German Reich in its unsuccessful legal action against Chancellor von Papen, who had deposed the legal government and instituted himself as a dictatorial "Reichskommissar" (Reich Commissioner) in Prussia. After his dismissal in 1933, he emigrated to Palestine, which he had visited several times before. Among other enterprises, he founded the Kinneret company to promote middle-class settlement on the land where kibbutz Ein Gev was founded.

ADD. BIBLIOGRAPHY: *Biographisches Handbuch der deutschsprachigen Emigration*, 1 (1980), 31; Y. Ilsar, in: TAJ, 20 (1991), 339–62.

[*Encyclopaedia Hebraica* / Marcus Pyka (2nd ed.)]

BADT-STRAUSS, BERTHA (1885–1970), writer, Zionist, feminist. Badt-Strauss was born in Breslau. She was descended from a well-known family of Jewish scholars and studied literature, languages, and philosophy in Breslau, Berlin, and Munich. One of the first women awarded a doctoral degree in Prussia, she worked as a researcher and publisher. She became a Zionist and deeply involved in the Jewish Renaissance: the creation of a Jewish community with a special Jewish culture. With her husband Bruno Strauss, a teacher and expert on Moses *Mendelssohn, she lived in Berlin from 1913 on. In 1921 their only son, Albrecht, was born. Shortly after his birth Badt-Strauss fell ill with multiple sclerosis. In spite of this she continued writing numerous articles for Jewish publications, such as the *Jüdische Rundschau* and the *Israelitische Familienblatt*, and also for leading non-Jewish newspapers. She also co-edited the first scholarly edition of Annette von Droste-Huelshoff's works and translated and edited volumes of works by Gertrud Marx, Profiat *Duran, *Suesskind von Trimberg, Heinrich *Heine, Rahel *Varnhagen, and Moses Mendelssohn. She contributed to the *Juedisches Lexikon* and the *Encyclopaedia Judaica*, wrote short stories, a serial novel, and a collective biography of Jewish women.

As a religious Jewess and a patriotic German, Badt-Strauss became not only one of the protagonists of the Jewish Renaissance, she also participated in the German women's movement, wrote about German literature and included (supposed) "*Assimilanten*" like Moses Mendelssohn or converts like Rahel Varnhagen in her agenda. She tried to reinterpret the return of prominent Jews to Judaism as a self-determined step in the right direction and offered new role models for identification.

Badt-Strauss' intensive engagement with Jewish women should also be mainly attributed to her aim of creating new role models. Her only belief was in the need to return to Judaism and eventually to Ereẓ Israel. By not specifying too narrowly what this return should be like and what role women had to play in Judaism and in the "*Jischuw*," she invited women to take part in the creation of a Jewish community that had not seen women's role in this context because of the rigid male definition of Jewish femininity. Badt-Strauss was most successful with her individual interpretation of the aims of the Jewish Renaissance – her list of publications includes more than 600 editions and articles.

In 1939 Badt-Strauss immigrated to the United States. She continued writing and published a biography of the American Zionist Jessie *Sampter.

BIBLIOGRAPHY: M. Steer, *Bertha Badt-Strauss (1885–1970)* (2005).

[Martina Steer (2nd ed.)]

BAECK, LEO (1873–1956), German rabbi and religious thinker, leader of Progressive Judaism. Baeck was born in Lissa (now Lenzno, Poland) the son of Rabbi Samuel Baeck. Leo Baeck first studied at the Conservative Jewish Theological Seminary of Breslau, and remained close to its approach throughout his life. From 1894 Baeck studied at the Liberal *Hochschule fuer die Wissenschaft des Judentums in Berlin. At the same time he also studied philosophy at the University of Breslau under J. Freudental and at the University of Berlin under the philosopher Wilhelm Dilthey. Baeck served as rabbi in Oppeln (1897–1907), Duesseldorf (1907–12), and Berlin (from 1912 on), and as an army chaplain in World War I. He began lecturing on midrashic literature and homiletics at the Hochschule in 1912 and became a close adherent of Hermann *Cohen.

Baeck was a member of the committee of the Central-Verein deutscher Staatsbuerger juedischen Glaubens and published numerous articles in its journal, *C.V. Zeitung*, and periodical, *Der morgen*, Baeck was a non-Zionist member of the Jewish Agency and occasionally contributed to the German Zionist weekly *Juedische Rundschau*. From 1922 he served as the chairman of the Rabbinerverband in Deutschland, which included Liberal as well as Orthodox rabbis. From 1933 he was president of the Reichsvertretung, the representative body of German Jews, and devoted himself to defending the rights remaining for Jews under the Nazis. He refused all invitations to serve as a rabbi or professor abroad, declaring that he would remain with the last *minyan* (prayer quorum) of Jews in Germany as long as possible. At Terezin (*Theresienstadt) concentration camp, to which he was deported in early 1943, he was named honorary president of the Aeltestenrat and continued the work of encouraging his people. Thus, he became a "witness of his faith," a theme that had long occupied a central position in his writings. According to a testimony he allegedly gave to Eric Boem, he was informed in 1943 of the death camps but decided not to share the information with the Jewish leadership of the camp in order not to undermine Jewish hope, a decision that was sharply criticized by some and provoked a bitter public debate. After the war, in July 1945, he moved to London, where he became president of the council of Jews from Germany and the chairman of the World Union for Progressive Judaism. From 1948 until his death he taught intermittently in the United States as professor of history of religion at Hebrew Union College in Cincinnati.

Thought and Works

Baeck saw himself primarily as a rabbi and a preacher, who understood his mission beyond the borders of his own Liberal affiliation, as shaped by his responsibility to the entire German Jewish community and the Jewish people at large. His philosophical-theological thought as well as his works on history of religion should be read and measured in light of his rabbinic mission. In 1901 he published a polemic article against *Wesen des Christentums* by the Protestant theologian Adolf von Harnack. Four years later Baeck published his main work *Wesen des Judentums* (1905; *The Essence of Judaism*, 1936). Many further editions and printings of it were published, as well as English (1948^{3}), Japanese, and Hebrew (1968) translations. The apologetic character that dominated the first edition was considerably modified in the second and the extreme rationalism was eliminated. This transformation was the result of the influence of mysticism and Jewish nationalism. He identified the essence of Judaism with biblical prophecy, namely the direct experience of God's presence and the command to worship Him, a view he adopted from Rabbi *Judah Halevi. Hence, the essence of Judaism is a dialectic polarity between "mystery" and "command." The commands, according to Baeck, do not necessarily form a system of commandments like the established *halakhah*, which imposes a required and fixed way of life; rather they appear from time to time in the form of instructions for action like flashes of lightning that break through the cloud covering the divine "mystery." Baeck adhered to Hermann Cohen's interpretation of Judaism as "ethical monotheism." He believed that piety is achieved by the fulfillment of the duties between man and man, but in contrast with Cohen he gradually developed a deep appreciation of mysticism, which he understood to be a creative, artistic imagination, based on myth and symbolic language, which point to a supreme spiritual sphere transcending art and imagination. Ritual observances are directed toward this ethical religious aim as well as the deepening of "mystical prophecy." His religious worldview was in that sense clearly liberal and deeply religious, though in practice he was quite traditionally observant.

Baeck sharply rejected Christianity, a religion that he regarded as a "romantic" one of the abstract spirit longing for redemption and as sharply distinguished from Judaism, the "classical" religion of the concrete spirit working for the improvement of this world. Judaism, in contrast with Christianity, is thus not aimed at the salvation of the individual soul but rather at the collective redemption of humanity and of the world. In line with his national and this-worldly view of Judaism and the Jewish people, Baeck had a sympathetic, although critical attitude towards Zionism. He thought that the building of Palestine was a valuable prospect for embodying the spirit of Judaism, but not a guarantee that it would be realized.

Other works of Baeck include *Wege in Judentum* (1933), a collection of essay and speeches; *Aus drei Jahrtausenten* (1938), a collection of scholarly papers destroyed by the Nazis and reprinted in 1958; *Die Pharisaeer* (1934; *The Pharisees and other essays*, 1947), *Maimonides, der Mann seine Werke und seine Wirkung* (1954) *Dieses Volk Israel* (2 vol., 1955–57; *This People Israel*, 1965), a work that he began to write in 1942 and whose first volume he completed while imprisoned in Terezin; *Judaism and Christianity* (1958). In 1954 Leo Baeck Institute for the study of the history of the Jews from German-speaking countries was established in his name, and he served as its first president. Other institutions carry his name, such as Leo Baeck College in London.

BIBLIOGRAPHY: T. Wiener, in: SBB, 1 no. 3 (bibliography of his writings); E. Simon, *Geheimnis und Gebot – Die Neue Wege* (1948); idem, in: L. Baeck, *Mahut ha-Yahadut* (1968); A.H. Friedlander, *Leo Baeck, Teacher of Theresienstadt* (1968). **ADD. BIBLIOGRAPHY:** *Leo Baeck – Werke*, ed. A.H. Friedlander et al. (1998–2003); E. Schweid, "'Prophetic mysticism' in Twentieth Century Jewish Thought," in: *Modern Judaism*, 14:2 (1994), 139–74; indem, *Ma'avak ad Shaḥar* (1991), 24–72; A. Barkai, "Von Berlin nach Theresienstadt – zur politischen Biographie von Leo Baeck (1933–1945)," in: *Hoffnung und Untergang* (1998), 111–40; M. Meyer, "The Thought of Leo Baeck – a Religious Philosophy for a Time of Adversity," in: *Modern Judaism*,

19:2 (1999), 107–17; W. Homolka (ed.), *Leo Baeck – Zwischen Geheimnis und Gebot* (1997); A. Barkai (ed.), *Leo Baeck – Manhigut ve-Hagut* (2000).

[Akiba Ernst Simon / Yehoyada Amir (2nd ed.)]

BAECK, SAMUEL (1834–1912), German rabbi and scholar. Baeck, who was born in Kromau (Moravia), the son and grandson of rabbis, served as rabbi of Leipa (Bohemia) and Lissa (Lezno, Poland) and was active in German-Jewish communal affairs. He successfully advocated the teaching of Jewish religion in Prussian high schools, for which he wrote some textbooks. His *Geschichte des juedischen Volkes und seiner Literatur…* (1888) went into three editions. To J. Winter and A. Wuensche (eds.) *Die juedische Literatur* (1894–96) Baeck contributed the sections on the halakhic, homiletic, and other literature from the 15th to the 18th centuries (also separately printed, 1893). Leo *Baeck was his son.

BAENA, JUAN ALFONSO DE (c. 1445), Spanish poet and scribe to Juan II of Castile. Most probably he was born a Jew and decided to convert. His conversion to Christianity enabled him to enter the court of Juan II and become one of his high officials. The *Cancionero de Baena*, an anthology of 14th- and 15th-century poetry which he compiled and presented to the king in 1445 deals with the social and political life of the period and includes many references to Jews and conversos. Hostility toward the conversos is expressed in several poems by Alfonso Alvarez de Villasandino (nos. 140–2, 183). Two *decires*, or poetic compositions, of the monk Diego de Valencia (probably a converted Jew himself) deal with conversos; the text of the first (no. 501) contains a number of Hebrew words. The *Cancionero* also includes poems celebrating the birth in 1405 of the future King Juan II. One of these (no. 230), the composition of a certain Don Mossé (described as surgeon to Henry III), indicates the part played by the Jews in Spanish cultural life. Baena's poetry is very rich and harmonious in its rhymes. Another Juan de Baena (also known as Juan de Pineda) rose from obscurity as a tailor in Córdoba to eminence at the court of Toledo. A converso, he was brought to trial and condemned to death in 1486.

BIBLIOGRAPHY: J.M. Azaceta (ed.), *Cancionero de Juan de Baena* (1966); A. Millares Carlo, *Literatura española hasta fines del siglo XV* (1950), 185–91; J. Amador de los Ríos, *Estudios… Judíos de España* (1848), 406–27; Baer, Spain, 2 (1966), 347ff. **ADD. BIBLIOGRAPHY:** B. Valverde, in: *Cuadernos del idioma* 9 (1968), 97–113; B. Blanco González, in: *Cuadernos de filología* (Mendoza, Argentina), 6 (1972), 29–75; J.M. Solá-Solé, in: *Sobre árabes, judíos y marranos y su impacto en la lengua y literatura españolas* (1983), 207–23.

[Kenneth R. Scholberg]

BAER, ABRAHAM (1834–1894), cantor. Baer was born in Wielen (Filehne), Poznan (Poland). He was a teacher and *ḥazzan* in various towns in western Prussia and in Posen, before becoming assistant cantor in Goteborg, Sweden, in 1857 and chief cantor in 1860. Collaborating with the organist of the synagogue, Joseph Czapek, he published a two-volume collection of hymns (principally those of *Sulzer) for choir, with organ accompaniment, *Musik till sångerna vid Gudstjensten* (2 vols., 1872). Five years later came his great work *Baal T'fillah*, a collection of melodies and recitatives according to the Polish, German, and Sephardi rituals, which became the basic manual for European cantors. The fruit of 15 years' work, it contains about 1,500 melodies which cover the liturgy of the year. Among them are several melodies of Sulzer, *Naumburg, and *Lewandowski, and some of his own. The collection went through five editions between 1877 and 1930.

BIBLIOGRAPHY: A. Baer, *Baal T'fillah oder der praktische Vorbeter* (1883²), xiii–xxviii; J. Schoenberg, *Die traditionellen Gesaenge des israelitischen Gottesdienstes in Deutschland* (1926); Sendrey, Music, indexes.

[Haim Bar-Dayan]

BAER, GABRIEL (1919–1982), historian. Born in Germany, Baer immigrated to Ereẓ Israel in 1933. His special field was the social history of the Middle East, particularly of Egypt, in modern times. A professor of Oriental Studies at the Hebrew University of Jerusalem, he was awarded the Israel Prize in 1976. His books include *A History of Landownership in Modern Egypt 1800–1950* (1962), *Egyptian Guilds in Modern Times* (1964), *Population and Society in the Arab East* (1964), *Studies in the Social History of Modern Egypt* (1969), and *Fellah and Townsman in the Middle East: Studies in Social History* (1982). Baer was also editor of two Middle Eastern quarterlies published in Jerusalem: *Hamizrah Hehadash* and *Asian and African Studies.*

ADD. BIBLIOGRAPHY: A list of Baer's published works appeared in *Asian and African Studies,* 17 (1983), 315–21. Obituaries: G.G. Gilbar, in: *IJMES,* 15, no. 1 (1983), 129–30; J.M. Landau, in: *Der Islam,* 41, no. 1 (1984), 8–9.

[Jacob M. Landau (2nd ed.)]

BAER, MAX (Maximilian Adelbert; 1909–1959), U.S. prizefighter, world heavyweight champion 1934–35, member of the World Boxing Hall of Fame and the International Boxing Hall of Fame. Born in Omaha, Nebraska, Baer dropped out of school in the eighth grade to work with his father on a cattle ranch in California, where he developed his muscles and a powerful right hand. He began to box in 1929 and won 22 of his first 24 fights, nine with first-round knockouts. In a fight on August 25, 1930, heavyweight Frankie Campbell was killed in a fight with Baer in San Francisco, which led to a grand jury investigation of local boxing. Baer was charged with manslaughter but was later cleared of all charges, though he was suspended from fighting in California for a year. He quit boxing for several months after Campbell's death and then lost four of his next six fights, partly, it was said, because of his reluctance to go on the attack.

Baer recorded a major victory on June 8, 1933, when he beat Germany's Max Schmeling, a former world champion, with a 10th-round TKO in front of 56,000 fans at Yankee Stadium. Baer won the heavyweight title on June 14, 1934, knocking down Italy's Primo Carnera 11 times in 11 rounds, before winning by a TKO in the 11th. Baer lost the title in his first defense on June 13, 1935, to Jim Braddock, "The Cinderella Man," who was listed as a 10–1 underdog. It is considered by many the greatest upset in boxing history. Baer then lost in his next fight in four rounds to Joe Louis on September 24, 1935, before 88,000 fans at Yankee Stadium. On June 1, 1939, Baer fought Lou Nova at Yankee Stadium in the first boxing match ever televised. Baer lost his last professional fight to Nova again in 1941, retiring with a record of 71 victories (53 by knockout), 13 defeats, and one no-decision. He later refereed boxing and wrestling matches. In *Ring Magazine*'s 2003 list of the 100 greatest punchers of all time, Baer was ranked 22nd.

Baer wore a *Magen David* on his boxing trunks beginning with his fight against Schmeling, whom he taunted with "That one's for Hitler" between blows. "I wore the insignia because I thought I should, and I intend to wear it in every bout hereafter," he said after the fight. Baer claimed "Jewish blood" through the paternal line of his immigrant father Jacob, a German-Jewish immigrant who worked as a butcher, cattle dealer and rancher in Colorado and California. Jacob's father, Aschill Baer from Alsace-Lorraine, married a non-Jew from Vienna, Fanny Fischiel. Baer became an actor while he was boxing and appeared in some 20 movies, including *The Prizefighter and the Lady*, which was banned in Germany because of Baer's Jewish grandfather. He also had a successful nightclub act both solo and with Slapsie Maxie *Rosenbloom. His son, MAX, JR. (1937–), was an actor famous for playing "Jethro" on the 1962–71 television series *The Beverly Hillbillies*.

BUDDY (Jacob Henry; 1915–1986), a brother, also boxed in the heavyweight division, fighting Joe Louis for the championship twice. Baer lost the first time on a disqualification in the seventh round on May 23, 1941, when his manager claimed a foul and refused to leave the ring; and again on January 9, 1942, when Louis knocked him out in the first round. These were Buddy Baer's last two fights, and he retired with a 50–7 record, with 44 KOs.

[Elli Wohlgelernter (2nd ed.)]

BAER, SELIGMAN ISAAC (1825–1897), Hebrew grammarian, masorah scholar, and liturgist. Born at Mosbach (Baden, Germany), Baer was a pupil of Wolf *Heidenheim, who left him many of his manuscripts. At the age of 19 he turned to masoretic studies. Franz *Delitzsch was impressed by Baer's scholarly approach and together they published the Psalms with masorah (1860) followed by most of the other books of the Bible with masorah texts. Delitzsch prefaced each book with a Latin introduction (except the last two, which appeared after his death, Jeremiah in 1890 and Kings in 1895). These masoretic editions were compiled by Baer from manuscripts representing the variants of the masorah of *Ben Asher, *Ben Naphtali, and other masorah texts. All his life, Baer remained in the humble position of a teacher in the Jewish community school at Biebrich (Rhineland), but on the initiative of Delitzsch he was awarded an honorary Ph.D. by the University of Leipzig (1876). Baer's masoretic Bible edition was generally regarded as a genuine rendition of the traditional masorah text although it also evoked some criticism, notably by C.D. *Ginsburg and E. *Kautzsch. Baer's masorah text was printed in the widely accepted Vilna edition of the rabbinic Bible (*Mikra'ot Gedolot*). He also wrote a book on the cantillation in the poetical books of the Bible (*Torat Emet*, 1852) and on the secondary accent, the *meteg* (*Die Methegsetzung*, 1867); and published Ben Asher's *Dikdukei Te'amim* (together with H.L. Strack, 1879) and *Zwei alte Thorarollen aus Arabien* (1870).

Baer's greatest achievement lay in the field of liturgy. His many editions of liturgical texts, in which he followed the example and standards set by Heidenheim, were not only a scholarly feat but added dignity and decorum to Orthodox synagogue services throughout Western Europe, where his editions gained great popularity. The most important of these is his *Avodat Yisrael* prayer book with a scholarly commentary *Yakhin Lashon* (1868, several times reprinted, the latest in 1937) which has been accepted as the standard prayer book text by most subsequent editions of the *siddur*. Besides this major work, Baer edited *Seliḥot, Kinot, Seder ha-Berakhot* (1858), a handbook for mourners, cemetery use, etc., in three versions (*Toẓe'ot Ḥayyim*, 1862; *Sefer Gemilut Ḥasadim*, 1880; *Derekh la-Ḥayyim*, 1926); *Tikkun ha-Sofer ve-ha-Kore*, a handbook for scribes and readers of the Torah (1875); a prayer book, *Tefillat Yesharim* (18765, with prayers in German at the end; these also appeared separately as *Kol Bat Ẓiyyon*, 18753); *Piyyutim* (1874); *Divrei ha-Berit*, circumcision service (1874). These handsome little books ran into several editions and were reprinted after World War II.

BIBLIOGRAPHY: A. Berliner, in: AZDJ, 59 (1902), 467; JC (March 12, 1897); ADB; H. Gullanz, *Shekel ha-Kodesh* (1919), with *Yesod ha-Yirah*.

[Isaak Dov Ber Markon]

BAER, YITZHAK (**Fritz**; 1888–1980), historian. Born in Halberstadt, where he obtained a thorough Jewish education, Baer studied philosophy, classical philology, and history (the latter under Heinrich Finke) at the universities of Berlin, Strasbourg, and Freiburg. From 1919 Baer was research associate of the Akademie fuer die Wissenschaft des Judentums in Berlin, under whose auspices he went twice to Spain (1925–26) to collect archival source material on the history of the Jews in Christian Spain. In 1928 he was appointed lecturer and in 1930 professor of medieval Jewish history at the Hebrew University in Jerusalem. From 1932 to 1945 he was professor of general medieval history; he served from 1930 to 1959 as head of the university's department of Jewish history. Baer was one of the founders and editors of the Jewish historical review *Zion*. A coeditor of the "Historiographical Library" and *Sefer ha-Yishuv*, he took a leading part in the Israel Historical Society and was one of the 20 founding members of the Israel Academy of Sciences. He also contributed important articles to the German *Encyclopaedia Judaica* and its Hebrew counterpart

(*Eshkol*). Baer's first extensive research was into the history of the Jews of Christian Spain. On this subject he wrote his dissertation *Studien zur Geschichte der Juden im Königreich Aragonien während des 13. und 14. Jahrhunderts* (Berlin, 1913); *Untersuchungen über Quellen und Komposition des Schebet Jehuda* (Berlin, 1923; second printing 1936); *Probleme der jüdisch-spanischen Geschichte* (in KAWJ, 6 (1925), 5–25); articles on Abner of Burgos (in *Tarbiz*, 11 (1939/40), 188–206), on the disputations of Paris, Barcelona, and Tortosa, on Isaac Abrabanel (in *Tarbiz*, 8 (1936/37), 241–59); *Die Juden im christlichen Spanien* (1929, 1936), an important two-volume collection of unpublished documents on Spain, which served as the basis for his *History of the Jews in Christian Spain* (Heb., 1945, 19592, repr. 1965; Eng. ed., 2 vols., 1961–66), which is regarded as the standard work on the subject. Baer's work is remarkable for its broad historical outlook, accuracy in detail, and scholarly synthesis. These qualities enabled him to throw new light on the economic, social, legal, political as well as the religious and cultural condition of Spanish Jewry. His works are a model of historiography. Especially important among his studies of the development and history of the Jewish communal organization are his *Das Protokollbuch der Landjudenschaft des Herzogtums Kleve*, 1 (1922, repr. 1936), and his article on the beginnings and fundaments of Jewish communal organization in the Middle Ages (*Zion*, 15 (1949/50, 1–41). His method seeks to bring to light the internal forces that fashioned the Jewish communities within the framework of general history and local conditions. Baer believed that the essential features of Jewish communal organization were already set during the early generations of the Second Temple period and that these forms of organization were a product of the religious and national experiences of the people, and not that the Diaspora gave birth to them, although there were changes reflecting special conditions of time and place. Baer also investigated the spiritual and religious world of the Jewish people from the Second Temple period and the Middle Ages. Among his studies in this area are a series of articles in *Zion* written between 1932 and 1961 dealing with the theology of the *Sefer Ḥasidim* (see also Baer's contribution to *G. Scholem… Festschrift*, 1968) and the *Ḥasidei Ashkenaz* in general; with the historical basis of *halakhah*; with the relations between Jews, the early Christian Church, and the Roman Empire until Constantine; and his books *Galut* (Ger. 1936; Eng. 1947, Port. 1952) and *Yisrael ba-Ammim* (1955), and the article "Social Ideals of the Second Commonwealth" (in *Cahiers d'Histoire Mondiale*, 11 (1967/68), 69–91). From all these emerges an original view of the entire course of Jewish history. According to Baer the driving force of Jewish history lies in the continuing socioreligious activity of groups of pious and practical men of faith who aimed at perfecting the world. They succeeded in influencing the active elements among the people, with their beliefs and teachings, maintaining close ties with the non-Jewish world, and participating in its religiocultural and socioethical development. Baer reveals keen understanding of hellenistic and Christian culture and society. From this vantage point he examined the history of the Jews in the days of the Second Temple. His conclusions may be evaluated from his above-mentioned works as well as from articles in *Molad* (21 (1963), 308ff.) and *Zion* (23–24 (1958–59), nos. 3–4) and on *Serekh ha-Yaḥad* ("The Manual of Discipline," *Zion*, 29, 1964), which he sees as a Judeo-Christian document of the beginning of the second century C.E. He also dealt with the image of Judaism in the synoptic gospels (*Zion*, 31, 1966) and came to the conclusion that the polemics reflect conditions of the period following the destruction of the Temple. Baer is recognized as one of the most fruitful students and teachers of Jewish history of modern times. A jubilee volume was published in his honor in 1961 on the occasion of his 70th birthday (including his bibliography up to 1959).

BIBLIOGRAPHY: I. Sonne, in: JSOS, 9 (1947), 61–80; L. Yahil, in: *Molad*, 21 (1963), 549–3: H.H. Ben-Sasson, in: *Religion and Society, Lectures of the Historical Society of Israel* (Heb., 1964), 23–40; J.M. Millás, in: KS, 9 (1932/33), 464–5; C. Roth, *ibid.*, 15 (1938/39), 200–1; F. Cantera, in: *Sefarad*, 1 (1941), 232–3; 26 (1966), 346–52; J.M. Millás, *ibid.*, 5 (1945), 417–40; 6 (1946), 163–88; 22 (1962), 178–80.

[Benzion Dinur (Dinaburg)]

BAERWALD, ALEX (1878–1930), one of the first Jewish architects in Ereẓ Israel. He was born in Berlin, and studied architecture at Charlottenburg. In 1910, he was invited by the Hilfsverein to plan the Technion buildings and the Reali school in Haifa. In these buildings, Baerwald tried to create a Jewish style of architecture, based on Muslim architecture.

Baerwald settled in Palestine in 1925, when he was appointed a lecturer at the Technion (which had been opened in 1924), and founded its Faculty of Architecture. He built many buildings in Haifa, Tel Aviv, and elsewhere in Palestine, in the same style that he developed in the Technion buildings (Bet Struck, the Anglo-Palestine Bank in Haifa). In spite of the quality of these buildings and their high architectural standard their influence on the development of architecture in Jewish Palestine was very limited. Baerwald himself designed a number of buildings in the contemporary modern European style. These include the Central Jezreel Valley Hospital and the Electricity Company's power stations at Haifa and Tiberias. He also planned two buildings in kibbutz Merḥavyah, combining rural European architecture with Middle Eastern motifs.

ADD. BIBLIOGRAPHY: A. Elhanani, "Israeli Architecture in the Twentieth Century" (Heb., 1998).

[Abraham Erlik]

BAERWALD, MORITZ (1860–1919), German lawyer and politician. Baerwald was born in Thorn, West Prussia, and founded a law firm in Bromberg, Posen, where Jewish business and professional men constituted the nucleus of the urban bourgeoisie and enjoyed privileges not easily available to them elsewhere in Germany. Baerwald was elected to the board of attorneys, to the Bromberg city government, and to the Prussian Diet in 1912. In 1919 he was elected to the German National Assembly but, like all the other deputies from

Posen, resigned when Posen was reincorporated in Poland. Baerwald was vice president of the assembly of representatives of the Jewish community of Bromberg.

BIBLIOGRAPHY: *Handbuch der Verfassunggebenden deutschen Nationalversammlung* (1919).

[Ernest Hamburger]

BAERWALD, PAUL (1871–1961), banker and philanthropist. Baerwald, born in Frankfurt, was the scion of a family of German bankers. He began his career with a banking firm in Frankfurt. In 1896 he immigrated to the U.S. and in 1907 became a partner in Lazard Frères of New York City. In subsequent years Baerwald held directorships in a number of corporations. Baerwald's Jewish communal work began in 1917 when he was asked to become associate treasurer of the *American Jewish Joint Distribution Committee (JDC) by his close friend, Felix M. *Warburg. He became treasurer (1920) and later chairman (1932). Baerwald's chairmanship of the JDC coincided with the Nazi period. During that time the JDC aided most of the European Jews who found haven in overseas countries. In 1938 Baerwald joined President Roosevelt's Advisory Committee on Political Refugees, which tried to find means to aid Nazi victims. He supervised the rescue work of the JDC during World War II and, risking its credit, sent money to Europe which had to be borrowed from New York banks. A high percentage of the President's War Refugee Board funds (1944–45) came from the JDC under Baerwald's direction. This financial policy was carried on in the postwar years when the JDC aided more than 500,000 refugees to reach Israel. In 1957 the American Jewish Joint Distribution Committee, the *Hebrew University of Jerusalem, and the Israel Ministry of Social Welfare founded the Paul Baerwald School of Social Work at the Hebrew University.

[Yehuda Bauer]

°**BAETHGEN, FRIEDRICH WILHELM ADOLPH** (1849–1905), German Bible critic and Semitic scholar, son of a Lutheran pastor in Lachem. After Baethgen completed his studies at Goettingen and Kiel, he was appointed lecturer in biblical studies at Kiel in 1878, and six years later became assistant professor of theology there. During this period he did pioneering work in the fields of biblical Hebrew poetry, Syriac grammar, and Peshitta on Psalms (*Die Psalmen*, 1897^2, 1904^3). In 1888, the year in which his *Beitraege zur semitischen Religionsgeschichte* first appeared, he went to Halle as assistant professor of theology. In the following year he became professor of theology at Greifswald, where he was also an influential member of the Pomeranian consistory. From 1895 until his death he was professor of theology in Berlin.

BAEYER, ADOLF VON (1835–1917), German organic chemist and Nobel Prize winner. Baeyer was born in Berlin. His mother was the daughter of J.E. *Hitzig, literature historian and authority on criminal law and his father, Johann Jacob Baeyer, a non-Jewish scientist. Adolf Baeyer made his first chemical discovery – a double carbonate of copper and sodium – when he was 12. He went to Heidelberg, where he came under the influence of his lifelong friend, August Kekulé, the German chemist, with whom he went to Ghent in 1858. In 1860 he returned to Berlin and was appointed professor of organic chemistry at the Gewerbeinstitut (later the Charlottenburg Technische Hochschule). There he worked on the study of uric acid, and began 20 years of research on indigo. This was the basis of synthetic indigo, which eventually completely displaced the natural product, and was the foundation of the German dyestuffs industry. His work on alizarin also led to alizarin dyes, driving the natural pigment off the market. His field then extended into physiological chemistry. In 1872 Baeyer became professor at Strasbourg and in 1875 in Munich, where he continued to teach and experiment until he was 80. His work covered many fields, including acetylenic compounds, strain within chemical molecules, the structure of benzene, the constitution of terpenes, oxygen compounds with quadrivalent oxygen, carbonium compounds, and the relationship between color and chemical constitution. His many papers in chemical journals helped to lay the foundations for the new science of organic chemistry. He was awarded the Nobel Prize in 1905 for "the advancement of organic chemistry and the chemical industry, through his work on organic dyes and hydroaromatic compounds." His numerous other awards included the Davy Medal of the British Royal Society in 1881 and a German patent of nobility in 1885.

BIBLIOGRAPHY: K. Schmorl, *Adolf von Baeyer, 1835–1917* (Ger. 1952), incl. bibl.; T. Levitan, *The Laureates* (1960), 27–29; Henrich, in: American Chemical Society, *Journal of Chemical Education*, 7 (1930), 1231–48; Perkin, in: Chemical Society (London), *Journal of the Chemical Society*, 123 (1923), 1520–46; G. Bugge, *Buch der grossen Chemiker*, 2 (1930), 321–35, index.

[Samuel Aaron Miller]

BAGHDAD, capital city of *Iraq. Baghdad was the capital of the *Abbasid dynasty from its foundation in 762. From then a Jewish community existed there which eventually became the largest Jewish community of Iraq, and the seat of the exilarch. During the gaonic period the Jews lived in a special quarter, Dār al-Yahūd (Jewish Quarter). The bridge in the western section of the town, which led to the Karkh quarter, was named Qanṭarat al-Yahūd (Bridge of the Jews). A tomb situated in this quarter was until recently the site of prayer gatherings. The local Jews believed it to be the tomb of Joshua son of Jehozadak, the high priest. By the end of the ninth century the famous yeshivot of Sura and Pumbedita were established in Baghdad. The Karaites also played an important part in the life of the city.

Early and Early Modern History

During the tenth century there were two distinguished Jewish families in Baghdad, *Netira and Aaron. They were both influential in the royal court and they showed concern for the welfare of the community. At the end of the tenth century R. Isaac b. Moses ibn Sakrī of Spain was the *rosh yeshivah*. He had traveled to Iraq and "had been ordained as *Gaon* in order to fill the position of Rav Hai, of saintly memory." During the 12th century, but beginning with the reign of Caliph al-Muktafī (902–908), the situation of the Jews in Baghdad greatly improved. A short while before 1170 *Benjamin of Tudela, the traveler, found approximately 40,000 Jews living peacefully in Baghdad, among them scholars and exceedingly wealthy people. He noted that there were 28 synagogues and ten yeshivot. During the reigns of Caliph al-Muktafī and his successors, the rights and the authority of the exilarch were increased and with it the prestige of the Baghdad community also grew. In that period the exilarch *Daniel b. Ḥasdai was referred to by the Arabs as "Our lord, the son of David." The Baghdad community reached the height of its prosperity during the term of office of *rosh yeshivah* *Samuel b. Ali ha-Levi (c. 1164–94), an opponent of *Maimonides, who raised Torah study in Baghdad to a high level.

During the late 12th century through the middle 13th century, some prominent poets, as well as the great scholars and the *rashei yeshivot* appointed by the caliphs, lived in Baghdad. The most important were R. Eleazar b. Jacob ha-Bavli and R. Isaac b. Israel, whom Judah *Al-Ḥarizi, the poet and traveler, referred to as the greatest Iraqi poet. Isaac b. Israel headed the Baghdad yeshivah from 1221 to 1247. There were many physicians, perfumers, shopkeepers, goldsmiths, and moneychangers among the Jews of Baghdad; however, Judah Al-Ḥarizi considered this period as one of decline in view of the past importance of the community.

In 1258 Baghdad was conquered by the *Mongols and the Jews were not maltreated, as was the case with the Muslims. Arghūn Khān (1284–91) appointed the Jew *Saʿd al-Dawla, who had previously been the sultan's physician, director of financial administration of Iraq. During the few years he held office, Saʿd al-Dawla developed the economic importance of Baghdad and as a result of this he was appointed chief vizier of the Mongol Empire in 1289. After the death of Arghūn, Saʿd al-Dawla was executed on the pretext that he had not given the khān the appropriate medical care. After their final conversion to Islam in the early 14th century, the Īl-Khānids reinstated decrees which they formerly had abolished, concerning the discriminatory dress of the Jews and Christians and the special taxes which applied to all "unbelievers" under Muslim rule. When Baghdad was conquered for a second time in 1393 by Tamerlane, many Jews fled to Kurdistan and Syria, leaving almost no Jews in Baghdad until the end of the 15th century.

During the struggle between the Ottomans and the Persian kings of the Safavid dynasty for the domination of Iraq, the political situation of the Jews of Baghdad underwent many changes. Generally, the Jews were oppressed by the Persians, who were fanatical Shiʿites and haters of non-Muslims; on the other hand they enjoyed fair treatment under the *Ottomans. The conquest of Baghdad in 1514 by Shah Ismāʿīl I did not worsen the situation of the Jews, but with the beginning of the reign of his son Ṭahmāsp I (1524–76), they suffered greatly from the hostile attitude of the Persian authorities. During the first part of the Ottoman rule, which lasted from 1534 to 1623, there was again an improvement in the situation for the Jews. Their economic position improved; their trade with foreign countries increased; and there were several wealthy merchants among them. In the early 17th century Pedro *Teixeria, the Portuguese Marrano explorer, found 25,000 houses in Baghdad, of which 250 belonged to Jews. In 1623 the Persians again conquered Baghdad, and during their rule, which lasted until 1638, there was a new deterioration in the situation of the Jews. Because of this, they gave their support to Sultan Murād IV, who conquered Baghdad in 1638. The day of the conquest, Tevet 16, 5399, was fixed as a *yom nes* (day of miracle). Additional evidence of the sympathy of the Jews toward the Ottomans is the custom fixing 11 Av, 5493 (1733), the day that the Persians were defeated trying to reoccupy Baghdad, as a *yom nes*. Carsten Niebuhr, a Danish traveler and scholar who visited Iraq some 30 years later, relates that there was a large Jewish community in Baghdad and that its influence was felt in the economic life of the city.

During the second half of the 18th century and the early 19th century Ottoman rule deteriorated in efficiency and the attitude of the government toward the Jews became harsh. Even so, some Jewish bankers were involved in the affairs of the governing circles, especially in the attempted rebellion of the governors.

During the reign of Sultan Mahmud II, the banker Ezekiel *Gabbai supported the removal of the governor of Baghdad, who had rebelled against the sultan in 1811. The last Mamluk governor, Dāʿūd Pasha (1817–31), who had also tried to rebel against the sultan, oppressed the Jews of Baghdad, and many of the wealthier ones fled to Persia, India, and other countries. Among them was David S. *Sassoon, a member of the distinguished Baghdad family.

The number of Jews at that time was still considerable. R. *David D'Beth Hillel, who visited the city in 1828, found 6,000 Jewish families there led by a pasha, also known as "king of the Jews," who was also responsible for the judicial affairs of the community. The English traveler Wellsted, who visited Baghdad in 1831, praised the remarkable moral conduct of the Jews, which he attributed to their religious upbringing. Wellsted made special note of the feeling of mutual responsibility among the Jews of Baghdad. According to him, there were no poor among them because anyone who lost his means of livelihood was assisted by his companions. R. Jehiel Kestelmann, an emissary from Safed, claims to have found 20,000 Jews in Baghdad in 1860. With the opening of the Suez Canal in 1869 and the improvement of the city's economic situation, the economic status of the Jews also improved. Many Jews from other localities settled in the city. According to the traveler Ephraim *Neumark, the Baghdad community numbered 30,000 in 1884; 50,000 in the early 20th century; and 100,000 in the 1930s.

Community Leaders

In the 18th and 19th centuries important changes in cultural and religious life occurred, because of the activities of outstanding rabbis in the community. A notable improvement took place with the arrival of R. Ẓedakah *Ḥozin from Aleppo in 1743. Ḥozin improved the educational system of the city and Jewish religious education improved. During the 18th century Palestinian emissaries visited the Baghdad community, strengthening its ties with the Palestinian population and reinforcing religious values within the community. Besides collecting funds for the communities of Jerusalem, Safed, and Hebron, these emissaries also delivered sermons and resolved halakhic problems. The most prominent of Baghdad's rabbis during the 19th century was R. ʿAbdallah *Somekh, who is considered the greatest Iraqi rabbi of the last generations. In 1840 he founded a rabbinical college, Beit Zilkha, whose graduates filled rabbinical positions in many different localities. Among the Jews of Baghdad in the 19th century were still some writers of *piyyutim*, such as R. Sasson b. Israel (1820–1885). In the same century there were wealthy philanthropists who contributed generously to the community projects, especially to educational and religious institutions. The most prominent of them were Jacob Ẓemaḥ (d. 1847), Ezekiel b. Reuben Manasseh (d. 1851), Joseph Gurji (d. 1894), Eliezer Kadoorie (1867–1944), and Menaḥem *Daniel (1846–1940).

Until 1849 the community of Baghdad was led by a *nasi*, who was appointed by the vilayet governor, and who also acted as his banker (*ṣarrāf bāshī*). The first of these leaders claimed to be descendants of the house of David and their positions were inherited by members of their families. Later, however, the position was purchased. The most renowned of these leaders were Sassoon b. R. Ẓalaḥ (1781–1817), the father of the *Sassoon family, and Ezra b. Joseph Gabbai (1817–24). From 1849 the community was led by the *ḥakham bashi* who represented the Jews to the Turkish authorities. The first one was R. Raphael Kaẓin. The *nasi*, and later the *ḥakham bashi*, were assisted by a council of 10 and later 12 delegates, which included three rabbis and nine laymen drawn from the wealthier members of the community. The council collected the taxes and dealt with community affairs. The collection of the *ʿaskarlī* ("military service ransom tax"), which replaced the *jizya* (poll tax), was sometimes the cause of violent conflicts within the community.

World War I and After

Until the British conquest of Baghdad in March 1917, the Jews were oppressed by the vilayet governor and the police commissioner, who attempted to extort money from them and to recruit their youth for the Turkish army. Hundreds of young men were recruited and the majority were sent to the Caucasus where many died of starvation and cold. Wealthy Jews were tortured and killed after being accused of devaluating the Turkish pound. The Jews naturally rejoiced when the British occupied Baghdad. The day of their entry was fixed as a *yom nes* (17 Adar, 5677, or February 3, 1917). From the conquest until 1929, the Jews of Baghdad enjoyed complete freedom. Many of them were employed in the civil service, while others were even appointed to important government positions. Zionist activities also prospered for some time. However, in 1929, when the British decided to grant independence to Iraq, many Jewish officials were dismissed from government services, Zionist activity was prohibited, and, in general, there was an increase of antisemitism. This was especially so after Dr. A. Grobbe, the German ambassador in Baghdad, began to propagandize in 1932.

In 1934 there were large-scale dismissals of Jewish civil servants, and from 1936 murders of Jews and bombing of their institutions were added to even more dismissals. These attacks reached a climax on Shavuot 5701 (June 1–2, 1941) with Rashīd ʿĀlī's pro-Axis revolution against the British. During those two days savage mobs massacred Jews and looted their property with the passive support of army and police officers. Neither the regent ʿAbd al-Ilāh, who had arrived in the city before the beginning of the riots, nor the British troops, who were stationed outside the city, made any effort to intervene. According to various sources 120 to 180 Jews, including women, elderly people, and children, were killed and 800 injured during some 30 hours. This was accompanied by cases of rape and abduction of women. The value of the looted property was estimated at 1,000,000 dinars (or 1,000,000 pounds sterling – then 4,000,000 dollars). Thousands of Jews left the city, most of them for India and Palestine. However, many of them returned before the end of the year after failing to integrate themselves in these countries and having heard that the situation in Baghdad had improved. A period of prosperity ensued and continued until 1945; even though the decrees concerning their employment in government service and their admission to public schools had not been repealed, the Jews lived in Baghdad at ease and without fear.

After 1945 there were frequent demonstrations against the Jews and especially against Zionism. With the proclamation of the partition of Palestine, November 1947, even greater danger threatened the Jews of Baghdad. There was fear of a massacre, and the Jewish underground defense, organized with help of Palestinian Jews, was in a state of preparedness; the catastrophe was averted when martial law was proclaimed by the government. Nonetheless, many Jews were brought before military courts and fines were levied on the majority of them.

Immediately after the establishment of the State of Israel, hundreds of Baghdadi Jews were arrested. Many of the detainees were accused of communist or Zionist activities. A few hundred Jewish youth had joined these clandestine movements, especially after 1948. Two communist and two Zionist leaders were hanged publicly in Baghdad. During the government of ʿAbd Al-Karīm Qassem (July 1958–February 1963) the attitude toward the Jews was more favorable. Even so, there were severe periodical restrictions on departure from Iraq, property confiscation, and a strengthening of economic pressure on the community.

Fourteen Iraqis, including nine Jews, were hanged publicly in Baghdad on January 27, 1969, after being convicted on charges of spying for Israel. Two other Jews were hanged in August of the same year. In April 1973 the total number of the innocent Jews who were hanged, murdered, or kidnapped and disappeared reached 46; dozens more were detained.

There were 77,000 Jews in Baghdad in 1947. After the mass exodus to Israel in 1950–51, approximately 6,000 Jews were left. Subsequently, Jews continued to leave Baghdad, so that only about 3,000 remained in 1963 when Qassem was toppled by ʿAbd al-Salām ʿĀrif. This figure remained nearly the same until 1971, when the Jews began to escape from the country to Iran via Kurdistan and the authorities began to issue passports to Iraqi Jews. From this point on, the number of Jews dropped steadily to be about 350 in 1975. In 2005 there were only a few Jews still living in Baghdad.

[Abraham Ben-Yaacob / Nissim Kazzaz (2nd ed.)]

Institutions and Community Life – 1917–1970

During the British administration and after World War II, the number of Jewish educational institutions, especially the secondary ones, increased. In spite of the restrictions on the number of Jews admitted to government secondary schools, their number in these institutions was higher in 1950 than in 1920; but, because of lack of data, only the number in Jewish educational institutions will be mentioned. In 1920 there were some 6,000 Jewish youngsters in Jewish educational institutions: 2,500 in *talmud torahs*, 3,350 in kindergartens and elementary schools, and 150 in secondary schools; for 1950, the total was 13,476 pupils, of which 1,800 were in the *talmud torahs*, 8,970 in kindergartens and elementary schools, and 2,626 in secondary schools.

During this period there were also important social changes within the Baghdad community. The majority of women removed the gown (Arabic, *ʿabaʾ*) and the veil (Persian, *pūshī*), which they formerly wore in the street. The number of girls engaged in teaching and in clerical work increased and some of them received a university education. There was also a change in the occupations of the Jews. Whereas in 1920 they were engaged in trade, banking, labor, and public services, in 1950 thousands earned their livelihood by clerical work or in the professions such as law. Immediately after the British conquest, the Jews began to leave their quarter to settle in all parts of the city. In the 1930s the Battāwīn and Karrāda quarters were established and inhabited by the wealthy. The attitude toward religion also underwent a change. During the first years after the British conquest there were only a few Jews who profaned the Sabbath or ate non-kosher food, whereas at the end of this period the number of Sabbath observers decreased.

From the end of the Ottoman period until 1931 the Jews of Baghdad had a "General Council" of 80 members, which included 20 rabbis and was led by the chief rabbi. The General Council elected a council for religious matters and a council for material welfare. The former dealt with ritual slaughter, burials, and the rabbinical courts, while the latter was responsible for the schools, hospitals, and charitable trusts. In 1926, however, a group of intellectuals gained the upper hand in the latter council and attempted to remove the chief rabbi, Ezra *Dangoor. After a stormy period, in 1931, the community passed the "Law of the Jewish Community." It deprived the rabbis of the community's leadership and made it possible for a nonreligious person to assume leadership. In spite of this in February 1933 R. Sasson *Kadoorie was elected chairman of the community. His position was, however, a secular one, while a rabbi without any community authority was elected to the position of chief rabbi. Just before the mass emigration of 1951, there were about 20 Jewish educational institutions in Baghdad; 16 were under supervision of the community committee, the rest were privately run. In 1950 about 12,000 pupils attended these institutions while many others attended government and foreign schools; approximately another 400 students were enrolled in Baghdad colleges of medicine, law, economy, pharmacy, and engineering. All but two of the Jewish educational institutions closed in 1952. These two had approximately 900 pupils in 1960, while about 50 Jewish pupils attended government schools. The Baghdad community also had a school for the blind, founded in 1930, which was the only one of its kind in Iraq. It closed in 1951.

Pupils in Jewish educational institutions in Baghdad in 1920 and just before the mass exodus of 1950–51

Year	Talmud Torah	Kindergartens and Elementary Schools	Secondary Schools	Total
1920	2,500	3,350	150	6,000
1950	1,880	8,970	2,626	13,476

The Jews of Baghdad had two hospitals; one, a general hospital named for Meir Elias, founded in 1910, and the second, an eye hospital named for Rima Kadoorie, founded in 1924. At both these hospitals, Jews received treatment, and operations were performed for the needy for little or no payment. Every school in town had a clinic. The community also had several philanthropic societies to provide dowries for girls without means, help to mothers, maintenance of yeshivah students, and for the vocational training of poor children. All these institutions, including the hospitals, eventually closed. Afterward, the community committee arranged for the sick to be admitted to various hospitals in the town.

Only seven synagogues remained in 1960 of the 60 synagogues of Baghdad in 1950. The community committee had subcommittees for religious affairs and administration. These two subcommittees were elected by the general committee, elected in turn by men of the community every four years. In November 1949, Sasson Kadoorie was forced to resign, when local Jewry blamed him for not acting to free the numerous young Jews arrested on charges of Zionism. He was replaced by Ezekiel Shemtob, who served until 1953, when Kadoorie again became president of the community. Kadoorie still presided in 1970. In accordance with an Iraqi law of 1954, a council elected every two years and supervised by the Ministry of Justice worked with the president. The subcommittees were abolished and a government law in December 1951 also abolished the rabbinical court in Baghdad.

[Hayyim J. Cohen]

Hebrew Printing

The first Hebrew (lithographic) printing press in Baghdad was founded by Moses Baruch Mizraḥi in 1863. The press printed a Hebrew newspaper named *Ha-Dover* (The Speaker) or *Dover Mesharin* (Upright Speaker) until 1870 and three small books. A second printing press with movable characters was founded in Baghdad in 1868 by Raḥamim b. Reuben, a resident of Baghdad, who had previously gained printing experience in Bombay. The brothers Moses and Aaron Fetaya later formed a partnership with Raḥamim, and after his death they continued his work until 1882. Fifty-five books were printed on this printing press.

In 1888 a new press was founded in Baghdad by Solomon Bekhor Ḥutz (1843–1892), a scholar, poet, author, journalist, bookseller, and communal worker. He brought his printing letters from Leghorn, Italy. Besides prayer books, he also printed many books which he considered useful to the members of his community. These included tales and works by Baghdad scholars which had been in manuscript until then. After his death, the printing press was taken over by his son, Joshua Ḥutz, and operated until 1913. Seventy-five books were printed on it.

In 1904 a new press was founded in Baghdad by R. Ezra Reuben Dangoor (1848–1930), who was also *ḥakham bashi* of Baghdad. This printing press was in existence until 1921 and over 100 books were printed on it. For the greater part they were books of prayers and *piyyutim* according to the custom of the Baghdad Jews, but there were also some popular books in the Judeo-Arabic jargon and a Hebrew weekly, *Yeshurun*, of which five issues were published in 1920. This was a second and last attempt at Hebrew journalism in Baghdad. During the British Mandate in Iraq, two small Hebrew printing presses were founded in Baghdad: the al-Waṭaniyya al-Isrāʾīliyya (The Israel Homeland) press, which printed about 20 books between 1922 and 1927; and the Elisha Shoḥet press, which printed more than 40 books between 1924 and 1937. When the British Mandate ended, these printing presses declined and finally ceased operation altogether.

[Avraham Yaari]

BIBLIOGRAPHY: Ben-Jacob, in: *Zion*, 15 (1951), 56–69; idem, *Toledot ha-Rav ʿAbdalla Somekh* (1949); idem, in: *Hed ha-Mizraḥ*, 2 (1943/44), no. 8, 13–14; idem, in: *Sinai*, 54 (1964), 95–101; idem, *Yehudei Bavel* (1965); A.S. Yahuda, *Bagdadische Sprichwoerter* (1906); S. Poznański, *Babylonische Geonim…* (1914); J. Obermeyer, *Die Landschaft Babylonien* (1929); D.S. Sassoon, *A History of the Jews in Baghdad* (1949); Yaari, Sheluḥei, index; Cohen, in: *Middle Eastern Studies* (Oct. 1966), 2–17; H.Y. Cohen, *Ha-Peʿilut ha-Ẓiyyonit be-Irak* (1969). HEBREW PRINTING: A. Yaari, *Ha-Defus ha-Ivri be-Arẓot ha-Mizraḥ*, 2 (1940), 100–59; idem, in: KS, 24 (1947/48), 71–72; A. Ben-Jacob, *ibid.*, 22 (1945/46), 82–83. **ADD. BIBLIOGRAPHY:** G. Bekhor, *Fascinating Life and Sensational Death* (1990); H.J. Cohen, *Ha-Yehudim be-Arẓot ha-Mizraḥ ha-Tikhon be-Yamenu* (1973); M. Gat, *Kehillah Yehudit be-Mashber* (1989); N. Kazzaz, *Yehudei Irak ba-Me'ah ha-Esrim* (1991); idem, *Sofa shel Golah* (2002); E. Kedourie, "The Jews of Baghdad In 1910," in: *Middle Eastern Studies*, 3 (1970), 355–61; E. Meir, *Ha-Tenuʿah ha-Ẓiyyonit ve-Yehudei Irak* (1994); idem, *Me-Ever la-Midbar* (1973); idem, *Hitpatḥut Ivrit Tarbutit shel Yehudei Irak* (1989); M. Sawdayee, *All Waiting To Be Hanged* (1974); A. Shiblak, *The Lure of Zion* (1986); N. Stillman, *The Jews of Arab Lands in Modern Times* (1991); S.G. Haim, "Aspects of Jewish Life In Baghdad under the Monarchy," in: *Middle Eastern Studies*, 12, (1976), 188–208; A. Twena, *Golim ve-Ge'ulim*, 5 (1975), 6 (1977), 7 (1979); I. Bar-Moshe, *Yawmān fī Ḥazirān* (2004); S. Somekh, *Bagdad Etmol* (2004); N. Rejwan, *The Last Jews in Bagdad: Remembering A Lost Homeland* (2004).

BAGINSKY, ADOLF ARON (1843–1918), German physician and founder of modern pediatrics. Baginsky was born in Silesia and in 1881 joined the faculty of Berlin University, being appointed associate professor in 1892. In 1890, with the assistance of Virchow, he founded the children's hospital, Kaiser und Kaiserin Friedrich Kinderkrankenhaus, of which he became director. His main contributions to pediatrics were in the fields of infectious diseases, the study of milk, and hygiene. Baginsky was a leader in the movement for the promotion of child welfare and his services in this field won him orders and decorations from many governments. He was founder and editor of the pediatric journal, *Archiv fur Kinderheilkunde* (1879). His works included *Lehrbuch der Kinderheilkunde* (1982; "Textbook of Pediatrics," translated into a number of languages), *Handbuch der Schulhygiene* ("Manual on School Hygiene," 1877), and *Praktische Beitraege zur Kinderheilkunde* ("Practical Contributions to Pediatrics," 1880–84), as well as many articles on physiological and chemical subjects.

Baginsky was an active member of the Jewish community in Berlin and of the movement to check antisemitism in Germany. He also wrote an interesting essay on the significance of hygiene in Mosaic legislation in which he expresses his admiration for the hygienic laws in the Bible.

BIBLIOGRAPHY: S.R. Kagan: *Jews in Medicine* (1952), 357–8.

[Suessmann Muntner]

BAGLEY, DAVID (1932–), *ḥazzan*. Bagley was born in Vilna where his musical talents were revealed at an early age. He spent the war years in Japan and China and studied in Mir Yeshiva in Shanghai. In 1947 he went to America, where he continued his religious studies and also furthered his cantorial learning. One of his outstanding teachers was Cantor Joshua Lind. His first post in the United States was in Atereth Zion Synagogue in Brooklyn, after which he went on to many important positions in the United States. He was chief cantor of the *Nidḥe Israel* congregation in Mexico City, and from 1967 to 1969 he was chief cantor in Ramat Gan, Israel. He has held posts in Johannesburg and Cape Town and has been chief cantor of Beth Shalom Synagogue in Toronto. He has produced many records of cantorial music (many under his own Shirei David label) and has composed several prayers, besides appearing in concerts throughout the world. Chanan Winternitz, a well-known Israeli liturgical arranger/accompanist, was for many years responsible for his concert repertoire. Besides two compilations of Recitatives and Melodies (*Ne'ilah* and *Hallel*), the Toronto Council of *ḥazzanim* together with the Council of Ḥazzanim of Greater Montreal has issued a volume of David Bagley's compositions entitled: *'Al Yedei David* (2000).

[Akiva Zimmerman / Raymond Goldstein (2nd ed.)]

BAGOHI (Gr. Βαγώας), governor of the Persian satrapy Yehud (Judea) in the time of Darius II and Artaxerxes II. Among the *Elephantine papyri there was found a letter sent in 408 B.C.E. by the Jews of Elephantine-Yeb to "Bagohi, governor of Judah," in which it is written that a similar letter had been sent to "Delaiah and Shelemiah, sons of Sanballat, governor of Samaria." In this letter they appeal for assistance in the reconstruction of their temple, which had been destroyed by the priests of the Egyptian god Khnub. This letter reveals that a similar appeal had been made three years earlier to "Bagohi, governor of Judah," to Johanan, the high priest in Jerusalem, to Ostanes the brother of Anani, and to the nobles of the Jews, but no reply had been received. It is probable that the reason for the failure of the high priest to reply was his negative attitude toward this temple, but it may also have been the tense relations existing between the Persian governor and the high priest. Josephus (Ant. 11:297–301) relates that when Johanan the high priest murdered his brother Joshua in the Temple (probably at the beginning of the fourth century B.C.E.), Bagohi forced his way into the Temple, declaring to the priests who opposed his entry (since he was a Gentile) that his defilement of the Temple was less than that of a person guilty of fratricide. The discovery of the Elephantine documents has disposed of the attempts of Wilrich and Wellhausen to dismiss the story as a legend on the grounds that no person of this name was known.

BIBLIOGRAPHY: E. Meyer, *Der Papyrusfund von Elephantine* (1912³); Cowley, Aramaic, 108ff., no. 30; A. Schalit, in *Sefer Yoḥanan Lewy* (1949), 252–72.

[Abraham Schalit]

BAGRIT, SIR LEON (1902–1979), British industrialist and automation pioneer. Bagrit was born in Kiev, Russia, but his family arrived in England as refugees from Belgium at the beginning of World War I. He studied engineering at London University, helping to support himself at college by playing the violin in a philharmonic orchestra. He was employed for several years by engineering companies for which he designed machinery but in 1935, in order to be free to use his patents, he established his own firm. In 1937 it was taken over by Elliott Brothers, Bagrit becoming managing director. In 1962, as chairman of the company, now renamed Elliott-Automation, he turned to the development of automated control systems for nuclear, aeronautical, and industrial purposes. The company was the first in Europe devoted to automation. In 1967 Elliott-Automation was taken over by the English Electric Company, with Bagrit as deputy chairman.

He was a member of the Council for Scientific and Industrial Research (1963–65) and the Advisory Council on Technology (from 1964). A director of the Royal Opera House, he founded the Friends of Covent Garden. He became a consultant on automation to the Israeli government. He was knighted in 1962. In 1964 Bagrit delivered the prestigious BBC Reith Lectures on "The Age of Automation."

ADD. BIBLIOGRAPHY: ODNB online.

[Moshe Eliahu Berman]

BAGRITSKI, EDUARD GEORGIYEVICH, pseudonym of **E.G. Dzyuba** (1895–1934), Soviet Russian poet. Bagritski, who was born into a middle-class Odessa family and had a traditional Jewish upbringing, was a dedicated communist. His verse, at first complex and influenced by Symbolism, gradually became simpler and more graceful, earning him a place among the leading Russian poets of the 20th century. Like his fellow writers from Odessa, *Babel, Olesha, *Ilf, and the Katayev brothers, Bagritski successfully combined literary sophistication with romantic naïveté in his perception and salutation of reality. This combination of highly polished craftsmanship and childlike wonder constitutes the most endearing quality of his lyric verse. It also accounts for the success even of his propagandist poems. Bagritski's most important work was the poem "Duma pro Opanasa" (1926; "The Lay of Opanas"), a blend of lyric and narrative verse which contains elements of Ukrainian folk poetry and of the old Slavic epic. "The Lay of Opanas" describes a Ukrainian peasant who deserts from a Red Army unit commanded by a Jew named Kogan, joins an anarchist band, captures his former commander, but later offers to release him. Kogan, a devoted Communist, proudly refuses, and is thereupon shot by Opanas, who is himself subsequently executed by the Reds. Bagritski's is one of the most successful treatments of the revolutionary theme in Soviet literature. Some of Bagritski's best poetry appeared in the collection *Yugo-zapad* (Southwest, 1928). He was also known for his Russian translations of English, French, Yiddish, and Ukrainian verse.

BIBLIOGRAPHY: G. Struve, *Soviet Russian Literature 1917–1950* (1951).

[Maurice Friedberg]

BAHIA, the first region to be colonized in *Brazil and today a state within the federal republic situated in the northeast of the country. In 2005 the general population was 13,085,769, and the Jewish population about 800.

Colonial Period

The presence of Portuguese *New Christians began with the discovery, conquest, and colonization of Brazil, then inhabited by dozens of groups of indigenous peoples. When the tribunal of the *Inquisition was established in Portugal (1536; operating until 1821), and after the first *auto-de-fé* (1540), the immigration of New Christians to the Brazilian colony grew, and many of them arrived in Bahia with the first governors. Some sources maintain that one New Christian, Gaspar da Gama, was part of Pedro Álvares Cabral's fleet, in 1500. There were a significant number of Jews involved in sciences and the art of navigation in Portugal during the period of overseas expansion in the early 1400s. The Tribunal do Santo Ofício da Inquisição, created in Portugal, did not settle permanently in colonial Brazil. As of 1591, the Tribunal do Santo Ofício made several visits to Brazil, powers were delegated to some bishops, like for instance the bishop of Bahia, and clergymen would indict people for Jewish practices directly in Lisbon.

In the second half of the 16th century, Bahia absorbed New Christians who contributed to the establishment of the first villages, to the mercantilist state, and to the Church struggle against the Indians, to the finance of and participation in the expeditions to the interior, and to cultivation of the land and of sugar cane in particular. Production and trade in sugar cane became the chief source of wealth of Brazil in the second half of the 16th and the 17th centuries. Besides sugar-mill lords, New Christians were slave merchants, farmers, and craftsmen, among other occupations. They ascended socially and economically, but they were faced with the restrictions of belonging to religious orders or political spheres, such as the Irmandades de Misericórdia and Câmaras Municipais.

News about the New Christian prosperity, their increasing numbers, and slight attachment to Catholicism led the inquisitors to set up a board of inquiry in Bahia to locate judaizers. Their sessions, known as *Visitações* (visitations), were held initially in 1591–95 and in 1618 aiming at judaizers, condemned sexual practices, witchcraft, and Holy Church slanderers. Between 1618 and 1619 a total of 134 people were indicted, of whom 90 were accused of being judaizers. Most of them were not taken to court and many fled from Brazil to other regions colonized by the Spaniards.

Between 1624 and 1625 the Dutch Colonial Empire conquered Bahia. Then religious tolerance was established, although just a few New Christians were in the region and a few Jews came to Bahia with the Dutch expeditionary forces.

An important investigation, known as the 1646 Inquiry, was carried out in Bahia in the 17th century, at the Jesuit seminary. With the aid of various testimonies, this inquiry revealed the role that the Portuguese of Jewish descent played in the political, economic, and administrative life in Bahia. In the 18th century many members of Brazilian families were still prevented from assuming public office because they were descendants of those denounced in 1646.

The New Christians continued to hold important positions in Bahian society until the end of the 18th century. In 1773, during the liberal government of Marques de Pombal, general governor of Brazil, the differentiation between new Christians and old Christians was abolished and the inquisitional procedures came to an end. Consequently the New Christians were then totally integrated into society at large, their descendants being among the prominent and ancient families of Bahia.

The Inquisition in Brazil was less systematic and more infrequent then its Portuguese counterpart, probably owing to the difficult control of the colony, the fact that a permanent tribunal was never established, and the greater permeability within the social and religious relations established in the Portuguese New World.

According to Wiznitzer, around 25,000 people were brought to court by the Portuguese Inquisition, out of whom 1,500 were condemned to capital punishment. In Brazil, approximately 400 judaizers were sued, most of them condemned to imprisonment, and 18 New Christians were condemned to death in Lisbon.

The presence of New Christians in colonial Bahia and Brazil has always been a controversial issue in both Brazilian and Portuguese historiography. More studies on Jewish history have been published in Brazil with regard to the colonial period than about modern times, which shows the broad interest aroused by the theme of the New Christians and the Inquisition in Brazil. Some historians believe that the interventions of the Inquisition Tribunal in Brazil, supported by the nobility and the Catholic clergy, aimed at expropriating the New Christians' possessions and impeding the social ascension of a group with bourgeois aspirations. Therefore, the Inquisition created a myth regarding origin and purity of blood which discriminated against those with "infected blood" according to the Statutes on Blood Purity. Other historians see strictly religious and political reasons related to the history of the Portuguese Catholic Church and Portuguese Empire.

Meanwhile, some historians maintain that Judaism or Crypto-Judaism was "fabricated" during the inquisitional processes (that is, by means of intimidating, indicting, menacing, and torturing, the inquisition "created" such Judaism ito justify its own existence and legitimacy); some others argue that New Christians deliberately and furtively professed Judaic or Crypto-Judaic elements inherited from their ancestors. According to Anita Novinsky, the New Christian was a "split human being," socially and existentially, with a differentiated identity in the Portuguese-Brazilian colonial world.

The antisemitism found in the Inquisition's procedures did not lead to the spread of antisemitism among the population in Bahia or Brazil, although the mental hold of the Inquisition and the terror it possessed can hardly be assessed. There are no apparent connections between the history of the New Christians and contemporary 20th-century Jewish history in Bahia. Nevertheless, the remote (and secret) Jewish origin of many traditional Catholic Portuguese families is quite well known, as a memory of the Jewish community and the Bahian population at large, specially among its elites.

Contemporary Period

The Jewish community in Salvador, the capital of Bahia, consisted of approximately 200 families with an active cultural and political life, which reached its peak between the 1930s and 1950s. Jewish immigrants coming from Eastern Europe started settling in Salvador in the 1920s.

Records show that small groups of Jewish immigrants also settled in Ilhéus and Itabuna, in the region where a local economy based on cocoa flourished, and in Bonfim, Petrolina, Juazeiro, and Jacobina, along the banks of the São Francisco River (the most important in the State). In Salvador, a synagogue started to function at a private household in 1924, in 1925 the Jewish Jacob Dinenzon school was created. During the 1930s, a second school was founded, Ber Borochov, with Zionist leanings, differing from the Jacob Dinenzon school in its progressive and Yiddishist orientation. The new school operated slightly over a decade, after which the community favored the older school. In 1970, there were 120 students registered at the latter, which closed down in 1978 because many families had immigrated to other cities. In addition, the Jewish community in Salvador opened a cemetery and ran the Sociedade Beneficente. Zionist women's organizations emerged, such as WIZO and Naamat-Pioneiras, and the Jewish minority organized itself around the Sociedade Israelita da Bahia, founded in 1947. In 1968 the Hebraica Club of Salvador was founded. In politics, Mário Kertesz was mayor of the capital and Boris Tabacof was finance secretary of the State of Bahia. In 2004, those who remained organized themselves around the synagogue.

BIBLIOGRAPHY: Documents of the Arquivo Histórico Judaico Brasileiro; A. Wiznitzer, *Os judeus no Brasil colonial* (1960); A. Novinsky, *Cristãos-Novos na Bahia* (1972); E. Lipiner, *Os judaizantes nas capitanias de cima. São Paulo – estudos sobre os Cristãos-Novos do Brasil nos séculos XVI e XVII* (1969); A.J. Saraiva, *Inquisição e Cristãos-Novos* (1969); M.C. Maio and C. Calaça. "Um balanço da bibliografia sobre anti-semitismo no Brasil," in: *BIB – Revista Brasileira de Informação Bibliográfica em Ciências Sociais*, no. 49 (2000) 15–50; *Os judeus na Bahia*, Special Supplement, in: *Shalom*, no. 296, n/d.

[Roney Cytrynowicz (2nd ed.)]

BAHIR, SEFER HA- (Heb. סֵפֶר הַבָּהִיר; "Book of Brightness"), kabbalistic, pseudoepigraphic and midrashic anthology which enigmatically depicts a sexualized, divine theosophy considered by scholarship to mark the literary emergence of Kabbalah at the beginning of the 13th century.

The Work and Its Titles

The *Sefer ha-Bahir* should not properly be considered a book as it has no known author and certainly no single author. It is comprised of numerous tradition-complexes, divided by Gershom *Scholem into 140 numbered passages. Many medieval Jewish esotericists contributed and revised the passages contained in this anthology, from its early and all but lost Ashkenazi version which lacked theosophic symbolism and on through its canonical status amongst kabbalists in Spain. The earliest manuscripts lack any title, although it was widely referred to in the 13th century as *Sefer ha-Bahir, or Midrash R. Nehunya ben ha-Kanah*, based upon the opening passages wherein this tannaitic figure interprets a verse from Job (37:21) which mentions the bright light (*Or Bahir*).

Historical Setting and Earliest Use by the Kabbalists

Scholem placed the *Bahir* historically after the German Pietists and before the emergence of the Provençal kabbalists, so that the *Bahir* stood out as the earliest kabbalistic text. However, it is now understood that the first known kabbalist who composed a kabbalistic work in Provence, R. *Isaac the Blind, did not know the *Sefer ha-Bahir.* Accordingly, traditions quoted in the name of R. Isaac the Blind conclude with citations of passages from the *Sefer ha-Bahir,* but these citations are additions. No evidence exists that the Provençal kabbalists of his circle used or even knew of the work, although if they did, they certainly ignored it, preferring their own traditions and esoteric sources. R. Isaac's nephew, R. *Asher ben David, possibly cites the *Bahir* once in his *Sefer ha-Yiḥud* by the name *aggadah*, but here too, even if so, the lengthy book draws on other sources. R. Isaac's students in Gerona incorporated the *Sefer ha-Bahir* into their canon and writings, but only into their later works, suggesting the independent sources and development of these literary and esoteric circles. The anti-kabbalistic polemicist, R. *Meir ben Simeon of Narbonne, distinguished between what he heard from or about the Provençal kabbalists from what he read in the *Sefer ha-Bahir,* once again separating the Provençal kabbalistic phenomenon from this work.

Composition and Redaction: Between Germany and Spain

Accretions or revisions to certain passages display the mark of Provençal Kabbalah, although it cannot be determined when and by whom these passages were altered. One view places the main redactional activity as late as the kabbalists of Gerona. The 13th-century kabbalist, R. Isaac ha-Kohen, reports that the *Sefer ha-Bahir* "came from the Land of Israel to the early pietists, the sages of Ashkenaz, the kabbalists of Germany and from there to the early wise men in Provence who chase after all sorts of written [records of] wisdom, those who know the divine, supernal knowledge. But they saw only part of the book and not all of it because they did not see it in its entirety, in its complete form." R. Isaac's testimony points to the Ashkenazi origin of some literary sources of the *Sefer ha-Bahir* as he denies that the Provencal kabbalists edited the work. Citations from the pre-theosophic version of the *Sefer ha-Bahir* by R. Ephraim bar Samson and other passages from *Sod ha-Gaddol* by R. Moses ben Eleazar ha-Darshan, both 13th-century German Pietists, point to the Ashkenazi origin of the textual sources to what later became the commonly accepted, theosophic version of the *Sefer ha-Bahir.* Scholem built an argument on the latter's quotations, suggesting that the work, *Sod ha-Gadol* can be traced back to the "Orient," based on the mention of the title *Raza Rabba* in a ninth-century Karaite polemic against some rabbinic, magical works. This claim has since been dismissed as no citations can be offered to compare the works, amongst a host of early and medieval works known by the title "Book of Secrets." Recent scholarship has suggested that some passages in the *Bahir* are based on the Babylonian vocalization, pointing to ancient sources in the East. These claims aside, the literary production and kabbalistic recension are the products of unidentified circles of medieval, European esotericists which did not feed into, nor cause, the apparent "eruption" of kabbalistic thinking and literature at the end of the 12th and the beginning of the 13th centuries.

Literary Character of the Bahir

The *Sefer ha-Bahir* was not intended and should not be seen as a primer for kabbalistic study nor should it be understood through the lenses of the highly structured sefirotic symbolism which crystallized in the decades following its final stages of its composition and editing. The *Bahir* is rudimentary in its literary style, as it offers very complex mythic images, defying simple and structuralist interpretations based on the term *sefirot*. Many of its passages are based on parables of a king and his son or sons and a daughter, pointing to the *sefirotic* understanding, but effectively elucidating only some of the relationships within the supernal world, more than explicating any one, set doctrine.

Influences and External Sources

Scholem argued that the *Bahir* is the product of a merging of rabbinic and Gnostic traditions, at one point claiming that the work contains a literal translation of the Greek term *male*, pleroma (or: fullness), in describing the godhead. These phenomenological or hermeneutical parallels aside, no evidence can be shown to suggest the literary influence of Gnostic works on these early Jewish esotericists and the emerging Kabbalah. More recent attempts to explain the appearance of the *Sefer ha-Bahir,* have sought to explain the work as the first text to feminize the **Shekhinah* and focus on Her as the grade of the divinity closest to the kabbalist adept. Accordingly, the 12th-century Christian rites which focus on Mary in Provence are seen to be the impetus and influence which informed the kabbalistic invention of the feminized theosophy. Here again, only impressionistic parallels can be suggested between the two corpora and religious traditions, which in any event are anachronistic as the literary sources of the *Seer ha-Bahir* predate this Christian phenomenon and the work emerges from a different geographical location, Ashkenaz. The *Sefer ha-Bahir* does offer many sexualized interpretations of the drama within the divine structure although it rarely mentions the *Shekhinah*. Locutions from *Sefer Yeẓirah* are central to a number of passages although no systematic attempt is made to transform the ancient esoteric work into a kabbalistic interpretation. The term "*sefirah*," taken from *Sefer Yeẓirah*, rarely appears and there is no systematic use of the sefirotic names more commonly found in the later works to depict the ten divine grades of the divine theosophy. The term "kabbalah" is also not mentioned as the proper name for the esoteric lore, although there are two important uses of the root in other forms.

The Text and its Editions

The earliest dated manuscript from 1298 formed the basis for Scholem's annotated German translation which comprised his doctoral dissertation in 1923. Scholem "corrected" or rather amended his Hebrew transcription, which formed the basis of his translation, with "better" readings from 13th-century kabbalists, changing the earliest textual witness in key places. The discrepancies between the earliest manuscript and the many citations which appear in later kabbalistic works, demonstrate that even the kabbalistic editing of the *Sefer ha-Bahir* was still in flux after the literary and social emergence of the Kabbalah. This process continued through the early modern period and on through the 20th century, when Reuven Margolioth edited a very popular edition of the Hebrew text by integrating all the readings from three late manuscripts, including words and phrases not found in the early manuscript witnesses. A number of passages cited as coming from the *Sefer ha Bahir* but not found in the main manuscripts are quoted in other kabbalistic works. Numerous commentaries and translations were prepared from the 14th century to the present. In 1994 an edition based on the earliest manuscripts was published including a facsimile of the first printed edition (Amsterdam 1651), the celebrated Munich manuscript copied in 1298, listings of the Bahiric passages not found in the *Sefer ha-Bahir,* variant readings from citations found in manuscript works, listings of all translations and commentaries and a bibliography of references to the *Sefer ha-Bahir* in printed works and modern scholarship.

BIBLIOGRAPHY: D. Abrams, *The Book Bahir: An Edition Based on the Earliest Manuscripts* (with intro. by M. Idel (Heb., 1994); J. Dan, "Midrash and the Dawn of Kabbalah," in: G. Hartman and S. Budick (eds.), *Midrash and Literature* (1986), 127–39; A. Green, "*Shekhinah,* the Virgin Mary and the Song of Songs: Reflections on a Kabbalistic Symbol in Its Historical Context," in: *AJS Review*, 26 (2002), 1–52; R. Meroz, "A Citation Attributed to the Book Bahir," in: *Kabbalah*, 7 (2002) 319–26; idem, "On the Time and Place of Some of *Sefer ha-Bahir,*" in: *Da'at*, 49 (2002), 137–80 (Heb.); H. Pedaya, "The Provençal Stratum in the Redaction of Sefer ha-Bahir," in: *Jerusalem Studies in Jewish Thought*, 9 (1990), 139–64 (Heb.); P. Schaefer, *Mirror of His Beauty: Feminine Images of God from the Bible to the Early Kabbalah* (2002); G. Scholem, *Das Buch Bahir* (1923); idem, *Origins of the Kabbalah*, trans. A. Arkush, ed. R.J.Z.Werblowsky (1987); M. Verman, *The Books of Contemplation: Medieval Jewish Mystical Sources* (1992), 166–73; E. Wolfson, "Hebraic and Hellenistic Conceptions of Wisdom in *Sefer ha-Bahir,*" in: *Poetics Today,* 19 (1998), 147–76; idem, *Language, Eros, Being* (2005), 46–166; idem, "The Tree That Is All: Jewish-Christian Roots of a Kabbalistic Symbol in *Sefer ha-Bahir,*" in: *Along the Path: Studies in Kabbalistic Myth, Symbolism and Hermeneutics* (1995), 63–88.

[Daniel Abrams (2nd ed.)]

BAHLUL, family of rabbis in Meknès, Morocco. DANIEL BEN JUDAH (second half of 17th century) was a halakhist, kabbalist, and preacher. He wrote copious notes on *Yazeḥ Yakar*, a work by Abraham Galanté on the Zohar to Exodus (Jerusalem National Library Ms.), and a volume of sermons which is frequently quoted in the work of his son Eleazar. His other sons were Samuel and Joseph.

SAMUEL was also a rabbi of Meknès. His signature occurs on the halakhic rulings of the community, one of which is dated 1732. ELEAZAR was one of the important scholars of Meknès. His signature appears on the decisions given in 1726 and 1730. Of his many works, which are extant in manuscript, the most important is *Sefer Mareh Einayim* (Jerusalem National Library), composed in Fez between 1710 and 1712, a collection of sermons by Castilian exiles and Moroccan rabbis from the 16th century, as well as sermons which Eleazar had heard from Ereẓ Israel emissaries. He also wrote *Pekuddat Elazar* on Proverbs, and a commentary on rabbinic maxims. In 1718 he edited and adapted *Refu'ot u-Segullot* and *Tivei Asavim* of Jacob Katan of Fez. JOSEPH was the secretary to the *bet din* of Meknès in 1834 and was later appointed *dayyan*.

BIBLIOGRAPHY: J.M. Toledano, *Ner ha-Ma'arav* (1911), 145; J. Ben-Naim, *Malkhei Rabbanan* (1931), 22b, 29a, 61b, 94a, 126a; G. Scholem, *Kitvei Yad be-Kabbalah* (1937), 102–4.

BAHRAIN (Bahrein), territory extending along the Arabian shore of the Persian Gulf southward from *Basra including many small islands. Talmudic references to ports and islands on the Persian Gulf indicate that Jews were already settled in this region. The Jews in the old capital of Bahrein, Hajar, are recorded in Arabic sources as having refused to accept Islam when Muhammad sent a force to occupy the territory in 630. In the 12th century *Benjamin of Tudela refers to 500 Jews living in Qays and to a Jewish population of 5,000 in al-Qatīfa (undoubtedly an exaggeration) who were said to control the pearl fishery. In the 19th century, Jewish merchants from Iraq, Persia, and India went to Bahrein, and there was a small Jewish colony. It has dwindled as a consequence of the political situation. In 1968 only some 100 Jews remained in the new capital city of Manama.

At the turn of the 20th century around 30 Jews remained in Bahrein, with services held in private homes on holidays. The Jewish community maintained its cemetery. Most of the Jews were prosperous and had good relations with their Muslim neighbors. Up until the Oslo Agreements (1993) between Israel and the Palestinians, the rulers of Bahrein had no official relations with Israel, but subsequently semi-official relations – commercial, in particular – were established.

BIBLIOGRAPHY: A.T. Wilson, *The Persian Gulf* (1954), 83–91; Fischel, in: *Alexander Marx Jubilee Volume* (Eng., 1950), 203–8; Gustinsky, in: *Edot*, 1 (1946), 238–40.

[Walter Joseph Fischel]

BAḤUR (Heb. בָּחוּר). In the Bible *baḥur* is first used to mean "selected for military fitness" and applied especially to hand-picked warriors (I Sam. 26:2; II Sam. 10:9; Judg. 20:15; I Chron. 19:10; et al.). Later, *ne'arim* was used for "youngsters," and *baḥur* came to mean young men in the prime of their life; cf. "The glory of young men is their strength" (Prov. 20:29). In many cases it is mentioned with *betulah* meaning virgin (Deut. 32:25) and Jeremiah contrasts *baḥur-betulah* with old-man-boy and with man-woman (51:22). Later the term was used for an unmarried man (Ket. 7a). The Talmud uses it also in the sense of an innocent young man who has not "tasted sin" (Pes. 87a), and eventually as a student at a talmudical school (yeshivah). In Yiddish, pronounced *boḥer*, it is also the term for an unmarried young man. In modern Hebrew it means a young man and the feminine *baḥurah*, an unmarried girl.

BAḤURIM (Heb. בַּחֻרִים, בַּחוּרִים), a biblical locality southeast of Jerusalem to which *Paltiel accompanied Saul's daughter Michal when he was forced to return her to her former husband, David (I Sam. 25:44; II Sam. 3:16). On his flight from Absalom, David passed Baḥurim after ascending the western slope of the Mount of Olives. He was cursed there by Shimei, son of Gera, a native of the place (II Sam. 16:5ff.; I Kings 2:8). Jonathan and Ahimaaz, who acted as intermediaries between David and his secret supporters in Jerusalem, hid there in a well when they fell under suspicion (II Sam. 17:18ff.). Its accepted identification is with Ra's al-Tamīm on the eastern slope of the Mount of Olives, where Iron Age pottery has been found.

BIBLIOGRAPHY: Voigt, in: AASOR, 5 (1925), 67ff.; EM, s.v.; Press, Ereẓ, 1 (1951), 65; Elliger, in: PJB, 31 (1935), 49ff., 70ff.

[Michael Avi-Yonah]

BAḤUẒIM (probably from the Hebrew בַּחוּץ, "outside"), name given by the Jews to the apparently Jewish tribes living in the 15th and 16th centuries along the Algerian-Tunisian border in the regions of Kabylia and Constantine in Algeria and of Le Kef in Tunisia, whom the Arabs named Yahūd al-ʿArab (Arab Jews). These seminomadic tribes were agriculturists in Tunisia, and peddlers and jewelers in Algeria. Completely illiterate, the Baḥuẓim observed the Sabbath and swore by *Sīdnā Mūsā* ("our Master Moses"). They had their sons circumcised by the rabbi of the nearest town, who also officiated at their marriages and funeral rites. The theory brought forward by N. *Slouschz that these tribes were originally Berbers who had adopted Judaism was followed by several authors; hence they used the term "Judaized Berbers." However, Ḥ.Z. *Hirschberg asserted that they were really marginal elements of the Jewish community living outside the Jewish centers. Their existence as such during the 16th century and their ignorance of the Berber language seem to confirm the latter's theory.

In 1852 there were about 1,500 Baḥuẓim in Algeria, and in 1912 there were still about a hundred Baḥuẓim tents in Tunisia. After the end of World War I these tribes steadily disappeared. Some of them converted to Islam, while others settled in the surrounding Jewish communities, which willingly accepted them.

BIBLIOGRAPHY: Netter, in: *Univers Israélite*, 7 (1852), 341–6; idem, in: MGWJ, 1 (1852), 377–82; J. Cohen-Ganouna, *Le Judaïsme Tunisien* (1912), 59–60; Bugéja, in: *Bulletin de la Société des Conférences Juives d'Alger*, 3 (1928/29), 101–25; Slouschz, in: *Keneset… le-Zekher Bialik*, 1 (1936), 443–64; Hirschberg, Afrikah, 2 (1965), 29–30.

[Rachel Auerbach]

BAḤYA (Pseudo), name given to the author of the Neoplatonic work *Kitāb Maʿānī al-Nafs* ("On the Essence of the Soul," Ar. version ed. by I. Goldziher, 1902; translated into Heb. by I.D. Broydé, 1896), at one time attributed to *Baḥya ibn Paquda. Nothing is known of the author. It appears that Pseudo-Baḥya wrote this work sometime between the middle of the 11th and the middle of the 12th centuries, since he cites *Avicenna and *Nissim ben Jacob who lived in the first half of the 11th century, but gives no indication that he was influenced by the late 12th-century developments in Islamic and Jewish philosophy.

On the Essence of the Soul presents the structure of the universe as a hierarchy of ten emanations created by God. These emanations are the active intellect, soul of the universe, nature, matter, bodies of the spheres, stars, fire, air, water, and earth. Each emanation is dependent on its predecessor for the divine power necessary to activate it. From the ten emanations are formed the composite substances of the sensual world to which the soul must descend. Criticizing the naturalist position that the soul is an accident of the body, the author maintains that the rational soul is spiritual, a product of the soul of the universe. While passing through each emanation in its descent, the soul acquires "outer garments" of impurities until it finally reaches earth and is embodied in man. Different degrees of impurity depending on the length of the soul's stay in each of the emanations through which it descends provide the differences between souls, which, however, are all similar in essence. Once it inheres in a body, the rational soul unites with the lower vegetative and animal souls, and it loses its original suprasensual knowledge. In order to reverse this process and ascend to the spiritual source from which it derived, the rational soul must purify itself by cultivating virtue and by governing the lower souls.

The author bases the immortality of the soul after death on the fact that all things composed of elements return back to their elements. Hence the soul returns to its origin, which is the spiritual soul of the universe, by means of an ascent which the soul can make once it has attained moral and intellectual perfection. Souls possessing only moral perfection can rise to an earthly paradise where they can acquire the knowledge necessary for their ascent to the suprasensual world. Souls possessing only intellectual perfection or no perfection at all are doomed to their earthly surroundings. As a part of their punishment these souls strive unsuccessfully to ascend to the suprasensual world. There is no direct evidence of the work having had any influence in medieval Jewish philosophy and it is not cited by other critics.

BIBLIOGRAPHY: A. Borrisov, in: *Bulletin of the Academy of Sciences of USSR, Class of Humanities* (Rus., 1929), 785–99; 41 (1897), 241–56; Husik, Philosophy, 106–13; Guttmann, Philosophies, 124–7.

[David Geffen]

BAḤYA BEN ASHER BEN ḤLAVA (13th century), exegete, preacher, and kabbalist. His great commentary on the Pentateuch (Naples, 1492) was written in 1291. According to tradition, he lived in Saragossa and served there as *dayyan* and preacher. He was a disciple of Solomon b. Abraham Adret, whom he called "my master," whenever he quoted from his commentaries. Curiously enough, Baḥya mentions neither his teacher's kabbalistic sayings nor his commentaries on the mystical teachings of Naḥmanides as did Solomon b. Adret's other disciples. There are also kabbalistic matters quoted anonymously by Baḥya which are attributed to Solomon b. Adret by other authors. This might confirm the assumption of J. Reifmann (*Alummah*, 1 (1936), 82) that Baḥya was not Solomon b. Adret's disciple in Kabbalah. It is also possible that he did not have his teacher's permission to quote him in kabbalistic matters. Isaac b. Todros of Barcelona, the commentator on Naḥmanides' esoteric teachings, is quoted by Baḥya only once, without the attribute "my teacher."

His Writings

Following *Botarel and for various reasons, spurious works (as well as writings whose authors are unknown) have been attributed to Baḥya. J. Reifmann's assumption that Baḥya wrote *Ha-Emunah ve-ha-Bittaḥon* (Korets, 1785), *Maʿarekhet ha-Elohut* (Mantua, 1558), and *Maʾamar ha-Sekhel* (Cremona, 1557), does not stand up to critical examination. Béla Bernstein has pointed out that a commentary on Job published in Baḥya's name was really a compilation made from two of his books: *Kad ha-Kemaḥ* (Constantinople, 1515) and *Shulḥan shel Arba* (Mantua, 1514). There was also the opinion that Baḥya's mention of *Ḥoshen Mishpat* was simply a printing error.

The clarity of Baḥya's style and his easy exposition have made his books (which draw their material from a variety of sources) popular with the public, particularly his commentary on the Pentateuch which has been published frequently from 1492 (with explanations and references, 2 vols., 1966–67). Additional testimony to its popularity are the numerous quotations from it in the book **Ẓeʾenah u-Reʾenah*. In his work Baḥya interprets the Pentateuch in four ways: literal, homiletical, rational, and according to the Kabbalah. He uses many different sources, beginning with talmudic and midrashic literature, exegetic and philosophic literature, and ending with kabbalistic literature. The way of *sekhel* ("reason") does not always mean philosophic-rationalistic interpretation. According to Baḥya, all that is outside the divine world, including demonological matters, belongs to "the way of reason," insofar as it is necessary to explain the verses or the *mitzvot* according to the subject. Baḥya is considered of great importance in Kabbalah and is one of the main sources through which the kabbalistic sayings of Naḥmanides' contemporaries have been preserved. As a rule, Baḥya does not divulge his kabbalistic sources. With the exception of the *Sefer ha-*Bahir*, which he considers an authentic Midrash, and Naḥmanides, who is his guide in Kabbalah, he rarely mentions other kabbalists, although he uses extensively the writings of Jacob b. Sheshet *Gerondi, *Asher b. David, Joseph *Gikatilla, and others. He treats the Zohar in a similar manner. Parts of the Zohar were known to him, and he copied from them. However, he mentions it only twice (as "Midrash Rabbi Simeon b. Yoḥai"). *Kad ha-Kemaḥ* contains alphabetically arranged clarifications on the foundations of faith and had a wide circulation. The best edition is that of Breit which contains a commentary (1880–92). A critical edition of *Kad ha-Kemaḥ, Shulḥan shel Arba*, and Baḥya's commentary to *Pirkei Avot* was published by C.B. Chavel (*Kitvei Rabbenu Baḥya*, 1970).

BIBLIOGRAPHY: J. Reifmann, in: *Alummah*, 1 (1936), 69–101; B. Bernstein, *Die Schrifterklaerung des Bachja B. Asher* (1891); Gottlieb, in: *Tarbiz*, 33 (1963/64), 287–313; idem, in: *Bar-Ilan Sefer ha-Shanah*, 2 (1964), 215–50 (Heb.), 27 (Eng. summary); 3 (1965), 139–85; 4–5 (1967), 306–23 (Heb.), 61 (Eng. summary); idem, *Ha-Kabbalah be-Khitvei R. Baḥya ben Asher* (1970).

[Efraim Gottlieb]

BAḤYA (Bahye) BEN JOSEPH IBN PAQUDA (second half of 11th century), moral philosopher. Little is known about the particulars of Baḥya's life beyond the fact that he lived in Muslim Spain, probably at Saragossa. Baḥya was also known as a *paytan* and some of his *piyyutim* are metered. Twenty *piyyutim*, either published or in manuscript, signed with the name Baḥya are assumed to be his. Baḥya's major work, *Kitāb al-Hidāya ilā Farā'iḍ al-Qulūb* (ed. A.S. Yahuda, 1912), was written around 1080. It was translated into Hebrew by Judah ibn *Tibbon in 1161 under the title *Ḥovot ha-Levavot* ("Duties of the Hearts"), and in this version it became popular and had a profound influence on all subsequent Jewish pietistic literature. Joseph *Kimḥi also translated portions of it, but his version gained no circulation and is still in manuscript. Several abridgments were made of the Hebrew translation, and the work was translated into Arabic, Spanish, Portuguese, Italian, and Yiddish. In more recent times it has been translated into English (*Duties of the Heart*, text and translation by M. Hyamson, 1962), German (*Choboth ha-L'baboth. Lehrbuch der Herzenspflichten*, tr. by M. Stern, 1856), and French *Introduction aux devoirs des coeurs*, tr. by A. Chouraqui, 1950). In his *Ḥovot ha-Levavot* Baḥya drew a great deal upon non-Jewish sources, borrowing from Muslim mysticism, Arabic Neoplatonism, and perhaps also from the *Hermetic writings. From Muslim authors he borrowed the basic structure of the book as well as definitions, aphorisms, and examples to illustrate his doctrines. In most cases his immediate sources cannot be identified, and the theory that he was influenced by *Al-Ghazali does not seem to be well-founded.

Despite the fact that Baḥya borrowed so liberally from non-Jewish sources, *Ḥovot ha-Levavot* remains an essentially Jewish book. In the introduction to this work Baḥya divides the obligations incumbent upon the religious man into duties of the members of the body (*ḥovot ha-evarim*), those obligations which involve overt actions; and duties of the hearts (*ḥovot ha-levavot*), those obligations which involve not man's actions, but his inner life. The first division includes the various ritual and ethical observances commanded by the Torah, e.g., the observance of the Sabbath, prayer, and the giving of charity, while the second consists of beliefs, e.g., the belief in the existence and unity of God, and attitudes or spiritual traits, e.g., trust in God, love and fear of Him, and repentance. The prohibitions against bearing a grudge and taking revenge are also examples of duties of the hearts. Baḥya explains that he wrote this work because the duties of man's inner life had been sorely neglected by his predecessors and contemporaries whose writings had concentrated on religious observances, that is, the duties of the members of the body. To remedy this deficiency Baḥya wrote his work, which may be considered a kind of counterpart to the halakhic compendia of his predecessors and contemporaries. Just as their halakhic compendia contained directions for the actions of the religious man, so Baḥya's work contained directions for his inner life. *Ḥovot ha-Levavot* is modeled after the works of Muslim mysticism, which attempt to lead the reader through various ascending stages of man's inner life, toward spiritual perfection and finally union (or at least communion) with God. In similar fashion *Ḥovot ha-Levavot* is divided into ten "gates" (chapters), each of which is devoted to a particular duty of the heart, which the Jew must observe if he is to attain spiritual perfection. The ten chapters deal with the affirmation of the unity of God (*yiḥud*), the nature of the world disclosing the workings of God (*beḥinat ha-olam*), divine worship (*avodat ha-Elohim*), trust in God (*bittaḥon*), sincerity of purpose (*yiḥud ha-ma'aseh*), humility (*keni'ah*), repentance (*teshuvah*), self-examination (*ḥeshbon ha-nefesh*), asceticism (*perishut*), and the love of God (*ahavat ha-Shem*).

In accordance with Platonic teachings (probably influenced partially by the Epistles of the Sincere Brethren), he maintains that man's soul, which is celestial in origin, is placed, by divine decree, within the body, where it runs the risk of forgetting its nature and mission. The human soul receives aid from the intellect and the revealed Law in achieving its goal. To elucidate this point Baḥya makes use of the Muʿtazilite (see *Kalām) distinction between rational and traditional commandments. He holds that the duties of the members of the body may be divided into rational commandments and traditional (religious) commandments, while the duties of the hearts are all rooted in the intellect. With the aid of reason and the revealed Law the soul can triumph over its enemy, the evil inclination (*yeẓer*), which attacks it incessantly in an effort to beguile it into erroneous beliefs and to enslave it to bodily appetites. Since the basis of religion is the belief in the existence of God, the first chapter of the work is devoted to a philosophical and theological explication of the existence and unity of God and a discussion of His attributes. In the second chapter Baḥya examines the order in the universe and the extraordinary structure of man, the microcosm. Such an examination leads to a knowledge of God, and to a sense of gratitude towards Him as creator. In the third chapter he discusses divine worship which is the expression of man's gratitude to God. To fulfill his duties to God without faltering and to achieve his true goal, man must diligently practice a number of virtues. One of these is trust in God, which is based on the belief that

God is good, and that he has a knowledge of what is best for man, and the power to protect him. To trust in God does not mean that one should neglect one's work, leaving everything to Him, but rather that one should conscientiously attempt to carry out one's duties, trusting that God will remove any obstacles which lie in the way of their fulfillment. While man has the freedom to will and choose, the realization of his actions is dependent on God's will. Further, a sound spiritual life requires sincerity, a perfect correspondence between man's conscience and behavior. Man's intentions must coincide with his actions in aiming toward the service of God. Humility, repentance, and self-examination are also essential. Another virtue is asceticism or temperance. Baḥya considers total asceticism, involving the breaking of all social ties, an ideal rarely attained in the biblical past and hardly to be recommended in the present. Actually, he recommends the pursuit of the middle way prescribed by the revealed Law, defining the genuine ascetic as one who directs all his actions to the service of God, while at the same time fulfilling his functions within society. The observance of these virtues leads to the highest stage of the spiritual life, the love of God. True love of God is the ardor of the soul for union with the Divine Light, a concept of a distinctly mystic character. Baḥya does not, however, develop this concept in all its implications. The love of God, in his view, is a synthesis of the degrees of perfection described above, but does not go beyond them. The lover of God, such as described by him, keeps at a distance from his loved one. Despite Baḥya's dependence upon Muslim mysticism, which is here more pronounced than elsewhere in the work, his teaching remains in the line of Jewish tradition, and he cannot be called a mystic in the strict sense of the term. It has been definitely established that the Judeo-Arabic Neo-platonic tract, *Kitāb Maʿanī al Nafs* (ed. by I. Goldziher, 1907; translated into Hebrew by I. Broydé as *Sefer Torat ha-Nefesh*, 1896) at one time attributed to Baḥya, was not written by him (see *Baḥya (Pseudo)).

BIBLIOGRAPHY: Husik, Philosophy, 80–105; Guttmann, Philosophies, 104–10; Kokowzoff, in: *Sefer Zikkaron… S. Poznański* (1927), 13–21; G. Vajda, *La théologie ascétique de Baḥya ibn Paquda* (1947); idem, in: REJ, 102 (1937), 93–104; M. Sister, in: *Bericht der Lehranstalt fuer die Wissenschaft des Judentums*, 50 (1936), 33–75; idem, in: MGWJ, 81 (1937), 86–93; D. Kaufmann, *Meḥkarim be-Sifrut Yemei ha-Beinayim* (1962), 11–77; Kaufmann, Schriften, 2 (1910), 1–98; D.H. Baneth, in: *Sefer Magnes* (1938), 23–30; Ramos Gil, in: *Archivo de Filologia Aragonesa*, 3 (1950), 129–80; idem, in: *Sefarad*, 11 (1951), 305–38; idem, in: *ME'AH*, 1 (1952), 85–148; J.H. Schirmann, *Shirim Ḥadashim min ha-Genizah* (1966), 203–8; Davidson, Oẓar, 4 (1933), 370.

[Georges Vajda]

BAIA-MARE (Hg. **Nagybánya**), mining and industrial town in Transylvania, Romania, within Hungary until 1918 and between 1940 and 1944. The prohibition against Jewish settlement in Hungarian mining towns (issued in 1693) was abolished in 1848. The oldest document indicating a Jewish presence dates from the year 1664 and mentions a Jew trading in the locally mined metal. In a document dated 1725 the absence of the Jews is noted. In 1850 Jewish artisans, businessmen, and farmers began to settle in Baia-Mare. Subsequently Jews did much to develop local commerce and industry. A community was organized in 1860, and a burial society founded in 1862. The first synagogue was opened in 1887. During the *Tisza-Eszlar blood libel case in 1882, a mob attacked the synagogue and pillaged it. The community always remained Orthodox, and Satmar Hasidism (see *Teitelbaum) had a strong following. There was also a flourishing Zionist movement. In the period between the two world wars there was increasing tension between the ḥasidic community and the Zionists. The Jewish population numbered 701 in 1890 (out of a total of 9,838); 1,402 in 1910 (out of 12,877); 2,030 in 1930 (out of 13,904); and 3,623 in 1941 (out of 21,404).

[Yehouda Marton / Paul Schveiger (2nd ed.)]

Holocaust Period

Between the two world wars the Jewish population suffered from attacks by the Romanian Iron Guard. Between 1941 and 1944, the town served as the headquarters of Labor Service Battalion No. x, the recruitment center for many of the Jewish males of military age in Northern Transylvania. The Battalion was under the command of Lt. Col. Imre Reviczky (1896–1957), a decent Hungarian officer who saved a large number of Jews after the German occupation in 1944 by recruiting them into labor service and thus rescuing them from deportation. In 1962 he was posthumously recognized by Yad Vashem as a Righteous Among the Nations.

The roundup of the Jews of Baia Mare began on May 3, 1944, together with those from Northern Transylvania. The ghetto for the Jews of Baia-Mare was established in the vacant lots of the Koenig Glass Factory; at its peak, it held close to 4,000 victims. The approximately 2,000 Jews from the communities in the District of Baia-Mare, including Alsófernezely, Hagymáslápos, Kapnikbánya, Láposbánya, Misztófalu, Nagysikárló, Tomány, and Zazár, were concentrated in a stable and barn in Valea Burcutului (Hung. Borpatak), which could accommodate only 200 people; the others had to be quartered outdoors. The 5,917 Jews concentrated in these two ghettos were deported to Auschwitz in two transports on May 31 and June 5, 1944, respectively.

[Randolph Braham (2nd ed.)]

The Jewish population in Baia-Mare numbered 950 in 1947. Subsequent emigration to Israel, Western Europe, and the United States reduced the community considerably. In 1969 it numbered 120 families. In 2004 a very small number of Jews remained in the town.

BIBLIOGRAPHY: *Magyar Zsidé Lexikon* (1929), 626. **ADD. BIBLIOGRAPHY:** R.L. Braham, *Politics of Genocide: The Holocaust in Hungary* (1994^2); PK Romanyah, 86–89.

BAIERSDORF, village in Bavaria, Germany, formerly the summer residence of the margraves of Kulmbach-Bayreuth. Tombstones in the Jewish cemetery indicate the presence of Jews in Baiersdorf at the end of the 14th century, although the first document in which they are mentioned dates from 1473. In 1632 they numbered 12 families. The synagogue, established before 1530, was rebuilt in 1651. After persecutions in 1680, the margrave issued an order in 1695 granting the Jews freedom of trade. In 1699 a "Jewish pharmacy" was opened in Baiersdorf. The community increased to 40 families (300 persons) in 1713 and 83 families in 1771. Baiersdorf was the seat of a district rabbinate in the 18th and 19th centuries. The Bavarian restrictions limiting Jewish households (*Matrikel-Gesetz*) led many of the younger sons to emigrate to England and America (for instance, the *Seligman family), and by about 1900 only 12 Jewish families remained. The rabbinate was dissolved in 1894. The synagogue built in 1711 was destroyed under the Nazi regime in November 1938; only three Jews remained in Baiersdorf at the time.

BIBLIOGRAPHY: ZGJD, 2 (1888), 95–96; A. Eckstein, *Geschichte der Juden im Markgrafentum Bayreuth* (1907); *Baiersdorf, Entwicklungsgeschichte einer fraenkischen Kleinstadt* (1953), 98–105, 143, 179. **ADD. BIBLIOGRAPHY:** *Aus der juedischen Geschichte Baiersdorfs* (1992).

[Ze'ev Wilhem Falk]

BAIERSDORF, SAMSON SOLOMON (d. 1712), son of Judah Selke, court agent of the margrave of Brandenburg-Bayreuth. Baiersdorf entered the margrave's service in 1670. He influenced him to issue a decree in 1695 granting the Jews in the margravate freedom of trade. In 1698 he bought real estate from the margrave. Although later involved in a court intrigue, Baiersdorf managed to retain his position. He donated the money for the synagogue of *Bayreuth, consecrated in 1711. Baiersdorf's daughter married Moses, the son of *Glueckel of Hameln, who became rabbi of *Baiersdorf in 1700. His sons, Veit and Solomon, known by the family name of Samson, and his son-in-law and brother also became court agents; the latter was permitted to retain an armed guard.

BIBLIOGRAPHY: H. Schnee, *Die Hoffinanz und der moderne Staat*, 3 (1955), 222–3; 4 (1963), 33; S. Stern, *The Court Jew* (1950), 100, 198, 251; Glueckel von Hameln, *Memoirs* (1932), 204–8, 220f., 232–5.

BAIGNEUX-LES-JUIFS, village northwest of *Dijon. Jews settled in the commune at its establishment in the middle of the 13th century, giving the locality its name. They were expelled with the other Jews in the duchy of Burgundy in 1306. The inventory made of their debts and property indicates that the community was fairly numerous and prosperous. Green and red wax, parchment, ink, and paint were taken from a Jew referred to as Rebi or Rabi – most probably the scribe of the community. The medieval synagogue was located on the present Rue Vergier-au-Duc.

BIBLIOGRAPHY: J. Garnier and E. Champeux, *Chartes de Communes... Bourgogne* (1898), 161f.; Gauthier, in: *Mémoires de la société d'émulation du Jura*, 3 (1914), 78, 225–32.

[Bernhard Blumenkranz]

°**BAIL, CHARLES-JOSEPH** (1777–1827), French soldier, publicist, and civil servant. Bail was in charge of the administration of the Bonapartist kingdom of *Westphalia, and thus had close contacts with the heads of the Jewish *Consistoire there. After the fall of Napoleon, he continued to defend the basic principles of the revolution. In this spirit he published a pamphlet on "The Jews in the 19th Century or Considerations of their Civil and Political Status in Europe" (*Les Juifs au XIXe siècle...* Paris, 1816). He here defended the basic principles of equality, ascribing the separatist characteristics of the Jews to their depressed civil and political status. The same year, following criticism from the Catholic Romantic side, Bail published a second edition in which he imputed some of the separatist characteristics of the Jews to their religion and form of society, although in the main still defending his original thesis. Bail took part in a competition held by the Académie des Inscriptions et Belles-Lettres on the history of the Jews in Europe in the Middle Ages. Although unsuccessful, Bail subsequently published his work "The Situation of the Jews in France, Spain and Italy" (*Etat des Juifs en France...* Paris, 1823).

BIBLIOGRAPHY: S. de Sacy, *Lettre à MXXX, relativement à l'ouvrage intitulé: Des Juifs au 19e siècle* (Paris, 1817); A.T. d'Esquiron de St. Agnan, *Considérations sur l'existence civile et politique des Israélites – suivies de quelques idées sur l'ouvrage de M. Bail... et trois lettres de M. de Cologna, grand rabbin du consistoire Israélite de Paris* (n.d.); *Dictionnaire de Bibliographie Française*, 4 (1948), s.v.; *Nouvelle Biographie Universelle*, 4 (1853), s.v.

[Baruch Mevorah]

BAILYN, BERNARD (1922–), U.S. historian. Born in Hartford, Connecticut, Bailyn received a B.A. from Williams College in 1945 and his M.A. (1947) and Ph.D. (1953) degrees from Harvard. Bailyn then joined the faculty of Harvard in 1953 and became professor of history in 1961. He was editor-in-chief of the John Harvard Library of American Cultural History from 1962 until 1970. He also served as coeditor of the journal *Perspectives in American History* (1967–77, 1984–86) and director of the Charles Warren Center for Studies in American History (1983–94).

Bailyn became Winthrop Professor of History in 1966, a position he held until 1981, when he became the first Adams University Professor. He was also named James Duncan Phillips Professor of Early American History, emeritus, at Harvard. He served as a senior fellow in the Society of Fellows and as director of the International Seminar on the History of the Atlantic World. In 1993 he received the Thomas Jefferson Medal and in 1994 the Henry Allen Moe Prize of the American Philosophical Society. In 1998 he was appointed the Jefferson Lecturer by the National Endowment for the Humanities and he delivered the first Millennium Lecture at the White House. In 2000 he was awarded the Bruce Catton Prize of the Society of American Historians for lifetime achievement in the writing of history, and in 2001 he received the Centennial Medal of the Harvard Graduate School of Arts and Sciences. He also received two Pulitzer Prizes in history (1968 and 1987).

Among his many publications, Bailyn wrote *The New England Merchants in the Seventeenth Century* (1955); *Massachusetts Shipping, 1697–1714* (with Lotte Bailyn, 1959); *Education in the Forming of American Society* (1960); *The Ideological Origins of the American Revolution* (1967), for which he received the Pulitzer and Bancroft prizes in 1968; *The Origins of American Politics* (1968); *The Ordeal of Thomas Hutchinson* (1974), awarded the National Book Award in History in 1975; *The Peopling of British North America: An Introduction* (1986); *Voyagers to the West* (1986), which won the Pulitzer Prize in history and other awards; *Faces of Revolution* (1990); *On the Teaching and Writing of History* (1994); and *To Begin the World Anew: The Genius and Ambiguities of the American Founders* (2003).

Specializing in American colonial and revolutionary history, Bailyn is known for meticulous research and for interpretations that sometimes challenge conventional wisdom, especially with regard to the causes and effects of the American Revolution. Bailyn taught his students that history is primarily about change and movement, and that however hard one has to work to understand what the past was like, the deeper challenge is to explain how one part of the past gave way to another. And because change can only be described through narrative, historians must be sensitive to all the matters of exposition that make narrative effective, which always involves understanding that expository decisions are as essential to historians as their mastery of sources and all the other technical skills on which historical scholarship depends.

[Ruth Beloff (2nd ed.)]

BAITLER, ZOMA (1908–1994), Uruguayan painter. Born and educated in Lithuania. Baitler, an impressionist, went to Uruguay in 1927 and exhibited for the first time at the "Free Artists Salon" in 1931. He was one of the founders of the atelier ETAP. Exhibitions of his work were held in North and South America as well as in Israel. In 1936 he issued the Art Magazine *Perseo* and wrote essays on art and on art criticism. In 1963 he was appointed cultural assistant to the Uruguayan Embassy in Israel for three years. His works are in the National and Municipal Museums of Uruguay and Israel.

BAITOS (Boethus) BEN ZONIN (beginning of second century), respected and wealthy resident of Lydda, whose home was a meeting place for scholars. It is related that the rabbis, headed by Rabban *Gamaliel of Jabneh, "reclined in the home of Baitos b. Zonin in Lydda and discussed Passover *halakhot* the whole of that night [of the *Passover Seder] until cockcrow" (Tosef., Pes. 10:12). He also discussed halakhic problems with the rabbis (TJ, Pes. 2:end of 4, 29c; Pes. 37a). Baitos conducted his life in accordance with the teachings of the rabbis, particularly *Eleazar b. Azariah (Meg. 27b; BM 63a; BB 13b), and his conduct is cited in tannaitic sources as evidence for the *halakhah* in both ritual and monetary matters (BM 5:3; Av. Zar. 5:2).

BIBLIOGRAPHY: Hyman, Toledot, 270.

[Zvi Kaplan]

BAIZERMAN, SAUL (1899–1957), U.S. sculptor. Baizerman was born in Vitebsk, the same Russian town in which Marc *Chagall was raised. At 13 he decided to become a sculptor. He received some artistic training in Russia; the first of his teachers there told him he was not talented enough to succeed as an artist. After escaping from an Odessa prison where he had been incarcerated for a year and a half for revolutionary activities, Baizerman arrived in America in 1910 at the age of 22. In 1911 he began classes at the National Academy of Design, and then continued his artistic training at the Beaux-Arts Institute of Design in New York for four years. He also studied at the Educational Alliance, where he became acquainted with Moses *Soyer and Chaim *Gross.

In the early 1920s Baizerman began a series of carved plaster figures, later cast in bronze, to inhabit a model of New York City. Until his death he worked on this project, titled *The City and the People.* Approximately 56 pieces show urban life on a small scale; some of the figures are only three inches high. The actual city is a nearly abstract, geometric form in which the laborers of the metropolis might toil. Even so, Baizerman exhibited the small sculptures as independent entities rather than creating a narrative for figures such as *Man with Shovel* (1921–23) and *Rabbi* (1922).

While *The City and the People* is Baizerman's most ambitious project, he is better known for the sculptural technique he adopted in 1926. He hammered copper sheets into representational forms, a physically exhausting procedure that displays the artist's labor as much as the subject represented. This approach had its roots in Baizerman's Russian childhood; his father, a harness maker, hammered leather into harnesses. Being concave as well as convex, Baizerman's sculptures are meant to be seen in the round. Although the sculptures appear solid and heavy, the hammered metal is thin. A January 1931 fire in his New York studio destroyed much of his sculpture, but with renewed energy he created a new body of work that was shown in exhibitions in the 1930s and 1940s, including one-man shows in 1933, 1938, and 1948. His work occasionally took on biblical themes, such as *Eve* (1949), *Crucifixion* (c. 1947–50), and *Creation* (1950–57), which stands eight feet high. He also did a portrait head of Albert Einstein (1940–49).

BIBLIOGRAPHY: S. Baizerman, *Saul Baizerman's Lifetime Project* (1998); M. Dabakis and D. Finn, *Vision of Harmony: The Sculpture of Saul Baizerman* (1989)

[Samantha Baskind (2nd ed.)]

BAJA, the seat of Bács (earlier Bács-Bodrog) county situated on the Danube in southern Hungary. Jews settled there in 1725. In 1753 there were ten and in 1773 16 families, mainly merchants in wool, leather, and tobacco. In 1773 the Jews, mostly immigrants from Moravia, received permission to build a synagogue and appoint a rabbi. In March 1840 the communal buildings, including the synagogue, were devastated in a fire that swept through the town. A new synagogue was built in 1842. The community opened a secondary school in 1878, complementing the primary school that had been in existence since 1771. In addition to several communal and charity organizations, the community also built a hospital in 1882. In 1885, the smaller Jewish communities of the neighboring villages, including those of Baracska, Bátamonostor, Borsód, Csátalja, Csávoly, Dantova, Felsöszentiván, Gara, and Vaskut, affiliated themselves to Baja organizationally. Baja's Jewish population ranged from 516 in 1840 (3.7% of the total) to 1,648 (5.9%) in 1930, with a maximum of 2,542 (13.2%) in 1880. Among the rabbis who served the Jewish community of Baja were József Márkus, who built the first synagogue in 1768; Rabbi Meir *Ash (Eisenstadt), a student of Ḥatam Sofer, who served from 1805 to 1815; and Rabbi Eliakim Schwerin Goetz Kohn, who served from 1815 to 1845.The latter also founded and headed a yeshivah. In 1941, Baja had a Jewish population of 1,378, representing 4.3% of the total of 32,369. In addition it had 149 (0.5%) converts who were identified as Jews under the racial laws then in effect. During the period of the Austro-Hungarian Empire, two Jews – Mór Hauser and Gyula Erdélyi – had served as the city's mayor. Hauser was also elected to the lower house of the Hungarian parliament.

After the German occupation of Hungary on March 19, 1944, the largely Neolog community numbered approximately 1,200 members. They were led by Zsigmond Weidinger and Rabbi József Klein. On April 14, the authorities arrested 150 prominent Jews, who were first taken to the Topolya internment camp and then deported to Grossrosen – a month before the start of the mass deportations from Hungary. Among the victims were Rabbi Klein, Lipót Kertész, the communal notary, and cantor Mór Rubovics. From Grossrosen, Rabbi Klein was eventually taken to Stettin (Szczecin), where he was beaten to death by German guards.

Baja served as a major concentration point for Jews rounded up in several neighboring districts, including those of Apatin, Baja, Hódság, Palánka, and Zombor. The roundup of the Jews was directed by Police Chief Béla Jeles. The Jews, including those brought in from the neighboring ghettos, were concentrated in three different locations, where they lived under miserable conditions until their deportation. Two of these ghettos were set up for the Jews of Újvidék (Novi Sad). The ghetto of Baja was led by a seven-member Jewish Council that included Ferencz Stein and László Biró. The approximately 8,200 Jews concentrated in Baja were deported to Auschwitz in two transports that left the town on May 28 and June 18, respectively. Prior to their deportation the Jews were subjected to still another round of expropriations under brutal conditions.

During the immediate post-liberation period, Baja had approximately 400 Jewish inhabitants, including those who moved in from the neighboring villages. The survivors reestablished the Neolog community in 1947 under the leadership of President Sándor Rostás, Rabbi József Rosenfeld, and Rabbi Tibor Klein. After 1948, the membership gradually declined. By 1953 only 180 identified themselves as Jews. This number had shrunk to 70 by 1964. By the turn of the century only a handful were still left in the city. In 1985 the synagogue was transformed into a public library.

BIBLIOGRAPHY: G. Dudás, *Bács-Bodrog vármegye monographiája*, 2 (1896), 254–15, 309–10; M. Pollák, *A bajai zsidó hitközség iskoláinak története*, (1896); S. Kohn, *Kohn Schwerin Götz* (Hung. 1899). **ADD. BIBLIOGRAPHY:** Braham, Politics; PK Hungaria, 168–70.

[Laszlo Harsanyi / Randolph Braham (2nd ed.)]

BAK (also **Pak**), a family of Jewish printers of Ashkenazi origin, who lived first in Venice and later in Prague. According to Zunz, the name represents the initials of *Benei Kedoshim* (Children of the Martyrs).

GERSON, the progenitor of the family, lived in Italy in the early 16th century, where his son JACOB followed the printing trade. Jacob printed the *Midrash Tanḥuma* in Verona (1595) and in Venice *Tanna de-Vei Eliyahu* (1598), and *Tiferet Yisrael* by *Judah Loew (the Maharal) of Prague in 1599. Apparently his connections with the latter brought him to Prague. From 1605 until his death in 1618 he printed numerous Hebrew and Judeo-German books. He was succeeded by his sons JOSEPH and JUDAH, who in 1623 set up a new printing house called "Jacob Bak's Sons." Their output was considerable, despite the temporary slowing down during the Thirty Years' War and the persecutions of 1648/49 and 1656. In about 1660 Joseph left the printing business, and Judah carried on alone. A libel action brought against the press led to its closing down in 1669. Judah died in 1671, and two years later his sons, JACOB (1630–1688) and JOSEPH (d. 1696), were authorized to resume printing books, as "Judah Bak's sons," but a special permit was required for each book. In 1680 Joseph completed a *maḥzor* at nearby Weckelsdorf – the only Hebrew work ever printed there. Between 1680 and 1683 Joseph apparently continued alone in Prague, while Jacob worked under the name "Judah Bak's Sons" (1682–88). Joseph was joined by Jacob's son MOSES (d. 1712), in 1686. From 1697 Moses ran the firm with his cousin, Joseph's son (later "The Bak Press"). Moses' son JUDAH (d. 1767/68), who was a compositor, managed the press from 1735 to 1756. In 1757 Judah's brother YOM TOV LIPMANN joined as his partner, and the firm became "Moses Bak's Sons." The firm later became "The Bak and Katz Press" (1784–89), and afterwards passed into other hands entirely. The Bak family members were pioneers in the field of Jewish printing, while also making an important contribution to the Jewish community of the time. Israel *Bak, the printer of Safed and Jerusalem, does not seem to have any connection with this Bak family.

BIBLIOGRAPHY: Zunz, Gesch, 264–6, 282–303; S. Hock, *Mishpeḥot K.K. Prag* (1892), 46–48; H.D. Friedberg, *Toledot ha-Defus ha-Ivri be-Arim... she-be-Eiropah ha-Tikhonah* (1937), 19–26; A. Tauber, *Meḥkarim Bibliografiyyim* (1932), 9–14; A. Yaari, *Ha-Defus ha-Ivri be-Arẓot ha-Mizraḥ* (1937), 14–15.

[Abraham Meir Habermann]

BAK, printers and pioneers in Ereẓ Israel. ISRAEL BAK (1797–1874) was born in Berdichev, Ukraine, into a family of printers. Later he owned a Jewish press in Berdichev, printing about 30 books between 1815 and 1821 when the press closed down. In 1831, after various unsuccessful efforts to reopen the works, he immigrated to Palestine and settled in Safed. There he renewed the tradition of printing Hebrew works, which had come to an end in the last third of the 17th century. During the peasant revolt against Muhammad Ali in 1834 his printing press was destroyed and he was wounded. Later he reopened his press, and also began to work the land on Mount Yarmak (Meron), overlooking Safed. His was the first Jewish farm in Ereẓ Israel in modern times. After the Safed earthquake in 1837 and the Druze revolt in 1838, during which his farm and printing press were destroyed, he moved to Jerusalem. In 1841 he established the first – and for 22 years, the only – Jewish printing press in Jerusalem. One hundred and thirty books were printed on it, making it an important cultural factor in Jerusalem. Bak also published and edited the second Hebrew newspaper in Ereẓ Israel, *Ḥavaẓẓelet* (1863). After a short time its publication stopped and was renewed only in 1870 by his son-in-law I.D. *Frumkin and others. Israel Bak was a leader of the ḥasidic community; as a result of his efforts and those of his son Nisan, a central synagogue for the Ḥasidim, called Tiferet Israel (after R. Israel of Ruzhin), came into being. In Jerusalem it was also known as "Nisan Bak's synagogue." It was destroyed in 1948 during the War of Independence.

NISAN (1815–1889), only son of Israel, was born in Berdichev and immigrated to Palestine with his father in 1831. Nisan managed the printing press after the death of his father until 1883, when he sold the business; thereafter he devoted himself exclusively to communal affairs in Jerusalem. He was an active worker in the ḥasidic community and the representative of the Ruzhin-Sadagura dynasty in Jerusalem. Through his contacts with the Turkish government he did much to modify decrees aimed against the *yishuv*. He initiated and executed several building projects in Jerusalem, such as the Kiryah Ne'emanah quarter, first named Oholei Moshe vi-Yhudit, but better known as Battei Nisan Bak. He and his brother-in-law I.D. Frumkin were pioneers of the Haskalah in Jerusalem; they also opposed the methods of **ḥalukkah* distribution. In 1884 Nisan and others founded the Ezrat Niddaḥim Society, which fought the missions and established the Yemenite quarter in Jerusalem.

BIBLIOGRAPHY: G. Kressel (ed.), *Mivḥar Kitvei I.D. Frumkin* (1954), index; A. Yaari, *Ha-Defus ha-Ivri be-Arẓot ha-Mizraḥ* (1937), 20–22 (list of books printed by Israel Bak in Safed); S. Halevi, *Ha-Sefarim ha-Ivriyyim she-Nidpesu be-Yrushalayim* (1963), index; G. Kressel, *Toledot ha-Ittonut ha-Ivrit be-Ereẓ Yisrael* (1964), index; Tidhar, 1 (1947), 64f.; M. Benayahu, in: *Aresheth*, 4 (1966), 271–95.

[Getzel Kressel]

BAK, SAMUEL (1933–), painter. Bak was born in Vilna. A few years later the area was incorporated into the independent republic of Lithuania. He was eight when the Germans occupied the city. Bak began painting while still a child and, prompted by the well-known Yiddish poet Abraham Sutzkever, held his first exhibition (in the Vilna ghetto) in 1942 at the age of nine. From the ghetto the family was sent to a labor camp on the outskirts of the city. Bak's father managed to save his son by dropping him in a sack out of a ground floor window of the warehouse where he was working; he was met by a maid and brought to the house where his mother was hiding. His father was shot by the Germans in July 1944, a few days before Soviet troops liberated the city. His four grandparents had earlier been executed at the killing site outside Vilna called Ponary.

After the war, the young Bak continued painting at the Displaced Persons camp in Landsberg, Germany (1945–48), where he also studied painting in Munich. In 1948, he and his mother immigrated to Israel, where he studied for a year at the Bezalel Art School in Jerusalem. After fulfilling his military service, he spent three years (1956–59) at the École des Beaux-Arts in Paris. He then moved to Rome (1959–66), returned to Israel (1966–74), and lived for a time in New York City (1974–77). There followed further years in Israel and Paris, then a long stay in Switzerland (1984–93). From 1993 Bak lived and worked outside Boston, in Weston, Massachusetts. In 2001 he published a detailed autobiography, *Painted in Words: A Memoir* (Indiana University Press).

Bak's paintings have been exhibited in museums and galleries and hang in public collections in England, the United States, Israel, Germany, and Switzerland. Many later works may be viewed at the Pucker Gallery (171 Newbury Street) in Boston. The editors of *Between Worlds: The Paintings and Drawings of Samuel Bak from 1946 to 2001* (Pucker Art Publications, 2002), a survey of more than a half-century of his work, summarize the sources of his vision as follows:

> Bak's life has inevitably influenced his choice of images and themes. The particulars of Vilna and the Holocaust, of surviving and being a wandering Jew, are part of his individual biography; but all are also aspects of our shared human condition. Bak has always sought to find the universal in the specific. His ongoing dialogues with the long-dead members of his family, with his early teachers, with the great masters of all epochs, with contemporary culture, and with the Bible and the diverse host of Jewish traditions – all come from his desire to represent the universality of loss and the endurance of man's hope for a *tikkun*.

The fragile balance between ruin and repair remained a central theme of his efforts to create for modern consciousness challenging visual images of our contemporary world.

BIBLIOGRAPHY: A. Kaufman and P.T. Nagano, *Samuel Bak: Paintings of the Last Decade* (1974); R. Kallenbach, *Samuel Bak: Monuments to Our Dreams* (1977); S. Bak and P.T. Nagano, *Samuel Bak: The Past Continues* (1988); J.L. Kornuz, *Chess as Metaphor in the Art of Samuel Bak* (1991); S. Bak, *Ewiges Licht (Landsberg: A Memoir 1944–1948)* (1996); L.L. Langer, *Landscapes of Jewish Experience*

(1997); *Samuel Bak Retrospektive 1946–1997*, Panorama Museum: Bad Frankenhausen (1998); L.L. Langer, *The Game Continues: Chess in the Art of Samuel Bak.* (2000); idem, *In a Different Light: The Book of Genesis in the Art of Samuel Bak* (2001); R. Cooper, *The Art of Speaking about the Unspeakable* (TV documentary about Samuel Bak; Pucker Art Publications, 2001); S, Bak, *Painted in Words: A Memoir* (2002); I. Tayler (ed.), *Samuel Bak: Between Worlds – Paintings and Drawings 1946 – 2001* (2002); C. Singer, *Samuel Bak: Painter of Questions* (TV documentary, Toronto, Canada) (2003); L.L. Langer, *New Perceptions of Old Appearances in the Art of Samuel Bak* (2005).

[Lawrence L. Langer (2nd ed.)]

BAKAN, DAVID (1921–2004), U.S. psychologist. Born in New York, Bakan held several university positions from 1961, teaching at the University of Chicago, Ohio State, Harvard, and York University in Toronto, Canada. Bakan wrote on a wide range of topics including psychoanalysis, religion, philosophy, and research methodology, as well as child abuse. In his book *Sigmund Freud and the Jewish Mystical Tradition* (1958) he attempted to trace the roots of early psychoanalytic concepts and methods in the Kabbalah, the Zohar, and talmudic interpretations. His *Duality of Human Existence: An Essay on Psychology and Religion* (1966) made important contributions to the history of psychology, especially in relation to the problem of introspection, research methodology, and the psychology of religion.

Other books by Bakan include *On Method: Toward a Reconstruction of Psychological Investigation* (1967); *Disease, Pain, and Sacrifice: Toward a Psychology of Suffering* (1968); *Slaughter of the Innocents: A Study of the Battered Child Phenomenon* (1971); *And They Took Themselves Wives: The Emergence of Patriarchy in Western Civilization* (1979); and *Maimonides on Prophecy* (1991).

Professor emeritus in York University's Department of Psychology, Bakan retired from teaching in 1991.

[Ruth Beloff (2nd ed.)]

BAKER, EDWARD MAX (1875–1957), U.S. investment broker and communal leader. Baker was born in Erie, Pennsylvania. His maternal grandfather was Rabbi David *Einhorn, and his uncles were Rabbis Emil G. *Hirsch and Kaufmann *Kohler, leaders of Reform Judaism. In 1901 Baker entered the brokerage business in Cleveland. He became resident manager of a national brokerage firm in 1911 and served as president of the Cleveland Stock Exchange for 14 years. Baker was a founder of the Cleveland Federation of Jewish Charities (1903), serving as its president (1923–27) and as a trustee for more than five decades. He was also a member of the national board of the American Jewish Committee and of other major Jewish institutions. Equally active in Cleveland civic affairs, Baker served as chairman of the Republican County Committee (1907–08). He was a founder of the Cleveland Legal Aid Society; a founder and president of the Cleveland City Club, a community forum; and member of the first Board of Trustees of the Associated Charities of Cleveland.

[Judah Rubinstein]

BAKHCHISARAI, town in Crimea, Ukraine. From the 16th to the 18th centuries it was the capital of the khans of Crimea. A settlement of Rabbanite Jews (Krimchaks) as well as of *Karaites evidently existed in Bakhchisarai in the second half of the 18th century. In the 1870s the Karaites abandoned *Chufut-Kale, approximately 1¼ mi. (about 2 km.) to the east, and moved to Bakhchisarai. A Jewish traveler in the 1870s found about 20 families of Rabbanite Jews and some 70 Karaite families there: in 1897 there were 210 Rabbanites and 967 Karaites. The Hebrew poet Saul *Tchernichowsky wrote several poems about Bakhchisarai. During the Soviet period the number of Jews remained stable, numbering 228 souls in 1939. Bakhchisarai was occupied by the Germans on November 2, 1941, and they soon murdered 90 Jews. In the first half of July 1943 they murdered over 1,000 from the town and the surrounding area. The Karaites were not considered Jewish by the Germans and were therefore not harmed by them.

BIBLIOGRAPHY: E. Deinard, *Massa ba-Ḥazi ha-I Krim* (1878), 104. **ADD. BIBLIOGRAPHY:** PK Ukrainah, s.v.

[Yehuda Slutsky and Eliyahu Feldman / Shmuel Spector (2nd ed.)]

BAKI (Heb. בָּקִי; "expert"), person possessing expertise in a particular field of ritual law, e.g., in divorce law (*"Baki be-tiv Gittin"*) or in dietary laws (*"Baki bi-terefot"*); also a person well versed in Talmud and rabbinic literature is called *"Baki be-Shas u-Fosekim."*

BAKKASHAH (pl. *bakkashot*; Heb בַּקָּשָׁה, בַּקָּשׁוֹת, "Supplication(s)"), liturgical compositions of the same type as *selihot. The word denotes a wide range of prayers in prose or verse, petitionary and abstract in content, mainly for recitation throughout the year. A number of *bakkashot* found at the beginning of the Sephardi prayer books from the 17th century onward are meant to be recited by congregants before dawn while waiting for the regular service to begin. Groups of Sephardim in Jerusalem called *Omerei Bakkashot* ("Sayers of Supplications") continue this practice every Sabbath from midnight until sunrise. At first these *bakkashot* had been said daily, but later, as a result of reduced attendance, they were confined to the Sabbath except during the month of Elul. The custom apparently originated in Safed among the followers of Isaac *Luria, and from there spread to other communities. It is first mentioned in a letter of Solomon Shlumal dated 1603 (S. Assaf, in: *Kobez al Jad*, 3 (1939), 123). This practice is not to be confused with Ashkenazi societies of Shomerim la-Boker ("Morning Watchers"), which recite hymns on Monday and Thursday mornings before dawn. The term was, however, often applied arbitrarily to certain hymns included in the service. Saadiah *Gaon's two *bakkashot*, that of *Baḥya ibn Paquda, and Solomon ibn *Gabirol's *Keter ha-Malkhut* (Venice, 1572) are examples. The term also refers to some of the short hymns by such poets as Abraham and Moses *Ibn Ezra and *Judah Halevi. Different collections of *bakkashot* exist, and all of them include the poem *Yedid Nefesh* by Eleazar *Azikri. Each composition concludes with a collection of scriptural verses beginning with "And Hannah prayed…" (I Sam. 2:1). Different collections have appeared, such as the volume of hymns published by Mordecai Ḥayyim Elijah Levi (1929) and the *Tehillat Yesharim ha-Shalem* (ed. by Z.J. Manẓur, 1954).

[Ernst Daniel Goldschmidt]

Musical Tradition

Under the influence of the *Zohar and 16th-century kabbalists of Safed, the custom developed of rising at midnight to chant hymns from the Psalms, refrains, and *bakkashot* until dawn. The concomitant for *piyyutim* stimulated the creativity of talented poets steeped in mystical doctrine. Although the singing of *bakkashot* is traditional in many communities, it evolved into an organized form of semi-religious activity particularly in Syria (Aleppo and Damascus) and Morocco. The first of the great poets whose hymns were introduced in the Syrian and Moroccan *bakkashot* was Rabbi Israel *Najara. The melodies set to the appropriate hymns are extremely varied and include sophisticated and popular idioms, the latest innovations, and traditional tunes, which have disappeared from contemporary cultures. The musical factor is prominent and often tends to overshadow the basically religious purpose of the meeting. The singing of *bakkashot* may thus be considered as half religious concert and half prayer meeting, attended equally for religious, aesthetic, and social reasons.

The Aleppo *bakkashot* consist of certain fixed *piyyuṭim* and optional ones, which are selected for the occasion according to circumstances and the character of the audience. Each *bakkashah* is performed antiphonally by two groups. Between one *bakkashah* and the next, a soloist or smaller group takes turns in singing the so-called *petiḥah* (opening), which may be a psalm or a verse which derives from the preceding *piyyut* or from the classical Hebrew poetry. Their melodies are improvised, highly melismatic, and constructed so as to establish a modulation from the **maqām* (melodic pattern) of the preceding to that of the following song. The concluding *bakkashah, Yedid Nefesh*, is sung in the *maqām* of the current Sabbath. In the Moroccan *bakkashot*, the repertoire is standardized, it is grouped into several series of different *piyyutim* – except for three or four recurring ones – for each series, which also has its own dominant musical mode (*nūbā'*). The general structure of each set is conceived in relation to the form of the "Andalusian" *nūba* of Moroccan art music, which is a kind of vocal and instrumental suite. Since instruments are not permitted, the singers add their own vocal imitations of instrumental passages. The Moroccan *bakkashot*, however, are also sung at celebrations outside the synagogue, and then the appropriate instruments are used. The *piyyutim* in the Moroccan *bakkashot* were collected into anthologies. One, entitled *shir yedidot*, which contains 550 *piyyutim* and was published in Marrakesh in 1921, is still used today.

After the establishment of an important community of Aleppo Jews in Jerusalem at the beginning of the 20th century, Aleppo *bakkashot* became a model for other Middle Eastern communities, but were themselves much modified by the participation of non-Aleppo singers. The result was the generalized *bakkashot* style now common to several ethnic groups. The Syrian community in Brooklyn, New York, also perpetuates the Syrian tradition.

See also *Aleppo, Musical Tradition and *Africa, North: Musical Traditions

[Amnon Shiloah]

BIBLIOGRAPHY: *Oẓar ha-Tefillot* (Ashkenazi rite, 1923), 56–63; Idelsohn, Liturgy, 157; Elbogen, *Gottesdienst*, 74, 229, 324; I. Davidson et al. (eds.), *Siddur Sa'adiah Ga'on* (1941), 47–81; R. Katz, in: *Acta Musicologica*, 40 (1968), 65–85 (Eng.). **ADD. BIBLIOGRAPHY:** P. Fenton, in: REJ, 134 (1975), 101–21; A. Shiloah, in: M. Abitbol (ed.), *Judaïsme d'Afrique du Nord* (1980), 108–13; E. Seroussi, in: *Pe'amim* 19 (1984), 120–29; K. Kaufman-Shelemay, *Let Jasmin Rain Down – Song and Remembrance among Syrian Jews* (1998).

°**BAKRI, MOHAMMED** (1953–), controversial Israeli Arab actor/director whose 2002 documentary *Jenin Jenin*, about the IDF incursion into Jenin, was banned by the Israeli censor. Although the ban was lifted later, it focused attention on the movie, which was widely distributed on DVD. Many pointed out its inaccuracies and accused Bakri of inciting hatred. Prior to directing this inflammatory film, Bakri, who was born in the village of Al Bineh in the Galilee, had a distinguished career as a film and theater actor. His most famous role was as the Palestinian inmate who joins forces with Israeli prisoners in the 1984 film *Beyond the Walls*. He has appeared in more than 25 other films, including several in which he portrays Israeli Jews. His film credits include *Hanna K.* (1983), *Esther* (1986), *Cup Final* (1991), *Desperado Square* (2001), and *Private* (2004). He subsequently concentrated on acting in and directing theater in Galilee.

[Hannah Brown (2nd ed.)]

BAKSHI, RALPH (1938–), U.S. animator and film director. Bakshi was born in Haifa, Israel, but moved with his family to Brooklyn, New York, when he was a year old. He showed an early talent for drawing, winning an award in animation upon graduation from high school. He went to work for Terrytoons, an animation studio, and during his ten years there he directed episodes of the television series *Deputy Dawg* and worked on the popular cartoons *Hekyll and Jekyll* and *Mighty Mouse*. By 1965 he was in charge of Terrytoons and was asked to put together a "superhero" TV cartoon series. He demonstrated disdain for the assignment by creating odd superheroes: Tornado Man, Cuckooman, Ropeman, and Diaper Baby. The CBS Television network, which then owned Terrytoons, loved the concept and broadcast *The Mighty Heroes*, a short-lived series.

After Terrytoons shut down, Bakshi moved to Paramount's cartoon division and stayed until 1967, when the studio closed it down. After working for Steve Krantz Productions on its adaptation of the Spider-Man comic book series in 1967, Bakshi produced his first theatrical animated feature, an obscenity-laced adaptation of Robert *Crumb's underground comic strip *Fritz the Cat* in 1972. The X-rated feline who uttered profanities onscreen stirred controversy. "There was talk about if I were a pornographer or not," Bakshi said. "What I did was anti everything animation was about." Animated characters, he felt, could elicit more powerful emotions than flesh-and-blood actors. His next feature, *Heavy Traffic*, was even more outrageous than *Fritz*, which went on to gross more than $90 million worldwide, creating a previously unknown market, adult animation. *Traffic* was a nihilistic, highly scatological tale of a young New York artist's drawing board fantasies. It featured several Jewish characters. In 1975 Bakshi released *Coonskin*, a savage attack on Hollywood racial stereotypes. It was one of the first animated features to depict black characters (drug dealers). Civil rights organizations boycotted the film to protest its unflattering portrayal of blacks.

After three urban animated dramas, Bakshi turned to fantasy in 1977 with *Wizards*, "about the creation of the State of Israel and the Holocaust, about the Jews looking for a homeland, and about the fact that fascism was on the rise again," he said. Bakshi withdrew from animated films but returned in 1981 with *American Pop*, a social history about four generations of Jewish-American immigrants. He devoted the next decade to painting but returned to animation with the 1992 film *Cool World*.

[Stewart Kampel (2nd ed.)]

BAKSHI-DORON, ELIAHU (1941–), rabbi, Sephardi chief rabbi of Israel. Bakshi-Doron was born in Jerusalem, where he studied at Hebron yeshivah and in the *kollelim* of Mosad Ha-Rav Kook and Kol Ya'akov.

He served as a neighborhood rabbi in Bat Yam, becoming the city's chief rabbi in 1972. In 1975 he was appointed chief Sephardi rabbi of Haifa, serving in that capacity until elected Sephardi chief rabbi of Israel in 1993. His ten-year term ended in April 2003.

On September 12, 2001, Chief Rabbi Bakshi-Doron called on the Islamic clerics who had published a *fatwa* (religious edict) ordering suicide-bombings and declaring the bombers *shahids* – martyrs – to rescind it and call on the world to preserve the sanctity of life, and to forbid large-scale attacks on innocent civilians. At times, Bakshi-Doron has taken controversial stands. At one point, he suggested that the Moslems retain their authority over the Temple Mount. However, he did decry the unsupervised Arab construction that has taken place on the Temple Mount in recent years. Bakshi-Doron also suggested that Israel's Marriage Law be rescinded, thus ending the Chief Rabbinate's monopoly on marriage and divorce. Since the rabbinic process was creating more enemies than friends of Judaism among secular Jews, perhaps the time had come for radical change. This particular statement caused a great uproar in religious circles.

Bakshi-Doron published dozens of articles reflecting his Torah learning, studies dealing with halakhic solutions to medical, economic, legal, and social problems as well as facets of political science. His work *Binyan Av* (vol. 1, 1982; vol. 2, 1989) deals with many facets of *halakhah* and also gives rabbinic responses to current issues. A third volume appeared following the order of the weekly Torah readings to which Rabbi Bakshi-Doron brings new light to *aggadah* and Jewish thought. The book also contains speeches given by the rabbi. Throughout his career, Rabbi Bakshi-Doron has worked for Torah education, establishing, among others, a *kolel* in Tel Aviv, an advanced *bet midrash* in Bat Yam, and a Torah learning center in Haifa. Bakshi-Doron also served as president of the Committee of Sephardi Communities and was a board member of numerous social and charitable foundations. He was also a member of the Board of Directors of LIBI.

[David Derovan (2nd ed.)]

BAKST, LEON (born **Lev Samuilovich Rosenberg**; 1864–1924), Russian artist. Born in St. Petersburg, he took the name Leon Bakst to honor his maternal grandfather. In his youth he was baptized but later returned to Judaism. At the age of 15, on the advice of the sculptor *Antokolski, he enrolled in the Academy of Fine Arts. In 1890 he met Alexander Benois, a Russian artist who introduced Bakst to the Mir Iskusstva ("World of Art") group that tried to overcome the prevailing provincialism of Russian art and to link Russia to the West. The impresario Serge Diaghilev was a member and he employed Bakst as chief designer of costumes and décors for his ballets. From its start in Paris, in 1909, until his death, Bakst was associated with Diaghilev's Ballets Russes. The subjects for the ballets were usually taken from Russian folklore, or from Oriental tales. Bakst, with his vivid imagination and his predilection for bright color, provided an atmosphere that carried the audience into a fairyland. While his creations are no longer in use on the stage, his sketches in pencil, pen-and-ink, crayon, watercolor, gouaches, or mixed media often appear in exhibitions of Russian art. They have become particularly appreciated since the recent revival of interest in *art nouveau*. As a teacher at the Svanseva School in St. Petersburg, Bakst had a strong influence on the young Marc *Chagall.

BIBLIOGRAPHY: A. Levinson, *Bakst* (Fr., 1924); R. Lister, *The Moscovite Peacock; A Study of the Art of L. Bakst* (1954).

[Alfred Werner]

BAKST, NICOLAI (Noah) IGNATYEVICH (1843–1904), Russian scientist, writer, and public figure. Born in Mir, Belorussia, Bakst studied at the rabbinical seminary in Zhitomir, where his father Isaac Moses taught Talmud, and thereafter at the University of St. Petersburg. After graduating, he was sent to Germany by the Russian Ministry of Public Instruction. There he continued his studies under the noted physiologist Hermann Helmholtz and others. In 1867 he was appointed lecturer in physiology at the University of St. Petersburg, specializing in the study of the nervous system. He wrote a number of works in German and Russian on physiology and the nervous system.

The emergence of antisemitism in Germany and the pogroms in Russia of 1881 awakened Bakst's interest in the Jewish question. For him the solution was to grant full civil rights to the Jews in Russia and improve their material and moral condition. Bakst became a highly esteemed public figure in Russian Jewry; he was one of the initiators of *ORT and active in its management. He served as an expert on the Pahlen Commission (1883–88), set up to examine the laws regulating Jewish life. This prompted Bakst to publish a series of articles on different aspects of Jewish life and thought in Jewish and non-Jewish journals.

BIBLIOGRAPHY: S.A. Wengeroff, *Kritiko-biograficheskiy slovar*, 3 (1892), 73–75; Galpern, in: *Voskhod*, 24 no. 27 (1904), 5–8; YE, 4 (c. 1910), 698–701.

BAKU, port on the western shore of the Caspian Sea, capital of Azerbaijan S.S.R. 1920–1991, from 1992 capital of *Azerbaijan. Jews are first mentioned in the area in the 13th century. A community of Persian Jews existed in Baku in the 18th century. The inhabitants, who were Muslims, harassed the Jews there and in 1814 threatened their lives following a blood libel. Although the Russian authorities offered them their protection, the Jews left and took refuge in *Kuba, also in the province of Baku, where there was a large community of *Caucasian Mountain Jews. Later, however, some returned to Baku.

A new chapter in the history of the community began in the 1870s with the development of the oil industry in Baku and its surroundings. Although restrictions were imposed to discourage Jews coming from European Russia, and on Jewish participation in the industry, the number of Jewish concessionaires and professional and skilled workers increased. Jews took a large share in initiating new enterprises and providing capital, in exploiting oil wells and setting up refineries, in developing transport facilities, and in marketing oil and oil products within Russia and abroad. Among pioneer industrial companies owned by Jews was that of Dembo and Kagan, founded by A. Dembo of Kovno and Ḥayyim Cohen of Brest-Litovsk. Also active in this sphere were the Dembot brothers, in collaboration with Baron H. Guenzburg, Bikhowsky, Leites, Ickowich, and A.M. Feigel. A central position in oil exploitation, transportation, and marketing was occupied by the *Rothschilds, who founded the Caspian-Black Sea Company and by the end of the 19th century headed a syndicate of many of the large oil companies. Another large company was Polak and Sons, owned by Grigori Polak and his sons Saveli (Shevaḥ) and Michael. Prominent in the field of technology was the chemical engineer Arkadi Beilin, who worked in a number of companies, including those of the Rothschilds, and after marrying the daughter of Grigori Polak joined Polak and Sons. In 1913–14 the share of the Jewish companies in kerosene production in Baku reached 44% while the proportion of Jews occupied in oil products marketing was even greater.

Jewish communal and Zionist institutions followed in the wake of the economic development. According to the 1897 census there were 2,341 Jews in Baku, of whom the majority were Caucasian with some from European Russia. The Jewish population continued to increase after the 1917 revolution through the influx of Mountain Jews who, deprived of their traditional livelihoods in the villages, moved to the towns. In 1926 the Jewish population numbered 21,995 (19,583 of European origin, 1,985 Caucasian Jews (Tats), and 427 Georgian Jews). In 1939 they numbered 31,050 and comprised about 4% of the total population. According to the 1959 census they numbered 29,179 (3% of the total) in Baku and its vicinity. In 1970 the Jewish population was 29,716 (2.2% of the total). Most of the non-European Jews resided in the old part of the city. The European, Tati, and Georgian communities each had their synagogue. The Tati synagogue was the oldest and largest. While *maẓẓot* could be obtained on Passover, ritually slaughtered meat was not available. Two local rabbis signed *Izvestia's* denunciation of the Sinai Campaign (on November 29, 1956). Consequently the European Jewish community was deprived of its rabbis who apparently were not replaced. In the 1990s most of the Jews emigrated to Israel and the West.

BIBLIOGRAPHY: J.J. Chorny, *Sefer ha-Massa'ot* (1884); H. Landau, in: *YIVO Bleter*, 14 (1939), 269–85.

[Simha Katz]

°BAKUNIN, MIKHAIL ALEKSANDROVICH (1814–1876), Russian revolutionary, one of the founders and theoreticians of Anarchism. While imprisoned in the Petropavlovsk fortress in St. Petersburg (1851), he wrote his "Confession" (*Ispoved*), in which he reproached the Polish independence leaders Adam *Mickiewicz and Joachim Lelewel for their favorable attitude toward Jews. Through his conflict with *Marx, *Hess, and other Jewish Socialists at the end of the 1860s, Bakunin's hatred of the Jews grew beyond bounds. In his answer to a letter of Moses Hess in the review *Le réveil* (October 20, 1869), he referred to the Jews as a nation of exploiters, entirely opposed to the interests of the proletariat. At another time he stated that the Jews were more dangerous than the Jesuits and constituted a real power in Europe: they reigned despotically over commerce and banking, and had taken over three-quarters of German journalism as well as a large portion of the press in other countries. Bakunin considered Marx as the modern Moses, a typical representative of the Jewish people.

BIBLIOGRAPHY: Yu.M. Steklov (pseud.), *Mikhail Aleksandrovich Bakunin*, 3 (Rus., 1927), 346–50, 388–404; Silberner, in: HJ, 14 (1952), 93–106; W. Polonski (ed.), *Materialy dlya biografii M. Bakunina*… 1 (1923).

°BAKY, LÁSZLÓ (1898–1946), Hungarian antisemitic politician. Baky was a leading member first of the Hungarian National Socialist Party and later of *Szálasi's *Arrow-Cross Party, which he left temporarily in 1941. In March 1944 he became undersecretary of state in the Ministry of the Interior, in charge of Jewish affairs. He presided at the secret meeting of April 4, 1944, where the arrangement for the deportations of Jews was drawn up, and was one of those who directed the setting-up of ghettos and the deportations. On June 29–30, 1944, Baky attempted an unsuccessful fascist coup against

Horthy. Nevertheless, he retained his position until September 5. Later he was one of the founders of a group of right-wing deputies who sought to give a legal framework to the Szálasi regime. Baky was sentenced to death by a Budapest People's Court and executed in 1946.

BIBLIOGRAPHY: J. Lévai, *Black Book on the Martyrdom of Hungarian Jewry* (1948), passim; A. Geyer, *A magyarországi fasizmus zsidóüldözésének bibliográfiája, 1945–1958* (1958), index.

[Bela Adalbert Vago]

BALAAM (Heb. בַּלְעָם, בִּלְעָם), son of Beor, a non-Israelite diviner famous for his effectiveness, enlisted by Balak, king of Moab, to pronounce curses over the Israelites. The pronunciation Balaam reflects the Greek rendering of the name in the Septuagint. Balaam's exploits are related in Numbers 22:2–24:25, known in modern research as "The Balaam Pericope," and traditionally recognized as a distinct literary unit within the book of Numbers. There we read that the numerous Israelites, encamped in the Steppes of Moab on their way to the land of Canaan, were feeding off the land, causing great apprehension in Moab. Balak despaired of driving them away by force, and he hoped to achieve victory by means of Balaam's execrations. To Balak's chagrin, however, Balaam refused to succumb to his offers of reward, and surprisingly, pronounced blessings over Israel instead of curses, predicting Israelite victories. His orations represent some of the most beautiful examples of early Hebrew poetry. Balaam's firm obedience to God's will is viewed with great favor. Similar praise is expressed in Micah 6:5, where Balaam's role in thwarting the design of one of Israel's enemies is evoked as a sign of God's providence over his people.

In contrast, Balaam is seen in a hostile light in several other biblical sources where he is mentioned. In a certain sense, the derogation of Balaam begins in the Tale of the Ass (Num 22:22–35), which mocks his reputed gifts as a seer (see further). And yet, as the tale unfolds, Balaam falls into line, and ends up obeying God's instructions. The attitude toward Balaam is decidedly unfavorable, however, in Numbers 31:8, 16, which report that Balaam's counsel had led to Israelite worship of Baal Peor, and that he was slain by the Israelites together with the kings of Midian in the course of the war against the Midianites. A resonance of the same episode is found in Joshua 13:22, where, in addition, Balaam is referred to as *ha-qôsem* ("the diviner"), as if to discredit him. In Joshua 24:9–10, within a narration of Israel's history, we read that God protected Israel, refusing to allow Balaam to curse the people, The underlying assumption is that Balaam had intended to do just that. Finally, according to Deuteronomy 23:5–6, the mere fact that Balaam had been retained by Balak, king of Moab, to curse Israel is adduced as a basis for prohibiting marriage with Ammonites and Midianites (cf. Neh. 13:2). It is difficult to explain this negativity toward Balaam against the background of the Balaam Pericope. Rather than following traditional explanations that Balaam's allegiances changed, it is more likely that subsequent Israelite misfortunes at the hands of neighboring nations, with whom Balaam was identified, brought him into disrepute.

Recent archaeological discoveries have added significant information about Balaam. In 1967, a Dutch expedition under H. Franken discovered fragments of inscriptions written on plaster at a Transjordanian site named Tell Deir ʿAlla, located about 5 mi. (8 km.) east of the Jordan, not far from the northern bank of the Jabbok (Zerqa) river that flows into the Jordan. In the Hebrew Bible this area is known as *cēmeq Sukkôt*, "the valley of Sukkoth" (Ps. 60:8, 108:8, cf. Gen. 33:17, Judg. 8, 1 Kings 7:46). Many of the plaster fragments were restored in the manner of a jigsaw puzzle, and the resulting "combinations" were published by J.A. Hoftijzer and G. van der Kooij in 1976. Composed in a language similar to biblical Hebrew, and dated in the late ninth to early 8th centuries B.C.E., the inscriptions attest the name of a seer, *blʿm brbʿr* – "Balaam, son of Beor"– for the first time in an extra-biblical source of the biblical period. Previously, Balaam had been known outside the Hebrew Bible solely from post-biblical sources (Baskin 1983).

The Deir ʿAlla inscriptions relate how a certain *blʿm brbʿr*, referred to as "a divine seer" (*ʾzh < lhn*), was visited at night in a dream by gods who revealed to him that an impending misfortune would devastate the land. The seer, greatly distressed at this news, assembles his people to disclose to them what he has learned. In these inscriptions Balaam is depicted as an heroic figure, who strove to save his people and the land. In content and style, the inscriptions noticeably resemble the Balaam Pericope of Numbers, and other biblical sources as well, so that any discussion of the role of Balaam in biblical literature must henceforth take the Deir ʿAlla inscriptions into account.

The Name Bilʿam and the Identity of the Person

There are essentially two ways of parsing the name *Blʿm*: (a) *Bil+ʿam*, whereby the component *ʿam* is a kinship term, and *bil* would represent the divine name Bel, yielding the sense: "Bel is my kinsman." As such, the Hebrew/Deir ʿAlla name has been compared with Akkadian *Bill-am-ma* and *Amma-baʾli* "Bel is a kinsman," or: "a kinsman of Bel" (*HALAT* 130, s.v. *Bilʿam* 1). (b) A name incorporating the verb *b-l-ʿ* "to swallow up, destroy," + *m*, an affix that can be represented as *åm* (elsewhere also *ån* and *–ôn*), and that characterizes the actor of the verb, hence: "the swallower, destroyer." Reference would be to the potency of Balaam's spells and execrations. This understanding of the name gains support from its uncanny similarity to the name of the first Edomite king, *Belaʿ*, son of *Beʿôr*, as recorded in Genesis 36:32. This resemblance can hardly be coincidental, and may argue for the identification of Balaam as a nearby Ammonite, Moabite, Midianite, or Edomite by origin, rather than as a more distant Aramean.

In fact, there appear to be two traditions concerning Balaam's homeland. One identifies Balaam as an Aramean, an extraction explicit in the opening verse of his first oration (Num. 23:7): "From Aram did Balak import me/ the king of Moab – from the mountains of Qedem." At the same time, there are indications that Balaam was perceived as a Transjordanian, or son of an inland nation. It is noteworthy that both the Vulgate and the Samaritan versions read in Num 22:5 *ʿereṣ benê ʿAmmô[n]* "to the land of the *Ammonites*." in place of Hebrew *benê > ammô*, "the land of his people."The attribution to a seer named Balaam of the inscriptions found at Deir ʿAlla which were, given their language and exposition, composed in the immediate area, would further endorse his identity as a figure who came from a neighboring, inland country. It is best, therefore, to allow for alternative traditions regarding Balaam's place of origin (Levine, 2000, 145–48).

The Structure and Contents of the Balaam Pericope

The Balaam Pericope consists of prose narratives that serve as a rubric for the poems of the pericope and poetic compositions.

(A) THE POETIC REPERTOIRE. There are four major orations, followed by a series of three, brief prophecies. Each oration is introduced as a *mashal* "balanced verse." Only the third and fourth orations explicitly identify Balaam as the speaker, though the first and second refer to Balak by name, making it virtually certain that Balak is the speaker. In the first oration (Num. 23:7–10), the speaker relates that he was called from Aram by Balak to pronounce curses over Israel, but was powerless to do so because Israel had been blessed by El/YHWH. Overlooking the Israelite encampment from the heights, Balaam was awed by its vast expanse, impressed that the Israelites needed no allies, and were capable of achieving victory on their own. He would willingly share the fate of such heroes! In the second (Num. 23:18–24), the speaker addresses Balak directly, insisting that El will not renege on his promise to bless Israel, and consequently his own mission could not be countermanded. YHWH would not countenance any misfortune overtaking Israel, a people strong as a lion and protected by a powerful deity who directly informs them of the future, thereby rendering divination unnecessary. In the third oration (Num. 24:3–9), entitled "The speech (Hebrew *ne'um*) of Balaam. Beor's son," the speaker's professional gifts are enumerated. He is "one who hears El's utterances," and "who beholds the vision of Shadday" (the fourth oration adds: "who is privy to Elyon's knowledge"). Balaam describes the beauty of the Israelite encampment in words that have become part of Jewish liturgy: "How lovely are your tents, oh Jacob/ your dwellings, oh Israel." Alluding to Saul, king of Israel, he predicts that Israel will prevail over the Amalekite king, Agag (I Sam. 15). In the fourth oration (Num. 24:15–19), similarly entitled, Balaam alludes to David's conquests of Moab and Edom.(II Sam. 8:2, 12–14), characterizing that king dramatically as a shooting star, as a meteor. In the three brief orations that follow (Num. 24:20–23) Balaam assumes the role of a "prophet to the nations" and predicts the ultimate downfall of the Amalekites and Kenites, and possibly of Assyrians, west of the Euphrates.

Viewing the Balaam orations in their entirety, it is clear that the agenda changes after the second poem. Having proclaimed Israel's victorious destiny on the way to the Promised Land, Balaam proceeds in the third and fourth orations to predict Israelite victories over the Canaanite peoples and over hostile neighboring peoples in the interior. This purview is expanded in the brief prophecies to the nations. It is also the case that after the second oration Balaam ceases to justify his refusal to carry out Balak's wishes, and, invoking his preeminent status as a seer, predicts without apology dramatic Israelite victories, including the subjugation of Moab itself.

The poetic sections employ several designations of divinity, in addition to YHWH and *ʾelōhîm*, namely, Shadday, Elyon, and most frequently, El. It has been customary to interpret these names as epithets of YHWH. Although originally the names of discrete deities, they had, so the argument goes, been synthesized with YHWH, thereby becoming merely another way of referring to the God of Israel. On this basis, we would translate Numberss 23:7 as follows: "How can I curse whom *the deity* has not condemned? How can I doom whom YHWH has not doomed?"

Though the El-YHWH synthesis (Eissfeldt, 1956) is indeed evident in biblical literature, it remains to be determined whether it is expressed in the Balaam orations, or in other poems that may hark back to a stage in the development of Israelite religion when the worship of the Syro-Cannanite deity, El, was regarded as acceptable. It is in this spirit, after all, that the worship of El, sometimes registered as El Shadday, is imputed to the Patriarchs (Gen. 28:3, 31:13, 35:11, 46:3), an attribution explained in so many words in Exodus 6:2–3. This is the view most recently adopted by Levine (2000, 217–34), who sees evidence of an El archive in biblical literature, parts of which were redacted so as to conform to the El-YHWH synthesis. In Levine's view, some of the El poems, most notably the Balaam orations, themselves were retained in their unredacted form, so that their references to El, in particular, should be understood as designations of the Syro-Canaanite deity by that name, not as epithets of the God of Israel. As will be observed, it is likewise El who presides over the gods in the Balaam inscriptions from Deir ʿAlla. Read in this manner, the biblical Balaam orations present a distinctive view of Israelite religion: YHWH is acknowledged as Israel's national God, their divine King, who is present in their midst to assure them victory. At the same time, it is powerful El who liberated Israel from Egypt, and who has blessed Israel irreversibly, keeping faith with them. This earlier religious outlook would be precisely what Exodus 6:2–3 was aimed at disavowing.

This understanding of the religious predicates of the Balaam orations, and of the posture of Balaam, explains why there is no battle projected between YHWH and the gods of Moab, and why Balaam is powerless to curse Israel. It is not only YHWH who is providential over Israel, but El, Shadday, and Elyon, as well. It is as if to say that Moab's own gods, members of the traditional West-Semitic pantheon, were arrayed against them. Most scholars, however, view the Balaam orations as expressing the El-YHWH synthesis, in essence proclaiming YHWH's exclusive providence over Israel, as well as his dominance over pagan seers like Balaam. In this perspective, the poetic orations are understood to express the same religious outlook as do the prose sections of the Balaam Pericope.

Just as the divine appellations in the Balaam orations are unusual, so are the designations of the Israelite collective. With only one exception (Num. 24:18–19), the consistent classification is (a) Jacob, (b) Israel, expressed in parallelism (Num. 23:7, 10, 21, 23, 24:5, 17). This nomenclature recalls the change of Jacob's name from *Yacaqôb* to *Yisra'el* after his combat with the angel, which, appropriately, occurred at Penuel, in the Valley of Sukkoth (Gen. 32), where the Deir ʿAlla inscriptions were found!

There has been considerable progress in the exegesis of the Balaam orations, which because of their relative antiquity and the dialectal features they manifest have resisted interpretation. They employ rare, even unique forms that afford little basis for comparison. W.F. Albright (1944) achieved a breakthrough by reducing the Masoretic text to its consonantal base, and reading the poems as West-Semitic epigraphy. Sh. Morag (1981) sought to shed light on unrecognized meanings through linguistic analysis. More recent attempts are presented in commentaries on the Book of Numbers by Milgrom (1990) and Levine (2000).

(B) THE PROSE NARRATIVES. The prose sections pursue a sequential narrative, except for the tale of the ass (Num. 22:22–35), which derives from a separate source. It was undoubtedly inserted as a satire, poking fun at Balaam's reputed clairvoyance as a seer. In a mode familiar to us from Aesop's fables, and from ancient Near Eastern wisdom literature, as well, it depicts Balaam as being blind to what even the ass he was riding was able to see! Its theme is that the God of Israel initially objected to Balaam's willingness to accompany Balak's messengers to Moab, and sent an angel to block his path. The ass made several attempts to avert the angel, and each time Balaam struck her, until God gave speech to the ass, so that she could explain to Balaam what was going on. Ultimately, God opens Balaam's eyes, as well, and he submits to God's will, offering to return home. Balaam is then told by the angel that he is permitted to accompany Balak's emissaries on condition that he speak only what YHWH communicates to him.

The Tale of the Ass is preceded in Numbers 22:2–21 by a narrative of Balak's invitation to Balaam to pronounce curses over Israel on his behalf. Balaam at first refuses, insisting that he is under the authority of Israel's God. However, God appears to him at night and authorizes him to accompany the men, but to speak only what he is told. The intervening tale effectively brings us back to this point, in Numbers 22; 35. In the ensuing narrative (Num. 22:36–23:6), we read that Balaam arrives in Moab and is welcomed by Balak, who offers him great rewards. After a feast prepared by Balak, Balaam proceeds to the mountain-top of Bamoth-Baal, where he is afforded a view of part of the Israelite encampment. There he pronounces his first blessings of Israel (Num. 23:7–10). When the prose narrative resumes, we read that Balak is furious, but Balaam repeats that he can speak only what YHWH instructs him to say. In an effort to achieve greater efficacy, Balaam is advised to move to a more propitious site, the peak of Pisgah, where he erects altars and offers sacrifice. YHWH encounters Balaam and places an oracle in his mouth. Balak asks him: "What has YHWH spoken?" which indicates that he now accepts Balaam's subservience to Israel's God (Num. 23:11–17). Then follows Balaam's second oration (Num. 23:18–24). At this point, Balak is all but ready to give up, but again suggests moving to a different site, the summit of Peor, where altars are erected and sacrifices offered, prior to a third attempt by Balaam, who now realizes that it pleases YHWH to bless Israel. Without further ado, he prepares to declaim his third oration (Num 23:25–30, 24:1–2), which predicts Israel's victory over the Amalekites of Canaan (Num. 24:3–9). When the prose narrative resumes, we read that Balak dismisses Balaam in anger, but that before returning to his own land, Balaam tells him that he will reveal what the Israelites will do to Moab (and Edom) in the future (Num. 24:10–14). This is the theme of Balaam's fourth oration (Num. 24:15–19). Numbers 24:20–29 present the three brief prophecies against neighboring nations.

Throughout the prose sections, YHWH and *'elohim* alternate exclusively as designations of the God of Israel, who is perceived as totally controlling the activities of Balaam from the outset. In fact, in Numbers 22:18 Balaam already refers to YHWH as *elohai* "my God," and in a manner not dissimilar from that of Pharaoh in the Moses sagas, Balak also becomes increasingly aware of YHWH's power, and of Balaam's subservience to it. In contrast to the Egyptian sagas, however, which repeatedly refer to the gods of Egypt, the prose sections of the Balaam Pericope nowhere refer to any other divine power, or use what would be regarded, in context, as epithets of YHWH or *'elohim.*

The Balaam Texts from Deir ʿAlla

Notwithstanding their poor state of preservation, the plaster texts from Deir ʿAlla add to our understanding of the Balaam Pericope, and in a reciprocal manner, the biblical sources enlighten us as to the meaning of the Deir ʿAlla texts. Like most new discoveries, the Deir ʿAlla texts raise problems of a literary and historical nature. The inscriptions were restored from plaster fragments that had fallen to the ground from the walls of a regional distribution center, where some cultic activity took place. (For transcriptions, translations, archaeological background and commentary see Levine, 2000, 241–75; idem, COS II, 140–45.)

COMBINATION I OF THE INSCRIPTION. Combination I relates that Balaam was visited at night by gods sent to convey to him a message from the high god, El. The message consisted of a celestial omen of disaster. A council (*mwʿd* = Hebrew *moʿed*)) of deities who opposed El had ordered the goddess Shagar-we-Ishtar, a Venus figure of light and fertility, to sew up the heavens, thereby producing darkness and dread. Upon hearing this, Balaam became greatly distressed, and took to weeping and fasting. He assembled his people and described the content of this revelation to them. Vultures will fly about shrieking, and wild beasts will occupy grazing lands. Although at this point the text becomes less clearly comprehensible, it is reasonable to read it as a recounting of Balaam's heroic attempt to free the goddess from the decree of the evil council, thereby saving the land from misfortune. Balaam admonishes the adversaries of Shagar-we-Ishtar, and takes the goddess to various diviners, oracles, priestesses, and magical practitioners to safeguard her from the punishment decreed upon her. His efforts were successful, and order was re-established in the land, which accounts for the commemorative installation of the inscriptions on the walls of the building at Deir ʿAlla.

COMBINATION II. Combination II, which is even more fragmentary, vividly describes a necropolis (*byt ʿlmn*) erected by El, a "house" where no traveler enters, nor any bridegroom. The portrayal recalls the Sheol oracle of Isaiah 14, and speaks of an unnamed, wise counselor, who will no longer be consulted, and who will be punished by being deprived of his ability to pronounce oracles and execrations. Although the name of Balaam does not occur in Combination II, it is suggestive to relate this text to Balaam. The opening title of Combination I, "The misfortunes of the Book of Balaam, the son of Beor," undoubtedly included Combination II, as well as additional compositions which may have been lost, or whose fragments have not as yet been restored in coherent form

Both Combinations exhibit shared vocabulary and diction with the biblical Balaam orations, and with other biblical poems of the El archive. Indeed, the Deir ʿAlla inscriptions resonate with biblical imagery.

The Phenomenology of Balaam's Performance

Now that we possess information from the Deir ʿAlla inscriptions, we can draw up a more complete profile of Balaam. Albright (1971), and others have compared him with the Mesopotamian *barû* ("diviner"). The parallel West Semitic functionary would be the *qosem*, a title given to Balaam only in Joshua 13:22, although Numbers 22:18 does in fact report that the elders of Moab (and Midian) brought to Balaam payment for *qesamim* ("divination"), indicating that he practiced that art. We are also told in Numbers 24:1 that for a time, Balaam also engaged in *nehashimā* ("augury"), but eventually gave that up (Num. 24:1).

For the most part, the biblical poems inform us that Balaam beholds visions, both while awake and asleep; he hears divine utterances, and possesses secret knowledge. He sees into the future and predicts events, and has a reputation for pronouncing effective curses. We may conclude that Balaam was expert at pronouncing effective blessings, which is what he actually did. The narratives provide additional information on Balaam's techniques: He offers burnt sacrifices as a means of attracting YHWH to particular sites, while also perambulating, walking around in search of an encounter with YHWH, and possibly in search of omens, as well. In this connection, one notes that visual access is a factor in Balaam's praxis. In the preparations for what Balak hoped would be effective curses, sites were sought out that afforded a partial, or complete, view of the Israelite encampment, which was the target of the curses.

There are two additional points to be made about Balaam's performance. First, as is true of ritual experts, polytheistic and monotheistic, Balaam acted under divine authority. Balaam could only do what he was authorized to do by the divine power, or powers, that controlled him. It was only after the gods signaled their approval that diviners and exorcists and other ritual experts could undertake the prescribed operations. Secondly, both the poems and the prose narratives portray Balaam in personal terms. In the poems, he is said to be awed by the strength and heroism of the Israelites, and by a realization, based on his own observation, that this people had been blessed and protected, and was not marked for misfortune. In the prose narratives and in the Tale of the Ass, Balaam is depicted as one given to anger and frustration, who is not tempted by wealth, and, above all, who is honest in accepting the limitations of his own powers. Balaam is also reactive; his acceptance of subservience to the God of Israel increases as his encounters with YHWH progress, until he becomes more than willing to bless Israel. Thus, the fourth, and final oration was not requested by Balak, but offered to him voluntarily, as were the three, brief prophecies.

The Deir ʿAlla texts shed further light on the performance of Balaam. We read more about his divinatory crafts, most notably his ability to interpret celestial omens, and of his admonitions directed at malevolent divine powersAlthough the atmosphere of the Deir ʿAlla inscriptions is polytheistic, and affords more attention to specific ritual practices, the difference between the Deir ʿAlla inscriptions and the biblical pericope is more a matter of degree than of kind, especially if we accept the interpretation that in the biblical Balaam orations, El, Elyon, and Shadday are proper names of West Semitic gods and not merely epithets of YHWH and *ʾelohim*.

The Sitz-im-Leben of the Balaam Pericope

According to the internal, Biblical chronology, the encounters related in the Balaam Pericope would have occurred during the late 13th century B.C.E., or thereabouts, but we must be careful not to confuse temporal setting with time of composition. There are problems in attempting to assign both the poetic and narrative sections of the Balaam Pericope to the usual documentary sources, J and E, as pointed out most clearly by A. Rofe (1981). It would be preferable to seek clues in the poems themselves as to their time and place of composition. As for the Balaam narratives, it is safe to say that they postdate the poems.

The Deir ʿAlla inscriptions help us to fix the context of the Balaam poems in more than one respect. For one thing, they raise the possibility that the biblical Balaam poems were also composed in Gilead, in central Transjordan, where an active Israelite community lived for several centuries until driven out after the Assyrian invasions of the late eighth century B.C.E. The Valley of Sukkoth, where Deir ʿAlla is located, figures notably in certain biblical traditions, such as the narratives of Genesis 32–33 and Judges 8. There is also a basis for seeing the Deir ʿAlla inscriptions themselves as Israelite compositions, notwithstanding the absence of any mention of the God of Israel, and despite their polytheistic character (Weippert 1991). In this connection, the highlighting of El in the Balaam poems fits in well with the veiled references to El worship in Hosea 6:8, 12:12 by the Israelites of Gilead. Perhaps these very Transjordanian Israelites, regarded as sinful by Hosea, were the ones, or similar to the ones, who installed the Balaam plaster inscriptions on the walls of the building at Deir ʿAlla.

Historically, the Balaam orations reflect a situation of conflict between Israel and Moab, wherein Israel is declared victorious. This context would suit conditions in the early to-mid-ninth century B.C.E., under the Omride dynasty, when northern Israel exercised hegemony over northern Moab. This would have been prior to Mesha's successful reconquest of that territory in the mid-ninth century, as recounted in the famous stele of that Moabite king. This is also the period during which the Heshbon Ballad of Numbers 21, which depicts the Israelite conquest of North Moab, would have been composed. As such, the biblical Balaam poems might have antedated the Deir ʿAlla inscriptions by about 50 years.

Thanks to the Deir ʿAlla discoveries we can now speak of Balaam as a biblical personage also known from external, Transjordanian sources. We know him better than we did before, whether we regard him only as a figure of legend or as an historical personage of legendary proportions.

[Baruch Levine (2nd ed.)]

In the *Aggadah*

Some rabbis inflated the importance of Balaam. They saw in him one of "The seven prophets who prophesied to the peoples of the world" (BB 15b; "God raised up Moses for Israel and Balaam for the peoples of the world" – Num. R., 20:1; Tanḥ., Balak, 1), and believed that in many respects he was greater than Moses: "No prophet like Moses had risen in Israel, but such a one has risen among the peoples of the world. Who is he? Balaam the son of Beor. But there is a difference between the prophecy of Moses and that of Balaam. Moses did not know who spoke with him but Balaam knew.... Moses did not know when [God] would speak with him till he was addressed by Him, whereas Balaam knew.... Moses did not speak with Him till he had stood up... whereas Balaam spoke with Him as he was falling" (Sif. Deut. end). They explained Balaam's power to curse by the fact that he could ascertain the exact hour of God's anger (Av. Zar. 4a–b; Sanh. 105b). Others, however, identified him with Elihu the son of Barachel the Buzite (Job 32:2) for Barachel means "God has blessed"; the epithet "Buzite" is derived from "*buz*" ("contempt"), hence it teaches that Balaam's prophecy was of a low order and contemptible (T.J. Sot. 5:8, 20d). Some rabbis saw in him an immoral figure: "An evil eye, a haughty spirit and a proud soul" are the marks of the disciples of "Balaam the Wicked" (Avot, 5:19). Balaam was one of Pharaoh's counselors and it was he who advised that the male children should be cast into the Nile (Sanh. 106a); and in the end he wished "to uproot an entire people for naught and for no reason" (Num. R. 20:1; Tanḥ. Balak, 1) and counseled Balak how to destroy them. It was this act which caused the departure of the holy spirit from the gentile peoples (*ibid.*), and since then prophecy was preserved in Israel alone. There is no basis for the theory put forward by some scholars that Balaam in the *aggadah* represents Jesus (but see *Jesus in Talmud and Aggadah).

[Yehoshua M. Grintz]

In Islam

Balaam is not mentioned by name in the Koran, and it is not even clear that he is intended by the inference in Sura 7 (lines 174–5), as read by several interpreters of the Koran, historians, and authors of *Legends of the Prophets* (*Qiṣaṣ al-Anbiyā*). The verses read: "Relate to them of him to whom we gave our signs, and who turned away from them; and Satan followed him, and he was of those who were led astray. But had it been our will, we would have exalted him through our signs, but he clung unto the earth, and followed his desire. He is like the dog who puts forth his tongue whether you chase him away or let him alone. That is the parable of the people who deny our signs. Tell them this history, that they may consider it."

It is the general opinion that the inference is to Balaam who acquiesced to the request of Balak, king of Moab (Num. 22–24), as related in the Bible and Jewish legend, and who was responsible for the going astray of the children of Israel with the daughters of Moab (*ibid.* 25). However, some interpret Muhammad's words as referring to *Umayya ibn Abī al-Salt, Muhammad's contemporary and competitor as a prophet who was sent to the Arabs. Others maintain that the inference is to Luqmān, an Eastern sage, to whom Muhammad dedicated Sura 31. Nevertheless, B. Heller presents a number of convincing arguments against this identification.

[Haïm Z'ew Hirschberg]

In the Arts

Balaam is regarded with general disfavor in Hebrew literature, and it was exclusively in Christian literature that he was accorded any importance – mainly because he was alleged to have predicted the advent of Jesus (Num. 24:17). By the Middle Ages, however, Balaam had become a figure of fun, and it is in this spirit that he is portrayed in such medieval miracle plays as the *Ordo Prophetarum*, the Chester and Stonyhurst cycles, and the *Mistère du Viel Testament*. Such treatment destroyed Balaam's literary standing, although the 16th-century French Christian kabbalist Guillaume Postel resurrected the "prophet of the Gentiles" in some of his patriotic visionary works. One rare later treatment is the dramatic poem *Balaam* (1787) by C. Davy.

Among artists, portrayal of the subject was largely influenced by Christian theological interpretation of Balaam's prophecy, that "a star rises from Jacob," which was seen as a prefiguration of the star of Bethlehem that according to the Gospels appeared to the Magi. Balaam is represented as a bearded figure wearing an antique tunic and mantle and a Phrygian cap or Oriental turban. Such early representations are found in third and fourth century catacombs. The figure of Balaam is sometimes placed next to the Madonna and Child and often appears on sarcophagi. In Byzantine art, Balaam is depicted as one of the foretellers of Jesus in a fresco on Mount Athos. There are similar treatments in the West, such as the 12th-century "Tree of Jesse" window at Chartres and the 14th-century ceiling of St. Michael's at Hildesheim. Balaam appears with his ass in a late 12th-century bronze door at Monreale and a 14th-century facade at Orvieto. There are other representations in illuminated manuscripts and incunabula, such as the Luebeck Bible (1494). Artists who painted the subject include Taddeo Zuccari (1529–66), Luca Giordano (1632–1705), and Rembrandt. There are also cycles covering Balak's command, his sacrifice, and Balaam and Balak on Mount Peor; a notable example of this is the illuminated Bible of San Paolo Fuori le Mura (c. 850). Others occur in later baroque Bible illustrations.

BIBLIOGRAPHY: W.F. Albright, in: JBL, 63 (1944), 207–33; idem, in: EJ 4:119–23; J. Baskin, *Pharaoh's Counselors* (1983); A. Caquot and A. Lémaire, in: *Syria*, 54 (1977), 189–208; O. Eissfeldt, in: JSS, 1 (1956), 25–37; HALAT, 130; J. Hoftijzer and G. van der Kooij, *Aramaic Texts from Deir ʿAlla* (1976); idem (eds.), *The Balaam Text from Deir ʿAlla Reevaluated* (1991); B.A. Levine, *Numbers 21–36* (AB; 2000); J. Milgrom, *Numbers JPS Torah Commentary* (1990); M. Moore, *The Balaam Traditions* (1991); Sh. Morag, in: *Tarbiz*, 50 (1981), 1–24; A. Rofe, *The Book of Balaam* (Heb., 1981); H. Rouillard, *La Péricope de Balaam* (1985); M. Weippert, in: Hoftijzer and van der Kooij, *Balaam*, 151–84. IN ISLAM: Ṭabarī, Tafsīr, 9 (1337 H), 83–84; Nīsābūrī, *ibid.*, 76ff.; Tabarī, *Taʾrikh*, 1 (1357 H), 308, 310; Thalabī, *Qiṣaṣ* (1356 H), 139–202; I. Eisenberg (ed.), Kisāʾī, *Qiṣaṣ* (1922), 227–9; A. Geiger, *Was hat Mohammed aus dem Judenthume aufgenomanen?* (1833), 176–7; Heller, *Shorter Encyclopaedia of Islam*, s.v. *Luqmān*; Vajda, in: EIS².

BALABAN, BARNEY (1887–1971), U.S. motion picture executive. Balaban was born in Chicago and worked at the age of 12 as a messenger for Western Union. In 1908, along with partner Sam Katz, he formed a company that developed a chain of deluxe movie and stage-show theater palaces. In 1917 they built what historians consider the city's first movie palace, the Central Park on West Roosevelt Road. Referred to as a "dream theater," it had a seating capacity of 2,200. It was here that they began working out the service system which soon spread to all quarters of the theater world. They outfitted their ushers in military-style uniforms, had them salute the theater patrons, and trained them to give quick, intelligent service.

At its peak, their cinema chain included 125 theaters in Chicago and the Midwest, such as the Riviera, the Tivoli, the Chicago, the Uptown, the McVickers, the Roosevelt, and the Norshore. The company introduced raked floors, comfortable seats, balconies, and air-conditioning. To keep patrons entertained, Balaban and Katz supplemented the theater's first-run motion pictures with lavish stage shows, a policy that would become standard at Chicago movie palaces during the 1920s. In 1926 they opened the Palace Theatre. Modeled after Versailles, the Palace had rose-marbled walls, crystal chandeliers, gold plaster ornamentation, and immense mirrors. That year they also opened the Oriental Theatre in Chicago's Loop area. A virtual museum of Asian art, the ornate three-level theater had a large domed ceiling graced by seahorses and goddesses. Turbaned ushers led patrons from the lobby – with polychrome figures and large mosaics of an Indian prince and princess – through an inner foyer with elephant-throne chairs and multicolored glazed Buddhas, to the auditorium's "hashish-dream décor."

In 1928 Balaban and Katz opened the Paradise on Chicago's West Side. Throughout their career the partners had been haunted by sentimental memories of the West Side, where they were born and raised and had first overcome poverty. Wanting to give their home turf the finest theater of all, they built the Paradise in the center of the city's population. Larger than any other theater outside of New York City, more daring and original in its architecture than any theater in the world at that time, their opulent 3,600-seat French Renaissance-style Paradise embodied the farthest reaches of their imagination.

Ultimately, Paramount Pictures bought a two-thirds interest in their cinema chain, and in 1936 Balaban was elected president of Paramount Pictures in Hollywood. Under his guidance, Paramount invested in television and pioneered the wide screen. Balaban was active in Jewish affairs.

Over the decades, many of the movie palaces fell into disrepair. The Paradise, for example, billed as "the world's most beautiful theater," was demolished in 1965. With the advent of talking pictures, fatal flaws in the acoustics and design of the building were exposed, so Balaban and Katz decided to demolish the theater and sell the land to a supermarket chain. Built to last forever, it took two years to tear it down.

In 1996 Chicago Mayor Richard Daley announced that the Oriental would be restored to its original grandeur for the presentation of live stage musicals. Renamed the Ford Center for the Performing Arts in 1997, the theater opened its doors to the public in 1998. Similarly, the Palace was purchased by General Motors and, renamed the Cadillac Palace Theater, opened in 1999 to present live stage productions.

[Ruth Beloff (2nd ed.)]

BALABAN, MEIR (**Majer**; 1877–1942), historian of Polish Jewry. The Balaban family had been active in Lemberg and Zolkiew (Zholkva) as Hebrew printers from 1830 to 1914. After studying law at the university of his native Lemberg, Balaban taught for seven years in Galician towns in schools founded by Baron de Hirsch. He later returned to the university, devoting himself to the study of history. In those years he was active in the Zionist movement and served on the editorial staff of the Zionist weekly *Wschód* (The East). After graduating, Balaban continued teaching religion in various secondary schools. During World War I he served as a military chaplain in Lublin and as an official of Jewish affairs for the Austrian occupation authorities in Poland. From 1918 to 1920 he was head of the Jewish High School in Czestochowa. From 1920 to 1930 he directed the rabbinical seminary Taḥkemoni in Warsaw, and from 1928 lectured on Jewish history at the University of Warsaw, becoming associate professor in 1936. He was one of the founders of the Institute for Jewish Studies in Warsaw (1927) and served as its director for several years.

Balaban published about 70 historical studies and about 200 short papers and reviews in various periodicals. He was justly considered the founder of the historiography of Polish Jewry, especially of its communal life. His studies were based on a wealth of source material found in government and municipal archives, as well as in the archives of the Jewish communities. His first book, *Zydzi lwówscy na przełomie XVI–XVII wieku* (The Jews of Lvov [Lemberg] at the Turn of the 17th Century, 1906), received a prize from the University of Lemberg. In this work he displayed a thorough grasp of his subject, scholarly meticulousness, and a capacity for presenting lucidly the various aspects of life in great detail. These characteristics also mark his second monumental work *Dzieje żydów w Krakowie i na Kazimierzu, 1304–1868* ("A History of the Jews of Cracow," 2 vols., 1931–36). His book on the Jews of Lublin, *Die Judenstadt von Lublin* (Berlin, 1919), is a vivid survey of history of the Jews in that city. A series of articles on the organization of the Jewish communities in old Poland reflect his vast legal knowledge. These papers first appeared in Russian but were later revised and published again in Polish in the monthly publication of the Jewish community of Warsaw (1937–39). To the 11th volume of *Istoriya yevreiskogo naroda* ("A History of the Jewish People," 1914), of which he was a coeditor, Balaban contributed an exhaustive study of the Council of the Four Lands. Collections of his articles and treatises, containing the biographies of rabbis, doctors, and communal leaders, and the history of printing houses, blood accusations, and the Karaites in Poland, were published in German, Polish, and Yiddish. Balaban contributed over 150 articles to the Russian-Jewish Encyclopedia *Yevreyskaya Entsiklopediya*. Particularly significant are his studies on the Shabbatean and Frankist movements, summarized in his *Le-Toledot ha-Tenu'ah ha-Frankit* (History of the Frankist Movement, 2 vols., 1934–35). He also wrote a book on the synagogues and other antiquities of the Jews in Poland, *Zabytki historyczne Żydów Polsce* (Jewish Antiquities in Poland. 1929). A summary of the history of the Jews in Poland until the end of the 18th century is contained in the second and third volumes of a textbook entitled *Historja i literatura żydowska* (The History of the Jewish People and its Literature, 1925; first of 3 vols. also in Hebrew, 1931); most of the historical chapters are included in *Beit Yisrael be-Polin* (vol. 1, 1948). His studies of the history of the Jews in 19th-century Poland are confined to Galicia. From the outset of his scholarly career Balaban applied himself to collecting a bibliography on the history of the Jews in Poland; his first prizewinning publication in this field appeared in Polish in 1903. The first part of his own bibliography for the years 1900–30 appeared in 1939. When the Nazis overran Poland, Balaban refused to flee. He died in Warsaw in November 1942 before the liquidation of the ghetto and was thus vouchsafed burial in the Jewish cemetery.

BIBLIOGRAPHY: N.M. Gelber, in: *Gazit*, 5 nos. 9–10 (1943), 7–10; R. Mahler, in: *Yidishe Kultur*, nos. 8–9 (1943), 56–59; H. Zeidman, in: S.K. Mirsky (ed.), *Ishim u-Demuyyot be-Ḥokhmat Yisrael* (1959), 223–74, includes bibliography. **ADD. BIBLIOGRAPHY:** I. Biderman, *M. Balaban – Historian of Polish Jewry* (1976).

[Raphael Mahler]

BALABANOFF, ANGELICA (1878–1965), European socialist and political activist. Balabanoff was born in Chernigov, near Kiev in the Ukraine, to a wealthy Jewish family. The daughter of a landowner and businessman, she was the youngest of 16 children, several of whom had died before her birth. Like most girls of her class and time, she was educated privately at home. At age 19 she left Chernigov to study at the Université Novelle in Brussels, Belgium, an institution noted for its radicalism. In her autobiography, *My Life as a Rebel*, Balabanoff asserted that a guilty awareness of her privileged background and a poor relationship with her mother, whom she considered dictatorial, motivated her to pursue goals of social justice. After receiving a doctorate in the philosophy of literature in Brussels, she began a wandering life of commitment to socialism which involved significant contact with prominent personalities and great historical events. In Brussels she came under the influence of George Plekhanov, a founder of the first Communist Party in Russia. Her acquaintances and comrades included Alexander *Berkman, Emma *Goldman, V.I. Lenin, Rosa *Luxemburg, Benito Mussolini, Leon *Trotsky, and Clara Zetkin. As an organizer and agitator, Balabanoff rejected feminism as a bourgeois philosophy. She was fluent in many languages, a firebrand speaker, and a talented journalist and editor. Balabanoff developed a close and lasting relationship with the Italian Socialist movement early in her political career. She also had a leadership role in the Swiss-based Zimmerwald Group, which attacked imperialism and demanded immediate peace. During and after World War I, Balabanoff became more sympathetic to the left wing of Socialism. After the Bolsheviks came to power, she returned to Russia, where she was appointed secretary of the Communist International. A year later, ousted from that position, she left Russia disillusioned, assailing the government and the movement it represented as corrupt and authoritarian. In response, the Bolsheviks attempted to malign her reputation. Balabanoff spent the interwar years in Paris and Vienna. During World War II, she found refuge in New York City where she became a friend of American socialist Norman Thomas and contributed occasionally to the *Socialist Review Journal*. Balanbanoff also spoke out against Italian Fascism. She settled in Rome after the war and was active in the Italian Socialist movement. Balabanoff was the author of *Impres-*

sions of Lenin (1934); *My Life as a Rebel* (1938); and *The Traitor: Benito Mussolini and the "Conquest" of Power* (1942–3); she also wrote poetry in English, French, German, Italian, and Russian.

BIBLIOGRAPHY: R. Florence, *Marx's Daughters: Eleanor Marx, Rosa Luxemburg, Angelica Balabanoff* (1975; Obituary, *New York Times* (Nov. 26, 1965); E. Wilson, "The Poetry of Angelica Balabanoff," in: *The Nation* (Nov. 27, 1943).

[Libby White (2nd ed.)]

BALAGUER, town in Aragon, northeastern Spain. At the time of the Christian reconquest at the end of the 11th century, several Jews already owned houses and land there. In 1280 Pedro III ordered an inquiry regarding violations of the interest laws by the local Jews. Efforts by the counts of Urgel to restore the community after the *Black Death and the anti-Jewish disorders accompanying it in 1348–49 were apparently successful. During the persecutions of 1391 the Jews in Balaguer took refuge in the citadel but were forced to leave by King John I. In 1416 Alfonso V, after suppressing a revolt, imposed a fine of 45 pounds of silver upon the Jews of the town, notwithstanding the fact that the community had become impoverished through migration to the estates of the nobility and the conversions to Christianity at the time of the *Tortosa disputation. New settlers were not granted exemption from taxes. The community existed until the expulsion of the Jews from Spain in 1492.

BIBLIOGRAPHY: J.M. Pou y Martí, *Historia de la ciudad Balaguer* (1913), 47ff.; 62, 116, 330; Baer, Urkunden, 1 pt. 1 (1929), index; Vendrell, in: *Sefarad*, 3 (1943), 137ff.; Piles, *ibid.*, 10 (1950), 179; Baer, Spain, 1 (1961), 115, 212.

[Haim Beinart]

BALAK (Heb. בָּלָק), son of Zippor; the first king of Moab whose name is known. Balak's memory survived only because of his ill-fated association with *Balaam, whom he had hired to curse Israel after the latter's victories over the Amorites (Num. 22–24; et al.). In Joshua 24:9 (cf. Judg. 11:25) he is described as having fought Israel. Micah 6:5 refers to the frustration of Balak's design as exemplifying God's kindness to Israel. No satisfactory explanation of the name has so far been advanced.

For bibliography, see *Balaam.

BALANCE (Heb. פֶּלֶס, *peles*; Isa. 40:12; Prov. 16:11; cf. *pilles* "make straight, level," Isa. 26:7; Ps. 78:50; synonomous by synecdoche with pair of scales, *moznayim* – Lev. 19:36; Isa. 40:12; Jer. 32:10; et al. – and with balance beam קָנֶה, *kaneh*; Isa. 46:6). The equal arm balance of the ancient Near East (as distinguished from the unequal arm balance with counterpoise introduced by the Romans) consisted of a horizontal beam moving freely on a central fulcrum, with the object to be weighed and standard weights suspended at opposite ends in pans or on hooks. In its earliest form the beam was suspended at its center by a cord held in the hand, and equilibrium was estimated visually. Under the 18th dynasty in Egypt larger balances were developed, supported by an upright frame resting on the ground. From the frame was suspended a weighing plummet (Heb. *mishkolet*, II Kings 21:13; Isa. 28:17) which could be compared with a pointer extending downward at right angles from the pivotal point of the beam.

The principle of the balance was probably derived from the yoke of the burden bearer (Isa. 9:3), with its two equalized loads. The earliest mechanical balances were small, and were used only for objects of high value in relation to their size, e.g., gold, silver, jewels, spices, etc. The oldest known example is a stone balance beam from the pre-dynastic Gerzean civilization in Egypt. Weights from the Sumerian and Indus civilizations show that the balance was in use there in the third millennium. Hand balances and large standing balances are illustrated in many Egyptian reliefs and wall paintings, the former also on a Hittite relief from Carchemish and the latter on one from ninth century Assyria. From ancient Israel a crude sketch of a man holding a pair of scales, incised on the base of a scale-weight of the seventh-sixth centuries B.C.E., is extant (unpublished). Biblical references to the balance are both literal (Lev. 19:36; Jer. 32:10; Ezek. 45:10; et al.) and figurative (Isa. 40:12; Ps. 62:10; Job 6:2; et al.). Fraudulent weighing is repeatedly denounced in the Bible, i.e., substandard weights (Amos 8:5), different sets of weights for buying and selling (Deut. 25:13), and false balances (Hos. 12:8; Prov. 11:1). An effort to standardize weights by marking them with an official shekel sign, attributable on archaeological grounds to Josiah, may have been accompanied by regulations for the construction and operation of balances. In later times the levites were made custodians of "all measures of quantity and size" (I Chron. 23:29).

BIBLIOGRAPHY: A.B. Kisch, *Seals and Weights* (1965), 26–78; F.G. Skinner, *Weights and Measures* (1967); EM, 4 (1962), 540–3 (incl. bibl.).

[Robert B.Y. Scott]

BALANJAR, town of the *Khazars located between *Bāb al-Abwāb and *Samandar in the north Caucasus region. It was formerly identified by Artamonov (see bibliography) with the ruins of Endere near Andreyeva, or as the site of present-day Buinaksk, but is now placed by him south of Makhachkala, where the remains of a town have been found (communication of November 1964). Balanjar is mentioned in Arabic sources as existing in the seventh and eighth centuries. Originally the name appears to have been an ethnic designation. A Pehlevi source cited by the historian al-Ṭabarī (vol. I, 895–6) states that in the time of the Sassanid ruler Khusraw Anūshirwān (531–79) a tribal group within the West Turkish empire was called Balanjar. According to the historian al-Masʿūdī (*al-Tanbīh*, 62), Balanjar was formerly the Khazar capital. It was the principal objective of the Arabs after they reached the Caucasus in 641 or 642. In 652 the Muslims attempted unsuccessfully to besiege Balanjar, then a fortified town, and were heavily defeated nearby. In 723, during the second Arab-Khazar war, it was captured by al-Jarrāḥ ibn ʿAbdallah al-Ḥakamī and is occasionally mentioned later.

BIBLIOGRAPHY: Dunlop, Khazars, index; M.I. Artamonov, *Istoriya Khazar* (1962), index.

[Douglas Morton Dunlop]

BALASSAGYARMAT, city in Nógrád county, northern Hungary. Jews first settled in the town toward the end of the 17th century. The poll of 1725 mentions only one Jewish family; in 1746 there were 19 families, and by 1778, 47 families. The number of Jews ranged from 529 in 1784 to 2,013 (17.4% of the total) in 1930, reaching a peak in 1920 with 2,401 (21.1%). According to the census of 1941, the town had 1,712 Jews, representing 13.9% of the total of 12,347. The Jewish community was organized in 1730, and its Chevra Kadisha in 1742. The community's first synagogue was destroyed in a fire in 1776; on its site a new synagogue was built in 1868. Among the rabbis who served the community were Judah Leb Engel (from 1730); Benjamin Ze'ev Wolf *Boskowitz; Mordecai and Ezekiel *Banet; and successive members of the Deutsch family (Aaron David, Joseph Israel, and David) from 1851 to 1944. The Jewish community, which was organized as Orthodox in 1868, was joined in 1885 by the smaller communities in the neighboring villages, including those of Dejtár, Érsekvadkert, Örhalom, Patak, and Szügy. During the interwar period, the community supported a number of social and welfare institutions, and together with the Jewish community of nearby Salgótarján published a Hungarian-language paper called *Szombati Értesitö* ("Sabbath News"). Located near the border with Slovakia, Balassagyarmat was a magnet for many Polish and Slovakian Jewish refugees who escaped persecution in their own countries.

After Hungary entered the war in June 1941, the Jews were subjected to ever harsher measures. Jewish males of military age were conscripted for labor service. The situation of the Jews took a turn for the worse after the German occupation of Hungary on March 19, 1944. According to a census conducted after the occupation, the Orthodox congregation had 1,516 members, led by President Mihály Lázár and Rabbi David Deutsch. The Jews were rounded up early in May 1944 under the direction of Mayor Béla Vannay. Balassagyarmat served as a major concentration and entrainment center for 5,820 Jews rounded up in Nógrád county. These Jews were concentrated in two ghettos: the approximately 2,000 local Jews were concentrated in the so-called "large ghetto," in and around Kossuth Lajos, Thököly, and Hunyadi Streets; the Jews brought in from the neighboring towns and villages in Nógrád county were concentrated in the so-called "little ghetto," located in Óváros Square. Among these were the Jews of Alsópetény, Apátújfalu, Becske, Bercel, Cserháthaláp, Diósjenö, Érsekvadkert, Galgaguta, Hugyag, Losonc, Noográdmarcal, Örhalom, Szécsény, Szügy, and several other locations. The Jewish Council was composed of Mihály Lázár (chairman), Dezsö Sándor, Pál Sándor, Ferenc Hajdú, Imre Léván, and János Weltner. Internally, the ghettos were guarded by a Jewish police force headed by Pál Sándor and András Fleischer. Externally, they were guarded by units of the police headed by László Eördögh and a gendarmerie unit from Miskolc. Just before their deportation, the Jews were relocated to the tobacco barns at Nyírjespuszta about 3 miles (5 km.) from the town. The Jews were deported to Auschwitz in two transports that left Nyírjespuszta on June 12 and June 14. The Germans used the synagogue as a munitions depot, and destroyed it prior to their departure.

Among the first survivors to return to the town were labor servicemen. They, together with the concentration camp survivors who returned in 1945–46, reorganized the community under the leadership of Rabbi Pinkász Kálmán. The Jews began to leave the town after 1948 and especially after the Hungarian Revolution of 1956. By 1970 only a handful of Jews were still in Balassagyarmat.

BIBLIOGRAPHY: M. Stein, *Magyar Rabbik*, 2 (1906), 7–8; 4 (1908), 3–4; 5 (1909), 5–6; M. Ladányi, *Nógrád és Hont vármegye* (1934), 139; MHJ, 5, pt. 1 (1959), 510. **ADD. BIBLIOGRAPHY:** Braham, Politics; PK Hungaria, 173–75.

[Laszlo Harsanyi / Randolph Braham (2nd ed.)]

BALÁZS, BÉLA (1884–1949), Hungarian author and motion picture critic. Balázs was born in Szeged and studied at Budapest. After the revolution in 1918–19 he moved to Vienna and Berlin and finally settled in the U.S.S.R., where he lectured at the Moscow Film Academy. He returned to Hungary after World War II and taught at the Budapest Academy of Dramatic Art. Balázs' interest in philosophy is evident in all his writing. His books include *Halálesztétika* ("Aesthetics of Death," 1907), *A tragédiának metafizikus teóriája* ("Metaphysical Theory of Tragedy," 1908), and *Dialógus a dialógusról* ("Dialogue about the Dialogue," 1913). He also wrote poems and several plays, of which *A kékszakállu herceg vára* ("Duke Bluebeard's Castle," 1912), provided the libretto for an opera by Béla Bartók. Bartók also set to music Balázs' fairy-tale ballet, *A fából faragott királyfi* ("Wooden Prince," 1912). Balázs was a pioneer of motion picture criticism, and wrote two books on film technique (1952, 1961). The Hungarian communist regime established a prize in his name for work in cinema art.

BIBLIOGRAPHY: E. Gyertyán, *Balázs Béla és a film* (1958); A. Komlós, in: B. Balázs, *Az én utam* (1960), introd.

[Jeno Zsoldos]

BALBO, MICHAEL BEN SHABBETAI COHEN (1411–after 1484), rabbi and poet in Candia (Crete). Although Candia was his permanent home, he is occasionally mentioned in nearby Canea and three sermons which he preached there in 1471, 1475, and 1477, are extant (Vatican Ms. 305). He functioned as *condostablo*, the leader of the Jewish community of Candia. Moses *Capsali in a responsum of 1458 refers to him as one of the communal leaders. Balbo's signature is found on many ordinances enacted in Candia between the years 1468 and 1479. He wrote letters and poems to many contemporary scholars, one poem dealing with the capture of Constantinople by the

Turks in 1453. In this lament on the fall of Constantinople, he associated the fate of the Jews with that of the defeated Greek-Orthodox. Balbo took issue with scholars on various topics; in his polemic against Moses Ashkenazi (who was known by the curious name of *Esrim ve-Arba* – "Twenty-Four") he vigorously attacked Ashkenazi for his rejection of the doctrine of metempsychosis. Balbo also wrote on behalf of the Candia community on such topical subjects as the ransoming of captives and *agunot*. These writings are valuable material for the history of his time. In a colophon at the end of a manuscript of the *Sefer Mitzvot Katan*, which he copied, he refers to the deaths of his son Isaiah and of Isaiah's son Michael in 1484.

BIBLIOGRAPHY: Freimann in: *Zion*, 1 (1936), 185–207; E.S. Artom and M.D. Cassuto (eds.), *Takkanot Kandyah*, 1 (1943), index; Urbach, in: KS, 34 (1958/59), 101; Malachi, in: KS, 41 (1965/66), 392f. **ADD. BIBLIOGRAPHY:** N. Stavroulakis, *The Jews of Greece, An Essay* (1990) 32; Z. Malachi, "The Balbo Family – Scholars of Hebrew Literature in Candia (15th Century)," in: *Michael*, 7:255–70.

[Yehoshua Horowitz]

BALCON, SIR MICHAEL (1896–1977), British film producer. Born in Birmingham, he began filmmaking in 1920 and during the next 40 years was responsible for many outstanding British films which opened new avenues in realism and humor. Among them were *The Captive Heart, It Always Rains on Sunday, Passport to Pimlico, Kind Hearts and Coronets, The Lavender Hill Mob, Whisky Galore, The Cruel Sea, Dunkirk*, and *The Long and the Short and the Tall.* His book *Michael Balcon Presents … A Lifetime of Films* was published in 1969. He was knighted for his services to the industry in 1948. Balcon was born and educated in Birmingham. He founded Gainsborough Pictures Ltd. in 1928, was director of production for Gaumont-British, director and producer at Ealing Studios, and chairman of British Lion Films.

ADD. BIBLIOGRAPHY: ODNB online; DBB, I, 110–15.

°**BALFOUR, ARTHUR JAMES, EARL OF** (1848–1930), British statesman, signatory of the *Balfour Declaration. In 1902, he became prime minister, but was defeated in the general election of 1905. He returned to Asquith's coalition as first lord of the admiralty in 1915 and served as foreign secretary in Lloyd George's coalition government, formed in December 1916. Balfour began to take an interest in the Jewish question in 1902–03, when *Herzl conducted negotiations with Joseph *Chamberlain, the British colonial secretary, and with Lord Lansdowne, the foreign secretary, regarding Jewish settlement in areas adjoining Palestine, such as the Sinai Peninsula. In 1906 he met Chaim *Weizmann in Manchester and was impressed by his personality. Balfour's interest in Zionism revived and grew more intense during World War I, when he became foreign secretary, in which capacity he signed the Balfour Declaration of Nov. 2, 1917. He was enthusiastically welcomed by the Jewish population when he visited Palestine in 1925 to attend the dedication ceremony of the Hebrew University in Jerusalem, at which he delivered the opening address. His anthology, *Speeches on Zionism* (1928), was translated into Hebrew. The motivation behind Balfour's attraction to Zionism has been the subject of conjecture. Being a rationalist it is doubtful whether religious tradition was a factor although his biographer Blanche *Dugdale introduces his Scottish ancestry with its Old Testament tradition. A more likely theory is that of Leonard Stein, who points out that Balfour had spoken out against the persecution of the Jews saying "The treatment of the race has been a disgrace to Christendom" and he saw the establishment of a Jewish state as an historic act of amends. Streets were named after him in Jerusalem, Tel Aviv, and Haifa. There is also a Balfour Forest at Ginnegar, and a moshav, *Balfouriyyah, founded in 1922 in the Jezreel Valley. The Balfour family continued the tradition of interest in the Zionist movement. Robert Arthur Lytton 3rd Earl of Balfour (1902–1969), his nephew, supported *Youth Aliyah. In 1939 he offered the family estate and home, Whittingham, to a Jewish committee as a training school for refugee boys and girls from Germany. Balfour's niece and biographer Blanche Dugdale worked in the political department of the Jewish Agency in London as a close collaborator of Chaim Weizmann.

BIBLIOGRAPHY: B. Dugdale, *A.J. Balfour*, 2 vols. (1939); K. Young, *A.J. Balfour* (1963); L. Stein, *Balfour Declaration* (1961).

[*Encyclopaedia Hebraica*]

BALFOUR DECLARATION, official statement which Arthur James *Balfour, the British foreign secretary, addressed to Lionel Walter Rothschild (2nd Baron Rothschild) on November, 2, 1917. It conveyed a declaration of sympathy with Jewish Zionist aspirations. The British government viewed with "favour the establishment in Palestine of a national home for the Jewish people."

The Declaration was a deliberate act of the British cabinet and part of its general foreign policy. It was a national policy in the sense that it represented the views of the three British political parties. It had acquired international status since the principal Allies – Russia, France, Italy, and the United States – had given it their prior approval. It was subsequently endorsed by the League of Nations and incorporated into the *Mandate.

The Balfour Declaration recognized the collective right of world Jewry to Palestine and the "Jewish People" became an entity in the context of international law. Recognition of Zionism was in line with the principle of self-determination and with the struggle of small nationalities for freedom and independence.

There were many hands, both Jewish and non-Jewish, which shaped the policy which led to the Declaration, but it was Chaim *Weizmann who emerged as the central figure in the struggle. His scientific achievements early in the war enabled him to render important services to the British government which brought him to the notice of David *Lloyd George, minister of munitions. The latter's personal admiration for Weizmann proved invaluable to the cause of Zionism when Lloyd George was serving as prime minister. Weizmann had met Arthur James Balfour for the first time in Manchester, in 1905. British statesmen, public men, and officials listened readily to Weizmann because he was able to show that he could influence Jewish opinion and that Zionism was advantageous to Britain.

C.P. Scott, the celebrated editor of the *Manchester Guardian*, was one of the leading public men whom Weizmann converted to Zionism. It was Scott who cemented Weizmann's relationship with Lloyd George and introduced him to Herbert *Samuel, then president of the Local Government Board, at that time the only Jewish member of the cabinet. Like Weizmann, Samuel realized that Turkey's entry into the war on November 5, 1914, opened up great possibilities. He went further than Weizmann and envisaged that, with the probable disintegration of the Ottoman Empire, the foundation of a Jewish state in Palestine could be laid. He confided his views first to Sir Edward Grey, the foreign minister, and found him favorably disposed towards the idea. Lloyd George was also keen to see the establishment of a Jewish state in Palestine; his interest predated Grey's.

However, several weeks later, Samuel concluded that, since the number of Jews in Palestine did not exceed one-sixth of the total population, the time was not ripe for the establishment of an independent and autonomous Jewish state. In a memorandum circulated in January 1915 (and in a revised version in March 1915), he advocated the annexation of Palestine to the British Empire, as only under British rule would Jewish colonization prosper and immigration be encouraged, so that in course of time when the Jews would become a majority they would be conceded "such a degree of self-government as the conditions of that day may justify."

On February 5, 1915, when Samuel met Grey again, he found him still anxious to promote Jewish settlement in Palestine but very doubtful of the possibility or desirability of the establishment of a British Protectorate. Neither Samuel nor Weizmann gave sufficient weight to the fact that Britain was disinclined to undertake new imperial responsibilities and that the wishes of the French in that region were to be respected. The inter-departmental committee, better known as the De Bunsen Committee, appointed in April 1915, recommended that maintenance of an independent Ottoman Empire, but with a decentralized system of administration, would serve British interests best. With regard to Palestine the committee suggested that it should be neutralized and placed under an international regime. This concept ran counter to Samuel's and Weizmann's wishes. It was not until early in 1917 that their doctrine began to appear relevant to British strategic interests. But during 1915–16 it was still condemned to the sidelines. Weizmann and Nahum *Sokolow, a member of the World Zionist Executive who arrived in England in December 1914, pursued their activity in a low key, and it was only in 1916 that a collection of essays, edited by Harry *Sacher, entitled *Zionism and the Jewish Future*, was published with the intention of enlightening public opinion on the essence of Zionism.

If the British government's interest in Zionism persisted, it was not in order to establish a claim to Palestine, as was manifested a year later, but in order to win over American Jewry, whose influence was thought to be considerable in the press, in finance, and in politics. Wooed by both belligerent camps, the attitude of the Jews in the United States was governed by the czarist government's hostile treatment of their kin in Russia. The British government regretted Russia's conduct but felt powerless to influence her. It was Horace *Kallen, a professor at the University of Wisconsin and an ardent Zionist, who first put to the Foreign Office (November 1915) an alternative method of winning over the American Jews to the Entente: should the Allies issue a statement similar to German promises in favor of Jewish national rights in Palestine, it would, he was convinced, counter German moves and elicit pro-British and pro-French sympathies among the Jewish masses.

Independently, a month later, Lucien *Wolf, a journalist and a historian, then secretary of the Conjoint Foreign Committee of the Board of Deputies of British Jews and of the Anglo-Jewish Association, made a similar proposal. Wolf was not a Zionist and deplored the Jewish national movement. But he was too much of a realist to ignore the shift in the balance of power which had taken place since the outbreak of the war. In America, he conceded, Zionism had captured Jewish opinion, and in view of the forthcoming American Jewish Congress he thought it important that "in any bid for Jewish sympathies ... very serious account must be taken of the Zionist movement ... This is the moment for the Allies to declare their policy in regard to Palestine." On March 3, 1916, he suggested a formula as a basis for a public pronouncement.

The Foreign Office was favorably disposed to the idea but had reservations about Wolf's eligibility to be the recipient of such a proclamation. Moreover, doubts later developed as to whether his suggested formula would make a strong enough appeal to Jewish communities all over the world.

While the matter was being considered, a rival proposition came from an unexpected quarter. Its author was Edgar Suarès, a prominent businessman and head of the Jewish community in Alexandria. Should the British government give concrete assurances on the Palestine question, he told Sir Henry McMahon, the High Commissioner in Egypt, it would "convert the indifference, if not hostility of American and other Jews into enthusiastic support." Suarès' scheme followed the familiar Zionist pattern but what made an impact on the Foreign Office, and particularly on Grey, was the allusion to the prospect of a German protectorate in Palestine.

On March 11, 1916, Lord Crewe, who was deputizing for Grey, drafted a cable to the British ambassadors in Paris and Petrograd asking them to sound out the French and the Russian governments about making a joint declaration with regard to Palestine which would satisfy Jewish aspirations. He quoted Wolf's formula but suggested instead a scheme which he thought would be far more attractive to the majority of Jews. It consisted of creating conditions which would enable Jewish settlers in Palestine to grow strong enough to cope with the Arab population and lay the foundation for Jewish self-government. Neither McMahon nor Grey, nor any other member of the Foreign Office, saw any inconsistency between this scheme and the British promise made to Sharif Hussein of Mecca at that time to recognize Arab independence. It was understood that, like Lebanon, Palestine was excluded from the deal.

Against all expectations, Sazonow, the Russian foreign minister, approved of Grey's *aide-mémoire* but Briand, the French premier and foreign minister, gave it its *coup de grâce*. The British gave the French arguments little credence but did not want to irritate their ally at a time when mutual trust was of supreme importance. The idea of a joint declaration was shelved but the need for it did not decrease, especially since German propaganda in the United States was gaining the upper hand. The situation was all the more critical since growing estrangement from England stood in a direct ratio to her increasing financial dependence on the United States. At this juncture, Sir Cecil Spring-Rice, the British ambassador to Washington, remarked: "The Zionist movement is growing in importance and we can well sympathize with it. Perhaps here would be a basis of common action."

With Lloyd George's accession to the premiership in December 1916, British policy in the Middle East altered radically. One of his primary objectives was the acquisition of Palestine. He had advocated its annexation since the outbreak of the war, and to him British and Jewish Palestine were almost synonymous. He had a long-standing interest in Zionism and Samuel's memorandum made a strong appeal to him. It also fitted in well with his strategic and political concepts. He had had no hand in making the *Sykes-Picot Agreement, which he regarded as an inconvenient legacy. The longer the war lasted, the stronger became his determination that Palestine, if recaptured, must be "one and indivisible."

However, the broader aim of Lloyd George's policy was to forestall the possibility of Turco-German predominance in Palestine. Herein lay the *raison dêtre* of the alliance with British Zionism. It provided a way to outmaneuver the French without breaking faith, and a useful card at the future peace conference to play against any German move to rally the German-oriented and Turcophile Jews to buttress her claim.

Late in 1916 the British began to suspect that Germany was bent on an aggressive course in the East. Events lent support to this suspicion. The resounding defeat of Serbia by the German army and Bulgaria's adherence to the Central Powers virtually opened the road from Hamburg to Baghdad. A German foothold on the eastern bank of the Suez Canal would have placed British imperial communications in grave jeopardy. In these circumstances destruction of the Ottoman Empire became an unavoidable necessity. It was also essential that Palestine come under sole British control. Samuel's thesis, expounded in his memoranda of January and March 1915, was now fully vindicated.

However, British strategic requirements clashed with the principle of non-annexation enunciated by President *Wilson and upheld by the Provisional Government in Russia. It constituted the most serious threat to British war aims. Henceforth, one of the greatest dilemmas of British diplomacy was how to achieve its desiderata without giving offense to its allies. This could be done only by marriage with the principle of self-determination. It was here that the importance of Zionism, as far as Palestine was concerned, came in. It provided a cloak under which Britain could appear free from any annexationist taint. The anti-Turkish crusade was essentially negative in nature, and as such could hardly commend itself to American and Russian opinion; but, when clothed in the ideological garb of struggle for the liberation of small nationalities, it acquired a different aspect.

The first step, which was to lead to a compact with Zionism, was taken by Sir Mark *Sykes, a leading expert on the East and a signatory to the Agreement with his French opposite number, François-Georges Picot. His conversion to Zionism was of particular importance. In January 1917 Lloyd George promoted him to the key position of assistant secretary to the war cabinet and delegated authority in Middle Eastern affairs to him. With his status enhanced he was in a position to play a major role in shaping British policy in that part of the world. His crucial meeting with the Zionist leaders, which included Rabbi Moses *Gaster, Lord Rothschild, Herbert Samuel, Harry Sacher, as well as Sokolow and Weizmann, took place on February 7, 1917. He heard from them what he had expected. The common denominator in the spectrum of their views was the desire for a British protectorate of Palestine. This played directly into his hands. He remained silent about the agreement reached with Picot and Sazonow in Petrograd in March 1916, but pointed to possible difficulties from France. He thought it would be useful if the Zionists appointed a representative to discuss the matter with them. The representative chosen to put the Zionist point of view to Picot, then in London, and subsequently to the Quai d'Orsay, was Sokolow. In the meantime, quite independently, the French government had changed its policy drastically and, when Sokolow arrived in Paris, he was told that France took a sympathetic interest in Jewish national aspirations, which, however, could be sanctioned only if France had a rightful share in the administration of Palestine. Nonetheless, Sykes considered it a step in the right direction. Thereafter, Sykes paved the way for Sokolow's visit to the Vatican. On May 1, he was received by Cardinal Gasparri, the papal secretary of state, who reassured him that the Zionists need fear no opposition from the Church. "On the contrary, you may count on our sympathy." Pope Benedict XV expressed himself in even warmer terms. "The return of the Jews to Palestine is a miraculous event. It is providential; God has willed it … I believe that we shall be good neighbors."

Sokolow's success did not go unnoticed by the Italian government and on May 8, Di Martino, the secretary-general of the Foreign Ministry, handed Sokolow an official declaration of sympathy with Zionist aspirations. Nor did the French government remain a passive onlooker. On June 4 Jules Cambon, the secretary-general of the French Foreign Ministry, gave Sokolow a letter which for the Zionists constituted a political victory of the highest order. The Italian and French declarations enabled the British to follow suit. Had the French government objected, as it did in 1916, there would have been no Balfour Declaration.

Another factor that told strongly in the Zionists' favor was the situation in Russia. Since April there were growing indications that Russia was drifting out of the war. Particularly disturbing was the demand by the Council of Workers' and Soldiers' Deputies for the early conclusion of peace. Russia's collapse or the conclusion of peace would have transformed the whole strategic situation and the moral effect would have been devastating. Propaganda therefore was badly needed but the British were handicapped in getting their message through. Anglophobia was deep-seated under the czarist regime. Nor did the March Revolution improve the situation. The Russians had an ingrained dislike of outside interference and Lloyd George's message to Prince Lvov enjoining the Russian people to strengthen their resolve in preventing the war failed to achieve the desired effect. This helps explain why the Zionists were *personae gratae* at the Foreign Office. In return for meeting their wishes, they could produce in Russia and elsewhere an army of voluntary propagandists, all the more effective since they had the obvious advantage of being citizens of their respective countries. Russian Jews disliked the war. It was not of their choosing and they had nothing to gain from its continuation. Both for political and economic reasons they were inclined more towards Germany than to England, but recognition of their rights in Palestine might make all the difference. Not only would it immunize them against German-inspired pacifist propaganda but their influence in the press and public life could be brought to bear. The military campaign in Palestine would be presented as an act of liberation and Britain's presence there linked to the principle of self-determination. Moreover, having a close interest in the success of Allied arms, they would be all the more eager to support the moderate element in the Provisional Government against the extremists and, considering the precarious balance of power within the coalition, this was not without significance.

After the March Revolution the position of Russian Jews, 5,000,000 strong, was transformed. The abolition of civic disabilities released tremendous sources of vitality which became manifest in all fields of cultural and political activity. Although they comprised only four percent of the total population, their influence far exceeded their numerical strength.

The most influential party in post-revolutionary Russia was the Zionist party. Its rise was spectacular. The number of enrolled members, which before the war amounted to 25,000, rose steeply in the spring of 1917 to 140,000. By the beginning of 1918 there were 1,200 registered local Zionist societies all over the country with 300,000 active members. The elections to an All-Jewish Congress held in Southern Russia showed that the Zionist movement enjoyed overwhelming support within the Russian Jewish community. These figures say nothing of those outside the movement, who by tradition and sentiment were attached to Palestine. British Military Intelligence estimated that "the great mass of the 6,000,000 Jews in Russia have been more or less in sympathy with the Zionist cause." Jehiel *Tschlenow was not exaggerating when, in his inaugural address to the Zionist Conference in Petrograd on June 6, 1917, he stated that Zionism had become a mass movement and as such, in a free country, was a formidable political factor.

In the United States, too, the Zionist movement had made much headway. Louis D. *Brandeis' leadership transformed it from a parochial organization into a significant force in Jewish communal life. One of its greatest assets was Woodrow Wilson, the president of the United States, who had come to believe that the Zionist program would help solve the Jewish question and had promised to lend his support to implement it.

In April 1917, when Balfour visited the United States, he thought it important to meet Brandeis, Palestinian policy being one of the subjects on which Balfour intended to explore American feeling. The broader aim of Balfour's mission was to prepare the ground for full Anglo-American co-operation and stimulate goodwill. He was fully aware that Brandeis' position in the President's Council might well facilitate friendship between the two countries. His meetings with Brandeis, both private and official (May 1), were rewarding. He gave Brandeis firm assurances of support for the Zionist cause but thought that the moment was not ripe to make a public pronouncement as Brandeis wished him to do.

International complexities apart, there was another difficulty that hindered Balfour from issuing an official statement. Aware of the strong opposition to Zionism among influential Jews, he was wary of antagonizing them. It was not before the controversy was resolved in the Zionists' favor at a meeting of the Board of Deputies on June 17 and the dissolution of the Conjoint Foreign Committee that the British government could move freely on the road to a public declaration.

The episode became a *cause célèbre* in Anglo-Jewish history. It resulted from mutual misunderstanding. The assimilationists feared that the recognition of Jews as a separate nationality would cause their alienation in the lands of their domicile and would play into the hands of antisemites. It was based on an erroneous assumption and was caused by misreading the term "nationality," mistaking conformity for civic loyalty.

On the other hand, the Zionists were guilty of indiscretions which tended to magnify their opponents' suspicions. Sensible enough to restrict the application of the concept of Jewish nationality to Palestine, they blundered in not making those most concerned aware of their thinking. A timely gesture might well have averted the crisis. With their diplomatic status in the spring of 1917 elevated, they chose to go it alone in their dealings with the British government. But since the agreement between the Conjoint Committee and the Foreign Office was still in force, such tactics could not lead them far. It is indeed doubtful whether the British government would have ventured to issue a declaration of sympathy with Zionism before consulting all sections of the Anglo-Jewish community.

By June it became clear that a public statement by the British government could no longer be delayed. For some time the German press, ranging from the Conservative *Reichsbote* to the Liberal *Frankfurter Zeitung*, had been urging the Reich government to show a more accommodating attitude to the Zionist movement. On June 12 Weizmann called on Sir Ronald Graham, the under-secretary of state for foreign affairs, and told him that he had received some disquieting information. For Zionism to fall under German influence would have been a serious blow to his efforts to anchor the movement firmly to Britain, particularly at a time when it was emerging as a leading force in the Jewish world. He insisted that it was essential for the British government to counter German moves and give public expression of its sympathy and support.

On June 19, Balfour invited Lord Rothschild and Weizmann to submit a draft proposal for a declaration of support. However, a month elapsed before they were able to forward a text to Balfour. Members of the Political Committee were remarkably modest in their claims. They refrained from using the words "Jewish state," on which some radical members like Harry Sacher insisted, and hit upon the more moderate "Jewish National Home." It originated in the *Heimstaette* of the Basle Program to which in November 1916 Sokolow prefixed the word "national." It was this word that infuriated leading British Jews so much. A term "home" or even "state" would have been less objectionable since such an entity would in no way have interfered with the loyalty of Jews outside Palestine.

After the dissolution of the Conjoint Foreign Committee, the attack was led by Edwin Montagu, a leading Jewish anti-Zionist who was secretary of state for India. The Zionist draft proposal filled him with horror. His memorandum, "The Antisemitism of the Present Government (August 23, 1917)," was the first in his campaign to suppress the proposed declaration. None of his memoranda convinced the cabinet. Ronald MacNeill, MP, subsequently under-secretary of state for foreign affairs, dismissed his views as unrepresentative and erroneous. However, in order to still his opposition and speed up the publication of the declaration, Leopold Amery (a member of the war cabinet secretariat) inserted (on October 3, 1917) two provisos. The first was to safeguard the rights of the native Moslem and Christian communities and protect them against possible dispossession; the word "in" (the national home was to be established "in Palestine") was the operative word intended to insure against the imposition of Jewish domination on other inhabitants of Palestine. The purpose of the second proviso was to dispel the misconception that Jews *qua* Jews, irrespective of their convictions and place of domicile, "belonged to Palestine" and owed allegiance to the National Home. The provisos, however, as Amery recorded, "gave away nothing that was not self-evident," and were not meant to impair the substance of the proposed declaration.

The Balfour Declaration

"His Majesty's Government view with favour the establishment in Palestine of a national home for the Jewish people, and will use their best endeavours to facilitate the achievement of this object, it being clearly understood that nothing shall be done which may prejudice the civil and religious rights of existing non-Jewish communities in Palestine, or the rights and political status enjoyed by Jews in any other country."

Brandeis was instrumental in convincing President Wilson to approve the proposed draft, whereas Sir Mark Sykes demolished Lord Curzon's contention that Zionism was "a dream incapable of realization." He pointed to the success of the Zionist colonization and felt certain that, given the proper conditions, the population in Palestine could be doubled within seven years without dispossessing anyone.

Sykes drew his information from Aaron *Aaronsohn, who, on October 1, had arrived in London. Both the War Office and the Foreign Office had a high opinion of his contribution to Military Intelligence and his presence weighed heavily in the Zionists' favor. Sykes did not flatter him unduly when acknowledging his share in Allenby's victory.

By October the news that the German government had begun to consider Zionism seriously instilled a sense of urgency in the Foreign Office and the cabinet. The British press was also clamoring for action. With the anti-Zionists' arguments defeated, Balfour was able, on October 31, to wind up the debate in the war cabinet, which had lasted for two months. None of the members present (Montagu was away in India) contested his motives for publishing the declaration in favor of the establishment of the Jewish National Home in Palestine. Nor did anyone disagree with his interpretation of its meaning. On November 2, 1917 a letter signed by Balfour was sent to Lord Rothschild but was made public only on November 9 so that it could be first published in the *Jewish Chronicle.*

The enthusiastic response to the Balfour Declaration among Jewish communities all over the world, especially in Russia, made the Foreign Office staff regret that the document had not been published earlier. Sir Ronald Graham, who throughout the latter part of 1917, had pressed unremittingly for an early statement, minuted: "It is a misfortune that our declaration was so long delayed." Belated as it was, London was still to reap some notable advantages from it. Zionism helped to legitimize Britain's position in Palestine, which otherwise would have been based solely on military conquest. Britain acquired a friendly base in Palestine and massive popularity among Jews everywhere.

BIBLIOGRAPHY: *The Letters and Papers of Chaim Weizmann*, vol. 8, Series A (1977); Ch. Weizmann, *Trial and Error* (1977); L. Stein, *The Balfour Declaration* (1961); M. Vereté, "*The Balfour Declaration and Its Makers*," in: Middle Eastern Studies (Jan. 1970); I. Friedman, *The Question of Palestine*, 1914–1918. *British-Jewish-Arab Relations* (1973, 1992[2]).

[Isaiah Friedman (2nd ed.)]

BALFOURIYYAH (Heb. בַּלְפוּרִיָּה), moshav in the Jezreel Valley, Israel. The settlement was founded on Nov. 2, 1922, north of Afulah, on land owned by the American Zionist Commonwealth Federation. Some of the founders were immigrants from the United States, the others from Eastern Europe. Balfouriyyah's economy was based on field and garden crops, cattle, and poultry. In 2002 the population was 287. The moshav's name refers to the date of its founding which was the fifth anniversary of the *Balfour Declaration.

[Efraim Orni]

BALI, ABRAHAM BEN JACOB (second half of the 15th to the beginning of the 16th century), Karaite author and physician living in Turkey. Bali was a pupil of the Rabbanite R. Shabbetai b. Malchiel ha-Kohen. Although disagreeing with the Rabbanites, Bali refers with respect to the contemporary Rabbanite scholars Mordecai *Comtino, Moses ha-Yevani Capuzato, and Solomon "Sharvit ha-Zahav" in his works. Most of them survived in manuscripts kept in various libraries. They include *Iggeret Issur Ner Shabbat*, upholding the Karaite prohibition against burning lights on the Sabbath (contrary to the reform introduced by Elijah *Bashyazi; non-critical print, Ashdod 2002); *Iggeret ha-Kohanim*, on the status of Rabbanites of priestly descent who become Karaites; *Perush Inyan Sheḥitah*, a commentary on the chapter dealing with ritual slaughter in *Aaron b. Elijah of Nicomedia's *Gan Eden* (non-critical print, Ashdod 2003); a commentary on al-*Ghazālī's *Maqāṣid al-Falāsifa*, in which Bali used a Hebrew translation of it and followed the commentary of Moses Narboni, which he much admired; and *Perush al Ḥamishah Perakim min ha-Haysharah le-Abu Nasr,* a commentary on the first five chapters of al-*Fārābī's *Logic*, translated into Hebrew under the title *Iggeret le-Petiḥat Sifrei ha-Higgayon*.

BIBLIOGRAPHY: Mann, Texts, 2 (1935), 1420; Danon, in: JQR, 15 (1924/25), 312–3; Steinschneider, in: HB, 20 (1880), 96–97; A. Neubauer, *Beitraege und Documente Zur Geschichte desKaraeertums* (1866); J. Gurland, *Ginzei Yisrael* (St. Petersburg, 1886); J-C. Attias, *Le commentaire biblique: Mordekhai Komtino ou l'hermeneutique du dialogue* (Paris, 1991), index.

[Isaak Dov Ber Markon]

BALI, MOSES BEN ABRAHAM, Karaite poet, physician, and *ḥakham* in Cairo in the late 15th and early 16th centuries. Two volumes of his liturgical poems have been preserved in the *Firkovich collection in Leningrad: the first, *Sefer Zeraḥ*, completed in 1489, consists of 224 *piyyutim* arranged in the order of the weekly lessons; the second, *Taḥkemoni*, contains 237 *piyyutim* for Sabbaths and festivals.

BIBLIOGRAPHY: Fuerst, Karaeertum, 2 (1865), 294; Geiger, in: WZJT, 3 (1837), 443, no. 9–10.

[Isaak Dov Ber Markon]

BALI, RIFAT (1948–), Turkish scholar. Bali was born in Istanbul and graduated from Sorbonne University, Ecole Pratique des Hautes Etudes. His fields of expertise are antisemitism, conspiracy theories, relations between the Turkish state and the non-Muslim minorities, the Jews in the Republican period, and the appearance of the new bourgeoisie in Turkey after 1980. His works include: *Cumhuriyet Yıllarında Türkiye Yahudileri Bir Türkleştirme Serüveni, 1923–1945* (1999); *Musa'nın Evlatları Cumhuriyet'in Yurttaşları* (2001), *Les Relations entre Turcs et Juifs dans La Turquie Moderne* (2001), *Tarz-ı Hayat'tan Life Style'a* (2002), *Cumhuriyet Yıllarında Türkiye Yahudileri, Aliya Bir Toplu Göçün Öyküsü, 1946–1949* (2003), *Devlet'in Yahudileri ve 'Öteki' Yahudi* (2004), *Anadolu'dan Yeni Dünya'ya* (2004), *Türkiye'de Yayımlanmış Yahudilikle İlgili Kitap, Tez ve Makaleler Bibliyografyası 1923–2003* (2004), *Avram Benaroya: Un Journaliste Juif Oublié suivi de ses Mémoires* (2004).

[Jacob M. Landau (2nd ed.)]

BALIDEH (al-Balideh), MOSES (15th century), Yemenite scholar. Balideh was the author of more than ten works on diverse subjects, mostly in the form of commentaries and expositions of rabbinic sayings. With the exception of his Midrash on the last chapter of Proverbs, *Sharḥ Eshet Ḥayil*, all his works are in manuscript in the British Museum (Margoliouth, Cat, no. 1101). Although he enjoyed a distinguished reputation, his works did not achieve wide circulation among Yemenite Jewry and were therefore almost unknown to succeeding generations. They include a commentary on the *Midrash Yelammedenu*, a commentary bearing a marked resemblance to the *Midrash ha-Gadol* in respect to sources, arrangement, and tenor. Balideh wrote a commentary concerning the ten items recounted as having been created on the (first) Sabbath at twilight (Avot 5:6) in addition to commentaries on some works of Maimonides.

BIBLIOGRAPHY: Ratzaby, in: KS, 28 (1952/53), 260, 263, 268, 277–8; Y.L. Naḥum, *Mi-Ẓefunot Yehudei Teiman* (1962), 206–22.

[Yehuda Ratzaby]

BALIN, MARTY (**Martyn Buchwald**; 1942–), U.S. singer and songwriter. Born in Cincinnati, Ohio, the young Balin and his family moved to San Francisco in 1948. Balin founded the seminal Bay Area rock group Jefferson Airplane (1965–71). In 1975, Balin re-formed the band under the new name of Jefferson Starship and immediately had a top-of-the-chart album, *Red Octopus.* He became president of the Great Pyramid Ltd. and owner of Diamondback Music Co.

Balin's distinctive, soulful voice became one of the hallmarks of the Airplane/Starship's sound, and he composed many of the band's most memorable songs, including "It's No Secret" (1966), "Plastic Fantastic Lover" (1967), "Young Girls" (1968), "Sunday Blues" (1969), "Volunteers" (1970), and Jefferson Starship's biggest hit, "Miracles" (1975).

Balin left the group in 1978, writing the rock opera *Rock Justice,* a fantasy about a rock star on trial for not having a hit. He then began a solo career with his 1981 album *Balin*, which generated the singles "Hearts" and "Atlanta Lady." After issuing *Lucky* in 1983, he joined former bandmates Paul Kantner and Jack Casady to form the KBC Band (1985–87). In 1989, all three participated in a Jefferson Airplane reunion, which yielded a new studio album and tour. In 1991, Balin issued *Better Generation* and two years later joined Kantner's Jefferson Starship – The Next Generation project, concurrently continuing his solo career with his 1997 album *Freedom Flight*. Balin's 1999 album *Marty Balin's Greatest Hits* was a compilation of re-recordings of past favorites.

With nine platinum and three gold records to his credit, Balin was inducted into the Rock & Roll Hall of Fame, and "Miracles" was inducted into BMI's Millionaires Club, having been played more than 2.7 million times.

Besides being a recording artist, Balin is a painter as well. His artwork depicts many of the musicians with whom he shared the stage, such as Janis Joplin, Jimmy Hendrix, Elton John, Jerry Garcia, John Lennon, Kiss, Bob Marley, and Grace Slick, as well his idols Otis Redding, Robert Johnson, and Jerry Lee Lewis. In 1999 his exhibit "World of Rock & Roll Legends" toured art galleries in the U.S.

[Jonathan Licht / Ruth Beloff (2nd ed.)]

BALINT, MICHAEL (1896–1970), psychoanalyst. Born Mihaly Maurice Bergmann in Budapest, the son of a physician, he changed his name to Michael Balint against his father's wishes. He also changed religion, from Judaism to Unitarian Christianity. In the 1930s Balint settled in Manchester, England, moving to London in 1945.

Balint devoted a lifetime of research and practice to the development of psychoanalysis as a science. Entering the field while it was still young and taking on form, Balint spent much time studying psychoanalytic technique as well as the patient's response to various forms of therapy. This work is discussed in his books *The Doctor, His Patient, and the Illness* (1957) and *Psychotherapeutic Techniques in Medicine* (1961). Balint also devoted much research to understanding the mechanisms of human sexuality, concentrating in large part on sexual perversions and their relation to neurotic and psychotic symptoms. In addition to writing *Problems of Human Pleasure and Behavior* (1957), he edited many anthologies on the subject of sexuality. In 1968 he was elected president of the British Psychoanalytical Society.

The Balint Society was founded in 1969 to continue the work begun by Balint in the 1950s. The aim of the society is to help general practitioners attain a better understanding of the emotional content of the doctor-patient relationship. The Balint method consists of regular case discussion in small groups under the guidance of a qualified group leader. Their objective is to reveal feelings unwittingly harbored by the doctor towards his or her patient, usually engendered by purely subjective factors, which interfere with the doctor's approach to a patient, thus jeopardizing not only the patient but also blurring or blinding the doctor's mind with regard to proper diagnostic procedures and further treatment. Balint societies have been formed in a number of countries. In 1972 the first international Balint conference was held in London.

[Maurice Goldsmith / Ruth Beloff (2nd ed.)]

BALKH, town in northern Afghanistan (within medieval Khurasan). Balkh was formerly the stronghold of Jewish settlements in Afghanistan. According to Persian and Muslim traditions, it was founded after the destruction of Jerusalem by Nebuchadnezzar (586 B.C.E.), who is said to have settled the exiled Jews there. It was to Balkh, according to Muslim tradition, that the prophet Jeremiah fled, and where the prophet Ezekiel was buried. According to the Muslim historian al-Ṭabarī, another Jewish prophet with the unidentifiable name of SMY conducted religious disputations with Zoroaster in Balkh. Reference by Arab geographers to a *Bāb al-Yahūd* (Gate of Jews) in Balkh, and to *"al-Yahūdiyya"* ("Jewish territory" or "Jewish town") provide additional evidence that a large Jewish settlement existed there. The name *al-Yahūdiyya* or *al-Yahūdān-al Kubrā* (the Great Jewry) was, however, later euphemistically changed to *al-Maymana* (the 'auspicious' town) since the term *"al-Yahūdiyya"* was rejected by the Muslims. It was at Balkh that the sectarian *Hiwi al-Balkhī was born in the ninth century. The Jews of Balkh were forced to maintain a public garden. Maḥmūd of Ghazna (1034) imposed special taxes on the Jews of the town, stipulating, however, that not more than 500 *dirham* should be accepted from them. The Jewish community continued well into the 13th century, when a Jewish merchant from Balkh named Khawāja Rashīd al-Dīn al-Ḥakīm went from Khurasan to India. However, the community was evidently destroyed during the Mongol invasions.

BIBLIOGRAPHY: Frye, in: EIS2, 1 (1960), 1000–02 (includes bibliography).

[Walter Joseph Fischel]

BALLAGI (formerly **Bloch**), **MÓR** (1815–1891), linguist and theologian. Born in Inocz, Hungary, he attended yeshivot and studied mathematics at Pest, continuing in Paris and Tuebingen. In 1843 he became a Protestant. During the Hungarian revolution in 1848, Ballagi served as secretary to General Görgey. He taught Hebrew, Greek, and biblical exegesis at the theological academy of the Reformed Church at Kecskemét from 1851, and in Pest from 1855 to 1877. While still a Jew Ballagi published a monograph, *A zsidókról* (1840), advocating the emancipation of Hungarian Jewry and the establishment of a rabbinical college. He translated into Hungarian the Hebrew prayer book (1841), the Pentateuch (1840–41), and the Book of Joshua (1842), and wrote a primer of the Hebrew language, *A héber nyelv elemi tankönyve* (1856; 2nd edition revised by Ignaz Goldziher in 1872), *Renaniana* (Hg., 1864), and biblical studies (*Bibliai tanulmányok*, 2 vols., 1865). Ballagi also compiled a dictionary of the Hungarian language, and published a Hungarian-German, German-Hungarian dictionary.

BIBLIOGRAPHY: S. Imre, *Emlékbeszéd Ballagi Mór rendes tagról* (1893); S. Csekey, *Budapesti Református Theológiai Akadémia története* (1955); Scheiber, in: *Református Egyház*, 7 (1955), 520.

[Alexander Scheiber]

BALLARAT, country town in Central Victoria, Australia. After the gold rush in 1851 a number of Jews went to Ballarat and in 1853 there was a *minyan* on the gold fields on the High Holidays and in 1859 there were 347 male Jews in the town. A Jew, Charles Dyte, took a leading part in the diggers' revolt in 1854 (known as the Eureka Stockade) against unjust government licensing. Later he became mayor of Ballarat. In 1855 a small synagogue was dedicated, the congregational president being Henry Harris. D. Isaacs was first minister, *shoḥet*, and teacher, followed in 1864 by S. Herman, I.M. Goldreich (1868), B. Lenzer (1905), M. Rosenthal (1922), L. Goren (1926), and Z. Mandelbaum (the last resident rabbi of Ballarat who ministered until 1942). A more commodious building, including rooms for a minister's residence and a Hebrew day school, was erected on land granted by the government in 1861. A *mikveh* was built and a burial plot consecrated. A Philanthropic Society, founded in 1857, was affiliated with the *Anglo-Jewish Association. In 1908 the congregation separated into two factions and the Central Hebrew Congregation was formed, with M. Levy as minister, but lasted only four years. In these early days Ballarat was regarded as the center of Orthodox Judaism in Australia.

Two Ballarat Jews achieved distinction in the arts: Nathan Spielvogel, a well-known short-story writer, and Abbey Alston, an artist whose works are found in most Australian national galleries. With the drift to Melbourne, the Ballarat community declined. In 1969 the Jewish population had dwindled to about 10–15 families. By the early 21st century a few families remained, as well as a historic Orthodox synagogue, open on High Holidays. Sovereign Hill, a popular local tourist attraction featuring a village from the Gold Rush era, includes Emanuel Steinfeld's Furniture Factory, an authentic recreation of the business of a prominent Jewish pioneer.

BIBLIOGRAPHY: N.F. Spielvogel, in: *Australian Jewish Historical Society*, 1, pt. 3 (1940), 92–94; 1, pt. 6 (1941), 206–7; 2, pt. 6 (1946), 350–8; L.E. Fredman, *ibid.*, 4, pt. 5 (1956), 279–80; L.M. Goldman, *ibid.*, 4 pts. 7 and 8 (1958), 440–1, 452–3, 459–60, 465–6, 477–8; D.J. Benjamin, *ibid.*, 4, pt. 3 (1960), 134. **ADD. BIBLIOGRAPHY:** H.L. Rubinstein, *The Jews in Victoria, 1835–1985* (1986), index.

[Shmuel Gorr]

BALLAS, SHIMON (1930–), Israeli writer. Born in Baghdad, Iraq, Ballas immigrated to Israel in 1951 without any knowledge of Hebrew. Like his colleague Sami *Michael, Ballas had been close to the Iraqi Communist Party and was not particularly interested in Zionist ideology. He began his literary career in Israel with the local Arab press and later spent four years in Paris, where he earned his Ph.D. from the Sorbonne. He is the author of a comprehensive study called "Arab Literature under the Shadow of War" (1978; French translation 1980) and taught Arab Literature at the University of Haifa. His first Hebrew novel, *Ha-Ma'abarah* ("The Transit Camp," 1964), is one of the first Hebrew novels to shed light on the harsh realities, tensions, and struggle for power in an immigrant settlement in Israel of the 1950s. This realistically narrated story was followed by novels and collections of stories. Among these are *Ḥoref Aḥaron* ("Last Winter," 1984), relating the experiences of a founding member of the Egyptian Communist Party who lives as an exile in Paris; *Ve-Hu Aḥer* ("And He is Different," 1991), depicting the fate of three protagonists in Iraq under a ruthless tyrant: the dictator's historian, a Jew who converted to Islam; a Communist; and an Arab-Jewish poet who later emigrates to Israel. The novel *Solo* (1998), set in Paris during the notorious *Dreyfus affair, is the story of an Egyptian-Jewish dramatist who fights for the independence of his homeland. Among his other prose works are the novels *Lo bi-Mekomah* ("Not in Her Place," 1994) and *Tel Aviv Mizraḥ* ("Tel Aviv East," 2003). The collections of stories include among others *Mul ha-Ḥomah* ("Facing the Wall," 1969) and *Otot Setav* ("Signs of Autumn," 1992). The stories in the latter collection are set – typically for Ballas – in Baghdad, Paris, and Tel Aviv: "Aya" tells of a Moslem nanny bidding farewell to the Jewish family for which she had worked; "Otot Setav" focuses on the complex identity of an old Egyptian intellectual torn between cultures. Ballas consciously abstains from Oriental exoticism and nostalgia. An English translation of "The Shoes of Tanboury" appeared in 1970.

BIBLIOGRAPHY: G. Shaked, *Ha-Sipporet ha-Ivrit*, 4 (1993), 166–87); N. Zach, in: *Haaretz* (May 17, 1991). Y. Orian, in: *Yedioth Ahronoth* (Jan. 16, 1981); E. Ben Ezer, "Through the Keyhole: S. Ballas' *A Locked Room*," in: *Modern Hebrew Literature* 7:1–2 (1981/1982), 28–30; I. Taha, "*Otot Setav be-Aviv Sifruti Na'eh*," in: *Alei Si'aḥ*, 34 (1994), 85–94; M. Yahil-Waks, "*Ha-Emdah ha-Shelishit*," in: *Itton*, 77, 92 (1987), 18–21; R. Snir, "'We Were like Those Who Dream'": Iraqi-Jewish Writers in Israel in the 1950s," in: *Prooftexts*, 11:2 (1991), 153–73; I. Taha, "Duality and Acceptance: The Image of the Outsider in the Literary Work of Shimon Ballas," in: *Hebrew Studies*, 38 (1997), 63–87; R. Snir, "*Boded be-Mo'ado – S. Ballas ve-Kanon ha-Sifrut ha-Ivrit*," In: *Itton* 77, 218 (1998), 16–21; H. Hever, "*Kinun Zehut bein Sippur le-Mapah: S. Ballas ba-Sipporet ha-Yisra'elit bi-Shenot ha-Shishim*," in: *Ẓiyyon ve-Ẓiyyonut be-kerev Yehudei Sefarad ve-ha-Mizraḥ* (2002), 561–73.

[Anat Feinberg (2nd ed.)]

BALLIN, ALBERT (1857–1918), German shipping magnate. He was the 13th child of a Danish Jew who settled about 1830 in Hamburg, where he opened a wool-dyeing shop. Later his father established an agency for shipping immigrants, which young Ballin expanded after his father's death. During the large-scale emigration of the 1880s, Ballin, as chief passenger agent for the English Carr Line, adapted the company's vessels for the transportation of steerage passengers. After keen competition with Hapag (the Hamburg–America Line), Germany's leading shipping line, the two companies merged in 1886; Ballin became head of the passenger department and in 1899 he started to lead the company. Hapag rapidly grew into one of the world's foremost shipping lines. This success was due mainly to Ballin's foresight and his setting of new standards of speed and comfort. His capacity for negotiation and compromise enabled him to form the first trans-Atlantic shipping conference, called the North-Atlantic Steamship Lines Association. In 1901 he established the International Mercantile Marine Company, in cooperation with Morgan's shipping interests. Kaiser William II frequently turned to him for counsel on economic matters. Ballin became a behind-the-scenes negotiator. He was one of the few Jews, like Emil *Rathenau and Walther *Rathenau, who could get close to the antisemitic emperor. As an unbaptized Jew he married a Protestant woman. Not being close to the Jewish community of Hamburg he followed the ideal of acculturation as a Jew. Before World War I he failed in his efforts, together with Sir Ernest *Cassel, to create the basis for German-British agreement on naval armaments. In 1914, Ballin undertook the organization of food supplies for the blockaded Reich and set up its central purchasing agency. During the war he remained a moderate in his ideas about "Mitteleuropa" and his plans concerning possible territorial gains by the Reich. These views conflicted with those of the military and reduced his influence with the Kaiser around 1917. In 1918 Ballin was entrusted with negotiations for an armistice and peace preparations. On Nov. 9, revolution broke out in Germany. Kaiser William II fled the country and Ballin – in despair over the collapse of his company and the loss of the monarchy that he admired – presumably committed suicide.

BIBLIOGRAPHY: P.F. Stubmann, *Ballin: Leben und Werk eines deutschen Reeders* (1926, 1927[2], abr. 1957, 1960[3]); L. Cecil, *Albert Ballin: Business and Politics in Imperial Germany 1888–1918* (1967); E. Rosenbaum, Albert Ballin: *A Note on the Style of his Economic and Political Activities*, in: YLBI, 3 (1958), 257–99. *Miscellany* ("…III. A Postscript to the Essay on Albert Ballin," in: YLBI 4 (1959), 267–70; H. Tramer, "Die Hamburger, Kaiserjuden," in: *Bulletin des Leo Baeck Instituts*, 3 (1960), 177–89; R. Hauschild-Thiessen, "Albert Ballin," in: G. Ahrens et al. (eds.), *Die Reeder: Laeisz. Ballin* (1989), 34–68; S. Wiborg, *Albert Ballin*, (2000); E. Straub, *Albert Ballin: Der Reeder des Kaisers* (2001); C. Schoelzel, *Albert Ballin: "Ein Schiffsherr ist's … ein Kaiser neigt sich vor dem jüdischen Mann…"* (2004).

[Joachim O. Ronall / Christian Schoelzel (2nd ed.)]

BALLIN, JOEL (1822–1885), Danish engraver and painter. He was born at Vejle, Jutland, and studied painting in Copenhagen, and engraving at Leipzig and Paris. His first painting was exhibited in 1841. Ballin lived from 1846 in Paris and London where he produced a series of reproductions of the paintings of Ostade and Protais and of some English and French artists. In 1861 he was awarded the gold medal of the Paris Salon. On his return to Denmark in 1883 Ballin was commissioned to engrave the works of prominent Danish artists. His "Procession on Simḥat Torah in the Synagogue of Copenhagen" is owned by the Copenhagen Jewish community.

BIBLIOGRAPHY: *Dansk Biografisk Leksikon*, 2 (1933), 54–55.

[Julius Margolinsky]

BALLIN, MOEGENS (1872–1914), Danish post-impressionist painter. Ballin settled in Paris in 1891. After meeting Jean Verkade, he was active in the Nabi group. In 1892 he went to Italy, where he converted to Catholicism. In 1894 he returned to Copenhagen. In 1943 Danish intellectuals organized a retrospective exhibition of his paintings as a protest against Nazi policies.

BALLIN, SAMUEL JACOB (1802–1866), Danish physician, best known for his efforts to combat Asiatic cholera. Born and educated in Copenhagen, he was early recognized as an expert in the treatment of Asiatic cholera and in 1831–32 traveled abroad by royal order to study the disease further. His published findings became a valuable source of information concerning the disease. During the great cholera epidemic in Copenhagen (1853) he was appointed chief physician of the cholera hospital and a member of the Board of Health. In honor of his achievements, he was appointed a member of the Royal Medical Society and given a professorship. Ballin was an active member of the National Liberal Party and an enthusiastic supporter of a Scandinavian union. Ballin was physician of the Jewish community for a number of years.

[Nathan Koren]

BALLMER, STEVE (1956–), U.S. business executive. As the first business manager hired by Bill Gates at the Microsoft Corporation, Ballmer, over 25 years with the computer giant, rose to become chief executive officer. In the process, he became one of the richest Jews in the world.

Steven Anthony Ballmer was born in Detroit, Michigan, the son of a Ford Motor Company employee. Shy as a child, he remembered hyperventilating before heading off to Hebrew school. His mother studied Hebrew with him. A scholarship student at Detroit Country Day School, he turned out to be a whiz in math, ranking in the top 10 among high school students on a statewide test. Thus he was able to fulfill his Protestant Swiss-born father's dream, a Harvard education. There he got his start as a leader, as manager of the football team, the student newspaper, the *Harvard Crimson*, and the literary magazine. It was at Harvard that Ballmer met Gates; they lived at opposite ends of a dormitory floor. Their shared passions for math and science brought them together.

In 1980 Gates persuaded Ballmer to drop out of Stanford University's business school to help run a fledgling Microsoft that was growing so fast it was nearly out of control. Gates valued Ballmer's management experience at Procter & Gamble, where he had helped market Duncan Hines cake mixes. Microsoft was then grossing $12.5 million in annual sales and had 43 employees. After taking over Windows in 1984, Ballmer drove engineers relentlessly to meet a launch deadline. But when Windows 1.0 was released, it flopped. It took Ballmer six more years to produce Windows 3.1, which took the world by storm. Ballmer played a classic role in tech start-ups: "He was the bottom-line–oriented grown-up," an article in the *New York Times* said, "who freed the computer nerds to focus on writing code." Gates was the code writer, Ballmer the hard-driving, charismatic, behind-the-scenes tactician, the arm twister and deal closer. Ballmer, and Microsoft, were highly competitive, and Ballmer was intimately involved in the company's tough tactics. In 2000, at the age of 43, Ballmer became executive vice president of sales and support, where he drove all activities related to Microsoft's sales, support, and marketing, and president, responsible for broadening the leadership of the company and positioning it to take advantage of future growth opportunities. But Ballmer also became known for his blunt, aggressive style. By 2002, Microsoft had a stock market valuation of $250 billion, and Ballmer was one of the leading businessmen in the world. He was also instrumental in making more than 10,000 Microsoft employees millionaires through stock options. According to F.A. Maxwell's biography, which was unauthorized, Ballmer "didn't turn his back on his Jewish heritage, even when doing so might have benefited him."

[Stewart Kampel (2nd ed.)]

BALLY, DAVICION (1809–1884), merchant and banker, a leader of the Sephardi community of Bucharest and its president for some time and a fighter for emancipation. Bally, who was self-educated, promoted *Haskalah among Sephardi Jewry in Romania, tending to favor assimilation into Romanian culture. In 1836 he was appointed treasurer of the police, a position which he held on an honorary basis for ten years; at the same time he was sympathetic to the national revolutionary movement in Walachia. Bally called for administrative reforms in the Sephardi community and for new methods of educating Jewish youth. In 1861, when a boys' school was founded in the Sephardi community of Bucharest, Bally was appointed president of the executive committee. He emphasized the study of Romanian in the community school and also proposed the establishment of an educational framework for girls. However, his proposals and reforms encountered strong opposition; some were not accepted at all, while the remainder were short-lived. Bally fought against antisemitism and published articles in defense of the Jews in the press; as a result of his intervention the governor (*Caimacam*) of Walachia withdrew a sharply anti-Jewish work from circulation in 1858. When anti-Jewish policy was enforced after 1866 by the government led by the former revolutionaries of 1848, Bally unsuccessfully attempted to influence them to abandon it. In 1882 Bally went to Ereẓ Israel to spend his last years there and died in Jerusalem.

ADD. BIBLIOGRAPHY: I. Massof, *Davicion Bally, revolutionarul de la 1848* (1935?); A. Niculescu, *Aux raciness de la democratie en Roumanie: "Pruncul Roman" (= L'Enfant Roumaine), premier journal libre roumain, chronique de la revolution valaque de 1848*, 1 (2002), 325–57.

[Eliyahu Feldman / Lucian-Zeev Herscovici (2nd ed.)]

BALLY, ISAAC DAVID (1842–1922), Romanian rabbi and educator, son of the banker Davicion *Bally. Born in Bucharest, Bally received a traditional Jewish Sephardi education together with a modern one. He later studied at the Rabbinical Seminary of Breslau and was ordained as a rabbi. He was influenced by the ideas of Rabbi Zacharias *Frankel and attempted to apply them to the Sephardi and general Jewish milieu of Romania. Bally also received a doctor of philosophy degree from Breslau University. After returning to Bucharest he taught Jewish religion and Hebrew language and became the principal of the modern girls' school of the Sephardi community and secretary of the Ḥevra Kaddisha Association of the Sephardi Jews. Because of his dual cultural background – Sephardi and Ashkenazi – he could serve institutions associated with both communities for the good of all Romanian Jews. In 1881 he became secretary of the "Infratirea Zion" Association, which later became *B'nai B'rith. In 1886 the Julius Barasch Jewish Historical Society was founded in his home and he became its librarian and treasurer. In these offices he fought for the emancipation of the Romanian Jews and for their return to Jewish life. In 1882–85 he published five textbooks on Judaism in the Romanian language for pupils of Jewish schools. Bally also published popular books on *halakhah* (marriage and family purity) and Jewish history for Romanian-speaking Jews, manuals of biblical Hebrew, and a manual of Judeo-Spanish for Sephardi Jewish children. He also published a translation and commentary in Romanian on the Passover Haggadah (1902). Some of his didactic and moralistic works remained unpublished.

BIBLIOGRAPHY: R. Siniol, *Portrete si schite sefarde* (1981), 95–101; L.Z. Herscovici, in: SAHIR, 8 (2003), 25–59.

[Lucian-Zeev Herscovici (2nd ed.)]

BALMES, ABRAHAM BEN MEIR DE (c. 1440–1523), physician, philosopher, translator, and grammarian. His grandfather, also called Abraham de Balmes (d. 1489), mentioned repeatedly in the royal records between 1463 and 1480, was court physician to King Ferdinand I of Naples (1472). Balmes was born in Lecce, southern Italy, and obtained doctorates in medicine and philosophy at the University of Naples in 1492 by special permission of Pope Innocent VIII. In 1510 when the Jews were expelled from Naples, Balmes appears to have gone to northern Italy. Later he became personal physician to Cardinal Domenico Grimani, who was deeply interested in Hebrew literature. Under Grimani's auspices, Balmes translated the works of a number of medieval Arabic authors from their Hebrew versions into Latin. These included the *Liber de Mundo* (On the Quadrant) of Ibn al-Hayham (11th century), the *Epistola expeditionis* based on a philosophical work by Avempace, Geminus' work on astronomy under the title "Introduction to Ptolemy's Almagest," *Averroes' "Epitome of Aristotle's Organon," "Middle Commentary on the Topics," and on "Sophistical Refutation," part of *De Substantia Orbis*, and logical questions by Averroes and other Arabic authors. The translation of the "Long Commentary on Aristotle's Posterior Analytics" published in Venice about 1520 seems to have been part of a more ambitious project which was to have included, besides other versions, an original philosophical work of his own (*Liber de demonstratione Abrami de Balmes*), no longer extant. Balmes' Averroistic materials were incorporated in the standard 16th-century edition of Aristotle, published in Venice in 1560. The Christian printer Daniel *Bomberg urged Balmes to write his famous Hebrew grammar *Mikneh Avram*. This appeared together with a Latin translation entitled *Peculium Abramae* in Venice at the end of 1523, some months after the author's death. The final chapter (on biblical accent marks) was completed by a fellow physician, Kalonymus b. David. In this work Balmes relied upon the grammarians *Ibn Janaḥ and Profiat *Duran. He mentioned Plato's *Cratylus* (which deals with semantics) – an indication of his interest in the philological conceptions of the Greek philosophers. His grammatical teachings lean too heavily on the theory of logic, and because of this and his attempt to use Latin philology to explain various aspects of Hebrew grammar, he exerted only limited influence upon Hebrew grammatical literature. Balmes' attempt to codify Hebrew syntax, to which he devoted a special section of his book (*Sha'ar ha-Harkavah ve-ha-Shimmush*) is, however, of some significance. The work was greatly used by Christian Hebraists of the ensuing period. According to Gedaliah *Ibn Yaḥya, who was present at Balmes' funeral, he had taught officially at the University of Padua, and many of his gentile students followed his bier.

BIBLIOGRAPHY: D. Amram, *Makers of Hebrew Books in Italy* (1909), 169–172; Gedaliah b. Joseph Yaḥya, *Shalshelet ha-Kabbalah* (Amsterdam, 1697), 49b–50a; C. Roth, *Jews in the Renaissance* (1959), 76; F. Secret, *Les Kabbalists chrétiens de la Renaissance* (1964), 107; N. Ferorelli, *Abramo de Balmes ebreo di Lecce e i suoi parenti* (offprint from *Archivio Storico per le Province Napoletane*, 31 (1906), 632–54); Steinschneider, Uebersetzungen, 972–3 and index s.v. *Abraham de Balmes*.

[Joseph Elijah Heller]

BALOGH, THOMAS, BARON (1905–1985), British economist whose main interests were planning, development, and labor economics. Born in Budapest, he worked as a Rockefeller Fellow at Harvard University, from 1928 to 1930. In 1931 he joined the economic staff of the League of Nations and settled in London, working as an economist until 1939, when he became associated with the Oxford University Institute of Statistics. From 1955 to 1960 he taught in England and in the United States. Balogh served as a consultant to various United Nations agencies and foreign governments, including India, Malta, Greece, Peru, and Turkey. In 1964 he became an economic adviser to the British Labour government under Harold Wilson. He received a life peerage in 1968. Balogh's publications include: *Dollar Crisis* (1949), *Unequal Partners* (1963), *Planning for Progress* (1963), and *Economics of Poverty* (1966). When Labour returned to office in February 1974, Balogh was appointed minister of state in the Department of Energy, a post he held until December 1975. In 1976–78 he served as chairman of the National Oil Corporation.

ADD. BIBLIOGRAPHY: ODNB online.

[Joachim O. Ronall / William D. Rubinstein (2nd ed.)]

BALSAM, spice designated in the Bible by various names: בֹּשֶׂם (*bosem*), בֶּשֶׂם (*besem*), צֳרִי (*ẓori*), נָטָף (*nataf*), and, in rabbinic literature, קָטָף (*kataf*), בַּלְסָם (*balsam*), אֲפּוֹבַּלְסָמוֹן (*appobalsamon*), אֲפַרְסְמוֹן (*afarsemon*), *afarsemon* occuring most frequently in the Talmud and Midrash and designating the perfume extracted from the sap of the *Commiphora opobalsamum*. It was the only tropical, and the most expensive, spice grown in Ereẓ Israel. According to Josephus (Ant., 8:174–5), balsam was originally brought to Ereẓ Israel by the Queen of Sheba as one of the gifts included in the "hundred and twenty talents of gold, and of spices very great store, and precious stones; there came no more such abundance of *bosem*" (I Kings 10:10). Generally, in the Bible, *bosem* signifies spices of all kinds. Yet in the Song of Songs, in the verses "I have gathered my myrrh with my *bosem*" (5:1) and "the beds of *bosem*" (5:13; 6:2), the reference is to balsam alone. At present the tree grows wild in the valley of Mecca where it is called *beshem*. Many strains of this species are found, some in Somalia and Yemen. As a perfume it is hardly used today. It serves in the Orient as a healing agent for wounds and as an antidote to snakebite and the sting of scorpions. Apparently, the *ẓori* of the Bible also signifies some remedy compounded of balsam sap and other ingredients. The "balm (*ẓori*) of Gilead" is mentioned as having healing properties. *Nataf* was one of the elements constituting the incense burned in the Tabernacle (Ex. 30:34) and is identified as *ẓori* in an early *baraita* dating back to the Second Temple (Ker. 6a). The word in another context designates balsam oil (Shab. 25b–26a), and this identification appears to be correct (see also *Storax). Balsam oil was highly regarded in rabbinic literature and by Greek and Roman writers. Among the latter, Theophrastus, Strabo, Diodorus, and Pliny the Younger lavished high praise on the balsam grown in orchards near the Dead Sea. Pliny's remarks are especially enlightening. In their struggle against the Romans, the Jews strove desperately to destroy the balsam orchards and prevent them from falling into the hands of the enemy. The Romans, however, captured them and, in his triumphal march in Rome, Titus displayed balsam trees brought from Judea. The orchards in Jericho and En-Gedi henceforth provided the Romans with an important source of revenue (*Historia Naturalis*, 12:25). Admiration was expressed in the Talmud for the balsam "of Rabbi (Judah ha-Nasi's) household and the household of the emperor." It was the best and most expensive spice of ancient times, and accordingly Rav, the Babylonian *amora*, composed for it a special blessing: "Who creates the oil of our land" (Ber. 43a). The perfume has a pungent odor and the Midrash cites it as one of the enticements of the sinful daughters of Zion: "She would place the balsam between her heel and her shoe and, when she saw a band of young men, she pressed upon it so that the perfume seeped through them like snake poison" (Lam. R. 4:18). Tradition has it that, after King Josiah hid away the "holy oil" with which the kings of Judah were anointed, balsam oil was used in its stead (Ker. 5b). In the messianic era, the righteous will "bathe in 13 rivers of balsam" (TJ, Av. Zar. 3:1, 42c). Remains of the terraces in the hills of En-Gedi, where balsam trees once grew, can still be seen. Excavations in the vicinity have uncovered a workshop complete with its ovens and its vessels. From his investigations in the Arabian Peninsula, the German botanist Schweinfurth has reconstructed the process of balsam production. The bark of the tree was split and the sap soaked up in cotton wool. The sap was then squeezed into oil which absorbed the pungent odor. The tree is a thorn bush with trifoliate leaves, and belongs to the genus *Commiphora* which includes several species, among them myrrh.

BIBLIOGRAPHY: Pauly-Wissowa, 4 (1896), 2836–39; O. Warburg, *Pflanzenwelt*, 2 (1916), 282ff.; Loew, Flora, 1 (1926), 299–304; J. Feliks, *Olam ha-Ẓome'aḥ ha-Mikra'i* (1968[2]), 246–8, 256–8. **ADD. BIBLIOGRAPHY:** J. Feliks, *Plants and Animals of the Mishna* (1983), 139.

[Jehuda Feliks]

BALTA, city in Odessa district, Ukraine. At the beginning of the 16th century, when Balta lay on the border between Poland and Turkey, there were Jews living in both sectors of the city (in the Józefgrod quarter on the Polish side). Many of the Jewish inhabitants together with refugees who had fled there from other districts were massacred by the *Haidamacks in 1768. The city was incorporated into Russia in 1791. Balta's importance as a commercial center increased after the construction of the Odessa-Kiev railroad in 1866. The Jewish population, which numbered 8,413 in 1863, mainly engaged in wholesale and retail grain dealing, the processing of agricultural products, tobacco and soap, tanning, flour milling, and liquor distilling. A pogrom broke out in 1882 in which over 1,200 Jewish houses and shops were pillaged; an attempt to organize Jewish *self-defense was suppressed by the police. Balta subsequently became the center of the Zionist movement in Podolia, Volhynia, and Bessarabia. The Zionist leader M. *Sheinkin served there as a government-appointed rabbi (*rav mi-ta'am*) in 1901–1904. Pogroms again broke out in the wake of the October revolution of 1905. The community was severely affected during the civil war of 1919, in which Balta repeatedly changed hands between the Bolsheviks and the troops of *Petlyura, the Ukrainian nationalist leader. Threatened by general pillage and massacre, many Jews fled to Odessa. The Jewish population, which numbered 13,234 in 1897 (57% of the total), had decreased to 9,116 by 1926 (39.6%). Owing to emigration to the big cities the Jewish population decreased further to 4,711 in 1939 (total population 17,945). At the beginning of the Soviet period the *He-Ḥalutz movement was still active and operated a farm, but during mass arrests on September 18–22, 1922, including He-Ḥalutz members, it was liquidated. In 1924 there were two Yiddish schools with 530 pupils in the city. Among the artisans there were many shoemakers. About 30 Jewish agricultural cooperatives operated in Balta county. Some were liquidated and the rest were turned into kolkhozes.

During World War II Balta was incorporated in the Romanian-occupied zone of *Transnistria. On August 8, 1941, 140 Jews were executed. About 1,500 who remained in Balta were confined in a ghetto together with deported Jews from Bessarabia and Bukovina, and a number were later executed. With the help of money received from Bucharest the Judenrat opened workshops. two orphanages, and inexpensive restaurants. About 1,795 Jews (including 175 from Bukovina) remained after the liberation on March 29, 1944. Fourteen hundred Jews were listed in Balta in the 1959 census. Most of the Jews emigrated in the 1990s. A number of small Jewish communities formerly existed in the vicinity of Balta, of which the largest were Bogopol, Krivoye Ozero, and Golovanevsk.

BIBLIOGRAPHY: Dubnow, Hist Russ, 2 (1918), 299–304, 314–7; S. Bernfeld, *Sefer ha-Dema'ot*, 2 (1920), 296–7; M. Altman, in: *He-Avar*, 3 (1955), 60–85; 10 (1963), 83–105; *Judenpogrome in Russland*, 2 (1909), 420–4. **ADD. BIBLIOGRAPHY:** PK Ukrainah, s.v.

[Yehuda Slutsky / Shmuel Spector (2nd ed.)]

BALTAZAR, CAMIL (pseudonym of **Leopold Goldstein**; 1902–1977), Romanian poet. Baltazar's first poems appeared in 1921 in *Sburatorul Literar*, a review edited by the Romanian critic Eugen Lovinescu, and his contributions were published thereafter in many of the leading literary periodicals. Baltazar's poetry was written mainly before World War II. His first collection, *Vecernii* (Vespers), appeared in 1923. This was followed by *Flaute de matase* (Silken Flutes, 1924), *Reculegeri in nemurirea ta* (Meditation on Your Immortality, 1925), *Biblice* (Biblical Poems, 1926, a volume of erotic poems with ancient Hebrew Biblical themes), *Strigari trupesti pe langa glesne* (Poems on Amorous Yearnings, 1927), and *Cina cea de taina* (The Last Supper, 1929). In his themes and mode of expression, Baltazar was, from the outset, hailed as an innovator. Though his sensitivity led to preoccupation with human suffering, he was widely known as "the poet of light" because of the serenity with which he transfigured the most somber themes. During the early 1930s, Baltazar published an anthology of Russian prose (1930) and translations from such German writers as Thomas *Mann, Franz *Werfel, and Jakob Wassermann. His completion of this work was marked by the verse collection *Intoarcerea poetului la uneltele sale* (The Poet's Return to his Tools, 1934), which are poems in prose about his work as a writer and a literary editor, written under the influence of Apollinaire and Blaise Cendrars. *Taram transcendent* (Trancendental Realm) appeared five years later. In 1928 he edited the literary review *Tiparnita literara* (The Literary Printer) and in 1932 was secretary of redaction of the literary weekly *Romania literara* (Literary Romania), edited by Liviu Rebreanu. After World War II, Baltazar became a contributor to the Romanian Jewish newspaper *Revista Cultului Mozaic* (c. 1965–77) and published further collections of his poems. He also published literary essays, memoirs, and publicistic writings in the volumes *Scriitor si om* (Writer and Man, 1947), *Contemporan cu ei* (Contemporary with Them, 1962), *Scrisori catre Camil Baltazar* (Letters to Camil Baltazar, 1965). Owing to the artistic dictates of the new (Communist) regime, Baltazar's "socialist" verse was largely devoid of literary value.

BIBLIOGRAPHY: E. Lovinescu, in: *Critice*, 7 (1922), 165; 9 (1924); idem, *Istoria literaturii romane contemporane* (1927), 415–24; G. Calinescu, *Istoria literaturii romane* (1941), 753–56. **ADD. BIBLI-**

OGRAPHY: A. Mirodan, *Dictionar neconventional*, 1 (1986), 90–98; A.B. Yoffe, *Bisdot Zarim* (1996), 208–11, 441–42.

[Dora Litany-Littman and Abraham Feller / Lucian-Zeev Herscovici (2nd ed.)]

BALTIMORE, city in Maryland, U.S. When Abraham *Rice of Bavaria accepted the rabbinic post at Baltimore Hebrew Congregation in 1840, the congregation became the first in America to employ an ordained rabbi. While Baltimore Jewry remains justly proud of this distinction, for Rabbi Rice, the experience was not a happy one: as he famously wrote his mentor in Germany, "The religious life in this land is on the lowest level, most people eat foul food and desecrate the Sabbath in public.... Under these circumstances my mind is perplexed and I wonder whether it is even permissible for a Jew to live in this land."

In Baltimore's defense, Rice's comment did not apply to Baltimoreans alone; his words pointed to the state of American Jewry in the mid-19th century. As an immigrant port of entry and border town between North and South, as a gateway to the nation's interior and a manufacturing center in its own right, Baltimore has been well-positioned to reflect developments in American Jewish life. Yet the Baltimore Jewish community has maintained its own distinctive character as well, reflective of the personality of Baltimore itself – a city known for its cohesive communities, periodically fractious citizenry, and occasional eccentricities.

Settlement Patterns and Demographics

Founded in 1729 on an inlet of the Chesapeake Bay in the colony of Maryland, Baltimore remained a small waterfront village until emerging as an important trading center in the late 18th century. Few Jews arrived in the early years. In addition to the town's slow start, they may have been deterred by Maryland's discriminatory constitution, which required that public office holders swear an oath of allegiance to Christianity. Not until the Maryland legislature passed the "Jew Bill" in 1826, enabling Jewish public officials to swear a substitute oath, did Jews achieve full civic equality in the state.

Greater religious toleration and a rising economy came at the right time to draw a good number of the Jewish immigrants beginning to stream into America from German lands. Baltimore's Jewish population surged from around 125 in 1825 to approximately 1,000 in 1840 and more than 8,000 in 1860. By 1880, Baltimore had some 10,000 Jews, mostly of Bavarian and Hessian origin. This profile would soon change dramatically, however. The mass migration of East European Jews that gathered force in the 1880s made an immediate impact, with Baltimore attracting many early arrivals, particularly from Lithuania. The city's Jewish population reached 24,000 by 1890, 40,000 by 1907, and 65,000 by 1920. Although Lithuanians continued to have a major presence, Baltimore received Jewish immigrants from across Eastern Europe between the 1880s and 1920s. The city also welcomed subsequent waves of Jewish migration, notably German-Jewish refugees from Nazism in the 1930s, Holocaust survivors in the post-World War II era, Iranians in the late 20th century, and Soviet and post-Soviet Jews in the late 20th century.

The diversity of Baltimore's Jewish population mirrored that of the city itself. As a busy immigrant port of entry, Baltimore became a multi-ethnic patchwork of neighborhoods. East Baltimore, the original site of German Jewish residence, became the area of settlement for most East European Jewish immigrants. American-born descendants of German Jews began moving to more affluent precincts on the city's northwest side by the late 19th century, where they tended to re-concentrate in predominantly Jewish enclaves. This pattern continued through the 20th century, as Jews moved away from the old East Baltimore neighborhood to a succession of residential areas in northwest Baltimore. As each Jewish sub-group moved up the economic ladder and into wealthier surroundings, its place was often taken by a less well-off sub-group.

At the turn of the 20th century, some 92,000 Jews lived in Baltimore: around one-quarter within the city limits, 70 percent in suburban Baltimore County, and the remainder in Carroll County. Most resided in predominantly Jewish areas in the northwest part of the metro region, in places such as Upper Park Heights, Mount Washington, Pikesville, Reisterstown, and Owings Mills. Jewish households made up 6 percent of households in the Baltimore area.

Economic Life

From the beginning, Baltimore's Jews found opportunity for economic advancement, though never without struggle. Widow Shinah Etting arrived in 1780 with five children and opened a boardinghouse; another widow, Judith Cohen, came with her children in 1803. Their sons rose to become prominent business and civic leaders. The German Jews who settled in Baltimore after the Ettings and Cohens started primarily as poor peddlers and small shopkeepers. In time, most achieved a measure of success. German Jewish entrepreneurs were the pioneering founders of Baltimore's most well-known retail establishments: Gutman's, Hutzler's, Hochschild Kohn's, Hamburger's, and Hecht's. Others established small clothing manufacturing firms that became the basis of Baltimore's nationally significant garment industry.

East European immigrants found a niche in the lowest rungs of that industry. Harsh conditions and low pay led them to forge a dynamic labor movement that met with bitter employer opposition, and for many years Baltimore's garment industry was wracked by strikes and lockouts. In 1914 the Amalgamated Clothing Workers and the Sonneborn firm, one of the nation's largest men's clothing factories, signed a landmark collective bargaining agreement. During the struggle, Orthodox leader Rabbi Avraham Schwartz interceded on behalf of workers about to be fired for refusing to work on the Sabbath, enlisting the support of the Sonneborn family's Reform rabbi, William Rosenau.

Many East European Jews left the sweatshops and factories (or avoided them altogether) to set up small family enterprises that relied on the labor of husbands, wives, and children. Pushcart peddlers and small shopkeepers reigned on Lombard Street, East Baltimore's bustling marketplace. Other entrepreneurs ranged well beyond the Jewish community. Lithuanian immigrant Jacob Epstein built the Baltimore Bargain House into a multimillion dollar wholesale business. The peddlers he sent out on the rail lines emanating from Baltimore became small shopkeepers and founders of Jewish communities from Pennsylvania to North Carolina. Louis *Blaustein and his son Jacob began selling kerosene door-to-door in 1910; their American Oil Company became one of the country's largest, pioneering the drive-in filling station. In less spectacular ways, many of Baltimore's East European Jews established successful businesses by the 1920s and began to exhibit an upward mobility that would extend in the coming decades despite reversals during the Great Depression.

Immigrants from later waves of Jewish migration also started low on the economic ladder, as door-to-door salesmen, cabdrivers, technicians, and the like. Coming from the upper professional levels in Germany, Iran, and the Soviet Union, most suffered a difficult loss of status, but their educated backgrounds helped many to advance. In the post-World War II era, Baltimore Jews increasingly gravitated to the professions, although business remained an important economic activity.

Religious Life

Abraham Rice would no doubt have been surprised to learn that Baltimore hosted the highest proportion of Orthodox Jews of any large American Jewish community at the end of the 20th century. The internationally known Ner Israel Rabbinical College and other highly regarded Orthodox institutions combined with Baltimore's relative affordability to enable the Orthodox community to attract new members from New York and other cities. But all branches of Judaism have been well represented in Baltimore. Jewish religious life has been marked by innovation as well as devotion to tradition, conflict as well as cohesion, and by leaders whose actions influenced the course of American Jewry.

With nationally prominent rabbis heading its congregations, Baltimore in the mid-19th century became the battleground of conflicting religious ideologies. The Baltimore Hebrew Congregation (incorporated as Nidchei Israel), the city's first, was established in 1830 by around 20 Jews of German and Dutch extraction. For the next 60 years, traditionalists and reformers clashed within the congregation or split off from it. Some German immigrants founded Har Sinai as a Reform counterpoint in 1842 and constructed America's first building specifically created as a Reform temple in 1849. Congregation Oheb Shalom formed in 1853 as a midway alternative to Baltimore Hebrew's Orthodoxy and Har Sinai's radical Reform. Its first rabbi, Benjamin *Szold, found himself in a bitter feud with Har Sinai's fiery Rabbi David *Einhorn shortly after arriving in Baltimore in 1859. Meanwhile, Baltimore Hebrew continued its slow but sure movement away from traditionalism. Rabbi Rice left in 1849 and two years later founded Shearith Israel, which upheld German-Jewish Orthodoxy for decades and remained an Orthodox congregation into the 21st century. In 1870, Baltimore Hebrew's remaining traditionalists, led by the Friedenwald family, split off to form the Chizuk Amuno Congregation. By the early 1900s, Baltimore Hebrew and Oheb Shalom had joined the Reform movement, while Chizuk Amuno became a founding member of the Conservative movement's United Synagogue of America.

Amidst all the *Sturm und Drang* among the Germans, a small congregation named Bikur Cholim opened in 1865, the first congregation in Baltimore to follow the Polish style of worship. As East Europeans began to trickle in, small *landsman*-based congregations sprang up, mostly in East Baltimore. Dozens of these shuls were established over the next several decades. Two of the most influential, B'nai Israel (founded by Lithuanians in 1873) and Shomrei Mishmeres (founded by Volhynians in 1892), took over the imposing synagogue buildings on Lloyd Street built by Chizuk Amuno and Baltimore Hebrew, respectively, after those congregations relocated to more upscale neighborhoods. A second phase of East European synagogue development began in the early 1920s when the first American-born generation founded several congregations in northwest Baltimore, including Beth Tfiloh, one of the nation's first "synagogue centers." In ensuing years, small immigrant shuls either merged into larger synagogues or disappeared. By 1999 Baltimore hosted more than 50 synagogues, representing every branch of Judaism.

Jewish Education and Philanthropy

Innovation has been a hallmark of Jewish education in Baltimore. The first known community Hebrew school opened as early as 1842, and community-operated schools such as East Baltimore's Talmud Torah flourished from the late 1880s to the 1940s. Samson *Benderly, the father of modern Jewish education in America, started his revolutionary experiments in Baltimore in 1900 and the city benefited from his direct influence until he left for New York in 1910. In 1917 Rabbi Avraham Schwartz of Shomrei Mishmeres founded the Talmudical Academy, the first Jewish day school outside of New York. In the late 20th century, a dramatic rise in Jewish day schools (16 by 2004) gave Baltimore one of the largest day school populations in the nation. The two institutions of higher Jewish learning have been *Baltimore Hebrew University, founded in 1919 by Israel *Efros, and the Ner Israel Rabbinical College, founded by Rabbi Jacob I. *Ruderman in 1933.

Baltimore Jewry's long tradition of philanthropy and mutual aid started with the United Hebrew Benevolent Society, founded in 1834. Two key institutions, Sinai Hospital and the Levindale Hebrew Geriatric Center, also date back to the 1800s. Some charities established by German and American-born Jews in the late 19th century focused on helping poverty-stricken East European immigrants. East European Jews started their own aid societies shortly after their arrival, and by the first decade of the 20th century, two parallel philanthropic networks had arisen: the German-sponsored Federated Jewish Charities and the East European-sponsored United Hebrew Charities. In 1921 the two combined into the Associated Jewish Charities. Ever since, the Associated has supported a comprehensive network of agencies offering social services, health care, and educational, recreational, and cultural programming. Widely recognized as one of the nation's leading Jewish federations, the Associated is known for its innovative programs, fundraising effectiveness, and leaders who have played important roles at the national Jewish communal level.

Community Life

Baltimore Jewry created a wide array of cultural, social, and recreational institutions through the years, as each wave of immigrants acted to meet the needs of its members. Several clubs and literary associations were established by the 1850s, including the first YMHA in the country (1854). A German-Jewish "high society" emerged by the 1880s, complete with debutante balls and exclusive social clubs. East European Jews developed a thriving Yiddish-based cultural scene in East Baltimore. Yiddish theaters, kosher restaurants, and bathhouses drew scores of neighborhood residents. Zionists and socialists, Orthodox and secularists aimed to enrich the immigrants' lives with classes, concerts, and lectures. Some *maskilim* collaborated with native Baltimorean Henrietta *Szold (daughter of Rabbi Benjamin Szold) to form the Russian Night School in 1889, a pioneering effort in immigrant education. The Jewish Educational Alliance, established in 1913, offered everything from youth sports leagues to adult English classes, and became a second home for thousands of newcomers.

For many decades the Jewish social scene was divided in two, with seemingly irreconcilable religious and cultural differences (as well as garment industry labor-management conflict) separating the "uptown" German Jews from the "downtown" Russian Jews. The rift began to heal in the post-World War II era. By century's end, new waves of Jewish immigration, generational change, and the emergence of a significant ultra-Orthodox community became more salient factors in shaping a pluralistic Jewish social and cultural life. A variety of sub-groups supported numerous organizations, activities, and newspapers – but all within relatively close proximity in northwest Baltimore, as the flowering of communal diversity did not alter the desire of most Jews to live in Jewish neighborhoods. Some institutions were shared by all, notably a popular two-campus Jewish Community Center and the well-read weekly *Jewish Times* (established in 1919). The Jewish Museum of Maryland remained in East Baltimore to preserve the legacy of the immigrant past. The nation's largest regional Jewish museum, its complex includes America's third-oldest surviving synagogue, the Lloyd Street Synagogue (1845).

National and International Jewish Issues

Baltimore Jews have provided leadership on the national Jewish stage since the mid-nineteenth century. David Einhorn launched his influential monthly *Sinai* in 1856, and America's first Hebrew weekly, *Ha-Pisgah*, appeared in Baltimore in 1891. Simon *Sobeloff was the inaugural president of the American Jewish Congress. Real estate magnate Joseph *Meyerhoff served as national chair of the United Jewish Appeal and State of Israel Bonds, demonstrating that the two organizations were complementary and not competitive. His son, Harvey Meyerhoff, became chairman of the United States Holocaust Memorial Museum in 1987 and, despite doubtful prospects, brought the Museum to its successful opening in 1993. Rabbi Arthur *Hertzberg's Orthodox upbringing in East Baltimore strongly influenced his contributions to national Jewish life.

Baltimore women have a history of "firsts." The first woman to head a major American Jewish congregation was Helen Dalsheimer, installed as president of Baltimore Hebrew Congregation in 1956. Shoshana Cardin became the first woman to lead a major Jewish federation when she assumed the presidency of Baltimore's Associated Jewish Charities in 1983. Cardin went on to be the first woman to preside over the national Council of Jewish Federations.

Baltimore has been an important center of Zionist activity. One of America's first *Ḥibbat Zion groups organized here in 1884, and the only American delegate to the First Zionist Congress was a Baltimorean, Shearith Israel's Rabbi Shepsel Schaffer. Henrietta Szold, founder of Hadassah, began her Zionist activities in this city. Harry *Friedenwald served as second president of the American Zionist Federation. In 1947, a group of Baltimore Zionists secretly acquired, rebuilt, and launched an old Chesapeake Bay steamer which picked up refugees in France and unfurled its new name, *Exodus 1947*, upon being attacked by the British on its way to Palestine.

The Baltimore Scene

From the beginning, Baltimore's Jews have actively engaged in their region's political, civic, and cultural life. Ettings and Cohens participated in the pivotal battle of Fort McHenry during the War of 1812. During the Civil War, Jews were as divided as the rest of the population in this border city. Rabbi Einhorn led the antislavery faction, Rabbi Bernhard *Illowy of the Baltimore Hebrew Congregation defended the status quo, and Rabbi Szold spoke for Jewish neutrality. Einhorn's tenure at Har Sinai was abruptly cut short in 1861 when his newspaper, *Sinai*, was destroyed by a pro-slavery mob and he fled with his family to Philadelphia. Jews have served throughout state and local government, from Solomon Etting and Jacob Cohen – elected to the City Council immediately after passage of the "Jew Bill" in 1826 – to popular 1970s Maryland governor Marvin *Mandel (whose political career was cut short by corruption charges).

Jews have played a critical role in Baltimore's cultural scene as patrons and participants. Jacob Epstein's personal art collection became a core holding of the Baltimore Museum of Art, while Etta and Claribel Cone gave the BMA the unparalleled collection of modern art they acquired in their European travels. Joseph Meyerhoff's philanthropy created Meyerhoff Symphony Hall, home of the Baltimore Symphony Orchestra, in 1982. Academy Award-winning film director Barry Levinson made significant contributions to American cinema with his three-part chronicle of Baltimore Jewish life, *Diner* (1982), *Avalon* (1990), and *Liberty Heights* (1999).

Jewish–Gentile Relations

Relations between Baltimore Jews and non-Jews have been generally amicable, though ethnic and religious prejudice, social snobbery, and discrimination occasionally vexed the Jewish community. In the 19th century, the city's large German population of Jews and non-Jews shared German-speaking clubs and many Jewish children attended Zion Lutheran Church's well-respected school, where instruction was in German. However, the local Catholic press, German and English, specialized in antisemitic articles until the appointment of Archbishop James Gibbons in 1877. Local antisemitism increased with the rise of Nazism in the 1930s, spurring the 1939 formation of the Baltimore Jewish Council, a community relations organization that continues to fight antisemitism, promote dialogue between Jewish and other local communities, and address broader urban issues.

The relationship of Jews to Baltimore's African American community has been complex. Jews participated in the civil rights movement, but the movement also targeted Jewish storeowners who maintained discriminatory policies. In one historian's words, a state of "intimate antagonism" existed between the two groups for much of the 20th century, as economic relations and geographic proximity promoted considerable interaction between Jews and blacks.

The close-knit nature of Baltimore's Jewish community arose from a combination of gentile prejudice and Jewish ties of kinship and culture. Residential discrimination kept Jews out of some areas until the mid-20th century, contributing to the emergence of intensely concentrated Jewish neighborhoods. Upper-class social and educational discrimination encouraged Jews to create separate clubs and "ecumenical" (largely Jewish) private schools. Such discrimination dissipated in the post-World War II era. By the dawn of the 21st century Baltimore Jewry emerged as a confident and assertive community determined to maintain its own distinct identity, neighborhoods, and institutions, while its members pursued ever-expanding ways to involve themselves in the broader society.

BIBLIOGRAPHY: I. Blum, *History of the Jews of Baltimore* (1910); *Cornerstones of Community: The Historic Synagogues of Maryland, 1845–1945* (Jewish Museum of Maryland, 1999); I.M. Fein, *Making of an American Jewish Community: The History of Baltimore Jewry from 1773 to 1920* (1971); *Jewish Community Study of Greater Baltimore* (The Association, 2001); G. Sandler, *Jewish Baltimore, A Family Album* (2000).

[Deborah Weiner (2nd ed.)]

BALTIMORE, DAVID (1938–), U.S. molecular virologist and Nobel laureate. Born in New York City, Baltimore received his B.A. with high honors in chemistry from Swarthmore College in 1960 and his Ph.D. from Rockefeller University, N.Y. He started his postgraduate work in 1963 at the Massachusetts Institute of Technology in biophysics, decided to work on animal viruses, moved to the Albert Einstein College of Medicine, Bronx, New York, and later to the Rockefeller Institute. After finishing his postdoctoral fellowships in 1965, he became a research associate at Salk Institute for Biological Studies, La Jolla, California (1965–68), and associate professor of microbiology at MIT (1968–72). From 1972 to 1997 he was an institute professor of biology at MIT and from 1973 he was an American Cancer Society professor of microbiology. He was founding director of the Whitehead Institute for Biomedical Research at MIT and served from the institute's creation in 1982 to 1990, when he became president of Rockefeller University. In 1997 Baltimore became president of the California Institute of Technology. His career has been distinguished by his dual contribution to biological research and to national science policy. Baltimore helped pioneer the molecular study of animal viruses, and his research in this field had profound implications for understanding cancer and, later, AIDS. As one of the nation's most distinguished biologists, he was awarded the 1975 Nobel Prize for his work in virology.

Baltimore has been a major figure in Washington as head of the National Institutes of Health AIDS Vaccine Research Committee from 1996 to 2002, and also in 1986 as co-chair of the National Academy of Sciences and Institute of Medicine's Committee on a National Strategy for AIDS. In 1999 he was awarded the National Medal of Science. He was a co-recipient of the 2000 Warren Alpert Foundation Prize and was awarded the 2002 AMA Scientific Achievement Award.

[Bracher Rager (2nd ed.)]

BALTIMORE HEBREW UNIVERSITY. The Baltimore Hebrew College and Teachers Training School was founded in 1919 by the noted Hebrew poet and scholar Israel *Efros. According to its charter, the purpose of the college was "to establish a College for Higher Hebrew and Semitic learning; to study the Hebrew and cognate languages and literature; to train and qualify teachers for Jewish religious schools; and for such cognate purposes as may from time to time be determined by the Board of Directors of this corporation, with power to confer degrees." The first class met on November 2, 1919, in the Chizuk Amuno synagogue and the first graduation took place in June 1923. Dr. Efros resigned in 1928, and in 1930 he was succeeded by Dr. Louis L. *Kaplan, who served as president until 1970. The college was housed at 1201 Eutaw Place from the mid-1920s until 1959, when it moved to Park Heights Avenue. The college became a constituent of the Associated Jewish Charities and Welfare Fund (now the Associated: Jewish Community Federation of Baltimore) in 1930. The college received accreditation from the state of Maryland in 1963 and from the Middle States Association of Colleges and Schools in 1974. It was renamed Baltimore Hebrew University in 1987 when Middle States conferred university status on it.

Over the years the university expanded its academic outreach to offer a number of degree programs. In 1971 the university opened its graduate school, which in 1975 was named the Peggy Meyerhoff Pearlstone School of Graduate Studies. In addition to the B.A. degree in Jewish Studies which is offered by the University's Bernard Manekin School of Undergraduate Studies, the graduate achool offers programs leading to the Masters and Ph.D. degrees in Jewish Studies. The graduate school also developed degree programs to train Jewish educators and communal professionals. These programs lead to the Master of Arts in Jewish Education or the Master of Arts in Jewish Communal Service. Graduates of these programs have become teachers, principals, and other educational specialists in the field of Jewish education and others have become executives in federations, Jewish Community Centers, community relations councils and in the field of Jewish family service. The university also maintains cooperative relations with Baltimore area colleges through the Baltimore Collegetown Network, which enables area colleges to share resources and jointly enhance the academic and social life of students.

While remaining committed to academic Jewish Studies and to the training of Jewish educators and communal professionals, the university also provides opportunities for Jewish learning to non-degree students through its program of Lifelong Learning. The program has featured weekend retreats with scholars, artists, and public figures; classes in Jewish Studies; a Distinguished Lecture series with major scholars, authors, playwrights, and filmmakers; and the Meah Program, a two-year 100-hour course of study covering the Jewish experience from biblical times to the present.

The University maintains the Joseph Meyerhoff Library, which contains over 70,000 books and periodicals in English, Hebrew, Yiddish, German, French, Russian, and other languages and includes a number of rare books going back to the 16th century. The library also houses the Baltimore Jewish Community Video Archive for Holocaust Testimonies and a collection of books that survived the Holocaust acquired through the Jewish Cultural Reconstruction Organization.

Among the distinguished scholars who have served on the faculty of the university are Moshe Aberbach, Joseph M. Baumgarten, Adele Berlin, Avram Biran, Cyrus *Gordon, Samuel Iwry, and Harry M. *Orlinsky.

The presidents who have served Baltimore Hebrew University are Israel Efros (1919–28), Louis L. Kaplan (1930–70), Leivy Smolar (1970–92), Norma Fields Furst (1992–95), Robert O. Freedman (1995–2001), and Rela Mintz Geffen (from 2001).

[George L. Berlin (2nd ed.)]

BAMBERG, city in Bavaria, Germany. There were Jews living in Bamberg before the First Crusade (1096), when they were forcibly baptized but later allowed to return to Judaism. Establishments in the medieval "Jewish Lane" (today Pfahlplaetzchen) included a dance hall for weddings, a hostel (*hekdesh*) for the needy sick and transients, a *mikveh*, and a synagogue. In 1298 during *Rindfleisch massacres 135 Jews were martyred in Bamberg. During the persecution following the outbreak of the *Black Death in 1348 the Jews there set fire to their homes and perished in flames. Between the 14th and 17th centuries Jews repeatedly attempted to settle in Bamberg, paying high "protection" taxes, only to be later attacked and expelled. In 1633 they numbered ten families, whose right of residence was recognized in 1644. An annual "plum fast" (*Zwetschgen Taanit*) was observed by the Bamberg community, to commemorate the preservation of the Jews there during the riots of 1699 by one of their number who averted greater damage by pouring plums over the mob. The community increased from 287 in 1810 to 1,270 in 1880 (4.3% of the total population), subsequently declining to 812 in 1933 (1.6%) and 418 in May 1939.

Prominent members of the community included the talmudist and *paytan* Samuel b. Baruch *Bamberg (13th century). Notable rabbis were Moses *Mintz who served there from c. 1469 to 1474; Samuel Meseritz (c. 1661–65), author of *Naḥalat Shivah*; and Joseph Kobak (1862–82), editor of *Jeschurun*. A. Eckstein, rabbi of Bamberg (1888–1935), wrote a number of studies on the history of the Jewish communities in Bavaria.

During the Nazi regime, the synagogue was burned down on Nov. 10, 1938, and 30 to 40 Torah scrolls were destroyed. In 1933–41, 443 Bamberg Jews left Germany and another 66 fled to other German cities. The 300 who remained at the end of 1941 were deported to Riga, Izbica/Lublin, Theresienstadt, and Auschwitz. After the war many displaced persons assembled in Bamberg (14,000 in 1947), but only 17 of the former Jewish residents were among them. In 1965 the cemetery was desecrated. The community then numbered 70. In 1989, there were 106 community members; their number rose to 893 in 2003 as a result of the immigration of Jews from the former Soviet Union.

BIBLIOGRAPHY: PK; Germ Jud, s.v.; H.F. Brettinger, *Juden in Bamberg* (1963); A. Eckstein, *Geschichte der Juden im ehemaligen Fuerstbistum Bamberg* (1898); idem, in: *Festschrift zur Einweihung der neuen Synagoge in Bamberg* (1910); idem, *Die israelitische Kultusgemeinde Bamberg, 1803–53* (1910); *Bilder aus der Vergangenheit der israelitischen Gemeinde Bamberg* (1933); R.M. Kloos, in: *Bericht des historischen Vereins Bamberg*, 103 (1967), 341–86. **ADD. BIBLIOGRAPHY:** N. Haas, *Juden in Bamberg 1868–1906;* H. Loebl, *Juden in Bamberg. Die Jahrzehnte vor dem Holocaust* (1999).

[Ze'ev Wilhem Falk]

BAMBERG, SAMUEL BEN BARUCH (first half of the 13th century), rabbi and *paytan*. Samuel was born in Metz, but lived in Bamberg, after which he was called. He studied under his father, *Baruch b. Samuel of Mainz, and *Eliezer b. Samuel of Metz. He corresponded on halakhic problems with *Eliezer b. Joel ha-Levi, *Simḥah b. Samuel of Speyer, and *Isaac b. Moses of Vienna, and was highly esteemed by leading contemporary scholars. Like his father, he was a talented poet, and fragments of his prayer book have survived. The name is mentioned in the *Memorbuch* of Nuremberg, but it is difficult to assume that he was one of the martyrs there. *Meir b. Baruch of Rothenberg was his pupil. For a time Samuel was regarded as the author of *Likkutei ha-Pardes* (Venice, 1519), but this view is no longer accepted. Of his works no more than excerpts and fragments of his responsa remain. His decisions are of a very independent nature, though his style is modest and austere.

BIBLIOGRAPHY: Michael, Or, nos. 1203, 1205; Urbach, Tosafot, 354–6, passim; A. Eckstein, *Geschichte der Juden im ehemaligen Fuerstbistum Bamberg* (1898), 140, 297–8.

[Itzhak Alfassi]

BAMBERGER, BERNARD JACOB (1904–1980), U.S. Reform rabbi, scholar, and author. Bamberger was born in Baltimore, Maryland, educated at Johns Hopkins University (1923), and ordained at Hebrew Union College (1926). After serving as rabbi of Temple Israel in Lafayette, Indiana, where he continued to study at HUC earning a D.D. (1929), Bamberger moved to Congregation Beth Emeth in Albany, where he remained until 1944. He next served as rabbi of Congregation Shaarey Tefila in New York City until his retirement in 1970. Bamberger combined his service as a pulpit rabbi with an active life of community service and scholarship. He wrote several scholarly and popular books. They include *Proselytism in the Talmudic Period* (1968^2); *Fallen Angels* (1952), a study of Jewish demonology and its influence on Christian thought; *The Bible: A Modern Jewish Approach* (1995); and *Story of Judaism* (1957). He served as president of the Synagogue Council of America (1950–51), and of the Central Conference of American Rabbis (1959–61) and later as president of the World Council for Progressive Judaism. He was a member of the interdenominational Jewish Publication Society's Bible translation committee that led to the new translation of the Bible and was the author of a modern commentary on Leviticus (1979) that served as part of the Union of American Hebrew Congregation's modern commentary published in its entirety after his death.

[Hillel Halkin]

BAMBERGER, EDOUARD-ADRIEN (1825–1910), French politician and physician. Born in Strasbourg, he moved in 1858 to Metz where he became vice president of the Metz Education League. He strenuously opposed the policies of Napoleon III and campaigned to bring about the anti-Empire majority in Metz in 1870. Elected as a Republican deputy in the National Assembly, Bamberger considerably influenced the votes on Napoleon III's responsibility for France's debacle and the subsequent deposition of the emperor. He voted against the treaty ceding his native Alsace to Germany and led the deputies from the annexed province out of the Assembly when the treaty was accepted. Recalled by Thiers following the 1871 insurrection, Bamberger resumed his seat at Versailles and voted regularly for the Republican majority. He was defeated in the 1881 elections, retired from politics, and became assistant librarian in the Museum of Natural History. During the parliamentary debates on the law concerning child labor, he moved an amendment – which was rejected – demanding that Jewish apprentices be exempt from working on Saturday.

BIBLIOGRAPHY: *Biographie complète des 534 députés...* (1876).

BAMBERGER, EUGEN (1857–1932), German chemist; a pioneer in the field of semi-microtechniques. Bamberger studied at Berlin University and in 1883 became an assistant to Baeyer in Munich, where he was appointed professor in 1891. From 1893 he was professor of general chemistry at the Zurich Polytechnic. From 1905 he was semi-paralyzed but continued his experimental work. Bamberger was meticulous in his work, and he inculcated clean and safe experimental techniques in his assistants. He insisted on following up not only the main product of any reaction under study, but also the minor products. He was an entirely "pure" chemist, his vast output covering most of the contemporary aspects of organic chemistry. His contributions were notable in the field of constitutions of natural products.

BIBLIOGRAPHY: *Berichte der deutschen chemischen Gesellschaft*, 66 (1933), 32; *Helvetica Chimica Acta*, 16 (1933), 644ff.

[Samuel Aaron Miller]

BAMBERGER, FRITZ (1902–1984), philosophical scholar and author. Born in Frankfurt, Bamberger from 1926 to 1933 was a research fellow of the *Akademie fuer die Wissenschaft des Judentums and until 1938 occupied various teaching posts in Berlin. Emigrating from Germany to the United States, he became professor of philosophy at the College for Jewish Studies, Chicago, from 1939 to 1942, and was on the staff and later editor in chief of *Coronet* magazine from 1942 to 1961. He was a founder of the Society of Jewish Bibliophiles. From 1962 Bamberger was professor of intellectual history and assistant to the president of the Hebrew Union College-Jewish Institute of Religion in New York. His collection of Spinoziana was considered to be the finest private collection of its kind.

Bamberger's main interest in the field of Jewish philosophy centered on Moses *Mendelssohn (*Moses Mendelssohns geistige Gestalt* (1929) and "Moses Mendelssohns Begriff vom Judentum," in: *Wissenschaft des Judentums im deutschen Sprachbereich*, ed. by K. Wilhelm (1967), 521ff.), and he edited three volumes of the bicentenary edition of Mendelssohn's writings (1929–32; cf. also *Denkmal der Freundschaft* (1929), and *Living Legacy* (1963), 86ff.). Other philosophers to whom he devoted studies were Spinoza (SBB, 5 (1961), 9ff.); Maimonides (*Das System des Maimonides*, 1935); Julius Guttmann (*Philosopher of Judaism*, 1960; also in German in: *Deutsches Judentum, Aufstieg und Krise* (1963), 85–119); and Leo Baeck (*The Man and the Idea*, 1958). Bamberger edited *Die Lehren des Judentums* (3 vols., 1928–30, together with S. Bernfeld); *Juedische Gestalten und ihre Zeit* (1936); *Das Buch Zunz* (1931; cf. also Zunz's *Conception of History* in PAAJR, 1941); and an anthology of ancient Jewish aphorisms (*Books Are the Best Things*, 1962).

BAMBERGER, HEINRICH VON (1822–1888), Austrian physician and teacher. Bamberger was born in Prague and studied medicine there. In 1854 he was appointed special professor of pathology at Wuerzburg University, where he remained until 1872, when he became professor at the University of Vienna. Bamberger became famous for his brilliant lectures and for his diagnostic techniques. He is especially known for his textbook on cardiac diseases and for his diagnoses of symptoms of cardiac diseases. His name was given to Bamberger's disease, Bamberger's bulbar pulse, and Bamberger's sign for pericardial effusion. He advocated the use of albuminous mercuric solution in the therapy of syphilis and reported albuminuria during the latter period of severe anemia. He also described muscular atrophy and hypertrophy. During the last two years of his life Bamberger was president of the Vienna Medical Association.

BIBLIOGRAPHY: S.R. Kagan, *Jewish Medicine* (1952), 292.

[Suessmann Muntner]

BAMBERGER, LOUIS (1855–1944), U.S. merchant and philanthropist. Bamberger was born in Baltimore, Maryland. As a boy, he began work in a dry goods store, but while still a young man he moved to New York to engage in wholesale merchandising. In 1892 he and his brother-in-law, Felix Fuld, founded L. Bamberger and Co., a small department store, in Newark, New Jersey. Adopting advanced methods of merchandising and the latest techniques of publicity, Bamberger's grew into one of the largest and most profitable American establishments. In 1929 R.H. Macy of New York took over the Bamberger firm but Louis Bamberger continued to serve as president of the Newark store until 1939. He gave his employees a cooperative interest in the firm, established a pension program for them, and marked his own retirement by distributing cash gifts and annuities to workers who had been employed for a minimum of 15 years. Another of Bamberger's successful enterprises was the Newark radio station WOR, which he built in the 1920s. Bamberger's philanthropies covered a wide range of interests. He gave generously to Newark's hospitals and Community Chest, and to the furtherance of the arts and sciences. The long list of Jewish causes and institutions to which he contributed included the *Jewish Theological Seminary of America. A charter member of the Newark Museum, and later its honorary president, he provided the funds for the new building, opened in 1926, and donated a vast quantity of art, archaeological, scientific, and industrial objects. Bamberger's greatest philanthropic act, which he shared with his sister, Mrs. Felix Fuld, was a gift of $5,000,000 for the establishment of the Institute for Advanced Study at Princeton. He and his sister also contributed to the Fuld House at Princeton, which provided quarters for the Institute.

BIBLIOGRAPHY: Newark Museum Association, *Louis Bamberger … a Tribute…* (1944); T. Mahoney, *Great Merchants* (1955), 167–70, 194.

[Morton Mayer Berman]

BAMBERGER, LUDWIG (1823–1899), German banker, politician, and economist; leading advocate of a gold standard for German currency. He studied law at Heidelberg and practiced as an attorney in his native city of Mainz. He joined the revolutionary movement of 1848 and edited the republican newspaper *Mainzer Zeitung* which advocated the unification of Germany and democratic government. He took part in the insurrection of 1849, fled to Switzerland, and was condemned to death in absentia. When, in 1866, a general amnesty was declared, Bamberger returned to Germany, and entered politics as a liberal, sitting in the German Reichstag from 1871 to 1893. During the years of his exile in London and in Paris he had entered the family firm of *Bischoffsheim where he acquired considerable knowledge of finance. In 1870 he was a leading founding figure of the Deutsche Bank (together with Adelbert Delbrueck) and became one of Bismarck's principal advisers on financial matters after the Franco-Prussian war of 1870. Later, Bamberger disagreed with Bismarck's policy of protective tariffs which he considered reactionary and in 1884 he and other followers seceded and formed the more liberal Freisinnige Partei. Though in opposition, he continued to exercise great influence on legislation of economic or financial character. He was an enthusiastic advocate of the gold standard and a champion of free trade and founded an association for its promotion. Bamberger was not a practicing Jew but in his memoirs he deplores German antisemitism. Stung by the antisemitic attacks of the German historian, Heinrich von Trietschke, he published a pamphlet "*Deutschtum und Judentum*" which was a vigorous rejoinder. He made numerous contributions to political and economic literature and his articles in the weekly *Die Nation* were published in book form under separate titles: *Wandlungen und Wanderungen in der Sozialpolitik* (1898); *Bismarck Posthumus* (1899). He also published his collected writings in five volumes (1894–98), and his memoirs appeared posthumously (1899).

ADD. BIBLIOGRAPHY: S. Zucker, *Ludwig Bamberger* (in English, 1975); L. Gall (ed.), *Die Deutsche Bank* (1995); M.-L. Weber, *Ludwig Bamberger* (in German, 1987); B. Koehler, *Ludwig Bamberger* (in German, 1999).

[Joachim O. Ronall / Marcus Pyka (2nd ed.)]

BAMBERGER, SELIGMANN BAER (Isaac Dov ha-Levi; 1807–1878), rabbinical scholar and leader of German Orthodoxy. Born in the Bavarian village of Wiesenbronn, Bamberger studied at the yeshivah of Fuerth and in his native village. Bamberger opposed the proponents of Reform at a meeting of Jewish communities of Lower Franconia in 1834, and at an assembly of notables called by the Bavarian government in 1836 where he represented A. *Bing, the district rabbi of Wuerzburg. In 1840 he was elected to succeed Bing in the face of fierce opposition from the Reformers. Bamberger continued the local yeshivah, founded an elementary school in 1855, and a teachers' training college in 1864.

By the middle of the 19th century, the Frankfurt Jewish community was dominated by the Reform movement. As a result, the community closed the *mikveh* and refused financial support to the Orthodox community. In response, the Orthodox Jews withdrew from the larger community and formed the *Religiongesellschaft*, appointed Samson Raphael *Hirsch their rabbi, and began a 25-year struggle for official autonomy. In July 1876, the Orthodox community was officially recognized by the State. The Reform-led general Jewish community offered to restore all the support it had previously rescinded, but the group led by Hirsch refused the offer. To help settle the controversy, Orthodox community members turned to Bamberger. Contrary to their expectations, Bamberger ruled that it was unnecessary to secede from the Reform-led community since it was providing for all of the needs of the Orthodox. Throughout the ensuing year, Hirsch and Bamberger engaged in a public, somewhat acrimonious polemic. The central issue of their argument was whether or not the Reform Jews were to be considered heretics. Hirsch said yes, while Bamberger said no. In the end, only a small portion of the entire Orthodox community seceded with Hirsch from the larger Reform-led community. Ironically, Hirsch, who represented the more modern Orthodox perspective, became the forerunner of 20th century ultra-Orthodox communities who try to cut themselves off as much as possible from the surrounding non-Orthodox and secular Jewish community. Despite his religious conservatism, Bamberger's position became the basis for modern Orthodox openness and acceptance of the surrounding non-Orthodox and secular Jewish community.

The "Wuerzburger Rav," as he was called, was one of the last great German-style talmudists, and his literary work was chiefly devoted to subjects of practical *halakhah; Melekhet Shamayim* (on the writing of Torah Scrolls etc., 1860²); *Amirah le-Veit Ya'akov* (laws of interest to women, originally German in Hebrew characters, 1858); *Moreh la-Zoveḥim* (handbooks for *shoḥatim*, 1864²); *Naḥalei Devash* (on the law of *ḥaliẓah*, 1867). Bamberger also wrote a commentary on Isaac ibn Ghayyat's halakhic compendium (*Sha'arei Simḥah*, 2 pts., 1861–62) and a treatise on the *Al Tikrei* formula in Talmud and Midrash (*Korei be-Emet*, 2 pts., 1871–78). His responsa appeared posthumously in *Zekher Simḥah* (1925), *Neti'ah shel Simḥah* (1928), and *Yad ha-Levi* (1965), all published by one or another of his descendants. Together with A. Adler and M. Lehmann, Bamberger published a German translation of the Pentateuch (1873, 1913⁷) on behalf of the Orthodox-Israelitische Bibelanstalt to counter L. Philippson's Bible translation, against which he had published a polemical pamphlet (1860).

Descendants

Bamberger became the founder of a widespread rabbinical family. Five of his six sons became rabbis, and his three daughters all married rabbis. His son SIMON SIMḤAH (1832–1897) was rabbi at Fischach and Aschaffenburg (Bavaria). He published *Ḥinnukh la-Ne'arim* (on the laws of *ẓiẓit* and *tefillin*; with Yiddish translation, 1882³); *Pekuddat ha-Levi'im* (Aaron b. Joseph of Barcelona's commentary on Alfasi, *Berakhot* and *Ta'anit*, with notes, 1874); *Avodat ha-Levi'im* (Jonathan b. David of Lunel's commentary on Alfasi, *Ḥullin*, 1871). SOLOMON (1835–1918) was rabbi at Lengnau, Niederlangenthal, and Sennheim (the latter two in Alsace). His talmudic research dealt mainly with Nathan b. Jehiel's *Arukh* (*Limmud Arukh* on various talmudic tractates, 1868–97; *Hegyon Shelomo*, 1878). MOSES LOEB (1838–1899) was district rabbi at Kissingen, Bavaria. SECKEL ISAAC (1839–1885) was *dayyan* at Frankfurt. NATHAN (1842–1919) succeeded his father as rabbi and seminary principal at Wuerzburg. He published *Likkutei ha-Levi*, on the religious customs of Wuerzburg (1907), and collaborated with his brother Simon Simḥah on *Pekuddat ha Levi'im*. He also wrote a memoir of his father (1897).

In the third generation: SECKEL (1863–1934), son of Simon Simḥah and district rabbi at Kissingen, wrote a halakhic tract on the immersion of vessels (*Tevilat Kelim*, with German translation, 1887); an edition of the *Midrash Lekaḥ Tov* on the Song of Songs and Ruth (1887); and a translation with commentary of *Avot* (1897, 1935³). MOSES LOEB (II; 1869–1924), also a son of Simon Simḥah, was rabbi at Schoenlanke (Pomerania, now Trzcianka, Poland). He edited J. Ettlinger's essays and addresses (1899) and Joseph ibn Naḥmias' commentary on Esther (1891–93), Proverbs (1911), and Jeremiah (1913). He also wrote on book censorship in the duchy of Baden (1902), on the history of the Jews of Wuerzburg (1905), and of Schoenlanke (1912). SELIG (1872–1936), son of Solomon and rabbi of the Hamburg *Klaus*, edited and translated into German a large number of halakhic, aggadic, and liturgical texts. He also edited Maimonides' commentary on tractate *Ḥallah* (1895). SOLOMON MENAḤEM (1869–1920), son of Seckel Isaac, was rabbi at Bingen, Burgpreppach, and Hanau. He was a cofounder of the *Juedisch-Literarische Gesellschaft. SIMON SIMḤAH (II; 1871–1961), son of Nathan and rabbi at Aschaffenburg (Bavaria), wrote on circumcision (*Beschneidungsakt*, 1913) and the creation (*Die Schoepfungsurkunde*, 1903).

The next generation included SIMON SIMḤAH (III; 1899–1957), son of Seckel Isaac, rabbi at Stuttgart and later in Israel, and his brother MOSES LOEB (III; 1902–1960), rabbi in Mainz and Nottingham and founder-principal of the Jewish Boarding School in Gateshead, England. Erich *Fromm, the social psychologist, and Saul Esh, the historian, were also descendants of S.B. Bamberger, as was the bookseller-publisher Nathan Wolf Bamberger (1888–1948), who in 1934 co-founded in Jerusalem the firm of Bamberger and Wahrmann which specialized in rare Jewish books.

BIBLIOGRAPHY: S. Esh (ed.), *Bamberger Family* (1964, with bibliographies); N. Bamberger, *Seligmann Baer Bamberger* (Ger., 1897); M. Auerbach, in: *Jeschurun*, 15 (1928), 524–38; H. Schwab, *History of Orthodox Jewry in Germany* (1951), 73–81; idem, *Chachme Ashkenaz* (Eng., 1964), 19–23; S. Bamberger, *Zekher... Yiẓḥak Dov Bamberger* (1958); M.L. Bamberger, in: L. Jung (ed.), *Jewish Leaders* (1964), 179–95. **ADD. BIBLIOGRAPHY:** L. Trepp, in: *Bits of Honey* (1993), 289–310; S. Robinson, in: *Le'ela*, 43 (1997), 16–19.

BAMBERGER, SIMON (1846–1926), U.S. mining industrialist, railroad builder, and governor of Utah. Born in Germany, Bamberger immigrated to the United States when he was 14. He worked first in the store of his elder brother, Herman, in Wilmington, Ohio, and later the brothers became clothing manufacturers in St. Louis, Missouri. In pursuit of a debtor, Simon Bamberger found himself at Piedmont, Wyoming, a Union Pacific Railroad work camp. He decided to stay, erected shacks and tents which he rented to workers on the new railroad, and cashed their paychecks at a discount. He then moved on to Ogden, Utah, where he bought an interest in a hotel, and in 1869 settled in Salt Lake City. He was joined there by his brothers and they tended to his business interests, leaving him free to seek his fortune in gold mining. He found it in the lucrative Centennial Eureka Mines. Subsequently he built a railroad to a coalfield in southern Utah, and after a struggle lasting 17 years against competing interests and harassing litigation, the Bamberger Railroad went into operation between Salt Lake City and Ogden, with Simon Bamberger as director and treasurer.

In 1898 Bamberger entered public service as a member of Salt Lake City's Board of Education, where he devoted himself to improving teachers' conditions. From 1903 to 1907 he sat in the State Senate and then was elected governor of Utah (1916–20), the first Democrat and non-Mormon to become governor. During his administration Bamberger sponsored legislation for the control and supervision of public utilities, improved public health services, guaranteed full-year salaries for teachers, the right of workers to voluntary association, benefits for farmers, and other liberal measures.

Bamberger was one of the founders of Utah's first Jewish congregation, Bnai Israel, and was later its president. He supported the Utah colonization fund established by the Jewish Agricultural Society which attempted to settle 140 Jews from New York and Philadelphia in the Clarion Colony. He was also prominent in several Jewish philanthropic and communal institutions.

BIBLIOGRAPHY: AJYB, 19 (1917/18), 249f.; N.Warrum, *Utah Since Statehood* (1919); L.L. Watters, *Pioneer Jews of Utah* (1952), 9f., 30f., 163–9; B. Postal and L. Koppman, *A Jewish Tourist's Guide to the U.S.* (1954), 608ff.

[Morton Mayer Berman]

BAMBUS, WILLY (1863–1904), one of the first German Jews to join *Ḥibbat Zion. He propagated the organization's ideas in the periodical *Serubabel*, edited by him in Berlin (1887–88). Bambus became a leading member of *Esra, a society founded in 1883 for the advancement of Jewish agricultural settlement in Palestine and Syria. Later, together with Hirsch *Hildesheimer, Emile *Meyerson, and Isaac Turoff, he established the central committee of Ḥovevei Zion in Paris, with branches in many countries. His intention was to transform the movement into a world organization. Herzl's creation of the Zionist Organization led him to abandon his idea and for a time he became a political Zionist. However, disagreeing with Herzl's rejection of the so-called "infiltration", i.e., small-scale settlement in Palestine without prior international agreement, he became strongly opposed to political Zionism. He expressed this primarily in the periodical *Zion* which he edited from 1895. In 1901 he was instrumental in the creation of the *Hilfsverein der deutschen Juden of which he became the first general secretary. After the Kishinev pogrom (1903) he worked in the defense organization against antisemitism (Komitee zur Abwehr Anti-semitischer Angriffe) in Berlin, and endeavored, unsuccessfully, to establish a bank for Jewish emigrants. His works included *Palaestina, Land und Leute* (1898), articles for *Die Welt* and the *Allgemeine Zeitung des Judentums,* as well as several works on Jewish settlement in Ereẓ Israel.

BIBLIOGRAPHY: A. Bein, *Theodor Herzl* (1962^2), 215–8, 227, 241; R. Lichtheim, *Geschichte des deutschen Zionismus* (1954), index; G. Herlitz, in: *Davar* (Nov. 8, 1954); J. Turoff, in: AZJ, no. 48 (Nov. 25, 1904), 567–68, no. 47 (1904), 3–4; H. Loewe, *Juedische Rundschau.*, no. 459 (1904), 6–8, 379–80. **ADD. BIBLIOGRAPHY:** R. Heuer (ed.), *Lexikon deutsch-juedischer Autoren,* 1 (1992), 344–45 (incl. bibl.).

[Oskar K. Rabinowicz / Marcus Pyka (2nd ed.)]

BA-MEH MADLIKIN (Heb. בַּמֶּה מַדְלִיקִין; "with what may one kindle?"), opening words of the second chapter of the Mishnah tractate *Shabbat* which deals with the oils and wicks proper to be used for the Sabbath lights, and with what must be done on Fridays before the commencement of the Sabbath. This chapter, which consists of seven paragraphs, is recited, according to traditional practice, during the Friday evening service either before the start of the *Arvit* prayer (Sephardi and Ashkenazi ritual in Ereẓ Israel) or at the end of it (Ashkenazi ritual). Some ḥasidic rites do not recite it at all. The reading of the chapter of the Mishnah was instituted in the geonic period as a reminder of the duty of kindling the Sabbath lights, as a precaution against any unintentional desecration of the Sabbath caused by adjusting the lamp, and as a safeguard for latecomers to the synagogue (the recital of this chapter by the congregation made it possible for latecomers to finish their prayers with the other congregants and to leave for home together without fear of injury in the dark). *Ba-Meh Madlikin* is not recited on a Sabbath falling on or immediately following a holiday because latecomers to the service would be few.

BIBLIOGRAPHY: Eisenstein, Yisrael, 3 (1909), 95; Eisenstein, Dinim, 46ff.; Baer, Seder, 192; Elbogen, Gottesdienst, 11ff.

BANAI, family of Israeli actors and pop-rock singer-songwriters. For over half a century the Banais provided the country with leading theater and film actors, directors and pop and rock stars.

Foremost among the clan was YOSSI BANAI (1932–2006), one of Israel's leading actors and comedians, who also released a number of big-selling albums based on the French *chanson* singing style, and published several books. Banai followed in the footsteps of his older actor brother Ya'akov, joining the Nahal entertainment troupe at the start of his military service in 1951. On his return to civilian life Banai enrolled at the *Habimah acting school and took part in numerous stage productions.

Banai always had a penchant for the comic side of his profession and in the 1960s joined forces with Rivka Michaeli in a program of humorous sketches and songs called *Yaldut Kashah* ("Difficult Childhood"). The songs from the show were later released on record. In 1968 Banai collaborated with Eli Gurelitzki in a comic-musical production, directed by Nissim *Aloni, called *Ḥakhamim ba-Layla* ("Smart Alecks") for which he wrote some of the sketches and two songs. A record of songs from this show, too, was subsequently released.

During the 1960s Banai spent some time in Paris and was later among the leading performers of French music, which was popular in Israel during the 1950s and 1960s. Banai performed translated versions of French hits in several of his productions, including *Tel Aviv ka-Ketanah* ("Little Tel Aviv") and *Yossiakhzakyuna*, and in 1969 he presented an entire show based on the music of popular French crooner Georges Brassens. In the early 1970s Banai released records that included the works of Belgian-born singer Jacques Brel and French singers Barbara and Georges Moustaki. Around this time he also put out several albums of original Hebrew compositions.

In 1973 Banai, Michaeli, and Aloni reunited for the comic production *Nissuin Nussakh Gerushin* ("Divorce-Style Marriage") which spawned two successful albums. It was around this time that Banai joined forces with one of Israel's top songstresses, Naomi *Shemer, with Banai providing the lyrics for Shemer's music to "Sefirat Mellai" ("Stock Taking").

In 1979 Banai created his most successful one-man show, *Ani ve-Shimon u-Moise ha-Kattan* ("Me, Shimon and Little Moise"), based on Banai's childhood in Jerusalem. The show closed with Naomi Shemer's composition *Al Kol Elleh* ("For All These") which quickly took on anthemic popularity. Throughout the 1980s Banai continued making popular albums, including teaming up with leading pop-rock figures such as Matti *Caspi and Yoni Rechter. In 1990 he recorded a song entitled *"Eyfo Ani ve-Eyfo Hem"* ("Where Am I and Where Are They"), written by his rock star son Yuval. Throughout this period Banai continued to be active in serious theater, participating in the Cameri Theater's *Gam Hu be-Aẓilim* (1989), *Mareh me-al ha-Gesher* (1990) for the Habimah Theater, and the 1999 production of *Melekhet Ḥayyim* for the Beit Lessin theater.

In 2000 Banai was awarded the Israel Prize in recognition of his contribution to the entertainment industry.

Other entertainers in the Banai clan include Yossi's younger brother GAVRI, who was a member of the country's leading comic team, *Ha-Gashash ha-Ḥiver, from its establishment in 1963.

Yossi's son, YUVAL (1962–), was a founder-member of rock band Mashina in 1984, following a stint as the soloist of short-lived rock band Shelom ha-Ẓibbur. Mashina soon found success and became the country's top rock act for much of its lifetime up to 1995. Yuval and Mashina were heavily influenced by British punk rock and American funk and started out performing cover versions of punk, funk, and blues numbers in small venues in and around Tel Aviv. There was also something revolutionary and anti-establishment about the band. The debut album, *Mashina 1*, included several hits, such as *"Rakkevet Layla le-Kahir"* ("Night Train to Cairo"), with lyrics written by Yuval's cousin Ehud, and *"Ha-Tottakh Meẓalzel Pa'amayim"* ("The Cannon Rings Twice"), the latter about a soldier who can't get the sounds of artillery out of his head after returning from battle. Mashina's material often touched on political and social issues, and its music had mass appeal as the band continued to fill the country's largest venues and its albums sold consistently well. The group disbanded in 1995, after a sell-out tour, reuniting in 2003. In the interim, Yuval released three solo albums and toured with Mashina members Iggi Dayan and Shlomi Brakha.

Yuval's cousin EHUD BANAI (1953–), the son of Yossi's brother Ya'akov, took cello lessons from the age of 10 and was inspired by the hits of Elvis Presley, Cliff Richard, and The Beatles. He began developing his guitar-playing skills as an IDF soldier and honed his craft entertaining on the streets of London after his release from the army. After his return home he started writing songs and worked as a stagehand for his uncle Gavri's Ha-Gashash ha-Ḥiver comedy team. Over the next few years Ehud wrote a number of hit songs and in 1982 tried, unsuccessfully, to start his own band together with vocalist Avi Mattos. At this time, his on-stage efforts received a welcome boost when he was hired to play guitar and provide backup vocals for his uncle Yossi's production *Kemo Ẓipporim* ("Like Birds") which was based on gypsy music. Ehud's first breakthrough came in 1985 when he recorded the hit single "Ir Miklat" ("City of Refuge") and the following year he established his Plittim (Refugees) band. Two years later, at the age of 34, Ehud finally got a recording contract and released his first album, *Ehud Banai ve ha-Plittim,* which was a smash hit. Ehud Banai became one of Israel's most popular rock artists, including a generous amount of ethnic material in his records and performances. He had put out seven albums by 2005, the last, the eagerly awaited *Anneh Lee*, being his first in six years and selling well.

Other successful members of the Banai "dynasty" include rock guitarist-vocalist MEIR (1961–); his younger brother, rock, dance, electronic music pianist-vocalist EVYATAR (1973–); and actress-comedienne ORNA (1969–).

[Barry Davis (2nd ed.)]

BANAT, region in the southwestern part of Romania which for many years was regarded as belonging administratively to Transylvania, though it also benefited from an independent administration in the framework of the medieval Transylvanian principality. It was inhabited for many centuries by Romanians, Hungarians, Germans (Swabians), Serbs, and Jews. The languages spoken there were German and Hungarian as the official languages and other vernacular languages.

The region is still considered to be a classical multicultural one.

The Jewish population of the region belonged to two principal Jewish groups, the Ashkenazim and the Sephardim, who coexisted under satisfactory conditions. However, the *Hapsburg authorities saw in the Jews of the region a certain danger because of the privileged relations they had with the Turks in the Ottoman Empire, who were contending for the region.

After 1867 there was a degree of competition between the Austrians and the Hungarians in the two-headed empire over who would better succeed in assimilating their Jews, a situation which had consequences for the Jews of Banat as the competing parties tried to Germanize and Hungarize them, respectively. After 1919, with the dismemberment of the Austro-Hungarian Empire, Banat became part of Greater Romania, which posed a language problem as most Jews did not speak the language. After the unification of Banat (as part of historical Transylvania) with Romania the region lost many of its multicultural specificities and a certain diversification set in. With the majority of Germans and Jews leaving the region under the Communist regime of Ceausescu, it underwent the most significant changes in its multinational history.

[Paul Schveiger (2nd ed.)]

BAND, ARNOLD (1930–), U.S. modern Hebrew literature scholar. Educated at Harvard University (where he trained as a classicist, writing a dissertation on Aristophanes) and Boston's Hebrew College, Band was the founding director of the Center for Jewish Studies at the University of California in Los Angeles and the founder of the Comparative Literature Department there. He also taught at Harvard College, Boston Hebrew College, Brandeis University, the Hebrew University, Tel Aviv University, Yale University, and the Jewish Theological Seminary of America. In the 41 years he spent teaching at UCLA, Band had a major impact on the historical and critical study of Hebrew literature, through his teaching, publishing, and training of graduate students, some of whom are now leading scholars in their own right. Band stressed historical contextualization in all his work; he was keenly aware of the need to place modern Jewish creativity in its broader contemporary context, as well as in its relation to earlier Jewish creative expression. Further, he insisted that 19th- and early 20th-century Hebrew literature is best appreciated when studied in tandem with literature written in Yiddish, the two literatures being seen as one cultural continuum. In more recent years he turned his attention to Kafka. Band's books, published in both Hebrew and English include *Ha-Re'i Bo'er ba-Esh* (a collection of Hebrew poetry), *Nostalgia and Nightmare: The Fiction of S.J. Agnon* (1968) and the *The Tales of Nahman of Bratlav* (1978). Band also published more than 125 articles in Hebrew and English on a range of topics in modern Jewish literature and Jewish cultural life. He was the recipient of many major awards, including a Guggenheim Fellowship, the UCLA Distinguished Teaching Award, and the National Endowment for the Humanities Award, and the National Foundation for Jewish Culture's award for lifetime achievement in social, literary and cultural studies.

[Jay Harris (2nd ed.)]

BANET (Baneth, Benet, Panet, Benedict, Binet, Bineter), family of Moravian rabbis and scholars. Its first known member, MORDECAI BEN YOM TOV, approved a *maḥzor* following the Polish ritual in Nikolsburg (Mikulov) in 1716. ABER (Aberl; d. 1758), possibly Mordecai's son, was *dayyan* in Nikolsburg. A responsum (*Noda bi-Yhudah, Mahadurah Tinyana* ḤM no. 12) was addressed by Ezekiel *Landau to JOHANAN BANET, a *dayyan* in Alt-Ofen (Budapest). Johanan's son JACOB (d. 1812) was *dayyan* in Alt-Ofen. One of Jacob's four sons was Ezekiel b. Jacob *Baneth. FRADL, a daughter of Aber, married Abraham Bia of Csurgo (Hungary). Their son Mordecai *Banet, who took his mother's family name, became head of the Nikolsburg branch of the family. In the 19th and 20th centuries members of the family distinguished themselves in various fields of modern Jewish scholarship.

BIBLIOGRAPHY: EJ, 4 (1929), s.v. *Benet* (with genealogy).

[Heinrich Haim Brody]

BANET (Benet), MORDECAI BEN ABRAHAM (1753–1829), Moravian rabbi, one of the leading talmudists of his time. Banet was born in Csurgo, Hungary. He studied at the yeshivah of Fuerth under Joseph Steinhardt, author of the responsa *Zikhron Yosef*. In 1784 he was appointed *dayyan* in Nikolsburg, Moravia. In 1787 and 1788 he served as rabbi of Lundenburg, Moravia, and subsequently of Sasvar, Hungary, and from 1789 as rabbi and head of the yeshivah of Nikolsburg, and district rabbi of Moravia. Banet's yeshivah attracted students from near and far, and during the 40 years that he headed it several thousands of students passed through. Banet fought vigorously against the Reform movement, particularly against Aaron *Chorin, and vehemently opposed the founding of the Reform Temple in Hamburg. At the same time he displayed a certain understanding of the spiritual needs of his contemporaries. At the request of the government, he prepared two courses of study for students for the rabbinate which included secular studies. His proposals were published in the *Toledot Mordekhai Banet* (1832) of his son Jacob Abraham. Under Banet's influence, his son Naphtali *Banet compiled a handbook (in Hebrew and German) on the fundamentals of the Jewish religion. Because of his great influence on his community, his talented leadership, and the support of the government, Banet succeeded in postponing the disintegration of Moravian Jewry for at least one generation later than that of the breakup of Bohemian Jewry. He was one of the chief opponents of Saul *Berlin in the controversy over his work *Besamim Rosh* (Berlin, 1793).

Of Banet's works, only *Be'ur Mordekhai* (2 vols. Vienna, 1805–13), novellae to the *Mordekhai* of Mordecai b. Hillel, was published during his lifetime. After his death the following were published: *Magen Avot* (Zolkiew, 1835; 1903^2; with notes by Shalom Mordecai ha-Kohen), on the main categories of work forbidden on the Sabbath; *Har ha-Mor* (Prague, 1861), responsa, published together with the *Hokhmat Shelomo* of Solomon Kwetsch, his pupil; *Parashat Mordekhai* (1889), responsa on the Shulḥan Arukh, together with notes by the publisher, Abraham Isaac Glueck; *Tekhelet Mordekhai* (1892), aggadic homilies and talmudic novellae, also containing a biography of the author; *Maḥashevet Mordekhai* (1902), aggadic novellae to the Pentateuch; *Sefer Maharam Banet* (also called *Divrei Mordekhai*; 1906), novellae on aspects of the dietary laws with notes by the publisher Abraham Jungreisz.

BIBLIOGRAPHY: R. Ferber, *Pe'er Mordekhai* (1951); R. Kestenberg-Gladstein, *Neuere Geschichte der Juden in den boehmischen Laendern*, 1 (1969), index S.V. *Benet; B. Mevorakh, in: Ẓion*, 34 (1969), 208ff.

[Moshe Nahum Zobel]

BANET (Benet), NAPHTALI BEN MORDECAI (1789–1857), Moravian rabbi and author, third son of Mordecai *Banet. Banet officiated as rabbi and principal of the yeshivah in Safov (Schaffa, Moravia) from 1836 to 1857. He enjoined a fast and a penitential prayer to be recited on the 24th of Sivan in memory of the great conflagration of 1822 which almost destroyed the entire Jewish quarter of Schaffa; the custom was adhered to by the community until the Holocaust. Banet's writings include *Berit Melaḥ* on *meliḥah* (salting) laws (Prague, 1816); *Emunat Yisrael*, a catechism of the fundamentals of Judaism for Jewish youth, in Hebrew and German (*ibid.*, 1832); *Torat Dat Moshe ve-Yisrael*, on the principles of Judaism, in Hebrew and German (*ibid.*, 1826). The latter were intended to serve as a substitute for Herz Homberg's catechism *Benei Ẓiyyon* and expressed a conservative point of view.

BIBLIOGRAPHY: A. Walden, *Sefer Shem ha-Gedolim he-Ḥadash* (1870), pt. 2, 8a, no. 97; D. Feuchtwang, in: *Festschrift Adolf Schwarz* (1917), 550; E. Faerber, *Pe'er Mordekhai* (1951), 55–58; B. Mevorakh, in: *Zion*, 34 (1969), 208ff.

[Moshe Nahum Zobel]

BANETH, family of scholars. EDUARD EZEKIEL BANETH (1855–1930), talmudic scholar, was a descendant of the well-known *Banet family of rabbis and scholars. He was born in Liptó-Szent-Miklós (Slovakia). From 1882 to 1895 he served as rabbi at Krotoszyn (near Poznan) and then as lecturer of Talmud at the Lehranstalt fuer die Wissenschaft des Judentums in Berlin. In 1919 the Prussian Ministry of Education awarded him the title of professor. Baneth's work was devoted mainly to talmudic and rabbinic literature, the development of *halakhah*, and the Jewish calendar. Among his published works are *Ursprung der Sadokaeer und Boethosaeer* (1882); *Maimunis Neumondberechnung* (4 vols., 1898–1903); *Der Sederabend* (1904); *Avot mit Maimunis arabischem Kommentar* (1905); *Maimonides als Chronologe und Astronom* (1914); *Soziale Motive in der rabbinischen Rechtspflege* (1922); *Bilder talmudischer Ethik* (1926); and *Der juedische und buergerliche Kalender* (1928). Baneth also contributed to the Samter-Hoffmann German translation and commentary of the Mishnah (order of *Mo'ed*, 1927²).

His son DAVID HARTWIG (ZVI; 1893–1973) was an Arabist. Born in Krotoszyn, from 1920 to 1924 he was an assistant at the Akademie fuer die Wissenschaft des Judentums. He then went to Palestine where he was a lecturer at the Hebrew University on Arabic philosophy, language, and literature. From 1946 he was professor of Arabic language and literature. In his earlier years David made important contributions to ancient Aramaic and Canaanite studies, but his life's work consisted in the study of Jewish thought as expressed in Arabic, Arabic as used by Jews, and medieval Hebrew. He wrote on the enigmatic Jewish rationalist *Ibn Kammuna (MGWJ, vol. 69, 1925), on the relationship between *Judah Halevi and the Muslim theologian *Ghazali (*Korrespondenzblatt*, vol. 5, 1929; see also *Keneset*, vol. 7, 1942), and on the use made by both Ghazali and the Jewish pietist Baḥya ibn Paquda of a passage in a book by a Christian author (*Magnes Jubilee Volume*, 1938).

Baneth was at his best in the editing and criticism of texts, such as his edition of Maimonides' letters (*Iggerot ha-Rambam*, 1946), his revisions of Maimonides' *Terminology of Logic* (edited by L. Roth, 1935) and of the *Book of Beatitude*, ascribed to Maimonides (prepared for publication by H.S. Davidowitz, 1939), as well as his discussion of the Hebrew translations of Maimonides' treatise on resurrection (*Tarbiz*, vol. 11, 1939/40, and vol. 13, 1941/42) and of Maimonides' Hebrew usage (*Tarbiz*, vol. 6, 1934/35 and vol. 23, 1951/52). He published many detailed reviews of Judeo-Arabic works in *Kirjath Sepher*. Of particular importance are Baneth's studies of the language and contents of the Cairo *Genizah* documents (cf. S. Shaked, *A Tentative Bibliography of Geniza Documents* (1964), 268–9). Most of the Arabic *Genizah* texts published by S. *Assaf were prepared for publication and translated into Hebrew by Baneth. By emphasizing that most deviations from classical Arabic grammar in the *Genizah* documents were not "mistakes," but represented the living language of the period, Baneth pointed the way for a sound approach to the understanding of those medieval writings.

[Moshe David Herr / Shelomo Dov Goitein / Samuel Miklos Stern]

BANETH (Benet, Paneth), EZEKIEL BEN JACOB (1773–1854), rabbi, born in Alt-Ofen (Budapest), Hungary. In 1810 Ezekiel was appointed rabbi of Szecseny. He became rabbi of *Paks in 1825 and subsequently of *Balassagyarmat, and from 1847 officiated at Nyitra. He corresponded on halakhic matters with Moses Sofer, Judah Aszód, and other rabbis. His yeshivah was attended by pupils from various parts of the country. One of his most talented students was his youngest son Jerachmeel Bernhard (1815–1871), rabbi of Liptoszentmiklos (Liptovsky Svaty Mikulas). Ezekiel was also an eloquent preacher. Recognized by his contemporaries as a halakhic authority, he left no written work, having destroyed his commentary on the Tosefta before his death. His grandson was Eduard Ezekiel *Baneth.

BIBLIOGRAPHY: M. Stein (ed.), *Magyar rabbik*, 4 (1908), 36, 74; D. Feuchtwang, in: *Festschrift Adolf Schwarz* (1917), 539–56.

[Jeno Zsoldos]

BANIAS, ruined city at the foot of Mount Hermon on the Hermon Brook, one of the sources of the River Jordan. The brook drains an area of about 60 sq. mi. (150 sq. km.), running swiftly for 2 miles (3.5 km.) and then dropping 600 ft. (190 m.). After another 5.5 miles (9 km.) it joins the Dan River and runs into the Jordan. The brook contains water all year round, with an annual total of 125 million cu. m. The city was called by the Jews *Dan or Mivẓar Dan ("the Fort of Dan"; a suggested identification with the biblical Beth-Rehob is uncertain). It stood over a cliff with a grotto dedicated to the Greek god Pan and the nymphs, and hence was named Paneas (Banias being an Arabic corruption). In 198 B.C.E., Antiochus III conquered Palestine from the Ptolemies by his victory near this place. Later the city belonged to the Itureans, from whom it was transferred by Augustus to Herod who named it Caesarea in honor of Augustus and to whom he erected a temple there. Philip the Tetrarch (*Herod Philip), Herod's son, developed the city, resided there, and struck coins with images of its buildings. It was generally known as Caesarea Philippi ("of Philip") to distinguish it from the better-known Caesarea-by-the-Sea. As such it is mentioned in the New Testament (Matt. 16:13; Mark 8:27) in connection with Jesus' visit to the area. In 61 C.E. *Agrippa II renamed it Neronias in honor of the emperor Nero, but it kept this name only until 68. In 70 *Titus held games there to celebrate his victory and many Jewish captives were put to death. In the Talmud, Caesarea is called Keissariyyon or Little Caesarea; the Mishnah also mentions the cave of Pamias referring to the same place. Caesarea's territory extended as far as Hadar and the Phiale Lake; the Ḥuleh Valley also belonged to it. A statue of Hadrian which stood there was regarded by the early Christians as representing Jesus healing a woman. The Talmud refers to the emperor Diocletian's oppression of the people of Paneas (Lieberman, in JQR, 36 (1946), 350ff.; TJ, Shev. 9:2, 38d). In Roman-Byzantine times Caesarea belonged to Phoenicia; its bishops took part in church councils from 325 to 451. In Crusader times it was called Belinas and a powerful castle (Qalʿat al-Subayba) was erected above it.

Banias and its rich archaeological remains were frequently visited by European and American explorers during the 19th century, who noted especially the rock escarpment to the north of the site with its caves, carved niches, and inscriptions. Small-scale Israeli excavations were conducted at the site in the 1970s and 1980s, with a very large ongoing archaeological project there since the 1990s, concentrating in two areas: the work directed by Z. Maoz in the area of the spring-cave and adjacent temples, and the other directed by V. Tsaferis in the central civic area of the site to the south of the springs. The Roman-period cultic compound next to the main spring comprised at least two temples, dedicated to the gods Pan and Zeus, with adjacent halls and installations. Among the finds was a good representation of Roman statuary. In other parts of the city, fragments of buildings from the Hellenistic period through medieval times were discovered. An important discovery close to the civic center was that of a large palace complex comprising underground vaulted chambers, halls, and courts and dating from the first century C.E. This palace was apparently built by one of Herod the Great's successors, i.e., Philip or Agrippa II. In addition to these finds, the expedition also brought to light remains of a bath house, a columned street from the Byzantine period, and a synagogue dating from the 11th century C.E.

[Michael Avi-Yonah / Gideon Biger and Shimon Gibson (2nd ed.)]

Since Banias was situated on the main road from Palestine to Damascus it served in the Middle Ages as an administrative center to a district with the same name. During the 11th century there was a relatively large Jewish community, whose members were called the Baniasites. They were frequently mentioned in *genizah* documents. A document of 1056 shows that the Banias community was well organized and had a *bet din*.

Since Babylonian Jews had settled in Banias, the community was split into two sections, the Palestinians and the Babylonians, who differed in their versions of prayers. These two sections existed to the beginning of the 12th century. A Karaite pseudo-messiah is reported in 1102. *Benjamin of Tudela mentions no community in Banias in 1170 and it is possible that it ceased to exist during the Crusades. Later, Banias was reinhabited by Jews. Even during the early Ottoman period, Jews still lived at Banias, as attested by a document from 1624 which mentions the murder of a Jewish physician, by the name of Elijah ha-Kohen of Banias, by an Arab sheik (Ben Zvi, in *Tarbiz*, 3 (1932), 442). From 1948 to 1967 Banias served the Syrians as a base for attacks on *Dan. In June 1967 it was occupied by the Israel Defense Forces. Later the area was declared a nature reserve, under the supervision of the Nature Reserves Authority. The reserve includes the river and its natural surroundings as well as the archaeological relics scattered around the river route.

BIBLIOGRAPHY: E. Orni and E. Efrat, *Geography of Israel* (1964), 74; Mann, Egypt, 2 (1922), 203; J. Braslavski, in: BJPES, 5 (1938), 128–31; Assaf, *ibid.*, 6 (1939), 16–19; Schuerer, Gesch, 2 (1906), 204ff.; M. Avi-Yonah, Geog, 150–2; Kuk, in: *Ha-Tor*, 6 (1926), no. 35, 8–10; no. 36, 8–9. **ADD. BIBLIOGRAPHY:** Y. Meshorer, "The Coins of Caesarea Paneas," in: *Israel Numismatics Journal*, 8 (1984–85), 37–58; V. Tzaferis, "Banias, la Ville de Pan," in: *Le Monde de la Bible*, 64 (1990), 50–53; J.F. Wilson, *Banias: The Lost City of Pan* (2004) s.v. Paneas; Y. Tsafrir, L. Di Segni, and J. Green, *Tabula Imperii Romani. Iudaea – Palaestina. Maps and Gazetteer* (1994), 199.

BANISHMENT, a form of punishment widely imposed throughout the ancient world. India, the Greek cities, the Roman republic, and the Teutonic peoples all used this practice to rid themselves of undesirables, ranging from criminals to political agitators who threatened the safety of the state and the authority of its rulers. Bereft of his property and prohibited from ever returning home, the victim was reduced to the level of an outcast, a permanent stranger or wanderer in foreign lands. The custom seems to have been known in Canaan, as attested by the *Ugarit texts (*Aqhat*, 1:152–5: T.H. Gaster, *Thespis* (1961), 365–6; cf. 366n.). In ancient Israel, too, banishment was not unknown, although it appears almost exclusively as a form of divine punishment. Thus Adam was expelled from the Garden of Eden (Gen. 3:23–24) and Cain was doomed to be a wanderer, hidden from the presence of God (4:14–16). Two notable cases in the Bible are the banishment by Solomon of Abiathar the high priest to his family estate in Anathoth (I Kings 2:26; cf. Jer. 1:1) and the banishment of Amos from the Northern Kingdom of Amaziah the priest (Amos 7:12). Collective banishment, or exile, was considered the ultimate punishment that could be meted out to the entire people for acts of defiance against God (cf. Deut. 28:64 ff.), which were variously interpreted in different times (see *Galut). *Karet was an extreme form of this divine punishment, involving the actual "cutting off" of the individual from life on earth (Lev. 20:2–6; cf. Zimmerli in bibl.). The only form of banishment still in existence in biblical society was that imposed on a man guilty of manslaughter or involuntary homicide, for whom *Cities of Refuge were provided (cf. Num. 35:10 ff.; Deut. 4:41–43; 19:1 ff.; Josh. 20). It has been conjectured that banishment was not otherwise sanctioned as a punishment because residence abroad was viewed as something that cut the victim off entirely from God (Hos. 9:3–5; cf. Gen. 4:14; Ezek. 11:15) and even forced him to worship idols (Deut. 4:27–28; I Sam. 26:19; Jer. 16:13). For this reason too, exile was dreaded (cf. Deut. 28:65; Ezek. 37:11) and deemed to have horrendous consequences. In later centuries, milder forms of banishment from the religious community were resorted to by means of excommunication, though, contrary to the view of some scholars, there does not seem to be any definite evidence of this practice in the Bible (cf. Greenberg in bibl.).

[David L. Lieber]

Second Temple and Talmud Periods

Banishment was resorted to by the Romans as part of their repressive policies. Thus *Archelaus the son of Herod I was banished by the Romans to Vienne in Gaul and probably remained there until he died. It is possibly to these administrative acts that *Avtalyon refers in his statement, "Ye sages, be heedful of your words lest ye incur the penalty of banishment [*galut*] and be banished to a place of evil waters" (Avot 1:11). Nevertheless the Pharisees seem also to have exercised this power. Josephus (Wars, 1:111) states that when they were in power they banished and brought back whomsoever they chose. The gravity of the punishment was not only that the victims would be exiled "to a place of evil waters and the disciples who come after you will drink thereof and die" (see above) but that they were also banished from the Divine Presence. On the verse, "For they have driven me out this day that I should not cleave to the inheritance of the Lord" (I Sam. 26:19), the Talmud comments that "he who lives outside the Land of Israel is regarded as worshiping idols" (Ket. 110b), and this sentiment is reflected in the words of the *Musaf* prayer for festivals: "But on account of our sins we were banished from our land and removed far from our country, and we are unable to appear and prostrate ourselves before Thee and to fulfill our obligations."

[Louis Isaac Rabinowitz]

Middle Ages to 18th century

In the Middle Ages banishment continued to be one of the punishments imposed on offenders in communities having a measure of criminal jurisdiction over their members (see Judicial *Autonomy) or able to withhold or withdraw domiciliary rights (*ḥezkat ha-yishuv*). Hence it was imposed most frequently in Spain and Poland and Lithuania, although also occasionally elsewhere. A distinction was drawn between banishment of the offender from the city and from the realm, as also banishment for a limited period and for life. The Spanish kingdoms, especially at the height of Jewish autonomy in the 13th century, recognized the right of the communal organizations to banish recalcitrants or exclude new members. James I of Aragon (1213–76) gave the communities the right to punish offenders by fine, ban, flagellation, or expulsion. Privileges accorded to the Barcelona community in 1241 and 1272 empowered the communal elders "to eject or expel [recalcitrant members] from the Jewish quarter or the entire city." A similar ordinance for Calatayud Jewry empowered the community in 1229 to expel two individuals of bad repute. In the 1280s the *kahal* of Alagon banished six butchers from the city for four years and excommunicated all members who ate meat purchased from them. James II of Aragon, on a complaint from the Valencia community in 1294, instructed the local prefect and judge to prevent influential Christians from concealing offenders condemned by the community to deportation. In 1280 Pedro III of Aragon, in a basic privilege granted to all Catalonian communities, empowered their elders to punish with incarceration and exile all crimes of assault and battery, libel, and the like, in accordance with Jewish law and their own judgment. The same privilege, granted by John I of Aragon to the Huesca community in 1390, provided that the elders could summarily sentence offenders to death, mutilation, flogging, or exile, without appeal. Offenses for which banishment was imposed included murder for which there was only one witness (Solomon b. Jehiel Luria, *Yam shel Shelomo le-Bava Kamma*, 8, no. 7), or for which no witness was available but where hearsay was convincing (Resp. Judah b. Asher, no. 58), and attack on a victim who dies after a lapse of a certain time (Resp. sent to Salamanca by Isaac b. Sheshet, no. 251). In Spain in particular banishment was meted out to delators and informers (communal statutes of the delegates of Castile, 1432). R. Menahem of Merseburg (early 14th century) banished a man for two or three years for viciously beating his wife (*Nimmukei Maharar Menaḥem me-Resburk* at the end of Resp. Jacob Weill, Venice,

1549). Prostitution and adultery were punished by life banishment by *takkanot* of Prague of 1612. There is even a report of a man who was excommunicated and "run out" of Ereẓ Israel by the Safed rabbis in 1548 for indulging in unnatural practices with his wife (Eleazar Azikri, *Sefer Ḥaredim* (1601), part 3, ch. 2). Forfeiture of domiciliary rights throughout Lithuania was applied by the Council of Lithuania to thieves, receivers, and forgers, and could be broadened also to any persons engaged in suspicious or prohibited dealings, infringing ethics, or disturbing the peace of the community. Since the whole community was liable to make good a claim by a gentile for money he had lent to a defaulting Jewish debtor, in Lithuania the Jew wishing to borrow from a gentile had first to obtain permission from the *av bet din*. A borrower who failed to do so could be banished, and his right of domicile forfeited (*Pinkas ha-Va'ad*, paras. 163 and 637). The Lithuanian Council also withdrew the right of domicile from and imposed banishment on a person provoking a gentile by quarrels or blows (idem, para. 21). Its regulations of 1623, when itinerant beggary and unlicensed behavior was widespread, lay down expulsion for a beggar, if necessary with the assistance of gentile officers. In 1628 the Lithuanian Council withheld the right of domicile from any Jew absent ten years from his community of origin who had failed to pay his fiscal contribution. Banishment was frequently applied in the Sephardi community of *Hamburg, its governing body (**mahamad*) being empowered by the Hamburg senate to expel from the community any of its members infringing morals or engaged in dishonest business dealings, among other offenses. The offender thus sentenced was served with a writ from the beadle (*shamash*). If he proved unable to travel for lack of funds, the *mahamad* lent his relatives money to defray the expenses of the journey. Sometimes the offender was sent abroad, mainly to Amsterdam, and if his conduct subsequently improved was permitted to return. This punishment was also meted out to juvenile offenders.

BIBLIOGRAPHY: IN BIBLE: Mak. 2:6; Sif. Num. 60; Jos., Ant., 4:172–3; Philo, Spec., 3:123; F. Rundgren, in: VT, 7 (1957), 400–4; W. Zimmerli, in: ZAW, 66 (1954), 10–19; M. Greenberg, in: JBL, 78 (1959), 125–23. MIDDLE AGES: S. Assaf, *Ha-Onashin Aḥarei Ḥatimat ha-Talmud* (1922), 35–38; Baron, Community, index; Baer, Spain, 1 (1961), 430.

BANJA LUKA (Banya Luka), city in northern Bosnia. The earliest reference to a Jewish community dates from 1713, when Jewish merchants of Banja Luka appealed to the French government to appoint one of them French mercantile consul in the town. The community had both a Sephardi and an Ashkenazi synagogue and numbered 226 persons in 1875, 336 in 1895, and 457 in 1927. A joint community center was built in 1936. It was damaged by Allied bombing in 1944. Each congregation had its own rabbi: Menachem Romano for the Sephardim, Pinchas Keller and Mavro Frankfurter for the Ashkenazim. There was some Zionist activity under the leadership of Judah Levy and Hans Bramer. Both synagogues were destroyed during the Holocaust, when most of the local Jews perished.

From the 1990s Banja Luka was the seat of the Republika Srpska (Serbian Republic) as part of the Federation of Bosnia-Herzegovina. A small Jewish community was reestablished.

BIBLIOGRAPHY: *Jevrejski Almanah*, 1–2 (1926–27), index. **ADD. BIBLIOGRAPHY:** *Spomenpca 400* (1966); Y. Eventov, *Toledot Yehudei Yugoslavia*, vol. 1 (1971), 97–99; Z. Loker (ed.), *Toledot Yehudei Yugoslavia*, vol. II (1991), 213–15.

BANKING AND BANKERS

Antiquity

There is little likelihood that financial transactions played a prominent role in the pre-Exilic epoch in Ereẓ Israel; according to the ethos of Jewish society, then founded on a pronounced agrarian structure, lending was part of the assistance a man owed to his neighbor or brother in need (cf. Deut. 23:21). During the Babylonian era Jews had greater opportunities to come into contact with a highly developed banking tradition and to participate in credit operations. After the Exile, commerce and credit certainly had a place in Ereẓ Israel. Though the society remained predominantly agrarian, Jerusalem had a number of wealthy families, including tax agents and landowners, who speculated and deposited their gains in the Temple, which had in some ways the function of a national bank (see *Heliodorus). Organized banking probably arose in connection with *Ma'aserot* ("tithes"), in particular *Ma'aser sheni*, and the pilgrimages to Jerusalem, through the activities of the *money changers. The use of Greek terms indicates a strong Hellenistic influence on the establishment of banking. Meanwhile, the Jewish communities forming in the Diaspora, the most important at first being that of *Babylonia, were given an impulse toward a new way of life by the long-standing traditions of a capitalist type of economy existing around them (see Nippur and *Murashu's sons). In Babylonia, Jews engaged in financial transactions: some were farmers of taxes and customs, and the wealthiest of them were landowners; among the latter were *Huna, the head of the academy of Sura, and Rav *Ashi. However, talmudic references show that the standards of an agrarian economy were still dominant and therefore gamblers and usurers were not thought trustworthy witnesses (see e.g., Sanh. 3:3).

Another important Jewish colony was to be found at *Alexandria, center of the trade between the Mediterranean and the Arabian and Indian world, where Jews were engaged not only in commerce and international trade but in moneylending too. According to *Josephus, a Jewish tax agent was able to make a loan of 3,000 talents. The *alabarch Alexander Lysimachus, who loaned King *Agrippa I 200,000 drachmas (Jos., Ant., 18:159–160), was also the steward of Antonia, mother of Emperor Claudius. Another Alexandrian Jew was treasurer to Candace, queen of Ethiopia.

Middle Ages

THE CALIPHATE. With the rapid development of city life and commerce in the caliphate of Baghdad from the late eighth century and the transition of the majority of Jews under caliphate rule from agriculture and a village environment to the cities, banking became one of the occupations of some upper-class Jews, especially in Baghdad and later under the Fatimids (from 968) in Egypt. This *Jahbadhiyya*, as it was called, was a form of banking based on the savings and economic activities of the whole Jewish merchant class and not only on the fortunes of the very rich: the bankers loaned to the state and its officers money deposited with them as well as from their own fortunes. The vast sums at the disposal of these Jewish bankers and their relative immunity from confiscation by the autocratic authorities both tend to confirm that these Jewish "court bankers" from the beginning of the tenth century onward were well-known to their Muslim debtors as a kind of "deposit banker" for Jewish merchants. Under the Fatimid caliph al-Mustanṣir the brothers *Abu Sa'd al-Tustarī and Abu Naṣr Ḥesed b. Sahl al-Tustarī (both died in 1048) were influential in the finances of Egypt. With the rise of *Saladin and the foundation of the Ayyubid dynasty in Egypt (1169), the position of the Jews deteriorated but they were able to continue their moneychanging activities at least. Toward the end of the Mamluk period (1517), Samuel, a moneychanger in Cairo, must have possessed considerable wealth, for the Arab chronicler Ibn Iyās tells that the sultan extorted from him more than 500,000 dinars. During the Muslim rule on the Iberian peninsula, Córdoba Jews were active in the financial administration in the tenth and eleventh centuries. The responsa of this period show a highly developed money economy existing before the First and Second Crusades.

EARLY MERCHANTS IN EUROPE. Persecution, such as occurred in Alexandria in 414 or the oppressive measures promulgated in the Byzantine Empire beginning with *Constantine and intensified under *Justinian, may have contributed to the fact that from the fifth century Jewish merchants followed their Greek and Syrian counterparts to Gaul and not only traded in luxury goods but also loaned money. With the disappearance of the Syrians and Greeks from Europe in the seventh century, the Jewish merchants were able to expand. Within the administration of the Merovingian kings (from 481) Jews possibly farmed taxes or advanced money on revenues to high officials; according to Gregory of Tours (c. 538–94), the count of Tours and his vicar were indebted to the Jew Armentarius. During the Carolingian period (from the mid-eighth century), Jews settled in the Rhineland again as they had done during the Roman Empire – some of them lending money on pledges or giving money to merchants in a kind of commenda partnership. Archbishop Anno of Cologne (d. 1075), as well as Emperor Henry IV (1056–1106), borrowed money from Jews.

THE MONEYLENDERS IN EUROPE. After the First Crusade (1096) the Jewish merchant, in his necessarily long journeys, no longer enjoyed even minimal physical security. In Western and Central Europe, especially in *Spain, the crystallization of the essentially Christian nature of the rising city communes combined with this insecurity to drive out the Jews from commerce and prohibit them from engaging in crafts. In France, England (up to 1290), Germany, Austria, Bohemia, Moravia, and northern and central Italy, Jews had to turn to loan-banking on a larger or smaller scale in order to make a living. The canonical prohibition against taking interest by Christians, which was stressed in successive *Church councils (especially the Fourth Lateran Council of 1215), and the vast opportunities for capital investment in land and sea trade open to the wealthy Christian made lending on interest for consumer and emergency needs virtually a Jewish monopoly in Western and Central Europe between the 12th and 15th centuries. By the 13th century the notion that the *Wucherer* ("usurer") was a Jew was already current, for example, in the writings of *Berthold of Regensburg, Walther von der Vogelweide, and Ulrich von Lichtenstein. The word *judaizare* became identical with "taking interest." Testimony from the 12th century shows that moneylending was then becoming the main occupation of the Jews; this was the case of those of Bacharach (1146) and of Muenzenberg (1188). However, there is little data to suggest that Jewish banking transactions were on a large scale even in the 13th century, but there is evidence that the bishop of Basle had debts with Basle Jews and that various monasteries had Jewish creditors.

The transition from a natural economy to a money economy in the course of the "commercial revolution," and the stabilization of territorial principalities opened new possibilities for Jewish banking activity, especially in the Rhineland and in southern Germany. Jews from Siegburg, Trier, Mainz, Speyer, Strasbourg, and Basle as well as from Ulm and Nuremberg appear as sources of credit. The most important banking transaction in the first half of the 14th century went through the hands of Vivelin the Red, who transmitted 61,000 florins in gold which King Edward III of England paid to Baldwin of Trier for becoming allied with him against France. Margrave Rudolf III of Baden was indebted to David the Elder, called Watch, and to Jekelin of Strasbourg and his partners. Muskin and Jacob Daniels served the archbishop of Trier in the administration of his finances; during the first half of the 14th century, Daniels was probably the most important Jewish banker of the Rhineland. He was followed in the service of the archbishop by his son-in-law Michael. At the same time Abraham von Kreuznach at Bingen had a similar position with the archbishop of Mainz. Gottschalk von Recklinghausen and his company was another group on the lower Rhine. Such banking activity is recorded in other parts of Central Europe as far as Silesia.

Moneychanging and coinage privileges were often combined with moneylending, and Jews were frequently the sole agents arranging loans. From the first half of the 12th century moneychanging as a special form of banking is supported by documentary evidence. To spread the risk, partnerships of between two and ten persons were formed. As security, custom at first recognized mainly pledges, but from the middle of the 13th century the letter of credit came into use, though princes still preferred to pledge jewels. Often, instead of a pawn, bail was given by several persons. In western Germany hypothecation of real estate was preferred, and in this way Jews acquired in pledge houses, vineyards, farms, villages, castles, towns, and even seigneuries. Interest rates do not seem to have exceeded 36% but in the case of deferred payment they could rise to 100% or beyond. From the 12th century popes and princes exploited the financial capacity of the Jews by frequent remission of debts or forced loans. The *Black Death and consequent persecutions of Jews gave rulers an opportunity forcibly to seize property and to restore pawns and letters of credit to debtors. The liquidation of Jewish debts by King *Wenceslaus IV of Bohemia around the end of the 14th century is a well-known example of such royal rapacity. With these and other measures and the rise of the merchant class, who gradually took over the function of loan-bankers to the princes and even to emperors during the 15th and early 16th centuries, the Jews were deprived of imperial protection and forced to leave the towns. They retired to the small seigneuries or migrated to Eastern Europe, where a less-developed economy offered them possibilities of making a livelihood. In Bohemia, Hungary, and in Poland and Lithuania both princes and nobility made use of their financial help. As the Eastern European kingdoms developed with the colonization of the forests, Jews played an increasing part in commerce and especially in the **arenda*. In the larger towns some engaged in moneylending and banking activities.

In 12th-century France moneylending was an important Jewish business, but in the 13th century Jewish lenders came up against the superior competition of the Lombards, a rivalry even more intense in the Netherlands. In England, where *Aaron of Lincoln and *Aaron of York were powerful bankers, a special *Exchequer of the Jews was set up to centralize Jewish transactions. However in the 13th century the crown began to rely on the greater resources of the Cahorsins and Italian bankers and in 1290 the Jews were expelled. In Italy Jewish bankers could expand their sphere of activity under the silent protection of the popes, despite resistance on the part of the Christian burghers (see *Popes and the Jews). From the second half of the 13th century they spread throughout central Italy and gradually expanded toward the north, migrating at first to the smaller and medium-sized towns. In Pisa and then in Florence the Da *Pisa family became important loan-bankers; in Florence in 1437 Cosimo de' Medici permitted a Jewish group to establish four loan-banks; in Venice in 1366 Jews, probably of German origin, obtained the right to lend on pledges. Here as in other places in northern Italy, Jewish loan-bankers from the south came into competition with Jews migrating from Germany or southern France. Finally only a few towns, such as Milan and Genoa, refused to admit Jewish loan-bankers. However, their activities were seriously challenged when the anti-Jewish preaching of the *Franciscans resulted in the establishment of branches of the *Monti di Pietà toward the middle of the 15th century.

The Iberian Peninsula after the Christian reconquest offers many examples of large-scale credit activities and tax farming by Jews. It is known that they provided money for armaments against the Moors. El Cid borrowed from Raquel and Vidas, Jews of Burgos, for his expedition against Valencia. King Alfonso VI of Castile (1072–1109) also obtained loans from Jews for his military expeditions. His successors employed Jews in the financial administration, especially as *almoxarifes* (revenue collectors), an activity combined with moneylending. Thus, Judah Ibn Ezra was in the service of Alfonso VII, Joseph Ibn Shoshan of Alfonso VIII, and Solomon *Ibn Zadok (Don Çulema) and his son Çag de la Maleha were *almoxarifes* in the service of Alfonso X, while Meir ibn Shoshan served as his treasurer. When Sancho IV (1258–95) came to the throne, *Abraham el-Barchilon was prominent in the financial administration, supervising the farming of the taxes. Generally, in Castile the Jews abstained from farming the direct taxes, which from 1288 the Cortes opposed. The Jews therefore tended to prefer the administration of the customs and other rights belonging to the office of *almoxarife*. The court of Aragon relied on Jewish financial administrators in a similar fashion. King James I employed *Benveniste de Porta as a banker, probably giving him as security for his advances the office of bailiff of Barcelona and Gerona. Judah de la *Cavalleria, the most powerful Jew in the Aragonese administration, had control over all the bailiffs of the kingdom. Under Pedro III the family of *Ravaya were most influential. Though during the 14th century the Jews in Aragon and Navarre were subjected to increasing pressures, Judah Ha-Levi and Abraham Aben-Josef of Estella were general farmers of the rents under Charles II and Charles III of Navarre. In Castile – in spite of the Cortes' opposition – Jews such as the *Abrabanel family in Seville continued to be active as *almoxarifes*. The young Alfonso XI appointed Joseph de *Écija as his *almoxarife mayor* (c. 1322); Pedro the Cruel (1350–69) made Samuel b. Meir ha-Levi *Abulafia of Toledo, known as the richest Jew of his time, his chief treasurer, and Henry of Trastamara had Joseph *Picho as his financial officer (*contador mayor*) despite his promise to remove all Jews from royal office (1367).

THE CONVERSOS. The persecutions of 1391 and the mass conversions which followed brought an important change. Some of the Conversos were able to use the act of baptism to climb to high positions in the financial administration: examples are Luis de la *Cavalleria, chief treasurer under John II of Aragon, Luis *Sánchez, royal bailiff of the kingdom of Aragon (c. 1490), and his brother Gabriel *Sánchez, who was treasurer-general. Under Henry IV of Castile (1454–74) Diego Arias de Avila was the king's secretary and auditor of the royal accounts; in spite of Diego's unpopularity his son Pedro succeeded him. Even Isabella the Catholic depended on the financial advice of the Jew Abraham *Senior, from 1476 chief tax gatherer in Castile, and Isaac *Abrabanel, who after having been banker of Alfonso V of Portugal served as the queen's private financial agent and loaned her a considerable sum for the war against Granada. The Converso Luis de *Santangel, chancellor and comptroller of the royal household and great-grandson of the Jew Noah Chinillo, loaned Isabella money to finance Columbus' expedition to America. Though some men like Isaac Abrabanel, who went to Naples, remained faithful to Judaism, a number of Jews of Spanish origin stayed in Portugal and, after accepting baptism, rose to financial influence there, especially in combination with the East Indian spice trade. Prominent among them were Francisco and Diogo *Mendes. The latter, who took up residence in Antwerp, became one of the most important merchant bankers there, lending money to the king of Portugal, the emperor, and Henry VIII of England. The firm "Herdeiros de Francisco e Diogo Mendes" was administered for some time after Diogo's death (1543) by Francisco's widow, Doña Beatrice de Luna (Gracia *Nasi) and her nephew João Miques (Joseph *Nasi). They subsequently immigrated to Turkey, where the latter combined commercial and banking activity with political influence. Another to rise to high position was Alvaro Mendes from Tavira, Portugal, who in Constantinople took the name Solomon *Abenaes. Jewish money-changers and tax farmers were to be found in many places of the Ottoman Empire. After the union between Spain and Portugal (1580), a number of influential Conversos took the opportunity to invest their capital in financing the various ventures of the crown, provisioning the army in Flanders and in the East Indies, and supplying contracts for Africa. Their activities expanded especially after the financial crisis of 1626 and continued until the Portuguese revolt of 1640 which restored independent sovereignty to the country. After this all members of the *gente de nação* (as Conversos were called) living in Spain became suspect. The last important financial venture by *New Christians in Portugal was the financing of the Brazil Company established in 1649. However, Jewish involvement in banking proper really begins with the activities of those Conversos who, fleeing the Inquisition in Portugal and Spain, settled in *Antwerp, *Hamburg, and *Amsterdam, some remaining nominally Christian and some openly returning to Judaism. In Antwerp the Ximenes and Rodrigues d'Evora families were outstanding among an important group of merchant bankers who had commercial relations extending as far as the East Indies and Brazil. While they remained Catholics (like the Mendes de Brito group in Portugal), those who emigrated to Hamburg and Amsterdam formed Sephardi communities. In Hamburg they participated in the founding of the bank in 1619; 30 (by 1623, 46) local Jews were among its first shareholders, and some of them were financial agents for various North European courts, especially those of Denmark and Schleswig-Holstein. Most famous in Antwerp were Diego Teixeira de Sampaio (Abraham *Senior), consul and paymaster general for the Spanish government, and his son Manuel (Isaac Ḥayyim Senior), who succeeded him as financial agent of Christina of Sweden. Manuel Teixeira was an outstanding member of the Hamburg exchange and participated actively in the transfer of Western European subsidies to the German or Scandinavian courts.

At Amsterdam at first only a few Jews were shareholders in the bank founded in 1609 and of the East India Company. One hundred and six Portuguese had accounts in 1620. Generally their resources were not sufficiently great to add any special weight to the formative stage of Amsterdam capitalism. Through Holland's developing overseas trade, especially with Brazil (until 1654) and then with the West Indies, as well as through the growth of the Amsterdam capital market and the transfer of subsidies and provisioning of armies through Amsterdam, Jewish financiers rose to importance in the exchange market, and were especially active in trading company shares. Outstanding were the *Pinto family and Antonio (Isaac) Lopez *Suasso (Baron d'Avernas le Gras); nevertheless the wealth of the Sephardi families remained far below that of their Christian counterparts. In the second half of the 18th century the Pinto family remained prominent, and another influential financier of Sephardi origin was David Bueno de *Mesquita.

Partly as a consequence of the marriage between Charles II of England and Catherine of Braganza (1662), and especially after William and Mary became joint sovereigns of England (1689), London, too, became a center of Sephardi banking, leading figures being Anthony (Moses) da Costa, Solomon de *Medina, and Isaac Pereira. In the reign of Queen Anne (1702–14), Manasseh *Lopes was a leading banker; during the 18th century Samson *Gideon, Francis and Joseph *Salvador, and the *Goldsmid brothers, leading members of the Ashkenazi community, were outstanding. In the middle of the 18th century Jacob Henriques claimed that his father had planned the establishment of the Bank of England (1694).

THE HOLY ROMAN EMPIRE. Only a few Jewish financiers, such as Joseph zum goldenen Schwan at Frankfurt or Michel *Jud, were active in the German principalities in the 16th century. In the early 17th century the Hapsburgs employed the services of Jacob *Bassevi of Treuenberg of Prague, Joseph Pincherle of Gorizia, and Moses and Jacob Marburger of Gradisca. The rise of the absolute monarchies in Central Europe brought numbers of Jews, mostly of Ashkenazi origin, into the position of negotiating loans for the various courts, giving rise to the phenomenon of *Court Jews. The most famous and most active of them in financial affairs were, in the second half of the 17th and the beginning of the 18th century, Leffmann *Behrends in Hanover, Behrend *Lehmann in Halberstadt, Bendix Goldschmidt in Hamburg, Aaron Beer in Frankfurt, and Samuel *Oppenheimer and Samson *Wertheimer in Vienna. Later Diego d' *Aguilar, and the *Arnstein and *Eskeles families became prominent. In the early 18th century Joseph Suess *Oppenheimer was the outstanding figure in southern Germany; his financial influence was widespread, especially in Wuerttemberg, until his fall and execution in 1738. Important court bankers around the end of the 18th century were Israel *Jacobson in Brunswick, the *Bleichroeder family in Berlin, Simon Baruch and Solomon Oppenheimer in Bonn, the *Rothschilds in Frankfurt, the Reutlinger, Seligmann, and *Haber families in Karlsruhe, the Kaulla family in Stuttgart, and Aron Elias Seligmann, later baron of Eichthal, in Munich.

ITALY. In the 15th and beginning of the 16th century the Italian loan-bankers reached their greatest eminence, including the Pisa, *Volterra, Norsa, Del Banco, *Rieti, and Tivoli families. In their wealth and style of life these men belonged to the Renaissance milieu as much as the artists and men of letters. However, with the expansion of the institution of the *Monte di Pietà* and the restrictive policy of the popes of the Counterreformation, their influence declined. The Da Pisa disappeared from Florence in 1570. However there were still between 60 and 70 loan-bankers operating in Rome toward the end of the 16th century and a century later about 20 were still in existence. In the first half of the 16th century about 500 loan-bankers were active throughout Italy; toward the end of the century about 280 remained in 131 places. Abraham del Banco was involved in the establishment of the famous Venetian Banco Giro in 1619.

[Hermann Kellenbenz]

WOMEN BANKERS. Jewish matrimonial and property laws permitted women to manage capital they acquired through dowry, inheritance, and, in case of innocent divorce or widowhood, their *ketubbah*. While *ketubbah* payments to a widow or divorcée might include real estate and houses, highly portable pawn pledges and bonds were particularly suitable. The percentage of women involved in moneylending was high: they were responsible for half of all loans in Northern France in the 13th and 14th centuries and in many communities in 13th century England, one-third in 41 German communities between 1350 and 1500, and from one-twentieth of the larger to one-third of the small loan sums in Austria. These figures represent loans granted by women alone (often widows) or at the head of a business consortium and do not include the many women who acted in conjunction with their husbands or relatives. Some women, most of them widows, were active in top-level business with the nobility or rulers. Such female "top bankers" with loans from 1,000 to 12,000 florins, like *Licoricia of Winchester (active 1242–77), Plume of Klosterneuburg (Austria, 1320–40), Reynette of Koblenz (1365–94), Zorline of Frankfurt (ca. 1380–95), Gentlin of Konstanz (ca. 1420–30), Eva (Hefe) *zum Buchsbaum* of Frankfurt (1401–52), Ricke of Frankfurt (1451–71), and Sara, called Gutlein of Wiener Neustadt (c. 1475–80), sometimes achieved considerable influence. Due to their high tax contributions, some gained administrative power as tax collector (Selda of Radkersburg, Styria, 1338) and even as *parnesset*, an elected officer of the local Jewish community (*Kaendlein of Regensburg 1354, Joseppine of Regensburg 1374). Like wealthy male Jews, women were arrested to extort high ransoms and became victims of burglary and murder (*Dulce of Worms 1196, Licoricia of Winchester 1277, Kaendlein of Regensburg c. 1364). In contrast to the Sephardi world, women's mobility was not restricted in Ashkenaz. Although contrary to halakhic standards of female personal modesty, contacts with Christians in connection with business dealings were permitted; businesswomen traveling alone were allowed to disguise themselves as men or as nuns for self-protection (*Sefer Hasidim*). Some women used their husband's seal (Reynette of Koblenz 1374, 1384, Ricke of Frankfurt 1451–71), others had their own seals (Disslaba of Regensburg 1398). Some signed their records with their Hebrew signature (Mirl of Friesach, Carinthia 1372, Plumel of Maribor 1442, Priba of Maribor 1468, Leah of Voitsberg, Carinthia 1496). Ricke of Frankfurt left a German will (1470). Many women submitted their financial cases to non-Jewish courts and took oaths. Although systematic research on women's business activities in early modern Europe has yet to be done, it appears that the rate of female involvement was not as high as in medieval times. The outstanding personality was *Glueckel of Hameln (1646/47–1724); also important were other wives and widows of the early "Court Jews," Brendele of Frankfurt (active c. 1541–60), Gertraud Munk of Vienna and Prague (1590–1614), and Esther *Liebmann of Berlin (1677–1713).

[Martha Keil (2nd ed.)]

19th and 20th centuries

Jewish banking in the 19th century begins with the rise of the house of *Rothschild in Frankfurt, a city which became the new banking center of Europe as a result of the political upheaval caused by the French Revolution and the Napoleonic Wars. The founder of the house (which became the symbol of the 19th-century type of merchant banking), Meyer Amschel Rothschild started as a banker to the elector of Hesse-Kassel. His sons rose to prominence as the major European bankers Amschel Mayer in Frankfurt, Solomon Mayer in Vienna, Carl Mayer in Naples, James Mayer in Paris, and Nathan Mayer in London. After the death of Abraham Goldsmid and Francis Baring in 1810, Nathan Rothschild became the dominant figure in the London money market. The majority of the English financial dealings with the continent went through the Rothschilds' offices. After the Congress of Vienna (1815) the Rothschilds extended their business into most European states, specializing in the liquidation of inflated paper currencies and in the foundation of floating public debts. In 1818 they made loans to European governments, beginning with Prussia and following with issues to England, Austria, Naples, Russia, and other stales, partly in collaboration with Baring, Reid, Irving and Company. Between 1815 and 1828 the total capital of the Rothschilds rose from 3,332,000 to 118,400,000 francs.

THE MERCHANT BANKERS. Prominent merchant bankers in Germany besides the Rothschilds were Joseph *Mendelssohn and Samuel *Bleichroeder. Mendelssohn founded his firm in Berlin in 1795, and was joined by his brother Abraham *Mendelssohn in 1804; they issued state loans for industrial development to several foreign countries, particularly Russia. Samuel Bleichroeder, Berlin correspondent of the Rothschilds, established his own business in 1803. His son Gerson Bleichroeder became a confidant of Bismarck and served as his agent for financing the war of 1866 and for the transfer of the French war indemnity in 1871. The Bleichroeder bank also made loans to foreign states. After the death of Gerson

Bleichroeder in 1893 his partner Paul Schwabach continued the business. The brothers Moses, Marcus, and Gerson *Warburg founded a bank in Hamburg in 1798. Its main business was concerned with the Hamburg overseas trade, especially transactions with England and the United States. Paul M. *Warburg, a brother of Max M. *Warburg, head of the Hamburg bank before World War I, established a branch office in New York. Toward the end of the 18th century J.M. *Speyer, through his bank's provisioning of armies and exchange business, had a capital of 420,000 florins, the largest Jewish fortune in Frankfurt at that time. In 1809 G.J. Elissen opened a banking house which took the name of J.L. Speyer-Elissen in 1818 and Lazard Speyer-Elissen in 1838. Philipp Speyer and Co., the U.S. branch, negotiated the American credit during the Civil War, participated in the development of the railroads in America, and conducted transactions in Mexico and Cuba, partly in association with the Deutsche Bank. In 1928 Speyer amalgamated with C. Schlesinger, Trier, and Company to form Lazard Speyer-Elissen K.a.A., Frankfurt and Berlin. The bank established by Solomon *Oppenheim in Bonn in 1789 acquired a leading position; at the beginning of the 19th century Solomon moved to Cologne, where his son Abraham became one of the most influential bankers in the Rhineland, financing insurance associations, railroad construction, and industrial investment.

Jewish bankers played an important part in the development of joint stock banks. Ludwig *Bamberger and Hermann Markuse were among the founders of the Deutsche Bank (1870), which was active in financing German foreign trade. The Disconto-Gesellschaft, established by David Hansemann in 1851, which amalgamated with the Deutsche Bank in 1929, had several Jewish partners. Eugen *Gutmann was the main founder of the Dresdner Bank, and Abraham Oppenheim was one of the founders of the Bank fuer Handel und Industrie (Darmstaedter Bank; 1853). The leading personality in the Berliner Handelsgesellschaft (established in 1856) was Carl *Fuerstenberg. Richard Witting, brother of Maximilian Harden, was one of the directors of the Nationalbank fuer Deutschland; when it merged with the Darmstaedter Bank in 1921, Jacob *Goldschmidt, then director of the latter, took control of the new enterprise. In 1932 the two other most important banks in Germany, the Deutsche Bank and the Dresdener Bank, were directed by Oskar *Wassermann and Herbert Gutman respectively.

In England, banks were established by Sir David *Salomons (London and Westminster Bank, 1832), the Stern brothers (1833), Samuel *Montagu (1853), Emile Erlanger (1859), the Speyer brothers, *Seligman brothers, and S. Japhet and Co., many of them immigrants from Frankfurt; the Speyer bank negotiated loans on behalf of Greece, Bulgaria, and Hungary, as well as for Latin American states. David *Sassoon and Company, established in Bombay in 1832, had branches throughout the Orient, handling extensive transactions. Sir Ernest *Cassel, partly in association with Sir Carl Meyer, established banks in Egypt and Turkey. Industrial banks were organized by Sir Moses *Montefiore and the Anglo-American Corporation, which was connected with the diamond and finance corporation of A. Dunkelsbueler, established by Sir Ernest *Oppenheimer. In South Africa the General Mining and Finance Corporation was set up by Hamilton Ehrlich and Turk, and one of the most important enterprises in South African financing was the Barnato brothers' company.

In France Achille *Fould, a competitor of the Rothschilds, was a supporter of Napoleon III and later his finance minister. Together with his brother Benoit he inherited the Paris firm of Fould, Oppenheimer et Cie., which had been established by his father. Meanwhile the brothers Emile and Isaac *Péreire, who moved to Paris from Marseilles in 1822, financed railway construction in France and Spain. Through the Crédit Mobilier, organized in 1852, they mobilized credit for various investment projects, but ran into difficulties in 1867. Among the other important Jewish banks was the Banque de Paris et des Pays-Bas (1872), with Henri Bamberger as one of the directors. The leading position among the private banks was held by Rothschild; from 1889 to 1901 all loans to Russia from Paris were issued through the Rothschild bank. Baron Maurice de *Hirsch from Munich, son-in-law of the Brussels banker Raphael Jonathan *Bischoffsheim, invested successfully in railroad construction. Other Jewish banks were those of Louis Dreyfus and Lazard Frères. In Italy, where Luigi *Luzzatti's agricultural associations were largely philanthropic, Jewish bankers played a leading part in the foundation of the Banca Commerciale Italiana and the Credito Italiano. The Rothschilds, Sterns, and Goldsmids also invested money in Spain and Portugal.

RUSSIA AND EASTERN EUROPE. A number of Jewish banks were established in Vienna during the 19th century, the most influential of which was Arnstein and Eskeles. This bank however was declared bankrupt in 1859. Weikersheim and Company and from 1821 Salomon Rothschild also established banks in Vienna. Jews participated in the foundation of the Niederoesterreichische Eskomptgessellschaft (1853) and the Kreditanstalt (1855), which made an essential contribution to the development of the Vienna stock exchange and extended international loan facilities, also investing in industry and railroads. Leading private banks in Hungary were of Jewish origin, such as the Ungarische Allgemeine Kreditbank (Hungarian General Credit Bank; established in 1867) with Siegmund Kornfeld as a general director, the Pester Ungarische Kommerzial-bank (Hungarian Commercial Bank at Pest), established in 1841 by Moritz Ullmann, and the Ungarische Hypotheken-bank (Hungarian Hypothecary Credit Bank; 1869) with Nándor (Ferdinand) Beck de Madarassy as its general director. In Prague the *Petschek family established a bank in 1920; in Galicia, under the Austrian regime, Brody (Nathanson, Kallir) and Lemberg had Jewish banks. Between the end of the 18th century and the beginning of the 19th Jewish banks of some importance rose in Russia. In St. Petersburg Nicolai and Ludwig *Stieglitz, immigrants from Germany, opened a bank in 1803, which under Ludwig (who with his brother was converted to Christianity in 1812) became one of the leading financial institutions in Russia. Otherwise Jewish banking activity was limited to southern Russia, especially to Berdichev and Odessa. In 1860 Yozel (Yerzel) *Guenzburg, originally a tax farmer, established the St. Petersburg bank J.Y. Guenzburg, and later the discount and credit bank there, managed by his son Horace; Guenzburg also established banks in Kiev and Odessa. Lazar (Eliezer) *Poliakoff opened a bank at Moscow in 1860 and participated in the foundation of the Moskowsky Zemelny Bank and other Moscow banks. Poliakoff and his two brothers also founded banks in southern Russia. Abram *Zak was director of the Petersburg Discount and Credit Bank (1871–93), and Soloveitchik established the Siberian Trade Bank. At the beginning of the 20th century private banks of some importance were those of H. *Wawelberg in St. Petersburg, and O. Chayes and R. Sonschein and Company in Odessa.

Toward the end of the 18th century several bankers such as Koenigsberger, Levy, and Simon Simoni emigrated from the west to Poland. Jacob *Epstein, court purveyor to King Stanislas II Augustus, founded an important dynasty of bankers. The Polish revolt of 1863 caused the bankruptcy of many Jewish banks. The bank of Wilhelm Landauer in Warsaw, established in 1857, closed in that year. However, Landauer returned to Warsaw some years later and opened a joint stock company in 1913. Mieczyslaw Epstein founded the Warsaw Discount Bank in 1871. Leopold *Kronenberg took part in the foundation of the Warsaw Credit Union in 1869 and the following year established the first joint stock bank in Poland, Bank Handlowy at Warsaw. The Natanson family bank was in operation between 1866 and 1932. In Romania, Maurice *Blank (d. 1921) established the house Marmorosch, Blank and Company, which his son, Aristide, directed after him.

SCANDINAVIA AND THE NETHERLANDS. The Goeteborgs Bank in 1848 was established in Sweden through the agency of L.E. Magnes, Morris Jacobsson, Edward Magnus, and others. Theodor *Mannheimer was the first managing director of Scandinaviska Kreditakteibolaget, and Louis *Fraenkel managed Stockholm's Handelsbank from 1893 to 1911. The Danish merchant financiers Joseph *Hambro and his son Carl Joachim *Hambro settled in London in 1832 and founded Hambro's Bank there. A leading Danish banker was Isaac *Glückstadt, who managed the Landsmans-Bank at Copenhagen from 1872 until his death in 1910; he was succeeded by his son Emil. A. Levy Martin was finance minister in 1870 and from 1873 till 1897 director of the Copenhagen Handelsbank. From 1913 until his death in 1923, Markus Rubin was director of the Danish Notenbank. In Holland the firm of Lissa and Kann was established in 1805. Another Dutch firm of the same era was Wertheimer and Gompertz, later known as the Bankassociatie. In 1859 the firm of Lippman, Rosenthal and Company was established as a subsidiary of the International Bank of Luxembourg. Its international activities were widespread, especially through Netherlands state loans. The bank of Elzbacher in Amsterdam later merged with the Amsterdamsche Bank. In Rotterdam Rothschild was represented by Moses Ezechiels en Zonen (liquidated in 1888). The bank of Benjamin Marx (established in 1869), later Marx and Company, was in existence until 1922. In Belgium Jacques Errera, Joseph Oppenheim, and Isaac Stern, all from Brussels, and the brothers Sulzbach and J. May from Frankfurt participated in the foundation of the Banque de Bruxelles in 1871. Private banks were those of F.M. Philippson and Company, the Societé Henri Lambert and Cassel and Company. Moving from Alsace to Switzerland in 1812, Isaac Dreyfus established a bank in Basle; after 1849 the firm was known as Isaac Dreyfus Soehne. It participated in the foundation of the Basler Handelsbank as well as the Basler Bankverein. The Hitler regime spelled the end of Jewish banking in the greater part of Europe; all Jewish banks in Germany were liquidated or transferred to a non-Jewish company (Solomon Oppenheim Jr. and Company in Cologne, for example, was changed into the firm of Pferdmenges and Company).

THE UNITED STATES. Already in early colonial times individual Jews were active in America as money brokers, such as Asser *Levy, who functioned in New York City during the second half of the 17th century. Often such figures were helped by their extensive family or fellow-Jewish contacts overseas, as was the case with David *Franks, who was instrumental in raising money for the British army during the French and Indian War with the aid of his brother Moses, a London financier. The best known Jewish financier of the times was the legendary patriot Haym *Salomon, an immigrant from Poland who succeeded under extremely trying conditions in raising large amounts of desperately needed cash for the American Revolution by negotiating bills of exchange with France and the Netherlands. Yet another figure who helped finance the war for American independence was Isaac *Moses, later among the founders of the Bank of New York. It was not until the middle of the 19th century, however, with the arrival in America of a large German-Jewish immigration, that Jewish banking houses on the European model came to exist in the United States. Some of the founders of these firms, like Philip and Gustav *Speyer of Speyer & Co., went to the United States as American representatives of already established European concerns; others, like August *Belmont, crossed the Atlantic with a degree of previously acquired banking experience; still others, like the *Lehman brothers, Meyer and Emanuel, were essentially self-made men. Among other Jewish banking houses started by immigrants from Germany that developed into financial powers during the years 1840–1880 were Kuhn, Loeb Co., Lazard Frères, J.W. Seligman Co., Goldman, Sachs & Co., and Ladenburg, Thalman & Co. All of these firms functioned essentially as investment bankers – the more established field of commercial banking offered relatively few opportunities to the German-Jewish immigrant – a capacity in which they helped to finance large numbers of American utilities and corporations whose rapid growth throughout the latter half of the 19th century created an insatiable demand for capital. To raise such funds these Jewish houses not only freely utilized their widespread European connections, particularly in France, England, and Germany, but created a chain of interlocking associations and directorates among themselves which enabled them quickly to mobilize sums many times larger than their individual holdings and to compete successfully with gentile firms several times their size. Not only was it common for the children and relatives of a given firm to marry each other, but marital alliances frequently occurred as well among different Jewish banking families, as was the case with the *Loebs, the *Kuhns, the *Schiffs, and the *Warburgs. Frequently too the children of such families married into families of large German-Jewish companies in a variety of other fields and the latter would then proceed to raise capital through the banking houses which they had joined. Socially, the result of such commercial and kinship ties was the creation of a German-Jewish banking and business aristocracy based in New York City whose descendants continued for over a century to play a dominant role in the financial, cultural, and political life of the American Jewish community, and to a lesser extent, of the nation at large. The contribution of such Jewish banking houses to the process of capital formation in the United States in the late 19th and early 20th century was considerable by any standard. Several of them, such as Speyer & Co., August Belmont & Co., and J. & W. Seligman, raised large sums for the federal government both during and after the Civil War (the Jewish house of Erlanger Co., on the other hand, obtained sizeable loans for the Confederacy); others, such as Kuhn, Loeb, were particularly active in the westward expansion of the railroads. In the late 19th century Seligman Co. alone was capitalized at an estimated $10,000,000, while during the Russo-Japanese War of 1905 Jacob *Schiff of Kuhn, Loeb was able on short notice to float a bond issue of $200,000,000 on behalf of the Japanese government. Although the total assets of such Jewish firms were nevertheless small when compared to those of the American banking system as a whole, their clannishness and ability to coordinate their actions made them the focus of antisemitic agitation from the 1890s on, when caricatures of ruthless Jewish oligarchs at the head of an international Jewish money conspiracy began to abound in the ranks of the Populist movement. In reality, however, the fiscal policies of the German-Jewish firms tended to be highly conservative and their owners exercised their fortunes with an unusual degree of social as well as fiscal responsibility. Although a number of the great 19th-century Jewish banking houses such as Lazard Frères and Kuhn, Loeb have survived into the present, none has continued as a family or even exclusively Jewish concern and even the most prosperous of them have lost their former importance as a result of the steady trend in the American financial market toward the predominance of ever larger and more impersonal corporations. At the same time, the general field of commercial banking in the United States has remained relatively closed to Jewish participation despite heavy Jewish involvement in such related fields as stock brokerage, investment analysis, and corporate management. A study undertaken by B'nai B'rith in 1939 revealed that out of 93,000 bankers in the United States only 0.6% were Jewish, and that even in New York City Jews formed only 6% of banking executives as compared to 28% of the general population. Similar statistics for a later period are unavailable, but reports of discrimination against Jews in major banks throughout the country persist and in 1968 the American Jewish Committee publicly filed a complaint before the Human Rights Commission of New York City charging the banking system with job bias against Jews.

[Hermann Kellenbenz]

In the latter years of the 20th century and the early years of the 21st, the banking industry consolidated, and some old-line "Jewish" firms were bought or incorporated into others as buyouts and mergers changed the landscape. As Jews assimilated into American life, many advanced in the workplace less along ethnic lines and more along lines of achievement. To be sure, there were many Jews in leadership positions in prominent financial institutions: Felix *Rohatyn at Lazard Frères, Bruce *Wasserstein at several large firms, Sanford *Weill at Citibank, and others, but their financial success was largely attributed to their business acumen rather than to their religious or ethnic background.

George Soros, a Hungarian immigrant, became one of the most successful investors and later spread his wealth to nonprofit organizations and to political causes. Michael Steinhardt and others made their mark in hedge funds or as independent venture capitalists, accumulating great wealth but also making large philanthropic contributions. Carl *Icahn and Irwin L. *Jacobs developed reputations as corporate raiders. Abby Joseph Cohen was the leading investment strategist for Goldman Sachs, and Henry Kaufman, a well-known economist, offered advice about the stock market that was followed by many. In addition, on Wall Street, such firms as Schwab & Co., headed by Charles *Schwab, achieved great success as a low-price stock-market firm.

Some investors – Ivan *Boesky, Michael *Milken, Marc *Rich – became infamous for their questionable financial activities, but whether their religion played a role is highly unlikely. They were perceived as corrupt financial figures, not corrupt Jewish financial figures.

In the last years of the 20th century, a number of Jews had important positions in the nation's economic community. Alan *Greenspan, a Republican, headed the Federal Reserve System for almost 20 years and became a powerful force in Washington. During the Clinton administration, Jewish economists, including Robert *Rubin, the Treasury secretary, and Lawrence *Sommers, his successor and later president of Harvard University, held Cabinet-level positions, and James D. *Wolfensohn headed the World Bank from 1995 to 2005. His successor, chosen by President George W. Bush, was Paul

D. Wolfowitz, a veteran foreign policy and defense official in Republican administrations.

[Stewart Kampel (2nd ed.)]

Assessment of the Role of Jewish Bankers

As shown above, Jewish activity, in particular in the late Middle Ages and in the 18th and 19th centuries, often played an important, sometimes a central, constructive role in the economy and social life of various countries, sometimes even internationally. However, banking always remained a subsidiary Jewish economic activity. Frequently, when Jews appeared to command large assets, they gave this impression because they mostly owned mobile property. The wealthy Jews always formed a small group, particularly in comparison with the wealthy nobles or Christian merchants. It was really only in the 19th century that Jewish financiers achieved remarkable wealth, largely resulting from the activities of some European courts in consequence of the upheavals brought about by the French Revolution and the Napoleonic Wars. With the growth of joint stock banks and of central banks in the middle of the 19th century the field of private banking became limited. Around the beginning of the 20th century, Jewish influence in finance and banking had reached its zenith; afterward it declined at an accelerating rate.

BIBLIOGRAPHY: ANTIQUITY: Baron, Social², index s.v. *Banking and bankers*; L. Herzfeld, *Handelsgeschichte der Juden des Alterthums* (1894²); V. Tcherikover, *Hellenistic Civilization and the Jews* (1959), 333–43. MIDDLE AGES–18th CENTURY: I. Schipper, *Toledot ha-Kalkalah ha-Yehudit*, 2 vols. (1935–36); W. Sombart, *Jews and Modern Capitalism* (1951); J. Guttmann, *Die Juden und das Wirtschaftsleben* (1913), review of W. Sombart; M. Hoffmann, *Geldhandel der deutschen Juden waehrend des Mittelalters* (1910); G. Caro, *Sozial-und Wirtschaftsgeschichte der Juden*, 2 vols. (1908–20), index s.v. *Bankiers*; H. Waetjen, *Das Judentum und die Anfaenge der modernen Kolonisation* (1914); H. Schnee, *Hoffinanz und der Moderne Staat*, 6 vols. (1953–67); S.D. Goitein, *A Mediterranean Society*, 1 (1967); L. Poliakov, *Les Banchieri juifs et le Saint-Siège du XIIIe au XVIIe siècle* (1965). **ADD. BIBLIOGRAPHY:** WOMEN BANKERS. J.R. Baskin, "Jewish Women in the Middle Ages," in: J.R. Baskin (ed.), *Jewish Women in Historical Perspective* (1998²), 101–27; A. Grossman, *Pious and Rebellious: Jewish Women in Medieval Europe* (2004), 114–22, 147–53, 259–62; D. Hertz, "The Despised Queen of Berlin Jewry, or the Life and Times of Esther Liebmann," in: V.B. Mann and R.I. Cohen (eds.), *From Court Jews to the Rothschilds. Art, Patronage and Power 1600–1800* (1996), 67–77; W.C. Jordan, "Women and Credit in the Middle Ages," in: *Journal of European Economic History* 17/1 (1988), 33–62; M. Keil. "She Supplied Provisions for her Household: Jewish Business Women in Late Medieval Ashkenaz," in: *The Jews of Europe in the Middle Ages*. Ed. Historisches Museum der Pfalz Speyer (2004), 83–89; idem, "Public Roles of Jewish Women in Fourteenth and Fifteenth-Centuries Ashkenaz: Business, Community, and Ritual," in: C. Cluse (ed.). *The Jews of Europe in the Middle Ages (Tenth to Fifteenth Centuries)*, Proceedings of the International Symposium held at Speyer, October 20–25, 2002 (Cultural Encounters in Late Antiquity and the Middle Ages, 4) (2004), 317–30; C. Tallan. "Medieval Jewish Widows: Their Control of Resources," in: *Jewish History*, 5 (1991), 63–74. 19th AND 20th CENTURIES: P. Emden, *Money Powers of Europe…* (1938); M. Lévy-Leboyer, *Les banques européennes…* (1964); J. Wechsberg, *Merchant Bankers* (1966); J. Riesser, *German Great Banks* (1911³); A. Marcus, *Die Wirtschaftliche Krise der deutschen Juden* (1931); idem, in: YIVOA, 7 (1952), 175–203; Goldberg, in: *Yivo Ekonomishe Shriftn*, 2 (1932), 56–92; S. Birmingham, *Our Crowd* (1967); K. Zielenziger, *Juden in der deutschen Wirtschaft* (1930); B.E. Supple, in: *Business History Review*, 31 no. 2 (1957); E.O. Eisenberg, in: *The National Jewish Monthly*, 53 no. 6 (Feb., 1939); Milano, in: JQR, 30 (1939/40), 149–86; Giuseppi, in: JHSEM, 6 (1962), 143–74; G. Myers, *History of the Great American Fortunes* (1910, 1937²); D.S. Landes, *Bankers and Pashas… in Egypt* (1958); K. Grunwald, *Hamizraḥ ha-Ḥadash: Ha-Banka'im ha-Yehudim be-Iraq*, 1 (1960), 160–5; H.-D. Kircholtes, *Juedische Privatbanken in Frankfurt/M.* (1969). See also bibliographies in articles on individual countries and families.

BANNER, a recognized symbol shared by a large group of people: a family, tribe, military unit, or nation. In the Bible, banner is denoted by the word *nes*. Although scholars differ concerning the exact meaning of another term, *degel*, this term apparently designates a military unit (perhaps originally the emblem of the group). The *nes* was composed of two parts: a long pole with a symbol, the *ʾot*, carved or drawn on it. Isaiah 30:17 gives a clear description of the pole: "Till you are left like a flagstaff on the top of a mountain, like a signal [*nes*] on a hill." Numbers 21:8 distinguished the *nes* from the symbol that it bears: "Make a *seraf* [fiery] figure and mount it on a standard [*nes*]…" The *nes* (and the *ʾot* which was on it) was positioned so that the community to whom it belonged could see it from a distance and converge around it. During the period of Israel's wandering in the desert, the special design of each tribe's *nes* and *ʾot* enabled each of them to recognize and gather around its own standard and unit (Num. 2:2). The motif drawn on the *ʾot* was apparently related to the tradition of the community, or was significantly associated with it, in a manner similar to the totem in use among certain present-day tribal societies. The term *nes* is also used symbolically in the Bible to denote a sign which can be seen from a distance and can serve as a summons not only for a tribe or the nation of Israel but also for the entire world (Isa. 5:26). When the people of Israel went into exile, this concept came to be the symbol for the gathering of the exiles scattered over the face of the earth, and for the redemption of Israel in general (Jer. 4:6). The verb derived from this noun, *nss*, serves as a metaphoric description for divine inspiration in the soul of man (Isa. 59:19). With a meaning closer to that of the word *nẓẓ*, this verb also describes the landscape in which precious stones are scattered (Zech. 9:16). Many Egyptian monuments from all periods depict standards or flags attached to poles which are carried by men. The symbols which appear on these standards or flags include illustrations of gods, cartouches, and other religious symbols. Some of the standards consist of a shield of metal or some other material mounted on a pole, with a group of ribbons attached to the join of the symbol and pole. Two different types of standards are depicted on Assyrian monuments from Nineveh. The first type, consisting of a pole bearing a ring to which streamers were attached, was placed on the side of a chariot, toward the rear, in a special place designated for it. The second, consisting of a pole with an opening at the top into which the symbol, probably of metal, was inserted, was carried by the charioteer. There are two recurring symbols on these monuments: one depicts two animals, and the other, a king or god standing on a bull. As is the case with other practical objects, these banners also served ritual needs. This type of ritual banner was found at Hazor (Stratum 1b). It consists of a silver-coated bronze tablet of approximately 4 in. (10 cm.). The snake goddess, surrounded by various other symbols, is depicted on it in relief. The base of the banner from Hazor was designed to be joined to the top of a pole as were the large banners.

BIBLIOGRAPHY: N. De G. Davies, *The Rock Tombs of El-Amarna*, 1 (1903), pls. xv, xx, 2 (1905), pl. xvii; J.G. Wilkinson, *The Manners and Customs of the Ancient Egyptians*, 1 (1878), 195; A.H. Layard, *The Monuments of Nineveh*, 1 (1853), pls. 10, 11, 19, 22, 27; Y. Yadin et al. (eds.), *Hazor*, 2 (1959), 109–110; Y. Aharoni, in: *Qadmoniot*, 1 (1968), 101.

[Ze'ev Yeivin]

BÁNÓCZI, Hungarian literary family. (1) JÓZSEF (1849–1926), Hungarian literary historian, philologist, and Jewish educator. József was born in Szentgál, abandoned his rabbinical studies for a university education, and graduated from Leipzig. In 1878 he became a lecturer in philosophy at Budapest University, and later an associate professor. From 1879 József was a corresponding member of the Hungarian Academy of Sciences. He was appointed principal of the Budapest Jewish Teachers' College in 1887 and held the post until his death. József distinguished himself mainly by his research into the history of the Hungarian language and literature. He also helped to create Hungarian terminology for philosophical expressions. He wrote biographies of Miklós Révai, the first Hungarian philologist (1879), and of the poet Károly Kisfaludy (1882–83). József encouraged Jewish studies and founded the *Izraelita Magyar Irodalmi Társulat* (the Hungarian-Jewish Society for Literature), whose annual he edited. József, together with Wilhelm *Bacher and Samuel *Krauss; published a Jewish-sponsored Hungarian translation of the Bible. (2) LÁSZLÓ (1884–1945), son of József Bánóczi, Hungarian playwright, author and translator. László graduated from the university of his native Budapest. He was responsible for the establishment of the Thália theater, which catered to working-class audiences and was its first director. László was prominent in the Hungarian Social Democratic Party, which he represented on the Budapest Municipal Council. His books on the drama included *Shakespeare a mai szinpadon* ("Shakespeare on the Contemporary Stage," 1910). During World War II, László was active in the theater fostered by the OMIKE, a Jewish association for popular education, and it was mainly due to his efforts that Hungarian-Jewish cultural life was maintained in a wide field of activities.

BIBLIOGRAPHY: *Magyar Zsidó Lexikon* (1929), 84–85; *Irodalmi Lexikon* (1927), 96; *Magyar Irodalmi Lexikon*, 1 (1963), 97.

[Alexander Scheiber]

BANSKA BYSTRICA (Hg. **Besztercebánya**; Ger. **Neusohl**), town in Slovakia. As Banska Bystrica was a mining town and settled partially by ethnic Germans, Jews were not permitted to live there until 1858. The Jewish congregation was established in 1868. The congregation chose the *Neolog (reform) rite. After World War I, Jews moved to the town from the neighboring village of Radvan, where a congregation had existed for about 100 years, and established an Orthodox congregation.

Local Jews engaged in intense Zionist and Jewish national activity. The local Zionist branch was established in 1897. In 1936 the *Maccabi World Union held its winter games in the town.

Most of the local Jews perished in the Holocaust after deportation to labor and concentration camps. During the Slovakian national uprising (Aug. 18–Oct. 28, 1944), thousands of Jewish refugees arrived in the town. About 1,000 were executed by the Germans near the neighboring village of Kremnička. A number of Jewish paratroopers from Palestine were among the victims, including Radvan-born Havivah Reik (Ada Robinson). After the fall of Communism in Czechoslovakia in 1994 a memorial was erected in Kremnička consisting of a Menorah and the Hebrew word ZAKHOR.

In 1947 there were 98 Jews in Banska Bystrica. Most emigrated to Israel in 1948–49. A small congregation continued to exist with prayer services for Jews in the vicinity on the high holidays.

BIBLIOGRAPHY: H. Iltis (ed.), *Die aussaeen unter Traenen…* (1959), 139–40; A. Nir, *Shevilim be-Ma'gal ha-Esh* (1967), 55; M. Lányi and H. Propper, *A szlovenszkói zsidó hitközégek története* (1933), 276–7; E. Bárkány and L. Dojč, *Židovské náboženské obce na Slovensku* (1991), 257–60; PK.

[Yeshayahu Jellinek (2nd ed)]

BANUS (first cent. C.E.), ascetic who according to Josephus "dwelt in the wilderness, wearing only such clothing as trees provided, feeding on such things as grew of themselves, and using frequent ablutions of cold water, by day and night, for purity's sake" (Jos., Life, 11–12). In his youth, Josephus claims to have been a devoted disciple of Banus, living with him for three years (c. 54–56 C.E.) before returning to the city to lead the life of a Pharisee. It is probable that Banus was an adherent of one of the many sects which were spread over the whole country, especially in the wilderness of Judea, not necessarily an *Essene or a member of the *Qumran sect. He may have been a hemerobaptist.

[Isaiah Gafni]

BANUS, MARIA (1914–1999), Romanian poet. Born in Bucharest, Banus' first poems were published in 1928. She gained fame with her first collection of verse, *Tara fetelor* ("The Maidens' Land," 1937), a lyrical description of the awakening sensuality of adolescence. Maria Banus came to be regarded as Romania's outstanding poet on feminine themes. Despite her early detachment from Judaism, she adopted a more positive attitude toward Jewish life in the shtetl as a result of her experiences during the Holocaust. *Bucurie* ("Joy," 1949) includes some important poems about Jewish suffering during the Holocaust. After World War II, Banus regarded the Communist Party as the savior of mankind. Social and humanitarian themes dominate her *Torentul* ("The Torrent," 1959) and *Magnet* ("The Lodestone," 1962), in which the poet denounces war and calls on mothers everywhere to join in the effort to secure lasting peace. In the "liberalization" period, she went back to writing personal poems, but as an aged woman. Her collections of verse include *Fiilor mei* ("To my Sons," 1949); *Versuri alese* ("Selected Poems," 1953); *Despre pamant* ("About the Earth," 1954); and *Se arata lumea* ("The World Shows Up," 1956). She also wrote two social dramas, *Ziua cea mare* ("The Great Day," 1951) and *Indragostitii* ("The Lovers," 1954), and published translations of Goethe, Pushkin, Rilke, and Shakespeare. Many of her poems have been translated into English, Russian, and Chinese, and some of them into Hebrew. She published *Din poezia de dragoste a lumii* ("Love Poetry in World Literature," 1965), including poems by Hebrew and Yiddish poets. In 1978 she published parts of her World War II journal, *Sub camuflaj* ("Under Camouflage"), which caused controversy because of its descriptions of her erotic experiences and her attitude to her Jewish identity. Although she identified with Jewish suffering, she preferred to be a Romanian, identifying with the Romanian language and culture.

BIBLIOGRAPHY: G. Calinescu, *Istoria literaturii romane* (1941), 847, 925; C. Baltazar, *Scriitor si om* (1946), 15–27; G. Calinescu, in *Contemporanul* (March 6, 1959); P. Georgescu, in: *Viata romaneasca* (Oct. 1964), 125–27; **ADD. BIBLIOGRAPHY:** A. Mirodan, *Dictionar neconventional*, 1 (1986), 99–112; A.B. Yoffe, *Bisdot Zarim* (1996), 218–21.

[Dora Litani-Littman / Lucian-Zeev Herscovici (2nd ed.)]

BAPTISM, FORCED. The nature of the Christian sacrament of baptism created special problems when it was carried out compulsorily, which differentiated it sharply from forced conversion to Islam (see *Anusim; *Jadid al-Islam). There is evidence that when Christianity established itself as the dominant religion in the Roman Empire, from the fourth century, large numbers of Jews were forcibly baptized: a detailed account is extant of the process in the island of *Minorca in 418. In due course, the church doctrine regarding this matter crystallized. From the time of Pope *Gregory I, it was generally agreed that by its very nature baptism should be accepted willingly and not imposed by force. Various problems however still remained. It was difficult to define what baptism by force actually implied, apart from sheer physical immersion: did it cover also "willing" acceptance of conversion under menace of death, or under a remoter anticipation of violence, or with the alternative of expulsion? Moreover, when baptism was illegally imposed, did it remain valid, or was the victim at liberty to return to his former faith unmolested? This last was a peculiarly complicated problem in the context of medieval Christianity, for if baptism was valid however conferred, the backsliding was an act of heresy, punishable by death according to the code later elaborated by the Inquisition. In any case, the conception of forcible baptism did not apply in the case of the children or grandchildren of the unwilling converts, who were frequently taken by their parents to church for baptism as a matter of routine when they were born (see *Conversos, *Marranos). Another problem presented itself in the case of infants: at what age could they be presumed to have minds of their own and to accept baptism "willingly" and not passively, or in return for some trivial temptation? On the whole, it may be said that whereas the church doctrine on the matter of forced baptism, which it theoretically condemned, remained unchanged, its attitude as regards *ex post facto* problems hardened through the centuries.

In the seventh century a wave of forced conversions spread over Europe, sparked off when in 614 Emperor *Heraclius forbade the practice of Judaism in the Byzantine Empire. He is said to have summoned his fellow sovereigns to follow his example; and similar steps were taken in Gaul in 626 by King Dagobert; in Italy in 661 by the Lombard sovereign Perctarit; and in Spain from 616 under successive Visigothic rulers. In the Byzantine possessions, including southern Italy, Heraclius' example was imitated in 873–4 under *Basil I. It is difficult however in most such cases to determine how effectively, and for how long a period, the edicts were put into execution; while on the other hand it is debatable how far baptism with the alternative of exile can be strictly considered in the category of "forced conversion." Moreover the mob sometimes took matters into its own hands and imposed baptism on the steadfast believers who had prepared themselves for the heroic alternative. This is what seems to have happened for example at the time of the campaign of the Byzantine emperor *Romanus I Lecapenus in 932–36 to suppress Judaism in his dominions, when a number of Jewish leaders died rather than submit.

Apart from such cases of mass baptism to escape expulsion as mentioned above, the earliest recorded instance of forced baptism in the more restricted sense seems to have been shortly after 820 in Lyons, where as part of his campaign to convert the Jews (described in his *Epistola de baptismo Judaicorum*), Archbishop *Agobard of Lyons assembled the children who had not been sent into safety by their parents and baptized all those who to his mind appeared to show some desire for conversion. When about 938 the archbishop of Mainz asked Leo VII whether he should force the Jews of his diocese to be baptized or expel them, the pope advised on the latter course. Many Jews, especially in the Rhineland, were baptized literally by force during the first and subsequent *Crusades, and the antipope *Clement III protested violently against their being permitted subsequently to revert to Judaism. On the other hand, after Benedict, the leader of the Jews of York was forcibly baptized on the day of Richard I's coronation (Sept. 3, 1189), the archbishop of Canterbury declared that if he desired to return to worship the devil he should be given free choice. One of the clauses in the *Constitutio pro Judaeis* issued by successive popes (including some of those least favorable to Jews) from the beginning of the 12th down to the close of the 15th century (see *Popes) declared categorically that no Christian should use violence to force Jews to be baptized so long as they were unwilling – though without specifying what was to happen if the illegal process actually took place. Indeed, Pope *Innocent III, in a letter of 1201 to the archbishop of Arles, considered that a Jew who submitted to baptism under threat of force expressed a conditional willingness to accept the sacrament, with the corollary that he was not at liberty to renounce it. On the other hand, Innocent IV in 1246 categorically forbade the forced baptism of children, the same presumably applying a fortiori to adults. However, in the last decades of the 13th century the strength of the Jewish communities of the Kingdom of Naples was broken by a wave of forced baptisms, sparked off by an apostate from Trani named Manuforte: the descendants of the victims, known as neofiti (see *Crypto-Jews), long remained a recognizable group, suspected of secret fidelity to their ancestral religion.

The events in the Kingdom of Naples in a way set the example for the wholesale wave of compulsory baptisms which swept Spain in and after 1391. This left in its train the phenomenon of the Marranos, which continued to be a problem in the Iberian Peninsula for centuries to come. It may be noted that a very large number, perhaps the majority, of these insincere conversions, especially after the initial episodes, were not the immediate result of actual violence, but were ostensibly quasi-spontaneous in anticipation of it or as the result of moral rather than physical pressure. This did not however apply to the large-scale happenings in Portugal in 1496/97, when practically the whole of the considerable Jewish community of that country were hounded into Christianity by actual violence or were baptized forcibly notwithstanding their protests. This explains the greater tenacity of Marranism in that country in subsequent generations, and down to the present day.

Pope *Martin V categorically forbade (c. 1419) the baptism of Jewish infants below the age of 12 without the parents' permission, to counteract an abuse which was at this time becoming widespread. But a new chapter in the history of forcible baptism began with the institution in Rome in 1543 of the House of *Catechumens (Casa dei Catecumeni), speedily followed in other cities. To justify their existence these institutions had to elaborate a system of propagating the faith, in which ultimately it became difficult to differentiate force from persuasion. Any person who could be imagined by whatever casuistry as having shown an inclination toward Christianity, or who could be considered to be under the authority of a person already converted, could be immured in the House of Catechumens in order to "explore his intention," meanwhile being submitted to unremitting pressure. In 1635 it was decided that the baptism of the head of a household could entail, if he expressed the desire, that of all those members of his family who were under age or dependent upon him, and this was subsequently extended to cover even more remote cases. There had moreover grown up a popular superstition that any person who secured the baptism of an unbeliever was assured of paradise, this leading to a spate of such ceremonies, verging on parody in execution though not in their tragic outcome, throughout the Catholic world.

At Reggio Emilia, during the plague of 1630, a barber summarily christened after his own style 17 or 18 Jewish children in the pest-house that had been set up – the survivors being thereafter brought up as Christians. In 1747 Pope *Benedict XIV decided that once baptized, even against the prescriptions of canon law, a child was to be considered a Christian and educated under church influence. In 1762, the son of the rabbi of Carpentras was pounced on and baptized in ditch water by a callous ruffian and thereafter lost to his family. The kidnapping for baptism of Terracina children in 1783, at the request of a remote relative, caused a veritable revolt in the Roman ghetto. Similar abuses took place in the Catholic lands of Central Europe and in Poland, where the *Jesuits were said to be the principal culprits in the mid-18th century. After the Napoleonic wars, the abuse in its worst form was restricted to those areas in Italy where the popes, now driven by circumstances into reaction, still wielded temporal power. The best-known instance was the *Mortara Case (1858) in Bologna; but it was neither the worst nor the last. In the Russian Empire in the second quarter of the 19th century the institution of the *Cantonists – involving the virtual kidnapping for military service of Jewish male children from the age of 12, or even 8 –was introduced in the expressed hope of compelling them to abandon Judaism. The number of forced or virtually forced baptisms which resulted probably exceeded all similar cases in other lands throughout history. During the Nazi persecutions in Central and Eastern Europe in 1940–45, many Jewish children were baptized by well-meaning Christians in order to help in saving their lives, or when contact with their parents was lost.

BIBLIOGRAPHY: B. Blumenkranz, *Juifs et Chrétiens dans le monde occidental* (1960), index s.v. *baptême*; S. Grayzel, *The Church and the Jews in the XIIIth Century* (1966²), index s.v. *Baptism, involuntary* and *Conversion, of Jews*; J. Parkes, *Conflict of the Church and the Synagogue* (1934), index; Roth, Italy, index; idem, *Personalities and Events in Jewish History* (1953), 256–74; idem, *Gleanings* (1967), 240–63.

[Cecil Roth]

BĀQĀ AL-GHARBIYYA; BĀQĀ AL-SHARQIYYA, two Muslim-Arab villages in central Israel, east of Ḥaderah. The first became part of Israel following the 1949 armistice agreement with Jordan. The village's economy was developed by the introduction of new farming methods and the establishment of workshops and preserves-industry enterprises. It served as an administrative center for the Arab villages of the vicinity and the seat of the Muslim Shariʿa Court for central Israel. In 1968 it had a population of 6,400, tripling to 19,800 by the end of 2002, with an area of 3.5 sq. mi. (9.1 sq. km.). In 1996

Bāqā al-Gharbiyya received municipal status. Bāqā al-Sharqiyya, which remained on the Jordanian side of the border in 1949, was occupied by Israel during the Six-Day War of 1967. In contrast to Bāqā al-Gharbiyya, its layout and economic and social structure remained largely traditional. Its population in 1967 was 1,205, rising to 3,054 in 1997.

[Efraim Orni]

BAʿQŪBA, town c. 25 mi. (40 km.) north of Baghdad. Under the Abbasid caliphate, Baʿqūba was a district center, with a prosperous Jewish community. At the end of the eighth century, Manasseh b. R. Joseph of Baʿqūba, was head of the academy of *Pumbedita. Even later, many Jews lived in the town. In the early 12th century, a self-styled herald of the messiah, Ibn Shadad, appeared in Baʿqūba and began a movement which was suppressed by the Muslim authorities. The community existed into the 19th century.

BIBLIOGRAPHY: J. Obermeyer, *Landschaft Babylonien* (1929), 144f.; Goitein, in: JJS, 4 (1953), 79; Mann, in: REJ, 71 (1920), 90f.; A. Ben-Jacob, *Yehudei Bavel* (1965), 13f., 222.

[Eliyahu Ashtor]

BAR, town in Vinnitsa oblast, Ukraine. Bar passed to Russia at the second partition of Poland in 1793, and from 1796 to the 1917 Russian Revolution was a district capital in the province (government) of Podolia. The Bar community was one of the oldest in the Ukraine. Jews are first mentioned there in 1542. By an agreement concluded in 1556 with the citizens of Bar, the Jews were permitted to own buildings and had the same rights and duties as the other residents; they were permitted to visit other towns in the district for business purposes but were forbidden to provide lodging for Jewish visitors in the city. The agreement was formally ratified the same year by the Polish king Sigismund II. The community grew during the second half of the 16th and the first half of the 17th century, and Jews from Bar engaged in trade in places as far away as Moldavia. According to a contemporary chronicler, the Bar community in 1648 numbered some 600 Jewish families, "men of wealth and standing." During the *Chmielnicki uprising in that year, many of the Jews in Bar were massacred. There was a further slaughter of the Jewish inhabitants by Cossacks and Tatars in 1651. There were 17 houses (out of 107) in Jewish ownership in Bar in 1565, 23 in 1570–71, and approximately 20 in 1661. In 1717, authorization to erect a synagogue in Bar was granted by the bishop. After 1793, under Russian rule, the community also developed. The Jewish population numbered 4,442 in 1847, 5,773 in 1897 (58% of the total), and 10,450 (46%) in 1910. Between 1910 and World War I, Jews opened factories based on agricultural products, such as sugar, linen, tobacco, and vodka. They owned most of the shops in town, and the only pharmacy and were the majority of artisans. Twenty Jews in Bar lost their lives during a pogrom in the summer of 1919. Religious and communal life came to an end with the establishment of the Soviet government. In the 1920s some 300 families lived from workmanship, 28 were clerks and workers, 150 heads of families worked in agriculture, some of them in a Jewish farm cooperative. The Jewish population totaled 5,270 in 1926 (55%) and 3,869 (total population – 9406) in 1939. In the 1930s 1,000 worked in various factories and 400 in industrial cooperatives; 53 families were members of a Jewish kolkhoz. The Germans occupied Bar on July 16, 1941. In December two ghettos were created, surrounded by barbed wire. On August 19, 1942, 3,000 Jews of the first ghetto were concentrated and kept for three days without food and water. In the nearby Jewish cemetery 1,742 Jews were killed, and the others, mostly young people, were taken to the abandoned ghetto, which turned into a working camp. On October 15, 1942, the 2,000 Jews of the second ghetto were murdered. Most of the working youngsters were killed one by one or died from hunger or diseases. Bar was liberated on March 25, 1944. In 1993 there were 199 Jews living there.

BIBLIOGRAPHY: *Bulletin of Rescue Committee of Jewish Agency for Palestine* (May 1946), 6–8; M. Carp, *Cartea Neagră*, 3 (1947), index; idem, *Transnistria, Lebn, Leidn un Umkum* (1950), 263.

[Yehuda Slutsky]

BAR, SHLOMO (1944–), singer, composer, drummer, and flutist. Bar was born in Morocco and came to Israel at the age of six. In 1977, against a background of social and cultural unrest in Israel, Bar founded a small ensemble which he called Ha-Breirah ha-T'ivit ("The Natural Selection"), whose very name hinted at the prevailing tensions. His first group included musicians of different origins: an American guitarist, an Indian Jewish violinist, and an Israeli-born Jew of Bokharian origin as contrabassist. They created an amalgamated, completely new style, dominated by his powerful personality. Bar supported the artistic ideals of the East in a broad sense, which stood in clear opposition to those of the West. In contrast to the complexity and sophistication of the architectonics of sound – the crowning achievement of Western musical art – Bar placed spontaneity at the center of his work, in improvisations characteristic of Eastern music. He created a style in which he integrated widely divergent musical traditions while endowing his work with a pervasive "Oriental" spirit. It thus represents a balance of stylistic plurality and stylistic fusion. From around the mid-1990s, the group evolved and changed, so that the music, like the group, came to represent a much greater range of cultures. The group made several tours, including trips to the U.S., Canada, and Europe, and participated in various international music festivals. Thus, Bar and some other musicians turned "Orientalization" into a conscious ideology, which reflected, in the field of music, the culturally as well as politically motivated aspiration to achieve "separate but equal" status for Oriental culture in Israel.

[Amnon Shiloah (2nd ed.)]

BARA, THEDA (**Theodosia Goodman**; 1885–1955), U.S. film actress. Born in Cincinnati, Ohio, Theda Bara was noted for her femme fatale roles. William Fox recognized her potential and cast her in *A Fool There Was* (1915) under the name by which she came to be known as the foremost "vamp" of the silent screen. Among her other films were *The Devil's Daughter* (1915), *The Serpent* (1916), *Heart and Soul* (1917), *The Forbidden Path* (1918), *Devil* (1918), *The Soul of Buddha* (1918), *When a Woman Sins* (1918), and *Lure of Ambition* (1919). However, of the more than 40 films she made from late 1914 through 1926, only three and a half remain.

Born in the wealthy, largely Jewish Cincinnati suburb of Avondale, Bara was close to her immigrant parents and siblings and had a happy childhood. Extremely intelligent and an avid reader, she attended college for two years. But she dropped out of school, dyed her blonde hair black, and set out to pursue her love of theater. Although she was not very successful on the Broadway stage, her role as the vampire in *A Fool There Was*, at the age of 30, made her an overnight success.

The first sex symbol for the masses, Bara was renowned for her portrayal of sinful, smoky-eyed women who lured proper husbands away from their wives, playing the relentless vamp in such films as *Sin* (1915), *Destruction* (1915), *The Vixen* (1916), and *The Rose of Blood* (1917). As the movie industry's first fabricated movie star, publicists billed Bara as "The Serpent of the Nile," who was born in the shadow of the Pyramids. They claimed that her first name was an anagram for "death" and her last name was "Arab" spelled backwards. Constantly being photographed with snakes, skulls, crystal balls, and opulent accouterments, Theda Bara epitomized evil at its most lavish. Because of her fatal allure for America's husbands and her influence on young women, clergymen across the country regularly denounced her from their pulpits.

After a while, Bara began to demand better roles and succeeded in playing such heroines as Cleopatra (1917), Salome (1918), Carmen (1916), Juliet (1917), Madame DuBarry (1917), and Marguerite Gautier in *Camille* (1918). But her two favorite parts were the staunch Foreign Legion girl in *Under Two Flags* (1916) and the innocent Irish peasant in *Kathleen Mavourneen* (1919). However, her film career ended with the latter, as Irish and Catholic groups protested not only the way Ireland was depicted but also the fact that a Jewish actress had been given the leading role. The film was pulled out of circulation after several bomb threats and movie-theater riots.

Undaunted and unscathed, Bara married successful director Charles Brabin in 1921. The wealthy couple lived well and traveled widely; and when they were at home, Bara's charm as a hostess and her skill as a gourmet cook made their Beverly Hills estate a haven for their friends in the film community. Bara wrote a memoir of her professional experiences entitled "What Women Never Tell," but it was never published.

BIBLIOGRAPHY: E. Golden, *Vamp: The Rise and Fall of Theda Bara* (1996).

[Ruth Beloff (2nd ed.)]

BARACS, KÁROLY (1868–1929), Hungarian communal leader and bibliophile. Baracs, the maternal grandson of Immanuel *Loew, was born in Budapest, where he studied engineering. On the completion of his studies he entered the service of a railway company, eventually becoming manager, and was regarded as an outstanding expert on public transport in the country.

Baracs had broad humanistic interests and his home served as a center for intellectuals and men of the spirit. Before World War I he was one of the founders of the Radical Party in Hungary and an intimate of Count Michael Karolyi, who headed the republican revolution of 1918 and became the first president of the Republic. After World War I he began to interest himself in Jewish communal affairs, serving as president of the Buda Community Synagogue, the oldest in the capital, from 1921 to 1926. He was responsible for the establishment of the Pro Palesztina Szovetsség (the Pro-Palestine Association), the purpose of which was, according to his definition, "to atone for the dissociation of contemporary [Hungarian] Jews from the work of upbuilding the Land of Israel." Through his advocacy, his congregation, unlike others in Budapest, contributed to the Jewish national funds. He engaged in other pro-Zionist activity, although there was no official government sanction for this at the time.

Baracs was also active in other spheres of communal life, particularly higher education, and was a member of the directorate of the Budapest Rabbinical Seminary. He was a noted bibliophile, particularly of the works of Goethe.

BIBLIOGRAPHY: P. Vidor, "Löw Immanuel es a budai község," in: *Semitic Studies in Memory of Immanuel Löw* (Budapest, 1947), 15–18; *Magyar Zsidó Lexicon* (1929), 85; *Magyar Eletrajzi Lexikon.* 1 (1967), 110.

[Baruch Yaron]

BARAITA, BARAITOT (Aram. בָּרַיְתָא, pl. בָּרַיְתוֹת), Aramaic for the Hebrew word *ḥiẓonah* ("external") and an abbreviated form of the phrase *matnita baraita* – "external mishnah," i.e., a tannaitic tradition which is not included in the Mishnah of Rabbi *Judah ha-Nasi (see *Mishnah). The term *baraita* occurs primarily in the Babylonian Talmud, where it is usually used in opposition to the Hebrew term *mishnatenu* or to the parallel Aramaic term *matnitin*, both meaning "our" Mishnah. The content of a given *baraita* may stand in opposition to the content of a parallel mishnah. Alternatively, it may provide additional information which supplements the tradition presented in the mishnah (Ber. 2b, Er. 2b). In this use, the term *baraita* is similar to the related Palestinian term *tosefet* ("addition" – see below). The content of a given *baraita* may in fact be unrelated to that of the mishnah under discussion, merely presenting another tradition for consideration (Ber. 34b). The term is sometimes used as a synonym for the general term *matnita* (Shab. 19b), without being juxtaposed to any particular mishnah at all. This more general sense is particularly characteristic of post-talmudic usage, where the term *baraita* is regularly used to designate any tannaitic source whatsoever – whether quoted in the *Talmudim,* or found in one of the original tannaitic works, like the *Tosefta, the *Sifra, *Sifrei, *Mekhilta, etc. In this sense, the *baraita* is often opposed to later and less authoritative traditions which derive from the amoraic period, which are usually referred to in the Talmud by the term *shemata* (tradition), or more rarely by the term *memra* (statement).

The term *baraita*, then, is used in a number of different ways, both within talmudic literature and in the post-talmudic commentaries. In order to minimize confusion, it will be necessary to clarify not only the meaning of the term itself, along with a number of related terms – *matnita, shemata, memra, tosefet* – but also the nature of the sources to which these terms refer, and particularly the way in which these sources function within the context of the talmudic *sugya* (discussion).

The Baraita as a Literary Source within the Talmudic Sugya

The vast literature of the Babylonian Talmud is made up of many distinct literary units, called *sugyot*. Taken as a whole, the Talmud is structured in the form of an elucidation and elaboration of the Mishnah of Rabbi Judah ha-Nasi, and the individual *sugya* usually takes the form of an extended commentary to, or discussion of, some particular mishnah. While the *sugya* as a finished literary unit usually has the appearance of a continuous and expansive dialectical discussion in Aramaic, one almost always finds embedded within it a number of discrete, relatively terse and well-defined literary sources, usually composed in rabbinic (mishnaic) Hebrew. These literary sources derive from the two primary historical periods of talmudic literature – the earlier tannaitic period (see *Tanna) and the later amoraic period (see *Amora). The Babylonian Talmud regularly distinguishes between its two primary types of literary source and employs certain terms in order to indicate this distinction.

An important terminological distinction is made between *matnita* (= tannaitic source) and *shemata* (= amoraic source). For example, in TB, Niddah 26a we are given a list of five related traditions, all terse and well-defined literary sources composed in identical rabbinic Hebrew. These five traditions are introduced by standard technical formulae, which indicate to which category they belong. The first tradition is introduced by the words *teno rabbanan*, two by the word *tanya*, and the last by the phrase "*teni Rav Ḥiyya*." These four formulae all include a form of the verb "*teni*" – "to repeat," "recite," or "relate" – and they are all understood to indicate tannaitic traditions, or in the words of the Talmud: *matniyata*. Only one of the five is introduced by the formula *amar Rav Yoḥanan* ("Rabbi Johanan said"), and it is therefore to be understood as an amoraic tradition – a *shemata*, or a *memra* (from the verb *amar*, "to say").

The continuation of this passage provides an important insight into the nature of the difference between these two categories. Following these five traditions, the Talmud provides a summary – more of their form than of their content – stating that three (!) of these five traditions are *matniyata*, and two (!) *shemata*. Now since four of the traditions were introduced by tannaitic formula, and only one was presented as an amoraic statement (*shemata*), the Talmud emends the wording of the fifth and final tradition, changing it from *teni Rav Ḥiyya* to *amar Rav Ḥiyya*. The only difference here is the change in the introductory formula from *teni* (= *matnita*) to *amar* (= *shemata*). In his commentary to this passage Rashi explains the difference between these terms: the words *teni Rav Ḥiyya* mean that Rabbi Ḥiyya related or transmitted the following tradition, whereas the wording *amar Rav Ḥiyya* indicates that Rabbi Ḥiyya was speaking in his own name, expressing his own opinion (*memra*), and not repeating an authoritative source (*matnita*).

From this we learn two important things. First, there is often no difference whatsoever between the actual wording of tannaitic and amoraic traditions. Secondly, the primary difference between the meanings of the verbs *teni* and *amar* lies in the fact that the former indicates the transmission of a received tradition, whereas the latter indicates that the rabbi whose name is linked to the tradition is expressing his own opinion and not reporting a received tradition. These two phenomena can, however, lead to certain ambiguities concerning the nature of the talmudic *baraitot*.

Baraitot and Memrot

First of all, the Talmud often introduces a given tradition by the following *double* formula: "Rabbi Abahu (or the name of some other *amora*) said and others report that it was recited as a *matnita*," etc. This formula reflects the first fact mentioned above, namely that there is often no difference between the wording of tannaitic and amoraic traditions. As a result, an identical halakhic tradition may circulate both as a *shemata* in the name of a specific *amora* and at the same time also as a *matnita* – usually transmitted anonymously but sometimes in the name of a specific *tanna*.

Similarly, the use of the verb "*teni*" as the sole criterion for identifying ancient and authoritative tannaitic traditions is complicated by an ambiguity inherent in the meaning of the term as explained by Rashi above. According to Rashi, the verb "*teni*" indicates that a given rabbi is reporting a tradition, whereas the verb "*amar*" indicates that the rabbi is expressing his own opinion. But what happens when the disciples of an *amora* "report" his words – when the *amora*'s "own opinion" becomes a tradition? This situation is reflected in the common talmudic formula in which a form of the verb "*teni*" is used explicitly with regard to an amoraic tradition: *matni la leha shemata* = "they reported the following amoraic tradition." This and other similar formulae reflect the obvious fact that amoraic traditions were also repeated, recited, studied, and transmitted alongside tannaitic traditions within the talmudic academies.

The Amoraic Baraita

When combined, these two phenomena give rise to a particularly difficult issue, namely, the amoraic *baraita*. We frequently find in the Talmud that the verb *teni* is used in association with the name of an *amora*, for example: *teni Rav Yosef*. This specific formula occurs dozens of times in the Babylonian Talmud, and there are many other similar formula. Does this formula intend to introduce an ancient tannaitic tradition, preserved and transmitted in the school of Rabbi Joseph? Or alternatively does it intend to introduce a later post-tannaitic tradition, first formulated and recited within the school of Rabbi Joseph himself, or within the school of one of his teachers? We may still accept Rashi's distinction and assume that the use of the introductory term *teni* serves to designate a "tradition" preserved and transmitted by Rabbi Joseph or by his school, and to distinguish it from the individual opinion of the *amora* himself. It does not, however, provide clear evidence as to the historical roots of that tradition, whether it derives from the tannaitic period, or from the later amoraic period.

The Baraita as a Legal Category

An important distinction emerges from the previous discussion: between the *baraita* as a literary category and the *baraita* as a legal category. Up to this point we have dealt mostly with the *baraita* as a literary phenomenon – a distinct and well-defined source, usually in Hebrew, appearing in the talmudic discussion and introduced by certain standard formulae which indicate that it reports a received tradition. The term is also used in a more specific sense, to designate a tradition deriving from sources of the tannaitic period and hence presumably possessing a greater legal authority than similar sources deriving from the later amoraic period – a *shemata* or *memra*. In order to clarify this point, we must return to our discussion of the role that these sources play in the talmudic *sugya*.

The legal sources which provide the foundation for the talmudic *sugya* can be divided (using standard post-talmudic terminology) into three categories: mishnah, *baraita*, and *memra*. While the sources belonging to all three categories are considered to be authoritative, they are not equally authoritative. A mishnah is usually (but not always) held to be more authoritative than a parallel *baraita*. On the other hand, either a mishnah or a *baraita* – as a tannaitic source – is generally considered more authoritative than any parallel amoraic *memra*. This question of relative authority, however, only becomes relevant when these sources come into conflict with each other. Thus two sources of equal authority (e.g. two *baraitot* or two *memrot*) can be treated as mutually contradictory (*rumya*, *raminhi*) for the purpose of talmudic analysis and interpretation, but one cannot be used to refute the other. A tannaitic source (a mishnah or a *baraita*), however, can be used to refute (*mativ*, *etive*, *tiyuvta*) the *memra* of an *amora*. Thus, in the case where there is no obvious way to resolve a contradiction between a *memra* and an alternative legal source, it becomes crucial to clarify whether that source is in fact a *baraita*, in the legal sense of an authoritative tannaitic source, or whether it is "merely" a *memra*, which the *amora* may dispute (cf. Git. 42b).

It is therefore significant that not all types of *baraitot* seem to possess equal authority in the context of the talmudic *sugyot*, as H. Albeck has shown in his classic study *Meḥkarim ba-Baraita u-va-Tosefta* (1944), pp. 15–60. He especially singled out the *baraitot* associated with the names of *amoraim* mentioned above (and similar groups of *baraitot*), pointing out that they seem to possess little authority in the eyes of some *amoraim*, who felt free to disagree with them.

The Baraita as a Historical Source

Having distinguished between the *baraita* as representing a literary form and the *baraita* as representing a tradition deriving from sources of the tannaitic period, we will now introduce a second distinction – between the *baraita* as a *legal category* and the baraita as an *historical category*. This is an issue which has occupied scholars in recent years, especially Shamma Friedman, who has devoted a number of important studies to it (see Bibliography).

The legal authority of a talmudic *baraita* – the fact that it can be used to refute the *memra* of an *amora* – depends to a large extent on the presumption that the tradition it contains actually derives from the tannaitic period. Does this mean that a *baraita* found in the Babylonian Talmud, which reports the opinion of a rabbi of the tannaitic period and which clearly is accepted by the Talmud as authoritative, can be assumed to reflect the original views of that rabbi as they were first formulated in second century Palestine? The difficulty of this question is compounded by the fact that these talmudic *baraitot* often differ significantly in both form and content from the parallel versions of the same traditions found in earlier Palestinian tannaitic collections, such as the Tosefta, Sifra, Sifrei, etc.

One of the most influential views concerning this issue was elaborated by H. Albeck. Basing himself on the conclusions of his previous work, *Untersuchungen zur Redaction der Mishna* (1923), Albeck assumed that tannaitic sources – once they had received final redactional form – were not changed substantially, either with regard to their form or to their content. Significantly different versions of the same tannaitic halakhic source must therefore reflect ancient parallel traditions which developed independently in different tannaitic schools (see *Mishnah). Given that the form and the content of the *baraitot* in the Babylonian Talmud usually differ from the parallel halakhic sources found, for example, in the Tosefta, he concluded that the Talmud neither knew nor used the Tosefta as a source for its *baraitot*. From this it follows that the Talmud must have had access to alternative collections of tannaitic halakhic sources – all of which were subsequently lost (*Meḥkarim ba-Baraita u-va-Tosefta*, 1944, 89–138).

A radically different understanding has emerged from the recent work of Shamma Friedman. In Friedman's view, "the *baraitot* in the Babylonian Talmud which have parallel versions in the Tosefta do not reflect a different tradition. On the contrary, they are very similar to their parallel texts in the Tosefta in content, order, language, and in structure. The differences are by and large localized, and derive from redactional considerations. In other words, there is no justification for the assumption that the differences in these *baraitot* are ancient, nor that they preserve independent traditions which originated in the tannaitic period. The opposite is the case. They do not present alternative traditions, but rather redactional parallels" (*Tosefta Atiqta*, 78). This position has been substantially confirmed in numerous case studies, carried out both by Friedman and by his students, which have examined in detail the development of individual traditions, tracing the various steps through which original tannaitic traditions passed on the way to their final and often significantly different form as *baraitot* in the Babylonian Talmud sources.

This of course does not mean that the phenomenon of ancient independent traditions is not to be found in many individual cases. But it does mean that this phenomenon is not the only legitimate explanation for the existence parallel tannaitic texts, as Albeck would have us believe. As a result, we may have to reexamine the assertion, put forward by a number of scholars of the last century, that many alternative collections of tannaitic *baraitot* circulated in later talmudic times, since much of the evidence for this assertion is valid only if one accepts Albeck's views regarding this issue. Friedman's approach also has consequences for the historian, who may no longer use talmudic *baraitot* as direct and independent historical evidence for the state of rabbinic law and lore as they existed in second century Palestine, without first examining the redactional history of the tradition included in the *baraita*.

The Development of the Terms Baraita and Tosefet

The *baraita*, both as a literary and as a legal phenomenon, provided the foundation for the development of amoraic halakhic literature, from the very earliest literary levels of the Palestinian and Babylonian *Talmudim* to the very end of the amoraic period. At the same time, it is striking that the term itself only appears in the Babylonian Talmud, the sole exception being the case of the Jerusalem Talmud, Nid. 3:3, 50d. Even in the Babylonian Talmud, it is found almost exclusively in the words of Babylonian amoraim from the fourth generation onwards, as pointed out by Neil Danzig. Danzig suggested that the use of the term *baraita*, meaning "external mishnah," as opposed to the more neutral term *matnita*, meaning "mishnah," reflected the growing establishment of the Mishnah of Rabbi Judah ha-Nasi as the central and uniquely authoritative source of tannaitic *halakhah* in the later Babylonian academies, after an extended transitional period in which the various collections of tannaitic *halakhah* were accepted on a more equal basis. It remains questionable whether this transitional period, documented by J.N. Epstein (*Mavo le-Nusaḥ ha-Mishnah*, 166–352), extended to the fourth generation of Babylonian *amoraim*. Moreover, the distinction between mishnah and *baraita* in the Babylonian Talmud is as often literary as legal, emphasizing the simple fact that a given tradition is part of the Mishnah of Rabbi Judah ha-Nasi – and so provides the literary foundation for a talmudic *sugya* – whereas some other tradition is not part of this foundational literary work. It would seem that the acceptance of the Mishnah of Rabbi Judah ha-Nasi as a unique literary document for the purpose of study preceded its acceptance as a unique legal source of authoritative halakhah by several generations.

Moreover, there may be a connection between the use of the term *baraita* in later Babylonian rabbinic literature and the use of the term *tosefet* ("addition") in earlier Palestinian rabbinic literature. In a number of places, tannaitic sources provide summaries of different categories of traditional study. Mishnah *Nedarim* (4:3), for example, mentions instruction in *mikra* (Bible) alongside instruction in *midrash*, *halakhot*, and *aggadot*. In another passage, Tosefta *Berakhot* (2:12) lists the same four categories of traditional study under two headings: the first category – *mikra* – is connected to the verb *likro* (= "to read"), while the other three (*midrash*, *halakhot*, and *aggadot*) are grouped together under the heading *mishnah* and connected to the verb *lishnot* (= "to recite"). In Palestinian rabbinic sources of the amoraic period (e. g. TJ, Hor. 3 5, 48c; Gen. R. 15, p. 147; Pesikta de-Rav Kahana 27, p. 405; cf. Ex R. 10, p. 225) we find similar lists, with the difference that the terms *tosefet*, *tosefot* have been added to the familiar list of tannaitic terms, *mikra*, *midrash*, *halakhot*, and *aggadot*. What is the significance of the inclusion of the term *tosefet* here, and how does it relate to the term *halakhot*, which was already a member of the original tannaitic list?

An answer to this question, as well as a possible connection to our term *baraita*, can be found in a midrash, which interprets the words of the Song of Songs (6:8): "There are sixty queens … and there is no end to [the number of] handmaidens." The version found in Song of Songs Rabbah (6 [9]:2) interprets the phrase "sixty queens" as a reference to the "sixty tractates of *halakhot*." It then interprets the second phrase, saying: "there is no end to handmaidens – there is no end to *tosefot*." When this tradition was restated in later midrashic collections (Num. R. 18:17, Tanḥuma Koraḥ 12), the first interpretation was abbreviated to "sixty tractates" (an obvious reference to the sixty tractates of the Mishnah of Rabbi Judah ha-Nasi); and the second interpretation was reformulated in the following words: "And there is no end to handmaidens – *mishnah ḥiẓonah*." As mentioned above, *mishnah ḥiẓonah* is the Hebrew translation of *matnita baraita*, and was one of standard ways of referring to *baraitot* in the early post-talmudic period (the period to which these late midrashic collections belong). It would seem therefore that the Palestinian term *halakhot* refers to the Mishnah of Rabbi Judah ha-Nasi, while the term *tosefot* ("additions") refers to that body of supplementary tannaitic *halakhot*, which is commonly referred to in the Babylonian Talmud by the term *baraitot*.

One additional factor may also have influenced the use of the term *baraita* in the Babylonian Talmud in place of the earlier Palestinian term *tosefet*. At some point in the development of the Babylonian talmudic tradition, the term *tosefet* – or more precisely its Aramaic equivalent *tosefta* – came to refer to a particular corpus of supplementary halakhic traditions (Meg. 28b, Kid. 49b, Sanh. 86a, Shavu. 41b), or perhaps even a particular literary work – like our Tosefta (see *Tosefta). As a result it may no longer have been able to serve as a "generic term" – as the name for an entire category of individual literary sources as well as a name for the individual sources themselves.

BIBLIOGRAPHY: B.M. Lewin (ed.), *Iggeret R. Sherira Ga'on* (1921), 6, 27, 34–47; Malachi b. Jacob, *Yad Malakhi* (18562); N. Krochmal, *Moreh Nevukhei ha-Zeman* (1928), ch. 73; idem, in: *He-Ḥalutz*, 3 (1856), 110–31; Weiss, Dor, vol. 2, 239–58; Halevy, Dorot, 2 (1923), 114–52, 162–216; Ch. Albeck, *Meḥkarim ba-Baraita…* (1944); M. Higger, *Oẓar ha-Beraitot* (1948), 9–134; Epstein, Mishnah (1948), 30–63, 171–4, 673–706, 726–803, 1291; Bacher, in: *Yerushalayim*, 10 (1913), 59–82; Bacher, Trad; E.Z. Melamed, in: *Sefer ha-Zikkaron M.Z. Ilan* (1959), 71–84; Neusner, in: PAAJR, 30 (1962), 79–127; **ADD. BIBLIOGRAPHY:** Danzig, in: *Sinai*, 85 (1979), 217–24; Sh. Friedman, *Tosefta Atiqta* (2002), idem, in: D. Boyarin (ed.), *Ateret le-Ḥayyim* (2000), 163–201; idem, in: Y. Elman et al. (eds.), *Neti'ot le-David* (2004), 195–274.

[Stephen G. Wald (2nd ed.)]

BARAITA DE-MELEKHET HA-MISHKAN (On the Building of the Tabernacle), ancient collection containing 14 chapters, giving a description of the building of the Tabernacle. The *baraita* is quoted by early authorities, including Hai Gaon, Rashi, the tosafists, and Naḥmanides, under the name *Baraita de-Melekhet ha-Mishkan* or *Mishnat Melekhet ha-Mishkan*. It is written in mishnaic Hebrew and contains practically no later additions. The sages quoted in it are *tannaim*, the latest of them being Judah ha-Nasi and his contemporaries. Extracts from it are cited in the amoraic literature. It was therefore evidently compiled at the same time as the other *beraitot*, i.e., after the close of the Mishnah but before that of the Babylonian Talmud. The chapter arrangement is as follows: chapter 1 – the dimensions of the Tabernacle, its boards, their appearance and arrangement; 2 – the curtains of *tekhelet* (blue), their preparation and the manner in which they were placed over the Tabernacle; 3 – the curtains of goats' skins and the other covers of the Tabernacle – the rams' skins dyed red and the *taḥash* (unidentified animal mentioned in the Bible) skins; 4 – the weaving of the veil and the screen at the entrance; 5 – the court of the Tabernacle; 6 and 7 – the ark of the covenant and the tablets which it contained; 8 – the table and the showbread; 9 and 10 – the candelabrum, its construction and manner of kindling; 11 – the altar of incense and the altar of burnt offerings; 12 – the laver; 13 – the work of the levites in the Tabernacle and the Israelite encampments in the wilderness; 14 – the clouds of glory. The priestly garments are not treated at all. Extracts from *Baraita de-Melekhet ha-Mishkan* are included in the *Baraita of 49 Rules*. Some are even of the opinion that the last two chapters, in which the aggadic element is considerable, originally belonged to the *Baraita of 49 Rules* (L. Gruenhut, *Sefer ha-Likkutim*, 2 (1898), 11–13). The *baraita* was first published in Venice in 1602, and a critical edition was published in 1908 by Meir Ish Shalom (Friedmann), on the basis of various manuscripts and editions, together with an introduction.

[Yitzhak Dov Gilat]

In 1992 Robert Kirschner published a new critical edition of *Baraita de-Melekhet ha-Mishkan*, based on early medieval manuscripts and *genizah* fragments, along with an introduction and translation. He raised a number of new issues and reexamined a number of old ones. The genre to which this work belongs is particularly problematic. On the one hand, it is similar to the literature of the Mishnah, in that it is organized by topic. On the other hand, it is closely tied to the biblical description of the Tabernacle and is concerned with the explication of the biblical text. It is somewhat similar to certain extended passages in tannaitic literature which restate biblical events and institutions. As a whole, it must be viewed as a unique synthesis, or hybrid, of these literary forms. Kirschner also reopened the question of its date of composition. He examined the character of the mishnaic Hebrew in which it is composed, the exegetical terminology it employs, the tradents quoted in it, and compared the text of the work to parallel passages found in rabbinic literature. Kirschner's conclusions confirm the view that the *Baraita de-Melekhet ha-Mishkan* is essentially an authentic work of the tannaitic period.

[Stephen G. Wald (2nd ed.)]

BIBLIOGRAPHY: A. Jellinek (ed.), *Beit ha-Midrash*, 3 (1938²), xxix–xxx; S. Buber, *Yeri'ot Shelomo* (1896), 15–16; L. Ginzberg (ed.), *Ginzei Schechter*, 1 (1928), 374–83. **ADD. BIBLIOGRAPHY:** R. Kirschner (ed.), *Baraita de-Melekhet ha-Mishkan* (1992).

BARAITA DE-NIDDAH, ancient work on ritual purity of sectarian character, already known in the early geonic period. It is mentioned in *Sefer ha-Mikẓa'ot* (cited in Aggur, sect. 1, Or Zaru'a esct. 360), and in Naḥmanides' commentary (Gen. 31:35), and is referred to by German-French talmudists of the 13th century, who were probably only indirectly acquainted with it in a fragmentary fashion and were not clearly aware of its sectarian nature. It was published in 1890 by C.M. Horowitz. The *baraita* consists of *aggadah* and *halakhah* concerning the biblical and post-biblical laws of the menstruant woman (*niddah*; Lev. 15:19–33). There is no mention of any Babylonian scholars and the chronology of *tannaim* and *amoraim* is ignored. The tendency of the *baraita* is to oppose the lenient rulings of the school of *Hillel and of R.*Akiva. The account in the Talmud (Er. 13b; TJ, Ber. 1:7, 3b) of a heavenly voice deciding in favor of the Hillelites is rendered in the *baraita* as follows: "Blessed be the strict. Both [Hillel and Shammai] speak the words of the living God; but we must regulate ourselves according to the teachings of the School of Shammai" (Horowitz, p. 21).

The *baraita* lays special stress on the laws of ritual cleanness, particularly with regard to food. B.M. Lewin (*Metivot* (1933), 108–12) points out that the stringencies referred to have no basis in the Talmud, but did exist among Jews in Ereẓ Israel. S. Lieberman, however, maintains that although some of the passages are difficult to understand and were not accepted as *halakhah*, a talmudic basis can be found for them (*ibid.*, addition to paragraph 78, p. 115–8). He is of the opinion that the laws concerning ritual cleanness and uncleanness contained in the *baraita* come from a rabbinic source in Ereẓ Israel and not from the Samaritans or the Sadducees. There appears to have been a section of the community in Ereẓ Israel that laid great stress on the laws of cleanness, as is reflected in Samaritan literature. It is possible that this *baraita* originated within such a framework. However, there may also be Sabaeen influences reflected in it. Thus, Maimonides, who rejects several of the rulings listed in it, describes customs of the late Zoroastrians (Guide 3:47) which bear definite affinities to some customs mentioned in the *baraita* (cf. W.W. Malandra, *An Introduction to Ancient Iranian Religion,* 1986, pp. 173–75). Its exact authorship and date of composition remain uncertain to the present day.

BIBLIOGRAPHY: C.M. Horowitz, *Tosefata Attikata*, 4 and 5 (1890). **ADD. BIBLIOGRAPHY:** S. Lieberman, *Shekiin* (1939); A. Aptowitzer, *Meḥkarim be-Sifrut ha-Ge'onim*, (1941), 166; *Sefer ha-Ḥillukim*, ed. M. Margaliot (1938), 135; M. Higger, *Alim* 3:3 (1938), 61–69; Y. Dinari, *Tarbiz* 49 (1980), 302–24; D. Sperber, *Masekhet Derekh Ereẓ Zuta* (1994), 136.

[Michael James Goldman / Daniel Sperber (2nd ed.)]

BARAITA OF 32 RULES, *baraita* giving 32 hermeneutic rules to be used in the aggadic interpretation of Scripture. Rashi makes frequent use of the *Baraita of 32 Rules* in his commentaries on the Bible and Talmud, referring to it by this name or as the *baraita* of Yose b. Eleazar, the Galilean. Until the 19th century it was known only from being quoted in the 14th century *Sefer Keritot*, the methodological work of *Samson b. Isaac of Chinon.

The *baraita* now appears at the beginning of the *Midrash Mishnat R. Eli'ezer* (discovered and published by H.G. Enelow (1933), 10ff.); and at the beginning of *Midrash ha-Gadol* to Genesis (ed. by M. Margaliot (1947), 22ff.). Although ascribed to Yose b. Eleazar, who lived about 150 C.E., many examples of the application of its rules are attributed to later *tannaim* and even to the *amoraim* Johanan, and Yose b. Ḥanina. It is therefore probable that the original *baraita* merely listed the rules, the examples being added later as a kind of *Gemara*. The *Midrash ha-Gadol* version contains the introductory statement, "These are the rules whereby the *aggadah* is to be understood," clearly indicating that these rules were to be applied only to the *aggadah* and not to the *halakhah*. The *baraita* deals mainly with the syntax, style, and subject matter of Scripture, and after each rule gives one or more examples of its application. Although the 13 halakhic rules of R. Ishmael (see *Hermeneutics) are included in the *baraita*, all the examples given are taken from aggadic passages, even Ishmael's rules being applied with less rigor. Under *ribbui* ("addition") for instance, the example given is that the word "and" in Genesis (Gen. 21:1) teaches that all the barren women in the world were blessed with children at the same time as Sarah. The word "also" in "I also saw in my dreams" (Gen. 40:16) teaches that in addition to his own dream the chief baker saw in his dream the interpretation of the chief butler's dream. Some of the rules are almost word games. Number 29 is *gematria* computing the numerical value of words. The numerical value of Eliezer, servant of Abraham, for instance, is 318. Hence, it is inferred that when Abraham went to war with 318 men to save Lot (Gen. 14:14) the reference is to Eliezer only. Number 30 is *atbash*, the substitution of the last letter of the alphabet for the first, of the penultimate letter for the second, etc. Thus לֵב קָמָי (Lev-Kamai; Jer. 51:1) becomes כַּשְׂדִּים (*Kasdim*; Chaldees). Number 31 is *notarikon*, the interpretation of each letter of a word or its breaking up as an anagram or acrostic. Thus אַבְרֵךְ (*avrekh*; "Abrech") applied to Joseph (Gen. 41:43) becomes the two words *av* ("father," in wisdom), and *rakh* ("tender" in years), describing the qualities of Joseph. Lieberman points out that some of these eccentric methods of interpreting texts were common literary devices among the Greeks, and were also used by them and by the rabbis in the interpretation of dreams. Being current literary devices, they were well-known and used by the rabbis both in aggadic interpretation and in finding some support in the biblical text for a decision. They were never used however, to derive halakhic decisions from the text. Lieberman finds support for this view in an anonymous Midrash, appended to the *Baraita of 32 Rules* in the *Midrash ha-Gadol*. Commenting on "For a dream cometh through a multitude of business" (Eccles., 5:2), the author says, "If the contents of dreams, which have no effect, may yield a multitude of interpretations, how much more then should the important contents of the Torah imply many interpretations in every case."

BIBLIOGRAPHY: Zunz, Vortraege, 90; Bacher, Tann, 2 (1890), 293–8; H.L. Strack, *Introduction to the Talmud and Midrash* (1945), 95–98, 289–96; S. Lieberman, *Hellenism in Jewish Palestine* (1950), 68–78.

[Barnet David Klien]

BARAK (Heb. ברק; "lightning"), Israelite military commander during the period of the Judges (Judg. 4–5), son of Abinoam, from Kedesh in Naphtali. It appears that Barak was well-known as a capable military leader before the prophet *Deborah encouraged him to go to battle against King *Jabin of Hazor. For this purpose Barak succeeded in organizing people mainly from his own tribe of Naphtali, along with warriors from the tribe of Zebulun. After mustering his forces on Mount Tabor, he advanced toward the vicinity of the Wadi Kishon, where the battle was waged under his command; in the ensuing battle, the army led by *Sisera, Jabin's military commander, was utterly routed.

There is no biblical datum available as to the nature and activities of Barak either before or after the aforementioned war. He is neither portrayed as endowed with the spirit of the Lord nor described as a judge. Because of a possible similarity in meaning between his name, Barak, and that of Deborah's husband, Lappidoth, some of the medieval commentators identified the two (David Kimḥi and Levi b. Gershom;

cf. *Midrash Yalkut Shofetim*, 42). However, this is not borne out by the context.

BIBLIOGRAPHY: EM, 2 (1965), 363–4 (incl. bibl.); Y. Amit, Judges (1996), 87; for further bibliography see *Deborah.

[Yehoshua M. Grintz]

BARAK, AHARON (1936–), Israeli jurist. Barak was born as Arik Brik in Kaunas (Kovno), Lithuania, where he was raised as a child and survived the horrors of World War II. During the war the Brik family lived in the ghetto. In 1943 his parents arranged for the six-year-old boy to escape the ghetto and stay with a family of Lithuanian farmers until the end of the war, when his family was reunited again. Shortly after the war, the Brik family planned to immigrate to Mandatory Palestine. After a long journey through Poland, Romania, Hungary, and Austria, it settled eventually in Rome, Italy, where Aharon attended formal school for the first time in his life. In 1947 the family finally immigrated to Israel and settled in Jerusalem, where Barak completed his elementary and high school education. While attending the Bet ha-Kerem high school, Barak met his future wife, Elisheva (later deputy president of Israel's National Labor Court). Upon the completion of his high school studies, Barak was selected to do his compulsory military service at the Academic Reserve (a military unit combining university studies with active military duty) and went on to study law, economics, and international relations at the Hebrew University of Jerusalem. During his military service, Barak completed a combat officers' course and received the rank of lieutenant. Between the years 1958 and 1963, he completed his LL.B., LL.M. and Ph.D. at the HU, followed by appointments there as lecturer in civil law (1963). In 1968 Barak was appointed associate professor of law and in 1974 full professor. Barak was also awarded the Israel Prize for law in 1974.

In the early 1970s Barak served as legal adviser to the UN Committee on International Trade Law. In 1974 he was appointed dean of the Hebrew University Law Faculty. A year later, however, Barak's career took a sharp turn when he was appointed attorney general and legal advisor to the government of Israel. Not only had Barak assumed public office but he also had to master public and criminal law. During Yitzhak *Rabin's first term as prime minister of Israel (1974–77), Barak was officially involved in several political affairs that turned out to be instrumental in bringing down Rabin's coalition and paving the way for the first transfer of power in Israel's history, in the elections of 1977. Barak had backed a series of investigations on charges of corruption involving the government's candidate for governor of the Bank of Israel, an acting minister, and finally the prime minister himself. When faced with the prospect of criminal charges for maintaining an illegal foreign bank account, Prime Minister Rabin resigned on the eve of the 1977 elections, thus providing the final blow to Labor's chances of retaining power. During that stormy period Barak had introduced into the legal culture the term "Buzaglo Test," a phrase pertaining to the principle of impartial equality before the law for ordinary people and influential officeholders alike.

Barak then served for another year as attorney general under newly elected Prime Minister Menaḥem Begin. During that time he was also a member of the Israeli delegation to the Camp David talks with Egypt in September 1978. Despite his resignation from the office of attorney general upon his return to Israel and his appointment as a justice of the Supreme Court of Israel, during the negotiations on the peace treaty with Egypt in October 1978, he was asked yet again by the government to join the negotiating team and special permission for this purpose was granted by the minister of justice and the president of the Supreme Court. In this role Barak proved to be a key figure in reaching and drafting the peace agreement with Egypt.

As a Supreme Court justice, Barak served on many public committees, the most notable one being the *Kahan Commission created in September 1982 to investigate Israel's involvement in the 1982 massacres at the Sabra and Shatilla refugee camps in Lebanon. The Kahan Commission found that no Israeli was "directly responsible" for the massacre, but determined that Defense Minister Ariel Sharon bore "personal responsibility." It ruled that he was negligent in ignoring the possibility of bloodshed in the camps following the assassination of Lebanese leader and president-elect Bashir Jumayyil on September 14, 1982.

As one of the youngest justices ever named to the Israel Supreme Court, Barak became the most influential figure in Israeli jurisprudence, creating new legal doctrines and becoming the object of praise and attack from different quarters in Israeli society. Barak's contention that every human dilemma can be answered by a legal doctrine led to the development of several such doctrines that gradually expanded the Court's powers of review. One judicial doctrine which played an important role in the expansion of the Court's review was the doctrine of *reasonableness*: In HC 389/80 Barak drew the lines of reasonableness as an independent standard, ruling that an administrative act may be invalidated if it is unreasonable. This legal doctrine was later used to strike down a government decision to appoint to a high post a senior ex-Secret Service officer who had been granted a pardon for his part in a cover-up related to the deliberate killing of two captured terrorists (HC 6163/92). By exercising this measure of reasonableness, the Court also forced the resignation of a cabinet minister who maintained the right to remain silent during a criminal investigation (HC 3094/93).

Barak was the driving force in lowering the standing requirement that served as a barrier preventing citizens from petitioning the High Court of Justice. In the landmark Ressler case (HC 910/86), the Court affirmed the existence of the "public petitioner," providing that whenever a petition raises an issue of constitutional merit, or when there is suspicion of serious executive violations of the principle of the rule of law, *any* person is entitled to bring the petition into court, *regardless* of one's personal standing or interest in the outcome of the litigation. In writing the Court's decision Barak also referred to the legal question of *judicability*, and outlined a legal theory that would haunt him in later years: "...Any [human] action is susceptible of determination by a legal norm, and there is no action to which there is no legal norm determining it."

Barak proved to be the mastermind in a series of decisions in the mid-1980s and early 1990s that redefined the power relations between the branches of government and established the Supreme Court as a key institute of Israeli politics. The initial success, however, brought with it political resentment against the court. Barak became the target of *ad hominem* attacks uniting all forces that resisted limits on political autonomy and the increased involvement of the Supreme Court in public affairs. These attacks intensified after the passage of two Barak-supported basic laws in 1992 that pertained to human rights (Basic Law: Freedom of Occupation and Basic Law: Human Dignity and Freedom). In his academic writings Barak defined this new legislation as a "constitutional revolution," thereby alarming the conservative and religious parties that traditionally resisted the adoption of a formal constitution. Those attacks have intensified following Barak's involvement in two court decisions viewed by many as interference with religious authority: In the Bavli case (HC 1000/92) Barak ruled that the Higher Rabbinical Court acted outside its jurisdiction by not applying a state law giving equal property rights to women and men in a case of divorce. Later, in the Danilowitz case (HC 721/94), Barak sat on the panel that granted the same-sex partner of an El Al male flight attendant the same privileges the company accorded the spouses of its other employees. Knowing that according to seniority, Barak was about to assume the office of president of the Supreme Court, personal attacks against him and against the alleged judicial activism of the Supreme Court became a common feature of Israeli public life, thereby eroding the Court's image as an institution standing over and above everyday political "squabbles." Barak received the appointment as president of the Supreme Court of Israel in 1995. During his term as president, the court turned out to be less active than before, showing more restraint and caution in political matters. Yet Barak was involved in several major decisions, among them the Ka'adan case (HC 6698/95), which accorded Israeli Arabs the same rights accorded to Jews to live on a communal settlement located on state land; the decision to outlaw torture during security-related investigations (HC 5100/94); a decision to release Lebanese detainees imprisoned in Israel as "bargaining chips" for securing the safe return of an Israeli air force navigator (Ron *Arad) captured on a combat mission (FH 7048/97); and redrawing the lines of the security fence in the West Bank (HC 2056/04) by taking the approach that the army's discretion related to lands under "belligerent occupancy" is not unlimited and that the fence's route must balance security considerations against the needs of local residents.

While serving as the president of the Supreme Court and head of the Judiciary, Barak continued to be active in academic writing, publishing numerous books and articles including several volumes in a series of books on "Interpretation in Law." "The Judge in a Democracy" (Heb.) was published in 2004.

Aharon Barak was a member of the Israeli Academy of Sciences and the American Academy of Sciences.

[Menachem Hofnung (2nd ed.)]

BARAK, EHUD (1942–), Israeli military commander and politician; member of the Fourteenth and Fifteenth Knessets and prime minister of Israel. Barak was born in Kibbutz *Mishmar ha-Sharon. He joined the IDF in 1959, beginning his military service in the Armored Corps. In the Six-Day War he fought as the commander of a reconnaissance unit and a year after the war received his B.Sc. in physics and mathematics from the Hebrew University of Jerusalem. From 1971 to 1973 he served in the legendary special forces unit at GHQ and was appointed its commander. In May 1972 he commanded the rescue operation to free the passengers of a Sabena plane that had been hijacked by members of Black September and landed at Lydda Airport. In the Yom Kippur War Barak commanded an armored battalion that fought on the southern front in the Sinai. In 1976 he was one of the planners of the Entebbe Operation, which freed the Jewish passengers of an Air France flight hijacked to Uganda, after all the non-Jewish passengers had been released by the hijackers.

Barak was promoted to the rank of major general in 1981 and became head of the Planning Branch of the General Staff. During Operation Peace for Galilee he served as deputy commander of the unit that fought in Baka'a. In 1983 he was appointed head of the Intelligence Branch, and in February 1986 commander of the Central Command. In 1987 he completed a second degree in systems analysis from Stanford University in California and in the same year was appointed deputy chief of staff under Dan *Shomron, serving four years. In 1991 Barak became Israel's 14th chief of staff, serving in that capacity until 1995. Though he did not participate in the Oslo talks, he was reported to have had reservations about the agreement reached with the Palestinians. After the signing of the Declaration of Principles in September 1993, he dealt with the implementation of the security arrangements and the redeployment of the IDF. Before leaving active service he met his Syrian counterpart twice in Washington. By the end of his military service Barak was the most highly decorated officer in the IDF.

After the mandatory six-month cooling-off period, Barak was appointed minister of the interior in *Rabin's government, and after Rabin's assassination was appointed by Shimon *Peres as foreign minister in his government. Barak was elected to the Fourteenth Knesset, and on June 4, 1997, won the Labor primaries for party leadership. In the elections to the Fifteenth Knesset and the premiership in 1999, Barak won a decisive victory over Binyamin *Netanyahu as head of the One Israel list, which included the Labor Party, Gesher, and Meimad. He set up a coalition that included *Meretz, *Shas, the Center Party, Natan *Sharansky's Yisrael be-Aliyah, and the *National Religious Party.

Barak fulfilled his election promise to take the IDF out of Southern Lebanon within a year of being elected prime minister. However, his attempts to reach a permanent settlement with Syria failed. Despite his willingness to make far-reaching concessions to the Palestinians, talks held with Yasir *Arafat under the auspices of President Bill Clinton in Camp David in July 2000 failed, and the second *intifada* broke out in the beginning of October. However, as a result of his willingness to reach an agreement with the Palestinians on the basis of far-reaching territorial concessions, Shas, the NRP, and Yisrael be-Aliyah left the government. Consequently Barak resigned and new elections for the premiership were held in February 2001, with Barak suffering a crushing defeat by Ariel *Sharon. After considering the possibility of joining Sharon's new government, Barak resigned from leadership of the Labor Party and his Knesset seat, deciding to take time out from political activity. In the beginning of 2004 he indicated that he was planning to make a political comeback towards the elections to the Seventeenth Knesset.

BIBLIOGRAPHY: B. Kaspit, *Barak: Ḥayal Mispar 1* ("Ehud Barak: Soldier Number 1," 1998); I. Kfir, *Barak: Ha-Biyographiah* ("Barak: the Biography," 1999); G. Sher, *Be-Merḥak Negi'ah: Ha-Masa u-Matan le-Shalom, 1999–2001, Edut* ("Touching Distance: the Negotiations for Peace, 1999–2001: Evidence," 2001); R. Edelist, *Ehud Barak: Milḥamto be-Shedim: Ma Kara le-Barak?* ("Ehud Barak: His War Against Devils: What Happened to Barak?" 2003); R. Drucker, *Harakiri: Ehud Barak be-Mivḥan ha-Totza'ah* ("Harakiri: Ehud Barak in the Test of Time," 2002).

[Susan Hattis Rolef (2nd ed.)]

BAR-AM, MICHA (1930–), Israeli photographer. Born in Berlin, Bar-Am immigrated with his parents to Palestine in 1936. He joined the Haganah and the Palmaḥ, and after the War of Independence became a member of kibbutz Malkiyyah and later of kibbutz Gesher ha-Ziv. Bar-Am began his photographic work with the 1954 archeological expedition to the Judean Desert led by Yigael *Yadin. His next large photographic venture, during the Suez Campaign in 1956, led to his first book of photographs, *Across Sinai.* This was followed by a nine-year engagement as staff photographer with the Israel army weekly *Ba-Maḥaneh.* In 1967 Bar-Am covered the Six-Day War with Cornell *Capa, and later was associated with the prestigious Magnum Agency. From 1968 he was a regular contributor to the *New York Times.* In 1974 Bar-Am embarked on a new phase of work in photography as curator and photo-historian, first at the Israel Museum in Jerusalem, and from 1977 until 1992 with the Tel Aviv Art Museum, where he staunchly promoted Israeli photography. He also established the first photography department at the Israeli Museum. His works are exhibited in various museums, such as the Israel Museum, Tel Aviv Museum, and Museum of Modern Art in New York. In 2003 he was awarded the Israel Prize.

Perhaps Israel's most prominent contemporary photographer, Bar-Am had his pictures praised for values that extended beyond reportage and photojournalism into the world of esthetic journalism. According to one critic, "Bar-Am's bromides transcend the realistic aspect of photography by wrapping the event into a comprehensive esthetic package." Another point of synthesis in Bar-Am's work was related to the particular conditions of his work and existence. The *New York Times* called him "a deeply committed Israeli and a fiercely independent journalist." Bar-Am expressed concern about being pigeonholed as a "combat photographer," being deeply interested in human beings and their behavior. He sought to take photographs that contain all the information related to a certain event but that are also elevated above the event.

Bar-Am was a brilliant student of world photography and succeeded in assimilating its achievements despite his lack of formal photographic education. He created his own unmistakably recognizable personal style. This transmits a strong sense of directness, an intuition for immediacy as well as for formal compositional qualities. His pictures prove that in photography a work of art maintains it umbilical link to its original context.

[Yeshayahu Nir]

BARAM, MOSHE (1911–1986), Israeli politician. Baram was born in Zdolbunov in Russia. As a boy, he joined the *He-Ḥalutz and the Freiheit Dror movement connected to *Po'alei Zion, and immigrated to Palestine in 1931, settling in Jerusalem. Baram was employed as a construction worker and was active in the *Histadrut and the *Haganah. In 1934 he started to work in the *Jewish Agency and in 1938 became a member of the Secretariat of the *Mapai branch in Jerusalem, becoming secretary in 1943. In 1944 he was a delegate to the Fourth Elected Assembly of the *Yishuv*. During the War of Independence he was a member of the Emergency Commission and of Haganah Headquarters in Jerusalem. In 1948 he was appointed secretary-general of the Jerusalem Labor Council and in 1955 was elected to the Jerusalem Municipal Council, serving as chairman of the coalition executive. Baram was first elected to the Fourth Knesset in 1959 and was appointed chairman of the Knesset Labor and Welfare Committee. In the Sixth Knesset he served as chairman of the Coalition Executive, chairman of the Unemployment Insurance Commission, and head of the Jerusalem branch of the Labor Party. In 1974 Baram was appointed minister of labor in Rabin's first government, holding this position until the elections in May 1977. In the government he chaired the Ministerial Committee on Wages and the Inter-Ministerial Committee on Employment. In 1975, despite Histadrut opposition, he introduced the Work Sanctions Bill.

Moshe Baram's eldest son, Uzi *Baram, was a member of the Ninth to Fifteenth Knessets for the Israel Labor Party.

BIBLIOGRAPHY: O. Betzer (ed.), *Moshe Baram: 1911–1986* (1987).

[Susan Hattis Rolef (2nd ed.)]

BARAM, UZI (1937–), Israeli politician. Member of the Ninth to Fifteenth Knessets. Born in Jerusalem and the son of Moshe *Baram, Uzi Baram studied political science and sociology at the Hebrew University of Jerusalem. In 1964–65 he was chairman of the Mapai National Students Union and in 1965 was one of the founders of the Young Guard in Mapai, serving as its secretary general in 1968–70. In 1970–72 Baram was responsible for the emigration of academics from North America in the Jewish Agency offices in New York and in 1972–74 he was chairman of the Future Generation Section in the Jewish Agency. In 1975–77 he was secretary of the Jerusalem Branch of the Labor Party. Baram was first elected to the Knesset in 1977. In the Tenth Knesset he served as chairman of the Knesset Immigration and Absorption Committee, and in the years 1984–89 as secretary general of the Labor Party, fighting for the internal democratization of the Labor Party and the adoption of primaries for the election of its leaders, Knesset list, and candidates for mayor. In 1984 Baram tried to get former President Yitzḥak *Navon to run for the Labor Party leadership against Shimon *Peres, but was unsuccessful. In 1988 he fought against Labor's entry into another National Unity Government under Shamir, believing that under the changed circumstances Labor would suffer ideologically and electorally. Baram, who supported Yitzḥak *Rabin in his leadership contest against Peres, was appointed minister of tourism in the government Rabin formed after the elections. He strongly supported the Oslo Accords. He served briefly as minister of the interior in 1995 but resigned for personal reasons. In the primaries for the Labor list towards the elections to the Fourteenth Knesset, Baram was unexpectedly elected to first place on the list after Shimon Peres. After Peres' defeat in the elections, Baram was one of those who demanded his resignation. He considered running for the party leadership, but finally decided not to and supported Ehud *Barak in the 1997 Labor leadership contest. He was not, however, appointed to a ministerial position in Barak's government. Like many other promising Labor politicians of his generation, Baram became disenchanted with developments in the party and decided to leave active politics towards the elections to the Sixteenth Knesset. Subsequently he was regularly invited by the media to act as a political commentator.

[Susan Hattis Rolef (2nd ed.)]

BARANGA, AUREL (**Leibovici**; 1913–1979), Romanian playwright and poet. Born in Bucharest, Baranga qualified as a physician and first published poems in the avant-garde review *Unu* (1928–32). In 1930–31 he edited *Alge*, a journal that cultivated the absurd. Later he wrote for the left-wing press. After World War II Baranga devoted himself entirely to writing: he became a reporter and wrote poems. When Romanian Nazis were put on trial in Bucharest in 1945, he was among the first to make the Romanian public aware of the full extent of Nazi crimes. His articles on the deportation of Romanian Jews to the Transnistria concentration camps were collected in *Ninge peste Ucraina* (Snow Falls over the Ukraine, 1945, 1946)

It was, however, in the theater that Baranga increasingly displayed his creative talents. From 1947 he wrote many stage successes, some of which were translated into English, French, Russian, and Chinese. Among them are *Iarba rea* (The Ill Weed, 1949), *Mielul turbat* (The Rabid Lamb, 1953), *Reteta fericirii* (Recipe for Happiness, 1957), *Sfantul Mitica Blajinul* (Saint Demeter the Kind-Hearted, 1965), *Opinia publica* (Public Opinion, 1967), *Simfonia patetica* (The Pathetic Symhony, 1969), *Travesti* (The Mask, 1968) and *Farsa infernala* (The Infernal Farce, 1969). These advocate a society based on the author's ethic of humanistic socialism and satirize Romanian inertia, bureaucracy, old-fashioned ideas, and insincerity. *Opinia publica*, which ran for a year in Bucharest, satirized "socialist realism" and parodied the Communist political trial, though it is evident that his satiric plays were written, performed, and published with the consent of the Communist Party, since Baranga was a privileged person. Nevertheless, his plays were popular with Romanian youth. Twice the winner of Romania's state prize for literature, Baranga was assistant director of the Bucharest National Theater, and coeditor of the periodical *Viata Romaneasca* (Romanian Life). In 1968 he published the verse collection *Poezii.* Some plays and verses contain "Jewish" allusions: a character speaks Yiddish, a poem is called *Kadis* (Kaddish), a play contains an allusion to the Six-Day War favorable to Israel.

BIBLIOGRAPHY: *Teatrul romanesc in contemporaneitate* (1964); D. Sararu, *Teatrul romanesc si interpreti contemporani* (1966); H. Kamm, in: *New York Times* (May 3, 1968). **ADD. BIBLIOGRAPHY:** A. Mirodan, *Dictionar neconventional*, 1 (1986), 116–26; A.B. Yoffe, *Bisdot Zarim* (1996), 270, 440.

[Dora Litany-Littman / Lucian-Zeev Herscovici (2nd ed.)]

BARANOVICHI (Pol., **Baranowicze**), capital of Baranovichi district, Belarus (from 1921–39 in Poland). After Baranovichi became a railroad junction at the end of the 19th century, Jews from the surroundings began to settle there without official permission (see *Russia). In 1897 the Jewish community of Baranovichi, then still a village, numbered 2,171 (total population 4,692). Jewish domicile was authorized in 1903 and the community rapidly expanded. In 1921 there were 6,605 Jews (57.5% of the total population). They were employed in the lumber, resort, and food industries.

After World War I Baranovichi became the center of residence of the *admorim* (ḥasidic rabbis) of the *Koidanovo and *Slonim dynasties. Educational institutions included Hebrew and Yiddish schools and two large yeshivot. Six Yiddish weeklies were published in Baranovichi between 1928 and 1939. The Zionist parties and youth movements and the Bund were very active. A kibbutz training center, Shaḥariyyah, of the He-Ḥalutz movement, was established near the city. In 1931 the Jewish population was 9,680. Jewish communal and cultural activities ceased and the economy was nationalized when Baranovichi became part of the U.S.S.R. in 1939. Jewish party activists and wealthy industrialists and merchants were exiled into the interior of the Soviet Union.

[Yehuda Slutsky]

Holocaust Period

On the eve of the Holocaust, 12,000 Jews lived in Baranovichi. Under Soviet rule (1939–41), Jewish community organizations were disbanded and any kind of political or youth activity was forbidden. Some youth groups organized flight to Vilna, which was then part of Lithuania, and from there reached Palestine. The Hebrew Tarbut school became a Russian institution. A Jewish high school did continue to function, however. In the summer of 1940 Jewish refugees from western Poland who had found refuge in Baranovichi after September 1939 were deported to the Soviet interior. When Germans captured the city on June 27, 1941, 400 Jews were kidnapped, leaving no trace. A *Judenrat was set up, headed by Joshua Izikzon. The community was forced to pay a fine of five kg. of gold, ten kg. of silver, and 1,000,000 rubles. The ghetto was fenced off from the outside on Dec. 12, 1941. The ghetto inhabitants suffered great hardship that winter, although efforts were made to alleviate the hunger. The Jewish doctors and their assistants fought to contain the epidemics. On March 4, 1942, the ghetto was surrounded. In a *Selektion* carried out by the Nazis to separate the "productive" from the "nonproductive", over 3,000 elderly persons, widows, orphans, etc., were taken to trenches prepared in advance and murdered. Resistance groups, organized in the ghetto as early as the spring of 1942, collected arms and sabotaged their places of work. Plans for rebellion were laid, but the uprising never came to pass, partly due to German subterfuge. In the second German *Aktion* on Sept. 22, 1942, about 3,000 persons were murdered. On Dec. 17, 1942, another *Aktion* was carried out, in which more than 3,000 persons were killed near Grabowce. Baranovichi was now declared **judenrein*. At the end of 1942 Jews were already fighting in groups among the partisans. A few survivors from the ghetto were still in some of the forced labor camps in the district, but most of them were liquidated in 1943. On July 8, 1944, when the city was taken by the Soviet forces, about 150 Jews reappeared from hiding in the forests. Later a few score more returned from the U.S.S.R.

[Aharon Weiss]

Postwar Period

In 1954 a monument was erected in the city as a memorial to the Jews murdered by the Nazis. Later it was destroyed and in its place a public latrine was built. The big synagogue was confiscated by the authorities, leaving a small one for the 3,000 Jews (1969 estimate). Most of the Jews emigrated in the 1990s. Societies of emigrants from Baranovichi function in Israel, the U.S.A., Argentina, Chile, and South Africa.

BIBLIOGRAPHY: *Bulletin of the Joint Rescue Committee of the Jewish Agency for Palestine* (April, 1945), 13–22; *Baranoviẓ: Sefer Zikkaron* (Heb. and Yid., 1953); *Baranovich in Umkum un Vidershtand*, 1 (1964); Ben-Mordekhai, in: S.K. Mirsky (ed.), *Mosdot Torah be-Eiropah be-Vinyanam u-ve-Ḥurbanam* (1956), 329–35.

BARANOWICZ, DAVID ELIEZER (1859–1915), Hebraist. Baranowicz, who was born in Vilna, lived in great poverty. He wrote several books on Hebrew grammar which were well received and published in several editions. He wrote the following books: *Oraḥ Selulah le-Dikduk Sefat Ever* (1883) on Hebrew grammar with an appendix in Yiddish on vocalization; *Luḥot ha-Pe'alim* (1889); *Kunteres Yefalles Nativ* (1909), which is an abridgment of his major unpublished work by the same name containing a critique of the Hebrew grammarian Koestlin's *Sefer ha-Maslul* ("Book of the Path") and of the methods of the ancient Hebrew grammarians; *Derekh Ḥadashah le-Ve'ur Kitvei ha-Kodesh* ("A New Way to Explain the Holy Scripture," 1910), a commentary on the Scriptures based upon a grammatical approach. His best-known works are *Messibbot ha-Shem* ("Rules of the Noun") and *Messibbot ha-Po'al* ("Rules of the Verb") which contain analyses of the Hebrew nouns and verbs (last edition, 1945). He also edited several books of Hebrew grammar. His autobiography was printed in *Ha-Toren* 3 (1915), 226–7.

BIBLIOGRAPHY: Kressel, Leksikon, 1 (1965), 365.

BÁRÁNY, ROBERT (1876–1936), Austrian otologist and Nobel Prize winner. Bárány qualified at the University of Vienna in 1900, and for the next five years did research in hospitals in Frankfurt, Heidelberg, and Freiburg, returning to Vienna in 1905. By 1914 his research encompassed all aspects of the physiology and pathology of the inner ear. His greatest innovation in the clinical study of ear diseases was the discovery of a method of examination of each of the two labyrinths separately, using cold and hot water. He was also the first to describe a practical operative procedure for otosclerosis ("hardening of the ear") cases. During World War I Bárány served as a surgeon in the Austrian Army. He was captured by the Russians in 1915. They released him after it became known that he had been awarded the Nobel Prize for medicine in 1914. Bárány was not made a full professor at Vienna because he was a Jew. However, in 1917 he was appointed professor of otology at the University of Uppsala, Sweden. Bárány only began to display interest in Judaism and Jewish questions toward the end of his life, when the Nazis came to power. In his will he left his valuable library to the National Library in Jerusalem. His major works are *Der primaere Wundnaht bei Schussverletzungen des Gehirns* (in: *Wiener klinische Wochenschrift*, 21 (1916)); and *Die Radikaloperation des Ohres ohne Gehoergangplastik bei chronischen Mittelohreiterungen* (1923).

BIBLIOGRAPHY: E. Wodak, *Der Báránysche Zeigeversuch* (1927); NDB, 1 (1953), 581.

[Yehiel G. Gumpertz]

BARASCH, JULIUS (Judah; 1815–1863), physician, writer, and communal leader from Walachia, Romania. Barasch, who was born in Brody, began his education in traditional Torah studies, but later came to the ideas of the *Haskalah and studied philosophy in Leipzig and medicine in Berlin. In the period of his studies, he published several articles in German and Hebrew in Jewish journals and became friends with Moritz *Steinschneider. In 1841, after becoming a doctor of medicine, he settled in Bucharest where he practiced. From 1843 he served as a government physician, at first in Calarasi and Craiova and from 1859 in Bucharest. In addition he taught science in several colleges, being the first teacher in this field in Walachia. Barasch did much to popularize science by organizing lectures and courses for the public and publishing textbooks and periodicals on popular topics. His Romanian-language book *Minunile Naturii* ("Natural Wonders," 1 vol., 1850; 3 vols., 1852) and periodical *Isis sau Natura* ("Isis or Nature," 1856–59) were the first of their kind in Romania. In these publications Barasch attempted to formulate a scientific terminology in Romanian. He played a decisive role in spreading Enlightenment (Haskalah) among Bucharest Jewry. Barasch initiated the establishment of the first secular Jewish school in Walachia, which opened in Bucharest in 1851. For a time he served as its principal. He polemicized against Orthodoxy and also against baptism, and advocated a Judaism for every Jew. From his point of view, reform had to be very moderate and mostly esthetic in order to attract wayward Jews to Jewish religious life. Barasch encouraged the founding of the Societatea de Cultura Israelita ("Association for Jewish Culture") in 1862, which he directed. In 1857 he helped to found the first Jewish periodical in Walachia, *Israelitul Roman*, which appeared in Romanian and in French and was established principally to further the cause of Jewish emancipation in Walachia. Barasch saw Hebrew as the unifying bond of the Jewish people and did much to promote Hebrew literature. He conceived the idea of publishing a scientific encyclopedia in Hebrew for East European Jews who were not fluent in West European languages, spreading scientific knowledge and Haskalah ideas among them, but only one volume, on philosophy, was published – *Oẓar Ḥokhmah*, 1856). Barasch wrote on Jewish subjects in German, describing Jewish communities in countries and localities he visited. The accounts are an important source of knowledge of Jewish life in the mid-19th century in the communities concerned and particularly of the history of the Jews in Romania.

BIBLIOGRAPHY: A. Zaltzman, in: *Iyyun* (1952), 151–68; M. Schwarzfeld, *Dr. Iuliu Barasch* (Rom., 1919), incl. bibl. **ADD. BIBLIOGRAPHY:** L.Z. Herscovici, in: *The Jews in Romanian History* (1999), 61–69; P. Cernovodeanu, in: *Jaloane pentru o viitoare istorie* (1996), 127–40.

[Eliyahu Feldman / Lucian-Zeev Herscovici (2nd ed.)]

BARASCH, MOSHE (1920–2004), Israeli art scholar. Barasch can be considered the father of art history in Israel, a fact acknowledged by the State in 1996 when it awarded him the first Israel Prize in art history. Born in Czernowitz, he was a child prodigy as a painter and writer. He had his first exhibition of Expressionist paintings in 1933, and in 1935 published his first book, *Die Glaubens schwere Wege*, stating his belief in Judaism and Zionism. During World War II, he joined the Romanian Resistance and later enlisted in the Red Army to fight the Nazis, as well as the Haganah's *Beriḥah organization. Arriving in Israel in 1948, he fought in the War of Independence and published in *Abysmal Reflections* (1948) drawings reflecting his reactions to World War II. In 1956 he began teaching art history at the Hebrew University of Jerusalem, and in 1965 inaugurated there a Department of Art History, the first in Israel. He believed that one should be able to teach all periods of art and stressed the importance of a broad knowledge of philosophy and culture in understanding art. He began to publish books on the Renaissance and Crusader Art, and later broadened his scope to include studies on the depiction of God, the iconography of gestures and facial expressions, aesthetics and the theory of color in Renaissance art, the ways that art communicates with the spectator, and the way the mental concept of blindness is imaged in art.

His published works on art history include *Michelangelo* (1961); *The Image of Man in the History of Art* (1967); *Introduction to Renaissance Art* (1968); *Crusader Figural Sculpture in the Holy Land* (1971); *Gestures of Despair in Medieval and Early Renaissance Art* (1976); *Approaches to Art 1750–1950* (1977); *Light and Color in the Italian Renaissance Theory of Art* (1978); *Icon: Studies in the History of an Idea* (1981); *Theories of Art: from Plato to Winckelmann* (1985); *Giotto and the Language of Gesture* (1987); *Modern Theories of Art,* vol. 1 (1990), vol. 2 (1998); *Imago Hominis: Studies in the Language of Art* (1991); *The Language of Art: Studies in Interpretation* (1997); *Das Gottesbild: Studien zur Darstellung des Unsichtbaren* (1998); *Blindness: The History of a Mental Image in Western Thought* (2001).

BIBLIOGRAPHY: M. Ebner, "Introduction to Moses Barasch," in: *Des Glaubens schwere Wege* (1935), 5–8; J. Assmann, Introduction to *Representation in Religion: Studies in Honor of Moshe Barasch*, J. Assmann and A.I. Baumgarten (eds.) (2001); Z. Amishai-Maisels, "Moshe Barasch (1920–2004)," in: *Ars Judaica*, 1 (2005), 156–58.

[Ziva Amishai-Maisels (2nd ed.)]

BARASH, ASHER (1889–1952), Hebrew writer. Born in Lopatin, Eastern Galicia, at an early age he was already well acquainted with modern Hebrew literature; however, most of his juvenilia was written in Yiddish, the rest in German and Polish. At the age of 16, Barash left home and wandered all over Galicia, returning from time to time to Lvov. This period is reflected in several of his more important works: *Pirkei Rudorfer* ("Rudorfer's Episodes," 1920–27), *Sippurei Rudorfer* ("Rudorfer's Stories," 1936–44), and other autobiographical stories. At that time, Barash began to publish his literary efforts, first in Yiddish and then in Hebrew, the latter in 1910 with a number of Hebrew poems in the second *Me'assef Sifruti*, edited by David Frischmann, and in *Shallekhet*, edited by Gershon Shofman. His first long story, "*Min ha-Migrash*" (1910), also appeared in *Shallekhet*. In 1914, Barash moved to Ereẓ Israel, where he taught, first at the Herzlia secondary school in Tel Aviv and, after World War I, at the Reali high school in Haifa. This period is described in his work *Ke-Ir Neẓurah* ("As a Besieged City," 1944).

After World War II he composed his best works in poetry and prose, wrote criticism, and edited several works. In conjunction with Ya'akov *Rabinowitz, he edited the prose volumes *Hedim*, the *Mizpeh Almanac*, and *Atidot*, a youth journal. He was also active in the organizational work of the Association of Hebrew Writers, and established the bio-bibliographical institute, Genazim, which now bears his name. Barash's works were collected in three volumes (*Kol Kitvei Asher Barash*, 1961^2). In 1931, he wrote *Torat ha-Sifrut* ("Theory of Literature," in two volumes) which was the first attempt in modern Hebrew literature to present the Hebrew reader with a systematic theory of literature.

It is, however, as an author of fiction that Barash left his impact. His works mainly highlight the world he left behind. His description, often touched by nostalgia, is at the same time indicative of the author's awareness that this world must inevitably disintegrate. Barash was also aware of the new life evolving in Ereẓ Israel, and this consciousness he conveyed in three works, *Ke-Ir Neẓurah, Ish u-Veito Nimḥu* ("The Man and His Home Perished," 1933–34), and *Gannanim* ("Gardeners," 1937–38). Among his historical fiction are two stories, "*Mul Sha'ar ha-Shamayim*" ("Facing the Gates of Heaven," 1924) and "*Ha-Nishar be-Toledo*" (1944; "Last in Toledo," in *Israel Argosy*, 8 (1962), 144–71).

Barash's literary works are characterized by a rather personal style, precise language, and a quiet tone tending to simplicity and clear and unsentimental description. He rejected both the traditional style of the school of *Mendele Mokher Seforim and the extreme impressionistic and psychological style of some modernists. These stylistic qualities rapidly won him the title of a cool realist, uninvolved in the world he creates.

Barash's affection for the "good people," who are mostly marginal characters in his stories, was interpreted as an "objective" description of the more pleasant aspects of life. This simplistic and superficial approach to his works, however, ignores the cracks in his seemingly tranquil world through which can be glimpsed the hidden abyss that he keenly sensed. In his essay on Barash (in *Arai va-Keva* (1942), 147–58) Halkin dwells on this hidden but basic aspect in Barash's writing. He points to the strange but consistent contrast between the seemingly realistic tranquility and the knowledge (which Barash may have tried to conceal from himself) that this pleasant existence is but a thin shell protecting the individual from the chaos which threatens to erupt at any moment and engulf him or her.

The early story "*Aḥim*" ("Brothers," 1911) describes two brothers, one anchored in the full life of a traditional Jewish family, and the other living in debauchery and poverty. When engaged on a mission of mercy to his brother's family, the rich brother finds himself strangely jealous of the other's way of life. In his early book, *Temunot mi-Beit Mivshal ha-Shekhar* ("Sketches from the Brewery," 1915–28), considered his best, the theme of the story of "The Burning Bed" sharply offsets the peaceful enterprise at a brewery and hints at the inevitable destruction of this idyllic setting.

In *Ammud ha-Esh* ("The Pillar of Fire," 1936) Barash depicts the contrast between a good, stable, and humdrum provincial life, with its lovable yet ridiculous Zionist activity, and the explosion of the oil well, a pillar of fire. The burning oil well transforms the small town and its industrious life into a hell, simultaneously attractive and repelling, which threatens the sanity of the people. The thematic juxtaposition, found in almost all of Barash's stories, lends them depth and ambiguity. The same is evident in his method of characterization. Some of his characters appear to serve his "healthy" realistic tendencies, while others result from his romantic affinity for the strange, the rare, and the threatening.

Structurally, Barash's stories and novels follow a conservative, ordered, and clear pattern that seems to avoid confusion. Each story opens with a systematic exposition that acquaints the reader with the significance of events and characters. At times, the author introduces an omniscient narrator who defines the characters clearly. The dramatis personae, however, do not conform to this characterization. In the denouement of the plot and events, their deeds and behavior, whether openly or secretly, contradict the authoritative evaluation of the narrator. What at first seemed a simple structure is actually a literary device through which the complexity of the characters, originally imagined to be much more artless, is revealed. Barash tends toward short and limited narratives. This is clearly evident even in his more extensive works which are composed of more or less independent "sketches" or "episodes." *Ke-Ir Neẓurah* is a collection of random contemporary historical fiction, narratives, and personal experiences which are organically disconnected. These portrayals may provide the main outlines of characters and events for a full-length novel, but they cannot sustain its necessary unity and complexity.

The novel *Ahavah Zarah* ("Alien Love," 1930–38) poignantly describes events and experiences characteristic of the problematic coexistence of Jews and non-Jews in a small Galician town. The "grandmother" is undoubtedly one of Barash's best-drawn satirical characters. Barash's simplistic solution to the love conflict of a Jew for a non-Jewish girl introduces a foreign tendentious element into the novel which reduces its tragic significance. Barash thus presents, but does not resolve, the problems in the sphere of human emotions. The girl marries a policeman who is an antisemite; the boy recognizes the evil that is rooted in the non-Jew, even in his own beloved. The solution is ideological and logical, stultifying the human elements in the story and the humanity of the characters.

In *Torat ha-Sifrut*, Barash attempts to guide the "novice poet" and the teacher of literature. His normative approach was undoubtedly useful and served as a guide to the teacher and the student of literature in the technique of writing. Today, however, Barash's dogmatic statements seem old-fashioned and at times even incorrect: they often unnecessarily limit literary concepts and terms. The anthology of Hebrew poetry edited by Barash, *Mivḥar ha-Shirah ha-Ivrit ha-Ḥadashah* (1938), attests to good taste and knowledgeable choice of material and is still a faithful and discerning reflection of the best of Hebrew poetry. In 1969, *Selected Stories of Asher Barash* appeared.

A list of his works translated into English appears in Goell, Bibliography, index.

BIBLIOGRAPHY: Halkin, in: *Arai va-Keva* (1942), 147–58; D. Sadan, *Bein Din le-Ḥeshbon* (1963), 226–33; Even, in: *Moznayim*, 22 (1966), 215–20; Kressel, Leksikon, 1 (1965), 383–6; S. Lachower, *Asher Barash, Bibliografyah, 1906–52* (1953); Waxman, Literature, 4 (1960^2), 173–4. **ADD. BIBLIOGRAPHY:** G. Shaked, *Ha-Sipporet ha-Ivrit*, 1 (1977), 341–55; N. Toker, *Ḥezyon Ḥolot ve-Yarkete Olam: Al Zikat ha-Makom ve-ha-Zeman be-Sippurei Asher Barash* (1980); N. Tamir-Smilanski, *Asher Barash, Mivḥar Ma'amrei Bikoret al Yeẓirato* (1988). **WEBSITE:** www.ithl.org.il.

[Yosef Ewen]

BARASH, EPHRAIM (1892–1943), head of the Judenrat in Bialystok. Barash, who was born in Volkovysk (then Russian Poland), was active from his youth in communal life, in Jewish self-defense, and the Zionist movement. During World War I he was a refugee in Russia. After the war he formed the municipal council of Volkovysk where he became president of the Jewish Trade Bank, a member of the community council, chairman of the local Zionist organization, and honorary chairman of He-Ḥalutz. In 1934 he settled in Bialystok and became general manager of the Jewish community council. When the Germans captured the town at the end of June 1941, Barash was appointed vice chairman of the Judenrat of which he was the guiding spirit. He represented a continuity of leadership of the Council. He organized ghetto life, established industrial enterprises, and, although well aware of German plans concerning the Jews, believed that the Jews would be spared if they could be employed in work essential to the German war effort, a view shared by Mordecai Chaim Rumkowski in Lodz. Unlike some other Judenrat leaders, including Rumkowski, Barash actively collaborated with the local Jewish fighting organization (led by Mordecai *Tenenbaum), and helped it financially and by providing material for manufacturing arms. Relations, however, broke off before the ghetto uprising in Bialystok. He was in personal contact with some of the Germans, and believed that they would give him ample warning of their intention to destroy – what the Nazis termed *liquidate* – the ghetto, at which time he intended to join the partisans. The Uprising commenced after the large deportations began on August 16, 1943. It took five days to suppress. The ghetto was destroyed on August 21–27, 1943, with the deportation of 25,000 Jews to Treblinka. For a short period of time Barash and his wife along with other Judenrat members and several hundred Jews were put in a small ghetto and from there they were sent to the Majdanek death camp, where he was killed.

BIBLIOGRAPHY: M. Einhorn (ed.), *Volkovyzker Yisker-Bukh*, 2 vols. (1949); N. Blumental, *Darko shel Yudenrat* (1962). I. Trunk, Judenrat (1972).

[Nachman Blumental]

BAR-ASHER (Ben Harosh), MOSHE (1939–), Hebrew scholar and linguist. Born in Ksar es-Suk (now Rashidiya), district of Tafilalt in southeast of Morocco, he immigrated to Israel in 1951 in the framework of *Youth Aliyah, studied in the Beiteinu "children's village" in Ra'anana (1951–53) and in Yeshivat ha-Darom, Reḥovot (1953–58), and served in the Israeli Army (1959–62). Bar-Asher received his academic training in Hebrew, linguistics, Bible, and Talmud, at the Hebrew University of Jerusalem (1963–76). He also studied at the Sorbonne and College de France (1967–68) and at Harvard (1977–79). Bar-Asher's major fields of research are Palestinian (esp. Syro-Palestinian) Aramaic, biblical, rabbinic, and modern Hebrew, Qumran texts, and the *sharh* (oral Maghrebian translations of the Bible and liturgical Jewish texts). Teaching at the Hebrew University of Jerusalem since 1964, he was appointed full professor in 1984 and chaired the Department of Hebrew Language (1981–83) and the Institute for Jewish Studies (1983–86). He was elected a member of the Hebrew Academy in 1977 and was appointed its vice president (1987–93) and president (from 1993). He taught as a visiting professor at various universities in France and the U.S. and lectured in many other universities around the world. He is regarded as the leading scholar in rabbinic Hebrew of the last generation and was the adviser of 28 Ph.D. students. He received the Israel Prize in 1993. Among his major publications are *Ha-Surit shel Eretz Israel u-V'ayot Nivḥarot be-Dikdukah* (1977); *La composante hebraïque du judeo-arabe algèrien* (1992); *Masorot u-lshonot shel Yehudei Tzefon Afrikah* (1998; 1999^2); *L'hébreu Mishnique: études linguistiques* (1999); and *Leshon Limmudum le-Rabbi Raphael Berdugo* (3 vols., 2001). A full list of Bar-Asher's works and scientific publications appeared in *Reshimat ha-Pirsumim shel Prof. Moshe Bar-Asher* (ed. S. Elkayam, 1999).

His father R. Abraham b. Harosh (d. 2003. in Jerusalem) was one of the last greatest informants of *sharh* and oral Hebrew and Arabic traditions, some of which are represented in the research of Bar-Asher; others are preserved as recorded materials in the Jewish Oral Traditions Research Center at the Hebrew University.

[Aharon Maman (2nd ed.)]

BARATZ, HERMANN (Hirsch; 1835–1922), jurist and historian born in Dubno, Volhynia. He graduated from the government rabbinical seminary in Zhitomir (1859) and from the law faculty of the University of Kiev (1869), and in 1863 was appointed adviser on Jewish affairs to the governor general of Kiev; from 1871 to 1901 he served as censor of Hebrew books. In 1881, with Max *Mandelstamm, he represented the Jews in the province of Kiev before the commission to investigate the causes of the pogroms in southern Russia. Baratz, who contributed to the Russian Jewish press from its beginnings in 1860, was one of the founders in 1904 of the Kiev branch of the *Society for the Promotion of Culture among the Jews in Russia. He wrote on the history of the Jews in Kiev, and published studies on the history of ancient Russian law; his chief work concerned the influence of the Bible and talmudic sources on ancient Russian literature. Three volumes of his studies were published posthumously by his sons, the first dealing with the Jewish sources of the ancient Russian chronicle *Povest vremyonnykh let* (1922), and the second and third with the Jewish element in ancient Russian literature (1926, 1927).

BIBLIOGRAPHY: KS, 2 (1925/26), 19–20.

[Yehuda Slutsky]

BARATZ, JOSEPH (1890–1968), Zionist labor leader; a founder of the collective settlement movement in Ereẓ Israel. Baratz was born in Kamenets, Ukraine. In Ereẓ Israel, where he settled in 1906, he worked as a laborer. In 1910, he became one of the founders of the first kevuẓah, *Deganyah. He was a leading figure in the *Ha-Po'el ha-Ẓa'ir Party (and later in *Mapai), and opened the founding conference of the *Histadrut in Haifa in 1920. During World War II and the Israel War of Independence, Baratz devoted himself to the welfare needs of the Jewish soldiers in Ereẓ Israel, becoming chairman of the Israel Soldiers' Aid Committee in 1948. The Soldiers' House (Beit ha-Ḥayyal) in Tel Aviv is named for him. He was a member of the First Knesset. His books include *A Village by the Jordan: the Story of Degania* (1954), which appeared in 13 languages; and *Im Ḥayyaleinu* ("With Our Soldiers," 1945). His wife, Miriam (née Ostrovsky), was one of the first settlers of the Second Aliyah, living and working in Deganyah from its founding.

BIBLIOGRAPHY: Tidhar, 3 (1958), 1402; B. Shohetman, *Divrei J. Baratz* (1950), incl. bibl.; D. Lazar, *Rashim be-Yisrael*, 2 (1955), 233–7.

[Abraham Aharoni]

BARAZANI, ASENATH, daughter of the eminent Rabbi Samuel b. Nethanel ha-Levi of Kurdistan (1560?–1625/1635?). Her father, a scholar and mystic with a large following, aimed to rectify a dearth of educated leaders by building a yeshivah in Mosul, where he hoped to train young men who would become community leaders and scholars. Since he had no sons, he trained his daughter to be a learned scholar of the highest order. Asenath was married to one of her father's finest students, Rabbi Jacob Mizraḥi, who promised her father that she would do no domestic labor and could spend her time as a Torah scholar. R. Mizraḥi, who succeeded Asenath's father as head of the yeshivah, became so involved in his studies that his wife essentially taught the yeshivah students and provided them with rabbinic training. Following her husband's death, the leadership of the yeshivah naturally passed to his widow in a painless transition. Since neither her father nor her husband had been successful fundraisers, the yeshivah was always in financial straits, and Asenath wrote a number of letters requesting funds in which she described the dire situation that had befallen herself and her children. Her home and belongings had been confiscated, as had their clothing and books. She was still teaching Torah, but the debts were adding up and, as a woman, she felt it was inappropriate to travel in search of financial support. In letters addressed to her, one sees the respect and admiration of fellow rabbis from far and near. Her few extant writings demonstrate a complete mastery of Torah, Talmud, Midrash, Kabbalah, and Hebrew, for her letters are lyrical as well as erudite. A recently discovered manuscript provides additional insight into her life, revealing inter alia an attempt to deceive her regarding transmission of contributions intended for her support. Nevertheless, she successfully ran a yeshivah which continued to produce serious scholars, including her son, whom she sent to Baghdad upon request, where he continued the dynasty of rabbinic scholars.

BIBLIOGRAPHY: M. Benayahu, "R. Samuel Barzani: Leader of Kurdistan Jewry,"in: *Sefunot* 9 (1965), 23–125 (Heb.); J. Mann, *Texts and Studies in Jewish History and Literature*, Vol. I (1972); A. Ben-Ya'akov, "Kurdistan Jewish Communities" (Heb., 1981); E. Brauer, *The Jews of Kurdistan* (R. Patai, ed.) (1993); U. Melammed Uri and R. Levine. "Rabbi Asenath: A Female Yeshiva Director in Kurdistan," in: *Pe'amim*, 82 (2000), 163–78 (Heb.); Y.Y. Rivlin, "Poetry of the Aramaic-Speaking Jews" (Heb., 1959).

[Renée Levine Melammed (2nd ed.)]

BARAZANI, MOSHE (1926–1947), Jew condemned to death by the British in Palestine. Barazani was born in Arbel, Syria, and came to Ereẓ Israel with his parents as a child and lived in Jerusalem. He joined Leḥi and was arrested in 1947 when, during a search, a hand grenade was found in his pocket. He was sentenced to death by a military court after a trial lasting less than two hours. Together with Meir *Feinstein, however, he cheated the gallows by taking his own life on the eve of his intended execution.

BIBLIOGRAPHY: Y. Nedava, *Olei-ha-Gardom* (1966); Y. Gurion, *Ha-Nizzaḥon Olei Gardom* (1971).

BARAZANI, SAMUEL BEN NETHANEL HA-LEVI (1560?–1630?), rabbi and kabbalist. His name derives from the town Barazan in Kurdistan, where he was probably born. His numerous wanderings were apparently the result of the political situation. He maintained yeshivot in Barazan, Akrah, Mosul, and Amadiyah. During his last years, he was the most distinguished scholar of Kurdistan and the acknowledged leader of Kurdistan Jewry. His authority was absolute though he held no official position. He revived the Jewish community of Kurdistan, where his disciples filled positions in many of the important communities. Barazani sent letters of rebuke and of comfort to the communities with the aim of preventing the prevalent religious laxity. He lived in great poverty and want. He was regarded as a saint, and his grave in Amadiyah became a place of pilgrimage. Barazani's books, many of which have been lost, are permeated with kabbalistic themes, and reflect an acquaintance with philosophy. Some of his *piyyutim*, festival prayers, and *reshuyyot* are included in the liturgy of Kurdistan, and some have been published. Among Barazani's works extant in manuscript are *Avnei Zikkaron* of which many copies exist, on the laws of ritual slaughter, *Sefer ha-Iyyun, Sefer Derashot*, and fragments of *Sefer Ḥaruzot*.

His daughter was Asenath *Barazani. The Barazani family included many rabbis of Mosul, other Kurdish towns, and until recently, Baghdad.

BIBLIOGRAPHY: Benayahu, in: *Sefunot*, 9 (1965), 21–125; A. Ben-Jacob, *Kehillot Yehudei Kurdistan* (1961), 33–38; idem, *Yehudei Bavel* (1965), 86.

BARBADOS, Carribean island. The uninhabited island of Barbados was visited in 1625 by Captain John Powel, who took possession of it in the name of James I, king of England. The first Jews reportedly arrived by the year 1628. Later on Jews arrived in three waves: (1) 1654 – after the Portuguese retook the province of Pernambuco in Dutch Brazil. The first official warrant of residence given to a Jew was to the physician from Dutch Brazil, Abraham de Mercado, and his son, the sugar production specialist David Raphael de Mercado; (2) 1664 – after the dispersal of the Jewish settlement in Remire on the island of Cayenne–French Guyana; (3) 1674 – when England surrendered Surinam to the Dutch and some Jews chose to leave with the English for Barbados.

In 1654 a Jewish community was founded in the capital Bridgetown and the Nidhei Israel synagogue was established. The Semah David synagogue was established in the second city, Speightown.

Jews, all of Spanish-Portuguese origin, also came from Hamburg and other Hanseatic cities in Germany, and from England, Guadeloupe, and Leghorn.

Jewish exiles from Brazil were needed in Barbados to help transform its lagging economy (its cotton plantations could not compete with the Carolinas; its tobacco was inferior to the product of Virginia) into a sugar-producing center. The Jewish newcomers introduced special modern methods of sugar refining and crystallizing sugar for export. The Jews, being Spanish-speaking, excelled in their commercial exchange with the Spanish colonies, mainly with Jews living in them as *Conversos.

The Jewish success and the support they received from the English governors Francis Lord Willoughby and his brother William Lord Willoughby stirred the envy and enmity of the local English colonists. This prompted the levy of special taxes on the Jews, disallowing them to employ Christians and limiting them to holding only one slave. This meant the Jews could not maintain plantations.

In 1739 the Jews left Speightown after a mob of English colonists attacked and destroyed the Semah David synagogue. As a result, a gradual abandonment of the island by the Jews began, with their new destinations being Nevis, Newport (Rhode Island), or England.

Jewish life was strictly Orthodox and distinguished owing to the prominent Hahams (rabbis) who served there: Eliahu Lopez, who was born in Malaga, Spain, as a Converso (1679); Meir Hacohen Belinfante (d. 1752), of a Dalmatian (Croatian) family; and Rafael Haim Isaac *Carigal from Hebron, who was in Barbados from 1774 to 1777. Jews only received full civil rights in 1820.

Nidhei Israel was finally abandoned in 1928 when the one remaining practicing Jew died. Led by Paul Altman, the synagogue, however, was rededicated by Jews from Trinidad and Eastern Europe, who reached the island in the 1930s. A group of Jews initiated the formation of a Caribbean Jewish Congress.

Israel is represented by its ambassador in Santo Domingo and an honorary consul in Bridgetown, Beny Gilbert. In the early 2000s the Jewish population numbered some 30 families.

BIBLIOGRAPHY: M. Arbell, *The Jewish Nation of the Caribbean* (2002); E.M. Shilstone, *Monumental Inscriptions in the Burial Ground of the Jewish Synagogue at Bridgetown, Barbados* (1956); W.S. Samuel, "Review of the Jewish Colonists in Barbados, 1680," in: TJHSE, 13 (1932–1935, 1936), 1–112; P.A. Farrar, "The Jews in Barbados," in: *The Journal of the Barbados Museum and Historical Society*, 9:3 (1942), 130–34; "The Lucas Manuscript Volumes in the Barbados Public Library (Nov. 1946–Feb. 1947).

[Mordechai Arbell (2nd ed.)]

BARBARA (**Monique Serf**; 1930–1997), French singer and songwriter. Daughter of an Alsatian Jew, André Serf, and a Jewess of Moldavian descent, Ester Brodsky, Monique Serf was born in Paris and raised in Marseille and Roanne in a state of relative poverty. During World War II, the family had to flee to Southern France and move several times after being denounced as Jews. Back in Paris after the war, the young girl was able to study music. In 1950 she ran away from home and found shelter in Brussells, then Charleroi, where she began singing in a small cabaret, L'etoile du Sud. With some bohemian friends and artists, she took part in the creation of a cabaret in Charleroi, "Le vent vert," but her piano playing and her voice were somewhat diffident and awkward and the audience was unappreciative. She persisted, and her style became more and more personal, and was soon to find a growing audience in various cabarets and concert halls in Paris and Brussels. She began working with France's major songwriters (Régine, Brassens, Georges Moustaki) and popular composers and arrangers like F. Rauber. Her songs were full of intimate childhood memories and uneasy feelings, and her long black clothing and thin silhouette earned her the nickname of "Dame en Noir" (Black Lady). Her relationship with her fans was passionate and immediate, as exemplified by the song "Ma plus belle histoire d'amour, c'est vous" ("You're My Most Beautiful Love Story"), which she would dedicate to her audiences. Often sad, even under a guise of lightness, sometimes humorous but never trivial, her songs ("Goettingen," "L'aigle noir," "Nantes," "Une petite cantate," "Perlimpimpin") deal with the departure of loved ones, the tragedy of incest, the deep, ambiguous mixture of sadness and joy that characterizes childhood. She was a committed supporter of the left-wing politics often associated in the collective memory with President Francois Mitterrand. Towards the end of her career, she became involved in the struggle against AIDS ("Sid'amour a mort"), and when she died of illness in 1997, the general feeling was that an icon of French song, "une grande dame de la chanson française," had disappeared.

BIBLIOGRAPHY: J. Garcin, *Barbara, claire de nuit*, Paris (1999).

[Dror Franck Sullaper (2nd ed.)]

BARBARIANS, people of the Germanic linguistic group (Vandals, Franks, Goths, Burgundians, Lombards, Angles, and Saxons), of the Indo-Iranian group (Alans and Sarmatians), and the Hunnic peoples who were recruited by, allied to, or invaded the Roman Empire during the fourth, fifth, and sixth centuries C.E. Most of the barbarians were pagans when they entered the empire but were eventually converted to orthodox Christianity. One important exception were the Goths who, when they settled in Italy, Gaul, and Spain were Arian Christians. Even these were eventually converted to orthodox Christianity. During the barbarian invasions the Jews, mostly city dwellers who were outwardly assimilated to their neighbors, no doubt suffered together with the rest of the population. Although no factual record survives, it may be assumed that this contributed to the numerical decline of the once prosperous Jewish communities of the Roman Empire. On the sack of Rome in 455, the Vandals carried off to Africa the spoils of the Temple brought back from Jerusalem by Titus.

When the barbarians entered the Roman Empire, they were profoundly influenced by the Christian-Roman population. In general it can be said that, while the barbarians were pagans, they treated the Jews well, probably better than the vanquished Christians who posed a threat to their power, since a community of interest existed between Jews and barbarians as a result of the opprobrium with which they both were regarded by the orthodox population. The same favorable attitude existed when they adopted Arian Christianity. Once, however, the barbarians became members of the Orthodox church, the position of the Jews rapidly deteriorated. Restrictions were placed upon them, they were persecuted, and they were ultimately faced, especially in Spain, with the choice of conversion, exile, or death. General expulsions were decreed in Gaul in 626, in Burgundy about the same time, and in Lombardy in 661. More is known of the long attempt of the Visigothic kings of Spain to suppress Judaism from 613 onward. In this the Jews suffered equally with all those minorities who were not Orthodox Christians.

BIBLIOGRAPHY: J.B. Bury, *The Invasion of Europe by the Barbarians* (1928); S. Katz, *The Jews in the Visigothic and Frankish Kingdoms of Spain and Gaul* (1937); B. Blumenkranz, *Juifs et chrétiens dans le monde occidental, 430–1096* (1960); J.M. Wallace-Hadrill, *The Barbarian West* (1962); J. Parkes, *Conflict of Church and Synagogue* (1934).

BARBASH, SAMUEL (c. 1850–1921), banker, leader of Ḥovevei Zion and of political Zionism in Russia. Barbash was born in Podolia. In the early 1880s he moved to Odessa, where he established a large bank, heading it until the Russian Revolution of 1917. He was one of the two guarantors to the Russian government for the legalization of the *Odessa Committee, the center of the Ḥovevei Zion movement, and served as its treasurer throughout the committee's existence. He was a member of the board of directors of the *Jewish Colonial Trust in its first years and its representative in Russia. He was active in many economic spheres affecting Zionism. Throughout his life he supported Hebrew cultural and literary projects.

BIBLIOGRAPHY: M. Kleinmann (ed.), *Enẓiklopedyah le-Ẓiyyonut*, 1 (1947), 176–7; M.b.H. Ha-Kohen, *Sefer Shemot* (1938), 81–82.

[Getzel Kressel]

BARBASTRO, city in northern Aragon, Spain. Ramón Berenguer IV, count of Barcelona, conferred an estate upon a Jew named Zecri of Barbastro in 1144 as a reward for his services. In 1179 the bishop of Huesca granted Benjamin Abenbitals and Joseph b. Solomon permission to erect shops near the cathedral. Toward the middle of the 13th century the Jews occupied the Zuda, the citadel of Barbastro, which became the Jewish quarter. The charter of privileges granted to them in 1273 allowed them to request the bailiff to execute informers (*malshinim*) and prosecute Jews of dissolute morals. During the 13th–14th centuries the community of Barbastro, with a population of 200–300 Jews, was one of the important Aragonese communities of the group following the leading Jewish centers in Saragossa, Calatayud, and Huesca.

In 1285 Pedro II endorsed new communal tax regulations. The Jews of Barbastro paid for the right to maintain a bureau in which the promissory notes for loans were drawn up. In 1330 Alfonso IV acceded to the request of the community to abrogate his instruction that a Christian burgher should be appointed to administer Jewish communal affairs, and endorsed the continuation of the former administrative system. The circumstances of the community were so straitened at this period that a special levy imposed by the king did not amount to more than 20 Jaca *sólidos*. In 1363, however, a levy of 500 Jaca *sólidos* was imposed by Pedro IV to meet the cost of the war with Castile. In 1383 the king renewed the privilege of the Barbastro community prohibiting apostates from entering the Jewish quarter and preaching missionary sermons there, while Jews could not be compelled to enter into religious disputations with Christians.

During the massacres of 1391 the Jews of Barbastro took refuge in the citadel, which was subjected to a siege and on August 18, King John I instructed the local authorities to take measures against the culprits. The Jews of Barbastro suffered little compared to other communities. The community evidently ceased to exist after the disputation of *Tortosa and as a result of the pressure exerted by the Dominican preacher Vicente *Ferrer. In 1415 Benedict XIII ordered the synagogue to be converted into a church, known as the hermitage of San Salvador, because all the Jews in the city had become baptized and left the faith. It remained, however, a *Converso center. Many Conversos lived near the plaza del Mercado.

BIBLIOGRAPHY: Baer, Studien, 146; Baer, Urkunden, 1 pt. 1 (1929), index; Baer, Spain, 1 (1961), 55, 142, 426; Neuman, Spain, 1 (1942), index; del Arco, in: *Sefarad*, 7 (1947), 273, 280–1, 329; Rius, *ibid.*, 12 (1952), 339–40, 348–9; Cabezudo, *ibid.*, 23 (1963), 265–84. **ADD. BIBLIOGRAPHY:** E. Martín Padilla, in: *Homenaje a Don José María Lacarra de Miguel*, 4 (1977), 213–33.

[Haim Beinart / Yom Tov Assis (2nd ed.)]

BARBIE, NIKOLAUS ("Klaus"), TRIAL OF, trial in Lyons, France, of SS Hauptsturmfuehrer (captain) Klaus Barbie (b. 1913). Known as "the Butcher of Lyons" for his wartime activities in France, Barbie joined the Nazi Party in 1932 and in 1935 became the personal adjutant to the head of the local Nazi Party office in Trier. In late September 1935 he also joined the SS, working in the SD (Security Service) main office and then as a specialist in the Duesseldorf region. On April 20, 1940, he was made an SS second lieutenant (Untersturmfuehrer). On May 29, 1940, shortly after the fall of the Netherlands. Barbie was assigned to the "culture" section of the SD in Amsterdam. His job was to monitor anti-Nazi tendencies in the fields of science, education, religion, sport, entertainment, and propaganda. In November of that year he was promoted to SS first lieutenant (Obersturmfuehrer); exactly two years later he would reach the rank of Hauptsturmfuehrer. During the disturbances in Amsterdam in February 1941, Barbie had acid thrown into his face by the Jewish owners of the Koko ice cream parlor. In reprisal over four hundred young Jewish men were arrested and sent to Mauthausen, where most of them perished.

Barbie was made the head of the Gestapo (KDS) in Lyons in November 1942 and remained in that post for nearly two years. To foil the Resistance, Barbie ordered that raids be conducted against arbitrary targets as well as places suspected of underground activity. His work was characterized by a combination of guile and cruelty. He was apparently responsible for the arrest of René Hardy, a resistance leader. Twice tried after the war, Hardy was found innocent of charges that he had divulged the names of French underground leaders to Barbie. Nevertheless, shortly after Hardy was interrogated, Barbie arrested Jean Moulin, Charles de Gaulle's representative in southern France. Moulin had unified the major undergrounds and resistance movements under the National Resistance Council, which was founded on May 27, 1943. During the course of Barbie's interrogation, Moulin was brutally tortured, but apparently gave away nothing before he died. Barbie was involved in the deportation of at least 842 other people from Lyons and its environs. Half of them belonged to the Resistance, and half of them were Jews. He also personally shot a number of persons and was responsible for the death of others from the villages of St. Rambert-en-Bugey, Evosges, Nivollet-Montgriffen, the Montluc prison in Lyons, and other places.

Perhaps his most ignominious act was the seizure and deportation of 41 children and five women who were found hiding in Izieu, a village about 44 miles (70 km.) east of Lyons on April 6, 1944. They were sent to Auschwitz on August 11, 1944. Barbie also was responsible for the deportation of 85 Jews taken in a raid on the headquarters of the Union Générale des Israélites de France (UGIF), on February 9, 1943, in Lyons.

In the spring of 1947, Barbie began working for the Counter Intelligence Corps of the U.S. Army in Germany. He became such a valuable informant that his superiors protected him from French attempts to extradite him and helped him escape to Bolivia. Arriving in Bolivia in 1951, he assumed the alias Klaus Altmann, eventually becoming an important advisor to several Bolivian governments. Barbie was tried in absentia in France in 1952 and in 1954. In the first trial he was charged with atrocities committed in the Jura region against the civilian population and the underground. In the second trial he was charged with committing a massacre at St. Genis-Laval and numerous shootings at the Montluc prison in Lyons. Both trials led to his conviction and sentences of death. In 1971 Barbie was found in La Paz, Bolivia, by Beate and Serge *Klarsfeld, French hunters of Nazis. It was not until 1983, however, following repeated appeals by the French, that he was expelled from Bolivia and brought to France for trial.

Barbie was charged with the raid on the UGIF office and the deportation of the Jews from Izieu, two acts for which he had not been previously tried. Coming under the rubric of "crimes against humanity," these acts were not subject to the statute of limitation in France. The main proceedings against Barbie took place between May 11 and July 4, 1987. The trial aroused a great deal of interest in France and the rest of the world. Many Frenchmen had mixed feelings about the trial or opposed it. Some Jews thought it might arouse antisemitism or become a forum for the denial of the Holocaust. Extreme right-wingers actually advanced the claim that Barbie's behavior was no worse than that of the Allies, who had bombed German cities and caused the death of civilians. Some feared it would raise the question again of events surrounding the death of Jean Moulin and of French collaboration with the Nazis.

Barbie himself, after making an early appearance in the courtroom, refused to be present for most of the trial. He was found guilty on July 4, 1987, and given the maximum penalty under French law, life imprisonment. He died in 1991.

BIBLIOGRAPHY: T. Bower, *Klaus Barbie, "Butcher of Lyons"* (1984); A.J. Ryan, Jr. (ed.), *Klaus Barbie and the United States Government* (1984).

[Robert Rozette]

BARBY, MEIR BEN SAUL (1729?–1789), rabbi of Pressburg. Barby took his name from his birthplace, Barby, a small town near Halberstadt. He studied under Ẓevi Hirsch b. Naphtali Herz Bialeh (Ḥarif) of Halberstadt and Jacob Poppers, rabbi of Frankfurt. On his return from Frankfurt, he was appointed *dayyan* of Halberstadt, was rabbi of Halle for a year, and was then appointed rabbi of Pressburg in 1763. In Pressburg he established a large yeshivah. Barby issued many community *takkanot*, some of them designed to prevent laxity in Jewish life – such as frequenting the theater and card playing. A vehement opponent of the *Shabbateans, he excommunicated one of their adherents, Nathan Erholz, and dismissed him from the post of rabbi of Stampen. In 1771 he was a candidate for the vacant post of rabbi of Frankfurt, but was not elected. He was in halakhic correspondence with many prominent scholars, including Ezekiel *Landau, Isaiah *Berlin, and Meir Posner, and he gave approbations to many works. Aside from his Torah erudition, Barby had a good knowledge of medicine and music. Though he opposed the publication of his responsa, many of his novellae are cited in the works of his contemporaries. His only published work is *Ḥiddushei Hilkhot Maharam Barby* (2 vols., Dyhrenfurth-Prague, 1786–92).

BIBLIOGRAPHY: *Arim ve-Immahot be-Yisrael*, 7 (1960), 41–45.

[Itzhak Alfassi]

BARCELONA, Mediterranean port in Catalonia, northeast Spain, seat of one of the oldest Jewish communities in the country. Amram *Gaon sent his version of the prayer book to "the scholars of Barcelona." In 876/7 a Jew named Judah (Judacot) was the intermediary between the city and the emperor Charles the Bald. Tenth- and eleventh-century sources mention Jews owning land in and around the city. The prominence of Jews in Barcelona is suggested by the statement of an Arabic chronicler that there were as many Jews as Christians in the city, but a list of 1079 records only 60 Jewish names. The book of *Usatges* ("Custumal") of Barcelona (1053–71) defines the Jews' legal status. Jewish ownership of real estate continued: the site of the ancient Jewish cemetery is still known as Montjuich. A number of Jewish tombstones have been preserved. From the end of the 11th century the Jews lived in a special quarter in the heart of the old city, near the main gate and not far from the harbor. The area known as Call, the name of the Jewish quarter throughout Catalonia, is still echoed in the names of some of its streets that contain the word, such as Carrer del Call. (The word *call* derives from the Latin *callum*). Barcelona's Jews were subject to the jurisdiction of the counts of Barcelona. The forms of contract used by Jews there from an early date formed the basis of the *Sefer ha-Shetarot* of *Judah b. Barzillai al-Bargeloni, written at the beginning of the 12th century. In the first half of the 11th century, some Barcelonan Jews were minters, and coins have been found bearing the name of the Jewish goldsmith who minted them. In 1104, four Jews of Barcelona received the monopoly to repatriate Muslim prisoners of war to southern Spain. Shortly afterward, *Abraham b. Ḥiyya was using his mathematical knowledge in the service of the king of Aragon and the counts of Barcelona, possibly assisting them to apportion territories conquered from the Muslims. Abraham's role in the transmission of Greco-Arabic culture to the Jews north of the Pyrenees who did not know Arabic was crucial. His encyclopedic works in Hebrew presented the scientific and philosophical legacy that was available in Arabic to the Jews of Christian Europe. It was probably due to his residence in Barcelona, a city that was for a very brief period under Muslim rule, but otherwise the most important city in Christian Spain in the early stages of the *Reconquista*, that Abraham b. Hiyya was so appreciative of the need to disseminate in Hebrew the treasures of the Greco-Arabic world. The Jewish community reached the peak of its prestige in the 13th century, when the Crown of Aragon, under James I, doubled the size of its territories. Besides the important members of the community who served the kings and counts, the community had very distinguished scholars who were among its political, financial, religious, and intellectual leaders.

Communal Life

Documents of the second half of the 11th century contain the first mention of *nesi'im* ("princes"; see *nasi) of the house of Sheshet (see Sheshet b. Isaac *Benveniste), who served the counts as suppliers of capital, advisers on Muslim affairs, Arab secretaries, and negotiators. From the middle of the 12th century the counts would frequently appoint Jews also as bailiffs (*baile*) of the treasury; some of these were also members of the Sheshet family. Christian anti-Jewish propaganda in Barcelona meanwhile increased. In 1263 a public *disputation was held at Barcelona in which *Naḥmanides confronted Pablo *Christiani in the presence of James I of Aragon. The bailiff and mintmaster of Barcelona at the time was Benveniste de Porta, the last Jew to hold this office. In 1283, as a result of the French invasion following the conquest of Sicily by Pedro I, "the Great," the Catalan noblemen, joined by their Aragonese and Valencian counterparts, forced Pedro to give up his Jewish civil servants who had occupied numerous positions throughout the Kingdom of Aragon. The Jews were subsequently replaced by Christian aristocrats and burghers and Jews from families whose ancestors had formerly acquired wealth in the service of the counts now turned to commerce and moneylending. Many of them returned to the communal political arena and aspired to hold important positions in the community leadership. However, learned Jews such as Judah *Bonsenyor continued to perform literary services for the sovereign. In 1294 Jaime II gave him the monopoly on all Hebrew and Arabic documents drawn up in the territory of Barcelona. By the beginning of the 13th century, a number of Jewish merchants and financiers had become sufficiently influential to displace the *nesi'im* in the conduct of communal affairs. In 1241, James I granted the Barcelona's Jewish community a constitution to be administered by a group of *ne'emanim* (*secretarii*, or "administrative officers") – all drawn from among the wealthy, who were empowered to enforce discipline in religious and social matters and to try monetary suits. James further extended the powers of these officials in 1272. The class struggle within the Jewish community that erupted in 1263 in Saragossa and spread throughout the communities in the Kingdom of Aragon did not greatly affect the political regime in Barcelona. Nevertheless, one of the institutions that served as the community's parliament, the Council of Thirty or *Eẓat ha-Sheloshim*, was established on the model of the municipal Council of the Hundred or Concell de Trente. Solomon b. Abraham *Adret was now the leading halakhic authority and public figure in Barcelona, a position he enjoyed for about 50 years. Under his guidance, the Barcelonan Jewish community became foremost in Spain in scholarship, wealth, and public esteem. He and his sons were among the seven *ne'emanim*, and he must have favored the new constitution. The *ne'emanim* did not admit to their number either intellectuals whose beliefs were suspect or shopkeepers and artisans. When the controversy over the study of sciences and philosophy took place in the years 1303–5 at the end of Adret's life, the intellectuals of Barcelona did not therefore dare to voice their opinions. In 1305, Adret prohibited, under ban, youth under 25 years of age from studying sciences and philosophy (except medicine): this provision was also signed by the *ne'emanim* and the 30 members of the Community Council.

A third constitution was adopted in 1327, by which time the community had been augmented, in 1306, by 60 families of French exiles. The privileges, such as exemption from taxes, enjoyed by Jews close to the court, were now abolished, and, alongside the body of *ne'emanim*, legal status was accorded to the "Council of Thirty," an institution that had begun to develop early in the 14th century. The new regulations helped to strengthen the governing body. Several Spanish Jewish communities used this constitution as a model. *Berurei averot* ("magistrates for misdemeanors") were appointed for the first time in 1338 to punish offenders against religion and the accepted code of conduct. In the following year *berurei tevi'ot* ("magistrates for claims") were elected to try monetary suits. The communal jurisdiction of Barcelona, which at times acted on behalf of all the communities of the Crown of Aragon, that is, Catalonia, Aragon, Valencia, Majorca, and Roussillon, extended to several communities, both small and large, which were included in its *collecta*. The *collecta* was an inter-communal organization originally created to facilitate the collection of the royal taxes but subsequently served other purposes as well. The *collecta* of Barcelona was headed by the community of Barcelona and included the communities of Tarragona, Montblanch, Villafranca, and Cervera. The other Catalan *collectas* were those of Gerona-Besalú, Léida (Lleida), and Tortosa. A nationwide body, consisting of seven members acting on behalf of Catalan Jewry, operated under the leadership of the community of Barcelona.

The community of Barcelona, called *aljama* as in the rest of the peninsula, had a number of institutions that were found in most communities throughout the medieval Jewish world. It had several synagogues, some of which had special characteristics. The *sinagoga mayor* was the Great Synagogue that was visited by James I during the *Barcelona Disputation. This synagogue has recently been restored. Another synagogue was the *sinagoga de les dones* (The Ladies' Synagogue), probably so called because it had special sections for women. The *sinagoga de los franceses* (The Synagogue of the French) was founded by the 60 Jewish families that were absorbed in Barcelona after the expulsion of 1306. The Jewish cemetery was situated on Montjuich (the Mountain of the Jews), where some tombstones with Hebrew inscriptions were found. An interesting inscription was discovered in a building in the *call* indicating that it was donated by the famous Rabbi Samuel ha-Sardi, probably to serve as a *talmud torah*.

The community suffered severely during the *Black Death of 1348. Most of the "thirty" and the *ne'emanim* perished in the plague, and the Jewish quarter was attacked by the mob. Despite protection extended by the municipality, several Jews were killed. In December 1354, delegates for the communities of Catalonia and the province of Valencia convened in Barcelona with the intention of establishing a national roof organization for the Jewish communities of the kingdom in order to rehabilitate them after the devastations of the plague. In the second half of the century R. Nissim *Gerondi restored the yeshivah of Barcelona to its former preeminence. Among his disciples were R. *Isaac b. Sheshet and R. Ḥasdai *Crescas, both members of old, esteemed Barcelonan families who took part in the community administration after the late 1360s.

Economic Life

The Jews of Barcelona owned extensive property in the city and its surroundings. In the 13th century they held quite a substantial part of the real estate in the region. This property was mostly in the hands of the wealthy class. The Jews were mainly occupied as artisans and merchants, some of them engaging in overseas trade. They played an important role in maritime trade thanks to their international connections with Jewish merchants throughout the Mediterranean basin, their easy communication in Hebrew, which was universally used by Jews, and their ability to have partners, agents, and hosts in many localities. They overcame some of the difficulties that Christian and Muslim merchants encountered in trade between their two worlds. Sources from the *Archivo Capitular* of Barcelona show the extent of the participation of the Jews of the city in the trade between Catalonia and Muslim countries in the eastern Mediterranean. The Catalans spared no effort in putting an end to the predominance of Jewish merchants from Barcelona in trade with Muslim countries. They turned to the law prohibiting trade of certain merchandise with the Muslims. When this failed they used the Papal Inquisition to make trade with the east risky and costly. Many Jews returning from the east found themselves arrested and charged as soon as they landed in Barcelona. The king yielded to the demands of the Christian merchants of Barcelona and practically put an end to the commercial activities of the Jews overseas, particularly in Egypt and Syria. By the beginning of the 14th century Jews no longer played an important role in the trade with Muslims. The elimination of Jewish competition in maritime trade was considered a vital goal that was finally achieved. In another field of economic activity where there was much criticism of the Jews but no alternative was found, the Jewish moneylenders continued their credit transactions.

Most of the Jews in Barcelona were engaged in crafts and other professions. We know that the Jewish bookbinders of Barcelona had their own confraternity. There were also some professionals, such as physicians, translators, and interpreters.

The Decline

Around 1367 the Jews were charged with desecrating the *Host, several community leaders being among the accused. Three Jews were put to death, and for three days the entire community, men, women, and children, were detained in the synagogue without food. Since they did not confess, the king ordered their release. However, Nissim Gerondi, Isaac b. Sheshet, Ḥasdai Crescas, and several other dignitaries were imprisoned for a brief period.

The community gradually recovered after these misfortunes. Jewish goldsmiths, physicians, and merchants were again employed at court. After Isaac b. Sheshet's departure from Barcelona and Nissim Gerondi's death, Ḥasdai Crescas was almost the sole remaining notable; he led the community for about 20 years. The main element in the Barcelona community was now the artisans – weavers, dyers, tailors, shoemakers, carpenters, blacksmiths, and coral-workers. These were organized into confraternities and now demanded their share in the communal administration. After the long period in which the ruling oligarchy had been exercising their authority to their own advantage, the 1327 charter was abolished by royal edict in 1386. A new charter was approved by which representatives of the two lower estates, the merchants and artisans, shared in the administration.

During the persecutions of 1391, the city fathers and even the artisans of Barcelona tried to protect the Jews of the city, but without success. The violence in Barcelona was instigated by a band of Castilians, who had taken part in the massacres in Seville and Valencia and arrived in Barcelona by boat. News of the onslaught on the Jewish quarter in Majorca set off the attack on Saturday, August 5. About 100 Jews were killed and a similar number sought refuge in the "New Castle" in the newer and second Jewish quarter. The gate of the *call* and the notarial archives were set on fire and looting continued throughout that day and night. The Castilians were arrested and ten were sentenced to the gallows. The following Monday, however, the "little people" (*populus minutus*), mostly dock workers and fishermen, broke down the prison doors and stormed the castle. Many Jews were killed. At the same time, serfs from the surrounding countryside attacked the city, burned the court records of the bailiff, seized the fortress of the royal vicar, and gave the Jews who had taken refuge there the alternative of death or conversion. The plundering and looting continued throughout that week. Altogether about 400 Jews were killed; the rest were converted. Only a few of them (including Ḥasdai Crescas, whose son, newly married, was among the martyrs) escaped to the territories owned by the nobility or to North Africa. At the end of the year John I condemned 26 of the rioters to death but acquitted the rest. In 1393 John took measures to rehabilitate the Jewish community in Barcelona. He allotted the Jews a new residential quarter and ordered the return of the old cemetery. All their former privileges were restored and a tax exemption was granted for a certain period, as well as a moratorium on debts. Ḥasdai was authorized to transfer Jews from other places to resettle Barcelona, but only a few were willing to move. The project failed. Reestablishment of a Jewish community in Barcelona was finally prohibited in 1401 by Martin I in response to the request of the burghers. Thus the Jewish community of Barcelona ceased to exist a hundred years before the expulsion.

The Conversos

While Jews no longer resided in the city, the *Conversos, those forcibly converted during the massacres, continued to live there. The renewed prosperity of Barcelona during the 15th century should be credited in part to the Conversos, who developed wide-ranging commercial and industrial activities. Despite protests by the city fathers, in 1486 Ferdinand decided to introduce the Inquisition on the Castilian model in Barcelona. At the outset of the discussions on procedure the Conversos began to withdraw their deposits from the municipal bank and to leave the city. The most prosperous merchants fled, credit and commerce declined, the artisans suffered, and economic disaster threatened. The inquisitors entered Barcelona in July 1487. Some ships with refugees on board were detained in the harbor. Subsequently several high-ranking officials of Converso descent were charged with observing Jewish religious rites and put to death. In 1492 many of the Jews expelled from Aragon embarked from Barcelona on their way abroad.

20th Century

At the beginning of the 20th century a few Jewish peddlers from Morocco and Turkey settled in Barcelona. After Salonika came under Greek rule in 1912 and the announcement by the Spanish government of its willingness to encourage settlement of Sephardi Jews on its territory (1931), Jews from Turkey, Greece, and other Balkan countries migrated to Barcelona. Other Jews arrived from Poland during World War I, followed by immigrants from North Africa, and by artisans – tailors, cobblers, and hatmakers – from Poland and Romania. There were over 100 Jews in Barcelona in 1918, while in 1932 the figure rose to more than 3,000, mostly of Sephardi origin. After 1933 some German Jews established ribbon, leather, and candy industries. By 1935 Barcelonan Jewry numbered over 5,000, the Sephardim by now being a minority. During the Spanish Civil War (1936–39), many left for France and Palestine. Some of the German Jews left the city after the Republican defeat in 1939, but during and after World War II Barcelona served as a center for refugees, maintained by the *American Jewish Joint Distribution Committee, and others returned to resettle.

The Barcelonan community, consisting of approximately 3,000 people in 1968 and 3,500 in 2000, is the best organized in Spain. The communal organization unites both Sephardi and Ashkenazi synagogues. There is also a community center, which includes a rabbinical office and cultural center. The community runs a Jewish day school and Chabad is active in the city. Youth activities include summer camps and a Maccabi movement. An old-age home supported by Jewish agencies outside Spain is maintained. The University of Barcelona offers courses in Jewish studies. Together with leaders of the Madrid community, Barcelona community heads were received in 1965 by General Franco, the first meeting between a Spanish head of state and Jewish leaders since 1492.

BIBLIOGRAPHY: J. Fiter Ingles, *Expulsíon de los judios de Barcelona* (1876); Loeb, in: REJ, 4 (1882), 57–77; F. de Bofarull y Sans, *Los judíos en el territorio de Barcelona* (1910); J. Miret y Sans and M. Schwab, *Documents de juifs Catalans des XIe, XIIe et XIIe siécles* (1915), 191; idem, in: *Boletin de la Real Academia de la Historia*, 69 (1916), 569–82; Baer, Urkunden, 1 pt. 1 (1929), index; Prevosti, in: *Sefarad*, 10 (1951), 75–90; A. López de Meneses, in: *Estudios de Edad Media de la Corona de Aragón*, 5 (1952), 677; idem, in: *Sefarad*, 19 (1959), 97–106, 323ff.; Madurell y Marimón, *ibid.*, 16 (1956), 369–98; 17 (1957), 73–102; 18 (1958), 60–82; 21 (1961), 300–38; 22 (1962), 345–72; 23 (1963), 74–104; 25 (1965), 247–82; 27 (1967), 290–8; Baron, Social², 4 (1957), 34, 249, notes 37f.; Cardoner, in: *Sefarad*, 22 (1962), 373–5; Suárez Fernández, Documentos, index; Baer, Spain, index; Millás Vallicrosa, in: *Sefarad*, 27 (1967), 64–70. **ADD. BIBLIOGRAPHY:** J. Shatzmiller, in: *Meḥkarim be-Toledot Am Yisrael*, 3 (1980), 121–37; J-L. Palos, in: *L'Aven*, 47 (1982), 21–31; L. Feldman, in: *Genuzot*, 1 (1984), 67–98; D. Abulafia, in: *Viator*, 16 (1985), 209–42; D. Romano, in: G. Dahan (ed.), *Les juifs au regard de l'histoire*, (1985), 195–99; E. Lourie, in: *Mediterranean Historical Review* 1 (1986), 187–220; E. Feliu i Mabres, in: *Calls*, 2 (1987), 145–79; Y. Assis, in: *Galut aḥar Golah* (1988), 257–83; idem, in: *Jornades d'história dels jueus a Catalunya* (1987), *Actes*, (1990), 77–92; M. Cinta Mañé, *The Jews in Barcelona, 1213–1291*; Y Assis (ed.), *Regesta of Documents from the Archivo Capitular* (1988); Y. Assis, *The Golden Age of Aragonese Jewry* (1997), index, s. v. Barcelona; idem, *Jewish Economy in the Medieval Crown of Aragon*, (1997), index, s.v. Barcelona. MODERN PERIOD: M. Fernández Matorell, *Estudio antropológico: una comunidad judía* (1984); M. Berthlot, *Historia oral de la comunidad israelita de Barcelona (Barcelona 1914–1954)* (2001).

[Zvi Avneri and Haim Beinart / Yom Tov Assis (2nd ed.)]

BARCELONA, DISPUTATION OF, religious disputation between Jews and Christians in 1263. The apostate Paulus [Pablo] *Christiani proposed to King James I of Aragon that a formal public religious disputation on the fundamentals of faith should be held between him and R. Moses b. Naḥman (*Naḥmanides) whom he had already encountered in *Gerona. The disputation took place with the support of the ecclesiastical authorities and the generals of the Dominican and Franciscan orders, while the king presided over a number of sessions and took an active part in the disputation. The Dominicans *Raymond de Peñaforte, Raymond *Martini, and Arnold de Segarra, and the general of the Franciscan order in the kingdom, Peter de Janua, were among the Christian disputants. The single representative for the Jewish side was Naḥmanides. The four sessions of the disputation took place on July 20, 27, 30, and 31, 1263 (according to another calculation, July 20, 23, 26, and 27). Naḥmanides was guaranteed complete freedom of speech in the debate; he took full advantage of the opportunity thus afforded and spoke with remarkable frankness. Two accounts of the disputation, one in Hebrew written by Naḥmanides and a shorter one in Latin, are the main sources for the history of this important episode in Judeo-Christian polemics. According to both sources the initiative for the disputation and its agenda were imposed by the Christian side, although the Hebrew account tries to suggest a greater involvement of Naḥmanides in finalizing the items to be discussed. The initiative in the debate remained on the Christian side throughout.

Basing himself on the Talmud as a whole, and in particular on the aggadic and homiletical passages, the Christian contestant sought to prove three points: that the Messiah had already appeared; that he was "both human and divine," and had died to atone for the sins of mankind; and that, in consequence, the precepts of Judaism had lost their validity. Against this Naḥmanides argued that the literal meaning of the passages quoted from the Talmud do not admit this christological interpretation. On the question of *aggadah* he claimed that the homiletical passages in the Talmud are not obligatory for Jews. Rabbis and eminent scholars, such as Yitzhak Baer, H.H. Ben-Sasson, and Martin Cohen maintained that Naḥmanides' claim was purely political, put forward in a disputation that had been imposed on him, so that he even had to use arguments in which he did not believe in order to overcome the Christian attack. Other scholars, such as Cecil Roth and Robert Chazan, expressed a more moderate opinion. Chavel, H. Maccoby, and B. Septimus suggested that Naḥmanides' view was fully compatible with a well-established Jewish tradition. Marvin Fox argues that this latter attitude is based on a complete misunderstanding of Naḥmanides' views and beliefs as they are found so clearly throughout his commentary on the Torah and that Nahmanides' view follows a Jewish tradition that, though paying full respect to the midrashic commentaries, does not accept them as necessarily binding, and avows that the main issue between Judaism and Christianity does not depend on belief in the Messiah. Naḥmanides even went on to attack the illogicality in Christian dogma concerning the nature of the Divinity. Some of his utterances hint at the future destruction of Christendom. He referred slightingly to the fate of Jesus, who was persecuted in his own lifetime and hid from his pursuers. Rome, which had been a mighty empire before Jesus lived, declined after adopting Christianity, "and now the servants of Muhammad have a greater realm than they." Naḥmanides also made the point that "from the time of Jesus until the present the world has been filled with violence and injustice, and the Christians have shed more blood than all other peoples." He similarly attacked the whole concept of the combination of human and divine attributes in Jesus.

A number of ecclesiastics who saw the turn the disputation was taking urged that it should be ended as speedily as possible. It was, therefore, never formally concluded, but interrupted. According to the Latin record of the proceedings, the disputation ended because Naḥmanides fled prematurely from the city. In fact, however, he stayed on in Barcelona for over a week after the disputation had been suspended in order to be present in the synagogue on the following Sabbath when a conversionist sermon was to be delivered. The king himself attended the synagogue in state and gave an address, an event without medieval precedent. Naḥmanides was permitted to reply on this occasion. The following day, after receipt of a gift of 300 *sólidos* from the king, he returned home.

The disputation had far-reaching consequences. It prompted the Dominican Raymond Martini to devise a better method of providing christological interpretations to the *aggadah*. In 1280 Martini concluded his book *Pugio Fidei* (Paris, 1651), and henceforward it was used indiscriminately by every Christian controversialist wishing to invalidate Judaism. The king cooperated with missionary activities throughout the realm and the Jews were forced to listen to the sermons preached by the Dominican friars. An order was issued by the latter between August 26 and 29 directing the Jews to erase from their copies of the Talmud any passages vilifying Jesus and Mary. Failure to do so was punishable by a fine, and books which had not been censored as required would be burned. The *Mishneh Torah* of *Maimonides was also condemned to be burned because of the references to Jesus in the chapter on the laws of kingship at the end of the work. Subsequently, the bishop of Gerona obtained a copy of Naḥmanides' own account of the disputation. Perhaps through his agency, proceedings were then instituted against Naḥmanides in 1265 before the court of the Inquisition on the charge that he had blasphemed Jesus. James' intention to sentence him to two years' banishment and to condemn his work on the disputation to be burned, evidently did not satisfy the Dominicans. He thereupon ordered the case to be tried before him personally, intending to adjourn it until the fanaticism had abated. The militant Christian religious mendicant orders acted as the instrument of the church in its war on Judaism. It was at the request of the friars that Pope Clement IV ordered the archbishop of Tarragona to collect all the Jewish books in the Kingdom of Aragon and surrender them to the Dominicans and Franciscans for examination; Paulus Christiani was recommended as a trustworthy and able assistant for this task. The bull *Turbato Corde*, also issued by Clement, became the basis of the Inquisition policy for prosecuting suspected Judaizers (see papal *bulls), and may also be regarded as an outcome of the disputation. The inference drawn by Naḥmanides is self-evident: he left Spain for Ereẓ Israel, arriving there in 1267. Judeo-Christian polemics continued in Barcelona in the days of *Adret, Nahmanides' outstanding disciple. On the Christian side Martini and Ramon Lull participated in the debates that took place in a more private forum. The use of Jewish classical texts by Paulus in his confrontation with the foremost rabbinic authority in Spain was an innovation in Judeo-Christian polemics. The Barcelona Disputation was the first arena where Paulus Christiani was able to try out his new technique of missionizing and where Naḥmanides provided Jewish counterarguments to the newly formulated Christian claims. While the Disputation may have been a great achievement for Paulus Christiani in his innovative use of rabbinic sources in Christian missionary efforts, for Naḥmanides it represented an additional example of the wise and courageous leadership which he offered his people.

BIBLIOGRAPHY: Baer, Spain, 1 (1961), 150–62; idem, in: *Tarbiz*, 2 (1930/31), 172–87; C. Roth, *Gleanings* (1967), 34–61; M.A. Cohen, in: HUCA, 35 (1964), 157–92; Ben-Sasson, in: *Molad*, 1 (1967), 363–5. **ADD. BIBLIOGRAPHY:** J. Forment, in: *Escritos del Vedat*, 7 (1977), 155–75; H. Grossinger, in: *Kairos n.F.*, 19 (1977), 257–85; 20 (1978), 1–15, 161–81; M. Orfali, in: *Sefarad*, 39 (1979), 111–20; R. Chazan, in *Speculum*, 52 (1977), 824–42; idem, in HUCA 51 (1980), 89–110; idem, in: HUCA, 61 (1990), 185–201; idem, *Barcelona and Beyond*, (1992); H. Maccoby, *Judaism on Trial* (1982), incl. text of the Disputation; H-G von Mutius, *Die christlich-jüdische Zwangsdisputation zu Barcelona* (1982); J. Riera I Sans and E. Feliu (eds.), *Disputa de Barcelona de 1263* (1985); S. Schreiner, in: *Judaica*, 42 (1986), 141–57; M. Fox, in: JJS, 40 (1989), 95–109.

[Haim Beinart / Yom Tov Assis (2nd ed.)]

BARCINSKY (Barczinsky), HENRYK (Henoch; 1896–1941?), painter and graphic artist. Barcinsky was born in Lodz, Poland. As a child, he received a traditional Jewish education and prior to World War I attended a private art school in Łodz. In 1915–16 he studied at Henryk Glitzenstein's studio in Warsaw. As a teenager, he became close to the circles of young Jewish writers and artists who made it their aim to develop "contemporary national art." These ideas were a formative influence on the development of Barcinsky's national and artistic *Weltanschauung*, and the artist maintained close ties with this environment all through his life. In 1918, he participated in the exhibition in Białystok organized by the Artistic Section of the local Kultur-Liga. In 1919, in Łodz, he joined the "Yung Yiddish" modernist group and published his drawings in its anthologies. In the same year, he moved to Dresden, where he attended the Academy of Arts. In 1924, upon completing his studies at the Academy, he traveled around Spain and then settled in Berlin. He joined Elsa Lasker-Schüeler's group, which brought together German-Jewish intellectuals and cultural figures. In the 1920s, he participated in a number of exhibitions in Berlin and Dresden. Living in Germany, he never broke ties with Poland and regularly sent his works to be shown at exhibitions there. In 1933, when Hitler came to power, Barcinsky returned to Poland and settled in Łodz. In 1934, the Jewish Society for the Encouragement of Artists organized his solo exhibition in Warsaw, in the Jewish community building. Barcinsky is one of the most remarkable and original representatives of expressionism in Polish art. He drew his themes from the Jewish life around him, as well as from Jewish folklore. When German occupation troops entered Poland and were approaching Łodz, Barcinsky fled to Tomaszow in the hope of finding refuge with friends there. After 1941, no trace of him remained..

BIBLIOGRAPHY: Y. Sandel, *Umgekumene Yidishe Kinstler in Poiln*, vol. 1 (1957), 47–53; J. Malinowski. *Grupa "Jung Idysz" i żidowskie środowisko "Nowej Sztuki" w Polsce. 1918–1923* (1987); idem, *Malarstwo i rzeźba Żydow Polskich w XIX i XX wieku* (2000), 158, 189–91.

[Hillel Kazovsky (2nd ed.)]

BARD, BASIL JOSEPH ASHER (1914–2002), English lawyer and chemist. Bard studied chemistry at the Royal College of Science and also became a barrister. During World War II he worked in the legal departments of various government ministries dealing with the production and supply of explosives and aircraft. In 1950 he entered the government National Research Development Corporation and successively served as commercial manager, technical director, executive director, and chief executive and was appointed its managing director in 1971. Bard became the first chairman of the British branch of the Licensing Executives Society and served on a number of government committees. Bard was actively interested in Jewish communal and Zionist affairs. From 1977 to 1981 he was chairman of the Birmingham Mint.

[Samuel Aaron Miller]

BARDACH, ISRAEL (Isaac ben Ḥayyim Moses; c. late 18th century), Hebrew grammarian. Bardach, who lived in Lithuania, is known as the author of *Ta'amei Torah* (Vilna, 1822), a book on the accents (cantillations) of the Torah which was published by his brother Meir Bardach. The second part of this work contains a treatise on Hebrew grammar. In the introduction to *Ta'amei Torah*, Bardach mentions that he had also written commentaries on the *Idra Rabba* (of the *Zohar), on the Babylonian and Jerusalem Talmuds, and on the Shulḥan Arukh. However, the existence of all of these is unknown.

BIBLIOGRAPHY: Benjacob, Oẓar, 211, no. 122.

BARDAKI, ISAIAH BEN ISSACHAR BER (1790–1862), Polish rabbi and later head of the Jerusalem community. Bardaki was born in Pinsk and settled in Ereẓ Israel in 1810, after the death of his first wife. In 1823 he married the daughter of R. *Israel b. Samuel of Shklov who mentions Bardaki with great affection. This marriage assured him of a leading position in the growing Ashkenazi community of Jerusalem. Upon the death of his father-in-law, he became head of the community. Wherever he went he was accompanied by his own interpreter and his personal attendant. Bardaki greatly strengthened the community, although he was opposed to all modern trends. Several buildings adjoining the Or ha-Ḥayyim Yeshivah were constructed under his auspices and the compound was named after him Ḥaẓar Rabbi Yeshayahu. He was a vice consul of Austria (a post of great importance in the *capitulations regime prevailing in Jerusalem), and received the title of *ḥakham bashi* ("chief rabbi"). Several of his works are extant in manuscript.

BIBLIOGRAPHY: A.M. Luncz, in: *Yerushalayim*, 5 (1898), 232–4; Y. Yellin, *Zikhronot le-Ven Yerushalayim* (1924), 8–10; Frumkin-Rivlin, 3 (1929), 227–9; A. Yaari, *The Goodly Heritage* (1958), 46, 53–4; J. Rimon and J.Z. Wassermann, *Yerushalayim ha-Attikah* (1958), 150–2.

[Itzhak Alfassi]

BARDANASHVILI, JOSEF (1948–), Israeli composer. Born in Batumi, Georgia, Bardanashvili studied at the Music Academy in Tbilisi under Alexander Shaverzashvili, where he graduated with a Ph.D. in composition in 1976. He was the director of the Batumi College (1986–91) and cultural vice minister of Adjaria (1993–94). He settled in Israel in 1995 and was composer-in-residence of the Israel Sinfonette Orchestra of Ra'anannah from 1996 to 1999. He taught at Camera Obscura College in 1998–99, at the Rubin Academy of Music, Tel Aviv, in 1998–2000, and at the Bar-Ilan University and Sapir Academy College. He served as musical director of the Tel Aviv Biennale for Contemporary Music in 2002 and 2004.

Bardanashvili composed the first Georgian rock-opera, *Alternative* (1976), and rock-ballet, *Tutor* (1982). Among his other works are three operas, *Moving Stars* (1982), *Eva* (1998), and *A Journey to the End of the Millennium* (2004); two ballets (1972, 1991); two symphonies (1980, 2001); concertos for guitar, flute, piano, and violin; a triptych for voices and orchestra, *Children of God*, with texts from the Talmud, Koran, New Testament, and Book of Psalms (1997); *Time to Love* with texts from the Song of Songs, the Evangelists, Samuel ha-Nagid, and Nahapet Kuchak (1999); string quartets, quintets, piano trios, piano sonatas, choir music, and music for over 20 films and 40 theater productions. Having been influenced by Schnittke's polistylistic music and Kancheli's music, Bardanashvili was one of the first postmodern composers in the former Soviet Union to build his compositions on Georgian folklore and the music of Caucasian Jews.

Bardanashvili's compositions have been successfully performed all over the world by famous soloists, conductors, and orchestras such as the Israel Philharmonic, the St. Petersburg Marinsky Theater, the Berliner Symphoniker, Jerusalem Symphony, Dochnanyi (Hungary), and festivals in Israel and abroad. Among his honors are the title of Honored Artist of Georgia (1988), the Paliashvili Award (1997), the AKUM Composer Prize (1998), the AKUM Prize for Lifetime Achievement (2002), the Margalit Prize (1999) for incidental music for the *Dybbuk*, the Israeli Prime Minister's Award (2000), and Israel Theater Music Oscar (2003).

[Dushan Mihakek (2nd ed.)]

BAR-DAROMA (Schermeister), ḤAYYIM ZE'EV (1892–1970), Israeli geographer. Bar-Daroma was born on a farm near Volkovysk, Poland, and in his youth studied in the famous Lithuanian yeshivot of Mir and Slobodka, secretly acquiring at the same time a knowledge of Russian and secular subjects.

In 1911 he joined his parents who had settled in the ICA settlement of Sejera (see *Ilaniyyah) and later moved to Petaḥ Tikvah. In 1918 he moved to Jerusalem where he adopted the name of Bar-Daroma and was one of the first students of the Hebrew University, studying among other subjects the geophysical history of Ereẓ Israel, geology, and archaeology. After receiving his M.A. in 1938, he proceeded to the United States where he continued his education at Dropsie College, receiving his doctorate in 1942.

Returning to Israel in 1946, he engaged in teaching until ill health forced him to relinquish it in 1951. Thereafter he devoted himself to research in the geography of Ereẓ Israel and published articles on topical subjects and literary criticism.

His first major work on the geography of Ereẓ Israel, *Ha-Negev*, was published in 1935. A physical geographical study of the area from Beersheba to the Suez Canal and the Red Sea, which according to Bar-Daroma was mistakenly called Sinai, this book won him the Bialik Prize from the City of Tel Aviv in 1936. In the same year his book *Jerusalem*, on the topography of the Old City, was published. His most important work, *Ve-Zeh Gevul ha-Areẓ* (1958), was awarded the Rabbi Ouziel Prize of the City of Jerusalem in 1959 and the Ramat Gan literary prize.

BARDEJOV (Hg. **Bartfa**; Ger. **Bartfeldt**), town in Slovakia, on the eastern Polish border. The first Jews probably appeared in Bardejov in the 13th century, after the Tartar invasion, when the Hungarian king Bela IV invited foreigners to settle in the devastated country. The Jews engaged in trade and established inns along the Tokay (Hungary)–Brody (Poland) highway. Jews again appeared in the town in the 18th century, and with them Ḥasidism and the *Halberstam (Sanz) dynasty. Several Halberstams served as local rabbis. In 1808 the Hevra Kaddisha (burial society) was founded and in 1830 the Great Synagogue was built. In all, there were five synagogues in Bardejov. Jews continued to engage in the export of wine to Poland as a principal occupation and Jewish enterprise helped develop Bardejov as a fashionable health resort in the early 19th century. Two printing shops published Hebrew books. Jews from Bardejov participated in the First Zionist Congress on 1897 and the *Mizrachi Zionist religious movement became a strong force in the town.

The Jewish population numbered approximately 300 in Bardejov and its surroundings in 1848, 181 in the town itself in 1851, 480 in 1862, 1,710 in 1900 (of whom, in 1901, 220 owned businesses, 24 kept taverns, and 89 worked as artisans), and 2,264 in 1930. Most of the local Jews were deported by the Germans to the Lublin area of Poland on May 15–17, 1942.

After the war Bardejov became a rehabilitation center for Jewish survivors from the concentration camps and a transit center for "illegal" immigration to Palestine. (See *Beriḥah). In 1947, 384 Jews lived in the town, including 79 children. Antisemitism was still rife and Jews were attacked in June 1947 without being protected by the police. In 1965 only one Jewish family remained. Ritual objects from Bardejov are preserved in the Divrei Ḥayyim synagogue in Jerusalem, named in honor of R. Ḥayyim *Halberstam, the founder of the Sanz ḥasidic dynasty.

The New York filmmaker Jack Gurfein, a native of Bardejov, produced a film on the Holocaust in his town called *The Journey Back*. In 2003 a volunteer group of architects from Israel restored a part of the former Jewish quarter of Bardejov, including the Great Synagogue.

BIBLIOGRAPHY: *Magyar Zsidó Lexikon* (1929), 92; M. Atlas, in: *Zeitschrift fuer Geschichte der Juden* (1966), 151–70; L. Rotkirchen, *Ḥurban Yahadut Slovakyah* (1961); P. Meyer et al., *Jews in the Soviet Satellites* (1953), 637; M. Lànyi and H. Propper. *A szlovenszkói zsidó hitközségek története* (1933), 142. **ADD. BIBLIOGRAPHY:** E. Bárkány and L. Dojč, *Židovské náboženské obce na Slovensku* (1991), 353–57; M. Atlas, "Die Juedische Geschichte der Stadt Bartfeld (Barfa) und des Bades Bardejov in der Tschechoslowakei," in: *Zeitschrift fuer die Geschichte der Juden*, 3 (1966), 151–71.

[Yeshayahu Jellinek (2nd ed.)]

BARDIN, SHLOMO (1898–1976), educator. Bardin was born Shlomo Bardinstein in Zhitomir, Ukraine, and emigrated to Palestine in 1918. After working as an administrative assistant at the Hebrew Secondary School in Haifa, he left to study at the University of Berlin in 1923 and University College in London in 1925. Returning to Haifa in 1926, Bardin taught at the Hebrew Boarding School before setting off for New York City and earning his M.A. at Columbia University's Teachers College in 1930 and his Ph.D. in 1932. In 1933, he returned to Haifa to establish the Haifa Technical Institute, to which he added the Haifa Nautical School in 1938. In 1939, he went back to the United States, where he remained when World War II broke out. He was naturalized as an American citizen in 1943. He was appointed concurrent director of the Youth Department of Hadassah and the newly established American Zionist Youth Commission (1939), under whose auspices he founded a summer leadership-training program for young adults in 1941. Located in Amherst, New Hampshire, the summer institute was an innovative leadership program styled on the kibbutz model; in addition to daily classes and study sessions, he instituted gardening and physical labor. Shabbat was the centerpiece of the week, celebrated in song, drama, pageantry, and egalitarian services. In 1943, Bardin moved the program to the Poconos, naming it the Brandeis Camp Institute in honor of the recently deceased Supreme Court justice, whose philosophy of American patriotism combined with the commitment to Judaism and Zionism Bardin espoused. Bardin recast his own definition of Zionism from physical relocation to a Jewish homeland to a return to "the spiritual center of one's mind." Bardin expanded his summer operations to comprise a western camp in the Simi Valley near Los Angeles (1947) and a southern camp in North Carolina (1949). He soon took the camps out of the Zionist fold and established a separate camp organization that attracted young people from the entire spectrum of Reform, Conservative, and Orthodox Judaism and gave them, as Bardin promised, "an experience that will last a lifetime." In 1951, he moved to Los Angeles and began transforming the west coast camp into an experiential educational center that comprised a summer camp program for youth and weekend institutes for young adults, couples, and families during the rest of the year. Enriched by the contribution of Hollywood writers and producers, the programming at the Brandeis Camp Institute in southern California became a model for Jewish educators everywhere. In 1974, Boston Hebrew College honored him with its Philip W. Lown distinguished service award. Bardin wrote two books, *Pioneer Youth in Palestine* (1932) and *Jews and the Sea* (1943). In 1977, the name of the institute in southern California was officially changed to the Brandeis-Bardin Institute, honoring its founder. It is now the largest Jewish institutional landholding outside of the State of Israel and features year round educational activities for Jews of all ages and all levels of learning and observance.

WEBSITE: www.americansforjews.org.

[Bezalel Gordon (2nd ed.)]

BAREKHI NAFSHI (Heb. בָּרְכִי נַפְשִׁי; "Bless the Lord, O my soul"), initial words of Psalm 104. The central theme of this psalm is the glorification of God as the Creator of the universe, the majesty and beauty of which testify to the wisdom of the Master of all creatures. This psalm is regarded as one of the loftiest and most beautiful examples of ancient Hebrew poetry and a magnificent expression of monotheism. According to traditional Ashkenazi custom, this psalm is recited in private, on the afternoons of the Sabbaths between Sukkot and Passover, together with the 15 "Psalms of Ascent" (120–134). The reason for this custom may well be the analogy of this psalm with the account of creation given in Genesis and read on the Sabbath following the Sukkot festival (*Shabbat Bereshit*). After Passover the recitation of *Pirkei *Avot* replaces that of the Psalms. The praise of the Creator and the creation is also the reason why Psalm 104 is recited on New Moons after the morning service (and in the Sephardi rite also before the evening service).

BIBLIOGRAPHY: Baer S., Seder, 266 ff.; Eisenstein, Dinim, 56.

BAREKHU (Heb. בָּרְכוּ), opening word of the call to worship by the *sheli'aḥ ẓibbur* at the formal beginning of the daily morning and evening services. The full invocation is *Barekhu et Adonai ha-mevorakh* ("Bless ye the Lord who is [to be] blessed"). The congregation responds *Barukh Adonai ha-mevorakh le-olam va-ed* ("Blessed be the Lord who is [to be] blessed for ever and ever"). "Bless," in this context, is the equivalent of "praise." *Barekhu* is also recited by the person who is called up to the Torah reading and is followed by the same congregational response. In the morning and evening services *Barekhu* also serves to introduce the reading of the *Shema*; this accounts for the absence of *Barekhu* before the **Minḥah* service which lacks the *Shema*. *Barekhu* is considered to be one of the *devarim she-bi-kedushah* (lit. "holy things") and may only be recited in the presence of a quorum of at least ten grown male Jews (*minyan*; Sof. 10: 7; Sh. Ar. OḤ 55:1). The invocation *Barekhu* possibly originated in the time of Ezra, as might have the practice of standing at *Barekhu*; compare with Nehemiah (9:5) "Then the Levites… said, 'Stand up [cf. the practice of standing at *Barekhu*] and bless the Lord your God from everlasting to everlasting and let them say: Blessed be Thy glorious Name, that is exalted above all blessing and praise.'" A shorter formula, *Barekhu et Adonai*, occurs in Psalms 134:1–2 and 135:19. In the opinion of R. Akiva, the liturgical invocation, in accordance with scriptural precedent, should consist simply of *Barekhu et Adonai*, whereas the formula *Barekhu et Adonai ha-mevorakh* was advocated by his contemporary, R. Ishmael (Ber. 7:3). The latter formula was preferred by most of the *amoraim* (Bet. 50a; TJ, Ber. 7:4, 11c), and became standard. There is evidence that in the early period *Barukh Adonai ha-mevorakh…* was the response to *Barekhu* only in the Torah reading, while different responses were used for *Barekhu* as the invocation to worship. These were *Barukh Shem kevod malkhuto le-olam va-ed* ("Blessed be His Name, whose glorious kingdom is for ever and ever"), the standard response when the Divine Name was mentioned in the Temple of Jerusalem; and *Yehe Shemeih rabba mevarakh le-alam u-le-almei almayya* ("Let His great Name be blessed for ever and to all eternity"; Sif. Deut. 306, ed. by M. Friedmann (1864), 132b). In the course of time, however, *Barukh Shem kevod…* became the response to the *Shema* only: *Yehe Shemeih rabba…* was reserved for the *Kaddish*; and *Barukh Adonai ha-mevorakh…* became the exclusive response to *Barekhu*. At one time *Barekhu* was also used as a summons to recite Grace after Meals, but in the amoraic period, it was felt that this second-person form of address removed the leader from group participation and the invitation was standardized to *Nevarekh* ("Let us bless"; Ber. 7:3 and 49b–50a; TJ, Ber. 7:2–3, 11b–c; Tosef. Ber. 5:18). This objection, however, did not apply to *Barekhu* in the synagogue. The Reader may employ the "you" form but only when inviting the congregation to join him in prayer. Even then, he repeats the congregational response, thus associating himself with the praise of God. The Sephardi rite, as well as some ḥasidic congregations, retained the paradoxical practice (Sof. 10:7) of reciting *Barekhu* at the conclusion of the daily morning and evening services when there is no Torah reading. The custom accommodates worshipers who arrive too late to hear *Barekhu* at the opening of the services.

BIBLIOGRAPHY: Liebreich, in: HUCA, 32 (1961), 227–37; M. Kadushin, *Worship and Ethics* (1964), 135–41; J. Heinemann, *Ha-Tefillah bi-Tekufat ha-Tanna'im ve-ha-Amora'im* (19662), English abstract, v–vi, and index, s.v.

[Herman Kieval]

BARENBOIM, DANIEL (1942–), Israeli pianist and conductor. Born in Buenos Aires to parents of Jewish Russian descent, Barenboim started piano lessons at the age of five with his mother, and then with his father, who remained his only other teacher. He gave his first public recital at the age of seven. Further education included Markevich's conducting classes in Salzburg (1954), and studies in Paris and Rome. Barenboim settled in Israel in 1952. Following his British and American debuts (1955, 1957), he toured widely and soon became known as one of the most versatile pianists of his generation. He first conducted in Israel (1962), and from 1965 was active as conductor and soloist with the English Chamber Orchestra. In 1967 Barenboim married the cellist Jacqueline *du Pré in Jerusalem. They performed and recorded together in the coming years until her career was tragically cut short by multiple sclerosis.

Following his debut as conductor with the New Philharmonia Orchestra (London, 1967), Barenboim was in demand by all the leading European and American symphony orchestras. He conducted opera for the first time at the Edinburgh Festival in 1973, and from 1981 was a regular visitor at the Wagner Bayreuth Festival. He was music director of the Orchestre National de Paris (1975–1989), the Chicago SO (1991), and the Deutsche Staatsoper Berlin (1992).

In 2000 the Staatskapelle Berlin appointed him chief conductor for life. He works on a regular basis with the Berlin and the Vienna Philharmonics. Barenboim has always been active as a chamber musician, performing with, among others, *Perlman, *Zukerman, and singer Fischer-Dieskau. His numerous recordings include the complete Beethoven sonatas and piano concertos and the Mozart concerti. As a conductor, he has been most successful with scores from the Romantic era. He also championed contemporary works, and in recent years moved into popular and crossover repertory, such as Argentine tango. He provoked an outcry in Israel by defying the country's ban on Wagner, playing the Prelude from *Tristan und Isolde* with the Berlin Staatskapelle as an encore in concert at the Israel Festival (2001). He has been a prominent advocate of peace in the Middle East. In the early 1990s, he met the Palestinian-born writer and Columbia University professor Edward Said, who shared his vision of peaceful coexistence in the area. This led to Barenboim's first concert on the West Bank, a piano recital at Bir Zeit University. Barenboim and Said established a foundation that promotes music and co-operation through projects targeted at young Arabs and Israelis. They jointly received Spain's Prince of Asturias Concord Prize (2002). Among Barenboim's other honors are the Tolerance Prize (2002) and in 2004 the Buber-Rosenzweig Medal, the Wolf Prize for the Arts, and the Haviva Reik Peace Award. A new version of Barenboim's autobiography, *A Life in Music*, was published in 2002, as was his book with Said, *Parallels and Paradoxes: Explorations in Music and Society*.

BIBLIOGRAPHY: Grove online; MGG²; Baker's Biographical Dictionary (1997); A. Blyth, "Daniel Barenboim," in: *Opera* 45 (Aug. 1994), 905–10; H. Kupferberg, "Daniel Barenboim: A 50-Year Career Just Keeps on Growing," in: *American Record Guide,* 63 (Nov.–Dec. 2000), 6–8.

[Naama Ramot (2nd ed.)]

BARGAS, ABRAHAM DE (c. 1740), Spanish Marrano author and physician. After escaping from Spain, Bargas settled first in France, where he was personal physician to the duke of Gramont, and later in Italy, where he became physician to the Leghorn Jewish community. There he composed a volume of ethical discourses on the Bible, *Pensamientos sagrados y educaciones morales…* (Florence, 1749). He also wrote an account of the earthquake of 1742, *Fiel relación de los terremotos…* (Leghorn, 1742), and translated into Spanish the order of service for the fast-day instituted to commemorate that event: *Traducción de la oración del ayuno y de los temblores de tierra…* (Pisa, 1746). He wrote some occasional poems, among them *El Casto Niceto* (Leghorn, n.d.).

BIBLIOGRAPHY: Kayserling, Bibl, 15–16; A.S. Toaff, *Cenni storici sulla communità ebraica e sulla sinagoga di Livorno.* (1955).

[Cecil Roth]

BAR GIORA, SIMEON, Jewish military leader in the war against Rome (66–70 C.E.). Simeon was born, according to Josephus, in *Gerasa, a large Hellenistic city in Transjordan, where the Jews lived in peace with the city's non-Jewish population. Some scholars, however, identify his birthplace with the village of Jerash in the neighborhood of Hartuv (Press, Ereẓ, 1 (1951²), 174, s.v. *Geresh*), others with Kefar Jorish near Shechem on the grounds that Simeon's activity began in its vicinity, i.e., in the province of Acrabatene. Since the word *giora* means proselyte in Aramaic, many scholars hold that his father was a convert to Judaism. The main source of information about Simeon is Josephus who is to be treated with circumspection, especially where an appraisal of the man and his activities are concerned, since Josephus entertained feelings of intense animosity toward him.

Simeon, already apparently known as a partisan leader, first distinguished himself in the battle at Beth-Horon against *Cestius Gallus (66 C.E.), in which the Jews inflicted a crushing defeat on the Roman army. Despite this achievement, however, Simeon was relegated to the background, since in Jerusalem the moderate party in control was disposed to come to terms with Rome. Simeon gathered around him a band of ardent patriots and, according to Josephus, engaged in brigandage. It is obvious, however, even from Josephus' own biased account, that these acts of "brigandage" were military operations conducted by the rebels under the leadership of Simeon against their internal enemies, opponents of the revolt, and sympathizers with Rome. In retaliation for these operations, the forces of the moderate government in Jerusalem compelled Simeon to take refuge among the *Sicarii who, under the command of *Eleazar b. Jair, had captured *Masada. For a time Simeon remained with them, taking part in their raids. Subsequently leaving them, he parted company, and "terrorized" the southern part of Ereẓ Israel. Although growing increasingly stronger, he was unable to capture Jerusalem. The Zealots in Jerusalem, who were fearful of him, seized his wife but released her because of his threats. In addition to his continuous war against the party in control in Jerusalem, Simeon also fought against the Idumeans and succeeded in occupying Idumea with the help of supporters among the Idumeans themselves. Hebron, too, fell into his hands. In April 69 C.E. he entered Jerusalem, the gates of the city having been opened to him by the enemies of *John of Giscala, who had called on

Simeon to come to their aid. Simeon thus gained control of the larger part of Jerusalem, both of the Upper and a considerable section of the Lower City.

The struggle between Simeon and John of Giscala continued. Constant hostilities were waged between them in the city, and came to an end only when Titus' forces reached the outskirts of Jerusalem (April 70 C.E.). Although all the rebels joined together during the siege to fight against the Romans and performed deeds of astounding bravery, the advantage enjoyed by the Roman army proved decisive. The Temple was burned and the devastated city captured by the enemy. Simeon and several of his most loyal friends hid in an underground passage among the ruins, but, unable to escape, Simeon finally surrendered to the Romans and was taken prisoner. The circumstances of his surrender were extremely strange. Josephus relates that Simeon suddenly appeared among the Temple ruins, as though out of the bowels of the earth, dressed in white and covered with a purple mantle. At the sight of him the Romans were terrified, but after recovering from their fear, bound him in chains. His strange appearance was probably connected with messianic expectations on his part; or by submitting to the victorious enemy he may have deliberately invited martyrdom.

Simeon was led as a prisoner in the triumphal procession held in Rome by Vespasian and his sons to celebrate their victory over the Jews. Scourged all the way, he was taken to the Mamertine prison, at the northeast end of the Forum, and executed at the moment of the culmination of the triumph. That he and not John of Giscala played this part in the triumphal procession shows that the Romans regarded him as the most important leader in Jerusalem and as the rebel commander. This is evident from other extant information as well. His army was far larger than that of his rivals, having numbered about 15,000 at the beginning of the siege of Jerusalem. His soldiers were also the best organized and disciplined. The fact that he was invited to Jerusalem by the priests and the people may have provided him with some legal basis for his leadership, although not all the patriot elements recognized his authority. Since information about them is very sparse, it is difficult to comprehend and explain the basis of the conflict between their different parties. At times it is even difficult to distinguish between the parties themselves. Nevertheless, from extant information it would appear that Simeon b. Giora was the leader of a clear eschatological trend in the movement of rebellion against Rome, and possibly filled the role of "king messiah" within the complex of eschatological beliefs held by his followers. His exceptional bravery and daring, mentioned by Josephus, undoubtedly attracted many to him, and won him preeminence among the rebel leaders. In contrast to the bitter hostility that existed between him and John of Giscala, there was a measure of understanding between him and the Sicarii at Masada.

Conspicuous among Simeon's characteristics was the enmity he bore toward the rich and the sympathy he showed to the poor, even to the extent of freeing slaves. This approach of his doubtless had its origin in his party's social outlook, opposed as it was to the existing order also in regard to the economic system and social justice.

BIBLIOGRAPHY: J. Klausner, *Ke-she-Ummah Nilḥemet al Ḥerutah* (1955⁹), 151–86; M. Hengel, *Die Zeloten* (1961), 303–4, 381–2; M. Stern, in: *Ha-Ishiyyut ve-Dorah* (1963), 70–78; O. Michel, in: *New Testament Studies*, 14 (1967/68), 402–8 (Ger.); C. Roth, in: *Commentary*, 29 (1960), 52–58.

[Uriel Rappaport]

°**BAR HEBRAEUS** (or **Bar ʿEbhraya** or **Ibn al-ʿIbri**), **JOHANAN** (later: **Gregorius** or **Abu al Faraj**; 1226–1286), the last of the important writers in Syriac. He was the son of an apostate Jewish physician, Aaron (hence the appellation Son of the Hebrew), and knew Hebrew. Born in Malaṭīya (in Asia Minor) he went with his father to Antioch, where he became a monk. He also pursued secular studies, at first under his father's tutelage and later with a Nestorian scholar in Tripoli (Syria). In 1246 he was ordained Jacobite (Monophysite) bishop of Gubos (near Mulafryn) and assumed the name Gregorius. In 1252 he was appointed Maphriyan (archbishop) of Mesopotamia and Persia. Bar Hebraeus traveled widely, supervising the congregations of his church. He died at Maghāra in Azerbaijan.

Bar Hebraeus was a prolific writer. His commentary *Oẓar Razei* ("Treasury of Secret Wisdom") on the Old and New Testaments, reveals the influence of traditional Jewish exegesis. In addition to theological works such as *Ḥokhmat Ḥokhmeta*, which contains a systematic exposition of Aristotle's teaching, he also wrote on Syriac grammar and composed a Syriac *Chronicle*, a history of the world from creation to his own time, in two parts: ecclesiastical history and secular history. It was translated into English by E.A.W. Budge in 1932, and became widely known. Bar Hebraeus also wrote many poems and compiled a collection of entertaining stories (English translation, *Oriental Wit and Wisdom, or the Laughable Stories*, 1889). In addition, he translated Arabic works into Syriac (including the philosophical work of *Avicenna, *Kitāb al-Ishārāt*), and also wrote works in Arabic, including an abridgment of the secular portion of his *Chronicle* with some revisions and addenda, and an epitome of the large work of al-Ghāfikī on medications (part published in the original with an English translation, with a commentary by M. Meyerhof and G.P. Sohby, 1932).

BIBLIOGRAPHY: A. Baumstark, *Geschichte der syrischen Literatur* (1922), 312–20; G. Graf, *Geschichte der christlichen arabischen Literatur*, 2 (1947), 272–81; Brockelmann, Arab Lit, 1 (1898), 349–50, 591; W. Wright, *Short History of Syriac Literature* (1894), 265–81.

[Eliyahu Ashtor]

BAR HEDYA (fl. first half of the fourth century), Babylonian scholar. Bar Hedya was one of the *neḥutei, amoraim* who moved between Babylonia and Ereẓ Israel, transmitting the rabbinical traditions of both countries. He testified, among other things, that in Ereẓ Israel care was taken to ensure that Hoshana Rabba (the 7th day of Tabernacles) did not fall on a

Sabbath (Suk. 43b). Known for his interpretations of dreams, *Abbaye and *Rava turned to him in this connection. Abbaye, who paid him, received favorable dream interpretations; Rava, who did not pay him, received unfavorable interpretations. Upon the materialization of Bar Hedya's predictions, Rava also began to pay him, whereupon his dreams were then favorably interpreted. It finally became clear to Rava that the secret of Bar Hedya's ability lay in the fact that "all dreams follow the mouth" (of the interpreter) (Ber. 56a).

BIBLIOGRAPHY: Hyman, Toledot, 285; Levy, Neuhebr Tal, 1 (1924^2), 258, no.2.

[Yitzhak Dov Gilat]

BAR-HILLEL, YEHOSHUA (1915–1975), philosopher and theoretical linguist. Bar-Hillel was born in Vienna, educated in Germany, and after 1933, at the Hebrew University. He served in World War II, and lost an eye fighting in the Israeli War of Independence. At the end of the war, he returned to the Hebrew University. He became a professor in 1961, a member of the Israel Academy of Arts and Sciences in 1963, and president of the International Union of History and Philosophy of Science in 1967. Bar-Hillel's early writings were concerned with the philosophy of mathematics, and culminated in the publication of his book with A.H. *Fraenkel, *Foundations of Set Theory* (1958). This sets out the major foundational approaches to mathematics and emphasizes their connection with broader philosophical issues. As distinct from Fraenkel's Platonism, Bar-Hillel's contributions stress that mathematical entities have only a pseudo-existence. Bar-Hillel's writings deal with the philosophy of language, philosophy of science, inductive logic, machine translation, mechanization of information retrieval, algebraic linguistics, and the semantics of natural languages. Some of these latter topics form the subject of his *Language and Information* (1964), which is concerned with the development of a science of language.

[Avrum Stroll]

BARI, Adriatic port in southern Italy. Bari was one of the flourishing Jewish centers of *Apulia which according to tradition were founded by captives brought to Italy by *Titus. However, no inscriptions have survived to show that the community may be traced back to the Roman period, as is the case in neighboring towns. The community in Bari evidently rose to importance somewhat later. An epitaph dating from the ninth century preserves the memory of Eliah ben Moses "strategos" and a stele (of uncertain date) commemorates Moses ben Eliah, devoted teacher of the law and poet, compared to the biblical Moses. In the ninth century the miracle-worker *Aaron of Baghdad visited Bari. The names of scholars who taught at the local rabbinical academy in the tenth and eleventh centuries are recorded, including Moses Calfo, who is mentioned in the *Arukh* of *Nathan b. Jehiel. Legend talks of "four rabbis," who sailed from Bari in 972, were captured at sea by Saracen raiders, and sold into slavery in Spain and North Africa; after being ransomed, they founded famous talmudic academies (see *Moses b. Hanokh). The legend at least indicates that Bari was known as a center of talmudic learning. This is confirmed by the adage cited by Rabbenu *Tam in the 12th century: "From Bari shall go forth the Law and the word of the Lord from Otranto" (a paraphrase of Isa. 2:3). The theological teaching of the Bari schools evidently attained a wide influence: Andrea, archbishop of Bari (d. 1078), actually became converted to Judaism (see *Obadiah the Proselyte).

The Jews of Bari underwent a number of vicissitudes. They were included in the edicts of forced conversion issued by the Byzantine emperors in the ninth and tenth centuries (see **anusim*). In about 932, the Jewish quarter was destroyed by mob violence and several Jews were killed. Between 1068 and 1465 the Jews in Bari suffered from the rival claims of the king and the archbishop on taxes levied on the Jews in the city. The Jews in Bari were also victims of the campaign to convert Jews to Christianity initiated by Charles of Anjou in 1290; in 1294, 72 families were forced to adopt Christianity, but continued to live in Bari as *neofiti* (see *Crypto Jews). There followed a century and a half of tranquility until the Jewish quarter was again attacked in 1463. A notable figure in this period is the physician David Kalonymus of Bari. In 1479 David Kalonymus and his family were offered Neapolitan citizenship along with exemption from commercial taxes, and in 1498 he requested the Sforza Duke of Bari to confer on him the same special rights in Bari as he already possessed in Naples. In 1495, during the unrest that accompanied the French invasion, Jewish property worth 10,000 ducats was pillaged. The expulsion of the Jews from the kingdom of Naples in 1510–11 sealed the fate of those in Bari: a small number were readmitted in 1520 and finally forced to leave in 1540–41. The Via della Sinagoga in Bari remains to attest the existence of the former community, and several early medieval tombstones are in the Museo Provinciale. Jewish communal life was briefly resumed during World War II, when in 1943 many Jews from other parts of Italy and from Yugoslavia took refuge in Bari from Nazi-occupied territories. Toward the end of the war a refugee camp was established at Bari. The beginning of the "illegal" immigration to Palestine movement in Italy was situated in the area around Bari. During this period Jewish soldiers, mainly from Palestine, were active in aiding and organizing the refugees.

BIBLIOGRAPHY: N. Ferorelli, *Gli Ebrei nell' Italia meridionale* (1915); E. Munkácsi, *Der Jude von Neapel* (1939); U. Cassuto, in: *Festschrift... Hermann Cohen* (1912), 389–404 (lt.); G. Summo, *Gli Ebrei in Puglia dall' XI al XVI secolo* (1939); Milano, Italia, index; Roth, Dark Ages, index; Roth, Italy, index. **ADD. BIBLIOGRAPHY:** V. Bonazzoli, "Gli ebrei del regno di Napoli all'epoca della loro espulsione. Il periodo aragonese (1456–1499)," in: *Archivio Storico Italiano,* 137 (1979), 495–539; C. Colafemmina, "Hebrew Inscriptions of the Early Medieval Period in Southern Italy," in: B.D. Cooperman and B. Garvin (eds.), *The Jews of Italy. Memory and Identity* (2000), 65–81; D. Abulafia, "The Aragonese Kings of Naples and the Jews," *ibid.*, 82–106.

[Attilio Milano / Nadia Zeldes (2nd ed.)]

BAR-ILAN, DAVID (1930–2003), Israeli journalist and pianist. Bar-Ilan was born in Haifa. A gifted pianist, he won a scholarship to Juilliard School of Fine Arts in New York at the age of 17. As a soloist he appeared with major orchestras and recorded six albums, including the works of Chopin, Beethoven, Mussorgsky, Tchaikovsky, and Brahms. In 1961 he was the first Israeli to perform in Germany. He began his writing career in the 1960s, becoming a staunch defender of Israel's case in articles he published in the American media. He also helped found Americans for a Safe Israel. Bar-Ilan was identified with Zionist Revisionist ideology and the Land of Israel Movement. He returned to Israel in 1990, where he joined *The Jerusalem Post*, first as editorial page editor and in 1992 as executive editor. Editorial policy under Bar-Ilan was characterized by right-wing positions on Arab-Israeli matters and support for the *Likud party. He wrote a weekly column, "Eye on the Media," castigating foreign media reporting on Israel. Yet, as editor he zealously kept the paper's op-ed pages open to a broad spectrum of political views. In 1996, after Netanyahu won the elections in Israel, Bar-Ilan joined Netanyahu's staff as his chief of information and policy planning. After Netanyahu's failure in the 1999 elections, he returned to *The Jerusalem Post*.

[Yoel Cohen (2nd ed.)]

BAR-ILAN (Berlin), MEIR (1880–1949), leader of religious Zionism. Bar-Ilan was born in Volozhin, Russia, the son of R. Naphtali Ẓevi Judah *Berlin. He completed his studies in yeshivot at Volozhin, Telz, Brisk (Brest-Litovsk), and Novogrudok. As a young man he joined the *Mizrachi movement, representing it at the Seventh Zionist Congress (1905), at which, unlike the majority of Mizrachi delegates, he voted against the *Uganda Scheme. In 1911 he was appointed secretary of the world Mizrachi movement, working in Berlin, and he coined the Mizrachi slogan *"Ereẓ Yisrael le-Am Yisrael al Pi Torat Yisrael"* ("The land of Israel for the people of Israel according to the Torah of Israel"). He moved to the United States in 1915, served as president of the U.S. Mizrachi, and from 1925 was a member of the Board of Directors of the *Jewish National Fund. In 1926 Bar-Ilan settled in Jerusalem where he served as president of the World Mizrachi center and as the Mizrachi representative in Zionist and *yishuv* institutions, including clandestine committees for defense. Between 1929 and 1931 he was a member of the Zionist Executive. A leading opponent of the Palestine partition plan in 1937, and of the British White Paper of 1939, he advocated civil disobedience and complete noncooperation of the Jewish population toward the British government. After the establishment of the State of Israel, he organized a committee of scholars to examine the legal problems of the new state in the light of Jewish law, and was an initiator of the National Religious Front, the group of religious parties that presented a united platform in the first Knesset elections. A central figure in the Zionist religious movement, Bar-Ilan founded and edited a religious Zionist weekly, *Ha-Ivri* ("The Hebrew"), which was published in Berlin from 1910 to 1914 and in New York from 1916 to 1921. Between 1938 and 1949 he was editor in chief of the Mizrachi daily, *Ha-Ẓofeh*, in Tel Aviv. Some of his articles were collected in his books *Bi-Shevilei ha-Teḥiyyah* ("In the Paths of Renaissance," 1940) and *Kitvei Rabbi Meir Bar-Ilan* (1950). His memoirs, *Mi-Volozhin ad Yerushalayim* ("From Volozhin to Jerusalem," 1939–40), were originally published in Yiddish. He also wrote a book about his father, entitled *Rabban shel Yisrael* ("Rabbi of Israel," 1943). He initiated and organized the publishing of the *Talmudic Encyclopaedia*, begun in 1947. He also founded the institute for the publication of a new complete edition of the Talmud. Bar-Ilan University near Tel Aviv, founded by the American Mizrachi movement, is named in his honor, as is the Meir Forest in the Hebron hills, and the moshav Bet Meir near Jerusalem.

BIBLIOGRAPHY: I. Avigur, *Ilan ve-Nofo* (1952); M. Krone, *Ha-Rav Meir Bar-Ilan* (1954); EZD, 1 (1958), 334–47; A. Hertzberg, *The Zionist Idea* (1960), 546–54.

[Zvi Kaplan]

BAR-ILAN UNIVERSITY, a religiously oriented university, founded in 1955. In the mid-1990s Bar-Ilan was the third largest university in Israel. The university's aim is to advance knowledge in both Jewish studies and general science in accordance with the ideology of *Torah im Derekh Ereẓ* ("Torah with general knowledge") and to serve as a bridge between religious and secular in Israel.

In the late 1940s a plan evolved to establish a religious university in Ereẓ Israel, supported by the *Mizrachi movement in the United States. The idea received further impetus under the leadership of Prof. Pinkhos *Churgin of Yeshiva University in New York, and the university was inaugurated in 1955. Classes opened with 80 students and 19 lecturers. At the opening ceremonies, Prof. Churgin said that Bar-Ilan would "demonstrate that Judaism is not a cloistered way of life, removed from scientific investigation and worldly knowledge." Named for Meir *Bar-Ilan (Berlin), Bar-Ilan received little encouragement in Israel at the outset. The government doubted the need for another university in addition to the Hebrew University in Jerusalem. *Agudat Israel and similar Orthodox groups were fearful of imperiling certain types of religious education, particularly the yeshivot. However, it gradually became clear that Bar-Ilan served an important function in combining modernity with tradition, and in expanding the country's scientific and Jewish studies' capabilities. Prof. Churgin served as first president of the University. In 2005 Moshe Kaveh was president. In 1957 Prof. Joseph Lookstein was appointed chancellor, holding the position until 1976. Under Lookstein's leadership the university grew rapidly and received a charter from the State of New York (the only institution of higher learning in Israel to do so).

The Bar-Ilan campus is located east of the city of Ramat-Gan and administers another five regional colleges throughout the country. The campus includes 63 buildings, 165 classrooms, 130 laboratories, and 25 libraries. It employs 1,650 academic staff, teaching in six faculties and 38 academic departments: exact sciences, natural sciences, social sciences, humanities, Jewish studies, and law. The campus also includes schools of education, social work, engineering, and business administration. In 2005 Bar-Ilan had 31,200 students and 59,000 alumni. Its annual budget was $130 million.

Bar-Ilan is the only Israeli university where all students benefit from a compulsory enrichment program in Jewish heritage (Bible, Jewish literature and history, ethics, culture, etc.), in addition to the full university curriculum. The university offers over 500 elective courses in Basic Jewish Studies. Degrees offered by Bar-Ilan's academic departments include: B.A., B.Sc., LL.B., M.A., M.Sc., M.S.W., LL.M., M.B.A., and Ph.D.; diplomas in communications, local government, music therapy, teaching, translation and interpreting. It has also taken a leading role in applied scientific research in the biomedical and pharmaceutical fields, and houses several national scientific centers, such as the Israel National Center for Magnetic Measurements. The university also houses high-level research centers in the fields of physics, medical chemistry, mathematics, brain research, economics, strategic studies, psychology, music, archaeology, and Jewish philosophy and law. Unique to Bar-Ilan are the Institute for Advanced Torah Studies and the counterpart Midrasha for Women, through which over 1,300 students combine intensive yeshivah-style studies with a full academic curriculum.

Bar-Ilan maintains academic cooperation agreements with 54 leading universities around the world. There are 64 endowed chairs and 66 research centers operating at the university, including several leading research institutes in physics, medical chemistry, mathematics, brain research, economics, strategic studies, developmental psychology, musicology, Bible, Talmud, Jewish education, Jewish law and philosophy. A special project of the university is the publication of responsa texts, historical and present, with special computer applications developed for this purpose. Bar-Ilan University Press published to the mid-1990s some 350 publications in addition to 20 periodicals and professional journals. The university owns the Bar-Ilan Research & Development Company aimed at marketing research results to private companies. The university sponsors many social and community outreach projects, including a prisoner rehabilitation effort, a big-brother program, legal aid, study programs for senior citizens, educational counseling, and a network of social counselors in development towns.

BIBLIOGRAPHY: Ben-Yosef, in: *Sefer ha-Shanah shel Bar-Ilan*, 4–5 (1967), 12–29. **WEBSITE:** www.biu.ac.il.

[David M. Weinberg / Shaked Gilboa (2nd ed.)]

BARISHANSKY, RAPHAEL (1864–1950), rabbi. Barishansky was born in Lipnishtok, Lithuania, and studied at the outstanding yeshivot of Eishishok and Mir as well as the kolel in Kovno and with the Gaon Rabbi Ḥayyim Lev. In Bialystok he studied with Rabbi Samuel *Mohilewer. Mohilwer influenced him to become a religious Zionist and Barishansky joined Hovovei Zion (see *Ḥibbat Zion).

For 30 years, beginning in 1893, Barishansky was the pulpit rabbi in a large congregation in the town of Gomel in Belorussia, even attracting non-observant Jews to Judaism. He worked to help Jewish soldiers in the Russian Army by sending them kosher food and ritual items for Jewish holidays.

Barishansky was a committed religious Zionist who sought to bring others to the cause; he attended several World Zionist Congresses. Barishansky's Zionism also brought him into conflict with the fairly large community of Lubavitcher Ḥasidim in Gomel. When *Mizrachi opened a chapter in Gomel, and there was community opposition, Barishansky vigorously defended the ideology of religious Zionism.

In the early 1920s, Barishansky publicly criticized Jewish communists for closing Jewish schools and discrediting Zionism. As a result, he was sentenced to two years in prison, but was released after six months, thanks to the intervention of several Zionists. By February 1924, he had fled Russia and arrived in New York. Because of his experiences in the "old country," when the American Jewish community wanted to ameliorate the conditions of the Jews in Soviet territories, he opposed attempts to keep them there, because even the Jewish communists were anti-religious and were suppressing Judaism, especially around the Jewish holy days.

Once in New York, Barishansky accepted a teaching position at the Talmud Torah Torat Moshe in the Bronx. He became an active member in the American Mizrachi movement and a member of the Agudat Harabbonim, but left when he disagreed with their policy of denying the certification of kosher meat in factories that also produced non-kosher meat. In 1926 he was a rabbi in Washington, D.C. When he retired in 1929, he returned to the Bronx. An autobiographical memoir of the trial in Russia in 1922 appeared in the *Morgen Journal* (Nov. 19, 1923) and was reprinted in M. Altshuler, "The Rabbi of Homel's Trial," in: *Michael*, 6 (1980), pp. 9–61.

BIBLIOGRAPHY: M. Sherman, *Orthodox Judaism in America: A Biographical Dictionary and Sourcebook*, (1996) 26–27; A. Rand (ed.), *Toledot Anshei Shem* (1950), 7; *Jewish Daily Bulletin* (Oct. 27, 1925)

[Jeanette Friedman (2nd ed.)]

BARIT, JACOB (1797–1883), Russian talmudist and communal leader. Born in Simno, Suvalki province, he left in 1822 for Vilna, where he kept a distillery. Attracted by the ideas of the *Haskalah, he studied foreign languages, mathematics, and astronomy. In 1850 he became principal of the yeshivah founded by R. Ḥayyim Naḥman Parnas, a position he held for 25 years. By the end of 1840 he was the acknowledged leader of the Vilna community. When Sir Moses *Montefiore visited Vilna in 1846 Barit advised him on his petition to Nicholas I. He was a member of the delegation sent to St. Petersburg in 1852 in connection with the oppressive new conscription law.

On several rabbinical committees summoned by the Ministry of the Interior, Barit was eloquent in advocating Jewish rights. In 1871 when the governor general of Vilna formed a committee to investigate the accusations made against the Jews by the apostate Jacob *Brafmann, Barit successfully convinced the committee of their falsehood.

BIBLIOGRAPHY: M.I. Barit, *Toledot Ya'akov* (1883); S.P. Rabbinovitz, *Kneset Israel*, 2 (1887), 157–62; H.N. Maggid-Steinschneider, *Ir Vilna* (1900), 62–67; Dinur, in: *He-Avar*, 15 (1968), 254–8.

BARKAI (Heb. בַּרְקַאי; "first morning light"), kibbutz in central Israel, at the western entrance of the Iron Valley, affiliated with Kibbutz Arẓi ha-Shomer ha-Ẓa'ir. It was founded on May 10, 1949, by pioneers from North America, joined later by newcomers from Romania and from English-speaking and other countries. In the mid-1990s the population was approximately 500, and by the end of 2002 it had decreased to 327. Farm branches included dairy cattle, poultry, avocado plantations, and field crops. The kibbutz runs a factory for polyethylene products.

WEBSITE: www.barkai.org.il.

[Efraim Orni / Shaked Gilboa (2nd ed.)]

BAR KAPPARA (beginning of third century C.E.), Palestinian scholar in the transition period between the *tannaim* and the *amoraim*. When quoted in *tannaitic* sources, he is called by his full name, "R. Eleazar ha-Kappar Beribbie." In his role as an *amora*, both when expressing his own opinion and when transmitting earlier tannaitic sources, he is referred to by the more informal title "Bar Kappara." The term "Beribbie," often used as a title of respect, may serve here as an abbreviation for "Beribbie Eleazar ha-Kappar," i.e., "the son of R. Eleazar ha-Kappar," as it seems that the father and the son were called by the same name. This fact has lead to some confusion as to which traditions, especially those mentioned in the later literary levels of the tannaitic works and in the talmudic *beraitot* are to be ascribed to the father and which to the son. Some scholars tend to ascribe almost all of the R. Eleazar ha-Kappar traditions to the father, and others to the son, while others have claimed that they are one and the same person. While there is clear evidence for the distinction between the father and the son – for example the use of the long form "R. Eleazar ben Eleazar ha-Kappar Berribie" (e.g., Tosef., Beẓah 1:7), to refer to the son – the notion that the two engaged in an halakhic dispute with each other (cf. Ḥul. 27b–28a) seems unfounded, as it fails to distinguish between Bar Kappara's role as a *tanna*, and his role in transmitting earlier tannaitic sources (cf. Sifra, Sheraẓim 10:1, Sifre Deut. 78).

Bar Kappara was a disciple of *Judah ha-Nasi and like his contemporaries, *Ḥiyya bar Abba and *Oshaya Rabbah, was the author of a compilation of *halakhot*. These were called "The Mishnah of Bar Kappara" or "The Great Mishnayot of Bar Kappara" (BB 154b; Eccles. R. 6:2). This collection, a supplement to the Mishnah of Judah ha-Nasi, was used to explain obscure passages in the standard Mishnah and brought to the knowledge of the *amoraim* various traditions and opinions that differed from the Mishnah of Judah ha-Nasi.

The academy of Bar Kappara was reported to be in the "south" (TJ, Nid. 3:2, 50c), perhaps in Caesarea or in nearby Parod (Av. Zar. 31a). It has also been suggested that it was in Lydda (Lieberman, p. 123). In 1969, however, a stone, which was apparently the lintel over the main entrance to a *bet midrash*, was found in the Golan area, inscribed with the words: "This is the *bet midrash* of Rabbi Eliezer ha-Kappar." It is unclear whether this inscription refers to the father or to the son. Some scholars have suggested that Bar Kappara was the final compiler of *Sifrei Zuta*, and, though a number of their proofs have been challenged, more research is still needed in order arrive at a definite conclusion in this matter. Among his associates were some of the outstanding scholars of the generation, such as *Oshaya and *Joshua b. Levi, who transmitted his *halakhah* and *aggadah* (Ker. 8a; Ber. 34a, et al.).

In addition to his role in the transmission of halakhic tradition, Bar Kappara's opinions on a number of important aggadic traditions have been preserved. For example, it is reported in his name: "Whosoever can calculate the movements of the solstices and planets, but fails to do so, to him is applied the verse [Isa. 5:12] 'But they regard not the work of the Lord; neither have they considered the operation of His hands'" (Shab. 75a). This tradition reflects the notion, common also among gentile sages of the time, that the celestial order reflects both divine wisdom and power, and so represents an early form of "natural theology." He apparently also looked favorably upon the use of Greek, even recommending it to his disciples: "Let the words of Torah be uttered in the language of Japheth [Greek] in the tents of Shem" (Gen. R. 36:8, in reference to Gen. 9:27). While permitting metaphysical speculation, he placed limitations on such speculations (Gen. R. 1:10; cf. Tos. Ḥag. 2:7. TJ, Ḥag. 2:1 77c), perhaps in response to the excesses of Gnostic teaching that were widespread at that time. Commenting on the verse, "For ask now of the days past, which were before thee, since the day that God created man upon the earth, and from one end of heaven unto the other" (Deut. 4:32), Bar Kappara stated: "You may speculate upon what came after creation and not upon what came before it. You may investigate from one end of heaven unto the other, but not what is beyond it." His opposition to asceticism is seen in the statement, "to what does Scripture refer when it says [of the Nazirite, Num. 6:11], 'Make atonement for him, for that he sinned by reason of the soul?' Against which soul did he sin? Against his own soul, in that he denied himself wine. And if one who denied himself only wine is termed a sinner, how much more so he who denies himself the enjoyment of all permitted things" (Ta'an. 11a, and parallel passages).

Bar Kappara showed great talent as a poet, and as an author of fables and epigrams. The Jerusalem Talmud (Ber. 1:8, 3d) quotes a beautiful prayer which he composed and which he used to recite during the repetition of the Thanksgiving blessing in the *Amidah*. It is related that during the marriage feast of Simeon, son of Judah I (or of his son, see Lev. R. 28:2),

Bar Kappara told 300 *fox fables, and so intently did the guests listen that they completely ignored the fact that their food was becoming cold. According to the Talmud, tensions existed between Bar Kappara and the house of Judah ha-Nasi: "On one occasion, Simeon, son of Judah, and Bar Kappara were studying together when a difficulty arose about a certain *halakhah*. Simeon said to Bar Kappara, 'Only my father, Rabbi Judah, can explain this.' Bar Kappara retorted, 'There is no rabbi in the world who understands it' [Rashi to MK 16a]. Simeon told his father, who was vexed, and when Bar Kappara next presented himself, Judah said to him, 'I have never known you'" (MK 16a), thus disowning him. On another occasion, Bar Kappara and Ben Elasah, the rich but ignorant son-in-law of Judah, were in the *nasi's* house at a gathering of scholars who were engaged in learned discourse. Bar Kappara proposed to Ben Elasah that he too take part in the discussion, and to this end composed for him a poetic riddle to present to his father-in-law as a genuine problem. The riddle was in fact a criticism of the conduct of Judah's household and of the fear which he inspired. The *nasi*, realizing from the smile upon Bar Kappara's face that he was the author of the riddle, exclaimed, "I do not recognize you as an elder" (i.e., "I do not wish to grant you recognition"), and Bar Kappara understood that he would not be ordained (TJ, MK 3:1, 81c). It is nevertheless told that Bar Kappara was the first to inform the sages, in moving words, of the *nasi's* death: "Mortals and angels have been wrestling for the holy ark; the angels have won and the ark has been taken captive."

BIBLIOGRAPHY: Y.M. Kahana, in: *Ha-Asif*, 3 (1886), 330–33; Graetz, Hist, 2 (1949), 455–6, 470; Bacher, Tann; Hyman, Toledot, 288–92; Alon, Toledot, 2 (1961), 145–7; S. Lieberman, *Sifrei Zuta al Sefer ba-Midbar* (1968), 104–24; Epstein, Mishnah 2 (1964[2]), 285–6, 288; Ch. Albeck, *Meḥkarim bi-Beraita ve-Tosefta* (1944), 69–70; S. Lieberman, *Sifrei Zuta* (1968), 104–29; *Ḥadashot Archeologiyot* (April, 1969), 1–2; D. Urman, in: IEJ, 22 (1972), 16–23; idem, in: *Beer-Sheva*, 2 (1985), 7–25 (Heb.).

[Yitzhak Dov Gilat / Stephen G. Wald (2nd ed.)]

BARKAT (Burstein), REUVEN (1906–1972), Israeli politician. Member of the Sixth and Seventh Knessets and speaker of the Knesset, 1969–72. Barkat was born in Tavrig (Taurage), Lithuania, where his father, Abraham Aaron Burstein, headed the local yeshivah. Barkat attended a Hebrew secondary school in Ponevezh (Panevezys). He was one of the founders of He-Ḥalutz ha-Ẓa'ir and chairman of Ha-Ivri ha-Ẓa'ir in Lithuania. He studied literature and law at the Sorbonne in Paris and was chairman of the Hebrew Students Union in the Diaspora. He immigrated to Ereẓ Israel in 1926 and immediately entered political life. In 1933–38 he was involved in the *Ha'avarah*. Subsequently, in 1940–46 he was secretary general of the National Committee for the Jewish Soldier, directing cultural and welfare activities for the members of the Palestinian Jewish units of the British Army and subsequently of the Jewish Brigade. At the end of the war these activities also involved clandestine activity connected with the rescue of Jewish survivors of the Holocaust (see *Beriḥah). In 1946 Barkat joined the Political Department of the *Histadrut. In 1949 he was appointed head of its International Department, a position he held until 1960. He was also appointed chairman of the Arab Department of the Histadrut. In 1961 Barkat was appointed ambassador to Norway. He was soon offered the position of ambassador to the Soviet Union, but finally he declined the post to become secretary general of *Mapai. He held this position in the years 1962–66, when the party was torn by internal dissension over the "Lavon Affair" (see Pinḥas *Lavon). Barkat was first elected to the Sixth Knesset on the Alignment list, serving in the Knesset Foreign Affairs and Defense Committee. He was elected to the Seventh Knesset and chosen to become speaker, a position which he held until his sudden death on the last day of Passover 1972.

BIBLIOGRAPHY: *Kovez shel Re'uven Barkat: Divrei Iyyun ve-Diyun bi-B'ayot Parlamentarism, Teḥikah u-Mimshal* (1977).

[Susan Hattis Rolef (2nd ed.)]

BAR KOCHBA ASSOCIATION, an organization of Jewish university students in Prague. It was founded in 1893 by students of the Prague German University and subsequently became a focal point of Zionist intellectual activities. Among the members who later played prominent roles in the Zionist movement were Shmuel Hugo *Bergman, Oskar Epstein, Hugo Hermann, Leo *Hermann, Hans Kohn, and Robert *Weltsch. The members of Bar Kochba contributed much to the deepening of Zionist ideology, particularly in the years preceding World War I. They were largely influenced by Martin Buber who, between 1909 and 1911, delivered his *Drei Reden über das Judentum* before this group. The Zionist outlook of these young men found expression in the weekly *Selbstwehr*, which they edited for a time, and in *Vom Judentum*, a collection of essays on the problems of Zionism and Judaism in general (1913). There were small-scale attempts at renewing the activities of Bar Kochba after World War I, including the publication of *Juedische Jugendblaetter* (jointly with *Blau-Weiss). Its functions were taken over by its sister society, Theodor Herzl, which consisted of Czech-speaking Jewish university students in Prague.

BIBLIOGRAPHY: H. Yachil, *Devarim al ha-Ẓiyyonut ha-Czekhoslovakit* (1967), 8–11; Y. Borman, in: *Gesher*, 15, no. 2–3 (1969), 243–50; *Semestralberichte des Vereins Bar-Kochba in Prag* (1910–13); F. Weltsch (ed.), *Prague vi-Yrushalayim* (1954), 77–121; H. Kohn, *Living in a World Revolution* (1965), 47–55.

[Oskar K. Rabinowicz]

BAR KOKHBA (d. 135 C.E.), leader of the revolt in Judea against Rome (132–135 C.E.).

The Man and the Leader

Bar Kokhba is known in talmudic sources as Ben Kozevah, Bar Kozevah, or Ben Koziva (Heb. בן כוזבה, בר כוסבא, בן כוזיבא; Sanh. 93b; BK 97b; TJ, Ta'an. 4:8, 68d), and in Christian sources as Βαρχωχεβας (Eusebius, *Historia Ecclesiastica*, 4:6, 2). In the recently discovered contemporary letters addressed to or originating from him, he is referred to as Simeon bar Kosevah, Bar or Ben Koseva (בר כוסבא שמעון בר כוסבה, בן כוסבא, the last form being found also in a contemporary Greek letter). The name שמעון (or its abbreviation שמע), which appears on coins of the revolt, undoubtedly refers to him. His original name was probably Bar Koseva, and it is doubtful whether it was derived from a settlement in the Judean mountains or whether it indicates his father's name or a general family name. The appellation Bar Kokhba was apparently given to him during the revolt on the basis of the homiletical interpretation, in a reference to messianic expectations, of the verse (Num. 24:17): "There shall step forth a star [כּוֹכָב, *kokhav*] out of Jacob." Bar Kokhba was general midrashic designation for the "king messiah" (see *Messiah), and customarily used before the destruction of *Jerusalem. Thus, in the verse "a star out of Jacob ... a scepter ... out of Israel" (*ibid.*), Onkelos renders "star" as *malka* ("king") and "scepter" as *meshiḥa* ("messiah"), a midrashic interpretation current among the *Zealots who joined in the war against the Romans. While this appellation became the popular one, his original name was retained in documents and letters. The disappointment that followed in the wake of the defeat (and perhaps even at the height of the revolt) may have led the people to give a derogatory turn to his original name of Bar Koseva by altering it to Bar Kozivah (בר כוזיבה) in a punning allusion to "a lie" (*kazav*). Even the homiletical interpretation of "a star out of Jacob" quoted by R. *Akiva was from then on interpreted ambiguously, as evidenced by R. *Simeon b. Yoḥai's statement: "'There shall step forth a star out of Jacob' – Kozeva stepped forth out of Jacob" (TJ, *loc cit.*). Similarly, in talmudic sources Bar Kokhba coins are referred to specifically as those of Ben Koziva. "A coin of one who rebelled, such as Ben Koziva," or "Koziva coins" (BK 97b; TJ, Ma'as. Sh. 1:1, 52d; Tosef., *ibid.*, 1:6).

Bar Kokhba's personality does not emerge clearly from the scant and obscure sources available, some of which, like those in the Talmud and Midrash, have legendary overtones, while later ones, such as the sparse references by Church Father Eusebius, are tendentious. The few traits of his personality that emerge from the administrative and economic documents found in the Judean Desert do not contradict the main features of his character as incidentally portrayed in the literary sources. He may be described as a leader who, in charge of both the economy and the army, ruled imperiously, concerned himself even with minor details, and did not refrain from threatening senior officers of his army with punishment or even from inflicting deterrent punishment.

Bar Kokhba's title in documents is נשיא ישראל or הנסי על ישראל ("*nasi* of Israel"), the former occurring also on coins of the revolt. According to the Talmud, Akiva said: "This is the king messiah" whereupon Johanan b. Torta answered him derisively: "Akiva, grass will grow in your cheeks and the son of David will still not have come" (TJ, Ta'an. 4:8; Lam. R. 2:2, no. 4). Eusebius states that Bar Kokhba regarded himself as the savior who had come down to the Jews like a star from heaven, to deliver them from their somber troubles. Some adduce proof of Bar Kokhba's messiahship from the *Vision of Peter*, a Christian work written a few years after the revolt, which refers to a deceiver who falsely represented himself as a messiah and was – according to this tendentious account – nothing but a murderer. But these are simply expressions of the Christian authors' hatred which distorted their outlook, and are devoid of real historical value. Nevertheless, the messianic hopes which were cherished by the nation centered on Bar Kokhba. As might be expected from such a powerful, dominant personality, he himself probably had pretentions to being a redeemer and fostered these hopes. That the very appellation Bar Kokhba expresses a messianic belief in the "star out of Jacob" as an ideal ruler can be seen from apocryphal literature (Test. Patr., Levi 18:3; and Judah 24:1; and cf. Rev. 22:16; *The Damascus Document*, 7:19–20; and *War of the Sons of Light with the Sons of Darkness*, 7:5, 1). *The Damascus Document* states that the "star out of Jacob" will be "the *nasi* of the entire community" and accordingly it might be contended that Bar Kokhba's title of *nasi* had a messianic allusion. But the documents contain no hint of a messianic reference, and the sway of the *nasi* applied to wholly mundane affairs such as the army, administration, and the economy. According to coins struck during the revolt, the *nasi* may have assigned in a compromise matters relating to worship and faith to Eleazar ha-Kohen (perhaps on the basis of the division between the *nasi* and the priesthood, as described in Ezek. 44–46). The basically authentic statement about a Sanhedrin at Bethar (Sanh. 17b) suggests that at a certain time a *bet din* participated in Bar Kokhba's rule. Therefore, the title *nasi* may itself have indicated a more restricted role than that regarded as implicit in "king messiah."

The *aggadah* which relates how Bar Kokhba's men were selected – by having a finger cut off or by uprooting a cedar tree (TJ, *loc cit.*; Lam. R. 2:2 no. 4) – reflects the exclusiveness of an elite rebel army and the harshness and even cruelty of its leader. The controversies between him and the sages, and his reliance on his own powers rather than on help from Heaven, are depicted in the *aggadah* as self-aggrandizement against God: "When he went forth to battle, he said 'Neither assist nor discourage us.'" To decide precisely the historical kernel that has been preserved in this tradition is difficult, but Bar Kokhba's letters to his subordinates (such as to Jeshua b. Galgolah or Jonathan and Masbelah) confirm that he was a stern leader who vigorously insisted on his views and with a firm hand controlled not only the population but also his senior officers. In contrast to the situation during the Jewish War (66–70/73 C.E.), the nation was now united under the leadership of a single commander-in-chief. This is evident from documents indicating that even in the final stages of the revolt he still exercised unlimited authority over his men. Presumably the unity of the nation in this war derived not only from the *nasi's* powerful personality, but also from the memory of past sufferings and the yearning for liberation. Geography, too, may have been a factor in this unity, for while the revolt spread to Galilee and Transjordan, it was mainly although not exclusively centered in Judea, making it both possible and practicable to exercise effective control.

Such was the background to the acceptance of a strong leader's authority, unopposed apparently by the soldiers. This unanimity of the nation can be inferred from Eusebius (as from the *Book of Revelation*) where Bar Kokhba is described as a murderer and bandit who deceived the people. Even in later generations, despite the disappointment engendered by his defeat, his image persisted as the embodiment of messianic hopes. This is evident from Maimonides who, in referring to the "king messiah," states: "Rabbi Akiva, the greatest of the sages of the Mishnah, was a supporter of King Ben Koziva, saying of him that he was the king messiah. He and all the contemporary sages regarded him as the king messiah, until he was killed for sins which he had committed" (Maim. Yad, Melakhim, 11:3).

The Bar Kokhba Revolt

Only sparse and fragmentary information exists, some of it late, on the Bar Kokhba revolt, its origins, course, and outcome. The main source consists of the scant statements of the Roman historian Dio Cassius in the 69th part of his history of Rome, written between 194 and 216 C.E. As for Bar Kokhba's documents, they contain nothing specific about the war itself or about its political and military significance, being mainly economic and administrative records. The revolt most probably broke out in 132 C.E. Dio Cassius states that before it began Hadrian had established a new city in Jerusalem, called Aelia Capitolina (after his own name Aelius and in honor of Jupiter Capitolinus). He built a temple to Jupiter in the new city, thereby infuriating the Jews and provoking "a fierce and protracted war." On the other hand, Eusebius declares that Aelia Capitolina was established after the revolt. Hadrian probably began to build Aelia Capitolina before the revolt, and its non-Jewish character inflamed the Jews against Rome, but the work was not completed until after the war (see *Hadrian and "New Archaeological Finds" below, for a contrary view). During 129–132 C.E. Hadrian stayed in Ereẓ Israel and its neighborhood, and his departure for Greece in the summer of 132 was the signal for the outbreak of the revolt. There were other factors that aggravated the situation, e.g., the harsh rule of *Tinneius Rufus, the new Roman governor of Judea; and the disillusionment of the Jews who had hoped that Hadrian would restore the ruins of Jerusalem, when rumors that he was rebuilding the Temple fostered messianic expectations. Their hopes, speedily shattered, were replaced by profound resentment. Agitation against Rome had, it seems, existed in Judea many years before the outbreak of the revolt, and the sages may have tried to mitigate it, as may be inferred from the account of the assembly in the valley of Rimmon at which *Joshua b. Hananiah calmed the turbulent mood of the people (Gen. R. 64:10). Ultimately, however, the revolt was a continuation of the uprisings of the Jews of the Diaspora against Rome in 115–117 C.E., which included "the war of *Quietus" ending

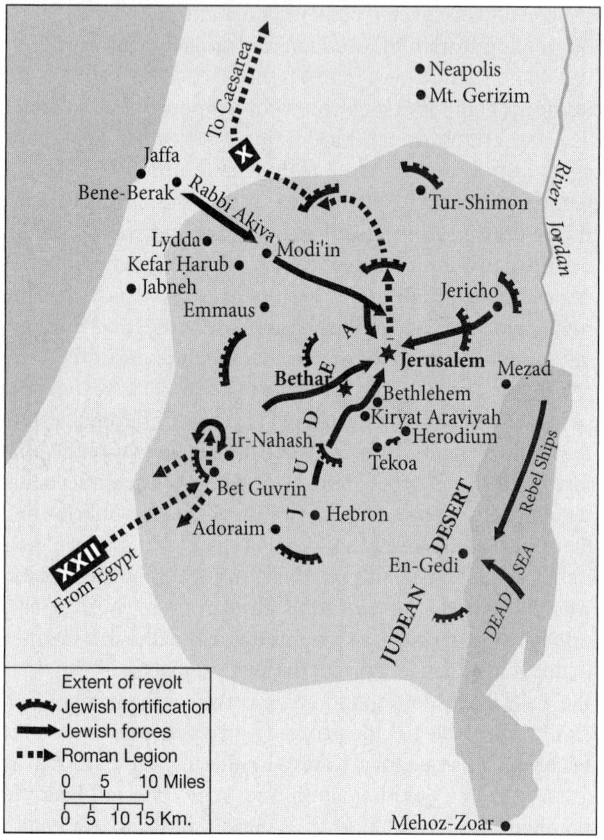

Map 1. Extent of the Bar Kokhba revolt in its first year, 132 C.E. After Y. Aharoni, Carta's "Atlas of the Bible," Heb. ed., 1966.

in 117. Even if Hadrian intended no particular enmity against the Jews and behaved in Judea with the same degree of cultural universalism that he adopted in other places, his innovations, bearing as they did a Hellenistic-Roman stamp, provoked the vehement opposition of the Jews both against non-Jewish culture and more especially against emperor-worship.

Dio Cassius gives a brief account of the course of the revolt. Accumulating arms by deceiving the Roman authorities, the Jews awaited a suitable opportunity, and when Hadrian left they openly rebelled. At first the Jews did not fight pitched battles. Instead they seized towns which they fortified with walls and subterranean passages. In an increasing number of clashes the rebels inflicted losses on the Romans. Hadrian was compelled to hurriedly send for one of his ablest generals, *Julius Severus, who specially came from Britain to Judea. Due to the large number of the rebels and their desperate fury, Severus refrained from waging open war and preferred to surround their fortresses and hem them in to prevent food from reaching them. Gradually he succeeded in wearing down the Judean fighters, on whom he inflicted heavy blows without respite until he reduced them to a state of complete submission. Dio Cassius relates that the Romans demolished 50 fortresses, destroyed 985 villages, and killed 580,000 people in addition to those who died of hunger, disease, and fire. He adds that many Romans perished as well, and when Hadrian informed

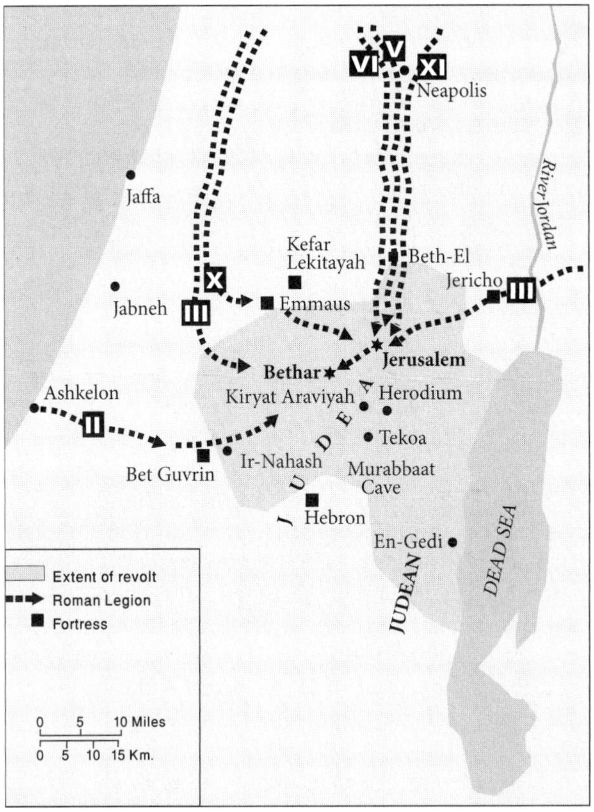

Map 2. Extent of the Bar Kokhba revolt in its third and fourth years. After Y. Aharoni, Carta's "Atlas of the Bible," Heb. ed., 1966.

the Senate of his victory he did not begin with the usual formula: "I and my army are well." Dio Cassius states that the insurrection, which was prepared in detail, spread until "the whole of Judea was in revolt" (he referred apparently to most of Ereẓ Israel, including Galilee and Golan). He further states that the Jews "throughout the world" supported the uprising as did non-Jews, too, and it was "as though the whole world raged." In its scope and vehemence, the revolt assumed the dimensions of a war which constituted a threat to the empire. As usual with Roman historians, Dio Cassius cites a supernatural omen, to show that the destruction of Judea was predestined, when he states that the "sanctified" tomb of Solomon had fallen down of itself.

Greek and Roman inscriptions mention the participation in the war of detachments of legions brought from all parts of the empire, from Egypt and as far away as Britain – the Tenth "Fretensis," the Third "Cyrenaica," the Fourth "Scythica," the Second "Trajana," the Twenty-Second "Diotrajana" legions, and perhaps also the Sixth "Ferrata" legion. The Syrian navy also presumably took part in the war. Although exact figures cannot be computed since these were auxiliary troops and detachments of legions, the magnitude of the Roman army indicates the dimensions of the war. Isolated evidence – an inscription on a tomb, third-century talmudic references to the destruction of Galilee (BK 80a; TJ, Pe'ah 7:1, 20a), the remarks of Sulpicius Severus (fourth century C.E.) on the rebellion of the Jews in Syria and Palestine in the days of Hadrian – shows the revolt spread to the north of Ereẓ Israel, to Beth-Shean and Galilee. However, the main conflict took place in Judea, the Shephelah, the mountains, and finally in the Judean Desert.

The war apparently lasted about three and a half years, during which Jerusalem was taken by the rebels, as evident both from the inscription לחרות ירושלים on coins of the revolt and perhaps also from the Judean Desert documents. Appian, a contemporary of the revolt, Eusebius, in his *De Theophania*, and Jerome (fifth century C.E.), in his commentary on Jeremiah 31:15, all state that Jerusalem was destroyed in the days of Hadrian. It would therefore appear that Bar Kokhba captured the city and only after his military defeat did Hadrian regain control and destroy it. There may be an allusion to this in Midrashim which tell of Hadrian's entry into Jerusalem and his desecration of the Temple Mount (Tanḥ. B., Ex. 128; Ex. R. 5:5, Deut. R. 3:13). Some maintain that the design on coins of the revolt, depicting a four-columned building surmounted by a star, symbolizes the Temple, and if the undated coins bearing the inscription לחרות ירושלים or simply ירושלים are indeed to be assigned to the third year of the revolt, Jerusalem was still in Bar Kokhba's hands toward the end of the revolt in the third year of the war, that is, in Tishri 134 C.E. This is confirmed by one of the Judean Desert documents which is dated (שנ)ת תלת לחרות יר(ו)שלים ("the third year of the freedom of Jerusalem"). This scant evidence shows that during the Bar Kokhba revolt Jerusalem not only symbolized the yearning for freedom but also served the political expression of the consolidation of the revolt and of its sway in Judea. There is, however, no evidence that the Temple was rebuilt at that time, nor is there any proof that Bar Kokhba was about to rebuild the Temple. However, an altar may have been erected for sacred worship.

Bar Kokhba made a final stand at *Bethar in the Judean Hills, but from the finds in the Judean Desert it would appear that after the fall of the last stronghold the flame of revolt continued to flicker in the desert and in the vicinity of the Dead Sea. Nevertheless, in talmudic and midrashic sources Bethar represents the fortress in which the rebels found refuge, and its fall, along with the defeat of Bar Kokhba who met his death there, symbolizes the end of the revolt. The place was apparently chosen as the rebels' main stronghold because of its strategic situation on the edge of a mountain overlooking the Valley of Sorek and dominating the important Jerusalem-Bet Guvrin road, and possibly also because of its fertile soil. Since it was not adequately fortified, Jerusalem could not serve as a stronghold. At that time Bethar was considered a large city (*kerakh*; TJ, Ta'an 4:8, 69a; Lam. R. 2:2 no. 4; cf. Mid. Hag. to Deut. 28:52), perhaps because numerous inhabitants from the entire neighborhood had gathered there, as attested by Jerome (in his commentary on Zech. 8:19), who mentions that many thousands of Jews found refuge in it – *Bether ad quam multa milia confugerant Judaeorum* (and cf. the midrashic references to 400 synagogues in Bethar).

The actual siege of Bethar began apparently after the recapture of Jerusalem. Whether Bar Kokhba's men had intended it from the outset to be their principal fortress or were driven there by the force of circumstances cannot be known. Even during the siege those in Bethar maintained contact with camps of fighters in the Judean Desert. One of the documents states: "Near the well of Ben Koseva, Nasi of Israel, in the camp," referring probably to the camp of Bethar, which is not mentioned, however, in the Dead Sea documents. Severus' strategy was to intensify the siege on the fortress, and a siege wall (*circumvallatio*) was built for this purpose. It was attacked by the besieged in desperate sallies, while the blockade grew tighter. A clear reminder of the Roman armies' presence in Bethar itself was preserved in a Latin inscription which was engraved on a rock near the well of Bethar and mentions detachments of the Fifth "Macedonica" and the Eleventh "Claudia" legions. The inscription is now illegible.

Eusebius states that Bethar was besieged in the 18th year of Hadrian's reign, that is, in 134 C.E., about two years after the outbreak of the revolt, and that its fall was caused by hunger and thirst. According to the talmudic account (TJ, Ta'an 4:8, 68d; Lam. R. 2:2, no. 4), Hadrian unsuccessfully laid siege to Bethar for three and a half years, until a Samaritan pretended that *Eleazar of Modi'in (ha-Moda'i) had conspired with him to surrender the city to the Romans. Incensed at this, Bar Kokhba killed Eleazar. "Immediately Bethar was captured and Ben Koziva met his death." Presumably great importance was attached in besieged Bethar to sages such as Eleazar of Modi'in, one of the leading rabbis of his generation, but whether he is identical with the Eleazar whose name appears on coins of the revolt cannot be determined. (In one of his letters, Bar Kokhba mentions a רבנו בטניה בר מיסה, whom he regarded as a great man.) These circumstances suggest that eventually a dispute broke out between the sages and the commander-in-chief and spread among the besieged. In any event these reports, like the statement of Eusebius, indicate that the capture of Bethar was difficult and was achieved under unusual circumstances.

The death of Bar Kokhba is enveloped in a legendary halo. The accounts of the massacre perpetrated in Bethar attest to the ferocity of the struggle (Git. 56a–b; Song. R. 2:17; cf. ARN 138, 115: "Not a soul escaped"). The sages state that on Av 15th the burial of the slain was permitted (Ta'an. 31a). Tradition has it that Bethar was taken on the Ninth of Av (*ibid.*, 29a), and Jerome (*loc. cit.*) also says that it occurred in August: *in hoc mense* (scil. *Augusto*). On the basis of the latest date – the fourth year of the liberation of Israel – mentioned in one of the documents, Bar Kokhba's rule lasted more than three years. In Jewish tradition the fall of Bethar was a disaster equal to the destruction of the First and Second Temples.

The Jewish population of Judea was largely exterminated in the period of repression which followed the fall of Bethar. The subjugation was associated with massacres and religious persecution, the sale of Jews into slavery, and uprooting of the people from the soil. The Jewish center of gravity now moved northward, chiefly to Galilee. Thus ended the final and perhaps greatest war of liberation of the Jews in ancient times. The independence of Judea had come to an end.

The Judean Desert Documents

The finds, dating from the days of Bar Kokhba and brought to light in the Judean Desert in 1952–61, contain additional facts of great importance for an understanding of the social and economic conditions prevailing during the Bar Kokhba war in 132–135 C.E. The first documents were found in 1952 in Wadi Muraba'at about 11 mi. (18 km.) southwest of *Qumran. Among them are commercial contracts, letters of divorce, two letters from Bar Kokhba, and one from the administrators of the community addressed to Jeshua b. Galgolah. An archaeological expedition undertaken in the Judean Desert south of En-Gedi in 1960–61 uncovered, alongside material finds such as skeletons, linen, remnants of clothes, metal and glass vessels, and remains of food, many documents of the time of the Bar Kokhba war, chiefly in one of the caves in Naḥal Ḥever, now named "The Cave of the Letters." The letters and economic documents in Hebrew, Aramaic, and Greek uncovered in the cave testify to the economic position in southern Judea on the eve of the revolt and at the height of the war (on the documents, their language, literary form, and historical significance see *Dead Sea Scrolls).

The letters, written apparently in Bar Kokhba's name but not personally by him, deal with everyday matters. Some of them are not entirely clear. The dates mentioned in them range from the second to the fourth year of the liberation of Israel (132–134 C.E.). The letters open with an almost identical formula:

> משמעון בן כוסבה לישע בן גלגולה לאנשי הכרך שלו. משמעון לישוע בן גלגולה שלום; שמעון בר כוסבה הנסי על ישראל ליהונתן ולמסבלה סלם; משמעון בר כוסבא לאנשי עינגדי למסבלא .בעין שלום; שמעון ליהודה בר מנשה לקרית ערביה (ר)ליהו(נ)תן ב(ו).
> "From Simeon ben Kosevah to Jeshua ben Galgolah and the men of his fortress!"; "From Simeon to Jeshua ben Galgolah, peace!"; "Simeon bar Kosevah the *nasi* ["prince"] of Israel to Jonathan and Masbela, peace!"; "From Simeon bar Koseva to the men of En-Gedi to Masbela (and) to Jonathan B(ar) Ba'ayan peace!" "Simeon to Judah bar Manasseh to Kiryat Araviyah."

In a letter to Jeshua b. Galgolah, one of his army commanders, Bar Kokhba refers to the גללאים (*gll'ym*), who are to be protected and, sternly reminding his men of this, threatens them with irons: "I call Heaven to witness against me … that I shall put your feet in irons." The actual occasion and the identity of the גללאים are not clear from the letter. In another letter to Jeshua, Bar Kokhba orders him to offer hospitality on the Sabbath to men who were bringing wheat to the camp and to provide them with accommodation until "after the Sabbath."

In other letters found in Naḥal Ḥever, the *nasi* writes to Masbelah b. Simeon and Jonathan b. Bayahu, who were apparently in command of the En-Gedi front, about the wheat supply, the grain harvest, the confiscation of property, the supervision of the men, and the mobilization of the men of *Tekoa on the border of the Judean Desert. His language is harsh, and he frequently threatens them with punishment if they fail to carry out his orders ("and if you will not do this, you will be punished"). In a Hebrew letter to Jonathan and Masbelah of En-Gedi, Bar Kokhba orders them to attend to the loading of a boat anchored in the harbor there. To the commanders in the rear and the population of the inhabited area of the desert, with whom he was incensed for having failed to supply food as he had commanded and who had neglected their duty, Bar Kokhba uses stern language: "You are living well, eating and drinking off the property of the house of Israel, and care nothing about your brethren."

In an Aramaic letter to Judah b. Manasseh of Kiryat Araviyah, Bar Kokhba orders Judah to supply him with the *Four Species for Tabernacles and apparently reminds him about separating the tithe: ותקן יתהן ("and give the dues from them"). Such references, made incidentally or hinted at in the letters, may indicate that Bar Kokhba's men, even under danger, strictly and quite naturally kept the commandments of Judaism, such as the sanctity of the Sabbath, the laws of the priestly and levitical dues, and the fullest observance of festivals.

The letters and other documents uncovered in the Judean Desert contain nothing specific about the attitude of the sages toward the rule of Bar Kokhba nor is there any mention in them of Bethar and of the war there. Nevertheless it is possible to comprehend from them explicitly and at first hand about Bar Kokhba's aggressive personality and his status, the economic straits in which the fighters of Judea found themselves, and the geographic extent of the revolt. The *nasi* was concerned about supply problems, food for his camp, and matters pertaining to real estate. The economic documents found in Wadi Muraba'at show that leases were made in the name and with the sanction of Bar Kokhba: "On the instructions of Simeon b. Koseva." Apparently the land belonged nominally to the *nasi*, it being clearly stated in a lease, "You have leased the ground from Simeon, the Nasi of Israel." In his name the lessors laid down the quota of grain that was to be given to them. As was to be expected in a time of war, the authorities insisted on the cultivation of the fields and confiscated the lands of those who neglected to till them. They "were dispossessed of the land and lost everything." In effect, Bar Kokhba regarded himself as holding the authority of the Roman emperor and transferred the lands of liberated Judea to his own possession. His orders concerning leases, sales, and confiscations were grounded on a juridical succession to the Roman rule, by virtue of which he was empowered to exercise control over the lands of Judea and confiscate property for the public good. Contracts found in Naḥal Ḥever indicate that Bar Kokhba wished to prevent the concentration of the lands of En-Gedi in the hands of a few owners in order to increase the supply of food in a time of stress.

From the names of the settlements mentioned in these documents, Bar Kokhba's men apparently controlled extensive areas, in the frontier regions of the Judean mountains, in the neighborhood of Bet Guvrin (Ir-Nahash), and in the Judean Desert, and maintained contact, it seems, with regions east and south of the Dead Sea, such as Ma'aleh ha-Luḥit in the district of Eglatin in Moab and Zoar in the Aravah. Herodium, the town of Herod about 6 mi. (10 km.) southeast of Jerusalem and mentioned in the documents, became an economic center in which the *nasi's* representatives were stationed; En-Gedi was an important supply harbor for the rebels. The settlements of Tekoa and Kiryat Araviyah in the vicinity of Bethlehem are mentioned in the documents. According to the reconstruction of ב ...שלים as Jerusalem, proposed by J.T. Milik who made a study of the Wadi Muraba'at documents, that city is referred to in two of them, one dating from the second, and the other from the fourth year "of the liberation of Israel" (Elul, 133 and Tishrei, 134, respectively). After the defeat, the fugitives from the war in Judea gathered in the Judean Desert, which then became the rebel center. The remains of Roman military camps found above the caves in Naḥal Ḥever show that the legions besieged the remnants of the fighters who, together with their families, had taken refuge in these hiding places. Surrounded by the Romans, there they met their death.

[Samuel Abramsky]

New Archaeological Finds

Since the writing of the above in the late 1960s new archaeological information concerning the Bar Kokhba revolt has emerged as a result of the intensive investigation of hundreds of refuge caves and underground hiding complexes. Refuge caves are found mainly in the Judean Desert and in the cliffs overlooking the Dead Sea, and were used as shelters for Jewish refugees at the close of the Bar Kokhba revolt. Underground hiding complexes, however, were subterranean warrens hewn artificially under or near residential buildings within Jewish towns and villages (some 125 sites according to a recent count). They have been found in the Judean Shephela, and in the Beth-El and Hebron Mountains, and reflect the general boundaries of the area that was under Bar Kokhba's administration. Excavations at the Abi'or Cave in the Judean Desert in 1986 and later in 1993 brought to light numerous fragments of new documents written on papyri in Greek and Aramaic. Additional finds from the cave consisted of textiles, ropes, and parts of sandals. These items were brought to the cave and hidden there towards the end of the revolt.

Excavations conducted in 1984 by Tel Aviv University confirmed that Khirbet al-Yahud (10 acres in size) is indeed *Bethar, the last bastion of Bar Kokhba. Hastily erected fortifications were uncovered and the discovery of slingstones and arrowheads indicates that a battle took place there. Roman siege camps were also identified in the vicinity of Bethar (present-day Battir).

Various artifacts dating from the time of the revolt have been unearthed at a number of sites and within underground hiding complexes, notably various forms of pottery, stone vessels, and coins. An important discovery was that of a lead weight found at Horvat 'Alim in the Shephela, bearing the name and title of Bar Kokhba, which was evidently used for administrative purposes. A signet ring bearing the name of Bar Kokhba is also reported from the vicinity of Quneitra in the Golan, and perhaps was brought to this destination by Jews fleeing persecution at the end of the Bar Kokhba revolt. A number of coin hoards have become known, many of them through clandestine digging, containing Jewish coins mixed with those produced in Aelia Capitolina. Clearly, Aelia Capitolina was founded before the outbreak of the revolt. There is no evidence that Bar Kokhba at any time held Jerusalem (see above for contrary view). Coins dating from the Bar Kokhba revolt have also begun emerging from controlled excavations, especially within the refuge caves and underground hiding complexes.

[Shimon Gibson (2nd ed.)]

BIBLIOGRAPHY: S. Abramsky, *Bar Kokhva, Nesi Yisrael* (1961), contains bibliography; S. Yeivin, *Milḥemet Bar Kokhva* (1952²); Allon, Toledot, 1 (1958³), 290–354; 2 (1961²), 1–83; BIES, 25 (1960/61), 5–108; Schuerer, Hist. 278, 299–304; Y. Yadin, *The Finds from the Bar Kokhba Period in the Cave of Letters* (1963); Y. Aharoni and B. Rothenburg, *Be-Ikkevot Melakhim u-Moredim* (1964³); P. Benoit et al., *Les grottes de Murabaʿat* (1961); Y. Yadin, *Bar Kokhba* (1972). **ADD. BIBLIOGRAPHY:** L. Mildenberg, *The Coinage of the Bar Kokhba War* (1984); A. Kloner and Y. Tepper, *The Hiding Complexes in the Judean Shephelah* (1987); Y. Meshorer, *The Coinage of Aelia Capitolina* (1989); A. Kloner, "Lead Weights of Bar Kokhba's Administration," in: *Israel Exploration Journal*, 40 (1990), 58–67; B. Isaac, *The Limits of Empire: The Roman Army in the East* (1990), 83–85; D. Ussishkin, "Archaeological Soundings at Betar, Bar-Kokhba's Last Stronghold," in: *Tel Aviv*, 20 (1993), 66–97; F. Millar, *The Roman Near East, 31 BC–AD 337* (1996), 372–374 and Appendix B; D. Urman, "A Signet Ring of Bar Kokhba (?) from the Vicinity of Quneitra in the Golan," in: *Bulletin of the Anglo-Israel Archaeological Society*, 15 (1996–1997): 51–54; H. Eshel, "The Contribution of Documents and Other Remains Found in the Judean Desert between 1979 and 1993 to the Understanding of the Bar Kokhba Revolt," in: *Bulletin of the Anglo-Israel Archaeological Society*, 15 (1996–1997), 107–110; H. Eshel and D. Amit, *Refuge Caves of the Bar Kokhba Revolt* (1998); P. Schäfer (ed.), *The Bar Kokhba War Reconsidered: New Perspectives on the Second Revolt Against Rome* (2003).

BARLAD (Rom. **Bârlad** or **Bîrlad**), town in Moldavia, E. Romania. The Jewish community there is first attested in 1738 when the prince of Moldavia, Grigore Ghica, appointed Marco (Mordechai) as leader (*staroste*) of the Jews of Barlad "according to ancient custom." "A row of Jewish stores" is mentioned in 1767 and a "Jewish street" in 1819; 53 Jewish households were recorded in 1803. In 1838 the Jews were accused of desecrating Christian holy objects, and 23 notables of the community, including three women, were imprisoned. They were released only after payment of a heavy fine. In December 1867, there was an outbreak of violence when the Jews were accused of murdering an antisemitic priest. The community numbered 2,000 in 1859; 5,883 (24% of the total) in 1899, about one-third of the merchants and artisans in the city being Jews; and 3,727 in 1930 (14% of the total), mainly occupied in commerce (many as clerks) and as artisans. There were then in Barlad a Jewish kindergarten and two Jewish schools, for boys and for girls. Aizic Taubes (1834–1920) was among the prominent rabbis. Barlad was also a Zionist center.

In November 1940, all Jewish men were sent to forced labor. However, the intellectuals were liberated due to protests by Romanian intellectuals. When the war against the U.S.S.R. broke out (June 22, 1941) the Jews from towns in the district were driven from their homes and sent to Barlad. The community founded a gymnasia and aided many pauperized Jews. After World War II Jewish life was reorganized for a short period only due to the considerable decrease in population through emigration, mainly to Israel. In 1969, 100 Jewish families lived in Barlad where there was one synagogue. In 2004, 46 Jews lived in Barlad.

BIBLIOGRAPHY: M. Carp, *Cartea Neagra*, 1 (1946), 115, 158; Filderman, in: *Sliha*, 1 no. 4 (1956). **ADD. BIBLIOGRAPHY:** PK Romanyah, I, 17–21; S. Rubinstein, *Me-Barlad ad Rosh Pinah* (1993).

[Eliyahu Feldman and Theodor Lavi / Lucian-Zeev Herscovici (2nd ed.)]

BAR-LE-DUC, capital of the Meuse department, northeastern France; former capital of the Duchy of Bar. The 12th-century Jewish community in Bar-le-Duc was reputedly expelled by the count of Bar, but Jews are again found there from 1220. They were expelled in 1309 but were allowed to return to the county in 1321, and settled in 30 localities. In 1322 the Jews were again expelled, but had returned by 1328 to be banished again in 1477. They resided in Bar-le-Duc in the Rue des Juifs, the present Rue de la Couronne. After the French Revolution Jews again settled in Bar-le-Duc. From 1808 the community was affiliated to the Consistory of Nancy and administered by the rabbinate of Verdun. It numbered 170 in 1892. During World War II 18 Jews living in Bar-le-Duc were deported or shot. In 1968, 40 Jews lived there.

BIBLIOGRAPHY: Weill, in: REJ, 125 (1966), 287ff.

[Georges Weill]

BAR-LEV (Originally **Brotzlewsky**), **HAIM** (1924–1994), eighth chief of staff of the IDF and Israeli politician; member of the Ninth to Twelfth Knessets. Bar-Lev was born in Vienna, and immigrated to Palestine in 1939 from Yugoslavia. In 1942 he graduated from the Mikveh Israel agricultural school and served in the *Palmaḥ until 1948. In 1946 he participated in the detonation of the Allenby Bridge near Jericho, as part of the struggle against the British. In the War of Independence he served successively as commander of the Eighth Battalion in the Negev Brigade, commander of a mechanized battalion, and brigade operations officer. In 1956, after attending the Senior Officers' School in Britain, he became director of training in the General Staff. During the Sinai Campaign he commanded an armored brigade which reached the Suez Canal. In 1958–61 he was commanding officer of the Armored Corps. He then went to the United States for two years and studied for an M.A. in economics and business administration at Columbia University. After returning to Israel, he served in 1964–66 as head of the Operations Branch in the General Staff, after which he went to Paris to study political science. He was recalled the following year, however, and appointed deputy chief of staff on the eve of the Six-Day War. In 1968–72 he served as chief of staff. In this period the Bar-Lev Line was constructed as Israel's defensive system along the Suez Canal – a system which collapsed in the first days of the Yom Kippur War, largely due to complacency. In the course of the Yom Kippur War Bar-Lev was recalled to active service as commander of the front with Egypt.

Even though he was not elected to the Eighth Knesset, Bar-Lev was appointed by Golda *Meir as minister of commerce and industry and development in the government she formed in March 1974 – a post he continued to hold under Yitzhak *Rabin. Bar-Lev was elected on the Alignment list to the Ninth Knesset, and after the Alignment's electoral defeat was appointed secretary general of the Labor Party – a position he held until 1984. In this period he acted together with Party Chairman Shimon *Peres to rehabilitate the party's organization and finances. In the National Unity Government of 1984–90 Bar-Lev served as minister of police. In 1992, following the resumption of diplomatic relations with Russia, Bar-Lev was appointed Israeli ambassador, a position he held until his death.

BIBLIOGRAPHY: K. Guy, *Bar-Lev* (1998).

[Susan Hattis Rolef (2nd ed.)]

BARLEY (Heb. שְׂעוֹרָה; *se'orah*), one of the seven species (see *Food) with which Ereẓ Israel was blessed (Deut. 8:8). In biblical times barley bread was a staple food and was extensively cultivated, especially as it grows even in poor soil and in areas with a low rainfall. The fact that barley was so widely sown accounts for the biblical ruling that the value of a field is to be estimated on the basis of the amount of barley required to sow it (Lev. 27:16). In the days of the Judges the farmer in Ereẓ Israel sustained himself mainly on barley, a cake of barley bread symbolizing the agricultural Israelites (in contrast to the nomadic Midianites) in the dream of the Midianite soldier (Judg. 7:13). It formed part of the diet of David's army (II Sam. 17:28) and also of the hewers of the timber in Lebanon for the Temple of Solomon (II Chron. 2:9).

In mishnaic times wheat largely replaced barley as human food, and barley was used mainly as animal fodder (it is referred to in this connection only once in the Bible (I Kings 5:8)) and the rabbis, therefore, in a homiletical view, give as the reason for the offering of barley meal in the ordeal of a woman suspected of adultery (Lev. 5:15) "that she had behaved like an animal" (Num. 5:15; cf. Sot. 9a). It became principally the poor man's food; hence the proverb, "Why do you eat barley bread? – Because I have no wheaten bread" (Sif. Num. 49). In the Bible the price of barley flour is given as half that of fine wheaten flour (II Kings 7:1), which was also the ratio of their prices in mishnaic times (Tosef., BM 9:10), the nutritive value of the former being regarded as half that of the latter (Pe'ah 8:5). The Karaite Anan held that for fulfilling the commandment on Passover unleavened bread made of barley was to be used, this being in his view, "the bread of affliction" and poverty. Of the cereals, barley ripens first (Ex. 9:31) and "the barley harvest season" is the designation of the spring (Ruth 1:22). On the second day of Passover, the *Omer* ("sheaf"), the first fruit of the harvest, was reaped (Lev. 23:9–15), and although there is no specific reference to its being barley, the rabbinic tradition to that effect is undoubtedly correct (Men. 84b) as the barley harvest begins at Passover time. One kind of beer was brewed from barley (BB 96b), another from a mixture of barley, figs, and blackberries (Pes. 107a), and yet another called "Egyptian *zythos*" from a third part of barley, a third part of safflower, and a third part of salt (*ibid.*, 42b). The brewing of beer has a long tradition in Egypt; it is depicted in ancient Egyptian drawings. *Se'orah*, the Hebrew name for barley, derives from the long hairs (Heb. *se'ar*, "hair") of its ears, and the cereal is designated by cognate words in almost all Semitic languages. The Greeks regarded barley as the very earliest crop grown in the world. In Ereẓ Israel there are at present cultivated species of two- and six-rowed barley (*Five Species). These species have been found in Egyptian tombs. A wild barley (*Hordeum spontaneum*) which grows in Ereẓ Israel is thought to be the origin of two-rowed barley. In excavations at Gezer four-rowed barley has been uncovered, and in the caves of En-Gedi and of the Judean Desert, two- and four-rowed barley of the mishnaic and talmudic periods has been found.

BIBLIOGRAPHY: Loew, Flora, 1 (1926), 707–23; J. Feliks, *Olam ha-Ẓome'aḥ ha-Mikra'i* (1957), 146–8, 318; idem, *Ha-Ḥakla'ut be-Ereẓ-Yisrael...*, (1963), 362 (index); idem, *Kilei Zera'im...* (1967), 23–27. **ADD. BIBLIOGRAPHY:** Feliks, Ha-Ẓome'aḥ, 164.

[Jehuda Feliks]

BARLIN, FREDERICK WILLIAM (fl. early 19th century), English portrait painter. Barlin, who worked in London, was the son of Berliner, the ḥazzan of the Chatham synagogue. Barlin exhibited at the Royal Academy in 1802 and 1807. Two of his portraits are of particular significance: that of Solomon *Herschel, chief rabbi of the Ashkenazi Jews in England, and that of the Sephardi haham Raphael *Meldola. The latter was painted wearing a three-cornered hat in a courtly, elegant, and typically English manner. This portrait was later engraved and published by Joshua Lopez.

BIBLIOGRAPHY: Roth, Art, 533; A. Rubens, *Anglo-Jewish Portraits* (1935), 53–55, 80.

BARMAS, ISSAY (1872–1946), violinist and teacher. Born in Odessa, Barmas studied with I. Grzimali in Moscow and with J. Joachim in Berlin. He made his debut as a soloist in Berlin in 1899 and toured Europe. He also formed his own quartet in 1919. From 1900 to 1929 he taught in Berlin (Stern Conservatoire, 1900–05; Klindwort-Scharwenki Conservatoire, 1905–29) and later moved to London. Among his publications are *Die Loesung des geigentechnischen Problems* (1913), *Ton-*

leiter-Spezialstudien, Doppelgriff-Spezialstudien, redactions, and editions of classical works.

BAR MITZVAH, BAT MITZVAH (Heb. masc. בַּר מִצְוָה, fem. בַּת מִצְוָה; lit. "son/daughter of the commandment," i.e., a person under obligation, responsible), term denoting both the attainment of religious and legal maturity as well as the occasion at which this status is formally assumed for boys at the age of 13 plus one day, for girls at 12 plus one day (Maim. Yad, Ishut, 2:9–10). Upon reaching this age a Jew is obliged to fulfill all the *commandments (Avot 5:1; cf. Yoma 82a). Although the term occurs in the Talmud for one who is subject to the law (BM 96a), its usage to denote the occasion of assuming religious and legal obligations does not appear before the 15th century (*Sefer Ẓiyyoni* of R. Menahem Ẓiyyoni to Gen. 1:5). A special celebration for a girl, the bat mitzvah, is not found mentioned before *Ben Ish Ḥai*, the legal code by Joseph Ḥayyim b. Elijah (19th cent.).

While the occasion of becoming bar/bat mitzvah was thus formalized only in later times, it is obvious from various sources that the status of obligation for boys of 13 was assumed in early times. According to Eleazar b. Simeon (second century C.E.), a father was responsible for the deeds of his son until the age of 13. For example the vows of a boy 13 and a day old are considered valid vows (Nid. 5:6). From then on a person can perform acts having legal implications, such as being a member of a *bet din*, being reckoned as part of a *minyan*, and buying and selling property. Yet there are notable exceptions, e.g., the testimony of a 13-year-old is not valid regarding real estate because he is "not knowledgeable about buying and selling" (Maim. Yad, Edut, 9:8).

Jewish law fixed 13 as the age of responsibility considering this the time of physical maturity for boys (and 12 for girls; Kid. 16b). At this age young people are thought to be able to control their desires (ARN² 16, 62–63). Rashi claims that bar mitzvah as a status of obligation was "in the category of biblical laws, as it was given to Moses at Sinai" (comment. to Avot 5:1). Midrashic literature gives many references for 13 as the turning point in the life of a young person, e.g., Abraham rejected the idols of his father at this age (PdRE 26), and at 13 Jacob and Esau went their separate ways, the former to study Torah, the latter to idol-worship (Gen. R. 63:10). Until 13 a son receives the merit of his father and is also liable to suffer for his parent's sin; after that each one bears his own sin (Yal. Ruth 600). This is also the time of transition from elementary school to the *bet ha-midrash* (*ibid.*). A tradition recorded in talmudic literature (Sof. 18:7, ed. M. Higger 1937) alludes to the fact that in Jerusalem during the period of the Second Temple, it was customary for the sages to bless a child who had succeeded in completing his first fast day at 12 or 13.

Being Called to the Torah

The calling up to the reading of the Torah is a symbol of a boy's attaining maturity. He is called up on the first occasion that the Torah is read following his 13th birthday according to the Jewish calendar. This is the first public demonstration of his new role as a full member of the community and, in modern times, it is to this occasion that the term bar mitzvah usually refers. When the boy's father is called to the Torah, he recites the benediction, "Blessed is He who has now freed me from the responsibility of this one" (Gen. R. *loc. cit.*). Among observant Jews in Eastern Europe the boy was usually called up to the Torah on the Monday or the Thursday following his birthday. In Western Europe, the occasion took on a more ceremonial importance, and it was customary for the bar mitzvah boy to be called up to the Torah to read the *maftir* portions and the *haftarah* on the first Sabbath after his birthday. For this task he had previously been prepared. According to an old Ashkenazi custom in Lithuania, Ereẓ Israel, etc., the boy recited the *maftir* on the Sabbath just before becoming fully 13, and immediately upon coming of age he received an ordinary *aliyah*. In the 17th and 18th centuries the custom was recorded in Worms, Germany, that those boys who were able and had pleasing voices conducted parts or all of the service. In some communities it was and still is customary for the young man to read the whole portion of the week. On a Sabbath when a bar mitzvah is celebrated, the morning service assumes a more festive atmosphere. Members of the boy's family are also called up to the reading of the Torah, and a special sermon is frequently delivered by the rabbi, stressing the boy's new responsibilities and privileges. In many modern synagogues, the rabbi ends his sermon by invoking the *Priestly Blessing or other blessing, and the bar mitzvah boy is given a gift from the congregation. After the service, a festive *Kiddush* is often held, with a banquet on the same or the following day. Some authorities ruled that parents must arrange a banquet when their son became bar mitzvah just as they do on the day of his wedding (see Magen Avraham on Sh. Ar., OḤ 225:2). Among the Jews of Morocco a special *piyyut* is recited when a bar mitzvah boy is called up to the Torah and, in most synagogues, a special **Mi she-Berakh* blessing is made at the end of the reading for the boy and his family.

Putting on Tefillin

The major ritual innovation obligatory on a boy reaching bar mitzvah is that henceforth he is required to put on *tefillin* for the morning prayer. He is usually coached in the forms of the rite some time before the bar mitzvah. The Sephardim and some of the Ḥasidim, interpreting the Kabbalah very exactly, insist that *tefillin* cannot be worn one day before bar mitzvah. Only when the boy has become fully 13 and one day does he keep this commandment. For the Sephardim the first occasion of putting on the *tefillin* was part of the celebration of the bar mitzvah itself. At that time a scholar or elder was honored with aiding the young man in donning the *tefillin*. Ḥasidim of the *Ḥabad* school taught that boys began putting on *tefillin* two months prior to the actual bar mitzvah, the first month without pronouncing the blessing, and the second month saying it.

The Bar Mitzvah Derashah

Solomon Luria (16th century) states that the bar mitzvah celebration was customary among Ashkenazim and that the boy was tutored to deliver a *derashah* ("talmudic discourse") during the banquet (*Yam shel Shelomo* BK 7:37). It usually dealt with some aspect of the rite; Sephardim call it the *tefillin derashah.* The discourse frequently serves as an occasion for the boy to thank his parents for their love and care, and the guests for their participation in his celebration. The custom is still observed today, with sons of traditional families giving a talmudic discourse, and others a more general talk. In Conservative, Reform, and some Orthodox synagogues a prayer before the ark is sometimes said by the bar mitzvah boy in place of the *derashah.*

Most congregational Hebrew schools have special classes for the preparation of bar/bat mitzvah students. In some congregations (notably the United Synagogue of Great Britain) the boy is not allowed to celebrate his bar mitzvah until after he passes an examination in Hebrew and the fundamentals of the Jewish religion.

Since 1967, some boys from Israel and abroad celebrate their bar mitzvah at the Western Wall. Some Jews from outside Israel make a special pilgrimage to celebrate their son's bar mitzvah there.

Confirmation

Reform congregations have instituted what is known as a Confirmation ceremony. This was originally in 19th century German Reform a substitution for bar mitzvah. The ceremony was held at a later age – 16 or 17 – on the grounds that before that age a young person cannot really understand the implications of the rituals. In modern times, especially in the U.S., confirmation has been adopted as a ceremony additional to bar mitzvah which is celebrated in a more traditional manner. The main intention of confirmation was to prolong the period of a child's Jewish education, and as such it is usually a ceremony with a "class" of young people being confirmed at the same time. The ceremony is usually held on or about Shavuot. The confirmands recite various sections from Scriptures and publicly declare their devotion to Judaism. The boys and girls frequently receive a special certificate, testifying their acceptance into the Jewish community.

[Zvi Kaplan]

Bat Mitzvah

The term bat mitzvah occurs only once in the Talmud (BK 15a), in reference to the time a girl becomes subject to the obligations of Jewish law incumbent on adults. While Avot 5:21 asserts that 13 is the age of adult responsibility, Niddah 5:6 rules that the vows of a girl who is 12 and one day are deemed valid, as are the vows of a boy who is 13 and one day. Similarly, after their respective 12th and 13th birthdays, girls and boys must fast on Yom Kippur (Yoma 85). Talmudic discussion in Kiddushin 16b clarifies that a boy is of age when physical signs of adulthood appear after he is 13 plus one day. Maimonides (Yad, Ishut 2:9–10) completes the equation and specifies that a girl's signs of adulthood are those that appear only after her 12th birthday plus one day. Aside from assuming ritual obligations, adult responsibility meant that a young woman was no longer dependent on her father, mother, or brother in marital arrangements and could act on her own behalf. Prior to the modern era this change in a female's status was rarely celebrated in a communal context. It is not until the 19th century that indications of ceremony or public recognition come from Italy, Eastern and Western Europe, Egypt, and Baghdad. These acknowledgements of female religious adulthood include a private blessing, a father's *aliyah* to the Torah, a rabbi's sermon and/or a girl's public examination on Judaic matters. Bat mitzvah as a female ceremony equivalent or identical to the male bar mitzvah is not found until the middle of the 20th century and is an American innovation, discussed in more detail below.

ITALY. The earliest source, from Verona on Passover 1844, refers to an *iniziazione religiosa delle fanciulle* and *la maggiorita delle fanciulle.* This reference to entrance "into minyan" was used for boys and girls. By the end of the century, this ritual had also spread to other cities such as Ancona, Bologna, and Rome. During this confirmation-like process the girl recited some biblical verses and a liturgical selection and a rabbi delivered a sermon. There was great debate in the 19th century Italian community as to whether this was a permitted rite. In Italy today a 12-year-old female is examined by a rabbi, usually on Shavuot or Purim, after which she reads special prayers in Hebrew and Italian in the synagogue; a celebratory party follows. Edda Servi Machlin describes her 1938 bat mitzvah experience in her cookbook, *The Classic Cuisine of Italian Jews* (1981), p. 69.

EUROPE. Some scholars have mentioned Rabbi Jacob *Ettlinger of Germany as favoring some form of puberty lifecycle event. It is clear, however, in Ettlinger's *Binyan Ẓiyyon* 107 (1867), p. 145, that he opposed confirmation or any similar celebration. Rather, in accordance with Danish regulations, he gave some girls a public exam on the completion of their religious studies (*limmudei kodesh*) and then delivered a sermon. All this took place in the synagogue. Intriguing references to bat mitzvah celebrations in various European cities include a confirmation in Warsaw in 1843 and a party in Lvov in 1902. Rabbi Musafiya notes that bat mitzvah celebrations were held in France towards the end of the 19th century. Anecdotal references to bat mitzvah celebrations include that of Charlotte Salomon (1917–1943) in Berlin (see Mary Lowenthal Felstiner, *To Paint Her Life* (1997)).

EGYPT. Rabbi Elijah Hazzan held a synagogue celebration for *benot mitzvah* (pl.) girls who had completed studies in religion and Jewish history in 1907 in Alexandria.

BAGHDAD. One significant early reference to a celebration for a girl is found in the book *Ben Ish Ḥai* by Rabbi *Joseph Ḥayyim b. Elijah of Iraq (1834–1909). In his discussion of *parashat Re'eh*, note 17, vol. 1, p. 132, Rabbi Ḥayyim posits that there is an equal sense of *simḥah* for boys and girls as they reach juridical responsibility; he recommends celebrating the girl's 12th birthday in some liturgical fashion. He declared that even though it was not the custom in his community (Baghdad) to make a *se'udat mitzvah*, nonetheless the event should be celebrated on that day and the girl should wear special (Sabbath) clothing. If at all possible, her father should buy her a new dress so that she could say the benediction *sheheḥeyanu* on the occasion of her bat mitzvah.

ISRAEL. In Israel it became customary to celebrate a girl's 12th birthday with a party. It was called a bat mitzvah but there was rarely any liturgical or synagogue component. In the early 21st century, often all the girls in a class prepare for a group celebration after studying relevant material throughout the school year. Some synagogues and schools do enable a ritual format for girls while some families go to Rachel's tomb or other sacred sites for a party. Tourists and Israelis who desire a liturgical and Torah element for a girl's bat mitzvah may go to the Western Wall to pray with the Women of the Wall.

NORTH AMERICA. There are reports of various forms of bat mitzvah ceremonies in the American Midwest as early as 1907, but the best-known bat mitzvah ritual was created in 1922 by Rabbi Mordecai *Kaplan for his daughter Judith Kaplan *Eisenstein. Although innovative in concept and held in a synagogue, it was not identical to a contemporary bar mitzvah which would have included an *aliyah* and the ritual recitation of a *haftarah*. Rather, Judith Kaplan read a section selected by her father from a printed *Ḥumash* (Five Books of Moses). The egalitarian bat mitzvah format, identical to a bar mitzvah, is not documented until 1940 and did not spread across North America until after the 1960s. The history of these ritual performances developed along denominational lines. Initially, the Reform movement was divided over any bat mitzvah rite as many congregations preferred a group confirmation ceremony for girls and boys at age 15 or 16. However, by the early 1960s, many North American Reform congregations offered prepared girls the option of bat mitzvah as well as confirmation. Although these early *benot mitzvah* generally read from the Torah scroll, their liturgical roles were often less than those of a bar mitzvah. Within the Conservative movement of the 1950s and 1960s there was debate as to where to place a ceremony for girls and what its content should be. During the 1970s and 1980s, the ritual celebration of bat mitzvah became ensconced within Reform, Conservative, and Reconstructionist congregations. At the beginning of the 21st century, most *benot mitzvah* in the Reform, Conservative, and Reconstructionist movements perform the same liturgical roles as a bar mitzvah, including reading from the Torah scroll and recitation of a *haftarah*. For some the ceremony is held on Friday night; but for most it takes place during Sabbath morning services.

By the 1970s many in Orthodox movements also sought ways to fit a bat mitzvah into the established order of worship in ways that were halakhically permissible. One option, established by Hebrew day schools in response to an Orthodox preference for home- or school-based rituals for girls, was a group bat mitzvah celebration. Another choice was to hold a ceremony in the synagogue at a time when no prayer services were taking place. An alternative possibility was to celebrate the bat mitzvah at a separate women's prayer service during which a non-liturgical reading from the Torah could occur. Even in contemporary ḥasidic and ḥaredi communities some format for the recognition and celebration of a girl's initiation as an adult Jew now exists

The major impact of bat mitzvah celebrations has been to increase the level of women's Jewish education and synagogue ritual participation. By the first decade of the 21st century adult bat mitzvah ceremonies had also become a common occurrence in synagogues of all denominations.

LEGAL RESPONSA. Rabbi Moses *Feinstein forbids the use of the sanctuary for an official bat mitzvah. He does allow a special birthday *kiddush* in the sanctuary, adding that the girl may say some appropriate words there after services; he also permits some form of public celebration in synagogue social halls or in the family home. Rabbi J.J. *Weinberg recommends a modest home-based celebration to strengthen the girl's education and attachment to Jewish traditions. A number of 20th century rabbinic decisors, including Rabbi Y. *Nissim, (*Noam* 7:4), Rabbi Ovadiah *Yosef (*Yabi'a Omer* 6:29.4, *Yehaveh Da'at* 2:29, 3:10), and Rabbi Chanoch Grossberg (*Ma'ayan*, 13:42), assert that a *se'udat mitsvah* (obligatory festive meal) is held in honor of a girl's bat mitzvah on her birthday. Rabbi Abraham Musafiya, writing in the latter part of the 19th century (first printed in *Noam* 7 (5724, 1964) p. 4), claims that there is no difference between a boy and a girl in terms of the obligatory nature of the festive meal and that this festive meal is customarily held for boys and girls in France.

RELATED BLESSING. At the time of a bar mitzvah blessing a father traditionally says *Barukh she-petarani me-onsho shel zeh*, indicating that he has been released from responsibility for his son's acts. There is disagreement within Orthodox Judaism whether this blessing is also recited for a girl. Some decisors claim that a father cannot say it on the occasion of a bat mitzvah since he is not obligated to teach his daughter Torah. Others claim that the girl's coming of age at 12 years requires the same parental blessing as that for a boy at thirteen years. Rabbi Ovadiah Yosef favorably quotes Rabbi A. Aburbia, who recommends saying the blessing without God's name (*Yabi'a Omer* OH 6:29, p. 98).

[Norma Baumel Joseph (2nd ed.)]

BIBLIOGRAPHY: L. Loew, *Lebensalter* (1875), 210–22, 410ff.; I. Rivkind, *Le-Ot u-le-Zikkaron. Toledot Bar Mitzvah* (1942), incl. bibl.; Assaf, *Mekorot*, 4 (1943), 108, 114, 127; Sadan (Stock), in: *Dat u-Medinah* (1949), 59ff.; ET, 4 (1952), 165–8; M.Z. Levinsohn-Lavi, in: *Sefer ha-Yovel shel Hadoar* (1952), 42–46; C. Roth, in: A.I. Katsh (ed.), *Bar Mitzvah* (1955), 15–22; J. Nacht, in: *Yeda-Am*, 17–18 (1955), 106–11; Joseph Manspach, *Minhag Bar Miẓvah*, ed. by A.M. Habermann (1958); B. Yashar, *Le-Vat Yisrael be-Hagiyah le-Mitzvot* (1963); S.B. Freehot,

Current Reform Responsa (1969), index. **ADD. BIBLIOGRAPHY:** BAT MITZVAH: J. Weissman Joselit, "Red-Letter Days," in: *The Wonders of America: Reinventing Jewish Culture 1880–1950* (1994), 89–133; S. Barack Fishman, *A Breath of Life* (1993); C. Koller-Fox, "Women and Jewish Education: A New Look at Bat Mitzvah," in: E. Koltun (ed.), *The Jewish Woman: New Perspectives* (1976), 31–42; A.S. Cohen, "Celebration of the Bat Mitzvah," in: *The Journal of Halakhah and Contemporary Society*, 12 (Fall 1986), 5–16; B. Sherwin, "Bar Mitzvah, Bat Mitzvah," in: B. Sherwin, *In Partnership With God: Contemporary Jewish Law and Ethics* (1990); P.E. Hyman, "The Introduction of Bat Mitzva in Conservative Judaism in Postwar America," in: *YIVO Annual*, 19 (1990), 133–46; idem, "Bat Mitzvah," in: Hyman and Moore (eds.), *Jewish Women in America,* (1998) pp. 126–128; Erica Brown, "The Bat Mitzvah in Jewish Law and Contemporary Practice," in: M. Halpern and Ch. Safrai (eds.), *Jewish Legal Writings by Women* (1998), 228–54; L. Katz, "Halakhic Aspects of Bar-Mitzvah and Bat-Mitzvah," in: *Journal of Jewish Music and Liturgy*, 9 (1986), 22–30. I.G. Marcus, *The Jewish Life Cycle: Rites of Passage from Biblical to Modern Times* (2004) 105–23; R. Stein, "The Road to Bat Mitzvah in America," in: P. Nadell and J. Sarna, *Women and American Judaism*, (2001), 223–34; S. Friedland Ben Arza (ed.), *Bat Mitzvah: Collected Writings and Reflections* (Heb., 2002). O. Wiskind Elper, *Traditions and Celebrations for the Bat Mitzvah* (2003); N. Joseph, "Ritual, Law, and Praxis: An American Response/a to Bat Mitsva Celebrations," in: *Modern Judaism*, 22:3 (Fall 2002); idem, "When Do I Get To Say Today I Am a Jew?" in: D. Orenstein (ed.), *Lifecycles*, vol. 1 (1994), 92–93; M. Meyer, *Response to Modernity: A History of the Reform Movement in Judaism* (1988). A. Reiner, "The Attitude Towards Bat-Mitzvah Ceremonies – A Comparative Study of Contemporary Responsa," in: *Netuim*, 10 (2003), pp. 55–77.

BARNA, VICTOR (**Vic**, formerly **Gyozo Braun**; 1911–1972), table tennis champion, winner of 22 world championships in singles, doubles, and team play. Born in Budapest to a printer, Barna learned table tennis playing at the local sports club before joining the Hungarian national team that won the 1929 Swaythling Cup. Barna won his first world singles title in 1930 in Berlin, eventually winning five world singles titles, including four consecutively in the 1930s, plus 17 others in men's and mixed doubles and team championships for Hungary. He also won several open tournaments in North America, Europe, and Australia. Barna's singles career ended when his right (playing) arm was severely injured in an auto accident in 1935, though he continued playing doubles and indeed won the 1939 world championships in mixed doubles. Barna moved to France in 1936 and played there professionally, before moving to England just before the outbreak of World War II. He adopted British nationality and competed for Britain the rest of his career. He played his last world championships in 1954, when he was runner-up in the men's doubles. Barna was noted for his legendary backhand drive, known as the "Barna Flick," and for being extremely agile on his feet, with terrific powers of anticipation and concentration. He is credited with popularizing the sport of table tennis worldwide. He was recognized in his native Hungary as "the most successful Hungarian sportsman of the twentieth century." He wrote *Table Tennis Today* (1962).

[Elli Wohlgelernter (2nd ed.)]

BARNACLE GOOSE MYTHS. The barnacle goose is a migratory bird, whose winter habitat is the Arctic region, when it is seldom seen outside the Arctic circle. In summer, however, large flocks are found on the western shores of the British Isles and other parts of the temperate zone. According to a popular medieval fable, the barnacle goose was produced out of the fruit of a tree, or grew upon the tree attached by its bill (hence called the tree goose), or was produced out of a shell. This fable – the origin of which is obscure – was taken quite literally by both Jews and non-Jews, and in consequence it was a matter of doubt whether it was to be regarded as bird, fish, or a completely distinct species. *Isaac b. Moses of Vienna (*Or Zaru'a*) quotes R. Tam – who was the first to deal with the subject – as ruling that it may be eaten after ritual slaughtering like poultry. This decision was in opposition to the views of contemporary famous scholars who permitted it to be eaten in the same way as fruit. Samuel he-Ḥasid and his son *Judah he-Ḥasid of Regensburg agreed with R. Tam. R. *Isaac b. Joseph of Corbeil forbade it (*Sefer Mitzvot Katan* no. 210), as he regarded it as a species of shellfish. The Zohar (3:156) states that R. Abba saw a tree from whose branches grew geese. The Shulḥan Arukh (YD 84:15) rules that birds that grow on trees are forbidden since they are regarded as creeping things. The fable was disputed, however, by various scholars but as late as 1862 R. Bernard Issachar Dov *Illowy in New Orleans quoted a conflict of authorities whether it might be eaten and vigorously denounced those who would permit it. He too referred to the belief of many early naturalists that it grows on trees.

BIBLIOGRAPHY: J.G.T. Graesse, *Beitraege zur Literatur und Sage des Mittelalters* (1850), 80; Lewysohn, Zool, 362f., no. 515; Ginzberg, Legends, 1 (1909), 32; 5 (1925), 50f.; Zimmels, in: *Minḥat Bikkurim… Arje Schwarz* (1926), 1–9.

[Harry Freedman]

BARNATO, BARNEY (**Barnett Isaacs**; 1852–1897), South African financier and mining magnate. Born in London, Barnato was educated at the Jews' Free School and went to Kimberley, South Africa, in 1873, during the diamond rush. He joined his brother Henry and they began buying diamonds as well as claims which were becoming unworkable as separate units. Within a short time the mines were bringing in an income of $9,000 a week. In 1881 the Barnato brothers formed the Barnato Diamond Mining Company, with capital of over $500,000. It soon rivaled the De Beers Mining Company of Cecil J. Rhodes, who was aiming at control of the diamond fields. The struggle between Rhodes and Barnato ended in 1888 with the amalgamation of the two companies into the De Beers Consolidated Mining Company, in which Barnato became a life governor. In the same year he was elected to the legislative assembly of Cape Colony. With the discovery of the Witwatersrand gold fields, Barnato acquired large holdings in Johannesburg, where the Barnato group eventually became one of the big mining units. In 1895 his optimism and business acumen saved the Rand from a serious slump. He denounced the Jameson Raid of that year which was aimed at overthrowing the government of Paul Kruger, but interceded with Kruger to reduce the offenders' sentences. Barnato was a colorful figure who loved to act in Shakespeare and sport fancy waistcoats. His wealth, financial shrewdness, and mode of living made him almost legendary. His vast interests, however, imposed a considerable strain on him and on a voyage to England in 1897, apparently emotionally disturbed, he jumped overboard and was drowned.

BIBLIOGRAPHY: H. Raymond, *B.I. Barnato* (1897); L. Herrman, *History of the Jews in South Africa* (1935), 228ff.; R. Lewinsohn, *Barney Barnato* (1937); S. Jackson, *The Great Barnato* (1970). **ADD. BIBLIOGRAPHY:** G. Wheatcroft, *The Randlords* (1985), index; ODNB online.

[Lewis Sowden]

BARNAY, LUDWIG (1842–1924), German actor. Son of the secretary of the Hebrew congregation in Budapest, Barnay had a remarkable career as a leading German actor, first in Bohemian Trautenau, then in Budapest, Graz, Leipzig, Vienna, and Frankfurt/Main. In 1874 he became member of the famous ensemble of Meiningen Hoftheater, with which he toured Europe and the U.S. several times. He distinguished himself in heroic roles in Schiller and Shakespeare, winning particular acclaim as William Tell and Mark Antony. Together with Adolph L'Arronge he founded the Deutsche Theater in Berlin in 1883. Despite his famous quarrels with the actor Joseph Kainz, he remained an influential and important figure in German theater life. In competition to L'Arronge, he was founding director of the Berliner Theater from 1887 to 1894 and later he acted in Wiesbaden as director at the Koenigliche Schauspielhaus Berlin and eventually at the Koenigliche Hoftheater in Hannover. His main achievement of lasting effect was the foundation for the union of professional actors (*"Genossenschaft deutscher Buehnenangehoeriger"*) in 1871, which considerably improved the position of actors in German society. Barnay published his memoirs, *Erinnerungen* (2 vols), in 1903.

BIBLIOGRAPHY: Ebert, *Schauspieler werden in Berlin* (1987), index; Brauneck, *Theaterlexikon* (1992), index.

[Marcus Pyka (2nd ed.)]

BARNEA, EZRA (1935–), ḥazzan, educator, and head of Renanot – Institute for Jewish Religious Music. Barnea was born in Jerusalem and from his youth was familiar with Sephardi cantorial music. He studied with Shaul Abbud, author of *Shirei Zimrah*, and with the Jerusalem cantor Moses Ner-Gaon. From the age of ten he was a chanter of the Torah readings and after his bar mitzvah a cantor in the Bukharan neighborhood in Jerusalem. In 1985 he opened a school for Sephardi cantorial music in Jerusalem and was appointed in 1986 the principal of Renanot in Jerusalem. In 1989 he received the Prize of the Ministry of Religious Affairs for his activities on behalf of Jewish music. Among his activities were the documentation and production of recordings of traditional Jewish music, especially liturgical pieces recorded from cantors and other knowledgeable individuals. He also organized a yearly conference on Jewish music during Hanukkah and published books and the periodical *Dukhan* on Jewish music.

[Gila Flam (2nd ed.)]

BARNEA, NAHUM (1944–), Israeli journalist. Barnea was born in Tel Aviv. and graduated in history and political science from the Hebrew University of Jerusalem, where he began his writing career on the university student newspaper. Subsequently, he joined **Davar*, where he worked first as the paper's Jerusalem affairs correspondent, then as the paper's representative in Washington, D.C., for six years, and later as a columnist. In 1981 he won the Sokolow prize for journalism. In 1982 he co-founded the **Koteret Rashit* news magazine. After its closure due to economic difficulties, Barnea joined **Yedioth Ahronoth* as a political columnist. He covered most important political, military, and economic stories in Israel. His reportage was characterized by broad knowledge, analytic acumen, and the ability to give a perspective to events. These qualities, together with his regular presence at news events and an easy pen, made him one of the most widely read newspaper journalists in Israel. His son was killed in a Jerusalem terrorist attack.

[Yoel Cohen (2nd ed.)]

BARNERT, NATHAN (1838–1927), U.S. businessman, public figure, and philanthropist. Barnert was born in Santomischel near Posen, Prussia, and was taken to the U.S. in 1849. After his travels in California during the gold rush, Barnert moved to Paterson, New Jersey, at 20, and opened a clothing establishment. During the Civil War, he filled large contracts for Union Army uniforms, using his profits for business expansion and acquisition of real estate holdings. Barnert retired from mercantile life at the age of 40 to devote all his attention to his profitable real estate interests. He used his capital to create a new industry in Paterson, the furnishing of supplies for paper mills. He also had great success in building large, modern textile mills as speculative projects. A Democrat in a normally Republican city, Barnert was elected to the Paterson Board of Aldermen in 1876 and 1879. He was elected mayor of Paterson in 1883 and 1889, and pursued a reform administration. An observant Jew, Barnert never appeared at City Hall on the Sabbath or festivals. He was a devoted worshiper at Congregation B'nai Jeshurun, to which, in 1889, he donated the land and assumed construction costs for a new synagogue building, whose dedication was attended by President William McKinley. Barnert built a Hebrew school (1904), and a nonsectarian hospital and nurses' home. Among his other philanthropic gifts were the construction of a synagogue for the Jewish community of Santomischel and an orphan asylum in Jerusalem. A statue of Nathan Barnert was dedicated in Paterson's City Hall Square in 1925.

BIBLIOGRAPHY: M. Baum, *Biography of Nathan Barnert* (1914).

[David H. Panitz]

BARNET, WILL (1911–), U.S. painter, graphic artist, and teacher. Barnet was born in Beverly, Massachusetts. He started drawing at age six, recording his childhood home and family. His artistic studies began at the Art School at the Boston Museum of Fine Arts in 1928. In 1931, the year he issued his first lithograph, he received a scholarship to study at the Art Students League (1931–34) in New York City. There he began classes with Stuart Davis and Charles Locke. By 1935 he began serving as the League's official printer, supervising editions by William *Gropper, among others; two years later he became an instructor of graphic art at the League. During these early years Barnet depicted social themes influenced by the work of the Mexican muralists, particularly José Clemente Orozco. He recorded city life in prints such as *Idle Hands* (1935), which shows the mind-dulling effect of the Depression on a homeless man, and in prints such as *Cafeteria Scene* (1934) and *Conflict* (1934). This latter scene depicts a group of bulky men storming a city building. Barnet held his first one-man show at the Eighth Street Playhouse in New York in 1935 and served as the technical adviser in graphic art for the Federal Art Project of the Works Progress Administration in 1936.

In the 1940s he showed his works in various venues in New York and beyond. At this time he began to focus on painting, making colorful, simplified canvases of his children and wife. He taught in several settings, most notably painting at the Art Students League (until 1980) and graphic art at the Cooper Union in New York. Other institutions at which Barnet taught include the Pennsylvania Academy of Fine Arts and the University of Minnesota at Duluth. Students who later went on to illustrious art careers include Mark *Rothko, Audrey Flack, and Donald Judd. In the 1950s, Barnet's printwork and painting became even more abstract, influenced by the simple design and balance of American Indian handicraft design. This interest relates to his goal of creating a "real American art." Throughout his career, Barnet oscillated between abstraction and figuration.

BIBLIOGRAPHY: R. Doty, *Will Barnet* (1984); G. Stavitsky, *Will Barnet: A Timeless World* (2000).

[Samantha Baskind (2nd ed.)]

BARNETT, JOEL, BARON (1923–), British politician. Educated in Manchester and by profession an accountant, Joel Barnett was a Labour member of Parliament from 1964 until 1983. After serving as an Opposition spokesman on economic affairs from 1970 to 1974, Barnett held office as chief secretary to the Treasury from March 1974 until the fall of the Labour government in May 1979. From February 1977 until May 1979 he served in James Callaghan's cabinet. Barnett is probably best known for devising the Barnett Formula, under which grants to Scotland and Wales were greater per capita than grants to England, in order to reflect the geographical problems of service provision in these two areas. He is the author of *Inside the Treasury* (1992) and was given a life peerage after he retired from the House of Commons in 1983.

[William D. Rubinstein (2nd ed.)]

BARNETT, JOHN (1802–1890), composer. Barnett was born in Bedford, England. His father Bernhard Beer, a cousin of Giacomo Meyerbeer, had changed his name to Barnett upon settling in England. John Barnett was a prolific composer for the London stage. In his opera *The Mountain Sylph* (1834) he reintroduced the composed recitative into English opera in place of the spoken dialogue. His attempt to establish an opera house at St. James's Theater was unsuccessful. In later life he settled at Cheltenham as a music teacher. He composed chamber music and songs, and published some writings on singing. His daughter, Clara Kathleen Rogers (1844–1931), became a well-known opera singer.

BARNETT, JOHN FRANCIS (1837–1916), composer. Born in London, nephew of the composer John *Barnett, he won the Queen's Scholarship at the Royal Academy of Music at the age of 12, and played Mendelssohn's piano concerto at a performance conducted by Louis Spohr. He was appointed professor at the Royal College of Music, London, in 1883. His works include piano, chamber, and orchestral music, and choral cantatas; the most successful were settings of Coleridge's *Ancient Mariner* (1867) and Keats' *Eve of St. Agnes* (1913).

BARNETT, LIONEL DAVID (1871–1960), British Orientalist. Barnett, who was born in Liverpool, was keeper of the department of Oriental printed books and manuscripts at the British Museum from 1908 to 1936. He was an authority on Indian literature, and lectured in Indian history at the London University School of Oriental and African Studies until 1946. He wrote *Antiquities of India* (1913) and *Hindu Gods and Heroes* (1922), and his translations included *A History of Greek Drama* (1900) and, from the Sanskrit, *Brahma-Knowledge* (1907). Barnett was an elder of the Spanish and Portuguese congregation in London, and in 1931 published *El libro de los acuerdos*, an English translation from the earliest records of the congregation, for the years 1663 to 1681. He also edited the Bevis Marks records of the contributions made to history by the congregation (2 vols., 1940–49).

Lionel Barnett's son, RICHARD DAVID BARNETT (1909–1986), like his father, made his career at the British Museum. Born in London, he began in 1932 as assistant keeper in the department of Egyptian and Assyrian antiquities and in 1955 was appointed head of the newly established department of Western Asiatic antiquities. From 1933 to 1935 he was secretary of the British School in Athens. Richard Barnett's research extended to Assyriology, the cultures of Syria, Phoenicia, and Asia Minor as well as biblical archaeology. In 1956 he organized the special exhibition at the Victoria and Albert Museum in London commemorating the tercentenary of the resettlement of Jews in the British Isles, and his catalog of the exhibition was one of his most distinguished publications. He was president of the Jewish Historical Society of England (1959–61) and contributed several important papers on the history of the Sephardim in England to its transactions. His publications include: *Carchemish: Report on the Excavations* at *Djerabis* (vol. 3 (with Sir L. Woolley, 1952)); *Catalogue of the Nimrod Ivories in the British Museum* (1957); *Assyrian Palace Reliefs and Their Influence on the Sculptures of Babylonia and Persia* (1960); *The Sculptures of Aššur-naṣir apli II...* (1962); and *Illustrations of Old Testament History* (1966). After his death the Jewish Historical Society of England established an annual lectureship in his honor.

ADD. BIBLIOGRAPHY: R. Loewe, "In Memoriam: R.D. Barnett (1909–86)," in: JHSET, 29 (1982–86), xv–xvii; "Richard David Barnett," in: ODNB online.

[Penuel P. Kahane]

BARNETT, SIR LOUIS EDWARD (1865–1946), New Zealand surgeon and professor. Barnett was born in Wellington, New Zealand, and in 1895 received a permanent lectureship in surgery at Otago University, where from 1905 to 1924 he was professor. He served with the rank of lieutenant-colonel in the Royal Australian and New Zealand Medical Corps (1915–17) and was knighted for his overseas war service. Barnett was one of the founders of the Radium Insitute in Dunedin and a pioneer in X-ray and radium research at Otago University. Most of his work was in the fields of cancer and hydatids research, and as a result of his efforts the incidence of hydatids in New Zealand was considerably reduced.

[Maurice S. Pitt]

BARNETT, ZERAH (1843–1935), pioneer of the modern Ereẓ Israel settlement and one of the founders of Petaḥ Tikvah. Barnett, who was born in Tytuvênai, Lithuania, settled in London in 1864 as a fur manufacturer and trader. There he organized communal life for the East European immigrants who remained outside the Anglo-Jewish community. After acquiring British nationality in 1871, he went to Ereẓ Israel for the first time and helped establish the Me'ah She'arim quarter outside the walls of Old Jerusalem. Having spent all his savings, Barnett returned to London to earn money and then went back to Ereẓ Israel – a process which he repeated 15 times. Wherever he went, he advocated Jewish settlement in Ereẓ Israel. In 1878 Barnett joined the group that established Petaḥ Tikvah. As London Ḥovevei Zion delegate to the *Katowice Conference (1884), he described the experiences and hardships of the new settlers from first-hand knowledge. Early in the 1890s Barnett settled in Jaffa, where, in order to improve living conditions, he built the Neveh Shalom quarter, and moved there with his family. He helped build the Sha'arei Torah school, introducing Hebrew as the language of instruction. He also founded the Or Zore'aḥ Yeshivah in Jaffa. Barnett published his memoirs, *Zikhronot*, in 1929. He died in Jaffa and was buried in Jerusalem.

BIBLIOGRAPHY: H. Trager, *Pioneers in Palestine* (1923); A. Yaari, *Goodly Heritage* (1958), 80, 89–93; Y. Churgin (ed.), *Sifriyyat Rishonim*, 1 no. 9 (1943); G. Kressel, *Em ha-Moshavot Petaḥ Tikvah* (1953), 56f.

[Getzel Kressel / Yehuda Slutsky]

BARNOWSKY, VIKTOR (1875–1952), German actor and theater director. Born in Berlin, Barnowsky became director of the Kleines Theater in 1905. From 1913 to 1924 he managed the Lessingtheater, and from 1925 to 1930 the Theater in der Koeniggraetzerstrasse and the Komoedienhaus, becoming one of the most important figures in the privately owned German theaters. He left Germany when Hitler came to power and went to the U.S., where he wrote film scripts and taught theater history at Fordham University and Hunter College, New York City.

BARNSTON, HENRY (1868–1949), U.S. Reform rabbi and scholar. Barnston was born Henry Barnstein in Dover, England, and ordained at Jews College, London. He attended University College in London and earned his Ph.D. in ancient Semitic languages at the University of Heidelberg, where he published *The Targum of Onkelos, According to the Yemenite Manuscripts* and collaborated on Aramaic and Chaldean dictionaries. In 1900, seeking an atmosphere more conducive to the practice of liberal Judaism, he immigrated to the United States to serve as the rabbi of Congregation Beth Israel in Houston, Texas. Beth Israel, the oldest and wealthiest synagogue in the city, had suffered a split when more traditional members left in protest against the congregation's move to Reform. Barnston, who changed his name after World War I in order to sound less German, took maximum advantage of his congregants' financial resources to build a temple widely considered to be the finest in the Southwest. At the same time, under Barnston's leadership, the congregation's membership increased tenfold to become the city's largest synagogue. Barnston's influence extended far beyond his congregation: he founded the Jewish Welfare Service, served as president of the local B'nai B'rith, and lectured on behalf of the Jewish Chautauqua Society and the Houston Conference of Christians and Jews. Statewide, he co-founded the Texas Kallah of Rabbis (comprising Orthodox, Conservative, and Reform members) and was elected president of the Texas Association of Rabbis. Over the course of his half-century in Houston – he became rabbi emeritus in 1943 and held that position until his death – Barnston emerged as a civic leader as well: he founded the Community Chest and is credited with forming the Houston Symphony Society and nurturing it into the renowned Houston Symphony Orchestra. He was also active in Houston's Ministerial Alliance and Rotary Club. While Barnston would not take any public stand on civil rights, he did join together with the First Methodist Church in an unprecedented gesture of ecumenical defiance of the Ku Klux Klan. Although he was a member and supporter of the anti-Zionist American Council for Judaism, he resisted his congregation's pressure for him to become a more outspoken activist in the organization. By the time Barnston was promoted to rabbi emeritus, he was the dean of Houston clergymen.

BIBLIOGRAPHY: D. Lefkowitz, *Central Conference of American Rabbis 61st Convention Publication* (1950); H.A. Weiner, *The Jewish Stars of Texas: Rabbis and Their Work* (1999).

[Bezalel Gordon (2nd ed.)]

BARON, BERNHARD (1850–1929), industrialist and philanthropist. Born in Rostov-on-Don, Russia, Baron immigrated to the United States as a boy and worked in a Maryland cigar factory. In 1890 he began manufacturing cigarettes by hand, to be sold at a cheap price. He opened a factory in Baltimore in 1894 and two years later perfected his own cigarette-making machine. In 1896 he took his invention to London, where he set up a company for manufacturing cigarettes. Seven years later he purchased Carreras, one of the oldest tobacco companies in England, and as a result of an extensive advertising campaign expanded it into one of the largest cigarette companies in the world. Within 20 years Baron had accumulated a fortune with over $20 million, much of which he proceeded to give away on an unprecedented scale. He set up two charitable trusts in his name, which distributed over £1 million to hospitals and children's homes, and made substantial gifts to the Jewish National Fund, the Keren Hayesod, and the Hebrew University of Jerusalem. He also made possible the erection of a new building for St. George's Jewish welfare settlement in the East End of London. Despite his enormous wealth – he left £4.9 million – Baron remained simple in his tastes and despised opulence. He refused a title but after his death his son, Louis Bernhard Baron (1876–1934), was made a baronet.

BIBLIOGRAPHY: P.H. Emden, *Jews of Britain* (1943), 491–5; DNB, *Concise Dictionary*, pt. 2 (1961), s.v. **ADD. BIBLIOGRAPHY:** G. Black, "Bernhard Baron: Tobacco and Philanthropy," in: TJHSE, 36 (1999–2001), 71–80; ODNB online; DBB, I, 177–81.

BARON, DEVORAH (1887–1956), Hebrew author. Daughter of a rabbi, she was born in Ozdah, Belorussia, and published her first Hebrew stories in Eastern European periodicals (**Ha-Meliẓ* and **Ha-Ẓefirah*). In 1911 she settled in Ereẓ Israel and later married Yosef *Aharonovitz, a prominent Labor Zionist leader and the editor of **Ha-Po'el ha-Ẓa'ir*, for which she was the literary editor.

She published *Sippurim*, her first volume of short stories in 1927, and in 1934, when the Bialik Prize was instituted, she was its first recipient. Following her husband's death in 1937, she edited his collected works together with Eliezer Shoḥat. She received awards for *Le-Et Attah* (1943), a volume of short stories drawn from her experiences as an exile in Egypt during World War I, and for her collected short stories *Parshiyyot* (1951). Childhood reminiscences and Jewish life in Eastern Europe are major themes in Devorah Baron's fiction. Her style, influenced by 19th-century European fiction, combines realism with impressionism. She writes movingly of her parents' home and her mother is often her favorite heroine. She is first described in "*Bereshit*" ("In the Beginning"), in "*Meẓulah*" ("Depths"), and in other stories, frequently portrayed as an unfortunate widow, struggling to maintain her orphaned children. Devorah Baron's Jewish town is permeated by a deep sense of loneliness experienced in the midst of an alien world and of the insecurity caused by poverty and anti-Jewish prejudice. At the same time, until the Holocaust, the Jewish town throbbed with a life which drew upon the inner resources of a deep faith. Its spirit was nurtured by a remarkable historical memory; its physical existence was safeguarded by the fertility of its families. The story "*Mishpaḥah*" ("Family"), for example, describes how an attempt to force divorce upon a childless couple is prevented, and ends with a miracle of triumphant motherhood. *Me-Emesh* ("Since Last Night," 1956), the last volume to be published during the writer's lifetime, contains four stories which describe Ereẓ Israel during World War II, the volunteers who joined the British Army, and an encounter with the remnants of European Jewry. The short story of one bereaved mother epitomizes the fate of the Jewish town and of all Eastern European Jewry, from the period of the slaughter of the defenseless in "normal" times to the "final solution" under the Nazis.

In her later years, while confined to her sickbed, Devorah Baron composed a group of stories depicting the world as seen through the window of an "invalid's room" ("*Be-Lev ha-Kerakh*," in *Parashiyyot*). Her perception remained sharp to the end, and her stories are animated by a deep empathy for the weak and the innocent. No other woman writer in Israel was as familiar with the sources of Judaism as Devorah Baron. Every human experience in her stories finds an echo in the age-old heritage of her people and in its literature. The rhythm of almost every period of Hebrew prose is clearly felt in the flow of her narrative. She is a true poet of the lost world of the Jewish town. In the wake of the growing interest in the works of Hebrew women writers, various academic studies and plays (e.g., those by Avivah Gali) have dealt with the life and writing of Baron. A selection of her stories translated into English appeared in 1969 under the title *The Thorny Path*, followed in 2001 by *The First Day and Other Stories*. A list of her works translated into English appears in Goell, Bibliography, 62. Bibliographical information and 118 letters appear in the posthumously published *Aggav Orḥa* (1960).

BIBLIOGRAPHY: J. Fichmann, *Benei Dor* (1952), 254–87; Y. Keshet, *Maskiyyot* (1953), 82–100; Y. Zmora, *Sifrut al Parashat Dorot*, 3 (1950), 113–30; R. Wallenrod, *The Literature of Modern Israel* (1956), index; R. Katznelson-Shazar, *Al Admat ha-Ivrit* (1966). **ADD. BIBLIOGRAPHY:** G. Shaked, *Ha-Sipporet ha-Ivrit*, 1 (1977), 452–66; N. Govrin, *Ha-Maḥzit ha-Rishonah: Devorah Baron, Ḥayyehah vi-Yeẓiratah* (1988); L. Rattok, *Ha-Kol ha-Aḥer: Sipporet Nashim Ivrit* (1994), 274–87; A. Lieblich, *Conversations with Dvora: An Experimental Biography of the First Modern Hebrew Writer* (1977); N. Seidman, *A Marriage Made in Heaven: The Sexual Politics of Hebrew and Yiddish* (1997); O. Lubin, *Ishah Koret Ishah* (2003), 116–59; 240–53. **WEBSITE:** www.ithl.org.il.

[Rachel (Katznelson) Shazar]

BARON, JOSEPH ALEXANDER (1917–1999), English novelist. Born Joseph Alexander Bernstein in Maidenhead, Berkshire, Baron's first work, *From the City, from the Plough* (1948), was inspired by World War II service during the invasion of Normandy. Anglo-Jewish tensions are explored in *With Hope, Farewell* (1952; reissued in 1962 as *The Thunder of Peace*); and the East London of Baron's childhood is the setting of *The Lowlife* (1963) and its sequel, *Strip Jack Naked* (1966). He also wrote a historical novel, *The Golden Princess* (1954), and *King Dido* (1969). During the 1930s, Baron was a Communist but increasingly broke with radical politics. His current reputation is that of an outstanding but neglected writer.

BIBLIOGRAPHY: ODNB online.

[William D. Rubinstein (2nd ed.)]

BARON, JOSEPH LOUIS (1894–1960), U.S. Reform rabbi and author. Baron was born in Vilna, Poland (then Lithuania), and immigrated with his family at the age of 13 to the United States, where they settled in New York City. He attended the Rabbi Isaac Elchanan Yeshiva and Columbia University, where he earned his B.A. (1914) and M.A. (1916). While at Columbia, he also studied at the Jewish Theological Seminary, helped found the Zionist youth movement *Young Judaea (1910), served on the staff of the New York Board of Education, and contributed articles to several New York newspapers and magazines. In 1920, Baron was ordained at *Hebrew Union College, having interrupted his rabbinical studies to serve Temple Sholom of Chicago when the congregation's rabbi entered the U.S. Army Chaplaincy during World War I. He had also attended the University of Cincinnati, edited the Hebrew Union College Monthly, and organized both the Young Judaea Council of Cincinnati and the Jewish Center of Norwood, Ohio. He earned a Ph.D. from the University of Chicago in 1932.

In 1920, Baron became rabbi of Tri-City Temple Emanuel, which served the Jewish populations of Davenport, Iowa, and Moline and Rock Island, Illinois. During his six-year tenure, he established the Tri-City Jewish Charities, the *Tri-City Scribe*, the Ezra School, the Emanuel Religious School, the Davenport Lodge of B'nai B'rith, and the local Council of Jewish Youth Clubs. He also taught at an extension of the University of Iowa and helped found Congregation Judah of Cedar Rapids, Iowa. In the summers, Baron traveled to New York City to work in social service under Rabbi Stephen *Wise of the Free Synagogue.

Baron's second – and last – congregation was Temple Emanu-El (later Emanu-El B'ne Jeshurun) in Milwaukee, Wisconsin, where he was to spend 35 years as a religious and civic leader (1926–51 as rabbi, 1951–60 as rabbi emeritus). Under his stewardship, the congregation grew to comprise a library, a museum, a modernized religious school, and auxiliary organizations. In the larger community, he was instrumental in establishing the Milwaukee Round Table of the National Conference of Christians and Jews, the Milwaukee Jewish Council, the Milwaukee Chapter of the American Jewish Committee, and the Yavneh School for Unaffiliated Jewish Children. In addition, he served on the boards of the Milwaukee Jewish Community Center, Federated Jewish Charities, and the Jewish Welfare Fund.

Statewide, Baron helped establish a number of synagogues and organizations. He also served on the Governor's Commission on Human Rights. On a national level, Baron was a member of the Board of Governors of Hebrew Union College (1937–40) and of the Joint CCAR-UAHC Commission on Religious Education (1926–27). In 1939, the Union of American Hebrew Congregations adopted his plan for a network of youth clubs that was to become, under the full-time guidance of Rabbi Samuel *Cook, the National Federation of Temple Youth (now called the North American Federation of Temple Youth).

Baron, who lectured on philosophy at State Teachers' College and the University of Wisconsin-Milwaukee, as well as for the Jewish Chautauqua Society, also developed a reputation as a scholar. A frequent contributor to academic journals and encyclopedias, he was the author of four books: *Death in Jewish Folk Religion* (1932); *In Quest of Integrity* (1936); *Candles in the Night* (1940); and *Stars and Sand* (1943). He is best known, however, for researching, compiling, and editing the valuable compendium of Jewish wisdom from throughout the ages, *A Treasury of Jewish Quotations* (1956, 1985). With its vast collection of 18,000 quotations, it remains one of the greatest Jewish reference resources of the 20th century.

[Bezalel Gordon (2nd ed.)]

BARON, SALO (Shalom) WITTMAYER (1895–1989), historian. Baron was born in Tarnow (Galicia) and taken to Vienna early in World War I. He studied at the university there and received doctorates in philosophy (1917), political science (1922), and law (1923); he was ordained by the Jewish Theological Seminary in Vienna in 1920. Baron taught history at the Jewish Teachers College (Juedisches Paedagogium) in Vienna during the years 1919–26. He went to the United States at the invitation of Stephen S. Wise to teach at the Jewish Institute of Religion in New York and remained at the Institute from 1927 until 1930. From 1930 to 1963 he taught at Columbia University, and served as director of the Center of Israel and Jewish Studies at Columbia from 1950 to 1968. From 1957 he also taught at the Jewish Theological Seminary. Baron was the first member of an American history faculty to teach Jewish studies. The many such chairs that now exist owe much to his example, and a substantial number of his former students are among their occupants.

Among Baron's many involvements in public and academic affairs were his presidency of the American Academy for Jewish Research (1940–43, 1958–66, and 1968 on); his presidency of the Conference on Jewish Social Studies (1941–54, 1963–67), and honorary presidency (1955–62 and 1967 on); his presidency of the American Jewish Historical Society (1953–55); his founding and presidency of Jewish Cultural Reconstruction, which after World War II worked in identifying and reclaiming the libraries and other cultural treasures despoiled by the Nazis; and his trusteeship of Tel Aviv University from 1967. From 1952 he was a corresponding member of the International Commission for a Scientific and Cultural History of Mankind. Baron's first major work, *Judenfrage auf dem Wiener Kongress* (1920), dealt with the Jewish question at the Congress of Vienna. He began to write articles as a youth and subsequently wrote many hundreds. Using his exceptional range of talents in many languages and disciplines,

Baron undertook the largest synthetic work of Jewish history in the contemporary period, *A Social and Religious History of the Jews* (3 vols., 1937; 2nd ed., vols. 1–17, 1952–80; index to vols. 1–8, 1960). His emphasis has been on the social history of the people, rather than on the achievements of individual figures; on elements and areas of cross-fertilization between Jews and their environment, rather than on pogroms and suffering; and on the Jewish Diaspora and Ereẓ Israel as the two centers of Jewish creativity, contrary to the views both of a Diaspora-oriented historian, such as Simon *Dubnow, and the new school of Israel-centered scholars, such as Ben Zion *Dinur. A bibliography that covers his works to 1955 appears in a Festschrift in his honor (*Essays on Jewish Life and Thought*, 1959). In addition to the works mentioned above, Baron's major publications are *Bibliography of Jewish Social Studies 1938–39* (1941), *The Jewish Community* (3 vols., 1942), *Modern Nationalism and Religion* (1947), *Jews of the United States*, 1790–1840, *A Documentary History* (edited with J.L. Blau) 3 vols., 1963, *Russian Jews Under Tsars and Soviets* (1964), and *History and Jewish Historians* (1964). Baron edited *Essays on Maimonides* (1941), *Judaism, Postbiblical and Talmudic Periods* (1954); he coedited *Freedom and Reason* (1951), a Festschrift in memory of Morris Raphael Cohen, and wrote the introductory essay for *Jerusalem: City Holy and Eternal* (1954). Baron's *Ancient and Medieval Jewish History* (1973) is a volume of essays written over a long period of time which deal in particular with the status of Jews in Christian lands during the Middle Ages. He was also one of the editors of the quarterly *Jewish Social Studies* from its appearance in 1939, and a consulting editor of the *Encyclopaedia Judaica*.

[Arthur Hertzberg]

BARON DE HIRSCH FUND, fund established by Baron Maurice de *Hirsch, the financier and philanthropist who dedicated his fortune to the welfare of East European Jews at a time when worsening conditions in Russia made mass emigration a stark necessity. Convinced that modern secular education could ameliorate the lot of his oppressed brethren, De Hirsch hoped to regenerate them into a class of independent farmers and handicraftsmen in the New World. In 1889, on the advice of Oscar S. *Straus and Michael *Heilprin, De Hirsch allocated the proceeds of a $2,400,000 fund toward agricultural colonies and trade schools in the United States. With the cooperation of Jacob Schiff and other American Jewish leaders, the Baron de Hirsch Fund was incorporated in New York in 1891. Judge Myer S. Isaacs became president; Schiff, vice president; and the trustees included Straus, Mayer Sulzberger, and William Hackenburg. A subsidized rural community, Woodbine, was established in southern New Jersey, with an agricultural school which functioned until 1917. In New York the Baron de Hirsch Trade School continued to serve a generation of immigrants. Significant also was the fund's support of the Jewish Agricultural Society and of classes in English, legal aid, and other services to integrate newcomers in America.

BIBLIOGRAPHY: S. Joseph, *History of the Baron de Hirsch Fund* (1935).

[Jehoshua Brand]

BARONDESS, JOSEPH (1867–1928), U.S. labor and communal leader. Barondess was born in Kamenets-Podolsk, Ukraine. He immigrated to the U.S. in 1888, working in New York City as a cloakmaker. Soon after, he joined the United Hebrew Trades and became a labor organizer in the garment industry, helping to lead the first great cloakmakers' strike in 1890. Indicted in 1891 on an extortion charge brought against him by the cloak manufacturers, Barondess was sentenced to a 21-month prison term but was released in a few weeks, after widespread protests and petitions for his pardon. His career as an organizer ended when he led an unsuccessful strike in 1894, but he remained active in the Socialist Labor Party, joining its moderate wing in 1898 in the battle against Daniel *De Leon, which led to the founding of the Socialist Party in 1901. By then, however, Barondess had retired from socialist politics and was devoting himself largely to an insurance business that he had started. In his new role as a successful businessman, Barondess accepted appointment to the National Civic Foundation in 1900 and to the New York City Board of Education in 1910. Partly as a reaction to the Russian pogroms of 1903, Barondess became active in the Zionist movement and during the last years of his life served as an honorary vice president of the Zionist Organization of America. He was also among the founders of the American Jewish Congress and a member of the American-Jewish delegation to the Versailles peace talks in 1919. His career typified that of many immigrants, whose process of integration in the U.S. was marked by initial disillusionment with American society, socialism, a higher economic status, and finally a retreat from radical political activity and a return to the Jewish fold.

BIBLIOGRAPHY: *New York Times* (June 20, 1928), 25; B. Weinstein, *Di Yidishe Yunions in Amerike* (1929), 116, 319–36.

BAROU, NOAH (1889–1955), economist. Born in Poltava, Russia, Barou became involved in revolutionary activities as a student and was exiled. After studying in Germany, he returned to Russia in 1913 and was general secretary of the central committee of the illegal left-wing Zionist organization, *Po'alei Zion. After the 1917 Revolution he was one of the three secretaries of the Ukrainian Trade Union Congress. In 1922 he left Russia and eventually settled in England, where he served from 1923 to 1936 as general secretary of the Po'alei Zion World Federation. He was one of the founders of the *World Jewish Congress and an active member of the *Board of Deputies of British Jews. In the early 1950s, Barou made the first contacts with representatives of the West German Federal Republic that led to the meeting of Nahum *Goldmann, president of the Jewish Material Claims Conference, with Chancellor Konrad Adenauer. This meeting laid the foundations for the *reparations eventually made to Jews for material losses at the hands of the Nazis. An authority on cooperative finance, Barou published numerous monographs in English. They include *Cooperative Banking* (1932), *Cooperation in the Soviet Union* (1946), and *British Trade Unions* (1947). He edited *The Cooperative Movement in Labour Britain* (1948).

BIBLIOGRAPHY: H.F. Infield (ed.), *Essays… in Memory of Dr. Noah Barou 1889–1955* (1962), includes bibliography.

[Cecil Roth]

BARR, ROSEANNE (1952–), U.S. actress and comedian. Brought up in Salt Lake City, Utah, Barr had a checkered youth and adolescence. Dropping out of high school, she worked as a waitress and regaled her customers with her brash, irreverent humor. She made her way into comedy, working punk clubs and motorcycle bars. She evolved an act that, in her own words, could "get inside the stereotype [of the housewife] and make it three-dimensional from within." She toured nationally on the comedy club circuit, where she fine-tuned her characterization of the frumpy, controlling, acid-tongued "Domestic Goddess." She made well-received appearances on late night talk shows before starring in her own comedy specials on HBO. In 1985 she successfully auditioned for the Comedy Store in Los Angeles. In 1986 the Carsey-Werner Company approached her with a proposal for developing a situation comedy based on her stand-up routines. By 1987 *The Roseanne Barr Show* had won cable television's Ace awards for best special feature and Barr herself was named best female in a comedy.

Barr rose to American media superstardom with *Roseanne* on ABC (1988–97). With John Goodman playing her husband in the series, Barr succeeded, as the eponymous mother of three, in presenting a realistic, no-holds-barred portrayal of working-class American life. In 1993 Barr won an Emmy and a Golden Globe award for outstanding lead actress in a comedy series.

The popularity of her sitcom broadened the audience for Barr as a public persona and greatly increased her power within show business. She pushed boundaries by having the series take risks and raising such issues as gender, homosexuality, and family dysfunction. The forthrightness of these dramatic moments was rare in primetime sitcoms, but the series continued to appeal to a wide audience. She did not write the scripts but had a good deal of artistic control. Many of the plots drew on aspects of her life prior to her success or referred to events in her own life at the time. Other episodes included dialogues that she proposed which addressed particular themes or issues.

In 1998 Barr was the host of her own daytime talk show, which lasted two seasons.

She appeared in several films: *She-Devil* (1989); the voice of Julie in *Look Who's Talking Two* (1990), *Freddy's Dead* (1991); *Even Cowgirls Get the Blues* (1994), *Blue in the Face* (1995), and the voice of Maggie in *Home on the Range* (2004).

Like certain other high-profile celebrities such as Madonna, Sandra Bernhard, Britney Spears, and Demi Moore, Barr became involved in Kabbalah, asserting that it was the force behind her own reinvention and helped her transform chaos into serenity. Barr has written two books – *Roseanne: My Life as a Woman* (1989) and *My Lives* (1994).

[Rohan Saxena and Ruth Beloff (2nd ed.)]

BARRASSA, JACOB (17th century), Marrano physician and writer. Born as Diego de Barros, probably in Portugal, he studied science, medicine, and astronomy in Spain, and published an annual "prognostication and calendar," *Prognóstico e lunario* (e.g. Seville, 1630 and 1635), based in part on Semitic sources. He embraced Judaism in Amsterdam shortly afterward and wrote a polemical work (still unpublished) on the ostensibly difficult passages of Scripture. He was one of the "Parnasim de Talmud Torah" in 1642, and a warden of the community in 1651.

BIBLIOGRAPHY: C. Roth, *Life of Menasseh ben Israel* (1934), 122–3.

[Cecil Roth]

BARRENNESS AND FERTILITY, the inability or ability of man and woman to procreate. Procreation is considered a blessing in the Bible and it is a commandment (Gen. 1:28; 9:7; Rashi, *ibid.*) applicable to all Jewish men, although not to Jewish women (Yev. 65b–66a). The world was created to be inhabited (Isa. 45:18) and God's blessings bestowed on Israel always included fecundity (Lev. 26:9; Deut. 28:11) and the absence of barrenness (Ex. 23:26; Deut. 7:14). Children are seen as the greatest blessing: "a heritage of the Lord" (Ps. 127:3–5); "Thy wife shall be as a fruitful vine… thy children like olive plants…" (*ibid.*, 128:3–4). The prodigious fertility of the Israelites in Egypt antagonized the Egyptians (Ex. 1:7, 12) and is interpreted by the Midrash (Tanh. and Rashi ad loc.) to imply that the women bore "six (children) at once." Procreation is one of the main purposes of marriage, and in later times an offspring (especially a male offspring) was also prized because it meant that *Kaddish* would be recited in one's memory; hence the popular phrase "to have a *Kaddish*" for a (male) child. Barrenness was a curse and a punishment (Lev. 20:20–21; Jer. 22:30, and MK 27b); Abimelech and his wives were punished, though only temporarily, with barrenness (Gen. 20:17–18), and so was Michal, Saul's daughter and David's wife (II Sam. 6:23). Sarah, Rebekah, Rachel, Samson's mother, Hannah, and the Shunamite woman were all barren at first, but God, who holds the key to fecundity (Ta'an. 2a; cf. Men. 98a), granted their and their husbands' prayers (cf. Ps. 113:9). The Midrash fully acknowledged the domestic suffering of childless women: even if the barren wife had no religious obligation to fulfill, she had failed to fulfill the primary expectation of her social role, since "it is children who assure a wife's position in her home" (Gen. R. 71:5). The childless matriarchs became important metaphors for consolation and comfort. Enumerations of these seven barren women whose yearnings for children were ultimately fulfilled included the personified Israel of some future time, based on the characterization of Zion as a barren woman in Isaiah 54:1 (Pesikta de-Rav Kahana 20:1).

Rachel preferred death to childlessness (Gen. 30:1), which prompted the comment of the *amora* Joshua b. Levi that to be without children is death (Ned. 64b). A childless scholar is not eligible to sit on the Sanhedrin (San. 36b. However, teaching Torah to the son of another person is equivalent to having fathered him (Sanh. 19b, 99b). Ben Sira said that it was better to die childless than to have children who were without the fear of the Lord (Ecclus. 16:1–4). According to a rabbinic story, King Hezekiah had refrained from procreation because he had foreseen that his children would be sinners but was rebuked by the prophet Isaiah, "What have you to do with the secrets of the All Merciful? You have to do your duty and let God do what it pleases Him" (Ber. 10a). The cause of sterility may lie as much with the husband as with the wife; this is suggested by Abraham (Gen. 15:2) and by the Talmud for both Abraham and Isaac (Yev. 64a; cf. Num. R. 10:5). A husband should divorce his wife after ten years of childless marriage; though she may marry again (Yev. 6:6; Sh. Ar., EH 154:6). Some men in childless marriages chose to take a second wife rather than divorce an apparently infertile spouse (Yev. 65a). Conversely, the Talmud records instances of childless wives who successfully petitioned rabbinic courts to compel their unwilling husbands to divorce them after 10 years of infertile marriages based on their fears of an impoverished widowhood and old age without the support of offspring (Yev. 65b). Aggadic texts generally deplore dissolution of marriages, even when male procreation is at stake, presenting preservation of a loving childless marriage as a situation where human needs and feelings overrule legal prescriptions. Such midrashic traditions emphasize instead the efficacy of prayer and the necessity of faith in God (*Pesikta de-Rab Kahana* 22:2; Song R. 1, 4:2).

Distinction ought to be made between accidental sterility and congenital or self-inflicted impotence or barrenness. Deuteronomy 23:2 prohibits an impotent man to marry a free-born Israelite (see Yev. 8:2) when the impotence is self-inflicted (*ibid.*, 75b; cf. Jos., Ant., 4:290). A priest who "hath his stones crushed" is unfit for Temple service (Lev. 21:20). The Talmud defines an *eilonit* ("ram-like, barren") as a woman who by the age of 18 or 20 is without the symptoms of feminity (ET, 1 (1947), 243–46 and ref.). According to some authorities, marriage to an *eilonit*, when contracted in ignorance of her condition, is invalid. Impotence and sterility may be only temporary, due to undernourishment (Ket. 10b). Certain foods, such as eggs, fish, garlic, wine, milk, cheese, and fat meat increase sexual potency (Ber. 40a; Sot. 11b; Yoma 18a–b, BK 82a), while salt, egg-barley, sleeping on the ground, bloodletting, and crying are detrimental to it (Git. 70a–b; ARN1 41:132). The *duda'im* (mandrakes, "love-flowers"), which Reuben brought to his mother Leah, who gave them to her sister Rachel (Gen. 30:14ff.), have been interpreted to be an aphrodisiac flower, though this is far from certain (see B. Jacob, Genesis, ad. loc.). The Talmud suggests that the suppression of the urge to urinate is a cause of sterility in men, and many pupils of the *amora* Huna (third century) became sterile on account of his over long lectures (Yev. 64b). See also *Birth Control; *Castration; *Vital Statistics.

ADD. BIBLIOGRAPHY: J.R. Baskin. *Midrashic Women: Formations of the Feminine in Rabbinic Literature* (2002); M. Callaway. *"Sing, O Barren One": A Study in Comparative Midrash* (1986); J. Cohen. *"Be Fertile and Increase, Fill the Earth and Master It." The Ancient and Medieval Career of a Biblical Verse* (1989); J. Hauptman, *Rereading the Rabbis: A Woman's Voice* (1998).

[Alexander Carlebach / Judith R. Baskin (2nd ed.)]

°BARRÈS, AUGUSTE MAURICE (1862–1923), French writer and politician. His extreme individualism and nationalism greatly influenced his generation. He contributed regularly to the nationalist antisemitic daily *La Cocarde* (founded in 1888), which he edited for a while, and there propounded many of the views on blood purity, the state, and the individual which were later developed and put into practice in Germany. He also expressed these opinions in his novels. Like Charles *Maurras, Barrès was influenced by H.A. Taine, who emphasized race and environment as the determinant factors in history, and by *Proudhon, who identified capitalists with bankers and bankers with Jews. With Maurras, Barrès laid the ideological foundations of the *Action Française, a forerunner of the Fascist movement. At the time of the *Dreyfus case, Barrès was among the most vehement of Dreyfus' accusers. During World War I, however, he became an ideologist of the "Union sacrée," and temporarily setting aside his prejudices accepted the Jews as members of the "spiritual family" of France.

BIBLIOGRAPHY: P. de Boisdeffre, *Maurice Barrès* (Fr., 1962), incl. bibl.; M.R. Curtis, *Three Against the Third Republic* (1959), incl. bibl. **ADD. BIBLIOGRAPHY:** Z. Sternhell, *Maurice Barrès et le nationalisme français* (1972); C.S. Doty, *From Cultural Rebellion to Counterrevolution: The Politics of Maurice Barrès* (1976).

BARRETT, DAVID (1930–), Canadian social worker, politician. Barrett was born in Vancouver, British Columbia, and raised in a secular Jewish home on the city's east side, where his father ran a produce market. Barrett studied philosophy and social work in the United States. He returned to Canada in 1957 and began work for the British Columbia Department of Corrections. Angered by what he regarded as wretched working conditions in an archaic prison system, he was soon an outspoken critic of the provincial penal system and organizer of a prison employee union. He was fired.

Carrying his battle into the political arena, in 1960 Barrett was elected to the provincial legislature for the Co-operative Commonwealth Federation (CCF), forerunner of the democratic socialist New Democratic Party (NDP). In 1969 he was elected leader of the British Columbia NDP and in 1972 led his party to victory with a major reform agenda. His was the first NDP government in British Columbia history and Barrett was the first Jewish provincial premier in Canadian history.

Defeated in 1975, he served for a time as leader of the opposition followed by a stint in broadcasting. He went on to become an NDP member of the federal Parliament from 1988 to 1993, when he retired.

[Harold Troper (2nd ed.)]

BARRIOS, DANIEL LEVI (Miguel) DE (1635–1701), Spanish poet and playwright. Barrios was born in Montilla, of a Portuguese Marrano family, and was one of the most eminent exiles who contributed to Spanish literature. Following the execution in 1655 of a relative, Marco (Isaac) de Almeyda *Bernal, Barrios' family left Spain, his parents settling in Algiers and he in Italy. After a sojourn at Nice and Leghorn (where he reverted to Judaism), he sailed with his first wife, Debora Váez, to Tobago, where she soon died. Barrios then moved to the Netherlands and in 1662 married Abigail de Pina in Amsterdam. At about the same time he took a commission as a captain in the Spanish Netherlands, and for the next 12 years lived outwardly as a Christian in Brussels, while simultaneously maintaining a connection with the Jewish community in Amsterdam. In 1674, Barrios renounced his military commission and thereafter lived openly as a professing Jew in Amsterdam. A follower of Shabbetai Ẓevi, Barrios had mystical delusions and often fasted for long periods. This so alarmed his wife that she hurried to R. Jacob *Sasportas on the first day of Passover, 1675, and pleaded for his assistance. Sasportas found Barrios prepared for the Messiah's advent before the New Year and convinced that the Christians, headed by the Dutch monarch, would convert to Judaism. As he dryly records in his *Ẓiẓat Novel Ẓevi* (1737), Sasportas found it necessary to remind the deluded poet of his immediate family obligations and of the perilous state of his health.

Barrios' work can be divided into two periods, before and after 1674. In Brussels, he emphasized classical and pagan allusions and in Amsterdam stressed his Jewishness, while retaining a great admiration for the Spanish poet Luis de Góngora. His first work, *Flor de Apolo* (Brussels, 1665), is a collection of poetry on varied themes; in the same volume he published three plays, *Pedir favor al contrario, El canto junto al encanto* and *El Español de Orán*, which were typical of the contemporary Spanish theater. An allegorical drama, *Contra la verdad no hay fuerza* (Amsterdam, undated, but before 1672), glorified the memory of three martyrs who died in an auto-da-fé in Cordoba in June while *Coro de las Musas* (Brussels and Amsterdam, 1672) contains poetic eulogies of the Spanish provinces and of famous people and cities, preceded by a panegyric on Charles II of England.

Barrios was one of the outstanding men of letters of 17th century Spain, who, together with other New Christians, contributed a great deal to the Spain's Golden Age. Like most Jews who left the Iberian Peninsula, as Jews in 1492 or as New Christians in subsequent years, Barrios retained the Spanish tongue as his language for every need and occasion. Whereas the Sephardi refugees developed Judezmo or Ladino, written in Hebrew script, the New Christians who returned to Judaism continued to use the Spanish and Portuguese languages as they were accustomed to in the Peninsula. Even though they returned to Judaism, many like Barrios continued to live in a culturally Spanish and Portuguese milieu, in Amsterdam or in Venice. Besides the cultural and linguistic legacy from the Peninsula, writers like Barrios brought with them into the Sephardi Diaspora certain concepts that can best described as Marranism. This consisted mainly of relying on the Old Testament part of the Bible as well as the apocryphal books, preserving certain very elementary dietary regulations, and celebrating in some way some Jewish festivals. Quite a number of Christian practices were adopted as a matter of course. To gain Jewish knowledge from books was difficult in Spain, but not impossible, thanks to the Spanish Hebraists. Poets of New Christian origin had different experiences once they returned to Judaism. Barrios had enough Jewish knowledge while a Crypto-Jew, but he found it rather difficult to adjust. He finally adopted messianic tendencies which might have been Christian-inspired. This affected the style and mood of his poetry.

The works of Barrios' Amsterdam period constitute five major collections. *Sol de la vida* (Antwerp, 1679) contains the *Libre albedrío*, a defense of the doctrine of free will. His *Triumpho del govierno popular y de la antigüedad holandesa* (Amsterdam, 1683), of which at least seven versions exist, includes sections on the history of the Amsterdam Sephardi community and its organizations. Some copies contain two religious poems: *La mayor perfección de Ley santisima* and *Triumpho canta la inmortalidad del Pueblo de Israel*. The undated treatise, *Relación de los poetas y escritores españoles de la Nación judaica amstelodama* (republished by M. Kayserling in REJ, 18 (1889), 276–89), is a rich, though sometimes highly romanticized, source of information on Sephardi literary figures. *Alegrías o pinturas lucientes de himeneo* (Amsterdam, 1686), a collection of wedding poems and panegyrics, commemorates some eminent Sephardi families. The most notable compositions in *Estrella de Jacob sobre Flores de Lis* (Amsterdam, 1686) are *"La Memoria renueva el dolor,"* on the death of the poet's wife, and two religious compositions, *"Providencia de Dios sobre Israel"* and *"Diás penitenciales."* *Metros nobles* (Amsterdam, 1675?) contains the religious poems also found in the (presumably earlier) *Triumpho del govierno popular*. Outstanding among Barrios' many other writings is his *Imperio de Dios en la harmonía del mundo* (Brussels, 1673?), the first part of a grandiose work intended as a poetic version of the Pentateuch. Barrios' literary output is uneven in quality, since he wrote to gain patronage to provide for himself and his family. As the poet laureate of Amsterdam Jewry he was a facile versifier, but some of his religious poems, thanks to their sincerity of feeling and elegance of expression, deserve wider recognition. Their general themes are the permanence and excellence of the Jewish faith, belief in free will, the author's repentance for the sin of posing as a Christian, and the harmony of Creation. Barrios glorified Sephardi culture (and its prime center, the Jewish community of Amsterdam), and perpetuated the memory of notable victims of the Inquisition. There is some evidence that Rembrandt's painting, "The Jewish Bride" (c. 1665) was a portrait of Barrios and his second wife.

BIBLIOGRAPHY: W.C. Pieterse, Daniel Levi de Barrios als geschiedschrijver... (1968); K.R. Scholberg, *Poesía religiosa Miguel de Barrios* (1962); idem, in: JQR, 53 (1962/63), 120–59; J. Amador de los Ríos, *Estudios históricos* (1848), 608–19; Kayserling, Bibl, 16–26; J.A.C. Zwarts, *Significance of Rembrandt's "The Jewish Bride"* (1929); H.V. Besso, *Dramatic Literature of the Sephardic Jews of Amsterdam* (1947), 73–84; J. Sasportas, *Ẓiẓat Novel Ẓevi*, ed. by J. Tishby (1954), 363ff.; Scholem, Shabbetai Ẓevi, 2 (1957), 446f. **ADD. BIBLIOGRAPHY:** E.M. Wilson, "Miguel de Barrios and Spanish Religious Poetry," in: *Bulletin of Hispanic Studies*, 40 (1963), 176–80; T. Oelman, *Marrano Poets of the Seventeenth Century: An Anthology of the Poetry of Joao Pinto Delgado, Antonio Enriquez Gomez, and Miguel de Barrios* (1982); J.L. Sanchez Fernandez, "Miguel de Barrios, un epíono olvidado," in: "M. Peléez del Rosal (ed.), *Conferencias del I curso de Verano de la Universidad de Cóndoba sobre "El Barroco en Andalucía,"* vol. 1 (1984), 103–13

[Kenneth R. Scholberg / Yom Tov Assis (2nd ed.)]

BARRIS, CHUCK (Charles; 1929–) U.S. television producer. Barris is known for his role as the producer of popular TV game shows, including some of the earliest forms of "reality television." Barris was born in Philadelphia, Pennsylvania, and attended the Drexel Institute of Technology. After graduating, he moved to New York, where he began his career in the television industry with a low-level job at NBC. Laid off a year later, Barris was unemployed for a year before being hired by ABC, where he worked with Dick Clark, the host of *American Bandstand*. Barris later sold the pilot of his own show, *The Dating Game*, to ABC. *The Dating Game* was an immediate hit, moving to primetime in 1966 and paving the way for Barris' popular *The Newlywed Game*. Barris continued to utilize the same formula in three more shows, *The Family Game*, *Dream Girl of 1968*, and *How's Your Mother-in-Law?* In 1968, he founded his own company, Barris Industries, which would produce television programs such as *The Game Game* and *Operation Entertainment*. *The Newlywed Show* was canceled in 1974, and Barris struggled to find a new niche in the television market until 1976, when he made his first appearance as the host of the talent competition *The Gong Show*. Barris' antics as the host of *The Gong Show* transformed the producer into a celebrity during the show's four-year run. Barris wrote his autobiography *Confessions of a Dangerous Mind* in 1986, which made the controversial claims that he had lived a double-life during the 1960s, working both as a TV producer and as an international CIA assassin. Barris also published a second autobiography, *The Game Show King* (1993), which made no reference to his alleged involvement with the CIA. In 2002, *Confessions of a Dangerous Mind* was made into a feature film of the same title directed by George Clooney.

[Walter Driver (2nd ed.)]

BARRON, JENNIE LOITMAN (1891–1969), U.S. lawyer, suffragist, judge, and community leader. Barron was born in Boston, the third of four daughters of Fannie and Morris Loitman. An outstanding student, she earned her undergraduate, law and master of law degrees from Boston University between 1908 and 1914 while working at night teaching Americanization classes. She opened a law practice in Boston in 1914. An active suffragist, Barron become the first president of the Boston University Equal Suffrage League and continued working for women's causes throughout her life, including women's rights to serve on juries, to become notaries, and to have uniform laws on marriage and divorce. Following her 1918 marriage to Samuel Barron, a graduate of Harvard Law School, she and her husband founded Barron and Barron, a law firm that continued until 1934 when Jennie Barron began a 30-year career in the judiciary when she was appointed a special judge for Norfolk County, Massachusetts. Barron and her husband had three daughters. Throughout her life she hosted Friday night Sabbath dinners at her home for her children and their growing families. Barron was awarded the National Mother of the Year Award by American Mothers, Inc. in 1959 when she was already a grandmother several times over.

In 1937, Barron was named an associate judge of the Boston Municipal Courts. In 1957 she was the first woman appointed as a full-time justice of the Massachusetts Superior Court. Active in numerous volunteer organizations, Barron was the president of the Massachusetts Association of Women Lawyers, the first president of the Women's Division of the American Jewish Congress, a national board member of Hadassah, and chair of the League of Women's Voters, among numerous other appointments.

BIBLIOGRAPHY: "Barron, Jennie Loitman," in: P.E. Hyman and D. Dash Moore (eds.), *Jewish Women in America* 1 (1997), 122–23; Obituary, in: *New York Times* (March 30, 1969).

[Judith R. Baskin (2nd ed.)]

BARROS BASTO, ARTURO CARLOS DE (1887–1961), leader of *Marrano revival in Portugal. Born at Amarante near Oporto, of a New Christian family, he was introduced to the secret practices of the Marranos by his grandfather, entered a military career in 1906 after he moved to Lisbon, where he tried to be accepted by the local Jewish community, and in the revolution in 1910 hoisted the Republican flag on the town hall of Oporto. On returning from World War I, he studied Hebrew, entering Judaism officially at the age of 33 in Tangiers, where he was circumcised, assuming the name Abraham Ben-Rosh. In Lisbon he married a member of a prominent Jewish family. He was the founder of the revivalist movement among the New Christians in Portugal that flourished under his leadership in the 1920s and 1930s. In 1923, together with some East European Jews he organized a community at Oporto, called *Mekor Haim*, secured foreign support for the construction of a monumental synagogue, set up a rudimentary seminary, called Yeshivat Rosh Pinnah in connection with it, and went on missionary journeys through the Marrano centers of northern Portugal. Two months after its establishment in June 1923, the community was officially recognized by the Portuguese authorities. Barros Basto served as the leader of the community in Porto. Barros Basto established a Portuguese periodical, *Ha-Lappid* ("The Torch"), to spread Jewish ideas among the Marranos. In some articles he published in *Ha-Lapid* he referred to the mysteries of the survival of Crypto-Jewish life in Portugal. He also edited various handbooks of religious guidance and wrote a history of the Jews of Oporto. He found in Samuel Schwarz (1880–1953), a mining engineer from Poland who settled in Portugal in 1915, an enthusiastic supporter for his plans to help descendents of New Christians return to normative Judaism. As a result of the activities of Barros Basto and Schwarz, some international Jewish organizations jointly sent Lucien *Wolf in 1926 to investigate the situation of Crypto-Jews. His report did not favor the intensive activity the Lisbon community or Barros Basto advocated. The latter continued to engage in an active educational and religious campaign designed to bring back to Judaism as many descendents of Crypto-Jews as possible. Barros Basto went on publishing his journal *Ha-Lapid*, which appeared until 1958. He attracted the attention of a number of Jewish personalities, such as Paul *Goodman, Cecil *Roth, and David de Sola *Pool. Rabbi Barukh Ben-Jacob, from Salonica, visited northern Portugal in 1931 and was deeply impressed by Barros Basto. It was in 1932 that the synagogue in Oporto was inaugurated, after the *Kadoorie family extended substantial financial support. Students and graduates of Rosh Pinnah helped Barros Basto in his task. He was able to establish communities in Bragança (*Sha'arei Pidyon* synagogue), in Covilhã (*Sha'arei Kabbalah* synagogue), and some religious activities were conducted in Belmonte. As anti-Jewish feelings increased in the early 1930s, opposition to the activities of Barros Basto spread. In December 1934 he was accused of homosexual relations with the students in Rosh Pinnah. In 1936 renewed accusations were leveled against him. In 1937 the Supreme Disciplinary Council declared him unfit to serve in the army. Although the military tribunal decided that the accusations were unfounded, he was not restored to the army. Even Schwarz no longer supported him. He died in 1961, almost blind, a disappointed man. He was buried, in accordance with his will, next to his grandfather in Amarante, his birthplace.

BIBLIOGRAPHY: Portuguese Marranos Committee, London, *Marranos in Portugal* (1938); C. Roth, *L'Apôrre des Marranes* (1929); *Jewish Guardian* (June 6, 1930); Roth, Marranos, 370–5; Friedenberg, in: *Midstream* (Spring, 1960), 2–4, 105–7. **ADD. BIBLIOGRAPHY:** H.P. Salomon, in: *Aquívos do Centro Cultural Portugês*, 10 (1976), 631–42; E.M. Baptista and I. Ferreira dev Oliveira, in: *História*, 54 (April 1983), 55–67; E. Rosenthal and R. Rosenthal, in: *Midstream* (Feb. 1987), 44–8; D.A. Canelo, *Os últimos criptojudeus em Portugal*, (2001); E. de Azevedo Mea and I. Steinhardt, *Ben-Rosh ...*, 1997.

[Cecil Roth / Yom Tov Assis (2nd ed.)]

°**BARRUEL, AUGUSTIN** (1741–1820), French Jesuit and anti-revolutionary polemicist. Barruel specialized in propagating fantastic stories about the part played by Freemasonry and secret societies in the Revolution. In 1807 Barruel alerted the French Government to an alleged world Jewish conspiracy. A mysterious Italian called Simonini (whose existence is doubtful) had delivered to Barruel the "plans of world Jewry" to become "masters of the world, turning the churches into as many synagogues, and reducing Christians to utter serfdom." Barruel's fantasies received the endorsement of Pope *Pius VII and were possibly the cause of *Napoleon's sudden decision to dissolve the French *Sanhedrin. In the longer perspective it was to have graver consequences, for the "Jewish plot" theme has served as a prototype for other deliberate fabrications, last but not least the Protocols of the *Elders of Zion.

BIBLIOGRAPHY: L. Poliakov, *Histoire de l'antisémitisme*, 3 (1968), index; DHGE, 6 (1932), 937; N. Cohn, *Warrant for Genocide; the Myth of the Jewish World Conspiracy and the Protocols of the Elders of Zion* (1967), 25–32, passim.

BARSHAI (Borisovich), RUDOLF (1924–), conductor, founder and leader of the Moscow Chamber Orchestra, viola soloist and orchestrator. Barshai was born in Stanitza Labinskaja in Russia. His grandfather was a high-ranking Cossack officer of the Subbotnik (Seventh Day Adventist) sect who had married a Jewish woman. During World War II his father fled to Central Asia and finally to the Moscow area. There, at the age of 15, Barshai started to play the violin. He entered the Special School for Musicians and later the Moscow Conservatory, where he became a pupil of the famous violinist Lew Zeitlin. He played the viola in the orchestra of the Bolshoi Theater and was a co-founder of the Borodin Quartet and the founder and leader of the Moscow Chamber Orchestra, which toured the world during the 1960s and 1970s. His soloists were Maria Judina, Svjatoslav Richter, David *Oistrach, and other well-known Russian musicians as well as Yehudi *Menuhin. Barshai and his orchestra produced numerous highly acclaimed recordings.

In 1967 Barshai begun to conduct major orchestras in the U.S.S.R. and in 1969 he conducted the premiere of Shostakovich's 14th Symphony. He made numerous transcriptions for small orchestra, notably of Shostakovitch's String Quartet No 8, Prokofiev's piano suite *Visions fugitives*, Bach's *Kunst der Fuge*, and Mahler's Symphony No 10. In 1976, Barshai decided to immigrate to Israel, where he worked with the Israel Chamber Orchestra. He then moved on to England, where he became chief conductor of the Bournemouth Symphony Orchestra. Subsequently he settled in Switzerland, touring the world and conducting well-known orchestras. He is the last of a generation of conductors with a singular and deep understanding of the great Viennese tradition of music.

[Bernd Feuchtner]

BARSHEFSKY, CHARLENE (1950–), U.S. lawyer and government trade representative. A native of Chicago, Barshefsky was born to Polish parents who did not speak English. She graduated from the University of Wisconsin, B.A. (1972) and the Catholic University, J.D. (1975). She was in private practice in the prestigious Washington firm of Steptoe and

Johnson from 1975 and 1993 and was then appointed by President Bill Clinton to serve as deputy trade representative under the president's key political ally, Mickey *Kantor. She was nominated to the office of trade representative when Kantor was named commerce secretary. Her nomination generated considerable controversy because as a private attorney Barshefsky had represented foreign governments in trade agreements. She was confirmed and was instrumental in negotiating agreements in China and Japan regarding piracy and movies. As the United States trade representative and a member of the president's cabinet, Ambassador Barshefsky was at center stage in global economic policymaking and international relations. As the administration's leader in the opening of foreign markets and the elimination of regulatory and investment barriers around the world, and as the architect of U.S. trade policy, she was a central figure for international business.

Barshefsky is best known for negotiating the historic market opening agreement with China on its entry into the World Trade Organization, which helped lead to the voluminous trade between the United States and China. She was an essential actor in the opening of foreign markets at the World Trade Organization and throughout the world, overseeing the negotiations of hundreds of complex trade and commercial agreements with virtually every major market, from Japan and the European Union to the smallest states of Latin America, Africa, and the Middle East. She negotiated agreements for the emerging information age, concluding global agreements covering the world's telecommunications markets, global financial services, information technology products, intellectual property rights, and cyberspace.

In addition to the China agreements, she was the architect of the negotiations to create a hemispheric free trade zone, the Free Trade Area of the Americas. She negotiated historic market opening agreements with Vietnam and Jordan that transcend international economic relations and are used as a basis for further regional integration. She also initiated free trade negotiations with Singapore and Chile, which further extended the broad trade agenda that she shaped.

After leaving the government, she became senior international partner at Wilmer, Cutler, Pickering Hale and Dorr, LLP and served on the corporate Board of Directors of the American Express Company; The Estee Lauder Companies Inc.; Intel, Idenix Pharmaceuticals, Inc., and Starwood Hotels & Resorts Worldwide, Inc.

[Michael Berenbaum (2nd ed.)]

BARSIMSON, JACOB, regarded as the earliest Jewish resident of New Amsterdam (later New York). Barsimson probably arrived there on July 8, 1654, aboard the ship *Peartree*, from Holland, thus preceding the 23 Jews who arrived in September of that year from Brazil. A man of small means, he was taxed below the majority of other New Amsterdam residents. In November 1655 Barsimson joined with Asser *Levy in petitioning for the right held by other inhabitants to stand guard and thus avoid payment of a special tax. The Dutch West India Company overruled Governor Peter Stuyvesant, who had rejected the petition. Barsimson may have returned to Amsterdam in 1659.

BIBLIOGRAPHY: Oppenheim, in: A.J. Karp (ed.), *The Jewish Experience in America*, 1 (1969), 37–50.

[Leo Hershkowitz]

BART, LIONEL (1930–1999), playwright and composer. Born Lionel Begleiter in London, Bart first won success with the lyrics and music of *Fings Ain't Wot They Used t'Be* (1959), which had a two-year run. This was followed by other shows, including *Blitz* (1962) and *Maggie May* (1964). His greatest success, *Oliver!* (1960), was made into a motion picture in 1968. *Oliver!* became probably the most famous musical ever written by an English composer. Its depiction of Fagin is notable for its balance and humanity. Bart was unable to repeat his success in later works.

BIBLIOGRAPHY: ODNB online.

[William D. Rubinstein (2nd ed.)]

BARTH, JACOB (1851–1914), Semitic linguist. Barth was born in Flehingen, Baden. Among his teachers in Talmud was his future father-in-law, Azriel *Hildesheimer. He studied Semitic philology at the universities of Berlin, Leipzig (under H.L. Fleischer), and Strasbourg (under Th. Noeldeke). From 1874 until his death he taught Hebrew, biblical exegesis, and Jewish philosophy at the Orthodox Rabbinical Seminary founded by Hildesheimer at Berlin. In 1876 he was appointed lecturer in Semitic philology at the University of Berlin, and in 1880 associate professor. Being a Jew, he was not appointed full professor, but he received the title of Geheimer Regierungsrat. Barth was one of the most important Semitic linguists of his time, and at least two of his works are still standard reference books: *Die Nominalbildung in den semitischen Sprachen* (1894), and *Die Pronominalbildung in den semitischen Sprachen* (1918). Despite Barth's tendency to adopt odd etymologies and to excessive schematization, these works, as well as others, show his genius in discerning linguistic analogies. Barth was also one of the outstanding Arabic scholars of his time. He edited grammatical, poetical, and historical texts as well as the commentary of Maimonides to Mishnah *Makkot* (1880). His contributions to the study of Hebrew include both linguistics and lexicography (especially his *Etymologische Studien zum semitischen, inbesonders zum hebraeischen und aramaeischen Lexikon* (1902). Being strictly Orthodox, he avoided higher criticism, but accepted the separate authorship of Isaiah 40 ff., which, in his view, was supported by the Talmud. Similarly, he usually refrained from emendation of the Bible text, although he had a natural tendency to text corrections (as exhibited in his Arabic studies). His commentary on almost all the books of the Bible, which originated in his lectures at the Hildesheimer Seminary, has not been published.

[Joshua Blau]

His son, AHARON (1890–1957), was an Israeli banker and Zionist leader. Born in Berlin, as a young man he became an active leader in the Mizrachi movement in Germany, representing it at most of the Zionist Congresses after 1920. From 1921 to 1938 he served as attorney for the Zionist Congress court, and from 1946 as its chairman. He settled in Palestine in 1933 and was appointed director-general of the Anglo-Palestine Bank (later Bank Leumi le-Israel) in 1947, retaining this post until his death. Of his articles and brochures on various Zionist and religious topics, the most important is *Dorenu mul She'elot ha-Neẓaḥ* published in 1954 and republished in 1955 (Eng. tr. *The Modern Jew Faces Eternal Problems*, Jerusalem 1956). In it, he summarized his views on traditional and modern aspects of Judaism. He is noted for his modern religious interpretation of Orthodoxy, stressing the contemporary relevance of Orthodox Jewish practice. He wrote the brochure *Letter to an English Friend* (1948), in which he propounds the religious basis for the Jewish claim to Palestine, and *The Mitzvoth: Their Aim and Purpose* (1949).

ELIEZER (LAZAR) (1880–1949), Aharon's elder brother, was a leader and central figure in the religious Zionist movement in Germany. Born in Berlin, he became a leader of the Zionist Organization of Germany, participated in most Zionist Congresses after 1903, and served as a member of the Zionist General Council. During 1929–31 he represented Mizrachi on the Zionist Executive in London. He published numerous articles on Zionist topics.

[Benjamin Jaffe]

BIBLIOGRAPHY: Rabbiner-Seminar zu Berlin, *Bericht ueber die ersten 25 Jahre* (1898), 9, 57; Eppenstein, in: *Jahresbericht des Rabbiner Seminars zu Berlin fuer 1914–5* (1915), 91–99; C.H. Becker, *Der Islam* (1916), 200–2; J. Fueck, *Die arabischen Studien in Europa* (1955), 242–3; EJ, 3 (1929), 1100–01; J. Blau, in: *Ḥokhmat Yisrael be-Ma'arav Eiropah*, ed. by S. Federbush (1959), 47–52; EẒD, 1 (1958), 227–33; S. Daniel, in: *Gevilin be-Maḥashavah Datit Le'ummit* (July 1957), 58–72.

°**BARTH, KARL** (1886–1968), Swiss Protestant theologian. From 1922, he served as professor of theology in various German universities. With the Nazi rise to power in Germany and the consequent split in German Protestantism, Barth helped to found the Confessing Church (Bekennende Kirche) which opposed Hitler and the National-Socialist ideology as incompatible with Christian commitment to the teaching and kingship of Jesus. In 1934, he drafted the theological declaration of Barmen, whereby the German Lutherans and Reformed united to define and defend their position against the totalitarian claims of the state. Expelled from Germany in 1935, he returned to his native Basle, where he was appointed professor of dogmatics.

His principal theological work, the monumental *Kirchliche Dogmatik*, which remained incomplete at his death, was published between 1932–53. While Barth took a courageous stand against antisemitism, seeing in hatred and persecution of the Jews an attack on the very foundations of the Christian message, his work evinces no understanding of actual Judaism. Throughout Barth's writings Judaism appears as a theoretical construction, a kind of figment of theological imagination, whose purpose it is to serve as a foil to the message of the gospel.

While not hostile in its intention, Barth's representation of Judaism is a complete caricature and falsification of Jewish reality. According to Barth, Israel is God's Chosen People and in spite of its obstinacy in assimilating to other peoples, the Divine election remains valid. Since the crucifixion of Jesus, there simply cannot be any normal existence for the Jewish people, for the Jew represents man as such, sinner, called by God's grace and rejecting this grace. In this exemplary role of man, the Jew necessarily irritates the nations of the world by acting as a kind of mirror in which the nations see their sinful humanity reflected. The Nazis sought to destroy the Jews, the people of Jesus, in order to liberate themselves from the rule of God and to break, as it were, the mirror in which fallen man sees himself reflected. Beside his numerous theological, literary, and political writings, Barth also wrote some works on the church in the Third Reich, and on the existence of Christians in the countries under communist rule.

BIBLIOGRAPHY: W. Pauck, *Karl Barth* (Eng., 1931); Taubes, in: JR, 34 (1954), 14, 231–43; R. Niebuhr, *Essays in Applied Christianity* (1959); F.W. Marquardt, *Die Entdeckung des Judentums fuer die christliche Theologie – Israel im Denken Karl Barths* (1967).

BARTHOLDY, JACOB (1779–1825), Prussian diplomat and art connoisseur. Born in Berlin into a prosperous Jewish family as Jacob Salomon, he was an uncle of the composer Felix Mendelssohn. He converted in 1805 and adopted the family name Bartholdy from a rented estate near Berlin. He was one of the group of gifted apostate Jews whose services were enlisted by von Hardenberg, the Prussian chancellor. Bartholdy studied law and philosophy, traveled extensively in Western Europe before becoming an officer in the Austrian army in the 1809 war against France. After entering the Prussian diplomatic service, he was appointed Prussian consul-general in Rome and took part in the conference of Aix-la-Chapelle (1818). In the same year he became Prussian chargé d'affaires at the court of Tuscany with the title of privy councillor of legation.

Bartholdy was an enthusiastic art patron and his home was decorated with frescoes by the Nazarenes, a group of contemporary German artists devoted to the revival of Christian art. After his death, the murals were bought by the Prussian government who also acquired his important collection of Etruscan vases, bronze, and ivory.

ADD BIBLIOGRAPHY: C. Lambour, "Quellen zur Biographie von Fanny Hensel, geb. Mendelssohn Bartholdy," in: G. Klein and R. Elvers (eds.), *Mendelssohn-Studien*, vol. 6. (1986), 49–105.

[Ernest Hamburger]

°**BARTOLOCCI, GIULIO** (1613–1687), Italian Christian Hebraist and bibliographer. Bartolocci was taught Hebrew by the convert Giovanni Battista Jonah Galileo (formerly Judah

Jonah of Safed), and in 1651 became professor of Hebrew language and rabbinic literature at the Collegium Neophytorum (for Jewish converts) in Rome; at the same time he served as *scriptor hebraicus* in the Vatican Library. He is remembered above all for his *Bibliotheca Magna Rabbinica... de scriptoribus et scriptis hebraicis, ordine alphabetico hebraice et latine digestis* (Heb. title *Kiryat Sefer*), a comprehensive bibliography of Jewish books (Rome, 4 vols., 1675–93). The last volume was edited by Bartolocci's student Carlo Giuseppe Imbonati, who added a fifth volume, *Bibliotheca Latina-Hebraica* (1694; all 5 vols. repr. 1969), containing a bibliography of Latin works by Christian authors on the Jews or on Judaism. Bartolocci's work is the first systematic, all-inclusive bibliography of Jewish literature. It served as the basis for Wolf's *Bibliotheca Hebraea* and for subsequent works in the field. Some of the works which Bartolocci regarded as most important he presents in full, in the Hebrew (or Aramaic) original and in Latin translation. Among these are the *Antiochus Scroll, Alphabet of Ben Sira*, and *Otiyyot de-Rabbi Akiva*. Occasionally, he gives biographies of important writers. His biographies of biblical commentators, such as Rashi, Ibn Ezra, David Kimḥi, Gersonides, and Abrabanel, were published also in A. Reland's *Analecta Rabbinica* (Utrecht, 1702). His work still retains some importance. Other works by Bartolocci remain in manuscript.

BIBLIOGRAPHY: G.M. Mazzuccheli, *Gli Scrittori d'Italia*, 2 (1763), 468; Roth, Italy, 394; Milano, Italia, 681; Steinschneider, in: ZHB, 2 (1897), 51 no. 99.

[Cecil Roth]

BARTOV, HANOCH (1926–), Israeli novelist. Bartov, who was born in Petaḥ Tikvah, served in the Jewish Brigade during World War II and during the War of Independence served in the Israel Army. Bartov was a member of kibbutz Ein ha-Ḥoresh, and a reporter for the daily *La-Merḥav*. He served as cultural attaché at the Israel Embassy in London, in 1966–68. A prolific writer, his writings include stories, novels, plays, and journalism, written in the more than five decades that have passed since the publication of his first novel, *Ha-Ḥeshbon ve-ha-Nefesh* ("The Reckoning and the Soul," 1953), in which he discussed the ideological disillusionment of Israeli youth when they returned to civilian life after the War of Independence. Problems of new immigrants are treated in the novel *Shesh Kenafayim le-Eḥad* (1954; *Everyone Had Six Wings*, 1974), which he later adapted for the stage. A visit to the U.S. is vividly recorded in the travel-book *Arba'ah Yisre'elim ve-Khol Amerikah* ("Four Israelis and All The U.S.A.," 1961). The subject of *Piẓei Bagrut* (1965; *The Brigade*, 1967) is the Jewish Brigade during World War II and the conflict between Jewish morality and the wish to avenge the Holocaust. For this novel, one of the finest Hebrew examples of an Israeli *Bildungsroman*, Bartov was awarded the Shlonsky Prize. Another novel in this genre is Bartov's *Shel Mi Attah Yeled?* (1988; *Whose Little Boy are You?*), recollecting childhood experiences in one of Israel's oldest moshavot. Bartov's realistic style is always suffused with humor and a touch of irony. The complex, dynamic Israeli identity is at the heart of all his works. Other works include: *Ha-Shuk ha-Katan* ("The Small Market," 1957); *S'a ha-Bayta, Yonatan* ("Go Home, Jonathan," 1962). *Be-Emẓa ha-Roman* ("In the Middle of It All," 1988), which won Bartov the Bialik Prize, tells the life story of Balfour Shub, a writer, as it is reconstructed by his son, who returns from the United States with his father's coffin and a literary inheritance consisting of 26 tapes. The gap between generations, the relations of fathers and sons, is a recurring motif in the prose of Bartov. The protagonist in *Zeh Ishl Medaber* ("Ishl Speaking," 1990), is yet another account of a life full of activity intertwined with political events in Israel. *Regel Aḥat Ba-Ḥuẓ* ("Halfway Out," 1994), describes the effects of World War II on life in British-ruled Israel, while the novella *Lev Shafukh* ("A Heart Poured Out," 2001) tells of an encounter between two men representing two worlds: Amos Gefen, a well-known Hebrew writer of Ashkenazi origin, and Sami Sasson, a house painter of Oriental origin, hired to whitewash the writer's apartment. The ups and downs of married life is one of the main issues in the novella, as in Bartov's 2004 novel *Mi-Tom ad Tom* ("From Innocence to Innocence").

In 1978 Bartov was awarded the Yiẓḥak Sadeh Prize for military literature for his *Dado*, a study of Lt.-General David *Elazar (Eng. trans. 1981). Other works include *Arba'a Yisra'elim be-Ḥazar Saint James* (1969); *An Israeli at the Court of St. James* (1971) and the travel account "A Fair in Moscow" (1988).

ADD. BIBLIOGRAPHY: G. Shaked, *Ha-Sipporet ha-Ivrit*, 4 (1993), 81–86; idem, in: *Haaretz, Sefarim* (Oct. 12, 1994); M. Gilboa, *Piẓei Zehut: Iyyunim bi-Yeẓirato shel H. Bartov* (1988); E. Shai, in: *Ma'ariv* (Oct. 7, 1994); A. Feinberg, in: *Modern Hebrew Literature* 11 (1985); M. Pelleg, in: *Haaretz, Sefarim* (Apr. 2, 2002); K. Feit, in: *Haaretz, Sefarim* (Jan. 28, 2004). I. Perlis, in: *Al ha-Mishmar* (Oct. 10, 1980); Z. Shamir, in: *Maariv* (Sept. 26, 1980); M. Pelli, "A Late Encounter with the Holocaust: Paradigms, Rhythm and Concepts in *The Brigade* by H. Bartov," in: *Hebrew Studies* 22 (1981), 117–254; E. Ben Ezer, in: *Al ha-Mishmar* (Jan. 16, 1981); A. Levit, in: *Maariv* (July 27, 1984); M. Gilboa, "*Amerika ke-Makom, ke-Metaforah ukhsemel bi-Shelosha Romanim*," in: *Migvan* (1988), 113–26; Z. Shamir, "*H. Bartov – Sofer 'Ba'al Maḥshavot*,'" in: *Moznayim* 64, 5 (1990), 53–55; H. Helperin, "*Mane'ul u-Vari'aḥ ve-Lev Shafukh*," in: *Moznayim* 76, 3 (2002), 14–16; A. Feldman, "*Sippuro shel Peẓa*," in: *Moznayim* 78, 2 (2004), 7–10.

[Gitta (Aszkenazy) Avinor / Anat Feinberg (2nd ed.)]

BARUCH (Heb. בָּרוּךְ; "blessed"), son of Neriah son of Mahseiah, scribe and trusted companion of the prophet *Jeremiah, who set down in writing all the latter's prophecies and may have composed the biographical narrative about Jeremiah (Jer. 36:4). Baruch's brother Seraiah was the quartermaster of Zedekiah (51:59), the last king of Judah. In the fourth year (or possibly the fifth) of the reign of *Jehoiakim, Baruch wrote down, at Jeremiah's dictation, all of the prophet's oracles and read them in the temple court before the entire community, which had assembled for a fast day proclaimed in Kislev of that year. Baruch then read them before the king's ministers

(36:4ff.). When the king was informed of these events, he ordered the scroll to be read before him. When he heard the prophet's message forecasting doom, Jehoiakim tore the scroll, cast it into the fire, and ordered Jeremiah and Baruch to be placed under arrest; they, however, succeeded in hiding from him. Then Jeremiah redictated the contents of the destroyed scroll and added to it (36:32). As a reward for Baruch's loyalty, Jeremiah declared that he would be saved (45:1ff.).

In the tenth year of Zedekiah's reign, when Jerusalem was under siege by the Babylonians, Jeremiah bought a field from Hanamel, his uncle's son. He entrusted the deeds of purchase to Baruch, asking him to place them in an earthenware vessel for safekeeping "that they may last for a long time" (32:1–16). The Babylonian commanders released Baruch together with Jeremiah and did not force him to go into exile to Babylon (40:1–7). Baruch apparently exerted a great influence over Jeremiah. When *Gedaliah son of Ahikam was killed and the remnant of the population that had escaped exile, fearing the vengeance of Nebuchadnezzar, asked Jeremiah whether they should stay in the country or go down to Egypt, he advised them to remain. But they suspected him of acting under Baruch's instigation, thinking that Baruch, out of hatred for them, planned to place them at the mercy of the Babylonian king. Baruch was then taken along with Jeremiah and the remnant of the population to Egypt.

In the *Aggadah*

Baruch is held to be a priest as well as a prophet and one of the descendants of Rahab (Meg. 14b; SOR, 20). He is identified with Ebed-Melech the Ethiopian, who saved Jeremiah from the dungeon (Sif. Num., on 12:1). Five years after the destruction of the Temple, Baruch (with Jeremiah) was taken from Egypt to Babylon, where he died (Meg. 16b; SOR 26:1; cf. Jos. Ant., 10:181–2). He is also said to have prophesied there in the second year of the reign of Darius, but was unable to return to Judah because of his advanced age. According to this tradition, Ezra was his pupil (Song. R. 5:5; Meg. 16b).

In the Middle Ages the Iraqi Jews possessed several legends about Baruch's grave, which was said to be near that of Ezekiel in Mushid A'li. A certain Arab ruler in Baghdad – at the time of the exilarch Solomon – wished to see the graves of Ezekiel and Baruch. When the grave was opened, Baruch's body was found in a marble coffin, looking as if alive. It was decided to transport him some distance from Ezekiel's grave, but, after a mile-long journey, the cart stopped and would not move, and he was buried at that spot (*Travels of R. Petachia of Ratisbonne*…, ed. and tr. by A. Benisch (1856), 21, 23, 49, 51). Jewish tradition extolled Baruch's piety and several apocalypses were attributed to him as well as an apocryphal letter.

Baruch came to have considerable importance in the apocryphal literature where a number of books were attributed to him. Moreover, there are apparently fragments of Baruch and Jeremiatic apocryphal literature among the Dead Sea Scrolls. According to the apocryphal books he received many visions and revelations of an apocalyptic nature. In II Baruch his assumption is foretold (II Bar. 25.1, 76:1).

BIBLIOGRAPHY: S. Yeivin, in: *Tarbiz*, 12 (1940/41), 260; de Vaux, Anc. Isr, 49, 120, 168; Noth, Personennamen, 183; EM, 2 (1965), 337–8 (includes bibliography); Ginzberg, Legends, index.

[Yehoshua M. Grintz]

BARUCH, name of several kabbalists.

BARUCH SHELI'AḤ ẒIBBUR TOGARMI. Baruch Sheli'aḥ Ẓibbur Togarmi, as is suggested by his cognomen Togarmi, was a cantor of eastern origin. He wrote a treatise, extant in several manuscripts (Paris, Oxford, New York), called *Maftehot ha-Kabbalah* ("The Keys to Kabbalah"), which contains a short, factually complete commentary on the Sefer *Yeẓirah, identical with the one described by Abraham *Abulafia in his *Oẓar Eden Ganuz* as being by his master, Baruch (no surname). In the early 14th century, *Isaac b. Samuel of Acre quotes a Baruch Togarmi in *Me'irat Einayim* in such a way as to suggest a scholar who lived at least one generation earlier. He says, "I saw written in the name of Baruch Togarmi" and ends with the eulogy for the dead. The three quotations display the same characteristic of short allusions to kabbalistic secrets through wordplay as the above-mentioned treatise, *Maftehot*. This is significant for the early history of the Abulafian current in the Kabbalah. The author already knows a distinct group of such kabbalists who are occupied with the (mystical) knowledge of the name of God. From his statements, it is to be understood that he belonged to a circle whose members believed themselves able to discover "by the three ways of the Kabbalah," i.e., *gematria* ("numerical value of words"), *notarikon* ("interpretation of each letter in a word as abbreviation of other words"), and *temurah* ("interchange of letters according to certain systematic rules") particularly profound mysteries of the mystic cosmology and theology. However, according to his testimony, he was not allowed either to divulge in public or even merely to set down in writing most of it. The treatise is full of obscure wordplay and peculiar *gematriot*. For example, the word "body" here means the evil principle, through the equation גוף רע (*guf ra*, "evil body" – 359) equals שטן (*satan* – 359). The work originates clearly from the same circle as the book *Sod ha-Levanah* (ed. by J. Klausner, in *Madda'ei ha-Yahadut*, 2 (1927), 240–1), which has survived in the name of Jacob Cohen (c. 1260–70, that is at the time of R. Baruch). According to this, Baruch would have lived in Spain. Thus, it is a plausible assumption that it was through him that Abulafia, during his stay in Barcelona in 1270–73, was introduced to the Kabbalah of this circle.

BARUCH THE KABBALIST. Baruch the Kabbalist was author of the book *Mafte'aḥ ha-Kabbalah* ("Key to Kabbalah") which was in Carmoly's possession (Cod. 249 of the Kirchheim Catalogue of Carmoly's Mss. of 1876). This book has no connection with the work of the above-mentioned Baruch Sheli'aḥ-Ẓibbur Togarmi. It belongs to an entirely different literary environment and it dates from the 14th century. This author already quotes the *Zohar and the *tikkunim*, and is familiar with the homily on Jeremiah 9:22 from the end of the 13th century and possibly later (preserved in the Berlin Hebr. Ms. 193, fol. 79–98 and dated by Steinschneider not before 1350; cf. also HB, 18 (1877), 20). He also copied several passages from Shem Tov *Ibn Gaon's work *Baddei ha-Aron*, which was completed in 1325. That is the origin of all the passages which are common to Baruch the Kabbalist's work, and that of Shem Tov's *Sefer ha-Emunot*. Since Baruch undoubtedly knew Shem Tov ibn Gaon's works, there is nothing to uphold Carmoly's assumption that Baruch's book was the one used in the *Emunot*. *Mafte'aḥ ha-Kabbalah* was not a comprehensive work (Carmoly's manuscript, which is incomplete, contains only 28 folios) and did not add anything novel to the doctrines of Kabbalah, only excerpts from other sources in defense of the Kabbalistic tradition. Moses Botarel relied apparently on this book when he quoted in length from a spurious work *Ḥoshen ha-Mishpat* in his *Yeẓirah* commentary (to ch. 4, mishnah 4). It is possible, however, that Botarel had in mind Baruch Togarmi as the author of a *Yeẓirah* commentary. Botarel also named Baruch among the authorities who dealt with the technique of *She'elat Ḥalom* ("Dream Queries") and, as a matter of fact, Baruch's exposition is still extant in manuscripts (Gaster 603, fol. 9 and in other manuscripts). Apart from this, an older kabbalist named Baruch, who could not have lived after 1400 since he is already mentioned in manuscripts from that period, is mentioned occasionally in manuscripts dealing with practical Kabbalah. In the old Paris manuscript no. 602, he is described as the "father-in-law of the kabbalist Menahem," who is himself unknown. In the Gaster manuscript no. 720, the theurgic use of the so-called *shem ha-kanaf*, i.e., of the mystic "name" *Ẓemarkad*, was transmitted "from the tradition of Baruch." In a work of similar character such as his *Yeẓirah* commentary (which is partly preserved in a Jerusalem manuscript), Botarel attributes a commentary on the *Ḥagigah* talmudic tract, particularly its second chapter, to a kabbalist called Baruch of Narbonne. It is to be assumed that he means by this the same person, who therefore belongs to the second half of the 14th century. S. Sachs, who mistakes this Baruch for the one mentioned above, ascribes *Ma'amar ha-Sekhel* (Cremona, 1557), which gives the 613 commandments a kabbalistic explanation, to him.

BARUCH ASHKENAZI. Baruch Ashkenazi who is called by Shem Tov *Attia, in the introduction to his commentary on the Psalms, an "old kabbalist," is, as clearly shown by his surname, a third person. There are no further details about him.

BIBLIOGRAPHY: Scholem, Mysticism, 127.

[Gershom Scholem]

BARUCH, prominent U.S. family.

SIMON (1840–1921)emigrated from his native Posen, Prussia, to America in 1855. He settled in South Carolina, where his first employers, impressed with his talents, assisted him in his studies at the medical colleges of South Carolina and Virginia. Baruch received his degree in 1862 and became a surgeon in Lee's Confederate Army, serving at the front for three years. Captured and interned at Fort McHenry, he wrote a book on military surgery, *Two Penetrating Wounds of the Chest*, which remained a standard work through World War I. In 1864 he was sent to Thomasville, North Carolina, to prepare hospital facilities for Confederate troops pursuing Sherman. After the war he lived in South Carolina, where he was elected president of the State Medical Association (1874) and chairman of the State Health Board (1880). In 1881 he moved to New York to escape the turbulence of Reconstruction, occupying the chair of hydrotherapy at Columbia University's College of Physicians and Surgeons. Credited with being the first doctor to successfully diagnose and remove a ruptured appendix, he also contributed to the treatment of malaria, childhood diseases, and typhoid fever. He edited the *Journal of Balneology*, the *Dietetic and Hygienic Gazette*, and *Gailland's Medical Journal*.

Simon's wife, the former ISOBEL WOLFE of Winnsboro, South Carolina, was a descendant of Isaac Rodriguez Marques, an early colonial settler. The couple had four sons, Hartwig, Bernard Mannes, Herman Benjamin, and Sailing Wolfe (1874–1962). HARTWIG (1868–1953), the eldest, became a Broadway actor. HERMAN (1872–1953) received a medical degree from the College of Physicians and Surgeons in 1895. He practiced medicine until 1903, when he joined his brother Bernard's Wall Street firm and became a member of the New York Stock Exchange. In 1918 Herman became a lifetime partner in H. Hentz and Company. He entered public service in 1943 when he participated in a Brazil conference sponsored by the board of Economic Warfare. After World War II Herman served as U.S. ambassador to Portugal (1945–47) and as ambassador to the Netherlands (1947–49).

BERNARD BARUCH (1870–1965), stock analyst, self-styled "speculator," and statesman, was born in Camden, South Carolina. He received a B.A. from the City College of New York, and in 1889 he joined the Wall Street firm of Arthur A. Housman. Bernard became a partner in 1896, and a member of the New York Stock Exchange. By 1902, by means of his financial wizardry and careful market research into raw materials such as gold, copper, sulfur, and rubber, he had amassed a fortune of over three million dollars.

Bernard first entered public life in 1916. Then, as a result of his keen knowledge of the raw materials market, President Wilson appointed him to the advisory commission of the Council of National Defense and made him chairman of the Commission on Raw Materials, Minerals, and Metals. During World War I he served as chairman of the War Industries Board with power to virtually mobilize the American wartime economy. At the war's end he served on the Supreme Economic Council at the Conference of Versailles, where he was President Wilson's personal economic adviser, and from that time on his advisory services were sought by every president of the United States. During World War II President Franklin Roosevelt named him chairman of a committee to report on the rubber shortage and to plan a solution. In 1943 he became adviser to War Mobilization Director James Byrnes, and in 1946 he was named the U.S. representative to the United Nations Atomic Energy Commission. In 1939 Bernard advocated a "United States of Africa" in Uganda, as a refuge for Jews and all victims of persecution. The founding of Israel he saw as only a part-way solution. No Zionist, he opposed the establishment of any state on the basis of religion, and looked upon himself always as first an American and then a Jew. Bernard was the formal author of the first official U.S. policy on the control of atomic energy, which he proposed before the United Nations on June 14, 1946. His plan called for the creation of an International Atomic Development Authority, empowered to universally control all dangerous uses of atomic energy and to inspect all atomic installations. It did not prohibit atomic weapons outright, which the Russians demanded, although they rejected inspection. It was vetoed by the U.S.S.R. in 1948 and it was never adopted. Bernard wrote *American Industry in the War* (1941), *My Own Story* (1957), and a sequel, *Public Years* (1960).

BIBLIOGRAPHY: SIMON: DAB; J.R. Marcus (ed.), *Memoirs of American Jews, 1775–1865*, 3 (1956), 269–81; H. Simonhoff, *Saga of American Jewry, 1865–1914* (1959), 125–9; BERNARD: C. Field, *Bernard Baruch* (1944); M.L. Coit, *Mr. Baruch* (1957), incl. bibl. **ADD. BIBLIOGRAPHY:** J.A. Schwarz, *The Speculator: Bernard M. Baruch in Washington, 1917–1965* (1981); J.L. Grant, *Bernard M. Baruch: The Adventures of a Wall Street Legend* (1983).

[Margaret L. Coit]

BARUCH, ADAM (1945–), Israeli columnist, writer, and editor. Born Baruch Rosenblum in Jerusalem to a rabbinical family of the old Yishuv, Baruch was brought up in Ramat Gan and educated at Midrashiyat Noam Yeshivah High School. He studied law at the Hebrew University of Jerusalem and later traveled extensively in the U.S. He began his journalistic career in the art section of *Haaretz* and in 1971 began writing a personal column in **Yedioth Ahronoth*. He edited *Mussag*, a periodical dealing with art and culture (1974–75) and the monthly magazine *Monitin* (1978–82). During the 1980s and early 1990s Baruch served as a senior editor at *Yedioth Ahronoth* and then at **Maariv* and was the editor of the business daily **Globes* (1992–96). From 1997 he wrote a weekly column in *Maariv* dealing with a wide range of issues but most notably with modern interpretations of rabbinical law. The column had a wide following in Israel and won him the Avi Hai Prize and the Yeshayahu Leibowitz Prize. The column's popularity also built his image as a spiritual mentor to many Israelis, and he became known as the *admor* (ḥasidic leader) of the *ḥilonim* (secular Israelis).

In addition to journalism, Baruch was active in Israeli art and photography. He was the curator of the Israeli exhibition at the international bianale for art in Venice (1988, 1990) and served as president of the Camera Obscura art school in Tel Aviv (1996–2002). Among his books are "Lustig" (1984), a political novel; an appreciation of the sculptor Yeḥi'el Shemi (1988); "He Was a Hero" (1998), a collection of short stories; a series of three books on contemporary Judaism and Jewish law; and "How Are Things at Home" (2004) on Israeli society.

[Anshel Pfeffer (2nd ed.)]

BARUCH, APOCALYPSE OF (Syriac) (abbr. II Bar.), an apocalyptic work ascribed to Jeremiah's scribe Baruch and purportedly containing the visions of Baruch on the eve of and subsequent to the destruction of Jerusalem. The work has been preserved partly in Greek and all of it in Syriac.

Contents

Chapters 1–4: In the 25th year of Jeconiah, king of Judah, Baruch is commanded to leave Jerusalem as its hour of destruction has come, and as long as he and his righteous companions are in the city, God is unable to destroy it. Baruch is informed in a vision that the destruction will be temporary, affecting only the earthly Jerusalem, the reflection of the heavenly and eternal Jerusalem. Chapters 5–8: The following day Baruch sees four angels with torches setting fire to the city at its four corners, while a fifth angel descends and stores away the sacred vessels of the Temple until the end of days. Chapters 9–12: After seven days Baruch is commanded to beg Jeremiah to accompany the exiles to Babylonia, but he himself is to remain with the ruined Temple. Baruch laments that Zion is destroyed whereas Babylonia is preserved. Chapters 13–20: Seven days later a mysterious voice informs Baruch that he will survive until the end of days. Chapters 21–30: After Baruch has fasted for seven days, the voice answers his question: "When will the messianic age come?" He is told that it will come in due time, but not before all the souls destined to be born will have been created. Chapters 31–34: Baruch prophesies to the people that the Temple will be rebuilt, destroyed again, and once more rebuilt for all eternity. Chapters 35–41: While Baruch sits on the ruins of the Temple, a vision is revealed to him. He sees a forest planted in a valley and surrounded by mountains. Opposite the forest is a vine, below which flows a spring. Rising to a mighty stream, the spring overturns the forest, leaving only a cedar standing, but it, too, is soon swept away by the waters of the spring. The interpretation of the vision is: The mountains and the forest are four future kingdoms, the forest being the fourth one; the spring represents the messianic age; the vine is the Messiah; and the cedar is the last ruler of the wicked kingdom (Rome). Chapters 42–52: Baruch goes to Hebron and after he fasts there for seven days, he is informed by the voice that the righteous will be resurrected at the end of days and exalted above the angels. Chapters 53–74: In a final vision, which the angel Ramiel explains to him, Baruch sees a cloud rising from the sea and shedding 12 times alternately dark and bright waters. Lightning, flashing above the black cloud, restores the places destroyed by the dark waters. Twelve rivers arise, but submit to the lightning. The interpretation of the vision is as follows: The six dark waters refer to the sins of man (those of Adam, the Egyptians, the Canaanites, Jeroboam, Manasseh, and the Babylonians), while the six bright waters represent the elect of the nation (Abraham and his progeny; Moses, Aaron, Joshua, and Caleb; David and Solomon; Hezekiah; Josiah; the restoration of Jerusalem in the Second Temple era). The last dark waters refer to the interval between the Second Temple and the advent of the Messiah, a period of causeless hatred and social revolutions, the final flash of lightning being the messianic kingdom. Chapters 75–87: Baruch thanks God for the revelations he has received and writes two letters, one to the ten tribes and the other to the two and a half tribes. Only the contents of the former are given. In this letter, carried by an eagle to the captives in Babylonia, Baruch promises a speedy redemption, if they make full repentance.

The Apocalypse of Baruch and Talmudic Literature

There are many parallels between the Apocalypse of Baruch and *aggadot* in the Talmud and Midrash. According to the *aggadah* (PR 26:131) God likewise commands Jeremiah to leave Jerusalem on the eve of its destruction (II Bar. 2:1); angels set fire to the city (*ibid.*, chs. 6–8); the priests hand over the keys of the Temple to Heaven (Ta'an. 29a; Lev. R. 19:6; PR *ibid.*; ARN[1] 4, 12; II Bar. 10:18); Baruch enters Paradise alive (II Bar. 13:3–4; cf. Sif. Num. 99). There are several other features common to the Apocalypse of Baruch and the *aggadah*, such as that Manasseh made an idol with five faces (II Bar. 64:3; Sanh. 103b; Deut. R. 2:13 (20)); that he was burnt to death by the Assyrians (II Bar. 64:7; PdRK 162); that some sacred articles of the Temple (missing subsequently in the Second Temple) were swallowed up by the earth (II Bar. 6:7–8; Yoma 21b; Num. R. 15:10); that the patriarchs knew the Torah (Yoma 28b); and that Abraham, when eating secular meals, observed the rules of levitical cleanness required for sacred food (BM 87a).

There are further parallels between the Apocalypse of Baruch and the *aggadah*: The Heavenly Jerusalem (the counterpart of the earthly Temple), revealed to Adam (II Bar. 4:3; Sif. Deut. 37) and to Abraham in "the covenant between the pieces" (Gen. R. 44:21; 56:10; II Bar. 4:4); the souls in the "treasury" (II Bar. 30:2; Yev. 62a; Sif. Num. 139; ARN ch. 12; Shab. 152b); and the abundance and fertility that would be in time to come (Ket. 100a–b). The language of many ancient prayers is very similar to that of Baruch (cf. 11:4 "those that sleep in the dust"; 54:13 – which resembles the language in the **Nishmat* prayer).

In form and purpose the Apocalypse of Baruch is close to IV *Ezra, but it is impossible to determine which was composed first. In any event the Apocalypse of Baruch was written shortly after the destruction of the Second Temple (see II Bar. 20:2–4) and before the Bar Kokhba revolt. The Syriac version, which is derived from the Greek translation, was published in 1861 in Latin by A.M. Ceriani (*Monumenta sacra et profana*, t. 1^2, I–IV, 73–98), as well as in facsimile (1876–83). The work was undoubtedly written originally in Hebrew (see II Bar. 21:14; see Greek Apocalypse of *Baruch; Rest of the Words of *Baruch).

BIBLIOGRAPHY: F. Rosenthal, *Vier apocryphische Buecher aus der Zeit und Schule R. Akibas* (1885); Ryssel, in: Kautzsch, *Apokryphen und Pseudepigraphen*, 2 (1900), 404ff.; M. Kmosko, *Patriologia Syriaca*, 2 (1907); Schuerer, Gesch, 3 (1909^4), 305–15; Charles, Apocrypha, 2 (1913), 470–526; Perles, in: REJ, 73 (1921), 182–3; B. Violet, *Die Apokalypsen des Esra und des Baruch* (1924); P. Riessler, *Altjuedisches Schrifttum ausserhalb der Bibel* (1928), 55–113; A. Kahana, (ed.), *Ha-Sefarim ha-Ḥiẓonim*, 1 (1936), 362–407; J. Klausner, *Ha-Ra'yon ha-Meshiḥi be-Yisrael* (1950^3); Klausner, Bayit Sheni, 5 (1951^2), 291–4.

[Yehoshua M. Grintz]

BARUCH, BOOK OF (abbr. I Bar.), an apocryphal book which together with the Epistle of *Jeremiah is associated in the Septuagint with the writings attributed to the prophet Jeremiah and is regarded as canonical in both the Eastern and Latin churches. It purports to be a letter sent by *Baruch, Jeremiah's amanuensis, from Babylonia to Palestine after the destruction of the First Temple (1:1–4). It contains five chapters which fall into two or three sections. The first (1:1–3:8) opens with Baruch's reading of the book to the people assembled in Babylonia on the banks of the river Soud (LXX Σοῦδ, Syriac *ṣwr*; cf. 4Qp Jer *swr*) and the assembled multitude's repentance and mourning (1:1–14). This is followed by a penitential prayer which comprises the remainder of the prose section. The first part of this prayer strongly resembles the prayer in Daniel 9:4–19 and a comparison leads to the conclusion that the prayer in Baruch is based on that in Daniel. The continuation of the prayer (2:20–3:8) is composed of a mosaic of biblical verses and some original sections. Prayers of repentance associated with public fasts and lamentation are mentioned in the literature of the period (cf. I Macc. 3:46–54; Judith 4:8ff.; and Ta'an 2:1). In form, the prayers in Baruch and Daniel show a strong resemblance to the liturgical texts from Qumran called *Divrei ha-Me'orot* (Baillet, in RB, 58 (1961), 195–250). The second section (3:9–44) is sapiential in character. It is addressed to Israel (3:9) and in part reproaches Israel for abandoning wisdom and in part praises wisdom. This poem contrasts the true wisdom known to Israel with that of the peoples of the East, famed for their wisdom. The passage, in common with Ben Sira and later wisdom writing, identifies true wisdom with that revealed to Israel, i.e., with the Torah. The final section of the book is composed of two poems of lamentation and comfort. The first (4:9–29) is a message of solace addressed to Israel by a personified Jerusalem, seen as a mother bewailing her children (4:10, 12, etc.). In 4:30 the speaker changes and Jerusalem is herself comforted with the message of the eventual redemption of Israel. The book is extant in Greek, Syriac, Syro-Hexaplar, three Old Latin versions, as well as Armenian, Arabic, Ethiopic, and Coptic. It has been suggested that the translation of the first section into Greek was the work of the translator of the second part of Septuagint Jeremiah (Thackeray, in: JTS, 4 (1903), 261–6). The question of the original language is intimately related to that of the literary unity of the work. A number of scholars have proposed that the book is a compilation of two or three original documents: the prayers of confession, the wisdom poem, and the laments. In general, all agree that the first section (1:1–3:8) was written in Hebrew, and most scholars who accept the documentary theory consider the third section (4:9–5:9) to be originally Greek and dependent on Wisdom of Solomon 11 (Charles, Apocrypha, 1 (1913), 572–3). This stance, modified by a vigorous defense of the coherence of the present form of the book as the work of a single "author-redactor" has been supported by Wambacq (*Biblica*, 47 (1966), 574–6), while A. Cahana in his Hebrew edition maintained the theory of literary unity and original Hebrew (*Ha-Sefarim ha-Ḥiẓonim*, 1 (1936), 350ff.). The book has been dated variously between the late Hasmonean period (*ante quem non* – dependence on Daniel) and the destruction of the Second Temple (the historical framework of the book). The existence of further Baruch-Jeremiah apocrypha at Qumran weakens this latter argument considerably.

BIBLIOGRAPHY: Charles, Apocrypha, 1 (1913), 569–95; J.J. Kneucker, *Das Buch Baruch* (1879); R. Harwell, *The Principal Versions of Baruch* (1915); B.N. Wambacq, in: *Sacra Pagina*, 1 (1959), 455–60; idem, in: *Biblica*, 40 (1959), 463–75; O. Eissfeldt, *The Old Testament, an Introduction* (1965), 592–4 (includes bibliography).

[Michael E. Stone]

BARUCH, GREEK APOCALYPSE OF (abbr. III Bar.), an apocalypse describing the journey of *Baruch through the heavens. Baruch, Jeremiah's scribe, weeps over the destruction of Jerusalem and questions God's righteousness. He is granted this heavenly journey in order to subdue his anger and console him in his grief. In the introduction, the angel of the Lord offers to show the mourning Baruch the secrets of God. He takes him to the First Heaven where they see men in monstrous form who are identified as the people who built the Tower of Babel. The angel also explains certain measurements of the First Heaven. In the Second Heaven they meet doglike human monsters who initiated the building of the tower. In the Third Heaven, the angel shows Baruch the dragon in Hades; he also tells him how it came about that God permitted Noah to plant the cursed vine which had been the cause of Adam and Eve's sin (the vine being identified with the forbidden fruit of the Garden of Eden – cf. Ber. 40a; Gen. R. 19:5). God promises him to change the curse into a blessing; the angel, however, warns against overindulgence in wine, for the most awful sins result from it. In this heaven Baruch also observes the coming and going of the sun and the moon. The sun's chariot is driven by four angels; other angels are busy purifying the sun's crown, defiled by men's daily sins. The phoenix absorbs with his wings most of the fiery rays of the sun, so as to prevent life on earth from burning up. Baruch is frightened by this spectacle and by the accompanying thunder. Next, the angel and Baruch pass the dwelling place of the righteous souls. In the Fifth Heaven, Baruch sees the archangel Michael weighing the good deeds of people, brought by the angel appointed over each individual, and sending them their reward. The angels who could not bring any good deeds from their protégés are ordered to attend upon the sinners until they repent, and if they do not, to inflict upon them all the prophesied evils. Baruch then returns to the earth and is instructed to reveal to the sons of men those of God's secrets which he has seen and heard.

In the present form the Greek Apocalypse of Baruch is the work of a Christian writer: the Christological interpretation of the vine in chapter 4; the citation from the New Testament in chapter 15; and the technical terms deriving from a Christian background, namely ἐκκλήσία ("church") and πνευματικοὶ πατέρες ("spiritual fathers") in chapter 13 are organic parts of the present story and cannot possibly be explained as mere interpolations. It is obvious however that this is not the original form of the book. The ultimate aim of the traveler through the heavens is to see the Glory of God, an aim usually attained in the Seventh Heaven (cf. Slavonic Enoch, ch. 9ff.; Test. Patr. Levi 3:8; Ḥag. 12b. etc.). Indeed, twice in the book (III Bar. 7:2; 11:2) the guiding angel assures Baruch, "Wait and you shall see the Glory of God," a promise which is never fulfilled, for Baruch reaches no further than the Fifth Heaven. This reinforces the probability that the present work is a later version of an apocalypse of Baruch which in an earlier version, mentioned by *Origen (*De principiis* 2:3, 6), included the Seven Heavens.

The main issues dealt with in the Greek Apocalypse of Baruch are the heavenly mechanisms of, and causes behind, cosmological matters, and man's just reward for his deeds. The latter brings it into the realm of the testament- and Adam-literature; it is in the light of this genre and not in that of direct New Testament influence (as M.R. James avers) that the lists of sins (III Bar. 4:7; 8:5; 13:4) should be understood. The uranological traditions of the Greek Apocalypse of Baruch are closely related to the Enoch books (cf. Ethiopic Enoch chs. 72, 73; Slavonic Enoch chs. 3–9, esp. 6); some stories have parallels in aggadic literature (see Ginzberg, and Artom's notes in Kahana); the theme that the souls of the righteous dwell as birds around a lake (ch. 10) might well be of Egyptian origin (in the hieroglyphics the bird designates the heavenly soul).

The Apocalypse is written in a very simple Koine-Greek of late antiquity; there is no evidence that it was translated from a Semitic language. Two Slavonic versions (see Picard, pp. 70–71 and Turdeanu) mainly follow the Greek text.

BIBLIOGRAPHY: S. Novaković, in: *Starine*, 18 (1886), 203–9; M.I. Sokolov, in: *Drevnosti*, no.4, 201–58; M.R. James, *Apocrypha Anecdota*, 2 (1897), li–lxxi, 83–102; V. Ryssel, in: E. Kautzsch (ed.), *Die Apocryphen and Pseudepigraphen*, 2 (1900),.446–57; L. Ginzberg, in: JE, 2 (1902), 549–51; W. Luedtke, in: ZAW, 31 (1911), 219–22; H.M. Hughes, in: Charles, Apocrypha, 2 (1913), 527–41; E.S. Artom, *Ha-Sefarim ha-Ḥiẓonim, Ḥazon Barukh* 2 (1967); idem, in: A. Kahana (ed.), *Ha-Sefarim ha-Ḥiẓonim*, 1 (1936), 408–25; E. Turdeanu, in: RHR, 138 (1950), 177–81; J.-C. Picard (ed.). *Apocalypse Baruchi graece* (1967), 61–96.

[Jacques Yakov Guggenheim]

BARUCH, JACOB BEN MOSES ḤAYYIM (late 18th century), editor and author. Baruch lived in Leghorn. In 1875 he edited (Leghorn, Castello & Saadun) *Shivḥei Yerushalayim* ("The Praises of Jerusalem"; or *Shabbeḥi Yerushalayim*, from

Psalms 147:12, "Praise, O Jerusalem"), an anthology of texts on the Land of Israel containing extracts from the following works: (1) *Tzaḥve-Adom* by Raphael Treves (Constantinople, 1740), on the holy places in the Land of Israel; (2) *Imrei Kadosh* from the *Sha'ar ha-Gilgulim* of Samuel ben Ḥayyim Vital, on the graves of sainted rabbis; (3) an Eretz Israel travelogue, whose author remained unknown until the scholarly edition of the manuscript by Izhak Ben-Zvi (1938), who identified him (after A. De Rossi's indication in *Meor Einayim*, ch. 46, ed. Cassel 449–50) with the rabbi Moses *Basola. Ben-Zvi criticized Baruch's publication, which omitted the beginning and the end of the manuscript, and was sometimes inaccurate; 4) *Masa'ot* of Benjamin of Tudela; (4) prayers of kabbalistic inspiration concerning the pilgrimage to the graves of the sainted rabbis, opposite the Temple Mount (also from Basola's travelogue), etc.; (5) *Kitzur Shenei Luḥot ha-Berit* of Yeḥiel Epstein; (6) a list of currencies and weights. *Shivḥei Yerushalayim* had considerable success and was published at least six times until the late 19th century.

In 1790 Baruch edited (and financed publication of) *Sha'ar ha-Ḥeshek* ("The Portal of Delight," Livorno, Falorni), a large part of *Shir ha-Ma'alot*, the introduction to Johanan *Alemanno's *Ḥeshek Shelomo* on Song of Songs, an elaboration on King Solomon's wisdom. Baruch added an introduction in which he praised the religious value of science (quoting Y. Del Medigo's *Sefer Elim*) and many notes to the text (under the name *Ashiv*, "Amar Shafel Ya'akov Barukh," "said the humble Jacob Baruch"), in which he emphasizes the Jewish origin of all the sciences (esp. p. 12a). These notes refer mainly to kabbalistic literature (from **Sefer Yetzirah* to Ḥayyim Joseph David *Azulai) but also take into account the Italian, rationalist tradition (A. De Rossi, p. 55a; A. *Portaleone, p. 23b). *Sha'ar ha-Ḥeshek* was published a second time in Halberstadt in 1862.

BIBLIOGRAPHY: I. Ben Zvi, *Masot Eretz Yisrael le-R. Moshe Basola* (1938), 7–11; A. David, *In Zion and Jerusalem. The Itinerary of Rabbi Moses Basola, 1521–1523* (1999), 7, 28–29; M. Steinschneider, *Hebraeische Bibliographie* 5 (1862), 28–29.

[Alessandro Guetta (2nd ed.)]

BARUCH, JOSEPH MARCOU (1872–1899), early Zionist propagandist in Western Europe and Mediterranean countries. Baruch, born in Constantinople, conducted an anti-assimilation campaign among Jewish students in Berne and was wounded in a duel with a non-Jewish student over an antisemitic remark. In 1893 Baruch went to Vienna and joined the student circle of the Zionist Kadimah association. In 1894, in Algeria, he edited the newspaper *Le Juge*, in which, despite the opposition of local Jewish leaders, he tried to awaken the national consciousness of Algerian Jewry. Registered with the police as an anarchist, Baruch was compelled to leave the country. In 1895, after returning to Vienna, he went to Bulgaria and established a Zionist group in Sofia. In Philippopolis (Plovdiv) he published a French-language newspaper with a Ladino supplement, called *Carmel*, and helped establish Zionist associations in various Bulgarian towns, until he was imprisoned. He was released under the protection of Prince Konstantinov, and in 1896 left Bulgaria for Egypt where he continued his Zionist activity in Port Said, Alexandria, and Cairo. Some of his ideas later reached Herzl, particularly his criticism of "infiltration" (i.e., small-scale settlement in Palestine without prior political guarantees), and his advocacy of the foundation of an internationally recognized Jewish state. Toward this end he proposed war with Turkey, even joining the group called Garibaldi's army, which eventually fought for the liberation of Crete from Turkish rule. When Herzl appeared on the Zionist scene, Baruch was among his supporters. He attended the Second and Third Zionist Congresses (1898, 1899), and went on Zionist propaganda tours. Herzl's feelings for Baruch alternated between sympathy and dislike, as a result of the latter's eccentric personality, and Herzl was even afraid he might make an attempt on his life. Baruch's last days were spent in Italy, where he published his book *Le Juif à l'Ile du Diable*, a defense of Alfred Dreyfus. He committed suicide in Florence.

BIBLIOGRAPHY: Y. Weinschal, *Marcou Baruch, Nevi Milḥemet ha-Shiḥrur* (1949); T. Herzl, *Complete Diaries*, ed. by R. Patai, 5 (1960), index; Molcho, in: *Haolam*, 33 (1946), 16–18; M.D. Gaon, *Yehudei ha-Mizraḥ be-Ereẓ Yisrael be-Avar u-va-Hoveh*, 2 (1938), 172–5.

[Getzel Kressel]

BARUCH, REST OF THE WORDS OF, apocryphal book, also called *Paralipomena Jeremiae* (Chronicles of Jeremiah) in its present form, a Christian reworking of a patently Jewish source. It is connected with the wider Baruch and Jeremiah literature represented also by the Syriac and Greek Apocalypses of *Baruch, the Greek Book of *Baruch, the Epistle of *Jeremiah, as well as fragments from Qumran Cave 4.

Its story opens with the destruction of the Temple, which is announced by God to Jeremiah. At God's orders, Jeremiah buries the Temple vessels beneath the Temple, where they are to remain until the coming of the Messiah. He also enquires what is to be done with the slave Abimelech (Ebedmelech of Jer. 38, and one Armenian recension) and is instructed to send him to Agrippa's vineyard where he would be hidden until the return from exile. Jeremiah was to go with the exiles of Babylon (cf. Jer. 43, but see SOR 26), while Baruch was to remain in Jerusalem.

The role played by Abimelech is unique to this book. He arrives in Agrippa's vineyard to pick some figs and, it being midday, lies down to rest and awakens only after 66 years. He examines his figs and finds them fresh. Going to Jerusalem, he does not recognize the city and, in his confusion, accosts an old man who tells him of what has happened while he slept. He is led to Baruch by an angel and they rejoice over the miracle of the figs in which they see a sign of redemption. Baruch prays for guidance in sending a letter to Jeremiah and the following morning a miraculous eagle appears and carries Baruch's letter and some of the figs to Jeremiah. To prove its genuineness, the eagle alights on the body of a dead man and he is restored to life. Jeremiah then reads the letter to the people in Babylon; they repent and weep, and the exiles set forth for

Jerusalem. Before they depart, however, Jeremiah examines them to ensure that there are no uncircumcised among them and none married to foreign women. Those who are thus disqualified desire to return to Babylon, but are not permitted to do so by the Babylonians, and so they build themselves the city of Samaria. The story concludes with the offering of sacrifices in Jerusalem and Jeremiah's death in the Temple. The sequel is Christian and, as generally agreed, not part of the original work. This story is extant in Greek, various Slavonic, Ethiopic, Coptic (P. Morgan Ms. 601), and three different Armenian recensions. The problem of textual history and the relationship between the various text forms have not been adequately studied. Klausner (EIV, s.v.) defends the primacy of the Ethiopic but, like most previous students of the work, he was not familiar with the Armenian recensions. The Jewish nature of the original is apparent from many distinctive features. Thus the approval of sacrifice, the rejection of foreign women, and the attitude to circumcision, to mention the most prominent, clearly disprove the theory of a Christian original.

It is probable that the book was composed after the destruction of the Second Temple, and some would even suggest that the hatred displayed toward the Samaritans indicates a date in the reign of the emperor Hadrian. It depends at many points on the Syriac Apocalypse of *Baruch. Recent studies have emphasized the prominence of Jewish religious ideas and terminology in this work.

BIBLIOGRAPHY: A. Dillmann, *Chrestomathia Aethiopica* (1866), 1–15; J.R. Harris, *The Rest of the Words of Baruch* (1889); J. Issaverdens, *Uncanonical Writings of the Old Testament* (1900); E. Kautzsch, *Apokryphen und Pseudepigraphen des Alten Testaments*, 2 (1900), 402ff.; DBI, suppl. 1 (1928), 454f. (incl. bibl.); J. Klausner, *Meḥkarim Ḥadashim u-Mekorot Attikim* (1957), 90–117; J. Licht, in: *Bar Ilan, Sefer ha-Shanah*, 1 (1963), 66–80; G. Delling, *Juedische Lehre und Froemmigkeit in den Paralipomena Jeremiae* (1967); W. Baars, in: VT, 17 (1967), 487ff.

[Michael E. Stone]

BARUCH BEN DAVID YAVAN (18th cent.), *Court Jew of the Polish king August III, financier of his minister Count Bruehl. He was a leader in the *Council of Four Lands and as **shtadlan* for the Council used his influence at court for furthering Jewish causes. Baruch received a talmudic education under R. Jacob Joshua *Falk and knew several languages. He was prominent in combating the remnants of *Shabbateanism and the *Frankists. In the controversy over Jonathan *Eybeschuetz' adherence to Shabbateanism he upheld Jacob *Emden (who was related to him by their children's marriage) in his condemnation of Eybeschuetz. Baruch did not hesitate to effect the removal of Ḥayyim b. Abraham, an adherent of Eybeschuetz, from his post of rabbi of Lublin and his imprisonment in 1751. Baruch took a leading role in Jewish diplomatic efforts to counter the Frankists. When the disputation between the talmudists and Frankists became in 1757 the occasion for an ecclesiastical order to burn the Talmud, Baruch, aided by the *shtadlan* Mordecai Merkil, sought the help of Count Bruehl. He obtained access to the papal nuncio and succeeded in saving many talmudic works. Baruch also persuaded Count Bruehl to use his influence at the papal curia to thwart the *blood libel instigated by Frank. In 1764 he frustrated Frank's intrigues with Russia, using his connections with the Russian nobility to convince the synodal authorities of the Russian Orthodox Church that Frank's application for acceptance into their faith was insincere.

BIBLIOGRAPHY: H. Graetz, *Frank und die Frankisten* (1868); A. Kraushar, *Frank i Frankiści* (1895); M. Balaban, *Le-Toledot ha-Tenu'ah ha-Frankit* (1934). **ADD. BIBLIOGRAPHY:** Halpern, Pinkas, 361 (Barukh me-Ereẓ Yavan).

[Nathan Michael Gelber]

BARUCH BEN ISAAC OF ALEPPO (c. 1050–c. 1125), scholar. Baruch appears to have been born in Spain, where he studied together with his younger kinsman *Baruch b. Samuel of Aleppo. From there he went to Aleppo where he was the head of a large yeshivah. From 1085 his signature appears on various documents, among them a letter of recommendation on behalf of Obadiah the Proselyte of Normandy. He wrote a commentary on the order *Kodashim*, of the Babylonian Talmud, which was highly recommended by *Joseph Rosh ha-Seder, who considered it equal to the commentaries of *Hananel b. Ḥushi'el on the orders *Mo'ed, Nashim*, and *Nezikin* and of *Isaac b. Melchizedek on *Zera'im* and *Tohorot*. He also wrote commentaries on other tractates, including *Shabbat* (quoted by Isaiah di Trani in his commentary on this tractate) and *Bava Meẓia* (see *Ginzei Kedem*, 5 (1934), 131–4). S. Assaf was of the opinion that the commentary on tractate *Zevaḥim* (Jerusalem, 1942), attributed to Hananel, was by Baruch, but this identification does not appear to be correct.

BIBLIOGRAPHY: Mann, in: *Ha-Tekufah*, 24 (1928), 337, 352–4; Epstein, in: *Tarbiz*, 16 (1944/45), 49–53; Assaf, *ibid.*, 19 (1947/48), 105–8.

[Israel Moses Ta-Shma]

BARUCH BEN ISAAC OF REGENSBURG (second half of 12th century), talmudic scholar. He was a member of the *bet din* of Regensburg, together with *Isaac b. Jacob Ha-Lavan of Prague, Abraham ben Moses of Regensburg, and *Judah he-Ḥasid b. Samuel (*Sefer Ḥasidim*, ed. by J. Wistinetzki (1924^2), 390). Baruch was one of the teachers of *Abraham b. Azriel, the author of *Arugat ha-Bosem*. There is record of a question addressed to Baruch and his two fellow judges by R. *Joel ben Isaac ha-Levi (*Sefer Ravyah*, no. 1031). Baruch engaged in disputations with his older contemporary *Eliezer b. Nathan of Mainz, who esteemed him highly, and with *Isaac b. Samuel ha-Zaken of Dampierre. Some scholars have incorrectly identified him with *Baruch b. Isaac of Worms, author of the *Sefer ha-Terumah*.

BIBLIOGRAPHY: H. Gross, in: MGWJ, 34 (1885), 558–60; idem, in: ZHB, 11 (1907), 179; J. Wellesz, in: MGWJ, 48 (1904), 442; V. Aptowitzer *Mavo le-Sefer Ravyah* (1938), 174, 326–9; Urbach, Tosafot, 286ff., 299, 334; idem, *Arugat ha-Bosem* (1963), index; idem, in: *Tarbiz*, 10 (1938/39), 86ff.

[Moshe Nahum Zobel]

BARUCH BEN ISAAC OF WORMS (late 12th–early 13th century), German tosafist. Although Baruch lived in Worms, he probably came from France and is sometimes referred to as Ha-Zarefati ("the Frenchman"). Baruch was a pupil of *Isaac b. Samuel the Elder of Dampierre, and after his teacher's death, spent a considerable amount of time in France with Judah of Paris. Baruch immigrated to Ereẓ Israel (1237?). It seems certain that he is not to be identified with *Baruch b. Isaac of Regensburg.

He is renowned as the author of *Sefer ha-Terumah* (written shortly before 1202; first published Venice, 1523), which comprises a summary of the established *halakhot* on several subjects, including the laws pertaining to Ereẓ Israel, combined and arranged according to the chapters of the relevant tractates of the Talmud. The whole work reflects the teachings of Isaac b. Samuel. In it Baruch mentions *Samuel b. Meir (Rashbam) and *Isaac b. Meir, as well as statements of Rabbi Jacob *Tam and his pupils; however, very few German scholars are referred to. By virtue of its wealth of material and its terse, easy style, well adapted to its purpose of leading, through discussion, to the practical *halakhah*, the book spread through France, Germany, Italy, and Spain, and was widely quoted by many later authorities among them, *Eliezer of Worms, *Isaac b. Moses Or Zarua, *Moses b. Jacob of Coucy, Zedekiah *Anav, *Aaron b. Jacob of Lunel, and *Naḥmanides. Entire halakhic passages from the work were inserted by copyists into the *Maḥzor Vitry. Numerous manuscripts of *Sefer ha-Terumah* and some manuscripts of an anonymous abridgment are extant. Baruch also wrote *tosafot* to several tractates of the Talmud, but only those on *Zevaḥim* have been preserved and they are printed in the standard editions of the Talmud. A. Epstein held that the anonymous commentary on *Tamid* attributed to Abraham b. David (Prague, 1725) should be ascribed to Baruch, but – despite a measure of similarity between the commentary and a number of quotations in Baruch's name which are known – this is unlikely. E.E. Urbach has maintained that the commentary on the *Sifra* ascribed to Abraham b. David was written by Baruch, but this too is uncertain.

BIBLIOGRAPHY: A. Epstein, *Das talmudische Lexikon "Yiḥusei Tanna'im ve-Amora'im"* (1895); Urbach, Tosafot, 263, 286–99, 511–2; V. Aptowitzer, *Mavo le-Sefer Ravyah* (1938), 327–8.

[Israel Moses Ta-Shma]

BARUCH BEN JEHIEL OF MEDZIBEZH (1757–1810), ḥasidic *ẓaddik*; grandson of *Israel b. Eliezer the Baal Shem Tov, the founder of modern *Ḥasidism. Baruch, who studied under Phinehas Shapira of Korets, officiated from 1780 as rabbi in Tulchin, but encountered opposition and returned to Medzibezh in 1788. He attributed great importance to his descent and regarded himself as the heir to the Ba'al Shem Tov's leadership. He held that the *ẓaddik* could save and lead the whole world; the duty of the common man was only "to destroy the evil impulses and abandon his desires." Regarding himself as the leader of Ḥasidism by hereditary right, he held "court" in Medzibezh in a highly autocratic and luxurious fashion, though preaching asceticism to others. He kept a "court jester," Hershele Ostropoler. His behavior aroused opposition from other ḥasidic leaders. In 1808 he met Shneur Zalman of Lyady in an effort to settle their differences. Baruch attached mystical importance to the custom practiced by Ḥasidim of giving presents to the rabbis (*pidyonot*). He encouraged Ḥasidim to immigrate to Ereẓ Israel. He took part in the assembly of ḥasidic rabbis at Berdichev (1802–03) that discussed the government's prohibition of Jewish settlement in the villages among other matters. His writings include *Amarot Tehorot* (1865; first published in his brother's (*Moses Ḥayyim Ephraim) *Degel Maḥaneh Ephraim*, Zhitomir, 1850) and *Buẓina di-Nehora* (1880).

BIBLIOGRAPHY: M. Bodek, *Seder ha-Dorot he-Ḥadash* (1865), 23; Horodezky, Ḥasidut, 3 (1953⁴), 12–17; Dubnow, Ḥasidut, 1 (1930), 205–8; M. Buber, *Tales of the Ḥasidim*, 1 (1947), 87–97; M.E. Gutman, *Mi-Gibborei ha-Ḥasidut*, 3 (1928).

[Nachum Arieli]

BARUCH BEN SAMUEL (d. 1834), adventurer and physician. Baruch was born in Pinsk and emigrated to Safed in 1819. The reports of a messenger who traveled from Safed to Yemen and back in 1825 gave rise to wondrous tales about a Jew from the tribe of Dan whom he allegedly met in Yemen and of stories about the "Sons of Moses" and the Ten Tribes. The community of Safed decided to send a messenger to these remote Jews to come to the aid of their brethren in Palestine. They chose Baruch who, in their opinion, possessed the qualities necessary for such a bold undertaking. They gave him a letter addressed to the Ten Tribes and made him swear to devote himself wholly to this task.

Baruch started his journey in 1831. His travels took him to Damascus, Aleppo, Kurdistan, Mesopotamia, Baghdad, Basra, Bushire, Muscat, and Aden. Toward the end of 1833 Baruch reached Yemen. The rabbis of San'a received him cordially and one of the members of the community (*dayyan* Māri Yiḥye al-Abyat) accompanied him to Ḥaydān at the northern extremity of Yemen, where, according to the rumor, the tribe of Dan lived. Baruch and his companion made their way into the desert where they met a shepherd, who appeared to them like a Danite. They gave him the letter and he promised to deliver the answer to them in Ḥaydān. Then Baruch and his companion hurried back to San'a for the autumn Holidays. The Jews of Ḥaydān promised to forward the anticipated answer to San'a, but it never came.

When Baruch returned to San'a, he offered to cure the sickly imam of Yemen, al-Mahdi. He hoped thereby to enlist the imam's aid in the completion of his mission. After his recovery, the imam appointed Baruch his court physician. Baruch began to behave haughtily toward the Muslims, and thus aroused their enmity and jealousy. In 1834 Ibrahim Pasha of Egypt attacked Yemen and captured Mocha. Baruch assured the imam that if he would give him an army, he would drive out the conqueror on condition that afterward he himself be appointed the ruler of that city. This proposal served Baruch's enemies as a pretext for charging him with spying for Egypt. The imam believed this false accusation and in February 1834, during his daily walk in the garden with Baruch, the imam shot his physician. The dying Baruch predicted that the Imam and his family would lose their kingdom. His prediction came true in less than a year.

BIBLIOGRAPHY: J. Saphir, *Even Sappir*, 1 (1866), 83–86; E. Brauer, *Ethnologie der jemenitischen Juden* (1934), 42–44; Yaari, Sheluḥei, 147ff.

[Yehuda Ratzaby]

BARUCH BEN SAMUEL OF ALEPPO (also called **Baruch of Greece**, or **the Sephardi**; 1070/80–1130/40), talmudic commentator. It is surmised that he was either from southern Italy or Spain. He immigrated to Ereẓ Israel and then to Aleppo, from where he sent questions to Samuel b. Ali, head of the Baghdad yeshivah. His commentaries are frequently quoted by the scholars of Germany, Italy, Provence, and Spain, among them *Isaac b. Moses of Vienna, author of *Or Zaru'a* and *Isaiah b. Mali di Trani. He is mostly quoted by Zechariah *Aghmati in his commentary on *Bava Kamma, Bava Meẓia* and *Bava Batra*. Baruch relied mainly on *Hananel's commentary and *Perushei Magenẓa* (Mainz) attributed to *Gershom b. Judah. He followed the method of giving a precis of the talmudic text and interweaving his own commentary. Like *Nissim b. Jacob and Hananel b. Ḥushiel he referred to the talmudic sources, *Sifra, Sifrei*, and Tosefta, and was meticulous with regard to variant readings. He also wrote *Ḥibbur Tohorot*, which is mentioned by Isaiah di Trani, and a book of halakhic decisions. Only his commentary to *Horayot* has survived and is printed in the Romm editions of the Talmud, although erroneously ascribed to Hananel.

BIBLIOGRAPHY: S. Assaf, in: *Tarbiz*, 1 no. 1 (1930), 126; Epstein, *ibid.*, 1 no. 4 (1930), 27–62; 16 (1944/45), 49–53.

[Josef Horovitz]

BARUCH BEN SAMUEL OF MAINZ (c. 1150–1221), scholar and *paytan*. Baruch was a pupil of Moses b. Solomon ha-Kohen, whom he succeeded as a member of the *bet din* of Mainz. There is no basis for Aptowitzer's statement that a dispute for the position between him and his kinsman, *Eliezer b. Samuel of Metz, took place. Baruch also studied under *Judah b. Kalonymus b. Meir of Speyer, and possibly *Ephraim b. Isaac of Regensburg. He was in halakhic correspondence with many contemporary scholars, including *Judah he-Ḥasid.

Baruch is best known for his *Sefer ha-Ḥokhmah*, a comprehensive work (now lost) covering the subject matter of *Nashim* and *Nezikin*, as well as the laws of *Issur ve-Hetter*; it also included his responsa. The work was still extant in the 16th century when Solomon *Luria and Bezalel *Ashkenazi used it. It is extensively quoted by the *rishonim*, particularly by *Mordecai b. Hillel and by *Meir b. Baruch of Rothenburg, sometimes being referred to as "The Book of Baruch of Mainz." Baruch is not mentioned at all by name in *tosafot*, although some ascribe to him the authorship of the printed *tosafot* to *Sotah*. Of Baruch's *piyyutim*, 33 of which have been preserved (published by Habermann – see bibl.), some deal with the persecutions in *Blois (1171), *Speyer and *Boppard (1196), and Wuerzburg (before 1221), and are a valuable historical source. One *piyyut* is devoted to the talmudic discussion "*ilan de-Ulla*" ("the tree of Ulla," BB 26b–27a), a rare phenomenon in *piyyut*. These *piyyutim*, some of which are rhymed, excel in their variety and their style – biblical language being interspersed with the language of rabbinical and early mystical literature. Baruch revised a number of his *piyyutim* in order to bring them up to date, as in the *seliḥot, Be-Terem Noledu Harim* and *Be-Terem Harve-Givah*. Highly popular among congregants, his *seliḥot* were affectionately termed "*berukhah*," "*mevorekhet*," and "*mevorakh*" ("blessed," a play on words from his name). His son, R. SAMUEL OF BAMBERG, the teacher of R. *Meir b. Baruch of Rothenburg, was also noted as an halakhic scholar and as a *paytan*.

BIBLIOGRAPHY: Urbach, Tosafot, 134–6, 352–4; Habermann, in: YMḤSI, 6 (1945), 47ff.; Epstein, in: *Tarbiz*, 12 (1940/41), 190–6; idem, in: MGWJ, 83 (1939, 1963²), 346–55; Davidson, Oẓar 4 (1933), 373; Germ Jud, 1 (1934), 201; V. Aptowitzer (ed.), *Mavo le-Sefer Rayyah* (1938), 313–4, 329–30.

[Israel Moses Ta-Shma]

BARUCH (BEN ABRAHAM) OF KOSOV (c. 1725/30–1795), kabbalist. He was a disciple of *Menahem Mendel of Vitebsk and also studied with *Menahem Mendel of Przemyslany for a short while. Baruch became *Maggid* in Kosov. In his sermons he tried to make the kabbalist doctrine, as taught mainly by Isaac *Luria and Ḥayyim *Vital, easily comprehensible by the use of explanatory metaphors. According to Baruch, Luria was the highest authority on Kabbalah. Therefore, he advised all who wished to study the *Zohar, first to read Luria and Vital. Baruch interpreted (as did Joseph *Ergas) Luria's doctrine of "*ẓimẓum*" (i.e., God's self-willed withdrawal), as a metaphor and not as an actual fact. On this point he argued against the realistic interpretation of Immanuel Ḥai *Ricchi. Baruch taught that the true life of every material entity was conditioned by its spiritual aspect. He therefore contended that full surrender and complete attachment to God was possible because this was an intellectual discipline originating in a love which knows no limits. He maintained that it was possible to attain a concept of things, first through the senses, then on a higher level, through the imagination, and finally, at the highest stage, through wisdom. It was only through wisdom that one could perceive the spiritual quality inherent in every material being. Only wisdom had the capacity to feel the pain which the soul inevitably felt when man committed a sin. Baruch conceded that the questions of predestination and free will were so difficult as to be unanswerable. Nevertheless he believed in both, and counseled unconditional belief in them (*Ammud ha-Avodah*, 54–55, 107; *Yesod ha-Emmunah*, 76–99). Baruch was totally and aggressively against the followers of *Shabbetai Ẓevi and Jacob *Frank. In 1760 his antagonism to the latter apparently motivated him to begin writing the above books with the aim of refuting the anthropomorphism applied by Frankists to the basic concepts of Kabbalah. From 1761 he had started to collect from learned authorities their written commentaries on the manuscripts of his books. However, it was only in 1854 that they were actually printed in Czernowitz: (1) *Yesod ha-Emunah*, on the Pentateuch and miscellanies; (2) *Ammud ha-Avodah*, on the basic questions of Kabbalah, including "a lengthy introduction to explain the essence of the spiritual entities."

BIBLIOGRAPHY: A. Yaari, *Meḥkerei Sefer* (1958), 453–4; I. Tishby, in: *Zion*, 32 (1967), 24–29.

[Samuel Abba Horodezky]

BARUH, BORA (1901–1941), Yugoslav painter. After studying law, he devoted himself to painting, moving to Paris in 1938. On returning to Belgrade in 1941, he joined the partisan movement in Serbia but was captured and executed. He painted landscapes, portraits, and Spanish Civil War scenes, mainly in oils.

BARUK, HENRI (1897–1999), French psychiatrist. In 1931 he was appointed chief physician at the Charenton mental institution, and in 1946 became professor at the Sorbonne. His early scientific studies concentrated on psychiatric disorders caused by tumors on the brain. He succeeded in creating, by artificial means, aggression psychoses in animals. This led him to study the connections between psychiatric illness and defective moral awareness in human beings, and he subsequently displayed a tendency to extend psychiatry into the area of general anthropology. In 1957 he became chairman of the French Neurological Society. Baruk compared biblical medicine with that of Greece and wrote studies on religious belief and medical ethics. He opposed scientific experiments on the human body and all methods of psychiatric treatment which suppress or diminish the personality. Deeply linked to Jewish tradition and texts, Baruk was active in Jewish affairs in France, as chairman of the Society for the History of Hebrew Medicine in Paris and of the French Friends of the Hebrew University of Jerusalem. His works include *Hebraic Civilization and the Science of Man*, 1961 (originally a lecture in Edinburgh in 1960); *Le Test Tzedek, le jugement moral et la délinquance* (1950); *Psychiatrie morale, expérimentale, individuelle et sociale; Psychoses et neuroses* (1965); *La Psychanalyse devant la médecine et l'idolâtrie* (1978); *La Psychiatrie et la crise morale du monde d'aujourd'hui* (1983); and *La Bible hébraïque devant la crise morale du monde d'aujourd'hui* (1987). He also published his memoirs: *Des hommes comme nous,mémoires d'un neuropsychiatre* (1975; *Patients are People Like Us: The Experiences of Half a Century in Neuropsychiatry*, 1977).

[Joshua O. Leibowitz / Dror Franck Sullaper (2nd ed.)]

BARUKH (Heb. בָּרוּךְ), initial word of the **berakhah* pattern of prayer. *Barukh* is conventionally translated "blessed," but the etymology is disputed. The root (ברך) seems to have meant originally "bend (or fall) upon the knees (*berekh* = knee)" in prayerful obeisance (Ps. 95:6; Isa. 45:23). Cassuto maintains, however, that it meant originally "bestow a gift" (Gen. 24:1, 35; 33:11, et al.). *Barukh* is a homonym expressing a reciprocal relationship: man can address God as *barukh* by expressing feelings of thanksgiving, reverence, love, and praise, while he is *barukh* by God who bestows His material and spiritual gifts. The person upon whom the divine blessing rests is called *berukh Adonai*, "blessed of the Lord" (Gen. 24:31, 26:29). *Barukh Adonai*, in the sense of man blessing God, occurs 24 times in the Bible.

The pattern *barukh Attah Adonai* ("blessed art Thou, Lord") occurs only twice in biblical literature (Ps. 119:12; I Chron. 29:10). This second person form attained currency no earlier than about the fourth century B.C.E. There is, however, no substantive difference between the second and third person forms. As applied to God "blessed" is identical with "praised" and the formula of blessing viz. benediction is, in fact, one of praise.

The prototype of the classical *berakhah* is to be found in the biblical formula, *barukh Adonai… asher…* (e.g., Gen. 24:27; Ex. 18:10), in which he who has experienced the marvelous or miraculous expresses adoration and awe. This pattern persisted for centuries and was eventually adapted for liturgical use as the Jew's response to "the miracles of every day." But the insertion of the pronoun *Attah* ("Thou") was slow in gaining exclusive acceptance. Some of the variant forms of the *berakhah* persisted until the third century C.E. when the standard pattern was fully established (Ber. 40b). In third-century Babylonia, Rav and Samuel were still debating whether *Attah* was required in the formula (TJ, Ber. 9:1, 12d). Rav's pattern, *barukh Attah Adonai*, became the standard opening phrase; but the old biblical formula in which *barukh* (*Attah*) *Adonai* was followed by the characteristic phrase, *asher* ("who," i.e., "performed some beneficent act") remained in use. This juxtaposition of direct address to God and a sequel in the third person created a syntactical paradox which has exercised commentators and theologians down to the present. Many commentators explain the juxtaposition of second and third person homiletically as indicating both God's nearness and transcendence. The second person address is referred to in traditional sources as *nigleh* ("revealed") and the third person as *nistar* ("hidden").

BIBLIOGRAPHY: Blank, in: HUCA, 32 (1961), 87–90; Bamberger, in: *Judaism*, 5 (1956), 167–8; M. Kadushin, *The Rabbinic Mind* (1965²), 266–70 (theological aspect); J. Heinemann, *Ha-Tefillah bi-Tekufat ha-Tanna'im re-ha-Amora'im* (1966²), 29–77 (textual criticism).

[Herman Kieval]

BARUKH SHE-AMAR (Heb. בָּרוּךְ שֶׁאָמַר; "Blessed be He who spoke"), benediction opening the section of *Shaḥarit called "passages of song," i.e., the morning psalms (*Pesukei de-Zimra* or *Zemirot*). In the Ashkenazi rite the benediction is placed at the beginning of the whole section, while in the Sephardi and other rites some verses and psalms are recited before *Barukh* *she-Amar.* In the original Sephardi prayer books (Leghorn, Amsterdam, and Vienna) there is a longer version, with additions for Sabbath. In the Eastern Sephardi rites – according to the Kabbalah – there is a shorter version of 87 words, which is similar to the Ashkenazi rite with slight variations. In its present form it is a combination of two separate prayers of which only the second part can be considered a benediction. The first part is a hymn praising God, the Creator and Redeemer. In spite of numerous variations and later accretions, the prayer may be of talmudic origin. It is first mentioned by Moses Gaon (c. 820) and is found in the prayer book of Amram Gaon (also ninth century), where the prayer is introduced as follows: "When Jews enter the synagogue to pray, the *ḥazzan* of the congregation rises and begins…" Nathan ha-Bavli reports a century later that at the ceremony of the installation of the exilarch *Barukh she-Amar* was sung antiphonally, and hence some scholars have suggested that the response *Barukh Hu* ("blessed be He"), was repeated as a refrain after every clause, and not only for the first one as in the present text. According to Saadiah's *Siddur* it was recited only on Sabbaths. The style of the hymn is midrashic and most of the phrases used are found in various passages of Talmud and Midrash (see S. Baer, *Siddur* (1868), 58). Eleazer b. Judah of Worms of the 12th–13th centuries, quoting from the *Heikhalot* texts of the early mystics, refers to the esoteric significance of the 87 words contained in *Barukh she-Amar* (at least in the Ashkenazi rite (Rokeaḥ 320)); the extant texts of the *Heikhalot* do not, however, have this passage. D. *Hoffmann has interpreted the first part of the prayer as an exposition of the various meanings of the Tetragrammaton. In Prague a Barukh she-Amar Society was active from the 16th century until World War II. The members rose early in order to be in the synagogue before the reciting of *Barukh she-Amar.*

BIBLIOGRAPHY: Abrahams, Companion, 31ff.; Elbogen, Gottesdienst, 82ff.; Idelsohn, Liturgy, 80f.; D. Hoffmann, *Das Buch Leviticus*, 1 (1905), 95ff.

BARUKH SHEM KEVOD MALKHUTO LE-OLAM VA-ED (Heb. בָּרוּךְ שֵׁם כְּבוֹד מַלְכוּתוֹ לְעוֹלָם וָעֶד; "Blessed be His name, whose glorious kingdom is forever and ever" (Singer, Prayer, and *Union Prayer Book*) or "Blessed be His glorious kingdom for ever and ever" (*Rabbinical Assembly Prayerbook*)), a doxology of ancient origin, based upon Nehemiah 9:5, "Stand up and bless the Lord your God from everlasting to everlasting; and let them say: Blessed be Thy glorious Name, that is exalted above all blessing and praise." Talmudic sources state that in the Temple it was not customary to respond "Amen" after blessings pronounced by the priests (Tosef., Ber. 7:22), but rather the aforesaid *Barukh Shem Kevod Malkhuto le-Olam va-Ed.* This was also the custom after the high priest pronounced the Holy Name (the Tetragrammaton) in his public confessions on the Day of Atonement (Yoma 35b, 39a, 66a; Ta'an. 16b; Tosef., Ta'an. 1:12; Sif. Deut. 306; see *Avodah*). This formula is pronounced in the daily prayers after the first verse of the *Shema* before continuing with the verses of Deuteronomy 6:4–9. In the Orthodox ritual, however, this formula is pronounced in a whisper, either because it is not biblical as is the rest of the *Shema* (Pes. 56a; Gen. R. 98:3) or because it is recited by the angels in heaven, corresponding to the people of Israel's reciting of the *Shema* (Deut. R. 2:36). It has also been suggested that precisely because the phrase was recited aloud in the Temple (Ta'an. 16b), it should be whispered after its destruction. For the second reason, this doxology is pronounced aloud in Orthodox synagogues only on the Day of Atonement, since on this day "Israel is as pure as the angels" (Deut. R. 2:36). Another explanation for uttering this formula in a whisper is that martyrs used to pronounce the *Shema* as they met their death while their relatives, out of fear of the oppressors, responded quietly. But on the Day of Atonement, when all are ready for martyrdom, it is pronounced aloud (see M.A. Mirkin's commentary to Deut. R. 98:3). In the Ashkenazi rite, at the close of the *Ne'ilah* service on the Day of Atonement, this formula is pronounced aloud three times as a solemn affirmation of the Jewish faith and in anticipation of the day when this belief will be realized by all mankind.

BIBLIOGRAPHY: J. Heinemann, *Ha-Tefillah bi-Tekufat ha-Tanna'im ve-ha-Amora'im* (1966²), 79, 84; E. Munk, *World of Prayer* (1961), 114; Werner, in: HUCA, 19 (1945–46), 282–9.

BARUKH SHE-PETARANI (Heb. בָּרוּךְ שֶׁפְּטָרַנִי; "Blessed be He who has relieved me," i.e., from the responsibility for my son's conduct), benediction pronounced by the father at his son's *bar mitzvah (see: Isserles, to Sh. Ar., OH 225:1; Maim. Yad, Teshuvah, 6:1). This benediction is based upon the Midrash: R. Eleazar said, "A man is bound to occupy himself with his son until the age of 13, thereafter he should say: Blessed be He who has released me from the responsibility (literally 'punishment') for my son's conduct" (Gen. R. 63:10), because from now on the boy assumed responsibility for his actions as a member of the community. At bar mitzvah ceremonies in Reform congregations, the *She-Heḥeyanu* blessing has been substituted for *Barukh she-Petarani* since they objected to the idea that parents are accountable for the religious transgressions of their offspring. In Yiddish *barukh she-petarani* became a familiar expression after getting rid of any annoying thing or person.

BAR-YEHUDAH (Idelson), ISRAEL (1895–1965), Israeli labor leader, born in Konotop, Ukraine. He studied mining engineering and joined the Ẓe'irei Zion movement. After he became secretary of its left wing (Ẓiyyonim Soẓialistim) in 1921, he was arrested by the Soviet authorities and exiled to the Arctic region. Released in 1923, Bar-Yehudah left for Berlin. There he served, with Berl *Locker, as secretary of the World Union of *Po'alei Zion. In 1926, upon settling in Palestine, he became secretary of the Petaḥ Tikvah Workers' Council and was imprisoned for leading a picket group that demanded the introduction of Jewish labor in the local citrus groves. After joining kibbutz *Yagur in 1930, he became a leading member of Ha-Kibbutz ha-Me'uḥad, mainly as coordinator of its defense committee. As a member of the *Mapai faction, Bar-Yehudah was active in the central institutions of the *Histadrut, the *yishuv*, and the Zionist organizations. When Mapai split, in 1944, he joined *Aḥdut ha-Avodah and became one of its leaders and later a member of its Knesset faction. During his term as minister of interior (1955–59) the question of "Who is a Jew" according to Israel law became a public issue in connection with identity-card registration. From 1962 until his death Bar-Yehudah served as minister of transport. During 1960–62 he was his party's secretary-general.

BIBLIOGRAPHY: D. Lazar, *Rashim be-Yisrael*, 1 (1953), 107–11.

[Abraham Aharoni]

BARYLKO, JAIME (1936–2003), Argentine educator and writer. Barylko was born in Buenos Aires and graduated from the Teachers Seminary in Moisesville. He taught in Jewish schools in the provinces of Argentina as well as in Buenos Aires. He directed the Rambam secondary school and, later, the Vaad Hachinuch Hamercazi (Central Council of Jewish Education). After obtaining a Ph.D. in philosophy from La Plata University, Barylko was appointed professor in various Argentine universities and dean of humanities in the private Maimonides University in Buenos Aires. He wrote a large number of books on Judaism, philosophy, psychology, and pedagogy, among them: *El aprendizaje de la libertad* (1982), *De Adán al mesías* (1989), *Usos y costumbres del pueblo judío* (1991), *El miedo a los hijos* (1992), *Los hijos y los límites* (1993), *Cábala de la luz* (1994), *Sabiduría de la vida* (1995), *Educar en valores* (1997), *Ética para argentinos* (1998), *El significado del sufrimiento* (2000), *El hombre que está solo y no espera* (2002), *Cómo ser persona en tiempos de crisis* (2002), *Jacob, drama y esencia* (2002), *La revolución educativa* (2002), *La Filosofía, una invitación a pensar* (2003), *Reflexiones filosóficas: Los múltiples caminos hacia la verdad* (2003). He also lectured for Jewish and non-Jewish organizations and frequently appeared on radio and television.

[Efraim Zadoff (2nd ed.)]

BAR-YOSEF, OFER (1937–), Israeli prehistorian of the southern Levant. Born in Jerusalem, Bar-Yosef undertook at the age of 18 his compulsory service with the Israel Defense Forces, and afterwards in 1960 began his studies at the Institute of Archaeology in the Hebrew University, concentrating primarily on prehistoric archaeology, which eventually led to his writing a Ph.D. (1966–70) on the Epi-Palaeolithic cultures of Palestine under the supervision of Moshe *Stekelis. During the 1970s Bar-Yosef taught at the Hebrew University, serving as associate professor between 1973 and 1979 and then as professor from 1979, influencing a generation of students of prehistoric archaeology in Israel.

Having first excavated with Stekelis at the Natufian and Neolithic site of Naḥal Oren in 1959–60, Bar-Yosef went on to participate in two other major projects associated with Stekelis at the important sites of Ubeidiya (1960–66) and Ein Gev I (1963–64). From the 1960s onwards Bar-Yosef directed numerous projects of field research, notably at Hayonim Cave in western Galilee, at Ubeidiya, in various parts of Sinai (including Gebel Maghara, Ain Hudeirah, and Kadesh Barnea), at the Qafzeh Cave at El-Wad Terrace and the Kebara Cave on Mount Carmel, and at the Neolithic site of Netiv Hagdud in the Lower Jordan Valley. Side by side with his continued excavations at Hayonim Cave in the 1990s and early 2000s, Bar-Yosef actively participated in excavations and researched materials from sites situated in different parts of the world: Turkey (Karain and Őkuzini Caves, Mezra'a Tleilat), China (sampling of the Zhoukoudian site, Yuchanyan Cave), Republic of Georgia (Dzudzuana Cave, Kotia's Klde), and the Czech Republic (Stranska Skala).

Bar-Yosef has numerous publications to his credit: 15 books and monographs and close to 300 research papers. He was a co-editor of *Geoarchaeology* and *Eurasian Prehistory* and served on the advisory board of numerous prestigious international scientific journals.

From 2005 Bar-Yosef was professor of prehistoric archaeology in the Department of Anthropology, Peabody Museum, Harvard University.

[Shimon Gibson (2nd ed.)]

BAR-YOSEF (Zenwirth), YEHOSHUA (1912–1992), Israeli novelist and playwright. Bar-Yosef was born in Safed and studied in yeshivot in Transylvania and Jerusalem. Bar-Yosef realistically describes the world of the old *yishuv*, the pre-Zionist Jewish settlers in Ereẓ Israel. His trilogy *Ir Kesumah* ("Enchanted City," 1949) is set in Safed. Bar-Yosef views life as a constant battle between the spiritual and the temporal, the Will to Evil and the Will to Good, the sacred and the profane. Bar-Yosef's plays *Be-Simta'ot Yerushalayim* ("In the Alleys of Jerusalem") and *Shomerei ha-Ḥomot* ("Guardians of the City Walls") were produced at the Ohel Theater. While his early work is graphically realistic, he later showed a tendency to symbolism. Recipient of the Bialik Prize (1984), his late works include the novels *Ha-Dag ve-ha-Yonah* ("The Fish and the Dove," 1989), *Utopi'ah be-Kaḥol Lavan* ("Utopia in Blue and White," 1990), and *Gevilim u-Besarim* ("Parchment and Flesh," 1993). Bar-Yosef's memoirs, *Bein Ẓefat li-Yerushalayim*, were published in 1972.

His son YOSEF (1933–) received an Orthodox education and later studied Jewish philosophy, Kabbalah, and English literature. He began publishing in 1962 and after the success of his play *Tura* (1963), which dealt with problems of an Oriental family´s integration into Israeli society, he continued to focus on playwriting. Among his plays, many of which were staged in Russia, Poland, Brazil, and Great Britain, are *Ha-Pardes* ("The Orchard," 1986), *Anashim Kashim* ("Difficult People," 1973) and *Ḥagigat Ḥoref* ("Winter Feast," 1992). An English translation of "Difficult People" is included in the volume *Modern Israeli Drama in Translation* (edited by M. Taub).

BIBLIOGRAPHY: S. Kremer, *Ḥillufei Mishmarot* (1959), 218–22. **ADD. BIBLIOGRAPHY:** B. Rubinstein, *Ha-Nistar ba-Nigleh: Tashti-*

yot Kabbaliyot bi-Yeẓirot shel Yehoshua Bar-Yosef ve-Yiẓhak Bashevis-Singer (1994); idem, *Ḥedvat ha-Ḥayyim mul Ḥedvat ha-Mavet* (1999); G. Shaked, *Ha-Sipporet ha-Ivrit*, 2 (1983), 338–51; B. Rubinstein, *Hashpaʿatam shel Gogol ve-Chekhov al ha-Iẓuv ha-Komi be-Maḥaẓotav shel Yosef Bar-Yosef* (1977).

[Yitzhak Julius Taub / Anat Feinberg (2nd ed.)]

BARZILAI, Italian family. GIUSEPPE (1824–1902), Orientalist. Born in Gradisca (Goerz), Giuseppe studied at Padua and was at one time secretary of the Trieste Jewish community. His work on the relations between the Semitic and Indo-Germanic languages (1885) won a prize from the *Académie Française*. He also translated the Song of Songs and Lamentations into Italian verse (1865 and 1867).

SALVATORE (1860–1939), son of Giuseppe, Italian politician, played no part in Jewish life. An ardent supporter of the Italian claim to Trieste, at the age of 18 he was found guilty of treason against Austria, but was acquitted on appeal after a year of imprisonment. Salvatore studied law at Bologna and began to practice in 1882, specializing in criminal law. Later he became recognized as an eminent legal authority. He was foreign editor of *La Tribuna* of Rome from 1883 to 1891, and entered the Chamber of Deputies in 1890 as an extreme left-wing republican advocating Italy's withdrawal from the Triple Alliance. His irredentism was so great that he became known as "the Deputy from Trieste." He strongly supported Italy's declaration of war against Germany and Austria in 1915, and was later appointed minister for the liberated territories. Salvatore was an Italian delegate at the peace conference in 1919 and became a senator in 1920. Among his writings are *La criminalità in Italia* (1885); *La recidiva* (1883); and *Il nuovo Codice Penale* (1889).

ADD. BIBLIOGRAPHY: E. Falco, *Salvatore Barzilai: un repubblicano moderno tra massoneria e irredentismo* (1996).

BARZILAI (Eisenstadt), YEHOSHUA (1855–1918), leader of the Ḥibbat Zion movement and writer. Barzilai was born in Kletsk, Minsk region, Belorussia, to a rabbinical family, and from an early age became active in the Ḥibbat Zion movement. He first visited Ereẓ Israel in 1887, but a year later returned to Russia, where he became one of the founders of the clandestine *Benei Moshe, which was led by *Aḥad Ha-Am and became a center of modern spiritual and national thought. He was elected deputy member of the Odessa Ḥovevei Zion Committee, which was then the central body for activities on behalf of the new settlements in Ereẓ Israel.

Barzilai returned to Ereẓ Israel in 1890 and was appointed secretary of the Executive Committee of Ḥovevei Zion in Jaffa. He was instrumental in the founding of several educational and community institutions, wrote numerous articles and reports on life in the Yishuv in various Hebrew papers in Russia, and from 1893 to 1895 edited, jointly with Yehudah Grasovski (*Goor) *Mikhtavim me-Ereẓ Yisrael* (Letters from Ereẓ Israel), a bulletin on the life and problems of the Jewish community in Ereẓ Israel. He was also active on behalf of the settlers in their disputes with the administration of Baron Rothschild.

Barzilai joined the Zionist movement and participated in the Minsk Conference of Russian Zionists (1902). He was among the opponents of the Uganda Plan. From 1904, he was an official of the Anglo-Palestine Bank in Jerusalem and was one of the founders of the Hebrew Gymnasium in Jerusalem, the first modern high school in Ereẓ Israel, and the Beit Ha-Am community center of Jerusalem. At the beginning of World War I he returned to Europe, and after a long illness died in Lausanne, Switzerland. His remains were reinterred in 1933 on the Mount of Olives. A collection of his writings was published in 1912.

BIBLIOGRAPHY: Tidhar, I, 150–1; M. Smilansky, *Mishpaḥat ha-Adamah*, II, 60–65; Rabbi Binyamin, *Keneset Ḥakhamim* (1961), 271–7

[Benjamin Jaffe]

BARZILLAI (Heb. בַּרְזִלַּי), name of two biblical persons.
(1) Barzillai the Gileadite (Heb. הַגִּלְעָדִי), a wealthy man of Rogelim. When David and his men fled to Mahanaim in Gilead because of *Absalom's rebellion, he, like two other prominent Transjordanians, Machir son of Ammiel of Lo-Debar and Shobi son of Nahash, the Ammonite, welcomed them with food. Barzillai also sustained David throughout his stay in Mahanaim. On David's return to Jerusalem, Barzillai accompanied him as far as the west bank of the Jordan; however, owing to his advanced age, Barzillai did not accept David's invitation to come to Jerusalem and reside at the royal court (II Sam. 17:27; 19:32–41). Instead, he sent his son Chimham (or Chimhan) with David and from this time Chimham and his family lived at the king's court (I Kings 2:7). It seems that a quarter near Bethlehem was set aside for Chimham and his relatives and was therefore called "Chimhan's (*keri*; *ketiv*: "Chemoham") Residence" (Geruth Chimham, Jer. 41:17). In post-Exilic Judah two priestly families, Habaiah and Hakkoz – which claimed descent from Barzillai, were disqualified from the priesthood. The sons of Hakkoz were readmitted in the same generation (Ezra 2:61; Neh. 7:63).

(2) Barzillai of Abel-Meholah (a city in Transjordan), the father of *Adriel, the husband of *Merab, the daughter of King Saul (II Sam. 21:8, where it reads Michal instead of Merab, cf. I Sam. 18:19). It has also been suggested that Barzillai from Meholah was Barzillai the Gileadite.

BIBLIOGRAPHY: de Vaux, Anc Isr, 121–2; B. Maisler (Mazar), in: *Tarbiz*, 12 (1940/41), 120; EM, 2 (1965), 342–3 (incl. bibl.).

[Israel Moses Ta-Shma]

BASCH, VICTOR GUILLAUME (1863–1944), French philosopher and a defender of human rights. Basch was born in Budapest and studied German at the Sorbonne. He served as a professor at the universities of Nancy, Rennes, and Paris. In 1918 he held the newly established chair of aesthetics at the Sorbonne. Basch became well-known when he championed Alfred Dreyfus. He was a founder of the League for the Rights of Man and its president in 1926. Basch was a socialist supporter of the left-wing coalition known as the Popular Front and a leader of the Alliance Israélite Universelle. During World War II, Basch was a member of the central committee of the French underground. He and his wife were executed by the Vichy government.

His writings include *Essai critique sur l'esthétique de Kant* (1896); *La guerre de 1914 et le droit* (1915); *Les doctrines politiques des philosophes classiques de l'Allemagne* (1927), and *Essais d'esthétique de philosophie et de littérature* (1934), as well as other works on literature, philosophy, and political issues.

ADD. BIBLIOGRAPHY: F. Basch, *Victor Basch ou la passion de la justice: de l'affaire Dreyfus au crime de la milice* (1994); F. Basch, L. Crips, and P. Gruson (eds.), *Victor Basch: un intellectuel cosmopolite* (2000).

BASCHKO, ẒEVI HIRSCH BEN BENJAMIN (1740–1807), rabbi and halakhist. Baschko was the last to occupy the position of rabbi (which he held from 1802) of the joint communities of Altona, Hamburg, and Wandsbek (the "Three Communities") before the union was dissolved. Born in Zamosc, Poland, of a distinguished family, he was rabbi first of Tischwitz (Tyszowce), then from 1771 of Brody, and from 1788 of Glogau, where he established an important yeshivah. He was one of the greatest rabbis of his day; among those who addressed halakhic questions to him were Isaiah Berlin, Solomon Zalman Fuerth, Phinehas Horowitz of Frankfurt, and Meir Posner, while Ezekiel Landau and Akiva Eger referred to him in unusually high terms of esteem. He wrote *Tiferet Ẓevi*, responsa on the Shulḥan Arukh in two parts, the first on *Oraḥ Ḥayyim* and *Yoreh De'ah* (Warsaw, 1816 (?)) and the second on *Even ha-Ezer* (Jozsefov, 1867). His responsa also appear in the works of contemporary rabbis. Some of his commentaries and homilies are still in manuscript. He died in Ottensen, near Altona, and was buried at Altona, his tombstone bearing the inscription, "There arose none, nor will there ever be another, like him." His sons were also rabbis: Moses at Tomaszow, and Judah Loeb at Komarno.

BIBLIOGRAPHY: E. Duckesz, *Ivvah le-Moshav* (1903), xxvii (Ger. pt.), 77–83 (Heb. pt.); I. Wolfsberg, in: *Arim ve-Immahot be-Yisrael*, 2 (1948), 33f.; N.M. Gelber, *ibid.*, 6 (1955), 59.

[Itzhak Alfassi]

BASEVI, Italian family of German origin, especially associated with Verona. In Hebrew, they called themselves Bath-Sheba and in abbreviation, Bash (ב"ש). The name Naphtali was common in the family, and therefore some of its members took a deer's head as their crest and became known as "Basevi Cervetto" (Italian: "little deer"), in accordance with the Blessing of Jacob (Gen. 49:21). Others took a boat as their crest, in accordance with the Blessing of Moses (Deut. 33:23), and became known as "Basevi della Gondola." It is not clear what precise relationship existed between this family and the Bassevi family of Prague (see *Bassevi, Jacob von Treuenberg). The brothers ABRAHAM and JOSEPH, sons of Sabbatai Mattathias Bath-Sheba, were printers in Salonika (1594–1605). Abraham subsequently became a printer in Damascus (1605–06), while his brother had been a proofreader in the Verona press, a Midrash *Tanḥuma* appearing with his name (1595).

GIOACCHINO (1780–1867), originally from Mantua, moved to Milan at the beginning of 19th century and was one of the earliest Italian Jews to attain distinction as a lawyer. He defended the Tyrolese hero Andreas Hofer in his trial for armed rebellion against Napoleon. In Milan, he wrote and published his principal works, *Il commento al Codice Civile Austriaco* (seven editions from 1845 to 1857) and *Il Trattato delle leggi attinenti al Processo Civile* (1850). EMANUELE (1799–1869) was a physician and medical writer from Pisa, where he took the university degree in 1817. In 1823 he published his first work, *Discorso*, and in 1824 *L'esposizione della Medicina Fisiologica di Broussais*. Among his other works were *Cenni sulla Medicina Fisiologica confrontata colla Dottrina Medica Italiana* (1825) and *Sugli uffici del medico* (1826). In 1825 the Grand Duke of Tuscany appointed him secretary of the Jewish community of Leghorn. ABRAMO (1818–1885), although a qualified physician, devoted himself to music, composed some operas, launched the publication of musical texts, and organized popular orchestral concerts. He founded in Florence the *Beethoven Matinées* (1859) and afterwards the well-known *Società del Quartetto*, which exerted a great influence on Italian music life. His writings (e.g., *Della Certezza*, 1842) anticipated the theories of the American programists. Giuseppe Basevi (?–1884) from Verona was a rabbi in Sabbioneta, Spalato and Verona.

In the 18th century some of the Basevi family emigrated to England. NATHAN or NAPHTALI (1738–1808), of Verona, settled in London in 1762 and was an early president of the *Board of Deputies of British Jews. His daughter, Maria, was the mother of Benjamin *Disraeli. The conversion of the Disraeli children in 1817 was followed by that of the family of JOSHUA, Maria's brother. A Lloyds underwriter, he moved to Brighton, where he was chairman of the magistrates from 1838 to 1843 and also a deputy lieutenant of the County of Sussex.

Joshua's son, NATHANIEL (1792–1869), was the first Jewish-born barrister to practice in England. Another son, GEORGE (1794–1845), an architect and a nephew of Maria d'Israeli, and himself a convert to Christianity, was articled to Sir John Soane, the most original British architect of his time. In 1816–19 Basevi traveled in Italy and Greece and his first buildings reveal the influences of classical architecture. These include St. Mary's Church, Greenwich, England, designed in 1823, when Basevi was 29 years old. His best-known building, the Fitzwilliam Museum, Cambridge, England, begun in 1836, already reveals a trend to more dramatic, baroque treatment which is fully evident in the famous building of the Conservative Club (now the Bath Club) of 1843, in St. James's Street, London, designed with Sydney Smirke. Earlier in his career Basevi designed several country houses and the main part of Belgrave Square, the largest and most elegant of early 19th century London thoroughfares. Basevi died as a result of a fall from the spire of Ely Cathedral, of which he was resident architect. Casts of a plaster bust of Basevi, attributed to T.I. Mazzotti, are in the Fitzwilliam Museum, Cambridge, the Soane Museum, London, and the Royal Institute of British Architects, London. Other members of the family include JAMES PALLADIO (1832–1871), Anglo-Indian surveyor and explorer; JACOB BASEVI CERVETTO (1682–1783), generally known as James Cervetto, musician, who introduced the playing of the cello into England, and his illegitimate son, JAMES CERVETTO (1746–1837), also a musician and one of the best cellists of his time. Both father and son composed various musical works, especially for the cello. Most of the members of this family were not professing Jews.

JOSEF BASEWI (b. 1840) founded the Giuseppe Basewi sugar firm in Trieste, which attained considerable importance in opening Oriental markets to Austrian export.

BIBLIOGRAPHY: A.M. Hyamson, *Sephardim of England* (1951), index; R. Blake, *Disraeli* (1966), index; Jamilly, in: JHSET, 18 (1953–55), 133–4; Roth, in: *Juedische Familien-Forschung*, 4 (1928), 57–60; G. Bedarida, *Ebrei d'Italia* (1950), index. GEORGE BASEVI: Roth, Art; Victoria and Albert Museum, *Anglo-Jewish Art and History (catalogue)* (1956); *The Penguin Dictionary of Architecture* (1966); N. Pevsner, *The Buildings of England*. **ADD. BIBLIOGRAPHY:** C. Roth, "La famiglia Basevi e le sue vicende," in: *La Rassegna mensile di Israel*, 36/2 (1970), 359–62; M. Mortara, *Indice alfabetico dei rabbini e scrittori israeliti di cose giudaiche in Italia con richiami bibliografici e note illustrative* (1886), 6.

[Vivian David Lipman / Federica Francesconi (2nd ed.)]

BASHAN (Heb. בָּשָׁן, הַבָּשָׁן), a region north of the Yarmuk River and east of the Jordan and lakes Ḥuleh and Kinneret. In biblical times, the city of *Salchah (Salcah) was at the eastern extremity of Bashan (Deut. 3:10; Josh. 13:11) and the city of Dan at its western (Deut. 33:22). Most of its area, some 4,334 sq. mi. (11,200 sq. km.) is covered with basalt as a result of lava eruptions occurring during the Pleistocene period or later. In some parts of Bashan, the volcanic material has eroded into fertile soil, but others are still covered with rocks.

The meaning of the name is not clear; by analogy with the Arabic word *batan* it may mean a rockless plain. Targum Onkelos and the Palestine Targum translate Bashan as *Matnan* (a possible variant of Batnan) and the Syriac Peshitta as *Matnin*. The Palestine Targum has *Butnaya* as a variant (Deut. 33:22) as does the Jerusalem Talmud, probably through Greek influence (cf. Ma'as 4:6, 51b, et al.).

With its sufficient rainfall in normal years and lava soil, Bashan is a very fertile region. Once possessing forests and pastures, it is praised in the Bible for its lofty trees (Isa. 2:13; Ezek. 27:6; Zech. 11:2), its cattle and sheep (Deut. 32:14; Amos 4:1; Ps. 22:13), and, with the Carmel, it is mentioned as an area of outstanding fertility (Isa. 33:9; Jer. 50:19; Nah. 1:4). Although its forests disappeared many generations ago, good pasture is still found in Upper *Golan and on Jebel Druze. The Plain of Bashan is noted for its hardy, superior wheat, but years of drought occur there more often than on the western side of the

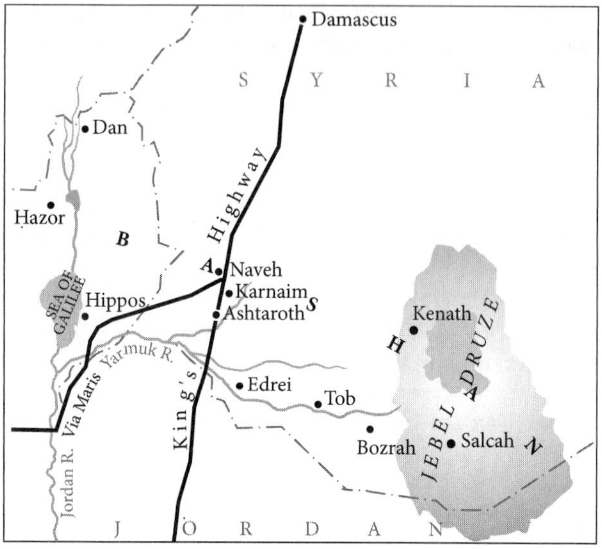

Map of the Bashan area in ancient times.

Jordan, with the exception of the Negev. The ancient "King's Highway" from Elath to Damascus passed through Bashan (Num. 20:17), merging with a branch of the Via Maris that crossed the Jordan near the Sea of Galilee; a second branch led to Damascus by way of Dan and Banias. Today Bashan is crossed by a highway that follows the same route and, in the east, also by the Hejaz railroad.

The ancient inhabitants of Bashan were the *Rephaim, one of whom was *Og, king of Bashan (Deut. 2:11; 3:11), whose 60 fortified cities were proverbial (Deut. 3:4; I Kings 4:13, etc.). Some of Bashan's important cities are mentioned in Egyptian documents from the Middle and New Kingdoms: Ashtaroth, Bozrah, Zer, Kenath, Tob, etc. Ashtaroth and *Edrei were the main cities of Og (Josh. 12:4–5), whom Moses defeated at Edrei (Num. 21:33). He allotted his land to the half-tribe of Manasseh (Num. 32:33–42), but most of the original inhabitants remained there (Num. 32:17). Foreign enclaves, such as those of the Geshurites east of the Sea of Galilee, and the Maacathites in Upper Golan south of Mt. Hermon survived into the early days of the monarchy (Josh. 13:13; II Sam. 10:6–8; 13:37). In the period of the First Temple, Damascus attacked Bashan and *Gilead and, from time to time, imposed its rule on them (I Kings 22:3). *Joash and his son *Jeroboam II were the last Israelite kings to hold Bashan (II Kings 13:25; 14:25). In 732 B.C.E. it was conquered by Tiglath-Pileser III who exiled many of its inhabitants (II Kings 15:29; cf. Isa. 8:23) and established two Assyrian provinces there – Karnini (Karnaim) and Hawrina (Hauran) – that evidently existed through Babylonian and Persian rule.

Under the Ptolemies, Bashan was divided into three provinces: Gaulanitis, Batanea, and Trachonitis. The Seleucids consolidated the whole of Transjordan north of the Arnon into a single unit called Galaditis (Gilead). In 164 B.C.E *Judah Maccabee went to the aid of the persecuted Jews of Bashan, defeated their enemies led by a certain Timotheus, and evacuated the Jews from Transjordan (I Macc. 5:9ff.;

Jos., Ant., 12:330ff.). Alexander *Yannai in 85 B.C.E. wrested Golan from the Nabateans, who, by the latter part of the second century, had spread out from their settlements in Edom and reached as far as Damascus. Some 20 years later, however, Pompey conquered Golan from the Jews and gave it to the Itureans, who controlled most of Bashan. He granted autonomy to the Greek cities Hippos (Susita) in Lower Golan and Raphana and Kanatha in the Plain of Bashan and included them in the *Decapolis. From 30 to 20 B.C.E. Herod gradually received all of Bashan from Emperor Augustus, and it remained the domain of his heirs Herod Philip and Agrippa I and II until about 100 C.E. In the days of Herod, Jews from Western Palestine and Babylonia were settled there. His army commander *Zamaris (Zimra), a Babylonian Jew, cleared Trachonitis (al-Lijā) of marauders and the area was later named for him – Terakhona de-Zimra, or Terakona. For halakhic purposes this region was considered part of Ereẓ Israel (Tosef., Shev. 4:11). In 106 C.E. Bashan was annexed to the Provincia Arabia, the capital of which was Bozrah.

In Byzantine times the al-Jafna dynasty of the Ghasān tribe ruled Bashan; its capital was Jabiyya, northwest of Nawe. Chosroes II, king of Persia, penetrated into Bashan in 614 and defeated the Byzantines near Edrei (Darʿa). The Muslims invaded in 634 and after the battle of the Yarmuk (Aug. 20, 636) Golan was included in Jund al-Urdun (Jordan Province), the capital of which was Tiberias. The rest of Bashan apparently became part of the district of Damascus – capital of the caliphate from 660 to 750. Because of its proximity to the centers of power and of Muslim culture, Bashan flourished under the Umayyad dynasty; thereafter it declined rapidly until, in Turkish times, it was inhabited by Bedouins, who plundered its few remaining villages. In 1711 Druze from Mt. Lebanon began to settle on Mt. Bashan, which was later renamed for them (Jebel Druze). Their number increased considerably there in 1860, when many Druze fled from Mr. Lebanon. Far from submitting to the Bedouin, the Druze established their authority over many tribes. The attempts of the Egyptians (from 1832 to 1840) and of the Turks (from 1840 to 1918) to extend their sovereignty over Jebel Druze were only partly successful. In 1925 the Druze rebelled against the French, who subdued the revolt, and subsequently granted the Bashan Druze area broad autonomy. Until the end of the British Mandate, Bashan was the most tranquil part of Syria; after 1944, it became part of the Republic of Syria. Attempts by the Damascus government to treat it like other provinces met with constant opposition and periodic rebellions.

On the Bashan Plain and in Golan, Turkish rule succeeded in enforcing its sovereignty over the inhabitants in the late 19th century. To strengthen its authority in these districts, the Turkish government settled Circassian refugees there in 1880–84. At the end of the 19th century, a French company laid a railroad line in Bashan from Damascus to al-Muzayyīb, north of the Yarmuk, to expedite the export of its wheat. In 1907 the Hejaz railway was built parallel to the French line as far as Edrei (Darʿa), and then branching off to cross the Yarmuk, thus connecting Bashan with Haifa. The French tracks were removed by the Turks during World War I. Good roads were constructed during the French Mandate, linking up with the road networks of Syria, Transjordan, and Palestine. During the 1890s, Baron Edmond de Rothschild purchased thousands of acres on both sides of Nahr al-ʿAllān and founded a Jewish settlement, but the pasha of Damascus expelled the settlers in 1899. A small private settlement called Benei Yehudah was founded in 1886 by Jews from Tiberias and Safed in the Golan, east of Lake Kinneret, but it was abandoned in 1920 as a result of the Arab riots and attacks after contact was broken between the two banks of the Jordan. In 1967 the area was captured from the Syrians and Israeli settlement there began. In 1981 the Golan Law declared the area part of Israel. In the early 2000s the Golan Heights included 33 settlements, mainly rural, with a population of 15,500 Jewish settlers and another 18,000 Druze concentrated in four large villages.

BIBLIOGRAPHY: Avi-Yonah, Land, index; Glueck, in: D.W. Thomas (ed.), *Archaeology and Old Testament Study* (1967), 450ff.; EM, s.v. (incl. bibl.). **ADD BIBLIOGRAPHY:** A. Heber-Percy, *A Visit to Bashan and Argob* (1895); R.P.A. Beaulieu, "la première civilization du Djebel Druze," *Syria*, 24 (1947): 232–250; G. Barkay, Z. Ilan, A. Kloner, A. Mazar and D. Urman, "Archaeological Survey in the Northern Bashan," *Israel Exploration Journal*, 24 (1974), 173–184; Z. Ilan, *Attempts at Jewish Settlement in Trans-Jordan, 1871–1947* (1984).

[Abraham J. Brawer / Shaked Gilboa (2nd ed.)]

BASHIRI, YAḤYA (**Yahya b. Abraham b. Sa'adiah al-Bashiri**; Heb. name **Abner bar Ner ha-Sharoni**; 17th century), Yemenite kabbalist and scribe. His extant work is characterized by accuracy and beauty. Later Yemenite scholars, particularly Yaḥya *Ṣaliḥ, refer to Bashiri in their writings, while popular legends extol his piety and the miracles he performed by virtue of his knowledge of practical Kabbalah. His two extant works, still in manuscript form, are *Ḥavaẓẓelet ha-Sharon*, a kabbalistic work on the letters of the Hebrew alphabet, and *Bashiri*, a pentateuchal commentary based on *gematria*. He is known to have written other works, which have not survived: two commentaries on the *Ein Ya'akov* of Jacob ibn Ḥabib and *Amirat ha-Emunot*, the contents of which are unknown. The numerous quotations from Bashiri in the *Ḥelek ha-Dikduk* of Ṣaliḥ reveal the *variae lectiones* collected by Bashiri in the course of copying the books of the Pentateuch, on which he may even have compiled a distinct work. His love of books is evidenced by his written vow (appearing in a colophon to the *Midrash ha-Gadol*, on Deuteronomy) never to sell a book "in his lifetime or thereafter," i.e., even if this be necessary to provide funds for his burial shroud.

BIBLIOGRAPHY: A. Elnadaf, *Seridei Teiman* (1928), 7a, 9b; Y. Ratzhaby, in: KS, 28 (1952/53), 260, 264, 268, 405; A. Koraḥ, *Sa'arat Teiman* (1954), 2.

[Yehuda Ratzaby]

BASHYAZI (Heb. בשיצי; traditional Rabbanite transcription for the Turkish name Bashyatchi), family of Karaite scholars in Adrianople and Constantinople. Although the family moved to Constantinople in 1455, they retained the cognomen "Adrianopolitans" even in later generations. The Karaite school of Adrianople tended toward liberalism. The Bashyazi family, its leading exponents, advocated the kindling of Sabbath lights contrary to the prevalent Karaite custom of spending Sabbath in darkness. MENAHEM B. JOSEPH BASHYAZI first permitted this practice around 1440. His grandson Elijah found support for this ruling in liberal Karaite halakhic sources and through his influence it was accepted in the Karaite communities of Turkey, Crimea, Poland, and Lithuania, although in Egypt, Syria, and Ereẓ Israel the Karaites continued to refrain from kindling lights on the Sabbath at least until the 19th century. Menahem also abolished the Karaite custom of starting the weekly Torah readings from the beginning of the Pentateuch in the month of Nisan and directed that the cycle should start in Tishri, conforming to Rabbanite practice. The more conservative Karaites opposed the change.

His grandson ELIJAH B. MOSES (c. 1420–1490) was the ideologist of the Karaite rapprochement with Rabbanism and a codifier of Karaite law. Elijah, in addition to upholding the rulings of his grandfather Menahem and father Moses, provided them with a theoretical basis and expanded them (e.g., concerning intercalation). He remains the supreme Karaite authority. Elijah is reported to have begun the compilation of his great code *Adderet Eliyahu* in about 1480, but the section on the calendar refers to the year 1457. After his death his pupil and son-in-law Caleb *Afendopolo attempted to complete the work. The *Adderet* was distributed chapter by chapter and its contents were recognized as binding even during the author's lifetime. It was also one of the first Karaite works to appear in print (Constantinople, 1530–31; Eupatoria, 1835; Odessa, 1870 [the latter repr. Ramle 1966]). Its Sabbath laws became the subject of much Karaite polemical literature. Other sections, especially those dealing with the sanctification of the new moon (Elijah was the first to draw up an official calendar for this, which was virtually a permanent one), the ten principles of faith (new and final formulation of the Karaite credo), and the laws of *sheḥitah* and incest were submitted to a series of adaptations, abridgments, and interpretations by Karaite religious leaders in different countries. Bashyazi's leniency on Karaite *halakha* stands in juxtaposition to the strict positions of *Aaron ben Elijah. In addition to reflecting the various schools of late medieval Karaite thought, the *Adderet* attests to Bashyazi's knowledge of both general and Jewish subjects. In the statements and sections concerning beliefs Bashyazi often tends towards Aristotelian positions.

Particularly noteworthy is Elijah's use of Rabbanite techniques and sources, even where they were antagonistic to Karaism. Elijah interpreted their hostility as a device to achieve publicity so as to cover their actual sympathy toward Karaism. However, he also polemicized against several Rabbanite scholars, including Mordecai *Comtino. While one of his three polemical works, *Iggeret ha-Yerushah* (published in the Eupatoria edition of *Adderet*), is directed against the Rabbanites, his *Iggeret ha-Ẓom* and *Iggeret Gid ha-Nasheh* are written to refute his Karaite opponents. Elijah's correspondence with Karaite leaders in Lithuania shows that his reputation had spread to the northern Karaite communities. He introduced the Lithuanian Karaites to his relaxation of Karaite *halakhah* and customs, recommending the establishment of a *bet din* of three in *Troki on the model of that in Constantinople, and the institution of kindling the Sabbath lights. His pupils included the Rabbanite *Moses of Kiev (with whom he also had sharp disputes), well-known among Lithuanian Karaites. The Karaite prayerbook contains several prayers and hymns composed by Elijah, including *Meliẓat ha-Mitzvot*, recited on Shavuot.

MOSES (first half of 16th century), great-grandson of Elijah, died relatively young. He renewed the connections with the Arabic-speaking Karaite communities. He also traveled to the East, returning with ancient Karaite manuscripts in Arabic and isolated pages of *Sefer ha-Mitzvot* by *Anan b. David in Aramaic on which he based his *Zevaḥ Pesaḥ* and *Sefer Re'uven* (in manuscript). His explanation of the laws of incest, *Sefer Yehudah*, was published by I. Markon, and an important part of his *Matteh Elohim*, on the history of the Karaite schism, was incorporated into *Mordecai b. Nisan's *Sefer David Mordekhai*.

BIBLIOGRAPHY: S. Poznański, *Karaite Literary Opponents of Saadiah Gaon* (1908), 82–85; idem, in: *Zekher Ẓaddikim* (1920), 33–34; R. Mahler, *Ha-Kara'im* (1949), 286–7: Danon, in: JQR, 15 (1926/27), 305–7, 311–2; 17 (1924/25) 168–9; Mann, Texts, 2 (1935), index s.v. *Elyah ben Moses Bashiatzi*; L. Nemoy (ed.), *Karaite Anthology* (1952), 236–70; Ankori, in: PAAJR, 24 (1955), 11; idem, in: *Tarbiz*, 25 (1955/56), 44–65, 183–201; idem, *Karaites in Byzantium* (1959), index; idem, *Beit Bashyazi ve-Takkanotav* (1966). **ADD. BIBLIOGRAPHY:** D. Lasker, in: *Jerusalem Studies in Jewish Thought*, 3 (1984), 405–425; S.B. Bowman, *The Jews of Byzantium (1204–1453)* (1985), index; J-C. Attias, *Le commentaire biblique: Mordekhai Komtino ou l'hermeneutique du dialogue* (Paris, 1991), index; M. Polliack (ed.), Karaite Judaism: A Guide to Its History and Literary Sources, (2003), index, s.v. "Bashyachi."

°**BASIL I**, Byzantine emperor 867–886. Basil first attempted to achieve the conversion of the Jews by persuasion and invited rabbis to a *disputation to defend their faith, vainly offering them material benefits if they would confess defeat. When this attempt failed he issued in 874 an edict ordering all his Jewish subjects to become converted to Christianity. The decree was also connected with his policy to propagate orthodox Christianity among the Bulgars, Russians, and other peoples, and forcible conversion of nonorthodox sects, notably the Paulicians, whom he probably associated with iconoclasm. His attempt to convert by force the Jewish communities in southern Italy then under Byzantine rule is recorded in the 11th-century Hebrew chronicle of *Ahimaaz b. Paltiel, which portrays Basil as a cruel and persistent enemy of the Jews and Judaism. Despite his decree, the legal status of the Jews remained unchanged and there was no curtailment of their existing rights. The decree, whether formally rescinded or not, eventually fell into disuse under Basil's son and successor Leo VI.

BIBLIOGRAPHY: J. Starr, *Jews in the Byzantine Empire* (1939), 4–6, 127ff.; A.A. Vasiliev, *History of the Byzantine Empire*, 1 (1964), 332–3; Baron, Social 2, 3 (1957), 180ff.; B. Klar (ed.), *Megillat Aḥima'aẓ* (1944), 20–23; A. Sharf, in: Roth, Dark Ages, 57ff.; A. Vogt, *Basile I* *empereur de Byzance, et la civilisation byzantine à la fin du* IX *siècle* (1908); Neubauer, Chronicles, 2 (1895), 111–24.

[Andrew Sharf]

BASILEA, SOLOMON AVIAD SAR-SHALOM (c. 1680–1749), rabbi and kabbalist in Mantua, Italy. Solomon received instruction from the most learned scholars in the city, including his father, Menahem Samson Basilea, Judah b. Eliezer *Briel (Bariel), Moses *Zacuto, and *Benjamin b. Eliezer Ha-Kohen Vitale of Reggio. He also studied geometry and astronomy. Solomon became rabbi of Mantua in 1729. At the age of 44 he began a methodical study of Kabbalah according to the system of Isaac *Luria. In 1733 he was accused by the Inquisition of having mocked Catholicism and of retaining unexpurgated Hebrew works, and was imprisoned for a year. He was subsequently confined to his house and finally to the ghetto. He courageously supported Moses Ḥayyim *Luzzatto against his accusers in the controversy over the latter's kabbalistic practices. Solomon Basilea's main work *Emunat Ḥakhamim* (Mantua, 1730) was intended to emphasize the continuity in Jewish tradition of the mystic significance of the Torah and the error of scholars opposing that interpretation. To support his thesis, Solomon reviewed not only the whole of Hebrew literature but also Greek, Arabic, and Renaissance philosophy. Basilea did not believe that the Zohar was written by Simeon b. Yoḥai, but that it nevertheless contained his esoteric doctrines as handed down to his disciples. Basilea also rejected the views which ascribed the authorship of the Zohar to *Moses b. Shem Tov de Leon. The book was very well received by the kabbalists, but opponents of the Kabbalah were critical of it. Jacob *Emden wrote a refutation of the *Emunat Ḥakhamim* in *Mitpaḥat Sefarim*, 2 (1768). Some rabbinical decisions of Solomon Basilea are included in the collections of his fellow student Isaac *Lampronti and others. He also wrote on the calendar and a commentary on Euclid's *Elements* as well as notes on the 1715 edition of *Tofteh Arukh* by Moses Zacuto. In his collections, he includes the responsa of his father MENAHEM SAMSON BEN SOLOMON (d. 1693), rabbi in Alessandria and from 1630 in Mantua. Menahem's responsa also appear in collections of his contemporaries, Moses Zacuto and Nethanel b. Aaron *Segrè.

BIBLIOGRAPHY: Ghirondi-Neppi, 36–39; S. Wiener, *Mazkeret Rabbanei Italyah* (1898), 37–40 (third pagination); Milano, Italia, 667; M. Mortara, *Catalogo dei manoscritti ebraici … di Mantova* (1878), 45–47; S. Simonsohn, *Toledot ha-Yehudim be-Dukkasut Mantovah* (1964), index.

[Attilio Milano]

BASILICA (Greek βασιλική, talmudic בָּסִילְקִי), elongated rectangular building divided by colonnades. During the Roman period this term was broadened from the narrow meaning of a meeting place for merchants to any assembly hall. In particular the term referred to a hall used in the philosophers' schools and in wealthy homes for reading and lectures. In these basilicas, the apse was the area set aside for the lecturer or teacher. The entire hall was oriented toward the podium set in the apse, which had a concave roof serving as an acoustical ceiling. This type of basilica was the prototype for the early synagogues and churches. Talmudic sources refer to three types of basilicas, which served as palaces, bathhouses, and treasuries (Av. Zar. 16b). They note that the basilica also served as a hall of justice (Gen. R. 68:12) and as a place for the sale of grain (as in Ashkelon, Tosef. to Oho. 18 end).

An early example of the basilica construction is found in the "Royal Stoa" which Josephus (Ant., 15:411–416) describes as having been erected along the southern wall of the Temple Mount by Herod when he had the Temple rebuilt. This basilica had four rows of pillars each 23 ft. (7 m.) high. According to Josephus, its length was one *stadion* (606 ft. (185 m.)), but it appears to have been longer – about 920 ft. (280 m.). The central hall was 30 cubits wide and 60 cubits high. The width of the side aisles was 20 cubits, and the height, 30 cubits, giving the structure a true basilical form. Two partially carved stone pillars have been found in Jerusalem which by their size indicate that they were destined for this basilica. However, they were cracked and therefore not used. It is possible that Herod modeled his stoa after the Great Synagogue in Alexandria which has been described as "a kind of basilica with a stoa within a stoa" (Tosef. to Suk. 4:6). Conceivably this expression refers to the central area which was constructed between two colonnades. Another interpretation is that this refers to an additional stoa which extended the width of the hall. Such construction was typical of the early synago-gues, remains of which have been found at Masada and in Galilee.

The Christians adopted the western form of basilica, and most of the early churches (fourth–sixth centuries) were built on that model, although the term "basilica" was no longer in common usage. In the early Christian basilicas, the apse served as the seat of the priests. The altar was set before it, and this part of the building was separated from the remainder by a grille which crossed the width of the church. Two or more rows of columns extended the length of the building, separating the main hall in the center from the narrower aisles at either side.

The first churches in Palestine and elsewhere, e.g., the Church of the Nativity in Bethlehem and the Church of the Holy Sepulcher in Jerusalem, were built according to this design. In the fifth century a vestibule (*narthex*) was added to the front facade of the basilica churches.

Basilicas were also used for secular purposes in the Jewish community in Palestine. One structure of this nature (135 × 49 ft. (40 × 15 m.)) was found in Bet She'arim. It consists of an enclosed paved court, a vestibule, and a basilica with two rows of five columns each. At the far end of the building, opposite the entry, is a low platform. It would appear that this was a hall of justice in the time of R. Judah ha-Nasi.

BIBLIOGRAPHY: C.M. Kaufmann, *Handbuch der christlichen Archaeologie* (1913); R. Cagnat and V. Chapot, *Manuel d'archéologie romaine*, 1 (1916), 128–34; H. Kohl und C. Watzinger, *Antike Synagogen in Galilea* (1916); S. Krauss, *Synagogale Altertuemer* (1922), 32–102; E.L. Sukenik, *Ancient Synagogues in Palestine and Greece* (1934); J.B. Ward Perkins, in: *Papers of British School at Rome*, 22 (1954), 69–89;

H.L. Gordon, in: *Art Bulletin*, 13 no. 3 (1931); M. Avi-Yonah and S. Yevin, *Kadmoniyyot Arẓenu*, 1 (1955), 200ff.; B. Mazar, in: YMḤEY, 21 (1957), 153–9.

[Michael Avi-Yonah]

BAṢĪR, JOSEPH BEN ABRAHAM HA-KOHEN HARO'EH AL- (**Yūsuf al-Basir**; first half of 11th century), Karaite halakhist and philosopher, who originated from Iraq or Persia. Because he was blind he was euphemistically called al-Baṣīr Abū Yūsuf Yaʿqūb "ha-Ro'eh" ("the Seeing"). Many Karaite authors confused him with Abū Yūsuf Yaʿqub al-*Kirkisani who lived 100 years prior to him. *Firkovich and later P. Frankl and *Harkavy have shown that he lived in the 11th century (he mentions in some of his works Samuel b. Hophni [d. 1013]). It is now known that he met Samuel b. Hophni in Baghdad. Though blind, he traveled extensively, probably as a Karaite propagandist. One of the most important Karaite scholars, he studied Talmud and rabbinic literature. He knew many languages and was well versed in Islamic philosophy. While in Baghdad he met also with Muslim theologians, with whom he had oral and written disputes. At the beginning of the 11th century he settled in Jerusalem, where he died around 1040.

In his philosophic views he followed the Baṣīran branch of the Muʿtazilites, notably ʿAbd al-Jabbār (see *Kalām). His teachings, with the additions and refinements of Yeshu'a b. Judah, became the recognized theology of Karaism for centuries to come. He strongly upholds the belief in the essentially rational character of ethics and gives priority to reason over revelation. He embraces the atomistic views of Islamic Kalām as the basis for the proof of the createdness of the world. Only reason can prove God's wisdom and omnipotence, which imply His existence. Other predicates of God are will, oneness and simplicity, incorporeality, and eternity. Of primary importance in al-Baṣīr's philosophy are the questions of God's justice, of the nature of good and evil, and of free will. God does good always because of His wisdom, not by necessity, and even if He inflicts pain it is for the good. Considering God's foreknowledge, al-Baṣīr has no doubt that man is free to determine his actions, though God knows beforehand how he will act. The commandments are God's means of guiding man in the right path and the obedient are eternally rewarded in the next world. If a sinner repents of his evil deeds, it is the duty of God to accept his repentance and remit his punishment. Al-Baṣīr authored two theological compendia, several theological and halakhic monographs and numerous epistles and response, some of which survived in manuscript fragments of various lengths in several libraries. His main works are the following:

(1) A concise work entitled *al-Tamyīz* ("The Distinction"), also *al-Manṣūrī*, consisting of 31 chapters. This work was translated with some additions by Tobiah b. Moses under the title *Maḥkimat Peti* (non-critical print Ashdod 2004). In a final chapter the author criticizes the esoteric book *Shi'ur Komah* and rejects the doctrine of Benjamin al-*Nahāwendī that the world was created by an angel.

(2) *al-Muḥtawī* ("The Comprehensive"). Divided into 40 chapters, the work tries to bring the main principles of the Muʿtazilite Kalām into agreement with the Karaite dogmas. The author polemicizes frequently against Christians, dualists, Magians, Epicureans, and other sects. A critical edition by Vajda was published with extensively annotated French translation (see bibl.). The book was translated from Arabic into Hebrew under the title *Sefer ha-Ne'imot* or *Zikhron ha-Datot*, probably by Tobiah b. Moses (non-critical print Ashdod 2004; individual chapters of the medieval Hebrew translation were published in critical editions, see Vajda).

(3) *al-Istibṣār* ("Careful Examination"), dealing with the precepts, includes also lengthy discussions of theological topics. It seems that the sections of the work had initially been composed as separate treatises and later compiled into one compendium. Several sections of the work are extant in the Russian National Library and the British Library. The section concerning the holidays, which contains a polemic in eight chapters against Saadiah, was translated by Tobiah b. Moses.

Several theological and halakhic works have been apocryphally ascribed to al-Baṣīr. The Karaites considered al-Baṣīr as one of their most important authorities. Judah *Hadassi, Aaron b. Joseph ha-Rofe, Bashyazi, and other Karaite authors often cite his halakhic views and his scriptural interpretations. His philosophic views were also esteemed by later Karaite scholars down to *Aaron b. Elijah in the 14th century, who often cites him in his *Eẓ Ḥayyim*. Of special significance is the reform, encouraged by him, of the Karaite law of consanguinity. This reform was developed further and made effective by his pupil *Jeshua b. Judah, who was likewise an important Karaite authority.

BIBLIOGRAPHY: P.F. Frankel, *Ein muʿtazilitischer Kalam aus dem 10. Jahrhundert* (1872); Steinschneider, Arab Lit, 89–91; S. Poznański, *Karaite Literary Opponents of Saadiah Gaon* (1908), 46–48; Guttmann, Philosophies, 78–81 and passim; Husik, Philosophy, 48–55 and passim. **ADD BIBLIOGRAPHY:** G. Vajda, *Al-kitab Al-Muhtawi de Yusuf Al-Basir / texte, traduction et commentaire*, ed. D.R. Blumenthal (1985) (Reviews: H. Ben-Shammai, in: *Kiryat Sefer*, 62 (1988–1989), 407–426 (Heb.); B. Chiesa, in: *Henoch*, 10 (1988) 355–376); C. Sirat, *A History of Jewish Philosophy in the Middle Ages* (1990), 54–55; D.E. Sklare, in: H. Lazarus-Yafeh et al (eds.), *The Majlis* (1999) 137–161; idem, in: D. Frank (ed.), *The Jews of Medieval Islam* (1995) 249–270; idem and H. Ben Shammai, *Judaeo-Arabic Manuscripts in the Firkovitch Collections: The Works of Yusuf al-Basir*, (1997, Heb.); M. Polliack (ed.), *Karaite Judaism: A Guide to Its History and Literary Sources*, (2003), index, s.v. "Yūsuf al-Baṣīr."

[Isaak Dov Ber Markon / Leon Nemoy]

BASKIN, JUDITH R. (1950–), U.S. scholar of women in late antiquity and the Middle Ages. Baskin was born in Hamilton, Ontario, Canada, the eldest child of Rabbi Bernard and Marjorie Shatz Baskin. Educated at Antioch College (B.A., 1971) and Yale University (Ph.D., 1976), she served as professor of religious studies and director of the Harold Schnitzer Family Program in Judaic Studies at the University of Oregon from 2000, where she was named Knight Professor of Humanities in 2002. Prior to that, she led the Department of Judaic Studies at the State University of New York at Albany and taught at the University of Massachusetts, Amherst. She is the author of *Pharaoh's Counsellors: Job, Jethro and Balaam in Rabbinic and Patristic Tradition*, (1983) and *Midrashic Women: Formations of the Feminine in Rabbinic Literature* (2002). The editor of several volumes, including the widely used collection of essays *Jewish Women in Historical Perspective.* (1991, 1998), she has written dozens of articles on various aspects of Jewish life and culture in late antiquity and the Middle Ages. In 2004 Baskin assumed the presidency of the *Association for Jewish Studies. She also served as editor of the Women and Gender division for the second edition of the *Encyclopaedia Judaica.*

[Jay Harris (2nd ed.)]

BASKIN, LEONARD (1922–2000), U.S. sculptor, printmaker, watercolorist, and illustrator.

Born in New Brunswick, New Jersey, Baskin was the son of a leading Orthodox rabbi. His earliest education was at a yeshivah in Brooklyn, where his family had moved when he was seven. After developing an interest in sculpture at age 14, he would attend day classes at the yeshivah and take evening art classes at the Educational Alliance (1937–39). Baskin also attended New York University (1939–41) and Yale University (1941–43). While at Yale, Baskin discovered William Blake. Impressed by Blake's role as a poet-artist-bookmaker, Baskin founded the Gehenna Press in 1942 and learned printmaking. The Press has published over 100 books, including Homer's *Iliad* (1962) and Dante's *Divine Comedy* (1969).

Three years in the Navy during World War II temporarily curtailed Baskin's artistic activity. After the war he completed his B.A. at the New School for Social Research (1949). In the early 1950s he also studied in Paris and in Florence. From 1953 to 1974, Baskin taught printmaking and sculpture at Smith College in Northampton, Massachusetts. He spent 10 years in England, in part to be close to Ted Hughes, with whom he collaborated on several books. Upon returning to the U.S., he taught at Hampshire College (1984–94).

Baskin's frequent subject is the human condition, often fragile and anxiety-ridden, rendered in a manner that shows the artist's debt to expressionist artists. Although he first gained acclaim for his printmaking, sculpture was his favored medium. He preferred printmaking over painting, and especially the medium of wood, because of the more democratic nature of prints, which can be reproduced widely. He often worked on a monumental scale; his 1952 woodcut *Man of Peace* measures five feet tall and *The Altar* (1977), a wood sculpture depicting the binding of Isaac, is nearly six feet long.

Many of Baskin's drawings and prints concern Jewish subjects. In 1974 he illustrated *A Passover Haggadah*, for which he provided watercolors, as well as hand lettering of much of the Hebrew text. Baskin received many important commissions, including a bas relief for the Franklin D. Roosevelt Memorial in Washington, D.C., and a seven-foot-tall bronze figure for a Holocaust Memorial in Ann Arbor, Michigan.

BIBLIOGRAPHY: L. Baskin, *Sculpture, Drawing, and Prints* (1970); I.B. Jaffe, *The Sculpture of Leonard Baskin* (1980); A. Fern and J. O'Sullivan, *The Complete Prints of Leonard Baskin: A Catalogue Raisonné, 1948–1983* (1984).

[Samantha Baskind (2nd ed.)]

BASLE (**Basel, Bâle**), Swiss city. The earliest information on a Jewish community dates from the beginning of the 13th century when Basle was still a German free city. The medieval Jewish cemetery was discovered in recent years and the remains were transferred in 1938 to the present Jewish cemetery. In the Middle Ages the Basle Jews were free to acquire and sell real estate. They engaged in commerce and money-lending, sometimes providing loans to the bishops of Basle. Juridically they were under imperial protection: according to a roster of 1242 the Jews of Basle had to pay the crown an annual tax of 40 marks. During the *Black Death they were accused of poisoning the wells; the members of the city council attempted to defend them, but finally yielded to the guilds who demonstrated before the town hall. Six hundred Jews, with the rabbi at their head, were burned at the stake; 140 children were forcibly baptized. This ended the first Jewish community in Basle (Jan. 16, 1349). In 1362 a Jew from Colmar in Alsace was permitted to settle in Basle; he was soon followed by others. In 1365 the emperor transferred his prerogatives over the Jews of Basle to the town. The second half of the 14th century was a period of prosperous growth despite restrictions imposed by the Church. However, in 1397, the slander of well poisoning was renewed. The Jews fled in panic and the community again came to an end. In 1434 a church council held in Basle introduced compulsory attendance of Jews at conversionist sermons. For four centuries there was no Jewish community in Basle. From the mid-16th century Basle authorities alternately issued residence permits to individuals and expulsion edicts. At the end of that century Basle became a center for Hebrew printing. The printing houses were owned by Christians, but they had to have recourse to Jewish proofreaders for whom they obtained residence permits. Johannes *Froben published the Psalms in 1516. His son Jerome in 1536 published a Bible in Hebrew. In 1578–80 Ambrosius Froben was permitted to print a duly censored edition of the Talmud, which had been banned under Pope Julius III in 1553 and placed on the Index in 1559. Also printed there were the works of Johannes *Buxtorf (father and son) who taught Hebrew at Basle University (1591–1664). From the 1560s Jews lived in rural communities in nearby Alsace.

In 1789, when anti-Jewish propaganda was rife in Alsace, many Alsatian Jews fled to Basle and were permitted to stay there temporarily. On the request of the French government the city authorities in 1797 exempted French Jews entering Basle from payment of the "body-tax" usually imposed on Jews, and in 1798 the tax was abolished completely in the whole of Switzerland. Under Napoleon several Jews, mainly French citizens from Alsace, settled in Basle. They numbered 128 in 1805 and were organized in a community. In 1835, however, Jews were expelled from the new separatist canton of Basle Land and the French government broke off relations. Some of the Jews returned after a brief interval, but in 1851–54 were again forced to leave both cantons of Basle. After the granting of free settlement to the Jews of Switzerland in 1866 Jews were able to return and live in Basle. A synagogue was consecrated in 1868. The first Zionist Congress was held in Basle in 1897 where the "*Basle Program" was adopted; other Zionist Congresses were subsequently held there: the second (1898), the third (1899), the fifth (1901), the sixth (1903), the seventh (1905), the 17th (1931), and the 22nd (1946). Prominent members of the Basle community were J. Dreyfus-Brodsky, representative of Swiss Jewry in the Jewish Agency (1859–1942), Rabbi Arthur Cohn, a leader of Agudat Israel, and his son, the lawyer Marcus Mordecai Cohn (1890–1953), an active Zionist and rabbinical scholar, who later became adviser on Jewish law to the Ministry of Justice in Israel. Other prominent Basle Jews were the chemist Markus Guggenheim (1885–1970) and Tadeus *Reichstein (1897–1996), who was awarded the Nobel Prize for Medicine in 1950. During World War II Basle served as a temporary refuge for many Jewish refugees. Most of them left after the war. In 2000 there were 1,421 Jews in Basle City and 318 in Basle Land The community maintained a community house from 1958 and an old-age home (Holbeinhof) from 2001, relocated in the city. A Jewish school was opened in 1961 and named after Rabbi Leo Adler. The Orthodox community (founded in 1927), with a membership of approximately 90 families, had its own network of services (e.g., a separate primary school and a small Jewish high school preparing students for yeshivah attendance). The Union of Jewish Women in Switzerland is centered in Basle and there are also WIZO and other Zionist organizations. Two youth movement are active in Basle, the unaffiliated Emuna and Bnei Akiva. From 1960 a small but excellent Jewish museum was open and from 1940 the weekly *Juedische Rundschau Maccabi* was published, later merging with the new Swiss Jewish weekly *Tachles*. In 1973 the community was formally recognized by the canton of Basle City, the first such case in Switzerland. Consequently, women received voting rights in 1975. An international congress honored the 100th anniversary of the first Zionist Congress in Basle (1997).

BIBLIOGRAPHY: A. Weldler-Steinberg, *Geschichte der Juden in der Schweiz* (1966), passim; A. Wolf, *Juden in Basel: 1543–1872* (1909); M. Ginsburger, in: REJ, 87 (1929), 209–11; idem, in: *Basler Zeitschrift fuer Geschichte und Altertumskunde*, 8 (1909); A. Nordmann, *ibid.*, 13 (1913); idem, in: *Basler Jahrbuch* (1914, 1929); *Jahresberichte der Israelitischen Gemeinde Basel* (1938–1953), Th. Nordemann, *Zur Geschichte der Juden in Basel* (1955). **ADD BIBLIOGRAPHY:** N. Guth-Biasini, *Synagoge und Juden in Basel* (1988), H. Haumann, *Juden in Basel und Umgebung* (1999), H. Haumann, *Der Erste Zionistenkongress von 1897* (1997); idem, *Acht Jahrhunderte Juden in Basel* (2005); *Israelitische Religionsgesellschaft Basel. Festschrift zum fuenfundsiebzigjaehrigen Jubiläum. 5688–5763 / 1928–2003* (2004); P. Kury, *Man akzeptierte uns nicht, man tolerierte uns! Ostjudenmigration nach Basel* (1998); E. Lang: *Aus den ersten fuenfzig Jahren. 5688–5738. 1927–1977. Israelitische Religionsgesellschaft Basel* (1977); A. Nolte, *Juedische Gemeinden in Baden und Basel* (2002); PRINTING: K. J. Luethi, *Hebraeisch in der Schweiz* (1926), 4ff., 21ff.; R.N.N. Rabinowitz, *Ma'amar al Hadpasat ha-Talmud* (1952), 75ff., 121; J. Prijs, *Die Basler hebraeischen Drucke (1516–1828)* (1952); idem, *Der Basler Talmuddruck (1578–80)* (1960); A.M. Habermann, *Ha-Sefer ha-Ivri be-Hitpatteḥuto* (1968), index; B. Friedberg, *Ha-Defus ha-Ivri be-Eiropah* (1937).

[Zvi Avneri / Uri Kaufmann (2nd ed.)]

BASLE PROGRAM, original official program of the Zionist Organization, named after the city where the First Zionist Congress (see *Zionism) was held (August 23–31, 1897), and where the program was formulated and adopted. Its first sentence, stating the objective of the Zionist movement, was followed by a four-point program: "Zionism seeks to establish a home for the Jewish people in Palestine secured under public law. The Congress contemplates the following means to the attainment of this end: (1) The promotion by appropriate means of the settlement in Palestine of Jewish farmers, artisans, and manufacturers; (2) The organization and uniting of the whole of Jewry by means of appropriate institutions, both local and international, in accordance with the laws of each country; (3) The strengthening and fostering of Jewish national sentiment and national consciousness; (4) Preparatory steps toward obtaining the consent of governments, where necessary, in order to reach the goal of Zionism." While the term "Basle Program" includes both the statement of aim and the enumeration of means, the phrase is frequently used to refer solely to the first fundamental sentence.

The text of the Basle Program was prepared by a special commission set up by the Preliminary Conference that met in Basle two days before the opening of the Congress. It consisted of Nathan *Birnbaum, Max *Bodenheimer, Siegmund Mintz, Siegmund Rosenberg, Saul Rafael *Landau, Hermann *Schapira and Max *Nordau – all except the last two being lawyers. The draft constituted a compromise between opposing viewpoints, and a synthesis of various elements. One of these was Herzl's London Program, proposed during his visit to London in July 1897, according to which the aim of Zionism was "the acquisition of a territory, in accordance with the Law of Nations, for those Jews who are not able or willing to assimilate themselves." Also of importance in the genesis of the Basle Program were Schapira's ideas on the colonization of Palestine and, in particular, the theses of the Cologne Nationaljuedische Vereinigung, headed by Bodenheimer, which postulated a Jewish commonwealth guaranteed by international law, the furtherance of the colonization of Palestine, dissemination of Jewish knowledge, and improvement in the social and cultural position of the Jews.

Not only Herzl in his *Judenstaat* (1896) but others, such as Bodenheimer, had expressly advocated a Jewish state, but the commission regarded it as prudent to refrain from using the word "state" in the official Zionist program. They felt that it was liable to antagonize Turkey, from which Herzl hoped to obtain the charter, and might also frighten certain Jewish circles. They therefore employed the term "*Heimstaette*" (home, or more exactly, homestead), suggested by Nordau, who submitted the draft proposal of the program to the Congress. This draft spoke of a "home secured by law" (*rechtlich gesicherte Heimstaette*).

Representatives of the younger generation, such as Fabius Schach and Leo *Motzkin – who spoke on this subject in the plenary session of the Congress – took exception to the term and proposed replacing it by "secured by International Law" ("*voelkerrechtlich gesicherte Heimstaette*"), wishing to emphasize the political character of the World Zionist Organization and to distinguish it clearly from the Ḥibbat Zion, whose cautious approach and exclusively philanthropic methods they strongly resented. It was Herzl himself who provided a compromise formula, which he had already used in his speeches – "*oeffentlichrechtlich gesicherte Heimstaette*" ("home secured by public law") and this formula met with universal approval. With this amendment the commission's draft proposal was unanimously passed by the Congress and became the official program of the World Zionist Organization for more than half a century. Parts of the first sentence of the Basle Program were incorporated into the *Balfour Declaration (1917) and the League of Nations Mandate over Palestine (1922).

After the declaration of Israel's independence (1948), it was felt that the Zionist program should be adapted to the new situation created by the establishment of the State of Israel, which had fulfilled the main postulate of Zionism. The most important among the proposals for a new Zionist program were those drafted by a committee established by the Zionist Organization of America and headed by the jurist Simon Rifkind, and another put forward by the American Section of the Jewish Agency Executive (both in 1949). These proposals assumed that the establishment of the state was a step toward, rather than a full realization of, the Zionist goal.

The question of the Zionist program figured high on the agenda of the 23rd Zionist Congress (Jerusalem, 1951), the first to meet after the proclamation of the state. The Congress committee charged with reformulating the Zionist program was headed by Ezra Shapiro (U.S.). Rather than abolishing the Basle Program and replacing it by a new one, the committee proposed completing it by a declaration that was officially styled "the task of Zionism." Generally known as the Jerusalem Program, this document reads as follows: "The task of Zionism is the consolidation of the State of Israel, the ingathering of the exiles in Ereẓ Israel and the fostering of the unity of the Jewish people." The Basle Program was retained and its first sentence – as well as the whole Jerusalem Program – was incorporated into the new constitution of the World Zionist Organization of 1960. There were several reasons for the affirmation of the Basle Program. First, a majority could not be found at the Congress for an entirely new reformulation of the goal and aim of Zionism. There were differences of opinion between the delegates from the United States and other English-speaking countries on the one hand and Israel and some Diaspora countries on the other, concerning the "Redemption of Israel through the Ingathering of Exiles" and other propositions. Further, it was felt that, at a time when little more than 10% of the Jewish people were living in the State of Israel, the "home" mentioned in the Basle Program could not be regarded as fully established. The desire to observe a time-honored tradition and to emphasize the continuity of the Zionist movement also played a part in the decision to retain the original platform of the Zionist Organization.

After the Six-Day War in 1967, when the Jewish people all over the world had shown its solidarity with embattled Israel, at least two points of the Jerusalem Program – those regarding the consolidation of the state and the unity of the Jewish people –had become common ground for the overwhelming majority of all Jews. It was felt, therefore, by many Zionists that the Jerusalem Program had lost much of its distinctive Zionist character, precisely because it was so widely accepted. The demand was increasingly voiced to keep the Basle Program unchanged but to revise the Jerusalem Program by making it more outspokenly Zionist. This revision, prepared by the Zionist Executive, was accomplished at the 27th Zionist Congress (Jerusalem, 1968). The Revised Jerusalem Program read as follows: "The aims of Zionism are: the unity of the Jewish people and the centrality of Israel in Jewish life; the ingathering of the Jewish people in its historic homeland Ereẓ Israel through *aliyah* from all countries; the strengthening of the State of Israel which is based on the prophetic vision of justice and peace; the preservation of the identity of the Jewish people through the fostering of Jewish and Hebrew education and of Jewish spiritual and cultural values; the protection of Jewish rights everywhere." This Revised Jerusalem Program was not merely an amplification and elaboration of the 1951 version; it introduced new points, some of which had been included in minority proposals at the 23rd Congress but had not been passed by the Plenary Session. These are the postulates of immigration from all lands; of Jewish and Hebrew education, as well as emphasis on the centrality of Israel in the life of the Jewish people and, consequently, of every Zionist.

BIBLIOGRAPHY: H.H. Bodenheimer, *Toledot Tokhnit Basel* (1947); A. Bein, *Theodor Herzl* (1962^2), index; B. Halpern, *Idea of the Jewish State* (1969^2), index; L. Jaffe (ed.), *Sefer ha-Kongress* (1950^2).

[Aharon Zwergbaum]

BASMAN BEN-HAYIM, RIVKE (1925–), Yiddish poet. One of the leading Yiddish poets of the post-Holocaust period, she was born in Vilkomir (Lithuania) and survived the Vilna Ghettto and the forced labor camps of World War II. In 1947 she immigrated to Palestine and participated in the War of Independence. After training as a teacher, she studied literature at Columbia University in New York and was a co-founder of the literary movement *Yung Yisroel*. Her poetry, which problematizes the tensions between an annihilated world and a new homeland, attempts to come to terms lyrically with the Holocaust while affirming life in all its manifestations. A sober poetic style and a boldly visual lexical metonymy express great sensitivity, quiet joy, and restrained sorrow. The poems on the death of her husband (Mulah ben Hayim) are elegiac and pantheistic. Her book publications include: *Toybn baym brunem* ("Doves at the Well," 1959), *Bleter fun vegn* ("Leaves on Paths," 1967), *Likhtike shteyner* ("Glittering Stones," 1972), *Tseshotene kreln* ("Scattered Pearls," 1982), *Onrirn di tsayt* ("Touching Time," 1988), *Di shtilkeyt brent* ("Burning Silence," 1992), *Di erd gedenkt* ("The Earth Remembers," 1998), and *Oyf a strune fun regn* ("On a String of Rain," 2002).

BIBLIOGRAPHY: I. Fater, in: *Nusakh Ashkenaz in Vort un Klang* (2002), 66–70; A. Spiegelblatt, in: *Toplpunkt*, 8 (2004), 11–14; Z. Kahan-Newman, in: J. Sherman (ed.). *Yiddish after the Holocaust* (2004), 266–85.

[Astrid Starck (2nd ed.)]

°BASNAGE, JACQUES CHRISTIAN (also called **Basnage de Beauval**; 1653–1725), Protestant divine and historian. Basnage was born in Rouen, France. In 1676 he became pastor there but after the revocation of the Edict of Nantes he accepted a call first to Rotterdam (1686) and later to the Hague (1691). He wrote several books, the most famous being *L'histoire et la réligion des Juifs depuis Jésus Christ jusqu'à present* (5 vols., 1706–11; Eng. *The History and Religion of the Jews from the time of Jesus Christ to the Present*, 1708), which was praised by Voltaire. The book was intended to supplement and continue the history of Josephus, but is marred by the author's inadequate knowledge of Hebrew, which obliged him to rely on Latin translations of Jewish sources and authors. He made use of the works of Buxtorf and Arias Montano and other Christian scholars. Despite Basnage's dry style and occasional inability to control the vast material, his book enjoyed great popularity and was the basis for later, more informed Jewish histories. In 1713 Basnage published another book on Jewish history *Antiquités judaïques ou Remarques critiques sur la république des hébreux*. His books are important as the first comprehensive and truly erudite history of the Jews in the Christian era, filling a gap between early Jewish historical writings and modern Jewish historical research.

BIBLIOGRAPHY: Bernfeld, in: *Ha-Shilo'aḥ*, 2 (1897), 198–201; E.A. Mailhet, *Jacques Basnage, théologien, controversiste, diplomate et historien: sa vie et ses écrits* (1880); Graetz, Hist, 6 (1949), index; *Dictionnaire de biographie française*, 5 (1951), 734.

[Benzion Dinur (Dinaburg)]

BASOLA, MOSES BEN MORDECAI (I) (1480–1560), Italian rabbi. Basola was apparently of French extraction, since he signed himself "Ẓarefati" ("The Frenchman"); it has been conjectured that his surname is identical with Basilea, i.e., Basle. From the age of nine he resided in Soncino. Basola served as teacher and tutor in the household of the banker Moses Nissim of Poligno in Pesaro. After he was ordained as a rabbi by R. Azriel *Diena of Sabionetta in 1535 he became a rabbi in Ancona and was the head of a Jewish academy (yeshivah) there and also a district rabbi of Marches. He was also involved in financial ventures with his son Azriel, and from 1554 owned a bank in the city of Rocca in the Marches. In the years 1557–58 he was a rabbi in Pesaro. Shortly afterward he immigrated to Ereẓ Israel and settled in Safed, where he died.

Although Basola's halakhic decisions have never been collected, some have been preserved as independent documents while others have been appended as approbations to rabbinic decisions issued in his day. Both types can be found in the collected responsa (published and manuscript versions) of his contemporaries. He had a central role in some of the halakhic debates and affairs that electrified Jewish society in Italy and elsewhere. For example, he took a strong stand against the planned international boycott of Ancona promoted by the Ottoman sultan's courtiers, Don Joseph *Nasi and Dona Gracia *Nasi. The courtiers' plan to shift the center of commerce between Italy and the East from Ancona to Pesaro was sparked by Pope Paul IV's execution of 25 *Conversos who had settled in Ancona. Basola joined other rabbinic figures and the Anconan and Levantine merchants whose livelihood was threatened (and who feared the wrath of the local authorities) in opposing the short-lived boycott that began in July 1556. He was deeply involved in the dispute over the printing of kabbalistic (Jewish mystical) works, which was significantly in Italy in the years 1557–58. Leone *Modena (1571–1648) testified that Basola was "a great sage in Kabbalah," but no kabbalistic works by Basola are extant. He even made a specific prediction that the "end of days," namely redemption, would occur between 1575 and 1578. Basola's contacts in the world of Kabbalah extended to Christian kabbalists. He was particularly close to the French-Christian kabbalist and Hebraist Guillaume *Postel. In 1521 Basola went as pilgrim from Venice to Ereẓ Israel, remaining there for a year and a half. His travelogue appeared as an anonymous text in Livorno (1785) in a collection of treatises called *Shivḥei Yerushalayim* ("Praises of Jerusalem") which was edited by Jacob b. Ḥayyim. With the publication of the Itzhak Ben-Zvi edition of this travel book in Jerusalem in 1938 the identity of its author was definitively established. The work is remarkable for its clarity, critical faculty, and clear delineation of economic and social conditions. At the end are appended an account of the organization of Jewish communal life in Jerusalem, reports on the (mythical) river *Sambatyon, and advice to Jewish sea travelers. Basola's book is not only a travel diary that records the impressions of the pilgrim as he prays at a venerated gravesite or enjoys Jerusalem's unique urban atmosphere. Rather, Basola envisioned his treatise primarily as a useful guide whose purpose was to provide European Jewish pilgrims and potential settlers in Ereẓ Israel with helpful information for planning their voyage.

MOSES BASOLA (II) (16th century), kabbalist originally from Safed and possibly the grandson of Moses Basola I, settled in Italy, where he edited, together with Gedaliah b.

Moses Cordovero, *Or Ne'erav* (a compendium of *Pardes Rimmonim*, Venice, 1587) and *Tomer Devorah* (Venice, 1589), both by Moses Cordovero.

MOSES BASOLA (III) (16th century), properly Della Rocca, was grandson through his mother of Moses Basola I. He was the teacher of Leone *Modena at Ferrara (1582–84). Subsequently he went to Cyprus where he died. Modena wrote a poem in his memory, which can be read either as Hebrew or Italian.

BIBLIOGRAPHY: C. Roth, *The House of Nasi: Doña Graciá* (1947), ch. 7; I. Ben-Zvi, *Masot Ereẓ Yisrael le-Moshe Basola* (1938); **ADD. BIBLIOGRAPHY:** R. Lamdan, in: *Michael*, 9 (1985), 171–93; idem, in: Z. Ankori (ed.), *From Lisbon to Salonica and Constantinople* (1988), 135–54; A. David, in: *Zion and Jerusalem: The Itinerary of Rabbi Moses Basola* (1999).

[Cecil Roth / Avraham David (2nd ed.)]

BASRA, port in southern Iraq, on the Shaṭṭ al-Arab, the outlet into the Persian Gulf of the rivers Tigris and Euphrates. Jews settled there under the *Umayyad regime and one of the nine canals near the town is called Nahr al-Yahūd ("River of the Jews"). Jews also settled in Ubulla, then the port of the town of Basra and now the site of Basra. Toward the end of the Umayyad caliphate, Māsarjawayh, a Jewish physician from Basra, gained fame for his Arabic translations of Greek medical books. In the first generation of *Abbasid rule, the court astrologer was the Jew Misha b. Abra, called Māshāallah. Besides many artisans and merchants, the Basra Jewish community comprised many religious scholars, including Simeon Kayyara of Ṣabkha (suburb of Basra), who wrote *Halakhot Gedolot* about 825 C.E. The sages of Basra were in close contact with the academy of *Sura, to which the community sent an annual contribution of 300 dinars. In the tenth century, when the academy closed, the last *Gaon*, Joseph b. Jacob, settled in Basra. But until about 1150 the Jews of Basra continued to direct their questions on religious matters to the heads of the yeshivah in Baghdad, and especially to *Sherira Gaon and his son *Hai Gaon. From these questions, it appears that the Jews of Basra had close commercial ties with the Jews of Baghdad. Both a Rabbanite and a *Karaite community existed in Basra. A Karaite, Israel b. Simḥah b. Saadiah b. Ephraim, dedicated a *Ben-Asher version of the Bible to the Karaite community of Jerusalem. In the 11th century, Basra was gradually abandoned as a result of civil wars in Mesopotamia; and many of its Jews emigrated. Solomon b. Judah (d. 1051), head of the Jerusalem yeshivah, mentions religious scholars and physicians from Basra in Palestine and Egypt.

However, throughout the Middle Ages there remained an important community in Basra. *Benjamin of Tudela (c. 1170) reports that approximately 10,000 Jews, including many wealthy men and religious scholars, lived in the town. He also mentions the grave north of the town, believed to be that of *Ezra and also venerated by the Muslims. According to an early 13th century letter by Daniel b. Eleazar b. Nethanel Ḥibat Allah, head of the Baghdad yeshivah, there was also a synagogue in the town named for Ezra. When the *Mongols conquered Iraq in the mid-13th century, Basra surrendered and was not severely damaged. However, when Tamerlane conquered Mesopotamia in 1393, many Jews were killed and all the synagogues in the town were destroyed. Nevertheless, a small community continued to exist.

The community regained its importance during the 18th century. Its wealth increased; rich landowners in the community liberally distributed alms and even sent contributions to Ereẓ Israel. The liturgical poem *Megillat Paras* ("Persian Scroll") by the emissary from Hebron, Jacob Elyashar, describes the siege of Basra by the Persians and the town's deliverance in 1775, when the Jewish minister of finance, Jacob b. Aaron, who had been captured, was released. Afterward, Nisan 2nd – the day on which the siege was lifted – was celebrated in Basra as the "Day of the Miracle." Jews played such a vital role in the commercial life of Basra that in 1793 the representative of the East India Company was forced to live in Kuwait for nearly two years, because he had quarreled with the Jewish merchants. In 1824 David d'Beth Hillel reported 300 Jewish households belonging to merchants and artisans in Basra and a Jewish finance minister. During the persecutions of Jews which took place under the rule of Da'ūd Pasha in the early 19th century, several wealthy members of the Basra community emigrated to India. The traveler, Benjamin II, mentions that in 1848, he found about 300 Jewish families in Basra. But in 1860 Jehiel Fischel, an emissary of the rabbis of Safed, reports 40 Jewish families in the town out of a population of 12,000. After the British occupation in 1914, the number of Jews increased from 1,500 to 9,921 in 1947, when Jews constituted 9.8% of the total population. Most of the Jews were traders and many worked in the administration service of the railroads, the airport, and the seaport. The legal status of the community was regulated by a 1931 law, according to which a president and a chief rabbi were assigned to head it. A boys' school was founded by the Alliance Israélite Universelle in 1903, and later became a high school. In 1950 it had 450 pupils. In 1913 an Alliance Israélite Universelle girls' school was founded, and attended in 1930 by 303 pupils. All schools were under the supervision of the community committee. In the 1930s, a theosophical group was formed and headed by the Jew Kadduri Elijah 'Aani (who went to Palestine in 1945 and died in Jerusalem). The community excommunicated this group, and its Jewish members were forced to establish their own synagogue, cemetery, and slaughter-house. A Zionist association, formed in Basra in 1921, was not allowed freedom of action.

[Eliyahu Ashtor]

Modern Period

In May 1941, under the pro-Nazi regime of Rashīd ʿĀlī al-Kailānī, Jewish shops were looted by an incited mob. In 1942 the newly founded Zionist movement of Basra trained Jewish youngsters to use arms in anticipation of further attacks and organized groups for *aliyah*. After a few years of relative calm, the Jews were again in danger. In 1948, with the declaration of the State of Israel, a military regime was declared in Iraq and many Jews were arrested and accused of cooperating with Israel. In September 1948, Shafiq Adas, a Jewish millionaire, was accused of selling arms to Israel via Italy. In fact he dealt with scrap metal left behind by the British forces. He was sentenced to death and fined L5 million; he was then hanged in front of his home in Basra. As the wave of arrests continued, thousands of Jews tried to leave Iraq and reach Israel using clandestine routes. Most of them arrived in Basra, and in 1949–50, the city served as a center for the flight of Jews to Iran, on their way to Israel, with the Jewish population rising to 13,000. Thousands were helped by smugglers to cross the Shatt al-ʿArab to the Iranian shore. Under ʿAbd al-Karīm Qāsim's military regime (1958–63), the Jews were given some freedom and civil rights, but after the Baʿathist counterrevolution, they were again persecuted. In 1969, many of Basra's Jews were arrested and transferred to *Baghdad. Nine of them were hanged. In 1968 fewer than 300 Jews were living in Basra. After American and British forces entered Iraq in 2003 and put an end to Saddam Hussein's dictatorship, the few remaining Jews in Basra and Baghdad emigrated to Israel, with the help of Jewish organizations.

[David M. Sagiv (2nd ed.)]

BIBLIOGRAPHY: Sassoon, in: JQR, 17 (1926/27), 407–69; A. Ben-Yaacov, *Yehudei Bavel* (1965), index (*Bibliography:* 388–415); S. Landshut, *Jewish Communities in the Muslim Countries of the Middle East* (1950), 44–45, passim; Y.F. Kestelman, *Masʿot Sheliʾah Ẓefat be-Arẓot ha-Mizraḥ* (1942), 56–58; H.J. Cohen, *Ha-Pe'ilut ha-Ẓiyyonit be-Irak* (1969), index. **ADD. BIBLIOGRAPHY:** H.J. Cohen, *Ha-Yehudim be-Arẓot ha-Mizraḥ ha-Tikhon be-Yameinu* (1972); M. Sawdayee, *All Waiting to be Hanged* (1974); N. Rejwan, *The Jews of Iraq* (1985), index; Y. Meir, *Hitpatḥut Ḥevratit-Tarbutit shel Yehudei Irak me-az 1830 ve-ad Yameinu* (1989); M. Ben-Porat, *Le-Bagdad ve-Ḥazarah* (1996); N. Kazzaz, *Sofah shel Golah* (2002), index; D.M. Sagiv, *Yahadut be-Mifgash ha-Naharayim* (2004).

BAṢRI, MEER (1911–), Iraqi author and economist. Active in Baghdad commercial life, Baṣri published a volume of essays on economics (1948) and two collections of short stories, notably *Rijāl wa-Ẓilāl* ("Men and Shadows," 1955). Unlike most of Iraq's Jewish writers, Baṣrī did not immigrate to Israel and made no mention of Jews or Judaism in his works of fiction.

[Shmuel Moreh]

BASS (Bezprozvany), HYMAN B. (1904–1983), Yiddish educator and essayist. Born in Vilnius (now Lithuania), Bass immigrated to New York in 1922 and taught in Yiddish schools. From 1953 he served as executive secretary of the *Congress for Jewish Culture and in 1966 as president of the Jewish Book Council of America. He edited textbooks for Yiddish schools and wrote extensively on Jewish education. His book of essays *Undzer Dor Muz Antsheydn* ("Our Generation Must Decide," 1963), embodied his ideas on Jewish education and cultural survival. S. *Dubnow, Y.L. *Peretz, and Chaim *Zhitlowsky were his mentors and he adapted their ideas to a mid-20th century American Jewish context.

BIBLIOGRAPHY: LNYL, 1 (1956), 355–6. **ADD. BIBLIOGRAPHY:** AJYB 85 (1985), 412–3.

[Sol Liptzin]

BASS (or Bassista; Heb. מְשׁוֹרֵר), **SHABBETAI BEN JOSEPH** (1641–1718), the first Jewish bibliographer. Bass's parents were killed in a pogrom in Kalisz (Poland) by the Cossacks in 1655, but he and his elder brother were saved and fled to Prague. Possessing a pleasant voice, Bass was engaged as an assistant singer (hence his nickname Bass) to the cantor Loeb at the Altneu synagogue (Altneuschul) in Prague. In Prague he acquired a thorough knowledge of the Talmud, and also a general education which included Latin. His love of books and a critical spirit drew him to publication and printing. In 1669 in Prague he printed a revised edition of the Yiddish commentary on the Pentateuch and the Five Scrolls by Moses Saertels, *Be'er Moshe*, with an appendix on "grammatical rules." As there was no complete list in Hebrew of Jewish literature, he undertook to compile one. Between 1674 and 1679 Bass visited libraries in Poland, Germany, and Holland. In Amsterdam he studied the art of printing and proofreading, and published *Massekhet Derekh Ereẓ*, a guide book for travelers (1680); the Pentateuch with a super-commentary on Rashi, *Siftei Ḥakhamim* (1680), a popular commentary often reprinted; and *Siftei Yeshenim* (1680), a list in Hebrew of some 2,200 Hebraica and Judaica. This was the first Jewish bibliography in Hebrew giving, apart from the names of the books, the name of the author, content, format, place and year of printing, and sometimes also where it could be found. He also listed manuscripts. In some copies a prayerbook was appended to the list. In 1688 Bass obtained a permit to set up a Hebrew printing press at Auras, and this was shortly afterward transferred to *Dyhernfurth. The first book printed by Bass was Samuel b. Uri Shraga's commentary *Beit Shemu'el* (1689), on Shulḥan Arukh *Even ha-Ezer*. He also successfully engaged in bookselling. When the Jesuits accused Bass of spreading hatred against the Christians and the government, he at first succeeded in refuting the accusations; but in 1712 the Jesuits repeated the accusations and he was arrested. In the trial he succeeded in proving the ignorance of his accusers and was released. His sons and grandsons continued to print books at Dyhernfurth up to the second half of the 18th century.

BIBLIOGRAPHY: Bloch, in: *Studies in Jewish Bibliography…* (1929), index; Shunami, Bibl, index.

[Abraham Meir Habermann]

BASSAN, ABRAHAM HEZEKIAH BEN JACOB (18th century), proofreader and poet. Abraham's father, JACOB, was the rabbi of the Spanish and Portuguese community of Hamburg. From 1735 to 1756 Jacob lived in Amsterdam and in 1755 published an order of service for the fast day proclaimed on the occasion of the great earthquake in Lisbon.

Abraham Hezekiah was proofreader for the Hebrew press in Amsterdam. He is mentioned as the proofreader of Benjamin Raphael Dias Brandon's *Orot ha-Mitzvot* (1753) to which his father wrote an approbation, and to which Abraham contributed an introduction and poem consisting of 13 stanzas. Other poems by Abraham were published in works by various authors: in the *Gemul Atalyah* (1770) of David *Franco-Mendes, in the *Se'ah Solet* (1757) of Raphael b. Gabriel Norzi, and in the *Maskiyyot Kesef* (1760) of Mordecai b. Isaac Tamah. In about 1773 he moved to Hamburg where he succeeded his father as rabbi of the local Spanish and Portuguese community. He was the author of a book of eulogies, *Sermões Funebres* (Amsterdam, 1753), written in Spanish. It is doubtful that he is the author of the *Yashresh Ya'akov* (Nuremberg, 1768), a work on grammar and the text of the prayer book, as has been conjectured (see Benjacob, Oẓar, 234 no. 503).

BIBLIOGRAPHY: Ghirondi-Neppi, 10 no. 40; Kayserling, Bibl, 26.

[Yehoshua Horowitz]

BASSANI, GIORGIO (1916–2000), Italian writer. Bassani, who was born in Bologna, lived for many years in Ferrara and was active in the anti-Fascist Resistance. After World War II he moved to Rome, but Ferrara, and especially its Jewish community, remained at the heart of Bassani's literary world. His first published work was a volume of stories and poems entitled *Una città di pianura* (1940), published under a pseudonym because of the Fascist antisemitic laws. In 1945 he made his reputation with a book of poems, *Storie di poveri amanti*. His collection of short stories *Cinque storie ferraresi* (1956) deals with provincial life in Ferrara. One of them, "Una lapide in via Mazzini" is the story of a Jewish survivor of a concentration camp: his presence is an embarrassing reminder to the people of his native town, who wish to forget the tragedy. *Gli occhiali d'oro* (1958; *The Gold-Rimmed Spectacles*, 1960) is the story of two men rejected by society, one because he is a homosexual, the other because he is a Jew. The Jewish theme is omnipresent in Bassani's fiction: Jewish identity is a paradigm of the malaise of modern man, who has lost his stable system of values. This theme is intertwined with the theme of memory, particularly in *Il giardino dei Finzi-Contini* (1962; *The Garden of Finzi Contini*, 1965), which has been translated into a number of languages, including Hebrew. Reality and fiction are mixed in this novel, which deals with the fate of an old and wealthy Jewish family during the Fascist years and the war, and stops just before its deportation. In *L'airone* (1968; *The Heron*, 1969) a Jewish bourgeois who leaves his property to his Christian wife and the Communist peasants represents the European bourgeois unable to establish a healthy relationship with the surrounding world. The association of a problematic Jewish identity with the crisis of the contemporary bourgeosie is also a key theme of *Dietro la porta* (1964; *Behind the Door*, 1972), the most autobiographical of his novels. Jewish characters are also present in *L'odore del fieno* (1972; *The Smell of Hay*, 1997). In 1980 Bassani revised his short stories and novels and published them in one volume under the title *Il romanzo di Ferrara*. His poems were collected in 1982 in *In rima e senza*; among them some texts dealing with the Jewish condition, such as "Le leggi razziali" (1974). *Di là dal cuore* (1984) is a collection all of Bassani's critical essays. From 1948 to 1961 he edited the literary review *Botteghe Oscure* and from 1948 to 1961 he was a vice president of Italian radio and television; for many years he was also president of Italia nostra, an association for the preservation of the country's artistic and natural heritage. In addition he taught the history of theater at the National Academy of Dramatic Art in Rome.

BIBLIOGRAPHY: M. Grillandi, *Invito alla lettura di Bassani* (1972); G. Bassani *Opere* (1998), with a chronology and bibliography; A. Dolfi, *Giorgio Bassani: una scrittura della malinconia* (2000); C. Kroha, "Judaism and Manhood in the Novels of Giorgio Bassani," in: T. Di Napoli (ed.), *The Italian Jewish Experience* (2000); P. Prebys, *Giorgio Bassani, Bibliografia sulle opere e sulla vita* (2002).

[Alessandro Guetta (2nd ed.)]

BASSANI, MORDECAI (**Marco** in Italian; the name **Hezekiah** was added on the occasion of his last illness, c. 1632–1703), Italian rabbi and polemicist. In 1666 he became preacher to the Ashkenazi community of Verona, and in 1680 he became its rabbi; in 1695 he was appointed rabbi of the entire Verona community. He was the author of *Sefer Bikkurim* (Venice, 1710) containing deathbed prayers and usages (adapted from *Ma'avar Yabbok* of *Aaron Berechiah ben Moses of Modena, and *Shenei Luḥot Ha-Berit* of Isaiah *Horowitz) written for the Bikkur Ḥolim fraternity of Verona, but later widely adopted. His treatise on divorce, entitled *Mikhtav le-Ḥizkiyyah*, and one on *ḥaliẓah*, entitled *Ma'amar Mordekhai*, were included by his great-grandson Menahem Navarra in his *Penei Yiẓḥak* (Verona, 1743). In his will he mentions a collection of "moral sermons" which he had compiled (*Avnei Binyan*, 1 (1938), 65). He was friendly with the Roman Catholic polemicist Fra Luigi Maria Benetelli. His criticisms of Benetelli's polemical work, *Le saette di Gionata…* (Venice, 1703) together with those of Samson *Morpurgo and Abraham Joel *Conegliano prompted Benetelli's rejoinder, *I dardi rabbinici infranti…* (Venice, 1705). In this work Benetelli speaks in the highest terms of the gentle manner, great charity, and admirable character of Bassani. Bassani is also the author of a lengthy responsum on the relationship between the Ashkenazi community of Verona and the smaller Sephardi community there.

BIBLIOGRAPHY: S. Baron, in: *Sefer… S. Krauss* (1936), 217–54; Sonne, in: *Zion*, 3 (1938), 123ff.; Simonsohn, in: KS, 35 (1959), 127 n. 1; 253 n. 109; C. Roth, *Gleanings…* (1967), 203, 206–7, 213.

[Cecil Roth]

BASSANO, small town in Veneto (Northern Italy). The first mention of Jews in Bassano is from a document of October 7, 1264; a certain Aicardo was said to own a vineyard. Only from the beginning of the 15th century, when Bassano passed over to

Venetian rule, is there more information. A certain Calimano had a bank in the town in 1404. Venetian authorities allowed Jews to settle in the town. However, moneylenders could only stay for a short time. Via Bricito was known as Via dei Zudei, because of the presence of many Jewish banking establishments. A notarial deed of 1435 reveals, however, that by then Jews resided in all parts of the city. Freedom of worship was granted by the Venetian Republic, but Jews were not allowed to have a synagogue and had to observe their festivals "in the houses in which they dwelled." Relations between the local population and the Jews were quite good. Once in 1486 some Bassano city dwellers attended a Jewish wedding. They were excommunicated by church authorities, but the town council had the excommunication repealed. It is not known if Bassano Jews had to wear the yellow badge, obligatory according to the Venetian decree of 1429. The preaching of Bernardino da Feltre and the creation of **monti di pietà* (savings and loan agencies) in 1423 brought a decline to the Jewish community. In 1468, a decree of perpetual banishment was issued against them. Nevertheless they returned. In 1475, following the ritual murder charge concerning Simon of *Trent, the municipality of Bassano requested permission from Venice to expel the Jews. They were banished again by the city council in 1481. However, they were soon readmitted. During the War of the League of Cambrai (1508), the Jews in Bassano paid a heavy tribute, but this did not prevent their expulsion from Bassano at the end of the war in 1509. The banks, however, closed completely only around 1510.

BIBLIOGRAPHY: G. Chiuppani, *Gli ebrei a Bassano* (1907); Roth, Italy, index; Milano, Italia, index. **ADD. BIBLIOGRAPHY:** F. Brandes, *Venice Jewish Itineraries* (1996), 24–27; A.M. Piattelli, "*Frammenti e manoscritti ebraici negli archivi di stato a Bassano e Verona,*" in: *Italia,* 11 (1994), 81–102.

[Attilio Milano / Samuel Rocca (2nd ed.)]

BASSANO (Bassan, Bassani), name of Italian family deriving from the town *Bassano. In the 17th and 18th centuries, it produced several rabbis and scholars, outstanding among whom are: MORDECAI *BASSANI (c. 1632–1703), rabbi of Verona and ISAIAH BEN ISRAEL HEZEKIAH (d. 1739), rabbi in Cento, Padua, Ferrara, and Reggio Emilia. Many of his responsa are included in the second volume of *Todat Shelamim* by his son Israel (see below) and in the *Paḥad Yiẓḥak* of Isaac *Lampronti and *Shemesh Ẓedakah* of Samson *Morpurgo. His other responsa, glosses on the Talmud, a number of poems, notes on the gospels, sermons, and a book, *Kur le-Zahav*, comprising critical notes on Solomon *Algazi's *Halikhot Eli*, remain in manuscript. His pupils included Moses Ḥayyim *Luzzatto. His son, ISRAEL BENJAMIN (1701–1790), one of the outstanding Italian Jewish poets of his day, published two collections of Hebrew poetry accompanied by Italian versions. He dedicated both to Francesco III of Este, duke of Modena (1750–53), calling the second *Corona Estense*. His *Todat Shelamim* (Venice, 1741, 1791) includes his own halakhic writings and responsa by his father. According to the Christian scholar G.B. *De' Rossi, he was highly esteemed in Jewish circles.

BIBLIOGRAPHY: I. Sonne, in: *Zion*, 3 (1938), 160–9 (where Israel Benjamin Bassano's will is published); Baron, in: *Sefer ha-Yovel... S. Krauss* (1937), 217–54; C. Roth, in: JQR, 15 (1924/25), 430 (= *Gleanings* (1967), 203, 206–7); Ghirondi-Neppi, s.v. **ADD. BIBLIOGRAPHY:** G. Badini, *Ricerche storiche* 73 (1993), 27–80; M. Benayahu, *Davar* (June 9, 1978).

[Cecil Roth]

BASSEVI OF TREUENBERG (Treuenburg), JACOB (1570–1634), Court Jew descended from a noted Prague family. He was probably the first European Jew outside Italy to be ennobled. Bassevi and his brother Samuel engaged in large-scale trading and in 1599 obtained a safe-conduct from the emperor exempting them from the restrictions imposed on most Jews. In 1611 Matthias II confirmed Bassevi's privileges and added the right of settling in Vienna. In 1622 because of the emperor's increased need of money during the Thirty Years War, Bassevi formed a consortium with Prince Liechtenstein and the imperial general Wallenstein, which leased the mint for an enormous sum and issued debased coinage. Bassevi, whose profit per silver mark was the lowest within the consortium, provided the financial expertise, and bought most of the necessary silver abroad. When currency dropped to one-seventh of its former value, the depreciated thaler was nicknamed the "Schmilesthaler," the Thaler of Shmil. In 1622 Ferdinand II granted Bassevi a coat of arms. This, however, evidently still did not endow Bassevi with unqualified noble rank, for shortly afterward he requested other privileges connected with his new status, which were nearly all granted.

Like other Court Jews, Bassevi took an active part in Jewish communal life. After the imperial troops left Prague in 1620, Bassevi organized a guard to defend the Jewish quarter from pillage. He obtained for the Jews in Prague in 1623 some 40 houses bordering on the Jewish quarter which had been confiscated from the rebels. He also paid 12,000 Reichsthaler toward the enormous indemnity demanded from Yom Tov Lipmann *Heller in 1629. As head of Prague Jewry for several years, Bassevi was largely responsible for apportioning the communal taxes, as a result of which the opposing faction complained about him to the authorities. After Prince Liechtenstein's death in 1627 the authorities took steps against the former members of the consortium, the complaints providing a welcome excuse for confiscating Bassevi's property and arresting him (1631). However, because of Bassevi's privileged status, Wallenstein succeeded in securing his release (1632). Bassevi then lived at Wallenstein's residence in Jicin, as fiscal administrator of his duchies. Bassevi survived the murder of Wallenstein in 1634 by only a few weeks and was buried at Mlada Boleslav. After his death all his privileges were declared illegal and abrogated.

Bassevi, who maintained his Jewishness while holding his high position, was considered a "princely Jew" ("Juden-fuerst") by his fellow Jews – a fact which seems to have been of some comfort to them in those dark days.

BIBLIOGRAPHY: S. Hock, *Die Familien Prags* (1892), 61–63, 367; Bondy-Dvorsky, 2 (1906), nos. 734, 818, 824, 948, 1044, 1045; Spiegel in: *Die Juden in Prag* (1927), 138–45; L.S. Porta, in: *Juedische Familien-Forschung*, 1 (1925–27), 12–15; H. Schnee, *Die Hoffinanz und der moderne Staat*, 3 (1955), 234–6; NDB, 1 (1953), 625; Hofmann, in: *Zeitschrift fuer die Geschichte der Juden in der Tschechoslowakei*, 4 (1934), 1–5; Polák-Rokycana, *ibid.*, 1 (1930–31), 253–6; Baron, Social², 14 (1969), 231–33.

[Ruth Kestenberg-Gladstein]

BASSIN, MOSES (**Moyshe**; 1889–1963), Yiddish poet. Bassin, who was born in Nivki, Belorussia, deserted the Russian army in 1907 and immigrated to New York. From 1909 he contributed lyrics, essays, folk ballads, and children's songs to American Yiddish journals. His reputation rests on two works: a two-volume, 600-page anthology, *Finf Hundert Yohr Yidishe Poezye* (1917, 1922²), with notes on the earlier selections by Ber *Borochov, which became a standard work; and an anthology of American Yiddish poetry *Amerikaner Yidishe Poezye* (1940), encompassing 31 poets. Bassin's own lyrics appeared in his anthologies but were never collected in book form.

BIBLIOGRAPHY: *Inzikh* (1940), 164–76; LNYL, 1 (1956), 228; J. Leftwich, *Golden Peacock* (1939), 411. **ADD. BIBLIOGRAPHY:** K. Hellerstein, in: *Shofar* 9/4 (1991), 9–23.

[Moshe Rosetti]

°**BASSUS, LUCILIUS** (d. 72 C.E.), Roman governor of Judea after the fall of Jerusalem in 70 C.E. Bassus was instructed to subdue the fortresses of *Herodium, *Machaerus, and *Masada, which still remained in Jewish hands. He first attacked Herodium, which fell without a battle. Then he marched on Machaerus, which was so strongly fortified as to "inspire its occupants with high hopes of security." The defenders fought bravely until one of their leaders, Eleazar, was captured and the Romans threatened to crucify him opposite the walls. The defenders then agreed to surrender the fortress if Eleazar's life were spared. Bassus kept his promise and allowed the occupants to escape, but followed some *Sicarii who had escaped to a forest called Jardes, where they were all killed. Bassus died as he was preparing to begin operations against Masada. It was during his administration of Judea that Jewish-held lands were confiscated to become imperial domain, and that the poll-tax of the *Fiscus Judaicus was put into operation.

BIBLIOGRAPHY: Jos., Wars, 7:163–5, 190–216, 252; Klausner, Bayit Sheni, 5 (1951²), 285ff.; Pauly-Wissowa, 26 (1927), 1640–42 (22).

[Edna Elazary]

BAS TOVIM, SARAH (18th century), author of highly popular *tkhines*, women's supplicatory prayers. Bas Tovim was born in Satanov in Podolia (present-day Ukraine), the great granddaughter of Rabbi Mordecai of Brisk. Her works contain a strong autobiographical voice: She refers to herself as "I, the renowned woman Sarah bas Tovim, of distinguished ancestry," and tells the story of her fall from a wealthy youth to an old age of poverty and wandering. Sarah composed two works published in the 18th century, *Tkhine shaar ha-yikhed al oylemes* (The *Tkhine* of the Gate of Unification concerning the Aeons) and *Tkhine shloyshe sheorim* (The *Tkhine* of Three Gates). Like other *tkhine* authors, Sarah often includes portions of earlier works; these excerpts from other sources date her *tkhines* to the middle of the 18th century. Because 18th-century *tkhines* published in Eastern Europe only rarely contain a notice of place or date of publication, it is very difficult to establish the bibliographic history of her works.

Tkhine shaar ha-yikhed al oylemes (a title with kabbalistic overtones) contains one long *tkhine* to be recited *Mondays and Thursdays (considered minor penitential days) and on fast days. The work concludes with a *tkhine* to be said before making memorial candles for Yom Kippur, a theme which recurs in *Tkhine shloyshe sheorim*, her better-known work. This composition contains *tkhines* for the three women's *mitzvot* (the first "gate"), the Days of Awe (the second "gate"), and the New Moon (the third "gate"). The most distinctive material is found in the second and third "gates." Sarah's powerful *tkhine* calls on the forefathers and foremothers of the Jewish people to aid their descendents with a healthy and prosperous New Year, and also to bring the Messiah, the end of death, and the resurrection of the dead. The *tkhine* for the Sabbath before the New Moon contains a great variety of material to be recited at the Blessing of the New Moon, much of it drawn from kabbalistic sources.

The figure of Sarah bas Tovim lived on in popular legend and in the literary imagination of Yiddish authors. Because her works were so popular, 19th-century *maskilim* who wrote *tkhines* to sell often attached her name to their own creations. In addition, Sholem Yankev *Abramovitsh (Mendele Moykher Sforim) mentions Sarah's *tkhines* in his fictional autobiography, *Shloyme, Reb Khayims* (*Ba-Yamim ha-Hem*, "In Those Days"), which includes a description of women making memorial candles before Yom Kippur, reciting a version of Sarah's *tkhine* for *kneytlakh legn*. Sarah also became the subject of a short story, "Der ziveg; oder, Sore bas Tovim," ("The Match; or, Sarah bas Tovim") by I.L. *Peretz, in which she appears as a sort of fairy godmother, helping those who faithfully recite her *tkhines*.

BIBLIOGRAPHY: Sarah bas Tovim, "*Tkhine* of Three Gates," in: T.G. Klirs et. al. (eds.), *The Merit of Our Mothers: A Bilingual Anthology of Jewish Women's Prayers* (1992), 12–45; Ch. Weissler, *Voices of the Matriarchs* (1998), 31–33, 76–85, 126–46.

[Chava Weissler (2nd ed.)]

BAT (Heb. עֲטַלֵּף; *atallef*). About 20 species of insect-eating bats are found in Israel and one, the *Rousettus aegyptiacus*, which feeds on fruit. The bat is actually a mammal, but because of its wings which enable it to fly, the ancients were in doubt whether it was to be classified with birds or mammals. In the Bible it is last in the list of the unclean birds (Lev. 11:19) but the Talmud declares that "although it lays eggs, it suckles" (Bek. 7b). Apparently the rabbis attributed to the bat the eggs laid by other birds in their caves. The bat is long-lived (up to 30 years) and many legends were woven about its development (BK 16a). The bat causes extensive damage to fruit trees, particularly the date palm, as is indicated in the Jerusalem Talmud (TJ, Pe'ah 8:1, 20d).

BIBLIOGRAPHY: Lewysohn, Zool, 102–5; F.S. Bodenheimer, *Ha-Ḥai be-Arẓot ha-Mikra*, 2 (1956), index; J. Feliks, *Animal World of the Bible* (1962), 47; S. Lieberman, in: *Leshonenu*, 29 (1965), 132–5.

[Jehuda Feliks]

°BAṬALYAWSĪ, ABU MUHAMMAD ABDALLAH IBN MUHAMMAD IBN AL-SĪD AL- (1052–1127), Arab grammarian, philosopher, and author. He was born in Badajoz (Arabic: Baṭalyaws), Spain, is known to have lived in Saragossa for some time, and died in Valencia. His main philosophical work is the *Kitāb al-Ḥadā'iq* ("The Book of Circles") which was translated independently into Hebrew, in whole or in part, three times. The book was quoted widely by Jewish religious philosophers down to the beginning of the 17th century. It is composed of seven chapters in each of which an explanation is given of a statement of the neoplatonic philosophers. The separate chapters center on the following themes:

(1) The procession of existing things from the First Cause imitates an imaginary circle. The explanation of this statement is that from God, the cause of all causes, all existing things emanate in hierarchically descending order, that is, the ten intellects, the soul, form, and matter. Then minerals, plants, animals, and man come into being in hierarchically ascending order. The souls of men are also arranged in ascending order from the vegetative, vital, rational, philosophic to the prophetic which contacts the divine and closes the circle. According to this doctrine, the soul of the prophet is intrinsically superior to that of the philosopher. (2) Man's knowledge imitates an imaginary circle. This may be understood in two ways. First of all, man begins his quest for knowledge with mathematics, and then rises to physics and metaphysics. He then descends to politics and reaches himself once again. Secondly, he descends from himself to the knowledge of animals, plants, minerals, the four elements, matter and then rises to contemplate form, the soul, and the Active *Intellect in which man's rationality has its source. (3) The individual soul may conceive the forms which are in the universal intellect. (4) Number is composed of imaginary circles in each of its stages. (5) The attributes of God should be expressed negatively. (6) The Creator knows Himself alone. (7) The soul is immortal. I. Brill's assertion that the work was wrongly ascribed to al-Baṭalyawsi is without foundation. The substitution of quotations from the Koran and Islamic traditional literature by citations from the Bible and Talmud is standard practice in the medieval Hebrew translations from Arabic which Moses ibn *Tibbon followed in his translation. Some quotations from the Koran are translated and introduced by the formula: "One of the founders of the religions says …"

BIBLIOGRAPHY: D. Kaufmann, *Die Spuren al-Batlajusis in der juedischen Religionsphilosophie* (1880); I. Brill, in: JE, 2 (1925), 593; A. Palacios, in: *Al-Andalus*, 5 (1940), 45–154; G. Vajda, in: *Semitic Studies… Immanuel Loeb* (1947), 202–4; A. Altmann, in: *Studies in Mysticism and Religion Presented to Gershom G. Scholem* (1967), 6ff. **ADD BIBLIOGRAPHY:** EIS², 1 (1960), 1092 (includes bibliography).

[Lawrence V. Berman]

°BATE, JULIUS (1711–1771), English Christian Hebraist. As a member of the Hutchinsonians (a Christian sect) he was involved in a controversy with Bishop William Warburton (1698–1779) on the latter's *Divine Legation of Moses* (1737), and with Benjamin Kennicott (1718–1783) on the published emendations of the masoretic text (1751). Bate's mastery of the Hebrew Bible is demonstrated in his most famous work *Critica Hebraica* (1767), a Hebrew-English dictionary in which the biblical words are reduced to their original roots and their specific forms illustrated and exemplified by passages cited at length from the Scriptures. A strong Christian piety pervades this work and his translation of the Bible which goes to the end of II Kings (1773). He wrote various pamphlets in defense of biblical mysticism.

[Zev Garber]

BATH, spa in Somerset, England. A fashionable resort from the 18th century, Bath early attracted Jewish residents, among them the physician Isaac *Schomberg, as well as visitors. Shortly after 1800, Moses Samuel, formerly warden of the Great Synagogue in London who had retired to Bath, organized a congregation there, and on his death in 1839 left money for building a synagogue. The community subsequently dwindled, and regular services had ceased by 1874. The synagogue closed in 1910. Short-lived congregations have since been set up more than once. By the 1960s there was no Jewish community in Bath, but in 2004 services were being revived under Progressive Jewish auspices.

BIBLIOGRAPHY: C. Roth, *Rise of Provincial Jewry* (1950), 27–29. **ADD. BIBLIOGRAPHY:** JYB, 2004; M. Brown and J. Samuel, "The Jews of Bath," in: JHSET, 29 (1982–86), 135–64.

[Cecil Roth]

BATH, BATHING. Bathing is referred to in the Bible not only for physical cleanliness but also for ritual purposes. Jacob charged his family to wash themselves before they built the altar at Beth-El (Gen. 35:3). Before the revelation at Sinai, the entire Jewish nation was bidden to sanctify themselves by washing their bodies and their garments (Ex. 19:10). Ritual immersion was associated with levitical purity and was stressed in the Book of Leviticus (see *Mikveh*). When Jeremiah described the sinfulness of Israel, he exclaimed, "For though thou wash thee with niter, and take thee much soap" (Jer. 2:22), it still would not remove the sins of the nation.

Talmudic Period

The Talmud declared it forbidden for a scholar to reside in a city which did not contain a public bath (Sanh. 17b). Rome was said to contain 3,000 public baths (Meg. 68) and despite the animosity to the Romans they were praised by the rabbis for constructing baths in Palestine (Shab. 33b). It is related that Rabban Gamaliel utilized the Bath of Aphrodite in Acre although the image of the idol adorned the bath (Av. Zar. 3:4). Originally the baths were communal institutions (Ned. 5:5). Afterward, smaller baths were also built by private individuals (BB 1:6; 10:7) and competition between them to attract customers was permitted (BB 21b). The bath attendants received checks or tokens from intending patrons so they would know in advance how many to expect and what preparations to make (BM 47b and Rashi ad loc.). The larger baths contained separate areas for bathing in lukewarm water, hot water, and steam baths (Shab. 40a). On entering the bathhouse, the rabbis ordained the following prayer: "May it be Thy will, O Lord, my God, to deliver me from the flames of the fire and the heat of the water, and to protect me from a cave-in." Upon leaving, the individual recited, "I thank Thee, O Lord, my God, for having delivered me from the fire" (TJ, Ber. 9:6, 14b; cf. Ber. 60a). Hillel the Elder told his disciples that he considered bathing in the communal bathhouse a religious duty for just as the custodians scour and wash the statues of the kings, likewise must man, created in God's image and likeness, do to his body (Lev. R. 34:3).

Middle Ages and Modern Times

The public bath and adjoining *mikveh* were maintained by Jewish communities throughout the Middle Ages as part of the institutions of Jewish social life and welfare. Hygienic habits and the ritual requirements of the Jewish religion made the Jews regard bathing as part of their living routine during a period when bathing was generally considered a form of rare luxury in Europe. By the end of the 11th century, some Jewish communities erected imposing buildings to house their baths and regularly attended to their servicing and upkeep. The refusal of Christians to allow Jews to share the municipal baths and the fear that Jewish women might be molested there increased the need for separate institutions. The fact also, that, with the exception of Poland, Jews were prohibited from bathing in the same river as Christians finally led them to build their own bathhouses, which often became landmarks, such as the *Badehaus* of the Jews of Augsburg, or "Bakewell Hall" in London, which was probably originally "Bathwell Hall." In Moslem Spain, Ramon Berenger IV allowed his court physician, Abraham, to build the only public bathhouse in Barcelona, which his family ran from 1160 to 1199. In the Middle East, and in modern times, particularly in Eastern Europe, Jews became addicted to the "Turkish bath" which has found its way into Jewish folklore. Several ancient baths have been discovered in Ereẓ Israel such as the swimming pool and hot baths that Herod built at *Herodium, which had waiting rooms, dressing rooms, hot rooms, and cool rooms with all the comforts of the baths at Rome. Among the best-preserved and beautifully finished baths that have been uncovered in Ereẓ Israel are those on Masada, where no less than four baths and one swimming pool were built by Herod. In the northern palace there is a small, private bathhouse finished in Roman style, and south of the palace there is a large swimming pool with cubicles for keeping clothes; Herod built a small bathhouse in the west palace as well, which was unusually heated by an oven in an adjoining room and fitted with a niche for an oil lamp. More important, however, are the remains of the large bathhouse near the north palace where more than 200 stands, the remnants of the piping system for the hot air, were discovered, as well as elaborate facilities for steam baths, cold baths, etc., adorned with frescoes and mosaics. At a later period the Zealots built a large bathhouse in the southern corner of Masada, consisting of a small *mikveh* and two connecting larger ones, which conform to *halakhah*. Near Tiberias are the remains of the hot, mineral baths of *Hamath of the Roman period.

BIBLIOGRAPHY: Y. Brand, *Kelei ha-Ḥeres ba-Sifrut ha-Talmudit* (1953), 27–35; G. Krauss, *Talmudische Archaeologie* (1910); U.E. Paoli, *Das Leben im alten Rom* (1948); J. Carcopino, *Daily Life in Ancient Rome* (1940); Th. Birt, *Zur Kulturgeschichte Roms* (1917); Baron, Social 2, 4 (1956), 37; I. Abrahams, *Jewish Life in the Middle Ages* (1932), 89, 426.

BAT ḤEFER (Heb. בת חפר; "Daughter of Ḥefer"), urban community located in the *Ḥefer Plain in central Israel. The settlement is located near the border of Samaria, near *Tūl Karm, and is part of the regional council of Emek Ḥefer. Its area is 0.4 sq. mi (1 sq. km.). The settlement was part of the "seven star" plan of Ariel *Sharon to establish settlements near the border of Samaria. Building began in 1994 and the first settlers arrived in 1996. At the end of 2002 the population of Bat Ḥefer was 4,610.

[Shaked Gilboa (2nd ed.)]

BATH-SHEBA (Heb. בַּת־שֶׁבַע, in I Chron. 3:5 בַּת־שׁוּעַ), wife of *David and mother of *Solomon. Bath-Sheba was originally the wife of *Uriah the Hittite, one of David's warriors. During the war against Rabbath-Ammon (II Sam. 11), David saw Bath-Sheba and ordered her brought to his palace. When David knew that she was pregnant by him, he attempted to return Uriah to his house (see II Sam. 11:6–13). Failing to do so, he sought and found a pretext to have Uriah killed in battle (11:14–27); he then married Bath-Sheba. The prophet *Nathan rebuked David for this act (12:1–12), but subsequently took Bath-Sheba's side and supported the enthronement of her son Solomon (I Kings 1:8ff.). She later agreed to present to Solomon *Adonijah's request for David's concubine *Abishag. In addition to Solomon, Bath-Sheba gave birth to at least three other sons, Shimea, Shobab, and Nathan (I Chron. 3:5). It seems that her first son, who died soon after his birth because of the sin of his father, is included in this list (II Sam. 12:13ff.).

According to II Samuel 11:3, Bath-Sheba was the daughter of Eliam, and according to I Chronicles 3:5, she was the daughter of Ammiel, who the rabbis of the Talmud (Sanh. 69b) identify with Eliam son of *Ahithophel the Gilonite (II Sam. 23:34); hence the opinion of early commentators (Kimḥi and Levi b. Gershom) and several recent scholars that the opposition of Ahithophel to David during the revolt of Absalom stemmed from his wish to avenge Uriah's death. Others believe that these opinions are unacceptable, because, if indeed Eliam was the son of the famous Ahithophel, the Bible would not have failed to mention the fact. It is also difficult to believe that Ahithophel, if he was the grandfather of Bath-Sheba, would have taken part in such an action which would undoubtedly have endangered the position of his granddaughter and her son in the royal court. On the other hand, there is reason to suppose that Bath-Sheba was of a family that existed in Jerusalem before its conquest by David.

[Yehoshua M. Grintz]

In the *Aggadah*

If she was Ahithophel's granddaughter, the prophecies which he believed foretold his own royal destiny, in fact applied to her (Sanh. 101b). Bath-Sheba was predestined for David; his sin was that he took her before the appointed time (Sanh. 107a). She was not guilty of adultery since it was the custom that soldiers going to war gave their wives bills of divorce which were to become valid should they fail to return and Uriah did fall in battle (Ket. 9b). She was a prophet in that she foresaw that her son would be the wisest of men. She is numbered among the 22 women of valor (Mid. Hag. to Gen. 23:1).

BIBLIOGRAPHY: Bright, Hist, 181, 188n., 189, 230; de Vaux, Anc Isr, index; M.Z. Segal, *Sifrei Shemu'el* (1964²), 299, 326–7; S. Yeivin, *Meḥkarim be-Toledot Yisrael ve-Arẓo* (1960), 198–207, 230–1; Noth, Personennamen, 146–7. IN THE AGGADAH: Ginzberg, Legends, 4 (1947), 94–95, 103–4; 6 (1946), 256–7, 264–5.

BATHYRA, place in the toparchy of Batanea (i.e., *Bashan, east of Golan) founded by Jewish military settlers from Babylonia. Desirous of defending his borders from attacks by the neighboring Trachonites, *Herod decided to settle a large number of Jews in the area of Bathyra with the further intention that it would serve also as a base for his own military offensives. Upon learning that *Zamaris, a Jew from Babylon, had crossed the Euphrates with five hundred horsemen and was staying near Antioch under the patronage of Saturninus, the governor of Syria, Herod offered them the territory for the proposed buffer-zone, promising to rescind all taxes and tributes. The Babylonians took possession of the land, building fortresses and a village named Bathyra. The settlers defended not only the local population from Trachonite brigandage, but also Jewish pilgrims from Babylonia on their way to Jerusalem.

The family of Zamaris became a major ally of Herod, supporting his policies as well as those of the two Agrippas. Although Bathyra remained their base, members of the family also resided throughout the neighboring territories. Relatives of Philip, grandson of Zamaris, were among the prominent residents of Gamala at the beginning of the Roman War (66 C.E.). Philip played a vital if somewhat ambiguous part during that uprising, as well as in the events in Jerusalem on the eve of the outbreak of the war in 66. It was his task to secure Batanea from insurrection against Agrippa II and the Romans. Numerous scholars have made the connection between Bathyra and the rabbis referred to in the Talmud as "the sons of *Bathyra," who held high offices in Jerusalem until they were superseded by Hillel. However, it is improbable that there was any connection between the warriors of Bathyra and the rabbinical "sons of Bathyra."

BIBLIOGRAPHY: Jos., Ant., 17:23ff.; Jos., Life, 46ff., 177ff.; H. Graetz, in: MGWJ, 1 (1851), 115ff.; Stern, in: *Tarbiz*, 35 (1965/66), 251–3; Neusner, Babylonia, 1 (1965), 38ff.

[Isaiah Gafni]

BATHYRA, SONS OF (according to TB; in TJ known as "Elders of Bathyra"), members of a famous Jewish family who were prominent from the first century B.C.E. to the second century C.E. Some scholars conjecture that the family was named after the city of *Bathyra in northern Transjordan. It is inferred from talmudic sources that members of this family were the religious authorities of their time, but that when Hillel demonstrated his superior knowledge of Torah (on the question of whether the paschal offering overrides the Sabbath) "they set him at their head and appointed him *nasi* over them" (TJ, Kil. 9:4, 32b; Pes. 66a; BM 85a). As a result of this abdication they were regarded exemplars of humility; Judah ha-Nasi said of them "whatever I am bidden I am prepared to do except what the Elders of Bathyra did for my ancestor (Hillel), namely abdicating from their high office in order to elevate him" (TJ, Ket. 12:3, 35a). The talmudic sources do not specify their names. According to the Jerusalem Talmud they were *nesi'im*. In other talmudic sources, while they were not specifically designated as such, it is implied that they held the patriarchate before Hillel was appointed. According to Halevy, the Sons of Bathyra carried out the functions of the patriarchate when the Sanhedrin was not functioning (possibly at the beginning of Herod's rule). Apparently members of this family exercised influence even after the destruction of the Temple, when the Sanhedrin was in Jabneh. Johanan b. Zakkai was said to have consulted the Sons of Bathyra in regard to certain legal rulings. A number of *tannaim* known by this patronymic, e.g., Judah b. Bathyra, Joshua b. Bathyra, and Simeon b. Bathyra, presumably belonged to this family.

BIBLIOGRAPHY: Halevy, Dorot, 1 pt. 3 (1923), 36–89; 1 pt. 5 (1923), 190–9; Hyman, Toledot, 365ff.; Graetz, in: MGWJ, 1 (1851), 115–20; Klausner, Bayit Sheni, 4 (1950²), 56, 143; Neusner, Babylonia, 1 (1965), index, s.v. *Bathyrans*.

[Zvi Kaplan]

BAT KOL (Heb. בַּת קוֹל; lit. "daughter of a voice," i.e., an echo of a heavenly voice, or a divine voice "once removed"), a heavenly or divine voice which revealed God's will, choice, or judgment to man. According to rabbinic tradition, the *bat kol* was already heard during the biblical period. It proclaimed Tamar's innocence; declared that the prophet Samuel had not materially benefited from his public position; and validated Solomon's judgment in awarding the child to the true mother (Mak. 23b). Before the death of Moses, a heavenly voice proclaimed that God Himself would attend to his burial (Deut. R. 11:10), and after his death a *bat kol* heard over an area 12 miles square announced his demise (Sot. 13b). A *bat kol* informed David that Rehoboam and Jeroboam would divide his kingdom (Shab. 56b); and when Solomon sought to emulate Moses a heavenly voice rebuked him (RH 21b). According to the Talmud a *bat kol* was often heard at the death of martyrs. After the death of the mother and her seven sons (see *Hannah and Her Seven Sons), a voice proclaimed: "A joyful mother of children" (Ps. 113:9; Git. 57b). When Ḥanina b. Teradyon was cruelly executed, a *bat kol* called out: "R. Ḥanina b. Teradyon and the Roman who hastened his death have been assigned to the world to come" (Av. Zar. 18a). After R. Akiva's execution, a "heavenly voice" resounded: "Happy art thou, R. Akiva, that thou art destined for the life of the world to come" (Ber.61b). When a Roman officer sacrificed his life so that R. Gamaliel II would be spared, a *bat kol* declared: "This high officer is destined to enter into the world to come" (Ta'an. 29a).

With the cessation of prophecy, the *bat kol* remained the sole means of communication between God and man (Yoma 9b). In most instances, where reference is made to a *bat kol*, it refers to an external voice which is heard by the recipient of the message. However, at times the *bat kol* was only perceived in dreams (cf. Ḥag. 14b). The "heavenly voices" mentioned in stories concerning R. Bana'ah (BB 58a) and Rabbah b. Bar Ḥana (BB 73b–74a) also were heard in dreams (see Chajes in bibl.).

The authority granted to a *bat kol* in determining *halakhah* is discussed in two different talmudic passages. In one instance, after three years of controversy between Bet Shammai and Bet Hillel, the sages accepted a *bat kol*'s pronouncement that "the words of both are the words of the living God, but the *halakhah* is in agreement with the rulings of Bet Hillel" (Er. 13b). However, R. Joshua refused to abide by a *bat kol* which ruled in favor of R. Eliezer in his dispute with the sages regarding the ritual purity of the oven of "*Akhnai*" (BM 59b). R. Joshua explained that the Torah "is not in heaven" (Deut. 30:12), and therefore no attention is given to a "heavenly voice," and it is rather the majority of the sages who determined the *halakhah*. Later commentaries accepted R. Joshua's viewpoint, and explained that the *bat kol* was only effective in determining the ruling in the Bet Shammai and Bet Hillel controversies, since the sages were themselves in doubt whether to rule in accordance with the larger school of Bet Hillel or the more profound thinkers of Bet Shammai (Tos. to Er. 6b s.v. כאן).

BIBLIOGRAPHY: A. Guttmann, in: HUCA, 20 (1947), 363–406; E.E. Urbach, in: *Tarbiz*, 18 (1946/47), 23–27; idem, *Ḥazal* (1969), 516; S. Lieberman, *Hellenism in Jewish Palestine* (1950), 194–9; Z.H. Chajes, *Student's Guide to the Talmud* (1960²), 212–3.

[Aaron Rothkoff]

BATLANIM (Heb. בַּטְלָנִים; "men of leisure"), originally an honorable title conferred on those who either wholly or partly abstained from work to free themselves for community service. In ancient as well as medieval times there existed the institution of the *asarah batlanim* ("ten men of leisure"). The Mishnah (Meg. 1:3) states that a town was regarded as large if it had "ten *batlanim*" who "frequent the synagogue" (TB Meg. 5a; TJ, Meg., 1:6, 70b) and "abstain from work" (TJ, *ibid.*). Among the population of 120 who make a town "eligible for a Sanhedrin" (Sanh. 1:6) are included "the ten *batlanim* of the synagogue" (Meg. 17b). The ten verses of the Torah read publicly on Mondays and Thursdays "correspond to the ten *batlanim*" (BK 82a). R. Judah, characterized the "ten *batlanim*" as "those who, like ourselves, have no need of our studies" (TJ, Meg. loc. cit.), meaning, probably that they needed no occupation in addition to their studies. The ten *batlanim*, at that time, were scholars. Rashi explains that they refrain from work and are supported by the community in order to attend prayers in the synagogue (Meg. 5a; cf. Rashi to Sanh. 17b). R. Nissim notes that they need not "abstain from work and be supported by the community" for their town to be reckoned a large one in connection with the variant practices concerning the reading of the scroll of Esther. It is sufficient if they attend prayers in the synagogue both mornings and evenings (commenting on Alfasi; beginning of *Megillah*). Elsewhere (BK 82a) Rashi states that an additional function of the ten *batlanim* is to occupy themselves with the needs of the community, and Maimonides sees them as "assigned to the synagogue for communal needs" (Yad, Megillah 1:8). Benjamin of Tudela records that in 12th-century Baghdad, the ten heads of the yeshivah "are called *batlanim*, their sole occupation being to engage in communal affairs.... They render decisions on legal and religious questions for all the Jewish inhabitants of the country." In later Yiddish usage the term became pejorative and meant a man who was lazy, loafed, and could not make his way in the world.

BIBLIOGRAPHY: R. Hutner, in: *Yavneh*, 1 (1946), 21–24.

[Zvi Kaplan]

BAT-MIRIAM (Zhelezniak), YOKHEVED (1901–1980), Hebrew poet. Born in Keplits, Belorussia, Yokheved Bat-Miriam attended the universities of Odessa and Moscow. Although her poems began appearing in 1923, her first volume of poetry *Me-Raḥok* ("From Afar") was published in 1932, four years after she settled in Ereẓ Israel; it was followed by six other volumes of poetry. The bulk of her poetry was written between the two world wars against the background of the Jewish tragedy of this period, and her personal experiences as a child in Russia and a settler in Israel. Influenced by Russian symbolist poetry, her verse is written against a dreamlike landscape, charged with symbols from nature drawn from the world of childhood. One image fades into another, with past and present merging. This coalescing of imagery is reinforced by a similar shifting of her idiom by means of assonance, alliteration, and other sonal devices. Her works include *Ereẓ Yisrael* (1937); *Re'ayon* (1949); *Demuyyot me-Ofek* (1942); *Mi-Shirei Rusyah* (1942); *1943 – Shirim la-Getto* (1946); and *Shirim* (1963). A list of her works translated into English appears in Goell, Bibl. She was awarded the Israel Prize in 1972.

BIBLIOGRAPHY: *Kitvei Shimon Ginzburg*, 1 (1945), 285–95; D. Miron, in: *Haaretz* (Feb. 22, 1963); A. Bernstein, in: *Keshet*, 8 (Winter 1966), 184–7; Band, in: S. Burnshaw et al., *The Modern Hebrew Poem Itself* (1965), 84–88. **ADD. BIBLIOGRAPHY:** A. Ukhmani, *Kolot Adam: Masot* (1967); R. Kartun-Blum, *Ba-Merḥak ha-Ne'elam: Iyyunim be-Shirat Yokheved Bat-Miriam* (1977); U. Agasi, *Bat Miriam: Dyukan Aẓmi* (1990).

BATO, LUDWIG YOMTOV (1886–1974), Zionist and writer. Bato was born in Dolní-Kubín in Slovakia (then Hungary) and in 1904 edited the first Zionist publication in Hungarian. While a student in Turin (1906–07), he founded the Piedmontese Zionist Federation. Returning to Hungary in 1908, he joined the editorial board of the Zionist newspaper *Zsidó szemle*. In 1910 he went to Vienna, where he lived until 1933. There he was one of the leaders of the Austrian Zionist Federation and from 1914 to 1918 edited its organ *Juedische Zeitung*. With O. *Abeles he published the literary almanac *Juedischer Nationalkalender* (6 vols., 1916–22). Between 1933 and 1940 Bato was director of the Jewish National Fund in Romania and in 1940 he settled in Tel Aviv. Bato wrote *Die Juden im alten Wien* (1928) and *Don Yosef Nasi* (Heb., 1942).

BIBLIOGRAPHY: MB (Feb. 11, 1966).

[Getzel Kressel]

BAT SHELOMO (Heb. בַּת שְׁלֹמֹה; "Daughter of Solomon"), Israel moshav in the Manasseh Hills northeast of Zikhron Ya'akov. It was founded in June 1889 by the administration of Baron Edmond de *Rothschild, to provide farmsteads for children of Zikhron Ya'akov settlers. The small village, with wine grapes as its principal branch of farming, made little progress. After the establishment of the State of Israel, immigrants from Hungary and Yemen settled in Bat Shelomo. In the mid-1990s the population was approximately 275, rising to 365 in 2002. The village was named for Baron James (Jacob) Rothschild's wife, whose father was Solomon Mayer Rothschild of Vienna.

[Efraim Orni]

BATSHEVA AND BAT-DOR DANCE COMPANIES. In 1964, Baroness Bethsabee de *Rothschild founded the Batsheva Dance Company, which has become the flagship of Israeli dance. Establishment of the troupe marked the beginning of the influence of American modern dance in Israel and contributed to the professional level of dance there. From the middle 1960s until the early 1970s, the troupe drew heavily on the techniques of Martha Graham, who was also its artistic adviser. The company's repertoire included seven important works by Graham: *Errand into the Maze*; *Diversion of Angels*; *Embattled Garden*; *Dark Meadow*; *Herodiade; Cave of the Heart*; and the *Learning Process*. In 1974, Graham created *Jacob's Dream* especially for Batsheva.

Graham and Bethsabee encouraged the dancers to create their own works, which was accomplished by Oshra Elkayam and Moshe Efrati, dancers and the troupe's outstanding choreographers.

The repertoire also included works by well-known choreographers, among them: Robert Cohan, Glen Tetley, Norman Morrice, Jerome *Robbins, and Jose Limon. Distinguished soloists were Rina Schenfeld, Rena Gluck, Nurit Stern, Ehud Ben-David, Moshe Efrati, and Rachamin Ron.

In spite of its many successful performances abroad and its great following in Israel, in the 1970s and 1980s the troupe went through a difficult period with a relentless turnover of artistic directors (Jane Dudley, Norman Walker, William Louther, Brian McDonald, Robert Cohan, Paul Sanasardo). Most of them came for short periods, their works were performed, and then they left. The guest list of choreographers who worked with the Batsheva Dance Company in that period, and whose creations the company staged, were: John *Cranko (*Song of My People*), Gene Hill Sagan, Anna *Sokolow, Daniel Ezralow, and Christopher Bruce. After Rothschild distanced herself from the troupe, its attitude of not accepting the works of Israeli choreographers who were not members of the company changed. In the second half of the 1970s, Caj Lottman was named its artistic director, the first Israeli one, soon followed by Moshe Romano, Sheli Shir, and David Dvir. In 1983 and 1986, they launched workshops for the purpose of encouraging original local creations. Discovered in those workshops was the young generation of choreographers: Yossi Tmim, Siki Kol, Alice Dor-Cohen, Tamar Ben-Ami, Nir and Liat Ben-Gal. Despite the fact that the company continued to be very much admired in Israel, it lost its intrinsic essence and novelty, lacking a clear and specific artistic direction.

In 1990, Ohad *Nahari was appointed artistic director of the Batsheva Dance Company and created a rich tapestry of productions for the troupe. His style greatly influenced Israeli dance. The troupe was rejuvenated and a young audience flocked to its performances. Among the prominent choreographers whose works were represented in its repertoire were: Wim Vandekeybus, Anjelin Prelojocal, Arvo Pärt, William Forsythe, and Jiri Kylian.

In 1991, the Batsheva Ensemble was founded. It is smaller, and most of its dance pieces are local choreographies which were auspicious beginnings for many Israeli artists, among them Itzik Galili, Inbal Pinto, and Anat Daniel.

The Baroness continued to support Batsheva financially until 1977, when the Israel Ministry of Education and Culture granted the troupe a subsidy.

Bat-Dor

In 1967, Rothschild established the Bat-Dor Dance Company for Jeannette Ordman, a classical ballet dancer from South Africa who captured the heart of the Baroness. Ordman was the artistic director, principal dancer, and headmaster of its dance school. From the beginning, Bat-Dor's style was a combination of modern dance with a strong emphasis on the technique of classical ballet. The Baroness gave her generous financial support to Bat-Dor, making it possible for the ensemble to purchase works of important artists all over the world.

Among the Israeli choreographers who worked with the ensemble were Domi Reiter-Sofer, Mirale Sharon, Gene Hill-Sagan, Yehuda Maor, Igal Perry, and, in the past decade, Tamir Gintz. The importance of Bat-Dor lies, essentially, in its school of dance in Tel Aviv and the branch in Beersheba, which have produced generations of young dancers who have permeated the dance companies in Israel. Rothschild's death (1999) brought an end to the stream of cash flowing into the company, and its ongoing work was soon in crisis. Requests for government subsidies were made subject to reorganization of the ensemble's management practices and, today, it only operates the school, which receives government support.

[Ruth Eshel (2nd ed.)]

BATTAT, REUBEN (1882–1962), Iraqi jurist. Battat studied law in Baghdad and in Constantinople and served as judge in various courts of Iraq. In 1923 as judge in Basra, he handed down a decision in favor of transferring the property of the Jewish philanthropist Gourji Shemtov to the Keren Hayesod. That decision was used against him in 1949, when he was tried by a military tribunal on charges of being a Zionist and sentenced to three years imprisonment. He was, however, released after four months. From 1924 Battat represented the Jews of Iraq for several terms in parliament; he was also one of the supporters of the Zionist organization in Baghdad. Before 1936 he published an important work about the constitution of the kingdom of Iraq (in Arabic). He died in Switzerland.

BIBLIOGRAPHY: *Hed ha-Mizraḥ* (Oct. 5, 1945).

[Haim J. Cohen]

BATTLE OF CABLE STREET, name popularly given to a major altercation in the East End of London, England, when Sir Oswald Mosley, leader of the British Union of Fascists, attempted to march with his supporters through this heavily Jewish area of London. On October 4, 1936, Mosley attempted to lead a march of 3,000 black-shirted British Fascists from the City of London through Whitechapel, where about 100,000 Jews lived. At Cable Street, at the edge of the East End, Mosley's men were forcibly prevented from advancing further by a large throng of left-wing protesters, comprised of local Jewish and Irish inhabitants as well as "cockney" dockers and other workers, organized in part by the British Communist Party, and they were forced to turn back. The term "Battle" is something of a misnomer, since the only violence occurred between anti-Mosley protesters and the police, on whom the anti-Fascists turned, and not between the Fascists and anti-Fascists. Nevertheless, the "Battle of Cable Street" has become legendary as one of the few times during the 1930s when the left and far right apparently clashed, and the far right was defeated. Since most of the anti-Mosley protesters were probably gentiles, "Cable Street" was also seen by many as a prime example of what a "popular front" could achieve to stop the seemingly irresistible spread of Fascism in Europe. It also probably enhanced the prestige of the British Communist Party, which attracted a significant level of support in the Jewish East End during the latter 1930s (but probably not earlier). Presumably in retaliation, the following week many windows of Jewish shops in Whitechapel were smashed by vandals.

BIBLIOGRAPHY: T. Kushner and N. Valman (eds.), *Remembering Cable Street: Fascism and Anti-Fascism in British Society* (2000); R. Skidelsky, *Oswald Mosley* (1990 ed.); J. Jacobs, *Out of the Ghetto: My Youth in the East End – Communism and Fascism* (1978); W. D Rubinstein, *Jews in the English-Speaking World: Great Britain*, 244, 315–16.

[William D. Rubinstein (2nd ed.)]

BATUMI (until 1936 **Batum**), port on the eastern shore of the Black Sea; capital of the Autonomous Adzhar Republic, within *Georgia. A Jewish community was established there in 1878 after the town was incorporated into Russia. In 1889 many of the Jews living there without official authorization (see *Pale of Settlement) were expelled. According to official statistics there remained 31 Jewish families, and according to unofficial sources about 100 Jewish families. The number, however, again increased rapidly. By 1897 there were 1,179 Jews living in Batum. One of the oil refineries was owned jointly by the Rothschild family and Jewish investors in Russia. The Jewish population numbered 3,700 in 1923 (6.1% of the total population) and 1,778 in 1939 (2,54% of the total population). Subsequent data are unascertainable.

[Abraham J. Brawer / Abba Ahimeir]

BAT YAM (Heb. בַּת יָם; "Daughter of the Sea"), city in central Israel, on the seashore south of Tel Aviv-Jaffa, founded in 1926 by 24 religious families who called themselves and the quarter they established "Bayit va-Gan" ("House and Garden"). In the 1929 Arab riots, this isolated group found refuge in Tel Aviv, returning to their homes in 1931. From 1933 the population increased as immigrants from Germany built their homes there. In 1937 the quarter received the status of a local council and changed its name to Bat Yam. In the War of Independence (1948), the town, then numbering approximately 1,000 inhabitants, had to defend itself against strong Arab attacks. With the mass immigration following the founding of Israel, the population grew rapidly. Receiving city status in 1958, it formed part of the Tel Aviv conurbation, bordering on the city of Tel Aviv-Jaffa in the north, Holon in the east, and Rishon le-Zion in the south. Manufacturing and recreation facilities were the mainstays of its economy. The food industry (light beverages, beer, ice cream) was a leading employer and the city was a popular resort with a seashore of 2 mi. (3.2 km.), three-quarters of it open for bathing. It also had a municipal museum, art galleries, and the Sholem *Asch House. Asch resided in Bat Yam in his last years.

The population of Bat Yam was 10,000 at the end of 1953, 62,000 in 1967, and 133,900 in 2002, making it the 11th largest city in Israel. It had a large concentration of recent immigrants from the former Soviet Union, Syria, and Ethiopia. The municipal area was 3.1 sq. mi. (8 sq. km.).

[Simha Moretzky / Shaked Gilboa (2nd ed.)]

°**BAUDISSIN, WOLF WILHELM, GRAF VON** (1847–1926), German Bible critic and historian of religion. Baudissin was born in Holstein and taught at the universities of Leipzig, 1874–1876; Strasbourg, 1876–1881; Marburg, 1881–1900; and Berlin, 1900–1921. He belonged to the Wellhausen school of thought in regard to the understanding of the Pentateuch as a whole, but he departed from its philosophy in his *Die Geschichte des alttestamentlichen Priesterthums* (1889) where he argued for the priority of P, the pre-Exilic Priestly Source, over the D, Deuteronomic, Source. In *Kyrios als Gottesname im Judentum und seine Stelle in der Religionsgeschichte* (4 vols., 1929), published posthumously, Baudissin championed the theory that the substitution of Adonai for YHWH first originated among Greek-speaking Jews. His main contributions in the area of comparative religion are *Studien zur semitischen Religionsgeschichte* (2 vols., 1876–78); *Jahve et Moloch* (1874); and *Adonis und Esmun* (1911). These studies deal with the influence of the Canaanite cult on the history of Israel.

BIBLIOGRAPHY: ZAWB, 33 (1918) (= *Festschrift ... Baudissin*) includes bibliography; O. Eissfeldt, *Kleine Schriften*, 1 (1962), 115–42, 234–8.

[Zev Garber]

°**BAUER, BRUNO** (1809–1882), German Protestant theologian, philosopher, and historian. He became influenced by the philosophy of Hegel while a student in Berlin, and because of radical criticism of the New Testament expressed in numerous works, was dismissed from his post as lecturer at Bonn in 1842. Bauer then returned to Berlin where he devoted himself to writing historical works and critical studies of the rise of Christianity. He also wrote on contemporary political issues, defending Prussian conservatism, and strongly opposed granting emancipation to the Jews in Germany. In his essay *Die Judenfrage* ("The Jewish Question," 1843), he stresses, like Hegel, the Oriental character of the "Jewish national spirit" (*Volksgeist*) which failed to comprehend the ideals of freedom and reason and saw its highest duty in fulfilling unreasonable ceremonies. In particular, Bauer attacked the representatives of Reform Judaism, who called for a return to a pure or purified "Mosaism." In his view, "pure Mosaism" was only possible in the land of Canaan, and only in a sovereign Jewish state. It was therefore impossible in contemporary circumstances. Bauer argued that the observance of Jewish laws made faith illusory and that Judaism was exclusive and unrealistic. As long as Jews were not ready to forsake their specific character, their emancipation was out of the question. The work gave rise to sharp controversy in which Abraham *Geiger, Gabriel *Riesser, Samuel *Hirsch, and Karl *Marx, among others, took part.

BIBLIOGRAPHY: N. Rotenstreich, in: YLBI, 4 (1959); 3–36; Ẓ. Rosen, in: *Zion*, 33 (1968), 59–76; K. Marx, *A World Without Jews* (1959).

[Reuven Michael]

BAUER, HANS (1878–1937), scholar of Semitic languages. Bauer, who was born in Bavaria, studied theology and Semitic languages and in 1922 was appointed professor of Semitic languages at the University of Halle. After working on medieval Arabic philosophy (especially Al-Ghazālī), and other Arabic studies, he turned to Hebrew grammar in the context of the other Semitic languages, employing the methods developed by Indo-Germanic linguists. In his book *Die Tempora im Semitischen* (1910), he dealt with the Semitic tenses. He worked on the assumption (which others had made before him) that the imperfect was in the early stages of the language the only defined verbal form (i.e., the all-tempora: Aorist), while the perfect was orginally a nominal form (i.e., a type of participle: nominal), and thus close in meaning to the present tense. The nominal participle has two temporal qualities, according to the meaning of each verb: an act done now or continuously; or an act, completed in the past, whose results are felt in the present. The second quality (*perfectum praesens*) is likely to develop into the *praeteritum*. In each of the Semitic languages, one of these qualities became the primary: in Akkadian, the former (Bauer equates the form *ikaššad* with the perfect of the other languages); in Aramaic, Arabic, Ethiopic, and even Phoenician, the latter. As a result, the semantic field of the all-tempora form became limited in its meaning. In Akkadian it is used as the perfect, but in the other languages as the present-future. Biblical Hebrew, which Bauer considered a mixed language, in this respect stands midway: the conversive tenses reflect the Akkadian usage, while the regular tenses are comparable to the use in other Semitic languages. His view of the mixed nature of Hebrew ("early Canaanite base," close to Akkadian, with a "late layer" which is closer to the other Semitic languages) derives from certain cases of phonetic inconsistency, such as the vowels after the *kof* in קָם (*kam*) as opposed to מָקוֹם (*makom*) which both are in Arabic *ā* (*qām, maqām*). This problem is discussed in his book *Zur Frage der Sprachmischung im Hebraeischen* (1924). With Pontus Leander, he wrote the *Historische Grammatik der hebraeischen Sprache des Alten Testaments* (1922; repr. 1965). They also collaborated in writing the *Grammatik des Biblisch-Aramaeischen* (1927). In 1930 he succeeded in deciphering most of the Ugaritic alphabet embodying the results of his study in *Die alphabetischen Keilschrifttexte von Ras Shamra* (1936); others followed him in completing this work. Bauer also wrote a book on the origins of the alphabet, *Der Ursprung des Alphabets* (1937).

BIBLIOGRAPHY: Wehr-Halle, in: ZDMG, 91 (1937), 175–84, obituary and bibliography; NDB, 1 (1952), 639.

[Hans Jacob Polotsky]

BAUER, JACOB (Jehiel ben Gershom; 1852–1926), *ḥazzan* of the Turkish-Israelite Temple in Vienna and adaptor of its liturgical music. Bauer was born in Szenice, Hungary, and went as a youth to Vienna. During his school days in that city, he was a soprano singer with the *ḥazzan* Pesaḥ Feinsinger. After regular training of his adult voice, Bauer was employed as *ḥazzan* at Ottakring, a suburb of Vienna, Szigetvar (Hungary, 1875), and Graz (1878). In 1880, the governors of the Vienna Sephardi congregation decided to adapt the musical part of their service "to the needs of modern times." They commissioned Bauer and the choir-director Isidor Loewit to arrange their melodies and to organize a temple choir. At first this modernized service was, more or less, in the common Ashkenazi style. In the course of time, Bauer and Loewit worked on arrangements of the original Turco-Sephardi melodies which were published as *Schir-Hakawod* in 1889.

Bauer founded and edited the *Oesterreichisch-Ungarische Kantoren-Zeitung* from 1881 to 1898 and was co-founder and temporarily chairman of the Oesterreichisch-Ungarischer Kantoren-Verband from 1883.

BIBLIOGRAPHY: Friedmann, Lebensbilder; E. Zaludkowski, *Kultur-Treger fun der Yidisher Liturgye…* (1930), 196.

[Hanoch Avenary]

BAUER, MARION EUGÉNIE (1882–1955), U.S. composer, teacher, and music critic. Bauer was the daughter of French Jewish immigrants to the U.S. Part of the "forgotten vanguard" of modernism, her work bridged the lush harmonies of French impressionism and the dissonant modernism of the late 1920s. She studied composition with Henry Holden Huss and Eugene Heffley and was Nadia Boulanger's first American pupil. Bauer taught composition and theory at New York University (1926–51) and the Juilliard School of Music (1940–55). Through teaching and mentoring, she maintained numerous ties to a younger generation of modernists including Milton *Babbitt and Ruth Crawford.

Bauer wrote reviews and criticism for the *Musical Leader* and *Musical Quarterly* and published four books on music, including the popular appreciation text *Twentieth Century Music* (1933). A fervent advocate of modern music, she helped found the American Music Guild, served as secretary for the Society for the Publications of American Music, and was on the executive boards of the League of Composers, the American Composers Alliance (ACA), and the Society of American Women Composers.

Aside from brief experiments in 12-tone writing in the 1940s and 1950s, Bauer's music never completely broke with tradition. Her impressive and frequently performed compositions include *Symphonic Suite* (1940), *American Youth* for piano and orchestra (1943), and *First Symphony* (1950). Her most successful work, *Sun Splendor* (1947), was premiered by the New York Philharmonic under Leopold Stowkowski.

BIBLIOGRAPHY: J.M. Edwards, "Marion Eugénie Bauer," in: S. Sadie (ed.), *The New Grove Dictionary of Music and Musicians* (2001^2); E.M. Hisama. *Gendering Musical Modernism: The Music of Ruth Crawford, Marion Bauer, and Miriam Gideon* (2001).

[Melissa de Graaf (2nd ed.)]

BAUER, OTTO (1881–1938), Austrian socialist leader; first foreign minister of the Austrian Republic (1918–19). Bauer, the son of a Jewish industrialist, became one of the most important Austro-Marxist theoreticians soon after joining the socialist movement along with many other young Jewish intellectuals of his time. In 1907, together with Karl Renner and Adolf *Braun, he founded the monthly *Der Kampf*, which became a forum for socialist discussion. In his famous study *Die Nationalitaetenfrage und die Sozialdemokratie* (1907), he contended that no socialist could disregard the problem of nationalities, and provided an original definition of the nation: "the totality of men united through a community of fate into a community of character." Bauer favored the granting of cultural autonomy to every national group in the Austro-Hungarian Empire. He praised the Jewish role in history, but argued that the Jews could not be regarded as a nationality, especially in Western Europe. He advocated assimilation and was sharply criticized by Zionists as a consequence. In November 1918, with the collapse of the Austro-Hungarian Empire at the end of World War I, Bauer became foreign minister of the new Austrian Republic. He resigned in 1919 when his main objectives, a merger with Germany and retention by Austria of the German-speaking parts of the Tyrol, failed to materialize. When the Dollfuss regime came to power in 1934, Bauer took a leading part in the uprising of the workers in Vienna and subsequently took refuge in Czechoslovakia after its suppression. In May 1938, he fled to Paris and died there a few weeks later – on the day the London *News Chronicle* published his appeal to world conscience to save the 300,000 Jews of Austria. Bauer was an outstanding figure within the Socialist International, where, although an opponent of Communism, he represented the Marxist left wing. He was a prolific writer on socialist problems, including the books *Bolschewismus oder Sozialdemokratie?* (1920), in which he contrasted the economic conditions of Soviet Russia and Western Europe, and *Kapitalismus und Sozialismus nach dem Weltkrieg* (1931), which was intended to be his magnum opus. After his death, his *Die illegale Partei* was published in Paris by Friedrich *Adler (1939).

BIBLIOGRAPHY: V. Reimann, *Zu gross fuer Oesterreich* (1958); J. Braunthal, *Eine Auswahl aus seinem Lebenswerk, mit einem Lebensbild Otto Bauers* (1961). **ADD. BIBLIOGRAPHY:** A. Barkai, "The Austrian Social Democrats and the Jews," in: *Wiener Library Bulletin*, 24 (1970); J. Bunzl, "Arbeiterbewegung, 'Judenfrage' und Antisemitismus: am Beispiel des Wiener Bezirks Leopoldstadt," in: *Bewegung und Klasse: Studien zur österreichischen Arbeitergeschichte* (1979); H. Gruber, *Red Vienna: Experiment in Working Class Culture 1919–1934*

(1991); J. Jacobs, *On Socialists and the "Jewish Question" after Marx* (1992); O. Leichter and O. Bauer, *Tragödie oder Triumph* (1970); R. Loew, *Otto Bauer und die Russische Revolution* (1980); A. Rabinbach, *The Crisis of Austrian Socialism: from Red Vienna to Civil War, 1927–1934* (1983); P. Riesbeck, *Sozialdemokratie und Minderheitenrecht: der Beitrag der oesterreichischen Sozialdemokraten Otto Bauer und Karl Renner zum internationalen Minderheitenrecht* (1996); R.S. Wistrich, *Socialism and the Jews: The Dilemmas of Assimilation in Germany and Austria-Hungary* (1982).

[Robert Weltsch / Lisa Silverman (2nd ed.)]

BAUER, SIMON HARVEY (1911–), U.S. physical chemist. Bauer was born in Kaunas, Lithuania, and immigrated to the U.S. in 1921. Awarded his Ph.D. degree from the University of Chicago (1935), he was a postdoctoral fellow at the California Institute of Technology (1935–37), and an instructor at Pennsylvania State University (1937–39) before being invited to join the Chemistry Department at Cornell University, where he became professor in 1950. Subsequently he was appointed adjunct professor at the Institute of Molecular Science in Okazaki and served as consultant to Los Alamos National Laboratory, Calspan, Arco-Harvey Tech Center, and Lockheed Cal. His research studies include structure determinations by electron and X-ray diffraction techniques; molecular spectroscopy in the IR measurements of rapid chemical conversions induced in shock tubes or via laser irradiation; measurements of physical, kinetic, and thermochemical properties of boron hydrides; and formulation of kinetics of condensation from supersaturated vapors.

[Bracha Rager (2nd ed.)]

BAUER, YEHUDA (1926–), historian of the Holocaust. Bauer was born in Prague, Czechoslovakia (now Czech Republic). He immigrated with his family to Palestine on March 15, 1939; the day German troops marched into Prague and Germany took control of Bohemia and Moravia. He later joined the Palmaḥ and fought in Israel's War of Independence. He completed his B.A. and M.A. at the University of Cardiff in Wales (1946–48; 1949–50) and then became a founding member of Kibbutz Shoval in the Negev, in Israel, in 1952. He completed his Ph.D. at the Hebrew University of Jerusalem in 1960 with a dissertation that focused on the Mandate period in Palestine. In 1961, Bauer joined the faculty of the Institute of Contemporary Jewry, where he began teaching about the Holocaust several years later and until his retirement in 1995. Bauer held many additional important positions in academia and research, among them: academic chairman of the Institute of Contemporary Jewry (1978–95); founding chair of the Vidal Sassoon International Center for the Study of Antisemitism at the Hebrew University (1982–95); chairman of the Study Circle at the Home of the President of Israel on the Jewish People in the Diaspora and the State of Israel (1980–95); founding editor of the *Journal of Holocaust and Genocide Studies* (1985–95); head of the International Institute for Holocaust Research at Yad Vashem (1995–2000); academic advisor at Yad Vashem (from 2000). In 1998 he was awarded the Israel Prize for his life's work in teaching and heightening awareness about the Holocaust, and in 2000 he was elected a member of the Israel Academy of Sciences.

Bauer's vast knowledge, sharp analytical capabilities, keen ability to synthesize many sources and much research into coherent observations, along with his written and spoken articulation and his dynamic teaching ability helped him reach broad audiences in Israel and around the world. He is considered to be one of the major scholars of the Holocaust, as well as one of the most important and influential voices to raise consciousness of the event and of its ongoing major impact on the world.

Bauer's approach to understanding the Holocaust is multifaceted. He believes that the Holocaust was an unprecedented event when it happened, but as an event that was part of human history, it is both accessible to human understanding and is an event that can be repeated once the precedent has been set.

Bauer has advocated and promoted meticulous empirical research in all relevant languages, both of official German and other documents, and of Jewish documents from the period and later, including oral history. Bauer argues that official government documents, and certainly Nazi documents, cannot automatically be taken as objective reflections of reality, or as being entirely true. He has cited numerous examples of German Nazi era documents that were sanitized or carefully edited (e.g., the Protocol of the Wannsee Conference, January 20, 1942) in order to create a particular impression at the time. Although oral testimony needs to be read critically and cross-referenced, in the same way as other documentation, such source material remains for Bauer an integral and necessary part of Holocaust research. Fundamentally, without a thorough examination of the story of the Jews in the Holocaust, our understanding of the event can be only partial.

Bauer has been influential in introducing a number of fundamental concepts to our understanding of the Holocaust, such as the distinction between information and knowledge of the event around the world as it unfolded. He has also advocated against mystification or glorification of the Holocaust or of those who played a role in it. He has kept his observations on the event grounded in human history, examining the participants in the event as human beings. In looking at the Jews, he has promoted the examination of their daily lives and struggles to get through to another day. He has always sought to keep the individual in perspective when discussing the mass of details and data. He frequently resorts to individual stories in his writing and speaking as a way to personalize the Holocaust and retain the humanity of its victims.

Bauer has also stood out in his willingness to engage in comparative analyses of the Holocaust with other genocides (e.g., of the Armenians by the Turks and of the Sinti and Roma by the Nazis), highlighting both their commonalities and their differences. Although he sees a number of basic common characteristics in all these events, the Holocaust remains for him a singular event, particularly in its totality and universality – attempting to murder all Jews everywhere – and in the central role played by race theory. It is fundamental in Bauer's understanding of the Holocaust that the Nazis saw in the Jews both a threat of cosmic proportions to human existence and the embodiment of the enlightened Western values that the Nazis despised. The Nazi attack on the Jews was an attack on the very foundations of Western civilization.

Bauer has published numerous books and articles. His research topics have included American Jewish responses to the Holocaust; the responses of the victims; the decision-making process in Nazi Germany; the events in Hungary, Romania, and Slovakia; Jewish attempts to rescue Jews via negotiations with the Nazis; events and Jewish life in the small and medium-sized towns of Eastern Europe, and more. A number of his articles have become basic introductory reading for students regarding a number of central subjects in the Holocaust (e.g., Jewish responses, rescue, Jewish leadership). Among his major books are *Flight and Rescue: Brichah* (1970), on the clandestine movement by survivors to Palestine; *My Brother's Keeper* (1974), on the Joint Distribution Committee through the 1930s; *The Holocaust in Historical Perspective* (1978), lectures delivered at the University of Washington; *American Jewry and the Holocaust* (1981); *A History of the Holocaust* (1982), a textbook (2001^{2}); *Jewish Reactions to the Holocaust* (1989); *Jews for Sale?: Nazi-Jewish Negotiations, 1933–1945* (1994); and *Rethinking the Holocaust* (2001), which is a collection and reworking of some of his major essays on the Holocaust and Holocaust historiography over the past decades.

BIBLIOGRAPHY: "Yehuda Bauer, Historian of the Holocaust," in *Dimensions: A Journal of Holocaust Studies*, vol. 18, no. 1 (2004, online); biography of Yehuda Bauer in *Israel Prize* (1998), 4–11.

[David Silberklang (2nd ed.)]

BAUM, HERBERT (1912–1942), German Communist and anti-Nazi fighter. Baum was a member of the German communist youth movement from 1932 and led a clandestine Jewish communist cell in Berlin from 1936. In 1937 he and his wife Marianne organized a political circle with communist leanings frequented by young Jews (both party members and others), including some Zionists. According to communist sources, this group continued its activities even after the outbreak of World War II by mimeographing leaflets and illegal newspapers and establishing contacts with French and Belgian forced laborers in Germany, mainly in the Siemens plant in Berlin where Baum worked. On May 18, 1942, Baum and a number of his comrades set fire to the Nazi propaganda exhibit *Das Sowjetparadies* ("The Soviet Paradise"). Shortly afterward Baum and members of his group were arrested. He died in jail, probably by his own hand, while his comrades were tried and sentenced to death or deported to death camps. At the request of the group's sole survivor, Charlotte Holzer, Baum and his comrades were buried in the Jewish cemetery at Weissensee, East Berlin.

BIBLIOGRAPHY: E. Maoz, *Yalkut Moreshet*, 3 (1944), 79–88; M. Pikarski, *Sie Bleiben unvergessen* (1968); L. Steinberg, *La revolte des justes – les juifs contre Hitler* (1970), 51–77; B. Mark, in: *Bleter far Geshikhte*, 14 (1961), 27–64 (Eng. summary in Y. Suhl (ed.), *They Fought Back* (1967), 55–68). **ADD. BIBLIOGRAPHY:** E. Brothers, in: W. Loehken and W. Vathke (eds.), *Juden im Widerstand* (1993), 83–93; M. Kreutzer, in: ibid., 95–158.

[Lucien Steinberg]

BAUM, MENAḤEM MENDEL BEN AARON OF KAMENETZ (1800?–1873), prominent member of the Ashkenazi community of Safed and Jerusalem, author of a travel book in Hebrew and Yiddish, and one of the first modern hoteliers in Ereẓ Israel. Baum was born in Kamenetz-Litovsk (Lithuania), but immigrated to Ereẓ Israel in 1833, settling in Safed, where he witnessed the anti-Jewish riots by the peasants who rebelled against Ibrahim Pasha (1834). He remained in Ereẓ Israel for a short period, visiting Tiberias, Jerusalem, and Hebron. He then traveled abroad both for personal economic considerations and also on a mission to collect funds for the community of *Perushim* (disciples of Elijah of Vilna) in Safed and Jerusalem. In 1842–43 he returned to Jerusalem and was active on behalf of the Grodno community (*kolel*). During this period he established a guesthouse, which evolved into the group of Kaminitz hotels of Jerusalem, Jaffa, and Hebron in the second half of the 19th century, and which reached their heyday in the lifetime of his son Eliezer Lipa Kaminitz. Run by members of the family, they supplied hostelry services on a European standard.

His travel book *Korot ha-Ittim li-Yshurun be-Ereẓ Yisrael* (Hebrew, 1839; Yiddish translation, 1841) was intended to serve both as a guide for East European immigrants and as a chronicle of the peasant revolt of 1834, so as to arouse concern about the fate of the Ashkenazi community of Safed and to encourage financial contributions. The historical section is essentially a description of the events of 1834, and is an authentic historical document, as the author himself witnessed many of the events described. The other two sections of the book briefly depict the process of immigration, as experienced by the author, and give a detailed guide to the professional, economic, and cultural conditions of the country. These sections are of great value for the study of the lifestyle of the period. The style of the Hebrew edition is simple and straightforward. The language of the Yiddish version is more popular and the trend of prayer and lamentation in it is more prominent. *Korot ha-Ittim* was reprinted in Hebrew by Meir Anshin (1931) and with an introduction and notes by G. Kressel, Jerusalem (1946). A new edition of the first printings in both languages with an introduction and indexes was issued in Jerusalem, 1975.

BIBLIOGRAPHY: Frumkin-Rivlin, *Toledot ḥakhmei Yerushalayim*, III 269; P. Grajewski, *Zikkaron la-ḥovevim ha-Rishonim* 19; J. Trivaks and A. Steinmann, *Sefer Me'ah Shanah* (1938), 164–76; A. Yaari, *Massa'ot Ereẓ Yisrael* (1946), 532–45, 777; D. Tidhar, *Enẓiklopediya le-Ḥaluẓei ha-Yishuv u-Vonav*, II, 560–61, III, 1200–01, XVIII, 5391–92, 5452–53.

[Israel Bar Tal (2nd ed.)]

BAUM, MORTON (1905–1968), U.S. lawyer, politician, and patron of the arts. Baum was born in New York City. He became a Republican district leader on Manhattan's West Side. In 1934 he was elected to the city council. As Mayor La Guardia's tax counsel, Baum devised New York City's first sales tax. He served as a tax consultant to subsequent New York mayors and to several governors. A lover of the performing arts, Baum was elected to the board of the Metropolitan Opera Company in 1941. In 1943 he helped found the New York City Center of Music and Drama, and was instrumental in developing its renowned ballet troupe and opera company. He was the first president of New York's Metropolitan Synagogue (1959).

BAUM, OSCAR (1883–1941), Czechoslovak author who wrote in German. Baum was a member of the Prague circle of Max *Brod and Franz *Kafka. Losing his sight as a boy, Baum was trained at the Vienna Institute for the Blind as an organist and pianist and subsequently became a music critic. Brod took down in shorthand his first short stories and persuaded Baum to publish them. *Uferdasein* (1908), *Das Leben im Dunkeln* (1909), and *Nacht ist umher* (1929), hailed by Stefan *Zweig as the "most moving document in German from the lightless world" were all taken from the life of the blind. They reflect his opposition to the compassion displayed by society and his call for equality of opportunity, which influenced modern education of the handicapped. Baum's *Die boese Unschuld* (1913) has acquired significance as a document of Jewish life in Bohemia against the background of the Czech-German nationality struggle. Baum also wrote a drama, *Das Wunder* (1920). His last novel, *Das Volk des harten Schlafes* (1937), ostensibly a story about the Jewish kingdom of the *Khazars, actually deals with problems of Jewry in the first years of Nazi rule. It was dedicated to Baum's "son and friend" Leo, who was later killed in the King David Hotel explosion in Jerusalem (1946).

BIBLIOGRAPHY: M. Brod, *Der Prager Kreis* (1966), 118–32; A. Schmidt, *Dichtung und Dichter Oesterreichs im 19. und 20. Jahrhundert*, 1 (1964), index.

BAUM, SHEPARD (c. 1900–1977), U.S. *kashrut* supervisor and Jewish community activist. Known to have been an amateur boxer in his youth, Baum was best known for his work as chief supervisor for Kosher Law Enforcement for the Department of Agriculture in the State of New York. Despite the separation of Church and State in the laws of the United States, the State of New York could have an official *kashrut* supervisor to ensure that consumers were not misled and fraud was not being practiced and that the food they were purchasing was indeed kosher.

An avid Zionist, he was national vice president of B'nai Zion, the American Zionist fraternal organization, and wrote many articles for B'nai Zion publications. Baum was also a founder of American Magen David Adom; president and chairman of The Bridge; president of the New York Jewish Conference; chaplain of the Bronx-Lebanon Hospital; member of the Commission on Synagogue Relations for the Federation of Jewish Philanthropies; chaplain for the Grand Lodge of Freemasons for the State of New York; and a U.S. Army chaplain during World War II.

BIBLIOGRAPHY: *The New York Times*, (July 23, 1977), 17.

BAUM, VICKI (1888–1960), novelist. Born in Vienna, Vicki Baum began her career as a professional harpist but her success as a short story writer led her to leave music. In 1921 she became an editor in the Berlin publishing house of Ullstein. Of her 25 novels, the best known is *Menschen im Hotel* (1929; *Grand Hotel*, 1930), which became a worldwide best seller and a popular film. In 1931 she settled in the United States. Vicki Baum often repeated the pattern of *Grand Hotel* – a montage of stories of interrelated characters – in her novels, for which she chose a wide range of historical, sociological, and psychological themes. Her autobiography, *Es war alles ganz anders* (1962), was published posthumously.

BIBLIOGRAPHY: J. Bithell, *Modern German Literature* (1959^3), 333–5; *Britannica Book of the Year 1961* (1962), 511.

[Samuel L. Sumberg]

BAUMAN, ZYGMUNT (1925–), sociologist. Born in Poznan, Poland, to assimilated Jewish parents. At the start of World War II Bauman escaped to the Soviet-occupied zone, where he fought in a Polish division of the Red Army. After the war, he entered the University of Warsaw and rose to the rank of professor of sociology. In 1948, Bauman married a survivor of the Warsaw ghetto. Following a wave of antisemitism in 1968, they left Poland for Israel and in 1971 Bauman became professor of sociology at the University of Leeds, U.K. A leading, prolific, and iconoclastic scholar in contemporary social thought, Bauman is best known for his theories of postmodernity, which he applied to the study of the Holocaust in his work *Modernity and the Holocaust* (1989). The book provoked considerable controversy as Bauman argues that the Holocaust was a result of modernity, that is, technology and bureaucracy, rather than specific German nationalism. While critics believe that his thesis absolves National Socialism of its responsibility, Bauman counters that blaming Germany exclusively – though clearly National Socialism is to blame – absolves all others who were complicit in adopting and promoting ideas such as eugenics, which were popular with well-respected thinkers at that time in both Europe and the U.S.

Professor emeritus at the University of Leeds from 1990, Bauman continued to write about the human condition in the postmodern age.

[Beth Cohen (2nd ed.)]

BAUME, PETER (**Erne**; 1935–), Australian politician. Born in Sydney, and a consulting physician, Baume served as a Liberal Party senator for New South Wales from 1974 to 1991. He held a number of cabinet posts under Malcolm Fraser (1975–82), including minister for aboriginal affairs (1980–82), minister for health (1982), and minister for education (1982–83). He was vice president of the Australia-Israel

Inter-Parliamentary Group from 1985 to 1991. After his political career, Baume went back to the medical academic world, becoming professor of community medicine at the University of New South Wales and, subsequently, chancellor of the Australian National University.

[William D. Rubinstein (2nd ed.)]

BAUMGARDT, DAVID (1890–1963), philosopher. In 1924 he was appointed lecturer in philosophy at the University of Berlin where he later was professor (1932–35). In 1935 he was visiting professor at the University of Madrid where he lectured on Maimonides at the congress organized by the Spanish government to commemorate the eighth centenary of Maimonides' birth. From 1935 Baumgardt taught at Birmingham (England) and from 1939 at Pendle Hill, Wallingford, Pennsylvania. From 1941 to 1954 he was consultant on philosophy to the Library of Congress in Washington, D.C. Baumgardt, a Zionist from his early youth, conceived the idea of founding a Hebrew philosophical journal. In his earlier works (particularly in his *Das Moeglichkeitsproblem der Kritik der reinen Vernunft, der modernen Phaenomenologie und der Gegenstandstheorie*, 1920) he treated the modalities (possibility, reality, and necessity) in the philosophy of Kant, Husserl, and Meinong (the late 14th-century German philosopher). He then turned his attention to historical studies, particularly to the history of philosophical romanticism in Germany at the beginning of the 19th century. This culminated in the publication of his book on Franz von Baader and philosophical romanticism (1929). Another work of Baumgardt is devoted to an investigation of the relations between Mendelssohn and Spinoza (1932). In *Der Kampf um den Lebenssinn unter den Vorlaeufern der modernen Ethik* (1933) he related the systematic study of ethics to the study of history. In this book he undertook a penetrating critique of Kant's system of ethics, showing that Kant's ethical system was derived from the basic idea of a Higher Unity pervading all human striving but that this derivation is merely a formal one, devoid of content. Baumgardt examined Hermann Cohen's attempt to rescue Kant's ethics but even here he arrived at negative conclusions. He likewise examined the attempts, undertaken by thinkers at the end of the 18th century (Herder, Hemsterhuis, Jacobi), to create a system of ethics possessed of content. In opposition to Kant, Herder extolled Hebrew ethics because they preserve man's unity. In connection with this investigation, Baumgardt assembled the literary material relevant to the relations between Herder and Spinoza. His search for ethical fundamentals possessing content led him to become particularly interested in Bentham's ethical system, to which he devoted a large volume on *Bentham and the Ethics of Today* (1952). In 1961 Baumgardt published *Great Western Mystics; Their Lasting Significance*. He sought a reconciliation of the ethics of force and the ethics of love.

BIBLIOGRAPHY: J. Frank, et al., *Horizons of a Philosopher: Essays in Honor of David Baumgardt* (1963); YLBI, 10 (1965), 239–65.

[Samuel Hugo Bergman]

BAUMGARTEL, ELISE J. (1892–1975), Egyptologist. Elise Baumgartel, who was born in Berlin, became a leading figure in the field of Egyptian prehistory. She left Germany for England during the Hitler era, and from 1948 to 1950 was keeper of the department of Egyptian antiquities at Manchester University. In 1951 she went to Oxford, where she engaged in research at the Griffith Institute until 1955. She then went to live in the United States, and became a member of the Oriental Institute at the University of Chicago. Elise Baumgartel's major publications are *Culture of Prehistoric Egypt* (2 vols., 1948–50) and the chapter on "Predynastic Egypt" in the *Cambridge Ancient History* (1963).

[Penuel P. Kahane]

BAUMGARTEN, EMANUEL MENDEL (1828–1908), Austrian economist, journalist and communal leader, Hebrew writer and poet. Baumgarten was born in Kremsier (Kroměříž), Moravia, into a traditional Jewish family of Talmud scholars. He first studied at Moravian yeshivot but also acquired secular knowledge. He heard lectures in economics at Pressburg and, from 1848, at Vienna University. While successfully devoting himself to commercial life, he also became active in the journalistic and literary fields, contributing to several political and Jewish papers in Vienna. With Mayer, he edited an economic paper, *Der Fortschritt*, and with I.H. Weiss the scientific Hebrew monthly *Beit ha-Midrash* (1865–66). In 1861, Baumgarten was elected to the municipal council of Vienna as one of the first Jews and later granted an order of merit by the emperor for his care for the wounded during the 1866 war. In 1870, he became warden of the Jewish Temple in Vienna. In 1872, he was elected to the council of the Jewish community (which he also represented in the state's boards of education), and in 1873 to the council of the newly founded Israelitische Allianz, assisting Jewish refugees from Russia and Romania. Though critical of Zionism, he also supported Jehiel *Brill's colonization plans in Palestine. In 1893, he was among the founders of the Israelitisch-theologische Lehranstalt in Vienna and was elected to its council. In honour of Baumgarten's 70th birthday (1898), his sons published a *Festschrift* (1899).

Among Baumgarten's published works are the first German translation of R. Bahya ibn Paquda's *Ḥovot ha-Levavot* ("Duties of the Heart"), on the basis of R. Judah ibn Tibbon's Hebrew translation, with an appendix by S.G. Stern, *Arugat Peraḥim*, containing biographies of Ibn Paquda, Ibn Tibbon, and Joseph Kimḥi (1854); several Hebrew poems, e.g., *Ruth*, with an introduction by M. Letteris (1864); *Einige Worte ueber den Weinhandel und die Weinkultur in Oesterreich* (1866); and *Die Juden in der Steiermark* (1903). In response to the new antisemitic movement, Baumgarten edited two apologetic works: *Die Blutbeschuldigung gegen die Juden. Von christlicher Seite beurtheilt* (1883) and *Gutmeinung ueber den Talmud der Hebraeer* by the Christian Hebraist C. Fischer (1883, originally completed in 1802). In addition, Baumgarten edited several sources for the history of Moravian Jewry: *Megillat Se-*

darim (1895), the memoirs of Abraham Broda Leipniker on the expulsion of the Jews from Usov (Maehrisch-Aussee) in 1722; *Yeshu'at Yisrael* (1898), the memoirs of Benjamin Israel Fraenkel from the 18th century; and *Maria Theresia's Ernennungsdekret für den Maehrischen Landesrabbiner Gerson Chajes* (1899).

BIBLIOGRAPHY: A. Frankl-Gruen, *Geschichte der Juden in Kremsier*, vol. II (1898), 153–56; *Unserem theuern Vater, Emanuel Baumgarten. Zur Erinnerung an seinen 70. Geburtstag, 15. Jänner 1898* (1899); *Neue Freie Presse* (Jan. 1898 and 1908); *Allgemeine Zeitung des Judentums* (May 29, 1908), *Der Gemeindebote*, Supplement, 3–4; J.S. Bloch, *Erinnerungen aus meinem Leben*, vol. I (1922), 207–211; R. Heuer (ed.), *Archiv Bibliographia Judaica*, vol. I (1992), 419–420; H. Schmuck (ed.), *Jewish Biographical Archive* (1995), F. 122, 209–28; Series II (2003), F. II/45, 348–51; S. Blumesberger et al. (eds.), *Handbuch oesterreichischer Autorinnen und Autoren juedischer Herkunft*, vol. I, no. 613 (2002), 80.

[Johannes Valentin Schwarz (2nd ed.)]

BAUMGARTEN, SÁNDOR (1864–1928), Hungarian architect. Baumgarten, together with Ö. Lechner, designed the building of the Postal Bank in Budapest (1900). Using Hungarian folkloristic motifs he built the Institute for the Blind and the Erzébet high school for girls.

[Eva Kondor]

°**BAUMGARTNER, WALTER** (1887–1970), Swiss Bible scholar and Orientalist. Baumgartner studied classical and Oriental philology and theology, and taught at the University of Marburg from 1916 (professor, 1928). From 1947, he was professor of Semitic languages at Basle. Baumgartner's position among biblical scholars and Orientalists is assured by the results of his work in the field of Bible and Semitic philology. His important studies on the Aramaic sections of the Bible include *Das Buch Daniel* (1926) and the Aramaic sections of L. Koehler and W. Baumgartner's *Lexicon in Veteris Testamenti Libros* (1953, 1958, 1967 ff.). In his doctoral dissertation, *Die Klagegedichte des Jeremia…* (1916), he employed critical methodology to prove that the monologues of Jeremiah were not later additions but may be attributed to the prophet himself. In his monographs *Alttestamentliche Religion* (1928) and *Israelitische und altorientalische Weisheit* (1933) he helped pioneer the study of ancient Near Eastern religion and wisdom literature. His book *Zum Alten Testament und seiner Umwelt*, a collection of previously published essays on the Bible and Oriental studies, was published in 1959 in honor of Baumgartner's 70th birthday (includes complete bibliography, pp. 1–26) and the jubilee volume *Hebraeische Wortforschung* was presented to him on his 80th birthday.

BIBLIOGRAPHY: Y. Kutscher, in: *Haaretz* (March 13, 1970).

[Zev Garber]

BAUMHORN, LIPÓT (1860–1932), Hungarian architect who built 25 synagogues in Austria-Hungary. Born in Kisbér, Baumhorn was educated at the Technische Hochschule in Vienna and started practicing in Ödön Lechner's office in Budapest, where he adopted the characteristic combination of plain plastered surfaces and red or yellow brick wavy decoration (string-courses, lysens, gables). Nevertheless, Baumhorn's style was slightly more conventional, using Moorish, Renaissance, or Gothic elements instead of the Hungarian national style.

His first building was the Neo-Moorish synagogue in Esztergom (1888), followed by synagogues at Rijeka (1895), Szolnok (1898), and Szeged (1903). The last is the most grandiose, expressing the aspirations of assimilated Hungarian Jewry with elaborated details and very rich ornamentation. It shows Baumhorn's typical nearly central floor plan with eastern *bimah*, emphasized central dome, and four subordinated corner-turrets containing the staircases for *ezrat nashim*.

Artistically the most noted synagogues are in Novi Sad (1906) and Budapest-Aréna-Út (1909) where affluent decoration disappears and the clarity of Proto-Modern architecture took over.

BIBLIOGRAPHY: J. Gerle, K. Attila, M. Imre, *A századforduló epiteszete Magyarországon* (1991), 33–35; A. Gazfa et al., *Magyarországi zsinagógák* (1989); R. Klein, chapter on synagogue architecture in Central and Eastern Europe, in G.S. Rajna, Z.A. Maisels, R. Klein, R. Reich, D. Jarasse, *L'art Juif* (1995).

[Rudolf Klein (2nd ed.)]

BAUMOL, JOSHUA (1880–1948), rabbi. Son of Nahum, the communal rabbi of Krachinka, who was his primary teacher, Baumol received rabbinical ordination from Rabbi Samuel Engel of Radomysl and Rabbi Benjamin Weiss of Chernovtsy, author of the *Even Yikarah*. Baumol taught Talmud in Vishnitz in the Bet Israel yeshivah from 1908 to 1911. He fled to Bohemia during World War I and became a pulpit rabbi in Brno at Congregation Maḥzekei ha-Dor.

Baumol arrived in the United States in 1920 and became the pulpit rabbi at Kehillath Adath Jeshurun in Williamsburg, Brooklyn, N.Y. As a member of the Agudat ha-Rabbonim, he became vice president of its Kashruth Committee. He was best known for handling issues confronting American Orthodox Jewry with tact and diplomacy. He was one of the founders and the first president of the *Agudat Israel of America, an umbrella group for Orthodox organizations and an advocacy organization. He was deeply involved in policymaking and administration of the Agudah and remained involved with the group until his death.

Baumol's peers respected him as a halakhic authority and often asked him for his opinions on contemporary matters. Among many things, he was asked about post-mortems, lie detector tests, and questions concerning survivors of the Holocaust. His two-volume set of responsa, *Emek Halakhah*, was published in 1934. In 1976, a revised edition, with addenda, was issued.

BIBLIOGRAPHY: B.-Z. Eisenstadt, *Dorot ha-Aḥaronim* (1937), 22; S. Elberg, *Sefer ha-Yovel ha-Pardes* (1951), 467–68; A. Rand (ed.), *Toeldot Anshei Shem* (1950), 8; M. Sherman, *Orthodox Judaism in*

America: A Biographical Dictionary and Sourcebook, (1996), 26–27; *Morgen Journal* (Sept. 9, 1948), 9; *New York Times* (Sept. 9, 1948), 27.

[Jeanette Friedman (2nd ed.)]

BAUR, HARRY (1883–1943), French actor. Born of poor Alsatian parents, Baur was compelled at the age of 12 to work on the Marseilles docks but managed to study at the Marseilles Conservatory of Music. He appeared briefly on the Paris stage but after the outbreak of World War I joined the army. Wounded, he returned to civilian life, continuing to act on the stage until movies became his chief interest. The French called Baur the "king of the character actors," and indeed, his heavy features and bushy brows lent themselves to a great range of parts including Beethoven in the *Life and Loves of Beethoven*. He also played in *Rasputin* and in *The Golem*. Baur was arrested in Berlin in 1942 on charges of forging a certificate of (Aryan) ancestry. Ironically, the Germans had to destroy a costly film because Baur had the main role. He was subsequently tortured for 4 months and died shortly after his release from prison.

[Louisa Cuomo]

BAUSKA (Yid. **Boysk**), town in S. Latvia, near the Lithuanian border. Originally in the duchy of *Courland, it was incorporated in Russia in 1795 and became a district town in the government (province) of Courland. Jews were permitted to settle there by a special law of 1799. At first their right of residence was restricted to a suburb on a bank of the river Aa (Lielupe), but the restriction was lifted in the 1820s. The community, most of whose members came from Lithuania, retained its "Lithuanian" character, with its stress on Torah learning and Orthodoxy. It numbered 2,669 in 1835 but by 1850 had decreased to 2,226 as a result of the settlement of 82 families (692 persons) from Bauska in the agricultural colonies in the province of Kherson in 1840 and of an outbreak of cholera in the area in 1848. The Jewish population numbered 2,745 in 1897 (42% of the total population). During World War I many Jews were forced by the Russian military authorities to evacuate Bauska, which was in the area of hostilities, for the Russian interior. Many did not return after the war and by 1920 there remained only 604 Jewish inhabitants. Their number rose to 919 in 1925. Most of the trade was in Jewish hands, supported by a Jewish cooperative bank. Well-known rabbis who officiated in the community in the second half of the 19th century were Mordecai *Eliasberg and Avraham Yitzḥak *Kook. During Soviet rule in 1940–1941 all Jewish life and trade was eliminated. Bauska was occupied by the Germans on June 26, 1941. On August 3, 50 Jews were murdered by Latvian police, and on September 30, 1941, all the remaining Bauska Jews, about 800, were executed.

BIBLIOGRAPHY: L. Ovchinski, *Toledot Yeshivat ha-Yehudim be-Kurland* (19112), 48–55; Z.A. Rabiner, in: *Yahadut Latvia* (1953), 244–76; M. Bove, *Perakim be-Toledot Yahadut Latvia* (1965). **ADD. BIBLIOGRAPHY:** PK Latvia ve-Estonia, s.v.

[Simha Katz / Shmuel Spector (2nd ed.)]

BAVA BATRA (Aram. בָּבָא בָּתְרָא, "last gate"), tractate of the Mishnah with *Gemara* in the Jerusalem and Babylonian Talmuds. The tractates *Bava Kamma, *Bava *Meẓia, and *Bava Batra* were originally one large tractate, *Nezikin*. The division into three apparently took place in Babylonia: in the Babylonian Talmud there are indications that the *Gemara* of each of the three sections was edited by a different hand, while in the Jerusalem Talmud they are uniform.

Chapters 1–3 of *Bava Batra* deal essentially with laws relating to ownership of real estate. Chapter 1 discusses the division of a courtyard held by joint owners whose homes open onto it. They may build a stone partition, each owner contributing an equal amount of land for its construction. Consequently, if the partition falls, "the place and the stones belong to them both." This law is similar to *Bava Meẓia* 10:1, for the last chapter of *Bava Meẓia* opens the discussion on ownership continued here. A courtyard containing several houses is a small community, and the Mishnah discusses the obligations of the individual to this community. Next, the mutual obligations of "neighbors" are presented for the dwellers of one city. The Tosefta adds to these communal obligations: "The citizens of a town can compel each other to build a synagogue, and to purchase a scroll of the Torah and the Prophets. The citizens are permitted to fix price ceilings and control weights and measures …" (Tosef., BM 11:23). In chapter 2, the Mishnah imposes limitations upon the actions of the property owner within the bounds of his own property, when such acts are a source of damage or nuisance to neighbors. Personal privacy is protected by a law prohibiting construction of windows which command a close-range view into a neighbor's windows. The section on ownership concludes with chapter 3, which discusses the rules of **ḥazakah*, according to which evidence of three years' undisturbed use of property can serve as proof of ownership. The Babylonian Talmud records many actual cases involving *ḥazakah* and disputed ownership, indicating the wide application of these laws in the area of Jewish real estate in Babylonia.

Concerning the acquisition of real estate, chapter 4 gives precise definitions of terms, so as to prevent a dispute between buyer and seller over what was included in the purchase. The list of legal definitions is continued in chapter 5 and extended to cover sale of movables. The variety of objects thus treated presents a wealth of precise Hebrew terminology and a rich description of the *realia* of Palestine during the mishnaic period. The remainder of this chapter expands on the requirement of justice in weights and measures (Lev. 19:35–36; Deut. 25:13–16), a topic related to purchase. Chapter 6 returns to definitions of objects of sale, not with regard to extent of inclusion but with regard to quality, i.e., to what degree the seller is required to replace inferior goods. The remainder of the chapter defines the minimum legal dimensions of various structures and tombs. Definitions of specific quantities of land mentioned in the sale of real estate are presented in chapter 7. This concludes the unit of "definitions," which began with chapter 6. The chapters discussed above deal with acquisition of property through purchase; chapters 8 and 9 consider acquisition of property by inheritance.

Chapter 10 contains rules for the proper preparation of legal documents by scribes, as well as the correct interpretation by the court of certain legal documents, especially bonds of indebtedness. This is a fitting conclusion to the tractate, since legal documents figure in acquisition, ownership, and other matters discussed in earlier chapters. The last Mishnah was intended, perhaps, as an apt conclusion for the entire tractate of *Nezikin* (the three *Bavot, Bava Kamma, Bava Meẓia,* and *Bava Batra*): "He that would become wise, let him occupy himself in cases concerning property, for there is no branch of law greater than they, for they are like a welling fountain" (10:8).

The Tosefta of *Bava Batra* contains 11 chapters. Generally the Tosefta follows the Mishnah, supplementing and paralleling it, but there are chapters where the material in the Tosefta is richer than the Mishnah and has an original and interesting order of its own.

The first chapter, dealing with the prevention of torts, parallels chapter 2 of the Mishnah (ch. 1 of which is paralleled by the second half of the Tosef., BM 11). Chapter 2:1–14, paralleling the Mishnah 2:1–6, deals with *ḥazakah*; while 2:14–17, paralleling Mishnah 2:2–8, is a supplement to chapter 1 of the Tosefta. It is probable that the connection between this supplement and the preceding section is *Samuel b. Meir's definition of a Tyrean window (14a) and the prohibition against opening a window facing that of a neighbor (14b). Chapters 3–4, paralleling Mishnah 4:1–5:5, deal with the regulations of selling; 5:1–6:21, paralleling Mishnah 5:6–6:3, deal with commercial honesty; the last part of this section differs from the Mishnah, in that the transition to the following two sections is clearly recognizable. Thus the subject of 6:22–23, paralleling the Mishnah at the end of chapter 6, deviates only slightly from the main discussion on commercial honesty, as it deals with the language used by a seller, a subject covered previously, and the subject of Tosefta 6:24–28 parallels the Mishnah of chapter 7. Chapters 7–10, discussing the *halakhot* of inheritance, contain a wealth of sources on details not mentioned at all in the parallel Mishnah (ch. 8 and 9). Chapter 11, dealing with deeds, parallels Mishnah chapter 10.

The rabbinic tradition regarding the order and authorship of the books of Scripture is recorded in *Bava Batra* 14b. The report of the travels of Rabbah bar Bar Ḥana (BB 73–74) contains fantastic descriptions of marvelous creatures and visions of the corpses of the Israelites who left Egypt and died in the wilderness of Sinai.

In the standard printed editions of the Babylonian Talmud more pages are found in this tractate than in any other (BB's last page is numbered 176). However, there are other tractates whose talmudic text is longer (see *Talmud). The size of the *Bava Batra* volume is due to the fact that the commentary of *Rashi is printed through page 29a only (in the Pesaro edition the termination of the commentary is marked: "Here died Rashi"), and the remainder of the tractate contains the more lengthy commentary of Samuel b. Meir. An English translation of the Talmud was made by I. Epstein (Soncino edition, 1935).

BIBLIOGRAPHY: Epstein, Amora'im, 187–270; A. Weiss, *Studies in the Law of the Talmud on Damages* (1966), 16–25; Ch. Albeck, *Shishah Sidrei Mishnah*, 4 (1959), 111–6; R. Yaron, *Gifts in Contemplation of Death in Jewish and Roman Law* (1960); D. Daube, in: *Tulane Law Review*, 18 (1944), 390–404.

[Shamma Friedman]

BAVA BEN BUTA (first century B.C.E.), sage and judge during the reign of *Herod. Bava, although a disciple of Shammai, agreed with Hillel, that the "Laying of Hands" (cf. Lev. 3:2) on sacrifices during festivals is permissible and was instrumental in establishing this law (Beẓah 20a–b). As a judge, Bava was noted for his thorough investigations and for his just decisions (Git. 57a). He offered daily guilt-offerings prescribed in cases of doubtful trespass, for fear that he had committed a sin (Ker. 6:3). This sacrifice came to be called "the guilt-offering of the pious." Bava overlooked an insult to himself to make peace between husband and wife (Ned. 66b). According to another legend Bava was the only Jewish sage who was not put to death by Herod; instead, Herod blinded him so that he could seek his counsel incognito. When Herod finally disclosed who he was and asked how he could make amends, Bava advised him to rebuild the Temple (BB 3b–4a). Josephus refers to "The Sons of Bava," who were among the noblemen of Jerusalem, and were beloved by the people. They were strong opponents of Herod, and for a long time "The Sons of Bava" remained in hiding for fear of him. Ultimately they were executed by him (Ant., 15:260–6).

BIBLIOGRAPHY: Schuerer, Gesch, 1 (1901[4]), 386–7; Klausner, Bayit Sheni, 4 (1950[2]), 27–28; Hyman, Toledot, 261–2.

[Zvi Kaplan]

BAVA KAMMA (Aram. בָּבָא קַמָּא), tractate of the Talmud, the first of the order *Nezikin*.

Name

Bava Kamma was originally not a separate tractate, but the first part of a larger tractate, whose name was identical with the name of the order. The title *Bava Kamma* is the abbreviated form for *Bava Kamma de-Massekhet Nezikin* ("the first gate (section) of the tractate *Nezikin*"). Tractate *Nezikin* ("torts") comprised 30 chapters, covering the entire range of pecuniary law (*dinei mamonot*). However, according to the Midrash, the size of *Nezikin* discouraged the student: "What does the fool say? 'Who can study the Torah? *Nezikin* has 30 chapters; *Kelim* has 30 chapters!'" (Lev. R. 19:2). For this reason *Nezikin* was divided into three sections, each consisting of ten chapters. The second and third parts are now called *Bava Meẓia* ("the middle gate") and *Bava Batra* ("the last gate"). The division seems to have taken place in Babylonia (*bava* as "gate" is unique to Babylonian Aramaic; see: Ned. 66b), where the size of *Nezikin* must have interfered with the regular practice of the academies to study one tractate each term. Palestinian sources indicate no division. (*Genizah* fragments of the Jerusalem Talmud treat it as one tractate.)

A similar division took place in the Tosefta, where the original tractate *Nezikin*, which contained 33 chapters, was divided into three sections of 11 chapters each. The mechanical nature of this division is evident from the fact that chapter 11 of Tosefta *Bava Meẓia* contains some material that parallels the last chapter of Mishnah *Bava Meẓia* and some that parallels the first chapter of Mishnah *Bava Batra*.

Contents

The first three *mishnayot* of *Bava Kamma* belong to one of the most ancient strata of mishnaic material, and contain, in succinct phrases, the underlying laws of *Torts (see *Avot Nezikin): "There are four *avot* (lit. 'fathers' or 'main categories') of torts – the *shor* ('ox'), the *bor* ('pit'), the *maveh* ('man' or 'tooth') and the *hever* ('fire').... If I am responsible for the care of a thing, it is I who make possible the injury it may do.... Assessment of the monetary equivalent [of an injury] must be made before a court of law, based upon the testimony of witnesses.... The laws of torts apply equally to women...." The antiquity of this section is indicated by the use of numerical listing (four *avot*), first person constructions, biblical phrases, archaic forms, and terse rules. One of the earliest of the Babylonian *amoraim*, Rav, alluded to the character of this section when he stated: "The *tanna* of this Mishnah was a Jerusalemite, who taught in a terse style" (BK 6b).

The list of four *avot* in the Mishnah is a convenient summary of the various sources of damage mentioned in Exodus 21:28–22:5. In the *beraitot*, other lists of *avot nezikin* are found, one containing 13, and others 24, according to varying schemes of inclusion (see BK 4b; Tosef. to BK 9:1).

CHAPTERS 1:4–3:7. Chapter 1:4 is another ancient Mishnah, again in the form of a numbered list, dealing, now in greater detail, with the *avot* of "horn," "tooth," and "foot," and, finally, "man." In chapter 2 each entry on the list in 1:4 is defined and expanded. For example, if an animal, while walking, kicks some pebbles, which hit another object and cause damage, this is "foot," only half of the damage is to be paid. Thus, chapter 2 of the Mishnah is a sort of "*Gemara*" on 1:4.

The first laws in chapter 3 come under the category of "pit": "If a man left a pitcher in the 'public domain,' and another stumbled over it... the owner is liable for the injury." The middle part of chapter 3 deals with "man": "If two pot-vendors [carrying their wares] were walking, one behind the other, and the first one stumbled...." The end of chapter 3 again deals with "horn" and appears to be a new discussion of the same subject covered in chapter 2. It has therefore been suggested by A. Weiss that 1:4–3:7 was originally an independent Mishnah section, dealing with the *avot* of "ox" ("horn," "tooth," "foot"), "pit," and "man." It would thus appear to be an expansion of the list of *avot* at the beginning of chapter 1, until *maveh*, in consonance with the interpretation that *maveh* is "man."

CHAPTER 3:8–6 END. This is another section, treating in detail the categories "horn," "pit," "tooth and foot," and "fire." It, too, is an expansion of 1:1, taking "ox" as "horn," and *maveh* as "tooth and foot." Thus the dispute between Rav and Samuel as to the meaning of *maveh* (BK 3b) did not originate with them; it had its origin in the underlying organizational scheme of early *mishnayot* which are independent expansions of the ancient Mishnah: "There are four *avot* ..."

CHAPTER 7. Chapter 7 is a comprehensive treatment of the laws of theft. It concentrates on the fines of "double," and "four or five" fold found in Exodus 22:3 and 21:37. Virtually each aspect of the theft and subsequent trial of the thief is scrutinized; each term of the pertinent scriptural verses is carefully defined and analyzed. In respect to the fine of "four or five" fold imposed by Scripture for the sale or slaughter of a stolen animal, the Mishnah determines that if the thief sold part of the animal but retained partial ownership, however minute, he is not liable to the fine of "four or five fold," but only to that of "double." Thus "sells it" in the scriptural verse is defined as the sale of the entire animal. Similarly, "if he slaughtered it and it became unfit under his hand [through a ritually improper slaughtering]" (7:5), he is exempt from the fine of "four or five" fold, such an act not being properly deemed "slaughter."

CHAPTER 8. This chapter is a comprehensive unit devoted to the laws of assault and battery.

CHAPTERS 9–10. Chapters 9 and 10 deal with laws of robbery. It would appear that a more natural position for these chapters would be after chapter 7, which deals with the related subject of theft. Their position is perhaps determined by their concentration upon the regulations governing transference of ownership of the stolen object through physical alteration or the original owner's despair of recovery, which makes them more closely related to the laws of acquisition and ownership in the succeeding chapters (see *Bava Meẓia) than to the laws of torts in the preceding ones.

It has been suggested that the function of "monetary law" in rabbinic sources is to prevent offenses of law, and to instruct the common man in moral behavior, rather than merely to provide for redress after a wrong has been committed (i.e., that such law is duty-oriented, rather than right-oriented, as explained by Silberg). Along these lines, types of damages are described in *Bava Kamma* for which one is "not liable according to human law, but guilty according to the laws of heaven" (55b–56a). Since there are acts which, even though not rendering one liable to suit, are morally wrong, it becomes an act of piety to take extreme care in preventing harm to the person or property of others. R. Judah held that the study of the laws of damages in *Bava Kamma* is a prerequisite for achieving true piety (30a).

Jerusalem Talmud

S. Lieberman has shown that the tractate *Nezikin* in the Jerusalem Talmud is of a different nature from the rest of that Talmud. The differences are attributed to its having been edited in Caesarea, no later than 350 C.E., while the rest of the Jerusalem Talmud was edited in Tiberias, some 50 years later. Among its distinguishing features are the short, pithy nature of the discussions, indicating a minimum of editing; a more primitive talmudic terminology; archaic Hebrew words; a relatively wider use of Greek and Latin (Caesarea was the seat of the Roman government in Palestine); and a distinctive orthography (e.g., -לָ for לָא). Anonymous statements in *Nezikin* are quoted elsewhere in the Jerusalem Talmud in the name of "the sages of Caesarea," or in the name of specific *amoraim* who lived in Caesarea. When points of law relating to *Nezikin* are discussed elsewhere in the Jerusalem Talmud, the treatment differs from the parallels in *Nezikin*. Conversely, sections of *Nezikin* which discuss matters relating to other tractates do not correspond to the material found in the relevant section of those tractates, although it is reasonable to assume that they were present in the corresponding tractates of the Talmud collection used by the editor of *Nezikin*. All this leads to the conclusion that *Nezikin* differs from the other tractates of the Jerusalem Talmud and constitutes the only existing remnant of the "Talmud of Caesarea." This issue has recently been reexamined by Y. Sussman, who arrived at different conclusions.

Aside from the regular editions, commentaries and translations, *Bava Kamma* has received special scholarly attention with the publication of a new critical edition of the Jerusalem Talmud of *Massekhet Nezikin*, edited by E.S. Rosenthal with commentary by S. Lieberman, and a comparative study of the Mishnah and Tosefta by Abraham Goldberg.

BIBLIOGRAPHY: A. Weiss, *Diyyunim u-Verurim be-Vava Kamma* (1966); S. Lieberman, in: *Tarbiz*, 2 (1931), Suppl. 4; L. Jacobs, *Studies in Talmudic Logic and Methodology* (1961), 132–5; M. Silberg, *Harvard Law Review*, 75 (1961), 307–31; Epstein, Amora'im, 279–87; S. Lieberman, *Sifrei Zutta* (1968); S. Friedman, (ed.), *Jonathan ha-Kohen's Commentary to Bava Kamma* (1969). **ADD. BIBLIOGRAPHY:** Y. Sussman, in: *Talmudic Studies* (1990), 55–133; *Yerushalmi Neziqin*, ed. E.S. Rosenthal (1983); A. Goldberg, *Tosefta Bava Kamma: A Structural and Analytical Commentary* (2001); A. Westreich, *Sidra*, 19 (2004), 77–100.

[Shamma Friedman]

BAVA MEẒIA (Aram. בָּבָא מְצִיעָא, "middle gate"), tractate of the Mishnah, with *Gemara* in the Jerusalem and Babylonian *Talmuds. Originally *Bava Meẓia* was not a separate tractate but the second part of the tractate *Nezikin* (see *Bava Kamma). Chapters 1 and 2 deal with the laws of *acquisition (*kinyan*) of lost or abandoned articles and describe the cases in which the article may not be acquired by the finder but must be held until claimed. These regulations are thus related to the laws of the last two chapters of *Bava Kamma*, which determine how and under what circumstances stolen articles may be legitimately acquired and under what circumstances they must be returned. Great religious importance is attached to the commandment of returning lost property: if a man returns a lost animal and it escapes again, he must continue to return it, even "100 times" (31a). Nonetheless, exemption is granted from this commandment if its performance would require violation of a ritual prohibition, entail behavior which is an affront to the personal dignity of the finder, or require the finder to neglect his own work and thereby sustain a financial loss greater than the object's value (30a). Chapter 2:9 reads like a new beginning and probably represents the incorporation of a new source, originally a Midrash on Deuteronomy 22:1. It closes with a section which is religious and moral in tone, thus marking the end of a unit.

An unpaid guardian, with whom goods were deposited for safekeeping, is discussed in chapter 3. He resembles one who guards found property (ch. 2), and also must, on some occasions, sell perishables deposited with him and hold the proceeds for the owner. If the guardian misuses the object, he is considered a robber and must assume all responsibility for subsequent damage. Chapter 4 opens with the general rules for acquiring movable property in a business transaction. Transfer of title to the buyer occurs, not at the time of payment, but only when the buyer takes the item (or symbolically "draws" it to himself). This means that the sale can be legally canceled even after payment, as long as the goods have not been "drawn"; but the sages said, "He that exacted punishment from the generation of the Flood … will exact punishment from him that does not abide by his spoken word" (4:2). However, R. Johanan held that originally payment of some amount of money effected the transfer of title, but that since this law led to abuse – the seller would not deliver but say, "Your wheat was destroyed by fire in the storeroom" – the rule was changed to its present form (46b). The remainder of the chapter contains a detailed section on *ona'ah*, unfair and illegal business practices (based on Lev. 25:17). Much attention is given to overcharging; the law guarantees redress to the party defrauded of one-sixth or more of the value of the purchase.

Chapter 5 is a self-contained unit dealing with the laws of interest (see Lev. 25:36); it appears here probably by virtue of its association with the regulations on commerce found in chapter 4, and closes with a section emphasizing the ethical seriousness of the prohibition (see Tosef. 6:17). Chapter 6 opens with cases of deception between employer and craftsmen, which can be considered a continuation of the theme of *ona'ah* found in chapter 4. The first Mishnah is followed by a series of *mishnayot* each beginning with the words, "If a man hired…." They deal with breach of contract in cases of hiring craftsmen or work animals. The final section concerns itself with craftsmen who work with others' material but on their own premises; they have the status of "paid guardian" and are responsible for loss or theft. Chapter 7 gives rules of labor relations and the right of the employee, especially the agricultural worker, to eat from the produce of the field. This law reflects the interpretation that Deuteronomy 23:25–26 refers specifically to the agricultural worker and not to any passerby, for granting to the latter the rights of eating the field's produce would not yield a viable situation for the owner (92a). The duty of the farmer to allow his animal to eat of the produce (Deut. 25:4) is also treated. The discussion of the right of those who guard produce (but do not work with it) to partake of the food is the occasion to introduce an ancient Mishnah delineating the laws of the four kinds of guardian: an unpaid guardian, a borrower, a paid guardian, and a hirer (Ex. 22:6–14). The beginning of chapter 8 continues the subject of guardians, specifically elaborating on Exodus 22:14 – that the borrower of an animal may not be liable for payment on unavoidable accidents when he had also borrowed or hired the personal services of the lender. The chapter closes with laws of renting houses (related to "hiring" above).

Chapter 9 opens with a related issue: leasing of a field where the lessee gives the owner a percentage of the produce, or a fixed amount of produce, instead of rental money. The last two parts of the chapter complement laws found earlier in the tractate; they deal with the duty to pay employees promptly and limitations of the creditor's right to exact a pledge from the borrower. The religio-moral tone of this section is typical of the close of a unit. Chapter 10 does indeed open a new topic, the ownership of real estate (continued through *Bava Batra), and deals basically with the property rights of neighbors whose properties are situated one above the other.

Among several aggadic passages in *Bava Meẓia*, the section beginning at the bottom of 59a is of special interest. R. Eliezer's arguments regarding the purity of a certain oven did not convince his colleagues. He then called for a series of miraculous acts to vindicate him. Although heavenly interventions were forthcoming, the miracles were deemed valueless in settling legal disputes. R. Eliezer then declared," If the law is according to my opinion, may it be proved from heaven." A heavenly voice (**bat kol*) issued forth saying, "Why do you challenge R. Eliezer, for the law is according to his opinion in all matters?" Whereupon R. Joshua rose and declared, "It is not in the heavens" (Deut. 30:12) "… since the giving of the Torah at Mt. Sinai, no attention is paid to a heavenly voice, but the opinion of a majority of the scholars determines authentic law." An English translation of the Talmud was made by S. Daiches and H. Freedman (Soncino edition, 1935). A students' edition, vocalized, with translation, commentary and notes in English, appeared as part of the *Talmud El-Am*.

[Shamma Friedman]

The Tosefta of *Bava Meẓia* contains 11 chapters. The *beraitot* in the Tosefta, in addition to giving supplementary and sometimes parallel passages to the Mishnah, also contain much more material than the Mishnah, dealing with entire subjects not mentioned in it.

Chapter 1 of the Tosefta parallels chapter 1 of the Mishnah, but it ends with a series of laws dealing with deeds and surety. They begin with the words (1:15), "if two have hold of a bill, the one saying it is mine but I lost it" etc., which are directly connected with the main subject of the chapter; since the editor did not want to fragment the source, he gives it in full on account of the first *halakhah*. Chapter 2 parallels Mishnah chapter 2, but from its last *halakhah* (33) it can be inferred to whom lost property need not be returned – "heretics, apostates, and informers" (cf. Av. Zar. 26b; and see Ch. Albeck, *Meḥkarim be-Varaita ve-Tosefta*, 1944, 138 n.4). Chapter 3:1–12, parallels chapter 3 of the Mishnah, and 3:13–29 parallels chapter 4 of the Mishnah. Chapter 5 of the Mishnah dealing with interest is paralleled by chapters 4–6 of the Tosefta. Tosefta 7:1–14 parallels 6:1–5 of the Mishnah, dealing with *ona'ah* in the hiring of laborers and cattle and the requirement not to deviate from traditional custom in the conditions of hire; while Tosefta 7:14–19 parallels Mishnah 6:6–8, dealing with the *halakhot* of craftsmen in respect of guarding articles in their care. It is probable that this chapter preserves richer and more original sources than those contained in the Mishnah.

Chapter 8:1–12, parallelling Mishnah 7:1–7, deals with the duties and rights of laborers, as well as the rights of cattle employed in work (in respect of eating the produce). Tosefta 8:13–26 deals with the four bailees and parallels Mishnah 7:8–8:5, but here too the Tosefta appears to preserve a more original order. It is not clear whether Tosefta 8:25–26 was brought in because of the previous cases of conflicting statements by the two litigants or whether it is merely the supplement of the body of *halakhot* in 7:1–14. Tosefta 8:27–33 parallels Mishnah 8:6–9 and discusses the laws of the hiring and borrowing of houses, inns, and shops. Tosefta chapter 9 deals with hiring and the renting and tenant-hiring of fields. (The Mishnah has nothing on hiring, whereas from the Tosefta the connection [in the Mishnah] between the renting of houses and the leasing of fields becomes clear.) Chapter 10:1 ("He who lends to his fellow") may be a supplement to the previous chapter (9:14, 20–21: "one may not deviate from local custom") or it may have been brought in because of the laws which follow dealing with remuneration for hire. Tosefta 10:2–7, dealing with the laws of hired men and their hire, parallels accordingly Mishnah 9:11–12, and subsequently 8–11 parallels Mishnah 9:13 in dealing with the taking of a pledge. Tosefta chapter 11, dealing with the laws of partners and neighbors, parallels chapter 10 of Mishnah *Bava Meẓia* together with chapter 1 of *Bava Batra*.

[Moshe David Herr]

Aside from the regular editions, commentaries and translations, *Bava Meẓia* has received special scholarly attention with the publication of a new critical edition of the Jerusalem Talmud of *Massekhet Nezikin*, edited by E.S. Rosenthal with commentary by S. Lieberman, and the monumental work *Talmud Arukh, Talmud Bavli Bava Meẓia VI*, by Shamma Friedman.

[Stephen G. Wald (2nd ed.)]

BIBLIOGRAPHY: Epstein, Amora'im, 279–87; D. Daube, in: *Tulane Law Review*, 18 (1944), 377ff.; Ch. Albeck, *Shishah Sidrei Mishnah*, 4 (1959), 57–63; A. Weiss, *Diyyunim u-Verurim be-Vava Kamma* (1966), 10–16, 26; B. De Vries. *Meḥkarim be-Sifrut ha-Talmud* (1968), 96–101; S. Albeck, in: *Sinai*, 62 (1968), 229ff. **ADD. BIBLIOGRAPHY:** *Yerushalmi Nezikin*, ed. E.S. Rosenthal (1983); S. Friedman, *Talmud Arukh, TB Bava Meẓia VI* (vol. 1. 1990, vol. 2 1996).

BAVARIA, *Land* in S. Germany, including Franconia. Jews are first mentioned there in the *Passau toll regulations of 906. Their settlement was apparently connected with the trade routes to Hungary, southern Russia and northeastern Germany. A Jewish resident of *Regensburg is mentioned at the end of the tenth century. The communities which had been established in *Bamberg and Regensburg were attacked during the First Crusade in 1096, and those in *Aschaffenburg, *Wuerzburg, and *Nuremberg during the Second Crusade in 1146–47. Other communities existed in the 13th century at Landshut, Passau, *Munich, and *Fuerth. The Jews in Bavaria mainly engaged in trade and moneylending. In 1276 they were expelled from Upper Bavaria and 180 Jews were burned at the stake in Munich following a *blood libel in 1285. The communities in Franconia were attacked during the *Rindfleisch persecutions in 1298. The *Armleder massacres, charges of desecrating the *Host at *Deggendorf, Straubing, and Landshut, and the persecutions following the *Black Death (1348–49), brought catastrophe to the whole of Bavarian Jewry. Many communities were entirely destroyed, among them *Ansbach, Aschaffenburg, *Augsburg, Bamberg, *Ulm, Munich, Nuremberg, Passau, Regensburg, *Rothenburg, and Wuerzburg. Those who had fled were permitted to return after a time under King Wenceslaus.

In 1442 the Jews were again expelled from Upper Bavaria. Shortly afterward, in 1450, the Jews in Lower Bavaria were flung into prison until they paid the duke a ransom of 32,000 crowns and were then driven from the duchy. As a result of agitation by the Franciscan John of *Capistrano, they were expelled from Franconia. In 1478 they were expelled from Passau, in 1499 from Nuremberg, and in 1519 from Regensburg. The few remaining thereafter in the duchy of Bavaria were expelled in 1551. Subsequently, Jewish settlement in Bavaria ceased until toward the end of the 17th century, when a small community was founded in *Sulzbach by refugees from *Vienna. During the War of the Spanish Succession (1701–14) several Jews from Austria serving as purveyors to the army or as moneylenders settled in Bavaria. In this period a flourishing community grew up in Fuerth, whose economic activities helped to bring prosperity to the city. After the war the Jews of Austrian origin were expelled from Bavaria, but some were able to acquire the right to reside in Munich as monopoly holders, *Court Jews, mintmasters, and physicians. Several Court Jews belonging to the Frankel and *Model families

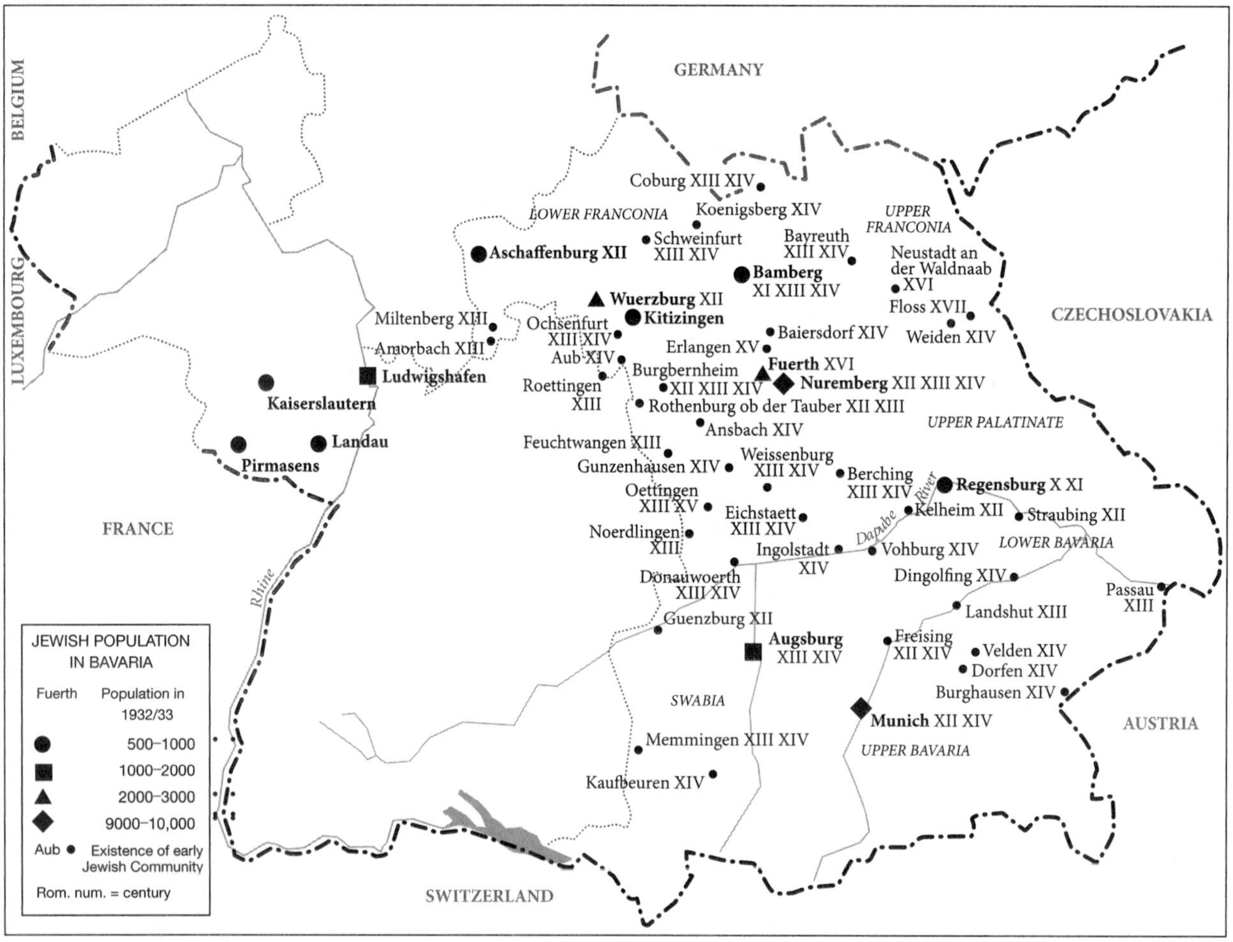

Map of Bavaria showing Jewish population centers from the tenth century to 1932-33.

became prominent in Ansbach and Fuerth for a while in the 18th century, particularly because of their services in managing the state's economy.

In the Napoleonic era Jewish children were permitted to attend the general schools (1804), the men were accepted into the militia (1805), the poll tax was abolished (1808), and Jews were granted the status of citizens (1813). However, at the same time their number and rights of residence were still restricted, and only the eldest son in a family was allowed to marry (see *Familiants Laws). In 1819 anti-Jewish disorders broke out in Franconia (the "*Hep! Hep!" riots). Owing to the continued adverse conditions and the restrictions on families a large number of young Bavarian Jews immigrated to the U.S. A second wave of emigrants left for the U.S. after the 1848 Revolution, which had been accompanied by anti-Jewish riots notably in rural Franconia. In 1861 the discriminatory restrictions concerning Jews were abolished, and Jews were permitted to engage in all occupations. However, complete equality was not granted until 1872 by the provisions of the constitution of the German Reich of 1871. Certain special "Jewish taxes" were abolished only in 1880. The chief occupation of Jews in 19th century rural Bavaria was the livestock trade, largely in Jewish hands (see *Agriculture). By the beginning of the 20th century Jews had considerable holdings in department stores and in a few branches of industry.

A number of Jews were active after World War I in the revolutionary government of Bavaria which was headed by a Jew, Kurt *Eisner, who was prime minister before his assassination in 1919. Another Jew, Gustav *Landauer, who became minister of popular instruction, was also assassinated that year. In the reaction which followed World War I there was a new wave of antisemitism, and in 1923 most of the East European Jews resident in Bavaria were expelled. This was the time when the National Socialist Movement made its appearance in the region, and antisemitic agitation increased. Jewish ritual slaughter was prohibited in Bavaria in 1931.

The size of the Jewish population in Bavaria varied relatively little from the Napoleonic era to 1933, numbering 53,208 in 1818 and 41,939 in 1933. A Bavarian Jewish organization, the Verband bayerischer israelitischer Gemeinden, was set up in 1921 and included 273 communities and 21 rabbinical institutions. In 1933 the largest and most important communities in Bavaria were in Munich (which had a Jewish population of 9,000), Nuremberg (7,500), Wuerzburg (2,150), Augsburg (1,100), Fuerth (2,000), and Regensburg (450). At this time the majority of Bavarian Jews were engaged in trade and transport (54.5%) and in industry (19%), but some also in agriculture (2.7% in 1925 compared with 9.7% in 1882). Over 1,000 Jews studied at the University of Bavaria after World War I, a proportion ten times higher than that of the Jews to the general population.

Regensburg was a center of Jewish scholarship from the 12th century. Regensburg was the cradle of the medieval Ashkenazi *Ḥasidism and in the 12th and 13th centuries the main center of this school. The traveler *Pethahiah b. Jacob set out from there in about 1170. Prominent scholars of Bavaria include *Meir b. Baruch of Rothenburg (the leading authority of Ashkenazi Jewry, 13th century); Jacob *Weil (taught at Nuremberg and Augsburg, beginning of the 15th century); Israel *Bruna (settled in Regensburg, mid-15th century); Moses *Mintz (rabbi of Bamberg, 1469–1474); and the Renaissance grammarian Elijah *Levita (a native of Neustadt). In the 19th/20th centuries there lived in Munich the folklorist and philologist Max M. *Gruenbaum; Raphael Nathan Nata *Rabinovicz, author of *Dikdukei Soferim*; and Joseph *Perles, rabbi of Augsburg, 1875–1910.

The Jews in Bavaria were among the first victims of the Nazi movement, which spread from Munich and Nuremberg. Virulent and widespread antisemitic agitation caused the depopulation of scores of the village communities so characteristic of Bavaria, especially after the **Kristallnacht* in 1938. The first concentration camp was established at *Dachau in Bavaria and many Jews from Germany and other countries in Europe perished there.

After World War II thousands of Jews were assembled in displaced persons' camps in Bavaria; the last one to be closed down was in Foehrenwald. Almost all of the 1,000 Bavarian Jews who survived the Holocaust were saved because they were married to Germans or were born of mixed marriages. A year after the end of hostilities a Nazi underground movement remained active in Bavaria, and the neo-Nazi anti-Jewish demonstrations of June 1965 started in Bamberg. Antisemitic sentiment was also aroused when the minister of Jewish affairs, Philip Auerbach, was prosecuted for misappropriation of funds in 1951.

In 1969 there were in Bavaria about 4,700 Jews, forming 13 communities, the majority from the camps of Eastern Europe. The largest communities were in Munich (3,486), Nuremberg (275), Wuerzburg (141), Fuerth (200), Augsberg (230), and Regensburg (150). There were smaller numbers of Jews in *Amberg, Bamberg, *Bayreuth, Straubing, and Weiden. In 1989 there were 5,484 community members. Due mainly to the emigration of Jews from the former Soviet Union, the number rose to 18,387 in 2003, the largest communites being those in Munich (8,917), Straubing (1,713), Augsburg (1,619), Nuremberg (1,286), and Wuerzburg (1,027).

BIBLIOGRAPHY: S. Taussig, *Geschichte der Juden in Bayern* (1874); Germ Jud, 1 (1963), 22–24; 2 (1968), 57–60; S. Schwarz, *Juden in Bayern im Wandel der Zeiten* (1963); R. Strauss, *Regensburg and Augsburg* (1939); H.B. Ehrmann, *Struggle for Civil and Religious Emancipation in Bavaria in the First Half of the 19th Century* (1948), 199; H.C. Vedeler, in: *Journal of Modern History*, 10 (1938), 473–95; P. Wiener-Odenheimer, *Die Berufe der Juden in Bayern* (1918), 131. **ADD. BIBLIOGRAPHY:** PK Bavaria; B.Z. Ophir (ed.), *Die juedischen Gemeinden in Bayern 1918–1945* (1979); J.F. Harris, *The People Speak* (1994); R. Kiessling (ed.), *Judengemeinden in Schwaben ...* (1995); G. Och (ed.), *Juedisches Leben in Franken* (2002).

[Zvi Avneri]

BAVLI (Rashgolski), HILLEL (1893–1961), Hebrew poet and educator. Bavli, who was born in Pilvishki, Lithuania, attended yeshivot in Kovno and Vilna. In 1912 he immigrated to the United States and studied at Canisius College and Columbia University. From 1918 he taught modern Hebrew literature at the Jewish Theological Seminary of America, after 1937 with the rank of professor. Bavli's first poems appeared in a children's periodical, *Ha-Peraḥim*, in 1908. His first book of poetry, *Neginot Areẓ* ("Melodies of the Land"), was published in 1929. Subsequent collections of his poetry, *Shirim* ("Poems," 1938), *Shirim le-Raḥelah* ("Poems for Raḥelah," 1950), and *Adderet ha-Shanim* ("The Mantle of Years," 1955), also appeared in Israel. Conservative in style and structure, Bavli covers a broad range of themes in his work: personal love; love of his people; love of Ereẓ Israel. He was one of the first Hebrew poets to deal with the American milieu. "Mrs. Woods" is an idyll about an American woman of simple tastes and honest demeanor. Bavli's critical essays *Ruḥot Nifgashot* ("Winds Meet," 1958) deal mainly with Hebrew and American writers. Bavli translated Dickens' *Oliver Twist* (1924) and Shakespeare's *Antony and Cleopatra* into Hebrew (1952). He also translated works by the black writers James D. Corrothers, W. Burghardt du Bois, and Claude McKay into Hebrew. He edited a miscellany, *Nimim* (1923); a yearbook, *Massad* (2 vols, 1933–36); the Ẓevi Scharfstein Jubilee Volume (1955); and several modern Hebrew classics for school use. He published a number of articles in English on modern Hebrew literature, including "The Growth of Modern Hebrew Literature" (1939) and "Some Aspects of Modern Hebrew Literature" (1958).

BIBLIOGRAPHY: A. Epstein, *Soferim Ivrim be-Amerika*, 1 (1952), 104–24; E.R. Malachi, *Zekher le-Hillel* (1962); J. Kabakoff, in: JBA, 20 (1962/63), 76–83; Waxman, Literature, 5 (1960^2), 190–2.

[Eliezer Schweid]

BAVLI, MENAHEM BEN MOSES (fl. 16th century), rabbi and kabbalist of the Safed school. There is little information about his descent. The title "*Bavli*" (Babylonian) probably stands for "Roman," and it is possible that he came from Italy. In 1522 and in 1525 he signed himself as *dayyan* in Trikkala, Greece. Later he immigrated to Ereẓ Israel and in 1531 he was in Safed together with his father and brother Reuben (responsa R. Moses b. Joseph di Trani, 1 (1641), no. 43). They made their living in the wool-dyeing trade. Menahem was considered one of the great scholars of the town. One of his responsa was published in the responsa collection *Maran le-Even ha-Ezer* (no. 14) and in it he quotes a ruling of R. Jacob *Berab, whom he calls "our teacher the Great Rabbi," which suggests that Bavli may have been a student at Berab's yeshivah in Safed. After 1553 he traveled to Egypt. From Safed Bavli went to Hebron probably in connection with the expansion of the Jewish settlement there, in which the scholars of Safed took part. In the introduction to his *Peri Ḥevron* (*Ta'amei ha-Mitzvot*) (Lublin, 1571), he wrote that he dedicated the income of this book to "Hebron, as a contribution for its reconstruction."

BIBLIOGRAPHY: Benayahu, in: KS, 29 (1954), 173f.; A.N.Z. Roth, *ibid.*, 31 (1956), 399; Benayahu, *ibid.*, 399–400; Dmitrovsky, in: *Sefunot*, 7 (1963), 67.

°**BAYAZID II** (c. 1447–1512), sultan of the Ottoman Empire (1481–1512), son and successor of Sultan Mehmet II, conqueror of Constantinople. Following the expulsion from Spain, great numbers of Jews streamed into the Ottoman Empire and settled in various towns of the Balkans and Anatolia. According to R. Elijah *Capsali, Sultan Bayazid issued an order to the governors of the provinces not to refuse those Jews entry or cause them difficulties but to receive them cordially and provide them with the help they needed to settle themselves. Nevertheless, according to the same source, Bayazid was a devout Muslim and was responsible for certain cases of forced conversion of Jews to Islam. He was also the only sultan to enforce the prohibition against building new synagogues. Immanuel *Aboab attributes to Bayazid the famous remark that the Catholic monarchs (Ferdinand and Isabella) were considered wise, but wrongly so, since they impoverished Spain (by the expulsion of the Jews) and enriched the Ottoman Empire. During the reign of Bayazid the position of rabbi in the capital was held by R. Moses *Capsali, who was succeeded by R. Elijah *Mizraḥi. Joseph *Hamon was the sultan's physician and influential at court. European sources accuse Hamon of complicity in the sudden death of Bayazid after his forced abdication in favor of his son Selim I.

BIBLIOGRAPHY: M. Franco, *Essai sur l'histoire des Israélites de l'Empire Ottoman …* (1897) 35–40; J.R. Hacker, "Ha-Rabbanut ha-Rashit ba-Imperiah ha-Ottomanit ba-Me'ah ha-15 ve-ha-16," in: *Zion*, 49, 3 (1984), 225–63; A. Shmuelevitz, "Capsali as a Source for Ottoman History 1450–1523," in: IJMES, 9 (1978) 339–44.

[Aryeh Shmuelevitz (2nd ed.)]

BAYEFSKY, ABA (1923–2001), Canadian artist and teacher. Bayefsky was born in Toronto, where he was first encouraged to paint by Canadian Group of Seven artist Arthur Lismer. In 1942 Bayefsky joined the Royal Canadian Air Force and became an official war artist in 1944. In May 1945 he was among the first to enter the newly liberated *Bergen-Belsen concentration camp. "For the first time," wrote Bayefsky," I had become aware of man's monstrous capacity for evil. It was the determining factor in everything I have done since." His camp images are part of the art collection of the Canadian War Museum. After the war Bayefsky returned to Europe to study at the Académie Julian in Paris and continued to paint and draw images based on the lives of Jewish displaced persons.

Back in Toronto, Bayefsky's drawings, paintings, watercolors, murals, and publications celebrated people and their everyday lives. Well traveled, he created works reflecting the diversity of human experience from the marketplaces of India to the traditional tattoo artists of Japan. Yet it was his Jewish heritage, his anger at what he witnessed during the Holocaust and at the resurgence of antisemitism during his later years that engendered Bayefsky's most vibrant work. "Tales from the Talmud" illustrated 18 talmudic folk tales and parables; large murals depicted scenes from Jewish history's joys and sorrows; "Epilogue," his last works, encompass 50 years of reflection on the Holocaust. "Epilogue" was donated to Yad Vashem in 1999.

Bayefsky exhibited in more than 45 one-man exhibitions and taught Fine Art at the Ontario College of Art from 1957 to 1988. He was also president of the Canadian Group of Painters and the Canadian Society of Graphic Art, a member of the Royal Canadian Academy, and appointed to the Order of Canada, the highest honor Canada bestows upon a citizen.

BIBLIOGRAPHY: A. Bayefsky, *Aba Bayefsky in Kensington Market* (1991).

[Paula Draper (2nd ed.)]

BAYER, BATYA (Bathja; 1928–1995), Israeli musicologist, music archeologist, and librarian. Born in Bingen, Germany, Bayer immigrated to Eretz Israel in 1936 with her family. She earned her Ph.D. at the University of Zurich in 1959. Subsequently she received a librarian's degree from the Hebrew University of Jerusalem. From 1964 to 1974, she was the director of the Music Department at the National and University Library and played a vital role in shaping the research of the major music research library in Israel. She was also a senior lecturer at the Department of Musicology of the Hebrew University. Bayer was a pioneer in the interdisciplinary study of music and archeology in relation to the ancient civilizations of the Near East, and one of the creators of a new field of study: music archeology. She made a significant effort to gather archeological and iconographical data from the biblical period in Palestine with a view to elucidating the musical passages and musical instruments mentioned in the biblical text and post-biblical writings. Her thorough investigation is exemplified by her monograph *The Material Relics of Music in Ancient Palestine and Its Environs* (1963), by the entry "*Neginah ve-Zimrah*" in the *Encyclopedia Biblica* 5 (1980), and, in particular, by her two extensive studies "The Biblical Nevel" (*Yuval* 1, 1968) and "The Titles of the Psalms" (*Yuval* 4, 1982).

Bayer was broadly cultured and an individual of enormous erudition and perfectionism. An eloquent example is her coverage of the extensive musical material related to biblical figures and stories for the first edition of the *Encyclopaedia Judaica* as well as her other entries on a wide variety of subjects.

[Amnon Shiloah (2nd ed.)]

BAYHAN (Bayḥān), county and its central city, Bayḥān al-Kaṣab, in South Arabia. This was a desert area with shifting sands on the ancient Perfume Road. In the Roman period the area flourished because of the perfume trade, but it deteriorated when Christianity became widespread. In *Nūr al-Ẓalām* by Rabbi *Nethanel ben Isaiah, Bayhan was referred to as Diklah (Gen. 10:27). At the end of the 15th century a Jewish false messiah orated in the area, but after he had been seized and killed by the authorities the area was evacuated of all Jews. In the 19th century the Jews suffered from the struggle between the Turkish and the British. Jews lived in Bayhan and in four villages in the area: Aylan, Shirka, Aliya, and Rawna, which were controlled by the Sheikh Husayn ibn Aḥmad. There were approximately 30 houses belonging to Jews in the town and about 20 families in the nearby villages. Most Jews were blacksmiths and weavers but some were merchants. A number of families had land in the neighboring city of Ḥarib. Jews and Muslims lived side by side and had good relations. There was one synagogue in Bayhan, established by R. Sa'id Kasha of Ṣan'a. Another rabbi from San'a was Salim Joseph Ṣan'ani. The cemetery was located in the western part of the city. One synagogue was situated in Aylan and was used by all Jews in the village area. The rabbibical court was staffed by the Mori and Menasheh families, which, according to their testimony, had lived in Bayhan for many generations, coming there from Bayda, Ḥabban, Rada', Suwadi, San'a, and other places. Jewish professions in the last generation included: blacksmithing, weaving, retail commerce, and some farming. The 88 Jews of Ḥabban were brought to Aden by a British air force flight in 1949 and from there immigrated to the State of Israel on December 4, 1949. They settled in the abandoned village of Ajur.

BIBLIOGRAPHY: R.B Serjeant, "Materials for South Arabian History," in BSOAS 13 (1950), 294; L.D. Loeb, "Jewish-Muslim Socio-Political Relations in Twentieth Century South Yemen," in: E. Isaac and Y. Tobi (eds.), *Judaeo-Yemenite Studies: Proceedings of the Second International Congress*, 71–99; R. Meissner, *Die suedjemenitischen Juden: Versuch einer Rekonstruktion ihrer traditionallen Kultur vor dem Exodus*, (1999), 47–51; Y. Kafiḥ, *Sefunot* 2 (1958), 249; Sh. Lahav, *Kehillat Yehudei Bayhan* (1996); Y. Tobi, in: *Pe'amim* 64 (1995), 28–31.

[Yosef Tobi (2nd ed.)]

BAYONNE, town in southwestern France. The first Jewish settlement in Bayonne, in the suburb of Saint-Esprit, consisted of *Marranos originally from Spain and Portugal, who settled there early in the 16th century. In 1550 they were granted rights of residence as "New Christians" by the central authorities, but the Bayonne merchants prohibited them from retail trading. In 1636 several Marrano families were expelled from Bayonne, and some of them found refuge at Nantes. From the middle of the 17th century, the Bayonne community organized a congregation, *Nefuẓot Yehudah* ("The Dispersed of Judah"). Their cemetery was established in 1660. The right of the community to observe Judaism openly was not officially recognized until 1723. Rabbis of Bayonne in this period included Ḥayyim de Mercado in the second half of the 17th century, succeeded by Raphael *Meldola (1730–1792) of Leghorn, and Abraham David Leon, author of *Instrucciones sagradas y morales* (1765). At the beginning of the 18th century the community numbered 700, and 3,500 in 1753.

The Bayonne community claimed jurisdiction over the small communities in Bidache, Peyrehorade, and other places in the vicinity. Marranos from Spain and Portugal continued to settle in Bayonne until late in the 18th century. The regulations of the community were drawn up in 1752, and confirmed by the "intendant du roi." Bayonne Jewry helped to introduce the chocolate industry into France; in the mid-18th century the import of salt and glue into Bayonne was in Jewish hands. Bayonne Jews were among the first to establish trade connections with the French West Indies. About one-third of the municipal tax revenue was derived from the Jewish residents. Despite opposition from their Christian neighbors, the Jews participated in the elections to the States-General in 1789. They were recognized as French citizens in 1790, with the rest of the "Portuguese, Spanish, and Avignonese" Jews in France. During the Reign of Terror, most of the members of the *Comité de surveillance* of Saint Esprit (known then as "Jean Jacques Rousseau") were Jews; it is noteworthy that no guillotinings took place. In the Napoleonic period the community benefited from the city's increasing prosperity. A new synagogue was built in 1837, using the Torah Ark erected during the reign of Louis XVI. The Jewish population nevertheless fell to 1,293 in 1844, and by 1926 had decreased to 45 families.

[Zvi Avneri]

Holocaust Period

After the Franco-German armistice (June 1940) Bayonne became a stopover for dozens of Jewish refugees, particularly from *Belgium and *Luxembourg. A great many could not get to Spain, and the official police census of March 15, 1942 registered 308 Jewish families there at that time. In April 1943 the majority of them were expelled, while 193 pieces of Jewish property were confiscated. Fortunately, the Ark, built in the style of Louis XVI, and the Torah scrolls, some of which were of Spanish origin, were hidden in the Basque Museum, and restored to the synagogue after the Liberation. Few of Bayonne's Jews survived the war. The rabbi of Bayonne, Ernest *Ginsburger (1876–1943) directed religious activities on behalf of the Jews interned in French concentration and labor camps. He was subsequently deported and murdered by the Germans. In April 1943, almost all the Jews in Bayonne and the surrounding district were forcibly evacuated.

After the war the community slowly rebuilt itself, with about 120 families recorded living in the city in 1960. With the arrival of immigrants from North Africa, the Jewish community more than doubled, so that in 1969 close to 700 Jews lived in Bayonne. The community maintained an old-age home. A rabbi was engaged to preside over regular community services, led according to the ancient Sephardic ("Portuguese") rites of the old synagogue, which was restored. The old Jewish cemetery, dating back to 1660, continued to be in use. The Basque Museum maintains two rooms with a large display of Jewish religious objects and historic documents relating to the Bayonne Jewish community. René *Cassin, the Nobel Prize winner and president of *Alliance Israélite Universelle, was born in Bayonne in 1887.

[Georges Levitte]

BIBLIOGRAPHY: L.F. de Beaufleury, *Histoire de l'établissement des juifs à Bordeaux et Bayonne* (1799); H. Léon, *Histoire des juifs de Bayonne* (1893); Gross, Gal Jud, 92f.; M. Schwab, in: REJ, 38 (1899), 272–4; Liber, *ibid.*, 64 (1912), 254–61; Genevray, *ibid.*, 74 (1922), 127–47; E. Ginsburger, *Le Comité de surveillance de Jean-Jacques Rousseau* (1934); Szajkowski, in: PAAJR, 24 (1955), 137–64; idem, in: HUCA, 30 (1959), 217–32; *Guide religieux de la France* (1967), 982f. **ADD. BIBLIOGRAPHY:** *Le Guide Culturel des Juifs d'Europe* (2002).

BAYRAMIÇ, town near *Çanakkale in Turkey in an area where many important ancient cities like Skamandros, Skepsis, called *Israillü* in the Ottoman Era, and Kebrene developed. Ottoman rule in this region started in the mid-14th century. Due to Jewish overpopulation in Çanakkale, some Jewish families emigrated to Bayramiç where they established a small quarter composed of 30 households in 1884 and 60 Jews in 1894. By 1910 the number of Jewish households had increased to 50. There were 800 Muslims, 190 Greeks, and 200 Armenians in the district in the 1890s. From time to time there were conflicts, as in the case of a Christian blood libel against the Jews in 1884. During the Gallipoli Campaign, the Jewish population in Bayramiç temporarily increased due to mass flight from the battlefields in Çanakkale. The Jews in Bayramiç had their own cemetery after the Gallipoli Campaign, whereas they had previously buried their dead in Çanakkale. The Jewish community was well organized in the sense that it had a synagogue, *talmud torah*, rabbis, and charitable institutions to provide relief for the needy. Economic activities like exporting cereal and bonito, small-scale manufacturing, and ironmongery were common among the Bayramiç Jews. According to the census of 1927, 93 Jews remained in the district. The Jewish presence in Bayramiç ended in the 1960s.

BIBLIOGRAPHY: *BOA (Başbakanlık Osmanlı Arşivi), TD* 166; *Karasi Vilayet Salnamesi* (H. 1305), 141; V. Cuinet, *La Turquie d'Asie*, 3 (1894), 696, 765; A. Galanté, *Histoire des Juifs d'Anatolie*, 4 (1987), 221–23; J.M. Cook, *Troad: An Archeological and Topographical Study* (1973), 279.

[M. Mustafa Kulu (2nd ed.)]

BAYREUTH, city in Bavaria, Germany, and former principality. Jews lived in the principality of Bayreuth at the beginning of the 13th century and are mentioned in *Meir b. Baruch of Rothenburg's responsa. In 1248 several Jews were admitted into the city of Bayreuth. In the course of the riots accompanying the *Black Death (1348–49) many Jews in the principality were killed. After this, the emperor Charles IV entrusted authority over the Jews of Bayreuth to the margrave. In 1372 the latter appointed a chief rabbi for all his territory, including at that time the communities of Kulmbach and Hof. Until the end of the 15th century the Jews were permitted freedom of movement and the right to bring claims against Christians before a mixed tribunal. In 1409 a charter was granted to the Jews of Neustadt an der Aisch (where 71 Jews had perished in the massacre of 1218) and in 1421 Jewish trade in the principality was regulated. In 1422 the Jews were compelled to renounce all claims against Christians and subsequently left the principality. However, six Jewish families resettled in the "Jewish lane" of the city of Bayreuth in 1441, and the position of the Jewish residents improved. A number of refugees from *Bamberg were admitted into the towns of Pegnitz, Steinach, *Baiersdorf, Erlangen, Neustadt an der Aisch, and Kulm (later called Chlumec in Czechoslovakia), and several *Court Jews were in the margrave's service at Bayreuth. In 1488 the Jews were again made to cancel all the debts owing to them as a condition for setting aside an expulsion order. Nevertheless, they were expelled several times from various parts of the principality during the 16th and 17th centuries, though most of the expulsion orders were short-lived.

Their position began to improve as a result of the influence of the Court Jew, Samson of Baiersdorf. In 1695 the margrave granted concessions and protection to Jewish tradesmen. The seat of the provincial rabbinate was Baiersdorf since Jews had been excluded from the city of Bayreuth from 1515. Further improvements followed after 1735, in the main a reflection of the liberal attitude of Margrave Frederick, who had a Jewish chess player and a Jewish painter at his court. The Jewish population of the principality rose from 135 families in 1709 to 346 families (1,727 persons) in 1771. Ten Jewish families were admitted into the city of Bayreuth in 1759, and there were 65 families (401 persons) resident in the city in 1771. In 1805 there were 2,276 Jews living in the principality, which was incorporated into Bavaria two years later. During the 19th and the beginning of the 20th centuries the number of the Jews declined. In spite of their shrill antisemitism, Richard *Wagner and his circle in Bayreuth did not affect the position of the Jews there. In 1933 the Jewish population of Bayreuth numbered 261 (0.7% of the total).

On Nov. 10, 1938, the synagogue (built in 1760) was ransacked and homes and shops were pillaged by the SA. The populace committed further acts of vandalism the next day, and the cemetery was desecrated beyond recognition. After flight and emigration, just 120 Jews remained in the city at the time. On Nov. 27, 1941, 60 persons were deported to *Riga; on Jan. 12, 1942, the last 11 were transported to Bamberg en route to *Theresienstadt. After World War II a new community was established which numbered 550 in 1949 and had decreased, through emigration, to 40 in 1967. As a result of the immigration of Jews from the former Soviet Union, the number of community members rose to 473 in 2003.

BIBLIOGRAPHY: A. Eckstein, *Geschichte der Juden im Markgrafentum Bayreuth* (1907); FJW (1928–29), 125f.; Germ Jud, 1 (1963), 24; 2 (1968), 60–61; Y.L. Bialer, *Min ha-Genazim*, 2 (1969), 54–58; PK. **ADD. BIBLIOGRAPHY:** E. Huebschmann (ed.), *Physische und behoerdliche Gewalt* (2000).

[Ze'ev Wilhem Falk]

BAY TREE. The *oren*, mentioned only once in the Bible (Isa. 44:14), is identified in the Talmud (RH 23a) with *ara*, the bay tree. It is mentioned in the Mishnah (Par. 3:8) as being among the trees that were used in preparing the fire for the burning of the red heifer. From it (according to one reading) long poles were made for the beacons that were kindled to announce the New Moon (RH 2:3). In Israel it is an important forest-tree that grows extensively on moist mountain slopes. An evergreen, its aromatic leaves are used for seasoning food, and were, according to the Talmud, an ingredient in a cure for intestinal worms (Git. 69b). In modern Hebrew *oren* denotes the pine tree, an identification that is based on the Septuagint, but the pine is the biblical *eẓ shemen*. The translation of *oren* as "ash" (AV) or as "cedar" (RV) is untenable, the latter being the biblical *erez*. In modern Hebrew the bay tree is called *dafnah* or *eẓ aẓil*.

BIBLIOGRAPHY: Loew, Flora, 2 (1924), 119–23; J. Feliks, *Olam ha-Ẓome'aḥ ha-Mikra'i* (1957), 92. **ADD. BIBLIOGRAPHY:** Feliks, Ha-Ẓome'aḥ, 21.

[Jehuda Feliks]

BAYUDAYA, group of adherents of Judaism in Mbale, Uganda. Numbering some 600 people who live in villages a few miles north of Mbale, this group owes its origins to a remarkable Ugandan soldier and traditional leader, Semei Kakungulu. At the beginning of the 20th century Kakungulu emerged as a powerful military leader on the British side against Muslim forces. Rewarded by the colonial authorities with a post as a semi-autonomous administrator in a large area around Mbale in the eastern part of the country, he decided to follow biblical teaching and become circumcised. In 1920 he declared of himself and his followers: "We shall be known as the Jews," and in 1922 published a book which was essentially a guide to Judaism. His followers in Mbale have maintained their Jewish practices (despite persecution at the time of Idi Amin). Orthodox conversions carried out in 2001 and 2002 have transformed the community into a substantially Orthodox community with links with western Jewry and Israel.

BIBLIOGRAPHY: M.Twaddle, *Kakungulu and the Creation of Uganda* (1993); A. Oded, "The Bayudaya of Uganda:a Portrait of an African Jewish Community," in: *Journal of Religion in Africa*, 6 (1974); T. Parfitt, *The Lost Tribes of Israel: The History of a Myth* (2002).

[Tudor Parfitt (2nd ed.)]

BAZA (Arabic **Basta**), town N.E. of Granada in S.E. Spain. Baza was annexed to Granada after Almeria's defeat by the army under *Samuel b. Joseph ha-Nagid's command (c. 1039). In the 11th century there was a Jewish community in Baza whose residents were employed mostly in the silk industry. The Jewish quarter was located opposite the present-day cathedral of Santiago. A *mikveh* with three bath chambers has been uncovered and is a good example of 11th-century Arabic bathhouse architecture.

BIBLIOGRAPHY: EI, 1 (1960²), S.V. *Basta*; M. Gómez-Moreno, in: *Al Andalus*, 12 (1947), 151–5; Ashtor, Korot, 2 (1966), 92–93.

BAZELON, DAVID L. (1909–1993), U.S. judge. Bazelon was born in Superior, Wisconsin, and was educated in Chicago. Admitted to the Illinois bar in 1932, he practiced law until 1949. In 1946 Bazelon was appointed an assistant attorney general of the U.S., and in 1949 President Truman appointed him judge of the U.S. Court of Appeals for the District of Columbia Circuit, often described as the country's most influential court next to the Supreme Court. At 40, he was the youngest judge ever appointed to that court. From 1962 to 1978 he served as chief judge, retiring in 1986 as a senior judge. From 1960 he was a member of the board of trustees of the Jewish Publication Society of America. In 1987 Bazelon's book *Questioning Authority* was published.

An authority on the relationship between law and psychiatry, Bazelon held several university lectureships, and in 1962 was elected honorary fellow of the American Psychiatric Association. As a member of the National Institutes of Health Advisory Commission, he was one of the key architects of early guidelines for genetic engineering. He expressed his particular interest in psychiatry related to the law as a lecturer in law and psychiatry at Johns Hopkins University, the University of Pennsylvania, and the Menninger Clinic. He was an active member of the American Orthopsychiatric Association, serving as its president from 1967 to 1970, and was the only non-psychiatrist included in the first U.S. Mission on Mental Health to the U.S.S.R. in 1967.

Rather than follow precedent set in a simpler time, Bazelon questioned the status quo and sought to apply new findings in the social sciences and psychiatry to issues the court faced. One of his landmark opinions from the appellate bench established the right of a mental patient to appropriate treatment in the least restrictive alternative setting.

At the forefront of the new legal advocacy was the Mental Health Law Project, formed by some of the lawyers and mental health professionals who worked on early cases. In 1993 MHLP celebrated its 20th anniversary by rededicating its mission to Bazelon and renaming itself in his honor. The Judge David L. Bazelon Center for Mental Health Law is a legal advocate for people with mental disabilities. Its precedent-setting litigation has outlawed institutional abuse and won protections against arbitrary confinement. For its clientele, the center's advocacy has opened up public schools, workplaces, housing, and other opportunities for community life.

[Ruth Beloff (2nd ed.)]

BDELLIUM (Heb. בְּדֹלַח) twice mentioned in the Scriptures, once in the description of the land of Havilah, which contained "gold, bdellium, and onyx stone" (Gen. 2:12), and again in the description of the manna, "its appearance was as the appearance of bdellium" (Num. 11:7). In both passages the Septuagint understands it as the name of some precious stone, as do Rashi, who interprets it as "a precious stone, crystal" and Saadiah Gaon, as "pearls." The Midrash gives two opinions. According to one, it is a precious stone, and according to the other the reference is to "the *bedolaḥ* of perfumers." In Genesis the Midrash decides in favor of the first interpretation because there it is associated with gold and onyx (Gen. R., 16:2). Josephus (Ant. 3:28) explains that "the manna resembled the spice bdellium." The reference is presumably to the sweet-smelling sap called in Greek βδέλλιον and in Latin *bdellium*, a semi-transparent resin extracted from trees of the genus *Commiphora*. According to Pliny (*Historia Naturalis*, 12:36) the best variety is Bactrian bdellium from Baluchistan, which is similar to that obtained from Nubia. In effect the sap of both the Bactrian, *Commiphora roxburgii*, and the Nubian, *Commiphora africana*, were used as incense. The former variety is known among Arabs as *mokul*, a name they also give to the resin issuing from the tree *Hyphaene thebaica*, a species of palm with a branching trunk that grows in the Arabah (at the approach to Elath), and in Sinai. The Arabs call it "Jewish bdellium." It is apparently this species that is referred to by Dioscorides as "the bdellium imported from Petra" (*De Materia Medica*, 1:80).

BIBLIOGRAPHY: Loew, Flora, 1 (1928), 304f.; J. Feliks, *Olam ha-Ẓome'aḥ ha-Mikra'i* (1968²), 259.

[Jehuda Feliks]

°BEA, AUGUSTIN (1881–1968), Catholic prelate. Born in Baden, Germany, Bea joined the Jesuit Order and had a distinguished ecclesiastical and scholarly career. From 1930 to 1949 he was rector of the Pontifical Biblical Institute in Rome, and editor of the periodical *Biblica* from 1930 to 1951. During World War II, he served as confessor to Pope Pius XII. He was created cardinal by Pope John XXIII in 1959. Pope John had already begun preparing for an ecumenical council to meet at the Vatican, and he appointed Bea head of the Secretariat for the Promotion of Christian Unity. Among his tasks was the preparation of a statement on the relation of the Catholic Church to non-Christian religions, including Judaism. The declaration, submitted to the Council's second session, met with considerable opposition on political and religiously conservative grounds. Bea accepted some changes, but continued to work for a forceful draft, which he submitted at the Council's third session in 1964. It was again deferred, over the protest of the large liberal element among the churchmen present. At the fourth session in November 1965, the statement, though weaker than Bea and other liberals had hoped for, was adopted by an overwhelming vote. Placed now in the context of friendly declarations on the church's attitude toward Islam and other religions, that on the Jews made two important points: that Jews of today should not be burdened with the guilt of the crucifixion of Jesus, and that the church "decried" antisemitism and hostility in any form. It further expressed the hope that friendly dialogue between Christians and Jews would in time eradicate all hostility. After the council's adjournment, Cardinal Bea wrote *The Church and the Jewish People* (1966), explaining the declaration and emphasizing its favorable aspects.

[Solomon Grayzel]

BEAME, ABRAHAM DAVID (1906–2001), first Jewish mayor of New York (but see *Lewis, Samuel). Beame was born in London, but was brought to New York by his parents before he was a year old. He grew up on the Lower East Side and graduated from the City College of New York in 1928. He practiced accounting during 1928–46, becoming a Certified Public Accountant in 1930, and from 1929 taught accounting and commercial law at Rutgers University. In 1946 he was appointed assistant budget director of the City of New York, and director in 1952, serving as a member of many city and state committees and commissions dealing with management, social services, the courts, city employees, the state constitution, and intergovernmental fiscal relationships.

In 1962, and again in 1969, Beame was elected comptroller and in 1965 won the mayoral nomination of the Democratic Party in a primary election. In 1967 he was a delegate to the New York State Constitutional Convention. In November 1973, at age 67, Beame defeated State Senator John Marchi and won the election for mayor of New York by a landslide victory, which included 63% of the Jewish vote and 68% of the black vote. He assumed office on January 1, 1974, as the 104th mayor of New York.

During his term of office, the city endured such crises as terrorist bombings, a citywide power failure that resulted in violence and looting, and the Son of Sam serial killings. At the same time, Beame faced the worst fiscal crisis in the city's history and spent most of his term trying to ward off bankruptcy. He slashed the city workforce, froze wages, and restructured the budget, which proved insufficient until reinforced by actions from newly created state-sponsored entities and the granting of federal funds. After a tumultuous four years as mayor, he ran for a second term in 1977 but was succeeded in 1978 by Edward *Koch, also a Jew. Despite criticism about his methods, Beame left office with a $200 million surplus for the city, having entered the mayoralty facing a $1.5 billion deficit.

Beame retired from politics but remained active as head of the Advisory Board of the UMB Bank and Trust, and later senior advisor of Sterling National Bank. He also served on the board of directors of a number of civic and corporate foundations.

BIBLIOGRAPHY: Chris McNickle, *To Be Mayor of New York* (1993).

[Ruth Beloff (2nd ed.)]

BEANS. Ancient Jewish sources refer to several species of beans under the Hebrew name of *pol* qualified by various epithets. *Pol* itself is the broad bean (*Vicia faba*) which was included in the food brought to David's forces by his loyal supporters from Ammon and Gilead (II Sam. 17:28). Its flour was added to the bread that Ezekiel was commanded to eat to symbolize the approaching destruction of Jerusalem (Ezek. 4:9). In mishnaic and talmudic times the broad bean was widely grown, being a cheap food popular especially among the poor (Tosef., BM 3:9; Sof. 21:4) and eaten with or without the husk. Another important plant was the *pol ha-miẓri* which, identified with the cowpea (*Vigna sinensis*), is a creeper which grows in summer. In mishnaic times it was highly regarded as a food for human consumption (Ned. 7:1; Shev. 2:8–9) but is now grown as fodder. To the botanical genus *Vigna* belongs another plant called *pol he-ḥaruv* which is the legume known as the yard-long bean (*Vigna sesquipedalis*), its Hebrew name being derived, according to the Jerusalem Talmud (Kil. 1:2, 27a), from the shape of its pods, which resembles that of the carob (*ḥaruv*). Another variety of the cowpea is called *she'u'it* (Kil. 1:1); this is the legume *Vigna nilotica*, which grows wild in Israel climbing river banks, or is sown as fodder. The Mishnah (*ibid.*) states that it is not a *mixed species (*kilayim*) with *pol ha-lavan*, the hyacinth bean (*Dolichos lablab*), the seed of which is used as food.

BIBLIOGRAPHY: Loew, *Flora* 12 (1924), 492f.; J. Feliks, *Olam ha-Ẓome'aḥ ha-Mikra'i* (1957), 156–8, 318; idem, *Kilei Zera'im* (1967), 41–43.

[Jehuda Feliks]

BEAR (Heb. דֹּב; *dov*). In ancient times the Syrian brown bear, *Ursus arctos syriacus*, had its habitat within the borders of Ereẓ Israel; it was found in the forests of Lebanon until World War I and is still occasionally reported in Lebanon and northern Syria. The bear is omnivorous, and when driven by hunger, it preys on large animals, including the ox or cow (cf. Isa. 11:7). In the Bible the bear is portrayed as an animal dangerous to man, like the lion. Especially emphasized is the danger of a (female) bear bereaved of its cubs (II Sam. 17:8; Hos. 13:8). This was a frequent occurrence as the cubs were taken from the dam to be trained. The bear was common in the period of the Mishnah, which forbids their sale to Gentiles (Av. Zar. 16a). One of the miracles ascribed to R. *Ḥanina b. Dosa was that after being attacked by bears, each of his goats came home with a bear on its horns (Ta'an. 25a). Because the second world kingdom of Daniel 7 was identified as the Persian one, the fact that it is represented by a bear (Dan. 7:5) is explained by the observation that the Persians "eat and drink like the bear, are fat like the bear, are hairy like the bear, and are restless like the bear" (Kid. 72a).

BIBLIOGRAPHY: Lewysohn, Zool, 99; Tristram, Nat Hist, 40–49; F.S. Bodenheimer, *Ha-Ḥai be-Arẓot ha-Mikra*, 2 (1956), index; J. Feliks, *Animal World of the Bible* (1962), 39. **ADD. BIBLIOGRAPHY:** Feliks, Ha-Ẓome'aḥ, 220.

[Jehuda Feliks]

BEARD AND SHAVING. The characteristic manner in which the beard and hair were shaved, cut, curled, or groomed identified specific peoples in the ancient world. Egyptian, Assyrian, and Babylonian monuments depict the unique way various peoples treated facial hair, thereby illustrating their ethnic identity. The Semites appear with thick beards or with thin and groomed beards; the Lybians are shown with pointed beards, while the Hittites, Ethiopians, and Sea Peoples are portrayed as clean-shaven. The Babylonians and Persians are represented with curly and groomed beards, and the majority of the images of Egyptian males reveal clean-shaven faces, with the exception of a number of pharaohs who appear with plaited beards extending from the chin only. Shaving was performed either by the individual himself or by a barber (Heb.

galav) who also attended to bodily ailments in a quasi-medical fashion. Razors were made entirely from metal or from flint blades fixed in a stone handle. Shaving was also connected with cosmetic treatment of the face (see *Cosmetics). According to Leviticus 19:27 and 21:5 in an apparent reference to the hair between the head and the cheeks (sidelocks) it is forbidden to destroy the "corners" of the beard. It is difficult to determine the reason for the ban, but it is possible that it was promulgated in order to differentiate Israelites from other peoples. Another possible explanation is that shaving specific areas of the face was associated with pagan cults or symbolized those who ministered to their gods and just as the Bible opposes imitation of pagan practices so it opposes this form of ritual shaving. In the Bible shaving of the head and beard is considered a sign of *mourning (e.g., Job 1:20) and degradation. Shaving was identified with the spontaneous plucking of the beard, an expression of great sorrow (Ezek. 5:1ff.). To humiliate a man, it was the practice to forcibly shave half of the beard as in II Samuel 10:4, where the elders, because of this humiliation, were commanded to hide in Jericho until their beards grew again. Shaving is also part of rituals of purification (Lev. 14:8; Num. 6:9; 8:7). Priests were forbidden to shave the "edges" of their beards (Lev. 21:5), and "the priests, the Levites, the sons of Zadok" (Ezek. 44:15) were allowed neither to shave their heads nor let their locks grow long, but only to trim their hair (*ibid.* 44:20).

[Ze'ev Yeivin]

In Talmudic Times

The Talmud regards the beard as "the adornment of a man's face" (BM 84a); a man without a beard was compared to a eunuch (Yev. 80b; Shab. 152a). Young priests whose beards had not yet grown were not permitted to bless the people (TJ, Suk. 3:14, 54a). *Sennacherib was punished by God by having his beard shaved off (Sanh. 95b–96a). Rabbinic authorities permitted only those who had frequent dealings with the Roman authorities to clip their beard with forceps (*kom*; BK 83a). Objection to the removal of the beard was on the ground that God gave it to man to distinguish him from woman; to shave it, was therefore an offense against nature (see Abrabanel to Lev. 19:27).

In the Middle Ages

Jews living in Islamic countries cultivated long beards whereas those in Christian Europe clipped them with scissors. This was permitted by *halakhah* (Sh. Ar., YD 181:10). Rabbinical courts punished adulterers by cutting off their beards (C.M. Horowitz, *Toratan shel Rishonim*, 1 (1881), 29; 2 (1881), 18). The post of *ḥazzan* was only bestowed upon a man with a beard (*Baḥ*, OH 53). Kabbalists ascribed mystical powers to the beard (and hair). Isaac *Luria refrained from touching his, lest he should cause any hairs to fall out (*Ba'er Hetev*, YD 181:5). With the spread of kabbalism to Eastern Europe, trimming the beard was gradually prohibited by leading rabbinic authorities (*Noda bi-Yhudah, Mahadura Tinyana*, YD 80) and with the rise of Ḥasidism, the removal of the beard became tantamount to a formal break with Jewish tradition. Nevertheless, from a strictly traditional point of view, shaving was permitted as long as it was done in a certain fashion. *Halakhah* forbids only the shaving proper of the beard; this is defined as the act of removing the hair with an instrument with one cutting edge. Chemical means (depilatory powder), scissors, or an electric shaver with two cutting edges, are permitted. Although it is customary not to use a single-edge razor to shave any part of the beard, the strict letter of the law forbids its use only for five parts of the face. Considerable difference of opinion among the rabbis as to the exact location of these five places had led to the practice of not using a single edge at all. In Western Europe and especially among Sephardi Jews, rabbinic authorities (S.D. *Luzzatto among others), consented both to the trimming of the beard and even of its entire removal by chemical agents. This became the accepted custom (from the second half of the 17th century). The question of cutting and shaving the beard on *ḥol ha-mo'ed*, prohibited by the Talmud (MK 3:1), was a matter of much controversy at the turn of the 19th century. R. Isaac Samuel *Reggio tried to prove that this talmudic injunction no longer applied because of changed circumstances (*Ma'amar ha-Tiglaḥat*, 1835) but the traditional opinion of the Shulḥan Arukh (OḤ 531) prevails among strictly observant Jews, who also refrain from cutting their beard (and from shaving) during the *Omer period (*Sefirah*) and the *Three Weeks (see also *Mourning Customs). To trim the beard (and have a haircut) in honor of the Sabbath and the festivals is regarded as a pious duty. Several rulers (e.g., Nicholas I of Russia) tried to force the Jewish population to cut off their beards and earlocks; others (e.g., Maria Theresa of Austria) ordered Jews to have beards so as to be easily singled out as a foreign element by their Christian neighbors.

BIBLIOGRAPHY: BIBLE: G.A. Reisner, *Mycerinus* (1931), pl. 45d; A.J. Tobler, *Excavations at Tepe Gawra*, 2 (1950), pl. 176, fig. 18; University of Pennsylvania Museum, *Buhen* (1911), pl. 64, no. 10313; E. Lefébure, *Le tombeau de Seti ler*, 2 (1886), pls. 4, 5; P.E. Newberry, *Beni Hassan*, 1 (1893), pls. 28, 30, 31; Chicago Oriental Institute, *The Epigraphic Survey; Medinet Habu*, 2 (1932), pl. 125A; E.F. Schmidt, *Persepolis I* (1953), plates 31B, 32B. POST-BIBLICAL: Benzinger, Archeologie, 94, 134, 351; J. Wellhausen, *Reste arabischen Heidentums* (1897^2), 195–200; ET, 11 (1965), 118–28; W. Mueller (ed.), *Urkundliche Beitraege... der maehrischen Judenschaft* (1903), 68–72; I. Abrahams, *Jewish Life in the Middle Ages* (1932).

BEARSTED, MARCUS SAMUEL, FIRST VISCOUNT (1853–1927), founder of the Shell Oil Company. Marcus Samuel was educated at Jewish schools in London and Brussels before joining the firm established by his father Marcus Samuel, who had prospered in the Far Eastern trade, principally from selling fancy shells and ornamental shell boxes. In 1878, the younger Marcus Samuel formed his own business partnership with his brother Sam (1855–1934), who later sat as a member of parliament for 20 years. Marcus Samuel successfully traded in the Orient, particularly Japan. Subsequently he became London banker to the Japanese government. Samuel entered the oil trade in 1892, built a fleet of tankers, and founded the Shell

Transport and Trading Company in 1897. His neglect of his business during his year as lord mayor (1902–03) resulted in Shell's amalgamation with the Royal Dutch Petroleum Company on what seemed disadvantageous terms, but he proved indispensable to the new organization. This move served Britain well in World War I. Another momentous war service was the supply of toluol, an essential ingredient in explosives. Marcus Samuel made generous donations to both Jewish and non-Jewish charities. The Bearsted Memorial Hospital, a maternity hospital in London, bears his name and was financed by him. Samuel was lord mayor of London in 1902–03, the fifth Jew to hold this office. In 1921, he was made baron, and in 1925, Viscount Bearsted. Although holding no important Jewish communal offices, Samuel used his influence to help persecuted Jews. While lord mayor of London he refused, in the face of opposition, to invite the Romanian ambassador to the lord mayor's banquet as a protest against Romania's treatment of its Jewish citizens. His brother Samuel Samuel was the founder of M. Samuel, a prominent City of London merchant bank.

His son WALTER HORACE SAMUEL, SECOND VISCOUNT BEARSTED (1882–1948) succeeded his father as chairman of Shell in 1920. A notable art collector, he was chairman of the trustees of the National Gallery in London. He also held various Jewish communal offices. The third viscount MARCUS RICHARD SAMUEL (1909–86) was chairman of the Bearsted Memorial Hospital and president of the Jewish Home and Hospital.

BIBLIOGRAPHY: R. Henriques, *Marcus Samuel, First Viscount Bearstead...* (1960); *Times* (Nov. 10, 1948); JC (Jan. 21, 1927 and Nov. 12, 1948). **ADD. BIBLIOGRAPHY:** ODNB online; DBB, V, 43–46.

[Vivian David Lipman]

BEATITUDE (Heb. הַצְלָחָה, *hazlaḥah*; *osher*), the blissful state of the soul in the World-to-Come (*Olam ha-Ba) that constitutes the ultimate end of human life. Medieval Jewish philosophy fused rabbinic religious ethics and eschatology with the teleological and rationalist conception of happiness (*eudaimonia*) as analyzed by Aristotle in the *Nicomachean Ethics*, thus investing them with new shades of meaning that were conceptual rather than pictorial. Within a rationalist teleological framework, Jewish philosophers maintained that the attainment of religious perfection requires the acquisition of moral and intellectual virtues through the study of philosophy, culminating in the knowledge of God or even in a mystical union of the rational soul, or intellect, with God. Within this broad framework, the interpretation of beatitude varied over time, reflecting changing anthropological schemas within Jewish philosophy, the interplay of Jewish philosophy with Islamic and Christian cultures, the rivalry between Judaism and the monotheistic religions concerning individual salvation, and the internal Jewish debate between rationalists and traditionalists about the ideal life for Jews. Jewish reflections on beatitude were part of the larger discourse on happiness in premodern Judaism.

*Saadiah Gaon, an exponent of the Jewish *Kalam school, was the first Jewish philosopher to reflect systematically about the ultimate end of human life and to articulate a philosophical anthropology as the basis for Jewish ethics. According to Saadiah human beings are a temporary combination of two substances – body and soul. Both are created by God and both are united by Him. The substance of the soul is refined, "comparable in purity to that of the heavenly sphere [and] like the latter, it attains luminosity as a result of the light which it receives from God" (*Beliefs and Opinions*, 242). After analyzing what people commonly consider the good life for humans, Saadiah shows that no social good can be pursued for its own sake and that the ultimate end of human life is intellectual – knowledge and devotion to God. Although the two substances, body and soul, separate at death and the soul of the righteous person continues to live on as an immortal substance, at the end of time, as a result of divine intervention, the individual soul will be recombined with its corresponding body. Saadiah interprets the rabbinic statement, "In the world to come... the righteous will sit with their crowns on their heads and enjoy the splendor of the *Shekhinah*" (Ber. 17a) to mean that life in the hereafter consists in the enjoyment of a specially created luminous substance which sustains the righteous and burns the sinners (*Beliefs and Opinions*, 9:4–5).

In Jewish neoplatonic philosophy, however, a different philosophical anthropology prevailed. Here the bliss of the World-to-Come is understood as the climax of the soul's ascent from its entanglement in matter to union with the supernal world. Isaac *Israeli was the first to link traditional Jewish eschatology with neoplatonic mysticism. Holding that the soul in its ascent passes through three stages, purification, illumination, and union with the supernal light, Israeli identifies the bliss experienced in the afterlife with the last of these stages. However, this union can already be achieved in this world, provided that man withdraws from the influence of the flesh and of the lower souls. The union achieved by the soul at its highest stage is not union with God (though Israeli speaks of the soul's being attached to God), but with "wisdom" which, together with "first matter," occupies a place just below God in Israeli's metaphysical scheme. Israeli identifies the soul's final stage with the religious notion of "Paradise" (*Book of Definitions*, in A. Altmann and S.M. Stern (eds.), *Isaac Israeli* (1958), 25–26). By contrast with his spiritual concept of human blessedness, he provides a more physical account of punishment in the hereafter. The soul of the sinner will be sad, in pain, tortured by fire (*ibid.*, 26–27). Some prominent features of Israeli's eschatology occur also in Joseph Ibn *Ẓaddik's *Olam Katan*.

In the 11th century, both Solomon ibn *Gabirol and *Baḥya ibn Paquda followed essentially the same pattern of neoplatonic thought, although they represent different social programs. Ibn Gabirol was a product of the Jewish courtier class and its commitment to the *adab* culture, whereas Bahya ibn Paquda was a jurist and a critic of a superficial adaptation of the *adab* culture by Jews who only cared about social advancement and worldly success. Ibn Gabirol saw the goal of the existence of man in the "attachment" of his soul to the supernal world that is the "return of like to like." This goal is to be reached by "knowledge," i.e., the contemplative life of the intellect, and by "work," i.e., the practice of the ethical virtues. The former is the exercise of intellectual virtues, whereas the latter pertains to the acquisition of moral virtues, which are linked to parts of the body. Ibn Gabirol explained the precise connection between specific moral traits and human physiology in his *Islah al-Akhlaq* translated into Hebrew as *Tikkun Middot ha-Nefesh* ("The Improvement of Moral Qualities"). This was a manual for the cultivation of proper character traits composed for the sake of the Jewish *adib* and reflecting the commitment of Jews to the social ideals of *adab* culture. Together moral and intellectual perfections free the soul from the captivity of nature, and purify it from its turbidity and darkness (*Mekor Ḥayyim*, 1:2). Ibn Gabirol holds that "knowledge" leads to "works," which, in turn, enable the soul to rise to the contemplation of the spiritual world. The highest level of contemplation consists in the ecstatic vision of the "first universal matter" in which all supernal forms are contained (3:56–58). There is, however, a still higher goal to be attained. Beyond universal matter (and universal form) there exists, in Ibn Gabirol's ontological scheme, the "will" of God and, in the final passage of his *Mekor Ḥayyim*, he speaks of a progress of knowledge leading to a knowledge of the "will." Holding that a still higher stage may be achieved, Ibn Gabirol calls for an ascent to the "will's" beginning and source, i.e., God. The fruit of this effort is freedom from death and man's "attachment" to the "fountain of life" (*mekor ḥayyim*), i.e., communion with God. Beatitude in the hereafter is, in Ibn Gabirol's view, not a mere continuation of the bliss of the contemplative life, but a gift of God (5:43, end).

With Ibn Gabirol, Baḥya shares the new intellectualist piety characteristic of Jewish philosophy in Muslim Spain. He too sees the upward way as the "road to felicity" (*Ḥovot ha-Levavot*, 1:7), passing through the stages of purification, illumination, and the vision of the "supernal and exalted forms" (8:4). He identifies the love of God with the soul's longing for union with the supernal light, i.e., supernal wisdom (10:1), holding that it arises from the purifying effects of the ascetic life (10:11) and from the scrutiny of the soul (10:8). According to Baḥya, man is an "exile" in this world (8:3), and the "bliss of the next world" should be his most cherished goal (4:4, end). The reward promised for the hereafter is said to consist in the "utmost distinction [conferred on man] by God" and in the "approximation to the supernal light" (4:4). This definition combines the notion of reward as a gift from God with the neoplatonic concept of illumination and union as a result of the soul's ascent. *Judah Halevi, another member of the courtier class in Muslim Spain who was critical of some of its tendencies, even though he absorbed the neoplatonic schema, teaches that the bliss of the World-to-Come is essentially identical with the supreme stage attainable in this world. This stage is conceived in neoplatonic terms as an "attachment" to the "supernal world" and to the "divine light" (*Kuzari*, 1:103; 3:20), and is more sharply defined as a suprarational prophetic stage. In Halevi's view the life of piety is essentially of the same order as the prophetic stage of illumination and communion with God. Accordingly, the pious man can achieve the bliss of attachment to God already in this world.

Discussions of beatitude became more sophisticated in Jewish Aristotelianism, but also more problematic from Jewish traditional perspective. While Jewish Aristotelians interpreted beatitude solely as a cognitive state in which the human intellect conjoins with the incorporeal intelligence, they disagreed on whether immortality is individual or collective, reflecting thereby a difference of opinion which also existed among Islamic philosophers. Among the Muslims, *al-Farabi (in his earlier works) and *Avicenna affirmed that the individual human intellect becomes immortal once it has achieved the stage of the "acquired intellect" (see *Intellect), while *Avempace and *Averroes held that in the afterlife there exists one intellect for all men, denying thereby that anything individual remains after death. Closely related to the question of immortality was that of man's "ultimate felicity," a state which Aristotelians generally identified with the "conjunction" of man's "acquired intellect" with the "agent intellect," or sometimes even with God. Reflecting the differences of opinion concerning immortality, those affirming that immortality was individual allowed for "ultimate felicity" in this world and the next, while the proponents of collective immortality held that "ultimate felicity" was possible only in this world.

The position of *Maimonides concerning immortality cannot be easily determined. In his *Guide of the Perplexed* (1:74, the seventh method), the discussion implies that he inclines to Avempace's doctrine of the unity of souls in the hereafter, which amounts to the denial of individual immortality. By contrast, he speaks of the "acquired intellect" as "separate from the organic body" (1:72), and sharply distinguishes the potential intellect with which man is born, and which is a "mere disposition," from the actual intellect, which remains after death, thus implying that immortality is individual (1:70; see also 1:41). Moreover, the whole tenor of his description of the state of man's attachment to God (3:51) points in the direction of an individual afterlife. Concerning beatitude, Maimonides holds that "ultimate felicity" is possible in this world, as well as in the next. While still in his bodily state a human being may achieve the state of continually being with God (whereby Maimonides seems to refer to "conjunction" with the agent intellect), by means of the intellectual worship of Him. Among humans, Moses achieved this state in the most excellent manner, but approximating this intellectual perfection is, in principle, also possible for others. This stage of ultimate felicity is continued in the afterlife. Maimonides' endeavor to impress his readers with the spiritual character of the bliss of the afterlife is particularly pronounced in his discussion in his commentary on the Mishnah (introd. to Sanh., *perek Ḥelek*), and reappears in his *Mishneh Torah* (*hilkhot Teshuvah*, ch. 8). Maimonides interprets the meaning of the previously cited rabbinic dictum: "In the world to come there is no eating, no drinking, no bathing, no anointing, no sexual intercourse; but the righteous sit with crowns upon their heads and enjoy the splendor of the *Shekhinah*" in the following manner: "'crowns upon their heads' means the survival of the soul by virtue of the survival of knowledge, the two being one and the same thing; 'enjoying the splendor of the *Shekhinah*' means taking delight in the intellection of the Creator, even as the holy *ḥayyot* and the other angelic orders delight in their comprehension of His existence." Maimonides, it should be noted, distinguished between the World-to-Come, which is an incorporeal state, and Paradise, which is a place here on earth. The treatise known as *Perakim be-Hazlaḥah* ("Chapters on Beatitude") has been wrongly ascribed to Maimonides, but it expresses views similar to his. Affirming that felicity is possible in this world and the next, the treatise distinguishes between the ecstatic experience of prophecy and the ultimate felicity of the soul's union with God in the next world. Prophecy is described as the stage of human perfection at which the rational soul, like a polished mirror, reflects the light of the supernal world. At this stage one is happy, though one's joy is tempered with the fear of God. Prophecy can be reached only after a search for wisdom and after subjecting the senses to a rigorous discipline. Imagination functions at this level under the complete control of the intellect (cf. Maimonides' letter in *Kovez Teshuvot ha-Rambam*, 2:39b, where the same motif is quoted in the name of Abraham Ibn Ezra's commentary on Ex. 23:20). The ultimate felicity, on the other hand, is the reward which all righteous may expect in the next world according to the measure of their worthiness. The author adds that this view of the afterlife is in agreement with the views of the philosophers, whereby he seems to refer to al-Farabi (in his earlier works) and Avicenna. The author assures his reader that every man can rise to a rank close to Moses' (for which there is a parallel in Guide, 3:51), and, echoing neoplatonic traditions, he states that ultimate felicity consists in the union with God following the purification of the soul and its illumination by the supernal light.

The meaning of beatitude and its implication for Jewish culture became a hotly debated issue, constituting the so-called Maimonidean Controversy of the 13th century. Its first phase (1202–4) concerned the fate of the human soul after death and the resurrection of the body; the second phase (1232–35) was about the composition of Jewish education; the third phase (c. 1290) pertained to the allegorical interpretation of the Torah; and the fourth (1303–5) to the validity of astrology, the discipline that most captured scientific naturalism, in traditional Jewish society. All of these debates were aspects of a larger question: what is the necessary and sufficient knowledge for the attainment of the ultimate end of human life defined as beatitude? The debates were exceptionally acrimonious because what was at stake was the salvation of the individual soul, a topic hotly debated not only among Jews but also between Judaism and Christianity. As Jewish rationalism spread in Spain, Provençe, and Italy during the 13th century, Jewish philosophers differentiated between two orders of felicity: one in this world and one of a still higher degree in the hereafter. This distinction is found in Shem Tov ibn *Falaquera's *Sefer ha-Ma'alot* (ed. L. Venetianer (1894), 15–19), where the "true happiness of the soul at its ultimate perfection" is said to lead to the eternal life. Invoking the notion of a twofold felicity, *Hillel b. Samuel in his *Tagmulei ha-Nefesh* (Lyck, 1874) states that humans, through the perfection of the moral and intellectual virtues, may achieve a rank even higher than that of the angels, but the beatific vision becomes possible only after death. The perfected human is then illumined by the "eternal light," rises from rank to rank, and at the end is granted the vision of God. This state, in Hillel's view, is the meaning of Paradise (*ibid.*, 23a–24a). Hillel's analysis of ultimate felicity manifests a familiarity with and influence of Christian scholastic discourse, especially of Thomas *Aquinas.

Jewish philosophers who accepted *Averroes' epistemology either openly or implicitly denied the validity of the belief in individual immortality. Thus, for example, Samuel ibn Tibbon appears to subscribe to Averroes' doctrine of the unity of souls, when in his *Ma'amar Yikkavu ha-Mayim* (ed. M. Bisliches, Pressburg, 1837) he says of the soul which has become perfect and separate from matter at death that it conjoins with the agent intellect, and that "they become one single thing, for now the soul becomes divine, of a superior and immortal order, like the agent intellect with which it is united" (p. 91). It may be assumed, especially in the light of his commentary on Ecclesiastes, that Ibn Tibbon speaks here of a "total fusion" which leaves no room for individual survival (see G. Vajda, *Recherches sur la philosophie et la Kabbale* (1962), 27 n. 3). *Levi b. Gershom, on the other hand, upheld the notion of individual immortality and of individual degrees of bliss in the hereafter. In his *Milḥamot Adonai* (1:13) he says that the "degrees of the happy ones" vary greatly according to the degree of unity achieved by the acquired intellect in its conception of the intelligibles. The degree of bliss in the hereafter – identified by him with Paradise – depends on the degree and type of knowledge achieved while on earth.

Traditionalist Reaction

The pronounced intellectualism of the philosophers' concept of beatitude provoked a great deal of indignant protest from the traditionalists who regarded the life of piety rather than intellectual pursuits as the gateway to eternal felicity. The kabbalist Jacob b. Sheshet *Gerondi (in his *Meshiv Devarim Nekhoḥim*; see Vajda, op. cit., 110–1) attacked Samuel ibn Tibbon's interpretation of the ladder in Jacob's dream as an allegory of man's intellectual progress. The Zohar was profoundly concerned with ultimate felicity and could be viewed as a dramatization of an ethical theory about the intrinsically good life as well as an implicit polemic against the systematic discourses of the rational philosophers. For the Zohar the Torah itself is considered as the source of the well-lived life in this world and the blissful life of the World-to-Come. Unlike the philosophers, for whom cognizing intelligibles culled from the observation of nature leads to enlightenment, for the Zohar, enlightenment comes only from fathoming those mysteries of the Torah that pertain to the inner life of the Godhead. The kabbalists, who possess this esoteric knowledge, are able to fathom the inner meaning of each and every mitzvah and perform it correctly, thereby producing holiness in the performer and in the world and even increasing the holiness of the Godhead, by bringing about the re-union of the masculine and feminine aspect of God. The ultimate end of the pursuit of religious perfection is thus the perfection of God. According to Zoharic anthropology the very fact of the afterlife is not a theoretical problem because the soul is an individuated entity even before its association with the particular body. When the body dies, the individual soul survives the event; its very existence as a separate substance does not depend on the body itself. The career of the soul after the death of the body depends on the balance between the merits and sins that one has accrued throughout life. If one lived a holy life, the soul returns to her divine source.

During the 14th century the path toward beatitude became the focal point of the Jewish-Christian polemics, when learned rabbinic Jews such as *Abner of Burgos, converted to Christianity and debated with their former coreligionists. Abner challenged his conversation partner, Isaac *Polleqar, to differentiate between faith and rational knowledge and argued that the highest expression of faith is the love of God but that love is not commensurate with the degree of intellectual perfection. Abner's position influenced Ḥasdai *Crescas, who was the main critic of the philosophic conception of beatitude. In his *Or Adonai* (3:3), he rejected the theory that the soul achieves its immortality only through the process of knowledge. The degrees of bliss in the hereafter correspond to the degrees of love of God and attachment to him. Crescas replaced the Maimonidean view of ultimate felicity with a non-intellectualist interpretation of human love that focused on the willingness of the individual to be committed to God. For Crescas ultimate felicity consists of a kind of life that is commensurate with the nature of the soul as in incorporeal substance; the happiness of the soul is predicated not on cognitive activity but on the ability of the will to freely choose the good. Human love for God is reflected not in the contemplation of intelligibles but in the actual performance of the commandments. The anti-intellectualist attitude gained ground in the last phase of Jewish life in Spain.

During the 15th and 16th centuries, philosophic reflections on beatitude changed in response to traumatic events in Jewish history: the persecutions and mass conversion of Jews in Spain in 1391 and the expulsions from Spain (1492) and Portugal (1497), growing Jewish familiarity with Christian scholasticism and Renaissance humanism, and increasing blending of rationalist philosophy and Kabbalah. In Italy the typical example of this intellectual syncretism was Johanan Alemanno, for whom the final end of human life was a mystical union with God's attributes, the *Sefirot*, or more particularly with the central sefirah, *Tiferet* ("Beauty"). Alemanno understood the mystical union with God in accord with his spiritual mentor, Abraham *Abulafia, who envisioned this state as prophecy. Using the Platonic characterization of "divine madness," Alemanno depicted this ecstatic state as the culmination of the erotic pursuit of wisdom. In that state the human soul loses any taint of corporeality and is able to become one with the form of the Good. The highest example of erotic spirituality, according to Alemanno, is the Song of Songs, which Alemanno read as a guide to the attainment of a mystical union with God in this life.

For Sephardi exiles in the Ottoman Empire reflections on ultimate felicity, or beatitude, became an obsession, looming large in their biblical commentaries, sermons, and systematic theology. Moses *Almosnino harmonized Jewish Arisotelianism and the Zohar in order to provide answers to Jewish perplexity after the expulsion from Iberia. His analysis of the pursuit of perfection agrees with Crescas that love of God is the ultimate end of human love. Through the love of God one attains the perfection of all virtues in this world for which one is rewarded with eternal life. The love of God is everlasting and inexhaustible because it is an unconditional love. This love is not a communication between two perfect intellects but the love of the infinite details of the beloved. Only a perfect will that can discern the infinite variations of particulars can love God, the most perfect Will, unconditionally. Therefore, those who unconditionally love the Torah, the manifestation of God's infinite love, love God and enjoy everlasting salvation. Love of God yields the blissful union of the separated soul with God, enjoying an incomparable spiritual delight. The bliss of personal immortality is reserved for perfect Jews, a community that includes men and women. Women could enter the World-To-Come, because for Almosnino, in contrast to the rationalist tradition, ultimate felicity does not depend on philosophical wisdom but on faith, the perfection of the will, and the actual performance of mitzvot. Almosnino did not ignore the traditional hope for the coming of the messiah but depoliticized it by spiritualizing its meaning. In the Messianic Age, a total transformation of human existence from corporeality to spirituality will take place so that all Jews will envision the "face of the *Shekhinah*" during their lifetimes because their bodies will no longer be material entities. The bliss of immortality could thus be enjoyed despite the continuation of political exile.

BIBLIOGRAPHY: A. Altmann (ed.), *Biblical and Other Studies* (1963), 222ff.; idem, in: *Harry A. Wolfson Jubilee Volume*, 1 (1965), 47–87; A. Altmann and S.M. Stern, *Isaac Israeli* (1958), index s.v. *union*; J. Guttmann, *Die Philosophie des Salomon ibn Gabirol* (1889), 165ff., 264, and passim; I. Heinemann, *Die Lehre von der Zweckbestimmung des Menschen* (1926), passim; S. Horovitz, in: *Jahresbericht des juedisch-theologischen Seminars* (Breslau, 1906), 146, 198ff.; (1912), 244ff.; D. Kaufmann, *Studien ueber Salomon ibn Gabirol* (1889), 19ff. and passim; S. Pines, in: *Tarbiz*, 27 (1957/58), 218–33; M.Z. Schreiner, in: *Mi-Mizraḥ u-mi-Ma'arav*, 4 (1889), 26ff.; G. Vajda, *La théologie ascétique de Baḥya ibn Paquda* (1947), 131ff.; idem, *L 'amour de Dieu dans la théologie juive du moyen âge* (1957), index s.v. *adhésion*. **ADD. BIBLIOGRAPHY:** M. Fishbane, "The Inwardness of Joy in Jewish Spirituality," in: L.S. Rouner (ed.), *In Pursuit of Happiness* (1995),

71–88; D. Frank, "The End of the Guide: Maimonides on the Best Life for Man," in: *Judaism*, 34 (1985): 485–95; W.Z. Harvey, "R. Hasdai Crescas and His Critique of Philosophical Happiness" (Heb.), in: *Proceedings of the Sixth World Congress of Jewish Studies*, vol. 3 (1977), 143–49; M.M. Kellner, *Maimonides on Human Perfection* (1990); H. Kreisel, *Maimonides' Political Thought: Studies in Ethics, Law, and the Human Ideal* (1999); E.I.J. Rosenthal, "The Concept of '*Eudaimoni*'" in Medieval Islamic and Jewish Philosophy," in: idem, *Studia Semitica*, 2 (1971), 127–44. N. Roth, "Attaining 'Happiness (*Eudaimonia*) in Medieval and Jewish Philosophy," in: *Centerpoint*, 4 (1981), 21–32; 37; H. Tirosh-Samuelson, *Happiness in Premodern Judaism: Virtue, Knowledge and Well-Being* (2003).

[Alexander Altmann / Hava Tirosh-Samuelson (2nd ed.)]

BEAUCAIRE (Heb. בלקיירי), town in France. Documents attest the existence of a Jewish community in Beaucaire in the 12th century; its Jews served the counts of Toulouse as fiscal administrators. After the death of Count Raymond in 1194 there were anti-Jewish outbreaks. With the annexation of lower Languedoc to France in 1229 the privileges formerly enjoyed by the Jews in Beaucaire were revoked. In 1294 Philip the Fair relegated the Jews to a special quarter, between the fortress and the present Rue Haute, today the Roquecourbe quarter. A year later he ordered the imprisonment of several Jews in order to extort money from them. The Jews had to leave Beaucaire when they were expelled from France in 1306. They were allowed to return in 1315, when their resettlement was supervised by Christian and Jewish agents sent by the king. In 1317 the Jews in Beaucaire were required to wear the Jewish *Badge. They were again expelled in 1322. The further rehabilitation of the community after 1359 came to an end with the general expulsion of the Jews from France in 1394; most of the exiles settled in Provence, then outside French administration, and in the Papal State of the *Comtat-Venaissin, where many Jews retained Beaucaire as a family name. The former Jewish quarter of Beaucaire was demolished during a siege in 1578.

The poet Judah Al-Ḥarizi, on his visit to Beaucaire in about 1210, found poets and philosophers living there. In about 1321, Samuel b. Judah of Marseilles (Marseilili) finished his Hebrew translation of *Averroes' "middle" commentary on Aristotle's *Ethics* while imprisoned in the fortress of Beaucaire. Moses b. Solomon of Beaucaire translated Averroes' long commentary on the *Metaphysics* (1342); Beaucaire was also the birthplace of the translator Tanḥum b. Moses.

BIBLIOGRAPHY: G.Saige, *Les Juifs du Languedoc* (1881); Steinschneider, Uebersetzungen, 171, 217, 666; Gross, Gal Jud, 119–21; Kahn, in: REJ, 65 (1913), 181–95; 66 (1913), 75–97; G. Caro, *Social-und Wirtschaftsgeschichte der Juden*, 1 (1924), 386–90, 510; Z. Szajkowski, *Franco-Judaica* (1962), index.

[Zvi Avneri]

BEBAI.

(1) Third-century Palestinian *amora*. Bebai studied under R. Johanan (BK 61a), Resh Lakish (TJ, Nid. 3:3, 50d), R. Eleazar b. Pedat (Zev. 70b), and R. Joshua b. Levi (Ber. 62b). He was a close associate of Ammi and Assi (Shab. 74a; TJ, Ter. 8:5, 45c). He interpreted Deuteronomy 28:66 in terms of his own poverty: "'The life you face shall be precarious' – this refers to him who purchases provisions from one year for the next; 'You shall be in terror night and day' – refers to him who purchases provisions from one Sabbath eve to the next, 'with no assurance of survival' – refers to him who is dependent upon the bakery." Although Bebai engaged chiefly in *halakhah*, his opinions being frequently cited in both Talmuds, he was also a competent aggadist. Particularly well-known is his application of the commandment, "You shall not swear falsely by the name of the Lord God" (Ex. 20:7), to hypocrites: "Do not don *tefillin*, wrap yourself in a *tallit*, and then commit a sin" (PR, 22:111b).

(2) Fourth-century Babylonian *amora*. Bebai studied under R. *Naḥman and the Talmud quotes halakhic problems that he discussed with his teacher (BM 23b; BB 36b). He taught *beraitot* in the school of Naḥman (Ḥag. 22b; Yev. 12b) and sat before Hamnuna (Nid. 27a). He transmitted teachings in the names of Rav and Samuel and was endorsed by R. Joseph: "Adopt the version of Bebai" (Meg. 18b). He was friendly with R. Joseph (Kid. 81a), who placed him in charge of religious affairs in his city (Kid. 76b). The exilarch Isaac was his sister's son (Yev. 115b).

BIBLIOGRAPHY: Hyman, Toledot, 264ff.

[Yitzhak Dov Gilat / Zvi Kaplan]

BEBAI BAR ABBAYE (fourth century), Babylonian *amora*. Bebai was a son of *Abbaye, head of the Pumbedita academy, and studied under him and R. *Joseph. He served as *dayyan* in Pumbedita and appears to have succeeded his father (Yev. 75b). According to the Talmud (Ket. 85a) his colleagues R. *Papi and R. *Huna b. Joshua, who sat with him as judges, at times opposed his rulings with the words, "Because you are a descendant of short-lived people your words are incomplete, lacking a beginning and making no sense" (referring to his descent from Eli the priest whose descendants were condemned to die young, cf. I Sam. 2:32; see *Arukh*, s.v. *mal*). However, R. Papi greatly respected him, referring to him as "master" even in his absence (Ḥul. 43b). Bebai was a prosperous farmer, leasing land in addition to his own (BM 109a; BB 137b). Many legends are related of him. According to one, the angel of death visited him frequently and disclosed to him the secrets of the other world (Ḥag. 4b–5a). Another relates that he perceived demons at work, and was stricken down, whereupon the scholars prayed for him and effected his recovery (Ber. 6a).

BIBLIOGRAPHY: Hyman, Toledot, 265f.

[Yitzhak Dov Gilat]

BEBE, PAULINE (1965?–), French reform rabbi. After studying the English and Hebrew languages in Paris, Pauline Bebe attended the rabbinical seminary at the London-based liberal Leo Baeck College, one of the few rabbinical institutions in Europe welcoming women. She completed her Hebrew cursus in Jerusalem (Hebrew Union College) and earned a degree from the Institut des Langues Orientales in Paris. Her first rabbinical appointments, while a student rabbi, were in Southport and Cardiff. Her academic interests were the attitude of Judaism towards proselytism and conversion and the ethics of language, both themes providing her with the background of a strongly liberal and passionate exploration of the dynamics of Jewish tradition.

Back in France, she became the country's first female rabbi in 1990, serving the MJLF (Mouvement Juif Liberal de France, the most liberal of the two branches of the Reform movement in France at the time), which she left in 1995 to start her own movement, the Communauté Juive Liberale, now embraced by more than 200 families. Her first book, *Le judaisme libéral* ("Liberal Judaism"), was published in Paris in 1993, followed in 2001 by an ambitious dictionary of women and Judaism (*Isha: un dictionnaire des femmes et du judaisme*).

[Dror Franck Sullaper (2nd ed.)]

°BECCARI, ARRIGO (1909–), priest and teacher at the Catholic seminary in Nonantola, near Bologna, Italy; Righteous Among the Nations. In July 1942, a group of 50 Jewish children arrived at the seminary, having fled from the war zone in Dalmatia, Yugoslavia, between Italian troops and local partisans. With the help of Delasem, the officially recognized Jewish emigration and welfare agency, the children were housed in the Villa Emma home. There, Josef Itai, the group's leader, became friendly with Father Arrigo Beccari. Nonantola seemed a safe place to sit out the war, but when Italy surrendered to the Allies on September 8, 1943, and the Germans overran the parts of the country not yet in Allied hands, a reign of terror began for the Jews. In order to keep the children at the Villa Emma from falling into German hands, Beccari, without necessarily consulting his superiors, took as many children as possible into the seminary for hiding and arranged for others to be housed with friendly villagers. Food for all of them was provided by the seminary's kitchen. As the Nazis and their local collaborators stepped up the search for Jews, it became urgent for the children and their adult leaders, a total of 120 persons, to be moved somewhere else. It was decided to take the whole group north and across the Swiss border. With the help of Dr. Giuseppe Moreali, Nonantola's physician, all 120 persons were provided with forged documents identifying them as Italians. Then they boarded a train for the Swiss frontier, a ride fraught with terrible but unavoidable risks, for most of them could hardly speak Italian and the forged papers may not have saved them during a police check. Luckily, no mishaps occurred during the long train ride, and on Yom Kippur eve of 1943 the group passed safely into Switzerland. The Gestapo, discovering the loss of the children, seized Beccari and imprisoned him in Bologna. Despite the tortures inflicted on him over the next few months, he refused to disclose the names of the persons who had helped him or to reveal the whereabouts of others Jews in hiding. His religious superiors interceded on his behalf and he was released. Years later he wrote: "It would be difficult for me to erase the memory of the terror and suffering of those days or of my joy at doing the small good which was my duty and which had to be done." In 1964, Don Beccari was awarded the title of Righteous Among the Nations by Yad Vashem.

BIBLIOGRAPHY: Yad Vashem Archives M31–35; M. Paldiel, *The Path of the Righteous* (1993), 356–57.

[Mordecai Paldiel (2nd ed.)]

BECHER, SIEGFRIED (1806–1873), Austrian economist. Becher was born in Plany (Bohemia) and educated in Prague and Vienna. After his conversion to Catholicism, he became professor of geography and history at the Vienna Polytechnic and was frequently consulted by the Austrian authorities on statistical and tariff questions, and represented his country in several international negotiations. In 1848 he was made a counselor at the Ministry of Commerce, and later was granted the title of "Hofrat" (court counselor). After a denunciation because of democratic inclinations he was dismissed in 1852 and died eventually in poverty. In addition to statistical investigations Becher's interests centered on labor and population economics. His publications include *Handelsgeographie* (2 vols., 1836–37); *Oesterreichisches Muenzwesen 1524–1838* (2 vols., 1838); *Die Bevoelkerungsverhaeltnisse der oesterreichischen Monarchie* (1846); *Organisation des Gewerbewesens* (1849); and *Die Volkswirtschaft* (1853).

ADD. BIBLIOGRAPHY: F. von Sommaruga, in: ADB, 2 (1875), 204; J. Baxa, in: NDB, 1 (1953), 691.

[Joachim O. Ronall / Marcus Pyka (2nd ed.)]

BECHHOLD, JACOB HEINRICH (1866–1937), German colloid chemist, born in Frankfurt. Bechhold was the director of the Institute of Colloid Research, Frankfurt, and took out several patents on filtration and on adhesives. He was the author of: *Die Kolloide in Biologie und Medizin* (1912; 1919⁵); *Handlexikon der Naturwissenschaften und Medizin* (1920); *Ultrafiltration* (1923); and *Einfuehrung in die Lehre von den Kolloiden* (1934).

BECHYNE (Get. **Bechin**), town in Bohemia, Czech Republic. Legends are connected with R. Ḥayyim, living in Bechyne in the 16th century, who apparently forbade the building of a burial hall at the cemetery. Five Jewish taxpayers are mentioned in 1570. In 1685 the representatives of Bohemian Jewry complained that the community of Bechyne had failed to comply with its ordinances. In 1695 the Jews there were prohibited from residing in the same building as Christians. The community numbered 81 persons (14 families living in six houses) in 1715, and 56 persons in 1725. In 1898 the community's German-language school was closed down. The community numbered 145 persons in 1902 and 32 in 1930. It was liquidated by the Nazis in 1942. Several of the Jewish houses in the Jewish street, and the cemetery with remarkable tombstones from the last quarter of the 17th century, were preserved. There were also Jewish communities in the vicinity in Bernartice and Stadlec.

BIBLIOGRAPHY: Chleborád, in: H. Gold (ed.), *Juden und Judengemeinden Boehmens* (1934), 23–25. **ADD. BIBLIOGRAPHY:** J. Fiedler, *Jewish Sights of Bohemia and Moravia* (1991), 42–43.

BECK, KARL ISIDOR (1817–1879), Hungarian-born poet, writing in German, who gave voice to the Hungarian people's struggle for liberation against the Austrian Empire. His work was filled with despair and disillusion with the state of Jewry and the world. His first poems, *Naechte, Gepanzerte Lieder* (1838), and *Stille Lieder* (1840), contained such glowing rhetoric, passionate imagery, and consuming love of freedom that he was hailed as a new Byron. When his *Lieder vom armen Mann* appeared in 1846, Friedrich Engels saw in him a future Goethe. The *Lieder vom armen Mann* are lyrics of great depth of feeling and clarity of vision, ranging from savage invective against social injustice to pathetic pictures of starvation in working-class homes. Beck prefaced the volume with the allegation that Rothschild had enslaved the masses with his gold and had failed to liberate his own unredeemed people. Beck was the first German lyric poet to write about slum conditions; in his lyrics there broods a vague hope of better days to come and a fear of impending social strife. Beck's Jewish despair found utterance in a cycle of poems entitled *Das junge Palaestina*, that bewail his unreciprocated love for Germany. His biblical drama *Saul* (1840) has as its climax David's vision of the Jewish people: he sees them as eternal fugitives who have become mere caricatures of a people that was once pure, simple, and glorious. His verse epic, *Jankó, der ungarische Rosshirt* (1841), contains some excellent descriptions of Hungarian life. The refrain of one of his poems, "an der schoenen blauen Donau" inspired Johann Strauss' famous "Blue Danube" waltz. Although he was baptized in 1843, Beck continued to be haunted by the fate of Jewry. He sank into a state of pessimistic resignation, which was intensified by the failure of the Hungarian rising of 1848. Filled with bitterness, he made his peace with the Austrian government, renounced his radical activities, and virtually ceased writing poetry for the rest of his life.

BIBLIOGRAPHY: S. Liptzin, *Lyric Pioneers of Modern Germany* (1928), ch. 3; E. Thiel, *Karl Becks literarische Entwicklung* (1938).

[Sol Liptzin]

°**BECK(IUS), MATTHIAS FRIEDRICH** (1649–1701), German Lutheran Orientalist. Born in Kaufbeuren (Swabia), Beck studied at Augsburg and Jena (1668–70), under the renowned philologist Johann Frischmuth. His competence in Oriental languages was very broad, Jewish interests being reflected in his translation into Latin of the Targum to Chronicles (1680–83) and publication of Jewish antiquities discovered in Augsburg (*Monumenta antiqua judaica Augustae Vindelicorum reperta*,1686). His voluminous unpublished works, now mostly dispersed, included translations of Benjamin of Tudela's and Petaḥiah of Regensburg's travelogues.

BIBLIOGRAPHY: J.B. Luhn, *M. Fr. Beckii Memoria* (Wittenberg, 1703); H. Pipping, *Memoria Theologorum* (Leipzig, 1705), 911f.; ADB, 2 (1875), 218. **ADD. BIBLIOGRAPHY:** Steinschneider, in: ZHB, 2 (1897), 102, F. Junginger in: *Kaufbeurer Geschichtsblätter*, 4 (1965), 121–124.

[Raphael Loewe / Giulio Busi (2nd ed.)]

°**BECK, MICHAEL** (1653–1712), German Lutheran theologian and Hebraist. Beck studied in Jena, like his namesake M.F. *Beck, under the apostate Frischmuth. He left a tract on the Masoretic accents as a hermeneutic device (Jena, 1678; repr. in G. Menthen, *Thesaurus theologico-philologicus*, 1, 1701), as well as *Hannahatan ve-Ḥalizatan shel Tefillin* or *Usus Phylacteriorum* (Jena, 1675), which is a public dissertation on phylacteries by Beck with the reply of Matthew Kreher.

BIBLIOGRAPHY: J.G.W. Dunkel, *Historisch-critische Nachrichten von verstorbenen Gelehrten*, 3 vols. (1753–57); A. Weyermann, *Nachrichten von Gelehrten… aus Ulm* (1798); ADB, 2 (1875), 218; J.C. Adelung, *Allgemeines Gelehrten-lexicon*, 1 (1784), 1580 (bibl.).

[Raphael Loewe]

BECK, MORITZ (**Meir**; 1845–1923), rabbi, educator, and leader of Romanian Jewry. Born at Pápa in Hungary, Beck studied at the University of Breslau and the Breslau rabbinical seminary. He went to Romania in 1873, and was appointed preacher (in 1900, rabbi) at the "Choir Temple" and principal of the Loebel Jewish School for Boys in Bucharest. Beck was considered rabbi of the progressive elements in the Bucharest community. He promoted the expansion of Jewish education in Romania, encouraging the formation of new schools with adequate financial support. He also helped establish social welfare institutions, and worked toward the renewal of the Bucharest community organization, which had disintegrated in the second half of the 19th century (see *Romania). Beck took a prominent part in the fight against antisemitism and discrimination in Romania and for the emancipation of Romanian Jews. He contributed to the general and Jewish press, and published the journal *Revista Israelită* from 1886 to 1892 and from 1908 to 1910. Aside from his sermons and numerous articles on various subjects, Beck compiled a Hebrew-Romanian dictionary of the Torah (1881). Toward the end of his life he was attracted by Zionism.

BIBLIOGRAPHY: *M. Beck, Cuvânt de omagiu: Viața și opera* (1925); A. Stern, *Insemnări din viața mea*, 2 (1921), passim.

[Eliyahu Feldman]

BECK, WILLY (1844–1886), Hungarian painter and cartoonist. He exhibited portraits and scenes from daily-life at the Budapest salon. He later earned his living by publishing the *Zeitgeist*, a humorous periodical in German, contributing all the prose and cartoons. In 1849 he settled in Vienna and edited the *Charivari*, a political and satirical journal, until the police suspended publication. He then returned to Hungary.

BECKELMAN, MOSES W. (1906–1955), U.S. social worker. Beckelman was born in New York City. He was a lecturer in social work at the City College of New York (1927–30), and managing editor of the *Jewish Social Service Quarterly* (1936–39). At the outbreak of World War II Beckelman was sent by the *American Jewish Joint Distribution Committee to Lithuania, where he helped large numbers of refugees to emigrate, until he was forced to leave in 1941. In 1942 Beckelman joined the U.S. Office of Strategic Services, and in 1943 directed a refugee camp in Morocco for UNRRA. After serving as an assistant director of the Intergovernmental Committee on Refugees, from February 1945, he rejoined the "Joint" in 1946 and became its director general in Europe in 1951. Until his death Beckelman supervised the liquidation of the displaced persons camps, the establishment of *Malben in Israel for the social care of immigrants, and extensive social work programs for Jews, especially in Morocco and Iran.

[Yehuda Bauer]

BECKER, U.S. family of bankers and philanthropists. ABRAHAM G. BECKER (1857–1925), U.S. banker and philanthropist, was born in Warsaw, Ohio, and eventually settled in Chicago. He organized his own commercial paper house, A.G. Becker and Company, which pioneered in the syndication of large loans. Active in communal affairs, Becker helped found the Associated Jewish Charities of Chicago and served as its president for eight years. He was a trustee of Hebrew Union College and the Chicago Orchestral Association and bequeathed large sums to the Chicago Art Institute and the Chicago Jewish charities. His son, JAMES HERMAN (1894–1970), was also a banker and communal leader. In 1914, while an undergraduate at Cornell University, he helped convoke the original Jewish War Relief Conference in Chicago. Becker served with the U.S. Army in Europe from 1918 to 1921, assisting war victims through the American Relief Association and later as director general of the American Jewish Joint Distribution Committee in Europe. Upon his return to America in 1921, Becker joined his father's firm, becoming director (1926), president (1947), and chairman (1961). He also directed several other companies and served with many Jewish organizations. In 1936 he was chosen president of the Chicago Jewish Welfare Fund, a post that he held for nearly 30 years.

[Edward L. Greenstein]

BECKER, AHARON (1906–1995), Israeli labor leader. Born in Kobrin, Belorussia, Becker grew up in Brest-Litovsk, where he joined the Zionist labor youth movement and *He-Ḥalutz. In 1925 he settled in Palestine. He was a construction worker in Petaḥ Tikvah and Tel Aviv and cofounder of Ha-Baḥarut ha-Sozyalistit ha-Ivrit, the union of young members of *Aḥdut ha-Avodah. He started his career as a *Histadrut worker in 1929 as the secretary of the workers' council in Ramat Gan; he later worked in Tel Aviv in various trade unions and was on its workers' council. He was an initiator of the cost-of-living scale for wages and salaries. In 1947 Becker was appointed by Ben-Gurion to organize the supply department of the Haganah and later of Israel's army, but in 1949 returned to Histadrut work, becoming the chairman of its executive's trade union department, a post he held for 12 years. From 1961 until 1969 he served as the Histadrut's secretary-general. He maintained many international contacts, and regularly attended the conferences of the International Labor Organization in Geneva, serving on its governing body from 1957 until 1971. Becker was elected to the Knesset (from the Third to the Seventh Knesset) on the Mapai and Labor Party ticket. He published a book entitled *Bi-Ymei Shilton ha-Labor* ("In the Period of Labor Government," 1955), after visiting Britain in the early 1950s, and *Ha-Oved be-Yisrael* ("The Worker in Israel," 1970).

[Shmuel Soler]

BECKER, EDWARD ROY (1933–), U.S. jurist. Becker was born in Philadelphia, Penn. He received his B.A. from the University of Pennsylvania in 1954 and his LL.B. from Yale Law School in 1957. He practiced law in Philadelphia with Becker, Fryman and Ervais from 1957 until 1970. In 1970, President Richard M. *Nixon nominated Becker, then only 37 years old, to the U.S. District Court, Eastern District of Pennsylvania. In 1981, President Ronald *Reagan nominated him to the U.S. Court of Appeals for the Third Circuit. He was Chief Judge from 1998 to 2003 and achieved a remarkable collegiality in the Court.

Federal appellate courts often decide cases with a single word: "Affirmed." Becker felt that this was a mistake, "that we owed the bar more." Providing a rationale for a judicial decision, Becker said, "was the right thing to do." When he began his term as Chief Judge, the Third Circuit resolved 53% of its cases without comment. By the end of 2002, the number was 3%. His passion for writing comprehensive opinions, leaving no hard issue behind and clarifying the law no matter how complex, led colleagues to chide him for his predilection for extensive footnotes In fact, his article "In Praise of Footnotes" has become a judicial classic.

He was deeply involved in efforts to improve the administration of justice, serving on the executive committee of the Judicial Conference and the board of the Federal Judicial Center. He helped simplify the management of complex litigation, improve the Federal Rules, and coordinate state and federal judicial efforts. He wrote and lectured extensively on cutting-edge legal issues and produced more than 1,000 opinions, a significant number of which were precedent-setting. His expertise – particularly in anti-trust, securities, class actions, scientific evidence, and tort law – is widely recognized, and his opinions are often cited by other judges, including justices of the Supreme Court.

In 2002, the American Judicature Society conferred its prestigious Devitt Distinguished Service Award upon him. This award honors a federal judge whose "career has been exemplary and who has made significant contributions to the administration of justice, the advancement of the rule of law, and the improvement of society as a whole." His nomination was co-signed by every judge on the Third Circuit.

Judge Becker served in leadership roles in his synagogue, but judicial rules precluded active participation in many Jewish organizations committed to fundraising, or to social issues that may come before the Court. Jewish leaders – cultural, philanthropic, civic, and entrepreneurial – have consulted with him often to benefit from his wisdom and insight.

BIBLIOGRAPHY: S.B. Burbank, "Making Progress the Old-Fashioned Way," in: *University of Pennsylvania Law Review* (2001), 1231; M.A. Hamilton, "A Truly Remarkable Judge," ibid., 1237; D.H. Souter, "Tribute to the Honorable Edward R. Becker," ibid., 1229.

[Jerome J. Shestack (2nd ed.)]

BECKER, GARY STANLEY (1930–), American economist, Nobel Prize winner. Born in Pottsville, Pennsylvania, Becker was educated at Princeton and the University of Chicago. He was the Arthur Lehman Professor of Economics at the University of Chicago and, from 1985, a columnist for *Business Week* magazine. A free-market philosopher, Becker applied the methods of economics to aspects of human behavior previously considered the domain of sociology, anthropology, and demography. Early in his career, for example, he decided that racial and ethnic bias could be maintained only if markets were not completely competitive. The idea that discrimination takes a financial toll on the discriminator is an accepted concept among economists today, thanks to Becker. And in his 1964 book *Human Capital*, he raised the idea of considering education as an economic decision.

In the late 1960s he postulated that the way to reduce crime was to raise the probability of punishment or make the punishment more severe. His insights into crime helped develop a new branch of economics. He also examined the family unit, considering the household as a small business the behavior of which could be analyzed by applying economic principles.

In 1967 Becker won the John Bates Clark Award of the American Economic Association and served as president of the association in 1987. In 1992 he was awarded the Nobel Memorial Prize in Economic Science "for having extended the domain of economic theory to aspects of human behavior which had previously been dealt with – if at all – by other social science disciplines such as sociology, demography, and criminology." Other books by Becker include: *The Economics of Discrimination* (1957), *The Allocation of Time and Goods Over the Life Cycle* (1975), *A Treatise on the Family* (1981), *The Economic Approach to Human Behavior* (1992), *The Essence of Becker* (1995), and *The Economics of Life: From Baseball to Affirmative Action to How Real World Issues Affect Our Everyday Life* (1996) – a collection of Becker's popular *Business Week* columns.

[Ruth Beloff (2nd ed.)]

BECKER, JULIUS (1881–1945), German Zionist journalist and politician. Becker was born in Gottesberg, Silesia, into an acculturated German-Jewish trading family. He studied at Berne University (Ph.D. in graphology). While in Switzerland, he joined the Zionist Democratic Fraction of Ch. *Weizmann, who had been appointed assistant lecturer at Geneva University in 1901. Shortly after, Becker moved to Berlin and joined the staff of the renewed Zionist weekly *Juedische Rundschau* (1895–1938), which, in Oct. 1902, had been taken over by H. *Loewe. Originally established as *Berliner Vereinsbote* (1895–1901) and first renamed *Israelitische Rundschau* (1901–02), it served as the official organ of the *Zionistische Vereinigung fuer Deutschland* (est. 1897). When Loewe resigned in Dec. 1908, Becker became editor-in-chief, followed by Felix Abraham in Oct. 1911. From 1906 to 1913, he also frequently contributed to the central Zionist organ *Die Welt* (1897–1914), signing himself "JB." In 1908, immediately after the Young Turk Revolution, he assisted R. *Lichtheim and V. *Jabotinsky in Constantinople to win the new regime's support for Zionism. Soon, Becker became a prominent figure in German Zionist organizations and was elected to both the Executive and Central Committee of the *ZVFD*. In addition, Becker contributed to political publications, especially those of the Ullstein company, such as *Berliner Morgenpost* (est. 1898) and *Vossische Zeitung* (taken over in 1913 and edited by G. *Bernhard). After 1919, Becker became correspondent of the *Vossische Zeitung* at the League of Nations in Geneva, for a time also chairing the assembly of press correspondents assigned to the League. From 1925, he extended considerable help to V. *Jacobson, the delegate of the Jewish Agency at the League, taking over this post on the latter's death in Aug. 1934. In 1935, Becker went to Shanghai to organize the Chinese Information Service for the Kuomintang government, returning to Switzerland in 1937. As a stateless person, he had to emigrate to the United States in 1941, where he continued his journalistic activities. In his *History of German Zionism* (1954), Lichtheim described Becker as "a very gifted journalist and a charming companion who, due to his numerous contacts, served Zionism a great deal."

BIBLIOGRAPHY: S. Rawidowitz (ed.), *Sefer Sokolow*, (1943), 353–60; *Aufbau*. No. 18 (1945); *MB* (June 29, 1945); M. Waldman, in: *Ha-Olam* (July 5, 1945); R. Lichtheim, *Geschichte des deutschen Zionismus* (1954), 157, 195; K. Blumenfeld, in: M. Sambursky and J. Ginat (eds.), *Im Kampf um den Zionismus* (1976), 299; Y. Eloni, *Zionismus in Deutschland* (1987), index; H. Schmuck (ed.), *Jewish Biographical Archive* (1995), F. 123, 303; Series II (2003), F. II/46, 330–36.

[Johannes Valentin Schwarz (2nd ed.)]

BECKER, JUREK (1937–1997), German writer of Polish-Jewish background. Born in Lodz, Becker grew up in the Lodz ghetto and the concentration camps of Ravensbrueck and Sachsenhausen. In 1945 he moved with his parents, who had survived the war together, to East Berlin. He joined the Freie Deutsche Jugend Communist youth organization and the Communist Party (SED) while studying philosophy. In 1960 he was ousted from the university for political reasons. After he studied at the Film School of Babelsberg he worked as a playwright and writer in East Berlin. Becoming more critical of the East German regime and defending dissidents publicly, he was thrown out of the Communist Party in 1976. A year later he left East Germany and, after a brief stay in the United States, settled in West Berlin.

Becker's best-known book is his first novel *Jakob der Lugner* (1968; *Jacob the Liar*, 1996), which tells the story of Jacob, who owns a radio in the Warsaw ghetto and invents hopeful stories about an imminent liberation. It became the basis of one of the most successful East German movies. *Der Boxer* (1976) describes the new existence of a concentration camp survivor, while *Bronsteins Kinder* (1986; *Bronstein's Children*, 1991) deals with the revenge of survivors against their Nazi torturers. In the 1980s and 1990s he became well known as a scriptwriter for many German TV comedies. Becker never denied his Jewish background, which is apparent in most of his major works, but stressed that in his life, Judaism played no active role.

BIBLIOGRAPHY: S.L. Gilman, *Jurek Becker: A Life in Five Worlds* (2003).

[Michael Brenner (2nd ed.)]

BECKER, LAVY M. (1905–2001), Canadian rabbi, communal official, businessman. Lavy Becker was born in Montreal to Russian immigrant parents. His father was a *shoḥet* and cantor there. Becker attended high school in Montreal and New York, where he studied Talmud at Yeshiva College (*Yeshiva University). He earned a B.A. at McGill University in 1926. In 1930 he was ordained by the *Jewish Theological Seminary.

While at JTS, Becker came under the influence of Mordecai *Kaplan, founder of Reconstructionist Judaism (see *Reconstructionism). Like his classmates and friends Ira Eisenstein and Milton Steinberg, Becker's career reflected a profound commitment to Kaplan's ideal of Judaism as a civilization, a Judaism more expansive than what was usually defined as the religious domain. After graduation, he became rabbi at the Sunnyside Jewish Center and over the next ten years he assumed executive positions at the Jewish Community Centers of Detroit and New Haven as well as taking on the position of executive director of the YM-YWHA in Montreal. Ever ready to assume significant communal challenges, in 1945–46 Becker became the country director for displaced persons in the American Zone of Occupation, under the auspices of the Joint Distribution Committee and UNRWA, responsible for the welfare of the thousands of Holocaust survivors.

After Becker's return to Montreal, he never again assumed a paid position within the Jewish community. He worked first in the family business and then went on to work for others and then himself, when he set up Lavy Becker Consultants. However, he remained deeply involved in Jewish communal life. In 1951, he was the founding rabbi at a new Conservative synagogue (Congregation Beth-El) in the new Jewish community of Mount Royal. Nine years later he realized his ideal of setting up a Reconstructionist synagogue in Montreal, Dorshei Emet, which he served as unpaid rabbi until 1977. During those same decades, Becker served on the executive of the Canadian Jewish Congress and the World Jewish Congress, where he had special responsibilities for smaller Jewish communities. He traveled extensively through the Caribbean and Latin America, including Cuba, as well as to Iceland. In Canada, he was appointed the chairman of the Centennial Interfaith Council, helping organize Canada's 1967 centennial celebrations.

Many regarded Lavy Becker's life as an embodiment of Mordecai Kaplan's Reconstructionist ideals. Within the Reconstructionist movement he was highly regarded, becoming president of the Federation of Reconstructionist Synagogues (1969–72) and chairman of the Board of Overseers of the Reconstructionist Rabbinical College (1969–74). In Montreal, the Jewish Community Federation established in his honor the Lavy M. Becker chair at the Reconstructionist College in Philadelphia.

[Richard Menkis (2nd ed.)]

BEDA (**Fritz Loehner**; **Fritz Loewy**; 1883–1942), Viennese journalist, satirist, and operetta librettist. Born in Wildenschwert, now Usti nad Orlici in the Czech Republic, the Loewy family changed its name to Loehner soon after moving to Vienna. There Beda, whose name is short for Bedrich, Czech for Friedrich, studied law, though already during his school days he had begun to write satirical verse, including some which ridiculed Jews who were attempting to assimilate into Austrian society. In the 1920s Beda became one of the most popular librettists in Vienna. Several of his works provoked scandals, and quotations from them became household words. The satires were published in contemporary Zionist periodicals, and subsequently collected in *Getaufte und Baldgetaufte* ("Baptized and Newly Baptized," 1908); and in *Israeliten und andere Anti-semiten* ("Israelites and Other Anti-Semites," 1909). A collection of personal lyrics is *Ecce ego* (1920). His best-known libretti (with co-authors) were for Franz Lehar's *Land of Smiles* (1929) and Paul Abraham's *Ball in Savoy* (1932); he also collaborated with Fritz Gruenbaum. He was active in the Zionist student organization *Kadimah, and president of the *Hakoah sports club, for whose benefit he organized the "Beda-Abende," one of the highlights of the Vienna season. In 1925 he married Helene Jellinek, with whom he had two daughters. In 1938 Beda was arrested and sent to Dachau, and subsequently deported to the *Buchenwald concentration camp. There he organized cultural activities and in a competition initiated by the camp commandant for a "camp song," Beda's entry (submitted in a "kapo's" name), the "Buchenwaldlied," was chosen as the winner and later became widely known as a reaffirmation that "whatever our fate we still say 'yes' to life." Beda's wife, her mother, and both their daughters were deported to Minsk in 1942. Beda himself died in *Auschwitz that same year.

BIBLIOGRAPHY: A. Baar (ed.), *50 Jahre Hakoah* (1959), 27, 227–8, 258–60; W. Barrel et al., *Buchenwald* (Ger. 1960), index; S. Czech, *Schoen ist die Welt* (1957), 34, 258–86, 292; MGG; G. Schwarberg, *Dein ist mein ganzes Herz. Die Geschichte von Fritz Löhner-Beda* (2000); B. Denscher and H.Peschina, *Kein Land des Laechelns. Fritz Löhner-Beda 1883–1942* (2002).

[Lisa Silverman (2nd ed.)]

BEDACHT, MAX (1883–1972), U.S. Communist leader. Bedacht was born in Munich, Germany. After an impoverished childhood and a career as a journeyman barber and trade union leader in Germany and Switzerland, he immigrated to New York City in 1908, where he supported himself as a barber and German-language newspaper editor. He moved to Detroit and then to San Francisco (1919), where he worked as an editor for the German press. In the same year he was made a member of the national executive committee of the newly formed Communist Labor Party, renamed the American Communist Party in 1921. In this capacity Bedacht was sent as a delegate to the Comintern Congress in Moscow (1921), from which he returned an apostle of the militant new line. While primarily a labor agitator, Bedacht rose to serve on the central executive committee's secretariat (1927–29), and in 1933 was named general secretary of the International Workers Order. He built its Jewish fraternal section into the party's largest auxiliary, while editing its publication *The New Order*. In 1946, following the post-World War II changes in Communist leadership, Bedacht was expelled from the party for factionalism, and retired to become a poultry farmer in New Jersey.

In 1949 he appeared before a hearing of the House Un-American Activities Committee to deny charges made against him by the former Russian espionage agent Whittaker Chambers that for many years he had served as a permanent link between Soviet military intelligence and the central committee of the American Communist Party. In his 1952 autobiography *Witness*, Chambers wrote: "About both brief, tidy men [Heinrich Himmler and Max Bedacht] there was a disturbing quality of secret power mantling insignificance – what might be called the ominousness of nonentity, which is peculiar to the terrible little figures of our time."

BIBLIOGRAPHY: D. Bell in: D. Egbert (ed.), *Socialism and American Life*, 1 (1952), index; T. Draper, *Roots of American Communism* (1957), index; Whittaker Chambers, *Witness* (1952), index.

[Edward L. Greenstein / Ruth Beloff (2nd ed.)]

BEDARIDA, GUIDO (1900–1962), Italian author and historian. Born in Ancona of a family of south French origin, Bedarida ultimately settled in Leghorn. The Jewish environment had a deep influence on him, inspiring his poetical and literary work and his eagerness to proclaim his Jewish and Zionist identity. Most of Bedarida's poems deal with Jewish subjects. His first collection of verse, *Io Ebreo* (1927), appeared under the pen name of Eliezer ben David, which he thereafter used frequently. Bedarida wrote plays such as *La casa vuota* (1928) and *Io t'ho chiamato* (1930), and three in the Jewish dialect of Leghorn: *Lucilla fa da sé* (1924), *Vigilia di sabato* (1934), and *Il siclo d'argento* (1935). In the verse dialogues *Alla "banca di Memo"* and *Il lascito del sor Barocas* (1950) and in a collection of sonnets, *Ebrei di Livorno* (1956), he gave a lively picture of the life of the Jews of Leghorn and the local Jewish dialect. His *Ebrei d'Italia* (1950) described the Jewish contribution to Italian culture.

BIBLIOGRAPHY: E. Toaff, in: *Scritti… in memoria di G. Bedarida* (1966), 5–13 (complete bibliography on p. 15).

[Giorgio Romano]

BÉDARRIDE, ISRAÉL (1798–1869), French jurist and historian. In 1823 Bédarride won a prize from the Institut de France for his essay on the Jews in the Middle Ages, which he later enlarged and published as *Les juifs en France, en Italie et en Espagne* (1859). The following year Bédarride became a lawyer in Montpellier and was reputed to be one of the best jurists of southern France. He wrote many articles on legal subjects, but Jewish history remained his main interest. In 1867 he published his *Etude sur le* "Guide des égarés" *de Maimonide*, and in 1869 his *Etude sur le Talmud*. Bédarride was also interested in contemporary Jewish life and wrote against proselytism and in favor of religious liberty, *Du proselytisme et de la liberté religieuse, ou le judaisme au milieu des cultes chrétiens dans l'état actuel de la civilisation* (published posthumously). He was the author of *Harcanot et Barcanot*, a comedy on life in Carpentras, written in the local Jewish dialect (1896, 2nd edition 1925).

BIBLIOGRAPHY: M.E. Lisbonne, *Etude nécrologique sur Israél Bédarride* (Montpellier, 1870); Felix, in: AI, 30 (1869), 717–23; Z. Szajkowski, *The Language of the Jews in the Four Communities of Comtat Venaissin* (New York, 1948), 32–36 (Yid. with Eng. summary).

BÉDARRIDES, village in the department of Vaucluse, near Avignon, S. France. The small Jewish community established in Bédarrides in the Middle Ages was expelled by the vice legate of Avignon in 1694. One of the prominent Jewish families of southern France originated in Bédarrides. Its members include: GAD BEN JUDAH OF BÉDARRIDES, who composed a hymn for a local Purim established at *Cavaillon to commemorate escape from rioters in 1713; JASSUDA BÉDARRIDE (1804–1882), jurist, who became mayor of Aix-en-Provence after the 1848 revolution; ISRAÉL (ISAIAH) *BÉDARRIDE; and GUSTAVE EMANUEL BÉDARRIDES (1817–1899), magistrate, the first French Jew to be appointed public prosecutor (*procureur général*) at Bastia, in Corsica (1862), and vice president of the Central Consistory from 1872. A branch of the family which established itself in Italy assumed the name-form *Bedarida.

BIBLIOGRAPHY: Bauer, in: REJ, 29 (1894), 254–65; Gross, Gal Jud, 105; *Dictionnaire de Biographie Française*, 5 (1951), 1256f.

[Cecil Roth]

BEDDINGTON, English family of businessmen, philanthropists, and soldiers, originally named Moses. HENRY MOSES (c. 1791–1875) became a wealthy wholesale clothing merchant in London, with links to the New Zealand wool trade, and left £500,000 at his death. In 1868, his children changed their surname to Beddington, a suburb in south London, giving rise to much humorous commentary. Henry Moses' son MAURICE BEDDINGTON (1821–1898), a London wool broker, left over £1 million. The family also branched out into the tobacco business and founded the Abdullah cigarette company. ALFRED HENRY BEDDINGTON (1835–1900) was active in the life of the London Jewish community. In World War I, 37 members of the family served in the British forces. They included Lieutenant-Colonel CLAUDE (1868–1940) who fought in the South African War and was in command of the Mounted Troops of the 20th Division in France in World War I. He became an enthusiastic yachtsman. SIR EDWARD HENRY LIONEL (1884–1966) was a career officer in the British cavalry and, after having taken part in World War I, retired from active service in 1920. At the outbreak of World War II he rejoined the army, became deputy director of Military Intelligence, and rose to the rank of brigadier. WILLIAM RICHARD (1893–1975) entered the British army shortly before World War I, served in France and the Mediterranean area, and was wounded in action. In 1939 he became officer commanding the 2nd Royal Dragoon Guards (The Queen's Bays). He held various staff appointments in the Middle East, Italy, and North Africa, and finally joined Supreme Headquarters, Allied Expeditionary Forces (SHAEF). In 1946 he rose to the rank of major general and retired in 1947. Henry Moses' grandson JOHN LOUIS ("JACK") BEDDINGTON (1893–1959) became one of the most famous advertising poster designers of the 20th century.

BIBLIOGRAPHY: P.H. Emden, *Jews of Britain* (1943), 447,449, 548; J. Ben Hirsh, *Jewish General Officers* (1967), 76–77. **ADD. BIBLIOGRAPHY:** L.D. Nathan, *As Old As Auckland* (1984); "John Louis Beddington," in: ODNB online.

BEDERSI, ABRAHAM BEN ISAAC (c. 1230–c. 1300), Hebrew poet in southern France. The designation "Bedersi" indicates that he originated from Béziers (Heb., בדריש). He may be identical with the Abraham Mosse de Montepessulano (Montpellier; otherwise Abram de Sala) mentioned in secular documents. Abraham settled as a youth in Perpignan where he was a pupil of Joseph Ezobi. He stayed for some time in Arles and once took refuge in Narbonne, but apparently lived most of his life in Perpignan, then under Aragonese sovereignty. The Jewish community there had been granted a charter of privileges by James I to protect them from molestation. Abraham is the conjectured author of a letter from the community to the Jews of Barcelona, appealing to them to persuade the king through the medium of the bishop of Huesca to uphold the rights granted under the charter and reduce the communal tax obligations. Letters of recommendation written by Abraham in the name of the Perpignan community on behalf of petitioners and fund-raising emissaries have also been preserved. In 1275 Todros b. Joseph ha-Levi *Abulafia, who had accompanied the Castilian monarchs to France, spent some time in Perpignan and the two exchanged verses. A well-known poem of Bedersi on the pen and the sword, inspired by Arabic verses, was written in his honor and sent to him on the occasion of this visit. Abraham also composed for Todros a poem in the style of the Passover *Haggadah*, the first attempt to parody it. He gave some financial assistance to the poet Isaac Gorni, although deriding his literary talents. Abraham wrote numerous poems and satires, apparently collected by his son *Jedaiah ha-Penini (mostly still in manuscript; the most complete manuscript is in the British Museum (Add. Ms. 27, 168); others are in Vienna, Amsterdam, and Leningrad). Despite his bombastic style, Abraham's works contain interesting historical details and provide an insight into the contemporary cultural scene. Between 1290 and 1295 he wrote *Ha-Ḥerev ha-Mithappekhet* ("The Revolving Sword"), a lengthy poem of 210 verses (according to the numerical value of the Hebrew letters in *ḥerev*). In it, Abraham mentions his birthplace and his father, and comments on the Hebrew poets who preceded him in Provence and Spain. He considered himself their inferior. He did, however, contend that he was the best poet of his generation and challenged his contemporaries to a competition for which he proposed judges. Abraham also composed *Ḥotam Tokhnit*, the first dictionary of Hebrew synonyms in the Bible. Both works were published in 1865, the latter with a commentary by Samuel David Luzzatto. There is some doubt whether Abraham or his son Jedaiah composed the prayer *Elef Alfin* (so called because its thousand (Heb. *elef*) words all begin with the letter *alef*; published in *Kerem Ḥemed*, 4 (1839), 57–65) and *Shir ha-Lamedin* (Frankfurt on the Oder, 1812), a *bakkashah* for the Day of Atonement, in which each word contains the letter *lamed*, and all subsequent letters of the alphabet are excluded.

BIBLIOGRAPHY: Baer, in: *Devir*, 2 (1924), 313–6; Baer, Spain, 1 (1961), 119, 142, 162; Schirmann, Sefarad, 2 (1956), 466–71, 695; idem, in *Sefer… Y. Baer* (1961), 154–73; Bergmann, in: MGWJ, 42 (1898), 507–17; I. Davidson, *Parody in Jewish Literature* (1907), 16ff.; Davidson, Oẓar, 4 (1933), 352; Regné, in: REJ, 62 (1911), 59ff.; Gross, Gal Jud, s.v. *Béziers*; Renan, Rabbins, 707–19; Doniach, in: JQR, 23 (1932/33), 63–69, cf. 349–56. **ADD. BIBLIOGRAPHY:** M. Thama, *Mashkiyot Kesef* (1765), 23b–26a; Schirmann-Fleischer, *The History of Hebrew Poetry in Christian Spain and Southern France* (1997), 469–90.

[Jefim (Hayyim) Schirmann / Zvi Avneri]

BEDFORD, English county town. In the Middle Ages a small community existed in Bedford, which housed one of the *archae* for registration of Jewish debts. Local Jews suffered from violence during the Barons' Wars in 1263 and again in 1274. Three Jews were hanged for coin clipping in 1278. By the time of the expulsion of the Jews from England in 1290, the community seems to have been almost extinct. Jews resettled in Bedford at the end of the 18th century, and a tiny community existed from 1803 to 1827 and from 1837 to c. 1879. Organized Jewish life was revived briefly in 1903 and again during the evacuation from London in 1939–45. In 1968 there were 55 Jews in Bedford and in 2004 the population was estimated at 45.

BIBLIOGRAPHY: C. Roth, *Rise of Provincial Jewry* (1950), 29–31; Roth, England, index; M. Lissack, *Jewish Perseverance* (1851); Rigg-Jenkinson, Exchequer. **ADD. BIBLIOGRAPHY:** JYB, 2004.

[Cecil Roth]

BEDIKAT ḤAMEẒ (Heb. בְּדִיקַת חָמֵץ; "searching for leaven"), ceremony of searching for leaven, instituted in order to ensure that not even the smallest particle of **ḥameẓ* remains in the house during Passover. The biblical injunction, "Even the first day shall ye put away leaven out of your house" (Ex. 12:15), was interpreted by the rabbis as referring to the eve of Passover, i.e., the 14th of Nisan. The ceremony of *bedikat ḥameẓ* takes place on the 13th of Nisan (or the 12th if the 13th should be on a Friday). It follows the *Ma'ariv* prayer immediately after nightfall and before any other kind of activity is undertaken. The ceremony is preceded by the blessing: "Blessed art Thou O Lord our God, King of the Universe, Who hast sanctified us by Thy commandments and commanded us concerning the removal of the leaven."

By the light of a wax candle, with a wooden spoon and a whisk made of several chicken or goose feathers tied together, the master of the house searches every corner in the house for stray crumbs. Every room into which *ḥameẓ* may have been brought during the past year has to be searched. Since a blessing must never be recited without good reason, a few crumbs of bread are deliberately left on window sills and in other obvious places. The ceremony of *bedikat ḥameẓ* takes precedence even over the study of Torah on that evening. If the husband is not available, the ceremony has to be performed by the wife or another member of the family. The kabbalistic school of R. Isaac Luria hid ten pieces of bread for *bedikat ḥameẓ*. Leaven to the mystics symbolized the ferment of base desires and evil impulses which had to be purged. Upon completion of *bedikat ḥameẓ*, the leaven collected is put away in a safe place and the master of the house recites these words: "May all leaven that is in my possession, which I have not observed, searched out or had cognizance of, be regarded as null and be common property, even as the dust of the earth." On the morning of the 14th of Nisan, no later than 10 A.M., the leaven is burned and a similar Aramaic formula is recited. This observance is called *Bi'ur ḥameẓ* – the removal or the burning of *ḥameẓ*. The laws concerning *bedikat ḥameẓ* are codified in Shulḥan Arukh (OḤ 431 to 445).

[Harry Rabinowicz]

BEDZIN (Yid. **Bendin**), town in the Zaglembie Dabrowskie area, Kielce district, Poland. A Jewish settlement existed in Bedzin from the beginning of the 13th century with a privilege from Casimir the Great and his successors to work as merchants The development of Bedzin was interrupted by the Swedish invasion of the mid-17th cent. In 1765 the Jewish population numbered 446; in 1856, 2,440 (58.6% of the total); in 1897, 10,839 (45.6%); in 1909, 22,674 (48.7%); in 1921, 17,298 (62.1%); and in 1931, 21,625 (45.4%). A large number of Jewish workers were employed in Bedzin's developing industries at the beginning of the 20th century, and the town became the center of Jewish and Polish socialist activity and Jewish workers parties like the Bund and Po'alei Zion during the 1905 Russian revolution. Zionist activities were begun in Bedzin by Ḥovevei Zion in the 1880s and expanded in interbellum Poland to comprise various Zionist youth organizations. After World War I Jews took a considerable part in iron-ore mining, metallurgy, zinc and tin processing, and the production of cables, screws, nails, and iron and copper wire. Jewish-owned undertakings included chemical works and factories for paints, candles, and bakelite products, in particular buttons for the garment industry, which expanded in the area during 1924–31. Most Jews earned their livelihoods as merchants and craftsmen.

Jewish schools and a gymnasium (secondary school) were supported by the community with the help of donations from local Jewish industrialists. The Jewish community was very active organizing social and cultural institutions. The first pioneers of the Third Aliyah came from Bedzin. Dr. S. Weinzier was elected as member of Parliament (Sejm). The chain of credit cooperatives and free loan societies established in Bedzin through the American Jewish Joint Distribution Committee had a membership of nearly 1,000.

[Nathan Michael Gelber / Shlomo Netzer (2nd ed.)]

Holocaust Period

The German army entered the town on Sept. 5, 1939, and five days later they burned the Great Synagogue in the Old City. About 50 houses surrounding the synagogue, which were inhabited exclusively by Jews, went up in flames and 60 Jews were burned to death. During 1940–41 the situation in Bedzin was considered somewhat better than in most other places in occupied Poland (Bedzin and its neighbor *Sosnowiec were for a long time the only large cities in Poland where no ghetto was established). For this reason thousands of Jews from central Poland sought refuge there. Several thousand Jews from the district were expelled and forced to reside in Bedzin, among them all the Jews from Oswiecim (German name – Auschwitz), who arrived in April–May 1941, prior to the construction of the Auschwitz camp. About 6,500 Jews in the town were sent to forced labor camps and others were put to work locally making clothing and boots for the German army. In May and June 1942 the first deportations took place in which 2,400 "nonproductive" Jews were sent to their death in Auschwitz. On Aug. 15, 1942, about 8,000–10,000 Jews were sent to Auschwitz, while others were shot on the spot for disobeying German orders. In spring 1943 a ghetto was established in the suburb of Kamionka. On June 22, 1943, 4,000 Jews were deported and on August 1, 1943, the final liquidation of the ghetto began. In all, about 30,000 Jews were sent to Auschwitz from Bedzin. Only a limited number of Jews survived the concentration camps by hiding. The Jewish underground resistance in Bedzin became active at the beginning of 1940. They circulated illegal papers and made contact with the Warsaw Ghetto underground. After the establishment of the ghetto, the underground concentrated mainly on preparations for armed resistance. A unified fighting organization came into being with strong ties with the Jewish Fighting Organization of the Warsaw Ghetto. On Aug. 3, 1943, during the last deportation, some armed resistance broke out. Among the fighters who fell in battle was the leading Jewish partisan Frumka Plotnicka. Deportees from Bedzin played a major role in the underground and uprising in the Auschwitz death camp (among them – Jeshajahu Ehrlich, Moshe Wygnanski, Ala Gertner, and Rosa Sapirstein). Although some Jewish survivors settled in Bedzin after the war (in 1946 the Jewish population numbered 150 people), all of them left after some time.

[Stefan Krakowski]

BIBLIOGRAPHY: *Yidishe Ekonomik* (1938), 488–90; A.S. Stein (ed.), *Pinkas Bendin* (Heb. and Yid., 1959). **ADD. BIBLIOGRAPHY:** Y.Rapaport (ed.), *Pinkas Zaglembie* (1972); D. Liver, *Ir ha-Meitim* (1946); *Hancia u-Frumka* (1945); PK.

BEE (Heb. דְּבוֹרָה). Beekeeping was practiced early in the Mediterranean region. However, there is no reference to it in the Bible where the bee is mentioned only four times and only once in connection with honey (Judg. 14:9). References to bees stinging those who approach them (Deut. 1:44; Ps. 118:12) may refer to the gathering of wild honeycombs, and the finding of honey is mentioned (I Sam. 14:25; Prov. 16:4). Bees swarm when the land is desolate and untilled, so that a child will then eat "butter and honey" (Isa. 7:22). On the other hand, the honey of "a land flowing with milk and honey" (Deut. 8:8) is date honey according to the rabbis. There are frequent references to beekeeping in the talmudic era. The rabbis give detailed accounts of the beehives which were made of wicker and attached to the ground with clay (Oho. 8:1; Uk. 3:10) and discuss the number of honeycombs which it was permitted to take from the hives in the case of a man who acquires them for one year only (BB 5:3). Bee honey is permitted as food and the rule "that which derives from the unclean is itself unclean" does not apply to it. The reason adduced is that the bee does not produce the honey but sucks it from the flowers and discharges it through the mouth (Bek. 7b). The bee referred to is the *Apis mellifica* whose sting is especially acute. For this reason in recent times the Italian species *Apis ligustica*, which is easier to handle, has been introduced into Israel.

BIBLIOGRAPHY: Lewysohn, Zool, 301; Dalman, Arbeit, 7 (1942), 291 ff.; F.S. Bodenheimer, *Ha-Ḥai be-Arẓot ha-Mikra*, 2 (1956), index; J. Feliks, *Animal World of the Bible* (1962), 120. **ADD. BIBLIOGRAPHY:** Feliks, Ha-Ẓome'aḥ, 215.

[Jehuda Feliks]

°**BEEK, MARTINUS ADRIANUS** (1909–1987), Dutch Bible scholar and Orientalist. He was minister of the Dutch Reformed Church and professor of the exegesis of the Hebrew Bible (in the Faculty of Theology) and of Hebrew language and literature (in the Faculty of Humanities) at the University of Amsterdam (1946–74). He was the successor to Judah L. *Palache, who was dismissed from his position in November 1940 and murdered in Auschwitz (1944).

Beek's books include works on Jewish apocalyptic literature, the literature and history of the Mesopotamian area, the history of Ancient Israel, a general introduction to the Bible, the modern State of Israel, and Martin Buber. Most of his books have been translated into English and/or German. From his many articles mention should be made of his "Saturation Points and Unfinished Lines in the Study of Old Testament Literature" (in Dutch, 1968; transl. in: *Voices from Amsterdam*, 1994) which became a stimulus for his students to explore new methods of interpretation. He was an initiator of the Societas Hebraica Amstelodamensis, which became known for the *Amsterdamse Cahiers* series and the translation of Ruth, Jonah, and other biblical books into Dutch ("to be read aloud"), published by the Dutch Bible Societies.

Of his many administrative activities outside the university mention should be made of his longstanding work for the Liberal Protestant radio corporation in the Netherlands (VPRO), the Netherlands-Israel Friendship League, the Bible Museum in Amsterdam, and the Praemium Erasmianum.

He was succeeded by Karel A. Deurloo (Faculty of Theology) and by Maas Boertien (Faculty of Humanities), who edited Tractate *Nazir* in the Giessener Mischna (1971).

BIBLIOGRAPHY: M.S.H.G. Heerma van Voss (ed.), *Travels in the World of the Old Testament* (1974), incl. bibl.; Suppl. to bibl. in: *Amsterdamse Cahiers voor exegese en bijbelse theologie* 5 (1984); M.A. Beek, *Wegwijzers en wegbereiders. Een halve eeuw oudtestamentische wetenschap.* (1975); L. van Reijendam-Beek (ed.), *'Hier blijven half alle ogenblikken'. Keuze uit het werk van M.A. Beek* (1988); M. Kessler (ed.), *Voices from Amsterdam* (1994); I.E. Zwiep, in: P.J. Knegtmans and P.T. van Rooden (eds.), *Theologie in ondertal* (2003); J. Siebert-Hommes, ibid.

[F.J. Hoogewoud (2nd ed.)]

BEER (Heb. בְּאֵר; "a well"), the name of several biblical localities. (1) One of the stations where the Israelites stopped during the Exodus, north of the Brook of Zered in Transjordan (Num. 21:16–18). It is possibly identical with Beer-Elim (Isa. 15:8) in southern Moab. (2) The place where *Jotham, son of *Gideon, sought refuge when he fled from his brother Abimelech (Judg. 9:21). As this place is associated with the history of *Gideon's family, it is generally located north of the Jezreel Valley. The Septuagint mentions Beeroth, in the inheritance of Issachar, between Shion and Anaharath, i.e., in the vicinity of Mount Tabor (Josh. 19:19), where the Arab village of al-Bīra is located. Nearby is Khirbat al-Bīra, where remains of the early Israelite period have been discovered. The village was abandoned by its inhabitants during the War of Independence.

BIBLIOGRAPHY: F.-M. Abel, in: JPOS, 17 (1937), 42ff. (Fr.).

[Michael Avi-Yonah]

BEER, AARON (1739–1821), German cantor, composer, and collector. Beer was born near Bamberg and was known as "*der Bamberger ḥazzan.*" He had a tenor voice of unusually wide range. While still a youth he became cantor of the Paderborn congregation and at the age of 26 was appointed chief cantor of the Heidereutergasse Synagogue in Berlin, a position he held until his death. Beer was known for his extensive repertory of liturgical melodies, including many of his own composition. Tradition credits him with 1,210 items. He made a habit of varying his tunes for regular prayers in order to discourage the congregation from joining in his singing, a practice he profoundly disapproved. Beer's collection of 447 festival prayer melodies was passed down to his successor, Asher Leon (1776–1863), and thereafter to Cantor Moritz Deutsch of Breslau (1818–92), H. Schlesinger, and Cantor E. Birnbaum (1855–1920). It is now in the library of the *Hebrew Union College in Cincinnati.

BIBLIOGRAPHY: Idelsohn, Melodien, 6 (1932), 1–194 (for Beer's preface in Hebrew, see after title page); Sendrey, Music, nos. 6042–43; Friedmann, Lebensbilder, 2 (1921), 27–29; J. Meisl et al. (eds.), *Pinkas Kehillat Berlin, 1723–1854* (1962), 229, 230, 232, 280; Idelsohn, Music, index.

[Joshua Leib Ne'eman]

BEER, BERNHARD (1801–1861), German scholar, community leader, and bibliophile. For nearly 30 years Beer served as head of the Dresden Jewish community and its schools. He founded various charitable organizations, and in 1829 joined in establishing a Mendelssohn Society for the furtherance of scholarship, art, and trades among Jewish youth. Through his writings and personal active efforts, Beer was able to wage an eventually successful struggle for the civic equality of the Jews in Saxony. Although he observed traditional practice and was emotionally attached to Jewish customs, Beer rejected Orthodoxy intellectually and aesthetically in favor of moderate reforms, especially in liturgy. He was the first Jew to give a German sermon in a Dresden synagogue. Beer's religious views were similar to those of his close friend, Zacharias *Frankel. Nevertheless the reformers *Geiger and *Holdheim also accorded him respect and admiration, and Beer was regarded as a mediating influence between the proponents of tradition and those of reform. Beer wrote numerous scholarly articles and reviews which appeared in Frankel's *Zeitschrift* and *Monatsschrift* as well as in *Orient, Kerem Ḥemed*, and other journals. His books include *Das Buch der Jubilaeen und sein Verhaeltniss zu den Midraschim* (1856), *Juedische Literaturbriefe* (1857), and *Leben Abrahams nach Auffassung der juedischen Sage* (1859). He also translated into German, with additions, Solomon Munk's *La Philosophie chez les Juifs* (Leipzig, 1852). The extensive and valuable library which Beer acquired during his lifetime was divided after his death between the Breslau Seminary and the University of Leipzig, where Beer received his doctorate in 1834.

BIBLIOGRAPHY: Frankel, in: MGWJ, 11 (1862); G. Wolf, *Ohel Issakhar*, Catalogue of B. Beer's Library in Dresden (Ger. and Heb., 1863). **ADD. BIBLIOGRAPHY:** R. Heuer (ed.), *Lexikon deutsch-juedischer Autoren*, 1 (1992), 435–40; A. Braemer, *Rabbiner Zacharias Frankel* (2000), index.

[Michael A. Meyer]

BEER, GEORGE LOUIS (1872–1920), U.S. historian and publicist. Born in Staten Island, N.Y., during his twenties he was successful in the tobacco business, from which he retired in 1903 to devote himself to research on the theme which commanded all his work as an historian: the economic features of 17th- and 18th-century British colonial policy. His writings include: *Commercial Policy of England toward the American Colonies* (1893); *British Colonial Policy, 1754–65* (1907); *The Origins of the British Colonial System, 1578–1660* (1908); and *The Old Colonial System, 1660–1754* (2 vols., 1912). Beer's basic theses were that English colonization had aimed at setting up a self-sufficient commercial empire of interdependent and complementary areas; that British commercial policy toward the American colonies had promoted their growth; and that the removal of the French from Canada encouraged the American colonies to assert themselves and seek independence. During World War I, Beer supported the British cause. He expressed the hope, particularly in *The English Speaking Peoples* (1917), that Great Britain and the U.S. would ultimately rejoin in a political union, to ensure the progress of the postwar world. He served as chief of the colonial division of the American delegation at the Paris Peace Conference, and helped draft the treaty provisions dealing with the former German colonies. He urged the establishment of "mandates" to promote the welfare of the natives. His *African Questions at the Paris Peace Conference* was published in 1923. A participant in many communal and charitable activities, Beer was a director of the Jewish Protectory and Aid Society.

BIBLIOGRAPHY: *George Louis Beer…* (1924); DAB, s.v.; Scott, in: *Marcus W. Jernegan Essays…* (1937), 313–22; Cockroft, in: H. Ausubel et al. (eds.), *Some Modern Historians of Britain* (1951), 269–85.

[Abraham S. Eisenstadt]

BE'ER, HAIM (1945–), Israeli writer. Born in Jerusalem, Be'er grew up in an Orthodox family, among deeply religious Jews whose conversations were studded with quotations from the Bible, the Talmud, and the later rabbinic literature. Following his army service in the military chaplaincy, he joined the Am Oved Publishing House in Tel Aviv, where he advanced from proofreader to member of the editorial board. Be'er's prose depicts the Orthodox milieu, a wide and colorful range of types, some eccentric or comic, others pitiable. His first novel, *Noẓot* (*Feathers*; Eng. trans. 2004) describes the experiences and observations of a boy growing up in Jerusalem and joining a military burial squad during the Yom Kippur War (1973). A sense of the grotesque, which underlines the portraits of a bizarre visionary leader, Esperantists, and vegetarians, also marks Be'er's second novel, *Et ha-Zamir* ("The Time of Trimming," 1987). It is the story of Naḥum Gevirẓ, serving in a rabbinical unit between 1965 and 1967, a period of messianic dreams and hopes of "liberating the Holy City from captivity." This merciless account, marked by parody and biting criticism, was described by critics as "the Israeli Catch 22." Be'er's personal experiences play an even more significant role in his third novel, *Ḥavalim* (1998; *The Pure Element of Time*,

2003), an autobiographical novel which has been praised as a pastiche of different styles. While the first part centers on the figure of the author's grandmother, a remarkable woman and a born storyteller, the second part depicts the marriage of his parents, his beloved mother and her much older, melancholy husband. The third part of this gripping epic triptych describes the protagonist's first steps as a writer. Other books by Be'er are a collection of poems *Sha'ashuei Yom Yom* (1970) and a study of the literary and personal relations between three outstanding Hebrew writers: Brenner, Bialik, and Agnon (*Gam Ahavtam, Gam Sinatam*, 1993).

BIBLIOGRAPHY: H. Halkin, "Three Men at the Hub," in: *The Jerusalem Report* (Dec. 17, 1992); J. Green, in: *The Jerusalem Post* (Oct. 16, 1998); H. Hever, in: *Haaretz, Sefarim* (Sept. 23, 1998); D. Rak, *Ha-Zhener ha-otobiyografi be-Sifrut ha-Olam u-Vituyo bi-Yeẓirat Haim Be'er u-vi-Yeẓirat Philip Roth* (2002); G. Shaked, "Between Utopia and Apocalypse: On H. Beer's *Noẓot*," in: *Modern Hebrew Literature* 6, 1–2 (1980), 14–18; idem *"Ha-Orev ha-Satiri be-Noẓot ha-Zamir,"* in: *Moznayim* 61, 10–11 (1988), 24–27; Z. Shamir, in: *Maariv* (Mar. 28, 1980); S. Katz, *"Yonim ba-Meiẓar,"* in: *Yerushalayim* 15, 2 (1981), 98–104; R. Lee, *"Od Noẓah al Noẓot,"* in: *Ha-Do'ar* 60,19 (1981), 299–300; G. Shaked, *"Ha-Orev ha-Satiri be-Noẓot ha-Zamir,"* in: *Moznayim* 61, 10–11 (1988), 24–27; Y. Oren, *"Ḥavalim,"* in: *Moznayim* 73, 4 (1999), 49–52; N. Ben Dov, *"Ḥevlei Ḥayyim,"* in: *Alei Si'aḥ* 42 (2000), 74–78. **WEBSITE:** www.ithl.org.il

[Anat Feinberg (2nd ed.)]

BEER, ISRAEL (1912–1966), military commentator and Soviet agent in Israel. Beer went to Palestine from Vienna in November 1938. He joined the *Haganah and was appointed to the Central Training Bureau. During the War of Independence he served on the General Staff with the rank of lieutenant colonel. After retiring from the army in 1949, he became noted as a military commentator in Israel and abroad. Later, when he held the chair of military history at Tel Aviv University, *Ben-Gurion commissioned him to prepare the official history of the War of Independence. In 1961 Beer was arrested and accused of having contact with a Soviet intelligence agent. He was found guilty of treason and sentenced to 15 years' imprisonment. He died in prison. The true facts of Beer's biography until his arrival in Palestine are difficult to establish, since he himself gave varying versions. Apparently, he was born in Vienna and studied literature and philosophy at the University of Vienna. He claimed to have simultaneously joined the Schutzbund (the military organization of the Austrian Social-Democratic Party) and the government militia, and to have graduated from a course at Wiener Neustadt Military Academy with the rank of lieutenant in 1935. He also alleged that, at the outbreak of the Spanish Civil War in 1936, he had been ordered by the Social-Democratic Party to join the International Brigade, being finally promoted to the rank of lieutenant colonel. He wrote *Der Nahe Osten, Schicksalsland zwischen Ost und West* (1960), and *Bitḥon Yisrael – Etmol, ha-Yom, Maḥar* (1966; "Israel's Security – Yesterday, Today, Tomorrow").

[Jehuda Wallach]

BEER, MAX (**Moses**; 1864–1943), German socialist historian and journalist. Beer was born in Tarnobrzeg, Galicia. Coming from socialist circles there, he emigrated to Germany via Vienna in 1889. He was first employed as a type-setter and printer, then became assistant editor of the social democratic daily *Die Volksstimme* ("Voice of the People") in Magdeburg. In 1893, as a result of a newspaper article, he was imprisoned for 14 months on the basis of the Sozialistengesetz (1878) and expelled from Prussia on his release. He stayed in London until 1915. In 1895–96, he enrolled at the newly founded London School of Economics, earning his living as a language teacher, lecturer, and correspondent for the social democratic paper *Post* in Munich and the Jewish *Arbeiter-Zeitung* in New York. From 1899 to 1901, he temporarily joined the latter's staff in New York and contributed to the *Jewish Encyclopaedia* (1901–06). Back in London, Beer became correspondent for the social democratic weekly *Neue Zeit* (est. 1898) and the Berlin daily *Vorwaerts*, the central organ of the German Social Democratic Party. In 1912, however, he resigned from his post due to political differences and intensified his historical research on British and international socialism. In 1913, his *Geschichte des Sozialismus in England* appeared which became a standard work (cf. *A History of British Socialism*, 2 vols., 1919–20). Considered an "enemy alien" during World War I, Beer was repatriated to Germany in 1915 where he continued his research and was naturalized as a German citizen in 1920 (revoked in 1934). In 1919–21, he edited *Die Glocke*, contributed book reviews to the *Times Literary Supplement*, and finally was invited by D. Ryazanov to serve as English librarian of the Marx Engels Institute in Moscow from 1927 to 1929. On his return, Beer was employed at the Frankfurt Institute for Social Research until, in 1933/34, almost 70 years old, he was forcibly divorced from his non-Jewish wife and expelled from Germany. Broken and impoverished, Beer again settled in London, continuing his research with the aid of the British Central Fund for German Jewry. In 1935, he published his autobiographical work *Fifty Years of International Socialism*. In 1943, almost forgotten, he died at the age of 78.

Due to his personal experience, Beer was considered one of the greatest experts on British and international socialism of his time. In 1918, on Karl Marx's centenary, Beer was commissioned to write *Karl Marx. Eine Monographie* (cf. *The Life and Teachings of Karl Marx*, 1921), followed by *Allgemeine Geschichte des Sozialismus und der sozialen Kaempfe*, 5 vols. (1919–23), which was published in several languages (cf. *General History of Socialism and Social Struggles*, 1922–26). Among Beer's other works are *Das Regenbogenbuch* (1915); *Jean Jaurès* (1915); *Sozialistische Dokumente des Weltkrieges*, nos. 1–5 (1915–16); *L'Entente annexionniste* (1917); *Der britische Sozialismus der Gegenwart 1910–1920* (1920); *Krieg und Internationale* (1924); *Die Reise nach Genf* (1932; *The League on Trial*, 1933); *Die auswärtige Politik des Dritten Reiches* (1934); and *Early British Economics from the Thirteenth to the Middle of the Eighteenth Century* (1938).

BIBLIOGRAPHY: R. Heinefling, in: *Universal Jewish Encyclopedia*, vol. II (1940), 133–34; W. Roeder and H.A. Strauss (eds.), *International Biographical Dictionary of Central European Emigrés 1933–1945*, vol. II (1983), 69; H. Schmuck (ed.), *Jewish Biographical Archive* (1995), F. 124, 165–71; Series II (2003), F. II/47, 124–34; S. Blumesberger et al. (eds.), *Handbuch oesterreichischer Autorinnen und Autoren juedischer Herkunft*, vol. I, no. 660 (2002), 86.

[Johannes Valentin Schwarz (2nd ed.)]

BEER, MICHAEL (1800–1833), German poet and playwright; brother of the composer Giacomo *Meyerbeer and of the astronomer Wilhelm *Beer. In one of his earliest works, the classical tragedy *Klytemnestra* (1823), he attempted to gain sympathy for a heroine who murders her husband. Beer's play was successfully performed in 1819 at the Berlin Hoftheater and later in Vienna. In 1825, he achieved a triumph with the poetic drama *Der Paria*, a disguised plea for Jewish emancipation, which won high praise from Goethe. Beer moved to Paris in 1824, and in 1827 settled in Munich, where he enjoyed the goodwill of King Ludwig of Bavaria and the friendship of Eduard von Schenk, the minister of interior. *Struensee*, generally regarded as his best play, was produced by the Bavarian Royal Theater in 1828, when it was favorably reviewed by Heine. The incidental music for *Struensee* was composed by his brother Meyerbeer. Beer's narrative poems include only one with a Jewish theme, a legend entitled *Der fromme Rabbi*. His collected plays and poems appeared in 1835, with an introductury biographical sketch by Eduard von Schenk and verse tributes by Schenk and M.G. *Saphir. Two years later, Schenk published Beer's collected letters.

BIBLIOGRAPHY: KAHN, IN: YLBI, 12 (1967), 149–60. **ADD. BIBLIOGRAPHY:** J. Stenzel, in: *Jahrbuch des freien deutschen Hochstifts* (1987), 314–35; R. Heuer (ed.), *Lexikon deutsch-juedischer Autoren*, 1 (1992), 442–44, bibl.; H. Olbrich, in: A. Kilcher (ed.), *Metzler Lexikon der deutsch-juedischen Literatur* (2000), 39–41.

[Sol Liptzin / Marcus Pyka (2nd ed.)

BEER, PETER (**Perez**; pen name: **Theophil Nikodem**; 1758 (or 1764)–1838), Austrian educator and author, representative of radical *Haskalah in the Habsburg Empire. Beer, who had a traditional Jewish education, also learned Latin and German. He attended the Prague and Pressburg (Bratislava) yeshivot, and from 1780 studied pedagogy at Vienna University, being one of the first Jews to train as a teacher within the educational reform program introduced by Emperor *Joseph II. From 1784 he taught at *Mattersdorf, then at his native Nový *Bydžov, and from 1811 until his death at the new Prague "Normalschule." Beer was also appointed "teacher of morals" to the Jewish pupils at Prague high schools in 1813, being probably the first Jew appointed to hold a government appointment and entitled to wear a government employee's uniform. In 1796 Beer published his *Toledot Yisrael*, a history of the Jews, omitting chapters likely to be unpalatable to enlightened circles, such as the slaying of the prophets of Baal by Elijah, as well as the entire talmudic period. It became the blueprint of biblical history textbooks used by teachers of the Enlightenment school in Europe for many years, both in the original and in translation (the last Russian translation was published in 1905). In 1809 Beer published *Dat Yisrael* and in 1810 *Emet ve-Emunah*, religious manuals in German. His two-volume *Geschichte, Lehren und Meinungen aller religioesen Sekten der Juden und der Geheimlehre oder Kabbala* (1822–23) is even now interesting for the material on the *Frankists and *Ḥasidism. In them, he developed an ideology of "Mosaism," which, parallel to "Christianity" that embraces Catholicism, Protestantism, etc., covers all different Jewish sects. Beer wrote several appeals, some anonymously, to the authorities on matters of public interest, including the question of military service and the establishment of a rabbinical seminary in Prague. He contributed to the periodicals **Sulamith, Ha-Me'assef* (see *Me'assefim), and **Bikkurei ha-Ittim*, and published a prayer book for "educated women" (1815). He was instrumental in opening the Reform synagogue in Prague and in inviting Leopold *Zunz to serve as preacher. He published a commentary on Genesis intended for readers of all creeds, drawing heavily on contemporary Protestant commentators. Only one installment of his translation of Maimonides' *Guide* was published (1834). It was sharply criticized by Joseph *Derenbourg. Beer was highly esteemed by the Austrian authorities and was awarded a decoration. However, his educational activities were viewed with suspicion by the majority of Jews. His autobiography, edited by Moritz Hermann, was published in 1839.

BIBLIOGRAPHY: Z. Scharfstein, *Toledot ha-Ḥinnukh*, 1 (1945), 135–6; R. Kestenberg-Gladstein, *Neuere Geschichte der Juden in den boehmischen Laendern*, 1 (1969), index; 39 (1963/64), 128; R. Mahler, *Ha-Ḥasidut ve-ha-Haskalah* (1961), index; G. Wolf, in: ZGJD, 5 (1892), 40–43; G. Scholem, in: YLBI, 7 (1962), 248–9; F. Roubík, in: JGGJČ, 5 (1933), 313–37;9 (1938), 411–47. **ADD. BIBLIOGRAPHY:** M. Brenner, "Between Kabbala and Haskala: Peter Beer's History of Jewish Sects," in: E. Carlebach and D.N. Myers (eds.), *History and Memory: Jewish Perspectives* (1998), 389–404; I. Schorsch, *From Text to Context: The Turn to History in Modern Judaism* (1995), index; V. Sadek and J. Šedinová, "Peter Beer (1758-1838): Penseur éclairé de la vieille ville juive de Prague," *in: Judaica Bohemiae*, 13 (1977), 7–28; R. Michael, *Ha-Ketivah ha-Historit ha-Yehudit me-ha-Renesans ad ha-Et ha-Ḥadashah* (1993), 155–67. L. Hecht, "How the Power of Thought Can Develop within a Human Mind – Salomon Maimon, Peter Beer, Lazarus Bendavid: Autobiographies of Maskilim Written in German," in: *LBI-Year Book*, 48 (2002), 21–38; idem, "The Clash of Maskilim in Prague in the Early 19th Century: Herz Homberg Versus Peter Beer," in: *Proceedings of the 12th World Congress of Jewish Studies* (Jerusalem 2000), Division B (History of the Jewish People), 165–74.

BEER, RACHEL (**Richa**; 1858–1927), owner and editor of the *Sunday Times*, London, 1893–1904. Rachel Beer was born in Bombay, the daughter of Sasson David *Sassoon and Flora (Farḥa) Reuben of Baghdad. She was an infant when the family settled in England. In an age which afforded women little scope, she displayed both character and talent. For two years she worked as an unpaid hospital nurse, and in 1887 married Frederick Arthur Beer, owner of the *Observer*. She became a contributor to the paper, and later its editor. In 1893 she bought its rival the *Sunday Times* which she edited while retaining her position on the *Observer*. Under her control the *Sunday Times* changed its outlook from independent liberal to non-partisan. She was also a composer and published a piano sonata and a piano trio. The first woman ever to edit a Fleet Street newspaper, in the 1890s she obtained one of the great "scoops" of the age for the *Observer* when she obtained proof that the documents used to convict Alfred *Dreyfus in France had been forged. Siegfried *Sassoon (1886–1967), the famous poet, was her nephew.

BIBLIOGRAPHY: C. Roth, *The Sassoon Dynasty* (1941); B. Falk, *Bouquets for Fleet Street* (1951). **ADD. BIBLIOGRAPHY:** D. Griffiths (ed.), *Encyclopedia of the British Press, 1422–1992* (1992), 98; S. Jackson, *The Sassoons: Portrait of a Dynasty* (1998); C. Bermant, *The Cousinhood* (1961), index; ODNB online.

BE'ER, RAMI (1957–), dancer, choreographer, and artistic director of the Kibbutz Contemporary Dance Company. He was born into a family of musicians in kibbutz Ga'aton in Israel. At a very early age, he began studying cello and later studied dance with Yehudit Arnon. Be'er joined the company as a dancer and choreographer in 1980.

His choreographic style is influenced by Central European expressionism and American modern dance. Generally, his works take up a full evening's program and are constructed as a collage around a central theme. His themes are connected to the reality in which we live and his choreographies reflect the tension between abstraction and expression. *Reservist Diary* (1989) reveals the ethical uncertainties of an Israeli soldier in the reserves during the *Intifada*. In *Real Time* (1991), Be'er deals with the kibbutz movement as the parting of ways. In *Angelos Negros* (1992), he addresses the Spanish Inquisition. In *Naked City* (1993), the dominant motif is the loneliness of the individual. The theme of *Aide Memoire* (1994) is strongly influenced by Be'er's being a member of a family of Holocaust survivors. The set and lighting designs are usually Be'er's own creations. In *On the Edge* (1999), the stage is designed as a huge fortress, and in *Screensaver* (2002), rays emitted by a television set are part of the production. He was awarded the Contributor to Cultural and Educational Creativity Prize in 2000.

BIBLIOGRAPHY: H. Rottenberg, "Rami Be'er – A Political Choreographer." Dissertation (1997).

[Ruth Eshel (2nd ed.)]

BEER, SAMUEL FRIEDRICH (1846–1912), Czech sculptor. Beer studied in Vienna and quickly gained some recognition as a portraitist. His friendship with Theodor Herzl inspired his Jewish subjects, such as the monumental group *Shema Israel*. He designed the medal issued on the occasion of the Second Zionist Congress at Basle. He later worked in Paris, Rome, and Florence.

BIBLIOGRAPHY: Roth, Art, 868; T. Zlocisti, in: *Ost und West*, 5 (1905), 78, 82, 83ff., includes reproductions.

BEER, WILHELM (1797–1850), German astronomer and brother of Giacomo *Meyerbeer, the composer, and Michael *Beer, the poet. Wilhelm Beer joined and later succeeded his father in the family banking house. His leisure hours were spent in studying astronomy in an observatory he had constructed in his garden. Together with J.H. Maedler, he studied the planet Mars during the 1828, 1832, 1835, and 1837 oppositions and their findings were published. Later they made a map of the moon; over many years they recorded every aspect of the moon surface and published their findings in *Der Mond nach seinen kosmischen und individuellen Verhaeltnissen, oder allgemeine vergleichende Selenographie* (2 vols., 1837). This was the standard work for many years. When Maedler left and joined a university, Beer went into politics and in 1846 was elected to the Prussian Chamber of Deputies. A mountain on the moon is named for him.

BEER-BING, ISAIAH (1759–1805), one of the leaders in the struggle for the "regeneration" of the Jews of France. He wrote a number of pamphlets including a refutation of an anti-Jewish pamphlet by Aubert Dufayet (*Lettre du Sr I.B.B.... à l'auteur anonyme d'un écrit intitulé: Le cri du citoyen contre les juifs*, 1787, 18052). Beer-Bing was appointed to the commission headed by Malesherbes to improve the status of the Jews in 1788. In 1799 he drew up a memorandum on the community of his birthplace Metz. He was a member of the municipal council of Metz from 1790 and became the administrator of the saltworks in eastern France. He was on the editorial committee of the *Décade philosophique*. Beer-Bing translated the *Phaedon* of Moses *Mendelssohn from German into French and Hebrew (*Sefer Hasharat ha-Nefesh*, 1786–87, republished many times), a *Song of Zion* by Judah Halevi from Hebrew into French, and a fragment from the *Beḥinat Olam* by *Jedaiah ha-Penini (in *Essai sur la régénération... des juifs* by his friend the abbé *Grégoire, 1789).

BIBLIOGRAPHY: E. Carmoly in: *Revue orientale*, 2 (1842), 337f.

[Moshe Catane]

BEER-HOFMANN, RICHARD (1866–1945), Austrian poet and playwright. The son of a Moravian lawyer, Beer-Hofmann was adopted by his uncle, the Viennese industrialist Alois Hofmann. After graduating in law at the University of Vienna, he was drawn into the "Young Vienna" literary group, which included many of his close friends, Arthur *Schnitzler, Peter *Altenberg, Hermann Bahr, Theodor *Herzl, Hugo von *Hofmannsthal, and Felix *Salten. He influenced the style of Viennese Décadence in his *Novellen* (1893) and in his earliest lyric poem, *Schlaflied fuer Miriam* (1898). His only novel, *Der Tod Georgs* (1900), depicts a main protagonist whose fascination with paganism and aestheticism is replaced in the end by a return to Jewish tradition. Self-sacrifice for the glory of God remains an enduring motif in Beer-Hofmann's oeuvre. His first drama, *Der Graf von Charolais* (1904), features a character – the "Rote Itzig" – who contrasts the Elizabethan tragedy of the narration with the ongoing suffering of Jewry. Beer-Hoffmann's work reveals the special message Judaism seems to offer the world when Nietzschean philosophy considers it lost to man.

If Beer-Hofmann's early works can be interpreted as seeing the rebirth of modernity out of the spirit of Judaism, his subsequent work may be viewed as seeing the rebirth of Judaism out of the spirit of modernity. Impressed and inspired by the Neo-Wagnerian theater concept of Max *Reinhardt, who had already staged *Der Graf von Charolais*, Beer-Hofmann tried to open to Jewry a space from which religious imperatives had banned it: the theater. In pursuit of a "Jewish national drama," he continued work on his biblical cycle, *Die Historie von Koenig David*, for decades. The prologue *Jaákobs Traum*, premiering in 1918, focuses on Israel's election by blending Jacob's dream of the ladder and his wrestling with the angel. In contrast to the pagan rituals of sacrifice in which contemporary dramatic theory identified the roots of tragedy, the play makes the sacrifice of Isaac the primal scene of Jewish theater. The transition play *Ruth und Boas* remained a fragment. The third part of a planned pentalogy, *Der junge David*, was completed in 1933 but never staged. The drama shows David in conflict between his destiny as king and his wish to leave royal dignity to God. Again, the action is linked to the sacrifice of Isaac. Jewish theater, in Beer-Hoffmann's conception, is legitimate only if it eschews idols and has no symbols or icons at its disposal, just as Abraham stood at Mount Moriah with nothing to sacrifice but his own offspring. Further theoretical reflection is provided by the prelude to a nonexistent fourth part, the *Vorspiel auf dem Theater zu Koenig David* (1936), where the stage is likened to an altar on which theater itself must be sacrificed to avoid idolatry. The only one of Beer-Hofmanns dramatical works to achieve sustained international attention was *Jaákobs Traum*, which was staged in Palestine as early as the early 1920s.

Beer-Hofmann emigrated from Austria to New York in 1939. *Verse* (1941) includes all the poems that he wished preserved. A posthumous fragment in tribute to his wife, *Paula* (1949), captures the autumnal mood of Austria as it influenced his own life and shaped his personality.

BIBLIOGRAPHY: S. Liptzin, *Richard Beer-Hofmann* (1936); E. Kahler, *Verantwortung des Geistes* (1952), 131–42. **ADD. BIBLIOGRAPHY:** R. Hank, *Mortifikation und Beschwoerung. Zur Veraenderung ästhetischer Wahrnehmung in der Moderne am Beispiel Richard Beer-Hofmanns* (1984); S. Scherer, *Richard Beer-Hofmann und die Wiener Moderne* (1993); M. Bunzl, "The Poetics of Politics and Politics of Poetics: Richard Beer-Hofmann and Theodor Herzl Reconsidered," in: *The German Quarterly* 69 (1996), 277–304, P. Theisohn, *Die Urbarkeit der Zeichen. Zionismus und Literatur – eine andere Poetik der Moderne* (2005), 129–80.

[Sol Liptzin / Philipp Theisohn (2nd ed.)]

BE'ERI (Heb. בְּאֵרִי), kibbutz in S. Israel, in the N.W. Negev, affiliated with Ha-Kibbutz ha-Me'uḥad. It was one of 11 settlements in the Negev and the south founded during the night of October 6, 1946. The founding settlers, members of Ha-No'ar ha-Oved (Israel Working Youth Movement), were joined by other settlers, mainly from Iraq. In the mid-1990s the population was approximately 850, dropping to 753 in 2002. The economy was based mainly on its printing press. The kibbutz cultivated around 3,000 acres of farmland, which included field crops and orchards, and raised dairy cattle and ostriches. The name commemorates the labor leader Berl (Be'eri) *Katznelson.

[Efraim Orni]

WEBSITE: www.beeri.org.il.

BEERI, TUVIA (1929–), Israeli painter and printmaker. Beeri was born in Czechoslovakia and immigrated to Israel in 1948. In 1957 he entered the "Oranim" art school, where he studied with Marcel *Janco and Jacob Wechsler, continuing his studies in Paris. From 1961 to 1963 he studied the technique of etching under Johnny *Friedlaender and attended the studio of lithography at the Ecole des Beaux-Arts, Paris. Returning to Israel, he taught at the Bezalel School of Arts and Crafts. From 1957 he taught printmaking at the Avni Institute of Art, Tel Aviv.

Beeri was one of Israel's leading graphic artists. He used etching-needle and drypoint, but was particularly in favor of aquatint print technique, which, by the creation of color and the variation of planes, makes it possible to introduce painting quality into graphic work.

Beeri's world is a dream world of color and form. His paintings remind one of mysterious landscapes of the Pyramids and of ancient times. Luminosity is achieved by printing bright colors one above the other, thus achieving transparency, depth, and plasticity of forms.

Beeri held many one-man shows and participated in group exhibitions in the United States, Canada, South America, Australia, Europe, and Israel. He also took part in some important Biennales of the graphic arts – in Paris, Florence, and Tokyo. His work is represented in the Museum of Modern Art, New York, the Bibliothèque Nationale, Paris, and in many museums both in Israel and abroad.

BIBLIOGRAPHY: G. Talpir, in: *Gazit*, 23, nos. 3–4 (1965), 17; M. Tal, in: *Ariel*, 15 (Summer, 1966), 72–79.

[Judith Spitzer]

BEERMAN, LEONARD (1921–), U.S. Reform rabbi. Beerman was born in Altoona, Pennsylvania, served in the U.S. Marine Corps during World War II, and entered Hebrew Union College in 1943. He interrupted his seminary education to volunteer for the *Haganah in 1947–48, returning to receive his rabbinic ordination in 1949. Beerman became the founding rabbi of Leo Baeck Temple in Los Angeles that year and remained there until his retirement in 1986. His career was marked by social activism on behalf of civil and human rights, as well as world peace. He was on the faculty of Claremont Men's College and Immaculate Heart College and served as president of the Pacific Association of Reform Rabbis and vice president of the Southern California Board of Rabbis.

[Bezalel Gordon (2nd ed.)]

BE'ER ORAH (Heb. בְּאֵר אוֹרָה), training camp of *Gadna (the Israel pre-military youth corps) founded in 1950 in the southern Negev, 14 mi. (20 km.) north of Eilat. Youth were brought here in groups for periods of a fortnight or longer to combine the study of nature and farming with excursions, sports, and small-arms training. In May 2001 a ceremony was held establishing a civilian settlement near the training camp, with the same name. However, in 2006 it was still not inhabited. Be'er Orah, meaning "Well of Light," is a reversal of the former Arabic Bīr (Be'r) Ḥindīs, "Pitchblack Well," so called by the Bedouin because the strong magnesia content of the local well's water was likely to cause illness.

[Efraim Orni]

BEEROTH (Heb. בְּאֵרוֹת; "wells"), one of the Gibeonite cities mentioned as part of a confederacy together with Gibeon, Chephirah, and Kiriath-Jearim (Josh. 9:17). Beeroth is listed with the cities of Benjamin (Josh. 18:25); part of its population had previously fled to Gittaim (II Sam. 4:3). One of David's heroes came from Beeroth (II Sam. 23:37; I Chron. 11:39), as did the assassins of Ish-Bosheth (II Sam. 4:2). The town was resettled after the return from Babylon (Ezra 2:25; Neh. 7:29). Birea, where Bacchides encamped in 161 B.C.E. before the battle with Judah Maccabee (I Macc. 9:4), has been identified with the biblical locality. Beeroth is commonly identified with the Arab town al-Bīra near Ramallah, 9 mi. (14 km.) north of Jerusalem; Bronze Age remains have been found nearby, at Ra's al-Ṭaḥūn. Several attempts to identify Beeroth with Tell al-Naṣb (Mizpeh?) or al-Jib (Gibeon) have been disproved by recent excavations. It has been proposed to locate Beeroth at Nebi Samwil, 1 mi. (1½ km.) south of el-Jib. Although this identification has not yet been confirmed by archaeological findings, it is strengthened by the statement of Eusebius (Onom. 48:9) that a village with this name was situated 7 mi. from Jerusalem on the road to Nikopolis (Emmaus; but according to Jerome, on the road to Neapoli, i.e., Shechem), and its possible appearance on the *Madaba Map.

BIBLIOGRAPHY: D.A. Alt, in: ZDPV, 69 (1953), 1–29; K. Elliger, *ibid.*, 73 (1957), 125–32; idem, in: *Mélanges… A. Robert* (1957), 82–94; EM, 2 (1965), 8–9; Albright, in: AASOR, 4 (1924), 102–11; Z. Kallai, in: *Eretz Israel*, 3 (1954), 111–5.

[Michael Avi-Yonah]

BE'EROT YIZḤAK (Heb. בְּאֵרוֹת יִצְחָק), kibbutz in central Israel on the Coastal Plain, east of Lydda. Affiliated with Ha-Kibbutz ha-Dati, it was originally founded on Aug. 9, 1943, southeast of Gaza by a group of religious pioneers from Germany and was the first settlement in the Negev. During the War of Independence in May 1948, it was all but razed by shelling from the Egyptian army. The settlers put up strong resistance and drove the attackers back from buildings they had already occupied. Although never abandoned during the fighting, it was so utterly destroyed that it was decided not to rebuild the place and in August 1948 the settlers reestablished their kibbutz on its present site, the former German Templar village of Wilhelma (whose inhabitants were interned there during World War II and later deported from the country). The economy of the kibbutz was based on highly intensive farming and a factory for coated steel pipes and fittings (Avrot Industries). In subsequent years it also operated a successful Subway-style sandwich service, supplying El Al, army bases, and schools. In the mid-1990s the population was approximately 480, while at the end of 2002 it was 417.

The name, meaning "Isaac's Wells," both refers to the wells sunk by the Patriarch (Gen. 26:18ff.) in the part of the Negev where the group first settled, and also commemorates Yizḥak *Nissenbaum.

[Efraim Orni / Shaked Gilboa (2nd ed.)]

BEERSHEBA (biblical: Beer-Sheba; Heb. בְּאֵר שֶׁבַע), city in the *Negev on the southern border of Judah; its name has been preserved in the Arabic form Bīr (Be'r) al-Saʿb. Beersheba was first settled in the Chalcolithic period. Excavations conducted in its surroundings by J. Perrot uncovered remains of cave dwellings dug in the earth from this age. The inhabitants of the caves engaged in raising cattle and the manufacture of metal tools. Their pottery and stone vessels and figurines carved out of ivory and bone display a highly developed craftsmanship. Evidence of the beginnings of a religious cult was also found.

According to the Bible, Abraham and Isaac dug wells at Beer-Sheba and also formed alliances there with *Abimelech "king of the Philistines." The allies bound themselves under oath to observe the treaties, and in one source Abraham set aside seven ewes as a sign of the oath, which the Pentateuch explains was the origin of the name of the city (*Be'er,* "well"; *Sheva*, "oath" or "seven"; see Gen. 21:31; 26:33). The sanctuary of "the Lord, the Everlasting God," which was apparently located there in very early times, was invested with great importance in the tales set in the patriarchal period (Gen. 21:33; 26:23–24, 32–33; 46:1). After the rise of Israel, Beer-Sheba became a city of the tribe of Simeon and was later incorporated into the tribe of Judah (Josh. 15:28; 19:2). It appears to have been a center of the Israelite settlement in the Negev in the time of Samuel since his sons were sent there as judges (I Sam. 8:1–3). The sanctuary at Beer-Sheba was regarded as the extreme southern point of the country in contradistinction to the sanctuary at Dan which was held to be the northern point (Amos 5:5; 8:14). Thus the phrase "from Dan to Beer-Sheba" (Judg. 20:1, etc.) was the customary designation, at least until the days of David and Solomon, for the entire area of the country. After the division of the monarchy, Beer-Sheba continued to be the southern frontier of the kingdom of Judah; the expression "from Dan to Beer-Sheba" was then replaced by "from Beer-Sheba to the hill-country of Ephraim" (II Chron. 19:4) or "from Geba to Beer-Sheba" (II Kings 23:8). Zibiah, the mother of Jehoash, king of Judah, originated from Beer-Sheba (II Kings 12:2). Elijah set out on his journey to Horeb from Beer-Sheba, the gateway to the desert (I Kings 19:3, 8). The city was settled by Jews after the return from Babylon (Neh. 11:27, 30). The biblical town of Beer-Sheba is to be sought at Tell al-Saʿb (Tell Beer-Sheba, a UNESCO World Heritage site (2005)), 2½ mi. (4 km.) NE of the new town, where remains of a fortress and potsherds from the Iron Age to the Roman period were found in excavations begun in 1969 by Y. Aharoni.

After 70 C.E. Beersheba was included in the Roman frontier-line defenses against the Nabateans and continued to be a Roman garrison town after the Roman annexation of the Nabatean kingdom. A large village existed then at its present site, where many remains have been found including mosaic pavements and Greek inscriptions (including a sixth-century C.E. ordinance regarding tax payments, which was issued to the south of the country, and a synagogue inscription). In the fourth and fifth centuries C.E., Beersheba first belonged to the district of Gerar and was later annexed to "Palaestina Tertia." The town was abandoned in the Arab period.

[Michael Avi-Yonah]

Modern Beersheba

The modern settlement dates from 1900, when the Turkish government set up an administrative district in southern Palestine separate from that of Gaza and built an urban center in this purely nomadic region. The Turks were motivated by the need to strengthen governmental authority over the Bedouin at a time when Turkey was struggling with Britain over the delineation of the Egyptian border in Sinai. German and Swiss engineers aided in laying out a city plan. Both a city and a district council were set up, and Bedouin sheikhs held seats on them. Until 1914, however, progress was slow, and Beersheba had about 800 Muslim inhabitants and some Jewish families, one of whom ran a flour mill. In World War I, the town became the principal base for the Turko-German Army fighting on the Suez and Sinai front. Fortifications were laid out around the town and more settlers, including Jews, came and provided services to the army. A branch of the Jerusalem-Jaffa railway line was constructed and led beyond Beersheba to the southwest. On Oct. 31, 1917, the town was taken by Allied forces under General *Allenby's command, with Australian and New Zealand units prominent in the battle. Allied losses were considerable; the British War Cemetery at Beersheba has about 1,300 graves. When Beersheba's strategic role ended, its economy dwindled and the railway was dismantled. In 1920, a few Jewish laborers planted a tree nursery and eucalyptus grove there and experimented with cultivating vegetables and other crops. In 1922, the population reached 2,356, among whom were 98 Jews. By 1931, the number of Jews had decreased to 11. The last Jews left during the 1936–39 riots, but efforts were intensified to purchase land for Jewish settlement in the Negev. During the *War of Independence the invading Egyptian army made Beersheba its headquarters for the Negev. When the town was taken by Israel forces on Oct. 21, 1948, it was totally abandoned by its inhabitants. Early in 1949, Jewish settlers, mostly new immigrants, established themselves there. The population, which totaled 1,800 at the end of 1949, reached 25,500 in 1956, 51,600 in 1962, and over 70,000 in 1968.

The vast majority of its inhabitants were originally new immigrants, mainly from North Africa, Iraq, India, Romania, Poland, Hungary, and South America. The first arrivals took over the abandoned houses, but from 1951 large new suburbs were built extending mainly to the north and northwest, while to the east a large industrial area sprang up. Arab Beersheba of Turkish times now became a small "old city" in a large modern town. The municipal area of about 10 sq. mi. (26 sq. km.) was doubled in 1967. Beersheba became the capital of Israel's Southern District, and a hub of communications linking up with the main roads and the railway lines Lydda-Kiryat Gat and Dimonah-Oron. A pumping station of the Eilat-Haifa oil pipeline was located there. Its largest industries (ceramics, sanitary ware, fire-resistant bricks, pesticides and other chemicals, and bromide compounds) exploited Negev minerals. There was also a large textile factory, flour mill, machine garage, and smaller plants for building materials, diamonds, metals, and other industries. The city had several academic, scientific, and cultural institutions, of which the Soroka Medical Center and the Municipal Museum were the first. In 1957, the Negev Institute for Arid Zone Research was established, which experiments with water desalination by electrodialysis, exploitation of solar energy, cloud seeding, adaptation of plants to aridity, hydroponics, and human behavior under desert conditions. The Institute for Higher Education, opened in 1965, was formally recognized as the University of the Negev in 1970 and had 1,600 students. Subsequently renamed Ben-Gurion University after Israel's first prime minister. It had 15,000 students in 2002. In 1973 the Beersheba Theater and the Symphony Orchestra were established. Beersheba also had a Biological Institute, mainly for the study of plant life in the desert. The city also served as a market center for the Negev's tens of thousands of Bedouin and had several large hotels. The traditional Thursday Bedouin market day was a noted tourist attraction.

In the 1970s the population of Beersheba passed the 110,000 mark, making it the fourth largest urban concentration in Israel after Jerusalem, Tel Aviv and Haifa. The original plan to make Beersheba an industrial center was not too successful, though there were several large industrial plants, such as Machteshim, which produced agricultural fertilizers and employed over 1,000 workers, and an Israel Aircraft Industries metal plant. The main sources of employment, however, were the Soroka Medical Center, employing over 2,000, and the university. The city thus continued to serve as a regional center and many workers in the Dead Sea chemical works and in the Nuclear Research Center near Dimona resided there. By the mid-1990s the population had risen to approximately 141,400, and in 2002 it was 181,500, making Beersheba the sixth largest city in Israel.

[George Schwab and Efraim Orni / Shaked Gilboa (2nd ed.)]

Another Beersheba was situated on the border of Upper and Lower Galilee (Jos., Wars, 3:39). It was fortified by Josephus, together with other places in Galilee in 66–67 C.E., for defense against the Romans during the Jewish War (*ibid.*, 2:573). It is located at Ḥorvat Beer-Sheba (Khirbat Abu al-Shabʿa) between Parod and Kafr ʿInān near the Acre-Safed highway, where remains from the Second Temple period have been found.

BIBLIOGRAPHY: G. Dalman, *Sacred Sites and Ways* (1935), index; S. Klein (ed.,) *Sefer ha-Yishuv*, 1 (1939) s.v.; Albright, in: JPOS, 4 (1924), 152; Alt, *ibid.*, 15 (1935), 320; L. Woolley and T.E. Lawrence, *Wilderness of Zin* (1915), 45ff., 107 ff.; Perrot, in: IEJ, 5 (1955), 17, 73, 167; Contenson, *ibid.*, 6 (1956), 163, 226; Dothan, in: *Atiqot*, 2 (Eng., 1959), 1ff.; EM, 2 (1965), 6–8 (incl. bibl.); Press, Ereẓ, 1 (1951), 62–63. **WEBSITE:** www.negevba.co.il.

BE'ER TOVIYYAH (Heb. בְּאֵר טוֹבִיָּה), moshav in the southern Coastal Plain of Israel, affiliated with Tenu'at ha-Moshavim. It was founded in 1887 by Jews from Bessarabia with the aid of Baron Edmond de *Rothschild and for years it was the southernmost Jewish settlement in the country. The village did not prosper, due to the scarcity of water, lack of capital and experience, distance from other Jewish centers, enmity of neighboring Arab villagers, and, particularly, the strained relations between the settlers and the Baron's administrators. It was nearly abandoned, but in 1896 the Ḥovevei Zion Association of Odessa (see *Ḥibbat Zion) purchased the land and new settlers came. They too endured hardships and in World War I were forced to leave temporarily by the Turkish authorities. The village was abandoned after it suffered losses in an Arab attack in the 1929 riots. The land was then taken over by the Jewish National Fund and the village was founded anew in 1930 by veteran agricultural laborers. Ground water was discovered and mixed farming introduced. Be'er Toviyyah soon became one of the most populous and prosperous moshavim in the country. In 1939 a second moshav, Kefar Warburg, was established on part of its land. After the Arabs abandoned the entire region during the Israeli *War of Independence (1948), Be'er Toviyyah became the center of a densely settled farming area, to which such urban agglomerations as Kiryat Malakhi and Ashdod were later added. Many of the settlers of Be'er Toviyyah came from Eastern Europe and Germany, others were Israeli-born. In 1968 the population was 645. The economy was mainly based on citrus and intensive farming. In 2002 the population was 763. The village was initially called Qastīna, after a neighboring Arab village. It became Be'er Toviyyah in 1896, the name being adapted from the Arabic name for the site, "Bīr (Bi'r) Taʿabya."

[Efraim Orni]

BE'ER YA'AKOV (Heb. בְּאֵר יַעֲקֹב), town in the Coastal Plain of Israel, W. of Ramleh, founded in 1907 by a group of 56 Jews from Russia (most of them "Mountain Jews" from Dagestan). Some of the settlers were peasants in their country of origin and preserved their picturesque dress and customs throughout the decades. Initially, almond orchards constituted Be'er Ya'akov's principal farming branch. In 1925, 20 families from Turkey settled in the village, but until 1948, its population did not exceed 400 inhabitants due to a scarcity of land. After the Israeli *War of Independence (1948), however, new immigrants were absorbed in local housing projects and in two moshavim, Be'er Ya'akov Pittu'aḥ and Talmei Menasheh, which were subsequently integrated into the municipal area. In 1949, it received municipal council status. Citrus orchards, poultry, and dairy cattle were originally prominent branches and constituted an important part of Be'er Ya'akov's economy. It was the site of three large hospitals (Asaf ha-Rofe, Shemu'el ha-Rofe, and a mental hospital) and industrial enterprises, among them a crate factory employing hundreds of laborers and a division of Israel Aircraft Industries. Be'er Ya'akov's educational institutions also attracted pupils from other localities, e.g., the Johanna Jabotinsky agricultural high school, a religious girls' teachers seminary, and yeshivot. The population rose to 3,950 in 1968, 6,960 in the mid-1990s, and 8,320 in 2002. The name, "Well of Ya'akov," commemorates the spiritual leader of the founders, Rabbi Ya'akov Yiẓhaki of Dagestan.

[Efraim Orni / Shaked Gilboa (2nd ed.)]

BEET. The plant referred to in rabbinic literature as *tered*, or *selek* (Er. 29a) is the spinach beet (*Beta vulgaris*, var. *Cicla*). The present varieties, red beet, sugar beet, and fodder beet, were unknown to the ancients. Although the long white root of the beet was sometimes eaten, it was the leaves which were mainly used as food. The rabbis, in common with the Greek and Roman naturalists, praised it highly for its nutritive and medicinal value. Thus the Talmud states: "A dish of beets is good for the heart and good for the bowels and especially for the small bowels" (Bet. 44b). It was also held to account for the absence of skin diseases and of leprosy in Babylonia (Ket. 77b). It is a winter plant, but due to its nutritive value, attempts were made to grow it also in summer, and Solomon's servants were said to have been able to supply summer beets for his table (Deut. R. 1:5).

BIBLIOGRAPHY: Loew, Flora, 1 (1926), 346–52; J. Feliks, *Kilei Zera'im…* (1967), 82–83. **ADD. BIBLIOGRAPHY:** Feliks, Ha-Tzome'aḥ, 173.

[Jehuda Feliks]

BEGGING AND BEGGARS. Although the Bible is concerned with the poor and the needy, there is hardly a reference to begging or to beggars, and there is, in fact, no biblical Hebrew word for it. The needs of the poor were provided by the laws of **leket*, *shikhḥah*, and *pe'ah* which were the perquisites of the *ani*, the "poor man," or the *evyon*, the "needy." The only possible references are not to actual begging and beggars but are contained in the complementary assurances that whereas the children of the righteous will not have to "seek bread" (Ps. 37:25), the children of the wicked will, after his untimely death, be vagabonds "and seek their bread out of desolate places" (Ps. 109:10).

During the talmudic period, however, the itinerant beggar who goes from house to house figures with some prominence. So characteristic does it seem to have been of social life in those times that the first Mishnah of tractate *Shabbat* employs the example of the beggar receiving his pittance from the householder, and the various ways in which it might be handed to him, to illustrate the important laws concerning the carrying of articles from a private to a public domain on the Sabbath. The Mishnah also deals with the rights of the beggar who "goes from place to place" and who had sometimes to be provided with lodging for the night (Pe'ah 8:7). It was regarded as immodest for women to beg, with the result that the Mishnah stipulates that if a man left insufficient means for his children, the daughters should remain at home and the sons go from door to door (Ket. 13:3). The New Testament describes the blind beggar Bartimeus sitting by the roadside and begging (Mark 10:46) and a lame beggar soliciting alms at the entrance to the Temple (Acts 3:2). The rabbis are censorious of those beggars who used to feign such afflictions as "blindness, swollen belly, and shrunken leg" in order to arouse the compassion of the charitable (Pe'ah 8:9; Tosef., Pe'ah 4:14). Nevertheless one rabbi takes a charitable view of those impostors, saying that they perform the useful function of exercising the charitable instincts of the people (Ket. 68a). Nor was the cheerful impudent beggar unknown, as the following story in the Talmud indicates: "A beggar once came to Rava who asked him 'What do your meals usually consist of?' 'Plump chicken and matured wine' answered the beggar. 'Do you not consider this a burden on the community?' asked Rava. The beggar retorted: 'I do not take from them – I take what God provides.' At that moment Rava's sister, who had not seen him for 13 years, appeared bringing him a fat chicken and matured wine. 'Just what I told you!' said the beggar" (Ket. 67b).

Nevertheless two factors tended to keep begging within bounds. One was the delicate custom of sending food to the poor in order to spare their feelings (see the examples, Ket. 67b), and the other was the highly organized system of collection for and distribution to the poor through the official *kuppah* ("charity fund") and *tamḥui* ("soup kitchen"). As a result, it was proclaimed that relief was actually to be withheld from those who went begging as they had forfeited their rights to organized charity, although a compromise was arrived at not to send such a mendicant away completely empty-handed (BB 9a).

In the early Middle Ages this was established as the actual *halakhah* (Yad, Mattenat Aniyyim 7:7; Sh. Ar., YD 250:3). *Rashi (to BB 9a) explains that it is "because he has accustomed himself to make the rounds, he must suffice with that." On the other hand, Solomon b. Adret, in answer to an enquiry from a community overburdened with beggars, ruled that although "the poor are everywhere supported from the communal chest, if they wish in addition to beg from door to door they may do so, and each should give according to his understanding and desire" (Responsa, pt. 3 no. 380). In Cracow, however, in 1595 and in the Spanish and Portuguese congregation in London in the second half of the 17th century, begging by mendicants was completely outlawed (Balaban, in JJLG, 10 (1913), 342; Barnett, *El Libro de los Acuerdos* (1931), 9).

This admirable system of organized relief for the poor (cf. Yad, loc. cit., 9:3: "We have never heard of a community which has no charity fund for the relief of the poor, though some have no *tamḥui*") seems almost to have eliminated beggars until the 17th century. Launcelot Addison (*The Present State of the Jews*, p. 212) goes out of his way to dispel the belief prevalent in his time that "the Jews have no beggars," which he attributed to the "regular and commendable efforts" by which the Jewish community supplied the needs of the poor. A notable literary description of the English Jewish beggar is Zangwill's *King of the Schnorrers*.

It would seem that an increase in Jewish mendicancy took place as an aftermath of the *Chmielnicki pogroms when hundreds of Polish communities were destroyed and thousands of penniless and destitute Jews roamed throughout Europe. From this time dates the word "*shnorrer*," the accepted Yiddish term for a beggar which became a characteristic feature of Jewish life. Sometimes the *shnorrers* openly collected for themselves, at other times for the dowry of a poor bride (see **Hakhnasat Kallah*) or to restore a house which had been burnt down in one of the many conflagrations of wooden houses. If the 18th century has been styled "a century of beggary" as a whole, it certainly applies to the impoverished Jewish communities of Central and Eastern Europe up to the dawn of the modern period.

Beggary, which was rife in Ereẓ Israel before the establishment of the State of Israel, has been largely eliminated in the streets, as a result of the increased activities of the Ministry of Social Welfare. It is still, however, a feature of the synagogues during the morning services. Beggars consist of two groups, genuine beggars and students of the old-fashioned yeshivot who are to some extent encouraged by the authorities of the yeshivah, not only as a source of subsistence but to afford the worshipers an opportunity of combining prayer with charity. A similar sentiment is held toward beggars in cemeteries. Despite objections that they disturb worshippers, opinion among the Orthodox is opposed to their removal.

See *Charity.

[Louis Isaac Rabinowitz]

Social Aspects

Begging as a social phenomenon is associated with migrations. It became prevalent in Jewish history during the period of the Mishnah and the Talmud and especially after the destruction of the Second Temple. This came about as a result of persecutions under Roman rule, as well as the physical and economic insecurity which impoverished the rural class and reduced the urban population to ruin. Yet, despite the increase in the numbers of poor and those reduced to begging, nothing is heard about Jewish mendicants forming a society and developing their own subculture, as did occur within the non-Jewish world at that time.

Jewish beggars wandering from place to place are more frequently found throughout the Middle Ages. In the Cairo *Genizah* a large number of letters from beggars complaining of their misfortunes and seeking support have been found. The documents indicate that these itinerant poor wandered from community to community, and from land to land. The *Or Zaru'a* (*hilkhot Ẓedakah* 11) of R. *Isaac of Vienna mentions that these destitute people customarily equipped themselves with "documents," i.e., letters of recommendation which they would present in their travels as proof of their trustworthiness.

In medieval times there was another class of wanderers who went from place to place, relying upon the hospitality of others, namely, the yeshivah students who moved from one center of Torah study to another. A parallel phenomenon (goliards, vagrant scholars) is found within the student community of Christian society of that time.

At the end of the 17th century, a relatively large class of Jewish beggars, called in non-Jewish sources *"Betteljuden,"* and *orḥei porḥei* ("flotsam and jetsam") in Jewish literature, developed throughout Europe, especially in Germany. The size of this class is not known exactly, but it has been estimated at as much as 20% of the total Jewish population. Although the reasons for the formation of this class are still not completely clear, it is assumed to have resulted from (i) the natural growth of the Jewish population; (ii) the limited number of Jews permitted to reside in any individual place by the local authorities; and (iii) the unstable economic conditions which brought about drastic changes from extreme wealth to great poverty. The *Betteljuden* constituted a section within the large class of non-Jewish itinerant poor. These Jewish vagabonds, like their Christian counterparts, eventually united into societies, religiously intermixed at times, developing their own subculture. This class became a source of manpower and information to the bands of thieves which were rampant at that time. The authorities treated these groups of Jewish mendicants very harshly. They condemned them for thievery and for causing diseases and plagues in various places. As a result of these accusations, local authorities sought to banish the beggars. The Jewish communities were very ambivalent vis-à-vis these mendicants. On the one hand, they strove to obey the local powers-that-be, for they also saw in the beggars a social danger, not only because of their associations with thieves, but also because of their licentiousness. Yet, on the other hand, they not infrequently had feelings of compassion and brotherliness toward these unfortunates. The manner in which the communities handled these *orḥei porḥei*, therefore, corresponded to their ambivalence toward them. In general, the community accommodated them in the homes of its residents for one night (for two nights over the Sabbath), and afterward sent them along with a sum of money for travel expenditures. Special lodgings for mendicants, particularly for the sick among them, were also set up in the *hekdesh* ("poor house"). After the Emancipation, with residence restrictions for Jews lifted, and areas in which Jews were permitted to work widened, this impoverished class was largely integrated with other social classes. However, the phenomenon itself did not disappear from Jewish communal life, and it continued to exist especially in Eastern Europe, if not to the same extent.

BIBLIOGRAPHY: I. Abrahams, *Jewish Life in the Middle Ages* (1932²), 331ff., 346f.; Baron, Community, 1 (1942), 131f., 363; 2 (1942), 321–5; Urbach, in: *Zion*, 16, nos. 3–4 (1951), 1–27; R. Glanz, *Geschichte des niederen juedischen Volks in Deutschland* (1968); Scheiber, in: M. Zohary and A. Tartakower (eds.), *Hagut Ivrit be-Eiropah* (1969), 268–75.

BEGHI, family of Karaite scholars in Constantinople (15th–17th centuries). Its members include: ELIJAH AFIDAH (AFDAH) BEGHI (d. before 1641). Elijah wrote *Hilkhot Sheḥitah*, on the rules of slaughtering; *Be'ur Asarah Ikkarim*, on the ten principles of Karaite faith; *Mikhtav Eliyahu*, poems, verse compositions and tales; several responsa (all these works survived in manuscripts kept in various libraries). JOSEPH BEN MOSES (15th–16th centuries). Joseph was the pupil of the Karaite scholar Abraham *Bali, who in 1505 wrote for Beghi and his fellow student, Joseph b. Caleb, his *Issur Hadlakat Ner be-Shabbat*, on the Karaite prohibition of kindling lights on the Sabbath. The cordial relationship between the Karaites and *Rabbanites at that period is attested by Joseph's correspondence with Rabbanite scholars. Two letters by Moses b. Jacob (evidently *Moses of Kiev "*ha-Goleh*") to Beghi are preserved. Joseph wrote *Iggeret Sukkah*, on Sukkot; *Keter Kehunnah*, six homilies; *Iggeret Kiryah Ne'emanah* especially directed against the identification of the Karaites with the Sadducees, a work of literary and historical value since it mentions a number of earlier Karaite scholars; *Iggeret Kelulah*, an explanation of a problem in marriage law. Simḥah Isaac b. Moses Lutzki mentions two important works of Joseph which are no longer traceable: *Shulḥan Ḥaverim*, a book of precepts, and *Safah Berurah*, a philosophical work. MOSES BEN BENJAMIN (second half of the 16th century), wrote *Mitzvot Moshe*, a book of precepts including two essays "*Ohel Moshe*" on the calendar, and "*Masat Moshe*" on the Sabbath laws, published in *Pinnat Yikrat* by the Karaite *Isaac b. Solomon (1834; non-critical print, 2 vols., Ashdod 2005). Benjamin also composed liturgical poems, several of which have been included in the Karaite prayer book.

BIBLIOGRAPHY: A. Neubauer, *Aus der Petersburger Bibliothek* (1866), 46n, 122; Danon, in: JQR 15 (1924/25), 337–39; HB, 17 (1877), 12; Mann, Texts, 2 (1935), 294n, 300, 302; Simḥah Isaac b. Moses (Lutzki), *Oraḥ Ẓaddikim* (1966), 98, 99, 107, 109; Z. Ankori, *Karaites in Byzantium* (1959), 36n, 58, 279. **ADD. BIBLIOGRAPHY:** M.L. Wilensky, in: PAAJR 40 (1972) 109–146; M. Polliack (ed.), *Karaite Judaism: A Guide to Its History and Literary Sources*, (2003), index.

[Isaak Dov Ber Markon]

BÉGIN, EMILE-AUGUSTE (1802–1888), French physician, historian, and librarian. Bégin, who was born in Metz, studied medicine at the Military College in Strasbourg. He soon gave up his position as a regimental physician in favor of a literary career. His early writing dealt mainly with the history of northeastern France. He became well known for his four-volume *Biographie de la Moselle* (1829–32) and his literary and political periodical *L'Indicateur de l'Est* (1830). His historical research embraced Jewish communities, and some of his findings appeared under the title *"Recherches pour servir l'histoire des Juifs dans le Nord-Est de la France"* in *Revue Orientale*, 1–2 (1841–42). Bégin settled in Paris in 1846 and became a contributor to publications of the Academy of Medicine. In 1850 he cooperated in the official edition of the papers of Napoleon I and in 1853–54 produced a laudatory five-volume biography, *L'Histoire de Napoléon Ier*, based on hitherto unpublished personal papers. Napoleon III rewarded him with an appointment as librarian at the Louvre, where he remained until 1871. In 1874 Bégin became librarian at the Bibliothèque Nationale, Paris.

BIBLIOGRAPHY: *Dictionnaire de biographie francaise*, s.v.; *L'Austraisie*, 7 (July, 1907), 3–26 (suppl.); Wininger, Biog, 1 (1925), 284.

[Herbert A. Strauss]

BEGIN, MENAḤEM (1913–1992), Israeli statesman and former commander of the Irgun Ẓeva'i Le'ummi (IẒL); prime minister of Israel. He served in the First to Tenth Knessets. Begin was born and educated in Brest-Litovsk. He graduated with a law degree from Warsaw University. After a short association with Ha-Shomer ha-Ẓa'ir he joined Betar, becoming a member of its leadership in Poland in 1931 and head of the movement there in 1938. During the disturbances in Palestine in the years 1936–38, Begin organized a mass demonstration near the British Embassy in Warsaw, and was imprisoned by the Polish police. When the Germans occupied Warsaw, Begin escaped to Vilna, where he was arrested by the Soviet authorities and sentenced to eight years of hard labor in the Arctic region. Because he was a Polish citizen, he was released at the end of 1941 and arrived in Palestine in 1942 with the Polish army formed in the Soviet Union. Toward the end of 1943, after having been discharged from the Polish ranks, Begin became commander of IẒL. He declared "armed warfare" against the British Mandatory Government at the beginning of 1944, and led a determined underground struggle against the British, who offered a reward for the disclosure of his whereabouts. On July 22, 1946, the IẒL under Begin's command, carried out an attack on British Headquarters in Jerusalem, in the King David Hotel, which resulted in numerous deaths. The original plan had been to cooperate in this operation with the *Haganah, but this attempt failed, and despite Begin's attempts to avoid violent clashes within the *Yishuv*, there was great animosity between the two camps. After the Proclamation of Independence, in the course of the first ceasefire in the War of Independence in June 1948, Begin was on board the IẒL ship *Altalena* when it approached Tel Aviv with a consignment of arms. The ship was shelled by order of the Israeli government (see *Irgun Ẓeva'i Le'ummi). In 1948 Begin founded the *Ḥerut movement and became its leader. He was to serve in the Knesset as leader of Ḥerut, and later *Gaḥal and the *Likud until 1983. David *Ben-Gurion refused to consider Begin as a partner in any of his coalitions, and it was only after Levi *Eshkol became prime minister in 1963 that the attitude of the ruling *Mapai towards him changed.

In 1952 he led the protest campaign against the Restitution Agreement with the Federal Republic of Germany, and after clashing with the police outside the Knesset building, was banned from participation in Knesset meetings for several weeks. In the course of his many years as leader of the main opposition party, Begin gained a reputation for his fiery speeches and acting as a watchdog for democracy. He unsuccessfully fought to have the Emergency Regulations, which Israel had inherited from the British, abolished, and objected to the special Military Administration to which the minority citizens of Israel were subjected until 1966, which was based on these regulations. Towards the elections to the Sixth Knesset in 1965 he was instrumental in establishing the Gaḥal parliamentary group with the Liberal Party. In May 1967, on the eve of the Six-Day War, Gaḥal was invited to join the government by Levi Eshkol, and Begin was named minister without portfolio in the Government of National Unity. As the head of Gaḥal, he jcined the government formed by Golda *Meir after the 1969 elections, but left the government the following year in protest against its acceptance of the American Rogers Plan for a settlement with Egypt, involving a withdrawal by Israel of territories occupied in the course of the Six-Day War (see *Israel, Historical Survey).

In 1977, after 29 years in the opposition, Begin, at the head of the Likud, won his first general election and was called upon to form a government. He established a coalition made up of the Likud (including Ariel *Sharon's Shlomẓion), the National Religious Party, Agudat Israel, and the Democratic Movement for Change. Five months after he became prime minister, President Anwar Sadat of Egypt came to Jerusalem for a historic visit, addressing the Knesset on November 20, 1977. In his response to the Egyptian President's speech Begin made his famous declaration: "No more war, no more bloodshed." After signing the Camp David Accords with Sadat on September 17, 1978, and with the help of Foreign Minister Moshe *Dayan and Minister of Defense Ezer *Weizman, Begin signed Israel's first peace treaty with an Arab state with Egypt on March 26, 1979, on the White House lawn in Washington. On December 10, 1978, Begin and Sadat jointly received the Nobel Prize for Peace in Oslo.

Despite many crises in his first government, and the resignation of numerous ministers, the Likud emerged victorious in the elections to the Tenth Knesset, and Begin formed his second government, made up of the Likud, the National Religious Party, Agudat Israel, and Tami, and despite misgivings he appointed Sharon as his defense minister. In June 1981

Sharon, with Begin's approval, embarked on Operation Peace for Galilee, which was meant at first to involve the occupation by the IDF of a 15-mi. (40-km.) strip in Southern Lebanon, and the ousting of the PLO from that land. Begin's slogan for the operation was: "No more Katyushas on Kiryat Shmonah." However, as the situation in Lebanon became more complex, and following the death of his beloved wife and his own failing health, Begin decided to resign from the premiership in October 1983. After his resignation Begin seldom left his home until his death in 1992.

His writings include *Ha-Mered* (1950; *The Revolt*, 1964), which describes the struggle of IẒL; *Be-Leilot Levanim* (1953; *White Nights*, 1957), reminiscences of his imprisonment in Russia; and *Ba-Maḥteret: Ketavim u-Te'udot* (4 vol., 1959–61), a collection of writings from his days in the underground.

Begin's son, Ze'ev Binyamin *Begin (1943–), was also active in politics.

ADD. BIBLIOGRAPHY: A. Golan and S. Nakdimon, *Begin* (Hebrew, 1978); U. Benziman, *Rosh Memshalah be-Maẓor* (1981); T. Preuss, *Begin la-Shilton* (1984); E. Silver, *Begin: the Haunted Prophet* (1984); S. Haydemann, *The Begin Era: Issues in Contemporary Israel* (1984); I. Peled, *Begin's Foreign Policy* (1987); A. Perlmutter *The Life and Times of Menachem Begin* (1987); S. Sofer, *Begin: An Anatomy of Leadership* (1988); Y. Aḥimeir, *Hamanhig she-Hevi et ha-Shalom* (1992); Arie Na'or, *Begin ba-Shilton: Edut Ishit* (1993); H.Z. Hurwitz, *Begin: His Life, Words and Deeds* (1994); M. Karniel, *Morashto shel Menaḥem Begin* (1995); S. Sandler (ed.), *Yisra'el ba-Mizraḥ ha-Tikhon: Moreshet Menaḥem Begin* (2000); M.H. Isaacson, *Begin* (Hebrew, 2003).

[Yohanan Bader / Susan Hattis Rolef (2nd ed.)]

BEGIN, ZE'EV BINYAMIN (1943–), Israeli geologist and politician. Member of the Twelfth to Fourteenth Knessets. Ze'ev Binyamin Begin was born in Jerusalem, the son of Menaḥem *Begin. He studied geology at the Hebrew University of Jerusalem and received his doctorate from the University of Colorado in the United States in 1978, later working in the Geological Survey of Israel as head of the environmental unit and the unit for the mapping of maritime geology. He entered politics in 1988 at the behest of his father. As a Knesset member. he was always noted for his modesty, and the fact that he usually arrived at the Knesset by public transportation. When Yitzḥak *Shamir invited Reḥav'am *Ze'evi to join his government in February 1991, he was one of several members of the Likud who objected, because of Ze'evi's advocacy of the transfer of land to the Palestinians.

Begin contested the leadership of the Likud in March 1993, following the party's defeat in the elections to the Thirteenth Knesset, but was defeated by Binyamin *Netanyahu. In the government formed by Netanyahu after the elections, he was appointed minister of science. Despite being part of the government, Begin strongly criticized Netanyahu's contacts with the chairman of the Palestinian Authority, Yasser *Arafat, and Netanyahu's willingness to fulfill Israel's undertakings under the Tab'a Agreement for a partial withdrawal from Hebron. He made constant efforts to prove that the Palestinians were systematically violating their commitments under the Declaration of Principles of September 1993, especially abrogation of the articles in the Palestine National Covenant that spoke of the destruction of Israel. After voting in the government twice within one week against resolutions proposed by the prime minister, Begin resigned from the government. Together with two additional members he left the Likud-Gesher-Tsomet parliamentary group and set up a new parliamentary group by the name of Ḥerut. Begin did not run for election in the Fifteenth Knesset and returned to his previous work as a geologist, on rare occasions coming out publicly on an issue, such as opposition to Prime Minister Ariel *Sharon's plan in 2004 to dismantle all the Jewish settlements in the Gaza Strip and several in Northern Samaria.

[Susan Hattis Rolef (2nd ed.)]

BEHAK, JUDAH (1820–1900), Hebrew writer. Behak, who was born in Vilna, was a member of the Vilna group (M.A. *Guenzburg, A.D. *Lebensohn, S.J. *Fuenn, and I.E. *Benjacob) which had a decisive influence on the Haskalah movement in Lithuania. He wrote for *Pirḥei Ẓafon*, the first Lithuanian Haskalah journal, and for *Ha-Karmel*. In 1848 he joined the staff of the newly established Vilna Rabbinical Seminary, and in 1856 moved to Kherson (most of his writings were signed *Ish Vilna be-Kherson*, "A Vilnaite in Kherson"). Behak devoted himself to the study of the Hebrew language. His main work was *Eẓ Yehudah*, linguistic studies of the Bible and the Talmud (5 vols., 1884–1901, Vilna, Odessa, Berdichev). His book *Yod ha-Rabbim*, a study of Aramaic, was published posthumously (1901). Behak also edited J.L. Ben-Ze'ev's *Talmud Lashon Ivri* (with Ẓ.H. Katznellenbogen, 1848) and S. Levisohn's *Meḥkerei Lashon* (with A.D. Lebensohn, 1849), and wrote commentaries for I.E. Benjacob's and A.D. Lebensohn's Bible, *Mikra'ei Kodesh* (1848–53).

BIBLIOGRAPHY: E.R. Malachi (ed.), *Kitvei P. Turberg* (1953), 52–62; P. Sandler, *Ha-Be'ur la-Torah shel M. Mendelssohn ve-Si'ato…* (1941), 178–9.

[Getzel Kressel]

BEHAR, LEON (1898–1957), Mexican Jewish community leader. Behar was born in Salonika, Greece, immigrated to Mexico in 1920, and a few years later started his communal activity, first among the Sephardim and later in the community at large. He took part in the establishment of the Asociación Israelita Sefaradí La Fraternidad (Sephardic Community) in 1924 and was its president for two years. In the 1930s he participated in the foundation of many important institutions, including the Sephardic Zionist Organization (serving as its president for several terms) and the Comité Central Sionista (as its vice president). Behar also presided over the joint aid committee for Jewish refugees in Europe and was active in other Jewish institutions. One of his most important activities was promoting the foundation of the Comité Central Israelita (the representative body of Mexican Jewry) in 1938, which he presided over for two years.

[Efraim Zadoff (2nd ed.)]

BEHAR, NISSIM (1848–1931), founder of modern Hebrew education in Ereẓ Israel and public figure in Jewish life in the U.S. Behar was born in Jerusalem. He graduated from the *Alliance Israélite Universelle teachers institute in Paris in 1869 and taught in Syria, Bulgaria, and Turkey. He headed the Alliance school in Constantinople from 1873 to 1882. There he introduced the direct method of teaching Hebrew, "*Ivrit be-Ivrit*." In 1882 Behar initiated the founding of the new Alliance school in Jerusalem, Torah u-Melakhah ("Torah and Work"), and became its headmaster. One of the teachers there was Eliezer *Ben-Yehuda, and its first students included David *Yellin and Yosef *Meyuḥas. Its modern methods were eventually applied in Hebrew schools throughout the country. Behar was an outstanding leader of the *yishuv*, especially as a liaison with the Turkish authorities. He attempted, with the help of Baron Edmond de *Rothschild, to regain the Western Wall for the Jewish community, but failed because of rabbinical opposition. The rabbis' hostility to Behar resulted from his educational innovations, and he was eventually relieved of his duties as headmaster (1897) and sent to represent the Alliance in the U.S. (1901). In his attempts to organize the work of the Alliance in the U.S., Behar encountered difficulties from Jewish institutions which looked askance at the activities of a large, foreign Jewish organization. American Jewish leaders did not approve of his intense propaganda, public meetings, and protests. Nevertheless, Behar soon became a public figure in American Jewry. He expounded the idea that political organizations should speak for American Jewry, and in 1906 founded the National Liberal Immigration League, directing it until 1924. In 1908 Behar traveled to Europe and back in order to learn how immigrants to the U.S. were treated on the boats. He was one of the founders of the Federation of Jewish Organizations. Behar was active in the *Histadrut Ivrit in the U.S. from its beginning. He died in New York and his remains were reburied in Jerusalem a year later.

BIBLIOGRAPHY: Z. Szajkowski, in AJHSP, 39 (1950), 406–43; A. Goldberg, *Pioneers and Builders* (1943), 188–93; H. Debrest, in: *Jewish Forum* (1928), 522–6; M. Ribalow, in: *Hadoar*, 6 (1925), 118; M.D. Gaon, *Yehudei ha-Mizraḥ be-Ereẓ Yisrael*, 2 (1938), 151–9; E. Cohen-Reiss, *Mi-Zikhronot Ish Yerushalayim* (1967²), index.

BEHEMOTH (intensive plural of Heb. *behemah*, "beast"), creature described in the Book of Job (40:15–24). It is depicted as an animal that eats grass like an ox, is all muscles and strength, lives in the marsh in the shade of the *ẓe'elim* ("*jujube"), eats huge quantities of food, and can swallow the waters of the Jordan. In the light of the description of other animals in these chapters, it would seem that the reference is to an existing animal, to which legendary details have been added. In later Jewish literature, however, it appears as a purely mythical creature. One of the mammoths fashioned on the fifth day of creation (Targ. Yer., Gen. 1:21; II Bar. 29:4), he is the male counterpart on land of the female *Leviathan in the sea (IV Ezra 6:49–52). He is said to dwell in the wilderness of Dendain (or Dudain), east of Eden (I Enoch 60:7–8), or else, by a fanciful interpretation of Psalm 50: 10, to span "a thousand hills" (IV Ezra 6: 49–52; Lev. R. 21). At the end of the world's existence he will be slain and served, along with his mate, at a banquet tendered to the righteous (*ibid.*; Targ. Yer., Num. 9:6; PdRE 11; cf. TB, BB 75a). It has been suggested that this reflects the Iranian belief that at the Resurrection the righteous will obtain immortality by drinking a nectar made out of the fat of the mythical ox Hadhayosh mixed with *haoma* (a plant; Bundahishn 19:13, 20:25; Dadistan-i-Denik 37:119); but it is undoubtedly inspired also by the statement in Psalms 74:14 that God once fed the flesh of Leviathan "to the people." The hippopotamus (*Hippopotamus amphibus*) has been identified with Behemoth. It is the largest land animal in the Middle East, weighing up to three tons. It has powerful sinews, an enormous head, and a wide mouth with huge molars. Once it inhabited Ereẓ Israel; skeletal remains of it have been found in the vicinity of the Yarkon River. In ancient Egypt it was a favorite quarry of hunters and its capture with spears is often depicted.

BIBLIOGRAPHY: Lewysohn, Zool, 355; Tristram, Nat Hist, 50–53; J. Feliks, *Animal World of the Bible* (1962), 24.

[Jehuda Feliks / Theodor H. Gaster]

BE-ḤOZAI, a district extending E. of *Mesene, S.E. of Babylon, and N. of the Persian Gulf. Geographically, Be-Ḥozai did not belong to Babylonia, but to Persia. Despite the great distance between them (Ta'an, 21b; BK 104b), very close ties (including commercial) existed between the Jews of Babylonia and those of Be-Ḥozai. The district had a plentiful supply of water, and rice, extensively grown there, was used for bread by its inhabitants (Pes. 50b). It was an important station for goods in transit between Babylonia and Persia (Shab. 51b; BK 104b; Ket. 85a). Many problems were addressed to the Babylonian scholars by its sages, the names of some of whom are known, e.g., Avimi (Nid. 5b), Aḥa (BM 39b), Beroka (Ta'an. 22a), Avram Ḥoza'ah (Git. 50a), Ḥanina (Shab. 130b). The Babylonians had a generally poor opinion of the common people of Be-Ḥozai (Ned. 22a). The Babylonian Talmud mentions, among other localities in the region, Be Lapet (Syriac for Be Shafat), where many Jews lived (Ta'an, 22a), and Shushan (Meg. 2b), or "Sus," its widely used Syriac abbreviation (Sanh. 94a).

BIBLIOGRAPHY: J. Obermeyer, *Landschaft Babylonien* (1929), 204–14. **ADD. BIBLIOGRAPHY:** B. Eshel, *Jewish Settlements in Babylonia during Talmudic Times* (1979), 58–59.

[Moshe Beer]

BEHR (Baer), ISSACHAR FALKENSOHN (1746–1817), Polish poet who wrote in German. Born in Zamosc, Behr was raised in a traditional, Yiddish-speaking home. He was a failure as a petty tradesman and, leaving his wife and family in order to seek an education, wandered to Koenigsberg and reached Berlin in 1764. There he learned German, Latin, and French, and studied mathematics, philosophy, and medicine. Daniel *Itzig became his patron and introduced him to the Berlin intellectuals. He soon wrote excellent German verse and in 1772 published his *Gedichte von einem polnischen Juden*, a pioneer achievement for an East European Jew. Goethe reviewed this strange collection of lyrics in the *Frankfurter Gelehrten-Anzeiger*. In 1773, Behr completed his medical studies at the University of Halle and devoted himself to medical practice in Courland; thereafter, he wrote no more poetry.

BIBLIOGRAPHY: M. Kayserling, *Der Dichter Ephraim Kuh* (1864), 43–47.

[Sol Liptzin]

BEHREND, JACOB FRIEDRICH (1833–1907), German jurist. Behrend became a law clerk in 1859, in 1864 he was appointed lecturer at the University of Berlin, and in 1870, associate professor of jurisprudence. From 1873 to 1887 he was professor of law at the University of Greifswald, and in 1887 became a member of the Supreme Court, one of the few Jews to achieve this distinction. He was an acknowledged expert on German and Roman law and specialized in the early sources of law. Behrend published many important works on jurisprudence which were highly regarded by scholars. His first published work was the *Magdeburger Fragen* ("Magdeburg Problems," 1863) which dealt with the jury system. Later Behrend edited numerous works on jurisprudence, including *Zeitschrift fuer die deutsche Gesetzgebung und fuer einheitliches deutsches Recht* ("Journal for German Legislation and for a Unitary German Law," 1880). His major work, *Lehrbuch des Handelsrechts* ("Textbook of Commercial Law"), was regarded as the first comprehensive work on this subject. Although he managed to complete only the first volume (in two parts, 1886–96), this was for many years an invaluable source of research.

BIBLIOGRAPHY: *Deutsche Juristen-Zeitung* 12 (1907), 170.

[B. Mordechai Ansbacher]

BEHRENDS (Behrens), LEFFMANN (1634–1714), Hanover Court Jew. Behrends, who began as a small merchant supplying luxuries to the court, gradually established himself as moneylender, diplomatic mediator, and coin minter. His position was strengthened under Duke Ernest Augustus (1679–98), for whom he procured the title of elector, and under George, elector of Hanover (1698–1727), the future George I of England. He established business and marital connections with the *Oppenheimers and *Wertheimers of Vienna and stationed his agents, usually his relatives, in the main German cities. An ardent talmudist, and father-in-law of David b. Abraham *Oppenheim, he supported talmudic studies. For many years he was head (*Vorsteher*) of the community of Hanover-Neustadt, the majority of whose members were connected with his household. In 1673 he acquired the right to open a cemetery, and in 1703 built a synagogue and presented it to the community. In 1687 at his request the duke agreed to permit the Jews of Hanover to appoint a *Landesrabbiner*. In 1700 he obtained the support of the elector in suppressing the writings of Johann *Eisenmenger. Behrends attempted to murder a relative of his who became an apostate, but he was able to use his influence to evade being brought to trial. His sons and grandsons, also Court Jews, carried on the family firm; their bankruptcy in 1721 shook the European financial world and took more than a century to settle legally. The trial revealed that Behrends had left his estate in a sorry condition. His descendants settled in Copenhagen.

BIBLIOGRAPHY: S. Stern, *The Court Jew* (1950), index; H. Schnee, *Die Hoffinanz und der moderne Staat*, 2 (1954), 13–67; 5 (1965), 54–81.

BEHRMAN, MARTIN (1864–1926), U.S. public official. Behrman was born in New York City and taken to New Orleans in 1865 by his parents, who died when he was 12. At 19 he became a traveling salesman for a large grocery concern. Turning to politics, Behrman was elected president of the State Board of Assessors, a member of the New Orleans Board of Education (1892–1906), state auditor (1904–05), and mayor of New Orleans in 1904, serving four terms until his defeat in 1920. Behrman was director of the American Bank and Trust Company. He was a leading state Democrat and was chairman of the Louisiana delegation to the national Democratic convention in 1908. Behrman was active in civic and Jewish affairs. He was a member of the Louisiana Constitutional Conventions of 1898 and 1921, and president of the League of American Municipalities (1917–18).

[Edward L. Greenstein]

BEHRMAN, SAMUEL NATHANIEL (1893–1973), U.S. playwright. Behrman was born in Worcester, Mass. His parents had emigrated from Lithuania, and his father often devoted himself to Hebrew Scripture. Behrman graduated from Harvard, where he joined G.P. Baker's Drama Workshop, and from Columbia University. It took him 11 years to sell his first play, *The Second Man* (1927). It was a great success and marked the beginning of a prolific and brilliant career. Intellect, technique, wit, and charm apparent in this early work marked his later writings. His plays, including *End of Summer* (1936), *No Time for Comedy* (1939), and *Jacobowsky and the Colonel* (in collaboration with Franz *Werfel; 1943), are distinguished by warmth and respect for human values. Behrman was far ahead of his fellow playwrights in showing awareness of totalitarian evils, as in *Rain from Heaven* (1935) and *Wine of Choice* (1938). Behrman turned to biography with *Duveen* (1952), the career of the famous British art dealer. This was followed by the autobiographical *Worcester Account* (1954), a charming description of an American Jewish boyhood with an immigrant background. In *Portrait of Max* (1960), he recorded his conversations with Sir Max Beerbohm. Behrman returned to the theater in 1958 with a dramatization of his autobiography under the title *The Cold Wind and the Warm*. He also adapted the Duveen biography as a play, *Lord Pengo* (1963). In 1964 he was one of three American authors whose new works were chosen for the opening season of the Lincoln Center Repertory Theatre in New York. Behrman's play was *But For Whom Charlie* (1964), a comedy about a conflict of temperaments. His novel *The Burning Glass* (1968) was set in pre-World War II Salzburg. Among other his works is *People in a Diary; A Memoir* (1972).

BIBLIOGRAPHY: S.J. Kunitz (ed.), *Authors Today and Yesterday* (1934^2), 56–57; B. Mantle, *Contemporary American Playwrights* (1941), 108–15; J. Mersand, *Traditions in American Literature* (1939), 51–67; O. Prescott, "Books of The Times" *New York Times* (November 5, 1954), p.19.

[Bernard Grebanier]

BEI AVIDAN, meeting place in talmudic times where scholars of various nations and faiths met for religious discussions and disputations. Enjoying the protection of the authorities, the institution was visited by some of the Jewish sages, while others, such as *Joshua b. Hananiah (Shab. 152a) and Eleazar b. Perata (Av. Zar. 17b), refrained from doing so, for which they were compelled to apologize to the authorities. Similarly, the *amora* Rav did not enter a *Bei Avidan*, whereas his colleague Samuel did (Shab. 116a). The *Bei Avidan* is mentioned in this context in association with a *Bei Niẓrefei* (or *Bei Naẓrufei*), to which neither Rav nor Samuel would enter, and which was apparently an idolatrous house of worship (cf. Er. 80a). R. Abbahu was asked whether it was permitted to save the books of a *Bei Avidan* from a fire on the Sabbath (Shab. loc. cit.). It apparently contained books of the Bible (see R. Hananel, ad loc.), but since it was not known whether a Jew or a sectarian had copied them, the doubt arose whether or not they could be saved on the Sabbath. Various theories have been advanced to explain the origin of the word. According to S.J.L. Rapoport (*Erekh Millin* (1852), 3), it derives from the Persian *abdan* ("a forum"), the meeting place there being called *Bei Avidan* (i.e., "house of"). L. Ginzberg (*Festschrift … Schwarz*, 1917, 329) suggests that the word derives from the name of a person, possibly the astrologer Abidas-Abidan, who was active in Persia at the beginning of the third century. L. Loew (*He-Ḥalutz*, 2 (1853), 100ff.) contends that the correct reading is "*Bei-Evyoni*," i.e., the meeting place of the Ebionites in the Land of Israel. However, the fact that the word "*Bei Avidan*" is not found in Palestinian sources and that, furthermore, the statement about Joshua b. Hananiah and Eleazar b. Perata is in Aramaic indicate that the *Bei Avidan* originated in Babylonia and that the term was adopted by the rabbis to apply to the institution in Ereẓ Israel. More recently, S. Shaked has suggested that the term is derived from a Persian word meaning "temple"; see Sokoloff, DPJA, p. 209b.

BIBLIOGRAPHY: Levy J., Neuhebr Tal, 1 (19242), 9; Jastrow, Dict. 1 (1950), 5; Neusner, Babylonia, 1 (1966), 73ff. (citing further literature).

[Yitzhak Dov Gilat]

BEIDER, CHAIM (1920–2003), Yiddish poet, journalist, and literary historian. Beider was born in the *shtetl* of Kupel, near the town of Proskurov (now Khmelnitski, Ukraine). After finishing the local Yiddish school, he studied in the Yiddish Department of the Odessa Teachers' Training Institute and, from 1933, published poems in periodicals. He graduated in 1940 and worked as a teacher. During the war he lived in Tadzhikistan. From 1946 he lived in Khmelnitski and Kamenets-Podolski, working on local Ukrainian dailies. In 1971 he moved to Birobidzhan and worked there as a staff journalist for the Yiddish newspaper *Birobidzhaner Shtern*. In 1973 he moved to Moscow and joined the editorial staff of *Sovetish Heymland*, first as an editor and later as associate editor. In 1998 he immigrated to New York.

His first poetic collection, *Khanukas Khabais* ("Housewarming"), appeared in Moscow in 1979. He also wrote numerous articles devoted to the history of Yiddish literature and culture, many of which were included in his collection *Di Vegn, Vos Mir Antdekn* ("The Ways That We Find," 1991). He was especially interested in such topics as the life and work of Sholem Jacob *Abramovitsh (Mendele Mokher Seforim), the cultural history of Birobidzhan, and biographies of Soviet Yiddish cultural and political activists. In New York, he briefly edited the Yiddish journal *Tsukunft* and regularly contributed to the Yiddish weekly *Forverts*.

BIBLIOGRAPHY: Ch. Beider (ed.), *Native Land* (1980); *Yiddish Writers Almanac: Year After Year* (1987).

[Gennady Estraikh (2nd ed.)]

BEIDERMAN, BERNARDO (1919–), Argentine criminologist. Beiderman was professor of criminal law at Buenos Aires University from 1957 to 1966, when he resigned because of government interference in the universities. He then became a lecturer on the same subject at the university Museo Social Argentino in Buenos Aires, and later dean of its faculty of communication sciences. As a member of the Argentinian Commission, he helped draft a model penal code for Latin America. Beiderman wrote on criminal theory, female criminality, obscenity and pornography, and penal reform.

BEILENSON, ANTHONY CHARLES (**Tony**; 1932–), U.S. congressman. Beilenson was born in New Rochelle, New York. His parents, Peter and Edna Beilenson, were both first cousins of the Hebrew journalist-writer-translator Moshe *Beilenson (1889–1936). Like their cousin, Peter and Edna Beilenson were involved in publishing; their firm, the Peter Pauper Press, was one of the most successful small presses operating in the United States from the 1930s to the 1950s.

At 16, Beilenson matriculated into Phillips Academy in Andover, Massachusetts – the alma mater of many U.S. lawmakers. Following his graduation in 1950, he entered Harvard, going on to graduate from both Harvard College (1954) and its school of law (1957) before striking out for California. Moving to the Los Angeles area, Beilenson spent two years working for a Beverly Hills law firm. A liberal Democrat, Beilenson was elected to the California State Assembly in 1963 and the State Senate in 1965. In his more than decade-long tenure in the California State Senate, he authored more than 200 pieces of legislation. Highly esteemed by both his fellow legislators and members of the press, Beilenson was named best all-around senator by the state capitol press corps and most effective senator in a poll of his Senate colleagues.

In 1976, Beilenson was elected to the U.S. House of Representatives, a post he would hold for the next 20 years. During his tenure in Congress, Beilenson served on the all-important House Rules Committee, where he became the point man on all Jewish and Israel-related issues. Within the House, Beilenson gained a reputation for being a "straight arrow, a man whose integrity is beyond reproach." Beilenson also served as chair of the House Permanent Select Committee on Intelligence. Beilenson's legislative interests ranged from budget reform and "covert-action language" for federal intelligence-gathering agencies to restrictions on U.S. imports of elephant ivory. Through Beilenson's efforts, the Convention on International Trade in Endangered Species eventually ordained a worldwide ban on trade in elephant ivory in 1989. On his many trips abroad, he always made it a point to have the U.S. State Department set up meetings with local Jewish groups and then have prominent Jews invited to American embassy dinners.

Beilenson voted against American involvement in the 1991 Gulf War. Reflecting on that vote, he said, "I don't like Americans systematically inflicting great violence and punishment on another people without absolutely compelling reasons for doing so. I don't like the fact that we are killing thousands of human beings who have not harmed any of us, and who have no capability of doing so. I regret that we didn't have the sense, the imagination, the wit, to deal with the problem in a way that could have produced the desired results without going to war." After serving ten two-year terms, Beilenson retired from Congress in January 1997.

BIBLIOGRAPHY: K.F. Stone, *The Congressional Minyan: The Jews of Capitol Hill* (2000), 12–15.

[Kurt Stone (2nd ed.)]

BEILIN, ASHER (1881–1948), Hebrew and Yiddish journalist, author, and editor. Beilin was born in Kiev. He worked intermittently as *Shalom Aleichem's secretary (1901–05). In 1906 he moved to London, where he engaged in journalism, and in 1933 settled in Jerusalem. Beilin contributed extensively to the Hebrew and Yiddish press, edited Yiddish papers, and in his later years wrote for the Tel Aviv Hebrew daily newspaper, *Davar*. His writings include reminiscences of J.Ḥ. *Brenner (1943), with whom he collaborated for many years, and Shalom Aleichem (1945), a novel *Al Belimah* ("On Nothing," 1928), and a play *Banim li-Gevulam* ("Sons to their Border," 1945). His selected works were published in 1956.

BIBLIOGRAPHY: *Kol Kitvei G. Shofman*, 4 (1960), 283; 5 (1960), 168; LNYL, 1 (1956), 287–8.

[Getzel Kressel]

BEILIN, YOSSI (1948–), Israeli politician and political scientist. Member of the Twelfth to Fifteenth Knessets. Beilin was born in Petaḥ Tikvah. He received his Ph.D. in political science at Tel Aviv University and taught there in 1972–85. In 1977–84 he served as the spokesman of the *Israel Labor Party and was part of the entourage of the Party Chairman, Shimon *Peres. When Peres served as prime minister in the National Unity Government in 1984–86, Beilin served as government secretary. In the following two years, after Peres became minister for foreign affairs, Beilin served as political director general at the ministry, making efforts to cool Israel's relations with South Africa, which still followed a policy of apartheid, and to establish relations with the African National Congress.

Within the Labor Party he formed the dovish Mashov Circle. He was elected to the Twelfth Knesset and, until the Labor Party left the National Unity Government, served under Peres as deputy minister of finance. In this capacity he expressed his opinion that only the needy, and not the whole population, should receive child suppport and other allowances from the state, provoking severe criticism within the party. He was also criticized for statements about the expected level of unemployment, which proved to be conservative.

When Yitzhak *Rabin formed his government in 1992, Beilin once again followed Peres to the Ministry for Foreign Affairs as his deputy. At this time he was one of the initiators of what came to be known as the Oslo Process with two colleagues – Dr. Ya'ir Hirschfeld and Dr. Ron Pundak. When he was convinced of the seriousness of the negotiations with the Palestinians, he approached both Peres and Rabin, who agreed to upgrade the talks, though until the end of August 1993 the talks were kept secret from the public.

In June 1995 Beilin was appointed minister of economics and planning. After Rabin's assassination, when Peres became prime pinister, Beilin brought about the dismantlement of the Ministry of Economics and Planning, which he thought was superfluous, and was appointed minister in the Prime Minister's Office.

Three days before Rabin's assassination Beilin concluded with the Palestinian politician Maḥmud Abbas (known as Abu-Ma'azen), who was later to become prime minister, a document that outlined the parameters of a permanent settlement between Israel and the Palestinians. The document, which was published by *Haaretz*, spoke of the establishment of a demilitarized Palestinian state in 90% of the West Bank and the Gaza Strip, with its capital in the Arab neighborhood of Abu-Dis, east of Jerusalem. Peres rejected the document, because he believed it would be harmful to the Labor Party in the forthcoming elections.

In June 1997 Beilin contested the leadership of the Labor Party, but lost to Ehud *Barak, receiving 28.5% of the party vote. In the government formed by Barak after the elections to the Fifteenth Knesset, he was appointed minister of justice. He resigned from the Knesset in November 1999, to enable the next member on the Labor list to enter the Knesset. After Shas left the government, he also assumed the portfolio for religious affairs. After failing to receive a realistic place in the Labor list for the Sixteenth Knesset, Beilin, together with Yael *Dayan, joined the Meretz list, but when Meretz received only six seats, he failed to enter the Knesset. With Palestinian leader Yasser Abed Rabbo, Beilin started to work on a new peace document that came to be known as the Geneva Initiative, signed in Geneva under the auspices of Swtizerland on December 1, 2003. On March 16, 2004, Beilin won the election for leadership of Meretz (which changed its name to "Yaḥad and the Democratic Choice") against MK Ran Cohen.

The following of his books have appeared in English: *Israel: A Concise Political History* (1993); *Touching Peace* (1999); *Dispatches from Palestine: The Rise and Fall of the Oslo Agreement* (1999); *His Brother's Keeper: Israel and Diaspora Jewry in the Twenty-First Century* (2000); *Manual for a Wounded Dove* (2003); *The Path to Geneva: The Quest for a Permanent Agreement, 1996–2004* (2004).

BIBLIOGRAPHY: S. Ben-Porat, *Siḥot im Yossi Beilin* ("Talks with Yossi Beilin," 1997).

[Susan Hattis Rolef (2nd ed.)]

BEILINSON (Belinson), MOSES ELIEZER (1835–1908), Hebrew and Yiddish writer and publisher. He was born in Dubrovna (Russia). In 1860 he published a brochure *Ẓevi la-Ẓaddik* containing an apologia for Judaism and an attack upon Christianity and Karaism. He translated Ludwig Philippson's novel *Die Vertreibung der Juden aus Spanien und Portugal* into Hebrew as *Galut Sefarad* in 1860. In the 1860s he established a Hebrew printing press in Odessa, and published *Alei Hadas*, a literary and scholarly periodical (1865), in which he printed his correspondence with Philippson on the situation of the Jews in Russia. Only four issues appeared. Perez *Smolenskin published his first pamphlets at Beilinson's press (1862–67); Beilinson wanted to "correct" Smolenskin's style, but most of his corrections were rejected. *Kol Mevasser* (1871), the first Yiddish weekly published in Russia, was also printed at Beilinson's press and Beilinson succeeded Moshe Leib *Lilienblum as its editor, using the pseudonym "M.E.B.N." He composed three genealogical histories (including one on his own family): *Megillat Yuḥasin* (1891), *Yalkut Mishpaḥot* (1892), and *Millu'im le-Kovez Yalkut Mishpaḥot* (1893). He published *Toledot ha-Rav Yosef Shelomo Rofe Delmedigo mi-Kandia* (1864), a biography based on Abraham Geiger's *Melo Ḥofnayim* (German section), and *Shelomei Emunei Yisrael*, three brochures dealing with literary and scientific topics (1898–1901). He also edited *Kovez Yagdil Torah* (1879–85) and *Kovez Mekhilta de-Rabbanan* (1885), dealing with halakhic matters. Beilinson adapted Longfellow's *Judas Maccabaeus* into a Yiddish Ḥanukkah play (1882), and also adapted Philippson's above-mentioned novel (1888). He additionally published *Nutslikher Fremdvorterbukh* (Part 1, 1887), a dictionary of foreign phrases used in Yiddish.

BIBLIOGRAPHY: Zeitlin, Bibliotheca, 18–19; Rejzen, Leksikon 1 (1928), 328–30; Wachstein et al., *Hebraische Publizistik in Wien*, 1 (1930), 11, 293.

[Gedalyah Elkoshi]

BEILINSON, MOSHE (1889–1936), Hebrew writer, journalist, and one of the chief spokesmen of the labor movement in Ereẓ Israel. Beilinson, who was born in Veprika, Russia, qualified as a doctor in 1913. A supporter of the Russian socialist movement, he was won over to Zionist socialism by Z. Shazar and B. Katznelson. After World War I he settled in Italy, where he became active in the Zionist movement. He also published a series of translations into Italian of books of Jewish interest, including: Buber's *Reden ueber das Judentum* (1923); R. Travers Herford's *Pharisees* (1925); and (with Dante *Lattes) Joseph Klausner's *Kizzur Toledot ha-Sifrut ha-Ivrit ha-Ḥadashah* (1926). In 1924 he settled in Petaḥ Tikvah and soon afterward joined the editorial board of the newly founded *Davar. Here Beilinson published articles and notes, discussing problems of the Palestinian labor movement. He first wrote in Russian but changed to Hebrew in 1926. His style was simple and fluent. Beilinson wrote: *Bi-Ymei Massah*, on the Jewish-Arab question (1930); *Bi-Ymei Teḥiyyat Italyah* (1930); *Be-Mashber ha-Olam* (published in 1940, with an essay on Beilinson by B. Katznelson) and *Ba-Derekh le-Aẓma'ut* (1949). One of the main hospitals in the Tel Aviv area was named after him.

BIBLIOGRAPHY: *Ẓiyyun le-Moshe Beilinson* (supplement to *Davar*, fasc. no. 3792, Nov. 9, 1937, includes a bibliography of his writings).

[Getzel Kressel]

BEILIS, MENAHEM MENDEL (1874–1934), victim of a *blood libel charge in Russia in 1911. On March 20, 1911, the mutilated body of Andrei Yushchinsky, a 12-year-old boy, was discovered in a cave on the outskirts of Kiev. The monarchist rightist press immediately launched a vicious anti-Jewish campaign, accusing the Jews of using human blood for ritual purposes. At the funeral of Yushchinsky, leaflets circulating the blood libel were distributed by members of the reactionary "Black Hundred" ("*Union of Russian People") organization. Meanwhile the police investigation traced the murder to a gang of thieves associated with a woman, Vera Cheberiak, notorious for criminal dealings. However, the reactionary antisemitic organizations led by the "Black Hundred" pressured the antisemitic minister of justice, I.G. Shcheglovitov, to conduct the investigation of the crime as a ritual murder. Accordingly, the chief district attorney of Kiev disregarded the police information and instead looked for a Jew on whom to blame the crime, through whom the entire Jewish people could be publicly indicted.

In July 1911, a lamplighter testified that on March 12, the day Yushchinsky disappeared, he had seen him playing with two other boys on the premises of the brick kiln owned by a Jew, Zaitsev. He also alleged that a Jew had suddenly appeared and kidnapped Yushchinsky, pulling him toward the brick kiln. On the strength of this testimony, Mendel Beilis, the superintendent of the brick kiln, was arrested on July 21, 1911, and sent to prison, where he remained for over two years. A report was submitted to Czar Nicholas II that Beilis was regarded by the judiciary as the murderer of Yushchinsky.

The case attracted universal attention. Protests and addresses by scientists, public and political leaders, artists, men of letters, clergymen, and other liberal-minded men were published in all the civilized countries of Europe and the United States affirming that the blood libel was baseless. The trial of Beilis took place in Kiev from September 25 through October 28, 1913. The chief prosecutor A.I. Vipper made anti-Jewish statements in his closing address and defended the Cheberiak gang against the charge of Yushchinsky's murder. Beilis was represented by the most able counsels of the Moscow, St. Petersburg, and Kiev bars: Vassily Maklakov, Oscar O. Grusenberg, N.P. Karabchevsky, A.S. Zarundy, and D.N. Grigorovitch-Barsky. The lamplighter and his wife, on whose testimony the indictment of Beilis rested, when questioned by the presiding judge, answered, "We know nothing at all." They confessed that both had been confused by the secret police and made to answer questions they did not comprehend. "Scientific" foundation for the blood libel was supplied at the trial by a Catholic priest with a criminal record, Justin Pranaitis, who stated that the murder of Yushchinsky had all the characteristics of ritual murder enjoined by the Jewish religion. His arguments were refuted by the rabbi of Moscow, Jacob *Mazeh, who proved that Pranaitis was ignorant of the talmudic texts cited. Two Russian professors of high standing, Troitsky and Kokovtzoff, also spoke on behalf of the defense in praise of Jewish values and exposed the falsity of the ritual murder hypothesis. The jury, composed of simple Russian peasants, after several hours of deliberation unanimously declared Beilis "not guilty."

Beilis, who still remained in danger of revenge by the "Black Hundred," left Russia with his family for Ereẓ Israel. In 1920, he settled in the United States. Bernard *Malamud's novel *The Fixer* is based on the Beilis case.

BIBLIOGRAPHY: M. Samuel, *Blood Accusation: the Strange History of the Beiliss Case* (1966); M. Beilis, *Story of My Sufferings* (1926); AJYB, 16 (1914/15), 19–89; A.D. Margolin, in: *Jews of Eastern Europe* (1926), 155–247; A.B. Tager, *The Decay of Czarism: The Beiliss Trial* (1935); M. Cotic, *Mishpat Beilis* (1978); Z. Szajkowski, in: PAAJR, 31 (1963), 197–218.

[Chasia Turtel]

BEIM, SOLOMON BEN ABRAHAM (1817?–1867), Karaite scholar and important public figure, a disciple of the Karaite scholar Mordecai *Sultansky. He also acquired a secular education and knew Russia, French, and German. In 1839 he accompanied Abraham *Firkovich in his voyages around the Crimea and Caucasus to help him search for antiquities. In the mid-1840s he conducted archaeological excavations in the Crimea and became a member of the Imperial Geographical Society. Beim first officiated as *ḥazzan* in Chufut-Kale, where he founded a Karaite school with tendencies of enlightenment. In addition to Bible and Hebrew, he also taught Russian and secular subjects. Beim was on friendly terms and corresponded with intellectuals of the Jewish Haskalah and Reform Movement. He attempted to ease the severe Karaite laws, but he met with strong opposition. In 1855, after the death of Simḥah *Babovich he was appointed as *ḥazzan* of the Crimea and Odessa. After the death of his father, the *ḥazzan* of the Odessa Karaite community, he moved to Odessa and continued his father's good relations with the Rabbanites. He died in the course of his visit to St.-Petersburg, where he came to deliver to Czar Alexander II samples of typical Karaite garments, on the Czar's request. He wrote *Pamiat' o Chufut-Qaleh* and several other treatises in Russian on the Karaites which, however, have limited value, being based solely on the findings of Firkovich.

BIBLIOGRAPHY: O.B. Beliy, in: MAIET 10 (2003), 639–66; R. Fahn, *Sefer ha-Keraim* (1929), 100–2; A. Gottlober, in: *Ha-Maggid*, 8, nos. 20–21 (1864); S. Pigit, *Iggeret Nidḥei Shemuel* (1894), 2f.

[Golda Akhiezer (2nd ed.)]

BEIMEL, JACOB (c. 1875–1944), *ḥazzan*. Beimel was born in Parichi, Belorussia, where his father was also a cantor; as a child, he sang in Bobruisk and Berdichev. He studied music in Odessa and Berlin, became cantor in Berlin, where he conducted the Mendelssohn Choir, and later served in Copenhagen. In 1915, he went to the U.S. and conducted choral concerts. He held posts in New York and later in Philadelphia. His works and adaptations of synagogue music, his folk songs and ḥasidic melodies, were published in the quarterly *Jewish Music Journal* (Eng. and Yid., 1934–35), which he edited in the U.S.

BEIN, ALEXANDER (1903–1988), archivist and historian of Zionism. Bein was born at Steinach and studied at Erlangen and Berlin. From 1927 to 1933 he served on the staff of the German State Archives. In 1933 he settled in Palestine where he became assistant director of the General Zionist Archives in 1936. In 1955 he was appointed director, and in addition from 1956 was state archivist of Israel. Apart from studies in general history, *Die Staatsidee Alexander Hamiltons in ihrer Entstehung und Entwicklung* (1927), Bein devoted his efforts to the history of Zionism and modern antisemitism. Among his works are *Toledot ha-Hityashevut ha-Ẓiyyonit* (1945²); *The Return to the Soil* (1952); his biography of Theodor Herzl (1934) which was translated into several languages; *Die Judenfrage* (1980; Eng., *The Jewish Question*, 1990). Bein also edited a new Hebrew edition of Herzl's writings in Hebrew which appeared in ten volumes in 1960–61. He contributed articles to scholarly journals on the history of modern antisemitism and Zionism. In 1987 he was awarded the Israel Prize for his contributions to Zionist historiography.

BIBLIOGRAPHY: Kressel, Leksikon 1 (1965), 230.

[Isaak Dov Ber Markon]

BEINART, HAIM (1917–), Jewish historian specializing in Spanish Jewry in the Middle Ages. Born in Pskow, Russia, Beinart received a traditional Jewish and general education at the Hebrew High School in Riga. He arrived in Palestine in 1937 as a student and commenced his academic studies at the Hebrew University of Jerusalem.

Concentrating on the history of the Jews in Spain, Beinart spent a research year in the Archivo Historico Nacional in Madrid and in the Archiva General de la Corona de Aragon in Barcelona. He received his Ph.D. in 1955 for his thesis on "The Trials of the Inquisition against the Judaizers in Toledo in the period of the Expulsion of the Jews from Spain."

Beinart taught in the department of Jewish history at the Hebrew University from 1952, becoming a full professor in 1972.

From 1965 to 1969 he served as academic adviser for the Faculty of Humanities and Social Sciences at what was to become the Ben-Gurion University of the Negev, and was dean of the faculty from 1969 to 1973. Beinart served also as the head of the Institute of Jewish Studies at the Hebrew University of Jerusalem. Beinart was awarded the Israel Prize in 1991 for Jewish history and in 2004 he received the Rothschild Prize.

Beinart's research work dealt extensively with the history of Spanish Jewry in the Middle Ages, based on original sources he uncovered through his meticulous searches in various libraries throughout the world. His research concentrated on the century before the expulsion of the Jews from Spain in 1492, although he investigated numerous other areas including studies on the Jews expelled from Spain and their search for refuge in other countries. This includes archival material about Marranos who formed the nucleus for the revival of Jewish communities outside of Spain.

Beinart published hundreds of scholarly articles in various journals in Spanish, Hebrew and English. His four-volume *Records of the Trials of the Spanish Inquisition in Ciudad Real*, which includes the reports of the trials against the Marranos during the Spanish Inquisition, his *Conversos on Trial*, and his *Expulsion of the Jews from Spain* made a major contribution to the study of the era.

Beinart founded and edited the *Hispania Judaica Series* (1978–) which publishes historical monographs on the Jewish community in Spain. He was a member of the editorial board of the quarterly *Zion* and of *The Shorter Jewish Encyclopaedia in Russian* and was editor of the history of the Jews in Christian Spain for the first edition of the *Encyclopaedia Judaica*.

[Elaine Hoter]

BEINISCH (Werba), DORIT (1942–), Israeli jurist. Born in Tel Aviv, Beinisch studied law at the Hebrew University of Jerusalem and from 1976 to 1982 served as director of the Department of Constitutional and Administrative Law at the State Attorney's Office. In 1982 she was appointed deputy state attorney and in 1989 she became state attorney. She served in this position for seven years, heading government litigation in the Magistrate, District, and Supreme Court. She also served as the official legal advisor to government departments and agencies. Beinisch gave special attention to ensuring that government institutions remain subject to legal restraints, with particular emphasis on the IDF, Police, and General Security Service. In 1995 she was appointed to the Supreme Court of Israel. Among her notable court opinions are her decision holding that parents cannot use corporal punishment against their children and decisions stressing the importance of protecting rights of women and children.

[Leon Fine (2nd ed.)]

BEI-RAV (Aram. בֵּי רַב), term in talmudic literature designating a place of elementary or advanced education (e.g., Sanh. 33b, 17b; Yev. 83b). A related term in Hebrew is *bet rabban* (e.g., Shab. 119b). The students at the *bei rav* also lived there (Ber. 25a). *De-Vei-Rav* is also used by some *amoraim* as a term for certain collections of tannaitic literature. *She'ar Sifrei de-Vei-Rav* ("Other Books of Bei-Rav") mentioned by some *amoraim* (Yoma 74a; BB 124b), are explained by Rashi as the tannaitic commentaries on Numbers and Deuteronomy, although Solomon b. Abraham *Adret and *Gershom b. Judah include the Midrash on Exodus as well. For them, the Midrash on Leviticus (*Sifra de-Vei Rav*) was the book of Bei-Rav as everyone was so well versed with it, whereas the other works were somewhat less well-known. Zunz identifies **Sifra* and *Sidra de-Vei-Rav* (also known as *Torat Kohanim*) with the commentary on Leviticus, and *Sifrei* and *Sifrei de-Vei-Rav* with the commentary on Numbers and Deuteronomy. Known under the single name of **Sifrei*, these midrashic commentaries were taught for the first time by Rav in Babylonia (Zunz, Vortraege, 49f.). Maimonides and Menahem Meiri after him considered Rav the author of these works. M. Friedmann, in his introduction to the **Mekhilta* (1870; xviff.), identifies *Sifra* with *Torat Kohanim* (i.e., the commentary on Lev.) and *Sifra de-Vei-Rav* with miscellaneous **baraitot* of Rav, or of the academy of Rav. D. Hoffman (*Zur Einleitung in die halachischen Midraschim* (1887), 13–20, and *Mar Samuel* (1873), 68f.), subscribes to the view that the term "*tanna de-Vei-Rav*" embraces the *Sifra* and *Sifra de-Vei-Rav*, a collection of the teachings of the sages at the academy of Rabbi Huna (cf. Sanh. 17b). For more on the halakhic midrashim, see **Midrashei Halakhah*.

BIBLIOGRAPHY: Weiss, Dor, 2 (1904⁴), 206f.; Bacher, Bab Amor, 2; idem, *Ergaenzungen und Berichtigungen*... (1913), 5; Gruenhut, in: *Sefer le-David Ẓevi (Festschrift... D. Hoffmann)* (1914), 1–11 (Heb.); J.Z. Lauterbach (ed.), *Mekhilta*, 1 (1933), xxiff. (Eng. and Heb.); J.N. Epstein, *Mevo'ot le-Sifrut ha-Tanna'im* (1957), 646ff., 728ff.; Ch. Albeck, *Mavo la-Talmudim* (1969), 102–6.

BEIRUT, capital city and chief port of Lebanon. From the second century B.C.E. Jews lived in its vicinity, and probably in the city itself. The Chronicle of Joshua the Stylite mentions the existence of a synagogue in Beirut at the beginning of the sixth century. *Abiathar b. Elijah (late 11th century) includes Beirut and Gebal (Byblos) among the cities subject to the gaonate of Palestine. At the time of the Crusader conquest (1100) Beirut contained 35 Jewish families and *Benjamin of Tudela (c. 1170) found 50 households there. According to Isaac of Acre, many Jews were killed during the Muslim capture of the city in 1291.

Jews frequently visited Beirut on their way to Ereẓ Israel, but a pupil of *Nahmanides who stopped there at the beginning of the 14th century did not note the presence of Jews in the city. An anonymous pupil of Obadiah *Bertinoro wrote in a letter (1495) "At Baroto (Beirut) there are no Jews, and I do not know the reason, because the Ishmaelites at Baroto are better than all the other people of the Kingdom and are very well-disposed toward the Jews." However Jews settled again in Beirut after their expulsion from Spain in 1492. Moses *Basola, who visited the city in 1521, found 12 Jewish families from Sicily. Abraham Castro was in charge of customs. During Basola's stay in the city, the activity of David *Reuveni, whom a Jewish merchant encountered at Gaza, excited the Jews. *David d'Beth Hillel, who visited Syria in 1824, relates "There are [in Beirut] some 15 families [of] Jewish merchants, natives of the country [i.e., the place] who speak Arabic and have a small synagogue, their customs resembling those of the Jews of Palestine."

In 1856 Ludwig August *Frankl stated that he found in Beirut 500 Sephardi Jews, mostly merchants and porters. In the course of time other Jews moved to Beirut from Damascus, Smyrna, Aleppo, Constantinople, and ultimately also from Russia. In 1878 the *Alliance Israélite opened a girls' school and the following year, one for boys. In 1901, 271 pupils were studying at the latter, and 218 at the former. In 1897 the Alliance opened a crafts school for girls.

In 1862 and in 1890 blood libels resulted in Christian attacks on the Jewish quarter. In 1890 order was restored by the Turkish authorities and the rioters were arrested. At that time Beirut contained a synagogue and 12 *batei midrash*. After World War I the Jewish population grew in Beirut, the newly established capital of *Lebanon.

The community was regarded as the most highly organized in Lebanon and Syria. The principal synagogue Magen Avraham was the center of the communal institutions, which included the schools of the Alliance and of the congregation, the B'nai B'rith Lodge, and the Maccabi Club.

The Jews of the city belonged mostly to the middle class, and the overwhelming majority of them engaged in commerce. They were not concentrated in special quarters, but the poorer Jews resided in streets formerly part of the Jewish quarter in Wadi Abu Jamil. When the State of Israel was established, the Lebanese security forces were ordered to protect the Jewish quarter, and when an anti-Jewish demonstration was held and infuriated mobs advanced on the Jewish quarter, members of the Maronite Christian Phalanges dispersed the demonstrators. The Jewish paper *al-ʿAlam al-Israili* ("The Israelite World") changed its name to *al-Salam* ("Peace"). The Jewish community was compelled to contribute a sum of money to the fund of the Arab League but in general the Jews were not mistreated.

In 1880 there were about 1,000 Jews in Beirut; in 1889, 1,500; between 1892 and 1906 there were 3,000; between 1907 and 1910 their number reached 5,000.

[Simon Marcus]

From 1948

The number of Jews rose from 5,000 in 1948 to 9,000 in 1958, as a result of the immigration of Syrian Jews to Lebanon. However, the numbers were subsequently depleted, especially from 1967; and in 1969 only about 2,500 were left. By 1970 the community had decreased to about 1,000–1,800.

Until the 1975–90 conflict (see *Lebanon), the Jewish community in Beirut, like the rest of the Jews living in the country, was considered to be an integral part of Lebanon's multiethnic society. During periods of crisis, such as the 1948 War, the first Lebanese civil war in 1958, and the 1967 War, the Lebanese authorities ordered the security forces to protect the Jewish quarter in Wadi Abu Jamil. The wealthy Jews living in new suburbs among members of other faiths were also unharmed. In contrast to other Arab countries, Jewish life in Lebanon continued almost normally: Jews were not discriminated against or arrested by the government in an arbitrary manner, and their property was not confiscated. In 1950 extremist Arab nationalists place a bomb beneath the *Alliance Israélite Universelle school building, causing it to collapse. The Alliance administered three other institutions, in which 950 pupils studied in 1965. In addition, 250 pupils attended the *talmud torah* and 80 studied at the Oẓar ha-Torah religious school. The Jewish scouts and Maccabi sports organization were closed by the government in 1953. The community council, which had nine members, was elected biennially. The Bikkur Ḥolim committee of the council was responsible for medical treatment of the poor, and their hospitalization if they were not Lebanese citizens. Its income derived from the *Arikha* (assessment) tax, paid by all males, as well as from endowments and from synagogues. Most Beirut Jews were merchants or employees of trading and financial enterprises.

[Hayyim J. Cohen]

During the early stages of Lebanon's second civil war (1975–90), the Jews in Beirut, like members of other minorities who resided in the Lebanese capital (e.g., Armenians and Kurds), found themselves caught in the crossfire between local and foreign forces that battled for control of the city and its neighborhoods. The proximity of the Jewish quarter to the "Green Line" separating Beirut's Christian and Muslim sectors exacerbated its inhabitants' insecurity. In the course of the fighting, many Jewish homes and businesses were damaged, as were their communal institutions, most notably the Magen Avraham synagogue (the building itself, which was reportedly hit by an Israeli shell in 1982, was, however, not destroyed). Jewish communal life was further disrupted when the local rabbi left the country in 1978. Meanwhile, impoverished Shiʿi Muslims, who had been driven from their homes by the war, began to settle in the Jewish quarter. The continued violence and chaos in Beirut encouraged most of the Lebanese Jews, whose number on the eve of the war was estimated at about 1,800 (of these, more than a thousand resided in Beirut) to leave the country, whereas others moved to safer areas in and around the capital. From 1975 on most

Lebanese Jews immigrated to France, Italy, the U.S., Canada, South America, and Israel.

In 1982 there were an estimated 150 Jews in the western part of Beirut and 100 in its eastern sector. But Israel's invasion into Lebanon and the siege imposed by its army on the Lebanese capital, combined with the chaos that prevailed in the city following the Israeli withdrawal and the failed attempt to reconstruct the Lebanese state in 1982–84, impinged on the situation of the country's remaining Jews, which were now estimated at 100–200. Radical Shi'i factions began to target the Jewish community in Beirut in order to exert pressure on the Israeli government and avenge attacks by the Israeli army in South Lebanon. Thus, in the period 1984–87, the Organization of the Oppressed on Earth, a radical Shi'i faction reportedly close to Hizbullah, abducted 11 prominent members of the local Jewish community, including its head, Isaac Sasson. The kidnappers claimed that their actions were part of their "resistance" to the Israeli occupation in Lebanon and demanded the release of Shi'i prisoners held by Israel and by its proxy, the South Lebanon Army. But Israel refused to comply. The bodies of four Jews were later recovered and the fate of the other seven remained unknown. These factors caused the Jewish community in Beirut to drop to about fewer than 100 members in the late 1980s and early 1990s.

In the 1990–2001 period, the number of Jews in Lebanon, who by then resided almost exclusively in Beirut and its vicinity, dropped even further. Wadi Abu Jamil was almost emptied of its Jewish residents, and the majority of the remaining Lebanese Jews resided in the eastern part of the Lebanese capital or in Mount Lebanon. During the 2004 municipal elections, only one of the registered Jewish voters in Beirut showed up at the polling booth. It was reported that most of the remaining Jews in Lebanon were elderly women.

[Oren Barak (2nd ed.)]

BIBLIOGRAPHY: S.D. Goitein, in: *Eretz Israel*, 4 (1956), 152; G. Scholem, in: KS, 2 (1925/26), 103; I. Ben-Zvi, *Masot Ereẓ Yisrael le-Moshe Basola* (1938), 38–40; A. Yaari, *Mas'ot Ereẓ Yisrael* (1946), 135f., 525f.; index; Ashtor, Toledot, 2 (1951), 121f.; S. Landshut, *Jewish Communities in the Muslim Countries of the Middle East* (1950), 54–56. **ADD. BIBLIOGRAPHY:** K.E. Schulze, *The Jews of Lebanon: Between Coexistence and Conflict* (2001).

BEIT, SIR ALFRED (1853–1906), South African financier and co-founder, with Cecil Rhodes, of Rhodesia. Born in Hamburg, Beit learned the diamond trade in Amsterdam and went to South Africa in 1875. He became prominent in the development of the Kimberley diamond fields and later of the Witwatersrand gold reefs. In 1889 he formed the partnership of Wernher, Beit, and Company, forerunner of one of the big Rand mining groups. Beit met Rhodes, and their careers became inseparable. His financial talents complemented those of Rhodes, and he became identified with Rhodes' imperial ambitions. Beit stood with Rhodes in the rivalry with *Barnato for the control of the diamond fields. He obtained the assistance of the London Rothschilds, and became a life governor in De Beers Consolidated Mines when it was formed in 1888. With Rhodes he established the British South Africa Company for the administration of the territory that became known as Rhodesia and had a part in the development of the country second only to that of Rhodes himself. He was implicated in Rhodes' plot against the Kruger regime that ended in the Jameson Raid of 1895. He made generous donations to South African war relief funds, founded the Beit professorship of colonial history at Oxford, and through the Wernher-Beit bequest stimulated university education in South Africa. Other bequests included £1,200,000 for education and communications in Rhodesia and thirty fellowships in medical research. Beit left a fortune of over £8 million, probably the largest personal fortune ever left in Britain until then. He left his entire estate to his brother, OTTO JOHN BEIT (1865–1930), who was associated with him in his financial and philanthropic activities.

BIBLIOGRAPHY: G.S. Fort, *Alfred Beit...* (1932); P.H. Emden, *Randlords* (1935), index; G. Saron and L. Hotz (eds.), *Jews in South Africa* (1955). **ADD. BIBLIOGRAPHY:** DBB, I, 253–55; ODNB online; G. Wheatcroft, *The Randlords* (1985), index.

[Dora Leah Sowden]

BEIT-HALLAHMI, BENJAMIN (1943–), Israeli psychologist and leading authority on the social psychology of religion. Born in Tel Aviv, Beit-Hallahmi served in the IDF in 1963–66. He was educated at the Hebrew University of Jerusalem (B.A. 1966) and at Michigan State University (M.A. 1968, Ph.D., clinical psychology, 1970). He taught at a number of American and Israeli universities, including the University of Michigan, the University of Pennsylvania, and the Hebrew University, and maintained membership in several American professional associations. From 1973 he was senior lecturer and professor of psychology at the University of Haifa.

The primary focus of Beit-Hallahmi's academic work (for which he acknowledged his debt to the work of William James) was the study of the social psychology of religion, with particular attention to religion and social identity; the appeal of New Religious Movements (or NRM, popularly known as "cults"), on which he was an acknowledged international authority; and the relationship between Jewish ideas of religious salvation and the Zionist project, and its social consequences. Among his influential publications in this area were his books *The Social Psychology of Religion* (1975, with Michael Argyle), *Prolegomena to the Psychological Study of Religion* (1989), *Despair and Deliverance: Private Salvation in Contemporary Israel* (1992), *The Psychology of Religious Behavior, Belief, and Experience* (1997, with Michael Argyle), several edited volumes and numerous journal articles.

Beit-Hallahmi, as a secular student of culture and "progressive" (his own word) citizen of Israel, brought his fundamental concerns to bear on public controversies regarding Israeli policy and Zionism, and published two important books examining their origins and history: *The Israeli Connection: Who Israel Arms and Why* (1987) and the classic *Origi-*

nal Sins: Reflections on the History of Zionism and Israel (1992; revised American edition 1993), a frank and hardheaded discussion of the permanent Israel/Palestine crisis: "Out of the original sins of the world against the Jews grew the original sins of Zionism against the Palestinians.... The problem is a moral one. Raising the moral question is not a mark of idealism but of realism."

[Drew Silver (2nd ed.)]

BEIT JANN, Druze village in Upper Galilee, Israel. Lying at 3,082 ft. (940 m.) above sea level on the western slope of Mt. Meron, it is one of Israel's highest inhabited places. Although the identification of the village with the town Beth-Dagon of the tribe of Asher is no longer regarded as correct, Beit Jann seems to be the Galilean village Bet Dagan, reported in talmudic times as producing a certain late-ripening vegetable (Tosef., Shev. 7:13). In 1839 Scottish missionaries found here a few Jewish families, who apparently had moved from Safed 6.2 mi. (10 km.) to the east after the 1837 earthquake. In 1964 Beit Jann received municipal council status. With 4,110 inhabitants in 1968, on an area of 1.8 sq. mi. (4.65 sq. km.), Beit Jann was one of the major Druze centers in Israel. Its economy was based on fruit, beef cattle, and tobacco. By the end of 2002 its population has risen to 9,430.

[Efraim Orni]

BEIT JIMĀL, monastery and agricultural school in the Judean Foothills, 3 mi. (5 km.) S. of Bet-Shemesh, founded in 1881 by Salesian Fathers from Italy on the supposition that R. *Gamaliel I had lived there and that the place was named after him. The site is supposed by some scholars to be identical to *Kefar Gamala, where the tomb of St. Stephen was located in the fifth century. Remnants of a church with a mosaic floor were discovered there in 1916. In 1988 a new monastery was built nearby for the Bethlehem Sisterhood, which houses about 30 nuns who choose to live their lives in solitude and silence.

WEBSITE: www.trekker.co.il/israel-monasteries.htm.

[Efraim Orni / Shaked Gilboa (2nd ed.)]

BEJA, town in S. Portugal, capital of the region of Alemtejo; one of the seats of the subordinate rabbinates set up under the general control of the *Arraby Moor in the 15th century. When the kingdom of Portugal was established in the 12th century, Jews are said to have been living already in Beja. In the charter (*foro*) granted to the town in the 13th century, nine clauses deal with the Jews, both resident and transient; most of them speak of established local usage. A tombstone found in the castle of Beja has a fragment of a Hebrew inscription referring to the death of R. Judah. Another tombstone from Beha was found in the 18th century and was brought to Evora in 1868. It is probably from 1378. After the expulsion of the Jews from Portugal in 1496–97, Beja became a center of crypto-Judaism and many natives of the city appeared at autos-da-fé or escaped abroad. In the early years of the 18th century, a physician named Francisco de Sá e Mesquita spitefully denounced persons from Beja – on one occasion 66, on another 92 – who, he said, had come together to observe Jewish rites. The name Beja was common among the Sephardim of the Orient: e.g., Ḥayyim Beja (c. 1810–1870) of Salonika, who subsequently became rabbi of Tyria in Asia Minor; and the scholar-preacher Isaac b. Moses *Beja.

BIBLIOGRAPHY: J. Mendes dos Remedios, *Os judeus em Portugal*, 1 (1895), 422f.; Rosanes, Togarmah, 3 (1938), 115–7; A.da Silva Carvalho, *Noticia sôbre alguns medicos judeus do Alentejo* (1930), 47–48. **ADD. BIBLIOGRAPHY:** F. Díaz Esteban, in: *Proceedings, 10th World Congress of Jewish Studies* (1990), Division B, Vol. 2, 122–3.

[Cecil Roth / Yom Tov Assis (2nd ed.)]

BEJA, ISAAC BEN MOSES (c. 1570–1628), preacher in Salonika and Nikopolis (Bulgaria). Beja studied in Salonika. He was compelled to wander from one community to another until he was invited to teach at the yeshivah of Nikopolis. He arrived there after the city had been damaged in the war between the Turks and the Walachians (1595–99). Beja's homilies and eulogies, blended with Kabbalah, were published under the title *Bayit Ne'eman* (Venice, 1621); he also wrote poetry, and four of his poems appear in this work. His work displays originality both in thought and in his homiletical approach. His homily on the building of the synagogue of Nikopolis was reprinted under the title "*Keter Torah*" in *Le-Ohavei Leshon Ever* (Paris, 1628). There were two contemporaneous Salonikan scholars both named Isaac Beja; one died in 1635, the other in 1647.

BIBLIOGRAPHY: Rosanes, Togarmah, 3 (1938²), 115ff.; M. Molḥo, *Be-Veit ha-Almin shel Yehudei Saloniki*, 4 (1933), 13; I.S. Emmanuel, *Maẓẓevot Saloniki*, 1 (1963), 250f., 270.

BEJERANO, family of Israeli industrialists. The brothers MOSHE (1902–1951) and SHIMON (1910–1971) BEJERANO were born in Plovdiv, Bulgaria, and educated in Switzerland. In 1921 they moved with their family to Milan, where they became active Zionists. Shimon settled in Palestine, in 1936, followed by Moshe three years later. Together they founded a cigarette factory, and acquired the Assis factory in Ramat Gan, which they developed into one of the largest syrup and canning enterprises in Israel. They became leaders of the Manufacturers' Association of Israel. Moshe served as Israel's first commercial attaché in Moscow and devoted himself to the development of commercial relations between Israel and the Far East. Shimon was active in the General Zionist Party, which he represented in the Second and Third Knessets.

[Abraham Aharoni]

BEJERANO, BEKHOR ḤAYYIM BEN MOSES (1850–1931), Bulgarian rabbi and scholar. Bejerano was born in Eski-Zagra, Bulgaria, and studied under Zechariah ha-Levi of Salonika. He learned, in addition to his regular Torah studies, languages and other secular subjects. In 1880, he moved to Rushchuk, where he served as head of the community and where Solomon *Rosanes was one of his pupils. During the Russo-Turkish War (1878), Bejerano found a haven in Choumla. He afterward moved to Bucharest, where he was both a *dayyan* and principal of the school of the Sephardi community. His years in Bucharest were his most fruitful, both in terms of literary productivity and of personal gratification. He maintained close ties with Queen Elizabeth of Romania and served as the official interpreter for Semitic languages of both the Romanian royal house and of the official government institutions. His publication of several books in Romanian earned him a government decoration. In 1908, Bejerano was chosen chief rabbi of Adrianople and in 1922, chief rabbi of Constantinople, a position he held until his death. Bejerano was famous for his generosity and was greatly honored in his lifetime. He was a corresponding member of the Spanish and French academies. His Hebrew articles appeared in *Ha-Maggid, Ḥavaẓẓelet, Ha-Me'assef and Ha-Mizpeh*, etc. He left many works in manuscript.

BIBLIOGRAPHY: M.D. Gaon, *Yehudei ha-Mizraḥ be-Ereẓ Yisrael*, 2 (1938), 143f.

[Itzhak Alfassi]

BEJERANO, MAYA (1949–), Israeli poet. Bejerano was born in Kibbutz Elon and spent her childhood in Jaffa. She studied literature and philosophy at Bar-Ilan University as well as violin and flute and was also an amateur photographer. Holding an M.A. in Library Science from the Hebrew University, she worked as a consultant at the Tel Aviv Municipal Library. She published 11 collections of poems, including *Bat Ya'anah* ("Ostrich," 1978), *Ibud Netunim* 52 ("Data Processing 52," 1983), *Livyatan* ("Whale," 1990), *Anaseh Laga'at be-Tabur Bitni* ("Trying to Touch My Belly Button," 1998). "Selected Poems 1972–1986" appeared in 1987 and 2005 saw a volume of collected works under the title *Tedarim*. While in "Trying to Touch My Belly Button" she movingly depicted her childhood experiences and her relationship with her parents, other poems address female concerns, the joys and anguish of love, and politics, and describe the sights and moods of Tel Aviv, especially the so-called "Shenkin myth." Descriptions of nature, states of consciousness, actions and moods blend in an attempt to transform poetry into "data processing" – the title of one of her collections. For Bejerano poetry writing is a kind of linguistic and emotional laboratory: "The Hebrew language is my friend", she writes. Bejerano was awarded the Bialik Prize (2002) and the Bernstein Prize (1988). Bejerano also wrote books for children, a collection of stories, and a play. Individual poems have been translated into various languages. Information is available at the ITHL website at www.ithl.org.il.

BIBLIOGRAPHY: M. Kobovy, "From 'Data Processing' to 'Sex, Car and Love Later,'" in: J.R. Baskin (ed.) *Women of the Word* (1994), 343–66; Y. Laor, in: *Haaretz* (May 6, 2005).

[Anat Feinberg (2nd ed.)]

BEKACHE, SHALOM (1848–1927), printer and publisher. He was born in Bombay of Baghdadi origin. After studying in Safed, he became a rabbi in Acre and then migrated to Algeria, where he was rabbi of the Ben-Thoa Synagogue, the oldest in Algiers, for 40 years. He contributed to the Hebrew periodicals *Ha-Maggid, Ha-Meliẓ*, and *Ha-Ẓefirah*. In 1885 he published in Leghorn in Judeo-Arabic *Mevasser Tov*, a historical, geographical, and literary miscellany, which was followed by a monthly bulletin, *Or ha-Levanah*, dedicated essentially to the history and geography of Ereẓ Israel; five issues were published. In about 1888 he established a small printing press in Algiers, which produced some 20 books in Judeo-Arabic, edited and translated by himself. These works, which deal with the history of the Jews of Babylonia and the kingdom of the Khazars in fictional form, were adapted to the intellectual standard of the Algerian Jews of that time and were useful in widening their historical knowledge. In 1891–93 Bekache published a weekly newspaper in Judeo-Arabic, *Beit Yisrael*. *Niẓẓaḥon ha-Or al ha-Ḥoshekh* ("Triumph of the Light over the Darkness," 1896) is a philosophical thesis in Hebrew presented in the form of a controversy between the Pharisees and the Sadducees.

BIBLIOGRAPHY: ZHB, 2 (1897), 37–38; 7 (1903), 153–4.

[Robert Attal]

BEKEMOHARAR, family of 18th–19th-century rabbis of Adrianople. MENAHEM BEN ISAAC ASHKENAZI (1666–1733) was born in Temesvár; he was two years old when his parents moved to Adrianople. He used to sign his name בכמוהר"ר (BKMOHRR= **B**en **K**evod **Mo**renu **h**a-**R**av **R**abbi), to which abbreviation each of his descendants appended the initial letter of his own father's name. When Abraham Gheron was appointed rabbi of Adrianople in succession to his father-in-law Abraham Ẓarefati, six of the 13 congregations, disapproving the appointment, appointed Menahem b. Isaac as head of the *bet din*. He headed a large yeshivah and wielded great influence, the surrounding communities subjecting themselves to his authority. His works on Maimonides' *Mishneh Torah*, on Jacob b. Asher's Arba'ah Turim, and on Isaac b. Abba Mari's *Ha-Ittur*, as well as a homiletic work, were destroyed in a fire that broke out in Adrianople after his death. Another homiletic work, responsa, and novellae on the Talmud were saved. A small portion of the responsa that were saved was published in *Mikhtav Shelomo* by his grandson Solomon Bekemoharar. Menahem was also a kabbalist and a poet; his poem recited at circumcisions is well known throughout Turkey and the Balkan states.

His son, MORDECAI B. MENAHEM (d. 1748), rabbi and halakhist, succeeded his father. Most of his *Ma'amar Mordekhai*, a commentary on Mordecai b. Hillel's commentary to tractates Yevamot and part of Ketubbot, was destroyed by fire. The first three chapters of Yevamot which were rescued were published (Salonika, 1874) with the text; appended are novellae on Maimonides' *Mishneh Torah* with assorted addenda. Still in manuscript form are homilies and a talmudic commentary. Several of his responsa were published in his son's *Mikhtav Shelomo.*

MENAHEM (II) B. MORDECAI (d. 1781) succeeded his father. He was a halakhist and kabbalist and his halakhic decisions survive in manuscript form. His son was Mordecai (II). NISSIM (a name added later) SOLOMON BEN MORDECAI (1732?–1770?) began to write halakhic responsa at an early age. His works include: *Ḥeshek Shelomo* (Constantinople, 1768) on the first 68 chapters of *Ḥoshen Mishpat, Mikhtav Shelomo*, responsa (vol. 1, Salonika, 1855; vol. 2, appended to his father's *Ma'amar Mordekhai*), and *Beit Shelomo*, only a small part published in his grandson Menahem (IV)'s *Devar Emet*. His *Mirkevet ha-Mishneh*, on Maimonides' Yad, was almost identical to Aaron *Alfandari's work of the same name, and as soon as Alfandari's work was published in Smyrna in 1755, Bekemoharar stopped working on his. His son, MORDECAI SIMEON BEN NISSIM SOLOMON (d. 1814?), rabbi and halakhist, traveled extensively between the communities in Turkey and the Balkans. He wrote *Matteh Shimon*, one of the most important works on the *Ḥoshen Mishpat* (until §258; in 3 vols.; Salonika, 1797–1819; vol. 3 consists of responsa).

MORDECAI (II) BEN MENAHEM (II) (d. 1821) succeeded his father. Some of his halakhic decisions were published in *Mera Dakhya* (appended to vol. 3 of Mordecai Simeon b. Solomon's *Matteh Shimon*). The Jewish concessionaires in Constantinople appealed against his monopoly of the laudanum concession. In 1802, after a controversy in which the rabbis of Constantinople and Adrianople took part, his rights to the concession were reaffirmed. His son, MENAHEM (III) (d. 1810), was a member of the rabbinate during his father's lifetime, from about 1800. In 1801 a new congregation was formed in Rushchuk, comprising settlers from Adrianople, Vidin (Bulgaria), Belgrade, and Niš (Yugoslavia), which chose Menahem as rabbi. He left several works in manuscript.

JOSEPH RAPHAEL B. MORDECAI (II) (d. 1849) also served in the rabbinate during his father's lifetime. In 1839 the sultan Abdul Mejid appointed him head of all the congregations in Adrianople and its environs. His eldest son, MOSES RAḤAMIM (d. 1878), succeeded him in his lifetime (1846). Moses wrote responsa to questions addressed to his father and published *Nitpal la-Kodesh*, a compendium of his own responsa, together with the *Ma'amar Mordekhai* of Mordecai (I) b. Menahem. During the Russo-Turkish War (1878), he escaped to Constantinople, where he died. He was succeeded by his son, RAPHAEL (d. 1899), who was a member of the Bulgarian parliament. When independent Bulgaria was founded, the communities that came under Bulgarian rule severed their ties with the Adrianople rabbinate.

His son, MENAHEM (IV) R. MORDECAI SIMEON (1810?–1887), preacher and halakhist, was productive as a writer and as a publisher of the works of his family. His works include *Devar Emet* (Salonika, 1843), on the laws of Torah scrolls; *Devar Menaḥem* (2 vols., 1866–69), on Oraḥ Ḥayyim; *Devar ha-Mishpat* (Smyrna, 1874); *Menahem Avelim* (1880), on the laws of mourning. He was employed in a bank. During the Russo-Turkish War (1878), he escaped to Constantinople; in 1880 he immigrated to Ereẓ Israel, where he died. His grandson, YOM TOV, a scholar and a *maskil*, contributed in his youth to *Ha-Maggid*, participated in communal endeavors, and was a Bulgarian Zionist leader.

BIBLIOGRAPHY: A. Danon, *Yosef Da'at* (1886), 66–67, 71–72, 82–88; Rosanes, Togarmah, 4 (1935), 252–3; 5 (1938), 34–40, 102–3, 149–52; 6 (1945), 109ff.; Marcus, in: *Mizraḥ u-Ma'arav*, 5 (1930–32), 173–84; idem, in: *Sinai*, 21 (1947), 48–63; Azuz, in: *Ḥemdat Yisrael... Ḥ.H. Medini* (1946), 164–7.

BÉKÉSCSABA, capital of Békés county, southeast Hungary. Jews first settled there at the end of the 18th century. The first Jewish community was organized at the beginning of the 1830s. The town, an agricultural and commercial center and later a railroad hub, attracted Jewish settlers, who helped develop the town's commercial life. Their number ranged from 110 (0.5% of the total) in 1840 to 2,458 (5.0%) in 1920. The first synagogue was built in 1850. Following the denominational rift of 1869, the community identified itself at first as Orthodox, but three years later as Status Quo. In 1883, the Orthodox seceded and formed their own congregation, building its own synagogue in 1894. The Status Quo community inaugurated its own synagogue in 1896. The community's Jewish elementary school opened in 1865. In the early 1940s the congregations operated separate high schools. The last two rabbis of the Orthodox community, Judah Wolf and Isaac Tiegermann, and Rabbi Jacob Silberfeld of the Status Quo community died in the Holocaust. Illés Szabó, who was elected rabbi in 1941, survived and eventually emigrated to Israel.

According to the census of 1941, the last before the Holocaust, the city had a Jewish population of 2,433, representing 4.6% of the total of 52,404. After the German occupation of Hungary on March 19, 1944, the Jews were first deprived of their rights and property. They were rounded up between May 7 and 14 and placed into a ghetto that was established in the local tobacco factory and its environs. At its peak the ghetto included 3,113 Jews, of whom about 2,500 were from the city proper. The others were brought in from the neighboring villages and towns, including Bánhegyes, Békés, Ebdröd, Gyula, Orosháza, Szarvas, and Tótkomlós. In addition, the Jews from three districts in the neighboring Csanád, Arad, and Torontál county – Mezökovácsháza, Battonya, and Elek – were brought to Békéscsaba. The approximately 350 Jews from Mezökovácsháza were first placed in the local ghetto situated in the Mentelep area. The 414 Jews from villages in the Mezökovácsháza, Battonya, and Elek districts were first taken to a temporary ghetto established on the so-called Mandel farm, near Magyarbánhegyes. The ghetto of Békéscasba was liquidated on June 25 and 26, 1944, with the deportation of the Jews in two transports: one, including the Jews of Orosháza, Kunágota, Battonya, Magyarbánhegyes, and Tótkmolós, was directed to Strasshof, Austria, where most of the Jews survived; the other, including the Jews of Békés, Békéscsaba, Csorvás, Gyula, and

Mezöberény, was directed to Auschwitz, where most of them perished.

The few hundred survivors – deportees and labor servicemen – reestablished their community after the war. But the anti-Jewish riot of November 30, 1946, coupled with the policies of the Communist regime that came to power in 1948, induced most of them to leave the city. In 1949, close to 500 Jews – 204 Neolog and 230 Orthodox – were still living in the city, but by 1968 their number had shrunk to 151. The Orthodox synagogue still exists; the Neolog was sold in 1961.

BIBLIOGRAPHY: F. Révész, *A békéscsabai izraelita hitközség multja és jelenje*, (1926); Braham, Politics; PK Hungaria, 180–82.

[Randolph Braham (2nd ed.)]

BEKHOROT (Heb. בְּכוֹרוֹת; "Firstborn"), fourth tractate in the Mishnah, in the order of *Kodashim*. Bekhorot is a striking instance of the weaving together of disparate strands to form a mishnaic tractate. The main unifying principle is biblical: "I consecrated every first-born in Israel, man and beast, to Myself, to be Mine, the Lord's" (Num. 3:13). The primary theme relating directly to the order Kodashim concerns the firstborn of "pure" animal species: ideally, it must be slaughtered at the Temple and consumed as a sacrifice. The firstborn of the impure ass, however, must be "redeemed" or killed; a ritual of redemption is ordained for human firstborns as well (Exod. 13:13. 34:20). A separate issue is the law of inheritance, in which the firstborn is entitled to a double share.

The opening clauses of the first two chapters introduce the tractate's two secondary subjects: the priests (kohanim) and the tithe of cattle. The paired clauses 1:1 and 2:1 relate the various laws concerning the firstborn to the special status of the priests, whose consecration replaced that of the firstborn Israelites (Num. 3:45). The priests are not the subject of a mishnaic tractate, (cf. *Kodashim*), but figure significantly in *Bekhorot*, above and beyond the entire chapter (Ch 7, see below) detailing the physical wholesomeness required for their service in the Temple. The ninth, concluding chapter is devoted to the cattle tithe, whose manner of consecration – by objective circumstance – is similar to that of the firstborn animal (as emphasized in 2:2). Although the chapter's opening formula continues the series of *Ḥullin* 5–12, the tithing of cattle is grounded (like the following tractates, *Arakhin* and *Temurah*) in Lev. Ch. 27, which is also the source for the automatic consecration of the firstborn (Lev. 27:26, 32–3).

The fact that – unlike other sanctified things – the *bekhor* (firstborn) does not require an act of consecration is key to the tractate's main legal issues. First, since the determinative conditions of birth may be in doubt – especially if the dam gives birth to multiple young – ownership may be contested between the original owner and the priest (who has a claim to the *bekhor*). Hence M 2:6–8 presents a series of tannaitic disputes regarding the disposition of this contested object, including R. Akiva's classical dictum: "Whoever seeks to extract property from his fellow, has the burden of proof." Second, after the destruction of the Temple, when people desisted from consecrating animals, the firstborn – holy at birth – becomes a terrible burden. Although it can no longer be actually offered and consumed at the Temple, it still must be treated with the full care and awe due to sanctified objects and animals. The only escape allowing the priest to consume it is in case the animal happens to contract a blemish that renders it unfit as a sacrifice. Thus the Mishnah carefully determines the manner and requisite authority for examining such blemishes, as well as the specifics of the blemishes themselves.

Chapters 4 and 5 are dedicated to the procedures for examining the firstborn and to safeguards against fraudulent permissions. This becomes the classical context for broader rules about mistaken rulings and about trustworthiness in general (M 4:4–10). The caption of chapter 6 is: "The following blemishes are grounds for slaughtering the firstborn" – that is, for non-sacral consumption. The chapter goes on to enumerate these blemishes in anatomical detail; this is, in effect, the catalog of blemishes that invalidate an animal for any kind of sacrifice. Chapter 7 applies the same rules to humans – that is, to priests, who may not serve if there is a blemish in their body – but goes on to define several differences, including the issue of what may be called moral blemishes (M 7:7).

As noted above, priests figure centrally in *Bekhorot*. As God's representatives, they are entitled to the firstborn animal, and it is from them that the firstborn Israelite son is redeemed. Chapter 8 is devoted to the human *bekhor*, "firstborn for the priest" (i.e., requiring redemption) and "firstborn for inheritance." It opens by distinguishing the definition of the maternal firstborn for this redemption ("first issue of the womb," Exod. 13:2, 12) from that of the paternal firstborn, entitled to a double inheritance ("the first fruit of his vigor," Deut. 21:17).

Tosefta *Bekhorot* follows the arrangement of the Mishnah especially closely, but adds several significant expansions. M. 1:2 discusses scenarios in which an animal of one species gives birth to a creature resembling another species – not only with regard to the sanctity of the firstborn, but also with regard to the animal's status as "pure" or "impure" for eating – and offers the rule: "Anything that emerges from the impure is impure; from the pure – pure." The Tosefta's extensive treatment of this rule (1:5–13) includes an explanation of why it is nevertheless permitted to eat honey, and a grounding of the rule in a firm biological principle that cross-species breeding is impossible. When discussing untrustworthiness, the Mishnah (4:10) emphasizes that it is context-specific. T. endorses this in its own extended discussion of the same topic (3:8–12), but posits an exception: "One who is suspect with respect to idolatry is [on that account] suspect with respect to the entire Torah [i.e., in all matters]" (3:12).

The Mishnah's discussion of the "firstborn for the priest" includes several cases in which two women give birth and doubts then arise as to whether their children were exchanged (8:4–6). It is only in the Tosefta's extended treatment of this theme (6:2–9) that the setting for these doubts becomes clear. The events are repeatedly described as having taken place "in a hideout," evidently reflecting the grim realities of the Hadrianic persecutions.

[Noam Zohar (2nd ed.)]

The role played by the mother in defining the firstborn for most matters leads the Babylonian Talmud to discuss the determination of a child's birth affiliation (to tribe or nation) by its father or mother (47a). A related discussion effectively recognizes a status of Levitess – the "daughter of a Levite" – whose son (even from a father who is an Israelite) is exempted, like the son of a Levite, from the toll of the firstborn (4a).

The Book of Numbers (Chs. 3 & 8) describes the Levites' dedicational ceremony, to serve in the firstborns' stead; B. explains the absence of the priests from this description by affirming that they are included in the collective group of the Levites (4a). B. concludes that prior to this replacement, the firstborn were appointed in charge of sacrificial worship (4b).

In the context of halakhic discussions of animal births, B. reports a battle of wits between R. Yehoshua b. Hanania and the "Elders of Athens," stemming from a disagreement regarding the duration of the pregnancy of the snake (8b–9a). The battle ends with the physical downfall of the Elders of Athens.

In the conclusion of its discussion of blemishes, the Mishnah (6:12) reports a debate as to whether or not androgynous and epicene (*tumtum*) animals are considered blemished. This leads B. into a lengthy discussion regarding the various possibilities to view the status of androgynous and epicene humans (41b–42b).

In the ninth chapter, the Mishnah defines the grouping of animals into a herd that should be counted and tithed together, both in terms of birthing cycles and in terms of physical spacing; R. Meir adds (9:2) that the Jordan River constitutes a boundary in this regard. B. discusses the status of the Jordan River as a border – whether it is considered part of the land of Israel, or a separate territory. B. then enters an extended discussion of rivers, focusing on the four rivers of Eden mentioned in the Creation account in Genesis (1:10–14): Pishon, Gihon and Tigris are said to be elevated above all other bodies of water; the Euphrates is the highest of all, and the source of all the world's water (55a–55b).

[Yedidah Koren (2nd ed.)]

BIBLIOGRAPHY: H.L. Strack, *Introduction to the Talmud and Midrash* (1945), 56, 263; P. Blackman (ed. and tr.), *Mishnayoth*, 5 (Eng., 1954), 241–2; J. Neusner. *A History of the Mishnaic Law of Holy Things*. (1978–80).

BEKHOR SHOR, JOSEPH BEN ISAAC (12th century), northern French exegete, tosafist, and poet. Referred to as Joseph Bekhor Shor, he has been identified with Joseph b. Isaac of Orleans, an identification which has been proved despite the doubts of various scholars. The designation Bekhor Shor ("Firstling Bullock") derives from the expression applied to Joseph (Deut. 33:17). He was the pupil of R. *Tam, who esteemed him greatly and referred to him in terms of high praise. Abraham b. Joseph of Orleans, mentioned several times in *tosafot*, was apparently his son. Joseph's commentary on the Pentateuch, parts of which previously appeared in various publications, was issued in its entirety by Joseph Gad (1956–60), while excerpts from his commentary on Psalms have been published in *Revue des Études Juives* (vol. 58 (1909), 309–11). In his exegesis, he adopted his French predecessors' method of literal interpretation – that of Rashi, Joseph *Kara, and particularly Samuel b. Meir upon whom he largely based himself. Nevertheless, in many respects he pursued a new and original course, although in his efforts to produce novel interpretations his comments are sometimes rather strange and pilpulistic, particularly in the manner in which he relates passages to one another. He dwells at length on the biblical figures and investigates the motives for their actions but at times interprets these somewhat in terms of contemporary social conditions (Gen. 27:40). In many respects his exegesis is similar to that of the Spanish commentators, this being apparent in his efforts to explain away anthropomorphic expressions (Gen. 1:2; Num. 23:19); in defending the actions of the Patriarchs and rejecting any calumnies against them (Gen. 30:33); in interpreting miracles as almost natural phenomena (Gen. 19:26; Ex. 9:8); and in giving, to a greater extent than his French predecessors, a rational basis for the Commandments (Ex. 30:1; Lev. 19:27).

He pays little regard to grammar, nor is he as extreme as Samuel b. Meir in his homiletical comments, adding these occasionally alongside the literal interpretation (Gen. 3:24; Ex. 25:29). He makes use of *gematria* (Ex. 22:16), and at times incorporates in his comment a lengthy halakhic discussion of a passage, in these two respects being close to the exegetical method of the tosafists. He sharply opposes the allegorization of the Commandments, any neglect of which he vehemently assails (Lev. 17:13), adopting a similar attitude as regards the precepts of the *tefillin* and *mezuzah* (Deut. 6:9). This did not however prevent him from giving a literal interpretation of some passages contrary to the accepted *halakhah* (Ex. 23:19), which he naturally neither repudiates nor controverts. Joseph knew Latin, and both in speech and in writing refuted the christological interpretation of biblical passages, attacking in his comments both apostates and Christians, against whom he argued a great deal rejecting all attempts to find in the Bible allusions to Christian dogmas. He similarly repudiated their allegorical explanations that deny the validity of the Commandments. "Although they have translated the Bible from the holy tongue into the vernacular, the Lord has given them neither a heart to understand, nor eyes to see, nor ears to hear" (Num. 12:18). In his commentary on Genesis and Exodus he adds at the end of each weekly portion a brief poem in which he expresses his hopes and those of the Jewish people. He also wrote *piyyutim* in the style of the German and northern French *paytanim*, describing in them the sorrows that afflicted his generation. Several of these were published by Habermann in *Tarbiz* (vol. 9, 1937–38); others have not yet appeared in print.

Joseph of Orleans, i.e., Bekhor Shor, is mentioned in the *tosafot*; four of his halakhic questions addressed to R. Tam are preserved in *Sefer ha-Yashar*, while excerpts of many others are quoted by earlier authorities.

BIBLIOGRAPHY: Liber, in REJ, 58 (1909), 307–14; N. Porges, *Joseph Bechor Schor* (Ger., 1908); S. Poznański (ed.), *Perush al Yeḥezkel u-Terei Asar le-R. Eli'ezer mi-Belganẓi* (1913), lv–lxxv; Urbach, Tosafot, 113–22; Abraham ben Azriel, *Arugat ha-Bosem*, ed. by E.E. Urbach, 4 (1963), index; G. Walter, *Joseph Bechor Schor, Der letzte nordfranzoesische Bibelexeget* (1890).

[Avraham Grossman]

BEKKER (Baruch), PAUL (1882–1937), German music critic and writer. Bekker started his career as a violinist and conductor in his native Berlin, and from 1906 wrote music criticism for Berlin papers and was chief music critic of the *Frankfurter Zeitung* from 1911 to 1925. He did much to promote acceptance of the works of Gustav *Mahler, Franz Schreker, and Paul Hindemith. As supervisor of the State Theater in Cassel (1925–29), and at Wiesbaden (1929–32), he continued to foster contemporary music, especially operatic. In his books on music history and aesthetics he pioneered the application of sociological criteria to the understanding of musical creation and performance. His critical biography of Beethoven (1911, first English translation 1926) is considered a major contribution to the analysis of the creative process in music. In 1934 Bekker immigrated to the United States and became music critic of the *New Yorker Staatszeitung und Herold*. His other books include biographies of Oscar Fried (1907) and *Offenbach (1909); studies of the symphonies of Beethoven (1911, Eng. trans. 1925) and Mahler (1921), and the life of Wagner (1924, Eng. trans. 1931); *Neue Musik* (1923); *Musikgeschichte als Geschichte der musikalischen Formwandlungen* (1926); *Materiale Grundlagen der Musik* (1926); *Wandlungen der Oper* (1934; *The Changing Opera*, 1935); and *The Story of the Orchestra* (1936).

BIBLIOGRAPHY: MGG s.v.; Baker, Biog Dict. S.V.

[Bathja Bayer]

BELAIS(H), ABRAHAM BEN SHALOM (1773–1853), Tunisian rabbi. At one time treasurer to the bey of Tunis, he had to leave the country following business reverses and settled in Jerusalem. For a time he was rabbi in Algiers, then, moving to Europe, he managed to secure the patronage of persons high in public life. He was appointed by the king of Sardinia rabbi of Nice, against the wishes of the community, with whom he promptly quarreled. In 1840, he went to London where before long he again got into financial difficulties and quarreled with the authorities. He was ultimately given a minor communal office and sat occasionally on the *bet din*. He published a large number of books, apart from his sycophantic odes in honor of European crowned heads and other influential persons. The following deserve mention: *Yad Avishalom* (1829), on *Oraḥ Ḥayyim; Peraḥ Shushan Beit Levi* (1844), sermons with English translation; *Petaḥ ha-Bayit* (1846), commentary and alphabetical index to part of the Shulḥan Arukh; responsa *Afrot Tevel* (1850); and an English translation of Ecclesiastes with his commentary. His undoubted scholarship was marred by his serious defects of character. Another Abraham (b. Jacob) Belaish (d. Jerusalem, c. 1828) was rabbi in Jerusalem and wrote a number of religious works.

BIBLIOGRAPHY: JC (Sept. 2, 1853); A.M. Hyamson, *Sephardim of England* (1951), 208–9, 291; D. Cazès, *Notes bibliographiques sur la littérature juive-tunisienne* (1893), 20ff.; G. Levi, in: RMI, 12, no. 3–4 (1937/38), 129–62.

[David Corcos]

BEL AND THE DRAGON, two stories appearing in different versions in the Apocrypha, the Septuagint, and Theodotion; they appear as a continuation of the Book of Daniel. In "Bel," Daniel challenged the divinity of the idol Bel, which was reputed to eat and drink. By scattering ashes on the temple floor, he revealed the footprints of the priests who secretly removed the sacrifices placed before the idol. As a result the Persian king, Cyrus, destroyed the idol and killed the priests. In "The Dragon," Daniel caused the death of a dragon worshiped by the Babylonians, by feeding it a mixture of pitch, fat, and hair. Thrown into the lion's den at the crowd's demand, Daniel was miraculously unharmed and survived for a week without food, after which he was fed by the prophet Habakkuk who was miraculously transported to Babylon (see Prophecy of *Habakkuk). The king thereupon praised God and had Daniel's accusers thrown to the lions who devoured them. The object of these stories is to portray the futility of idolatry. The suggestions that they are either a "Jewish version" of the Babylonian Marduk and Tiamat legend, or propaganda against Hellenistic idolatry, seem improbable. They appear to be popular works composed in Babylon when Bel was no longer worshiped, i.e., between the destruction of the temple of Babylon by Artaxerxes (485–465 B.C.E.) and its rebuilding by Alexander the Great (332 B.C.E.). Snakes (= dragons) were used in the Babylonian cult, and the stories were perhaps a midrashic elaboration of Jeremiah 51:34, 44. The two Greek versions seem to be translations from an Aramaic original. A version from the *Midrash Bereshit Rabbati* of R. Moses ha-Darshan (published by A. Neubauer, Book of Tobit (1878), Hebrew portion p. 39–40) as well as by Ch. Albeck (1940, p. 175) is found in the *Pugio Fidei* of Raymond *Martini (p. 957). These two versions are almost identical with the Syriac *Peshitta*. An Aramaic version of Bel and the Dragon in the *Chronicle of Jerahmeel* is based on Theodotion. A Hebrew fragment is preserved in Genesis R. 68:20 and a Hebrew version is found in *Josippon (3).

[Yehoshua M. Grintz]

BELARUS, C.I.S. republic. For the region's earlier history, see *Belorussia.

Developments from the 1970s

In 1979 Belorussia's Jewish population amounted to 135,400 and in 1989 to 112,000 (with 39,100 in Minsk, 31,800 in Gomel province, and 18,400 in Mogilev province). Nearly 70,000 emigrated in the 1989–93 period, mainly to Israel and the United States, and the Jewish population was further reduced through emigration to 27,798 in 1999 and 24,300 in 2002. The main umbrella organization coordinating all Jewish activities in the country was the Belarus Union of Jewish Organizations and Communities, operating in 20 cities, most of them with synagogues and Jewish schools. Minsk had a Jewish People's University operating as an evening school and affiliated with the Belarus State University. In 1994 a Center for Jewish National Culture was opened in Minsk, as was a Center for the History of the Jews of Belarus in Vitebsk. In all, over 100 Jewish organizations were in operation throughout the country.

One Jew was elected to the republic's Supreme Soviet in 1990. Antisemitism within the Belorussian national movement militated against its receiving support from Jewish organizations. Antisemitic propaganda was rife in such publications as *Politicheskii sobesednik, Slavianskie vedomosti, Semʾdnei, My I vremia, and Prognoz*. The year 1991 saw the desecration of the Jewish cemetery in Borisov and in 1994 cemeteries were desecrated in Gomel, Mogilev, and Haradok, Vitebsk region. Antisemitic incidents continued to occur sporadically throughout the decade. Right-wing organized antisemitic activities in Belarus came mainly from pan-Slavic organizations which advocated a close union with Russia and were supported by their counterparts there. Such organizations included "Slaviane" (The Slavs), "Bratsva Slavian" (Brotherhood of Slavs), "Slavianskii Sobor – Belaia Rus" (Slavic Council – White Russia), On Independence Day in 1994 about 1,000 extremist nationalists marched through Minsk bearing slogans such as 'Belarus only for the Belorussians."

The monthly Jewish newspaper *Aviv* began to appear in 1992 and by 1993 there were five Jewish periodicals appearing in Belarus. In 1992 Rabbi Yitzḥak Volpin came from New York to occupy the long vacant pulpit in the Minsk synagogue. In the spring of the same year Belarus established diplomatic relations with Israel.

BIBLIOGRAPHY: U. Schmelz and S. DellaPergola, in: AJYB, 1995, 478; S. DellaPergola, "World Jewish Population 2002," ibid. (2002), 623ff.; *Supplement to the Monthly Bulletin of Statistics*, 2 (1995); Y. Florsheim, in: *Jews in Eastern Europe*, 1:26 (1995), 25–33; M. Beizer and I. Klimenko, in *Jews in Eastern Europe*, 1 (24) 1995, 25–33; *Anti-Semitism Worldwide* (1994), Tel Aviv University, 132–134. **WEBSITE:** www.worldjewishcongress.org; www.fjc.ru.

[Daniel Romanowski and Michael Beizer]

BELASCO, DAVID (1859–1931), U.S. theatrical producer and playwright. Born in San Francisco, Belasco came from a Portuguese-Jewish family named Valasco. He was educated in a monastery, which may have accounted for the way he dressed later in life, a free-flowing style that earned him the epithet "the Bishop of Broadway." As a boy in Victoria, British Columbia – where his father, a one-time clown, owned a store – he joined a circus. At the age of 11 he appeared at the Victoria Theater in Charles Kean's production of *Richard III*. Working as a stage manager on the Pacific Coast, he devised melodramas with fires and battles and a passion play with real sheep. In 1879 he went to New York, where his name became associated with sensational scenic effects. He was a pioneer in the use of electricity for stage lighting. Belasco's first melodrama, *La Belle Russe*, was produced at Wallack's Theater in 1882. He established the Lyceum School of Acting and produced successes such as *Du Barry* and *Zaza*. In 1902 he opened the first of two theaters, both called the Belasco, where he introduced innovations such as footlights sunk below stage level. His 374 productions displayed a passion for flamboyant realism. His greatest successes as a playwright were *Madame Butterfly* (1900, based on a story by J.L. Long) and *The Girl of the Golden West* (1905), both turned into operas by Puccini. Belasco's work was primarily in melodrama, and though the literary worth of his plays was slight, he was able to satisfy the contemporary demand for spectacular staging. His production of *The Merchant of Venice* (1922), with David *Warfield as Shylock, was regarded as the finest artistic achievement of his career.

ADD. BIBLIOGRAPHY: W. Winter, *The Life of David Belasco* (1918); L. Marker, *David Belasco: Naturalism in the American Theatre* (1975).

[Bernard Grebanier / Ruth Beloff (2nd ed.)]

BELAYA TSERKOV (Heb. שְׂדֵה לָבָן; "White Field"), ancient town in Kiev district, Ukraine, center of a fertile agricultural region. A community was formed there toward the end of the 16th century; 100 houses in Jewish ownership out of a total of 800 are recorded in 1646. The community was destroyed during the *Chmielnicki rising in 1648, and again suffered at the beginning of the *Haidamack rising in 1703. Subsequently, Jews again began to settle there, in 1765 numbering 1,876 poll-tax-payers in the town and its vicinity. After Belaya Tserkov had been attacked by the hordes under Cossack general Gonta (1768), only 223 Jewish inhabitants remained. The community increased to 1,077 in 1787; 6,665 in 1847; and 18,720 in 1897 (54% of the total population). The grain trade and sugar industry contributed to the growth of the town during the 19th century. In 1904, Jews owned 250 workshops and 25 factories engaged in light industry employing 300 Jewish workers. The Jews there suffered from pogroms in 1905. During the civil war of 1919–20, about 850 Jews were massacred in Belaya Tserkov by Ukrainian troops, bands of peasants, and soldiers of the White Army. The religious and cultural life of the community, which numbered 15,624 (36.4%) in 1926, came to an end with the establishment of the Soviet government. Under the Soviets in 1929, 240 artisans were organized in cooperatives and 3,628 were unemployed. Of these, 2,655 were sent to the local sugar refinery and 847 went to work in the nearby kolkhozes. Two Yiddish schools operated in Belaya Tserkov, one of them a vocational school. In 1939, Jews numbered 9,284 (20% of the total population). The town was occupied by the Germans on July 16, 1941. They confiscated all Jewish belongings in October, and later they assembled 6,000 Jews from Belaya Tserkov and its environs in prisoner-of-war camp No. 334, and murdered all of them. There were 5,600 Jews listed as residents in Belaya Tserkov in the 1959 census. Its sole synagogue was closed in 1962 and thereafter Jews conducted private prayer services. During the 1965 High Holidays, militia broke into such *minyanim*, arrested participants and confiscated religious articles. In 1970, the Jewish population was estimated at 15,000. Most left in the 1990s. In Jewish folklore Belaya Tserkov is also referred to as the "Black Abomination" (Yid. *Shvartse Tume*), a play on its name in Russian ("White Church").

BIBLIOGRAPHY: S. Ettinger, in: *Zion*, 21 (1956), 107–42; *Die Judenpogrome in Russland* 2 (1909), 406–8; A.D. Rosenthal, *Megillat ha-Tevaḥ* 1 (1927); 78–81; *Eynikeyt*, no. 24 (1945). **ADD. BIBLIOGRAPHY:** PK Ukrainah, s.v.

[Yehuda Slutsky / Shmuel Spector (2nd ed.)]

BELCHATOW (Pol. **Bełchatów**), small town 28 mi. S. of Lodz, central Poland, in the district of Piotrkow. Seven Jews are recorded as living in Belchatow in 1764. Jewish settlement increased after the formation of Congress *Poland. By 1897 there were 2,897 Jewish residents out of a total population of 3,859, mainly engaged in the flourishing textile industry which developed in the 19th century. In 1921 the Jewish population numbered 3,688 (59% of the total), and in 1939, 6,000, constituting one-third of the total population.

Holocaust Period

The German army took the town during the first week of the war, during the High Holidays. Many Jews dressed in *tallit* and *kittel* were humiliated in the streets and photographed by German soldiers. The Torah Scrolls and other liturgical objects were taken from the local synagogues and burned while the congregation was forced to dance around the pyre. Jewish property was looted, goods in Jewish warehouses were confiscated, and the Jews were evicted from their homes and sent on forced labor. There was no formal ghetto, but a few streets were earmarked as the Jewish district. Numerous refugees from the smaller towns and villages were crowded into this small area. Frequent German raids took place in which able-bodied men were kidnapped and deported.

The final liquidation of the Jewish community took place in August 1942 when close to 1,000 able-bodied Jews were sent to the *Lodz ghetto and 5,000 Jews were deported to the death camp in *Chelmno. No Jewish community was established in Belchatow after the war.

[Danuta Dombrowska]

BIBLIOGRAPHY: I. Trunk, in: *Bleter far Geshikhte*, 2 no. 1–4 (1949), 64–166; D. Dabrowska, in: BŻIH, no. 13–14 (1955); idem (ed.), *Kronika getta łodzkiego*, 2 vols. (1965–66), passim; *Belkhatov Yisker Bukh* (Yid., 1951). **ADD. BIBLIOGRAPHY:** *Piotrkow Trybunalski veha-Sevivah* (1965), 113–15, 192, 202.

BELED, village in Györ county (in 1944, iKapuvár district of Sopron county), western Hungary. The first Jewish settlers came to Beled in the mid-18th century, mainly from the neighboring village of Vásárosfalu. Their number ranged from 61 in 1784 to 336 in 1930. According to the census of 1941, the last before the Holocaust, their number was 320, representing 11% of the total of 2,909. The community was organized in 1785; its synagogue and cemetery were established around 1790. A Jewish school was established in 1861 and a *ḥevra kaddisha* under the leadership of Lipót Kohn in 1884. The congregation identified itself as Orthodox in 1876. Among the rabbis who served the community were Joel Fellner (1902–22) and Áron Silberstein (1925–44). Organizationally, the Beled congregation also served the spiritual and communal needs of the Jews in the neighboring smaller villages, including Babot, Bogyoszló, Cirák, Csapod, Csáfordjánosfa, Dénesfa, Egyed, Garta, Iván, Kapuvár, Kisfalud, Mihályi, Szil, and several others.

In May 1944, the Jews were first placed in a local ghetto set up in and around the synagogue. The ghetto also included the Jews from the neighboring communities of Csapod, Mihályi, Páli, and Vitnyéd. At its peak the ghetto held 360 Jews. It was liquidated on June 17, when about half of the ghetto population was transferred to Szombathely and the other half to Sopron, from where they were deported to Auschwitz on July 5, 1944.

Forty-two survivors returned in 1945. Most emigrated or relocated soon thereafter; in 1968 there was still one Jewish resident in the village. The synagogue was destroyed during the German occupation.

BIBLIOGRAPHY: M. Stein, *Magyar Rabbik*, 3 (1907), 1f.; 5 (1909), 3f.; M. Raab, in: *Soproni Szemle* (1957), 244–52. Braham, Politics; PK Hungaria, 170–71.

[Randolph Braham (2nd ed.)]

°**BELEV, ALEXANDER** (1900–1944), first commissar for Jewish affairs in *Bulgaria (1942–43). He was one of the founders of the antisemitic organization Ratnik and became an official of the ministry of the interior. Belev was sent in 1941 to Germany to study methods of enforcing anti-Jewish legislation and, in September 1942, he became head of the Commissariat for Jewish Affairs. He collaborated closely with Dannecker, *Eichmann's representative in Bulgaria, with whom he signed an agreement on February 22, 1943, to deport 20,000 Jews. Belev implemented the antisemitic "Law for the Protection of the Nation" (which had been passed on December 24, 1940) with cruelty and sometimes exceeded his authority in order to gain his end – the deportation of all Bulgarian Jewry, but he succeeded only in deporting "to the East" the Jews from the Yugoslav and Greek territories under Bulgarian military occupation. His wide powers earned him the nickname "King of the Jews." When Bulgaria was conquered by the Soviet Army in September 1944, Belev attempted to flee with the Germans, but he was caught by the militia and disappeared without a trace. He was sentenced to death in absentia by a People's Court in Sofia in 1945.

BIBLIOGRAPHY: B.J. Arditi, *Yehudei Bulgaryah bi-Shenot ha-Mishtar ha-Naẓi 1940–44* (1962), index; EG, 10 (1967). **ADD. BIBLIOGRAPHY:** M. Bar-Zohar, *Beyond Hitler's Grasp. The Heroic Rescue of Bulgaria's Jews* (1998), 179–84.

[Ora Alcalay]

BELFAST, capital of Northern Ireland. The earliest reference to Jews in Belfast dates from 1652. Mention of a "Jew Butcher" in 1771 suggests the existence of the nucleus of a community. Jews are again recorded in the 1840s. D.J. Jaffe, who settled in Belfast in 1851, established a congregation in 1869 and built its first synagogue in 1871–72. Joseph *Chotzner was the first minister (1869–80; and again 1893–97). After 1881 the community increased with the arrival of Jewish refugees from Russia. These at first formed their own congregation but in 1903 joined the main congregation. A municipal Jewish elementary school was established in 1898. Sir Otto *Jaffe, twice lord mayor and once high sheriff, served for many years as the congregation's president and built its second synagogue in 1904. Isaac *Herzog served as rabbi of Belfast from 1915 to 1919, followed in 1926 by Jacob Shachter, and in 1954 by Alexander Carlebach (who served until 1965). In 1967 the Jewish population numbered about 1,350. In that year, a new synagogue building was consecrated. In the mid-1990s the Jewish population dropped to approximately 550, and in 2004 to about 500. An Orthodox synagogue and a Jewish community center continue to exist.

BIBLIOGRAPHY: B. Shillman, *Short History of the Jews in Ireland* (1945), 134–6; Carlebach, in: JHSET, 21 (1968), 261ff.; idem, in: JC, Suppl. (July 30, 1965); L. Hyman, *Jews of Ireland* (1972). **ADD. BIBLIOGRAPHY:** JYB, 2004.

[Cecil Roth]

BELFORT, capital of the territory of Belfort, eastern France. A grant of privilege conferred on the city in 1307 authorized Jewish residence. Persecutions of Jews living in Belfort are recorded in 1336. They were subsequently expelled and readmitted in 1689. During the French Revolution anti-Jewish excesses took place in the region, but the Jews in Belfort remained unharmed. The Jewish population increased considerably after the Franco-Prussian war (1870–71) with the arrival of Jews from Alsace-Lorraine (then annexed to the German Empire) who wished to remain French.

Holocaust and Postwar Periods

The Belfort Jewish community was destroyed under Nazi occupation. Out of a total of 700 Jews, about 245 were killed. A monument bearing the names of those who perished was erected in the Jewish cemetery after the war. The community was rebuilt after World War II, and together with the Montbeliard Jewish community it numbered 1,200 in 1987. It had a synagogue with an acting minister, a communal center, a network of institutions, and a quarterly bulletin.

BIBLIOGRAPHY: Salfeld, Martyrol, 68, 240; A. Corret, *Histoire pittoresque et anecdotique de Belfort* (1855), 263–72; Z. Szajkowski, *Analytical Franco-Jewish Gazetteer* (1966), 165.

[Roger Berg]

BELFORTE, SOLOMON (1806–1869), printer of Leghorn. Belforte belonged to an Italian Jewish family that settled in Leghorn (Livorno) at the end of the 17th century. He started to edit Hebrew prayer books in 1821 and established his own printing house in 1834. In 1843, the local government authorized the printing of Italian translations of Hebrew liturgical texts. The activity of Salomone Belforte & Co. was continued by the family – with the forced hiatus of the period of Fascist antisemitic laws and the war – until 1961, when all the equipment of the printing house was sold to an Israeli company. For almost 100 years, Salomone Belforte & Co. was one of the most prestigious publishers of Hebrew books, meeting the intellectual and religious needs of Italian, Sephardi, and also Ashkenazi communities. Beside this, the Belforte printing house published Italian literary works and school books.

BIBLIOGRAPHY: M. Luzzatti (ed.), *Ebrei di Livorno tra due censimenti (1841–1938)* (1990), 90–106.

[Alessandro Guetta (2nd ed.)]

BELGIUM, West European kingdom.

The Medieval Community

Jews first appeared in the southern Netherlands during the early 13th century, although the exact date of their settlement there cannot be ascertained. They arrived from the east, most probably from the large Rhenish communities, and did not migrate further south than *Brussels and Mechlin (*Malines). Most of the immigrants settled along, or within proximity of, the Cologne-Bruges axis. Jews are mentioned in Jodoigne (in Brabant province) in about 1200; in Louvain, where a small community lived precariously, in about 1220; in Tirlemont in about 1230; and in Brussels shortly before 1260. In his will (1261) Duke Henry III ordered that "all Jews and usurers be expelled from the province of Brabant. They are to be totally extirpated until not even one remains, unless they undertake to engage in commerce after the fashion of other merchants and agree to cease their practice of moneylending and usury." Apparently their expulsion was not implemented. When consulted, Thomas *Aquinas recommended that the Jews should be taxed moderately, so as not to deprive them of the necessary means to lead a decent existence. He added that it was preferable to compel them to earn their livelihood by manual labor rather than become wealthy by the practice of usury. The fact remains that they were not disturbed in any of their occupations. The organization of a crusade in 1309 brought this comparative tranquillity to an end. After the massacre of Jews in Louvain who had refused baptism, Duke John II took the survivors under his protection. Jews later returned to Louvain, and in 1311 had their own rabbi. The number of Jews throughout Brabant during this period was not large.

As a result of the expulsion from France in 1306, a number of exiles found refuge in the province of Hainaut. They were scattered in about ten localities, the community in Mons being the most important. In 1326, a converted Jew was put to death in Cambron, on a charge of stabbing an image of the Virgin. In 1337, the count of Hainaut renewed his protection of the Jews. A census on this occasion showed 18 Jewish families, comprising 35 adults. They subsequently scattered in other cit-

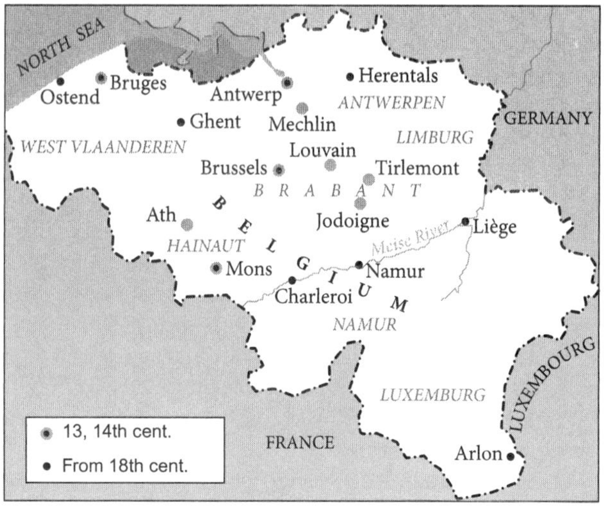

The Jewish communities of Belgium.

ies in Hainaut, but their numbers remained small. The *Black Death (1348–49) calamitously disrupted the existence of these communities. Accused of having introduced the plague by poisoning the wells, the Jews were either massacred by the populace or executed by the authorities. Almost all the Jews in Brabant were put to death. In Brussels the community ceased to exist. The massacre may have spread to *Antwerp, and few communities in Hainaut remained unscathed.

Thus the Jews disappeared almost completely from Hainaut. In Brabant, however, tiny communities were reestablished. There were seven families living in Brussels in 1368 and two in Louvain. In 1370 the Jews in Brussels and Louvain were accused of desecrating the Host, and after confessions extracted by torture a number were burned at the stake. The Jews thus disappeared also from Brabant. The role and number of the Jews in medieval Belgium were unimportant. Mainly petty moneylenders, their restricted numbers prevented them from wielding any influence in the economic life of the country. They were generally regarded as foreigners and as such exposed to violent hostility.

The Resettlement Period

It is only in the early 16th century that Jews again appeared in the southern Netherlands. At that time, Portuguese merchants made their way to the north, attracted by the economic development of the Netherlands, first to Bruges and then to Antwerp. Possibly the majority of them were *Marranos whose presence was sanctioned by a safe-conduct accorded to the New Christians in 1526. The newcomers consolidated their presence in Antwerp, notwithstanding a number of inconsistent measures concerning them. For a number of them, such as the future Duke of Naxos, Joseph *Nasi, or the physician *Amatus Lusitanus, Antwerp was only a place of transit en route to the hospitable Turkish haven. The Marrano population of Antwerp gradually increased with the intensification of their persecution in Portugal. However, with the establishment of an open Jewish community in *Amsterdam, the main tide of Marrano settlement was diverted to that place and to Holland generally. On the other hand, the Dutch Jews now not infrequently visited Brussels or Antwerp, sometimes for prolonged periods, without suffering serious inconvenience. When Antwerp came under Austrian rule in 1713, the community was at last able to profess Judaism more openly. With the occupation of the Netherlands by the French revolutionary armies in 1794, Jews were able to settle freely in Brussels and Antwerp. From the early 18th century, there was also a slight immigration of Ashkenazi Jews to Belgium. The authorities took care to limit their numbers by the imposition of special taxes which aroused vehement protests by the Dutch Jews, who rejected this attempt at discrimination.

Under French domination, Belgian Jewry, which then numbered some 800 persons, was incorporated into the *Consistory of Krefeld; the administrative framework disappeared with the downfall of Napoleon's empire. The principal communities in Belgium at the time were in Antwerp, Brussels, Herentals, Liège, and Mons. From 1831, once Belgian independence was achieved, the Jewish religion received official recognition, religious freedom being an integral part of the constitution guaranteed by the Concert of Europe. However, the synagogue councils were not officially recognized until 1870. The organization of Belgian Jewry remained strongly influenced by the Napoleonic prototype. Centralized in Brussels, it was administered by the Consistoire Central Israélite de Belgique.

Throughout the 19th century, Belgian Judaism developed on the French pattern. At the end of the century, however, as a result of the influx of immigration from Central and Eastern Europe, Belgian Jewry underwent a process of bipolarization which has lasted to the present day. Brussels was the center of French influences while in the Antwerp community Yiddish influences, and accessorily Flemish, were equally strong; occasionally conflicts arose between the two. In 1900, Antwerp numbered some 8,000 Jews, the greater part intending emigrants en route to the United States. The sudden impetus given to the diamond industry by the discovery of mines in South Africa opened numerous possibilities of employment in Antwerp. After an interruption during World War I, when part of the Jewish population migrated to Holland, the Jewish community again began to grow. Massive immigration to Antwerp, as well as the local particularism, rapidly resulted in a marked difference in character between Antwerp Jewry and the main body in Belgium, not only from the economic aspect, but also from the aspect of Antwerp Jewry's anxiety to retain the traditional forms of Jewish life. The Antwerp community resisted assimilation with more success than neighboring Brussels. This was also due to the care taken to ensure that almost every child should attend a Jewish school. The Jewish community of Antwerp remained faithful to its East European origins and was rightly considered as a bulwark of European Judaism. The Brussels community, as well as the smaller communities, had also benefited from a strong numerical contribution from Eastern Europe, but this had little effect on its structure or character. The Belgian government's restrictive naturalization policies encouraged the continued cohesion of the Antwerp community, whose members represented some 75% of the local manpower employed in the diamond industry and commerce.

[Simon R. Schwarzfuchs]

Holocaust Period

The study of the Holocaust in Belgium has been complicated by lack of unified research and by contradictory accounts. Furthermore, as the Belgian Constitution does not allow any mention of religion in documents of civil status, exact official data are lacking.

When the German army invaded on May 10, 1940, between 90,000 and 110,000 Jews lived in Belgium, among whom there were probably about 20,000 German refugees. Only 5–10% of the Jews in Belgium were of Belgian nationality, while the majority of Jews who immigrated to Belgium from other countries had to remain foreign nationals. Antwerp had at that time at least 55,000 Jews, forming Belgium's largest, and economically, socially, and culturally most closely knit Jewish community, and thus suffered more heavily than the loosely knit community in Brussels (at least 35,000) and the other smaller communities: Charleroi, with at least 2,000 Jews; Liège, 2,000; Ghent, 300; and Namur, 50. At the time of the invasion, the adult males among the German-Jewish refugees were treated as suspect aliens although many had volunteered for the Belgian Army. They were rounded up by the Belgian police and interned in the Gurs camp in France. Their families remained behind, many reliant on the social welfare committees of the Jewish communities.

The majority of Jews in Belgium fled the country, mainly southward toward France. Some managed to escape German occupation and emigrated overseas; others were overtaken by the German armies and ordered to turn back. Many who reached unoccupied France were lured back to Belgium a few months later in accordance with Nazi policy at the time to assuage the fears of the Jews and prevent the rise of antagonism among the non-Jewish population. Belgium capitulated on May 28, 1940, and was held under military rule until the liberation in September 1944. The German military occupation set up a Belgian administration in charge of civilian affairs, which was instructed by the Wehrmacht to carry out anti-Jewish measures. This situation was more favorable than that for the Jews in the *Netherlands, where the *Gestapo was in charge of carrying out anti-Jewish measures. The anti-Jewish policy was executed in two stages. The preparatory phase circumscribed the Jewish population, ordered their geographic fixation, and brought about gradual economic and social paralysis. The exterminatory phase, which began on July 22, 1942, consisted of labor call-ups, followed by roundups and razzias for internment in the Dossin assembly camp near Mechlin (Malines). From there, the inmates were deported to extermination camps in the east.

The succession of edicts followed that in other Nazi-occupied countries, though what the Germans termed the "lack of understanding of the local population," and the courageous and well-supported Jewish resistance did slow up the persecution somewhat. The tragic and still not forgotten experience in Belgium of German occupation during World War I brought about more immediate and efficient resistance than in the Netherlands. The first edicts were issued in October 1940. Ritual slaughter was forbidden (Oct. 23, 1940). The first sign of racial discrimination was the ordinance of Oct. 28, 1940, which defined who was a Jew and prohibited the further return of Jews to Belgium. It required all Jews above the age of 15 to register at the communal administration and have the letter J stamped on their identity cards. The registration affected about 42,000 Jews; apparently 10,000–13,000 Jews did not register at all. Jewish property had to be registered, and was not transferable. Notices of Jewish ownership in three languages (Flemish, French, and German) had to be posted. Jews in the fields of law, education, and communication were prohibited from practicing their professions. The first protest was raised by the Belgian associates of Jewish professional men and the Belgian administration in the case of discriminatory legislation bearing on Jews in the professions. They objected to the anti-constitutional character of the anti-Jewish legislation and claimed they were unable to carry it out. The Belgian government in exile, residing in London, laid down a decision on Jan. 10, 1941, that all laws imposed by the German occupation which contradict the Belgian Constitution would be annulled at the time of liberation.

In 1941, further edicts were issued to restrict and paralyze Jewish life: edicts for confiscation of radios (May 31); enforced declaration of bank holdings (June 10); prohibition against residing outside the four large cities of Antwerp, Brussels, Liège, and Charleroi (August 29); and a curfew between 8 P.M. and 7 A.M. (August 29). On Nov. 25, 1941, the German military commander for Belgium and northern France ordered the formation of a Judenrat, called Association des Juifs en Belgique (AJB), under the pretext of organizing Jewish social welfare for the community and furthering Jewish emigration. A national committee of seven representatives was to encompass all Jews and take over existing Jewish bodies and their property. Rabbi T.S. Ullman, the only rabbi of Belgian nationality, accepted the presidency only after consultation with high Belgian authorities. Local committees were formed in Brussels, Antwerp, Charleroi, and Liège. Although no documents attest to the modes of constitution of these committees, there are indications that the Germans held sway over the choice of their members. In the course of time, the members of the AJB committees were utilized by the Germans as a front for carrying out their own aims. On Dec. 1, 1941, the Judenrat was ordered to set up an educational system for Jewish children who were expelled at that time from the public schools by the Germans.

The AJB was ordered to hold another census of the Jews and, by March, forced to take charge of the distribution of call-ups to be accompanied by covering letters pressing for conformance to the orders. In September 1942, the AJB leaders were interned in the concentration camp of Breendonck and charged with insufficient diligence in carrying out German orders. The AJB president was released after a week and resigned. Razzias now replaced call-ups, and the AJB's job was largely limited to mitigating the suffering of the deportees. Officially, however, they were permitted to continue their activities. They set up children's homes and old-age homes, and their employees and administrators were "protected," i.e., not liable for deportation. The underground took advantage of this status by introducing some of its people into positions within the AJB and utilized its resources, despite all the risks involved.

On May 27, 1942, the Nazis issued an order for every Jew to wear the yellow badge. The Belgian administration refused to promulgate the order and the Germans were forced to do it themselves, but a few days later they imposed the task on the AJB. The Belgian population showed its hostility to this discriminatory measure, expressing its sympathy in various ways. By June 1, 1942, Jewish doctors, dentists, and nurses were forbidden to practice on gentile patients. Previously (March 2 and May 8), forced labor for the Nazi organization Todt had been imposed theoretically on all the unemployed, but was in fact aimed at the Jews, who had been evicted from all economic pursuit. The underground issued pleas not to submit to these labor call-ups. By July 1942, summonses were issued to unemployed Jews to report to Malines for "work in the east." At first the summonses were meekly obeyed, but the resistance movements' warnings started taking effect and people went into hiding. As the call-ups provided insufficient numbers of "volunteers," the Germans commenced their razzias. The first convoy of 1,000 Jews left on Sept. 2, 1942. Within five weeks, 10,000 had been deported. Later, the deportations slowed down. By July 31, 1944, 25,631 victims had been deported in 31 convoys. Only 1,244 of the deportees returned after the war. Belgian leaders, among them the queen mother Elisabeth and Cardinal van Roey, intervened on behalf of the small number of Jews of Belgian nationality, and the Germans agreed to omit them from expulsion as long as they would not transgress German laws. This show of tolerance was short-lived. On Sept. 3, 1943, Jews holding Belgian citizenship were all rounded up and deported.

Resistance

The Jewish population required time to organize resistance. Some Jews individually joined the ranks of the Belgian underground. But after the dissolution of Jewish organizations, the former social and political groups started regrouping, mainly for the purpose of mutual social help. Anti-fascist elements grasped the significance of the persecutions sooner and formed a group of about 70 Jewish armed partisans, many of whom fell in the line of duty. An estimated 140 fell, including those who fought as individuals in the general armed resistance. The Committee for Jewish Defence (CDJ, recognized officially after the war as a civilian resistance group affiliated to the Front de l'Indépendance) comprised a complete range of Jewish groups and individuals. It soon realized the need to hide Jews, and called upon all the Jews to resist and disobey any German edicts as well as instructions from the AJB. The Committee developed a vast, well-organized network of activity for hiding children (an estimated 3,000 children were thus saved) and adults (an estimated 10,000). In fact, in Belgium a high proportion of Jews was saved compared to other occupied countries. Places of hiding, identity papers, food ration tickets, and money were obtained, and escape routes established toward Switzerland and Spain. The cultural aspect of the Jewish resistance groups was remarkable. They distributed information and propaganda material, established a lending library, and maintained a Jewish illegal press. The Yiddish paper *Unzer Vort* appeared 28 times, and *Flambeau* in French and the *Vrije Gedachte* in Flemish appeared with the help of the Belgian illegal press.

Contacts were made with numerous non-Jewish organizations that helped, including Oeuvre Nationale de l'Enfance, Jeunesse Ouvrière Catholique, the Red Cross, a number of Catholic institutions, and underground resistance movements. As time went on, more and more money was needed to keep alive those in hiding. Millions of francs were contributed by local Jews and non-Jewish organizations and credit was allotted. Later, large sums were secretly obtained through Switzerland, and some came from the Belgian government-in-exile. A number of people managed to escape from deportation trains in a feat unique to occupied Belgium. The 20th convoy departing on April 19, 1943, was attacked in a well-organized action initiated by the CDJ together with Georges Livchitz and partisans of Group "G" (an armed resistance group). It enabled several hundred to escape, although many of them were caught or killed by the Germans. Another Jewish underground group, the Ninth Brigade, was organized under the aegis of the Mouvement National Belge, a more rightist group. A little-known and rather circumscribed resistance activity was carried out by the federation of the Zionist parties, which succeeded in obtaining through Switzerland a few immigration certificates to Palestine which protected the holders from deportation. At one point (1941–42) a *hakhsharah* (agricultural training program) for members of Zionist youth movements was provided. According to partial studies and reports by former participants, there were innumerable cases (not generally known) of underground activity, including armed attacks on collaborators, sabotage, and withdrawing those children in hiding who were exposed and in danger of arrest by the Gestapo.

The Catholic Church on many occasions intervened on behalf of the Belgian Jews through the work of Cardinal van Roey, who acted mainly through his secretary Canon Leclef. On Aug. 4, 1942, he alerted the Vatican to the inhumanity of the racial laws, pointing out that even Catholics of Jewish origin were affected. The Church was largely efficacious through its request to Catholic institutions to hide Jewish children and to refrain from baptizing them, unless specific permission was given. When the German-Jewish refugees in Antwerp were deported at the end of 1940 to the province of Limburg, the priests instructed the local population to help them. When the Jews were compelled to wear the yellow badge, priests denounced this discriminatory act and elicited the sympathy of large parts of the population. The Belgians made attempts to allay Jewish suffering, though prior to the invasion, the Germans had encouraged Flemish nationalism and separatism and fanned antisemitism. For this reason the persecutions met with greater success in the mostly Flemish Antwerp region.

[Rivka Irene Banitt]

Early postwar years

In 1945 the Jewish population was composed of those who had remained in the country, had returned from exile, or were liberated from prisons and camps. Until about 1955, thousands of Jewish refugees from Eastern and Central Europe resided in Belgium for a limited time, awaiting immigration permits to other countries of permanent settlement. In the 1960s both emigration and immigration considerably decreased. The number of Jews in Belgium in 1970 was about 40,000. This population, essentially urban, was distributed approximately as follows: Brussels, 18,000; Antwerp, 12,000; Liège, 1,000; Charleroi, 500; Ghent, Ostend, and Arlon, 1,000; the remainder was dispersed among other cities. As the Jewish population became stable, social and economic integration within Belgian society improved in many respects. It was not especially difficult to obtain citizenship, and a great number of immigrants and their descendants were therefore Belgian citizens. Although many arrived in the country without independent resources, within a short period they displayed great social mobility. The majority came to belong to the middle class and were active in the fur and textile industry, wholesale and retail trade, crafts, and the manufacture of clothing and leather goods. Antwerp Jewry has been professionally concentrated for a long time in the diamond industry and trade. Since the end of World War II, more young people have undertaken university studies, resulting in the growth of the professional and white-collar classes. Though the country's economic progress benefited the Jewish population, there was still a small number of underprivileged persons and social cases, most of whom were cared for by the community. The favorable attitude of the government and communal authorities, as well as the population as a whole, facilitated the integration of Jews in Belgium, though from time to time in the first two decades after World War II certain manifestations of antisemitism were provoked by small factions of the extreme right.

The Jewish religion is legally recognized along with the Catholic and the Protestant religions. Belgian laws also guarantee public Jewish worship. In 1970 there were 12 recognized Jewish communities in the country: four in Brussels, three in Antwerp, and one each in Liège, Charleroi, Ghent, Ostend, and Arlon. Two of these communities were Sephardi, the others Ashkenazi. The rabbis, cantors, and synagogue boards were elected by the members of the community. Each community has proportional representation at the Consistoire Central Israélite de Belgique, which represents the communities in their relations with the state. Though this institution, of Napoleonic origin, supervises the administration of synagogue properties and examines their budgets and accounts, it generally does not intervene in their internal affairs but is called to ratify the nomination of rabbis and *ḥazzanim*.

Until 1980 the chief rabbi was appointed by the Consistoire to act as the supreme authority on Jewish religious affairs. Since that time the post has been formally vacant, though Albert Guigui, rabbi of Brussels from 1983, acted as rabbinic adviser to the Consistoire and in effect fulfilled the function of chief rabbi. In addition, at the outset of the 21st century, four government-recognized regional rabbis, including Guigui, were in office. Cultural differences between communities represented in the Consistoire were evident. Some older communities reflected many formal aspects of the Reform movement, which spread through Belgium during the 19th century, but whose influence was reduced by East European Jews. The result of the contact between the two elements was the widespread practice of Conservative Judaism. Other communities remained faithful to an Orthodoxy imbued with Yiddish Ashkenazi traditions. In spite of the differences, most blatant in the contrasting character of the Brussels and Antwerp communities, the Consistoire preserved a sense of unity. The state paid the salaries of the regional rabbis, cantors, and state-recognized teachers who provide religious instruction in public primary, secondary, and technical schools throughout the country. The state also subsidized Jewish day schools in which courses of Jewish content were taught in addition to the compulsory general curriculum. The state's contribution to various religious and educational institutions illustrates concretely the recognized position of the Jewish religion, which gives observant and nonobservant Jews a feeling of security and confidence.

About 100 Jewish organizations, either revolving around the recognized communities or developing on the fringe, are active in every facet of Jewish life. The main types of organizations are welfare and philanthropic, Zionist and pro-Israel, communal bodies, youth movements, and independent religious, political, cultural, and sports-oriented groups. Welfare and philanthropic organizations are united for fund-raising purposes in Brussels and are absorbed into a central body in Antwerp. These two centralizing institutions collaborate at the national level in La Conférence Permanente des Oeuvres Sociales Juives de Belgique. Youth movements are grouped in La Fédération de la Jeunesse Juive de Belgique. Very influential before the war, the Zionist Federation of Belgium continues to concern itself with the renewal of its structure and with the aim of expanding its membership; but since the creation of the State of Israel, the distinction between Zionists and non-Zionists within the community has lost much of its acuteness. Indeed, most Belgian Jews express their support of Israel, and for many of them it has developed into a component of their identity. Manifestations of this support are shown in various ways: financial contributions, collective trips to Israel, the study of modern Hebrew, and hosting Israel experts on communal and educational matters. The favorable attitude toward Israel is widely shared by non-Jews as well. During the Six-Day War (1967), non-Jews walked side by side with Jews in public demonstrations to proclaim solidarity with Israel, and the Belgian press as a whole supported Israel's point of view.

[Max Gottschalk / Willy Bok]

Later Developments

The Jewish population of Belgium in 2002 was estimated at 31,400, equally divided between French and Flemish speakers, with around 15,000 Jews each in Brussels and Antwerp and the rest in such shrinking communities as Liege, Charleroi, Arlon, Mons, Ghent, and Ostend.

COMMUNITY LIFE. An important merger of community organizations began in 1971 to unify divergent organizations under a central umbrella organization, which would serve as spokesman for Belgian Jewry. As a result, in 1977, 21 Belgian Jewish organizations banded together, as well as the communities of Liege, Charleroi and Ghent. In September 1977 the Coordinating Committee and the Belgian Section of the World Jewish Congress merged into the Coordinating Committee of Belgian Jewish Organizations, affiliated with the WJC with the president of the Belgian Section as its head. By 2002 it had 41 members and, together with the Consistoire, was recognized as an official representative of the Jewish community for political matters. A parallel organization, Forum oder Joodse Organisaties, founded in 1994 and based in Antwerp, represented Flemish-speaking Jews before the authorities.

The Consistoire remained the central authority for Belgian Jews in religious matters, with 16 member congregations in 2002. In all, around 50 synagogues and places of worship were in operation (around 30 in Antwerp). A Jewish chapel opened (1986) at the Brussels international airport, following the request of Orthodox travelers. Religious life continued to be much more intense in Antwerp with its largely Orthodox population than in Brussels. However, starting in the late 1980s Brussels witnessed a strengthening of its more traditionalist religious life – the creation of two new Orthodox communities, the suppression of the organ and the mixed choir at the principal synagogue, the opening of a kosher restaurant and a yeshivah. The Israelite Community of Waterloo and of Southern Brabant, which belonged also to this current, was recognized (1992) by the Cult Administration only four years after its creation. The new congregation is the result of changes in the urbanization of the Brussels area; its membership consists largely of English-speaking expatriates. The Liberal congregation has grown steadily and in 1984 founded its own burial society with its own cemetery.

A reorganization of the Belgian Zionist Federation took place in 1976. Following an intensive nationwide membership campaign in 1975–76, some 5,000 Jews enrolled as members of the Zionist Federation, which has branches in five communities, all of which were directly represented on the directorate.

The World Conference of Jewish Communities on Soviet Jewry convened in Brussels in 1971 and 1976. The congress was hosted by the Coordinating Committee of Belgian Jewish organizations, the Jewish Secular Community Center of Brussels, and the National Belgian Committee for Jews in the Soviet Union. The congress, sponsored by the World Zionist Federation, World Jewish Congress, B'nai B'rith, the Public Councils for Soviet Jewry, the Conference of Presidents of Major Jewish Organizations in the United States, and various national committees for Soviet Jewry, was attended by 1,200 representatives from 35 countries throughout the world, and hundreds of leading Jewish and non-Jewish personalities.

Jewish education in Belgium continued to benefit from the national educational system, providing for diverse religious studies in all State schools where a significant number of parents request them. Such classes are attended by 60 percent of Jewish public school children in Brussels and 30 percent in Antwerp. Though paid for by the State, teachers are hired by the Consistoire and supervised by its religious inspectors. In addition, the State subsidizes the general curriculum of Jewish day schools, attended by around 7,000 children in the early 2000s. There were three such schools in Brussels (Maimonides Athenaeum, Ganenou Athenaeum, Beth Aviv) with around 2,000 children, and three in Antwerp (Tachkemoni, Yesode Hatora, Yavne) which together with a number of ḥasidic *ḥadarim* and some other institutions accommodated around 5,000 children. Extracurricular studies were conducted through the community *talmud torah* in Brussels and youth groups at the community centers, and through the Zionist youth movements. Adult Jewish education continued to improve, with Hebrew courses taught in conjunction with the Jewish Agency. The Ministry of Education also largely supported a free faculty of Jewish studies called "Institut Universitaire d'Etudes du Judaïsme" founded in 1972 and operating under the auspices of the Brussels Free University, which since the academic year 1986–1987 has recognized Institut degrees in Jewish history, thought, and civilization. The Flemish section (created in 1983 at the Vrije Universiteit te Brussel) was later moved to the Instituut voor Joodse Studies in Antwerp.

POLITICAL DEVELOPMENTS. In December 1974, the Volksunie Party submitted a bill to Parliament granting amnesty to former Nazi collaborators. The bill was strongly opposed by the Belgian Jewish community, led by the national Jewish organizations of ex-servicemen, former resistance fighters, and deportees, as well as by their Christian counterparts, and on March 25, 1976 the bill was defeated by a vote of 98 to 81 with 3 abstentions.

Belgium has been the site of a number of Arab terrorist attacks on Jewish or Israel-connected objectives. In 1979 there was an attempted attack on El Al passengers at Brussels airport. In July 1980 a hand grenade was thrown into a group of children about to leave Antwerp for summer camp; one boy was killed and others were injured. In October 1981 a car bomb exploded in Antwerp near a small Sephardi synagogue shortly before services were to begin; over 100 passers-by were injured, two of them fatally. There was vociferous public protest over these incidents.

After the municipal (October 1988) and European elections (June 1989), the general elections (October 1991) confirmed the success of the right-wing parties by electing politicians openly against immigration as well as against Jews (in Antwerp 20 percent of the population voted for them). This was not a specifically Belgian phenomenon but an international one, as was stressed at the conference of the World Jewish Congress held in Brussels in July 1992, called "My Brother's Keeper."

Also giving rise for concern were the killing in 1989 of Professor Joseph Wybran, president of the political body of Belgian Jewry; the release (July 1990) of a Palestinian terrorist in exchange for the freedom of four Belgian hostages held by the Abu Nidal group; and antisemitic slogans painted on walls. All these events brought protests from Jewish bodies to the government, which reacted positively.

Antisemitic outbursts became particularly widespread with the onset of the second Intifada in Israel in 2000, which, coupled with pro-Palestinian terror throughout Europe and the local anti-Israel press, made life for Belgium's Jews distinctly uncomfortable. Among the incidents recorded in the early 2000s were the firebombing of synagogues, including rifle fire in one case, and Nazi and antisemitic graffiti. In 2001 Rabbi Guigui was attacked in the street by young Muslims of Moroccan origin.

INTERFAITH RELATIONS. Jewish-Christian relations remained essentially cordial. The Consistoire worked together with the National Catholic Commission in Belgium, a subcommittee of the National Commission for Ecumenism, and the Belgian Protestant Council for Relationship between Judaism and Christianity, sponsored by the Federation of Protestant Churches in Belgium. A regular interfaith scholastic dialogue, "Institutum Judaicum," was conducted as well as more general lectures and study groups on Judaism, and an Interfaith Bulletin published.

Following the end of the Carmelite Convent affair in Auschwitz (August 1993), a Judeo-Christian Consultation Group was organized. It had to deal with two exhibitions illustrating anti-Jewish prejudice like the Bible des Communautés Chrétiennes which was uncovered by a researcher of the Leuven Catholic University.

As to the Israel-Vatican Agreement, it was in Brussels that the World Jewish Congress held a seminar with the main negotiators (Monsigneur Celli from the Vatican and Israel's Deputy Foreign Minister Yossi *Beilin) to assess the situation one year later (December 1994).

From December 1985 to May 1993 the "Yarden affair" provided a bad image in the media of the ḥasidic community and of the Jews. Thanks to the work of the FBI, the three children born of a mixed marriage and kidnapped by the father (a member of the Satmar ḥasidic group) before he was put in a Brussels jail were given back to their mother.

On the official level the Consistoire also maintained cordial relations with Muslim representative bodies in Belgium.

REMEMBERING THE HOLOCAUST. Holocaust consciousness was heightened among Belgian Jewry. The case of the Carmelite convent in Auschwitz (see *Auschwitz Convent) was first taken up in Belgium. Actions around this affair froze official interfaith relations, although in 1993 a "Committee of Consultations between Jews and Christians in Belgium" was set up. After the publication of Professor M. Steinberg's thesis on "The History of Jews in Belgium between 1940 and 1944," an international colloquium on "The Holocaust Period in Belgium" was organized in Bar-Ilan University in Israel (1989). Belgium television (French and Dutch channels) produced and broadcast several documentaries on this subject followed by discussions.

As approximately 20,000 Jews were hidden by Christians during the last period of the Holocaust, several memorials were opened in remote places by different associations, one of which, the Belgian Hidden Children Association, helped organize the first congress in New York on this subject.

The 50th anniversaries of several historical events were commemorated by impressive ceremonies attended by thousands of Jews and non-Jews. For the 45th celebration of VE-day, King Baudouin attended a gathering in the Jewish National Memorial; it was the first time in the history of Belgium that the ruling king ever came to a Jewish monument.

Paradoxically the right-wing political successes occurred during the period of the 50th anniversary of the events linked to the end of the World War II. From King Albert II, who attended the opening of the museum in Mechelen (May 7, 1995) to his son Philippe, who was at the commemoration of the Warsaw Ghetto and the attack of the XXth convoy (April 1993), from the prime minister, who visited Auschwitz with a former Jewish Belgian deportee (January 1995) before the official pilgrimage (March 1995), to the Ministry of Education, which launched a nationwide campaign entitled "Democracy or Barbarism … 50 Years After," everyone tried to do something to remember what had happened 50 years before. Numerous exhibitions attended by millions of people, TV series, books, new plays, movies, operas, and classical music programs were presented on the subject. Most of the time the fate of the Jews was underlined.

A memorial to Belgian Jews who perished in the Holocaust was dedicated in Antwerp (November 13, 1994).

The first European meeting of hidden children was organized at the University of Brussels (April 30–May 1, 1995) and three ceremonies were held for Righteous Gentiles during 1995.

Belgium also created a commission in 1997 to investigate the fate of Jewish assets seized during the war. Subsequently, in

2001, a National Commission for Restitution was established to examine claims and facilitate compensation.

[Daniel Dratwa]

Relations with Israel

Important circles in Belgium displayed sympathy for Zionism and supported the struggle of the Zionist movement almost from its beginning. Noteworthy were the active support of Queen Elisabeth and various Socialist leaders, including Emile Vandervelde, Camille Huysmans, de Brouquère, and Paul Henri Spaak. On Nov. 29, 1947, Belgium voted in the UN in favor of the establishment of a Jewish state and it was among the first countries to establish diplomatic relations with Israel (de facto Jan. 31, 1949, and de jure in January 1950). These relations were subsequently elevated to the ambassadorial level. The Israel ambassador in Brussels is also accredited in Luxembourg, which is tied to Belgium through a customs' pact, and is attached to the European Economic Community, whose seat is in that city. Trade relations between Belgium and Israel developed satisfactorily and tourism also increased, reaching 8,000 people in 1968. Belgium filled a specific role in Israel's foreign relations because of its special position in the process of European integration and the fact that Brussels had become a sort of "capital of Europe." Many of Israel's diplomatic efforts directed toward the European Community passed through Belgium, which was either a host or an active participant in the creation of the new European identity. The official ties between the two countries included the visit of Queen Elisabeth and a short visit of King Baudouin, which was mainly a pilgrimage to the Holy Land, and the visits of President Izhak Ben-Zvi and prime ministers David Ben-Gurion and Levi Eshkol to Belgium.

[Yohanan Meroz]

During the 1970s trade between Israel and Belgium continued to grow. Exports from Belgium (including Luxembourg) to Israel rose from $115 million in 1972 to $404 million in 1980, while imports from Israel rose from $49 million to $236 million. By 2004 the figures were $955 and $695 million, respectively, excluding diamonds. The movement of diamonds between the two countries reached $5.5 billion.

In March 1992, elections were held in Belgium to the Zionist Congress: 3,140 voted (25 percent more than in 1987). The results showed a shift to the right, possibly because the leader of the left was involved in organizing a meeting with Palestinians. The anti-Israel feelings prevailing in the media since the Lebanon War were still felt among the population and the flow of tourists going to Israel dropped. One consequence was the closing of the Israel Tourist Office in Brussels. The Oslo Accords brought a resurgence of goodwill but the onset of the second Palestinian Intifada produced a dampening of official relations, fueled by a hostile press and the presence of half a million Muslims in the country, as the Belgian government, professing evenhandedness, regularly voted for anti-Israel resolutions in international bodies, including the UN. In 2002 Belgium suspended arms sales to Israel and in 2001 and 2002 the Brussels and Flemish Regions of Belgium suspended their cooperative agreements with Israel. Tensions came to a head when war crimes charges were brought against Israeli Prime Minister Ariel *Sharon in Belgium for his part in the Lebanon war under Belgium's "universal jurisdiction" legislation. Israel withdrew its ambassador. Subsequently the Belgian Supreme Court ruled that Sharon could not be tried while serving as prime minister of Israel.

Since 1992, Israel has had two ambassadors in Brussels, one for the EEC, the other for Belgium.

BIBLIOGRAPHY: E. Ouverleaux, *Notes et documents sur les Juifs de Belgique sous l'ancien régime* (1885); S. Ullmann, *Studien zur Geschichte der Juden in Belgien bis zum XVIII. Jahrhundert* (1909); idem, *Histoire des Juifs en Belgique jusqu'au 19e siècle* (1934); E. Ginsburger, *Les Juifs en Belgique au XVIIIe siècle* (1932); J. Stengers, *Les Juifs dans les Pays-Bas au moyen âge* (1950); E. Schmidt, *Geschiedenis van de Joden in Antwerpen* (1963). HOLOCAUST PERIOD: R. Hilberg, *Destruction of the European Jews* (1961), 382–9; C. Reitlinger, *Final Solution* (1968²), 398–408; Belgium, Commission d'enquête sur la violation des règles du droit des gens…, *Les crimes de guerre commis sous l'occupation de la Belgique 1940–1945: la persécution antisémitique* (1947); Gutfreund, in: Yalkut Moreshet, 2 no. 4 (1965), 43–55; Liebman, in: *Centrale* (Bruxelles, March 1964); B. Garfinkels, *Les Belges face à la persécution raciale 1940–1944* (1965); Steinberg, in: *Regards*, nos. 29 and 30 (Aug.–Oct. 1968); E. Schmidt, *Geschiedenis van de Joden in Antwerpen* (1963). CONTEMPORARY JEWRY: Centre National des Hautes Études Juives, *La vie juive dans l'Europe contemporaine* (1965), with Eng. summ.; J. Gutwirth, in: JJSO, 10:1 (1968), 121–37; idem, in: *Les Nouveaux Cahiers*, no. 7 (1966), 56–63; C. Lehrer, in: *L'Arche*, no. 62 (1962); S. Brachfeld, *Het Joods Onderwijs in België* (1966); A. Tartakower, *Shivtei Yisrael*, 2 (1966), 225–37. **ADD. BIBLIOGRAPHY:** AJYB (2003).

BELGOROD-DNESTROVSKI (formerly **Akkerman**; Rum. **Cetatea-Albă**), city in Ukraine, in the region of *Bessarabia, on the river Dniester; in Romania 1918–40 and 1941–44. It is referred to in Jewish sources as Weissenburg and *Ir Lavan* (both meaning "White City"). Karaite scholars, including apparently Caleb *Afendopolo, lived there in the early 16th century, attesting to the existence of a cultured Karaite settlement during this period. A Rabbanite community is first recorded in Belgorod-Dnestrovski in 1591. In 1808, 18 heads of Jewish families were registered there. According to tradition, a *bet midrash* was built there in 1815 and a synagogue in 1828. The community grew considerably in the 19th century with the arrival of Jews in Bessarabia from other regions of the *Pale of Settlement. The Jewish population numbered 2,422 in 1864 and 5,613 in 1897 (19.9% of the total). The Jews in Belgorod-Dnestrovski were influenced in social and cultural spheres by the important Jewish center in *Odessa. Most of the Jews earned their living in the grain trade, which was mainly concentrated in Jewish hands, but many engaged in crafts. In 1905, there was a pogrom in which eight Jews were killed. After Bessarabia passed to Romania in 1918, the Jews in Belgorod-Dnestrovski developed a flourishing communal and cultural life, and established cultural and welfare institutions. Jewish institutions before World War II included a hospital (founded in 1882), an old-age home, a kindergarten, and a Hebrew elementary *Tarbut school. In 1930, 4,239 Jews resided in Belgorod-Dnestrovski (12.3% of the total population).

[Eliyahu Feldman]

Holocaust Period and After

In July 1940, during the Soviet occupation, all Jewish life was disbanded, and a few months later, the great Remasline synagogue became a government archive. Prominent and wealthy Jews were arrested and tried or disappeared altogether. On the night of June 13, 1941, dozens of families were exiled to Siberia, most of whom did not survive. When the fighting drew near, in 1941, about 4,000 Jews fled the city, mostly for nearby Odessa. Most of them were caught in the German siege of the city and shared the fate of local Jews, being later executed or deported by the Romanians. Those who remained were the sick and the old and pious Jews. The entry of German and Romanian troops was preceded by the murder of Jews and the plunder of Jewish property on the part of the local peasants. As soon as the town was occupied, all the remaining Jews were gathered in the Remasline synagogue where they were kept for three days without food and water. They were then taken to the Liman River where they were all shot to death; about 800 Jews were killed in the slaughter. Approximately 500 of the prewar population of Belgorod-Dnestrovksi survived the war, and about half of these eventually returned. In 1970, the Jewish population was estimated at 300 families. Most emigrated in the 1990s but Jewish life revived in the 21st century with Rabbi Fishel Chichelnitzky heading a kindergarten, Sunday school, and the new Chabad synagogue.

[Jean Ancel]

BIBLIOGRAPHY: I. Feldman, *Toledot ha-Yehudim be-Besarabyah ad Sof ha-Me'ah ha-Tesha-Esreh* (1970), index; idem, in: *Tarbiz*, 38 (1968/69), 61–74; Y. Schildkraut, *Al Ḥurvot Besarabyah* (1954), 17–191.

BELGRADE (Serb. **Beograd**), capital of Serbia. Several Jews from Italy and Hungary settled in Belgrade in the 13th and 14th centuries. They were joined by Sephardi Jews after the Turkish conquest in 1521. They lived mostly in the Jewish *mahala* ("quarter") near the citadel, and were physicians, weaponsmiths, tanners, and merchants. The Jews lived in comfortable circumstances and were allowed to own land. The community enjoyed a degree of judicial autonomy. It numbered 800 in 1663. Between 1642 and 1688, the Belgrade yeshivah became widely known under the rabbis Judah *Lerma, Simḥah b. Gershon Kohen, and Joseph *Almosnino.

With the start of the decline of the Turkish Empire in the late 17th century, a long series of catastrophes befell the Jews of Belgrade. In 1688, at the approach of the Austrians, Turkish janissaries plundered and burned the Jewish quarter. After the capture of the city, Austrian soldiers burned, looted, and killed the Turkish and Jewish population. The community was totally destroyed; some Jews managed to flee to Bulgaria, but the majority were taken prisoner and deported to Austria to be sold as slaves or offered to Jewish communities for ransom.

Shortly after, a number of Jews returned to the city and rebuilt the synagogue. However, since Belgrade became the key fortress against the Turks, under Austrian rule (1717–39) Jewish residence was restricted. The town was captured again by Turks in 1739 and by 1777 the number of Jews had increased to 800. In 1795 irregular troops of Pazvan Oglu, pasha of *Vidin, attacked Belgrade, burning the synagogue and many Jewish houses in the *mahala* Nevertheless, the Jews remained prosperous: in 1798 all the Belgrade guilds together paid 1,600 grush in taxes, while the Jewish community alone paid 10,000 grush.

A series of rebellions and wars by the Serbs against the local Turkish despots, who had made themselves semi-independent of Constantinople, began in 1803, continuing intermittently for nearly 30 years. Belgrade changed hands many times, the Jews suffering each time. In 1807 the Serbs expelled the Jews from Belgrade. The anti-Jewish measures were revoked at Russian intervention. Some Jews had been allowed to stay, and more returned between 1811 and 1813, but were forced to leave once more when an abortive rebellion broke out in 1813. When in 1815 Milosh Obrenovich was recognized ruler of Serbia the situation of the Jews improved. There were some 1,300 Jews (200 Ashkenazim) in 1831. Prince Milosh's Serbian State Press, founded in 1837, had Hebrew type too. The works, mostly liturgical or ritual, were printed in Ladino, or in Hebrew with a Ladino translation. The Ladino periodical *El Amigo del Pueblo* was established in 1888 and appeared in Belgrade throughout the 1890s. Milosh's successor, Alexander Karageorgevich (1842–58), introduced a series of restrictions on Jewish residence, professions, and acquisition of property.

After obtaining full rights following the Congress of Berlin in 1878, the wealthier Jews gradually became absorbed into Serbian society. They spoke Serbian, their children went to state schools and universities, and became physicians, civil servants, etc. In 1907 they built the new Sephardi synagogue, Bet Yisrael, in the upper town. There was a Hebrew school from the 1850s. Most Jews lived in the *mahala* until World War I when it was partly destroyed. After World War I, when Belgrade became the capital of independent Yugoslavia, the younger generation gradually left the *mahala* to enter the professions, banking, the stock exchange, and the garment industry.

Holocaust Period

When the Germans entered Belgrade in April 1941, 12,000 Jews were living there. The 20,000 Volksdeutsche (ethnic Germans) of Belgrade led the Germans to Jewish shops and homes, looting all that the Germans left. Jews were evicted and their property confiscated. The Ashkenazi synagogue was turned into a brothel; the Bet Yisrael synagogue became a storehouse for looted Jewish property and was blown up before the German retreat. All communal activities were forbidden, but the *Vertretung* ("Representation"), nominated by the Germans, contrived to organize public kitchens, medical services, etc. for the local Jews and for the 2,500 Jews from the Banat region who were expelled to Belgrade. All men between the ages of 14 and 60 and all women between the ages of 14 and 40 were forced to work in the town, not only without payment but also providing their own food.

With the beginning of armed resistance in Serbia, the Germans began executing hostages, mostly Jews. The first mass execution took place on July 29, when 122 "Communists and Jews" were shot. The "final solution" began with the mass arrest of some 5,000 Jewish men in July and August. After being imprisoned in two camps in Belgrade, the men were then taken in groups of 150 to 400 "to work in Austria" and shot in nearby forests by regular German army units. The remaining 6,000 Jewish women and children were arrested in December 1941 and transported to the Saymishte camp, a former commercial fairground on the left bank of the Sava. Food was scarce, and many froze to death in the winter of 1941–42. Between February and May 1942, the remainder were killed in gas vans and buried in the village of Jaintsi. Patients of the Jewish hospital in the *mahala* were also liquidated in 1942.

Resistance

Immediately after the German occupation Jewish youth, mainly from Ha-Shomer ha-Ẓa'ir, joined the resistance movement, sabotaging enemy installations, disseminating propaganda, and collecting funds and medical supplies. In August 1941 they joined partisan units in the forests, but not before considerable numbers of them had been arrested and shot. A monument to fallen Jewish fighters and victims of Fascism was set up after the war in the central cemetery of Belgrade.

Contemporary Period

Immediately after the liberation of Belgrade in October 1944 the Jewish community resumed its activities by opening a soup kitchen, a center for returnees, and medical services. The Ashkenazi synagogue was reconsecrated in December 1944, with the Ashkenazi and the Sephardi communities merging. In 1947 the community had 2,271 members, half of whom emigrated to Israel shortly after. In 1969 there were 1,602 Jews in Belgrade and in 2000 around 1,500. The community center ran an internationally known choir, a youth club, and a kindergarten. It also housed the Federation of Jewish Communities of Yugoslavia. The Yugoslav Jewish Historical Museum founded in 1948 and officially opened in 1952, contains material on all Jewish communities in Yugoslavia. and their artistic creativity. The J. community remained stable demographically with natural increase and returning émigrés offsetting those leaving for Israel and other countries. Jewish holidays were celebrated and J. events noted in a regularly appearing monthly publication. In 1995 an impressive sculpture cast in brass, the work of Nandor Glied, entitled "Menorah in Flames," was erected near the Danube at the site of the ancient Jewish quarter.

BIBLIOGRAPHY: A. Hananel and E. Eškenazi, *Fontes Hebraici…* 1 (1958), 219, 468–71, and index; 2 (1960), 177–8, 258–60, and index; D. Djurić-Zamolo, in: *Jevrejski Almanah 1965–67*, 41–76; A. Alkalay, in: *Jevrejski Almanah 1961–62*, 82–97; Moses Kohen, *Et Sofer* (Fuerth, 1691). HOLOCAUST PERIOD: Savez Jevrejskih Opština, *Zločini fašističkih okupatora…* (1952), 1–9 (Eng. summary); G. Reitlinger, *Final Solution* (1961), 385–92; R. Hilberg, *Destruction of European Jewry* (1961), 435–42. **ADD. BIBLIOGRAPHY:** Z. Loker (ed.), *Pinkas ha-Kehillott Yugoslavia* (1988); Ž. Lebl, *Do "konačnog rešenja" – Jevreji u Beogradu 1521–1942* (2001).

[Daniel Furman / Zvi Loker (2nd ed.)]

BELGRADO, DAVID FERNANDO (1918–), rabbi and *ḥazzan*. Born in Florence, Italy, Belgrado was appointed third *ḥazzan* to the Great Synagogue of Florence at the age of 18. He went on to become the second *ḥazzan* and ultimately the chief *ḥazzan* of the Florentine community. He was ordained as rabbi in Rome and was appointed chief rabbi of Florence in 1961. Belgrado studied music and singing at the municipal theater of Florence and has sung in operas and concerts of Jewish and general music. He has made recordings of his renditions of cantorial chants in the Florentine style.

[Akiva Zimmerman]

BELIAL (Heb. בְּלִיַּעַל; lit. "worthlessness"). In the Bible a common noun characterizing persons who behave in a dissolute manner, give false testimony, or hatch infamous plots. It is used in apposition to such words as "son" (Deut. 13:14; I Sam. 2:12), "daughter" (I Sam. 1:16), "man" (I Sam. 30:22; Prov. 16:27), "witness" (Prov. 19:28), and "counselor" (Nah. 1:11). A "matter of *beliyya'al*" is a base thought (Deut. 15:9), and "rivers of *Belial*" (Ps. 18:5) are hellish currents of adversity. In post-biblical literature – especially in the pseudepigrapha – Belial (usually written Beliar) is the name of the Prince of Evil, i.e., *Satan – a view which no doubt underlies the practice of the Vulgate (and of Theodotion, Judg. 9:22) to reproduce the word by transliteration in certain passages of Scripture. Belial is the spirit of darkness (Test. Patr., Levi 19:1; 1QM 13:12). Evil men are dominated by him or his attendant spirits (Test. Patr.: Ash. 1:8; Levi 3:3; Joseph 7:4; Dan. 1:7; Ben. 6:1), and the world is currently under his sway (1QS 1:18, 24; 2:5, 19; 1QM 14:9; Mart. Isa. 2:4). His will opposes God's (Test. Patr., Naph. 3:1), and he wields a sword which causes bloodshed, havoc, tribulation, exile, death (or plague?), panic, and destruction (*ibid.*, Ben. 7:1–2), or catches men in the snares of lewdness, lucre, and profanity (Zadokite Document 4:13ff.). Belial will ultimately be chained by God's holy spirit (Test. Patr., Levi 18:12) or cast into the all-engulfing fire (*ibid.*, Judah 25:3), and his attendant spirits will be routed (*ibid.*, Iss. 7:7; *ibid.*, Dan 5:1), and discomfited by the Messiah (*ibid.*, Dan 5:10; *ibid.*, Ben. 3:8). There will be a final war in which he and his partisans will be defeated by God and God's partisans, aided by heavenly cohorts (1QM 1:5; 15:3; 18:1, 3). The latter now abide in the second of the seven heavens (Test. Patr., Levi 3:3). The concept of Belial as the opponent of God probably owes much to Iranian dualism, where the eternal antagonists Asha (Right) and Druj (Perversity) are portrayed as destined to engage in a final "*Armageddon," aided respectively by heavenly and earthly partisans, *ashovans* and *dregvants*. (In 1QS (2:20–21; cf. 4:23; 9:21), these terms are reproduced exactly as *benei ẓedek*, "sons of righteousness," and *benei ʿawel*, "sons of perversity.") The Iranian picture was validated, however, by the authority of the biblical text Zechariah 14:5, "The Lord my God will come and all the holy ones [will be] with you" (LXX: "and all His holy ones with Him"). In the third book of the *Sibylline Oracles* (65–74), Belial is identified with a deceiver and miracle-monger whose line hails from Sebaste, i.e., Samaria. This is thought to refer to Simon Magus.

BIBLIOGRAPHY: Tur-Sinai, in: EM, 2 (1965), 132–3; Gaster, in: IDB, 1 (1962), 377.

[Theodor H. Gaster]

BELIEF

The Bible

In the Bible there are no articles of faith or dogmas in the Christian or Islamic sense of the terms. Although trust in God is regarded as a paramount religious virtue (Gen. 15:6; Isa. 7:9; cf. Job 2:9), there is nowhere in Scripture an injunction to believe. Even a verse like II Chronicles 20:20 "believe (*haʾaminu*) in the Lord your God, and you will be established; believe His prophets, and you will succeed" expresses only King Jehoshaphat's advice to the people; it is not a religious commandment. Furthermore, the verb *heʾemin* (האמין "to believe"), the noun *ʾemunah* ("belief"), and other forms derived from the stem *ʾmn* (אמן) mean to trust, have confidence; and faithfulness; and in this sense are used both of God and of man (Gen. 15:6; Deut. 32:4; Prov. 20:6; Job 4:18). This usage is in striking contrast to the concept of "belief" in the New Testament (e.g., John 3:18). It is only in the Middle Ages, when Jewish theologians began to formulate articles of faith, that derivations of the root *ʾmn* came to be used in a dogmatic sense.

The reason for the absence of a catechism in both the Bible and the rabbinic tradition is probably twofold: in Judaism the primary emphasis is not on profession of faith but on conduct (Avot 1:17); and speculative and systematic thinking is not characteristic of the biblical or the rabbinic genius. Dogmatics entered Judaism as a result of external pressure; contact with alien religious systems, which had formulated theological doctrines, compelled Jewish thinkers to state the basic creeds of their own faith. In a sense, Jewish dogmatics forms part of the larger category of Jewish apologetics.

No religion, however, is conceivable without fundamental doctrines or axiomatic principles, and Judaism, in its scriptural as well as rabbinic aspects, is no exception. Indeed, the Bible contains certain summary statements that might be considered incipient dogmas. The *Shemaʿ (Deut. 6:4), underscoring the unity of God; the Ten Commandments (Ex. 20:1 ff.; Deut. 5:6 ff.), providing an epitome of Jewish precepts; the formulation of the divine attributes in Exodus 34:6–7; Micah's sublime summary of human duty (6:18); and the majestic simplicity of the Lord's assurance to Habakkuk "but the righteous shall live by his faith" (2:4) are a few examples culled from many. But valuable as these formulations are, they do not embrace the complete range of fundamental biblical teachings. Only an analysis of scriptural doctrines against the background of the entire complex of biblical thought can yield the essential religious beliefs, moral ideals, and spiritual truths that underlie the faith expounded by the Scriptures.

That "God is" is axiomatic. He is One (Deut. 6:4) and incomparable (Isa. 40:18); there are no other gods (Deut. 4:39). He is omnipotent (Job 42:2), omnipresent (Ps. 139:7–12), omniscient (Job 28:23 ff.), and eternal (Isa. 40:6–8; 44:6). Even more important is the doctrine that He is the God of justice and love (Ex. 34:6–7); it is His moral nature that makes Him holy (Isa. 5:16). In His might He willed the creation of the universe (Gen. 1), and in His love He continues to sustain it (Ps. 104; 145:14 ff.). He made the laws of nature; the miracles are exceptions to these cosmic rules, but both the normal and the abnormal conform to the Divine Will. Mythology, except for idiomatic phrases, is excluded from biblical teaching. Magical practices are forbidden (Deut. 18:10); unlike miracles, they do not issue from the will of God, but seek to overrule divinely established laws of nature.

The apex of creation is man, created in the divine image. This "image" is reflected in the moral and spiritual qualities of human nature. In man creation achieves a new dimension – a moral personality endowed with freedom of will. The relationship between God and man has a voluntaristic ethical character. It is an encounter between the Divine Person and His human counterpart, between Father and child. Ideally it is an "I–Thou" relation. But man may disobey; sin is spiritual treason, which transforms the "nearness" of God into "estrangement." The divine "Thou" then becomes "It."

Human freedom of choice (Deut. 30:15, 19) is the source of man's responsibility, upon which are predicated rewards and penalties, both collective and individual. Divine retribution is a corollary of God's righteousness; but its purpose is primarily not punitive but educative and reformative; it aims to restore the "I–Thou" nexus. Thus God does not desire the destruction of the wicked, but their return to the path of goodness (Ezek. 18:23, 32), and heaven's grace far exceeds the measure of divine punishment (Ex. 20:5–6; Deut. 5:9–10). Hence all the predictions of the prophets are conditional (cf. Jonah). The Heavenly Father hopes for His punitive decrees to be nullified. Conceptually there appears to be a contradiction between God's omniscience and omnipotence on the one hand, and man's freedom of action on the other. But the Bible harmonizes them in a supreme historic event. Human rebellions will ultimately end in a great reconciliation. In the messianic era Zion's teaching will become a universal heritage (Isa. 2:2 ff.; Mic. 4:1 ff.). "In the end of days" the divine design of history will be realized as perfectly as His cosmic plan.

Human waywardness was manifest from the beginning of history. Man has constantly been tempted to do wrong: "every imagination of the thoughts of his heart was only evil continually" (Gen. 6:5). To aid humanity to persevere along the path of righteousness, divine revelation was necessary. Its purpose was to direct and supplement the basic sense of right and wrong innate in every human being (cf. Gen. 39:9). Certain spiritual geniuses – the patriarchs, the prophets – learned to know the will of God in given situations. But the complete revelation was vouchsafed to the Children of Israel at Sinai. It comprised many elements – legal and ritual, moral and spiritual, national and universal – each component being necessary to its educative and purifying intent. The precepts were neither to be augmented nor diminished (Deut. 4:2); the law was immutable. Intrinsically the prophets did not add to the Torah. The glory of Hebrew prophecy consists not in preaching new ideas, but in elucidating the historic covenant and applying its teachings to the circumstances of their time. In particular they stressed the moral and spiritual values of religion, and the universal conception of the consummation of history in the kingdom of God.

By accepting the Torah, Israel became the "treasured people" of the Lord, a holy nation in the service of the Holy God (Ex. 19:5; Lev. 19:2). They entered into a covenant with Him (Ex. 24:7; Deut. 29:11, 12), calling for unswerving obedience on their part and protective providence on the part of God. The election of Israel was not an act of favoritism. On the contrary, it represented a mission involving special responsibility and corresponding retribution. "You only have I known of all the families of the earth; therefore I will visit upon you all your iniquities" (Amos 3:2). Nor was God's providential care limited to Israel; there was a Philistine and Aramean exodus comparable to that of Israel (*ibid.* 9:7). The covenant with Israel was an integral part of God's universal historic plan of salvation (Isa. 49:6). Hence the Israelites were as indestructible as the cosmos (Jer. 33:25–26). Their sins would be punished, but redemption would succeed every disaster. The national hope of restoration and return to the Land of Israel is thus indivisibly linked with the redemption of all mankind. Jewish nationalism and universalism are not opposed but complementary biblical ideals.

Since ethics occupies a central position in scriptural theology, theodicy greatly exercised the minds of the prophets and sages of Israel. The thought "shall not the Judge of all the earth do justly?" (Gen. 18:25) is echoed in various forms throughout the Scriptures. It is an essential aspect of the dialogue between man and God. To criticize and challenge God in sincerity is not viewed by Scripture as a sin (witness Abraham, Moses, Jeremiah, Habakkuk, and Job); only hypocrisy and smugness are iniquitous (Job 42:7). The biblical answers to the problem of suffering are varied: it is accounted for by sin, by the concept of "the suffering servant," by the limitations of human knowledge. Man's view is too short; however long the process, righteousness triumphs in the end (Ps. 92:8). In the final analysis God's purpose is beyond man's understanding (Isa. 55:8; Job 42:3). Until the ultimate reconciliation at "the end of days," the Incomprehensible God can be apprehended only in faith (Hab. 2:4).

Hellenistic Literature

The encounter with Greek culture in the Hellenistic period brought the challenge of new concepts and philosophic methodology to Judaism. But the impact was transitory, and *Philo, "the first theologian," was the only one among the Greco-Jewish writers to formulate Jewish dogmas. He enumerates five tenets: (1) God exists and rules the universe; (2) He is one; (3) the world was created; (4) creation is one; (5) Divine Providence cares for the world (Op. 61). Josephus asserts that the antagonism between the Sadducees and Pharisees was based on doctrinal differences, such as the question of providence, the immortality of the soul, and the belief in resurrection with the concomitant idea of the final judgment (Wars, 2:162–5). Modern scholarship, however, is inclined to give a political and national interpretation to these disputes.

Rabbinic Literature

Rabbinic theology is marked by an overwhelming diversity of opinion. Since the sages' method of study was essentially based on argumentation and controversy, it is by no means easy to determine at all times its fundamental ideas. Furthermore, while the rabbis sought to give clear definition to the *halakhah*, the *aggadah* remained vague, unsystematized, and contradictory. Nevertheless in Talmud and Midrash, as in Scripture, it is possible to discern ground patterns of thought and basic concepts that constitute the foundations of the tannaitic and amoraic ideology. It is axiomatic that rabbinic teaching rests firmly on biblical doctrine and precept. Here, as in the Bible, God is the transcendent Creator; the Torah is the unalterable embodiment of His will; providence is motivated by moral principles; there is an "I–Thou" relationship between man and God; the election of Israel, linked to the immutable covenant of the Torah, is a paramount idea; and the prophetic promise of Israel's ultimate redemption and the establishment of the kingdom of God upon earth is the national-universal denouement of the drama of history. But rabbinic theology is a superstructure founded on scriptural faith, not a copy of it; there are evolutionary differences in talmudic Judaism that distinguish it from biblical norms and give it its distinctive qualities.

Rabbinic Judaism produced no catechism; but external cultural pressures and internal heresies gave rise to certain formulations of a dogmatic character. Sanhedrin 10:1, for example, in defining those who have no share in the world to come, gives to the belief in resurrection and in the divine origin of the Torah credal status. Similarly Hillel's dictum "That which is hateful to thee do not do unto others" (Shab. 31a) constitutes in its context the principal Jewish dogma. In discussing the precepts of the Torah the rabbis spoke of various figures who reduced the number of precepts (from the traditional 613), ending with Habakkuk who subsumed them all under one fundamental principle, "but the righteous shall live by his faith" (Hab. 2:4; cf. Mak. 24a). But in rabbinic, as in scriptural, literature, the root-ideas can be reached only by a careful examination of the complete compass of the tradition and a comparative study of its beliefs.

A new mysticism, emanating from the doctrines of *ma'aseh bereshit* ("work of creation") and *ma'aseh merkavah* ("work of the chariot"), now attaches to the concept of God. Gnostic influence, despite the general opposition of the sages to Gnostic ideas, is discernible. But these esoteric notions were reserved for the few only (Ḥag. 2:1). On the other hand, the broad-based popular approach, found in numerous *aggadot*, inclines toward an anthropopathic presentation of the Deity. The Holy One of Israel suffers all Israel's tribulations; He too is exiled (Sif. Num. 84; Ber. 9b). Man is conceived as a dualism: his soul, which is immortal, gives him a place among the angels; his body makes him akin to the beasts (Sif. Deut. 309). But the body is not condemned as a source of evil, nor may the material things of this world be left unenjoyed (TJ, Kid. 4:12, 66d). They are the work of God and inherently good. Indeed, God is to be served with both lower and higher impulses (Sif. Deut. 32; Ber. 54a). Man's freedom of choice, however, is fully recognized: "All is in the power of heaven except the reverence of heaven" (Ber. 33b), though the omniscient God foresees all (Avot 3:15). But this freedom is the basis of responsibility and the justification of retribution. To err is human, but penitence is the great shield that protects man (*ibid.* 4:13). Hence it was created even before the world (Pes. 54a).

The Torah, as the will of God, is immutable, and the sages regarded it as their supreme task to expound and determine its provisions, giving precedence, where needed, to moral principles over strict legalism (e.g., TJ, BM 2:5, 8c). To be holy and to walk in the Lord's ways implied in particular the practice of lovingkindness (Sifra 19:1; Sif. Deut. 49), which was equal to all the precepts put together (TJ, Pe'ah 1:1, 15b). The purpose of the commandments is to purify man (Gen. R. 44:1), and the true spirit of observance seeks no reward beyond the service of God (Avot 1:3). But there are two Torahs: the Oral Law, which was also revealed at Sinai, supplements and elucidates the Written Law. On the basis of Deuteronomy 17:11 (Ber. 19b), the sages claimed the right to enact laws of their own (*mi-de-rabbanan*), chiefly with a view to their serving as a "fence" (protection) to the biblical ordinances (*mi-de-orayta*). The most daring principle of all originated by the rabbis was their right to interpret the Torah in conformity with their understanding and to decide (by majority vote) accordingly. It was they, not the heavenly court (*familia*), that fixed the calendar (TJ, RH 1:3, 57b). Even if a halakhic ruling ran counter, so to speak, to the view of heaven, the rabbis still maintained that theirs was the right to decide, for the Torah, having been vouchsafed to man, was now subject to human judgment. Nor did this principle displease the Holy One, Blessed Be He, for He smiled indulgently when His children outvoted Him (BM 59b). The sages went so far as to declare "the suppression of the Torah may be the foundation thereof" (Men. 99). Thus the rabbis evolved theological machinery for adapting the *halakhah* to historical changes and needs without discarding an iota of the scriptural tradition. Theologically they justified this procedure by the theory that all that the rabbis taught was already inherent in the Sinaitic revelation (Lev. R. 22:1; TJ, Pe'ah 2:6, 17a), that the sages did not innovate but discovered already existing truths.

The rabbinic exaltation of Torah study was a natural corollary of their attitude to the Scriptures. The Mishnah lists the things whose fruits a man enjoys in this world, while the capital is laid up for him in the world to come, and declares "the study of the Law is equal to them all" (Pe'ah 1:1). The rabbis (BB 12a) elevate the sage (with his restrained, reflective approach) above the prophet (with his incandescent, intuitive consciousness). Nevertheless the truth that Judaism is life and that learning must lead to deeds was not lost sight of: "Great is the study of the Torah, because it leads to [right] action" (Kid. 40b).

Israel's election is a leading theme in rabbinic thought. It brought comfort and renewed courage to a suffering people. God's ultimate salvation was never doubted. The messianic era, despite the preceding tribulation, would bring redemption to Israel and the land. This belief suffuses the entire aggadic literature and inspires every facet of the liturgy. Great emphasis is placed on the importance of Ereẓ Israel in Talmud and Midrash and the prayer book. The rabbis exhaust the language of praise and indulge in unrestrained fantasy in depicting the future glories of the land. One dictum even avers that "he who dwells outside the Land of Israel is as one who serves idols" (Ket. 110b). This hyperbole was intended not only to encourage Jewish settlement in Ereẓ Israel, but also to strengthen the hope of national restoration. Jewish nationalism did not, however, exclude universalist ideals. "The pious of all nations have a share in the world to come" (Tosef., Sanh. 13:10). "Whoever repudiates idolatry is called a Jew" (Meg. 13a); and the greatest Torah principle is enshrined in the verse "This is the book of the generations of Adam" – the brotherhood of man (TJ, Ned. 9:4, 41c).

In the Talmud, as in the Bible, the problem of theodicy is a major theme. The sages range the entire gamut of possible explanations for human suffering. In the ultimate analysis they propound the profoundest conception of all: suffering deriving from divine love (Ber 5a). Human suffering is an essential element in human spiritual advancement. It is an aspect of God's grace. Another cardinal rabbinic belief offered a collective historical solution to the question of divine justice. The concept of resurrection (Sanh. 10:1) was closely linked with the advent of the Messiah and the last judgment (Shab. 152b; Ḥag. 12b; Sanh. 91a–b). Bygone generations would, if worthy, share in the sublime joy of the kingdom of God upon earth. Maimonides, however, interprets the resurrection in a purely spiritual sense (*Ma'amar Teḥiyyat ha-Metim*). Going beyond biblical theology, the rabbis envisaged yet another world, where the imbalance of earthly justice is rectified. The immortal soul is judged after the death of the body in the hereafter ("world to come") and is requited according to the individual's deeds upon earth (Sif. Deut. 307; Ber. 28b; Shab. 153a; Ber. 17a). In this solution time is transcended. God's ultimate justification is a function of eternity.

These norms of rabbinic faith provided the basis of medieval Jewish theology and philosophy. Their lack of definition gave later Jewish thinking flexibility and their emphasis a firm framework.

[Israel Abrahams]

Medieval Jewish Philosophy

In medieval philosophy belief is a general philosophical category belonging to the theory of knowledge, of which religious belief is one specific kind. The medieval philosophers distinguished between two activities of the mind: the formulation of propositions, and the affirmation that propositions in the mind correspond to a reality outside the mind, and identified belief with the latter activity. In line with this account *Maimonides defines belief as "… the notion that is represented in the soul when it has been averred of it that it is in fact just as it has been represented" (*Guide of the Perplexed*, 1:50). In somewhat less technical language *Saadiah defines belief as "… a notion that arises in the soul in regard to the actual character of anything that is apprehended. When the cream of investigation emerges, and is embraced and enfolded by the minds and, through them acquired and digested by the souls, then the person becomes convinced of the truth of the notion he has acquired" (*Book of Beliefs and Opinions*, introd.). Belief defined in this manner may still be true or false, and hence it is necessary to add criteria by means of which true beliefs may be distinguished from false ones. Saadiah, discussing this issue, lists four criteria which enable one to establish that a belief is true: sense perception, self-evident propositions, inference, and reliable tradition (*ibid.*, introd.; cf. Maimonides, "Letter On Astrology," in: R. Lerner and M. Mahdi (eds.), *Medieval Political Philosophy: A Sourcebook* (1963), 228). This conception of belief as the affirmation or conviction that propositions within the mind correspond to reality outside the mind can be traced to Greek philosophy, particularly to the Stoics.

Belief for medieval Christian, Muslim, and Jewish thinkers meant, in the first instance, religious belief, that is, the conviction that the teachings of Scriptures are true and that their truth is guaranteed by the authority of their respective traditions. At the same time they noted that philosophers also investigated some of the same issues that interested them, e.g., the existence of God, the creation of the world, principles of human morality, and they further noted that there was a similarity between the teachings of religion and human reason. Hence the question arose how the teachings of religion, that is, religious beliefs, are related to the teachings of philosophy, that is, philosophical beliefs. There were essentially three views concerning this interrelation. There were those who, denying that the term belief applies to philosophic teachings, affirmed that this term in its strict sense refers only to propositions accepted on the basis of religious authority; there were those who permitted the application of the term only to propositions known by way of demonstration; and there were still others, who were prepared to use the term belief for describing both. In line with these distinctions H.A. *Wolfson classifies the attitudes toward religious belief in a threefold fashion: the double faith theory, according to which the acceptance of propositions based both on religious authority and rational demonstration constitutes belief; the single faith theory of the authoritarian type, according to which the acceptance of propositions based on authority alone constitutes belief; and the single faith theory of the rational type, according to which the acceptance of propositions based on demonstration alone constitutes belief (JQR, 33 (1942), 213–64).

Saadiah, a proponent of the double faith theory, accepts the notion of belief as applying to things known both by way of authority and by way of demonstration. He maintains that the doctrines of Scripture coincide with those of philosophy, and that an affirmation of these doctrines, whether based on revelation or on rational demonstration, constitutes belief. While Saadiah advocates speculation about the truths of religion, he, nevertheless, maintains that it is forbidden to ignore Scripture entirely and to rely solely on one's reason, for the reason is not infallible, and may lead to erroneous conclusions.

*Judah Halevi, a representative of the single faith theory of the authoritarian type, maintains that belief applies only to things known by means of authority. According to him, belief is an acceptance of the doctrines of Scripture based on authority, i.e., on the fact that these doctrines of Scripture were divinely revealed. For example, in connection with sacrifices Halevi states categorically that "… he who accepts [sacrifices], without examination or reasoning is better off than he who resorts to research and analysis" (*Kuzari*, 2:26; see also 1:64–65, and 3:7).

Maimonides, on the other hand, is a representative of the single faith theory of the rationalist type. He maintains that belief applies only to things known by way of demonstration. While he does not state categorically that an acceptance of the doctrines of Scripture based on authority is not belief, he definitely considers an acceptance based on demonstration to be a more perfect form of belief. Belief is more than verbal acceptance; it requires understanding and a rational basis. Providing an example, Maimonides writes that someone who utters with his lips that he believes in the unity and incorporeality of God, while at the same time maintaining that God has positive attributes, cannot be said to believe truly in God's unity. That he can maintain that God has attributes indicates that he does not understand the principle of God's unity, and there is no belief without understanding (*Guide*, 1:50). According to Maimonides the precept "You shall love the Lord, your God," cannot properly be fulfilled without an understanding of metaphysics. Love of God, according to Maimonides, is "proportionate to apprehension" (*Guide*, 3:51; cf. Yad, Yesodei ha-Torah, 4:12).

*Levi b. Gershom shares the view of the Maimonidean school that there is no opposition between reason and belief. He holds that priority should be given to reason where its demands are unambiguous, for the meaning of Scripture is not always clear and is subject to interpretation (*Milḥamot Adonai*, introd.).

See also *Allegory, *Revelation, *Philosophy.

[Jacob Haberman]

Maimonides' aforementioned definition of belief (Arab.: *i'tiqâd*; Hebrew: *emunah*) may be called the "cognitive" sense of *emunah*, i.e., opinion or position held. The positive evaluation of *emunah* in its cognitive sense dominates Jewish philosophy until the late 14th century, when the influence of scholastic philosophy is felt, especially in Spain. There one can distinguish three new approaches: *emunah* as non-volitional and of little religious significance; as non-volitional yet superior to rational knowledge; as volitional and hence of supreme religious significance. The view of *emunah* as non-volitional is adopted by Hasdai *Crescas, who still adheres to the cognitive sense. Because *emunah* is non-volitional, its religious significance is of little value according to Crescas; God does not reward and punish humans solely on the basis of their belief-states. Crescas responds here to the Jewish Aristotelians who considered the possession of rationally justified *emunot* to be a necessary (and perhaps sufficient) condition for the immortality of the soul. Crescas' student Joseph *Albo defines *emunah* as "a firm conception of the thing in the mind, so that the latter cannot in any way imagine its opposite, *even though it may not be able to prove it*" (*Ikkarim* 1.19, trans. Husik). According to Simeon *Duran, *emunot* are proved by miracles or by a reliable tradition concerning them, whereas according to Isaac *Abrabanel, *emunot* are distinct from both knowledge *and* opinion. Isaac *Arama views *emunot* not only as superior but as often contrary to reason. True wisdom is attained only when one assents to the Torah's commands that are *opposed* to speculation. The language of *emunah* that dominates these discussions is most probably influenced by Christian treatments of *fides*, "faith."

The most telling example of this influence is found in Abraham *Bibago's *Derekh Emunah*, which should be translated, *The Way of Faith*. Bibago distinguishes between attaining knowledge via rational inquiry and via faith. In the case of Judaism the latter method is superior to the former because it is guaranteed by a reliable tradition that stretches back to Moses, whereas many philosophical doctrines are debatable. The point is as old as Halevi, but the language is that of *emunah*. Since rational knowledge is not as certain as knowledge acquired through faith, the mind of the faithful is superior to that of the philosopher. Moreover, Bibago implies that *emunah* is fundamentally different from rational knowledge, for *emunah* is the "assent to unseen things" (a similar definition is found in *Aquinas) whereas rational knowledge is of revealed things. Divine science, i.e., theology and metaphysics, can be attained only through *emunah* (*Derekh Emunah* 2:7).

[Charles Manekin (2nd ed.)]

Modern Jewish Philosophy

While in medieval philosophy the description of faith formed an integral part of the theory of knowledge, the rise of modern science and the concomitant decline of the belief in the divine revelation of Scriptures have made faith a matter of trusting in God rather than of the affirmation of certain propositions. Characteristic of this attitude in recent Jewish thought are the views of Franz *Rosenzweig, according to whom religious belief arises from the experience of personal revelation, for which man must always strive and be prepared. This view was anticipated by Hermann *Cohen in his theory of correlation. Similarly, Martin *Buber and Abraham *Heschel see faith as a relationship of trust between man and God, which arises from, and manifests itself in, personal encounters between man and God, and man and man, which Buber calls I–Thou relationships.

Another tendency among modern thinkers, which reflects the influence of psychology, is to view belief as a psychological state which is valuable insofar as it motivates man to act in an ethical manner. Mordecai *Kaplan, a representative of this naturalistic view, implies that faith is a kind of "self-fulfilling prophecy" insofar as it leads to the redemption of human society. According to the others embracing a naturalistic view, faith is good in that it infuses meaning and purpose into an otherwise meaningless and cruel existence. This point is taken up strongly by Richard *Rubenstein, who has been concerned with the challenge to Jewish faith posed by the Holocaust.

BIBLIOGRAPHY: S. Schechter, *Studies in Judaism*, 1 (1911), 147–81; I. Efros, in: JQR, 33 (1942/43), 133–70; A. Heschel, *ibid.*, 265–313; G.F. Moore, *Judaism*, 2 (1946), 237–8; H.A. Wolfson, *Philo*, 1 (1948), 155–6; M. Buber, *Two Types of Faith* (1951); W. Eichrodt, *Theology of the Old Testament*, 2 (1967), 277–90; E.E. Urbach, *Ḥazal* (1969), 15–28; S.H. Bergman, *Jewish Philosophy in Modern Times* (1968), 177–9. **ADD. BIBLIOGRAPHY:** S. Rosenberg, "The Concept of *Emunah* in Post-Maimonidean Jewish Philosophy," in: I. Twersky (ed.), *Studies in Medieval Jewish History and Literature* (1984); M. Kellner, *Dogma in Medieval Jewish Thought* (1986); idem, *Must a Jew Believe Anything?* (1999); C.H. Manekin, "Jewish Philosophy in the Thirteenth and Fourteenth Centuries," in: D. Frank and O. Leaman (eds.), *Routledge History of Jewish Philosophy* (1997), 350–59; M. Shapiro, *The Limits of Orthodox Theology: Maimonides' Thirteen Principles Reappraised* (2004).

BELINFANTE, Sephardi family. Its paterfamilias, JOSEPH COHEN BELINFANTE, fled Portugal in 1526 because of the persecution of the Jews. The family settled in the Balkans, in the city of Belgrade. After the Austrian conquest of Belgrade, the Jews were denied access to that city, and for this reason a part of the family came over to the Netherlands.

One example is ELIJAH HEZEKIAH, born in 1699. He played an important part within the Portuguese community in Amsterdam. Isaac *Belinfante (d. 1780), son of Elijah Hezekiah, was a Hebrew poet and writer. Elijah Hezekiah's brother, MEIR ḤAYYIM (d. 1721), settled permanently in Amsterdam. His son, SADDIK (1675–1750), became the chief rabbi of the Portuguese community and was the author of several Bible commentaries and some halakhic writings: *Simḥat Ẓaddik, Neḥamot Ẓaddik, and Peri Ẓdadik.*

The son of Saddik, MOSES COHEN BELINFANTE (The Hague, 1761–1827), was actively involved in the struggle for Jewish emancipation in the Netherlands. In 1806, Moses moved to Amsterdam, where he became the editor of the official newspaper published in the Netherlands. Moses' brother, JACOB COHEN (1780–1845), was editor between 1807 and 1837. He also published several Jewish almanacs as well as the *Jaarboeken voor de Israelieten in Nederland* between 1835 and 1840. Their sister SARA BELINFANTE was the headmistress of an Amsterdam school for Jewish girls.

In the 19th century, the Belinfantes were primarily active in the field of journalism. ARON BELINFANTE (1811–1881) became a member of the editorial staff of the *Dagblad van Zuid-Holland en 's Gravenhage,* which was merged with the *Nieuwe Dagblad.* ISAAC BELINFANTE (1814–1892) worked for the *Nederlandsche Staatscourant* and the *Algemeen Handelsblad'* and was also a co-founder of the *Weekblad van het Regt.* His brother JOSEPHUS JUSTUS (1812–1882) was co-director of the Nederlandsch Correspondentie Bureau and compiled the *Rijks- en Residentie Almanak.* MAURITS ERNST BELINFANTE (1849–1903), son of Josephus Justus, succeeded his father at the Bureau and worked as a journalist for several newspapers, among which were the *Revue des Deux Mondes* and the *Chronique Politique.* GEORGE BELINFANTE (1837–1888), son of Isaac, became known for his polemical writings in the *Haagsche Courant* and his political letters in the *Zaanlandse Courant.* In the field of politics, he became known after 1870 as the writer of the chamber reviews for the *Nieuwe Rotterdamse Courant.*

ARY BELINFANTE (1870–1925) became famous in Dutch music circles as a pianist and a teacher at the Amsterdam school for orchestra, and as the founder of the first private school of music. He published several studies on the history of music and on the science of music education.

In the 20th century, also the female members of the family stepped more into the limelight. EMILIE JOSEPHINE (or Emmy), BELINFANTE (1875–1944) was educated as a primary schoolteacher, but she became famous as a journalist. In 1901 she became the chief editor of *Het Familieblad – 's Gravenhaagsch Nieuws – en Advertentieblad.* She was in charge of her own section, using "May" as a pen name. In 1905, she started working for a daily paper called *Land en Volk,* in which she ran her own women's section. In 1908 she was appointed to work as a regular member of staff of the *Nieuwe Courant*, in which she reported extensively on the emerging women's movement and on women's issues. Her work as a reporter focused mainly on the women's movement until World War II. In February 1944 she was arrested and a few months later she was murdered in the concentration camp at Auschwitz-Birkenau.

JUDITH BELINFANTE (1943–) was prominent in the cultural and political life of the Netherlands. In 1976, she was appointed director of the Jewish Historical Museum in Amsterdam. From 2003 she was chief curator of Special Collections of the Amsterdam University Library. She was a member of parliament for the PvdA (Dutch Labour Party) from 1998 to 2000.

BIBLIOGRAPHY: S. Boas, in: *Habinjan*, 38 (1984) 22–23; E. Carmoly, in: *Revue Orientale* III (1843–1844), 134–38; J. Divendal, in: H. Berg (ed.), *Gelykstaat der Joden. Inburgering van een minderheid* (1996) 35–45; idem, in: *Studia Rosenthaliana*, 31 (1997) 94–138; C. de Greef and J. Salman, in: *Historisch Tijdschrift*, VII (1991) 35–53; S. Jacobus, in: *Hakehilla* 42 (1996), 4, 10–11; *Nieuw Nederlands Biografisch woordenboek* I (1911) 281–82; H. Lakmaker, in: *Biografisch Woordenboek van Nederland* (2002); J. Meijer, in: *Maandblad voor de Geschiedenis der Joden in Nederland* 1 (1947–1948), 50–57, 90–94, 141–48, 243–52, 279–86; P.M. Netscher, *Levensschets van Josephus Justus Belinfante* (1883); L. Shirah, in: *Levend Joods Geloof*, 43 (1996), 21–22.

[Monika Saelemaekers (2nd ed.)]

BELINFANTE, ISAAC BEN ELIAH COHEN (d. 1780), man of Hebrew letters. A younger contemporary of David *Franco Mendes, Belinfante was probably born in the early 1720s. From the 1750s he participated in the burgeoning Hebrew literary life of the Amsterdam Portuguese-Jewish community. Besides his work as a *darshan*, he took an active part in preserving and disseminating contemporary Hebrew culture, by compiling manuscript anthologies (e.g., of the literary society Shomrim la-Boker) and by bringing to press compositions of his fellow literati. His own work, some of which was written under the pseudonym Pi ha-Medabber, includes sermons, occasional and ethical-didactic poetry, and historical-documentary material (e.g., the bibliographical *Si'aḥ Yitzḥak*, i.e., *Sifte Yeshenim Ḥadash*), which testifies to a new cultural self-awareness among the Amsterdam Sephardim. The majority of these writings remained in manuscript.

BIBLIOGRAPHY: H. Azulay, *Ma'agal Tov* (ed. 1879), *passim*; H.G. Enelow, in: *Studies… A.S. Freidus* (1929), 5–30; Z. Malachi, in: *Tagim* (1969), 78–87; idem, in: *Studies in the History of Dutch Jewry* (1975), 123–50; L. Fuks and R.G. Fuks-Mansfeld, *Hebrew and Judaic Manuscripts in Amsterdam Public collections,* II (1975), *passim.*

[Irene E. Zwiep (2nd ed.)]

BELINKOV, ARKADII VIKTOROVICH (1921–1970), Russian literary critic and writer. Belinkov was born and educated in Moscow. In 1944 he was arrested and condemned to death on charges of writing an "anti-Soviet novel," *Rough Copy of Feelings*, and for founding an anti-Soviet literary group, but the sentence was commuted and he spent only 13 years in prison. In 1960 his book on Y.N. Tynyanov (second editon, 1965) was published; the work had a considerable influence on Soviet literature. In 1968 Belinkov immigrated to the U.S., where he lectured at Yale and Indiana Universities and published his works in the emigré editions of the *Novyi Zhurnal* and *Novoe Russkoe Slovo*, as well as the *Russian Review.* In the middle of the 1960s, his literary career moved from pure literary criticism to the journalistic genre, which he maintained was a continuation of the tradition of fierce opposition of the prerevolutionary underground press. He opposed the political trends of both the West and the censored Soviet press. Belinkov's central theme is the place of the intelligentsia in history and its attitude toward the revolution, society, and the state. He asserts the everlasting opposition of intellectuals (as the only social group that needs spiritual freedom) to the state, which suppresses this freedom, and society collaborating with the state. Belinkov was deeply aware of his Jewish identity and stressed his sympathy for Israel. He died in the U.S.

[Lazar Fleishman]

BELISHA, Moroccan family of merchants and financiers. In 1817 MOSES BELISHA (1788–1851) settled in Marseilles where he acquired a large fortune. He became "Merchant of the sultan of Morocco" and a benefactor of the Jewish community. His activities extended to Gibraltar and to Manchester. Moses was assisted by his son BARROW who traded with India, Egypt, and Mogador, where the philanthropists JESHUA and SOLOMON had remained. Moses' nephew, ISAAC, merchant and industrialist, became president of the Manchester Sephardi community in 1872. Isaac's grandson was Leslie *Hore-Belisha.

BIBLIOGRAPHY: J.L. Miège, *Maroc*, 1 (1961), 94, 144, 574; A. Hyamson, *Sephardim of England* (1951), 359, 397.

[David Corcos]

BELKIN, ARNOLD (1930–), Mexican painter. Born in Canada, Belkin settled in Mexico in 1948. Belkin saw the possibilities of the mural as expanding into multiple viewpoint conceptions which changed and shifted as the spectator moved. The most important of Belkin's murals were at the Federal Penitentiary (1960), at the Children's Welfare Institute (1963), and at the Jewish Cultural Center (1966). From 1954 to 1960 he was assistant professor of mural techniques at the Universidad Motolinia, Mexico City. During this time, his etchings and aquatints included a series of biblical themes, a number of large black and white paintings grouped under the theme "Earth Creatures" and drawings on "Love and War."

BELKIN, SAMUEL (1911–1976), U.S. rabbi, educator, and scholar. Born in Swislocz, Poland, Belkin studied at the yeshivot of Slonim and Mir, and was ordained in Radun (1928). He immigrated to the U.S. in 1929 and received his Ph.D. at Brown University in 1935. He joined the Yeshiva College faculty as instructor in Greek and Talmud (1935–37), becoming secretary of its graduate school (1937) and member of the College Executive Committee (1939). Appointed professor and dean of Yeshiva's Rabbi Isaac Elchanan Theological Seminary in 1940, Belkin became president of the RIETS and Yeshiva College in 1943. He launched a far-reaching program of academic and physical expansion which enlarged Yeshiva University from 850 students and a faculty of 94 to 8,000 students and a faculty of some 2,200 with teaching centers throughout New York City. Fourteen constituent schools were founded, and in 1945 the college became *Yeshiva University.

Belkin, an authority on Jewish law and Hellenistic literature, especially Philo and early Midrashic sources, published many scholarly studies. In his major work, *Philo and the Oral Law* (1940), he stressed that "the oral law which originated in Palestine was also known and practiced among the Jews who lived outside of Palestine, and that Philo's *halakhah* is based upon the Palestinian oral law as it was known in Alexandria." He further showed that "there prevailed a great interdependence of thought between the Alexandrian and Palestinian Jewish communities and that we cannot regard them as two entirely separate forms of Judaism." His later works also demonstrate Philo's dependence upon ancient rabbinic traditions. Belkin wrote *Essays in Traditional Jewish Thought* (1956) and *In His Image* (1960), in which he formulated a religious philosophy of Judaism as reflected in the *halakhah*. Numerous articles of his were published in learned periodicals, both in Hebrew and in English.

As an educator, Belkin stressed that "Torah is the source from which all human obligations spring." He especially enunciated the religious philosophy of Judaism as reflected in the *halakhah*. To him its basic principles are the sovereignty of God and the sacredness of the individual. Hence, many legal and spiritual institutions in Judaism can be understood only by these fundamental teachings based on belief in divine kingship and the finite worth of the human personality. Though recognized as a modernist Orthodox spokesman, Belkin generally maintained rapport with all groups in Judaism, promoting the unity of peoplehood.

BIBLIOGRAPHY: G. Klaperman, *History of Yeshiva University* (1969); *Hadoar* (Kislev 6, 5728); *Hapardes* (Tammuz 5728); Yeshiva University, *The Inauguration of Rabbi Samuel Belkin* (1945). ADD. BIBLIOGRAPHY: V.B. Geller, *Orthodoxy Awakens: The Belkin Era and Yeshiva University* (2003).

[Sidney B. Hoenig]

BELKIN, SIMON (1889–1969), Canadian political activist, community leader, and historian. Belkin was born in Smoljanka, a small village near Kiev in the Ukraine. A committed reformer who deeply identified as a Jew, he participated in the 1905 struggle for radical social change in the czarist empire before he joined the Zionist *Po'alei Zion movement. He immigrated to Montreal in 1911 but retained a strong emotional attachment to his region of origin. When, during the civil war following the Russian Revolution, the White forces organized large-scale pogroms against the Jewish communities of the Ukraine in 1920, Belkin traveled to Moscow to help organize relief efforts and arrange for the emigration of Jewish orphans from Russia to Canada.

But it was Belkin's involvement in the creation of the Canadian Jewish Congress in 1919 that established his reputation as a forceful community leader and committed socialist. In the years preceding the founding of the Canadian Jewish umbrella organization, Belkin campaigned tirelessly in favor of Canadian Jewish unity and a left-wing nationalist approach to solving community problems. A spokesperson for the Yiddish-speaking Zionist population in Montreal, he campaigned for Jews to retain their culture in their new country and to express solidarity with the Zionist movement.

In 1921 Belkin became director of the *Jewish Colonization Association. The JCA was founded in 1906 as the Canadian wing of Baron Maurice de *Hirsch's effort to resettle displaced East European Jews on agricultural lands in the New World. Although several such Canadian rural colonies predate the JCA, most were organized by the JCA. All these efforts eventually failed. By the end of World War II, most Jewish farm settlements were being abandoned as farmers moved to cities. Belkin left the employment of the organization in 1954.

Belkin turned to chronicling the Canadian Jewish experience. In 1956 he published his benchmark study of the Labor-Zionist movement in Canada entitled *Di Poale-Zion Bavegung in Kanade (1904–1920)*, which served to establish his reputation as a leading researcher in the field of Jewish Canadiana. To this day this work has not been surpassed in scope or in the thoroughness of its documentation. Belkin also wrote an important study on Canadian Jewish immigration history entitled *Through Narrow Gates* (1966). Belkin retired to California.

[Pierre Anctil (2nd ed.)]

BELKIND, Ereẓ Israel family of the First *Aliyah.

MEIR BELKIND (1827–1898), one of the first teachers of the modern Hebrew school system in Ereẓ Israel, was born in Logoisk, Belorussia, and followed his sons, Israel and Shimshon, to Ereẓ Israel at the beginning of the 1880s. He settled first in Jaffa and later in *Gederah, where he served as rabbi for the new settlers. Although a traditional Jew himself, he defended the *Bilu'im against the attacks of the religious zealots. When his son Israel established the first Hebrew school in Jaffa in 1889, Belkind became its teacher for religious subjects, thus molding the method of religious instruction in the modern schools of Ereẓ Israel.

ISRAEL (1861–1929), one of the founders of Bilu, was born in Logoisk. In 1882, while studying at Kharkov University, he was among the students who founded the Bilu movement and went to Ereẓ Israel at the head of its first group. He led the opposition against Baron Edmond de *Rothschild's officials and, on being expelled by them from Rishon le-Zion, settled in Gederah. In 1889 Belkind opened a private Hebrew school in Jaffa. He was accepted as a teacher at the *Alliance Israélite Universelle in Jerusalem in 1892, and there published several textbooks. In 1903 he founded an agricultural training school at Shefeyah (near Zikhron Ya'akov) for orphans of the Kishinev pogroms whom he brought to Ereẓ Israel. However, the school was forced to close down in 1906 because of lack of funds. During World War I Belkind resided in the U.S., where he published his memoirs in Yiddish, *Di Ershte Shrit fun Yishuv Erets Yisroel* ("The First Steps of the Jewish Settlement of Palestine," 1918).

Apart from numerous articles and popular pamphlets, Belkind published a geography of Palestine, *Ereẓ Yisrael ba-Zeman ha-Zeh* ("The Land of Israel Today," 1928). He died in Berlin, where he had gone for medical treatment. His remains were interred in Rishon le-Zion.

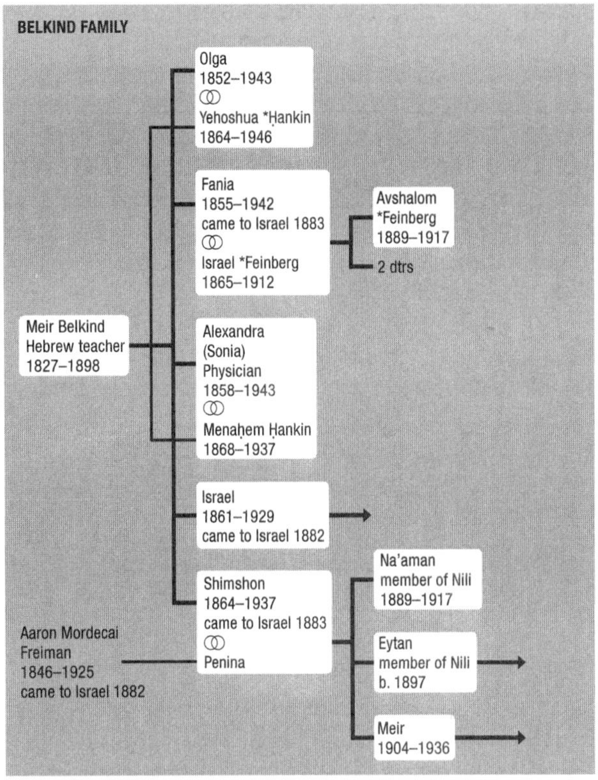

SHIMSHON (1864–1937), a Bilu pioneer, was born in Logoisk. He joined the Bilu movement in Russia and settled in Ereẓ Israel in 1883. He worked at various crafts in Jerusalem, Mikveh Israel, and Rishon le-Zion, and in 1888 moved to Gederah, where he was a farmer. His sons Na'aman and Eytan were members of *Nili.

NA'AMAN (1889–1917) was a member of Nili and was executed by the Turks. He was employed in the Rishon le-Zion wine cellars, where he came into contact with visiting Turkish officers. He joined Nili together with his cousin Avshalom *Feinberg. In September 1917, while attempting to reach Egypt to investigate the circumstances of Feinberg's death, he was caught by Bedouin who handed him over to the Turkish authorities. He was taken to Damascus, tried, convicted for spying, and hanged in the winter of 1917, together with Yosef *Lishansky. He was later buried in Rishon le-Zion.

BIBLIOGRAPHY: D. Idelovitch (ed.), *Rishon le-Ẓiyyon* (1941), 76–81; M. Smilansky, *Mishpaḥat ha-Adamah*, 2 (1944), 128–32; A. Yaari, *Goodly Heritage* (1958), index; A. Engle, *Nili Spies* (1959), index.

[Yehuda Slutsky]

BELKOWSKY, ẒEVI HIRSCH (Grigori; 1865–1948), Zionist leader and jurist. Belkowsky was born in Odessa, where his father died of wounds received during the 1881 pogroms. He was admitted to a Russian high school and graduated cum laude from the University of Odessa law school. He was offered a post at the university on the condition that he convert to Christianity. He refused and became a lecturer and later professor at the University of Sofia in Bulgaria (1893–97). As a university student, he had joined the *Ḥibbat Zion movement, and from 1891 was in contact with the pre-Herzl Zionist circle surrounding Nathan *Birnbaum in Vienna. When Herzl's *Judenstaat* was published in 1896, Belkowsky joined Herzl's group and helped organize the First Zionist Congress (1897). At the Third Congress he was elected to the General Council and appointed representative to the St. Petersburg district of the movement. He was among the leaders of the opposition to the *Uganda Scheme. Belkowsky published a series of pamphlets on Zionist subjects. He also initiated the publication of a bibliographical work in Russian entitled *Ukazatel literatury o sionizme* ("A Guide to Zionist Literature," 1903). Belkowsky continued his Zionist activity during the Russian Revolution. He was adviser to the British consul in Moscow on matters regarding Palestine immigration certificates, and chairman of the Zionist Central Committee of Russia (1920–22). In 1924 he was arrested for his Zionist activities and sentenced to deportation to Siberia, but the sentence was commuted to banishment from the Soviet Union. He settled in Palestine in 1924 and was active in the Federation of General Zionists. He later wrote his memoirs, *Mi-Zikhronotai* (1940).

BIBLIOGRAPHY: *Enẓiklopedyah le-Ẓiyyonut*, 1 (1947), 143–6; A.L. Jaffe (ed.), *Sefer ha-Congress* (1950²), 299.

[Yehuda Slutsky]

BELL, DANIEL (1919–), U.S. sociologist. Like many New York intellectuals, Bell, who was born to Polish immigrants, was deeply affected by the Great Depression. He grew up in the slums of the Lower East Side and his first language was Yiddish. He always viewed Zionism with a skeptical eye and Socialism, not Judaism, was his real religion as a boy.

Bell read widely, attending the Socialist Sunday School, and was tempted to join the Communist Party. His anarchist relatives in Mohegan Colony, N.Y. were horrified. Bell was handed pamphlets on the Russian sailors' rebellion at Kronstadt that Leon Trotsky had brutally suppressed. They dispelled any illusions he might have harbored about the true nature of Bolshevism. When Bell continued his studies, he was the only member of his circle who resisted the lure of Trotskyism.

In 1940, he became managing editor of the socialist weekly *The New Leader*, which featured the writings of a number of future liberal cold warriors including Melvin J. Lasky and Sidney *Hook. Bell excoriated industry for war profiteering and revered the magazine's editor, Sol M. Levitas, a Menshevik who had fled the Bolsheviks and who exposed the delusions of many New York intellectuals about the true nature of Stalin's Russia. Bell went on to write for many years for Henry M. Luce's *Fortune* magazine, but always felt the academic tug. In the late 1940s, he taught at the University of Chicago before moving to New York, where he taught at Columbia University and was close friends with scholars such as Lionel *Trilling and Richard *Hofstadter. Bell also wrote for the journal *Encounter* and worked for the Congress for Cultural Freedom in Paris from 1956 to 1967.

Bell's legacy rests with his books, which traverse immense terrain and are studded with footnotes that themselves often constitute minor essays. In 1960 Bell's book *The End of Ideology* created a sensation by declaring that the old categories of left and right were becoming defunct. Next Bell turned his attention to the unresolved tension between capitalism and morality. In the *Coming of Post-Industrial Society*, Bell prophesied the shift away from a manufacturing to a knowledge society that has taken place in the U.S. and Europe. But Bell did not believe that the quest for control over information would fundamentally alter the nature of human beings. He noted that "what does not vanish is the duplex nature of man himself – the murderous aggression, from primal impulse, to tear apart and destroy; and the search for order, in art and life, as the bending of will to harmonious shape."

If ideology was at an end, the *Public Interest*, which Bell co-founded with Irving Kristol in 1965, was supposed to supply sound social science solutions to the problems that faced the U.S. But politics intruded. Like other New York intellectuals, Bell was horrified by the aggression and primal impulses displayed by student radicals who rioted at Columbia in 1968. He and others saw the New Left as totalitarian, hedonistic, and jejune. It was indulging in revolutionary rhetoric that almost irreparably damaged the university – the institution that had offered a passport to the wider intellectual world for Bell and others. Nothing filled Bell with more contempt than the daydreamers about revolution and utopia who ended up creating bloodshed and tyranny.

But unlike Kristol, Bell never moved to the right or accepted the term "neoconservative." Instead, he remained focused on his academic work and moved to Cambridge, Mass., to become a professor of sociology at Harvard in 1969. In 1976, he amplified his observations about capitalism and hedonism in his classic *The Cultural Contradictions of Capitalism*. In a sweeping historical tour de force, Bell sought to show how capitalism had over the centuries inexorably weakened the authority of the very bourgeois societies it had brought into being. Where self-denial had allowed the Fuggers in Europe to amass great wealth, the bounty created by postwar American capitalism had created an unmoored individual indulging mainly in self-gratification. The individual, he concluded, "can only be a cultural wanderer, without a home to return to." The result is to threaten the vitality of capitalism itself.

Though he retired from teaching, Bell continued to write on politics and cultural matters in journals such as *Dissent*. Bell described himself as a socialist in economics, a liberal in politics, and a conservative in culture. His profound insights have ensured that his own works are beyond ideology and have become classics.

[Jacob Heilbrunn (2nd ed.)]

BELL, SIR FRANCIS HENRY DILLON (1851–1936). New Zealand politician and prime minister. Francis ("Harry") Bell was the son of a Protestant father and a Jewish mother, Margaret Hort. His Jewish background was well known in his lifetime. Born in Nelson, New Zealand, Bell was educated at Cambridge University and became a barrister in London until 1875, when he returned to Wellington, New Zealand, to practice law. After an extremely successful legal career, he entered politics and served as mayor of Wellington three times. In 1893 he was elected to the New Zealand parliament, serving until 1896, when he resumed his legal career. In 1912 Bell was appointed to the Legislative Council, New Zealand's upper house, serving until his death. A forceful and well-respected politician, he held numerous government posts and served as acting prime minister several times before becoming New Zealand's prime minister for two weeks in May 1925 following the death of Prime Minister William Massey. Bell was New Zealand's first native-born prime minister and the second Jew, after Julius *Vogel, to hold the office. Bell received a knighthood in 1915. Originally a radical, he later described himself as a "Tory socialist."

BIBLIOGRAPHY: W.J. Gardiner, "Bell, Francis Henry Dillon," in: *The Dictionary of New Zealand Biography* (2003; online update).

[William D. Rubinstein (2nd ed.)]

BELL, JOSHUA (1967–), U.S. violinist. Born in Bloomington, Indiana, Bell studied with Mimi Zweig, and with Josef Gingold (1980–89). Winning the grand prize of the *Seventeen Magazine* / General Motors competition (1981) led to a highly acclaimed orchestral debut with Riccardo Muti and the Philadelphia Orchestra. In 1985 he made his Carnegie Hall debut. In 1987 he received an Avery Fisher Career Grant and made his first recordings, creating a sensation throughout the music world. His playing combined a virtuoso technique with sweetness of tone and phrasing. He performed with leading conductors and orchestras, made recordings of the concerto repertory and also composed his own cadenzas for the major violin concertos. In 1993 Bell gave the premiere of Maw's Concerto, of which he is the dedicatee. A chamber music enthusiast, Bell initiated a chamber music series in London and Paris. A multifaceted musician, he also teamed up with artists such as Chick Corea and Bobby McFerrin. He continued to explore all sides of the musical spectrum in concerts and recordings (such as *Gershwin Fantasy* and *West Side Story Suite*, a deconstruction of *Bernstein's original score). He is known widely for his brilliant performance on the soundtrack to the film *The Red Violin*. The Indiana Historical Society named Bell an Indiana Living Legend (2000). He also received the Indiana Arts Council Governor's Award (2003), and recordings awards. Bell holds an Artist Diploma from Indiana University. In 1998, he began teaching master classes at London's Royal Academy of Music. He plays an Antonius Stradivarius.

BIBLIOGRAPHY: Grove online; MGG². *Baker's Biographical Dictionary* (1997); D. Templeton. "Fresh Prince: Joshua Bell on Composition, Hyperviolins, and the Future of Music," in: *Strings* 17 (Oct. 2002), 46–53;

[Naama Ramot (2nd ed.)]

BELLELI, LAZARUS MENAHEM (1862–1940?), Greek polyglot writer and philologist. Born in Corfu, by the early age of 15 he was already a serious author. In 1877 he edited *Atteret Baḥurim* ("The Crown of the Young"), a Hebrew-Greek vocabulary for the Book of Genesis supplemented by a sketch of Hebrew grammar. Afterward he contributed to the *Vessillo Israelitico*, the *Famiglia Israelitica*, *Mose*, and *Corriere Israelitico*. Belleli graduated from the University of Athens, but was forced to leave in 1883 due to antisemitic discrimination. Then, he went to study at the Instituto di Studi Superiori at Florence, where he obtained his doctorate in philology in 1890. During part of this period he served as principal of the Jewish school in Leghorn.

In 1890 Belleli returned to Corfu where he was the secretary of the local Alliance Israélite Universelle chapter.

Belleli had already sensed for several years the dangers that the Jewish population was to face in the future. He tried to combat the antisemitic instigation of the local press. He was unsuccessful in his talks with local politicians to get political equality for the Jews, for the latter only reiterated that the Jews enjoyed protection. At best this "protection" was feeble and soon to be shattered.

Belleli witnessed the violent outbreak against the Jews in Corfu in 1891 that followed the murder of the seven-year-old Jewish girl Rubina Sarda and a vicious blood libel against the Jews. He represented the Alliance as an observer and reported back to them extensively at the ensuing trial in Patrás.

In response to the spread of anti-Jewish literature Lazarus Belleli translated into Greek Theodore Reinach's *Histoire des Juifs* (1895).

In 1895 Belleli left for England. In 1908 while still living in London he received the Corgialegno Prize from the University of Athens for his study "President Capodistrias as a Propagator of Education in Greece." This was the first time that a Jew had been awarded such a high honor in Greece. In 1909 he published *Examination of the Assuan and Elephantine Aramaic Papyri*.

He eventually returned to Greece. From 1929 to 1930 he taught Jewish studies at Aristotle University, Salonika.

[Yitzchak Kerem (2nd ed.)]

BELLISON, SIMEON (1881–1953), clarinetist. Bellison studied first with his father and then, from 1894 to 1901, in the Moscow Conservatory with J. Friedrich. He performed from the age of nine and organized his own ensembles. Bellison played first clarinet in the Moscow Opera Orchestra (1904–14) and the Petrograd Opera Orchestra (1915). He served in the Russian army during the Russo-Japanese War and WWI. Bellison organized the Zimro woodwind ensemble (1918), which went on tour in Asia and the U.S. In 1920 he joined the New

York Philharmonic Orchestra as first clarinetist (until 1948). He transcribed many Jewish compositions for his ensemble. The Bellison archives and a collection of his instruments are housed at the Rubin Academy of Music, Jerusalem.

BIBLIOGRAPHY: P. Weston, *More Clarinet Virtuosi of the Past.* (1977), 45–7

BELLOW, SAUL (1915–2005), U.S. novelist. Author of 11 novels and numerous novellas and stories, Pulitzer Prize winner for *Humboldt's Gift* (1975), Nobel Prize winner for literature in 1976, and the only novelist to win three National Book Awards, for *The Adventures of Augie March* (1953), *Herzog* (1964), and *Mr. Sammler's Planet* (1970), Bellow brilliantly captured the Jewish-American experience and voice of the mid-20th century.

Born Solomon Bellow, the youngest of four children of Abraham (Abram) and Liza (Lescha) Belo, Russian Jewish immigrants to Canada, Bellow changed his name as the Bellows assimilated, from Shloimke to Solomon to Sol to Saul. He was born in Lachine, Quebec, two years after his family immigrated to Canada, and was raised in Montreal and Chicago, Illinois. He spoke fluent Yiddish, French, and English as a child, and studied Hebrew. Bellow's trilingual childhood is evident in Bellow's vivid stylistic mix of high and low registers, of classical English and the uniquely Jewish dialect of his Chicago childhood.

The Bellows, owing to poverty and Abram's troubles with the law as a result of his bootlegging, moved to Chicago when Saul was nine. Bellow later in life had a nostalgic love for the Chicago of his youth, and he explored Chicago's history, diverse ethnic cultures, unique American dialect, and Jewish immigrant society in much of his literature. In his later works he contrasted his nostalgia for the Chicago of his youth with his mounting anxiety concerning what he saw as the city's rapid urban decay. This concern may help account for his growing conservatism, which was a dominant theme of such later books as *Mr. Sammler's Planet* (1970), in which Bellow brought together, through the Holocaust survivor Sammler, the Shoah and his dark satirical rejection of 1960s radicalism. His conservatism can also be seen in *The Dean's December* (1982), Bellow's depiction of contemporary Chicago as a violent, barbaric dystopia.

Bellow's religious childhood had a profound impact on his works, for Jewish American issues and culture permeate his novels. His religiously observant mother had hopes that he would become a rabbi or talmudic scholar; at four he could recite whole passages from the Torah in Hebrew or Yiddish. Bellow used both vernacular Yiddish and Yiddish cadences and syntax throughout his works. In early works such as *The Adventures of Augie March* and later works such as "Cousins" from his short story collection *Him with His Foot in His Mouth* (1984), Bellow also depicted Jewish immigrant family life with vividness and affection. In his use of Jewish irony and humor and in his introspective, morally focused protagonists, Bellow is recognizably a Jewish writer. He referred to his Jewish upbringing as a literary "gift, a piece of good fortune with which one doesn't quarrel." Nevertheless, he rejected the label "Jewish American author," preferring to say that he was "an American, a Jew, a writer by trade," perhaps due to a fear that being identified as too Jewish would relegate him to a literary ghetto. Bellow was not religiously observant as an adult. Nonetheless, he never denied his Jewishness, and he spoke out in support of oppressed Jews in the Soviet Union and against antisemitism everywhere, spoke often to Jewish groups, and visited Israel often, including going to Israel in 1967 to report on the imminent war. Bellow went to Israel again in 1970 and in 1976, eventually writing about his experiences there and about the global political problems facing Israel in his well-reviewed nonfiction book *To Jerusalem and Back* (1976).

Jewish themes are central to many of Bellow's major works, as are autobiographical elements. For example, Bellow's Kafkaesque *The Victim* (1947) is an original treatment of the theme of antisemitism and the first of his attempts to confront the meaning of the Holocaust, with the secular Jewish protagonist Asa Leventhal confronted by the antisemitic Kirby Allbee; his award-winning *The Adventures of Augie March* (1953) is a picaresque novel about the adventures of a Jewish boy from Chicago during the Depression of the 1930s. In his powerful novella *The Bellarosa Connection* (1990), Bellow told the story of a Holocaust survivor while at the same time delved into Jewish issues of memory and the ethical and psychological problems faced by American Jews living safe lives while their European brothers suffered and died. Bellow's final novel *Ravelstein* (2000), a moving fictionalized treatment of his friendship with the conservative Jewish intellectual, Allan *Bloom, author of the controversial *The Closing of the American Mind*, is also arguably Bellow's most overtly Jewish novel, with discussions concerning the Holocaust, Jewish history and identity, Israel, and the fate of the Jewish people.

While his father and brothers were business-minded, Bellow was always more interested in books and culture, and this conflict between pragmatism and idealism, the real world and the inner or ideal world, is central to much of his fiction. Bellow was introspective and death-obsessed from an early age, partly due to childhood illnesses including six months spent in the tuberculosis ward at Royal Victoria Hospital when he was eight, where he saw many die and came near death himself. He later described his mother's early death when he was 18 as the greatest loss in his life; fears of death and loss thus dominate much of Bellow's canon. His early loss of his mother may also help to explain his problematic relationship to women, including his five marriages and four unpleasant divorces, themes that reoccur throughout his novels.

Bellow entered the University of Chicago in 1934, but transferred the following year to Northwestern, where he studied anthropology with Melville Herskovits. Upon graduation in 1937, Bellow entered the University of Wisconsin to pursue a graduate degree in sociology and anthropology, but soon left to marry his first wife, Anita Goshkin, and then left for New York to become a writer. The Bellows quickly returned to Chicago. In 1940 he and his wife traveled to Mexico with the hopes of meeting his boyhood hero, Leon Trotsky, only to discover that Trotsky had been killed the day before they arrived. Bellow's early attempts at writing novels proved frustrating. He abandoned an early novel set in Mexico and threw away the manuscript for *The Very Dark Trees*, a novel about a Southern white man turning black, after the publisher for the book canceled its publication for the duration of the war.

Bellow wrote his first published novel, the semi-autobiographical *Dangling Man* (1944), while waiting to enter the army. During this period Bellow's first marriage began to collapse while he waited to be conscripted (he finally joined the merchant marines toward the end of the war) and worked at various jobs, including three years (1943–46) on the editorial staff of the *Encyclopaedia Britannica*. In *Dangling Man*, the Kafka-inspired protagonist, Joseph, a young Jewish would-be writer, waits to be drafted as he experiences Romantic isolation, studies classic writers, has an affair, and suffers from death anxieties and emotional turmoil. In this way Bellow set the pattern for many of his major works, works focused on semi-autobiographical, introspective, intellectual, Jewish protagonists searching for meaning in a savage, irrational universe.

Bellow followed *Dangling Man* with *The Victim* (1947) and with *The Adventures of Augie March* (1953), which Salman Rushdie referred to as the best candidate there was for the Great American Novel. Bellow then published *Seize the Day* (1956), a study of loneliness, failure, and the onset of middle age, and *Henderson the Rain King* (1959), an excursion into the fantastic about a wealthy American's search for ultimate reality among primitive African tribesmen. Bellow's most widely acclaimed work was *Herzog* (1964), an international best seller that gained Bellow fame and numerous awards. Its protagonist, Moses Herzog, is a ruminating, near-mad Jewish professor who writes letters to everyone, including dead relatives, Jung, Nietzsche, and God. Herzog struggles comically but futilely to relate with humanistic values to a dehumanized modern world; like all Bellow's protagonists, he is doomed to live out the contradiction between an inner world of romantic aspiration and an outer one of less than romantic fact.

Bellow was a prolific writer throughout his life, publishing his first play, *The Last Analysis*, in 1964; a volume of short stories, *Mosby's Memoirs and Other Stories* (1968); *Mr. Sammler's Planet* (1970); *Humboldt's Gift* (1975), after which he was awarded the Nobel Prize for literature for 1976; *To Jerusalem and Back* (1976); The *Dean's December* (1982); a short story collection, *Him with His Foot in His Mouth* (1984); *More Die of Heartbreak* (1987); a collection of three novellas, *Something to Remember Me By* (1991); an essay collection, *It All Adds Up* (1994); *The Actual* (1997); and *Ravelstein* (2000). He also edited *Great Jewish Short Stories* (1963). Bellow led a largely itinerant life, moving from university to university as he moved from marriage to marriage; however, he did remain married to his final wife Janis for the last 16 years of his life, and was a professor for the Committee on Social Thought at the University of Chicago from 1962 to 1993. He also maintained close friendships with a large number of Jewish friends from Tuley High School in Chicago and with such eminent writers as Ralph Ellison, John Berryman, Allan Bloom, John Cheever, Philip *Roth, and the Jewish poet Delmore *Schwartz, the model for Von Humboldt Fleisher of *Humboldt's Gift*. Widely considered one of mid-century America's leading novelists, Bellow died leaving behind a powerful canon of literature.

BIBLIOGRAPHY: J. Atlas, *Bellow: A Biography* (2000); J.J. Clayton, *Saul Bellow: In Defense of Man* (1968); I. Malin (ed.), *Saul Bellow and the Critics* (1967); idem, *Saul Bellow's Fiction* (1969); K.M. Opdahl, *The Novels of Saul Bellow: An Introduction* (1967); E. Rovit (ed.), *Saul Bellow: A Collection of Critical Essays* (1975).

[Craig Svonkin (2nd ed.)]

BELMONT, AUGUST (1816–1890), U.S. banker, diplomat, and politician. Belmont was born in Alzey (Hesse), but claimed descent from the distinguished *Belmonte family of Portugal. His enemies later circulated the story that his original name was Schoenberg. He began his career as an apprentice in the Frankfurt banking house of *Rothschild and was soon transferred to the Naples office, where he conducted the Rothschilds' financial negotiations, including those with the Vatican. After an assignment to Havana, Cuba, in 1837, Belmont served the Rothschild interests in New York. Later he opened his own banking house, August Belmont & Co., which continued to represent the Rothschilds in the United States until the beginning of the 20th century. In 1844 he was appointed honorary Austrian consul general in New York, but resigned in 1850 in protest against the Vienna regime's brutal treatment of the Hungarian rebels, particularly their leader, Louis Kossuth. Belmont represented the United States at The Hague as chargé d'affaires (1853–55), and as minister (1855–58). At the conclusion of his foreign service, Belmont returned to New York and became active in political life. He supported the Union during the Civil War and raised and equipped the first German-born regiment in New York. He enlisted the support of European bankers and merchants for the Union cause during visits to Europe in 1861 and 1863. As Democratic National Committee chairman from 1860 until his retirement from politics in 1872, he exercised great influence in his party and American society. He became the founder of the U.S. Racing Club. One of America's best-known racetracks bears his name. Belmont severed his Jewish ties and married the daughter of Commodore Matthew C. Perry. One son, PERRY (1850–1947), became a lawyer, diplomat, congressman, and an author on United States history and politics. The other, AUGUST (1853–1924), succeeded his father as head of the bank, and played an important role in financing public transportation in the United States.

BIBLIOGRAPHY: R.J.H. Gottheil, *The Belmont-Belmonte Family* (1917), 173–5; I. Katz, *August Belmont…* (1968).

[Joachim O. Ronall]

BELMONTE, town in northern Portugal near the Spanish frontier. Its medieval community is seldom mentioned in the contemporary records, but there is preserved a Hebrew synagogal inscription of 1296–97, probably originally intended to be placed above the synagogue Ark. After the forced conversion of the Jews in Portugal at the end of the 15th century, Belmonte became a major center of New Christian life. A number of well-known families of the Crypto-Jewish Diaspora bearing this name originally derive from this place. It was here that S. Schwarz first established contact with the surviving Crypto-Jews in 1917. The Crypto-Jewish traditions have been more faithfully preserved here than in any other place in Portugal. Reforms that were introduced by Pombal may have caused paradoxically a decline in Crypto-Jewish practices, although prejudice against the descendants of the New Christians persisted in Portugal. In Belmonte, Crypto-Jewish identity remained very strong. During the 19th century there is evidence that some Jews were aware of the existence of New Christians who considered themselves Jewish or felt a certain affinity towards Jews and Judaism. Some scholars at that time, such as M. Kayserling and J. Latouche, drew attention to this fact. The newly established Jewish community in Lisbon showed little interest in New Christians who visited their synagogue. Arthur Carlos de Barros Basto, a New Christian who was a high-ranking officer in the army, found no warmth there. In 1912, after his visit in Portugal, Nahum Slousch reported that many in Portugal led Jewish lives in secret. It was Schwarz, however, who discovered the Crypto-Jews of Portugal, and especially those of Belmonte. He wrote a full and emotional account of his encounter with the Belmonte Crypto-Jews in his book, published in 1925. Schwarz made efforts to have the Crypto-Jews of Belmonte and others return officially to Judaism. Several Jewish organizations, such as the Alliance Israélite Universelle, and individual Jews like Cecil Roth and Lucien Wolf, joined these efforts with enthusiasm. Barros Basto, who returned to Judaism, and Schwarz at first cooperated but finally ended up as bitter rivals. In 1989 the Jewish Community of Belmonte was officially established. In 1996 the Bet Eliahu synagogue was inaugurated. The return of some Crypto-Jews to normative Judaism was no simple matter, since the rabbis who came to instruct and guide them brought normative Judaism as a definitive alternative to the entire body of practices, prayers, and beliefs that had been considered as authentic Judaism practiced in secret.

BIBLIOGRAPHY: Roth, Marranos, index; A. Novinsky and A. Paulo, in: *Commentary* (May, 1967), 76–81; S. Schwarz, *Os Christãos-Novos em Portugal no século XX* (1925), 9–12 (Heb. trans. with intro. and notes by D. Stuczynski, 2005); idem, *Inscrições hebráicas em Portugal* (1923), 23–28; N. Slouschz, *Ha-Anusim be-Portugal* (1932), 94–99; ESN, 1 (1949), 59. **ADD. BIBLIOGRAPHY:** F.A.A. Mourâo, "Um caso de persistência socio-cultural," *Revista de História* (São Paulo), 56 (1977), 589–96; A. Paulo, I. Steinhardt, and A. Kasselman, "The Hidden Jews of Belmonte," in: *Jewish Chronicle Colour Magazine* (March 17, 1978), 6–19; D.A. Canelo, *The Last Crypto-Jews of Portugal,* trans. W. Talmon-l'Armee, (1990); J. Adler, "The Road Back," in: *Jewish Chronicle Magazine* (March 22, 1991), 26–30.

[Cecil Roth / Yom Tov Assis (2nd ed.)]

BELMONTE, Dutch Sephardi family of poets and diplomats of Marrano extraction. The first member of the family to figure in Jewish life was JACOB ISRAEL (1570–1629). Born in Madeira as a Marrano under the name of Diego Nuñez Belmonte, he was one of the founding members of the Amsterdam Jewish community. According to Daniel Levi (Miguel) de *Barrios, he wrote a satire in Spanish directed against the Inquisition and a poem on Job, both now lost. His son MOSES (17th century) drew and engraved a portrait of his mother Simḥah (Gimar) Vaz. It is impossible to establish their family relationship with ISAAC NUÑEZ (alias MANUEL) BELMONTE (d. 1705), a wealthy merchant who served from 1664 as Spanish agent general in the Netherlands and from 1674 as resident minister or consul. In 1684/5 his community dues amounted to 50 fl, making him sixth in the taxpayers list. In 1693 be was created count palatine by Emperor Leopold III, while at the same time the king of Spain conferred on him the title of baron. In 1676 Isaac Nuñez Belmonte founded a poetic society in Amsterdam, the *Academia de los Sitibundos* and in 1685 the *Academia de los Floridos*. Meetings of the *Academia* were held in his mansion. In 1684 he was appointed one of the two deputies to represent the Sephardi community in cases before the Dutch authorities. From 1700 he lived in the splendid house now at 586 Herengracht. He wrote two poems in memory of the Crypto-Jew Abraham Bernal, who was burned in the auto de fé in Córdoba in 1655. He was *parnas* of the community on and off between 1697 and 1704 and also served as a member of the committee for the redemption of the captives. Unmarried, he was succeeded after his death, both in his title and his diplomatic post, by his nephew Baron FRANCISCO (ISAAC) XIMENES (d. 1713) who, in turn, was followed by his son, MANUEL XIMENES (d. 1730) who died childless, and the title became extinct. JACOB ABRAHAM BELMONTE (alias Franz van Schoonenberg; b. 1757), Dutch diplomat, also was connected with this family, but it is impossible to establish the exact relationship. ISAAC NUÑEZ BELMONTE (18th–19th centuries), a scholar of Smyrna, presumably belonged to a branch of this family which had emigrated to Turkey. He was author of *Sha'ar ha-Melekh* (Salonika, 1771; Bruenn, 1801; Lemberg, 1859), a commentary on the first and second parts of Maimonides' *Mishneh Torah*.

BIBLIOGRAPHY: Brugmans-Frank, 1 (1940), 455; Roth, Marranos (1959), 304, 332, 337f.; J. Caro Baroja, *Los Judíos en la España moderna y contemporanea*, 2 (1961), 152; ESN, 1 (1949), 59; I. da Costa, *Israel en de Volken* (1848), 287; idem, *Noble Families among the Sephardic Jews* (1936), index; R.J.H. Gottheil, *The Belmont-Belmonte Family* (1917). **ADD. BIBLIOGRAPHY:** Y. Kaplan, *From Christianity to Judaism* (1989), index.

[Kenneth R. Scholberg]

BELOFF, MAX, BARON (1913–1999), English historian and political scientist. Beloff, who was born in London, graduated in modern history from Oxford in 1935. From 1939 he taught history at Manchester University and returned to Oxford in 1946 as reader in the comparative study of institutions. During World War II he served in the Royal Signal Corps. In 1957 he became professor of government and public administration at Oxford and a fellow of All Souls' College. The author of numerous works on European history, American government, and Soviet foreign policy, Beloff also wrote extensively about developments in contemporary international relations, particularly concerning Western Europe after World War II. In *The United States and the Unity of Europe* (1963) he considered the prospects of European unity and the interdependence of Western Europe and the U.S. Two works on Soviet foreign policy, *The Foreign Policy of Soviet Russia 1929–41* (1947–49) and *Soviet Policy in the Far East 1944–51* (1953) were among the pioneering attempts to present a documentary and historical assessment of the Soviet Union's role and aims in international politics and are considered standard works in this field. Beloff's studies of American government, including *The American Federal Government* (1959), concentrated on the historical roots of American federalism and how its evolution shaped the structure and functioning of contemporary American politics and institutions. Among his other works are: *The Age of Absolutism, 1680–1815* (1954); *Europe and the Europeans...* (1957), a report prepared at the request of the Council of Europe; *The Great Powers: Essays in 20th Century Politics* (1959); and *The Balance of Power* (1967). In 1992 Beloff produced an autobiography, *An Historian in the Twentieth Century.* In the early 1970s Beloff was instrumental in founding University College, Buckingham, Britain's only purely private university, and served as its principal from 1974 to 1979. An outspoken Conservative, Beloff was knighted in 1980 and given a life peerage by Margaret Thatcher in 1981.

His sister NORA BELOFF (1919–1997), political correspondent of *The Observer* in 1964–76, was the first woman political correspondent of a Fleet Street newspaper. A brother, JOHN BELOFF (b. 1920), became probably the best-known serious investigator of parapsychological phenomenon in Britain, and is the author of *The Existence of Mind* (1962) and *Parapsychology: A Concise History* (1993). Another sister married the Nobel Prize-winning scientist Sir Ernest *Chain.

ADD. BIBLIOGRAPHY: ODNB online, s.v. "Sir Max Beloff" and "Nora Beloff."

[Brian Knei-Paz (Knapheis) / William D. Rubinstein (2nd ed.)]

BELORUSSIA, territory located between the rivers Neman (west) and Dnieper (east) and the rivers Pripet (south) and Dvina (north). Between the 14th and 18th centuries part of *Poland-Lithuania, from the partitions of Poland (1772–95) until the 1917 revolution it was part of the "northwestern region" of Russia, and much of it was included in the three "guberniyas" (provinces) of Minsk, Mogilev, and Vitebsk. Under Soviet rule Belorussia became a political entity as the Belorussian Soviet Socialist Republic. After the dissolution of the Soviet Union, the area was called Belarus and was a C.I.S. republic.

Up to Soviet Rule

In Jewish history Belorussia is part of "Lita" (Lithuania), its Jews being considered "Litvaks." Jewish merchants apparently first visited Belorussia in transit between Poland and Russia as early as the 15th century. Jews were acting as toll collectors in Nowogrodek (1445), *Minsk (1489), and *Smolensk (1489). In 1495 the Jews in Belorussia were included in the expulsion of Lithuanian Jewry, returning with it in 1503. As large-scale farmers of customs dues and wealthy merchants, Jews from *Brest-Litovsk played an important role in the development of Belorussia. Their agents were often the pioneers of the communities of Belorussia. A community was established in *Pinsk in 1506. By 1539 Jews had settled in *Kletsk and Nowogrodek, and subsequently in Minsk, *Polotsk, *Vitebsk, *Mogilev, and *Orsha. The Christian citizenry consistently opposed the permanent settlement of Jews within the areas of the cities and towns under municipal jurisdiction. In Vitebsk, for instance, Jews were not granted permission to build a synagogue until 1630. Within the framework of the Council of Lithuania (see *Councils of the Lands), Pinsk was one of the three original principal communities; most of the communities in Belorussia came under the jurisdiction of the Brest-Litovsk community, while several were subject to that of the Pinsk community. In 1692 the *Slutsk community achieved the status of a principal community. Smaller communities also grew up under the protection of landowners who rented their towns, villages, taverns, or inns to Jewish contractors (see *Arenda). These made constant attempts to break away from the jurisdiction of older communities and manage their communal affairs independently.

Until the partitions of Poland the communities in Belorussia were constantly exposed to the danger of Russian incursions, which were accompanied by wholesale massacres and forced conversions. Such events occurred in 1563 in Polotsk, and in many other communities between 1648 and 1655.

The relative strength of the Belorussian communities in the middle of the 18th century is shown by the amounts levied on them as listed in the tax register of the Council of Lithuania for 1761: for the communities in the eastern part of Belorussia, 16,500 zlotys; Polotsk and environs, 3,000 zlotys; the area around Minsk (including 40 small communities), 4,260 zlotys; Slutsk and its environs, 2,420 zlotys; Druya and its environs, 750 zlotys; Nowogrodek, 300 zlotys. According to the government census of 1766, there were 62,800 taxpaying Jews living in Belorussia, forming 40% of Lithuanian Jewry. The largest communities were in Minsk (1,396 Jewish inhabitants) and Pinsk (1,350).

After Belorussia passed to Russia in the late 18th century, *Shklov became an important commercial center on the route between Russia and Western Europe. Although a small group of Jews acquired wealth as building contractors, army suppliers, and large-scale merchants, the vast majority of Jews in the region of Belorussia were relatively destitute. Nevertheless, their numbers grew. There were 225,725 Jews living in the three "guberniyas" of Belorussia in 1847, and 724,548 in 1897

(13.6% of the total population), forming the majority in the principal cities of the region. There were 47,561 Jews in Minsk (52.3% of the total population); 34,420 in Vitebsk (52.4%); 32,369 in *Daugavpils (46.6%); 21,539 in Mogilev (50%); 21,065 in Pinsk (74.2%); 20,759 in *Bobruisk (60.5%); and 20,385 in *Gomel (54.8%). The Jews in the cities and townships of Belorussia had associations with the village and rural economy in a variety of ways. Both the wealthy and poorer Jews engaged in the development and trade of forest industries, and established small- or medium-sized timber enterprises. They also developed leather and allied industries on a similar scale. Another Belorussian Jewish occupation was peddling combined with the buying up of village produce, such as flax, hemp, and bristles, which the Jewish peddler sold to Jewish merchants who exported these commodities to the West. Because of the prevailing conditions of poverty, large numbers of Jews emigrated from Belorussia to the Ukraine or southern Russia, and, from the 1880s, to the United States.

In the cultural sphere, the Jews of Belorussia were influenced by the centers in Vilna, Volhynia, and Podolia. In general the *Mitnaggedim* trend predominated in the north and west of the region. Most of the celebrated Lithuanian yeshivot were in Belorussia, those of *Volozhin and *Mir, among others. Ḥasidism penetrated Belorussia from the south. Two of the fathers of Ḥasidism, *Menahem Mendel of Vitebsk and *Shneur Zalman of Lyady, were active there. Belorussia was the cradle of *Ḥabad Ḥasidism. In southern Belorussia the influence of the ḥasidic rabbis of the *Karlin and *Stolin dynasties was strong. By the mid-19th century Haskalah penetrated the larger towns from Vilna. The pogroms in Russia from 1881 to 1883 did not spread to Belorussia. The Ḥovevei Zion found adherents mainly in the larger and average-size communities. Toward the end of the 19th century Zionism and the Bund movement began to spread among Belorussian Jewry. Zionism found its main adherents among middle-class professionals and white-collar workers or working men from the ranks of traditional Judaism. It was in Belorussia that Labor Zionism originated, its centers being Minsk, Bobruisk, Gomel, and Vitebsk. The second convention of Russian Zionists was held in Minsk in 1902. The Bund won converts mainly among Jewish artisans and workers, but also among radicals of the intelligentsia. During the revolution of 1905 the Bund headed the revolutionary movement in Belorussia. Self-defense organizations to protect the Jews during the wave of pogroms in this period were established by the Bund and Labor Zionists in every town in the region. The first move toward organized Jewish self-defense was made to combat a gang of rioters in Gomel in the fall of 1903. As a result, only a few communities in Belorussia experienced harm.

The revolution precipitated far-reaching changes in the internal life of the Jews of Belorussia which contributed to the breakup of traditional Jewish social and spiritual patterns and loyalties. Zionism resulted in the development of modernized *ḥadarim* and Hebrew schools. After the outbreak of World War I a stream of refugees and émigrés from Poland and Lithuania passed through Belorussia, and were warmly received by the Jews there. The 1917 February Revolution aroused great expectations among the Jewish public, and Jewish political parties emerged from underground. A number of Jewish journals were issued in Minsk, including the Zionist *Der Yid* and the Bundist *Der Veker*. In the Minsk district the Zionists received 65,400 votes in the elections to the All-Russian Constituent Assembly, with 16,270 votes cast for the Bund and the Mensheviks. After the October Revolution and the Peace of Brest-Litovsk, Belorussia became a battlefield between the Red Army and the Polish army. The Jewish communities suffered severely both from general wartime conditions and from attacks by the Polish Army when Jews were killed indiscriminately on the charge of spying and helping the Red forces. The victims of these atrocities included 35 Jews in Pinsk in April 1919. Russian volunteers under the command of General Bulak-Balakhovich terrorized the Jews in the small towns and villages. After the Treaty of Riga in March 1921, Belorussia was divided between the Soviet Union and Poland.

Under Soviet Rule (until 1941)

During the first years of Soviet rule, the Jews of Belorussia found themselves in an exceptional situation. Among the Belorussian people, mainly poor and uneducated peasants, nationalist feelings were just beginning to crystallize. The anti-Jewish tradition, which poisoned relations between the Jews and non-Jews in Poland and the Ukraine, was little felt among the peasant masses of Belorussia. On the other hand, there were no cultural ties between the Belorussians and the Jews. The Jewish poet Samuel Plavnik (1886–1941), writing under the pseudonym Zmitrok *Byadulya, who was one of the creators of Belorussian literature even before the October Revolution was a rare phenomenon. The Jewish population in Belorussia existed in conditions conducive to a flourishing cultural and social life of its own. Relatively, the largest concentration of Jews in the Soviet Union was that of the Belorussian Republic, with a solidly based social structure and culture, Yiddish being its main language. According to the census of 1926, the 407,000 Jews in Belorussia formed 8.2% of the republic's total population. A considerable proportion of the urban population was Jewish. There were 53,686 Jews (40.8%) in Minsk; 37,745 (43.7%) in Gomel; 37,013 (37.5%) in Vitebsk; and 21,558 (42%) in Bobruisk. The Belorussian government, in its policy of reducing the predominance of the Russian language in towns, which was to no small extent a language used by the Jews, encouraged the use of Yiddish among the Jewish population. For some time the slogan "Workers of the World Unite!" was also inscribed in Yiddish, in addition to Belorussian, Russian, and Polish, on the emblem of the Belorussian Republic.

With the consolidation of the Soviet regime in Belorussia, the old economic structure of the Jewish population was overturned. The abolition of private trade and restrictions on small artisans created a large class of citizens "deprived of rights" ("*Lishentsi*"). Attempts to integrate these elements into the agricultural and industrial sectors failed to solve the problem. A partial solution was however achieved by the continuous Jewish emigration from Belorussia to the interior of Russia, especially to Moscow and Leningrad. According to the census of 1939, there were only 375,000 Jews living in Belorussia, and their proportion in the general population had decreased to 6.7%.

The *Yevsektsiya (Jewish section of the Communist Party) was particularly active in Belorussia in its violent campaign of propaganda and persecution against the Jewish religion and way of life and Jewish national solidarity. *Ḥadarim* and yeshivot were closed down, and synagogues turned to secular use. Yet, even in the late 1920s religious Jews still fought courageously for the right to publish *siddurim*, calendars, etc., and to maintain synagogues. *Ḥadarim* and yeshivot were maintained secretly. A relentless war was also waged on Zionism, which was deeply entrenched in Belorussia. Underground Zionist youth movements (*Kadimah, *Ha-Shomer ha-Ẓa'ir, *He-Ḥaluẓ) continued their activities in Belorussia until the late 1920s. It was only after repressive measures and systematic arrests that the movements were suppressed.

On the other hand, Jewish Communists attempted to create a framework for promoting a Soviet-inspired secular national-Jewish culture in Belorussia. A network of Jewish schools giving instruction in Yiddish was established, which, in 1932–33, was attended by 36,650 children, 55% of the Jewish children being of school age. A number of Yiddish newspapers were also established, the most important of which were the daily *Oktyaber* and the literary journal *Shtern*. In 1924 a Jewish department was established at the Institute of Belorussian Culture of Minsk, with philology, literature, and history sections. There was also an institute for Jewish teachers at the Belorussian University. In 1931 proceedings were conducted in Yiddish in ten Soviet law tribunals. A center for Yiddish literature was created in Minsk, of which the most outstanding members were the writers Izzie *Kharik, Moshe *Kulbak, and Selig *Axelrod. During the 1930s there was a sharp decline in this cultural activity with the abolition of the Yevsektsiya. The Jewish cultural and educational institutions gradually degenerated, and toward the end of this decade most were liquidated. The systematic "purge" of Jewish intellectuals in Belorussia also began in the late 1930s (Izzie Kharik and Moshe Kulbak in 1937, and Selig Axelrod in 1941).

Western Belorussia under Polish and Soviet Rule

In the western part of Belorussia, which was under Polish rule from 1920 to 1939, Jewish life developed along entirely different lines. The old economic order was maintained, and the Jews continued to engage in commerce and crafts, most living in great poverty. Jewish culture, however, was able to develop freely. *Ḥadarim* and yeshivot, including yeshivot whose members had fled from the Soviet sector, such as the yeshivah of Slutsk that transferred to Kletsk, continued to expand. A Hebrew school network (Tarbut, Yavneh) was established. The Zionist movement was well organized and many of the local youth joined Zionist bodies, from Ha-Shomer ha-Ẓa'ir to Betar. Many were also members of the illegal Communist movement which was rigorously repressed in this border region. Yiddish remained the spoken language of the Jewish masses and knowledge of Hebrew was widespread. In the cultural sphere the Jews of Western Belorussia looked to the important centers of Vilna, Brest-Litovsk, Bialystok, and Warsaw.

In September 1939, when western Belorussia was annexed by the Soviet Union, hundreds of thousands of Jews in whom religious and nationalist feelings were strong augmented the numbers of Belorussian Jewry already under Soviet rule. They also included groups of refugees from the Nazi-occupied zone. Even though the Soviet authorities immediately began to liquidate the practice of religion and the Zionist movement, signs of awakening were evident among the "older," "Soviet" Jews. In Bialystok a nucleus of Jewish writers and intellectuals was formed. The Hebrew schools were converted to Yiddish institutions. The higher authorities, however, were quick to liquidate this "reactionary evolution." Arrests of "bourgeois elements" and expulsions to the interior of Russia soon followed, and every effort was made to press forward with the liquidation and assimilation carried out over 20 years in eastern Belorussia. The German invasion of Belorussia in June 1941 interrupted this activity, then at its height. The Jews in Belorussia, most of whom had not succeeded in escaping eastward, were now caught in the trap of the Nazi occupation.

For their subsequent history, see *Russia, Holocaust Period, Contemporary Period; *Belarus.

BIBLIOGRAPHY: Dubnow, Hist Russ; N.P. Vakar, *Belorussia – the Making of a Nation* (1956); idem, *Bibliographical Guide to Belorussia* (1956); W. Ostrowski, *Anti-Semitism in Belorussia and its Origin* (1960); H. Shmeruk, *Ha-Kibbutz ha-Yehudi ve-ha-Hityashvut ha-Yehudit be-Belorussia ha-Sovietit – 1918–1932* (1961), Eng. summ.; *Vitebsk Amol* (Yid., 1956); *Slutzk and Vicinity* (Heb., Yid., Eng., 1962); *Sefer Bobruisk* (Heb., Yid., 1967); *Sefer Pinsk* (1969).

[Yehuda Slutsky]

BELOV, A. (pen name of **Abraham Joshua Elison**; 1911–2000), Soviet Russian writer, translator, and journalist. Belov was born in the town of Mogilev on the Dnieper. He received a traditional Jewish education before entering a Soviet public school. In 1927–28 he was a member of the underground Zionist youth organization and escaped arrest by moving to Leningrad. In 1933–36 he studied at the Leningrad Conservatory. From 1932 he contributed to Soviet periodicals and in 1934–49 he was on the staff of *Leningradskaya pravda*. He was fired from the newspaper during the campaign against the "cosmopolitans." After World War II Belov coauthored several volumes of popular history that were translated into a number of languages. Together with the semitologist L. Vilsker (1919–88) he translated works from the Syrian (Aramaic) and Hebrew languages. His translations of Israeli writers are collected in *Rasskazy izrailskikh pisateley* ("Stories of Israeli Writers," 1965) and *Iskatel' zhemchuga* ("The Pearl Diver,"

1966). He was the only translator of *Shalom Aleichem from Hebrew into Russian (*Za granitsey i doma* ("At Home and Abroad") and *Shimele*, both in 1959). These were the first legal translations from Hebrew in the Soviet Union since 1923. In 1964 Belov published an essay on A. *Shlonsky's translation of Pushkin's *Eugeni Onegin* in an anthology called *Masterstvo perevoda* ("The Mastery of Translation"). He also translated from Yiddish. Publication of Belov's book on the trial of Adolf *Eichmann and his book on the Dead Sea were banned by the Party censor. The latter book was later published in Jerusalem as *Dno mira* ("The Bottom of the World," 1978).

Belov was one of the first teachers of Hebrew in Leningrad. From 1974 he lived in Israel. He continued to work as a translator, translating works by S.Y. *Agnon, Y. *Burla, A. *Meged, and others into Russian. He also worked as a journalist and published 153 letters written to him by Shlonsky and B. *Gaponov. In 1990 his memoirs were published in a Hebrew translation as *Eikh hayiti kushi* ("How I Was a Blackamoor"). In 1998 he published his book on Hebrew writers, poets, journalists, scholars, and teachers in the Soviet Union under the title *Rytsari ivrita v byvshem Sovetskom Soyuze* ("The Knights of Hebrew in the Former Soviet Union").

[Naftali Prat (2nd ed.)]

BELSHAZZAR (Heb. בֵּלְשַׁאצַּר, בֵּלְאשַׁצַּר; the Akkadian name *Bel-šar-uṣur,* "O Bel, guard the king"; LXX, Βαλτασάρ), son of *Nebuchadnezzar and the last king of Babylon, according to the Book of Daniel. The biblical account (Dan. 5) relates that Belshazzar gave a banquet for his high officials at which the wine was drunk from the sacred vessels captured by Nebuchadnezzar from the Temple in Jerusalem amid songs to the idols of gold, silver, etc. While they were thus engaged, a mysterious hand appeared and wrote on the wall words which none of the Chaldeans was able to read or interpret but which Daniel, on being summoned by the king, read as **Mene Mene, Tekel Upharsin*, and interpreted as a warning to Belshazzar of the impending downfall of his kingdom. That night Belshazzar was killed and was succeeded as world ruler by *Darius the Mede (5:30; 6:1). Two of Daniel's visions are dated as occurring in the first and third years of Belshazzar's reign (7:1; 8:1). While the details given in Daniel appear historically inaccurate, Babylonian texts mention a Bēl-šar-uṣur as the son, crown prince, and regent of *Nabonidus, the last king of Babylon (556–539 B.C.E.). In Nabonidus' absence, Babylon was captured by the armies of *Cyrus, king of Persia. Neither Nabonidus nor Belshazzar was directly descended from Nebuchadnezzar. Presumably because he was a regent, Belshazzar's name is coupled with that of Nabonidus in Babylonian prayer formulae (in the prayer for the king's health in I Bar. 1:11, it is coupled – unhistorically – not with Nabonidus but with Nebuchadnezzar) and in two legal documents (12th and 13th years of Nabonidus), where an oath is sworn by their lives. While the Greek historians Herodotus (1:191) and Xenophon (*Cyropaedia*, 3:5, 15) do not mention Belshazzar, they share with Dan. 6 the – hardly historical – tradition that the Babylonians were engaged in revelry at the time when the Persians entered the city (corresponding to the time when Belshazzar was killed in the biblical account).

In the *Aggadah*

Belshazzar is often linked in the *aggadah* with two of the other Babylonian rulers mentioned in the Bible, Nebuchadnezzar and *Evil-Merodach. Thus the "three-year-old heifer" that Abraham was commanded to offer up (Gen. 15:9) is said to be a reference to these three kings (Gen. R. 44). The occasion of Belshazzar's feast was his miscalculation that the "seventy years" (Jer. 25:11–13) of exile before the redemption had passed without any sign of God's help to His people, a calculation that he made from the date of Nebuchadnezzar's accession to the throne, instead of from the destruction of the Temple (Dan. 9:2; Meg. 11b). Darius and Cyrus were the doorkeepers of Belshazzar's chamber. On the night after he had seen the handwriting on the wall, the king commanded them to kill anyone who tried to enter, even if he should claim to be king. Belshazzar himself, however, had cause to leave the room during the night by a private entrance, and when he attempted to reenter through the usual entrance, Darius and Cyrus, in accordance with his own instructions, slew him (Song. R. 3:42).

In the Arts

Christian writers and artists of the Middle Ages saw in Belshazzar a prefiguration of the antichrist. Belshazzar's feast is described in the *Ordo Prophetarum*, a medieval mystery cycle, in the section dealing with the prophet Daniel. From Renaissance times onward, however, the theological aspect of the story faded, and its dramatic and spectacular character was invariably emphasized. The great Spanish playwright Pedro Calderón de la Barca (1600–1681) devoted one of his innumerable *autos sacramentales* to the theme, his *La Cena de Baltasar* (written c. 1634), combining fine poetry with excellent stagecraft. In England Hannah More included a *Belshazzar* in her *Sacred Dramas* (1782); Lord *Byron wrote the poem "Vision of Belshazzar" (in his *Hebrew Melodies*, 1815); and the poet and historian Henry Hart Milman, who became dean of St. Paul's Cathedral, produced *Belshazzar; a Dramatic Poem* (1822), a melodramatic verse-play not intended for the stage. Another English work inspired by the biblical story was *The Impious Feast* (1828), a poem by Robert Eyres Landor. Lord Byron's interpretation is said to have inspired the poem *Belsazar,* one of the earliest works of Heinrich *Heine, which appeared in his *Buch der Lieder* (1827). Another writer who dealt with the theme was the Spanish playwright and novelist Gertrudis Gómez de Avellaneda, author of the romantic tragedy *Baltasar* (1858).

In the visual arts treatment of the Belshazzar episode followed the same pattern as in literature. The antichrist interpretation occurs in medieval manuscript illumination, notably the 11th-century *Saint-Sever Apocalypse*, and in sculpture at Vézelay, France (12th century), and Amiens and Magdeburg (13th century). By contrast, the spectacular aspect is dominant in later painting, notably the dramatic portrayal by *Rembrandt (1634).

The biblical story has also inspired orchestral and vocal music. Handel's powerful oratorio *Belshazzar* (1745; text by Charles Jennens) did not deter later composers from attempting versions of their own. The most successful of these was William Walton's oratorio *Belshazzar's Feast* (1931; text arranged by Osbert Sitwell). Other treatments of the theme were Sibelius' *Belsazars gästabud* (1906), written as incidental music to a drama by the Finnish-Swedish poet Hjalmar Procopé and reworked as an orchestral suite in 1907; and a setting of Heine's *Belsazar* by Bernard van Dieren (1884–1936). The incidental music to a play on the theme which Joseph *Achron composed in 1928 was later reworked as two tableaux for large orchestra.

[Bathja Bayer]

BIBLIOGRAPHY: IN THE BIBLE: J.A. Montgomery, *Daniel* (ICC, 1949[2]), 66, 261; R.P. Dougherty, *Nabonidus and Belshazzar* (1929), passim; H.L. Ginsberg, *Studies in Daniel* (1948), 25–26. IN THE ARTS: L. Réau, *Iconographie de l'art chrétien*, 2 pt. 1 (1956), 408–9; Sendrey, Music, nos. 7504, 9083.

BELTESHAZZAR (Heb. and Aram. בֵּלְטְשַׁאצַּר; בֵּלְטְאשַׁצַּר; LXX, Βαλτασάρ; Vulg., Baltassar), name given to *Daniel in Babylonia (Dan. 1:7). Foreigners introduced into court life were often given native names; e.g., in Egypt *Joseph became known as Zaphenath-Paneah (Gen. 41:45). Popular etymology related the name Belteshazzar to Bel (Dan. 4:5) but it probably derived from *Balaṭ-šarri-uṣur* ("Protect the life of the king").

BIBLIOGRAPHY: J.A. Montgomery, *The Book of Daniel* (ICC, 1949[2]), 123; W. Baumgartner, *Hebraeisches und aramaeisches Lexikon zum Alten Testament* (1967), 127.

[Bezalel Porten]

BELTSY (Rum. **Bălti**), city in Bessarabia, Moldova; in Romania 1918–40 and 1941–44. Jews were invited there in 1779 when an urban nucleus was formed in the village. Their rights and obligations were established by an agreement in 1782. By 1817 there were 244 Jewish families living in Beltsy. The community subsequently increased through immigration; after the *May Laws were issued in 1882, many Jews expelled from neighboring villages settled in Beltsy. The community numbered 3,124 in 1864 and had grown to 10,348 in 1897 (56% of the total population) even though Jewish domicile was limited by legislation and Jews were often expelled from the city as illegal residents. As an outcome of these expulsions, coupled with economic difficulties, many Jews from Beltsy emigrated toward the end of the 19th century, including a group who journeyed to Ereẓ Israel.

In 1847 a Jewish state school was opened in Beltsy. A *talmud torah*, founded in 1889, provided instruction in both Jewish and general subjects. By the 1930s Jewish educational institutions included a kindergarten, three elementary schools, and two secondary schools, for boys and girls. Welfare institutions included a hospital and old-age home. The Jews in Beltsy were mainly employed in commerce and crafts; some living in the vicinity engaged in agriculture. The 1,539 members of the local Jewish cooperative loan-bank in 1925 included 656 engaged in business, 441 in crafts, and 156 in agriculture. The Jewish population numbered 14,259 (46% of the total) in 1930. When Bessarabia became part of Soviet Russia in June 1940, the communal organization was disbanded.

[Eliyahu Feldman]

Holocaust Period and After

In June 1941 about two-thirds of the town's buildings were destroyed in German and Romanian air raids. The Jews fled to nearby villages, mainly to Vlad. On July 7 a gang of Vlad peasants seized homes sheltering the refugees, murdered the occupants, and set fire to the houses. The next day a group of Romanian soldiers encountered 50 Jews on the road to Beltsy, drove them into the swamps, and shot them to death. Beltsy was captured by the Germans on July 9 and those Jews who had returned were deported to a concentration camp. The same day 10 Jews who had been taken as hostages were executed. The Gestapo also asked the ghetto committee to furnish it with a list of 20 "Jewish communists" who were to be put to death. When they refused to do so, all the committee members, together with another group of 44 Jews, were forced to dig their own graves and shot. Twenty more Jews were shot by the Germans on July 16. On July 11, 1941, all surviving Jews were assembled in the courtyard of the Moldova Bank. Romanian troops transferred them to an internment camp in the Răuţel forest, some 7½ mi. (12 km.) from the town. Many of the inmates died from starvation and disease. By August 30, 1941, only 8,941 Jews were left in the entire district (compared to the 31,916 who resided there according to the 1930 census). They were concentrated in three camps, and later on all were deported to *Transnistria. Even the Jewish tombstones were removed from the cemetery in Beltsy to erase all traces of the Jewish inhabitants of the town. Jews returned to Beltsy after the war. The only synagogue was closed by the authorities in 1959 and the Jewish cemetery was badly neglected. In 1962 militia broke into a house where Jews had assembled for prayer; those attending were taken to the public square where communist youth had been gathered to jeer at them. Their children were expelled from school. The city has retained a certain Jewish character and Yiddish is often heard on its streets. Its estimated Jewish population in 1970 was 15,000 and 1,000 in the early 2000s.

[Jean Ancel]

BIBLIOGRAPHY: E. Schwarzfeld, *Din istoria evreilor ... in Moldova* (1914), 36–39; M. Carp, *Cartea Neagr*, 3 (1947), index; Feldman, in: *Sefer Yahadut Besarabyah* (in press); M. Mircu, *Pogromurile din Basarabia* (1947), 5, 17, 160.

BELY, VICTOR ARKADYEVICH (**Aronovich**; 1904–1983), composer and musicologist. Born in Berdichev, Bely studied at the Kharkov Conservatory (violin and composition, 1919–21) and at the Moscow Conservatory with G. Konyus and N. Myaskovsky (composition, 1922–29). From 1935 to 1948 he taught composition there. After working at the Minsk Conservatory in 1949–52 he returned to Moscow and became editor in chief of the Moscow journal *Muzykalnaya Zhizn*. He replaced his early expressionistic style through participation in *Prokoll* (the production collective) with poster-like music for revolutionary masses and then songs for the masses. A vocal piece, *Orlyonok* ("Young Eagle," 1936), was followed by successful war songs, including a popular "Ballad of Captain Gastello." His collection of songs won the Stalin Prize in 1952. Bely was awarded the titles of Honored Art Worker of the RSFSR and Honored Artist of the Belorussian SSR.

BIBLIOGRAPHY: Yu. Korev, *Bely* (1962); I. Mangur, *Viktor Bely* (1979); *Sovetskaya kultura*, (17 March 1983).

[Marina Rizarev (2nd ed.)]

BELZ, small town in the Lvov district, Ukraine (between the world wars, in Poland). The Jewish settlement in Belz dates from the beginning of the 15th century. About 200 Jews inhabiting 32 houses are recorded in 1550. Two hundred Jews died during the *Chmielnicki uprising in 1648–49 and 60 children subsequently during the Swedish invasion (1660). The community later revived and became famous as a center of Ḥasidism. The *rebbes* of the Rokeaḥ dynasty (see next entry) officiated as rabbis of the community. Other noted rabbis of Belz include Joshua *Falk, Joel *Sirkes, Zechariah *Mendel, and Jonah Te'omim. In 1921 the Jews numbered 2,104 (50.7% of the total population). In May 1942, during the Nazi occupation, there were 1,540 Jews in Belz. About 1,000 were deported to the Sobibor death camp via *Hrubieszow. The remaining Jews were put to work on farms and after the harvest were deported to Sobibor, also via Hrubieszow. In 1970, Jews were living in the town and there was one synagogue there, but there was no community by the early 21st century.

BIBLIOGRAPHY: *Bleter far Geshikhte*, 1–2 (1950), 78, table 5. **ADD. BIBLIOGRAPHY:** PK Ukrainah, s.v.

[Nathan Michael Gelber / Shmuel Spector (2nd ed.)]

BELZ, one of the most important ḥasidic dynasties of Galicia, so called after the township where it took up residence (see previous entry). The founder of the dynasty, SHALOM ROKE'AḤ (1779–1855), came from a distinguished family descended from R. Eleazer *Roke'aḥ of Amsterdam. Orphaned as a child, Shalom studied under his uncle, Issachar Baer of Sokal whose daughter he married. At Sokal he was introduced to ḥasidic teachings by Solomon of *Lutsk, a devoted follower of *Dov Baer, the *Maggid* of Mezhirech. Later Shalom became a disciple of *Jacob Isaac Horowitz, ha-Ḥozeh ("the Seer") of Lublin, Uri of *Strelisk, the *maggid* Israel of *Kozienice, and *Abraham Joshua Heschel of Apta. On the recommendation of Horowitz, Shalom was appointed rabbi in Belz. After Horowitz' death in 1815, Shalom was recognized as a *ẓaddik* as his following increased. He built a splendid *bet midrash* in Belz. Thousands of Ḥasidim flocked to him, including rabbis and well-known *ẓaddikim*, and Belz became the center of Galician Ḥasidism. Many legends tell of the miracles he performed. Shalom was also considered an authoritative talmudist; he stressed the importance of talmudic study and strengthened the principle of learning in Ḥasidism. Active in public affairs, he served as a spokesman for Galician Jewry, taking part in the struggle to improve the severe economic conditions, and opposing Haskalah. Excerpts from his teachings have been frequently quoted. They are collected, with legends and tales of his activities, in *Dover Shalom* (1910). Many of Shalom's descendants served as *ẓaddikim*, including his son-in-law ḤENIKH OF OLESKO and his son JOSHUA (1825–1894) who succeeded him. The latter provided Belz Ḥasidism with the organizational framework which maintained it as the focus of Ḥasidism in Galicia, and ruled his community strictly. One of the leaders of Orthodox Jewry in Galicia, he was prominent in the opposition to Haskalah. He initiated the establishment of the Maḥazikei ha-Dat organization and the Orthodox newspaper *Kol Maḥazikei ha-Dat.*. As a result of the cultural and social tensions in Galician Jewry, the Belz *ẓaddikim* adopted an extreme stand and resisted every new idea emanating from non-Orthodox circles. Some of Joshua's teachings are published in *Ohel Yehoshu'a* (printed with *Dover Shalom*, 1910). Joshua's successor ISSACHAR DOV (1854–1927) was greatly influenced by Aaron of Chernobyl although Aaron taught a form of Ḥasidism that differed radically from that of the Belz school. Issachar Dov was an exacting leader of Galician Orthodoxy and also headed the Maḥazikei ha-Dat. In particular he opposed the Agudat Israel and denounced any innovations. He strongly opposed Zionism in any form. In 1914, when the war front reached Belz, he fled to Hungary and lived in Újfehértó where he succeeded in winning many Hungarian Jews to Belz Ḥasidism. In 1918 he moved to Munkács (*Mukacevo) and became embroiled in a bitter quarrel with the *ẓaddik* of Munkács which gave rise to a voluminous exchange of polemics. In 1921 Issachar Dov returned to Galicia and settled first in Holschitz, near Jaroslaw, moving back to Belz in 1925.

His son and successor AARON (1880–1957) deviated little from the pattern set by his father. He lived an ascetic life, and instituted a lengthy order of prayers. The influence of Belz Ḥasidism had considerable impact on Jewish life in Galicia because its adherents entered all spheres of communal affairs and were not afraid of the effects of strife within the community. Many rabbis accepted the authority of the Belz *ẓaddikim*. In the parliamentary elections the Belz Ḥasidim did not join the Jewish lists, but voted for the Polish government party. On the outbreak of World War II, Aaron escaped to Sokol and then to Przemysl where 33 members of his family were murdered. After confinement in the ghettos of Vizhnitsa, Cracow, and Bochnia, he was sent to Kaschau (now *Kosice), then in Hungary, at the end of 1942 and subsequently to Budapest. In 1944 he managed to reach Ereẓ Israel. There he revised his political views and directed his followers to support the Agudat Israel. He established yeshivot and *battei midrash* throughout the country. His home in Tel Aviv became the new center for the followers of Belz Ḥasidism throughout the world. His grave is a place of pilgrimage where many gather on the anniversary of his death. He was succeeded by his nephew, ISSACHAR DOV (1948–), who established a *bet midrash* in Jerusalem and an independent *kashrut* system. Large numbers of Belz ḥasidim also inhabit the Boro Park section of Brooklyn, New York.

BIBLIOGRAPHY: L.I. Newman, *Hasidic Anthology* (1934), index; M.I. Guttman, *Rabbi Shalom mi-Belz* (1935); A.Y. Bromberg, *Mi-Gedolei ha-Ḥasidut*, 10 (1955); M. Prager, *Hazzalat ha-Rabbi mi-Belz mi-Gei ha-Haregah be-Polin* (1960); Y. Taub, *Lev Same'aḥ Ḥadash* (1963); N. Urtner, *Devar Ḥen* (1963); B. Landau and N. Urtner, *Ha-Rav ha-Kadosh mi-Belza* (1967); M. Rabinowicz, *Guide to Ḥassidism* (1960), 93–96.

[Itzhak Alfassi]

BELZBERG, SAMUEL (1928–), Canadian financier and philanthropist. Belzberg was born in Calgary to Abraham and Hilda, who immigrated to Canada from Poland in 1919. His father was clearly imbued with an entrepreneurial spirit. He moved from working on the floor of an abattoir to owning a secondhand furniture store and then successfully shifted into real estate. Samuel was clearly his father's son. Together with his brothers Hyman and William, he embarked on a remarkable and sometimes controversial career in business and finance. Basing himself in Edmonton, Belzberg first made money on oil leasing, and investing the proceeds in real estate, set up what would grow into First City Financial Corporation to finance the acquisitions. In 1968 he moved to Vancouver, where he expanded his finance and real estate holdings. In the rough-and-tumble world of corporate takeovers in the United States of the 1980s, Samuel and his brothers (elder brother Hyman remained in Calgary, while his brother William moved to the United States) scored a number of successes. First City Financial Corporation was, at its height in the 1980s, a powerhouse in the Canadian financial world valued at more than $5 billion. First City and Samuel Belzberg suffered reversals in the early 1990s. In a bitter and much publicized dispute with his two brothers, Samuel was forced out of the financially slumping business. Under the weight of enormous debt, the firm crashed as dramatically as it had soared. Samuel's subsequent business activities were relatively modest.

Paralleling his business rise, Belzberg was heavily involved in philanthropic and community activities in both Edmonton and Vancouver, with much emphasis on support for Jewish causes. In Vancouver, he made substantial donations of time and expertise to both Simon Fraser University (where he was honored with an honorary doctorate) and the University of British Columbia. He and his wife, Frances, established the Dystonia Medical Research Foundation in 1976, after their daughter Cheri was diagnosed with the genetic disease that disproportionately affects Ashkenazi Jews. The Belzbergs became friendly with Rabbi Marvin Hier when he served in Vancouver as rabbi in the Orthodox synagogue Schara Tzedeck. In 1977 Belzberg supported Hier in his establishment of the Simon Wiesenthal Center in Los Angeles and the Center's Museum of Tolerance, which opened in 1993. In 1988 Belzberg was appointed a member of the Order of Canada and in 2001 was promoted to officer in the Order. He married Frances Cooper, who was also a member of the Order of Canada for her efforts on behalf of dystonia research and an HIV Care Unit in Vancouver and for her active support of the Simon Wiesenthal Center.

[Richard Menkis (2nd ed.)]

BELZEC (Pol. **Bełżec**), one of the six Nazi death *camps in German-occupied Poland, situated in the southwest corner of the country on the Lublin–Lvov railway line. Between February and December 1942, close to half a million Jews were killed in its gas chambers by the German SS and their collaborators.

During the ten months of its operation, Belzec was the most lethal of all Nazi camps established in occupied Poland. The overwhelming number of those murdered there came from *Lublin and surrounding areas as well as from the provinces of *Cracow, *Lvov, *Stanislav (Stanislawow), and *Tarnopol – the heart of Galician Jewry. Victims also included Jews from Austria, Germany, and Czechoslovakia. Once the Nazis concluded that all the Jewish communities of *Galicia had been destroyed, they dismantled the death camp and tried to remove all traces of their crime.

Virtually no one brought to Belzec survived, and only two of its victims bore witness to the horrors that took place there. Rudolph Reder of Lublin was the lone survivor to give extended testimony; a second survivor, Chaim Hirszman, was murdered after his first day of testimony.

Unlike some other death camps, the Nazis situated Belzec in a relatively populated area, close to the heavily traveled railway line. Poles and Ukrainians in the area witnessed the systematic murder of Jews; they saw ghetto liquidations and trains arriving at the killing center. Poles lived in terror that the fate of the Jews could soon be theirs. With the scarcity of Jewish eyewitnesses local Poles became a valuable source for learning what occurred.

Belzec, together with *Treblinka and *Sobibor, were the three death camps that operated under the German codename *Aktion Reinhard*, devoted to murdering the Jews in General Gouvernement territory.

Belzec was first established as a forced labor camp for the Jewish and gypsy prisoners who worked on antitank ditches along the German-Soviet border in 1940. This was more than a year before Belzec assumed any role in the killing process. Later, when the killing center at Belzec became operational, these antitank ditches were used as mass graves.

During a conference held in Lublin on October 17, 1941, *SS-Brigadefuehrer* (Brigadier-General) Obidio Globocnik, who was assigned by Heinrich *Himmler to organize *Aktion Reinhard*, informed gathered Nazi officials about the decision to murder the Jews of the General Gouvernement. Within two weeks the first three SS men of the future camp crew arrived to Belzec and requested 20 workers from the local mayor. By

November 1, 1941, construction had begun on the Belzec killing center. The timing of the creation of Belzec coincided with the creation of *Chelmno, one of the six Nazi killing centers where murder by gassing became operational on December 8, 1941. Gassing was by mobile gas canisters of the same type that were built by SS men stationed at Belzec, which were used to kill mental patients in *Zamosc county in December–January 1941–42.

By the end of February 1942 about 120 Jews from Lubycza Krolewska had become the first victims of gassing at Belzec. Between March 17, 1942, and April 14, 1942, "the great action" of killing Jews began as some 70,000–75,000 Jews, most of them from Lublin and Lvov, were murdered. The first gassing installations consisted of three gas chambers located inside a small 26 × 13 foot barrack. The floor of the gas chamber and the walls were covered with tin and the door was made of hard wood to prevent it from being broken open from the inside. The pace of killing overwhelmed the camp's facilities, so on April 17 the gassing ceased, resuming only in the middle of May 1942 when transports from the Cracow district start arriving again to a functioning camp. Once again the speed of deportation outpaced the camp's facilities. So deportations were halted again and murder by gassing ceased in mid-June to permit the old gas chambers to be torn down and replaced with much larger and more efficient ones. They were made of brick and concrete with one door for entering the gas chambers and another for clearing out the bodies. The size of each gas chamber was 13 × 16 feet. At the entrance to the building was a sign: "Shower and Disinfection Room." Their capacity was 1,000–1,200 bodies at a time, or those incarcerated in ten freight cars of arriving prisoners.

By the second week of July deportations and the gassing that followed resumed, continuing uninterrupted until December when the gassing operations were halted. Work detachments of Jewish forced laborers excavated mass graves and burned the bodies to remove all evidence of the crime. When the work was completed, the Germans murdered virtually all surviving forced laborers at *Sobibor. Chaim Hirszman jumped from the train to Sobibor and survived until liberation. He was killed in Lublin, in 1945. A third escapee, Sylko Herc returned to Belzec, where he remained for 2–3 days before going to Cracow. His fate is not known.

In spring 1943–summer 1944, German officials and *Trawniki-trained auxiliaries plowed under the site of the Belzec camp, planted trees, and built a manor house nearby in order to conceal any traces of the killing center. At the end of July 1944, the Soviet Army overran Belzec

The staff of Belzec consisted of between 14 and 30 SS officials, many of whom were veterans of the T-4 operations: the murder of mentally retarded, physically infirm, and emotionally disturbed Germans, where the Nazis pioneered murder by gassing. Some 90–120 Trawniki-trained guards joined them. Trawniki was the camp where 2,500 captured Soviet soldiers and 2,200 civilians became police auxiliaries for the *Aktion Reinhard* killing centers. These troops worked throughout the camps and supported deportations throughout German-occupied Poland.

Christian Wirth, the commandant of Belzec, first developed the killing center. In 1942 Globocnik appointed him inspector of the SS Special Detachments with overall responsibility for the *Aktion Reinhard* camps. Nicknamed the "Wild Christian" by his fellow SS men, his "ideas" for Belzec were also used in Sobibor and Treblinka. He was suceeded as Belzec's commandant by Gottleib Hering in August 1942.

The design of the gas chambers is credited to SS-*Hauptscharfuehrer* (Master Sergeant) Lorenz Hackenholt, who first served as a mechanic in the T-4 program operating the mobile gas vans. After his experience at Belzec he constructed the gas chambers at Sobibor and Treblinka. The gas chambers were euphemistically called *Stiftung Hackenholt* (Hackenholt Foundation).

Only one Belzec official faced charges after the war, Wirth's deputy, Josef Oberhauer, a veteran of T-4, who supervised the construction of Belzec. In 1965 he was sentenced to four years and six months in prison.

Number of Victims

Until recently, historians cited 600,000 as the number of Jews killed at Belzec. First established in 1946, the figure was based on the prewar population of Jewish communities presumably deported to Belzec. Because this estimate does not account for Jews murdered in the ghetto deportation operations, or shot in other locations, it is too high.

To date, only one known document, a report dated January 11, 1943, from the coordinator of *Aktion Reinhard*, Hermann Hoefle, to SS-*Obersturmbannfuehrer* Adolf *Eichmann in Berlin, gives a specific figure for Jews killed in Belzec: 434,508. The report, intercepted by the British during World War II, and recently discovered as a declassified document, purports to be a statistical summary of the actual number of Jews arriving at Belzec up to December 31, 1942. It had been radioed on January 11, 1943, by Hoefle for the attention of SS-*Obersturmbannfuehrer* (Lieutenant Colonel) Franz Heim, commander of Security Police in Cracow, and to Eichmann, in Berlin.

As Rudolph Reder reported, there was no detailed count of Belzec's victims and some transports may even not have been included in Hoefle's figures. The Belzec Memorial estimates that the actual death toll for Jews at Belzec may have been as high as 500,000. Groups of non-Jewish Poles and Roma and Sinti were murdered at the Belzec death camp as well. Their number, according to testimonies, could range from dozens to several hundred, but a specific number could not be determined. Poles have argued that several of the Poles were killed for the "crime of saving Jews," but to date no evidence has been found to substantiate this claim.

Rudolph Reder, the only known survivor of Bełzec who lived to tell his story, escaped his captors in November 1942 when he was taken outside the camp by them.

Reder described the killing process as follows:

> Receiving of the train began. Dozens of SS men would open the wagons yelling "*Los!*" ("Get out!"). With whips and their rifle butts, they pushed people out. The doors of the wagon were a meter or more above the ground. Driven out by whips the people had to jump down: everybody, old and young; many broke their arms and legs falling down. They had to jump down to the ground. The children were mangled in the bedlam. Everybody pouring out – dirty, exhausted, terrified....
>
> With each transport it was the same as with the one that I arrived on. People were told to undress, leave their things in the courtyard.... People always showed a spark of hope in their eyes that they are going to work. But seconds later, babies were torn away from their mothers, the old and the sick were thrown on stretchers, and the men, little boys and girls were pushed with rifle butts further and further down the path.
>
> While the women were rounded up naked and shaved, whipped like cattle into a slaughterhouse, the men were already dying in the gas chambers. It took two hours to shave the women and two hours to murder them. Many SS men using whips and sharp bayonets pushed the women toward the building with the chambers.
>
> Then the askars [Trawniki-trained guards] counted out 750 persons per chamber....
>
> I heard the noise of sliding doors, moaning and screaming, desperate calls in Polish, Yiddish – blood-curdling screams. All that lasted 15 minutes.
>
> After the doors were closed, the Jews in the gas chambers realized what was about to happen with them and started to cry and scream. But after a few minutes everything went quiet. After 20 minutes the outer doors of the gas chambers were opened again and the corpses of the Jews were disposed of in the mass graves.

The *Sonderkommando* were Jewish prisoners who were selected to live in order to facilitate the camp's function as a killing center. They escorted the victims from the trains to the gas chambers and disposed of the bodies after the victims were murdered. The crucial tasks of the camp were restricted to the Germans. They alone decided "who shall live and who shall die." They started the diesel engines.

How did the *Sonderkommando* personnel, whom the Germans periodically murdered and replaced with new deportees, cope? Reder reported:

> We moved like automated figures, just one large mass of them. We just mechanically worked through our horrible existence ... Every day we died a little bit together with the transports of people.
>
> When I heard children calling [in the gas chamber]: "Mommy, haven't I been good? It's dark," my heart would break. Later we stopped having feelings.

Another valuable source of historical information was Kurt Gerstein, who was both a perpetrator and informant. An anti-Nazi by conviction, he nevertheless served as an SS-*Untersturmfuehrer* in the Technical Disinfections Department in the Hygienic Institute of the Waffen SS, working directly with Zyklon B. Yet he was so appalled by what he saw in the *Aktion Reinhard* camps of Belzec and Treblinka in August 1942 that he passed on information to a neutral Swedish diplomat, to the Vatican, and to a bishop in the anti-Nazi German Confessing Church. His depiction of the dead is as follows:

> Inside [the gas chamber] the people were still standing erect, like pillars of basalt, since there had not been an inch of space for them to fall in. ... Families could still be seen holding hands, even in death. It was a tough job to separate them as the chambers were emptied to make way for the next batch. A couple of dozen workers checked the mouths of the dead, which they tore open with iron hooks.... Other workers inspected anuses and genital organs in search of money, diamonds, gold, etc. Dentists moved around hammering out gold teeth, bridges, and crowns. In the midst of them stood Captain Wirth, in his element.

There were a few outside sources who made information available to the Polish underground. Among them was Janusz Peter, M.D., a Tomaszow physician who obtained information from local members of the underground as well as SS and Trawniki-trained camp guards who were his patients. This information made its way to London and Washington. Peter alone reports on an instance of resistance on June 13, 1942, that resulted in the killing of several SS guards. No other source for resistance has been found.

For many years Jan Karski, the Polish underground courier, maintained that he had visited Belzec. His description of the camp he visited comports with the contours and function of Izbicia, which was a way station to Belzec. Szlamek Bajler, an escapee from Chelmno shortly after it opened, obtained information regarding the camp that was transmitted to the Oneg Shabbat group in Warsaw. A document sent to the West, based on local eyewitness testimony, notes that killing was by electrocution for local Poles.

Postwar History of the Camp

In 1945–1946, the District Commission on the Investigation of Nazi Crimes in Poland in Lublin investigated the crimes committed in Belzec and concluded that the Nazis murdered about 600,000 Jews at Belzec between March and December of 1942. In 1946, the eyewitness account of Rudolph Reder was published by the District Jewish Historical Commission of Cracow. This is the lone account by a victim of Belzec.

In 1963, a monument was unveiled at the Belzec site, the first commemoration of Belzec's victims.

In 1965, the trial of the former SS man of the Belzec crew Josef Oberhauser took place. He was the only SS guard convicted for the crimes committed in Belzec. His sentence was 4½ years in prison. The other seven SS men tried together with Oberhauser were acquitted by the Munich court. The Main Commission for the Investigation of Nazi Crimes in Poland conducted the second investigation of Belzec crimes but did not find any new information about the camp.

In 1967–1968, at the request of the KGB, the Polish secret police investigated Trawniki-trained Ukrainian guards in Belzec. The documentation was only recently declassified after 30 years.

In 1995, the *United States Holocaust Memorial Museum entered into an agreement with the Council for the Protection of Monuments of Combat and Martyrdom in Poland to erect a new monument at the Belzec site. In May 1997 an international jury chose a design by Andrzej Solyga and his team. Over the next two years archeological surveys were conducted at the Belzec site marking down 33 graves as well as remnants of the building structures and in 2002 construction began on a new monument constructed as a joint effort by the Polish government and the American Jewish Committee.

On January 1, 2004, the Belzec memorial became a division of the State Museum of Majdanek in Lublin in anticipation of the opening on June 2 of a new monument consisting of an evocative environment sculpture together with an adjacent museum explaining how the camp functioned.

BIBLIOGRAPHY: Y. Arad, *Operation Reinhard Death Camps: Belzec, Sobibor and Treblinka* (1987); A. Donat (ed.), *The Death Camp Treblinka* (1979); R. Reder, *Bełżec* (Pol., 1946).

[Michael Berenbaum (2nd ed.)]

BELZYCE (Yid. and Heb. **Belzitcz, Belshic, Ba'al Shitz**), small town in Lublin province, Poland. A charter of privileges granted to Belzyce in 1432 designated it a compulsory halting stage for merchants traveling to the Lublin fair. Jews settled there at the beginning of the 16th century, probably connected with this traffic. The physician Jacob *Naḥman lived in Belzyce at the end of the 16th century. The Council of Four Lands convened in Belzyce in 1643. The community suffered heavy losses during the *Chmielnicki massacres of 1648–49. The ḥasidic rabbi Gedaliah Samuel Jacubson lived in Belzyce in the second half of the 19th century. In 1764 the Jewish population numbered 949; in 1897, 1,705 (out of 3,182); in 1921, 1,882 (over half the total population); and in 1939, 2,100.

[Nathan Michael Gelber]

Holocaust Period

The German army entered the town in mid-September 1939, and the Jewish population became subject to the persecution and terror carried out throughout Lublin Province. In February 1940 about 300 Jews from Stettin (then Germany) were deported to Belzyce. In February and March 1941 about 500 Jews from Cracow and another 500 from Lublin were forced to settle there. On May 12, 1942, several thousand Jews from central Germany (Sachsen and Thuringen) arrived. The town's Jewish population grew to about 4,500 by the time the mass deportations to the death camps began. In spring 1942, the Germans conducted an *Aktion* to liquidate the remaining Jews in Belzyce. They rounded up over 3,000 Jews for extermination at Sobibor. Subsequently the Germans established a concentration camp in Belzyce in a few houses around the destroyed synagogue. In May 1943 the Belzyce camp was liquidated. Several hundred Jews, mostly women and children, were shot, while another 250 women and 350 men were sent to Benzin, where only a handful survived. After the war the Jewish community in Belzyce was not reconstituted.

[Stefan Krakowski]

BIBLIOGRAPHY: T. Bernstein, in: *Bleter far Geshikhte* (Jan.–June 1950), 51–78. **ADD. BIBLIOGRAPHY:** Halpern, Pinkas, index; R. Jakov, in: *Galed* 1 (1973) 13–30; PK.

BE-MOẒA'EI MENUḤAH (Heb. בְּמוֹצָאֵי מְנוּחָה; "at the close of the rest (day)," i.e., the Sabbath), name of a *piyyut* in acrostic style of unknown authorship. It forms part of the *Seliḥot service on the first day of the *Seliḥot* cycle preceding Rosh ha-Shanah. It consists of eight verses which close with the refrain "Hear our supplication and our prayer." The initial words of the first stanza as well as other expressions indicate that it was composed for the first day of *Seliḥot*, which always falls on a Saturday night-early Sunday morning. A song of a similar name, *Be-Moẓa'ei Yom Menuḥah*, forms part of the traditional hymns for the closing of the Sabbath. Its author is the liturgist Jacob de *Lunel ("Ya'akov min Yeriḥo").

BIBLIOGRAPHY: English translation in *Seliḥot*, published by the Rabbinical Assembly, N.Y. (1964), 33–35; I.G. Glickstein and S. Braslavsky, *Midnight Service* (1931), 15 ff.; A.J. Rosenfeld, *Authorized Selichot* (1957), 13; Text and melody in A. Nadel, *Zemirot Shabbat, Die haeuslichen Sabbatgesaenge* (1937), 44 (Hebrew part 16).

[Meir Ydit]

BEMPORAD, AZEGLIO (1875–1945), Italian astronomer. Bemporad, who was born in Siena, was appointed director of the Capodimonte Observatory near Catania in Sicily in 1912. Some of his first publications were of a purely mathematical nature, and until c. 1924 his main interest was the complex study of the extinction of starlight within the earth's atmosphere. He was also concerned with observational and theoretical studies of solar radiation, of variable stars, solar and lunar eclipses, and occultations. From 1925, he published discussions on the progress of the compilation of the *Catalogo astrofotografico… di Catania* as part of the international enterprise of mapping the sky. Bemporad wrote about the history of astronomy. In 1946, a commemorative volume of his life work was published.

[Arthur Beer]

BEMPORAD, ENRICO (1868–1944), Italian publisher. At an early age he joined the Florentine publishing company of the brothers Alessandro and Felice Paggi. After the death of his father, Roberto, in 1891, he became the head of the firm which had, in the meantime, changed its name into R. Bemporad and son. Under his direction the publishing house became one of the most important in Italy. Bemporad established branch offices in many towns and extended the company's activities from educational and scholastic publications to wider literary fields. His company published the works of Giovanni Verga and Luigi Pirandello as well as the initial edition of Dante's works for the Italian Dante Society. Bemporad was at various times president or managing director of other Italian publishing companies, including Lattes of Turin, Sansoni of Florence, and Zanichelli of Bologna. During the Nazi occupation Bemporad was compelled to abandon his publishing work. He went into hiding and died a few days after Florence was liberated.

[Giorgio Romano]

BEN (Benista), ZEHAVA (1968–), Israeli popular singer. Ben was brought up in a poor neighborhood in the city of Beersheva; her father had been an *'ud* (lute) player in Morocco. As a teenager, Ben admired and studied the songs of Yemenite singer Zohar *Argov and was inspired by his Middle Eastern vocal style. When Argov died in 1987 she sang his hit "*Peraḥ be-Ganni*" in his memory at an anti-drug concert.

Ben's first major success came in 1990 when she took part in a film called *Tippat Mazzal* ("A Drop of Luck"). The song she sang derived from a Turkish folk tune and became a hit all over Israel. She also made her commercial cassette debut that year, selling 80,000 copies.

Her mainstream vocal breakthrough continued with "*Ketourna Masala*," an east-west duet with the popular Ethnics rock band. The song climbed to first place in the 1992 Israeli hit parade. A turning point in Ben's career came in 1994, when she decided to sing the songs of the most famous singer in the 20th-century Arab world, the legendary Umm Kulthum. Ben's interpretation of the latter's sophisticated and classic songs "*al-Atlal*" and "*Inta 'umri*" won over her most fanatical fans. She performed this repertoire accompanied by the Haifa Arab Music Orchestra, conducted by Suheil Radwan, at a Palestinian gathering in Nablus, in Jericho during Ramadan, at public concerts in Israel, and at memorial ceremonies for Yitzhak *Rabin. She was also invited with the orchestra to a number of festivals in Europe, including Stockholm, Monpelier, and Paris (Theatre de la ville). In 1995, Ben issued a CD of Umm Kulthum songs called *Zehava Ben Sharah Aravit.*

[Amnon Shiloah (2nd ed.)]

BENA'AH (Benaiah; third century C.E.), Palestinian scholar in Tiberias at the end of the tannaitic and the beginning of the amoraic era. Most of his dicta are transmitted in the Talmud by his disciple *Johanan Nappaḥa, but some are also cited in collections of tannaitic literature. His extant sayings are chiefly of an aggadic character: e.g., "Whoever occupies himself with the Torah for its own sake makes learning an elixir of life" (Ta'an. 7a); "The Pentateuch was given scroll by scroll" (Git. 60a). Bena'ah acquired a great reputation for wisdom, juridical ability, and the unraveling of complex legal cases, as a result of which the Roman authorities appointed him a judge. He was the author of an enactment according to which any judge found guilty even in a civil case was deemed unworthy of continuing in his judicial office (BB 58a–b). According to the biographer of the emperor Alexander Severus, the introduction of a similar statute in Roman law was the result of the Jewish precedent (*Scriptores Historiae Augustae*, Alexander Severus, 45:7). Bena'ah used to mark burial caves to keep the unsuspecting from defilement. In this connection, the talmudic aggadah relates some wondrous tales such as that of his visit to the grave of Adam (BB 58a). Bena'ah was the head of an academy in Tiberias, which apparently continued to function after his death. His disciple, Johanan, taught there (TJ, Shab. 12:13c). Some scholars maintain that it was because of this college that Tiberias was selected as the site of the central academy in Palestine.

BIBLIOGRAPHY: Bacher, Tann; Hyman, Toledot, 280–1.

[Zvi Kaplan]

BEN-ABRAHAM, ZVI (1941–), geologist. Born in Jerusalem, he received his B.Sc. in geology in 1968 from the Hebrew University and his Ph.D. from the Massachusetts Institute of Technology and at the Woods Hole Oceanographic Institution in 1973. Upon his return to Israel in 1973, after six months as a postdoctoral fellow at Woods Hole Oceanographic Institution, he began working at the Israel Oceanographic and Limnological Research Institute in Haifa and later at the Weizmann Institute of Science in the Department of Applied Mathematics. In 1982, after a two-year sabbatical at Stanford University, Ben-Avraham joined the Department of Geophysics and Planetary Sciences at Tel Aviv University, holding the Nebenzahl and Grossberg Chair in Geodynamics, and heading the Minerva Dead Sea Research Center. That same year, he was appointed professor of geophysics at Stanford University. In 1989 Ben-Avraham accepted an offer to hold the Max Sonnenberg Marine Geosciences Chair at the University of Cape Town. He conducted detailed measurements on the sea floor, magnetic field, gravity field, sub-bottom, and heat flow of the Sea of Galilee, Dead Sea, and the Gulf of Eilat using different geophysical methods. He made numerous geophysical studies of the Levant continental margin and the Levant basin, eastern Mediterranean. He also researched the evolution of the Pacific oceanic margins and ways in which continents grow and compared the San Andreas and Dead Sea faults, which are tectonically similar. As a result, a number of advances were made in understanding the Dead Sea fault valley. Ben-Avraham gained extensive academic experience at various universities in the U.S. and Europe and conducted scientific studies of numerous seas. He is a fellow or member of numerous scientific societies and recipient of the Israel Prize (2003) and the L. Meitner-A.V. Humboldt Research Award (2004).

[Bracha Rager (2nd ed.)]

BENACERRAF, BARUJ (1920–), physician and Nobel Prize laureate in medicine. Benacerraf was born in Caracas, Venzuela. He moved to the United States in 1939 and graduated in science from Columbia University, New York, in 1942 and in medicine from the Medical School of Virginia in 1945. His life-long research interest was immunology. He worked at Columbia University in 1948–49, the Broussais Hospital in Paris in 1949–56, and the New York University School of Medicine in 1956–68, where he became professor. He was director of the immunology laboratory at the National Institute of Allergy and Infectious Diseases, Bethesda, in 1968–70 and Fabyan Professor of Comparative Pathology, Harvard Medical School, from 1970. In 1980 he was awarded the Nobel Prize in medicine (jointly with George Snell and Jean Dausset) for establishing that immune responses are genetically controlled. This and his other discoveries have profound implications for understanding immunity in infections, allergy, and cancer. Among his many awards is the Rabbi Shai Shacknai Prize in immunology and cancer research of the Hebrew University in 1974. He was a member of the board of governors of the Weizmann Institute of Science. He had a special interest in the training of young scientists. He abandoned a successful business career to concentrate on research and his pride in his Sephardi origins was expressed in his Nobel Prize acceptance speech.

[Michael Denman (2nd ed.)]

BEN-ADIR (pen name of **Abraham Rosin**; 1878–1942), writer and Jewish socialist leader, born in Krucha, Belorussia. He received a traditional Jewish education from his grandfather Jacob Aaronson and his uncle Solomon Aaronson. At the age of 16 he went to Odessa to sit for the university examinations as an external student, and then moved to Minsk. In 1896–97 he became influenced by A. *Liessin who advocated a Jewish national brand of socialism. After the First Zionist Congress in 1897, Ben-Adir published an article advocating political Zionism in opposition to the ideology of *Aḥad Ha-Am. In 1901 he moved to Paris where he studied at the Free Russian University, and later returned to Russia. After the *Kishinev pogrom of 1903 Ben-Adir published a call for the formation of a Jewish party which would combine the aims of revolutionary socialism with national Jewish aspirations. Ben-Adir was one of the founders and ideologists of the *Vozrozhdeniye group, and of its successor of the Sejmists (*Jewish Socialist Workers' Party) whose program included Jewish national-political autonomy while envisaging *Territorialism as a remoter aim. He edited its organs *Serp* (Russian) and *Folksshtime* (Yiddish). After the February 1917 Revolution, Ben-Adir became a leader of the *United Jewish Socialist Workers' Party. Also in 1917 he published *Kehile Fragen*, a pamphlet envisaging the *kehillah* as an instrument of national Jewish *autonomy. Ben-Adir withdrew from the united party in 1919 when the communist trend predominated, and in 1921 left Russia for Berlin. His *In Khaos fun Lebn un Denken* ("Whirlwind of Life and Thought"), a collection of essays on socialist problems, in particular an argument against communism, was published in 1925. Ben-Adir stayed in Ereẓ Israel between 1925 and 1927 but returned to Berlin, leaving for Paris in 1933. After the French defeat by the Nazis in 1940 he went to the United States. In Paris and New York he coedited the *Algemeyne Entsiklopedye* ("General Encyclopedia" in Yiddish) to which he also contributed.

BIBLIOGRAPHY: LNYL, 1 (1956), 336–9; Rubin, in: *Asufot*, 1 (1945), 21–25.

BENADOR, URY, originally **Simon Schmidt** (1895–1971), Romanian novelist. One of his best known novels, *Ghetto veac XX* ("20th-Century Ghetto," 1934), presents a picture of Romanian-Jewish life. A short story, *Appassionato* (1935), describes expressionistically the ecstatic and mystic fascination that Beethoven's music exercises on a young ḥasid from an East European shtetl. During the Communist period, the writer became a conformist supporter of the regime, publishing anti-Zionist and anti-religious pamphlets. A novel, *Gablonz "Magazin Universal"* (1961), is a violent attack on the Jewish bourgeoisie. He also wrote a biography of Beethoven (1964).

[Leon Volovici (2nd ed.)]

BEN-AHARON (Nussenbaum), YITZḤAK (1906–) Israeli labor leader and politician. Member of the First to Fifth, Seventh and Eighth Knessets, on behalf of Mapam, Aḥdut ha-Avodah-Po'alei Zion, and the Alignment lists. Ben-Aharon was born in Zoinitza, then Austrian Bukovina. He studied political science and economics in Berlin and was also a leader in the *Ha-Shomer ha-Ẓa'ir movement. Ben-Aharon immigrated to Palestine in 1928, and in 1933 was one of the founders of Kibbutz Givat Ḥayyim, where he remained a member. In 1932–38 he was secretary of the Tel Aviv Labor Council, and in 1939 secretary of *Mapai. In 1940 Ben-Aharon joined the British Army and was taken prisoner by the Germans in Greece in 1941, remaining in a German prison camp until the end of the war. After the war he took part in the struggle of the Yishuv against the British and was among the Jewish leaders arrested on "Black Saturday" on June 29, 1946.

When *Aḥdut ha-Avodah seceded from *Mapai, and established Aḥdut ha-Avodah–Po'alei Zion, he became one of its leaders, representing it in the *Histadrut. In 1948, Aḥdut ha-Avodah–Po'alei Zion united with Mapam and the two parties ran in a single list in the Knesset elections. Ben-Aharon was elected on behalf of Mapam to the First and Second Knessets, and after that on behalf of Aḥdut ha-Avodah–Po'alei Zion. In 1959–62 he served as minister of transportation, resigning due to differences of opinion within his own party on the need for unification with Mapai, and with other members of the government over social and economic issues. In 1965 he was one of the driving forces for the establishment of the first Alignment with Mapai, and in 1968 for the establishment of the Israel Labor Party. From 1969 to 1973 Ben-Aharon served as secretary general of the Histadrut. In this position he encouraged wage claims, particularly on behalf of the lower-paid workers, frequently in contravention of the economic policy of Minister of Finance Pinḥas *Sapir, and spoke out strongly against the high earnings and luxurious living of the wealthy in Israel. He also advocated having the governing bodies of the Histadrut elected by the districts rather than on a national basis and called for an increase in the proportion of representatives elected by the workers directly instead of by the party and trade union functionaries. In this period he strongly criticized the political positions of Prime Minister Golda *Meir, and within *Ha-Kibbutz ha-Me'uḥad clashed with Yitzḥak *Tabenkin, who supported the Greater Israel idea. Ben-Aharon did not run for the Ninth Knesset but continued to act behind the scenes within Ha-Kibbutz ha-Me'uḥad and the Labor Party, while expressing dovish views with regard to the peace process with the Palestinians.

Throughout his career Ben-Aharon was considered not only a political leader but an ideologue as well. His articles and speeches appeared in various collections.

ADD. BIBLIOGRAPHY: *Siḥot Im Ben-Aharon* (1984); Y. Gvirtz, *Yeled Lo Ratzu'i: Yizḥak Ben-Aharon: Biografyah* (2003).

[Susan Hattis Rolef (2nd ed.)]

BENAIAH (Heb. בְּנָיָהוּ, בְּנָיָה; "YHWH has built"), son of Jehoiada, one of David's warriors and Solomon's commander in chief. Benaiah came from Kabzeel in Judah. Famous for his individual acts of valor, the killing of two warriors, the slaying of a lion in a pit in the snow, and the defeating of an Egyptian giant, he was one of David's most honored warriors (II Sam. 23:20–23; I Chron. 11:22–25). It is reasonable to attribute some of these deeds to the period of David's outlawry or to the first part of his reign. David appointed Benaiah as the head of his bodyguard (II Sam. 23:23; I Chron. 11:25), identified by some scholars with the Cherethites and Pelethites (II Sam. 20:23, according to the *keri*; I Chron. 18:17; cf. II Sam. 8:18; I Kings 1:38), whose commander was also Benaiah. After the death of *Ahithophel, he served as counselor to David, together with the priest *Abiathar (I Chron. 27:33–34, where the order of the names should be reversed according to some versions: "Benaiah son of Jehoiada" instead of "Jehoiada son of Benaiah"). Benaiah opposed *Adonijah's attempt to seize the crown at the end of David's reign and, together with the priest *Zadok and the prophet *Nathan, he proclaimed Solomon king (I Kings 1:8–44). He later carried out the liquidation of *Shimei, of Solomon's rival *Adonijah, and of the latter's supporter *Joab (2:25–46), in whose stead Solomon appointed Benaiah commander in chief.

BIBLIOGRAPHY: Bright, Hist, 189–90; de Vaux, Anc Isr. 127–8, 220–1; Dinaburg (Dinur), in: *Zion*, 11 (1946), 165 ff.; Mazar, in: *Sefer D. Ben Gurion* (1964), 248–67.

[Yehoshua M. Grintz]

BENAIM (Heb. בן נאיים), name of North African families of rabbis and merchants. JACOB ḤAYYIM BENAIM (d. 1803), rabbi in Fez, Morocco, author, and halakhic authority, left Fez about 1760 for Algeria on his way to Ereẓ Israel, but remained in the city of Mascara, where he was appointed rabbi and *dayyan*. In 1764 he moved to Algiers to become *av bet din*, a position he held for 18 years; eventually, however, his harsh exercise of this office provoked opposition from noted scholars in the community and he left. He settled in Leghorn in 1782 and there had his works printed, including *Zera Ya'akov*, responsa (1784); *Yeshu'ot Ya'akov*, sermons (1795); and an edition of the Zohar (1795). His novellae to the Talmud were published posthumously in *Ḥesed ve-Emet* (Salonika, 1813). He also composed *piyyutim* for a local Purim of Algiers to commemorate the victory over the Spanish.

MOSES (19th century), merchant, emigrated from Algiers to Marseilles, France. In 1819 he established the Dramont commercial house for Franco-Moroccan trade; his good relations in the two countries proved beneficial to the business affairs of his Jewish compatriots. His son Makhluf founded another commercial company with the later Rif rebellion leader Abd el-Kader. RAPHAEL ḤAYYIM MOSES (c. 1850–1920), was born in Tetuan but emigrated to Palestine in his youth. He was a member of the *bet din* of Tiberias. In the 1870s he traveled to Turkey and North Africa as an emissary to collect charitable funds for Palestine. In Gibraltar he was chosen chief rabbi (1881), and held this position until his death. His publications include *Raḥamim* [initials of Raphael Ḥayyim Moses (son of) Isaya (and) Masudah] *Peshutim*, responsa (Tunis, 1910; but according to the preface not published before 1914), and other rabbinical works.

JOSEPH (1882–1961), rabbi and clerk to the *bet din* of Fez, Morocco, was a lifelong bibliophile, who collected the largest library of books and manuscripts in Morocco. His own works include a bio-bibliographical dictionary of rabbis of Morocco, *Malkhei Rabbanan, Kevod Melakhim* (Jerusalem, 1931); a collection of sermons, *Millei Me'alyata* (in manuscript); and many other writings left in manuscript. After his death his library was sold to the Jewish Theological Seminary of New York. DAVID (1888–1968), son of Raphael Ḥayyim Moses, was the leader of the Jewish community in Gibraltar after his father's death. He became a member of the Government Council of the Colony, and in 1954 he was appointed honorary consul of Israel for Gibraltar.

BIBLIOGRAPHY: J.M. Toledano, *Ner ha-Ma'arav* (1911), 185, 193; Yaari, Sheluḥei, 656, 859; R.H.M. Benaim, *Raḥamim Peshutim* (1910), preface; A. Cahen, *Juifs dans l'Afrique septentrionale* (1867), 105–6; Hirschberg, Afrika, 2 (1965), index; H.Z. Hirschberg, *Me-Ereẓ Mevo ha-Shemesh* (1957), 212–4; *Oración Fúnebre… J. Ibn Naim* (Leghorn, 1803); Miège, Maroc, 2 (1961), 160, 156.

[David Obadia]

BEN ʿALĀN, JOSHUA (ninth century?), author of a Hebrew treatise on the Jewish calendar. Excerpts from the treatise are found in a polemical essay by the Karaite scholar Hasan b. Mashi'aḥ (Ms. Leningrad), in which the latter refers to Ben ʿAlān as "the rabbinical scholar who is the best versed in the science of the calendar." This is the only source for Joshua's name; a grammarian by name of Judah b. ʿAlān, who lived in Tiberias at the beginning of the tenth century, may have been Joshua's brother, as Harkavy assumes.

BIBLIOGRAPHY: Harkavy, in: *Ha-Goren*, 4 (1903), 75–80; Poznański, in: REJ, 44 (1902), 176–7; Bornstein, in: *Ha-Tekufah*, 9 (1921), 224–5; Z.H. Joffe, *Korot Ḥeshbon ha-Ibbur* (1931), 86 ff., 94 ff., 129 ff.

[Moshe Nahum Zobel]

BEN-AMI (Shieren), JACOB (1890–1977), actor and director. Ben-Ami's long stage career began in his native Minsk, Belorussia, before he was a teenager. After traveling with many Yiddish acting companies through Eastern Europe, Ben-Ami went to the United States in 1912 to appear with Rudolf Schildkraut and Sarah Adler in Yiddish plays. In 1918, together with Maurice *Schwartz, he founded the Yiddish Art Theater in New York. Ben-Ami's reputation as an actor and director grew, and in 1920 he made his English-language acting debut in *Samson and Delilah*, a drama written by a Dane, Sven Lange, that Ben-Ami had played and directed in Yiddish in New York and in Russia. The following year he made his Broadway debut in Peretz Hirshbein's *The Idle Inn*, and many leading roles followed. Ben-Ami played more parts on the English-speaking stage than on the Yiddish, but he did not appear in a commercial success until almost 40 years later, when he played a grandfather in Paddy Chayefsky's *The Tenth Man* (1959). In the interim, Ben-Ami toured extensively in South America, in South Africa, and in the United States where he did Yiddish plays and Yiddish translations of Russian, European, and American plays.

[Stewart Kampel]

BEN-AMI (Dankner), OVED (1905–1988), founder and longtime mayor of Netanyah. Ben-Ami, who was born in Petaḥ Tikvah, served as secretary of Benei Binyamin (1924–28), an organization of the sons of early Jewish settlers, which was instrumental in establishing several new settlements. Ben-Ami founded the town of Netanyah in 1928–29, and the settlement of Even Yehudah in 1932. He was mayor of Netanyah continuously from 1930 with minor interruptions. During that time Netanyah became a major resort and the center of Israel's diamond industry. In 1947 Ben-Ami and other Jewish mayors and *yishuv* leaders were arrested by the British Mandatory authorities in reprisal for Jewish underground activities. Ben-Ami was a member of the Liberal Party and a part owner of *Ma'ariv*, the daily evening paper. From 1958 to 1961 he was active in the establishment of the new town of Ashdod, heading the Ashdod Development Company. He wrote the books, *Netanyah, Birat ha-Sharon* (1940), and *Unbreakable Spirit of Our Jewish Heritage* (1964).

BIBLIOGRAPHY: Tidhar, 2 (1947), 1024–25.

[Benjamin Jaffe]

BEN-AMITAI, LEVI (1901–1980), Hebrew writer. He received a general education in his native Belorussia and in 1917 joined the He-Ḥalutz movement. In 1920 he emigrated to Palestine, where he worked as a manual laborer. He became a member of kibbutz Deganyah Bet in 1925, and worked there first as an agricultural laborer, then as a teacher. His stories and sketches in Hebrew periodicals began to appear in 1925. His books of poetry include *Ha-Shibbolim Penimah* (1934); *Leilot ba-Maẓor* (1939); *Ba-Kevuẓah* (1938); *Sadot she-ba-Emek* (1950); *Oholivah* (1959); *Mi-Midbar Mattanah* (1962), poems about the Essenes; and *Osfei Kayiẓ* (1966). He edited the anthologies *Deganiyyot* (1955) and *Ha-Sofer ba-Kevuẓah* (1956), and was coeditor of a collection of short stories by writers in cooperative agricultural settlements, entitled *Al Admatam* (1959). Ben-Amitai's poetry is distinguished by its short verses, and restrained, almost prosaic style. The agricultural-folk setting takes on symbolic dimensions by virtue of the connotative language he chooses. Much of his writing is charged with strong religious accents that evoke a prayerful mood.

ADD. BIBLIOGRAPHY: R. Peled, *Yaḥid ve-Yaḥad be-Shirat Levi Ben-Amitai ba-Shanim 1925–1939* (1993).

[Getzel Kressel]

BEN-AMMI (Rabinowicz), MORDECAI (1854–1932), author and journalist writing in Russian. A traditional Jewish education and the harsh circumstances of his life after he lost his father at a young age are reflected in his stories. At Odessa he attended a yeshivah where the curriculum included languages and sciences. Influenced by Perez *Smolenskin, he became a *maskil*, and entered a Russian secondary school and thereafter the University of Odessa. When pogroms broke out in southern Russia in 1882, Ben-Ammi took part in organizing Jewish self-defense in Odessa. He campaigned against the czarist regime for organizing the pogroms and the Russian press for condoning them, also castigating the Jewish intelligentsia for failing to defend its people. In 1882 he went to Paris to obtain assistance from the Alliance Israélite Universelle for the victims of the pogroms. From there he sent his "Letters from Paris" to the Russian-Jewish monthly *Voskhod* (signed "Resh Galuta"), which reflect his deep appreciation of Jewish values. The same year Ben-Ammi moved to Geneva, where he began to write stories depicting the joyous spirit of Jewish festivals and the legends associated with them. In 1883 he completed the stories "*Priezd Tsadika*," and "*Ben Yukhid*," the latter reflecting the atmosphere of the days of the Cantonists, and in 1884 a long story "*Baal Tefila*." The stories became popular among Jews who read Russian. In 1887 Ben-Ammi returned to Odessa, where he remained until 1905, and published the autobiographical story *Detstvo* ("Childhood"), in which he describes the Jewish background of his youth. In articles published in *Voskhod*, he attacked the czarist authorities for their anti-Jewish discrimination. He also criticized the Jewish intelligentsia for having renounced Jewish values and for leaving their persecuted brethren to suffer an unfortunate fate. He also published a collection of stories for Jewish juvenile readers with illustrations, as well as a series of stories in Yiddish. Ben-Ammi became a member of the committee of Ḥovevei Zion in Odessa upon its formation in 1890, and was a delegate to the First Zionist Congress and other congresses convened by Theodor Herzl. His esteem for Herzl was so great that on his death Ben-Ammi mourned him as though he were a close relative. While living in Odessa, he taught in the Jewish school directed by Mendele Mokher Seforim, whose faithful friend he remained throughout his life. On the outbreak of the

Russian revolution of 1905, Ben-Ammi returned to Geneva. In 1923 he settled in Ereẓ Israel. Ben-Ammi's stories portray the traditional Jewish way of life from the inside. Despite a certain sentimentality and romanticization, their pervasive sincerity and spirit of piety give them a unique appeal, especially among the young. Several were translated into Hebrew by Ḥ.N. Bialik.

BIBLIOGRAPHY: Aḥad Ha-Am, *Al Parashat Derakhim*, 3 (1921), 64–65; J. Klausner, *Yoẓerei Tekufah u-Mamshikhei Tekufah* (1956), 107–17; *Haolam*, no. 17 (1911), 2–3; LNYL, 1 (1956), 349; I. Klausner, *Mi-Katoviẓ ad Basel*, 2 (1965).

[Israel Klausner]

BEN-AMOTZ, DAHN (**Moshe Tehilimzeiger**; 1923–1989), Israeli author and humorist. Born in Poland, he was taken to Palestine with a group of children in 1938, escaping the fate of his parents, who were murdered in the Holocaust. He joined the British Navy during World War II. After the war he volunteered for the Palyam, the marine branch of the Palmaḥ, where he first established himself as a humorous writer. Though his earliest publication is a volume of "serious" stories *Arba'ah ve-Arba'ah* (1950), he won fame with a collection of Palmaḥ lore – half fact, half tall story – entitled *Yalkut ha-Kezavim* ("Bag of Lies," 1956), which he wrote jointly with the poet Ḥayim *Ḥefer. His other humorous writings, initially published in the Hebrew press, are collected in *Mah Nishma* ("What's New," 1959) and *Eikh La'asot Mah* ("How to do What," 1962). In 1968 he published his first full-scale novel, *Lizkor ve-Lishko'aḥ* ("To Remember and To Forget") which, though laced with humor, is basically a return to serious writing. A semi-autobiographical story, it constitutes the author's attempt to confront a past he had tried to ignore, his non-*sabra* origin, the murder of his parents, and his own responsibility as their son. The questions of the German people's guilt, the existence of the "other Germany," and the moral justification for accepting German reparations are all widely explored in this book. An English translation of *To Remember and To Forget* was published in 1973.

Besides writing, Ben-Amotz made a reputation for himself as a witty radio personality, starting with the popular *Three in One Boat* program, as a sharp-tongued interviewer, as manager of the Ḥamam satirical cabaret, organizer of happenings, lexicographer of Hebrew slang, sometime actor (a small part in *A Streetcar Named Desire* – during his Hollywood phase – and the part of Uzi in *Exodus*), and as the quintessential Israeli, an exemplar of the "New Jew," the sabra, combining charm and brashness with a highly visible bohemian lifestyle and left-wing politics. Dying of cancer, he arranged a now legendary farewell party for himself, receiving the accolades of Israel's cultural and political elite with customary good cheer.

ADD. BIBLIOGRAPHY: A. Dankner, *Dahn Ben-Amotz, Bi'ografyah* (1992); Z. Yaniv, *Sippurav ha-Mukdamim shel Dahn Ben-Amotz, 1945–1948* (1992); Z. Chafets, in: *The Jerusalem Report* (Jan. 23, 1992). **WEBSITE:** www.ithl.org.il.

[Miriam Arad / Fred Skolnik (2nd ed.)]

BENAMOZEGH, ELIJAH BEN ABRAHAM (1822–1900), Italian rabbi and kabbalist. Benamozegh was born in Livorno (Leghorn) of Moroccan parents. His father died when he was three years old and his Jewish education was seen to by his mother's brother, the kabbalist Judah Coriat. Destined for a commercial career, Benamozegh soon revealed extraordinary intellectual ability and from 1846 could devote himself entirely to study. He served as a preacher at the synagogue of Livorno, as a professor of theology in the rabbinical school of the city, and as a member of the local rabbinical court. He also founded a printing house for Jewish religious books. Benamozegh's intellectual energy was directed mainly to the defense of the Kabbalah, and he may be considered the last important kabbalist in Italy. He considered the Kabbalah as a genuine part of Jewish dogma, paralleling the tradition of the Oral Law. Hostile to Ḥasidism (which he saw as a superstitious degradation of pure Jewish theology), Benamozegh tried to show the affinities between Kabbalah and philosophy (as had a century before another kabbalist from Livorno, Joseph *Ergas), arguing that the former took precedence. Embracing Eastern and Western elements, the will to both unity and to multiplicity, the Kabbalah could moreover represent a solution to the religious crisis of modern Europe. Benamozegh wrote numerous books and articles in Hebrew, Italian, and French. Among his works are (1) Exegesis: *Ner le-David* (1858), a commentary on Psalms; *Em la-Mikra* (1862–65), a commentary on the Pentateuch in five volumes incorporating the findings of comparative philology, archaeology, and ancient history, in which the influence of the Italian philosopher G. Vico is particularly prominent. This commentary was condemned by the rabbis of Aleppo and Jerusalem, who attacked it for being too open to "external sciences" and to mythology; (2) Theology: *Spinoza et la kabbale* (1864), on the possible kabbalistic origins of Spinoza's thought; *Teologia dogmatica e apologetica* (1877), in which Benamozegh starts to build a comprehensive Jewish theology based on the Kabbalah. Benamozegh saw in Hegel's philosophy the most dangerous enemy of a religious philosophy and considered the thought of the Catholic V. Gioberti a powerful weapon in the fight against "modern pantheism," i.e. German idealism; *Israël et l'Humanité* (revised and published postumously in 1914 by his Christian disciple Aimé Pallière; *Israel ve-ha-Enoshut* (1967; *Israel and Humanity*, 1994), on the universal potential of Judaism. (3) Apologetics: *Ta'am le-Shad* (1863), a refutation of Samuel David *Luzzatto's *Vikku'ah al Ḥokhmat ha-Kabbalah*, in which Luzzatto denied the antiquity of the *Zohar* and the theological interest of Kabbalah; *Morale juive et morale chrétienne* (1867; *Jewish and Christian Ethics*, 1873; *Bi-Shevilei Musar*, 1966), on the superiority of Jewish ethics, which concerns itself with the political sphere while Christian ethics sees ascetism as its supreme value. In the second part of this work, *L'origine des dogmes chrétiens*, Benamozegh tries to show that Christianity derives from an incorrect interpretation of Kabbalah. (4) History: *Storia degli Esseni* (1865), a collection of lectures on the *Essenes, seen as the forerunners of the kabbalists.

BIBLIOGRAPHY: G. Lattes, *Vita e opere di Elia Benamozegh* (1901). **ADD BIBLIOGRAPHY:** D. Lattes, *"Ani Ma'amin shel Filosof Yehudi: heḤakham Elijah Benamozegh"* (1943); Y. Colombo, "Il dibattito tra Luzzatto e Benamozegh intorno alla Kabbalà," in: RMI, 8 (1934), 471–97, 32 (1966), 179–204; M. Idel, *"Al ha-Kabbalah eẓel ha-Rav Elijah Benamozegh,"* in: *Pe'amim* 74 (1998), 87–96; A. Guetta, *Philosophie et Cabbale. Essai sur la pensée d'Elijah Benamozegh.* (1998), with bibliography; idem (ed.), *Per Elijah Benamozegh* (2000); L. Amoroso, *Scintille ebraiche* (2004), 85–151.

[Alessandro Guetta (2nd ed.)]

BENARDETE, MAIR JOSÉ (1895–1983), philologist. Benardete was born in Turkey and emigrated to the United States in 1910. He was a long-time professor of Spanish and Sephardic Studies at Brooklyn College in New York City. Benardete and Federico de Onis, who founded Columbia University's Hispanic Institute in 1920, are well known for effecting a reconciliation between Hispanics and Sephardim in America. Benardete was director of the institute's Sephardic Studies Section in the late 1920s. Under his direction, the section sponsored lectures on Sephardi civilization, generated articles for the institute's *Revista Hispanica Moderna*, published a Ladino/Spanish commemorative volume on medieval Spanish-Jewish poet *Judah Halevi, and staged plays in Judeo-Spanish.

Benardete wrote a number of volumes in the field of Spanish literature and civilization. Several Loyalist ballads are presented in English translation in *And Spain Sings* (1937), which he prepared in collaboration with the poet Rolfe Humphries. His *Hispanic Culture and Character of the Sephardic Jews* (1952; Spanish, 1963) is an analysis of the Sephardi Jews.

Benardete retired from City University of New York / Brooklyn College in 1965. As a tribute to the renowned scholar, his colleagues Louis Levy and David Barocas formed the Committee for the Advancement of Sephardic Studies and Culture to publish the testimonial book *Studies in Honor of M.J. Benardete*. They then joined forces with other Sephardi leaders to continue publishing books on Sephardi history and Sephardi life in the U.S.

In the late 1970s Benardete, along with Rabbi Marc *Angel, Levy, and Barocas, initiated the idea of a cultural center that would fill the void in information and programming regarding Sephardi history and culture. To that end, Sephardic House was established in 1978 at Congregation Shearith Israel in New York City.

BIBLIOGRAPHY: H.V. Besso, in: I.A. Langnas and B. Sholod (eds.), *Studies in Honor of M.J. Benardete* (1965), 459–86 (including bibliography).

[Victor A. Mirelman / Ruth Beloff (2nd ed.)]

BENARES, capital of Benares district, India. This sacred city of the Hindus became the residence of Anglo-Jewish merchants toward the end of the 18th century because of its proximity to the diamond mines. Among these early Jewish merchants was Jacob Barnet, an English diamond merchant who moved from Madras to Benares in 1780. His clients in London included the merchant-house of Israel Levin Solomons. In 1786 Lyon Prager was sent by this firm to Bengal and established his headquarters in Benares. Prager also became inspector and purchaser of drugs, indigo, and other commodities for the English East India Company. After his death in 1793 his activities were continued by his brother George Prager, who moved from Benares to Calcutta. The Jewish association with Benares was maintained by the affluent Anglo-Portuguese Jewish diamond merchant Benjamin d'Aguilar (d. 1813), and Pellegrine Treves (d. 1825), who obtained permission to settle in Bengal in 1774.

BIBLIOGRAPHY: W.J. Fischel, in: REJ, 123 (1964), 433–98.

[Walter Joseph Fischel]

BEN-ARIEH, YEHOSHUA (1928–), Israeli geographer specializing in historical and cultural geography and the Middle East. Considered one of the most important researchers of Ereẓ Israel and Jerusalem in the modern era, Ben-Arieh was born in Tel Aviv, and received his Ph.D. from the Hebrew University of Jerusalem in 1963. He began to lecture at the Hebrew University in 1965 and became a professor in 1979. From 1982 until 1985 he served as dean of the Faculty of Humanities. In 1997 he became rector of the Hebrew University. He was a research fellow at the University College of London and was visiting professor at the University of Maryland, Carleton University, and University College of London. In 1971 he received the Ben-Zvi Prize and in 1977 the Bialik Prize. In 1999 he was awarded the Israel Prize for geography. Among his books in English are *Rediscovery of the Holy Land in the Nineteenth Century* (1980), *Jerusalem in the Nineteenth Century: The Old City* (1985), and *Jerusalem in the Nineteenth Century: Emergence of the New City* (1987). Volumes edited include *Jerusalem in the Mind of the Western World, 1800–1948* (1997) and *Painting the Holy Land in the Nineteenth Century* (1997).

[Shaked Gilboa (2nd ed.)]

BEN-AROYA, AVRAHAM (1887–1979), Greek socialist and one of the founders of the labor movements in Salonika and Macedonia. Born in Vidin, Bulgaria, Ben-Aroya was a teacher and in 1908 went to Salonika, then under Turkish rule, where he taught Bulgarian and worked as a printer. Already an enthusiastic socialist, Ben-Aroya found in Salonika's large Jewish working class a ready audience for his doctrines. While his views were close to those of the small revolutionary Bulgarian group, he was drawn to the exploited and unorganized Jewish workers in the city, especially the tobacco workers with whom he shared common interests. In 1909 he formed the Salonika workers' organization later known as the *Federación Socialista Laboradera* ("Socialist Workers' Federation"). Under Ben-Aroya's direction the Federation founded the first workers' newspaper in Turkey, *El Journal del Laborador*, and later a weekly Ladino newspaper, *Solidarità Oberadera*. After the Balkan war, Ben-Aroya joined with Greek socialists in Athens. He formed *La Bursa del Laboro* ("Jewish Syndicate Center") and was elected chairman of its executive. He was also a leader of the Greek Socialist Party, but when the Party split in 1924 Ben-Aroya helped to found the Social Democratic Party and its newspaper *The New Period* (in Greek). Subsequently, Ben-Aroya published numerous political pamphlets including tracts on *Social Democracy and the Jewish Question* (Bulgarian) and *The Workers' Movement in Turkey* (Hebrew tr. 1910). In 1953 Aroya emigrated to Israel. Although bitterly opposed to Zionism for many years, the rise of Nazism and World War II changed his views, while his decision to emigrate to Israel reflected his disillusionment with socialism, which he had previously believed would resolve the Jewish question.

[Baruch Uziel]

BENAROYA, AVRAM (1888–1955), journalist and first teacher of stenography in Turkey. Born in Edirne, Benaroya studied in the Ecole Normale Israélite in Paris. His first teaching position was in Hasköy, Istanbul, and then in Damascus. From 1911 he taught French and stenography at the Turkish Lycée Galatasaray and the High School of Commerce. His stenography method was adopted by the Ministry of Education. In 1925 the Ministry of Commerce decided to introduce stenography in the commercial schools and Benaroya was responsible for the curriculum. In 1928 Benaroya started working as a stenography teacher in the Turkish Parliament. His journalistic career began in *Le Jeune Turc*. Later he wrote in *Ikdam*, *Stamboul*, *La République*, and *Le Journal d'Orient*. In 1948 he started publishing *L'Etoile du Levant*, a weekly newspaper in French which appeared until shortly after his death. His books include: *Basit ve Vatani Kıraat: Lectures Patriotiques Faciles* (1916), *Türkçe Lisanına Mahsûs Stenografya Usûlü*, Istanbul (1918), *Türkçe'ye Mahsûs Stenografya Usûlü* (1929), *Istenografi Esas Kuralları ve Kısaltmalar Ders 1–2* (1943), *İstenografi: Esas Kurallar ve Kısaltmalar (12 ders)* (1944), *Istenografi Dersleri* (1947).

BIBLIOGRAPHY: R.N. Bali, *Un Journaliste et un Journal méconnu: Avram Benaroya et L'Etoile du Levant* (2004).

[Rifat Bali (2nd ed.)]

BENARUS, ADOLFO (1863–1958), Portuguese writer. His grandfather David Bensabat, born in Morocco, was the first Jew to settle (1815) in the Azores Islands. Benarus was born there, at Angra do Heroísmo. He was a painter and philologist and taught English in the faculty of letters of the University of Lisbon and in other educational institutions. He was active in communal life and was honorary president of the Jewish community of Lisbon. He wrote *Israel* (1924); *Os Judeus, Historia Estranha deste Povo* ("The Jews, the Strange Story of This People," 1927); *A Tragédia da Historia* ("The Tragedy of History," 1937); *Anti-semitismo* (1948) as well as pamphlets on Jewish festivals.

[Moses Bensabat Amzalak]

BENAS, BARON LOUIS (1844–1914), English banker and communal worker. Born in London, he settled in Liverpool early in life where he carried on the family banking business. He established in 1867 the Liverpool branch of the *Alliance Israélite Universelle, which later became the local branch of the *Anglo-Jewish Association, serving as its president until his death. He was chairman of a commission set up in 1882 by the London Russo-Jewish Committee to supervise the emigration via Liverpool to the United States of refugees from Russia. He was elected president of the Liverpool Literary and Philosophical Society in 1890 and wrote several papers for that and other learned societies, including *Records of the Jews in Liverpool* (1899) as well as an article on the history of Liverpool Jewry for *The Jewish Encyclopedia* of 1909. His son, BERTRAM BENJAMIN BARON (1880–1968), practiced as a chancery barrister from 1906. A well-known figure in legal circles, he was appointed bencher of the Middle Temple in 1953 and was also chairman of the Liverpool Bar Association. He served as president of the Merseyside Jewish Representative Council (1944–46) and of the Jewish Historical Society of England (1951–53). He was the author of a number of books and papers, including supplements to his father's pioneering monograph on Liverpool Jewish history.

BIBLIOGRAPHY: JC (Feb. 6, 13, 1914, on Baron Louis; Dec. 13, 1968, on Bertram Benjamin); Roth, Mag Bibl, index; Lehmann, Nova Bibl, index. **ADD. BIBLIOGRAPHY:** B. Benas, "A Survey of the Jewish Institutional History of Liverpool and District," in: JHSET, 17 (1951–52).

[Sefton D. Temkin]

BEN-ASHER, AARON BEN MOSES (called **Abu Saʿid** in Arabic; first half of tenth century), last and most important of a family of masoretes active in Tiberias for five generations, from the second half of the eighth century. That Ben-Asher lived in the first half of the tenth century may be deduced from a list in the *Keter*, a biblical manuscript formerly in Aleppo, now in Israel. This states that Ben-Asher vocalized and *masar* (i.e., wrote the *Masorah of) the *Keter*, which was written by Solomon b. Bouya'a, a well-known scribe, who wrote another Bible dated 930. It is also known that Ben-Asher was no longer alive in 989, since the scribe of the manuscript of the Former Prophets from that date says of him: "may he rest in the Garden of Eden" (Leningrad, Firkovich II, Ms. 39). Ben-Asher was apparently an elder contemporary of *Saadiah Gaon, who wrote the anti-Karaitic critique "*Essa Meshali*," against Ben-Asher.

The controversial question, as to whether or not Ben-Asher was a Karaite, was seemingly settled when this reply of Saadiah (mentioned in Dunash's objections on Saadiah, p. 21, no. 72) was discovered. In this reply it is clear that the Ben-Asher who was Saadiah's opponent worked on masorah, and it seems, therefore, that he was identical with Aaron Ben-Asher, the well-known masorete. The assumption that he was a Karaite serves to explain his attitude to the Bible and its authoritativeness in matters of *halakhah* (for example, *Dikdukei ha-Te'amim*, ed. A. Dotan (1967), ch. 2: "The prophets… complete the Torah, are as the Torah, and we decide

Law from them as we do from the Torah") and to vocalization, opinions rooted in Karaite thought. It appears from the parallel ideas and style used in the *Maḥberet Ben-Asher* (see below), from the "Wine Song" written by his father, and from the list which his father appended to the codex of the Prophets (kept in the Karaite synagogue, Cairo), which he wrote "827 years after the destruction of the Second Temple" (i.e., in 895), that his father, Moses Ben-Asher, was also a Karaite, and it is probable that Karaism was a family tradition. (Note, however, that Dotan (*Sinai*, 41 (1957), 280ff.) and M. Zucker (*Tarbiz*, 27 (1957/58), 61ff.) hold that Aaron Ben-Asher and his family were not Karaites.) It is noteworthy that the founder of the family, "Asher the Great Sage," apparently lived in the first half of the eighth century and was a contemporary of Anan, a precursor of Karaism.

Ben-Asher rapidly gained fame as the most authoritative of the Tiberias masoretes, and in 989, the scribe of the abovementioned manuscript of the Former Prophets vouched for the care with which his copy was written by the fact that he had vocalized and added the masorah "from the books that were [vocalized] by Aaron ben Moses Ben-Asher." Maimonides, by accepting the views of Ben-Asher (though only in regard to open and closed sections), helped establish and spread his authority. Referring to a Bible manuscript then in Egypt, he writes: "All relied on it, since it was corrected by Ben-Asher and was worked on (*ve-dikdek bo*) by him for many years, and was proofread many times in accordance with the masorah, and I based myself on this manuscript in the *Sefer Torah* that I wrote" (Yad, Maim. Sefer Torah, 8:4). It is generally agreed that the codex used by Maimonides is that formerly in Aleppo.

Proof for this is adduced from Saadiah b. David Al-Adni, who wrote in his commentary on the Yad (*ibid.*): "The Codex that the Gaon [i.e., Maimonides] used is in Zoba, called Aleppo, and is called the *Keter*... and at the end is written, 'I Aaron Ben-Asher proofread it... I saw and read it'" (Oxford, Bodleian Library Ms. Hunt. 372, fol. 138b; cf. P. Kahle, *The Cairo Genizah* (1947), 58). However, Cassuto, who studied the *Keter* in Aleppo, was doubtful. An attempt was made to refute these doubts by M. Goshen-Gottstein (*Textus*, 1 (1960), 1ff.), but A. Dotan further supported Cassuto's position (*Tarbiz*, 34 (1964/65), 136ff.) It now appears likely that it was Ben-Asher who vocalized and added the masorah to the *Keter* of Aleppo, despite the fact that the note in the manuscript was written after his death. The masorah has been vocalized and added by "the lord of scribes, the father of wise men and the first of teachers... the unique Rabbi Aaron ben Rabbi Asher, may his soul be bound up in the bond of eternal life" (the latter being an epithet applied to a person who has died)

The tradition of Ben-Asher is the one accepted in the Jewish Bible, but this does not mean that the version of the Bible found in the common editions is exactly the same as that which Ben-Asher produced. The differences between the printed editions and the various manuscripts assumed to be written in the Ben-Asher tradition are mainly in the placing of the accents, especially the use of the *meteg*, different uses of the *sheva* and *ḥataf* in certain grammatical forms, all differences that are unimportant for the average reader. These differences developed over the years, usually as a result of grammatical assumptions that were not always correct. Furthermore, certain divergences in vocalization and masorah are found even in manuscripts that are accepted as Ben-Asher codices. This fact, combined with the evidence of Mishael b. Uzziel in his *Kitab al-Khulaf*, indicates that Ben-Asher used different systems of vocalization at different times in specific words. It may be said, therefore, that different Ben-Asher manuscripts reveal a continual development in his method of vocalization.

Ben-Asher was one of the first to lay the foundations of Hebrew grammar. His *Sefer Dikdukei ha-Te'amim* (or the *Maḥberet Ben-Asher*, as David *Kimḥi called it in his commentary on Judg. 6:19) is a collection of grammatical rules and masoretic information. Grammatical principles were not at that time considered worthy of independent study. The value of this work is that the grammatical rules presented by Ben-Asher reveal the linguistic background of vocalization. The book was first published in *Biblia Rabbinica* edited by Pratensis, the format later called *Mikra'ot Gedolot* (1516–18), and again in 1879 by S.I. Baer and Strack, who edited the material according to topics, in a manner different from that in the first edition. Until recently all studies relating to Ben-Asher's system of grammar and masorah were based on this edition. A. Dotan's edition (1967), which includes a commentary and studies on the content of the book, changed the previous conception of *Dikdukei ha-Te'amim* as it had been understood for 90 years. Many of the phonological and morphological topics which had been commonly attributed to *Dikdukei ha-Te'amim* are not included. The main theme discussed in the book is the relationship of the biblical accents to the rules of vocalization and pronunciation. The *sheva* and its pronunciation play a major part in this work.

Except for certain parts, including masoretic lists, the book is written in a rhymed poetic style, using paytanic language. It can be assumed that the parts not written in this style were not by Ben-Asher. The language of the book shows a certain Arabic influence, particularly with regard to grammatical terms. Even in its more limited form *Dikdukei ha-Te'amim* is important not only for showing how the different vocalizers determined the correct vocalization, but also for a clearer understanding of the grammatical world of the later masoretes, who laid the foundations for Hebrew grammar in later generations.

BIBLIOGRAPHY: Fuerst, Karaeertum, 1 (1862), 112; Graetz, in: MGWJ, 20 (1871), 1–12, 49–59; Bacher, in: ZAW, 15 (1895), 293–304; Mann, Egypt, 2 (1922), 43–49; P. Kahle, *Masoreten des Westens*, 1 (1927); idem, in: VT, 1 (1951), 161–8; idem, in: *Donum Natalicium H.S. Nyberg* (1955), 161–70; L. Lipschuetz, *Der Bibeltext der Tiberischen Masoretenschule* (1937); K. Levy, *Zur masoretischen Grammatik* (1936); Teicher, in: JJS, 2 (1950/51), 17–25; S. Pinsker, *Likkutei Kadmoniyyot*

(1860), 32; Schorr, in: *He-Ḥalutz*, 6 (1862), 67ff.; J. Saphir, *Even Sappir*, 1 (1866), 11–20; 2 (1874), 185ff.; B.Z. Bacher, *Niẓẓanei ha-Dikduk* (1927), 27–41; D. Yellin, *Toledot Hitpatteḥut ha-Dikduk ha-Ivri* (1945), 6–29; M.H. Segal, *Mevo ha-Mikra*, 4 (1952[3]), 896–9 and esp. notes 15, 17; *Ben-Ḥayyim*, in: *Leshonenu*, 18 (1953), 92–94; B. Klar, *Meḥkarim ve-Iyyunim* (1954), 276–319; Cassuto, in: *Haaretz* (April 15, 1949). **ADD. BIBLIOGRAPHY:** E.J. Revell, in: ABD, 4: 593–94; J. Penkower, in: DBI, 1:117–19.

[Zeev Ben-Hayyim]

BEN-ASHER, MOSES (second half of ninth century), scribe and masorete. Moses was the fourth in the line of well-known masoretes descended from Asher the Elder, and the father of the last, Aaron. A manuscript by him of the Former and Latter Prophets has survived, written, pointed, and furnished with accents and masoretic notes. Found today in the Karaite synagogue in Cairo, it has been photographed a number of times (one photocopy is in Jerusalem). A colophon by Ben-Asher at the end of the manuscript testifies that he wrote it in Tiberias in the year 827 after the destruction of the Second Temple (i.e., 896 C.E.). The manuscript is a beautiful one, embellished with drawings and illuminations, the work of an expert artist, in a style which, according to the latest investigations, constitutes an ancient specimen of Islamic decorative art, older than any extant surviving Koran and thus perhaps the most ancient of this type.

The vowel-points, the accents, and the masoretic notes are marked with the stamp of antiquity, but deviate greatly from the method of pointing of his son Aaron, whose method is nowadays called "the school of Ben-Asher" (see *Ben-Asher, Aaron). A comparison of the readings in the manuscript with the list of variants in the *Kitāb al-Khulaf* of Mishael b. Uzziel shows that in almost two-thirds of the cases the manuscript follows the reading of *Ben-Naphtali, and only in one-third, that of Aaron Ben-Asher (see *Masorah). At times it also maintains its own independent reading. In about a quarter of the cases in which the two authorities agree, according to Mishael, he differs from both their readings. He points בִּישְׂרָאֵל (Jer. 29:23) and לִירְאָה (Jer. 32:39). Accordingly the Ms. displays a great measure of affinity with what was later termed "the school of Ben-Naphtali." On the other hand it contains a great number of *ge'ayot* (i.e., *metegs*; "secondary stress"), more than was usual in other manuscripts of his time, particularly *ge'ayot* in open syllables (known as *ga'ayah gedolah* "major *ga'ayah*"). There are also other anomalies in the pointing, such as some *degeshim* in the letter א (בּ/תלוּאִי, Jer. 38:12; תלוּאִים, Hos. 11:7). It follows that the actual tradition of pointing was not uniform throughout the generations of the Ben-Asher family; it was only the occupation with the masorah that they had in common. Another possibility, suggested by A. Dotan, is that the pointing and accents of the manuscript are by a different scribe and that Moses Ben-Asher only wrote the consonantal text. In any event the fragment entitled "The order of Scripture," which he copied at the end of the manuscript (p. 583), was certainly not written by him.

No other works by Moses have survived, but his name is mentioned in an Arabic *genizah* fragment (Cambridge, Ms. T.-S. Arabic 9/5): "and Moses Ben-Asher, may God have mercy upon him, has already written a large book…." Because that fragment also mentions, though without any connection with M. Ben-Asher, the expressions מצותה ("vowel"), אלז' מצותאת ("the seven vowels"), Allony conjectured that the large book attributed here to M. Ben-Asher is the anonymous *Kitāb al-Muṣawwitāt* mentioned in several places in the writings of Jonah *Ibn Janaḥ. Mention of it has also been discovered in Nissim Gaon's *Megillat Setarim* (see *Nissim b. Jacob b. Nissim), where it is ascribed to Ben-Asher (with no first name). At present there is not sufficient evidence to accept this conjecture. It would appear that he also wrote *piyyutim* and composed the "Song of the Vine," in which the people of Israel is compared to a vine whose roots are the patriarchs, and from which come forth the prophets and sages. Mention is also made there of the masorah, the accents, and the work of the masoretes. Most of the poem is extant, in three manuscripts (one of which is Ms. Leningrad B 19a); only its end is missing. The initial letters of the remnant verses form the acrostic ... משה בן אש ("Moses Ben-Ash…"). This poem contains one of the decisive proofs that M. Ben-Asher was not a Karaite.

In some places the name has been corrupted as a result of a faulty completion of the abbreviation "Ben-Asher," as in the commentary *Migdal Oz* on Maimonides' Yad, Sefer Torah 8:4, where "Moses Ben-Asher" occurs instead of Aaron, and as in the British Museum manuscript (Or. 4227, p. 274b) where "Moses b. Aaron Ben-Asher, the great scribe," occurs instead of Aaron b. Moses.

BIBLIOGRAPHY: J. Saphir, *Even Sappir*, 1 (1866), 14a–17a; 2 (1874), 185–91; R. Gottheil, in: JQR, 17 (1905), 639–41; E.S. Artom (Hartom), in: *Ha-Kinnus ha-Olami le Madda'ei ha-Yahadut*, 1 (1952), 190–4; B. Klar, *Meḥkarim ve-Iyyunim* (1954), 309–14; Pérez Castro, in: *Sefarad*, 15 (1955), 3–30; A. Dotan, in: *Sinai*, 41 (1957), 288–91, 295–9, 357–62; idem (ed.), *The Diqduqé Haṭṭĕʿamim of Ahăron ben Mōse ben Ašér*, 1 (1967), 70f.; M. Zucker, in: *Tarbiz*, 27 (1957/58), 61–82; P.E. Kahle, *The Cairo Geniza* (1959[2]), 82–86, 91–105; idem, *Der hebraeische Bibeltext seit Franz Delitzsch* (1961), 51–76; R.H. Pinder Wilson and R. Ettinghausen, *ibid.*, 95–98; N. Allony, in: HUCA, 35 (1964), 1–35 (Heb. pt.); idem, in: *Sefer Segal* (1964), 271–91; idem, in: *Leshonenu*, 29 (1964/65), 9–23, 136–59; I. Yeivin, *Keter Aram-Ẓovah* (1968), 360f. **ADD. BIBLIOGRAPHY:** D. Levit-Tawil, in: JNES, 53 (1994), 157–93.

[Aron Dotan]

BENATZKY, RALPH (1884–1957), composer. Benatzky was born in Moravske-Budejovice and studied in Prague and Munich. A composer of light music, he wrote about five thousand songs and 92 operettas. The best known was *Im Weissen Roessl* (1930), which became famous throughout the world as *White Horse Inn*. Benatzky went to live in the United States in 1938, but later returned to Europe and settled in Zurich. He wrote the scores for about 250 films.

BIBLIOGRAPHY: Riemann-Gurlitt; Baker, Biog. Dict.

[Dora Leah Sowden]

BEN-AVI, ITHAMAR (1882–1943), Hebrew journalist and Zionist. He was the son of Eliezer *Ben-Yehuda, from the initials of whose name Ben-Avi formed his Hebrew name. Ben-Avi was one of the first modern Jews whose mother tongue was Hebrew. In his early youth he began publishing in Hebrew periodicals edited by his father. He studied at the Teachers' Seminary of the Alliance Israélite Universelle in Paris and at the Institute for Oriental Studies at the University of Berlin. On his return to Ereẓ Israel in 1908, he joined the editorial board of Ben-Yehuda's *Ha-Ẓevi* and *Ha-Or*, bringing to them something of the flamboyant spirit of popular European and American journalism. During World War I he lived with his family in the U.S.A. Returning after the war he founded the daily **Do'ar ha-Yom* in Jerusalem in 1919 and continued to edit it until 1929. He also served as the Jerusalem correspondent for the London *Times* and *Daily Mail* and several French newspapers. An accomplished speaker in several languages, Ben-Avi visited various countries on behalf of the Jewish National Fund and the settlement projects of the native generation of moshavot farmers, of whose organization, *Benei Binyamin, he was a co-founder. In 1939 he went to the U.S.A., where he later died. His remains were interred in Jerusalem in 1947. Impetuous by nature, Ben-Avi advocated bold innovations, such as the writing of Hebrew in Latin characters, in which he published the weekly *Dror* (1933–4) and a biography of his father (*Avi*, 1927). In the 1930s he campaigned for the partitioning of Palestine into Jewish and Arab cantons. His political and cultural aim was the transformation of the Jewish people into an independent "western" nation.

BIBLIOGRAPHY: Ḥ. Ben-Yehuda, *Nosei ha-Degel* (1944), includes bibliography.

[Gedalyah Elkoshi]

BENAYAH, family of scribes living in San'a, Yemen, in the 15th–16th century. Between 1450 and 1483 the patriarch of the family, BENAYAH BEN SAADIAH BEN ZECHARIAH BEN BENAYAH BEN ODED, known as Ben Merjaz, copied dozens of books, most of which were copies of the Bible (*tījān*, sin. *tāj*). In the margins of the pages of these copies there was the *mesorah and at the beginning the *Maḥberet ha-tījān,* which included the rules of reading. These copies, however, did not include the Aramaic *targum* of *Onkelos or the Arabic *tafsīr* of *Saadiah, as was customary in ancient Yemenite copying. Benayah's inscriptions are considered to be accurate and concise, which make him the most important of Yemen's scribes. His children were also scribes: DAVID (1484–1510), JOSEPH (1486–1508), SAADIA (b. 1489), the daughter MIRIAM (!), and the grandchildren ME'ODED and AVIGAD, the sons of David. Y. Sappir, who visited Yemen in 1859, tells of the beautiful and accurate copying done by Miriam. At the end of the manuscript she wrote: "Do not bring punishment upon me if you discover mistakes since I am a nursing mother, Miriam the daughter of Benayah the scribe" (*Massa' Teiman,* 1945, 174; the manuscript was never found). The sons of Benayah also copied the *haftarot*, prayer books which preserves the ancient Yemenite tradition, and other books such as the *Kitāb Mi'yār al-'Ilm* of Abū Ḥāmid al-*Ghazālī by Sa'adia. The connection between the tradition of the scholars of Tiberian tradition and the writings of the Benayah family was a subject of debate among scholars in 1961. According to an ancient tradition, Benayah copied over 400 texts. Today 33 manuscripts of the Benayah family are documented. Most texts are owned by public libraries and a few by private collectors (Rigler, 1991, 163–65). The texts were usually ordered by wealthy men, and after a while were donated to synagogues. In the colophon of a copy of the Early Prophets from 1475 Benayah dedicated a poem honoring the man who had ordered the book, a certain Avraham (Ratzaby, 1975). The Benayah family controlled the copying profession in San'a, which was the most important Jewish center in Yemen between 1460 and 1540.

BIBLIOGRAPHY: Y. Sappir, *Massa' Teiman* (ed. A. Ya'ari, 1945), 173–74; *Haaretz*, May 26, June 2, 16, July 14, 1961; Jan. 5, Feb. 2, 1962; Y. Ratzaby, in: *Sinai* 76 (1975), 273–76; M. Beit Arié and C. Sirat, *Oẓar Kitvei Yad Ivriyyim* (1972–86), 3 vols; M. Rigler, in: *Y. Ratzaby Jubilee Volume* (1991), 161–79.

[Yosef Tobi (2nd ed.)]

BENAYAHU, MEIR (1926–), Israeli scholar. The son of the Israel chief rabbi Isaac *Nissim, Benayahu was a member of the team of senior workers at the *Ben-Zvi Institute for Research on Oriental Jewish Communities, which was founded in 1947, and from 1964 he was its director. A prolific researcher, he published numerous studies and documents. His works include: *Marbiẓ Torah* ("Propagator of the Torah"), on the authority, functions, and status of the bearer of the title *Marbiẓ Torah* in Oriental countries (1951); *Rabbi Ḥayyim Yosef David Azulai* (1959), a comprehensive monograph; *Rabbi Ya'akov Elyashar ve-Ḥibburo Megillat Paras* ("R. Jacob Elyashar and His Work 'The Scroll of Persia'," 1960); *Sefer Toledot ha-Ari* ("Biography of R. Isaac *Luria", 1967). He also published a new edition of *Zimrat ha-Areẓ* of Jacob *Berab (the Third) on the beginnings of the Jewish settlement in Tiberias during the mid-18th century. Benayahu was an editor of the yearbook *Yerushalayim* (Jerusalem), comprising studies on Ereẓ Israel (vols. 3–5; 1951–55). The first seven volumes of the scientific periodical of the *Ben-Zvi Institute, *Sefunot* (begun in 1957), were jointly edited by Izhak *Ben-Zvi and Benayahu, while from the eighth volume onward he was the sole editor. From 1985 he was director of the Nissim Research Institute and in 2004 he was awarded the EMET Prize for work that integrated traditional Torah learning with modern scholarship.

BEN AZZAI, SIMEON (early second century C.E.), *tanna*, generally referred to in talmudic literature simply as "Ben Azzai." In three places in the Mishnah (Zev. 1:3, Yad. 3:5, 4:2) he is referred to by his full name: Rabbi Shimon ben Azzai (according to Parma de Rossi 128 and others). Presumably a disciple of *Joshua b. Hananiah, he transmitted rulings in his name (Yoma 2:3), brought a proof in support of R. Joshua's position (Yev 4:13), and interpreted an obscure tradition before R. Joshua (Par. 1:1). He is found disagreeing with R. Akiva (Shek. 3:1, 4:5) and he transmitted a tradition in the name of R. Joshua in the presence of R. Akiva, who changed his ruling in line with this tradition (Taan 4:4). In the Bavli he is called a "disciple-colleague" of R. Akiva (BB 158b). It was said of him: "With the passing of Ben Azzai, diligent scholars passed from the earth" (Sot. 9:15). According to tradition Ben Azzai was one of the four "who entered the Garden" (*pardes*). According to Tosefta Ḥag. 2:3, "he caught a glimpse and died," while his companion Beb Zoma went mad as a result of this mystical experience. In the Jerusalem Talmud (Ḥag. 2:1 77b) their roles are reversed. Although he declared that whoever abstains from procreation is regarded as though he had shed blood (Tos. Yev 8:7), he himself never married so as not to be distracted from his studies. When accused of not practicing what he preached, he answered: "What shall I do if my soul yearns for Torah? The world can be perpetuated by others" (*ibid.*). The Bavli, nevertheless, reports in one place that he married, but separated from his wife (Sot. 4b), and according to another tradition he was betrothed to Akiva's daughter who, as her mother had done, made it a condition of marriage that her husband devote himself to the study of the Torah (Ket. 63a, but cf. S. Friedman, *JSIJ*, 3 (2004) 1–39, and Tosefot to Ket. 63a). His aphorisms included: "Be quick in carrying out a minor commandment as in the case of a major one, and flee from transgression; for one good deed leads to another good deed and one transgression leads to another transgression; for the reward for a good deed is another good deed and the reward for a transgression is another transgression" (Avot 4:2). While R. Akiva said that the verse "Thou shalt love thy neighbor as thyself" (Lev. 19:18) is a great principle of the Torah, Ben Azzai declared that the verse "This is the book of the generations of man" (Gen. 5:1) embodied an even greater principle, i.e., of the common origin of mankind (Sifra 7:4 and parallel passages). Ben Azzai was not referred to as "rabbi" and was not described as one of the "sages," but rather as one of the "disciples" who argued in the presence of the sages (Sanh. 17b). Because of his reputation, later generations of scholars used to underscore their own scholarship by claiming: "I am like Ben Azzai in the marketplace of Tiberias" (Kid. 20a). Ben Azzai was renowned for his saintliness; it was said: "He who sees Ben Azzai in his dreams may look forward to achieving saintliness" (Ber. 57b). He is numbered by some among the *Ten Martyrs (Lam. R. 2:2, no. 4).

BIBLIOGRAPHY: Bacher, Tann; Hyman, Toledot, 1206–09.

[Zvi Kaplan]

BEN BAG BAG, *tanna*, apparently of the first century C.E. His most famous dictum: "Turn it and turn it [the Torah], for everything is in it, and contemplate it, and grow grey and old over it, and stir not from it, for you can have no better rule than this" (Avot 5:25) is elsewhere attributed to Hillel (ARN 12, 11). A number of halakhic statements are reported in Ben Bag Bag's name in various *baraitot* (e.g., Er., 27b; Tosef., BK 10:38). On the question whether a person is permitted to take the law into his own hands he states: "do not enter your neighbor's courtyard in stealth to take what belongs to you without his permission, lest you appear to him a thief; rather break his teeth [i.e., enter openly] and say to him, 'It is my own property that I take'" (BK 27b). Some scholars identify Ben Bag Bag with Johanan b. Bag Bag, who sent a question to Judah b. Bathyra in Nisibis, and whom the latter eulogized as "an expert in the chambers of the Torah" (Tosef., Ket. 5:1). Some incline to the view that the name is symbolic like that of *Ben He He (Avot 5:26) with whom he has been identified, and that he was a proselyte (Ḥag., 9b and Tos., s.v. *Bar He He*). Some identify him with the proselyte who came to Hillel and asked to be taught the Torah "while standing on one leg," which occasioned the famous reply of Hillel: "What is hateful to thee do not do to thy fellow."

BIBLIOGRAPHY: Bacher, Tann; Frankel, Mishnah, 100f.; Hyman, Toledot, 672 s.v. *Yoḥanan b. Bag Bag.*

[Zvi Kaplan]

BEN CHANANJA, the first Hungarian Jewish learned periodical, published in German between 1844 and 1867. *Ben Chananja* was founded and edited by Leopold *Loew. It first appeared in Leipzig as a quarterly in 1844; resumed publication in Szeged, Hungary, in 1858; and became a weekly in reduced format in 1861. *Ben Chananja* advanced the scientific development of Jewish studies and stimulated interest in Jewish questions. Its contributors were scholars of prestige in Hungary and abroad. The periodical presented biblical exegesis, commentary on the Talmud, historical studies, educational information, and literary news. It also considered religious and social problems, advocating the establishment of a rabbinical seminary and legislation for Jewish emancipation. Among the contributors were Simon Bacher, Abraham Hochmuth, Solomon Buber, S.D. Luzzatto, and Leopold Dukes. The academic material was supplemented with topical articles, editorials, Jewish communal news, and occasional poems. *Ben Chananja* had correspondents in Jerusalem, Berlin, New York, and in most cities with large Jewish communities in Europe and America.

[Jeno Zsoldos]

BENCHETRIT, AARON (1886–1967), physician and communal leader. Born in Tetuan, Spanish Morocco, Benchetrit spent his childhood in Caracas, Venezuela, and studied in Paris and Caracas. He was the medical director and administrator of the Leproserías de Venezuela (1921–26). In 1927 he moved to Bogotá, Colombia, where he was in charge of all leprosy cases in the country from 1927 to 1935 and directed many scientific researches on leprosy. He published several medical works including *Disertaciones de un estudiante de medicina* (1917), *La epidemia febríl de Caracas* (1919), *Nuevas disertaciones* (1921), and *Disertaciones acerca de la lepra* (1922). He also wrote on Zionism in *Disertaciones acerca del sionismo*. Benchetrit was president of the Centro Israelita of Bogotá and was president of the Zionist Federation of Colombia, 1943–44.

BENCHIMOL, Moroccan family. The descendants of ABRAHAM BENCHIMOL, one of the leaders of the community in *Fez (1700), established a business of international repute in Tangiers at the end of the 18th century. For four generations the family played a leading role in Morocco's political and economic life. As diplomats, they were entrusted with many missions by the French or the sultans. ḤAYYIM (1834–1915), who lived in Tangiers, was the founder of freemasonry in Morocco. There he organized and supported the *Alliance Israélite Universelle. He also established the first newspapers in Tangiers for the defense of human rights and of the Jews in particular. His influence provoked attacks by the anti-Semite Edouard *Drumont. A philanthropist and founder of charitable institutions, Ḥayyim headed the Jewry of northern Morocco.

BIBLIOGRAPHY: J.M. Toledano, *Ner ha-Ma'arav* (1911), 124, 133; F. Rey, *De la protection diplomatique et consulaire dans les échelles du Levant et de Barbarie* (1899), 515–7; A. Laredo, *Memorias de un viejo Tangerino* (1935), 435–449; Miège, Maroc, 2 (1961), 85ff.; 210; 3 (1962), 443, 498; 4 (1963), 49–50; Hirschberg, Afrikah, 2 (1965), 313.

[David Corcos]

BEN-CHORIN, SCHALOM (1913–1999; until 1931 **Fritz Rosenthal**), German philosopher, journalist, and writer. Ben-Chorin grew up in an assimilated family in Munich. Causing severe conflicts with his family, he discovered Judaism in 1928, showing an interest in the Jewish religion, Zionism, and modern Jewish literature at the same time. He also took on the name "peace, son of freedom" (Schalom Ben-Chorin). Following Martin *Buber he sought an alternative to Orthodoxy and secular Zionism, which he finally found in Reform Judaism (cf. *Jenseits von Orthodoxie und Liberalismus*, 1937). Having left his apprenticeship as a bookseller at the Jewish Ewer bookstore and studying German literature, theater, and religion, he was arrested and mistreated in the streets of Munich in 1933, a turning point in his life (cf. his autobiography *Jugend an der Isar*, 1974). In 1935 he immigrated to Palestine and started working as journalist for German newspapers (articles collected in *Begegnungen*, 1991) as part of a group of German-Jewish intellectuals and writers in Palestine. Together with the writer Gerson Stern he edited an early anthology of German-Jewish literature in Palestine and himself wrote novels and poetry (*Menora. Eine Auswahl literarischen Schaffens in Erez-Israel*, 1941). Ben-Chorin was much better known, however, as a thinker in Reform Judaism – he also laid the foundation of the Reform community in Jerusalem in 1958 (the Har-El-Synagogue) – and as philosopher of religion mediating between Judaism and Christianity. On the one hand, he wrote several fundamental and introductory works on Jewish theology, anthropology, and ethics, such as for example *Juedischer Glaube* (1975), which is based on a series of lectures at Tuebingen and aims at portraying the theology of Judaism according to Maimonides' classic model of the 13 *Articles of Faith, though more for a non-Jewish audience (cf. also *Die Tafeln des Bundes*, 1979; *Juedische Theologie im 20. Jahrhundert*, 1988). On the other hand, he reflected upon the relation between Judaism and Christianity, seeking not only the differences but much more the links. While still in Munich and under the name Rosenthal he wrote the poem *Der Rabbi von Nazareth* (in *Das Mal der Sendung*, 1935). In this spirit, from 1940 he wrote several books promoting the Jewish-Christian dialogue (*Die Christusfrage an den Juden*, 1941; *Das christliche Verstaendnis des Alten Testaments und der juedische Einwand*, 1941), an endeavor which he stepped up after the war, traveling to Germany from 1956 and still writing in German (*Theologia Judaica*, 1/2, 1982, 1992; *Weil wir Brueder sind*, 1988). In this context, he made clear the Jewish origins of Christianity, interpreting some of the central figures of Christianity like Jesus, Paul, and Miriam (cf. the trilogy *Die Heimkehr*, consisting of *Bruder Jesus*, 1967; *Apostel Paulus*, 1970, *Mutter Mirjam*, 1971). As a catch-phrase symbolizing his approach, the often-quoted sentence from his book on Jesus might be cited: "Der Glaube Jesu einigt uns, aber der Glaube an Jesus trennt uns" ("The faith of Jesus unifies us but the belief in Jesus separates us"). At the same time he tried to answer a central theological question which came up after the Holocaust: the meaning of suffering and the absence of God (e.g., *Als Gott schwieg*, 1986). He was highly esteemed for his efforts at bringing about a new Jewish-Christian and Jewish-German dialogue after 1945. Ben-Chorin died in Jerusalem.

BIBLIOGRAPHY: G. Mueller (ed.), *Israel hat dennoch Gott zum Trost* (1978); H. Bleicher (ed.), *Der Mann, der Friede heißt* (1983); T. Vasko, *From the Creation to the Kingdom of God: The Concept of God's Revelation by the Reform Jew Schalom Ben-Chorin in Dialogues with Christianity and Islam* (2003).

[Andreas Kilcher (2nd ed.)]

BENDA, JULIEN (1867–1956), French writer and philosopher. Benda studied history and philosophy at the Sorbonne. His first book, *Dialogues à Byzance* (1900), offered a bold analysis of the manifestations of corruption in French society, which formed the background of the Dreyfus Trial. Benda wrote several novels, especially in the first years of his literary activity, including *L'Ordination* (1911), which reveal his rationalistic outlook and rigorous morals. But Benda was first and foremost a philosopher who preferred to express his ideas in essays defending reason, science, and responsible thinking against the cult of intuition. In *Le Bergsonisme, ou une philosophie de la mobilité* (1912) and in other works, Benda attacked Bergson's irrationalism; in *Belphégor* (1919; Eng. tr. 1929), Benda rejected most contemporary writers, such as Romain Rolland, Paul Claudel, Maurice Barrès, George Sorel, and Charles Péguy, his former friend. Benda's militancy increased in his most famous book *La trahison des clercs* (1927; *The Great Betrayal*, 1928), in which he castigated contemporary thinkers and writers, including the intellectuals and the professionals. He accused them of having sold reason or of having left it to the state, to society, to the parties, to the family, etc. He charged them with having forsaken service to reason and to the perennial truth, all for the sake of temporary success. The rigorous conclusions which oppose any compromise are the basis of his views in theology, history, and aesthetics, in his last books such as *Essai d'un discours cohérent sur les rapports de Dieu et du monde* (1931) and *La France byzantine; ou Le triomphe de la littérature pure...* (1945). This last work was sharply criticized. Although Benda did not convert to Christianity, he was completely isolated from Jewish life, and considered his Jewish origin a burden. He had to seek refuge during World War II in southern France. However, he regarded the Jewish problem as only a minor aspect of the war.

BIBLIOGRAPHY: H.E. Read, *Julien Benda and the New Humanism* (1930); P. Brodin, *Maîtres et témoins de l'entre deux guerres* (1943); C. Mauriac, *La trahison d'un clerc* (1945); R.J. Niess, *Julien, Benda* (Eng., 1956).

[Hiram Peri]

BEN-DAVID, JOSEPH (1920–1986), Israeli sociologist. Ben-David was born in Gyor, Hungary, and immigrated to Israel in 1941. He studied at the London School of Economics from 1947–1949. He received his M.A. in history and sociology in 1950 and Ph.D. in sociology in 1955, both from the Hebrew University.

In 1951 he was appointed George Wise Professor of Sociology at the Hebrew University, in 1968 research associate and visiting professor of sociology at the University of Chicago, and in 1979 the Stella M. Rowley Professor of Education and professor of sociology at the University of Chicago.

Ben-David's sociological research and publications reflected his interest in the interaction between macrolevel historical events and microlevel sociological processes in the areas of the development of science, higher education, and the professions and social stratification.

His publications included *Fundamental Research and the Universities: Some Comments on International Differences* (1968), *The Scientist's Role in Society: A Comparative Study* (1971); *American Higher Education: Directions Old and New* (1972), and *Centers of Learning: Britain, France, Germany and the United States* (1971).

[Beverly Mizrachi (2nd ed.)]

BENDAVID, LAZARUS (**Eleazar**; 1762–1832), German mathematician, philosopher, and educator. He attended the universities of *Göttingen* and Halle, and spent from 1792 to 1797 in Vienna where he delivered public lectures on Kantian philosophy. In 1802 he became political editor of the newspaper *Haude- und Spenersche Zeitung*. In 1806 he was appointed honorary director of the Juedische Freischule in Berlin, which he headed until 1825. The school attained a high reputation and a large proportion of its students were Christian until 1819, when the government forbade the enrollment of non-Jews. The school offered a revolutionary model of modern Jewish education combined with a high level of German and secular classic culture that represented the educational and philosophic notions of the Jewish Haskalah. Bendavid began his scientific work in 1785 with an investigation of the theory of colors. In 1786 he published *Ueber die Parallellinien*, and in 1789 *Versuch einer logischen Auseinandersetzung des mathematischen Unendlichen.*

In 1795 his *Vorlesungen ueber die "Kritik der reinen Vernunft"* appeared. Bendavid held that philosophy had attained the pinnacle of its development in the Kantian system. From 1796 to 1798 he wrote a series of works explaining Kant's philosophy. In 1799 he published *Versuch einer Geschmackslehre*, containing his theory of aesthetics based on Kant. In 1801 the Royal Academy of Sciences in Berlin awarded him a prize for his study, *Ueber den Ursprung unserer Erkenntnis*, and published it in 1802.

With this work, Bendavid's philosophical labors came to an end. During his remaining thirty years he wrote solely on Jewish problems. These writings reflect the struggles of the first post-Mendelssohnian Jewish generation with the problem of being Jewish. Bendavid regarded Reform Judaism as the only means of stemming the tide of conversion to Christianity. In his work *Etwas zur Charackteristick der Juden* (1793), he advocated the abolition of the ritual laws and the cultural and social assimilation of Jews. Nevertheless, he eschewed conversion to Christianity. Kant wrongly interpreted Bendavid's attitude as counseling Jews to accept Christianity and advised them, on the strength of Bendavid's views, openly to adopt the religion of Jesus and thus at long last attain a religious ethic and through it a religion (cf., Kant, *Der Streit der Fakultäten*; also, the pertinent remarks of Hermann *Cohen in his *Kants Begruendung der Ethik* (1901), 49). Bendavid's biblical studies are in the spirit of extreme Haskalah rationalism. In an essay in 1797 he attempted to show that the Ark of the Covenant was an electrical device which helped to kindle the wood on the altar. He published studies on the jubilee year, the prohibition of usury, the mixture of wool and linen, the belief in the Messiah, and the written and oral Law. In his article on the Messiah he sought to demonstrate, by investigating the theory of the transmigration of the Messiah's soul, that the belief in the coming of the Redeemer is not a dogma of Judaism and that the bestowal of equal rights upon the Jews would signify that the "Messiah" had come.

ADD. BIBLIOGRAPHY: D. Bourel, "Eine Generation Später – Lazarus Bendavid (1762–1832)," in: M. Albrecht (ed.), *Moses Mendelssohn und Kreise seiner Wirksamkeit* (1994), 363-80; idem, "Lazarus Bendavids Bildungsweg und seine Tätigkeit als Direktor der jüduschen Freischule in Belin," in: B.L. Behm, U. Lohmann, and I. Lohmann (eds.), *Jüdische Erziehung und aufklärerische Schulreform – Analysen zum späten 18. und frühen 19. Jaherhundert* (2002), 359–67; I. Lohmann, "Die juedische Freischule in Berlin im Spiegel ihrer Programmschriften (1803–1826)," in: A. Herzig, H.O. Horch, and R. Jütte (eds.), *Judentum und Aufklärung* (2002), 66–90.

[Samuel Hugo Bergman / Yehoyada Amir (2nd ed.)]

BENDEMANN, EDUARD JULIUS FRIEDRICH (1811–1889), German painter. Born in Berlin as the youngest child of Anton Bendemann and Fanny, née von Halle, a burgeois Jewish family who later converted to Protestantism, Bendemann revealed his talent early in a portrait he painted of his grandmother before he was 20. After having studied under Johann Gottfried von Schadow, he followed the son of Johann Gottfried, Wilhelm von Schadow, to Duesseldorf in 1827 and enrolled in the Duesseldorf School of Painting, whose head was Wilhelm Schadow. In 1830 he accompanied Schadow to Italy, where for one year he devoted himself exclusively to the study of Raphael, Michelangelo and the Nazarenes. There he apparently formed his taste for painting monumental historical scenes in a classicist style. Bendemann produced his best-known paintings between 1831 and 1835, among them *The Exiles of Babylon* (1832), *Two Girls at the Well* (1833), *Jeremiah at the Destruction of Jerusalem* (1836) and *Die Kuenste am Brunnen der Poesie* (1837). In 1835 Bendemann married Schadow's sister Lida. He was appointed professor at the Academy of Fine Arts of Dresden in 1838 and executed a number of murals for the royal palace there. In the revolution of 1848 he was an active member of pro-revolutionary leagues. In 1859 he succeeded his former teacher and brother-in-law as director of the Academy in Duesseldorf, but resigned in 1867 due to ill health. He was commissioned to paint portraits of well-known figures, and a large number of his works are exhibited in Berlin museums. In addition, his illustrations in the neo-classical style appear in such literary works as the *Nibelungenlied* (published 1840 in Leipzig) and Lessing's *Nathan the Wise*. His son RUDOLF (1851–1884) was also a well-known painter. His elder son FELIX (1848–1915) was an admiral and chief of Naval Staff.

BIBLIOGRAPHY: Roth, Art, 544; J. Schrattenholz, *Eduard Bendemann* (Ger., 1891). **ADD. BIBLIOGRAPHY:** W. Aschenborn, *Eduard Bendemann (1811–1885). Das Direktorat an der Düsseldorfer Kunstakademie 1859–67* (1998); L. von Donop (ed.): *Ausstellung der Werke von Eduard Bendemann in der Koeniglichen Nationalgalerie* (1890); W. von Kalnein (ed.), *Die Duesseldorfer Malerschule* (1979); *Die Handzeichnungen des 19. Jahrhunderts. Duesseldorfer Malerschule. Die erste Jahrhunderthaelfte* Teil 1: Tafeln;. 1978. Teil 2: Textband. 1980. Bearb. v. Ute Ricke-Immel. (1980); B. Maaz, *Johann Gottfried Schadow und die Kunst seiner Zeit* (1995).

[Pnina Nave / Sonja Beyer (2nd ed.)]

BENDER, ALFRED PHILIP (1863–1937), South African minister. The son of a minister of the Dublin Hebrew Congregation in Ireland, he was the recognized leader of Cape Town Jewry for many years, both in religious and secular affairs. He was minister of the Cape Town Hebrew Congregation, the "mother congregation" of South Africa, from 1895 for 42 years and was responsible for initiating many educational, social, and cultural activities, including special services for children, confirmation services for girls, Sunday morning classes for women, and debating and social clubs for young men, taking a special interest in Jewish university students. Although very English in outlook and not sympathetic to the ways of "foreigners," he always gave generous assistance to East European immigrants in their settlement problems. He was long opposed to the principle of a representative lay body for South African Jewry, and in consequence his congregation did not affiliate with the Board of Deputies until 1919. He was also unsympathetic to the Zionist movement, but supported it after the Balfour Declaration. In the general community he was prominent in numerous educational and philanthropic endeavors, giving long service to the Cape Town hospital board, the school board, the council of the Cape Town University, and a variety of nondenominational philanthropic organizations.

BIBLIOGRAPHY: I. Abrahams, *Birth of a Community* (1955), index; G. Saron and L. Hotz (eds.), *Jews in South Africa* (1955), index.

[Gustav Saron]

BENDER, MORRIS BORIS (1905–1983), U.S. neurologist. Bender, who was born in Russia, was taken to the United States in 1914. After graduating in medicine he trained in neurology and psychiatry in several New York hospitals. He was research fellow in neurophysiology at Yale University (1936–38) and New York's Mount Sinai Hospital (1938–42). He then served as head of the laboratory of experimental neurology at New York University (1942–50). He joined the faculty of neurology at the New York University College of Medicine in 1938, becoming professor of clinical neurology in 1953. In 1966 he was appointed professor and chairman of the department of neurology of the Mount Sinai School of Medicine. He was also clinical professor of neurology at Columbia University's College of Physicians and Surgeons from 1953 to 1967. Bender's major research interests were the physiology of the visual and oculomotor systems and behavioral neurology, especially consciousness and perception. His major works are *Disorders in Perception* (1952) and *Visual Field Defects after Penetrating Missile Wounds of the Brain* (in collaboration with others, 1960); he also edited *The Oculomotor System* (1964) and *The Approach to Diagnosis in Modern Neurology* (1967).

[Fred Rosner]

BENDERLY, SAMSON (1876–1944), U.S. educator. Benderly, who was born in Safed, Palestine, emigrated to Baltimore in 1898. He received a medical degree at Johns Hopkins University. During his internship Benderly became interested in modern Jewish education in Baltimore and abandoned his medical career. In 1910 he was appointed director of the first Bureau of Jewish Education in the United States, in New York. This agency outlasted its parent body, the *kehillah* of New York City, and was molded by Benderly's lifework. Benderly conceived of a comprehensive educational program to raise the level of Jewish life in America. He was the American organizer of *Ivrit be-Ivrit* pedagogy – the use of Hebrew as the language of instruction. He initiated pilot schools that developed curricula and experimented with new ideas. He organized school board representatives, formed principals' and teachers' study groups, and initiated a leadership-training program to make Jewish education a profession. Benderly also pioneered in the education of Jewish girls, and in adolescent and secondary Jewish schooling. He experimented with Jewish educational camping, initiated home-study projects for the preschool child, and designed extension programs for the unschooled. His bureau structure was the prototype for similar agencies throughout America, and the personnel he trained became foremost leaders of Jewish education in America.

BIBLIOGRAPHY: N.H. Winter, *Jewish Education in the Pluralist Society* (1966), incl. bibl.

[Nathan H. Winter]

BENDERY (Rom. **Tighina**), city in Bessarabia (in Romania 1918–40; 1941–44), Moldova. The presence of Jews there is first recorded in 1769 and a burial society, whose *pinkas* (register) is still extant, was founded in 1793. There were 101 Jewish families living in Bendery in 1808 (out of 331). In 1814 the *ẓaddik* Aryeh Leib Wertheim, son of Simeon Solomon of *Savran, became rabbi of Bendery; the descendants of the dynasty of *ẓaddikim* which he founded served as rabbis of Bendery until World War II. The Jewish population increased with the influx of immigrants into Bessarabia in the 19th century, numbering 4,297 in 1864 and 10,644 in 1897 (33.5% of the total population). Institutions of the community included a hospital founded in 1885, an old-age home, a secondary school founded in 1912, and an elementary school. In 1925, of the 1,526 members of the local Jewish cooperative loan-bank, 701 were employed in commerce, 363 in handicrafts, and 49 in agriculture. The economic situation of the Jews detoriated as a result of growing antisemitism, as the city was the center of Alexander *Cuza's Fascist Party. According to the official census, the community numbered 8,294 (26.4% of the total population) in 1930. The communal organization was dissolved and its institutions were abolished or nationalized when Bessarabia became part of Soviet Russia in June 1940.

[Eliyahu Feldman]

Holocaust Period

Under Soviet occupation (1940–41), wealthy Jews were exiled to Siberia, as were wealthy non-Jews. With the beginning of the German-Romanian invasion, the Soviet authorities provided transport and many Jews fled to the interior of Russia. On July 4, 1941, the Romanian army assembled the remaining 700 Jews in the local castle, and shot them. After the liberation in September 1944, some 800 Jews returned, reestablishing the community, but they eventually left for Romania and from there Israel. In Bendery an agreement was signed between Germany and Romania, on August 31, 1941, concerning the plan to deport Jews to Transnistria.

[Jean Ancel / Shmuel Spector (2nd ed.)]

BIBLIOGRAPHY: Taubman, in: *Kovez Besarabyah* (1941), 90–96; Feldman, in: *Sefer Yahadut Besarabyah*. **ADD. BIBLIOGRAPHY:** PK Romanyah, s.v.

BENDIX, BENEDICT HEINRICH (1768–1828), German engraver, known for his portraits of leaders of German Jewry in the early 19th century. Bendix was born in Berlin and studied engraving. He portrayed various contemporaries such as the Duke and Duchess of Mecklenburg and the mathematician Abraham Wolff. He exhibited his works at the Academy of Berlin in 1788 and 1793. His only mezzotint (1808) portrays Aron Beer, the first cantor to be appointed to the Berlin Jewish community. Among his most important works are two plates, each consisting of three medallions: one depicting Napoleon I, Frederick William III, and Alexander I of Russia, and the other Empress Josephine, Queen Louise, and Empress Elizabeth of Russia. Bendix also executed an engraving of Nathan and the Templar (1806), a subject taken from Lessing's play *Nathan the Wise*. When the Berlin Jewish community opened a school in 1825 Bendix was engaged as teacher of drawing. He remained in that position until his death by suicide.

ADD. BIBLIOGRAPHY: U. Thieme, "Felix Becker," in: *Allgemeines Lexikon der bildenden Künstler von der Antike bis zur Gegenwart*, vol. 3 (1992).

BENDIX, OTTO (1845–1904), pianist, oboist, composer, and teacher. Born in Copenhagen, the brother of the conductor Victor *Bendix, he studied with Niels Gade and then with Kullak in Berlin and Franz Liszt in Weimar. Bendix taught piano at the Copenhagen Conservatory and was oboist in a theater orchestra.

In 1880 he immigrated to the United States to teach at the New England Conservatory in Boston, and in 1895 he founded his own music school in San Francisco. He also appeared as a concert pianist in the United States and Europe and published some piano pieces.

BIBLIOGRAPHY: *Baker's Biographical Dictionary of Musicians* (1991⁸); W. Lyle, *A Dictionary of Pianists* (1985).

[Naama Ramot (2nd ed.)]

BENDIX, REINHARD (1916–1991), U.S. sociologist. Born in Berlin, Bendix left Germany after Hitler's rise to power and emigrated to the U.S.A. In 1943 he began his academic career as an instructor at the University of Chicago. He taught at the University of Colorado (1946–47) and then at the University of California at Berkeley. In 1956 he became full professor and chairman of the Department of Sociology. In 1959 he was elected president of the American Sociological Association. He served as director of the University of California Education Abroad Program in Gottingen, Germany (1968–70), and in 1972 he joined the Department of Political Science at Berkeley.

Bendix approached sociological problems typologically. His first published work, *Social Science and the Distrust of Reason* (1951), began to build bridges between European and American sociological traditions. He used the theories of Max Weber as a basis for his sociological explorations and refined and advanced them considerably. His book *Max Weber: An Intellectual Portrait* (1960) is largely biographical but his primary interests, as is shown in most of his books and numerous articles in sociological journals, were in political and industrial sociology, social stratification, and sociological theory.

His book *Class, Status and Power* (1953; 1967²), a collection of readings in stratification edited jointly with Seymour Martin *Lipset, became a standard work in the field. A later publication was *Social Mobility in Industrial Society*, which he also co-authored with Lipset. His best-known book, for which he received the MacIver award, is *Work and Authority in Industry: Ideologies of Management in the Course of Industrialization* (1956). It is based on historical data from England, the United States, Russia, and East Germany. Another work, *Nationbuilding and Citizenship* (1964), analyzes the processes leading to the formation of new nations. Bendix was the author of numerous scholarly papers, chiefly on topics of a theoretical nature. Throughout his career, Bendix saw himself living between cultures, building connections between academic disciplines in the United States and Germany. In his honor, the Institute of International Studies established the Reinhard Bendix Memorial Research Fellowship for graduate students in the field of political and social theory or historic studies of society and politics. Other books by Bendix include: *Kings or People: Power and the Mandate to Rule* (1978); *Force, Fate, and Freedom* (1984); *From Berlin to Berkeley*, (1986); *Embattled Reason, Vol. 1* (1988); *Embattled Reason, Vol. 2* (1989); and *Unsettled Affinities* (1993, published posthumously).

[Werner J. Cahnman / Ruth Beloff (2nd ed.)]

BENDIX, VICTOR EMANUEL (1851–1926), pianist, conductor, and composer. Born in Copenhagen, the brother of the pianist Otto *Bendix, Victor Bendix studied at the Copenhagen Conservatory with composer Niels Gade and as a pianist with, among others, Liszt (from 1881). He was répétiteur at the Copenhagen Royal Theater and later piano teacher at the Royal Academy of Music. Bendix was an excellent conductor, and in this role he made great contributions to the musical life of Copenhagen. He was the conductor of the choral society, which he founded in Copenhagen (1872–76), and of the Copenhagen Philharmonic Concerts (which he established in 1897). His concert performances of *Siegfried* and *Tristan und Isolde* and his staged performances of Verdi's *Don Carlos* were welcome innovations in the usual repertory of the Copenhagen Musical Society. From 1892 to 1893 he conducted the *Volkskonzerte* in Berlin. Bendix wrote many songs but his important works were his compositions for the piano; among them are Piano Trio op. 12, Piano Concerto op. 17, and Piano Sonata op. 26. He also composed *Psalm 33* for chorus and orchestra and four symphonies.

BIBLIOGRAPHY: Grove online.

[Israela Stein (2nd ed.)]

BEN-DOR, IMMANUEL (1901–1969), archaeologist. Ben-Dor, who was born at Okopy, Poland, was a member of the archaeological expeditions of the University of Pennsylvania in Beth-Shean, Egypt, Mesopotamia, and Italy and also took part in the American School of Oriental Research excavation at Beth-El and that of the University of Liverpool at Jericho. He served as assistant keeper (1935) and librarian (1939) of the Palestine Archaeological Museum and conducted excavations at Nahariyyah and al-Zīb. From 1948 to 1954 he was assistant director of the Israel Department of Antiquities and was also archaeologist to the Link Underwater Expedition at Caesarea. From 1958 to 1968 he was professor of biblical archaeology and Semitics at Emory University, Atlanta. He published articles on aspects of Palestinian archaeology.

[Michael Avi-Yonah]

BEN DOV, YAAKOV (1882–1968), photographer and Israeli pioneer. Ben Dov was born near Zhitomir, Russia and studied photography in Russia. Emigrating to Palestine in 1908, he was one of the first students and graduates of the Bezalel School of Arts (now the *Bezalel Academy of Arts and Design), supporting himself during his studies by working as a photographer and publishing illustrated postcards and albums of life in the country. At the outbreak of World War I he was mobilized in the Austrian army and served as a medical photographer in the Austrian military hospital in Jerusalem. After acquiring equipment from Austria he made several documentary films, including one of General Allenby's entry into Jerusalem. He thus became one of the pioneers of film in Israel, but abandoned filmmaking upon the advent of sound movies.

After the liberation of Jerusalem from Ottoman rule in 1918 he devoted himself to communal matters and helped organize the artisans' center and their Savings and Loan Bank, and was one of the representatives of the artisans on the First Jewish Municipal Council. In this capacity he was invited to be present at the official announcement of the Balfour Declaration.

Ben Dov was a founder of the Talpiot Quarter of Jerusalem and initiated other projects for building new suburbs in and around Jerusalem. In 1966 he was appointed a *Yakir Yerushalayim* (an honored citizen of Jerusalem). His works have been exhibited at the Israel Museum.

BIBLIOGRAPHY: *Tidhar*, 4:1629–30.

BENE-BERAK (Heb. 1) .(בְּנֵי בְּרַק) A biblical city 5 mi. (8 km.) E. of Jaffa. It is included in the territory of the tribe of *Dan together with Jehud and *Gath-Rimmon (Josh. 19:45), but it was no doubt in the area controlled by the Philistines until the period of the united monarchy. Assyrian sources describing Sennacherib's invasion in 701 B.C.E. speak of Bene-Berak as subject to *Ashkelon (together with Jaffa, Beth-Dagon, and Azur). After the destruction of the Second Temple, Bene-Berak became a center of Jewish learning when R. *Akiva established his school there, which was attended by such well-known pupils as Judah, Meir, and Simeon b. Yoḥai (Tosef., Ber. 2:14; Tosef., Shab. 3:3; Sanh. 32b; Gen. R. 95:30). The Passover *Haggadah* preserves an account of a famous *seder* held there by R. Akiva. When Eleazar b. Azariah accompanied Akiva to the public baths at Bene-Berak, it gave rise to a halakhic query (Tosef., Shab. 3:4). Echoes of religious persecution by the Romans (under Hadrian) are contained in both the passage in the *Haggadah* and in the Tosefta (Tosef., Ber. 2:14). Even after the *Bar Kokhba War (132–35 C.E.), Bene-Berak remained a Jewish city; Judah ha-Nasi visited it and was impressed by the extraordinary fertility of its orchards and vineyards (Mid. Tanḥ. to 26:9; TJ, Pe'ah 8:4, 20b). The same impression is reported by the *amora* Rami b. Ezekiel (third century C.E.), who applied to it the biblical phrase "a land flowing with milk and honey" (Ket. 111b). The Crusaders called the city Bombrac and built a fortress there to protect the approaches to Jaffa.

[Michael Avi-Yonah]

(2) One of the ten towns in Israel which form the metropolitan area of Tel Aviv, about 3 mi. (5 km.) northeast of downtown Tel Aviv, bordered on the north by the Yarkon River, on the east by the main highway to the south and north, and on the south and west by Ramat Gan. Bene-Berak was established in 1924 by a group of 13 Orthodox families from Warsaw, Poland, under the leadership of Rabbi Y. Gerstenkorn, who later became the town's first mayor. Until 1936 affairs were run by a local committee, and from 1936 to 1949 by a local council, but since 1950 Bene-Berak has been a township, comprising about 1,775 acres (7,100 dunams). The founders engaged mostly in farming and by 1929 the settlement grew to 100 families. It had 4,500 inhabitants in 1941, 8,800 in 1948, 25,000 in 1955, and 64,700 in 1968. In the mid-1990s the population was approximately 125,000 and in 2002 about 138,900, making it the tenth largest city in Israel, with a municipal area of 2.7 sq. mi. (7 sq. km.). Its dynamic growth was due to its proximity to Tel Aviv, and its special position as a place for a thoroughly Orthodox population and way of life. As a suburb, Bene-Berak is interrelated with the Tel Aviv nucleus for its public transportation, wholesale and retail trade, entertainment, education on the university level, and for employment – especially for white collar workers in Tel Aviv who live in Bene-Berak. Bene-Berak is known for its numerous yeshivot, headed by the Ponevezh Yeshivah, founded in 1941 by Rabbi Joseph *Kahaneman. It is also known for the strict public observance of the Sabbath, holidays, and Jewish laws, one consequence of which is that all its roads are closed to traffic on the Sabbath and holidays. There are more than 200 synagogues, many of them for ḥasidic *rebbes*, and closed ḥasidic neighborhoods like Zikhron Meir, Vizhnitz, and Satmar (see *Satu Mare). Bene-Berak was the home of Ḥazon Ish (Rabbi Abraham I. *Karelitz), who established Tiferet Zion yeshiva. A Haredi College for academic studies geared to observant students was founded in 1999. It had around 100 students in 2002. The special character of the city as a bastion of ultra-Orthodoxy, with most men studying in the yeshivot rather than working, makes the city a center of poverty as well. The city includes one secular neighborhood – Pardes Katz.

Bene-Berak became one of Israel's important industrial areas and in 1969 had about 150 factories and numerous workshops for food preserves, cigarettes, wool textiles, and other branches, among them several of the country's largest such enterprises, employing about 8,000 workers. At the beginning of the 21st century, the city had five industrial areas, with some of the largest plants in Israel.

[Alexander Cohn / Shaked Gilboa (2nd ed.)]

BIBLIOGRAPHY: D.D. Luckenbill (ed.), *The Annals of Sennacherib* (1924), 31; S. Klein (ed.), *Sefer ha-Yishuv*, 1 (1939), s.v.; EM, 2 (1965), 174; Press, Ereẓ, 1 (1951), 109; A. Cohn, "The Development of Bene-Berak as a Satellite Town of Special Features" (Thesis, Technion Haifa, 1969), Hebrew with English synopsis.

BENEDEK, THERESE F. (1892–1977), U.S. psychoanalyst and psychiatrist. Born in Eger, Hungary, Benedek obtained clinical experience in Budapest and Leipzig, and emigrated to the United States in the early 1930s. She was appointed a staff member at the Chicago Institute for Psychoanalysis in 1936. In her research she concentrated on studying the psychological implications of female sexual functions and the personal disturbances associated with their impairment. She wrote (with B.B. Rubenstein) *The Sexual Cycle in Women* (1947), *Psychosexual Functions in Women* (1952), and *Insight and Personality Adjustment* (1946).

°**BENEDICT**, name of 16 popes, several of whom had significant contacts with Jews. BENEDICT VIII (1012–1024) ordered the execution of a number of Roman Jews in 1020 or 1021, on a charge that they had mocked the cross and thereby caused an earthquake which killed a number of Christians. BENEDICT XII (1334–1342) gave proof of his conversionary zeal when in 1320, while still bishop of Pamiers, he argued with a certain Baruch who had been forced into Christianity during the *Pastoureaux persecutions. He displayed the same zeal in 1338 by urging all Christians to aid in the pursuit of converted Jews who changed their places of residence in order to revert to Judaism. In 1335 he ordered the destruction of a synagogue in Posen because it had been erected too near a Cistercian chapel. He complained to King Pedro of Aragon in 1340 that Jews and Muslims were erecting too many synagogues and mosques and were enjoying too many contacts with Christians. At the same time, he was deeply concerned over the report by Albert II, duke of Austria, in 1338, that the Jews of *Passau had been falsely accused of having desecrated the *Host. A similar charge in *Nuremberg a few years previously had also proved false. The pope now ordered the bishop of Passau not to permit the Jews to suffer if they had been unjustly accused. BENEDICT XIII (Peter de Luna, 1394–1417) does not belong to the apostolic succession, since he is counted as an anti-pope during the Great Schism of the Church. His hostility to Jews and Judaism was evident during his period in Avignon (1394–1411). In 1396 he acted upon the accusation that the Jews of Geneva were enjoying many privileges under the protection of the local authorities; he also charged the leaders of the Avignon Jews with exceeding their powers. In 1403 he granted a three-year moratorium on debts owed by Christians to Jews. He did grant the Jews of Toro (Castile), in 1404, the right to have a synagogue in place of the two they had had before the persecutions in

Spain in 1391, but this had already been granted them by the king of Castile. His attempt in 1410 to calm the excessive zeal of the inquisitors in Majorca may also have been due to the exigencies of diplomacy rather than to personal good will. His really spectacular anti-Jewish activity began when, expelled from Avignon, he moved to his native Spain, still claiming to be the only legitimate pope. The depressed condition of the Spanish Jews at the time persuaded him that he could startle Christendom by obtaining the conversion of all Spanish Jewry. The Disputation of *Tortosa was the result. When it was concluded in May 1415, Benedict issued his Bull *Etsi doctoribus gentium* imposing every conceivable restriction on Jewish life. It condemned the Talmud and ordered it expurgated of every statement that might appear uncomplimentary to Christianity, and it made contact between Jews and Christians all but impossible. The Bull's enforcement lapsed after Benedict XIII was deposed by the Council of Constance in 1417; but its spirit remained alive and found echoes in a number of *Bulls by later popes. BENEDICT XIII (1724–1730) used every pressure, especially economic, on the inhabitants of the Roman ghetto to become converted to Christianity. He personally participated in the ceremonious baptism of 26 of them. He tried to limit Jewish trade to nonessentials. BENEDICT XIV (1740–1758) was deeply interested in the rigid interpretation and enforcement of Canon Law. Consequently, while reaffirming the right of the Jews of Avignon to trade in cloth, he increased the onus of the Jewish badge for the Jews of Rome by ordering them to wear it even when on a journey. A mere suspicion of consent was now enough to declare a Jew properly baptized; while a child, even if baptized without parental consent, was compelled to remain a Christian. Converts were limited to marrying only born Christians. Twice during his pontificate, in 1753 and 1755, Jewish books were confiscated and examined for anti-Christian statements. Yet he recognized that Jewish taxation was too heavy. Moreover, it was under his auspices that Lorenzo Ganganelli (later Pope *Clement XVI) drew up his memorandum concerning the *blood libel, and Benedict subsequently wrote to the authorities in Poland deploring the recent wave of accusations.

For Benedict XVI, see *Popes; *Vatican.

BIBLIOGRAPHY: BENEDICT VII: Roth, Dark Ages, 76, 119; Vogelstein-Rieger, 1 (1896), 213. BENEDICT XII: Grayzel, in: HJ, 17 (1955), 89–120; MHJ, 1 (1903), 62, no. 36; Baron, Social², 11 (1967), 170f., 267. BENEDICT XIII (anti-pope): Baer, Spain, 2 (1966), 155, 167, 229ff., 393f.; M. Simonsohn, *Kirchliche Judengesetzgebung im Zeitalter der Reformkonzilien von Konstanz und Basel* (1912). BENEDICT XIII: E. Rodocanachi, *Le Saint-Siège et les Juifs* (1891), 220, 284; Roth, Italy, 381. BENEDICT XIV: C. Roth, *Ritual Murder Libel and the Jew* (1934); Roth, Italy, 379, 411; Rodocanachi, op. cit., 266, 284, 292; Vogelstein-Rieger, 2 (1895), 242, 245ff.; *New Catholic Encyclopedia*, index.

[Solomon Grayzel]

BENEDICT, SIR JULIUS (**Isaac**; 1804–1885), composer and conductor, born in Stuttgart. After conducting in Vienna (1823–25) and later in Naples, he settled in London in 1835. He accompanied Jenny Lind on her American tour (1850–52) and conducted at Drury Lane and Covent Garden. Of his operas, the most successful was *The Lily of Killarney* (Covent Garden, 1862). Although a convert to Protestantism (1826), he set to music Psalm 84 (first verse) for the inauguration of the first British Reform Synagogue (West London) in 1840. His works include cantatas, symphonies, and piano concertos. He wrote biographies of Felix Mendelssohn (1853²) and Carl Maria von Weber (1881), whose pupil he was. He was knighted in 1871.

BIBLIOGRAPHY: P.H. Emden, *Jews of Britain* (1943), 514–15; Raphael, in: BLBI, 11 no. 41 (1968), 32–37; Grove, Dict; Riemann-Gurlitt; Baker, Biog Dict; Sendrey, Music, indexes.

[Dora Leah Sowden]

BENEDICT BEN MOSES OF LINCOLN (d. 1278), English financier, in secular records called Magister Benedictus filius Magistri Mossei de Lincolnia. Benedict came from a family of scholars: his great-grandfather, Moses of Bristol (later of Oxford), had been a patron of letters; his grandfather, Yom Tov (apparently also known as Simeon), composed the lost *Sefer ha-Tena'im*; and his father, R. *Moses b. Yom Tov of London, was the leading Hebrew and talmudic scholar of his day in England. One of Benedict's brothers was Hagin (Ḥayyim), *archpresbyter of English Jewry from 1257 until his death in 1280; another was R. *Elijah Menahem b. Moses of London. Benedict's business activities in Lincoln date from 1252 and are often referred to in the records of subsequent decades. It is conjectured that the *blood libel at Lincoln in 1255 took place when a number of Jews from all over England were assembled to celebrate the marriage of Benedict's daughter Bellasset. Benedict was among those arrested. After his family had procured the intervention of the Castilian ambassador, Benedict was released in December 1255 and his sequestered property restored to him. In Hebrew Benedict was known as R. Berechiah of Nicole (Lincoln). He was regarded as one of the outstanding Anglo-Jewish halakhic scholars of his day and was mentioned with veneration long after his death. R. Berechiah was also known as an exegete. His name occurs along with those of other English rabbis of the 13th century in the works of several tosafists.

BIBLIOGRAPHY: J. Jacobs, in: JHSET, 1 (1893–94), 101–2; C. Roth, *ibid.*, 15 (1946), 29ff.; idem, in: JJS, 3 (1952), 56–61; Rigg-Jenkinson, Exchequer, index; Urbach, Tosafot, 402; J. Ḥazzan, *Eẓ Ḥayyim*, ed. by I. Brodie, 1 (1962), 141, 310; 2 (1964), 179; E.E. Urbach, in: *Sefer ha-Yovel Tiferet Yisrael... Brodie* (1967), 1ff.

BENEDICTIONS (Heb. sing. בְּרָכָה, *berakhah*; pl. בְּרָכוֹת, *berakhot*), formulas of blessing or thanksgiving, in public and private services. The Hebrew noun *berakhah* is derived from the verb *brk* ברך ("to fall on one's knees"). The Talmud ascribes the institution and formulation of the benedictions to "the Men of the Great *Synagogue" (Ber. 33a), to the sages of old (Sif. Deut. 33:2; Mid. Ps. 17:4), or to the "120 elders" at the head of the community in the time of *Ezra (Meg. 17b; TJ, Ber. 2:4, 4d). These references, however, cannot be considered historically authentic, although they are indicative of the fact that benedictions were known to have been instituted in very ancient times. In the Bible, mention is made of a number of individual benedictions (Gen. 24:27; Ex. 18:10; Ruth 4:14; I Sam. 25:32; II Sam. 18:28; I Kings 1:48; 5:21; 8:15, 56; I Chron. 16:36; II Chron. 2:11; 6:4; Ps. 28:6; 31:22). After the victory of the Maccabees over Nicanor, the people exclaimed, "Blessed be He who has kept His holy place undefiled" (II Macc. 15:34). According to the Book of Enoch (36:4), each time Enoch beheld some of the wonders of nature, he "blessed the Lord of Glory, Who had made great and glorious wonders to show the greatness of His work to the angels and to spirits and to men, that they might praise His work and all His creation."

The Origin of the Berakhot

Elbogen and other scholars have shown that the various benedictions probably originated in different congregations and localities. The formulas ultimately adopted by all Jews were selections from, and combinations of, local customs and traditions. The attempts of other scholars to establish a definite date for the formulation of each benediction and to reconstruct an "original" wording appear to lack foundation. There are indications which suggest that different formulas were known and used simultaneously. Similarities to the 18 benedictions which comprise the **Amidah* prayer are, for instance, to be found in various sources: the hymn recorded in Ecclesiasticus 51:12, and the prayer found in Ecclesiasticus 36:1ff. The latter contains a series of benedictions petitioning for the ingathering of the exiles and the salvation of Israel. It also expresses the hope that Zion and the Temple may be filled with God's glory. The "eight benedictions," recited by the high priest on the Day of Atonement (Yoma 7:1; TJ, Yoma 7:1, 44b), and the order of the morning service of the priests in the Temple (Tam. 5:1), are also examples of this procedure.

THE END OF THE SECOND TEMPLE PERIOD. By the end of the Second Temple period, certain "orders of benedictions" had become the generally accepted custom in most communities. Prominent among these were the seven benedictions which comprise the *Amidah* for Sabbaths and festivals, the nine for Rosh Ha-Shanah (Tosef., Ber. 3:14), and most likely also the 18 benedictions for the weekday *Amidah*. The number and contents of the benedictions before and after the *Shema, and the three benedictions of the *Grace after Meals, were also standardized about this time. The "redaction" of the regular, prescribed prayers and benedictions under Rabban *Gamaliel II at Jabneh (Ber. 28b ff.), at the end of the firstcentury C.E., gave official sanction to what had been in essence the prevailing custom for a considerable time, and probably established the order and content of the benedictions. It did not, however, become the single, authoritative version.

THE TALMUDIC PERIOD. At the earliest, prayers were written down by the end of the talmudic period, and many alternative formulations of the same benediction are known from talmudic sources (some are in use in different rites to the present day). The order of prayer was still relatively flexible, for while the general outline and the motifs of the prayers and blessings were well defined, their recital involved an element of improvisation and free composition. The latter was seen as a safeguard against mechanical prayer. Some *amoraim* were singled out for praise because they recited "a new prayer" or "a new benediction" every day (TJ, Bet. 4:3, 8a). During talmudic times, however, only the requirements for the wording of each benediction were fixed in greater detail, and various subsidiary motifs which had to be included in some of them were enumerated. Consistent attempts at establishing one single authoritative version of all prayers only came later.

The Benediction Formula

Every blessing opens with the words *Barukh Attah Adonai* ("Blessed art Thou, O Lord"). When the benediction occurs at the beginning of a prayer, the words *Eloheinu Melekh ha-Olam* ("our God, King of the Universe") are added. There are three types of formulas for benedictions: The first is a short blessing (*matbe'a kaẓar,* "short formula") which, after the above opening, is followed by a few words of praise specific to the occasion, e.g., the benediction over bread: *ha-moẓi leḥem min ha-areẓ* ("who brings forth bread from the earth"). The second is a long blessing (*matbe'a arokh*, "long formula"), in which the opening is followed by a more elaborate text, e.g., in the first section of the Grace after Meals, after which a concluding benediction formula must be recited at the end of the prayer, e.g., *Barukh Attah Adonai ha-zan et ha-kol* ("Blessed art Thou O Lord, Who feedest all"). The third type of benediction forms part of a series (*berakhah ha-semukhah le-ḥavertah*, "contiguous blessings"). The opening formula is omitted (except in the first benediction of each series), and only the conclusion is phrased in the benediction style. The second section of the Grace after Meals, for instance, begins with the words *Nodeh Lekha* ("We thank Thee"), and ends with the benediction *Barukh Attah Adonai al ha-areẓ ve-al ha-mazon* ("Blessed art Thou O Lord, for the land and the food"; TJ, Bet. 1:8, 3d). The mention of God as "King of the Universe" (known as *Malkhut*) occurs only in the first two forms, and not in the third. It is totally absent from the *Amidah*, and probably did not become customary before the second century C.E. (Ber. 40a). The introduction of *Malkhut* into the opening phrase of the formula may have been motivated by the desire to stress the exclusive kingship of God, as a protest against the Roman cult of emperor worship. Since most of the obligatory prayers, e.g., the *Amidah*, and the benedictions preceding and following the *Shema*, consist of a series of blessings, the form occurring most frequently in the synagogue service is the third, in which the benediction formula is used only as a conclusion.

The standard benediction formula occurs only twice in the Bible (Ps. 119:12; I Chron. 29:10); other formulas such as *Hodu la-Adonai* ("Praise God"), *Odekha Adonai* ("I will thank Thee, O Lord") are more frequent, as is the phrase *Barukh Attah* (without *Adonai*). The benedictions in Ecclesiasticus 51:12, for instance, are introduced by *Hodu la-Adonai*, and in the Dead Sea Scrolls the benediction formula is used interchangeably with *Odekha Adonai*, and the like (e.g., Thanksgiving Scroll, cf. 2:20, 31; 4:5, with 11:28, 30; 16:8; and especially 5:20, where the latter formula has been struck by the scribe and replaced by the former). Nor do the Dead Sea Scrolls yet distinguish between the use of the divine names *Adonai* and *El* in benedictions. The Talmud also retains some traces of formulas other than the standard ones (Ber. 40b and 54b; Tosef., Ber. 4:4–5). The ultimate choice of the formula containing both the Tetragrammaton and the direct address of God in the second person was deliberate. It reflects the personal and even intimate relationship of the worshiper with God. It also ensures that supplications and petitions (such as the intermediary benediction of the *Amidah*) invariably conclude with words of praise. After asking for forgiveness, the prayer concludes: "Blessed art Thou ... who dost abundantly forgive."

Laws of Benedictions

The Talmud (Ber. 40b) quotes Rav as saying that every benediction must include the name of God, and R. Johanan as saying that each benediction must also contain the attribute of God's kingship. It is also obvious from this talmudic passage that a benediction could be recited in the vernacular and did not have to be an exact translation of the Hebrew formula. A shepherd, Benjamin, is quoted as having said in Aramaic, "Blessed be God, the master of this bread," and Rav agreed that it was sufficient (Ber. 40b). Particular stress is laid upon the closing formula (Ber. 9:5; Ta'an. 2:3; Tosef., Ber. 7:21–22). While the benediction formula is obligatory in every one of the prescribed prayers, its use is precluded in spontaneous free prayers: "He who recites a blessing which is not necessary is considered to transgress the prohibition 'Thou shalt not take the name of the Lord Thy God in vain'" (Ex. 20:7; Ber. 33a). Maimonides (Yad, Berakhot 1:4) divides the benedictions into three types: those which are recited before enjoying a pleasure (e.g., food); those which are recited for the performance of a religious duty (e.g., hearing the *shofar*); and those which are forms of liturgical thanksgiving and praise (e.g., Grace after Meals).

*Abudarham distinguished four classes or types of benedictions: those recited in the daily prayers; those preceding the performance of a religious duty; blessings offered for enjoyments; and those of thanksgiving or praise (*Abudarham ha-Shalem, Berakhot*).

Many benedictions, though obligatory and therefore couched in the characteristic *berakhah* formula, are not recited in congregational worship but by the individual in private prayer. Prominent among them are three groups: benedictions before and after the partaking of food and drink; benedictions to be recited before the performance of most *mitzvot*; and benedictions of praise for various occasions (the morning benedictions which express man's gratitude for awakening in possession of all his faculties were originally of this type). Since all three types of benedictions are essentially of a private character, no *minyan* is required for their recital. (The Grace after Meals is, however, preceded by a special introduction when said in company.)

BENEDICTIONS RECITED BEFORE THE PERFORMANCE OF A MITZVAH. All benedictions recited before the observance of a *mitzvah* begin with the formula "Blessed ... who has sanctified us through his commandments and commanded us...," and mention the specific *mitzvah* about to be performed. The same formula is also used before the performance of commandments of rabbinic origin (e.g., the lighting of candles on the Sabbath or on Ḥanukkah) since such commandments are implied in the biblical injunction to observe the teaching of the sages (Deut. 17:10; Shab. 23a). The actual benediction over the *mitzvah* is sometimes followed by further benedictions (e.g., on kindling the Ḥanukkah candles, the benediction "who has performed miracles for our fathers in days of old at this season" is recited). When a *mitzvah* is performed for the first time in the year, the *She-Heḥeyanu* benediction ("who has kept us alive and preserved us and enabled us to reach this season") is also added. No blessings are recited after the observance of *mitzvot*, unless they involve public reading from the Scriptures (e.g. Torah, Prophets, *Hallel*). It is, however, recorded that Palestinian scholars recited one on removing the *tefillin*.

In practice, a benediction is not recited before the performance of every *mitzvah*. Some commentators have suggested that the determining principle is that no benediction should be recited before *mitzvot* which do not involve any action (e.g., leaving the corner of the field for the poor; Lev. 19:9), or the observance of which is possible only in undesirable circumstances (e.g., divorce, or the return of stolen goods). In the case of other *mitzvot* (e.g., the giving of alms), however, the reason for the absence of a benediction is not readily apparent, and there is no general agreement regarding the underlying principles. Custom on the matter seems to have varied as late as geonic times.

BENEDICTION OF PRAISE ON VARIOUS OCCASIONS. Among the many benedictions prescribed for various special occasions, those to be recited on hearing good and bad tidings, on witnessing awesome natural phenomena, on visiting a place where miracles have been performed in the past (in Ereẓ Israel) are prominent. The blessing *Ha-tov ve-ha-metiv* ("Blessed is He Who is good and does good") is recited by an individual upon hearing good news which will also benefit others, such as when hearing news that one has received an inheritance or when rain begins to fall after a drought. It is also recited when partaking of additional wine which is different in kind from that drunk previously. The *Birkat ha-Gomel*, a blessing recited upon individual salvation from danger, is included in this category. Known generally as "blessings of praise," the main purpose of these benedictions is "to make us remember our Creator at all times" (Maim. Yad, Berakhot 1:4). While the benedictions over food are evidently intended to sanctify the physical act of taking nourishment, and those recited before *mitzvot* serve to prevent the performance of the *mitzvah* in a thoughtless routine manner, the recital of the "benedictions of praise" is practically an end in itself. These benedictions serve to illuminate the educational function of blessings which transform a variety of everyday actions and occurrences into religious experiences designed to increase awareness of God at all times. R. Meir went so far as to declare that it is the duty of every Jew to recite 100 benedictions daily (Men. 43b), a custom which, according to one tradition, was instituted by King David (Num. R. 18:21). The rabbinical discussions of benedictions are contained in the Mishnah tractate *Berakhot, and the *gemara* in both Talmuds.

BIBLIOGRAPHY: Abrahams, Companion; Ch. Albeck (ed.), *Shishah Sidrei Mishnah: Berakhot* (1952); Elbogen, Gottesdienst; Finkelstein, in: JQR, 16 (1925/26), 1–43, 127–70; 19 (1928–29), 211–62; L. Ginzberg, *Perushim ve-Ḥiddushim ba-Yerushalmi*, 4 vols. (1941–61); J. Heinemann, *Ha-Tefillah bi-Tekufat ha-Tanna'im ve-ha-Amora'im* (1966²); idem, in: JSS, 5 (1960), 264–80; idem, in: JJS, 13 (1962), 23–29; Idelsohn, Liturgy; Kohler, in: HUCA, 1 (1924), 387–425; Liebreich, *ibid.*, 21 (1948), 176–209; 34 (1963), 125–76; idem, in: PAAJR, 18 (1948/49), 255–67; Liber, in: JQR, 40 (1949/50), 331–57; Mann, in: HUCA, 2 (1925), 269–338; A.I. Schechter, *Studies in Jewish Liturgy* (1930); Zunz, Vortraege; Petuchowski, in: HUCA, 37 (1966), 175–89.

BENEDIKT, MORITZ (1835–1920), Austrian neurologist, anthropometrist, and criminologist. Born in Eisenstadt, Hungary, Benedikt served as a surgeon in the Austrian army during the wars with Italy and Prussia in 1859 and 1866. Appointed a lecturer at the University of Vienna, he rose to become professor of neurology. He achieved eminence for his varied contributions to neuropathology, the localization of brain function, and electrotherapeutics, a field in which he made important innovations. His interest in electricity was not confined to its medical application but extended to generic physics, and he produced a number of significant studies on magnetism and electric current. He contributed to various branches of medical research, including the physiology and pathology of the circulatory system, and was one of the founders of electrotherapy.

Benedikt also engaged in anthropometric studies of criminals, devoting particular attention to cephalometry and brain pathology and to criminal psychology. His studies in physical anthropology are to be found in his *Anatomische Studien an Verbrecher-Gehirnen* (1879; *Anatomical Studies upon Brains of Criminals*, 1881) and *Kraniometrie und Kephalometrie* (1888). These made him, together with Cesare Lombroso, one of the pioneers of criminal anthropology.

Of diverse cultural interests and activist liberal propensities, he wrote on current affairs and contemporary literature and aesthetics, and participated actively in various reformist movements, notably the extension of women's suffrage. His memoirs, *Aus Meinem Leben*, appeared in 1906.

BIBLIOGRAPHY: S.R. Kagan, *Jewish Medicine* (1952), 374.

[Ephraim Fischoff]

BENEDIKT, MORITZ (1849–1920), Austrian journalist and politician. Born into an acculturated German-Jewish trading family in Moravia, Benedikt was sent to Vienna to be educated at the *Schottengymnasium* and later studied at Vienna University, especially economics. His interest in politics was sparked by the battle of Koeniggraetz (1866). He soon turned to journalism, contributing to various economic newspapers, periodicals, and yearbooks. In 1872, like E. *Bacher, he joined the staff of the liberal Vienna daily *Neue Freie Presse* (est. 1864 by Max Friedlaender and Michael Etienne), then the most influential newspaper in the Austro-Hungarian Empire. In 1879, after the death of Etienne, he was appointed editor of its economic section, publishing a widely read series of articles on financial, commercial, and economic affairs of Austria-Hungary. In 1881, he joined Bacher as editor-in-chief (and later part owner). Even before the death of his partner in 1908, he determined the editorial policy, trying to modernize the paper, from 1904 especially against the competing Vienna daily *Zeit* (est. 1896 as a weekly). With the financing of the Rothschild and *Creditanstalt* banks, he was able to engage prominent writers to contribute to the paper. Like Bacher, he made the *Neue Freie Presse* an organ of the German Liberal Party in Austria. He violently opposed the new Jewish national movement of Zionism, keeping *Herzl, then literary editor, from writing anything in support of Zionism in the paper. As stated in Herzl's diaries, Benedikt desperately tried to prevent him from publishing *Der Judenstaat* (1896) and later *Die Welt* (1897). Benedikt's fiercest Jewish opponent was K. *Kraus, regularly attacking him in his satirical magazine *Die Fackel* (from 1899). Through his editorials, Benedikt managed to achieve considerable influence in Austro-Hungarian politics, advocating peaceful solutions and a compromise between Austria and Hungary (cf. the "Benedikt formula"). His journalistic style was clear and precise. Though Benedikt served as a political adviser in financial affairs, as a Jew he never really succeeded in party politics. Only in May 1917, at the age of 68, was he appointed to the Upper House (*Herrenhaus*) of the Austrian parliament by Emperor Karl I. After 1918, with the end of World War I and the breakup of the old Austro-Hungarian Empire, Benedikt's paper lost in importance. Dismayed by the deteriorating political, economic, and social situation in Austria and especially Vienna, he failed to accommodate himself to the new era. The *Neue Freie Presse* was carried on by his son Ernst Benedikt (1882–1957).

BIBLIOGRAPHY: *Neue Freie Presse* (March 1920); *Allgemeine Zeitung des Judentums* (Apr. 8, 1920), supplement *Der Gemeindebote*, 3–4; I. Walter, "Moriz Benedikt und die *'Neue Freie Presse'*" (Ph.D. thesis, 1950); A. Wandruszka, *Geschichte einer Zeitung. Das Schicksal der* "Presse" *und der* "Neuen Freien Presse" *von 1848 zur Zweiten Republik* (1958); T. Herzl, *Briefe und Tagebuecher* (ed. A. Bein et al.), 7 vols. (1983–96), index; W.R. Langenbucher (ed.), *Sensationen des Alltags. Meisterwerke des oesterreichischen Journalismus* (1992), 27–37, 363–69, 402–3; H. Schmuck (ed.), *Jewish Biographical Archive* (1995), F. 46, 47–48 / 130, 93–109; Series II (2003), F. II/53, 90–96; S. Blumesberger et al. (eds.), *Handbuch oesterreichischer Autorinnen und Autoren juedischer Herkunft*, 1, no. 79 (2002), 95.

[Johannes Valentin Schwarz (2nd ed.)]

BENE EPHRAIM, name adopted by a Judaizing movement of Telugu-speaking Indians from Andhra Pradesh. There is no historic element to the Bene Ephraim. They have come to a kind of Judaism for reasons which are somewhat obscure, but the ambitions of their religious leaders – the Sadoc brothers – or the brothers' disappointment with the Baptist Church – may figure among them. Nonetheless, the community as it is presently constituted has a genuine sense of Jewish identity: for the children and young people it is their main identity in the villages where they live. They are sincere in their desire to be recognized as Jews both by their neighbors and by foreign Jews; they practice Judaism as best as they can and learn Hebrew as best as they can. They feel embittered that they have been ignored by Jews elsewhere and point to their Christian neighbors who receive sustenance from overseas Christian churches in the U.S. and elsewhere. The community, which maintains two synagogues, seems to be marked by piety, a desire to better their lot, and a determination to raise the flag of Judaism in Andhra Pradesh. Because of their vague idea of descent from Israelites they feel ethnically as well as religiously Jewish.

BIBLIOGRAPHY: J. Francisco, "'Discovering' the Telugu Jews of India," in: K. Primack, *Jews in Places You Never Thought Of* (1998); T. Parfitt, *The Lost Tribes of Israel: The History of a Myth* (2002).

[Tudor Parfitt (2nd ed.)]

BENEI AISH (Heb. בְּנֵי עַיִשׁ), community in central Israel. The settlement is located a little over a mile (3 km.) south of *Gederah. It was founded in 1957 on land that had served as a British military base during the Mandate period. The first settlers were mainly new immigrants from Yemen, Persia, Iraq, and Morocco who were removed from nearby transit camps (see **ma'abarah*). In the beginning, they worked in the nearby moshavim. In 1981 Benei Aish received municipal status and during the 1990s it absorbed many new immigrants, with 1,500 new apartments built. By 1998, 65% of the inhabitants were recent immigrants. The absorption of the immigrants, mainly secular, led to tensions with the old-time religious settlers. Subsequently the municipality sponsored culture activities aimed at integrating the two populations. However, the result of demographic and social changes was to make Benei Aish less religious than before, though it still maintained religious services. Its population in 2002 was 7,570. The settlement is named after R. Akiva Joseph *Schlesinger, a leader of *Po'alei Agudat Israel and one of the founders of *Petaḥ Tikvah.

[Shaked Gilboa (2nd ed.)]

BENEI BINYAMIN (Heb. בְּנֵי בִּנְיָמִין, "Sons of Benjamin"), association of second-generation farmers in the veteran moshavot of Palestine, active from 1921 to 1939. It engaged mainly in promoting economic and cultural interests, along with matters of security and self-defense. Benei Binyamin was founded by Alexander *Aaronsohn and was named in tribute to Edmond (Binyamin) de *Rothschild and Theodor (Binyamin Ze'ev) *Herzl. The association had as its motto: "To preserve the existing and to rebuild the destroyed." It was active in such veteran settlements as Petaḥ Tikvah, Rishon le-Zion, Nes Ẓiyyonah, Ekron, Ḥaderah, Zikhron Ya'akov, Rosh Pinnah, Mishmar ha-Yarden, and Yesud ha-Ma'alah. The Benei Binyamin Cooperative Bank, opened in 1924, loaned money to members for agricultural development, which the association constantly encouraged. In the same year Benei Binyamin began publication of its own newspaper, *Yedi'ot ha-Va'ad ha-Merkazi shel Histadrut Benei Binyamin*. Netanyah, Kefar Aharon, Even Yehudah, and part of Herzliyyah were founded by Benei Binyamin. Its active supporters in the U.S. included Nathan *Straus (in whose honor Netanyah was named). Alexander Aaronsohn was its president, and Oved *Ben-Ami served as its secretary for a number of years.

BIBLIOGRAPHY: Dinur, Haganah, 2 pt. 3 (1964), index; Benei Binyamin, *Likerat ha-Binyan* (1922).

BENEI DAROM (Heb. בְּנֵי דָּרוֹם), moshav shittufi east of Ashdod, Israel, affiliated with the Ha-Po'el ha-Mizrachi Moshavim Association. It was founded in 1949 by members of *Kefar Darom who had defended it during the War of Independence, until it fell and remained within the Egyptian-controlled Gaza Strip. In 1961 the settlers decided to change from the kibbutz to the moshav shittufi form of settlement. Some settlers originated from Germany and North America, others were born in Israel. Its economy was based on intensive farming including citrus orchards and irrigated field crops. Later it added pasta and preservative factories and a visitor's center for tourists. In 1968 its population was 144, doubling to around 300 in the mid-1990s and maintaining its size into the 21st century.

[Efraim Orni]

BENEI DEROR (Heb. בְּנֵי דְּרוֹר, "Sons of Freedom"), moshav in the southern Sharon, Israel, affiliated with Tenu'at ha-Moshavim, founded in 1946 by World War II veterans who were joined by immigrants from Turkey in 1949. Its economy was based on avocado plantations, citrus groves, a plant nursery, and milch cattle. In 1968 its population was 231, in the mid-1990s it increased to 300, and by 2002 it stood at 841. **WEBSITE:** www.bnei-dror.co.il.

[Efraim Orni]

BENEI MOSHE (Heb. בְּנֵי מֹשֶׁה; "Sons of Moses"), secret order of Ḥovevei Zion founded in Russia in 1889 to ensure personal dedication to the spiritual renaissance of the Jewish people and the return to Ereẓ Israel. Benei Moshe, founded on the seventh of Adar, the traditional birth date of Moses, was active in Russia and Ereẓ Israel until 1897. Its originator was Yehoshua *Barzillai (Eisenstadt), who returned from Ereẓ Israel dissatisfied with the situation of Jewish agricultural settlement and the general state of depression in the small new *yishuv*. Barzillai's views conformed with those of *Aḥad Ha-

Am, as expressed in his historic article *"Lo Zeh ha-Derekh"* ("The Wrong Way"), then still in manuscript but known to a limited circle. Barzillai and Avraham *Lubarsky persuaded Aḥad Ha-Am to accept leadership of the order. In his article *Derekh ha-Ḥayyim* ("Way of Life," 1889) and its supplements, Aḥad Ha-Am outlined the aim of the association: the return of the Jews to their historic homeland, but with prior spiritual preparation. The name Moshe (Moses) was to serve "as a sign to all members ever to keep in mind this chosen son of our people," a symbol of humility and morality. In this spirit, the order attempted "to broaden the scope of nationalism, elevating it to an ethical ideal based on the love of Israel, and embracing moral values."

Benei Moshe chapters consisted of at least five members, headed by leaders and advisers. A member was initiated in a ceremony in which he vowed to adhere faithfully to the group's statutes. The language used was Hebrew, and knowledge of Hebrew was a prerequisite for membership eligibility. The minimal eligibility age was 20. Members were called "brothers." Despite its very small membership (about 160), the order exerted considerable influence on the Ḥibbat Zion movement, whose leaders were, in fact, members of Benei Moshe. However, it had many opponents, namely those who advocated the primacy of practical settlement work in Ereẓ Israel above everything else (among them Moses Leib *Lilienblum), as well as Orthodox circles that conducted a fierce campaign against what they regarded as the secular ideology of Benei Moshe (among them Jehiel Michael *Pines and Ze'ev Wolf Jawitz).

Benei Moshe's practical achievements were in the field of modern Hebrew education in Ereẓ Israel and elsewhere (e.g., the modernized Hebrew-speaking *ḥeder* called *ḥeder metukkan*); in helping to found the settlement *Reḥovot; and in the establishment of the Hebrew publishing house Aḥi'asaf. The order helped publish the Hebrew anthologies *Kavveret* (1890) and *Pardes* (2 vols., 1892, 1895) in Russia. In Ereẓ Israel they published *Mikhtavim me-Ereẓ Yisrael* ("Letters from Ereẓ Israel," 1893–94), edited by Barzillai under the pen name Beit ha-Levi.

In 1891 Aḥad Ha-Am left the leadership of the order, although he remained its spiritual guide throughout its existence. The Benei Moshe headquarters moved to Jaffa in 1893. The order gradually abandoned its secret form, and in 1895 Aḥad Ha-Am suggested that it become a political party. By this time, however, the order was embroiled in bitter controversy both with its opponents and within its own ranks. Neither changes in the statutes nor the opening of the association could remove the feeling of frustration and reinvigorate it, and in 1896 Aḥad Ha-Am himself suggested that Benei Moshe be dissolved. This came about naturally with the rise of political Zionism, particularly with the convening of the First Zionist Congress in Basel (1897), which gave a new impetus to the Jewish national movement. The aims of Benei Moshe were sustained in Aḥad Ha-Am's continued opposition to Herzl's political Zionism.

BIBLIOGRAPHY: Aḥad Ha-Am, *Essays, Letters, Memoirs*, ed. by L. Simon (1946), index; *Kol Kitvei Aḥad Ha-Am* (1947), index; Aḥad Ha-Am, *Iggerot*, 6 (1960), index; idem, *Selected Essays*, ed. by L. Simon (1962); B. Halpern, *The Idea of the Jewish State* (1969²), 26, 83f.; S. Tchernowitz, *Benei Moshe u-Tekufatam* (1914); Malachi, in: *Hadoar* (1955/56), nos. 37–42; Kressel, Leksikon, 1 (1965), 60–71; I. Klausner, *Mi-Katoviẓ ad Basel*, 2 (1965), index.

[Getzel Kressel]

BENE ISRAEL, Jewish community in India.

In India

The original tradition, as related to Christian missionaries early in the 19th century, is that the Bene Israel are the descendants of the survivors (seven men and seven women) of a shipwreck off the Konkan coast at Navgaon, about 26 miles south of Bombay. Their ship was said to have come "from northern parts" and the date was "some sixteen to eighteen hundred years ago" (J. Wilson, *Lands of the Bible* (1847) II, 667). In the 19th century various theories were propounded by Europeans about Bene Israel origins conjecturing that the Bene Israel were an offshoot of the Jewish settlements in Yemen, refugees from the persecution of the Jews by Muhammad, or descendants of the Babylonian-Persian Diaspora. Later, in the light of the study of the Bible, of other Jewish literature, of ancient history sources relating to India, the Middle East, etc., some members of the Bene Israel community itself delved into details of possible Bene Israel origins. H.S. Kehimkar (*History of the Bene Israel of India* (1937) written in 1897) favored the theory that the ancestors of the Bene Israel left the Galilee because of persecutions by Antiochus Epiphanes (175–163 B.C.E.). D.J. Samson's argument for Bene Israel arrival in India at some time between 740 and 500 B.C.E. appeared in 1917 in an issue of the Bene Israel periodical The *Israelite* (I, no. 4,68–70) in an article entitled *The Bene Israel: Who, Where, Whence.* In any case their descendants remained for centuries isolated from Jewish life elsewhere. Thus they forgot much of the Hebrew language, prayer and ceremonies, and adopted customs and dress of their Konkan neighbors, and their language, Marathi, as their mother tongue. Throughout the centuries they clung, however, to some fundamentals of the Jewish tradition and observed circumcision, dietary laws, the Sabbath, and most fasts and festivals prescribed in the Torah, and recited the *Shema*. But they were otherwise unaware of Torah, or of talmudic and halakhic lore. In their new surroundings the Bene Israel turned to the pursuit of oil-pressing and agriculture and became known to their neighbors as *Shanwar Tells* ("The Sabbath-observing oilmen"), indicating both their occupation and their religious observance. The presence of a special Jewish group in the Konkan region remained unknown to outsiders, except for casual references to them.

Bene Israel tradition tells of a Jew, David Rahabi, who about the year 1000 C.E. (or, some say around 1400 C.E.) discovered the Bene Israel in their villages, recognized their vestigial Jewish customs, and taught them about Judaism, preparing certain young men among them to be the religious preceptors of the Bene Israel. They were called *Kajis* and their position became hereditary. They were also recognized officially as judges in disputes within the Bene Israel community. Somewhere along the line the Bene Israel formed a special attachment to the Prophet Elijah. They invoke his blessings on all auspicious occasions. Another typically Bene Israel feature is their custom called *Malida*, i.e., the preparation of a ceremonial food offering (composed of special ingredients) accompanied by recitation of Jewish prayers, psalms, and other appropriate biblical quotations on the occasions of purification after childbirth; preparation for a wedding; when taking, and after completing, a vow; after a circumcision, and for all other auspicious occasions; whenever there is a crisis or need for divine help; for the expression of gratitude to God; and on Tu Bi-Shevat to celebrate the first fruits of their locale, and also to give respect to the Prophet Elijah at Kandala, the place where he is believed to have appeared to the Bene Israel.

In mid-18th century, many Bene Israel moved from their villages into the rapidly developing new city of Bombay. Here the horizons of the Bene Israel were widened as they benefited from the educational and employment opportunities offered under British rule. The British authorities were anxious to recruit reliable soldiers to their "native" regiments. Some Bene Israel had already served in the army or in the navy of other Konkan potentates, and many enlisted under the British. Most of these rose to officer rank and established a reputation as good fighters in the Anglo-Mysore, Anglo-Afghan, and Anglo-Burmese wars of the 18th and 19th centuries. They were also efficient civil servants.

An impetus to their return to traditional Judaism was given to the Bene Israel through the cooperation of Cochin Jews who visited Bombay and the Konkan villages, and through the new wave of immigration of Arabic-speaking Jews from Baghdad to Bombay in the early decades of the 19th century. The secular education of the Bene Israel was considerably influenced by Congregational missionaries from America who opened schools both in Bombay and in the outlying towns and villages. They trained Bene Israel to become teachers in these schools, and it was in these schools that the Bene Israel got their first understandable introduction to be Bible. Then, in 1826 a Jew from Cochin, who had been converted to Christianity, Michael Sargon, was deputed to work among the Bene Israel. He not only devoted his energy to teaching them in the Marathi language, without any attempt at proselytization, but also mediated in their disputes. Somewhat later the most celebrated of all Christian missionaries to work among the Bene Israel, the Rev. John Wilson of the Scottish Presbyterian Mission, started his educational activities among them. In 1832 he published a Hebrew Grammar in Marathi, and Bene Israel studied Hebrew in the high school and in the college founded by him. Gradually the missionaries withdrew from the field of primary education and the Bene Israel took their education into their own hands. H.S. Kehimkar, in collaboration with his brother and A.D. Pezarkar, started a small primary school in 1875. It later became necessary to solicit for funds, and generous aid was given by the Anglo-Jewish Association of London, Jewish philanthropists in England and France, members of the *Sassoon family, and the Government of Bombay. The school, with its own building, grew into a high school teaching Marathi, English and Hebrew. Originally called the Israelite School, the name was changed in the early 1930s to the Elly Kadoorie School, in recognition of a large donation (earmarked for the reconstruction and extension of the old school building) by Sir Elly *Kadoorie of Hong Kong.

Religious development was also very much facilitated for the Bene Israel by translations of the Old Testament by an association of Protestant Christian missionaries of all denominations beginning in the early twenties of the 19th century. Since its establishment in 1857 Bombay University included Hebrew in its curriculum.

Originally, the communal organization, religious as well as secular, of the Bene Israel was headed by the *Kajis*. With the establishment of synagogues (the first was established in 1796 in Bombay by Bene Israel army officer Samuel Ezekiel *Divekar and was named Sha'ar ha-Rachamim ("Gate of Mercy")), the secular functions of the *Kajis* were gradually taken over by the *Muccadams*, who either were the most prominent persons in the local community, or who succeeded their fathers in the office. In large synagogue congregations the *Muccadams* were aided by *Choglas*, or councilors. Eventually the ritual functions of the *Kajis* came to be performed by the *ḥazzanim* who were initially recruited from Cochin but later also from among the Bene Israel themselves.

The Bene Israel established additional synagogues in Bombay – Sha'ar Razon (1839), Etz Hayim (1888), and Magen Chassidim (1931) – and also several prayer halls. From 1848 onwards Bene Israel synagogues were also established in 12 different towns on the Konkan coast; and far afield in the cities of Poona, Ahmedabad, Karachi (now in Pakistan) and New Delhi.

The relations between the Bene Israel and the Hindu and Muslim communities of the Konkan coast proved to be very peaceful. The only thing that the Bene Israel found upsetting was that their neighbors did not always identify them as Jews, and until well into the second half of the 20th century associated them with the caste of oil-pressers because of the traditional occupation of their ancestors, though already in the later British period the occupations of the Bene Israel were quite diverse.

Apart from serving in the British "native" regiments they were employed as civil servants in government, railway, postal and customs offices; as teachers, hospital assistants, nurses; many were skilled carpenters, masons, and mechanics; but very few were engaged in trade or commerce. Many Bene Israel who attended Elphinstone, Wilson and other colleges affiliated to Bombay University became well known as engineers, lawyers, physicians, educators, architects, writers and social workers. Prominent among the leaders and educators of the 19th century were Hayim Samuel *Kehimkar, historian of the community, and Joseph Ezekiel *Rajpurkar, writer and translator of Hebrew liturgical works into Marathi. One of the earliest liturgical works to be printed was by a Yemenite Jew from Cochin, Solomon Shara'bi, *Seliḥot According to the Sephardi Rite* (1841). It was followed by the publication of the Hebrew calendar (*Luaḥ*, 1845) and the first Passover *Haggadah* (1846, facsimile reprinted by W.J. Fischel, 1968) with a Marathi translation. From the last decade of the 19th century the Bene Israel published a number of journals and periodicals in Marathi and English. Some of them were short-lived, but *The Israelite* continued from 1917 to 1927; *The Friend of Israel* lasted from 1916 to 1921; *The Maccabi* from 1946 to 1971.

In the first half of the 20th century some Bene Israel participated in the Indian nationalist movement.

Bene Israel who have received the *Padma Shri*, one of the highest awards of the Government of India, awarded on Indian Independence Day to outstanding individuals in various fields of endeavor are (1) Dr. (Miss) Jerusha Jacob Jhirad, in 1966, for her work in gynecology and for her services in social welfare; (2) Mr. David Abraham Cheulkar, in 1969, for his character acting in Indian films; and (3) Dr. Reuben David Dandekar, in 1975, for his outstanding work and originality as superintendent of the Ahmedabad Zoo. (A fourth Indian Jew to receive the *Padma Shri* Award is a member of the Baghdadi Jewish community of Bombay: Mr. Ezra Mir, in 1970, for his outstanding work in making Indian documentary films and children's documentaries.) Among the many other Bene Israel who have achieved careers of distinction in India are Khan Bahadur Jacob Bapuji Israel, who as chief administrator in the State of Aundh, made specific innovations for rural development many decades before similar reforms were begun elsewhere; Shalom Bapuji Israel, who from ordinary police constable rose to be Dewan of Janjira State; Dr. Abraham Solomon Erulkar, an ardent nationalist, who had attended upon Mahatma Gandhi during almost all of his fasts (not as Gandhi's personal physician) especially in his capacity as then president of the Indian Medical Council; David Solomon Erulkar who was the Junior Council for-the-defense in the famous trial of the freedom-fighter Lokamanya B.G. Tilak (a Hindu), working together with the Senior Council in the case, a famous Muslim, Muhammed Ali Jinnah. Erulkar was also on the governing body of the International Labor Organization of the League of Nations. He founded *The Israelite* magazine. David Ezra Reuben secured first place in the competitive examination for admission to the Indian Civil Service in 1917. He was the only Bene Israel ever to serve in the ICS. He was made Chief Justice in 1951 of the Patna Court (in Bihar State). Miss Rebecca Reuben obtained her T.D. degree from London University; was principal of the Israelite School 1922–1950; issued a monthly journal for Jewish children, called *Nofeth* (written in Marathi it served as an excellent tool for education in things Jewish); authored highly successful series of English readers for secondary schools, also a grammar, and guides for teachers; Dr. Elijah Moses, Mayor of Bombay 1937–1938. Several officers in the Indian Army, Navy and Air Force, notably including Vice Admiral Benjamin Abraham Samson, former Commandant of the Indian Defense Academy, who commanded the Western Fleet during hostilities with Pakistan in 1965, subsequently managing director of the Mazagaon Docks where he supervised the construction of the first two Indian-built frigates; Major General Jonathan Reuben Samson of the Indian Engineers, now general manager of the Armored Vehicle Factory at Avadi, Madras; Dr. Sarah Jacob, principal of the Jaipur Government Medical College; Dr. Eliezar Moses Best, dean of B.J. Medical College and superintendent of Civil Hospital, Ahmedabad; Mrs. Meera Jacob Mahadevan, author and innovative social worker who conceived of and developed a network of Mobile Creches and Schools for the impoverished, neglected children of itinerant laborers; Solomon Shalom Aptekar, popular author and playwright of the 1920s; Joseph David Penkar, pioneer in the Indian screen industry, script and song writer; Nissim Ezekiel, highly rated Indian poet writing in English, editor, art critic, playwright, reader in American Literature at Mumbai (formerly Bombay) University; Dr. Esther Solomon, Ph.D., Sanskritist at Gujarat University; Samuel Israel, director of the National Book Trust of India since 1974; Ezra Kolet, formerly in government service in the Finance Ministry, later in the Ministry of Shipping and Transport as chief comptroller of chartering and as additional secretary to the ministry, the moving spirit of the Delhi Jewish community, and founder, secretary and violinist of the Delhi Symphony Orchestra; and Judah Reuben, India's only Jewish umpire (cricket), member of the All India Panel of Umpires.

Most Bene Israel congregations became affiliated (in reality very loosely) either with the World Council of Synagogues (Conservative) or with the Union of Orthodox Jewish Congregations. A significant development in the religious field was the establishment in 1925 of the Jewish Religious Union in Bombay by Dr. Jerusha Jhirad who, upon her return from medical training in England, used the London organization as the prototype. In Bombay this was an entirely spontaneous move without outside financial help, though prayer books and other literature were obtained from the Liberal Jewish Synagogue of London. The Bombay Jewish Religious Union was one of the founder members of the World Union for Progressive Judaism (established in 1926) and made a small annual contribution toward its expenses. In the 1950s the Bombay congregation's own funds were supplemented with financial aid from circles of Progressive Judaism outside India and from Sassoon Trust Funds, all of which enabled the Bombay Jewish Religious Union, now called Congregation Rodef Shalom, to obtain premises of its own and the services of two young rabbis, both graduates of *Hebrew Union College. In August 1957 Rabbi Hugo Gryn (for more than two full years), followed by Rabbi Elisha Nattiv (for about three years) ministered to this congregation and exerted an influence among the Jews of Bombay far beyond the three hundred members of Congregation Rodef Shalom.

The first contacts of the Bene Israel with the modern Zionist movement go back to the time of Theodor Herzl. In

1897 the Bene Israel were invited to participate in the First Zionist Congress. They refused with the explanation that the community was waiting for "the Divine Hand" to bring them back to Zion. The first Zionist association was founded in Bombay in 1919. Visits of Zionist leaders such as Israel *Cohen in 1921, the first Zionist emissary to India on behalf of the World Zionist Organization, and subsequently of Immanuel Olsvanger, and others, stimulated the community's interest in and support of the Jewish National Home.

In the second half of the 20th century the numbers of the Bene Israel community have significantly decreased due to the emigration of its members to Israel, Europe, and the Americas. In the early years of the 21st century there were approximately 4,000 Bene Israel left in India, most of them living in Maharashtra State. Other Bene Israel communities functioned in Ahmedabad and New Delhi. Communities maintained a number of synagogues and prayer halls, such as the Magen Hassidim and Tiferet Israel synagogues in Mumbai (formerly Bombay), and the Shaar Hashamaim synagogue in Thane. In some places, there was a regular *minyan*; in others there were services on Saturday mornings and not on Friday nights, or on High Holidays only. The first synagogue in Bombay celebrated its bicentenary in February 1996.

[Walter Joseph Fischel, Shirley Berry Isenberg, and Benjamin J. Israel / Shalva Weil and Yulia Egorova (2nd ed.)]

In Israel

Between 1948 and 1952, approximately 2,300 Bene Israel emigrated to Israel. As a result of sit-down strikes and hunger strikes (see below), the Jewish Agency returned a total of 337 individuals, in several groups, between 1952 and 1954. Most of them were brought back to Israel by the Jewish Agency after several years. From the establishment of the state until 1969, over 12,000 Bene Israel emigrated to Israel. They were mainly absorbed into the branches of industry in which they were occupied in India, such as textiles and metals, as well as into public services. They settled mainly in Beersheba, Dimonah, Ashdod, and Eilat. Some settled in kibbutzim and moshavim.

SOCIAL-RELIGIOUS CRISIS. The Bene Israel became the focus of a controversy which arose in 1954 over the basic question of the personal status of the Bene Israel regarding marriage with other Jews. Although the Chief Rabbinate had laid down in essence that "the sect of the Bene Israel in India is of the seed of the House of Israel without any doubt," several rabbis in Israel refused to marry Bene Israel to other Jews. This standpoint was based on halakhic decisions that had been given for Jews from Baghdad who had settled in India, and who denounced intermarriage with those whom they considered to belong to an inferior caste. On first coming to India in the 18th century, the Baghdadi Jews had prayed in the synagogues of the Bene Israel and buried their dead in their cemeteries. However, as they became more settled and acquired a higher status and education, they began to keep apart and to question whether the Bene Israel were legitimately Jewish. They considered that association with the Bene Israel should be debarred for fear of illegitimacy (*mamzerut*), since the latter were unfamiliar with the Jewish laws of divorce (*gittin*), absolved themselves from levirate marriage, and did not practice *ḥaliẓah*. Not one of the rabbis outside India who returned a negative decision concerning the Bene Israel in previous generations had ever visited there or met representatives of the Bene Israel community in order to obtain knowledge of their customs or information directly from them. In Israel the controversy arose between those who rejected the Bene Israel and those who regarded them as Jews in every respect. In 1962, the Israel Chief Rabbinate appointed a commission of four rabbis who were charged with meeting representatives of the Bene Israel. From the evidence of the leaders of the community who appeared before the rabbis and from earlier sources, it became clear that the Bene Israel had not been accustomed to divorce women at all, in the same way that divorce was not practiced among Indians other than Muslims until about a century ago. It was only on the arrival in India of rabbis from Baghdad and Yemen who were experts on the Jewish laws of divorce that a number of Bene Israel had approached them. Concerning widows the Bene Israel generally followed the custom of their Indian neighbors and did not permit them to remarry, so that the question of levirate marriage or *ḥaliẓah* did not arise. On Oct. 18, 1962, the council of the Chief Rabbinate decided that marriage with Bene Israel is permissible. However, the rabbi registering the marriage was bound to investigate, as far back as three generations at least, the maternal ancestry of every applicant of the Bene Israel, man or woman, wishing to marry outside the community, in order to establish to what extent there were not intermixed in the family persons who were non-Jews or proselytes. The rabbi concerned was also bound to establish as far as possible that neither the parents of the applicant nor his grandparents had remarried after a previous divorce, and that they were not within the prohibited degrees of kinship.

These directives aroused fierce resentment, culminating in a stormy strike in Jerusalem in the summer of 1964, in which several hundred of the Bene Israel from all over Israel participated. Subsequently, the prime minister, Levi Eshkol, issued the statement that "the government of Israel reiterates that it regards the community of the Bene Israel from India as Jews in every respect, without any restriction or distinction, equal in their rights to all other Jews in every matter, including matters of matrimony."

To these troubling afflictions had been added the difficulties of absorption of the Bene Israel into a society totally different from that to which they had been accustomed in India, and the difficulties of finding employment and of language. When the first groups of Bene Israel encountered the difficulties of absorption, they reacted by sit-down strikes of groups and individuals. The presence of Bene Israel strikers at the doors of the offices of the Jewish Agency became a regular feature of the 1950s. In the Indian Parliament, a debate upon discrimination against Indian Jews in Israel took place at the beginning of the crisis. On Sept. 8, 1952, a statement of the Indian deputy minister for external affairs, Shri Anil R. Chanda, was read in answer to a question in the Indian Council of States in New Delhi, as follows: "The government of India has received complaints from some Indian Jews who had returned from Israel that there was discrimination against them on account of their color. The government has not verified any of these complaints, and in any event, such individual complaints do not justify a general statement that there is a color bar in Israel." The young generation of Bene Israel has become integrated into Israel society and found its place in all fields of Israel life. Their communal attachment is still strong and finds particular expression at meetings on festivals.

[Naftali Bar-Giora]

As a result of natural increase, the Bene Israel in Israel number over 50,000. They tend to live in well-defined communities such as Dimonah, Ashdod, Yeruḥam, Kiryat Gat, and Lydda (Lod); there are large communities in Ashkelon, Beersheba, Ramleh, and Kiryat Ata. Many Bene Israel are employed in the transportation and communications industries as skilled workers and clerks; others work in the armed forces and police. More than half the women are employed outside the home. Social life is organized around the synagogue, which acts as a community center in each urban settlement. Communal events are arranged by nearly 30 voluntary associations around the country; two associations are national and the rest serve local interests. Activities are conducted in Hebrew, English, and Marathi, the native tongue of the immigrant generation. A Marathi quarterly called *Mai Bolli* has been published in Israel since 1989. In 1995, the Indian Women's Organization celebrated its quartercentary celebration in Lydda.

[Shalva Weil (2nd ed.)]

BIBLIOGRAPHY: H.S. Kehimkar, *History of the Bene Israel of India* (1937); M. Ezekiel, *History and Culture of the Bene Israel in India* (1948); R. Reuben, *Bene Israel of Bombay* (1913); L.I. Rabinowitz, *Far East Mission* (1952); N. Bar-Giora, *Massa be-Hodu* (1953); W.J. Fischel, *Ha-Yehudim be-Hodu* (1960); idem, in: *Essays… Abba Hillel Silver* (1963), 170–85; S. Strizower, *Exotic Jewish Communities* (1962), 48–87; I. Nissim, *Benei Yisrael, Piskei Halakhah* (1962); B.J. Israel, *Religious Evolution among the Bene Israel of India since 1750* (1963); S. Shellim, *Treatise on the Origin and Early History of the Bene Israel* (1963); R. Dafni, *Indian Jews in Israel* (1969). **ADD. BIBLIOGRAPHY:** S. Samuel, *Treatise on the Origin and Early History of the Bene Israel of Maharashtra State* (1963); J.H. Lord, *The Jews of India and the Far East* (1907); S. Strizower, *The Children of Israel: The Bene Israel of Bombay* (1971); S.B. Isenberg, *India's Bene Israel, A Comprehensive Inquiry and Sourcebook* (1988); J. Roland, *The Jewish Community of India* (1998).

BENEI ZION (Heb. בְּנֵי צִיּוֹן), moshav in central Israel, in the southern Sharon, affiliated with Ha-Iḥud ha-Ḥakla'i middle-class settlements association. It was founded in 1947 by veteran farmers, who were later joined by immigrants from Poland, Romania, and North Africa. Its economy was based on citrus plantations and intensive farming. The moshav is named after the B'nai Zion Order of America, which contributed funds toward the acquisition of the land. In the mid-1990s the population was approximately 430, increasing to 742 in 2002 after upscale expansion.

[Efraim Orni]

BEN-ELIEZER, BINYAMIN (**Fuad;** 1936–), Israeli military commander and politician, member of the Eleventh to Sixteenth Knessets. Ben-Eliezer was born in Basra in Iraq and immigrated to Israel on his own in 1950, when he was only 13. During the Six-Day War he served as the deputy to the Bedouin commander of the Shaked unit in the Southern Command. During the Yom Kippur War he was deputy commander of a brigade. In the mid-1970s he was appointed Israel's first commander in Southern Lebanon and was in charge of the opening of the "Good Fence" between Israel and Lebanon and creating the foundations for the Southern Lebanese Army under Major Haddad. In 1978 he was appointed military administrator of Judea and Samaria, a position he held for close to four years. In that period he participated in the effort to establish an alternative Palestinian leadership to the PLO in the form of the village leagues. He left the army in 1982 and for a brief period served as the secretary general of the ethnic Tami party established by Aharon Abuhazeira. However, he was recalled to active service by Minister of Defense Moshe *Arens in 1983 and appointed coordinator of operations in Judea, Samaria, and Gaza. In the course of his military service Ben-Eliezer graduated from the IDF Command and Staff Academy and the College for National Security.

After his final discharge from the IDF in 1984 Ben-Eliezer joined Ezer *Weizman in establishing a new party, Yaḥad, which was elected to the Eleventh Knesset and joined the Alignment before the formation of the National Unity Government. When not serving as a minister, Ben-Eliezer served on the Knesset Foreign Affairs and Defense Committee. In the government formed by Yitzhak *Rabin in 1992, he was appointed minister of construction and housing, a position he also held in the government formed by Shimon *Peres after Rabin's assassination. During this period he shifted the focus back to construction within the Green Line. In the government formed by Ehud *Barak in 1999, he was deputy prime minister and minister of communications, and after the NRP resigned from the government also served as minister of construction and housing. Following Barak's defeat in the elections for prime minister held in February 2001 and Labor's entry into the government formed by Ariel *Sharon, Ben-Eliezer was appointed minister of defense but resigned from the government with the Labor Party in November 2002.

As minister of defense he had to contend with the growing violence of the *Intifada* and was in charge of Operation Defensive Shield in the territories in the spring of 2002. As the violence escalated he favored the construction of a fence between Israel and the Palestinian territories, but continued to believe in a negotiated settlement which would lead to the establishment of a Palestinian state. Already in June 2001 he advocated the need to remove outposts of the settlers in the territories. In primaries held for the Labor Party leadership in December 2001 Ben-Eliezer ran against Avraham *Burg, winning by a narrow majority. However, just before the elections to the Sixteenth Knesset, Amram Mitzna defeated him in another round of primaries for the party leadership.

[Susan Hattis Rolef (2nd ed.)]

BEN ELIEZER, MOSHE (1882–1944), Hebrew editor, author, and translator. Ben Eliezer, who was born in Shchuchin, near Vilna, became attracted to the Haskalah while studying at Mir yeshivah, and joined the staff of the Hebrew daily *Ha-Zeman*. From 1906 to 1910 he lived in the United States, where he established *Shibbolim* (1909), a journal devoted to modern Hebrew literature. Returning to Poland he edited several Hebrew journals for young people, and spent some time after World War I in Kovno as press officer for the Lithuanian Ministry for Jewish Affairs. Immigrating to Palestine in 1925, he joined the editorial staff of the newspaper *Haaretz*. His stories, feuilletons, and translations appeared in the Hebrew press of various countries and he also wrote and edited several series of books for children. His works include the historical novels *Yerovam u-Reḥavam* ("Jeroboam and Rehoboam," 1939) and *Don Yosef Nasi* (1945), the novel *Gavri'el* (1945), and translations of works by Scott, Dickens, Conrad, Hawthorne, and others.

BIBLIOGRAPHY: N. Goren, *Demuyyot be-Sifrutenu* (1953), 69–74; H. Weiner, *Pirkei Ḥayyim ve-Sifrut* (1960), 94–95; F. Lachower, *Shirah u-Maḥashavah* (1953), 236–8; Rabbi Binyamin, *Mishpeḥot Soferim* (1960), 312–3.

[Getzel Kressel]

BENE MENASHE, name given to Judaizing groups from northeast India mainly in the two Indian states of Mizoram and Manipur. The Bene Menashe claim descent from the tribe of Manasseh, one of the ten tribes exiled from the Land of Israel by the Assyrians over 2,700 years ago. Members of the group include ethnic Chins, Lushais, Kukis, and Mizos. Collectively they are often referred to as Shinlung. The movement, if one can call it such, started in the 1950s as a by-product of the experience of colonialism and Christian missions. Remarkably, by the end of the 20th century several hundred Shinlung had formally converting to Orthodox Judaism. Many thousand more practiced a kind of Judaism. Others practiced Christianity while thinking of themselves as descendants of the ancient Israelites. By 2005 some 800 converts had settled in Israel, helped by an organization called Shavei-Israel, a Jerusalem-based group that attempts to give help and succor to "lost Jews" seeking to return to the Jewish people. For the most part the Shinlung do not see themselves as converts in the usual sense of the term: like other such groups – one might cite the *Bene Ephraim Telugu-speaking Jews of Andhra Pradesh who believe themselves to be descended from the Tribe of Ephraim – they believe that they are historically of Jewish descent. This controversial claim has found little support among scholars, although a gifted Israeli essayist and translator – Hillel Halkin – took up their cause in a colorful account published in 2002. He was joined in 2005 by the Sephardi chief rabbi of Israel, Shlomo Amar, who decided to formally recognize the Bene Menashe as "descendants of Israel" and agreed to dispatch a *beit din* from Israel to northeast India to convert them.

BIBLIOGRAPHY: S. Weil, "Double Conversion among the 'Children of Menasseh,'" in: *Contemporary Society: Tribal Studies* (Satya Narayana Ratha Festschrift Volumes), vol.1, *Structure and Progress*, ed. G. Pfeffer and D. Behera (New Delhi, n.d.); T. Parfitt, *The Lost Tribes of Israel: The History of a Myth* (2002); T. Parfitt and E. Trevisan-Semi, *Judaising Movements: Studies in the Margins of Judaism* (2002); H. Halkin, *Across the Sabbath River: In Search of a Lost Tribe of Israel* (2002); M. Samra, "Judaism in Manipur and Mizoram: By-Product of Christian Mission," in: *The Australian Journal of Jewish Studies*, 6, no.1 (1992); idem, "The Tribe of Menasseh: 'Judaism' in the Hills of Manipur and Mizoram," in: *Man in India*, 71/1 (1991); idem, "Buallawn Israel: The Emergence of a Judaising Movement in Mizoram, Northeast India," in: L. Olson (ed.), *Religious Change, Conversion and Culture* (1996).

[Tudor Parfitt (2nd ed.)]

BENESCH, ALFRED ABRAHAM (1879–1973), U.S. attorney and civic leader. Benesch was born in Cleveland, Ohio, the son of Bohemian immigrants. He established a law practice in Cleveland and was elected to the Cleveland City Council in 1912. In 1914–15 he served as public safety director in Mayor Newton D. Baker's cabinet. Under Benesch's direction the first electric traffic signal lights were installed in Cleveland on August 5, 1914, by the American Traffic Signal Company. In 1922 Benesch gained prominence as a libertarian for his fight against a proposed quota system for Jews at Harvard. His public career was highlighted by 37 years of continuous service on the Cleveland Board of Education (1925–62); he was its president in 1933–34. Benesch made an immediate impact on school policy when he successfully opposed compulsory reserve military training in the city's public high schools. He was Ohio State Director of Commerce during 1935–39. Benesch held many public and civic offices and was equally active as a Jewish communal leader, serving as a trustee of many local Jewish agencies.

[Judah Rubinstein]

BENEŠOV (Ger. **Beneschau**), town in Bohemia, the Czech Republic. The community, first mentioned in 1419, was among the earliest to be established in a seignorial town in *Bohemia. Five Jewish families were living there in 1570. A community is again mentioned there in 1845, numbering seven families in 1852. It was officially registered in 1893 with 786 persons (including those living in 27 surrounding villages). Benešov was a center of the Svaz *čechů-židů, Czecho-Jewish movement, and of the struggle against the German-language Jewish school at the end of the 19th century. In 1930 the community numbered 237 (2.8% of the total population), 24 of whom declared their nationality as Jewish. The anti-Jewish laws imposed during the

German occupation were sometimes not enforced in Benešov. Most of the community was deported by the Nazis to the Maly Trostinets extermination camp near Minsk in 1942. Only two Jews returned. The synagogue equipment was sent to the Central Jewish Museum in Prague; two cemeteries still remain. No community has been reconstructed.

[Jan Herman]

BENEVENTO, town in southern Italy. Epigraphical evidence may indicate that Jews were living in Benevento already in the fifth century. Around 950 the miracle worker *Aaron of Baghdad visited the town. Later, members of the *Ahimaaz family resided in Benevento, Hananeel b. Paltiel establishing his yeshivah there. In 1065, Landolfo VI, prince of Benevento, forced a number of Jews to become converted to Christianity, being reproved for this by Pope *Alexander II. In 1077 Benevento became part of the Patrimony of St. Peter and its Jews passed under the rule of the pope. When *Benjamin of Tudela visited Benevento about 1159 he found 200 Jewish families. Two Hebrew inscriptions on a sepulchral stone from 1153 also attest to the existence of a Jewish community in this period. The Jews were living in a fairly ample quarter; in 1198 three churches in Benevento were known as "de Judeca." Jewish economic activities included weaving and especially dyeing, on which taxes were paid to the archbishop. Later Jews engaged in moneylending. In the early 16th century they also dealt in corn. When in 1442 Alfonso of Aragon became king of Naples, he also occupied Benevento. The Holy See compromised by nominating Alfonso apostolic vicar in the city, recognizing his rule *de facto*. In 1452 Alfonso accorded the Jews of Benevento the same privileges enjoyed by the Jews living in the Kingdom of Naples, in return for a thousand ducats. In 1458, upon Alfonso's death, Benevento returned to pontifical rule. Benevento being a Papal enclave, the Jewish community which now maintained two synagogues was not disturbed at the time of the general expulsion from southern Italy in 1541. Nevertheless, after the election of Pope *Paul IV in 1555, their position sharply deteriorated and several Jews converted, among them a rich banker, Raphael Usiglio. In 1569 they were expelled from Benevento as from the other small towns in the Papal States. The municipal council readmitted Jews in 1617, but in 1630 they were accused of poisoning the wells. Thereafter, the organized Jewish community ceased to exist.

BIBLIOGRAPHY: P.M. Lonardo, *Gli ebrei a Benevento* (1899); idem, in: *Vessillo Israelitico*, 67 (1917); Roth, Dark Ages, index; Milano, Bibliotheca, no. 1041 and index. **ADD. BIBLIOGRAPHY:** C. Colafemmina, "Gli ebrei a Benevento," in: *Italia Judaica*, 6 (1998), 204–27.

[Attilio Milano / Nadia Zeldes (2nd ed.)]

BENEVENTO, IMMANUEL BEN JEKUTHIEL (died c. 1560), Italian grammarian and kabbalist. Benevento, who lived in Mantua, was the pupil of R. Moses *Basola of Pesaro. He wrote *Livyat Hen* (Mantua, 1557) on Hebrew grammar and poetry and published *Ma'arekhet ha-Elohut*, the kabbalistic work of Perez b. Isaac Gerondi (of Barcelona), which he annotated with his own commentary (Mantua, 1558). He was also one of the publishers of the first printed edition of the Zohar (Mantua, 1558–60), and went to the Ottoman Empire in search of new Zohar manuscripts for this edition. Benevento was also involved in the dispute about printing the Zohar, justifying it in the introductions to his books. He died before the printing was completed.

BIBLIOGRAPHY: Steinschneider, Cat Bod, 541, no. 3492, 1055, no. 5266; J. Perles, *Beitraege zur Geschichte der hebraeischen und aramaeischen Studien* (1884), 220; G. Scholem, *Bibliographia kabbalistica* (1927), 166, 177. **ADD. BIBLIOGRAPHY:** I. Sonne, *Mi-Paolo Harevi'i ad Pius ha-Hamishi* (1954), 110–17, 127–29; I. Tishby, "Studies in Kabbalah and Its Branches" (Heb., 1982), 79–130.

[Umberto (Moses David) Cassuto / Moti Benmelekh (2nd ed.)]

BENEVENUTUS GRAPHEUS HIEROSOLYMITANUS (c. 12th century), the most famous medieval non-Arab oculist. Probably Jewish, he practiced and lectured in Southern Europe. His work on ocular diseases was the best-known textbook until well into the 16th century. Twenty-two manuscripts and 18 printed editions are still in existence, differing in length and completeness. According to a Vatican Latin codex, the work was "translated from the Hebrew into Latin." The Latin *editio princeps* is the Ferrara incunabulum (1474). Benevenutus' knowledge of anatomy and his physiological and pathological conceptions follow closely Galen's teachings. In therapy, however, he reflects ophthalmological knowledge of his own time. His description of seasonal ophthalmia is an indication of his having been a "Hierosolymitanus" (Jerusalemite), since it conforms surprisingly well with the summer and autumn epidemics of conjunctivitis in Ereẓ Israel. His therapy is empirical and free from irrational elements. Among his numerous remedies some carry the adjective "Jerusalem." From his descriptions of couching for cataract, the radical treatment of trichiasis, dacryocystitis, and "scabies" of the eyes (trachoma), Benevenutus must have been an experienced and skillful surgeon. He describes an astonishingly modern method for dealing with ocular injuries; embryos from freshly embryonated eggs, removed and reduced to a pulp, and regularly used as an ointment, "bring about a good consolidation of the wound." Of the many names of Benevenutus, Grapheus seems to be the correct one. It would appear to be a stylized derivation of the Hebrew *rofe* ("physician"). In the Paris codex he is called "*Bien Venu Raffe.*" The various Christian invocations in his writings were probably later insertions and are not proof that he was not Jewish, nor does the frequently repeated assertion "nos Salernitani" prove that Benevenutus taught in Salerno.

BIBLIOGRAPHY: J. Hirschberg, in: A. Graefe-T. Saemisch, *Handbuch der gesamten Augenheilkunde*, 13 (1908); C.A. Wood (ed.), *Beneventus Graffus, De Oculis* (Eng., 1929); H. Friedenwald, *Jews and Medicine*, 2 (1944), 539–40; Feigenbaum, in: *Acta Medica Orientalia*, 14 (1955), 26–29, 75–82.

[Aryeh Feigenbaum]

BENFELD, town south of Strasbourg, eastern France. In 1349, a regional assembly of feudal lords was held in Benfeld to finalize measures to be taken against the Jews who were accused of spreading the *Black Death. Shortly afterward the Jews living in Benfeld were murdered or expelled. A new community was established in 1830, numbering 236 in 1836. A synagogue was built in 1845. It was one of the few in Alsace not desecrated during World War II under the German occupation, when 31 Jews were deported from Benfeld. In 1968, the community numbered 75 persons.

BIBLIOGRAPHY: E. Scheid, *Histoire des Juifs d'Alsace* (1887), 36–37, 286–7; R. Berg, *La persécution raciale* (1947), 181.

[Roger Berg]

BENFEY, THEODOR (1809–1881), German comparative philologist and Sanskritist. Benfey was born in Noerten, near Goettingen, and lived in Goettingen from his childhood. His first works in classical philology were produced hastily and contained many inaccuracies (as in his *Griechisches Wurzellexikon*, 1839–42). As a young scholar he interested himself in the relationship of Egyptian to Semitic languages, on which he wrote *Ueber das Verhaeltniss der aegyptischen Sprache zum semitischen Sprachstamm* (1844), his sole work on Semitic linguistics. He also dealt extensively with the recurrence of certain motifs in narrative literature, tracing their derivation from Oriental, especially Indian, sources. His work turned increasingly to Indian linguistics, a field in which he became a recognized authority. His two Sanskrit grammars, the complete (1852) and the short (1855), for many years served as basic texts in this field. Though Benfey was a pioneer in the study of the language of the Veda, he never completed the Vedic grammar on which he worked for many years. In 1834 Benfey was appointed a lecturer at the University of Goettingen; in 1848, after converting to Christianity, he was appointed associate professor; and in 1862 full professor. A noted teacher, his students included Jacob Wackernagel and Theodor Noeldeke. For the Bavarian Academy's history of sciences in Germany, Benfey wrote the volume *Geschichte der Sprachwissenschaft und orientalischen Philologie*… (1869), with an outstanding chapter on the beginnings of comparative linguistics and its spiritual background.

BIBLIOGRAPHY: T. Benfey, *Kleinere Schriften*, 1 (1890), biography by M. Benfey; 2 (1892), 133–56 (bibliography).

[Hans Jacob Polotsky]

BENGALIL (Abengalel), family which flourished in Spain and North Africa in the 13th century. JOSEPH BENGALIL was a rabbi probably living in Ceuta, Morocco, who corresponded with Solomon b. Abraham *Adret. His sons ABRAHAM and SAMUEL both served on diplomatic missions for the Aragonese kings to Granada and Morocco. Abraham resided in Valencia, and was authorized to conduct business there in 1276 by James I at the request of the sultan of Tunis, apparently also using his official journeys for business purposes; in 1280, when his goods were impounded by the Castilian authorities, Pedro III retaliated in kind against Castilian merchants visiting Aragon. In 1291 Abraham took his family with him on a mission to Tlemçen (Algeria).

BIBLIOGRAPHY: J.M. Toledano, *Ner ha-Ma'arav* (1911), 41; J. Ben-Naim, *Malkhei Rabbanan* (1931), 57; Baer, Spain, 1 (1961), 410; Corcos, in: JQR, 54 (1963/64), 65; Hirschberg, Afrikah, 1 (1965), 281–2.

[David Corcos]

BEN-GAVRIEL, MOSHE YA'AKOV (originally **Eugen Hoeflich**; 1891–1965), Israeli author who wrote in German. Born into a bourgeois Viennese family (his mother was a cousin of pianist Arthur *Schnabel), he began studying Arabic at Vienna university, but after three years was expelled because of his socialist views. Wounded in Poland during World War I, Ben-Gavriel went to Palestine as an Austrian liaison officer with the Turkish forces in Jerusalem. After just a few months he was dismissed for his "pansemitic" activities and he had to return to Vienna. From there he contributed to Martin Buber's *Der Jude* and became an active Zionist. In *Der Weg in das Land* (1918), *Feuer im Osten* (1920), and *Die Pforte des Ostens* (1923), Ben-Gavriel presented Zionism as a pan-Asian movement, the *yishuv* being the link between East and West. Later he adopted the outlook of the Berit Shalom without actually joining the group. Returning to Palestine in 1927, Hoeflich changed his name to Ben-Gavriel. There he was the local representative of the Deutsches Nachrichtenbuero until 1933 and later worked for the Swiss press. His World War II experiences in a Palestinian unit of the British Army inspired the Schweik-like hero of *Frieden und Krieg des Buergers Mahaschavi* (1952; *Mahaschavi in Peace and War*, 1960). After 1948 Ben-Gavriel, living in Jerusalem, was successful in writing and broadcasting about the State of Israel in West Germany, where his many books on the Middle East, many of them styled as Oriental tales, such as *Kumsits* (1956), were bestsellers. Among his outstanding works is his novel *Das Haus in der Karpfengasse* (1958), set in Nazi-occupied Prague, which appeared in Hebrew in 1944. Two volumes of early recollections were *Zahav ba-Ḥuẓot* (1946) and *Die Flucht nach Tarschisch* (1963). A critical edition of Ben-Gavriel's 1915–27 diaries appeared in 1999.

BIBLIOGRAPHY: E. Benyoetz, in: NDB, 9 (1972), 314–16; J. Schmidt, *Der Unterhaltungsschriftsteller Moshe Ya'akov Ben-Gavriel* (1979); A. Wallas, in: M.H. Gelber et al. (eds.), *Von Franzos zu Canetti* (1996), 305–44; A. Wallas (ed.), *Eugen Hoeflich: Tagebuecher 1915–1927* (1999, with extensive commentary); idem, in: A. Eidherr and K. Mueller (eds.), *Jiddische Kultur und Literatur in Oesterreich* (2003), 72–102.

[Marcus Pyka (2nd ed.)

BENGHAZI, port city in the district of Cyrenaica (see *Cyrene), Libya. In ancient times it was called Hesperides, but was later renamed Berenice. After 74 B.C.E. it was part of Roman Cyrenaica, but according to an inscription of 13 B.C.E., found at Benghazi, the Jews of Berenice were considered citizens (as in the rest of Cyrenaica) but were ruled by their own Jewish archons and not by an ethnarch as in other parts of the Diaspora. Furthermore they are described as a "municipal community," and appear from the inscription to be observant of the festivals (CIG 3:2, no. 5361). Another inscription found in 1938, gives thanks to certain donors for helping to dedicate a synagogue in Berenice in 56 C.E. In both this and the previous inscription the majority of the names mentioned are non-Jewish, testifying to a fair degree of hellenization, as in Egypt. During the revolt of the Jews of Cyrene in 115 and during the Byzantine era the Jews of Berenice suffered the same fate as those of Cyrene in general. After the Arab conquest in 660, Berenice was mostly deserted. In the 14th century it was called by its Arabic name Benghazi (*Bin Ghāzī*). In the beginning of the 16th century, many Jews from Tripoli helped to repopulate it, earning their livelihood by trade with North Africa and the Mediterranean area, or as smiths or tailors.

Following the Ottoman occupation of 1640, Jewish families from Tripoli were attracted to the city. In 1745 epidemics and poverty drove out the inhabitants, but about 1750 some members of the previous Jewish community returned and reorganized the community, which began to flourish about 1775 with the arrival of Jewish families from Italy. In the 18th and 19th centuries Benghazi had 400 Jewish families divided into two groups: those of the town and the surrounding region (*Kahal Bengazi*) and those who were born in *Tripoli and Italy. Although both groups recognized the authority of one rabbi, each had its own synagogue. The Muslim brotherhood of the Sanusiya, whose influence was considerable in Cyrenaica from the 1840s onwards, was well disposed toward the Jews of Benghazi, appreciating their economic-mercantile contributions and peaceful attitude. The Jews enjoyed complete freedom and were not forced to live in a special quarter. They lived in affluence, and because of their commercial activity the town became an important trading center for Europe and Africa. Several wealthy families occupied high positions in the service of the Ottoman authorities. Among scholars of this community were Elijah Lavi (1783–1883), author of *Sefer Ge'ullot Adonai* (1864) and other works written in Hebrew or Judeo-Arabic; Moses Ḥakmon; and Isaac Khalfon. A modernized *talmud torah* was organized under the leadership of Elia Juili (1890), Ḥai Teshuba, and others. In 1909 when a large fire broke out in the bazaar, the Ottoman soldiery, who were supposed to extinguish it, looted and attacked the population, especially the Jews. Because of this, several families moved back to Tripoli. From 1911 Italian rule attracted more Jews from the interior of the country, as well as from Italy, to Benghazi, and in 1935 the Jewish population numbered 2,236. Until 1936 life under Italian rule proceeded peacefully for the Jews. In 1936, however, the Italians began to enforce fascist legislation aimed at modernizing social and economic structures based on conditions current in Italy. With the implementation of anti-Jewish racial legislation in late 1938, Jews were removed from municipal councils, public offices, and state schools and their papers stamped with the words "Jewish race." When Benghazi fell to the British on Feb. 6, 1941, the Jews were overjoyed, but suffered in attacks by hostile Muslim youth when the city was recaptured by the Italians on April 3, 1941. On Dec. 24, 1941 the British retook the city but Italian-German forces once again conquered it on Jan. 27, 1942. This again resulted in anti-Jewish attacks, the systematic plunder of all Jewish shops, and the promulgation of a deportation order. Almost all the Benghazi Jews were deported to Giado, 149 miles (240 km.) south of Tripoli, a camp in the desert where they lived under severe climatic, health, and living conditions. Consequently, 562 of them died of starvation and typhus. Forced labor, however, was not general, and food distribution was not conditional upon it. The condition of the Jews in Giado improved only when the British entered the camp in January 1943. In November 1945 and June 1948 the Jews of Benghazi did not suffer anti-Jewish pogroms at the hands of Arabs similar to the Jews of Tripoli, though small-scale incidents did occur. Thus, several Jews were beaten up in mid-June 1948, a shop was looted, and a fire broke out in a synagogue, but the local police introduced order and there was no need for the British Army to intervene. Emergency measures were introduced, demonstrations and gatherings were forbidden, and a curfew was instituted. Still, the Jews felt unsafe and feared for their life and property. Violence against individuals as well as cases of kidnapping and forced Islamization of young Jewish women took place, especially in the countryside. As a result, once emigration to Israel was permitted in early 1949, the majority of the community of 2,500 persons emigrated to Israel through the end of 1951, with approximately 200 Jews left in Benghazi in 1967. During the Six-Day War of 1967, unlike other areas of Jewish settlement in Libya, the authorities reacted fairly rapidly to protect the Jews in Benghazi. Almost immediately after word of Israel-Arab fighting came, the Jews were rounded up and put into protective custody in army barracks outside the city. Subsequent to the Six-Day War most of the remaining Jews in Benghazi emigrated, mainly to Italy.

For bibliography see *Libya.

[David Corcos / Rachel Simon (2nd ed.)]

BENGIS, SELIG REUBEN (1864–1953), Lithuanian rabbi. Bengis studied in Volozhin under Naphtali Ẓevi Judah *Berlin and Ḥayyim *Soloveichik. In 1894 he was appointed rabbi of Bodki and, in 1912, of Kalvarija, Lithuania. At the outbreak of World War I he went to Smolensk, but in 1915 he returned to Kalvarija. In 1938 he was appointed head of the *bet din* of the separatist Orthodox community Ha-Edah ha-Ḥaredit of Jerusalem, and in 1949, on the death of Joseph Ẓevi *Duschinsky, became its rabbi. Despite the fact that his community consisted of active religious extremists, he succeeded in directing its affairs into practical channels and in curbing its most extreme wing, the *Neturei Karta. He also served as head of the Ohel Moshe Yeshivah in Jerusalem. Bengis' mastery of rabbinic literature, and his memory, were phenomenal; he could unhesitatingly give the source of any random quotation from the Talmud, Rashi, or *tosafot*. He published *Li-Felagot Re'uven* (in 7 parts, Kaidan, Riga, Jerusalem, 1924–46), consisting of **hadranim*, i.e., discourses delivered on completing the study of a talmudic tractate, interwoven with his novellae. He justified the unusual form of his work by maintaining that while novellae are little read, there was a considerable interest in this form of talmudic learning. Bengis himself stated that he had written, under the same title, a commentary on Alfasi, and sermons, which remained in manuscript. Some of his halakhic articles appeared in *Tevunah* (Jerusalem, 1941).

BIBLIOGRAPHY: S. Schurin, *Keshet Gibborim* (1964), 40–43.

[Itzhak Alfassi]

BEN-GURION (Gruen), DAVID (1886–1973), Zionist leader, Israeli statesman, first prime minister and defense minister of Israel; member of the First to Eighth Knessets.

Early Years

Ben-Gurion was born in Plonsk (then in Russian Poland). His father, Avigdor Gruen, was a member of Ḥovevei Zion and his house was the center of Zionist activity in the town. His mother Sheindel (née Friedman) died when he was 11 years old. He was educated in a modern Hebrew-language *ḥeder*, and studied secular subjects with private tutors. At the age of 14, Ben-Gurion was among the founders of a Zionist youth group "Ezra." He joined the *Po'alei Zion movement in 1903, traveling and speaking on its behalf in Plonsk, Warsaw, and smaller towns. During the 1905–06 revolution he was arrested twice but released at the intervention of his father. In September 1906 Ben-Gurion immigrated to Ereẓ Israel, working in the orange groves of Petaḥ Tikvah and in the wine cellars of Rishon le-Zion. He was elected to the Central Committee of Po'alei Zion. In 1907 he managed to have the sentence "the Party aspires for political independence for the Jewish people in this country" included in the party's first platform, which was drafted in the spirit of Ber *Borochov's writings. Ben-Gurion's ideological positions during this period combined Jewish nationalism with pragmatic socialism, which stressed the obligation of every member of the movement to settle in Ereẓ Israel and the right of the settlers to manage their own affairs without interference from the Diaspora. He demanded that Hebrew be the sole language of all Jewish public life in Ereẓ Israel, including Po'alei Zion, and refused to collaborate with the Yiddish party organ *Der Anfang*. In the 1907–10 Ben-Gurion was an agricultural worker and watchman in Sejera and Milḥamiyyah in the Lower Galilee, Kinneret, and Zikhron Ya'akov. In these years he became convinced that "the settlement of the land is the only true Zionism, all else being self-deception, empty words, and merely a pastime." In 1910 Ben-Gurion joined the editorial staff of the new party organ *Aḥdut* ("Unity") in Jerusalem, together with Izhak *Ben-Zvi and Raḥel Yanait. It was in this publication that he printed his first articles under the name "Ben-Gurion," which he adopted from one of the last Jewish defenders of Jerusalem against the Roman legions. The central theme of these articles was that the *yishuv* must organize politically, together with Jews in other parts of the new Ottoman state following the Young Turk Revolution of 1908, and strive for Jewish autonomy in Ereẓ Israel. In 1911 he and Ben-Zvi were elected as delegates to the Eleventh Zionist Congress and participated in the third world conference of Po'alei Zion in Vienna. The same year Ben-Gurion joined a group of young Zionists who enrolled at Turkish universities, with the object of establishing close ties with the educated ruling circles in Turkey. At first he lived in Salonika, and established contacts with the large Jewish community there, but after Salonika was taken over by the Greeks in 1912, he moved to Constantinople to continue his law studies

1914–1921

When World War I broke out, Ben-Gurion and his party advocated loyalty to Turkey and the adoption of Ottoman citizenship. However, when the Turkish administration started persecuting the Zionists, both he and Ben-Zvi were arrested and accused of conspiring against Ottoman rule in order to establish a Jewish state. In March 1915 they were exiled to Egypt, where they met Joseph *Trumpeldor, who was engaged in forming the "Zion Mule Corps" within the British army, an activity to which both Ben-Gurion and Ben-Zvi objected, because they feared that it endangered the *yishuv* without benefiting the Zionist cause.

Later in 1915 Ben-Gurion and Ben-Zvi proceeded to New York, where their main efforts were directed to the establishment of the *He-Ḥalutz organization, preparing young Jews for settlement in Palestine after the war. In 1917 Ben-Gurion married Paula Munweis (born in Minsk, Russia, 1892), who was a nurse in New York, and an active member of Po'alei Zion. After the *Balfour Declaration Ben-Gurion was among the first in the United States to call for the formation of Jewish battalions to participate in the liberation of Palestine, writing that "England shall not return the country to us.... A country is acquired by a people only through the pain of labor and creation, construction efforts and settlement. The Hebrew people itself must turn this right into a living and existing fact." Volunteering for the British Army in May 1918, he reached Egypt in August as a soldier in the *Jewish Legion – the 39th Battalion of the Royal Fusiliers. There he met volunteers from the labor movement in Palestine and with them started planning for the establishment of a united workers' movement in Palestine after the War that would prepare for the mass Jewish immigration expected to follow the liberation of the country from Ottoman rule. However, they did not manage to see active service, since their unit arrived in the country after the British had already conquered it.

At the 13th conference of Po'alei Zion in Jaffa in February 1919, Ben-Gurion called upon Jewish workers in Palestine and abroad to unite in forming a political force that would direct the Zionist movement toward the establishment of a Jewish socialist society in Palestine, based on the collectivist principles embodied in the *kevutzot* (see *Kibbutz Movement). In 1919 Ben-Gurion opened the founding conference of *Aḥdut ha-Avodah in PetaḥTikvah. He also participated in the world delegation of Po'alei Zion which prepared a blueprint for the future development of Ereẓ Israel. After the Jerusalem riots of Passover 1920, Ben-Gurion traveled to London, where he and Shelomo *Kaplansky headed the Political Bureau of Po'alei Zion, which established contacts with the British Labour Party.

Building the Histadrut

On his return to Palestine at the end of 1921, Ben-Gurion was elected as the first secretary of the *Histadrut, which had been founded in 1920 – a position which he was to hold for the next 14 years. He was active on all levels – the struggle for the improvement of workers' conditions, the organization of strikes, the employment of Jewish workers in all sections of the economy, including government works, and provision for the unemployed. Since Ben-Gurion's objective was to turn the Histadrut into an instrument for settlement, as well as an economic and political body, he proposed that it become a cooperative "workers' society" (*ḥevrat ovedim*), which would undertake agricultural settlement, the promotion of industry and construction, as well as providing workers with all the financial and welfare services that they required. A version of this vision was adopted by the second Histadrut conference in 1923. In the early 1920s Ben-Gurion tried to develop economic relations between the Histadrut and the Soviet trade unions and economic bodies, in the hope that such relations would facilitate the operation of the He-Ḥalutz movement in the Soviet Union and Jewish emigration from there to Palestine. He visited the Soviet Union in 1923, when the Histradrut participated in the Moscow Agricultural Exhibition, but his efforts to gain Soviet support failed.

During the 1920s the non-socialist middle class within the Zionist Movement and in the *yishuv* gained in strength, and the *Revisionist movement declared its opposition to the idea of an all-embracing socialist workers' organization. The Revisionist leader Ze'ev *Jabotinsky called for the "breaking" of the Histadrut (*"ja brechen"*). Ben-Gurion's reaction was to strive to unite the various Zionist workers' parties, with the goal of attaining hegemony for the labor movement in the World Zionist Organization. In 1930 he was instrumental is getting Aḥdut ha-Avodah and *Ha-Po'el ha-Ẓa'ir to unite into a single party that assumed the name *Mapai – an acronym for *Mifleget Po'alei Ereẓ Yisrael.* In the next four years Ben-Gurion concentrated on efforts to prevent the Revisionists from gaining ascendancy in the Zionist Movement. At the 18th Zionist Congress in 1933, in which the workers parties comprised close to 50% of the delegates, Ben-Gurion became a member of the Zionist and *Jewish Agency Executive. In an attempt to prevent a split in the Zionist movement, he reached a tentative agreement with Jabotinsky which would establish a *modus vivendi* on labor matters between the Histadrut and the Revisionist workers. To Ben-Gurion's great regret, however, this agreement was rejected by the members of the Histadrut. Ben-Gurion regarded the rejection as a "grave error" but accepted the verdict. In 1935 Ben-Gurion was elected chairman of the Zionist Actions Committee and the Jewish Agency, and during the next 11 years, he and the president of the Zionist Organization, Chaim *Weizmann, were to run all Zionist affairs. These two very different leaders frequently clashed over both strategy and tactics, but together they saw the movement through its most fateful years. After 1946 Ben-Gurion bore most of the burden on his own.

In the 1930s Ben-Gurion held talks with various leaders of the Arab national movement, but finally reached the conclusion that an agreement with the Arabs would be attained only after the latter became convinced that they could not defeat the Zionist endeavor by force of arms.

Toward the Founding of the Jewish State

Together with Weizmann and Moshe *Sharett, who after the murder of Chaim *Arlosoroff was appointed head of the Political Department of the Jewish Agency, Ben-Gurion accepted the plan for the partition of Palestine into an Arab and a Jewish state, as recommended by the Peel Commission Report in June 1937, believing that even a small Jewish state was better than none, and that the Zionists should accept whatever was offered. This position was opposed by Berl *Katznelson and Yiẓhak *Tabenkin. When the British government abandoned the partition plan, Ben-Gurion participated in the St. James Round Table Conference held by the British in London in 1939, with separate Jewish and Arab delegations, since the Arabs refused to sit with the Jews. Following these talks, and with the clouds of war already looming on the horizon, the British declared their White Paper policy, which called for limited Jewish immigration to Palestine in the next five years, with future immigration dependent on Arab consent, and restrictions on Jewish land acquisitions. Ben-Gurion condemned the White Paper as a betrayal, and called for active resistance to its implementation, by means of intensified "illegal" immigration and enhanced land settlement in restricted areas. Upon the outbreak of World War II Ben-Gurion declared that the *yishuv* would fight on the side of the British against the Nazis as if there were no White Paper, and continue to fight against the White Paper as if there were no war against the Nazis. Active protests against the British policy continued until June 1940, when Italy entered the war, opening a second front against the British in the Mediterranean. Many members of the *yishuv* joined the British army, and in September 1944 the Jewish Brigade was formed. But at the same time Ben-Gurion started to plan for the struggle that would follow the war, and turned to the United States for moral and material support. In May 1942, while in New York and contrary to Weizmann's wishes, he was instrumental in drawing up the *Biltmore Program, which called for the opening of Palestine to free Jewish immigration and settlement, and defined the Zionist goal as the establishment of a Jewish Commonwealth in Palestine that would be integrated into the structure of the new democratic world. When, towards the end of the war, the dissident underground organizations – the Irgun Ẓeva'i Le'ummi (IẒL) and Loḥamei Ḥerut Israel (Leḥi) – carried out armed attacks against British targets in Palestine, Ben-Gurion ordered the Haganah to act against them. He even went so far as to cooperate with the British authorities in apprehending members of the dissident organizations, a policy nicknamed the "*Saison*" (i.e., the hunting season) that aroused much controversy within the ranks of the Haganah and the *yishuv*.

When, following the war, it became clear that the British government had no intention of abandoning the White Paper policy, Ben-Gurion led the active struggle against the British, for a time in cooperation with the dissident organizations, which came to be known as the Hebrew Resistance Movement (Tenu'at ha-Meri ha-Ivri), and intensified "illegal" immigration. In the meantime he embarked on a policy of acquiring arms from all available sources in preparation for a possible armed clash with the Arabs.

On June 29, 1946, known as "Black Saturday," when members of the Jewish Agency Executive in Palestine were arrested by the British, Ben-Gurion was in Europe. Though he refused to reach a compromise with the British, he ordered a pause in the armed struggle in Palestine. Ben-Gurion's policy was approved at the 22nd Zionist Congress held in December 1946, which failed to reelect Weizmann as president of the World Zionist Organization but reelected Ben-Gurion as chairman of the Jewish Agency Executive, to whom the defense portfolio was added. After returning to Palestine, he started planning for the possibility of an armed clash not only with the Arabs in Palestine but also with the armies of the Arab states that had started to organize in the Arab League. Ben-Gurion was one of the chief Zionist spokesmen before the Anglo-American Inquiry Commission in 1946 and the United Nations Special Commission on Palestine (UNSCOP) in 1947.

War of Independence, 1947–1949

When the *War of Independence broke out in December 1947, following the adoption of the partition plan by the UN General Assembly on November 29, Ben-Gurion stood at the head of the defense effort, involving the raising of funds, the acquisition of arms, the recruitment of military experts, and the outlining of military goals, though he did not direct the actual military operations. It was he who, at the end of the war, ordered a withdrawal from the Sinai Peninsula, and refused to allow Yigal *Allon to conquer the West Bank from the Arab Legion. In his determination to free the newly established IDF from all separatist influences, Ben-Gurion ordered the disbanding of the *Palmaḥ command and the complete integration of all its units in the general framework of the new army, which was led by officers, most of whom were veterans of the British Army. He also had to deal with the dissident organizations – the IẒL and Leḥi. In the case of the IẒL, any chance for independent activity on its part was ended with the controversial order given by Ben-Gurion in June 1948 to sink the *Altalena,* an IẒL arms ship, while the fate of Leḥi was decided by the assassination of the Swedish UN emissary, Count Folke *Bernadotte, by its men.

1948–1963

As the termination of the British Mandate drew near in the spring of 1948, Ben-Gurion decided, despite the doubts of many of his colleagues and pressure from the American government to the contrary, to declare the establishment of the Jewish State. This he did in the Proclamation of the State of Israel on May 14, 1948. He became prime minister and minister of defense in the Provisional Government, and after the elections to the Constituent Assembly on January 25, 1949, continued to serve in these posts as the head of a coalition government. By 1963, when he resigned for good, Ben-Gurion had headed eight coalition governments, frequently using the tool of resignation from the premiership in order to get his way vis-à-vis his unruly coalition partners. In December 1949 Ben-Gurion declared Jerusalem the capital of Israel, even though there were few states that were willing to recognize it as such. As minister of defense, Ben-Gurion devoted most of his efforts to strengthening Israel militarily while introducing civilian control over it. In the international arena he struggled to win international support for Israel's right to security. In his domestic policy he insisted on *mamlakhti'ut* – a statist as opposed to a partisan approach.

In 1951 he traveled to the United States, where he launched the first *Israel Bond Drive. He used his full weight to get the emotionally loaded *Restitution Agreements with the Federal Republic of Germany approved, and this primarily because of Israel's grave foreign reserves situation.

Ben-Gurion was instrumental in making the in-gathering of the exiles a supreme principle in the ideology of the state; introducing a free, unified national education system; using the army as a means of integration and social consolidation; and making the advancement of science and research a central factor in the development of the state and its people.

In December 1953 Ben-Gurion announced his resignation from the premiership and retirement from active politics, citing his need for a rest after 18 years at the helm as his main reason for doing so. As part of his advocacy for the settlement of the Negev, he joined Kibbutz *Sedeh Boker. During his period in retirement Moshe Sharett was chosen by Mapai as prime minister, even though Ben-Gurion preferred Levi *Eshkol.

In February 1955, following the collapse of an Israeli intelligence network in Egypt, in what came to be known as the "*esek bish*" or "mishap," and the resignation of Defense Minister Pinḥas *Lavon, Ben-Gurion returned to active politics, at first as minister of defense under Sharett. In this period Israel's international position deteriorated as a result of the Bandung Conference of Nonaligned States of April 1955, which refused to accept Israel into its ranks, and the Czechoslovak-Egyptian arms deal concluded with the blessing of the Soviet Union in September 1955. Terrorist activities from across Israel's borders increased, and Ben-Gurion decided on a policy of military reprisals across the armistice lines. Following the elections to the Third Knesset in November 1955, Ben-Gurion once again assumed the twofold position of prime minister and minister of defense. He now concentrated on the development of close relations with France, which due to its own struggle in Algeria, viewed Egyptian President Gamal Abdul *Nasser as a bitter enemy. These ties became even closer when Nasser nationalized the Suez Canal in July 1956. In October 1956 Ben-Gurion went to France for a secret meeting with representatives of the French and British governments. At this meeting an agreement was reached on concerted military action against Egypt. On October 29, 1956, the Israeli Army moved into the Sinai Peninsula (see *Sinai Campaign), while Britain and France closed in on the Suez Canal. However, under international pressure Britain and France were forced to give up their effort to reverse Nasser's actions, and Israel was compelled to agree to the withdrawal of its forces from the Sinai Peninsula and the Gaza Strip. This withdrawal was completed in March 1957, and relative quiet was attained after UN forces were stationed in the Gaza Strip and the sea route to Eilat through the Straits of Tiran was reopened to Israeli shipping. Following the Sinai Campaign, and the election of Charles de Gaulle as president of France, Israel's relations with France remained cordial. However, Ben-Gurion increased Israel's efforts to diversify its sources of arms to include West Germany and the United States.

During the election campaign for the Fourth Knesset at the end of 1959, Ben-Gurion raised the issue of electoral reform. He advocated a system of personal elections in constituencies, which he believed would cure Israel's political ills by reducing the number of parliamentary groups in the Knesset. His opponents argued that Ben-Gurion's intention was to "gerrymander" the constituencies in such a way that Mapai would win an absolute majority of Knesset seats. The elections, however, produced no significant change in the composition of the Knesset, and Ben-Gurion did not have the power to change the electoral system.

In the years 1960–62 Ben-Gurion traveled a great deal, visiting the United States, where he met with President John *Kennedy, Western Europe, where he met with German Chancellor Konrad *Adenauer and French President Charles de Gaulle, and Burma. Towards the elections to the Fifth Knesset, what now came to be known as the Lavon Affair, concerning responsibility for the bungled intelligence operation in Egypt back in 1954, reemerged, not least of all because Ben-Gurion wanted the truth to be uncovered as to who had given the order for the operation. Ben-Gurion believed that Pinḥas Lavon, now secretary-general of the Histadrut, was responsible. Ben-Gurion's obsession with this affair was severely criticized by his opponents both within Mapai and outside of it. However, a commission of seven ministers, set up to examine the relevant documents acquitted Lavon of responsibility, a verdict that Ben-Gurion refused to accept. He submitted his resignation in January 1961 and, before new elections were held for the Fifth Knesset, demanded that the Mapai Central Council make a choice between himself and Lavon. On February 4 the Central Council decided by 159 votes to 96 to remove Lavon from his office as Histadrut secretary-general. However, this was a Pyrrhic victory for Ben-Gurion, whose position in the party was greatly undermined. In the elections Mapai was greatly weakened and Ben-Gurion experienced much difficulty forming a new coalition. He would not let the crisis over the Lavon Affair subside, and in June 1963 once again resigned from the premiership – this time for good.

Ben-Gurion in Opposition

Eshkol became prime minister upon Ben-Gurions' recommendation and Ben-Gurion once again retired to Sedeh Boker and devoted himself to writing. But soon he was back, once again advocating a reform of the electoral system, and expressing his opposition to the establishment of the Alignment between Mapai and Aḥdut ha-Avodah. However, the Lavon Affair was still under his skin. In the autumn of 1964 he submitted a dossier of documents that he had prepared to Minister of Justice Dov *Joseph and to the attorney general and demanded that a judicial inquiry be opened on the issue. At a meeting of the Mapai Central Committee party conference in January 1965, a majority voted against Ben-Gurion's demands. Though it was only a minority that supported Ben-Gurion, Eshkol decided to put an end to the matter and resigned from the premiership, with the demand that the government be allowed to decide on the matter without party interference. He then formed a new government, with the same makeup as the outgoing one. Ben-Gurion's response was to leave Mapai with a group of his followers, who included Moshe *Dayan, Shimon *Peres, and Yosef *Almogi, and set up a new parliamentary group called *Rafi (Reshimat Po'alei Yisrael), which ran in the 1965 Knesset and Histadrut elections. While Rafi gained 10 seats in the Sixth Knesset, and Ben-Gurion was to remain a member of the Knesset until May 1970, to all intents and purposes he had lost his political clout and influence. Rafi rejoined Eshkol's government on the eve of the *Six-Day War, with Dayan assuming the Defense portfolio, and shortly after the war joined with Mapai and Aḥdut ha-Avodah to form the *Israel Labor Party, a move to which Ben-Gurion objected, leaving him as a single Member of Knesset when the other nine members of Rafi joined the new parliamentary group. In the elections to the Seventh Knesset Ben Gurion ran at the head of a new party – the State List – which received four seats. Half a year after the elections, at the age of 84, he resigned from the Knesset and returned to Sedeh Boker, where he once again dedicated himself to writing and studying, and occasionally expressing his views on the political situation, generally advocating an Israeli withdrawal from the territories occupied during the Six-Day War. Though in his last years Ben-Gurion cut a solitary figure, he continued to be admired as the most influential Zionist and Israeli leader in the modern age, an individual who had made some of the most fateful decisions in the history of the Jewish nation in its early years, more or less on his own. Though he had little formal education, he was a learned man, and throughout his life he never ceased to study the Bible, Greek philosophy, Buddhism, the philosophy of Baruch *Spinoza, and many other subjects. Though he was frequently accused of having resorted to undemocratic methods to get his way, he had a deep belief in democracy, and his well-known statement in the early years of the State that the communists and the Ḥerut movement could not be members of his government stemmed from his belief that neither was truly democratic. To the end of his life he believed that all Jews should immigrate to Israel, and expressed contempt for those who considered themselves Zionists but remained in the Diaspora. After his death Beersheba University, Lydda International Airport, the government compound in Jerusalem, and many other Israeli institutions and locations were named after him.

BEN-GURION'S WORKS. *Rebirth and Destiny of Israel* (1952); *Israel: Years of Challenge* (1963); (ed.), *The Jews in Their Land* (1966); *Anaḥnu u-Shekheneinu* (1931); *Mi-Ma'amad le-Am* (1933); *Ba-Ma'arakhah*, 5 vols. (1947–49); *Be-Hillaḥem Yisrael* (1950); *Ḥazon va-Derekh*, 5 vols. (1951–57); *Ẓava u-Vittaḥon* (1955); *Ma'arekhet Sinai* (1959); *Pegishot im Manhigim Arviyyim* (1967); *Mikhtavim el Paula ve-el ha-Yeladim* (1968; *Letters to Paula*, 1971); *Medinat Yisrael ha-Meḥuddeshet* (1969; *Israel: A Personal History* 1971); *Negotiations with Nasser* (1970); *Memoirs* (1970); *My Talks with Arab Leaders* (1972); *Ben-Gurion Looks at the Bible* (1972); *Iggerot David Ben-Gurion* (1972); *David Ben-Gurion – Rosh ha-Memshalah ha-Rishon: Mivkhar Te'udot 1947–1963* (David Ben-Gurion – The First Prime Minister: A Selection of Documents 1947–1963) (1996).

BIBLIOGRAPHY: S. Lachower, *Kitvei David Ben-Gurion* (a bibliography, 1960); R. St.-John, *Ben-Gurion* (Eng., 1959); B. Litvinoff, *Ben-Gurion of Israel* (1954); M. Edelman, *Ben-Gurion, A Political Biography* (1964); M. Pearlman, *Ben-Gurion Looks Back* (1965); O. Zmora, *Days of David Ben-Gurion* (1967); M. Bar-Zohar, *The Armed Prophet: A Biography of Ben-Gurion* (1967); J.Comay, *Ben-Gurion and the Birth of Israel* (1967). **ADD. BIBLIOGRAPHY:** R. St.-John, *Ben-Gurion: A Biography* (1971); S. Peres, *With Strength and with Spirit* (1974); M. Bar-Zohar, *Ben-Gurion: A Biography* (1978); D. Kurzman, *Ben-Gurion: Prophet of Fire* (1983); S. Teveth, *Ben-Gurion and the Palestinian Arabs: From Peace to War* (1985); Y. Navon, *David Ben-Gurion, Builder and Warrior* (1986); S. Teveth, *Ben-Gurion: The Burning Ground* (1987); R.W. Zweig (ed.), *David Ben-Gurion: Politics and Leadership in Israel* (1991); S. Teveth, *Ben-Gurion and the Holocaust* (1996); idem, *Ben-Gurion's Spy: The Story of the Political Scandal That Shaped Modern Israel* (1996); J. Heller, *The Birth of Israel 1945–1949: Ben-Gurion and His Critics* (2000); G. Goldberg, *Ben-Gurion Against the Knesset* (2003).

[Yehuda Slutsky / Susan Hattis Rolef (2nd ed.)]

BEN-GURION UNIVERSITY OF THE NEGEV, Israeli university with campuses in Beersheba and Sede Boqer. Established in 1969 as the Negev University, it became Ben-Gurion University (BGU) after the death of David Ben-Gurion. The university is Israel's youngest and smallest university, but it has become a major center of education and research. Ben-Gurion University, headed by Avishai *Braverman as president, is known for its rapid growth. More than 10,000 students enrolled for the 1995/6 academic year in its four faculties, and by 2003 it already had 16,000 students.

Ben-Gurion University is intimately involved in the development of Israel's southern arid region, the Negev, which comprises nearly 60% of the country, but contains only 10% of its population. It plays a central role in the educational, social, and industrial developments of the region. The university promotes academic research with commercial applications as the key to economic development in the Negev. Through its pioneering research in arid zone communities, BGU has established a basis for cooperation with countries sharing a similar climate, particularly in the Middle East.

Approximately 50% of the students originate from the Negev, 40% from the center of the country, and 10% from the north. New immigrant students are absorbed in all BGU departments.

The university has four faculties:

(1) The Faculty of Health Sciences, founded in 1974, is located on the campus of the Soroka Medical Center, in close proximity to the university. Its establishment brought about major changes in health care in the Negev while developing an innovative medical education program. From the first year, students integrate academic theory with clinical care. The orientation of the school is strongly focused on community medicine. The faculty and students work in Beersheba at the Soroka Medical Center and travel to development towns, kibbutzim, and Bedouin encampments.

There are three Divisions: Health in the Community; the Division of Basic Medical Sciences, and the Division of Clinical Medicine. The faculty offers graduate degrees in Medical Science. The Recanati School of Nursing and Physiotherapy is also part of the faculty.

(2) The Faculty of Engineering Sciences comprises six departments: Nuclear Engineering, Materials Engineering, Chemical Engineering, Mechanical Engineering, Electrical and Computer Engineering, and Industrial Engineering and Management and the Program for Biotechnology.

(3) The Faculty of Natural Sciences consists of five departments: Mathematics and Computer Sciences, Physics, Chemistry, Life Sciences, and Geology and Mineralogy. Its scientists pursue both basic and applied research projects, many of which have served to advance the growth of science-based industry and the agricultural development of the Negev.

(4) The Faculty of Humanities and Social Sciences has eleven departments: Behavioral Sciences; Bible and Ancient Near Eastern Studies; Economics; Education; Geography and Environmental Development; Hebrew Language; Hebrew Literature; Foreign Literature and Linguistics; History; Philosophy; and Social Work. The unit for teaching English as a Foreign Language is also part of the faculty. The Department of Behavioral Sciences integrates psychology, sociology, and anthropology. The Hebrew Literature Department has the only Master's Program in Creative Writing in the country, and in the Department of Social Work all third-year stu-

dents are required to develop active projects within the Negev community.

The Overseas Student Program is given in English for either one semester or a full academic year. The curriculum focuses on Human Resettlement (Russians, Ethiopians, and Bedouin), Desert Studies and Archeology, and Pre-Med. The School for Continuing Education offers a wide variety of courses to the Negev community at large.

Since the beginning of BGU activities, its scientists have engaged in basic and applied research. This covers widely ranging areas as desert research, alternative energy, development of water resources, chemistry, biotechnology, agriculture, and medicine, regional development, social ecology, the David Ben-Gurion era, and medical education.

Originally found in 1957 as the Institute for Arid Zone Research, the Institutes for Applied Research became part of the university in 1973. Comprising the institutes are the Institute for Chemistry and Chemical Technology and the Institute for Agriculture and Applied Biology. The institutes for applied research are geared toward tapping the various natural resources for the region's development. Numerous plant species with industrial and agricultural value have been selected and developed for desert growth. Experiments with underground brackish water irrigation have resulted in new cash crops for Negev settlements. Other projects include research on food technology, desalination, recycling of waste water, the application of waste heat and solar energy for refrigeration and direct-contact cooling, and the synthesis of organic compounds for chemical industries.

The Jacob Blaustein Institute for Desert Research was established in Sede Boqer as a national center for arid zone research. Its goal is to provide the knowledge and skills to transform arid lands of low productivity, human deprivation and famine into areas that are productive and self-sustaining.

Members of the institute's 15 units work together to explore a wide array of problems relating to the settling of the desert. The fields of study touch on man's habitat and social organization, climate and the desert environment, water resources and natural energy sources, such as solar energy, the adaptive mechanisms to climatic extremes of plants and animals, and the development of unique biotechnologies suitable for desert areas.

By government decision, BGU was entrusted with some 750,000 documents associated with the late David Ben Gurion, founding father and first prime minister of Israel. These papers form the Ben-Gurion Archives and serve the Ben-Gurion Research Center. They reflect the ideology, political activities, and spiritual testament of Ben-Gurion – the man, the Zionist, and the statesman – and constitute an invaluable record of the creation of the State of Israel. At the Ben-Gurion Research Center scholars study the Ben-Gurion era, Zionism, the history of Israel, and related subjects. The center publishes and disseminates relevant studies and, in conjunction with the Faculty of Humanities and Social Sciences, provides academic courses and educational programs.

BGU sponsors a host of innovative programs as part of its outreach service to the community. All students who receive financial aid from BGU commit themselves to participating in one of the university's wide range of social action programs, which include the Open Apartments Project, in which the students live in underprivileged neighborhoods and serve as part-time community workers; the "Kidma" (Progress) Program, which promotes the advancement of new immigrants from Ethiopia; a special program of Assistance for the Elderly; and the Matriculation Examination Program for the Bedouin Sector.

WEBSITE: www.bgu.ac.il.

[Linda Livna]

BEN-HADAD (Heb. בֶּן הֲדַד; "Son of [the god] Hadad"), the name of two, or perhaps three, kings of *Aram-Damascus (see *Damascus), as Hebraized in the Bible. In Aramaic inscriptions the name appears as *Brhdd* (ברהדד), with the native Aramaic word for "son," *br* (then pronounced *bir*, later *bar*), instead of the Hebrew *ben*.

BEN-HADAD I. Ben-Hadad I lived in the early ninth century B.C.E. He was the son of Tabrimmon and grandson of Hezion (I Kings 15:18), and contemporary with King *Asa of Judah and King *Baasha of Israel. Like his father (cf. I Kings 15:19; II Chron. 16:3), he was bound by alliances to the kings of both Israel and Judah. However, when war broke out between Baasha and Asa, the latter won Ben-Hadad to his cause by sending him treasures from the Temple and the royal palace. Ben-Hadad invaded the kingdom of Israel, conquering *Ijon, *Dan, *Abel-Beth-Maacah, the region of Chinneroth, and all the land of Naphtali (I Kings 15:20). (The Ben-Hadad who set up the votive stele, found in the vicinity of Aleppo, which was dedicated to the Tyrian god Melqart (COS II, 152–53) is probably not identical with Ben-Hadad I the son of Tabrimmon. This other Ben-Hadad seems to have ruled another Aramean kingdom, perhaps Arpad.)

BEN-HADAD II. Scholars (see bibliography in Pitard, ABD I, 665) have debated the identity of the Ben-Hadad referred to in I Kings 20–22 through II Kings 8. In I Kings 20 and 22, chapters which raise numerous critical probems, the royal protagonists in the battles between Aram-Damascus and Israel are *Ahab and Ben-Hadad. Chapters 5–8 of II Kings deal with relations between Ben-Hadad and Ahab's sons, Ahaziah and Joram. W. Albright identified the Aramean king as Ben-Hadad the son of Tabrimmon (= Ben-Hadad I) and assigned him a reign of 40 years. Others viewed the Aramean king of these chapters as a successor of Ben-Hadad son of Tab-rimmon, to be designated Ben-Hadad II. That designation would make Hazael's son and successor (see below) Ben-Hadad III. However we designate him, this Ben-Hadad is described as a dominant ruler who could muster 32 vassals against Israel (I Kings 20:1). On three occasions he waged war against Ahab, succeeding in the first conflict in besieging Samaria (20:2ff.). Ahab resolved to resist when the demands of Ben-Hadad became excessively harsh, and managed to defeat him. Later

Ben-Hadad again opened hostilities against Ahab, but was defeated a second time at *Aphek and taken prisoner (I Kings 20:26ff.). By the terms of the friendly alliance that he subsequently concluded with Israel, Ben-Hadad undertook to return the Israelite towns under his dominion and to put bazaars in Damascus at the disposal of the merchants of Israel. After three years of peace, Ahab, with the assistance of *Jehoshaphat, the king of Judah, embarked on a new war against Aram in Ramoth-Gilead, during which he met his death (I Kings 22, where the king of Aram is referred to only by his title). It seems that between the second and the last war against Ahab, Ben-Hadad (who is referred to in Assyrian inscriptions as Adad-Idri, i.e., Hadadezer, perhaps his personal name as distinct from his throne name; but cf. Pitard in Bibliography) led an alliance consisting of the kings of Syria, Phoenicia, and Palestine (including Ahab) in a war against Shalmaneser III, king of Assyria, near *Qarqar in 853 B.C.E. After the war of Qarqar the coalition split up and the last war with Israel took place. Afterward Ben-Hadad resumed the leadership in an alliance against Assyria and thus succeeded in temporarily removing the Assyrian threat (848, 845 B.C.E.). Shortly after *Jehu's accession to the throne of Israel, Ben-Hadad was assassinated on his sickbed by Hazael (II Kings 8:15), who seized the throne of Aram (II Kings 8:7–15; cf. I Kings 19:15). The biblical depiction of Hazael as a usurper appears to be reflected in an Assyrian inscription of Shalmaneser III (858–24 B.C.E.) that describes him as "son of a nobody." (See Cogan and Tadmor in Bibliography.)

BEN-HADAD III. Ben-Hadad III, son of Hazael, was the contemporary of *Jehoahaz and *Joash, kings of Israel (814–800 and 800–784 B.C.E.). During the early years of his reign the greater part of the kingdom of Israel was occupied by Aram. It is also possible that Ben-Hadad added to the conquests of his father because he headed an alliance of north Syrian and neo-Hittite kingdoms (e.g., *Que, *Sam'al) that attacked Zakkur, king of Hamath and Luath, and besieged Hadrach, though without success (COS II, 155). In 806–805, Adad-Nirari III, king of Assyria (810–782), renewed the war against Aram, besieged Damascus in 802, and imposed a heavy tribute on Ben-Hadad (whom the Assyrian inscriptions refer to by the Aramean title of *Mari*, "Lord"). It was this setback of Aram that enabled Israel to throw off the Aramean yoke. In the reign of this Ben-Hadad, Damascus lost its dominant position in Syria, and for a generation after, the kings of Israel and Judah were the predominant force there.

[Isaiah Gafni]

H. Winckler and E. Meyer (followed in the 1940s by W.F. Albright) believe that there were only two kings of Aram by the name of Ben-Hadad, the Aramean contemporary of Baasha being identical with that of Ahab.

Moreover, while the chronology of the books of Kings has been followed above, H.L. Ginsberg has suggested that, though there are bound to be differences as to just what adjustments need to be made, the distribution of the incidents during the Aramean wars among the various kings of Israel cannot be correct in all respects. If the Aramean incident of I Kings 20 took place under the dynasty of Jehu, the above Ben-Hadad II is identical not with the above Ben-Hadad I but with the above Ben-Hadad III, and Ahab's Aramean ally had only the one name Adad-Idri / Hadadezer, for there is no difficulty in assuming that this legend in II Kings 8:15 is in error regarding the name of Hazael's predecessor. Also, the elaborate story in I Kings 20:1–35 about the anonymous king of Israel who dies in his chariot of an arrow wound sustained in a battle with the Arameans, in which he was assisted by King Jehoshaphat of Judah, at Ramoth-Gilead, bears a strong resemblance to the palpably historical account in II Kings 8:25–9:24. This tells of how King Jehoram of Israel, while recuperating (at Jezreel) from wounds sustained in a battle with the Arameans, in which he was assisted by King Ahaziah of Judah, at Ramoth-Gilead, is shot dead in his chariot with an arrow from the bow of Jehu, who follows him (to Jezreel) from the camp at Ramoth-Gilead. Thus one wonders if the suspicion that the former is a legendary parallel to the latter and has nothing to do with Ahab has not been voiced before. (The incident in the former, with the various prophets, probably contains a core of history, but also pertains to Jehoram and Ahaziah, not to "Ahab" and Jehoshaphat.)

See also *Ahab, *Jehoahaz, *Joash, *Jehoram, and *Jehu, and the bibliography below under Jepsen.

[Harold Louis Ginsberg]

BIBLIOGRAPHY: Bright, Hist, 215, 221, 223–4, 228, 235, 237; A. Dupont-Sommer, *Les araméens* (1949); E. Kraeling, *Aram and Israel* (1918); M.F. Unger, *Israel and the Arameans of Damascus* (1957); A. Jepsen, in: AFO, 14 (1941–4), 153–72; W.F. Albright, in: BASOR, 87 (1942), 23–40; 90 (1943), 32; 100 (1945), 10–22. **ADD. BIBLIOGRAPHY:** W. Pitard, ABD I, 663–65; M. Cogan and H. Tadmor, II *Kings* (1988), 92; M. Cogan, I *Kings* (AB; 2000) 471–74.

BEN-HAIM (Frankenburger), PAUL (1897–1984), Israeli composer, one of the leading founders of Israeli art music. Ben-Haim was born in Munich. His father, Heinrich, was a respected professor of law. In 1920 Ben-Haim graduated from the Munich Academy of Music as conductor, composer, and pianist, and then was assistant to Bruno *Walter at the Munich Opera. In 1924 he became Kapellmeister of the Augsburg Opera. While in Germany he composed about 80 lieder as well as chamber and orchestral works (e.g., *Concerto Grosso*, 1931) which were very well received. In 1929 he met the Jewish composer Heinrich Schalit (1886–1976), who encouraged him to write a series of Jewish-oriented choral works to biblical verses. In October 1933 he settled in Tel Aviv and changed his name to Ben-Haim. He dedicated himself to composition and to teaching at the Jerusalem Academy of Music and at the Music Teachers Training College in Tel Aviv. Some of Israel's best composers were his private composition students. As a highly prolific and inspired composer, Ben-Haim found the way to retain his cherished European heritage, with his admiration for J.S. Bach (as in his *Metamorphosis on a Bach*

Chorale) and special liking for Debussy and Ravel (*Sonatina*) and with his commitment to the ideology of the vision of the East (his striking *Sonata à tré* for mandolin, guitar, and harpsichord). From 1939 until 1955 he collaborated with the unique Yemenite singer Bracha *Zephira as pianist and arranger of 35 of her traditional songs, most of which he quoted in his chamber and orchestral works. His music was well received and frequently performed worldwide by great conductors and soloists, among them Leonard *Bernstein, Yehudi *Menuhin, Jascha *Heifetz, and Menahem *Pressler. Ben-Haim's orchestral works include two symphonies (1940 and 1945); concertos for piano (1949), violin (1960), and cello (1962); the symphonic movements *Sweet Psalmist of Israel* (1953), which were awarded the Israel Prize in 1957; *Liturgical Cantata* (1950); the cantatas *Vision of a Prophet* (1959), *Three Psalms* (1952), and *Kabbalat Shabbat* (1967). Ben-Haim founded the genre of the Hebrew Lieder to poems by prominent poets such as *Bialik, Sh. *Shalom, Lea *Goldberg, and *Raḥel. He composed a *String Quartet*, a *Clarinet Quintet*, a *Piano Trio (Variations on a Hebrew Tune)*, a *Piano Sonata* (1953) and several suites for piano, and a *Solo Violin Sonata*.

ADD. BIBLIOGRAPHY: Grove online; MGG²; P. Gradenwitz, *The Music of Israel* (1996), 351–57; J. Hirshberg, *Paul Ben-Haim, His Life and Works* (1990).

[Peter Emanuel Gradenwitz / Jehoash Hirshberg (2nd ed.)]

BEN-HAIM, YIGAL (1935–), *ḥazzan*. Born in Jerusalem, Ben-Haim was the 11th generation in a family of cantors originally from Bukhara. His early cantorial education was from his father. As a child he sang in the Jerusalem Taḥkemoni school under the direction of Cantor Mendel Tirnover and Ẓvi *Talmon. He sang in the Mizmor Shir choir established by Kol Yisrael. When 18 he debuted as the cantor of the Baba Tamma Synagogue in the Jerusalem Bukharan neighborhood. He studied cantorial theory and *maqamat*. He led services and appeared in concerts in Israel, the United States, South America, Europe, and the Far East. Ben-Haim sings on cassettes presenting selections from the prayers as rendered by the Oriental Jewish communities. He was an instructor of Sephardi cantorial skills in the Jerusalem Renanot cantorial school and Bat Yam school, thus continuing his longstanding activity of shaping cantors. In a CD called *Avot u-Banim* issued recently he and family members perform cantorial pieces

[Akiva Zimmerman]

BEN HA-MELEKH VE-HA-NAZIR (Heb. בֶּן הַמֶּלֶךְ וְהַנָּזִיר "The Prince and the Hermit"), Hebrew version by Abraham b. Samuel ha-Levi *Ibn Ḥasdai of an original Hindu tale about a prince who eventually became an ascetic. Balauhar and Budasaph, the names of the heroes of the tale in the old Pahlavi version, became Barlaam and Joasaph in the Greek version and Barlaam and Josaphat in the oldest Latin version (1048) and in later European translations. The Hebrew work is based on an Arabic version, but whether it is a translation or an adaptation cannot be determined until the Arabic text is established. *Ben ha-Melekh ve-ha-Nazir* is the account of a prince, Joasaph, sent by his father to a luxurious palace on an island in an effort to avert the fulfillment of a prophecy that he would become a Christian monk. When the prince discovers the reason for his confinement, he implores his father to allow him to return to the mainland. The king yields, and the son soon becomes aware of evil in the world, with consequent unrest in his heart. A monk, Barlaam, who comes disguised as a merchant (monks being prohibited in the land) gains access to the prince and gradually teaches him to realize the vanity of this world and the advantages of the ascetic life. Unlike the Greek and the Arabic tales, the Hebrew does not reintroduce the father, nor does it relate his efforts to undo the effects of the monk's instruction. Instead, it continues the discussion on philosophic and theological questions until the monk is obliged to leave and the prince feels bereft and lonely. The course of transmission of the original tale until it evolved into a world classic is complicated, with many problems still unresolved. In the European texts, the prince adopts the Christian faith of his preceptor. The Hindu original is obviously modeled after the life of Buddha. The Hebrew version is attractively written, and the prose narrative is interspersed with versified aphorisms. There is a Catalan translation by T. Calders (1987).

BIBLIOGRAPHY: H. Peri (Pflaum), *Der Religionsdisput der Barlaam-Legende* (1959); Abraham b. Ḥasdai, *Ben-ha-Melekh ve-ha-Nazir*, ed. by A.M. Habermann (1951); F. Liebrecht, *Zur Volkskunde* (1879), 441–60; Steinschneider, Uebersetzungen, 863–7; E.A.W. Budge, *Barlaam and Jewâsaf* (1923); D.M. Lang, *The Wisdom of Balahvar* (1957); J. Jacobs, *Barlaam and Josaphat* (1896). **ADD. BIBLIOGRAPHY:** T. Calders, *El Príncep i el monjo d'Abraham ben Semuel ha-Levi ibn Hasday* (1987).

BEN ḤAYYIM (Goldmann), ZE'EV (1907–), Hebrew scholar and linguist. Born in Mościska, Galicia, he emigrated to Palestine in 1931 and in 1934 became secretary of the Va'ad ha-Lashon. In 1948 he was appointed lecturer (1955, professor) of Hebrew language at the Hebrew University and in 1961 was elected vice president of the *Academy of the Hebrew Language in Jerusalem and in December 1973 was appointed its president, succeeding the late Prof. Naphtali *Tur-Sinai.

Ben Ḥayyim specialized in the Samaritan Hebrew dialect, literature, etc., on which he published *Ivrit ve-Aramit Nusaḥ Shomeron* ("The Literary and Oral Tradition of Hebrew and Aramaic among the Samaritans," 5 vols., 1957–77; volume 5 was translated and slightly updated as *A Grammar of Samaritan Hebrew*, 2000) and *Tevat Marka – Asuppat Midrashim Shomroniyyim*, 1988. In these books, he discusses the evolution and historical development of the Samaritan languages (Hebrew and Aramaic), starting from their earliest literary sources through the linguistic tradition preserved in the modern idioms. They contributed not only to the recognition of these particular dialects, but also to the clarification of important aspects of the history of the Hebrew and Aramaic languages and their development.

In his pamphlet *Lashon Attikah bi-Meẓi'ut Ḥadasha* ("Ancient Language in a New Reality," 1953) he deals with problems of the growth and development of modern Hebrew as the living language in the State of Israel. This article was republished along with most of his articles on modern Hebrew during the long period of his activity at the Academy in *Be-Milhamtah shel Lashon*, 1992. He was the editor of the historical dictionary of the Hebrew language – one of the major projects of the Academy. He also edited Hebrew dictionaries containing modern Hebrew terms in the fields of mathematics, anatomy, technology, etc., and contributed articles to leading linguistic journals on problems of Hebrew grammar and on the systems of Hebrew grammarians. Ben Ḥayyim was the *Encyclopaedia Judaica*'s divisional editor for Hebrew and Semitic languages. He received the Israel Prize in 1964. A full list of Ben Ḥayyim's works and scientific publications appeared in *Leshonenu* (vol. 32, Tishri–Tevet 1967/68), the publication of the Academy, edited by Ben Ḥayyim from 1955 to 1965; updated in *Leshonenu* 65 (2003), 201–26 with an assessment of his scientific achievements, ibid., p. 227–38.

BEN HE HE (c. first century), *tanna*. In *Avot* (5, end) appears a maxim in the name of Ben He He: "According to the labor is the reward." The same maxim is quoted as a popular saying in the name of Hillel the Elder (ARN[1] 12:28; ARN[2] 27:28), while a similar version occurs in Samaritan literature (see S. Liberman, *Greek in Jewish Palestine* (1942), 160, p. 113). The Talmud (Ḥag. 9b), implying that he may have been a pupil of Hillel, contains questions addressed to Hillel by Bar He He (see *Seder ha-Dorot*, s.v. *Ben Bag Bag*; cf., however, Liberman, loc. cit.). His name is said to have originated from his having been "a proselyte, i.e., the son [*ben*] of Abraham and Sarah, to each of whose names the letter ה [*he*] was added" (cf. Gen. 17:5, 15; Tos. to Hag. 9b; *Maḥzor Vitry*, ed. Hurwitz (1923), 563–4). Bacher (Tann, 1 (1903[2]), 8–9) suggests that he was converted under the influence of Hillel. He is also identified with *Ben Bag Bag (Tos. and *Maḥzor Vitry*, loc. cit.),

BIBLIOGRAPHY: Hyman, Toledot, 285.

[Zvi Kaplan]

BEN-HORIN (Zelig Bidner), ELIAHU (1902–1966), Zionist activist, journalist and writer. Ben-Horin was born in Balta, Ukraine and studied at the University of Odessa where he was chairman of the Zionist Students' Union. He was active in Zionist and self-defense clandestine organizations during the early years of the Soviet regime. Immigrating to Palestine in 1921, he joined the Histadrut and was among the founders of the collective settlement Ha-Sharon (later to become Kibbutz Yifat). He broke away from the Labor movement in 1928 to join the *Revisionist party and served on the editorial boards of the Revisionist press (*Do'ar ha-Yom* and *Yarden*). In 1931 he left the Haganah, and joined the *Irgun Ẓeva'i Le'ummi (IZL), in which he served as *Jabotinsky's personal representative on its Supervisory Board. He participated in collecting funds and in the purchase of arms for the organization. He was a Revisionist delegate to the 17th Zionist Congress (1931), and when the New Zionist Organization (NZO) was founded in 1935, he was elected to its presidency. During 1944–50 he cooperated with ex-President Herbert Hoover in formulating the "Hoover Plan" for settling Palestinian Arabs in Iraq. He also served as advisor on Middle Eastern affairs to the American Zionist Emergency Council. His works include *The Red Army* (1942) and The *Middle East: Crossroads of History* (1943).

BIBLIOGRAPHY: *Tidhar*, 10 (1959), 3470–71; Dinur, Haganah, 2, index.

[Joseph Nedava]

BEN-HORIN, MEIR (1918–1988), U.S. Jewish educator. Born in Koenigsberg, East Prussia, Ben-Horin was assistant professor of education at the Boston Hebrew Teachers College from 1951 to 1957. From 1957, he headed the department of education of Dropsie College (now *Dropsie University) in Philadelphia, with the rank of professor from 1962. Ben-Horin wrote *Max Nordau: Philosopher of Human Solidarity* (1956) and *Common Faith – Uncommon People* (1970). Together with Judah *Pilch he coedited *Judaism and the Jewish School* (1966). In applying to Jewish education the Reconstructionist view of Judaism as a religious civilization, Ben-Horin follows the educational and philosophical thinking of Dewey, M.M. Kaplan, and Theodore Brameld.

[Leon H. Spotts]

BENICHOU, PAUL (1908–2001), French literary critic and historian of literature. Born in Tlemcen to a Jewish Algerian family, Benichou, was soon recognized as a brilliant student and sent to study in Oran and then Paris' prestigious Lycée Louis-le-Grand high school. While teaching literature in Paris, he began the research and the writing on his first major essay on French classicism, *Morales du Grand Siècle*, but was barred from teaching in 1940 as a result of the antisemitic legislation of the Vichy regime, which stripped him, as an Algerian Jew, of French citizenship and forced him to flee to Argentina, where he pursued his teaching career. *Morales du Grand Siècle* was eventually published by Gallimard in 1948 and Benichou came back to France in 1949. During his Argentinean years, Benichou, unable to access French archives, began a critical study of the romancero, whose brilliant originality was highly praised, and became acquainted with writer Jorge Luis Borges, whom he would later translate into French. In five independent but interrelated essays tracing back the origins of French romanticism (*Le Sacre de l'écrivain*, 1973; *Le Temps des prophètes*, 1977; *Les Mages romantiques*, 1988; *L'École du désenchantement*, 1992; *Selon Mallarmé*, 1995), Benichou tried to account for the pessimism of most major 19th century French writers, as opposed to the general euphoria of the time. This series of essays, which Benichou began to publish only at the age of 65, renewed the vision of French romanticism and its link to classicism, and taken together they provide a panorama of French literature from 1750 to 1900, as well as a milestone in the general theory of literature. Benichou characteristically linked literary theory to the history of ideas, thus providing insights on the relation of the writer to contemporary society whose far-reaching implications earned him recognition as one of the major scholars of the 20th century.

[Dror Franck Sullaper (2nd ed.)]

BENIDER, Moroccan family. ABRAHAM BENIDER (first half of 18th century), a native of Tetuan, later a resident of Gibraltar and Tangiers, was chandler to the British fleet and official interpreter. His son JACOB, born in Gibraltar, served as interpreter in the British consulates in Tetuan, Tangiers, Salé, Mogador, Safi, and Agadir. In 1768 he was vice consul in Salé. In 1772 the sultan of Morocco sent him as his ambassador to London on a special mission. However, Benider was not successful in his mission. Apparently he did not return to Gibraltar or Morocco.

BIBLIOGRAPHY: C. Roth, in: JHSEM, 2 (1935), 84–90; Hirschberg, Afrikah, 2 (1965), 285, 288–91; idem, in: *Essays... I. Brodie*, 2 (1967), 165–81.

[David Corcos]

BENIOFF, HUGO (1899–1968), U.S. seismologist. Born in Los Angeles, Benioff was assistant at the Mount Wilson observatory from 1917 to 1924. In 1923–24, he carried out seismological research at the Carnegie Institute in Washington. He then joined the staff of the California Institute of Technology in the seismological research department, where he was professor from 1950. He designed instruments for measuring movements of the earth's crust on land and in the sea. Benioff applied his knowledge as consultant to building firms to help plan against earthquake destruction and to the U.S. Navy submarine section. He was adviser to the geophysical department of the U.S. Air Force.

BENISCH, ABRAHAM (1814–1878), author, scholar, and precursor of Zionism. Benisch was born in Drossau, Bohemia. As a student of medicine at the University of Prague he joined Moritz *Steinschneider, who founded a student organization for the purpose of "reestablishing Jewish independence in Ereẓ Israel." Continuing his studies in Vienna in 1838, Benisch, and Albert Loewy, established a secret society, *Die Einheit*, whose purpose was to initiate organized Jewish immigration to Ereẓ Israel. With this aim in mind he talked to Adolphe *Crémieux and, in 1841, proceeded to London with a letter of recommen dation from the House of Rothschild to influential Jewish circles. Receiving no tangible support, Benisch nevertheless continued to promote his views in the periodical *The Voice of Jacob* (1841–48), and in 1853 started the *Hebrew Observer* as a rival to the then 12-year-old *Jewish Chronicle*. In 1854 the paper was merged with the *Jewish Chronicle*, which for the next 13 years, and again from 1875 to 1878, was edited by Benisch, under the title *Jewish Chronicle and Hebrew Observer*. During these years Benisch utilized every opportunity, including the *Damascus Affair and the Crimean War, to raise the question of Jewish revival in Ereẓ Israel. He collaborated with Charles *Netter in founding the *Mikveh Israel agricultural school. He was one of the founders and first directors of the *Anglo-Jewish Association and carried on an unceasing campaign for the rights of the Jews in Russia and the Balkan countries. In his articles before and during the Congress of Berlin (1878), Benisch stressed the importance of Jewish settlement of Ereẓ Israel as integral to the solution of Near Eastern problems. Benisch published a Hebrew commentary on the Book of Ezekiel (1836), and wrote *Two Lectures on the Life and Writings of Maimonides* (1847). He translated the Bible into English (1851), and in the same year also translated into English the *Travels* of *Pethahiah b. Jacob of Regensburg. He wrote a Hebrew grammar and a scripture manual in 1852, entitled *Bikkurei ha-Limmud*, and *An Essay on Bishop Colenso's Criticism of the Pentateuch and Joshua* (1863). A collection of his lectures entitled *Judaism Surveyed* appeared in 1874.

BIBLIOGRAPHY: *Jewish Chronicle: 1841–1941* (1949), ch. 5; S.W. Baron, in: *Jewish Studies in Memory of G.A. Kohut* (1935), 72–85; N.M. Gelber, in: *Prague vi-Yrushalayim* (1954), 42–44; idem, *Shivat Ẓiyyon*, 1 (1950), 106–30. **ADD. BIBLIOGRAPHY:** J.M. Shaftesley, "Dr. Abraham Benisch as Newspaper Editor," in: TJHSE, 21 (1968), 214–21; Katz, England, 356–68; ODNB online.

[Nathan Michael Gelber]

BEN-ISRAEL, RUTH (1931–), Israeli legal scholar. Born in Port Said, Egypt, Ben-Israel received her LL.B. and LL.M., magna cum laude, and a Ph.D. degree from the Hebrew University of Jerusalem. She taught labor law, civil procedure, social security, and occupational equality at Tel Aviv University from 1975 and served as dean of the Law Faculty in 1990–91. Her extensive publications include nine books, one of which is *Israel Labor Law* (Heb., 1989), and many articles. She was a member of many international organizations and edited the *Israel Labor Law Year Book* in 1998–2000. She was awarded the Bar Niv Prize in Labor Law (1988), the Minkoff Prize for Excellence in Law (2000), the Israel Prize in law (2001), and the Israel Bar Association Prize for Women in Law (2001). She served as special legal adviser on labor legislation to the Labor and Welfare Committee of the Knesset (1985–92); public representative on the National Labor Court (1988–2000); special legal adviser to the minister of labor and welfare (1993–95); and chaired numerous public and government committees on women's rights and labor laws.

[Leon Fine (2nd ed.)]

BENJACOB, ISAAC (1801–1863), first modern Hebrew bibliographer. He was born near Vilna and spent most of his life in that city. After publishing original works and republishing several medieval writers, including *Ḥovot ha-Levavot* by *Baḥya ibn Paquda (with a commentary of his own), Benjacob published, with Abraham Dov *Lebensohn (Adam ha-Kohen), a 17-volume edition of the Hebrew Bible (1848–53). It included Rashi's commentary, Mendelssohn's German translation (in Hebrew script), a new commentary by Lebensohn as well as Benjacob's own *Mikra'ei Kodesh*, an abridged version of *Tik-*

kun Soferim ("the scribes' emendations to the biblical text"). This edition helped spread Haskalah among Russian Jewry and was utilized not only for the study of Scriptures, but also for learning German. Benjacob then began his magnum opus of 20 years' duration, *Oẓar ha-Sefarim* (Vilna, 1880; repr. New York, 1965), one of the greatest bibliographic achievements in Hebrew literature. The work lists approximately 8,480 manuscripts and approximately 6,500 books published up to 1863, with a description of their contents. Benjacob also wrote a collection of epigrams, poems, and literary essays, *Mikhtamim ve-Shirim Shonim* (1842). His son JACOB (1858–1926) was a merchant, banker, and Zionist. After first publishing his father's work *Oẓar ha-Sefarim* with the assistance of M. *Steinschneider (1877–80), he began expanding it, using new bibliographical methods but retaining its original chronological limit (1863). His son-in-law Moses *Schorr reported that the new edition contained 60,000 entries and comprised 12 volumes. Both Benjacob and Schorr tried unsuccessfully to have it published. The manuscript was lost during the Holocaust in Poland.

BIBLIOGRAPHY: Benjacob, Oẓar, xxi–xxvii; B. Nathanson, *Sefer ha-Zikhronot* (1876), 112–5; Habermann, in: *Yad la-Kore*, 3 (1952/53), 1–6; Schorr, in: YIVO *Bleter*, 8 (1935), 138–46; idem, in: *Soncino Blaetter* (1927), 38–40; Waxman, Literature, index.

[Benzion Dinur (Dinaburg)]

BENJAMIN (Heb. בִּנְיָמִין), youngest son of *Jacob by *Rachel (Gen. 35:16–18), and the eponym of the tribe of Benjamin. Benjamin was the only one of Jacob's sons to be born in Canaan. Little is told of his life and personality. Our preserved texts attribute no words to him, though he is frequently mentioned in the stories about Jacob, because he was the youngest son and born of the beloved wife Rachel and also because he was, as *Joseph's only full brother, closest to him. Jacob did not send Benjamin to Egypt with the other brothers to procure food during the famine, but when they applied to Joseph for rations he insisted that Benjamin should be sent for. Much against Jacob's will, Benjamin eventually accompanied his brothers to Egypt after Judah had undertaken to be responsible for him. When Benjamin was presented to him, Joseph was so overcome with feeling that he went into a private room and wept there. He invited his brothers to dine and favored Benjamin with extra portions. Joseph, however, put his brothers' integrity to the test and did not make himself known to them. He instructed his steward to conceal a silver goblet in Benjamin's bag and later to overtake the brothers on their journey home and accuse him of stealing it. The brothers interceded for Benjamin, and Judah declared himself ready to sacrifice his liberty in exchange for Benjamin's release to spare their father's grief if he failed to return. Then Joseph finally disclosed his identity to them, and sent an invitation to his father to settle in Goshen with his family (Gen. 42–45).

Rachel had named her son Ben-Oni which could mean either "son of my vigor" or "son of my suffering," though the second meaning better fits the context as her labor was hard

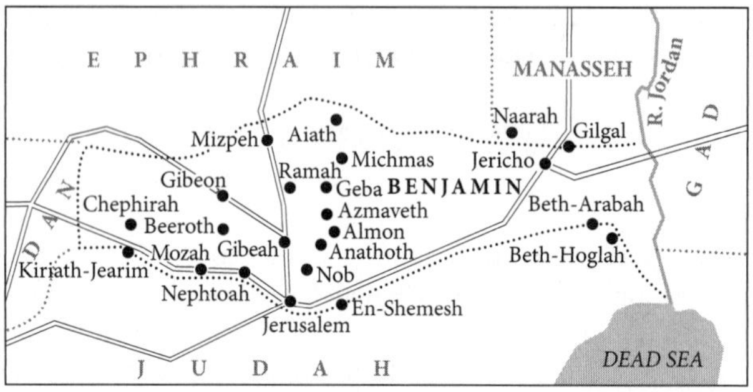

Territory of the tribe of Benjamin.

and she died in childbirth. The father, however, named the baby Benjamin, which literally means "son of the right hand," and can be understood as having an auspicious sense. It could also mean "son of the south" (cf. Ps. 89:13), either because this son was the only one born in the south, that is in Canaan (all his brothers were born in Aram-Naharaim), or because the legacy of Benjamin was south (i.e., to the right) of that of his brother Joseph. A parallel to the name Benjamin used in the sense of "southerners" is to be found in the *Mari documents referring to West Semitic tribes called Dumu. Meš (= *binī*-) *Yamina*, meaning "southerners," literally, "sons of the right," in contrast to another group of tribes called Dumu. Meš (= *binī* -) *Sim'all*, "northerners," literally, sons of the left." There is a linguistic connection between the Hebrew term "Benjamin" and the Bini-Yamina tribes of the Mari documents (18th century B.C.E.) but no apparent historical connection.

The Genealogies

The Bible contains genealogical lists of the tribe of Benjamin which in part do not correspond with one another either in respect of the number of clans or their names (Gen. 46:21; Num. 26:38–41; I Chron. 7:6–12; 8:1–40; 9:35–44). The variations arise from the fact that some are fragmentary and that the lists may reflect differing traditions about the lineage of the tribe as well as periodic changes in its composition and in territorial boundaries. Beriah, for example, appears in the genealogical lists of Benjamin (I Chron. 8:13–16), Ephraim (*ibid.* 7:21–23), and Asher (Gen. 46:17; Num. 26:44–45). If in each case the reference is to the same clan then this reflects a movement of Beriah from south to north or the reverse. Huppim and Shuppim are included in the genealogical lists of the tribes of both Benjamin (Gen. 46:21, where the latter is Muppim; Num. 26:39; I Chron. 7:12) and Manasseh (I Chron. 7:15). In view of the close ties between Benjamin and the east bank of the Jordan (see below) it seems that the duplication reflects the migration of one or two clans from Benjamin to Manasseh or the reverse. I Chronicles 8:29–40 and 9:35–44 preserve two parallel lists of the family of Saul, which place "the father of Gibeon" in the genealogical records of Benjamin. The city of Gibeon was inhabited by the Gibeonite descendants of the Hivites and included in the territory of Benjamin, and the relationship of Saul to Gibeon in these lists indicates the intermingling of the Gibeonite population with the Benjaminites.

However, some scholars believe that "Gibeon" is a scribal error for "Gibeah," the city of Saul (I Sam. 11:4).

The Tribal Territory

The territory of Benjamin, which extended from the hill country of Ephraim to the hill country of Judah, is described in great detail in Joshua 18:11–28. The description of its southern border fits that of the northern border of Judah (Josh. 15:5–11), while the picture of its northern border accords with that of the southern border of the House of Joseph (Josh. 16:1–3, 5). The northern boundary began at the Jordan and continued in an almost straight line westward to Jericho, which it bypassed to the north; it then ascended the mountains in a west-northwesterly direction, encompassing Beth-El, turning south and continuing to the southwest, and circumventing lower Beth-Horon on the south. The western border of Benjamin is unclear; however, from the description of the territory of Dan, it would seem that it did not reach the sea, but ended in the vicinity of the valley of Aijalon, with the area of lower Beth-Horon and Kiriath-Jearim marking its northern and southern extremities (cf. Josh. 18:28 with 15:60). The southern border ran "from the outskirts of Kiriath-Jearim" (Josh. 18:15), eastward via the "spring of the Waters of Nephtoah" (Lifta) to Jerusalem, which was included in the territory of Benjamin; for the border passed Jerusalem on the south and descended east by way of En-Rogel, En-Shemesh, "the Stone of Bohan son of Reuben," and Beth-Hoglah to the Dead Sea, near where the Jordan enters it. The eastern border was the Jordan.

The list of Benjaminite towns (Josh. 18:21–28) does not accord with the northern border of the tribe as described in Joshua 18:12–13 since Beth-El, Zemaraim, Ophrah, and Mizpeh are elsewhere included in the territory of Ephraim (cf. Josh. 16; II Chron. 13:4, 19). Possibly the list of cities and the list of border points are not from the same period and reflect fluctuating territorial and historical situations. It is generally believed that the list of border points antedates the period of the monarchy, whereas the list of cities is of later date. A westward expansion of the Benjaminites – possibly as early as the end of the period of Judges, but perhaps taking place during the monarchy – can be inferred from the list of Benjaminite towns in Nehemiah 11:31–35. Non-Israelite enclaves existed within the territory of Benjamin; the Jebusites dwelt in Jerusalem (Josh. 18:28), and there were four cities of the Hivites in the western portion. Echoes of the conflicts between the Benjaminites and the indigenous population are discernible in II Samuel 21:1–2 and possibly in I Chronicles 8:6–8.

The History of the Tribe

Despite the fact that the territory of Benjamin was smaller than that of most of the other tribes and although Benjamin was regarded as the youngest tribe (see the *Tribes of Israel), it played an important part in the history of the unification of the tribes of Israel during the period of the Judges and the beginning of the monarchy. One of the first judges who arose to save Israel was *Ehud son of Gera, of the tribe of Benjamin (Judg. 3:15), and the first king to rule Israel was *Saul the Benjaminite (I Sam. 9:1). Benjamin's importance was due to the strategic position of its territory, through which the divide (watershed) of the central hill country passed. The territory's main north-south road ran along the divide; a main highway connecting Transjordan with the west also passed through Benjamin's territory. It was this road that the Israelites used after they crossed the Jordan. When *Eglon king of Moab extended the boundaries of his rule westward, the oppressive effects were felt mainly by the tribe of Benjamin, since the corridor connecting regions on the banks of the Jordan was situated in its territory. Therefore it was not just by chance that the judge who saved Israel from Moab came from the tribe of Benjamin (Judg. 3:12ff). The close ties between the Benjaminites and the people of Jabesh-Gilead (Judg. 20–21; I Sam. 11; 31:11–13; Obad. 19) are also explained in part by the Benjaminites' easy access to Transjordan. In the days of *Deborah the Benjaminites joined in the war against Jabin and Sisera (Judg. 5:14). After forcing the tribe of Dan to move northward, Philistine pressure focused upon the territory of the Benjaminites because of the strategic importance of the area. The *Philistines dominated the entire central part of the country and placed a garrison in Gibeath-Benjamin (I Sam. 10:5; 13:3). Opposition to Philistine rule was thus centered in Benjamin, and so it is hardly surprising that the first king, Saul, whose primary task it was to save Israel from the Philistines (cf. I Sam. 9:16), was a Benjaminite. This is also in keeping with Benjamin's reputation for military prowess, as expressed in Jacob's blessing: "Benjamin is a ravenous wolf; in the morning he consumes the foe, and in the evening he divides the spoil" (Gen. 49:27).

A count of Benjaminites made before the intertribal war that followed the affair of the concubine in Gibeah (Judg. 19–21) revealed "twenty six thousand men that drew the sword… Among all these were seven hundred picked men who were left-handed; every one could sling a stone at a hair and not miss" (Judg. 20:15–16; cf. I Chron. 8:40; 12:1–2). According to the account, Benjamin was defeated and its civilian population massacred. The survival of the tribe was only insured by seizure as wives for the 600 remaining warriors of the unmarried women of Jabesh-Gilead and Shiloh (Judg. 21). The kingdom of Judah established by David did not include Benjamin (see *Ish-Bosheth), and when Israel also chose David as its king, Benjamin continued to belong to "the House of Joseph" (II Sam. 19:17–21). The tribe retained some rancor against David as the supplanter of the House of Saul, as is shown by the episode of *Shimei son of Gera and the revolt of *Sheba son of Bichri (II Sam. 16:5–13; 20:1–2). Under Solomon, too, the territory of Benjamin constituted one of the administrative divisions of Israel (I Kings 4:18). After Solomon's death and the revolt of Israel, the Davidides tried to regain as much of Israel as they could, and according to II Chronicles 13 for a time pushed the northern limit of their dominion well beyond Benjamin. Ultimately, however, they had to be content with the Benjaminite watershed as a buffer between Israel and their place of residence, Jerusalem (I Kings 15:22).

[Bustanay Oded]

In the *Aggadah*

Benjamin, according to one opinion, was the image of his mother, Rachel (Tanḥ. B. 1:197), and according to another resembled his father (Tanḥ., Mi-Keẓ 10). He alone of all the brothers took no part in the sale of Joseph; as a result he was privileged to have the Temple built on the territory of his tribe (Gen. R. 99:1). Another reason is that he was not yet born when his father and brothers prostrated themselves before Esau (Targ. Sheni to Esther 3:3). Although he knew of Joseph as having been sold into slavery, he never revealed it to his father (Mid. Ps. 15:6). The four additional portions given by Joseph to Benjamin (Gen. 43:34) consisted of one each from Joseph, Asenath, and their sons, Ephraim and Manasseh (Gen. R. 92:5). After Joseph's silver cup was found in Benjamin's sack, his brothers struck Benjamin on the shoulder saying, "O thief and son of a thief, thou hast brought the same shame upon us that thy mother brought upon our father when she stole the teraphim that were her father's" (Tanḥ. B. 1:198). Jacob's deathbed blessing to Benjamin contained the prophecy that his tribe would provide Israel with its first and its last ruler, both Saul and Esther being of the tribe of Benjamin (Gen. R. 99:3). He was untainted by sin (Shab. 55b), and when he died his corpse was not exposed to the ravages of worms (BB 17a).

In Islam

Though Muhammad does not mention the name Benjamin in the Sura of Yūsuf (Sura 12, verse 69ff.), there is no doubt concerning the identity of the brother whom Joseph wishes to bring to him in Egypt. The Koran continues with the biblical account (cf. Gen. 42–43), according to the version derived from the *aggadah*. Not only Reuben but all the brothers guarantee Jacob that they will bring Benjamin back (sura 12, 66; cf. Tanḥ. *Mi-Keẓ*, 8). There are many accounts in Muslim legends of the threats made by Benjamin's brothers when Joseph wanted to imprison him (cf. Gen. 44:17).

[Haïm Z'ew Hirschberg]

BIBLIOGRAPHY: W.F. Albright, in: AASOR, 4 (1922–23), 150–5; J. Muilenburg, in: JBL, 75 (1956), 194–201; Z. Kallai, in: VT, 8 (1958), 134–60; E.A. Speiser, *Genesis* (1964), 273–4; K.D. Schunck, *Benjamin* (Ger., 1963); idem, in: ZDPV, 78 (1962), 143–58; H.L. Ginsberg, in: *Fourth World Congress of Jewish Studies, Papers*, 1 (1967), 91–93. IN THE AGGADAH: Ginzberg, Legends, index. IN ISLAM: Ṭabarī, *Tafsir*, XIII, 6–20; al-Kisā'ī, *Qiṣaṣ* (1922), 169–76; Vajda, in: EIS², s.v. *Binyamin*. **ADD. BIBLIOGRAPHY:** A. Ben-Tor (ed.), *The Archaeology of Ancient Israel* (1992), 286, 289, 372; S. Ahituv, *Joshua* (Heb., 1995), 294–97.

BENJAMIN II (originally **Israel Joseph Benjamin**; 1818–1864), Romanian explorer and writer born in Falticeni, Moldavia. He engaged first in the lumber trade (for this reason he was nicknamed Chiristigiu or "Lumberjack") but after some initial success, he lost his fortune at the age of 25. Influenced by his failure and by the romantic trends of the time, he decided to emulate the medieval traveler Benjamin of Tudela. He styled himself Benjamin II and, in 1845, took to the road in search of the remnants of the Ten Lost Tribes. He traveled first to Egypt, from there through Ereẓ Israel and Syria, and then to Armenia, Iraq, Kurdistan, Persia, India, and China. He came back by way of Afghanistan to Vienna (1851) and from there went on to Italy and to Tripoli, Tunisia, Algeria, and Morocco. Wherever his travels took him, he made a point of assembling information concerning the Jewish settlement in that place – the number of Jews of that community, how they earned their livelihood, their customs, and folklore. Although unscientific, his approach was simple and direct, and earned the praise of scholars like A. von Humboldt and A. Petermann. He described his experiences in a Hebrew travelogue, first published in French under the title *Cinq années de voyage en Orient 1846–1851* (1856; Eng. 1859). The Hebrew edition of the book, *Sefer Mas'ei Yisrael*, as revised by David *Gordon, was published in Lyck in 1859. He published at his own expense in 1863 Nathan Hannover's *Yeven Meẓulah* on the 17th-century Chmielnicki massacres in Poland. Over and above his literary endeavors, Benjamin undertook to ease the plight of the Jews of Morocco. He also appealed to Turkey, France, and England in an attempt to ameliorate the condition of the Jews of Kurdistan and Persia. In 1859 Benjamin II began a three-year journey through the United States, describing his travels in *Drei Jahre in Amerika* (1862; republished in English in 1956 by the JPSA). He died in London in poverty while preparing another trip to the Orient.

BIBLIOGRAPHY: JC (May 13, 1864), 5; I.J. Benjamin, *Three Years in America* (1956), introduction by O. Handlin. **ADD. BIBLIOGRAPHY:** PK Romanyah, I, 190.

BENJAMIN, BARUCH BEN ISRAEL (17th century), Jerusalem rabbi. After studying under his father, Baruch proceeded to the yeshivah of Isaac Gaon, where Kabbalah was included in the curriculum. He was a signatory to the regulation of 1646, which exempted rabbinic scholars from taxation (A. Ankawa, in *Kerem Ḥemed*, 2 (1871), 22b). In 1657 he, together with other Jerusalem kabbalists, endorsed the certificate which declared that Baruch Gad, the Jerusalem messenger to the East, had visited the Ten Lost Tribes. Some of his responsa were published in *Mishpetei Ẓedek* (1945, nos. 66, 95, 98, 100, 131, 133) of his friend, Samuel *Garmison. While serving as *dayyan* in Jerusalem he wrote a work on divorces (Jerusalem Ms. Heb. 8°199). Toward the end of his life he traveled to Egypt, possibly as an emissary, and he died there.

BIBLIOGRAPHY: J. Sambari, *Likkutim mi-Sefer Divrei Yosef*, ed. by A. Berliner (1896), 66; Frumkin-Rivlin, 2 (1928), 29; A. Yaari, in: *Sinai*, 6 (1940), 170–5.

BENJAMIN, BARUCH BENZION (1904–?), Indian government official. Born in Bombay, of the *Bene-Israel community, Benjamin joined the Indian government service following independence in 1947 and was made deputy chief controller of imports and exports in 1953. From 1955 until his retirement in 1959 he was an undersecretary in the Indian Ministry of Finance. Active in Jewish affairs, Benjamin was a vice president of the World Council of Synagogues and president of the Delhi Jewish Welfare Association.

BENJAMIN, ERNEST FRANK (1900–1969), British army officer and commander of the *Jewish Brigade in World War II. Born in Toronto, Canada, Benjamin was educated in England at the Royal Military Academy, Woolwich, and at the Staff College, Camberley. He was commissioned in 1919 and served in Turkey, Malaya, and Madagascar. During World War II Benjamin commanded the marine division of the Royal Engineers and later the Combined Training Center for the Middle East and Italy. From 1944 to 1946 he commanded the Jewish Brigade which went into action in north Italy in 1945 as part of the Eighth Army. Brigadier Benjamin later served in Hong Kong and retired in 1950. He was joint honorary treasurer of the Jewish Lads Brigade.

BIBLIOGRAPHY: J. Ben Hirsh, *Jewish General Officers* (1967), 78; E. Rubin, *140 Jewish Marshals, Generals and Admirals* (1952), 252–6.

BENJAMIN, ISRAEL (c. 1570–1649), *posek* and kabbalist, who was among the greatest of Egyptian and Jerusalem scholars of his century. According to David *Conforte he was also called "Israel Eliakim." Benjamin was a disciple of R. Eleazar Monzalavi and his friend Samuel b. *Sid, and corresponded with Jacob Castro of Egypt (*Oholei Ya'akov*, 1738, no. 58). According to Conforte a collection of more than a hundred legal decisions and a book of scriptural exegesis by Benjamin were in the possession of his son Baruch Benjamin in Jerusalem. Ḥ.J.D. Azulai also saw a manuscript of his responsa. Abraham Azulai quotes new rulings by Benjamin in his annotations. He was a disciple of the kabbalist *Joseph ibn Tabul in Egypt. In the manuscript *Oẓerot Ḥayyim* by Ḥayyim *Vital (Ms. Jerusalem 80 370) there are annotations by Benjamin as well as statements of Ibn Tabul which the latter heard from Isaac *Luria. Benjamin taught Kabbalah in Egypt and Jerusalem. His disciples include Meir *Anaschehon and Meir *Poppers. They had Benjamin's annotations to other writings of Isaac Luria, as well as a *maḥzor* based on the Kabbalah; these are found in *Beit Mo'ed* in the manuscripts of Solomon b. Benjamin ha-Levi. Ḥayyim Vital's *Sefer ha-Gilgulim* contains glosses by Benjamin. An immigrant from Carpi who went to Jerusalem in 1625 found manuscripts of Luria in the possession of Benjamin. He served in Jerusalem as *dayyan* and was one of the prominent scholars in the town. In 1623 he signed an agreement not to cause division in the community and in 1625 he signed an agreement to exempt the scholars from taxes. In that year the Jews of Jerusalem suffered from the oppressive rule of Ibn Farruk, and Benjamin signed a circular entitled *Ḥurvot Yerushalayim* which was handed to emissaries who were sent to the Diaspora with the aim of collecting money for the reconstruction of the community. His signature is also found in a letter to Fez in 1630. In 1646 he was the head of the Jerusalem rabbis. In 1649 he signed first on the endorsement (**haskamah*) of Joseph *Caro's *Maggid Meisharim* (vol. 2, Venice 1649).

BIBLIOGRAPHY: Conforte, Kore, 48b–49a; S. Ḥazzan, *Ha-Ma'alot li-Shelomo* (1894), 45a–b; *Yerushalayim* (ed. by A.M. Luncz), 2 (1887), 147–8; 5 (1901), 73–85; Azulai, 1 (1852), 114, no. 406; J.M. Toledano, in: HUCA, 4 (1927), 464–6 (Heb.); Frumkin-Rivlin, 2 (1928), 27–29; 3 (1929), 13.

BENJAMIN, JUDAH PHILIP (1811–1884), U.S. lawyer and statesman. Benjamin was undoubtedly the most prominent 19th-century American Jew. He was a noted lawyer, whose services were requested in connection with some of the most significant legal disputes of the time, a powerful politician who was a leader in the cause of Southern rights and on behalf of the short-lived Confederacy.

Born in St. Croix in the West Indies, of British parents, Benjamin was a British subject. His family moved to Charleston, South Carolina, while he was still a boy. He was at Yale University for two years, but studied law privately in New Orleans while earning a meager living as a tutor in English and as a clerk in a business establishment. Deprived of a happy home through an unsuccessful marriage to a non-Jewess, Natalie St. Martin, a high-spirited Creole who left him to live in Paris after their only child was born after ten barren years, he was free to devote himself to law and politics. His legal eminence brought him wealth, and his political activity fame. He was the first professing Jew to be elected to the United States Senate, as a Whig in 1852, and as a Democrat (after the Democratic Party espoused the cause of Southern rights) in 1856. He became a leading member of the school of Southern politicians which favored secession from the Union as the only safeguard for Southern survival and delivered a number of major addresses in the Senate defending slavery. When Louisiana seceded, he withdrew from the Senate, and was immediately called to the cabinet of the newly created Confederate government (March 1861) as attorney general. President Jefferson Davis relied heavily upon Benjamin's companionship and counsel and appointed him to the more important position of secretary of war in September 1861. Benjamin quickly succeeded in antagonizing Davis's high-strung generals with his complacent lawyerly manner and became a convenient scapegoat for a number of military disasters and chronic supply problems, causing him to resign in March 1862. Loyal to Benjamin despite antisemitic attacks, Davis promptly appointed him secretary of state, a position which he held until the collapse of the Confederacy. In this role Benjamin came close to obtaining recognition of and help for the Confederacy from England and France. But the Confederacy's cause was doomed from the first, and after Lee's surrender to Grant (April 1865) Benjamin was the only leading Confederate to choose permanent exile rather than live in the defeated South, convinced that as both a rebel and a Jew he had little future in America. He parted ways with the fleeing president in South Carolina and escaped to England through Florida and Nassau, and there made for himself a distinguished career as barrister (he was appointed Queen's Counsel), which in many ways outshadowed his prewar American legal career. Ill health forced his retirement from active work in 1882 and he died two years later in Paris where he had finally rejoined his wife and daughter.

Benjamin took no discernible interest in Jewish affairs, although he never denied his origin and was never converted to the Catholic faith of his wife. There is no record of membership on his part in any synagogue, nor did he ever give support to any Jewish cause or organization.

BIBLIOGRAPHY: B.W. Korn, *American Jewry and the Civil War* (1951), index; idem, *Eventful Years and Experiences: Studies in Nineteenth Century American Jewish History* (1954); R. Douthat Meade, *Judah P. Benjamin, Confederate Statesman* (1943). **ADD. BIBLIOGRAPHY:** E.N. Evans, *Judah P. Benjamin: The Jewish Confederate* (1988).

[Bertram Wallace Korn]

BENJÁMIN, LÁSZLÓ (1915–1986), Hungarian poet, born in Budapest. His first poems were published in the left-wing press and in such anthologies of working-class poetry as *Tizenkét költő* ("Twelve Poets," 1940). Benjámin's early poetry was based on the hopelessness preceding World War II and, during and immediately after the war itself, on the class struggle. The collections of this period include *A csillag nem jött fel* ("The Star Did Not Come Forth," 1939), *Betüöntók diadala* ("The Victory of the Typecasters," 1946), and *A teremtés után* ("After the Creation," 1948). When the Hungarian Communist government was formed in 1949, Benjámin became one of its chief literary spokesmen. From 1953 his writing changed, and he turned to themes of self-criticism and personal confusion. This later poetry appears in *Éveink múlása* ("The Passing of our Years," 1954), *Egyetlen élet* ("Only During One Lifetime," 1956), and *Ötödik évszak* ("The Fifth Season," 1962).

BIBLIOGRAPHY: *Magyar Irodalmi Lexikon*, 1 (1963), 136–7; *Hét évszázad magyar versei*, 3 (1966), 686–740.

[Itamar Yaos-Kest]

BENJAMIN, MOSES (first half of the 18th century), rabbi and kabbalist in Baghdad. He was the first of the Baghdad scholars known to have studied much Kabbalah and was an expert in Lurianic Kabbalah. Very little is known about his life; his wife and children died in an epidemic before 1737, and he never fulfilled his desire to immigrate to Jerusalem. He apparently served as rabbi, because he mentions among his writings "some legal rulings." His book *Ma'aseh Rav* (Constantinople, 1736) is a kabbalistic commentary on the sayings of *Rabbah b. Bar Ḥana. In the introduction he mentions the following of his own works: *Matteh Moshe*, a commentary on the masorah as well as an explanation of rabbinic verses and sayings; *Ho'il Moshe*, a homiletical interpretation of the Pentateuch; and a collection of sermons which he preached on Sabbaths and various occasions. His kabbalistic works are *Tefillah le-Moshe* and *Sha'arei Yerushalayim*, completed in 1731 (author's manuscript; Sassoon Library, 771). The latter contains kabbalistic principles according to the *Zohar and Isaac *Luria. These two books were stolen while en route to the publishers and the author was left with only the first draft.

BIBLIOGRAPHY: D.S. Sassoon, *Ohel Dawid*, 1 (1932), 442–3; A. Ben-Jacob, *Yehudei Bavel* (1965), 95–96.

BENJAMIN, RAPHAEL (1846–1906), U.S. Reform rabbi. Benjamin was born in London, England, received his B.A. degree from the University of London, and was ordained by the chief rabbi of the British Isles. In 1874, he was elected assistant minister and reader of the Melbourne Hebrew Congregation (Bourke Street Synagogue) in Melbourne, Australia as well as master of the Jewish schools of that city. He earned his M.A. from the University of Melbourne. In 1882, he was named rabbi of K.K. Benai Israel (the Mound Street Synagogue) in Cincinnati, Ohio, where he also served as vice president of the Young Men's Hebrew Association. In addition, Benjamin lectured and served as governor and examiner at Hebrew Union College. In 1889, he became rabbi of Congregation Shaarei Shomayim (the Fifteenth Street Temple) in New York. When his congregation merged with the Fifty-Fifth Street Synagogue (Congregation Ahavath Chesed), he ministered at large in New York City, serving as secretary of the Board of Jewish Ministers (later the New York Board of Rabbis) and conducting services at the Hebrew Orphan Asylum. In 1902, he became rabbi of the Keap Street Temple in Brooklyn (Congregation Beth Elohim). Benjamin was also a fellow in the American Association for the Advancement of Science.

[Bezalel Gordon (2nd ed.)]

BIBLIOGRAPHY: M.A. Meyer, *Publications of the American Jewish Historical Society*, Number 17, 1907.

BENJAMIN, RICHARD (1938–), U.S. actor and director. Born in New York City, Benjamin attended the New York High School of Performing Arts and then Northwestern University, where he met his actress wife Paula Prentiss; he graduated in 1960. While Prentiss' film career took off immediately, Benjamin focused his attention initially on the stage; his Broadway debut was *Star-Spangled Girl* (1966). Benjamin's first on-screen appearance was opposite Prentiss in the television series *He & She* (1967), while his film turn came with the adaptation of Philip Roth's *Goodbye, Columbus* (1969), which was followed by Mike Nichols' *Catch 22* (1970) and another Roth adaptation, *Portnoy's Complaint* (1972). He was first nominated for the Golden Globe for *The Marriage of a Young Stockbroker* (1971) and won the award for his supporting role as Walter Matthau's nephew in Neil Simon's *The Sunshine Boys* (1975). In 1982, Benjamin turned his attention to directing with *My Favorite Year*, followed by *City Heat* (1984), *The Money Pit* (1986), *My Stepmother is an Alien* (1988), *Mermaids* (1990), and a made-for-television update of Neil Simon's *The Goodbye Girl* (2004).

[Adam Wills (2nd ed.)]

BENJAMIN, WALTER (1892–1940), German philosopher and literary critic. Born in Berlin, Benjamin attended Haubinda, a country educational establishment, where he met the radical school reformer Gustav Wyneken. From 1910 to 1914 Benjamin took an active part in the youth movement influenced by Wyneken and was for some time the students' president at Berlin University. He published his first articles under the pseudonym Ardor in *Der Anfang* edited by Wyneken. In 1915 Benjamin broke off with Wyneken and his movement because of their acceptance of World War I. Benjamin studied philosophy in Freiburg, Berlin, Munich, and Berne. He returned to Germany in 1920 and lived there till 1933. His thesis written to obtain the qualification to teach aesthetics and history of literature at the university in Frankfurt was not accepted. Today, however, this work on the origin of the German drama (Berlin, 1928) is regarded as one of the most important philosophical interpretations of this field. In 1929 Benjamin joined Bertold Brecht (*Versuche ueber Brecht*, 1966), with whose ideas he identified himself to a large extent. Benjamin felt his Jewishness intensely and had for several years toyed with the idea of going to Palestine. When the Nazis came to power he first went to the Balearic Isles and then to Paris. At the outbreak of World War II he was interned as a German citizen, but was released in November 1939. He fled to the south of France and, with a group of refugees, crossed the Spanish border. When the police chief of the border town Port-Bou threatened to send them back to France, Benjamin took his own life.

Between 1914 and 1924, he did not publish much. Then he wrote a long essay, *Goethe's Wahlverwandtschaften* (publ. by H. v. Hofmannsthal in *Neue deutsche Beitraege*, 1924–25; in book form 1964), and continued his intensive activity as essayist and literary critic, especially in the *Frankfurter Zeitung, Literarische Welt*, and *Die Gesellschaft*. During his lifetime, Benjamin published only two books: a volume of philosophical aphorisms *Einbahnstrasse* (Berlin, 1928), and, during the Nazi era, under the pseudonym Detlev Holz, *Deutsche Menschen, eine Folge von Briefen* (Lucerne, 1936), an annotated collection of 25 letters from 1783–1883), in which he discussed the flowering and the first decadence of German bourgeois culture. The first collection of his writings appeared posthumously in 1955 (*Schriften*, 2 vols., Frankfurt), edited by Theodore Adorno who had always stressed Benjamin's importance as a philosopher. *Illuminationen* (1961; *Illuminations*, 1969), *Angelus Novus* (1966), *Das Kunstwerk im Zeitalter seiner technischen Reproduzierbarkeit* (1963), *Staedtebilder* (1963), and *Zur Kritik der Gewalt* (1965) contain more of his essays, some taken from his literary legacy. G. Scholem and Th. Adorno published a selection of his correspondence (2 vols., 1966).

Benjamin is considered as the most important critic in the German language between the two wars, and his importance is growing. His thought, formed by Kant and the religious-philosophical current, had been metaphysically oriented in the beginning. Later, especially from 1930 on, Benjamin showed an inclination toward Marxism, whose ideas he, however, interpreted in a highly personal way. Benjamin considered himself as a philosophical commentator of important literary events, stressing especially historical, philosophical, linguistic, and social motives. Intellectually, he was extremely independent, a fact felt in everything he wrote, even in the short book reviews. His concentrated prose makes him difficult to read. He had a strong poetic streak, expressed clearly in his *Berliner Kindheit um Neunzehnhundert* (first published in Frankfurt, 1950). Benjamin was also important as a translator, especially of French literature, which attracted him deeply. He translated from Baudelaire (*Tableaux Parisiens*, 1923), several volumes of Proust (1927–30), and several novels by M. Jouhandeau.

[Gershom Scholem]

It was Gershom *Scholem who quoted the following remark by his friend Walter Benjamin: "Whenever I will find my own philosophy, it will be somehow a philosophy of Judaism" ("Wenn ich einmal meine Philosophie haben werde, so wird es irgendwie eine Philosophie des Judentums sein"). Scholem wished to point to Benjamin's hidden commentary on Judaism when he dealt with the philosophical question of language and translation (since Benjamin's early Essay *Über die Sprache überhaupt und über die Sprache des Menschen*, 1916), the question of a philosophy of history (e.g., in Benjamin's theses which promote a messianic philosophy of history), and also when he discussed German-Jewish writers like Karl Kraus and Franz Kafka (cf. Benjamin/Scholem, *Benjamin über Kafka*, 1980). In his philosophical as well as in his critical works Benjamin remains ambivalent, however: On the one hand he avoids the construction of Jewish or even less Zionist perspectives, on the other hand he engages in a subtextual and also critical dialogue with Judaism and Zionism, his philosophical starting point being the Neo-Kantianism of Hermann *Cohen, his early letters to Ludwig Strauß and, from summer 1916, his friendship with Scholem. Both Scholem and Benjamin agreed in taking a critical attitude towards assimilation as well as towards Buber's type of cultural Zionism and his legitimization of war during the World War I period. But whereas Scholem found a clear Zionist alternative, Benjamin placed himself intellectually between universal Judaism and Marxism. And whereas – after the failure of Benjamin to qualify as a teacher in 1925 at the University of Frankfurt with his thesis *Der Ursprung des deutschen Trauerspiels* – Scholem tried to convince him to come to Jerusalem between 1926 and 1930, Benjamin became inspired by the syndicalist French thinker Georges Sorel, the communist Asja Lacis, whom he met in Capri 1924 and in Moscow 1926, and approached the Frankfurter Institut für Sozialforschung and later on Bert Brecht, whom he joined in his Danish exile in 1934.

Already in the last years of the Weimar Republic, Benjamin moved to Paris, "the capital of the 19th century," where he also spent the most time after March 1933. Here (in the Paris National library) he worked on an encyclopaedic historiographical project on the modernity of Paris in the 19th century, the so-called *Passagen-Werk*, which was not published until 1982 (in two volumes) and since then has come to be considered one of Benjamin's most important scientific works. Here he was combining the Marxist analysis of the "Warenwelt," the psychoanalytic method of "Traumdeutung," and the surrealist techniques of writing and quoting. On this basis he found a new method of performing history and by this means "saving" its neglected aspects much better than telling its linear story as the 19th century "Historismus" did. In the *Passagen-Werk* as well as in his thesis *Ueber den Begriff der Geschichte* (1940) he developed a philosophy of history which is apocalyptic and messianic at the same time: The historiographer is entitled to save the forgotten and the dead. Benjamin has seen here also a Jewish conception of history, which understands time not as "empty" and "homogeneous" but every "now," every "second" as "the little gate through which the Messiah may enter."

[Andreas Kilcher (2nd ed.)]

BIBLIOGRAPHY: G. Scholem, *Walter Benjamin* (= Leo Baeck Memorial Lecture, no. 8, 1965); R. Tiedemann, *Studien zur Philosophie Walter Benjamins* (= *Frankfurter Beitraege zur Soziologie*, vol. 16, 1965), includes bibliography; W. Kraft, in: *Merkur*, 21 (Ger., 1967), 226–32; H. Heissenbuettel, ibid., 232–44; R. Alter, in: *Commentary* (Sept. 1969), 86–93; H. Holz, in: *Sinn und Form*, 8 (1956), 514–49; P. Missac, in: *Critique* (Aug.–Sept. 1966), 692–710 (Fr.). **ADD. BIBLIOGRAPHY:** H. Arendt, *Benjamin, Brecht, Zwei Essays* (1971); G. Scholem, *Walter Benjamin – die Geschichte einer Freundschaft* (1975); idem, *Walter Benjamin und sein Engel* (1983); W. Menninghaus, *Walter Benjamins Theorie der Sprachmagie* (1980); St. Mosès, *Der Engel der Geschichte* (1994); S. Weigel, *Entstellte Ähnlichkeit. Walter Benjamins theoretische Schreibweise* (1997); A. Deuber-Mankowsky, *Der fruehe Walter Benjamin und Hermann Cohen* (2000); H. Peukert, *Wissenschaftstheorie, Handlungstheorie, Theologie* (1980); H. Ruttnies and G. Smith, *Benjaminiana* (1991); S.B. Plate, *Walter Benjamin* (2005).

BENJAMIN, YEHOSHUA (1920–), Indian government official and scholar. Born in Lonavla, Maharashtra, of the *Bene-Israel community, by the time he retired he was the chief architect of India's Ministry of Works and Housing. His scholarly interests are reflected in his book *The Mystery of the Lost Tribes* (New Delhi, 1989).

[Tudor Parfitt (2nd ed.)]

BENJAMIN BEN AARON OF ZALOZCE (late 18th century), East European homilist. In his sermons he commented pointedly on the social and religious life of his time. His didactic works include instructions on personal behavior and on the conduct of Jewish community leaders. He was involved also in the controversy concerning the spiritual value of immigration to Ereẓ Israel, which was a main issue among Jewish thinkers in the 1760s and 1770s. His writings include some important quotations from *Israel b. Eliezer Ba'al Shem, the founder of Ḥasidism, and other early ḥasidic teachers. His three main works are *Amtaḥat Binyamin*, a homiletic exegesis on Ecclesiastes (Minkowitz, 1796); *Ahavat Dodim*, on Song of Songs (Lvov, 1795); and *Turei Zahav*, a major collection of sermons on the weekly portions of the Pentateuch, and on the holy days (Mogilev, 1816).

BIBLIOGRAPHY: B. Dinur, *Be-Mifneh ha-Dorot* (1955), index s.v. *Binyamin me-Zeloziẓ;* I. Werfel *Ha-Ḥasidut ve-Ereẓ Yisrael* (1940), 39–46.

BENJAMIN BEN AZRIEL (11th century), liturgical poet, who apparently lived in France. His name and his father's are known only from his *piyyutim*, which are written in the spirit of the earlier *paytanim*. While the influence of Joseph *Bonfils and *Moses b. Kalonymus is apparent in the language of his *piyyutim*, Benjamin at times introduced new terms into the vocabulary of the *paytanim*. His hymns are found in the old French *maḥzor* and have not as yet been published. It is almost certain that a number of hymns signed merely "Binyamin" are his.

BIBLIOGRAPHY: Zunz, Lit Poesie, 144–5; Davidson, Oẓar, 4 (1933), 371.

[Abraham Meir Habermann]

BENJAMIN BEN ELIEZER HA-KOHEN VITALE OF REGGIO (1651–1730), Italian kabbalist. Benjamin, who was among the leading disciples of Moses *Zacuto in Mantua, was rabbi in his native town of Alessandria, Piedmont, until 1682 and afterward in Reggio. He became well-known as a preacher and poet, but in particular as a kabbalist; he was considered one of the major exponents of Isaac *Luria's Kabbalah in Italy. Most of his *piyyutim* (*Etha-Zamir,* Venice, 1707) were kabbalistic. He also wrote numerous notes and glosses on Luria's works, some of which were published together with the writings of Luria (particularly in the Korets editions). His books are written in the spirit of ascetic kabbalah. Benjamin was a close friend of Abraham *Rovigo in Modena, and desired to immigrate with him to Ereẓ Israel. However, these plans failed. Both he and Rovigo were among the believers in *Shabbetai Ẓevi even after the latter's apostasy and for decades he was among the leading secret Shabbateans in Italy, without, however, relinquishing his ascetic way of life. Benjamin was among the chief proponents of a modern "ḥasidic" Shabbateanism which sought to combine traditional Judaism with the belief in the messianic character of Shabbetai Ẓevi. He did not openly express his Shabbatean views in print, but in *Allon Bakhut* (on Lamentations, Venice, 1712) he dared to explain the lamentations as joyful hymns on the Redemption, on the Shabbatean supposition of the change in their meaning in "the days to come." Many leading Shabbateans met in his home; he also made a point of collecting information about the "faith" and was greatly interested in every new manifestation of a Shabbatean prophet. While his Shabbateanism was still moderate, Benjamin was the teacher of Ḥayyim *Malakh. In his writings Benjamin kept apart the Lurianic Kabbalah from the new Shabbatean Kabbalah of *Nathan of Gaza. He refused to join in the persecution of the Shabbatean Nehemiah *Ḥayon (1714). One of his Shabbatean pamphlets, *Sod Adnut Adonenu* ("The secret of the Lordship of our lord [Shabbetai

Ẓevi] according to Nathan"), was published by A. Freimann. Isaiah Bassan, his son-in-law and successor as rabbi of Reggio, was Moses Ḥayyim *Luzzatto's teacher. When the aging Benjamin learned of Luzzatto's revelations in Kabbalah, he wrote asking him about the root (*"shoresh"*) of his soul, and its restitution (*"tikkun"*). A small part of the correspondence between Benjamin and Moses Zacuto, is extant in *Iggerot ha-Remaz* (Leghorn, 1780). Others are still in manuscript. A large collection of his sermons (*Gevul Binyamin*) was published in his old age (Amsterdam, 1727). Some of his halakhic rulings were published in *Lampronti's *Paḥad Yiẓḥak*. Benjamin's responsa, *She'elot u-Teshuvot ha-Re* (1970) were published by Chief Rabbi Yitzḥak *Nissim.

BIBLIOGRAPHY: A. Freimann (ed.), *Inyanei Shabbetai Ẓevi* (1912), 93–108; G. Scholem, *Ḥalomotav shel ha-Shabbeta'i R. Mordekhai Ashkenazi* (1938), chs. 7, 11; I. Tishby, *Netivei Emunah u-Minut* (1964), 95–98, 230–32; S. Ginzberg, *Ramḥal u-Venei Doro* (1937), 5–8, 36–40, 45–48, 56; Sonne, in: *Sefer ha-Yovel... A. Marx* (1943), 93–95; D. Kaufmann, in: MGWJ, 41 (1897), 700–8.

[Gershom Scholem]

BENJAMIN BEN ELIJAH (18th century), *Karaite pilgrim to Ereẓ Israel. A resident of *Chufut-Kale (Bakhchisarai), in the Crimea, Benjamin made a vow to "cross seas and deserts and brave great hardships" in order to visit Jerusalem, where a small Karaite community had been revived in 1744. He embarked with six other Karaites from Eupatoria on June 27, 1785, and reached Jerusalem on October 18. After a month's stay there Benjamin returned by way of Jaffa and Constantinople. Benjamin described his nine-month journey in his account, in which he relates, among other matters, that contributions from Crimean Karaites to those in Jerusalem were concealed from the Turkish authorities in order to prevent extortion of money. Some hymns by Benjamin are included in the Karaite liturgy.

BIBLIOGRAPHY: H.J. Gurland, *Ginzei Yisrael be-St. Petersburg*, 1 (1865), 44–54; J.D. Eisenstein, *Oẓar ha-Massa'ot* (1926), 212–8; A. Ya'ari, *Masot Ereẓ Yisrael* (1946), 459–78, 775f.

[Avraham Yaari]

BENJAMIN BEN ELIJAH DUWAN (1747–after 1816), leader of Karaite community in Eupatoria (Yevpatoriya) and its *ḥazzan*. He was also the *dayyan* of the local *bet din*. In 1782–83 in the course of his visit in Constantinople he studied astronomy in order to deepen his knowledge of the calendar. In 1785 he made a pilgrimage to Ereẓ Israel with four other Karaites. He described his impressions in his travelogue. In Jerusalem they stayed with the Karaite community, under the leadership of *ḥakham* Mordecai ben Samuel ha-Levi, which numbered 16 houses. They also visited Hebron, and stayed at Rabbanite houses which he claimed had once been Karaite houses.

In 1881, after a calendar dispute that lasted 18 years, Benjamin came to Chufut-Qaleh at the head of several Eupatorian Karaite dignitaries in order to confront the Karaite scholar *Isaac ben Salomon. According to Isaac's report, Benjamin was defeated, but he did not give in, and Yom Kippur was kept by him and his group on a Sunday against Isaac's calculation which was supported by the majority. Benjamin authored a number of liturgical poems, some of which are included in the Karaite *Siddur*. He was familiar with Rabbanite books and was interested in Kabbalah.

BIBLIOGRAPHY: G. Akhiezer, in: M.Polliack (ed.), *Karaite Judaism* (2003), 741; E. Deinard, *Masa Krim* (1878), 70–71; H.Y. Gurland, *Ginzei Yisrael*, 1 (1865), 44–54, 88–89; A. Yaari, *Masa'ot Ereẓ Yisrael* (1976), 459–78; Mann, Texts 2, (1935), 1535, index.

[Golda Akhiezer (2nd ed.)]

BENJAMIN BEN ḤIYYA (**Jehiel**; 11th–12th century), liturgical poet. Benjamin lived in Germany during the First Crusade and was among the refugees from Neuss, Bacharach, and Speyer. The horrors of the Crusade constitute the theme of his poetry. According to a 13th-century commentary, his three-line *seliḥah* beginning *"Berit Kerutah"* refers to the claim made by two monks to have brought back from the Holy Sepulcher a document in which the extermination of the Jews is urged. It is probable that other *piyyutim* which bear the name Benjamin are attributable to him.

BIBLIOGRAPHY: Zunz, Lit Poesie, 158; Zunz, Poesie, 139, 166, 197; Landshuth, Ammudei, 52; Davidson, Oẓar 2 (1929), 77, no. 1717.

BENJAMIN BEN JAPHETH (fl. third century), Palestinian *amora*. Benjamin studied under R. Johanan and transmitted legal rulings in his name (Ber. 33a, et al.). R. Zeira praised him for a report he transmitted in the name of Johanan (Shab. 53a). However, he would not rely upon him when he contradicted the tradition of Ḥiyya b. Abba in whom Zeira placed greater trust (Ber. 38b). Benjamin also transmitted many sayings in the name of R. Eleazar b. Pedat, noteworthy among them his comment on the fact that Jacob bowed to his son Joseph (Gen. 47:31), viz., "Bow to the fox in his season" (i.e., if you behold fortune favoring the fox, bow down to him, meaning that one should submit to an inferior person when he is in a position to convey a favor; Meg. 16b).

BIBLIOGRAPHY: Hyman, Toledot, 282f.

[Yitzhak Dov Gilat]

BENJAMIN BEN SAMUEL HA-LEVI (of Coutances; early 11th century), rabbi and liturgical poet. Benjamin lived in Coutances, Normandy. His poems are composed in the style of the old *piyyutim* and are, at times, of considerable artistic distinction. Benjamin wrote *piyyutim* for the three pilgrimage festivals, Rosh Ha-Shanah, and the Day of Atonement. Some of his poems are included in the *Maḥzor Romania*. Benjamin was regarded as a talmudic authority and was often quoted by contemporary talmudic scholars.

BIBLIOGRAPHY: Landshuth, Ammudei, 53; Zunz, Lit Poesie, 115ff.; Graetz, Gesch, 6 (1894^3), 53 (calls him Benjamin b. Samuel of Constance); Gross, Gal Jud, 553; Davidson, Oẓar, 4 (1933), 371; Moses b. Jacob of Coucy, *Sefer Mitzvot Gadol* (1905), no. 42; Mordekhai, RH, no. 720; Tos. to Ḥag. 12a; Shelomo b. Yiẓḥak (Rashi), *Pardes*, ed. by Ehrenreich (1923), 229; S. Bernstein, *Piyyutim u-Faytanim Ḥadashim me-ha-Tekufah ha-Bizantinit* (1947), 44–57; H. Merḥaviah, in: *Sefer Ḥayyim Schirmann* (1970), 195–212.

BENJAMIN BEN ZERAH (c. 1050), liturgical poet. Benjamin probably lived in France or in Germany. He composed liturgical poetry of various sorts in the style of the earliest *paytanim*, but his works already contain the names of angels and other holy appellations. Because of the esteem accorded to him, he was designated *Ha-Gadol* ("the Great"). He was also called *Ba'al ha-Shem* ("Master of the Divine Name"), possibly on account of the numerous names of God and the angels in his poems. About 60 of his *piyyutim* are known, many being included in the Ashkenazi and Italian liturgies.

BIBLIOGRAPHY: Landshuth, Ammudei, 52; Davidson, Oẓar, 4 (1933), 371; Zunz, Lit Poesie, 120–3, 239–43, 615.

[Abraham Meir Habermann]

BENJAMIN NEHEMIAH BEN ELNATHAN (16th century), Italian Jewish chronicler. Exiled from Naples, and later a resident or perhaps rabbi of Civitanova near Ancona, he was arrested with five other members of the Jewish community in the summer of 1559 on a charge of being implicated in the conversion of a Catholic priest. They were sent to Rome for trial by the Inquisition but were released with the other prisoners of the Holy Office on the death of Pope *Paul IV. On Benjamin's return he wrote a vivid account of his experiences, viewing them in the historical context of Paul IV's persecution of the Jews and Marranos of Ancona, which he apparently witnessed. He wrote his account in fine, idiomatic Hebrew, and it is an important contribution to Hebrew literature as well as to Jewish history. The chronicle was discovered by I. Sonne and published in *Tarbiz* (vol. 2, 1930/31), and again in his *Mi-Paolo ha-Revi'i ad Pius ha-Hamishi* (1954).

[Cecil Roth]

BENJAMIN OF BRODY (18th-century), preacher. Benjamin was the official preacher of the Jewish community in Berdichev for 17 years, after which he moved to Brody. His sermons were collected in the book *Imrei Binyamin* (Tarnopol, 1814) by his grandson, Meir Eliezer b. Phinehas. Benjamin's sermons, which follow the order of the weekly Torah portions, are undoubtedly edited versions of those he had originally delivered orally. Rabbinic in character, they deal frequently with halakhic problems, interpretations of talmudic sayings, and moralistic preaching.

BENJAMIN OF CAMBRIDGE (12th–13th century), English scholar, pupil of R. *Tam. A number of Benjamin's opinions on *halakhah*, grammar, and exegesis are preserved in scattered secondary sources. He is referred to as "Benjamin of קנטברייא," formerly interpreted as Canterbury, but without doubt designating Cambridge ("Caunbrigge"). His English origin is confirmed by the citation of one of his opinions by *Elijah Menahem b. Moses of London. He is to be identified with "Magister Benjamin" of Cambridge, mentioned in English records, who maintained the local synagogue.

BIBLIOGRAPHY: C. Roth, *Intellectual Activities of Medieval English Jewry* (1948), 136, 149; H.P. Stokes, *Studies in Anglo-Jewish History* (1913), 113–4; J. Jacobs, *Jews of Angevin England* (1893), 54, 281; S. Eppenstein, in: MGWJ, 40 (1896), 178; 41 (1897), 222; Urbach, in: *Essays ... I. Brodie* (Heb. vol., 1966), 13ff.

[Cecil Roth]

BENJAMIN OF TIBERIAS, leader of Palestinian Jewry at the beginning of the seventh century C.E. At the time of the Persian invasion of Ereẓ Israel in 614, Benjamin appears to have been among the Jewish leaders who negotiated with the Persians; as a result of these contacts, the Persian armies received Jewish military support. Benjamin then considered the Christians to be the enemies of his people; however, when the armies of Heraclius, the Byzantine emperor, reconquered the country in 628, he was compelled to receive them on friendly terms. Benjamin, who was exceedingly wealthy, accomodated the emperor in Tiberias and then succeeded in obtaining a general pardon from him for those Jews who had committed offenses against Christians under Persian rule. Benjamin accompanied Heraclius to Jerusalem in 629, and on the way the emperor succeeded in persuading him to be converted. He was baptized in the house of Eustathios, an influential Christian living in Neapolis (now Nablus). In Jerusalem the members of the Christian clergy influenced Heraclius to break the promise which he had given to the Jews through the intervention of Benjamin; the emperor condemned many of them to death, and prohibited the Jews from living in Jerusalem or within a three-mile radius of the city. There is no further mention of Benjamin in historical sources.

BIBLIOGRAPHY: M. Avi-Yonah, *Bi-Ymei Roma u-Bizantyon* (1952^2), 190, 200f.

[Michael Avi-Yonah]

BENJAMIN (Ben Jonah) OF TUDELA (second half of 12th century), the greatest medieval Jewish traveler. Nothing whatsoever is known about him except that which emerges from his famous *Sefer ha-Massa'ot* (*Book of Travels*). (See Map: Benjamin of Tudela's Travels.) He is frequently called "Rabbi" by non-Jewish writers, but there is no authority for this except that the conventional abbreviation "ר" is prefixed to his name in the Hebrew sources. From internal evidence the beginning of his journeys has been dated either about 1159 or about 1167, and he returned to Spain in 4933 (1172/73). His journeys lasted therefore a minimum of 5 and a maximum of 14 years. Since he spent at least a year on the last lap of his journey, from the time he left Egypt to the time of his return to Spain, the latter conjecture is more probable. In any case, he obviously had leisure to spend some time in the places he describes. The object of his journey is unknown, though it has been suggested that he was a gem-merchant – he more than once shows an interest in the coral trade. His *Book of Travels*, largely impersonal,

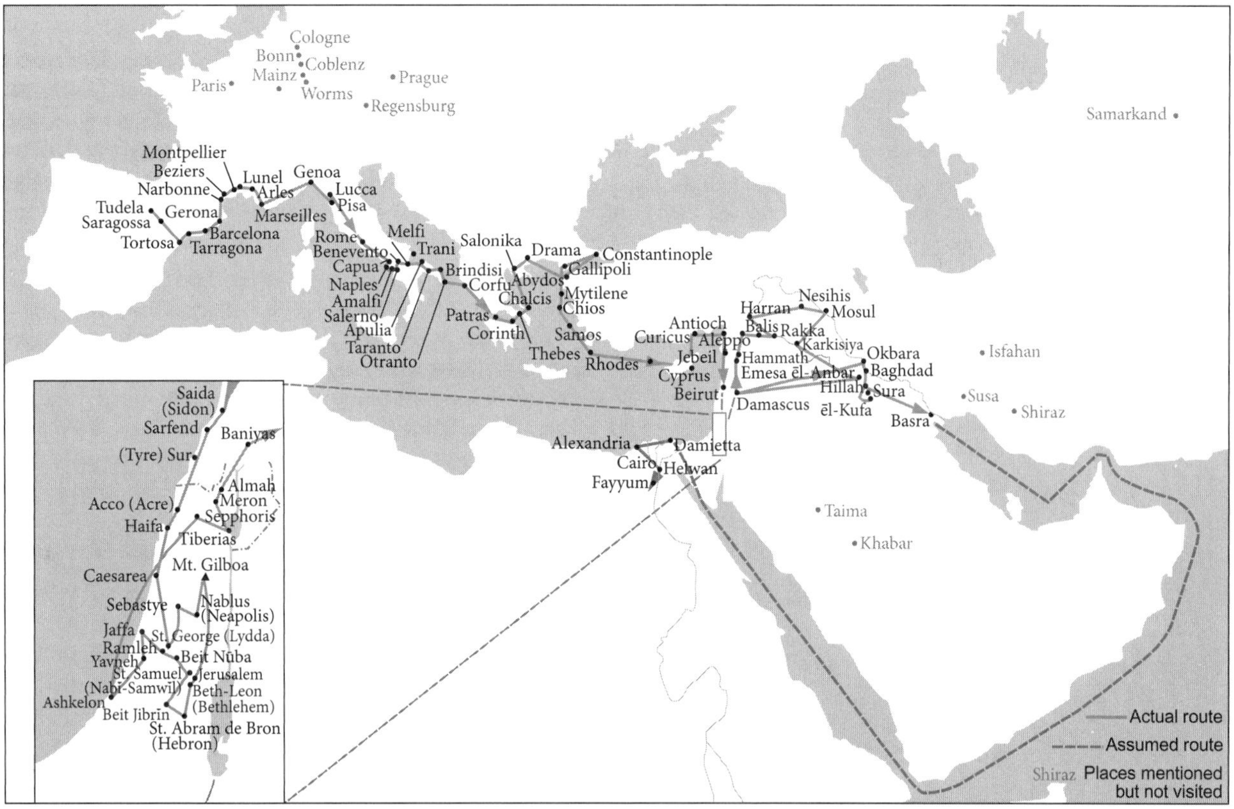

Map showing the travels of Benjamin of Tudela.

was based on the materials which the author noted down in the course of his travels. From Tudela in northern Spain Benjamin traveled by way of Saragossa and Tarragona to Barcelona, and thence via Gerona into Provence. He gave a fairly full account of the cities and especially the scholars of this region (Narbonne, Beziers, Montpellier, Lunel, Posquières, Arles), paying adequate attention to economic life. From Marseilles he went by sea to Genoa, and thence through Pisa to Rome. Here he must have spent a fairly long time, for he has a detailed description of the antiquities of the city. Many of these he, like other writers of the period, interpreted as being associated with Jewish history. He also writes about the Rome Jewish community and their relations with the much-opposed Pope Alexander III. It is clear therefore that he was there either shortly after the beginning of Alexander III's pontificate in September 1159, or in the brief period between November 1165 and July 1167, when this pope was again securely established in the city. From Rome, Benjamin went southward, traveling throughout southern Italy and describing, sometimes at length, conditions in many places in this region such as Salerno, Amalfi, Melfi, Benevento, Brindisi. He embarked at Otranto, sailing by way of Corfu to Arta, and then through Greece, where he noted the Jewish silkweavers in various places, and the agricultural colony at Crissa on Mt. Parnassus. He seems to have spent a particularly long time in Constantinople, where his lively picture, excelled by no other medieval traveler, is of great importance for knowledge of non-Jewish as well as Jewish conditions. Thence by sea through the Aegean archipelago (Mytilene, Chios, Samos, Rhodes) to Cyprus whence he crossed to the mainland, making his way south via Antioch, Sidon, Tyre, and Acre into Ereẓ Israel, at that time under the rule of the Crusaders. He traveled throughout the country, giving a detailed account of the Holy Places (which he calls in many instances by their French names: thus Hebron is St. Abram de Bron). It is a document of primary importance for the Palestinian history of this period. His record of the Samaritans, although highly disapproving, is characteristic. On the whole, his descriptions are far more objective than those of Christian pilgrims of the age, and he shows himself to peculiar advantage in his account of Jerusalem and its monuments. On leaving Tiberias he traveled north to Damascus, and thence through Aleppo and Mosul – it is not easy to trace his precise route – to Baghdad. His account of the Druze is the first in the non-Arabic literature. Of Baghdad he gives a longer account than of any other city on his itinerary. He draws a graphic picture of the court of the caliph and the charitable foundations of the city. He also tells us of the organization of the still-surviving talmudic academies and the glories and functions of the Exilarchate. He seems to have traveled widely about Mesopotamia and into Persia, though his account of conditions here contains much legendary material. A good deal of space is devoted to the story of the pseudo-Messiah

David *Alroy which was, until recently, almost the sole historical source about his career. It is not probable that he ventured beyond this area, but he speaks with some fantastic detail of China, India, and Ceylon. His personal impressions are obviously resumed in his admirable and detailed account of Egypt in general and its Jewish life in particular, especially in Cairo and Alexandria, which he visited on his return voyage. After this he reembarked for Sicily, his account of Palermo being both accurate and picturesque. From here he probably made his way back to Spain by sea, though the itinerary as we have it ends with an idealized picture of Jewish life in northern France and Germany, presumably based on hearsay. He reentered Spain, as is specifically stated, through Castile, having left it by way of Aragon.

There is no general account of the Mediterranean world or of the Middle East in this period which approaches that of Benjamin of Tudela in importance, whether for Jewish or for general history. Most of his record is concise and clear, presumably only a precis of the ampler material he brought back with him. He indicates the distances between the various towns he visited, tells who stood at the head of the Jewish communities, and who were the most notable scholars. He gives the number of Jews he found in each place, though it is not clear in many instances whether he is speaking of individuals or of householders, and in some cases such as Baghdad, the figures seem to be exaggerated. This may be due to the corrupt state of the text as we now have it. He notes economic conditions, describing the activity of merchants from various lands in Barcelona, Montpellier, and Alexandria, and speaking frequently of the occupations of the Jews – the dyers in Brindisi, the silkweavers in Thebes, the tanners in Constantinople, and the glassworkers in Aleppo and Tyre. He was deeply interested in Jewish scholarship, and his account of intellectual life in Provence and Baghdad is of singular importance, as is his characterization of the organization of synagogal life in Egypt. Sects, too, engage his attention, not only the Samaritans in Palestine, but also the Karaites in Constantinople and a heretical sect in Cyprus which he relates observed the Sabbath from dawn to dawn. His characterizations of non-Jewish life are vivid, and sometimes very important. He speaks of the internecine fighting at Genoa and Pisa, the constant wars between these two republics, the embarkation ports of the Crusaders in south Italy, the palaces and pageants of Constantinople and the wealth and the weaknesses of the Byzantine Empire. His somewhat highly colored account of the Assassins of Lebanon and of the Ghuzz Turks are primary historical sources, and he is said to be the first European of modern times to mention China by the present name. The importance of the work can be gauged from the fact that it has been translated into almost every language of Europe, and is used as a primary source-book by all medieval historians

BIBLIOGRAPHY: The *Itinerary of Benjamin of Tudela* was first published at Constantinople in 1543 and, according to a much-differing manuscript, at Ferrara in 1556. The standard editions are those edited by A. Asher, with very valuable notes and excursus and much additional material (London, 1840–41; reprinted New York, 1927, includes list of editions); and by M.N. Adler (London, 1907, with critical Heb. text and Eng. tr.; reprinted from JQR, vols. 16–18, 1904–06; reprinted 1964); there is also an edition by L. Gruenhut and M.N. Adler (Jerusalem-Frankfort, 1903–04) and another edition by H. Haddad (Baghdad, 1945). See also E. Carmoly, *Notice historique sur Benjamin de Tudèle* (1852), followed by J. Lilewel, *Examen géographique de ses voyages*; R. Luria, in: *Vessillo Israelitico*, 36 (1888), 56–58; Borchardt, in: JJLG, 16 (1924), 139–62; idem, in: *Journal of Roman Studies*, 26 (1936), 68–70; C.R. Beazley, *Dawn of Modern Geography* 2 (1897), 218–64; Andréadès, in: *Byzantinische Zeitschrift*, 30 (1929–30), 457–62; Reissner, in: *Zeitschrift fuer Religions-und Geistesgeschichte*, 6 (1954), 151–5; E. García de Herreros, *Quatre voyageurs espagnols à Alexandrie d'Egypte* (1923). Most works dealing with the history of the Jews in Italy, Palestine, Byzantium, Mesopotamia, and the Middle East in the 12th and 13th centuries use and comment upon Benjamin's material.

[Cecil Roth]

BENJAMIN ZE'EV BEN MATTATHIAS OF ARTA (early 16th century), *dayyan* and halakhist. He first engaged in business but later became a member of the *bet din* at Arta (Epirus). After living at Larissa (1528) and Corfu (1530), Benjamin Ze'ev settled in Venice; but toward the end of his life returned to Arta (1538). As a result of his lenient decisions on an *agunah*, Benjamin Ze'ev was severely criticized by David ha-Kohen, Joseph Taitaẓak, and others. He replied in his *Binyamin Ze'ev*, containing 450 legal decisions and responsa, completed in 1534 at Venice, where it was published five years later. It constitutes an important source for a knowledge of the economic conditions and religious life of the Jews of Greece, Turkey, and Asia Minor. His legal decisions reflect his independence in halakhic matters, which led to the opposition of German and Italian rabbis to his book. He was hostile to Marranos who willingly "follow the laws of the Gentiles and transgress all the commandments of the Torah," and stated that "they are less than the Gentiles" (*Binyamin Ze'ev*, 203, end). Contemporaries, such as Isaac Gershon of Venice and David ha-Kohen, questioned his authority in legal decisions; while Solomon Luria (*Yam shel Shelomo*, BK 78) expressly states that "no one should follow Benjamin Ze'ev, unless he has made a thorough study of the relevant talmudic passages and the halakhic authorities." Several prominent rabbis, among them the rabbis of Salonika, agreed with Benjamin. Following the intensification of the dispute between Benjamin and his opponents at Arta (1530), the views of the Italian rabbis were sought by both sides. Some, including Azriel Diena (Dayyena), favored Benjamin Ze'ev's dismissal from the rabbinate. The dispute continued until 1532, but Benjamin nevertheless continued as rabbi at Arta after that date. His son Mattathias, who died in 1541, wrote a poem to mark the completion of his father's book (*Binyamin Ze'ev*, 573a).

BIBLIOGRAPHY: Graetz, Gesch, 8 (c. 1900⁴), 70, 443–7; Bruell, Jahrbuecher, 1 (1874), 88–90; Rosanes, Togarmah, 1 (1930), 114, 155–8; Assaf, in: KS, 15 (1938/39), 113–9.

[Yehoshua Horowitz]

BEN KALBA SAVU'A (1st century C.E.), according to tradition he was a wealthy man of Jerusalem, who was renowned for his generosity. The Bavli relates that during the Roman siege of Jerusalem, he and his two wealthy friends, Nakdimon b. Guryon and Ben Ẓiẓit ha-Kassat, provided food and other necessities for the inhabitants over a number of years, until the zealots set fire to their stores, in an attempt to force the people to make a desperate effort to break the siege (Git. 56a). Josephus mentions the burning of "provisions that would have sufficed … for a long siege," although he does not mention Ben Kalba Savu'a or his associates (Wars, 5:25). The Bavli also relates that Rachel, Ben Kalba Savu'a's daughter, married R. *Akiva, who in his youth had been Ben Kalba Savu'a's shepherd. This was against the wishes of her father, who disinherited them. When Akiva had become famous as a great scholar, his father-in-law was reconciled to him and bequeathed him half of his wealth (Ket. 62b–63a; Ned. 50a). Regarding the historicity of these traditions, see S. Friedman, "A Good Story Deserves Retelling: The Unfolding of the Akiva Legend."

BIBLIOGRAPHY: Hyman, Toledot, 274; Z. Vilnay, *Maẓẓevot Kodesh be-Ereẓ Yisrael* (1963), 281–5: **ADD. BIBLIOGRAPHY:** S. Friedman, in: JSIJ, 3 (2004), 1–39.

[Zvi Kaplan]

BEN-KIKI (Quiqui), Moroccan family. REUBEN (late 17th and 18th century) participated in 1719 in negotiations with Great Britain; in 1721 he assisted Ibn Attar, the Moroccan royal treasurer, in concluding a peace treaty with Great Britain. After the death of the king of Morocco, Ahmad al-Dhahabi, in 1729, he became one of the ministers of the new king, Abdullah. His brother ELEAZAR had been appointed ambassador to Holland by Ahmad al-Dhahabi to take charge of the peace talks, and was in Gibraltar, on his way to Holland, when the king died. He was not allowed to continue his journey, nor to return to his country until 1730. After Reuben was appointed a minister in Morocco, he succeeded in sending his brother to Holland, but the latter was unable to negotiate a treaty.

BIBLIOGRAPHY: Hirschberg, Afrikah, 260, 269–71, 280; idem, in: *Essays… I. Brodie* (1967), 161–2, 164.

[Abraham David]

BENKOW, JO (**Josef Elias**; 1924–), Norwegian politician. Born in Trondheim, he was a photographer by profession like his father and grandfather. Towards the end of the 1920s the family settled in Bærum, a municipality near Oslo. In World War II he and other male members of his family (his father, brother, and uncle) succeeded in fleeing to Sweden. The female members of his family were deported to Auschwitz, where they were killed on arrival. In March 1944 he left Sweden for service in the Norwegian Air Force in England and Canada.

In the 1950s his political interests brought him posts in the liberal conservative party Høyre, the second-largest political party. He was elected a member of the Bærum local council in 1959 and the first Jewish-born member of the Storting (the Norwegian parliament) in 1965. He was the vice chairman of Høyre from 1973 to 1980 and the chairman from 1980 to 1984. He was then elected president of the Storting, a post he held until 1993. His Jewish connection has been expressed through his interest for Israel (e.g., as a speaker) and his involvement in the cause of Soviet Jewry. After leaving his post at the Storting he worked extensively to promote human rights and combat antisemitism and racism. From 1983 to 1984 he served as president of the Nordic Council. He was also the president of the International Helsinki Federation for Human Rights from 1993 to 1998. He spent two years (1994–1995) as visiting professor at Boston University and in 2000–04 he was a judge on the Oslo Conciliation Board. In honor of his contribution to society Benkow received titles and medals from the Norwegian King, the Finnish president, and the Austrian president.

In 1985 Benkow published his autobiography *Fra synagogen til Løvebakken* ("From the Synagogue to Lion Hill," a popular name for the Storting), which was a great success, over 240.000 copies being sold. In it, he describes his childhood and youth, his Jewish family and Jewish connections, his opinions concerning religious faith and absence of faith and tells about his political life. He also writes about general prejudices and touches on Jewish history (the history of his own family), Jewish customs, discrimination against Jews in the Soviet Union, and tells about his relations with Israel ("a turning point in Jewish self-understanding," as he says). He also published *Folkevalgt* ("Popularly Elected," 1988), an account of his life in parliament; *Vendepunkt – 9. april i vår bevissthet* ("Turning Point – April 9th in Our Consciousness"), written together with Prof. Ole Christian Grimnes, about the German occupation of Norway in 1940–45 and its aftermath; *Olav – Menneske og monark* ("Olaf – Human Being and Sovereign," 1991), a biography of the late king Olaf V; *Det ellevte bud* ("The Eleventh Commandment," 1994), a polemic directed against racisim; and *Hundre år med konge og folk* ("A Hundred Years with King and People," 1998), an historical account of the 20th century in Norway. Through his objectivity, command of language, and calm and dignified manner, Benkow won widespread respect and recognition.

[Oskar Mendelsohn / Lynn Feinberg (2nd ed.)]

BEN LA'ANAH (Heb. בֶּן לַעֲנָה), name of the author of an unknown apocryphal work. The Jerusalem Talmud (Sanh. 10:1, 28a), includes the book of Ben La'anah among the works forbidden to be read (cf. Eccles. R. 12:12 where the reading is Ben Tiglah). However, except for a reference by David Messer Leon in the 16th century to an apocryphal work called *Ben Ya'anah* (בֶּן יַעֲנָה), which may be identical with Ben La'anah, nothing is known about the book or the author. Various scholars have tried to identify him either with the pagan philosopher Apollonius of Tyana (M. Joel), or with the author of a collection of fox fables *Mishlei Shu'alim* (J. Fuerst), but none of these theories is regarded as satisfactory.

BIBLIOGRAPHY: Perles, in: REJ, 3 (1881), 116–8; Kaufmann, *ibid.*, 4 (1882), 161; Klein, in: *Leshonenu*, 1 (1928/29), 340, 344.

BEN MEIR, AARON (early tenth century), scholar and *rosh yeshivah* in Ereẓ Israel. Aaron lived apparently in *Ramleh, and traced his descent to the former *nesi'im* ("patriarchs") of Palestinian Jewry. His relations with the *Karaites in Palestine were extremely strained. In about 920 he went to Baghdad to complain to the central authorities of the malicious Karaite attacks upon the Rabbanites. After his return, Aaron conceived the idea of strengthening the religious hegemony of Palestine, which had been weakened by the Babylonian yeshivot. To achieve this, Aaron attempted to restore to the Palestinians the sole authority to fix the calendar, as they had had until the middle of the ninth century. On Hoshana Rabba 921 he proclaimed on the Mount of Olives to all communities of Palestine and of the Diaspora that the months of Marḥeshvan and Kislev would be defective, i.e., consisting of only 29 days. As a result, Passover of 922 would fall on Sunday and the New Year of 922 would fall on a Tuesday instead of on the following Thursday as it would have done were these months to contain the full 30 days (see *Calendar).

This proclamation aroused the opposition of several scholars, notably of *Saadiah, who was on his way to Baghdad. The latter tried repeatedly to convince Aaron that there was no justification for opposing the Babylonian calendar calculations. Aaron stood his ground, however, and gave publicity to his proclamation. Fearing that the Jewish festivals might be celebrated at different times in different places, Saadiah addressed himself to the Diaspora communities warning them against acceptance of Aaron's proclamation, but he could not prevent a split. In 922 the Jews of Palestine, and, apparently, also those of Egypt, celebrated Passover two days before the Jews of Babylonia, fixing also the date of the following Rosh Ha-Shanah accordingly. This split caused considerable agitation throughout Jewry. References to it are to be found even in Syriac literature. Thus, the Syrian, Elias of Nisibis, wrote: "The year 309 [of the Hijra] began on the Sabbath, Iyyar 12, 1232 of the Seleucid era; in that year dissension broke out between the Jews of the West [Palestine] and those of the East [Babylon] with regard to the calculation of their holidays. The former fixed the New Year on a Tuesday and the latter on a Thursday" (Baethgen, *Fragmente syrischer und arabischer Historiker* (Leipzig, 1884), 84). The Karaite Sahl b. Maẓli'aḥ sought to prove from this controversy that the Rabbanite calendar calculations were altogether groundless.

The controversy between Aaron and his opponents on this issue continued for some time thereafter, ending in Aaron's defeat, and with it the failure of the attempt to strengthen the sole religious authority of the Palestinian scholars.

BIBLIOGRAPHY: H. Malter, *Saadia Gaon* (Eng., 1921), 69–88, 409–19; Mann, Egypt, 1 (1920), 50–55, 61–66; 2 (1922), 49–57; Mann, Texts, 2 (1935), index; American Academy for Jewish Research, *Saadia Anniversary Volume* (1943), index; Abramson, Merkazim, 29 33; H.J. Bornstein, *Maḥaloket Rav Sa'adyah Ga'on u-Ven Me'ir* (1904), printed also in *Sefer ha-Yovel… N. Sokolow* (1904), 19–189.

[*Encyclopaedia Hebraica*]

BENN (Benzion Rabinovich; 1905–1989), painter and graphic artist. Benn was born in Bialystok, Poland, and finished the Hebrew gymnasium there, where he later started his education in art at the private studios of local artists. He also studied at the Academy of Arts in Warsaw. He made his debut in 1927 with his first solo exhibition, shown first in Białystok and then in Warsaw. During this period, he designed the typography for collections of Yiddish poetry. In Białystok, his native town, he became a leading figure in local cultural life. He was among the founders of the modernist group "3F" ("Forma-Farba-Faktura"), where most of the members were Jewish artists. In 1928, he organized the first Autumn Salon for Białystok and Vilna artists. In 1926–29, he designed the scenery for the performances of several Yiddish theater companies in Białystok. In 1929, the Białystok municipality awarded him a scholarship for a trip to Paris. On the eve of his departure, Benn arranged a "farewell" solo exhibition that was later shown in Warsaw with the assistance of the Jewish Society for Encouragement of Artists. In Paris, he studied with Fernand Leger. From 1932, Benn regularly exhibited in Paris art salons. His works were highly praised by critics and won public recognition. Six one-man shows in the 1930s at private art galleries in Paris are yet another indication of his success. During this period, he was also active in book design. During the German occupation of France, Benn went into hiding. However, not long before the end of the occupation, he was finally seized by the Gestapo and deported to the Drancy concentration camp. By sheer luck, he not only survived but also escaped further deportation to Auschwitz. In 1945, Benn returned to Paris. In the post-war years, having rejected the cubist and expressionistic techniques that had so strongly attracted him in the 1920s and 1930s, Benn crystallized his individual manner based on an organic combination of "metaphysical painting" techniques and surrealism. From the 1950s through the 1970s, while mainly active in painting, he also engaged in book design and, among other works in this field, executed a series of illustrations for The Song of Songs (1950, 1974) and other books of the Bible (1948, 1954, 1971), as well as for an edition of "*Ḥad Gadya*" (1956). In these years, he had numerous one-man shows in France and other West European countries as well as in Canada and Israel.

BIBLIOGRAPHY: P. Learsin, "Ben-Tsiyon Rabinovitsh," in: *Illustrierte Voch* (Warsaw), 16, 98 (1928), 14; C. Aronson, *Scenes et visages de Montparnasse* (1963), 561–65; S. Roi, *Benn* (Yid., 1967); *Jubilé du peintre Benn* (Paris, 1975); J. Malinowski. *Malarstwo i rzeźba Żydow Polskich w XIX i XX wieku* (2000), 398.

[Hillel Kazovsky (2nd ed.)]

BENN, BEN (Benjamin Rosenberg; 1884–1983), U.S. painter. Benn was born in Russia and immigrated to New York with his family in 1889. After studying drawing in high school, he attended the National Academy of Design in New York City from 1904 to 1908, where he received traditional art training with Jewish classmates Benjamin *Kopman and William *Zorach. His first exhibition, "Oils by Eight American Artists," showed in New York at the Artist's Gallery. A 1915 El Greco exhibition at the Knoedler Gallery made an important impact on Benn, after which time he began to gently distort the human figure and employ a more painterly approach. Benn participated in the *Forum Exhibition of Modern American Painters* in 1916, organized by avant-garde artists of the period, including Alfred *Steiglitz. Although at times his palette would darken, throughout his career Benn painted simplified portraits, stilllifes, and landscapes, influenced by the vibrant and colorful fauvist tendencies of Henri Matisse and the vigorous brushstroke of Chaim *Soutine. He had several one-man shows, notably an exhibition at the Jewish Museum in 1965. His works can be found in the permanent collections of the Whitney Museum of American Art and the Metropolitan Museum of Art.

BIBLIOGRAPHY: B. Benn, *Ben Benn: An American Painter, 1884–1983* (1983); S. Geist, "Ben Benn," in: *Art Digest*, 28 (Oct. 1953): 15, 25–28.

[Samantha Baskind (2nd ed.)]

BEN-NAPHTALI, MOSES (Or Jacob) BEN DAVID, masorete. He is assumed to have been a contemporary of Aaron b. Moses *Ben-Asher, who dates from the ninth or tenth century C.E., and an inhabitant of Tiberias. Although nothing about him is known, except his name, there survives a list of some 850 minor differences from the reading of Ben Asher in vowels and accents in the Hebrew Bible. The list notes only eight variants in the consonantal text. The differences in vocalization and accents, especially as recorded by Mishael b. Uzziel (10th–11th centuries) with considerable deviations in detail in the different traditions (published by L. Lipschuetz), reveal no systematic features, and may be nothing but a gathering of traditional variants. Penkower (in bibliography) argues that the high level of agreement proves that Ben-Naphtali and Ben-Asher do not represent two rival schools regarding the biblical text, but rather the contrary. Some scholars have observed that the very name Ben-Naphtali is suspect: Naphtali in the Bible is the son of Jacob born after Asher, and the series "Ben-Asher, Ben-Naphtali" resembles the standard series of random names, "Reuben, Simeon." In Western and Central Asia in that period it was a common feature to systematize differences by assigning them to two "schools," only one of which existed. The closest parallel, as shown by Gotthold *Weil, is the invention of a Kufan School of Arabic grammar as a foil for the Basrian School.

There are, indeed, a number of Bible manuscripts with a type of Tiberian vocalization rather different from that of the Ben-Asher school (which itself is not entirely monolithic), but the slight similarity these manuscripts share with some variant readings ascribed to Ben-Naphtali in Mishael's list is not sufficient to substantiate the claim that they are representative of the Ben-Asher School.

See also: *Masorah.

BIBLIOGRAPHY: C.D. Ginsburg, *The Massorah* (1880–1905); idem, *Introduction to the Massoretico-Critical Edition of the Hebrew Bible* (1897), 241–86; Mann, Egypt, 2 (1922), 43–49; Edelmann, in: P. Kahle, *Masoreten des Westens*, 2 (1930), 45–68; idem, *The Cairo Geniza* (1947), 67–76; L. Lipschuetz, in: *Textus*, 2 (1962), Heb. pt. 3–58; 4 (1964), 1–29; Morag, in: JSS, 4 (1959), 216–37; idem, *The Vocalization Systems of Arabic, Hebrew, and Aramaic* (1962), 34, 38–41; idem, in: *Leshonenu*, 29 (1965), 203–9; G. Weil (ed.), *Abu'l-Barakāt ibn al-Anbāri, Die grammatischen Streitfragen der Basrer und Kufer* (1913), 48–93. **ADD. BIBLIOGRAPHY:** J. Penkower, in: DBI I, 119–20.

[Chaim M. Rabin]

BEN-NATAN, ASHER (1921–), Israeli diplomat. Ben-Natan was born in Vienna and immigrated to Ereẓ Israel as an "illegal" immigrant in 1938. He was one of the founders of the group which established kibbutz *Dobrath (Dovrat). In 1944 Ben-Natan joined the Aliyah Department of the Jewish Agency and was delegated to the British Department, which, in liaison with the Allied Forces, specialized in the interrogation of Nazi war criminals and in compiling lists of them and their crimes. In October of that year he was transferred to Vienna, where he was in charge of the *Beriḥah movement in Austria, holding the position until 1947. During this period he established a special group to search for war criminals. In 1947 Ben-Natan was a special assistant to David Ben-Gurion and in 1948 was appointed chief of special operations in the Political Department of the Israel Ministry for Foreign Affairs. From 1951 to 1953 he studied at the Institute of Higher International Studies in Geneva, and in 1956 was appointed special delegate of the Ministry of Defense for Europe, taking up the post in Paris in 1957. From 1960 to 1965 he served as director general of the Ministry of Defense and from 1965 to 1969 was first Israel ambassador to the Federal Republic of Germany. In 1970 he was appointed Israel ambassador to France. Ben-Natan was a candidate for mayor of Tel Aviv in Nov. 1978 but was not elected.

BEN-NER, YITZHAK (1937–), Israeli writer. Born in Kefar Yehoshua, Ben-Ner studied literature and drama at Tel Aviv University before spending a couple of years in New York. His first novel, *Ha-Ish mi-Sham* (1967; *The Man from There*, 1970), tells of a young Israeli soldier who is trapped in a small Egyptian border town. An Egyptian doctor protects and hides him in his fiancée's house. An ambiguous relationship develops, full of tension and surprises. The novel, which gained Ben-Ner much acclaim, was followed by prose works – novels and collections of stories – as well as by books for children (e.g. *Kishona*, 1977; *Jeans*,1991), film and television scripts, and plays (e.g., the monodrama *David August*, 1983, *Ta'atuon*, performed at the Cameri Theatre in 1990, and *Uri Muri*, performed there in 1999). The collection *Sheki'ah Kafrit* (1976; *Rustic Sunset*, 1997) comprises eight short stories, tales of childhood and maturity, depicting urban life in Israel and looking critically at the seemingly heroic officers of the Israeli army. *Malakhim Ba'im* ("The Angels Are Coming," 1987) is a sophisticated parody on contemporary Israeli society through the story of David Halperin, a hedonistic Tel Aviv bachelor.

Boker shel Shotim ("Morning of Fools," 1992) is structured as a series of monologues by the mentally retarded Uzai, who observes life around him in his moshavah; the monologue technique, one of the characteristics of Ben-Ner's prose, is used also in the four stories entitled *Ta'atu'on*, dealing mostly with soldiers torn between duty and the desire for self-fulfillment. *Mitḥam Oyev* ("Enemy Territory," 1997) was written in the wake of Yitzhak Rabin's murder: A bodyguard of the assassinated prime minister seeks to assuage his guilt by penetrating a secret underground organization in the West Bank. As in most of his works, Ben-Ner introduced political and moral issues perturbing Israeli society. *Ir Miklat* ("City of Refuge," 2000) is yet again a cruel and barbed portrait of contemporary society, with seven monologues representing different aspects of life in a troubled, decadent Tel Aviv. Ben-Ner is also known for his radio and television work. He was awarded the prestigious Agnon Prize and the Bernstein Prize.

BIBLIOGRAPHY: S. Brosh, *Ke-Mikhvat Esh: Iyun bi-Yeẓirot Ben-Ner* (1979); H. Barzel, *Megamot be-Sipporet ha-Hoveh: Y. Ben-Ner* (1979); A. Karinski, *Sheki'ah Kafrit* (1984); G. Shaked, *Ha-Sipporet ha-Ivrit*, 5 (1998), 410–44; R. Furstenberg, "After the Rain," in: *Modern Hebrew Literature* 6, 1–2 (1980), 68–71; R. Furstenberg, "Here and Now: Ben Ner's *A Distant Land*," in *Modern Hebrew Literature* 7, 1–2 (1981/82), 78–81; Y. Mazor, "*Ha-Makom bo ha-Sipporet Meshikah la-Shirah*," in: *Moznayim* 56, 6 (1983), 46–51; Y. Berlovitz, in: *Davar* (Sept. 2, 1983); R.L. Kofman, "In Egypt, in Exile: Studies in Two Works by Ben Ner," in: *Hebrew Studies* 24 (1983), 107–19; A. Lipsker, in: *Alei Si'aḥ* 27–28 (1990), 143–51; N. Gertz, "Amos Oz and Izhak Ben Ner: The Image of Woman in Literary Works and as Transvalued in Film Adaptations," in: *Israeli Writers Consider the "Outsider"* (1993), 57–81; G. Morahg, "Subverting Dystopia: Ben Ner's Fiction of the Future," in: *Prooftexts* 13, 3 (1993), 269–87; L. Yudkin, "Y. Ben Ner, Israeli Novelist," in: *Jewish Book Annual* 51 (1993), 71–81; Y. Zerubavel, "Revisiting the Pioneer Past," in: *Hebrew Studies* 41 (2000), 209–24.

[Anat Feinberg (2nd ed.)]

BENNETT, ARCHIE (**Aaron Baehr**; 1891–1980), Canadian community leader. Bennett was born in Malech in the Brest-Litovsk district of Belorussia and was taken to Canada as a child. He was raised in Kingston, Ontario, where he became co-owner of a large real estate and building firm. In the summer of 1912 Bennett served as editor of the *Canadian Jewish Times* in Montreal. He began writing in Yiddish in that same year for the *Keneder Adler*. At this time in Montreal he became part of the circle of young intellectuals around Reuben *Brainin and wrote for the latter's short-lived *Der Veg* in 1914. In 1914 he settled in Toronto. In 1919 he was a delegate to the first Canadian Jewish Congress in Montreal, where he delivered a paper on nationality minority rights. In 1922 Bennett reorganized the structure of the Zionist movement in Ontario and instituted the province's first Keren Hayesod campaign. Bennett, in that same year, began writing for the *Canadian Jewish Review*, then published in Toronto. He helped establish the Menorah Society at the University of Toronto and from 1922 to 1924 was a faculty adviser to the Jewish students. In 1933–34 he led in the reorganization of the Canadian Jewish Congress and in the World War II years was president of its central region, Ontario, active in refugee aid, war efforts, and community relations. Writing for the Jewish press was Bennett's lifelong avocation. In 1914 he began writing editorials for the *Canadian Jewish Chronicle* which absorbed the *Canadian Jewish Times*. During the 1930s and until the early 1940s he wrote regular columns for the *Canadian Jewish Review*; and from the mid-1940s in the *Jewish Standard*.

[Ben G. Kayfetz]

BENNETT, AVIE J. (1928–), Canadian property developer; best known as a philanthropist, dedicated supporter of the arts, and former owner of several Canadian publishing companies, foremost among them McClelland & Stewart of Toronto. Described as a "Maecenas with the courage of his convictions and the money to back them up" (MacSkimming, 314), Bennett worked tirelessly and creatively throughout his career to enrich the cultural landscape of Canada.

As a business pioneer, Bennett made his fortune as a developer of shopping malls, acting as chairman and president of First Plazas Inc., the successful commercial real estate company that has helped finance many of Bennett's ventures in the arts.

In January 1986, Bennett purchased McClelland & Stewart from the charismatic Jack McClelland, whose father had founded the company together with his colleague Frederick Goodchild in 1906. Following years of financial difficulty, with M&S on the brink of bankruptcy, Bennett stepped in to rescue a company that had become known as "the Canadian publishers." Bennett's infusion of cash was a stabilizing force, and his energy and vision ensured M&S's standing as a premier publisher of Canadian trade titles.

While at the helm of M&S, Bennett acquired Hurtig Publishers of Edmonton (in 1991); Tundra Books of Montreal (1995); and Macfarlane Walter & Ross of Toronto (1999). With Penguin Canada, he created Canbook, a joint warehouse and distribution center. In 2000, in an unprecedented move, Bennett donated 75 percent of M&S to the University of Toronto. As he proclaimed, "[t]o achieve the survival of one great Canadian institution, I have given it into the care of another great Canadian institution" (MacSkimming, 357). He sold the remaining 25 percent of the company to Random House of Canada. Bennett remains chairman of the board of M&S.

Bennett was a board member of many arts organizations in Canada. In 2005, he was vice chairman of the Historica Foundation and co-chair of the Canadian Democratic and Corporate Accountability Commission. He was made Officer of the Order of Ontario in 1996 and Officer of the Order of Canada in 1997. From May 1998 to June 2004, Bennett served as chancellor of York University in Toronto.

BIBLIOGRAPHY: R. MacSkimming, *The Perilous Trade: Publishing Canada's Writers* (2003).

[Ruth Panofsky (2nd ed.)]

BENNETT, MICHAEL (1943–1987), U.S. producer, writer, choreographer, director, performer. Michael Bennett DiFiglia, whose mother was Jewish, was born in Buffalo, N.Y., and became the most influential director and choreographer of his generation as the creator in 1975 of *A Chorus Line*, once the longest-running show in Broadway history. In a career that spanned more than two decades, he received Tony Award nominations for every musical with which he was associated, and won eight.

A former chorus dancer, Bennett's talent emerged in the 1970s, first in his collaborations with Hal *Prince and then on his own as Broadway and Off Broadway director, choreographer, and producer. The dances in *Company, Follies, A Chorus Line, Ballroom,* and *Dreamgirls* flowed from the action of the plays and the motivations of their characters, and that seamlessness marked Bennett's work.

Bennett had started dance lessons at three and by 12 he was versed in tap, ballet, modern, and folk dancing. Just before he was to graduate from high school, he joined a company of *West Side Story* and spent a year in Europe with the show. When the tour ended, he went to New York and danced in the choruses of *Subways Are for Sleeping, Here's Love*, and *Bajour*. He participated in several commercial failures but with Neil *Simon's *Promises, Promises*, in 1968, his career took off. It was also his first work with Donna McKechnie, a dancer to whom he was briefly married and who became a noted actress and choreographer after stopping the show in *A Chorus Line*. In 1969 Bennett choreographed Andre *Previn and Alan Jay *Lerner's musical *Coco*, starring Katharine Hepburn as the fashion designer Coco Chanel. The play ran for more than 300 performances but was a commercial failure. By 1970, Bennett was collaborating with Prince on Stephen *Sondheim and George Furth's *Company*, which became a signature musical of the decade. A year later, Bennett won the first of his two Tony Awards, as choreographer and co-director, with Prince, of Sondheim and James Goldman's *Follies*, a homage to the Ziegfeld era and the first backstage musical Bennett came to be identified with. As one of Broadway's most celebrated show doctors, he took over the Cy *Coleman–Dorothy *Fields musical *Seesaw* and changed every element, from the choreography to the sets, costumes, and lighting. The show opened in 1973 and won for Bennett his second choreography Tony.

In 1974 Bennett held a late-night session with a group of dancers with whom he had worked, talking about the experience of being a Broadway gypsy. Discerning the potential of a show about Broadway's most-overworked and least heralded performers, Bennett persuaded Joseph *Papp, the theatrical Pied Piper, to finance a workshop to develop the material. Bennett hired Marvin *Hamlisch to compose the music, Ed Kleban to write the lyrics, and James Kirkwood and Nicholas Dante to write the book. After two five-week workshops at Papp's Public Theater, the show, *A Chorus Line*, inaugurated Lincoln Center's Newman Theater and moved to the Shubert Theater on Broadway a few months later. The show won nine Tony Awards, including best direction and choreography for Bennett and best musical, as well as the Pulitzer Prize, which Bennett shared, and the New York Drama Critics Circle award. The final number in *A Chorus Line*, "One," became Bennett's signature: a company of disparate individuals emerging into a triumphant whole.

In 1981 Bennett won wide acclaim for *Dreamgirls*, a musical based loosely on the careers of the Supremes, a group of black women singers. "When Broadway history is being made, you can feel it," wrote Frank Rich, chief theater critic of the *New York Times*. "What you feel is a seismic jolt that sends the audience, as one, right out of its wits. Broadway history was made at the end of Michael Bennett's beautiful and heartbreaking new musical."

Bennett's death at 44 was attributed to lymphoma, a form of cancer, as a result of AIDS.

[Stewart Kampel (2nd ed.)]

BENNETT, SALOMON YOM TOV (1761–1838), English engraver and writer. Bennett was born in Polotsk, Belorussia. In 1792 he went to study in Copenhagen. Three years later he moved to Berlin, where he was admitted to the Royal Academy and engraved portraits of Frederick the Great, the king and queen of Prussia, and others. In 1799 he settled in London. However, as his standard of religious observance was open to criticism he found himself cold-shouldered in official circles. He began to attack the chief rabbi, Solomon *Hirschel, in books and pamphlets. Bennett produced a series of polemical, theological, and exegetical works, including: *The Constancy of Israel* (1809); *Discourse on Sacrifice* (1815); *The Temple of Ezekiel* (1824); *The Molten Sea* (1824); *Critical Remarks on the Authorized Versions of the Old Testament* (1824); and *A Theological and Critical Treatise on the Primogeniture and Integrity of the Holy Language* (1835). He began to prepare a new English translation of the Bible of which only the first two parts, comprising Genesis chs. 1–41, appeared (1841). As a frontispiece to the *Temple of Ezekiel* Bennett included an engraved portrait of himself painted by another artist. The work is illustrated by a fine and erudite reconstruction of the general view and ground plan of the Temple.

BIBLIOGRAPHY: Barnett, in: JHSET, 17 (1951–52), 91–111; S. Kirschstein, *Juedische Graphiker aus der Zeit von 1625–1825* (1918), 15–27; Roth, Mag Bibl, index; A. Barnett, *The Western Synagogue Through Two Centuries* (1961), 51–54; Roth, Art, 532–3. **ADD. BIBLIOGRAPHY:** Katz, England, 328–29.

BENNY, JACK (formerly **Benny Kubelsky**; 1894–1974), U.S. vaudeville, film, radio, and television entertainer. Benny won virtually every award in the entertainment industry, including an Emmy as television's outstanding comedian. Benny portrayed an unyielding skinflint, an atrocious fiddler, and a demanding boss. A steady cast of characters, including his wife, Mary Livingstone (née Sadye Marks, 1909–1983), and valet, Rochester (Eddie Anderson), ran through his shows.

Born in Chicago, Illinois, Benny was raised in Waukegan, a place he made reference to during his entire career. Although there is now a school named after him in Waukegan (Jack Benny Junior High School), Benny's education consisted of one term at Central High School. He worked in his father's haberdashery shop, then at age 16 he got a job playing violin in the pit of the town's Barrison Theater. After spending several years on the road with various partners in piano-violin duos he joined the Navy, where his talent for stand-up comedy was revealed. After his naval stint he created a solo vaudeville act, which ultimately got him noticed by the film industry. In 1928 he appeared in the short film *Bright Moments* and in 1929 headlined in the films *Hollywood Revue of 1929* and *Chasing Rainbows,* and in *Medicine Man* (1930). With this national exposure in film, Benny became a star.

In 1932 Benny hit the radio waves, featured on his friend Ed Sullivan's talk show. Two months later, Benny was the host of his own radio program. Over the next eight years, he became one of the biggest names in radio with his weekly half-hour comedy show. According to Benny, comedy was based on seven principles: the joke, exaggeration, ridicule, ignorance, surprise, the pun, and the comic situation. Fine-tuning those principles as he went along, Benny added a regular cast to his show. In addition to Rochester and his wife, Mary, they included Phil Harris, Dennis Day, and Don Wilson.

In 1950 Benny advanced to television. The Jack Benny Show entertained 18 million viewers for 15 years. Some of the classic recurring themes were his stinginess, his vanity about his supposed age of 39, a basement vault where he kept all his money, and a feigned ineptness at playing the violin. Added to Benny's famous pregnant pause and exasperated "Well!" were a mincing walk, an affected hand to the cheek, and a sustained look of disbelief when confronted by a problem. During that time he starred in several films as well: *The Big Broadcast of 1937*, *Buck Benny Rides Again* (1940), *Love Thy Neighbor* (1940), *Charley's Aunt* (1941), *To Be or Not to Be* (1942), and *Who Was That Lady?* (1962). When his TV show ended in 1965, the perennial 39-year-old was 71. But he did not retire from his beloved show business. He appeared in the films: *It's a Mad, Mad, Mad, Mad World* (1967), *A Guide for the Married Man* (1967), and *The Man* (1972). He returned to NBC once a year to do a TV special, performed with symphonies, and made numerous live appearances in theaters in the U.S. and abroad.

Although the character he portrayed on radio and tv was as miserly as they come, the real Jack Benny was extremely generous. And at age 60, he began to take violin lessons to perfect his craft. He played benefit concerts to sell-out audiences to raise money for musicians and concert halls. In 1961 his benefit concert helped save New York's Carnegie Hall from being demolished. In addition, he raised $20,000 for the construction of a music center near Waukegan, and $838,000 for a conservatory at the University of Hartford.

In 1974, his final year, he was working on his third TV Farewell Special for NBC and preparing for his first starring role in a film in 30 years. He was to co-star with Walter Matthau in the comedy *The Sunshine Boys*. However, when the movie was completed, Benny's best friend George Burns played the part in his place. In 1989 Jack Benny was inducted into the Radio Hall of Fame. With his daughter, Joan, he co-wrote his memoirs, entitled *Sunday Nights at Seven*, which was published posthumously in 1990.

BIBLIOGRAPHY: I. Fein, *Jack Benny: An Intimate Biography* (1976); M. Josefsberg, *The Jack Benny Show* (1977).

[Ruth Beloff (2nd ed.)]

°**BENOÎT, PIERRE-MARIE** (1895–1990), French priest and Righteous Among the Nations. Born Pierre Péteul, in Bourg d'Iré (Marne-et-Loire), France, to a family of flour millers, Benoît entered the Capuchin-Franciscan order in 1913. After a tour of duty in the French army during World War I, where he was wounded, he took up theological studies, earning a doctorate in theology and teaching at the Capuchin college in Rome. With Italy's entry into World War II in June 1940, he was sent back to France, and took up residence at the Capuchin convent in Marseilles, at 51 Croix-de-Regnier Street. This eventually became a beehive of activity to help Jews in flight to acquire lodgings, identity documents, and baptismal certificates as well as aid in crossing to Switzerland or Spain. In this he was coopted by local Jewish and non-Jewish religious and lay leaders. After the German occupation of the Vichy zone, in November 1942, Benoît traveled regularly to Nice, then under Italian occupation. There the Jewish-Italian banker Angelo Donati introduced Benoît to Guido Lospinoso, the newly appointed Italian commissioner for Jewish affairs, who agreed to Benoît's request to be allowed to continue his rescue activity of Jews. Fearing a German takeover of the Italian zone, Donati and Benoît devised a plan to remove the approximately 30,000 Jews there to Italy proper, and for this Benoît went to Rome to make arrangements. In an audience with Pope Pius XII, on July 16, 1943, Benoît requested the Vatican's intercession with the Italian government to facilitate the transfer plan. In addition, he asked the Vatican for aid in obtaining news of French Jews deported to Germany and improvement of the situation of Jews in French detention camps as well as intervention with Spain to allow the repatriation of Jews claiming Spanish ancestry. It is not known if the Vatican acted on these requests. In the meantime, with the overthrow of Mussolini, on July 25, 1943, the transfer plan was amended to move the Jews by ships to North African havens. The new Italian government of Marshal Badoglio was prepared to provide four ships and requisition trucks, and the U.S.-based Joint to underwrite the cost of this large-scale operation. Benoît also received support for this undertaking from Francis Osborne and Myron Taylor, the British and American diplomatic representatives to the Vatican. Italy's surrender to the Allies, however, on September 8, 1943, and the immediate occupation of Italy and its zone in France by the Germans scuttled this rescue operation. Benoît, now under the name of Padre Benedetto, worked closely with Delasem (*Delegazione per l'Assistenza dei Emigranti Ebrei*), originally created to deal with facilitating Jewish emigration, and presently occupied with helping Jews in hiding. Elected to Delasem's executive board, when its president Settimio Sorani was arrested, Benoît replaced him as head. At first, Delasem's activities were centered in the Capuchin offices, on 159 Via Sicilia; then, for security reasons, it moved it operations from place to place. It dealt mainly with obtaining various forms of forged documents, food, ration cards, and residencies for the thousands of Jews in Rome, many of whom had fled there from other regions in Italy, and originating in various countries. Benoît, together with his Jewish aide Stefan Schwamm, also solicited the aid of the Swiss legation, as well as the Romanian and Hungarian legations, countries allied to Nazi Germany, in obtaining various documents, including "letters of protection." Financing came from from Delasem funds, the Joint, and Genoa-based Cardinal Pietro Boetto. It is estimated that as many as 4,000 Jews benefited from Benoît's aid. As his fame spead among Jewish refugees, many sought out the "Father of the Jews." Benoît escaped several attempts to arrest him, and he eventually went into hiding for about a month, and returned to Rome to witness the city's liberation on June 4, 1944. Afterwards, Benoît was hailed by the Italian Jewish community. In 1966, Yad Vashem awarded him the title of Righeous Among the Nations. In 1978, he wrote: "What I did for the Jewish people, what I did to merit being called 'Father of the Jews' is but an infinitesimal contribution of what should have been done to prevent this most heinous and satanic slaughter of some six million Jews, which will undoubtedly remain mankind's foulest disgrace – a shame affecting all those who participated or allowed it to happen.… It is by divine providence that the Jewish people wishes to live and fulfill its divine goals – first, for its own good, then, for the good of all humanity."

BIBLIOGRAPHY: Yad Vashem Archives M31–201; P.-M. Benoît, "Résumé de mon activité en faveur des Juifs persécutés (1940–1944)," in: *Livre d'Or des Congregations Françaises, 1939–1945* (1948); S. Zuccotti, *Under His Very Window* (2000), index; F. Leboucher, *Incredible Mission,* (1969); M. Paldiel, *The Path of the Righteous* (1993), 56–59; J. Rorty, "Father Benoît, Ambassador to the Jews," in: *Commentary,* 2 (Dec. 1946), 6; I. Gutman (ed.), *Encyclopedia of the Righteous Among the Nations: France* (2003), 68–70.

[Mordecai Paldiel (2nd ed.)]

BENOLIEL, Moroccan family. ELIEZER, a leading citizen of *Fez (1730), established his family in Gibraltar; there JUDAH (d. 1839) was consul-general of Morocco (1817), the only agent of the sultan in the service of the European powers, signed the treaty with Austria in 1830, and was later the representative of that country. Judah negotiated with Sweden, Norway, Denmark, and Belgium and reestablished peace between Sardinia and Morocco. As president of the Gibraltar Chamber of Commerce, he enjoyed the confidence of European financiers. His financial interests were widespread and at his death he left a fortune estimated at about three million gold dollars. He was president of the Jewish community in Gibraltar and founded charitable institutions in Morocco. At his request the sultan authorized the reconstruction of the synagogue in Tangiers. Joseph *Benoliel was a scholar and bibliophile.

BIBLIOGRAPHY: J. Davidson, *Notes Taken During Travels in Africa* (1839), 3–6; H. de La Martinière, *Souvenirs du Maroc* (1919), 26, 123; *Report of Anglo-Jewish Association* (1877/78), 113; Miège, Maroc, 2 (1961), 29, 89, 161, 191–3, 249; Kayserling, Bibl, 26–27; A.I. Laredo, *Memorias de un viejo tangerino* (1935), 262–5.

[David Corcos]

BENOLIEL, JOSEPH (**José**; 1888–1937), Portuguese scholar and bibliophile. Benoliel was born and died in Tangiers but spent most of his life in Lisbon. He was a distinguished philologist, fluent in Hebrew, Arabic, Spanish, French, and Portuguese. After studying in a yeshivah in Morocco and in the Oriental School of the Alliance Israélite Universelle in Paris, he taught for a time at Mikveh Israel in Palestine. He then became professor of French and Hebrew at the University of Lisbon as well as official translator for the Portuguese Ministry of Foreign Affairs. He wrote many books, including French grammars and French and Portuguese dictionaries;, a volume of poetry entitled *Echos de solidão* which came out in 1897; a volume of liturgical pieces entitled *Porat Yosef,* published in 1887; and studies on the *Lusiadas* of Camões, parts of which he translated into Hebrew.

[Moses Bensabat Amzalak]

BEN PETURA (also **Ben Peturi**, **Ben Peturin**; early second century), *tanna*. He is best known for his dispute with R. Akiva: "Two men are traveling in the desert; one has a pitcher containing enough water to enable one of them to reach a place of habitation. If they share the water both will die; if one drinks, his life will be saved." Ben Petura taught: "It is better that both drink and die than one witness the death of his companion." But R. Akiva expounded: "It is written: that thy brother may live with thee (Lev. 25:36) this means that 'thy life takes precedence over that of thy brother'" (BM 62a; Sifra 9:5, with slight variations).

BIBLIOGRAPHY: Bacher, Tann; Aḥad Ha-Am, *Al Parashat Derakhim*, pt. 4 (1947³); Kaminka, in: *Keneset le-Zekher Bialik*, 4 (1939), 352–3, no. 41; S. Pines, in: *Tarbiz* 16 (1944/45), 238–40.

[Zvi Kaplan]

BEN-PORAT, MIRIAM (1918–), Israel jurist and state comptroller. Born in Vitebsk, Russia, Ben-Porat grew up in Lithuania and emigrated to Palestine in 1931. In 1945 she completed her law studies. She joined the Ministry of Justice in 1948, and from 1950 to 1958 served as deputy state attorney at the Ministry of Justice and from 1958 to 1975 as judge of the District Court of Jerusalem, appointed its president in December 1975. In November 1976 she was appointed acting judge of the Supreme Court and a permanent justice in 1977; from 1983 to 1988 she was vice president of the court. During these years, from 1964 to 1978, she held an academic position as associate professor in the Hebrew University and also wrote commentaries on the laws of assignments and contracts. In 1988 she retired from the court and became state comptroller, a position she held for 10 years, until 1998, when she retired after two terms. During her time in office, she strengthened the institution of state comptroller as the "watchdog of Israel's democracy," closely examining the activities of government ministries and the public sector. In 1991 she was awarded the Israel Prize for special contribution to society and the State.

[Shaked Gilboa (2nd ed.)]

BEN-PORAT (Kazaz), MORDEKHAI (1923–) Israeli politician, member of the Sixth to Eighth and Tenth Knessets. Ben-Porat was born in Baghdad. In 1942 he joined the Ḥalutz movement in Iraq and immigrated to Eretz Israel in 1945. In 1947 he joined the *Haganah. He fought in the War of Independence, and finished the first officers' course in the IDF in 1948. In 1949 he returned to Iraq to prepare over 120,000 Iraqi Jews for immigration to Israel. He remained in Iraq for two years and was detained by the Iraqi authorities four times, each time managing to escape – the last time after being tortured.

In 1955 he was elected as head of the Or-Yehuda local council, a position he held until 1969. He was the founder and first chairman of the Center for the Heritage of Babylonian Jewry in Or-Yehuda. He was one of the founders of *Rafi and was elected on its list to the Sixth Knesset in 1965. Following the foundation of the Israel Labor Party in 1968, he was elected to the Knesset on the Alignment list, and in 1970–72 was deputy secretary general of the Labor Party. He was elected on the Alignment list to the Seventh and Eighth Knesset, but left the parliamentary group in March 1977 and continued to serve as an independent MK. In 1975 he was one of the founders of the World Organization of Jews from Arab Countries, becoming one of its chairmen. In 1977 he was member of the Israeli delegation to the United Nations. In 1979, after the rise to power in Iran of the Ayatollah Khomeini, Ben-Porat was sent to Teheran to help Jews leave the country. In 1981 he was elected to the Tenth Knesset on behalf of Telem, a party formed by Moshe *Dayan a short time before his death, and a year later was appointed minister without portfolio in Menaḥem *Begin's second government. In June 1983 Telem broke up, and Ben-Porat established a parliamentary group by the name of the Movement for Social Zionist Renewal. In January 1984 he resigned from Yitzḥak *Shamir's government, demanding that a National Unity Government be formed. He joined the Likud in 1988.

He wrote *Le-Bagdad ve-Ḥazarah* (1996; *To Baghdad and Back: The Miraculous 2000-Year Homecoming of the Iraqi Jews*, 1998).

[Susan Hattis Rolef (2nd ed.)]

BENREMOKH (Rimokh, Remoch, Rimoc, Ramukh), family in Spain and Morocco. SOLOMON BENREMOKH (1285) was a communal leader in Lerida, Spain. The exegete ABRAHAM BEN ḤAYYIM was born in Barcelona. He wrote a commentary on Psalms, to which he appended an autobiography containing information on the situation of the Jews in southern Europe. In 1391 his home was pillaged, his possessions stolen, and he himself imprisoned. He participated in the disputation of *Tortosa in 1413–14. In the 15th century the Benremokh family fled to Morocco, where it attained a position of leadership in the community before 1492. ḤAYYIM BEN SHEM TOV (d. after 1526) was one of the spiritual leaders of the indigenous communities of the kingdom of Fez, and SHEM TOV BEN ABRAHAM was their *nagid*. A dictatorial person, his dispute with the Spanish exiles of 1492 on questions concerning ritual slaughter created a friction of long duration between them and the native Jewish community. Dismissed from office in 1527, he was replaced by his relative SAUL BEN SHEM TOV who remained *nagid* until after 1563. YAMIN, confidential adviser to King Mūlay Zaydān, was sent on a mission to London in 1615 and in 1624 to Holland, where he remained until 1628. SHEM TOV (II) was *nagid* of Fez until his death in 1648. In 1650 his brother bought the position from the king against the will of the community, to which he caused great suffering. Thereafter, the family gave up political activity but remained among the most respected members of the Fez community. Part of the family settled in Gibraltar in 1785 and in London.

BIBLIOGRAPHY: Baer, Urkunden, 2 (1927), index, s.v. *Rimoch*; Baer, Spain, 2 (1966), 131, 218ff., 472, 484, 500; SIHM, Angleterre, 2 (1925), 490; Pays-Bas, 3 (1912), 498; 4 (1913), 72, 111, 143–6, 202–3; J.M. Toledano, *Ner ha-Ma'arav* (1911), 65–80, 101; Hirschberg, Afrikah, 2 (1965), 235–6.

[David Corcos]

BENRUBI, ISAAC (1876–1943), philosopher. Born in Salonika, he was a member of a well-known Turkish family which produced rabbis and rabbinic emissaries. After serving as a teacher in a public school in Philippopolis (Plovdiv) in Bulgaria, he left for Jena, Germany, where he studied philosophy with Rudolf Eucken. In 1900, while attending the Sorbonne, he became interested in contemporary French philosophy. His participation in the Second International Congress of Philosophy in Geneva (1904) brought him into personal contact with the leaders of the philosophic schools in France. Benrubi decided to devote himself to the study of modern French philosophy and to disseminate its ideas abroad, especially in Germany, where almost nothing was known of French philosophy after Comte. In addition, he was eager to spread knowledge of the German philosophy of idealism in France. From 1907 to 1914 he attended the lectures of Bergson in Paris, where he was asked to prepare a German translation of Bergson's book *Matière et Mémoire* (1896). Benrubi undertook this task with the assistance of Bergson. He engaged in frequent conversations with Bergson on philosophical, religious, social, and political questions, keeping current notes of these conversations, which took the form of his book *Souvenirs sur Henri Bergson* (1942), an important source for an understanding of Bergson's personality. During World War I, he lectured at the University of Geneva on contemporary French and German philosophy. After the war, he finally completed the first part of his original project: an exposition of modern French philosophy, which was first published in an abridged version both in English, *The Contemporary Thought of France* (1926), and in German, *Philosophische Stroemungen der Gegenwart in Frankreich* (1928). In 1933 the complete work appeared in French, under the title, *Les sources et les courants de la philosophie contemporaine en France*. Benrubi wrote this book, on the basis, among other things, of the comprehensive conversations he had had with the thinkers of whom he wrote. After his death, his friend, Axel Stern, published a book of selections illustrating his views on epistemology and ethics, *Connaissance et Morale* (1947).

[Samuel Hugo Bergman]

BENSANCHI, MENTESH (**Mordecai**; 1882–1943), Greek journalist and member of parliament. Born in Salonika, he worked as a journalist for the Judeo-Spanish newspaper *La Epoca*, and the French newspaper *Salonique*. With the termination of *La Epoca*, in 1912 he was the founding editor of *El Liberal*. He also worked for the government newspaper *La Liberta*. Later, he became editor of several Salonika newspapers, including *El Imparcial* and *L'Indépendant*. As a Zionist, he was active in the *Kadima* society, which promoted Hebrew culture and language, and as its general secretary he was active in Zionist propaganda and took an interest in problems of Jewish settlement in Ereẓ Israel. He was one of the editors of the Zionist weeklies *La Esperansa* and *El Congreso Jidyo*, which appeared in French and Judeo-Spanish during WWI. During the years 1926–30, he was the head of the *Jewish National Fund in Salonika. A liberal Zionist and an outstanding orator, he was sent by Salonika Jewry as its representative to the Greek parliament. In the 1925 Greek national elections he was elected as a Kafandarist (Progressive Liberal). He was reelected in 1928. As an active Jewish-Zionist public figure, he often clashed with ultra-Greek nationalists. After the 1931 antisemitic Campbell riots in Salonika, he gave a strong speech in parliament against the disturbances and the support of the local government for the rioters. Before WWII, the Jewish Agency decided to make him an emissary to Eastern Jewish communities for fundraising and Zionist propaganda. He was an eloquent speaker in Judeo-Spanish and French. In the 1930s, in the press, he exposed the antisemitic Kleiber, who had infiltrated into local Salonikan Jewish circles and eventually became a Nazi collaborator. Bensanchi wrote numerous articles against Germany and was blacklisted by the Germans. In the summer of 1942, he was caught by the Germans hiding with his family in a village in Crete, was interned in Larisa and Salonika, released, and in 1943 finally was deported to Auschwitz, where he died.

BIBLIOGRAPHY: D. Recanati (ed.), *Zikhron Saloniki, Gedulatah ve-Ḥurbanah shel Yerushalayim de-Balkan* (1972), 329; *Saloniki, Ir ve-Em be-Yisra'el* (1967), 103, 115, 328; M. Molho and J. Nehama, *Sho'at Yehudei Yavan* (1965), 34, 54.

[Yitzchak Kerem (2nd ed.)]

BEN-SASSON, HAIM HILLEL (1914–1977), Israeli historian. Ben-Sasson was born in Volozhin, Lithuania, and immigrated to Palestine in 1934. He taught at the Hebrew University, Jerusalem, from 1949 and became a full professor in 1970. Among Ben-Sasson's published works are *Millon le-Munaḥei ha-Politikah* (1941), a Hebrew political dictionary; *Perakim be-Toledot ha-Yehudim bi-Ymei ha-Beinayim* (1958), a history of the Jews in the Middle Ages; and *Hagut ve-Hanhagah* (1959), on the social concepts of Polish Jewry at the end of the Middle Ages. He also edited the textbook of Jewish history *Toledot Am Yisrael* (3 vols., 1969–70; *A History of the Jewish People*, 1976). From 1966 served as one of the editors of the Hebrew historical quarterly *Zion*; he was also editor (first edition) of the *Encyclopaedia Judaica*'s history division for Jewish history in Central and Eastern Europe and the departmental editor for general articles on Jewish history, Jewish economic history, and the history of the Jews in Poland and Lithuania.

BENSAUDE, Moroccan-Portuguese family. ABRAHAM BENSAUDE (1790–1868) left Morocco after the creation of a mellah in his hometown of Rabat in 1807. In 1819, he settled in São Miguel, in the Azores and founded the first Jewish community on the island. He was joined by his brother ELIAS and his cousin SOLOMON, who established the firm of Bensaude and Company. Under the direction of the latter's son, ABRAHAM, this became one of the most important enterprises in Portugal, with its head office in Lisbon. By the mid-19th century the Bensaude family had established a network of commercial relations between branches in Mogador, Gibraltar, Hamburg, London, Manchester, and Lisbon. The family of the first Abraham Bensaude contributed to the economic development of San Miguel for over a century. His son JOSÉ (1835–1922) established the tobacco industry and promoted the culture of pineapples, tea, and flax. José's son JOAQUIM (1859–1952) was a distinguished Portuguese historian, noted for his research into the history of Portuguese scientific navigation, *L'astronomie nautique au Portugal à l'époque des grandes découvertes* (Berne, 1912). He disproved Alexander von Humboldt's thesis concerning the German origin of scientific navigation in Portugal. In particular, he pointed out the important part played by Jewish astronomers and astrologers in the Iberian Peninsula during the Middle Ages, from which scientific navigation in Portugal originated.

BIBLIOGRAPHY: A. Bensaude, *Vida de José Bensaude* (1936); Miège, Maroc, 2 (1961), 96, 574.

[John Alfred Nathan]

BEN-SHABETAI, ARI (1954–), Israeli composer. Born in Jerusalem, Ben-Shabetai studied at the Guildhall School of Music in London, England and graduated cum laude in composition and theory of music; with Mark *Kopytman at the Jerusalem Rubin Academy of Music and Dance (1983); and with George Crumb and Richard Wernick at the University of Pennsylvania, U.S. (1984–87), where he received a Ph.D. in music composition.

Ben-Shabetai has won many awards and prizes. His *Sinfonia Cromatica* won first prize in the 1994 Israel Philharmonic Orchestra Composition Competition and was included in the program of its tour to Germany, France, Italy, and the U.S. with Zubin *Mehta conducting. *Magreffa* for symphony orchestra was commissioned in 1995 by Lorin *Maazel for the Pittsburgh Symphony Orchestra and performed both in Pittsburgh and Jerusalem. In 1990 Ben-Shabetai was awarded the AKUM Composition Prize for *Yehezkel* (Concerto for Cello and Orchestra). In 1996 he received the Prime Minister's Prize for composers. His *Elegy For Anna Frank* won the Israel Sinfonietta Prize (1982) and his *Three Romances* for piano the AKUM Prize (1991).

Influenced by contemporary music of the 1980s and 1990s and Oriental music, Ben-Shabetai can be categorized as one of the earliest composers of the postmodern style. His individual style incorporates influences of heterophony, post-impressionistic harmony, and minimalism as well as modern rock and jazz music (*Blues and White* for piano, *Deus Ex Machina* for electric violin and DJ).

From 1987 he was a professor at the Jerusalem Academy of Music and Dance. He also served as chairman of the Israel Composers League for four years, during which period he founded the Israeli Music Center publishing house and produced the *Anthology of Israeli Piano Music* published by this organization. His chamber opera *Aya No Tsuzumi* (*The Damasc Drum*), composed to a gibberish libretto and based on the Noh Theater play was commissioned by and premiered at the Tel Aviv Biennale 2004).

[Dushan Mihalek (2nd ed.)]

BEN-SHAKHAR, GERSHON (1942–), Israeli cognitive psychologist and president of Israel's Open University. Ben-Shakhar's fields of inquiry are cognitive psychophysiology, psychophysiological detection of information, psychological testing and individual differences, and the confirmation bias in expert opinions. Ben-Shakhar completed his academic studies at the Hebrew University of Jerusalem, receiving a B.A. in psychology and statistics in 1966, an M.A. in psychology in 1970, and a Ph.D. in psychology in 1975. In 1976, after a postdoctoral year at Northwestern University, he joined the department of psychology at the Hebrew University; he was head of the department 1987–90, becoming a full professor in 1991. Between 1992 and 1995 he was the dean of the Faculty of Social Sciences at the Hebrew University, and from 1995 until 1998 he was pro rector of the university. During these years he was visiting professor at Stanford, Toronto, and Brandeis universities. In 2003 he was appointed president of the Open University. Ben-Shakhar wrote many articles and a number of books, among them *Theories and Applications in the Detection of Deception: A Psychophysiological and International Perspective* (with J.J. Furedy, 1989) and *Studies in Psychology: Volume in Honor of Sonny Kugelmass* (edited with A. Lieblich, 1995).

[Shaked Gilboa (2nd ed.)]

BEN SHEMEN (Heb. בֶּן שֶׁמֶן), youth village and moshav in central Israel, in the northern Judean foothills, 1.8 mi. (3 km.) east of Lydda. Land bought here in 1904 by the Anglo-Palestine Bank was transferred to the *Jewish National Fund in 1907, thus becoming one of its first holdings in the country. "Atid," a Jewish company for oil and soap production, founded a factory here in 1905. A year later, Kiryat Sefer, a children's village, was established for orphans of the *Kishinev pogrom, under the direction of Israel *Belkind. In 1908 the Palestine office of the Zionist Organization set up a training farm for agricultural workers; they planted groves of olives and other fruit trees. These plantations were then named "Herzl Forest." Ten Yemenite families were settled at Ben Shemen in 1911 to combine farming with arts and crafts in the style of the *Bezalel School of Jerusalem. During World War I Ben Shemen was a battlefront between the German-Turkish and the Allied armies. It was abandoned and largely destroyed. In 1921 one of the first moshavim was founded at Ben Shemen. In 1927 an agricultural school was opened under the direction of Siegfried *Lehmann and in 1934 it was among the first institutions to be included in the framework of *Youth Aliyah. Early in 1948, during the War of Independence, both the school and the moshav came under siege and the school was evacuated to the Ḥefer Plain until the end of the year, there constituting the basis for the Ne'urim Youth Village. In 1952 a new moshav (affiliated with Tenu'at ha-Moshavim) was established by settlers from Romania, whose main occupation was dairy and citrus farming. In 1968 Ben Shemen had 920 inhabitants, of whom 720 were in the youth village. In the mid-1990s Ben Shemen had approximately 1,360 inhabitants, of whom 990 were in the youth village. In 2002 the population of Ben Shemen (moshav) was 550 residents with another 638 in the youth village. The school includes an elementary and high school with dormitories. The name is taken from Isaiah 5:1.

[Efraim Orni]

BENSHEN, Ashkenazi term, probably derived (via Old French) from the Latin *benedicere*, meaning "bless" or "pronounce a benediction." It is mainly used for *Grace after Meals which, when recited by three adult males, is introduced by a formula, of which the Yiddish version is *Raboysay, mir volen benshen* ("Gentlemen, let us say Grace"). It is also used as a designation for the Prayer for the New Moon, *Rosh Ḥodesh benshen*, and for the benediction recited by a person who has survived a perilous escape, *gomel benshen*. The kindling of Sabbath and festival lights is called *likht benshen*. The blessing of children by parents is also called *benshen*. The term corresponds to the Sephardi *bencao*.

BEN SIMEON, RAPHAEL AARON (1848–1928), rabbi. Ben Simeon, who was born in Jerusalem, became chief rabbi of Cairo in 1891. Toward the end of his life he returned to Palestine and settled in Tel Aviv. Ben Simeon wrote a number of works, mainly dealing with questions of *halakhah* and ritual. They include *Nehar Miẓrayim* (1908), on the ritual followed by the Jews in Egypt, and *Sha'ar ha-Mifkad* (1908–19), on the various rituals observed by the Jerusalem communities. His collection of responsa, *U-mi-ẓur Devash* (1912), includes rulings by his father David; *Tuv-Miẓrayim* (1908) gives genealogies of Egyptian rabbis.

BIBLIOGRAPHY: Frumkin-Rivlin, 3 (1929), 307–8.

[Eliyahu Ashtor]

BEN SIRA, ALPHABET OF, a narrative, satirical work, written probably in the geonic period in the East. The *Alphabet of Ben Sira* is one of the earliest, most complicated, and most sophisticated Hebrew stories written in the Middle Ages. Four versions of the work have been printed: (a) the usual text found in most editions and manuscripts, edited with notes by Steinschneider and published in Berlin in 1858; (b) a fuller version of part of the work that was discovered by Steinschneider in a manuscript in Leiden (parts of it were added as notes to his edition); (c) a totally different version printed by Loewinger and Friedman from a Kaufmann manuscript in Budapest, published in Vienna in 1926; and (d) part of a fourth version discovered by Habermann in a manuscript in Jerusalem and published in 1958. There are more than 50 extant manuscripts of the work, in full or in part, many of which contain different versions and additional stories.

There is no reason to doubt the unity of the work as a whole, despite the fragmentary character of the different versions. All the versions share a special, satirical, and even heretical, character, and this indicates that they all were written by a single hand. They seem to reflect varying degrees of censorship on the part of editors and copyists. The complete work contains four parts. The first part is the biography of Ben Sira from his conception until the age of one year. This story, omitted in many editions, explains how Jeremiah, the prophet, was simultaneously Ben Sira's father (the numerical value of Ben Sira's name equals that of Jeremiah), and grandfather. Ben Sira's mother was Jeremiah's daughter. The old prophet was forced to an act of onanism by wicked men, and his daughter conceived from his emissions when she came to bathe. The form of this story is based on a biblical verse that tells the glories and wonders of God's deeds; thus the story satirizes not only Jeremiah, but God's deeds as well.

The second part is more sophisticated in form. It tells how Ben Sira, now one year old, meets with his teacher, who tries to teach him the alphabet. Instead of repeating each letter of the alphabet after his teacher, Ben Sira responds with an epigram beginning with that letter. The epigrams lead the teacher to tell the story of his life. It may be assumed that the original structure of this part was 22 + 12 paragraphs, each containing a letter, an epigram, and a part of the story.

The third part is the longest and contains most of the narrative material in this work. It recounts the story of Ben Sira's life and adventures in the court of Nebuchadnezzar, king of Babylonia. It also includes stories told by Ben Sira himself as answers to the king's questions. These stories often include pornographic elements, as well as derogatory descriptions of biblical figures, like King Solomon or Joshua. Some of the stories in this section contain motifs from international folklore and may be based on folktales, but they were adapted to the special framework of the work and satirical elements were added to them. Examination of the various versions indicates that here, too, there were 22 stories, arranged according to the letters of the alphabet, to which 12 other stories were added.

The fourth part, which is found in most versions and gave the work its name, contains 22 alphabetically arranged epigrams attributed to Ben Sira that serve as material for discussion and interpretation by Ben Sira's son, Uzziel, and his grandson, Joseph b. Uzziel. The contents are satirical and even heretical. It may be assumed that this part was constructed in the same manner as the two previous ones – 22 + 12 sections. The work, therefore, displays elements of unity both in structure and in its ideological aims. It is all but impossible, however, to discover the background upon which such a work could have been written. Some scholars (L. Ginzberg and others) believe that it aimed at ridiculing the story of Jesus' birth; but the basis for such a conclusion may be found only in the first part, and even this is not very clear, for the irony seems to be directed more against God than against Jesus. It is hardly possible that the author was a Karaite, as some of the abusive stories are directed against biblical figures, and not only against the Talmud and Midrash. It seems likely that the author did not belong to any organized group or definable ideological movement, but was merely a writer with an anarchistic tendency who used satire to ridicule all the institutions of established religion in his day.

Another difficult problem is the relationship between this pseudepigraphal work and the original proverbs of Ben Sira. Some of the proverbs and epigrams included in the work are originally in the work of Ben Sira, but many such proverbs are found in talmudic literature, and the author probably took them from there. The author of the pseudepigraphal work did not even know Ben Sira's first name. There is only one slight connection that might be accidental: the Wisdom of *Ben Sira has a preface written by the author's grandson, who edited the work, and in the pseudepigraphal work the figure of a grandson is also present.

It is impossible to fix even the approximate date of this work. It has been suggested that a quotation from the work is included in the tenth-century *Arukh*, but this now seems very doubtful. The *Alphabet*, however, seems to have been written in the East after the rise of Islam.

Maimonides and other authorities attacked the work vigorously, but it was generally accepted as part of the midrashic tradition, to the extent that a circle of Ashkenazi ḥasidic mystics in the 12th and 13th centuries attributed some of their mystical compilations to works and theories received from Joseph b. Uzziel, who inherited the wisdom of Ben Sira and Jeremiah. The anarchistic and heretical elements in the work went unrecognized, probably because of the censorship exercised by copyists, who prevented the full version from being known to readers.

BIBLIOGRAPHY: M. Steinschneider (ed.), *Alpha Betha de-Ben Sira* (1858); D.Z. Friedman and D.S. Loewinger (eds.), *Alpha Betha de-Ben Sira* (1926) (= HHY, 10 (1926), 250–81); A.M. Habermann in:

Tarbiz, 27 (1957/58), 190–202; I. Reifman, in: *Ha-Karmel*, 2 (1873), 123ff.; A. Epstein, *Mi-Kadmoniyyot ha-Yehudim* (1957), 111–5; J.L. Zlotnick, in: *Sinai*, 18 (1946), 49–58; S. Lieberman, *Sheki'in* (1939), 32–42.; J. Dan, in: *Molad*, 23 (1965), 490–6; Lévy, in: REJ, 29 (1894), 197–205; Zunz, Vortraege, 106–11; S.H. Kook, *Iyyunim u-Meḥkarim*, 1 (1959), 231–3.

[Joseph Dan]

BEN SIRA, SIMEON BEN JESUS (second century B.C.E.), Hebrew aphorist, sage, and scribe, the author of Wisdom of *Ben Sira (Ecclesiasticus). Ben Sira was a younger contemporary of the high priest Simeon (50:1ff.), apparently Simeon the Just, who according to the Talmud and Josephus (Ant., 12:43, 157) lived at the beginning of the third century B.C.E. In the introduction to the Greek translation of the Wisdom of Ben Sira, the author is referred to as Jesus, by which name he is generally known in the Christian tradition. In the more authoritative Hebrew version, however (50:27; 52:end), his full name is given as Simeon b. Jeshua b. Eleazar b. Sira. The book was translated into Greek by Ben Sira's grandson after his arrival in Egypt in 132 B.C.E. From this date, given by the grandson in the preface to his translation, it may be reckoned that Ben Sira completed the book about 170 B.C.E. Apparently Ben Sira's life was at one time in jeopardy because of a false charge leveled against him, from which, however, he was saved (51).

BIBLIOGRAPHY: S. Schechter and C. Taylor, *The Wisdom of Ben Sira* (1899); R. Smend, *Die Weisheit des Jesus Sirach erklaert* (1906–07); M.H. Segal, *Sefer Ben-Sira ha-Shalem* (1958²); E.S. Hartom, *Ha-Sefarim ha-Ḥiẓonim: Ben-Sira* (1963).

[Moses Zevi (Moses Hirsch) Segal]

BEN SIRA, WISDOM OF (also called **Ecclesiasticus**), a work of the Apocrypha, which, though usually known by this name, may have been called by its author, "The Words of Simeon b. Jeshua," the title found on the Hebrew fragments. In Greek the book is called Σοφία (Ἰήσου υἱοῦ) Σειράχ), "Wisdom of (Jesus son of) Sirach," and hence in Latin it was known as Siracides (i.e., Sira's son). Its common name in modern times, Ecclesiasticus (abbr. Ecclus.) dates from the 4th-century custom of naming certain homiletical books *libri ecclesiastici* (i.e., books for (reading in) the church). The book is divided into eight sections, each introduced by a poem in praise of wisdom or of the wise man. The last section (Hebrew version 44–50), called "The Praise of the Fathers," eulogizes the great figures of the Bible, with the exception of the final chapter which is devoted to praise of Simeon b. Johanan the priest, i.e., *Simeon the Just. The greater part of the work consists of maxims, poetic in form, like those in the book of Proverbs. It also contains psalms of supplication and of thanksgiving (36:1–17 (33:1–13; 36:16–22); 42:21–35 (15–25), 43, et al.), these latter being characterized by a lofty poetic style and by elevated thought (cf. 42:21 (15); 43:33 (58). (References are given to two editions: the first to the Hebrew edition by M.H. Segal (19582), the second to the standard edition in the Greek text of the Apocrypha). The work also includes didactic poems on subjects of daily life and on historical events, after the manner of certain psalms (13; 15; 16; 18; 34:19–35; 40:41; et al.), and concludes with an epilogue comprising two poems of praise and thanksgiving, and an alphabetic poem on the importance of acquiring wisdom.

The Wisdom of Ben Sira directs man to the love of wisdom and ethical conduct, teaches him virtue and good deeds, and proper behavior in eating and drinking, speech and silence, work and commerce, studying and teaching, poverty and wealth, health and sickness. It also seeks to instruct man to perform all his actions with intelligence and understanding, moderation, care and wisdom, so that his deeds may bring to him and others the appropriate benefit. It teaches man how to behave within his family circle: toward his father and mother, his wife, his sons, and his daughters. It guides him in his conduct toward all men. It stresses, as does the book of Proverbs, that the fear of the Lord is the beginning and the end of all wisdom. The work, though written in the spirit of the Bible and in the language of the later biblical books, bears a contemporary impress of the second century B.C.E., and its faith, in general, is that of subsequent Pharisaic Judaism (everything is foreseen but man has freedom of choice: 15:15–17; cf. Avot 3:15). It also reveals some influence of Greek literature and idiom: men grow and fall like leaves on a tree (14:19; cf. Iliad 6:146–9); he becomes wise who is unfettered by affairs, corresponding to the σχολαστικός, the Greek man of leisure. The work also contains a trace of the Greek gnosis and perhaps also of its philosophical thought (cf. 42:29–33 (20–23)). Unlike other books of proverbs, in which the authors address themselves to youth, the Wisdom of Ben Sira attaches prime importance to the well-ordered family, the effective basis of which is the father. It is primarily to him that the author addresses himself, advising and instructing him. A man should marry a suitable wife, beautiful and kindly-spoken, who, assisting him, will bring him supreme happiness. He should rear his sons in the Torah, marry off his daughters while they are young, and deal faithfully with his fellow man.

From a literary viewpoint, the work is well constructed. Most of the maxims are arranged according to subject matter, and the various sections have headings such as "The fear of the Lord," "Honoring parents," "Humility," "Lovingkindness," and the like. For the rabbis of the early talmudic period the work had an importance almost equal to that of the book of Proverbs. Its aphorisms, quoted either in Ben Sira's name or anonymously, are scattered throughout talmudic literature and are cited by both *tannaim* and *amoraim*, such as R. Levitas of Jabneh (Avot 4:4, cf. Ecclus. 7:13), Akiva, and Rav. Several of Ben Sira's maxims are to be found in other books of the Apocrypha, the New Testament, the Syriac version of the book of *Aḥikar as well as in the writings of early medieval Jewish scholars. Ben Sira's influence on ancient Hebrew prayers and *piyyutim* is particularly great. Although the Wisdom of Ben Sira is quoted in talmudic literature with the introductory phrase "as it is written," ordinarily reserved for biblical quotations, and is once explicitly mentioned among the books of the Hagiographa (BK 92b; cf. Ecclus. 27:9), it was not included in the canon. Some *amoraim* even forbade it to be read (Sanh. 100b; TJ, Sanh. 10:1, 28a). In the book of Proverbs the ethics are personal and worldly, and its general character is bound up with its secular origin, even though the religious content of the book is of prime importance. In the Wisdom of Ben Sira there is a notable difference. Wisdom, which is spoken of in the book of Proverbs as a primordial fascinating entity, is in Ben Sira identified with the Torah given to Israel, emphasizing that it is the true basis of all divine and human wisdom. In the Wisdom of Ben Sira there occur for the first time a number of ideas subsequently found in the *aggadah*, such as that Israel as well as the Torah was among the first acts of God's creation (cf. Ecclus. 36:15 and Gen. R. 1:4) and that the people of Israel (37:29 (25)), the Temple (17:20 (13)) and the priesthood of Aaron and of Phinehas (45:26, 45 (15, 24)) will endure forever (cf. Sif. Num. 92; Lev. R. 2:2). Ben Sira is also the original source for several customs which are later found in the *halakhah* (e.g., the blessing on seeing a rainbow – 43:13 (11)), and contains the earliest reference to the accepted basis of the Eighteen Benedictions and the like. The sages delivered homilies based on Ben Sira's maxims, but changing their form and language. They were even rendered at times in the mishnaic Hebrew or Aramaic spoken by the sages. Excerpts from these maxims, current among the masses, were collected in small compilations, not always in the original order, and they included not only biblical verses but some aphorisms which were not Ben Sira's. As a result these verses and aphorisms were erroneously ascribed to Ben Sira by the rabbis.

The original Hebrew text was no longer extant after the time of Saadiah Gaon (10th century). In the 19th century the work was translated from the Greek into Hebrew by Judah Leib *Ben-Zeev S.I. Fraenkel, and others. In 1896, however, S. Schechter discovered among the **Genizah* fragments in Cairo a page of the original Hebrew work. During the next four years, Schechter and other scholars found many other fragments from various manuscripts, comprising about two-thirds of the entire book. In 1929 Joseph Marcus found a fragment from a fifth manuscript containing 46 verses; in 1957 J. Schirmann found a new folio, and in 1959 yet another folio of manuscript B, as well as two folios of manuscript C. These fragments consist at times of no more than portions of verses, and contain many mistakes, omissions, and corruptions, as well as numerous additions and repetitions. Nonetheless, they presumably preserve an early or even original version. Some fragments of the Hebrew original (6:20–31) were discovered in Qumran Cave II. In 1964 Yigael Yadin discovered at Masada fragments containing chapters 39:27–44:25, which indicate that manuscript B of the *Genizah* represents substantially the original Hebrew version of the book. The Wisdom of Ben Sira was included in the Septuagint, from where it made its way into the Christian Bible. It was translated into Syriac in about 300 C.E. by a Christian (apparently a Jewish apostate). Although these versions contain very many mistakes, by comparing them with the Hebrew version it is generally possible to establish the original text of the work.

[Moshe Zevi (Moses Hirsch) Segal]

A critical edition of *Ben Sira*, giving the Hebrew original, including fragments from the Genizah, the Dead Sea Scrolls, and Masada, with facsimiles, was published (1973) by the Historical Dictionary of the Hebrew Language, under the aegis of the Hebrew Language Academy, with Professor Z. Ben *Ḥayyim as chief editor. It provides a complete concordance of all the words in these texts, with textual notes.

On the question of the date of the author and the book, see *Ben Sira, Simeon son of Jesus.

See also *Apocrypha and *Bible, Canon.

In the Arts

In literature and art the Wisdom of Ben Sira has not inspired great creativity. In music, by contrast, Ben Sira's work has proved to be of considerable importance. The use of its texts may be considered under three headings: (a) The Priestly Office. The text beginning *Ecce sacerdos magnus* ("This is the high priest"), a paraphrase based on the praises of Moses and Aaron in chapters 44 and 45, is used in the Catholic liturgy for the commemoration or welcome of high ecclesiastical dignitaries, especially popes and bishops. The traditional plainchant melody was used by Palestrina as a *cantus firmus* (compositional foundation) in the first of his published masses (1554), which was dedicated to Pope Julius III; and also for festive motets on the text itself, such as those written by Constanzo Porta (book of motets for 6 voices, 1585, dedicated to Pope Sixtus V) and Tomas Luis de Victoria (4 voices, in his *Motecta festorum totius anni* … 1585). The last, like the Palestrina mass, has since been sung at many papal coronations. An *Ecce sacerdos* motet appears in the *Opus musicum* by Jacob Handl (Gallus; 1550–1591), in which other settings of Ben Sira texts also appear. It may be assumed that the attention of composers was drawn to Ben Sira as a text-source by the feeling of obligation, which the Counter-Reformation inspired, that no part of the liturgical cycle be neglected by composers. (b) "Now praise the Lord." The short hymnic passage in ch. 50:22–24, adopted by the Anglican *Book of Common Prayer*, was set by William Byrd (1545–1623) as an impressive six-voiced anthem, *Behold now praise the Lord*. The rhymed German paraphrase *Nun danket alle Gott*, by Martin Rinkart (first published by him in 1636 as a grace at table), became famous as the "German *Te Deum*" when it was sung on the occasion of the peace treaty ending the Thirty Years' War in 1648 to a chorale-melody composed by Johann Crueger (first published in the same year). Translated by Catherine Winkworth in 1858 as *Now thank we all our God*, it became popular in the English-speaking church; and both the German and the English versions have been sung on many historic occasions. Bach used the chorale-melody for his cantata no. 192, *Nun danket alle Gott*, and at the conclusion of his cantata no. 79. Felix *Mendelssohn adapted it for the *Festgesang* which he wrote for the 400th anniversary of the invention of printing, celebrated at Leipzig on June 25th, 1840.

(c) "Let us now praise famous men." The opening passage of the "Praise of the Fathers," ch. 44, in the English version of *The Book of Common Prayer*, has been set for choir by Ralph Vaughan Williams (1923), Cyril Scott (1935), and other English-speaking composers.

Settings of other texts include those by Heinrich Schuetz; the rhymed Dutch paraphrase *Ecclesiasticus* by Jan Fruytier (1965), which used the tunes of Clemens non Papa's famous *Souterliedekens* ("Little Psalter Songs," 1556); and the three-voiced canon on "Non impedias musicam" ("Do not impede the music," ch. 32, 5^2), in G.B. Martini's *Storia della Musica* (vol. 1, 1757).

[Bathja Bayer]

BIBLIOGRAPHY: M.H. Segal, *Ḥokhmat Ben Sira* (1933); idem, *Sefer Ben Sira ha-Shalem* (1958^2), contains detailed bibliography; idem, in: *Tarbiz*, 29 (1959/60); Grinz, in: *Beḥinot*, 6 (1953/54), 85–93; Schirmann, in: *Tarbiz*, 27 (1957/58), 440–3; A. Kahana *Ha-Sefarim ha-Ḥiẓonim*, 2 (1959); Charles, Apocrypha; A.A. Di Lella, *Hebrew Text of Sirach* (1966); C.C. Torrey, in: *Alexander Marx Jubilee Volume* (1950), 585–602; Yadin, in: *Eretz Israel*, 8 (1967), 1–45.

BENSON, ROBBY (Robin David Segal; 1956–), U.S. actor, director, voice-over artist. The son of a writer and a stage actress, Benson was born and raised in Dallas, Texas. He started his career in show business at the age of three, acting in commercials and community theater productions. At age 12 he made his Broadway debut starring in a production of *Zelda*, where he exhibited a natural talent for portraying sensitive adolescent characters. As a teenager Benson's good looks and sympathetic talents landed him in a string of roles in romantic films in the 1970s and 1980s, most notably *Jeremy* (1975), *Ode to Billy Joe* (1976), *One on One* (1977), *Ice Castles* (1978), and the TV production of *Our Town* (1976). Some of these roles exhibited darker and more complex performances such as his memorable portrayal opposite Jack Lemmon in *Tribute* (1980) and his performance as Danny Saunders in Chaim *Potok's *The Chosen* (1981). After recovering from open-heart surgery in 1984, Benson began writing and directing for TV, film, and theater. In 1988 he directed his first feature, *Crack in the Mirror*, and went on to become one of the most successful sitcom directors of the 1990s, directing multiple episodes for such hit shows as *Friends*, *Dream On*, and *Ellen*. He also performed as the gruff voice of Beast in Disney's Oscar-nominated *Beauty and the Beast*, and continued to voice characters for animated films. In addition, Benson composed scores for numerous films and received two gold records for songwriting with his wife and collaborator, Karla DeVito. Benson also taught in film and theater departments at several universities.

[Max Joseph (2nd ed.)]

BENSOUSSAN, GEORGES (1952–), French historian and Holocaust scholar. After completing a doctorate in modern history, Bensoussan began teaching history in high school while pursuing a parallel career in historical research and writing. An active militant against antisemitism and Holocaust denial, to which he sought to oppose precise historical knowledge and provocative reflections on the transmission of memory (*Génocide pour mémoire: des racines du désastre aux questions d'aujourd'hui*, 1989; *Auschwitz en héritage? Du bon usage de la mémoire*, 2003), Bensoussan collaborated on several journals (*Raison Présente* in 1989; *Le débat* in 1994), and was eventually appointed chief editor of the *Revue d'Histoire de la Shoah*, a major publication first issued in 1946 as *Le Monde Juif* and renamed in 1997 to better suit its scientific purposes. Later, reacting to the resurgence of antisemitism in France against the background of the Israeli-Palestinian conflict, Bensoussan wrote several pamphlets (some under a pseudonym) and books about the new antisemitism (*Anti-Semitism in French Schools: Turmoil of a Republic*, published by the Hebrew university of Jerusalem, Vidal Sassoon International Center for the Study of Antisemitism, 2004), which echo his previous reflections on the convergence and relationship between antisemitism, anti-Zionism, and Holocaust denial ("Négationnisme et antisionnisme: récurrences et convergences des discours du rejet," in: *Revue d'Histoire de la Shoah*, May–Aug. 1999), and his academic work on the history of antisemitism in France since the Dreyfus affair (*L'idéologie du rejet: enquête sur "Le monument Henry" ou archéologie du fantasme antisémite dans la France de la fin du XIXe siècle*, 1993). Bensoussan also wrote a general history of the Holocaust (1996) and an intellectual and political history of Zionism (2002).

[Dror Franck Sullaper (2nd ed.)]

BEN SṬADA, or **Ben Sṭara**, a person mentioned in two apparently unrelated passages in the Tosefta, identified in later tradition with Ben Pandira (Jesus). The first passage is found in Tosefta *Shabbat* (11:15), which reports a dispute concerning someone who made markings on his flesh. R. Eliezer held such a person liable for the desecration of the Sabbath, while his colleagues considered him exempt from punishment, since this is not the normal way of writing. In support of his position, R. Eliezer said: "Isn't it true that Ben Sṭara (other readings: Siṭra, Soṭra, Sṭada) learned in this way?" To this the Sages replied: "And because of one idiot, we should hold all of the normal people liable?" The second passage concerns the halakhah in Mishnah *Sanhedrin* (7:10) which permits the authorities to "entrap" someone who seeks to persuade a Jew to engage in idolatry. The Tosefta (San. 10:11), commenting on this halakhah, states: "And that is precisely what they did to Ben Sṭada (other readings: Sṭara) in Lydda – they placed two scholars in hiding [to testify against him] and stoned him." (The spelling of his name is uncertain also in the parallel passages in the Talmudim (see below, and cf. Lieberman, *Tosefta ki-Feshuta*, 1 (1955), 179–80).)

The second baraita, which tells of Ben Sṭada's execution, is brought in the Jerusalem Talmud (Yev. 16:6, 15d) virtually verbatum. The first *baraita*, which describes his practice of writing on his flesh, is brought in the JT *Shabbat* (12:4, 13d) in a form very similar to the text of the Tosefta. It differs, however, in one important respect: the rather obscure allusion to Ben Sṭara's eccentric behavior ("Ben Sṭara, 'learned' in this way") is expanded and explained: "Isn't it true that Ben Sṭada [brought witchcraft out of Egypt] in this way?" While it is possible that the Jerusalem Talmud is preserving here an ancient tradition concerning Ben Sṭada, it is equally likely that this is a harmonistic interpretation of Tosefta *Shabbat* in an attempt to explain why he was executed in Tosefta *Sanhedrin*.

Both of these traditions were originally brought in the Babylonian Talmud, but they were eliminated in part from later editions as a result of Christian censorship, for reasons that will be made clear immediately. The later printed texts of TB Shabbat 104b read as follows: "R. Eliezer said to the Sages: Isn't it true that Ben Sṭara brought witchcraft out of Egypt by marking on his flesh? They said to him: He was an idiot, and one does not bring proofs from idiots". Here the *sugya* ends in the later printed editions. The continuation of the *sugya*, as represented by all manuscripts and the earliest printed text, reads as follows: "[Was he] the son of Sṭara (or: Sṭada)? Wasn't he rather the son of Pandira! Rav Ḥisda said: Sṭara was [his mother's] husband; Pandira was [his mother's] lover. [But his mother's] husband was Papos the son of Judah! Rather, his mother was Sṭara (or Sṭada), his father was Pandira. [But] his mother was Mary the hairdresser (*magdala*)! Rather [she was called Sṭada] because of what they say in Pumbedita: She cheated (*saṭa da*) on her husband." The name "Ben Pandira" was understood in the Babylonian Talmud as a euphemism for Jesus (cf. Tosefta Ḥul. 2:24, TB Av. Za. 16b-17a). It is fairly clear, therefore, that this entire talmudic passage is an anti-Christian polemic, ridiculing the doctrine of the virgin birth of Jesus (see D. Rokeah, "Ben Sṭara is Ben Pantira"). In keeping with this anti-Christian tendency, the version of the second *baraita* as brought in the uncensored text of TB *Sanhedrin* 67a reads as follows: "And that is precisely what they did to Ben Sṭada (or: Sṭara) in Lydda, and they hung him on the day before the Passover" – apparently a reference to the crucifixion. The text then continues as in *Shabbat* ("Was he the son of Sṭara? Wasn't he rather …").

While the Babylonian tradition clearly seems to identify Ben Sṭada with Ben Pantira (Jesus), it is highly unlikely that this reflects any historical tradition deriving from the tannaitic period. On the contrary, it is almost certainly a classic example of the Babylonian Talmud's "creative historiography" which seeks to identify obscure and unknown figures (like Ben Sṭada) with significant and well known figures (like Ben Pantira = Jesus). The Babylonian Talmud here as elsewhere reworks early sources (Tosefta and TJ) in order to achieve its own literary and polemical ends. It is therefore not surprising that inconsistencies remain between the older, more original elements, and the more recent trends and interpretations which coexist in the Babylonian Talmud's final retelling of these stories. Attempts to relate all of these various elements to a particular concrete historical figure will therefore almost always result in contradiction.

For example, Rabbenu Jacob b. Meir *Tam (in early editions of *tosafot* to Sanhedrin) mentions an interpretation which identifies Ben Stada with Jesus. This suggestion is based on the allusion to Pandira and strengthened by the mention of a Passover execution and of a mother named Miriam (Mary). R. Tam, however, rejects this view, pointing out that Pappos b. Judah lived a century after Jesus. Furthermore, Jesus was executed in Jerusalem and not in Lydda. Modern scholarship has suggested that Ben Stada may have been the Egyptian prophet who, during the administration of the Roman procurator Felix, persuaded "large crowds to follow him to the Mount of Olives," where at his command, "Jerusalem's walls would fall down and he would provide an entrance to the city" (Jos., Ant., 20:169ff.; Acts, 21:38). The only real link between the two, however, is the mention of Egypt. Josephus claimed that the prophet disappeared, whereas Ben Stada (according to the earliest and most reliable evidence) was executed in Lydda, possibly in the second century C.E. (see Derenbourg, *Essai sur les formes des pluriels arabes* (1867), 468–71). Given the scanty evidence concerning Ben Stada which is preserved in the earliest sources, it is unlikely that any definite identification of the historical figure that stands behind these traditions can be made.

BIBLIOGRAPHY: R.T. Herford, *Christianity in Talmud and Midrash* (1903), 37, 344ff.; J. Klausner, *Jesus of Nazereth* (1929), 20–23; Schoeps, in: HUCA, 21 (1948), 258ff.; Chajes, in: *Ha-Goren*, 4 (1903), 33–37; D. Rokeah, in: *Tarbiẓ*, 39 (1970), 9–18.

[Isaiah Gafni / Stephen G. Wald (2nd ed.)]

BENSUSAN (Ibn Sūsān or **Shoshan**, also **Cohen ibn Sūsān** and **Levy Bensusan)**, Moroccan family that can be traced to the 12th century. JUDAH IBN SŪSĀN (d. 1165) was *Maimonides' teacher in *Fez; he was martyred there by the *Almohads. During the 13th and 14th centuries, members of the Ibn Sūsān family held important posts as rabbis, astronomers, physicians, financiers, and diplomats in Christian Spain. Their descendants returned to Morocco after 1391. Some time before 1539, the Moroccan mathematician ISSACHAR B. MORDECAI IBN SŪSĀN settled in Jerusalem and later in Safed, where he wrote *Tikkun Yissakhar* (Salonika, 1564), which was reedited under the title *ʿIbbur Shanim* ("Intercalation of the Years," Venice, 1578). The book includes two treatises on the rituals to be followed according to yearly variations of the Jewish calendar, and the apportioning of the *haftarot* according to the rites of different communities. NATHAN LEVI BENSUSAN was a leader of the *toshavin* ("native") community in Morocco in the early 16th century. Several of his descendants were scholars who were often named in the statutes of the Fez community.

The family constituted a powerful merchant clan in Rabat-Salé, and often acted against the interests of other members of the community. During the 17th and 18th centuries their activities extended to London, where they were active in the Sephardi community. In the 19th century they reinforced their position in trade in Morocco, especially in Mogador and Marrakesh, where JOSHUA LÉVY-BENSUSAN (19th cent.) represented France in about 1881. SAMUEL LÉVY BENSUSAN (1872–1958), who lived in Essex, England, wrote a number of books about the English countryside, such as *Annals of Maychester* (1936), and also published studies of great artists. He traveled widely and wrote about Morocco, Spain, Paris, Germany, and the haunts of Shakespeare. Bensusan edited a weekly newspaper, *The Jewish World* (1897–98), and *The Theosophical Review* (1925–28).

BIBLIOGRAPHY: A. Hyamson, *Sephardim of England* (1951), 247, 336, 397; J.M. Toledano, *Ner ha-Ma'arav* (1911), 25ff., 41, 63, 109, 191; REJ, 6 (1941), 12–25; Miège, Maroc, 2 (1961), 550; 3 (1962), 208; 4 (1963), 304.

[David Corcos]

BEN TEMALYON, name of a demon. According to talmudic legend it accompanied R. *Simeon b. Yoḥai on his journey to Rome where he pleaded with the authorities to annul the decree compelling the Jews to have intercourse with their menstruating wives, to desecrate the Sabbath, and not to circumcise their children. The demon entered into the Roman emperor's daughter and when Simeon b. Yoḥai exorcised it, his request was granted (Me'il. 17b). A more detailed account of this miracle is contained in **Halakhot Gedolot* (ed. Hildesheimer, 603–4), where, however, the demon is called "Shamdon" or "Ashmedai." The story frequently recurs in medieval folklore, sometimes with an anti-Jewish bias. Some scholars have attempted to identify Ben Temalyon (or Bar Temalyon) with the apostle Bartholomew about whom a similar legend is related in connection with his missionary voyage to India.

Ben Temalyon (or Telamyon) is also the name of a person who technically avoided perjury by concealing a hundred dinars which he owed to a plaintiff, in a hollowed cane which he asked the latter to hold, and taking an oath that he had returned him the money (cf. Ned. 25a).

BIBLIOGRAPHY: I. Lévi, in: REJ, 8 (1884), 200–2; 10 (1885), 66–73; Halevy, *ibid.*, 60–65; R. Margoliouth, *Malakhei Elyon* (Jerusalem, 1945), p. 222.

BENTOR, JACOB (1910–2002), geologist specializing in the geology, petrology, and tectonics of the Middle East. Bentor was born in Koenigsberg, Germany, and after studying linguistics at the Sorbonne in Paris and physical science there and in Berlin immigrated to Ereẓ Israel in 1933, where he continued his studies, including geology, at the Hebrew University as well as in Switzerland and France. Back in Palestine in 1940 he completed his Ph. D. theses at the Hebrew University in 1945 and in Clermont-Ferrand in 1952. During World War II he was a consultant to the British administration on various geological projects and in 1949 he joined Ḥemed Gimmel (the Israeli army science corps) and headed the national efforts to map the Negev's natural resources and evaluate its economic potential. One of the major products of this activity was the Geological Map of the Negev, 1:100,000, which included the mapping of Israel's major mineral deposits – the Negev phosphates and the Timna copper. For this achievement Bentor and his colleague A. Vroman were awarded the Israel Prize for science in 1953. Until 1966 he was at the head of all national mineral and energy resources enterprises, including the Dead Sea resources, the Negev phosphates, Timna copper ore, and petroleum exploration. During his work he also discovered new geological phenomena, such as combustion metamorphism, a contribution in the field of mineralogy that has been recognized by the international mineralogical community, with the mineral "bentorite" being named in his honor. He introduced many new scientific disciplines, such as geochemistry, marine geology, and seismology to the entire earth science community in Israel, and especially to his many students at the Hebrew University, where he was appointed associate professor in 1957 and full professor in 1963. In 1967–74 he headed a large-scale geological study of the Sinai Peninsula. Focusing on the Precambrian Basement of this area, he made a major contribution to the understanding of the Precambrian Arabian Massif and guided many research projects in the framework of this study. He also had a long-term interest in the possible geological origin of many events chronicled in myth and history and wrote on geological events in the Bible. Bentor headed many national and international scientific committees, including the Council for Oceanographic Research, the World Geological Map Project, and the Council of the International Committee for the Scientific Research of the Mediterranean.

He retired from the Hebrew University in 1977 and was associated with the Scripps Institution of Oceanography, where he remained active in his studies on the Precambrian realm and on the combustion metamorphism of the Hatrurim Formation in Israel ("Mottled Zone") as well as of similar phenomena in California. He was a recipient of the Freund Prize of the Israel Geological Society (1986).

[Yossi Bartov (2nd ed.)]

BENTOV (Gutgeld), MORDEKHAI (1900–1985). Israel politician, member of the First to Fifth Knessets. Bentov was born in Grodzisk, near Warsaw. He immigrated to Ereẓ Israel in 1920, working for several years in road construction and draining swamps. He graduated from the government law classes in Jerusalem and later became a member of kibbutz *Mishmar ha-Emek, where he lived for the rest of his life. As a leader of the *Ha-Shomer ha- Ẓa'ir movement, Bentov served as its representative in central bodies of the *Histadrut and the Zionist Movement. He was one of the members of Ha-Shomer ha-Ẓa'ir active from the late 1930s in trying to find a peaceful solution to the Arab-Israeli conflict on the basis of bi-nationalism, and was an active member in the League for Jewish-Arab Rapprochement and Cooperation. He was a member of the Jewish delegation to the 1939 Round Table Conference with the British Government to discuss the future of Palestine. Following the failure of the Conference, Bentov was chairman of a League of Nations committee that prepared a report published in June 1941 on a future constitution for Palestine, which came to be known as the "Bentov book." In 1947 he became a member of the Political Committee representing the Jewish Agency in the UN. In 1943–48 he served as editor of the Mapam daily, *Al ha-Mishmar.* In the 1948 Provisional Government of Israel Bentov was minister of labor and reconstruction. He was a member of the Knesset for Mapam in 1949–65, minister of development in 1955–61, and minister of housing in 1966–69. He wrote *Constitutional Development of Palestine* (1941); *The Road to Bi-national Independence for Palestine* (1947); *Yisrael, ha-Palestina'im ve-ha-Semol* ("Israel, the Palestinians and the Left," 1971); and a 1984 memoir.

[Benjamin Jaffe / Susan Hattis Rolef (2nd ed.)]

BENTWICH, English Zionist family who settled in Palestine during the 1920s.

HERBERT BENTWICH (1856–1932), British Zionist leader and lawyer. An authority on copyright law, for many years he edited the *Law Journal.* Bentwich was born in London. He became a leading member of the English Ḥovevei Zion and one of the first followers of Theodor *Herzl in England. In 1897 Bentwich organized the first pilgrimage to Ereẓ Israel of the Order of the Ancient Maccabeans, on whose behalf, in 1923, he acquired land for settlement at Gezer, near Ramleh. Bentwich was a founder of the English Zionist Federation in 1899 and for some time served as its vice chairman. He was a legal adviser for the *Jewish Colonial Trust. From 1916 to 1918 he served on the Zionist political advisory committee under Chaim *Weizmann. Bentwich settled in Palestine in 1929, spending most of his time at the family home in Zikhron Ya'akov.

His son, NORMAN DE MATTOS BENTWICH (1883–1971), English Zionist, lawyer, and scholar, was born in London, where he practiced law from 1908 to 1912. In 1913 he was appointed commissioner of courts in Egypt and lecturer at the Cairo Law School. During World War I he served in the British Army on the Palestine front and was demobilized with the rank of major. From 1920 until 1931 Bentwich was attorney general of the Mandate government in Palestine, and in this capacity was active in modernizing the country's courts and introducing British law and procedure to replace those of the former Turkish regime. In 1930 an attempt was made on his life by an Arab terrorist. The Mandate government's anti-Zionist policy led him to resign in 1931.

The following year Bentwich was appointed professor of international relations at the Hebrew University of Jerusalem. He advocated Arab-Jewish rapprochement, sharing the views of the *Berit Shalom group. He served as director of the League of Nations' Commission for Jewish Refugees from Germany between 1933 and 1936. In 1951 he retired from the Hebrew University and returned to England where he was active on behalf of the Hebrew University.

Bentwich was a prolific writer. His books on Zionism and Israel include *Palestine of the Jews: Past, Present and Future* (1919), *England in Palestine* (1932), *Fulfillment in the Promised Land* (1938), *Palestine* (1946^2, *Jewish Youth Comes Home, 1933–1943* (1944), *Israel* (1960^2), *Israel and her Neighbors* (1955), *Legislation of Palestine* (1926), and *The Criminal Law of Palestine* (1928); on international relations: *The Religious Foundations of Internationalism* (1959^2), *From Geneva to San Francisco* (1946), *A Commentary on the Charter of the UN* (1950), and *The Mandates System* (1930); on Hellenism: *Hellenism* (1919), *Josephus* (1914), and *Philo-Judaeus of Alexandria* (1910); biographies: *Solomon Schechter* (1938), *For Zion's Sake* (on J.L. *Magnes, 1954), and on Brigadier F. Kisch. *Wanderer in the Promised Land* (1932), *Wanderer Between Two Worlds* (1941), and *Wanderer in War* (1946) are all autobiographies as is *My 77 Years* (1961). *Mandate Memoirs 1918–1948* (1965) was written in collaboration with his wife Helen, and a biography of his father, *The Pilgrim Father* (1940), in collaboration with his sister Margery (d. 1976). Bentwich's wife, Helen Caroline (née Franklin; 1892–1972), was chairman of the London County Council in 1956–57, and alderman from 1958 to 1965. She wrote *Our Councils, the Story of Local Government* (1962).

JOSEPH BENTWICH (1902–1982), another son of Herbert Bentwich, was an Israeli educator. Bentwich was born in London and settled in Palestine in 1924. From 1928 to 1948 he served as inspector of schools for the Mandate government, and from 1943 to 1948 as assistant director of the Department of Education. Bentwich was principal of the Reali High School in Haifa from 1948 to 1955, and from 1955 to 1958 he lectured on education at the Hebrew University. In 1962 he was awarded the Israel Prize for his contribution to Israel education. Bentwich was a leader of the Amanah ("Covenant") group, established to study and promote new interpretations of Judaism. He edited *Yalkut ha-Datot* ("Anthology of Religions," 1964) and *Yahadut, Mikra'ah* ("Judaism, a Reader," 1967). He published several textbooks for teaching English and mathematics and *Education in Israel* (1965).

Herbert Bentwich's ninth child, Thelma (1895–1959), was a cellist (see *Yellin-Bentwich, Thelma).

[Benjamin Jaffe / Cecil Roth]

°**BENTZEN, AAGE** (1894–1953), Danish biblical scholar, He was appointed professor of biblical studies at the University of Copenhagen in 1929. He was the first president of the International Organization of Old Testament Scholars, which was established in Leiden in 1950, and was instrumental in helping to establish its journal, *Vetus Testamentum*, in the same year.

Bentzen was a prolific scholar, expert in all phases of biblical exegesis. Since he observed little agreement between the J and E documents, and regarded them as independent of one another, he preferred to write in terms of etiological legends, myths, and cultic songs. He almost completely ignored the older classification of literary criticism, including the Documentary Hypothesis, and was inclined instead to emphasize historical narrative, historiography, and strata of traditions. Typical of Bentzen's methodology and thought is his *Messias – Moses redivivus – Menschensohn* (1948; *King and Messiah*, 1955), where he attempts to assess the contributions of the

English and Scandinavian myth and ritual schools in regard to the cultic situations in the life of the king of Israel. Bentzen criticizes both schools and argues for the impact of history on the cultic myth. Furthermore, it is the "Urmensch" idea which underlies the role of the king, the priest, the prophet, and the messiah in Israel. He also wrote *Introduction to the Old Testament* (2 vols., 1948–49, 1961^6).

BIBLIOGRAPHY: VT, *Congress Volume* (1953), vii–xv (incl. complete bibliography).

[Zev Garber]

BENVENISTE (also **Bienveniste, Benvist, Abenbenist**, etc.), personal name and surname of a widespread Sephardi family. The name originated in Spain and Provence and means "welcome." It is first mentioned in documents from Barcelona in 1079. After the expulsion from Spain in 1492, the family was dispersed, especially throughout the Ottoman Empire.

Prominent members, in addition to those to whom separate articles are devoted, include BENVENISTE IBN BENVENISTE (early 14th century), translator of medical works from Arabic into Catalan during the reign of James II, king of Aragon (1291–1327); IZMEL (ISHMAEL) of Barcelona (early 14th century), physician, father of the physician Samuel *Benveniste; ADZAY (=ḤASDAI) BENVENIST (mid-15th century), member of the communal council in Saragossa; JUDAH B. ABRAHAM (1460–1515), born in Toledo, a descendant of Abraham *Benveniste of Soria, who, after the expulsion from Spain, was active in Salonika; and NISSIM (15th century), a scholar whose halakhic queries to Isaac *Aboab were published by Abraham Meldola in *Ziv ha-Einayim*.

BIBLIOGRAPHY: Baer, Urkunden, 1 pt. 2 (1936), index, s.v. *Bienvenist*; Baer, Spain, index; Cantera-Millás, Inscripciones, 180, 193–4; *Sefarad*, index to vols. 1–15 (1957), 399, 401.

BENVENISTE, ABRAHAM (1406–1454), "court rabbi" in Castile mentioned in crown documents dating from about 1430. The young king, John II, handed over the government of Castile to two noblemen, who appointed Benveniste, a native of Soria, to restore its shaky fiscal administration. Benveniste acted as tax farmer general of the realm and organized the levy of the taxes and customs duties with the assistance of subordinates, mainly Jews. He also supplied the army with money and grain. In 1432, at the request of the Jewish communities of the Castile, the king appointed Benveniste chief justice and tax superintendent of Castilian Jewry, with the title of *Rab de la Corte*. The same year he convened the representatives and scholars of the Castilian communities in Valladolid, and framed a number of ordinances designed to strengthen the status of Spanish Jewry, which had been undermined by the recent tragic events. These enactments were directed toward maintaining religious instruction, the fair administration of justice in Jewish courts, equitable tax apportionment, defense against informers, and curbs on extravagance in dress and entertainment. Benveniste was conservative in his approach to religious problems. He opposed the rationalist philosophical trends widespread among Jewish scholars, and strove for the rehabilitation of Jewish communal life through strict observance of the precepts of Judaism.

BIBLIOGRAPHY: Graetz, Hist, 4 (1949), 228–9, 280, 341, 351; Baer, Urkunden, 1 pt. 2 (1936), 305–6, 309; Baer, Spain, index; Neuman, Spain, index; Finkelstein, Middle Ages, 103, 349.

[Zvi Avneri]

BENVENISTE, ABRAHAM (18th century), rabbi and communal leader in Smyrna. Benveniste was a son-in-law of Ḥayyim Ventura and of Abraham Ibn Ezra, both outstanding scholars of Smyrna. His communal activity brought him into contact with the scholars of Italy, and his correspondence with Moses Ḥayyim Morpurgo of Ancona during the years 1746–50 is extant. Morpurgo asked him to supply a list of books recently published in Turkey and to keep him informed of any new publications, while Benveniste on his part sent Morpurgo a list of books which he asked him to acquire for him in Venice. It is possible therefore that Benveniste was in the book trade.

BIBLIOGRAPHY: M. Benayahu, in: *Aresheth*, 1 (1958), 224–6, 231–9.

BENVENISTE, EMILE (1902–1976), French scholar of language theory and comparative grammar. Holding a chair at the College de France from 1937 to his death, Benveniste was extremely influential on French theorists in various domains of linguistics and literary criticism, such as Gerard Genette for narrative discourse and Roland Barthes, Tzetan Todorov, and Michel Riffaterre in the field of poetry theory. Benveniste's linguistics perpetuates the heritage of his master, Antoine Meillet, and that of Ferdinand de Saussure, though his theory of communication notably diverges from Saussure's. Benveniste published profusely, but his most influential essays and theories are collected in the two volumes of his *Problèmes de linguistique générale*, in the first volume of which key dichotomies are proposed: "*je/non-je*" (I/non-I), "*histoire/discours*" (story/discourse). These concepts are central to modern narrative discourse as well as communications theory: they help define the larger dichotomy between objective and subjective utterance.

Another crucial dichotomy is to be found in the chapter "Sémiologie de la langue" in the second volume: the dichotomy of "semiotic" (related to the sign) and "semantic" (related to discourse).

[Dror Franck Sullaper (2nd ed.)]

BENVENISTE (or **Benvenist**), **ḤAYYIM BEN ISRAEL** (1603–1673), Sephardi rabbinic scholar and codifier. Benveniste studied in his native Constantinople mainly under Joseph b. Moses of Trani, and also under Joseph *Samegah. In 1624, when he was only 21, he began to write his detailed commentary on the *Sefer Mitzvot Gadol* of *Moses b. Jacob of Coucy, which he called *Dina de-Ḥayyei* ("Law of the Living"). The same year he was appointed to decide cases dealing with ritual law (*Issur ve-Hetter*). Benveniste was rabbi in Tirya, near Smyrna, from 1643 to 1655 when he settled in Smyrna. When Chief Rabbi Joseph Escapa of Smyrna reached an advanced age, Benveniste was appointed in 1661 to act for him in matters of ritual and matrimonial law, and succeeded him after his death the following year. In 1665 the council of the city's scholars (with Benveniste's consent) appointed Aaron *Lapapa in charge of civil cases, but at the end of the same year the latter was deposed by the many admirers of Shabbetai Ẓevi, whom Lapapa had excommunicated and condemned to death. After Shabbetai Ẓevi's conversion to Islam a small section of the Smyrna community unsuccessfully attempted to reinstate Lapapa. As a result, Benveniste became involved in a dispute with Lapapa. Benveniste's attitude to the Shabbatean movement as a whole was entirely negative, but he sought to avoid controversy in the interest of communal harmony, and was not resolute enough in certain instances to oppose openly the majority of his community, who followed Shabbetai Ẓevi and his followers.

Benveniste's role in this episode however did not detract from his dignity and authority as one of the greatest of the Jewish codifiers. Among his many disciples were Solomon ibn Ezra, Isaac Algazi, Ḥayyim Algazi, and Abraham b. Aaron de Boton. His principal work *Keneset ha-Gedolah*, was accepted by both Ashkenazi and Sephardi rabbis as an authoritative work of great practical value. In his work, which comprises eight large volumes, Benveniste cites and methodically explains all the conclusions and legal novellae to be found in the responsa and other halakhic works of the outstanding authorities after the time of Joseph *Caro, as well as some of the decisions of earlier scholars whom Caro had failed to cite.

In Benveniste's lifetime only three parts of the work were printed: on *Oraḥ Ḥayyim* (Leghorn, 1658); *Sheyarei*, addenda on *Oraḥ Ḥayyim* (Smyrna, 1671); and on *Ḥoshen Mishpat* (part 1, Smyrna, 1660). After his death there appeared the volume on *Yoreh De'ah* (3 parts, Constantinople, 1711–17); on *Even ha-Ezer* (Smyrna, 1731, new ed. Lemberg, 1861); on *Ḥoshen Mishpat*, part 2, with several appendixes by other authors (Smyrna, 1734). Also his *Dina de-Ḥayyei* was published posthumously from a defective manuscript (Constantinople, 2 pts. 1747). Additional legal novellae on the *Ḥoshen Mishpat* are to be found in Ḥayyim b. Menahem Algazi's *Benei Ḥayyai* published in Orta-koi (near Constantinople) in 1712. Benveniste also wrote important responsa (*Ba'ei Ḥayyei*, "Needs of the Living"), on the four parts of the *Turim*, the following of which have been published: on *Oraḥ Ḥayyim* (part 2, Salonika, 1783), on 211 sections of *Yoreh De'ah* and on 24 of the *Even ha-Ezer* (*ibid.*, 1788), as well as on the *Ḥoshen Mishpat*, in two parts (*ibid.*, 1791). Benveniste also wrote novellae on a number of tractates: that on *Sanhedrin* which he called *Ḥamra ve-Ḥayyei*, only part of which is extant, was published, together with notes and extracts from the manuscripts of the novellae of the earlier halakhic authorities, under the title of *Ḥemer Ḥivver Attik* (Leghorn, 1802). Benveniste's son Israel (1644–1729) succeeded him as chief rabbi of Smyrna.

BIBLIOGRAPHY: J.J. Emden, *Torat ha-Kena'ot* (1752), 4b; J. Sasportas *Ẓiẓat Novel Ẓevi*, ed. by I. Tishby (1954), index, S.V. *Benvenisti, Ḥayyim*; Conforte, Kore, 51a; Bernfeld, in: *Kobez al Jad*, 9 (1899), 1–11 (third pagination); A. Freimann (ed.), *Inyanei Shabbetai Ẓevi* (1912), 142, no. 20; Rosanes, Togarmah, 4 (1935), 42–47, 160–4; Benayahu, in: *Zion*, 12 (1946/47), 44–48; idem, in: *Reshumot*, 5 (1953), 197–211; idem, in: *Sinai*, 34 (1954), 167, 200–2; Scholem, Shabbetai Ẓevi, index; Sonne, in: *Sefunot*, 34 (1960), 48, 50, 57 s.v. *Benvenest*; Molho and Amarijlio, *ibid.*, 214–6 (Eng. summ.).

[Moshe Nahum Zobel]

BENVENISTE, IMMANUEL (**Manoel**; Venice? c. 1608–Amsterdam c. 1660), Hebrew printer in Amsterdam. Benveniste's name appears in an entry in the *Puiboken* of that city, dated Feb. 10, 1640: "Immanuel Benveniste of Venice, 32 years old, parents still living…" Among the approximately 50 works he printed between 1640 and 1659 are *Midrash Rabbah* (1641–42), *Mishnah* (1643), and Alfasi's *Halakhot* (1643). His outstanding production, however, was the Babylonian Talmud (1644–48), which restored some passages expunged by the censor in previous editions. As correctors Benveniste employed Moses di Cordova b. Isaac of Constantinople (for the *Midrash Rabbah*) and the Amsterdam rabbi Abraham b. Joshua of Worms (for the Alfasi edition). Benveniste's editions can usually be recognized by the title page frame of a gate of prism-shaped stones with his printer's mark, a castle flanked by a lion with a star superimposed.

BIBLIOGRAPHY: J.S. da Silva Rosa, *Geschiedenis der portugeesche Joden te Amsterdam 1593–1925* (1925), 29–30.; ESN 1 (1949), 62; Brugmans-Frank, 469, 476. **ADD. BIBLIOGRAPHY:** L. Fuks and R.G. Fuks-Mansfeld, *Hebrew Typography in the Northern Netherlands 1585–1815*, 1 (1984), 146–84; M.J. Heller, in: *Studies in Bibliography and Booklore*, 19 (1994) 3–20.

[*Encyclopaedia Judaica* (Germany) / A.K.Offenberg (2nd ed.)]

BENVENISTE, ISAAC BEN JOSEPH (d. c. 1224), physician to James I of Aragon and *nasi* of Aragonese Jewry. He was the leading figure in the representative congresses of the Jewish communities convened at Montpellier and Saint-Gilles in 1214 and 1215 to consider protective measures in view of the approaching *Lateran Council. Subsequently he secured for the Aragonese communities a temporary suspension of the obligation to wear the Jewish *badge. In 1220, he received from Pope Honorius III a warm letter of recommendation to the king and the archbishop of Tarragona notwithstanding Isaac's "erroneous" views in matters of religion.

BIBLIOGRAPHY: Neuman, Spain, index; Solomon ibn Verga, *Shevet Yehudah*, ed. by A. Shochat (1947), 147, 223; S. Grayzel, *The Church and the Jews* (1966^2), index.

[Cecil Roth]

BENVENISTE, JOSEPH BEN MOSES DE SEGOVIA (second half of the 16th century), rabbi and author. Benveniste spent most of his life in Safed but died in Brusa, Turkey. His principal teacher was Elisha *Gallico, but he also studied under Isaac *Luria and Samuel b. Isaac de *Uceda. Joseph

*Ganso, rabbi of Brusa, was his pupil. He wrote many works which were lost. Benveniste mentions two of them: *Be-Ẓel ha-Kesef*, an ethical work modeled on the *Kad ha-Kemaḥ* of *Baḥya b. Asher, and *Yakhol Yosef* (also erroneously called *Yevul Yosef*) containing various novellae. A number of his biblical comments, including interpretations he learned from Isaac *Luria, are quoted in the *Dovev Siftei Yeshenim* (Smyrna, 1671) of his grandson Nissim Solomon *Algazi.

BIBLIOGRAPHY: Scholem, in: *Beḥinot*, 9 (1956), 82; Tamar, in: *Tarbiz*, 27 (1957/58), 105–8; M. Benayahu, *Sefer Toledot ha-Ari* (1967), 362–4.

[Abraham David]

BENVENISTE, JOSHUA RAPHAEL BEN ISRAEL (1590?–1665?), Turkish rabbi, physician, grammarian, and poet; brother of Ḥayyim *Benveniste. Joshua was born in Constantinople and was a disciple of Joseph b. Moses *Trani and Abraham *Alegre. He studied grammar under Isaac *Uzziel, and medicine under Isaac Caro, the physician. While serving as rabbi in Constantinople, he accepted the rabbinate of Sophia, after the community had agreed to all of his conditions, but the Constantinople community objected and prevailed upon him to remain. For some years Joshua was rabbi of Bursa. Many communities, even Karaites, addressed their problems to him, and responsa written by him, as early as 1610, are extant. Benveniste was a versatile author and many of his works are still regarded as basic in their fields. He devoted himself particularly to the Jerusalem Talmud, which was largely neglected in his day. His commentary on it, *Sedeh Yehoshu'a*, was published with the text. Joshua's method was first to explain all difficult words according to the Babylonian Talmud, the *Arukh*, etc., and then to explain the passage, comparing it with the parallel passage in the Babylonian Talmud or explaining it according to the context where no such parallel exists. Where the *halakhah* differs in the two Talmuds he decided according to the Babylonian, "since it is the essential one." He also collected explanations which he found in works of *rishonim* and halakhists and added his own. He deals only with the halakhic portions, ignoring the *aggadah*. His language is very prolix. This may explain why the commentary did not become widespread among the scholars of Eastern and Western Europe.

His commentary to the following tractates was published: *Berakhot, Pe'ah, Orlah, Ḥallah*, and *Bikkurim* of the order *Zera'im* (Constantinople, 1662); a number of tractates of *Mo'ed, Nashim*, and *Nezikin* (Constantinople, 1749). The commentary has frequently been reprinted together with the text. His *Seder ha-Get* and *Seder Ḥaliẓah* were published in *Get Pashut* (Constantinople, 1719) of Moses ibn Ḥabib. According to Ḥayyim Joseph David *Azulai, his four volumes of responsa, *Sha'ar Yehoshu'a*, were destroyed by fire after 1677. Some of his 97 responsa on *Ḥoshen Mishpat*, which have remained in manuscript (Jewish Institute, Warsaw, no. 13), were published in Husiatin in 1904 and many of his responsa were published in the books of his contemporaries. His other published works are *Oznei Yehoshu'a* (Constantinople, 1677), sermons, and *Avodah Tammah* (Constantinople, 1691–95), an exposition of the *Avodah in the Day of Atonement liturgy, and a clarification of the variant readings. The following remain in manuscript: *Mishmeret ha-Mitzvot* (JTS, Ms. 0347), a poetic arrangement of the commandments in accordance with the enumeration of Maimonides; *Levush Malkhut*, describing the greatness of the Creator as evinced in the human anatomy, written in the style of the *Keter Malkhut* of Solomon ibn Gabirol; *Perek be-Shir* (Montefiore Ms. 377), on prosody and meter; and a treatise on medicine.

BIBLIOGRAPHY: L. Ginzberg, *Perushim ve-Ḥiddushim ba-Yerushalmi*, 1 (1961), introduction (Eng.) liii–liv; N. Allony, *Mi-Torat ha-Lashon ve-ha-Shirah bi-Ymei ha-Beinayim* (1944), 85–92; idem, *Mi-Sifrut Yemei ha-Beinayim* (1945), 39–42; Benayahu, in: *Aresheth*, 3 (1961), 151.

BENVENISTE, MOSES (second half of the 16th century), Turkish physician. As medical attendant to the grand vizier, Siavouch Pasha, Benveniste attained considerable influence in Turkish politics; in 1582 he was largely responsible for reinstating Peter the Lame as *gospodar* (ruler) of Moldavia. In 1583, in conjunction with Nissim, the Jewish director of the mint, he recommended the currency reform which led to a revolt of the Janissaries. Later, he was associated with the Jew David *Passi and the Italian Paolo Maria in unsuccessful intrigues with the English ambassador Barton against Solomon *Abenaes, Duke of Mytilene. In 1598 Benveniste, who had always favored the pro-Spanish party in Turkish politics, was one of the three Turkish plenipotentiaries in the peace negotiations with Spain. Having exceeded their instructions, they were banished. It is possible that Benveniste unsuccessfully tried to escape this sentence by embracing Islam, but died a political prisoner, probably in Rhodes. The poet Yehudah Zarko, a native of Rhodes, wrote a long poem about the exile of Benveniste to Rhodes. His son, Rabbi Israel Benveniste, visited him there. It seems that he became one of the leaders of the Jewish community in Rhodes. Rabbi Israel died after 1695 and we have the poem which was written on his tombstone. His well-known grandchildren were Rabbi Ḥayyim *Benveniste and Rabbi Moses Benveniste.

BIBLIOGRAPHY: Rosanes, Togarmah 3 (1938²), 8, 13, 356–8, 363; C. Roth, *House of Nasi, Duke of Naxos* (1948), 200, 204, 211, 215; A. Galanté, *Turcs et Juifs* (1932), 101; idem, *Juifs de Rhodes* (1935), 109f.; E. Charrière (ed.), *Négociations de la France dans le Levant*, 4 (1966), 246f. **ADD. BIBLIOGRAPHY:** Graetz-Shefer, 7, 309, 428. Benayahu, in: *Sefunot* 12 (1971–78), 123–45; C.M. Kortepeter, *Ottoman Imperialism during the Reformation: Europe and the Caucasus* (1972), 214–26; F. Braudel, *The Mediterranean and the Mediterranean World in the Age of Philip II* (1973), 1143–85.

[Cecil Roth / Leah Bornstein-Makovetsky (2nd ed.)]

BEN-VENISTE, RICHARD (1943–), U.S. lawyer. A native New Yorker, Ben-Veniste is from a Sephardi family on his father's side, with its roots in northern Spain and Greece, and has a German and Russian background on his mother's side. He earned his undergraduate degree magna cum laude from Muhlenberg College and returned to New York to get his law degree from Columbia University, where he was the Harlan Fisk Stone Scholar. He joined the United States Attorney's office in New York straight from Northwestern University's law school, where he received his master of law degree in 1968. He stayed on, assigned first to the Special Prosecutions Section and then as chief of the Official Corruption Section (where he prosecuted several celebrated cases), from June 1972, until, at the age of 30, joining the main Watergate task force, investigating the activities of President Richard M. Nixon, and questioning witnesses in connection with the White House tape recordings.

It was Ben-Veniste, an assistant special prosecutor, who presented the opening statement on behalf of the seven-member prosecution team in the Watergate cover-up trial, portraying Nixon as one of the central conspirators. In a four-hour presentation, Ben-Veniste told the jury that Nixon held a "multitude of meetings" in April 1973 with John D. Ehrlichman and H.R. Haldeman, then his chief aides and two of the five defendants in the trial. He also laid out details of the case against the other defendants, including Attorney General John N. Mitchell. Ben-Veniste thus had one of the key roles in the unraveling of the Nixon presidency and Nixon's resignation before he could be impeached.

Ben-Veniste practiced law in Washington, specializing in litigation involving high-profile white-collar clients, including, in the 1990s, the investigation of President Bill Clinton and his wife, Hilary, concerning the failed land deal known as Whitewater. That investigation found no evidence of criminal activity on the part of the Clintons.

In 2004, Ben-Veniste was a Democratic member of the independent commission investigating the Sept. 11 attacks, engineered by Osama Bin Laden and Al-Qaeda, on the World Trade Center in New York and on the Pentagon. As such he harshly questioned Condoleezza Rice, President George W. Bush's national security advisor, on her and the president's assessment of a briefing on Aug. 6, 2001, that carried the title "Bin Laden Determined to Attack Inside the United States." Rice described it as "historical information based on old reporting – there was no new threat information," a contention Ben-Veniste disputed. Ben-Veniste played a major role in shaping the commission's final report, in which it asserted that the Clinton and Bush administrations failed to grasp the gravity of the threat from Al Qaeda.

[Stewart Kampel (2nd ed.)]

BENVENISTE, SAMUEL (d. after 1356), physician and translator, who lived in Tarragona and Saragossa, Spain. Benveniste was a familiar figure at the court of King Pedro IV of Aragon, being physician to his brother, Don Manuel. In about 1300 he translated into Hebrew Maimonides' *Sefer ha-Kaẓẓeret* ("Treatise on Asthma"), apparently from a Latin translation; his rendering is colloquial and fluent, although the surviving manuscripts were carelessly copied. Some scholars ascribe to Benveniste a translation of Boethius' *Consolations of Philosophy.*

BIBLIOGRAPHY: HB, 8 (1865), 85, 125f.; 9 (1869), 91; 10 (1870), 84; Steinschneider, Uebersetzungen, 496, 767; Baer, Urkunden, 1 (1929), 172, 434; Sanchez Real, in: *Sefarad*, 11 (1951), 347.

BENVENISTE, SHESHET BEN ISAAC BEN JOSEPH (also called "**Perfect de Pratis**"; c. 1131–1209), Spanish financier, physician, and poet; grandson of Sheshet ha-Nasi of Barcelona. In his youth, Benveniste entered the service of the count of Barcelona. Subsequently, he served the kings of Aragon Alfonso II and from 1196 Pedro II as physician, translator into Arabic, political adviser, and diplomatic envoy. He also took an active part in the fiscal administration, and received certain state revenues in return for loans to the royal treasury. Like the nobility of the kingdom, Benveniste was exempted from taxes and enjoyed legal immunity from the jurisdiction of both the crown authorities and the local Jewish community. He received a royal grant of privileges on the basis of which he regulated the affairs of the Barcelona synagogue. His signature in Hebrew figures on official documents. Benveniste apparently had a wide knowledge in many subjects. He wrote Hebrew poetry, was in touch with Muslim scholars, knew general history, and wrote medical works still preserved in manuscript. Benveniste regarded the *Mishneh Torah* of Maimonides as the basic authority on *halakhah* and vigorously championed the latter's philosophical views. *Benjamin of Tudela and Judah *Al-Ḥarizi, who met Benveniste in Barcelona, praise him highly. He was a patron of poets and scholars, such as *Isaac b. Abba Mari, and Joseph *Ibn Zabara, who dedicated to him his *Sefer ha-Sha'ashu'im.*

BIBLIOGRAPHY: Baer, Spain, 1 (1961), 91, 100; D. Kaufmann, in: REJ, 39 (1899), 62–63; Marx, in: JQR, 25 (1934/35), 406–7.

[Zvi Avneri]

BENVENISTE DE PORTA (d. 1268), financial official in Aragon during the reign of James I, from Villafranca del Panadés. Benveniste dealt in grain and owned flour mills in Barcelona. In the 1250s and 1260s he served the crown as *baile* (bailiff) in Barcelona and elsewhere, such as Gerona, Perpignan, and Lérida. In exchange for the sums he lent to the king and his ministers, Benveniste received concessions on royal revenues in Catalonia and the Balearic Islands. At one time, he provided the silver for the Barcelona mint. In 1264 his brother Astrug de Porta was accused of blaspheming Jesus during a religious discussion but, through Benveniste's influence, the sentence of banishment was commuted to a fine.

BIBLIOGRAPHY: F. de Bofarull y Sans, *Los judíos en el territorio de Barcelona* (1910); Neuman, Spain, index; Baer, Spain (1961), 146, 156.

[Zvi Avneri]

BENVENISTI, DAVID (1897–1993), Israeli geographer and educator. Born in Salonika, Greece, Bevenisti immigrated to Ereẓ Israel with his parents in 1913 and studied at the Jerusalem Teachers' Seminary under David *Yellin. After serving in the Jewish Legion during World War I, he taught the geography of Ereẓ Israel and was pedagogical adviser at the Jerusalem Teachers' Seminary from 1925 until 1963. Devoting himself to educational problems as much as to geography, Benvenisti distinguished himself by promoting an interest in the topography of Ereẓ Israel and a love of nature. To popularize hiking, he was active in founding both the Israel Hikers' Association and the Israel Youth Hostels Federation. He wrote a number of textbooks and teaching guides on the subject of Israeli geography and also became interested in the folklore of the Jews of Salonika, publishing books on this subject, and in 1977 published a guide to the street names of Jerusalem. He was awarded the Israel Prize in 1982 for teaching an appreciation of the Land of Israel and its lore.

BENWAISH, ABRAHAM (16th–17th centuries), banker to the sultan of Morocco Aḥmad al-Manṣūr in Marrakesh (south Morocco) and later superintendent of finances (until 1627). Benwaish was extremely influential and it was because of him that members of the *Pallache family were appointed ambassadors of Morocco to Holland. He was responsible for one of his relatives, Abraham Buzaglo-Azulay, being sent to Venice in 1606 to buy expensive goods for the ruler. Benwaish was appointed **nagid* of the Jews of the kingdom of *Marrakesh and promoted study there. In his capacity as superintendent of finance he discriminated against the English and Dutch Christians in favor of his coreligionists, a policy which brought protests from the European governments. Accused of embezzlement, he had no difficulty in clearing himself. His descendant SAMUEL (1738–1817), *dayyan* of *Meknès, was renowned for his piety. His responsa are extant in manuscript.

BIBLIOGRAPHY: SIHM, Angleterre, 2 (1925), 233, 363, 441, 468; 3 (1936), 64, 66, 68–70; Pays-Bas, 1 (1906), 343, 500; J.M. Toledano, *Ner ha-Ma'arav* (1911), 106, 111, 196; J. Ben-Naim, *Malkhei Rabbanan* (1931), 121; Hirschberg, Afrikah, 2 (1965), 225.

[David Corcos]

BEN-YEḤEZKI'EL, MORDEKHAI (1883–1971), Hebrew essayist and adapter of folktales. Born in Galicia, he moved in 1906 to Lvov where he was both student and tutor. After visiting Western Europe, he taught for a time in Lvov, and immigrated to Palestine in 1920. At first he taught at the Tel Aviv Teachers' Seminary and from 1925 was an instructor of Hebrew, Bible, and Literature at the Mizrachi Teachers' Seminary in Jerusalem. After the publication of his first article on *Ḥasidism in **Ha-Shilo'aḥ* in 1904, he wrote regularly on language, literature, Ḥasidism, etc., in the Hebrew press and was encouraged by Ḥ.N. *Bialik to publish his adaptations of various folktales, which appeared as *Sefer ha-Ma'asiyyot* ("Book of Folk Tales"; four volumes 1926–29; expanded edition in six volumes, 1957).

BIBLIOGRAPHY: G. Bader, *Medinah va-Ḥakhameha* (1934), 76; *Kitvei A. Barash* (1957), 131; A. Korekh, *Kehillat Glina* (1950), 77–80; E.M. Lipschuetz, *Ketavim*, 3 (1957), 181–4.

[Getzel Kressel]

BEN-YEHUDA, ELIEZER (1858–1922), Hebrew writer and lexicographer, generally considered the father of modern Hebrew, and one of the first active Zionist leaders. Born Eliezer Yiẓhak Perelman in Luzhky, Lithuania, he officially adopted the pseudonym Ben-Yehuda, which he had previously used in his literary activities, when he went to Palestine. Ben-Yehuda's father, a *Ḥabad Ḥasid, died when Eliezer was five years old. At the age of 13, he was sent to his uncle to attend the yeshivah in Polotsk. The head of the yeshivah, a *maskil* in secret, introduced him to secular literature. To save him from heresy, his uncle sent him to study in Glubokoye, in the Vilna district, where Ben-Yehuda made the acquaintance of Samuel Naphtali Herz Jonas, also a Ḥabad Ḥasid, who was writing for Hebrew periodicals. Jonas persuaded him to prepare for secondary school matriculation, and his eldest daughter, Deborah, taught him Russian. After a year of preparation he entered the Dvinsk Gymnasium from which he graduated in 1877.

The Russo-Turkish War (1877–78) and the struggle of the Balkan nations for liberation planted in Ben-Yehuda the idea of the revival of the Jewish people on its ancestral soil. He maintained that the Jewish people, like all other peoples, had a historic land and a historic language. What was needed was to actuate a national movement that would restore Israel to its land and to its language. He wrote in the preface to his dictionary: "In those days it was as if the heavens had suddenly opened, and a clear, incandescent light flashed before my eyes, and a mighty inner voice sounded in my ears: the renascence of Israel on its ancestral soil." He determined to settle in Ereẓ Israel, and in 1878 went to Paris to study medicine so that he might have a profession to sustain himself. He discussed his plan for a Jewish national movement with some Hebrew writers; they, however, were not interested. His article "*She'elah Lohatah*" ("A Burning Question") was published in P. *Smolenskin's *Ha-Shaḥar* in 1879 (after *Ha-Maggid* had refused to accept it) under the name "E. Ben-Yehuda." For the first time the idea of a national spiritual center in Ereẓ Israel was clearly propounded. Ben-Yehuda linked the Jewish national revival with the general European awakening and said that the Jewish people should learn from the oppressed European peoples that were fighting for political freedom and national revival. The Jewish people must establish a community in Ereẓ Israel that would serve as a focal point for the entire people, so that even those Jews who would remain in the Diaspora would know that they belong to a people that dwells in its own land and has its own language and culture. In this essay, the fundamental principles of spiritual Zionism are anticipated: the settlement of the land not for the return of the entire people from the exile, but for the creation of a national center designed to save from assimilation those Jews that are scattered all over the Diaspora.

In Paris, Ben-Yehuda met George (Getzel) *Selikovitch, a Jewish journalist, who told him that in his travels through Asia and Africa he had spoken Hebrew with the Jews of these lands, so that in fact Hebrew was not dead. When Ben-Yehuda contracted tuberculosis in the winter of 1878, he decided to discontinue his medical studies and make his home in the more favorable climate of Ereẓ Israel. He enrolled in the teachers' seminary of the Alliance Israélite Universelle, to qualify for a teaching post in *Mikveh Israel. There he attended the lectures of the Assyriologist Joseph *Halevy who in the periodical *Ha-Maggid* had advocated the coinage of new Hebrew words as early as the 1860s. As his health deteriorated, Ben-Yehuda entered the Rothschild Hospital in Paris, and there he met the Jerusalem scholar A.M. *Luncz who spoke Hebrew to him in the Sephardi pronunciation and told him that the members of the various Jewish communities in Jerusalem were able to converse with one another only in Sephardi Hebrew. This reinforced Ben-Yehuda's opinion that the Jews could not hope to become a united people in their own land again unless their children revived Hebrew as their spoken tongue. The Hebrew living language must have Sephardi phonetic sounds because that was the pronunciation which served in the transliteration of biblical names in ancient and modern translations of the Bible. In 1880 he published two articles in *Ha-Ḥavaẓẓelet* in which he advocated that Hebrew rather than the various foreign languages become the language of instruction in the Jewish schools in Ereẓ Israel. In 1881, he left for Palestine. He traveled by way of Vienna, where he was joined by his childhood acquaintance, Deborah Jonas, whom he married in Cairo. In October 1881, they arrived in Jaffa where Ben-Yehuda informed his wife that henceforth they would converse only in Hebrew. The Ben-Yehuda household thus was the first Hebrew-speaking home established in Palestine, and his first son, Ben-Zion (later called Ithamar *Ben-Avi), the first modern Hebrew-speaking child.

To ingratiate himself with the Orthodox Jews who knew written Hebrew and could, therefore, readily learn to speak the language, Ben Yehuda at first adopted their customs. He grew a beard and earlocks, and prevailed upon his wife to wear a *sheytl* ("wig"). This did not last very long because the Orthodox Jews of Jerusalem soon sensed that for Ben-Yehuda Hebrew was not a holy tongue, but a secular, national language, and that his purpose for introducing spoken Hebrew was solely nationalist and political. They began to suspect him, and Ben-Yehuda became an extremist in his antireligious attitude. He registered as a national Jew "without religion."

As early as 1881 Ben-Yehuda, together with Y.M. *Pines, D. *Yellin, Y. *Meyuḥas, and A. Masie, founded the society Teḥiyyat Israel based on five principles: work on the land and expansion of the country's productive population; revival of spoken Hebrew; creation of a modern Hebrew literature and science in the national spirit; education of the youth in a national and, at the same time, universal humanistic spirit; and active opposition to the **ḥalukkah* system. During the period 1882–85, Ben-Yehuda worked on *Ha-Ḥavaẓẓelet* and put out a supplement to the periodical under the name *Mevasseret Ẓiyyon*. At the same time, he taught in the Jerusalem Alliance school, which post he accepted only after he was permitted to use Hebrew exclusively as the language of instruction in all Jewish subjects. The school was thus the first in which at least some subjects were taught in Hebrew. In 1885, Ben-Yehuda published a geography of Palestine, called *Ereẓ Yisrael* (only part 1 appeared). Toward the end of 1884, he founded a weekly, *Ha-Ẓevi*, which later became a biweekly, under the new name, *Ha-Or*. In 1908, it became a daily, known first as *Ha-Ẓevi*, and from 1910 onward as *Ha-Or*; it appeared until 1915. For several years, from 1897, Ben-Yehuda also published a weekly (from 1904, biweekly) called *Hashkafah*. In his periodicals he fought against the *ḥalukkah* system, championed agricultural labor, the new settlement, and, especially, the revival of spoken Hebrew. He spared no effort to enrich the language by coining new terms and introducing transliterations from foreign tongues. Financial difficulties in the economically poor Jerusalem environment were mainly responsible for the shortcomings of his magazine. Despite all its defects, however, Ben-Yehuda's periodical was the first in Hebrew to meet European standards. It removed the barrier between strictly Jewish topics and secular subjects, and discussed, insofar as the strict Turkish censorship permitted, all aspects of general political and cultural life.

In 1891, Ben-Yehuda's wife died, and about six months later he married her younger sister. She adopted the Hebrew name Ḥemdah. A constant companion to her husband in his literary activity, Ḥemdah Ben-Yehuda published translations and original Hebrew stories in his periodicals. It was she who incited Ben-Yehuda's extremism against the Jewish tradition. Ben Yehuda's unorthodox behavior, and the campaign which he waged in the columns of his periodicals against the *ḥalukkah* system and its administrators, aroused the vehement opposition of the extreme Orthodox Jews. Seeking a pretext for revenge, they found it in an article by Jonas in the 1894 Ḥanukkah number of *Ha-Ẓevi*, which contained the phrase "let us gather strength and go forward." Some of Ben-Yehuda's more bigoted enemies distorted its meaning and interpreted it to the Turkish authorities as "let us gather an army and proceed against the East." Ben-Yehuda was charged with sedition and sentenced to a year's imprisonment. The affair created a great stir throughout the Jewish world; an appeal was lodged and he was released.

Turkish censorship of *Ha-Ẓevi*, however, became more stringent from then on. As a result, Ben-Yehuda began to concentrate more on linguistic questions to which the censors could make no objection. He became increasingly engrossed in his dictionary for which he had begun to collect material from the day he arrived in Ereẓ Israel. In order to conduct research and raise funds for its publication, Ben-Yehuda traveled several times to Europe, and later also to the United States where he worked in American libraries. In 1910, assisted by various sponsors, he began to publish his *Complete Dictionary of Ancient and Modern Hebrew* volume by volume; after his death, his widow and his son Ehud continued his publication which was completed in 1959 (17 vols.), with an introductory volume, *Ha-Mavo ha-Gadol* ("Prolegomenon").

In 1890, together with David Yellin, Aaron Masie, and others, Ben-Yehuda founded the Va'ad ha-Lashon over which he presided until his death. This *va'ad* was the forerunner of the *Academy of the Hebrew Language which Ben-Yehuda had also suggested in 1920.

Ben-Yehuda was among the supporters of the *Uganda scheme; he wrote articles in *Ha-Ẓevi* advocating the idea, and even a special pamphlet called *Ha-Medinah ha-Yehudit* (1905). His views incurred many enemies for him among those who were not prepared to exchange Zion for any other country. On the other hand, he won general respect when he led the fight (1913–14) against the plan of the *Hilfsverein der deutschen Juden to introduce German as the language of instruction in its secondary schools in Palestine and in the technical college which was about to be established in Haifa.

During World War I, when Jamal Pasha, the Turkish commander in Palestine, outlawed Zionism, Ben-Yehuda left for the United States. There he wrote his book *Ad Eimatai Dibberu Ivrit?* ("Until When was Hebrew Spoken?" 1919). He returned to Palestine in 1919. Together with M. *Ussishkin, he prevailed upon Herbert *Samuel, the British high commissioner, to declare Hebrew one of the three official languages of the country. He founded Sefatenu, a society for the propagation of Hebrew, and also served as secretary of the Planning Committee of the Hebrew University. A number of his writings were collected and published posthumously: the anthology *Yisrael le-Arẓo ve-li-Leshono* (1929) and *Avot ha-Lashon ha-Ivrit*; part 1: *Rabbi Akiva* (1945).

Ben-Yehuda's cultural activities and achievements fall into four divisions: (1) The revival of spoken Hebrew. Hebrew was spoken before the days of Ben-Yehuda but only intermittently. The very sanctity with which the language was invested prevented its daily use. Ben-Yehuda made Hebrew speech a national goal. He was convinced that a living Hebrew, spoken by the people in its own land, was indispensable to the political and cultural rebirth of the nation. In this view Ben-Yehuda differed from *Smolenskin, *Lilienblum, and *Herzl, who were able to envisage a Jewish homeland without Hebrew as its mother tongue. Ben-Yehuda fought untiringly and uncompromisingly for this ideal. He lived to see his vision realized: the revival of the *Hebrew language as a spoken tongue after more than two thousand years. (2) The creation of a simple, popular style in Hebrew literature. Ben-Yehuda fought against the use of inflated rhetoric and the archaic expressions and forms which had lost their appeal. He demanded simplicity and concreteness in Hebrew prose which, until then, had been rhetorical and florid. With this objective in mind, he translated a number of stories from various languages into plain, unadorned Hebrew. (3) Ben-Yehuda was the first to make a regular and systematic practice of coining Hebrew words. Neologism was not new to Hebrew, but it had never been done methodically and specifically to meet the practical demands which were constantly being made on the language in daily speech, in journalism, in science, and in literature. (4) His dictionary complemented his achievement of the revival of spoken Hebrew. The dictionary attempts to include all the Hebrew words used in the different periods and developmental stages of the language. It is also arranged in the manner of modern European language dictionaries, and not according to word roots, as was customary in former Hebrew dictionaries. A characteristic feature of the dictionary is its bold omission of all Aramaic words, as well as other foreign words found in the Bible, Talmud, Midrash, and other works that are not of Semitic origin.

BIBLIOGRAPHY: R. St. John, *The Tongue of the Prophets* (1952); R. Brainin (ed.), *Sefer Zikkaron le-Eliezer Ben Yehuda* (1918); D. Yellin, *Ben Yehudah and the Revival of the Hebrew Language* (c. 1924); I. Ben-Avi, *Avi* (1927); J. Kena'ani, *Eliezer Ben Yehuda* (Heb., 1929), contains bibl.; Ḥ. Ben Yehuda, *Ben Yehuda, Ḥayyav u-Mifalo* (1940); idem, *Ha-Loḥem ha-Me'ushar* (1932); J. Klausner, *Eliezer Ben Yehuda, Toledotav u-Mifal Ḥayyav* (1939); A. Herzberg, *The Zionist Idea* (1960), 158–65; J. Fichman, *Be-Terem Aviv* (1959), 195–203, 215ff.; R. Sivan, in: *Leshonenu la-Am*, 12 (1961/62), 35–77; G. Kressel (ed.), *Ḥol va-Ru'aḥ* (1964); idem, *Toledot ha-Ittonut ha-Ivrit be-Ereẓ Yisrael* (1964[2]), 67–100; Kressel, Leksikon, 1 (1965), 275ff. (includes bibl.). **ADD. BIBLIOGRAPHY:** J. Fellman, *The Revival of a Classic Tongue: Eliezer Ben-Yehuda and the Modern Hebrew Language* (1973).

[Joseph Gedaliah Klausner]

BEN-YEHUDA, ḤEMDAH (1873–1951), Hebrew author; wife of Eliezer *Ben-Yehuda. Her sister Deborah was Ben-Yehuda's first wife. After she died, Ḥemdah went to Jerusalem from Lithuania and married Ben-Yehuda in 1892. She aided her husband in his literary work, wrote articles and stories for his papers, and after his death in 1922 concerned herself with the continued publication of his multi-volume dictionary. Her two main works were *Ben Yehuda, Ḥayyav u-Mifalo* (1940), a life of Ben Yehuda, and *Nose ha-Degel* (1944) on her stepson Ithamar *Ben-Avi.

BIBLIOGRAPHY: J. Harari, *Ishah va-Em be-Yisrael* (1959) 273–7.

[Getzel Kressel]

BEN YEHUDA, NETIVA (1928–), Israeli military officer, writer, and scholar of spoken Hebrew, who embodied the heroic voluntarism and utter loyalty to the "Jewish national rebirth in its homeland" that was the hallmark of the *Palmaḥ from the 1940s. Fearlessness, physical prowess, and total devotion were some of the features that distinguished this young officer, whose military specialties included topography, reconnaissance, and demolition. Born in Tel Aviv and educated at the Herzlia Hebrew Gymnasium, where her father, Baruch (1894–1990), served as teacher and principal (he later became the first director general of Israel's Ministry of Education and Culture), Ben Yehuda volunteered for the Palmaḥ and later served as an officer in the Israel Defense Forces. She married in 1950 and gave birth to a daughter, Amal, in 1953. Ben Yehuda and her husband separated in 1962 and later divorced.

She worked as an editor of the *Encyclopedia Hebraica* and as a spokeswoman in the Ministry of Labor.

Ben Yehuda's lifelong devotion to the cause of spoken Hebrew began a few years after independence. After study both at home and abroad (art, Hebrew language, linguistics, and philosophy), she became a freelance editor who mediated between the spoken Hebrew developed in the Palmaḥ, marked by humorous slang and linguistic inventiveness, and the elevated, highly stylized standards then required by Hebrew *belles lettres*. Her dedication to this issue resulted in the 1972 publication of *Millon Olami le-Ivrit Meduberet* ("The World Dictionary of Hebrew Slang"; a second volume appeared in 1982), a hilariously irreverent book which she co-authored with another Palmaḥ member, writer, and satirist Dahn *Ben Amotz (1924–1990).

Traces of this early work can be found in her later Palmaḥ Trilogy, which consists of *Between the Calendars* (1981); *Through the Binding Ropes* (1985); and *When the State of Israel Broke Out* (1991). Unique both stylistically and generically, the trilogy, which preserves slang and idiomatic Hebrew of days gone by, is a subversive revision of a major chapter in the Israeli national narrative. By reducing the myth of a glorious past to human and at times petty proportions, the Palmaḥ Trilogy contributed to the "new historical" de-mythologization of the 1948 War of Independence. At the same time, the trilogy also coincided with Israeli feminist research of the 1980s that exposed the gap between the Palmaḥ's promise of "sexual equality" and the sexist reality in its ranks. A personal trauma caused by this fissure emerges as the hidden motivation behind Ben Yehuda's narrative and explains the "writer's block" underlying the author's 30-year-long reticence. Ben Yehuda's other books include *Autobiography in Shir va-Zemer* (1990).

BIBLIOGRAPHY: Y.S. Feldman, *No Room of Their Own: Gender and Nation in Israeli Women's Fiction* (1989).

[Yael S. Feldman (2nd ed.)]

BEN-YEHUDAH, BARUKH (1894–1990), Israeli educator. Ben-Yehudah, who was born in Marijampole, Lithuania, settled in Ereẓ Israel in 1911. During World War I he joined *kevuẓat* Deganyah, teaching there and at Rosh Pinnah. He then studied at the University of Brussels and, after receiving a degree in mathematics and physics in 1924, returned to teaching. He became principal of the Herẓlia Gymnasium in Tel Aviv. In 1927 he helped found the pioneering high school youth movement Ḥugim (later known as Maḥanot Olim). He also founded the Teachers' Council for the Jewish National Fund. He was director of the education department of the Va'ad Le'ummi in 1947, and the first director-general of the Ministry of Education and Culture of the State of Israel (until 1951). In 1979 he was awarded the Israel Prize for education. His books include *Toledot ha-Ẓiyyonut* ("The History of Zionism," 1943); *Ha-Keren ha-Meḥannekhet: Tenu'at Morim Lema'an Ẓiyyon u-Ge'ulatah* ("The Educating Fund: The Teachers' Movement for Zion and its Redemption" 1949, 1952); *Ta'amei ha-Mikra le-Vattei Sefer* ("Biblical Cantillation for Schools," 1968); *Kol ha-Ḥinnukh ha-Ẓiyyoni* ("The Voice of Zionist Education," 1955); and *Yesodot u-Derakhim* ("Fundamentals and Ways," 1952). He also wrote on teaching mathematics: *Hora'at ha-Matematikah be-Veit ha-Sefer ha-Tikhon* ("The Teaching of Mathematics in High School," 2 vols., 1959–60) and mathematics texts.

[Abraham Aharoni]

BEN YIẒḤAK, AVRAHAM (pen name of **Avraham Sonne**; 1883–1950), Hebrew poet. Born in Galicia, Ben Yiẓḥak received a traditional Jewish and secular education, and then studied at the universities of Vienna and Berlin. From 1913 to the summer of 1914, he was visiting lecturer in Hebrew literature and psychology at the Jerusalem Teachers' Seminary. After a brief career in the Zionist organization, he served as teacher and later principal at the Hebrew Pedagogium (Teachers' Academy) in Vienna, founded by *H.P. Chajes. After the Nazi Anschluss of Austria in 1938, he emigrated to Ereẓ Israel and settled in Jerusalem. Although he published only 11 poems during his lifetime Ben Yiẓḥak is considered a distinguished figure in modern Hebrew poetry. Most of his poems appeared before World War I and immediately attracted attention. His first poem, "*Ḥoref Bahir*" ("Bright Winter") was published in *Ha-Shilo'aḥ* in 1908. His last poem, "*Ashrei ha-Zore'im ve-Lo Yikẓoru*" ("Happy Are They That Sow But Shall Not Reap") in 1928, a farewell to his craft, concludes with the words, "And their everlasting lot shall be silence." His refusal to publish further remains a mystery. Later poems were found among his effects, but others, which he had read to his friends, are lost. Some of his work has been translated into English and various European languages. Ben Yiẓḥak wrote according to the Sephardi pronunciation (the one adopted in Ereẓ Israel) long before it was adopted by other Hebrew poets, who wrote in the Ashkenazi accent used by Hebrew-speaking European Jews. Ben Yiẓḥak's lyrics, with their terse style and biblical diction, focus on nature, meditation, and love. Though the form of Ben Yiẓḥak's poems is occasionally reminiscent of the Psalms, their content expresses a modern outlook on life and poetry, and he is considered by many to be the first truly modern Hebrew poet. His prose works included anonymous articles in German-Jewish periodicals and an essay on *Mendele Mokher Seforim in *Der Jude*, 3 (1918–19). One of the most scholarly and sensitive thinkers of his generation, Ben Yiẓḥak's personal influence on both Jewish and non-Jewish writers and philosophers was profound, yet he always declined to publish his obiter dicta. His collected poems appeared posthumously.

BIBLIOGRAPHY: A. Ben Yiẓḥak, *Shirim* (1957), original poems with English translation, biography and essay by Benzion Benshalom Katz; L. Goldberg, *Pegishah im Meshorer* (1952); S. Burnshaw et al. (eds.), *Modern Hebrew Poem Itself* (1965), 50–53. **ADD. BIBLIOGRAPHY:** L. Hakak, *Im Arba'ah Meshorerim: Ben Yiẓḥak, Gilboa, Zach ve-Zamir* (1979); L. Goldberg, *Pegishot im Meshorer: Al Avraham Ben Yiẓḥak Sonne* (1988); Ḥ. Ḥever, *Periḥat ha-Dumiyah: Shirat Avraham Ben Yiẓḥak* (1993); G. Ganiel, *Haggut u-Poetikah be-Shirat Avraham Ben Yiẓḥak* (1997).

[Lea Goldberg]

BEN-YOSEF (Tabachnik), SHELOMO (1913–1938), first Jew executed by the British in Palestine. Ben-Yosef, who was born in Lutsk, Poland, joined *Betar in 1928. In 1937 he reached Palestine as an "illegal" immigrant and joined the Betar work brigade at Rosh Pinnah. Ben-Yosef and two of his comrades, Shalom Zurabin and Avraham Shein, decided to retaliate for the murder of Jews by Arab terrorists, and on April 21, 1938, tried to attack an Arab bus on the Rosh Pinnah-Safed road. The attack failed and the three were arrested and brought before a military court. Ben-Yosef and Shein were sentenced to death and Zurabin to imprisonment. Shein was reprieved because of his youth. All efforts to save Ben-Yosef from execution were in vain. He went to the gallows at Acre prison on June 29, 1938, singing Betar songs. On the day of his execution, riots broke out in Tel Aviv when demonstrators clashed with the British police. Ben-Yosef was buried at Rosh Pinnah, and after the establishment of the State of Israel a monument was erected in his memory on the Rosh Pinnah-Safed road.

BIBLIOGRAPHY: Y. Nedava, *Sefer Olei ha-Gardom* (1952); Dinur, Haganah, 2 pt. 3 (1964^2), index; Tidhar, 4 (1950), 1764–66; D. Niv, *Ma'arkhot ha-Irgun ha-Ẓeva'i ha-Le'ummi*, 2 (1965), 61–74.

[David Niv]

BENZAMERO, Spanish-Moroccan family. Its best-known members in Spain lived chiefly in Seville. JUDAH BEN EPHRAIM (1245–1330); MOSES (I) and his son EPHRAIM, were 14th-century financiers; and SOLOMON (I) and MEIR (I), 14th-century physicians. ISAAC (I) settled in Badajoz, Spain, where shortly before the 1492 expulsion Ferdinand and Isabella intervened to ensure that the large sums he had advanced them for the war against Granada would be repaid. He was probably the same Isaac Benzamero who after 1496 settled in Safi (Morocco). He became the treasurer of the Portuguese governors there, exercising important political influence, and was entrusted with many diplomatic missions, both to the king in Lisbon and to the Moroccan leaders. With his relative ISHMAEL he led 200 Jewish soldiers who took part in the defense of Safi when it was besieged by the sharif of Marrakesh in 1510.

Isaac's brother ABRAHAM BEN MEIR (d. c. 1530), paytan, physician and diplomat, lived in Granada and Malaga, and then in Tlemcen and Oran. In 1493 in Oran he wrote philosophic poems, quoted by Abraham *Gavison in his *Omer ha-Shikhḥah*. Later he settled in Safi, and there, in 1510, by decree of King Emmanuel I, was appointed chief rabbi with wide powers. Abraham b. Meir's political role in Portuguese affairs in Morocco was preeminent. He was highly regarded both by his coreligionists and the Muslims. He was also esteemed by King John III of Portugal, who received him at his court, and by the sultans of Fez and the sharifs of Marrakesh. David *Reuveni made his acquaintance in Lisbon.

In the 16th century JUDAH and SLIMAN held eminent positions in commerce. A letter is extant from their nephews SAMUEL and his brothers, which mentions the existence of independent Jewish warrior tribes in the western Sahara, a fact which is confirmed in other sources. AARON (16th century) was deputy governor of Agadir (Morocco), where he built a synagogue that received the former Marranos from the Canary Islands. ABRAHAM, who was official interpreter in Mazagan (1527), was evacuated to Arzila when the Portuguese lost their southern Morocco territories (after 1541).

The Benzameros then settled in Fez. Even before 1560 SOLOMON (II) had undertaken official functions, for which he received secretly large sums of money from Jeanne d'Autriche. MOSES (II) converted at the Escorial (the Spanish royal palace), took the name Pablo de Santa-Maria, and became a royal councillor. This caused a great scandal but the family continued to hold a leading position in Moroccan Jewish affairs. ISAAC (II), rabbi and *dayyan*, signed *takkanot* of Fez, when DAVID was *nagid* (1600–05). JOSEPH published *Divrei David* by *David b. Solomon ibn Abi Zimra at Leghorn in 1828, when his own work *Hon Yosef* appeared also. In Safi the family burial vaults, called the "Seven Zamero sons," were until recent years the site of frequent pilgrimages.

BIBLIOGRAPHY: I. Loeb, in: REJ, 22 (1891), 104; Baer, Urkunden, 1 pt. 1 (1929), 182, 404; 1 pt. 2 (1936), 127, 162, 384–9; J. Caro Baroja, *Los judíos en la España moderna*, 1 (1962), 80; Suárez Fernández, Documentos, 401; J.M. Toledano, *Ner ha-Ma'arav* (1911), 88–89; J. Ben-Naim, *Malkhei Rabbanan* (1931), 25, 31–32, 72; SIHM, Portugal, 1–5 (1934–53), passim; SIHM, Espagne, 3 (1961), 11–13; Hirschberg, Afrikah, 1 (1965), 319–21; Corcos, in: *Sefunot*, 10 (1966), 57, 59–69.

[David Corcos]

BEN ZAQEN, Moroccan family descended from Spanish exiles. SAMUEL BEN ZAQEN (c. 1670–1745) lived in Fez, and studied under R. Judah Uzziel and R. Judah b. Attar. His works include *Peri Eẓ ha-Gan* (2 volumes, 1904), on the Bible and Midrash, *Gefen Poriyyah* (1904), also on the Midrash, and responsa. A part of the family emigrated from Morocco to Gibraltar in 1741, and from there some went to America, where, before 1750, they were well-established merchants in New York. JACOB BEN SAMUEL BEN ZAQEN was a communal leader in Gibraltar between 1834 and 1851. His cousin ISAAC BEN VIDAL BEN ZAQEN sent financial assistance to the Jewish poor in Rabat, Morocco. JOSEPH BEN ZAQEN served as *nagid* and was appointed the Swedish and Norwegian consul in Tetuan c. 1836. LEON BEN ZAQEN (1905–1977) studied medicine in Paris and became an ophthalmologist. He was much respected by his fellow Jews and had considerable influence with King Mohammed V of Morocco. When Morocco gained independence he was appointed minister of posts (1956–58).

BIBLIOGRAPHY: Rosenbloom, Biogr Dict, 12; J.M. Toledano, *Ner ha-Ma'arav* (1911), 76, 144, 188; Samuel b. Zaqen, *Gefen Poriyyah* (1904), introd.; J. Ben-Naim, *Malkhei Rabbanan* (1931), 123a; Miège, Maroc, 2 (1961), 91, 95, 168.

[David Obadia]

BENZAQUÉN, SAADIA (1925–1986), rabbi of the Jewish Moroccan community in Argentina. Born in Tetuan, Morocco, he immigrated to Argentina in 1951 and was appointed chief rabbi of the Asociación Comunidad Israelita Latina de Buenos Aires, serving until his death. In 1974 he succeeded in uniting all the synagogues and institutions of the Moroccan Jews in Buenos Aires in one central organization – ACILBA (Asociación Comunidad Israelita Latina de Buenos Aires).

[Efraim Zadoff (2nd ed.)]

BEN ZE'EV, JUDAH LEIB (1764–1811), grammarian and lexicographer; the first Jewish scholar to apply Western research methods to the study of Hebrew. Born near Cracow, Ben Ze'ev received a traditional Jewish education, but covertly, on his own, studied Hebrew philology and secular subjects. He belonged to the group of Polish-Jewish writers that published *Ha-Me'assef*, a literary organ in the spirit of the early Haskalah. Later, in 1787, when he moved to Berlin, he was admitted to the circle of Haskalah scholars there. In Berlin, he devoted himself to secular studies but returned to his native city which he was forced to leave when persecuted by Orthodox Jews because of his liberal opinions. He settled in Breslau and worked as a proofreader in a Hebrew publishing house. Later he moved to Vienna where he was employed in the same capacity, in the Hebrew printing establishment of Anton von Schmid.

Ben Ze'ev's versatile literary activities spread over a number of fields: grammar and phonetics, lexicography, Bible exegesis, translations, poetry, parodic works, and the editing of medieval texts. *Talmud Leshon Ivri* (Breslau, 1796), probably his best-known work, is a grammar that served as the main source for the study of Hebrew in Eastern Europe for a hundred years; it was frequently reissued and exerted considerable influence on subsequent grammarians. In it, Ben Ze'ev discusses phonetics (and vocalization); the theory of forms (parts of speech); the noun, the verb, the particles; selected aspects of syntax (particularly the combination of sentences); aspects of literary theory (parallelism, rhyme, and meter); and the theory of *ta'amei ha-mikra* ("biblical accentuation and cantillation"). In his study of phonemes, he followed the line of thought of S.Z. Henau; in the definition of the parts of speech that of M. Mendelssohn; in his description of the noun and the verb the ideas of Elijah *Levita, and in his discussion on syntax the foundations of David Kimḥi in *Sefer ha-Mikhlol*. Ben Ze'ev applied the methods used in the study and research of European language grammars; his rules, based on logic, are organized in a manner suitable for instruction. Many of the concepts in his books are original, not to be found in any previous grammatical work: especially, a new terminology in the field of composition and syntax; innovations in syntax; and the study of poetry. His most important achievement is *Oẓar ha-Shorashim* (Vienna, 1807–08), a Hebrew-German and German-Hebrew dictionary which was inspired by the works of David Kimḥi. It is arranged in alphabetical order, e.g., in the German section, verbs with prefixes are listed alphabetically according to the prefixes; the definitions of the terms often include synonyms and examples of usage taken either from the Bible directly or cited in sentences formulated in biblical style; the German terms are written in Hebrew characters. Ben Ze'ev laid the basis for the modern Hebrew terminology in linguistics, translating grammatical terms from German into Hebrew and indicating their German equivalent.

Among his translations is Ecclesiasticus rendered into Hebrew (Breslau, 1798; at a time when the Hebrew text had not yet been discovered). When later parts of the Hebrew text were recovered it was found that Ben Ze'ev's translation in a biblical gnomic style was imbued with the very spirit of the author. *Meliẓah le-Furim*, a collection of ironic prayers and *seliḥot* for Purim (Breslau, 1800), containing also many clever parodies on well-known Jewish texts and poetic writings, mainly in the genre of the fable, are among his literary creative works. Ben Ze'ev lacked a poetic flair and it is in his grammatical studies that he excelled.

BIBLIOGRAPHY: Klausner, Sifrut, 1 (1952^2), 178–90; R. Fahn, *Tekufat ha-Haskalah be-Vinah* (1919), 38–46; G. Bader, *Medinah va-Ḥakhameha* (1934), 44–46; Waxman, Literature, 3 (1960^2), 125–7.

[Menachem Zevi Kaddari]

BENZER, SEYMOUR (1921–), U.S. neuroscientist. Born in New York, Benzer graduated from Brooklyn College (1942) and received his Ph.D. from Purdue University, Indiana (1947), in physics where he progressed to distinguished professor (1945–67). During this period he collaborated with outstanding contemporary scientists, including M. Delbrueck (California Institute of Technology), F. Jacob and J. Monod (Pasteur Institute), and F.H. Crick and S. Brenner (Cambridge, U.K.). In 1967 he joined California Institute of Technology, first as professor and latterly as emeritus professor. Benzer moved from physics to molecular genetics followed by neuroscience. His initial discoveries concerned the molecular organization of genes, which he exploited to analyze the development of the nervous system and genetically controlled behavior in fruit flies (*drosophila*). This research has potential implications for understanding degenerative diseases of the nervous system in man and human behavior. His recent research concerned the genetic control of aging, notably muscle strength. His many honors included the Gairdner Award (1964), the Lasker Award (1971), the Harvey Prize of the Haifa Technion (1977), the Wolf Prize (1991), and the Neurosciences Award of the U.S. National Academy of Sciences. He is a member of the U.S. National Academy of Sciences and foreign member of the Royal Society of London.

[Michael Denman (2nd ed.)]

°BENZINGER, IMMANUEL (1865–1935), German Protestant theologian and Orientalist. Benzinger was born in Stuttgart and served as lecturer in biblical studies at Berlin University from 1898 to 1902. He taught in Jerusalem at various Christian institutes and at the Ezra Society School from 1902 to 1911. Thereafter he was professor of Bible in Toronto, Canada (1912–15), Meadville, Pa. (1915–18), and Riga, Latvia (from 1921 until his death). His principal work, *Hebraeische Archaeologie* (1894, 1927^3), is a comprehensive reference book of biblical archaeology. His *Buecher der Koenige* (1899) and *Buecher* *der Chronik* (1901) are commentaries on the books of Kings and Chronicles. His other major works include *Bilderatlas zur Bibelkunde* (1905), *Geschichte Israels bis auf die griechische Zeit* (1904, 1927^3), and *Jahvist and Elohist in den Koenigsbuechern* (1921). At the outset of his scholarly career, Benzinger followed the *Wellhausen school of biblical criticism, but later became an adherent of the Pan-Babylonian school.

[Michael Avi-Yonah]

BEN-ZION (1897–1987), U.S. painter, graphic artist, and sculptor. Born Ben-Zion Weinman in the Ukraine, he was the son of a cantor and at one time planned to enter the rabbinate. His father discouraged his early artistic interest, but Ben-Zion prevailed and by the age of 17 traveled to Vienna to study art. After the art academy rejected him because of antisemitism, he wrote poetry, plays, and fairy tales in Hebrew.

In 1920 he settled in America, where he found little interest in his writing. He began teaching Hebrew to support himself and then in the early 1930s returned to painting. He used his art to comment on the rise of fascism in Europe, events he felt could not be adequately explored with words. Largely self-taught, Ben-Zion visited the museums of New York City to learn his new trade. His first painting on a large scale, *Friday Evening* (1933, Jewish Museum, New York), depicts a Sabbath dinner table as recalled from his family home. Ben-Zion supported himself by working odd jobs until the establishment of the Works Progress Administration's Federal Art Project. Under the auspices of the WPA, Ben-Zion thrived and galleries began to show his work. In 1936, after his first one-man show at the Artists' Gallery in New York, Ben-Zion joined "The Ten," which included such progressive artists as Mark *Rothko and Ilya *Bolotowsky. The group exhibited together until 1942.

His work steers away from pure representation, but even when eschewing academic modes, Ben-Zion maintains elements of realism. He imaginatively reinterpreted biblical scenes, a staple of the art world for centuries. His first biblical painting, *The Prophet in the Desert* (1935), was followed by many others, such as *Ruth and Boaz* (1948). Indeed, over 150 of Ben-Zion's paintings are of biblical subjects, reflecting the yeshivah education of his early years in Eastern Europe. Thirty-nine of these paintings were shown at the Jewish Museum in New York in 1948, and he had a retrospective there in 1959.

A series of 17 works, given the title *De Profundis* (Out of the Depths), express the artist's distress at the events of the Holocaust, while also functioning as a memorial to the Jews murdered under the Nazi regime. These paintings show only the figures' heads, often distorted and painted in muted color. The suffering of these figures is rendered by a strong linear structure.

His etchings of biblical subjects were collected in several volumes, including *Biblical Themes* (1951), *Prophets* (1952), and *The Book of Ruth, Job, and Song of Songs* (1954).

In 1959 Ben-Zion began sculpting in iron, one of the most difficult media in which to work. The sculptural quality of the figures in his paintings seems to have led to this new medium. As with his painting, Jewish themes preoccupy his sculptures, such as *Sacrifice of Isaac* (1961) and *Moses Dropping the Tablets* (1979).

BIBLIOGRAPHY: Ben-Zion and S. Kayser, *Ben-Zion, 1933–1959: A Retrospect* (1959); E. Grossman, *Art and Tradition* (1967); L. Dubin and T. Shalem, *Ben-Zion: Iron Sculpture* (1985).

[Samantha Baskind (2nd ed.)]

BEN-ZION, S. (pseudonym of **Simhah Alter Gutmann**; 1870–1932), Hebrew and Yiddish author. Ben-Zion, who was born in Teleneshty, Bessarabia, settled in Odessa in 1889. He taught there with Bialik, at the modern elementary school, where modern Hebrew was the language of instruction. With Bialik and *Rawnitzki, he founded the publishing house *Moriah and was editor of its juvenile division. The three also collaborated in the writing of Bible stories for children. Ben-Zion published the widely used reader, *Ben Ammi* (3 parts, 1905–11). From 1905 until his death he lived in Palestine, where he edited various journals and miscellanies; *Ha-Omer* (Jaffa, 1907–09); *Moledet* (1911); *Shai* (1918–19), the literary supplement of the weekly *Ḥadashot me-ha-Areẓ*; *Ha-Ezraḥ* (1919); and, for a short period (1930–31), the weekly *Bustanai*. Ben-Zion was also active in public life and was one of the founders of the Aḥuzzat Bayit suburb, out of which Tel Aviv developed. Ben-Zion's main achievement was as a short story writer. He began as a realist, influenced by *Mendele Mokher Seforim, but his realism had none of Mendele's social satire. The main theme of his early works is the decline of the Bessarabian small Jewish town at the end of the 19th century. The younger generation longed to escape from the poverty and ignorance of their parents, but found themselves unequipped to do so. Their approach to life was blighted by an excessive leaning toward abstraction and they lacked a realistic approach to everyday problems. Ben-Zion's memories of his own childhood and youth occupy a prominent place in these stories. In *Nefesh Reẓuẓah* ("A Crushed Soul," 1952), he denounces the anguish inflicted upon the Jewish child, crushed in the stifling atmosphere of the *ḥeder*. Ben-Zion's emigration to Palestine marked a turning-point in his writing. Sensing that the true essence of Zionism at the time was to be found not in the reality but in the vision, he abandoned his realism for poetic lyricism and visionary symbolism. In this vein, he wrote his prose-poems *Raḥel* and *Leviyyim* which, though artistically imperfect, nevertheless represent a milestone in modern Hebrew literature. Toward the end of his life Ben-Zion wrote two lengthy historical novels, *Megillat Ḥananyah*, set in the period of the Second Temple, and *Ma'aseh ha-Nezirah*, the story of Judith and Holofernes. He also excelled as a translator and rendered several of the classical works of German poetry into Hebrew: Goethe's *Hermann und Dorothea* (1917); Schiller's *Wilhelm Tell* (1924); *Ẓelilim*, a selection of Heine's poems (1923); Heine's *Deutsch-*

land, ein Wintermaerchen (1938), published posthumously. In addition, Ben-Zion wrote monographs on the Biluim and the colonies of Nes Ẓiyyonah and Gederah, edited an anthology entitled *Ha-Kotel ha-Ma'aravi* ("The Western Wall," 1929), and published *Zemirot li-Yladim* ("Songs for Children") with music by Joel *Engel (1923). His collected writings were first published in 1914 (in two volumes), and were later reissued in a single large volume (1949), with a complete bibliography, and illustrations by his son, Naḥum *Gutmann (1949).

BIBLIOGRAPHY: I. Klausner, *Yoẓerim u-Vonim*, 2 (1929), 183–99; J. Rawnitzki, *Dor ve-Soferav*, 2 (1937), 106–14.

[Gedalyah Elkoshi]

BEN ẒIẒIT HA-KASAT (or **ha-Kassaf**; "silversmith"), wealthy and prominent citizen of Jerusalem at the time of the destruction of the Second Temple (Git. 56a; Gen. R. 42:1; Lam. R. 1:5, no. 31). It is related that Ben Ẓiẓit and his associates undertook to provide the needs of the inhabitants of Jerusalem throughout the war with Rome, but the Zealots burned their stores (see also *Ben Kalba Savu'a). Ben Ẓiẓit is possibly the Hebrew equivalent of the Latin *crispus* ("curly-headed").

BIBLIOGRAPHY: Graetz, Gesch, 3 pt. 2 (1906^5), 528; Epstein, in: MGWJ, 63 (1919), 262ff.; Klein, in: *Leshonenu*, 1 (1928/29), 343.

[Zvi Kaplan]

BEN ZOMA, SIMEON (second century), *tanna*. A contemporary of *Akiva, he appears to have studied under *Joshua b. Hananiah (Naz. 8:1, and cf. Tos. Ḥag. 2:6). The Mishnah says that he was the last of the authoritative biblical expositors (Sot. 9:15). According to Tosefta Ber. 6:2, when Ben Zoma was convinced that the scholar was the "crown of creation," and when he would see the multitude of different kinds of people and professions which populated the world, he would declare: "Blessed be He who created all of them to serve me." In further explanation of his position he continued: "In what labors was Adam involved before he obtained bread to eat? He had to plow, sow, reap, bind the sheaves, thresh and winnow and select the ears of corn; he had to grind them and sift the flour, to knead and bake, and only then could he eat; whereas I get up and find all these things prepared for me. And how much Adam had to labor before he found a garment to wear. He had to shear, wash the wool, comb it, spin and weave it, and only then did he acquire a garment to wear; whereas I get up and find all these things done for me. All kinds of craftsmen come early to the door of my house, and I rise in the morning and find all these things before me" (Ber. 58a, cf. Tos. Ber. 6:2). Many of his sayings became proverbs, such as "Who is wise? – he who learns from every man. Who is mighty? – he who subdues his evil inclination. Who is rich? – he who rejoices in his lot. Who is honored? – he who honors his fellow men" (Avot 4:1). He was one of the *tannaim* who occupied themselves with cosmological speculation, the *ma'aseh bereshit* (Tos. Ḥag. 2:6). According to Tos. Ḥag. 2:4 he was one of the four sages who "entered paradise," it is said (ibid.) that "he cast a look and went mad," while his companion Ben Azzai died as a result of this mystical experience. In the Jerusalem Talmud (Hag. 2:1, 77b) their roles are reversed. According to the Bavli he was regarded as "a disciple of the sages" (Kid. 49b and Rashi *ibid.*), and as one of those "who discussed before the sages" (Sanh. 17b and Rashi *ibid.*). Nevertheless, he was considered an outstanding scholar, so that it was said that whoever sees Ben Zoma in a dream "may hope for wisdom" (Ber. 57b).

BIBLIOGRAPHY: Bacher, Tann; Hyman, Toledot, 1172–73; S. Lieberman, *Tosefta ki-Feshutah*, 5 (1962), 1294.

[Zvi Kaplan]

BEN ZUTA (Ben Zita), ABU AL-SURRĪ (tenth century), Karaite exegete. A number of his explanations of the Scripture are sarcastically dismissed by Abraham *Ibn Ezra in his commentary on the Pentateuch (e.g., on Ex. 20:23; 21:35; 22:28) and his *Sefer ha-Ibbur*. In the absence of corroboration from Karaite sources, Ibn Ezra's citations remain a principal source for particulars about Ben Zuta's life. A passage in an anonymous Arabic commentary on Samuel suggests, however, that Ben Zuta lived in Jerusalem and at a somewhat later period than had been conjectured. Judah *Ibn Bal'am also mentions Ben Zuta and cites his objection to an interpretation of Anan b. David, the founder of Karaism, to Ezra 18:6.

BIBLIOGRAPHY: M. Friedlaender, *Essays on the Writings of Abraham Ibn Ezra*, 4 (1877), 70 (Heb. appendix); J. Israelsohn, in: REJ, 23 (1891), 132–3; S. Poznański, in: MGWJ, 41 (1897), 203–12; Mann, Texts, index, s.v. *Alī Surri Hakkohen b. Zuta*.

BEN-ZVI (Shimshelevich), IZHAK (1884–1963). Labor leader in the Yishuv, historian, Israeli politician, second president of the State of Israel; member of the First and Second Knessets. Ben-Zvi was born in Poltava, Ukraine, the eldest son of Ẓevi Shimshelevich. His father, a member of *Benei Moshe, visited Ereẓ Israel in 1891 to explore the possibility of settling there. Ben-Zvi was educated in both a traditional and a modern *ḥeder*, and in 1901–05 studied at a Russian gymnasium. He visited Ereẓ Israel for the first time in 1904 for a period of two months. He entered the University of Kiev in 1905, but studies were interrupted due to a general strike. During the November pogroms he was active in the Jewish self-defense organization in Poltava. In 1906 he attended the founding conference of *Po'alei Zion (Zionist Social Democrats) of Russia, held in Poltava. Ben-Zvi served on the committee of three that formulated the final version of the party's program drafted by Ber *Borochov and contributed the section dealing with Palestine.

In June 1906 a search of Ben-Zvi's parents' home by the Russian police revealed a cache of weapons belonging to the self-defense organization that Ben-Zvi headed. His father was sentenced to lifetime exile in Siberia, serving 16 years before being allowed to leave the Soviet Union and settle in Ereẓ Israel. His aunt, his sister, and his brother Aaron *Reuveni were also imprisoned, but Ben-Zvi himself escaped to Vilna where he participated in the clandestine activities of the central committee of Po'alei Zion. He traveled to Germany, Austria, and Switzerland to try to influence Jewish students there. In Vienna he organized the first ties between Po'alei Zion branches in different countries. At the end of 1906 he returned to Vilna, which, after Borochov's imprisonment, had become the center of the movement.

Ben-Zvi settled in Ereẓ Israel at the beginning of 1907. In the same year he was a Po'alei Zion delegate from Ereẓ Israel to the Eighth Zionist Congress held in The Hague. He participated in the founding of the Bar Giora organization in Jaffa in 1907, and in 1909 of *Ha-Shomer, along with Raḥel Yanait (*Ben-Zvi), who had settled in Ereẓ Israel in 1908, and was to become his wife in 1918.

After the second Turkish revolution (1909), Ben-Zvi traveled to Turkey on behalf of Po'alei Zion. He visited Smyrna, Constantinople, and Salonika, as well as Beirut and Damascus, establishing ties with the Jewish communities and leaders. In Salonika he first encountered the remnants of the Shabbatean sect, later to become a subject for his research.

In 1910 Ben-Zvi, together with Raḥel Yanait, Ze'ev Ashur, and others, founded the first Hebrew socialist periodical in Ereẓ Israel, *Aḥdut* ("Unity"). Upon the outbreak of World War I, Ben-Zvi interrupted his studies at the University of Constantinople and returned to Ereẓ Israel. During the persecution of Jews by Jamal Pasha, the Ottoman governor, *Aḥdut* was closed down, and Ben-Zvi, together with David *Ben-Gurion, was imprisoned. They were both deported, and eventually made their way to New York. There they founded in 1915 the He-Ḥalutz movement of America.

Before the British offensive on the Palestine front, Ben-Gurion and Ben-Zvi initiated a volunteer movement for Jewish battalions in the U.S., and were among the first volunteers. They arrived in Egypt in 1918, and from there they went to Ereẓ Israel as soldiers of the *Jewish Legion in the British Royal Fusiliers. During the disturbances of 1920, 1922, and 1929, Ben-Zvi was active in the ranks of the *Haganah, while also representing the *Yishuv* in negotiations with the British authorities.

He was elected to the Central Committee of the *Aḥdut ha-Avodah Party at its founding convention. During the summer of 1920 he participated in the world conference of Po'alei Zion held in Vienna, in which the movement split under the impact of the Bolshevik revolution in Russia. Ben-Zvi was instrumental in its reorganization on a firm Zionist platform.

In October 1920 he was appointed by the British High Commissioner to Palestine, Sir Herbert *Samuel, to the Palestine Advisory Council. But with the Jaffa riots of May 1921 and the subsequent temporary suspension of Jewish immigration, he resigned from the Council in protest against Mandatory government policy.

Ben-Zvi was elected to the Secretariat of the *Histadrut when it was founded in 1920. He devoted a considerable part of his public activity to Jerusalem and its Jewish population. He was first elected to the Jerusalem Municipal Council in 1927, but after the riots of 1929 he resigned from the municipality in protest against the stand of the city's Arab administration. In September 1934 he was reelected to the municipality.

In 1920 Ben-Zvi was elected to the Va'ad Le'ummi, first as a member, then in 1931 as its chairman, and in 1945 as its president. He participated as a delegate in all the Zionist Congresses during the 1920s, and as chairman of the Va'ad Le'ummi he represented the Yishuv at the coronation ceremonies of King George VI in 1937, and at the Round Table Conference on Palestine in London in 1939.

After the establishment of the State of Israel, Ben-Zvi was elected as a *Mapai member to the First and Second Knessets. Upon the death of President Chaim *Weizmann in 1952, he was elected president of the State. He was elected to a second term in 1957, and to a third term in 1962. He died in office on April 23, 1963.

Ben-Zvi headed the Institute for the Study of Oriental Jewish Communities in the Middle East, which he founded in 1948, and which was renamed the Ben-Zvi Institute in 1952. His research on the history of the people of Israel was a lifelong endeavor. The scholarly works that he published were devoted mainly to research on communities and sects (such as the Samaritans, Karaites, Shabbateans, Jewish communities in Asia and Africa, the mountain Jews, and others) and to the geography of Ereẓ Israel, its ancient populations, its antiquities, and its traditions. He was also a prolific journalist, publishing articles under his own name as well as under various pseudonyms.

His brochure *Ha-Yishuv ha-Yehudi bi-Kefar Peki'in* ("The Jewish Yishuv in Peki'in Village," 1922) was the beginning of series of studies on the Jewish villages in Ereẓ Israel that preceded modern Jewish settlement, most of which were included in his book *She'ar Yishuv* ("The Remnant of the Yishuv," 1927) and in vol. 2 of his writings. His studies of communities were greatly facilitated by his direct contact with the subjects and by their willingness to reveal historical documents previously unpublished. Ben-Zvi's collected surveys on the non-Jewish communities of Israel appear in *Ukhlusei Arẓenu* ("Populations in our Land," 1932), which, together with his book on the Jewish population of Israel, *Ukhloseinu ba-Areẓ* ("Our Population in the Land," 1929), is included in vol. 5 of his writings (1937). His studies on the history of the Samaritans, *Sefer ha-Shomeronim* (1935, and new enlarged edition 1970), is a basic work. Ben-Zvi also published *Masot Ereẓ Israel le-Rav Moshe Basola* ("Journeys of R. Moses Basola in Ereẓ Israel"), based on an original manuscript. This study, he believed, had enabled him to identify the unknown traveller in the *Masot ha-Nose'a ha-Almoni mi-Livorno mi-Shenat Resh Peh Bet* ("Journeys of an Unknown Traveler from Leghorn, from the Year 1521/22"). His book *Niddeḥei Yisrael* was translated into English (*The Exiled and the Redeemed*, 1958 and 1961), Spanish, French, Italian, Swedish, and Yiddish. The most important of his many studies on the history of the *yishuv* is *Ereẓ Yisrael ve-Yishuvah bi-Ymei ha-Shilton ha-Ottomani* ("Ereẓ Israel and

Its Yishuv during the Ottoman Empire," 1955), which is based on Turkish documents and rabbinical responsa of the period. A large part of this work appears in English translation in L. Finkelstein (ed.), *The Jews, their History, Culture and Religion* (1960), pp. 602–88. His book *The Hebrew Battalion Letters* (1969) also appeared in English. A volume of his memoirs, *He-Ḥazon ve-Hagshamato* appeared in 1968. His complete works, including diaries, letters, and articles were republished, starting in 1965, by Yad Izhak Ben-Zvi, a memorial institute founded to perpetuate Ben-Zvi's interests and works.

BIBLIOGRAPHY: Yad Izhak Ben-Zvi, *In Memoriam* (1965); R. Ben-Zvi, *Coming Home* (1963); S. Shunami, *Bibliografyah shel I. Ben-Zvi* (1958), with a biography by S.Z. Shazar; Y. Carmel, *I. Ben-Zvi: mi-Tokh Yoman Beit ha-Nasi* (1967).

[Shneur Zalman Shazar]

BEN-ZVI, RAḤEL YANAIT (1886–1979), labor leader and writer; from 1918, wife of Izhak *Ben-Zvi. Born in Malin, Ukraine, Raḥel Yanait was educated in Russia and in Nancy, France, where she pursued studies in agronomy. After helping to create the *Po'alei Zion labor movement in Russia, she settled in Ereẓ Israel as a teacher in 1908, and was a cofounder of the Hebrew Gymnasium in Jerusalem, the second modern high school in the country. She played a pioneering role in *Ha-Shomer and Tenu'at ha-Po'alot (Women's Labor Movement), and coedited the weekly *Aḥdut*, the first Hebrew organ of the Po'alei Zion movement in Ereẓ-Israel, from its founding in 1910. After World War I, she became a founder of *Aḥdut ha-Avodah labor party and a leader of the *Haganah in Jerusalem, continuing her career as an educationist, and in 1920 established near Jerusalem's Talpiot quarter a girls' agricultural high school of which she was the first principal. In 1948, she was the guiding spirit behind the founding of an agricultural youth village in Ein Kerem. After her husband became president of Israel in 1952, she assisted him in his official duties and worked particularly to make the president's home a popular meeting place for all the communities of Israel. Upon her husband's death in 1963, she became an active member of Yad Ben-Zvi, his memorial institute. She was the recipient of the Israel Prize for special contribution to Israel state and society in 1978. Her memoirs have been published: *Anu Olim* (1959; *Coming Home*, 1963) and *Eli* (Heb., 1957), a book written together with her husband about their son, who died in the Israeli War of Independence. She also coedited her husband's writings, which began to appear in 1965.

BIBLIOGRAPHY: H.M. Sachar, *Aliyah: The Peoples of Israel* (1961), 115–51.

[Getzel Kressel]

BEN-ZVI, SHLOMO (1964–), media owner. Born in London as Michael Goldblum, Shlomo Ben Zvi was educated at Netiv Meir Yeshivah High School in Jerusalem and various other national-religious yeshivot in Israel and studied philosophy at the Hebrew University of Jerusalem. After making a substantial fortune in real estate and the technology sector in Europe, he decided to become active in the Israeli media at the start of the 21st century. His first venture was the Tekhelet cable TV channel, whose programming concentrated on different aspects of Jewish life and which began broadcasting in 2003. He also purchased 20 per cent of Israel's Channel Ten together with cosmetics heir Ronald *Lauder, who purchased 40 per cent.

He went on to concentrate his holdings in the right-wing and religious media, buying the weekly *Makor Rishon* in 2003 and acquiring control of the national-religious daily **Ha-Ẓofeh* and the monthly of the settlers movement, *Nekudah,* in 2004. His plans called for a relaunch of an expanded *Makor Rishon* in early 2005 and the start-up of a new right-wing daily newspaper. Ben Zvi was critical of the Israeli media for not being patriotic enough and for showing the IDF in a negative light. He was a member of the right-wing "Jewish Leadership" faction of the *Likud Party.

[Anshel Pfeffer (2nd ed.)]

BEN-ZVI, ZEEV (1904–1952), Israeli sculptor, whose work influenced a generation of sculptors. Ben-Zvi was born in Ryki, Poland and studied at the Warsaw Academy of Art before immigrating to Palestine in 1924. He entered the *Bezalel School in Jerusalem that year and studied under Boris *Schatz. Ben-Zvi specialized in portrait heads in beaten copper and molded plaster, which he treated in a cubist manner. When the New Bezalel School was opened in 1936 Ben-Zvi was appointed teacher of sculpture. During 1937 he visited France and England. On the outbreak of World War II, he executed the first model of *Outcry* – a hand lifted to the heavens. *Outcry* symbolized the horror and rebellion of Jews against the Holocaust in Europe – a subject to which Ben-Zvi frequently returned. In 1947, he executed his moving monument, *In Memory of the Children of the Diaspora*, at Mishmar ha-Emek. From 1947 to 1949 he tried to alleviate the hardships of the illegal immigrants detained by the British government in the Cyprus detention camps by teaching them art. Ben-Zvi's works are to be found in museums and private collections in Israel and Great Britain. He won the Israel Prize for art in 1953 and the Dizengoff Prize in 1952.

BIBLIOGRAPHY: H. Gamzu, *Ben-Zvi, Sculptures* (1955).

[Fritz Schiff]

BEN ZVI INSTITUTE FOR THE STUDY OF JEWISH COMMUNITIES OF THE EAST, Israeli research institute. The Institute was founded in 1947 by Izhak *Ben-Zvi, who later became Israel's second president. His public career was highlighted by passionate concern for Jews of Muslim countries and the East, who in the 20th century were uprooted from their ancient communities. Their rich literature, traditions, and customs might have been completely lost were it not for the great efforts made to preserve them. The institute devotes itself to preserving the precious cultural legacy of these communities of the East. The scholars, scientists, poets, and communal leaders of Sephardi and Eastern communities made an indelible mark on Jewish history. Their communal documents provide critical information to scholars in many fields. Furthermore, over half of Israel's population is rooted in these cultures. Their thorough appreciation is their entitlement and is essential to dealing with contemporary social and cultural issues.

The Ben-Zvi Institute is a fertile common meeting ground for scholars from all of Israel's universities and from abroad. The institute maintains a prestigious research staff, publishes books and periodicals, and holds lectures and symposia. It is affiliated with the Hebrew University of Jerusalem and Yad Izhak Ben-Zvi (see below). It cooperates with all of Israel's universities and enjoys the support of the Center for the Integration of the Oriental Jewish Heritage of Israel's Ministry of Education (since its establishment in 1977) and of the Israel Academy of Sciences. The institute initiates and supports research, publishes texts, periodicals, and monographs, and organizes academic conferences and lectures on the Jewish communities of the East.

Its specialized collection on Oriental Jewish communities, housed in the Yad Izhak Ben-Zvi library, contains the most comprehensive collection of its kind in the world. It is open to scholars and advanced students, who enjoy easy access to books on open shelves and individual attention by expert librarians. The Israel Prize was awarded to the Ben-Zvi Institute in recognition of its contribution to the study of Sephardi and Eastern Jewish history and culture.

The Institute publishes two periodicals: (1) *Pe'amim: Studies in Oriental Jewry* (a quarterly publication in Hebrew). Established by the Ben-Zvi Institute in 1979, *Pe'amim* provides scholars, teachers, and students with the best of recent academic research on the Jews of the East. The periodical has revolutionized the study of Oriental Jewry and the teaching of the subject. In recognition of its achievements *Pe'amim* received the Jerusalem Prize in 1982. (2) *Sefunot: Studies and Sources on the History of the Jewish Communities in the East* (Hebrew periodical). Appearing since 1956, this series is addressed to a scholarly audience and publishes textual studies of importance for the history, culture, language, and literature of Oriental Jewry. Among its research projects are (a) *Oriens Judaicus* – Sources for the History of the Jews in Muslim Lands. The purpose of this long-term project is to collect all the sources pertinent to the history of the Jews in Muslim lands. Materials are edited and published in volumes arranged by region and period. (b) *Archives in the Former Soviet Union.* The opening of libraries and archives in the former Soviet Union has offered scholars unprecedented opportunities to explore hitherto inaccessible archival sources. Scholars affiliated with the Ben-Zvi Institute are examining materials found in St. Petersburg (the Firkovich archive) and other sites. (c) *Ethiopian Jewry Legacy.* Initiated before the mass *aliyah* from Ethiopia, this project seeks to document the written and oral heritage of Ethiopian Jewry. Three issues of *Pe'amim* have been devoted to the subject and an annotated bibliography was published. The Institute hosts the Secretariat of the International Society for the Study of Ethiopian Jewry. (d) *The Karaite Jews.* Several aspects of the history and culture of the *Karaite Jews are being investigated. These include an encyclopedia of Karaite personalities, a bibliography of Karaism, and a study of the inscriptions of the Karaites in Crimea. (e) *Judeo-Arabic Culture and Literature.* This consists of three projects: (i) Judeo-Arabic halakhic literature; (ii) Judeo-Arabic biblical exegesis; and (iii) Judeo-Arabic philosophical, theological, and polemical works.

There is also the ongoing project to catalogue the Judeo-Arabic manuscripts in the Firkovitch Collection.

Yad Izhak Ben-Zvi

Yad Izhak Ben-Zvi was established in 1963 by a decision of the Israel government. During the first years of its existence its main activities were focused on gathering and consolidating the archives of Izhak and Raḥel Ben-Zvi and the publication of the writings of Izhak Ben-Zvi. In 1969 the Knesset adopted a law determining the aims of the Yad, which was charged with advancing research on the history of the Land of Israel and the dissemination of information about it and its various settlements and the heritage of the Jewish communities of Muslim lands. The law which defined Yad Ben-Zvi's objectives and modus operandi placed responsibility upon it to further study and education in this field. In addition, a few years later (1973), the study of the Jewish communities in Oriental countries and in the Sephardi Diaspora was added to its responsibility. In 1972 the Yad moved to its permanent headquarters in the building which had served as the residence of the president of Israel in Jerusalem. Yad Ben-Zvi has from its very inception involved leading scholars from all of Israel's universities in its activities. It has established joint centers for the study of Ereẓ Israel with each of these universities. The basic principle which has guided Yad Izhak Ben-Zvi since its inception has been not to limit itself to academic activities for the benefit of small elite groups but to spread knowledge in these fields among all strata of Israeli society – senior officials and junior staff in government offices, the religious and the secular, veteran residents and new immigrants, the elderly and the young, teachers and pupils – throughout the entire country.

BIBLIOGRAPHY: S. Rubinstein, "The Establishment and Beginnings of the Institute for the Study of Jewish Communities in the East," in: *Pe'amim*, 23 (1985), 127–49; A. Bar-Levav (ed.), *Pe'amim* (2002–2004), 92–94.

[Menahem Ben-Sasson (2nd ed.)]

BEOBACHTER AN DER WEICHSEL (Ger., "The Watcher by the Vistula"; Pol. title *Dostrzegacz Nadwislański*), the first Polish Jewish newspaper; published in Congress Poland from 1823 to 1824. Its editor was Anton *Eisenbaum, who approached the authorities for permission to publish a paper to serve the ideals of the Enlightenment (see *Haskalah). Permission and financial backing were granted, but only on the condition that a translation into Polish would be provided. The first issue of the paper accordingly came out at the end of 1823 with a Polish translation accompanying the Yiddish text (which was in fact German in Hebrew transcription). Some items, calculated to please the authorities, were printed in Polish only. The paper was divided into five sections: official announcements and general news from Poland; foreign news and descriptions of Jewish life in other countries (including descriptions of Jewish agricultural settlement in Kherson province); commercial news; miscellaneous items including biographies of famous Jews such as Josephus, Maimonides, Moses Mendelssohn, and Rothschild; announcements. Official announcements were published without comment or criticism. Discussion of actual problems facing Jewry seems to have been deliberately avoided. Eisenbaum had no assistants and virtually produced the paper by himself. It was apparently difficult to find suitable candidates since the few Jewish writers who could write in Polish seem to have preferred non-Jewish platforms. The paper appeared for less than a year, from Dec. 3, 1823, to Sept. 29, 1824: altogether there were only 44 issues, with the circulation never exceeding 150. The paper had to close down when the grant it had received from the government was exhausted. It failed to gain increased circulation because the typical advocates of the Enlightenment were not particularly interested in Jewish problems, while the Jewish masses found the quasi-Yiddish incomprehensible. The extreme assimilationist views of the paper and its negative attitude toward Jewish religious traditions made it objectionable to the majority of the Jewish population of Warsaw.

BIBLIOGRAPHY: J. Shatzky, *Geshikhte fun Yidn in Varshe*, 1 (1947), 290–1; S. Łastik, *Z dziejó oświęnia żydowskiego (1961)*, 176–8. **ADD. BIBLIOGRAPHY:** *M. Fuks, Prasa zydowska w Warszawie*, 1823–1939 (1979) 21–40, index; P. Glikson, *Preliminary Inventory of the Jewish Daily and Periodical Press Published in the Polish Language, 1823–1982* (1983); J. Fraenkel, "Prasa Zydowska w Warszawie XiX w.Dostrzegacz Nadwislanski," in: BŻIH, 1/89 (1974), 19–45

[Moshe Landau]

BERAB (Beirav), JACOB (c. 1474–1546), halakhic authority and leader of the Jewish communities of Palestine, Egypt, and Syria during the first half of the 16th century. Berab was born in Maqueda near Toledo, Spain, and went to Morocco after the expulsion of Jews from Spain in 1492. According to his own statement, he was only 18 years old when he was appointed rabbi of Fez. A few years later Berab left Fez and traveled to Egypt, Palestine (Jerusalem, Safed), and Syria (Aleppo, Damascus) in connection with business concerns, which proved very successful. During these sojourns Berab also taught Torah, gathering wide circles of pupils, who respected him greatly. He considered himself superior to the majority of scholars in Egypt, Palestine, and Syria, and tried to impose his authority on questions of *halakhah* that were brought before him, or that he undertook on his own initiative. Although Berab had close associations with many of his contemporaries, his domineering tendency brought him into conflict with scholars who would not submit to him.

Berab was swept along with the messianic current of the early 16th century, which resulted in large measure from intensive study of the Kabbalah. Berab himself gave some impetus to messianic anticipation by trying to revive the institution of **semikhah* ("rabbinical ordination"). According to Maimonides (Yad, Sanhedrin 1:3), the establishment of a "great *bet din*" will take place before the coming of the messiah. Since an institution competent to give *semikhah* had not existed for several hundred years, Maimonides provided instructions for its establishment. He authorized the rabbis of Ereẓ Israel to nominate one among them who would be the first *samukh* (ordained rabbi). In turn, that rabbi would have the authority to ordain others, who could then form a Sanhedrin (Yad, Sanhedrin 4:11). The Spanish expulsion and the ingathering of many Jews in Ereẓ Israel was interpreted as a sign that redemption was imminent.

Berab, while still in Egypt, conceived the idea of renewing *semikhah*. As the Palestinian settlement became stronger and the number of scholars increased, Safed became the seat of the messianic impetus. In 1538 Berab, who had been living in Safed periodically from at least 1524, succeeded in winning over the scholars there, including R. Joseph *Caro and R. Moses of *Trani, to his point of view. The scholars of Safed decided to renew the *semikhah* and they designated Berab as the first *samukh*. Immediately after this decision was taken, a messenger was sent to R. *Levi b. Ḥabib in Jerusalem, asking him to give his consent to the renewal of the *semikhah* and to accept the ordination of Berab. Not only did Levi b. Ḥabib, with whom Berab had had various disputes, refuse to accept the *semikhah* of Berab, he also opposed the decision of the rabbis of Safed on halakhic grounds. He also insisted that Maimonides' statement concerning the reestablishment of *semikhah* did not represent a decision but only an opinion, and that Maimonides had retracted it later (Yad, Sanhedrin 4:2). The protests of Levi b. Ḥabib delayed Berab's project. Discussions on the question of *semikhah* among the rabbis of both towns had been in progress for three months when Berab was forced by the Turks to leave Palestine. Apparently, he had become embroiled in a private affair, as a result of which his enemies denounced him to the Turkish authorities in Safed.

According to *halakhah, semikhah* could not be given outside Palestine. Berab feared that he might not be able to return and that all his plans would come to an end. Before he left, therefore, he gave *semikhah* to four rabbis of Safed, among whom were Joseph Caro and Moses of Trani. Levi b. Ḥabib, considering this to be a disregard of his protests, then publicly opposed the *semikhah*. From Damascus Berab conducted the discussion of the question in a vigorous manner, even by personal attacks on his adversary. Levi b. Ḥabib replied in kind and he was supported by an important ally – R. *David b. Solomon ibn Abi Zimra, who lived in Egypt. Thus, the project of establishing the "great *bet din*" came to an end; even the validity of the *semikhot* already given was in doubt. Nevertheless, those who had been ordained by Berab ordained other scholars after his death.

Berab wrote a commentary to all those parts of Maimonides' work not dealt with in the *Maggid Mishneh* commentary by *Vidal Yom Tov of Tolosa. However, only a small part was published (by Y.L. Maimon (Fishman) in *Sinai*, 36 (1955), 275–357). His responsa and his novellae to tractate *Kiddushin* were published together (1663). These novellae were republished from a manuscript in an enlarged form by Michael Rabinowitz (in Y.L. Fishman (eds.), *Sefer ha-Yovel… B.M. Levin* (1939), 196–299). Many of his halakhic decisions are reported in the works of his contemporaries, especially Joseph Caro.

Berab's grandson, JACOB BEN ABRAHAM (d. 1599), rabbi and halakhic authority, studied under Joseph Caro and was ordained by him. From 1563 he is mentioned in documents with the more important rabbis of Safed. By 1593 he was the most prominent of Safed's scholars and it was he who gave *semikhah*. He ordained R. Moses Galante, R. Eliezer Azikri, his own brother R. Moses Berab, R. Abraham Gabriel, R. Yom Tov Ẓahalon, R. Ḥiyya ha-Rofe, and R. Jacob Abulafia, all of Safed. In 1599 these seven rabbis reached an agreement not to ordain any other person without his approval. None of his writings remains, but his approvals of the decisions of his contemporaries, as well as some of his responsa scattered in the works of contemporary scholars, are known.

BIBLIOGRAPHY: J. Newman, *Semikhah* (Eng., 1950), includes bibliography; Graetz, Hist, 6 (1949), index, s.v. *Jacob Berav*, Gruenhut, in: *Ha-Ẓofeh me-Ereẓ Hagar*, 2 (1912), 25–33; Katz, in: *Zion*, 16:3–4 (1951), 28–45; Benayahu, in: *Sefer Yovel… Y. Baer* (1960), 248–69; Dimitrovsky, in: *Sefunot*, 6 (1962), 117–23; 7 (1963), 41–102; 10 (1966), 113–92; *Teshuvot RalbaḤ* (Venice, 1565), including a report of the controversy at the end.

BERAB (Beirav), JACOB BEN ḤAYYIM (end of 17th–18th century), poet and hymnologist. A descendant of R. Jacob *Berab, Berab was born in Safed. He left Palestine with his father-in-law R. Ḥayyim b. Moses *Abulafia before 1710 and settled in Smyrna (Izmir), Turkey. In 1740 they returned to Palestine and helped found the new Jewish settlement at Tiberias. Berab recorded all the events of the journey to Tiberias and their subsequent settlement in *Zimrat ha-Areẓ* (Mantua, 1745, etc). He also noted interesting details of the wars between the governor of Damascus, Soliman Pasha (1741–43), and the sheikh of Galilee, Dahr al ʿAmr. The purpose of his work was to call to the attention of the Diaspora the importance of the resettlement in Tiberias. Appended to the published editions were 12 of his poems in Hebrew and Ladino praising the resettlement and Tiberias. Some of these poems were, until recently, sung to a special folk tune in the Balkan countries.

BIBLIOGRAPHY: J.b.Ḥ. Berab, *Zimrat ha-Areẓ*, ed. by M. Benayahu (1946), introduction; Shalem, in: *Hed ha-Mizraḥ*, 2 no. 9 (1943), 9; Baron, in: *Sefer ha-Yovel… A. Marx* (1943),79; Ben Zvi, Ereẓ Yisrael, 308–11.

[Abraham David]

BERAḤ DODI (Heb. בְּרַח דּוֹדִי; "make haste my beloved," Song of Songs 8:14), *ge'ullah piyyut* in the morning prayer of the first day of Passover in the Ashkenazi rite. It consists of three stanzas based upon the allegorical interpretation of the central motif of *Song of Songs according to which "the beloved" is the people of Israel and the "lover" is God. Israel implores the "lover" to hasten his return to his "beloved." It made use, at the end of each stanza, of the text of Song of Songs: "Behold he standeth behind our wall" (2:9); "Hark! my beloved! behold, he cometh" (2:8); "This is my beloved, and this is my friend" (5:16). On the basis of the initials interwoven in this *piyyut* (שלמה יגדל בתורה חזק), the authorship has been ascribed to the 10th-century liturgical poet Solomon b. Judah ha-Bavli. Another *ge'ullah piyyut* in the morning prayer of the second day of Passover recited outside Ereẓ Israel (Ashkenazi rite), and composed by *Meshullam b. Kalonymus (c. 1000 C.E.), bears the same name. This *piyyut* of four stanzas is based upon the same motif as the aforementioned one. A third *piyyut* by the same name is recited on the Sabbath during the Intermediate Days of Passover. This was composed by Simeon b. Isaac, who also lived in the 10th century.

BIBLIOGRAPHY: *Service of the Synagogue*, tr. by I. Zangwill (London, 1954), 202.

BERAJA, RUBEN EZRA (1939–), Argentinean community leader and Zionist activist. Born in Ciudadela, Province of Buenos Aires, to a family from Aleppo, Syria, from an early age Beraja was active in Jewish public life and after graduating as a lawyer from the University of Buenos Aires he joined the management of the Cooperativa Mayo, a credit cooperative established in 1961 that used its profits to support the Sephardi Jewish school network and for other beneficial activities. Beraja, who was the youngest member of the board, was soon appointed president of the cooperative. He continued to fill this position when the cooperative was transformed into the Banco Mayo (1978), acting in this capacity until the bank went bankrupt in 1998.

In the late 1960s Beraja was invited by Rabbi Itzhak Schehebar, the spiritual leader of the Aleppine community, to join the board of directors of the Congregación Sefaradí Argentina, becoming an active promoter of its educational and religious activities. At the same time he became one of the promising leaders of the Zionist Sephardi movement.

Using the financial success of the Banco Mayo, Beraja expanded its assistance to the educational, cultural and Zionist institutions of the Jewish community at large, increasing the influence of the Orthodox sector and the prestige of the Sephardi leadership.

In 1991 Beraja was elected president of the *DAIA, becoming the political representative of Argentinean Jewry. He was reelected in 1993 and 1996. Acting during the presidency of Carlos Saúl Menem, he was involved (1992) in the opening of the archives dealing with the immigration to Argentina of Nazi criminals in the postwar years under Peron's presidency. He also acted in defense of the Jewish community following the two dramatic events that shook its existence – the explosion of the Israeli Embassy in March 1992 and of the AMIA community building in July 1994.

However, the conflicting interests of his financial and political careers led to his downfall, caused by the collapse of Menem's economic policy and the political and economic crises that ensued. Beraja was held responsible for the losses of the Banco Mayo, which had bitter consequences for the Jewish community. Beraja was placed in preventive custody in December 2003 and at the beginning of 2005 was still awaiting trial. He accused the president of the Argentinean Central Bank during the crash of Banco Mayo – Pedro Pou – of discrimination and antisemitism.

Beraja served in several international Jewish organizations and was the vice president of the World Jewish Congress and the president of the Latin American Jewish Congress and the Fedración Sefaradí Latinoamericana (FESELA). He promoted the creation of important new projects, like the Universidad Hebrea Bar Ilan and a Jewish video-cable station (ALEPH), which did not last. He was the recipient of the Jerusalem Award for Jewish Education in the Diaspora from the World Zionist Organization and the Jewish Agency for Israel.

[Efraim Zaidoff (2nd ed.)]

BERAKHAH, ISAAC (d. 1772), rabbi and preacher in the Aleppo community. The support and encouragement of Elijah Silbirah enabled Berakhah to pursue his studies until he became a noted scholar. His *Berakh Yiẓḥak* (Venice, 1763), a book of homiletics, contains several sermons for each weekly Reading of the Law; they deal mostly with halakhic problems. He often mentions Maimonides' *Yad ha-Ḥazakah*, Samuel Eliezer *Edels, the *tosafot*, and the responsa of *Isaac b. Sheshet. In addition to halakhic problems, he deals with such questions as the *kavvanah* and joy with which one should perform the *mitzvot*. Some of Berakhah's responsa were published in S.R. Laniado's *Beit Dino shel Shelomo* (Constantinople, 1775). Abraham Antibi, one of his many pupils, eulogized him at his death. Berakhah's sons Ḥayyim and Elijah were also rabbis in Aleppo.

BIBLIOGRAPHY: Steinschneider, Cat Bod, 1096 no. 5321; D. Laniado, *Li-Kedoshim Asher ba-Areẓ* (= Aram-Zobah, i.e., Aleppo; 1952), 37.

BERAKHOT (Heb. בְּרָכוֹת: "Benedictions, Blessings"), first tractate of the Mishnah, Tosefta, Palestinian and Babylonian Talmuds. On its placement at the head of the order *Zera'im*, which deals with agricultural laws, see *Zera'im*.

The tractate deals with aspects of the daily liturgy (as distinct from the prayers of holy days, ritual readings of scripture, etc.). In keeping with the general objectives of the Mishnah, it is concerned primarily with the laws governing formal prayers and blessings, and deals only rarely or peripherally with the content, theology, or rationales for these prayers. These latter dimensions are discussed more extensively in the Tosefta, Talmuds, and cognate passages in midrashic works. Although the Talmud was able to identify some biblical foundation for the liturgical topics dealt with in the tractate, the Mishnah organizes the material according to a topical sequence, with only occasional allusions to scriptural sources. Study of other literature from the Second Commonwealth, especially the liturgical texts from Qumran, allows us to better understand the place of rabbinic prayer in the broader evolution of Jewish worship of the time.

Mishnah *Berakhot* focuses primarily on three liturgical categories: (1) the *Shema*; (2) the *Tefillah*; (3) miscellaneous blessings to be recited on specified occasions, especially on the enjoyment of food and other physical pleasures. A "blessing" is a formal liturgical unit that is usually recognizable by its opening "Blessed are you, Lord our God [Sovereign of the Universe] …."

Shema

Early rabbinic and apparently pre-rabbinic tradition interpreted the command (Deut. 6:6, 8) "And these words, which I command thee this day, shall be upon thy heart … when thou liest down, and when thou risest up" and the similar expressions in Deuteronomy 11:18–19 as explicit directives to recite the passages in which those expressions occur (Deut. 6:4–9, 11:13–21) daily in the evening and morning. This obligation was understood to be the fulfillment either of a separate precept, of the broader requirement to study Torah, or as a declaration of one's acceptance of the "yoke of the kingship of Heaven" in declaring "the Lord is one" (Deut. 6:4) and the "yoke of commandments" in Deuteronomy 11:1, as understood by Rabbi *Joshua ben Korḥa (Ber. 2:2). A third section was added to the *Shema*, at least in its morning recitation: Numbers 15:37–41, dealing with the commandment of ritual fringes. The Mishnah (1:5) sees this as fulfillment of the obligation to mention the Egyptian Exodus daily, though this seems doubtful. In both its morning and evening versions, the *Shema* is embedded in a framework of blessings that relate to the natural transition of the times of day, the divine love for Israel that was expressed in the giving of the Torah (of which the *Shema* is a part), and hopes for redemption.

The first three chapters of the Mishnah deal with the regulations for reciting the *Shema*. Topics include: the designated times when it may be recited, the appropriate physical postures, the accompanying blessings, laws about interruptions and irregularities in the recitation (e.g., if it was inaudible or in the incorrect sequence), and instances when a person is exempted from the obligation.

Tefillah

Mishnah chapters 4–5 deal with the *tefillah*, the central rabbinic prayer whose standard version consists of 18 blessings and was to be recited in the evening, morning, and afternoon. The structure and text of the prayer are presupposed, but not set out, in the Mishnah. Although the sages linked the institution of prayer at fixed times to the practices of the biblical patriarchs and the schedule of daily sacrificial offerings, the content and set times of the mandatory *tefillah* are considered to be of rabbinic origin, albeit influenced heavily by biblical themes. Topics dealt with by the Mishnah include the designated times for the three services, occasions when the full 18 blessings or an abbreviated versions should be recited, occasions when one may forgo the normal physical requirements of standing facing towards the Jerusalem Temple, aggadah-like traditions about the preference for spontaneity and a reverent state of mind, and some prayer customs that are forbidden, evidently because of heterodox associations.

Blessings

Chapters 6 through 9 of the Mishnah are devoted to the blessings that accompany specified occasions. The Tosefta (4:1) supplies theological and scriptural rationales for this practice: "A person should not taste anything before reciting a blessing, as it says [Ps. 24:1] 'The earth is the Lord's, and the fullness thereof.' One who enjoys the benefits of this world without a blessing has committed a trespass," etc. The *halakhah* in the Mishnah requires that the precisely appropriate blessing be recited for each occasion. Accordingly, different blessings are designated for fruits of the earth, fruits of trees, bread, other baked goods, wine, "the seven species" of Deuteronomy 8:8; and guidelines are provided for choosing the correct blessings when there are numerous foodstuffs.

Chapter 7 discusses the procedures for the concluding blessing after a formal meal or banquet, especially the "invitation to bless" (*zimmun*).

Chapter 8 consists of a list of disputes between the Houses of Shammai and Hillel related to blessings recited at meals. Some of these disputes, or the reasons underlying the respective positions, remain obscure, and several were transmitted in differing versions in *baraitas* in the Tosefta and Talmuds.

Chapter 9 contains a miscellaneous collection of blessings for various occasions, including places of religious significance, wonders of nature, life-milestones, and deliverance from danger.

The Mishnah contains traditions covering the full range of the tannaitic generations, including material dating from the Second Temple era (e.g., 1:1 cites the evening purification practices of the priests as a reliable sign of the advent of nightfall).

Both the Palestinian and Babylonian Talmuds contain full tractates for *Berakhot*. The Babylonian is the longest in the Talmud (by word count), owing to its extensive collection of aggadic material, much of it appearing as loosely connected digressions. Although some of these passages offer valuable insights into the rabbis' attitudes towards prayer (often defined as a plea for divine mercy), the material covers a vast assortment of themes, including biblical expositions, hagiographical narratives, dream interpretation, and a great deal of folklore.

BIBLIOGRAPHY: N. Sacks, *The Mishnah with Variant Readings: Order Zera'im* (1971); A. Houtman, *Mishnah and Tosefta: A Synoptic Comparison of the Tractates Berakhot and Shebiit* (1996); Tz. Zahavy (trans.), *Berakhot* (1989); A.Z. Ehrman, *The Talmud: With English Translation and Commentary. Berakhot* (1965); J. Heinemann, *Prayer in the Talmud: Forms and Patterns* (1977); I. Elbogen, *Jewish Liturgy: A Comprehensive History* (1993).

[Eliezer L. Segel (2nd ed.)]

BERBERS, indigenous North African tribes who originally spoke dialects of the Berber language. Medieval Arab writers ascribed the ancestry of the Berbers to *Goliath the Philistine and maintained their Canaanite origin. The Phoenician colonization of Africa, the long Carthaginian domination, and the survival of Punic, a language closely related to Hebrew, supported these legends which spread among the Berbers themselves. Similar tales are found in the writings of Greek and Latin authors and in the Talmud which spread the legend that the Canaanites immigrated of their own free will to North Africa. It is said that the survivors of the Jewish revolt in *Cyrenaica (115–116 C.E.) found refuge among the Berbers of Western *Libya. Scholars have frequently claimed that the Jews' desire to proselytize found a favorable atmosphere among the Berbers from the first to the seventh centuries. African Christianity, whose early converts were Jews, clashed with Jewish proselytism. Archaeological discoveries, epigraphs, and writings of the Christian scholars Tertullian and St. Augustine, indignant at the growing Berber conversions to Judaism, attest to these facts. The persecutions by the Byzantines forced Jews to settle among the Berbers in the mountain and desert regions. Ibn Khaldun confirmed the existence of a large number of proselyte Berbers at the time of the Arab conquest of Africa. The Islamization of these countries, however, did not abolish all previous beliefs. Christianity was abandoned rapidly; Judaism continued to exist and – from Tripolitania to *Morocco – modern ethnographers and anthropologists encountered small groups whom they called "Jewish Berbers." These isolated groups of Jews lived in the high mountains of North Africa until the last few decades. Some scholars designated them as the descendants of Berber proselytes. In most cases they eventually intermingled with the rest of the population. However, the survival of such groups to the present is now doubted.

It is difficult to evaluate Jewish life in Berber society because Berbers did not have a written history. Berber history was completely oral. Thus, information on Jewish life comes from travelers who visited the Atlas Mountains, from a few written sources, and from interviews with people who lived in these areas. Two main sources are *Higgid Mordechai*, written by *Mordechai Hacohen*, a Jewish scholar from Tripoli who wrote about the Jews in Jabel Nafusa, south of Tripoli, and a statistical study carried out between 1961 and 1964 by the Mossad, the Israeli secret service, during the "Yachin Operation," in which the Mossad organized the *aliyah* of the Jews in the area.

Jews coexisted within Berber society. They had complete autonomy, communal organizations, and the possibility of practicing their religion. Jews were mainly occupied in trade and the crafts and did not work in agriculture. There was some kind of understanding between Berbers and Jews about the occupational structure of each group, enabling each to earn a livelihood. They also shared religious rituals and customs. For example, at Shavuot the Berbers of Libya poured water on Jews as one of their customs.

The Mossad study referred to Jewish life in Berber society at the end of its existence. In the village of Gourama in southeast Morocco, for example, there were 285 Jews, 73% of them below the age of 30. About 20% of the families had eight members, 50% fewer that seven persons. Seven Jews were tailors, seven farmers, five merchants, and two butchers. Although more research is needed it seems that these figures characterize Jewish life in the Berber villages.

BIBLIOGRAPHY: H. Fournel, *Les Berbères* (1875), 32–41; S. Gsell, *Histoire ancienne de l'Afrique du Nord*, 1 (1920), 236–343; E.F. Gauthier, *Le passé de l'Afrique du Nord* (1942), 140ff., 225–44, 270ff., 439; Simon, in: *Revue d'histoire et de philosophie religieuses* 26 (1946), 1–31, 105–45; M. Simon, *Verus Israel* (Eng. 1948), index; Hirschberg, in *Zion*, 22 (1957), 10–20; idem, in: *Journal of African History*, 4 (1963), 313–39; Hirschberg, Afrikah, 2 (1965), 9–36; N. Slouschz, *Hébraeo-Phéniciens et Judéo-Berbères* (1908); idem, *Travels in North Africa* (1927), 453–88, passim; A.N. Chouraqui, *Between East and West* (1968). **ADD. BIBLIOGRAPHY:** M. Shokeid, "Jewish Existence in a Berber Environment," in: Sh. Deshen and W.P. Zenner (eds.), *Jews among Muslims…* (1996), 109–20; E. Goldberg, "Ecologic and Demographic Aspects of Rural Tripolitanian Jewry 1853–1949," in: *International Journal of Middle East Studies*, 2 (1971), 245–65; E. Goldberg and H. Goldberg, *Cave Dwellers and Citrus Growers: Jewish Community in Libya and Israel (1972)*; E. Goldberg, "Communal Organization of the Jews of Tripolitania during the Late Ottoman Period," in: *Jewish Political Studies Review*, 5:3–4, (Fall 5754/1993), 77–95; idem, "The 'Maskil' and the 'Mequbbal'; Mordecai Ha-Cohen and the Grave of Rabbi Shim'on Lavi in Tripoli," in: H.E. Goldberg (ed.), *Sephardi and Middle Eastern Jewries* (1996), 168–80.

[David Corcos / Haim Sadoun (2nd ed.)]

BERCOVICI, KONRAD (1882–1961), U.S. novelist. Born in Romania, Bercovici used his experiences as an investigator for a controversial exposé, *Crimes of Charity* (1917). He wrote several books about the gypsies, including *Ghitza and Other Romances of Gypsy Blood* (1919) and *Story of the Gypsies* (1928). His other works include *Savage Prodigal* (1948), a biography of Rimbaud; *Dust of New York* (1919), set in the Lower East Side; *Main Entrance* (1932); and *Exodus* (1947), the story of Moses. His autobiography, *It's the Gypsy in Me*, appeared in 1941.

BERCOVITCH, PETER (1879–1942), Canadian labor lawyer, politician, and Jewish community leader. Bercovich was born in Montreal. The son of Romanian immigrants, he attended Université Laval à Montreal and McGill University before entering legal practice. He was an activist on behalf of Montreal's underprivileged Jewish workers and was soon a favorite speaker at many community political meetings and rallies of fraternal, charitable, and social organizations in the city's Jewish quarters. He represented the workers during the protracted and bitter strikes in the Montreal men's clothing industry in 1916 and 1917, forcing improvement in labor conditions from the mostly Jewish manufacturers.

Bercovich became the first president of the Jewish Immigrant Aid Society and in the 1920s joined the Jewish community's court battle for equal rights for Jews in Quebec's schools, insisting on an accommodation within existing structures rather than a separate Jewish school system. A prominent Liberal Party member, Bercovich was elected to the Quebec Legislative Assembly for Montreal's Saint-Louis constituency in 1916 and was re-elected six times. He fought for a solution to the school question and supported measures to help the disadvantaged. He also shepherded a bill through the Quebec Assembly which validated Jewish marriages and authorized rabbis to keep registers of civil status. In 1938 Bercovich was elected to the federal House of Commons, where he served until his death.

[Gerald Tulchinsky (2nd ed.)]

BERCOVITCH, SACVAN (1933–), U.S. literary scholar. Bercovitch was born in Montreal of poor Ukrainian immigrant parents, both of whom were idealistic communists. His mother, Bryna, enlisted in the Red Army in 1917 and fought in the civil wars following the Revolution; his father, Alexander, an artist who had studied in Palestine, St. Petersburg, and Munich, had been conscripted into, and deserted from, the Russian Army during World War I. They immigrated to Canada in 1926. Bercovitch, who spoke Yiddish and French in childhood before learning English, was named after Sacco and Vanzetti.

Bercovitch began his higher education at the New School in New York and at Reed College in Oregon, but dropped out to live for four years in a left-wing kibbutz in Israel, where he met his first wife. He returned to Canada in 1958 and while working at a supermarket in Montreal attended night classes at Sir George Williams College (today Concordia College), where he earned his B.A. in 1961. He received his M.A. in 1962 and Ph.D. in 1965 from Claremont Graduate School in California. He taught at Brandeis (1966–68), the University of California, San Diego (1968–70), Columbia (1970–83), and finally Harvard (1983–2002), where he subsequently became professor emeritus and Powell M. Cabot Research Professor of American Literature. He was a visiting professor or lecturer at many universities around the world.

Bercovitch's scholarly work, growing out of his fascination with (and resistance to, in his words) American culture, has focused primarily on the formation of the American character and of American myth, what he has called the "symbolic construction of America," through an examination of classic American literature from the 17th through the 19th centuries. He is the author of several influential works of scholarship, including *The Puritan Origins of the American Self* (1975), *The American Jeremiad* (1978), and *The Office of "The Scarlet Letter"* (1991); editor or coeditor of the equally influential collections *The American Puritan Imagination: Essays in Revaluation* (1974), *Reconstructing American Literary History* (1986), and *Ideology and Classic American Literature* (1986, with Myra Jehlen); and author of numerous important essays, some of which are collected in *The Rites of Assent: Transformations in the Symbolic Construction of America* (1993). (The essay "The Music of America," printed as the Introduction to this book, contains Bercovitch's reflections on his personal and intellectual relationship to American culture as well as the Canadian and "Yiddishist-leftist" culture in which he grew up.) He was also the editor of the ongoing new multivolume *Cambridge History of American Literature* and published English translations of Yiddish writers.

Sacvan Bercovitch characterizes his work as "cultural close reading," and its subject as the "American 'consensus.'" "America was a venture in exegesis," he says, "… a corporate identity built on fragmentation and dissent" whose "function was partly to mystify or mask social realities. Nonetheless it denoted something equally real: a coherent system of symbols, values, and beliefs, and a series of rituals designed to keep the system going" (*The Rites of Assent*, 29–30). His great erudition, intellectual depth, and skepticism of doctrinaire interpretation won him widespread respect and made him one of the most influential Americanists of his time.

[Drew Silver (2nd ed.)]

BERDICHEV, town in the historic region of Volhynia, now in Zhitomir district, Ukraine. Apart from two single references to individual Jews from Berdichev in 1593 and 1602, there is no evidence that a Jewish community existed in Berdichev before 1721. In 1732, the owner of the town granted a charter to the Jewish guild of tailors freeing them from interference by the communal authorities (*kahal*). The Jewish population gradually increased with Berdichev's development as a fair town from 1765. According to the census of 1765, the Jews in Berdichev numbered 1,220 (out of a total population of 1,541) including Jews living in the vicinity; they numbered 1,951 in 1789 (out of 2,460). In 1794, Prince Radziwill, the owner of the town, deprived the rabbis of their right of civil jurisdiction, which was transferred to a court to be elected by majority Jewish vote. Berdichev had become an important center of Volhynian *Ḥasidism in the last quarter of the 18th century, and the Ḥasidim were thus able to secure the election of *dayyanim* so as to free themselves from the jurisdiction of the *kahal* and its *Mitnaggedim* rabbis. As the town grew, a number of noted scholars served as rabbis of Berdichev, including Lieber "the Great," Joseph "the Ḥarif," and, from the end of the 18th century until his death in 1809, *Levi Isaac of Berdichev.

In 1797, Prince Radziwill granted seven Jewish cloth merchants the monopoly of the cloth trade in Berdichev, and in the first half of the 19th century the town's commerce was concentrated in Jewish hands. Jews founded scores of trading companies and banking establishments there, with agencies in the Russian interior and even abroad. Jews also served as agents of the neighboring estates of the nobility, whose agricultural produce was sold at the Berdichev fairs. The expatriation of Polish nobles and decline of the Polish nobility after the uprising of 1863 dealt a blow to Jewish commerce in Berdichev. The economic position of most of Berdichev's Jews was further impaired by the restrictions imposed on Jewish settlement in the villages by the "Temporary Regulations" (*May Laws) of 1882 and other restrictive government measures.

The main increase in the Jewish population of Berdichev occurred in the first half of the 19th century. There were 23,160 Jews living in Berdichev in 1847, and 46,683 in 1861. It was then the second-largest Jewish community in Russia. Shortly afterward the numbers began to decline, and in 1897 Berdichev had 41,617 Jewish residents (80% of the total population). The 1926 census shows 30,812 Jewish residents (55.6% of the total); about the same number were probably living there in 1939. Until World War I, emigration was balanced by the natural increase in the Jewish population; after the 1917 Revolution the proportion of Jewish residents steadily decreased through emigration.

At the end of the 19th century, about half of the Jewish wage earners were employed in manual trades, mostly in tailoring, shoemaking, carpentry, metalwork, etc. About 2,000 were hired workers, while the remainder gained their livelihood from trade. Berdichev became one of the foremost centers of the *Bund. After the 1917 Revolution, the proportion of hired workers increased, while a considerable number of Jews were absorbed by the state administration.

The ideas of the Enlightenment (*Haskalah) began to spread in Berdichev early in the 19th century, especially among wealthier families. The Galician Haskalah pioneer and Hebrew author Tobias *Feder Gutmann settled in Berdichev toward the end of his life. Influenced by Isaac Baer *Levinsohn, a group of *maskilim* was formed there in the 1820s, in which the physician Israel Rothenberg was particularly active. Among the opponents of the *maskilim* was the banker Jacob Joseph Halpern, who had great influence in ḥasidic circles and close ties to the government. The first public school in Berdichev giving instruction in Russian was opened in 1850. With the economic decline of Berdichev, the wealthier *maskilim* left for the larger cities. Because of the poverty of the majority of the Jewish population, a large number of children were even unable to attend *ḥeder*. According to the 1897 census, only 58% of Jewish males and 32% of Jewish females were able to read or write any language.

In Russian and Jewish literature and folklore, Berdichev epitomizes the typical Jewish town. It had some 80 synagogues and *battei midrash* and its cantors were celebrated throughout the Ukraine. It served as the model for the town depicted in the writings of *Mendele Mokher Seforim and *Shalom Aleichem (*Gants Berdichev*), as well as in *Der Nister (*Mishpokhe Mashber*). During the 1917 Revolution and the civil war of 1917–19, the head of the community and mayor of the town was the Bundist leader D. Lipets. In early 1919, the Jews in Berdichev became victims of a pogrom perpetrated by the Ukrainian army.

Under the Soviet government, most of the synagogues were closed. Yiddish continued to receive official acknowledgment and Yiddish schools were opened in Berdichev. In 1924, a government court of law was established there, the first in Ukraine to conduct its affairs in Yiddish. According to the 1926 census, of the 30,812 Jews in Berdichev 28,584 declared Yiddish as their mother-tongue. However, by the early 1930s, complaints were heard about curtailment of the use of Yiddish in government offices in Berdichev. A Yiddish periodical *Der Arbeter* appeared in Berdichev about twice weekly until the middle of the 1930s. The number of Yiddish schools dropped in the 1930s. By 1939, the number of Jews had fallen to 23,266 (37.5% of the total). All Jewish cultural activities there were suspended before World War II.

The Germans captured Berdichev on July 7, 1941; 1,000 Jews succeeded in fleeing from the city. In July around 1,300 were murdered. Thousands more were crowded in a closed ghetto. In late August 2,000 Jews were executed, and on September 5, 1941, another 4,300. In October the 15,000 remaining ghetto inhabitants were murdered near the village of Radianskoye. The few remaining artisans were killed by mid-1942. About 6,500 Jews lived in Berdichev in the late 1950s.

Although *mazzah* baking was prohibited in the early 1960s, it resumed after a few years. In 1970, there were an estimated 15,000 Jews in Berdichev with a synagogue, a cantor, and a ritual poultry slaughterer. The cemetery was reported to be neglected, but the Jews had erected a fence around the grave of Levi Isaac of Berdichev. Most of Berdichev's Jews left for Israel and the West in the 1990s.

[Shmuel Ettinger / Shmuel Spector (2nd ed.)]

Hebrew Printing in Berdichev

In 1807, Samuel C. Isachar Ber, who had established printing presses in several towns, set up a press in Berdichev, initially as a branch of his Ostraha house. Samuel and, after 1817, his son Jacob Funkelmann operated the press until 1820, when the business was transferred to Szdelkow. Altogether they printed over 30 works on Ḥasidism, Kabbalah, and *halakhah* in addition to prayer books and popular books in Yiddish. Another printing house was established by Israel *Bak in 1815–21. Before his immigration to Ereẓ Israel in 1831, he produced 26 works on roughly the same subjects, most of them set in a new typeface designed and cut by Bak himself, with his own illustrations. Other Berdichev printers were M.H. Rothenberg (1834–36) and H.J. Sheftel (1885–1910); the latter published a great number of scholarly works, including a popular edition of the Babylonian Talmud (with Rashi) in one volume (1894).

[Avraham Yaari]

BIBLIOGRAPHY: Horodezky, in: *Ha-Me'assef* (1902), 106–9; A. Zederbaum, *Di Gehaymnise fun Berdichev* (1870); M. Morgulis, in: *Voskhod*, 15 no. 4 (1895), 21–35; Lestschinsky, in: *Blaetter fuer demographische Statistik und Wirtschaftskunde der Juden*, 2 (1923), 37–48; M. Osherowitch, *Shtet un shtetlekh in Ukraine*, 1 (1948), 92–104; *Yalkut Volin*, 2 (1951), 12–13; Yaari, in: KS, 10 (1934/35), 100ff., 296f.; H.D. Friedberg, *Toledot ha-Defus ha-Ivri be-Polanyah* (1950^2), 133ff. **ADD. BIBLIOGRAPHY:** PK Ukrainah, s.v.

BERDICHEVSKY SCHER, JOSE (d. 2000), general of the Chilean army born in Santiago (Chile). He realized a brilliant military career. In 1952 he was the personal pilot of President Gabriel Gonzalez Videla and rose to the rank of general in the Air Force, becoming the first Jewish general there. During the military regime of Augusto Pinochet (1973–89) he was named chief of staff of the Air Force, chief of the garrison of Santiago, and a member of the Military Junta. As chief of the garrison of Santiago he commuted death sentences handed down in court martial proceedings. He retired from the Air Force in 1978 and then served as ambassador to Israel.

[Moshe Nes El (2nd ed.)]

BERDUGO, family name of many distinguished rabbis in Morocco, chiefly in Meknès. According to tradition, the family was of Davidic descent through the exilarch Bustanai. *YAḤYA (or Ḥiyya) BERDUGO (d. 1617) endorsed an ordinance in Fez in 1605, later left for Tetuán and was nominated deputy rabbi there in 1614. A Yaḥya Berdugo was known in Meknès about the same time but it is not certain whether they are identical or not. MOSES BEN ABRAHAM, called "Mashbir" (c. 1679–1730), was head of the rabbinical court in Meknès, where the Berdugos settled after leaving Fez. Famous for his sense of justice (compilation *Or ha-Ḥayyim* to Deut. 1:15), he was the author of *Rosh Mashbir*, novellae on the Pentateuch and on some of the Talmud tractates (1840); *Kenaf Renanim I*, commentaries and novellae to the Bible (1909), and *Kenaf Renanim II*, an anthology of homilies (1932); and *Divrei Moshe*, responsa (1947). Other unpublished writings are at the National Library, Jerusalem (Ms. Heb. 8^0 1446), Ben-Zvi Institute, Jerasalem (Ms. 736), and in private possession. JUDAH BEN JOSEPH I (1690–1744), *dayyan* in Meknès (1730) following Moses b. Abraham Berdugo the Mashbir, was the author of *Mayim Amukkim*, a commentary on the Pentateuch and *haftarot* (1937). Some of his responsa have been published in the responsa of Jacob ibn Ẓur. MORDECAI BEN JOSEPH, "Ha-Marbiẓ" (1715–1762), brother of Judah, was the grandnephew, pupil, and son-in-law of Moses b. Abraham, and a noted *dayyan* (after 1748) in Meknès. He wrote many works, of which, however, only *Mordekhai* has been published (1948); others are still extant in manuscript. RAPHAEL (1747–1821), son of this Mordecai, *dayyan* and scholar, was the author of the following works: *Mishpatim Yesharim*, responsa (2 vols., 1891), *Torot Emet*, commentary on the Shulḥan Arukh (1939); bound with the latter are *Kiẓẓur ha-Takkanot* and *Minhagei Terefot*; and *Mei Menuḥot*, a commentary on the Pentateuch (2 vols., 1900–42). Other works are still in manuscript, including translations of the Bible from Genesis to the end of Isaiah into Arabic, under the title *Leshon Limmudim*. MAIMON "the Mevin" (1767–1824), son of Raphael, was a *dayyan* and the author of responsa and other works, including *Lev Mevin* and *Penei Mevin* (issued together 1951). His novellae to the Talmud are in manuscript.

PETHAHIAH MORDECAI BEN JEKUTHIEL (1764–1820), the author of *Nofet Ẓufim*, responsa (1938), and *Pittuḥei*

Ḥotam, a commentary on the Talmud (unpublished). JACOB (1783–1843), his brother, *dayyan* and poet, was known for his stand against the rabbis of Tiberias in favor of the Jerusalem rabbis in the controversy of 1836 over participation in the *ḥalukkah*. His works include *Shufrei de-Ya'akov*, responsa (1910); *Gallei Amikta*, a commentary on *Mayim Amukkim* of Judah Berdugo (1911); *Kol Ya'akov*, liturgical poems (1844). *To'afot Re'em* or *Karnei Re'em*, on Rashi and Elijah *Mizraḥi, is still in manuscript (Ms. Jerusalem National Library, Ms. Heb. 80 3839, and 1448). JOSEPH (1802–1854), *dayyan* in Meknès, was a scholar whose works include a lexicon of Hebrew grammatical roots and their derivatives, *Ketonet Yosef* (3 vols. 1922–43). Other works are unpublished. JACOB BEN MORDECAI (d. 1901), brother of Joseph, was an *av bet din* in Meknès. SOLOMON BEN DANIEL (1854–1906), halakhic authority and poet, was a rabbi in Meknès and in 1897 was appointed rabbi of the community. He was the author of *Dei Hasher, Em le-Masoret*, responsa, a collection of laws and Torah novellae; appended are *Musar Haskel* and *Shirei Shelomo* (1950). JEKUTHIEL ḤAYYIM BEN ELISHA (1858–1940), great-grandson of Mordecai b. Joseph, was born in Rabat, and appointed *dayyan* there in 1893. The French government appointed him in 1922 a member of the supreme *bet din* (court of appeal) which had its seat in Rabat, the capital of Morocco. In 1934 he deputized for Raphael *Ankawa, chief rabbi of Morocco, during his illness, and he succeeded him after his death. In 1935 he was made president of the Supreme *bet din*. JOSHUA BEN JACOB (1878–1953) became chief rabbi of Meknès in 1904 and in 1941 chief rabbi of Morocco, where he served until his death. He had a strong personality and on a number of occasions was in conflict with the leaders of the Church and with members of the French government, by whom he was respected. The communal rules and regulations adopted during this time were published in the pamphlets of "The Council of Moroccan Rabbis" (Casablanca). None of his books was published.

BIBLIOGRAPHY: J.M. Toledano, *Ner ha-Ma'arav* (1911), index; idem, *Oẓar Genazim* (1960), 167; J. Ben-Naim, *Malkhei Rabbanan* (1931), passim; Yaari, Sheluḥei, index; M. Benayahu, in: *Minḥah le-Avraham Elmaleḥ* (1959), 35. See also introductions to published works of members of the family.

[David Obadia]

BERDYANSK (in 1827–30 **Kutur-ogly**, in 1830–42 **Novo-Nogaisk**, in 1939–58 **Osipenko**), town in the Zaporozhie region of the Ukraine. Berdyansk was founded as a village by order of the governor-general of Novorossia, Count M.S. Vorontsov, whose attitude to Jews was fairly liberal. In 1842 it became a district capital. From the beginning the Jews formed part of its population, employed as tailors and merchants. In 1847 the Jewish population was 572 and in 1860 a Talmud Torah school was founded. In 1864, 703 Jews were registered in the town and 744 in the district. In April 1881, concerned over anti-Jewish acts in the wake of the assassination of Alexander II (see *Pogroms), the Jews requested the authorities to dispatch troops to prevent pogroms.

In 1890 there were three Jewish schools in Berdyansk. A vocational branch of the Talmud Torah was also founded. According to the 1897 census the number of Jews in the town was 3,306 (including 258 *Karaites), i.e., 12.9% of the total population; while in the district it was 9,171 (3% of the population). During World War I new schools were opened for the children of the Jewish refugees from the frontline area. In the period of the Civil War Berdyansk changed hands a number of times and the Jewish population suffered from violence and pillage. In June 1920 seven members of the Jewish Communist Party, *Po'alei Zion, volunteered for the Red Army. According to the 1926 census there were 2,138 Jews in Berdyansk in 1926 and 2,393 in 1939 (4.6% of the population). Berdyansk was occupied by German troops in October 1941. About a thousand Jews were shot in a gorge near the town; the rest were annihilated in 1942. Little is known about Jewish life under subsequent Soviet rule. However, in the early 1990s a Jewish cultural society was founded and a synagogue congregation was active. According to the *Jewish Agency there were 2,000 Jews in Berdyansk in 1994 (1.3% of the total population).

[Naftali Prat (2nd ed.)]

BERDYCZEWSKI (Later: **Bin-Gorion**), **MICHA JOSEF** (1865–1921), Hebrew writer and thinker. Born in Medzibezh, Podolia, Berdyczewski was the descendant of a line of ḥasidic rabbis. His father served as the rabbi of Medzibezh during Berdyczewski's childhood. Berdyczewski began to read Haskalah writers in his adolescence and the ensuing struggle between modern ideas and the concepts and forces of traditional Judaism was to animate his writings throughout his life. His first marriage (1883–85) ended when his father-in-law would not tolerate his preoccupation with modern Hebrew books. Shortly thereafter he moved to the yeshivah of Volozhin to study for over a year. Here he began his literary career and incurred the wrath of his teachers with his writings.

His first article was "*Toledot Yeshivat Eẓ Ḥayyim*" (in *Ha-Asif*, 1887) and his first story "*Heẓiẓ ve-Nifga*" (in *Ha-Meliẓ*, 1888). Most of his publications in this period were polemical articles, some popular and some scholarly, which contain many of the ideas he developed later. He often expressed his views in lyrical outbursts rather than in connected logical statements – a style which marked much of his writing throughout his life.

Berdyczewski left Russia for Germany (1890) and stayed two years in Breslau, studying at the rabbinical seminary and the university. He met frequently with David *Frischmann who strove to expand Berdyczewski's intellectual horizons and cultivate his literary taste. In 1892 he moved to Berlin and combined both Jewish and secular studies but continued the lonely existence of the poor, foreign university student. In Germany Berdyczewski's chaotic, revolutionary ideas were given shape under the impact of his studies in philosophy. The influence of Schopenhauer can be noticed in his famous article "*Reshut ha-Yaḥid Be'ad ha-Rabbim*" ("The Individual and the Community," in *Oẓar ha-Sifrut*, 1892), in which he defended the claims of individual freedom and creativity against the stultifying demands of such abstractions as tradition, religion, public consensus and will, history, and ideology. Here and in other articles, Berdyczewski attacked the limited scope of much of Hebrew literature, the inadequacies of Haskalah, Aḥad Ha-Amism, and Ḥibbat Zion. After two years of studies in Berne, Berdyczewski returned to spend four years (1896–1900) in Berlin, one of the most productive periods in his life. Stimulated by his opposition to both *Aḥad Ha-Am and *Herzl, and encouraged by his friends and other Hebrew writers there, Berdyczewski published in many of the leading Hebrew journals, vigorously attacking all accepted ideological positions and calling for a "transvaluation" – in the Nietzschean sense – of Judaism and Jewish history, and the expansion of the canons of Hebrew literary taste. His impulsive tone won him the admiration of the young and the scorn of the older, more conservative readers, mostly the admirers of Aḥad Ha-Am. The famous Aḥad Ha-Am versus Berdyczewski debate appeared in *Ha-Shiloaḥ* (1897). In 1900 Berdyczewski firmly established himself in the history of Hebrew literature with the publication of nine volumes of articles and stories.

The year 1900 was also significant in Berdyczewski's personal life; he married Rachel Romberg, a dentist. During the next 20 years she assisted him in his literary and scholarly work and together with their son Immanuel Bin-Gorion continued to edit his writings after his death. With his bride he returned home for a brief visit to the Russian Pale of Settlement for the first time in ten years. The renewed confrontation with the harsh realities of Jewish life in the Pale both modified his stridency and rekindled his interest in the narrative possibilities afforded by this rapidly disintegrating organic community.

After a short stay in Warsaw, he returned to Germany and Breslau (1901–11) and, in self-imposed isolation from colleagues and current affairs, devoted himself to intense literary work which he carried out through many periods of poverty and infirmity until his death. In Breslau, where some of his finest works were written between 1906 and 1909, he continued to write in Hebrew, but embarked upon several new ventures – he wrote articles and stories in Yiddish; systematically collected rabbinic legends; studied the origins of Judaism with particular emphasis upon the Samaritan tradition; and began a still unpublished diary in German. His collected Yiddish writings were published in 1912. After moving to Berlin in 1911, he edited anthologies of legends, reworked his previous writings for the Stybel edition (1921–25), and studied Jewish history of the biblical and Christian period. The years after 1914 were particularly difficult: his health failed; his travel was restricted since he was a Russian citizen; and after the war he was deeply shocked at the news of the pogrom in Doubovo and his father's murder. Nevertheless, Berdyczewski wrote some of his major stories after the war, notably his short novel *Miryam*, which he completed shortly before his death.

Though Berdyczewski's writings are commonly divided into four groups: essay, fiction, folklore anthologies, and scholarship, the borders between them are often quite arbitrary. Written over a period of 35 years and edited by the author for the Stybel edition, Berdyczewski's literary output is rich but its ambivalent attitudes are the mark of an uprooted, marginal man capable of simultaneously embracing logically contradictory positions and emotions. Many of Berdyczewski's paradoxes can be understood in terms of the dialectical stages of his development, each a reflection of *fin de siècle* European moods.

In his literary criticism, Berdyczewski derided exhibitionistic mannerism and the submission of a writer's artistic individuality to the demands of ideology. He showed little appreciation for the outstanding literary figures of his day, *Mendele Mokher Seforim, Aḥad Ha-Am, Ḥ.N. *Bialik, and J. *Klausner, but supported younger writers like J.H. *Brenner and M.Z. *Feuerberg and others devoted to their art. He held literature to be one of the vital forces in human experience and reacted to it impressionistically in often fragmentary critical essays, replete with intemperate outbursts and bitter irony; hence his critical point of view is far from consistent.

Berdyczewski wrote more than 150 Hebrew stories, many in Yiddish, and several in German. These stories deal with two central subjects: life in the Jewish towns of Eastern Europe in the last decades of the 19th century and the life of the Eastern European Jewish students in the cities of Central and Western Europe. Heavily autobiographical, many of his pre-1900 stories are often impressionistic, emotional monologues with essayistic digressions.

The *shtetl* ("Jewish town") served as the background for dramatic situations embodying Berdyczewski's philosophical outlook. He was obsessed with exceptional, individualistic types – lonely, rebellious, and ostracized, and the inevitable clash between them and the intolerant community. The archetypal topography of the town with its Jewish and gentile quarters separated by a river is symbolic of the psychological and social tensions in dozens of stories. Often there is an implied protest against pre-arranged marriages and other forms of coercion within the Jewish community which cause misery, particularly for the women. Life is often depicted as a struggle between light and darkness, beauty and ugliness, refinement and crudeness, and in this struggle the good and beautiful are vanquished. The stories after 1900 consciously strive to erect a literary monument to a fading society or to comprehend human existence in literary terms. Increasingly, the *shtetl* is comprehended as a society in the grip of a blind, cruel force.

In his fiction one can discern basic patterns and archetypal figures which appear in various forms: the gracious woman who is callously given to a commonplace or vulgar husband; the uprooted student; the undistinguished, almost impotent male; the virile, ruddy man. Berdyczewski attempted to discover the basic psychological features of his protagonists as they function in plausible, realistic situations and thus added a new dimension to the Hebrew short story. The recurring typology, however, and the use of key epithets and motifs organized his more successfully integrated stories and opened them to symbolic interpretation. In their structure they resemble the rabbinic legends whose concrete situations and symbolic implications had always fascinated Berdyczewski. During his most rebellious period (1896–1900) he collected ḥasidic legends which he published as a separate volume in 1900. The vitality, individuality, and aesthetic sensibility of the Ḥasidim attracted him since they were the antithesis of rabbinic Judaism. Both the Hebrew and the German editions of these anthologies substantially expanded the library of Jewish literature available to the average reader.

One of the most seminal figures in both modern Hebrew literature and Jewish thought, Berdyczewski exerted a subtle yet crucial influence upon many readers after the turn of the century because he embodied, both in his personality and in his writing, the painfully ambivalent attitudes toward both traditional Judaism and European culture shared by many Jewish intellectuals. Characteristically, Berdyczewski rebelled against his religious background, but could never completely reject it.

Berdyczewski's collected works are *Kol Kitvei*, Stybel edition (20 vols. (1921–25) and various other later editions; collected Yiddish works *Yidishe Ksurim* (1924); rabbinic legends; *Me-Oẓar ha-Aggadah* (2 vols., 1913; *Mi-Mekor Yisrael* (5 vols., 1930–45). A list of his works translated into English appears in Goell, Bibliography, 63, 94. An English translation of *Miriam* appeared in 1983. Among recent collections in Hebrew are A. Holtzman, Y. Kafkafi (eds.), *Kitvei M.J. Berdyczewski* (1996) and A. Holtzman (ed.), *Meḥkarim u-T'eudot* (2002)

His son IMMANUEL BIN-GORION (1903–1987), writer and translator, was born in Breslau. In 1936 he settled in Tel Aviv where he served as director of Bet Mikhah Yosef (a municipal library based on his father's collection). His writings in Hebrew and German include essays, literary criticism, and studies of folklore. He edited and published his father's writings. His Hebrew books include *Shevilei ha-Aggadah* (1950) and *Ḥidot ha-Sheloshah*, ancient Indian legends.

BIBLIOGRAPHY: Waxman, Literature, 4 (1960), 113–24, 382–93; Kressel, Leksikon, 1 (1965), 322–5; S. Spiegel, *Hebrew Reborn* (1930), 331–74; Y.A. Klausner, *Major Trends in Modern Hebrew Fiction* (1957), 124–43; *Kol Kitvei J.Ḥ. Brenner*, 3 (1967), 34–54; Fishmann, in: *Kol Sippurei Bin-Gorion (Berdyczewski)* (1951), 13–28; Y. Kaufmann, *Golah ve-Nekhar*, 2 (1954), 386–404; Y. Keshet, *M.J. Berdyczewski* (Heb., 1958); Lachower, Sifrut, 3 (1963), 71–139, bibliography 217–9; Meron, in: *Moznayim*, 19 (1954), 248–58; I. Rabinovitz, *Major Trends in Modern Hebrew Fiction* (1968), 124–44. **ADD. BIBLIOGRAPHY:** N. Govrin (ed.), *M.J. Berdyczewski: Mivḥar Ma'amrei Bikoret al Yeẓirato ha-Sippurit* (1973); G. Shaked, *Ha-Sipporet ha-Ivrit*, 1 (1977), 163–205; Z. Kagan, *Me-Aggadah le-Sipporet Modernit bi-Yetzirat Berdyczewski* (1983); Y. Oren, *Aḥad Ha-Am, M.Y.Berdyczewski ve-Ḥavurat "Ẓe'irim"* (1985); E. Bin-Gorion, *Olam ve-Olamot bo: M.J. Berdyczewski, Mored u-Meshorer* (1986); Y. Ben Mordechai, *Shivḥei ha-Eyvah: Iyyunim bi-Yeẓirato shel M.J. Berdyczewski* (1987); D. Miron, *Boah Laylah: Iyyunim be-Yeẓirot Bialik u-M.J. Berdyczewski* (1987); A. Holtzman, *Hakarat Panim: Masot al M.J. Berdyczewsi* (1993); idem, *El ha-Kera she-ba-Lev* (1995); H. Bar-Yosef, *Magga'im shel Dekadans: Bialik, Berdyczewski, Brenner* (1997); N. Govrin (ed.), *Boded be-Ma'aravo: M.J. Berdyczewski be-Zukhronot benei Zemano* (1997); W. Cutter, *Relations between the Greats of Modern Jewish Literature: M.Y. Berdyczewski's Complicated Friendship with Martin Buber* (2000); A. Holtzman, *"Ha-Sefer ve-ha-Ḥayyim"* (2003); M. Bergman, in: D. Stern (ed.), *The Anthology in Jewish Literature* (2004).

[Dan Almagor / Arnold J. Band]

BERECHIAH (fourth cent.), Palestinian *amora*; sometimes referred to in the Midrash as R. Berechiah ha-Kohen. His father's name was apparently Ḥiyya (Tanḥ. B. Gen. 60, cf. Lev. R. 31); was a pupil of R. *Ḥelbo, whose aggadic sayings, as well as those of other scholars, he reported. His many aggadic sayings are found mostly in the Midrashim and in the Jerusalem Talmud, but he is also mentioned in the Babylonian Talmud. R. Berechiah preached and taught in his own *bet midrash* (TJ, Ber. 7:6, 11c). In his homilies he stresses the virtues of charity and the uniqueness of the Jewish people (Lev. R. 27:7; Ta'an. 4a). "God said to Israel: 'My children: If you see the merit of the patriarchs declining and the merit of the matriarchs diminishing, go and cleave to acts of charity'" (TJ, Sanh. 10:1, 27d). He gave voice to the expectation that God would exact vengeance upon Israel's enemies (Lam. R. 5:1). Although only a few of his *halakhot* are mentioned, it is clear that his views in the field of *halakhah* were regarded as authoritative (TJ, RH 3:1, 58d). Some scholars think that there was an earlier Palestinian *amora* (third century) called Berechiah or Berechiah Sabba ("old").

BIBLIOGRAPHY: Bacher, Pal Amor, s.v.; Hyman, Toledot, 296–8; Z. Rabinowitz, *Sha'arei Torat Bavel* (1961), 368; Frankel, Mevo, 69.

[Zvi Kaplan]

BERECHIAH BEN NATRONAI HA-NAKDAN (end of 12th–13th century), fabulist, translator, thinker, copyist, and grammarian. Some have identified him with Benedictus le Puncteur of Oxford, who presented a gift to Richard I in 1194, though many deny this. Berechiah lived in Normandy and at a certain period also in England. His title *ha-Nakdan* testifies to the fact that he punctuated Hebrew books. He also knew foreign languages and translated and adapted several books into Hebrew, including *Quaestiones Naturales* by Adelard of Bath, a popular 12th-century book on natural sciences. Berechiah entitled it *Dodi ve-Nekhdi* or *Ha-She'elot* (ed. by H. Gollancz, 1920). His collections of ethical treatises *Sefer ha-Ḥibbur* and *Sefer ha-Maẓref* (ed. by Gollancz, *The Ethical Treatises of Berachyah, son of Rabbi Natronai Ha-Nakdan*, 1902) summarized the opinions expressed in Saadiah Gaon's *Emunot ve-De'ot* (of which Berechiah used the old, unprinted translation in Hebrew), as well as the opinions of other *geonim*. In these essays he invented several Hebrew terms for philosophical concepts. He also wrote *Ko'aḥ Avanim* (unpublished), a translation-adaptation of a Latin book about the magical powers in stones.

His most famous work is *Mishlei Shu'alim* (English translation by M. Hadas *Fables of a Jewish Aesop*, 1967), a collection of fables translated mostly from the French fable collection *Ysopet* by Marie de France (c. 1170), and also from the lost Latin translation of Aesop, *Romulus*, as well as from other collections of Oriental origin. Berechiah writes in his preface: "These fables are well-known to all mankind and are in books by people of all languages, but my faith differs from theirs." The preface contains an appraisal in rhyming puns of the low moral state of English Jewry as seen through Berechiah's eyes: "The wicked are saved, the righteous groan, the bitter are sweetened, the evil rise, while the great are cast down, and prayer is tasteless, glory is folly, and the sacrifice is wicked." He concludes, "I would prefer toil and a dry crust to sharing my lot with them." *Mishlei Shu'alim* has appeared in 18 editions, most of them, including the first (Mantua 1557–59), being incomplete. Berechiah has been identified with Krespia or Crispia (Heb. קרשפיא, קרישפיה, קרישפיהו) the grammarian, one of whose fables (Fable 119) was included in *Mishlei Shu'alim*, but this identification is unfounded. Berechiah's son, Elijah, who lived in "the city of Radom" (Darom, i.e., Dreux) was a copyist and grammarian. In those of his texts which have survived he expresses his feeling of honor at his father's respected position and refers to him as "the *tanna* and pedant."

BIBLIOGRAPHY: A.M. Habermann (ed.), *Mishlei Shu'alim* (1946), complete edition, based on manuscripts; Davidson, Oẓar, 4 (1933), 373; W.I.H. Jackson, in: *Fables of a Jewish Aesop* (ed. M. Hadas, 1967); C. Roth, *Jews of Medieval Oxford* (1951), 118–9; idem, *Intellectual Activities of Medieval English Jewry* (1949), 48–50; J. Jacobs, *Jews of Angevin England* (1893); Steinschneider, Uebersetzungen, 958–62; Porges, in: HB, 7 (1903), 36–44; Gross, Gal Jud, 180–5; Fuenn, Keneset, 202–3. **ADD. BIBLIOGRAPHY:** M.M. Epstein, in: *Prooftexts* 14, 3 (1994), 205-31.

[Abraham Meir Habermann]

BERECHIAH BERAKH BEN ELIAKIM GETZEL (c. 1670–1740), rabbi and author. Born in Cracow, Berechiah Berakh served as a rabbi in Klementow and later as a preacher in Yaworow (Yavorov). The leader of Polish Jewry, Abraham Isaac *Fortis (Ḥazak), allowed him to preach in every place without previously obtaining the permission of the local rabbi. His eloquent sermons belong to the end of the period of the Council of Four Lands. He spoke out against the low moral standards prevailing in the upper strata of Polish Jewry in the first half of the 18th century. He criticized rabbis who took gifts from the parents of their pupils, judges who accepted remuneration beyond that permitted by law, and preachers and communal leaders who accepted gifts in return for their efforts. He also criticized the practice of lending money at interest. His outspokenness earned him many opponents. Isaac Eisik of Szydlowiec withdrew an approbation he had given to Berechiah's book of responsa when he learned that the latter, whose words were misinterpreted, prohibited a certain marriage permitted by Solomon *Luria. As a result, the above-mentioned book, together with four others on which Berechiah had labored for more than 22 years, was forcibly taken from him and he had to flee. Only a small part of his works (on the Pentateuch, Psalms, Talmud, and *Turim*) survived, and was published by Berechiah in two volumes, entitled *Zera Berakh* as a supplement in two parts to the work of the same name in two volumes by his grandfather *Berechiah Berakh b. Isaac Eisik. The first consists of explanations and homilies to Genesis (Halle, 1714), and the second of novellae to the tractate, *Berakhot* (Frankfurt on the Oder, 1731). A commentary on the Pentateuch, *Zera Berakh*, part 4 (mentioned *ibid.*, part 3) has remained in manuscript.

BIBLIOGRAPHY: Michael, Or, 299, no. 647; H.N. Dembitzer, *Kelilat Yofi*, 2 (1893), 50a–52b; Halpern, Pinkas, 477–9; A. Yaari, *Meḥkerei Sefer* (1958), 445–9.

[Samuel Abba Horodezky]

BERECHIAH BERAKH BEN ISAAC EISIK (d. 1663), called "the Elder" in differentiation from his grandson *Berechiah Berakh b. Eliakim Getzel; rabbinical scholar, *dayyan*, and preacher in Cracow; his father-in-law was Yom Tov Lipmann *Heller. Berechiah studied under the kabbalist Nathan Shapiro, and became a *dayyan* of the *bet din* of Joshua Hoeschel of Cracow. He officiated as chief preacher to the community in Cracow, belonging to a category of preachers held in high esteem. His sermons were published under the title *Zera Berakh* in two parts: the first (Cracow, 1646) includes Berechiah's exposition of Genesis, concluding with the portion *Masei*, and the second (1662) completes the commentary to the end of Deuteronomy and includes sermons on the Five Scrolls and the Passover *Haggadah*. His commentaries are not only representative of homiletics in 17th-century Poland-Lithuania, but provide wide-ranging disquisitions on central problems of Jewish society, such as the causes of the Chmielnicki massacres in 1648–49. He also composed a special elegy, entitled "*El Male Raḥamim*," on the martyr's death suffered by *Mattathias in Cracow in 1663, which was introduced into the Cracow liturgy. Berechiah died in Constantinople on his way to Ereẓ Israel.

BIBLIOGRAPHY: H.H. Ben-Sasson, *Hagut ve-Hanhagah* (1959), index.

BEREGI, ÁRMIN BENJAMIN (1879–1953), Hungarian Zionist. Born in Budapest, Beregi was a relative of Theodor *Herzl and knew him from childhood. He graduated as an engineer in 1901 and worked in factory construction in various parts of Europe and later in Palestine. At Herzl's request he organized a Zionist student movement in Hungary. He served as president of the Hungarian Zionist Organization from 1911 to 1918. A Jewish defense force that he organized in 1918 for protection against pogroms was authorized by the Hungarian government. Beregi headed the Palestine Office (see *Jewish Agency) in Budapest from 1925 to 1935, when he settled in Palestine. The last years of his life were spent in Tel Aviv as construction manager of a brick factory. In 1933 he published a two volume novel about life in Palestine, entitled *Isten árnyékában* ("In the Shadow of God").

BIBLIOGRAPHY: *Ha-Olam* (Feb. 28, 1950); Tidhar, 13 (1963), 4223–24.

[Getzel Kressel]

BEREGI, OSZKÁR (1876–1966), Hungarian actor, famous for his Shakespearean roles. Beregi worked for three years with Max Reinhardt in Berlin and became a member of the Pest National Theater in 1899. Nationalist elements brought about his dismissal in 1910 and he went to Vienna. By 1925 he was acting in Hollywood and appeared in *Anything Can Happen* (1952), *Call Me Madam* (1953), and *Desert Legion* (1953).

BEREGOVO (Cz. **Berehovo**; Hg. **Beregszász**), city in Sub-Carpathian Ruthenia (now in Ukraine). Toward the end of the 18th century Jews were first permitted to settle there on the estates of the counts Schoenborn and to pursue trade. Most of them originated from Poland. By 1795 there was an organized community with a synagogue and *ḥevra kaddisha*. Abraham Judah ha-Kohen *Schwarz officiated as rabbi from 1861 to 1881, and Solomon Sofer (Schreiber) from 1884 to 1930. A Hebrew elementary school was opened after 1918, while Beregovo was within Czechoslovakia. There were 4,592 Jews living in Beregovo in 1921 and 5,865 (out of a total population of 19,379) in 1941. They owned 16 factories, three flour mills, and two banks, and were represented in the professions by 22 doctors and 17 lawyers. Most of the Zionist parties and youth were active in Beregovo. A number of Jews owned vineyards, and supplied the international market as vintners. After the Hungarian takeover in 1938, the Jews were deprived of their business licenses. Five hundred males were drafted into labor battalions and perished on the eastern front. In 1941 about 250 local Jews without Hungarian citizenship were deported to the German-occupied Ukraine and murdered there. In the winter of 1944 a ghetto and Judenrat were established, and in mid-May 1944 about 11,000 Jews were deported to Auschwitz, among them 3,600 from Beregovo with the others from the surrounding area. The big synagogue was confiscated while a service was being held during Passover 1959 in order to house the local theater. After that time, services were held in a rented room. The number of Jewish families was estimated at 300 in 1970. Presumably most left in the 1990s.

BIBLIOGRAPHY: Y. Erez (ed.), *Karpatorusyah* (1959); *Yedi'ot Yad Vashem*, nos. 10–11 (1956), 20, 31. **ADD. BIBLIOGRAPHY:** PK Tshekhia, s.v.

[Oskar K. Rabinowicz / Shmuel Spector (2nd ed.)]

BEREGOVSKI, MOSHE (1892–1961), Soviet Russian musicologist. Born in the Ukraine, Beregovski was the son of a *melammed* and reader (*ba'al kore*) and sang in the synagogue choir, where he received his first musical training. He studied composition at the Leningrad Conservatory and participated in the field expeditions of the late 1910s. He taught music and conducted a choir at the Jewish folk music society in Kiev. In 1918 he founded and directed the music section of the Jewish Culture League in Kiev and in 1927 began to collect and study Jewish folk music at the Faculty of Jewish Culture of the Ukranian Academy of Sciences. From 1928 to 1941 he was the head of the Folk Music Division of the Jewish Culture League and the Folklore Department of the Kiev Conservatory. By the beginning of World War II the folk music department had more than 1,200 cylinder recordings of 3,000 items and more than 4,000 transcriptions, of which more than 600 were recorded by Beregovski, as well as the collections of *An-Ski and Joel *Engel. In 1944 he received his diploma in music in Moscow for his thesis on Jewish instrumental music. In 1946 his doctoral work on musical theater and his thesis were rejected because of elements of Western culture which he described. In 1949 the department of Jewish culture was closed and in 1950 Beregovski was arrested and imprisoned for five years. After his release he tried to publish his work but could not do so for political reasons. He had written most of his projected five-volume study of East European Jewish folk music and given it to his family before his arrest. Most of his recordings and writings survived WWII and are kept in several institutions in the Ukraine. His five volumes include: (1) workers' and revolutionary songs of the 1905 period, domestic and army songs (published in 1934 under the title *Yevreyskiy musikalny folklor* and in its Yiddish edition (in Latin characters) as *Jidisher Muzik Folklor*); (2) love and family songs; (3) klezmer music; (4) songs without words; (5) music of the *Purimshpil*. These are all being published in the U.S., Russia, and Israel. In 1938 Beregovski published another collection of Yiddish songs from several sources under the tittle *Yidishe Folkslider*, edited with Itzik *Fefer (1938), which contained 298 items influenced by Soviet ideology.

Beregovski was the first ethnomusicologist to record in the field with a recording machine the oral traditions of East European Jews. The material he collected between 1914 and 1948 includes songs of the Holocaust. He was a pioneer in addressing the question of modes and context in the study of Jewish folk music. Beregovski's extensive work represents the rich musical life of Jews in Russia and the Ukraine before the Holocaust and established the basis of modern studies of this material. The following of his works appeared posthumously: *Old Jewish Folk Music* (ed. M. Slobin, 1982); *Jewish Instrumental Folk Music* (ed. M. Slobin, R. Rothstein. and M. Alpert, 2001); *Evreiske Narodnye Musikalno-Teatralnye Predstavlenia* (2001).

[Gila Flam (2nd ed.)]

BERENBAUM, MICHAEL (1945–), U.S Holocaust scholar who played a prominent role in what he describes as the "Americanization" of the Holocaust: the transformation of a sacred Jewish memory into a significant part of the conceptual and physical landscape of the American public culture.

Berenbaum was born in Newark, New Jersey, and educated at Hebrew-speaking New York yeshivot, Queens College (B.A., 1963), the Jewish Theological Seminary, the Hebrew University of Jerusalem, Boston University, and Florida State University, completeing his Ph.D. as a student of Richard Rubenstein, whose influence was apparent in Berenbaum's text of the President's Commission on the Holocaust (PCOH) Report presented to President Carter on September 27, 1979. Influenced by the magisterial work of Raul *Hilberg, Rubenstein and Berenbaum understood the Holocaust in large measure as a bureaucratic triumph of a Nazi society of total domination. Among the recommendations to the president offered in Berenbaum's text was a "living memorial," to consist of a memorial and museum space, an educational foundation, and a committee on conscience. The commission's recommendation would eventually become the conceptual blueprint for the United States Holocaust Memorial Museum in Washington, D.C., which opened in April 1993. Berenbaum played a major role in the creation of the museum and the content of its permanent exhibition, serving as project director from 1988 to 1993 and director of the Museum's Research Institute from 1993 to 1997. Berenbaum directed a design team that created an exhibition narrative focusing on careful inclusion of non-Jewish victims, a balance between Jewish life before the Holocaust, the extermination, the return to life after, and an emphasis on Americans as bystanders (often complicit ones) and liberators.

In recent years, Berenbaum has served as president and chief executive officer of the Survivors of the Shoah Visual History Foundation (1997–99) and director of the Sigi Ziering Institute: Exploring the Ethical and Religious Implications of the Holocaust at the University of Judaism. He consults widely on the development of Holocaust museums and films. He was one of three American representatives to the international competition that chose the memorial at the Belzec death camp and a member of the team that created the accompanying and highly acclaimed museum. His many film projects include co-producing *One Survivor Remembers: The Gerda Weisman Klein Story,* which received an Academy Award for Best Short Documentary and an Emmy Award in 1995. He was historical consultant to *The Last Days,* which won the Academy Award in 1998.

Berenbaum has written or edited 16 books, including *After Tragedy and Triumph: Modern Jewish Thought and the American Experience* (1990); *Holocaust: Religious and Philosophical Implications* (co-edited with John Roth, 1989); *A Mosaic of Victims: Non-Jews Persecuted and Murdered by the Nazis* (1990); *The World Must Know: The History of the Holocaust as Told in the United States Holocaust Memorial Museum* (1993); *The Holocaust and History: The Known, the Unknown, the Disputed and the Re-examined* (co-edited with Abraham Peck, 1998); and *Bombing of Auschwitz: Should the Allies Have Attempted It?* (co-edited with Michael Neufeld, 2000). He also served as executive editor for the second edition of the *Encyclopaedia Judaica.*

Holocaust memory has become a compelling, volatile, sometimes controversial element in American public culture. Berenbaum's career, particularly his many years of service to the United States Holocaust Memorial Museum project, has been dedicated to ensuring that Holocaust memory moved beyond ethnic boundaries into a wider culture in the hope that Holocaust memory – expressed through cultural representations of so many kinds – will offer a sober reminder of what is possible in a modern society.

[Edward T. Linenthal (2nd ed.)]

BERENBLUM, ISAAC (1903–2000), pathologist specializing in cancer research. Berenblum was born in Bialystok, Poland, and was taken to England in 1914. In 1923 he received his B.Sc. with honors in physiology and biochemistry, his M.B. and Ch.B. in 1926, his M.D. with distinction in 1930 and his M.Sc. (1936) all from Leeds University. As a student he became interested in cancer research, and from 1936 to 1948 was a member of the Dunn School of Pathology at Oxford University and in charge of the Oxford Research Center of the British Empire Cancer Campaign. During this period he developed the theory of the two-stage mechanism for the production of tumors. He found that in addition to the chemical that causes cancer, another chemical is required for the promotion of a tumor. He continued the development of this research theme at the National Cancer Institute at Bethesda in the United States from 1948 to 1950. In 1950 he joined the staff of the Weizmann Institute at Rehovot, where he set up the department of experimental biology. He developed an internationally recognized school of cell biologists and cancer workers. He served for three years (1965–68) as a member of the scientific council of the international agency for cancer research. Berenblum was deeply interested in the public aspects of cancer, and was chairman of the Israel Cancer Society. In 1974 Berenblum was awarded the Israel Prize for science, and in 1980 the Alfred B. Sloan Prize and Gold Medal. He wrote *Science Versus Cancer* (1946; U.S. ed. *Man Against Cancer,* 1952) and *Cancer Research Today* (1967).

[Jack Gross]

BERENDSOHN, WALTER A. (1884–1984), literary historian and critic. Berendsohn was born in Hamburg. He taught literature at Hamburg University, from 1921 until 1933, when the Nazi racist legislation forced him into exile. He then made his home in Copenhagen. While still in Germany he published works on Selma Lagerloef and Knut Hamsun, and his first work in his new home was *Der lebendige Heine im Germanischen Norden* (1935) in which he investigated the influence of the various translations of Heinrich Heine's writings into Danish, Swedish, Norwegian, Finnish, and Icelandic.

Berendsohn fled from Denmark to Sweden in 1943. There he continued his literary work, devoting extensive studies, inter alia, to August Strindberg, some of whose works he translated into German. Shortly after World War II he published *Die Humanistische Front* (1946), the first part of a two-volume work on "exile literature," created by refugees from the Third Reich all over the world. This work – with a title that marks the contrast between humanism and the Hitler regime's adoration of power and violence-laid the foundations for what later became a subject of study and research at many academic institutions in Europe and the U.S.A. In Sweden this research was for many years headed by Berendsohn himself at the Institute for German Studies at Stockholm University.

Berendsohn later devoted much special research to Thomas Mann. While his book *Thomas Mann – Kuenstler und Kaempfer in bewegter Zeit* (1965; *Thomas Mann, Artist and Partisan in Troubled Times*, 1973) is a general introduction to his life and work, *Thomas Mann und die Seinen* (1974) also includes essays on the work of Mann's five children, his author brother Heinrich and his wife Katja. He also issued, with a preface, *Sieben Manifeste zur Juedischen Frage* (1966) – essays written by Thomas Mann between 1936 and 1948 in protest against Nazi persecutions of the Jews and in support of the Jewish renaissance in the Land of Israel, which he himself enthusiastically supported. Berendsohn visited Israel fourteen times and dedicated several articles and one major book (*Volk der Bibel im Land der Vaeter*, 1962) to it. Stockholm University issued his *Die kuenstlerische Entwicklung Heines im "Buch der Lieder"* (1970) and *Lion Feuchtwanger – Der Meister des politischen Romans* (1974). Amsterdam University published his *August Strindberg: Der Mensch und seine Umwelt – Das Werk – Der schoepferische Kuenstler* (1974) – perhaps the first work to concentrate on Strindberg's artistic achievement, rather than his biography. In the same year there appeared in Darmstadt his *Die Dichterin Jüdischen Schicksals Nelly Sachs: Ekstatischer Aufstieg und kuenstlerische Entwicklung.*

A comprehensive bibliography of Berendsohn's books and articles (over 800 titles), edited by Brita von Garaguly, was published by the Royal Library in Stockholm in 1974.

BIBLIOGRAPHY: D. Stern, *Werke juedischer Autoren deutseher Sprache* (1969); *Allgemeine Wochenzeitung der Juden in Deutschland* (Sept. 12, 1960); *Neue Zuercher Zeitung* (Sept. 11, 1974). **ADD. BIBLIOGRAPHY:** R. Heuer (ed.), *Lexikon deutsch-juedischer Autoren*, 2 (1993), 141–62.

[Erich Gottgetreu]

BERENDT, GOTTLIEB MICHAEL (1836–1920), German geologist. Berendt was born in Berlin, where he studied mining geology. The results of his early field work in the Berlin area were published in his first major book *Die Diluvialablagerungen der Mark Brandenburg* (1863). This research made him an ardent protagonist of the new, and at the time controversial, glacial theory, for which he adduced additional evidence by a study of the Harz Mountains. In 1873 he was appointed professor at the University of Koenigsberg, and in 1875 professor at the University of Berlin. He was one of the first Jews to join the Prussian Geological Survey, where he directed the department for the North German Lowlands. Berendt engaged in extensive geological mapping, particularly of glaciated areas. His geological map of the province of Brandenburg was the first of its kind. Notwithstanding his open mind on modern geological theory, he was an opponent of Darwin whose theory of evolution he tried to refute in *Die Theorie Darwins und die Geologie* (1870).

BIBLIOGRAPHY: NDB, 2 (1955), 69–70.

[Yakov K. Bentor]

BERENICE (1) (last half of first century B.C.E.), daughter of *Salome, sister of *Herod and of Costobar the Edomite. She was the wife of *Aristobulus (son of Herod and Mariamne). Berenice bore Aristobulus three sons (*Herod, who became king of Chalcis; Agrippa, who became *Agrippa I; and *Aristobulus) and two daughters (Mariamne and *Herodias, the second wife of *Antipas (Herod Antipas)). Berenice did not live harmoniously with her husband, who was proud of his descent from the Hasmonean Mariamne. She was used by Salome to obtain information about her husband so as to arouse Herod's enmity against him. After Aristobulus had been put to death in 6 B.C.E., Berenice was given in marriage to Theudian, brother of *Doris, the first wife of Herod and mother of his son Antipater. She spent her last years in Rome, where she gained the friendship of the emperor *Augustus and *Antonia, the widow of Drusus. On the strength of this friendship Antonia was well disposed toward the young Agrippa I, even to the extent of assisting him with large sums of money when he was heavily in debt.

(2) (b. 28 C.E.), the oldest daughter of Agrippa I. At the age of 13 she was married to Marcus, son of the *alabarch Alexander Lysimachus. After the death of Marcus she was married to *Herod, king of Chalcis, her father's brother. Two sons were born of this marriage – Berenicianus and Hyrcanus. On the death of her husband in 48 C.E., Berenice went to stay with her brother *Agrippa II, who had succeeded Herod. The residence of brother and sister under one roof gave rise to calumny. Berenice was married a third time, c. 65 C.E., to Polemon II, then king of Olba in Cilicia. However, she left him after a short time and returned to the house of her brother. She was in Caesarea with Agrippa in 60 C.E. when Paul was put on trial before the governor Festus (Acts 25:13–26;30). The Jerusalem riots of 66 C.E. found Berenice in the city in fulfillment of a Nazirite vow made when she was ill. She risked her life in an attempt to keep Gessius Florus from provoking the multitude, but was unsuccessful. When she attempted to pacify the rioters, they burned down her palace, forcing her to flee. Later, when the Syrian governor *Cestius and his

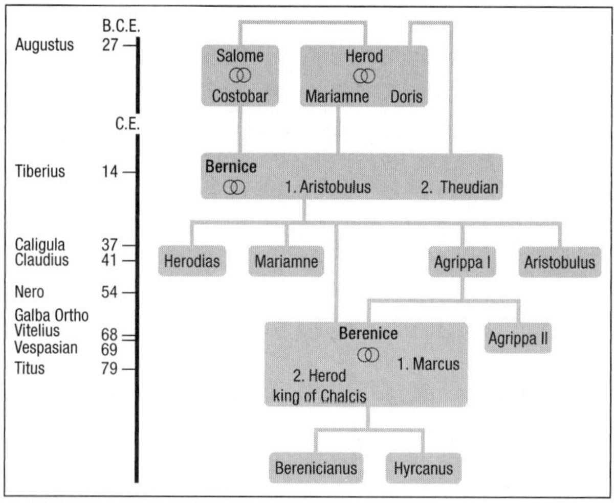

army marched on Jerusalem, she went over to him with her brother. She remained in the Roman camp even when Vespasian commanded the army fighting against the rebels. Titus, son of Vespasian, fell in love with Berenice who was 39 years old at the time. She was with him during the siege of Jerusalem and witnessed the horrors of its destruction. In 75 C.E. Titus established her in the royal palace at Rome and conducted himself toward her as if she were about to become his legal wife. The ruling circles in Rome, however, did not look favorably upon the affair and when Berenice began to act like an empress, the opposition to her deepened and Vespasian compelled Titus to send her away. After Vespasian's death in 79 C.E., she returned to Rome. However, her previous relationship with Titus was not renewed. The Greek inscription in honor of Berenice by the civic leaders of Athens dates apparently from the period of her travels between Italy and Judea.

Her story has been the subject of fiction as in Leon Kolb's *Berenice, Princess of Judea* (1959) and Lion Feuchtwanger's *Josephus* trilogy.

BIBLIOGRAPHY: BERENICE DAUGHTER OF COSTOBAR: Schuerer, Hist, 152, 215f.; Pauly-Wissowa, suppl. 3 (1918), 203, no. 19; A. Schalit, *Hordos ha-Melekh* (1964[3]), 287, 292; Klausner, Bayit Sheni, 4 (1950[2]), 270. BERENICE DAUGHTER OF AGRIPPA I: Pauly-Wissowa, 5 (1897), 287 9, no. 15; Schuerer, Hist, 238–42, 245, 248; Klausner, op. cit., 35; 5 (1951[2]), 20, 140–4, 265, 281; A.H.M. Jones, *Herods of Judea* (1938), index.

[Abraham Schalit]

BERENIKE (Gr. Βερενίκη, the name of several ancient cities founded (or restored) by the Ptolemaic kings and named in honor of Egyptian queens. One of these cities, in the territory of Israel, was Ailane on the Gulf of Eilat (Jos., Ant., 8:163). Another was in Cyrenaica (see *Benghazi).

BIBLIOGRAPHY: Pauly-Wissowa, 5 (1897), 280–2; Avi-Yonah, Geog, 175.

BERENSON, BERNARD (1865–1959), U.S. art historian and art connoisseur. Berenson was born Valvrojenski in the Lithuanian village of Baltramentz, where his father, an ironmonger and grain and lumber merchant, was one of the leaders of the Jewish community. When Berenson was ten, the family emigrated to the United States, where they changed their name. Berenson was sent to the Boston Latin School and, with the financial assistance of the art collector, Isabella Stewart Gardner, was able to go to Harvard University. After graduating he went to London, Oxford, Berlin, and finally Italy, where he made his home for the rest of his life.

Berenson made a thorough study of Italian Renaissance art, and was soon able to purchase important masterpieces for his patron. Through his books – his earliest, *The Venetian Painters of the Renaissance*, appeared in 1894 – he became known as an authority. In 1907 he began his long association with the English art dealer, Joseph (later Lord) *Duveen. This connection enabled Berenson to amass a fortune by providing Duveen's pictures with "Berenson passports," certifying the expensive paintings as genuine. He and his wife, who came from a wealthy American Quaker family, acquired an old villa near Florence and filled it with art treasures and a vast library. Here Berenson's research into Renaissance art came to fruition in a number of important books, among them *The Study and Criticism of Italian Art* (in three series, 1901, 1902, and 1916), *Essays in the Study of Sienese Painting* (1918), and *Italian Pictures of the Renaissance* (1932). Berenson was a prolific writer. His bibliography, published on his 90th birthday, listed 73 pages of books and articles. Although he destroyed some time-hallowed attributions, he also rediscovered artists forgotten for hundreds of years whose works had been credited to better-known masters. He managed to bring light into the jungle of naïve or careless credits that prevailed in Renaissance connoisseurship when he began his career.

Berenson experienced a certain conflict in his relationship to Judaism. As a young man he contributed essays on Jewish topics to the *Harvard Monthly*, and throughout his long life never denied being a Jew and even boasted of carrying on the Jewish "traditions of great learning." However, he joined the Episcopalian church as a young man, and later became a Catholic, although he never publicized these conversions. As an American citizen he was not affected by the antisemitic legislation in Italy before and during the Nazi domination. However, he became apprehensive for the safety of his art treasures, and in 1942 went into hiding until the German retreat from the country. In his autobiographical writings he vacillated between an enormous racial pride and a sharp condemnation of the Jewish people. One of his last autobiographical books was *Sketch for a Self-Portrait* (1949), which contained reminiscences of his childhood in Lithuania. For many years he was an anti-Zionist, but in his old age he accepted Zionism and the necessity for a Jewish state. He bequeathed his villa "I Tatti," with all its treasures, to Harvard, to be available to young scholars so that they could "live" art there as he had lived it.

BIBLIOGRAPHY: S. Sprigge, *Berenson* (1960); N. Mariano, *Forty Years with Berenson* (1966); H. Kiel (ed.), *Bernard Berenson Treasury* (1962).

[Alfred Werner]

BERENSON, LEON (1885–1943), Polish lawyer and diplomat. Berenson was born in Warsaw, and started his legal practice there in 1905 as defense counsel in political cases in which he showed himself a brilliant and courageous fighter for social justice. He soon became one of Poland's most famous lawyers. In 1914 he joined the Organization for the Civic Equality of Jews and Poles (later the Organization of Poles of the Jewish Faith, Wyznania mojzeszowego), which favored Jewish assimilation. He was elected to the Warsaw Municipal Council in 1916 as the representative of this party. When the Polish state was established in 1918, Berenson, as an official in the Ministry of Justice, helped to organize the Polish judiciary. In 1920 he entered the Foreign Ministry and served in Washington until 1923 and later in the U.S.S.R. Berenson resigned from the foreign service in 1930, when the National Democratic Party (N.D. = Endeks) became a powerful force in the ruling Pilsudski regime. He resumed his legal practice and was defense counsel in several political trials of historical significance. He died in the Warsaw ghetto. His writings include *Z sali śmierci: Wrażenia obróncy politycznego* ("From the Death Cell: Memoirs of a Defense Counsel in Political Cases," 1929).

BIBLIOGRAPHY: Hafftka, in: I. Schiper et al. (eds.), *Żydzi w Polsce odrodzonej*, 2 (1933), 250; EG, 1 (1953), 249–50. **ADD. BIBLIOGRAPHY:** E. Ringelblum, *Kronika getta warszaskiego*, 491–92, 624–25; idem, *Polish-Jewish Relations during the Second World War* (1974), 82.

BERENSON (Abbott), SENDA (Valvrojenski; 1868–1954), "Mother of Women's Basketball" and a member of the Basketball Hall of Fame and the Women's Basketball Hall of Fame. Born in Baltramentz (Butrimonys), a town near Vilna, Lithuania, Berenson's family immigrated to Boston when she was seven, changing the family name from Valvrojenski to Berenson. She became the first director of physical education at Smith College in Northampton, Massachusetts, in January 1892, a month after James Naismith invented basketball in nearby Springfield. Berenson visited Naismith to learn the game and adopted it for her female students, organizing the first official game of women's basketball on March 22, 1893. It featured the Smith sophomores against the freshmen, with no male spectators allowed. Berenson introduced the first rules of women's basketball (1899), adapted to avoid the roughness of the men's game and stressing a refined game that favored socialization and cooperation over competition and winning. Her rules included dividing the court into three areas, with two players permanently designated for each area; eliminated stealing the ball; limited dribbling to three bounces; and restricted a player from holding the ball longer than three seconds. She was editor of *Spalding's Official Basketball Guide for Women* (1901–17) and chairwoman of the U.S. Women's Basketball Committee (1905–17). She left Smith in 1911 after marrying Herbert Vaughan Abbott, a professor of English at Smith, and chaired the physical education department at the Mary A. Burnham School in Northampton until 1921. In 1934, she moved to Santa Barbara, Calif., where she died. She was one of first three women elected to the Basketball Hall of Fame (1985). Her brother was the art historian Bernard *Berenson.

[Elli Wohlgelernter (2nd ed.)]

BERENSON, ZVI (1907–2001), Israel Supreme Court justice. Berenson was born and educated in the Galilee. He received a grant for excellence from the British High Commissioner to study mathematics in England, where he also studied law. Returning to Israel, he served as legal adviser of the Histadrut (General Labor Federation) from 1934 until the creation of the State of Israel in 1948. At the request of Prime Minister David Ben-Gurion, he drafted the Declaration of Independence. In 1950, he was named director general of the Labor Ministry, and in 1954 he became a justice of the Supreme Court, where he served for 23 years until his retirement in 1977. His decisions were characterized by clarity, innovation, and a liberal approach to protection of individual rights. His major contributions were in administrative law, public tenders, torts, and labor and family law. He emphasized the legal basis of High Court of Justice decisions and judicial review of Knesset legislation and government decisions. He played a key role in the development of the Supreme Court ruling that administrative decisions of the government require it to state the grounds for them, the government's obligation to carry out court decisions and the right of the Supreme Court sitting as a court of equity to award administrative damages. His name is associated with several judicial precedents of public interest, such as the interim order compelling Prime Minister Golda Meir to allow television broadcasts on the Sabbath, equal allocation of assets between a married couple, and simplification of judicial procedures.

After retirement from the Supreme Court bench, Berenson served as chair of the arbitration board for the public sector for 17 years, until 1994.

[Leon Fine (2nd ed.)]

BERÉNY, RÓBERT (1887–1953), Hungarian painter and graphic designer. Born and educated in Budapest, Berény studied in Paris and Italy. On his return he joined the *"Nyolcak,"* a progressive group of artists searching for new forms of pictorial expression. In 1948 he was appointed professor at the Academy of Creative Arts in Budapest. Berény's early work reflects the influence of Cézanne, while his later work is more expressionistic. He painted a wide variety of subjects, including life studies and landscapes. He was an outstanding graphic artist whose posters maintained a high standard. His *Self-Portrait with Straw Hat* (1906), *The Lady Cellist* (1929), *The Scrawl* (1933), *Ice-Carrying* (1937), and *The Student Painter* (1947) are in the Hungarian National Gallery. His portrait of Béla Bartók is in the Bartók Archives, New York.

[Jeno Zsoldos]

BERESTECHKO (Pol. **Beresteczko**), small town in Volhynia, Ukraine; until 1795 and from 1919 to 1939 within Poland. Jewish settlement there is first mentioned in a document dated 1569. Until 1648 the number of Jews exceeded 1,000. About 200 families perished in Berestechko during the *Chmielnicki massacres in 1648 -49. In the battle fought at Berestechko between the Cossacks and Poles in 1651 some 1,000 Jews fought on the Polish side, according to Nathan Nata *Hannover. There were 872 Jews registered in the community in 1765, of whom 632 lived in the town. It was devastated by a pestilence at the end of the 18th century. Rehabilitated shortly afterward, the community numbered 1,927 in 1847, 2,251 in 1897 (45% of the total population), and 2,210 in 1931 (total population 6,514). Between the World Wars the economic situation deteriorated. Most Jewish industry consisted of small enterprises processing agricultural produce for the local market. In addition, 177 shops of the town's 234 belonged to Jews, and they were the majority among artisans, accounting for 28 of 30 tailors and 18 of 19 furriers. A Hebrew school and a public library functioned and served as a cultural center for local Jews.

Holocaust Period

In September 1939 the Soviets annexed Berestechko, nationalized the economy, closed all Jewish communal institutions, and disbanded all parties and organization. The Hebrew school was turned into a Yiddish one.

On June 23, 1941, the Germans captured the city. On August 8 German police with the help of local Ukrainians rounded up 300 Jewish men and executed them near the local castle. A Judenrat was chosen from among former public activists and a heavy tax was levied on the Jews. From October 5 to 14 a ghetto was set up , surrounded by barbed wire. Some needed artisans were housed in separate quarters. Later Jews from nearby villages were brought in, causing great crowding in living quarters. From September 7 to 9, 1942, the ghetto population was murdered, with only a few managing to escape and hide. Berestechko was recaptured by the Soviet Army on April 24, 1944. The few survivors who returned from the Soviet Union found their homes in ruins.

ADD. BIBLIOGRAPHY: PK Polin: Volhin ve-Polesie, s.v.

[Aharon Weiss / Shmuel Spector (2nd ed.)]

BERETTYÓÚJFALU, town in Hajdú (in 1944 Bihar) county, eastern Hungary. Jews first settled in the town at the beginning of the 19th century, having moved in mostly from neighboring Zsáka. Their number ranged from 125 (2.5% of the total) in 1840 to 1,083 (9.9%) in 1930. According to the census of 1941, the last before the Holocaust, the town had a Jewish population of 982, representing 8.3% of the total of 11,781. The community established a *ḥevra kaddisha* in 1807, and built its first synagogue in 1840 and a *mikveh* in 1866. After the communal rift of 1868–69, the community identified itself as Orthodox. In 1876, the community established a Jewish elementary school. In 1885, several small Jewish communities in the neighboring villages, including that of Csökmö, joined the larger community of Berettyóújfalu. By 1920 the town also boasted a ḥasidic congregation. Among the rabbis who served the community were Amram *Blum (1883–1907), Mordechay Friedmann (1912–30), and Béla Benzion Blum, Amram's son (1930–44). Rabbi Béla Blum perished in the ghetto of Budapest.

During World War II, the Jews were subjected to drastic discriminatory measures, and many of the Jewish males were conscripted for forced labor. Shortly after the German occupation of Hungary in March 1944, the Jews were rounded up and first concentrated in a local ghetto. The ghetto also included the Jews from the neighboring villages in the district of Berettyóújfalu, including those of Bakonszeg, Csökmö, Hencida, Váncsod, and Zsáka. On June 7, the ghetto population was first transferred to the local brickyard, and a day later to the ghetto of Nagyvárad (Rom. Oradea), from where they were deported to Auschwitz a few days later.

After the war 150 survivors, many among them former labor servicemen, returned. According to the census of 1949, the town had 221 Jews. These continued to maintain a congregation until 1956. The synagogue was sold in 1964. Most of the Jews either moved to other places or emigrated. In 1968 there were some 20 Jews living in the town; by the end of the century only two.

BIBLIOGRAPHY: M.M. Stein, *Magyar rabbik*, 3 (1907), 12; 5 (1909), 5f.; Z. Nadányi, *Bihar vármegye*, (1938), 454; S. Kiss, *Berettyóujfalu és környéke*, (1940), 6, 15; Braham, Politics; PK Hungaria, 183–84.

[Randolph Braham (2nd ed.)]

BEREZA (also **Kartusskaya Bereza**; Pol. **Bereza Kartuska**), town in Brest district, Belorussian S.S.R.; until 1795 and between the two world wars in Poland; today in Belarus. A Jewish community existed there from the beginning of the 17th century. Erection of a synagogue was authorized in 1629. The community numbered 242 in 1766, 515 in 1847, and 2,623 in 1897 (42.1% of the total population). At the end of the 19th century barracks were built for the Russian army, which benefited Jewish tradesmen. Although their number decreased to 2,163 by 1921, the Jews still formed 61.3% of the total population. The main occupation of the Jews was in the lumber industry: sawmills, furniture, and other wood products, which were mostly exported. A number of noted rabbis served in Bereza, including Isaac Elhanan *Spektor who officiated there when a young man (1839–46), and Elijah *Klatzkin (1881–94). In the 1920s Jews served as the mayor and deputy mayor of the town. Jewish children studied in three schools: Hebrew, Yiddish, and a *talmud torah*.

[Shmuel Spector (2nd ed.)]

1939–1941

After the outbreak of World War II and the Soviet-German agreement on the division of Poland, Bereza fell to Soviet rule. All public, independent political activity of a national character was forbidden. The Jews' sources of livelihood were reduced by the creation of a network of government-owned stores, cooperatives, and services.

Holocaust Period

On June 23, 1941, a day after the outbreak of war between Germany and the U.S.S.R. German forces entered Bereza. On June 26 the synagogue and houses nearby were burned down. The community faced kidnappings for forced labor, starvation, and disease throughout that winter (1941–42). In July 1942 a ghetto was established, comprising two sections: ghetto "A" for "productive" persons employed by the Germans; and ghetto "B" for the "nonproductive," nonworking members of the community. On July 15, 1942, the inmates of ghetto "B" were taken to Brona Góra and murdered. Some of the Jews in ghetto "A" attempted to flee to the forests, or to *Pruzhany Ghetto, which was still free from deportations. On October 15, 1942, the Germans carried out an *Aktion* to liquidate ghetto "A" In defiance, the Jews set the ghetto ablaze. That day some of the members of the *Judenrat committed suicide at their last meeting. Many of the inmates were murdered in the ghetto itself, while about 1,800 were taken and killed outside the town. The community was not reconstituted after World War II.

[Aharon Weiss]

BIBLIOGRAPHY: *Słownik geograficzny krolestwa polskiego*, 1 (1880), 140–1; *Regesty i nadpisy*, 1 (1899), no. 781; NLYL, 1 (1956), 18–19; *Pinkes fun Finf Fartilikte Kehiles* (1958), 687–91, 327–464. **ADD. BIBLIOGRAPHY:** PK Polin: Volhin ve-Polesie.

BEREZHANY (Pol. **Brzeżany**), town in Ukrainian S.S.R. and Republic (formerly in E. Galicia). Jews had settled there by the 18th century. Jewish representatives from different communities met at the fairs held in Berezhany, e.g., in September 1740. There were 90 Jews living in Berezhany in 1765, in 1900, 4,305 (over 40% of the total population), and 3,580 in 1921. Of the 825 pupils attending the German high school in Berezhany in 1908, 186 were Jews. Before World War I the flour trade was mainly in Jewish hands. The community had a hospital and old-age home. Among the rabbis of Berezhany was Shalom Shvadron.

During the Holocaust, on Oct. 1, 1941, 500–700 Jews were executed by the Germans in the nearby quarries. On Dec. 18, another 1,200, listed as poor by the *Judenrat*, were shot in the forest. On Yom Kippur 1942 (Sept. 21), 1,000–1,500 were deported to Belzec and hundreds murdered in the streets and in their homes. On Hanukkah (Dec. 4–5) hundreds more were sent to Belzec and on June 12, 1943, the last 1,700 Jews of the ghetto and labor camp were liquidated. Few survived the war.

BIBLIOGRAPHY: J. Kermisz, *"Akcje" i "Wysiedlenie"* (1946), index; *Bleter far Geshikhte*, 4 no. 3 (1953), 104; Bauer, in: *Midstream*, 4 (1968), 51–56. **ADD. BIBLIOGRAPHY:** M. Katz (ed.), *Brzeżany Narayov ve-ha-Sevivah* (1978); S. Redlich, *Together and Apart in Brzezany: Poles, Jews and Ukrainians, 1919–1945* (2002); PK.

BEREZINO, small town in Mogilev disrtrict, Belorussian S.S.R., today Belarus. The Jews there suffered during the *Chmielnicki uprising in 1649. In 1702, during the Swedish campaign, the Jews were fined for failing to pay their post duties which had been imposed by the Polish Sejm (diet) in 1673. The community numbered 208 in 1766; 1,289 in 1847; and 3,377 in 1897 (69.3% of the total population). It suffered in 1920 when Berezino was on the front line between the Polish and Soviet armies. In 1926 there were only 1,565 (53%) Jews. They worked in cooperatives, with 20 families in a multinational kolkhoz (farm). The Jews numbered 1,536 in 1939. Berezino was occupied by the Germans on July 3, 1941. In August they murdered 150 Jews and on December 25–27 another 1,000 Jews, with most infants thrown alive into mass graves.

BIBLIOGRAPHY: *Yevrei v SSSR*, 4 (1929[4]). **ADD. BIBLIOGRAPHY:** Jewish Life, s.v.

[Shmuel Spector (2nd ed.)]

BEREZOVKA, town in Odessa district, Ukraine. A Jewish community was established there by the first half of the 19th century. On April 26–27, 1881, the Jews were attacked in a pogrom and out of the 161 buildings owned by Jews only the synagogue and pharmacy were undamaged. The local population prevented another pogrom from occurring in October 1905. The Jewish population numbered 3,458 (56.2%) in 1897 and 3,223 (42.6%) in 1926, dropping to 1,424 in 1939. During the Soviet period Jews were employed in artisan cooperatives and Jewish kolkhozes. A Yiddish elementary school, a Yiddish evening school, a club, and a library were in operation. Berezovka was taken by the Germans on August 10, 1941. On August 14 they murdered 41 Jews and on August 25 another 100. By September, 211 were dead. Subsequently the town was included in Romanian Transnistria, and Jews from Bessarabia and Odessa were deported to the Berezovka area, with nearly 7,000 perishing.

BIBLIOGRAPHY: *Yevrei v SSSR* (1929[4]), 50; *Eynikeyt* (May 4, 1945). **ADD. BIBLIOGRAPHY:** PK Romaniyah, PK Ukrainah, s.v.

[Shmuel Spector (2nd ed.)]

BEREZOVSKY, BORIS ABRAMOVICH (1946–), Russian tycoon and political figure. Born in Moscow, Berezovsky graduated from the Moscow Timber Institute (Department of Electronics and Computer Engineering) and subsequently from Moscow State University (Department of Mechanics and Mathematics), pursuing postgraduate studies in the theory of decision making and receiving a doctorate at the age of 37. He published over 100 scientific papers and a number of monographs, some of them in the U.S., U.K., Japan, Germany, and France. From 1991 he was a corresponding member of the Russian Academy of Sciences and a member of the International Scientific Society for the Theory of Decision Making.

Berezovsky worked as an engineer at a research institute connected to the Ministry of Instrument Making, Automation and Control Systems (1968–69). In 1969 he was an engineer at the Hydrometeorological Research Center and in 1969–87 worked at the Institute of Control Science of the Academy of Sciences.

Political and economic changes in Russia made it possible for Berezovsky to go into private business. He was active in the automobile industry and in 1989 organized LogoVaz, which became a holding company in 1994. Subsequently he gained control of ORT (Obshchestvennoe Rossiyskoe Televidenie, Russian State Television) and the Siberian Oil Company (Sibneft), ultimately being called the richest man in Russia by *Forbes*. He also became influential in the political life of the new Russia. He became close to President Yeltsin and rose to the position of deputy secretary in Yeltsin's National Security Council in 1996 and executive secretary of the Commonwealth of Independent States (Sodruzhestvo Nezavisimykh Gosudarstv) in 1998, contributing to the settlement of the Chechnya crisis and the cessation of hostilities. Called the "grey eminence" by his enemies and represented as a typical "oligarch," a tycoon who made his fortune by illegal means

A bar mitzvah boy surrounded by family and friends carries the Torah Scroll as part of the Torah reading at the Western Wall, one of the favored sites in Israel to commemorate a boy's Jewish coming of age. *Photo: Z. Radovan, Jerusalem.*

For a Jew the stages of life are accompanied by various rituals and ceremonies, from birth through education and bar/bat mitzvah to marriage and family to death. Items may relate to an individual, such as birth amulets, *tefillin* bags, and dowries, or to the community, such as the *ḥevra kaddisha* (burial society) appurtenances. The locale of each community influenced the materials and styles reflected in the various objects and events shown here.

LIFE CYCLE

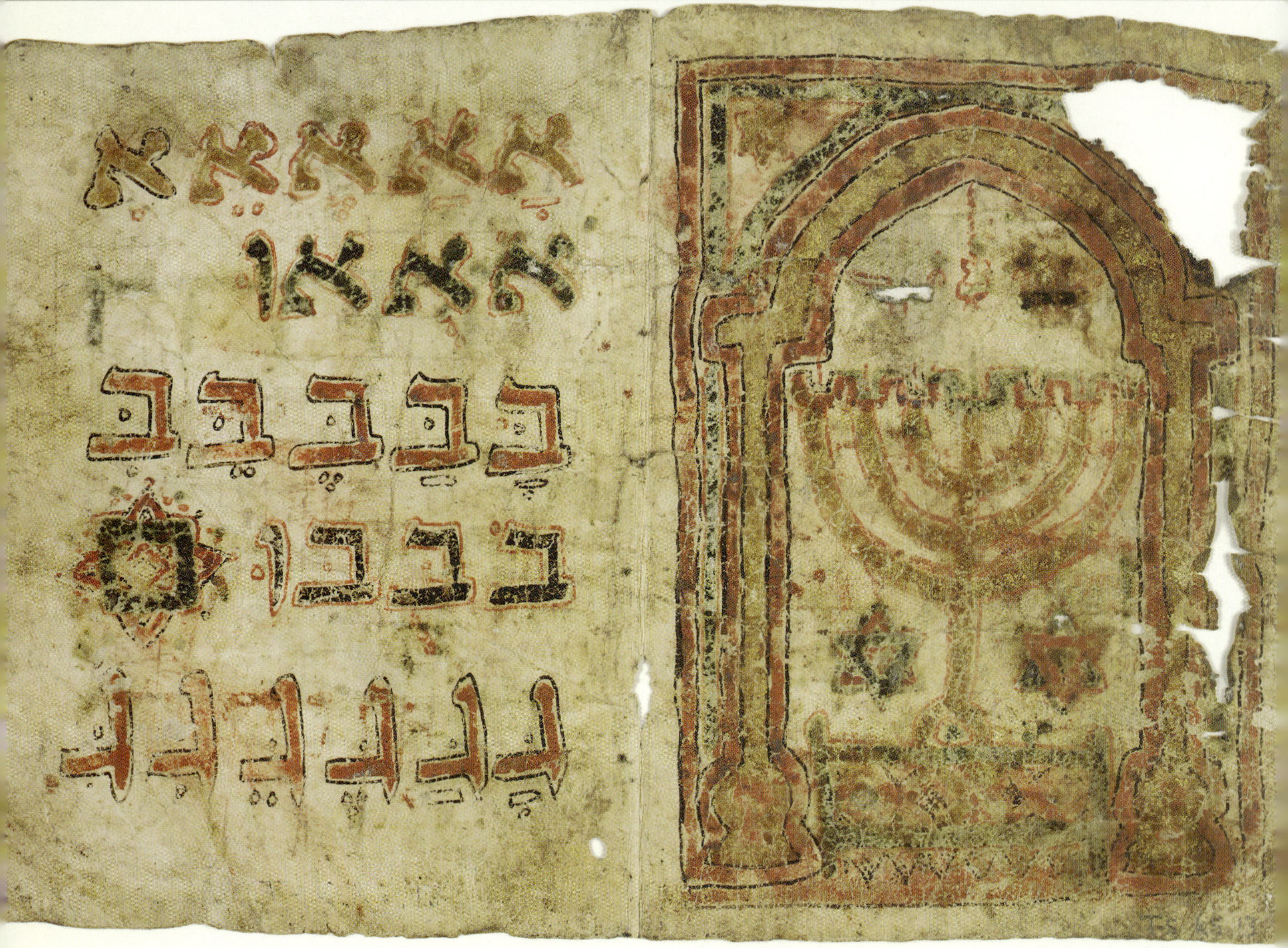

A tenth-century children's alphabet primer from a Hebrew manuscript. Cambridge University Library, T-S K5.13.

ABOVE: Ethiopian boys and girls learn Hebrew in a makeshift classroom in Addis Ababa. *© Ricki Rosen/Corbis SABA.*

LEFT: Children studying Torah in a ḥeder (elementary level Jewish class), end of 20th century, Jerusalem. *Photo: Z. Radovan, Jerusalem.*

(opposite page):
The Jewish Wedding,
1861, by Moritz Daniel Oppenheim, (1800–1882), German painter. Oil on canvas, 37 x 27.5 cm.
Collection, The Israel Museum, Jerusalem. Photo © The Israel Museum, Jerusalem, by David Harris.

(this page) LEFT:
A bat mitzvah girl wearing a yarmulke and *tallit* (prayer shawl) reads the Torah.
© Israel images/Alamy.

A man prays the kaddish (mourning prayer) at the Western Wall wearing a *tallit* (prayer shawl), and *tefillin* (phylacteries). Jewish people from around the world make pilgrimages to the Wall, especially during the festivals of Passover, Shavuot, and Sukkot. *Photo: Z. Radovan, Jerusalem.*

Dowry of a Jewish bride, made from costly items and containing several sets of dresses, coats, underpants, scarves and ornate leather boots. Bukhara, Central Asia, 19th century. *Collection, The Israel Museum, Jerusalem. Photo © Israel Museum, Jerusalem, by David Harris.*

A rabbi holds up a couple's *ketubbah* (marriage contract) during a wedding ceremony in the central square of the Jewish Quarter of the Old City of Jerusalem, 1994. *© Bojan Brecelj/Corbis.*

Wedding rings, Germany and Italy, 17th century. Engraved, filigree, and enameled gold. *Collection, The Israel Museum, Jerusalem. Photo © The Israel Museum, Jerusalem, by Avi Ganor.*

Yemenite Jewish bride and groom in their traditional finery. *Photo: Z. Radovan, Jerusalem.*

and interferes in Russian politics with the aim of furthering his narrow interests, he became a convenient target for antisemitic attacks in Russia's nationalist press. In March 1999 he was relieved of his post, accused of overstepping the bounds of his authority and not following instructions. In December 1999 Berezovsky was elected to the State Duma for the Karachai-Cherkess Autonomous Region. He opposed the new course of centralization inaugurated by President Putin, though he actively contributed to Putin's election victory. In July 2000 Berezovsky resigned from the State Duma in protest over Putin's policies and became active in the opposition as co-chairman of the Liberal Russia Party. Under criminal investigation, Berezovsky left the country in 2002, losing control of ORT and being granted political asylum in the U.K. in 2003.

Berezovsky always represented himself as a Jew "by nationality" although he converted to Russian Orthodoxy. To be elected to the State Duma he renounced his Israeli citizenship, which he acquired in accordance with Russian legislation allowing dual citizenship. He supported the arts through the Triumph Foundation and in 2000 set up the International Foundation for Civil Liberties, which supported liberal causes.

[Naftali Prat (2nd ed.)]

BERG, former duchy in Germany. After their expulsion in 1424, Jews from *Cologne are thought to have settled in Berg. The Jews were temporarily expelled from the duchy in 1461. Early in the 15th century, after the amalgamation of Berg with *Juelich, a joint communal organization was established for both communities. Assemblies were held at specified intervals to deliberate questions of tax allocation, rabbinical appointments, the prohibition of resort to the general law courts, and the maintenance of adequate facilities for Torah study. In the 18th century they were held every four years, except in time of war. The Grand Duchy of Berg established by Napoleon comprised a number of localities with ancient communities such as *Duisburg and Siegburg (dating from the early 12th century), *Dortmund, *Essen, *Soest, and Hamm (13th century), and *Recklinghausen and Unna (14th century). After the dissolution of the grand duchy in 1815, its territory was incorporated into *Prussia.

BIBLIOGRAPHY: Kaufmann, Schriften, 1 (1908), 199–200; idem, in: *Oẓar ha-Sifrut*, 3 (1889), 7–16; C. Brisch, in: *Der Israelit* 20 (1879), 97ff., 145f., 174f. **ADD. BIBLIOGRAPHY:** D.J. Cohen, *Die Landjudenschaften in Deutschland als Organe Juedischer Selbstverwaltung*, vol. 1 (1996), 93–98.

[Zvi Avneri]

BERG, GERTRUDE (**Edelstein**; 1899–1966), U.S. actress, scriptwriter, and creator of the popular radio family the Goldbergs. Born in New York, Gertrude Berg wrote, directed, and performed in *The Goldbergs* on radio for 17 years, in which she played Jewish housewife Molly Goldberg.

Berg began writing and performing skits at her father's resort hotel in the Catskill Mountains, later studying playwriting at Columbia University. In 1929, she submitted a script to NBC for a daily radio show called *The Rise of the Goldbergs*, which was an instant hit. Shortened to *The Goldbergs*, it was on the air six days a week, and in 1931 it picked up a sponsor and ran until 1934. As the writer and producer as well as star of the show, Berg created an entire neighborhood of characters and a series of situations that won an audience which eventually numbered in the millions. Producer Sol Lesser called her to Hollywood, where she wrote screenplays for him. In 1938, Berg received a five-year, million dollar contract to write and star in the Goldberg series, which aired on the radio from 1938 to 1945.

Concerned about the growth of Fascism in the 1930s and the welfare of European Jews, Berg became active in many Jewish groups and during World War II participated in the larger war effort.

Berg wrote a Broadway play, *Me and Molly* (1948), and a film version entitled *Molly* in which she herself acted (1951). From 1949 *The Goldbergs,* sometimes referred to as the earliest soap opera, had a five-year run on television. An idealized vision of the American melting pot, the show centered on the dreams and aspirations of a lower-class Jewish family in the Bronx. The older members of the family, including Molly, her husband, Jake, and Uncle David, spoke with thick Yiddish accents, while the two children sounded like typical young Americans. In 1950 Berg won an Emmy for her comedic performance. In 1951 she took a stand against the blacklist, refusing to fire her long-time co-star Philip Loeb, who resigned to prevent the show's cancellation.

In later years Berg appeared in Broadway plays, including *A Majority of One* (1959), for which she won a Tony Award. In 1961–62 she starred as Sarah Green in the TV sitcom *The Gertrude Berg Show*.

In 1989 *The Goldbergs* was inducted into the Radio Hall of Fame. Berg wrote *The Molly Goldberg Cookbook* (1955) and her autobiography *Molly and Me* (1961).

[Ruth Beloff (2nd ed.)]

BERG, JACKIE "KID" (**Judah Bergman**; 1909–1991), professional boxer, junior welterweight champion 1930–31, member of the International Boxing Hall of Fame and World Boxing Hall of Fame. Born in the Whitechapel section of London's East End to Orthodox immigrant parents from Poland, Berg was one of nine children and had to quit school early to earn a living to help feed the family. Yiddel, as he was known, fought his first professional fight on June 8, 1924, 20 days before his 15th birthday, thus justifying his nickname "Kid." When Yiddel Bergman introduced himself to the fight's promoter, Lewis Kurtz, the latter said, "You can't go in there with a respectable Jewish name. We'll change it around a bit and call you Jack Berg."

Kid Berg spent his early career fighting in London, winning his first 20 fights and 56 of his first 59, with 25 knockouts. He gained the sobriquet "The Whitechapel Whirlwind" from his perpetual motion, piston-shooting style of fighting, which was neither boxing nor punching.

At 19, he moved to the U.S., winning 10 of his first 11 fights with his only loss to Billy Petrolle, the first time Berg was knocked out in 62 fights. He proceeded to win his next 18 fights, including one on October 21, 1929, against Bruce Flowers at Madison Square Garden in New York, in a benefit fight on behalf of the "Palestine Relief Fund," which raised $101,000 from the crowd of 20,000.

Berg beat Tony Canzoneri on January 17, 1930, and then defeated fellow countryman and Jew Mushy Callahan in London on February 18, 1930, for the junior welterweight title, defending it six times over the next 14 months. Berg was considered by then one of the five best, if not the best, pound-for-pound fighter in the world.

On April 24, 1931, Berg again fought Canzoneri, who was now world lightweight champion. Berg was 88–4–5 coming into the fight at Chicago Stadium, having won 58 of his previous 59 fights over a five-year stretch. But Canzoneri scored a KO in the 3rd round, retaining his lightweight belt and winning Berg's junior welterweight title, as both fighters were under 135 pounds. Berg fought and won six more fights before challenging Canzoneri in a rematch at New York's Polo Grounds on September 10, 1931. Berg was fouled at least three times, was knocked down twice, and suffered a terrible gash below the eye, and lost the fight on points in 15 rounds. Berg was never the same champion boxer after his two losses to Canzoneri, though he continued fighting for another 14 years. The last fight of his 21-year-career was May 19, 1945, when he won a fifth-round KO over rookie fighter Johnny McDonald to retire a month shy of his 37th birthday. His record was 157 wins with 61 KOs, 26 losses, and 9 ties, with 14 of his wins coming on disqualifications – an all-time record for winning on fouls; he was knocked out eight times.

Berg was proud of his Jewishness, and, as many Jewish fighters have done in history, would wear a Star of David on his trunks, with his Hebrew initials "Yod-Bet" in the center. But Berg added a singular Jewish touch – he would also wear *tzitzit* into the ring, hanging them on the ring post. "It's comforting to have God on your side no matter what you are doing," he said.

[Elli Wohlgelernter (2nd ed.)]

BERG, LEO (1862–1908), German essayist. A founder of the Berlin literary group *Durch* (1887) and editor of its *Akademische Zeitschrift*, he popularized the aesthetic principles of German naturalism. Berg called attention to the importance of Ibsen's innovations in *Henrik Ibsen und das Germanentum in der modernen Literatur* (1887). Five years later, he distanced himself from naturalism in his book *Der Naturalismus*. In the essays of *Zwischen zwei Jahrhunderten* (1896) he maintained his skeptical attitude toward all established writers. He defended *Heine against antisemitic detractors, and espoused the cause of Tolstoy. Berg prophesied that national literatures would give way to a common European literature as the expression of the emerging "good European." In his volume, *Der Uebermensch in der modernen Literatur* (1897; *Superman in Modern Literature*, 1916), he revealed his adoption of Nietzschean doctrines.

ADD. BIBLIOGRAPHY: R. Heuer (ed.), *Lexion deutsch-juedischer Autoren*, 2 (1993), 162–78, bibl.

[Sol Liptzin]

BERG, MOE (**Morris**; 1902–1972), U.S. baseball player, spy, scholar, linguist. Once called "the strangest fellah who ever put on a uniform" by Casey Stengel, Berg was an anomaly in the world of baseball, where few players had any formal education and where he was recognized as the best-educated man ever to play the game. He was born in a cold-water tenement in East Harlem in New York City, the third child of Bernard and Rose (Tashker). Bernard was himself of keen intellect and attended public school, which was rare for a Russian Jew in that era. He fled the pogroms of Russia in 1894 at the age of 24, arriving in New York with $10 dollars in his pocket, and two years later sent for Rose, from the Kamenets-Podolski region of the Ukraine, to join him.

When Berg was nine months old, the family moved to Newark, New Jersey, where Bernard opened a pharmacy. The family was not religious, never went to synagogue, and the children never celebrated their bar mitzvah, though Bernard did teach Hebrew and Yiddish to his son, whose photographic memory retained everything. Berg became a star player at Barringer High School, where he began learning languages, excelling in Latin, Greek and French. Graduating at 16, he spent a year at New York University before transferring to Princeton. He was the star there as well, playing shortstop for three years and becoming captain his senior year, when he hit .337 and the team won 18 straight games. He majored in languages, adding Spanish, Italian, German, and Sanskrit to his growing list, and graduated in 1923 magna cum laude and 24th in his class of 211.

Berg began his baseball career with the Brooklyn Dodgers the day after his last game for Princeton, playing 15 years with the White Sox, Indians, Senators, and Red Sox, first as a shortstop and third baseman before settling in as a third-string catcher. With his lifetime average of only .243 and six home runs, it was to Berg that the classic expression "good field, no hit" was first applied.

Berg pursued his scholarly interests while he continued playing baseball, attending the Sorbonne in Paris, graduating from Columbia Law School second in his class, and adding Japanese, Chinese, Korean, Indian, Arabic, Portuguese, Hungarian, and a few regional dialects to his linguistic arsenal. While it was never established exactly how many languages Berg spoke, they were of no use to him in baseball. Said one player, "He can speak twelve languages, but he can't hit in any of 'em."

Berg's life changed in 1934, when he accompanied a team of baseball all-stars to Japan on a baseball barnstorming tour. While there, he went to the roof of the tallest building, a hospital, and photographed the Tokyo skyline, the harbor, and munitions facilities, which may have helped U.S. General Jimmy Doolittle in his bombing raids over Tokyo in 1942.

Moe's celebrated academic knowledge received national attention in February 1938, when he appeared on *Information, Please*, the intellectual's radio quiz show. Moe amazed all of America when he answered questions about the derivation of words and names in Greek and Latin, historical events in Europe and the Far East, and current international conferences.

After his career was over in 1939, Berg spent two years as a coach with the Red Sox. In 1942 he was named Goodwill Ambassador to Latin America by Nelson Rockefeller, head of the Office of Coordinator of Inter-American Affairs, and subsequently worked for the Office of Strategic Services (OSS), the forerunner of the CIA. His first assignment was to assess the political and military situation in embattled Yugoslavia. He spoke to the forces under Tito and to the Serbian camp of Mihajlovic, reporting back – correctly – that the Yugoslav people supported Tito. His most notable mission was to Switzerland, with instructions to kill top German scientist Werner Heisenberg, who was lecturing there and suspected of working on the A-bomb. Questioning Heisenberg with a loaded gun in his pocket, Berg determined that the Germans were not building the bomb, and his invaluable report was read by British Prime Minister Winston Churchill, U.S. President Franklin Roosevelt, and the scientists working on America's Manhattan project to develop the nuclear bomb.

Berg was also a loner and an eccentric, known among other things for always wearing a black suit and not letting people touch his newspapers until he had finished reading them. "Berg's was a life of abiding strangeness," wrote Nicholas Dawidoff in his definitive biography of Berg, *The Catcher Was a Spy*. Berg died seconds after asking a bedside nurse: "How are the Mets doing today?"

[Elli Wohlgelernter (2nd ed.)]

BERG, PAUL (1926–), U.S. biochemist and Nobel laureate. Berg was born in New York and received his undergraduate degree in biochemistry from Pennsylvania State University in 1948 after serving in the U.S. Navy during World War II. He was awarded a doctorate from Western Reserve University in 1952 and then studied for a year in Copenhagen with Herman Kalckar at the Institute of Cytophysiology and for a second year with Arthur *Kornberg at Washington University in St. Louis, where he stayed until 1959, when he moved to Stanford Medical School. In 1960 he was appointed professor of biochemistry at Stanford.

Gradually making a transition from classical biochemistry to molecular biology, Berg's interests shifted from studies with microorganisms to mammalian cells, and he spent a year experimenting with Polyoma and SV40 tumor viruses in mammalian cell culture at the Salk Institute. He served as chairman of Stanford's Department of Biochemistry from 1969 to 1974, in 1970 being appointed Willson Professor there. From 1973 to 1983 he was a non-resident fellow of the Salk Institute. He served as director of Stanford University's Beckman Center for Molecular and Genetic Medicine from 1985 to 2000 and from 1994 to 2000 as Cahill Professor in Biochemistry and Cancer Research. From 2000 he was Cahill Professor in Biochemistry, Emeritus, and director of the Beckman Center for Molecular and Genetic Medicine, Emeritus.

In the course of his career Berg succeeded in developing a general way to join two DNAs together *in vitro*, work that led to the emergence of recombinant DNA technology, a major tool for analyzing mammalian gene structure and function. This was the basis of his being awarded the 1980 Nobel Prize in chemistry. That same year he received the Albert Lasker Award for basic research, along with Dr. Stanley N. *Cohen and Dr. Dale A. Kaiser, fellow Stanford University researchers, and Dr. Herbert W. Boyer of the University of California in San Francisco. They were cited for their work in manipulating the genetic material in cells.

Berg is a member of the Institute of Medicine, the National Academy of Science (member of the council since 1979), the American Academy of Arts and Sciences, the American Society of Biological Chemists (president, 1974–1975), and the American Society of Microbiology. He is an honorary member of the Academy of Natural Sciences of the Russian Federal Republic (1991) and a Foreign Member of the Royal Society, London (1992).

His most recent appointments include chairman of the National Advisory Committee to the Human Genome Project, chairman of the board of the National Foundation for Biomedical Research, member of the advisory panel to the Human Genome Education Program, and member of the NAS-CSIS Roundtable on Biotechnology and Bioterrorism.

[Ruth Rossing (2nd ed.)]

BERG, PHILIP (**Gruberger**; 1929–), founder and director of The Kabbalah Center, a controversial organization dedicated to the popular dissemination of a modern synthesis of Kabbalah and New Age religion. Berg was born in Williamsburg, New York, studied at Beth Medrash Govoha in Lakewood, New Jersey, and was ordained at Torah VaDaat in Williamsburg. During the 1960s, Berg studied Kabbalah with disciples of kabbalist Yehudah *Ashlag (1886–1955), such as Levi Isaac Krakovsky (1891–1966) and Yehudah Ẓevi *Brandwein (1903–1969). Berg claims to have been appointed by Brandwein to carry on Ashlag's mission, namely, to spread kabbalistic knowledge to a wide audience and to assume the leadership of Kol Yehudah, Ashlag's kabbalistic yeshivah. Inspired by his wife KAREN (1945–), Berg established The Kabbalah Centre in 1969 to propagate their distinctive approach to Kabbalah to men and women of all faiths, ages, and ethnic backgrounds throughout the world. In the early 2000s there were over 50 centers internationally offering lectures, courses, spiritual counseling, and ceremonies to adults and children, as well as an extensive and sophisticated presence on the World

Wide Web. The Kabbalah Centre publishes popular literature on Kabbalah and translations of classic works in 10 languages. The Bergs' sons, born during their parents' 10-year sojourn in Israel, are important contributors to the Kabbalah Centre mission. They were educated at the Hafetz Hayyim and Shaar Hatorah yeshivot in New York and received ordination at Knesset Yehezkel in Jerusalem. In addition to writing popular literature, YEHUDAH (1972–) produced (with his father) a prayer book according to the Lurianic tradition that includes meditations from later kabbalists; MICHAEL (1973–) authored a full English translation of the Zohar with Ashlag's commentary *Ha-Sulam*.

Distinctive Kabbalah Centre teachings acknowledge that God designed Kabbalah as a gift to all humanity, even though it was preserved by and limited to Jews for centuries and was embedded within a Jewish society that advocated strict adherence to biblical and rabbinic Judaism. According to Philip Berg, the scientific advances of the 20th century and the beginning of the astrological Age of Aquarius fulfilled the preconditions for the inevitable worldwide spread of kabbalistic knowledge. Kabbalistic knowledge, he teaches, contains the foundation principles of all science, the structure for achieving spiritual perfection, the path to world peace, and the means to success in such earthly pursuits as business, personal relationships, and health. The *mitzvot* of the Torah are tools designed by God for humanity to achieve these ends, as are special kabbalistic devices (holy water, the red *bendel*) and ritual practices (meditations using divine names and Zohar texts). The Kabbalah Centre ignores the traditional Jewish context of these concepts and practices, as well as the many restraints upon and critiques of these practices voiced by Jewish teachers over the centuries. Kabbalistic teachings are synthesized with modern, particularly New Age, themes such as astrology, reincarnation, holistic healing, and spiritualism. In its effort to reach the widest possible audience, the Kabbalah Centre uses mass-market advertising and showcases its celebrity followers, the most prominent of whom is Madonna.

[Jody Myers (2nd ed.)]

BERGAMO, city in northern Italy; ruled mainly by Venice between 1430 and 1797. Jewish moneylenders in Bergamo are mentioned in the 15th century. The anti-Jewish sermons preached there by the Franciscan Bernardino da *Feltre in 1479 led to the temporary expulsion of the Jews. By the beginning of the 16th century, Jews in Bergamo still owned houses and real estate. When Louis XII of France captured the city in 1509 the Jewish inhabitants were expelled, but they were permitted to return when it reverted to Venice in 1559. There has been no Jewish community in Bergamo in recent times.

BIBLIOGRAPHY: Milano, Italia, 208, 277. **ADD. BIBLIOGRAPHY:** G. Antonucci, "*Per la storia degli ebrei in Bergamo*," in: *Bergomum* 15 (1941), 52–54.

[Umberto (Moses David) Cassuto]

BERGEL (Abergel), Moroccan family. The Bergels came from Safi. They settled in Tangiers, Marseilles, and Gibraltar, where before 1810 MOSES founded a powerful commercial organization. His son YOM TOV (1812–1894), an outstanding figure in western Mediterranean Jewry, served as president of the Gibraltar community from 1860. He helped the Péreire family in establishing the Compagnie Générale Transatlantique in Morocco. Yom Tov and his son MOSES of Marseilles obtained the monopoly for the sale of specialized Moroccan products in Europe.

BIBLIOGRAPHY: JC (Oct. 26, 1894); Miège, Maroc, 2 (1961), 121, 250, 511; 3 (1962), 487.

[David Corcos]

BERGEL, BERND (1909–1966), Israel composer. Bergel was born in Hohensalza, Germany, the nephew of Sammy *Gronemann, one of the principal leaders of the Zionist movement in pre-World War II Germany. He studied at the Berlin Music Academy where he was a student of Arnold *Schoenberg. He settled in Tel Aviv in 1938. Bergel was invited by the Music of the Twentieth Century Festival 1954 in Rome to compose his *Prayer of a Man in the Year 2100* for solo voice and 11 instruments. His works include *Divertimento* for small orchestra, *Variations* for orchestra (Israel Philharmonic Orchestra Prize), and the opera *Jacob's Dream* (1961) based on text by Richard Beer-Hoffmann.

[Ury Eppstein (2nd ed.)]

BERGEL, JOSEPH (1802–1884), physician, poet, and author. Bergel, who was born in Moravia, was a practicing physician, publishing papers in medical journals. He was a Hebrew poet of note and his poems appeared in the journals *Bikkurei ha-Ittim* and *Kokhevei Yiẓhak* and in a collection *Pirkei Leshon Ever* (1873). In these poems he was the first to scan by Ashkenazi word accent. He also translated German and Latin poems into Hebrew, including those of Goethe and Schiller. Probably his most important contribution to Jewish scholarship was *Medizin der Talmudisten* (1885), with an appendix on *Anthropologie der alten Hebräer*. He also wrote *Studien über die naturwissenschaftlichen Kentnisse der Talmudisten* (1880); *Eheverhältnisse der alien Juden im Vergleich mit den griechischen und römischen* (1881); *Der Himmel und seine Wunder…* (also published under the title *Mythologie der alten Hebräer*, 1882); and a history of Hungarian Jewry, *Geschichte der Juden in Ungarn* (Ger. and Hg., 1879).

BIBLIOGRAPHY: Carmilly-Weinberger, in: *Aresheth*, 4 (1966), 400–1.

BERGELSON, DAVID (1884–1952), Russian Yiddish writer. Born in Okhrimovo (Sarna), near Uman, in the Ukraine, Bergelson was the son of a pious Talner ḥasid and prominent lumber and grain merchant, who died when Bergelson was only nine; his mother died five years later. He then went to live with older brothers in Kiev, Odessa, and Warsaw. His traditional *ḥeder* education was supplemented by private instruction in secular subjects. In 1901 and again in 1907–08, he studied as an external student in Kiev, but failed the examinations, and then audited courses in dentistry, without taking a diploma.

Bergelson read Hebrew and Russian literature before he was in his teens, and began writing in both those languages. His early literary efforts, a Hebrew story *"Reikut"* ("Emptiness") and a Yiddish story *"Der Toyber"* ("The Deaf Man"), submitted to several periodicals, initially did not meet with success. *"Der Toyber,"* however, was later published in the first edition of his collected works (Berlin, 6 vols., 1922–23); it was dramatized under the title *Di Broyt Mil* ("The Mill," 1930), and was staged with some success in both Russia and America. His first full-length work, *Arum Vokzal* ("At the Depot"), published in Warsaw in 1909 at his own expense, was warmly received by major critics; Bergelson thereafter wrote only in Yiddish, devoting himself to Yiddish literature and *belles lettres*. The novel *Nokh Alemen* ("After All is Said and Done,"1913) was justly hailed as a masterpiece and established his reputation as both a gifted author of prose and the leading modernist prose writer in Yiddish, whose major theme was the slow decay of the Jewish bourgeoisie in village and town.

Bergelson was very active in Jewish cultural circles and one of the founding directors of the dynamic Kultur Lige, a Jewish cultural organization established in Kiev immediately after the Russian Revolution. He coedited two of its most influential publications: the literary miscellanies *Oyfgang* (1919, in which his work *"In Eynem a Zumer,"* "During One Summer," appeared) and *Eygns* (1920, in which his novella *Opgang*, "Descent," was first published).

In 1920, Bergelson moved to Berlin where he coedited the journal *Milgroym* with *Der Nister, and then two issues of the short-lived literary journal *In Shpan* ("In Harness"), the title of which suggested a new leftist political orientation. In Berlin, he also published a series of short stories dealing with the theme of exile. Writing for the New York Jewish daily *Forverts* until 1925, he later became a correspondent for the Moscow *Emes* and the New York communist newspaper, *Morgn-Frayhayt*. In marked contrast to his earlier views, in which he originally argued that art should not provide "naked abstractions" for propaganda purposes, his writings of this period came increasingly to identify with Soviet ideology, and in his critical writing as well as his fiction he insisted that literature should be committed to the cause of the Revolution, the Communist Party, and the interests of the proletariat. His short novels and stories of those years dealt with revolutionary themes.

Bergelson traveled widely: in 1924, through the Jewish communities of Romania, under the auspices of ORT; to the Soviet Union in 1926, where he declared himself a "Soviet writer"; to Paris; to the United States for six months during 1929 where he was able to witness at first hand the Wall Street crash and the beginning of the Great Depression; through Poland on a lecture and reading tour; and to Copenhagen for a brief stay, in 1933. In 1934, he settled in Moscow after a visit to the Jewish autonomous region of Birobidzhan. His major work of the 1930s, *Baym Dnieper* ("On the Dnieper"), is a modified, partly autobiographical *Bildungsroman* (2 vols., 1932–40). Like most Jewish and other Soviet writing of the decade, Bergelson's work adapted itself increasingly to the thematic and stylistic demands of Socialist Realism.

After 1941, and for the duration of World War II, Bergelson was active in the Jewish *Anti-Fascist Committee; his wartime stories appeared in its publication, *Eynikeyt*. Two dramas, *Prints Reuveni* ("Prince Reuveni") and *Mir Viln Lebn* ("We Want to Live"), were written during this time: the first was never performed in Russia; the second was staged by the Habimah Theater in Tel Aviv. Early in 1949, Bergelson was imprisoned (apparently without trial) with other leading Yiddish writers – including P. *Markish, I. *Feffer, D. *Hofstein – and together with them was shot on August 12, 1952, his 68th birthday. A Soviet edition of selected works from his *oeuvre*, published in 1961, indicated the extent of his subsequent "rehabilitation."

Bergelson's early theme – the decline of individual initiative in a period of widespread stagnation – finds its precise tonal correlative in his style: indirect quotation, passive verb forms, adjectival repetition, periodic sentences, and similar devices create a fatalistic atmosphere in his fiction that subtly suggests character while foregrounding the pessimistic curve of the plot. This style persists even in his "revolutionary" writing of the 1920s, but becomes more straightforwardly dramatic in his stories about Birobidzhan and Soviet progress. His wartime fiction, collected in *Naye Dertseylungen* ("New Stories," 1947), shows an interesting variation of his early impressionism. Yiddish criticism considers Bergelson one of its foremost modern prose writers.

BIBLIOGRAPHY: Rejzen, Leksikon, 1 (1926), 347ff.; LNYL, 1 (1956), 379–83; Y. Dobrushin, *David Bergelson* (1947); B. Finkelstein, in: *Sovetish Heymland*, 4 (1964), 148–50 (bibliography); Kressel, Leksikon, 1 (1965), 317–8; B. Harshav, et al. (eds.), *A Shpigl oyf a Shteyn* (1964) (complete bibliography on life and works); I. Howe and E. Greenberg (eds.), *A Treasury of Yiddish Stories* (1953); C. Madison, *Yiddish Literature* (1968). **ADD. BIBLIOGRAPHY:** A. Novershtern, in: *Di Goldene Keyt*, 94 (1977), 132–43; 115 (1985), 44–58; J. Sherman (ed. and trans), *Opgang/Descent* (1999).

[Ruth Wisse / Joseph Sherman (2nd ed.)]

BERGEN, POLLY (**Nellie Paulina Burgin**; 1930–), U.S. actress, singer, entrepreneur. During her long professional life, Bergen distinguished herself as an extremely versatile entertainer and business executive. She enjoyed enduring success as an actress on the stage and screen, as a singer, and as the founder of her own cosmetic and jewelry lines. Born in Bluegrass, Tennessee, Bergen began working in radio at the age of 14. She arrived in Hollywood at age 19, making her feature film debut in *Across the Rio Grande* (1949). Bergen subsequently starred in three films alongside legendary comedy duo Dean Martin and Jerry *Lewis, including *At War With the Army* (1950), *That's My Boy* (1951), and *The Stooge* (1953) as well as making her Broadway debut with a starring role in the revue *John Murray Anderson's Almanac.* Bergen released the first two of her 17 musical albums, *Polly Bergen* and *Little Girl Blue*, on the Jubilee record label in 1955. She became a household name as a regular on the TV game show *To Tell The Truth* (1956–61). Bergen's many film and television credits over the following half-century include two memorable performances opposite actor Robert Mitchum. The first as Peggy Bowden in the classic film *Cape Fear* (1962), and again two decades later as Rhoda Henry in the mini-series *The Winds of War* (1983), for which she was nominated for an Emmy Award. Bergen was also nominated for a Tony Award for her role in *Follies* (2001). She acted as the CEO and public face of several corporations, including Polly Bergen Cosmetics, Polly Bergen Shoes, and Polly Bergen Jewelry. Bergen is the author of three books, *The Polly Bergen Book of Beauty, Fashion and Charm* (1962), *Polly's Principles* (1974), and *I'd Love to, but What'll I Wear?* (1977). Continuing to perform, she made a notable TV appearance in 2004 on *The Sopranos*.

[Walter Driver (2nd ed.)]

BERGEN-BELSEN, Nazi concentration camp near Hanover, Germany. It was established in July 1943 as an *Aufenthaltslager* ("transit camp") in part of a prisoner-of-war camp, Stalag 311, and intended for prisoners whom the German government wished to exchange for Germans in allied territory. The camp was run by the SS, whose commandants were Adolf Haas, Siegfried Seidle, and Josef Kramer. It was built by Jewish prisoners from Buchenwald and Natzweiler. Five satellite camps were created: a prisoner camp for those constructing the camp; a special camp for Jews brought from Poland who possessed passports or citizenship papers of Latin American states, entry visas for Palestine (or the official promise of visas), hostages, prisoners who had paid a ransom, collaborators, and others; a neutral camp for Jewish citizens of neutral countries such as Turkey, Argentina, and Spain; a "star" camp for Jews who would be exchanged; and a Hungarian camp which was established at the conclusion of the deportations from Hungary on July 8, 1944, and held the 1,684 prisoners on the *Kasztner transport. During the war, two prisoner exchanges took place: 301 persons were sent to Switzerland (165 were detained on their way, and only 136 arrived in Switzerland) and 222 to Palestine. In August 1944, 318 Jews from the Kasztner transport reached neutral Switzerland and in December the remaining 1,365 reached freedom. There was room in Bergen-Belsen for 10,000 inmates, and conditions, though difficult, were at first better than in other camps. But during 1944 there was a significant deterioration in conditions. Food rations were reduced to below the minimum nutritional requirement, and the prisoners were forced to do hard labor and were cruelly beaten. In addition, whether from intent, incompetence or simply overwhelming conditions, the camp authorities failed to provide even essential services.

Bergen-Belsen became a destination point for prisoners sent inland away from the advancing Soviet front during what became known as the death marches of the winter of 1944–45. Just when most of the prisoners had reached the point of physical and spiritual collapse, they were joined by prisoners removed from other camps as a result of the German retreat. Twenty thousand women arrived from Auschwitz and Buchenwald and thousands of male prisoners from Sachsenhausen and Buchenwald. The camp population swelled rapidly from 15,257 in December 1944 to 41,000 in March 1945; during the last few weeks there was an additional massive influx of prisoners from the East. The new prisoners, who arrived after forced marches sometimes lasting weeks, were starved and disease-ridden. Epidemics broke out, but there was no medical attention. Overwhelmed by the influx of arriving prisoners, the camp simply ceased to function. One survivor contrasted the orderly Auschwitz with the collapsing Bergen-Belsen after the arrival of the death march survivors. She recalls:

> At least there [in Auschwitz] we worked. And every once in a blue moon, we … we went into the showers. As much as we were afraid to go to the showers, because we didn't know if the showers would give us water or gas. Over there [in Bergen-Belsen], we had no showers.
>
> As to the dead:
>
> In Auschwitz there were well-planned facilities for cremation. When these did not suffice, bodies were burned in open fields and their ashes scattered.
>
> At Auschwitz they took away the dead people. They gassed them and they burned them; and in the camps we didn't see any dead people. We only saw the people being hit or being dragged away, but we never saw any dead people lying around … Bergen-Belsen was nothing but dead people. Skeletons, skin and bones. They piled them up as they died. They just piled them up, like a mountain.

The death rate was high: in March 1945 just weeks before liberation, nearly 20,000 people died (including Anne *Frank). A total of 37,000 died before the liberation.

Bergen-Belsen was the second major camp in Germany to be liberated by the Allies. The British entered on April 15, 1945. The horrors, which deeply shocked the British soldiers, received widespread publicity in the West. Among the arriving liberating troops were British filmmakers who recorded the scene of bulldozers burying the dead and filmed the burning of the camps. These films were shown widely in movie newsreels throughout the world and are emblematic of the liberation and of the Nazi crimes for those who saw them then and many years later. The British arrested the SS administrators, including the commandant, Josef Kramer, and almost all were put to work clearing and burying the thousands of corpses. Twenty of them died doing this work, probably from infectious diseases. The rest were tried at the end of 1945. Eleven were condemned to death, 19 to imprisonment, and 14 were acquitted.

When British troops entered the concentration camp of Bergen-Belsen they encountered more than 10,000 corpses and around 58,000 surviving inmates – the overwhelming majority of whom were Jews – who suffered from a combination of typhus, tuberculosis, dysentery, extreme malnutrition, and other virulent diseases.

Brigadier H.L. Glyn Hughes, deputy director of medical services of the British Army of the Rhine appointed Dr. Hadassah (Ada) Bimko, a 32-year-old Jewish dentist from Sosnowiec, Poland, to organize and head a team of 28 doctors and 620 female and male volunteers from among the survivors, only a few of whom were trained nurses, to help the military medical personnel care for the camp's thousands of critically ill inmates. Despite their desperate efforts, however – it was not until May 11 that the daily death rate fell below 100 a day – the Holocaust claimed 13,944 additional victims at Bergen-Belsen during the two months after liberation.

To contain the different epidemics rampaging through Bergen-Belsen, the British evacuated the survivors to the military barracks of a Panzer training school located about a mile away which in short order became the *displaced persons (DP) camp of Bergen-Belsen. On completion of the relocation on May 21, 1945, the British set fire to the concentration camp's wooden barracks.

Bergen-Belsen became the largest DP camp in Europe. From 1945 until 1950, it was an autonomous, self-governed, and largely self-contained Jewish community. Within days after the liberation, the camp's Jewish survivors elected their own political leadership headed by Josef *Rosensaft, a Polish Jew who had also survived Auschwitz, Birkenau, and Dora-Mittelbau. They focused on four main tasks: the physical rehabilitation of the survivors, the search for relatives, spiritual rehabilitation and – often against the will of the British military authorities – the political fight for rights and immigration to Palestine, or Ereẓ-Israel.

The Jewish population of Bergen-Belsen was in constant flux, numbering approximately 12,000 within a few weeks of liberation, remaining around 10,000 through 1947, and then steadily declining as emigration from Germany became more feasible. While Jewish survivors from Western Europe and Czechoslovakia were repatriated in a matter of weeks after liberation, most Jewish survivors from Poland and many from Hungary chose not to return to their native countries. In 1946, when the British sought to prevent thousands of additional Polish Jewish refugees from entering the British zone, Rosensaft and his colleagues openly defied the Military Government by giving them sanctuary in Bergen-Belsen.

By June 1945, the Jewish Committee of the Bergen-Belsen DP camp was enlarged to represent all Jewish DPs throughout the British zone of Germany. In September 1945 the first Congress of Liberated Jews met at Belsen and elected the Central Jewish Committee for the British Zone, representing both the Jewish DPs from Eastern Europe and the newly reconstituted German Jewish communities of cities such as Hamburg, Cologne, Bremen, Duesseldorf, and Hanover. Josef Rosensaft served as its chairman and Norbert Wollheim, an Auschwitz survivor originally from Berlin who had organized the *Kindertransport*, was vice chairman. Rosensaft headed both the Central Committee and the Bergen-Belsen Jewish Committee until the DP camp was closed in the fall of 1950.

As Rosensaft explained 20 years later, "Our feelings and ideas, unfortunately, were at variance with the political climate in 1945, and the calculations of those who held our fate in their hands. There were political factors in Germany that attempted to deny the Jewish character of the problems, which confronted the world as a result of the Hitler catastrophe. They sought by all means at their command to loosen the strong grip that Jewish pain and suffering and the tragic Jewish situation had on world conscience."

When the British officially renamed the DP camp "Hohne" in an attempt to at least nominally sever its relationship with the notorious concentration camp and thereby dilute the impact of the survivors' struggle for Jewish rights in international public opinion, Jewish leadership simply ignored the new designation. They understood full well the dramatic news value of the Bergen-Belsen name and were not about to surrender it. Official communications sent by the British military authorities to Rosensaft at "Hohne" were responded to on stationery that gave "Bergen-Belsen" as the Central Committee's address.

Yiddish was the official language of the Bergen-Belsen DP camp and Zionist politics were the order of the day. The first handwritten and mimeographed issue of the Bergen-Belsen newspaper, *Undzer Shtimme* (Our Voice), appeared on July 12, 1945. At first declared illegal by the British military authorities, it soon received official sanction and then appeared regularly. The first book published in Bergen-Belsen (on September 7, 1945) was a listing, in English and German, of the camp's Jewish survivors to facilitate the reunification of family members and friends, and some 60 other publications followed.

Several hundred children were liberated at Bergen-Belsen, and many more came there from Poland and other parts of Eastern Europe during 1945 and 1946. As early as June 1945, the first school was opened in Bergen-Belsen with separate classes in Polish, Romanian, and Hungarian. Jewish children from different parts of Eastern Europe soon joined them. In due course Bergen-Belsen had a kindergarten; an elementary, high, and vocational training school; and a full complement of Jewish religious educational institutions. In addition, the camp had a rabbinate, a hospital, its own Jewish police force, a library, two theater companies, an orchestra, and a host of youth and sports clubs.

Determined to create new lives for themselves, the Jewish DPs of Bergen-Belsen began to marry soon after liberation. More then 2,000 children – a vertitable population explosion – were born in the DP camp between 1946 and 1950.

Bergen-Belsen was at the heart of the Zionist struggle to establish a Jewish state, resulting in frequent confrontations with the British authorities. At the September 1945 Congress of Liberated Jews, the Jewish DPs formally adopted a resolution calling for the establishment of a Jewish state in Palestine and expressing their "sorrow and indignation that almost six months after liberation we still find ourselves in guarded camps on British soil soaked with the blood of our people. We proclaim that we will not be driven back into the lands which have become the graveyards of our people."

Both the Anglo-American Committee of Inquiry on Palestine and the United Nations Special Committee on Palestine (UNSCOP) paid official visits to Bergen-Belsen. Following the establishment of the State of Israel in May 1948, many of the Bergen-Belsen DPs immigrated there. Others immigrated to the United States, Canada, and elsewhere, and the Bergen-Belsen DP Camp was officially closed in September 1950.

The World Federation of Bergen-Belsen Associations, based in New York and led by Josef Rosensaft, Norbert Wollheim, Sam E. Bloch, and Hadassah Bimko Rosensaft, was one of the first and most active organizations of Holocaust survivors, organizing commemorative events in the U.S., Israel, and Canada as well as frequent pilgrimages to the mass-graves of Bergen-Belsen, and publishing numerous memorial volumes about Bergen-Belsen and the Holocaust generally. In Israel, the survivors of Bergen-Belsen are represented by the Irgun She'erit ha-Pletah me-ha-Ezor ha-Briti (Organization of Survivors from the British Zone).

The *Gedenkstätte* (Memorial Site) of Bergen-Belsen includes the mass graves, the Jewish and International monuments erected there, a museum, and a major research center and archive. In May 1985, U.S. President Ronald Reagan visited the site in an attempt to alleviate the opposition to his decision to pay tribute to fallen German soldiers, including members of the *Waffen-SS*, at the *Bitburg military cemetery.

BIBLIOGRAPHY: Irgun She'erit ha-Pletah me-ha-Ezor ha-Briti, *Belsen* (Eng., 1957). **ADD. BIBLIOGRAPHY:** S.J. Goldsmith, "Yossl Rosensaft: The Art of Survival," in: *Twenty 20th Century Jews* (1962); H. Lavsky, *New Beginnings: Holocaust Survivors in Bergen-Belsen and the British Zone of Germany, 1945–1950* (2002); S.E. Bloch (ed.), *Holocaust and Rebirth: Bergen-Belsen 1945–1965* (1965); A. Königseder and J. Wetzel, *Waiting for Hope: Jewish Displaced Persons in Post-World War II Germany* (2001); J. Reilly, *Belsen: The Liberation of a Concentration Camp* (1998); H. Rosensaft, *Yesterday: My Story* (2004); M.Z. Rosensaft, "Bergen-Belsen: The End and the Beginning," in: *Children and the Holocaust: Symposium Presentations* (2004); B. Shephard, *After Daybreak, The Liberation of Belsen, 1945* (2005).

[Jozeph Michman (Melkman) and Yehuda Bauer / Menachem Rosensaft (2nd ed.)]

BERGEN COUNTY, district located in the northern part of the state of New Jersey, U.S., bordering the Hudson River, and including 70 individual municipalities. Bergen County's population in 2000 was about 897,500, of whom approximately 100,000 were Jews. The first Jewish settlers in Bergen County arrived in Englewood in the 1880s and the 1890s. They came primarily from Lithuania and Russia and made their living as farmers and small businessmen. The first religious service in Bergen County was held on Rosh Hashanah, 1896, in Englewood and was conducted by Benjamin Sher, a native of Lithuania. This group became the first congregation, Congregation Ahavath Torah, in Bergen County. Early Jewish settlers in other towns eventually built their own synagogues, most them immediately after World War I, in Park Ridge, Hackensack, Ridgefield Park, and Westwood. The Hackensack Hebrew Institute, which later became Temple Beth El, was founded in 1913. A number of descendants of the early settlers still live in the county. The Jewish population of Bergen County grew slowly, with some spurts after World War I, until the completion of the George Washington Bridge in 1931, which opened the door for a huge migration from New York City. The first services for Jews in Teaneck, which has become a major hub of Jewish life in Bergen County, took place in the 1932. The High Holiday services were held in the studio of Israel Doskow, and they were led by Rabbi David Pearlman. This group began religious school classes in 1933, and 400 people attended High Holiday services that year at the Masonic Square clubhouse in Teaneck. The congregation dedicated the Teaneck Jewish Community Center in 1949. Temple Emeth, a Reform Congregation, began in 1947 when members of 50 families met in the Hackensack YMHA. This temple's current home was dedicated in 1959 and the sanctuary was completed in 1965. Congregation Beth Shalom, Teaneck's second Conservative synagogue, was formed in 1950 through the efforts of 28 families and Rabbi and Mrs. Barry Schaeffer. B'nai Yeshurun, Teaneck's first Orthodox congregation, was formed in 1958. Congregation Beth Am, Teaneck's second Reform temple, was formed in 1964 by 31 families. Congregation Beth Aaron was organized in 1971 by several women who felt the need for an Orthodox congregation in the Cedar Lane area of Teaneck.

The greatest increase in Jewish population took place after World War II with the housing boom. By 1950 there were approximately 20,000 Jews in the general population of 540,000. In the following two decades the Jewish population more than quintupled, whereas the general population has not quite doubled. In 2000 Teaneck, the largest municipality in Bergen County, had nearly 40,000 people and 15,000 Jews; Fair Lawn with a general population of 32,000 had an estimated Jewish population of 13,000; Englewood with 27,000 residents had 5,500 Jews. The Jewish community is affluent and well educated. According to the 2001 Jewish Community Study of Bergen County & North Hudson, Bergen is the 19th largest Jewish community in the United States. It has become an increasingly observant community. Nearly 30% of households keep a kosher home and 39% of Jewish children age 6–17 are enrolled in Jewish day schools – both being the highest percentages among any recently surveyed Jewish community in the United States. The strong connection between the Bergen County Jewish community and Israel is reflected by the 32% of households with Jewish children up to age 17 who have sent at least one Jewish child to Israel. This is by far, the highest percentage of any Jewish community in the United States.

Political Activity

Jews have been prominent in the political life of the county. Matthew Feldman, a native of neighboring Hudson County, who served as mayor of Teaneck, 1959–66, and as state senator, 1966–67, was chairman of the County Democratic Party in 1969. Nelson Gross of Upper Saddle River was appointed chairman of the County Republican Party in 1966 and chairman of the State Republican group in 1969. Nat Feldman was elected councilman in Englewood in 1969 and was mayor of Englewood (1970). Alvin Moskin, a descendant of one of the earliest settlers, served as mayor of Englewood, 1956–59. Martin Kole of Fair Lawn and Abraham Rosenberg of Bogota were appointed to judgeships on the county bench in 1966. Franklin H. Cooper was elected to the Bergen County Board of Freeholders on the Republican ticket (1969). Loretta Weinberg, a Democrat from Teaneck, was first elected to the New Jersey Assembly in 1992 and was elected in 2002 to be the Majority Conference Leader for the Democratic Party in the Assembly. State Senator Byron M. Baer (D) has served in the State Senate since 1994 and was elected Senate Leader Ex-Officio in 2004. Congressman Steven Rothman is a Democrat from Fair Lawn who was first elected to the U.S. House of Representatives in 1996. He is now in his fourth term of representing the Ninth District, which includes a portion of Bergen County. Congressman Rothman served as the two-term mayor of Englewood (1983–89) and as the Bergen County Surrogate Court judge (1993–96). Robert M. Gordon of Fair Lawn was elected to the New Jersey State Assembly in 2004. In the early 2000s, Bergen County had many Jewish mayors, including Michael Wildes of Englewood, Jacqueline Kates of Teaneck, Jack Alter of Fort Lee, David Ganz of Fair Lawn, Michael Kaplan of Norwood, Sandy Farber of Palisades Park, Peter Rustin of Tenafly, and Fred Pitofsky of Closter. United States Senator Frank *Lautenberg, who served in the Senate from 1982 to 2000 and was elected to a fourth term in 2002, was born in neighboring Paterson, New Jersey, and now resides in the Bergen County town of Cliffside Park. The growing political power of Jews in Bergen County, and the community's active participation in the area's social and cultural life, represents a radical change from the 1930s and the early 1940s. During this earlier period, the county was a hotbed of activity for pro-German Bundists. Country clubs that once discriminated against Jews are now fully integrated with all minority groups, and there is very little overt antisemitism in the county.

Organizational Life

Organizational life is very active, with over 185 known Jewish organizations. There are 23 Conservative synagogues, 15 Reform, 30 Orthodox, one Reconstructionist, and one unaffiliated. The Rabbinical Council of Bergen County (Orthodox) and the North Jersey Board of Rabbis (Conservative and Reform) seek to enhance the life of the North Jersey Jewish community by furthering the interests of the professional rabbinate and the congregations in the area. The umbrella organization for the community is the UJA Federation of Northern New Jersey, which was formed on July 1, 2004, by the merger of the UJA Federation of Bergen County & North Hudson and the Jewish Federation of North Jersey. The Federation is now the 18th largest UJA Federation out of the 186 major Federations in North America. It serves a Jewish population of 100,000 people living in 35,000 households in 90 communities in Bergen County, Passaic County, and parts of Hudson County. In 2005, the Federation aimed to raise $15 million to support 84 beneficiary agencies and community services funded by its Annual Campaign. In 2004, the Federation's Endowment Foundation went over $50 million in holdings. The Bergen County Federation was founded on September 19, 1977. It was one of the leading Federations in the United States in raising the most money for the Operation Exodus Campaign on a per capita basis. Over $15 million was donated to its Operation Exodus to help the Jews of the former Soviet Union make **aliyah* to Israel in the early 1990s. Among the Federation's major beneficiary agencies in Bergen County are the JCC on the Palisades in Tenafly, the Bergen County Y, a Jewish Community Center in Washington Township, the Jewish Family Service of Bergen County in Teaneck, and the Jewish Home at Rockleigh: Russ Berrie Home for Jewish Living. The Home opened its new state-of-the-art facility in 2001, after serving the Bergen County older adult community from its Jersey City site since the 1930s. The Bergen County YJCC, which began as the Hackensack YM-YWHA in the 1920s, opened its new building in 1987 to meet the recreational and cultural needs of the growing Jewish population in the Pascack Valley area of Bergen County. The JCC began in Englewood in 1950. The JCC's membership expanded so greatly that an expansion became necessary. In 1981, it opened it present-day facility – the JCC on the Palisades – in Tenafly, where it has become a major cultural and educational resource in Bergen County. The Jewish Family Service, which began in the 1950s, oversees counseling services, Kosher Meals on Wheels, a Job Search Network, New American services, and a Schony.com Computer Training Center. The Jewish Association of Developmental Disabilities established New Jersey's first kosher group home (Nathan and Naomi Berrie Group Home) in 1988. As of 2004, J-ADD oversees nine kosher group homes for Jewish people with developmental disabilities. There are 13 Jewish day schools, two regional Jewish high schools, and four educational programs for Jewish children with special needs. These schools are served by the Jewish Educational Services of the UJA Federation, which provides teacher training, and centrally organized programs and services. Israel Programs Center of the UJA Federation provides educational programs about Israel to schools and organizations in the community. In 1998, the UJA Federation launched a Synagogue Leadership Initiative, in partnership with the Henry & Marilyn Taub Foundation, to help strengthen the 70 synagogues in Bergen County. The Jewish Community Relations Council, which was created in 1969, is the public policy, community relations, and advocacy arm of the UJA Federation.

[Max M. Kleinbaum / Alan J. Grossman (2nd ed.)]

BERGER, ARTHUR VICTOR (1912–2003), U.S. composer, critic, and educator. Born in New York, Berger studied at the Longy School of Music, at Harvard (M.A. in musicology, 1936), in Paris with Boulanger and composition with Darius

*Milhaud. He taught at Mills College, Brooklyn College, the Juilliard School, and Brandeis University. In 1979 he became a member of the New England Conservatory, from whose composition faculty he retired in 1998.

In the 1940s and 1950s Berger wrote musical criticism for the *Boston Transcript*, *New York Sun*, and *New York Herald Tribune*. He served as editor of the *Musical Mercury* (1934–37) and was co-founder and editor of *Perspectives of New Music* (1962–63). He contributed to many music journals (including pieces on Stravinsky, Ives, and *Babbitt), produced a monograph on the music of Aaron *Copland (1953; reissued 1990), and wrote *Reflections of an American Composer* (2002). He was a member of the American Academy of Arts and Sciences and the Institute of Arts and Letters.

As a composer, Berger was distinguished for his economy of means, vigor of expression, and strong formal structures. His music in the 1940–57 period shows the influence of Stravinsky's neo-classicism; later works categorizes him as a serial or post-Webern composer. He evolved his own characteristics, especially an interest in musical space, both vertical and horizontal. From 1958 Berger showed increasing stylistic independence and paid increased attention to the use of instrumental color and to revisions of earlier works, utilizing a variety of techniques which range from re-composition to the simultaneous overlay of new materials. His compositions include works for orchestra (such as *Ideas of Order*, 1952; *Polyphony*, 1956), chamber music, vocal works, and many piano pieces.

BIBLIOGRAPHY: *Grove online, s.v.; Baker's Biographical Dictionary* (1997); B. Boretz, in: *Perspectives of New Music* 41 (2003).

[Max Loppert / Naama Ramot (2nd ed.)]

BERGER, DAVID (1943–), historian and Orthodox thinker. Berger was educated at Yeshiva College (B.A., 1964) and Columbia University (M.A., 1965; Ph.D., 1970). Primarily a medievalist, he has written about the history of medieval Jewry, Jewish-Christian relations and polemics, messianic ideas and movements, and the intellectual history of the Jews throughout the Middle Ages. In the 1990s he turned his attention to the contemporary Orthodox world, coming to castigate it for its indifference in the face of the "scandal" of the messianic claims surrounding the last Lubavitcher rebbe. He argued that Lubavitch messianism stands outside the acceptable range of messianic claims and must be opposed by the contemporary Orthodox world.

Berger was active in the major institutions of American Jewish academic life, having served as president of the Association for Jewish Studies and as a member of the Executive Committee of the American Academy of Jewish Research and vice chair of the Academic Advisory Committee of the National Foundation for Jewish Culture.

Among his publications are *The Rebbe, the Messiah, and the Scandal of Orthodox Indifference* (2001); *The Jewish-Christian Debate in the High Middle Ages: A Critical Edition of the Nizzahon Vetus with an Introduction, Translation, and Commentary* (1979); and, as editor, *History and Hate: The Dimensions of Anti-Semitism* (1997).

[Jay Harris (2nd ed.)]

BERGER, ELMER (1908–1996), U.S. Reform rabbi and anti-Zionist propagandist. Berger was born in Cleveland, Ohio, and ordained at Hebrew Union College in 1932. He had begun his career serving two congregations in Michigan as rabbi when, in 1942, he wrote a widely circulated essay *Why I Am A Non-Zionist*, in which he challenged the Zionist claim "to represent something called 'the Jewish people.'" As a result of his manifesto, which set forth the case for a universal and prophetic Judaism, he became executive director in 1943 of the American Council for Judaism, the leading U.S. Jewish organization opposed to the creation and existence of the State of Israel. As executive vice president of the ACJ from 1956, the pro-Arab Berger lobbied vigorously in the national media against Israel. After the Six-Day War in 1967, Berger fell afoul of the ACJ leadership and left to form a splinter group, American Jewish Alternatives to Zionism, which remained marginal. He summarized his life's crusades in his autobiographical *Memoirs of an Anti-Zionist Jew*, published in Beirut in 1978. His other books include *The Jewish Dilemma* (1945); *Judaism or Jewish Nationalism* (1957); *A Partisan History of Judaism* (1951); *United States Politics and Arab Oil* (1974); and *Who Knows Better Must Say So* (1956). Upon his death, Berger was eulogized as a hero in Arab scholarly publications.

BIBLIOGRAPHY: K.M. Olitzky, L.J. Sussman, M.H. Stern, *Reform Judaism in America: A Biographical Dictionary and Sourcebook* (1993).

[Bezalel Gordon (2nd ed.)]

BERGER, ISAAC ("**Ike**"; 1936–), U.S. Olympic weightlifter, winner of one gold and two silver Olympic medals, member of U.S. Weightlifters Hall of Fame. Born in Jerusalem to a rabbi, Berger was lightly wounded by shrapnel during Israel's War of Independence in 1948, a year before his family moved to New York. Measuring only five feet tall as a teenager, Berger started lifting weights and soon began competing, winning the national AAU championship from 1955 to 1961 and in 1964. He was the first featherweight to lift over 800 pounds and press double his own body weight. Berger won the gold medal at the 1956 Olympics, setting a record in the featherweight class (776.5 lbs. / 352.5 kg). The next year he won the gold medal at the 1957 Maccabiah Games and became the first athlete to establish a world record in Israel by pressing 258 pounds (117.1 kg.) in the featherweight class. He finished third that year in the world championships in the featherweight class but won the following year and again in 1961, while finishing second in 1959, 1963, and 1964. Berger also won the gold medal at the Pan American Games in 1959 and 1963. At the 1960 Olympic games, Berger won the silver medal lifting 798.75 pounds (362.6 kg.), losing to Yevgeny Minayev of the Soviet Union in a face-off that lasted 10 hours, until 4:00 A.M. Berger set an Olympic record at the 1964 games with a jerk of

336 pounds (152.5 kg.), which at a bodyweight of 130 pounds made him pound-for-pound the strongest man in the world, a record that stood for nine years. He also won a silver medal in the featherweight class (841.5 lbs. / 382.5 kg.). Berger was inducted into the U.S. Weightlifters Hall of Fame in 1965 and that same year started a program at the New York College of Music to become a cantor.

[Elli Wohlgelernter (2nd ed.)]

BERGER, LILI (1916–1996), Yiddish author and essayist. Born in Malkin, Poland, Berger settled in Paris in 1936, where she married the Jewish Communist leader Louis Gronowski. In 1949 she returned to Warsaw where she began publishing articles and stories in both Yiddish and Polish, followed by collections of literary criticism, short stories, and novels. In 1968 she resumed her literary activity in Paris. Many of her articles and essays are personal recollections replete with historical detail. Her award-winning fiction reflects the Polish Jewish experience in the 20th century. Among her books are *Ekhos fun a Vaytn Nekhtn* ("Echoes from Long Ago," 1986); *Eseyen un Skitsn* ("Essays and Sketches," 1965); *Fun Vayt un Noent* ("From Far and Near," 1978); *In Loyf fun Tsayt* ("In the Course of Time," 1988); *Oyf di Khvalyes fun Goyrl* ("On the Waves of Fate," 1986).

BIBLIOGRAPHY: B. Gryn, in: *Morgn Frayhayt* (July 16, 1967), 11; F. Forman et al. (eds.), *Found Treasures* (1994), 223–35, 353; B. Kagan, *Leksikon fun Yidishe Shraybers* (1986), 104–5; L. Domankievich, in: *Tsukunft* (May-June 1971), 202–4; P. Hyman and D. Ofer (eds.), *Jewish Women: A Comprehensive Historical Encyclopedia* (CD-ROM, 2005).

[Vivian Felsen (2nd ed.)]

BERGER, MEIR (1901–1981), Mexican Jewish educator. Born in Suwalki, Poland, he studied in a yeshivah and in a teachers' seminar in Lithuania. Later he taught in a Hebrew school. He immigrated to Mexico in 1924 and in the same year founded the first modern Jewish school there: Colegio Israelita de Mexico – Yiddishe Shul. This school imparted Jewish and general knowledge and Berger was its principal until 1944. In that year he was replaced by the educator Avraham *Golomb. Berger participated in the establishment of the first Zionist institutions in Mexico: in 1925 he was secretary of the Zionist Organization and in 1926 he headed the local Keren Kayemet le-Israel office. He was also the first editor of the Zionist periodical *Farn Folk* and he published numerous essays and articles in the Yiddish newspaper *Der Veg*.

[Efraim Zadoff (2nd ed.)]

BERGER, MEYER (1898–1959), U.S. journalist. During his career on *The New York Times* (1928–59), he wrote frequently on New York lore and life. In 1950 he won the Pulitzer Prize for his report on the shooting of 13 persons by an insane war veteran in New Jersey, and sent the prize money to the killer's mother. A collection of his writings was published as *The Eight Million* (1942). Berger also wrote *The Story of the New York Times, 1851–1951*.

BERGER, SAMUEL R. (**Sandy**; 1945–), U.S. foreign affairs specialist. Born in Sharon, Conn., Sandy Berger, as he was usually known, became national security adviser to President Bill Clinton in his second term, serving from 1996 to 2001 as the senior White House aide on all international issues. Berger grew up in Millerton, N.Y., a rural community in dairy country. He father died when he was eight and his mother ran a struggling surplus clothing store. The Bergers stood apart from the Millerton mainstream as Democrats in a very Republican county and as Jews in an upper-income Republican area. Berger took his religious training from a rabbi in a nearby hospital for the mentally retarded. "Where I grew up is very important to what I am," he said. "My perspectives are still more Millerton 1960 than Washington 2000. The small-town sense of community and social responsibility – that's the lasting imprint of Millerton on me."

At Cornell University, from which he graduated in 1967, he was active in student politics. He got a job as a student intern in Washington for Representative Joseph Resnick. At Harvard Law School, from which he graduated in 1971, he volunteered in the presidential campaigns of Eugene McCarthy and then for Robert F. Kennedy. Four years later, in the presidential campaign of George McGovern, he met Bill Clinton, and they became friends.

Berger joined one of Washington's premier law firms, Hogan & Hartson, where he represented Japanese and other clients and talked often with the firm's most eminent figure, former Senator J. William Fulbright. When Jimmy Carter was elected president, Berger served as deputy director of the Policy Planning Staff in the State Department, where he was involved in a wide variety of international economic, security, and foreign policy matters. During the 1980s Berger formed an alliance with Pamela Harriman, the Washington social doyenne, writing speeches for her and benefiting from her wealth and connections. When Clinton lost a re-election bid as governor of Arkansas, Berger persuaded Mrs. Harriman to put him on the board of her political action committee, which came to be a major fund-raising arm of the Democratic Party. When Clinton ran for president in 1992, Berger joined him as a senior foreign-policy adviser. After Clinton won, Berger persuaded him to send Mrs. Harriman to Paris as ambassador. Berger was offered the national security adviser's job but demurred on the grounds of limited experience, suggesting Anthony Lake. Berger became Lake's deputy and replaced him after Clinton's first term.

Intimately involved with all aspects of Clinton foreign policy, Berger, considered the most influential foreign-policy adviser since Henry A. *Kissinger, was at the nexus of the Clinton strategy to end the war in Kosovo.

After leaving the White House, Berger served as chairman of Stonebridge International, a Washington-based strategy firm that he started to help build business relationships through Asia, Europe, and Latin America, and also had a senior position with *Lehman Brothers, the international investment firm.

[Stewart Kampel (2nd ed.)]

BERGER, VICTOR (1860–1929), U.S. journalist, socialist leader, and congressman. Berger was born in Nieder-Rehbach, Austria. In 1880 he immigrated to the United States and settled in Milwaukee, where he taught German and also taught Sunday School at the Bnei Yeshuron synagogue. In 1892 Berger became editor of the *Milwaukee Daily Vorwaerts*, a German-language socialist paper, and in 1897 he helped to found the American Socialist Party. A conservative socialist influenced by the writings of Eduard Bernstein, Berger joined ranks with Morris *Hillquit in opposing the influence of the communists and such radicals as Daniel *De Leon in the socialist camp. In 1908 he became editor of the weekly *Social Democratic Herald*, which was later replaced by the daily *Milwaukee Leader*, a newspaper that he then headed until his death. In 1911 Berger was elected to Congress from Wisconsin, thereby becoming the first avowed socialist to serve in the U.S. House of Representatives, where he was known for his advocacy of labor legislation and social reform. His opposition to America's entry into World War I led the postmaster general to revoke the mailing privileges of his *Milwaukee Leader* on the grounds of its being a subversive journal, and Berger himself was indicted under the Espionage Act. A court conviction led to a 20-year sentence, as a result of which the House refused to seat him when he won the off-year election in 1918 and again the following year when he won in a rerun. In 1921, however, the Supreme Court reversed his conviction, and a year later, in consequence of this ruling and the general abatement of war hysteria, the House allowed him his seat which he continued to hold until 1928. At the time of his death he was chairman of the National Executive Board of the American Socialist Party.

BERGER-BARZILAI, JOSEPH (original name **Isaac Zelaznik**, from 1922 **Barzilai**; 1904–1978), Israeli political scientist. Berger-Barzilai was born in Cracow. In 1920, having joined the newly created Zionist youth movement Ha-Shomer ha-Ẓa'ir, he went to Ereẓ Israel. Two years later he joined the small founding group of the illegal Palestine Communist Party, of which he was appointed secretary.

In 1924 he visited Moscow and the Comintern Executive there. On his return he helped organize Communist groups in Syria, Lebanon, Egypt, and Transjordan, and in his capacity as party secretary made contact with Arab leaders in Ereẓ Israel, notably Jamal al-Husseini. He secretly visited Moscow several times and in March 1929 had a five-hour talk with Stalin on Ereẓ Israel and Near Eastern affairs. During the Arab riots of 1929 he hid in the Arab village of Beit Safafa near Jerusalem, whence he directed Communist propaganda. In 1931 he was sent by the Comintern to Berlin to serve as secretary of the Anti-Imperialist League, whose chairmen were then Albert Einstein and Henri Barbusse. In 1932 he was called to Moscow to head the Near East Department of the Comintern and was given the name Joseph Berger. Two years later he was suddenly dismissed and expelled from the party, and in 1935 arrested for "Trotskyist agitation." Though he denied the charge, he was sentenced to five years' hard labor. In 1936 he was brought to Moscow as a potential witness against *Zinoviev; refusing to give evidence, he was sentenced to death. The sentence was unexpectedly commuted to eight years' imprisonment; 20 years later Berger-Barzilai learned that his life had been saved by his Jewish interrogator's sympathy for his Palestinian past. For more than 15 years Berger-Barzilai was sent from prison to prison and from camp to camp, undergoing such ordeals as a renewed death sentence which was later repealed, long hunger strikes, and physical torture. In 1951 he was released but condemned to exile for life in Siberia. Only in 1956, after the 20th Congress of the Soviet Communist Party, was Berger completely "rehabilitated" and accepted again into the party ranks. He left, however, with his family for Poland and worked for a while in the Polish Institute of Foreign Affairs in Warsaw. In 1957 he settled in Israel, and henceforth assumed the double name Berger-Barzilai. During the long years of imprisonment Berger-Barzilai returned to his Jewish loyalties and religious faith. In 1968 he was appointed senior lecturer in political science at Bar-Ilan University, and rapidly became an international authority on Communist and Soviet affairs, publishing numerous interviews and articles in journals and the daily press. He was invited to lecture at learned institutions and appeared as a commentator on Israel radio.

He described some of his experiences in the Soviet Union in several books: in Hebrew, *Zohar ba-Ḥaẓot* ("Light at Midnight," 1962), *Ha-Tragedyah shel ha-Mahpekhah ha-Sovyetit* ("The Tragedy of the Soviet Revolution," 1968); and in a more comprehensive volume in English: *Shipwreck of a Generation* (American title, *Nothing but the Truth*, 1971).

His wife, ESTHER FELDMAN (1898–1972), described her life in the U.S.S.R. as the Jewish wife of an "enemy of the people" in *Kele Beli Sogar* ("Prison without Bars," 1964).

[Binyamin Eliav (2nd ed.)]

BERGGRÜN, HEINRICH (1838–1889), *ḥazzan* and composer. Born in Warsaw, Berggrün was a music teacher in Vilna, and later a violinist at the Grand Theater, Warsaw. He studied singing in Milan, became choirmaster in Odessa, was appointed *ḥazzan* in Posen, and chief cantor in Hanover in 1870. His compositions include: "Festival *Kaddish*" for *ḥazzan* and choir on the occasion of the jubilee of the Hanover synagogue, 1892; "Complete *Kaddish*" for *ḥazzan* and choir, 1889.

BERGH, VAN DEN, Dutch family of industrialists. ZADOK VAN DEN BERGH (1769–1857) was a merchant and leader of the Brabant Jewish community, living in the small village of Geffen. His son DANIEL VAN DEN BERGH (1794–1866) headed a textile factory from 1836, which under the name Bergoss (1856–1986) made Oss into a center of the textile industry. His younger brother SIMON VAN DEN BERGH (1818–1907) continued their father's business, bartering groceries and dry goods for butter supplied by peasants from the surrounding countryside. In 1872, Simon, helped by his sons Samuel, Arnold, Henry, Isaac and Jacob, started production of "artificial butter," or oleomargarine, in a factory in Oss, in 1890 replaced by a bigger one at Rotterdam. Henry and Jacob opened a branch in London, while in 1888 a margarine factory was opened in Cleve (Germany). A few years later, in 1895, a factory was opened in Brussels. Subsequently, the firm developed rapidly and became one of the leading margarine manufacturers in Europe. In 1930 the Van den Bergh Margarine Union Ltd. merged with Lever Bros. Ltd., forming Unilever Ltd., which expanded into a giant international concern. Simon's son, SAMUEL VAN DEN BERGH (1864–1941), obtained a leading position in the firm, but was active in politics as well and within the Jewish community. He was a Member of Parliament for the Liberal Party from 1905 to 1909, and a Member of the First House from 1923 to 1938. He was also the Dutch delegate to the International Jewish Agency and a member of the board of the Dutch branch of Keren Hayesod. His son, the lawyer and professor GEORGE VAN DEN BERGH (1897–1966), was active in the Socialist Party and was a Member of Parliament from 1925 to 1933. As the chairman of the board of the Zionist agricultural project in the Wieringermeer, he served the Jewish community. George's brother, SIDNEY JAMES VAN DEN BERGH (1898–1978), was also active in public affairs. After serving as a commissioner for UNICEF, he was appointed minister of defense in 1959. The next generation too produced a Member of Parliament: George's son ROBERT VAN DEN BERGH (1913–1997) represented the Socialist Party from 1963 to 1971. Thereafter he became a member of the Council of the State (1972–83).

BIBLIOGRAPHY: C. Wilson, *Story of Unilever* (1954); J. Becker, *Het smouse kerkhof te Geffen 1643–1908* (1987) 44–77; F.J.M, van de Ven, "Bergh, Samuel van den (1864–1941)," in: *Biografisch Woordenboek van Nederland* 3 (1989); J. Mulder, *Sidney van den Bergh, een liberaal* (1975).

[Bart Wallet (2nd ed.)]

BERGHEIM, village N. of Colmar in Alsace, E. France. Jews are first mentioned there in connection with the persecutions in the 14th century by the *Armleder gangs and following the *Black Death. During the Burgundian wars (1476–78) they again suffered severely. By the beginning of the 16th century, however, Bergheim had the largest Jewish community in Alsace. The Jewish settlement was pillaged by rebel peasants in 1525, and an anti-Jewish outbreak in 1784 followed the abolition of the "body tax" on Jews. The Jewish population declined from 327 in 1784 to 40 in 1926. In 1968 there were no Jews living in Bergheim.

BIBLIOGRAPHY: M. Ginsburger, *Les Juifs à Ribeauvillé et à Bergheim* (1939).

[Zvi Avneri]

BERGMAN, ALAN (1925–) and **MARILYN** (1929–), U.S. songwriters, composers. Alan and Marilyn Bergman (Katz), a prolific husband-and-wife team, are best known for their many film score classics such as the Academy Award-winning songs "The Way We Were" (*The Way We Were* (1973)) and "The Windmills of Your Mind" (*The Thomas Crown Affair* (1968)). The couple received the Academy Award for Best Musical Score for *Yentl* (1983), writing the lyrics to accompany Michel Legrand's music for the film. They were nominated for 16 other Academy Awards.

Alan Bergman was educated at the University of California-Los Angeles and received a B.A. from the University of North Carolina. His career began during WWII when he wrote and directed Special Services shows for American troops. After the war, he directed television shows for CBS from 1945 until 1953. He joined ASCAP in 1955 and began writing songs for television, revues, and nightclub acts, for performers such as Fred Astaire and Marge and Gower Champion. His notable stage scores include *That's Life, Ice Capades of 1957*, and *Something More!*, while his albums include *Never Be Afraid* and *Aesop's Fables*. He married his wife and songwriting partner, Marilyn, in 1958. Marilyn attended New York University. She joined ASCAP in 1953, two years before her husband. She also wrote songs for revues and nightclub performances and is credited with several television theme songs. Some of the couple's other most memorable songs include "Nice 'n' Easy," "Yellow Bird," "The Way You Make Me Feel," "It Might Be You," "Moonlight," "Cheatin' Billy," "Don't Know Where I'm Goin'," "I've Never Left Your Arms," "That Face," "Baby, the Ball Is Over," "Ol' MacDonald," "Sentimental Baby," "If I Were in Love," and "That's Him Over There."

[Walter Driver (2nd ed.)]

BERGMAN, ANDREW (1945–), U.S. writer, director, producer. Born in Queens, N.Y., Bergman attended Harper College before earning his doctorate in American history at the University of Wisconsin. His doctoral dissertation, "We're in the Money: Depression America and Its Films" (1971), earned him respect as a trenchant sociologist and film historian and led to a job as a youth contact in the PR department at United Artists. After writing the critically acclaimed Broadway comedy *Social Security*, Bergman received his first screenwriting credit for the Mel Brooks blockbuster farce *Blazing Saddles* (1974), which was based on Berman's treatment for a film called "Tex X." Bergman earned the sole screenwriting credit for the 1979 comedy *The In-Laws*, starring Alan *Arkin and Peter *Falk. He made his directorial debut two years later with *So Fine*, a Madison Avenue satire about a professor who conquers the garment industry with an idea for transparent jeans. Bergman was widely praised for his adaptation of Michael Ritchie's novel *Fletch* (1985), featuring Chevy Chase as droll newspaper reporter Irwin Fletcher. Bergman continued to write and direct during the 1990s while also producing a number of films in conjunction with producer Michael Lobell and their joint venture Lobell/Bergman Productions. The versatile Bergman both wrote and directed *The Freshman* (1990), starring Marlon Brando and Matthew Broderick, as well as the features *Honeymoon in Vegas* (1992) and *Striptease* (1996), while writing the screenplays for *Soapdish* (1991) and *The Scout* (1994). His production credits include *Chances Are*

(1989), *Undercover Blues* (1993), *Little Big League* (1994), and *Striptease* (1996).

[Walter Driver (2nd ed.)]

BERGMAN, SAMUEL HUGO (1883–1974), philosopher. Bergman studied philosophy in Prague and Berlin. During his student days at Prague, he was a member and leader of the Zionist student circle, Bar Kochba, and in 1903 began to publish articles on Zionist and Judaic themes. From 1909, when Martin *Buber began to give his lectures on Judaism in Prague and other European cities, Bergman became his close disciple, although he sometimes was very critical of Buber, whose influence on him lasted throughout his entire life. The Bar Kochba circle and his close association with Buber were the pivotal and formative factors of Bergman's personality and philosophy. During World War I, he served as an officer in the Austro-Hungarian army. In 1919 he was nominated a member of the "National Council of Jews of the Czechoslovakian Republic" and of the "Committee of Delegations" for the Versailles peace treaty negotiations. He also served as the World Zionist's Organization's secretary of education in London and in 1920 emigrated to Palestine, where he became the first director of the Jewish National and Hebrew University Library in Jerusalem, a position he held until 1935. He was involved in founding the *Histadrut ha-Ovedim, and was elected a member of its executive council. In 1928 he became a lecturer in philosophy at the Hebrew University, and in 1935 was promoted to professor. From 1935 until 1938 he served as its first rector. One of the founders and editors of *Kiryat Sefer*, he was the editor of general philosophy for the *Encyclopaedia Hebraica*, and an editor of the philosophical quarterly *Iyyun*. Bergman was a member of *Ha-Po'el ha-Ẓa'ir, being the first philosopher to delve seriously into the writings of the party's spiritual master, A.D. *Gordon. Later Bergman also became involved in *Berit Shalom and *Iḥud, of which he became the main spokesman. He headed the Jewish delegation from Palestine to the Pan-Asian Conference held in New Delhi in 1947.

Bergman's main intellectual interests were scientific knowledge and religious experience. He saw reason and faith as two sources of truth and as grounds for human moral orientation, which endow life with significance. Throughout his entire life Bergman strove for a comprehensive approach to these two sources of truth, an approach which would resolve the mutual context of rationality and of mysticism, of knowledge of being with the human longing for sanctity and eternity.

In Bergman's early years, his philosophical views were influenced by Brentano, and he applied himself chiefly to an analysis of the phenomena of perception and evidence. From the early 1920s on, he turned to Kantian philosophy and devoted quite a few of his studies to a critical analysis of the philosopher's struggle for evidence and for causality (see his *Ha-Filisofiyah shel Immanuel Kant* ("The Philosophy of Immanuel Kant," 1937, 1970²)). His approach to these questions was deeply influenced by the neo-Kantian school, especially that of Hermann *Cohen, who became one of his main sources in philosophy and religion. Among his contributions to the study of philosophy are *Mavo le-Torat ha-Hakarah* ("Introduction to Epistemology," 1940); *Mavo le-Torat ha-Higayon* ("Introduction to Logic," 1954); *Ha-Filosofiyah shel Shelomo Maimon* ("The Philosophy of Solomon Maimon," 1932; Eng. trans., 1967); *Toledot ha-Filosoiyah ha-Ḥadashah* ("History of Modern Philosophy," 4 vols., 1970–77).

Bergman's intention, as stated in the opening remark of his *Hogei ha-Dor* ("The Philosophers of Our Time," 1935), was to show how scientific-philosophic discourse found itself at a dead end at the beginning of the 20th century and how philosophy "seeks in the last generation, in various directions and with the assistance of a variety of tools, to find the way out of it." The different directions he referred to, are mostly existential-religious ones, some of which he called "*Dialogical Philosophy*" (Heb. *Ha-Filosofiyah ha-Dialogit mi-Kierkegaard ad Buber*, Intro. N. Rotenstreich, 1973; Eng., 1991). Under this umbrella Bergman included the philosophies of some of his main masters, namely, besides Buber and Cohen, Franz Rosenzweig and A.D. Gordon. Of no less import for him was Abraham Isaac *Kook, on the Jewish side as well as Rudolf Steiner and Sari Aurobindu on the Christian and Hindu side.

Bergman's own religiosity combined a naive faith and a constant striving for God-experience and guidance, with highly sophisticated humanistic restrictions. Although he deeply believed in personal spontaneous prayer, he participated in the traditional public prayer prescribed by the *halakhah*. Although he believed in the central role and the necessary authority of *halakhah*, he was open to the need for change and personal autonomy. Bergman was a devoted Jew, but rejected the exclusiveness of the idea of the election of Israel, and affirmed the unity and messianic cooperation of all religions. He delved all his life into the literary sources of Judaism but was fully convinced that human consciousness should be the final authority for religious decisions and determinations.

This dynamic balance between religious commitment, human responsibility, and devotion to philosophic deliberation marks Bergman's attitude in the many areas in which he was active. He saw the human as being constantly called upon to live in covenant with God, to be His partner, and yet to be fully aware of God's sovereignty over humanity. This approach shaped his political Zionist view and led him to seek dialogue and compromise with the Palestinian people. It permeated his commitment to social justice and pluralism, and his understanding of philosophy and religion as endless journeys towards the truth, which one can progressively approach, but which always remains transcendingly divine, and cannot be possessed by the human mind or deed.

Bergman's observations on religion are to be found, among his many publications, especially in his *Hogim u-Ma'aminim* ("Thinkers and Believers," 1959), *Faith and Reason: An Introduction to Modern Jewish Thought* (ed. A. Jospe, 1961), and *Anashim u-Derakhim* ("Persons and Paths," 1967). He also wrote *Ba-Mishol*, ed. N. Rotenstreich, 1976.

BIBLIOGRAPHY: B. Shohetman and Sh. Shunami (eds.), *The Writings of Shemuel Hugo Bergman, A Bibliography* (1903–1967) (1968); **ADD. BIBLIOGRAPHY:** S.H. Bergman, *Tagebuecher & Briefe*, ed. M. Sambursky (1985); Y. Amir, "*Teguvot Ereẓ Yisre'eliot le-Haguto shel Franz Rosenzweig*" (diss., Jerusalem, 1993), 129–248; (incl. supp. bibl. of Bergman's publications and secondary sources, 490–591); Z. Bar-On (ed.), *On Shmuel Hugo Bergman* (1986); W. Kluback, *Courageous Universality – the Work of Schmuel Hugo Bergman*, (1992); Z. Maor, "*Mistikah Yeẓirah ve-Shivah el ha-Yahadut: Ḥug Prag bi-Teḥilat ha-Me'ah ha-Esrim*" (diss., Heb. Univ., 2005); M. Schwarz, *Hagut Yehudit Nokhaḥ ha-Tarbut ha-Klalit* (1976), 145–64.

[Nathan Rotenstreich / Yehoyada Amir (2nd ed.)]

BERGMANN, ERNST DAVID (1903–1975), Israeli organic chemist. Bergmann was born in Karlsruhe, Germany, the son of Judah *Bergmann. He obtained his doctorate at the University of Berlin and joined the staff of the Chemical Institute of the university. In 1933 he moved to London and began his long and close association with Chaim Weizmann. After working in the Featherstone Laboratories in London, he was made responsible for the planning of the Daniel Sieff Research Institute in Reḥovot, Palestine, and in 1934 went there to become its scientific director. In 1939 Bergmann went to France to work in the Ministry of Armaments and in 1940 to London, to work in the Grosvenor Laboratories of the Ministry of Supply. Weizmann and Bergmann developed the "catarole process" for making aromatic hydrocarbons from petroleum, and also worked on fermentation and a process for making isoprene. Bergmann returned in 1946 to the Daniel Sieff Institute and, when this was incorporated in the Weizmann Institute in 1949, was named scientific director. In 1948 he became scientific director of the science department of the Israel Ministry of Defense, a position he held for nearly 20 years. He resigned his position at the Weizmann Institute in 1951 and the following year was appointed professor of organic chemistry at the Hebrew University in Jerusalem. From 1953 to 1966 he was chairman of Israel's Atomic Energy Commission. He was a member of Israel's National Council for Research and Development and the Israel Academy of Sciences and Humanities. In 1968, he was awarded the Israel Prize for Natural Sciences. His output of scientific work covered a wide range of topics, including polycyclic aromatic hydrocarbons, carcinogenic agents, the addition of sodium to double bonds, dipole moments, molecular rearrangements, photochemistry, and insecticides. Bergmann and W. Schlenk wrote *Ausfuehrliches Lehrbuch der organischen Chemie* (2 vols., 1932–38; Bergmann's name was deleted from the title page). In 1948 he published *The Chemistry of Acetylene Compounds* and *Isomerisation of Organic Compounds.*

BIBLIOGRAPHY: *Israel Journal of Chemistry*, 1 (1963), 323–50 (includes list of publications until 1962); D. Lazar, *Rashim be-Yisrael*, 2 (1955), 211–5.

[Samuel Aaron Miller]

BERGMANN, FELIX ELIEZER (1908–2002), Israeli organic chemist and pharmacologist. Born in Frankfurt on the Oder, Germany, to Hedwig (née Rosenzweig) and Dr. Judah Bergmann, who was a rabbi in Berlin and wrote on Jewish subjects, he received his Ph.D. in organic chemistry in 1933 from the Humboldt University in Berlin. Concurrently, he studied medicine, but received his diploma only after World War II. An active Zionist from his youth, he left for Palestine in 1933.

Bergman, belonged to the founding generation of science in Israel. Together with his eldest brother, Ernst David *Bergmann, he was among the founders of the Sieff Institute in Reḥovot in 1934. Immediately upon his arrival in Israel, he was approached by the *Haganah, to find an explosive that would be safer than the gelignite then in use. Thus, concurrently with his research on polycyclic carcinogens at the Sieff Institute, he developed an efficient industrial method for producing the explosive PETN, nicknamed in Hebrew "Ten." His devotion to scientific research was rivaled only by his dedication to the security of Israel. He conducted weapons research for the Haganah, developing, with a team of brilliant young Jewish scientists he recruited abroad, rocket fuel for the first locally made rockets, which were used effectively in the War of Independence. He was a key-figure in the founding of Ḥemed, the Army Science Corps, before the establishment of the State; after its dissolution, he continued as adviser to the Ministry of Defense and the Biological Research Institute in Nes Ẓiyyonah. Bergmann was also a scientific advisor to the chemical and pharmaceutical industries. In 1950 he joined the newly founded Hebrew University and Hadassah Medical School in Jerusalem, where he established the Department of Pharmacology (1956) and its teaching curriculum. Bergmann served as head of department until his retirement (1976). His background in both chemistry and medicine enabled him to engage in a broad spectrum of research areas, ranging from organic chemistry to biochemistry, and from pharmacology to physiology and neurology. Already during World War II, he was instrumental in synthesizing an anti-malarial drug for the British army. Notable among his varied fields of research was his extensive work on the function of the neurotransmitter acetylcholine, particularly in the elucidation of the mechanism of action of its degrading enzyme, acetylcholinesterase. Later on, he was engaged in the characterization of the activity of xanthine oxidase, another enzyme of major biological and medical importance. He trained generations of Ph.D. and M.Sc. students in chemistry, pharmacology, and biology who later held key positions in universities and in industrial research. Bergmann was a member of the Israeli Academy of Sciences.

[Hanna Scolnicov (2nd ed.)]

BERGMANN, JUDAH (1874–1956), rabbi and author. Born in Brzezany (Galicia), Bergmann served as rabbi at Karlsruhe and Frankfurt on the Oder and from 1908 with the Berlin Jewish community. Bergmann took an early interest in Jewish scholarship and published various articles on Jewish history and folklore in Jewish scholarly journals. Among his published works are *Juedische Apologetik im neutestamentlichen Zeitalter* (1908), in which he described the self-defense of Palestinian

Judaism against emerging Christianity; *Legenden der Juden* (1919), a study on the nature and sources of *aggadah*; *Ha-Am ve-Ruḥo* (1938), studies and essays on the problems of scholarship and life; *Ha-Ẓedakah be-Yisrael* (1944), a study on the history and institutions of charity among the Jews; and *Ha-Folklor ha-Yehudi* (1953), about the popular knowledge, beliefs, characteristics, and customs of Jewish people. He was one of the founders of the Freie Juedische Volkshochschule in Berlin. When the Nazis seized power in 1933, he emigrated to Jerusalem. His son was E.D. *Bergmann.

[Abraham Meir Habermann]

BERGMANN, MAX (1886–1944), chemist, best known for his research in leathers. Bergmann was born in Fuerth, Bavaria. He obtained his doctorate in 1911 at Berlin, where he became the assistant to the organic chemist Emil Fischer. In 1920, Bergmann was appointed head of chemistry at the Kaiser-Wilhelm Institut fuer Faserstoff-Forschung in Berlin, and in 1921, director of the Kaiser-Wilhelm Institut fuer Lederforschung in Dresden and professor of the Technische Hochschule there. He held these positions until forced to leave Germany in 1934. His main area of research was in the chemistry and structure of proteins. Bergmann went to the United States where he became a member of the Rockefeller Institute for Medical Research.

BIBLIOGRAPHY: *Journal of the Chemical Society* (1945), 716–8; H.T. Clarke, in: *Science*, 102 (1945), 168–70; J.C. Poggendorff, *Biographisch-litterarisches Handwoerterbuch der exakten Naturwissenschaften*, 7B (1967), 335–7.

[Samuel Aaron Miller]

BERGMANN, RICHARD (1920–1970), table tennis player, winner of seven world championships, including four singles crowns. Born in Vienna, Bergmann began playing table tennis at age 12 and won his first world championship in 1936 at the age of 16 as a member of the Austrian Swaythling Cup team. He also won the bronze medal that year in the men's singles event. A year later in 1937, Bergmann became and remains the youngest player in history to win the gold medal in the men's singles competition; he won the silver in 1938. When the Nazis invaded Austria in March, Bergmann fled to England. In 1939, he won his second world singles crown and the world doubles title with Victor *Barna. Following World War II, he reclaimed his title in 1948 as world singles champion and won the bronze in doubles again with Barna. In 1949 Bergmann and Barna helped England win the bronze in team competition, and Bergmann won the bronze in doubles with Tage Flisberg. In 1950 Bergmann won his fourth world championship singles 13 years after his first and led England to a team bronze. In 1952 he won silver in doubles (with Johnny Leach) as well as in team competition, and his seventh and final world championship was in team play in 1953. Bergmann won the bronze in singles and team in 1954, and his final medal was bronze with England in 1955. Bergmann also finished first in the English singles championships six times and the doubles four times. Bergmann became the world's first professional table tennis player in the mid-1950s, touring extensively with the Harlem Globetrotters basketball team. Sometimes referred to as Richard the Lionhearted, Bergman was the author of *Twenty-One Up* (1950).

[Elli Wohlgelernter (2nd ed.)]

BERGNER, ELISABETH (1897–1986), actress. Born as Ella Ettel in the Galician town of Drohobycz (today Ukrainian Drogobyc), she came in her youth to Vienna, where she studied. She acted there and in Berlin for Victor Barnowsky, Max Reinhardt, and her future husband, Paul Czinner. Especially as Rosalind in *As You Like It* on stage and in many films of the 1920s and early 1930s, she gained an international reputation, bolstered by her interpretation of the title role of Shaw's *Saint Joan*. Her androgynous type, which combined sex appeal with a female aspiration for emancipation, made her an idol on stage and screen in interwar Europe. Bergner toured the Continent and made her first appearance in Great Britain in Margaret Kennedy's *Escape Me Never* (1933). This was an immediate success, which she repeated two years later in New York. She remained there as an émigré until 1950, when she returned to London. Under the direction of her husband, Paul Czinner, she appeared in a number of films. Her films included *Der traeumende Mund* and *Stolen Life* (1939). She was not a success in Hollywood films. After World War II she toured Germany and Austria. In 1978 she published her memoirs, *Bewundert und viel gescholten – Elisabeth Bergners unordentlichen Erinnerungen*.

ADD. BIBLIOGRAPHY: K. Voelker, *Elisabeth Bergner* (Ger., 1990); D. Wuensche: *Elisabeth Bergner.* Dokumente ihres Lebens (1990); Historisches Museum der Stadt Wien, *Unsere schwarze Rose* (catalogue, 1993).

[Pnina Nave / Marcus Pyka (2nd ed.)

BERGNER, HERZ (1907–1970), Yiddish novelist. The younger brother of Melech *Ravitch, Bergner grew up in Radimno, Galicia. After a short stay in Warsaw, he immigrated to Melbourne in 1938. From 1928 he published short stories in leading Yiddish periodicals in Europe, Israel, Australia and the United States. In Warsaw he published the collection *Shtubn un Gasn* ("Houses and Streets," 1935) and was co-editor of *Shriftn* (1936). His novels, *Tsvishn Himel un Vaser* (*Between Sky and Sea*, 1946) dealing with a boatload of Jewish refugees, and *Likht un Shotn* (1960; *Light and Shadow*, 1963) describing the struggle of a Jewish family for acceptance in an Australian community, were translated into English. Bergner's Australian short stories, especially his volume *Vu der Emes Shteyt Ayn* ("Where the Truth Lies," 1966), realistically mirror various aspects in the life of Jewish immigrants in Melbourne.

BIBLIOGRAPHY: LNYL, 1 (1956), 379; M. Ravitch, *Muyn Leksikon* (1945), 43–45. **ADD. BIBLIOGRAPHY:** I. Kahan, in: *Australian Jewish Historical Society*, 7/4 (1973), 286–90; I. Turkov-Grudberg, in: *Di Goldene Keyt*, 56 (1966), 248–50.

[Sol Liptzin]

BERGNER YOSSL (**Yosef**; 1920–), Israeli painter. Born in Vienna, the son of the singer Fania Bergner and the Yiddish poet Melech *Ravitch. Bergner immigrated to Australia in 1937 and studied at the art school of the National Gallery of Victoria in Melbourne. He arrived to Israel in 1950 and settled in Safed. During his career Bergner exhibited his work all over the world. He represented Israeli art in international exhibitions such as the Biennale in Venice and the Biennale of Sao Paulo. In addition to painting Bergner produced book illustrations and designed theater sets and costumes for the Yiddish and Hebrew stage, particularly for plays written by Nissim *Aloni. In 1980 Bergner was awarded the Israel Prize. Bergner is married to the painter Audrey Bergner.

In his unique way Bergner remained a Jewish cosmopolitan refugee in spite of his Israeli citizenship and spending most of his life in Israel. Bergner's art consists of a large variety of subjects: Jewish, Australian aborigines, children of Safed, wall paintings, masks, angels and kings, still lifes, toys and flowers, paintings inspired by the Bird's-Head *Haggadah*, Kafka's images, Brighton Beach, chairs and tables, Zionists figures and pioneer images (*Pioneer's Funeral*, 1977, Israel Museum, Jerusalem). Bergner described himself as someone who has to express everything that goes through his head, in a very eclectic way.

Bergner's style moves freely between extremes, from compact compositions and minimal coloration to richness and dramatic style. He always maintained a rare combination between figurative description and surrealistic atmosphere. At the heart of his approach lies the understanding that the visual image is a more or less aesthetic representation of the meaning beyond it.

More then once Bergner has been defined as a literary painter, in his case meaning a painter who is as comfortable with world literature as he is familiar with Jewish literature. As the son of a Yiddish poet, the stories of Mendele Mokher Seforim (Sholem Yankev *Abramovitsh), *Shalom Aleichem, and I.L. *Peretz were a part of his life. At the same time Bergner's art has been an inspiration to many Israeli poets like Dan *Pagis, Tuvia Rivner, and Ḥayim Hefer. They were drawn to the characteristic images of Bergner's art, referring to them as an integral part of their poems.

During the years 1971–72 Bergner dealt with the theme of the Crucifixion. The cross looms high in the foreground of a cloudy sky. Instead of a human being crucified there are graters or a white fabric. The atmosphere in these paintings is dramatic and magical (*Messenger – The Dismantled Cross*, 1972, Private Collection, Tel Aviv).

Bergner's paintings are very popular among religious people because of the absence of human figures and the focus on objects.

BIBLIOGRAPHY: C. Rubin (ed.), *Yosl Bergner – A Retrospective* (2000).

[Ronit Steinberg (2nd ed.)]

BERGSON (**Berkson**), assimilated Warsaw family, descended from the court factor Samuel *Zbitkower (d. 1800). Most of the children of his second wife, Judith Levi of Frankfurt on the Oder, were given a secular education, and converted to Christianity, founding the Fraenkel, Oesterreicher, and Flatau families which played an important role in Polish economic life. BER (Berek), Zbitkower's son by his first wife, alone remained Jewish, and under Prussian rule adopted the family name Sonnenberg. He and his wife, Tamar (Temerl), built a synagogue in the Praga suburb of Warsaw in 1807. Their home became a meeting place for the Ḥasidim in Poland. Their sons, Jacob, Leopold, and Michael, took the name Bergson (or Berkson, "son of Berek"). Members of the family included JOSEPH BERGSON (1812–?), a lecturer in medicine at Warsaw University (1841–61), and the musician MICHAEL *BERGSON (1820–1898), father of the most celebrated member of the family, the philosopher HENRI *BERGSON. Active in the Warsaw community was MICHAEL BERGSON, the son of Leopold, who served as president of the community from 1896 to 1918. Other family members were bankers and manufacturers.

BIBLIOGRAPHY: A.N. Frenk, *Meshumodim in Poyln*, 1 (1923); I. Schipper (ed.), *Żydzi w Polsce odrodzonej*, 1 (1932), 481; J. Shatzky, *Di Geshikhte fun Yidn in Varshe*, 3 vols. (1947–53), index; A. Levinson, *Toledot Yehudei Varshah* (1953), 204; EG, 1 (1953), 235–54. **ADD. BIBLIOGRAPHY:** A. Guterman, *Kehillat Varshah bein Shetei Milḥamot Olam* (1977), Index.

[Nathan Michael Gelber]

BERGSON, ABRAM (1914–2003), U.S. economist and expert on the Soviet Union. Born in Baltimore, Maryland, Bergson earned his B.A. degree from Johns Hopkins University in 1933 and his M.A. and Ph.D. from Harvard in 1935 and 1940, respectively. While he was a graduate student, he and his brother Gustav, a physicist, decided to change their name to Bergson because they felt the name they were born with – Burk – did not convey their Jewish heritage.

From 1937 to 1940 Bergson was an instructor at Harvard, and from 1940 to 1942 assistant professor at the University of Texas. He spent 1942 to 1946 as an economist in various agencies of the U.S. government, and as chief of the division for the Office of Strategic Services, was a U.S. delegate to the Moscow Reparations Conference (1945). For the next ten years he was at Columbia University but returned to Harvard in 1956 as professor of economics, where he remained for the rest of his career.

He began his academic life as a theorist, publishing an extremely influential paper at the age of 23 on the measurement of well-being across society. His best-known work later became linked with that of Paul A. *Samuelson, a classmate at Harvard who won the Nobel in economic science. The Bergson-Samuelson social welfare function, which combines individual gauges of well-being, has been a fixture in economic analysis for decades.

Bergson was director of the Russian Research Center (now the Davis Center) from 1964 to 1968 and acting director from 1969 to 1970. He remained involved in activities at the center until 2002, frequently leading off the question-and-answer period at lectures and symposia. His knowledge of Soviet economic policies and practices qualified him as the outstanding expert before congressional committees dealing with the Soviet economy. As the world's leading authority on the subject, he was consulted and cited far more than any other expert about the assessment and evaluation of Soviet economic performance. After the Soviet Union collapsed in 1991 Soviet scholars, once forced to adjust their findings to the "Party line," were free to express their esteem for Bergson's work. "They would make pilgrimages to see him as if they were coming to consult the oracle," observed Marshall Goldman, associate director of the Davis Center for Russian and Eurasian Research.

In 1983 Bergson received the Distinguished Fellow award of the American Economic Association.

Bergson was the editor of *Economic Trends in the Soviet Union* (1963). He wrote extensively on his special field of interest; his published works include *The Structure of Soviet Wages* (1944), *Soviet National Income and Product in 1937* (1953), *Soviet Economic Growth, Conditions and Perspectives* (1953), *Soviet National Income and Product 1940–48* (1954), *The Real National Income of Soviet Russia Since 1928* (1961), *The Economics of Soviet Planning* (1964), *Essays in Normative Economics* (1966), *Planning and Productivity Under Soviet Socialism* (1968), *Productivity and the Social System: The U.S.S.R. and the West* (1978), *Welfare, Planning, and Employment* (1982), and *The Soviet Economy: Towards the Year 2000* (co-editor with Herbert Levine, 1983).

[Joachim O. Ronall / Ruth Beloff (2nd ed.)]

BERGSON, HENRI LOUIS (1859–1941), French philosopher. His father, Michael *Bergson, came from a distinguished Warsaw family; his mother from England. He was born in Paris and from 1881 taught philosophy at the Angers Lycée and subsequently at Clermont-Ferrand, where he gave his famous lectures on laughter, and where, after long meditations in the countryside, he first devised the idea of the vital, continuous, and generative impulse of the universe. From the age of 25, Bergson devoted himself to elaborating this theory in various forms. In 1889 he returned to Paris, published his Ph.D. thesis *Essai sur les données immédiates de la conscience* (*Time and Free Will*, 1910), and lectured at the Lycée Henri IV and the Ecole Normale Supérieure. In 1900 he was appointed professor of philosophy at the Collège de France. His lectures were popular and were attended by the elite of Paris society. These lectures, like his books, especially *L'Evolution créatrice* (1907; *Creative Evolution*, 1911), were distinguished by their lucid and brilliant style and established his fame in France and throughout the world. In 1914 he became a member of the French Academy and in 1928 was awarded the Nobel Prize for literature. Bergson was also politically active, especially in foreign affairs, and headed a French delegation to the U.S. He was president of the League of Nations' Committee for Intellectual Cooperation. In 1940, after the French surrender to the Nazis, Bergson returned all his decorations and awards, and, rejecting the French authorities' offer to exclude him from the edicts against the Jews, queued for many hours to register as a Jew although he was weak and ill. In his latter years he was attracted to Catholicism but remained a Jew in order to maintain his identification with the persecuted. He died a Jew in 1941.

Most of his works deal with the conception and explication of the notions of "duration" and "movement," not as static concepts defined by the mind but as experiences, conceived by the intuition when it is freed from the limitations which the intellectual consciousness imposes upon the conceiver and the conceived. According to Bergson, the dynamic element of the duration, the flowing time, is the sole penetrator of real existence. "Time" abolishes the static world of the conscious mind and the concept of "duration" may be defined as the continual change which takes place in time. This change is not transcendentally motivated but results from an inner energy – the vital impulse (*élan vital*) which derives from an unlimited source. The actual duration of the vital impulse is the basic element of the universe, while matter and awareness are only momentary manifestations or creations of the central stream. The consciousness can grasp the essence of reality, both in its primary purity as a duration and in its consolidation and objectification as matter in space. In the same manner consciousness can also reach self-knowledge in two different ways: through intellectual static self-consciousness, and through an intimate awareness of its essence as a conscious duration, a vital and fluctuating spirit, regenerating and developing continuously. From this it follows that the factor fashioning consciousness is memory. Memory comprises the duration for it accumulates all past achievements and within it "the past grows into the present." Through the intuition, which is the essence of the memory, man grasps his personal essence as a vital and conscious duration, and, similarly, grasps the creative duration, which is absolute reality.

Bergson's view also appears in his theories on the functions of instinct, intellect, and intuition. Life evolution advances in three directions: vegetative, instinctive, and rational. The instinct is the capability of utilizing organic instruments, but this function is merely a blind practical knowledge. The intellect has the ability of execution and of utilizing inorganic instruments, and it introduces, therefore, the knowledge of the qualities of objects, accompanied by self-knowledge. When the intellect has time enough to develop its knowledge, it judges all objects as if they were inorganic instruments, thus viewing the living reality itself in a mechanical, devitalized mirror. This perverted conception can be corrected by intuition, which is a developed instinct with self-awareness. Bergson conceived the intuition as the only means by which it is possible to inject a primary flexibility into fossilized scientific methods and draw them closer to reality.

Bergson recognized that the potential capability for immediately grasping reality is actualized only in a few select men. Strong fetters of habit tie man down to the social, moral, and conceptual reality of his environment, and only an elite few are capable of extricating themselves. Therefore, Bergson admired the great mystics (see his *Les deux sources de la morale et de la religion*, 1932; *Two Sources of Morality and Religion*, 1935).

BIBLIOGRAPHY: A.D. Lindsay, *The Philosophy of Bergson*, 1911; H. Wildon Carr, *Henri Bergson: The Philosophy of Change*, 1912; Hugh S. Elliot, *Modern Science and the Illusions of Professor Bergson*, 1912; V. Jankelevitch, *Henri Bergson*, 1931; A. Keller, *Eine Philosophie des Lebens* (1914); J. Maritain, *La philosophie Bergsonienne* (1914); A. Thibaudet, *Le Bergsonisme* (1923); J. Chevalier, *Bergson* (Fr., 1948); A. Pallière, *Bergson et le Judaïsme* (1932); I. Benrubi, *Souvenirs sur Henri Bergson* (1942); B. Scharfstein, *Roots of Bergson's Philosophy* (1943); A. Cresson, *Bergson, sa vie, son oeuvre* (1950); R.M. Mossé-Bastide, *Bergson éducateur* (1955); idem, *Bergson et Plotin* (1959); I.W. Alexander, *Bergson, Philosopher of Reflection* (1957). **ADD. BIBLIOGRAPHY:** B. Gilson, *L'individualité dans la philosophie de Bergson* (1985); G. Deleuze, *Bergsonism* (1988); F. Burwick and P. Douglas (eds.), *The Crisis in Modernism: Bergson and the Vitalist Controversy* (1992); K. Ansell-Pearson, *Philosophy and the Adventure of the Virtual: Bergson and the Time of Life* (2002); L. Lawlor, *The Challenge of Bergsonism: Phenomenology, Ontology, Ethics* (2003).

[Pepita Haezrahi]

BERGSON, MICHAEL (1820–1898), Polish pianist and composer, born in Warsaw. He was the father of the French philosopher Henri *Bergson. Michael's opera *Luisa di Montfort* was produced in Florence (1847) and in Hamburg (1849); his operetta *Qui va à la chasse, perd sa place* in Paris (1859). For ten years he was piano professor, then director of the Geneva Conservatory. In 1873 he settled in London, where he collaborated with M. Hast in the compilation and editing of synagogue music. A pupil of Chopin, he composed in Chopinesque style, for which Schumann criticized him. One of his works, *Scena ed Aria*, is still widely played by military bands.

BIBLIOGRAPHY: Baker, Biog Dict; Grove, Dict; Sendrey, Music, indexes.

[Dora Leah Sowden]

BERGSTEIN, FANIA (1908–1950), Hebrew poet. Born in Szczuczyn, near Lomza, Poland, she received a Hebrew and a Russian education. In her youth she became active in the Zionist youth movement He-Ḥalutz ha-Ẓa'ir, immigrated to Palestine in 1930, and joined kibbutz Gevat. Her books include *Baẓir* (1939), poems; *Avim Ḥolefot* (1950), poems; *Asif* (1955), collected poems; and *Reshimot* (1952), collected prose, edited by M. Poznański. Among her ten volumes of poems, stories, and plays for children is *Tekhelet ve-Adom* (1961). A list of her works that have been translated into English appears in Goell, Bibliography, index.

BIBLIOGRAPHY: *Fania* (Heb., 1950), memorial brochure, issued by Kibbutz Gevat; N. Goren, *Demuyyot be-Sifrutenu* (1953), 144–9; Y. Harari, *Ishah va-Em be-Yisrael* (1959), 455–7. **ADD. BIBLIOGRAPHY:** S. Even Shoshan, *Fania Bergstein: Parashat Ḥayyim vi-Yeẓirah* (1971).

[Getzel Kressel]

°**BERGSTRAESSER, GOTTHELF** (1886–1933), German Semitic scholar and linguist. Bergstraesser was born in Oberlosa (Thueringen). During World War I, while professor at the University of Constantinople, he studied the spoken dialects in Palestine and Syria on which he later published several scholarly works: *Sprachatlas von Syrien und Palaestina* (1915); *Zum arabischen Dialekt von Damaskus* (1924); *Neuaramaeische Maerchen und andere Texte aus Maʿlula* (1915); *Glossar des neuaramaeischen Dialekts von Maʿlula* (1921). Bergstraesser began to work on an edition of Gesenius' *Hebraeische Grammatik* of which only two parts appeared (*Einleitung, Schrift-und Lautlehre*, 1918; *Verbum*, 1929). He also edited a Hebrew reader *Hebraeische Lesestuecke aus dem Alten Testament* (1920). In addition to the linguistic studies which earned him international repute (*Einfuehrung in die semitischen Sprachen*, 1928), Bergstraesser engaged in research on textual criticism and reading of the Koran, Arabic translations from Greek, especially of Galen, and on Islamic law. A fierce opponent of Nazism, Bergstraesser spoke out strongly against antisemitism.

BIBLIOGRAPHY: M. Meyerhof, in: *Isis*, 25 (1936), 60–62 (Eng.); H. Gottschalk, in: *Der Islam*, 24 (1937), 185–91 (with partial bibliography).

[Martin Meir Plessner]

BERGTHEIL, JONAS (1819–1902), pioneer in Natal, South Africa. Bergtheil emigrated to Cape Colony from Bavaria in 1834 and moved in 1843 to Durban, where he formed a company to bring settlers from Europe and grow cotton for the first time in South Africa. To encourage immigration to South Africa he took a Zulu to Germany in 1847 as an example of the indigenous population and recruited 188 non-Jewish settlers whom he took to Natal. The 47 families concerned were each given 250 acres of land at New Germany in the Pinetown district some 15 mi. (24 km.) from Durban. Although cotton growing was initially a failure, the settlement prospered. Bergtheil was also director of a company which built the first railway line in South Africa, a short stretch starting in Durban. He was elected in 1857 to the first legislative council in Natal, holding the seat until 1866. He was one of the founders of the Cape Town Hebrew Congregation in 1841. In 1866 he left to settle in England.

BIBLIOGRAPHY: G. Saron and L. Hotz (eds.), *Jews in South Africa* (1955), index; *Jewish Affairs*, 9 (Johannesburg, 1954), no. 6.

[Louis Hotz]

BERIḤAH (Heb. בְּרִיחָה; "flight"), name of an organized underground operation moving Jews out of Poland, Hungary, Czechoslovakia, Romania, Yugoslavia, the Baltic countries, and the U.S.S.R. into Central and Southern Europe between 1944 and 1948 as a step toward their – mostly "illegal" – immigration to Palestine: also name of the spontaneous mass movement of Jewish survivors from Europe toward Ereẓ Israel.

In 1939, Jewish refugees fleeing from the Germans were illegally crossing frontiers into Soviet-occupied Poland and thence to Lithuania or, in the south, to Romania. While this movement was in the main chaotic, Zionist, Bundist, and Orthodox groups provided some organized nuclei. The same holds true of Jews fleeing from Slovakia to Hungary in 1942, and from Hungary back into Slovakia and into Romania in 1944. At the end of World War II, tens of thousands of Jews found that they could not remain in the countries of Central Europe either because of their memories of the *Holocaust and the destruction of their homes or because of the antisemitic atmosphere that prevailed in these countries. A mass migration of the remnants of the Holocaust began. It was partially spontaneous and partially organized as an attempt to find a way to reach Palestine. The first initiators of the organized Beriḥah came from among the leaders of Jewish resistance groups, partisans, and organizers of Zionist underground groups who already had participated in illegal border crossings in Nazi-occupied Eastern Europe during the war years.

In 1944, with the liberation of Rovno in Volhynia and Vilna by the Soviet Army in February and April, respectively, illegal groups of former Jewish partisans were formed independently of each other. Their aim was to take out the remnants of the Jewish population and bring them to Ereẓ Israel. They were joined by Zionist groups returning from Soviet Asia, and met in Lublin in December 1944 under the leadership of Abba *Kovner. In January 1945, they were joined by the remnants of the Warsaw ghetto fighters under Yiẓḥak *Cukierman, and founded the Beriḥah organization under the leadership of Kovner. The first groups were sent to Romania in the middle of January 1945, in the hope of reaching Ereẓ Israel with the help of emissaries (*sheliḥim*) of the *yishuv* staying at the time in Bucharest. During the first months after the war, before the borders of Central European countries were redrawn and closed and when millions of *Displaced Persons were returning to their homes, the movement of Jews searching for a way to Palestine also began. An event connected with this mass movement was the "Rescue Train," which, under the auspices of the International Red Cross, set out for Poland to return to Romania Jews who had been deported by the Germans. This project succeeded in returning from Poland to Romania about 5,000 Jews, including many children. But hopes of reaching Palestine from Romania had soon to be discarded, and in May, Kovner had instead established transit points in Hungary and Yugoslavia, moving his people toward Italy, which he himself reached in July. Polish Jews were now coming via Slovakia to Budapest, and thence to Graz in Austria, hoping to cross the Italian border from there. In August, however, the British occupation forces stationed there closed the border and 12,000 people were stranded in the Graz area. They managed to cross the border in small groups only in the winter of 1945/46.

A center (*Merkaz la-Golah*) for smuggling Jews into Italy from the liberated concentration camps in Germany and Austria was established by Palestinian Jewish soldiers stationed in Europe, both from the *Jewish Brigade and from other army units. It started its activities in June 1945 and brought in some 15,000 people till August, when British forces sealed the border. Financing in this early period was from *Jewish Agency funds. The first attempt to organize the migration of Jewish survivors throughout Europe was made at a meeting of Beriḥah activists in Bratislava in March 1946. A central committee of the Beriḥah was chosen with Mordechai Surkis from the Jewish Brigade and Pinḥas Rashish (d. 1978), head of the Palestine aid delegation to Poland, as its heads. This committee exercised an ill-defined and shadowy control over Beriḥah activities in Europe until the end of 1946.

From August 1945 onward, a movement started out of Poland into the Displaced Persons (DP) camps of Czechoslovakia; the various routes led to the U.S. zone in Austria and into Bavaria. From October onward an alternative route operated via Szczeczyn (Stettin), Berlin, and the British zone (northern Germany) to the U.S. zone in the south. Transit through Czechoslovakia, Austria, and Hungary was controlled by Levi Kopelevich (Argov), a *shali'aḥ* from Palestine, who from March 1946 headed the Beriḥah secretariat in Bratislava. Movements were coordinated with the Beriḥah in Poland under Isser Ben-Ẓvi, a *shali'aḥ* who had taken over in October 1945. In the winter of 1945/46, funds began to be received from the *American Jewish Joint Distribution Committee for food and clothing for stranded refugees. The control over Beriḥah exercised heretofore through Surkis was now acknowledged to be in the hands of the "Mosad le-Aliyah Bet" (or "Mosad," center for "illegal" immigration) in Palestine, whose head, Shaul *Avigur, moved his office to Paris in 1946.

The movement was largely organized by Zionist youth movements whose representatives in Poland formed the Beriḥah "center," to which the commander was responsible. The movements and Zionist parties formed groups, many of which were influenced by the kibbutz idea and therefore known as "kibbutzim." The groups were directed to border towns where Beriḥah teams accommodated them in "stores" (temporary lodgings). There they were provided with slips of paper containing a code ("*parol*") and sent to the actual border station ("point") where the local Beriḥah team smuggled them across. Until 1946, forged Red Cross documents were employed to identify people as Greek refugees. In Czechoslovakia, an informal agreement was obtained not to hamper the movement of Jews, and UNRRA and the Czech government paid the train fares from the Polish border to either Bratislava or As on the Czech-German frontier. On the Szczeczyn-Berlin route, Soviet or Polish truck drivers were bribed into smuggling people in, and exit from Berlin to the British zone was effected either through UNRRA officials whose sympathy was obtained or with the help of forged documents. From October 1945 onward, the operation in Austria was under Asher Ben-Nathan, and in Germany under Ephraim Frank, both *sheliḥim* from Palestine. In Vienna a series of transit camps were clustered around the Rothschild Hospital, receiving refugees passing from Bratislava to the U.S. zone of Austria. From the U.S. zone of Austria transit was effected either to Italy (until about May 1946), directed by Issachar Haimovich, or to the U.S. zone in Germany.

The U.S. Army did not encourage entry of Jewish refugees into their zones. However, poor conditions in DP camps in these zones had caused an investigation to be made by Earl G. Harrison in August, 1945, and the report that was published on Sept. 30, 1945, reflected badly on the army. To avoid arousing public opinion in the United States the army acquiesced in Jewish refugee movements, provided no very large numbers were involved. Simon H. Rifkind and Philip S. Bernstein, advisers on Jewish affairs to the U.S. command in Germany, played a large part in persuading the army to maintain its tolerant attitude.

The murder of 41 Jews in a pogrom at *Kielce (Poland) on July 4, 1946, created a wave of panic among Polish Jews, who now included the 150,000 repatriates from the U.S.S.R. who came out from February 1946 onward (before that there had been only 80,000 Jews in Poland). Pressure was exerted on Beriḥah by panic-stricken Jews to take them out of Poland. In July this was still done by the usual illegal means. But the Polish government, which arrived at the conclusion that it would not be able to restrain the outbursts against the Jews, saw their exodus from Poland as a solution to the problem. In late July, negotiations conducted by Yiẓḥak Cukierman with Polish government agencies led to an oral understanding whereby Jews were allowed to leave Poland without hindrance through the Silesian border into Czechoslovakia. Simultaneously (on July 26) the Czech government, largely through the influence of Jan Masaryk, the foreign minister, decided to open its frontier to Jews fleeing from Poland. In the three months of July, August, and September 1946 more than 70,000 Jews fled through Czechoslovakia. Transport was paid for by the Czechs, against an UNRRA promise to return the money later; food was obtained largely from the JDC and UNRRA. The exodus of those months was joined by 15,000 Hungarian Jews and some 1,000 Romanian and Czech Jews. Despite Polish insistence that only the Silesian route should be used after the July agreement, Beriḥah continued to send also large numbers of Jews via Szczeczyn to Berlin, a route which was controlled by Jewish Brigade soldiers. Others went from Szczeczyn to Luebeck and Hanover in the British zone by train or boat through PUR, the Polish agency expelling Germans from Poland: the Jews posed as Germans and were thus enabled to leave by "being expelled." The total number leaving Poland from July 1945 to October 1946 was estimated at 110,000, excluding PUR and a large number of people who came out not with the organized Beriḥah but with professional smugglers, Jews as well as non-Jews. From the beginnings of the Beriḥah until October 1946 no less than 180,000 people were involved in the migratory movements.

After some hesitation, and due again largely to the intervention of Rabbi Philip Bernstein, the U.S. Army allowed the large scale move into the U.S. zones of Germany and Austria to take place in the summer of 1946. Movements out of Germany into Italy were limited, especially during the second half of 1946, until the route was reestablished in early 1947 through the Valle Aurina. In early 1947 the Polish government terminated the arrangement at the border; movement via Szczeczyn had almost come to a standstill in November 1946. During 1947, less than 10,000 Jews managed to leave Poland via Beriḥah routes. In Germany, Beriḥah cooperated with the committees of Jewish DPs to arrange for social and political absorption of the refugees into the camps. Beriḥah's orientation was clearly Zionist, but there were refugees who declared their preference for migration to countries other than Palestine.

The Beriḥah movement from the Soviet Union was a special case. Many Jews who had lived in prewar Poland left the U.S.S.R. with their families as part of the Polish repatriation program. The position of veteran citizens of the Soviet Union was a more difficult one. Nonetheless, activities of the Beriḥah were organized by a number of bodies, which, inter alia, brought out many Lubavitch Ḥasidim from the Soviet Union. When the new Soviet border was definitely sealed in 1946, the Soviet authorities began to seize the Beriḥah organizers, some of whom were arrested and sentenced to long prison terms. At the end of 1946 a meeting of Beriḥah commanders was held at Basle during the 22nd Zionist Congress. Shaul Avigur, head of the "Mosad," was present. There a new European commander of the Beriḥah, Ephraim Dekel, a former head of *Haganah Intelligence in Palestine, was nominated. Under Dekel Beriḥah became more closely linked with the "Mosad," but the numbers coming in from Eastern Europe were falling. In the spring of 1947 economic crisis and fear of antisemitism caused a panic flight of some 15,000 Romanian Jews to Hungary and Austria. On April 21, 1947, the U.S. Army decreed that no more Jews would be accepted into existing DP camps, but Beriḥah poured the refugees into the Viennese transit camps until the American authorities relented and allowed the people entrance into camps in the U.S. zone in contravention of the decree. The tension in Palestine between the *Haganah and the dissident underground organizations, *Irgun Ẓeva'i Le'ummi (IẒL) and *Loḥamei Ḥerut Israel (Leḥi), sometimes influenced the work of the Beriḥah as well, and in September 1947 a Beriḥah man was murdered at a "point" near Innsbruck by IẒL members. In general, however, the *Revisionists were part of the current of the Beriḥah and the "illegal" immigration to Palestine.

In 1948, Meir Sapir took over from Dekel as Beriḥah commander, and Beriḥah was slowly wound up, though Beriḥah points still operated on certain eastern borders in 1949. In the west, Beriḥah points existed on the German-French and, briefly, on the Belgian, frontier, and the 4,500 *Exodus* passengers passed through these in June 1947. However, entry into France was regulated by the "Mosad" rather than Beriḥah. The total number of people who left Eastern Europe between 1944 and 1948 can be estimated at about 250,000, and of these about 80% at least came with the organized Beriḥah. The Beriḥah was a prime factor in the struggle for the establishment of the Jewish State from 1945 to 1948. It dramatically underscored

President Truman's demand for a speedy admission of 100,000 Jewish refugees to Palestine (August 1945) and was reflected in the conclusions of the Anglo-American Committee (May 1946). It created a reservoir of people from which came the masses of immigrants that fought together with the *yishuv* to open the gates of Palestine to Jewish immigration and to establish the State of Israel.

BIBLIOGRAPHY: Y. Bauer, *Flight and Rescue* (1970); J. and D. Kimche, *The Secret Roads* (1954); *"Brycha" 1945–1948* (Pol., 1950?), an album; E. Dekel, *Bi-Netivei ha-"Beriḥah"* (1958); idem, in: *Seridei Ḥerev* (1963); A. Gefen, *Poreẓei ha-Maḥsomim* (1961); L.W. Schwarz, *The Redeemers* (1953), 232–45; R. Korchak, *Lehavot ba-Efer* (1965), 303–7.

[Yehuda Bauer]

BERINSKI, LEV (1939–), Yiddish poet. Berinski was born in Kauschan (Bessarabia) and became one of the most inventive of the post-Holocaust Yiddish poets. During World War II his family fled to Tadzhikistan, returning to Moldavia in 1945. In 1963 Berinski moved to Smolensk in order to study German, then to Moscow to study poetry and poetic translation. Initially he wrote poems in Russian, then later in Yiddish, and translated into Russian from Romanian, Spanish, German, and Yiddish. In 1991 he immigrated to Israel, and settling in Acre. In 1992 he founded and became the editor of the literary almanac *Naye Vegn*; in 2000 he published an anthology of contemporary literature and became co-editor of *Toplpunkt*, a quarterly journal of literature, art, and social issues. In 1997 he won the David Hofstein and Itzik Manger Prize, the most distinguished prize for Yiddish literature, and the following year he became chair of the *Fareyn fun Yidishe Shraybers un Zhurnalistn in Yisroel*. Berinski's Yiddish work comprises poems and poem cycles, stories, and essays. He is a postmodern poet who expresses the chaos that results from annihilation through collage, montage, intertextuality, quotation, proverb, aphorism, and mathematical formula, thus creating bold metaphors that connect the traditionally Jewish and philosophically enlightened with the surrealistically cosmic, while the whole opens up into the realm of the absurd and ironic. In addition to two volumes of Russian poetry (1992, 1997), he has published several volumes in Yiddish: *Der Zuniker Veltboy* ("Sunny Construction of the World," 1988); *Rendsburger Mikve* ("Rendsburger Ritual Bath," 1994); *Calystegia Sepium* ("Bindweed," 1995; *Fischfang in Venetsye* ("Fishing in Venice," 1996); *Luftblumen* ("Flowers in the Air," 1999).

BIBLIOGRAPHY: I. Fater, in: *Nusakh Ashkenaz in Vort un Klang* (2002), 83–92.

[Astrid Starck (2nd ed.)]

BERIT HA-BIRYONIM (Heb. בְּרִית הַבִּרְיוֹנִים), an underground group operating in Palestine from 1930 to 1933 against the Mandatory regime. Its founder and chief ideologue was Abba *Aḥimeir, and two other leading members were Uri Ẓevi *Greenberg and Yehoshua *Yeivin. The group comprised about 30 active members and a few score of sympathizers. Ideologically the Berit stood on the extreme right of the *Revisionist movement, and in Palestine it dominated the party organ *Ḥazit ha-Am*. The activities of the Berit were of limited scope: it demonstrated against the visit to Palestine of the British Under-Secretary for the Colonies, Drummond Shiels; called for a boycott of the official census; organized the blowing of the Shofar at the end of the Day of Atonement service at the Western Wall; and pulled down the swastika flags from the German Consulates in Jerusalem and Jaffa. Berit ha-Biryonim disintegrated shortly after the murder of *Arlosoroff, as a result of persecution by the Mandatory authorities.

BIBLIOGRAPHY: A. Aḥimeir, *Berit ha-Biryonim* (1972): Y. Aḥimeir, Sh. Shatzki, *Hinnenu Sikarikim* (1978).

[Joseph Nedava]

BERIT SHALOM ("Covenant of Peace"), society founded in Jerusalem in 1925 to foster relations of rapprochement between Jews and Arabs in Palestine, on the basis of a bi-national solution to the conflict between them, with Jews and Arabs having an equal share in the administration regardless of the size of their respective populations (see *Bi-Nationalism). Bi-nationalism for Berit Shalom was not an ideal but a function of reality. The trigger for the establishment of the society was a lecture at the opening of the Hebrew University in Jerusalem by the Orientalist Professor Joseph Horowitz of the University of Frankfurt on the Main. The initiative for founding Berit Shalom came from Arthur *Ruppin. The active members in the society belonged to several groups. The first, which was predominant in the early years, was made up of men who had immigrated to Palestine before World War I and were all (except Ruppin himself) of East European origin, had an academic education, and shared a practical political approach to Zionism. They included, in addition to Ruppin, Dr. Jacob *Thon, Dr. Joseph *Lurie, Dr Yitzḥak Epstein, Haim *Margolis-Kalvaryski, and *Rabbi Binyamin. The second group, which became predominant after 1929, was made up of intellectuals of a Central European liberal background, was much more ideological than the first group, and its members were all strongly influenced by the philosophy of Martin *Buber. They included Prof. Samuel Hugo *Bergmann, Prof. Hans *Kohn, Prof. Gershom *Scholem, Prof. Ernst *Simon, and Dr. Robert Weltsch. Finally there was a group of so-called "Anglo-Saxons," mostly men who were employed by the Palestine Administration, including Edwin Samuel, son of the first High Commissioner to Palestine, Herbert *Samuel, and the attorney general of Palestine, Norman *Bentwich, who did not become full members until 1929. Prof. Judah Leon *Magnes, who also advocated bi-nationalism in this period, was never a member of the society, even though his name was frequently identified with it. Berit Shalom never numbered more than 200 members. From the start there were differences concerning the purpose of the society. Ruppin wanted it to be a research group that would present the results of its studies to the Zionist leadership, while others urged that it formulate and attempt to implement its own political program. Ruppin was chairman of the society until 1929, and the more activist line was carried out by his successor, Joseph Lurie. Rabbi Binyamin, the first editor of Berit Shalom's monthly, *She'ifoteinu* ("Our Aspirations"), who demanded an agreement with the Arabs on the basis of unlimited Jewish immigration, was replaced when a majority of the members declared themselves ready to accept a temporary limitation of immigration to facilitate an agreement with the Arabs. In 1930 senior members of Berit Shalom published a series of memoranda, the first of which – *Memorandum by the Brit Shalom Society on an Arab Policy for the Jewish Agency* – was submitted to the Zionist Executive in London in February. The second memorandum, entitled *Practical Proposals for Cooperation Between Jews and Arabs in Palestine*, was prepared as a response to a suggestion by one of the members of the 1929 Shaw Commission. The third memorandum was a personal endeavor by Ernst Simon, and was distributed to the members of the Conference of the Administrative Committee of the Jewish Agency in London. The fourth and last one was a "Judeao-Arab Covenant" prepared by Kalvaryski in August (apparently unknown to his colleagues at the time), and submitted by him to a member of the Arab Executive. Berit Shalom was attacked by most of the Zionist parties, who viewed its members as defeatists at best and traitors and worst. By 1933 it had virtually ceased to exist, after many of its members deserted it, and it ran out of funds.

BIBLIOGRAPHY: *She'ifotenu* (1930–33); S. Hattis, *The Bi-National Idea in Palestine in Mandatory Times* (1970).

[Susan Hattis Rolef (2nd ed.)]

BERK, FRED (1911–1980), dancer and exponent of Jewish and ethnic dance in the U.S. Born in Vienna into an Orthodox Jewish family, he studied dance there at the studio of Gertrud *Kraus and performed in her modern dance troupe. The Nazi annexation of Austria forced him to flee in 1939. He arrived in the U.S. in 1941. In 1950 Berk founded the Jewish Dance Division at the 92nd Street YMHA-YWHA, New York. Cofounder of the Merry-Go-Rounders, a children's dance group, he did the choreography for their *Holiday in Israel* and *Wedding in Austria*. He formed Hebraica Dancers in 1958. He wrote *The Jewish Dance* (1959).

BERKLEY, ROCHELLE (1951–), U.S. congresswoman. Rochelle (Shelley) Berkley, the elder of William and Estella (Colonomos) Levine's two daughters, was born in New York City. She was raised in the Catskill community of South Fallsburg, where her father worked at the famed Concord Hotel. In the early 1960s the family moved to Las Vegas, Nevada, where William found employment with the Sands Hotel; he would remain at the Sands for 36 years, the last ten as the hotel's maître d'.

During Berkley's formative years in Las Vegas, the city had a Jewish population of no more than 2,500. Berkley's mother served as president of the local Hadassah, while Shelly was elected president of the Las Vegas chapter of B'nai B'rith Girls. Berkley attended the University of Nevada at Las Vegas, where she was elected student body president, and graduated from the law school of the University of California at San Diego. Returning to Las Vegas, she worked as deputy director of the Nevada State Commerce Department and as counsel for the Southwest Gas Corporation. Following a two-year stint (1982–84) in the Nevada State Legislature, Berkley became vice president for government and legal affairs for the Sands Hotel. In this position, she served as in-house counsel for Sands' chairman Sheldon Adelson, the man who virtually invented the computer trade show.

In 1998 Berkley ran as a Democrat for one of Nevada's two seats in the United States House of Representatives. Elected by a small margin, Berkley continued to be reelected by the people of Las Vegas. Her campaign brought her to the attention of national Democratic party leaders. Once elected, she was given a seat on the prestigious House International Relations Committee. As a member of the subcommittee on the Middle East, Berkley was an ardent supporter of Israel. Berkley also served on the Congressional Task Force on Antisemitism. During her first campaign for Congress Berkley was diagnosed with osteoporosis. Shocked to discover that her medical insurance did not cover the costs of a bone scan, she became an ardent supporter of the "Patients' Bill of Rights." This measure, which eventually fell short of passage, would have guaranteed that medical decisions be made by doctors and patients rather than by medical insurance carriers.

BIBLIOGRAPHY: K.F. Stone, *The Congressional Minyan: The Jews of Capitol Hill* (2000), 26–29.

[Kurt Stone (2nd ed.)]

BERKLEY, WILLIAM R. (1945–), U.S. insurance holding company executive. Berkley received a B.S. from New York University (NYU) (1966) and an M.B.A. from Harvard (1968). During his business career, he founded a number of public and private companies which he continues to control or of which he serves as chairman or director. He also chairs or serves on the board of several banks and other financial institutions.

The W.R. Berkley Corp. was founded in 1967 and is headquartered in Greenwich, Connecticut. In 2005 it had 32 subsidiaries operating in the U.S. and globally and was ranked 431 by Fortune 500. Berkley serves as chair of the Board of Overseers of the NYU Stern School of Business; as vice chairman of the Board of Trustees of NYU, where he serves on the Executive and Finance Committees; on the Board of Directors of Georgetown University; as vice chairman of the Board of Trustees of the University of Connecticut; and as co-chairman of the Albert B. Sabin Vaccine Institute, Inc.

Berkley has received many awards for his business, civic, and philanthropic activities, including, most recently, an honorary doctor of law degree from Mercy College. In 1999, he was awarded the Medallion for Entrepreneurship by Beta Gamma Sigma, which honors outstanding individuals who combine innovative business achievements with service to humanity.

BERKOFF, STEVEN (1937–), English actor, director, and writer. Born in Stepney, London, he studied drama at the Webber-Douglas School in London and mime at the Ecole Jacque le Coq in Paris.

He established himself as one of the most innovative theater personalities in the last quarter of the 20th century. As a writer he adapted many works for the stage including Kafka's *The Trial* and "Metamorphosis" and Poe's "The Fall of the House of Usher." His first professional production was an adaptation of Kafka's "In the Penal Colony."

His personal acting style is original and highly physically controlled – the expression both hypnotic and threatening; although controlled, his stage rages are full of hurt and foreboding leaving an audience little solace. Each performance is unique.

He is a prolific playwright whose original works include *Decadence, Greek, West,* and *East.* Much of his work is based on the vernacular of the present day – *West* with the social language and mores of the West End; *East* with the East End of London, for example. *Kvetch* is, at the same time, amusing and discomfiting; it received the London drama critics' award as the best comedy of 1991. The language of his works is acerbic, clear, intelligent, and unpretentious. Many of his chosen characters as writer or actor are either disturbed or social misfits. He is also a master in the transposition of mythology on to modern life.

He has appeared in a number of films and TV productions, such as *Octopussy, Beverly Hills Cop, Rambo,* and *The Krays,* playing "baddies" (film villains) with relish and undisguised glee.

Berkoff has toured and acted in his own productions of *Hamlet, Macbeth, Salome,* and *Coriolanus* throughout Europe, Israel, and Australia. In his book on the theater *Coriolanus in Deutschland* he describes his unease as a Jew in Munich. Other publications include *I Am Hamlet, A Prisoner in Rio, The Theatre of Steven Berkoff* (1992), and an autobiography, *Free Association* (1996). In 1983 Steven Berkoff received the Los Angeles Drama Critics Award for directing.

ADD. BIBLIOGRAPHY: *R. Cross, Steven Berkoff and the Theatre of Self-Performance* (2004).

[Sally Whyte]

BERKOVITS, ELIEZER (1908–1992), theologian and Jewish philosopher. Berkovits was born in Oradea, Romania, in 1908. He received his rabbinical ordination in 1934 at the Berlin ("Hildesheimer") Rabbinical Seminary, where he studied under Rabbi Jehiel Jacob *Weinberg, (author of the *Seridei Esh*); as well as from the Mir yeshivah and the rabbinate of Hungary. In parallel, he earned a doctorate in philosophy at the Friedrich-Wilhelms (now Humboldt) University of Berlin, where he studied under Wolfgang Kohler, one of the founders of Gestalt psychology. After escaping Germany in 1939, Berkovits served as a communal rabbi in Leeds, England (1940–46); Sydney, Australia (1946–50); and Boston, Massachusetts (1950–56). In 1958 he accepted the chair of the philosophy department at the Hebrew Theological Seminary in Skokie, Illinois, which he held until 1975. At that time, at the age of 67, Berkovits relocated to Jerusalem, where he lived and worked until his death. During his lifetime, Berkovits wrote 19 books and hundreds of essays and articles, covering every major area of Jewish philosophy.

Berkovits' philosophy of Judaism places a heavy focus on the role of man in history. In his view, classical Judaism, as embodied in the Hebrew Bible and the Talmud, presents a coherent critique of Western culture and its ideas about man – a critique which can be applied to the most pressing questions of modern life. Building on both his philosophical training and talmudic background, Berkovits saw the task of Jewish philosophy to "make Judaism a significant philosophy of life in the intellectual climate of our age … [and to] equip it with the truth of God in relationship to the vital issues of present-day human existence." Thus, in addition to his constructive philosophy of Judaism, his work includes explicit critiques, from a Jewish perspective, of many of the leading streams of thought in his time, including existentialism, radical theology, the 1960s drug culture, and situation ethics; of non-Jewish writers like Rudolf Otto and Arnold Toynbee, and of Jewish thinkers like Hermann *Cohen, Martin *Buber, and Franz *Rosenzweig.

Theology and the Holocaust

Berkovits' most important theological work appears in *God, Man, and History* (1959), which offers the central framework for his entire philosophy of Judaism. The essence of Judaism, he wrote, is found in the personal encounter of the prophet with God; it is through the memory of that encounter, no less than through rational speculation, that one understands the nature of God and his covenant. In this regard, he followed the tradition of the medieval thinkers *Saadiah Gaon and *Judah Halevi, and in modern times Samson Raphael *Hirsch, who viewed revelation as axiomatic to any philosophy of Judaism. He thus challenged the Maimonidean approach to divine attributes, for example, according to which it is reason alone that allows one to comprehend the Absolute; in Berkovits' view, memory of the encounter is primary and irreducible to reason. Reason can only help one describe the nature of God; however, it is only through the encounter that one discovers the central principle of Jewish religion – that God cares about the fate of humankind. "The foundation of religion is not the affirmation that God *is*, but that God is concerned with man and the world; that, having created this world, he has not abandoned it, leaving it to its own devices; that he cares about his creation." God created the universe with man as its capstone; man is endowed with the capacity to take responsibility for creation, and therefore is charged by God with a duty to care for the world and for human history. Berkovits quotes, in this regard, the statement in Genesis 2:15 that God placed Adam in the Garden of Eden "to work it and to keep it." God's central concern for man is that he take responsibility for history, improving the world and caring for it. He developed these points further in his *Man and God: Studies in Biblical Theology* (1969).

In our own time, the most significant theological question in this regard concerns the problem of evil, especially in the wake of the Holocaust. Berkovits treated this subject most extensively in his *Faith After the Holocaust* (1973) and *With God in Hell: Judaism in the Ghettos and Death Camps* (1979). In these works, he offered a significant defense of the classical notion of the covenant, in the face of major theological opposition to it in modern Jewish writing, and established human responsibility as the focal point of any approach to dealing with the destruction of European Jewry. In this context, he also developed a highly critical view of the role that Christianity played in promulgating antisemitism in Europe throughout history, seeing this role as a significant antecedent to the Holocaust which cannot be discarded when considering the future of Jewish-Christian relations.

Morality and Halakhah

Berkovits' most developed statement on the nature of Jewish law appears in his *Not in Heaven: The Nature and Function of Halacha* (1983). Whereas the main streams of Western morality focus on the intentions of the individual, Judaism, he argued, is concerned principally with the outcome of one's actions. For this reason, Jewish law developed over time, showing flexibility of its rules in light of their effects within communal life. Jewish law, while a system of rules, nonetheless is guided by a higher set of moral values which are themselves concerned with providing real-world fairness, stability, economic prosperity, and concern with the fate of the unfortunate. He developed these themes further in *Crisis and Faith* (1976), where he discussed the issues of conversion and Jewish sexuality; *Jewish Women in Time and Torah* (1992), which offers a modern reconsideration of the role of women in Judaism; and his three Hebrew-language halakhic treatises: *Tenai be-Nisu'in u-ve-Get* ("Conditionality in Marriage and Divorce," 1966), a controversial attempt to address the problem of **agunot*, or refused divorce; as well as *Halakhah: Koḥah Ve-Tafkidah* ("*Halakhah*: Its Authority and Function," 1981), and *Higayon ba-Halakhah* ("Logic in Halakhah," 1986).

Nationhood and Zionism

Because of the nature of human morals, Berkovits wrote, it is not enough to hope for the improvement of humankind through the teaching of good principles of conduct. Rather, Judaism insists on the creation of a "holy nation," a people that dedicates itself to righteousness in every realm of its life, and which may thereby serve as an example for humankind. But to fulfill this mission, such a people requires sovereignty in its own land. "A people in control of its own life, capable of implementing Judaism by applying it to the whole of life, is a people in its own land. Judaism, as the religion of the deed, requires a people in its land." For this reason, the State of Israel represented for Berkovits not only the salvation of the Jews from the trials and horrors of exile, but an opportunity to apply Judaism in its fullest sense. Berkovits' developed his Zionist philosophy most thoroughly in *Towards Historic Judaism* (1943) as well as the final section of *God, Man, and History*. His critique of the modern Israeli reality in light of this ideal appears in *Mashber ha-Yehadut bi-Medinat ha-Yehudim* ("The Crisis of Judaism in the Jewish State," 1987).

Other Writings

Berkovits' doctoral dissertation, "Hume und Der Deismus" ("Hume and Deism," 1933) examines the epistemological issues concerning revelation and natural religion in the thought of David Hume. In *Was Ist Der Talmud?* ("What is the Talmud?" 1938), he offered an introduction to the methods and aims of the oral tradition. Other significant works include *Judaism: Fossil or Ferment?* (1956), a book-length response to Arnold Toynbee's depiction of the Jews; *Prayer* (1962), a monograph on the uniqueness of prayer in Judaism; *Major Themes in Modern Philosophies of Judaism* (1974), in which he offered extensive critiques of the philosophies of Hermann Cohen, Franz Rosenzweig, Martin Buber, Abraham Joshua *Heschel, and Mordecai *Kaplan; and *Unity in Judaism* (1986), in which he called for the rediscovery of Jewish collective identity above denominational divisions. His collected sermons from the war period appear in *Between Yesterday and Tomorrow* (1945).

A collection of his major essays was published in 2002 (Shalem Press), titled *Essential Essays on Judaism* (ed. David Hazony), which includes a bibliography of his writings.

[David Hazony (2nd ed.)]

BERKOW, IRA (1940–), U.S. sportswriter. Born and raised in Chicago, Berkow attended Sullivan High School (1957), Miami University (Oxford, Ohio, B.A., 1963), and Northwestern University (M.S.J., 1965). He worked as a sportswriter and book reviewer for the *Minneapolis Tribune* (1965–67), and a sportswriter, sports columnist, general columnist, and senior writer for the Newspaper Enterprise Association (1967–76) before joining *The New York Times* as a sports feature writer, sports columnist, and senior writer in 1981. Berkow won a Pulitzer Prize for national reporting in 2001 as part of a *Times* team for the series "How Race is Lived in America," contributing an 8,300-world essay on "The Minority Quarterback," and was a finalist for the Pulitzer for distinguished commentary in 1988. Berkow is the only sportswriter to have been represented for five decades in the respected annual anthology *Best Sports Stories*, and its successor, *Best American Sportswriting*. He was also reprinted in the *Best American Sports Writing of the Century* anthology. Berkow is the author of *Oscar Robertson: The Golden Year 1964* (1971); *Rockin' Steady: A Guide to Basketball and Cool* (with Walt Frazier, 1974); *Beyond the Dream: Occasional Heroes of Sports* (1975); *Maxwell Street: Survival in a Bazaar* (1977); *The DuSable Panthers: The Greatest, Blackest, Saddest Team from the Meanest Street in Chicago* (1978); *Carew* (with Rod Carew, 1979); *Red: A Biography of Red Smith* (1986); *The Man Who Robbed the Pierre: The Story of Bobby Comfort* (1987); *Pitchers Do Get Lonely, and Other Sports Stories* (1988); *Hank Greenberg: The Story of My Life* (with Hank Greenberg,

1989); *How to Talk Jewish* (with Jackie Mason, 1990); *The Gospel According to Casey: Casey Stengel's Inimitable, Instructional, Historical Baseball Book* (with Jim Kaplan, 1992); *To the Hoop: The Seasons of a Basketball Life* (1997); *Court Vision: Unexpected Views on the Lure of Basketball* (2000); and *The Minority Quarterback, and Other Lives in Sports* (2002).

[Elli Wohlgelernter (2nd ed.)]

BERKOWICZ, JOSEPH (**Józef**; 1789–1846), Polish army officer, the son of Berek *Joselowicz. In 1809 he joined Napoleon's Polish Legion, and took part in the battle of Kock, where his father was killed. For his distinguished service in Napoleon's Russian campaign of 1812, in which he was severely wounded, Joseph was awarded two crosses for valor. Retiring because of his war injuries he was employed in forestry, becoming chief forester in various localities in Poland. At the time of the 1830–31 uprising he called upon the Jews to take up arms and fight for their Polish fatherland. After the Polish defeat, he left with his son Leon for France, where he lived in Besançon. He later moved to Liverpool, England, where he wrote a novel which he himself translated into English, *Stanislaus or the Polish Lancer in the Suite of Napoleon*… (published posthumously by his sons, 1846).

BIBLIOGRAPHY: A. Kraushar, *Syn Berka Joselowicza*… (1889); E. Tuniński, *Berek Joselewicz i jego syn* (1909), 51–109; M. Balaban, in: *Nowy Dziennik* (April 12, 1933); *Polski Słownik Biograficzny*, 1 (1935), 454–5; A. Levinson, *Toledot Yehudei Varshah* (1953), 122–3.

BERKOWITZ, HENRY (1857–1924), U.S. Reform rabbi. Berkowitz was born in Pittsburgh, Pa. He was a member of the first graduating class of *Hebrew Union College in 1883. After occupying pulpits in Mobile, Alabama, where he organized the Humane Movement for the Protection of Children and Animals from Cruelty and wrote *Judaism on the Social Question* (1888) on labor-capital relations. His family did not fare well in Mobile; a son died of yellow fever and his wife Flora wrote an article in Isaac Mayer *Wise's *Israelite* describing their plight. It resulted in a job offer from Kansas City, where he succeeded his brother-in-law Joseph *Krauskopf. Berkowitz became rabbi of Congregation Rodeph Shalom, Philadelphia (1892), succeeding the distinguished Talmud scholar Marcus Jastrow. Despite opposition he eliminated many traditional forms from the practice of his congregation and brought it within the mainstream of advanced Reform. Berkowitz established in Philadelphia the Jewish Chautauqua Society in 1893, an educational and interfaith organization modeled after Methodist teacher training and adult education programs, and was its chancellor until his death. After 1910 its focus was changed to educating non-Jewish college students about Judaism. He took an active part in the establishment of the Federation of Jewish Philanthropies in Philadelphia in 1901 and the Philadelphia Rabbinical Association in the same year. He was a member of the Mayor's Vice Commission in order to deal with the rise in prostitution among East European immigrant girls. He helped develop playgrounds throughout the city. During World War I, he toured army bases and was chaplain to soldiers. His efforts led to the development of a heart condition and forced retirement. He was the first secretary of the Central Conference of American Rabbis. Among his publications are *Kiddush or Sabbath Sentiments in the Home* (1898) and *Intimate Glimpses of a Rabbi's Career* (1921).

BIBLIOGRAPHY: W. Rosenau, in: AJYB, 26 (1924/25), 448–58; M.E. Berkowitz, *Beloved Rabbi* (1932); O. Levitas, in: AJA, 14 (1962), 3–19.

[Sefton D. Temkin / Michael Berenbaum (2nd ed.)]

BERKOWITZ, MICKEY (1954–), Israeli basketball player. Born in Kefar Sava, Berkowitz joined the Maccabi Tel Aviv youth club at age 11, played with the junior squad at 15, and joined the senior team at 17 in 1971. He helped the Israeli team beat the U.S. team at the 1973 Maccabiah games, 86–80, and subsequently became the first Israeli to play NCAA Division I basketball, joining the third-ranked University of Nevada, Las Vegas in 1975. Though he had a guaranteed contract offer from the Atlanta Hawks and the New Jersey Nets, Maccabi Tel Aviv would not release him from his contract.

Berkowitz, a 6′ 3″ guard, returned to Maccabi Tel Aviv after the 1975–76 season and subsequently became one of the team's stars. Teaming up with Tal *Brody, Berkowitz helped lead the team to the European Championship in 1977 and 1981, scoring 17 points in the 78–77 win over Mobilgirgi of Varese, Italy, on April 7, 1977, and 20 points in the final against Sinudyne, Bologna, on March 26, 1981. Berkowitz played 17 seasons for Maccabi Tel Aviv, also winning 17 Israeli league championships and 13 Israeli State Cups. He also played on the Israeli national team that won a gold medal at the 1974 Tehran Asian Games and a silver medal at the 1979 European championships in Torino, Italy. Berkowitz's highest-scoring game in international competition occurred at the 1975 European championships in Belgrade, Yugoslavia, when he scored 44 points against Turkey. Berkowitz retired in 1996 and remained active on the basketball scene as a general manager and team owner. He was named Israel's Sportsman of the Year in 1975 and chosen Best Sportsman in the history of Israeli sports on the country's 50th anniversary.

[Elli Wohlgelernter (2nd ed.)]

BERKOWITZ, YITZḤAK DOV (1885–1967), Hebrew and Yiddish novelist, editor, and translator of *Shalom Aleichem. Born in Slutsk, Belorussia, Berkowitz studied in *ḥeder* and educated himself in secular subjects. In 1903 he made his way to Lodz. He became friendly with Itzhak *Katzenelson. One of his first stories, "*Moshkele Ḥazir*," was printed in *Ha-Ẓofeh* in 1903 and won a literary prize. In 1905 he became literary editor of *Ha-Zeman*, and his articles and stories appeared in most of the Hebrew and Yiddish journals of the day. In 1906 Berkowitz married Shalom Aleichem's daughter, Ernestina, spent 18 months in Switzerland, and visited the U.S. in 1908. While there, he contributed to the local Yiddish and Hebrew press. In 1909 he moved to Warsaw, where he edited the literary page of the Yiddish journal, *Di Naye Velt*. Several volumes of his collected stories were published in Hebrew and Yiddish from 1910 onwards.

In 1913 he went to the United States where he edited the weekly *Ha-Toren* as well as *Miklat* (1920–21). He settled in Palestine in 1928, and became one of the first editors of the weekly, *Moznayim*. Berkowitz published his translation of the collected works of Shalom Aleichem and his masterfully written reminiscences of the great Yiddish writer and his generation, under the title *Ha-Rishonim ki-Venei Adam* (1933–48).

While his contemporaries, G. *Schoffman, J.Ḥ *Brenner, and U.N. *Gnessin revolted against the style of *Mendele Mokher Seforim and Ḥ.N. *Bialik, Berkowitz remained true to the older prose writing tradition, displaying his individuality in the choice of subject, methods of characterization, and structure of the story. Although his less conformist contemporaries were not always accepted by the literary establishment, he himself was praised by Bialik. Berkowitz's stories, novels, plays, and memoirs appeared in Yiddish and Hebrew. The bulk of his work was written in Hebrew.

Berkowitz is important as a writer of short stories. In his early years he wrote realistic stories under the influence of Mendele, Bialik, and Chekhov but soon was captivated by the technique and style of Shalom Aleichem. The influence of the greater writer tended to weaken Berkowitz's originality. Berkowitz's stories were written out of the context of the social crisis which shook Eastern European Jewry in his day. Among his central themes are (1) the weakening of parental authority: "*Lifnei ha-Shulḥan*" ("Before the Table"); "*Pere Adam*" ("The Ill-Mannered One"); "*Malkot*" ("Lashings"); "*Ba'al Simḥah*" ("The Feted"); "*Maftir*"; "*Moshkele Ḥazir*"; (2) the problems resulting from changes in the protagonists' social status and from their cultural isolation: "*Viddui*" ("Confession"); "*Talush*" ("Severed", in *Israel Argosy*, 1936); "*Kelei Zekhukhit*" ("Glass," in *Reflex*, 1927); (3) problems resulting from emigration: "*Karet*" ("The Outcast," in *The Jewish Standard*, 1936); "*El ha-Dod ba-Amerikah*" ("To Uncle in America," in *B'nai Brith Magazine*, 1930); "*Yarok*" ("The Greenhorn," in *The American Jewish Chronicle*, 1917); "*Mi-Merḥakim*" ("From Afar"); (4) problems from the social pressure of a strange world: "*Pelitim*" ("Refugees"); "*Ruḥot Ra'ot*" ("Evil Spirits"). The characters, generally unable to face up to the crisis, are "anti-heroes" who collapse under pressure, victims of social and psychological situations beyond their control. It is not the plot, but the social and psychological situation expressed through the plot, which is the main point of Berkowitz's stories. His characterization is not introspective (as is the case with J.Ḥ. Brenner and U.N. Gnessin), but external. The inner world of the protagonists is revealed through mannerism, habits, and dialogue. In many cases wider basic situations are implied through the specific case by the symbolic expansion of landscapes or verbal hints, extending the significance of the dialogue or characters. The background of most of Berkowitz's stories is Russia at the turn of the century, and the effect of the social and general crisis of the time on the country's Jews. Some of the stories deal with the place of immigrants of the old generation in the U.S., others with the impact of Ereẓ Israel on new immigrants: "*Amerikah Olah le-Ereẓ Yisrael*" ("America Comes to Ereẓ Israel," 1946); "*Ha-Nehag*" ("The Heart of a Chauffeur," in *Commentary*, 1953).

There is a change in direction as regards technique and theme in Berkowitz's novels. In the first of these, *Menaḥem Mendel be-Ereẓ Yisrael* ("Menahem Mendel in Ereẓ Israel," 1936) he attempted to transfer one of Shalom Aleichem's characters to the new environment of Ereẓ Israel, continuing the epistolary technique. The correspondence is one-sided; Menahem Mendel writes to his wife, Sheine Sheindel; she does not reply. The theme is the ideological struggle between fathers, who still belong to the Diaspora in their way of thinking and try to make easy money out of the building boom in the Tel Aviv of the 1930s, and the sons, who are committed to the ideal of pioneer labor. The mode is satirical rather than humoristic. *Yemot ha-Mashi'aḥ* ("Messianic Days," 1938) is a description of the emigration of Dr. Menuḥin, a Zionist intellectual, from the United States to Ereẓ Israel. At times it reads like a *roman à clef*, in which the writer hints at real characters and at the struggle between the *Revisionist (right-wing Zionist) and the Labor movement. His hero, Menuḥin, is searching for a new truth and a new way of life, and he eventually finds a wife (Yehudit), after overcoming various prejudices, and discovers the attractions of "labor Palestine." The ideology of the labor movement is one of the important aspects of the novel and events are judged by its light.

Berkowitz also wrote several plays of different types, some of which appeared in a separate volume in 1928. The fourth, *Mirah*, was published in 1934. His play, *Ba-Arazot ha-Reḥokot* ("In the Distant Lands," 1928), is a comedy on the life of immigrants to the United States. The appearance of Anton, a Russian farmer, in the midst of a Jewish family, causes various romantic complications and errors. *Oto ve-Et Beno* ("He and His Son," 1928), a realistic "somber drama," is a continuation of the story "*Moshkele Ḥazir*" – Moshke, a convert to Christianity who had a son, Jacob, by a non-Jewish wife, is nevertheless still tied to his Jewish origins. During a pogrom in the midst of the Russian Revolution, Moshke hides Jews in his home and this act brings about a clash between him and his son, in which Moshke murders Jacob and commits suicide. The play is written in realistic, Ibsenesque style and is well made; it was produced by the Habimah Theater in 1934. *Mirah* was influenced by Ibsen's *A Doll's House*, and deals with the status of women in the United States immigrant society, contrasting the heroine's moral qualities, despite her sin, with her husband's imperfections. In old age, Berkowitz published reminiscences, both of his childhood in Russia, *Pirkei Yaldut* ("Childhood Episodes," 1966), and of Ereẓ Israel in the 1930s, *Yom Etmol Ki Avar* ("Yesterday," 1966). He also translated Tolstoi's *Childhood* (1912) and Chekhov's *Youth* (1922).

Berkowitz was received with enthusiasm by the critics of his time. Bialik praised him warmly while Brenner regarded him with mixed feelings, praising his clarity and freshness but noting his limitations. A later generation dealt with the relationship between naturalism and realism in his work (Y. Keshet), emphasized the central psychological dilemma in his work, which confronts the little man with a situation beyond his control (D. Sadan), and described the alienation of his intellectual heroes (S. Halkin). The young Israeli critics have not devoted much attention to his work. Some have stressed the sociological aspect in his work (i.e., the breakup of the home – G. Katznelson) and others have studied in detail his technique in story and playwriting (G. Shaked). He has had little influence on the writers of his own and the subsequent generation or on the young Israeli writers. A list of his works translated into English appears in Goell, Bibliography.

BIBLIOGRAPHY: I. Holt, *Isaac Dov Berkowitz, Voice of the Uprooted* (1972); Ḥ.N. Bialik, *Iggerot*, 1 (1938), 263; idem, *Devarim she-be-al-Peh* (1935), 188–90; *Kol Kitvei J. Ḥ. Brenner*, 2 (1960), 380; D.A. Friedman, *Iyyunei Perozah* (1966), 143–60; S. Halkin, *Arai va-Keva* (1942), 95–112; D. Sadan, *Bein Din le-Ḥeshbon* (1963), 163–8; J. Fichmann, *Benei Dor* (1952), 226–53; Y. Koplewitz (Keshet), *Be-Dor Oleh* (1950), 13–24; G. Katznelson, in: *Gilyonot*, 30 (1954), 239–43; G. Shaked, *Al Arba'ah Sippurim* (1964), 11–33; idem, *'Oto ve-Et Beno' ve-ha-Maḥazeh ha-Re'alisti: Al Sheloshah Maḥazot* (1968), 9–38; A. Komem-Kominkovsky, in: *Me'assef le-Divrei Sifrut*, 4 (1964), 243–53; R. Wallenrod, *Literature of Modern Israel* (1956), 162–6, 169. **ADD. BIBLIOGRAPHY:** G. Shaked, *Ha-Sipporet ha-Ivrit*, 1 (1977), 327–41.

[Gershon Shaked]

BERKSON, ISAAC BAER (1891–1975), U.S. educator and philosopher. Berkson, who was born in New York, began his teaching career at the Central Jewish Institute in New York, of which he was appointed director in 1917. From 1918 until 1927 he supervised the schools and extension program of the city's Bureau of Jewish Education. In 1927 he began teaching education at the Jewish Institute of Religion (later merged with the Hebrew Union College), and in the same year accepted the invitation of Henrietta Szold, who headed the Palestine Executive's department of education, to survey Jewish schools in Palestine. After completing his survey, he remained in Palestine from 1928 to 1935 as superintendent of the Jewish school system. In 1938 Berkson began lecturing in the philosophy of education at the City College of New York (professor, 1955). Though a follower of the progressive education ideas of John Dewey and W.H. Kilpatrick, Berkson only partially accepted their pragmatic-instrumentalist philosophy. His merger of these views with his own, which were a reflection of the ideals and values of his Jewish heritage, was given expression in his book *The Ideal and the Community* (1958). In dealing with the specific problems of Jewish education he advanced the "community theory." According to him, the Jewish communities of the world constitute the "Knesset Israel," which has its own "heritage of cultural, social, and spiritual values." The cultivation of the individual's Jewish personality must therefore combine loyalty to his own community – the "Knesset Israel," including the State of Israel – and sharing with his fellow men in the "realm of universal ideals." Berkson's *Theories of Americanization* (1920) was an important influential statement of the American theory of cultural pluralism which he applied specifically to the problems of Jewish education. Berkson's other works include: *Preface to an Educational Philosophy* (1940), *Education Faces the Future* (1943), *Ethics, Politics and Education* (1968), and *The Ideal and the Community: A Philosophy of Education* (1970).

BIBLIOGRAPHY: S. Dinin, in: *Jewish Education*, 32 (1962), 134; E. Schwarcz, *ibid.*, 29 (1958), 56; J. Pilch (ed.), *Judaism and the Jewish School* (1966), 42.

[Ernest Schwarcz]

BERL, EMMANUEL (1892–1976), French author. A relative of *Bergson and *Proust, Berl was a passionate political essayist and critic of the French bourgeoisie. His works include *Mort de la pensée bourgeoise* (1925), *La politique et les partis* (1932²), *Discours aux Français* (1934), *La culture en péril* (1948), and *Nasser tel qu'on le loue* (1968). Berl was chief editor of the weekly, *Marianne* (1933–37). He also wrote short stories and novels including *Sylvia* (1952) and *Rachel et autres grâces* (1965), notable for their insight and an incisive style. Deeply affected by World War I after serving for two years, Berl, a convinced anti-fascist, adopted pacifist views that led him in June 1940 to write some of future Vichy leader Pétain's speeches. He quickly put an end to this cooperation when he became aware of the antisemitic direction of the new regime. After the war, he left politics and devoted himself exclusively to literature. In 1967, he was awarded the French Academy's *Grand Prix de Literature*.

BIBLIOGRAPHY: B. Morlino, *Emmanuel Berl: Les trbulations d'un pacifiste* (1990); L.-A. Revah, *Berl, un juif de France* (2003).

[Dror Franck Sullaper (2nd ed.)]

BERL, ERNST (1877–1946), Austrian-U.S. chemist. Berl was born in Silesia and worked at the Zurich Polytechnicum (1898–1907) and in a Belgian artificial silk factory (1910–14). In World War I he directed an Austrian explosives factory. Berl was professor of chemical technology and electrochemistry, Technische Hochschule, Darmstadt (1919–33); he emigrated to the U.S.A. and became research professor at Carnegie Institute of Technology, Pittsburgh. He worked on lead chamber process, nitration of cellulose, and combustion problems and was coauthor of *Chemisch-technische Untersuchungsmethoden* (4 vols., 1921–23) and *Chemische Ingenieur-Technik*.

BERLE, MILTON (formerly **Mendel Berlinger**; 1908–2002), U.S. comedian, known as "Mr. Television" and "Uncle Miltie." Born in New York, Berle played in nightclubs, films, and Broadway shows, including the *Ziegfeld Follies* of 1943. From 1948 to 1956 he did a weekly variety show on television in modern slapstick style. In the 1960s he also appeared in serious parts, including a role in the film *The Loved One*.

Berle's career began when he was five years old and spanned more than 80 years on stage, film, radio, and television. At the age of five, Berle won a Charlie Chaplin look-alike contest. And as a child he appeared in the silent films *The*

Perils of Pauline and *Tillie's Punctured Romance*. He moved up through the vaudeville circuit, finding his niche in the role of a brash comic known for stealing the material of fellow comedians. In 1931, he played the Palace Theater in New York, becoming the youngest master of ceremonies on Broadway. He also wrote some 400 published songs. But it was on television in the 1940s and 1950s that he made his most enduring mark. *The Texaco Star Theater*, featuring Berle and guest stars in what would become legendary comic skits, debuted in 1948 and caught on with the public almost immediately. It became a Tuesday night fixture in homes across America and was credited with helping sell millions of first-time TV sets to a nation just getting acquainted with the new medium. Known for his trademark cigars and for occasionally donning women's clothes to get a laugh, Berle, who hosted the show, was a mainstay on network television for nearly two decades. Even before his television success, he was reportedly one of the highest-paid comedians in show business. But *Texaco Star Theater* cemented Berle's fame. NBC gave him a "lifetime contract" of 30 years in 1951, paying him $200,000 a year. In 1954 the show, replete with singers, comedians, acrobats, and comedy skits, was renamed *The Milton Berle Show*.

In 1965, Berle renegotiated his 30-year contract with NBC, allowing him to appear on any network. He later made guest appearances in dramas as well as comedy programs. In addition to television, Berle's career in later years included film, nightclubs, and benefit shows. He was the subject of nearly every show business tribute and award, including TV specials devoted to his contributions and legacy in broadcasting. He won an Emmy award in 1949 for Most Outstanding Kinescope Personality and received another Emmy in 1979 for Lifetime Achievement. He was one of the first members of the Academy of Television Arts & Sciences Hall of Fame, and for more than a decade he was president of the Friars Club. In 1984 he was inducted into the Television Hall of Fame, and he was the first entertainer to be inducted into the International Comedy Hall of Fame (1991). In 1996 he was awarded the American Comedy Lifetime Achievement Award.

Berle also wrote a number of books: *Laughingly Yours* (1939); *Out of My Trunk* (an autobiography, 1945); *Earthquake* (1959); *Milton Berle: An Autobiography* (with Haskel Frankel, 1974); *B.S. I Love You: Sixty Funny Years with the Famous and the Infamous* (a collection of stories and anecdotes, 1987); *Milton Berle's Private Joke File* (1989); and *More of the Best of Milton Berle's Private Joke File* (1993).

BIBLIOGRAPHY: S. Allen, *The Funny Men* (1956); D. Glut and J. Harmon, *The Great Television Heroes* (1975); W. Berle and B. Lewis, *My Father Uncle Miltie* (1999); J. Forray, *I Laughed Until I Cried: My Life with Milton Berle, Broadway, Hollywood, and Beyond* (2002).

[Ruth Beloff (2nd ed.)]

BERLEWI, HENRYK (1894–1967), painter, graphic artist, stage designer, art critic, and theorist of art. Berlewi was born in Warsaw and as a child attended a *ḥeder* for a short period of time. He started his art education at the Warsaw Art School (1906–9), while at the same time studying at a local gymnasium. In 1909–10, he attended the Art Academy in Antwerp, where in addition he completed a course at a lyceum. In 1911–12, Berlewi lived in Paris and studied at the École de Beaux Arts. It was during this period that he established close ties with groups of Dadaists and futurists and was influenced by cubism and expressionism. In 1913, he returned to Warsaw and became acquainted with the young Jewish artists who combined a keen interest in avant-garde art with the pursuit for "a new Jewish style" in literature and art. After World War I, he participated in a number of epatage events initiated by Polish Futurist poets (e.g., the Futurist "Subtropical Evening" in Warsaw, 1918). Berlewi became a prominent figure in modernist artistic circles and was a member of various groups. In 1919, he showed his work at the Kultur-Liga exhibition in Białystok. He was close to the "Yung Yiddish" group and was part of its activities; from 1920, he collaborated with a group of Yiddish modernist authors who rallied around the Warsaw *Ringen* journal, did its cover drawings, and published articles on contemporary European and Jewish art. Berlewi was among the founders of the Jewish Society for the Encouragement of Artists and organized exhibitions of Jewish artists. His work in this period is guided by the idea of developing "contemporary Jewish art" by way of synthesizing the discoveries of the European avant-garde and Jewish folk art traditions. Utilizing scenes of Jewish life in most of his paintings, he treated them in a cubist and expressionist manner, thinking of these works as exemplars of "Jewish expressionism." As a book designer, he made an impressive contribution to contemporary Yiddish typography. In addition, he collaborated with Yiddish theater companies in Warsaw and designed the scenery for several of their productions. In 1921, Berlewi made his acquaintance of El Lissitsky, who introduced him to the theory of suprematism developed by Kazimir Malevich (1878–1935) and aroused his interest in non-figurative art. In 1922–23, Berlewi lived in Berlin and collaborated with the leading constructivist artists. Inspired by the environment, he started developing his personal version of constructivism, which he later called "*mechano-faktura*." He showed his work at the "Novembergruppe" exhibition and at the First International Exhibition in Duesseldorf. Together with Jankel *Adler, he represented East European Jewish artists in organizing the Congress of the Union of Progressive International Artists (Duesseldorf, May 29–31, 1922). In this period, he maintained close ties with the activists of the Jewish modernist movement who resided in Berlin. In 1922, he did the cover drawing for the second issue of the *Albatros* Yiddish journal under the editorship of Uri Zevi *Greenberg. He published a number of articles on new trends in European and Russian art in the Berlin *Rimon-Milgroim* Jewish journal. In 1923, Berlewi returned to Warsaw. To promote the "new Jewish art" within a broader universal and cosmopolitan context, he became an organizer and standard-bearer of the "Block" group that united Polish constructivist artists and adherents of non-figurative art, among them many Jewish artists. In 1924, he published his "*Mechano-faktura*" manifesto in Polish (the German translation was published the same year in *Der Sturm* journal). Also in the same year, the first exhibition of his constructivist works was shown in the "Ausrto-Daimler" Auto Salon. In addition, he founded "Reklama-Mechano," a functional design bureau. At the same time, he remained active in book design and designed the typography for several books in Yiddish and Hebrew and published articles on art in Yiddish and Polish. His two one-man exhibitions took place in 1926 and 1928 in Warsaw, showing his figurative works and those inspired by Jewish themes. From 1928, Berlewi made his permanent residence in Paris. In the early 1930s, he returned to figurative painting and produced portraits and still lifes in the manner of the "Neue Sachlichkeit." In the 1930s, his exhibitions were held in France, Belgium, and Holland. During World War II Berlewi joined the French Resistance. In the 1950s, he returned to his experiments in abstract art and developed a new version of "*Mechano-faktura*" which he called Op Art. In 1960, Berlewi founded "Les Archives de l'Art Abstrait et de l'Avant-garde Internationale." He published articles in the Paris press in French as well as in Yiddish on European and Jewish art.

BIBLIOGRAPHY: H. Berlewi, *Mechano-faktura* (1924); H. Colleye. *Henryk Berlewi: Poolsch Schilder* (1937); *Retrospective Ausstellung Henryk Berlewi: Gemälde, Zeichnungen, Graphik, Mechano-Fakturen, Plastic von 1908 – bis Heute*, exh. cat., Berlin (1964); J. Malinowski, *Grupa "Jung Idysz" i żidowskie środowisko "Nowej Sztuki" w Polsce. 1918–1923* (1987); S.A. Mansbach, *Modern Art in Eastern Europe. From the Baltic to the Balkans, ca. 1890–1939* (1999), 121–23; J. Malinowski. *Malarstwo i rzeźba Żydow Polskich w XIX i XX wieku* (2000), 170–80, 199–205, 214–16, 221–26.

[Hillel Kazovsky (2nd ed.)]

BERLIAND, SHLOMO MEIR (1868–1941), one of the first members of the Ḥovevei Zion in Bessarabia and a founder of the *Odessa Committee, the center of the Ḥovevei Zion in Russia (1890). Berliand was born in the Ukraine. In 1920 he became the secretary of the committee for aiding Jewish refugees from the Ukraine and in 1921 was a member of the delegation sent to Bucharest to the Romanian prime minister Averescu to ask for help. From 1926 until 1940 he served as chairman of the Zionist Federation and the central committees of *Keren Hayesod, of *Tarbut in Bessarabia, Romania, and of the Committee for Education and Culture of the Jewish community of Kishinev. He was also a member of the Municipal Council of Kishinev. Berliand was an advocate of *Aḥad Ha-Am's "cultural Zionism." Head of the Wissotzky Tea Company's agency throughout this period, he worked for the Zionist movement wherever he traveled, and aided Jacob Bernstein-Kogan in his Zionist activities. At the outbreak of World War II Berliand refused to join his sons in London. When Bessarabia was occupied by the USSR (June 1940), he was forced to leave Kishinev. In June 1941, a week before the German attack on the USSR, he was arrested in Czernowitz, where he was living in his daughter's home. Although he declared that he had ceased all political activity, he was sent to a forced labor camp in Kom along with a group of Zionists, and died there. His wife, daughter, and son-in-law were also arrested and deported.

BIBLIOGRAPHY: *Haolam* (Feb. 24, 1938); M. Landau et al. (eds.), *Al Admat Bessarabia*, 2 (1962), 13–14. **ADD. BIBLIOGRAPHY:** M. Slipoi, in: *Yahadut Bessarabia* (EG, 11), 873; D. Vinitzky, *Bessarabia ha-Yehudit be-Ma'arekhoteihah bein Shetei Milḥamot ha-Olam 1914–1940* (1973), 125–27, 130–32, 157.

[David Vinitzky / Lucian-Zeev Herscovici (2nd ed.)]

BERLIGNE, ELIYAHU MEIR (1866–1959), *yishuv* leader and a founder of Tel Aviv. Berligne was born in Mogilev, Russia. He was a delegate to several Zionist congresses and at the Fifth Congress in 1901 joined the Zionist *Democratic Fraction under the leadership of Chaim *Weizmann. In 1907 Berligne settled in Ereẓ Israel, where he established industrial plants producing olive oil and soap. He was one of the founders of Tel Aviv, served on its first administrative committee, of which he was appointed chairman in 1909, and was made an honorary citizen of the city in 1946. Berligne was a member of the board of Herzliah High School in Tel Aviv. In 1919 he was a member of the *yishuv* delegation to the Paris Peace Conference. He was active in the Provisional Council of Palestinian Jewry (Ha-Va'ad ha-Zemanni), was a member of the Va'ad Le'ummi from 1920 to 1948, also serving as its treasurer, and was a signatory of Israel's Declaration of Independence in 1948. He was a member of the General Zionists ("A" Group) which later (1949) became the Progressive Party.

BIBLIOGRAPHY: Tidhar, 4 (1950), 1736–38; M. Attias (ed.), *Sefer ha-Te'udot shel ha-Va'ad ha-Le'ummi* (1963), index; A. Druyanow (ed.), *Sefer Tel Aviv* (1936).

[Benjamin Jaffe]

BERLIJN, ANTON (**Aron Wolf**; 1817–1870), Dutch composer, born in Amsterdam. He was for many years conductor and director of the Royal Theater, and was made a member of the Order of Merit by King William III of the Netherlands. Other monarchs (of Belgium, Denmark, Greece, Sweden, and Austria) also decorated him. He founded many choral groups, wrote liturgical works for the synagogue, and composed a large body of other music. His compositions included nine operas (of which *Die Bergknappen* and *Proserpina* became popular), an oratorio *Moses auf Nebo*, a symphony (performed by Spohr at Cassel, 1857), seven ballets, and a cantata. His archives, including correspondence with Mendelssohn and Meyerbeer, among others, are preserved at the National and University Library, Jerusalem.

BIBLIOGRAPHY: Grove, Dict; Baker, Biog Dict; Riemann-Gurlitt; Sendrey, Music, index.

[Dora Leah Sowden]

BERLIN, largest city and capital of Germany.

The Old Community (1295–1573)

Jews are first mentioned in a letter from the Berlin local council of Oct. 28, 1295, forbidding wool merchants to supply Jews with wool yarn. Suzerainty over the Jews belonged to the margrave who from 1317 pledged them to the municipality on varying terms, but received them back in 1363. Their taxes, however, were levied by the municipality in the name of the ruler of the state. The oldest place of Jewish settlement in "Great Jews' Court" (Grosser Judenhof) and "Jews' Street" had some of the characteristics of a Jewish quarter, but a number of wealthier Jews lived outside these areas. Until 1543, when a cemetery was established in Berlin, the Jews buried their dead in the town of Spandau. The Berlin Jews engaged mainly in commerce, handicrafts (insofar as this did not infringe on the privileges of the craft guilds), moneychanging, moneylending, and other pursuits. Few attained affluence. They paid taxes for the right to slaughter animals ritually, to sell meat, to marry, to circumcise their sons, to buy wine, to receive additional Jews as residents of their community, and to bury their dead. During the *Black Death (1349–50), the houses of the Jews were burned down and the Jewish inhabitants were killed or expelled from the town.

From 1354, Jews again settled in Berlin. In 1446 they were arrested with the rest of the Jews in *Brandenburg, and expelled from the electorate after their property had been confiscated. A year later Jews again began to return, and between 1454 and 1475 there were 23 recorded instances of Jews establishing residence in Berlin in the oldest register of inhabitants. A few wealthy Jews were admitted into Brandenburg in 1509. In 1510 the Jews were accused of desecrating the *Host and stealing sacred vessels from a church in a village near Berlin. One hundred and eleven Jews were arrested and subjected to examination, and 51 were sentenced to death; of these 38 were burned at the stake in the new market square together with the real culprit, a Christian, on July 10, 1510. Subsequently, the Jews were expelled from the entire electorate of Brandenburg. All the accused were proved completely innocent at the Diet of Frankfurt in 1539 through the efforts of *Joseph (Joselmann) b. Gershom of Rosheim and *Philipp Melanchthon. The elector Joachim II (1535–71) permitted the Jews to return and settle in the towns in Brandenburg, and Jews were permitted to reside in Berlin in 1543 despite the opposition of the townspeople. In 1571, when the Jews were again expelled from Brandenburg, the Jews of Berlin were expelled "for ever." For the next 100 years, a few individual Jews appeared there at widely scattered intervals. About 1663, the Court Jew Israel Aaron, who was supplier to the army and the electoral court, was permitted to settle in Berlin.

Beginnings of the Modern Community (to 1812)

After the expulsion of the Jews from *Vienna in 1670, the elector issued an edict on May 21, 1671, admitting 50 wealthy Jewish families from Austria into the mark of Brandenburg and the duchy of Crossen (Krosno) for 20 years. They paid a variety of taxes for the protection afforded them but were not permitted to erect a synagogue. The first writ of privileges was issued to Abraham Riess (Abraham b. Model Segal) and Benedict Veit (Baruch b. Menahem Rositz), on Sept. 10, 1671, the date considered to mark the foundation of the new Berlin community. Notwithstanding the opposition of the Christians (and also of Israel Aaron who feared competition) to any increase in the number of Jewish residents in Berlin, the community grew rapidly, and in the course of time the authorities granted letters of protection to a considerable number of Jews. In addition, many *unvergleitete* Jews (i.e., without residence permits) infiltrated into Brandenburg. The first population census of 1700 showed that there were living in Berlin at that time 70 Jewish *vergleitete* families with residence permits, 47 families without writs of protection, and a few peddlers and beggars (about 1,000 persons). The refugees from Austria now became a minority, and quarrels and clashes broke out within the community (see below). The Jews of Berlin engaged mainly in commerce. The guilds and merchants were bitterly opposed to them and they were accused of dealing in stolen goods. The Christians demanded the expulsion of the foreign Jews or restriction of their economic activity to dealing in secondhand goods and pawnbroking, not to be conducted in open shops. The government responded only partly to such demands, being interested in the income from the Berlin Jews. It imposed restrictions upon the increase of the Jewish population in the city and issued decrees increasing their taxes, making the community collectively responsible for the payment of protection money (1700), for prohibiting Jews from maintaining open shops, from dealing in stolen goods (1684), and from engaging in retail trade in certain commodities except at fairs (1690). Nevertheless, the number of Jewish stores grew to such an extent that there was at least one in every street. The Jews were subsequently ordered to close down every store opened after 1690, and all other Jews were forbidden to engage in anything but dealing in old clothes and pawnbroking. They could be exempted from these restrictions on payment of 5,000 thalers.

Elector Frederick III, who became King Frederick I of Prussia in 1701, began a systematic exploitation of the Jews by means of various taxes. The protection tax was doubled in 1688; a tax was levied for the mobilization and arming of an infantry regiment; 10,000 ducats were exacted for various misdemeanors; 1,100 ducats for children recognized as *vergleitete*; 100 thalers annually toward the royal reception in Berlin; 200–300 thalers annually in birth and marriage taxes; and other irregular imposts. Frederick William I (1713–40) limited (in a charter granted to the Jews on May 20, 1714) the number of tolerated Jews to 120 householders, but permitted in certain cases the extension of letters of protection to include the second and third child. The Jews of Berlin were permitted to engage in commerce almost without restriction, and in handicrafts provided that the rights of the guilds were not thereby infringed. By a charter granted in 1730, the number of tolerated Jews was reduced to 100 houscholders. Only the two oldest sons of the family were allowed to reside in Berlin – the first, if he possessed 1,000 thalers in ready money, on payment of 50 thalers, and the second if he owned and paid double these amounts. *Vergleitete* Jews might own stores, but were forbidden to trade in drugs and spices (except for tobacco and dyes), in raw skins, and in imported woolen and fiber goods, and were forbidden to operate breweries or distilleries. They were also forbidden to engage in any craft, apart from seal engraving, gold and silver embroidery, and Jewish ritual slaughter. Land ownership by Jews had been prohibited in 1697 and required a special license which could be obtained only with great difficulty. Jews might bequeath their property to their children, but not to other relatives. On Jan. 22, 1737, Jews were forbidden to buy houses in Berlin or to acquire them in any other fashion. In 1755 an equal interest rate was fixed for Jews and Christians.

The Jews in Berlin in the 18th century primarily engaged as commercial bankers and traders in precious metals and stones. Some served as *court Jews. Members of the *Gomperz family were among the wealthiest in Berlin. In the course of time, all trade in money in Berlin was concentrated in Jewish hands. One of the pioneers of Prussian industry was Levi Ilf, who established a ribbon factory in Charlottenburg in 1718. At the same time the royal policy continued of restricting the Jewish population of Berlin, and even decreasing it as far as possible. When in 1737 it became evident that the number of Jewish families in Berlin had risen to 234, a decree was issued limiting the quota to 120 families (953 persons) with an additional 48 families of "communal officers" (243 persons). The remainder (584) were ordered to leave, and 387 did in fact leave. However in 1743 Berlin had a Jewish population of 333 families (1,945 persons).

*Frederick the Great (1740–86) denied residence rights in Berlin to second and third children of Jewish families and wished to limit the total number of protected Jews to 150. However, the revised *Generalprivilegium* and the royal edict of April 17, 1750, which remained in force until 1812, granted residence rights to 203 "ordinary" families, whose eldest children could inherit that right, and to 63 "extraordinary" families, who might possess it only for the duration of their own lifetime. A specified number of "public servants" was also to be tolerated. However, during his reign, the economic, cultural, and social position of the Jews in Berlin improved. During the Seven Years' War, many Jews became wealthy as purveyors to the army and the mint and the rights enjoyed by the Christian bankers were granted to a number of Jews. In 1763, the Jews in Berlin were granted permission to acquire 70 houses in place of 40. While their role in the retail trade decreased in importance because of the many restrictions imposed, the number of Jewish manufacturers, bankers, and brokers increased. On May 2, 1791, the entire *Itzig family received full civic rights, becoming the first German Jews to whom they were granted. At the same time, the king compelled the Jews to supply a specified quantity of silver annually to the mint at a price below the current one (1763), to pay large sums for new writs of protection (1764), and, in return for various privileges and licenses, to purchase porcelain ware to the value of 300–500 thalers from the royal porcelain factory and sell it abroad.

As a concomitant of economic prosperity, there appeared the first signs of cultural adaptation. Under the influence of Moses *Mendelssohn, several reforms were introduced in the Berlin community, especially in the sphere of education. In 1778 a school, *Juedische Freischule (Ḥinnukh Ne'arim), was founded, which was conducted along modern comprehensive principles and methods. Mendelssohn and David *Friedlaender composed the first German reader for children. The dissemination of general (non-Jewish) knowledge was also one of the aims of the Ḥevrat Doreshei Leshon Ever ("Association of Friends of the Hebrew Language"), founded in 1783, whose organ *Ha-Me'assef* (see *Me'assefim) began to appear in Berlin in 1788. Mendelssohn's home became a gathering place for scholars, and Berlin became the fount of the Enlightenment movement (*Haskalah) and of the trend toward *assimilation. The salons of Henrietta *Herz, Rachel *Varnhagen, and Dorothea *Schlegel served as rendezvous for both Jews and Christians of the social elite of Berlin. However, progress toward legally recognized civil equality was slow. After the new Exchange building was erected in Berlin in 1805, a joint "corporation" of Christians and Jews was established in which the latter were in the majority and had equal rights. In 1803–04, during the literary controversy over the Jewish question, the government took no action whatever on behalf of the Jews, but after the Prussian defeat by Napoleon the Municipal Act of Nov. 19, 1809, facilitated their attainment of citizen status. Solomon *Veit was elected to the Berlin municipal council and David Friedlaender was appointed a city councilor. The edict of March 11, 1812, finally bestowed Prussian citizenship upon the Jews; all restrictions on their residence rights in the state, as well as the special taxes they had to pay, were now abolished.

Internal Life (17th–18th Centuries)

The fierce controversies that had broken out in the Jewish community during the communal elections in 1689 resulted in governmental intervention in the administrative affairs of the community. Thus the decree of January 24 and the statute of Dec. 7, 1700, included government-approved regulations for the Jewish community. The communal leaders (*parnasim*), elected for three years, were empowered to impose fines (two-thirds of which went to the state treasury and one-third to the communal charity fund) and to excommunicate members with the consent of the local rabbi and government. The "chief *parnas*" acted as mediator between the Jews and the state. In 1717, complete anarchy in the conduct of communal affairs became evident; the *parnasim* were deposed and a fine was imposed on the community amounting to 10,000 thalers, later reduced to 6,500. In 1722 and in 1723 new statutes were promulgated regulating the organizational structure of the community. Apart from the chief *parnasim*, who were appointed by the king and functioned under the supervision of a Jewish commission, a communal committee of three, four, or five *parnasim* was set up which would coopt to itself two optimates (*tovim*) and two alternates (*ikkurim*) for handling particularly important matters. To decide on matters of extreme importance larger committees were appointed of 15, 18, or 32 members. In 1792 a supervisory committee was created consisting of three members to supervise the fiscal aspect of communal administration. The first rabbi, elected at the time of the erection of the Berlin synagogue in the Heiderentergasse, was Michael Ḥasid (officiated 1714–28). His successors include Jacob Joshua b. Ẓevi Hirsch *Falk of Cracow (1731–34), author of *Penei Yehoshu'a*, David *Fraenkel (1743–62), author of *Korban ha-Edah* on the Palestinian Talmud and teacher of Moses Mendelssohn, and Ẓevi Hirsch b. Aryeh Loeb (Hirschel *Levin, 1772–1800), known for his opposition to Haskalah.

From the Edict of Equality to the Accession of the Nazis

The political history of the Jews of Berlin after 1812 becomes increasingly merged with that of the Jews of *Prussia and *Germany as a whole. In the 1848 Revolution the Jews played an active role as fighters on the barricades and members of the civic guard, as orators and journalists, and the like. Despite the edict of 1812 Jews continued to be hampered by a number of restrictions, and formal civic equality was not attained until July 1860. Subsequently, Jews began to enter Berlin's political and social life in increasing numbers, and the Berlin municipality was for a long time a stronghold of liberalism and tolerance. About one-fifth of Berlin's newspapers were owned by Jews. The *Berliner Tageblatt* and the *Vossische Zeitung*, whose publishers and editors were Jewish, were read abroad with particular attention, although it was known that they did not express the opinions of circles close to the government. Berlin Jews played a prominent part in literature, the theater, music, and art. Their successes aroused fierce reaction among the more conservative elements and Berlin became a center of antisemitism. The "Berlin Movement" founded by Adolf *Stoecker incited the masses against the Jews by alleging that they were the standard-bearers of capitalism and controlled the press (see *Antisemitic Political Parties and Organizations).

The Jewish population of Berlin numbered 3,292 in 1812; 11,840 in 1852; 108,044 in 1890; and 172,672 in 1925. Thus, within a century it had increased more than fiftyfold. The Jews comprised about 2% of the total population in 1840, 5.02% in 1890, and 4.29% in 1925. The Jews in Berlin comprised 1.4% of German Jewry in 1811–28, 7.03% in 1871, and 30.6% in 1925. Despite the increasing instances of intermarriage, renunciation of Judaism, and conversion to Christianity, and the decline in the Jewish birthrate, the Jewish population of Berlin continued to grow through the arrival of Jews from provincial centers, especially from the province of Posen (Poznan) and from Eastern Europe. As Berlin grew in importance as a commercial and industrial center, Jews played an increasingly important role in the city's economic life, especially as bankers (*Mendelssohn, *Bleichroeder, and others), owners of department stores (*Wertheim, *Tietz, Jandorf), and in the grain and metal trades, the textile and clothing industries, building construction, the manufacture of railway engines and cars, the brewing of beer, and other branches of the economy. Ludwig *Loewe headed a large armaments factory in Berlin. The General Electric Company (AEG) was founded by the Jewish engineer Emil *Rathenau, and both his son Walter *Rathenau and Felix Deutsch were active in it. In 1861 53.17% of the Jews in Berlin engaged in commerce, and 17.3% in industry and the manual trades; by 1910 the percentage of those occupied in commerce had decreased to 41.61%, while 35.16% earned their livelihood in industry and the manual trades.

Internal Life of the Berlin Community (1812–1933)

Following the partitions of Poland-Lithuania, 1772–95, the Berlin community became increasingly influenced by the steady stream of Eastern European Jews (*Ostjuden*) who first arrived from the Posen district. This influx made up for the losses to the Jewish communities through assimilation and apostasy. Later there was growing immigration from the *Pale of Settlement. From the second half of the 19th century the increasing colony of Russian, mainly Jewish, students exerted a powerful cultural influence in Berlin. The organizational structure of the Jewish community was undermined after the emancipation of the Jews in 1812. The old regulations were abolished by the 1812 edict and no new regulations were instituted. For some time the community was not allowed to collect dues and faced disintegration. A statute issued in July 1837 permitted the renewal of normal communal life, and from then on the Berlin community was administered by a committee of seven members and three alternates and a council of 21 members and ten alternates. The first elections to the council took place in February 1854, and the community's first constitution was ratified in August 1860. During this period, the community was thrown into a ferment as a result of the aspiration of David Friedlaender and others for extreme liturgical reforms. The *Reform program was temporarily restrained by a decree of Dec. 9, 1823, which laid down that all divine worship was to take place in the local synagogue and according to accepted custom without any innovations in the language, ritual, prayers, and liturgy.

In 1819, the *Verein fuer Kultur und Wissenschaft des Judentums ("Society for Jewish Culture and Learning"), was founded in Berlin by Leopold *Zunz, I.M. *Jost, and Eduard *Gans, with Heinrich *Heine among its members (see *Germany). In the meanwhile, far-reaching changes had been introduced in education. The Ḥinnukh Ne'arim school was closed at the end of 1825 for lack of funds, and was replaced in 1826 by a new school for boys, founded by the community; Zunz was principal of this school until 1830. In 1835 the community founded a school for girls. There were also several Jewish private schools in Berlin, such as that of H.M. Bock (founded in 1807), whose principals were Jost (1816–35) and Sigismund *Stern (1835–45). R. Meir b. Simḥah Weyl, who charted a conservative course in education, opened a teachers' seminary in 1825. From 1840 to 1850 a teachers' seminary functioned under the direction of Zunz. A teachers' training institute was established in 1859 under the rectorship of Aaron *Horowitz.

In 1844 Michael Jehiel *Sachs was invited to be the third *dayyan* and preacher of the community. Although a Conservative, he was not opposed to moderate reform. In the wake of the foundation of the second Kulturverein ("cultural association"; 1840), Aaron *Bernstein founded the Reform Society in 1845, and later the Reform Congregation, which introduced far-flung liturgical reforms, especially during the rabbinate of Samuel *Holdheim (1847–60). At first, divine worship was held both on Saturdays and Sundays and later only on Sundays. The Reform Congregation was unsuccessful in its attempt to secede from the official community, but the latter was obliged to give very substantial financial support to the Reform Congregation since many of its members were among the largest taxpayers. The Berlin community was again violently shaken when many of its members pressed for the introduction of an organ and modification of the liturgy in the New Synagogue. The appointment of Abraham *Geiger as rabbi of the Berlin community (officiated 1870–74) met with strong opposition from Orthodox circles, and in 1869 Azriel (Israel) *Hildesheimer and his adherents left the main community and established the Adass Yisroel congregation, which received official recognition in 1885. Abraham Geiger had stipulated as a condition of his appointment that an institute for Jewish research be established in Berlin, and in 1872 the *Hochschule fuer die Wissenschaft des Judentums was opened there. A year later, Hildesheimer opened a rabbinical seminary for Orthodox Judaism (*Rabbinerseminar fuer das orthodoxe Judentum). Between 1880 and 1930, eight large synagogues were erected by the Berlin community, among them that in the Fasanenstrasse which was one of the most magnificent synagogues in the world. In all, the community owned 16 synagogues, seven of them Orthodox and the remainder Liberal and Reformist. Thirty rabbis served in Berlin after Abraham Geiger (12 Orthodox and the remainder liberal). In addition, most religious groups which were supported by the community had their own rabbis.

Berlin was the center of the national German-Jewish organizations, such as the *Deutsch-Israelitischer Gemeindebund (founded in 1869), Verband der deutschen Juden (1904), the *B'nai *B'rith (1883), *Central-Verein deutscher Staatsbuerger juedischen Glaubens (1893), *Hilfsverein der deutschen Juden (1901), Zentralwohlfartsstelle der deutschen Juden (1917), and others. Likewise, Jewish newspapers and periodicals were published in Berlin, including the communal organ, whose circulation reached 60,000 copies. The Berlin communal institutions and their activities in every field served as a model for Jewish communities throughout the world. The annual communal budget in the 1930s was about 10,000,000 marks (as against 5,000,000 marks in 1914). About 70,000 Jews in Berlin paid dues to the community.

For about 80 years the Liberals were predominant in the Berlin community. But Liberals and Orthodox worked together in full harmony in the central organizations in which, at least for a certain period, the Zionists also participated. The *Ḥibbat Zion movement met with but a lukewarm reception in Berlin, especially among the Orthodox, and the opposition to political Zionism was particularly keen. The Berlin rabbi S. *Maybaum was among the leaders of the "*Protest Rabbis," and the Central-Verein and the *Vereinigung fuer das liberale Judentum launched a concerted effort against the Zionistische Vereinigung fuer Deutschland and its organ, the *Juedische Rundschau. When the procedure for communal elections was changed after World War I, four representatives of the *Juedische Volkspartei (a coalition of Zionists, *Mizrachi, and the Verband der ostjuedischen Organizationen) and one of the *Po'alei Zion were elected in 1920 to the representative council (Repraesentantenversammlung), which consisted of 21 members; two Zionists sat on the communal committee (Gemeindevorstand). In the 1926 election, a coalition of the Juedische Volkspartei, the Conservatives, and the Mittelpartei won a majority. For three years, the Zionist Georg Kareski headed the communal committee. However, in the elections of November 1930, 24 Liberals were elected to the representative council, 14 from the Juedische Volkspartei, and three from among the small parties; seven Liberals, three Zionists, and one Conservative sat on the communal committee. Max Naumann and his faction were the spearhead of the extremist anti-Zionist faction which rejected all cooperation with non-German Jews and demanded that the Zionists be deprived of their German citizenship and permitted to reside in Germany only as aliens. In 1922, at the initiative of the Berlin community, the Preussischer Landesverband juedischer Gemeinden was founded, comprising 655 communities, not including the Orthodox communities which formed their own association. A great boon to the Berlin community was the government support which was granted for the first time during the inflation of late 1923, without which it could not have survived. In later years, the government subsidy to the community was insufficient.

After the murders of Karl Liebknecht and Rosa *Luxemburg in January 1919, antisemitic propaganda in Berlin increased. The Kapp Putsch (March 1920) had blatant anti-Jewish undertones. Walter Rathenau, the German foreign minister, was assassinated by antisemitic nationalists on June 24, 1922. On Nov. 5, 1923, antisemites attacked the Jews living in Grenadierstrasse and Dragonerstrasse, which were centers of Jewish residence. In 1926, after the appointment of Joseph *Goebbels as *Gauleiter* in Berlin, anti-Jewish rabble-rousing increased. On the eve of the Jewish New Year (Sept. 12, 1931), Jews returning from synagogue in Kurfuerstendam were assaulted by gangs of Nazis, organized by Count Wolff Heinrich von Halldorf (later chief of police in the Third Reich).

[Joseph Meisl]

1933–39

At the time the Nazis came to power, Berlin's organized Jewish community numbered about 172,000 persons. In the preceding years as the Nazi movement was growing in influence, the rate of Jewish affiliation had increased. With Hitler's ascent to power on January 30, 1933, street demonstrations were immediate and made Jews feel deeply uncomfortable. In 1933 the Nazi boycott (April 1) affected Jewish shop owners; April 7th legislation against non-Aryans led to dismissal of Jewish professionals and civil servants, including physicians and professors; while "aryanization" of Jewish firms and the dismissal of their Jewish employees was carried out by the exertion of steady economic pressure. The response of the community was mixed. There was a wave of suicides but also an attempt by the community to respond to deteriorating conditions. Economic assistance was provided to those in need; new vocations were found for youth, legal counseling and housing advice was provided. In response to the April 1st boycott of Jewish businesses,Robert Weltsch wrote an editorial in the *Judische Rundschau* called "Wear the Yellow Badge with Pride." Synagogue attendance increased, as did Zionist activities. Still the community did not formally encourage emigration. It thought of Germany as the land of its fathers and its children, a perspective that was to dramatically change. Eight new Jewish elementary schools were founded in 1933. Jewish officials – "Jewishness" was soon defined to refer to one's parents and grandparents and not one's own identity – not affected by these early measures were eventually ousted under the provisions of the *Nuremberg Laws (1935). During this early period, such incidents as the murder of a Jewish physician, Dr. Philippsthal (spring 1933), and the suicide of Rudolf S. Mosse after mistreatment in prison (fall 1933), the first such instances of their kind, caused great consternation among the Jews. In these initial years, when the members of the Jewish community were being methodically deprived of their economic standing and civil rights, Jewish religious and cultural life in Berlin underwent a tremendous upsurge. Jewish children, most of them excluded from the public schools, attended schools set up and maintained by the Jewish community or private schools. In addition to the eight Jewish elementary schools that were maintained at one period to meet the community needs, the famous college for Jewish studies, the *Hochschule fuer die Wissenschaft des Judentums, was sustained to train leadership and its program greatly expanded. Jews were later forbidden to attend theaters and public places of entertainment. The Juedischer Kulturbund ("Jewish Cultural Society") was established. In the summer of 1935 yellow benches for the segregation of Jews were set up in parks and inscribed *nur fuer Juden* ("only for Jews"). Signs inscribed *Juden unerwuenscht* ("Jews not wanted") were displayed in public places. The economic condition of Jews in Berlin deteriorated rapidly. By 1935 welfare assistance was a significant responsibility of the community. Signs discriminating against Jews were removed for the duration of the Olympic Games held in Berlin (summer 1936). Antisemitic propaganda was reduced only to return with a vengeance once the Games were over and the tourists had returned to their native lands. Throughout this period from 1933 to 1938, raids and arrests became frequent occurrences and were accelerated in 1938. Until November 1938 Jewish newspapers and books were published on an unprecedented scale. Notable among the newspapers was the *Berliner juedisches Gemeindeblatt*, a voluminous weekly published by the community. Zionist work was in full swing, especially that of He-Ḥalutz, and in February 1936, a German Zionist convention was held in Berlin (the last to meet there), still reflecting in its composition the vigorous party life of German Zionists. From March 28, 1938, the Jewish community was deprived of its status as a recognized public corporate body. The Berlin community was made a "private" organization, denied the right to collect dues from the community, and renamed the Juedische Kultusvereinigung Berlin ("Jewish Religious Society").

In June 1938, mass arrests of Jews took place on the charge that they were "asocial," e.g., had a criminal record, including traffic violations, and they were imprisoned in the *Sachsenhausen concentration camp. On November 9–10, *Kristallnacht marked a turning point in the affairs of Berlin Jewry: synagogues were burned down, Jewish shops destroyed, Jewish institutions were raided and closed, including libraries and museums, and Jewish manuscripts and documents were destroyed. In the wake of **Kristallnacht*, 1,200 Jewish businesses were put up for Aryanization and 10,000 Jews from Berlin and other places were arrested and imprisoned in Sachsenhausen. The "*Bannmeile*" was decreed, which restricted Jews to an area within a certain radius from their place of residence; banished them from most of the main thoroughfares, and the area in which government offices were located; and evicted Jews from their apartments, a step which had begun earlier, but was now accelerated. Jewish newspapers had to cease publication. The only paper was the new *Das juedische Narchrichtenblatt* which was required to publish Gestapo directives to the Jews. Meetings of bodies of the Jewish community were no longer permitted, and the Jewish community's executive council had to conduct its affairs from then on without consulting any representative group. Religious services, when resumed, were now restricted to three synagogues (on Levetzow, Luetzow, and Kaiser Streets) and a few small halls. The pace of Aryanization accelerated as did the rate of emigration. Most of Berlin's rabbis left Berlin before *Kristallnacht*: the last three rabbis to stay were Felix Singerman (died in Riga in 1942), Martin Salomonski (died in Auschwitz in 1944), and the most prominent of all, Leo *Baeck, who was offered the opportunity to leave but decided to stay with his flock and was sent to Theresienstadt camp in early 1943. As the Germans arrived in his home, Baeck asked for half an hour, during which time he posted a letter to his daughter in England and with an unyielding sense of honor paid his gas and electric bills. At the end of January 1939, the Gestapo established a Zentralstelle fuer juedische Auswanderung ("Central Bureau for Jewish Emigration") in Berlin. The Berlin community, presided over by Heinrich *Stahl, was the largest and most dynamic German-Jewish community, and was incorporated along with the Reichsvertretung der deutschen Juden into the Nazi-imposed Reichsvereinigung der Juden in Deutschland – the change in name from German Jews to Jews in Germany was essential, not incidental – established on July 4, 1939. After its incorporation into the Reichsvereinigung, the Berlin community maintained its autonomous function for some time.

1939–45

After the outbreak of war, some 82,000 Jews were living in Berlin – about half having left between 1933 and 1939. The living conditions and situation of the Jews worsened. Emigration was still permitted and even encouraged, and existing organizations and institutions (the Kulturbund, Jewish schools) were able to continue functioning. However, Jews were drafted for forced labor at wages far below the prevailing rate and with no social benefits, but this at least provided them with a minimum income and delayed their deportation. Many were employed in armament industries, which also slowed their deportation. On Jan. 31, 1940, a special Arbeitsamt fuer Judenarbeiter ("Labor Exchange for Jew-Workers") was set up. In the spring of 1940 Stahl was removed from his post in the Reichsvereinigung by the Nazi authorities and replaced by Moritz Henschel, a former attorney. In September 1941, a drastic turn for the worse came about. First the *Judenstern* ("Jewish star," i.e., yellow *badge) was introduced. Two weeks later, on the Day of Atonement, in the middle of a sermon by Rabbi Leo Baeck, the president of the community was summoned to the Gestapo and told that the community would have to prepare for a partial evacuation from the city, that large apartments still occupied by Jews would have to be cleared, that many additional parts of the city would now be out of bounds to Jews, and that the Levetzowstrasse synagogue would be turned into a *Sammellager* ("assembly camp") for 1,000 persons. In due course more such assembly camps were added. Legal emigration was prohibited on October 23. The last transport of legal emigrants left Berlin on October 18 for Lisbon. In the preceding months (May–October), 1,342 emigrants had been permitted to leave. Between October 23 and the end of the year only 62 persons managed to leave, and in 1942 only nine Jews were permitted to go abroad. To make Berlin **judenrein*, deportations began. There were five major phases in the process of deportation, the destination of Berlin's Jews reflecting the changes in German policy from forced emigration to resettlement in the East and then to murder by gassing: (a) between fall 1941 and January 1942 the deportees were sent to Riga, Minsk, Kovno, and Lodz, sometimes directly to the killing fields; (b) those deported in spring 1942 were sent to Lublin (Trawniki); (c) between summer 1942 and February 1943 their destination was Theresienstadt, Auschwitz, Riga, and Tallinn (Rasiku); (d) Auschwitz was the destination of the deportees of March–April 1943; (e) those deported from spring 1943 until the end of the war were sent to Bergen-Belsen, Ravensbrueck, Sachsenhausen, and Auschwitz. Altogether there were 63 *Osttransporte* carrying some 35,000 victims to death camps in the east, and 117 *Alterstransporte*, transporting some 15,000 (mainly older) persons to Theresienstadt. It is believed that about 95% of the first and 90% of the second group perished. (For lists of transport numbers, dates, numbers of deportees and destinations, see bibliography, Sellenthin, 84–85.) All through 1942 the deportations were kept up, although community employees and persons employed on forced labor were still excluded. In November and December 1942, the infamous commissar Alois Brunner (see Adolf *Eichmann) from Vienna was employed in Berlin and was responsible for organizing the picking up of the candidates for deportation in their homes, distinguishing himself by his extraordinary cruelty. Eventually, the deportations came to include groups of community employees, and from the fall of 1942, only those Jewish laborers who were employed in vital war production were still safe from deportation. At the beginning of 1943, the Gestapo persuaded the military administration to relinquish these workers, which resulted on February 27–28 in the so-called "*Fabrikaktion*" – marked by exceptional cruelty – in which all the workers were taken straight from the factories and deported from Berlin. Those Jews arrested in this "action" who had gentile wives were taken to a special camp for onward deportation, but when their wives carried out violent street demonstrations, the Gestapo yielded and set their husbands free. Even at that late date, the Nazis were seemingly responsive to public opinion. On May 13, 1942, an anti-Jewish exhibition, *Soviet Paradise*, was opened in Berlin, and was attacked by a group of Jewish communists, led by Herbert *Baum. The group was caught and hardly any of them survived. The Germans imposed collective – and disproportionate – reprisal. Two hundred and fifty Jews – 50 for each German who had been killed in the attack – were shot, and another 250 were sent to Sachsenhausen and perished there. The community offices were closed down on June 10, 1943, and six days later the "full" Jews among the members of its executive council were deported to Theresienstadt. The remaining Jews were looked after by the Neue Reichsvereinigung, which took up its seat in the Berlin Jewish Hospital, which together with the Jewish cemetery were the two Jewish institutions that continued to function throughtout the war. While the deportations went on, many Jews tried to stay on illegally, a very difficult undertaking, owing to the need for frequent change of hideouts and the lack of ration cards; many were caught and deported. The "illegals" were given temporary help on an organized basis, by groups of people who were of mixed parentage (*Mischlinge*) and as such were not liable for deportation themselves; there were also some Germans who at the risk of their lives put their apartments at the disposal of the Jews who were hiding out. One group of Jewish youngsters and their instructor managed to hide in Grunewald for an extended period, spending their time in the study of Zionist subjects. No exact figure is available for the number of "illegal" Jews who survived in Berlin, and estimates vary from 2,000 to 5,000. Berlin became officially "*judenrein*" ("clean of Jews") on June 16, 1943. On June 30, 1943, there were in fact 6,700, and on March 31, 1945, 5,990 Jews, comprising 4,790 Jews who had non-Jewish spouses, 992 "*Geltungsjuden*" (persons of mixed parentage, professing Jewish religion), 46 Jews from non-enemy countries, and 162 "full" Jews, most of whom were employed in the Jewish Hospital. The Jewish cemetery had remained in use – several Torah

Scrolls were hidden there during the years of the Nazi persecution in a concerted organized activity which encompassed over 500 scrolls to be restituted after the war.

Number of Jews in Berlin – 1816–1945

	Absolute Numbers	Percentages
1816	3,373	1.20
1837	5,648	1.98
1855	12,675	2.93
1871	36,326	4.15
1895	94,391	4.48
1905	130,487	4.30
1910	142,289	4.05
1925	172,672	4.30
1933	160,564	3.80
1939[1]	82,788	1.70
Jan. 1942[2]	55,000	—
Dec. 1942[2]	33,000	—
Apr. 1943[3]	18,315	—
1945	9,000	—

1 Including Jews by "race" – decrease due mainly to emigration but in small measure also due to a mortality rate higher than the birth rate. Emigration figures were actually higher for Berlin Jewry, but were offset by the influx of Jews from the provinces.
2 Decrease due to deportation.
3 Decrease due to final mass deportations.

Dashes denote unavailability of information.

Size of the Jewish Population

The Table: Jewish Population of Berlin shows the decrease in the Jewish population of Berlin between 1925 and 1945. The statistics before 1933 refer to persons designated as members of the Jewish faith, whereas the later figures for the most part also include Jews "by race" (as defined by the Nuremberg Laws):

[Kurt Jakob Ball-Kaduri / Michael Berenbaum (2nd ed.)]

Contemporary Period

On July 15, 1945, the Jewish community was officially reconstituted. At first it was headed by Erich Nelhans, a former *Mizrachi leader, and from the fall of 1945 by Hans Erich Fabian, who had returned from Theresienstadt, the only member of the Reichsvereinigung to survive the war. Also active in the leadership of the community were Alfred Schoyer, a member of the Berlin Jewish Community Council before his deportation; Heinz Galinski, who had returned from Bergen-Belsen; and Julius Meyer, a survivor of Auschwitz. At the beginning of 1946, the community had a registered membership of 7,070 people, of whom 4,121 (over 90% of all married members) had non-Jewish spouses, 1,321 had survived the war by hiding, and 1,628 had returned from concentration camps. The Jews were dispersed throughout Berlin, a third of them living in the Soviet sector. The community was assisted by the military government, as well as by the *American Jewish Joint Distribution Committee (JDC), which initiated its activities in Berlin in the autumn of 1945. Several synagogues were opened, the Jewish Hospital resumed its work (although most of its patients and staff were not Jews), and three homes for the aged and a children's home were established. There was no local rabbi or religious teachers, but American Jewish army chaplains volunteered their services. The general assumption at this time was that the Jews would not be able to reestablish themselves in Berlin (or anywhere else in Germany) and that the community's principal task was to help them to emigrate from the country. The community was thus defined as a "liquidation community" (*Liquidationsgemeinde*).

In addition to the organized Jewish community, Berlin also became a center for Jewish *Displaced Persons (DPs). Toward the end of 1945 and during the first half of 1946, the main *Beriḥah route from Poland led through Stettin and the Soviet Zone to Berlin, from where it continued through the remaining part of the Soviet Zone and the British Zone to the American Zone. It was a very arduous route, especially during the harsh winter months, and temporary shelter had to be provided in Berlin. A small camp was established in the Wittenau district of the French sector of the city in the autumn of 1945 with a capacity of 200; at the beginning of 1946 a large camp was established at Schlachtensee in the American sector, which could hold 4,000 refugees, and a third camp was established in the summer of 1946 in the Tempelhof district of the American sector. In July 1946, however, the Beriḥah from Poland took on a quasi-legal character and was rerouted through Czechoslovakia and Vienna to the American Zone in Germany and Austria. As a result the refugee population of Berlin became fairly stabilized. By the end of 1946, there were 6,785 DPs in the three Berlin camps. When the Soviet blockade of Berlin was lifted, the Occupation authorities decided to evacuate the DPs, and between July 23 and Aug. 1, 1948, 5,456 Jewish refugees were airlifted from Berlin to various camps in the American Zone.

By this time the Jewish community had reached a measure of consolidation, in spite of the difficult economic and political conditions in the city. Although a few hundred members had emigrated overseas and mortality exceeded the birthrate, the total number of Jews had increased as a result of the influx of Jews returning from abroad. Prominent among the returnees was a group of 500 refugees who had spent the war years in *Shanghai. The welfare services extended by the community were greatly improved; the return of confiscated property, a process which was initiated at this time, also helped raise the standing of the community. In 1946, upon the initiative of Fabian, the community established its own weekly, *Der Weg*, later to be merged with the Jewish weekly appearing in Duesseldorf. Jewish organizations in the United States arranged for American rabbis to undertake several years' service in Berlin. In 1949 Galinski was elected as chairman of the community council.

The growing tension between the Western and Soviet Occupation authorities also had its effect upon Berlin Jewry. In 1947 Nelhans was arrested by the Soviets on the charge of aiding Soviet military personnel to desert; he was sentenced to 15 years imprisonment and was not heard of subsequently. Although the city administration was split in two, the Jewish community remained unified until the end of 1952, when its own split became inevitable. In the following years, the situation of the Jews and the community in West Berlin was greatly improved as a result of the rising economic prosperity in West Germany (which also affected West Berlin) and the return of confiscated property and the indemnification of victims of Nazi persecution. The Berlin City Senate showed great concern for the rehabilitation of the community and its individual members; Joachim Lipschitz, the senator for internal affairs (who was the son of a Jewish father and a Christian mother), in particular did his utmost to help the development of the community. Four synagogues were operating in Berlin. In 1959, the City of Berlin erected a large Jewish community center on Fasanenstrasse at the site on which one of Berlin's most magnificent synagogues had stood until 1938. In 1954 the Zionist Organization and the Israel Appeal renewed their activities in Berlin. A Jewish women's organization, a B'nai B'rith lodge, a Jewish students' organization, and a youth organization as well as several organizations dedicated to the fostering of interfaith relations were established.

In 1954 the community had a membership of about 5,000 and by January 1970 this figure had risen to 5,577. The demographic composition of the community was marked by relatively high average age (4,080 were above the age of 41), a low birthrate, and a great number of mixed marriages.

EAST BERLIN. In 1946 the number of Jews in the Soviet sector was 2,442, while in 1966 it was estimated at 850 (according to figures given by the community's president, Max Schenk). Although there was officially no restriction on religious practice and the authorities supported the community (the great synagogue on Rykestrasse was reconstructed), the prevailing anti-religious atmosphere of a communist state had a detrimental effect upon the community. By 1990 the number of community members had fallen to 200.

[Chaim Yahil]

SINCE 1989. After the German reunification of 1989, the Jewish communities of former West and East Berlin merged in 1990. The community maintains six synagogues, an elementary school, and other educational institutions. Since 1995 the magnificent building of the former synagogue on Oranienburger Strasse has housed the Centrum Judaicum, which serves as a museum and a center of documentation and research. Jewish cultural institutions and initiatives are manifold and an integral part of Berlin's cultural life. A Jewish museum was opened in 2002 and has since been among the museums drawing the largest numbers of visitors in Germany. The number of community members has risen from 6,411 in 1989 to 11,167 in 2003, with many coming from the former Soviet Union.

[Stefan Rohrbacher (2nd ed.)]

Hebrew Printing in Berlin

The first Hebrew printer in Berlin was the court preacher and professor D.E. Jablonsky, as Jews could not obtain the necessary license; nevertheless, the manager J.L. Neumark, and most of the setters and proofreaders were Jews. The first book published by them was the Book of Psalms (1697), followed by the complete Bible (1699), and other scholarly and liturgical works. An application by Rabbi Mirels for permission to print the Talmud in Berlin was refused by Frederick I, king of Prussia; the permission to publish Maimonides' Code was not taken up, as this was just being printed in Amsterdam by J. *Athias. But a Talmud edition was issued by Gottschalk and Jablonski, in partnership with a Frankfurt on the Oder printer, 1715–22. Among other printers to be mentioned are Baruch Buchbinder (Radoner) of Vilna (1708–17), who printed a number of important works such as the *Tzena Urena* and works by the Shabbatean Nehemiah *Ḥayon (1713), a Mishnah with Rashi and Jacob Ḥagiz's commentary (1716–17), and a *Ḥoshen Mishpat* (1717). Nathan, son of the aforementioned J.L. Neumark, was active 1719–27, while his son-in-law Aaron b. Moses Rofe of Lissa built up an important press, 1733–62, publishing a series of well-known rabbinic works, above all the second Berlin Talmud edition 1734–39. Aaron's press was continued for a while by his grandson Moses b. Mordecai. An annual *Lu'aḥ* began to appear probably from 1725 but not later than 1738. Of some importance was the press of Isaac b. Jacob Speyer (1764–70), a son-in-law of the Berlin rabbi David Fraenkel, who printed notable rabbinic works – Steinschneider calls it "the highlight of Hebrew printing in Berlin"; and that of Mordecai Landsberg, also from 1764. The prolific writer and editor Isaac *Satanow took over Landsberg's press in 1772 and issued a considerable number of books, particularly his own (until 1804). In 1784 David Friedlaender and his friends founded the Verlag der juedischen Freischule, managed by A. *Wolfsohn-Halle, who bought the Landsberg press and obtained a license to print and sell books. Pupils of the society were taught the craft of printing and a number of books were published from 1796 with the imprint "Orientalische Druckerei." During these years Berlin became the center for the printing of Enlightenment literature, notably the writings of M. Mendelssohn, N.H. Wessely, D. Friedlaender, etc. Mendelssohn's edition of the Pentateuch appeared here in 1783.

In 1830 the Landsberg press was bought by Isaac Levent. In that year the printer Trevitsch and son moved to Berlin from Frankfurt on the Oder. In 1834, the year of his death, David Friedlaender founded his own press and published a number of important books; the scholar D. *Cassel worked there as a proofreader. In 1836 the apostate Julius Sittenfeld set up a printing house which published the complete Talmud (1862–68), Maimonides' Code (1862), and other works. In the late 19th and early 20th century H. Itzkowski and Siegfried, Arthur and Erich Scholem were active as general, Jewish, and also Hebrew publishers and printers in Berlin. In 1930 a Pentateuch was printed for the *Soncino-Gesellschaft by the "Officina Serpentis" with a new Hebrew type cut for this occasion.

[Abraham Meir Habermann]

BIBLIOGRAPHY: J. Meisl (ed.), *Pinkas Kehillat Berlin 1723–1854 – Protokollbuch der juedischen Gemeinde Berlin* (Heb. and Ger., 1962); idem, in: *Arim ve-Immahot be-Yisrael*, 1 (1946), 80–140; H.G. Sellenthin, *Geschichte der Juden in Berlin* (1959); Germ Jud, 2 (1968), 68–73; E.L. Landshuth, *Toledot Anshei Shem* (1884); P. von Gebhardt (ed.), *Das aelteste Buergerbuch 1453–1700* (1927); L. Geiger, *Geschichte der Juden in Berlin* (1871); D. Kaufmann, *Die letzte Vertreibung der Juden aus Wien* (1889), 206–21; L. Davidsohn, *Beitraege zur Sozial- und Wirtschaftsgeschichte der Berliner Juden vor der Emanzipation* (1920); M. Stern, *Beitraege zur Geschichte der juedischen Gemeinde zu Berlin*, 6 vols. (1926–34); *Gemeindeblatt der juedischen Gemeinde zu Berlin* (1911–38); *Juedisches Jahrbuch fuer Gross-Berlin* (1926–28) and *Juedisches Jahrbuch* (1929–33); D. Friedlaender, *Akten-Stuecke, die Reform der juedischen Kolonien in den Preussischen Staaten betreffend* (1793); I. Freund, *Die Emanzipation der Juden in Preussen*, 2 vols. (1912); S. Stern, *Der preussische Staat und die Juden*, 2 vols. (1925, repr. 1962); W. Heise, *Die Juden in der Mark Brandenburg bis zum Jahre 1571* (1932); H. Rachel, *Das Berliner Wirtschaftsleben im Zeitalter des Fruehkapitalismus* (1931); H. Rachel et al., *Berliner Grosskaufleute und Kapitalisten*, 3 vols. (1934–39); J. Jacobsohn (ed.), *Die Judenbuergerbuecher der Stadt Berlin, 1809–1851* (1962); M. Sinasohn (ed.), *Adas Jisroel, Berlin* (1966); H. Seeliger, in: YLBI, 3 (1958), 159–68; I. Eisenstein-Barzilay, in: PAAJR, 25 (1956), 1–37; 29 (1960–61), 17–54; idem, in: *Essays on Jewish Life and Thought* (1959), 183–97; Barzilay, in: PAAJR, 29 (1960–61), 17–54; idem, in: JSOS, 21 (1959), 165–92; E. Hurwicz, in: YLBI, 12 (1967), 85–102. HOLOCAUST PERIOD: P. Littauer, *My Experiences During the Persecution of the Jews in Berlin and Brussels, 1939–44* (1945); Irgun Olej Merkas Europa, *Die letzten Tage des deutschen, Judentums* (1943); Ball-Kaduri, in: *Yad Vashem Studies*, 3 (1959), 261–81; 5 (1963), 271–316; H. Gaertner, in: YLBI, 1 (1956), 123–42; F. Friedlaender, *ibid.*, 3 (1958), 187–201; S. Shiratzki, *ibid.*, 5 (1960), 299–307. **ADD. BIBLIOGRAPHY:** *Nachrichtenblatt der juedischen Gemeinde von Gross-Berlin D.D.R.* (1961); A. Brass, *Aufbau* (March 12, 1971); idem, *Geschehnisse auf dem Friedhof Berlin-Weissensee in den Jahren 1936–45*; B. Scheiger, in: S. Jersch-Wenzel (ed.), *Von Zuwanderern zu Einheimischen* (1990), 153–488; W. Gruner, *Judenverfolgung in Berlin* (1992); B. Meyer, in: H. Simon (ed.), *Juden in Berlin 1938–1945* (2000); A. Nachama (ed.), *Juden in Berlin* (2001). HEBREW PRINTING: H.D. Friedberg, *Toledot ha-Defus ha-Ivri be-Arim Augsburg…* (1935), 87ff.; R.N. Rabinowitz, *Ma'amar al Hadpasat ha-Talmud* (1952), 108f., 152f.; Steinschneider, in: ZGJD, 1 (1887), 377ff.; 2 (1888), 200ff.; 3 (1889), 84ff., 262ff.; A.M. Habermann, *Ha-Sefer ha-Ivri be-Hitpattehuto* (1968), index.

BERLIN, ARYEH LOEB BEN ABRAHAM MEIR (1738–1814), German rabbi. Berlin, the younger brother of Noah Ḥayyim Ẓevi Hirsch *Berlin, was born in Fuerth where his father, a well-to-do merchant, was communal leader of Franconian Jewry. Like his brother, he was appointed *dayyan* in Fuerth but Aryeh Loeb was at the same time rabbi of Baiersdorf in Bavaria. From 1789 he was rabbi of Bamberg, where his duties included that of civil judge. While there he was involved in an unpleasant lawsuit when the heirs of a large estate of which he was appointed executor accused him of abusing his office, exacting illegal fees, and not accounting for certain expenditure. He was acquitted of dishonesty, but made to pay a fine. The publication of the relevant documents by Eckstein (see bibl.) shows that the charges were groundless. In 1794 Berlin was appointed chief rabbi of Hesse-Kassel, but owing to the opposition of his detractors in Bamberg he was unable to leave and did not assume his post until the following year. When the kingdom of Westphalia, with Kassel as its capital, was created by Napoleon in 1807 and given to Jerome Bonaparte, Berlin delivered a sermon in Hebrew welcoming the new king and composed a hymn of praise in Hebrew (published under the title *Davar be-Itto Mah Tov*, with a German translation, Kassel, 1807). In 1808, when the Jewish *consistory was organized on the basis of the French consistories he was appointed chief rabbi of the kingdom. The president of the consistory was Israel *Jacobsohn, and Berlin, despite the protests of the more extreme rabbis, agreed to certain relaxations of the strict laws of Passover, in particular permitting the eating of peas and beans on Passover.

Berlin's annotations to the Talmud appear in the three volumes of the Fuerth edition (1829–32) which were published, and his annotations to the tractate *Shevu'ot* are in the Romm-Vilna edition. Some of his novellae appear as an appendix to his brother's *Aẓei Almuggim* (Sulzbach, 1779).

BIBLIOGRAPHY: A. Eckstein, *Geschichte des Juden im ehemaligen Fuerstbistum Bamberg* (1898), 176–9, and Nachtraege (1899), 3–44; E. Kohn, *Kinat Soferim* (1892), 896f.

BERLIN, CONGRESS OF, gathering of the great European powers in 1878 to settle problems concerning the Balkans and Near East arising after the war between Russia and Turkey in 1877. Held between June 13 and July 13, 1878, it was attended by representatives of Austria-Hungary, France, Great Britain, Italy, Russia, and Turkey, with some participation of representatives of the Balkan states (Greece, Montenegro, Romania, and Serbia). Among its most influential members was the head of the British delegation, Benjamin *Disraeli (Lord Beaconsfield). The position of the Jews in the Balkan countries (Romania, Serbia, and Bulgaria) was also placed on the agenda on the initiative of the "Zion" society in Bucharest, led by Adolf Weinberg and Adolf *Stern; these joined with the *Alliance Israélite Universelle in Paris and the Council for the Defense of Romanian Jews in Berlin, led by Moritz *Lazarus. The Jewish community of Berlin petitioned the chairman of the congress and head of the German delegation, Count *Bismarck, on Feb. 28, 1878, to raise the question of equal rights for Romanian Jews at the congress. As a result, the German representatives were instructed to demand equal civil rights for the members of all religions in the Balkan countries and the inclusion in the peace treaty of special paragraphs to this effect explicitly providing for their implementation. The question of equal rights for the Jews in these countries was also discussed in the parliaments of France, Italy, Austria, and Hungary, and the representatives of these countries at the congress were requested by special resolutions to ensure an appropriate settlement.

To deal with the Jewish questions a special council was established in Berlin consisting of the representatives of the Committee for Jewish Affairs in Berlin (Gerson von *Bleichroeder, M. Lazarus, Jacob *Bernays, and Berthold *Auerbach), representatives of the Alliance (Sacki Kann, Charles *Netter, and Emanuel *Veneziani), the delegation of Romanian Jews (Adolf Stern, Marco Brociner, Taussig, and Hermann *Hirsch), and representatives of the Alliance in Berlin (Salomon Neumann, the banker Julius Platho, and Hermann Goldschmidt). This committee formulated a memorandum which was submitted to the entire congress, followed by a second memorandum to Bismarck. The memoranda contained a description of the plight of the Jews in the Balkan countries accompanied by a request that the members of all creeds and races should be guaranteed equal civil rights in the peace treaty (stipulated in special clauses). Special steps were also taken to submit the Jewish requests to the representatives of the different governments. To this end Baron Maurice de *Hirsch and Sir Moses *Montefiore began negotiations with the representatives of England and France, and Bleichroeder turned his attentions to Bismarck and the Russian representative, Count Shuvalov.

The members of the united committee also visited the representatives of the Balkan countries (Romania, Serbia, Bulgaria), who were not officially represented at the congress but were working behind the scenes. The Romanian representative, Kogălniceanu, endeavored to persuade the Jewish representatives not to appeal to the congress since the question of equal civil rights for Jews was an internal affair of the Romanian government. Threats against the Jews of Romania appeared in Romanian newspapers which also attempted to influence the Western Jews to withdraw their demands. These tactics, however, were vehemently condemned and rejected by the representatives of the Alliance.

On June 24, 1878, the Jewish problem came up for discussion as part of the general consideration of Bulgarian affairs. The French representative, Waddington, proposed that a clause be inserted in the peace treaty recognizing the independence of Bulgaria on condition that it granted equal civil rights to members of all races and religions. The proposal was accepted. On June 28, during the discussions on Serbia, the Turkish representative, Karatheodori (Caratheodory) Pasha, and the English representative, Lord Salisbury, demanded that a similar clause be inserted in the peace treaty as a condition for the recognition of Serbian independence. The Russian representative, Prince Gorchakov, opposed this resolution on the ground that the Jews of Serbia, Romania, and Russia could not be put in the same category with the Jews of Paris, London, Berlin, and Vienna. Despite his opposition it was decided to insert in the peace treaty a clause (par. 35) guaranteeing equal rights.

Also during the discussions on Romania it was proposed by Waddington that recognition of that country's independence should be made contingent on her granting equal rights to the members of all religions within her borders. The proposal received the full support of Beaconsfield, Count Andrássy of Austria Hungary, and Bismarck, and even the agreement of Shuvalov. By a separate resolution, introduced into paragraph 44 of the peace treaty, equal rights were granted to the members of all religions in Romania. This principle was also to be binding, according to a resolution introduced by Salisbury, on Turkey, Greece, and Montenegro.

The question of the future of Palestine was also touched upon by the congress indirectly. In June 1878 a group of Jews submitted a memorandum to the congress (addressed to Bismarck and Beaconsfield) requesting that the Jews in Palestine should be given their independence (in the same manner as had been restored to the Balkan peoples) and permitted to establish a constitutional Jewish monarchy in that country. This memorandum was listed in the protocol of documents submitted to the congress but was not discussed on the floor. Before the congress assembled, there were discussions in the English press concerning the political resurgence of the Jews in Palestine. After the congress was concluded, Serbia and Bulgaria complied with the clauses of the peace treaty obliging them to grant equal rights to their minorities, and even incorporated these clauses in their constitutions. Romania refused to meet her obligation, and the struggle to implement paragraph 44 of the peace treaty in this country extended over decades.

BIBLIOGRAPHY: Kohler and Wolf, in: AJHSP, 24 (1916), ix; 1ff.; 40; J. Brociner, *Die Judenfrage in Rumaenien und ihre Loesung* (1879); B. Segel, *Rumaenien und seine Juden* (1918); L. Wolf, *Notes on the Diplomatic History of the Jewish Question* (1919), 23–26, 52; Gelber, in: HJ, 2 (1940), 39–48; idem, in: YLBI, 5 (1960), 221–48; idem, in: *Sefer Yovel… S. Federbush* (1960), 117–64; idem, in: *Sefer Yugoslavyah* (Tel Aviv, 1962); J. Meisl, *Die Durchfuehrung des Artikels 44 des Berliner Vertrages in Rumaenien und die europaeische Diplomatie* (1925); N. Leven, *Cinquante ans d'histoire…*, 1 (1911).

[Nathan Michael Gelber]

BERLIN, DAVID BEN (Judah) LOEB (d. 1771), German rabbi and talmudic authority. The brother of Isaiah *Berlin, he was probably born in Eisenstadt (Hungary). After serving as rabbi of Dessau and Marktbreit (Bavaria) and as chief rabbi of Schwarzburg, Berlin was appointed rabbi of the three united congregations of Altona, Hamburg, and Wandsbeck. In 1769 when the Danish government, at the instance of the Hamburg Town Council, sought to separate the Altona Jewish community from that of Hamburg, Berlin was elected a member of the delegation whose successful intercession with the Danish king resulted in the continuation of the status quo. His learned correspondence with his brother-in-law, Joseph Steinhardt, was published in the latter's work, *Zikhron Yosef* (EH 4:11; ḤM 1:2); a number of his responsa have been published in *Or Yisrael* of Israel b. Eliezer *Lipschuetz (Cleves, 1770) and in *Beit Evel u-Veit Mishteh* of Samuel Palaggi (Altona, 1770). Some of his talmudic novellae and homilies are in manuscript at the Bodleian Library.

BIBLIOGRAPHY: A. Berliner, *Rabbi Jesaja Berlin* (Ger., 1879), 8; Fuenn, Keneset, 227f., s.v. *David b. Aryeh Leib Berlin*; E. Duckesz, *Ivah le-Moshav*, 59–63; Neubauer, Cat, no. 526; L. Loewenstein, *Index Approbationum* (1923), 47, no. 825.

[Joseph Elijah Heller]

BERLIN, ḤAYYIM (1832–1912), Lithuanian rabbi, eldest son of R. Naphtali Ẓevi Judah *Berlin, head of the yeshivah at Volozhin for some 40 years. Ḥayyim Berlin received his education from his father and became conversant with all aspects of rabbinic literature as well as being well versed in Jewish subjects. At the age of 17 he married into the wealthy Zeitlin family of Shklov (see Zeitlin, *Joshua), and later used part of his wealth to amass an excellent library which was acquired by the Yeshivat *Eẓ Ḥayyim of Jerusalem after his death.

In 1865 Berlin became the rabbi of Moscow. In 1889 he returned to Volozhin at the request of his aged father, who wanted his son to succeed him as head of the yeshivah. However, he was opposed by many of the Volozhin yeshivah students, who favored the election of his niece's husband, R. Ḥayyim *Soloveichik, who was renowned for his unique analytical approach to talmudic study. The controversy soon ended with the forced closing of the school by the Russian government on January 22, 1892.

With the closing of the yeshivah, Berlin became the rabbi of Yelizavetgrad (*Kirovograd), where he remained until 1906, when he settled in Jerusalem. His erudition, family heritage, and patriarchal appearance gained for him a leading role on the Jerusalem scene, and in 1909 he was elected to succeed R. Samuel *Salant as chief rabbi of the Ashkenazi community of Jerusalem.

R. Meir *Bar-Ilan (Berlin), who was nearly 50 years his junior, was his half-brother.

BIBLIOGRAPHY: M. Bar-Ilan, *Mi-Volozhin ad Yerushalayim*, (1971), 314–24; *ibid.*, 2 (1971), 632; S.K. Mirsky (ed.), *Mosedot Torah be-Eiropah be-Vinyanam u-ve-Ḥurbanam* (1956), 72–74; E. Leoni (ed.), *Sefer Volozhin* (1970), 155ff.

[Aaron Rothkoff]

BERLIN (Baline), IRVING (Israel; 1888–1989), U.S. popular songwriter. Berlin was born in Kirghizia, Russia, the son of a cantor, and was taken to New York in 1893. His first regular job was as a "singing waiter," and it was then that he wrote the lyrics of his first song "Marie from Sunny Italy" in 1907. His second song, "Dorando" (1908), brought him $25 and a job with a music company. He became a partner in the firm and later established his own music publishing house. Berlin had no musical training and never learned to read music. His technique remained primitive, and when he composed at the piano he did it only in one key; modulations were effected by a special set of pedals. After composing a tune, Berlin either sang or played it for an assistant, who would then transcribe it into musical notation.

His first big success was the song "Alexander's Ragtime Band" (1911), which sold more than a million copies in just a matter of months. His melodies, for which he wrote the lyrics, were infectious, sentimental, and have maintained their popularity. He composed more than 1,000 songs, 19 musicals, and the scores for 18 movies. Among his most popular songs are "White Christmas," "Easter Parade," "There's No Business Like Show Business," "Blue Skies," "Puttin' on the Ritz," "Cheek to Cheek," "Say It with Music," "What'll I Do?" "A Pretty Girl Is Like a Melody," and "Always." Films for which he wrote the songs include *The Cocoanuts* (1929), *Puttin' on the Ritz* (1930), *Top Hat* (1935), *Follow the Fleet* (1936), *On the Avenue* (1937), *Holiday Inn* (1942), *Easter Parade* (1948), and *White Christmas* (1954). Among the Broadway shows for which he wrote the music, the best known are *Annie Get Your Gun* (1946) and *Call Me Madam* (1950). Among his many awards were an Academy Award for Best Original Song for "White Christmas" in 1942 and a special Tony Award in 1963.

As such a prolific writer and the rare combination of both a composer and a lyricist, Berlin was haunted all his life by the rumor that his songs were written by other people or were plagiarized from other material. Many people thought it was impossible for one person to write as many songs in as many styles as he did or for an untrained musician to write so many works of genius. But no evidence has ever been found that he ever plagiarized anything.

In 1918 Berlin wrote the stirring "God Bless America," which he revamped two decades later as war loomed large over Europe. Kate Smith sang it on her radio broadcast on Armistice Day in 1938, and the song was an immediate sensation. It sold millions of copies, won numerous awards, earned immense royalties, and threatened to replace the national anthem because of its patriotism and popularity. Berlin donated all the royalties from the song to the Boy Scouts, Girl Scouts, and Campfire Girls, saying that he refused to capitalize on patriotism. He composed numerous other patriotic songs during the war that benefited the Navy Relief, Red Cross, March of Dimes, and Bond Drives and contributed all the royalties to war charities.

His altruistic acts were acknowledged with such accolades as the Army's Medal of Merit from President Truman in 1945; a Congressional Gold Medal for "God Bless America" and other patriotic songs from President Eisenhower in 1955; and the Freedom Medal from President Ford in 1977.

Berlin also supported Jewish charities and organizations and donated generously to worthy causes. In 1944 he was honored by the National Conference of Christians and Jews for "advancing the aims of the Conference to eliminate religious and racial conflict." Five years later, he was honored by the New York YMHA as one of "12 outstanding Americans of the Jewish faith."

In 2002, the U.S. Army at Fort Belvoir, Virginia, named the Army Entertainment Division (AED) World Headquarters "The Irving Berlin Center" in his honor. Also that year he was commemorated on a U.S. postage stamp.

An intuitive businessman, Berlin was a co-founder of ASCAP (American Society of Composers, Authors, and Publishers), founder of his own music publishing company, and with producer Sam Harris, builder of his own Broadway theatre, The Music Box.

BIBLIOGRAPHY: A. Woollcott, *Story of Irving Berlin* (1925); D. Ewen, *Story of Irving Berlin* (1950); Baker, Biog Dict; Sendrey, Music, nos. 3605–07. **ADD. BIBLIOGRAPHY:** L. Bergreen, *As Thousands Cheer: The Life of Irving Berlin* (1990).

[Nicolas Slonimsky / Ruth Beloff (2nd ed.)]

BERLIN, SIR ISAIAH (1909–1997), English philosopher and political scientist. Born in Latvia, Berlin was taken to England as a boy. He later studied at Oxford, where he lectured in philosophy from 1932 and became the first Jewish Fellow of All Souls College in 1938. During and after World War II he served with the British Information Services in New York and with the British embassies in Washington and Moscow. From 1957 Berlin was professor of social and political theory at Oxford, and in 1966 he was appointed the first president of the newly founded Wolfson College in Oxford. Berlin was awarded the Order of Merit in 1971. In 1974 he was elected president of the British Academy, of which he had been vice president from 1959 to 1961, the first Jew to be appointed to this office. In November 1978 he was awarded the Jerusalem Prize.

His work was characterized by a strongly liberal attitude to social and political questions. His *Karl Marx* (1939) examines Marx's thought within the context of the intellectual atmosphere of the 19th century. In his *The Hedgehog and the Fox* (1953), Berlin considers Tolstoy as a writer who vainly sought some unifying thread in history. In *Historical Inevitability* (in: *Auguste Conte Memorial Lectures 1953–62*, 1964) he opposes the notion that events are inevitable and therefore predictable, and that political conditions are not capable of being changed by individuals. In *Two Concepts of Liberty* (1958), Berlin distinguishes between those thinkers who have sought to found liberty within a framework of mutual restraints while at the same time recognizing the diversity of human needs and behavior, and those who, espousing one all-embracing and dogmatic notion of liberty, seek to "force men to be free" and thus end by enslaving them. Among his other writings are *The Age of Enlightenment* (1956), *The Life and Opinions of Moses Hess* (1959), *Four Essays on Liberty* (1969), and numerous essays. Berlin earned a considerable reputation as a scholar, teacher, and conversationalist, and influenced generations of students in Britain and in the United States, where he was visiting professor at several universities. His long-standing ties with Israel and Zionism were distinguished by personal friendships with a number of Zionist leaders including Chaim *Weizmann. He was a member of the editorial board publishing the Weizmann letters and was a governor of the Hebrew University of Jerusalem. Berlin also served as president of the Jewish Historical Society of England and was the first president of Wolfson College, Oxford. He was certainly one of the most famous public intellectuals in the English-speaking world at the time of his death. In 1998 he published his reminiscences of 17 famous people, *Personal Impressions*.

ADD. BIBLIOGRAPHY: J. Cray, *Isaiah Berlin* (1996); M. Ignatieff, *Isaiah Berlin: A Life* (1998); H. Hardy, *Flourishing: Letters 1928–1946* (2004); M. Lilla (ed.), *The Legacy of Isaiah Berlin* (2001); ODNB online.

[Brian Knei-Paz (Knapheis)]

BERLIN, ISAIAH BEN JUDAH LOEB (Isaiah Pick; 1725–1799), rabbi and author. Berlin was known also as Isaiah Pick after his father-in-law, Wolf Pick of Breslau, who supported him for many years. He was born in Eisenstadt, Hungary, but his father, an eminent talmudic scholar (who later became rabbi of Pressburg), moved to Berlin where the young Berlin studied under him. Later he studied under Ẓevi Hirsch Bialeh (Ḥarif), the rabbi of Halberstadt, at the latter's yeshivah. In 1755 Berlin moved to Breslau where he engaged in business. In 1793, when already advanced in years, he was elected to a rabbinical post, being appointed to succeed Isaac Joseph Te'omim as rabbi of Breslau. His election was marked by a dispute between the members of the community and the local *maskilim*, who had begun to organize themselves as a body and opposed Berlin, who, despite his love of peace, openly attacked their ideas. Berlin was elected by an overwhelming majority. According to ḥasidic sources, Berlin was sympathetically disposed toward that movement and extended a friendly welcome to one of its emissaries, Jacob Samson of Spitsevka. Berlin was renowned for his conciliatory attitude and for his avoidance of all disputes. Characteristically, he called a work *She'elat Shalom* ("A Greeting of Peace"), for "all my life I have been careful not to treat my fellow men with disrespect, even to the extent of not slighting them by faint praises." As a result of this moderation, leaders of the Breslau *maskilim*, such as Joel Brill and Aaron Wolfsohn, frequently visited him. Berlin corresponded on halakhic subjects with his brother-in-law Joseph *Steinhardt, Ezekiel *Landau of Prague, Eleazar b. Eleazar *Kallir, and Ephraim Zalman *Margolioth of Brody, among others. His chief claim to fame rests not on his rabbinic and halakhic but rather on his extensive literary activities devoted to glosses and textual notes on talmudic literature. He commented on the Bible, Mishnah, Talmud, Alfasi, Maimonides, the *Arukh*, and the whole corpus of the earlier halakhic authorities. Of his collated texts, in which he notes parallel passages and variant readings, the most important is that on the Talmud, entitled *Masoret ha-Shas* ("Talmud Tradition"), which supplements an earlier work by Joseph Samuel, rabbi of Frankfurt. First published at Dyhernfurth (1800–04), it has since been printed in every edition of the Talmud. Berlin not only cites parallel passages, but also amends and compares texts, displaying an acute critical faculty and a profound grasp of history.

His other works are (1) *She'elat Shalom* (Dyhernfurth, 1786), a commentary on Aḥai of Shabḥa's *She'iltot*, with sources and notes entitled *Rishon le-Zion*; (2) *Hafla'ah sheba-Arakhin*, glosses and annotations to Nathan b. Jehiel of Rome's *Arukh* (first published, part 1, Breslau, 1830, part 2, Vienna, 1859), and thereafter in many editions of the *Arukh*; (3) *Minnei Targima*, expositions on Targum Onkelos (Breslau, 1831); (4) *Tosefot Rishon le-Ẓiyyon*, notes and brief comments on the Mishnah (first published at Sulzbach, 1783–85, and often reprinted); (5) *Kashot Meyushav* (Koenigsberg, 1860), in which all talmudic passages concluding with the word *kashya* ("difficulty") are answered; (6) *Omer ha-Shikḥah*, containing talmudic *halakhot* not mentioned by the codifiers. This work, first published as an addendum to *Kashot Meyushav*, was later printed separately (Johannisberg, 1866).

There was no early work to which Berlin did not write glosses and explanations, as he was in the habit of annotating every book that he read. Thus he wrote glosses to (7) the Bible (Dyhernfurth, 1775; Lemberg, 1861); (8) the prayer book in *Tikkun Shelomo* (Dyhernfurth, 1806); (9) Alfasi (Pressburg, 1836); (10) Maimonides' Yad (Dyhernfurth, 1809); (11) Elijah Baḥur's *Tishbi* (his annotations appearing in Moses Koerner's *Birkat Moshe*, Berlin, 1834); (12) Malachi b. Jacob's *Yad Malakhi* (Berlin, 1852); (13) Elijah b. Moses de Vidas' *Reshit Ḥokhmah* (Dyhernfurth, 1811).

His unpublished works include (14) *Yesh Seder la-Mishnah*, a commentary in several volumes on the Mishnah; (15) *Tena Tosefta*, a commentary on the Tosefta; (16) *Keneset Ḥakhmei Yisrael*, responsa; (17) *Shetarei ha-Me'uharin*, novella on Rashi and *tosafot* to the Talmud, dealing with those passages where proof was deduced from later biblical verses but could equally well have been inferred from earlier ones; (18) glosses and notes on the minor tractates.

Berlin was the first in Germany to interest himself in the history of post-talmudic literature. He was also the first to offer a solution to the problem of the identity and the period of the *paytan* Eleazar *Kallir, and although his conclusions are not accepted by scholars, they all use the extensive material cited by him (see J. Steinhardt's *Zikhron Yosef* to OḤ 13–15).

BIBLIOGRAPHY: A. Berliner, in: MWJ, 6 (1879), 65–89; Y.A. Kamelhar, *Dor De'ah* (1935^2), 87–89.

[Itzhak Alfassi]

BERLIN, ISRAEL (1880–?), Russian-Jewish historian, descended from a distinguished ḥasidic family. Berlin was educated at a Lithuania yeshivot and moved to St. Petersburg, where he became a member of the editorial board of the Russian Jewish Encyclopedia (*Yevreyskaya Entsiklopediya*, vols. 9–16) for which he edited the sections on the geonic period and rabbinic literature. He also contributed many basic articles on other topics, among them the Hebrew language, the Zohar, Ḥasidism, the Khazars, and Judaizers. He also contributed to the periodical *Yevreyskaya Starina*. In his fundamental study "Historical Settlements of the Jewish People on the Territory of Russia" (1919), Berlin attempted to explain the origins of Jewish settlements in Russia and trace their history up to the end of the 16th century. This work, based on copious literary and documentary material, was not completed. Berlin's fate under Soviet rule is not known.

BIBLIOGRAPHY: B.Z. Dinur, *Be-Olam she-Shaka* (1958), 151–3.

[Yehuda Slutsky]

BERLIN, MOSES (1821–1888), Russian scholar and civil servant, born in Shklov, Belorussia. Berlin wrote his first paper in Hebrew under the Latin title *Ars logica* (1845). In 1849 he was appointed teacher in the government school for Jews in Mogilev and in 1853 he became adviser on Jewish affairs to the governor-general of Belorussia. He subsequently held the post of adviser on Jewish matters at the Department of "Foreign Religions" (1856–66). Berlin translated into Russian Joshua b. David's *Ẓok ha-Ittim* on the *Chmielnicki massacres. For his work on the ethnography of the Russian Jews, *Ocherk etnografii yevreyskogo naseleniya v Rossii* (1861), Berlin was elected a member of the Imperial Russian Geographical Society. Berlin responded to the attacks on Jews and the Talmud, made in Russian literature and the press by antisemites. He was also active in the St. Petersburg community.

BERLIN, NAPHTALI ẒEVI JUDAH (known as **ha-Neẓiv** from the initials of his name; 1817–1893), one of the leading rabbis of his generation, and head of the yeshivah at *Volozhin for some 40 years. He was born at Mir and already in his early youth was famed as a great talmudic scholar. In 1831 he married the daughter of R. Isaac b. Ḥayyim *Volozhiner who headed the large and important yeshivah in that town. When R. Isaac died in 1851 he was succeeded by his elder son-in-law Eliezer Isaac. When the latter died in 1854, Berlin succeeded him, transforming that institution of learning into a spiritual center for the whole of Russian Jewry. In his day, the yeshivah at Volozhin was attended by more than 400 students, among whom were many men of great talent and unusual intellectual caliber. He taught the whole of the Babylonian Talmud in the order of its arrangement, without omission and with a commentary of his own, in which he followed the system and method of R. Elijah b. Solomon the *Gaon* of Vilna. He avoided hairsplitting *pilpul*, being concerned only with determining the plain meaning of the text as well as establishing its accuracy by reference to parallel passages in the Jerusalem Talmud and in the halakhic Midrashim. Early in life he wrote a commentary on *Sifrei* (published 1959–61 in Jerusalem, in three volumes, under the title *Emek ha-Neẓiv*). He ascribed great importance to the study of geonic literature and the works of the early authorities who lived close to the time of the Talmud. This accounts for his special interest in the *She'iltot* of R. *Aḥa of Shabḥa which he published with a commentary. It was the most comprehensive of its kind on this work, and was titled *Ha'amek She'elah* (Vilna, 1861, 1864, 1867; second edition with addenda and corrigenda from Berlin's manuscripts, Jerusalem, 1948–53). Berlin also devoted considerable attention to the interpretation of the Scriptures, following again in the footsteps of the Vilna *gaon*. In the yeshivah he gave a daily lesson in the weekly portion of the Reading of the Law, an unusual innovation in the yeshivot of his day. His commentaries on the Torah, *Ha'amek Davar*, were published (Vilna, 1879–80; second edition with addenda from manuscripts, Jerusalem, 1938) as were those on the Song of Songs, *Rinnah shel Torah* (Warsaw, 1886). In his Bible commentaries, he sought to demonstrate the consonance of the interpretations of the Pentateuch as transmitted in talmudic sources with the plain meaning of the Written Law and the rules of Hebrew grammar and syntax. While steeped in Talmudic and midrashic lore, the Neẓiv's comments were also highly original.

In the course of his long years as head of the yeshivah at Volozhin, Berlin dedicated his energies to that institution. He adamantly opposed any modernization of the yeshivah and the introduction of secular studies in its curriculum, as demanded by the *maskilim* in Russia, who were supported by the authorities. He feared that such innovation might detract from the purpose and mission of the yeshivah – the education of scholars of the traditional type. He did not negate secular learning per se, but regarded the study of the Torah and the production and maintenance of talmudic scholars as the very foundation of Jewish existence. He exhibited the greatest solicitude over any form of neglect of Torah study and professed a fatherly love for all his students, who in turn admired and revered him greatly, including those who later departed from his way of life and outlook. Bialik's poem *"Ha-Matmid"* reflects in large measure his personal impressions of his student days at Volozhin. Bialik describes the heart-warming personality of the "head of the yeshivah," and stresses his great love for the students of the Torah.

Berlin was keenly interested in the general community and its needs. He wrote many detailed responsa to questions arriving from various communities throughout the world on matters of *halakhah* and on general public affairs. A small part of his responsa was collected in his *Meshiv Davar* (2 vols., Warsaw, 1892) which revealed his general breadth of outlook. He completely rejected the demand of certain religious circles to establish separatist orthodox communities, stressing that "such advice is as painful as a dagger in the body of the nation," for all Jews are commanded to form "one union" (*Meshiv Davar,* vol. 1 responsum 42). He joined the *Ḥibbat Zion movement from its very inception, and at the Druzgeniki Conference (1887) was elected "counseling member" of its executive. In many letters he urged observant Jews to join the movement and to support the settlement of Jews in Ereẓ Israel, even though some were nonobservant. At the same time, he stressed that "our contributions do not go to settle the land of the Philistines, but to restore the desolation of our Holy Land… so that the Torah and the precepts be observed among its inhabitants" (*Meshiv Davar,* vol. 2, responsum 50, on *shemittah*). With that end in view, he urged that a religious person be appointed supervisor of the settlers in the colonies in Ereẓ Israel to ensure they conduct themselves in accordance with the Torah and the precepts. He also suggested that "secular" members of the Jewish settlements (referring to the Bilu'im in Gederah) be enabled to return to their countries abroad and that their place be taken by observant Jews from the old *yishuv* in Jerusalem. Later, however, he withdrew this suggestion, and even defended the Bilu'im because they had "improved their ways." Berlin was opposed to the permission granted by other rabbinic authorities for fields to be worked during the sabbatical year by means of the legal fiction of "selling" the land to non-Jews.

In his last years, he came into conflict with the Russian authorities as a result of their instructions both for a reduction in the number of students at the yeshivah of Volozhin and the introduction of secular subjects, especially the study of Russian, in the curriculum. Very much against his will, he reduced the student roll somewhat and introduced the study of Russian. However, even after these steps, the number of students at the yeshivah remained double that permitted by the Government, with few students among them attending the lessons in Russian. As a result the yeshivah was closed down by government decree in 1892 and Berlin and his family were exiled. They moved first to Minsk and later to Warsaw. The closing down of the yeshivah seriously affected his health and he was unable to carry out his desire to settle in Ereẓ Israel. He died in Warsaw about 18 months after his departure from Volozhin. His sons were R. Ḥayyim Berlin and R. Meir *Bar-Ilan.

BIBLIOGRAPHY: Berdichevsky, in: *Ha-Asif*, 3 (1886), 231–42; A.J. Slutzky (ed.), *Shivat Ẓiyyon*, 1 (1891), 17–18; 2 (1891), 5–8, 18–19, 28–30; I. Rivkind, *Ha-Neẓiv ve-Yiḥuso le-Ḥibbat Ẓiyyon* (1919); idem, *Iggerot Ẓiyyon* (1923), 73–103; idem, in: *Reshumot*, 5 (1927), 262–375; M. Berlin, *Mi-Volozhin ad Yerushalayim*, 1 (1939); idem, *Rabban shel Yisrael* (1943); S.Y. Zevin, *Ishim ve-Shitot* (1958), 9–37; J. Litvin, in: L. Jung (ed.), *Men of the Spirit* (1964), 285–99; Waxman, Literature, 3 (1960), 730–3. **ADD. BIBLIOGRAPHY:** B. ha-Levi Epstein, *My Uncle the Netziv* (1988); H. Adler Sosland, in: *Judaism*, 51:3 (2002), 315–27.

[Zvi Kaplan]

BERLIN, NOAH ḤAYYIM ẒEVI HIRSCH (1734–1802), German rabbi and halakhist. Berlin was born in Fuerth and was the son of Abraham Meir Berlin, the communal leader of Franconia. He became a *dayyan* at Fuerth in 1764 and later served as rabbi in Bayersdorf and Bayreuth. In 1783 Berlin was appointed rabbi of Mainz and the surrounding district. His appointment was ratified by the prince elector. He established a yeshivah at Mainz, and lived there until 1799 when he succeeded Raphael ha-Kohen as the rabbi of the united communities of Altona, Hamburg, and Wandsbeck. Berlin showed skill and tact in uniting the various elements in these communities. Wolf *Heidenheim was his most outstanding pupil. Berlin wrote *Aẓei Almuggim* (1779), a commentary on the hand-washing ritual, *eruvei ḥaẓerot*, and marriages forbidden by rabbinical enactment; *Aẓei Arazim* (1790), a commentary on the Shulḥan Arukh, *Even ha-Ezer; Ma'yan ha-Ḥokhmah* (1804), on the 613 commandments (in verse and with a commentary). This work, unfinished by Berlin, was completed by his brother Aryeh Loeb *Berlin. Two further works, *Aẓei Besamim* and *Aẓei Levonah*, remained unpublished. He wrote glosses to the tractates of *Berakhot* (1829), *Shabbat* (1832), and *Shevuot*. The last was published in the Vilna edition of the Talmud. There is a rational basis to his explanation of the *halakhah*, and he makes use of the Jerusalem Talmud.

BIBLIOGRAPHY: Fuenn, Keneset, 346; E. Duckesz, *Ivah le-Moshav*, 1 (1903), 74–77, 139–40, xxvi; I. Wolfsberg, in: *Arim ve-Im-*

mahot be-Yisrael, 2 (1948), 33; idem, *Die Drei-Gemeinde* (1966), 66; A. Eckstein, *Nachtraege zur Geschichte der Juden im ehemaligen Fuerstbistum Bamberg* (1899), 5; Loewenstein, in: JJLG, 3 (1905), 233; *ibid.*, 8 (1910), 72.

[Yehoshua Horowitz]

BERLIN, RAYNA BATYA (c. 1817–c. 1875), learned East European woman remembered for her concern with the status of women in traditional Judaism. Berlin lived her entire life in the orbit of the Volozhin Yeshivah. Her grandfather, R. Ḥayyim *Volozhiner, founded the yeshivah, and her father, R. Isaac *Volozhiner, would later take over. In 1831 Rayna Batya married R. Naphtali Ẓevi Judah Berlin (Neẓiv), a promising student who became leader of the yeshivah in 1854. The couple had four children, R. Hayyim, who married Rivka Zeitlin and was a rabbi in Moscow and later in Jerusalem, Michael, who died in his youth, and Sarah Resha and Dreyzl, who were married consecutively to R. Raphael Shapira.

In this environment of intense engagement with Jewish texts, where knowledge of Torah was honored above all else, it is not surprising that some of the women in the family would also take an interest in Jewish study and knowledge. Family stories about Berlin's grandmother, as well as Berlin and her sister, describe sharp-witted and sharp-tongued women committed to upholding the rabbinic world view. By far the most complete picture of Berlin comes from the memoirs of her nephew, R. Barukh ha-Levi Epstein. Epstein, whose mother was the Neẓiv's sister, spent the middle years of the 1870s as a student at the Volozhin Yeshivah. During these years he was also a frequent visitor at the home of his uncle and aunt. In a volume of his memoirs devoted to R. Naftali Ẓevi Judah Berlin, Epstein included one chapter on his aunt, entitled, "Wisdom of Women." The portrait of Rayna Batya Berlin produced by Epstein is of an unusually learned Jewish woman, frustrated by the limits imposed on her by gender and Jewish law. According to Epstein, Berlin spent her days sitting in her kitchen surrounded by Jewish texts including volumes of the Mishnah and *aggadah* as well as historical and other works. On his visits, she would frequently engage him in discussions about women in Jewish law, especially with regard to the study of the Torah. In recent years a number of scholars have taken an interest in Rayna Batya Berlin and her anomalous position in Orthodox Judaism.

BIBLIOGRAPHY: M. Bar-Ilan, *Fun Volozhin biz Yerushalayim* (1933); idem, *Raban shel Yisrael* (1943); B. Epstein, *Mekor Barukh* (1954); D. Seeman, "The Silence of Rayna Batya: Torah, Suffering, and Rabbi Barukh Epstein's 'Wisdom of Women,'" in: *Torah U-Madda Journal*, 6 (1995–96); D. Seeman and R. Kobrin, " 'Like One of the Whole Men': Learning, Gender and Autobiography in R. Barukh Epstein's *Mekor Barukh*," in: *Nashim*, 5 (1999); S. Zolty, *'And All Your Children Shall be Learned': Women and the Study of Torah in Jewish Law and History* (1993).

[Eliyana R. Adler (2nd ed.)]

BERLIN, SAUL BEN ẒEVI HIRSCH LEVIN (also called **Saul Hirschel**; 1740–1794), German rabbi. His father was Hirschel *Levin (Ẓevi Hirsch) and his brother, Solomon *Hirschel. At the age of 20, he was ordained by some of the greatest rabbis of the time. In 1768 he was serving as *av bet din* in Frankfurt on the Oder. In 1778 he wrote an approbation for Moses Mendelssohn's commentary on the Torah *Biur* (*Be'ur*; Berlin, 1783). Some time before 1782 Berlin, becoming disenchanted with what he considered antiquated rabbinical authority, retired from the rabbinate and settled in Berlin. There he joined the Haskalah group whose members, known as the *Me'assefim*, were the pupils and admirers of Mendelssohn. He was also an ardent supporter of Naphtali Herz *Wessely at a time when the most eminent rabbis of Germany violently opposed him. After the publication of Wessely's *Divrei Shalom ve-Emet* (Berlin, 1782), Berlin wrote a satire *Ketav Yosher* (published anonymously after his death, 1794), in which he sharply criticized the methods of education and the scholarship of his time as well as the customs and superstitions which had spread among the people. It also sought to dispel the rabbis' opposition to the work of Wessely. In 1784 he traveled to Italy, ostensibly to seek a cure for his rheumatism, but, quite conceivably, to meet those rabbis who had placed themselves in Wessely's camp. In Italy Berlin wrote a provocative anonymous pamphlet of objections to the *Birkei Yosef* of R. Ḥayyim Joseph David *Azulai (Leghorn, 1772), to which the latter replied in his book *Maḥazik Berakhah* (*ibid.*, 1785). Interesting himself in manuscripts, Berlin began to edit the *Or Zaru'a* of *Isaac b. Moses of Vienna, to which he added his own notes and novellae; these were omitted, however, from the posthumously published version in 1862. In 1789 his book *Miẓpeh Yokte'el* appeared in Berlin under the pseudonym of Obadiah b. Baruch Ish Polonyah. It contained the most extreme criticism of the novellae to *Yoreh De'ah*, entitled *Torat Yekuti'el*, by Raphael b. Jekuthiel Susskind *Kohen, rabbi of the united communities of Altona, Hamburg, and Wandsbeck. Berlin's book, in which Raphael is accused of plagiarism and of condoning corruption, stirred up a storm among the rabbis, including Berlin's own father, who placed a ban upon the book and upon its author. When the identity of the author became known, his father regretted his action and tried to protect his son. However, before the storm had subsided, another of his books, *Besamim Rosh*, appeared in Berlin in 1793 and touched off a new tempest. The book contains 392 responsa purporting to be by Asher b. Jehiel and his contemporaries: on the title page it was stated that these responsa had been collected and prepared for publication by R. Isaac di Molina. Although Berlin maintained that he had copied the book from a manuscript in Italy and that he had only added his own notes and novellae (*Kassa de-Harsana*), it soon became evident that the statements attributed to Asher and the other rabbis quoted were full of strange leniencies which actually bordered on antinomianism. The suspicion was soon raised that the whole book was fictitious and that its author was Berlin. The first to attack him was R. Wolf Landsberg in his pamphlet *Ze'ev Yitrof* (Frankfurt on the Oder, 1793). After him came R. Mordecai Benet, who wrote to Berlin's father and to other rabbis. A massive rabbinical campaign then followed which branded Berlin as an atheist who sought to uproot the foundations of the Torah. Berlin's father came again to his aid, requesting the rabbis to retract their accusations against his son, and even attempting to establish the genuineness of the manuscript and R. Raphael ha-Kohen and his circle as the source of the libel. It seems that he succeeded in appeasing the rabbis, but not those scholars who held no rabbinical position. Disappointed, Berlin began to wander from one country to another. According to his relative Ẓevi Horowitz (*Kitvei ha-Ge'onim*, 1928), Berlin went to London in 1794 to take up the position of rabbi of the Ashkenazi community there but died before he was able to assume the office. His literary remains present many bibliographical problems, some of which have not yet been solved. He left critical essays which have been published in various places. He is probably the author of *Ha-Orev* (Vienna, 1795), attributed to R. Baruch *Jeiteles.

BIBLIOGRAPHY: C. Roth, *The Great Synagogue London 1690–1940* (1950), 108–24, 180–201; Samet, in: KS, 43 (1967/68), 429–41; M. Wunder, *ibid.*, 44 (1968/69), 307–8.

[Abraham David]

BERLINER, ABRAHAM (1833–1915), scholar and author. Berliner's vast knowledge of rabbinic literature and of ancient and modern languages was mostly self-taught (cf. his autobiographical *Aus meiner Knabenzeit*, JJGL, 16 (1913), 165ff.). After succeeding his father as teacher in his native Obersitzko, he became preacher and teacher in Arnswalde (both in the province of Posen, then Germany). From 1858 to 1865 he lectured at the *bet ha-midrash* of the Berlin Talmudic Society out of which developed the Rabbinical Seminary, founded by Azriel *Hildesheimer in 1873. Here Berliner lectured in Jewish history and literature and was also librarian. In subsequent years he paid frequent visits to the important libraries of Germany, England, Holland, France, and, above all, Italy, in search of their Jewish treasures. He prepared the first critical edition of Rashi's commentary on the Pentateuch, giving Rashi's sources and explanatory notes (1866); this book was accepted by Leipzig university as a Ph.D. thesis. In the completely revised second edition (1905) he added a vocabulary of foreign words used in the commentary. Berliner pursued his Rashi studies in a number of important monographs and also turned his attention to other medieval commentators (*Peletat Soferim*, 1872, 1966[2]). He also provided a modern edition of *Targum Onkelos* (1884). Berliner's historical studies were chiefly devoted to Italian Jewry, as shown by his three-volume *Geschichte der Juden in Rom* (1893). On the history of German Jewry, he wrote *Aus dem Leben der deutschen Juden im Mittelalter* (1861, second revised and enlarged edition 1900, 1937[3]; Hebrew translation, 1900). Complementary to this work was a monograph *Persoenliche Beziehungen zwischen Juden und Christen im Mittelalter* (1882). Berliner also wrote biographies of Israel *Isserlein and of Isaiah *Berlin and a defense of *Maimonides against the accusation of apostasy (*Moses ben Maimon, sein Leben…* 2 (1914), 103ff.). Berliner published many bibliographical studies and works on liturgy and Talmud. He discovered in Rome parts of commentaries on the Bible and the Talmud by *Hananel b. Ḥushi'el and *Gershom b. Judah and was instrumental in the inclusion of both commentaries in the Vilna (Romm) Talmud edition. In 1874 Berliner began to publish a *Magazin fuer juedische Geschichte und Literatur* which two years later became the *Magazin fuer die Wissenschaft des Judentums* (with a Hebrew supplement, *Oẓar Tov*), which he edited with David *Hoffmann until 1893. In 1885 he revived the *Mekiẓe Nirdamim society. On his 70th birthday he was awarded the title of professor by the Prussian government. On that occasion too appeared a *Festschrift* in his honor, edited by A. Freimann and M. Hildesheimer (*Birkat Avraham*, 1903) with a bibliography of his writings. A three-volume collection of Berliner's writings was planned but only the first appeared in 1913. A two-volume collection was published in Hebrew (1945–49). Berliner was a staunch supporter of Orthodoxy and an opponent of Reform. He supported Hildesheimer in the establishment of the *Adass Jisroel* secessionist congregation and acted as the chairman of its council for many years. Yet in his *Randbemerkungen* he suggested certain changes in prayer texts and customs, which were not to the liking of some of his Orthodox friends.

BIBLIOGRAPHY: Eppenstein, in: *Jeschurun* (new series), 2 (1915), 457ff. **ADD. BIBLIOGRAPHY:** *Biographisches Handbuch der Rabbiner*, 1:1 (2004), 186–87 (bibl.).

[Alexander Carlebach]

BERLINER, EMILE (1851–1929), inventor. Born and educated in Wolfenbuettel, Germany, Berliner emigrated to the U.S.A. in 1870. He worked in New York and Washington, D.C., as a clerk, salesman, and assistant in a chemical laboratory. He studied electricity and in 1876 began experimenting with Bell's newly invented telephone, which he succeeded in refining with his invention of the loose-contact telephone transmitter or microphone and the use of an induction coil. The Bell Telephone Company immediately purchased the rights to his invention, which for the first time made the telephone practical for long-distance use. Berliner was appointed chief electrical instruments inspector of the company. In 1887 he improved Edison's phonograph by introducing a flat disc instead of a cylinder and the use of a shallow groove. The patent was acquired by the Victor Talking Machine Company and served as the basis for the modern gramophone. In his later years he engaged in aviation experiments and introduced the use of a revolving cylindered light engine. Between 1919 and 1926 he built three helicopters which he tested in flight himself. Berliner also interested himself in public matters, particularly in the field of health and hygiene. In 1890 he founded the Society for the Prevention of Sickness. In 1907 he organized the first milk conference in Washington, whose efforts contributed to the pasteurization of milk and an improvement in its quality. He played a leading part in the fight against the spread of tuberculosis and wrote a number of articles on hygiene and preventive medicine. He set out his agnostic ideas on matters of religion and philosophy in his book *Conclusions* (1902). Toward the end of his life Berliner supported the rebuilding of Palestine and was active on behalf of the Hebrew University of Jerusalem.

[Grete Leibowitz]

Emile's son HENRY ADLER BERLINER (1895–1970), aeronautical engineer, did pioneering work with his father on helicopter construction during and after World War I. He was president of Berliner Aircraft, Inc. in Washington and from 1930 to 1954 chairman of Engineering and Research Corporation. In 1955 he became president of the Maryland firm of Tecfab Inc. In World War II, during which he lost an arm, he was chief of war plans for the Eighth Air Force.

[Samuel Aaron Miller]

BIBLIOGRAPHY: F.W. Wile, *Emile Berliner, Maker of the Microphone* (1926); C.J. Hylander, *American Inventors* (1934).

BERLINER, ISAAC (1899–1957), Mexican Yiddish poet. Born in Lodz, Berliner immigrated to Mexico in 1922 and earned a precarious livelihood as a peddler in the Mexican provinces. In 1927 he and two other Mexican Yiddish poets, Moses Glikovski (d. 1980) and Jacob *Glantz, published a volume of lyrics *Dray Vegn* ("Three Roads," Spanish transl. *Tres Caminos*, 1997). His second volume *Shtot fun Palatsn* (1936), illustrated by the Mexican painter Diego Rivera, appeared in English as *City of Palaces* (1996). His national elegies *Ad Mosay* ("Until When?" 1941) were followed by *Shtil Zol Zayn* ("Let There Be Silence," 1948) and *Gezang fun Mentsh* ("The Song of Man," 1954). In style, imagery, use of neologisms, and rich rhythms, Berliner was influenced by his Lodz fellow poet Moses *Broderzon, but Berliner was more socially conscious. In many lyrics he cries out vehemently against the abysmal poverty of the Mexicans around the Tepito Market in the heart of the "city of palaces."

BIBLIOGRAPHY: LNYL, 1 (1956), 392–3; S. Kahan, *Yidish-Meksikanish* (1945), 211–23; idem, *Meksikaner Viderklangen* (1951), 106–201; idem, *Meksikaner Refleksn* (1954), 228–31.

[Melech Ravitch / Alan Astro (2nd ed.)]

BERLINSKI, HERMAN (1910–2001), composer. Born in Leipzig, Berlinski studied piano, composition, and conducting at the Leipzig Conservatory (1927–32). He left Germany in 1933 and went to Paris, studying piano with Alfred Cortot and composition with Nadia Boulanger at the Ecole Normale de Musique (1934–38). In 1939 he joined the French Foreign Legion but on the fall of France he emigrated to the United States (1941). Berlinski's style combines twelve-tone techniques with traditional Hebrew cantillation. His works include a cantata, *Habakkuk*, pieces for organ and piano, *Flute Sonata* (1941), *Violin Sonata* (1949), *Symphonic Visions* (1949) and liturgical Jewish compositions – *Kaddish* (1953), *Avodat Shabbat* (1957), and *Kiddush ha-Shem* (1958).

ADD. BIBLIOGRAPHY: *Baker's Biographical Dictionary*; M. Kayden, "The Music of Herman Berlinsky," in: *Bulletin of the American Composers Alliance* 3 (1959).

[Israela Stein (2nd ed.)]

BERMAN, ADOLF ABRAHAM (1906–1978), socialist Zionist. Born in Warsaw, he was the son of Isser Berman, a well-known Zionist and member of the Ḥovevei Sefat Ever society, and a brother of Jacob *Berman. Adolf Berman joined the Left Po'alei Zion as a student and edited both its Polish language organ and its Yiddish weekly, *Arbeter Tsaytung*. After the outbreak of World War II he was for some time chief director of "Centos," the organization for social welfare in Warsaw, and was active in the Polish underground movement. Upon the establishment of the Anti-Fascist Bloc in 1942, he became one of its leaders and coeditor of its paper *Der Ruf*. He left the ghetto after the mass deportation of Jews to Treblinka in the summer of 1942 and established himself in the so-called Aryan side of Warsaw, where he cooperated with left-wing political groups. He was a member of the presidium of the Jewish National Committee and its representative with the Polish underground organization. He fought in the Warsaw uprising of 1944 and after the liberation of Poland was a member of the Polish temporary parliament.

In 1947 Berman became president of the central committee of Polish Jews, but three years later he immigrated to Israel. Here he joined Mapam, and in 1951 was elected to the Knesset. In 1954 he left Mapam and became a member of the Communist Party. He was elected to the party's central committee and edited its Yiddish language weekly, *Frei Israel*. In 1956 he became a member of the general council and bureau of the International Resistance Organization.

ADD. BIBLIOGRAPHY: A. Berman, *Mimei ha-Makhteret* (1971); idem, *Be-Makom asher Yo'ad li- ha-Goral* (1978; Yid. *Wos der Goyrel Hot Mir Bashert*, 1980); I. Gutman, Yehudei Varshah 1939–1943 (1977), index; A. Berman, *Dzialalnosc komunistow wsrod Zydow w Polsce, 1944–1949* (2004), index.

[Abraham Wein]

BERMAN, HOWARD LAWRENCE (1941–), U.S. congressman. Raised in a traditional home in Beverlywood, Los Angeles, by an Orthodox Polish-immigrant father, Berman spent several summers at Machene Yehuda, a Jewish camp in the hills northeast of Los Angeles' San Fernando Valley. The camp's head counselor was the young Rabbi Chaim *Potok (1929–2002). Berman always considered his summers at Machene Yehuda to be "the single-most important Jewish experience" in his life.

Berman entered the University of California at Los Angeles (UCLA) in 1958, where he majored in political science and became active in the California Federation of Young Democrats, where he was befriended by the head of the Draft Stevenson campaign, fellow Angelino Henry Waxman. The two became fast friends, eventually forming (along with Howard's brother Michael) an informal political alliance known as "The Waxman-Berman Machine." After graduating from UCLA in 1962, Berman went to the university's School of Law, receiving his LL.B. in 1965.

By 1965, Waxman had become president of the California Federation of Young Democrats (CFYD). Along with Waxman, Berman and the CFYD gravitated toward the party's insurgent faction, led by future United States Senator Alan Cranston, and against the party's more established wing, controlled by California Assembly Speaker Jesse ("Big Daddy") Unruh. By 1967, when Howard became a VISTA (Volunteers in Service to America) volunteer, he was irrevocably hooked on politics. Following his year with VISTA, Berman went into private practice, specializing in labor law. Meanwhile, brother Michael was masterminding Henry Waxman's election to the California State Assembly. Named chair of the Assembly committee that oversaw reapportionment in 1972, Waxman hired Michael Berman to help him draw up district lines. Part of their plan was to create an Assembly district for Howard right in his own backyard of Beverlywood. When California Governor Ronald Reagan vetoed the Waxman-Berman reapportionment plan, Howard moved from Beverlywood into a district that ran along the Santa Monica Mountains from Hollywood to the San Fernando Valley and successfully ran against a twenty-six-year incumbent Charles Conrad, the Assembly Republican leader.

Within days, the freshman legislator was named Assembly majority leader – the youngest in California history. As majority leader, Berman passed legislation that imposed stiff penalties on California banks that joined the Arab boycott against Israel. In 1980, after five years as Assembly majority leader, Berman narrowly lost a bid to become that body's speaker. After his defeat, Berman allied himself with San Francisco-area Congressman Phillip Burton in the 1982 congressional reapportionment plan. Burton, working alongside Michael Berman – who, by then had become a major player in California Democratic politics – managed to secure a congressional seat for Howard. Howard Berman was elected with 60 percent of the vote.

Upon entering the House of Representatives, he quickly broke out of the freshman pack by getting himself a seat on the Democratic Steering and Policy Committee. Berman managed to get himself seated on both the House Committee on Foreign Affairs (later renamed "International Relations") and House Judiciary – two plum assignments for a newly minted legislator. In Congress he forged a reputation for being "one of the most aggressive and creative members of the House – and one of the most clear-sighted operators in American politics."

In Los Angeles, Berman was one half of the powerful "Waxman-Berman Machine" that raised enormous sums of money, mainly from Jewish liberals. The Waxman-Berman Machine changed the face of American politics: they were the first to make contributions to the campaigns of other like-minded candidates.

Berman was one of Israel's strongest voices in the halls of Congress. He arranged tens of thousands of visas for immigrants without close relatives in the United States. These visas, selected randomly by computer, came to be known as "Berman visa applications" and were a boon to thousands and thousands of Soviet Jewish émigrés who settled in America in the 1980s and 1990s.

BIBLIOGRAPHY: K.F. Stone, *The Congressional Minyan: The Jews of Capitol Hill* (2000), 30–34; *Almanac of American Politics* (1982–2004).

[Kurt Stone (2nd ed.)]

BERMAN, JACOB (1878–1974), rabbi, educator, and communal worker. Berman was born in Salant, Lithuania. He studied rabbinics at Telz Yeshivah and law at St. Petersburg University. While in St. Petersburg he played a part in the founding of the Baron Guenzburg Jewish Academy. In 1902 he was a delegate to the Zionist Conference in Minsk and the first Mizrachi Conference in Lida, where he lectured on the need for modernizing the yeshivot and initiated the founding of the Lida yeshivah of Isaac *Reines. He was principal of the yeshivah of Odessa, and rabbi in Berdichev, where he was active in saving and aiding refugees. In 1921 he immigrated to Ereẓ Israel, and from 1924 to 1944 he was head of Mizrachi religious education, served as deputy director of the Keneset Yisrael education department, and was chief inspector of religious schools. He was active in enlarging and developing the state religious education network and founded and directed the Religious Pedagogical Institute for yeshivah graduates. He wrote *Torat ha-Medinah be-Yisrael, Pirkei Shulḥan Arukh le-Talmidim*, and *Halakhah le-Am.* He was awarded the Israel Prize for Education in 1968.

BERMAN, JAKUB (1901–1984), Polish Communist leader. Born in Warsaw, a brother of Adolf *Berman, Jacob graduated in law and then undertook research into the economic and social history of Poland. Some of his articles on these subjects dealt with Jewish problems, and in 1926 he published a dissertation on the tasks of the historical section of the Jewish Scientific Institute (YIVO). From 1928 to 1939 he worked for the Jewish Telegraphic Agency. Berman joined the Polish Communist Party in 1928, becoming one of its most active workers. During World War II he took refuge in the Soviet Union, and in 1943 helped to organize the Soviet-sponsored Union of Polish Patriots. He was a member of the political staff of the Polish Army in the U.S.S.R. and of the Polish National Liberation Committee. After the war he returned to Poland and was undersecretary of state in the presidium of the Council of Ministers from 1945 to 1952. From 1952 to 1956 he was a deputy premier. In these years Berman was a leading figure in the Political Bureau and a close colleague of the Polish president, Boleslaw Bierut. In 1956, when Wladislaw Gomulka came to power, Berman was accused of Stalinism and removed from all his government and party posts. From 1958 to 1968 he worked as editor in a publishing house but in 1968, during the antisemitic campaign, he was forced to retire.

ADD. BIBLIOGRAPHY: C. Kozlowski, *Zarys Dziejow Polskiego Ruchu Robotniczego do roku 1948* (1980), index; D. Stola, *Kampanja antysjonistyczna* (2000), index; J. Eisler, *Marzec 1968* (1991), index; K. Nusbaum, *Ve-hafakh lahem le-Ro'ez, Ha-Yehudim be-Ẓava ha-Amami ha-Polani bi-Berit ha-Mo'eẓot* (1984), index.

[Abraham Wein]

BERMAN, JULIUS (1935–), U.S. lawyer, rabbi, and communal leader. Berman was born in Dukst, Lithuania. Despite the German occupation the family managed to immigrate to the United States in April 1940 and settled in Hartford, Connecticut. After earning a B.A. at Yeshiva University (1956), Berman attended Yeshiva's Rabbi Isaac Elchanan Theological Seminary (in the daytime) and NYU Law School (at night). In 1959 he received his rabbinic ordination from the seminary and in 1960 he graduated first in his class from law school, having been named a member of the law review and the legal honor society.

Choosing to pursue a legal career rather than practicing as a rabbi, Berman joined the New York firm of Kaye, Scholer, Fierman, Hays & Handler (now Kaye Scholer LLP) in August 1959, where in the course of a career spanning more than 40 years he was an accomplished litigator in state and federal courts, a renowned negotiator, and a highly respected counselor for numerous clients throughout the United States, particularly those with Orthodox affiliations.

Berman was a pioneer among Sabbath-observing Jews in the New York legal world, particularly the larger law firms. By working Sundays and carrying a workload even greater than many of his colleagues, Berman was able to demonstrate that Sabbath observance did not hinder success; and his diligence and skill were rewarded in July 1969 when he was made a partner in the firm. Indeed, it was through his efforts (and those of a small number of others) that hiring observant Jews became a matter of routine in New York and other major cities. Unlike the Kaye, Scholer of the early 1960s, today many of the firm's attorneys wear *kippot* in the office and, due largely to Berman's efforts over the years, the firm today boasts a daily *minhah/ma'ariv minyan* and a weekly advanced Talmud lecture.

Berman's service to the American Jewish community began with an Orthodox focus. He was a founder and president of the National Jewish Commission on Law and Public Affairs (COLPA), which provided legal representation with respect to issues of interest to the Orthodox community; and the founding president of Camps Mogen Avraham, Heller, Sternberg, Inc., which operated four camps serving some 3,000 Orthodox campers. Berman was active in the Union of Orthodox Jewish Congregations of America (the Orthodox Union) from the outset of his career and ultimately was elected its president.

Berman was heavily involved in representing Orthodoxy in the broader Jewish community, in such organizations as the multidenominational Synagogue Council of America and the National Jewish Community Relations Advisory Council. While serving as Orthodox Union president, he became the first Orthodox lay leader to become chairman of the *Conference of Presidents of Major American Jewish Organizations, which propelled him into a prominent role on the national and international Jewish scene. Other national positions included the chair of the American Zionist Youth Foundation, chair of the Jewish Telegraphic Agency, and board member of the Joint Distribution Committee. He was also a member of Yeshiva University's Board of Trustees and Executive Committee and chairman of the Isaac Elchanan Theological Seminary's Board.

Among the significant attachments in Berman's life was his close relationship with Rabbi Joseph *Soloveitchik, who had been his teacher at the seminary during his rabbinic studies. Over time, Berman became the "Rav's" lawyer, literary agent, and personal confidante. When Soloveitchik decided to publish many of his lectures and manuscripts, he entrusted the pertinent materials (including a large number of audio tapes of lectures) to Berman for safekeeping.

In the early 21st century Berman became chairman of the *Conference on Jewish Material Claims Against Germany, serving a rapidly aging survivor population. His role forced him to balance the needs of survivors, diminishing in numbers but in greater need of assistance, with the Claims Conference's commitment to use some of the funds for Holocaust education, scholarship, and remembrance. This placed him in an unenviable and certainly not an uncontroversial position.

[Michael Malina (2nd ed.)]

BERMAN, MORTON MAYER (1899–1986), U.S. Reform rabbi and organization executive. Berman was born in Baltimore, Maryland. He was a graduate of Yale (1921) and was ordained by the Jewish Institute of Religion in 1926, where he was deeply influenced by its president, Stephen S. *Wise. He attended the Hebrew University of Jerusalem as the school's first Guggenheimer Fellow in 1926 and then studied in Berlin in 1927; he served as rabbi in Davenport, Iowa (1927–29), the Free Synagogue in New York City (1929–37), where he was an assistant to Wise and director of education, and Temple Isaiah Israel in Chicago (later KAM Isaiah Israel; 1937–57), a synagogue that had fallen upon hard times during the Depression, its membership depleted to 150 dues-paying members from 1,000 and which he brought back to its former prominence. During World War II Rabbi Berman was a chaplain in the Pacific with the U.S. Navy, where he won a Bronze Star for service on Okinawa. Berman was a political activist serving communal, national, and Zionist causes. From 1939 to 1957 he played leading roles in such national organizations as the Jewish National Fund, the Zionist Organization of America, and the American Jewish Congress. He edited the *Congress Courier*, now the *Congress Bi-Monthly*. A life-long Zionist, he took his own teaching to heart and in 1957 he moved to Jerusalem, where he became director of the department of English-speaking countries for Keren Hayesod. Rabbi Berman wrote *Jew's*

View of the Crucifixion (1929), *Role of the Rabbi* (1941), and *For Zion's Sake: A Personal and Family Chronicle* (1979).

[Michael Berenbaum (2nd ed.)]

BERMAN, MYRON R. (1928–), U.S. Conservative rabbi. Berman was born in New York, educated at the City College of New York, and ordained at the Jewish Theological Seminary. He also received a B.H.L. from its seminary college as well as an M.H.L. and an honorary D.D. degree. He served as chaplain in the United States Air Force, serving in New Mexico and Japan. He received his Ph.D. from Columbia University in 1963. From 1965 until his retirement in 1993, he served as rabbi of Temple Beth-El of Richmond, Virginia, a community he served as an educator, a civil rights activist, and a historian. His writings include *Richmond's Jewry, 1769–1976: Shabbat in Shockoe* (1979) and *The Attitude of American Jewry Towards Eastern European Jewish Immigration, 1881–1914* (1980), in which Berman demonstrated that American Jews, while helping individual immigrants, acquiesced in restrictive immigration laws in the late 19th century; it was only after the *Kishinev pogrom in 1903 that American Jews sought to liberalize immigration policies for their East European brethren. Berman came to Temple Beth-El in Richmond, Virignia, in August 1965 after serving as associate rabbi for Beth-El in Cedarhurst, New York, for seven years. He was the first rabbi to serve as president of the Richmond Area Clergy Association, He received the Richmond City Medallion for communal service and later was honored by the National Conference of Christians and Jews. He received a citizen's award from the Henrico Police Department. Berman had served as chairman of the board of education for the seaboard region of the United Synagogue.

Berman was a member of the Virginia-Israel Commission, appointed by Governor Baliles. He wrote the introductions to both Holocaust curricula published by the State of Virginia, and he was also a consultant to the state's commission on social studies. More recently, he served as a member of the Henrico 2000 Committee, which forecast trends in education for the next decade. He was cited by *Hadassah Magazine* and *Surroundings* as among Richmond's most influential citizens.

BIBLIOGRAPHY: P.S. Nadell, *Conservative Judaism in America: A Biographical Dictionary and Sourcebook* (1988).

[Bezalel Gordon (2nd ed.)]

BERMAN, PANDRO S. (1905–1996), U.S. film producer. Born in Pittsburgh, Pennsylvania, Berman was responsible for the production of 85 films for RKO, including the Ginger Rogers-Fred Astaire musicals.

Born into the film industry, Berman's father, Henry, was general manager of Universal Pictures during Hollywood's formative years. Pandro spent most of the 1920s learning the business. He started out as a script clerk and then rose to film editor. By 1931, the 26-year-old Berman was an assistant director at RKO when David O. *Selznick took over the floundering studio. Selznick fired many people at RKO, but he saw something in Berman and made him his assistant. Berman was a success and, as a producer, brought to the screen many stars and great films. It was he who paired Rogers with Astaire, made Katherine Hepburn a star, and brought Elizabeth *Taylor to public attention. In 1940 he signed a contract with MGM. In 1963, when an MGM power play diminished his authority, Berman left to do independent work.

Berman's productions include *The Gay Divorcee* (1934); *Top Hat* (1935); *Shall We Dance* (1937); *Stage Door* (1937); *The Hunchback of Notre Dame* (1939); *National Velvet* (1945); *The Seventh Cross* (1944); *The Picture of Dorian Gray* (1945); *Of Human Bondage* (1948); *Madam Bovary* (1949); *Father of the Bride* (1950); *The Prisoner of Zenda* (1952); *Ivanhoe* (1952); *The Blackboard Jungle* (1955); *Tea and Sympathy* (1956); *Something of Value* (1957); *Jailhouse Rock* (1957); *The Brothers Karamazov* (1958); *Butterfield 8* (1960); *Sweet Bird of Youth* (1962); *The Prize* (1963); *A Patch of Blue* (1965); *Justine* (1969); and *Move* (1970). In 1977 Berman received the Irving Thalberg Award at the 49th annual Academy Awards.

ADD. BIBLIOGRAPHY: M. Steen, *Hollywood Speaks: An Oral History* (1974).

[Ruth Beloff (2nd ed.)]

BERMAN, SHELLEY (1926–), U.S. actor, comedian, author. Berman was trained as an actor at the Goodman Theater in his native Chicago before joining stock companies in Chicago and New York. In the mid-1950s he joined the Chicago Compass Players, the famed performance group now known as The Second City. Berman's first breakthrough as a comedian came in 1957 when he began performing at Mr. Kelly's in Chicago. His success as a comedian, including 21 appearances on *The Ed Sullivan Show*, led to three best-selling comedy records and the distinction of winning the first Grammy Award for a non-musical recording, as well as becoming the first stand-up comedian to perform at Carnegie Hall. His stage credits include starring roles in the Broadway musical *Inside Outside and All Around Shelley Berman* and Neil *Simon's touring musical production *Two by Two*. On television Berman appeared on both variety shows such as *The Ed Sullivan Show* and *The Jack Paar Show*, and scripted programs such as *L.A. Law, Friends, Arliss, Walker, Texas Ranger, Dead Like Me,* and *Curb Your Enthusiasm*, on which he played the role of Larry David's father. His major film credits include *The Best Man*, *Every Home Should Have One*, *Divorce American Style*, *Teen Witch*, and *The Last Producer*. Berman is the author of three books (*Cleans and Dirtys*, *A Hotel is a Funny Place*, and *Up in the Air*), two plays (*First is Supper* and *Silver Sonata*). He was also a professor in the University of Southern California's Professional Writing Program and was awarded an honorary doctorate of humane letters from the Spertus Institute of Jewish Studies.

[Walter Driver (2nd ed.)]

BERMAN, SIMEON (1818–1884), precursor of Jewish agricultural settlement in Ereẓ Israel. Berman, who was born in Cracow, founded a Jewish agricultural settlement society there in 1851. He immigrated to the United States in 1852 and settled in New York. There and in other cities he attempted to found societies for agricultural settlement, but received no support. In 1870 he went to Ereẓ Israel and proposed that Mikveh Israel land be set aside for an agricultural settlement, but his proposal was rejected. Berman sent a request, through the U.S. consul, to the Ottoman government asking to be allowed to buy land in Ereẓ Israel. The request was granted, and Berman moved to Tiberias, where he founded the cooperative Holy Land Settlement Society. He received messages of encouragement from rabbis Ẓevi Hirsch *Kalischer and Elijah *Guttmacher, who also promised funds. A parcel of land on the shores of Lake Kinneret was chosen for settlement, and Berman went abroad to propagate the scheme. His Yiddish book *Masot Shimon*, published in 1879, relates his experiences in Ereẓ Israel. In 1882 Berman returned to Tiberias where he died. Toward the end of his life he witnessed the establishment of the first settlements in Judea and Galilee. Their founders, as the early settlers David Schub and Moshe *Smilansky testify in their memoirs, had been influenced by his book.

BIBLIOGRAPHY: A. Yaari, *Masot Ereẓ Yisrael* (1946), 593–610, 780; E ẒD, 1 (1958), 420–8 (includes bibliography); *Hadoar*, May 16, 1958.

[Avraham Yaari]

BERMAN BERMAN, NATALIO (1907–1959), Chilean politician and Zionist leader. Born in Podolia (Russia), Berman immigrated to Chile in 1915 when he was eight years old. His family settled in Valparaíso, where he graduated from high school. From early childhood he demonstrated his qualities as a leader, organizing the Jewish youth of the small community of Valparaíso. At the age of 15 he was named a delegate from Valparaíso to the Zionist Congress of Chile. He studied medicine at the University of Santiago, working as an assistant in anatomy. During his studies he engaged in broad communal activity, founding the periodical *Nosotros*, which became the organ of the entire Chilean Jewish community. He was active in merging the four existing Jewish youth groups into one organization – the Asociación de Jóvenes Israelitas (AJI).

In 1930 Berman was elected president of the Federación Sionista de Chile. After his graduation in medicine he moved to Concepción, continuing his Jewish communal activities. At the same time, however, he was extremely active among the poor Chilean classes, starting his political career in the N.A.P. (Nueva Acción Pública), which later united with the Socialist Party.

In 1936 Berman led a public campaign against higher taxes, as a consequence of which the government exiled him to a remote island in the south of Chile and revoked his Chilean citizenship. This act provoked the general indignation among the Chilean public, and the Parliament passed a law restoring Berman's Chilean citizenship.

In 1937 Berman was elected a member of Parliament for Concepción. During his term of office, which lasted until 1949, he was very active in the struggle against Nazism and in obtaining entry permits for Jewish refugees. Berman participated in the Popular Front government. In 1941 he withdrew from the Socialist Party, forming the Partido Socialista de Trabajadores (Socialist Workers' Party), which later united with the Communist Party. He abandoned the CP, however, due to Stalin's antisemitic policy. Throughout his political career he continued his activities on behalf of the Jewish community.

[Moshe Nes El (2nd ed.)]

BERMANN, RICHARD ARNOLD (1883–1939), Austrian author and journalist. Bermann was born in Vienna to an assimilated Viennese Jewish family, but spent much of his childhood in Prague. In 1906 he received his doctorate in philology; he began his career as a writer while still a student. From 1912 he was correspondent of the *Berliner Tageblatt* under the pseudonym of Arnold Hoellriegel; he traveled widely as a foreign reporter and "pacificist" war correspondent for the newspaper *Die Zeit* during World War I. After the war he continued his career as a journalist, travel writer, and film critic. He visited Palestine with Arthur Rundt, and their book *Palaestina* (1923) was a glowing account of early Zionist achievements. Both men were careful, however, to disclaim any personal adherence to Jewish nationalism. In Vienna, he maintained a close friendship with author Leo *Perutz, and also knew *Freud, Viktor *Adler, and Otto *Bauer. Bermann's most popular book, *Das Urwaldschiff* (1927; *The Forest Ship*, 1931), described an adventurous trip up the Amazon. The subject of *Derwischtrommel* (1931), which appeared in English as *The Mahdi of Allah* (1931) with an introduction by Winston Churchill, was the Sudanese struggle against the British in the days of General Gordon and Lord Kitchener. After the Nazis occupied Vienna in 1938, Bermann attempted to flee three times to the United States. After being arrested and imprisoned, he was finally able to find refuge in the U.S. that same year, where he continued his resistance to the Nazis as director of the American Guild for German Cultural Freedom in New York, an organization which supported persecuted authors. He died in 1939 in the artists' colony of Yaddo in Saratoga Springs, N.Y.

ADD. BIBLIOGRAPHY: R.A. Bermann (alias A. Hoellriegel, "Die Fahrt auf dem Katarakt. Eine Autobiographie ohne einen Helden," H.-H. Mueller (ed.), *Deutsche Intellektuelle im Exil. Ihre Akademie und die "American Guild for German Cultural Freedom"* (1993); idem, Oesterreicher – Demokrat – Weltbürger (1995); H.-H. Mueller, "Arnold Höllriegel – der Journalist Richard A. Bermann," in: *Relation. Medien – Gesellschaft – Geschichte* (1996), 73–78.

[Sol Liptzin / Lisa Silverman (2nd ed.)]

BERMANN, VASILI (**Ze'ev Wolf**; 1862–1896), one of the first members of Ḥovevei Zion in Russia. He was born in Mitava, Russia (today Jelgava, Latvia) and studied at the Russian-Jewish school run by his father Eliezer Bermann, who published the Russian-Jewish newspaper *Russkii Yevrei* in St. Petersburg. He graduated as a lawyer from St. Petersburg University. After the 1881 pogroms in South Russia, he joined the Ḥibbat Zion movement. He published and edited the Russian-language anthologies *Palestina* (1884, with A. Flekser, Volynsky) and *Sion*, which expounded the intellectual basis for the Ḥibbat Zion ideology. Bermann attended the Ḥovevei Zion Druskiniki conference (1887) and aided in the efforts to obtain an official permit for the Ḥovevei Zion society to operate in Russia. He was secretary of the founding assembly of the society in Odessa (1890). Convinced that organized emigration was essential for Russian Jewry, Bermann supported Baron de *Hirsch's plans to organize the mass exit of Jews from Russia, and regarded this as supplementing the settlement project in Ereẓ Israel. He became secretary of the ICA (*Jewish Colonization Association) founded by Baron de Hirsch, conducted a comprehensive survey of the problem of Jewish emigration, and established and headed the ICA's emigration department. Bermann was also a founder of the Historical-Ethnographical Committee of the Society for the Spreading of Enlightenment among the Jews in Russia. He contracted tuberculosis and went to live in Cairo, where he died.

BIBLIOGRAPHY: *Lu'aḥ Aḥi'asaf*, 4 (1896), 46–50; Katznelson, in: *Ha-Meliẓ*, no. 76 (1896), 3–4; A. Raphaeli (Zenziper), *Pa'amei ha-Ge'ullah* (1951), 28, 88.

[Yehuda Slutsky]

BERMANT, CHAIM ICYK (1929–1998), Lithuanian-born Scottish humorist and journalist noted for his gently satirical sketches of British Jewry. His short novels, which reflect a traditional upbringing, include *Jericho Sleep Alone* (1964), *Diary of an Old Man* (1966), and *Swinging in the Rain* (1967). He also published a guidebook, *Israel* (1967), and *Troubled Eden: An Anatomy of British Jewry* (1969). Possibly Bermant's most valuable work was his biographical history of England's "grandee" Jewish families like the Rothschilds and Montefiores, *The Cousinhood* (1961). Bermant also published a biography of England's Chief Rabbi, *Lord Jakobovits* (1990). Bermant wrote a weekly column in the *Jewish Chronicle* (of which he was Features Editor in 1964–66), which was widely noted and often controversial. Two volumes of Bermant's best weekly columns appeared, *Murmurings of a Licensed Heretic* (1990) and *On the Other Hand* (2000), which was published posthumously. Bermant also wrote a volume of autobiography, *Genesis: A Latvian Childhood* (1998).

[William D. Rubinstein (2nd ed.)]

BERMUDA CONFERENCE, Anglo-American Conference on Refugees in 1943. During World War II, Jewish and general public opinion in the U.S. and the British Commonwealth urgently demanded that the Allied governments rescue the victims of the Nazi regime. Under pressure from parliament, churches, and humanitarian organizations, the British Foreign Office, on Jan. 20, 1943, proposed joint consultation between Britain and the U.S.A. to examine the problem and possible solutions. After an exchange of diplomatic notes, the Anglo-American Conference on Refugees was held in Bermuda from April 19 to 30, 1943. The American delegation was headed by Harold Willis Dodds, president of Princeton University; the British delegation, by Richard Law, parliamentary undersecretary of state for foreign affairs. No private organizations or observers were admitted but interested Jewish organizations in America and England prepared memoranda proposing rescue measures. Chaim *Weizmann submitted a document on behalf of the *Jewish Agency for Palestine, underlining the importance of Palestine in the solution of the problem of Jewish refugees, and demanding abandonment of the policy based on the British White Paper policy of May 1939. The delegates, however, anxiously avoided referring to the Jews as the Nazis' major victims. Disagreement between the two governments about continuing the Intergovernmental Committee of Refugees, founded at the *Evian Conference in July 1938, took up most of the time but it was decided eventually to extend its mandate to deal with postwar problems. British plans for opening up camps in North Africa as a haven for refugees during the war proved impracticable. After seven months – on Dec. 10, 1943 – the report of the conference was published. Its only positive decision – to revive the Evian Committee – came too late to save a single Jew from the Nazi Holocaust.

BIBLIOGRAPHY: M. Wischnitzer, *To Dwell in Safety* (1948), 245–8; Adler-Rudel, in: YLBI, 11 (1966), 213–41; A.D. Morse, *While Six Million Died* (1968), index; World Jewish Congress (Australian Section), *Bermuda Conference on Refugees* (1943); A. Tartakower and K.R. Grossmann, *The Jewish Refugee* (1944), index.

[Shalom Adler-Rudel]

°BERNADOTTE, FOLKE, EARL OF WISBORG (1895–1948), Swedish statesman. Bernadotte was the youngest son of Prince Oscar August of Sweden, a brother of King Gustav V. During World War II he organized an exchange of disabled prisoners of war between Germany and the Allies on behalf of the Swedish Red Cross. He became vice chairman in 1943, and president in 1946, of the Swedish Red Cross. Stimulated by Norwegian and Danish intervention on behalf of their civilian prisoners in German concentration camps, he negotiated on behalf of the Swedish Red Cross with *Himmler who was persuaded to release more than 7,000 Scandinavians during March and April 1945, including over 400 Danish Jews, from *Theresienstadt. Following negotiations with a representative of the *World Jewish Congress in Sweden, Norbert Masur, he also effected the release of several thousand Jewish women from various countries interned in the Ravensbrueck concentration camp. Most of those released were transferred to Sweden. Subsequently, at a meeting in Luebeck on April 24, 1945, Himmler tried to use Bernadotte's good offices to forward peace proposals to the Allies. Bernadotte transmitted the Allies' rejection of these proposals to Himmler on April 27, in Flensburg.

On May 20, 1948, six days after the proclamation of the State of Israel and five days after the commencement of military action, the Security Council of the United Nations appointed Bernadotte mediator in the Arab-Israel conflict. He succeeded in bringing about the first four-week truce on June 11, but failed to achieve Arab consent for its prolongation. Overextending his assignment as mediator, Bernadotte worked out a peace plan that deviated substantially from the UN partition resolution, suggesting, *inter alia*, the incorporation of Jerusalem and the whole Negev in Transjordan in exchange for the inclusion of Western Galilee in Israel. These proposals, which became public a few days after Bernadotte's death, met with stiff opposition by Israel and failed to achieve endorsement by the UN General Assembly in November 1948. On Sept. 17, 1948, Bernadotte was assassinated in Jerusalem. His assailants have not been identified but are believed to have been connected with *Loḥamei Ḥerut Israel. A forest named in his honor has been planted by the *Jewish National Fund in the Judean Hills. Among his books are *The Curtain Falls: Last Days of the Third Reich* (1945) and *To Jerusalem* (1951).

BIBLIOGRAPHY: R. Hewins, *Count Folke Bernadotte: His Life and Work* (1950); Yachil, in: *Yad Vashem Studies*, 6 (1967), 181–220; B. Nadel, *Reẓaḥ Bernadotte* (1968); M. Sharett, *Be-Sha'ar ha-Ummot 1946–1949* (1958), index.

[Leni Yahil]

BERNAL, Sephardi family of Marrano extraction. Its members included ABRAHAM (Manuel Nuñes) BERNAL (c. 1612–1655), a native of Almeida in Portugal, who was the leader of the crypto-Jewish group at Écija (Spain). After trial by the Inquisition at Córdoba he was burned at the stake for his faith, proclaiming his adherence to Judaism to the end. When the news reached Amsterdam the local Jewish poets collaborated in a volume in his memory under the title *Elogios que zelosos dedicaron á la felice memoria de Abraham Nuñez Bernal*, which was published by his cousin JACOB BERNAL. This volume also includes a sermon in honor of Abraham by Isaac *Aboab da Fonseca, and a prose account of the imprisonment and death of Abraham's nephew MARCO (Ishac de Almeida) BERNAL who was martyred also in 1655 at the age of 22. It ends with a sermon by Jacob Abendana in honor of both martyrs. In the course of the 18th century, some of the family settled in London. JACOB ISRAEL BERNAL, a West Indian merchant (d. 1766), served as a warden of the Spanish and Portuguese Jewish community there in 1745, but resigned in protest in 1752 when the synagogue authorities objected to his marriage to an Ashkenazi woman. His son JACOB (d. 1811) dissociated himself from the community and denounced its methods as inquisitorial when he failed to be elected to office; he did not formally abandon Judaism. In the course of time, however, the family left the Jewish community. His son RALPH (1783–1854), brought up as a Christian, was a politician and member of parliament from 1820 to 1853. In 1853 he was president of the British Archaeological Society and a renowned art collector. His son RALPH BERNAL-OSBORNE (1808–1882) was a noted wit and Liberal politician, who was secretary to the admiralty (1852–58). The physicist John Desmond *Bernal (1901–1971) is also descended from this family. The Jewish origin of MESTRE BERNAL, who accompanied Columbus' first expedition to America, is hypothetical.

BIBLIOGRAPHY: A.M. Hyamson, *Sephardim of England* (1951), 170–1, 197–8; C. Roth, in; REJ, 100 (1936), 38–51; Roth, Marranos, index; I.S. Revah, in: REJ, 124 (1965), 368, 426; P.H.D. Bagenal, *Life of Ralph Bernal Osborne* (1884); DNB, 2 (1921–22), 373–4; A.B. Gould, in: *Boletín de la Real Academia de la Historia*, 90 (1927), 532–60; J. Picciotto, *Sketches of Anglo-Jewish History* (1956²), 149, 198–201.

[Kenneth R. Scholberg]

BERNAL, JOHN DESMOND (1901–1971), physicist. Bernal was born in Nenagh, County Tipperary, now in the Irish Republic, and graduated in science from Cambridge University (1923). After research at the Royal Institution, London (1923–27), he returned to Cambridge as a lecturer in structural crystallography before his appointment as professor of physics at Birkbeck College, London (1937). His main research achievements concerned the crystallographic study of proteins, an essential step in the emergence of molecular biology. His pupils included Rosalind *Franklin, Aaron *Klug, and Max *Perutz. Known as the "Great Sage of Cambridge," he was a polymath to the detriment of his personal achievements. His interests included the origins of life on Earth and the creation of the Mulberry harbors indispensable for the 1944 D-Day landings. He was deeply interested in the social concerns of science and he lectured and wrote prolifically in this field and on popular science and the history of science. His honors included election to the Royal Society of London, the Lenin Prize of the U.S.S.R., and the U.S. Medal of Freedom. The precocious child of Sephardi Jews on his father's side and an American mother, he became a Marxist and, with the rise of fascism in the 1930s, briefly a member of the Communist Party.

[Michael Denman (2nd ed.)]

°**BERNARD, EDWARD** (1638–1697), English Orientalist and bibliographer. He had already studied Hebrew at school (in London), and at Oxford, when his mathematical ability secured him the professorship of astronomy at Oxford, first as Wren's deputy, and for one year (1676) he acted as tutor to Charles II's sons. He was devoted, however, to the study of Oriental languages. Bernard was one of the earliest students of Samaritan; he traced all alphabets to this script as putative parent (1689). His planned edition of Josephus foundered after the early books of the *Antiquities* (Oxford, 1700); he had written on the Septuagint and Letter of Aristeas (*ibid.*, 1692) and published W. Guise's translation of part of Mishnah *Zera'im* (*ibid.*, 1690). The wider scholarly world knows Bernard as author of the still important combined catalog of English and Irish manuscript collections (*ibid.*, 1697). His publications and manuscript *reliquiae* are listed by A. Wood (*Athenae Oxonienses*, ed. by P. Bliss, 4 (London, 1813–20), 703), and a printed auction-catalog of his library survives in the British Museum.

ADD. BIBLIOGRAPHY: ODNB online.

[Raphael Loewe]

BERNARD, ḤAYYIM DAVID (1782–1858), Polish physician and ḥasidic leader. Born in Dzialoszyce, near Piotrkow, Bernard is reputed to have been the son of the poet and physician Issachar Falkensohn *Behr. At the age of 14 Bernard arrived in Berlin and later qualified as a physician in Erfurt. The liberal policies of King Frederick William II enabled him to become court physician at Potsdam and a medical officer in the Prussian Army – a considerable achievement for a Jew. After Napoleon's conquest of Poland, Bernard was appointed medical inspector for the western regions of the Grand Duchy of Warsaw (1807–15). A typical product of the German-Jewish Enlightenment, he at first remained aloof from Polish Jewry, but a spiritual crisis led him to approach R. David of *Lelov, who introduced him to R. *Jacob Isaac ha-Ḥozeh mi-Lublin, the Seer of Lublin. Bernard, known thereafter as R. Ḥayyim David, became a strictly Orthodox Jew and a follower of the Seer. He grew a beard, although he retained western dress, and never mastered Yiddish. As the Warsaw Jewish archives have shown, he was a leading communal figure and later worked in collaboration with R. *Simḥah Bunem of Przysucha. Among the Jews and Christians whom he treated, Bernard was venerated as a saint and he spent the rest of his life in Piotrkow, both as head of the local hospital and as a "wonder-working" Ḥasid. Although his wife opposed the Seer's wish to designate her husband as his successor, Bernard was widely regarded as the Seer's spiritual heir and for decades after the physician's death his grave was a center of ḥasidic pilgrimage.

BIBLIOGRAPHY: *Maḥanayim*, no. 123 (1969), 174–8.

BERNARD, JESSIE (1903–1996), U.S. sociologist and feminist. Born Jessie Sarah Ravitch in Minneapolis, Minnesota, the daughter of Jewish-Romanian immigrants, Bernard received B.A. (1923) and M.A. (1924) degrees from the University of Minnesota. Her M.A. thesis was entitled "Changes of Attitudes of Jews in the First and Second Generation." In 1935 Bernard earned a Ph.D. from Washington University in St. Louis. In some of her work Bernard collaborated with her husband, Luther Lee Bernard, a professor of sociology whom she had met at the University of Minnesota. Bernard spent many years on the faculties of Washington University and Pennsylvania State University. In her early career she researched issues relating to Jewish life. Later, her concerns focused on the family, sexuality, and gender. In her sixties Bernard became an ardent advocate of feminism; she was an influential figure who was regarded as a role model for younger women. She served as president of the Eastern Sociological Association and president of the Society for the Study of Social Problems; in retirement Bernard was a visiting professor at Princeton University. Among awards established in her name are the Jessie Bernard Wise Women Award of The Center for Women's Policy Studies and The American Sociological Association's Jessie Bernard Award for scholarly works dealing with the role of women in society, presented at the group's annual meeting. Among Bernard's publications are *Academic Women* (1964); *The Future of Marriage* (1972); *The Future of Motherhood* (1975); and *The Female World* (1981). Bernard's books were often best sellers and frequently controversial. *The Future of Marriage*, for example, concluded that, while men thrived emotionally in marriage, women were oppressed.

BIBLIOGRAPHY: R.C. Bannister, *Jessie Bernard: The Making of a Feminist* (1991); M.J. Deegan, "Jessie Bernard," in: *Women in Sociology: A Bio-bibliography Sourcebook* (1991); Obituary, *New York Times* (Oct. 11, 1996).

[Libby White (2nd ed.)]

BERNARD, TRISTAN (1866–1947), French playwright and novelist. Born in Besançon, Bernard began his career as a sports writer, but soon turned to the theater, where he was able to exercise his talent for comedy, good-humored satire, and witty observation of the man in the street. His *bons mots* were so famous that for three decades he was credited with many of the jokes current in France. Bernard wrote several novels, notably *Mémoires d'un jeune homme rangé* (1899), *Amants et voleurs* (1905), and *Mathilde et ses mitaines* (1912). He is best remembered, however, as the author of such hilarious comedies as *Les pieds nickelés* (1895), *L'anglais tel qu'on le parle* (1899), *Le petit café* (1911), *Le prince charmant* (1923), *Jules, Juliette, et Julien* (1929), *Le sauvage* (1931), and *Que le monde est petit* (1935). Tristan Bernard combined the wit of the French with the bitter humor of the Jew. *Le Juif de Venise* (1936) attempts to reinterpret the character of Shakespeare's Shylock. He was arrested by the Nazis during World War II but was released, following the intervention of influential friends. His son, JEAN-JACQUES BERNARD (1888–1972), also wrote a number of popular plays including *Martine* (1922) and *L'invitation au voyage* (1924). Though a convert to Catholicism, he was imprisoned at Compiègne for part of the Nazi occupation. His war experiences were recorded in *Le camp de la mort lente* (1945) and are reflected in the story, *L'Intouchable* (1947).

BIBLIOGRAPHY: R. Blum, *Tristan Bernard* (Fr., 1925); P. Blanchart, *Masques*, 11 (1928); idem, *Tristan Bernard, son oeuvre* (1932); J.J. Bernard, *Mon père, Tristan Bernard* (1955).

[Moshe Catane]

BERNARDI, HERSCHEL (1924–1986), U.S. actor. Born in New York City, Bernardi was the product of a long-established family of Yiddish performers. On stage from childhood, he made his first on-camera appearances in 1939 in the Yiddish-language films *Green Fields* and *The Singing Blacksmith*. Bernardi toured in a one-man program of Shalom Aleichem stories and performed in *The World of Sholom Aleichem*, 1954. Along with many fellow entertainers, he was blacklisted by

Hollywood in the early 1950s for alleged Communist ties. Bernardi's first part on Broadway was in the musical *Bajour* in 1965. He then played Tevye in the Broadway production of *Fiddler on the Roof* (1966–67), as well as in a revival run at Lincoln Center in 1981. He also performed in the Broadway productions *Zorba* (1968–69) and *The Goodbye People* (1979).

In addition to his many television guest appearances and roles in TV movies, Bernardi is well remembered for his characterizations of Lt. Jacoby on the *Peter Gunn* detective series (1958–61) and Arnie Nuvo in the sitcom *Arnie* (1970–72). Bernardi also provided voiceovers for hundreds of cartoons and commercials, most notably the wisecracking Charley the Tuna and the laughing Jolly Green Giant. At one point in his career, he had strained his vocal chords so severely that his doctor ordered him not to speak for a full year or he might lose his voice permanently.

He appeared in a number of films over the years, among them *Murder by Contract* (1958); *The Savage Eye* (1960); *A Cold Wind in August* (1961); *Irma La Douce* (1963); *Love with the Proper Stranger* (1963); and *The Front* (1976). Bernardi was one of the main interviewees in the 1984 documentary *Almonds and Raisins*, written by Wolf *Mankowitz and narrated by Orson Welles. The film examines the dozens of Yiddish-language talking films made in the U.S. and Europe between the release of *The Jazz Singer* in 1927 and the outbreak of World War II.

BIBLIOGRAPHY: J. Bernardi, *My Father the Actor* (1971).

[Ruth Beloff (2nd ed.)]

°**BERNARDINO DA FELTRE** (1439–1494), *Franciscan friar, born at Feltre, N. Italy. From 1471 Bernardino began to attain a great reputation throughout northern Italy as a preacher, especially of the Lenten sermons urging the people to repentance. Pursuing the policy of his order, Bernardino inveighed against the Jews and supported the foundation of public loan-banks (*Monte di Pietà) in order to displace Jewish moneylenders. His preaching was mainly responsible for the blood libel at *Trent in 1475. In the following year, he made a similar attempt at Reggio, and then in Bassano and Mantua; in 1485 he instigated the expulsion of the Jews from Perugia, and in 1486 from Gubbio. In 1488 he was expelled from Florence to prevent disorders. In 1491 in Ravenna he succeeded in having the Jews expelled and the synagogue destroyed. In 1492 he secured the expulsion of the Jews from Campo San Pietro, and from Brescia in 1494. Shortly after his death he was beatified.

BIBLIOGRAPHY: E. Lazzareschi, *Il beato Bernardino da Feltre, gli Ebrei e il Monte di Pietà in Lucca* (1941), Roth, Italy, 170–6, passim; Milano, Italia, index; U. Cassuto, *Gli Ebrei a Firenze nell' età del Rinascimento* (1918), 52–53, 56–60, 62–63.

[Cecil Roth]

°**BERNARDINO DA SIENA** (1380–1444), Franciscan friar, celebrated for his powerful oratory. One of the main themes urged by Bernardino in his sermons was the return of the Church to its original purity and the exclusion of any form of association between Christians and Jews. Hence, Bernardino ruthlessly upheld the application of anti-Jewish restrictions, including segregation, exclusion from money-lending, limitation of economic activities, and wearing of the Jewish badge. He preached throughout Tuscany, Umbria, and Abruzzi, culminating in inflammatory sermons delivered at Aquila in 1438, attended by King René of Anjou. Almost everywhere, Bernardino's sermons resulted in a deterioration of the relationships between Christians and Jews and often provoked disorders. The circle of disciples which formed around Bernardino assiduously propagated his anti-Jewish doctrine. Most important of those whom he influenced were Barnabas of Terni, Giacomo della Marca, and *Bernardino da Feltre.

BIBLIOGRAPHY: V. Facchinetti, *Bernardino da Siena* (It., 1933); Roth, Italy, 162ff.; Milano, Italia, 162f., 684.

[Attilio Milano]

°**BERNARD OF CLAIRVAUX** (1090–1153), French Cistercian, homilist, and theologian. In 1146, when preaching the Second Crusade, he intervened orally and in writing to protect the Jews in the Rhineland from persecution incited by a certain monk Radulph, declaring that an attempt on the life of a Jew was a sin tantamount to making an attempt on the life of Jesus. A letter addressed by Bernard to the Germans implicitly repudiates the policy urged by *Peter the Venerable, abbot of Cluny, against the Jews (although without expressly naming the abbot) by emphasizing the difference between Jews and Muslims; Bernard, while considering it right to take up arms against Muslims, maintains that it is forbidden to attack Jews. While Peter wished to expropriate the wealth of the Jews to finance the Crusade, Bernard limited himself to recommending the abolition of interest on credit they had advanced to crusaders. He finally recalled in his epistle the fate of Peter the Hermit and his followers, who had persecuted the Jews during the First Crusade and led his supporters into such peril that practically none had survived. Bernard warned that the present crusaders might well suffer similar Divine retribution: "It is to be feared that if you act in like manner, a similar fate will strike you." Jewish chroniclers stress Bernard's disinterestedness in his defense of the Jews.

BIBLIOGRAPHY: A. Neubauer (ed.), *Hebraeische Berichte…* (1892), 58ff., 187ff.; Blumenkranz, in: K.H. Rengstorf and S. von Kortzfleisch (eds.), *Kirche und Synagoge* (1968), 119ff.

[Bernhard Blumenkranz]

BERNAYS, family originating in Germany with branches elsewhere in Central Europe and the U.S.

ISAAC BEN JACOB BERNAYS (1792–1849), rabbi of Hamburg, Germany, was born in Mainz, studied at Wuerzburg University and at the yeshivah of Abraham Bing and was appointed rabbi of Hamburg in 1821. While Bernays, who preferred the Sephardi designation of ḥakham, was committed to the preservation of inherited customs and ceremonies, he did modernize the curriculum of the local *talmud torah* and regularly gave sermons in the German vernacular. In his struggle against Reform in the community, Bernays formulated elements of a "modern orthodoxy" which influenced the views of his disciple, Samson Raphael *Hirsch. In 1842 Bernays interdicted the Reform siddur, then republished by the Hamburg Temple Congregation, stating that a Jew did not fulfill his religious duties if he read his *tefillot* from this prayer book. *Der biblische Orient*, the only work attributed to him, is considered by many to have been written by or in cooperation with J.A. von Kalb, a Christian friend of his from Munich.

Isaac's eldest son JACOB (1824–1881), born in Hamburg, was a philologist and classicist. He taught Greek at Bonn University (1848–53), at which time he published the Teubner edition of Lucretius' *De Rerum Natura* (1850), *Heraklitische Studien* (1850), and *Ueber Spinozas hebraeische Grammatik* (1850). Unlike his younger brother, Michael, Jacob was attached to Judaism and when, because of it, he could not gain promotion at Bonn he left and helped to found the Breslau *Jewish Theological Seminary in 1853/54. Jacob mainly taught classics, history, German literature and Jewish philosophy. He encouraged the publication of treatises with the annual report, himself contributing three (on the poetic fragments of Phocylides, 1856; on the *Chronicle* of Sulpicius Severus, 1861; and Theophrastus' lost work *On Piety*, 1886). His greatest work, *Grundzuege der verlorenen Abhandlung des Aristoteles ueber die Wirkung der Tragoedie* (1857), on Aristotle's treatise which preceded the *Poetics*, aroused considerable criticism. In 1866 Jacob finally overcame the prejudices at Bonn and was appointed (extraordinary) professor and chief librarian, but still maintained an interest in the seminary at Breslau. His collected works were issued in 1885 (edited by Usener; reprinted in 1971).

[Yehoshua Horowitz]

Isaac's younger son, MICHAEL BERNAYS (1834–1897), was a distinguished literary critic and historian. He was professor of German literature at the University of Munich (1874–90) and wrote pioneering textual studies of Goethe. After his indifference towards Judaism led him to convert to Protestantism in 1856 his family broke with him completely. Isaac's other son BERMAN BERNAYS (d. 1879), merchant and secretary to the Viennese economist, Lorenz von Stein, was father of MARTHA BERNAYS (1861–1951) who married Sigmund *Freud.

[George Schwab]

PAUL ISAAC BERNAYS (1888–1977), mathematician, is best known as the coauthor with D. Hilbert of *Grundlagen der Mathematik* (2 vols., 1934–39), which is considered a classic work. Bernays, who was born in London, became Hilbert's assistant in Goettingen in 1917, and was appointed professor in 1922. In 1934 Bernays left Nazi Germany for Zurich, Switzerland, where he taught at the Polytechnicum. In the postwar era, Bernays was mainly concerned with the philosophy of mathematics. In "Some Empirical Aspects of Mathematics" (1965), he argued that his discipline has an objective ("phenomenological") reality distinct from the natural world. Bernays wrote numerous papers on this subject, coauthored with Abraham Fraenkel *Axiomatic Set Theory* (1958), and coedited *Information and Prediction in Science* (1965). A book in his honor entitled *Logica, Studia Paul Bernays Dedicata* was published in Switzerland in 1959. Edward L. *Bernays (1891–1995), was a public relations expert whose methods revolutionized the field of public relations.

[Paul G. Werskey]

BIBLIOGRAPHY: Fuerst, in: MGWJ, 58 (1914), 516–8; Bach, *ibid.*, 83 (1939), 533–47; Duckesz, in: JJLG, 5 (1907), 297–322; Heinemann, in: *Zion*, 16 (1951), 44–90; M. Fraenkel, *Jacob Bernays* (Ger., 1932); L. Wickert, in: *Historische Zeitschrift*, 205 (1967), 269–94. **ADD. BIBLIOGRAPHY:** H.I. Bach, *Jacob Bernays* (1974); Poppel, in: LBIYB, 28 (1983), 453–61; L. Tye, *The Father of Spin: Edward L. Bernays and the Birth of Public Relations* (1998).

BERNAYS, EDWARD L. (1891–1995), U.S. public relations executive. Born in Vienna, a nephew of Sigmund *Freud, Bernays is regarded by many as the "father" of public relations. His efforts helped popularize Freud's theories in the United States. He also was responsible for molding public opinion on a variety of cultural issues in the United States in the 20th century. He was public relations adviser for the Ballet Russe of Sergei Diaghilev, the Metropolitan Opera, Enrico Caruso, Procter and Gamble, President Calvin Coolidge, Henry Ford, Conde Nast Publications, David *Sarnoff, William *Paley, Clare Booth Luce, Samuel *Goldwyn, Mack Trucks, United Fruit (bananas), American Tobacco, United Brewers Association, the National Association for the Advancement of Colored People, the American Civil Liberties Union, the Waldorf-Astoria hotel, General Electric, General Motors, Westinghouse Electric, and Columbia University. His mother, Anna (Freud) Bernays, was Sigmund Freud's sister. His first cousin was Sigmund's daughter, Anna *Freud, the renowned child psychologist, and his daughter, Anne *Bernays, was a novelist and the wife of Justin Kaplan, a Pulitzer Prize-winning author and biographer of Walt Whitman.

Bernays was raised in New York City from the age of one. He attended public schools and graduated from Cornell University's College of Agriculture in 1912. After World War I (Bernays volunteered to aid the American effort, working in President Woodrow Wilson's Office of War Information), he and his future wife opened an office to promote various clients and causes. Some of his efforts became legendary. To promote Ivory soap and make bathing more popular with children, he set up a national small-sculpture panel that for years oversaw soap-carving competitions. He enlisted "third party authorities" to plead for his clients' causes: to promote the sale of bacon, he conducted a survey of physicians and reported their recommendations that people eat hearty breakfasts, including bacon and eggs.

In the early 1920s, Bernays arranged for the American publication of Freud's *General Introduction to Psychoanalysis*. Bernays used his association with his uncle to establish his own reputation as a thinker and theorist. He wrote several landmark texts, notably *Crystallizing Public Opinion* (1923), *Propaganda* (1928), and "The Engineering of Consent" in *Annals of the American Academy of Political and Social Science* (1947).

Several of his social ideas have had long-lasting effects. He helped make it acceptable for women to smoke in public, sponsoring demonstrations in which debutantes gathered on street corners to light up "torches of freedom." In his later years, Bernays was a public opponent of smoking and took part in antismoking campaigns.

In his autobiography, *Biography of an Idea*, in 1965, Bernays recalled a dinner at his home in 1933 where Karl von Weigand, foreign correspondent of the Hearst newspapers, was talking about Joseph *Goebbels and his propaganda plans to consolidate Nazi power. "Goebbels had shown Weigand his propaganda library," Bernays wrote. "Goebbels, said Weigand, was using my book *Crystallizing Public Opinion* as a basis for his destructive campaign against the Jews of Germany. This shocked me ... Obviously the attack on the Jews of Germany was no emotional outburst of the Nazis, but a deliberate, planned campaign."

[Stewart Kampel (2nd ed.)]

BERNBACH, WILLIAM (1911–1982), U.S. advertising executive. Born in the Bronx, N.Y., he served in the U.S. Army in World War II and then worked at Grey Advertising, one of a few Jewish-owned advertising agencies in New York. His modest upbringing during the Depression and public school education instilled a strong sense of gratitude for the achievements that lay before him during his remarkable career in advertising.

In 1949, seeking to develop an environment based on the primacy of creativity, he joined with Ned Doyle, another Grey vice president, and with Maxwell Dane, a small agency owner, to form Doyle Dane Bernbach (DDB). They specialized in subtle, intelligent copy and graphics. So successful were these efforts that in less than 20 years the agency had become the sixth largest in the U.S. Bernbach's influence on the contemporary advertising industry was profound. His creative leadership won him many awards.

One of his most famous slogans was "You don't have to be Jewish to love Levy's" (rye bread). That campaign elevated Levy's to the largest seller of rye bread in New York and helped Bernbach and his partners acquire the first of many national and international clients. Other well-known slogans were "Think Small" for a small-car manufacturer and "We Try Harder Because We're Only Number 2" for the Avis car-rental company. In 1954 DDB determined that the uniqueness of Dr. Edwin Land's Polaroid breakthrough could best be demonstrated on live television, so they hired some of the most popular celebrities (Steve Allen, Jack Paar, Johnny Carson, and later Mariette Hartley and James Garner) to demonstrate the benefits of the Polaroid instant camera. The relationship between Polaroid and DDB lasted almost 30 years, and the campaign became one of DDB's most widely recognized.

In its early years, DDB gained its reputation from its ad campaigns for Jewish clients. Orbach's department store, Levy's, and El Al airlines provided the ad agency the opportunity to develop noticeable work, which would eventually gain the attention of Volkswagen. Soon to follow was El Al Israel Airlines' introduction of its trans-Atlantic service from Europe to the U.S. While most airlines would never have shown an image of the ocean in its advertising, for fear of reminding readers of the possibility of a crash, Bernbach faced this fear head on. El Al was the only airline at the time that could offer non-stop service between the two continents. Turning that to El Al's advantage, DDB created the "torn ocean" ad with the headline "The Atlantic Ocean will be 20% smaller." The one-time ad was so powerful, that within one year, El Al's sales tripled.

Bernbach and his partners raised Jewish and other minority advertising agencies into the mainstream of the medium. In 1969 alone, more than 100 new Jewish and Italian agencies opened, ensuring Bernbach's legacy for decades to come. Largely due to Bernbach's business acumen, DDB's $775,000 off-Madison Avenue business in 1949 evolved into a multibillion-dollar international powerhouse by the mid-1980s, when it merged with Needham Harper Worldwide to create DDB Needham. Bernbach was one of the first inductees into the Copywriters Hall of Fame in 1961 and is in the Advertising Hall of Fame.

BIBLIOGRAPHY: J.W. Young, *A Technique for Producing Ideas* (1965); D. Higgins, *The Art of Writing Advertising* (1986); B. Levenson, *Bill Bernbach's Book* (1987); N. Millman, *Emperors of Adland* (1988); K. Stabiner, *Inventing Desire* (1993); S. Fox, *The Mirror Makers* (1997).

[Isadore Barmash / Ruth Beloff (2nd ed.)]

BERNE (Ger. Bern), capital of Switzerland. Jews in Berne, engaged in moneylending, are first mentioned in a document of 1262 or 1263. In 1293 or 1294 several Jews were put to death there in consequence of a *blood libel, and the remainder expelled from the city. However, an agreement was made with the citizenry through the intervention of Adolf of Nassau permitting the Jews to return, against a payment of 1,500 marks and a moratorium on debts owed to them. During the *Black Death (1348) the Jews in Berne were accused of poisoning the wells, and a number were burnt at the stake. The Jews were expelled from Berne in 1392 after Christians were permitted to engage in moneylending (1384). Although between 1408 and 1427 Jews were again residing in the city, the only Jews to appear in Berne subsequently were transients, chiefly physicians and cattle dealers. After the occupation of Switzerland by the French revolutionary armies and the foundation of the Helvetian Republic in 1798, a number of Jews from Alsace and elsewhere settled in Berne. They required a special license to engage in commerce and were obliged to keep accounts in German or French instead of their customary Alsatian Judeo-German. These restrictions were removed in 1846. An organized Jewish community was officially established in 1848: a synagogue was consecrated in 1855, and a cemetery in 1871.

In 1906 a beautiful Moorish-style synagogue was built, which was still in use at the beginning of the 21st century. For some 30 years, there was a separate East European Jewish community. Berne University was one of the first German-speaking universities (1836) to allow Jewish lecturers without requiring a change of professed faith, and many Jews subsequently held academic positions there. The university was attended by numerous students from Russia and Hungary before World War I, including Chaim Weizmann. The first Jewish woman lecturer in Switzerland, Anna Tumarkin, was active at Berne University. The famous trial in which evidence was brought that the *Protocols of the Learned *Elders of Zion* was a forgery was held in Berne in the 1930s. In the 1990s the Jewish communities of Berne and *Biel were jointly granted state recognition. In 2000 there were 807 Jews in the canton of Berne.

BIBLIOGRAPHY: M. Kayserling, in: MGWJ, 13 (1864), 46–51; Tobler, in: *Archiv des historischen Vereins des Kantons Bern*, 12 (1889), 336–67; *Festschrift zur Jahrhundertfeier der juedischen Gemeinde zu Bern* (1948), **ADD. BIBLIOGRAPHY:** E. Dreifuss, *Juden in Bern. Ein Gang durch die Jahrhunderte* (1983).

[Zvi Avneri / Uri Kaufmann (2nd ed.)]

BERNFELD, SIEGFRIED (1892–1953), psychoanalyst and educator. Born in Lemberg (Lvov), he studied at the universities of Freiburg and Vienna. A pupil of Sigmund Freud, Bernfeld was also influenced by Gustav Wyneken, the German educator and philosopher. He practiced and taught psychoanalysis in Vienna and Berlin and later in Menton, France. Leaving France in 1936, he settled in San Francisco, California. Bernfeld was active in Austrian and German youth movements, applying in practice the conclusions he drew from his psychoanalytic studies. During World War I, he organized the Zionist youth movement in Austria, and published the Zionist youth periodical *Jerubaal* in Vienna (1918–19). Among his other works of Jewish interest are *Das juedische Volk und seine Jugend* (1920). He was a founder of the Hebrew Paedagogium at Vienna and the Jewish children's home at Baumgarten. Bernfeld wrote extensively on a variety of topics. His examination of infant psychology and of Freud's childhood, and also his attempts at educational reform, are noteworthy.

ADD. BIBLIOGRAPHY: K. Fallend and J. Reichmayr (eds.), *Siegfried Bernfeld, oder die Grenzen der Psychoanalyse* (1992), bibl.; J. Bunzl, in: N. Lassar (ed.), *Juedische Jugendbewegungen* (2001), 62–79; P. Dudek, *Fetisch Jugend* (2002).

[Shnayer Z. Leiman]

BERNFELD, SIMON (1860–1940), rabbi, scholar, and author. Bernfeld was born in Stanislav, Galicia, and was educated in Koenigsberg and Berlin. In 1886 he was appointed chief rabbi of the Sephardi community of Belgrade, Serbia; he remained there until 1894, when he returned to Berlin and devoted himself to scholarly pursuits. He continued his literary work until his death, despite blindness in his later years. Bernfeld wrote several monographs in Hebrew on Jewish history and philosophy, the earliest published when he was only 19 (in *Ha-Maggid*, 1 (1879), 91ff.). His best-known work is *Da'at Elohim* ("Knowledge of God," 2 vols., 1897), a history of religious philosophy. He also wrote *Toledot ha-Reformazyon ha-Datit be-Yisrael* (1900), a history of the Reform movement; *Benei Aliyyah* (2 vols., 1931), a collection of monographs on famous Jews of various periods; *Sefer ha-Dema'ot* ("Book of Tears," 3 vols., 1923–26), an anthology of historical sources in prose and verse on the persecution of Jews from the earliest periods until the Ukrainian pogroms of 1768, still an important reference work; and *Mavo Sifruti-Histori le-Khitvei ha-Kodesh* (3 vols., 1923–25), an introduction to the Bible from the viewpoint of biblical criticism. Bernfeld also wrote in Hebrew on the history of the Haskalah in Germany and Galicia, *Dor Tahapukhot* (1897–98) and monographs on Muhammad (1898) and on the Crusades (1899). Bernfeld's works in German include *Juden und Judentum im neunzehnten Jahrhundert* (1898); *Der Talmud, sein Wesen, seine Bedeutung und seine Geschichte* (1900); and *Kaempfende Geister in Judentum* (1907). His German translation of the Bible, which follows traditional translations, was published in several editions. Bernfeld edited *Die Lehren des Judenthums* (4 vols., 1920–24 and later editions; Eng. tr. of vol. 1 by A.H. Koller, *Teachings of Judaism* (1929), vol. 1: *Foundations of Jewish Ethics*, with new introduction by S.E. Karff, 1968). Although not original in his ideas, Bernfeld popularized and disseminated much important literary and scientific knowledge.

BIBLIOGRAPHY: I. Klausner, *Yoẓerim u-Vonim*, 1 (1944²), 290–8; idem, *Yoẓerei-Tekufah u-Mamshikhei Tekufah* (1956), 153–61; EIV, 9 (1958), 870–2; M.J. bin-Gorion, *Kitvei... Bi-Sedeh-Sefer*, 2 (1921), 52–63; Voyeslavsky, in: *Gilyonot*, 2 (1934/35), 478–84; S.B. Weinryb, in: *Bitzaron*, 1 (1939/40), 502–11; Hodess, in: *New Judea*, 16 (1940), 73–74.

[Joseph Gedaliah Klausner]

BERNHARD, GEORG (1875–1944), German political economist and journalist. Born into an acculturated German-Jewish trading family in Berlin, Bernhard first went into in the banking business from 1892 to 1898, then turned to professional journalism. In 1896, he joined the financial staff of the Berlin *Welt am Montag* as "Gracchus." In 1898, he was appointed editor of the economic section of the *Berliner Zeitung* by L. *Ullstein and in 1902 created the first popular financial column of its kind at the *Berliner Morgenpost* (est. 1898). In addition, from 1901 to 1903, he contributed to M. *Harden's periodical *Die Zukunft* (est. 1892) as "Plutus." At the same time, he enrolled at Berlin University in 1899, completing his studies in economics and public law in 1902. As a revisionist Social Demokrat, Bernhard was elected a member of the Reichstag in 1903 and thus had to resign from all journalistic posts. Instead, he founded his own financial weekly *Plutus. Kritische Zeitschrift fuer Volkswirtschaft und Finanzwesen* (1904–25). After a dramatic dispute with A. Bebel in 1903, he was eventually excluded from the Social Democratic Party. In 1908, he returned to the Ullstein company as publisher-editor of the dailies *Berliner Morgenpost* and *B.Z. am Mittag*. When Ullstein took over the prestigious *Vossische Zeitung* in 1913, Bernhard became its editor-in-chief from 1914 to 1930 (until 1920 together with Hermann Bachmann). He was also appointed lecturer at the Berlin *Handelshochschule* (1916–30, from 1928 as honorary professor). As one of the most influential journalists of the German Empire and Weimar Republic, Bernhard was deeply involved in communal and national politics. After 1918, he strongly supported a reconciliation between Germany and France, which, however, made him a public enemy of the political right, including the NSDAP. Subsequently, Bernhard was appointed to the National Economic Council and, as a leading member of the DDP (from 1924), again to the Reichstag (1928–30). Between 1913 and 1930, he was elected council member of several press associations and was active in German-Jewish communal organizations, e.g., as a council member of the Central-Verein, ORT, and, though critical of Zionism, the Pro-Palaestina-Komitee. At the end of 1930, Bernhard resigned from all journalistic and political posts, engaging in commerce instead. In February 1933, he managed to flee via East Prussia and Denmark to Paris, where he founded the influential emigrant paper *Pariser Tageblatt* (1933–36, continued as *Pariser Tageszeitung* until 1940). At the end of 1937, however, he had to resign as editor-in-chief, instead working as a representative of the World Jewish Congress in Paris. In addition, from 1933, he engaged in numerous emigrant organizations (e.g., Volksfront, FEAF, ZVE, etc.), and served as an adviser to the French government. In 1940, he was interned at Bassens near Bordeaux but, after a dramatic flight to Spain, succeeded in escaping to the United States in 1941. On his arrival in New York, he was employed at the Institute of Jewish Affairs of the American Jewish Congress, continuing his restless activity for several German-American emigrant organizations. Among Bernhard's published works are numerous studies on politics, economics, and finance (cf. ABJ II (1993), 274–279). He published *Die Deutsche Tragoedie* (1933); *Meister und Dilettanten am Kapitalismus* (1936); *Warum schweigt die Welt?* (ed. B. Jacob, 1936, in collaboration with others), etc.

BIBLIOGRAPHY: R. Schay, *Juden in der deutschen Politik* (1929), 267–72; "Un grand journaliste allemand," in: *Revue mondiale* (Jan. 1931), 198–202; *Aufbau* (Feb. 18, 1944); MB (Feb. 18, 1944); K.H. Salzmann, in: *Neue Deutsche Biographie*, vol. II (1955), 117–18; W. Roeder and H.A. Strauss (eds.), *International Biographical Dictionary of Central European Emigrés 1933–1945*, vol. I (1980), 58; R. Heuer (ed.), *Archiv Bibliographia Judaica*, vol. II (1993), 271–79, incl. bibl.; H. Schmuck (ed.), *Jewish Biographical Archive* (1995), F. 138, 22–57; Series II (2003), F. II/59, 419–28; J. Mikuteit, *Georg Bernhard (1875–1944), Ein deutscher Journalist in Presse und Politik vor*, Diss. phil., Europa-Universität Viadrina Frankfurt (Oder), 1998 (Microfilm, 2002); M. Klein, *Georg Bernhard. Die politische Haltung des Chefredakteurs der 'Vossischen Zeitung' Frankfurt a. M.* (1999).

[Johannes Valentin Schwarz (2nd ed.)]

BERNHARD, SANDRA (1955–), U.S. actress, comedian, vocalist, author. Born in the suburbs of Flint, Michigan, the daughter of a proctologist and an artist, Bernhard's first public performance was singing "Hello Dolly" at a bar mitzvah. She spent eight months working on a kibbutz in Israel. At 18 she moved to California, where she first worked as a manicurist for clients such as Tina Louise. Her comedy career began in the late 1970s in Los Angeles' comedy clubs and led to a spot as a regular on the short-lived *Richard Pryor Show*. Her first major film role was opposite Robert DeNiro in Martin Scorcese's *King of Comedy* (1983). Her other major film credits include *Hudson Hawk*, *The Apocalypse*, and *Inside Monkey Zetterland*. Bernhard has received critical acclaim for her distinctive one-woman shows, a format particularly well suited to her wide-ranging caustic social commentary and extremely personal performances. Her most notable one-woman shows are "Without You I'm Nothing" (1988), which was later adapted into film, and "I'm Still Here … Damn It!" (1998). Throughout her career, Bernhard's controversial personal life has been deeply intertwined with her professional success. Her highly publicized relationship with Madonna coincided with her appearance in Madonna's 1991 video *Truth or Dare*, and she also received great attention for her regular role on the television show *Roseanne* as the title character's lesbian friend. Bernhard has released seven albums, winning high praise in particular for her 1985 debut album *I'm Your Woman*. Bernhard is also the author of three books, including her autobiography *Confessions of a Pretty Lady* (1988) as well as *Love, Love, and Love* (1993) and *May I Kiss you on the Lips, Miss Sandra?* (1998).

[Walter Driver (2nd ed.)]

BERNHARDT, SARAH (**Rosine Bernard**; 1844–1923), French actress. Fathered by a Frenchman (Edouard Bernard), she was the eldest of three illegitimate daughters born to Judith Van Hard, a Dutch-Jewish music teacher. When Sarah was ten years old she was sent to the convent of Versailles and baptized. However, she remained proud of her Jewish heritage. She made her debut at the Comédie Française in 1862 as Iphigénie in Racine's *Iphigénie en Aulide*. She acted at the Odéon from 1866 to 1872, and achieved popular acclaim in Coppée's *Le Passant* as the page Zanetto, her first male role. Returning to the Comédie Française, she became one of the greatest interpreters of Racine, playing *Andromaque* in 1873 and *Phèdre* in 1874. Temperament and impatience with authority ended her career at the Comédie in 1879. She embarked on a series of tours abroad and drew crowds wherever she appeared. She acted in a London season almost annually until as late as 1922. She visited the U.S. nine times, and acted in Germany, Russia, Latin America, and Australia. Everywhere she conquered her audience with *La Dame aux Camélias* by Alexandre Dumas, fils. Forming her own company, she appeared in both classical and modern works, and excelled in Sardou's *Fédora* (1882), *Théodora* (1884), and *La Tosca* (1889), all of which he wrote for her. Almost every role she acted became her personal triumph. In Edmond Rostand's *L'Aiglon* she played the part of Napoleon's 21-year-old son when she was herself 55. In 1899 she took over a large Paris theater, renamed it Théâtre Sarah Bernhardt, and directed it until her death. Here she presented *Hamlet* and herself played the title role. A neglected knee injury resulted in complications, and in 1914 Bernhardt was obliged to have her right leg amputated. She continued to appear in roles which permitted her to sit, such as Racine's *Athalie*. The "Divine Sarah," as she was called by Victor Hugo, died while at work on a film. Her autobiography *Ma Double Vie* was published in 1907.

BIBLIOGRAPHY: L. Verneuil, *Fabulous Life of Sarah Bernhardt* (1942); J. Agate, *Madame Sarah* (Eng., 1945); J. Richardson, *Sarah Bernhardt* (Eng., 1959); C.O. Skinner, *Madame Sarah* (Eng., 1967).

[Linda Gutstein]

BERNHEIM, GILLES (1952–), French Orthodox rabbi and philosopher. Bernheim simultaneously completed rabbinical studies at the Seminaire Israelite de France and higher studies in philosophy. As a rabbi, he was first appointed chaplain for students (from 1978) and academics (until 1996). He gained recognition in the Jewish as well as the non-Jewish world through his effort to combine Jewish tradition and Western philosophy, an endeavor that he tried to convey through numerous articles, conferences, and books. From 1996 he headed the Torah Committee at the Consistory of Paris, and was appointed in 1997 chief rabbi of Paris' main synagogue, the Grande Synagogue de la Victoire. Committed to interfaith dialogue, Bernheim was deputy president of the Amitie Judeo-Chretienne de France, an association founded in the aftermath of World War II following in the footsteps of Jules Isaac's work. Ethics and social problems were also central to Bernheim's commitment, and he developed expertise on problems of medical ethics which led him to be chosen as an honorary member of the Conseil National du Sida, a government body dedicated to fighting the AIDS epidemic and helping its victims. Bernheim was also deputy president of the Medical Ethics Committee at the Consistory of Paris. According to him, "in the philosophy of Israel, there is neither dissociation nor a gap between ethics and religion. Concern and care for the other is the way to meet the divine." Such a vision of Judaism has deep implications for the life of the city (as clearly developed in his book *Un rabbin dans la cite*). Hence Bernheim's dedication to meeting the face of the other, in the sense defined by Emmanuel *Levinas, and his attitude of openness and dialogue towards Gentiles as well as Jews, with emphasis on reception and transmission, mutual teaching and enrichment. This commitment ran counter to ultra-Orthodox tendencies in modern-day French Jewry, which may explain his failure to be elected as France's chief rabbi in 1994.

[Dror Franck Sullaper (2nd ed.)]

BERNHEIM, HIPPOLYTE (1840–1919), French neurologist. Born in Alsace, he was appointed professor of internal medicine at Nancy University in 1878. In 1884 he began to devote himself to nervous and mental disease and was one of the first to concentrate systematically on the problems of psychotherapy. His methods included suggestion and hypnosis. He was regarded as head of the Nancy school of psychiatry, as opposed to the Paris school headed by Charcot, which saw hypnosis as an investigative method and not as a method of treatment. Bernheim based treatment on persuasion – the doctor's psychological influence on the course of the neurosis. His methods became outdated but his activities were instrumental in winning acceptance for psychotherapy by the medical profession. Bernheim's most important work was *De la suggestion et de ses applications à la thérapeutique* (1886). His other works include *Hypnotisme, suggestion et psychothérapie* (1890). His work laid the foundation for an understanding of the human personality in the light of psychopathology rather than of philosophy. Bernheim recognized "automatisms" which were not under conscious control. He absolved the will as being the origin of mental disease and crime – thus attacking the stigma attaching to insanity and opening the road to the principle of "irresistible impulse" in the penal code.

BIBLIOGRAPHY: S.R. Kagan, *Jewish Medicine* (1952), 375–6; Zilbourg, *A History of Medical Psychology* (1941), 367–9.

[Joshua O. Leibowitz]

BERNHEIM, ISAAC WOLFE (1848–1945), U.S. distiller and philanthropist. Bernheim was born in Schmieheim, Baden. He emigrated to the U.S. in 1867 and settled in Paducah, Kentucky, where he worked as a salesman and bookkeeper. In 1872 Bernheim, together with a brother, established a distillery. The business was moved to Louisville, Ky., in 1882, and became one of the most important in the country. Bernheim made several gifts to public causes. In 1889 he organized the first YMHA in Louisville and contributed its first home. He contributed to Hebrew Union College its first library building (1912), and later helped subsidize its second. Other benefactions included an addition to the Louisville Jewish Hospital (1916), sculpture for Louisville and the Statuary Hall in Washington, a 13,000-acre nature reserve near Louisville, and gifts to the village of his birth. Bernheim was rigid and autocratic in temperament. Particularly hostile to Zionism, in 1918 he addressed a letter to the Central Conference of American Rabbis urging the founding of a "Reform Church of American Israelites" to consist of "100 percent Americans." In a 1921 address to the Union of American Hebrew Congregations, of which he was a vice president and for over 40 years member of the executive board, he called for a Sunday Sabbath and argued that the terms "Jew and Judaism" were a "reservoir from which is fed the perennial spring of hatred, malice, and contempt." Likewise he urged that foreign terms such as "temple" and "synagogue" strengthened the accusation that the Jews were a "foreign and indigestible element." From 1906 to 1921 Bernheim was treasurer of the American Jewish Committee. He wrote two autobiographical works, *Bernheim Family* (1910) and *Closing Chapters of a Busy Life* (1929). He also wrote *History of the Settlement of the Jews in Paducah and the Lower Ohio Valley* (1912).

[Sefton D. Temkin]

BERNHEIM, LOUIS (1861–1931), Belgian army officer. Born in Saint-Josse-ten-Noode, Bernheim was commissioned in the Grenadiers and was transferred to the general staff in 1888. Later he returned to the Grenadiers and on the outbreak of World War I commanded the 7th Infantry Regiment at Antwerp. At the battle of the Marne, Bernheim commanded a Belgian brigade in the First Division and later defended Antwerp against German attacks. He subsequently took command of the First Division. He was seriously wounded in September 1915 but was promoted to lieutenant general in the following year and in 1918 commanded three Belgian divisions in Flanders in the final advance on the German lines. Bernheim received numerous awards and honors and was given a state funeral. After his death a statue was erected in his honor in a Brussels square.

BIBLIOGRAPHY: *New York Times* (Feb. 14, 20, 21, 22, 1931).

BERNHEIMER, CARLO (1877–?), Italian scholar. Born in Leghorn, Bernheimer taught Sanskrit at the University of Bologna from 1906 to 1938, when he was dismissed under the Fascist racial laws. Bernheimer devoted himself especially to the study of Hebrew paleography, and bibliography. In his *Paleografia ebraica* (1924) he set himself the task "of illustrating… everything that concerns Hebrew manuscripts." He also published catalogs of the Hebrew and cognate manuscripts in the *talmud torah* of Leghorn (1915), in French, the Ambrosian Library of Milan (1933), and the Biblioteca Estense of Modena (1960).

[Alfredo Mordechai Rabello]

BERNHEIMER, CHARLES SELIGMAN (1868–1960), U.S. social worker. Bernheimer, who was born in Philadelphia, Pa., served with Jewish welfare and educational organizations during six decades, holding such posts as business secretary of the *Jewish Publication Society of America (1890–1906), executive director of the Hebrew Educational Society of Brooklyn (1910–19), and director of community studies for the *National Jewish Welfare Board (1921–40). He also edited the information bulletin of the Jewish Welfare Board, *The Jewish Center*, for many years. As assistant head worker of the University Settlement in New York City (1906–10), Bernheimer played a prominent role in support of the workers in the Shirtwaist Strike of 1909 that helped establish modern trade unionism in the garment trades. Bernheimer edited the pioneer study *The Russian Jew in the United States* (1905), in which he wrote the chapters on Philadelphia. He was coauthor of the book *Boys' Clubs* (1914) and contributed to many periodicals. His memoirs *Half a Century in Community Service* were published in 1948.

[Irwin Yellowitz]

BERNHEIM PETITION, petition against Nazi anti-Jewish legislation, signed by Franz Bernheim on the initiative of Emil *Margulies and submitted to the League of Nations on May 17, 1933, by representatives of the *Comité des Délégations Juives (Leo *Motzkin, Emil Margulies, and Nathan Feinberg). At the same time they presented to the League a similar petition signed by the Comité, the American Jewish Congress, and other Jewish institutions. Since there was a special procedure regarding petitions addressed by inhabitants of German Upper Silesia, Bernheim's petition alone was immediately considered by the League. When the Nazis came to power, Bernheim, a warehouse employee in Upper Silesia, was dismissed from work as a result of racial discrimination, and took up temporary residence in Prague. In his petition he complained that the anti-Jewish legislation of the Third Reich was also being applied to Upper Silesia, in violation of the German-Polish Convention of May 15, 1922 (Geneva Convention), which guaranteed all minorities in Upper Silesia equal civil and political rights. The petition requested the League to state that all the anti-Jewish measures, if and when applied in Upper Silesia, infringed upon the Geneva Convention and were therefore null and void, and that the rights of Upper Silesian Jews be reinstated and that they receive compensation for damages. Bernheim's petition was placed on the agenda of the 73rd session of the League Council on May 22, 1933. The German representative, von Keller, lodged an objection denying Bernheim's right to submit the complaint, a plea that was rejected by an ad hoc committee of jurists. Four days later von Keller declared in the name of his government that internal German legislation did not in any way affect the General Convention and that if its provisions had been violated, this could only have been due to errors and misconstructions on the part of subordinate officials. The purpose of this public apology was to prevent a general debate on the petition, but these tactics failed, and in two public sessions (May 30 and June 6) the persecution of Jews in Germany was fully discussed. Many of the speakers severely censured Germany for the treatment of its Jews and demanded that they be accorded minimum human rights. In a unanimous decision, Germany and Italy abstaining, the Council adopted a resolution noting the German government's declaration and requesting it to furnish the Council with information on further developments. On September 30, 1933, the German government submitted a letter in which it claimed to have fulfilled its obligations, and that the rights of the Jews of Upper Silesia had been restored. The main objective of the Comité des Délégations Juives in bringing the petitions before the League was to focus world attention on the anti-Jewish legislation of Nazi Germany and the persecution of its Jews, and to have it condemned. The discussions in the League Council, and especially the declaration of the German government, helped the Jews of Upper Silesia in their struggle for their rights before such local bodies as the Mixed Commission established under the Geneva Convention. Until the expiration of the Convention on July 15, 1937, the Jews of Upper Silesia continued to enjoy equality of rights, and even *sheḥitah*, forbidden in the Third Reich, was permitted them.

BIBLIOGRAPHY: G. Kaeckenbeck, *International Experiment in Upper Silesia* (1942); *Question des Juifs allemands devant la Société des Nations* (1933); G. Weissmann, in: BLBI, 61 (1963), 154–98; N. Feinberg, *Ha-Ma'arakhah ha-Yehudit neged Hitler al Bimat Ḥever ha-Le'ummim* (1957).

[Nathan Feinberg]

BERNSTEIN, ABRAHAM MOSHE (1866–1932), *ḥazzan* and composer. Born in Shatsk, in the Russian province of Minsk, Bernstein was a cantor in Bialystok and choir director for cantor Baruch Leib Rosowsky in Riga before being appointed cantor of the Taharas Kodesh synagogue in Vilna (1893–1923). A prolific composer, he set to music more than 150 Hebrew and Yiddish poems, the best known being *Zamd und Stern* and *Hemeril* ("The little hammer"). He compiled a collection of folksongs, *Muzikalisher Pinkos* (1927) and a cantorial collection, *Avodas Haborei* (3 vols. 1931). His son was the Israeli composer Aviassaf Bernstein (Barnea; 1903–1957).

BERNSTEIN, ALINE (1881–1955), U.S. stage designer. Born in New York City, Aline Bernstein worked at Neighborhood Playhouse from 1915, did settings for *The Dybbuk* and costumes for Max Reinhardt's *The Miracle*, 1924. Later she designed for the Theater Guild and Civic Repertory, and did settings in the 1930s for *Reunion in Vienna, Animal Kingdom, The Cherry Orchard, Romeo and Juliet,* and other plays. With Irene Lewisohn, she founded in 1937 the Museum of Costume Art in Rockefeller Center, which is now housed in the Metropolitan Museum of Art. She wrote her autobiography, *Actor's Daughter* (1941), and wrote and illustrated *Masterpieces of Women's Costume of the 18th and 19th Centuries* (1959).

BERNSTEIN, ARNOLD (1888–1971), German shipbuilder. Born in Breslau, Germany, Bernstein served in the German Army during World War I and was awarded the Iron Cross. After the war he began a small shipping business. His first successful venture came as a result of his construction of ships, called "floating garages," on which uncrated automobiles could be shipped without risk of damage. The process involved a substantial saving in automobile transportation, and at one time his ships carried more than half the automobiles exported from America to Europe. With the sharp decline in tourism in the difficult economic period of the early 1930s, Bernstein converted his ships into combined freight-passenger vessels and introduced one-class tourist cabins. He bought the Red Star Line with the profits from this venture. Shortly thereafter he established the Palestine Shipping Company, which included the *Tel Aviv*, the first ship fully manned by a Jewish crew. After difficult negotiations with the Nazi government and in cooperation with Zionist organizations Bernstein was able to rescue many Jewish emigrants from Germany to Ereẓ Israel on his ships beginning from 1935. During a visit to Germany in 1937 he was arrested by the Nazis on the charge that he had violated currency regulations. A prison sentence and a fine of $400,000 were imposed on him. The Holland-America Line gained control of all his ships in return for payment of the fine, except those belonging to the Palestine Shipping Company. Some months later the latter went into bankruptcy. Upon Bernstein's ransom in 1939 he moved to New York where he organized the Arnold Bernstein Shipping Company and in the 1950s, the Atlantic Banner Line. This failed because it could not meet the competition of the airlines. In 2001, his autobiography was published posthumously in German translation (*Von Breslau ueber Hamburg nach New York*).

BIBLIOGRAPHY: *Biographisches Handbuch der deutschsprachigen Emigration nach 1933*, 1 (1999), 59. **ADD. BIBLIOGRAPHY:** A. Kludas, *Geschichte der deutschen Passagierschiffahrt*, 5 (1990), 100–9.

BERNSTEIN, ARON DAVID (1812–1884), German political and scientific writer and one of the founders of the Jewish Reform community in Berlin. Born in Danzig (Gdansk), he had a thorough religious education in a yeshivah in Fordon, but no secular schooling of any kind. At the age of 20 he went to Berlin, where he taught himself the German language, and literature and science. He earned his living for some years as an antiquarian bookseller, but began publishing in German in 1834 with an annotated translation of the Song of Songs. Bernstein combined progressive thought in politics, science and religion with a nostalgic affection for Jewish ghetto life. His main interest was natural science, of which he became a successful popularizer. He promoted the Jewish Reform Movement in Berlin, proclaiming that change is the basic principle of Judaism. In addition he edited the community monthly, *Die Reform-Zeitung*. Bernstein's widely read stories, written in the German-Jewish dialect *(Judendeutsch)* – *Voegele der Maggid* and *Mendel Gibbor* (1860; reissued 1934, 1935, 1994) – were forerunners of a literary genre which sentimentalized the Jewish lower middle class in small-town ghettos. They were translated into several languages. During the Prussian liberal era, Bernstein, who wrote under the pseudonym of A. Rebenstein, was influential as a political journalist. A champion of democracy, he fought on the barricades during the Prussian revolution of 1848. In 1849, when the revolutionary tide receded, he founded the *Urwaehlerzeitung*, an organ advocating moderate political reform. This brought him into conflict with the authorities, and in about 1852 the newspaper was suppressed and he was sentenced to four months' imprisonment. As a successor to the *Urwaehlerzeitung*, Bernstein founded the influential daily, the *Berliner Volkszeitung*, where his political editorials and articles on popular science appeared for nearly 30 years. A selection of his political articles was published in 1883–84. His essays on science, *Naturwissenschaftliche Volksbuecher*, were published in 21 volumes (1855–56), and a Hebrew translation (mainly by David Frischmann) entitled *Yedi'ot ha-Teva* appeared in Warsaw from 1881 to 1891. Bernstein himself was a practical scientist and experimented widely in telegraphy and photography.

ADD. BIBLIOGRAPHY: J.H. Schoeps, *Buergerliche Aufklaerung und liberales Freiheitsdenken* (1992); R. Heuer (ed.), *Lexikon deutsch-*

juedischer Autoren 2 (1993), 289–300 (bibl.); G. von Glasenapp, *Aus der Judengasse* (1996).

[Robert Weltsch / Marcus Pyka (2nd ed.)]

BERNSTEIN, ARYEH LEIB (1708–1788), chief rabbi of Galicia, and merchant; born in Brody. While a young man he served for a brief period as rabbi of Zbarazh, subsequently returning to Brody where he entered commerce. The 1740s was a period of prosperity for Brody; the Jews there began to establish commercial links abroad. Bernstein succeeded in concentrating a large part of the trade in his hands. When in 1776 the election of a chief rabbi (*Oberlandesrabbiner*) of Galicia was about to take place, the rabbi-designate Ezekiel *Landau remained in Prague, and Bernstein was appointed. At his new place of residence in Lemberg, Bernstein took over control of the religious functionaries and the administration of taxes in the communities under his jurisdiction. His authoritarian ways and interference in the administration of the communities aroused opposition which was exacerbated by his financial dealings, which he continued while serving as chief rabbi. His opponents complained bitterly against him, and in 1785 an investigation was begun. However, through his influence, the charges were dropped and his accusers were punished. Despite this, his authority was undermined. The increasing dissatisfaction among the mass of Jews, coupled with the inclination of the authorities to abolish the centralistic chief rabbinate, led to its abrogation on Nov. 1, 1786. Bernstein, who was permitted to retain the title only, did not succeed in his intention to continue to manage religious affairs. He subsequently devoted himself mainly to commerce and left a large fortune to his heirs.

[Moshe Landau]

His father, ISSACHAR BER (d. 1764) was also a distinguished scholar, rabbi, and communal leader. Issachar Ber's first position was as a rabbi of the Kehillat Ḥayyatin ("Congregation of the Tailors") in Brody. In 1750, he was elected *rosh ha-medinah* ("head of the province") of Brody, and also was appointed "a trustee of the Council of Four Lands and *parnas* of Rydzyna Province." Despite the intense opposition of some communities, he remained a trustee until 1763.

[Itzhak Alfassi]

BIBLIOGRAPHY: N.M. Gelber, *Aus zwei Jahrunderten* (1924), 14–37; idem, in: JQR, 14 (1923/24), 303–27; S. Buber, *Anshei Shem* (1895), xixff.

BERNSTEIN, BÉLA (1868–1944), Hungarian Jewish historian. Bernstein was born in Várpalota; he graduated in 1892 from the Jewish Theological Seminary of Budapest, and received his doctorate in 1890 in Leipzig. He served as rabbi in Szombathely from 1892 to 1909 and then became rabbi in Nyiregyháza. He tried to introduce a uniform religious education in Hungary in 1901. Bernstein wrote works devoted to the history of the Jews in Hungary: *Az 1848–49-iki magyar szabadságharc és a zsidók* ("The 1848–49 Hungarian Revolution and the Jews" (1898), preface by Mór Jókai); "The History of the Jews in Vasmegye," in: *Magyar Zsidó Szemle*, vols. 30–32 (1913–15); and "*Die Anfaenge der Judengemeinde inNyiregyháza*" in *Semitic Studies in Memory of Immanuel Loew* (1947). In his last years Bernstein worked on his memoirs. He was deported to Auschwitz by the Nazis in 1944 and died there.

BIBLIOGRAPHY: *Magyar Zsidó Szemle*, 49 (1932), 235–8.

[Alexander Scheiber]

BERNSTEIN, CARL (1944–), U.S. investigative reporter. Born in Washington, D.C., Bernstein, with Bob Woodward, succeeded, with their disclosures of the Watergate scandal in the 1970s, in helping to end the presidency of Richard M. Nixon, who resigned in disgrace rather than face impeachment.

After attending the University of Maryland from 1961 to 1964, Bernstein worked as a reporter for the *Washington Star*. He joined the *Elizabeth* (N.J.) *Daily Journal* in 1965 and worked until the following year as a reporter and columnist before joining the *Washington Post*, where he worked as a reporter for ten years, ending in 1976. Bernstein was a reporter for six years before he began work on one of the most important news stories of the 20th century. He covered local county and municipal governments, and liked to write long articles about Washington's people and neighborhoods. Although he was not assigned to the story of the break-in at the Watergate complex headquarters of the Democratic National Committee on June 17, 1972, he wrote an accompanying story about the five burglary suspects to complement Woodward's coverage of the break-in. He then persuaded his editors to let him cover leads that Woodward was not following. After Bernstein traced the origin of a $25,000 payment to the burglars back to the Republican re-election committee, he and Woodward began working together. At first the relationship was testy but they agreed they had to discover more about the story, and began to cooperate. They labeled one anonymous source Deep Throat and vowed not to disclose his/her identity. As the Watergate stories began to implicate high officials in the Nixon administration, White House officials denied the stories vigorously. The pair worked on the story almost alone for a year. In March 1973, a letter from one of the burglars, James McCord, to the judge presiding over a grand jury, implicated highly placed administration officials in perjury and use of political pressure, confirming Woodward and Bernstein's reporting. The reporters wrote *All the President's Men*, recounting their exhaustive and exclusive reporting, and the account was a huge bestseller. It became a major motion picture, with Robert Redford portraying Woodward and Dustin *Hoffman playing Bernstein.

Within a week of Nixon's resignation, Woodward and Bernstein began writing *The Final Days,* a chronicle of the last 15 months of Nixon's presidency, culminating in the resignation in August 1974. The book was heavily criticized for its use of "backstairs gossip" and for alleged tastelessness. And some denied their quoted statements, although Bernstein, backing the reporting, said that some of these sources were likely to deny that they had been interviewed. Both books had major sales in the United States and abroad.

His marriage to the writer-turned-film director Nora *Ephron ended in divorce, as did his first marriage. Ephron used the marriage as the basis of her novel *Heartburn*, which became a film of the same name. Bernstein was portrayed in that movie by Jack Nicholson.

After Bernstein left the Post, he worked for the American Broadcasting Company and wrote for a number of magazines. With Marco Politi he wrote *His Holiness: John Paul II and the Hidden History of Our Time*, published in 1996.

[Stewart Kampel (2nd ed.)]

BERNSTEIN, EDUARD (1850–1932), German socialist theoretician, spokesman for the so-called revisionist group which challenged orthodox Marxist doctrines. Born in Berlin, Bernstein was the son of a Jewish engine driver. He joined the Social Democratic Party in 1872 and participated in the creation of the important Gotha program (1875). In 1878, Bernstein was forced to leave Germany after the enactment of the anti-socialist legislation. He lived first in Switzerland, where he edited the *Sozialdemokrat*, and then in London. It was while he was in London that he published his principal work *Die Voraussetzungen des Sozialismus und die Aufgaben der Sozialdemokratie* (1899; *Evolutionary Socialism*, 1909), in which he set out his nonconformist Marxist interpretation of history. Bernstein contested the view of the inevitable collapse of capitalism and urged the socialists to become a party of reform. His views were vehemently opposed as heretical by most of the party but gained numerous adherents, the so-called "revisionists." In 1901 Bernstein returned to Germany and sat in the Reichstag from 1902 to 1906 and from 1912 to 1918. In World War I his pacifist views led him to disassociate himself from the right-wing faction and join the left-wing independent socialists who opposed the war. He returned to the majority party in 1918 and sat in the Reichstag again as a Social Democrat from 1920 to 1928. Concerning Judaism, Bernstein grew up in a Reform-oriented environment; Aaron David *Bernstein was his father's brother. Thus, Eduard Bernstein was aware of Jewish traditions and ideas, but not interested in them. Nevertheless, throughout his tenure as a deputy in the Reichstag, he was an active fighter for Jewish emancipation and against antisemitism. In common with many Jewish socialists of the time, Bernstein left the Jewish community because the party disapproved of all religious affiliations. During World War I, however, he began to rethink his conception of being Jewish in the modern world. In his book *Die Aufgaben der Juden im Weltkriege* (1917) he argued that because of their dispersion and universalist ideas, the Jews should be the pioneers of an internationalism which would unite nations and prevent war. Towards the end of World War I, he got in touch with the *Po'alei Zion movement, and established close contacts with Zalman Rubashov (later *Shazar, third president of Israel). During the Weimar Republik, Bernstein became an active supporter of East European Jews. Because of their specific situation he accepted a distinct Jewish nationalism among them, while he disapproved of the same for Western and Central European Jews. Toward the end of his life, he came to support the concept of a Jewish national home in Palestine and became a leader of the "International Socialist Pro-Palestine Committee." Bernstein's writings include his autobiography *Erinnerungen eines Sozialisten* (1918; *My Years of Exile*, 1921), *Ferdinand Lassalle* (1919); *Die Deutsche Revolution* (1921), and *Sozialismus und Demokratie in der grossen Englischen Revolution* (1922; *Cromwell and Communism*, 1930).

BIBLIOGRAPHY: G. Lichtheim, *Marxism* (1961), index; P. Angel, *Eduard Bernstein et l'évolution du socialisme allemand* (1961); P. Gay, *The Dilemma of Democratic Socialism: Eduard Bernstein's Challenge to Marx* (1952); E. Silberner, in: HJ, 15 (1953), 3–48. **ADD. BIBLIOGRAPHY:** R. Heuer (ed.), *Lexikon deutsch-juedischer Autoren*, 2 (1993), 301–38, bibl.; L. Heid, in: E. Bernstein, *Texte in juedischen Angelegenheiten* (2004), 13–56.

[Robert Weltsch / Marcus Pyka (2nd ed.)]

BERNSTEIN, ELMER (1922–2004), U.S. composer. A prolific composer known primarily for his work in film and television, Bernstein was born in New York City. His musical compositions appeared in more than 200 films and television shows, receiving 14 Academy Award nominations, including an Academy Award in 1967 for *Thoroughly Modern Millie*, as well as an Emmy Award and several Golden Globe and Tony Awards. During the McCarthy era, Bernstein's alleged leftist sympathies led to a spot on Hollywood's "gray list," a designation that kept him from working on major studio projects during the 1950s but did not result in a full ban from participating in the film industry. Despite being relegated to low-budget films during this period, Bernstein's career is distinguished for both his endurance as well as his versatility. His compositions have appeared in films of virtually every genre, from the epic *Ten Commandments* (1956) to popular comedies like *Animal House* (1978) and *Ghostbusters* (1984), dramas such as *To Kill a Mockingbird* (1962), the Western *True Grit* (1969), the action/WWII film *The Great Escape* (1963), and the musical comedy *The Blues Brothers* (1980). Among Bernstein's many other credits, his music appeared notably in *The Man with the Golden Arm* (1955), *Birdman of Alcatraz* (1962), *Hud* (1963), *The Sons of Katie Elder* (1965), *Meatballs* (1979), *Airplane!* (1980), *My Left Foot* (1989), *The Age of Innocence* (1993), and *Wild Wild West* (1999).

[Walter Driver (2nd ed.)]

BERNSTEIN, HAROLD JOSEPH (1914–1984), Canadian physical chemist. Born in Toronto, Bernstein completed his Ph.D. from the University of Toronto in 1938. A scholarship from the University of Copenhagen brought him to Denmark that year. In 1940, when Germany occupied Denmark, Bernstein was arrested and interned in Germany until 1945. He returned to Canada after the war and, in 1946, joined the National Research Council of Canada in Ottawa and established a molecular spectroscopy section, opening up the study of nuclear magnetic resonance. In 1959, together with W.G. Schneider and J.A. Pople, Bernstein coauthored *High Resolution Nuclear Magnetic Resonance Spectroscopy*, a pioneering text in the field of Raman spectroscopy. In 1973 he cofounded the *Journal of Raman Spectroscopy* and served as coeditor until 1978.

Among other honors, Bernstein was awarded a fellowship in the Royal Society of Canada in 1953 and, the next year, in the Chemical Institute of Canada. He received the Herzberg Award from the Spectroscopy Society of Canada in 1978. In 1980 the International Conference on Raman Spectroscopy established the Harold Bernstein Award in Physical Chemistry for graduate students at Ottawa's two universities.

[Ruth Rossing (2nd ed.)]

BERNSTEIN, HARRY (1909–1993), U.S. historian. Born and educated in New York City, in 1958 he became professor of history at Brooklyn College. Bernstein's historical interests covered the post-18th century in geographical areas such as Mexico, Brazil, and the Caribbean. He emphasized regional factors in historical development. This approach appears in his textbook *Modern and Contemporary Latin America* (1952). Among his other works are *Origins of Inter-American Interest, 1700–1812* (1945), a pioneer study of economic and political ties between Pennsylvania, New York, and New England and portions of the Spanish Empire in America; *Dom Pedro II* (1973); *Venezuela and Colombia* (1974); *The Brazilian Diamond in Contracts, Contraband, and Capital* (1988); and *The Lord Mayor of Lisbon* (1989).

BERNSTEIN, HENRI-LEON (1876–1953), French playwright. Bernstein was born in Paris, and during his early period (1900–1914) wrote powerful, realistic plays depicting the cruelty of modern life and society. The best known of these are *La Rafale* (1905), *Le Voleur* (1907), *Samson* (1908), *Israël* (1908), and *Le Secret* (1913). Some of his plays deal with the Jew's position in modern society. There are echoes of the *Dreyfus case in *Israël*, which deals with one of the tragic results of assimilation. The young leader of an antisemitic movement discovers that his own father is a Jew. Overwhelmed by the revelation and unable to accept his new status, the young man is eventually driven to suicide. The plays written from 1918 to 1938 place increasing emphasis on the psychological problems of their heroes. To this period belong *Judith* (1922), *Félix* (1926), *Mélo* (1929), and *Espoir* (1936). The theme of antisemitism periodically recurs, and Nazism is attacked in *Elvire* (1940). During World War II, Bernstein lived in the United States. Although he continued writing after 1945, tastes had changed, and his plays declined in popularity.

BIBLIOGRAPHY: L. Le Sidaner, *Henri Bernstein* (1931); P. Bathile, *Henri Bernstein, son oeuvre* (1931); H. Clovard, *Histoire de la littérature française du symbolisme à nos jours*, 1 (1947).

[Denise R. Goitein]

BERNSTEIN, HERMAN (1876–1935), U.S. journalist, born in Neustadt-Schirwirdt (Vladislavov), Lithuania; one of the first to expose the *Protocols of the *Elders of Zion* forgery. Bernstein went to the United States from Russia in 1893 and wrote in Yiddish and English. His first book was *With Master Minds* (1912), a collection of interviews with European personalities. In 1914 he founded the Yiddish daily *Der Tog* (*The Day*), which became a recognized organ of liberal Jewish opinion. He was its editor until 1916 and editor in chief of the *American Hebrew until 1919. During World War I, Bernstein made an on-the-spot study of Jewish conditions in Eastern Europe and stimulated the organization of relief for Jewish war victims. In 1917, when he was correspondent of the *New York Herald*, he discovered 65 telegrams which had been exchanged between the German kaiser and the czar between 1904 and 1907, and published them as *The Willy-Nicky Correspondence* (1918). In 1921 Bernstein published *The History of a Lie* (1928), a book which was among the first exposures of the notorious *Protocols of the Elders of Zion* as a forgery. He also instituted legal proceedings against Henry Ford, who had helped to circulate the *Protocols* and had allowed anti-Semitic articles based on them to appear in his weekly *The Dearborn Independent*. Bernstein's postwar interviews for the daily press were reprinted as *Celebrities of Our Times* (1925) and *The Road to Peace* (1926). He wrote a study of Herbert Hoover in 1928. Bernstein served as United States envoy to Albania from 1931 to 1933.

[Sol Liptzin]

BERNSTEIN, IGNATZ (1836–1909), Yiddish folklorist and collector of proverbs. Born in Vinnitsa (now Ukraine), Bernstein was the son of a wealthy family of sugar merchants, and as a rich industrialist in Warsaw he was able to indulge in his hobby of collecting the folklore of many cultures. He accumulated one of the world's richest libraries in this field. Bernstein published a two-volume illustrated catalog of his collection of books and manuscripts (1900, 1968^2). He traveled through Europe, North Africa, and Palestine, and for 35 years collected Yiddish proverbs current among the Jews of Russia, Poland, and Galicia. He published 2,056 Yiddish proverbs in Mordecai Spector's annual *Hoyzfraynd* ("Family Friend," 1888–89). Two decades later the number of proverbs had grown to 3,993, which he published in a magnificent volume *Yidishe Shprikhverter un Rednsartn* ("Jewish Proverbs and Sayings," 1908, 1912, 1948, 1988). In the same year he published his collection of 227 Yiddish proverbs concerned with sex under the Latin title *Erotica et Rustica* (1908, 1918^2, 1975). Bernstein helped to found, and also supported, the central Jewish library in Warsaw.

BIBLIOGRAPHY: Rejzen, Leksikon, 1 (1928), 373–5; LNYL, 1 (1956), 407–8; J. Shatzky, *Geshikhte fun Yidn in Varshe*, 3 (1953), 325–8. **ADD. BIBLIOGRAPHY:** G. Weltman and M. Zuckerman (eds.), *Yiddish Sayings Mama Never Taught You* (1975 repr. and trans. of *Erotica et Rustica).*

[Sol Liptzin and Charles Cutter / Benjamin Sadock (2nd ed.)]

BERNSTEIN, ISSACHAR BERUSH BEN ARYEH LOEB (1747–1802), German rabbi and author. Bernstein studied under his father, the son of Jacob Joshua *Falk, and Ẓevi Hirsch Levin of Berlin. In 1788 he succeeded his father as rabbi of Hanover. Legend attributes Bernstein's untimely death to his having insulted the son of Jonathan *Eybeschuetz, R. Wolf Eybeschuetz, who, as a young man, had held heretical views but had subsequently recanted. Several of Bernstein's novellae were included in his father's *Penei Aryeh* on *Bava Kamma* (printed with Jacob Joshua Falk's *Penei Yehoshu'a*; Fuerth, 1780, together with Bernstein's rejoinders to critical comments made by R. Judah Leib Friedenburg on this work). His *Hadrat Ḥakhamim*, discourses delivered on the conclusion of the study of talmudic tractates, is still in manuscript. Of his sons, the best known is SAMUEL (d. 1839) who succeeded his father-in-law, Jacob Moses b. Saul, as rabbi in Amsterdam, becoming the fifth member of the family to hold this position. Samuel wrote an approbation to the *Arẓot he-Ḥayyim* of Malbim (1836), and corresponded with Moses *Sofer on halakhic matters. Samuel's son BERUSH was a *dayyan* in Amsterdam and later rabbi in The Hague.

BIBLIOGRAPHY: A. Walden, *Shem ha-Gedolim he-Ḥadash* (1864), 116, no. 33; H. Dembitzer, *Kelilat Yofi*, 1 (1888), 115a; S. Knoebil, *Gerem ha-Ma'alot* (1921^2), 55; De Vries, in: *Ba-Mishor*, 271 (1945), 8.

[Itzhak Alfassi]

BERNSTEIN, JACOB NAPHTALI HERZ (1813–1873), Polish communal leader born in Lvov, descendant of a distinguished rabbinical family. Bernstein led the Orthodox Jews in Lvov in resisting the establishment of a *Reform temple and a secular Jewish school. He opposed the reforms introduced into the community in 1848 and its first Reform rabbi, Abraham *Kohn. However, his efforts to force Kohn to resign were unsuccessful. Kohn was later poisoned, and Bernstein, who was included among the suspects, remained in custody for a year. After his release he continued to oppose the Reform and Germanizing trends, with the backing of the Polish nobility. A street has been named after him for the services he rendered to the Lvov municipality. Bernstein was the grandfather of the Jewish scholar J.N. *Simchoni. The play *Herzele Meyukhes* by M. Richter is based on Bernstein's life.

BIBLIOGRAPHY: M. Balaban, *Dzieje Żydów w Galicyi i w Rzeczypospolitej Krakowskiej 1772–1868*, (1914); F. Friedman, *Die galizischen Juden im Kampfe um ihre Gleichberechtigung* (1929), 51, 60–63; N.M. Gelber, in: EG, 4 pt. 1 (1956), 247–64; J. Tenenbaum, *Galitsye Mayn Alte Heym* (1952), 50.

BERNSTEIN, JOSEPH (1945–), Israeli mathematician. Bernstein was born in Moscow. He received a M.Sc. in mathematics in 1968 and his Ph.D. in 1972 from the University of Moscow. He left the Soviet Union in 1981, teaching at the University of Maryland before joining Harvard University's Department of Mathematics, where he spent 10 years (1983–93). In 1993 he immigrated to Israel and joined Tel Aviv University, where he is became a professor in the School of Mathematical Sciences. Bernstein's fields of interest include algebraic geometry, representation theory, number theory, and automorphic forms. From the very beginning of his academic career in the early 1970s, his research was unique and his impact profound. First with his teachers, and later with his students and independently, Bernstein wrote on a broad spectrum of mathematical areas, including representation theory of Lie algebras and Lie groups, theory of *D*-modules, representation theory of p-adic groups, and automorphic forms, to mention only a few. The concepts incorporated in his numerous papers have become cornerstones of modern-day mathematics theory, and his classic article on the localization of *D*-modules, written jointly with A. Beilinson in 1981, remains one of the most widely cited articles in mathematics today.

Bernstein was elected to the Israel Academy of Sciences and Humanities in 2002 and to the National Academy of Sciences (U.S.) in 2004. He was awarded the Israel Prize in mathematics in 2004.

[Ruth Rossing (2nd ed.)]

BERNSTEIN, JULIUS (1839–1917), German physiologist and medical educator, who laid the foundations of neurophysiology. Bernstein, the son of Aron *Bernstein, was born in Berlin and began his research career under Du-Bois Reymond in his native city, continued his investigations into electrophysiology at Heidelberg, and was appointed professor of physiology in Halle in 1872. Through his novel application of physical instrumentation, such as differential rheotome and photography, to the study of nerve and muscle function, Bernstein developed the concept of the polarized membrane as the major focus of the excitation process. His view that the impulse is a self-propagating wave of depolarization deriving from permeability changes forms the foundation of modern neurophysiology. Though best known for his *Untersuchungen ueber den Erregungsvorgang im Nerven- und Muskelsystem* (1871), Bernstein also published books on medical education, toxicology, electrobiology, and the significance of mechanism in biology.

[George H. Fried]

BERNSTEIN, LEONARD (1918–1990), U.S. composer and conductor. Bernstein was born in Lawrence, Mass., and studied at Harvard (1935–39), the Curtis Institute (1939–41), and the Berkshire Music Center (summers of 1940 and 1941), where he took composition with Walter Piston among others, orchestration with Randall Thompson, and conducting with Fritz *Reiner and Serge *Koussevitzky. In 1943 he was appointed Artur Rodzinski's assistant at the New York Philharmonic; he attracted national attention by acquitting himself brilliantly when called upon to conduct a difficult program at short notice. In 1953 he conducted Cherubini's *Medea* at the Teatro alla Scala in Milan with Maria Callas – the first time an American conductor had appeared there. From 1958 to 1969 he was the music director and conductor of the N.Y. Philharmonic, the first American-born musician to occupy this post.

He also succeeded Igor Stravinsky as president of the English Bach Festival. In 1989, on the occasion of the fall of the Berlin Wall, he conducted Beethoven's Ninth Symphony with an orchestra drawn from German musicians from both East and West. In his latter years he had a close association with the Vienna Philharmonic Orchestra.

Bernstein was closely associated with Israel from 1947, when he conducted for the first time in the country. After the establishment of the State of Israel he was instrumental in creating the Koussevitzky music collection at the JNUL in Jerusalem. In 1967 after the Six-Day War, he conducted the Israel Philharmonic Orchestra on Mount Scopus celebrating the reunification of Jerusalem in a program including symbolic work such as Mahler's Resurrection Symphony. In 1978 the Israel Philharmonic Orchestra decided to devote its World Festival entirely to the works of Bernstein to honor the 30th anniversary of his first appearance in Israel. The Israel Philharmonic also bestowed on him the lifetime title of Laureate Conductor in 1988. Over the years he made periodic guest appearances with the Israel Philharmonic Orchestra, both in Israel and on its tours abroad.

Bernstein was an innovator in using television to educate the audience. He produced programs for adults and children where he lectured about composers (such as Beethoven and *Mahler, whom he identified as the central figure of 20th-century music) and their music in a fascinating way. His lecture series started with the *Omnibus* program in 1954, followed by the Young People's Concerts with the N.Y. Philharmonic in 1958, which extended over 14 seasons (53 concerts). These programs, which were broadcast live and for which Bernstein would often feverishly prepare his script all through the previous night with the help of family and friends, became a centerpiece of his work, part of what he described as his educational mission. He also used the programs to introduce young performers to the musical world, among them the 16-year-old Andre Watts.

Bernstein, one of the dominant musical personalities of his time, soon became a celebrity. His private life came under scrutiny and he was known for his liberal political sympathies, supporting the Black Panthers in the 1960s. As a composer-conductor, Bernstein came closer than anyone since Mahler to achieving equal eminence in both spheres. His reputation as a composer began in 1943 with the ballet *Fancy Free*. His musical language never abandoned tonality, although in his later works he used serial devices (in "The Pennycandy Store beyond the El"). Among his works are the *Jeremiah Symphony*, with a vocal solo to the Hebrew text of Lamentations (1944); *The Age of Anxiety*, after a poem by W.H. Auden, utilizing jazz rhythms; *Kaddish* (in Hebrew), oratorio for narrator, chorus, and orchestra, which he conducted for the first time in Tel Aviv in 1963; *Chichester Psalms* (also in Hebrew), for chorus and orchestra (1965); the ballet *Dybbuk* (1974); three symphonies (1942, 1949, 1963); and the music for the film *On the Waterfront* (1954). Bernstein contributed substantially to the Broadway musical stage. He had his greatest popular triumph with *West Side Story* (1957), an adaptation of the Romeo and Juliet story using youthful gang rivalry in New York City as the backdrop, which owed much of its success on both stage and screen to his dynamic music. Other shows for which he wrote the music were *On the Town* (1944), *Wonderful Town* (1953), *Candide* (1956), and *1600 Pennsylvania Avenue* (1976). His *Missa Solemnis* (1971), about the celebration of the Mass, aroused wide comment. He also published books on music, *The Joy of Music* (1959), *The Infinite Variety of Music* (1971), and *Findings / Fifty Years of Meditations on Music* (1982). Among his many honors were the Kennedy Center Honor for a lifetime of contributions to American culture, the Academy of the Arts Gold Medal for music, the Sonning Prize, the Siemens Prize, the Lifetime Achievement Grammy Award, and 11 Emmy Awards. Festivals of Bernstein's music have been produced throughout the world, such as a Bernstein Festival in 1986 produced by the London Symphony Orchestra and the Beethoven/Bernstein Festival in 1989 produced by the city of Bonn.

BIBLIOGRAPHY: D. Ewen, *Leonard Bernstein* (Eng., 1960, 1967), includes bibliography; J. Briggs, *Leonard Bernstein, the Man, his Work and his World* (1961); A.L. Holde, *Leonard Bernstein* (Ger., 1961); J. Gruen (text) and K. Heyman (phot.), *The Private World of Leonard Bernstein* (1968). **ADD. BIBLIOGRAPHY:** Grove online; MGG2; M. Cone, *Leonard Bernstein* (1970); J.W. Weber, *Leonard Bernstein* (1975), discography; J. Gottlieb, *Leonard Bernstein: a Complete Catalogue of his Works* (1978); I. Nerius, *L. Bernstein: Ausdruck eines grossen Musikers* (1978); P. Robinson, *Bernstein* (1982); P. Gradenwitz, *Leonard Bernstein* (1984; Eng. trans., 1987); J. Peyser, *Bernstein, a Biography* (1987); S. Chapin, *L. Bernstein: Notes From a Friend* (1992); M. Secrest, *L. Bernstein: A Life* (1994/95).

[Nicolas Slonimsky / Israela Stein (2nd ed.)]

BERNSTEIN, LOUIS (1927–1995), U.S. Orthodox rabbi and Zionist leader. Bernstein was born in New York City, received his B.A. from Yeshiva University in 1947, and was ordained at the Rabbi Isaac Elchanan Theological Seminary of Yeshiva University in 1950. In 1977, he earned his Ph.D. from Yeshiva University, which also awarded him an honorary D.D. degree in 1994. Bernstein began his rabbinic career at the Glenwood Jewish Center in Brooklyn (1947–50) and then served as a chaplain in the United States Army during the Korean War (1951–53). In 1953, he became rabbi of Young Israel of Windsor Park in Bayside, Queens, New York, where he was to remain until his death. Under his guidance, the congregation grew from a small *minyan* meeting in a house to the most prominent Orthodox synagogue in eastern Queens. Concurrently, he was professor of Jewish History at Yeshiva University's College of Hebraic Studies, specializing in American Jewish history. After teaching at the high school and college levels for 40 years, he was granted the title professor emeritus in 1994.

Bernstein made his mark writing with a passion that carried him to the highest levels of leadership in the world of modern Orthodox Judaism. As a graduate student, he was editor of the Yeshiva University newspaper *The Commentator*, on whose pages he exhorted the Orthodox community to support the burgeoning movement for a Jewish state. From that point on, Bernstein made it a point to be the editor of the house organ of each and every organization he was to head, including *The Rabbinical Council Record* (published by the *Rabbinical Council of America), *Jewish Horizons* (the publication of the Religious Zionists of America), and even the newsletter of the Yeshiva College Alumni Association. He reached a larger, general audience as a columnist for *The Jewish Press*, the mass-circulation Brooklyn-based weekly.

A man of action as well as words, Bernstein was an effective lobbyist for Jewish causes. In the 1960s, when Congress was debating a humane treatment of animals bill whose provisions threatened the practice of **sheḥitah* (Jewish ritual slaughter), he met personally with influential politicians and galvanized opposition that succeeded in derailing the legislation. This kind of initiative and savvy led to his election as president of the Rabbinical Council of America, the foremost association of Orthodox rabbis in the United States. While his provocative editorials in the RCA's in-house publication occasionally sparked controversy, his popularity remained so high that he was re-elected to two additional terms as president, and ultimately died in office.

Bernstein was also president of the combined rabbinic-laity organization Religious Zionists of America, the U.S. affiliate of the worldwide *Mizrachi-Hapoel Mizrachi movement. Subsequently, he moved up to the position of chairman and represented the RZA as a member of the Board of Governors of the *World Zionist Organization and of the executive of the *Jewish Agency. His diplomatic skills were sorely tested during those stormy years, when he was called on to defend the traditional ideologies of religious Zionism even as many of its followers in Israel spearheaded the ultra-nationalist settlement movement in Israel

Combining his devotion to Zionism with his dedication to the education of young people, Bernstein served as chairman of the board of the Rabbinical Council's *yeshivot* in Israel (1958–93), helping transform two small schools into burgeoning campuses. As director and spiritual leader of Camp Massad Bet in the Pocono Mountains of Pennsylvania, he promoted Zionist values and a love for modern spoken Hebrew in a unique atmosphere of tolerance embracing campers from Reform, Conservative and Orthodox backgrounds alike. During the rest of the year, back in his home community, he served as chairman of the Board of Education of Yeshiva of Central Queens, one of the largest day schools in North America.

In 1973 he received Yeshiva University's Samuel Belkin Award for Community Service Leadership. In 1993, the World Zionist Organization awarded him the Jerusalem Prize; he was one of only two recipients worldwide – and the only North American – to win the biennial prize that year. Also in 1993, he was honored by the Union of Orthodox Jewish Congregations of America with the organization's National Rabbinic Leadership Award.

A prolific writer, Bernstein wrote *Challenge and Mission: The Emergence of the English-Speaking Orthodox Rabbinate* (1982), a history of the first 25 years of the Rabbinical Council of America that also chronicles the story of the formative years of modern Orthodox Judaism in the United States.

[Bezalel Gordon (2nd ed.)]

BERNSTEIN, LUDWIG BEHR (1870–1944), U.S. social worker. Bernstein was born in Jelgava (Mitau), Latvia, and emigrated to the United States in 1892. Bernstein taught languages in the New York City public schools for several years, and in 1903 became managing director of the Hebrew Sheltering Guardian Orphan Asylum in Pleasantville, New York. His contributions to Jewish child welfare administration included the development of a cottage home plan and the organization of the Home Bureau of the Hebrew Sheltering Guardian Society – a pioneer experiment in foster home placement. In 1919–20 Bernstein served as executive director of the Bureau of Jewish Social Research, supervising studies in child welfare and delinquency in the Jewish communities of Chicago, Philadelphia, and New York. He moved to Pittsburgh in 1921 as executive director of the Federation of Jewish Philanthropies. During the 1930s Bernstein was a pioneer in the movement to establish Jewish community councils in American cities.

[Roy Lubove]

BERNSTEIN, MOSHE (1920–), Israeli painter and draughtsman. Bernstein was born in Bereza Kartuskaya, Poland. He completed his studies at the Vilna Art School in 1939 and, immigrating to Israel in 1948, he took part in the exhibition of "Immigrant Art" held in Tel Aviv that year. In his paintings and pen drawings, Bernstein displayed his deep attachment to the Jewish world and which constituted an inseparable part of his life. He expressed the emotional experiences of his childhood, depicting the *bet ha-midrash* and the Jewish street. Like Chagall, he used in his pen drawings cubist form and compositional language. However, instead of using colors, he made skillful use of black pen and created effects of light and shadow and the impression of a colorful picture which is composed of juxtaposing layers, thus producing the illusion of depth.

Since his first one-man show in Tel Aviv in 1950, Bernstein had many exhibitions and participated in various group exhibitions, such as the 1974 Cyprus exhibition with Zeev *Ben-Zvi. He won the City Medal of Tel Aviv in 1980.

BIBLIOGRAPHY: M. Tal, in: *Israel Magazine* (Oct. 1972), 62–66.

[Judith Spitzer]

BERNSTEIN, NATHAN OSIPOVITCH (1836–1891), Russian physiologist and civic leader. The grandson of Solomon Eger, chief rabbi of the Posen provinces, Bernstein moved to Odessa in 1849 with his parents. He studied medicine at the University of Moscow. From 1871 he lectured without official appointment at the New-Russian University at Odessa (1865). He wrote a textbook on physiology, and succeeded Leo Pinsker as editor of the Russian-Jewish periodical *Zion*. Bernstein was president of the Medical Society of Odessa for 14 years, and became both a city councillor and an honorary Justice of the Peace. He was a director of the Odessa Talmud Torah.

BERNSTEIN, ORI (1936–), Israeli poet. Bernstein, who was born in Tel Aviv, studied law at the Hebrew University, serving as an attorney in the army and later in the private sector. For 23 years he acted as managing director of one of Israel's largest corporations. His first poems, *Be-Oto ha-Ḥeder, be-Oto ha-Or* ("Same Room, Same Light") appeared in 1962, followed by a dozen collections of poems, three books for children, and a volume of essays on poetry entitled *Isuk bein Ḥaverim* ("Among Friends," 1998). While his early poetry is influenced by N. Alterman and N. Zach, Bernstein later developed his own, very intimate style, contemplating the dialectics of life and death, the yearning for love and friendship and, on the other hand, loneliness and bereavement. *Im Mavet* ("With Death," 1982) deals with the death of his mother, the sequel *Ẓafonah le-Tamid* (1987) with the death of his father. A selection of Bernstein's poems was published under the title *Shirim 1962–2002* (2004). Bernstein's only novel, *Safek Ḥayyim* ("A Dubious Life," 2002), is an autobiographical account in the tradition of Proust: The recollection of experiences from childhood and adolescence, hours of friendship and love, is interwoven with literary echoes. Bernstein is a professor at the Ben-Gurion University in Beersheba, where he teaches poetry and the theory of writing. He also translates English, Italian, and French poetry into Hebrew.

BIBLIOGRAPHY: Z. Luz, *Shirat Ori Bernstein* (2000); Y. Oppenheimer, in: *Haaretz* (Dec. 20, 2002); N. Calderon, in: *Maariv* (May 25, 2004); Z. Shamir, "*Siḥot im Erev*," in: *Itton* 77, 64 (1985), 13; Y. Bachur, "*Meshorer Ḥushani, Neziri u-Mufnam*," in: *Moznayim* 60:4 (1986), 55–57; Y. Mazor, "*Kifninim Mitpazrot be-Zerem Iti*," in: *Moznayim* 73:8 (1999) 17–20. **WEBSITE:** www.ithl.org.il

[Anat Feinberg (2nd ed.)]

BERNSTEIN, OSIP SAMOILOVICH (1882–1961), Russian-French chess master, born in Zhitomir. Bernstein placed second to Tchigorin in the Russian championship (Kiev, 1903) and tied with Akiva *Rubinstein for first place in a tournament at Ostend, Belgium (1907). He settled in France after 1916 and shared a first prize with Miguel *Najdorf, at Montevideo, Uruguay, when 72.

BERNSTEIN, PEREZ (**Fritz**; 1890–1971), Zionist leader, publicist, and Israel politician. Bernstein, who was born in Meiningen, Germany, studied commerce. In his youth he went to Rotterdam, Holland, where he entered business. In 1917 he joined the Dutch Zionist organization, and soon attained a prominent position. He later served as secretary of the Dutch Zionist Federation and as its president for four years. From 1930 to 1935 he was chief editor of the Dutch Zionist weekly, in which he fought for "unconditional Zionism," both in relations with non-Jews and in debate with the socialist and the religious Zionists. In his major work *Der Anti-semitismus als Gruppenerscheinung* (1926; *Jew-Hate as a Sociological Problem*, 1951) he tried to prove that antisemitism is a sociological phenomenon which cannot be eliminated by better knowledge, by persuasion, or by education. He also rejected the theory that the Jews in the Diaspora have negative traits which encourage antisemitism. Another of his books is: *Over Joodsche Problematiek* (1935). In 1936 Bernstein settled in Palestine and became editor of the General Zionist newspaper *Ha-Boker*. From 1941 he was chairman of the Union of *General Zionists which, in 1946, elected him a member of the Jewish Agency, where he was responsible for commerce and industry. Bernstein was a member of the Knesset from its inception until 1965, and minister of commerce and industry in 1948–49 and from 1952 to 1955. When the Liberal Party was established he was elected one of its two presidents. Following the party split in 1964, he became honorary president of the larger faction which retained the name of the Liberal Party. Bernstein continued his journalistic activities during his political career. He often opposed the left wing in his articles and advocated a business-oriented policy.

BIBLIOGRAPHY: Y. Nedava (ed.), *Sefer Perez Bernstein: Mivḥar Ma'amarim u-Massot* (1962); D. Lazar, *Rashim be-Yisrael*, 1 (1953), 62–66; Tidhar, 3 (1958^2), 1395.

[Jozeph Michman (Melkman)]

BERNSTEIN, PHILIP SIDNEY (1901–1985), U.S. rabbi. Bernstein was born in Rochester, N.Y., and was ordained in the first graduating class of the Jewish Institute of Religion (1926). He served as rabbi of Rochester's Congregation B'rith Kodesh for half a century. Bernstein was a committed pacifist until the German invasion of Poland, which forced him to rethink his views. During World War II he was executive director of the committee on army and navy religious activities of the Jewish Welfare Board, a position he held until 1946. He was responsible for supervising the 300 rabbis of all denominations serving in the U.S. Armed forces. His service propelled him into national Jewish life. He served as a member of the Zionist Emergency Council and helped form the American Christian Palestine Committee. In 1946 he returned to his congregation in Rochester, only to leave again when he was appointed by President Truman as Jewish adviser to U.S. Army commanders in Europe (1946–47), where he played a significant role at the time in alleviating the conditions of Holocaust survivors and making conditions in the Displaced Persons camps less deplorable. In his non-military role, he assisted in moving Jews from Russian-occupied Poland to American-occupied Germany, working directly with *Beriḥah. In 1947 he returned to Rochester once again. He was president of the Central Conference of American Rabbis (1950–52). He was chairman (1954–68), and subsequently honorary chairman, of the American Israel Public Affairs Committee, then in its formative years. He was the author of *What the Jews Believe* (1951), which grew out of a series of articles published in *Life* Magazine. He also wrote *Rabbis at War* (1971), an account of his war years and the service of his colleagues to 600,000 American Jews who served in World War II.

ADD. BIBLIOGRAPHY: Y. Bauer, *Flight and Rescue: Brichah, the Organized Escape of Jewish Survivors of Eastern Europe* (1970); T.P. Liebschutz, "Rabbi Philip S. Bernstein and the Jewish Displaced Persons," Rabbinic Thesis, HUC-JIR (1965).

[Malcolm H. Stern / Michael Berenbaum (2nd ed.)]

BERNSTEIN, SID (1918–), U.S. music promoter, agent, and manager; most famous for bringing the Beatles to the United States in 1964. Bernstein was born in New York City, the only child and adopted son of Israel and Ida Bernstein, Russian immigrants who came from Lukshivka, a village near Kiev. His parents called Bernstein by his Hebrew name, Simcha. His career already showed promise in high school, when he landed a fellow student a spot on the Major Bowes Amateur Hour, a popular radio program in the 1930s and 1940s.

After serving as a soldier in France in World War II, Bernstein's show business career started in the Catskill summers of the early 1950s, working as activities director at the Brown's Hotel. Bernstein produced musical shows in New York at the Paramount, the Palace, the Brooklyn Paramount, and the Apollo, and the comeback tour for Judy Garland, but went broke promoting the Newport Jazz Festival in 1961. Bernstein suggested to Tony Bennett that he perform at Carnegie Hall, a performance that was instrumental in boosting Bennett's singing career. In early 1963, reading about a group called the Beatles and the hysteria they were causing in England, he called their manager, Brian *Epstein, to arrange for them to perform in America, and on February 12, 1964, the esteemed Carnegie Hall hosted its first-ever rock concert. On August 15, 1965, Bernstein promoted the Beatles concert at sold-out Shea Stadium in New York, the largest crowd (55,000) for which the Beatles ever played and the first rock concert ever held in a sports stadium. It changed the face of the music business, and Bernstein himself.

Bernstein's instinctive vision was evident throughout the era of rock and roll's "British Invasion," when he brought over to the United States other English bands like the Rolling Stones, Dave Clark Five, the Kinks, the Animals, Manfred Mann, Herman's Hermits, and the Moody Blues. Bernstein also helped promote the careers of James Brown, Ray Charles, John Denver, Joan Baez, Miles Davis, Tito Puente, Muddy Waters, Ella Fitzgerald, Frankie Valli, and Frank Sinatra, and was the personal manager of the Rock Hall of Fame group The Young Rascals. But it was for his promotional work with the Beatles that Bernstein will always be remembered. "You know, Sid, at Shea Stadium I saw the top of the mountain," John Lennon once told him. "You know John, so did I," answered Bernstein.

[Elli Wohlgelernter (2nd ed.)]

BERNSTEIN, SIDNEY LEWIS, BARON (1899–1993), British television pioneer and publisher. Born in Ilford, Essex, Bernstein inherited his interest in show business from his father, Alexander Bernstein (d. 1921), who owned a group of cinemas. Sidney Bernstein was a founder of the Film Society in 1924, and started his Granada chain of cinemas at Dover in 1930. During World War II he was film adviser to the British Ministry of Information (1940–45) and chief of the film section, SHAEF (Supreme Headquarters, Allied Expeditionary Force; 1943–45). Bernstein introduced additional entertainments into his cinemas, including art exhibitions, and established links with Hollywood. However, his most important interest eventually became the Granada group of television companies operating mainly from Manchester. Bernstein had seen the possibilities of television in 1948 but could not obtain a license until the British Television Act of 1954. The Granada companies made many endowments to universities. He and his brother, Cecil Bernstein (a fellow director), gave £300,000 in 1965 for the establishment of a Northern Arts and Sciences Foundation. After 1961 he acquired a substantial interest in the publishing companies of Rupert Hart-Davis, McGibbon and Kee, and several others. A Labour supporter, he was awarded a life peerage in 1969.

ADD. BIBLIOGRAPHY: C. Moorehead, *Sidney Bernstein: A Biography* (1984); J. Tinker, *Television Barons* (1980); ODNB online.

[John M. Shaftesley]

BERNSTEIN, SIMON (1884–1962), journalist and Hebrew scholar. Bernstein was born in Latvia. From 1908 to 1911 he was Hebrew secretary of the Society for Spreading Enlightenment Among the Jews of Russia. In 1912 he joined the staff of the World Zionist Organization, being attached to the head office in Berlin until 1915, to the Copenhagen Bureau 1915–20, and to the London office 1921–22. In 1922 he settled in the United States, becoming editor of *Dos Yiddishe Folk*, organ of the Zionist Organization of America. He held this post until 1953. Bernstein was a prolific writer. Apart from his newspaper articles and Zionist pamphlets, he devoted himself to scholarly research, especially in the field of Hebrew poetry. He brought to light unpublished *piyyutim* of Spanish, Italian, and Byzantine poets; altogether he published over 3,000 such poems. Bernstein's major books are *Be-Ḥazon ha-Dorot* (1928), a volume of Hebrew essays; editions of *Divan Rav Immanuel ben David Frances* (1932); *Divan Yehudah Aryeh mi-Modena* (1932); *Shirei Yehudah ha-Levi* (1944), selected liturgical and secular poems; *Divan Shelomo Da Piera* (1942); *Al Naharot Sefarad* (1956), lamentations in the Sephardi rite on the destruction of Jerusalem and other calamities; and *Shirei ha-Kodesh* (1957), the collected liturgical poetry of Moses ibn Ezra.

BIBLIOGRAPHY: J. Modlinger, *Simon Bernstein* (1949); M. Glenn, in: *Or ha-Mizraḥ*, 11 (April 1963), 40–42; A. Ben Ezra, *ibid.*, 43–44; M. Schmelzer, in: *Hadoar*, 42 (1963), 195.

BERNSTEIN, THEODORE M. (1904–1979), U.S. editor and author. Born in New York, Bernstein joined the *New York Times* in 1925, became foreign-news editor, and in 1952 assistant managing editor. He was a founding editor of the newspaper's international edition in Paris. He taught at the Columbia School of Journalism, and wrote on English usage in such books as *Watch Your Language* (1958), *Headlines and*

Deadlines (1961), *Watch That Word* (1962), *More Language That Needs Watching* (1962), *The Careful Writer: A Modern Guide to English Usage* (1965), *Bernstein's Reverse Dictionary* (1975), and *Dos, Don'ts & Maybes of English Usage* (1977).

BERNSTEIN, THERESA (1890–2002), U.S. artist. Born in Philadelphia to cultured immigrant parents, Bernstein showed an interest in art as a child. She took some classes at the Pennsylvania Academy of Fine Arts and earned a degree at the Philadelphia School of Design for Women. By 1912 she was living in New York City, where she briefly studied at the Art Students League with William Merritt Chase. In these early years she painted in an Ashcan style, influenced by John Sloan and other artists of the period who depicted the everyday life of the city in dark tones. *New York Street* (1912) and *Waiting Room: Employment Office* (1917) exemplify Bernstein's realist tendency of this period. She had her first solo exhibition at the Milch Gallery in New York City in 1919, the same year that she married the artist William Meyerowitz.

An expressionist technique pervades Bernstein's work in the 1920s and 1930s, during which time she added jazz musicians to her large repertoire, a subject naturally in accord with her new style and her lifelong love of music. Beginning in the 1920s, she spent summers in Gloucester with her husband. These vacations produced paintings of beaches, harbors, and fish. In the 1930s she continued painting a wide range of subjects, including portraits, still lifes, and beach scenes. Under the auspices of the Works Progress Administration's Federal Art Project, Bernstein created a mural, *The First Orchestra in Americas* (1938), for the Manheim, Pennsylvania Treasury Department. While many artists in the 1930s joined the Communist Party, Bernstein's political consciousness centered around Zionism. Although *Zionist Meeting, New York* (1923) comes from an earlier period, the subject matter indicates her political sympathies.

Bernstein's Jewish identity was reinforced by her husband, the son of a cantor. *Prayer* (1938), Bernstein's most obviously religious canvas, shows the energy of the worshippers through a gestural brushstroke. After the establishment of the State of Israel, Bernstein and Meyerowitz visited there 13 times during a 30-year period. In her 1991 autobiography Bernstein devotes a full chapter to her experiences in Israel and her attraction to the land, of which she painted several canvases. She also published a journal dedicated to her Israeli trips in 1994.

BIBLIOGRAPHY: T. Bernstein, *Theresa Bernstein* (1985); P.M. Burnham, "Theresa Bernstein," in: *Woman's Art Journal*, 9:2 (1989), 22–27; T.B. Meyerowitz, *The Journal* (1991); T.B. Meyerowitz, *Israeli Journal* (1994).

[Samantha Baskind (2nd ed.)]

BERNSTEIN, ZALMAN CHAIM (1927–1999), U.S. businessman and philanthropist. Zalman Bernstein, or, as he was known for most of his 72 years, Sanford C. Bernstein, was born in New York City to middle class parents. He enlisted at 18 in the Navy, seeing service in World War II. After graduating from New York University where he majored in economics, he was accepted by Harvard Business School and earned his M.B.A. He then spent three years in France, working with the Marshall Plan, becoming fluent in French, and marrying the first of his three wives. Upon returning to the United States, he worked at several security firms and in 1967 launched Sanford C. Bernstein & Co. by placing full-paged advertisements in major newspapers containing a single word in bold type, "Bernstein." Investors were attracted by a reputation for integrity, reliance on careful research, prudent risk-taking and successful results. Though strongly opinionated, he tolerated and even welcomed and respected contrary views. At his death, his company was a respected name on Wall Street, managing more than $80 billion for 25,000 private and institutional clients.

The turning point in Bernstein's Jewish life came with the passing of his father in 1977. Though then scarcely able to read Hebrew, he was determined to say *kaddish*, which led him to Lincoln Square Synagogue in Manhattan and Rabbi Shlomo Riskin, who was a major influence in his Jewish development. In 1984, collaborating with two friends more knowledgeable about Jewish life, he established the Avi Chai Foundation which became the prime focus of his philanthropy. In his lifetime, he contributed hundreds of millions of dollars to the foundation as well as Jewish causes in Israel and the United States. Avi Chai's mission was predicated on the teachings of Rabbi Abraham I. Kook, which Bernstein understood superficially, yet with a sincerity that ran deep. The Kookian principles that he embraced are an encompassing attachment to the land of Israel, recognition of the Covenant between God and Abraham as an eternal legacy of the Jewish people, and a commitment to Judaism's religious heritage that includes mutual understanding and sensitivity among Jews of different religious backgrounds and commitments to observance.

Originally functioning in North America, by the early 1990s Avi Chai expanded into Israel where Bernstein in his later years became a citizen and made his home. In Israel, he developed other notable philanthropic initiatives. In North America, day school education has been the major beneficiary of Avi Chai support. Projects have included widespread innovations in Hebrew language instruction and Judaica curriculum as well as a program, unmatched in scope, to encourage new day school construction through interest-free loans. In Israel, the goal of promoting mutual understanding has been manifested by a network of programs known as Tzav Pius.

He died in 1999 and left nearly his entire substantial estate to charity. Bernstein provided instructions that he not be eulogized and that no facility or project be named in his memory. He arranged in his life, with characteristic determination, to be buried in Jerusalem on the Mount of Olives, near the grave of Rabbi Kook.

[Marvin Schick (2nd ed.)]

BERNSTEIN, ZVI HIRSCH (1846–1907), publisher, editor, and pioneer of the Yiddish and Hebrew press in the United

States. Born in Russia, he received a traditional education and contributed articles to Hebrew literary magazines. In 1870 he emigrated to the United States and founded the first Yiddish paper *Di Post*. (J.K. Buchner's *Di Yidishe Tsaytung*, although published earlier in 1870, appeared only three or four times.) In 1871 Bernstein founded the first Hebrew newspaper in the United States, *Ha-Ẓofeh ba-Areẓ ha-Ḥadashah*, which survived until 1876. Afterward he became a successful businessman and a patron of the Yiddish theater.

BIBLIOGRAPHY: B.Z. Eisenstadt, *Ḥakhmei Yisrael ba-Amerikah* (1903), 20–22; M. Davis, in: *Sefer ha-Yovel li-Khevod Alexander Marx* (1950), 115–41; Kressel, Leksikon, 1 (1965), 374.

[Eisig Silberschlag]

BERNSTEIN-COHEN, MIRIAM (1895–1991), actress and pioneer of the theater in Israel. Born in Romania, the daughter of Jacob *Bernstein-Kogan, she was educated in Russia and took a degree in medicine. Turning to the stage she worked for a time in the Russian theater. In 1921 she went to Palestine and joined David Davidow's (d. 1976) company known as the "Hebrew Theater." When the group dissolved in 1923, she and other members went to Germany to study stage work. In Berlin she met Menahem *Gnessin and helped him to organize the Teatron Ereẓ Israeli. She returned with the company to Palestine in 1924 and worked with it until its merger with the *Habimah Theater a few years later. Subsequently she appeared with various companies, gave solo performances in Palestine and abroad, and eventually joined the Cameri Theater in Tel Aviv. She translated plays and stories by de Maupassant, Tolstoy, Henri Barbusse, and Pearl Buck. In 1975 she was awarded the Israel Prize for the arts.

[Mendel Kohansky]

BERNSTEIN-KOGAN (Cohen), JACOB (1859–1929), Russian Zionist leader. Bernstein-Kogan, who was born in Kishinev, studied medicine in St. Petersburg and Dorpat. After the wave of pogroms in southern Russia in 1881, he devoted himself to Ḥibbat Zion and Zionism. As a delegate to the First Zionist Congress, he was elected to the Zionist Actions Committee. He administered an information center called the Zionist "post office," which informed Zionist branches in Russia, numbering about one thousand, of developments in the movement. He was a leading member and ideologist of the *Democratic Fraction (1901) and was one of the leaders of the Russian Zionist opposition to the *Uganda Scheme. Settling in Ereẓ Israel in 1907, he worked as a doctor in Lower Galilee and in Petaḥ Tikvah. He was a founder of the Medical Association of Ereẓ Israel (1908). Conflicts with the conservative settlers of Petaḥ Tikvah induced him to return to Kishinev in 1910. He moved to Ereẓ Israel again in 1925, but accepted a proposal of the *American Jewish Joint Distribution Committee to serve as a physician in the Jewish agricultural settlements in the Ukraine.

BIBLIOGRAPHY: M. Bernstein-Cohen (ed.), *Sefer Bernstein-Cohen* (1946); I. Klausner, *Oppoziẓyah le-Herzl* (1960), index; D. Smilansky, *Im Benei Dori* (1942), 51–59; Tidhar, 1 (1947), 192–3; A.L. Jaffe (ed.), *Sefer ha-Kongress* (1950^2), 307–10; J. Yaari-Poleskin, *Ḥolemim ve-Loḥamim* (1964^3), 89–92.

[Yehdua Slutsky]

BERNSTEIN-SINAIEFF, LEOPOLD (1867–1944), French sculptor. He was born in Vilna to an Orthodox family. He began to study drawing before moving to Paris at the age of fourteen. In Paris he studied under Rodin and Dalou and first exhibited at the Salon des Champs Elysées in 1890. He executed statues, portraits, groups of figures, and funerary monuments, and made busts in bronze and marble of important figures such as Pope Leo XIII. He received the Order of the Legion of Honor and his sculpture *Ezra Mourning* was acquired by the French nation. When the Germans occupied France they destroyed the sculpture *Youth and Age* to which Bernstein-Sinaieff had devoted over ten years. The Nazis arrested him and sent him to the prison camp at Drancy. Two weeks later he was released, only to be reinterned and sent to an extermination camp where he was killed.

BEROR ḤAYIL (Heb. בְּרוֹר חַיִל), place in southern Israel, 8½ mi. (14 km.) S.E. of Ashkelon. In Byzantine times the town was called Bouriron (Vita Sabeae, 10). It was the place where R. *Johanan b. Zakkai moved and taught after his stay in Yavneh. When the performance of Jewish marriages was prohibited under Emperor Hadrian, in the second century C.E., the inhabitants of Beror Ḥayil announced a clandestine marriage ceremony by putting a candle on the window sill (Sanh. 32b). Beror Ḥayil is now a kibbutz affiliated with Iḥud ha-Kibbutzim. It was founded on May 4, 1948, during the War of Independence, with the aim of reestablishing contact with the Jewish settlements spread over the northern Negev at a point where the Arabs had repeatedly cut off Jewish traffic to and from the south. The kibbutz was set up overnight. The initial settling group, pioneers from Egypt, was later joined by immigrants from Brazil, Uruguay, and other countries. In 1968 the kibbutz had a population of 520, dropping to 462 in 2002. Its economy was based on intensive farming (field crops, greenhouses, dairy cattle, orchards) and various small enterprises (software, a frozen pastry plant, and an educational tourist center). In the early 1960s, the *Ḥeleẓ oilfield expanded southward when reserves were discovered at Beror Ḥayil (their exploitation was in no way connected, however, with the economy of the kibbutz).

[Efraim Orni]

BEROSUS (**Berossus** = Bel-Usur?; c. 330–250 B.C.E.), priest of Bel (Marduk) at Babylon, author of a history in Greek of Babylon (*Chaldaika* or *Babyloniaka*) in three books. This work, dedicated to Antiochus I, is extant only in fragments, particularly in *Alexander Polyhistor, *Josephus, the Church Father *Eusebius, and the Byzantine compiler George Syncellus. The first book described Babylonia and the creation and explained Chaldean astrology, the second covered the kings before the

Flood, the Flood itself, and the dynasties down to Nabonassar (747 B.C.E.), and the third brought the account down to Alexander. Recent discoveries of cuneiform texts on the Flood show that Berosus was faithful to his sources, and that in fact his account is in large part taken from the Gilgamesh epic.

Berosus was particularly important to Samaritan, Jewish, and Christian writers for apologetic purposes, since his chronology contradicted that of the Greek historians and since he appeared to confirm the antiquity of, and thus lent credibility to, certain portions of the Bible. But inasmuch as Berosus, under the influence of astrological theory, spoke of 600 periods of 3,600 years each, whereas the Bible mentions a much shorter period since creation, writers such as the Samaritan Eupolemus tried to reconcile these discrepant chronologies. Unfortunately, however, only part of Berosus' chronology has been transmitted, and his lists of dynasties have often been mutilated by those who cite him or by later copyists of the manuscripts.

Berosus was similarly found useful in confirming the biblical narrative of the Tower of Babel, since he too mentions a tower near Babylon built by men who gloried in their own strength and size and despised the gods, whereupon, as in the Bible, the gods brought about a confusion of their languages, though they had hitherto all spoken one tongue. Alexander Polyhistor later apparently attempted to synchronize this account with those of the Bible and the Greek poet Hesiod's story of Prometheus. Berosus is of great importance as a source for Josephus, although questions are still raised as to whether he used him directly or through some compilation such as that of Alexander Polyhistor or perhaps that of King Juba of Mauretania. Josephus cited Berosus in support of his statements that a portion of the ark of Noah (*Xisouthros* in Berosus) still survives in Armenia (Ant. 1:93; cf. Apion 1:130), that the patriarchs lived unusually long lives (Ant. 1:107), and that Abraham lived ten generations after the Flood and was well versed in astronomy (Ant. 1:158). In his polemic against Greek historians he cites with approval (Apion 1:142) Berosus' criticism of their reports of Semiramis' achievements. The fact that on two occasions (Ant. 10:219–28; Apion 1:134–44) he cites the same passage on Nebuchadnezzar from Berosus, together with precisely the same confirmatory references from *Philostratus and *Megasthenes, would indicate that at least here he was using a handbook. The accuracy of this passage from Berosus, particularly the description of the battle of Carchemish, has now been confirmed by Wiseman's publication of a chronicle of Chaldean kings on cuneiform tablets; but it must be noted that Josephus' account (Ant. 10:96–102) of the events leading to the fall of Jerusalem and the capture of Jehoiachin differs in several details from the Chronicle.

The attribution (Suidas, 10th century) of the Babylonian (or Egyptian) Sibylline books to him has been disputed. The founder of the astrological school on the Greek island of Cos to whom the Athenians erected a statue (Pliny, *Natural History*, 7:123) is pseudo-Berosus.

BIBLIOGRAPHY: F. Jacoby, *Die Fragmente der griechischen Historiker*, 3C (1958), no. 680, 364–95 [fragments in Greek]; I.P. Cory, *The Ancient Fragments ... of ... Berossus ...* (1828), 19–38 [English translation of some important fragments]; E. Schwartz, in: Pauly-Wissowa, 3.1 (1897), 309–16; P. Schnabel, *Berossos und die Babylonisch-hellenistische Literatur* (1923), esp. 67–93 [on Berosus and Hellenistic-Jewish literature]; D.J. Wiseman, *Chronicles of Chaldean Kings (626–556 B.C.) in the British Museum* (1956), 24ff.; W. Spoerri, in: *Der Kleine Pauly*, 1 (1964),

[Louis Harry Feldman]

BERR, JACOB (c. 1760–1855), French physician and publicist, nephew of *Berr Isaac Berr de Turique. Besides gaining a reputation as a surgeon, Berr was a fervent advocate of equal rights for French Jews. In 1789 he published a refutation of an anonymous pamphlet which contested the right of Alsatian Jews to enlist in the National Guard. Later, in a letter addressed to the bishop of Nancy (1790), he criticized his uncle's project to preserve a special status for French Jews. According to E. Carmoly, *Historie des médecins juifs* (1844), Berr was the first French Jew to marry a Christian without forsaking Judaism.

BERR (de Turique), MICHEL (1781–1843), French lawyer. Born in Nancy, he was the son of *Berr Isaac Berr and became the son-in-law of Isaiah *Beer-Bing. Like his father, Berr was an advocate of Mendelssohnian Enlightenment. He sided with its radical exponents, however, and tended to disregard the national and religious aspects of Judaism while concentrating on the struggle for civic equality for the Jews in their different countries. In this spirit he defended persecuted Jews in a pamphlet entitled *Appel à la justice des nations et des rois* (1801). Berr was the first Jewish lawyer to practice in France. In 1806 he and his father were deputies at the *Assembly of Jewish Notables, and in 1807 Berr was appointed secretary of the Napoleonic *Sanhedrin. He then held an official appointment in the Kingdom of Westphalia and subsequently in the Préfecture of La Meurthe, but his later career was disappointing and he dissipated his talents.

Many important non-Jewish personalities regarded Berr as the ideal type of modern Jew. Berr translated a number of works from Hebrew including panegyrics to Napoleon. His most voluminous work was *Abrégé de la Bible et choix de morceaux de piété et de morale à l'usage des Israélites de France* (1819). At first Berr's attitude toward Judaism tended to be radical and rationalist. He held that once Judaism had detached itself from "talmudic quibbling" it would appear as the universal truth, while Christianity, also freed from its superstitions, would simply merge with Judaism. Later Berr insisted on the retention of what, in his opinion, were essential Jewish practices, which he explained in his *Nouveau précis élémentaire d'instruction réligieuse et morale à l'usage de la jeunesse française israélite* (1839), thus adhering in his eclectic way to Jewish religious reform.

BIBLIOGRAPHY: Terquem (Tsarphaty), in: AI, 4 (1843), 721–7; AI, 5 (1844), 109–16, 168–80; Barcinski, in: *Euphorion*, 15 (1908); *Dic-*

tionnaire de biographie française, 6 (1954), 141; Szajowski, in: JJS, 14 (1963), 53–66.

[Moshe Catane]

BERR ISAAC BERR DE TURIQUE (1744–1828), leader in the struggle for Jewish *emancipation in France, born in Nancy. His father Isaac Berr had been appointed Jewish "syndic" by King Stanislaus of Poland, duke of Lorraine. Berr himself, a naturalized French citizen, was a tobacco manufacturer and banker. In August 1789 he was chosen as one of six members of a Jewish delegation sent to Paris from Alsace and Lorraine to put the case for granting Jewish civic equality, acting as their spokesman at the bar of the National Assembly. He was a member of the Nancy municipal council from 1792, and in 1806 was a leading delegate in the *Assembly of Jewish Notables, sitting on its "Committee of Twelve." He later became a member of the Napoleonic *Sanhedrin. In 1816 he purchased an estate in Turique, adding "de Turique" to his name by royal permission. Berr translated N.H. *Wessely's proposals for Jewish educational reform into French under the title *Instructions Salutaires Adressées aux Communautés Juives de l'Empire de Joseph II* (Paris, 1790). He also published letters in defense of Jewish rights, demonstrating the moral value of the Talmud. While supporting certain reforms in Jewish life and customs, including the abolition of Jewish communal and judicial autonomy, Berr did not advocate religious Reform (*Réflexions sur la Régénération Complète des Juifs en France*, 1806).

BIBLIOGRAPHY: E. Carmoly, in: *Revue Orientale*, 3 (1843/44), 62–63; L. Kahn, *Les Juifs de Paris pendant la révolution* (1898), 27; Graetz, Hist, 6 (1949), index.

[Moshe Catane]

BERSHAD, small town in *Vinnitsa district, Ukraine. Jews started to settle there at the end of the 16th century. They were butchered by one of the Cossack bands during the *Chmielnicki massacres, and in the 18th century by the *Haidamak gangs. The community numbered 438 in 1765; 650 in 1787; 3,370 in 1847; 6,600 (out of a total of 8,885) according to the 1897 census; and 7,400 (61%) in 1910. At the beginning of the 19th century, when the *ẓaddik* *Raphael of Bershad lived there, Bershad became a center of Ḥasidism. It became celebrated for its *tallit* weaving industry which came to an end after many of the weavers immigrated to the United States. Most of the plants for sugar refining and distilling, flour mills, and tanneries established in Bershad toward the end of the century were owned by Jews. Of the town's 175 artisans, 163 were Jewish. During the civil war of 1919–20, 150 Jews in Bershad were massacred by Ukrainian gangs and soldiers of *Denikin's army. In 1926 they numbered 7,016 (total population 11,847), dropping to 4,271 in 1939. During this period, under the Soviets, many Jews worked in artisan cooperatives, some of which later developed into factories; about 20% of the Jews were blue-collar workers and clerks, and 20% were unemployed. A Yiddish high school had 621 students. Bershad was occupied by the Germans and Romanians on July 29, 1941, and included in Transnistria on September 1. A ghetto was established in the town and 25,000 Jews deported from Bessarabia and Bukovina were sent there. Many died of hunger and disease as up to 25 people were packed into a room. By August 1942, 10,000 Jews remained. The situation improved after financial aid arrived from Jewish organizations in Bucharest. A hospital, pharmacy, soup kitchen, and orphanage were opened. Local Jews organized an armed underground and later took to the forest and joined Soviet partisan units. The Jews numbered 2,200 in 1959 and 553 in 1993. There was a synagogue, and both a rabbi and kosher poultry were available.

BIBLIOGRAPHY: A.D. Rozenthal, *Megillat ha-Tevaḥ*, 1 (1927), 100–2, 110; Y. Midrashi, *Bershad ve-ha-Haganah Shellah* (1935); N. Huberman, *Bershad* (Heb., 1956). **ADD. BIBLIOGRAPHY:** PK Romanyah, PK Ukrainah, s.v.

[Shmuel Ettinger / Shmuel Spector (2nd ed.)]

°BERSHADSKI, SERGEY ALEXANDROVICH (1850–1896), historian of Lithuanian Jewry. He became interested in the history of the Jews in Lithuania through his teacher, F. Leontovich. Bershadski, who for many years worked in official archives, in particular those of the archduke of Lithuania, also lectured in law at the University of St. Petersburg. His first historical study of Lithuanian Jewry was published in the series *Yevreyskaya Biblioteka*, where he also published a collection of sources relating to Jewish history in southwest Russia and Lithuania. In 1882 he published two volumes of documents relating to Jewish history in Lithuania from 1388 to 1569, and in 1883 his book *Litovskiye Yevrei* ("The Lithuanian Jews"), a history covering the same period. His other works on this subject include a Russian history of the Jewish community in Vilna from 1593 to 1649 (*Voskhod*, nos. 10, 11, 1886, and nos. 3–8, 1887), and studies on Abraham Jesofovich, the Lithuanian treasurer (1888), and on Saul Wahl (*ibid.*, nos. 1–5, 1889).

In the 1890s Bershadski began to interest himself in the history of the Jews in Poland, for which he collected material from the central archives in Warsaw. He published several articles on the subject, the documents upon which he drew being published posthumously in *Russko-Yevreyskiy Arkhiv* (vol. 3, 1903). In response to the growing antisemitism of the time, Bershadski also undertook a study of the blood libel in Poland and Lithuania in the 16th to 18th centuries, published in *Voskhod* (nos. 1, 9, 11, 12, 1894). Before his death he began publication of a work on the "Jewish Statute" of 1804, but did not complete it.

After he began his researches, Bershadski, who had been formerly radically anti-Jewish, developed an appreciation of the Jewish people and became their warm supporter. In his wish to promote their integration into the Russian state and culture, he attempted to show the antiquity of the Jewish settlement there and that the Jews had made a positive contribution to Russian life and the Russian language. He attributed the isolation of the Jews by the rulers of Poland to the annexation of Lithuania in 1569. Bershadski considered that the union had brought Lithuania "the Talmud, Jewish autonomy, and *Kahal* solidarity." He was, however, not an expert in the internal developments in Jewish history.

BIBLIOGRAPHY: M. Vinaver, in: *Voskhod*, 17 no. 5 (1897), 49–54 (second pagin.); Vengerov, in: *Kritiko-Biograficheskiy slovar'*, 3 (1892), s.v.

[Shmuel Ettinger]

BERSHADSKY (Domashevitzky), ISAIAH (1871–1908), Hebrew novelist. Bershadsky, who was born in Zimoshti, Belorussia, received the traditional Jewish education of the period, and also acquired a knowledge of Russian. His novel *Be-Ein Mattarah* ("To No Purpose") appeared in 1899 (under the pseudonym Bershadsky, an abbreviation of the Hebrew for Ben Reb Shimon Domashevitzky) in the *Biblioteka Ivrit* series founded by Ben Avigdor. It proved a landmark in Hebrew literature. For the first time in the 20 years since the foundation of the Ḥibbat Zion movement a novel was published in Hebrew giving a comprehensive view of contemporary society. *Be-Ein Mattarah* is a psychological realistic novel of the type prevalent in the European literature of the period. The background is the Jewish middle class in a town in the Pale of Settlement, and the main characters are the Hebrew teachers. The plot deals with their social and ideological problems arising from the question of a Jewish national rebirth. The hero, Admovitz, in common with Bazarov, Turgenev's nihilist archetype of Russian literature, rejects idealism and favors theorizing and philosophizing. He thus reacts negatively to Zionism and to the concept of a resurrection of the Hebrew language, both of which threw the Pale of Settlement into a ferment in the 1890s. However, his rejection does not lead to any constructive alternative. His attempts to immerse himself in materialistic pleasures are accompanied by agonies of conscience, a result of his religious education. These he tries to hide beneath a mask of cynicism and mockery. His life is joyless and purposeless. In the character of Admovitz, who shares many personality traits with his author, Bershadsky created the prototype of the Jewish social misfit, who became the anti-hero of Hebrew fiction in the first quarter of the 20th century. A two-volume anthology of Bershadsky's stories and sketches was published during 1899 and 1902 under the title *Tippusim u-Ẓelalim* ("Types and Shadows"). His second novel, *Neged ha-Zerem* ("Against the Stream") appeared in 1901 in four parts. Written before *Be-Ein Mattarah*, it depicts the collapse of traditional Jewish life. The hero, Israelson, the representative of Zionist orthodoxy, discovers that the bourgeois youth has surrendered to anarchy, cynicism, and hedonism. He eventually reached the conclusion that no Diaspora-based system of education can contain assimilation. Bershadsky is one of the first modern Hebrew authors to describe the relationship between the sexes realistically. In general, his works mark the entry of realism into Hebrew fiction, ending its tradition of over-moralizing. There are, however, defects in his writing. These include weakly traced plots, an excess of propaganda, usually put into the mouths of the heroes during their numerous arguments, and a dry, unimaginative style, lacking lyrical finesse.

Bershadsky was a member of the editorial board of the periodical *Ha-Zeman* in 1904–05 in St. Petersburg and later in Vilna. He died in Warsaw. His later stories and sketches and his early and unpublished writings were collected and published posthumously in two volumes under the title *Ketavim Aḥaronim* ("Last Writings," 1910).

BIBLIOGRAPHY: I. Bershadsky, *Be-Ein Mattarah* (1967), introduction (contains a selected bibliography); I. Bershadsky, *Ketavim Aḥaronim*, 1 (1910), 7–22 (biography by P. Kaplan); A. Sha'anan, *Ha-Sifrut ha-Ivrit ha-Ḥadashah li-Zerameha*, 3 (1964), 322–6; Waxman, Literature, 4 (1960), 85–92.

[Gedalyah Elkoshi]

BERSOHN, MATTHIAS (1823–1908), Polish art collector and historian. Bersohn was active in the Warsaw Jewish community. He assembled an important collection of Jewish and Polish art in his own home and made generous presents to Polish museums. Since all his children converted to Christianity, he presented his collection and library to the Warsaw Jewish community, which established the "Bersohn Museum for Jewish Antiquities" to house it, at the time the only institution of its kind in Poland. In March 1940 the Germans broke into the museum and robbed it of its treasures. Bersohn's general collection was given to Polish museums. One of the earliest researchers of the history of art in Poland, he wrote a study on the wooden-structured synagogues in Poland (Pol., 3 vols., 1895–1903; Ger., in MGJV, 8 (1901), 159ff.). He also wrote a study of Joseph Nasi (MGWJ, 18 (1869), 422ff.) and one of Tobias Cohen and other Polish-Jewish doctors (1872). His lexicon of Jewish scholars in Poland, 16th–18th centuries (Pol., 1906), and his collection of documents on Polish Jewish history from 1388 to 1872 (1910, ed. posthumously by his son-in-law A. Kraushaar) are not too reliable.

BERSON, ARTHUR JOSEPH STANISLAV (1859–1942), Austrian meteorologist. Born in Neu-Sandec, Galicia, he worked at the Prussian Aeronautic Observatory later transferred to Lindenberg and Friedrichshafen. In 1899 he introduced new methods for the study of the air strata structure at heights of tens of miles above the earth. Berson employed kites and balloons of rubber and paper filled with hydrogen gas and attached them to thin metal threads. Berson, in balloons of his own design, rose to the upper atmosphere a number of times with instruments for the measurement of the air pressure, the air temperature, and the relative humidity. Berson also carried out his observations over Spitzbergen, the Arctic Ocean, East Africa, Brazil, the Indian Ocean, and Indonesia. From these observations of Berson, the notion of the troposphere and the stratosphere were accepted generally. In 1901 Berson and a companion reached a height of about seven miles without oxygen masks. Berson also sent up unmanned balloons to heights of 18 miles. These balloons contained recording instruments which, if the balloon exploded, would come down by means of small parachutes. He also used red balloons sent up at a fixed rate which could be tracked and thus determine the direction of the wind. During World War I this knowledge of the direction of wind at high altitudes was of great importance to the fighter planes. The observations and studies of Berson were first published in three volumes, together with those of R. Assmann, under the title *Wissenschaftliche Luftfahrten* (1899–1900).

[Dov Ashbel]

°**BERTHOLD OF FREIBURG** (13th century), Dominican preacher and theologian. In his *Summa*, completed in about 1295, the oldest known textbook of canon law in the German language, Berthold contests the validity of forced conversion to Christianity, obtained by "use of arrow or lance," or by "pushing people under the baptismal font against their will." He further prescribes that converts should be allowed to retain their property after baptism, in opposition to the fiscal policy followed by certain princes who commonly confiscated the property of the new converts to compensate for the loss of the Jewish tax.

BIBLIOGRAPHY: R. Stanka, in: *Theologische Studien der oesterreichischen Leo-Gesellschaft*, 36 (1937), 146; *Monumenta Judaica* (1963), 162, 165.

[Emmanuel Beeri]

°**BERTHOLD OF REGENSBURG (Ratisbon**; before 1210–1272), Franciscan friar, the most celebrated preacher in Germany in the Middle Ages. From 1240 Berthold traveled throughout the German-speaking countries. In 1263 he began to preach the crusade. His sermons, delivered in fields or public squares, drew huge crowds. While preaching against Christian heresies, such as those held by the Cathari and Waldenses, he included the Jews in his attacks. Berthold declared that the heretics together with their allies the Jews, were so powerful that, but for the emperor's opposition, they would have gained control over Germany. He even predicted that a time would come when Christians would have to defend themselves against them in the same way as against the "infidels" (the Muslims). Berthold strongly opposed the practice of usury by the Jews whom he also accused of proselytizing among Christians.

BIBLIOGRAPHY: DHGE, 8 (1935), s.v. *Berthold de Ratisbonne*; R. Iannucci, *Treatment of the Capital Sins and the Decalogue in the German Sermons of Berthold von Regensburg* (1942), includes bibliography.

[Bernhard Blumenkranz]

°**BERTHOLET, ALFRED** (1868–1951), Swiss Bible scholar and theologian, who taught biblical exegesis at the University of Basle.

Bertholet wrote extensively on the canonical and extracanonical books of the Bible. His works include commentaries on Leviticus (1901), Deuteronomy (1899), Ezekiel (1897), Ruth (with E.F. Kautzsch, 1923), and Ezra and Nehemiah (1902). His Appendix on the Apocrypha and Pseudepigrapha in the *Geschichte der althebraeischen Literatur* (ed., K. Budde, 1906, 1909^2) is considered one of the best in the field. In his works *Der Beitrag des Alten Testaments zur allgemeinen Religionsgeschichte* (1923) and *Das Dynamistische im Alten Testament* (1926) Bertholet maintained that the religion of ancient Israel, characterized by a strong personal conception of the Deity, was unique in a world dominated by dynamistic theories which viewed the universe as essentially constituted by natural and supernatural forces. His other works in biblical studies include: *Die Stellung der Israeliten und der Juden zu den Fremden* (1896), *Die juedische Religion von der Zeit Esras bis zum Zeitalter Christi* (1911), *Kulturgeschichte Israels* (1919), and a second commentary on the Book of Ezekiel (1936). His works in the field of comparative religion include *Buddhismus und Christentum* (1902, 1909^2), *Dynamismus und Personalismus…* (1930), *Goetterspaltung und Goettervereinigung* (1933), *Das Geschlecht der Gottheit* (1934), *Der Sinn des kultischen Opfers* (1942), *Die Macht der Schrift in Glauben und Aberglauben* (1949), and the posthumous *Grundformen der Erscheinungswelt der Gottesverehrung* (1953).

BIBLIOGRAPHY: *Festschrift A. Bertholet* (1950), 564–78, includes a complete bibliography; Baumgartner, in: *Schweizerische Theologische Umschau*, 21 (1951), 121ff.

[Zev Garber]

BERTINI, GARY (1927–2005), Russian-born Israeli conductor and composer. After training in Israel and Italy, he studied in the Paris Conservatoire and at the Sorbonne. Among his teachers were Boulanger and Messiaen. In 1954 he returned to Israel and taught conducting in Tel Aviv at the Music Teachers' College, and later at the Rubin Academy, where he was appointed professor in 1975. He played an important role in the development of Israeli music. He founded and directed many of Israel's leading musical institutions such as the Rinat Choir (1955), the Israel Chamber Orchestra (1964–75), the Musical Evenings for Contemporary Music (1962–65), the Liturgical Festival (1978), and the Israel Festival. He was musical director of the Symphony Orchestra of Jerusalem (1978–86) and artistic and musical director of the New Israel Opera in Tel Aviv (1994–97). Bertini regularly conducted the major orchestras of the world and held appointments as conductor, musical advisor, and director with leading orchestras, among them the Scottish National Orchestra (1971–78), the Detroit Symphony Orchestra (1981–83), the Cologne RSO (1983–91), the Frankfurt Opera (1987–90), and the Tokyo Metropolitan Symphony Orchestra. He was later appointed musical director of the San Carlo Theater.

Bertini is known for a wide repertory ranging from Josquin des Près to contemporary composers. He is noted for his interpretation of Mahler and French music. He has given the premieres of many works of Israeli composers (such as *Partos, *Ben Haim, *Orgad, *Avni, *Seter, and *Tal) and others. His compositions include incidental scores, works for orchestra, chamber music, songs, and choral arrangements. Bertini is the recipient of the Israel Prize (1978), the Frank Pelleg Prize (1999), and the Grand Prix of the French music critics. He also wrote an essay on Anton Webern.

BIBLIOGRAPHY: Grove online; MGG[2]; *Baker's Biographical Dictionary* (1997).

[Naama Ramot (2nd ed.)]

BERTINI, K. AHARON (1903–1995), poet and editor. Bertini, who was born in Bessarabia, began to publish poetry in 1924, and taught in Hebrew high schools in Bessarabia from 1927. He immigrated to Ereẓ Israel in 1947, where he resumed his teaching career. From 1965 he served as an editor of *Moznayim*, the literary magazine of the Hebrew Writers' Association. His volumes of poetry include *Temol Deheh* (1939), *Mi-Layil ad Boker* (1951), *Marot al ha-Efer* (1954), *Shevil Kaḥol* (1961), *Bakbuk al Penei ha-Mayim* (1969), *Maḥshakim u-Derakhim* (1974), *Me'aḥorei ha-Pargod* (1985), *Le-Orekh ha-Yamim, le-Orekh ha-Mayim* (1988) and the essays *Seder Re'iyah: Masot Sifrutiyot* (1977). With Z. Rosenthal and D. Vinitsky he edited the literary anthology *Min ha-Ẓad* (1939–40). He translated from French, Romanian, and Yiddish into Hebrew. Among the last are David *Bergelson's play *Prince Reuveni*, Moshe Altman's short story collection *Be-Omek Ha-Re'i* (1967, and H. Leivick's dramatic poem *Abelar un Heluiz*. Bertini also edited an anthology of translations from Yiddish literature for high schools (1958) and prepared an anthology of works by Romanian Jewish writers (1972). Dan Miron edited a collection in two volumes of Bertini's poems (2003) with a supplementary essay. His son Gary *Bertini is a noted composer and conductor.

BIBLIOGRAPHY: M. Avishai, *Bein Olamot* (1962), 153–6. **ADD. BIBLIOGRAPHY:** B.J. Michali, *Mishbeẓot Bikoret* (1980); Y. Peles, in: *Haaretz* (Aug. 27, 2004).

[Getzel Kressel]

BERTINORO, OBADIAH BEN ABRAHAM YARE (Di or Of; c. 1450–before 1516), Italian rabbi and Mishnah commentator. The name Yare is an acrostic of the Hebrew יְהִי רְצוּי אֶחָיו (*Yehi Reẓui Eḥav*; "Let him be the favored of his brethren"; Deut. 33:24). Little is known of his family, which derived from the town Bertinero in northern Italy. At some time he apparently lived in Città di Castello, where he was a banker. His best-known teacher was Joseph *Colon. Much more is known about Bertinoro, after he left this place, from three letters he wrote during 1488–91 in which he described his travels and his early impressions of Ereẓ Israel. (See Map: Journey from Italy to Israel). Leaving his home at the end of 1486, he went on via Rome to Naples and stayed there and at Salerno for four months, where he taught (probably Jewish matter). In 1487 he reached Palermo where he stayed three months, preaching every Sabbath. Though pressed to become rabbi, he refused, and sailed by way of Messina and Rhodes for Alexandria, where he arrived early in 1488. He describes at length the Jewish communities of these places and their customs. He proceeded to Cairo, and the *nagid* Nathan ha-Kohen *Sholal received him with great honor. Sholal asked Obadiah to remain in Cairo but he refused and continued his journey via Gaza, Hebron, and Bethlehem, reaching Jerusalem just before Passover in 1488. Jacob of Colombano, an Ashkenazi rabbi who had come to

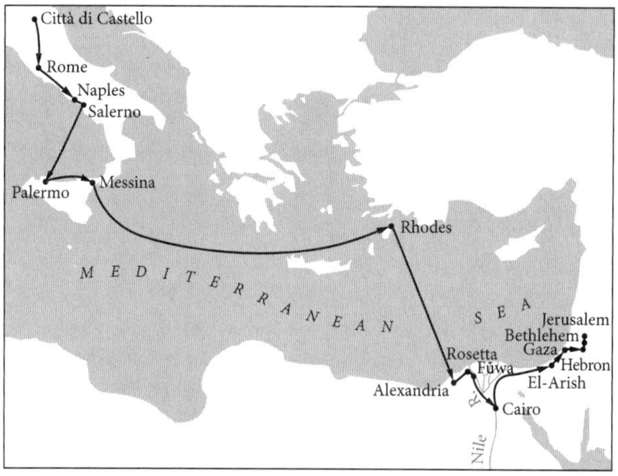

Obadiah di Bertinoro's journey from Italy to Ereẓ Israel, 1485-1488.

Jerusalem from Italy, welcomed him warmly. On his arrival Bertinoro became the spiritual leader of Jerusalem Jewry, and was embroiled with the local communal leaders, in his words – "*zekenim*" (elders). However, he was successful in uniting the oppressed and divided community. He established regular courses of study and preached twice a month in Hebrew. He even occupied himself with the burial of the dead since no one else was ready to undertake this religious duty. He enacted communal regulations and made himself responsible for the collection of funds from Italy for the support of the poor. Emanuel Ḥai Camerino of Florence, to whom Bertinoro had entrusted his property and who had promised to send 100 ducats a year, added an additional 25 ducats for charity. Bertinoro's wealthy brother also sent contributions. Nathan Sholal put his house in Jerusalem in Bertinoro's charge and authorized him to manage the communal affairs. It seems also that he officially served as a deputy **nagid* in Jerusalem. With the repeal of the communal tax and the arrival after 1492 of refugees from Spain, the community began to grow. An anonymous traveler testifies in 1495 to Bertinoro's fame in Ereẓ Israel and in the Diaspora. From his third letter in 1491 from Hebron it appears that he left Jerusalem for a while and became rabbi of Hebron. By 1495, however, he was back in Jerusalem. He was buried on the Mount of Olives.

Bertinoro's fame rests on his commentary on the Mishnah which was completed in Jerusalem and published in Venice (1548–49). It has become the standard commentary on the Mishnah as is Rashi's on the Talmud. This commentary was published with the text in almost every edition of the Mishnah. Written in an easy, lucid style, it draws largely on Rashi, often quoting him literally, and on Maimonides, whose rulings he cites. For the sections of Mishnah which have no Talmud he drew on the commentary of *Samson b. Abraham of Sens and of *Asher b. Jehiel. Falsely attributed to him is *Amar Neke* (published: Pisa, 1810), a commentary on Rashi on the Pentateuch. The three letters mentioned above were written in a flowing, limpid Hebrew to his father, his brother, and possibly his friend, Camerino. They have frequently been published under the title *Darkhei Ẓiyyon* or *Ha-Massa le-Ereẓ Yisrael* and translated into many languages, such as, German, French, English, Italian, and Spanish. Other works remain in manuscript: responsa, novellae on R. Moses of Coucy, *Sefer Mitzvot Gadol,* and Maimonides' *Mishneh Torah,* as well as an exchange of letters, poems, and prayers.

BIBLIOGRAPHY: Luncz, *Ha-Me'ammer,* 3 (1919), 93–174; Sachs, in: *Jahrbuch fuer die Geschichte der Juden und des Judenthums,* 3 (1863), 193–270; Marx, in: *Sefer ha-Shanah shel Ereẓ-Yisrael,* 2–3 (1926), 97–99; Cassuto, in: *Ha-Ẓofeh le-Ḥokhmat Yisrael,* 10 (1926), 296–302; P. Grojewski, *Rabbenu Ovadyah Yare mi-Bartenura* (1938); E.N. Adler, *Jewish Travellers* (1966²), 209–50; Artom, in: *Yavneh,* 3 (1942), 112–24; A. Yaari, *Iggerot Ereẓ Yisrael* (1943), 98–144; M.A. Shulvass, *Roma vi-Yrushalayim* (1944), 31ff.; Ch. Albeck, *Mavo la-Mishnah* (1959), 249ff. **ADD. BIBLIOGRAPHY:** Shochetman, in: *Pe'amim,* 37 (1988), 3–23; Toaff, *ibid.,* 24–30; Horowitz, *ibid.,* 31–41; G. Busi (ed.), *Ovadyah Yare da Bertinoro e la presenza ebraica in Romagna nel quattrocentro* (1987); I.D. Lerner, *Rabenu Ovadiah mi-Bartenura* (1988); Reiner, *Shalem,* 6 (1992), 23ff.; M.E. Artom and A. David, *Me-Italyah li-Yerushalayim* (1997).

[Abraham David]

BERTONOFF, DEBORAH (1915–), mimic-dancer, teacher, and researcher of dance; one of the pioneers of dance in Israel. Daughter of Yehoshua Bertonoff, a veteran of the *Habima Theater, she was still a child in Russia when she danced "*The Beggars' Dance*" in *The Dybbuk* directed by Vakhtangov. She immigrated to Israel in 1928 with Habima. In 1929 she went to Berlin and studied dance at the school of Trumpy Skoronel. Upon her return to Israel in 1932, she produced recitals concentrating on the description of individual personalities and the dramatic stories of people's lives: *Individuals at a Jewish Wedding, Two Jews Are Conversing,* and *The Maker of Magic.* In 1934, she went to study in England at the schools of Kurt Jooss and Sigurd Leeder. Bertonoff was awarded a first prize for mimic-dancing in Paris in 1936.

She opened a studio in Tel Aviv and produced *Exodus from Egypt* (1946) to the music of Yosef *Tal. This was a work of solo dances and readings whose subjects were national-biblical and which later (1957) became *Memories of a Nation.* Her first Broadway performance was in 1948. She represented Israel in the Theater of Nations in 1962. Thanks to a scholarship from UNESCO, she was able to go on research trips to Ghana in 1960 and 1965 and to India in 1966. Bertonoff left the stage in 1970 and, after a 15-year hiatus, returned to the stage in a recital that was a reconstruction of her dancing from the past. In 1991, she received the Israel Prize for dance. She wrote *Dance Towards the Earth* (1965), *Spirit Possessed* (1965), *Dance Towards the Horizons* (1968), *Dance, Drums, Drama* (1979), and *Journey to the World of Dance* (1982).

BIBLIOGRAPHY: R. Eshel, *Dancing with the Dream – The Development of Artistic Dance in Israel 1920–1964* (1991), 23–24 (Hebrew).

[Ruth Eshel (2nd ed.)]

BERUREI AVERAH/AVEROT (Heb. בְּרוּרֵי עֲבֵרָה / עֲבֵרוֹת; "the elected [to control] sin"), an institution of Catalonian origin found in the Jewish communities in Spain from the second half of the 13th century and later in the *Sephardi Diaspora in the 16th and 17th centuries. The *berurim* were the leaders of the community, some of whom were especially appointed for special tasks. The *berurei averot* were responsible for people's behavior in general. Officers so appointed mainly had the authority to deal with religious and moral transgressions. There were also similar officers (*berurei tevi'ot*) to investigate monetary suits. *Berurei averot* had the authority to impose punishments such as expulsion, excommunication, and flogging on guilty persons. The communities of Catalonia, Valencia, and Majorca had two or three such officers, while in Aragon this function was included in the duties of the *adelantados. A legend about Isaac b. Solomon *Luria in 16th-century Safed conveys the atmosphere in which this body practiced its activities: "It happened that the sages of Safed appointed ten men concerning transgressions, all of them learned and wise." One of them looked out of his window early in the morning and saw a well-dressed woman. He followed her, and seeing her enter the courtyard of a man of light morals, "immediately after the end of the morning prayers ordered the beadle to call together his fellow appointees over transgressions, and [stated that] he would testify before them concerning a transgression that he had himself seen." While they were in assembly Luria proved miraculously to the accuser that his suspicions were unfounded.

BIBLIOGRAPHY: Baer, Urkunden, 1 pt. 1 (1929), index s.v. *berurim do avero*; Baer, Spain, index; M. Benayahu (ed.), *Sefer Toledot ha-Ari* (1967), 159–60. **ADD. BIBLIOGRAPHY:** Y. Assis, *The Golden Age of Aragonese Jewry* (1997), 87, 104, 111, 315.

BERURYAH (second century), a learned woman mentioned once in the Tosefta, and identified in the aggadot of the Talmud Bavli as the daughter of R. *Hananiah b. Teradyon and wife of R. *Meir. Beruryah is the only woman mentioned by name in tannaitic sources whose view on an halakhic matter was taken into account by the scholars of her time. Tosef., Kelim, BM 1:6 reports a dispute between R. Ṭarfon and the Sages, in the context of which Beruryah expressed an opinion. The Tosefta goes on to state: "When this matter was reported to R. Judah, he said: 'Beruryah spoke well.'" Significantly, the daughter of R. Hananiah ben Teradyon is also mentioned in Tosefta *Kelim* (BK 4:17), where her halakhic opinion also is quoted with approval, and in a very similar fashion: "When this matter was reported to R. Judah ben Bava, he said: 'His daughter spoke better than his son.'" Aside from the similarity of the two cases and their proximity to each other in the Tosefta, there is no positive reason to identify these two figures. Moreover, if we assume that R. Ṭarfon was alive and active during the final years of the Second Temple (cf. Tosef. Soṭ. 7:16), it does not seem likely that a woman who was old enough to debate with Ṭarfon could have been R. Hananiah ben Teradyon's daughter, let alone R. Meir's wife. Indeed, one source mentions R. Meir's wife, but without mentioning her by name (Mid. Prov. to 31:1). It would seem, therefore, that the figure of Beruryah – talmudic scholar, daughter of R. *Hananiah b. Teradyon and wife of R. *Meir – is in fact a conflation of a number of distinct figures, mentioned either by name or without name in earlier sources. The fascinating and problematic figure of Beruryah, therefore, must be seen as a synthetic literary product of the Talmud's method of "creative historiography," as was shown by David Goodblatt in his classic study, "The Beruriah Traditions." The notion that Beruryah was largely a product of the talmudic "collective consciousness" only increases the significance of her figure for an understanding of the talmudic mind and its problematic attitude toward scholarly and assertive female figures (Tal Ilan, 3–8). We will therefore summarize the basic elements of the Bavli's Beruryah aggadot in outline:

The Talmud tells of her great knowledge (Pes. 62b). It describes her as restraining her husband Meir in a moment of moral weakness. When certain evil persons antagonized her husband and he prayed for their death, she rebuked him, interpreting Psalms 104:35 as expressive of God's desire for the destruction of sin, and not of sinners, and exhorting him to pray, rather, that they repent of their evil ways (Ber. 10a). The *aggadah* also tells of her mocking wit. Once, when R. Yose the Galilean, meeting her along the way, asked, "By which road should we travel in order to reach Lydda?" she replied: "Galilean fool! Did not the rabbis say, 'Talk not overmuch with women?' You should have asked: 'How to Lydda?'" (Er. 53b). Another instance of her sharpness is her reply to a sectarian concerning the interpretation of a verse from the Prophets (Ber. 10a). Beruryah also guided students in their study. When she found a student studying in an undertone, she rebuked him, saying: "Is it not stated (II Sam. 23:5) 'Ordered in all things, and sure'? – If the Torah be ordered in the two hundred and forty-eight organs of your body, it will be sure, and if not, it will not be sure" (Er. 53b–54a). Finally, Rashi, in explaining the obscure phrase "the story of Beruryah," mentioned in Av. Zar. 18b, quotes a legend to the effect that as a result of her exaggerated self-confidence – feeling that she was above "feminine weakness" – she ultimately was led astray, with tragic consequences. Beruryah was also the heroine of a number of belletristic works and plays in Hebrew and in other languages.

BIBLIOGRAPHY: Hyman, Toledot, 294–5; Graetz, Gesch, 4 (1908[4]), 172–3; D. Goldblatt, in: JJS, 26:1–2 (1975), 68–85; T. Ilan, in: AJS Review, 22:1 (1997), 1–17.

[Stephen G. Wald (2nd ed.)]

BESALÚ (Latin **Bisuldunum, Bisuldum**; Heb. ביואלדו, ביסאלו, בסלו), town in Catalonia, N.E. Spain. Its Jewish community was one of the oldest in Catalonia, a tombstone dating from 1090 having been found there. In 1258 James I gave permission to the Jews of Gerona and Besalú, then forming a single *collecta* ("tax administrative unit"), to appoint five representatives to act in financial and administrative matters. In 1258 the two communities together paid a tax of 15,000 sólidos. In the 13th century there were 18 Jewish families (about 130 persons) in Besalú, and in the 14th century between 38 and 49 families (170–220 Jews). The Zabara and Corvida families were among the leading members of the community of Besalú in the 13th through 15th centuries. Several of their number were baptized in 1391. Other important families were the Monells, the Payrusa, the Astrucs, the Caracausas, the Bonanasms, the Bellcaires, and the Benvenists. As in the rest of Catalonia some rich Jews were moneylenders, very often in addition to their occupations or financial enterprises. Considering the size of the community, there were many Jewish physicians in Besalú – in the 14th century there were no fewer than 15. Among the best known there were the Castlars, Abraham and David, who were father and son, Bendit Deuslogar, Belshom Maymon, Moshe Abraham de Portal, Samuel Cabrit, Salamon Caravida, and Ishaq Adret. In 1271 the Jews of Besalú were empowered by the Infante Pedro to execute legal contracts in the same way as Christians and Moors. During a heresy hunt in Besalú in 1292 the Dominicans tried to interfere in Jewish affairs, but were prevented by the king. An outbreak against the Jews at Gerona during Easter 1331 had repercussions there. During the anti-Jewish outbreaks that swept Spain in 1391 the Jews were protected by the local authorities. Thus between 1392 and 1415, a period of general decline of the Jewish population in Catalonia, 36 Jewish families, around 160 Jews, lived there. Nevertheless the number of Jews who converted to Christianity increased significantly in the 15th century. A small Jewish community continued to exist in Besalú in the 15th century, until the expulsion from Spain. It had its own synagogue, cemetery, and *mikveh*. The *mikveh* was discovered in 1964 in the old Jewish quarter.

BIBLIOGRAPHY: Baer, Studien, 42ff.; Neuman, Spain, index; Cantera, in: *Sefarad*, 9 (1949), 481–2; Millás Vallicrosa, *ibid.*, 25 (1965), 67–69; Cantera-Millás, Inscripciones, 264. **ADD. BIBLIOGRAPHY:** M. Grau Montserrat, in: *Revista de Girona* 82 (1978), 49–54; idem, in: *Anuario de Filología*, 5 (1979), 125–83; 7 (1981), 285–307; idem, in: *Annals* [*Olot*] (1978), 49–120; (1979), 91–115; (1980–1), 111–24; X. Barral I. Altet, in: M. Mentrú (ed.), *L'art juif au moyen âge* (1988), 127–28; E. Lourie, in: *Michael*, 11 (1989), 62–78.

[Haim Beinart / Yom Tov Assis (2nd ed.)]

BESANÇON, capital of the department of Doubs, eastern France; from the 13th century a free city, annexed to France in 1674. The first reference to Jews in Besançon is found in 1245. The Jewish street was in the present Rue de Richebourg, and the cemetery in front of the present Porte de Charmont. Jewish bankers of Besançon are mentioned in the chronicles of the Anglo-French war of 1296–1301. In 1321, and between 1393 and 1404, Jews expelled from *Franche-Comté and *Burgundy reached the city. The Jews left Besançon in the 15th century, and in 1465 the cemetery was sold by the municipality. Jews were denied free access to Besançon from the end of the 17th to the end of the 18th century, a few permits of temporary residence for a limited period being granted to a small number of merchants. A permit of longer duration was issued to an engraver of semiprecious stones.

After the French Revolution the community in Besançon was reestablished. It numbered 20 families in 1807, and sent a delegate to the Assembly of Jewish notables and to the Sanhedrin convened by Napoleon. The community was administered by the *Consistory of Nancy until 1858, and then later by Lyons. The present synagogue, in Moorish style, was consecrated in 1869. In 1872 an independent consistory was set up at Besançon. The community was increased by Jews who left Alsace after the Franco-Prussian war of 1870. At the beginning of the 20th century there were 170 families living in Besançon.

[Zvi Avneri]

Holocaust and Postwar Periods

The community was largely destroyed and dispersed under the German occupation during World War II. In May 1940, over one hundred Jews were deported by the Germans. After the war, the Jewish community slowly revived, and had 120 families in 1960. By 1969 their number had practically doubled, largely as a result of the influx of Jewish immigrants from North Africa. The community engaged a rabbi and cantor and maintained a number of institutions.

[Georges Levitte]

BIBLIOGRAPHY: J. Morey, in: REJ, 7 (1883), 2f., 19f.; 49 (1904): 2–7, 257–61; J. Auscher, in: AI, 31 (1870), 441ff., 472ff., 592ff.; M.A. Gerson, *Essai sur les juifs de la Bourgogne au moyen âge* (1893); A. Castan, *Notes sur l'histoire municipale de Besançon* (1898), 210, 278, 316, 348, 351; Z. Szajkowski, *Analytical Franco-Jewish Gazetteer* (1966), 185; R. Berg, et al., *Guide Juif de France* (1968), 148.

BESDIN, MORRIS J. (1913–1982), U.S. rabbi, pioneer in *keruv*. Besdin was born in Lithuania. His family immigrated to America when he was three years old. After completing his elementary schooling at Yeshiva Chaim Berlin, he continued his studies at the Rabbi Isaac Elchanan Theological Seminary, where he was ordained in 1936. He began his career as a pulpit rabbi in Scranton, Pa., and then as the successor to his father, who had died, on the Lower East Side. He became the rabbi of the Beis Medrash HaGadol in Washington Heights, a prominent congregation of first and second generation immigrants. The Beis Medrash HaGadol also had a tradition of scholarship which Besdin addressed with confidence. Living in the neighborhood at the time was Samuel *Belkin, the new president of RIETS. It was the beginning of a lifelong association.

The advent of World War II marked Besdin as a quiet "doer." He gave up his pulpit and volunteered for military service as a chaplain in the South Pacific. In 1950, the Kew Gardens Synagogue invited Besdin to become their spiritual leader. This synagogue was the first Orthodox synagogue established and built in New York shortly after the war. The lay leadership was a group of strong, assertive German and Belgian Jews who had immigrated to the United States shortly before the beginning of World War II, just in the nick of time. They were reconstituting on American shores a community they were forced to leave behind. They soon fell in love with their modest, Yiddish-speaking Litvishe rav. Eight years later he was to leave them for a second career in Jewish education.

In a pioneering venture into what later became known as *keruv*, Yeshiva University established in 1958 the James Striar School. The new school was an attempt to capture the hearts and minds of inquiring, college-age young men for Judaism. Belkin did not like boisterous people. Spotlight seekers disturbed his sense of decorum. Having followed Besdin's career, Belkin knew that Besdin was the man he needed for this new school. Even as a pulpit rabbi, Besdin had been in the forefront of Jewish education. As one of the founders of the Yeshiva Dov Revel in Forest Hills, he had made his mark. Having been trained by talmudic giants, Moses *Soloveitchik and Bernard *Revel, Besdin was very conscious of the failure of the "about" theory of Jewish education. He believed in the "it" of Jewish learning. The student had to know – and had to be proud that he knew – the original text. He did not countenance false piety, premature piety. When his newly religious students would walk around with their *ẓiẓit* outside their shirts, Besdin would say: "A man in a tuxedo is elegant, but if his shirt is hanging out of his pants and his hat is on the side of his head, what is he?" He would answer his own question: "A clown." He would advise: learn Hebrew, read the text well, and then decide on the externals.

[Victor Geller (2nd ed.)]

BESEKOW, SAMUEL (1911–2001), Danish actor, director, and author. After training in Berlin with Max *Reinhardt and Erwin Piscator he became director of a workshop theater in Copenhagen, *Riddersalen*, where he presented works by modern playwrights. During the last years of World War II Besekow was a refugee in Stockholm. After the war be worked as director in theaters in Copenhagen and abroad. Besekow staged Brecht's *Galileo* in Tel Aviv, in 1962, and Molière's *The Miser* for the *Freie Volksbuehne* in West Berlin in 1967. He wrote books about the theater, novels depicting the artist's life; *Guds Gölere* ("God's Jesters," 1954), a novel dealing with Jewish life in Russia, Denmark, and Germany; *Ild brander, eng gror* ("Fire Burns, Meadow Grows," 1958); *Letters to a Theater-Crazy Professor* (1959); *Skrevet i Vand* ("Written in Water," 1962); *Skrédderens søn* ("The Tailor's Son," 1964); *Syvtallet* ("The Number Seven," 1966); *Komedianter* ("The Comedians," 1969); *Det musiske faenomen* ("The Aesthetic Phenomenon," 1979); *Fra majonaesekvarteret til det konglige teater* ("From the Neighborhood of Mayonnaise to the Royal Theater," 1993).

[Torben Meyer / Bent Lexner (2nd ed.)]

BESICOVITCH, ABRAM SAMOILOVITCH (1891–1970), mathematician. Besicovitch was descended from a Karaite family. He began his academic career at St. Petersburg where he worked under Markoff. Owing to difficult conditions caused by the Revolution he moved to Perm in the Urals. Besicovitch left the Soviet Union in 1925 and in 1926 settled in Cambridge. He was elected a Fellow of the Royal Society in 1934 and received its Sylvester medal in 1952. Kekeya's famous problem, the determination of the least area swept out by a straight line which is reversed in direction by a continuous motion in the plane, was solved by Besicovitch who proved the surprising result that there is no least area. He made important contributions to the theories of measure, sets of points, real analysis, surface area, and also to the additive theory of numbers. He was known for producing apparently simple problems which were extremely difficult to solve. His publications include *Almost Periodic Functions* (1955^2).

BIBLIOGRAPHY: J.C. Poggendorff, *Handwoerterbuch zur Geschichte der exakten Wissenschaften*, 8 (1966).

[Barry Spain]

BESOR, BROOK OF (Heb. נַחַל הַבְּשׂוֹר), a river valley (wadi) in the Negev that David crossed in pursuit of the Amalekites after their attack on Ziklag (I Sam. 30:9–10, 21). It is commonly identified with Wadi Ghazza-al-Shallāla southwest of Beersheba.

BIBLIOGRAPHY: Abel, Geog, 1 (1933), 405; Press, Ereẓ, 4 (1955), 806–7, s.v. *Ziklag*.

[Yohanan Aharoni]

BESREDKA, ALEXANDER (1870–1940), French immunologist, known for his research on anaphylaxis, local immunization, and immunization in contagious disease. Besredka was the son of a Hebrew writer, Elimelech Ish-Naomi. He first studied in Russia, but when it was proposed to him that he convert to Christianity in order to further his scientific career, he refused and moved to France. He completed his medical studies in Paris, became a French citizen, and was appointed a member of the Pasteur Institute of which he was later a director. Besredka maintained his contacts with Judaism all his life, was active in Jewish organizations such as *OSE, and wrote for Jewish scientific journals, including the Hebrew *Ha-Refu'ah*. His anaphylaxis research was based on original concepts, different from the accepted beliefs in immunology. In 1907 he discovered the possibility of eliminating hypersensitivity to foreign serum. His desensitization method was accepted throughout the world as the pretreatment of patients who had acquired a sensitivity toward a serum, in order to prevent anaphylactic shock by repeated serum treatment. Besredka was closely associated with the biologist Metchnikoff and in 1910 was appointed professor at the Pasteur Institute in Paris. His book *Immunisation locale, pansements spécifiques* was published in 1925.

BIBLIOGRAPHY: Adler, in *Ha-Refu'ah*, 19 (July–Aug. 1940), 13.

[Aryeh Leo Olitzki]

BESSARABIA, region between the rivers Prut and Dniester; before 1812 part of Moldavia, with several districts under direct Ottoman rule; within Russia 1812–1918; part of Romania 1918–40; returned to Russia 1940, and together with the Moldavian Autonomous S.S.R. became the Moldavian S.S.R. After the disintegration of the Soviet Union, the state of Moldova was established.

Up to 1812

From the 15th century onward, Jewish Sephardi merchants from Constantinople frequented Bessarabia while using the trade route which crossed the length of the territory, connecting the countries of the East and the Black Sea shores with Poland. Later, Jewish merchants from Poland also began coming to Bessarabia. Some of them settled there, thus laying the foundation of the first Jewish communities in northern and central Bessarabia; in southern Bessarabia Jewish communities were found already in the 16th century. By the early 18th century, permanent Jewish settlements had been established in several commercial centers. Toward the end of the century, relatively large numbers of Jews were living in most of the urban settlements and in many villages. Their number was estimated at 20,000 in 1812. The legal status of the Jews in the part of Bessarabia under Moldavian rule was similar to that of the rest of Moldavian Jewry. They were organized in autonomous communities subject to the authority of the *ḥakham bashi* in Jassy. In the parts under Ottoman rule they were subject to the same laws as the other communities under this regime. In the 18th and 19th centuries, the Jews in Bessarabia mainly engaged in local commerce and liquor distilling; some traded on a considerable scale with neighboring countries. In the villages main occupations were leasing activities and innkeeping. In the cultural sphere, Bessarabian Jewry during this period was not advanced. The most prominent rabbis of the early 19th century were *Ḥayyim b. Solomon of Czernowitz, rabbi of *Kishinev, and David Solomon *Eibenschutz, rabbi of Soroki. Jacob *Frank exerted an influence from Podolia, and Khotin became a center for Frank and his adherents. Toward the end of the 18th century, Ḥasidism penetrated Bessarabia.

1812–1918

After the Russian annexation in 1812, Bessarabia was included in the *pale of Settlement, and many Jews settled there from other parts of the Pale. The Jewish population, mainly concentrated in Kishinev and its district and in the northern part of the region, grew from 43,062 in 1836 to 94,045 in 1867 (excluding New Bessarabia, see below), and to 228,620 (11.8% of the total) in 1897. Of these 109,703 (48%) lived in the towns (of them 50,237, or 22%, in Kishinev), 60,701 (26.5%) in small towns, and 58,216 (25.5%) in the villages. They formed 37.4% of the town population, 55.7% of the population of the small towns, and 3.8% of the village population. Regulations governing the legal status of the Jews of Bessarabia after the annexation were issued in 1818. In conformance with the Russian pattern, Jews were required to join one of three classes: merchants, townsmen, or peasants. All their former rights were confirmed, while the existent Russian legislation concerning the Jews did not apply, since Bessarabia had autonomous status. The regulations even expressly authorized Bessarabian Jews to reside in the villages and engage in leasing activities and innkeeping, in contradiction to the "Jewish Statute" of 1804 (see *Russia). Because of this regional autonomy, the Jews of Bessarabia were spared several of the most severe anti-Jew-

Main centers of Jewish settlement in Bessarabia in 1897, showing total Jewish population according to districts.

ish decrees issued in the first half of the 19th century. By 1835, when the liquidation of Bessarabian autonomy began, the "Jewish legislation" then promulgated in Russia was equally applied to Bessarabian Jewry, although the prohibition on Jewish residence in border regions was not enforced in Bessarabia until 1839, and compulsory military service until 1852. In the second half of the 19th century, the restriction on Jewish residence in the border area assumed special importance for the Jews of Bessarabia. According to the terms of the Treaty of Paris (1856), a territory in the southern part of the region was allocated to Romania, and many localities, including Kishinev, now fell in the border area. The restrictions were not strictly enforced and thousands of Jews settled in this region, although decrees of expulsion were issued in 1869, 1879, 1886, and 1891. Of these the most severe and extensive was that of 1869. Expulsions of individual Jews also became frequent. The Jews in New Bessarabia – the area incorporated within Romania by the Treaty of Paris – shared the fate of the other Jews in the country. The anti-Jewish riots which broke out in the towns of this region – *Izmail, Kagul, and Vilkovo – in 1872 aroused both Jewish and non-Jewish public opinion in Europe, and diplomatic intervention was enlisted to alleviate the position of the Jews. When New Bessarabia reverted to Russia in 1878, the Jews who were then recorded on the Romanian tax registers were permitted to remain there. The "*May Laws" of 1882 severely affected Jews in Bessarabia as a considerable proportion lived in the villages, and frequent expulsions ensued. In 1903 a frightful pogrom broke out in Kishinev. The wave of pogroms in 1905 swept Bessarabia. Three towns and 68 other localities were struck and 108 Jews were murdered. The damage was estimated at 3,500,000 rubles. The 1917 Revolution in Russia brought civic equality for the Jews of Bessarabia.

During the 19th century, the economic structure of Bessarabian Jewry remained basically unchanged. In their old occupations Jews played an important role within the agrarian economy of the region. An increasing number of Jews entered agriculture, and between 1836 and 1853, 17 Jewish agricultural settlements were established in Bessarabia, mostly in the northern districts, on lands purchased or leased from Christian or Jewish landowners. There were 10,859 persons living on these settlements in 1858; 12.5% of Bessarabian Jewry were farmers, and the region became among the largest and most important centers of Jewish agriculture in Russia. There were 106,031 *dessiatines* (276,283 acres) in Jewish ownership in 1880 (representing 2.5% of the arable land in Bessarabia) and an additional 206,538 *dessiatines* (557,652 acres) leased by Jews. In time, especially after the application of the "May Laws," most of the settlements were liquidated. According to a survey carried out by the *Jewish Colonization Association (ICA) in 1899, there were 1,492 families (7,782 persons), of whom 53% were landowners, on the six settlements still in existence. Of these families only 31.5% were engaged in agricultural work. The land in Jewish ownership also diminished. In 1897, 7.12% of the Jews in Bessarabia were engaged in agriculture; 26.81% in crafts and industry; 3.65% in transport; 2.34% in commercial brokerage; 39.53% in commerce (of these 58% engaged in the trade of agricultural produce); 8.9% as clerks or employees in private enterprises, domestics, daily workers, or unskilled laborers; 4.9% in public or government services or the liberal professions; and 6.75% in miscellaneous occupations. The 22,130 Jews engaged in commerce constituted 81.2% of the total number of merchants in the region, and 95.8% of the grain dealers. The proportion of Jewish artisans, mainly tailors, was lower (39%). From the early 1880s, the economic situation of Bessarabian Jewry deteriorated as a result of the frequent expulsions from the villages and border areas, and the agrarian crisis in Russia during this period. Many impoverished Jews emigrated overseas. The principal factor in Jewish spiritual life was Ḥasidism. Many of the village Jews of no marked learning adopted much of the way of life and customs of the Moldavian peasantry. A major influence was wielded by the *ẓaddikim* of the Friedman (see *Ruzhin) and *Twersky families. During the 1830s and 1840s, Haskalah began to penetrate into Bessarabia. From the end of the 1840s, Jewish government schools were opened in Bessarabia. In 1855 there were six such schools, in *Beltsy, Khotin, *Brichany, and Izmail, and two in Kishinev, with 188 pupils. Private secular Jewish schools also began to appear, and from the 1860s Jews in Bessarabia, especially wealthier ones, began to send their children to the general schools. During the 1870s, 30% to 40% of the pupils in some of the secondary schools of the region were Jewish. In 1894, however, 60.9% of Jewish children of school age still attended *ḥeder*. The population census of 1897 revealed that only 27.8% of Bessarabian Jews above the age of ten could read Russian. After the pogroms of the 1880s, Ḥovevei Zion societies were founded in Bessarabia as elsewhere, the most important in Kishinev, led by Abraham *Grunberg and Meir *Dizengoff. Toward the end of the 1880s and early 1890s, there was some movement toward pioneer settlement in Ereẓ Israel (*aliyah*). Seven delegates from Bessarabia, of whom six were from Kishinev, took part in the founding meeting of the Ḥovevei Zion Odessa Committee (April 1890). The Zionists of Bessarabia were represented at the First Zionist Congress in 1897 by Jacob *Bernstein-Kogan of Kishinev. Toward the close of the 19th century and the beginning of the 20th, a line of poets and authors emerged on the cultural scene in Bessarabia, many of whom were to play an important role in Yiddish and Hebrew literature, including Eliezer *Steinbarg, Judah *Steinberg, S. *Ben-Zion, Jacob *Fichman, Samuel Leib *Blank, and Ḥayyim *Greenberg. The chief rabbi of Bessarabia, Judah Loeb *Zirelson, wrote halakhic works.

1918–1941

After the incorporation of Bessarabia into Romania in 1918, the Jews there automatically received Romanian citizenship, in accordance with the commitments of Romania under the Treaty of Paris. However, as a result of the Nationality Law of 1924, many Bessarabian Jews who could not fulfill its requirements were deprived of Romanian nationality, and defined as aliens. According to a census taken in 1920, there were 267,000 Jews in Bessarabia. As in the other parts of Romania, they encountered popular hostility, anti-Jewish measures and suspicion on the part of the government, and petty administrative harassment. In 1938, 21,844 Jewish heads of families in Bessarabia were deprived of Romanian nationality (according to official statistics). The economic situation of Bessarabian Jewry also deteriorated. The separation of the region from its former Russian markets, the drought which struck Bessarabia three times during this period, the world economic crisis, and the government's policy of exploitation, all resulted in a severe crisis in the agricultural economy. Assistance from abroad was provided principally by the *American Joint Distribution Committee and ICA. The savings and credit cooperatives set up before the war supported by ICA also played an important role in this period. In 1930 there were 41 savings and loan banks operating in 39 localities with a membership of 30,202, i.e., two-thirds of Jewish breadwinners in Bessarabia. Of these 12% were farmers, reflecting the development of Jewish agriculture in this period. At the time of the agrarian reform in Bessarabia (1920–23), between 4,000 and 5,000 Jews received 7 to 10 acres of land each – altogether approximately 120,000 acres were cultivated. In Bessarabia agriculture as a Jewish occupation ranked second after Ereẓ Israel. In 1935 about 3,000 families cultivating a total of approximately 20,000 hectares were supported by ICA. Two new agricultural settlements were established with assistance from ICA. Under Romanian rule, Jewish communal life flourished and leadership revived. A number of political parties, prominent among them the Zionist movements, were active, as well as other organizations. The first conference of Bessarabian Zionists was convened in 1920 in Kishinev, and a central office for the Zionist Organization of Bessarabia was set up in Kishinev. On the basis of the minority treaties signed by Romania, a ramified network of Jewish elementary and secondary schools with instruction in Yiddish or Hebrew was established in Bessarabia at the beginning of Romanian rule. In 1922 there were 140 Jewish schools with 19,746 pupils (105 giving instruction in Hebrew with 16,456 pupils). A teachers' seminary was established in Kishinev. However, by the end of 1922 government policy changed. Many of the schools were deprived of their Jewish character and converted into Romanian schools. By 1929–30 there remained 64 Jewish educational institutions in 30 localities (15 kindergartens, 37 elementary schools, 11 secondary schools, and one vocational school) with 6,381 pupils and 312 teachers. Social welfare institutions in Bessarabia during this period included 13 hospitals, a sanatorium for tubercular patients, societies for assistance to the sick in 25 localities, 13 old-age homes, and four relief institutions for children. From 1923 the *OSE society was also active in Bessarabia where it maintained stations in eight localities. After the entry of the Red Army into Bessarabia on June 28, 1940, life for the Jews of Bessarabia was gradually brought into line with the general pattern of Jewish existence under the Soviet regime. On June 13, 1941, a comprehensive "purge" was carried out throughout the region. Thousands of Jews – communal leaders, active members of the Zionist movement, businessmen, and persons suspected of disloyalty to the regime – were arrested and deported to internment camps or exiled to Siberia.

[Eliyahu Feldman]

From 1941

The first Soviet occupation of the area lasted from 1940 until the beginning of hostilities between Germany and Russia in June of the following year. Romania was an ally of Germany. Bessarabia was reconquered by German and Romanian troops by July 23, 1941, and remained under Romanian authority until August 1944, when it was reoccupied by the Russians. Central and northern Bessarabia, as well as a narrow strip on the west side of the Dniester, became the Moldavian Soviet Socialist Republic with the capital in Kishinev. When Bessarabia was reoccupied by the Soviets, only a few Jews were still alive. The great majority had been massacred by the Einsatzkommandos of Einsatzgruppe D, and by the German and Romanian soldiers, while others were deported to *Transnistria, where more than half of them died. Many of the deported Jews preferred to slip back into Romania, and from there to leave for Israel.

For further information on the Holocaust in Bessarabia and subsequent events, see articles on *Russia and the various towns. For the period after the breakup of the Soviet Union, see *Moldova.

[Theodor Lavi]

BIBLIOGRAPHY: *Die Judenpogrome in Russland*, 1 (1910), passim; 2 (1910), 5–37; N. Sharand, *A Dritl Yorhundert Yidisher Kooperat-*

sye in Besarabye (1934); J. Starr, in: JSOS, 3 (1941), 57–80; *Besarabyah* (Heb., 1941), essays; A. Ettinger, *Im Ḥakla'im Yehudim ba-Tefuẓot* (1942), 110–70; Sh. Hillels, in: *Shevilei ha-Ḥinnukh* (1943), 3–16, 67–73; idem, in: *Ha-Tekufah*, 30–31 (1946), 786–806; Z. Scharfstein, *Toledot ha-Ḥinnukh be-Yisrael ba-Dorot ha-Aḥaronim*, 3 (1949), 248–59; M. Ussishkin, in: *Pirkei Besarabyah*, 1 (1952), 32–50; *Al Admat Besarabyah*, 3 vols. (1959–63), essays; E. Feldman, *Toledot Ha-Yehudim Be-Bessarabia ba-Me'ah ha-19* (1970); idem, in: *He-Avot*, 12 (1965), 102–20; idem, in: *Zion*, 30 (1965), 206–33; Vol. 11 of the *Enẓiklopediah shel Galuyot* (1971) is devoted to Bessarabia.

BESSELS, EMIL (1847–1888), German physician, Arctic explorer and naturalist. After his graduation from the University of Heidelberg in 1865, Bessels was appointed custodian of the Stuttgart Museum of Natural Science. In 1869 he was a member of a German Arctic expedition which studied the influence of the Gulf Stream on areas east of Spitzbergen. Bessels served as a surgeon in the German army in 1870. The following year Bessels sailed on the U.S. vessel *Polaris* as surgeon and naturalist with Captain Charles Francis Hall's expedition to the North Pole. Hall died unexpectedly in 1871 at Thank God Harbor, Greenland, after the *Polaris* had traveled farther north than any other ship. In the following year, the *Polaris* was caught in the polar ice and wrecked near Littleton Island. Nineteen members of the expedition, including Bessels, became separated from the rest of the crew and floated 1,300 miles on an ice-floe to the Bay of Melville off the Labrador coast, before they were rescued by a sealer. On his return to the U.S. in 1873, Bessels was accused by one of the crew of murdering Hall by administering morphine. An inquiry conducted by the surgeon-generals of the U.S. Army and Navy ruled that Hall had died of apoplexy and that Bessels was innocent. Subsequently, Bessels prepared the scientific results of this Arctic expedition (1876), wrote on natural history for scientific journals, and edited reports of the United States Naval Institute. Bessels was a member of an ethnological expedition which sailed on the steamship *Saranac* to the northwest coast of America. The vessel was wrecked in Seymour Narrows, British Columbia. Bessels died in Stuttgart.

BIBLIOGRAPHY: C.H. David, *Narrative of the North Polar Expedition, U.S. Ship Polaris, Capt. Charles Francis Hall Commanding* (1876); J. Mirsky, *To The North* (1934).

BESSER, CHASKEL O. (1923–), Orthodox rabbi. Besser was born in Katowice, Poland. His father, Naphtali Besser, was a successful businessman who was the right-hand man to the *Radomsko rebbe, Solomon Rabinowich, and tried to get him to escape occupied Poland, but the rebbe refused to leave his people. As a child, Chaskel Besser studied in the Radomsker Keter Torah Yeshivah both in Katowice and in Lodz. He escaped Poland on September 1, 1939, as the Germans entered the country, and reached Ereẓ Israel five days later. He continued his studies with Rabbi Herschel Eisenstadt (originally of Poland) of Jerusalem, who was the disciple of Rabbi Ḥayyim Brisker. He was ordained in 1942 by Rabbi Joseph Blumenfeld, the head of the Bet Din of Tel Aviv.

Besser moved to New York in 1946, where he became a successful businessman in real estate. However, his real devotion was to working for the benefit of the Jewish people and labored on behalf of common causes. He was friendly with presidents and prime ministers as well as a diverse group of Jewish leaders including Nahum *Goldmann and Menaḥem *Begin as well as such rabbinic leaders as Moses *Feinstein and *Aaron Kotler and a variety of ḥasidic leaders.

Besser was instrumental in popularizing the *daf yomi* (study of the daily Talmud page in a 7½-year cycle) starting. He was one of three rabbis invited to the inauguration of President George H. Bush. In 1987, he was appointed to the U.S. Commission for the Preservation of American Heritage Abroad.

In 1987, Rabbi Besser met Ronald S. *Lauder, a leading businessman, philanthropist, and Jewish leader while Lauder was serving as U.S. ambassador to Austria. The following year, Lauder established the Ronald S. Lauder Foundation to develop and nurture Jewish life in former Communist countries. Besser quickly became Lauder's mentor and spiritual guide for the activities of the Foundation. Besser was already active in fighting for the preservation and restoration of Jewish cemeteries in Poland and in surrounding countries. This dedication led him also to seek out the remaining Jews of Poland and other countries, especially those who had only recently discovered their true Jewish identities. Being one of the first Jews to recognize that there were many more Jews remaining in Poland than previously thought, he labored ceaselessly to enable any Jew who wanted to return to the Jewish people to be able to so. Today, there are more than 20,000 practicing Jews in Poland, in large measure due to the groundwork laid by Besser in the late 1980s on.

Besser became the rabbi of Bnai Israel Chaim on Manhattan's West Side. He was also one of the closest allies and confidants of Rabbi Moses Sherer, the executive director of Agudat Israel for several decades, helping him strengthen and expand the activities and the impact of the organization.

BIBLIOGRAPHY: W. Kozak, *The Rabbi of 84th Street* (2004).

[Michael J. Schudrich (2nd ed.)]

BESSIS, ALBERT (1885–1972), Tunisian politician. Born in *Tunis into a distinguished family of writers and *dayyanim*, Bessis qualified as a lawyer and was elected to the Grand Council of *Tunisia in 1934 where he became chairman of the committee on legislation. He participated in the negotiations with the French government in the early 1950s that led to the granting of autonomy to Tunisia in 1955. Bessis was minister of housing and town planning from 1954 to 1955 when he became minister of public works. He retained his post following the independence of Tunisia in 1956. He resigned in the following year and retired from public life. Bessis was an active figure in the Jewish community and was president of the Tunisian *ORT and other communal organizations.

[David Corcos]

BESSIS, JESHUA (1773–1860), Tunisian scholar. Bessis was appointed chief rabbi of Tunis in 1847 and served in this office until his death. He wrote responsa and a work on the Shulḥan Arukh, only the section on *Yoreh De'ah* being published, part of it under the title *Avnei Ẓedek* (1902) and part as *Avnei Ẓedek u-Me'orot Natan* (1903). Bessis wrote introductions and approbations for the books of Tunisian scholars. He engaged in practical Kabbalah and was regarded as a saint; his grave became a place of pilgrimage.

BIBLIOGRAPHY: Arditti, in: *Revue Tunisienne*, 3 (1932), 102–3; Hirschberg, Afrikah, 2 (1965), 148.

BESSO, HENRY (1905–1993), scholar of Sephardi studies. Born in Salonica, Besso went to the College St. Jean Baptiste de la Salle. He moved to New York after the death of his parents, where he joined his brothers and worked with an export-import firm while pursuing his education in the evening at the City College of New York, where he earned his B.A. (1931) and later at Columbia University (1935). Because his firm collapsed he became eligible for work under the provisions of the WPA and began working as a teacher of French and Spanish in New York's Adult Education department and was soon training teachers and creating curricula to assist his students. With the world war looming, he was moved to Washington to train Army Air Force and Navy officers and government officials for their missions abroad and then became a research analyst and speech writer for the Voice of America beginning many decades of service to that agency.

In 1945 he was sent to Biarritz American University in France and then to the Command School in Germany to teach Spanish and French. While in Europe he lectured on Hispanic and Judeo-Spanish language and culture. He became a respected lecturer on Sephardi culture and a communal activist in the Sephardi Jewish Brotherhood of America and was for a time executive director of the World Sephardi Federation. In 1963, he researched and edited a listing of 289 Judeo-Spanish works he had uncovered at the Library of Congress in Washington, D.C. To this day *Ladino Books in the Library of Congress: A Bibliography* is still considered one of the definitive bibliographic listings of the world's great collections of Judeo-Spanish literature. In 1967 he became one of the founders of the American Society for Sephardic Studies at Yeshiva University.

On the eve of his retirement in 1976, the Foundation for the Advancement of Sephardic Studies and Culture devoted its *Tract XI* to him. Entitled *Study of the Meaning of Ladino, Judezmo and the Spanish-Jewish Dialect*, it included reprints of many of Besso's articles and writings, with an extensive and thorough bibliography of his works. The volume was dedicated to Besso as "a most distinguished contemporary scholar, whose numerous and varied works on Sephardic culture and folklore will always be remembered."

[Efraim Zadoff (2nd ed.)]

BET (Heb. בֵּית ;ב), second letter of the Hebrew alphabet: a voiced bilabial plosive [b] and voiced labiodental fricative [v] (a positional variant); its numerical value is 2.

The earliest form of *bet* – in the Proto-Sinaitic inscriptions – is the acrophonic pictograph of a house (*bayit*) ⊏⊐ While in South Arabic its shape is ⊓ and in Ethiopic በ, in the Proto-Canaanite script the main stages of development are → ⊏ → ⊐ → 𐤁. Variants of the latter form survive in the Phoenician (𐤁, 𐤁), Hebrew (𐤁, 𐤁), and Samaritan (ࠁ) as well as in the Greek (8 → B) and Latin scripts.

The Aramaic *bet* like the *dalet, resh,* and *'ayin* has an open top already in the seventh century B.C.E. While in the fifth century B.C.E. the downstroke has a diagonal flourish, from the fourth century B.C.E. onward the downstroke is vertical curving into a horizontal base; at the same time there is a tendency to straighten the top of the letter: ב. In the early Jewish script the tick on the left side of the top ב is the only remnant of the half-circled head. Already in the Herodian period, the base of the Jewish *bet* is written occasionally with a separate left-to-right stroke ב. This fashion prevails, becomes common in the Jewish bookhand, and the *bet* does not change its basic shape during the ages: In some cursive trends, as in the period of Bar Kokhba and today, the *bet* is written without lifting the pen: ב. However, the Ashkenazi cursive developed as follows: ב → ב → ב → ב.

Palmyrene *bet* follows the third-century B.C.E. Aramaic ב and develops through ב into Syriac ܒ. The Nabatean *bet* loses its top ; this form is adopted for Arabic *ba,* which later is distinguished by a diacritic sign ب from ت (*ta*), ن (*nun*), and ي (*ya*). See *Alphabet, Hebrew.

[Joseph Naveh]

BET AGLAYIM, a place mentioned by Eusebius (Onom. 48:19) 8 mi. (13 km.) S. of Gaza, near the sea coast, which he erroneously identified with the biblical Beth-Hoglah (Josh. 15:6; 18:19–21). Bet Aglayim is most probably the ancient name of the important Tell al-'Ajjūl located about 4½ mi. (7 km.) southwest of Gaza, which was excavated from 1929 to 1931 by Sir Flinders Petrie (who identified it with ancient Gaza). The remains at Tell al-'Ajjūl date mainly from the Middle and Late Bronze Ages and include Hyksos fortifications and graves, and the palace of an Egyptian governor. Rich finds of gold, silver, and jewelry were discovered in the tombs.

BIBLIOGRAPHY: W.M.F. Petrie, *Ancient Gaza*, 5 vols. (1931–52); Maisler, in: ZDPV, 56 (1933), 186ff.; Abel, Geog, 2 (1938), 265; Albright, in: AJSLL, 55 (1938), 337–59.

[Michael Avi-Yonah]

BETA ISRAEL, ethno-religious group in Ethiopia which claims to be of Jewish origin and which is attached to a form of the Jewish religion based on the Bible, certain books of the Apocrypha, and other post-biblical Scripture; living in the provinces surrounding and to the north of Lake Tana and now in Israel. The Beta Israel, as the group calls itself, were known until recently by others as the Falashas, a term regarded by the group as one of contempt.

Although Beta Israel have long fascinated scholars, many features of their history remain little known and inadequately studied. This article seeks to present a survey of the political history of the Beta Israel from earliest time. It seeks to reveal the dynamic character of Beta Israel society and the manner in which patterns of leadership changed throughout the group's recorded history. Special attention is given to the competing claims concerning different types of leadership: secular/religious; traditional/modernizing; externally/internally selected.

Early History and Legends

Given the dearth of reliable historical material concerning the earliest Jews in and Jewish influences on Ethiopia, it is virtually impossible to offer any detailed analysis of their political structure. Nevertheless, a number of tentative generalizations can be offered which shed some light on the character of their communal organization. On the basis of the available evidence it does not appear likely that the earliest Jews entered Ethiopia in a single united group. It seems far more probable that they arrived in the country in small groups alongside other non-Jewish merchants, settlers, soldiers, etc. In a similar fashion, since Judaized elements could have entered Ethiopia from Arabia at any time from the 1st to the 6th century, there appears to be no reason to confine the entry of Jewish elements to a single brief period. Finally, the widespread impact of Jewish practices and influences on Ethiopian culture is only understandable if we assume that the Jewish immigrants did not live in isolation from their neighbors.

While a number of scholars have claimed that the introduction of Christianity to Ethiopia in the 4th country led to the persecution of local Jews, there is no direct evidence to support this.

In fact, it appears unlikely that the earliest Christian emperors had either the political mandate or the religious zeal to pursue such a policy. A strong possibility does exist, however, that the 6th-century Ethiopian emperor Kaleb, who sent troops to punish the Judaized Arabian ruler *Yusuf Dhu Nuwas, may also have taken action against the Jews of the Aksumite (Ethiopian) kingdom. It is most interesting to note that during his reign we hear for the first time of the Semien region (later a Beta Israel stronghold) as "that country [to which] the King of the Aksumites exiles anyone whom he has sentenced to be banished."

None of the sources on the period between the 6th and 13th centuries is of sufficient historicity to permit anything more than the most tentative of conclusions. This is particularly the case with regard to the legendary "Beta Israel queen" Judith (Gudit). While Bruce and Rathjens treated stories concerning this ruler with considerable enthusiasm, Conti Rossini and Ullendorff have more soberly concluded that they "possess no basis in historical fact." Even if the existence of a medieval queen is conceded, there is little evidence that she was a Jewess, much less a Beta Israel. Certainly, no Jewish dynasty ruled Ethiopia in this period. In the Hebrew sources for this period, neither *Eldad ha-Dani nor *Benjamin of Tudela appears to possess any first-hand knowledge concerning Ethiopia. Clearly we must wait for the "Early Solomonic" period in Ethiopian history (from 1270 onward) before we encounter any truly reliable sources on the Beta Israel polity.

WAR AND ADAPTATION. 1270–1632 The year 1270 marks a turning point in Ethiopian history. In that year a new dynasty which traced its descent to King Solomon and to the ancient Ethiopian Kingdom of Aksum came to power. Once these "Solomonic" Kings had consolidated their rule in the traditionally Christian areas of Ethiopia, they set out to impose their hegemony on all of the independent peoples of the Ethiopian highlands. Beginning with the reign of Amda Siyon (1314–1344) almost all these kings were to a greater or lesser extent concerned with the political subjugation of the Judaized population in the regions of Semien, Woggara, and Dambiya. In the middle of the 16th century, after the Ethiopian Christians had (with Portuguese assistance) successfully repulsed a major Muslim invasion, they turned their full attention to the Beta Israel. King Minas (r. 1559–1563) and his son Sarsa Dengel (r. 1563–1597) fought major battles against the Beta Israel and inflicted heavy losses upon them. Hostilities were renewed in the reign of Susenyos (1607–1632) and under his leadership the Ethiopian army totally defeated the Beta Israel who were led by their ruler Gideon. This defeat marked the end of Beta Israel independence.

A BETA ISRAEL KINGDOM. Although it has for many years been claimed that an independent "Beta Israel" kingdom existed in Ethiopia during this period, and the Beta Israel themselves claim to have been ruled by a long line of kings, these contentions should not be accepted without careful scrutiny. There is little support in the contemporary primary sources for the idea that the Beta Israel were united into a single political framework earlier than the 16th century. As was noted above, none of the sources from the period prior to the 14th century is of sufficient historicity for firm conclusions to be drawn. Nor is there any evidence for the existence of a unified Jewish kingdom in the 14th and 15th century reports. Judaized groups are invariably referred to in the contemporary hagiographic texts and chronicles by the region they inhabited. Their rulers are depicted as local governors, members of the regional nobility. Thus we read of people "like Jews" in Semien, Wagara, Salamt, and Sagade," of "sons of Jews" in Enfraz; of the governor of Semien and Cambiya, etc. Even James Bruce, who perhaps more than any other writer deserves credit for popularizing the exploits of the Jewish "kings" of Ethiopia, makes no mention of a monarchy in this period. It is therefore difficult to escape the conclusion that in the 14th and 15th centuries the Beta Israel were politically divided and geographically dispersed.

The recognition of this reality has several important consequences for the interpretation of Beta Israel history. Firstly, it serves as a caution against attempts to artificially impose unity on the sources by treating scattered events in specific regions as if they affected all Beta Israel. The Christian Emperor Yeshaq's (r. 1413–1430) victory over the Beta Israel governor of Semien and Dambiya was not, for example, a defeat for all Beta Israel. Some were allies of the Emperor and benefited from his victory. In a similar fashion, the reported conversion to Christianity of much of the population of Salamt province by the 15th-century Christian missionary St. Takla Hawaryat must be evaluated in its proper geographic context. His successes in that region left the population of Semien at least temporarily untouched.

A recognition of the decentralized character of Beta Israel society during this period is also of crucial importance to the proper understanding of the dynamics of Beta Israel political history. If one accepts the existence of an ancient Beta Israel kingdom with its origins shrouded in the undocumented past, the rest of Beta Israel history appears almost automatically to be little more than an account of their decline from this mythical peak. In fact, the story is much more complex. According to the extant sources, a centralized relatively unified political organization existed among the Beta Israel only from the 16th and early 17th centuries. The effective military-political structure described in Ethiopian royal chronicles of this period was not, therefore, an aboriginal characteristic of Beta Israel society. Rather it developed relatively late, probably in response to the external threat posed by the Christian empire. Their history is not accordingly a story of continuous and unremitting decline but rather a gradual process of consolidation and unification followed by a series of catastrophic defeats.

Even when applied solely to the period of the 16th and 17th century the term Beta Israel kingdom should not be applied too casually. Even those later sources which portray a far more centralized polity than existed in earlier periods are far from unanimous as to the precise character of the group's political structure. It is, for example, of interest to note that while many medieval Hebrew sources (none of them eyewitness accounts) accept the existence of a kingdom as axiomatic, the first-hand reports of Ethiopian, Portuguese, and Muslim observers are far more restrained. The claim put forward in the *Chronicle* of Emperor Sarsa Dengal that the 16th-century Beta Israel leader Radai lived from his own labor ("he was a tiller of the soil, who ate his bread by the sweat of his brow"; cf. Gen. 3:19) is difficult to reconcile with the idea of a fully developed monarchy.

Nor should James Bruce's detailed reports on the Jewish kings be accepted uncritically. Bruce, it must be remembered, visited Ethiopia almost a century and a half after Susenyos' victory over the Beta Israel. He was, therefore, at least in this case, a recorder of traditions and not an eyewitness. In addition, his claim that a Beta Israel king and queen still ruled at the time of his visit scarcely enhances his credibility.[8]

THE RISE OF MONASTICISM. The gradual evolution of a more centralized political structure was only one of the responses engendered by the Christian threat to the Beta Israel. During the same period a major revolution took place within the structure of Beta Israel religious life. A new form of religious leadership began to emerge. Faced with increasing political and military pressure from the Christian Ethiopian emperors, the Beta Israel adopted the Christian institution of monasticism as a means of consolidating and developing their unique communal identity. Beginning with Abba Sabra and Sega Amlak, who lived in the 15th century and are credited with founding Beta Israel monasticism, monks played a vital role among the Jews in Ethiopia.

According to Beta Israel traditions, the introduction of monasticism was accompanied by a number of other religious innovations including the introduction of new religious literature, the composition of prayers, and the adoption of important laws of ritual segregation and purity. The Beta Israel monks can thus be justly claimed to have been the chief carriers of their people's distinctive religious heritage. It appears probable that it was they who provided the ideological basis for the creation of a unified political structure among their people. Just how successful the monks were in assuming a central position in Beta Israel society is evidenced not only by the fact that they survived the demise of the autonomous political leaders but also by the fact that nearly all the figures commemorated by the Beta Israel as holy men at various holy places in Ethiopia were monks.

1632–1860

Any doubts one might have with regard to the finality of the Beta Israel's defeat at the hands of Susenyos are resolved by the decision of his son Fasiledes (1632–67) to build his capital at Gondar near the heart of Beta Israel territory. The site would only have been chosen after the local people had been totally subdued. According to both Christian and Jewish traditions, Beta Israel soldiers and artisans were speedily incorporated into the military and economic life of Christian Ethiopia. Although the Beta Israel no longer ruled themselves, the Gondarine period (1632–1769) is remembered as a period when the "(Beta) Israel lived in peace and welfare." Beginning in 1769, however, Ethiopia was plunged into an extended period of conflict and internal struggle. Known as the *Zemane Masafent* (the era of the princes or judges), because it resembled the period of the Old Testament judges when "there was no king in Israel: every man did that which was right in his eyes," this period brought fresh sorrows to the Beta Israel. During a period of almost 100 years (1769–1855) Ethiopia lacked effective imperial rule and local rulers vied with each other for supremacy. The Beta Israel, whose well-being was largely dependent upon royal patronage and protection, suffered accordingly. Their decline from independence to imperial appointees to despised artisans is clearly visible in their changing patterns of leadership.

AZMACH AND BEJEROND. Following their loss of independence in the 17th century, the structure of Beta Israel political leadership underwent a dramatic change. Autonomous rulers no longer exercised control over the community or the regions in which the Beta Israel lived. Political power passed into the hands of royal-appointed governors, none of whom was chosen by virtue of their traditional roles among their own people. Rather they acquired land and titles through their ability to render services to the Christian Emperors who resided in Gondar. The principal secular leaders of the Beta Israel became those who were recognized as such by the dominant society, rather than those related to their own previous ruling families. A new elite of soldiers, masons, and carpenters emerged.

The Beta Israel leaders of the Gondarine period are remembered as having held two titles: *azmach* (commander) and *bejerond* (treasurer). The former, which was the higher of the two ranks, was used to refer to military leaders and local officals. The latter appears to have had connections with tax collection, although as applied to the Beta Israel it seems to have referred primarily to the "chief of the workers" – especially potters, carpenters, masons, and blacksmiths. While the *azmach* might exercise leadership over a heterogeneous community, the *bejerond*'s authority was confined to the Beta Israel. One informant stated, "The *azmach* was government administrator for many people, but the *bejerond* was only concerned with the Beta Israel."

One of the clearest indications of the deterioration of the status of the Beta Israel in the late 18th and 19th century is the gradual disappearance of the *azmach*. In the Gondarine period Beta Israel were appointed both *azmach* and *bejerond*, by mid-19th century those few Beta Israel who had any titles at all were exclusively *bejerond*. As James Quirin has noted, this transition was symptomatic of their social-political decline and increasing identification as a low-status artisan group.

COMMUNAL ORGANIZATION. One immediate consequence of the Beta Israel's loss of autonomy was a return to the decentralized pattern of communal organization which had characterized their political structure prior to the 16th and 17th century. While it may be convenient to continue to speak of the Beta Israel "community," no evidence exists for the survival of formal centralized communal institutions. Rather a large number of scattered communities existed with informal economic, political, marital, and religious ties. Halévy observed when he visited Ethiopia in 1867, "Chaque commune est autonomie et indépendante. C'est seulement dans les cas òu un grand danger menace la religion qu'on se reunit, afin de repousser l'ennemie commun" (J. Halevy, in: *Bulletin de l'Alliance israélite universelle* (1868), 95).

The Beta Israel's lack of autonomy and of an effective political-military leadership also resulted in a sharp decline in the communities' coercive power. Abba Yeshaq, one of the Beta Israel's outstanding religious leaders of the 19th century, told the French explorer Antoine d'Abbadie that originally the Beta Israel would stone to death any member of the community who ate leavened products on Passover. Following their loss of independence, however, they were compelled to change the punishment. "Mais aujourd'hui, comme on n'a pas de roi juif, on se contente d'infliger une pénitence qui est le don d'une chèvre d'un an."

Abba Yeshaq's words serve as a reminder that however great the authority of the Beta Israel clergy, neither they nor any other group in post-independence Beta Israel society had the power to enforce its will upon the population. On the whole, the means of coercion in their hands were largely limited to steps such as ostracism, which depended upon the support of community opinion. As Halévy wrote, "Chaque province, chaque ville se soumet *volontairement* à la decision de son prêtre et de ses debteras."

At the heart of the daily functioning of the voluntary system described by Halévy stood the village elders (*shmagilotch*). On their role he observed, "La justice est exercée par les anciens (chimaguelié). Les plaintes et les différends sont portes devant eux. Leurs jugements sont toujours respectes par les deux partis. Personne n'ose s'y opposer ni faire appel a l'autorité amharique."

Although Halévy appears to have been the first witness to mention the role of the elders in Beta Israel society, the phenomenon he describes was probably of considerable antiquity. Certainly we can presume that it existed at least from the time when the Beta Israel lost their independence. More importantly, it formed an integral part of Beta Israel life throughout the 19th and 20th centuries, and thus forms a vital element in any comprehensive picture of their traditional leadership in the modern era.

Although we possess no specific information of the Beta Israel clergy during the Gondarine period, it appears likely that their importance was increased by the decline of the autonomous political leadership. In particular, the monastic clergy who became virtually the only leaders not dependent upon the Christian kings for their position, probably rose in status. The further decline of the secular leaders during the "era of the princes" could only have further enhanced their standing.

By the time we begin to receive detailed accounts of Beta Israel life in the first half of the 19th century, the paramount position of the monastic clergy is clearly established. Antoine d'Abbadie, one of the most important of the early European visitors to Ethiopia wrote, "Bien qu'il n'y ait pas de hierarchie ecclesiastique, les Falachas reconnaissent pour chef les plus savent ou le plus habile de leurs moines." The centrality of the monastic clergy during this period receives further confirmation in the Beta Israel's own sources according to which their religion survived a severe crisis in the early 19th century due to the efforts of the monk, Abba Wedaje. Significantly it was also the monastic clergy who served as communal spokesmen when the first efforts to communicate with world Jewry were made. Finally, it was upon the monastic clergy that the main responsibility fell to defend their people against the temptations of foreign missionaries.

1860–1905: The Missionary Challenge

By the middle of the 19th century a small number of Westerners had visited the Beta Israel and brought reports about them back to Europe. Although a number of these travelers were themselves missionaries, it was only in 1859 that organized Western missionary activity amongst the Beta Israel began. In that year the London Society for Promoting Christianity among the Jews established its Ethiopian mission. It is difficult to overestimate the impact of the mission's activities upon the Beta Israel. While the number of converts they procured was never very large, the educational opportunities they offered and the vernacular scriptures they distributed significantly disrupted the Beta Israel communities. Existing divisions between regions and groups within the population were exacerbated. New tensions were also created. For the monastic clergy in particular, the missionary intervention proved fateful.

THE DECLINE OF MONASTICISM. A crucial feature of the missionary program was a concerted effort to undermine the Beta Israel's confidence in their priests and monks. These clerics attracted the ire of the missionaries for a variety of reasons. Firstly, as evangelical Protestants the missionaries had a deep aversion to any monastic religious hierarchy. (They were, for example not less bitter in their condemnation of the clergy of the Ethiopian Orthodox Church.) The Beta Israel religious leaders were, moreover doubly blameworthy in their opinion, because they claimed biblical sanction for their office. Typical of their hostility to the monks was the encounter of the missionary Henry Aaron Stern with a "wild fanatical looking monk with a grin of contempt which imparted to his black face and capacious mouth a repulsive expression with an air of pride and self-complacency."

Stern and his colleagues not only attacked the priesthood and monasticism as institutions, but also exploited every opportunity to demonstrate their superiority by engaging individual clerics in disputations. Their task was not a difficult one. The Beta Israel clergy were honored by their people because of their piety and the communal and ritual roles they performed; not for their skill as debaters. Few, if any, Beta Israel priests possessed a complete Bible. The arts of citation and argumentation, at which the missionaries were so skilled, was totally foreign to them. Inevitably, they came out second best in the confrontations engineered by the missionaries.

The deleterious effects of the missionaries' direct attacks upon the monastic clergy were further supplemented by other activities with less immediate but no less important consequences. In particular, the opening of the mission schools and the distribution of Amharic Bibles (and religious tracts) set in motion a mini-reformation among the Beta Israel. Young men and secondary clerics (*debtera*) attracted by the mission's offer of education and an alternative avenue to achievement and status were among the most prominent early converts. The missionaries themselves drew a clear connection between literacy and familiarity with the biblical text, and the decision to defy clerical authority.

The missionary attempt to undermine the Beta Israel's trust in their religious leaders was based upon a shrewdly accurate assessment of their centrality to their people. In the mid-19th century as today most Beta Israel possessed only a rudimentary understanding of the symbols and rituals which comprised their religious traditions. The clergy, especially the monks, were not only the paramount ritual experts, but also the chief guardians of the community's traditions and beliefs. It thus, for example, fell to them to defend the community's interests before the king when in 1862 the missionaries succeeded in temporarily curtailing Beta Israel sacrifices. The monks moreover held tremendous sway over their followers. On no less than three occasions during the first decades of the missionary enterprise (1862, 1874, 1879) groups or individual monks succeeded in leading large bands of Beta Israel on ill-fated exoduses out of Ethiopia. Given such devotion, it becomes clear that the missionary assault on clerical prestige and status held the promise of totally undermining the Beta Israel religious system. In fact, the missionaries seem to have been confident that this was, in fact, happening.

"Respecting the Jews, or Falashas, one remarkable feature is at present observable, namely, that they have been greatly divided in their religious opinions, as also in respect of their adherence to the monks... Hence, a great division has arisen, and although we must not as yet be too sanguine, yet we may freely say that the balance is in our favor" (*Jewish Record* (January 1862), 2).

The earliest period of missionary activity also saw the creation of another sort of division among the Beta Israel, with the establishment of a major settlement in the Tigre province of northern Ethiopia.

Although Beta Israel villages appear to have existed in Tigre province during the Middle Ages, the modern Tigrean communities appear to have originated in 1862. In that year a large number of Beta Israel inspired by a prophet set out for the Promised Land. Their attempt ended not in a miraculous crossing of the Red Sea, but in disaster and starvation. Many died, some straggled back to Gondar, others settled in Tigre especially in the Shire region. As time passed they acquired many of the characteristics of their Tigrean neighbors, most notably the language Tigrinya. Their economic situation and historical experience also diverge significantly from their brethren further south. During the late 19th and early 20th century contact between the Jews of Gondar and Tigre was irregular, and no common leadership united the two regions.

While the activities of the missionaries may have posed a serious challenge to the religious authority of the Beta Israel monks, this problem pales in comparison to the threat to their survival created by the great famine of 1888–1892. During this four year period Dervish invasions, rinderpest, drought, locusts, and disease devastated most of northern Ethiopia. It appears likely that between a third and a half of the Beta Israel died during this period. Those who survived left their normal places of residence and scattered far and wide. Traditional village life and the customary separation from non-Jews broke down in face of the danger of starvation. Beta Israel monks seem to have been especially hard hit. Certainly, none of the travelers who visited Ethiopia in the late 19th or early 20th century viewed them any longer as the central pillars of Beta Israel religiosity. Priests (*qessotch*) and elders had, by this time, become the new communal leaders.

1904–1936: Faitlovitch and His Students

The arrival of Jacques *Faitlovitch in Ethiopia in 1904 marks another turning point in the history of the Beta Israel. Although Faitlovitch's teacher, Joseph *Halévy, was the first practicing European Jew to visit the Beta Israel, it was only through the activities of Faitlovitch himself that they were slowly introduced into the mainstream of world Jewish history. He was moreover similarly instrumental in beginning the gradual trend towards the "normalization" of their religious belief and practice. Processes set in motion by Faitlovitch in the early 1900s were to reach their culmination in the *aliyah* of the majority of the Beta Israel in the decade of the 1980s.

Faitlovitch's activities were central for an understanding of the history of the Beta Israel in the 20th century even if his immediate effect on the majority of the Beta Israel population should not be overestimated. Either the symbolic impact of Faitlovitch's presence in the capital and his closeness to the *Negus* or the circulation of his letters written in Amharic, kept as precious relics by the families that possessed them, played a role creating imaginary links with the Jewish world among Beta Israel population living in the villages. The total number of students who studied in Addis Abeba. Asmara and small villages' schools Faitlovitch founded was never very large but information about new possibilities in education circulated even among distant villages.

Twenty-five young Beta Israel were educated mostly in Europe, ten in Palestine and 1 in Egypt. The boys were received by local Jewish communities and individual rabbis in different ways, sometimes strongly supported to adapt to the Western world and other times abandoned due to a lack of money, interest or commitment. Some of them contracted illnesses and died such as Solomon Isaac, Yizkiahu Finkas, Abraham Baroch, Abraham Meir. While, some students such as Ghetié Yirmiahu, Taamrat Emmanuel, and later Bayyu (Reuben) Isayyas, Menghestu Isaac, Taddesse Jacob and Yona Bogale used their education on behalf of their people, many never returned to the villages which they had left behind. Some of them took advantage of the opportunities they were offered when Haile Sellasse regained his power in 1941 and offered them to work in different ministries in Ethiopia. The primary significance of Faitlovitch's efforts for the Beta Israel political structure may well lie in his attempt to develop a new modernized elite. The fact that Faitlovitch was very paternalistic and authoritarian in his decisions regarding the fate of the young Beta Israel he brought to Europe, imposing the adoption of new Western Jewish codes and the abandon of the entire Beta Israel culture for sure influenced the behavior of the future Beta Israel elite that didn't always act as expected by Faitlovitch. Certainly, from Faitlovitch's time onward an ever-increasing gap existed between those perceived by outsiders as Ethiopian leaders and the internal realities of Beta Israel society. In part at least this gap reflects the differing rates of development between European and Ethiopian Jewry. The increasingly modernized and cosmopolitan world Jewish leadership sought their counterparts in Ethiopia and found them among Faitlovitch's students. Thus, a tiny group of urbanized, educated Beta Israel came to be seen as community representatives. At the same time in rural Ethiopia the priests and elders continued to dominate village life and a decentralized pattern of communal organization persisted. (T. Parfitt, E. Trevisan Semi (eds.) *The Beta Israel in Ethiopia and Israel*, Richmond (Surrey) 1999; T. Parfitt, E. Trevisan Semi (eds.), *The Beta Israel: the Birth of an Elite among the Jews of Ethiopia*, 2005)

[Steven Kaplan / Emanuela Trevisan Semi (2nd ed.)]

1935–1941: The Italian Conquest

The Italian invasion of Ethiopia in 1935/36 put a dramatic end to Faitlovitch's educational efforts. As Mussolini's troops approached Addis Ababa in the spring of 1936, the pupils of the Faitlovitch school took refuge in the French Legation. After Taamrat Emmanuel in 1937 was forced to flee the country Menghestu Isaac took his place as school's director. The Addis Ababa school continued to exist in bad conditions until the end of the occupation maintained by pupils working in the town. During the period of the Italian occupation a number of Beta Israel (such as Taamrat Emmanuel and Taddesse Jacob) distinguished themselves in the patriotic resistance. Others collaborated with the Italian authorities.

Since Italian policy towards the Beta Israel varied during the period of their occupation and was itself somewhat self-contradictory, its effects on community leadership and organization were complex. Although the Italians initially considered the possibility of pursuing a policy towards the Jews of Ethiopia similar to that exercised in Libya, it soon became clear to them that the absence of a formal community structure made this impossible. In the end they were forced to conclude that "if and when the Jews of Ethiopia will be organized in a community, they will be required to join the Union of Italian Jewish Communities." After promulgating "racial laws" in 1938 in Italy the Minister of Africa "no longer allowed the involvement of foreign Jewish organizations in the affairs of the Falashas" and there was no more an interest in that policy (D. Summerfield, *From Falashas to Ethiopian Jews: The External Influences for Change c.1860–1960*, London and New York, 2003, p.96). In the meantime, the Beta Israel were considered an oppressed tribal group "liberated" from the Christian Amhara. Bayyu (Reuben) Issayas, a former student with administrative experience, was appointed their chief and awarded the traditional Ethiopian title of *Gerazmach* (Commander of the Left Flank). The Italians appeared to have abolished the land restrictions that denied the Beta Israel to own land and established an area for Beta Israel to settle, near Gondar (Wuzeba and Ambober), linked by the building of roads. During the massacre of 120

Ethiopians in Mereba, a crime committed by the Italian occupants in 1937, thirty-two Beta Israel were killed (Taamrat's letter to Faitlovitch, 19.9.1937, in: E. Trevisan Semi, *L'epistolario di Taamrat Emmanuel: un intellettuale ebreo d'Etiopia nella prima metà del XX secolo* (Torino, 2000), 250–256.

1941–1974

Prior to the liberation of Ethiopia in 1941 only a handful of Western Jews had visited the Beta Israel. In the next three decades, their numbers were to swell dramatically. Trends which first became apparent in the period of Faitlovitch, such as outside intervention, education, and normalization of religious practice, escalated significantly. In a similar manner the pressure upon the Beta Israel to speak with one voice grew. The traditional religious leadership was increasingly challenged by Western-educated members of the community and contact with outsiders became an ever more important route to status.

No description of Beta Israel leadership and the influence of outside forces on community organization in the period after World War II would be complete without a discussion of the figure of Yona *Bogale. Born in Wolleqa, Gondar in 1910, Yona studied with Faitlovitch and Taamrat Emmanuel in Ethiopia. Later he pursued further studies in Jerusalem, Frankfurt, Zurich, and Paris. After his return to Ethiopia he worked as a teacher and a civil servant. In 1953 he left the imperial service and from that time on, until he left Ethiopia in 1979, he involved himself with various projects connected with the Beta Israel community.

During the more than 25 years of Ato Yona's activities as a spokesman for the Beta Israel, foreign involvement with the community in Ethiopia steadily increased. The Israel government, the Jewish Agency, ORT, JDC, political activists and casual travelers all made their impact felt upon the Jews of Ethiopia. From the perspective of the various Jewish organizations, which sought to aid their co-religionists in Ethiopia, the Beta Israel's lack of political unity and their tradition of village-level politics appeared inefficient and wasteful. In an attempt to rationalize and simplify the giving of assistance, such organizations sought to impose an artificial unity on the Beta Israel whereby a single individual represented all the communities and coordinated the distribution of assistance.

Despite, or perhaps because of, his unique background, Ato Yona came to represent the Beta Israel community to much of the outside world, especially to various Jewish organizations. As the interest and financial involvement of world Jewry with the Beta Israel grew, Ato Yona became a well-known and idealized figure. Yet, his position within the community was often a far cry from that depicted by outsiders.

Throughout the period of the 1970s, for example, an open dispute existed between Yona Bogale and the leading priest of the Gondar area, Abba Uri Ben (Berhan) Baruch. In part, the quarrel was based upon a disagreement as to how funds from the various "pro-Beta Israel" committees should be divided among different villages. However, it soon developed beyond this specific issue to a more general dispute over the nature of community leadership and society: a conflict between internal religious leadership and external/political power. On the one hand, the religious leader was known, trusted, and respected throughout the Gondar region; and on the other hand the political leader, was educated and experienced, and had gained prestige and influence through both the money he received from abroad, and the recognition of foreign committees.

The quarrel also appears to have had a generational component as well, for it pitted the young Israeli-educated Hebrew teachers against the priests and elders. In the words of Uri ben Baruch "the young teachers want to lead the people, but the priests and the head of the elders don't want to surrender their leadership… But, because the young teachers have access to the government, Beta Israel follow them, and only adults and the elderly continue to obey the priests as of old."

The divisions which arose in this case can as we have seen be analyzed on a variety of levels. Religious, political, and generational factors all appear to have been of relevance. There was, moreover, a minor geographical component insofar as the leadership struggle appears to have originated in the competition between villages for scarce resources. However, the importance of the geographical factor was relatively insignificant, when compared to the major role it assumed in the division between Amharan and Tigrean Beta Israel. In this case a major regional division developed whose repercussions are being felt to this day in Israel.

Despite the earlier visits of Faitlovitch and Rabbi Ḥayyim *Nahoum world Jewry remained largely ignorant of the Tigrean Jews. In a census undertaken in the 1950s the number of Jews in Tigre province was underestimated by more than two thirds (1,250 est. versus 4,000). Moreover, the Jews of Tigre benefited far less than those in the Gondar region from the relief and educational efforts of world Jewry. Thus existing social, economic, and linguistic differences were exacerbated by a growing gap in modernization, education, and secularization. By the time the Beta Israel were brought *en masse* to Israel in the 1980s (and here too the experience in the two regions varied tremendously) a latent hostility existed between many members of the Gondar and Tigrean communities.

[Steven Kaplan]

Developments in the Later 1970s

JEWISHNESS OF THE FALASHAS. The first major statement affirming the Jewishness of the Beta Israel was made in the 16th century by Rabbi David ibn Zimra, the Radbaz. After an intensive study, he declared the Beta Israel as "of the seed of Israel, of the Tribes of Dan." He further stated that marriage to one of the Beta Israel is permissible as long as that person accepts the more modern practices of rabbinic Judaism. And in later responsum, he became explicit and even more emphatic in stating the Beta Israel are unquestionably Jews.

Recognizing that the Beta Israel, because of their isolation, practiced a more biblical Judaism than the rabbinic Judaism of his time, the Radbaz wrote: "These who came from the land of Cush (Ethiopia) are without doubt of the Tribe of Dan and because there are not among them scholars, masters of tradition, they seize unto themselves the literal meaning of Scripture… they are as a child who has been held captive among idolators."

Thus spoke the great rabbi from Cairo, who lived in North Africa and was perhaps closer to the Beta Israel people and their issues than any rabbi of his time or since then.

After the Radbaz, a few other noted rabbis such as Rabbi Ya'akov Castro, also declared the Beta Israel as descendants of the Tribe of Dan. But it was not until Christian missionaries, especially the apostate Jew, Henry Stern, started to make inroads among the Beta Israel in the mid-19th century, that the western Jewish world once again became concerned about the Jews of Ethiopia.

It was the revered Rabbi Azriel Hildesheimer of Eisenstadt, founder of the Agudat Israel, who made a bold statement in favor of the Beta Israel in 1864. Rabbi Hildesheimer, described in the *Jewish Chronicle* as "one of the foremost leaders of the strictly orthodox party on the (European) continent," urged that a special mission be undertaken to them. "Do not lose courage, my brethren, but be full of confidence; never yet have the unfortunate knocked at the door of a Jewish house without having found assistance."

Yet little happened until the Alliance Israélite Universelle of Paris sent the semiticist Joseph *Halévy to investigate the situation in Ethiopia. Convinced that the Beta Israel were Jews by religion who wanted to be recognized as part of the Jewish people, Halévy inspired his pupil, Professor Jacques *Faitlovitch, to concern himself with the Beta Israel.

Faitlovitch, who probably more than any other single person was responsible for keeping interest in the Beta Israel alive, obtained a very important document. It was a letter written in 1906 addressed to the Beta Israel as "our brethren, sons of Abraham, Isaac, and Jacob, who dwell in Abyssinia." It refers to the Beta Israel as "our flesh and blood," and it assures them of help in religious education. It expressed hope that G-d" will gather us from the four corners of the earth and bring us to Zion." The letter was signed by 44 leading rabbis from Europe, America and Egypt. Included in the list were Herman Adler (Chief Rabbi of London), H. Gaster, S. Daiches, Moritz Gudemann (Chief Rabbi of Vienna), Raphael Meir Panigel (Sephardi Chief Rabbi of Jerusalem and of Palestine), and Jacob Reines of Russia (the first head of the Mizrachi movement).

Among the many documents Faitlovitch obtained was a letter, dated December 4, 1921, from Abraham Isaac *Kook, the highly respected Ashkenazi chief rabbi of Palestine. Rav Kook called out to World Jewry "to save our Beta Israel brethren from extinction and contamination… and to rescue 50,000 holy souls of the House of Israel from oblivion. A holy obligation rests upon our entire nation to raise funds with a generous hand to improve the lot of the Falashas in Ethiopia and to bring their young children to Jewish centers in Palestine and the Diaspora…"

It was on February 9, 1973, that the plight of the Ethiopian Jews was brought once more to the attention of world Jewry. Rabbi Ovadiah *Yosef, Sephardi chief rabbi of Israel, in a letter addressed to Mr. Ovadia Hazi, former spokesman for the Ethiopian Jews living in Israel, gave a ruling on the status of the Beta Israel as Jews according to the *halakhah*.

After quoting the views of a number of eminent religious authorities, including those of the Radbaz, Rabbi Hildesheimer, and the Ashkenazi chief rabbis of Israel, Rabbi Abraham Isaac Kook and Isaac Halevi *Herzog, in favor of their being in fact Jews, Rabbi Ovadiah Yosef wrote:

> I have therefore come to the conclusion that Falashas are descendants of the Tribe of Israel who went southward to Ethiopia, and there is no doubt that the above sage established that they (the Falashas) are of the Tribe of Dan… and (these sages) relached the conclusion on the basis of the most reliable witnesses and evidence.
>
> I, too… have investigated and inquired well into… (these matters)… and have decided that in my humble opinion, the Falashas are Jews, whom it is our duty to redeem from assimilation, to hasten their immigration to Israel, to educate them in the spirit of our holy Torah and to make them partners in the building of our sacred land…
>
> I am certain that the government institutions and the Jewish Agency, as well as organizations in Israel and the diaspora, will help us to the best of our ability in this holy task… the mitzva of redeeming the souls of our people… for everyone who saves one soul in Israel, it is as though he had saved the whole world.

Rabbi Ovadia Yosef's letter refers to the Beta Israel as descendants of the Tribe of Dan. Support for this view can be traced back as far as the 9th century C.E. in the writings of the Jewish traveler Eldad Ha-Dani. Such rabbinic luminaries as Rashi cite Eldad as an unquestioned authority on these issues.

On March 11, 1975, it was reported that an Interministerial Committee had ruled that Israel recognized the Ethiopian Jews entitled to automatic citizenship and full benefits as prescribed under the 1950 Law of Return.

Chief Ashkenazi Rabbi Shlomo Goren expressed disapproval of this ruling, but after the winter of 1978 when he met a group of new immigrants from Ethiopia with the greeting, "You are our brothers; you are our blood and our flesh. You are true Jews… You have returned to your homeland," he too joined the ranks of the long list of rabbis affirming the Jewishness of the Beta Israel.

Nonetheless, Rabbis Yosef and Goren requested a symbolic ceremony which is called a *ḥidush ha-yahadut*, meaning "renewal of Judaism." This ceremony consists of a ritual immersion without the necessity of a blessing for the women. The men are also immersed because they are already circumcised. They need only a ceremonial *milah*.

This symbolic ceremony is not a conversion. It does not require any study period. The rabbis request that it be done within a few days of the Ethiopian Jews' arrival in Israel. Rabbi Ovadia Yosef expressed it best when he defined the ceremony as "an act of renewing their covenant with the Jewish people" (*Jerusalem Post*, August 1977).

Some Ethiopian Jews, who have suffered much as a people to preserve their Judaism against almost insurmountable odds, felt the ceremony was an insult. Nonetheless, all went through with it until 1985 when they started to oppose to it. This opposition culminated in a month-long strike in the autumn of 1985 that ended with an agreement (S. Kaplan "The Beta Israel and the Rabbinate: Law, Politics and Ritual," *Social Science Information* 27, 3, 1988, pp. 357–70). Nevertheless this issue continued to be considered very sensitive and when in 1989 rabbi David Chelouche was appointed marriage registrar for all Ethiopians in the country the question was settled by a compromise: "Since he did not believe that Ethiopians needed to undergo any form of conversion, those married under his auspices were exempted from any preconditions not imposed on other Israelis" (S. Kaplan and H. Salomon, "Ethiopian Jews in Israel: a Part of the people or Apart from the people?" in U. Rebhun and C. Waxman (eds.), *Jews in Israel: Contemporary Social and Cultural Patterns*, Hanover and London, 2003, pp. 118–148: 131)

[Howard M. Lenhoff / E. Trevisan Semi (2nd ed.)]

ORGANIZATIONAL EFFORTS. In the U.S. during April 1974, the old American Pro-Beta Israel Committee started by Professor Jacques Faitlovitch and another committee merged to form the American Association for Ethiopian Jews. This new organization, founded by Dr. Graenum Berger, has brought the plight of the Ethiopian Jews to the forefront of issues in American Jewry, and supports many absorption programs in Israel. Also in the U.S., the National Jewish Community Relations Advisory Council in 1980 formed a Committee on Ethiopian Jewry.

In 1977, the ORT World Union established a nonsecular training program in Addis Ababa and in the province of Gondar that affected a number of Ethiopian Jews.

ETHIOPIAN JEWS IN ISRAEL. In Israel, the Ethiopian Jews demonstrated against the government, the Jewish Agency and world Jewish leadership on January 1, 1979, and again on October 30, 1979, for not doing enough to bring their people to Israel. Following these demonstrations, Prime Minister Begin met with the leaders of the Ethiopian Jews of Israel and pledged his full support to save their people and to bring them to Israel. Renewed demonstrations took place in December 1981. At the end of the 1970s there were about 1,000 Ethiopian Jewish residents of Israel, whereas estimates of the number of Beta Israel remaining in war-torn Ethiopia ranged from 20,000 to 25,000.

[Howard M. Lenhoff]

1982–1992

In a decade of dramatic changes for World Jewry, the Beta Israel stood out as the Jewish community that had undergone the most dramatic transformation. At the end of 1982 the number of Ethiopian immigrants in Israel stood at about 2,300 and the vast majority of community members were still in Ethiopia. Ten years later the Beta Israel as a diaspora community had ceased to exist. By the end of 1992 over 45,000 Ethiopian immigrants had settled in Israel. When those born in Israel are included and those who have died subtracted, the total number of Ethiopian Jews in Israel exceeds 50,000. (See Table: Ethiopian Jews in Israel).

Despite the relatively short period within which the Beta Israel were brought to Israel, each period in their immigration had different characteristics. Most of those who came prior to 1984 were from the Tigre and Walqayit regions of northern Ethiopia. They arrived in small numbers through the Sudan and were gradually settled throughout Israel. In 1984 over ten thousand Jews from the Gondar region of Ethiopia flooded into Sudanese refugee camps. Initially they were brought out a few hundred at a time, but deteriorating conditions necessitated a more dramatic approach. During a period of less than two months starting in mid-November 1984, more than 6,500 Beta Israel were airlifted to Israel in what became known as "Operation Moses." Premature publicity brought the operation to a halt, but in March 1985 a further 650 Jews were rescued in "Operation Joshua." During the period from March 1985 to October 1989 only a relatively small number of Jews managed to leave Ethiopia. The renewal of diplomatic relations between Israel and Ethiopia, however, paved the way for legal emigration on the basis of family reunification. By the summer of 1990 over twenty thousand Ethiopian Jews had migrated to Addis Ababa in the hope of being taken to Israel. During 36 hours between May 24 and 25 as rebel troops threatened to conquer the capital, over 14,000 Beta Israel were airlifted to Israel in "Operation Solomon." In the succeeding year and a half, several thousand more Beta Israel were brought to Israel. By the end of 1992 only a handful of Beta Israel remained in Ethiopia. A large number (estimates vary between 30–250,000) of *falas moura* (Christians of Beta Israel descent) remained in Ethiopia.

Although all the Beta Israel have left Ethiopia, their resettlement in Israel is far from complete. Virtually every aspect of their absorption process remains fraught with difficulties, and a clear danger exists that Ethiopian Jews in Israel will find themselves marginalized geographically, socially, and religiously.

Despite clearly stated criteria for dispersing Ethiopian immigrants around the country, settling them in permanent apartments has always proven difficult. Housing in the designated sites has not always been available, while local authorities and residents have not necessarily welcomed the influx of a dependent population. For their part the Ethiopians have been reluctant to abandon the protection of immigrant housing and have often refused to do so unless provided with housing that meets all of their criteria regarding cost, proximity to relatives, climate, and employment opportunities. Only after immigrants have been settled in permanent apartments can issues such as children's education and long-term employment be seriously confronted.

As of September 1992 almost half the Ethiopian immigrants in the country were still in temporary housing: 2,500 were in hotels, 7,600 were in regular absorption centers, and 15,000 were living in mobile homes. Each of these groups presents officials with a different set of difficulties, but the last is probably the most problematic. Mobile homes for Ethiopian immigrants (as well as a relatively small number of Russians and veteran Israelis) were situated in 22 sites around the country. Most were located in isolated areas far removed from other Israelis, schools, and employment opportunities. It was anticipated that many immigrants would continue to live in such quarters for at least 3 or 4 years.

So long as the Ethiopians remained in temporary quarters, it was extremely difficult to complete their educational, social, and occupational absorption. Although official statistics were never released, it was generally estimated that prior to 1991, 80% of Ethiopian immigrants eligible for work had found jobs. Those who have arrived in the following two years had a much harder time finding employment both because of their geographic isolation and difficult conditions in the Israeli economy.

Although more than two decades have passed since Rabbi Ovadiah Yosef (at the time Sephardi chief rabbi) ruled that the Beta Israel were Jews, many details of their religious status remain unresolved. Despite recurrent demonstrations and court appeals, most Israeli marriage registrars continue to follow the Chief Rabbinate's guidelines and require Ethiopian immigrants wishing to marry to undergo ritual immersion. Rabbi David Chelouche of Netanya and other rabbis designated by him require no such ceremony and continue to perform weddings for Ethiopian Jews throughout the country. Some Ethiopian activists have demanded that *qessotch* (priests), the community's religious leaders, be allowed to conduct weddings and perform divorces as in Ethiopia. The Chief Rabbinate has firmly rejected this demand. Instead it has agreed to allow the *qessotch* to serve on religious councils in areas with large Ethiopian populations and has suggested that they study to become marriage registrars.

The ongoing controversy concerning marriages and the status of the *qessotch* is not merely a halakhic-legal issue. It is also symptomatic of the vast changes that have shaken the Ethiopian family in the past decade. Couples have divorced and remarried, children have asserted an unprecedented degree of independence, and women have redefined their roles. Changes have, moreover, not been limited to the restructuring of relations within the family. The family's relationship to the surrounding society has also been radically changed. In Ethiopia families and households were the foundation of rural communal life and served as schools, workshops, clinics, reformatories, and credit organizations. In Israel most of these functions have become the primary responsibility of other institutions. Thus, the past decade has witnessed not only a dramatic and irreversible change of location (in a geographic sense) for the Ethiopian family. It has also produced a no less revolutionary transformation of its place (in a social-economic sense) and its relationship to its surroundings.

[Steven Kaplan]

1992–2005

The Ethiopian Jews continued to undergo dramatic changes in a very short period of time. In 2005 there were approximately 85,000 in Israel, of whom 23,000 were Israeli-born. Official Israeli absorption policy aimed to prevent the development of Ethiopian ghettos and thus encouraged Ethiopians not to concentrate in the same areas and to purchase homes in towns where employment and social services were available. This policy failed to some extent because immigrants wished to be housed near relatives and chose to live were it was cheapest, often preferring not to leave absorption centers. In 1993 the Ministry of Absorption initiated a special program to encourage immigrants to buy houses and apply for mortgages outside peripheral areas. Between 1988 and 2001, 10,542 Ethiopians purchased apartments with the help of government mortgages. If the special mortgage program permitted many Ethiopian families to own their homes, the goal of settling them in the center of the country was not achieved, because the Ethiopians concentrated in a few selected areas while Jerusalem and Tel Aviv remained with very small Ethiopian populations.

The State acted in the process of absorption of Ethiopians according to a model of "mediated absorption" and the Jewish Agency was responsible for the process. This policy encouraged employees to treat immigrants as a social problem, which led immigrants to conform to expectations and behave accordingly. In 1999 there were 14,778 Ethiopians aged 25–54 in the country but only 53 percent participated in the labor force (compared to 76 percent of all Israelis of the same age). Only 38 percent of the Ethiopians in the labor force were women (compared to 68 percent of all Israeli women). Most of the Ethiopians were employed in manufacturing (especially men) and in public services (especially women). Few of the Ethiopians were in academic and liberal professions (4 percent of men and 15 percent of women).

The Israeli education system planned to have all young Ethiopians attend state religious schools in the first year of their arrival. Government policy sought to restrict the percentage of Ethiopian students in classes to no more than 25 percent, but this program too was not achieved. Many students went to *Youth Aliyah boarding schools.

In 1996 *Maariv* revealed that the Magen David Adom blood bank had for years systematically thrown out blood donated by Ethiopian Israelis without informing the donors. This occurred because Ethiopian immigrants were considered a high-risk group for AIDS (especially those who arrived in Operation Solomon). The "blood scandal" was accompanied by many demonstrations covered by the international media and by a commission of enquiry. At the outset of the 21st century the absorption of Ethiopian Jews remained the most problematic, economically, socially, and culturally, among all immigrant groups.

[E. Trevisan Semi (2nd ed.)]

BIBLIOGRAPHY: W. Leslau (ed.), *Beta Israel Anthology; Black Jews of Ethiopia* (1951), incl. bibl.; A.Z. Aescoly, *Sefer ha-Falashim* (1943); idem, *Recueil de Textes Falachas* (1951); C. Conti Rossini, in: *Rivista degli Studi Orientali*, 8 (1919–20), 563–610; idem, in: *Rendiconti della Reale Accademia Nazionale dei Lincei*, 31 (1922), 221–40; J. Faïtlovitch, *Notes d'un Voyage chez les Falachas* (1905); idem, *Mota Musē* (Heb. and Fr., 1906); J. Halévy (ed.) *Tēēzaza Sanbat* (Fr. and Ethiopian, 1902); C. Rathjens, *Die Juden in Abessinien* (1921); L. Stein, *Die Juden in Abessinien* (1851); H.A. Stern, *Wanderings among the Falashas in Abyssinia* (1862, 1968^2); E. Ullendorff, *The Ethiopians* (1960); idem, in: *Bulletin of the School of Oriental and African Studies, University of London*, 24 (1961), 419–43; M. Wurmbrand, *ibid.*, 25 (1962), 431–7; idem, in: JA, 242 (1954), 83–100; idem, in: *L'Orient Syrien*, 8 (1963), 343–94; C.A. Viterbo, in: *Annuario di Studi Ebraici* (1935–37), 113–23; F. Altheim and R. Stiehl, *Araber in der Alten Welt*, 1 (1964), 127–30; 3 (1966), 18–21, 22; 5 pt. 1 (1968), 2, 133. **ADD. BIBLIOGRAPHY:** L. Anteby-Yemini, *Les Juifs éthiopiens en Israel: les paradoxes du paradis* (2004); E. Hertzog, *Immigrants and Bureaucrats: Ethiopians in an Israeli Absorption Center* (1999); S. Kaplan, "Black and White, Blue and White and Beyond the Pale: Ethiopian Jews and the Discourse of Color in Israel," in: *Jewish Culture and History*, 5, 1 (Summer 2002), 51–68; S. Kaplan and H. Salomon, "Ethiopian Jews in Israel: a Part of the People or Apart from the People?" in: U. Rebhun and C. Waxman (eds.), *Jews in Israel: Contemporary Social and Cultural Patterns* (2003), 118–48; T. Parfitt and E. Trevisan Semi (eds.) *The Beta Israel in Ethiopia and Israel: Studies on the Ethiopian Jews* (1999); idem (eds.), *The Beta Israel: the Birth of an Elite among the Jews of Ethiopia* (2005); T. Shwartz, *Ethiopian Jewish Immigrants: the Homeland Postponed* (2001); Sh. Swirski and B. Swirski, "Ethiopian Israelis: Housing, Employment, Education," in: *The Israel Equality Monitor*, 11 (June 2002), 1–45: E. Trevisan Semi, "Hazkarah, a Symbolic Day for the Refoundation of the Jewish Ethiopian-Community," in: *Jewish Political Science Review*, 17, 1–2 (Spring 2005); Sh. Weil, "Religion, Blood and the Equality of Rights: the Case of Ethiopian Jews in Israel," in: *International Journal on Minority and Group Rights*, 4 (1997), 397–412.

BET ALFA (Heb. בֵּית אַלְפָא), place in Israel in the eastern Jezreel Valley at the foot of Mount Gilboa. The name is historical and has been preserved in the Arab designation of the site, Beit Ilfa, which may have some connection with the proper name Ilfa or Hilfa which occurs in the Talmud (Ta'an. 21a). The foundations of an ancient synagogue were discovered in 1929 near Bet Alfa by E.L. *Sukenik and N. *Avigad, who were conducting excavations on behalf of the Hebrew University. The synagogue covered an area of 46 × 92 ft. (14 × 28 m) and included a courtyard, narthex, basilica-type hall with a nave and two side aisles, and, apparently, a women's gallery. The apse at the end of the hall was oriented south toward Jerusalem, and a small cavity in its floor probably served as a *genizah*; above it once stood an ark for Scrolls of the Law. The entire floor of the structure is paved with mosaics: the courtyard, narthex, and aisles in simple geometric designs, while the floor of the nave is decorated with mosaic panels surrounded by a broad ornamental border. Two inscriptions were found at the entrance to the hall: one (in Aramaic) states that the mosaic was made during the reign of Emperor Justin (undoubtedly Justin I, 518–27); the other (in Greek) gives the names of the mosaicists, *Marianos and his son Ḥanina. Symbolic animals are depicted on either side of the inscriptions: a lion on the right and a bull on the left. The three mosaic panels in the center of the hall depict (from north to south): (1) *The Offering of Isaac*, which shows Abraham pointing a drawn knife at Isaac who is bound near an altar; behind Abraham a ram is tied to a tree, and alongside it appears the inscription "And behold a ram." The hand of God is seen between the sun's rays above; Abraham's two servants and donkey stand behind him; a band of palm trees separate this scene from the next one. (2) *The Signs of the Zodiac*, with the sun in the center in the form of a youth riding a chariot drawn by four horses; each sign has its Hebrew designation inscribed above it. In the corners appear the four seasons of the year (Tishri, Tevet, Nisan, Tammuz), each in the form of the bust of a winged woman adorned with jewels. (3) *The Ark of the Synagogue*, in which the ark has a gable roof with an "eternal light" suspended from its top and two birds perched at its corners; on either side is a lion with a seven-branched *menorah* (candelabrum) and above it and between them are depicted *lulavim* (palm branches), *etrogim* (citrons), a *shofar*, and censers. Curtains adorn the scene on the left and right sides.

The simple but strong style of the mosaic pavement represents a folk art that appears to have developed among the Jewish villagers of Galilee. The figures are depicted frontally and the artist took great pains to make each scene expressive. The mosaics of Bet Alfa are striking in their coloring and stylization and are among the finest examples of Jewish art in the Byzantine period. In 1960 the synagogue structure was renovated and the pavement repaired by the Israel Government.

[Michael Avi-Yonah]

The kibbutz of Bet Alfa was founded in 1922 by pioneers from Poland. It was the first settlement of the Kibbutz Arẓi ha-Shomer ha-Ẓa'ir movement. For over 14 years it was the easternmost village of the Jewish region in the central valleys and was exposed to Arab attacks in the 1936–39 riots. In 1968 it numbered 670 inhabitants, in the mid 1990 its population increased to 785 residents, and at the end of 2002 it was 589. Its economy is based on intensive and diversified farming (field crops, dairy cattle, and fishery) and industry (thermostats, trailers, and a quarry).

[Efraim Orni]

BIBLIOGRAPHY: E.L. Sukenik, *Ancient Synagogue of Beth Alpha* (1932); N. Avigad, *Bikat Beit She'an* (1964), 63–70; E.R. Goodenough, *Jewish Symbols in the Greco-Roman Period*, 1 (1953), 241–53; Roth, Art, 209–13.

BET(H)-ANATH (Heb. בֵּית עֲנָת), Canaanite city named after the goddess Anath. Beth-Anath may possibly be mentioned in the list of cities conquered by Thutmosis III in c. 1469 B.C.E.

(no. 97) but it definitely appears in the records of the campaigns of both Seti I in c. 1300 B.C.E. (between Tyre and Kadesh) and of Rameses II in c. 1280 B.C.E. (before Kanah). Although it is listed with the cities in the territory of the tribe of *Naphtali (Josh. 19:38), this tribe could not overcome it and only imposed tribute on the inhabitants (Judg. 1:33). Some scholars locate it in Lower Galilee at Bu'eina in the valley of Beth-Netophah or at el-Bina in the Bet ha-Kerem valley, but the archaeological survey makes a location in Upper Galilee more probable and its identification with Safd el-Batikh has been suggested. In talmudic times a Beth-Anath is mentioned as a city outside Ereẓ Israel with a mixed Jewish-gentile population (Tosef., Kil. 2:16). The Zeno Papyri from 259 B.C.E. contain a reference to a vineyard at Baitoanaia. It has also been suggested that the Batnaea mentioned by Eusebius (Onom. 30:5; 52:24) refers to the same site. (If so, the Caesarea 15 mi. (24 km.) distant would be Caesarea Philippi.)

BIBLIOGRAPHY: Aharoni, Land, index; Avi-Yonah, Land, 143; EM, 2 (1965), 96f.; Press, Ereẓ, 1 (1951^2), 95–96; S. Lieberman, *Tosefta ki-Feshutah, Zera'im* (1955), 620.

[Michael Avi-Yonah]

BETAR (abbreviated name of **Berit Trumpeldor**, Heb. ,בֵּיתָ"ר בְּרִית תְּרוּמְפֶּלְדוֹר), an activist Zionist youth movement founded in 1923 in Riga, Latvia, and attaining significant proportions in the 1930s, mainly in Eastern Europe. Betar played an important role in Zionist education, in teaching the Hebrew language and culture, and methods of self-defense. It also inculcated the ideals of *aliyah* to Ereẓ Israel by any means, legal and "illegal," and of personal dedicaton to the creation of a Jewish state "on both sides of the Jordan." The Betar ideology originated in a fusion of Vladimir *Jabotinsky's "legionism" with the ideas of personal pioneering and defense exemplified in Joseph *Trumpeldor's life and death.

1923–1935

At its inception Betar was a variation of the Zionist trend in East European Jewish youth that led to the Third Aliyah. The group of students and young workers that founded the movement declared themselves a "part of the Jewish Legion to be established in Ereẓ Israel." They organized a farm for the agricultural training of pioneer settlers in Palestine. The first Betar immigrants to Palestine (1925–29) joined the Histadrut and the Haganah as a matter of course. In the 1930s, however, with the growing rift and exacerbated conflict between the Revisionists and the Zionist-Socialist majority, Betar gradually became a bitter rival of Zionist-Socialist youth, both in the Diaspora and in Palestine. Sometimes relations deteriorated into physical clashes on the streets of Tel Aviv. Zionist-Socialist circles pointed to the brown shirts of the members of Betar as tangible proof of its "fascist character," and called for its speedy elimination from public life, whereas Betar spokesmen asserted that the "red-brown" shade of their uniform symbolized the earth of Ereẓ Israel, and in any event its adoption in the early 1920s preceded the rise of the German Nazis.

Betar members constituted a major part of the rank and file of the Union of Zionist Revisionists (from 1935, the New Zionist Organization) and also of the National Labor Federation and the *Irgun Ẓeva'i Le'ummi in Palestine. In 1926 the second world congress of the Union of Zionist Revisionists in Paris recognized the Latvian group as the sponsor and provisional center of its youth movement. The first world conference of Betar, which convened in Danzig in 1931 with 87 delegates representing 21 countries, formulated the principles of the movement and elected Jabotinsky as *rosh Betar* ("head of Betar"), empowering him to appoint the overall leadership ("*shilton*").

Defense training was proclaimed the foremost duty of every member, and those going to Palestine were to enlist for two years in special work brigades. At the second world conference of Betar in Cracow, in 1935, Jabotinsky proposed a codified text of the Betar ideology called *Ha-Neder* ("the Oath"), which stipulated in its first paragraph: "I devote my life to the rebirth of the Jewish State, with a Jewish majority, on both sides of the Jordan." It demanded, in addition to the basic tenets of all Zionist youth movements, a "monistic" conception of Zionism, rejecting any fusion with "alien" creeds (meaning mainly socialism). It also urged the inculcation of a mode of thought and deed called *hadar*, defined by Jabotinsky as "beauty, respect, self-esteem, politeness, and faithfulness."

Betar in Palestine

In Palestine the Betar work brigades (from 1934 called mobilized groups) grew into a network of disciplined units based in villages and settlements. Most of these were in Upper Galilee but, after the outbreak of the Arab riots in 1936, such units were established also in the Jewish quarter of the Old City of Jerusalem and at Naḥalat Yiẓḥak, near Jerusalem. These groups engaged in clandestine defense training within the framework of Irgun Ẓeva'i Le'ummi, maintaining themselves collectively as laborers on the farms of old-time Jewish settlers or as wage earners in town. Some members eventually formed the nuclei of the first Betar settlements (Ramat Tiomkin near Netanyah, Tel Ẓur near Binyaminah, and in Mishmar ha-Yarden).

Systematic defense training was introduced in Betar in many Diaspora countries during the early 1930s by Yirmiyahu Halpern, who established training courses and camps where self-defense, drill, street-fighting, the handling of small arms, boxing, and military tactics were taught. In Poland members of Betar also underwent training in the official paramilitary units of the state. In Shanghai Betar members organized a separate Jewish unit as part of the international force which policed the non-Chinese sections of the city.

The first Betar instructors' school was set up in Tel Aviv in 1928 and its trainees took part in the defense of the city during the riots of 1929. In 1931 Betar units joined dissident Haganah members in Jerusalem in setting up the separate underground organization Irgun Ẓeva'i Leummi. In 1930 a Betar naval unit was founded in Tel Aviv, training with sailboats. A central naval school of Betar was established in Civitavecchia, Italy, functioning there from 1934 to 1937 and graduating 153 cadets. About 50 sailors were also trained by Betar in Latvia between 1935 and 1939. These men later played important roles in the establishment of the Israel Navy and the Merchant Marine. In 1935 Jabotinsky's son Eri, heading a unit of mobilized Betar members in Palestine, constructed the first glider in the country. Flying courses were introduced later by the Irgun Ẓeva'i Le'ummi in Palestine; by 1939, 13 members had graduated as pilots.

Betar underwent rapid expansion during the 1930s as illustrated by the growth of its total world membership from 22,300 in 1931 to nearly 90,000 in 1938. In the late 1930s Betar was actively engaged in the Revisionists' "illegal" *aliyah* operation which, by 1939, took thousands of Jews to Palestine, among them many members of Betar. During World War II many Betar members in Palestine volunteered for the Palestinian units of the British Army and, later, the Jewish Brigade.

After the Holocaust

Most of the European branches of Betar were destroyed in the Holocaust. A few thousand members escaped by joining the anti-Nazi partisans, while Betar and Revisionist units took part in the ghetto uprisings, notably in Warsaw, Vilna, and Bialystok. With the loss of European Jewry, Israel became the center of the movement, which in the late 1960s numbered about 8,000 members, of whom over 4,000 were in Israel, and the rest in 13 other countries, mainly in Latin America, the United States, South Africa, and Australia. By the early 21st century its membership had grown to around 12,500 in Israel and 8,500 in the rest of the world.

Many members of Betar in Israel, upon joining the army, went into *Naḥal units. The movement in Israel also maintains youth towns in collaboration with *Youth Aliyah. Between 1948 and the late 1960s Betar, in cooperation with the Ḥerut movement, established 12 collective and cooperative settlements, some of them border settlements, such as Amaẓyah in the Lachish area, Mevo Betar near the site of historical *Bethar, *Ramat Raziel in the hills of Jerusalem, and Ẓur Natan in Central Israel.

Betar's membership in Palestine grew rapidly and by 1937 it had its own sports center which enabled its members to play, among other sports, football, basketball, and table tennis, engage in gymnastics, and train as boxers. Betar in Israel is affiliated with the Israel Football Association and the Israel Sports Federation.

BIBLIOGRAPHY: H. Ben Yeruḥam, *Sefer Betar, Korot u-Mekorot*, 1 (1969); Brith Trumpeldor, *This is Betar* (1956[2]); J.B. Schechtman, *V. Jabotinsky Story*, 2 vols. (1956–61); B. Lubotzky, *Ha-Ẓohar u-Vetar* (1946); E. Even, *Songs of Betar* (1966); Brith Trumpeldor, *Generation to Generation* (1958); D. Niv, *Ma'arekhot ha-Irgun ha-Ẓeva'i ha-Le'ummi*, 3 vols. (1965–67), passim.

[David Niv]

BET(H)-ARABAH (modern Bet ha-Aravah) (Heb. בֵּית הָעֲרָבָה; "House of the Steppe"), place in southern Ereẓ Israel, in the Jericho Desert of the Lower Jordan Valley. The ancient name is preserved in ʿAyn al-Gharaba, southeast of Jericho near the Jordan River, but no corroborative archaeological remains have been thus far discovered in the vicinity. According to the Bible it belonged to the tribe of Judah on the border of Benjamin (Josh. 15:61; 18:22). More recently it was a kibbutz situated 1,235 ft. (380 m.) below sea level, 1.8 mi. (3 km.) north of the Jordan mouth of the Dead Sea. It was founded on Oct. 8, 1939, by a group of the Maḥanot ha-Olim youth movement and young immigrants from Germany and other Central European countries, on land of the Palestine Potash Company. Bet ha-Aravah was affiliated with Ha-Kibbutz ha-Me'uḥad. The kibbutz succeeded in sweeping its extremely saline soil with fresh Jordan water, making it capable of producing abundant farm crops. The land thus won yielded out-of-season vegetables, fruit, fodder, and other farm products. Carp ponds were also installed. A number of members worked in the potash plant. Members of the kibbutz cultivated friendly relations with the Arab inhabitants of Jericho and even with the nearby villages of Transjordan. Bet ha-Aravah proved that both adults and children could overcome the health hazards of the torrid climate. In the Israel War of Independence (1948) the completely isolated settlement held out for six months. Eventually the settlers were evacuated by boat to Sodom, at the south end of the Dead Sea. Later its members erected two new settlements in Galilee, *Kabri and *Gesher ha-Ziv. The Arab Legion completely razed the empty settlement. Its soil again became saline and hardly any vestige of the village could be discerned when Israel forces reached the site in 1967. The following year a *Naḥal group set up a new settlement, Naḥal Kallia, in the general vicinity. In 1977 another Naḥal group settled about a mile (2 km.) west of the original settlement. In 1986 it was affiliated with Ha-Kibbutz ha-Me'uḥad. In 2002 the population of Beit ha-Aravah was 52. The main economic branch was farming, mainly dates, vineyards, and field crops. In addition, the kibbutz operated a food stall at its nearby gas station.

BIBLIOGRAPHY: Abel, Geog, 2 (1938), 267; EM, s.v.; Aharoni, Land, 235,302. **WEBSITE:** www.megilot.org.il/arava.htm.

[Efraim Orni]

BET(H)-CHEREM (Heb. בֵּית הַכֶּרֶם, "*Bet ha-Kerem*," "The House of the Vineyard"), settlement west of Jerusalem in the First and Second Temple periods. It is first mentioned at the time of the Judean kingdom in an appendix of the Septuagint to the list of Judean cities in Joshua 15:49 (as Karem), situated between Suba (Tzova), Gallim (Beth Jala), Baither (Battir) and Manahath (Malcha). Judging by a passage in Jeremiah (6:1), the town was the capital of the district west of Jerusalem in the Iron Age, where beacons were lit in times of danger. Jeremiah warned of the pending destruction from the north with the approach of the Babylonians: "O ye Children of Benjamin [in the north], gather yourselves to flee out of the midst of Jerusalem, and to blow the trumpet in Tekoa [in the south], and to set up a sign of fire [i.e., beacons, *massa'ot*] in Beth-Cherem [in the west]; for evil appeareth out of the north, and great destruction." Jeremiah referred specifically in this passage to the ultimate territory of Jerusalem (a radius of five kilometers around the city), demarcated specifically by the furthermost sites of Tekoa and Beth-Cherem, to the south and west, respectively, and with the northern limit set at the border between Judah and Benjamin (probably at Gibeah/Tell el-Ful). It again appears during the time of Nehemiah as the center of one of the Judean districts; Malchijah, son of Rechab, the ruler of the district of Beth-Cherem, took part in building the walls of Jerusalem under Nehemiah (Neh. 3:14). The valley of Beth-Cherem appearing in later sources should apparently be sought next to the town. According to the Mishnah (Mid. 3:4: Biq'at Beth-Cherem), the stones for the temple altar and its ramp were brought from the valley of Beth-Cherem (Ex. 20:25 (JPS 20:22); Deut. 27:5–6). The fertile valley in the proximity of Ain Karim was also noted as a source of a specific kind of flat stone, still seen there today. Elsewhere we hear that the bright color of the valley soils was discussed by the sages in reference to menstrual blood (Niddah 2:7). The town and its valley are also mentioned in two Dead Sea Scrolls from the end of the Second Temple period. In the Genesis Aprocryphon on Genesis 14:17, the "vale of Shaveh – the same is the King's Vale" is thought by some scholars to be the same as "the valley of Beth-Karma." The Copper Scroll, which contains a list of hiding places for treasure, describes Beth-Cherem as a depository for treasure in a large water system (*asyw*). In Jerome's commentary on Jeremiah 6:1 (from the fifth century C.E.), Bethacharma is incorrectly situated on a mountain between Jerusalem and Tekoa. An attempt was made by Y. Aharoni to identify Beth Cherem with Ramat Rahel – a site which he excavated – in southern Jerusalem, based mainly on Jerome's misidentification.

Beth-Cherem should be identified as Ain Karim ("spring of the vineyard"), situated within the western suburbs of modern Jerusalem. In antiquity it was a major town in the hills east of a broad valley basin, with excellent sources of natural water and surrounded by rich agricultural lands. The main spring, known as the Spring of the Virgin, provided 1,135 cubic meters of water per day. Archaeological finds in the present village date back to the Middle Bronze Age II, Iron Age II and Persian periods. Later remains from the Roman, Byzantine and medieval parts are also known. Ain Karim is important in Christian sources as the birthplace of John the Baptist. Two churches in the village – the Nativity and the Visitation – are associated with the tradition of John the Baptist. In the hinterland is the traditional Monastery of John in the Wilderness, and nearby recent excavations have uncovered a Byzantine memorial cave dedicated to the Baptist, with earlier remains connected to baptism rituals dating back to the Roman period.

BIBLIOGRAPHY: M.T. Petrozzi, *Ain Karim* (1971); 392–93 in Z. Kallai, *Historical Geography of the Bible: The Tribal Territories of Israel* (1986); Y. Aharoni, "Beth-Haccerem," 171–84 in T.D. Winton (ed.), *Archaeology and Old Testament Study: Jubilee Volume of the Society for Old Testament Study 1917–1967* (1967); Y. Tsafrir, L. Di Segni, and J. Green (eds.), *Tabula Imperii Romani. Iudaea – Palaestina: Maps and Gazetteer* (1994), 82; M. Piccirillo, "Ain Karim: les sanctuaries de l'enfance de Jean," *Le Monde de la Bible*, 89:24–5; S. Gibson, *The Cave of John the Baptist* (2004), 26–43.

[Shimon Gibson (2nd ed.)]

BET(H)-DAGON (Heb. בֵּית דָּגוֹן), several biblical places, named after a house (shrine) of the god Dagon (cf. the Temple of Dagon in Ashdod, I Sam. 5:1ff.). (1) An unidentified city in the southern Shephelah district of Judah (Josh. 15:41). (2) A place in Galilee on the eastern border of the tribe of Asher, northeast of Mount Carmel (Josh. 19:27), which is possibly mentioned in a list of cities of Pharaoh Ramses III. (3) A city mentioned as Bit-Daganna, near Jaffa, in the inscriptions of Sennacherib, king of Assyria, in whose time (701 B.C.E.) it was under the rule of Ashkelon. The Tosefta in reference to it (Oho. 3:9) specifies that it is located "in Judah," and distinguishes it from Beth-Dagon located by Eusebius (Onom. 50:16) "between Diospolis (Lydda) and Jamnia (Jabneh)," but called by him Kefar Dagon. The original name appears on the Madaba Map in the form (Bet)odegana. It was populated by Samaritans, who built a synagogue there in the fourth century; their presence is still attested to in the tenth century. The crusaders erected a castle there, known as Casal Moyen or Castellum de Maen, i.e., "midway" between Jaffa and Ramleh, which was destroyed by Saladin in 1187, but rebuilt by Richard the Lion-Hearted four years later.

[Michael Avi-Yonah]

Modern Period

This site is now the small town of Bet Dagan. In modern times the Arab village Beit Dajan existed there, which increased in population and wealth due to the development of nearby Tel Aviv. Heavy fighting took place there during the War of Independence (1948) to secure Jewish traffic to Jerusalem and the south, and the village was abandoned. It was settled by immigrants from Bulgaria at the end of 1948 and called Bet Dagan ("House of Corn"). This soon developed from a moshav into a semi-urban community. In 1953 Bet Dagan received municipal council status. In 1962 the Israel Institute for Meteorology was opened there along with a state-owned agricultural experimental station. The town had 2,680 inhabitants in 1968 and 4,830 in 2002, occupying a municipal area of 0.6 sq. mi. (1.5 sq. km.).

[Efraim Orni / Shaked Gilboa (2nd ed.)]

BIBLIOGRAPHY: M. Avi-Yonah, *Madaba Mosaic Map* (1954), 62; Avi-Yonah, Land, 157; 107; Abel, Geog, 2 (1938), 269; G. Beyer, in: ZDPV, 56 (1933), 227; E. Dhorme, in: RHR, 138 (1950), 130–1; Press, Ereẓ, 1 (1951), 79; Aharoni, Land, 337. **WEBSITE:** www.beitdagan.muni.il.

BET DIN AND JUDGES (Heb. בֵּית דִּין; lit. "house of judgment"). *Bet din* (pl. *battei din*) is the term, in rabbinic sources, for a Jewish court of law. In modern times it usually refers to an ecclesiastical court dealing with religious matters such as divorce, and supervision of the dietary laws, and acting, with the consent of all concerned, as a court of arbitration. In Israel the term has come to mean the rabbinic court (as opposed to the secular court known as the *bet mishpat*) which has, by act of the Knesset, jurisdiction in matters of personal status in addition to its normal religious function. This article deals with the general meaning as found in rabbinic sources.

In Jewish Law

ORIGINS. The Bible records that Moses sat as a magistrate among the people (Ex. 18:13) and, either on the advice of Jethro, his father-in-law (Ex. 18:17–23), or on his own initiative (Deut. 1:9–14), he later delegated his judicial powers to appointed "chiefs of thousands, hundreds, fifties, and tens" (Ex. 18:21; Deut. 1:15) – reserving to himself jurisdiction in only the most difficult, major disputes (Ex. 18:22 and 26; Deut. 1:17). It is therefore probable that Israel was one of those civilizations in which the judicature preceded the law, and that some of the later, codified law may have originated in judicial precedents. The earliest reports of such legal decisions already indicate a high standard of judicial practice and qualifications. Judges had to be "able men, such as fear God, men of truth, hating unjust gain" (Ex. 18:21) and "wise men, and understanding and full of knowledge" (Deut. 1:13). They were charged to "hear the causes between your brethren and judge righteously between a man and his brother and the stranger," not be "partial in judgment," but to "hear the small and the great alike; fear no man, for judgment is God's" (Deut. 1:16–17). When the children of Israel settled in their land, the allocation of jurisdiction on a purely numerical basis ("thousands, hundreds, fifties, tens") was to be replaced by allocation on a local basis, i.e., that judges were to be appointed in every town within the various tribes (Deut. 16:18 and Sif. Deut. 144; Sanh. 16b). It is disputed whether this injunction to establish courts in every town applied only in the land of Israel or also in the Diaspora. Some hold that outside the land of Israel courts ought to be established in every district, but need not be established in every town (Mak. 7a); whereas others hold that the injunction applies only in Israel, viz. "in all the settlements that the Lord your God is giving you," but not "in foreign countries in which He has dispersed you" (Maim. Yad, Sanh. 1:2). However, later authorities regard as obligatory the establishment of a court in every community (cf., e.g., *Arukh ha-Shulḥan* ḤM 1:18). In towns with less than 120 inhabitants, there was only a court of three judges – three being the minimum number – so that where opinions were divided, a majority could prevail (Sanh. 3b; Yad. Sanh. 1:4). In towns with 120 inhabitants or more, the court should have 23 judges and be designated as a "Sanhedrin Ketannah" (Sanh. 1:6; Yad, Sanh. 1:10). Courts of 23 judges also sat in the Temple precincts in Jerusalem (Sanh. 11:2; Yad. Sanh. 1:3). The highest court was the "Sanhedrin Gedolah" of 71 judges which sat in the Temple (*Lishkat ha-Gazit*) in Jerusalem (Mid. 5:4; Sanh. 11:2; Yad, Sanh. 1:3 and 14:12), corresponding to the 70 elders and officers who took their place with Moses to "share the burden of the people" (Num. 11:16–17).

The jurisdiction of the various courts was as follows.

(1) Courts of three judges exercised jurisdiction in civil matters generally (Sanh. 1:1), including those which might involve the imposition of *fines (Sanh. 1:1; Sanh. 3a). They also had jurisdiction in matters of divorce (Git. 5b) and *ḥaliẓah* (Yev. 12:1). A court of three judges was required for the conversion of non-Jews (Yev. 46b); for the absolution from vows (Ned. 78a; TJ, Ḥag. 1:8, 76c and Ned. 10:10, 42b); for the circumvention of the law annulling debts in the Sabbatical year ("prosbul"; Shev. 10:4; Git. 32b); for the non-release of slaves after six years (Ex. 21:6; Mekh. Mishpatim 2; Yad, Avadim 3:9); for the enslavement of one who commits a theft and does not have the means to pay for the principal (Ex. 22:2; Yad, Sanhedrin 1:1; Genevah 3:11); and also for the taking of any evidence, even in noncontroversial cases (Yev. 87b; Resp. *Ha-Meyuḥasot la-Ramban* 113; Resp. Rashba vol. 1, no. 749). Compulsory orders in matters of ritual would also require the concurrence of three judges in order to be valid (Ket. 86a; Ḥul. 132b), as would the imposition of any sanction for disobedience (*Mordekhai* Git. 384).

(2) Courts of 23 judges exercised jurisdiction in criminal matters generally, including capital cases (Sanh. 1:4). They also exercised jurisdiction in quasi-criminal cases, in which the destruction of animals might be involved (e.g., Lev. 20:15–16; Ex. 21:28–29; Sanh. 1:4). Where a case was originally of a civil nature, such as slander, but might in due course give rise to criminal sanctions, such as slander of unchastity (Deut. 22:14), it was brought before a court of 23 (Sanh. 1:1); if the slander was found to be groundless, the matter would be referred to a court of three for civil judgment (Maim. Yad, Sanh. 5:3). According to one view, the imposition of the penalty of *flogging required a court of 23 (Sanh. 1:2), but the prevailing view is that a court of three is sufficient (Sanh. 1:2; Yad, Sanh. 5:4), as it is really a penalty that is not necessarily for criminal offenses (see *Contempt of Court), as well as being the accepted method of judicial admonition (*makkot mardut*).

(3) The court of 71 judges had practically unlimited judicial, legislative, and administrative powers but certain judicial and administrative functions were reserved to it alone. Thus, the high priest (Sanh. 1:5), the head of a tribe (Sanh. 16a), and presumably also the president of the Sanhedrin (*nasi*), could, if accused of a crime, only be tried by the court of 71. Certain crimes were also reserved to its jurisdiction, such as the uttering of false prophecy (Sanh. 1:5), rebellious teaching by an elder ("*zaken mamre*"; Sanh. 11:2; see *Majority Rule), and the subversion of a whole town or tribe (Sanh. 1:5); and certain death penalties had to be confirmed by it before being carried out (such as of the rebellious son, the enticer to idolatry, and false witnesses; Tosef., Sanh. 11:7). The *ordeal of a woman suspected of adultery took place in the Great Court at Jerusalem only (Sot. 1:4).

Among the administrative functions reserved to the Great Sanhedrin were the appointment of courts of 23 (Sanh.

1:5; Maim. Yad, Sanh. 5:1); the election of kings (Yad, loc. cit. and Melakhim 1:3) and of high priests (Yad, Kelei ha-Mikdash 4:15); the expansion of the limits of the city of Jerusalem and of the Temple precincts (Sanh. 1:5), and the partition of the country among the tribes (according to Ulla; Sanh. 16a); the declaration of war (Sanh. 1:5); the offering of a sacrifice for the sin of the whole community (Lev. 4:13–15; Sanh. 13b); and the appointment and control of priests serving in the Temple (Mid. 5:4; Tosef., Ḥag. 2:9). The legislative functions of the Great Sanhedrin cannot easily be enumerated. It has been authoritatively said that the Great Court of Jerusalem was the essential source of all Oral Law (Yad, Mamrim 1:1). The law as laid down (or as interpreted) by the Great Sanhedrin is binding on everybody, and any person contravening or repudiating it was liable to the death penalty (Deut. 17:12; Sif. Deut. 155; Yad, Mamrim 1:2), even where the law as laid down (or interpreted) by the court might appear misconceived: "even though they show you as right what in your eyes is left or as left what is right – you must obey them" (Sif. Deut. 155; but cf. Hor. 1:1 and TJ, Hor. 1:1, 45d; and see *Rabbinical Authority). As a corollary of their legislative powers, the Great Sanhedrin also exercised advisory functions: wherever in any court any question of law was in doubt, the final and binding opinion of the Great Court at Jerusalem would have to be taken (Sanh. 88b; Yad, Sanh. 1:4). For the question of appeals see *Practice and Procedure.

(4) Apart from the regular courts mentioned above, there sat in the Temple a special court of priests charged with the supervision of the Temple ritual and with civil matters concerning the priests (cf. Ket. 1:5). Mention is also made of a special court of levites, presumably with similar functions (cf. Tosef., Sanh. 4:7). Originally, the priests performed general judicial functions: they were the sole competent interpreters (or diviners) of God's judgment (Ex. 28:15, 30, 43; Num. 27:21; Deut. 33:8–10); later, they adjudicated matters together or alternately with the judges (Deut. 17:9; 19:17; 21:5), and it seems that the litigants had the choice of applying to the priest for the dictum of God or to the judges for judgment according to law; eventually, the judicial functions of the priests were reduced to their simply being allotted some seats in the Great Sanhedrin (Sif. Deut. 153).

(5) While no regular court could consist of less than three judges (Sanh. 3b), recognized experts in the law (*"mumḥeh la-rabbim"*) were already in talmudical times admitted as single judges (Sanh.5a), albeit in civil cases only and not without express reservations and disapproval – there being no true single judge other than God alone (Avot 4:8; Yad, Sanh. 2:11). No litigant could be compelled to submit to the jurisdiction of a single judge (Sh. Ar., ḤM 3:2).

APPOINTMENT OF JUDGES. The appointment of judges presupposed the *"semikhah"* ("laying of hands") by the appointer upon the appointee, as Moses laid his hands upon Joshua (Num. 27:23) thereby making him leader and supreme judge in succession to himself. The tradition is that throughout the ages judges received their authority from their immediate predecessors who "laid their hands" upon them; so it came about that in law the president of the Great Sanhedrin would be the authority conferring judicial powers on graduating judges (Sanh. 5a), in a formal procedure before a court of three in which he participated or which he appointed (Yad, Sanh. 4:5). But judges were also appointed by kings (e.g., II Chron. 19:5–6), a power which appears to have eventually devolved on the *exilarch in Babylonia (Yad, Sanh. 4:13), but was superseded even there by the overriding authority of the heads of the academies (*rashei yeshivot*; cf. A. Harkavy (ed.), *Zikhron… Kammah Ge'onim*, 80f., no. 180). Courts need not be composed of authorized judges only: any duly authorized judge could form a court by co-opting to himself the necessary number of laymen (Yad, Sanh. 4:11).

The original practice of *semikhah* ceased about the middle of the fourth century and at the present time *battei din* exercise their judicial functions only as agents of, and by virtue of, an implied authority from the Ancients (Git. 88b; BK 84b; Yad, Sanh. 5:8). This "agency" does not extend to capital cases; even for cases involving fines nonauthorized judges would not be qualified (Sh. Ar., ḤM 1:1). It is only because of force of circumstances that the scope of jurisdiction was in practice never restricted, but extended to whatever causes local conditions required (cf. *Netivot ha-Mishpat*, Mishpat ha-Urim, ḤM 1:1; Nov. Ramban Yev. 46b).

One of the consequences of the cessation of the traditional authorization of judges was the adoption in many (mostly Western European) communities of a system of election of judges; in Spain, the judges were elected every year, along with all other officers of the community (cf. Resp. Ribash 207). The leading rabbinical authorities of the period were time and again consulted about election procedures (cf., e.g., Resp. Rashba vol. 3, nos. 417, 422–5; vol. 5, no. 284), so as to ensure that the best and most impartial candidates would be elected. It seems that, when elected, they could not refuse to serve, even though they had not put up their candidature (cf. *Rema* ḤM 25:3; see Judicial *Autonomy; *Mishpat Ivri).

In the State of Israel today, the procedure for appointing rabbinical judges is similar to that for appointing secular judges (*Dayyanim* Act, 5715 – 1955), but while the qualifications of secular judges are laid down in the law, those of rabbinical judges are in each individual case to be attested to by the chief rabbis on the strength of examinations.

No authorization (*semikhah*) and no appointment of a judge will be valid where the appointee did not possess the necessary qualifications (Maim. Yad, Sanh. 4:15); and the sin of appointing unqualified judges is said to be tantamount to erecting an **asherah* beside the altar of the Lord (Sanh. 7b); and where the man was appointed because he was rich, it was like making gods of silver or gods of gold (*ibid.*), not only causing miscarriages of justice but idolatry (Maim. loc. cit., 3:8); and it is reported that judges appointed because of their money were treated with open contempt (TJ, Bik. 3:3, 65d). "The Sages have said that from the Great Court messengers were sent out all over the country of Israel, and they looked for judges who were wise and feared sin and were humble and clearsighted and of good appearance and good manners, and first they made them judges in their towns, and then they brought them to the gates of the Temple, and finally they would elevate them to the Great Court" (Maim. loc. cit., 2:8).

QUALIFICATIONS. The judicial qualifications have been enumerated by Maimonides as follows: judges must be wise and sensible, learned in the law and full of knowledge, and also acquainted to some extent with other subjects such as medicine, arithmetic, astronomy and astrology, and the ways of sorcerers and magicians and the absurdities of idolatry and suchlike matters (so as to know how to judge them); a judge must not be too old, nor may he be a eunuch or a childless man; and as he must be pure in mind, so must he be pure from bodily defects, but as well a man of stature and imposing appearance; and he should be conversant in many languages so as not to stand in need of interpreters. The seven fundamental qualities of a judge are wisdom, humility, fear of God, disdain of money, love of truth, love of people, and a good reputation. A judge must have a good eye, a humble soul, must be pleasant in company, and speak kindly to people; he must be very strict with himself and conquer lustful impulses; he must have a courageous heart to save the oppressed from the oppressor's hate, cruelty, and persecution, and eschew wrong and injustice (Yad, Sanh. 2:1–7). Playing cards for money or other games of chance and lending money on interest also disqualify a person from judicial functions (Sanh. 3:3). A judge who is a relative of one of the litigants, or has any other personal relationship toward him ("loves him or hates him"), must disqualify himself from sitting in judgment over him (Sanh. 3:4–5). A judge should not engage in manual work, so as not to expose himself to popular contempt (Kid. 70a).

PRINCIPLES OF JUDICIAL CONDUCT. A judge must show patience, indulgence, humility, and respect for persons when sitting in court (Yad, Sanh. 25:1; Sh. Ar., ḤM 7:2–5); he must always hear both parties to the case (Sanh. 7b; Shev. 31a; and Codes); he may not in any way discriminate between the parties (Lev. 19:15; Shev. 30a–31a; Yad, Sanh. 21:1–2; 20:5–7; Sh. Ar., ḤM 17:1 and commentaries ad. loc.); nor may he act under the possible pressures of any undue influence, including *bribery by money or by words (Deut. 16:19; Sanh. 3:5; Shab. 119a; Ket. 105b; and Codes); he must, on the one hand, proceed with deliberation and care, and reconsider again and again before finally pronouncing his verdict (Avot 1:1; Sanh. 35a; Sif. Deut. 16 and Codes), but may not, on the other hand, unduly delay justice (Yad, Sanh. 14:10 and 20:6); and he must so conduct himself that justice is not only done but is also manifestly seen to be done (Yoma 38a; Shek. 3:2) and readily understood by the litigants (ḤM 14:4). Before joining a court, a judge must satisfy himself that the judges sitting with him are properly qualified (Yad, Sanh. 2:14); and no judge should sit together with another judge whom he hates or despises (Sh. Ar., ḤM 7:8). Nor may a judge – especially in criminal cases – instead of considering and deciding the issue before him on his own, rely on the opinion of greater judges in the court and try thus to disburden himself of his judicial responsibility (Tosef., Sanh. 3:8; Yad, Sanh. 10:1).

[Haim Hermann Cohn]

Talmudic Period

The rabbis ascribe the development of *battei din* to leading biblical personalities such as Shem, Moses, Gideon, Jephthah, Samuel, David, and Solomon (Mak. 23b; Av. Zar. 36b; RH 2:9; RH 25a). Historical evidence of the existence of a *bet din* in the time of Jehoshaphat is found in *Deuteronomy Rabbah* 19:8. However, the *bet din* belongs essentially to the period of the Second Temple, and its establishment is attributed to *Ezra. He decreed that a *bet din*, which was to sit on Mondays and Thursdays (BK 82a), be established in all populated centers. These were local courts, while the Great Sanhedrin of Jerusalem served as the supreme court (Deut. 17:8–13; Sot. 1:4: Sanh. 1:6). The Sanhedrin existed for the duration of the Second Temple. A decree against immoral behavior is ascribed to the *bet din* of the Hasmoneans (Av. Zar. 36b).

After the destruction of the Temple, *Johanan b. Zakkai established his *bet din* in Jabneh as the cultural and political center of the Jews, and it succeeded the previous Sanhedrin Gedolah. The Jabneh *bet din* was responsible for regulating the calendar and thereby became the religious and national center not only of Ereẓ Israel, but also of the Diaspora. In addition to this central *bet din*, local *battei din* continued to function, particularly in the vicinity of the academies. The Talmud speaks of the courts of R. Eliezer in Lydda, R. Joshua in Peki'in, R. Akiva in Bene-Berak, and R. Yose in Sepphoris (Sanh. 32b). Under R. Johanan's successor, *Gamaliel II, the power and influence of the central *bet din* increased. The summit of its authority was reached under *Judah ha-Nasi I. His grandson, Judah Nesia, may be regarded as the last *nasi* under whose direction the *bet din* was still the actual center of the Jewish people. The Talmud therefore refers to Gamaliel and his *bet din* (Tosef., Ber. 2:6) and to Judah ha-Nasi and his *bet din* (Av. Zar. 2:6), thereby indicating the central civil and religious authority of the Jews.

Toward the middle of the third century, the *bet din* of the *nasi* gradually lost its importance due to the rise of Jewish scholarship in Babylonia and the increased oppression of Palestinian Jewry under Roman rule. Although the office of the *nasi* continued until the end of the fifth century, his *bet din* was no longer the center of the Jewish people. In Babylonia, no *bet din* ever achieved preeminent authority, even for Babylonia alone. This situation continued throughout the geonic period, as no central *bet din* could be established because of the rivalry between the two academies.

Medieval and Modern Period

The *bet din* became the stronghold of Jewish *autonomy in the Middle Ages, and continued with reduced powers into modern times. It experienced many changes in the various centers of Jewish life in the Diaspora, while retaining the continuity of the principles of talmudic law. A vast literature of rabbinic responsa grew out of the written judgments passed by the scholars of every age on actual cases, thus setting precedents and affording an orderly development of Jewish jurisprudence.

In some exceptional cases Jews resorted to non-Jewish courts. Such occurred in Egypt and Ereẓ Israel in the 11th and 12th centuries, following the decline of the gaonate, and in Spain, Majorca, Tunis, and Algeria in the 14th century. In Germany, Jewish and Christian judges met in the synagogue to adjudicate cases between Jews and Gentiles.

The general rule in the Middle Ages, however, was that Jews were strictly prohibited from taking litigation among themselves to gentile courts. This was achieved partly by the control exercised by the community over the individual and by the conception that "Judgment is God's" and hence that recourse to gentile courts meant "aggrandizing the honor of alien gods," as well as by the fairness, incorruptibility, and swiftness of Jewish justice in the majority of countries and most of the time.

In the first half of the geonic period local judges were appointed centrally in Babylonia by the *exilarchs. Later the country was divided into three domains: one was under the jurisdiction of the exilarch, and the other two under the academies in *Sura and *Pumbedita respectively. The local court usually consisted of three judges, one appointed by the exilarch or by the *Gaon* and two more local associates co-opted by him. In Egypt the *nagid* selected local judges.

In the absence of a central authority in the newly developing Jewish settlements in Europe the judiciary became part of the local government of each community. Either the elders themselves constituted a court of justice, or special *dayyanim* ("judges") were selected. In the days of *Gershom b. Judah (tenth century) these local courts were invested with full judicial authority to impose fines and exact penalties. They were mostly constituted of laymen, not necessarily versed in the law. Later, when communities began engaging rabbis, the lay judges were expected to consult them on talmudic law.

In Spain the *bet din* achieved its fullest growth and widest powers. The prerogatives of every *alijama* ("community council") were often defined by a royal charter. The *bet din* thus derived its authority from the king through the *kahal*. The king often appointed a chief rabbi for the realm who was a grandee not necessarily expert in Jewish law, the judiciary being included within his competence. He usually sought the advice and guidance of trained Jewish jurists. The authority of the *bet din* extended to all spheres of Jewish life, social as well as individual, its judgments resting on rabbinic law. It developed a rigorous system of punishments, some of which were far removed from the legacy of ancient Jewish jurisdiction. It assumed, for instance, the right to mete out flagellation, fines (which generally went to the royal treasury), excommunication, chains, imprisonment, exile, and even bodily mutilation, such as cutting off hands or the nose, or cutting out the tongue, as well as the death penalty for *informers (*malshinim*). Hence on the basis of temporary emergency legislation many local Christian legal mores were adopted by the Jewish *bet din*.

During the period when the *Councils of the Lands had jurisdiction over the communities in Poland and Lithuania these bodies included a supreme judiciary selected from among the talmudic scholars of the main communities. In general, appellate Jewish courts existed in many lands, including Spain, Italy, Moravia, Bohemia, Austria-Hungary, and Bulgaria.

Whereas the traditional *bet din* for civil cases consisted of three judges, there were other compositions of this court ranging from one person, usually the local rabbi, to the seven *tovei ha-ir*, the elders of the community. Large cities had more than one *bet din*. A court of arbitration whereby each litigant selected one judge and these two judges appointed the third was very common. Small rural settlements which were administratively allied with a neighboring *kahal* took their litigation to the *bet din* of that *kahal*. Associations within a community, mainly those of artisans, had their own *bet din* for their members by permission of the *kahal*. On the arrival of the Spanish exiles in Turkey after the Expulsion of 1492, each congregation established its own *bet din*.

In Russia the *bet din* was especially powerful until the latter part of the 19th century. Before the abolition of the *kahal* there in 1844 the *bet din* not only applied strict penalties to guilty individuals but also had jurisdiction over the *kahal* itself in claims of individuals against it. There is even a record of the imposition of capital punishment upon two informers in Novo-Ushitsa in 1836.

The distinguishing characteristic of the medieval *bet din* was that it served as an arm of the self-governing *kahal* which possessed powers of law enforcement. As emancipation of the Jew in the modern era dissolved the corporative structure, Jews tended increasingly to resort to the general courts. Wherever the *bet din* has survived to this day it enjoys the prerogatives only of a court of arbitration whose decisions are generally upheld by the law of the country. In many countries, in particular in England and its dominions, and to a lesser degree in France, the *bet din* system, headed by the *bet din* of the chief rabbi of the country, still plays a central role in Jewish life. In Ereẓ Israel, under the mandatory government, an elaborate network of *bet din* courts was established under the Supreme Rabbinical Court in Jerusalem. The State of Israel has taken over this system, giving the *bet din* exclusive jurisdiction over the Jewish population in matters of personal status.

[Isaac Levitats]

In the State of Israel

GENERAL. A system of rabbinical courts operates in the State of Israel. In the legal system of the State, the rabbinical courts have jurisdiction over matters of marriage and divorce and additional matters related to family law. Furthermore, in an arbitration capacity they also preside over other issues in the area of civil and public law, when the both parties consent to their jurisdiction.

HISTORICAL BACKGROUND. Already during the Ottoman rule in the Land of Israel the authorities conferred official recognition on the Jewish Rabbinical Courts, (at that time the regime was based on the capitulation system in which judicial jurisdiction was determined in accordance with religion or citizenship). The head of the Rabbinical Courts system was officially recognized by the Ottoman authorities.

After the Ereẓ Israel was conquered by the British, in 1922, the Kings Order in Council was enacted, conferring exclusive jurisdiction in family matter to the religious courts: Jewish, Islamic, and Christian. Jewish Rabbinical Courts were already in existence; they functioned for the duration of Jewish history. In the Ereẓ Israel the Rabbinical Courts system was established by Chief Rabbi Abraham Isaac ha-Kohen Kook of blessed memory in conjunction with the establishment of the Chief Rabbinate of the Land of Israel, established in 1921 (see remarks of Justice Z.A. Tal in HC 3269/95 *Katz v. Regional Rabbinical Court*, 50 (4) PD 590, 617, hereinafter *Katz*).

This arrangement remained in force during the first years of the State's existence, in accordance with the constitutional principle established on the day of the State's establishment. Accordingly, the Mandate Law, which had been in force in Mandate Palestine (the Land of Israel) from its conquest in 1917 and until the termination of the Mandate in 1948, would remain in force (see sec. 11 of the Law and Administration Ordinance, 5708 – 1948).

POWERS OF THE RABBINICAL COURT IN ACCORDANCE WITH THE JURISDICTION LAW. In 1953 the Knesset enacted the Rabbinical Courts Jurisdiction (Marriage and Divorce) Law, 5713 – 1953 (hereinafter – "the Jurisdiction Law"). The substantive provision of section 2 provides: "Marriages and divorces of Jews shall be performed in Israel in accordance with Jewish religious law" (*din torah*). The term "Jewish religious law" includes biblical law, rabbinic law, and regulations according to the *halakhah*. Section 1 of the aforementioned law establishes the jurisdiction of the Rabbinical Courts: "Matters of marriage and divorce of Jews in Israel, being citizens or residents of the State, shall be under the exclusive jurisdiction of the rabbinical courts."

The term "matters of marriage and divorce" includes the validity of the marriage and divorce. Accordingly the rabbinical court is the only forum competent to adjudicate and decide the personal status of a Jew, i.e., whether he is married or unmarried. This jurisdiction is limited to cases in which both of the spouses are Jewish. Where one of the spouses is Jewish and the other belongs to another religion, the judicial forum with jurisdiction to dissolve the couple's marriage is determined by the President of the Supreme Court.

Both or either of the parties file an application to the President of the Supreme Court, and the latter exercises his power only after the Attorney General gives him the written opinions of the relevant religious courts. These religious courts give their opinions in each particular file regarding whether the religious court would give a divorce judgment, or dissolve the marriage, or declare the marriage void *ab initio*. After the President of the Supreme Court receives the opinions of the relevant religious courts (of both spouses, respectively) by way of the attorney general, he decides, at his own discretion, whether to refer the matter to one of the religious courts of the spouses or to the family court (see: Matters of Dissolution of Marriage (Jurisdiction in Special Cases) Law, 5729 – 1969; Regulations for Dissolution of Marriage (Special Cases) (Procedures) 5745 – 1984).

The Law further determines the substantive law to be applied by the family court in the event that it acquires jurisdiction pursuant to the decision of the President of the Supreme Court, under the aforementioned law (sec. 5 of the Law). Where a religious court acquires jurisdiction established pursuant to the decision of the President of the Supreme Court, it will then adjudicate the case in accordance with the religious law applicable in that court. Hence, where the rabbinical court acquires jurisdiction, it will decide the matter in accordance with the Jewish Law, i.e., the *halakhah*. For example, where the case concerns a mixed marriage of a Jew with a non-Jew, the halakhic position is that the marriage is not valid, and thus in terms of the *halakhah*, there is no need for an act of divorce – because the marriage was not valid in the first place.

In 2005 the legal position applying to mixed marriages changed (see: Matters of Dissolution of Marriage (Special Cases and International Jurisdiction) (Legislative Amendments), 5765 – 2005. Section 1 of this Law comprises all of the amendments to the Dissolution of Marriage Law, from 1969. Due to the tremendous volume of applications for dissolution of marriages filed with the President of the Supreme Court, it was decided that the family court would henceforth be empowered to decide which forum would adjudicate the matter, and that the family court would have residual jurisdiction over the matter, "unless in accordance with the provisions of this Law, the religious court has jurisdiction" (section 1 (a) of the 1969 Law, as amended in section 1 (2) of the law of 2005. The 2005 amendment did not affect the procedure for requesting the opinions of the respective religious courts, except that in accordance with the amendment, the application was made by the deputy president of the Family Court, who would apply directly to the head of the relevant religious courts. Accordingly, where one of the spouses is Jewish, an application is made to the president of the Rabbinical Court of Appeals (see section 3 (a) and section 3 (g)(1) of the 1969 Law, as amended in 2005). The purpose of the application for the head of the religious court was to determine *"whether there is a need for a divorce under the religious law by which he adjudicates, even by reason of a doubt, so that the spouse to whom that religious law applies will be able to remarry"* (*section 3 (a)(1), concluding passage*). If the head of the rabbinical court rules that a divorce is required under religious law, the family court will transfer the application for the dissolution of a marriage to that rabbinical court. On the other hand, the Law further emphasizes that in such a case the conferral of application does not as such confer the rabbinical court with jurisdiction over matters included in the divorce (section 3 (c) of the Law, in the concluding passage). In this regard the Law specifies that the general rules governing jurisdiction and inclusion will continue to apply. These rules will be explained below. Should the head of the rabbinical court rule that there is no need for divorce, or if he fails to respond within three months, then the family court has jurisdiction to adjudicate the matter of dissolution of the marriage (section 3 (d) of the Law). In this respect, the new law introduced a significant innovation, because until that time the rabbinical court had exclusive jurisdiction for the determination of marital status in matters concerning Jews, and according to the new law of 2005, in such cases, the family court has jurisdiction.

For the sake of efficiency, the Law allows the head of the religious court to give a general notification to the President of the Supreme Court, stating that under specific circumstances there is no need for divorce under the religious law by which he adjudicates, as a condition for the ability of the party subject to that law to remarry. This condition obviates the need for an application to the religious court in such cases in the future (section 3 (f)). This power can be exercised in the case of a marriage between a Jew and someone who is not Jewish, for as stated above, according to the *halakhah*, mixed marriages are prohibited and invalid (see *Mixed Marriege). In the 1969 Law, the President of the Supreme Court was conferred the power to avoid determining jurisdiction for spouses belonging to different religions, "if he deems that under the circumstances, it would not be appropriate to grant a remedy to the applicant" (sec. 3 of the 1969 Law). This section was repealed in the 2005 Law. Nonetheless, upon application of one of the litigants, or the Attorney General, the President of the Supreme Court can order that the jurisdiction to dissolve the marriage should be conferred to the family court or the religious court (including, naturally, the rabbinical court) if the President is convinced that it is justified under the circumstances (section 3 (e) of the Law, as amended in 2005.

An additional condition for the jurisdiction of the rabbinical court is that the parties are "Jews in Israel, being citizens or residents of the State" (sec. 2 of the Jurisdiction Law). According to the Supreme Court's ruling it is not sufficient that both spouses be Jewish; there is a need for an additional link connected them to the State of Israel, by force of their being (physically) in Israel, and by virtue of their personal link to Israel, by being residents or citizens of Israel (see, e.g., the decision of Justice Zamir, in CA 3868/95 *Werber* v. *Werber*, 52 (5) PD 817, 843); decision of Justice M. Cheshin in HC 1480/01 *Hagag v. Rabbinical Court of Appeals*, 55 (5) PD 214, 225–226). A decision recently given by the Supreme Court (HC 6751/04 *Sabag* v. *Rabbinical Court of Appeals* (not yet published) (hereinafter – *Sabag*), concerned a Jewish couple who were married in Monaco, in both a civil and a religious ceremony. They were divorced civilly, and the women petitioned to compel her husband to give her a *get* in accordance with religious Jewish law, because according to the *halakhah*, she was still married, and hence – an *agunah*. She turned to the Israeli rabbinical court. The majority view in the Supreme Court, sitting as the High Court of Justice, was that insofar as neither of the spouses had any connection to Israel, the rabbinical court lacked jurisdiction to rule on their case, both on the question of marriage and divorce, and on the question of maintenance (per Justices A. Proccaccia, concurred with by Justice Y. Adiel). The minority view was that in order to prevent the woman becoming from an *agunah*, the rabbinical court was authorized to adjudicate the issue of maintenance, which includes the maintenance awarded under the rule of "*me'ukevet me-ḥamato le-hinaseh*" (a woman prevented from marrying for reasons dependent on the husband). For the same reason the rabbinical court was also empowered to delay the husband's departure from Israel and to make his return to Monaco conditional upon him giving high financial securities (decision of Justice E.Rubinstein in *Sabag*). The minority viewed relied on the previous ruling in HC 1796/03 *Cobani* v. *Rabbinical Court of AppealsI* (not yet published).

In 2005, a major change was introduced into the issue of the rabbinical court's jurisdiction over divorce, and its jurisdiction was extended so that it was no longer limited to spouses resident in Israel, but was also extended to six additional cases in which Jewish spouses had married under *din torah* (Jewish religious law) and in respect of which one of the following connections to the State of Israel sufficed for purposes of conferring jurisdiction to the rabbinical court, to adjudicate their divorce: (1) the defendant's place of residence is in Israel; (2) both of the spouses are Israeli citizens; (3) the plaintiff's place of residence is in Israel, provided that he/she lived there for at least one year immediately prior to the filing of the action; (4) the plaintiff's place of residence is in Israel, provided that the most recent spousal residence was in Israel; (5) the plaintiff is an Israeli citizen, and his place of residence is in Israel; (6) the plaintiff is an Israeli citizen, and lived in Israel for at least one of the two years immediately preceding the filing of the action (see section 4A (a) of the Rabbinical Courts Jurisdiction (Marriage and Divorce) Law, 5713 – 1953, which was added under section 2 of the Matters of Dissolution of Marriage (Special Cases and International Jurisdiction) (Legislative Amendments), 5765 – 2005). In addition, the Law stipulates that where a Jewish couple was married in accordance with *din torah*, and was already divorced under the laws of the external state, the rabbinical court has jurisdiction to adjudicate an action for divorce in accordance with *din torah*, and an action to remove an impediment to remarrying in accordance with *din torah*, even where only the plaintiff is an Israeli citizen (see section 4A (c) of the aforementioned law). A classic example of this kind of case is where the Jewish spouses were married outside Israel both civilly and in accordance with *din torah*, and the court of that country issued an order for civil divorce. In these cases the husband may regard himself as being at liberty to remarry who ever he wishes (under the law of that state) whereas, in the absence of a *get*, the woman continues to be a married women according to Jewish Law and therefore she prevented from remarrying, and any conjugal relations with another man will be deemed as an act of adultery, and any child born from such relations will be regarded as a *mamzer. In such a case the rabbinical court is empowered to adjudicate her divorce, provided that the wife is an Israeli citizen, even if her husband is not an Israeli citizen. This is in addition to the other six possibilities, any one of which suffices to confer jurisdiction to the rabbinical court to adjudicate the divorce action. It should further be noted and emphasized that the Law confers jurisdiction for religious divorces only. The rabbinical court is not empowered to adjudicate and rule on matters of civil divorce (section 4A (b) (2) of the aforementioned law), if an action for a civil divorce was filed in the foreign state prior to the delivery of the *get*.

Furthermore, the conferral of jurisdiction to the rabbinical court over matters of divorce is exclusively for purposes of solving the problem of *aggunot*, and accordingly the new law does not "*confer the rabbinical court with jurisdiction over matters included in divorce*" (section 4A (e) of the Law) such as maintenance, property, or child custody.

The jurisdiction conferred to the rabbinical court under the 2005 law is not only the jurisdiction over divorce, but also enables it to adopt measures prescribed by the Rabbinical Courts Law (Upholding Divorce Rulings) 5755 – 1995. These measures range from the authority to prevent the husband's exit from Israel to the authority to order imprisonment of a recalcitrant husband (see in detail in entry on *Divorce (Enforcement of Divorce in Israel). In this way the rabbinical court in Israel functions as the exclusive forum in the world that has jurisdiction to resolve the *agunah* problems of Jews who were married under *din torah*, by using the enforcement mechanism of the State of Israel including preventing exit from the State, and imprisonment.

Where the plaintiff is not in Israel, the rabbinical court still has jurisdiction to adjudicate divorce, if one of the conditions enumerated above exists. However, the Law provides that in such a case, the action must be served to the defendant outside Israel, together with a translation certified by a notary. Even where a judgment is issued due to the defendant's absence, he is permitted to apply for rehearing of the action (see section 4B of the aforementioned law).

The amendment of 2005 enables the Rabbinical Court of Appeals or one of its *dayyanim* to give a halakhic opinion regarding a *get pitturin* (divorce writ under Jewish Law) or a permit to marriage in a state abroad, provided that the rabbinical court receives a request for its halakhic opinion regarding one of these matters, and even if the Jewish spouses are not subject to the exclusive jurisdiction of the rabbinical court, but were married in accordance with *din torah*.

In order to resolve practical problems concerning *aggunot*, the law of 2005 provides that it will also apply to currently pending claims (section 3 (d) of the 2005 law). Conceivably, these could be regarded as retroactive application, but a reasonable interpretation of the law is that the issue concerns the conferral of jurisdiction in order to solve problems of *agunot*, and the impeding party has no vested right to continue impeding his /her spouse and there is therefore a moral and substantive reason for the immediate application of this Law, even with respect to currently pending actions.

The jurisdiction law also addresses additional matters pertaining to the rabbinical courts' jurisdiction:

(a) The divorce action can also include additional matters (such as maintenance and property), in which case the rabbinical court will have exclusive jurisdiction over those matters too (section 3 of the Jurisdiction Law). The case-law recognized two categories of inclusion (or attachment): (1) a matter which according to its nature and essence is included in the divorce action; (2) a matter which although not necessary a matter of personal status, but regarding which a decision is necessary for the efficient dissolution of the relations between the couple being divorced (decision of Justice M. Silberg in CA 8/59 *Goldman* v. *Goldman*, 13 PD 1085, 1091). Child custody is a matter which by its nature and essence is included in the divorce action, and therefore belongs to the first category, placing it under the jurisdiction of the rabbinical court, even if not expressly mentioned in the divorce action. (ST 1/60 *Winter* v. *Beeri*, 15 PD. 1457. in the decision of Justice M.Silberg and *dayyan* (judge in rabbinical court), Rabbi Goldsmith). To the extent that it concerns the second category of inclusion, under case-law there is a need to explicitly include the particular matter (for example maintenance for the wife, or property) in the divorce action, and in addition, according to the interpretation of the Israeli Supreme Court, the rabbinical court's exclusive jurisdiction is dependent on the fulfillment of three cumulative conditions: (1) the divorce suit filed in the rabbinical court must be *bona fide*; (2) the inclusion of the woman's maintenance or of property must be lawful; (3) the inclusion must also be *bona-fide*. The burden of proof for the fulfillment of these three conditions lies with the litigant claiming that jurisdiction resides in the rabbinical court and not the family court, because in the view of the Supreme Court, that person is attempting to deny the general jurisdiction of the territorial courts of the State and transfer it to a particularistic religious court (see e.g., decision of Justice M. Shamgar in CA *Givoli* v. *Givoli* 34 (4) PD 155). On the other hand, if the parties had already litigated the matter of maintenance and property in the rabbinical court, then the rabbinical court has jurisdiction, even if the three conditions were not fulfilled (see HC 5679/03 *Anon.* v. *State of Israel*, per President A. Barak with the concurring opinions of Y. Tirkel and Y. Adiel (not yet published). Notably, since the adoption of the principle of good faith in Israeli Law (see sec.39 of the Contracts (General Part) Law, 5733 – 1973), it has also been applied and implemented with regard to the jurisdiction of the rabbinical courts and the aforementioned criterion for inclusion (see, e.g., CA 700/81 *Paz* v. *Paz*, 38 (2) PD 736, 742 per Justice M. Elon).

(b) Section 4 of the Jurisdiction Law provides that when a woman files a claim for maintenance, unconnected to a divorce suit, or for maintenance from an estate, "the defendant's plea that the rabbinical court has no jurisdiction in the matter shall not be heard." The courts interpreted this section as meaning that the rabbinical court and the civil courts have parallel jurisdiction over the wife's maintenance when the case is unrelated to divorce. In these cases, the wife is entitled to apply to either court at her own discretion, and the forum that she turns to first acquires exclusive jurisdiction to adjudicate the matter of her maintenance. Having chosen either of these forums, she is no longer permitted to switch to another forum at a later stage.

(c) In matters of *ḥaliẓa* (levirate marriage, see *Levirate Marriage and Ḥaliẓa) and maintenance until the day of the *haliẓa* – the rabbinical court has exclusive jurisdiction (sec. 5 of Jurisdiction Law).

(d) The jurisdiction law enables consensual jurisdiction: In the specific matters of personal status over which the rabbinical court does not have exclusive jurisdiction under the Jurisdiction Law, the rabbinical court can acquire jurisdiction provided that all the parties concerned have expressed their consent to its jurisdiction (sec. 9 of the Jurisdiction Law).

The rabbinical court also has jurisdiction under other laws. For example, section 155 (a) of the Succession Law 5725 – 1965 provides that the rabbinical court is authorized to issue a succession order, a probate order, and to rule on maintenance from an estate, if all the parties concerned have given their written consent thereto (for the interpretation of this section, see also in decision of Justice M. Elon, CA 807/77 *Sobol* v. *Goldman* 33 (1) PD 789, 798 (hereinafter: *Sobol*). Similarly, the rabbinical court has exclusive jurisdiction in any matter relating to the creation or the internal management of a Wakf or a religious endowment that was established in accordance with Jewish Law (see sec. 53 (a) of the Kings Order in Council, 1922.)

THE STATE'S AUTHORIZATION FOR DECISIONS OF THE RABBINICAL COURT. In all of the matters under rabbinical court jurisdiction, the decisions and orders of the rabbinical court are enforced by the executive authority of the State, the Police and the Execution (civil) framework pursuant to section 1 of the Execution Law, 5727 – 1967. The court decisions enforced and executed by the Execution Office include decisions of a religious tribunal (including the rabbinical court). The rabbinical courts system is also empowered to summon witnesses and litigants, to issue restraining orders against leaving the country, and to impose liens. All of these powers are conferred by Knesset legislation, which even imposes the sanctions under the Contempt of Court Ordinance for a person who refuses to comply with the orders of the rabbinical court. (See: Religious Courts (Summons) Law; sections 6 and 7 of the Contempt of Court Ordinance, which applies to the rabbinical court by force of section 7A of the aforementioned law.)

In 1995 the Knesset adopted a law empowering the rabbinical courts to impose a series of sanctions, extending to imprisonment, in order to enforce a divorce judgment. (see at length in the entry *Divorce (Enforcement of Divorce in Israel).

THE LAW APPLYING IN THE RABBINICAL COURTS. Since their establishment during the period of Ottoman rule, under the British Mandate, and even after the establishment of the State of Israel, the rabbinical courts have applied and implemented Jewish Law, i.e., the Jewish religious law, which rabbinical courts have applied since ancient times. Where it concerns laws of personal status and ritual law, this phenomenon is anchored in the very act of conferring jurisdiction to rabbis, the assumption being that they will operate in accordance with the dictates of their religious convictions and will not deviate from the dictates of the *halakhah*. Hence, in the case of *Skornik v. Skornik* (CA 191/51 8 PD 141, per Justice S. Agranat) the rabbinical courts did not apply the rules of private international law, exercising instead the evidentiary and procedural rules of the halakhah (traditional Jewish law).

Both the Mandate Legislature and the Israeli Legislature recognized the rabbinical court's subordination to the Jewish religious law, and consequently they significantly curtailed the number of laws directed at the rabbinical courts. In the isolated laws containing provisions directed at the rabbinical court, the rabbinical court had a monopoly over its interpretation Nonetheless, in 1994 the Supreme Court ruled that the rabbinical courts were obligated to apply the doctrine of joint matrimonial property, a doctrine based in Israeli common-law and not the provisions of Jewish law on the matter (HC 1000/92 *Bavli* v. *Rabbinical Court of Apeals*), 48 (2) PD 221). This signaled a new direction in High Court policy, curtailing the powers of the rabbinical court by compelling it to apply Israeli Law, and as such was criticized

CIVIL LAW IN THE RABBINICAL COURTS AND A WRIT OF REFUSAL. Apart from its powers in defined areas of personal status in which Israeli Law confers jurisdiction to the rabbinical courts, it must also be remembered that throughout Jewish history rabbinical courts have always adjudicated disputes brought before them by two Jews. Today too, the rabbinical courts continue to function in this format. In such cases, from the perspective of Israeli law, these cases have the status of arbitration cases, and following the confirmation of the civil courts, the decisions are enforceable. Absent an arbitration agreement, the rabbinical court has no jurisdiction (see HC 2174/94 *Kahati* v. *Rabbinical Court of Appeals*, 50 (2) PD 214). On the other hand, signing an arbitration agreement is not required under Jewish Law, and in the State of Israel this measure is only adopted as a means of making the rabbinical court's decision enforceable under the Arbitration Law, 5728 – 1968 (see decision of Dayyan, Harav Dickhovsky, File 14603/5743, as cited in the *Weiss* case, *ibid.*, 619)

Throughout Jewish history, where people refused to litigate before the Jewish rabbinical courts, an excommunication order (*ketav siruv*) was issued against them, intended to compel the *defiant litigant* to appear before the rabbinical court and accept its jurisdiction over the case, owing to fear of the pain of excommunication should he refuse to do so. When a decision had already been given, the excommunication order was issued to enforce the compliance of the party against whom the decision was given. The ostracizing and excommunication components of the order meant that the order "served as an important sanction for the Jewish court, which while enjoying judicial autonomy all over the Jewish dispersion, nonetheless lacked the requisite coercive powers that are at the disposal of a sovereign state" (per Justice M. Elon, *Sobol, ibid.*, p. 803).

Despite the fact that the issue of an excommunication order by a rabbinical court had always been an accepted measure under Jewish law for ensuring compliance with a rabbinical decision, the Israeli High Court was unwilling to recognize this practice. When the Israeli rabbinical court issued a writ of refusal, and a person regarded himself as aggrieved by the order, he applied to the High Court of Justice and the latter ruled by majority opinion that the rabbinical court was not empowered to issue such orders. The High Court ruled that the rabbinical court lacked the power to issue writs of refusal, because matters of that nature exceeded the powers of the rabbinical court, as a body established by the State and operating under its laws (the view of Justices Y. Zamir and Justice D. Dorner in the aforementioned *Katz* case).

On the other hand, in his minority opinion Justice Z. Tal demurred, noting that the *ketav seruv* had been issued by rabbinical courts throughout Jewish history and there was no reason for not maintaining the institution in the State of Israel. Concededly, recourse to the *ketav seruv* should be cautious and measured, but the litigants had been directed to the rabbinical court to adjudicate their case, and the High Court of Justice was therefore unable to prevent the rabbinical court from making the declaration and issuing the excommunication order.

HIGH COURT SUPERVISION OVER THE RABBINICAL COURTS. The Rabbinical Courts are part of the Israeli Judiciary. Section 1 (b)(1) of the Basic Law: Judiciary provides stipulates: "Judicial power is vested also in the following: …a religious court (*bet din*). Section 15 (d)(4) of the same Basic Law empowers the Supreme Court, sitting as the High Court of Justice, "to order religious courts to hear a particular matter within their jurisdiction or to refrain from hearing or from continuing to hear a particular matter not within their jurisdiction, provided that the court shall not entertain an application under this paragraph if the applicant did not raise the question of jurisdiction at the earliest opportunity."

In fact, the Supreme Court exercised its supervisory powers over the rabbinical courts system when the latter exceeded the limits of their jurisdiction (ultra vires). To cite a few examples: Rabbinical adjudication where one of the parties is not Jewish, or not an Israeli resident (see: *Sabag, ibid.*), or adjudication by an incomplete panel (HC 7/83 *Biares v. Haifa Regional Rabbinical Court*, 38 (1) PD 673, *per* Justice M. Bejsky; *Katz,* p. 626). Moreover, if the rabbinical court operates in defiance of the rules of natural justice, and does not give each party the opportunity of submitting evidence and pleading, or acts with bias, its ruling under such circumstances will be annulled by the High Court of Justice (see, e.g., HC 10/59 *Levi* v. *Tel Aviv-Jaffa Regional Rabbinical Court*, 13 PD 1182, *per* Justices M. Silberg and Y. Zussman; HC 323/81 *Vilozni* v. *High Rabbinical Court of Appeal*, 36 (2) PD 733, 739, *per* Justice M. Elon).

In addition to the High Court of Justice, every judicial forum has jurisdiction to decide whether or not it has jurisdiction over a particular matter. Thus, both the rabbinical courts and the family courts rule on the question of their jurisdiction when the question is raised before them. In a previous decision Supreme Court held that "where one judicial body has adjudicated and ruled in good faith on a particular matter, no other judicial body has the power to entertain another claim on the same matter – regardless of the formal jurisdiction" (CA 359/75 *Yahalomi* v. *Yahalomi*, 31(2) PD 25, 27, *per* Justice Chaim Cohn). The philosophical underpinning of this rule is "the principle of mutual respect that the civil courts and the religious courts must accord each other. This mutual respect is not a question of good manners and proper behavior alone; it is vital for the existence of a properly functioning legal system, especially in the sensitive legal area of matters of personal status, in which two judicial systems have parallel jurisdiction within the same legal system" (ST 1/81 *Nagar v. Nagar*, 38(1) PD 365, 397–398, *per* Justice M. Elon). When one judicial forum rules on a jurisdictional question, it is not proper for another forum to consider the matter further, and it must abide by the decision of the first forum. Recently, the Supreme Court ruled in a majority opinion that only when there is a special reason (e.g., when there was no preliminary hearing regarding the question of jurisdiction or where the ruling of the first forum on the jurisdiction is illegal or deviates from the rules of natural justice), the other judicial forum has no jurisdiction to rule again on the question of jurisdiction (see HC 8497/00 *Feig-Felman v. Felman*, 57(2) PD 118, *per* Justice D. Beinisch, and concurring opinion of Justice T. Strassberg Cohen). The dissenting opinion was that even in these exceptional cases there was no place for conflicting rulings of the rabbinical and the family courts and that the proper procedure was to petition to the High Court of Justice it order for it to render a decision in the matter (see opinion of Justice D. Dorner, *ibid.*, pp. 142–143).

When the question is whether a particular matter falls within the jurisdiction of the rabbinical court or of the civil court, Article 55 of the King's Order in Council, 1922 sets forth a mechanism for resolving the matter, i.e., the establishment of a special tribunal composed of two Supreme Court justices and one judge from the highest level of the Rabbinical Court of Appeals (see entry Special Tribunal (*Bet Din Meyuḥad*).

RABBINICAL COURTS – COMPOSITION. The rabbinical courts comprise two levels: A regional court is located in each of the major cities in Israel. The regional court sits in panels of three judges, known as *dayyanim* (Section 8(e) of the *Dayyanim* Law). In matters that do not involve a dispute, and with regard to temporary orders, the law provides that the proceedings will be conducted before one *dayyan* only (Section 8(e), *ibid* and The *Dayyanim* Regulations (Matters that May Be Adjudicated Before a Single *Dayyan*), 5750 – 1990).

The Rabbinical Court of Appeals in Jerusalem serves as a court of appeals regarding decisions and judgments of the regional rabbinical courts. The Rabbinical Court sits in panels of no fewer than three *dayyanim*.

This structuring of trial and appellate courts is a result of the initiative of the Mandatory Government. There were those who opposed this system, citing the situation throughout all of the years of exile, in which there were rabbinical courts in every city, with no hierarchical system. Others found support for the establishment of a court of appeals in the commentary of Sforno regarding Jethro's suggestion to Moses that he appoint officers of thousands, officers of hundreds, officers of fifties and officers of tens (Exodus 18:21): "There should be four levels, each higher than the previous one: The lowest will judge first, and he who is dissatisfied with the ruling will complain to the one above him, and from the second to the third and from the third to the fourth. And thus there will be only a few who will come before you for a judgment."

During the period of the Mandatory government, an appellant argued before the Rabbinical Court that Jewish Law does not recognize a right of appeal, the Rabbinical Court ruled that the appellant had a right of appeal on the judgment "because the right of appeal was accepted as an enactment of the sages (*takkanat ḥakhamim*), and it has the same validity as our holy Torah, and one who accepts its adjudication is considered to be aware of this" (File 1/4/705, *B.* v. *A.* Collection of Rabbinical Judgments, Z. Wehrhaftig, ed., 1950, p. 71).

There was another approach in the rabbinical courts, whereby each *dayan* was entitled to maintain his independence, as part of his obligation to rule in accordance with Jewish law. Consequently, even when a judgment of that *dayyan* was overruled by the Rabbinical Court on appeal, he was of the opinion that he was not obligated to obey the Rabbinical Court of Appeals. A similar case came before the Supreme Court, and the Court expressed astonishment and reservation with respect to that opinion. The Supreme Court held that in establishing the Rabbinical Court of Appeals, a hierarchical structure was created in the rabbinical court system, under which a lower level court is not empowered to disobey the appellate level, and this was expressed in the procedural regulations of the rabbinical court (see CA 682/81 *Fried* v. *Fried* 36(2) PD 695, pp. 697–699 *per* Justice M. Landau).

APPOINTMENT OF DAYANIM. The *Dayyanim* Law, 1955, sets forth the manner of appointing *dayyanim*. The *dayyanim* are appointed by the President of the State (Section 5 of the Law), according to the recommendations of the Appointments Committee, whose composition is set forth in Section 6 of the Law, as follows: The two chief rabbis of Israel, two *dayanim* of the Rabbinical Court of Appeals, two ministers, two members of the Knesset, and two practicing advocates. The composition of this committee is very similar to the composition of the Committee for the Appointment of Judges in Israel. It is evident that the representatives of the rabbinical court system do not command a majority on the committee, and great weight attaches to the sovereign bodies of the State of Israel.

The Appointments Committee chooses *dayyanim* from among those who are qualified to serve as *dayyanim*. The first condition for qualification is Israeli citizenship (Section 3a of the *Dayanim* Law). In addition, the conditions for qualification include rabbinical ordination under the auspices of the Chief Rabbinate Council, and passing the examinations for *dayyanut* (see: Section 1 of the *Dayanim* Regulations (Conditions and Procedures for Rabbinical Ordination), 1955). The regulations even set forth the subjects of the examinations, including knowledge of Talmud and the *Posekim*, the Shulḥan Arukh, *Even ha-Ezer* and *Ḥoshen Mishpat*, drafting of a judgment in a hypothetical case and knowledge of the rules and procedures (Section 8 of the Regulations, *ibid*).

A person appointed to serve as a *dayan* by the Appointments Committee must make a declaration of allegiance before the President of the State, in the presence of the Chief Rabbis of Israel, as follows: "I pledge allegiance to the State of Israel, to dispense justice fairly, not to pervert the law and to show no favor" (Section 10 of the *Dayanim* Law).

In the State of Israel there are two chief rabbis, one Ashkenazi and one Sefaradi, who are chosen by an electoral assembly of the rabbis of the various cities and neighborhoods, mayors and public figures, as set forth in Sections 6–8 of the Chief Rabbinate of Israel Law, 1980. Pursuant to Section 16 of the law, Chief Rabbi serves for a term of 10 years, and Section 17 provides that for half of the term of office of the Chief Rabbis one of them serves as the President of the Council of the Chief Rabbinate and the other serves as the Head of the Rabbinical High Court, and in the second half of their term they exchange these positions.

STATUS OF THE DAYYANIM. The *dayyanim* enjoy the same degree of independence as any one serving in a judicial capacity in the State of Israel. Section 12 of the *Dayyanim* Law provides that "The *dayyan* shall be subject to no authority other than that of the law according to which he judges" The *dayyanim* are also accorded salaries and other benefits and pension terms similar to those of judges; the decisions regarding their salaries are made by the Knesset Finance Committee, as is the case regarding judges (Section 17 of the *Dayyanim* Law).

In this context it should be pointed out that until 2003 the rabbinical courts were part of the Ministry of Religious Affairs. With the dissolution of this ministry in 2004, the rabbinical courts were transferred to the Justice Ministry, placing them, from an administrative perspective as well, in their natural and appropriate place, i.e., the Ministry of Justice, which is responsible for the courts in the State of Israel.

An additional example of the Israel legislature's treatment of the *dayyanim* as part of the judicial system of the State of Israel is in the Commissioner for Public Complaints Against Judges Law, 2002. This law also grants the Commissioner jurisdiction over matters concerning *dayyanim* in the rabbinical courts (see Section 1 (5), the definition of "judge"). It bears emphasis that following his investigation of a complaint filed against a person serving in a judicial capacity, the Commissioner is authorized to act in one of several ways. The most serious of these is the referral of the matter to the Committee for the Appointment of Judges, in order for it to decide whether to terminate the appointment of the judge (Section 22(e) of the aforementioned law). This authority exists with respect to *dayyanim* as well, as set forth in Section 33(2) of the law, which amended the *Dayyanim* Law in this respect (see Section 16a(a) of the *Dayyanim* Law).

When the question arose before the High Court of Justice regarding whether a *dayyan* in the Rabbinical Court of Appeals could concurrently take part in political activity, the High Court of Justice ruled that a *dayyan*, as a judge, is obligated to be impartial and to merit the confidence of the public at large. Political activity is deleterious to this status and it is therefore forbidden for one serving in a judicial capacity (including a *dayyan* in a rabbinical court) to fulfill a political position, and to proffer advice to political parties (H. Cdi 732/84 *Tzaban* v. *The Minister of Religious Affairs*, 40(4) PD 141, *per* Justice A. Barak).

PROCEDURAL RULES. Even before the establishment of the State, during the British Mandatory rule, in 1943, the Council of the Chief Rabbinate established procedural rules for the rabbinical courts in Ereẓ Israel. The preparation of these rules began when Rav *Kook and Rav Jacob *Meir were serving as chief rabbis. Most of these rules have their source in the Shulḥan Arukh and the other halakhic authorities, while others were set forth by the Council of the Chief Rabbinate for Ereẓ Israel for the purpose of organizing the proceedings and as *takkanat ha-rabbim*. These rules were replaced and amended in 1960. An updated version of the rules, including amendments and improvements, was enacted in 1993. The rules cover numerous matters related to procedure, including: local jurisdiction, the means of filing a claim and submitting a defense, provisions regarding courtroom procedures and hearing evidence, temporary orders and appeals.

In 2004, the Knesset enacted a law dealing with the disqualification of a judge. This law stipulates identical provisions for judges in the general court system in the State of Israel and *dayyanim* in the religious courts, including the rabbinical courts (see Section 19A of the *Dayyanim* Law as amended pursuant to the 2004 law).

The provisions of this law are unusual, inasmuch as until it was enacted, the starting point of all reference to the rabbinical courts was the autonomy of the rabbinical courts, both regarding application of the religious law and the promulgation of procedural rules. The civil courts also operated according to internal rules or rulings of the court itself with respect to the disqualification of a judge. However, when the Knesset decided to enact legislation dealing with the disqualification of judges in the civil courts, it did so with respect to the religious courts as well, using the same terms and nearly identical provisions for all of the judicial forums in Israel, in order to achieve uniformity regarding the subject of disqualification of judges.

JUDGMENTS OF THE RABBINICAL COURTS. The rabbinical courts have handed down many judgments since the period of the Mandatory government. The early decisions did not include the reasons for the decision, but gradually the rabbinical courts, especially the Rabbinical Court of Appeals, began to provide the reasons for their decisions, even at length.

A collection of the rabbinical judgments during the Mandatory government was published by Z. Warhaftig in 1950. After the establishment of the State of Israel, the rabbinical judgments were published as official publications, under the auspices of the Ministry for Religious Affairs under the title *Piskei Din Rabbaniyyim* (PDR). Twenty volumes of the PDR have been published thus far. Since 1995, the judgments are published in *Shurat ha-Din* with eight volumes published to 2005. During the last year Rabbinical Court decisions have been published on the website: www.rbc.gov.il/judgment

A number of *dayyanim* publish their judgments in collections such as *Teḥumim*. There are *dayyanim* who write responsa including judgments that they gave while serving as *dayyanim* in the rabbinical courts (see, e.g., *Ẓiẓ Eliezer* (Rav. Eliezer Waldenburg), *Binyan Av* (Rav Eliyahu Bakshi Doron), *Shema Shelomo* (Rav. Shelomo Amar), *Mishpateha le-Ya'akov* (Rav Ẓevi Yehudah ben Ya'akov).

CONCLUSION. The *dayyanim* in the rabbinical courts in the State of Israel make up the high-quality human cadre that transmits the Jewish tradition and *halakhah* from generation to generation. In this context we will remark that two of the foremost scholars of the generation (*gedolei ha-dor*), Rabbi Ovadia Yosef and Rabbi Yosef Shalom Elyashiv, served for many years as *dayyanim* on the Rabbinical Court of Appeals and their judgments are included in the PDR.

The rabbinical courts constitute an important part of the judicial system in the State of Israel, and they deal primarily with issues of family law. As we pointed out, the status of the *dayyanim* of the rabbinical courts is very similar to that of Israel's judges, both with respect to their independence, as well as other symbols of their status.

In the framework of the overall picture, it must be remembered that aside from the rabbinical courts, which operate according to the law of the State, as explained above, there are many private rabbinical courts operating in Israel, some of them under the auspices of political or quasi political parties (such as the *Beit Din Ẓedek* of Agudath Israel; the *Beit Din Ẓedek* of *Ha-Eidah ha-Ḥaredit*), some under the auspices of the religious councils (the rabbinical court for civil matters under the auspices of the religious council in Jerusalem, which has even published numerous collections of its judgments), and some of which are rabbinical courts that have achieved renown because of the head of the court (such as the rabbinical court of Rabbi S. Wuzner and the rabbinical court of Rabbi Nissim Karlitz, both of them in Bnei Brak).

In conclusion, it may be stated that from many perspectives, the rabbinical courts in the State of Israel constitute a continuation of the Jewish judicial system that has existed throughout history. These rabbinical courts have exclusive jurisdiction in the area of marriage and divorce, and accordingly they are on the frontline regarding the need to solve practical modern problems according to *halakhah*. Even in instances in which they deal with civil matters and questions of public law, their contribution to Jewish law is great.

BIBLIOGRAPHY: D. Hoffmann, Der Oberste Gerichtshof in der Stadt des Heiligthums (1878); J. Jelsky, Die innere Einrichtung des Grossen Synedrions zu Jerusalem und ihre Fortsetzung im spaeteren palaestinensischen Lehrhause… (1894); A. Buechler, Das Synedrion in Jerusalem und das Grosse Beth-Din in der Quaderkammer des Jerusalemischen Tempels (1902); Schuerer, Gesch, 4 (1911^4), index, s.v. Gerichtswesen; Gulak, Yesodei, 4 (1922), index; S. Assaf, Battei ha-Din ve-Sidreihem Aḥarei Ḥatimat ha-Talmud (1924); idem, in: Ha-Mishpat ha-Ivri, 1 (1925/26), 105–20; A. Feldman, in: Juridical Review, 41 (1929); D.M. Shohet, The Jewish Court in the Middle Ages (1931); A.A. Neuman, The Jews in Spain, 2 (1942), index, s.v. Courts, Jewish; Ḥ. Albeck, in: Zion, 8 (1942/43), 85–93; I. Levitats, Jewish Community in Russia 1772–1844 (1943), 198–217; A. Weiss, in: Sefer ha-Yovel… Ginzburg (1946), 189–216; Albright, in: A. Marx Jubilee Volume (1950), 61–82; Gershoni, in: Ha-Torah ve-ha-Medinah, 2 (1950), 72–75; ET, 1 (1951^3), 117–9; 2 (1949), 253; 3 (1951), 150–74, 174–80, 181; 8 (1957), 510–2; S.B. Hoenig, The Great Sanhedrin (1953); H. Mantel, Studies in the History of the Sanhedrin (1961); Silberg, in: Molad, 23 (1965/66), 265–74; Baron, $Social^2$, index, s.v. Courts, Jewish; Elon, Mafteaḥ, 12–16; J.S. Zuri, Mishpat ha-Talmud, 7 (1921), 1–12. **ADD. BIBLIOGRAPHY:** M. Elon, "Developments in the Rabbinic Judiciary of Israel," in: *Dinei Israel*, 5 (1974), lxxi; idem, *Ha-Mishpat ha-Ivri* (1988^3), 676–77; 1337–45, 1473–1536; idem *Jewish Law* (1994), 2:835–836, 4:1596–1606, 1752–1826); idem, *Jewish Law (Mishpat Ivri): Cases and Materials*, (Matthew Bender Casebook Series; 1999), 391–420 (See, e.g., M.Elon "These Statements Are Obiter Dicta… They Are Based on Error and It Is Appropriate Not To Follow Them": Critiques and Reflections on the Bavli and Lev cases); M: Mautner et al (ed.) *Multiculturalism in the Democratic and Jewish State, the Ariel Rozen-Tzvi Memorial Book* (1998), 361–407; M. Silberg, *Ha-Ma'amad ha-Ishi be-Yisrael* (1958); M. Silberg, P. Shifman, *Ha-Ma'amad Ha'Ishi Be-Yisrael – Miluim ve-Hashlamot al pi ha-Pesika ha-Ḥadashah* (1967); M. Shaveh, *Ha-Din ha-Ishi Be-Yisrael* (2001^4); P. Shifman, *Dinei ha-Mishpaḥah be-Yisrael*, vol. 1 (1995^2), esp. 11–135; A. Rosen Tzvi, *Dinei ha-Mishpaḥah be-Yisrael – Bein Kodesh le-Ḥol* (1990), esp. 25–188; B.Z. Sharshavski, *Dinei Mishpaḥah* (1994^4); A. Shochetman, *Seder ha-Din le-Or Mekorot ha-Mishpat ha-Ivri, Takkanot ha-Din u-Pesikat Batei ha-Din ha-Rabbaniyyim be-Yisrael* (1988); S. Dihovsky, "*Samkhut Batei ha-Din ha-Rabbaniyyim Bi-Re'i Pesikat Batei ha-Din,*" *Dinei Yisrael*, 10–11 (1981–83), 9; idem, "*Batei Din Rabbaniyyim-Mamlakhtiyyim: Be'ayotehem ve-Hesegeihem,*" *Dinei Israel*, 13–14 (1986–88), 7; idem, "*Ma'amado shel Beit Din Rabbani ha-Dan be-Dinei Mamonot ke-Borer,*" *Shenaton ha-Mishpat ha-Ivri, 16–17* (1990–1991), 527; Y. Cohen, "*Shipput Rabbani ve-Shipput Ḥiloni,*" *Dinei Israel*, 7 (1976), 205 (see: M.Drori, "The Duty to Testify, in: *Gilyon Parashat ha-Shavua, Parashat Vayikra* (2001), www.daat.ac.il); idem, "Decision of the Rabbinical Court in Civil Matters and Their Ramifications for Israeli Law," in: *Madai Yehadut*, 39 (1999), 121–31); idem, "Who is Empowered to Interpret a Secular Law Directed at a Religious Court?" in: *Tel Aviv Law Review*, 3 (5734 – 1974), 941–46.

BET(H)-EDEN (Heb. בֵּית עֶדֶן), the biblical name for Bît Adini, an Aramean kingdom some 200 mi. (320 km.) northeast of *Damascus that extended along the banks of the Euphrates from the mouth of the Sâjūr River in the north to the mouth of the Balikh River in the south (see *Aram). Its capital was Til-Barsip. The name Beth-Eden appears in its entirety in Amos 1:5; the short form Eden is found in Ezekiel 27:23; and the phrase children of Eden (*benei Eden*) appears in II Kings 19:12 and Isaiah 37:12. The identification of Beth-Eden with Bît Adini is based on the fact that Beth-Eden is mentioned because of its importance along with the kingdom of Damascus (Amos 1:5). The kingdom was founded in the tenth century B.C.E., and during the first half of the ninth century was the most important Aramean kingdom in Mesopotamia. It was probably named for the father of the dynasty that founded it, and is first mentioned in the Annals of Adad-nirari II around the year 900. The biblical references to Beth-Eden belong to the period when the kingdom was an Assyrian province after being captured by Shalmaneser III (859–824) in 855 B.C.E.. A. Malamat views the expression "one who holds the scepter [i.e., a ruler] from Beth-Eden" (Amos 1:5) as a reference to Shamshši-ilu, the Assyrian governor, who, as is known from a document discovered at Til Barsip, was appointed over Beth-Eden in the time of Amos. (The toponym *byt* > *dn* in KAI 233: 14–15, a seventh century Aramaic letter, refers to a different locale.) The words spoken by the messengers of Sennacherib about "children of Eden who were in Telassar" (II Kings 19:12; Isa 37:12) refer to the conquests of Shalmaneser III, who resettled the children of Eden in Telassar, perhaps located in the far-away Zagros region.

BIBLIOGRAPHY: A. Malamat, in: BASOR, 129 (1953), 25–26; Pritchard, Texts, 275. **ADD. BIBLIOGRAPHY:** M. Cogan and H. Tadmor II *Kings* (AB; 1988), 235; S. Paul, *Amos* (Heb., 1994), 34; P. Dion, *Les Araméens*…(1997), 85–98

BET(H)-EL (Heb. בֵּית אֵל), Canaanite and Israelite town, 10½ mi. (17 km.) N. of Jerusalem, located at the intersection of the north-south mountain road along the watershed and the east-west road leading to the plains of Jericho and to the Coastal Plain (cf. Judg. 20:31). At present its site is occupied by the small Muslim village of Baytīn, 2,886 ft. (880 m.) above sea level. Excavations were conducted at Beth-El by W.F. *Albright and J.L. Kelso in 1927 and 1934 and resumed by Kelso in 1954, 1957, and 1961.

Settlement at Beth-El apparently began at the turn of the third millennium B.C.E., when it inherited the position of neighboring *Ai (al-Tell), which already lay in ruins. In the 16th century B.C.E. the settlement was enlarged and surrounded by an 11 ft. (3⅓ m.) thick stone wall. The biblical account of Abraham's building an altar to the Lord between Beth-El and Ai (Gen. 12:6–8) is usually assigned to this period. Beth-El's main importance, however, is derived from its traditional association with Jacob's dream. Fleeing from his brother Esau, Jacob spent the night there and dreamed he saw a ladder reaching to heaven with angels of God ascending and descending it. A voice then spoke to him and assured him of God's protection and confirmed the promise that the land on which he rested would be given to him and his descendants (*ibid.*, 28:10–22). Arising the next morning, Jacob erected a *mazzevah* ("sacred pillar") over which he poured oil as a thanksgiving sacrifice. The name of the place, which was formerly Luz, was now called Beth-El (i.e., "home of God"; *ibid.*, 5:19; 35:6, 15; 48:3; Josh. 18:13; according to Josh. 16:2, however, Beth-El was east of Luz).

Canaanite Beth-El continued to flourish in the Late Bronze Age (15th–14th centuries, B.C.E.), when it had commercial relations with Cyprus, indicated by the pottery finds. The remains of a house with rooms built around a large courtyard, plastered or stone flooring, and masonry sewage channels belong to this period. A burnt layer indicates that the city was captured and burned down around the first half of the 13th century B.C.E. and resettled by an Israelite population (cf. Judg. 1:22ff.; Josh. 12:16). The city was on the southern border of Ephraim (Josh. 16:1–2; 18:13; I Chron. 7:28), but it is also listed as a Benjamite town (Josh. 18:22). There was a decline in the standard of living at Beth-El during the Israelite period, when the building became cruder, but a recovery is noticeable during the reigns of David and Solomon. The stormy epoch of the Judges is reflected in three building phases, while the relatively calm period of the United Monarchy is represented in a single building phase. The Tabernacle and the Ark were set there for a while, and in the conflict with Benjamin the Israelites prayed, fasted, and offered sacrifices there. They invoked the oracle of the Urim and the answer was provided by Phinehas (Judg. 20:18, 28). Deborah lived near the city (Judg. 4:5), and Samuel visited it periodically to judge the people (I Sam. 7:16). During Saul's war with the Philistines, he concentrated his forces in the mount of Beth-El (I Sam. 13:2).

With the division of the Monarchy, Beth-El passed into the possession of Jeroboam I. In order to wean his people away from making pilgrimages to Jerusalem, he erected one of the two principal shrines of his kingdom there (the other one was at Dan), with its own priesthood. The golden calf he set there was apparently designed to serve as a substitute for the cherubim in the Temple of Jerusalem. In the same spirit he ordered the 15th day of the eighth month to be celebrated instead of the Feast of Ingathering (Sukkot), which was observed on the 15th of the seventh month in Jerusalem as the main pilgrim festival (I Kings 12:29–33). This schism aroused vehement opposition among the prophets (I Kings 13) and caused a rift between Jeroboam and Ahijah the Shilonite (I Kings 14:7ff.). The biblical story of Hiel the Bethelite, who ignored the curse of Joshua and rebuilt Jericho on its ruins (I Kings 16:34), and that of the children of Beth-El who mocked Elisha (II Kings 2:23) may serve as proof of the strained relations existing between the inhabitants of Beth-El and the prophetic circles. This antagonism assumed its most acute form in the days of Amos (3:14; 4:4; etc.) and Hosea (10:15), both of whom call Beth-El Beth-Aven ("The House of Iniquity"; Amos 5:5; Hos. 4:15; cf. Jer. 48:13).

Beth-El and its surroundings were conquered by Abijah, king of Judah, in his war against Jeroboam (II Chron. 13:19), but it was returned to Israel not later than the reign of *Baasha and remained there until the fall of the kingdom. In the eighth century B.C.E., Beth-El was enclosed by a thick wall with towers that was repaired in the following century. Even after the destruction of Samaria (721 B.C.E.), priests still served at Beth-El (II Kings 17:28) until Josiah captured it, broke down its altar, destroyed its high place, and defiled the site (II Kings 23:15). Beth-El was destroyed during the Babylonian invasion (587 B.C.E.) and remained in ruins until the Persian period. In the time of Nehemiah, it was included in the territory of Judah (Ezra 2:28; Neh. 7:32). During the Hasmonean revolt, it was fortified by the Syrian general Bacchides (I Macc. 9:50). Beth-El is not mentioned again until its capture by Vespasian in 69 C.E. (Jos., Wars, 4:551). Coins found there date only from the period between 4 B.C.E. and its capture. In the Byzantine period, Beth-El was a village in the territory of "Aelia Capitolina" (Jerusalem), located 12 (Roman) miles from the capital "on the right, as one goes to Neapolis" (Eusebius, Onom. 192 etc.). The Christian traveler the Pilgrim of Bordeaux (333 C.E.) and the Christian writer Theodosius (c. 503 C.E.) also refer to it. According to Jerome (fifth century) a church was erected at Beth-El. On the Madaba Map "Luzah, which is also Beth-El" is also represented as a village north of Jerusalem. Very few remains of the Roman and Byzantine periods have been discovered at the site.

[Michael Avi-Yonah]

Modern Beit El

Beit El (Heb. בֵּית אֵל) is a settlement in the Judean hills, northeast of Ramallah. The first settlers, numbering 17 families, took over an army base in 1977. Subsequently the community divided into two settlements: Beit El Alef was a residential religious community and Beit El Bet a yeshivah community. Over the years, new religious settlers joined both settlements, until in 1997 the two were united again under a single municipal council. In 2002 the combined population was 4,410. As the seat of a regional council, Beit El provided a variety of social and educational services. There were also some private businesses, stores, restaurants, and light industry, most notably the Beit El tefillin factory.

[Shaked Gilboa (2nd ed.)]

BIBLIOGRAPHY: Y. Kaufmann, Religion, index; N.H. Tur-Sinai, *Ha-Lashon ve-ha-Sefer*, 2 (1950), 307; Alt, in: PJB, 21 (1925), 28ff.; Noth, in: PJB, 31 (1935), 7–29; Albright, in: BASOR, 55 (1934), 23–25; 56 (1934), 2–5; 57 (1935), 27–30; 74 (1939), 15–17; U. Cassuto, *La Questione della Genesi* (1934), 284–6, 291–7; Galling, in: ZDPV, 66

(1943), 140–55; 67 (1944), 21–43; H.H. Rowley, *From Joseph to Joshua* (1950), 19, 111, 138; Kelso, in: BASOR, 137 (1955), 5–10; 151 (1958), 3–8; 164 (1961), 5–19; Bright, Hist, index; Aharoni, Land, index.

BET ESHEL (Heb. בֵּית אֶשֶׁל), former Jewish settlement in southern Israel, southeast of Beersheba. It was founded in 1943 as one of the first three observation outposts in the Negev. The settlers, immigrants from Central Europe, lived as a kibbutz but intended to make Bet Eshel a moshav. They succeeded in growing grain crops with dry farming methods. A water well drilled at the spot enabled them also to grow vegetables and plant fruit orchards, thus proving the feasibility of agricultural settlement in the northern Negev. In the Israel War of Independence, Bet Eshel was besieged for over 10 months (December 1, 1947–October 21, 1948). It suffered heavy losses and was destroyed by continuous shelling. After the lifting of the siege, the settlers consented to leave and they established moshav Ha-Yogev in the Jezreel Valley. "Bet Eshel" means "House of the Tamarisk," this tree being characteristic of the Beersheba desert flora.

[Efraim Orni]

BET GARMU, family of bakers who supervised the preparation of the showbread (*leḥem ha-panim*) in the Temple (Shek. 5:1; Tosef., Yoma 2:5). The Mishnah states that the memory of the family was held in disrepute because they would not teach others how to prepare the showbread (Yoma 3:11). According to one *baraita*, "the sages sent for specialists from Alexandria of Egypt, who knew how to bake as well as they, but they did not know how to remove the loaves from the oven as well as the Bet Garmu," and some report that "their bread became moldy" (Tosef., loc. cit., Yoma 38a). According to Tosefta *Yoma* 2:5, Bet Garmu agreed to return to work only after their remuneration was doubled. Other traditions report that they justified their refusal to teach their art to others, saying: "Our family knows that the Temple will be destroyed and perhaps an unworthy man will learn the process and use it for idolatrous worship" (Tosef., loc. cit.). The same source praises the family for never using bread made of fine quality flour, lest they be suspected of eating the holy showbread.

BIBLIOGRAPHY: A. Buechler, *Die Priester und der Cultus…* (1895), 52ff.; Schuerer, Gesch, 3 (19074), 333; S. Klein, in *Leshonenu*, 1 (1928/29), 347.

[Isaiah Gafni]

BET GUVRIN (Heb. בֵּית גּוּבְרִין).

(1) A prominent city in the period of the Second Temple, located in the southern Shephelah. Ancient Bet Guvrin rose to importance after the destruction of Maresha (Marissa) by the Parthians in 40 B.C.E. Betabris, mentioned by Josephus (Wars, 4:447) as one of two villages taken by the Romans in 68 C.E. "right in the heart of Idumea," may possibly refer to Bet Guvrin. The city began expanding following the Bar Kokhba revolt, during the second half of the second century C.E., with the construction of public and administrative buildings. In 199/200 C.E. Septimus Severus conferred on it the privileges of a Roman city and called it Eleutheropolis ("the city of freemen"). The city of that period covered an area of about 160 acres, and topographically it extended mainly over a hill located south of the present-day highway between Bet Shemesh and Ashkelon, with the northern extension of the city built on a low plain. Two aqueducts and an underground tunnel supplied water to the city. The Midrash (Gen. R. 41:10) interprets Mt. Seir of the "Horites" (Gen. 14:6) as Eleutheropolis – an interpretation based on a play of words, since *Ḥori* means both "freeman" and "cave dweller" and the Bet Guvrin region abounds in large caves. Severus also granted the new city a large area encompassing the districts of Bethletepha, western Edom, and Hebron as far as En-Gedi, which made it the largest single region in Roman times, with over a hundred villages. Bet Guvrin also had its own system of dating and coinage. The wealth of its inhabitants is attested to by a mosaic pavement of a Roman house from the fourth century C.E. which depicts a hunting expedition, with representations of animals and the personifications of the four seasons. Public buildings have been uncovered in recent excavations, including a bath house with double arches and a system of vaults made of ashlars with Severan-type stone dressing, and an amphitheater which was built on flat ground on the northwest edge of the city. The amphitheater has an elliptical plan and was erected during the second half of the second century C.E. Eleutheropolis suffered a severe earthquake in 363 C.E., at which point the amphitheater fell into disuse. The *tanna* Judah b. Jacob (Tosef., Oho. 18:15, 16) and the *amora* Jonathan (TJ, Meg. 1:11, 71b) resided at Bet Guvrin and there were still Jewish farmers in its vicinity in the fourth century. The place was regarded as being outstandingly fertile and the rabbis applied to it the verse from Isaac's blessing of Esau: "And the dew of the heaven above" (Gen. 27:39; Gen. R. 68:6). In matters of *halakhah*, Bet Guvrin was regarded as belonging to Edom and was therefore exempt from the commandments applying only to Ereẓ Israel (TJ, Dem. 2:1, 22c; TJ, Shev. 8:11, 38b). The talmudic region Darom (Gr. *Daromas*) was within the area of Bet Guvrin. An inscription found there records the donation of a column to the local synagogue in Byzantine times. Eleutheropolis appears on the Madaba mosaic map of the mid-sixth century C.E. Excavations have uncovered the mosaic pavements of two churches from this period; it was an Episcopal see from the fourth century or earlier. The city flourished in the Early Islamic period as archaeological finds testify. Clusters of burial caves from the Late Roman, Byzantine, and Early Islamic periods have been uncovered in excavations around the city. The castle of Bayt Jibrin was apparently constructed around 1134 and was granted to the Hospitalers by King Fulk of Anjou late in 1136; a civilian settlement subsequently developed around the castle. Sacked by the Moslems in 1158, the castle was eventually abandoned to Salah-a-Din (*Saladin) in 1187. A church belonging to this castle has recently been uncovered. In 1171, Benjamin of Tudela reported three Jewish families living there.

[Michael Avi-Yonah / Efraim Orni / Shimon Gibson (2nd ed.)]

(2) Kibbutz in the southern Judean Foothills, on the Ashkelon-Hebron road. Bet Guvrin is affiliated with Ha-Kibbutz ha-Me'uḥad. In 1949, after the large Arab village of Beit (Bayt) Jibrīn was abandoned by its inhabitants in the War of Independence, the present settlement was established. Most of its settlers were Israeli-born and its economy was based primarily on field crops, orchards, milch cattle, and poultry. Over the years the kibbutz also developed a tourist industry, which included visits to the Bet Guvrin caves, catering, a swimming pool, three hostels, and outdoor activities. In 2002 the population of the kibbutz was 231.

[Efraim Orni / Shaked Gilboa (2nd ed.)]

BIBLIOGRAPHY: Neubauer, Géogr, 122–4; Y.Z. Horowitz, *Ereẓ Yisrael u-Shekhenoteha* (1923), s.v.; S. Klein (ed.), *Sefer ha-Yishuv* (1939), s.v.; Vincent, in: RB, 31 (1922), 259ff.; Abel, *ibid.*, 33 (1924), 593; Beyer, in: ZDPV, 54 (1931), 209ff. **ADD. BIBLIOGRAPHY:** E.D. Oren and U. Rappaport, "The Necropolis of Maresha-Beth Govrin," in: *Israel Exploration Journal*, 34 (1984): 114–153; Y. Dagan, M. Fischer and Y. Tsafrir, "An Inscribed Lintel from Bet Guvrin," in: *Israel Exploration Journal*, 35 (1985): 28–34; D. Urman, "Beth Govrin: A History of a Mixed Population During the Mishnah and Talmud Period," in: E. Stern and D. Urman (eds.), *Man and Environment in the Southern Shepelah: Studies in Regional Geography and History*," (1988), 151–162; D. Pringle, *The Churches of the Crusader Kingdom of Jerusalem*. vol. 1: A–K. (1993), 95–101, s.v. Beit Jubrin; Y. Tsafrir, L. Di Segni, and J. Green, *Tabula Imperii Romani. Iudaea – Palaestina. Maps and Gazetteer* (1994), 118–119; A. Kloner and A. Hubsch, "The Roman Amphitheatre of Bet Guvrin: A Preliminary Report on the 1992, 1993 and 1994 Seasons," in: *Atiqot*, 30 (1996), 85–106; J. Magness and G. Avni, "Jews and Christians in a Late Roman Cemetery at Beth Guvrin," in: H. Lapin (ed.), *Religious and Ethnic Communities in Late Roman Palestine* (1998), 87–114.

BET HA-EMEK (Heb. בֵּית הָעֵמֶק), kibbutz in northern Israel, northeast of Acre, affiliated with Iḥud ha-Kibbutzim. Bet ha-Emek was founded on Jan. 4, 1949, by young survivors of the Holocaust from Hungary and Slovakia. Later, immigrant youth from England and Holland joined the settlement to form the majority of its members. The kibbutz has a number of cultural institutions set up with contributions from England and other countries. In addition to highly intensive farming (field crops, fruit plantations, dairy cattle and poultry), Bet ha-Emek had a plant laboratory and biomedical, silk, and shoe factories. A nearby mound is supposed to be identical with biblical Beth-Emek (Josh. 19:27), which belonged to the tribe of Asher and was also inhabited in the time of the Talmud. The village ʿAmqa, abandoned by its Arab inhabitants during the War of Independence (1948), preserved the ancient name; and antique columns, capitals, ashlars, etc. were used in the construction of its dwellings. In 1970 Bet ha-Emek numbered 286 inhabitants; in 2002 the population was 444.

[Efraim Orni]

BET HA-LEVI (Heb. בֵּית הַלֵּוִי), moshav in central Israel in the Ḥefer Plain, founded in 1945 by settlers from Bulgaria. Its economy was mainly based on citrus plantations, garden crops, and milch cattle. In 2002 the population of Bet ha-Levi was 502. The village bears the name of *Judah Halevi.

[Efraim Orni]

BET ḤANAN (Heb. בֵּית חָנָן), moshav in central Israel, west of Nes Ẓiyyonah, founded in 1930 by settlers from Bulgaria. Its economy was based on citrus plantations, poultry, milch cattle, and other farm products. In 2002 the population of Bet Hanan was 534. The village's name resembles the former Arabic denomination of the site "Wadi Ḥanīn."

[Efraim Orni]

BETHANY (Heb. **Bet Aniyya**, **Bet Hananyah**), a village about 1¾ mi. (3 km.) E. of Jerusalem, frequently mentioned in the Gospels (Mark 11:1; 14:3; Matt. 21:17; Luke 19:29; etc.). According to Christian tradition, it was the home of the sisters Mary and Martha, with whom Jesus lodged, and the scene of the resurrection of their brother Lazarus after he had been interred for four days (John 11). At the end of the fourth century, the Byzantines built a church and adjoining monastery at Bethany which was renovated in the following century. It was named after Lazarus, and from this comes the Arabic name of the village, al-ʿAzariyya. During the Crusader period, the church was regarded as the property of the Church of the Holy Sepulcher, and it underwent extensive alterations. It was destroyed in the 16th century and a Greek monastery stands in its place. The ancient site of the church was apparently near the present Catholic monastery Raʾs al-Shayyāḥ. Remains of ancient buildings and tombs dating from the period of the Second Temple and later have been uncovered there. A cistern from the Second Temple period, which served as a shrine in Byzantine times, has Christian-Greek graffiti on its plastered walls. It was discovered in 1949–53 together with oil presses, cisterns, and numerous tombs of later periods.

BIBLIOGRAPHY: G. Dalman, *Sacred Sites and Ways* (1935), index; Benoit and Boismard, in: RB, 58 (1951), 200–50; S.J. Saller, *Excavations at Bethany* (1957).

[Michael Avi-Yonah]

BETHAR (**Betar**) (Heb. בֵּיתָר), *Bar Kokhba's last stronghold in his war against Rome. It is identified with Khirbet al-Yahūd ("ruins of the Jews"), an area of ruins on the summit of a steep hill, northwest of the Arab village of Battīr which has preserved the ancient name. Bethar is mentioned in the Septuagint in a verse added after Joshua 15:59 (Βαιθηρ) together with several other cities of Judah, including Beth-Lehem. It also appears in a manuscript of the Septuagint (Version "A") after Beth-Shemesh in the list of Levitical cities in I Chronicles 6:44. The various transliterations of the name in the Septuagint and in Eusebius (*Historia Ecclesiastica* 4:6) – Bitter, Better – seem to indicate that it was originally called Bet-Ter (בֵּית־תֵּר). In aggadic literature the name has been preserved in the Aramaic Bei-Ter (בֵּי־תֵר).

Bethar lies on a rocky spur 7 mi. (11 km.) southwest of Jerusalem; it is bounded by the Rephaim Valley on the east, north, and west. The upper part of the hill, c. 2,300 ft. (700 m.) above the level of the Mediterranean, constitutes the tongue of a plateau, sloping gradually to the north to the steep drop of the Sorek Brook c. 490 ft. (150 m.) above the bottom of the valley. The northern half of the spur may have served as an area of orchards of the ancient town and contains few building remains. A spring, the source of water of ancient Bethar and at present of the Arab village of Battīr, flows from a rock southeast of the spur. Part of a defaced Latin inscription on the rock near the mouth of the spring mentions the Roman legions V Macedonica and XI Claudia, which participated in the siege of Bethar. Since Hadrian was forced to bring these legions from the northern part of the Empire this probably indicates the extent of the difficulties that the Romans suffered in overcoming the revolt. The site has been investigated by various explorers since the 19th century, notably by V. Guérin in 1863, who made the identification of Battir with Bethar, and by C. Clermont-Ganneau in the 1870s, who was the first to note the Latin inscription at the spring. Explorers and archaeologists who studied the site include: Germer-Durand (1894); Zickermann (1906); Caroll (1923); Alt (1927); Reifenberg (1950); S. Yeivin (1944–46); Kochavi (1968); and Z. Yeivin (1970s). This work indicated that the summit of Khirbet el-Yehud was surrounded by a fortified wall, with aerial photographs and ground surveys showing the existence of a Roman siege system, comprising a surrounding circumvallation wall and two Roman camps to the south, and with pottery evidence suggesting that archaeological remains at the site date not just from the Roman period but also to as early as the Iron Age II (7th–6th centuries B.C.E.).

In 1984 excavations were conducted at the site by Tel Aviv University under the direction of D. Ussishkin, and the history of the site and its features are now more or less clear. Access to the site was from the southeast with a path linking it to its agricultural hinterland and to the spring and its irrigated terraces. The fortifications visible around the site of Khirbet el-Yehud, encompassing an area of about 10 acres (40 dunams), did indeed date from the time of Bar Kokhba and showed evidence of having been hastily built. The surrounding defense wall had at least six semi-circular towers and three square ones. Segments of the curtain walls and three towers were uncovered during the excavations. Pottery, slingstones, iron arrowheads, and a few coins dated from the time of Bar Kokhba.

With the outbreak of the revolt, Bethar was chosen as Bar Kokhba's headquarters because it was situated close to Jerusalem, it was strategically located above the main road running between Jerusalem and Gaza, it had a spring with an abundant source of water, and it was provided with natural defenses by deep valleys on three sides. The settlement could have had a population of between 1,000 and 2,000 individuals. Bethar was Bar Kokhba's last bastion, but it appears from the careless and inconsistent way that the fortifications were built that they were erected not long before the siege by the Romans. It would appear that most of the defenders' efforts went into cutting a moat at the southern approach to the site to render difficulties to the attacking Romans. The reference to the men "who went down to the rampart of Bethar" (Tosef., Yev. 14:15) may refer specifically to the southern side of the site. No archaeological evidence however exists at the site for a siege ramp. The Romans built a surrounding circumvallation siege wall and two rectangular camps, and it would appear that one section of the siege wall succeeded in cutting off the settlement from its spring. No historical account exists relating to the actual battle at Bethar, but the discovery of unused slingstones on the top of the wall suggests that the subjugation of Bethar may have been quite rapid. Following the conquest of Bethar, its inhabitants were slaughtered and the town was razed and never rebuilt.

In Israel's 1949 armistice agreement with Jordan, most of the village, together with the historical mound, remained on the Jordanian side, but the railway line at the bottom of the gorge and a narrow strip of land with a number of houses and gardens on its southern side were included in Israel territory. A certain area with a few dozen inhabitants belonged to Israel from 1948 but from 1967 the bulk of the village, with 1,445 inhabitants, became part of the territory under Israel administration. In recent years the village has been designated as part of the territory falling under Palestinian administration.

[*Encyclopaedia Hebraica* / Shimon Gibson (2nd ed.)]

A town with a similar name, Bethar Illit, was established nearby, 6 miles (10 km.) from Jerusalem, on the southwest side of the Judean hills. The settlement was the first town established under the program for public housing for the ultra-Orthodox population. Founded in 1988, it received municipal council status in 1990 and absorbed newcomers mainly from Jerusalem and Bene-Berak. In 2003 the population was 22,926.

[Efraim Orni / Shaked Gilboa (2nd ed.)]

BIBLIOGRAPHY: J.K. Sepp, *Jerusalem und das Heilige Land*, 1 (1873), 647ff.; Zickermann, in: *ZDPV*, 29 (1906), 51ff.; Schuerer, Gesch, 1 (1901³), 693ff.; Carroll, in: AASOR, 5 (1925), 77ff.; Schulten, in: *ZDPV*, 56 (1933), 180ff.; Reifenberg, in: *Archaeology*, 3 (1950), 40ff. D. Ussishkin, "Betar: The Last Stronghold of Bar-Kokhba," *Bulletin of the Anglo-Israel Archaeological Society*, 6 (1986–87): 49–50; idem, "Archaeological Soundings at Betar, Bar-Kokhba's Last Stronghold," in: *Tel Aviv*, 20 (1993): 66–97; B. Bagatti, *Ancient Christian Villages of Judaea and Negev*, (2002), 27–28; P. Schäfer (ed.), *The Bar Kokhba War Reconsidered. New Perspectives on the Second Revolt Against Rome* (2003); Y. Tsafrir, L. Di Segni, and J. Green, *Tabula Imperii Romani. Iudaea – Palaestina. Maps and Gazetteer.* (1994), 86–87.

BET(H)-HARAM (or **Haran**) (Heb. בֵּית הָרָם, הָרָן), town in the Jordan Valley, N. of the Dead Sea, allotted by Moses to the tribe of Gad and included in the list of its cities (Num. 32:36; Josh. 13:27). It is possibly mentioned in the Egyptian Execration Texts of the 18th century B.C.E. In the Talmud, Beth-Haram is identified with Bet ha-Ramta (TJ, Shev. 9:2, 38d; cf. Shab. 26a) which is also mentioned by Eusebius (Onom. 48:14) as Betharamphtha. *Herod Antipas, who fortified the city, called it Livias, in honor of the empress Livia, and also Julias, as soon as Livia became a member of the Julian imperial family. In 56 C.E. *Agrippa II received Livias and its district from the emperor Nero (Jos., Wars, 2:59, 168, 252; Jos., Ant., 18:27; 20:159). Beth-Haram was the headquarters of a region as late as the Byzantine period. Springs and groves are reported to have existed in its vicinity. The Hellenistic and Roman cities are situated on Tell al-Rāma, in the lower Jordan Valley, which has preserved the ancient name; the Israelite city has been located by Nelson Glueck at Tell Iktanū nearby.

BIBLIOGRAPHY: EM, S.V.; Glueck, in: AASOR, 25–28 (1951), 389–95; Press, Ereẓ, 1 (1951), 82; Aharoni, Land, index.

[Michael Avi-Yonah]

BET ḤARODON, locality 3 mi. (5 km.) S. of Jerusalem. It was on the road leading to Bukei'a in the wilderness where the he-goat that was allotted to *Azazel in the Temple ritual on the Day of Atonement was pushed to its death from a cliff (Yoma 4:2ff.; Yoma 66bff.). It has been identified with Khirbat Ḥarazān near the wilderness of Ẓuq. Bet Ḥarodon is also mentioned (in the form Ḥarodona) in a marriage contract from 117 C.E., written in Aramaic, found in the *Murabbaʿat cave.

BIBLIOGRAPHY: Avi-Yonah, Geog, 104, 226; P. Benoit et al., *Les Grottes de Murabbaʿat* (1961), 111.

[Michael Avi-Yonah]

BETHBASI (Βηθαλαγα), locality in Judea identified with Khirbat Beit Bassa southeast of *Bethlehem, where *Simeon b. Mattathias the Hasmonean was besieged by the Syrian general *Bacchides. Simeon managed to raise the siege by burning Bacchides' war engines (I Macc. 9:62–64; cf. Jos. *Antiq.* XIII, 26). Bethbasi is also mentioned in a document from Murabbaʿat (115, 2). The ruins of Khirbat Beit Bassa consist of fragmentary structures, terraces, cisterns, and at least one rock-hewn stepped *mikveh* with a double entrance from the Second Temple period. No fortifications are discernible.

BIBLIOGRAPHY: Abel, in: RB, 34 (1925), 211ff.; P. Benoit, et al., *Les Grottes de Murabbaʿat* (1961), no. 24. **ADD. BIBLIOGRAPHY:** M. Kochavi (ed.), *Judaea, Samaria and the Golan: Archaeological Survey 1967–1968* (1972), 42, Site 29; D. Amit, *Ritual Baths from the Second Temple Period in the Hebron Hills* (1996); Y. Tsafrir, L. Di Segni, and J. Green, *Tabula Imperii Romani. Iudaea – Palaestina. Maps and Gazetteer.* (1994), 80.

[Michael Avi-Yonah / Shimon Gibson (2nd ed.)]

BETHE, HANS ALBRECHT (1906–2005), nuclear physicist and Nobel Prize laureate in physics (1967). Bethe was born in Strasbourg, Alsace-Lorraine. He studied physics at Frankfurt-am-Main University and received his Ph.D. in theoretical physics at Munich University in 1928. He held successive appointments at the universities of Munich, Stuttgart, and Tubingen. He emigrated to England in 1933 because his mother was Jewish, but he never acknowledged any personal Jewish affiliation. After a temporary appointment at Manchester University and a fellowship at Bristol University, he became assistant professor at Cornell, Ithaca, in the U.S., in 1935. He was full professor in 1937–75 and then professor emeritus. In 1943–46 he worked in Los Alamos on the Manhattan Project as director of the theoretical physics division. His work in theoretical physics led to the Nobel Prize for his studies on atomic structure in general and more specifically for elucidating the sequence of energy-creating nuclear reactions in stars which culminate in helium production. His many awards include the Presidential Medal in 1948 and the Max Planck Medal in 1955. He was a member of the President's Science Advisory Committee in 1956–64 and in 1958 was scientific adviser to the U.S. at the Geneva test ban talks. In the 1980s and 1990s he campaigned for international control and peaceful use of nuclear energy. The books he wrote between 1955 and 1964 remain important sources of information on nuclear particle interactions and quantum theory.

[Michael Denman (2nd ed.)]

BET ḤERUT (Heb. בֵּית חֵרוּת; "Home of Freedom"), moshav in central Israel, in the Ḥefer Plain, founded in 1933. The settlers, mostly from East and Central Europe, transformed their village in 1966 from a regular moshav into a moshav shittufi. Its economy was based on citrus plantations, garden crops, and milch cattle. In 1970 Bet Ḥerut numbered 290 inhabitants, more than doubling to 616 by 2002.

[Efraim Orni]

BETH HATEFUTSOTH – The Nahum Goldmann Museum of the Jewish Diaspora.

The idea of a museum to depict the Jewish Diaspora throughout the ages, and in all its various phases, was first suggested by Dr. Nahum Goldmann at a meeting of the World Jewish Congress held in Stockholm in 1959. The museum was opened in Tel Aviv on May 15, 1978, the 30th anniversary of the State of Israel.

Beth Hatefutsoth is unique among museums in the world in the field of the humanities. It contains no artifacts or historical relics and aims at presenting a kaleidoscope of Jewish history and life during 2,500 years of Diaspora through the use of the most varied and innovative techniques.

The permanent exhibit is not presented in chronological or geographical order but is divided into six thematic sections, the originator of which was the Israeli poet Abba Kovner, and it conveys a comprehensive picture of the spiritual and social life of Diaspora Jewry. The six sections are The Family, The Community, Faith, Culture, Among the Nations, and The Return. A seventh section, the Chronosphere, is a hall resembling a planetarium on whose dome and walls an audio-visual display of Jewish history is projected by a battery of 35 synchronized projectors, providing an overall historical and chronological frame of reference.

Four study areas are installed in various sections of the permanent exhibit. Each contains five two-seat booths in which short documentary films on topics related to the subject-matter of the museum can be selected by the visitor from a catalogue and viewed on TV-size screens. Each study area has also a booth containing a computer screen terminal. The computer's memory contains information on Jewish Diaspora communities around the world, and the visitor can "converse" with the computer and request information concerning these communities.

A central architectural feature of the four-story building is the Memorial Column, suspended from the museum's roof. At the base of the somber pillar is a specially illustrated volume, *Scrolls of Fire*, recounting episodes of Jewish martyrdom.

In addition to the permanent exhibit, Beth Hatefutsoth presents several temporary exhibitions every year, all related to Diaspora Jewish life and history. These exhibitions are displayed in the Temporary Exhibitions Gallery and in the Foyer. In 1981 the "Jewish Heritage in the Eye of the Camera" attracted entries from Jewish communities the world over.

The exhibitions at Beth Hatefutsoth have become the basis for a dynamic network of educational and cultural activities. Lectures, symposia, study-days and seminars take place regularly in the museum's B'nai Zion auditorium. Thousands of Israeli high school children regularly visit Beth Hatefutsoth for special study programs led by the museum's Youth Division. A special department is charged with organizing study days and seminars for Jewish youth from the Diaspora. This operation, involving thousands of students each year, is run jointly with the World Jewish Congress and is conducted in English, French, Spanish and Portuguese. As such, the museum functions not as an Israeli museum but as a museum of the Jewish people.

Organizations of Friends of Beth Hatefutsoth have been established in various countries to assist the museum with special projects. The major portion of the finance for the establishment of the museum was donated by the Council of Organizations of the United Jewish Appeal in New York. The building was designed by the Israeli architects Eliahu Gwircman and Itzhak Yashar, following an international competition in which the renowned architect Mies van der Rohe headed the panel of judges. The planning of the museum's contents was entrusted to a team consisting of Karl Katz of the Metropolitan Museum of Art, New York (chairman), Abba Kovner, Professor Bezalel Narkiss, head of the Fine Arts Institute at the Hebrew University in Jerusalem, Paul Kedar, later Israel consul-general in New York, and Jesaja Weinberg, director-general of Beth Hatefutsoth who was in charge of the entire project from 1970. Dr. Geoffrey Wigoder and Dr. Ely Ben-Gal also participated in programmatic planning. An Academic Committee drawn from the faculty of Tel Aviv University and headed by Professor Shlomo Simonsohn, then rector of the university, guided the planning work. Advisory contacts were maintained with Professors Salo W. Baron and Meyer Schapiro of Columbia University. The exhibit was designed by two noted international experts – Charles Forberg of New York and James Gardner of London. Dozens of artists and craftsmen from Israel, England, and the United States were involved in the production of the exhibits.

In 1996 Beth Hatefutsoth launched its online site, aiming to serve as a link between Jews in the Diaspora and Israel. The site includes virtual exhibitions and information about the museum's activities as well as various data bases.

WEBSITE: www.bh.org.il.

[Geoffrey Wigoder]

BET HILLEL (Heb. בֵּית הִלֵּל), moshav in northern Israel, in the Ḥuleh Valley, founded in 1940 as one of the settlements then being established on the periphery of the then Ḥuleh swamp. It suffered heavy damage in the War of Independence (1948) and was subsequently rebuilt by a group of demobilized soldiers. The population was composed of immigrants from Eastern Europe and other areas. Its economy was based on milch cattle, field crops, and fruit orchards. Guest facilities were also opened there. In 2002 the population of Bet Hillel was 550. The settlement was named after Hillel *Joffe.

[Efraim Orni]

BET HILLEL AND BET SHAMMAI, two schools of exposition of the Oral Law, named after *Hillel and *Shammai who lived at the end of the first century B.C.E. and the beginning of the first century C.E. These two schools existed from the time of these two sages, their founders, until the second generation after the destruction of the Second Temple, i.e., until the beginning of the second century C.E. Tannaitic literature, the *halakhah*, the halakhic Midrashim, and the *aggadah* record the numerous controversies which took place between Bet Shammai and Bet Hillel. These debates comprise the principal content of the Oral Law in the last two to three generations of the Second Temple period. Very little is extant of the teachings of individual scholars as they are frequently cited as part of the overall teachings of Bet Shammai and Bet Hillel. Many of the *halakhot* and tannaitic controversies dating from the generation of Jabneh (c. 70 C.E.) are probably, and a large number are explicitly, based on the views of Bet Hillel which were adopted as the *halakhah* in opposition to those of Bet Shammai (see below), while numerous anonymous *halakhot* are extant which may once have been the subject of dispute between Bet Shammai and Bet Hillel.

Their controversies are concerned with four areas.

(1) Halakhic decisions based on judgment and on logical reasoning. For example, in discussing the order of the blessings in the *Kiddush* for Sabbaths and festivals, Bet Shammai declares that the blessing is to be said first over the day (i.e., the Sabbath or festival) and then over the wine; whereas Bet Hillel maintains that the blessing is to be said first over the wine and then over the day (Ber. 8:1). Again, Bet Shammai contends that a woman may not remarry on the evidence of a "mere voice" (i.e., the voice of someone who, testifying to the death of the husband, cannot be identified), while Bet Hillel holds that she may remarry on the basis of such evidence (Yev. 122a).

(2) Determining the "fences" around prohibitions, and the extent to which a prohibition is to be applied. For exam-

ple, with regard to spiced oil, Bet Shammai declares it liable to tithing by one who buys it from an *am ha-areẓ* (a person who in his ignorance is not scrupulous in observing the laws concerning priestly and levitical dues), whereas Bet Hillel exempts it (Dem. 1:3). If one slaughters with a scythe with a forward movement (i.e., not against the serrated edge), Bet Shammai maintains that the slaughtering is invalid, while Bet Hillel declares it valid (Ḥul. 1:2).

(3) Halakhic Midrashim. For example, Bet Shammai maintains that in the evening a man should recline (on his side) and recite the *Shema*, and in the morning he should stand, according to the verse (Deut. 6:7), "When thou liest down, and when thou risest up." Bet Hillel, however, declares that a man should recite it as it suits him, since it states (*ibid.*), "When thou walkest by the way." Why then does the biblical verse state, "When thou liest down, and when thou risest up?" This means at the times when people customarily lie down and at the time they rise up (Ber. 1:3). Again, Bet Shammai states: "A man should not divorce his wife unless he finds some unchastity in her, since it says: 'because he hath found some unseemly thing in her" (Deut. 24:1), but Bet Hillel states: even if she has merely spoilt his food, since it says: "because he hath found something unseemly in her" (i.e., anything the husband personally finds unfitting) (Git. 9:10).

(4) *Aggadah*, religious philosophy, and ethics. For example, Bet Shammai asserts that it were better if man had not been created at all, whereas Bet Hillel maintains that it is better for man to have been created than not (Er. 13b).

Only three controversies between Hillel and Shammai themselves have been preserved, but more than 350 are reported between Bet Hillel and Bet Shammai, most of which are in the *Zera'im*, *Mo'ed*, *Nashim*, and *Tohorot* sections of the Mishnah. They deal with personal life, with blessings and prayers, the separation of priestly dues and tithes, marriage and divorce, levitical cleanness and abstinence, and in a very few instances with sacrifices and the priestly service, and with civil and capital cases. In some of these controversies Shammai himself disputes the opinions of both Bet Shammai and Bet Hillel (Eduy. 1:7, 8, 10, 11). In several instances where the view opposed to that of Bet Shammai is quoted anonymously (*tanna kamma*) or in the name of the sages (Ber. 6:5; Dem. 3:1), the version is late as this is how the opinion of Bet Hillel was recorded after it had been adopted as the definitive ruling. Proof of this is found in a number of cases where the view of the *tanna kamma* or of the sages quoted in a Mishnah occurs in a *baraita* as that of Bet Hillel (cf. Ter. 4:3, with Tosef., Ter. 5:3, et al.). Generally, Bet Shammai is mentioned before Bet Hillel, and tradition sees in this an expression of the latter's humility (Er. 13b).

Many of the controversies between the two schools took place in Second Temple times. There is, for example, the argument whether on a festival hands could be laid on burnt and peace offerings, a subject on which Hillel and Shammai themselves held conflicting views (**Semikhah* on Sacrifices). A dispute concerning this *halakhah* took place in the forecourt of the Temple between Hillel and the pupils of Bet Shammai, and between them and those of Bet Hillel. On this question, the *halakhah* was decided during the existence of the Second Temple (Ḥag. 2:3; Tosef., Ḥag. 2:10–12; and parallel passages). During this period Bet Shammai once achieved ascendancy over Bet Hillel in the Temple Chamber of Hananiah b. Hezekiah b. Garon with the adoption of the "Eighteen Measures" – restrictive decrees that increased the barrier between Jews and non-Jews (TJ, Shab. 1:7, 3c; and parallel passages). This event is believed by several scholars to have taken place shortly before the destruction of the Second Temple. The early date of other controversies is evident from the conflicting views of *tannaim* living in the period of the destruction of the Second Temple in formulating the disputes between Bet Shammai and Bet Hillel (Tosef., Pe'ah 3:2). There are, however, controversies about problems raised by the destruction of the Temple, e.g., procedure at the time of removal of **ma'aser sheni* (Ma'as. Sh. 5:7).

Very little is known about the identity of the pupils of Hillel and Shammai. A *baraita* states that "Hillel the Elder had eighty disciples… the greatest of them was *Jonathan b. Uzziel, the least *Johanan b. Zakkai" (Suk. 28a). None of the teachings of Jonathan b. Uzziel has been preserved, and while Johanan b. Zakkai's statements reflect the outlook of Bet Hillel, it is difficult, as a matter of chronology, to assume that he studied under Hillel himself. Several of Shammai's pupils are known, most of them from the period of the Second Temple, their connection with Bet Shammai being stressed in tannaitic literature. They are Bava b. Buta, a contemporary of Hillel (Tosef., Ḥag. 2:11; and parallel passages); Dostai of Kefar Yatmah who transmitted a tradition he had heard from Shammai (Or. 2:5); Joezer, master of the Temple, who once put a question to Gamaliel the Elder in the Temple court (Or. 2:12); and Johanan b. ha-Ḥoranit of the generation of the destruction of the Temple (Tosef., Suk. 2:3). Sometimes "the elders of" Bet Shammai and Bet Hillel are mentioned (Suk. 2:7; Tosef. RH 4:11; Men. 41b et al.). According to a *genizah* fragment of *Sifrei Zuta* on *Ḥukkat* (*Tarbiz*, 1 (1930), 52), Bet Shammai had Idumean pupils, their halakhic statements corresponding to those of R. Judah who taught the view of Eliezer b. Hyrcanus "*ha-Shammuti*" (Men. 18a). According to Rashi, Nid. 7b, this refers to the fact that R. Eliezer was excommunicated, but this interpretation is inacceptable. As Tos. *in loc* points out, it means "a Shammaite" (cf. also Rashi to Shab. 132b, where he gives this as an alternative). Eleazar b. Hananiah, the general for Idumea in the Jewish War against the Romans (Jos., Wars, 2:566), also followed the line of Shammai (cf. Mekh., Ba-Ḥodesh, 7 with Beẓah 16a).

The circumstance that gave rise to the two schools is given in a tannaitic tradition: "At first there were no controversies in Israel…. When anyone had need of a *halakhah* he went to the Great Sanhedrin…. If they had heard (such a *halakhah*), they informed him of it, but if not, they decided the matter by taking a vote…. From there the *halakhah* would spread in Israel. With the increase in the pupils of Shammai and Hillel who had not sufficiently 'ministered to sages' (i.e., inadequately studied the Torah), controversy increased in Israel" (Tosef., Sanh. 7:1; and parallel passages). Even if the deficient learning of the pupils of Shammai and Hillel is ascribed to various historical factors, such as the dissolution of the Sanhedrin under Herod, or the Sadducean majority in the Sanhedrin which precluded any halakhic decisions being submitted to it by the sages, it is doubtful whether this tannaitic tradition adequately explains the numerous controversies which spanned almost a century. A more likely explanation is in terms of the expansion and crystallization of the *halakhah* involving a clash between different opinions and approaches in interpreting earlier traditions and in creating new *halakhot*. Tannaitic tradition presumably saw in the two views a legitimate expression of conflicting opinions: "Both of them are the words of the living God" (TJ, Ber. 1:7, 3b). It was reasonably permitted to follow the views either of Bet Shammai or of Bet Hillel but "a man who wishes to impose additional restrictions upon himself by adopting the stricter practices of Bet Shammai as well as the stricter practices of Bet Hillel, can be characterized by the verse 'the fool walketh in darkness'" (Eccles. 2:14; Tosef., Eduy. 2:3). It was furthermore stated that "although one school prohibited what the other permitted, or forbade what the other declared eligible, nonetheless Bet Shammai did not refrain from marrying women from [the families of] Bet Hillel, nor Bet Hillel from [the families of] Bet Shammai.... Nor did either refrain from borrowing the utensils of the other for the preparation of food under conditions of levitical cleanness" (Yev. 1:4). In all this there is no indication that the controversies originated from "insufficiently ministering to sages," but rather have their basis in the process whereby the *halakhah* was created.

Tannaitic tradition emphasizes that Bet Shammai adopted the stricter, Bet Hillel the more lenient view. The Mishnah (Eduy. 4) enumerates 23 (or 24) of their controversies that differ from the others in that they are "instances of Bet Shammai's lenient and of Bet Hillel's restrictive rulings." To these, various sages added a further 17 examples (*ibid.*). There are others concerning which the Talmud and the commentators try to find an explanation as to why they too were not similarly cited. The total of all of these is about 50. Of Bet Shammai's restrictive rulings the bulk extends the application of a prohibition, Bet Shammai, adopting the stricter view (i.e., the wider application of the prohibition). Bet Hillel usually adopts the more lenient approach.

Many scholars have sought to define the basic principles underlying the divergences between the two schools. Some have explained this divergence by claiming that they reflect the individual traits of their founders, of Hillel who was gentle and kind, and of Shammai who was stern and short-tempered. But this is inadequate, particularly since only a few controversies took place between Hillel and Shammai personally. Another interpretation regards their disputes as a social and economic conflict, holding that Bet Shammai belonged to the upper or middle landed classes, whereas the sages of Bet Hillel were from the lower strata of society with their respective views reflecting the needs and life of these strata. However, this point of view has been attacked by some scholars on the grounds that there is scanty proof that Bet Shammai belonged to the wealthy middle class. It is moreover difficult to accept the interpretation given to the *halakhot* listed by these scholars. It is similarly difficult to accept theories such as that which attributes the difference to the divergent halakhic outlook, conception, and apprehension of the two schools, with Bet Shammai adopting a uniform, systematic approach to the *halakhah*, as against the particularized, heterogeneous viewpoint of Bet Hillel. It has also been suggested that Bet Shammai represented the continuation of an early halakhic tradition which was strict in its interpretation of the law. Some have even suggested that the differences between Bet Hillel and Bet Shammai can be found in the political tensions that existed towards the end of the Second Temple period. Bet Shammi represented a more extreme political position, possibly tracing its origins back to the Hasmoneon rebellion and even serving as the inspiration for some of the more extreme elements in the rebellion against Rome, while Bet Hillel was representative of a more realistic and moderate approach which might have sought some sort of accommodation with Rome. A difficulty for all of the above mentioned theories is that many of the traditions of Bet Hillel and Bet Shammai were themselves subject to editorial revision and products of different time periods; therefore each source must be examined individually and critically before any attempted conclusions are made. Various factors and traditions, as well as different approaches and tendencies, probably combined to produce the divergent views. Difficult though it is to find the social or conceptual bases for the rise of the two schools, a certain line is evident in their homiletical exegesis of biblical passages and in their discussions of many *halakhot*. Bet Shammai tends in the former to the plain and sometimes even to the narrow, literal interpretation of a verse, as opposed to the wider significance assigned by Bet Hillel. Because of the limited number of controversies involving the exegesis of biblical verses it is impossible to ascertain what relation their disputes bear to the seven exegetical principles laid down or formulated by Hillel (Tosef., Sanh. 7:11). Insofar as the *halakhah* is concerned it is evident in many cases that the view of Bet Hillel is characteristic of theoretical *halakhah* which differentiates between principles of jurisprudence and that they decided in *halakhah* in accordance with such principles, in contrast to the view of Bet Shammai which is characteristic of the literal and even the conservative approach, conservative not in the sociological sense but in creativity and in halakhic innovation (cf. Pe'ah 6:1; Eduy. 4:1 and 5; Er. 1:2; Beẓah 1:2). With the publication of the halakhic works from the Dead Sea Scrolls, some scholars have claimed that there can sometimes be found a similar approach to halakhic sources and reasoning in both the Dead Sea Scrolls and the halakhah of Bet Shammai. It is thus possible that the reasons for the gradual triumph of the halakhah of Bet Hillel over that of Bet Shammai is similar to those reasons for the ascendance of Rabbinic halakhah over that found in the Dead Sea Scrolls.

The Mishnah reports several instances in which Bet Hillel retracted its opinion and agreed with that of Bet Shammai (Yev. 15:3; Eduy. 1:12, et al.) But there is only a single instance in which Bet Shammai retracted and agreed with Bet Hillel (Ter. 5:4), when it is stated "after they agreed," i.e., Bet Shammai with Bet Hillel. In matters relating to the Temple the *halakhah* was decided according to the opinion of Bet Hillel on only one occasion (Tosef., Ḥag, 2:11, cf. Pes. 8:8; Tosef., *ibid.*, 7:13, et al.). At Jabneh, in the generation after the destruction of the Temple, Bet Hillel gained the ascendancy (first–second century), whereupon the *halakhah* was laid down according to Bet Hillel. It was then stated that the possibility of making a choice between the two schools applied only "before a **bat kol* [heavenly voice] went forth, but once a *bat kol* went forth, the *halakhah* was always according to Bet Hillel, and whoever acted contrary to the views of Bet Hillel deserved death. It was taught: A *bat kol* went forth and declared, 'The *halakhah* is according to the words of Bet Hillel.' Where did the *bat kol* go forth?… At Jabneh" (TJ, Ber. 1:7, 3b; and parallel passages). The determination of the *halakhah* according to Bet Hillel was probably not accomplished in a single act but was rather a process that continued during the entire Jabneh period, commencing with Johanan b. Zakkai, soon after the destruction of the Temple (70) and ending with the death of Rabban Gamaliel before the Bar Kokhba war (c. 135). This process was strongly opposed by the last adherents of Bet Shammai (Tosef., Eduy. 1:1; Tosef., Yev. 1:9–10; TJ, Shev. 4:5, 35b). In the amoraic period the *halakhah* of Bet Hillel was accepted in the schools of the *amoraim* who declared: "The opinion of Bet Shammai when it conflicts with that of Bet Hillel is no Mishnah" (Ber. 36b, et al.). Several *halakhot* were, however, decided according to Bet Shammai (see Ber. 51bff.; Tos. to Suk. 3a, s.v. *de-amar*), and traces of the decision of Bet Shammai are to be found in various passages in tannaitic and even amoraic literature. The Kabbalah and following it Ḥasidism explained the differences between the two schools in terms of their philosophies: Bet Shammai has its origin in *gevurah* ("might") and Bet Hillel in *ḥesed* ("mercy"); in the future (i.e., the world to come) the *halakhah* will be according to Bet Shammai (Zohar, *Ra'aya Meheimna* 3:245a; Moses b. Menahem (Graft) *Sefer va-Yakhel Moshe* 2 (1699)).

BIBLIOGRAPHY: A. Schwarz, *Die Erleichterungen der Schammaiten und die Erschwerungen der Hilleliten* (1893); Bacher, Tann 1 (19032), 11–22; Buechler, in: *Sefer… M. Bloch* (1905), 21–30 (Heb. part); Weiss, Dor, 1 (19044), 167–76; M. Guttmann, *Zur Einleitung in die Halacha*, 1 (1909), 36ff.; D. Hoffmann, *Ha-Mishnah ha-Rishonah* (1913), 12–59; Frankel, Mishnah, 47–57, 94; L. Ginzberg, *Perushim ve-Ḥiddushim ba-Yerushalmi*, 1 (1941), 146–7, 152–60; idem, *On Jewish Law and Lore* (1962), 88–124; Sonne, in: *Louis Ginzberg Jubilee Volume* (1945), 275–91; Guttmann, in: HUCA, 28 (1957), 115–26; Gilat, in: *Bar-Ilan Sefer ha-Shanah*, 4–5 (1967), 104–16; L. Finkelstein, *The Pharisees* (19623), index s.v. *Hillel and Shammai*. **ADD. BIBLIOGRAPHY:** I. Konovitz, *Bet Shammai-Bet* Hillel (1965); Y. Gilat, *Sefer Bar-Ilan*, 4–5 (1967), 104–116; idem., *Yad le-Gilat* (2002), 156–166; J. Neusner, *The Rabbinic Traditions about the Pharisees Before 70* (1971), vol. 2; S. Safrai, in: WCJS, 7 (1981), 21–44; M. Weiss, in: *Sidra*, 4 (1988), 53–66, idem, in: *Sidra*, 6 (1990), 41–62; Y. Zusman, in: *Tarbiz*, 59 (1990), 11–76; Y. Ben-Shalom, *Beit Shammai u-Ma'avak ha-Kannaim Neged Romi* (1993); J. Schwartz, in: *Zion*, 59:4 (1994), 515–520; V. Noam, in: *Jewish Studies*, 41 (2002), 45–70.

[Shmuel Safrai]

BETH JACOB SCHOOLS, network of religious schools for girls organized in Poland in the post-World War I era with the aid of *Agudat Israel, an ultra-Orthodox organization whose schools for boys were to be found in every community. While the boys' schools were of the old traditional type, the newly formed schools for girls combined Jewish traditional studies and industrial training.

The first school was founded in Cracow in 1917 by Sara Schnirer. The school in Cracow had an enrollment of only 30 pupils, but the success of this early venture in imparting religious Jewish studies, some secular learning, and vocational training led to the formation of a large number of schools in a number of countries. By 1929 there were 147 such schools in Poland, and 20 schools in Lithuania, Latvia, and Austria. The Beth Jacob school system included teachers' training institutes founded in 1931 and post-graduate courses (1933). Two periodicals were published: *Beth Jacob Journal* and *Der Kindergarten*.

With the invasion of Austria, Poland, Lithuania and Latvia by the Nazis and subsequently by the Russians, the activities of the Beth Jacob schools were discontinued. At the end of World War II Beth Jacob schools were opened in Israel, England, Switzerland, Belgium, France, Uruguay, Argentina, and the United States. In Israel there are over 100 schools serving 15,000 girls. These schools, with their teacher-training programs at the post-high school seminary level, have become more flexible in recent years, allowing girls to study there simultaneously for technical degrees in such fields as computers, architecture, and interior design.

In the U.S. the Beth Jacob National Council was organized in 1943. By 1947 there were eight schools under their aegis. In 1951 two teacher-training schools were established and in the late 1950s two high schools were founded. At the turn of the century about 25 schools were in operation.

BIBLIOGRAPHY: Z. Sharfstein (ed.), *Ha-Ḥinnukh ve-ha-Tarbut be-Eiropah Bein Shetei Milḥamot ha-Olam* (1957), 61–83; J. Pilch (ed.), *A History of Jewish Education in the United States* (1969), 140. **ADD. BIBLIOGRAPHY:** J. Lupu, *New Directions in Haredi Society: Vocational Training and Academic Studies* (2004).

[Judah Pilch]

BETHLEHEM (Beth-Lehem) (Heb. בֵּית לֶחֶם; Arab. *Bait Laḥm*), city in Judah located five mi. (eight km.) S. of Jerusalem. Bethlehem may be mentioned in the *el-Amarna letters (14th century B.C.E.) as a city in the territory of Jerusalem (*Bit ilu Nin. Ib* = the house of the god Ninib = Lahamu?; EA, 290; however, the meaning of the ideogram *Nin. Ib* is not certain). Tradition placed the tomb of *Rachel in the vicinity of Ephrath/Beth-Lehem where Jacob is said to have buried her (Gen. 35:19). Together with its neighboring cities (I Chron. 2:51, 54), Beth-Lehem became the center of the tribe of *Judah and was settled by an important clan claiming descent from Perez, son of Tamar and Judah, among whose descendants were Boaz and Jesse the father of David. In the period of the Judges, the fields of Beth-Lehem were the scene of the idyll of Ruth and Boaz as related in the Book of Ruth. The levite youth in the story of Micah and the graven image (Judg. 17:7), as well as the levite's concubine mentioned in Judges 19, came from this city. *David and some of his warrior-kinsmen, sons of Zeruiah, were also born at Beth-Lehem, and it was there that Samuel anointed David king (I Sam. 16:1–13). The sacrificial act performed by Samuel on that occasion suggests that Beth-Lehem may have been a center for the worship of the Lord. At the end of Saul's reign, Beth-Lehem was occupied for a time by a Philistine garrison. The story of David's men bringing him water from the "well of Beth-Lehem, that was by the gate" (II Sam. 23:15) implies that it was even then a fortified city. Some of the assassins of Gedaliah son of Ahikam, Nebuchadnezzar's governor in Judea after the destruction of the Temple, came from the neighborhood of Beth-Lehem (Jer. 40:8); the remnants of his followers withdrew to the same region before their flight to Egypt (Jer. 41:16–17). With the return from Babylonia, the exiles from Beth-Lehem went back to their city (Ezra 2:21; Neh. 7:26), and Jews inhabited the city until the time of Bar Kokhba. In 135 C.E. a Roman garrison was stationed there to root out the remnants of Bar Kokhba's army (Lam. R. 1:15). Later a gentile population resided in Bethlehem and erected a temple to Adonis (Tammuz) in a grove at the edge of the city (Jerome, Epistle 58 to Paulinus).

On the basis of Micah 5:1, the early Christians identified Jesus' birthplace with Bethlehem (Matt. 2:1, 5; Luke 2:4, 15; John 7:42). The location of this event in a cave east of the city is first mentioned by Justin Martyr (155–160) and by the time of Origen (third century) the site of the cave already corresponded to its present position. At the beginning of the reign of Constantine, his mother *Helena erected a Christian church over the cave. The church was destroyed during the Samaritan uprising against Byzantine rule (529): it was rebuilt by Justinian in the form that it has kept to the present time. On the facade of the building, over the entrance, were depicted the birth of Jesus and his adoration by the kings of the East. Because this picture portrays people in Oriental costume, the Persians are said to have spared the building when they captured Bethlehem in 614. In the fifth century *Jerome settled in Bethlehem and built a monastery there. In preparing his Latin translation of the Bible, the basis of the Vulgate, he was assisted by Jewish scholars who apparently lived in villages in the neighborhood of the city. The grotto in which he is reputed to have lived is still to be seen under the Church of the Nativity. Further evidence of the resumption of Jewish settlement in the hills of Jerusalem is also found in an extant account of the Persian campaign, according to which the invaders were aided by Jewish inhabitants of the hill country.

In the early Arab period Bethlehem suffered no damage. The city fell to Tancred's forces during the First Crusade without fighting. Baldwin I and II, the crusader kings of Jerusalem, were crowned in the church of Bethlehem. The crusaders built a fort in the city that was demolished in 1489 during clashes between the Christians of Bethlehem and the Muslims of Hebron. *Benjamin of Tudela visited the city (c. 1160) and found 12 Jewish dyers there. The church of Bethlehem remained in Christian hands during the rule of the Mamluks and the Turks, even though the Muslim rulers oppressed the Christian minority. The Christians continually reduced the size of the entrance to the church for security reasons, so that by now it is just a low and narrow opening. From time to time, the Christian rulers in Europe concerned themselves with the maintenance and repair of the church. The conflicts between the various Christian communities in Bethlehem caused damage to the church and served to motivate international friction; the theft of the Silver Star from the church in 1847 was one of the factors behind the outbreak of the Crimean War. In the middle of the 19th century, the Turkish authorities determined the division of the church among the various Christian communities and the order of their ceremonies, according to previous tradition; this decision has been observed, almost without amendment, to the present.

[Michael Avi-Yonah]

Modern Bethlehem

Until 1948, Bethlehem was a city with a Christian majority. Of its 8,000 inhabitants in 1947, 75% were Christians and the rest Muslims; this ratio, however, subsequently changed as a result of the influx of Arab refugees from Israel who settled there. During the Six-Day War (1967), Bethlehem surrendered to the Israel army without a fight. In the 1967 census taken by Israel authorities, the town of Bethlehem proper numbered 14,439 inhabitants, its 7,790 Muslim inhabitants represented 53.9% of the population, while the Christians of various denominations numbered 6,231 or 46.1%. The 1,874 inhabitants of the refugee camp, lying within the municipal confines, raised the percentage of Muslim citizens to 58.2%. However, the three townships of Bethlehem, Beit (Bayt) Saḥur (the traditional Field of Ruth), and Beit (Bayt) Jala can be considered as a unit, as in 1967 they formed a continuous built-up area and a social and economic entity. Their total population amounted to 27,000, of whom 14,400 were Christians, constituting a 55% majority. The main Christian denominations are the Latins (Roman Catholics) and the Greek Orthodox. Other communities with over 100 adherents include the Syrian-Orthodox, the Syrian-Catholics, and the Melkites. There are also Protestants of various denominations, Maronites, and Armenians. Throughout most of its history, Bet (Bayt) Jālā was an exclusively Christian town. It has numerous churches and Christian institutions, including the Greek Orthodox St. Nicholas Church, the Catholic Patriarchate's Seminary, and a Lutheran secondary school. Nearby is the Cremisan Monastery of the Salesian fathers.

The Bethlehem town group has close economic and social ties with Jerusalem. In 1968 farming, trade, and tourism continued to constitute the mainstay of Bethlehem's economy. Inhabitants of the town own olive groves, vineyards, and deciduous fruit orchards. Bethlehem is a market town where Bedouin from the nearby Judean Desert trade their produce for local and imported goods. The town has a number of small hotels and restaurants catering to tourists and, more important, many workshops producing Christian souvenirs. Christian institutions contributed to raising the educational level and provided employment to a large number of inhabitants. The main building in Bethlehem is the Church of the Nativity (sections of which are maintained by the Greek Orthodox and the Catholics, the latter holding St. Catherine's Church adjacent to the main basilica). It is a major attraction for Christian pilgrims, especially at the Christmas celebrations of the Latins (Dec. 24 and 25), Orthodox (Jan. 6 and 7), and Armenians (Jan. 19 and 20). Bethlehem has numerous other Christian buildings, including convents of the Franciscans and the Rosary Sisters, edifices above the Milk Grotto, the Syrian-Orthodox Church, the Lutheran Church, parish schools, orphanages, and a French hospital. Near Bethlehem is the traditional "Shepherds' Field." Between Bethlehem and Jerusalem is the Greek Orthodox monastery of Mar Elias, the traditional resting place of Elijah the prophet when he fled from Jezebel.

In 1997 the populations of Bethlehem numbered 21,673, among them 6,568 refugees, while the population of Beit Jala was 11,957, including 5,329 refugees, and the population of Beit Saḥur 11,285 with 1,913 refugees. The city was transferred to the Palestinian Authority after the Oslo agreements. In 2002 a group of Palestinian terrorists took over the Church of the Nativity and held hostages there for more than a month under siege by the Israeli army. During the second ("al-Aqsa") Intifada Beit Jala sheltered snipers firing at the nearby Jerusalem residential neighborhood of Gilo, consequently taking return fire from the Israel Defense Forces and in effect turning the once tranquil area into a frontline battleground.

[Efraim Orni / Shaked Gilboa (2nd ed.)]

BIBLIOGRAPHY: Lewy, in: JBL, 59 (1940), 519–22; EM, 2 (1965), 86–88; Press, Ereẓ, 1 (1951), 88–89; R.W. Hamilton, *Guide to Bethlehem* (1939); L.H. Vincent and F.M. Abel, *Bethléem* (Fr., 1914). **WEBSITE:** www.bethlehem.org.

BETHLEPTEPHA, town in Judea which, in the time of Herod, replaced Keilah as the headquarters of one of the toparchies into which the province was divided. It is sometimes written "Betholeptephon" and is mentioned by Josephus (Wars, 4:445) as "Pella." Schuerer regards the name as a distortion of the Hebrew *Bet Netofah (Beit Nattif) a village six miles (10 km.) north of Bet Guvrin. The identification has now been generally accepted, though some identify it with Bet le-Tappu'aḥ (the Tappuah of Josh. 15:34). Vespasian destroyed Bethleptepha and killed all its inhabitants on his way from Emmaus to Edom. A mosaic floor of a fifth-century Byzantine church was discovered there as well as other mosaics, tombs, cisterns, and pillars from the Roman-Byzantine period.

BIBLIOGRAPHY: A. Reland, *Palaestina...* (1714), 648; Schuerer, Gesch, 2 (1907^4), 232n.; S. Klein, *Ereẓ Yehudah* (1939), 214; A. Schalit, *Hordos ha-Melekh* (1964^3), 111ff.

[Michael Avi-Yonah]

BET(H)-HORON (Heb. בֵּית חוֹרוֹן; Upper, עֶלְיוֹן (*Elyon*), and Lower, תַּחְתּוֹן (*Taḥton*)), two adjacent biblical towns named after the Canaanite deity Horon mentioned in Ugaritic literature and other texts. The towns, known as Upper and Lower Horon, were strategically located on the Gibeon-Aijalon road and guarded the important "ascent of Beth-Horon." Biblical tradition attributes their founding to Sheerah, daughter of Beriah, son of Ephraim (I Chron. 7:24). They were located on the border between the territory of the tribe of Ephraim and that of Benjamin (Josh. 16:3; 18:13–14). One or both of the towns was a levitical city (Josh. 21:22; I Chron. 6:53). Solomon fortified Beth-Horon (the lower town only, according to I Kings 9:17; both towns according to II Chron. 8:5). Beth-Horon is mentioned together with Gibeon in the list of towns conquered by Pharaoh *Shishak (tenth century B.C.E.). It then became part of the kingdom of Judah (cf. II Chron. 25:13). In the Persian and Hellenistic periods, Beth-Horon was in Judea. During the Hasmonean Wars, *Bacchides fortified both towns (I Macc. 9:50). The Mishnah (Shev. 9, 2) states that the Maritime Plain begins at Beth-Horon. It is located by Eusebius (Onom. 46:21) 12 (Roman) mi. from Aelia Capitolina (i.e., Jerusalem) and within its territory; on the *Madaba Map the two villages are marked as one place. Upper Beth-Horon is now identified with the Muslim Arab village ʿUr al-Fawqā (pop. 298 in 1967) and Lower Beth Horon with Beit ʿUr al-Taḥtā (pop. 920 in 1967). The road passing the two and the ascent between them were of military importance in ancient times. *Joshua pursued the Canaanite kings along this ascent after the battle of Gibeon (Josh. 10:10–11); the *Philistines passed this way after their setback at Michmas (I Sam. 13:18); here also *Judah Maccabee defeated Seron, the Seleucid general (I Macc. 3:16), and a Zealot force defeated the Roman governor *Cestius Gallus on his retreat from Jerusalem (Jos., Wars, 2:538ff., 546ff.). Archaeological finds indicate that Lower Beth-Horon, where potsherds from the Late Bronze Age onward have been uncovered, was established before Upper Beth-Horon, where the finds date only from and after the Iron Age (the Monarchy). An ostracon found at Tell el Qasīle (north Tel Aviv) mentions a consignment of gold for "Beth-Horon," but it is uncertain whether the name of the place Beth-Horon is meant or "the temple of [the god] Horon."

[Michael Avi-Yonah]

BIBLIOGRAPHY: Abel, Geog, 2 (1938), 274; B. Maisler (Mazar), in: JNES, 10 (1951), 266ff.; Mazar, in: VT, Suppl., 4 (1957), 61; Aharoni, Land, index; J. Garstang, *Joshua-Judges* (1931), 224; EM, 2 (1954), 73–75.

BETHPHAGE, village on the Mount of Olives in the immediate vicinity of *Jerusalem; it is named for green figs (*paggim*). In ancient times, it was surrounded by a wall. Bethphage marked the eastern confines of Jerusalem in the Second Temple period (Men. 11:2; Men. 75b). In the New Testament (Matt. 21:1–9; Mark 11:1–10; Luke 19: 29–38; John 12:12–19) it is mentioned as the place where *Jesus found the ass on which he entered Jerusalem. A church existed at this spot in the Byzantine period, and many pilgrims used it as a final stopping point on their journey to Jerusalem. The Crusaders put up many buildings in Bethpage, notably the Chapel of the Savior. It has been identified with the village of et-Ṭūr, on the southern of the three hills of the Mount of Olives. According to an ancient tradition the prophetess *Huldah was buried there. Recent excavations have uncovered the lower part of a Byzantine building, largely rock-hewn, which was used as an oil press.

BIBLIOGRAPHY: Abel, Geog, 2 (1938), 279; Press, Ereẓ, s.v. **ADD. BIBLIOGRAPHY:** S. Saller and E. Testa, *The Archaeological Setting of the Shrine of Bethphage* (1961); J. Wilkinson, *Jerusalem Pilgrims Before the Crusades*, (1977), 152–3; D. Pringle, *The Churches of the Crusader Kingdom of Jerusalem*, 1, (1993), 157–9; Y. Tsafrir, L. Di Segni, and J. Green, *Tabula Imperii Romani. Iudaea – Palaestina. Maps and Gazetteer.* (1994), 85.

[Michael Avi-Yonah / Shimon Gibson (2nd ed.)]

BETHSAIDA (Heb. בֵּית צַיְּדָא, **Bet Zayyada**), fishing village that was situated on the northeast shore of the Sea of Galilee near the mouth of the Jordan River in the Second Temple period. Philip the son of Herod (*Herod Phillipus) renamed it Julias in 30 C.E. in honor of Livia-Julia, the wife of the emperor Augustus and mother of Tiberius. It was Philip's second capital and he was buried there in 34 C.E. (Jos., Ant., 18:28, 108; Wars, 2:168; 3:515; Life, 398; cf. Pliny, *Historia Naturalis* 5:15). *Nero later presented it to *Agrippa II. The city is mentioned several times in the New Testament (Matt. 11:21; John 1:44, Luke 10:13, etc.) in accounts of visits of *Jesus and his disciples to villages on the shores of the Sea of Galilee and as the birthplace of the apostles Peter, Andrew, and Philip. It was the place to which Jesus withdrew on hearing of John the Baptist's death (Luke 9:10). It is also mentioned by Eusebius (Onom. 58:11) and the sixth-century pilgrim Theodosius (ch. 2, ed. Geyer). In the 19th century scholars suggested identifying Bethsaida with the site of et-Tell, a large mound situated inland and not far from where the Jordan flows into Lake Kinneret. Sixteenth-century travelers reported a Jewish fishing village there. The explorer Schumacher suggested the alternative sites of el-Araj, not far from the mouth of the Jordan River, and el-Mesadiyeh, an additional ruin located to the southeast of el-Araj. New excavations were commenced by Rami Arav and his associates at the site of et-Tell, bringing to light significant remains of settlements from Early Bronze I and II, as well as the remains of a well-fortified Iron Age II city with a well preserved gate with a carved stele and a large public building of *bit hilani* type. Impressive remains of a Hellenistic period fishing village were uncovered at the site as well as poorly preserved remains dating from the time of Jesus, with some pottery and stone vessels. Stone looting occurred at the site during later periods.

BIBLIOGRAPHY: Alt, in: PJB, 27 (1931), 40; Schuerer, Gesch, 2 (1907), 208; Avi-Yonah, Land, 105; Press Ereẓ, 1 (1951), 99; G. Schille, in: ZDPV, 73 (1957), 142. **ADD. BIBLIOGRAPHY:** C.C. McCowen, "The Problem of the Site of Bethsaida," in: *Journal of the Palestine Oriental Society*, 10 (1930): 32–58; A. Kindler, "The Coins of the Tetrarch Phillipus, Son of Herod I, and the Renaming of Bethsaida/Julias," in: *Cathedra*, 53 (1989): 24–26; R. Arav, *Bethsaida. A City by the Shore of the Sea of Galilee* (1995).

[Michael Avi-Yonah / Shimon Gibson (2nd ed.)]

BETHUEL (Heb. בֵּית אֵל = בְּתוּאֵל; "house of God," cf. *Batiilu* in the *Tell el-Amarna letters or – מתואל, "man of God"), the youngest son of *Nahor and Milcah (Gen. 22:21–22) and the father of Laban and *Rebekah (22:23, 24:15, et al.). In the list in Genesis 22, Bethuel appears as head of a tribe of Nahor's descendants and brother of Kemuel the father of Aram. Bethuel does not play as important a part in the biblical story of Rebekah as does Laban (24:28ff., et al.), and it appears that Bethuel was no longer alive, this being the reason that Laban received Abraham's servant, since in the organization of the patriarchal society that emerges from this story, the firstborn brother was regarded as head of the family. Bethuel is only mentioned in the discussion of the marriage and, even there, only after Laban (24:50). It is quite possible, as has been suggested by scholars, that this is a later addition, for even when Rebekah commences her journey, the members of the family salute her as "Our sister!" (24:60).

In the *Aggadah*

Bethuel was the king of Haran (Yal., Gen. 109). Bethuel's apparent disappearance in the middle of the negotiations with regard to Rebekah (cf. Gen. 24:50, 55) is explained by the assumption that he died suddenly while they were in progress. There are two Midrashim. According to one, when Bethuel saw the treasures Eliezer had brought with him, he tried to kill him by placing poisoned food before him. While he was telling his story, however, the angel who accompanied Eliezer changed the dishes so that the dish intended for Eliezer was set before Bethuel, who ate it and died (Yal., Gen. 109). According to the other account, Bethuel had introduced the *jus primae noctis* and his subjects declared themselves ready to submit to this outrage on the condition that his own daughters should not be exempt from it. He was about to exercise this right on Rebekah, but to spare her this shame, God caused his death (*ibid.*). With her approval Eliezer refused to let Rebekah remain in her father's house during the week of mourning (Gen. R. 60:12). From the fact that Rebekah was consulted before she accompanied Eliezer, the rabbis conclude that a fatherless minor girl may not be given in marriage without her consent (*ibid.*).

BIBLIOGRAPHY: E.A. Speiser, Genesis (Eng., 1964), 181, 184; de Vaux, Anc Isr, 29; Maisler (Mazar), in: *Zion*, 11 (1946), 7–8 (incl. bibl.); W.W. Baudissin, *Kyrios als Gottesname…*, 3 (1929), 300, 304. IN

THE AGGADAH: Ginzberg, Legends, 1 (1942), 294–6; 5 (1947), 261–2; L. Rabinowitz, in: JQR, 58 (1967/68), 143–61.

BETHULIA, the home of *Judith, the heroine of the apocryphal Book of Judith, in which it is described as a Jewish city that was besieged by the Assyrian general Holofernes. His death brought the siege to an abrupt end. The name of the city is apparently a form of Beth-El ("House of God"), and the geographic context of the story indicates a location on the northern edge of the hills of Samaria, near Dothan, and Ibleam. Some scholars have identified Bethulia with Jerusalem, Bemeselis (Mithiliyya), or with other localities such as Shechem or Sheikh Shibl above Kafr Qūd. It seems most probable, however, that Bethulia was an imaginary city that was endowed with a theophoric name for the purposes of a historical romance.

BIBLIOGRAPHY: Abel, Geog, 2 (1938), 283; J.M. Grintz, *Sefer Yehudit* (1957), 30 ff.

[Michael Avi-Yonah]

BET (Bayt) IKSA (بيت اكسا), Muslim-Arab village in the Judean Hills, west of Jerusalem; population (1967) 633. Located in mountainous terrain, its economy is mainly based on orchards of olives, almonds, and other fruit trees. In the Israel War of Independence (1948), hard battles were fought over the village which lies close to the Jerusalem–Tel Aviv highway. Israel forces captured Bet Iksā but under the terms of the 1949 Armistice Agreement the village was returned to Jordan, in exchange for small areas elsewhere given to Israel. The stipulation to keep the village demilitarized was not observed by the Jordanians. Bet Iksā was taken by Israeli forces in the Six-Day War.

[Efraim Orni]

BET KESHET (Heb. בֵּית קֶשֶׁת), kibbutz north of Mount Tabor, affiliated with Ha-Kibbutz ha-Me'uḥad. Bet Keshet was founded on Aug. 15, 1944, as the first settlement of the then clandestine *Palmaḥ. Most settlers had received agricultural training in the nearby Kadoorie School, while others were demobilized soldiers who had served in World War II. South African immigrants and others joined the kibbutz after 1948. In the War of Independence (1948) hard battles raged around Bet Keshet and a monument was subsequently erected to its members who fell. Its economy was based on field crops, deciduous fruit, vines, beef cattle, and other farm products. In 2002 the population of Bet Keshet was 297. The name, "House of the Bow," refers to the village being founded by pioneer soldiers (cf. II Sam. 1:18).

[Efraim Orni]

BET(H) LEḤEM (Ha-Gelilit), place located in western Galilee, near Kiryat Tivon, in the lower Zebulun region (Jos. 19:15; perhaps also Judges 12:8f.). It is referred to as Beth-Leḥem Ẓeriyah (TJ, Meg. 1, 70a), however this name has not yet been given a definitive explanation. Dalman believes that it means the Beth Leḥem which once belonged to Tyre. According to the list of priestly places of residence in Galilee, members of the Malkiya priestly division lived in Beth Leḥem in the 3rd and 4th centuries; it may also have been the home of the amora Kahana bar Malkiya (of the Malkiya priestly division). The biblical name was preserved by an Arab site called Beit Laḥm, southeast of Haifa. At present there is a moshav affiliated with Tenu'at ha-Moshavim near the site. This was founded in 1948 on the land of the former German Templar colony Bethlehem whose inhabitants were interned during World War II and later deported from the country. The population was composed of immigrants from Central and Eastern Europe and native-born Israelis. Its population in 1968 was 270, rising to around 425 in the mid-1990s and 570 in 2002. The moshav's residents earned their living in farming, tourism, and employment outside the moshav.

BIBLIOGRAPHY: IDB, 1 (1962), S.V. Bethlehem, no. 2; *Enẓiklopediyah le-Geografiyah Mikra'it* 1 (1963), 281–2.

[Efraim Orni]

BET(H)-MAON (Heb. בֵּית מָעוֹן).

(1) See *Baal-Meon.

(2) A locality ½ mi. (¾ km.) from Tiberias (Tell Mā'ūn) where Josephus conferred with the men of Tiberias during the Jewish War in 66 C.E. (Life, 64, 67). In talmudic times Beth-Maon is frequently mentioned as a center of opposition to the Patriarchs residing in Tiberias and as a refuge for rabbis antagonistic to them (Gen. R. 80:1, 24; 31:2). The priestly family of Huppah settled there after the destruction of the Temple (ha-Kallir: *Yashevah Eikhah*). The sources mention a synagogue there (cf. TJ Ta'an, 4:2, 68a).

BIBLIOGRAPHY: Avi-Yonah, Geog, 139; Press, Ereẓ, 1 (1951), 90. Y. Tsafrir, L. Di Segni, and J. Green, *Tabula Imperii Romani. Iudaea – Palaestina. Maps and Gazetteer* (1994), 84.

[Michael Avi-Yonah]

BET MEIR (Heb. בֵּית מֵאִיר), Israel moshav in the Judean Hills, west of Jerusalem, affiliated with Ha-Po'el ha-Mizrachi moshavim association. In the War of Independence (1948) the Arab garrison entrenched in the then-Arab village had cut off Jewish Jerusalem. The capture of the village by Israel forces opened the "Jerusalem Corridor." Bet Meir was founded in 1950. Its inhabitants came mainly from Hungary, Romania, and Poland. The settlers made use of hydroponics in order to conform with the religious prescription of the *sabbatical year. In 2002 the population of Bet Meir was 527. The moshav lies in the center of the Martyrs' Forest. It is named after Meir *Bar-Ilan.

[Efraim Orni]

BET (HA)-MIDRASH (pl. *battei (ha)-midrash*) (Heb. בֵּית (הַ)מִדְרָשׁ, pl. בָּתֵּי (הַ)מִּדְרָשׁ; "house of study"), study center where people assembled to listen to words of wisdom and exposition of the Law from very early in the Second Temple period. Esau and Jacob are said to have attended *beit ha-sefer* together until the age of 13, when Jacob continued his studies at *bet ha-midrash*; Esau, instead, frequented idolatrous shrines (Gen. R. 63:10). The Talmud described the 394 courts of law in Jerusalem and the equal number of synagogues, *battei midrash*, and *battei sefer* that existed there (Ket. 105a). Simeon *Ben Sira in the second century B.C.E. invited people to "dwell in my *bet midrash*" (Ecclus. 51:47). In the mishnaic period it was an institution independent of the synagogue and regarded as being more holy. R.*Joshua b. Levi stated that a synagogue may be turned into a *bet midrash*, but not the contrary, for it is "a place where Torah is exalted" in contradistinction to the synagogue which is "a place where prayer is exalted" (Meg. 27a). Sleeping in a *bet ha-midrash* was prohibited, although an exception was made for scholars who spent all their time there (Meg. 28a; Ber. 25a). It was considered ill-omened for a family to eat its Sabbath repast while public study sessions met at the local house of study (Git. 38b). Mothers were praised for sending their children to the synagogue to study, and for waiting up for their husbands who returned late from *bet ha-midrash* (Ber. 17a). One who goes directly from the synagogue (after services) to *bet ha-midrash* (to study) is deemed worthy to welcome the Divine Presence (Ber. 64a); and whosoever enters synagogues and houses of study in this world will be privileged to enter synagogues and houses of study in the world to come (Deut. R. 7:1). The *bet ha-midrash* was the center of instruction for scholars and the common people alike and contributed to disseminating culture widely in Jewish society. In the Middle Ages it tended to be merged with the synagogue, but its specific characteristic was preserved: in the *bet ha-midrash* prayer was a secondary activity, while the study and discussion of Jewish Law and problems concerning Judaism were its main concern, and usually open to all who cared to attend. The *bet ha-midrash* normally had a library with works on various branches of rabbinical literature intended for all sectors of the public. Attendance at the *bet ha-midrash* was not limited as at the **ḥeder* and *yeshivah, and the instructors were often itinerant preachers engaged by the community. The *battei midrash* serving the yeshivot acquired a somewhat cloistered character. The rabbi prayed there with his students when he was not required to join the communal worship. The *bet ha-midrash* also afforded lodging to yeshivah students, and occasionally was used as a hostel for impecunious travelers.

In some *battei midrash* independent study was pursued. In some communities the *bet ha-midrash* became identical with the yeshivah or the synagogue, where scholars taught immediately after morning and evening prayers. Some *battei midrash* were established and maintained by the community, while others were built by philanthropists who bequeathed funds for their maintenance. In Germany, such *battei midrash* were known as *Klaus* (from Lat. *clausura*), and in Eastern Europe as *kloyz*. The *Ḥasidim developed a new combination of public instruction and prayer in the **shtibl* ("small room"). In Islamic countries, and some Sephardi communities, the *bet midrash* is called simply *midrash*.

BIBLIOGRAPHY: Baron, Community, index; H.H. Ben-Sasson, *Hagut ve-Hanhagah* (1959), index; J. Katz, *Tradition and Crisis* (1961), index; ET, 3 (1951), 210–3.

[Natan Efrati / Aaron Rothkoff]

BET NEḤEMYAH (Heb. בֵּית נְחֶמְיָה), moshav northeast of Lydda. Bet-Neḥemyah is affiliated with Ha-oved ha-Ẓiyyoni moshavim association. It was founded in 1950 on the site of the former Beit (Bayt) Nabālā camp of the Arab Legion where a decisive battle was fought in the War of Independence in 1948. Bet Neḥemyah was initially a "work village" whose settlers, immigrants from Iran, were engaged in land reclamation. On its grounds is the site of the Second Temple village Nebellat. The village is named for Nehemiah. In 1970 Bet Neḥemyah numbered 227 inhabitants, expanding considerably to 632 in 2002.

[Efraim Orni]

BET NETOFAH (Heb. בֵּית נְטוֹפָה), village in Lower Galilee, north of Sepphoris. It was known in talmudic times as a place where the vetch plant grew later than in other places (Shev. 9:5). Bet Netofah is identified with Khirbat al-Nāṭif, on the northeastern edge of the plain known in Arabic as Sahl al-Baṭṭūf and in Hebrew as the Bet Netofah Valley. Josephus (Life, 207) calls it the Valley of Asochis. High quality clay was found in this valley. In modern times, one of the reservoirs of the National Water Carrier (see *Israel, State of: Economic Affairs – Water and Irrigation) was built in the valley and is now called the Eshkol Reservoir in honor of Levi *Eshkol.

BIBLIOGRAPHY: Abel, Geog, 1 (1933), 410; Press, Ereẓ, 1 (1951), 92, 120–1.

[Michael Avi-Yonah]

BET(H)-NIMRAH (Heb. בֵּית נִמְרָה), biblical locality in the Jordan Valley opposite Jericho, in the area allotted to the tribe of Gad (Num. 32:36; Josh. 13:27; called Nimrah in Num. 32:3). It is mentioned in the form Bethnambris in the time of the Jewish War with Rome (66–70/73; Jos., Wars, 4:420), after which it continued to exist as a Jewish settlement and is frequently mentioned in talmudic sources (e.g., Pe'ah 4:5, etc.). In Byzantine times it was known as Bethnambris (Eusebius, Onom. 44:17; Johannes Moschus, *Pratum Spirituale*, PG, 87, pt. 3, 2952) and it is mentioned in the Rehov Synagogue inscription as well. The biblical town of Beth-Nimrah has been identified with Tell Balaybil, and the later settlement with Tell Nimrīn, 11 mi. (18 km.) S.W. of *Gadara. The nearby Wadi Nimrin may very well be the "'waters of Nimrin" (Isa. 15:6; Jer. 48:34). Explored in the 19th century by C.R. Conder, the site was visited by many scholars including W.F. Albright and N. Glueck. Following a new survey of the site in 1976, a sixth-century three-aisled church was uncovered by M. Piccirillo in 1980 with magnificent decorated mosaic floors. Since 1989 large-scale excavations have been conducted at the site, revealing the archaeological remains of settlements from the

Early Bronze IV, Middle Bronze II, Iron Age I–II. Destruction levels found in the Iron Age levels at the site date from the late 10th century B.C.E., late 9th century B.C.E., and the 7th century B.C.E. Persian through to Mamluk strata were also uncovered at the site.

BIBLIOGRAPHY: Glueck, in: AASOR, 25–28 (1951), 367–71; Abel, Geog, 2 (1938), 278; Press, Ereẓ, 1 (1951), 92–93; 3 (1952), appendix, 10. **ADD. BIBLIOGRAPHY:** M. Piccirillo, "A Church at Shunat Nimrim," in: *Annual of the Department of Antiquities of Jordan*, 26 (1982); J.W. Flanagan, D.W. McCreer, and Kh. N. Yassine, "Preliminary Report on the 1990 Excavation at Tell Nimrin," in: *Annual of the Department of Antiquities of Jordan*, 36 (1992).

[Michael Avi-Yonah / Shimon Gibson (2nd ed.)]

BET OREN (Heb. בֵּית אֹרֶן; "House of Pine Tree"), kibbutz on Mount Carmel, affiliated with Ha-Kibbutz ha-Me'uḥad. Founded in 1939, the settlement was initially isolated and had little land, so that its members had to work as hired laborers in Haifa. During the Mandate regime Bet Oren served as a clandestine training camp of *Haganah. After irrigable land on the Carmel coast was allocated to Bet Oren, it raised dairy and beef cattle, fodder, field crops, deciduous fruit, and other products. The kibbutz had a large rest house amid the natural pine and oak forests and nature reserves of the surrounding area. In 1970 Bet Oren numbered 220 inhabitants; in 2002, 299.

[Efraim Orni]

BET OVED (Heb. בֵּית עוֹבֵד), moshav in central Israel, southeast of Nes Ẓiyyonah. Bet Oved, affiliated with Tenu'at Ha-Moshavim, was founded in 1933 by workers from Russia. Its economy was based on citrus plantations, garden crops, and dairy cattle. In 1970 Bet Oved numbered 195 inhabitants, increasing to 285 in the mid-1990s and 304 in 2002.

[Efraim Orni]

BET(H)-REHOB (Heb. בֵּית רְחוֹב), biblical city, dynasty, or district, that gave its name to one of the *Aramean states existing at the time of David. In Num. 13:21 we have the phrase "to Rehob at Lebo-Hamath." The city Laish-Dan is placed specifically in the "valley that belongs to Beth-Rehob" (Judg. 18:28) but its exact location remains unknown. The Arameans of Beth-Rehob were among the mercenaries hired by the Ammonites to fight Israel; they were thoroughly routed first by Joab at Medeba and then by David (II Sam. 10:6ff.; I Chron. 19:6ff.). It has been assumed that *Aram-Zobah, which is closely associated with Beth-Rehob/Rehob (II Sam. 10:6, 8; and see II Sam. 8:3, 12), already held the other Aramean kingdoms under its sway at that time; the period of Israelite control was broken by *Damascus, who took the lead in revolting against Solomon. The last appearance of Rehob may be in an inscription of Shalmaneser III (853 B.C.E.), which mentions a certain Ba'sa son of Ruhubi from Amana, in a list of Syrian-Palestinian kings.

BIBLIOGRAPHY: EM, s.v.; Bright, Hist, 181. **ADD. BIBLIOGRAPHY:** B. Levine, *Numbers 1–20* (1993), 354; G. Herion, in: ABD, 1, 692; S. Bar-Efrat, *II Samuel* (Heb., 1996), 86.

[Michael Avi-Yonah / S. David Sperling (2nd ed.)]

BETROTHAL (Heb. שִׁדּוּכִין, *shiddukhin*).

Definition

In Jewish law *shiddukhin* is defined as the mutual promise between a man and a woman to contract a marriage at some future time and the formulations of the terms (*tena'im*, see below) on which it shall take place. In general parlance, as opposed to legal terminology, it is known as *erusin* (Kid. 63a, Tos.), which is in fact part of the marriage ceremony proper (see *Marriage, Ceremony of). The concept of *shiddukhin* can entail either a promise by the intending parties themselves or one made by their respective parents or other relatives on their behalf (Kid. 9b; Sh. Ar., eh 50:4–6 and 51). The sages regarded *kiddushin* (consecration; see *Marriage) without prior *shiddukhin* as licentiousness and prescribed that "he who enters into a marriage without *shiddukhin* is liable to be flogged" (TJ, Kid. 3:10, 64b; TB, Kid. 12b; Maim. Yad, Ishut, 3:22 and Issurei Bi'ah, 21:14; Sh. Ar., EH 26:4). *Shiddukhin* as such has no immediate effect on the personal status of the parties – it being only a promise to create a different personal status in the future (Resp. Rosh 34:1; *Beit Yosef* EH 55). Nor does the promise give either party the right to claim specific performance from the other – since a marriage celebrated in pursuance of a judgment requiring the defendant to marry the plaintiff is repugnant to the basic principle that a marriage requires the free will and consent of both the parties thereto.

Gifts

(Heb. סִבְלוֹנוֹת, *sivlonot*). The Talmud (Kid. 50b) discusses the question whether the bride's acceptance of gifts from her bridegroom is to be regarded as an indication that *kiddushin* has already been celebrated between them – thus making it necessary for her to receive a divorce, on the grounds of "doubt," in the event she does not marry him and wishes to marry someone else. The *halakhah* was to the effect that the matter be left dependent on local custom so that any "doubt" as to whether or not *kiddushin* had already taken place would depend on whether or not there was any custom in the particular place where the parties resided to send such gifts before or after *kiddushin*. From the time that it became the general custom for parties to initiate their intended ties with each other by way of *shiddukhin* (when the bridegroom would send gifts to his bride) and for the *kiddushin* and *nissu'in* (the marriage proper; see *Marriage) to take place simultaneously at a later date, there would usually be no opportunity for the bridegroom to send such gifts to the bride after the *kiddushin* but before the *nissu'in*, so the *halakhah* was then to the effect that the giving of gifts per se implied no suspicion of *kiddushin* as mentioned above (Sh. Ar., eh 45:2; *Arukh ha-Shulḥan* EH 45:16–18. See also **Minhag*.

Tena'im

(Heb. תְּנָאִים, "conditions"). It is customary, but not generally or necessarily so, for the *tena'im*, or conditions of the *shiddukhin*, to be reduced to writing – whereby such matters would be prescribed as the date and place of the proposed marriage, the financial obligations of the parties, i.e., the *dowry (Heb. נְדֻנְיָה, *nedunyah*) to be brought by the bride, or the period for which her father undertakes to provide for the couple. All such obligations undertaken at the time of the *shiddukhin* are valid and binding, even without a formal or symbolic *kinyan* (see Modes of *Acquisition), as obligations of this nature are "in these matters effected by mere verbal arrangement" (Ket. 102a; Kid. 9b; See also *Contract). It is also customary to stipulate a sum of money as a penalty to be paid in the event of a breach of promise without good cause. In the Talmud such written instruments are termed *shetarei pesikta* – abbreviated by the *posekim* to "*shetarei*" or "*tena'ei shiddukhin*" or simply "*tena'im*" (Rashi, ad loc.; Sh. Ar., eh 51: *Arukh ha-Shulḥan*, EH 51:13; see also forms: A.A. Rudner *Mishpetei Ishut*, 178f, and Gulak, Oẓar 1–19 (nos. 1–4), 362 (no. 403); see also **Shetar*).

Breach of the Shiddukhin

CONSEQUENCES OF BREACH. The party committing a breach of promise, i.e., by not marrying the other party, may be liable to compensate the other party for any actual damage sustained, such as the expenses of the preparations for the marriage, and may also be obliged to return the gifts he received on the occasion of the *shiddukhin*, whether from the other party or from relatives and friends (Sh. Ar., EH 50:3–4; Resp. Rosh, 35:8; *Arukh ha-Shulḥan*, EH 50:20). The offending party may further be liable to pay the penalty stipulated in the *tena'im* – or, if not so stipulated, such amount as a court may determine as proper in the circumstances – having particular regard to the degree of mental suffering, shame, and public degradation suffered by the other party as a result of the breach of promise (Tos. to BM 66a; Sh. Ar., EH, 50:3–4; *Ba'er Heitev* 15). In cases where the sum stipulated in the *tena'im* to be paid by way of compensation exceeds the value of the actual damage caused, so as to make it a real penalty, the *posekim* debate the legal validity of such a condition on the grounds that the promise is tainted with **asmakhta*, i.e., that a promise to pay such a sum by way of compensation might possibly not have been meant seriously, since both parties would have been at the time so certain and confident of fulfilling their respective commitments. Some of the authorities, mainly Ashkenazi, took the view that the law requiring one who shamed another to compensate the latter should be strictly applied in these cases as well, and that the plea of *asmakhta* avails only if the stipulated sum is a highly exaggerated one (Tos. to BM 66a and to Kid. 8b; Resp. Rosh 34:2,4; *Rema* EH 50:6 and *Beit Shemu'el, ibid.*; *Arukh ha-Shulḥan*, EH 50:21f.; *Rema* ḤM 207:16 and *Siftei Kohen, ibid.*). Other sages, primarily Sephardi, held that the plea of *asmakhta* would avail the offending party even in a breach of promise case involving *shiddukhin* (Maim. Yad, Mekhir 11:18; Sh. Ar., ḤM 207:16; *Beit Yosef* EH 50; see also PDR 3:131–154). In order to avoid any doubts, however, in the Middle Ages the Sephardi authorities introduced the practice of two separate agreements between the parties – one whereby each party unconditionally undertook to pay to the other a fixed sum in the event of breach of promise and another whereby each party released the other from the former undertaking upon the fulfillment of all the obligations stipulated in the *tena'im* (Sh. Ar., ḤM, *ibid.*, and EH 50:6; Resp. Maharit, 131). Even if the *tena'im* had not been reduced to writing the court would adjudge the offending party to pay such compensation as may seem proper in the circumstances, having regard to the standing of the parties, provided the terms of the *shiddukhin* had been evidenced by *kinyan* between the parties.

DEFENSES AGAINST LIABILITY. Any justifiable reason for withdrawing from the *shiddukhin* is a valid defense to a claim for compensation. Since the matter in issue is a promise to marry, involving a personal tie between the parties, the court will tend to regard any ground for not entering the marriage as reasonably justified, even if it is not directly attributable to the defendant. For example, if the *tena'im* were agreed by the parents and subsequently the son or the daughter involved refused to accept them, such refusal would be regarded as justified and would not involve him or her in any liability (Resp. Rosh 34:1; Tur and Sh. Ar., eh 50:5, *Arukh ha-Shulḥan*, EH 50:29; pdr 5, 322–9). However, if the grounds on which the defendant bases his withdrawal were known to him prior to the *shiddukhin* or if they became known to him thereafter and he did not immediately withdraw, he will be regarded as having waived his objections and such grounds will not later avail him as a defense.

Validity of the Tena'im after Marriage (Nissu'in)

Noncompliance with the terms of the *tena'im* after the marriage has taken place does not exempt the parties from the duties imposed on them by law vis-à-vis each other as husband and wife. Thus, the husband is not absolved from his duty to maintain and provide a home for his wife because she or her parents may have failed to honor their undertaking to provide a home for the couple – the husband's duty being imposed on him by law (see *Marriage) and being unconnected with any rights deriving from the *shiddukhin* (*Bayit Ḥadash* EH 52; *Rema* EH 52:1, and *Ba'er Heitev* 5). On the other hand, the existence of the marriage is not necessarily to be regarded as constituting a waiver and cancellation of the obligations created by the *shiddukhin*. In order to avoid such a contention, it is customary for the parties to draw up "secondary" or "new" *tena'im* at the time of the *kiddushin*, whereby they reaffirm the original *tena'im* – or else stipulate specifically in the **ketubbah* that the marriage is based on the terms of the original *tena'im*; the latter form being the customary procedure in the *ketubbah* adopted in the State of Israel (A.A. Rudner, *Mishpetei Ishut*, 179). Such procedures provide either party with a clear cause of action for claiming the specific performance of all obligations undertaken in the *tena'im* after the marriage has taken place. According to some *posekim*, there is no need for the original *tena'im* to be specifically recalled at the time of the *kiddushin* – as it is presumed that the *kiddushin* was entered upon in accordance with the terms of such *tena'im* (PDR 1:289–313; 4:193–9, 289–304).

Customs

The ceremony and the writing of the agreement is called in Yiddish *teno'im shrayben*. The term *knas-mahl* ("penalty meal") was also used because of the penalty (usually 50% of the promised dowry) stipulated in the document to be paid by the party guilty of breach of the promise to marry (Sh. Ar., EH 51).

Though of secondary importance from an halakhic point of view, the "betrothal" remains a significant ceremony in marriage arrangements. According to *Elijah b. Solomon, the Gaon of Vilna, a bridegroom, rather than break the engagement, should marry and then divorce his bride. In certain Jewish circles, a marriage is not contracted with a person who was a party to a broken engagement.

Among the Oriental Jews, the engagement ceremony is a very elaborate affair. Kurdish Jews had the custom of *hatlabba* ("bidding the bride") and those of *Djerba indulged in great festivities. After the engagement, bride and bridegroom would exchange presents, and on Passover, Shavuot, and Sukkot, the groom would send his bride clothing, jewelry, and choice fruits. Similarly among Ashkenazi Jews, as *sivlonot* the groom usually sent the bride clothing or jewelry, and she reciprocated with a new *tallit* or a richly embroidered *tallit* bag she had made herself. At the Ashkenazi *tena'im* ceremony, it is customary to break a plate; the act is parallel to the crushing of the glass at the wedding ceremony.

BIBLIOGRAPHY: Buechler, in: *Festschrift... Lewy* (1911), 110–44; Gulak, Yesodei, 2 (1922), 82; 3 (1922), 14–19, 22, 29, 45; Gulak, Oẓar, 1–19 (nos. 1–14), 362 (no. 403); idem, in: *Tarbiz*, 3 (1931–32), 361–76; 5 (1933–34), 126–33, Herzog, Instit, 1 (1936), index; Ch. Albeck, in: *Kove... M. Schorr* (1944), 12–24; ET, 2 (1949), 114; 6 (1954), 610; 7 (1956), 138–49; PD 12:1121–204; 16:2737–40; B. Schereschewsky, *Dinei Mishpaḥah* (1967^2), 22–31; idem, *Kenas u-Fiẓẓuyim Ekev Hafarat Ḥozim le-fi Dinei Yisrael* (1960); B. Cohen, in: PAAJR, 18 (1949), 67–135; republished in his *Jewish and Roman Law*, 1 (1966), 279–347, addenda 777–80; H. Schauss, *The Lifetime of a Jew* (1950), 129–31, 150–2, 158–61, 165–9, 182–6; Elon, Mafteaḥ, 326ff. M. Elon. *Ha-Mishpat Ha-Ivri* (1988) 1: 371, 438, 533, 633: idem, *Jewish Law* (1994) 1, 449, 2: 535, 648, 784-5. **ADD BIBLIOGRAPHY:** B. Lipshitz, *"Matanah Lehud, Bein Kinyan le-Hithayvut,"* in: *Dinei Yisrael*, 12, (1984), 125.

[Ben-Zion (Benno) Schereschewsky]

BET(H)-SHEAN (Heb. בֵּית שְׁאָן), biblical city whose name is preserved in the former Arab town of *Beisan* (Josh. 17:11, 16; Judg. 1:27; I Sam. 31:10, 12; 2 Sam. 21:12; I Kgs. 4:12; I Chron. 7:29). Written sources mention Beth-Shean as being in a plain close to the Valley of Jezreel (Josh. 17:16) and Mt. Gilboa (I Sam. 31:8, 10), and in close proximity to the Jordan River (Papyrus Anastasi I), Rehov, and Pella (Stele of Seti I). Beginning in Hellenistic times the city was called Scythopolis (II Macc. 12:29–30; Judith 3:10; Josephus, *Antiquities* V, i:22) or Nysa-Scythopolis in imperial coinage. C.R. Conder and H.H. Kitchener (1883, 101–4) and G.A. Smith (1894, 357–64) were the first to provide historical summaries on the site based on classical, medieval, and early modern sources.

Origin and Meaning of the Name

The origin and meaning of Beth-Shean is obscure. When part of a city name, *bet(h)* often refers to a sanctuary where a local deity is worshipped. In this particular case, *Shean* may be the name of such a deity. However, the only god we know to have been worshipped at Beth-Shean is Mekal, a Canaanite deity whose name and seated image was found carved on a small Egyptian stele dating to the 19th Dynasty (13th century B.C.E.). The god is mentioned a second time in a Hellenistic inscription from Cyprus.

During the time of the Diadochi, the successors of Alexander the Great, Beth-Shean took on the name Scythopolis, "City of the Scythians." The origin of the name is obscure, but it may refer to a colony of Scythian mercenaries serving under Ptolemy II. The city was also known as Nysa or Nysa-Scythopolis. According to a legend mentioned by the ancient historians Pliny and Solinus, Dionysus (the Greek god of wine and revelry who the Romans called Bacchus) founded the city in honor of his nursemaid, Nysa, who he buried in this spot. He then apparently settled Scythian archers there to stand watch over her grave. In the Arabic period, following a destructive earthquake in 749 C.E., the name reverted back to its ancient Semitic name in the form of Beisan. This change supports the view that even after decades of Greco-Roman rule the local dialects were still spoken; thus the town's Semitic name was never forgotten.

Historical Importance

The town's historical importance derives from its strategic location at the junction of major roads that pass through the Jezreel and Jordan Valleys (Levant Grid 1977.2124). Moreover, throughout much of the Bronze Age, the international trunk road that linked Egypt with Syria and Mesopotamia passed by way of Beth-Shean to continue northwards to the Sea of Galilee region and points further north.

The summit of the mound is c. 10 acres (4 hectares/40 dunams). However, as excavations have shown, the Middle Bronze Age through Iron Age occupation was limited to the highest part of the tell in the south and did not exceed 5 acres (2 hectares/20 dunams). Thus, despite its strategic importance, Beth-Shean remained a small town throughout the biblical period. The main center at this time was at nearby Rehov (Tell ec-Sârem), c. 3.5 mi. (6 km.) to the south.

The site's location on a naturally high hill defended on two sides by deep ravines carved by the Harod (Jalud) and Asi Rivers gave it an advantage that may have influenced its Arabic name, *Tell el-Husn*, "mound of the fortress." Moreover, an abundance of water and rich soil made the surrounding region attractive to human settlement throughout history. This may have inspired the comment by Rabbi Shimon ben Lakhish (ca. 350 C.E.) to write that if Paradise is in the Land of Israel, then its entrance is Beth-Shean (Er. 19a). Today, a number of agriculturally oriented kibbutzim dot the landscape.

History of Exploration

Beth-Shean was first investigated in 1921–33 by archaeologists from the University Museum of the University of Pennsylvania: C.S. Fisher (1921–23), A. Rowe (1925–28), and G.M. FitzGerald (1930–31, 1933). As a result of their work, Beth-Shean became the first tell in Palestine to produce a complete stratigraphic sequence spanning more than 18 layers of occupation from the late Neolithic period (fifth millennium B.C.E.) through medieval times. University Museum archaeologists also explored the Northern Cemetery on the northern bank of the Harod River opposite Tell Beth-Shean, as well as the nearby Byzantine period Monastery of Lady Mary.

For 50 years no work was done on the tell until Y. *Yadin of the Hebrew University of Jerusalem returned in 1983 to carry out a short three-week season to explore the Iron I period. This was followed by a longer project in 1989–96 headed by A. Mazar of the Hebrew University of Jerusalem, whose goal was to further study the Iron Age and Bronze Age remains.

While the tell saw a cessation of activity for half a century following the University of Pennsylvania excavations, work continued on Late Antiquity remains. At the foot of the mound, S. Applebaum (1961–62) and A. Negev (1962) excavated the second century C.E. Roman theater. A Byzantine-era synagogue known as the "House of Leontis" was excavated by N. Zori (1964) and D. Bahat and A. Druks (1970–72) for the Israel Department of Antiquities and Museums. Exploration of the Roman-Byzantine city of Scythopolis at the base of the tell began on a small scale in 1980–81, and developed into a large-scale project in 1986 under G. Mazor of the Israel Antiquities Authority and G. Foerster and Y. Tsafrir of the Hebrew University of Jerusalem. Today, Beth-Shean is part of the Israel National Parks Authority.

Beth-Shean in History and Archaeology

THE EARLY PERIODS (LEVELS XIX–XI). The earliest evidence for occupation on the mound is during the Pottery Neolithic period (Level XIX following E. Braun, fifth millennium B.C.E.) and Chalcolithic period (Level XVII, fourth millennium B.C.E.) at the bottom of FitzGerald's deep sounding. Above this, several strata from Early Bronze Age I-III (Levels XVI-XI, 3500–2000 B.C.E.) reach a total depth of 25 ft. (8 m.). This must have been an impressive time of occupation; not only was Tell Beth-Shean occupied, but so was nearby Tell Ictaba directly opposite Beth-Shean on the north, creating twin tells separated from one another by the flow of the Harod River. The end of the Early Bronze Age, now called EB IV by many scholars, is characterized by seasonal occupation on the mound and shaft tombs in the Northern Cemetery.

THE MIDDLE BRONZE AGE (LEVEL X). Following the end of Early Bronze Age there is a gap in occupation for most of MB I–II (ca. 2000–1750 B.C.E.). Resettlement occurred in the time of transition between MB II–III and continued until the end of the period around 1550 B.C.E. Strangely, at a time when most settlements in Palestine were fortified, it seems that Beth-Shean was not. Renewed excavations on the mound have verified that city walls are missing throughout the Bronze and Iron Ages. The well-known gate and city wall at the northwest corner of the mound dates to Crusader times. Either the mound was sufficiently high to protect the inhabitants, or as B. Arubas has argued, any pre-existing fortifications may have been removed by the Roman architects of Scythopolis who quarried away parts of the mound to make room for the grid pattern of streets. Whether with or without city walls, Beth-Shean remained its modest 5 acre size throughout the biblical period.

THE LATE BRONZE AGE (PRE-LEVEL IX–LEVEL VII). There are five settlement phases on the tell from the Late Bronze Age (1550–1200 B.C.E.). The earliest phase (Pre-Level IX, ca. 1550–1450) belongs to the beginning of the Late Bronze Age (LB IA) before the Egyptian garrison was established in Level IX. The four subsequent phases (Levels IXB, IXA, VIII, and VII) are from when the town functioned as an Egyptian stronghold.

The Hebrew University excavations introduced two important changes to the older Penn stratigraphy. The first is that Level IX comprised not one, but two, phases of occupation – Level IXB (LB IB) and Level IXA (LB IIA). The second is that the initial phase of Late Bronze Age occupation below Level IX was missed by the University Museum, even though some had suspected its existence based on the pottery. In this phase, Mazar revealed a modest tripartite Canaanite temple in a clear stratigraphic context above Level X (MB III) and below Level IXB (LB IB). To date, this is the earliest in a series of five sanctuaries that would continue into Iron Age IB (Upper VI). In this same vicinity, the Roman inhabitants of Scythopolis built a temple to Zeus and the Byzantine Christians a church. As the familiar maxim says, "once a holy place, always a holy place."

THE EGYPTIAN GARRISON (LEVELS IX–LOWER VI). *Level IX (c. 1450–1300 B.C.E., Late Bronze Age IB–IIA).* With the establishment of Level IX around 1450 B.C.E., Beth-Shean was transformed into an Egyptian garrison; a role that it would maintain for some 300 years until Egypt pulled out of the country in the second half of the 12th century B.C.E. The key figure in bringing about this change in status from Canaanite settlement of Egyptian garrison was Thutmose III, an 18th Dynasty pharaoh who fought some 300 Canaanite rulers allied with the Hurrian kingdom of Mitanni against Egypt. The showdown between them at Megiddo in the mid-15th century B.C.E. is recorded in the Annals of Thutmose III (Aharoni, 1979, 153–54); the earliest and most detailed record to date of a military campaign.

After his victory at Megiddo, Thutmose III makes a follow-up campaign in which he claims to have subjugated 119 cities. The topographic list is inscribed on the walls of the temple of Amen-Re at Karnak (Aharoni, 1979: 154–65). It is here that Beth-Shean is mentioned for the first time as *bt š'ir* (No. 110). It is probably after this that Thutmose III built the garrison of Level IXB (ca. 1450–1375 B.C.E.). Dating to a time slightly after this, when the settlement goes through renovations in Level IXA, Beth-Shean is mentioned a second time in Amarna Letter 289:20 (ANET 489) as *bit ša-a-ni*. The town is described as an Egyptian garrison staffed by Canaanite mercenaries loyal to Tagi the son-(father?)-in-law of Lab'ayu (see other references to these individuals in EA 252–54; 264–66). Additional testimony to these rulers came to light in 1993 when excavators of Roman-Byzantine Scythopolis found a small clay cylinder bearing the names Tagi and Lab'ayu in the spoil heaps of the University of Pennsylvania excavations at the foot of the mound.

Even though the settlement of Level IX in both of its phases was an Egyptian garrison as indicated in the textual references and from the various finds of Egyptian inspiration, the town nevertheless remained largely Canaanite in character. All the buildings, the temple complex, and most of the artifacts were typical of northern Palestine. The well-known basalt slab depicting a lion and dog (lioness?) in combat is regarded by most as a prime example of Late Bronze Age Canaanite art.

Levels VIII–VII (c. 1300–1200 B.C.E., Late Bronze Age IIB). At some point towards the end of the 18th Dynasty, the settlement of Level IX was destroyed and rebuilt on a new plan (Level VIII). This change reflects an intensification of Egyptian control, perhaps beginning with Seti I, ca. 1300 B.C.E. The explanation for this may lie in the growing Hittite threat to the north. To counter this, Egypt not only strengthened its hold on the Beth-Shean garrison, but increased the number of Egyptian outposts and exercised its influence in other ways as well. Level VII probably represents renovations to the original Level VIII settlement in the time of Ramesses II.

As noted above, the Ramesside period settlement was built on an entirely new plan with only the temple in the same location as the earlier sanctuary of Level IX. Residential units organized into city blocks with an orthogonal street configuration stood east of the temple. To the west of the temple were two large Egyptian-style structures that probably served the interests of the garrison – the so-called "Migdol" (fortified building) and the "Commandant's House." The first was probably an administrative building and the second a Three Room House. A third building revealed by Mazar further to the north below Building 1500 of Lower VI resembles in part the square fortress at Deir el-Balah from the same period. This building may have been the residence of a high official. In contrast to the garrison of Level IX where Egyptian-style pottery comprised only 1% of the assemblage, the Ramesside era settlement produced around 25 times that amount.

During this time, Beth-Shean appears in the topographic lists of Seti I and Ramesses II (Aharoni, 1979, 176–83), as well as in *Papyrus Anastasi I* from the end of the 13th century (ANET, 477). Three stelae were also found in later reuse by the University Museum. Two belong to the time of Seti I and the third to his son Ramesses II. The first stele of Seti dates to the first year of his reign and describes an extensive campaign that included the rescue of Beth-Shean and Rehov (Tell ec-Sârem) from Pella (Pexel) and Hammath (Tell el-Ammeh) (ANET, 253; Rowe, 1930, 24–29). The second stele mentions a skirmish involving the 'Apiru (ANET, 255; Rowe, 1930, 29–30). A third stele from the ninth year of Ramesses II mentions a campaign that probably passed by way of Beth-Shean (ANET, 255; Rowe, 1930, 33–36). A small stone stele dedicated to "Mekal, the god, the lord of Beth-Shean" was mistakenly attributed to Level IX; it actually belongs to the 13th century (James and McGovern,1993, 240, Appendix, No. 8).

Late VII–Lower VI (c. 1200–1125 B.C.E., Iron IA). The 20th Dynasty, the final stage of Egyptian control in Palestine, begins with an ephemeral phase called "Late VII" (12th century B.C.E.). The main stratum of this period is Level VI, which the University of Pennsylvania divided into "Lower VI" (12th century B.C.E.) and "Upper VI" (11th century B.C.E.). The Level VI temple was rebuilt on the same spot as the Level VII sanctuary, while the Migdol and the Commandant's House were replaced by probable storehouses. The square administrative building of Level VII was replaced in Lower VI by Building 1500, the "Governor's Residence," a square building with a central hall surrounded by rooms. In Egypt, this type of structure is known as a "Center Hall House." Architectural fragments from this and other buildings included lotus-shaped column capitals, inscribed doorjambs, a life-sized statue of a seated Ramesses III which was found in the following level, and inscriptions. The most important inscription was a carved limestone lintel depicting Ramesses-Weser-Khepesh, who is identified as "commander of the troops," with cartouches of Ramesses III next to him. These finds, as well as a high percentage of locally produced Egyptian pottery, attest to an intensive Egyptian presence at this time.

In the Hebrew Bible, Beth-Shean was assigned to the tribe of Manasseh, but they were unable to hold onto it because of the military superiority of the Canaanites (Josh. 17:11, 16; Judg. 1:27). According to the conventional chronology, this period in biblical history would correspond to Lower VI when the Egyptians were in control of Beth-Shean. It is uncertain when the Egyptians finally abandoned the site, but many scholars suggest the second half of the 12th century in the time of Ramesses VI or Ramesses VIII. In the ashes of the destruction of Lower VI were found sherds of Mycenean IIIC probably imported from Cyprus. This type of pottery is typical to the period of the Sea Peoples migration from the Aegean to the east.

IRON AGE IB (UPPER VI). With the construction of Upper VI emerges a new material culture typical to the 11th century B.C.E. and lacking the Egyptian component. The plan of the settlement represents a significant departure from that of the Egyptian garrison. Important buildings from this time include the twin temples, identified by the University Museum archaeologists with "the House of Ashtaroth" (I Sam. 31:10) and "the House of Dagon" (I Chron. 10:10). Both temples produced numerous cylindrical and house-like cult stands decorated with snakes and birds. The excavators assigned these two buildings to Level V, but they probably belong to Upper VI.

According to the biblical accounts of Saul's death the Philistines killed Saul and his three sons in a battle at the foot of Mt. Gilboa. They cut off his head and placed it in the temple of Dagon, stripped off his armor and placed it in the "temple of their gods" (Chronicles) or in the "temple of Ashtaroth" (Samuel). Then they fastened his body and those of his sons to the city walls of Beth-Shean (I Sam. 31:10–12; I Chron. 10:9–10), or as I Samuel 21:12 reports, hung them in the public square. Following the original excavators, most commentators have assumed that the two temples were in Beth-Shean, but this is unclear from the text. They could just as easily have been in Philistia. No significant Philistine presence has ever been identified at Beth-Shean, although we can assume on the basis of the biblical narrative that they exercised some sort of political control over the region as the self-declared successors of the Egyptians.

IRON AGE II (LEVELS V–IV). It is generally assumed that Beth-Shean was brought under Israelite control by David, since by Solomon's time, it was part of the fifth administrative district under Baana ben Ahilud (I Kgs. 4:12). If so, then David may have been the one who destroyed Upper VI. Excavations at the highest point of the tell (Level V) have produced the remains of an administrative complex from this era, hinting to the town's continued strategic importance. The impressive building compound might also explain why Beth-Shean was singled out in the Kings passage with Megiddo and Taanach, since it may have been a regional center for the fifth administrative district.

The severe destruction that characterized the end of Level V is difficult to date with certainty, but one possibility is Pharaoh Shishak (Egyptian, Shoshenq), who lists Beth-Shean on the walls of the temple to Amen-Re at Karnak as one of the cities he conquered. Shishak's campaign took place after the division of the United Monarchy in the fifth year of Rehoboam, ca. 925 B.C.E. (I Chron. 12). While the town's final destruction in Israelite times (Level IV) is not mentioned in any biblical or extra-biblical source, the cumulative historical and archaeological evidence supports its capture by the Assyrian monarch Tiglath-Pileser III in 733/2 B.C.E.

The Hellenistic Period

Following the destruction of the Israelite town there is a gap in settlement until the site is resettled in the third century B.C.E. While there is evidence for settlement on the tell (Level III), for the most part, it seems that the city developed on Tell Ictaba to the north where Hellenistic structures were found, though badly damaged by later Roman ones.

Under the Seleucid ruler, Antiochus IV, Scythopolis was granted the status of a Greek city (*polis*). Beth-Shean is also mentioned in the context of the Maccabean wars (I Macc. 5:52; 12:40–42; II Macc. 12:29–31). In 107 B.C.E., during the Hasmonean period, it was conquered by John Hyrcanus I and made into an important administrative center. Later, perhaps after the conquests of the Roman general Pompey in 63 B.C.E. Scythopolis became the chief city of the Decapolis. It was the largest city of this group according to Josephus (*Wars* III, ix, 7), and the only one west of the Jordan River. The Decapolis is mentioned several times in the New Testament gospels, e.g. Matt 4:25; Mk 5:20.

The Roman Period

By the first century B.C.E., the city expanded around the foot of the mound where a number of remains were uncovered. On the summit of the tell (Level III) which served as the city's acropolis stood a Roman temple probably dedicated to Zeus Akraios, god of the "High Mountain," who is mentioned in inscriptions found in the lower city. The temple to Nysa appears to have been originally constructed in the first century C.E., but continued to stand until the 749 C.E. earthquake. Roman tombs were found in the Northern Cemetery, including a stone sarcophagus inscribed with the name of Antiochus, son of Phallion, possibly a cousin of Herod the Great. When the Great Revolt broke out in 66 C.E., Jewish rebels attacked Beth-Shean. Although the Jewish inhabitants stood alongside the Gentile population in resisting their countrymen, Josephus writes that the Gentiles later became suspicious and through an act of deception massacred around 13,000 inhabitants (*Wars* II, xviii, 3–5).

The vast civic center that one sees today started to flourish in the second century C.E., though not all of the buildings can be dated with precision. Late Roman period projects of the 2nd–3rd centuries C.E. included the theater, amphitheater, and nymphaeum (water fountain). Behind the nymphaeum, the Hebrew University excavated a basilica built sometime after the first century C.E. Inside the basilica was found a six-sided stone altar dedicated to Dionysus. The accompanying inscription identified him as the founder of the city. Its date in Year 75 of the Scythopolis era translates to 12 C.E. No city wall is known from this time, and it is quite possible that the city remained unfortified. Written sources indicate that Beth-Shean was a key center for making and exporting textiles. The Talmud mentions the manufacture of linen garments from locally-grown flax, farming, and olives as principal occupations (TJ, Pe'ah 7:4, 20a).

The Byzantine Period

In Byzantine times the city reached its greatest extent of 100 hectares. At this time the city was surrounded by a wall and had a population of 30,000–40,000. At the beginning of the fifth century C.E., Scythopolis became the capital of the province of Palestina Secunda, as well as the seat of the commissioner and the tribunal. Scythopolis was also the seat of a Christian episcopate and had numerous churches. The round church on the summit of the tell (Level II) was dated by the University of Pennsylvania to the early fifth century C.E.

Several features of the city first established in the Roman period were refurbished and continued into the Byzantine period. The *cardo* (main north-south street) averaging 24 ft. (7.5 m) wide and the *decumanus* (main east-west street) were probably built in Roman times, but what one sees today is Byzantine. Flanking both sides of the cardo were two large bath house complexes. At the crossing point of the main streets stood a temple that may have been dedicated to Nysa; in any case, it would have been part of the cult of Dionysus or Tyche. While its superstructure no longer exists, two of four columns that supported the gabled roof of the facade to a height of 45 ft. (15 m.) still lie knocked down from the 749 C.E. earthquake. A cylindrical limestone pedestal in front of the temple has an inscription indicating that a statue or bust of the Roman emperor Marcus Aurelius Antoninus (161–180 C.E.) stood on it. The inscription also states how the citizens of Nysa-Scythopolis, a Greek city of Coele-Syria, had dedicated the statue of the ruler. Not far from the temple to Nysa is the Nymphaeum which brought water into the city by means of an aqueduct from the Sachne springs c. 2 mi. (3 km.) to the southwest. The theater, originally built in late Roman times, continued to be used in the Byzantine period and could seat up to 8,000 people. The amphitheater also continued in use and was capable of seating up to 7,000 spectators. At the western end of Tell Ictaba stood the sixth century C.E. Monastery of Lady Mary (in honor of a donor, not the Virgin Mary). A beautiful mosaic inside depicts the 12 months and the sun and moon as human figures. Numerous tombs from the Byzantine period were excavated in the Northern Cemetery.

SYNAGOGUES ON TELL ICTABA. Ancient sources indicate that Scythopolis was a mixed population of pagans, Jews, Samaritans, and Christians. Approximately 200 m northeast of the Monastery of Lady Mary, outside the city wall, is what may be a Samaritan synagogue dating to the 5th–early 7th centuries C.E. It is built in the form of a basilica. Its apse is oriented northwest (not south towards Jerusalem). The floor is covered by a beautiful mosaic depicting geometric and plant motifs, but no human images. The portion of the mosaic in front of the apse depicts a Torah shrine flanked by menorahs, shofars, and incense shovels. There are three Greek inscriptions, one of which refers to Marianos and Hanina, the artists who made the mosaic in the *Bet Alpha synagogue. Another inscription is in Samaritan script, but in the Greek language. Nearby, mosaics from a second synagogue of the sixth century C.E. also has ritual vessels and a menorah, as well as Greek, Hebrew, and Aramaic inscriptions.

THE HOUSE OF LEONTIS. A short distance from the civic center of Nysa-Scythopolis and still within the city walls is another synagogue from the Byzantine period known as the "House of Leontis." Based on its plan and a Greek inscription that refers to "Jose the innkeeper," some have suggested that the synagogue was part of an inn. The synagogue is paved with a mosaic floor depicting geometric, animal, and plant motifs, and in the center, a medallion containing a menorah and the Hebrew word *Shalom* (peace). The mosaic also includes four dedicatory inscriptions – two in Aramaic and two in Greek. One Aramaic inscription refers to the "members of the holy community" who contributed to the synagogue's renovation. The other refers to the unnamed artist who carried out the work. One of the Greek inscriptions invoke divine blessing on all those who names were known to God, while the other refers to "Jose the innkeeper" mentioned above. Another mosaic in the complex from Hall No. 3 depicts scenes from Homer's *Odyssey*. It is in the center of this mosaic, adorned with birds, that a Greek inscription refers to Leontis and his brother Jonathan, who donated this mosaic and wished to be remembered for their act. Other depictions in the mosaic include a five-branched menorah and Nilotic scenes: the Nile River is personified as a bearded god, a building symbolizing a city that is identified as "Alexandria" in Greek, and a nilometer.

VILLA. East of the "House of Leontis" is a private house that probably stood two-stories high and contained some 25 rooms. The villa produced a rich collection of pottery and other objects made of stone, metal, glass, and bone.

The Islamic Period

In 636 C.E., Islamic forces conquered the city after the defeat of the Byzantine army at the Battle of Yarmuk. During this time the city ceased to be called Scythopolis and reverted back to its original Semitic name in the slightly altered form of Beisan. To honor their defeat of the Byzantine army, the Arab forces called their day of victory "Beisan Day."

The excavations in Scythopolis have provided ample testimony to continued life in Beisan during the Umayyad period, including occupation on the tell (Level I), until the huge earthquake struck on January 18, 749, bringing this ancient and glorious city to an end. The city was rebuilt in the Abbasid period (750–969), but only as a mere shadow of its former glory.

In Crusader and Mamluk times the city declined in size and clustered mainly along the valley road leading to Tell Ictaba. The Crusaders fortified the summit of the tell (Level I) with a city wall and gate that was mistakenly attributed by the University Museum excavators to the Byzantine period. The Crusaders also built a square fortress south of the tell. It seems that the Crusaders were not too kind to the region. The Muslim geographer Yakut writes that as of 1225, the many date palms that used to exist in the area had been reduced to two.

In the 14th century, Beth-Shean was chosen by Estori ha-Parhi as the center for his historical and topographic research.

[Robert A. Mullins (2nd ed.)]

The Modern Period

In September 1918, Beth-Shean was captured by British forces. In the 1920–1930s Bedouin from the Beth-Shean Valley settled in the town, which numbered 2,000 inhabitants in 1921 and over 3,000 during the Israel *War of Independence (1948). From the beginning of the 20th century, Jews, mainly from Kurdistan and other Muslim countries, also took up residence in Beth-Shean, but temporarily left during the 1929 Arab riots; the Jewish population of Beth-Shean numbered 94 persons in the spring of 1936. Most of them abandoned the town immediately upon the outbreak of the 1936 riots. The town became a headquarters for Arab bands attacking Jewish villages in the neighboring Harod Valley, but the marauders' position was weakened when Jewish *tower and stockade settlements were established on all sides of Beth-Shean in the years to follow. In the War of Independence, Beth-Shean capitulated on May 12, 1948, to Jewish forces, who found it deserted by its former inhabitants. The settlement of Beth-Shean by Jewish immigrants began in 1949. In 1950, the town numbered 1,200 inhabitants, and in 1968, 12,800 – of whom half originated from North Africa (mainly from Morocco), 30% from other Muslim countries (Iran, Iraq, and Turkey), while 20% came from Europe or were Israel-born. In 2002 the population was approximately 15,900, occupying an area of 2.7 sq. mi. (7.1 sq. km.). As the town had no industry in the initial phase of its resettlement, the inhabitants had to subsist in the 1950s mainly on small trade and on doing hired farm work in the vicinity. Later, a number of industries were established, the largest being a textile mill, followed by a clothing factory, a plastics plant, and by smaller enterprises. A few factories in Beth-Shean were run by local kibbutzim, while the inhabitants of the town were also employed in industry and agriculture in the rural communities of the Beth-Shean Valley. Social and living standards were not satisfactory, however, particularly during the 1965–67 recession, and income remained considerably below the national average over the years.

After the *Six-Day War (1967), Beth-Shean, exposed to the Jordanian artillery positions beyond the Jordan River, suffered from occasional shelling. In addition, the city suffered from terrorist infiltration from Jordan, but since 1975 the area has been quiet. After the peace agreement with Jordan in 1994, a border station was opened nearby.

[Efraim Orni / Shaked Gilboa (2nd ed.)]

BIBLIOGRAPHY: Y. Aharoni, *The Land of the Bible: A Historical Geography*, tr. and ed. A.F. Rainey (1979); D. Bahat, "The Synagogue at Beth-Shean," in: *Qadmoniot*, 5 (1972), 55–58, Heb.; R. Bar-Nathan, and G. Mazor, "Beth-Shean during the Hellenistic Period," in: *Qadmoniot*, 27:3–4 (1994), 87–91, Heb.; E. Braun, *Early Beth Shan (Strata XIX–XIII): G.M. FitzGerald's Deep Cut on the Tell*. University, Museum Monograph 121, University of Pennsylvania Museum of Archaeology and Anthropology (2004); C.R.Conder and H.H. Kitchener, *The Survey of Western Palestine. Memoirs of the Topography, Orography, Hydrography, and Archaeology*. Volume 2: Samaria. Palestine Exploration Fund (1882; reprinted 1998, Archive Editions and Palestine Exploration Fund); G.M. FitzGerald, *Four Canaanite Temple of Beth-Shan. The Pottery (Beth-Shan II/2)* (1930); idem, *Beth-Shan Excavations, 1921–1923: The Arab and Byzantine Levels (Beth-Shan III)* (1931); idem, "Excavations at Beth-shan in 1933," in: *Palestine Exploration Fund Quarterly Statement*, 65 (January 1934), 123–34; "The Earliest Pottery of Beth-Shan," in: *Museum Journal*, 24 (1935), 5–32; idem, *A Sixth Century Monastery at Beth-Shan (Beth-Shan IV)* (1939); G. Foerster, "Beth-Shean at the Foot of the Mound," in: E. Stern, A. Lewinson-Gilboa, and J. Aviram (eds.), *New Encyclopedia of Archaeological Excavations in the Holy Land*, vol. 1 (1993), 223–35; G. Foerster and Y. Tsafrir, "Glorious Beth Shean: Huge New Excavation Uncovers the Largest and Best-Preserved Roman/Byzantine City in Israel," in: *Biblical Archaeology Review*, 16:4 (July/August 1990), 16–31; W. Horowitz, "A Letter of the El-Amarna Period on a Clay Cylinder from Beth Shean," in: *Qadmoniot* 27:3–4 (1994), 84–86, Heb; F.W. James, "Beth Shan," in: *Expedition* 3:2 (1961), 31–36; idem, *The Iron Age at Beth Shan: A Study of Levels VI–IV* (1966); F.W. James and P.E. McGovern, *The Late Bronze II Egyptian Garrison at Beth Shan: A Study of Levels VII and VIII*, 2 vols. (1993); A. Mazar, "The Excavations at Tel Beth Shean (1989–1990): Preliminary Report," in: *Eretz-Israel*, 21, Ruth Amiran Volume (1991), 197–211; idem, "The Excavations of Beth Shean in 1989–90," in: A. Biran and J. Amiran (eds.), *Biblical Archaeology Today: Proceedings of the Second International Congress on Biblical Archaeology, Jerusalem, June-July 1990* (1993a), 606–19; idem, "Beth Shean in the Iron Age: Preliminary Report and Conclusions of the 1990–1991 Excavations," in: *Israel Exploration Journal*, 43 (1993b), 201–29; idem, "Beth Shean: Tel Beth-Shean and the Northern Cemetery," in: E. Stern, A. Lewison-Gilboa, and J. Aviram (eds.), *New Encyclopedia of Archaeological Excavations in the Holy Land* (1993c), 214–23; rev. ed., Israel Exploration Society and Carta (1994); idem, "Four Thousand Years of History at Tel Beth Shean," in: *Qadmoniot*, 27:3–4 (1994), 66–83, Heb.; idem, "Beth Shean, in: E. Meyers, *The Oxford Encyclopedia of Archaeology in the Near East*, vol. 1. (1997a), 305–9; idem, "The Excavations at Tel Beth Shean During the Years 1989–94," in: N.A. Silberman and D. Small (eds.), *The Archaeology of Israel: Constructing the Past, Interpreting the Present*, Journal for the Study of the Old Testament Supplement Series 237 (1997b), 144–64; idem, "Four Thousand Years of History at Tel Beth-Shean: An Account of the Renewed Excavations, in: *Biblical Archaeologist*, 60, 2 (1997c), 62–76; idem, Beth Shean (Tel); Husn (Tell el-), in: A. Negev and S. Gibson, *Archaeological Encyclopedia of the Holy Land* (2001), 81–85; idem, "Beth Shean in the Second Millennium BCE: From Canaanite Town to Egyptian Stronghold," in: *The Synchronization of Civilization in the Eastern Mediterranean in the Second Millennium B.C. II: Proceedings of the SCIEM 2000 – EuroConference, Haindorff, 2nd of May – 7th of May 2001* (2003), 323–40; idem, *Tel Beth Shean I. The Iron Age* (2005); A. Mazar and R. Mullins, *Tel Beth Shean II. The Middle Bronze II and Late Bronze I-IIA Periods* (2005); B. Mazar, "The Valley of Beth Shean in Biblical Times, in: *The Beth Shean Valley: The 17th Archaeological Convention*, Israel Exploration Society (1962), 9–20, Heb.; A. Mazar, A. Ziv-Esudri, and A. Cohen-Weinberger; "The Early Bronze II–III at Tel Beth Shean: Preliminary Observations," in: G. Philip and D. Baird (eds.), *Ceramics and Change in the Early Bronze Age of the Southern Levant (Levantine Archaeology 2)* (2000), 255–78; G. Mazor and R. Bar-Nathan, "Scythopolis – Capital of Palaestina Secunda, *Qadmoniot*, 27:3–4 (1994), 117–37, Heb.; P.E. McGovern, *Late Bronze Age Palestinian Pendants: Innovation in a Cosmopolitan Age*. JSOT/ASOR Monograph Series No. 1 (1985); idem, Beth-Shan," in: *Anchor Bible Dictionary*, vol. 1 (1992), 693–96. W.L. Moran (tr. and ed.), *The Amarna Letters* (1992); R.A. Mullins, "Beth

Shean during the Eighteenth Dynasty: From Canaanite Settlement to Egyptian Garrison," Ph.D. dissertation, Hebrew University of Jerusalem 2 vols. (2002); *Level IX Revisited: The Palestine Expedition of the University of Pennsylvania Museum to Beth Shan (1927–1931)*, BAR International Series (2005); E.D. Oren, *The Northern Cemetery at Beth Shan* (1973); A. Rowe, *The Topography and History of Beth Shan (Beth Shan I)*. (1930); *The Four Canaanite Temples of Beth Shan. The Temples and Cult Objects (Beth Shan II/1)* (1940); J. Seligman, "Excavations in the Crusader Fortress at Beth-Shean," in: *Qadmoniot*, 27:3–4 (1994), 138–41; G.A. Smith, *The Historical Geography of the Holy Land*. (1894, 1931[2]); H.O. Thompson, "Tell el-Husn: Biblical Beth-shan," in: *Biblical Archaeologist*, 30:4 (1967), 110–35; *Mekal: The God of Beth-Shan* (1970); N. Tzori, "The House of Kyrios Leontis at Beth Shean," in: *Israel Exploration Journal*, 16 (1966), 123–34; Y. Tzafrir and G. Foerster, "The Hebrew University Excavations at Beth-Shean, 1980–1994," in: *Qadmoniot*, 27:3–4 (1994), 93–116, Heb.; Y. Yadin, Y. and S. Geva, *Investigations at Beth Shean: The Early Iron Age Strata* (Qedem 23), Monographs of the Institute of Archaeology, Hebrew University of Jerusalem (1986).

BET SHE'ARIM (Heb. בֵּית שְׁעָרִים; Gr. **Besara**), ancient city on the southern slopes of Lower Galilee situated on the hill of al-Sheikh Burayk (near Kiryat Tivon on the Nazareth–Haifa road). Although settlement at Bet She'arim apparently started during the period of the divided monarchy (Iron Age II), the first mention of the city occurs at the end of the Second Temple period, when it was a center of the estates of Berenice (the daughter of Agrippa I and sister of Agrippa II) in the Plain of Esdraelon. Josephus speaks of it as Besara (Life, 118–9). According to talmudic sources, important *tannaim* and *amoraim* lived there (Tosef., Ter. 7:14; Nid. 27a). Bet She'arim reached a position of great importance and prosperity in the late second century, when *Judah ha-Nasi took up residence there and made it the seat of the Sanhedrin (RH 31a–b). From the beginning of the following century the necropolis of Bet She'arim became a central burial place for Jews of Palestine and the Diaspora (TJ, MK 3:5, 82c). The city was thought to have been destroyed by Gallus during the suppression of the Jewish revolt in 352 C.E., but recent research suggests that the impact of the revolt may have been overstated. Although clearly affected by the earthquake of 363 C.E., the town quickly recovered and flourished during the Byzantine and early Arab periods.

The hill of al-Sheikh Burayk has been partly excavated by B. Mazar (1935–40; 1960) and N. Avigad (1953–58) under the auspices of the Israel Exploration Society. An inscription found there contains the name Besara, confirming the identification of the site with Bet She'arim. Additional excavations were conducted at the site by F. Vitto (1983) for the Israel Department of Antiquities.

The city of Bet She'arim extended over the entire summit of the hill – an area of some 25 acres (100 dunams), 450 ft. (137 m.) above sea level. It was surrounded by a wall, two sections of which were exposed. Remains of various large buildings were uncovered on the northeastern part of the hill. The most important of these was a spacious basilical-type synagogue, 115 × 49 ft. (35 × 15 m.), built of ashlar blocks, of which only two courses have survived. The front of the synagogue was oriented toward Jerusalem and contained three entrances that led into the large columned hall; the bases of the columns have been preserved. The synagogue was decorated in the style characteristic of Galilean synagogues and was dated by the excavators to the third century C.E., though scholars now prefer dating it to the early fourth or fifth centuries C.E. many architectural fragments derived from this synagogue were found scattered among its ruins: column drums, capitals, jambs, lintels, and decorated friezes. The ruins of other buildings and courtyards were found in the vicinity of the synagogue, including a large two-story building with an outer wall 99 ft. (30 m.) long, built of fine ashlar blocks, as well as the remains of what was apparently a glassmaking workshop. Many small artifacts were found: metal, pottery, and glass vessels, inscribed marble slabs, and some 1,200 bronze coins, all of which were struck in the first half of the fourth century C.E. These coins suggested to the excavators the date of the destruction of all the buildings in the area. A gate and an oil press, used chiefly in the Byzantine period, were also found nearby.

The excavations, however, were concentrated mainly in the extensive ancient necropolis that stretched over the slope of the hill northeast, north, and west of the city and over the slopes of adjacent hills to the north and west. Rock-cut catacombs that were prepared to provide burial places to sell to people from outside Bet She'arim were found in all these areas. Some were family vaults, but the majority were for the general public. Each catacomb contained an open court and a number of tomb halls that were connected by a series of chambers to some of the branch burial compartments containing graves. The openings between the chambers are arched. The usual form of a grave is the *arcosolium* – an arched niche cut into the wall with trough-like graves hewn at the bottom. *Kukhim* (*loculi* – "burial recesses") are also found frequently. Some of the catacombs lack all decoration, but many possess chambers that display a variegated ornamentation. The soft rock easily lent itself to carving and incision. The many reliefs, graffiti, and drawings adorning the walls are generally executed in the primitive style of the Jewish folk art popular in the Roman period. Jewish symbols and ritual objects are very common motifs, particularly the seven-branched candelabrum and the Ark of the Law, complete with columns and steps. The *shofar, lulav, etrog*, and incense shovel are also represented. But secular motifs also occur: human figures, animals, ships, geometric patterns, etc., as well as architectural ornaments that were carved in the rock (columns, capitals, arches, and niches). Ornamental stone doors were decorated to imitate wooden ones, complete with panels, nailheads, and knockers. These were locked by bolts, and lifted by keys. The doors still turn on their hinges. Some of the main entrances are adorned with built arches resting on pillars. The facades of two catacombs (nos. 14 and 20) are built of smooth ashlar stones in the form of an arcade of three arches. Over these facades are structures of monumental steps with prayer niches. A mausoleum was built over catacomb no. 11 and contained rich architectural decorations and reliefs.

Of special importance are the epitaphs, of which some 300 have been discovered. The majority are in Greek and the others are written in Hebrew, Aramaic, and Palmyrean. They are incised in the soft rock of the chamber walls, on the sides of the tombs, on lintels, on stone or marble slabs, or are painted in red or black. Their contents are generally restricted to the name of the deceased and his patronymic (or other family descent), with the addition of a word of affection or praise. The rank or occupation of the deceased, and occasionally his place of origin, are sometimes mentioned. Among the callings and titles are teacher, kohen, banker, goldsmith, government official, perfumer, chief warden of a community, chief of a synagogue, and rabbi (written *ribbi* and *bi-ribbi*). Typical examples of Hebrew inscriptions read: "Shalom to Judah," or "This tomb is (of) Rabbi Isaac bar Makim, shalom." An unusual Aramaic epitaph was found: "He who is buried here [is] Simeon, son of Johanan, and on oath, whoever shall open upon him shall die of an evil end." In catacomb no. 14 the following epitaphs were found: "Rabbi Simeon"; "This is the burial place of Rabbi Gamaliel"; and "Anina [Ḥanina] the Small." As it is known from the Talmud that before his death Judah ha-Nasi appointed his son Simeon *ḥakham*, Gamaliel (his second son) patriarch, and his most outstanding pupil, *Ḥanina b. Ḥama, head of the yeshivah (TB, Ket. 103b), one may assume that this catacomb was the burial place of the patriarch and his family. There are 218 Greek inscriptions and Greek was apparently the common language of the Jews at the time. Pure Greek names occur beside Hebrew ones in Greek transliteration. Some inscriptions express a belief in eternal life. The places of origin appearing in the epitaphs indicate that Bet She'arim was a central burial place for the Jews of Palestine-Elath (Exion-Geber), nearby Arabah and Baka, and of the Diaspora – Tadmor (Palmyra), Antioch, Byblos, Tyre, Sidon, and Beirut in Syria, Meishan in northern Mesopotamia, and Himyar in southern Arabia. Two inscriptions found incised on marble slabs in the mausoleum over catacomb no. 11 and in catacomb no. 18 are arranged in the form of Greek epigrams in the Homeric style. The former reads:

> Here lie I, son of Leontius, dead, son of Sappho-Justus,
> And after I had plucked the fruit of all wisdom
> I left the light, the miserable parents who mourn ceaselessly
> And my brothers. Woe to me, in my Besara!
> After descending to Hades, I, Justus, lie here
> With many of my people, for so willed stern fate.
> Be comforted, Justus, no man is immortal.

The mausoleum also contained a reused sarcophagus on which Greek mythological scenes were depicted.

The largest catacomb excavated (no. 20) was comprised of 24 burial chambers with over 200 coffins made of local limestone and many fragments of imported marble sarcophogi decorated with mythological figures. On the coffins birds and animals and even human beings were depicted. These coffins were not apparently used for Jewish burial and were brought into the tomb in the Islamic period as raw material for the purpose of lime burning. The inscriptions found in the catacomb (almost all in Hebrew) reveal that it was occupied by members of the patriarchal family, "holy" rabbis, and other sages.

Additional information on the industrial activities of Bet She'arim was supplied by the discovery of a huge glass slab (11 × 7 ft. (c. 3⅓ × 2 m.) and 18 in. (45 cm.) thick, weighing nine tons) in an underground cistern. It possibly served as raw material for village glassmakers in the region. The slab must have been heated for several days at about 1922 °F (1050 °C) in order to melt it. Recent research suggests that the slab should be dated to the ninth century C.E. Numerous lamps from this period were found within the necropolis, notably in Catacomb no. 20.

Modern Bet She'arim

A moshav named after ancient Bet She'arim, lies 3 mi. (5 km.) further west of it in the northwestern corner of the Jezreel Valley, founded in 1936 by a group of Israel-born and East European settlers. In 1968 the moshav's economy was based on livestock and crops. Its population was 320 in 1968. In the mid-1990s the population was approximately 370.

BIBLIOGRAPHY: B. Mazar, *Bet She'arim... 1936–40*, 1 (Heb., 1957[2]); Avigad, in: IEJ, 4 (1954), 88–107; 5 (1955), 205–39; 7 (1957), 73–92, 239–55; 9 (1959), 205–20; Mazar, *ibid.*, 10 (1960), 264; Brill, *ibid.*, 15 (1965), 261f.; Avi-Yonah, in: *Eretz Yisrael*, 8 (1967), 143–8; Frey, Corpus, 2 (1952), 177–212; M. Schwabe and B. Lifschitz, *Bet She'arim*, 2 (Heb., 1967). **ADD. BIBLIOGRAPHY:** J. Geiger, "The Last Jewish Revolt Against Rome: A Reconsideration," in: *Scripta Classica Israelica*, 5 (1979/80), 250–57; F. Vitto, "Byzantine Mosaics at Bet She'arim: New Evidence for the History of the Site," in: *Atiqot*, 28 (1996), 115–46.

[Nachman Avigad / Shimon Gibson (2nd ed.)]

BET(H)-SHEMESH (Heb. בֵּית שֶׁמֶשׁ; "the house [temple] of [the sun-god] Shemesh"), name of a number of places mentioned in the Bible.

(1) A city in the Shephelah on the northern border of the tribe of Judah, between Chesalon and Timnah (Josh. 15:10). Beth-Shemesh appears on the list of cities of the tribe of Dan (Josh. 19:41, as Ir-Shemesh), but it was apparently never actually conquered by it (Judg. 1:35, if the identification of Harheres with Beth-Shemesh is correct). In the list of levitical cities, it is mentioned as belonging to the tribe of Judah (Josh. 21:16; I Chron. 6:44). Beth-Shemesh was located close to the border of Philistia, and the archaeological excavations there have shown that in the period of the Judges, the Philistines exerted a strong influence on the city. The Samson narratives all take place in the vicinity of Beth-Shemesh; his birthplace, Zorah, lay just to the south of it, and the Philistine city Timnah is to the west of it. It has even been suggested that the name Samson itself (Heb. *Shimshon*) indicates a connection with the city. When the Philistines returned the "Ark of God," which they had captured at the battle of Eben-Ezer, on an ox-driven cart, it was sent along the road that led straight from Ekron to Beth-Shemesh (I Sam. 6). In the period of the monarchy, the city was part of Solomon's second administrative district, which included the former cities of the territory of Dan (I Kings 4:9). The war between Amaziah and Jehoash,

kings of Judah and Israel, in about 790 B.C.E. was fought near Beth-Shemesh, and Amaziah was taken prisoner there (II Kings 14:11–13; II Chron. 25:21–23). The last reference to Beth-Shemesh in the Bible occurs during the reign of Ahaz, king of Judah, from whom it was captured by the Philistines in about 734 B.C.E. (II Chron. 28:18).

Beth-Shemesh is identified with Tell al-Rumayla, astride the Wadi al-Ṣarār (biblical Sorek Valley?) on one of the major highways connecting Jerusalem with the seacoast (the modern Jerusalem-Tel Aviv railroad follows this ancient route). The site was excavated by D. Mackenzie (1911–12) and E. Grant (1928–33); G.E. Wright assisted in analyzing the results. The excavations revealed that the first city (stratum VI) of Beth-Shemesh was established toward the close of the third millennium B.C.E. (end of the Early Bronze Age). The next city (stratum V), dating to the Hyksos period (c. 1750–1550 B.C.E.), is characterized by a high level of development. This Middle Bronze Age city was fortified by a massive wall with insets and offsets and towers. In the southern part of the wall, a strong gate was discovered with the entrance between two guardrooms, a style typical of the period. The city continued to flourish in the Late Bronze Age (stratum IV, c. 1550–1200 B.C.E.). In this stratum plastered water cisterns, installations for the manufacture of bronze, numerous imported vessels from the Aegean area and Egypt, an inscription in the Ugaritic cuneiform alphabet, and an ink-inscribed ostracon in early Canaanite-Phoenician script were found. The following stratum (III) dates to the period of the Judges (Early Iron Age). This city shows signs of a decline in the material culture as is also evident in other sites from this period. The decline, however, did not affect the metal industry, which continued to operate at its previous high level. The abundance of Philistine pottery found in this stratum is proof of the strong influence of the Philistines in the area during this period. The destruction of the city by fire in the second half of the 11th century B.C.E. was a result of the wars with the Philistines that preceded the establishment of the monarchy. The city was rebuilt (stratum IIa) sometime in the tenth century and was surrounded by a casemate wall – the typical fortification of Israelite cities in the period of the united monarchy. The large store house and granary erected in the city confirm the biblical description of the important administrative role held by Beth-Shemesh.

Settlement at Beth-Shemesh continued until the end of the First Temple period (strata IIb and IIc). The last city was unfortified. Between IIb and IIc there appears to have been some interruption in the occupation of the site, which may explain the absence of Beth-Shemesh from the detailed city list of Judah, where it would be expected to appear in the Zorah-Azekah district (Josh. 15:33–36). Scholars disagree as to whether the date of this gap in the history of Beth-Shemesh should be ascribed to Pharaoh Shishak's campaign in c. 924 B.C.E. or to the capture of the city by Jehoash, king of Judah, in the eighth century. In Roman times the settlement moved to nearby Ayn Shams, which preserves the ancient name. Talmudic sources describe Beth-Shemesh as a small

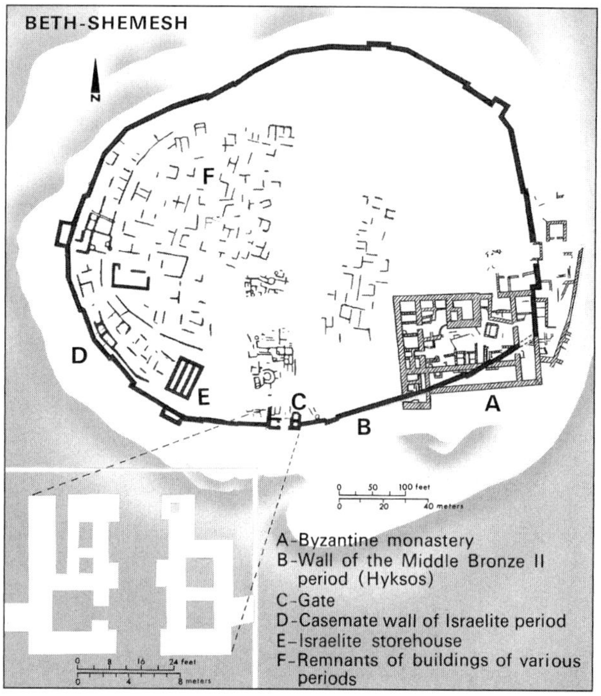

Plan of the excavations at Beth-Shemesh. Courtesy, Mosad Bialik, Jerusalem.

village (Lam. R. 2:2; etc.) and Eusebius (Onom. 54:11–13) accurately locates it 10 miles from Eleutheropolis (Bet Guvrin) on the road to Nicopolis (Emmaus).

(2) A Canaanite fortress town listed as part of the inheritance of Naphtali (Josh. 19:38) but not settled by the tribe in the early stages of the Israelite occupation of the country (Judg. 1:33). It was most likely located in the northern part of Upper Galilee, where remains of strong Canaanite settlements have been discovered. Some scholars identify it with the Beth-Shemesh of Issachar ((3) below) and accordingly place it in Lower Galilee on the border between Issachar and Naphtali.

(3) A city in the territory of Issachar, apparently close to the northern border of the tribe (Josh. 19:22). Khirbat Sheikh al-Shamsāwī in the southern part of the valley of Naphtali may preserve the ancient name. Some scholars, however, identify it with al-ʿUbaydiyya, farther east near the Jordan River, on the assumption that it is identical with (2) above.

(4) The city On-Heliopolis in Egypt whose temple to the Egyptian sun-god Re is mentioned in Jeremiah's prophecies against the nations (Jer. 43:13; cf. Isa. 19:18). It is the present-day el-Matariyeh, east of Cairo.

[Yohanan Aharoni]

Modern Period

In the vicinity is the modern town of Bet-Shemesh. Its beginnings go back to the village of Hartuv, founded in 1895 by Jews from Bulgaria who bought the land from a training farm set up 12 years earlier by the English Mission of Jerusalem which had tried unsuccessfully to convert Jerusalemite Jews working there. Hartuv made little progress due to its isolation and the lack of water and good soil. In the 1929 Arab riots, the few inhabitants had to leave the village temporarily but soon returned. Shortly before 1948, the Tel Aviv municipality opened a youth training farm there, and construction of the large "Shimshon" cement factory was begun. Bet-Shemesh was abandoned for a few months during the 1948 War of Independence, but finally fell to Israeli forces on September 19, 1948. A *ma'barah* ("immigrant transit settlement") was set up there in 1950, and in 1951 a permanent urban settlement was begun as part of the program of populating and securing the "Jerusalem Corridor."

Bet-Shemesh grew to serve as an urban center providing community and commercial services to 60 rural settlements. The city had two large industrial areas, but some of its residents commuted to Jerusalem and Tel Aviv. It numbered 10,000 inhabitants in 1969 and received municipal status in 1991. In the mid-1990s the population was approximately 20,900 and by 2002 the fast-growing city had increased its population to 53,400, 50% among them under the age of 21. It occupied an area of 20 sq. mi. (50.5 sq. km.). In this latter period the city absorbed many new immigrants, mainly from the former Soviet Union. The majority of them were secular and their presence in the city led to a degree of cultural-religious tension. The Ramat Bet-Shemesh suburb south of the city attracted a religious population, including many English-speaking immigrants.

[Efraim Orni / Shaked Gilboa (2nd ed.)]

BIBLIOGRAPHY: (1) Press, Ereẓ, 1 (1951), 104–5; EM, 2 (1965), 110–8 (includes bibliography). (2) Y. Aharoni, *Hitnaḥalut Shivtei Yisrael ba-Galil ha-Elyon* (1957), 52, 74–5. (3) Abel, Geog, 2 (1938), 282–3; Aharoni, Land, index. (4) EM, 1 (1965), 147; 2 (1965), 119. **WEBSITE:** www.betshemesh.muni.il.

BET(H)-SHITTAH (modern Bet ha-Shittah; Heb. בֵּית הַשִּׁטָּה), biblical locality mentioned in the description of the Midianites' flight after their defeat by Gideon (Judg. 7:22). Some scholars locate it at the small village of Shata' (site of a prison), east of the hill of Moreh but most prefer to place it in the immediate vicinity of the Jordan. There is a kibbutz in the Valley of Jezreel named after the biblical locality of Beth-Shittah. The kibbutz is affiliated with Ha-Kibbutz ha-Me'uḥad. Bet ha-Shittah was founded in 1935 by sabras and pioneers from Germany, later joined by immigrants from other countries. In 1968 Bet ha-Shittah had 885 inhabitants, maintaining its size over the years (pop. 900 in 2002). Its economy was based on farming (field crops, particularly cotton, fodder, fishery, dairy cattle, and other farm products) and industrial enterprises such as farm machinery and preservatives, the latter plant subsequently sold to the Osem food company. The kibbutz also operated a small shopping center at the nearby road junction.

WEBSITE: www.bethashita.org.il.

[Efraim Orni]

BETTAN, ISRAEL (1889–1957), U.S. rabbi. Born in Kovno and educated in yeshivot in Lithuania, Bettan came to the United States at the age of 18 where he enrolled at Rabbi Isaac Elchanan Rabbinical Seminary, but soon transferred to Hebrew Union College. He received his B.A. from the University of Cincinatti (1910), his ordination from HUC in 1912, and his D.D. three years later writing on early Reform in rabbinic responsa.

He then went to a Congregation B'nai Israel in Charleston, West Virginia, where he established his reputation as an excellent preacher and congregational leader. He served with the American Forces in France in World War I, having taken leave of his congregation, and then returned to Charleston, where he was rabbi until 1922, when he was named chairman of the Department of Homiletics of HUC. He taught at HUC for 35 years, including midrash. As a professor of homiletics it was his task to prepare future rabbis for the life cycle and communal events that they were to lead, from weddings to funeral, bar mitzvah to invocations and benedictions. He believed in the power of the pulpit and taught his students how to use that power to motivate their congregations. His unique style of teaching made him very popular among students who valued the practical experience as well as the intellectual guidance he offered.

Active in the Reform movement, he was twice named a member of the committee that revised the *Union Prayer Book*. He also served as president of the Central Conference of American Rabbis in 1956 and retired from teaching the next year to continue his presidency.

Among his writings was *The Five Scrolls: A Commentary* (1950) and *Studies in Jewish Preaching* and *Opposition of Orthodoxy to Early Reform* (1914).

BIBLIOGRAPHY: M. Meyer, *Response to Modernity* (1988); S. Karff, *Hebrew Union College-Jewish Institute of Religion at One Hundred Years* (1976); K. Olitzky, L. Sussman, and M.H. Stern, *Reform Judaism in America: A Biographical Dictionary and Sourcebook* (1993).

[Michael Berenbaum (2nd ed.)]

BETTAUER, HUGO (1872–1925), Viennese journalist and novelist. Bettauer converted to Protestantism at the age of 18 and after a period in Zurich went to the United States, where he first worked in business and later taught German literature. In 1899 he returned to Europe as an American citizen, settled in Berlin, and became a journalist for the *Berliner Morgenpost*, a newspaper of the *Ullstein publishing house. He was several times imprisoned for offending Emperor William II and the Prussian police, causing him finally to be expelled from the country. Back in New York, he worked on German newspapers published by the Hearst group. In 1908 he returned to Vienna, where he worked for the *Zeit* and the *Neue Freie Presse*. He wrote several novels, successful in their time, which were also filmed, the most noteworthy of these being *Stadt ohne Juden* (1922; *The City without Jews*, 1926). The novel dealt with the extreme antisemitic atmosphere in Vienna after World War I, which was mainly directed at Jewish war refugees from Eastern Europe: A utopian state, akin to the first Austrian republic, expels all Jews for economic and antisemitic reasons; as a result it breaks down completely and decides to call its Jewish population back. The novel, as well as the film version by Hans Karl Breslauer (1924), aroused controversy in Vienna and Berlin. In 1924 Bettauer founded the periodical *Er und Sie: Wochenschrift fuer Erotik und Lebenskultur* (later *Bettauers Wochenschrift*), advocating sex education, abortion, and homosexuality, but also calling attention to unemployment and poverty. His views made him the focus of attacks from right-wing newspapers. In March 1925 he was murdered in his office by the National-Socialist Otto Rothstock.

BIBLIOGRAPHY: M.G. Hall, *Der Fall Bettauer* (1978); F. Krobb, "Vienna Goes to Pot without Jews: Hugo Bettauer's Novel *Die Stadt ohne Juden*," in: *The Jewish Quarterly* 42 (1994), 17–20. **ADD. BIBLIOGRAPHY:** *Die Stadt ohne Juden*, ed. G. Geser and A. Loacker (2000).

[Mirjam Triendl (2nd ed.)]

BETTELHEIM, family originating from Pozsony (*Bratislava, Pressburg), formerly in Hungary. According to tradition, one of its forebears frustrated a plot by the count of Bethlen to abduct his wife, and for this feat was called "Bethlen-Jude," which later became Bettelheim. The first noted member of the family, LOEB BETTELHEIM, served as *dayyan* in Pozsony in 1709. LIPOT LEOPOLD (MEYER LEB) BETTELHEIM (1777–1838) was physician to the count in Galgoc (now Hlohovec) and a noted Hebraist. MOSES BETTELHEIM (beginning of the 19th century) was head of the Jewish community in Pozsony. His son, FÜLÖP (RAPHAEL), represented the Orthodox Jews in Pozsony at the assembly of Jewish delegates held in Pest in 1868. Samuel *Bettelheim was a journalist and editor. Prominent members of the family outside Hungary include Albert (Aaron) Siegfried *Bettelheim, rabbi, publicist, and physician. KARL BETTELHEIM (1840–1895), also a physician, became head of a Vienna clinic and the editor of *Medizinisch-Chirurgische Rundschau* (1870–78).

BIBLIOGRAPHY: EẒD, 1 (1958), 272–4; S. Federbush, *Ḥokhmat Yisrael be-Ma'arav Eiropah*, 2 (1963), 371–2.

[Jeno Zsoldos]

BETTELHEIM, ALBERT (Aaron) SIEGFRIED (1830–1890), U.S. rabbi. Bettelheim was born in Galgoc, Hungary. He served as correspondent on Jewish affairs for several periodicals, director of a network of Jewish schools, editor of a political weekly *Elöre* ("Forward"), and rabbi of a small congregation. Bettelheim's progressive political views brought him into trouble with the government, and he emigrated to America in 1867. He served as rabbi in Philadelphia, and on the faculty of the short-lived Maimonides College. He also acquired a medical degree. In 1875 Bettelheim accepted a pulpit in San Francisco. There he organized a society for Hebrew study for Christian clergymen, and was active in civic affairs, especially prison reform. He coedited a weekly, the *Jewish Times and Observer*, which represented the traditionalists' views. In 1887 he returned East to a pulpit in Baltimore. A foundation to aid needy scholars in Vienna was established in his memory by his daughter Rebekah, wife of Alexander *Kohut. Bettelheim left no complete scholarly work but he wrote many articles on art, medicine, and other subjects and some of his notes and suggestions were incorporated into Kohut's *Arukh*. His son, FÉLIX ALBERT BETTELHEIM (1861–1890), a physician, also moved to the United States and initiated the establishment of the first hospital in Panama, serving as head physician between 1883 and 1889.

BIBLIOGRAPHY: M. Davis, *Emergence of Conservative Judaism* (1963), 329–31.

[Jack Reimer]

BETTELHEIM, BRUNO (1903–1990), U.S. psychologist and educator, best known for his pioneering techniques in the treatment of emotionally disturbed children and his analysis of the psychological aspects of racial prejudice. Born in Vienna, Bettelheim studied at the university there. In 1938 he was sent to the Dachau concentration camp and then to Buchenwald. In 1939 he was released and permitted to leave for the United States. In 1943 he published a highly influential essay on the psychology of concentration camp prisoners.

Bettelheim worked with the Progressive Education Association and, for a short period, with Rockford College in Illinois. He was subsequently appointed principal of the University of Chicago's Sonia Shankman Orthogenic School, a residential institution devoted to the education and treatment of children with severe emotional disorders. In that capacity, he placed special emphasis on the treatment of autism. From 1944 to 1973 he was professor of educational psychology at the University of Chicago.

In a number of essays and reviews and in a volume entitled *The Informed Heart* (1960), Bettelheim, basing himself on limited documentation, appears as a stern judge of the Jewish masses who did not revolt against the Nazi terror.

Bettelheim wrote prolifically on the diagnosis and therapy of emotionally disturbed children. He wrote *Dynamics of Prejudice* (1950) in collaboration with Morris Janowitz, which was regarded as a vital work in its field. His other major publications included *Love Is Not Enough* (1950); *Truants from Life* (1955); *The Empty Fortress* (1967); *The Children of the Dream* (1969), an analysis of the rearing of kibbutz children; and *The Uses of Enchantment* (1976), which looks at fairy tales from a Freudian perspective.

Suffering from depression most of his life, Bettelheim committed suicide in 1990 at the age of 86.

During his lifetime Bettelheim was well respected for his work. However, after his death his credibility began to be questioned. Not formally trained in analysis, Bettelheim and his theories, as well as his biographical data, were challenged in journalist Richard Pollak's controversial book *The Creation of Dr. B: A Biography of Bruno Bettelheim* (1998).

BIBLIOGRAPHY: J. Robinson, in: *Yad Vashem Studies*, 8 (1970); M.J. Blumenthal, in: *Conservative Judaism* (Spring 1970), 16–19; D.

Dempsey, in: *New York Times Magazine* (Jan. 11, 1970), 22–23, 107–11; N. Sutton, *Bruno Bettelheim: The Other Side of Madness* (1995); N. Sutton, *Bettelheim: A Life and a Legacy* (1996); R. Pollak, *The Creation of Dr. B: A Biography of Bruno Bettelheim* (1998).

[Abraham J. Tannenbaum / Ruth Beloff (2nd ed.)]

BETTELHEIM, SAMUEL (1872–1942), early Zionist and Mizrachi leader in Hungary, later in Czechoslovakia. Bettelheim was born in Pressburg (later Bratislava), where he received a religious and secular education. Under Herzl's influence, he formed the first Zionist association in Hungary. When the Mizrachi movement was founded in 1904, he became one of its leaders. From 1908 he published and edited in Pressburg a Zionist weekly, *Ungarlaendische Juedische Zeitung*. During World War I, the Austro-Hungarian government sent him on a mission to the United States to influence American Jewry in its favor. After the war, he became a leading Zionist in Czechoslovakia. However, Bettelheim, who opposed the political and cultural activities of the Zionist Organization, soon joined Agudat Israel, taking an extreme anti-Zionist stand. He edited their newspaper *Juedische Presse* in Bratislava and Vienna and from 1922 *Juedische Zeitung* in Bratislava, where he propounded Agudat Israel. In 1934–35, he published in Bratislava a German-language monthly called *Judaica*, devoted to Jewish literature and history and containing material on Jewish and Zionist history in Hungary. In his last years he lived in Budapest.

BIBLIOGRAPHY: S.H. Weingarten, *Toledot Yehudei Bratislava* (1960) 139–40; EẒD, 1 (1958), 272–4.

[Samuel Weingarten-Hakohen]

BETTMAN, GARY (1952–), commissioner of the National Hockey League since 1993. Bettman was born in Queens, New York, and raised by his mother. He graduated from Cornell in 1974 and New York University Law School in 1977. After law school he worked at Proskauer Rose, a prestigious sports law firm in New York, where he met David *Stern, who went on to become commissioner of the National Basketball Association. Bettman joined Stern at the NBA as assistant general counsel in 1981 and worked in the NBA league office for 12 years.

Bettman became commissioner of the NHL on February 1, 1993, the sixth man to run the NHL since 1917. When he arrived, the league had teams in only 14 U.S. cities, league sponsorships were almost nonexistent, and the NHL had not had a network television agreement in almost 20 years. Bettman expanded the league from 24 to 30 teams, including teams in new locales such as Dallas, Anaheim, Miami, Phoenix, Carolina, Nashville, and Columbus, and new teams in former NHL cities such as Denver, Atlanta, and Minnesota. He increased revenues from $400 million to over $1.6 billion, and negotiated two network television contracts, including a $600 million deal with ABC and ESPN in 1998. In 1998, Bettman allowed NHL players to participate in the Olympic Winter Games, marking the first time NHL players had played in the Olympics. The NHL also suspended the regular 2001–2 season for 10 days to allow 125 players to participate in the Olympic Winter Games in Salt Lake City. Bettman made changes to the game itself, realigning and renaming the league's divisions to reflect geography; adopting a two-referee system; moving goal lines, blue lines, and defensive-zone circles; and changing the playoff formats.

However, his term in office was also marked by labor strife, first in 1994 when owners voted to lock out the players at the start of the season, which wiped out 32 games of the 80-game season; and in the 2004–5 season, which was canceled altogether.

[Elli Wohlgelernter (2nd ed.)]

BETTMANN, BERNHARDT (1834–1915), U.S. Reform lay leader. Born in Germany, Bettmann immigrated to the U.S. in 1850, settling in Cincinnati and building a successful clothing business. Early on, he formed a close relationship with Reform leader Rabbi Isaac Mayer *Wise, who tapped him to serve the Zion Collegiate Association. An active leader of the Reform movement throughout its formative years, Bettmann joined the first executive board of the *Union of American Hebrew Congregations upon its founding in 1873. In 1875, he became the first chairman of the Board of Governors of the *Hebrew Union College, a position he held until becoming its honorary president in 1910. Ideologically, Bettmann was a non-Zionist, contending that while Palestine could possibly serve as a haven for the oppressed Jews of Russia, there was no need for a general return to a Jewish homeland. Spurning Jewish nationalism, he believed that the mission of Judaism was to spread the word of God and the brotherhood of man. A noted philanthropist, Bettmann was a pioneer in the development of community-wide social services. He was instrumental in founding the United Jewish Charities of Cincinnati and served as the organization's first president (1896–1903).

BIBLIOGRAPHY: K.M. Olitzky, L.J. Sussman, and M.H. Stern, *Reform Judaism in America: A Biographical Dictionary and Sourcebook* (1993).

[Bezalel Gordon (2nd ed.)]

BET YANNAI (Heb. בֵּית יַנַּאי), coastal moshav in the Ḥefer Plain, affiliated with Tenu'at ha-Moshavim; founded in 1933. Its settlers came from Poland, Lithuania, and North America. Its economy was based on farming (mostly citrus plantations) and tourism (the moshav also became a seaside resort). In 1968 its population was 229, increasing to 330 in the mid-1990s and 370 in 2002. It is named after the Hasmonean king Alexander Yannai.

[Efraim Orni]

BET YEHOSHU'A (Heb. בֵּית יְהוֹשֻׁעַ), moshav shittufi in central Israel, in the southern Sharon, affiliated with Ha-Oved ha-Ẓiyyoni. It was founded as a kibbutz in 1938 by pioneers from Poland. Its economy was based mainly on citrus plantations and dairy cattle. In 1968 its population was 260, rising with expansion to 420 in the mid-1990s and 652 in 2002. The village's name commemorates the Zionist leader Osias (Yehoshu'a) *Thon.

[Efraim Orni]

BET YERAḤ (Heb. בֵּית יֶרַח), large Canaanite city on the shore of the Sea of Galilee extending over a tell of approximately 50 acres, from the site of the present-day moshavah *Kinneret, to the outlet of the *Jordan River from the lake near *Deganyah. This location is based on the Jerusalem Talmud (Meg. 1:1, 70a) which speaks of two autonomous cities surrounded by walls, Bet-Yeraḥ and Ẓinabri (*Sennabris), in the vicinity of the Sea of Galilee. An additional reference is found in *Bekhorot* 51a, which states that the Jordan River "began" at Bet Yerah. Inasmuch as Sennabris is usually identified with Ḥaẓar Kinneret, it is probable that Bet Yeraḥ was situated on the site known to the Arabs as Khirbat al-Karak. Although not mentioned in the Bible, the name points to an ancient Canaanite settlement whose deity was a moon god. Excavations were conducted there in 1944–46 by the Jewish Palestine Exploration Society and, from 1949, by the Department of Antiquities and the Oriental Institute, University of Chicago.

The earliest settlement at Bet Yeraḥ is dated at the end of the Chalcolithic and the beginning of the Early Bronze Age I (c. 3200 B.C.E.). The inhabitants lived in huts some of which were sunk into pits dug to a depth of about 11½ ft. (3.5 m.). Traces of pavements and ovens were found in the pits. The

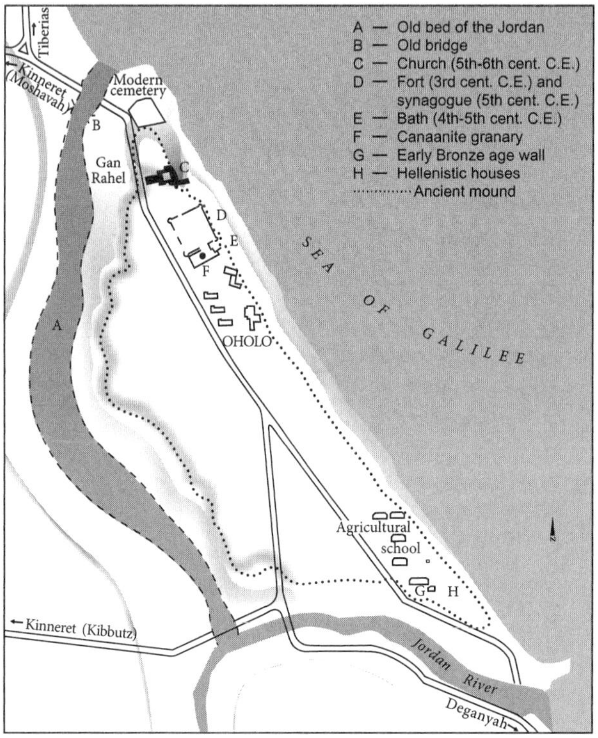

Map showing the site of the Canaanite city of Bet Yeraḥ in relation to the modern Oholo. After P. Delougaz and R.C. Haines, A Byzantine Church at Kirbat Al-Karak, *1960.*

erection of a brick wall, the first of Bet Yeraḥ's fortifications, was followed by the building of mud-brick houses and in the 29th century B.C.E. (Early Bronze Age II), stone houses made their appearance. A tomb from this period found at moshavah Kinneret contained gold ornaments in the style of Asia Minor. The settlement reached its zenith in the Early Bronze Age III (26th–24th centuries B.C.E.), when a large granary, 3,936 sq. ft. (1,200 sq. m.) in area, was constructed to the north of Bet Yeraḥ, indicating that at that time it was already the center of a large region of irrigated farmlands. The pottery of this epoch is light red or red-black burnished ware (a type common in Syria and Asia Minor) and its presence is apparently to be attributed to influences of northern peoples who penetrated through trade or invasion. In the Middle Bronze Age I the settlement was concentrated in the southern part of Bet Yeraḥ. No settlement existed there after that for about 1,500 years until the Persian period; to this period belong several graves found there. The city's location in ancient times east of the Jordan, on a narrow tongue between the river and the Sea of Galilee, necessitated building the main fortifications on the southern side. Here, where the Jordan now flows, the city lacked natural defenses in ancient times. The settlement at Bet Yeraḥ flourished again in the Hellenistic period. It has been identified with Philoteria, a Ptolemaic center, captured by *Antiochus III in 198 B.C.E. and also mentioned among the cities conquered by *Alexander Yannai (according to George Synkellus, 1:559). Remains uncovered from this period include a stone wall with vaulted openings and several houses, some with floors, plastered and painted walls, and windows overlooking the lake; numerous Rhodian stamped jar handles were also discovered.

In the early Roman period, a large Roman structure, covering an area of 105 × 59 ft. (32 × 18 m.), was erected on the ruins of the Hellenistic houses on the south. A large rectangular fort built of dressed masonry with towers at its corners was constructed on the northern part of the tell in the third century C.E. From this period there are several reports of a mixed Jewish-gentile population at Bet Yeraḥ (TJ, Meg. 1:1, 70a). After the Bar Kokhba war, priests of the Haaziah family settled there. The verse "Naphtali is a hind let loose" (Gen. 49:21) was interpreted by rabbis of the time as referring to Bet Yeraḥ, the territory of which was "entirely irrigated" (Gen. R. 98:22). The statement in the Jerusalem Talmud (loc. cit.) "The city was destroyed and became the possession of gentiles" also alludes to some event which occurred in the third century at Bet Yeraḥ or in its vicinity. In the fourth and fifth centuries, the fort seems to have been abandoned and its southern wall was used as the northern wall of a bathhouse. Excavations have shown that the bathhouse, the water for which was conducted through earthenware pipes from the aqueduct of *Tiberias, had a central hall with a circular pool in the center and heated rooms. In the fifth century, a synagogue was built within the fort. It was basilical, with an apse oriented to Jerusalem, and was one of the largest contemporary synagogues in the country, 121 × 72 ft. (37 × 22 m.). Its foundations have survived as well as part of its mosaic floor depicting a citron tree, a man and a horse (possibly a representation of the story of Mordecai and Haman), and also the base of a column incised with a seven-branched candelabrum.

North of the synagogue, a Christian church was built, basilical in form, with a central hall and two aisles; an atrium containing a well lay on its west side. The church had been enlarged to the north by a baptistery with a mosaic pavement dating from 529 C.E. Bet Yeraḥ was resettled in the seventh century after having been destroyed during the Persian or Arab invasion, but it was abandoned shortly afterward and reoccupied only in recent years. In 1945 an agricultural secondary school for the settlements of the Jordan Valley was built south of the tell and in 1949 Oholo, a conference and study center in memory of Berl *Katznelson, was erected north of it. Oholo opened in 1957 on the initiative of Ben Zion Yisreeli of Kevuẓah Kinneret, a leading personality of the labor and kibbutz movement. It houses courses for soldiers after their discharge; a teachers' seminary, principally for students hailing from Middle Eastern countries who intend to teach in immigrant villages and development towns; and a field school of the Society for the Preservation of Nature.

BIBLIOGRAPHY: Maisler et al., in: IEJ, 2 (1952), 165–73, 218–29; P. Bar-Adon, in: *Eretz Israel*, 4 (1956), 50–55; Albright, in: AASOR, 6 (1926), 27ff.; idem, in: JPOS 15 (1935), 200; Sukenik, in: JPOS, 2 (1922), 101ff.; P. Delougaz and R.C. Haines, *Byzantine Church at Khirbat al-Karak* (1960).

[Michael Avi-Yonah / Efraim Orni]

BET YIẒḤAK (Heb. בֵּית יִצְחָק), moshav in central Israel, in the Ḥefer Plain. It was founded in 1940 as an unaffiliated middle-class settlement by immigrants from Germany, many of whom were formerly members of academic professions. Later, Bet Yiẓḥak merged with the neighboring moshav Nirah, most of whose settlers came from Czechoslovakia and Austria. In 1968 Bet Yiẓḥak had a population of 825. Its economy was based on citrus orchards, a natural fruit preserve factory, and intensive farming. In the mid-1990s the population was approximately 1,440, increasing to 1,560 in 2002. Its name commemorates the German Zionist Yiẓḥak Feuerring, whose bequest was instrumental in financing the settlement.

[Efraim Orni]

BET YOSEF (Heb. בֵּית יוֹסֵף), moshav in Israel, in the north of the Beth-Shean Valley near the Jordan River, affiliated with Tenu'at ha-Moshavim; founded on April 9, 1937 as a "*tower and stockade" settlement. Its inhabitants came from Kurdistan. Its economy was based mostly on livestock and field crops, including cotton. Following the Six-Day War in June 1967, Bet Yosef frequently suffered from Jordanian artillery fire and acts of sabotage. In 2002 the population was approximately 350. Its name commemorates the Israel labor leader, Yosef *Aharonovitch.

[Efraim Orni]

BET ZAYIT (Heb. בֵּית זַיִת), moshav west of Jerusalem, affiliated with Ha-Mo'aẓah ha-Ḥakla'it association of "middle-class" settlements. Bet Zayit was founded in 1949 by immigrants from Yugoslavia, Romania, and Hungary. Later, immigrants from Egypt settled in the village. Its economy was based on fruit orchards, vegetables, poultry, and other farm products. Situated on the fringe of the Jerusalem Forest Park it operated a swimming pool and guest house as well. Near the village is the Ein Kerem dam built to store winter flood waters. The name, "House of the Olive Tree," refers to the extensive olive groves on the slopes around the village. In 1970 Bet Zayit numbered 468 inhabitants, in the mid-1990s the population was 840, while by 2002 it had increased still further 1,110. A place of the same name mentioned in the books of the Maccabees stood further north, possibly at the site of the Arab village Bīr al-Zayt, north of Ramallah.

[Efraim Orni]

BET ZEKHARYAH (Heb. בֵּית זְכַרְיָה), site 10 mi. (16 km.) S.W. of Jerusalem and 6 mi. (9½ km.) N. of Beth-Zur, where the Hasmonean army clashed with that of Antiochus V Eupator, king of Syria, in 162 B.C.E. In this battle *Eleazar, a brother of *Judah Maccabee, was crushed to death by one of the enemy's elephants whom he attacked, believing it to be carrying the king. The Jewish force was compelled to retreat (I Macc. 6:32–3; Jos., Ant., 12:369ff.). Bet Zekharyah is present-day Khirbat Beit Zakarya, 2.2 mi. (4 km.) S.W. of Solomon's Pools.

BIBLIOGRAPHY: Jos., Wars, 1:41ff.; Avi-Yonah, Geog, 103; Abel, in: RB, 33 (1924), 212ff.; Ploger, in: ZDPV, 79 (1958), 173.

[Michael Avi-Yonah]

BET ZERA (Heb. בֵּית זֶרַע, "House of Seed"), kibbutz in Israel, 1¼ mi. (2 km.) S. of Lake Kinneret, affiliated with Kibbutz Arẓi ha-Shomer ha-Ẓair, founded in 1927 by pioneers from Germany who had previously participated in establishing *Mizra in the Jezreel Valley. It received part of the Umm Jūnī lands (among the first acquired in the country by the Jewish National Fund), ceded by nearby *Deganyah when it intensified its farming methods. The settlers developed a farming economy adapted to the hot climate, based on field crops, bananas, and other tropical fruit. In addition, it raised dairy cattle. In the mid-1970s, industry began to replace farming as the main source of livelihood, with the kibbutz manufacturing a variety of plastic goods. In 1968 Bet Zera had 660 inhabitants, increasing slightly to 715 in 2002. In its initial years, the settlement was named also Kefar Nathan Laski, after the English communal leader. The site is supposed to be that of Kefar Agun of talmudic times, home of R. Tanḥum b. Ḥiyya (Gen. R. 100:7).

WEBSITE: www.betzera.org.il.

[Efraim Orni]

BET ẒERIFA, Jewish family of the Second Temple period. According to the Mishnah "there was a family of Bet Ẓerifa in Transjordan and Ben-Zion rejected it by force" (Eduy. 8:7; see also TJ, Yev. 8:3, 9a: TJ, Kid. 4:1, 65c). Scholars are divided as to whether this implies that Ben-Zion (of whom nothing more is known) had it ejected from the priesthood because he questioned its legitimacy. Possibly the learned Judah, son of Sariphaeus (Ẓerifa), who – according to Josephus – incited his disciples to pull down the golden eagle erected by Herod the king over the temple gate, belonged to this family, as well as R. Judah son of Ẓipporai, also known as Ben Ẓerifa.

BIBLIOGRAPHY: Jos., Ant., 17:149; Jos., Wars, 1:648; Buechler, in: *Festschrift A. Schwarz…* (1917), 137ff.; S. Klein, in: MGWJ, 64 (1920), 180ff.; J.N. Epstein, *ibid.*, 65 (1921), 89–90.

[Isaiah Gafni]

BET(H)-ZUR (Heb. בֵּית צוּר), ancient city in Ereẓ Israel, 4½ mi. (7 km.) N. of Hebron, and, according to Eusebius (Onom. 52:1–2), 20 Roman miles south of Jerusalem, on the Hebron-Jerusalem road. The name has been preserved at Khirbat Burj al-Ṣūr but the ancient city was located nearby at Khirbat al-Tubayqa, on a high isolated plateau. Beth-Zur seems to have first been settled during the Early Bronze Age (third millennium B.C.E.). The earliest city, however, was apparently established by the *Hyksos in the second half of the Middle Bronze Age (c. 18th century B.C.E.). Only meager traces of the Late Bronze Age have been discovered. The site was rebuilt during the period of the Israelite settlement and appears to have been associated with the rule of the sons of *Caleb and the tribe of Judah (Josh. 15:58; I Chron. 2:45). The Israelite city was destroyed by fire c. 1,000 B.C.E., apparently in one of the Philistine attacks. Rehoboam included Beth-Zur in his system of fortifications (II Chron. 11:7). In the days of *Nehemiah, it was the capital of a sub-district. Its ruler, Nehemiah, son of Azbuk, took part in the rebuilding of the walls of Jerusalem (Neh. 3:16). From this time onward, Beth-Zur served as a defense post on the southern frontier of Judea against the Idumeans in the Hebron district. It played an important role in the Hasmonean wars; a Seleucid garrison stationed there from 175 B.C.E. was routed by Judah *Maccabee in 165 B.C.E. This victory and Judah's fortifications of Beth-Zur as a border stronghold of Judea made possible the resumption of the service in the Temple and its rededication (I Macc. 4:29). Two years later, the Syrians regained control of the city and thereby of the road to Jerusalem (I Macc. 6:60). Their general *Bacchides rebuilt its fortifications, c. 160 B.C.E. (I Macc. 9:52), but after a prolonged siege it was finally captured by the Hasmonean *Simeon son of Mattathias in the mid-forties of the second century B.C.E. and its defenses were strengthened. Remains of the Maccabean fortress, containing large rock-hewn cisterns, were uncovered in excavations conducted in 1931 and resumed in 1957. The city was destroyed and abandoned, apparently during *Vespasian's campaigns, but as shown by the Madaba Map, it was reestablished in the Byzantine period, probably on the opposite hill, Khirbat Burj al-Ṣūr, whose ruins date from Crusader times.

BIBLIOGRAPHY: O.R. Sellers, *Citadel of Beth Zur* (1933); Lapp, in: BASOR, 151 (1958), 16–27; Aharoni, Land, index; Avi-Yonah, Geog, index.

[Michael Avi-Yonah]

BET-ẒURI, ELIAHU (1922–1945), Jew executed in Egypt in the Mandate Period. Bet-Ẓuri was born in Tel Aviv. He became a member of *Leḥi after its secession from IZL. Together with Eliahu *Ḥakim he was sent by his organization to Cairo to assassinate Lord Moyne, then British minister of state for the Middle East, whose seat was in Cairo. The attempt was successful, but Bet-Ẓuri and Ḥakim were apprehended. They were sentenced to death by a military court in Cairo on Jan. 1, 1945, and executed on Mar. 22. Their remains were interred in the Jewish cemetery of Cairo.

BIBLIOGRAPHY: Y. Nedava, *Olei-ha-Gardom* (1966); Y. Gurion, *Ha-Nizzaḥon Olei Gardom* (1971).

°**BEUGNOT, AUGUSTE ARTHUR** (1797–1865), French lawyer, senator (1841), and delegate to the National Assembly (1848). Beugnot was keenly interested in the improvement of the situation of the Jews in France. In 1822, together with J.B. Capefigue and G.B. Depping he won a French Academy competition for a paper *Juifs d'occident, ou recherches sur l'état civil, le commerce, la littérature des Juifs en France, en Espagne et en Italie, pendant la durée du moyen âge* (Paris, 1824). Beugnot showed thorough knowledge of Jewish history and concluded his study with an exposition of the contributions of the Jews to the growth of European economies and culture. He asserted that whatever negative traits the Jews possess can be blamed on the Christians. In 1824 the Institute of Science, Agriculture, and Art in Strasbourg announced a competition under the patronage of an anonymous Jew, which had as its purpose to find "the most helpful ways in enabling the Jewish population of Alsace to enjoy the accomplishments of civilization." Beugnot won first prize but his submitted work never appeared in print. A resumé of his "Quels sont les moyens les plus propres à faire jouir la population israélite de l'Alsace des bienfaits de la civilisation?" appeared in *Journal de la Société des Science, Agriculture et Arts du Departement du Bas Rhin* (1 (1824), 114–6; 2 (1825), 297–320). He proposed that a council of Alsatian Jews be formed, under state sponsorship, to form committees for schools, publication of textbooks, experimental farms, trade, and charity. He argued that it was necessary to found a modern theological school and also proposed changing the Sabbath to Sunday.

[Noe Gruss]

°**BEVAN, EDWYN ROBERT** (1870–1943), historian and philosopher. He was educated at Oxford and became lecturer in Hellenistic history and literature at King's College, London. Bevan's main publications of Jewish interest are *The House of Seleucus*, 2 vols. (1902) and *Jerusalem under the High Priests* (1904), still a standard work. He also was coeditor (with Israel Abrahams and Charles Singer) of the *Legacy of Judaism* (19282), to which he contributed the article on Hellenistic Judaism. Bevan was a close friend of Claude *Goldsmid-Montefiore and an active member of the Society of Christians and Jews. Paradoxically, his sister was the notorious conspiracy theorist Nesta Webster. His brother, ANTHONY ASHLEY BEVAN (1859–1933), taught Oriental languages at Cambridge University. His chief interests were Arabic and Hebrew and he wrote a commentary on the Book of Daniel (1892).

ADD. BIBLIOGRAPHY: ODNB online.

°**BEVIN, ERNEST** (1881–1951), British trade union leader and statesman. He was a member of the British War Cabinet in World War II (1941–45), and foreign secretary in the Labor government (1945–50) when Palestine was transferred de facto from the aegis of the Colonial Office to that of the Foreign Office. Bevin's Palestine policy was based on two premises: first, he felt that since the vast majority of the Middle East population was Arab, nothing should be done against their will, lest this set the Arab world against Great Britain and the West in their global struggle with the U.S.S.R. and Communism; second, he believed that Palestine could not essentially solve the Jewish problem as Jews should continue residing in Europe and contributing to its welfare. Rather than impose a Jewish state on the Arabs, he desired some kind of settlement between Jews and Arabs. In an attempt to obtain U.S. government approval for his Palestine policy, Bevin proposed appointing an Anglo-American commission whose task would be to plan a solution to the Palestine question. In the summer of 1946 he rejected the committee's proposals for the immediate admission of 100,000 Jewish refugees from Europe and the annulment of the provisos in the Macdonald White Paper restricting the acquisition of land by Jews. As a result, the situation in Palestine deteriorated, and Bevin began applying severe repressive measures against the *yishuv*. Leading members of the Jewish Agency and the Va'ad Le'ummi were arrested, "illegal" immigrants were deported to detention camps in Cyprus, and the *Exodus*, bearing 4,500 such immigrants, was shipped back to Germany. At the same time, Bevin proposed other ways of solving the problem. One of these was the cantonization of Palestine, better known as the Morrison Scheme, which allocated about 17% of the country to the Jews; another was the Bevin Plan to give the British government a five-year trusteeship over Palestine with the declared object of preparing the country for independence. On Feb. 15, 1947, after both plans had been rejected by Jews and Arabs, Bevin announced that he was referring the entire matter to the United Nations. As a result, the United Nations Special Committee on Palestine (UNSCOP) was appointed and, on Nov. 29, 1947, the UN voted to divide Palestine into a Jewish and an Arab State. Bevin gradually became reconciled to the idea of a Jewish state; in January 1949, eight months after the proclamation of the State of Israel, he granted it de facto recognition.

BIBLIOGRAPHY: F. Williams, *Ernest Bevin* (Eng., 1952); J.C. Hurewitz, *The Struggle for Palestine* (1950); R.H.S. Crossman, *A Nation Reborn* (1960), ch. 2; idem, *Palestine Mission* (1946); B.C. Crum, *Behind the Silken Curtain* (1947); Jewish Agency, *The Jewish Plan for Palestine* (1947). **ADD. BIBLIOGRAPHY:** A. Bullock, *Ernest Bevin: Foreign Secretary* (1984); ODNB online.

[Moshe Rosetti]

BEYTH, HANS (1901–1947), *Youth Aliyah leader. Beyth, who was born in Bleicherode, Germany, was active in his youth in the *Blau-Weiss Zionist youth movement. In 1935 he went to Palestine, where he worked as Henrietta *Szold's assistant in Youth Aliyah. His resourcefulness in rescuing and warmth in educating the Youth Aliyah wards made him an outstanding personality in the organization. He was instrumental in the establishment of Youth Aliyah institutions in communal settlements, and in the absorption of many wards into kibbutz life. Beyth was sent to Europe at the end of World War II to prepare the emigration and absorption of surviving Jewish children. In the last year of his life he arranged for the care of 20,000 wards. Beyth was murdered by Arabs in December 1947 while on his way home to Jerusalem from Haifa and Athlit, where he had been welcoming children on their arrival from a youth village in Cyprus.

BIBLIOGRAPHY: *Hans Beyth, Ish Aliyyat ha-No'ar* (1951); *Im Gedenken an Hans Beyth*, (1948), published by the Jewish Agency.

[Arye Lipshitz]

BEẒAH (Heb. בֵּיצָה; "egg"), a tractate (so called after its opening word) of the order *Mo'ed*, in the Mishnah, Tosefta, Babylonian Talmud, and Jerusalem Talmud. The tractate deals with the laws of festivals, but whereas other tractates of the order *Mo'ed* deals with specific festivals, *Beẓah*, in the main, discusses the laws common to festivals in general; for this reason this tractate is also called *Yom Tov* ("festival"). The tractate consists of five chapters in both the Mishnah and the Talmud, but of only four in the Tosefta. The first two chapters of the Mishnah consist chiefly of differences of opinion between Bet Shammai and *Bet Hillel (e.g. 2:7; 3:8; 5:5) but also includes traditions from the period of Jabneh (2:6). The Mishnah ascribes most of the halakhot to various *tannaim* who were disciples of R. *Akiva, but it also contains many anonymous mishnayot of later *tannaim* who were contemporaries of Judah ha-Nasi. *Beẓah* in the Babylonian Talmud contains many teachings of Palestinian scholars who reached Babylon by way of the **neḥutei*, but which do not appear in the Jerusalem Talmud. Conversely, the text of the tractate in the Jerusalem Talmud contains statements of Babylonian scholars which are not found in the Babylonian Talmud. *Beẓah* contains many additions of the *savoraim* (26a, 27a, 35b), as well as older material revised by them. Aside from the regular editions and commentaries, one of the earliest commentaries on the Jerusalem Talmud has been preserved for *Beẓah*, that of R. Eleazar Azikri, edited by Israel Francis (1967).

BIBLIOGRAPHY: P. Blackman (ed. and tr.), *Mishnayot*, 2 (Eng., 1952), 349–75 (with introd. and notes); H.Strack, *Introduction to the Talmud and Midrash* (1959[2]), 39–40; Epstein, Tanna'im, 354–62; Epstein, Amora'im, 24–44; H. Albeck, *Shishah Sidrei Mishnah, Seder Mo'ed* (1958), 281–6.

[Zvi Kaplan]

BEZALEL (Heb. בְּצַלְאֵל; "in the shadow [under the protection] of God," cf. Ps. 91:1; similar to the Akkadian *ina-ṣilli-Bēl* ("in the shadow of Bel"), *ina-ṣilli-Nabû*, "in the shadow of Nabu," and the like), son of Uri, son of Hur of the tribe of Judah; an expert in metalwork, stonecutting, and woodcarving. Moses appointed Bezalel head of the artisans who were employed both in the construction of the *Tabernacle and its equipment and in designing the priests' vestments (Ex. 31:1–11; 36–39). He was assisted by *Oholiab son of Ahisamach the Danite, who was an expert craftsman and embroiderer (31–6; 35: 34–35).

The Bible views Bezalel's construction of the Tabernacle and its equipment as the execution of a plan that the Lord detailed to Moses on the Mount (Ex. 25:9, 40; 26:30; 27:8; Num. 8:4). The idea that the Temple's construction should be detailed according to a divine plan is also found in Ezekiel's vision concerning Jerusalem and the Temple (40:2ff.). Similarly, the author of I Chronicles (28:19) asserts that the instructions for building the First Temple were given "in writing, by His hand." Parallel notions are to be found in the literature of other nations as, for example, in the inscriptions of Gudea, king of Lagash, concerning certain structures he erected in his land, and in Babylonian inscriptions dealing with the temple of Marduk. Drawing upon Exodus 31:3, which describes Bezalel as being endowed with "… a divine spirit of skill, ability, and knowledge…. "Philo viewed Bezalel as a symbol of pure knowledge (II Gig. 23). He inferred from the name "Bezalel" that he knew God by seeing the divine shadow, that is, by seeing only God's works, and not God Himself, as had Moses (ILA 3: 102).

[Yehoshua M. Grintz]

In the *Aggadah*

When Moses was instructed to erect the Sanctuary and fashion its vessels, God showed him the name of Bezalel written in the Book of the Generations of Adam (Gen. 5:1), in which are inscribed all the deeds of future generations, as the divinely appointed architect. Nevertheless he was told to obtain the approval of the Children of Israel for the appointment, in order to teach that no leader should be appointed without the consent of the people (Ber. 55a; cf. Jos., Ant., 3:104). At the side of Bezalel, who belonged to the aristocratic tribe of Judah, worked Oholiab, of the lowliest tribe, that of Dan, to show that before God "the great and the lowly are equal" (Ex. R. 40:4). God filled Bezalel with wisdom (Ex. 31:3) "because he already possessed wisdom," since "God does not grant wisdom save to those who already have wisdom" (Tanḥ. Va-Yakhel, 2; Ber. 55a). Bezalel had five other names: Reaiah ("the seer"), Shobal ("the builder of the dovecote," a synonym for the Tabernacle), Jahat ("the dreadful"), Ahumai ("the unifier of Israel"), and Lahad ("one who beautified Israel," or "one who was near to the poor"; Ex. R. 40:4).

[Elimelech Epstein Halevy]

BIBLIOGRAPHY: Ginzberg, Legends, index.

BEZALEL, Academy of Arts and Design in Jerusalem. The Bezalel Academy of Arts and Design was founded in 1906 by Boris *Schatz, first named the Bezalel School of Arts and Crafts. It was named after the artist in charge of the construction of the *Tabernacle, Bezalel ben Uri (Ex. 31:1–5, 35:30–32). Schatz, who had a utopian vision, believed that the students would be able to help build a Third Temple in Jerusalem. In 1903 Schatz broached his idea to Theodor Herzl, and the decision to establish Bezalel was confirmed at the Seventh Zionist Congress (Basel, 1905).

From the beginning the institute contained three divisions: a school for painting, workshops, and the Bezalel Museum. In 1908, when the school moved to new premises it already taught 30 different crafts, such as silverwork, weaving, woodcarving, ivory inlaying, etc. In 1913 the number of students was around 500. In 1911–14 a separate branch for Yemenite goldsmiths operated in *Ben Shemen. The works of art created in the workshops were displayed by Schatz in Europe and New York as means of getting financial support.

The Bezalel style in crafts was a combination of Art Nouveau, the Oriental style, and the Art and Crafts Movement. Most of the objects were Judaica artifacts utilizing images from Jewish tradition, from the Bible as well as from the Zionist ideology (*Elijah's Chair*, 1916–25, Israel Museum, Jerusalem).

Economic factors in the main caused the closure of the Bezalel institute in 1929. A basic argument about its artistic style was one of the reasons its influence on Israeli art declined. The leading opponents were a group of young artists from Tel Aviv who desired a connection with modern Western art styles such as Expressionism, Primitivism, and Cubism.

German-influenced teachers founded the New Bezalel in 1935, and it was directed in that spirit by Josef *Budko, Erich *Mendelson, and Mordecai *Ardon. At that time the influence of modernism and the aesthetics of the Bauhaus became dominant. Since the 1970s Bezalel has been the major institute for fine arts and design in Israel.

BIBLIOGRAPHY: O. Gideon, "The Utopian Art of Bezalel," in: *Ariel*, 51 (1982), 33--63; N. Shilo-Cohen (ed.), *Bezalel shel Schatz – 1906–1929* (1983).

[Ronit Steinberg (2nd ed.)]

BEZALEL BEN MOSES HA-KOHEN (1820–1878), Lithuanian rabbi and unofficial rabbi of Vilna. At the age of 11, Bezalel already knew by heart two of the six orders of the Talmud; at 13, he had covered the entire Talmud and amazed his listeners with his original halakhic discourses. A sermon which he delivered before the rabbis of Vilna at the age of 18 was subsequently published in his *Reshit Bikkurim*. His novellae were collected in a work *Torat Yisrael* which is no longer extant. In 1843 although only 23 years of age, Bezalel was chosen as one of the rabbis of Vilna in succession to Joseph Shiskes. He soon became the leading "*moreh ẓedek*" of Vilna, an office equivalent to that of rabbi of the city. Bezalel was well versed in secular subjects, particularly mathematics and engineering. *Reshit Bikkurim*, responsa and comments on the *Sifra* (1868), reveals his extensive scholarship and his firm attitude in halakhic questions. His glosses on the Talmud, *Mareh Kohen*, bearing the same title as his notes on *Yoreh De'ah*, were published in the Vilna edition of the Talmud (1884). His commentary on the *Sefer ha-Mitzvot* of Maimonides appeared in the Vilna edition of 1866. He also published a pamphlet entitled *Hora'at Hetter*, dealing with the permissibility of using *etrogim* from Corfu on Sukkot (1876). Many of Bezalel's responsa appear in the works of his contemporaries and a number of his writings are still in manuscript.

BIBLIOGRAPHY: H.N. Maggid-Steinschneider, *Ir Vilna*, 1 (1900), 55–61; J.L. Maimon, *Middei Ḥodesh be-Ḥodsho*, 4 (1958), 12–16.

[Itzhak Alfassi]

BEZALEL BEN SOLOMON OF KOBRYN (17th century), preacher and author. Bezalel was active in Slutsk (Minsk region), Boskowitz (Moravia), and Przemysl. The following of his books are worthy of note: (1) *Pelaḥ ha-Rimmon* (Amsterdam, 1659), consisting of 20 different expositions of various Midrashim; (2) *Ammudei ha-Shivah* ("Seven Pillars," Lublin, 1666), sermons on obscure Midrashim. The "Seven Pillars" are Abraham, Isaac, Jacob, Moses, Aaron, David, and Solomon, and each section has in its title a biblical verse containing the respective names of these worthies. In his introduction the author states: "I found favor in the eyes of the rulers and leaders of the country [Lithuania], who were moved to make a large contribution toward the publication of the book, and it also received the approbation of the Council of the Four Lands." Selections from the book were published by Joshua Abraham b. Israel of Zhitomir under the title *Nofet Ẓufim* (Lemberg, 1804). (3) *Korban Shabbat* (Dyhernfurth, 1691), homilies on the Sabbath precepts and customs, compiled from the halakhic authorities and works of Kabbalah. Other of his works are still in manuscript.

BIBLIOGRAPHY: Michael, Or, 289, n. 613; Halpern, Pinkas, 78–79, 99; *Pinkas Slutsk*... (1962), 19, 33, 272.

[Yehoshua Horowitz]

BEZEK (Heb. בֶּזֶק), place-name mentioned in the Bible. Saul mustered his army there before undertaking his campaign to relieve *Jabesh-Gilead, which was being besieged by the Ammonites under Nahash (I Sam. 11:8). Bezek has been identified (following Eusebius, Onom. 54:8) with Khirbat lbzīq, 15 mi. (24 km.) north of Shechem on the road leading to Beth-Shean. Its position on the road descending from the hill country of Ephraim to the Jordan Valley would explain its choice as a mobilization point.

A Bezek is also mentioned in Judges 1:4–5, as the place where the tribe of Judah defeated the Canaanites and Perizzites. Their dying overlord, Adoni-Bezek, was taken to Jerusalem. Attempts to locate this Bezek in the vicinity of Jerusalem have so far been unsuccessful. Some scholars accept its identification with the other Bezek, assuming that the tribe of Judah crossed the Jordan Valley in the direction opposite to that taken by Saul and then continued south to its inheritance.

BIBLIOGRAPHY: Clermont-Ganneau, Arch, 2 (1899), 239ff.; Alt, in: PJB, 22 (1926), 48ff.; EM.

[Michael Avi-Yonah]

BEZEM, NAFTALI (1924–), Israeli painter. Born in Essen, Germany, the youngest son of a Polish-Jewish immigrant family, Bezem immigrated to Eretz-Israel with the assistance of *Youth Aliyah. His parents were murdered in Auschwitz. In 1943 Bezem began his studies at the Bezalel Academy of Art and Design in Jerusalem under the guidance of Mordecai *Ardon, whom he adopted as a father figure. Later Bezem himself became a teacher in the institute. In 1949 he traveled with his wife, Hannah Liberman, to Paris and studied at the Centre d'Art Sacre, a Catholic art school specializing in modern sacred art. Over the years Bezem had many one-man shows and produced a number of reliefs for public buildings, wall paintings, stained glass, and tapestries. In 1975 his eldest son was murdered in a terrorist attack in Jerusalem's Zion Square. Bezem divided his life between Israel and Switzerland.

Besem's art was much involved in the history of Israel. Some of his art works are located in official institutes of the State of Israel, such as the ceiling painting in the President's Residence in Jerusalem and the metal relief at the Yad Vashem Holocaust Memorial in Jerusalem. In his symbolic style he integrated Jewish and Zionist contents with the formal requirements of these institutes.

During the years Bezem devised a symbolic language. The *beheaded fish* or the *rooster* were symbols of atonement and in the context of the Holocaust served as a symbol of the victim being sacrificed. *Boats with oars* were the means of transport by which he arrived to Israel; the forward motion symbolized progress with the boat a protective device. The *lion* was his characteristic symbol for Jewish objects and *stones* represented an old city on which a new city is built. The *Sabbath candles* symbolized the happiness of his childhood and the candles of his mother but also the light that went out when his son died.

For several years after the death of his son Isaac, Bezem, the mourning father, dedicated himself to the theme of Isaac's sacrifice (the **Akedah*). In these paintings he created an analogy between the sacrifice of the father and sacrifice of the son, without a ram for redemption.

BIBLIOGRAPHY: Z. Amishai-Maisels, *Naftali Bezem* (1986).

[Ronit Steinberg (2nd ed.)]

BEZIDUL NOU (Hg. **Bőződújfalu**), village in Transylvania, Romania, inhabited by Szeklers, a distinctive ethnic group of Hungarian origin who speak a specific Hungarian dialect. In the 17th century it was an important center of the Sabbatarians, who practiced their religion mostly in secret. There were other centers of Sabbatarians in 18th century Transylvania, but they disappeared in the face of Christian hatred and enmity towards them. In 1868–69, after equal rights had been granted to Hungarian Jewry, the Sabbatarians, then numbering approximately 100, mostly poor farmers, openly practiced

Judaism. The seal of the community they established was inscribed the "Proselyte Community Congregation of Jeshurun." At the beginning of the 20th century a few Jews by birth settled in the village and intermarried with the proselytes. In 1940 Bezidul Nou passed from Romania to Hungary and there followed a period of disaster because of the strong racial laws which existent in Horthiite Hungary. The authorities ordered the demolition of the synagogue; under pressure from the local Christian clerics and the Hungarian Horthiite authorities, most of the community became converted to Unitarianism. From 1940 the leaders of the congregation tried to obtain exemption for their members from the anti-Jewish racial laws. On Oct. 3, 1941, the Hungarian minister of justice signed an order enabling the descendants of Sabbatarians to obtain certificates of exemption. There were then 94 proselytes living in Bezidul Nou, while an additional 30–40 persons originating from the village or the vicinity also obtained certificates. These were still being issued by the Hungarian ministry of justice in spring 1944, a few days before the German occupation. When ghettos were established, the proselytes were deported to the Marosvasarhely ghetto together with the other Jews who lived in the region. Some of their leaders succeeded in reaching Budapest and obtained certificates for a small number already confined in the ghetto, who were subsequently released. Those who did not wish to accept the certificates were deported to *Auschwitz.

After World War II Bezidul Nou reverted to Romania; those who survived the Holocaust remained formally Christians, although some continued to follow Jewish observances. In 1960 they began to emigrate to Israel, where by 1968 they numbered approximately 50. Only five families, all aged persons, remained in the village in 1969, formally belonging to the Unitarian Church. But they observed the Sabbath and their wives lit candles on Sabbath eve as they had learned from their forefathers; they also maintained close contact with their relatives in Israel for some time. A small cemetery with a few hundred tombstones attests to the past existence of the community. The Hebrew inscription (*Ger Ẓedek*, "proselyte") appears next to the name on many of the tombstones, most of which bear the *menorah* and a *Magen David*. Today these are almost the only memory of the existence of a specific Sabbatarian community among the Szeklers, though even today there are stories about these the "Jewish" predecessors.

BIBLIOGRAPHY: S. Kohn, A *szombatosok* (1889), 336–7; Beck, in: *Dr. Blochs Oesterreichische Wochenschrift* (1912), 704–5, 738–40, 754–6; Gy. Balázs, in: *Libanon*, 6 (Hg., 1941), 18–22.

[Yehouda Marton / Paul Schveiger (2nd ed.)]

BÉZIERS (Heb. בדרש; based on the Latin form), city in the department of Hérault, France. Natives of the city were known as בדרשי normally transliterated as "Bedersi." An estate near Béziers belonging to Jews (*Guardia Judaica*) is mentioned in a document of 990. In the 11th century, the Jews lived in both parts of the city, which was divided between the bishop and the count. They paid the count taxes on honey, cinnamon, and pepper. The synagogue was built in 1144 or 1164 in the present rue de la Promenade. Its mosaic pavement, with Hebrew inscriptions and its foundation stone, were discovered in the first half of the 19th century. The cemetery was situated outside the city walls to the east and two Hebrew tombstones have been discovered there. A rue de la Juiverie recalling one of the medieval Jewish quarters still exists. Both the count and the bishop made use of Jewish commercial and financial agents. In 1160 the bishop abolished the ancient local custom of stoning the houses of the Jews on the Sunday before Easter. In return, the Jews undertook to pay an annual tax. Count Roger II was kindly disposed toward the Jews, even entrusting them with administrative functions. The Christian inhabitants of Béziers, who had *Albigensian leanings, were also, as a rule, favorably disposed. About 200 Jews were among the victims of the massacre of the Albigenses in Béziers in 1209. Most of the Jewish population had previously fled from the city. Some of the refugees settled in Narbonne; some apparently in *Gerona, Spain; an inscription apparently intended for the synagogue they founded there has been discovered in Gerona. The revenues formerly derived by the counts of Béziers from the Jews now went to the king. The bishop however retained his right, and even built a new synagogue in the part of the city under his jurisdiction in an effort to attract Jews from the area. In 1278, however, the king compelled him to destroy the synagogue and ordered the Jews who had moved to the bishop's territory to return.

Béziers was known to the medieval Jews as "the little Jerusalem." Abraham *Ibn Ezra stayed there for some time in about 1155; he dedicated his *Sefer ha-Shem* to two scholars of Béziers. *Benjamin of Tudela, visiting the town in about 1165, remarked on "a congregation of learned men." The best known of these are the liturgical poet Abraham b. Isaac *Bedersi, his son *Jedaiah ha-Penini, and *Meshullam b. Moses. The poets Eleazar Hanan Ezobi, Astruc of Béziers, and Meshullam Ezobi also lived in Béziers. Samuel Ibn *Tibbon lived there for some time. Solomon b. Joseph ibn Ayyub of Granada and Jacob b. Moses, translators of Arabic works into Hebrew, settled at Béziers.

The Jews were expelled from Béziers in 1306. An indication of the scope of the Jewish settlement there is provided by three deeds of sale which have been preserved concerning the subsequent liquidation of their real estate on the king's behalf. The documents mention at least 13 houses which had belonged to some ten Jews. In 1367 the community was renewed by an agreement made by a number of Jews with the bishop. The general expulsion of the Jews from France in 1394 again forced them to leave. During World War II, 300 Jewish refugees stayed in Béziers, where they had two prayer rooms at their disposal, until 1943. A new community was formed after the war which in 1968 comprised some 400 persons, mostly from North Africa.

BIBLIOGRAPHY: Graetz, Hist, 6 (1949), index; Roth, Dark Ages, 136, 146; Gross, Gal Jud, 96–105; Z. Szajkowski, *Franco-Judaica* (1962), no. 309; idem, *Analytical Franco-Jewish Gazetteer* (1966), 198;

Millás Vallicrosa, in: *Sefarad*, 10 (1950), 341–3; Catane, in: *Tarbiz*, 24 (1954/55), 232f.; H. Vida, *Episcopatus… Béziers* (1951).

[Zvi Avneri]

BIALA, town in W. Galicia, S. Poland, on the river Biala opposite the Silesian town *Bielsko with which it was amalgamated in 1950 to form Biala-Bielsko. The two were closely connected through their joint textile industry. In 1765 the Jews were expelled from Biala. Many of them subsequently returned and formed a community in conjunction with the Jews in the suburbs which until the middle of the 19th century remained under the jurisdiction of the Oswiécim community. A cemetery was established in 1849 and an independent congregation constituted in 1872. The Jews in Biala numbered about 2,600 in 1929. With the exception of the *ḥevra kaddisha* the charitable and cultural institutions were maintained jointly with those of the Bielsko (Bielitz) community. For Holocaust period see *Bielsko.

BIAŁA PODLASKA, town in Lublin province, Poland. The first mention of Jewish settlement in Biała Podlaska dates from 1621 when 30 Jewish families were granted rights of residence there. In 1841 there were 2,200 Jews out of a total population of 3,588; in 1897, 6,549 out of 13,090; in 1921, 6,874 out of 13,000., and in 1939, 7,439 (36.9% of the total population). The main Yiddish newspaper, *Podlasyer Leben* was published there between the two world wars.

Holocaust Period

On September 26, 1939, the Soviet army entered the town, but withdrew a month later when the Soviet-German boundary agreement was reached. About 600 Jews left the town together with the Soviet army. The remaining Jewish population was immediately subjected to Nazi persecution and terror. At the end of 1939 about 2,000 Jews from Suwalki and Serock were forced to settle here. A few months later about 1,000 Jewish prisoners of war who had served in the Polish army were brought to Biała Podlaska from the prison camp in Czarne near Chojna. Several score of them were murdered during the march on foot to Biała Podlaska. They were imprisoned on arrival in a forced labor camp and about a year later were transferred to a Lublin prisoner of war camp. During 1940 and 1941 further deportations to Biała Podlaska took place. Several hundred Jews from Cracow and Mlawa were dispatched there. As a result of all the "resettlements" the Jewish population in the town grew to about 8,400 in March 1942. At the end of June 1941 a number of Jews were sent to the concentration camp in *Auschwitz for giving bread to Soviet prisoners of war marching through the town. They were among the first Jewish victims to perish in Auschwitz.

On June 11, 1942, the first deportation from Biała took place. About 3,000 people were sent to *Sobibor death camp and exterminated. In late September and early October 1942, a second deportation was carried out in which the entire remaining Jewish population was sent to the ghetto in Miedzyrzecz, and from there to *Treblinka death camp in November. Only 300 Jews were left in Biała Podlaska in a newly established forced labor camp. This was liquidated in May 1944 and all its inmates transferred to *Majdanek concentration camp, where only a few survived. Several hundred Jews fled to the woods during the deportations, but only about 30 of them survived in hiding until the liberation of the region in July 26, 1944. After the war the surviving Jewish remnant, together with a few hundred former residents who came back from the Soviet Union, tried to rebuild the Jewish community, but were forced to leave the town in the summer of 1946 because of antisemitic manifestations among the Polish population. In June 1946 Polish antisemites killed two young Jews and destroyed the monument which the Jewish survivors had erected in memory of the murdered Jewish community. Societies of former Biała Podlaska residents were active in Israel, the U.S., Argentina, France, Canada, and Australia.

BIBLIOGRAPHY: M.I. Feigenbaum (ed.), *Sefer Biała-Podlaska* (1961). **ADD. BIBLIOGRAPHY:** Halpern, Pinkas, index; B. Wasiutynski, *Ludnosc Zydowska w Polsce w wiekach xix i xx w.* (1930).

[Stefan Krakowski]

BIALE, DAVID (1949–), U.S. historian of Jewish culture, religion, and politics. Biale was educated at Harvard University, the University of California at Berkeley, the Hebrew University, and UCLA, where he received his Ph.D. in history in 1977. He taught Jewish history at the State University of New York, Binghamton, and Graduate Theological Union in Berkeley, and from 1999 served as Emmanuel Ringelblum Professor of Jewish History at the University of California at Davis.

He is the author of a number of books, among them *Gershom Scholem: Kabbalah and Counter-History* (1979), *Power and Powerlessness in Jewish History* (1986), *Eros and the Jews: From Biblical Israel to Contemporary America* (1992), and is the editor of *Cultures of the Jews: A New History* (2002), a significant re-conceptualization of the entirety of Jewish history.

Biale's work is characterized by attention to the broad sweep of Jewish history; while he is primarily a specialist in modern European Jewish history, his investigations took him to all periods and geographic centers. Especially significant is his edited volume, *Cultures of the Jews*, a work designed to re-focus the discipline of Jewish history on everyday matters, on the multifaceted interaction of Jews with their social and political environments, and on neglected groups within the Jewish community.

[Jay Harris (2nd ed.)]

BIALEH, ẒEVI HIRSCH BEN NAPHTALI HERZ (1670–1748), German rabbi and *rosh yeshivah*. Bialeh was born in Lemberg. He served as rabbi of Biała (hence his name) and then as head of a yeshivah in Lemberg. In 1718 he was appointed to Halberstadt (hence his other appellation Ẓevi Hirsch Halberstadter) where he remained until his death. Because of his acumen he was also called Hirsch Ḥarif ("sharp"). He established a large yeshivah in the town and among its pupils were such outstanding rabbis of the following generation as Akiva *Eger, Isaiah *Berlin, and Mordecai *Halberstadt. He refused to publish his novellae on the grounds that through the continual publication of works by *aḥaronim*, students would neglect the *rishonim*, but glosses and responsa by him can be found scattered in various works of his contemporaries. His works, which were published only after his death, are *Ateret Ẓevi* (1804), comprising responsa, sermons, eulogies, and novellae; *Kos Yeshu'ot* (1902), Part 1 novellae on *Bava Kamma* and *Shevu'ot*, Part 2 on *Bava Meẓia* and other material. He preferred to penetrate deeply into the understanding of the sources, stress the plain meaning of the Talmud, and avoid excessive *pilpul*. Five of his children were rabbis: Solomon Dov Berush in Glogau; Naphtali Herz in Dubno; Abraham in Rawicz; Samuel in Halberstadt; and Simḥah in Dessau. His brother, Israel b. Naphtali Herz (d. 1744) lived in Cleves, Offenbach, and Hanau. His talmudic novellae are contained in his brother's *Ateret Ẓevi*.

BIBLIOGRAPHY: Michaelson, in: Ẓevi Hirsch Ḥarif, *Kos Yeshu'ot*, 1 (1902), appendix (*Toledot ha-Meḥabber*); Israel Moses b. Ḥayyim Joshua, *ibid.*, 2 (1910), appendix (*Toledot ha-Meḥabber*); B.H. Auerbach, *Geschichte der israelitischen Gemeinde Halberstadt* (1866), 64–70; S. Buber, *Anshei Shem* (1895), 196, 240, 247f., I.T. Eisenstadt and S. Wiener, *Da'at Kedoshim* (1897–98), 141f.; Loewenstein, in: JJLG, 14 (1921), 19; Frankel, in: *Naḥalat Ẓevi*, 7 (1937), 321f.; Meisl, in: *Reshumot*, 3 (1947), 190; *Sefer Biala-Podlaska* (1961), 19, 270.

[Yehoshua Horowitz]

BIALIK, ḤAYYIM NAḤMAN (1873–1934), the greatest Hebrew poet of modern times, essayist, storywriter, translator, and editor, who exercised a profound influence on modern Jewish culture. Born in the village of Radi, near Zhitomir (Volhynia), Bialik's development as a poet was influenced by his environment – the simplicity and fervor of a folk spirituality – which characterized Volhynian Jewry, and the ḥasidic ambience, alive with mystic lore, in which it was steeped. His father, Isaac Joseph, came of scholarly stock and had been engaged in the family timber trade and in flour milling before coming down in life through his impracticality. For his father as well as his mother, Dinah Priva, this was a second marriage, both having been widowed previously. Despite his family's dire economic circumstances, Bialik retained many happy memories of the first six years of his childhood in Radi. In some of his best poems, "*Zohar*" ("Radiance," 1901) and "*Ha-Berekhah*" ("The Pool," 1905), attempting to recapture the lost paradise of childhood, he idealizes the enchanted hours which he spent romping in the dazzling light of the fields and in the secret shade of the forest. Others have fewer happy references and are marked by loneliness, parental neglect, and the almost narcissistic withdrawal of a sensitive, artistic child, e.g., the prose poem "*Safi'aḥ*" ("Aftergrowth," 1908).

Childhood Period (1880–1890)

When Bialik was six, his parents moved to Zhitomir in search of a livelihood and his father was reduced to keeping a saloon on the outskirts of town. Shortly thereafter, in 1880, his father died and the destitute widow entrusted her son to the care of his well-to-do paternal grandfather, Jacob Moses. For ten years, until he went to yeshivah in 1890, the gifted, mischievous Ḥayyim Naḥman was raised by the stern old pietist. At first he was instructed by teachers in the traditional *ḥeder* and later, from the age of 13, pursued his studies alone. He was a lonely figure in the almost deserted house of study on the edge of town, for the expanding modernization of Jewish life had restricted the traditional study of Torah to a secluded nook. Passionate and solitary dedication to study shaped traits of character that Bialik was to exalt: "A fertile mind, lively logic, a trusting heart when the knee falters." From this experience of his adolescence stems the sense of vocation of the chosen individual who dedicates his life to an ideal, sacrificing youth and the delights of the world in order to remain faithful to the last. This theme of vocation was to become central to Bialik's thinking and his poetry is a spiritual record of the paradoxical struggle to free himself from his calling and at the same time to remain faithful to it. During this period too his reading of medieval theology and Haskalah works stimulated ambitions for secular knowledge, moving him to seek a more comprehensive education. He dreamed of the rabbinical seminary in Berlin, and of acquiring the cultural tools that would give him entrance to modern European civilization.

Volozhin Period

Convinced by a journalistic report that the yeshivah of *Volozhin in Lithuania would offer him an introduction to the humanities, as well as a continuation of his talmudic studies, Bialik persuaded his grandfather to permit him to study there. In Volozhin, a center of *Mitnaggedim*, his hopes for a secular academic training were not fulfilled since the yeshivah concentrated only on the scholarly virtues of talmudic dialectic and erudition. For a short time Bialik immersed himself in the traditional disciplines. In some of his poems the image of his stern grandfather merges with the image of the uncompromising *rosh yeshivah*, becoming a symbol of the burning imperatives of traditional Judaism. In the end, however, modernist doubts triumphed over traditionalist certainties. Bialik began to withdraw from the life of the school and lived in the world of poetry. At this time, he read Russian poetry and started his acquaintance with European literature. During the following year in Volozhin and later in Odessa, he was deeply moved by Shimon Shemuel Frug's Jewish poems, written in Russian, and many of Bialik's early motifs echo him. His first published poem, "*El ha-Ẓippor*" ("To the Bird"), was written in Volozhin. In the yeshivah Bialik joined a secret Orthodox Zionist student society, Neẓaḥ Israel, which attempted to synthesize Jewish nationalism and enlightenment with a firm adherence to tradition. Bialik's first published work (in *Ha-Meliẓ*, 1891) is an exposition of the principles of the society and reflects the teachings of Aḥad Ha-Am's spiritual Zionism.

Aḥad Ha-Am's Influence

*Aḥad Ha-Am, whose thinking had a profound impact on Bialik and his generation, first began publishing his essays in 1889. They provided a framework of ideas that helped his contemporaries translate their Jewish loyalties from a religious context into a modern, philosophically oriented humanist rationale for Jewish existence. Bialik recognized Aḥad Ha-Am as his great teacher. He wrote of this period, "... the day a new essay of Aḥad Ha-Am's appeared was a holiday for me. " Bialik later wrote a poem in tribute to his mentor: "Receive our blessing for each seed of... idea/That you have sown... in our desolate hearts." But Aḥad Ha-Am also had an inhibiting influence on Bialik's poetic imagination. Preferring a classical and lucid style, Aḥad Ha-Am discouraged many of Bialik's ventures into more modernist or more experimental poetry.

First Stay in Odessa

The break with tradition occurred in the summer of 1891 when amid disruptions in the yeshivah, Bialik left for Odessa, the center of modern Jewish culture in southern Russia. He was attracted by the literary circle that formed around Aḥad Ha-Am and harbored the dream that in Odessa he would be able to prepare himself for the entrance to the modern Orthodox rabbinical seminary in Berlin. Penniless, alone, unemployed, and hungry, he earned a livelihood for a while by giving Hebrew lessons. He continued to study Russian literature, reading and admiring the poetry of Pushkin and Frug, as well as the stories and novels of Dostoevski and Gogol. He was tutored in German grammar and read works of Schiller and Lessing. At first the shy youth did not become involved in the literary life of the city but when he showed his poetry to Moses Leib *Lilienblum the latter commended the poem "*El ha-Ẓippor*" to Aḥad Ha-Am who passed it on to Yehoshua Ḥana *Rawnitzki to be published in the first volume of *Ha-Pardes* (1892, p. 219f.). The poem, a song longing for Zion written in the style of the poets of the Ḥibbat Zion era, was favorably received by the critics. During the six months he spent in Odessa, Bialik wrote several poems and made the acquaintance of prominent literary figures with whom he was to establish lasting relationships. He was especially close to Rawnitzki and their friendship was to develop into a unique collaboration in literary and publishing endeavors.

Return to Zhitomir

When Bialik learned, early in 1892, that the yeshivah of Volozhin had been closed, he cut short his stay in Odessa and hurried home in order to spare his dying grandfather the knowledge that he had forsaken his religious studies. On returning home he found that his older brother too was dying. Dejected by the whole atmosphere, which for him embodied the chronic despair and spiritual squalor of Jewish life, he wrote "You have not changed from what you were/Old oldness, nothing new/Let me join your company, my brothers,/Together we will rot till we stink" ("*Bi-Teshuvati*" ("On My Return"), 1892). Another poem of this period which is reminiscent of Frug "*Mi-Shut ba-Merḥakim*" ("From Wandering Afar") also develops the theme of unfulfilled return. The alienated son, full of youthful vitality, is repelled by the melancholy of a moribund traditionalist society. The death of Judah Leib *Gordon, the last significant poet of the Haskalah period, in the summer of 1892, closed an era. Rawnitzki asked Bialik to compose an elegy for the second volume of *Ha-Pardes* (1893, p. 248f.), and he complied with "*El ha-Aryeh ha-Met*" ("To the Dead Lion"). Like other early poems, it still showed the influence of the Haskalah poets and was omitted from the collected poems. The elegiac mood characterizes a considerable part of Bialik's early work and tears are a recurring motif in the first volume of poems (1901). Before leaving Odessa he wrote "*Hirhurei Laylah*" ("Night Thoughts," 1892; "My song is a bottle of tears, a bottle of tears"), and in a later poem "*Shirati*" ("My Song," 1901) he describes his mother's tear falling into the dough she is kneading and it is this tear that enters his bones and is transformed into poetry.

1893–1896

In the spring of 1893, after the death of his brother and grandfather, Bialik married Manya Averbuch (d. 1972) and for the next three years joined her father in the timber trade in Korostyshev, near Kiev. Since business kept him in the forest for long stretches, he read widely and broadened his education considerably during this lonely period. At that time he wrote "*Al Saf Beit ha-Midrash*" ("On the Threshold of the House of Study," 1894) which predicts the ultimate triumph of Israel's spirit. While the themes of the poem, which poignantly speaks of the abandoned house of study, are vocation and return, the underlying priestly symbolism, relating to the Ninth of Av, the date on which the poem was written, endows the house of study with the universal metaphor of ancient ritual. In the hymn "*Birkat Am*" ("The Blessing of the People," 1894), written several months earlier, which is permeated by intricate allusions to Temple ritual, the poet metamorphoses the builders of Ereẓ Israel into priests and Temple builders. Temple imagery seems to be a predominant symbol both of Bialik's thought and of his poetry and is a basic point of reference of his brilliant cultural interpretation of the two Jerusalems – the earthly and the celestial – in his address at the opening of the Hebrew University (1925).

1897–1900

In the spring of 1897, failing in business, Bialik found a position as a teacher in Sosnowiec, near the Prussian border. The pettiness of provincial life depressed him and he wrote several satires that were published under pseudonyms. During this period he started to write stories (e.g., "*Aryeh Ba'al Guf*," 1899) and to experiment with Yiddish writing. Some of his poems appear to reflect the life-affirming themes of the "new way" embraced by the writers of the 1890s, although Bialik remained wary of what he felt was the literary pretensions of its members. The poet's ire against Jewish apathy toward the rising national movement found expression in "*Akhen Ḥaẓir ha-Am*" ("Surely the People is Grass," 1897) in which he called out to the people, "Even when the horn be sounded and the banner raised/Can the dead awaken, can the dead stir?" Widely acclaimed, it was the first of his poems of wrath and reproof in which he speaks to the people in the tones of prophetic visions. While biblical themes were not uncommon in the period, Bialik's unequaled mastery of the prophetic diatribe added a dimension of authenticity to his utterances, and he began to be considered the national poet. Other poems indicate his preoccupation with the implications of the First Zionist Congress. Welcoming the high tide of national enthusiasm, as in "*Mikra'ei Ẓiyyon*" ("Convocation of Zion," 1898), he was at the same time faithful to Aḥad Ha-Am's spiritual ideology and wrote a satire against Herzl's political Zionism, "*Rabbi Zeraḥ*" (1912), which, because of its tone of levity, Aḥad Ha-Am refused to print in *Ha-Shilo'aḥ*. "*Al Levavkhem she-Shamem*" ("On Your Desolate Hearts," 1897), his most profound response to the Zionist Congress, gives vent to Bialik's despair with contemporary Jewish life. In it he develops his own set of symbols which were to recur throughout his poetry; the cat, which first appears in "*Levadi*" (1902), as a symbol of boredom and despair; the sanctuary as the symbol of tradition; and the spark of fire, appearing in many poems in various forms (a burning coal or candle, a twinkling star, or flaming torch), representing the true ideal. "*Ha-Matmid*" ("The Talmud Student," 1894–95), his first long poem, apparently begun in Volozhin, was an immediate triumph. In the poem Bialik traces the inner struggles of the dedicated student who represses his natural inclinations and sacrifices life, movement, change, nature, and family for the ascetic study of Torah. This was an ideal figure who captured the imagination of the reader. He embodied the moral qualities that build societies and preserve cultures. The ability to sublimate for the sake of higher values was a basic idea in Bialik's conception of vocation. The key metaphor of the poem is, characteristically, the twinkling light.

Settling in Odessa

In 1900 Bialik finally succeeded in finding a teaching position in Odessa where he lived until 1921, except for a year's stay in Warsaw (1904), where he served as literary editor of *Ha-Shilo'aḥ*. He was drawn into the circle of writers and Zionist leaders that gathered around Aḥad Ha-Am, *Sholem Yankev *Abramovitsh, and Simon *Dubnow. Other members of the group were Mordecai (Ben-Ami) Rabinowicz, Ḥayyim *Tchernowitz, and Alter Druyanov. As Bialik gained a reputation, young poets such as Zalman Shneour, Jacob *Fichmann, and Jacob *Steinberg went to Odessa to meet him. Working with Mendele, he translated the latter's "*Fishke the Lame*" into Hebrew from the original Yiddish. He had tried his hand at Yiddish poetry before leaving Sosnowiec and now his work with Mendele, a master in Hebrew and Yiddish literatures, turned him to Yiddish again. His realistic stories in Hebrew, "*Aryeh Ba'al Guf*" and "*Me-Aḥorei ha-Gader*" ("Behind the Fence," 1909), were influenced by Mendele's realism of style – indeed they came into being because Mendele had forged a new and pliant Hebrew idiom. Bialik's poetry, however, including the prose poem "*Safi'aḥ*," was relatively free of his mentor's influences. Together with Rawnitzki, Simḥah *Ben-Zion, and Elḥanan Leib Lewinsky he founded the Moriah Publishing House which produced suitable textbooks for the modern Jewish school written in the spirit of Aḥad Ha-Am's educational ideals. In his dark rooms in Odessa Bialik created nature poems that evoke a childhood intoxicated with light (e.g., "*Zohar,*" 1901). During this period also a self-imposed challenge to cast folk expression into Hebrew, only a literary language then, led the poet to write the first of a series of folk songs. In his first decade in Odessa he wrote poems of wrath in Yiddish ("*Fun Tsa'ar un Tsorn*" ("Of Sorrow and Anger"), 1906) and in Hebrew ("*Ḥazon u-Massa*" ("Vision and Utterance"), 1911). Both were products of that critical period in Jewish life when the initial impetus of Zionism was retarded and other movements and ideologies, such as Yiddishism and territorialism, offered different solutions to national problems. When Bialik's first volume of poems appeared in 1901, Joseph Klausner hailed him as "the poet of the national renaissance." In 1902 he wrote "*Metei Midbar*" ("The Dead of the Desert"), a long descriptive poem whose motifs are taken from the legend that the generation of the Exodus did not die but slumbers in the desert. Gigantic in stature, they awaken from time to time to utter defiance against the divine decree which consigned them to their state of living death, and to fight for their own redemption. It may also reflect the universal predicament of modern man whose struggle for the right to determine his own destiny involves the desperate rejection of the divine imperative.

Kishinev

The Kishinev pogroms in 1903 deeply shocked the whole civilized world. Bialik, on behalf of the Jewish Historical Commission in Odessa, went to Kishinev to interview survivors and to prepare a report on the atrocity. Before leaving he wrote "*Al ha-Sheḥitah*" ("On the Slaughter," 1903) in which he calls on heaven either to exercise immediate justice and, if not, to destroy the world, spurning mere vengeance with the famous lines "Cursed is he who says 'Revenge'/Vengeance for the blood of a small child/Satan has not yet created." Later he wrote "*Be-Ir ha-Haregah*" ("In the City of Slaughter," 1904), a searing denunciation of the people's meek submission to the massacre, in which he is incensed at the cowardliness of the people, bitter at the absence of justice, and struck by the indifference of nature – "The sun shone, the acacia blossomed, and the slaughterer slaughtered."

Influence of Warsaw

In 1904 Bialik became the literary editor of *Ha-Shilo'aḥ* and moved to Warsaw, where, among the members of the circle of Isaac Leib *Peretz, he found a lighter mood. They were less cautious and less involved with higher principles than the Odessa group. In Warsaw he wrote several memorable love poems. The symbolist emphasis of Peretz may have influenced the poem "*Ha-Berekhah*" ("The Pool," 1905), most of which was written during the Warsaw stay. The pool, guarded by the forest, reflects the changing moods of nature and the observer, meditating on the "riddle of the two worlds," objective reality and reality as it is reflected in the pool, ponders which is primary – the external manifestation, or the inner conception of the soul (of art). This was Bialik's most prolific period and "*Ha-Berekhah*" was followed by his most enigmatic and experimental work, "*Megillat ha-Esh*" ("The Scroll of Fire," 1905). The work is a prose poem which fuses elements drawn from Jewish legend (*aggadah*) and Jewish mysticism. Its overt theme is the destruction of the Temple and of Jerusalem, and the exile which followed. The destruction of the Temple appears to represent the destruction of the poet's soul on one level and that of the religious faith of an entire generation on the other. The youths, marooned on the island, as they are transported into exile may symbolize spiritual isolation; at the same time the two youths represent the struggle between faith and despair which is the poem's central theme. The chosen youth himself is caught between the call to preserve the last spark of redemption and the lure of *eros*, the girl. Torch in hand, he moves toward the girl and plunges into the abyss.

Silence

After "*Megillat ha-Esh*" Bialik fell into a period of silence, writing few poems and becoming occupied with manifold cultural activities: public lectures, essays, criticism, translating, and editing. The growing tension and the stark dichotomies in his poetry point to an inner crisis; the lonely poet can no longer find solace either in his individual talent or in his God. The radical split of personality in the autobiographical prose poem "*Safi'aḥ*" (1908), in which the child's inner self is abandoned by its double, who accompanies the crowd, marks the farthest development of Bialik's ambivalent attitude to tradition and religion. Baruch Kurzweil has shown that the change in the motif of return in "*Lifnei Aron ha-Sefarim*" ("Before the Book Case," 1910) marks a turning point in Bialik's poetry. The poet desperately realizes that his attempt to return and to repent fails because there is no one to return to, and no condition of dialogue with God or the world. The flame of the study candle has died, the people's past is a graveyard that offers nothing, and the returning son, despairing, welcomes death and departs. Bialik's poetry now becomes acutely personal. The poet, sensing his strangeness in the world, retreats and longs for death. Having lost the purity of childhood and the grace of the chosen, he is preoccupied with death – a broken, useless twig, dangling from its branch ("*Ẓanaḥ lo Zalzal*" ("A Twig Fell"), 1911). Before his death Bialik wrote the cycle "*Yatmut*" ("Orphanhood" poems, c. 1933) in which the existential predicament is fused with the poignancy of his own orphaned childhood.

Berlin and Palestine

Bialik lived in Odessa until 1921 when Maxim Gorki interceded with the Soviet government to permit a group of Hebrew writers to leave the country. Bialik went to Berlin, which had become a center of Jewish émigré writers, engaging in publishing and editing, until he settled in Tel Aviv in Palestine in 1924 where he spent the rest of his life. He died in Vienna where he had gone for medical treatment.

Essays

A series of essays written between the years 1907 and 1917 secures Bialik's place as a distinguished essayist. In it he charts the course of modern Jewish culture: the state of Hebrew literature, the condition of Hebrew journalism, the development of language and style, the existential function of language, and the role of authority in culture. "Ha-Sefer ha-Ivri" ("On the Hebrew Book," 1913) propounds his basic idea of selecting and collecting the best of classic Jewish literature.

Cultural Role

After 1905, he became more active in public affairs, devoting his abundant vigor, vision, and charm to the preservation and advancement of Jewish culture. He participated in Zionist Congresses (1907, 1913, 1921, and 1931) and the Congress for Hebrew Language and Culture (1913). His cultural missions took him to the United States (1926) and to London (1931). From 1928 on, ill health forced him to spend his summers in Europe and these trips became occasions for the promotion of Jewish culture. He was active in the work of the Hebrew University, served as president of the Hebrew Writers Union and of the Hebrew Language Council, and initiated the popular *Oneg Shabbat*, a Sabbath study project.

Editor and Translator

Bialik was the literary editor of several periodicals, *Ha-Shilo'aḥ* (1904–09), *Keneset* (1917), and *Reshumot* (1918–22), and he founded *Moznayim* in Palestine (1929). Together with Rawnitzki he compiled a selection of rabbinic lore, *Sefer ha-Aggadah* (1908–11) and the collected works of the medieval poets Solomon ibn *Gabirol (1924) and Moses *Ibn Ezra (1928). In 1932 he published a commentary to the first order of the Mishnah. His masterful translations of *Don Quixote* (1912) and *Wilhelm Tell* (1923) are an integral part of his work. After his death some of Bialik's lectures and addresses were collected in *Devarim she-be-Al Peh* (2 vols., 1935) and part of his huge correspondence was published in *Iggerot* (5 vols. 1938–39).

For English translations of his work see Goell, Bibliography, index.

[Samuel Leiter]

Evaluation

Bialik's literary career is a watershed in modern Hebrew literature; when he arrived on the scene, Hebrew poetry was provincial and by and large imitative. It could not free itself of the overwhelming biblical influence which had dominated it for centuries and, except for the poetry of a few, the stylized florid biblical *meliẓah* (ornate phrase) had a stifling effect on the creativity of the Haskalah poets. At the same time most of these poets slavishly imitated in subject and in genre the European models – mainly German romantic poetry. Bialik, who more than any other Hebrew poet since *Judah Halevi had a thorough command of Hebrew and the ability to use the many resources of the language, forged a new poetic idiom which enabled Hebrew poetry to free itself from the overwhelming biblical influence and yet, at the same time, retain its link with "the language of the race." While his Hebrew remained learned and "literary," he anticipated the conversational verse which was to become the hallmark of the Palestinian poets (e.g., in his folk poems and children's verse). Not an experimenter, Bialik nevertheless opened new vistas when on rare occasions he abandoned the accepted accented syllabic meter for purely biblical cadences, or when he developed the Hebrew prose poem. While he wrote his serious verse in the Ashkenazi accent, he was among the first to try out the Sephardi accent in his children's verse. He freed Hebrew poetry from its didactic and propagandistic tendency. Although his works are often filled with fervent Jewish hopes, memories, and ideals, content is always subordinate to aesthetic criteria. Early Bialik criticism invariably reads all his poems as expressions of national ideas, but many of his poems are purely lyrical and have been misinterpreted by critics whose love of ideals exceeded their literary taste. Lyric poems like "*Ẓanaḥ lo Zalzal*" or "*Im Dimdumei ha-Ḥamah*" are among the finest in Hebrew literature. Bialik's dominant theme is the crisis of faith which confronted his generation as it broke with the sheltered and confined medieval Jewish religious culture of its childhood and desperately sought to hold on to a Jewish way of life and thought in the new secularized world in which it found itself. He adopted the ethico-humanist reading of Judaism which was proffered by Aḥad Ha-Am, but as Kurzweil has pointed out, he often had grave misgivings as to its efficacy in bridging the traditional and the modern. His doubts find conscious and unconscious expression in his writings. Despite his moments of despair, Bialik did not completely abandon the Aḥad Ha-Amian hope of reconciling modernism with tradition within the context of a new national Jewish culture (Kurzweil's view on this is to the contrary).

Bialik's poetry, growing out of the cultural milieu of Eastern European Jewry in a particular area, is in a sense regional, but because of its great artistic merit has become the concrete expression of the general crisis of faith which faced an entire generation of Europeans. His poetry can be read on three levels: the individual, the Jewish, and the universal. As an individual, the poet emerges as a sensitive artist who seeks to preserve the purity of his "calling" in the face of the materialism and the erotic drive of modern man. He loses his purity as he leaves the security of his childhood Eden and vainly attempts to recapture it. At times he is not sure whether his preoccupation with society, with his people and its ideals, may not actually hinder his self-fulfillment as an artist. On the Jewish level, the poet becomes the spokesman of his generation. Born in the pious world of the East European Jewish town, he is cast into a secular materialist world which questions the old values. He strives to reconstruct a way of life in which he can survive as a Jew and thus fulfill Judaism's historical mission. On the universal level, the poet, a product of a preindustrial rural world, is driven into the secular city, driven out of the Eden of good order and faith. He is left to agonize about his loneliness, his barrenness, and his ultimate death.

Searching out new and further vistas yet rooted in the rich Jewish heritage, Bialik is both the product and the dominant motivator of the cultural revolution of his age, embodying its very essence – to carve out of the past the foundation on which the people might build with dignity in the future. In answering the silent cry of a people needing articulation in a new era, he has gained its permanent recognition. As a poet his genius and spirit have left an indelible imprint on modern Hebrew literature.

[Ezra Spicehandler]

BIBLIOGRAPHY: I. Efros, *Ḥayyim Nahman Bialik* (Eng., 1940), incl. bibl.; F. Lachower, *Bialik, Ḥayyav vi-Yẓirotav* (1950²); J. Fichmann, *Shirat Bialik* (1946); Z. Shapiro, *Bialik bi-Yẓirotav* (1951); idem, *Derakhim be-Shirat Bialik* (1962); J. Klausner, *Bialik ve-Shirat Ḥayyav* (1951); D. Sadan, *Avnei Boḥan* (1951), 60–77; E. Kagan, *Marot Shetiyyah be-Shirat Bialik* (1959); R. Zur, *Devarim ke-Ḥavayatam* (1964); A. Zemach, *Ha-Lavi ha-Mistatter* (1966); B. Kurzweil, *Bialik re-Tchernichowsky* (1967); E. Schweid, *Ha-Ergah li-Mele'ut ha-Ḥavayah* (1968); J. Haephrati, in: *Ha-Sifrut*, 1 (1968/69), 101–29; M. Perry, *ibid.*, 607–31; I. Avinery, *Millon Ḥiddushei Ḥ.N. Bialik* (1935); A. Avrunin, *Meḥkarim bi-Leshon Bialik ve-Yalag* (1953); B. Benshalom (Katz), *Mishkalav shel Bialik* (1945); A. Avital, *Shirat Bialik ve-ha-Tanakh* (1952); A. Even Shoshan and Y. Segal, *Konkordanẓyah le-Shirat Bialik* (1960); Z. Fisman, in: *En Hakore*, 2–3 (1923), 97–134, incl. bibl.; M. Ungerfeld, *Ḥ.N. Bialik vi-Yẓirotav: Bibliografyah le-Vattei ha-Sefer* (1960); E.H. Jeshurin, in: Ḥ.N. Bialik, *Oysgeklibene Shriftn* (1964), Bialik's bibliography; Shunami, Bibl, nos. 3261–72. **ADD. BIBLIOGRAPHY:** B. Kurzweil, *Bialik ve-Tschernichowsky* (1967); I. Biletzky, *H.N. Bialik ve-Yiddish* (1970); S. Zemah, *Al Bialik: Asarah Ma'amarim* (1977); M. Genn, *The Influence of Rabbinic Literature on the Poetry of H.N. Bialik* (1978); Z. Luz, *Tashtiyot Shirah: Ikkarim ba-Po'etikah shel Bialik* (1984); S. Werses, *Ben Gilu'i le-Kisu'i: Bialik be-Sippur u-ve-Masah* (1984); Z. Shamir, *Ha-Ẓarẓar Meshorer ha-Galut: Al ha-Yesod ha-Amami bi-Yeẓirat Bialik* (1986); U. Shavit, *Ḥevlei Niggun* (1988); D. Aberbach, *Bialik* (1988); D. Sadan, *H.N. Bialik ve-Darko bi-Leshono u-Leshonotenu* (1989); S. Shva, *Ḥozeh Beraḥ: Sippur Ḥayyav shel Bialik* (1990); D.S. Breslauer, *The Hebrew Poetry of H.N. Bialik and a Modern Jewish Theology* (1991); E. Nathan, *Ha-Derekh le-"Metei Midbar": Al Poemah shel Bialik ve-ha-Shirah ha-Russit* (1993); U. Shamir and Z. Shamir (eds.), *Al Sefat ha-Brekhah: Ha-Poemah shel Bialik bi-Re'i ha-Bikkoret* (1995); D. Miron, *H.N. Bialik and the Prophetic Mode in Modern Hebrew Poetry* (2000); A.M. Rubin, *From Torah to Tarbut: H.N. Bialik and the Nationalization of Judaism* (2000); Z. Luz and Z. Shamir (eds.), *Al Gilu'i ve-Kisu'i ba-Lashon: Iyyunim be-Masato shel Bialik* (2001); R. Shoham, *Poetry and Prophecy: The Image of the Poet as a "Prophet," a Hero and an Artist in Modern Hebrew Literature* (2003); Y. Bakon, *Ẓofeh Hayyiti be-Eyno shel Olam* (2004). **WEBSITE:** www.ithl.org.il.

BIALKIN, KENNETH J. (1929–), U.S. lawyer. Born in the Bronx, N.Y., to immigrant parents, Bialkin graduated from the University of Michigan in 1950 with a degree in economics and then earned a J.D. degree from Harvard in 1953. His law practice encompassed a broad range of corporate and securities law matters, first when he was senior partner in the law firm of Willke, Farr & Gallagher and then with Skadden, Arps, Slate, Meagher & Flom. At the same time, he taught securities law at New York University School of Law for 18 years and became involved in a number of Jewish organizations. As such he was frequently quoted in the press on issues of Jewish interest. He was national chairman of the Anti-Defamation

League; president and chairman of the American Jewish Historical Society, president of the Jewish Community Relations Council of New York; chairman of the Conference of Presidents of Major American Jewish Organizations, and chairman of the America Israel Friendship League. He also served for 30 years as vice chairman of the Jerusalem Foundation.

In his law practice, Bialkin represented insurance companies, broker-dealers, investment bankers, and other financial institutions. In 1998 he represented Travelers Group in its merger with Citicorp. The year earlier, he represented Travelers in its acquisition of Salomon Inc., and he represented the stock exchange Nasdaq in its restructuring to separate it from the NASD in 2000 and 2001. He was involved in some of the largest insurance company mergers and acquisitions in the United States, including the Metropolitan Life Insurance Company in its merger with New England Mutual Life Insurance Company. He also represented Travelers Group in its $4 billion acquisition of Aetna's property-casualty operations.

Bialkin is a former editor of *Business Lawyer* magazine and was chairman of the American Bar Association's committee on federal regulation of securities. His wife, Ann Bialkin, who earned a master's degree in social work from Columbia University, established Elem (a Hebrew acronym for "youth in distress"), a foundation that assists teenagers in Israel who commit crimes or use drugs and who are apparently overlooked by the judicial system.

In recognition of his 16 years as a member of its board of directors, Citigroup established the Kenneth J. Bialkin/Citigroup Public Service Award at the American Jewish Historical Society.

[Stewart Kampel (2nd ed.)]

BIALOBLOCKI, SAMUEL SHERAGA (1888–1960), talmudic scholar born in Pilwiszki (western Lithuania). Bialoblocki studied for many years at the Lithuanian yeshivot of Telz, Slobodka, and Ponevezh; at the last he studied under Isaac Jacob Rabinowitz and Isaac *Blaser. After World War I he entered the Bet Midrash Elyon of Ḥayyim *Heller in Berlin. He also attended various universities and graduated from Giessen with a thesis on *Materialien zum islamischen und juedischen Eherecht...* (1928) and became instructor in modern Hebrew. Between 1928 and 1934 he was one of the contributors on talmudic subjects to the German *Encyclopaedia Judaica*. With the advent of the Nazis he emigrated to Palestine where first he taught at the Mizrachi Teachers' Training College in Jerusalem but later ventured into the real estate business, though continuing to devote most of his time to his studies. When Bar-Ilan University was opened in 1955, Bialoblocki was appointed head of its Talmud department; he also served as chairman of the university's Senate.

Bialoblocki, though a profound scholar of vast erudition, did not publish much; his importance lay chiefly in his influence as a teacher. His method, both in teaching and writing, expressed a spirit of conservative criticism. He began to prepare an anthology of early commentaries on the Talmud with notes on the variants and sources for the Makhon ha-Talmud ha-Yisre'eli ha-Shalem, of which a first part was published posthumously (*Bar Ilan, Sefer ha-Shanah*, 2 (1964), 65–69). In Germany he published his *Beziehung des Judentums zu Proselyten und Proselytentum* (1930, Heb. tr., 44–60). Various learned articles of his appeared in: *Keneset*, 6–8 (1942–44); *Yovel Shai... S.J. Agnon* (1958); and *Alei Ayin* (*Sefer Yovel... S. Schocken* 1952). He contributed the article on Personal Status (*Ishut*) to the *Encyclopaedia Hebraica*. Bialoblocki also contributed articles on the Torah centers in Lithuania and on his teacher I.J. Rabinowitz in: *Yahadut Lita*, 1 (1960), 185ff., 394ff.

BIBLIOGRAPHY: H.Z. Hirschberg and S.J. Agnon, in: *Bar-Ilan, Sefer ha-Shanah...*, 2 (1964), 7–43 (Eng. summaries); Ungerfeld, in: *Ha-Ẓofeh* (Jan. 2, 1970).

[Yehoshua Horowitz]

BIALOBLOTZKY (Bialloblotzky), CHRISTIAN HEINRICH FRIEDRICH (1799–1869), hebraist and missionary. Bialoblotzky converted to Christianity as a young man and studied ecclesiastical history and philosophy at Goettingen, where he also was active as preacher. He traveled in Asia and Africa on behalf of different Protestant missions, and after serving as head of a private school in England, became lecturer at the University of Goettingen. Among his published works are *Das Biblische Unterrichtswesen* (1828); *The Chronicles of Joseph b. Joshua Meir the Sephardi* (2 vols., 1835–36), a translation with introduction and notes of Joseph *ha-Kohen's *Sefer Divrei ha-Yamim*; a Hebrew lexicon, *Oẓar ha-Shorashim* (*Lexicon radicum hebraicarum*, 1843), in Hebrew and Latin as well as in Hebrew and English; and *Psalms* (first book 1846), Hebrew, Greek, and English, as part of Origen's *Hexapla*.

ADD. BIBLIOGRAPHY: K.H. Voigt, in: F.-W. Bautz (ed.), *Biographisch-Bibliographisches Kirchenlexikon* 15 (1999), 132–42; N.M. Railton, "Transnational Evangelicalism: The Case of Friedrich Bialloblotzky 1799–1869," in: M. Brecht et al. (eds.), *Arbeiten zur Geschichte des Pietismus*, 41 (2002).

BIALOSTOTZKY, BENJAMIN JACOB (1893–1962), Yiddish poet, essayist, and folklorist, born in Pumpenai (Pumpian), Lithuania. Bialostotzky was the son of the famed "Posvoler Maggid." He immigrated to the United States in 1911 and studied at the City College of New York. From 1914 a member of Poale Zion, he helped found Yiddish schools, was active in various organizations, co-edited Yiddish journals and, from 1922, wrote for the Yiddish daily *Forverts*. His works were first collected in *Lider un Eseyen* ("Poems and Essays," 1932). In 1953 he edited the memorial volume for the poet David *Edelstadt. His own volume of poetry *Lid tsu Lid* ("Poem to Poem," 1958), includes his bibliography by E.H. Jeshurin. His folklore studies resulted in several collections of legends: *Fun Golus Bovl bis Roym* ("From the Babylonian Exile to Rome," 1949), *Di Mesholim fun Dubner Magid* ("Parables of the Maggid of Dubno," 1962); *Yidisher Humor un Yidishe Leytsim* ("Jewish Humor and Jewish Jesters," 1963).

BIBLIOGRAPHY: LNYL, 1 (1956), 277–8.; S.D. Singer, *Dikhter un prozaiker* (1959), 105.

[Melech Ravitch]

BIALYSTOK (Rus. **Belostok**), industrial city in N.E. Poland; latterly one of the principal Russian/Polish Jewish centers; incorporated into Russia between 1807 and 1921 and administered by the U.S.S.R. between 1939 and 1941, reverting to Poland in 1945. Originally the Bialystok community formed part of the *Tykocin (Tiktin) community. Jewish settlement in the village of Bialystok was encouraged by the manorial overlords, the counts of Branicki. In 1745 the Bialystok community became self-governing, although remaining within the Tykocin province. The heads of the Jewish community were permitted to take part in municipal elections in 1749. In 1759 the Jews had to contribute two-thirds of the funds required to provision the armies in transit through Bialystok. The character of the craft guilds explicitly admits Jewish membership. Communal affairs were regulated by the counts in 1749 and 1777. By 1765, there were 765 Jews living in Bialystok. (See Table: Jewish Population of Bialystok, 1765–1948.)

The Jewish Population of Bialystok, 1765–1948

	Absolute Numbers	Percentages
1765	765	22.4
1808	4,000	66.6
1856	9,547	69.0
1861	11,873	69.8
1895	47,783	76.0
1910	52,123	68.5
1913	61,500	68.6
1929	43,150	47.8
1932	39,165	60.5
1936	42,880	43.0
1945	1,085	n.a.
1948	660	n.a.

The position of the Jews deteriorated when Bialystok passed to Prussia (1795), and subsequently to Russia. Its situation on the western border was favorable for developing trade with Russian markets, however, and the Jews were able to earn a livelihood as army purveyors or importers of tea and other commodities. The economic situation deteriorated when there was an influx of Jews expelled from the neighboring villages in 1825–35 and 1845, under the 1804 discriminatory legislation (see *Russia), who crowded into Bialystok. There was a steep increase in the Jewish population which in 1856 numbered 9,547 out of a total population of 13,787, many of them homeless or unemployed. Welfare institutions were established in an attempt to alleviate matters.

The development of the large textile industry in Bialystok after the Napoleonic wars owes much to Jewish enterprise. A number of the soldiers from Saxony were expert weavers and spinners who settled in Bialystok and established workshops largely financed by Jews; textile mills were erected by two Jews in 1850. As they acquired spinning, weaving, knitting, and dyeing skills, Jews replaced the German specialists. In 1860, 19 of the 44 textile mills in Bialystok were Jewish owned, with an output valued at 3,000,000 rubles; in 1898, of the 372 mills in Bialystok, 299 (80.38%) were Jewish owned, while 5,592 (59.5%) of the workers were Jewish. Of the total output of the Bialystok mills for this year, valued at 12,855,000 rubles, the Jewish share amounted to 47.3%.

The Jewish labor movement found strong support in Bialystok, and in 1897 many Jewish workers there became members of the *Bund. The Bialystok Jewish workers issued an underground newspaper, *Der Byalistoker Arbayter*, the same year. The intensive activities of the labor movement in Bialystok during the Russian revolution of 1905–06 provoked savage acts of reprisal by the Russian authorities. The *pogroms in Bialystok that occurred between June 1 and 3, 1906, were the most violent of the mob outbreaks against Russian Jewry that year, resulting in 70 Jews being killed and 90 gravely injured. The commission of inquiry later appointed by the Duma to investigate the circumstances surrounding the pogrom held both the local police and the central authorities to blame for the tragedy. A prolonged crisis in Bialystok's trade and industry followed.

The contacts with German Jewry during the period that Bialystok was governed by Prussia had introduced the spirit of Enlightenment (*Haskalah) into Jewish circles in Bialystok. Prominent in the movement were members of the *Zamenhof family; Abraham Schapiro, author of *Toledot Yisrael ve-Sifruto* (1892); Jehiel Michael Zubludowsky, a contributor to *Ha-Karmel* and author of *Ru'aḥ Ḥayyim* (1860); and the poet Menahem Mendel *Dolitzki. A Ḥovevei Zion group was formed in Bialystok in 1880. Zionism in its manifold ideological ramifications subsequently gained numerous supporters. The Bialystok Zionists were led by Samuel *Mohilewer, and later by Joseph *Chasanowich. Rabbis living in Bialystok in the 19th century included Aryeh Leib b. Baruch Bendit (1815–20), author of *Sha'agat Aryeh*; Yom Tov Lipmann Heilpern (1849–79); and Samuel Mohilewer (1883–98).

Modern Jewish elementary schools, such as the modern *ḥeder* (*ḥeder metukkan*), a girls' school, and institutes for commerce and crafts were founded while Bialystok was part of Russia; the language of instruction was Russian, but Hebrew was also taught. The first Hebrew kindergarten was founded in 1910. Hebrew elementary and high schools were established after World War I.

In 1895 the Jewish population numbered 47,783 (out of 62,993). Of the 3,628 merchants and shopkeepers in the city in 1897, 3,186 (87.8%) were Jews. In 1913 the Jewish population numbered 61,500 (out of 89,700). In 1921, 93% of the businessmen were Jewish, and 89% of the industrial plants were Jewish owned; later the proportion of Jews in business decreased (to 78.3% in 1928). In 1932 there were over 39,165 Jews (out of 91,207) in Bialystok.

[Nathan Michael Gelber]

Holocaust Period

Shortly after the outbreak of the war, the Germans entered Bialystok, first occupying it from September 15 until September 22, 1939, when it was transferred to the Soviets. The second German occupation was from June 27, 1941, to July 27, 1944. At that time some 50,000 Jews lived in Bialystok, and some 350,000 in the whole province. On the day following the second German occupation, known as "Red Friday," the Germans burned down the Jewish quarter, including the synagogue and at least 1,000 Jews who had been driven inside. Other similar events followed in rapid succession: On Thursday, July 3, 300 of the Jewish intelligentsia were rounded up and taken to Pietrasze, a field outside the town, and murdered there; on Saturday, July 12, over 3,000 Jewish men were put to death there. Their widows were later known in the ghetto as *"die Donnershtige"* ("the ones from Thursday") and *"di Shabbesdige"* ("the ones from Saturday"). A *Judenrat was established on German orders (July 26, 1941), and chaired by Rabbi Rosenmann, but his deputy, Ephraim *Barash, was the actual head and served as its liaison with the German authorities. On August 1, some 50,000 Jews were segregated into a closed ghetto. The three gates in the barrier were guarded by armed gendarmes.

For administrative purposes, Bialystok was incorporated into the Reich (end of July 1941), as an autonomous district (*Bezirk*) of East Prussia under *Gauleiter* and *Oberpraesident* Erich Koch, one of Hitler's trusted men. Under this setup various Nazi authorities in Berlin, Koenigsberg, and Bialystok issued frequently contradictory orders concerning the fate of the Jews of the ghetto. The first year, there was relative quiet and order in the ghetto (except for the deportation of 4,500 of the poorest Jews to Pruzhany) as the Germans wished to exploit the ghetto to a maximum in industrial production for the army. Every Jew in the 15–65 age group was forced to work, and the Germans meted out physical punishment, including death sentences, to anyone attempting to avoid or resist forced labor. The only remuneration was a daily bread ration of 500 grams, which was later reduced to 350 grams. In addition, the Germans confiscated property, imposed forced "contributions," and collected a head and apartment tax; the Judenrat collected its own taxes to cover its expenses. There were private factories in the ghetto, owned by a German in-

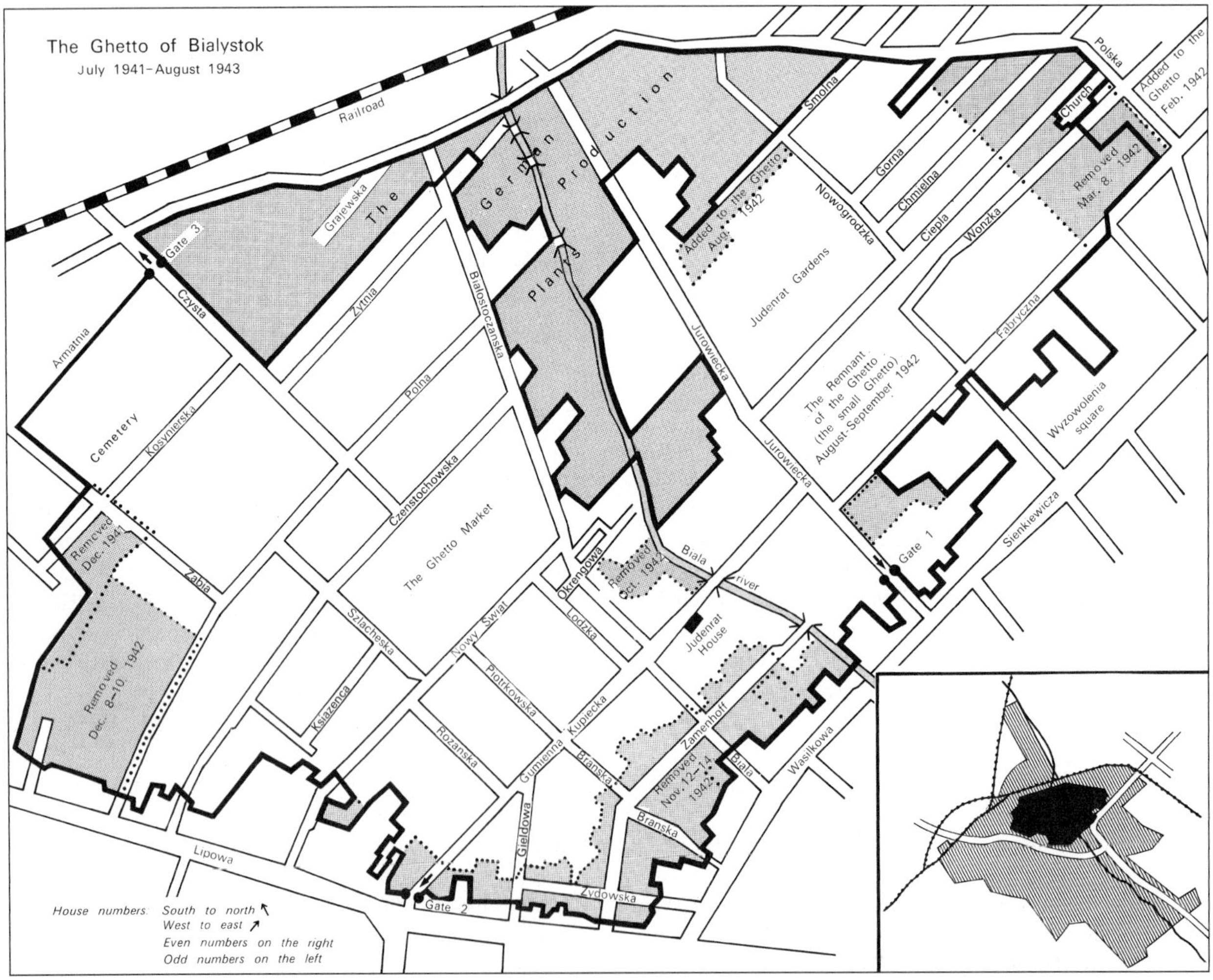

dustrialist, Oskar Stefen; Jews were also employed in various German enterprises outside the ghetto. Two thousand persons were employed by the Judenrat, not including those in charge of the ghetto's economic enterprises. Over 200 men served in the "Jewish Police." The Judenrat maintained important departments: industry and artisans, labor, finances, and supply; its other departments dealt with health, welfare, housing, culture, and vegetable gardening for staples for a small segment of the ghetto; in the main, however, the Judenrat concentrated on factories engaged in war production in the hope of thus prolonging the survival of the ghetto inhabitants. The deputy chairman of the Judenrat, Barash, knew the truth about the deportations and death camps and had also read German documents containing plans to liquidate the ghetto. Nevertheless, up to his last day, he trusted in the idea that the inmates' hard work and economic "usefulness" would delay their destruction or even save them. Most of the inhabitants of the ghetto trusted Barash and shared his illusions. He stayed at his post until he was deported to Majdanek and murdered.

The Germans embarked upon the liquidation of the Jews on Feb. 5–12, 1943, when the first *Aktion* in the ghetto took place. The Jews were dragged from their homes and hiding places. One thousand of them were killed on the spot, while 10,000 were deported to Treblinka death camp. The period following the first *Aktion* was marked by Jewish underground preparations for armed resistance in the event that the deportations would be resumed. At this time the local German authorities, who were interested in prolonging the existence of the ghetto for economic reasons, were negotiating with the Berlin and Koenigsberg authorities on the date for the liquidation of the ghetto. The differences of opinion were resolved in the latter's favor, leading to the final destruction of the ghetto on Aug. 16, 1943.

RESISTANCE. An underground came into existence in the early days of the ghetto and expressed itself mainly through sabotage acts at the members' places of work. It lacked, however, a uniform plan of action and a clear idea of its aims. Finally, in November 1942, Mordecai *Tenenbaum (Tamaroff), sent by the *Warsaw Jewish Fighting Organization to organize resistance in Bialystok Ghetto, arrived in the city and gave the movement direction. The underground's main problems were the lack of arms and disunity in the ranks. The ghetto stood alone in its struggle, for no help could be expected from the Polish underground. Arms had either to be stolen from the German armories or purchased at high prices outside the ghetto; only the hand grenades were of home manufacture.

In the early stage, Barash supported the ghetto underground and supplied it with finances and information through Tenenbaum. Barash also passed on copies of the Judenrat's minutes and proclamations as well as copies of German documents for the underground's secret archives. These archives were established by Tenenbaum on the model of the *Ringelblum *Oneg Shabbat* archives in the Warsaw Ghetto. Tenenbaum wrote a great deal himself and also collected diaries, depositions, historical articles, folklore, and Judenrat and German documents. These archives were hidden outside the ghetto and uncovered after the war; most of its contents are now in the custody of *Yad Vashem in Jerusalem. Until January 1943, the Bialystok underground maintained regular contact with the Jewish Fighting Organization in Warsaw, *Vilna, and other ghettos.

Barash supported the underground, however, only as long as the Germans were unaware of its existence. When the first *Aktion* took place, in February 1943, the underground was not yet ready. However it stepped up its activities. The men were trained in the use of arms, more weapons were acquired, and attempts were made to establish contact with the partisans in the forests. Several sentences of death were also carried out on Jews who acted as informers or otherwise cooperated with the Gestapo. The ghetto youth were greatly attracted to the forests, where there was a chance of fighting and personal salvation. Three small groups left the ghetto for the forests (January, March, and June 1943). But the Jewish partisan groups there were in a difficult situation, for they had few arms, and there was no Soviet partisan activity in the vicinity in this period. The ghetto therefore remained the base for the provision of food, medical aid, clothing, and arms to the small number of Jewish partisans.

One of the weaknesses of the underground, disunity, stemmed from differences in the members' political background and views on the underground's character and goals. Some were convinced that the minimum conditions necessary for military operations could not exist inside the ghetto, and that in fighting in the forests, side by side with the other partisans, the Jews could contribute to the common struggle against the Nazis. Tenenbaum on the other hand, adhered to the view that the underground had to concentrate on the struggle inside the ghetto, and that only after they had carried out this national duty could the members of the underground continue the struggle in the forests. It was not until July 1943, after the break with the Judenrat chairman, that the various underground movements in the ghetto united, on the basis of Tenenbaum's views, in a united fighting organization. Tenenbaum was elected its chairman, and Daniel Moszkowicz deputy chairman. Other prominent members of the underground were Zerach Zylberberg, Hershel Rosenthal, Haika Grosman, and Israel Margulies.

The united Jewish underground called upon the Jews to disregard the orders for deportation, and join the active resistance. Most of the Jewish population, however, stupefied by the Germans' surprise attack, which launched the final liquidation of the ghetto on Aug. 16, 1943, obeyed the orders given. The Germans were aware of the existence of the underground and therefore made careful secret preparations for the *Aktion*, for which a special commando unit from *Lublin was brought under the command of Odilo *Globocnik. The Jewish Fighting Organization tactics were to open battle, prevent the Jews from leaving the ghetto for the deportation trains, break through the German ranks, and seek refuge in the forests. German fire, however, supported by tank action, crushed the rebellion. After a day of fighting, 72 fighters retreated to a bunker in order to organize their escape to the forests. The Germans discovered the bunker and killed all the fighters, with a single exception. The ghetto fighters held out for another month, and night after night the gunfire reverberated through Bialystok. The commanders, Tenenbaum and Moszkowicz, presumably committed suicide when the revolt was quashed. A month later the Germans announced the completion of the *Aktion*, in which some 40,000 Jews were dispatched to Treblinka and Majdanek. The members of the Judenrat were among the last group to be deported. A few dozen Jews succeeded in escaping from the ghetto and joined the partisans in the forests. The revolt made a deep impression upon the Poles and the Germans. After the ghetto's liquidation, six Jewish girls remained who had posed as "Aryans." They acted as underground couriers, and now helped those who escaped to reach the partisans. After suffering many losses, the Jewish partisans in the forests united to form a single group, "Kadimah." They in turn were absorbed into a general partisan movement led by Soviet parachutists at the end of 1943.

After the war there remained 1,085 Jews in Bialystok, of whom 900 were local inhabitants, and the rest from the neighboring villages. Of the ghetto inhabitants 260 survived, some in the deportation camps, others as members of partisan units. The community presumably dwindled and dissolved.

[Bronia Klibanski]

BIBLIOGRAPHY: A.S. Hershberg, *Pinkas Bialystok* (1949); J. Lestschinsky, in: EJ, 4 (1928), 471–9; I. Schipper (ed.), *Zydzi w Polsce odrodzonej*, 2 (1933), 495–6, 523; B. Wasiutyński, *Ludność żydowska w Polsce w w. xix i xx* (1930). HOLOCAUST PERIOD: Klibanski, in: *Yad Vashem Studies*, 2 (1958), 295–329; M. Tenenbaum-Tamaroff, *Dappim min ha-Delekah* (1948); H. Grossman, *Anshei ha-Mahteret* (1965^2); N. Blumental, *Darko shel Yudenrat: Te'udot mi-Getto Bialystok* (1962); R. Raizner, *Umkum fun Byalistoker Yidentum 1939–1945* (1948); B. Mark, *Oyfshtand in Byalistoker Geto* (1950); D. Sohn (comp.), *Byalistok Bilder Album…* (1951), with English captions; S. Datner, *Walka i zaglada bialostockiego getta* (1946).

BIARRITZ, coastal town in southwestern France. The Jewish community dates to the beginning of the 17th century. In 1619, after disorders in St. Jean-de-Luz, many *Marranos left that town to settle in Biarritz; according to the contemporary Pierre l'Ancre they numbered 2,000. In the census of Jews taken in 1942, 168 families were registered in Biarritz. The present synagogue, built in 1904, contains the Torah scrolls, the Ark, and the silver candelabrum from the former synagogue of Peyrehorade. In 1968, the Biarritz community had 150 members, many of whom originated from North Africa.

BIBLIOGRAPHY: Roth, Marranos, 223ff.; Laborde, in: *Le Républicain du Sud Ouest* (1963); Loeb, in: REJ, 22 (1891), 111; Z. Szajkowski, *Analytical Franco-Jewish Gazetteer* (1966), 241.

[Roger Berg]

BIBAGO, ABRAHAM BEN SHEM TOV (15th century), Spanish scholar, religious philosopher, commentator on Aristotelian works, and preacher. His name is also spelled Bivach. Bibago was born in the province of Aragon. He first resided in Huesca, where, in his youth, he completed a commentary on Aristotle's *Posterior Analytics*, and where there is reference to his having a wife and children (1446). Bibago seems to have been forced out of his community; in his own words, "for they suspected me for my studying the books of the Greeks … and I was wandering and alone, away from my land and the place of my desire, exiled among the nations." Bibago presumably outgrew or overcame his reputation as a radical. In 1465 he participated in the conversion of a Maranno in Huesca. He later settled in Saragossa, where he was head of the yeshivah (c. 1470), and preached publicly on Sabbaths and festivals. He engaged in numerous disputations with Christian scholars at the court of Juan II, king of Aragon, on the Trinity and other Christian tenets, and for this reason kept abreast of Christian theology and scholastic philosophy. He died before the Inquisition's trial and execution in 1489 of the participants in the Huesca conversion years before, including Bibago's brother Isaac, a physician.

Works

Bibago knew Arabic and Latin, and his works are replete with references to Greek, Latin, and Arabic as well as a wide variety of Hebrew sources, including the Kabbalah. He knew the works of Aristotle and wrote commentaries to several of his books, including *Posterior Analytics* (preserved in Vatican ms. 350 and Paris ms. 959), *Physics* (no longer extant), and *Metaphysics* (Munich ms. 357), based on the Middle Commentaries of *Averroes. Among the Greeks, he quotes Euclid, Galen, Ptolemy, Alexander of Aphrodisias, Themistius, Apollonius of Perga and others. Among Christian sources, he quotes the Gospels, Eusebius, Duns Scotus, William of Ockham, and Thomas Aquinas. Among the Arabic philosophers, besides Averroes he mentions, Al-Farabi, Avicenna, Al-Ghazali, Ibn Tufayl, and Avempace. Many of his numerous works, including on medicine and astronomy, and some of his philosophical works, have not survived.

Bibago's *Eẓ Ḥayyim* ("Tree of Life") has survived in a single manuscript (Paris ms. 995), dealing with the creation of the world, and presenting arguments against the doctrine of eternity. Several of Bibago's letters to Moses *Arondi (who had also participated in the 1465 conversion) have survived (Parma ms. 457), as have a treatise on the multiple forms, which M. Steinschneider and A. Nuriel attribute to Bibago (Paris ms. 1004/1), and *Zeh Yenaḥamenu* ("He will comfort us," Gen. 5:29; printed in Salonika, 1522/3, and also found in Paris ms. 995 and Adler ms. 28), a homily for the first Sabbath of the year. Bibago's most important work is his *Derekh Emunah* ("Path of Faith"), probably written in Saragossa around 1480, and printed in Constantinople in 1521/2. (A defective photo-offprint, Jerusalem, 1970, is missing pp. 98–101). Annotated selections were published by Chava Fraenkel-Goldschmidt (Jerusalem, 1978). Four manuscripts of the book exist (Paris ms. 747 and ms. 995; Munich ms. 43; Cambridge Trinity College). The book is divided into three treatises. The first discusses the acts of God, His knowledge, and His providence; the second the intellect and its objects, faith and reason, sin, and related topics; and the third, the principles of the Jewish religion, miracles, creation, and special articles of faith.

His "Derekh Emunah" and Philosophy

M. Steinschneider called Bibago "a rational believer" ("*Denkglaubigen*"), and A. Altmann described him as a "staunchly … Orthodox thinker." Perhaps the experiences of his youth, when he felt his faith and piety were wrongly doubted, led him to insist on the supremacy of faith (thus, the name of his book, "the Path of Faith"), although he accepted the view of many of his predecessors that the ancient prophets and rabbis originally knew the sciences, and that in fact science had originated as Jewish wisdom, which subsequently became forgotten in exile. Since the ancient Jewish authors knew the rational truth, by accepting their truth on the authority of faith one shares in their rational knowledge without having to resort to speculation. Faith and reason thus differ in method but not in content. Indeed, since it is the conclusion that matters, once we have true conclusions, we do not need the speculative principles which led to those conclusions (DE 70c).

Faith is thus both rational in content and superior to reason, because "faith itself is that by which the soul becomes actualized and immortal, and is thus the immortality itself … For the path of faith (*derekh emunah*) is what saves (*moshi'ah*) and provides immortality to the faithful nation … and gives perfection to conception and verification" (DE 59c–60a). Rational speculation can only provide the basis of salvation for a few intellectuals, "but in faith, every person is saved, 'for the just will live by his faith' (Hab. 2:4)" (DE 49d). Faith is thus the highest human perfection, and "I say that the ultimate purpose of miracles is the imparting of faith" (DE 85b). In an interesting collective twist on Maimonides' intellectual theory of providence, Bibago suggests that since the Torah, teaching true faith, actualizes the Jews' intellects, the Jewish people enjoys special national providence. Faith thus provides for national as well as individual salvation.

Faith being both superior to reason and rational in content, Bibago opposed both the extreme opponents and proponents of philosophy. On the one hand, he sharply denounced the bigoted zealots "who retain the shell but reject the kernel, posing as pious before the multitude, while vilifying and mocking the master [i.e., Maimonides] and his disciples" (*Derekh Emunah* 45:4). On the other hand, however, he sharply criticized the destructive tendency of some of the rationalists in their pursuit of philosophy and free enquiry.

Influence

Bibago's views influenced Isaac *Arama, who refers to them, without, however, mentioning the author's name. It appears that Arama gained this knowledge through personal contact rather than through reading the *Derekh Emunah* (Wilensky, *Yiẓhak Arama*, 44–5; cf. J.S. Delmedigo, *Maẓref la-Ḥokhmah*, 8b). Arama describes Bibago as "one of the most important scholars and philosophers of our people" (*Akedat Yiẓhak, Gate 80*). Isaac *Abrabanel quotes the *Derekh Emunah* in his *Rosh Amanah*, without, however, mentioning its author's name. Jacob *Ibn Habib speaks highly of Bibago's scholarship, although he objects to his allegorical interpretation of talmudic passages (*Ein Ya'akov*, end of tractate Berakhot).

BIBLIOGRAPHY: Baer, Spain, index, s.v. *Abraham Bivach*; Munk, Mélanges, 507; Graetz, Gesch, 8 (1890^3), 219ff.; Steinschneider, in: MGWJ, 32 (1883), 79ff., 229; Steinschneider, Uebersetzungen, 89ff., and passim; S. Wilensky (Heller), *Yiẓhak Arama u-Mishnato ha-Filosofit* (1956), index; Y. Hakker, in: *Fifth World Congress of Jewish Studies*, vol. 3 (1969); A. Altmann, "Moses Narboni's 'Epistle on Shi`ur Qoma,'" in: *Studies in Religious Philosophy and Mysticism* (1969), 209; A. Lazaroff, *The Theology of Abraham Bibago* (1981); A. Nuriel, *Concealed and Revealed in Medieval Jewish Philosophy* (Heb., 2000); idem, in: *Tarbiz*, 52 (1983), 154–66; C. Sirat, *A History of Jewish Philosophy in the Middle Ages* (1985), 384–89; R. Jospe, in: *A.J.S. Newsletter*, 33 (1983), 8–9.

[Raphael Jospe (2nd ed.)]

BIBAGO (Bivach), ISAAC (d. 1489), physician in Huesca, Spain; brother of Abraham *Bibago. In the 1460s he and others of his circle helped to bring back to the faith Jews who had been forcibly converted to Christianity (see *Anusim). These included the wealthy Converso *Juan de Ciudad, who spent some time as a guest of the Bibago brothers in order to be instructed by them in the principles of Judaism. In 1489 the Inquisition uncovered the Huesca community's proselytizing activities, and Isaac was among the few suspects still living at the time. He was arrested and was condemned to be burned at the stake. However, as he accepted baptism he was strangled before his body was consigned to the pyre; his fellow prisoners were burned alive.

BIBLIOGRAPHY: Baer, Spain, 2 (1966), 297–9, 385–9; Baer, Urkunden, 1 pt. 2 (1956), 488ff.

BIBAS, family of rabbis and physicians originating in Spain. After 1492 the Bibas family fled to Morocco where its members became spiritual leaders of important communities. ABRAHAM BIBAS was one of the leaders of the Castilian community in Fez in 1526. ḤAYYIM became *dayyan* of Tetuan in 1575; there he built the Great Synagogue, which was destroyed by the Muslims in 1667. His direct descendants succeeded him as leaders of the community until after 1700. Other members of the family were *dayyanim* in Salé. Known for their piety and learning, they exercised great influence and had many disciples. Their decisions and responsa were collected and many of them were published with others of their works. Members of the Bibas family settled in Safed, Jerusalem, Cairo, Leghorn, Amsterdam, and Gibraltar. SHEM TOV was a member of Joseph Caro's *bet din* in Safed. JOSEPH was one of the leading rabbis in Safed at the end of the 17th century. He was the father-in-law of the Shabbatean Nehemiah Ḥayyon who found in his library an old manuscript of the Zohar, attributed to Benjamin ha-Levi. SAMUEL (d. 1793), a friend of Ḥ.J.D. *Azulai, was *dayyan* in Salé. His son JUDAH (1780–1852), a prominent rabbi and precursor of Zionism, was born in Gibraltar, and studied there and in Leghorn, Italy. He received a secular education in Italy and was apparently granted a doctoral degree by an Italian university. Between 1805 and 1832 he lived in Gibraltar, London, and Leghorn, gaining a reputation as a Jewish scholar. In 1832 he was appointed rabbi of Corfu, where he reorganized the Jewish community and its education system, and introduced reforms which aroused opposition from some of the heads of the community. He traveled through Europe in 1839, visiting Turkey, the Balkans, Vienna, and Prague. In Zemun he met Judah *Alkalai, from whom he learned of the new concept of *teshuvah* as a return to the Land of Israel, and not merely as "repentance." Alkalai incorporated his impressions of Bibas in his book *Darkhei No'am*. Two Scottish missionaries, A. Bonar and R.M. M'Cheyne, relate of a visit to the Holy Land in their book *Narrative and Mission of Inquiry to the Jews in 1839* (1878), that Jews in Romania quoted Bibas as saying: "The Jews must be instructed in sciences and in arms so that they may wrest the land of Palestine from the Turks under the conduct of the Messiah, as the Greeks wrested their country." It appears that Bibas conceived the idea of the return to Zion in active, contemporary terms, on a religious basis. In 1852, after a stay in London and another ten-year period in the rabbinical post in Corfu, Bibas went to Ereẓ Israel and settled in Hebron.

BIBLIOGRAPHY: I.R. Molho, *Ha-Rav Y. Bibas* (1957); I. Ben-Walid, *Va-Yomer* (1875), 11, nos. 103–5. J.M. Toledano, *Ner ha-Maarav* (1911), 60, 89–90, 152–3, 158; J. Ben-Naim, *Malkhei Rabbanan* (1931), passim; I.R. Molho, in: *Oẓar Yehudei Sefarad*, 3 (1960), 112–5; M. Benayahu, *ibid.*, 95–111; Hirschberg, Afrikah, 1 (1965), 314; EẒD, 1 (1958), 276–80; T. Preschel, in: *Sinai*, 53 (1963), 174–5.

[David Corcos / Getzel Kressel]

BIBLE. This entry is arranged according to the outline below. Bibliography for a section is indicated by (†).

THE CANON, TEXT, AND EDITIONS

CANON

- **General Titles**
- **The Canon**
  - THE SIGNIFICANCE OF THE CANON
  - THE PROCESS OF CANONIZATION
  - CONTENTS AND TITLES OF THE BOOKS
- **The Tripartite Canon**
  - THE CANONIZATION OF THE TORAH (PENTATEUCH)
  - THE CANONIZATION OF THE PROPHETS
  - THE CANONIZATION OF THE KETUVIM (HAGIOGRAPHA)
- **The Hellenistic Canon**
- **The Number of Books**
- **The Order of the Books**
- **The Languages of Scripture**

TEXT

- **The History of the Biblical Text**
  - THE EARLIEST PERIOD
  - THE SECOND PERIOD
  - THE THIRD PERIOD †

PRINTED EDITIONS (HEBREW) †

TRANSLATIONS

ANCIENT VERSIONS

- **Aramaic: the Targumim**
  - ORIGIN OF THE TARGUMS
  - MANNER OF USAGE
  - DATE OF TARGUM
  - LITURGICAL USE OF THE TARGUM
- **Targums to the Pentateuch**
  - TARGUM ONKELOS
  - PALESTINIAN PENTATEUCH TARGUMS
    - *Codex Neofiti I*
    - *Targum Yerushalmi I (Pseudo-Jonathan)*
    - *Targum Yerushalmi II (the Fragmentary Targum)*
- **The Targums to the Prophets**
  - TARGUM JONATHAN
  - TARGUM YERUSHALMI TO THE PROPHETS
- **Targums to the Hagiographa**
  - JOB
  - PSALMS
  - PROVERBS
  - FIVE SCROLLS
  - CHRONICLES
  - R. JOSEPH AND THE AUTHORSHIP OF THE HAGIOGRAPHA TARGUMS †
- **Greek: The Septuagint †**
- **Old Latin / Vulgate †**
- **Samaritan †**
- **Syriac Aramaic: Peshitta and Other Versions**
  - THE CHRISTIAN-PALESTINIAN VERSION
  - THE PHILOXENIAN VERSION
  - THE SYRO-HEXAPLA †
- **Ethiopic †**
- **Egyptian (Coptic) †**
- **Armenian †**
- **Arabic**
  - PRE-SAADIAN TRANSLATIONS
  - SAADIAH'S TRANSLATION
  - KARAITE TRANSLATIONS
  - SHARḤ
  - GLOSSARIES †

MODERN VERSIONS

- **Introduction**
  - FEMINIST SENSITIVITIES OF TRANSLATION
  - JEWISH SENSITIVITIES OF TRANSLATION (NEW TESTAMENT)
  - TRANSLATING THE NAME OF GOD
  - THE NATURE OF BIBLE TRANSLATION
- **Jewish Languages**
  - JUDEO-PERSIAN
  - JUDEO-TARTAR

THE CANON, TEXT, AND EDITIONS

CANON

General Titles

There is no single designation common to all Jews and employed in all periods by which the Jewish Scriptures have been known. The earliest and most diffused Hebrew term was *Ha-Sefarim* ("The Books"). Its antiquity is supported by its use in Daniel in reference to the prophets (Dan. 9:2). This is how the sacred writings are frequently referred to in tannaitic literature (Meg. 1:8; MK 3:4; Git. 4:6; Kelim 15:6; et al.). The Greek-speaking Jews adopted this usage and translated it into their vernacular as τά βιβλία. The earliest record of such is the Letter of *Aristeas (mid-second century B.C.E.) which uses the singular form (v. 316, ἐν τῇ βίβλε) for the Pentateuch. The translator of The Wisdom of *Ben Sira into Greek (c. 132 B.C.E.) similarly employs "The Books" to designate the entire Scriptures (Ecclus., prologue, v. 25 "καὶ τά λοιπά τῶν βιβλίων"). It is from this Hellenistic Jewish usage of τά βιβλία, which entered European languages through its Latin form, that the English "Bible" is derived.

The term *Sifrei ha-Kodesh* (*Sifre ha-Qodesh*; "Holy Books"), although not found in Hebrew literature before the Middle Ages, seems to have been used occasionally by Jews even in pre-Christian times. The author of I Maccabees (12:9), who certainly wrote in Hebrew (c. 136–135 B.C.E.), speaks of "the Holy Books". In the early first century C.E., the Greek writer of II Maccabees 8:23 mentions "the Holy Book" (… τὴν ἱεράν βίβλον) and toward the end of that century, both Josephus (Ant., 20:261) and Pope Clement I (*First Epistle*, 43:1) refer to "the Holy Books" (αἱ ἱεραὶ βίβλοι). The appelation is rare, however, since the increasing restriction of *sefer* in rabbinic Hebrew to sacred literature rendered superfluous any further description. On the other hand, *Kitvei ha-Kodesh* (*Kitve ha-Qodesh*; "Holy Writings"), is fairly common in tannaitic sources as a designation for the Scriptures (Shab. 16:1; Er. 10:3; Yad. 3:2, 5; 4:6; BB 1:6; Par. 10:3). Here the definition is required since the Hebrew כתב (*ktb*) did not develop a specialized meaning and was equally employed for secular writing (cf. Tosef., Yom Tov 4:4). The title "Holy Writings" was also current in Jewish Hellenistic and in Christian circles, appearing in Greek as αἱ ἱεραὶ γραφαὶ (Philo, Fug. 1:4; Clement's *First Epistle* 45:2; 53:1), as τά ἱερά γράμματα (Philo, Mos. 2:290, 292; Jos., Ant., 1:13; 10:210; et al.). Closely allied to the preceding is the title *Ha-Katuv* ("The Scripture"; Pe'ah 8:9; Ta'an. 3:8; Sanh. 4:5; Avot 3:7, 8, et al.) and the plural *Ha-Ketuvim* ("The Scriptures"; Yad. 3:5 et al.). These, too, were taken over by the Jews of Alexandria in the Greek equivalent, probably the earliest such example being the Letter of Aristeas (vv. 155, 168, διά τῆς γραΦῆς). This term was borrowed by the early Christians (ἡ γραΦή John 2:22; Acts 8:32; II Tim 3:16 et al.; αἱ γραφαί Mark 12:24; I Cor. 15:34 et al.; τά γράμματα John 5:47).

These uses of the Hebrew root *ktb* ("to write") to specify the Scriptures have special significance, for they lay emphasis on the written nature of the text in contradistinction to the oral form in which the rabbinic teachings were transmitted. In the same way, *Mikra* (*Miqra'*; lit. "reading"), another term for the Bible current among the rabbis, serves to underline both the vocal manner of study and the central role that the public reading of the Scriptures played in the liturgy of the Jews. The designation is found in tannaitic sources (Ned. 4:3; Avot 5:21; TJ, Ta'an, 4:2, 68a), but it may be much older, as Nehemiah 8:8 suggests. It is of interest that *Miqra'* as the Hebrew for "Bible" achieved wide popularity among Jews in the Middle Ages The acronym תנ"ך (*TaNaKh*), derived from the initial letters of the names of the three divisions of the Bible (*Torah, Nevi'im, Ketuvim*), became similarly popular.

Still another expression for the Scriptures is *Torah, used in the widest sense of the term as the revelation of religion. While it is only occasionally so employed for the Bible in rabbinic literature (cf. MK 5a with respect to Ezek. 39:15; Sanh. 91b citing Ps. 84:5; PR 3:9, in reference to Eccles. 12:12), the fact that νόμος, the Greek rendering of Torah, is found in the New Testament in the same way (John 10:34, quoting Ps. 82:6) indicates that it may once have been in more common use among Jews.

Thoroughly Christian is the characterization "Old Testament" (i.e., Covenant; II Cor, 3:14; cf. Heb. 9:15–18). This term is used to distinguish the Jewish Bible from the "New Testament" (i.e., Covenant; I Cor. 11:25; II Cor. 3:6; Christian interpretation of Jeremiah 31:30–32). At the same time, it is possible that the designation "Testament" (i.e., "Covenant," Gr.: διαθήκη) may have been a reflection of an extended use among Jews of the Hebrew *berit* ("covenant") or *Sefer ha-Berit* ("Book of the Covenant"; Ex. 24:7; II Kings 23:2, 21). Jeremiah (31:30–32) himself uses "covenant" and "Torah" synonymously, and the "Book of the Torah" found in the Temple (II Kings 22:8, 10) is alternatively styled the "Book of the Covenant" (*ibid.* 23:2, 21). The Wisdom of Ben Sira (24:23) actually uses the latter term βιβλως διαθήκης) parallel with Torah (νόμος), and a similar usage is found in I Maccabees 1:56–57.

[Nahum M. Sarna]

The Canon

The term as applied to the Bible designates specifically the closed nature of the corpus of sacred literature accepted as authoritative because it is believed to be divinely revealed. The history of the word helps to explain its usage. "Canon" derives ultimately from an old Semitic word with the meaning of "reed" or "cane" (Heb. קנה), later used for "a measuring rod" (cf. Ezek. 40:5), both of which senses passed into Greek (κάννα, κανών). Metaphorically, it came to be used as a rule or standard of excellence and was so applied by the Alexandrian grammarians to the Old Greek classics. In the second century, κανών had come to be used in Christian circles in the sense of "rule of faith." It was the Church Fathers of the fourth century C.E. who first applied "canon" to the sacred Scriptures.

No exact equivalent of this term is to be found in Jewish sources although the phrase *Sefarim Ḥiẓonim* ("external books"; Sanh. 10:1), i.e., uncanonical, is certainly its negative formulation. However, tannaitic literature does employ the phrase *mettame et ha-Yadayim* ("rendering the hands unclean") to convey what is commonly understood by "canonical." According to rabbinic enactment, hands that came into direct contact with any biblical book contracted uncleanness in the second degree, so that if they then touched *terumah* without prior ritual washing they rendered it unfit for priestly consumption (Kelim 15:6; Yad. 3:2; 4:6). Whatever the true origin and purpose of this legislation (Yad. 3:3–5; Tosef., Yad. 2:19; Shab. 13b–14a; TJ, Shab. 1:6, 3c), the effect was to make the phrase "rendering the hands unclean" synonymous with canonical. Hence, rabbinic discussions about the full canonicity or otherwise of Ecclesiastes, Song of Songs (Eduy. 5:3; Yad. 3:5; Tosef., Yad. 2:14), Esther (Meg. 7a), Ben Sira, and other books (Tosef., Yad. 2:13) are expressed in terms of this formula.

THE SIGNIFICANCE OF THE CANON. The concept enshrined in the "canon" is distinctively and characteristically Jewish. Through it the canonized Scriptures were looked upon as the faithful witness to the national past, the embodiment of the hopes and dreams of a glorious future, and the guarantee of their fulfillment. They constituted, in time, the main source for the knowledge of Hebrew and typified the supreme standard of stylistic excellence. Through the instrumentality of the Oral Law they represented the force of truth, wisdom, law, and morality. In short, the development of the canon proved to be a revolutionary step in the history of religion, and the concept was consciously adopted by Christianity and Islam.

THE PROCESS OF CANONIZATION. It should be noted, however, that the above refers to the canon solely in respect of its religious connotation. There is evidence that as early as the second half of the second millennium B.C.E., the classical literary texts of Mesopotamia were beginning to assume standardized form. There emerged a widely diffused, recognizable body of literature with fixed authoritative texts, the sequence and arrangement of which were firmly established. This discovery is significant because it provides an important precedent for the external features of canonical literature, and it means that the process of canonical development could have begun quite early in Israel's history. Unfortunately, there is no direct information about the origins of the canon, nor can the criteria of selectivity adopted by those who fixed it be ascertained.

It is clear that the books that make up the Bible cannot possibly have contained the entire literary production of ancient Israel. The Scriptures themselves bear testimony to the existence of an extensive literature which is now lost. The "*Book of the Wars of the Lord" (Num. 21:14) and the "*Book of Jashar" (Josh. 10:13; II Sam. 1:18) are certainly very ancient. Prophetic compositions are ascribed to Samuel, Nathan, and Gad (I Chron. 29:29) of the early monarchy period and to Ahijah, Jedo/Iddo, and Shemaiah from the time of the division of the kingdom (II Chron. 9:29; 12:5; 13:22). The references to the chronicles of King David (Chron. 27:24), of Solomon (I Kings 11:41), and of the Kings of Israel and Judah (*ibid.* 14:19, 29; I Chron. 9:1; II Chron. 16:11; 20:34; 27:7; 32:32; 33:18) all bear witness to royal annalistic sources no longer extant. A category of literature called "Midrash" (II Chron. 13:22; 24:27) is also ascribed to the times of the monarchy, and a book of dirges to the end of that period (II Chron. 35:25). While it is true that in many of these instances it is possible that the same work has been referred to under different titles and that the caption *sefer* might indicate a section of a book rather than the whole, it cannot be doubted that numerous other works must have existed which were not mentioned in the Bible. In fact, the very concept of a scriptural canon presupposes a process of selection extending over a long period.

The quantitative disproportion between the literary productions and the literary remains of ancient Israel is extreme. The main factor at work was the natural struggle for survival. The absence of mass literacy, the labor of hand copying, and the perishability of writing materials in an inhospitable climate all combined to limit circulation, restrict availability, and reduce the chances of a work becoming standard. In addition, the Land of Israel was more frequently plundered and more thoroughly devastated than any other in the ancient Near East. At the same time, in the historical realities of the pre-Exilic period Israel's cultural productions had scant prospects of being disseminated beyond its natural frontiers. Developments within Israel itself also contributed. The change of script that occurred in the course of Persian hegemony doubtless drove out of circulation many books, while the mere existence of canonized corpora almost inevitably consigned excluded compositions to oblivion.

Certainly there were other books, including some of those cited above, which were reputed holy or written under the inspiration of the divine spirit, but why they did not enter the canon cannot be determined. The possibility of chance as a factor in preservation cannot be entirely dismissed. Some works probably survived because of their literary beauty alone. A very powerful instrument must have been scribal and priestly schools which, by virtue of their inherent conservatism, would tend to transmit the basic study texts from generation to generation. Similarly, the repertoire of professional guilds of Temple singers would be self-perpetuating, as would the liturgies recited on specific occasions in the Jerusalem Temple and the provincial shrines. Material that appealed to national sentiment and pride, such as the narration of the great events of the past and the basic documents of the national religion, would, particularly if employed in the cult, inevitably achieve wide popularity and be endowed with sanctity. Not everything that was regarded as sacred or revealed was canonized; but sanctity was the indispensable ingredient for canonicity. It was not, in general, the stamp of canonization that conferred holiness upon a book – rather the reverse. Sanctity antedated and preconditioned the formal act of canonization, which in most cases, simply made final a long-existing situation. Of course, the act of canonization, in turn, served to reinforce, intensify, and perpetuate the attitude of reverence, veneration, and piety with which men approached the Scriptures, and itself became the source of authority that generated their unquestioned acceptance as the divine word.

CONTENTS AND TITLES OF THE BOOKS. The Jewish Bible is composed of three parts, designated in Hebrew: *Torah* (תורה), *Nevi'im* (נביאים), and *Ketuvim* (כתובים). The earliest name for the first part of the Bible seems to have been "The Torah of Moses." This title, however, is found neither in the Torah itself, nor in the works of the pre-Exilic literary prophets. It appears in Joshua (8:31–32; 23:6) and Kings (I Kings 2:3; II Kings 14:6; 23:25), but it cannot be said to refer there to the entire corpus. In contrast, there is every likelihood that its use in the post-Exilic works (Mal. 3:22; Dan. 9:11, 13; Ezra 3:2; 7:6; Neh. 8:1; II Chron. 23:18; 30:16) was intended to be comprehensive. Other early titles were "The Book of Moses" (Ezra 6:18; Neh. 13:1; II Chron. 35:12; 25:4; cf. II Kings 14:6) and "The Book of the Torah" (Neh. 8:3) which seems to be a contraction of a fuller name, "The Book of the Torah of God" (Neh. 8:8, 18; 10:29–30; cf. 9:3).

With the widespread dissemination of the Torah in the generations following the activities of *Ezra and *Nehemiah, it became customary, for strictly nonliturgical purposes and for convenience of handling, to transcribe the work on five separate scrolls; hence the Greek name ἡ πεντάτευχος (βίβλος), "the five-volumed [book]," which has passed into English as Pentateuch. In rabbinic literature the Hebrew equivalent is "The Five Books of the Torah" (*Ḥameshet Sifrei Torah*; TJ, Meg. 1:7, 70d; *Ḥamishah Sifrei Torah*; TJ, Sot. 5:8, 20d), or "The Five Fifth-parts of the Torah" (*Ḥamishah Ḥomshei* (popularly, but inaccurately called *Ḥumshei*) *Torah*; Ḥag. 14a; TJ, Sanh. 10:1, 28a; Sanh. 44a).

The English names for the books of the Torah – Genesis, Exodus, Leviticus, Numbers, and Deuteronomy – derive from those of the Latin Bible which, in turn, have their origins in titles current among the Greek-speaking Jews, who translated Hebrew designations in use among their coreligionists in Palestine. These titles are descriptive of the contents or major theme of the respective books and they have partly survived in rabbinic literature and medieval Hebrew works in these forms: *Sefer Beri'at ha-Olam* ("The Book of the Creation of the World"); *Sefer Yeẓi'at Miẓrayim* ("The Book of the Exodus from Egypt"); *Torat Kohanim* ("The Book of the Priestly Code"); *Ḥomesh ha-Pekuddim* (*Ḥomesh ha-Pequddim*; "The Book of the Numbered"), *Mishneh Torah* ("The Repetition of the Torah"; cf. TJ, Meg. 3:7, 74b et al.). Another method of naming was to entitle a book by its opening word or words, or by its first significant word; cf. the Babylonian "When on High" and "Let me Praise the Lord of Wisdom." This was common in rabbinic sources (*Elleh ha-Devarim*; "These Are the Words" = Deuteronomy, Sot. 7:8; Gen. R. 3:5; TJ, Meg. 3:1, 74a) and has remained the most popular mode of designation in Hebrew to the present time. Finally, there is also evidence that ordinal numbers were used (cf. Gen. R. 3:5; TJ, Meg. 3:1, 74a).

The second division of the Bible is known as *Nevi'im* ("Prophets"), later subdivided into "Former Prophets" and "Latter Prophets." This distinction, one of convenience only, serves to differentiate between the narrative, historical works – Joshua, Judges, Samuel, and Kings – and the (largely poetic) literary creations of the prophetic orators Isaiah, Jeremiah and Ezekiel, and the Twelve "minor" prophets – Hosea, Joel, Amos, Obadiah, Jonah, Micah, Nahum, Habbakuk, Zephaniah, Haggai, Zechariah, and Malachi. The popular epithet "minor" in connection with these twelve has a solely quantitative connotation and is no indication of relative importance. The names of the books are based upon the central figure or reputed author. The subdivision of the Prophets into "Former" and "Latter" was not known in the modern sense in talmudic times. The rabbis employed "former" in reference to the prophets up to the destruction of the First Temple (Sot. 9:12; Ta'an. 4:2; Sot. 48b; cf. Zech. 1:4; 7:7, 12), and reserved "latter" exclusively for the postexilic prophets; Haggai, Zechariah, and Malachi (Tosef., Sot. 13:2; Sot. 48b).

The *Ketuvim* ("Writings," Hagiographa), the third division of the Bible, is a varied collection composed of liturgical poetry – Psalms and Lamentations; secular love poetry – Song of Songs; wisdom literature – Proverbs, Job, and Ecclesiastes; and historical works – Ruth, Chronicles, Ezra, Nehemiah, Esther, and a blend of history and prophecy in the Book of Daniel.

This tripartite division of the Scriptures is simply a matter of historical development and does not, in essence, represent a classification of the books according to topical or stylistic categories. The Hellenistic Jews, apparently sensitive to the more or less random nature of the organization of biblical literature, attempted to effect a more systematic arrangement (see Hellenistic Canon, below).

The Tripartite Canon

The earliest sources consistently refer to the three corpora of scriptural books. *Ben Sira, approximately 180 B.C.E., speaks of "the Law of the Most High," "the wisdom of the ancients," and "prophecies" (Ecclus. 39:1). His grandson who wrote the Prologue to the Book of Ben Sira (c. 132 B.C.E.) refers explicitly to "the Law and the Prophets and the others that followed them," "the law and the prophets and the other books of our fathers," "the law…, the prophecies and the rest of the books." The author of II Maccabees (2:2–3, 13) mentions "the Law," "the kings and prophets, the writings of David…." *Philo is familiar with the Law, the "Prophets and the Psalms and other Writings" (Cont. 25). Josephus knows of the "five books of Moses," "the Prophets" and "the remaining… books" (Apion, 1:39–41). The same threefold arrangement is specified in the New Testament. To the author of Luke (24:32, 44) the Scriptures consist of "the Law of Moses and the Prophets and the Psalms."

From these sources it becomes clear that the third collection of Scriptures was not known by any fixed name. In fact, it was often not referred to by any name at all. IV Maccabees (18:10) mentions simply the "Law and the Prophets" even though Daniel, Psalms, and Proverbs are included in the designation (18:13–16). It must have been a widespread practice to refer to the entire Bible in this manner for it is encountered in the most diverse sources, rabbinic (Tosef., BM 11:23), New Testament (Matt. 5:17 7:12; 11:13; 22:40; Luke 16:16; John 1:45; Rom. 3:21), and the Scrolls from the Judean Desert (1QS 1:2–3). All this can mean only one thing: the *Ketuvim* were canonized much later than the Prophets and the tripartite canon represents three distinct and progressive stages in the process of canonization. This is not to say, however, that there is any necessary correlation between the antiquity of the individual books within a given corpus and the date of the canonization of the corpus as a whole. Further, a clear distinction has to be made between the age of the material and the time of its redaction, the period of its attaining individual canonicity and the date that it became part of a canonized corpus.

THE CANONIZATION OF THE TORAH (PENTATEUCH). Where is this differentiation more applicable than in respect of the Torah. A clear distinction must be made between the literature of the Torah and the Torah book. Whatever the details of the incredibly complex history of the pentateuchal material, it is beyond doubt that much of it is of great antiquity and was venerated at an early period. The traditional doctrine of Mosaic authorship of the entire Torah has its source in Deuteronomy 31:9–12, 24, more than in any other passage. But the reference here seems more likely to be to the succeeding song (Deut. 32), as is indicated by verses 19 and 22. The Torah itself contains no explicit statement ascribing its authorship to Moses, while Mosaic attribution is restricted to legal and ritual prescription and is hardly to be found in connection with the narrative material. Moreover, the term "Torah" (which means "teaching," as well as "rule" and "law," has to be examined in each case in its own context and in no instance can it be unequivocally understood in its later, comprehensive sense. In fact, the phrase "Torah of Moses" is not pentateuchal.

An important stage in the history of the pentateuchal canon is the tale of the chance finding of the "book of the Torah" in 622 B.C.E. as described in II Kings 22–23; II Chronicles 34. It is highly significant that there is no suggestion that the book is new. Indeed, given the renewed interest in antiquity, and the veneration of the past that marked the Near East of the seventh century B.C.E. and the following two or three centuries, newness would have been no virtue. The enquiry of the prophetess Huldah and her reply serve to authenticate the book and its message. The "Torah" was publicly read and accepted as binding in a national covenant ceremony. The identity of the book is not given, nor is it termed Mosaic in direct speech (II Kings 23:25 and II Chron. 34:14 are editorial remarks). Yet insofar as the ensuing reform of the cult expresses precisely the leading motifs of *Deuteronomy, it may be assumed that the ceremony described represents the beginning of the formation of the Pentateuch, not as literature, but as a sacred book.

Division	Subdivision	Book	Chapters	The Twelve Prophets	Chapters
The Law *Torah* **Pentateuch**		Genesis	50 Chapters		
		Exodus	40		
		Leviticus	27		
		Numbers	36		
		Deuteronomy	34		
The Prophets *Nevi'im*	Former Prophets	Joshua	24		
		Judges	21		
		I Samuel	31		
		II Samuel	24		
		I Kings	22		
		II Kings	25		
	Later Prophets	*Isaiah	66	Hosea	14
		Jeremiah	52	Joel	4
		Ezekiel	48	Amos	9
		The Twelve Prophets		Obadia	1
				Jonah	4
				Micah	7
				Nahum	3
				Habakkuk	3
The Writings *Ketuvim* **Hagiographa**		Psalms	150	Zephaniah	3
				Haggai	2
		Proverbs	31	Zechariah	14
		Job	42	Malachi	3
	Five Scrolls *Megilot*	Song of Songs	8		
		Ruth	4		
		Lamentations	5		
		Ecclesiastes	12		
		Esther	10		
		Daniel	12		
		Ezra	10		
		Nehemiah	13		
		I Chronicles	29		
		II Chronicles	36		

The first report of the reading of the Torah in public assembly subsequent to Josiah comes from the post-Exilic period, namely, the ceremony conducted in Jerusalem by Ezra, approximately 444 B.C.E. (Neh. 8–10). This ceremony cannot be the occasion of the canonization of the Pentateuch, as has often been claimed, since the initiative for the public reading comes from the people and there is no hint that the promulgation of a new law is involved. The book is called "the book of the Torah of Moses which the Lord commanded Israel" (Neh. 8:1) and the emphasis is on its dissemination and exposition. It would appear that the Torah, or at least some form of it, had achieved canonical status.

Further evidence that the Torah had already been canonized by this time is provided by the Chronicler and by Samaritan tradition. The former, writing approximately 400 B.C.E., frequently appeals to the "Torah of Moses" and shows familiarity with every book of the Pentateuch. The Samaritans adopted the entire Torah together with the belief in its Mosaic authorship. Since hostility to the Judeans was already acute in Ezra's time and since the Samaritan-Jewish schism could not have taken place much after this, it follows that the canonization of the Pentateuch could not then have been a very recent event.

It may safely be assumed that the work of collection, fixing, and preservation of the Torah took place in the Babylonian exile (cf. Ezra 7:14, 25). But our extant sources preserve no recollection of a formal canonization.

THE CANONIZATION OF THE PROPHETS. The existence of the Torah Book served as a stimulus to the collection and organization of the literature of the prophets. A consistent tradition, repeatedly formulated in rabbinic sources, regards Haggai, Zechariah, and Malachi as the last of the prophets, the "divine spirit" having ceased to be active in Israel with their death (Tosef., Sot. 13:2; Sot. 48b; Yoma 9b; Sanh. 11a). Indeed, the absence of prophecy was regarded as one of the features that characterized the Second Temple period as opposed to the First (TJ, Ta'an. 2:1, 65a; Yoma 21b). Josephus, too, reflects this same tradition (Apion, 1:39–41). By the middle of the second century B.C.E., the institution was accepted as having lapsed (I Macc. 9:27; cf. 4:46; 14:41).

That contemporary prophecy was falling into discredit soon after the return from the exile is clear from Zechariah 13:2–5, and it is quite likely that the closing verses of the last prophetic book (Mal. 3:22–24) are actually an epilogue to the entire collection indirectly expressing recognition of the cessation of prophecy and the hope of its eschatological renewal (cf. I Macc. 4:45; 14:41; 1QS 9:11). The cessation of prophecy could thus be understood ideologically as part of the spiritual punishment that Israel must endure for its sins (Jer. 18:18; Ezek. 7:26; Amos 8:11–12; Micah 3:6–7). More important was the ironic fact that once the writings of the great prophets of the past became immortalized in written form, it became increasingly difficult for living prophets to compete with them.

The tradition declaring the prophetic canon to have been closed during the era of Persian hegemony, i.e., by 323 B.C.E., can be substantiated by several unrelated facts. That Chronicles belongs to the *Ketuvim* and neither displaced nor supplemented Samuel-Kings in the Prophets is best explained on the assumption that the latter were already sealed at the time Chronicles was canonized. Similarly, the omission of Daniel from the Prophets (cf. Sanh. 94a) would be inexplicable if their canonization occurred in Hellenistic times. The absence from the Prophets of Greek words or of any reference to the historical fact of the downfall of the Persian empire and the transition to Greek rule provides further evidence. Notwithstanding assertions to the contrary, the tannaitic discussions about Ezekiel (Ḥag. 13a) have nothing to do with the history of canonization. The suggestion to relegate the book to the bibliocrypt (*lignoz*) was intended solely to remove it from common use. In fact, only sacred things could be so treated. Apparently, some time must have elapsed between the canonization of the Torah and that of the Prophets, since only the former and not the latter were publicly read at the great assemblies described in Nehemiah 8–10, while the Samaritans, who became schismatic in the days of Ezra or soon after, received the Torah but not the Prophets.

THE CANONIZATION OF THE KETUVIM (HAGIOGRAPHA). The third collection of biblical books does not constitute a unified entity either contextually or ideologically. Many of the books were certainly written while prophets were still active and the books were individually canonized quite early. They were excluded from the prophetic collection because their inspiration appeared to be human rather than Divine, or because they did not otherwise conform to the special ideological content or historical-philosophic framework of that corpus. This would be true of such works as Psalms and Proverbs. Other books, like Ezra, Chronicles, and Daniel, must have been written too late for inclusion in the Prophets. They were certainly canonical, as was Job too, by the generation before the destruction of the Second Temple (Yoma 1:6). At the same time, there is plenty of evidence to show that the collection of the *Ketuvim* as a whole, as well as some individual books within it, was not accepted as being finally closed until well into the second century C.E. As noted above, the practice of calling the entire Scriptures the "Torah and Prophets" presupposes a considerable lapse of time between the canonization of the second and third parts of the Bible. The fact that the last division had no fixed name points in the same direction. Even the finally adopted designation "*Ketuvim*" is indeterminate, since it is also used in rabbinic Hebrew in the two senses of the Scriptures in general and of individual texts in particular.

Other indications of lateness in *Ketuvim* are that the Song of Songs contains two Greek words (3:9, אַפִּרְיוֹן = palanquin; 4:4, תַּלְפִּיּוֹת = τηλῶπις = far-off), as does Daniel (3:5, 15, סוּמְפֹּנְיָה = συμφωνία = bagpipe; 3:5, 7, 10, 15, פְּסַנְתֵּרִין = Ψαλτήριον), קיתרס = κίθαρις which even refers to the break-up of the Greek empire (by name 18:21; 11:2) and which most likely did not achieve its final form before approximately 167 B.C.E. (For the influence of Persian and Greek on the Book of Ecclesiastes see *Ecclesiastes.) Ben Sira (c. 180 B.C.E.), who shows familiarity with all other biblical books, does not mention Daniel or Esther. The latter book, in fact, seems not to have been accepted among the sectarians of Qumran; at least no fragments of it have yet turned up among the scrolls from the Judean Desert. Indeed, that there was once a certain reserve in respect of the sanctity of the Book of Esther is apparent from rabbinic discussion (Meg. 7a; cf. Sanh. 100a).

The ambivalent attitude on the part of the rabbis to the

Wisdom of Ben Sira is highly significant. The fact that in the middle of the second century C.E. it was necessary to emphasize the uncanonical status of this book (Tosef., Yad. 2:13) and to forbid its reading (TJ, Sanh. 10:1, 28a) proves that the corpus of *Ketuvim* was still fluid at this time, and that Ben Sira had acquired a measure of sanctity in the popular consciousness. Despite the ban, the book continued to achieve wide circulation. The *amoraim* even quote from it, employing the introductory terminology otherwise exclusively reserved for Scripture (cf. Nid. 16b *di-khetiv*; Ber. 55b *she-ne'emar*). In one instance, a third-generation Babylonian *amora* actually cites Ben Sira as *Ketuvim* as opposed to Torah and Prophets (BK 92b).

It is true that in the generation after the destruction of the Temple the author of IV Esdras 14:41–46 (cf. Joseph., Apion, 1:39–41) seems to imply a closed biblical canon of 24 books; nevertheless, tannaitic and amoraic disputes about the canonicity of Proverbs, Song of Songs, and Ecclesiastes (Eduy. 5:3; Yad. 3:5; ARN 1:2), as well as of Esther (Meg. 7a), show that the widely held, though unsupported, view that the formal and final canonization of the *Ketuvim* occurred at the Synod of Jabneh (c. 100 C.E.) has to be considerably modified. More probably, decisions taken on that occasion came to be widely accepted and thus regarded as final in succeeding generations.

The Hellenistic Canon

The needs of the Hellenistic Jews, whether of Alexandria in particular or of the Greek-speaking Diaspora in general, led to the translation of the Bible into Greek. Beginning with the Torah about the middle of the third century B.C.E. the process took many centuries to complete. The formation of much of the Greek canon was thus coeval with the emergence of the Hebrew Bible as a sealed collection of sacred literature. The final product, however, diverged from the Hebrew – apart from the problem of the text – in two important respects. It adopted a different principle in the grouping and sequence of the biblical books, and it included works not accepted into the normative Hebrew canon. It must be understood, however, that, with the exception of a few fragments, all extant manuscripts of the Greek Bible are of Christian origin, and while it is reasonable to assume a Jewish prototype, the content and form of the Hellenistic Jewish canon cannot be known with certainty.

The Greek Ben Sira (prologue) clearly shows that the Palestinian tripartite division of the Bible was known in Alexandria in the second century B.C.E.; yet the Greek Bible does away with the *Ketuvim* as a corpus and redistributes the books of the second and third divisions according to categories of literature, thus creating a quadripartite canon of Torah, history, poetic and didactic writings, and prophecy. The sequence of books in the Greek Bible varies greatly in the uncial manuscripts and among the different patristic and synodical lists of the Eastern and Western churches. The Torah, however, always takes priority, followed by the Former Prophets. Ruth is attached to Judges, sometimes before, sometimes after it. The Minor Prophets invariably appear as a unit, though in slightly different order (Hosea, Amos, Micah, Joel, Obadiah, Jonah, etc.) and frequently preceding the three major prophets. Lamentations is affixed to Jeremiah, its reputed author. Of those books excluded from the Hebrew canon but included in the Greek Bibles, the number varies, but the following are found in the fullest collections: I Esdras (Ezra), Wisdom of Solomon, Wisdom of Ben Sira, Judith, Tobit, Baruch, the Letter of Jeremiah, I–IV Maccabees, and the Psalms of Solomon.

The order of the books in the Greek Bibles is illustrated in the table below:

Order of the Books in the Greek Bibles
(the Hebrew Codex Aleppo is given for comparison)

CODEX VATICANUS (B)	CODEX ALEXANDRINUS (A)	CODEX ALEPPO (C)
4th century	5th century	10th century
Genesis-Judges	Genesis-Judges	Genesis-Judges
Ruth	Ruth	I–II Samuel
I–IV Kings	I–IV Kings	I–II Kings
(Samuel, Kings)	I–II Chronicles	
I–II Chronicles	Isaiah	
I Ezra (apochryphal)	Hosea	Jeremiah
II Ezra	Amos	Ezekiel
(Ezra-Nehemiah)	Micah	Hosea
Joel	Joel	
Psalms	Obadiah	Amos
Proverbs	Jonah	Obadiah
Ecclesiastes	Nahum	Jonah
Song of Songs	Habakkuk	Micah
Job	Zephaniah	Nahum
Wisdom of Solomon	Haggai	Habakkuk
Wisdom of Sirach	Zechariah	Zephaniah
Esther	Malachi	Haggai
Judith	Isaiah	Zechariah
Tobit	Jeremiah	Malachi
Baruch		
Hosea	Lamentations	I–II Chronicles
Amos	Letter of Jeremiah	Psalms
Micah	Daniel	Job
Joel	Ezekiel	Proverbs
Obadiah	Ruth	
Jonah	Esther	Ecclesiastes
Nahum	Tobit	Lamentations
Habakkuk	Judith	Esther
Zephaniah	I Ezra	Daniel
Haggai	II Ezra	Ezra
Zechariah	I–IV Maccabees	
Malachi	Psalms	
Isaiah	Job	
Jeremiah	Proverbs	
Baruch	Ecclesiastes	
Lamentations	Song of Songs	
Letter of Jeremiah	Wisdom of Solomon	
Ezekiel	Wisdom of Sirach	
Daniel	Psalms of Solomon	

The Number of Books

By dividing Samuel, Kings, and Chronicles into two books each, and by individually enumerating Ezra, Nehemiah, and the twelve minor prophets, English Bibles usually list 39 books. This reckoning, however, is not traditional, for the twelve were written on a single scroll and counted as one; Ezra and Nehemiah were likewise treated as a unit, and the convenient bisection of Samuel, Kings, and Chronicles was unknown in Hebrew Bibles before the Bomberg edition of 1521 (see Editions, below). In this way the traditional total of 24 books is obtained.

This number is consistently specified in the literature of the *amoraim* (cf. Ta'an. 5a) and is implicit in the tannaitic listing of the biblical books (BB 14b). It must be quite ancient for it is expressly mentioned as something well understood n IV Ezra 14:45, a passage deriving from about 100 C.E. From about this same period derives a variant tradition of Josephus limiting the canon to 22 books (Apion 1:39–41). It is possible that the Song of Songs and Ecclesiastes were not yet included in Josephus' Bible. More likely, however, the difference is to be explained by the practice of attaching Ruth to Judges or Psalms, and Lamentations to Jeremiah. Since many of the Church Fathers also mention a 22-book canon (cf. Origen in Eusebius, *Historia Ecclesiastica* 6:25, 1), it must be assumed that the observation of Josephus reflects a fairly widespread, if minority, Jewish scribal tradition that persisted for several centuries. Either way, the specified number really refers to the sum of separate scrolls used in transcribing the corpus of canonized literature. The artificiality of the number 24 and the absence of any authentic tradition to explain its origin are clear from the homiletics of the *amoraim*, who variously connected it with the like number of ornaments in Isaiah 3:18–24 (Ex. R. 41:5; Song. R. 4:11; Tanḥ. B., Ex. 111–117), of priestly and levitical courses in I Chron. 23:28; 24:4 (Num. R. 14:18; Eccles. R. 12:11; PR 3:9), and of the bulls brought as dedicatory offerings by the chieftains of the tribes (Num. 7:88; Num. R. 14:18).

It has been suggested, but with little probability, that Jewish practice may have been influenced by the pattern set by the Alexandrian division of the Odyssey and Iliad of Homer into 24 books each, an innovation itself dictated as much by the practical consideration of avoiding the inconvenience of handling a scroll containing more than 1,000 verses as by the desire to create a correspondence with the number of letters in the Greek alphabet. The 24-book division may have been regarded as a model for the national classics, especially because it is a multiple of 12, a number which was charged with special significance in the ancient world, even in the literary sphere. This is evidenced by the 12-tablet division of the Gilgamesh Epic, the 12 sections of the Theogony of Hesiod and the Laws of the Twelve Tablets. The 22-book division might well have been an adaptation of Greek practice to the Hebrew alphabetic enumeration.

The Order of the Books

In considering the arrangement of the biblical books in a specific sequence, two distinct problems have to be differentiated. The first relates to the very meaning of "order," the second to the underlying rationale of the diverse arrangements found in literary sources and manuscripts. The earliest list of biblical books is that preserved in an anonymous tannaitic statement (BB 14b):

> Our Rabbis taught: the order of the Prophets is Joshua, Judges, Samuel, Kings, Jeremiah, Ezekiel, Isaiah, and the Twelve…; the order of the Ketuvim is Ruth, the Book of Psalms, Job, Proverbs, Ecclesiastes, the Song of Songs, Lamentations, Daniel, the Scroll of Esther, Ezra, and Chronicles.

The question of "order" would normally apply to books produced as codices, rather than scrolls. However, the above-cited *baraita* cannot be later than the end of the second century C.E., whereas the codex was not accepted by Jews until many centuries later. Sarna seeks the solution in the library practices of the Mesopotamian and Hellenistic worlds.

The steady growth of collections, whether of cuneiform tablets or papyrus rolls, necessitated the introduction of rationalized and convenient methods of storing materials in ways that facilitated identification and expedited usage. At the same time, the requirements of the scribal schools engendered an established sequence in which the classic works were to be read or studied. This combination of library needs and pedagogic considerations would then be what lies behind the fixing of the order of the Prophets and *Ketuvim* as recorded in the list above. The reference would be to the order in which the individual scrolls in these two corpora were shelved and cataloged in the Palestinian archives and schools. Haran has challenged Sarna's theory on the grounds that the small number of the books of the Bible made literary cataloguing unnecessary. It would have been simple to follow Roman practice and lay out the scrolls on shelves divided by panels. Alternatively, scrolls might have been tagged as they were

The Order of the Latter Prophets

1. Talmud and three mss.	2. Two mss.	3. Eleven mss.	4. Five Early Editions
Jeremiah	Jeremiah	Jeremiah	Jeremiah
Ezekiel	Ezekiel	Ezekiel	Ezekiel
Isaiah	Isaiah	Isaiah	Isaiah
The Twelve	The Twelve	The Twelve	The Twelve

1. (1) The Babylonian Talmud; (2) 1280 C.E. Madrid, National Library, ms. no. 1; (3–5) London, British Museum, mss. Orient. 1474, Orient. 4227, Add. 1545.
2. (1) 1286 C.E. Paris, National Library; (2) London, British Museum, Orient. 2091.
3. (1) 916 C.E. Leningrad codex; (2) 1009 C.E. Leningrad ms.; (3–11) London, British Museum, mss. Orient. 1246 C.E., Arund. Orient. 16, Harley 1528, Harley 5710–11, Add. 1525, Add. 15251, Add. 15252, Orient. 2348, Orient, 2626–8.
4. (1) The first printed edition of the entire Bible, 1488 Soncino; (2) The second edition, 1491–93 Naples; (3) The third edition, 1492–1494 Brescia; (4) The first edition of the Rabbinic Bible, edited by Felix Pratensis, 1517 Venice; (5) The first edition of the Bible with the Masorah, edited by Jacob b. Ḥayyim, 1524–25 Venice.

The Order of the Hagiographa

	1. Talmud and Six mss.	2. Two mss.	3. Add. 15252	4. Adat. Devorim and three mss.	5. Ar. Or. 16	6. Or. 2626–28	7. Or. 2201	8. Five Early Editions
1	Ruth	Ruth	Ruth	Chronicles	Chronicles	Chronicles	Psalms	Psalms
2	Psalms	Psalms	Psalms	Psalms	Ruth	Psalms	Job	Proverbs
3	Job	Job	Job	Job	Psalms	Proverbs	Proverbs	Job
4	Proverbs	Proverbs	Proverbs	Proverbs	Job	Job	Ruth	Song of Songs
5	Ecclesiastes	Song of Songs	Song of Songs	Ruth	Proverbs	Daniel	Song of Songs	Ruth
6	Song of Songs	Ecclesiastes	Ecclesiastes	Song of Songs	Song of Songs	Ruth	Ecclesiastes	Lamentations
7	Lamentations	Lamentations	Lamentations	Ecclesiastes	Ecclesiastes	Song of Songs	Lamentations	Ecclesiastes
8	Daniel	Esther	Daniel	Lamentations	Lamentations	Lamentations	Esther	Esther
9	Esther	Daniel	Esther	Esther	Esther	Ecclesiastes	Daniel	Daniel
10	Ezra-Nehemiah	Ezra-Nehemiah	Ezra-Nehemiah	Daniel	Daniel	Esther	Ezra-Nehemiah	Ezra-Nehemiah
11	Chronicles	Chronicles	Chronicles	Ezra-Nehemiah	Ezra-Nehemiah	Ezra-Nehemiah	Chronicles	Chronicles

1. (1) The Talmud; (2) 1280 C.E. Madrid, University Library, codex no. 1; (3–7) London, British Museum, mss. Harley 1528, Add. 1525, Orient. 2212, Orient. 2375, Orient. 4227.
2. (1) 1286 C.E. Paris, National Library, mss. no. 1–3; (2) London, British Museum, Orient. 2091.
3. London, British Museum, Add. 15252.
4. (1) 1009 C.E. Leningrad ms.; (2) 1207 C.E. Adat Devorim; (3–4) London, British Museum, mss. Harley 5710–11, Add. 15251.
5. London, British Museum, Arund. Orient. 16.
6. London, British Museum, Orient. 2626–28.
7. 1246 C.E. London, British Museum, Orient. 2201.
8. The five early editions, see Table 1, note 4.

at Qumran, and much earlier in Mesopotamia. Haran suggests instead that the *baraita* reflects a time when scribes had begun to resort to larger scrolls containing several books rather than using one scroll per book. This technological change would have necessitated a fixed order. The silence about the Pentateuch in the *baraita* is due to the fact that its priority in its long fixed order was so universally known as to make it superfluous. As to the underlying principles that determined the sequence, it is clear that the historical books of the prophetical division are set forth as a continuous, consecutive narrative with Jeremiah and Ezekiel following in chronological sequence. The anomalous position of Isaiah after Ezekiel (reflected also in some manuscripts) (see Table: Order of the Latter Prophets) has been variously explained. According to the *Gemara* (BB 14b) contextual considerations were paramount:

> The Book of Kings ends with a record of destruction; Jeremiah deals throughout with destruction; Ezekiel commences with destruction and closes with consolation, while Isaiah is entirely consolation. Therefore, we juxtapose destruction to destruction and consolation to consolation.

This explanation is hardly adequate since Jeremiah contains prophecies of comfort and the observation on Isaiah applies only to chapters 40–66. Nor is it likely that the late exilic origin of the last 27 chapters of Isaiah determined its place after Ezekiel, since there is no evidence that the rabbis recognized the heterogeneous nature of the book. More persuasive, perhaps, is the thesis that the sequence Jeremiah, Ezekiel, Isaiah, and the Twelve was conditioned by their respective lengths in decreasing order. There may have been a tendency to place in close proximity prophets who were considered to have been contemporaries so that the great similarity between Isaiah 1:1 and Hosea 1:1 might well have been responsible for the juxtaposition of the books of Isaiah and the Twelve.

The *baraita* gives no list of the Minor Prophets. It simply designates them "the Twelve," implying that the order was well-known and universally accepted. The same conclusion is to be drawn from Ben Sira's reference to "the twelve prophets" (Ecclus. 49:10). Doubtless, the arrangement of the 12 small books, always written on a single roll, was based on chronological principles as understood by the religious authorities responsible for the canonization of the prophetic corpus. The present sequence is uniform in all Hebrew manuscripts and printed editions.

No reason for the tannaitic order of the *Ketuvim* is given in the *Gemara*, but it may be noted that the 11 books are arranged chronologically in groups according to rabbinic notions of their authorship. Ruth, which closes with the genealogy of David, precedes Psalms, which was ascribed to that king. Job follows, probably because of a tradition assigning the book to the time of the Queen of Sheba (BB 15b; cf. Job 1:15). Proverbs, Ecclesiastes, and Song of Songs were all attributed to Solomon; Lamentations was thought to have been written by Jeremiah; Daniel was credited to the exilic period and the last two to the Persian era. Notwithstanding the tannaitic notice, it would seem that the sequence of the *Ketuvim* was never really fixed, for the manuscripts and printed editions exhibit a variety of systems (see Table: Order of the Hagiographa). Nevertheless, the differences are restricted to specific books or clusters of books. In the manuscripts and early editions, Chronicles never appears other than at the beginning or end of the corpus. Ezra-Nehemiah is invariably either the penultimate or final book depending on the position of Chronicles. The three larger works: Psalms, Job, and Proverbs, always constitute a group, with Psalms invariably first and the other two interchanging. The Talmud itself lists the "three larger books of the *Ketuvim*" as Psalms, Proverbs, and Job (Ber. 57b), a variant possibly conditioned by the view that Job was among those who returned from the Babylonian exile (BB 15a).

The most unstable books in respect of their order in the *Ketuvim* are the five Scrolls (*Megillot*). Their position varies in the manuscripts and printed editions both as part of the corpus of *Ketuvim* and as separately attached to the Pentateuch (see Table: Order of the Megillot). Nowhere in rabbinic sources are all five listed in immediate succession, nor is the term "Five *Megillot*" used. The chronological sequence, according to reputed author, that underlies the tannaitic listing is essentially reflected in another talmudic source which identifies "the three smaller books of the *Ketuvim*" as the Song of Songs, Ecclesiastes, and Lamentations, in that order (Ber. 57b). In fact, six of eight main variations basically preserve this chronological principle (see Table: Order of the Hagiographa, cols. 1–5, 7). The practice of grouping all five *Megillot* together has its origin in the custom of reading these books on festival days: the Song of Songs on Passover, Ruth on Pentecost, Lamentations on the Ninth of Av, Ecclesiastes on Sukkot, and Esther on Purim (cf. Soferim 14:1, ed. Higger, p. 251–2). This is the order as it crystallized in the early printed Hebrew Bibles and in some manuscripts and early printed editions of the Pentateuch, to which all five *Megillot* have been attached.

The Order of the *Megillot* after the Pentateuch

1. mss. Nos. 1,2,3	2. mss. Nos. 4,5,6	3. mss. Nos. 7, 8	4. mss. No. 9	5. Early Editions
Song of Songs	Esther	Ruth	Ruth	Song of Songs
Ruth	Song of Songs	Song of Songs	Song of Songs	Ruth
Lamentations	Ruth	Ecclesiastes	Lamentations	Lamentations
Ecclesiastes	Lamentations	Lamentations	Ecclesiastes	Ecclesiastes
Esther	Ecclesiastes	Esther	Esther	Esther

The nine mss. collated for this Table are the following in the British Museum: (1) Add. 9400; (2) Add. 9403; (3) Add. 19776; (4) Harley 5706; (5) Add. 9404; (6) Orient. 2786; (7) Harley 5773; (8) Harley 15283; (9) Add. 15282.
The fifth column represents the order adopted in the first, second and third editions of the Hebrew Bible, as well as that of the second and third editions of Bomberg's Quarto Bible (Venice 1521, 1525), in all of which the five Megillot follow immediately after the Pentateuch

The final position of Chronicles is most remarkable since Ezra-Nehemiah follows naturally in continuation of the narrative. The anomaly is emphasized by the widespread support it received in the manuscripts and early printed editions. It would appear that the New Testament, too, reflects this arrangement (Matt. 23:35; Luke 11:51). As an explanation, it might be suggested that the position of Chronicles represents the chronology of canonization, though there is no evidence to support this. More likely, it resulted from a conscious attempt to place the biblical books within a narrative framework. Genesis and Chronicles both begin with the origin and development of the human race and both end with the promise of redemption and return to the Land of Israel. The two books actually employ the same key verbs in this connection (Gen. 50:24–25; II Chron. 36:23; פקד, עלה; *pkd* (*pqd*), *ʿlh*). Indeed, the messianic theme of the return to Zion as an appropriate conclusion to the Scriptures was probably the paramount consideration in the positioning of Chronicles. Further evidence that the arrangement of the Scriptures was intended to express certain leading ideas in Judaism may be sought in the extraordinary fact that the initial chapter of the Former Prophets (Josh. 1:8) and of the Latter Prophets (Isa. 1:10) and the closing chapter of the prophetical corpus (Mal. 3:22), as well as the opening chapter of the *Ketuvim* (Ps. 1:2), all contain a reference to Torah, a conscious assertion of the theological priority of the Torah.

The Languages of Scripture

The books of the Bible have come down in the Hebrew language with the exception of two words in Genesis (31:47), a single verse in Jeremiah (10:11), and sections of Daniel (2:4b–7:28) and Ezra (4:8–6:18; 7:12–26), all of which are in Aramaic. The problem of the language of Scripture is, however, more complicated than would appear on the surface and it constitutes part of the larger issue of the history of the growth and formation of the canon. Some scholars, for instance, regard Job, Ecclesiastes, and Chronicles, as well as the Hebrew sections of Daniel and Ezra-Nehemiah as translations, in whole or part, from Aramaic. This implies that the original is lost, and at once raises the possibility of error in the course of rendition from language to language. It should be noted, though, that in dealing with the problem of translation care must be taken to distinguish between Aramaisms and Aramaic influence on Hebrew style on the one hand, and a translation that may betray its Aramaic substratum on the other.

Even works unquestionably composed in Hebrew are not without their linguistic history. In dealing with biblical Hebrew it must be remembered that the language of Scripture represents a period of creativity covering several hundred years during which internal development inevitably took place. In general, it may be said that the poetic texts in the historical books have preserved the earliest strata of the language (Gen. 49; Ex. 15; Num. 23–24; Deut. 32; 33; Judg. 5), while the Hebrew of those works deriving from the postexilic period – like Haggai, Zechariah, Malachi, Ecclesiastes, Chronicles, Ezra-Nehemiah, and Daniel – exhibits features that distinguish the known characteristics of postbiblical Hebrew. In between there are several linguistic layers, the isolation of which is complicated by the relatively small amount of material available for comparison, the difficulties in dating the different documents, and the problem of distinguishing between the age of the material and the period of the final stage of its redaction. Much scholarly effort in recent years has been directed to identifying the specific linguistic features of Late Biblical Hebrew (LBH). Also, it is not known to what extent the editors "modernized" the language of the material they worked with. Comparative Semitic phonology and morphology make it certain that the present system of vocalization of the Hebrew consonants reflects the stage of Hebrew pronunciation more or less as it had crystallized in the Second Temple period. It can be said from internal biblical evidence (cf. Judg. 12:6) and from several inscriptions that there were important differences in dialect between northern Israel and southern Judah. Consequently, since much of the biblical literature originated in the north but was mediated through the Judean scribes, it must have been stylistically transformed to conform to the standard Jerusalemite dialect. Finally, in evaluating the language of the Bible, the problem of the reliability and integrity of the Hebrew consonantal text tradition cannot be overlooked.

TEXT

The History of the Biblical Text

In the medieval codices of the Hebrew Bible, as in the printed editions to the present times, the text generally comprises three distinct components. These are the consonants, the vowel symbols, and the liturgical, diacritical notations. The latter two elements were invented by the masoretes (see *Masorah) while the history of the consonantal text, with which this section is exclusively concerned, represents the crystallization of a textual critical process of very great antiquity and of remarkable complexity. The second edition of the Rabbinic Bible, edited by Jacob b. Ḥayyim and published by Daniel *Bomberg (Venice 1524/25), served as the model for all future printed editions (see Printed Editions, below). Between this date and that of the most ancient fragments of the Hebrew Scriptures found in the Judean Desert intervenes a period of approximately 2,000 years, and many more centuries of textual transmission separate the earliest documents from the *editio princeps* of a biblical book.

THE EARLIEST PERIOD (up to c. 300 B.C.E.) It is no longer possible to reconstruct the textual evolution of the Hebrew Scriptures between the time of the composition of an individual work and the age of the first known witnesses, approximately 300 B.C.E. The existence of divergent texts of the same books may be postulated since this is the only way to explain the variants in the many passages duplicated in the Bible. (II Sam. 22 = Ps. 18; II Kings 18:13–20:19 = Isa. 36–39; II Kings 24:18–25:30 = Jer. 52; Isa. 2:2–4 = Micah 4:1–3; Ps. 14=53; 40:14–18=70; 57:8–12 = 108: 2–6; 60:7–14 = 108; 7–14; 96 = I Chron. 16:23–33; Ps. 105:1–15 = I Chron. 16:8–22; 106:1, 47–48 = I Chron. 16:34–36; the parallels between Sam.–Kings and Chron.).

As late as the 13th century traditions were still preserved about a period of disorder in biblical texts and the textual-critical activities of the "Men of the Great Assembly" (David Kimḥi, preface to his commentary on Joshua). This conclusion is reinforced by the findings from caves in Qumran. Here a plurality of text-types has been discovered – a situation which must represent a state of affairs much older than its earliest documentation. Indeed, it may be argued that the very idea of canonicity carries with it an attitude of reverence for the text and fosters care and accuracy in its transmission. This would be particularly true of a written text since scribal activities would naturally be restricted to a relatively small circle of specialists. Furthermore, the use of sacred literature in public worship and in the curriculum of influential schools would tend to endow a certain version of a scriptural text with greater prestige. All these factors would tend to work in the direction of inhibiting the multiplication of textual versions and would serve to give some text-types greater prominence than others.

The situation presupposed here finds support in the history of Mesopotamian literature, where all the evidence points to the emergence of authoritative standard versions of the classical texts by the end of the second millennium B.C.E. As a consequence of this development, the great cuneiform literary texts appear in very limited editions despite wide geographic distribution and considerable chronological variability. A similar state of affairs is discernible in connection with the Greek classics. As early as the sixth century B.C.E. the production of a definitive text of the Odyssey and the Iliad was commissioned by Pisistratus, tyrant of Athens, though this is not necessarily the text that finally became predominant. From the third century B.C.E. on, considerable textual-critical work on the manuscripts of Homer to determine the correct readings was undertaken by scholars at the museum library of Alexandria. There is no reason why the textual history of the sacred Scriptures of Israel should have been more anarchic than that of the Mesopotamian and Greek classics. In fact, the existence of a fixed text of at least part of the Torah before the close of the pentateuchal canon is presupposed by the injunction in Deuteronomy (17:18–19) that the king have a copy of the law transcribed for himself for purposes of regular study, as well as by the prescription to hold a periodic public reading of the Law from an official copy deposited in the central sanctuary (Deut. 31:9–12, 26). There is no way of knowing, however, whether any one recension achieved greater national importance or prominence within this period. It can only be concluded that since the prototype of the text-family that ultimately achieved hegemony is present at Qumran, the history of that text must be much older.

THE SECOND PERIOD (c. 300 B.C.E.–First Century C.E.) The starting point, it should be noted, is somewhat arbitrary and is conditioned by the fortuitous existence of manuscript documentation; and the limiting point is fixed by the observation of a radical change after the destruction of the Temple. The evidence for development within this period involves Hebrew sources and Greek translations and is both direct and indirect. It is characterized by the diversity of text-types, though the number seems to have been very limited and each family of manuscripts appears to have maintained its homogeneity over a long period of time.

Until the discovery of the *Dead Sea Scrolls, the evidence of textual diversity in this period consisted mainly of the Samaritan *Pentateuch and the Septuagint; the latter must have been translated from a Hebrew source at variance with the received text. Further evidence for a still fluid state of the text is provided by the citations of Scripture found in the books of the *Apocrypha and by rabbinic traditions about the activities of the **soferim*. These latter are credited with responsibility for textual emendations (*tikkunei soferim*, Mekh., Shira, 6; Sif. Num. 84), for marking dislocated verses (*ibid.*; Shab. 115b–116a) and suspect readings (ARN[1] 34, 100–1; ARN[2] 37, 97; Sif. Num. 69), as well as for deletions (*itturei soferim*, Ned. 37b). Other rabbinic traditions tell of the need for "book correctors" (*maggihei sefarim*) in Jerusalem attached to the Temple (Ket. 106a; TJ, Shek. 4:3, 48a) and even of divergent readings in pentateuchal scrolls kept in the Temple archives (TJ, Ta'an 4:2, 68a; Sif. Deut. 356; ARN[2] 46, 65; Sof. 6:4).

This fluidity of text is precisely the situation that was revealed at Qumran, particularly Cave IV which has yielded about 100 manuscripts, complete or fragmentary. The outstanding phenomenon is the ability of the sect to tolerate, with no apparent disquiet, the simultaneous existence of divergent texts of the same book, as well as verbal and orthographic variety within the scope of a single recension. Clearly, an inviolable, sacrosanct, authoritative text did not exist at Qumran. Whether the identical conclusion is also valid for the normative Jewish community of Palestine in this period is less certain. It is true that there is nothing specifically sectarian about the Qumran Bible scrolls, either in the scribal techniques and conventions employed or in the nature of the divergent readings, which are decidedly neither tendentious nor ideological. Nevertheless, caution must be exercised in the use of the Qumran evidence for reconstruction of a generalized history of textual development in this period. The lack of more examples of the masoretic text-type may be solely accidental. It is also possible that this is less a library than a *genizah* which would tend to preserve discarded texts and so present a distorted picture. In many instances, the fragments are very small and are only *disjecta membra*, making the derivation of overall characteristics very hazardous. Finally, the isolated, cloistered, and segregated existence led by the sect of "covenanters," with its implacable hostility to the Jerusalem religious establishment, could well have insulated Qumran from normative developments elsewhere in Judea, where a less tolerant approach to textual diversity may have prevailed.

In fact, the rabbinic testimony cited above demonstrates the existence of a movement away from a plurality of recensions and toward textual stabilization. The textual-critical activities of the *soferim* are all directed to this end and they are expressly reported to have worked on a text fixed even in respect of the number of its letters (Kid. 30a). Whatever its intrinsic worth this talmudic tradition could not have arisen among the rabbis had the fixing of the text been recent. The presence of Temple-sponsored "book correctors" implies the acceptance at some point in the Second Temple period of an authoritative text by which the accuracy of other scrolls was measured (Ket. 106a; TJ, Shek. 4:3, 48a; Sanh. 2:6, 20c). The record of the variant Temple scrolls is a tradition concerned with an attempt to ensure just such a standardized recension. Indeed, that there existed an official Temple Scroll (*Sefer ha-Azarah*) which enjoyed high prestige is amply attested in rabbinic sources (TJ, Sanh. 2:6, 20c; Shek 4:3, 48a; MK 3:4; Kelim 15:6; cf. Jos., Wars, 7:150, 162), though it is not possible to tell exactly to what period they refer. Certainly, the seven rules of biblical hermeneutics, compiled but not invented by Hillel the Elder (Tosef., Sanh. 7:11; ARN[1] 37, 110; cf. Pes. 66a; TJ, Pes. 6:1, 33a), take the history of the attempt at textual stabilization at least back to the time of Herod.

Soon after the destruction of the Temple, Josephus (Apion, 1:8) wrote about the inviolate nature of the text of the Jewish Scriptures and it is clear that he regarded this as a virtue of long standing. Further proof for the existence of the notion of an authoritative text is provided by the Letter of Aristeas which is well aware of the circulation of carelessly written books of the Law (Arist. 30) and has Ptolemy send to the high priest in Jerusalem for a Hebrew text from which to make the Greek translation (*ibid.*, 33–40, 46; cf. 176). Once produced, this translation itself came to be regarded as sacrosanct by the Jews of Alexandria (*ibid.*, 311). Nevertheless, there is evidence from Qumran that the Greek translation was the object of much recensional activity, the purpose of which was to bring it into line with developments in the Hebrew texts current in Palestine. This phenomenon reveals, once again, both that the Hebrew text was still fluid and that there was a movement toward textual stabilization.

Within this period the notion of an authoritative text was well rooted outside the Qumran community. A very limited number of textual families is discernible, probably each having achieved local authority. Each family, however, exhibits internal textual variety. The religious leadership in Jerusalem appears to have recognized a fixed text and to have been engaged in textual-critical activity aligning divergent exemplars with it. The beginnings of this movement may possibly be traced to the Maccabean victories. At any rate, the recensional family that ultimately crystallized into what came to be known as "masoretic" is well represented among the Qumran collection, the most outstanding example being the Isaiah scroll (1QIsb).

THE THIRD PERIOD (First Century C.E.–Ninth Century C.E.) The existence of an official text with binding authority from the generation of the destruction of the Temple is clearly reflected in halakhic discussions. Zechariah b. ha-Kaẓẓav, who was apparently a priest in the Temple (cf. Ket. 2:9), based legal decisions on the presence of a conjunctive *vav* (Sot. 5:1). *Nahum of Gimzo, of the first generation of *tannaim*, employed the principle of "extension and limitation" in the interpretation of certain Hebrew particles (Ḥag. 12a; Pes. 22b), a hermeneutical system later developed to the full by R. *Akiva to whom not a word of the Torah, nor even a syllable or letter, was superfluous. Hence, he could derive a multiplicity of rules from each tittle on the letters of the Torah (Men. 29b). He, too, warned against teaching from "uncorrected" books (Pes. 112a) and emphasized the importance of the protective devices (*masoret*) for the Torah text (Avot 3:13). Further, it was in Akiva's day that the question arose as to whether the established consonantal text or the traditional manner of reading was to determine the halakhic interpretation (Mak. 7b; Sanh. 4a; Pes. 86b; Kid. 18b). R. *Ishmael, his contemporary, formulated the 13 *hermeneutical norms (Sifra 1:1) which presuppose a fixed recension. He also advised R. Meir to be extraordinarily meticulous in his work of transcribing sacred texts lest he omit or add a single letter (Er. 13a). This period is distinguished from its predecessors in that a single stabilized text attained unimpeachable authority and achieved hegemony over all others. This development seems to have occurred in the course of the first century C.E., probably as a consequence of the need for religiocultural cohesion and national unity following the destruction of the Temple. Before long, all other Hebrew recensions were discarded and passed into oblivion, leaving only a few traces behind.

It is true that in the generation after R. Akiva copies of the Torah made by R. Meir might still contain a few textual oddities (Gen. R. 9:5; 20:12), and medieval tradition could retain a record of variant readings found in a Torah scroll stored in the synagogue of Severus in Rome (*Bereshit Rabbati*, ed. Albeck, p. 209). It is also true that rabbinic literature has preserved several hundred deviations from the received text in scriptural quotations and in reconstructed readings underlying a specific piece of midrashic exegesis, while the same phenomenon may be discernible in citations in Jewish Palestinian apocryphal and pseudepigraphical literature, in the New Testament, and in the Church Fathers. Even in the third century C.E., R. Ammi, a Palestinian *amora*, might still find it necessary to warn against the retention of "uncorrected books" for more than 30 days (Ket 19b). Nevertheless, at this period all this constitutes a survival and not a living tradition.

The hegemony of the masoretic-type text is amply attested, apart from halakhic sources, by two independent classes of witnesses. On the one hand, the Hebrew biblical scrolls and fragments discovered at Masada (66–73 C.E.), at Wadi Murabbaʿat, and at Naḥal Ḥever (both from c. 132–35 C.E.) are all practically identical with the received text. On the other hand, the Jewish Greek translation of the Minor Prophets found in Naḥal Ḥever, and the second-century Greek translations of the Bible attributed to *Aquila, *Symmachus, and Theodotion all testify to revisions of the Septuagint attempting to bring it closer to a masoretic-type Hebrew text which had become exclusively authoritative. Whether this development resulted from an official promulgation by accepted religious authorities, or whether it was the culmination of a long period of growth during which the masoretic type had always represented the mainstream of tradition can no longer be determined. Whatever the case, no further developments of any significance in the biblical Hebrew consonantal text took place during the 600 years that elapsed between the latest manuscripts from the tannaitic period (c. 200 C.E.) and the earliest medieval ones (c. ninth century C.E.). None of the medieval manuscripts and codices, and not even the thousands of Bible fragments from the Cairo *Genizah* represent a recension different from the received text.

See also **Masorah*, **Poetry* in the Bible.

BIBLIOGRAPHY: F. Buhl, *Canon and Text of the Old Testament* (1892); C.D. Ginsburg, *Introduction to the Massoretico-Critical Edition of the Hebrew Bible* (1897), repr. 1966 with a prolegomenon by HM Orlinsky; V. Aptowitzer, *Das Schriftwort in der rabbinischen Literatur* (1906–15); H.E. Ryle, *The Canon of the Old Testament* (1909); H.B. Swete, *An Introduction to the Old Testament in Greek* (1968²); L. Ginsberg, in: JBL, 41 (1922), 115–36; M.L. Margolis, *Hebrew Scriptures in the Making* (1922); G.F. Moore, *Judaism…* (1927–30); A. Geiger, *Urschrift und Uebersetzungen der Bibel…* (1928); S. Zeitlin, in: PAAJR, 4 (1932), 169–223; R. Gordis, *Biblical Text in the Making* (1937); J. Ph. Hyatt, in: BA, 6 (1943), 71–80; E. Urbach, in: *Tarbiz*, 17 (1945/46), 1–11; B.J. Roberts, *Old Testament Text and Versions* (1951); Y. Kaufmann, Toledot; E.A. Parsons, *The Alexandrian Library* (1952); M.H. Segal, in: JBL, 72 (1953), 35–47; idem, *Mevo ha-Mikra* (1956); L.J. Liebreich, in: HUCA, 25 (1954), 37–40; C.H. Robert, in: *British Academy Proceedings* (1954), 169–204; M. Weitemyer, in: *Libri*, 6 (1955–56), 217–38 (Eng.); M. Greenberg, in: JAOS, 76 (1956), 157–67; P. Katz, in: ZNW, 47 (1956), 191–217; M. Haran, in: *Tarbiz*, 25 (1955/56), 245–71; I.L. Seligmann, *ibid.*, 118–39; P.W. Skehan, in: VT Supplement, 4 (1957), 155–60; W. Hallo, in: IEJ, 12 (1962), 13–26; idem, in: JAOS, 83 (1963), 167–76; 88 (1968), 71–89; S. Lieberman, *Hellenism in Jewish Palestine* (1950); D. *Barthélemy, Les Devanciers d'Aquila* (1963); F.M. Cross, in: HTR, 57 (1964), 281–99; idem, in: IEJ, 16 (1966), 81–95; idem, in: BA, 28 (1965), 87–100; E. Wuerthwein, *Text of the Old Testament* (1957); M.H. Goshen-Gottstein, *Text and Language in Bible and Qumran* (1960); idem, in: *Textus*, 2 (1962), 28–59; 5 (1966), 22–23 (Eng.); idem, in: A. Altmann (ed.), *Biblical and Other Studies* (1963), 79–122; idem, in: *Biblica*, 48 (1967), 243–90 (Eng.); P. Kahle, *The Cairo Geniza* (1959²); S. Talmon, in: *Textus*, 1 (1960), 144–84; 2 (1962), 14–27; 4 (1964), 95–132 (Eng.); F.G. Kenyon, *Our Bible and the Ancient Manuscripts* (1965⁴); N.M. Sarna, in: *Essays in Honor of I.E. Kiev.* **ADD. BIBLIOGRAPHY:** Traditional commentaries on the Torah: *Torat Ḥayyim: Ḥamisha Ḥumshe Torah* (Genesis-Deuteronomy complete in 7 vols), Jerusalem: Mosad Harav Kook: 1986–1993; The English translation of the Bible by the Jewish Publication Society of America was completed as follows: *Torah*: 1962; *The Prophets*: 1978; *The Writings*: 1982. The entire work is now in one volume: *Tanakh: A New Translation of the Holy Scriptures According to the Traditional Hebrew Text*, Philadelphia/New York/Jerusalem: Jewish Publication Society, 1985. All of the following contain extensive bibliographies. The most recent work on the textual history and criticism of the Bible is: Emanuel Tov, *Textual Criticism of the Hebrew Bible*, Minneapolis: Fortress Press and Assen/Maastrict: Van Gorcum, 1992. A major reference work in biblical studies is the now-complete *Enẓiklopediyyah Mikra'it* in Hebrew: E.L. Sukeinik (dec.), U.M.D. Cassuto (dec.), H. Tadmor, and Sh. Ahituv, editors, *Enẓiklopediyyah Mikra'it* (= Encyclopaedia Biblica), Vols. 1–9, Jerusalem: Mosad Bialik, 1950–1988. Other reference works in biblical studies are: David Noel Freedman, editor-in-chief, *Anchor Bible Dictionary*, complete, Vols. 1–6, New York/London/Toronto/Sydney/Auckland: Doubleday, 1992; G.J. Botterweck, Helmer Ringgren and, Heinz-Josef Fabry, editors, *Theological Dictionary of the Old Testament*, Volumes 1–7 covering א through ל, Grand Rapids, MI: Eerdmans, 1974–1995 (trans. of *Theologisches Wörterbuch zum Alten Tes-*

tament, Volumes 1–4, Stuttgart: Kohlhammer, 1970–1984). The most accurate Hebrew text of the Bible to have been produced to date is Mordecai Breuer, *Torah Nevi'im Ketuvim*, Jerusalem: Mosad Harav Kook, Torah, 1977; Nevi'im, 1979; Ketuvim, 1982; 1 A series of original Hebrew commentaries on the biblical books written from the perspective of Jewish tradition is *Daat Mikra*, Jerusalem: Mosad Harav Kook, most of planned 24 volumes completed 1970–1989. Scholarly commentaries on the individual books of the Bible have included: David A. Hubbard and Glenn W. Barker, General Editors; John D. Watt, Old Testament Editor, *Word Biblical Commentary*, Word Books, Waco, TX (volumes 1–32 cover the entire Old Testament; NT is also covered), 1983–1992; R.K. Harrison, General Editor, *The New International Commentary on the Old Testament*, William B. Eerdmans, Grand Rapids, MI (commentaries on most of the books of the OT now complete), 1976–1993; Bernhard W. Anderson, *et al.*, general editors, *The Old Testament Library*, includes commentaries (some original, some translations) on most of the books of the OT, as well as: *Introduction to the Old Testament* (J.A. Soggin), *Israelite and Judaean History* (ed. John H. Hayes and J. Maxwell Miller), *Near Eastern Religious Texts Relating to the Old Testament* (ed. Walter Beyerlin), *A History of Israel* (John Bright), *Theology of the Old Testament* (Walther Eichrodt) and more. London: SCM Press and Philadelphia/Louisville, KY: Westminster/John Knox Press, 1962–1993; *Biblischer Kommentar, Altes Testament*, Neukirchen: Neukirchener Verlag, (most of planned of 24 volumes completed), 1966–1991; William Foxwell Albright (dec.) and David Noel Freedman, editors, *The Anchor Bible*, New York, Garden City: Doubleday (most of planned 25 volumes on OT already complete; also volumes on Apocrypha and NT), 1962–1993; *The JPS Torah Commentary*, Philadelphia: Jewish Publication Society, Genesis-Numbers completed 1989–1991; Deuteronomy expected; Menaḥem Haran (General editor), [*Enẓiklopediyyah*] *Olam ha-Tanakh*, Earlier volumes: Ramat Gan: Revivim 1982–1989; later volumes: Tel Aviv: Davidson-Ittai, 1993–1995. The following are some general works on the Hebrew Bible: Richard Elliot Friedman, *Who Wrote the Bible*, New York: Harper & Row, 1987; Brevard S. Childs, *Introduction to the Old Testament as Scripture*, Philadelphia: Fortress Press, 1979; Robert Alter and Frank Kermode, *The Literary Guide to the Bible*, Cambridge, MA: Harvard University Press, 1987. The following works are on the history of biblical exegesis and scholarship: Martin J. Mulder, editor, *Mikra: Text, Translation, Reading and Interpretation of the Hebrew Bible in Ancient Judaism and Early Christianity*, Philadelphia: Fortress Press and Assen/Maastricht: Van Grocum, 1988; Ezra Zion Melammed, *Mefarshei ha-Mikra: Darkhehem ve-Shitotehem*, Volumes I–II, Jerusalem: Magnes Press 1975; Douglas A. Knight and Gene M. Tucker, *The Hebrew Bible and Its Modern Interpreters*, Philadelphia: Fortress Press and Chico, CA: Scholars Press, 1985

[Nahum M. Sarna / S. David Sperling (2nd ed.)]

PRINTED EDITIONS (HEBREW)

The story of the printing of the Hebrew Bible begins with the 1477 edition of the Psalms, most probably produced at Bologna. Each verse is followed by the appropriate passage from David *Kimḥi's commentary, an arrangement which does not appear again in Hebrew Bibles. Since the first printers had considerable difficulty with the vowel-points, they abandoned them after Psalm 4:4, excepting only three consecutive verses, 5:12–6:1. Many words are printed *plene* (with vowel letters (*matres lectionis*, Heb. *immot ha-keri'ah*)), including even *yod* for *segol*. There are frequent errors, whole verses (108), half verses (3), and odd words (43) are omitted, and there are dittographs both of letters and of words.

The next venture was due to the *ẓedakot* ("charities") of the rich and pious Joseph b. Abraham Caravita. Knowing that the vigor of Judaism depends on serious and continued reading and study of the Bible, many wealthy Jews employed scribes to copy manuscripts in order to foster this study. In Spain they continued using scribes, but Jews in Italy quickly realized that the invention of printing with movable type would enable them to ensure the more effective dissemination of the Bible. In 1479–80 Joseph b. Abraham invited from Ferrara to Bologna Abraham b. Ḥayyim di Tintori, a master craftsman who had largely solved the problems of both vowel-points and accents. The result of this move was the Bologna Pentateuch of 1482, which set the pattern for many future editions, culminating in the Bomberg rabbinic Bibles of the next century. The folios consist of Rashi's commentary across the page, top and bottom, with the Hebrew text in the inner and wider column and Targum Onkelos in the outer column. The type is larger than that of the 1477 psalter, but, as in some Ashkenazi manuscripts, the final letters *kaf, nun*, and *pe* do not extend below the base-line of other consonants, so that it is virtually impossible to distinguish between *dalet* and final *kaf.*

A little later, a certain Israel Nathan b. Samuel moved to Soncino, a small town in the duchy of Milan. There he set up a printing press for his son, and this was the beginning of the great firm of Joshua Solomon *Soncino and his nephews, Moses and Gershom. Attracting Abraham b. Ḥayyim from Bologna, they produced the first complete Bible, the Soncino Bible of 1488, with vowels and accents, but without a commentary, as was the custom of the Soncinos. The Soncino brothers also were responsible for the 1491–93 Naples Bible, in which the vowel-points and accents are better placed than before. Gershom Soncino moved to Brescia, where he produced the 1495 Brescia Bible, an improved edition of the 1488 Soncino Bible, but, more important, in small octavo format, making it a pocket edition specifically produced for the persecuted Jews who, perpetually moving from place to place, found it difficult to carry the huge and costly folio Bibles. It was this edition which Martin Luther used when he translated the Bible into German.

In Spain a Hebrew Pentateuch with Targum and Rashi was printed by Solomon Salmatic b. Maimon in 1490 at Ixar (Hijar). There were also printing presses in Portugal, where in 1487 the Faro Pentateuch was produced. In this edition the printer was unable to solve the problem of placing a dot in the middle of a consonant, so there is no *dagesh*. This was followed in 1491 by the Lisbon Pentateuch in two volumes with the Targum and Rashi's commentary, and in the next year by Isaiah and Jeremiah at Lisbon and Proverbs at Leira. The expulsion of the Jews from Spain (1492) put an end to the printing of new editions of the Bible, both in Portugal and Italy, for wealthy Jews needed all their means to help the refugees, over a quarter of a million of them. The Portuguese tradition was revived in Salonika 23 years later in an edition of Psalms, Proverbs, Job, and Daniel with Don Judah Gedaliah as patron and Joseph b. Mako Golphon as printer. The first Bible to be printed in Spain was the 1514–17 Complutensian Polyglot printed at Alcalde Henares (Lat. *Complutum*) under the patronage of Cardinal Ximenes de Cisneros, founder of the university there, regent of Castile, and archbishop of Toledo. The project was completed in 1517, but it was nearly three years before Pope Leo x authorized the work and a further two years before publication, by which time Cardinal Ximenes had been dead for five years. Accents were deliberately rejected; other signs were introduced to mark the colons and the penultimate accented syllables. The vowel-points are far from reliable.

By the year 1511 the Soncinos, now at Pesaro, were able to make a new start and in stages they completed a fourth edition of the complete Bible. Gershom had used the interval to perfect his technique and this edition is the best produced by Ashkenazi Jews in Italy. Around this time Daniel *Bomberg, a Christian merchant of Amsterdam, arrived in Venice and established his printing office there. In 1516–17 he published the first Great Rabbinic Bible, edited by Felix Pratensis, who was born a Jew but was baptized in 1506. The work is in four volumes, with Targums and commentaries. For the first time the *kerei* is given, but in the variants in the margin (see *Masorah). The last volume contains additional material, notably Maimonides' "Thirteen Articles" and the treatise on accents entitled *Dikdukei ha-Te'amim* said to be by *Ben Asher and here printed for the first time. Here also for the first time in Hebrew Samuel and Kings were each divided into two books in imitation of the Vulgate. The strangest thing about this edition is the statement made to the pope when his *imprimatur* was sought; it claimed that the many previously printed Bibles "contain as many errors as words" and that "no one had attempted it before." Daniel Bomberg and Felix Pratensis duly received the pope's blessing, though it proved more of a hindrance than an asset. Even before this four-volume Bible was published, Bomberg realized that he had made two bad mistakes: employing an apostate Jew as his editor, and requesting the pope's *imprimatur.* He therefore remade the columns as soon as the folios of the large Bible had been run off and issued a quarto edition at the same time, this time without any mention of either editor or pope. A second edition was called for within four years, when the whole was reset; on this occasion the two sons of Baruch Adelkind were mentioned as printers, and great emphasis was laid on the fact that they were Jews, thoroughly Orthodox and already engaged in printing the whole of the Talmud. However, something had to be done about the Great Rabbinic Bible, and, as though divinely guided and certainly opportunely, Jacob b. Ḥayyim ibn Adonijah arrived in Venice after his family had been driven out of Spain and again out of Tunis. After seven penurious years of wandering Jacob b. Ḥayyim found work with Bomberg in Venice. The chief fruit of the partnership was the second Great Rabbinic Bible of 1524–25, the text of which became the standard masoretic text and continued as such for 400 years. Jacob b. Ḥayyim was very conscious of the importance of the masorah as the guarantee of the correct text, and he went to great pains and undertook several journeys to secure as many codices with a masorah as possible. Thus, for the first time, there was a printed Hebrew Bible with a marginal masorah. As the editor discovered that "the masorah did not harmonize with the majority of the codices," he had to exercise his discretion. The edition was in four volumes, with Targums, and with commentaries by Rashi, Ibn Ezra, David and Moses Kimḥi, and Levi b. Gershom. A third Bomberg quarto edition appeared in 1525–28, the text being a combination of that of Felix Pratensis and that of Jacob b. Ḥayyim.

Daniel Bomberg's tribulations were not over, for soon after 1525 Jacob b. Ḥayyim became a Christian. In 1527 Elijah *Levita, a refugee originally from Neustadt near Nuremberg, came to Venice and found employment with Bomberg. No more is heard of Jacob b. Ḥayyim, Elijah Levita being henceforth chief adviser to the Bomberg firm. In subsequent reprints of the 1524–25 Bible, there is no mention of the editor. Bibles printed after 1525 all follow substantially the text of Jacob b. Ḥayyim ibn Adonijah until *Buxtorf's small-format Bible of 1611 and his four-volume rabbinic Bible of 1618–19, printed at Basle, in which the text was influenced by Sephardi traditions, and not dominated by the Ashkenazi ones as were all previous editions printed under Jewish auspices. The text was edited by Jablonski in 1699, but the most important edition based on the Buxtorf text is that of J.H. Michaelis in 1720. It is a critical edition, quoting 19 printed editions and five Erfurt manuscripts, especially the very important Erfurt 3 with its masorah, and containing also *Okhlah ve-Okhlah*, an 11th-century masoretic work of great importance then printed for the first time. The critical notes and the variants provided by Michaelis indicate a masoretic tradition different from that of the 1524–25 Bible of Jacob b. Ḥayyim. They form a pattern, already discernible in Jablonski's 1699 edition, but more clearly in *Lonzano's *Or Torah* and *Norzi's *Minḥat Shai.* Norzi depended mostly on the de'Rossi codex 782, which had a strange, disturbed history, though *de'Rossi (vol. 1, p. 128) recognized it as "the most perfect examplar of the masoretic text." This tradition must have come to Spain at a comparatively early date, and it is firmly established in Sephardi tradition. It is responsible for at least some of the differences between the Complutensian Polyglot and the standard text based on Ashkenazi codices. Michaelis' critical edition is an early and neglected precursor of the modern editions of the Hebrew Bible, those by P. Kahle and N.H. Snaith.

The story of modern times begins with Seligmann *Baer, who published the Hebrew Bible in single volumes with notes, except for Exodus to Deuteronomy (for which see the Roedelheim Pentateuch, a popular edition without notes). The dates of these volumes are 1869–1895. Baer believed that the masorah is supreme, that firm rules can be established, and that these must be rigidly followed, whatever the manuscripts may say. In this he is the literary descendant of Elijah Levita and his *Masoret ha-Masoret*. Baer, who regularly followed a masorah or a rule against the codices and frequently "corrects an error," worked according to the rules laid down by Jekuthiel in *Ein ha-Kore*, and later by Heidenheim. Baer was supported by Franz *Delitzsch, whose authority was immense. In his books on the accents, W. Wickes (*Verse Accents*, 1881; *Prose Accents*, 1888), similarly makes and adopts fixed and rigid rules. In contrast, C.D. *Ginsburg (British and Foreign Bible Society edition, 1911–26) followed Jacob b. Ḥayyim; where the various masorah traditions disagreed either with the text or with each other, he exercised his judgment, with the result that he paid more attention to the manuscripts than to either masorah or to Jacob b. Ḥayyim. With the third edition of R. Kittel's *Biblia Hebraica* (BH3; 1936), a new signpost was erected. P. Kahle was responsible for the text, based on the Leningrad codex (Firkovich collection B19a) which Kahle claimed was a true, accurate, and genuine Ben Asher codex. (The Leningrad codex itself is now available in an affordable photographic reproduction edited by D.N. Freedman (1998).)Ever since Maimonides supported the Ben Asher tradition against *Saadiah b. Joseph Gaon, who favored the *Ben Naphtali tradition, it had been agreed that a true masoretic Bible must follow Ben Asher.

The 1928 Foreign Society (N.H. Snaith) edition was based mainly on British Museum's mss. Orient. 2626–28, a beautifully illustrated codex, close to the notes of Lonzano, Norzi, and the tradition found in the 1720 Michaelis Bible. The text, though compiled from completely different sources, is very close to the Kahle text. This indicates that the Ben Asher text is to be found not only in Leningrad manuscript but also in the best Sephardi manuscripts (in the first hand, and not as corrected by a second hand to the Ben Ḥayyim tradition, as often happened after 1492 when the exiled Jews came into close contact with the other traditions).

Recent years have witnessed great progress towards the production of a truly critical edition of the Hebrew Bible. Despite its superiority to previous efforts the numerous shortcomings of BH3 pointed out by reviewers necessitated a fourth edition (including variants from biblical manuscripts from Qumran), *Biblia Hebraica Stuttgartensia* (BHS) published in 1977. Differing in kind from its predecessors a new Biblia Hebraica edition Quinta (BHQ) is appearing in fascicles. (*Megilloth* appeared in 2004). In the manner of of its predecessors BHQ uses Leningrad as a base text, but includes the large and small masorah with the text accompanied by a single critical apparatus. When completed BHQ will be printed as a single volume, accompanied by a separate volume with translations, notes, and commentary on the masorah. Even more ambitious is the multi-volume Hebrew University Bible Project (HUBP), based on the excellent but incomplete Aleppo codex (ca. 925). HUBP has four separate apparatuses and suggests no conjectural emendations. Of special note is the inclusion of variants recovered from biblical citations in rabbinic literature. Thus far three volumes have appeared: Isaiah (1995), Jeremiah (1997), and Ezekiel (2004). Of interest too is N. Ben-Zvi (ed.), Jerusalem Crown: The Bible of the Hebrew University of Jerusalem (2000), Not to be confused with HUBP, Jerusalem Crown is an aesthetically pleasing "scholarly manipulation" (Sanders 2004) of the Aleppo and Leningrad codices into a rabbinic Bible.

Bibles containing the original Hebrew text (or Greek in the case of New Testament) together with the important ancient versions arranged in parallel columns are termed polyglots. They were at one time important in ascertaining correct readings or meanings of the text. The oldest one in print is the *Complutensian Polyglot*, mentioned above containing the Hebrew masoretic text, the Vulgate, the Aramaic Targum (with a Latin translation), and the Septuagint (with a Latin translation). The most comprehensive are Brian Walton's *London Polyglot* (1654–57) which contained texts in Hebrew, Samaritan, Aramaic, Greek, Latin, Ethiopic, Syriac, Arabic, and Persian (all with Latin translations), and Samuel Bagster's *Polyglot* (1831) in Hebrew, Greek, Samaritan, Latin, Syriac, German, Italian, French, English, and Spanish. More modern polyglots have contented themselves with giving the texts in Hebrew, Greek, Latin, and a modern language.

BIBLIOGRAPHY: C.D. Ginsburg, *Introduction to the Massoretico-Critical Edition of the Hebrew Bible* (1897), repr. 1966 with introd. by HM Orlinsky; E. Levita, *Massoreth ha-Massoreth and the Introduction of Jacob ben Chayyim ibn Adoniyah to the Rabbinic Bible of 1525*, ed. by C.D. Ginsburg, introd. by N.H. Snaith (1967). **ADD. BIBLIOGRAPHY:** M. Haran, in, JANES, 22 (1993), 51–61; M. Cohen, www.cs.anu.edu/au…cohen art; A. Hurvitz, in, SVT, 80 (2000), 143–60; L. McDonald and J. Sanders (eds.), *The Canon Debate* (2002); J. Sanders, in: JBL, 118 (1999), 518–26; idem, Review of Biblical Literature 03/2004 (at www.bookreviews.org); E. Tov, "Writing of Ancient Biblical Texts," in: C. Cohen et al (eds.), *Sefer Moshe* (FS Weinfeld; 2004), 445–58.

[Norman Henry Snaith / S. David Sperling (2nd ed.)]

TRANSLATIONS

ANCIENT VERSIONS

Aramaic: the Targumim

The word *targum* (תַּרְגּוּם) means "translation," corresponding to the verb *tirgem* (תרגם; "translate"), of which passive participle, *meturgam*, occurs in Ezra 4:7: "The letter was written (*katuv*) in Aramaic and translated" (*meturgam*; the second mention of "Aramaic" in the verse is a note to the reader that the Aramaic version of the letter follows (Blenkinsopp 109–10)). There are no other biblical attestations of *trgm*. In Jewish Babylonian Aramaic the verb *trgm* means "translate into Aramaic," "explain." In Syriac the verb means "explain," "translate" (Sokloff DJBA, 1231–32). In Jewish Palestinian Aramaic *trgm* means "translate" into any language (Sokoloff, DJPA, 591). In Samaritan the verb means "translate," "relay the message" (Tal, DSA, 963). *Tirgem* is a denominative verb, being derived from the noun *turgeman*. The term may have entered Hebrew and Aramaic through Akkadian *targumānu* ("interpreter") whence, ultimately, the English *dragoman*. The

Akkadian noun itself has been connected by some scholars with the verb *ragāmu*, "call out," "summon," "prophesy," "sue" (CAD R, 62–7), and with Ugaritic *rgm*, "speak," "say." Others have argued for a non-semitic origin (details in Starke). In Aramaic and Hebrew the word *turgeman* exists alongside a more native-looking Hebrew adaptation, *meturgeman*. In tannaitic and amoraic Hebrew *tirgem* is said of translating from Hebrew into any other language (TJ, Kid. 1:1, 59a; TJ, Meg. 1:11, 71c), but the noun *targum* does not seem to occur with reference to any but Aramaic versions of the Bible (Shab. 115a; TJ, Kid. 1:1, 59a; TJ, Meg. 1:11, 71c). In fact, the Mishnah (Yad. 4:5) refers to the Aramaic originals of certain sections of Daniel and Ezra as *targum*.

ORIGIN OF THE TARGUMS. The Jewish diaspora in Babylonia must have exchanged Hebrew for Aramaic as its vernacular in only a few generations. In Palestine the process was much more gradual, but Aramaic was probably the language of the majority of Jews there before the end of the Persian period. During the period of Persian domination (539–333 B.C.E.), Aramaic was the language of the Persian administration and the lingua franca of southwestern Asia. The bilingual character of the books of Ezra and Daniel is due to the attempt to make these books more "biblical" by providing them with Hebrew beginnings, but they reflect a period of Aramaic dominance. The practice of translating the Bible reading into Aramaic in the synagogue is attributed to Ezra by *Rav (third century C.E.), who interprets the word *meforash* in Nehemiah 8:8 to mean an interpretation of the Hebrew text of the Bible in Aramaic translation (Meg. 3a; Ned. 37b; cf. TJ, Meg. 4:1, 74d), but both the meaning of the word and the reliability of the account in Nehemiah 8 are subjects of controversy. At any rate the custom of interpreting the synagogue reading of the Bible text with the Targum after each verse (or after each three verses) in the presence of the congregation, so as to permit a translator to repeat it in Aramaic, is attested in the Mishnah (Meg. 4:4).

MANNER OF USAGE. The professional translator of the Hebrew Bible text in the synagogue was called *meturgeman* (Meg. 4:4). His oral explanations were given along with the reading of the Sabbath lesson. The rules for reading the Targum are formulated in the *halakhah* (Meg. 4:4–10; Meg. 23b–25b; Tosef., Meg. 4:20–41). The Targum was to be read after every verse of the *parashah* of the Pentateuch and after every third verse of the reading from the Prophets. There is no mention in this source of reading from a written Targum, and elsewhere (TJ, Meg. 4:1, 74d) the use of such writings was forbidden, at least for the Pentateuch, for the Sabbath worship service, but the preparation and use of them by individuals for private study and school instruction was permitted. Although certain portions of the Bible were read but were not translated (as Gen. 35:22), others were neither read nor translated (as Num. 6:24–26; II Sam. 11–13). *Judah b. Ilai, a *tanna*, and a pupil of Akiva rhetorically expressed the difficulty faced by all Bible translators in his declaration that whoever translates (*ha-metargem*) a verse of Bible literally is is a fictionalizer, while he who makes additions is a blasphemer (Tosef., Meg. 4:41; Kid. 49a). A later anonymous opinion (Kid. 49a) cites Judah's statement as proof that one may not translate the Bible on one's own but must translate only from "our targum," i.e., Onkelos (see below). In *Sifrei* (Deut. 161), the Targum is mentioned as a branch of study that falls between the Bible and the Mishnah. The Targums as a whole are not always primarily literal translations of the corresponding Hebrew text; they are often intermingled with various paraphrases and aggadic supplements such as one meets in exegetical or homiletic works like the Talmud and the Midrash. They also contain explanations and alterations adapted to secure the sense of the masoretic text current among the rabbinical authorities, offering it to the people in an intelligible form. In this period an important concern of Jewish criticism and exegesis was the need to remove or tone down all references to God that could lead to misunderstanding in the popular mind. The Targum thus employs various devices to obviate the appearance of a very distinct anthropomorphic character of God. These, however, are not consistently applied. Indeed at times anthropomorphic phrases are translated literally or even amplified, e.g., PT to Exod. 15:17 (Klein, 1982; 1986, xxxii).

DATE OF TARGUM. There are early indications that the Targum was committed to writing, although for private use only. A tannaitic tradition refers to an Aramaic translation of the book of Job which existed in written form at the time of *Gamaliel I (first century C.E.) and which, after being withdrawn from use, reappeared in the lifetime of his grandson Gamaliel II. Targum Onkelos, which was made the official Targum of the Babylonian schools, was committed to writing and redacted as early as the third century C.E., since there is a masorah to it which dates from the first half of that century (see below). The official recognition of a written Targum and the final redaction of its text, however, belong to the post-talmudic period, thus not earlier than the fifth century C.E.

LITURGICAL USE OF THE TARGUM. Two Palestinian *amoraim* of the third century C.E. (Ber. 8a–b) urged that in private worship the Hebrew text of the weekly *parashah* be read twice and the Targum once, exactly as was done in public worship. There are still pious Jews who do this before the Sabbath, although Aramaic is no longer the vernacular of the Jews. The Yemenite Jews have even retained the public reading of Targum Onkelos (see below). Targums to all the books of the Bible except Daniel and Ezra-Nehemiah (this constituting in Jewish tradition a single book of Ezra) have survived to this day.

Targums to the Pentateuch

TARGUM ONKELOS. The official Targum to the Pentateuch, the only such Aramaic version that was subjected to a unified and scholastic redaction, is known by the name of Targum Onkelos. The origin of this name is derived from the Babylonian Talmud (Meg. 3a), where the Targum to the Torah is attributed to the proselyte *Onkelos, who is said to have composed it (literally, "spoke it," "declaimed it") under the guidance of R. Eliezer and R. Joshua (An anonymous statement (*ibid.*) goes so far as to say that the original targum was given at Sinai, subsequently forgotten, and then restored by Onkelos.) The Palestinian Talmud, however (Meg. 1:11, 71c), contains the statement: "Aquila the proselyte translated (*tirgem*) the Pentateuch in the presence of R. Eliezer and R. Joshua," in a context which shows that a translation into Greek is meant. These accounts are obviously related: in the Babylonian Talmud only the name Onkelos occurs, while Aquilas (= Akylas, the Greek adaptation of the Latin Aquila) alone is found in the Jerusalem Talmud. The latter is historically reliable – Aquila did compose a scrupulously exact and literal Greek translation of the Bible, and Targum Onkelos, however, is almost a literal Aramaic translation of the Pentateuch. In addition to this, a great deal of what is revealed about Onkelos in Babylonian sources is attributed to Aquila in the Jerusalem ones. Important works that discuss the identity of Onkelos and Akylas (= Aquila) are those of M. Friedmann, A.E. Silverstone, and D. Barthélemy. Silverstone argues that Aquila was identical with Onkelos, and that this one individual produced both a Greek and an Aramaic translation. Friedmann believes that they were two different personalities. Barthélemy argues that the Babylonian Jewish scholars possessed an anonymous Aramaic translation to which they gave the name Targum Onkelos. This was based on mistakenly transferring the western tradition of Aquila's Greek translation of the Torah into Greek to the Aramaic Targum of the Torah that the Babylonians possessed.

The Aramaic of this Targum exhibits a mixture of the Western (e.g., *yat* as nota accusativi) and Eastern (e.g., *ḥzy*, "to see") features. This combination gave rise to a variety of opinions about the Targum's place of origin. A. Berliner, T. Noeldeke, G. Dalman, and E.Y. Kutscher believe that it originated in Palestine, while its final redaction took place in Babylonia. The opposing view is held by P. Kahle and his followers, who consider this Aramaic version to have originated entirely in Babylonia. Adherents of Palestinian origin have argued from the content of the Targum that it was composed in Palestine (particularly in Judea) sometime in the second century C.E., since both the halakhic (legal) and aggadic (non-legal) portions betray the influence of the school of Akiva. In addition, they have maintained that the western Aramaic elements, e.g., preservation of the absolute state, are much stronger. Kutscher (11–13) argued that the Aramaic of Onkelos is quite close to that of the Genesis Apocryphon found at Qumran in Palestine; and Greenfield, in the same vein classified both as examples of Standard Literary Aramaic. After the destruction of the Second Temple and the suppression of the Bar Kokhba revolt, which destroyed the cultural centers of Judea, Targum Onkelos disappeared from Palestine. The old Standard Literary Aramaic was superseded by the local Western Aramaic dialects, and since the center of Jewish life shifted to Galilee, a new Targum in the Galilean dialect evolved in the course of time. At the beginning of the Amoraic period (end of second century C.E.), before it had disappeared from Palestine, Targum Onkelos was imported, the argument continues, along with the Mishnah to Babylonia. There it underwent final revision during the third century C.E. and was recognized as the authoritative Aramaic version of the Pentateuch for the local Jewish population. In the Babylonian Talmud (Kid. 49a) it is mentioned as "our Targum" or by the expression "as we translate." A special masorah prepared for it contains statements concerning the divergencies between the Babylonian academies of *Sura and *Nehardea. More recently, however, Mueller-Kessler has argued that the similarity between the language of the targums and the Aramaic literary dialect of the Mesopotamian Jewish Aramaic magic bowls of the fourth-seventh centuries C.E. points to a Babylonian origin of both the Targum Onkelos and Jonathan.

This Targum Onkelos is the most literal translation of the Pentateuch. The text from which it was prepared was in all essentials the masoretic one. The principal objective was to conform the Targum as closely as possible to the original text, and the grammatical structure of the Hebrew was thus followed closely. One prominent example of this is the use of the particle *yat* as a sign of the accusative for the corresponding Hebrew particle *ʾet*. Yet there are numerous exceptions where the Targum does not adhere to the original. Paraphrase occasionally takes the place of translation: in the poetic portions (e.g., Gen. 49) there are aggadic (non-legal) supplements of moderate size, while halakhic (legal) regulations are often read into the legal portions (e.g., Ex. 21:16). Offensive or disagreeable material is paraphrased or rendered by some sort of circumlocution (e.g., Gen. 20:13; Ex. 24:11). The paraphrastic style of translation affected by the Targums in general, in order to obviate anthropomorphisms and anthropopathisms in reference to God, is quite prominent in the Targum Onkelos. Thus, the embarassing Genesis 20:13 "when the gods (*elohim*) caused me to wander" (plural verb *hitʿû* following *elohim*) is rendered "when the gentiles (*ṭʿô* with *tet*) strayed after the works of their hands." The rhetorical Exodus 15:11, "Who is like you among the gods Yahweh?" is translated as "There is none other than you, you are God, Adonai." Nonetheless, Onkelos has no problem with the plurals in Genesis 1:26, "let us make the human in our image." Figurative language, as a rule, is not translated literally but is explained (e.g., Gen. 49:25; Ex. 15:3, 8, 10; 29:35). Geographical names are sometimes replaced by those current at a later time (e.g., Gen. 10:10; Deut. 3:17). Apart from *Megillah* 3a (previously mentioned), all the references to Onkelos as the author of the Aramaic translation of the Pentateuch originated in the post-talmudic period, although they are all based on this passage in the Babylonian Talmud. The earliest of those is in the late midrashic work known as *Pirkei de-R. Eliezer* (38), where the targumic passage on Genesis 45:27 is cited in the statement "Onkelos has translated." The ninth-century *gaon* *Sar Shalom (*Shaʿarei Teshu-*

vah, 29) names Targum Onkelos as the Targum that was in circulation in the Jewish community at that time and as having more claim to sanctity than any other existing Targums. The *gaon* *Natronai (*Seder Rav Amram*, Warsaw (1865), p. 29) attributes this Targum to the rabbis of the Talmud and attaches a canonical value to it. Accordingly, the designation "Targum Onkelos" was firmly established in the early part of the geonic period.

Noteworthy is the fact that the Jews of Yemen received this Targum, like that of the Prophets, with the Babylonian supralinear punctuation. A critical edition of Targum Onkelos to the Pentateuch (as well as Targum Jonathan to the Prophets) with supralinear punctuation according to Yemenite manuscripts has been edited by A. Sperber (see bibliography. See also Cohen, *Haketer: Joshua–Judges*, 79*–82). Yemen and Yemenite synagogues in Israel were the only places where the reading of Targum Onkelos continued to accompany that of the Pentateuch on Sabbaths into the 20th century. Elsewhere, some pious Jews still observe the custom of going over the weekly portion of the Torah privately on the eve of the Sabbath, verse by verse in Hebrew, Targum, and Hebrew again (Ber. 8a–b; Sh. Ar., OḤ, 285).

PALESTINIAN PENTATEUCH TARGUMS. *Codex Neofiti I.* Since 1930, there has been great progress in the recovery of the old "Jerusalem," properly speaking, Galilean, Targums. In that year Kahle edited for the first time some *genizah* fragments of such Targums (see bibliography) dating from between the seventh and ninth centuries C.E.

Because they overlap, they exhibit divergences which show that their text, unlike that of Targum Onkelos, was never fixed. Further texts have since been published by A. Diez-Macho, Y. Komlosh, W. Baars, and M. Klein. In 1956 Diez-Macho, who had studied with Kahle, announced the discovery of a complete Palestinian Targum to the Pentateuch called Neofiti I, which he had found in the Vatican Library (VT Supplement, 7 (1960), 222–245). The text had been incorrectly catalogued as Targum Onkelos.

Prior to the discovery of Neofiti I, the Galilean Targum was represented by two main recensions: Targum Yerushalmi I (TY I), also known as Targum Jonathan or Targum Jonathan b. Uzziel in Hebrew and hence as Pseudo-Jonathan in Western languages; and Targum Yerushalmi II (TY II), the so-called Fragmentary Targum. More correct than Targum Yerushalmi, "Jerusalem Targum," is Targum Ereẓ Israel, "the Palestinian Targum," by which it is designated in a responsum by R. Hai Gaon, but it is already called "the Targum of the People of the Holy City" by *Menahem b. Solomon, the 12th-century author of the *Midrash Sekhel Tov*. With the appearance of Neofiti I, three principal Galilean Aramaic versions of the Pentateuch are now in existence. Whereas Neofiti I is complete, 15 verses are missing from Targum Yerushalmi I, and Targum Yerushalmi II contains only 850 verses of the Pentateuch. Codex Neofiti I differs from other Galilean Targum manuscripts in orthography, grammar, and range of paraphrase. It also contains a large number of marginal and interlinear variants.

Targum Yerushalmi I (Pseudo-Jonathan). This targum is quite expansive, being almost twice as long as the Hebrew original.The ascription of this Targum to *Jonathan b. Uzziel is believed to date back to the 14th-century commentator Menahem b. Benjamin Recanati, who erroneously analyzed the abbreviation, ת״י (Targum Yerushalmi) as Targum Jonathan. W. Bacher believed that Recanati probably misinterpreted a passage in the Zohar (1:89a) according to which Jonathan translated *ha-mikra* (הַמִּקְרָא), which in this case refers to the Prophets rather than to the whole Bible (hence the Pentateuch). The name Targum Ereẓ Israel is found in writers of the 11th century. The Tosafot cite the Galilean Pentateuch Targum variously as Targum Jonathan (to Ḥag. 27a), Jonathan b. Uzziel (to Av. Zar. 59a), and Targum Yerushalmi (to Ber. 8b). The language of this version of the Pentateuch is Galilean Jewish Aramaic (outside the manuscript it was not transmitted in its pure form). Its most distinctive characteristic is the free aggadic handling of the text. Like the other Targums, it sets aside figurative speech and eliminates most anthropomorphic expressions referring to God. Early geographical names are replaced by those current in a later age. This Targum contains abundant information on most of the religious and dogmatic teachings of Judaism of the talmudic period. One finds the Jewish (not always biblical) doctrines of the being of God, His dwelling place, His revelation in the Torah, angels, creation, sin, death, the messianic kingdom, resurrection of the just and the future life, gehenna, and the world to come.

This Targum is not earlier than the seventh century C.E., although it contains material which is much earlier than the date of its final compilation and redaction. A very ancient date has been claimed for the following passages: Genesis 15:19, Numbers 24:21, the interpretation of "Kenites" as Salmeans, contemporaries and allies of the Nabateans, and Deuteronomy 33:11, the reference to Johanan (b. Hyrcanus) the high priest. Indications of a late date of composition, however, occur in Exodus 26:9, in which reference is made to the Six Orders of the Mishnah; in Genesis 21:21, where the Hebrew names of the two wives of *Ishmael (regarded as the ancestor of the Arabs) are rendered respectively by עיישא or חדישא, i.e., the name of Muhammad's wife Ayesha or of his wife Khadijah, and פטימא, the name of his daughter Fatima; and in Genesis 49:26 and Deuteronomy 33:2, where Edom (i.e., Byzantium or Christian Europe) and Ishmael are spoken of as world powers in a way that was possible only in the seventh century at the earliest.

Targum Yerushalmi II (the Fragmentary Targum). This Targum contains renderings of only certain verses, phrases, or words of the Pentateuch, estimated at about 850 verses altogether. Three-fourths of these are on the historical sections of the Pentateuch, while the remaining fourth is on the legislative sections in Exodus, Leviticus, and Numbers. There are about 14 chapters which have no translation at all, while for some 90 verses there are translations of only a single word of the Hebrew text. The earliest known fragments were first published in Bomberg's Great Rabbinic Bible in 1516–17, based on Vatican Codex 440 (a good portion of the fragments had already appeared under the title "Tosefta Yerushalmi" in the Lisbon Bible of 1491). In 1899 M. Ginsburger edited a number of other fragments from manuscript sources, expecially from Paris Codex 110, as well as from quotations from the Targum Yerushalmi found in early works, under the title *Das Fragmententhargum*. This work also contained numerous fragments that occur under the title *Nusḥa Aḥarena* in the Venice Bible of 1591. These plus other variants are sometimes referred to as Targum Yerushalmi III. The language of this Targum is Galilean Jewish Aramaic, and it includes many foreign loan words. Its fragmentary condition has been accounted for in various ways.

The fragments are not all contemporaneous. The text of the majority of them is older than Pseudo-Jonathan. Many of these fragments, especially the aggadic paraphrases, agree with Pseudo-Jonathan, which may, on the other hand, be older than some of them. Similarly, aggadic additions were made to the text of the Targum in later centuries, so that a North African manuscript of 1487 alludes to the capture of Constantinople by the Turks in 1453. Early in the 12th century, *Judah b. Barzillai wrote of these additions: "The Jerusalem Targum contains aggadic sayings added by those who led in prayer and who also read the Targum, insisting that these sayings be recited in the synagogue as interpretations of the text of the Bible." These numerous additions to the Jerusalem Targum and the majority of the fragments are all of a later date than Onkelos, yet both Pseudo-Jonathan and the Fragmentary Targum contain much that has survived from a very early period. According to W. Bacher, the nucleus of the Jerusalem Targum is older than the Babylonian one, which was, in his opinion, redacted from it.

The Targums to the Prophets

TARGUM JONATHAN. This Targum gradually became recognized as the official Aramaic version of the Prophets. According to P. Churgin, its final redaction was accomplished by the seventh century C.E. in the form in which it is now known. Like the Targum to the Pentateuch, it originated in the synagogue, where it was recited after every three verses from the Hebrew text of the Prophets during that part of the service. According to the Babylonian Talmud (Meg. 3a), it was written by Jonathan b. Uzziel "at the dictation of Haggai, Zechariah, and Malachi." The talmudic account thus traces the origin of the Targum of the prophets to the last prophets, making for an unbroken chain of transmission. The account continues to relate that because of this translation the entire land of Israel was shaken and a voice from heaven cried out: "Who has revealed my secrets to man?" The story adds that Jonathan wished to translate the Hagiographa as well, but that a heavenly voice bade him to desist. According to W. Bacher the Targum to Job, which was withdrawn from circulation by Gamaliel I, may have resulted from Jonathan's attempts to translate the Hagiographa. Jonathan b. Uzziel is named as *Hillel's most prominent pupil in the first century B.C.E. and was a contemporary of Gamaliel I. In the Babylonian Talmud, this Targum is quoted quite frequently by R. Joseph b. Ḥiyya (270–333 C.E.), head of the Pumbedita Academy (MK 28b; Sanh. 94b; Meg. 3a). Thus, as early as the beginning of the fourth century, the Targum to the Prophets was recognized as being of ancient authority. Hai Gaon (commentary to *Tohorot*, quoted in *Arukh ha-Shalem*, 2 (1926), 293a) regarded R. Joseph as its author, since he cited passages from it with the words "Rav Joseph has translated."

Targum Jonathan contains Eastern as well as Western Aramaic linguistic traits. It has a few Persian loan words, such as *dasteqa / disteqa* ("hilt," "handle." = Syriac *dasteqa*. Cf. Pahlavi *dast*, "hand," *dastag*, "bundle," Farsi *daste*, "handle," Judg. 3:22) and *idron* (Persian; *andarōn*, "inside," "within," Joel 2:16). Its style is very similar to that of Targum Onkelos, especially in the Former Prophets – the historical narratives. In the prose sections one meets an occasional reading which is not in the masoretic text (Josh. 8:12) or an apparent conflation of two variants (*ibid.* 8:16). Proper names are sometimes transformed into their (often, surely, merely guessed) up-to-date appellations (*ibid.* 7:21, where Shinar is interpreted as Babel and Jer. 46:25, where No (נֹא) is interpreted as Alexandria), but for the most part they are taken over unchanged from the Hebrew text. The usual rules of targumic interpretation are observed in the rendering of anthropomorphic expressions and figurative language (Hos. 1:3). Poetic passages are drastically paraphrased (e.g., Judg. 5; I Sam. 2:1–10). The same holds true for difficult passages, where paraphrasis is specially employed in an attempt to explain the Hebrew text (cf. I Sam. 15:23; 17:8; II Sam. 14:11; 20:18). The rendering in the Latter Prophets is more paraphrastic on the whole than the Former Prophets, which is to be expected in view of their more exalted and rhapsodic style (cf. Targum Jonathan's amplification of the Heb. text of Isa. 29:1 and Jer. 10:11; for instances of *aggadah* in this Targum see Isa. 12:3; 33:22; 62:10; Micah 6:4). This Targum is noteworthy for its unity of style and character throughout the historical as well as the prophetic books. This can be seen, as Gesenius pointed out, from a comparison of the passages II Kings 18–19 (= Jer. 36–39) and Isaiah 2:2–4 (= Micah 4:1–3), which are translated alike with only slight variations, and from other features, such as the rendering of Tarshish by Yama, which is common to Jonah, Jeremiah, and Ezekiel.

A conspicuous affinity exists between Targum Jonathan and Targum Onkelos, as seen from certain passages which are identical word for word. Most of the early writers on this subject recognized this identity but differed in their conclusions. Thus, while de'Rossi and Herzfeld were certain that Onkelos knew the Targum to the Prophets, L. Zunz took the view that Jonathan and Onkelos before him had quoted it in Judges 5:8 (= Deut. 32:17), I Samuel 12:3 (= Num. 16:15), II Kings 14:6 (= Deut. 24:16), and Jeremiah 48:46 (= Num. 21:28–29).

TARGUM YERUSHALMI TO THE PROPHETS. The existence of such a Targum is inferred mainly from the frequent citations from it by early authors, especially Rashi and David Kimḥi. Fragments from the books of Joshua, Judges, Samuel, Kings, Isaiah, Jeremiah, Amos, Jonah, and Zechariah are contained in Codex Reuchlinianus, written in 1105 (ed. Lagarde, *Prophetica Chaldaica*, 1872), in the form of 80 extracts. W. Bacher investigated their character in his detailed article "Kritische Untersuchungen zum Prophetentargum" (in ZDMG, 28 (1874), 1–58). The language is Palestinian in character, yet its aggadic additions are frequently traceable to the Babylonian Talmud. This Targum thus belongs to a later period, when the Babylonian Talmud began to exercise a considerable amount of influence on Palestinian literature. There are also "Toseftas" (additions) to the Prophet Targum that are similar to the Targum Yerushalmi and are also cited by Kimḥi (see esp. A. Sperber, *The Bible in Aramaic*, 2 (1959), ix–x, 3 (1962), xi, 23–25, 462–5, 479–80; for Tosefta to Targum Onkelos, see 1 (1959), xvii–xviii, 354–357). For a list of targumic Toseftas see Klein, *Genizah*, xxix.

Targums to the Hagiographa

Although there are extant Targums to the Hagiographa, they did not enjoy official recognition. They did not originate until a later period, and were written at different times by various authors, yet they contain old material. W. Bacher considers them to have originated in Palestine, since they contain expressions known in the Jerusalem Talmud and the Midrash, although in the Targums to the Five Scrolls many linguistic features of the Aramaic of the Babylonian Talmud occur. Their unofficial status was probably due to the fact that they were not used in the public synagogue service (with the exception of Esther, though in later times all Five Scrolls were used in the liturgy of the synagogue) or school. The Targum to the Book of Job, which existed in the first century C.E. according to the Babylonian Talmud (Shab. 115a), cannot be identified with the Targum to this biblical book in existence now, which is a product of a much later period. Its relation to the Aramaic translation of Job from Qumran (see below) is a matter for speculation. The various Targums of this part of the Bible may be conveniently classified into three categories: Targums of Job, Psalms, and Proverbs; of the Five Scrolls; and of Chronicles.

JOB. This Targum and that of Psalms may have had a common origin, in view of the many similarities between them. Both aim at giving a fairly faithful rendering of the Hebrew text, and although aggadic additions are present from time to time, they are brief and can easily be separated from the translation itself. Each Targum contains a number of double renderings (Job has between 40 and 50, Psalms has fewer); the second rendering is introduced by ת"א (*targum aḥer*) and is considered by some the original one. In such cases, one of the translations is generally aggadic, while the other is more literal. About six verses in Job even have a third rendering. An indication of an early date is contained in Job 4:10, where the word שני which the masoretic pointing interprets, in accordance with the context, as *shinnei* ("the teeth of") is interpreted by the translator as *shenei* ("the two"), apparently alluding to Rome and Constantinople as the two capitals of the Roman Empire – a fact which would indicate that the work was composed before the fall of Rome in 476 C.E. (cf. the Targum on Ps. 108:10). Another common feature of these two Targums is the fact that between them they contain about a hundred variants in vowels and even consonants from the masoretic text, a feature not found with such frequency in the other Targums. Since a number of these same variants also occur in the Peshitta and the *Septuagint, they offer adequate proof of an early date of composition for these two Targums. In both the two constant themes are the law of God and its study as well as the future life and its retribution. A Targum to Job was among the many finds discovered among the Dead Sea *Scrolls in 1947. A preliminary study on some of the fragments was published by J.P.M. van der Ploeg (see bibliography; see also A.S. van der Woude, in VT Supplement, 9 (1962), 322–31). This was followed by their editio princeps, and then byan edition by Sokoloff (bibliography) in 1974. A neglected fragment was rediscovered by Reed and Zuckerman in 1992.

PSALMS. This Targum is partly allegorical and partly literal; thus it was probably the work of more than one hand. The paraphrase in it is explanatory rather than simply expansive (e.g., 29:1; 46:4). An indication of an early date is Psalms 108:10, which still mentions the Western Roman Empire. In Psalms 18 the targumist has availed himself of the Targum to II Samuel 22, although without adopting the linguistic peculiarities of the Babylonian recension of Targum Jonathan

PROVERBS. A unique feature of this Targum is its striking similarity to the Peshitta. Various explanations have been offered for this phenomenon (Komlosh, 31–32). Some think that the Targum was influenced by the Peshitta and was actually a Jewish recension of it; others consider the possibility of both versions being separate reworkings of an older Aramaic version. About one third of the verses in this Targum agree with the Peshitta against the reading of the Hebrew original (e.g., 1:7; 4:26; 5:9; 7:22, 23; 9:11; 12:19; 16:4, 25)

FIVE SCROLLS. The Targums of these books are essentially a collection of Midrashim, and consequently they are exclusively paraphrastic and verbose in form. Only in a few instances, where no Midrash can be utilized, are they literal in their approach. The exception is the text of the Targum Esther in the Antwerp Polyglot, which is almost a literal translation; the text of the London Polyglot, which is essentially the same as that of the Antwerp Polyglot but has many aggadic additions, is now the standard Targum text to Esther. The Targums of Ruth and Lamentations are somewhat less paraphrastic than those of Esther, Ecclesiastes, and Song of Songs. An additional Targum exists to the Book of Esther (Targum Sheni). It is much more voluminous than the first Targum of this scroll and is regarded as an amalgam from other Targums and Midrashim. The commentators refer to it as *"aggadah"* and as "Midrash." The earliest mention of Targum Sheni occurs in tractate *Soferim (13:6), and it was probably not completed before 1200 C.E. The Targum of Song of Songs interprets the biblical book as an allegory on the relation between God and Israel and on the history of Israel. The types of paraphrase employed by the various Targums to the Five Scrolls may be summarized as follows: historical parallels; motives and reasons to explain the occurrences of events; etymology and explanation of proper names; figurative language rendered into prose and allegory in the place of narrative; the Sanhedrin, as well as the study of the law, frequently mentioned; appendance of elaborate genealogies to names; and general statements related to names of particular individuals, such as the Patriarchs, Nimrod, Pharaoh, Nebuchadnezzar, Titus, Alexander, and the Messiah.

CHRONICLES. No Targum to this book was known to exist until the appearance of the Polyglot Bibles. It was first published, in a somewhat incomplete form, in 1680–83 from an Erfurt manuscript of 1343 and edited with notes and translation by M.F. Beck. In 1715 a more complete form of the text was edited by D. Wilkins on the basis of a Cambridge manuscript of 1347, which contained a later revision of the targumic text. This Targum is essentially a literal rendering of the Hebrew original, although midrashic amplifications are also employed at times (e.g., I Chron. l:20, 21; 4:18; 7:21; 11:11, 12; 12:32; II Chron. 2:6; 3:1; 23:11). Instances where the author made use of "Jerusalem" Targums to the Pentateuch are Genesis 10:20 and I Chronicles 1:21, and Genesis 36:39 and I Chronicles 1:43. Similarly, acquaintance with Targum Jonathan to the Prophets is suggested when one compares the readings from the books of Samuel and Kings to the readings from the Targum in the synoptic passages in Chronicles, only slight variations occurring between them. The date of the Targum may be surmised from the translation of geographical names, as well as their rendering into modern forms. The final redaction of the Erfurt manuscript has been assigned to the eighth century, and that of the Cambridge manuscript to the ninth century C.E. (M. Rosenberg and K. Kohler in bibliography).

R. JOSEPH AND THE AUTHORSHIP OF THE HAGIOGRAPHA TARGUMS. The 1680–83 Augsburg edition of Targum to Chronicles carries the title "Targum Rav Yosef." This fact is related to the view that prevailed in early times that R. Joseph b. Ḥama, the Babylonian *amora* who had the reputation of being thoroughly versed in the Targums of the Prophets, was the author of the Targum of the Hagiographa. Thus, a quotation from Targum Sheni to Esther 3:1 is introduced as *kedimtargem Rav Yosef* in tractate *Soferim* 13:6. Furthermore, the Breslau Library manuscript of 1238 appends the following statement to apocryphal additions to Esther known as "*Ḥalom Mordekhai*": "This is the end of the book of the Targum on the Hagiographa, translated by R. Joseph." The 12th-century commentator *Samuel b. Meir quoted passages on Job and Proverbs in the name of R. Joseph (see Ex. 15:2; Lev. 20:17). In the Talmud, the phrase *kedimtargem Rav Yosef*, "as R. Joseph has translated," occurs frequently, but it occurs only with reference to passages in the Prophets and once in the Pentateuch (cf. Sot. 48b). It was inferred that R. Joseph was also the author of the known Hagiographa Targums, but on the basis of the basically Palestinian linguistic character of the Hagiographa Targums, as well as the variety of the translation techniques, which mitigate against the view of one author for all of them, this opinion has been rejected as historically without basis. Furthermore, the *Tosafot* (Shab. 115a) assign the origin of the Hagiographa Targums to tannaitic times (cf. Meg. 21b).

BIBLIOGRAPHY: EDITIO PRINCEPS: Targum Onkelos: Bologna, 1482, Sabbioneta, 1557; Targum Pseudo-Jonathan: Venice, 1591; Fragmentary Targum: *Rabbinic Bible*, Venice, 1518; Targum Jonathan: Leira, 1494, Venice, 1518; Targum to Hagiographa: Venice, 1517; *Ms. Neofiti I-Genesis* (A. Diez-Macho), Madrid-Barcelona, 1968. CRITICAL EDITIONS: A. Sperber, *The Bible in Aramaic*, 1–3 (1959–62); M. Ginsburger, *Pseudo-Jonathan* (1903); idem, *Das Fragmententhargum* (1899); A. Diez-Macho, *Biblia Polyglotta, Matritensia IV/5 Deuteronomium Caput I* (1965), 1–23; P. Kahle, *Masoreten des Westens*, 2 (1930), 1–65; J.F. Stenning, *The Targum of Isaiah* (1953²); P. de Lagarde, *Hagiographa chaldaica* (1873); R.H. Melamed, *The Targum to Canticles According to Six Yemen Mss.* (1921). LEXICONS, TRANSLATIONS, GRAMMARS, AND CONCORDANCES: Jastrow, Dict; S. Krauss, *Griechische und Lateinische Lehnwoerter im Talmud, Midrasch und Targum*, 2 vols. (1898–99); J.W. Etheridge, *The Targums of Onkelos and Jonathan ben Uzziel on the Pentateuch with the Fragments of the Jerusalem Targum* (1862–65, 1968); G.H. Dalman, *Grammatik des Juedisch-Palastinischen Aramaeisch* (1905, 1960); H.J. Kassovsky, *Oẓar ha-Targum* (1940). GENERAL WORKS: Geiger, Urschrift, 159–70; M. Ginsburger, *Die Anthropomorphismen in den Thargumim* (1891); H.Z. Hirschberg, in: *Sefer ha-Shanah shel Bar-Ilan*, I (1963), 16–23; M.R. Lehman, in: *Revue de Qumran*, 1 (1958), 249–63; M. Mc-Namara, in: CBQ, 28 (1966), 1–19; M. Martin, in: *Orientalia et Biblica Lovaniensia*, 4 (1962), 425–51; S. Maybaum, *Die Anthropomorphien und Anthropopathien bei Onkelos und die spaeteren Targumim* (1870); A. Sperber, *The Bible in Aramaic*, 4 (1969); G. Vermes, in: *Annual of the Leeds University Oriental Society*, 3 (1960–61), 81–114; Zunz, Vortraege; P. Nickels, *Targum and New Testament, a Bibliography* (1967). TARGUM ONKELOS: A. Berliner, *Targum Onkelos*, 1–2 (1884); M. Friedmann, *Onkelos und Akylas* (1896); S.D. Luzzatto, *Ohev Ger* (1830); A.E. Silverstone, *Aquila and Onkelos* (1931); A. Sperber, in: *Jewish Studies in Memory of G.A. Kohut* (1935), 554–64, PALESTINIAN TARGUM: Geiger, Urschrift, 451–80; A. Diez-Macho, in: VT Supplement, 7 (1960), 222ff.; idem, in: CNFI, 13 pt. 2 (1962), 19–25; M. Mc-Namara, *The New Testament and the Palestinian Targum to the Pentateuch* (1966). TARGUM JONATHAN: Z. Frankel, in: MGWJ, 21 (1872), 192ff.; P. Churgin, *Targum Jonathan to the Prophets* (1907). HAGIOGRAPHA TARGUMIM: W. Bacher, in: MGWJ, 21 (1872), 408–16, 463–73; 20 (1871), 208–23, 283–4; P. Churgin, *Targum Ketuvim* (1945); Y. Komlosh, in: *Sefer M.H. Segal* (1964), 265–70; J.P.M. van der Ploeg, *Le targum de Job de la grotte 11 de Qumran* (1962); M. Rosenberg and K. Kohler, in: JZWL, 8 (1870), 72–80, 135–63, 263–78; J. Shunary, in: *Textus*, 5 (1966), 133–44; A.S. van der Woude, in: VT Supplement, 9 (1963). **ADD. BIBLIOGRAPHY:** D. Barthélemy, *Les devanciers d'Aquila* (1963); A. Diez Macho, *Neophyti I, Targum Palestinense ms. de la Biblioteca Vaticana* Vols. I–VI (1968–79); R. le Déaut and J. Robert, *Targum des Chroniques* (1971); J. van der Ploeg et al., *Le Targum de Job del la grotte xi* *de Qumran* (1971); B. Grossfeld, *A Bibliography of Targum Literature* (1972); S. Kaufman, in: JAOS 93 (1973), 317–27; idem, ABD IV, 173–78; idem (ed.), "CAL Bibliographic Resources," electronically available at: CAL1.cn.huc.edu; E.Z. Melammed, *Mefarshei ha-Mikra* (detailed description and analysis of targumic techniques; 1978), 131–352; E.Y. Kutscher, *Hebrew and Aramaic Studies* (1977); M. Sokoloff, *The Targum to Job from Qumran Cave XI* (1974); idem, *A Dictionary of Jewish Palestinian Aramaic of the Byzantine Period* (DJPA; 1990); idem, *A Dictionary of Jewish Babylonian Aramaic* (DJBA; 2002); Y. Komlosh, in: C. Rabin (ed.), *Bible Translation An Introduction* (1988), 5–44; A. Tal, *The Language of the Targum of the Former Prophets and its Position within the Aramaic Dialects* (1975); M. Klein, in: JJS, 26 (1975), 61–67; idem,*The Fragment-Targums of the Pentateuch* (1980); idem, *Anthropomorphisms and Anthropopathisms in the Targumim of the Pentateuch* (1982); idem, *Genizah Manuscripts of Palestinian Targum to the Pentateuch* (1986); B. Levy, *Targum Neofiti I: A Textual Study*, 2 vols. (1986, 1987); J. Blenkinsopp, *Ezra-Nehemiah* (1988); P. Alexander, in: M. Mulder (ed.), *Mikra* (1988), 217–53; idem, in: ABD, 321–31; S. Fassberg, *A Grammar of the Palestinian Targum Fragments from the Cairo Genizah* (1990); M. Cohen (ed.), *Mikra'ot Gedolot "Haketer"* (1992ff.); S. Reed and B. Zuckerman, in: CAL *Newsletter* 10 (1993), 1–7; M. McNamara et al. (eds.), *The Aramaic Bible* (ongoing series of English translations of the Aramaic Targums; 1987ff);,idem, in: A. Hauser and D. Watson (eds.), *A History of Biblical Interpretation* (2003), 189–90; F. Starke, in: *WdO*, 24 (1993) 20–38; D. Stec, *The Text of the Targum of Job: An Introduction and Critical Edition* (1994); J. Greenfield, in: *Al Kanfei Yonah..Collected Studies... J.C. Greenfield...* (2001), 361–65; C.Mueller-Kessler, in: *Journal for the Aramaic Bible* (JAB) 3 (2001), 181–98; C.M. Brady, *The Rabbinic Targum of Lamentations* (2003): D. Shepherd, *Targum and Translation: A Reconsideration of the Qumran Aramaic of Job* (2004).

[Bernard Grossfeld / S. David Sperling (2nd ed.)]

Greek: The Septuagint

The Septuagint (or LXX) is an important corpus of ancient Jewish writings that includes Greek translations of all of the books of the Hebrew Bible and of other works originally composed in Hebrew or Aramaic, plus several original compositions in Greek. It functioned as Sacred Writ for Greek-speaking Jewish communities from the mid-third century B.C.E. until sometime in the early centuries of the Christian Era. At an early period, Christians adopted the Septuagint as their Old Testament, which led to its losing favor, although not all of its status, among Jews. The Septuagint is important as the first written translation of the Hebrew Bible; as a repository of otherwise unobtainable data about the beliefs, practices, and language of Hellenistic Judaism; and as an influence on the thinking of subsequent, primarily (although not exclusively) Christian religious thinkers.

Evidence of the origins of the Septuagint can be found in documents such as the Letter of *Aristeas, which probably dates to the early or mid-second century B.C.E. Although it purports to be an eyewitness account of the events it describes, in all probably it is separated from them by about a century. As related in the Letter, the reigning king of Egypt, *Ptolemy II Philadelphus (285–246 B.C.E.), sought to include in his growing Library at Alexandria, a Greek copy of the Jewish Law; that is, the Torah. To accomplish this, he invites the High Priest in Jerusalem to send 72 elders, of unblemished moral character and outstanding linguistic skills in both Hebrew and Greek, to Alexandria to prepare the desired Greek text. After a series of lavish banquets, distinguished by the depth of conversation as much as the breadth of foodstuffs – the elders/translators go off to palatial quarters to accomplish their task. They work in teams, as is often the case to this day, preparing preliminary drafts and arguing back and forth to arrive at renderings on which they could all agree. When their finished version is read before the assembled Jews of Alexandria, it elicits great acclaim and an anathema/curse is pronounced on anyone who would change even a word of it.

This narrative, which describes only the origins of the Greek Pentateuch, contains sufficient historical inaccuracies and inconsistencies to render it impossible to consider the work a product of the reign of Ptolemy II. Over the past century, there has been considerable scholarly debate on how much, if anything, can be salvaged from the Letter that is historically reliable or at least probable. On the positive side, there is firm consensus that the LXX Pentateuch does originate in Alexandria and from a period prior to the mid-third century B.C.E. It is also clear that its translators were indeed Jews who were reasonably well versed in Hebrew and in koine Greek. Additionally, it is certain that the books of the Torah were the first to be translated and that they served as a model (sometimes followed, sometimes ignored) by those responsible for subsequent books of the LXX.

Serious doubt, however, has been cast on the Letter's portrayal of royal initiative as the decisive factor in the creation of the text. Does it not, it might be asked, make more sense to seek LXX origins within the Alexandrian Jewish community itself, which saw the need for an authoritative Greek version of Sacred Writ, as fluency in, or even familiarity with, Hebrew became rarer and rarer? But it is most likely that both internal and external causes were responsible for this groundbreaking endeavor (this was the first time, so far as we know, that a "barbarian text" such as Hebrew Scripture was rendered into Greek); such a confluence of interests accords better with both the history of the times and later developments in Bible translation than does a dogmatic either/or formulation.

Although Aristeas pictures the LXX Pentateuch as the result of committee actions at one particular time and place, modern scholars detect at least five (and perhaps six) different translators at work on the Five Books of Moses. They are different enough to be identifiable, but all five (or six) were working within the same general parameters: what might be termed reasonable and somewhat flexible literalism, on occasion bending the Greek rather far in the direction of the Hebrew original, at other times showing a deep concern for a Greek-speaking audience.

The author of the Letter of Aristeas sees little of what might be called "miraculous" in the production of the LXX Pentateuch. He does note, somewhat sheepishly, that the 72 translators worked exactly 72 days (and nights). Later on, within both Judaism and especially Christianity, this relatively restrained account was embellished in many directions. Within the Jewish world, it is primarily to the first century C.E. philosopher *Philo, himself a native of Alexandria, that we owe several significant additions to Aristeas' narrative. For example, Philo names the Island of Pharos as the location at which the translators worked, and he describes an annual festival, still observed in his day, to honor their work. Moreover, he speaks of those responsible for the Septuagint as prophets rather than (mere) translators. In this way, he is able to account for material that was found in the Greek but not in the Hebrew text.

As fully elaborated in the work of the fourth century Christian writer Epiphanius, each of the translators was isolated in a cell and cut off from discussion or comparisons with his colleagues – and yet all 72 produced texts that were identical in every detail (in other forms of the tradition, the translators worked in pairs). This and other "miraculous" occurrences served to demonstrate the sacredness of the text produced and the role it was to play as Scripture for Christians.

It is not entirely clear what the author of Aristeas intended in this regard. On the one hand, as noted above, the deliberations of the elders proceeded in much the same way as modern teams of Bible translators operate. Nonetheless, what they produced was accepted as somehow authoritative by the Alexandrian Jewish community and, by extension, the larger Jewish world. This is seen not only in the curse uttered against all who might change it, but also in the deliberate way in which the reception of the Septuagint is modeled on the reception of the Ten Commandments and accompanying laws in the biblical book of Exodus.

It is likely that when the author of the Letter of Aristeas fashioned a communal curse on those who would change the Greek Pentateuch, he had some specific concerns in mind that were relevant to his own second century B.C.E. context; that is to say, as early as that date, if not even before then, there were individuals who were revising the Septuagint of the Pentateuch and of other books subsequently translated. Such individuals, who may have come from or worked in Jerusalem, judged most, if not all, differences between the LXX and their Hebrew text as deficiencies in the Greek, and they therefore sought to "correct" the LXX in the direction of the Hebrew text of their community. Although they probably also had some linguistic interests, their goal, as well as their motivation, was primarily what may be described as theological.

As noted above, Philo, while also recognizing differences between the Greek and the Hebrew, devised another explanation entirely; namely, that these divergences were as much a part of God's inspired message as were the far more numerous places where the Greek and the Hebrew were in agreement. It may be that the author of the Letter of Aristeas had, in some inchoate sense, a similar intimation; if so, he did not explicitly express it. For most early Christians, the creators of the LXX, whether they knew it or not, were prophetic in the sense that much of their distinctive wording looked forward to the coming of Jesus as Christ. And this was in spite of the fact that the LXX was created for Jews by Jews, almost three centuries before Jesus' birth!

We are, it would seem, without much, if any, external information (that is, outside of the text of the LXX itself) on the location, order, or modus operandi of those responsible for the LXX beyond the Pentateuch. With few exceptions, it is reasonable to place these translators within the context of Alexandria. It is also likely that the book of Joshua was translated next after the Pentateuch. Beyond that, there are a few, but only a few, references to historical figures or events that can be gleaned from any of the LXX books; more numerous are likely examples of dependence of one LXX book (or, better, its translator) on another, thereby allowing for some tentative relative, although not absolute, ordering of books chronologically.

The task of discerning the history of the creation of the LXX is further complicated by the nature of the evidence. For the most part, our earliest texts for this Greek material derive from codices (manuscripts in book form, rather than scrolls) from the third and fourth centuries C.E.; in particular, Codex Vaticanus, Codex Alexandrinus, and Codex Sinaiticus. The codices are uncials (that is, written in all capital letters) from important Christian scriptoria; therefore, they contain the LXX as part of their "Bible" (the New Testament completes it for them). There is no reason to think that Christian scribes deliberately changed the originally Jewish text for tendentious, theological reasons, although it is certain that all sorts of scribal changes led to many differences, some substantial, between what the codices contain and what the earliest Greek (or Old Greek) read. We are not without earlier evidence in the form of a limited number of Greek texts from Qumran and other Dead Sea locales; citations, allusions, and reworkings in the New Testament; and Qumran scrolls that preserve in Hebrew the likely *Vorlage* or text that lay before the LXX translators (which, as noted above, is sometimes close to our received or Masoretic Text, but on occasion quite different from it).

A reasoned and important conclusion from an analysis of all of this material is that what we term *the* Septuagint is in fact an almost accidental gathering together of texts from diverse sources. Some of the books of the Septuagint, as in the Pentateuch, appear to be quite close to the Old Greek. In other cases, the earliest form of the translation is lost in almost all sources (as in Daniel), or is entirely lost (as for Ecclesiastes), or is combined with later material (as in Reigns [that is, the books of Samuel and Kings]). Even when due allowance is made for this diversity of origins, scholars are struck by the very different ways in which translators approached their Hebrew. The range runs the gamut from almost wooden literalism to recontextualizing to paraphrase. It used to be argued that the translators of Ketuvim were freer inasmuch as those books were considered somewhat less important that the Torah and Nevi'im. Such a contention does not, however, stand up under close scrutiny. The point needs to be made that we simply do not know why translators treated their material as they did or why one Greek version of a book was chosen over another (when competing versions were available).

We cannot even be sure of exactly what the LXX "canon" contained. Surely, all the books of the Hebrew Bible were included, as well as additions to Daniel and to Esther that, although attached in one way or another to the earlier Hebrew material, have been preserved only in Greek (whether they were translations of now lost Hebrew or Aramaic texts or original Greek compositions). Other books that apparently were never part of the Hebrew Bible are also found in the fully developed LXX corpus. For the most part, this material is found in the Old Testament of Roman Catholics and Orthodox Christians; Protestants tend to refer to it as the Apocrypha. It is likely that for some communities, this assemblage reflected Scripture. Whether or not that determination comes from Christians, it is important to keep in mind the Jewish origins and early development of the LXX.

In the third century C.E., the Church Father *Origen gathered together in his *Hexapla* as many examples as he could find of the Greek Bible. Among them were three apparently continuous Greek texts later than the Old Greek, all of which seem to have originated within Jewish communities (although ancient evidence and modern scholarship remain ambivalent on key issues). One of these texts is attributed to *Aquila (traditionally dated to the second century C.E.); it is hyperliteral and can almost serve as a primer to the Hebrew language as well as to biblical thought and teaching. Another version is associated with Symmachus (late second century C.E.); it reads well in Greek, but at the cost of linguistic and other departures from the Hebrew original. A third version, attributed to Theodotion (second century CE), seems to balance the often-competing interests of source language (in this case, Hebrew) and target language (here, Greek).

It is entirely likely that all three of these individuals, about whom very little can be definitely said, were Jewish, although the ancient (and sometimes modern) connection of each with a particular rabbi or school of rabbinical thought can no longer be held. The case of Theodotion is particularly interesting, since some of his distinctive language found its way into the New Testament – almost two centuries earlier than the "historical" Theodotion is said to have lived. This has led to the supposition of a "Proto-Theodotion," who would have been active in the first century B.C.E. In the case of Aquila, it is accurate to describe him as a reviser; that is to say, he started with an older form of the Greek, which he changed only when he saw a theological or linguistic reason for doing so. Theodotion was also a reviser in some instances; elsewhere as in Daniel, where his text supplanted the Old Greek in nearly all manuscripts, Theodotion appears as a fresh translation, as seems often to be the case with Symmachus as well.

The observation that at least some of these later Greek texts are the result of Jewish revision should cause the rejection or at least serious modification of the often-expressed view that Jews abandoned the Septuagint when Christians adopted (or co-opted) it. The very fact that at least some Jewish translators chose to revise the older Greek demonstrates their allegiance to it, even when circumstances led them to change it in a given number of instances. Moreover, as can be seen from fragments preserved in the Cairo Genizah and elsewhere, Greek-speaking Jews continued to rely on a Greek "Bible," in particular a developed form of Aquila, well into the Byzantine era.

Nonetheless, it is true that the Septuagint ceased to be a concern for most Jews from the first century of the common era until early in the 19th century, when some Jewish scholars (such as Z. *Frankel) began to look seriously at it as a heritage of their past. In so doing, they uncovered many places where interpretative material in the LXX reflected concerns found in rabbinic discussions. Also fairly numerous are instances of what might be termed rabbinic-like midrash.

These findings alert scholars once again to the fact that the Septuagint, as a document of Hellenistic Judaism, is a repository of thought from that period. It is very difficult, often impossible, to determine whether distinctive elements of LXX presentation are the results of "creative activity" on the part of the translators themselves or accurately reflect their *Vorlage,* which in these cases differed from the MT. Caution is strongly advised when making statements that characterize LXX thought in one way or another, since, as noted above, the LXX is not a unified document, and its translators did not adopt a standardized approach to their Hebrew text. Moreover, it is inappropriate to describe the "world of the LXX or LXX thought" solely in terms of differences between it and our received Hebrew Text, for this would leave out their many points of near or total convergence.

It is then not surprising that the rabbis of the early common era had decidedly negative things to say about the LXX (see, for example, Tractate *Soferim* 1:8) as well as some positive statements about its value (as in Meg. 9 a–b); see also the passages within rabbinic literature that cite a tradition according to which between 10 and 18 alterations were inserted into the Greek translation of the Pentateuch. It is not easy to organize these differing opinions chronologically or geographically – or in any other way. The rabbis, or at least some of them, were open to extra-Jewish (re)sources so long as they were kept subservient to what the rabbis understood as the core values of Judaism. But, as has often been pointed out, a given language cannot be completely separated from the values of the society in which it is spoken. Thus, whatever acceptance the LXX found among the rabbis can be aptly described as grudging.

Today the LXX is studied by a growing number of Jewish scholars worldwide. As part of their heritage, Jews in general should not be averse to learning about the Septuagint, its development, and its distinctive features. It is a priceless reminder of a time and place, not unlike our own, when Jews struggled to varying degrees of success with issues of self-identification and accommodation within a cosmopolitan world in and of which they were a creative minority.

BIBLIOGRAPHY: S. Jelllicoe. *The Septuagint and Modern Study* (1968); H.M. Orlinsky, in: *Hebrew Union College Annual*, 46 (1975): 89–114; S. Tov, in: *Journal for the Study of Judaism*, 15 (1984): 65–89; M.K.H. Peters, in: *Anchor Bible Dictionary* 5 (1992): 1093–1104; M. Harl et al. (eds.), *La Bible grecque des Septanate: Du Judaïsme hellénistique au Christianism ancien* (1994[2]); C. Dogniez, *Bibliography of the Septuagint = Bibliographie de la Septante (1970–1993)* (1995); J.W. Wevers, in: M. Saebø (ed.), *Hebrew Bible*, OT: *The History of Its Interpretation*, vol. 1 (1996), 84–107; E. Tov, *The Text-Critical Use of the Septuagint in Biblical Research* (1997[2]); N. Fernández Marcos, *The Septuagint in Context: Introduction to the Greek Version of the Bible* (2000); L.J. Greenspoon, in: A.J. Hauser (ed.), *A History of Biblical Interpretation*, vol. 1 (2003), 80–113; L.J. Greenspoon, in: A. Berlin and M.Z. Brettler (eds.), *The Jewish Study Bible* (2004), 2005–20; J.M. Dines. *The Septuagint* (2004).

[Leonard J. Greenspoon (2nd ed.)]

Old Latin / Vulgate

The earliest evidence for a Latin translation of the Bible comes from the scriptural quotations of the Christian writer Cyprian of Carthage in the middle of the third century C.E. By the end of the following century, different recensions of the Latin Bible were circulating in Italy, Gaul, and Spain. Whereas some modern scholars believe the evidence indicates that there was a single original Latin text that underwent various developments (corruption, revision, expansion) to produce these recensions, the evidence is inconclusive and there remains no consensus. In the face of such historical obscurity and textual uncertainty, the term "Old Latin" or *Vetus Latina* (OL) refers not to a single and complete translation of the Bible but rather to the various Latin texts prior to Jerome's new translation from the Hebrew, production on which began in the late fourth century. Until the late fourth century, the OL was constantly being revised based on a growing number of Greek versions produced during the first centuries C.E. (e.g., those of Aquila, Symmachus, and Theodotion). Indeed, Augustine of Hippo complained that in his day so many Christians were inserting Greek-based corrections into the Latin text that there appeared to be as many Latin versions as codices.

In contrast to the LXX and the Masoretic Text (MT), the OL has not enjoyed rigorous and systematic study. Thus much of what may be said about the OL in relation to these other ancient translations is subject to revision, particularly as scholars continue to study these ancient translations in light of the biblical texts of the Dead Sea Scrolls. While the OL Pentateuch is assumed to have direct Jewish and Hebrew origins, in general the OL is considered to be a translation of the LXX, and as such, constitutes a secondary witness to the text of the Hebrew Bible. Like the LXX, the OL is not a unified translation, varying from book to book. At times, some texts of the OL can preserve earlier forms of the LXX, often referred to as the Old Greek (OG), that have not survived in Greek manuscript form. It is here that the OL can be an important witness to the textual criticism of the OG. Furthermore, the study of the OL can be particularly valuable when considering a book for which the LXX and MT may vary greatly like Samuel. In these situations, it is possible that the OL can contain an earlier Hebrew text than that found in the MT.

In 383, Pope Damasus I commissioned *Jerome (c. 347–420), the leading biblical scholar of the day and his personal secretary, to revise the OL Gospels in light of the LXX. He continued, on his own initiative, by revising the Psalter according to the LXX. This recension became known as the Gallican Psalter because of its use by Charlemagne in Gaul. In 386, shortly after relocating to Bethlehem, where he spent the last part of his life, Jerome discovered Origen's *Hexapla* in the library of nearby Caesarea. The *Hexapla* was Origen's edition of the Hebrew Bible / Old Testament presenting most of the books in six parallel columns, the fifth consisting of a critical text of the LXX with signs indicating where the Greek differed from the Hebrew. Jerome used these signs in his amended edition of the Latin versions of the Psalms, Job, Chronicles, and the books attributed to Solomon (viz., Proverbs, Ecclesiastes, Song of Songs). Through this work, Jerome found the LXX increasingly unsatisfactory and became convinced of both the supreme authority of the Hebrew and the necessity of producing a fresh translation based on the original "Hebrew truth" (*Hebraica veritas*). Jerome embarked on his new Latin translation "according to the Hebrew" (*iuxta Hebraeos*) around 390 and by 405 had completed his work on the Hebrew Bible.

Because he accepted the Hebrew canon as authentic Scripture (i.e., as *Hebraica veritas*), Jerome did not translate the deuterocanonical books (with the exception of Tobit and Judith). Thus, the Latin version of the Bible that became the official text of the western Church from the early Middle Ages and that was given the name Vulgate in the 16th century was not produced entirely by Jerome. Rather, the Vulgate includes Jerome's translations from the Hebrew text (the Psalter excepted), his versions of Tobit and Judith, his revision of the Gospels, and his revision of the Psalter made from the *Hexapla* (i.e., the Gallican Psalter). It is now generally believed that the Vulgate version of the epistles, Acts, and the Apocalypse is not the work of Jerome himself but rather that of an unknown hand or hands.

From the early medieval period, the biblical text of the Vulgate has exerted an incalculable influence not only on Roman Catholic teaching and piety, but also on the languages and literature of western Europe. This text remains the basis for some modern translations (e.g., that of Ronald Knox into English). In 1979, Pope John Paul II promulgated a new official revision of the Vulgate according to the Hebrew and the Greek. Furthermore, in 1987 Benedictine monks of the Monastery of St. Jerome completed a critical edition of the Vulgate that includes the most certain findings of modern biblical scholarship and exegesis.

BIBLIOGRAPHY: J. Trebolle Barrera, *The Jewish Bible and the Christian Bible: An Introduction to the History of the Bible*, tr. W.G.E. Watson (1998); A. Kamesar, *Jerome, Greek Scholarship, and the Hebrew Bible* (1993); J.N.D. Kelly, *Jerome: His Life, Writings, and Controversies*

(1975); W. McKane. *Selected Christian Hebraists* (1989); E. Ulrich, *The Dead Sea Scrolls and the Origins of the Bible* (1999).

[Franklin T. Harkins and Angela Kim Harkins (2nd ed.)]

Samaritan

The Samaritan Bible contains only the *Pentateuch. In many Pentateuch manuscripts the Samaritan Hebrew text is accompanied by a targum into Samaritan, a western Aramaic dialect. Sometimes the targum was copied separately. Tal, who provided the first reliable critical edition, dates the production of the Samaritan targum to the middle of the third century. No manuscripts survive from the time that Samaritan Aramaic was a spoken language. As a result much of the ancient text was corrupted by the penetration of Arabic, which replaced Aramaic as the spoken language, and by Hebrew. Nonetheless, several manuscripts preserve the older Samaritan Aramaic, which is very close to that of the Palestinian targums. The Samaritan targum is more literal than the Jewish targums and usually has one Aramaic word for each Hebrew word. Tal (1988) has shown, nonetheless, that subtle midrashic and paraphrastic interpretations are to be found, especially when it comes to apologizing for the actions of biblical heroes and defaming unpopular characters like Esau and Nimrod, a penchant it shares with Jewish midrash. The younger manuscripts tend to be more paraphrastic than the older. Similarities between the Samaritan targum and Onkelos are probably due the late activity of learned Samaritan scribes (Tal 1989).

BIBLIOGRAPHY: A. Tal, *The Samaritan Targum of the Pentateuch*, 3 vols. (1980–83); idem, in: Rabin (ed.) *Bible Translation* (1984), 45–8; idem, in: Mulder (ed.), *Mikra* (1988), 189–216; idem, in: A. Crown (ed.), *The Samaritans* (1989), 413–67; idem, in: JAB 1 (1999), 297–314; idem, *A Dictionary of Samaritan Aramaic* (2000); R. Macuch, *Grammatik des Samaritanischen Aramäisch* (1982); R. Anderson, *Encyclopedia of Religion*, 13:33–6.

[S. David Sperling (2nd ed.)]

Syriac Aramaic: Peshitta and Other Versions

There is no unanimity as to the precise meaning of the term "Peshitta" (*pšyṭt'*), the Syriac Bible translation in use in the Church of the East ("Nestorian"), the Syrian Orthodox ("Jacobite") Church, and the Maronite Church. Until the late Middle Ages the Peshitta was also the Bible of the Byzantine Syrian Malkite Church. The Peshitta comprises the Old Testament (*diatiqi atiqta*), the New Testament (*diatiqi ḥdata*), and the Apocrypha or deutero-canonical books (on the classification of Syriac within the dialects of Late Aramaic see S. Kaufman, ABD IV, 174–75). Once confined in the main to Asia, Syriac-speaking churches that use the Peshitta are now found in the United States and Europe as well. Grammatically, the feminine form of the passive participle of the verb *pešaṭ*, "stretch out," "extend," "make straight," "Peshitta" has been taken to mean "simple," as opposed to paraphrastic; "in common use," as against the Syro-Hexaplaric translation (see below) and "monolingual edition." (Unlike its Jewish-Aramaic and Middle Hebrew cognate *pšṭ*, the Syriac verb does not mean "explain.") The Peshitta conforms closely to the Hebrew text though it often makes additions for the sake of clarity. (For translation techniques see Weitzman 1996.) Although this version was used by the fourth-century scholars Aphrahat and Ephraim the Syrian and Theodore of Mopsuestia (d. 428) the name Peshitta was first used by Moses b. Kefa (d. 913) and then in the 13th century by *Gregory Bar Hebraeus. Almost every assertion regarding the authorship of the Peshitta and the time and place of its origin is the subject of controversy among scholars. Jacob of Edessa (eighth century) ascribes the origin of the Peshitta to the efforts of Abgar, "the believing" king of Edessa, and Addai the apostle, who are said to have sent scholars to Palestine to translate the Bible into Syriac (cf. Bar Hebraeus, Commentary to Ps. 10). However, this tradition apparently conflates Abgar IX (179–216), who may have been history's first Christian king, with the first century Abgar V, to whom later specious documents attributed epistolary correspondence with Jesus. Addai the apostle is completely legendary. J Other legendary traditions with no historical value assign the work to the time of Solomon, and ascribe the translation to an order of Hiram, king of Tyre, or to the priest Assa (alternative: Asya) sent by an Assyrian king to Samaria (a legend based on II Kings 17:27–28).

Although the Peshitta is the Bible of eastern Christians, at least parts of it were known to medieval Jews. *Naḥmanides in his introduction to Genesis cites and translates into Hebrew a long passage that he had seen in a book he calls "The Great Wisdom of Solomon," which he refers to as *ha-sefer ha-meturgam*, "the translated book." The citation, in Syriac in Hebrew characters, is essentially identical with a verse from Wisdom of Solomon in Peshitta. This same scholar in his commentary to Deuteronomy 21:14 cites a passage from Peshitta Judith 1:8 which he describes as being "in the Aramaic language." As to the origin of Peshitta's Old Testament section, some scholars argue for Jewish translators, others for Christian translators, and still others for Jewish-Christians. The general contemporary consensus that the Peshitta's Old Testament section was directly translated from the Hebrew indicates strongly that the translators had a Jewish background. There are very few obvious Christological elements. For example, the translation, *betulah*, "virgin," for Hebrew *almah*, "young woman," in Isaiah 8:14 in line with Matthew 1:23, "behold the virgin shall conceive," may be seen in the light of Biblical Hebrew *betulah*, "virgin," "young woman," and Greek *parthenos* with the same meanings. Even if *virgo intacta* is meant, Peshitta *betulta* could be a late Christian adaptation (Vööbus 1958), as are the superscriptions of certain Psalms. Evidence for Christian origins has also been adduced from the indifference or negative attitude of the translators to rabbinic and even Pentateuchal legal norms relating to the calendar, sacrifice, and, possibly, the dietary laws. This too is not conclusive. The last few decades of new discoveries and refined scholarly methods have shown the diversity in both Judaism and Christianity and the porousness of the borders between the two religions. Weitzman (1999) concludes that the Old Testament Peshitta is of non-rabbinic Jewish origin, the work of translators in Edessa, somewhat estranged from the larger Jewish community. The gradual absorption of the Jewish community of Edessa into Christianity could have facilitated the adoption of the Peshitta by Syriac-speaking Christians as their Bible. The Peshitta itself was probably complete by the third century.

The literary relation among the Peshitta and the Jewish Targums has been debated by scholars for 150 years. In his dissertation of 1859 published as *Meletamata Peschitthonia*, J. Perles collected cases in which Peshitta's translation could only be understood as reflective of Jewish legal and non-legal exegesis, an indication of Jewish origins (e.g., Ex. 22:30 and Ḥul. 102b; Lev. 16:7 and Ḥul. 11a; Lev. 18:21 and Meg. 25a; Lev. 24:8 and Men. 97a). Perles goes as far as to say that the text was used in the synagogue since it was divided into weekly lessons for the Palestinian triennial cycle; the portions read in the synagogue on the festival are indicated (Lev. 23:1; cf. Meg. 30b); and the superscriptions to Exodus 20:1 עסרא פתגמין ("Ten Commandments") and Leviticus 17 נמוסא דקורבנא ודדבחא ("The Law of Offerings and Sacrifices") are in the rabbinical spirit (cf. Meg. 30b). According to Perles, the shared Aramaic Jewish exegetical tradition was available orally. Others (Baumstark, Kahle) accounted for these relations by positing a written west Aramaic Jewish Targum that was brought east and rewritten in Syriac. Vööbus accepted the western origin but saw the transformation as gradual. Still others (Sperber) posited an originally Jewish targum geographically and dialectally closer to Syriac. More recently, in his studies of the Peshitta to the Pentateuch, Maori agreed with Perles that Peshitta did not depend on any particular targum but made use of stylized written literary material as well as oral traditions that had already been stylized.

Recent research into the history of the Peshitta text indicates that it was the accepted Bible of the Syrian Church from the end of the third century C.E. Ephraem Syrus, who died in 373, speaks of it as an old translation. In the fifth century theological differences divided the Syrian Christians into two distinct groups, the Nestorians and the Jacobites. Differences were exacerbated by the use of different Syriac scripts. Each group then proceeded to formulate its own Peshitta text based upon previous versions, with the result that there are two different text forms of the Peshitta: Western Syriac and Eastern Syriac. In the fifth and sixth centuries the Melchites (Palestinian Syrians) attempted to make the Eastern Syriac version conform with the Septuagint, the official text of the region, thus creating a text which was a mixture of the Peshitta and the Septuagint.

Knowledge of these versions, recently augmented by finds of textual fragment, is important for an understanding of the evolution of the Peshitta and subsequently in the assessment of the masoretic text. The oldest manuscript dates back to 464. It was first published in the Paris Polyglot Bible of 1645. This edition did not contain the Apocrypha, which were later added in the London Walton Polyglot of 1657. In 1823, the Peshitta was printed separately by the British Foreign Bible Society in London and known as the Lee Edition. This edition, in Jacobite characters, practically reproduces the London Polyglot which itself was based on the Paris Polyglot. Two editions were prepared by American missionaries: The Urmia edition of 1852, and the Mosul edition of 1887–91 (1951^2), both in Nestorian characters: the first work was proved to be influenced by the Lee edition, while the second is dependent on the Lee and Urmia editions and corrected according to the Vulgate. Attempts to publish the Peshitta in Hebrew characters include Hirsch's edition of the Five Scrolls (1866), Eisenstein's edition of the first two chapters of Genesis (1895), and Heller's Genesis (1928). A new era in Peshitta studies began in the late 20th century with the production of reliable texts. The Peshitta Institute in Leiden, Netherlands, is well on the way to the publication of a critical edition of the Peshitta, *Vetus Testamentum Syriace* (1972ff.) as well as monographs on specific books. The text is based in the main on the Ambrosian manuscript 7a1 accompanied by an apparatus of variants from manuscripts through the 12th century. The project is under the general editorship of K. Jenner and A.v.d. Kooij.

THE CHRISTIAN-PALESTINIAN VERSION. Around the fifth century the Melchite Christian in Palestine published a Bible translation in the local western Aramaic dialect, referred to in earlier Anglophone scholarship as Syro-Palestinian but now more accurately referred to as Christian Palestinian Aramaic (CPA). (To refer to this dialect as "Syriac," or "Palestinian Syriac," is erroneous.) The script of CPA is a development from Syriac Estrangelo, which distinguishes it from the closely related western Aramaic dialects of Samaritan and Palestinian Jewish Aramaic. The distinction served to set boundaries among the speakers of these dialects. It is generally admitted that this translation was made from the Greek, rather than the Hebrew, but Jewish Aramaic targums were influential, and perhaps, secondarily, the Peshitta. On the estimate of Mueller-Kessler and Sokoloff only about ten percent of the CPA text of the Old Testament has survived. The apocrypha are represented by fragments of Wisdom of Solomon, Ecclesiasticus, and the Epistle of Jeremiah.

[S. David Sperling (2nd ed.)]

THE PHILOXENIAN VERSION. In an attempt to displace the Peshitta, Philoxenus, the Jacobite bishop of Mabbugh, ordered a translation of the Septuagint (Lucian's version) and the Greek New Testament. Polycarp, his coadjutor, finished the work in 508. Of this translation only fragments from the Old Testament (Isaiah) were preserved, while five books from the New Testament entered into the printed edition of the Peshitta. A century later a version with marginal notes, taking into account various Greek manuscripts, was published by Thomas of Heraclea. It is not known whether in this work Thomas revised the Philoxenian Version completely or confined himself to adding the marginal notes.

THE SYRO-HEXAPLA. Commissioned by the patriarch Athanasius I, Paul, the bishop of Tella (near Alexandria), prepared a translation based on the fifth column of Origen's Hexapla. The translations of Aquila, Theodotion, and Symmachus were taken into account in marginal notes. This translation was completed in about 617. A manuscript of this work from the eighth or ninth century is extant in Milan. Paul of Tella's Syro-Hexapla, as it is called, is of great importance since Origen's Hexapla, upon which it was based, was almost completely destroyed.

BIBLIOGRAPHY: TEXTS OF THE PESHITTA: A.M. *Ceriani Biblia Sacra juxta versionem simplicem, quae dicitur Pschitta* (1951^3); The Peshitta Institute of the University of Leiden, *Vetus Testamentum Syrice et Neosyrice* (1954); idem, *Peshitta... Specimen edition* (1969); for biblical Peshitta manuscripts see VT vol 12 and following; T. Noeldeke, in: *Archiv fuer wissenschaftliche Erforschung des Alten Testaments*, 2 (1871), 246–9; STUDIES: R. Duval, *Anciennes Littératures Chrétiennes*, vol. 22: *La Littérature Syriaque* (1899); F.C. Burkitt, *Early Eastern Christianity* (1904), 39–78; H. Mager, *Die Peschittho zum Buche Joshua* (1916); A. Baumstark, *Geschichte der syrischen Literatur* (1922), idem, in: BZ, 19 (1931), 257–70; P. Kahle, *Masoreten des Westens*, 2 (1930); idem, *The Cairo Geniza* (1959^2), 265–313; C. Moss, in: *Le Muséon*, 46 (1933), 55–110; C. Peters, *ibid.*, 48 (1935), 1–54; 52 (1939), 275–96; idem, in: *Biblica*, 22 (1941), 25–34; P. Churgin, in: *Horeb*, 2 (1935), 259–79; I. Nobel, in: *ibid.*, 10 (1948), 77–104; M. Black, in: BJRL, 33 (1950/51), 203–10; A. Vogel, in: *Biblica*, 32 (1951), 32–56, 198–231, 336–63, 481–502; M. Goshen-Gottstein, in: BJRL, 37 (1954/55), 429–45; idem, *Text and Language in Bible and Qumran* (1960); A. Vööbus, *Peschitta und Targumim des Pentateuchs* (1958); idem, in: *Le Muséon*, 68 (1955), 215–8; E.R. Rowlands, in: VT, 9 (1959), 178–91; J.A. Emerton, *The Peshitta of the Wisdom of Solomon* (1959); W. Baars, in: VT, 10 (1960), 224–7; 13 (1963), 260–8; 18 (1968), 548–54; P. Wernberg-Møller, in: *Studia Theologica*, 15 (1961), 128–80; idem, in: JSS, 7 (1962), 253–66; J.A. Emerton, *ibid.*, 204–11. **ADD. BIBLIOGRAPHY:** J. Bloch, in: AJSL, 35 (1919), 215–22; P. Dirksen, in: M. Mulder (ed.), *Mikra* (1984), 255–97; idem, *An Annotated Bibliography of the Peshitta of the Old Testament* (1989); idem and A. van der Kooij, *The Peshiṭta as a Translation* (1995); S.P. Brock, ABD VI, 794–99; idem, *Syriac Studies: A Classified Bibliography (1960–1990)* (1996); idem, "Syriac," in: S.D. Sperling (ed.), *A New Handbook of Aramaic and its Dialects* (2006); Y. Maori, *The Peshitta Version of the Pentateuch and Early Jewish Exegesis* (Heb., 1995); M. Weitzman, in: M. Sæbø (ed.), *Hebrew Bible / Old Testament* (1996), 587–611; idem, *The Syriac Version of the Old Testament* (1999); P. Borbone et al. (eds.), *The Old Testament in Syriac. Concordance: The Pentateuch* (to be extended to cover entire OT; 1997); D. Walter, in:DBI II, 264–67; R. Taylor, in: JAB 2 (update of Peshitta research; 2000), 119–139. THE CHRISTIAN PALESTINIAN VERSION: J.P.N. Land, in: *Anecdota Syriaca*, 4 (1862–75), 103–224; A.S. Lewis, *A Palestinian Syriac Lectionary ...* (1897); J.T. Milik, in: RB, 60 (1953), 526–39; L. Delekat, in: ZAW, 71 (1959), 165–201. **ADD. BIBLIOGRAPHY:** F. Schlthess, *Grammatik des christlich-palästinischen Aramäisch* (1924); M. Goshen-Gottstein, *The Bible in the Syropalestinian Version* (1973); C. Müller-Kessler, *Grammatik des Christlich-Palästinisch- Aramäischen* (1991), incl. extensive bibl.; idem and M. Sokoloff, *A Corpus of Christian Palestinian Aramaic I: The Christian Palestinian Aramaic Old Testament...* (1997), incl. glossary. THE PHILOXENIAN VERSION: A.M. Ceriani (ed.), *Monumenta Sacra et Profana* vols. 1, 2, 3, 5, 7 (1866–74); L. Delekat, in: ZAW, 69 (1957), 21–54. THE SYRO-HEXAPLA: Ceriani, op. cit. vols. 2, 5, 7; A.P. de Lagarde, *Veteris Testamenti ab Origene recensiti fragmenta* (1880); J.M. Vosté, in: *Biblica*, 26 (1945), 12–36. **ADD. BIBLIOGRAPHY:** S. Brock, ABD, VI, 795.

[Bernard Grossfeld / S. David Sperling (2nd ed.)]

Ethiopic

Christianity arrived in Ethiopia in the fourth century, and the need for a translation of the Bible and the New Testament was felt not long afterward. The original translation into classical Ethiopic (Ge'ez), beginning with the New Testament gospels and the psalms, was probably made during the fifth and sixth centuries, and completed by the mid-seventh century. The translation of the Bible was based on the Greek (Septuagint), the underlying Greek text types varying from book to book. It has commonly been believed that there were also Syriac-speaking missionaries involved in the translation, but this is not proven, and seems unlikely; most of the Aramaic loanwords in early Ethiopic likely derived not from Syriac but rather from a "pre-Christian Jewish element in early Christianity" (Polotsky; Knibb). While there are a few 13th- or possibly 12th-century manuscripts of New Testament gospels, there are no known manuscripts of the Ethiopic Old Testament that survive from before the 14th century, at which time, especially during the literary renaissance under King Amda Sion (1314–44), the text was much revised under the influence of a Syriac-based Arabic version of the Bible; this revised text is known as the "vulgar recension." It was probably later still, during the 15th or 16th century (when there was an Ethiopian community in Jerusalem) that further revisions were made to bring the text closer into alignment with the Hebrew masoretic text; manuscripts of this "academic recension" exhibit a number of Hebrew words simply transliterated into Ethiopic (Knibb). In addition to canonical and apocryphal books, the Ethiopic Bible often contains pseudepigraphic works as well, such as Enoch and Jubilees, which are held in the same regard. Translations of the Bible into modern languages of Eritrea and Ethiopia, such as Tigrinya, Tigre, and Amharic, have been produced over the past century, generally by European missionaries.

BIBLIOGRAPHY: Ludolf, *Psalterium Davidis aethiopice et latine...* (1701); A. Dillmann, *Biblia Veteris Testamenti Aethiopica* (1853–94); J. Bachmann, *Dodekapropheton Aethiopum oder die zwölf kleinen Prophenen der aethiopischen Bibelübersetzung*. I. *Der Prophet Obadia* (1892); J. Bachmann, *Der Prophet Jesaia nach der aethiopischen Bibelübersetzung* (1893); J. Bachmann, *Die Klagelieder Jeremiae in der äthiopischen Bibelübersetzung* (1893); R.M.J. Basset, *Les apocryphes éthiopiens* (1893–1900); F.M. Esteves Pereira, *Le livre de Job: version éthiopienne* (1907); J.O. Boyd, *The Octateuch in Ethiopic*. Part I: Genesis; Part II: Exodus and Leviticus (all published; 1909–11).; J. Schäfers, *Die äthiopische Übersetzung des Propheten Jeremias* (1912); F.M. Esteves Pereira, *Le livre d'Esther: version éthiopienne* (1913); F.M. Esteves Pereira, *O livro do profeta Amós e a sua versão etiópica* (1917); F.M. Esteves Pereira, *Le troisième livre de 'Ezrâ (Esdras et Néhémie canoniques): version éthiopienne* (1919); F. Da Bassano (ed.), *Beluy*

Kidån (4 vol., 1922/23–1925/26); O. Löfgren, *Die aethiopische Uebersetzung des Propheten Daniel* (1927); O. Loefgren. *Jona, Nahum, Habakuk, Zephanja, Haggai, Sacharja und Maleachi aethiopisch* (1930); S.A.B. Mercer, *The Ethiopic Text of the Book of Ecclesiastes* (1931); S. Grébaut, *Les Paralipomènes. Livres I et II: version éthiopienne* (1932); H.C. Gleave, *The Ethiopic Version of the Song of Songs* (1951); A. Vööbus, "The Ethiopic Versions," in: *Early Versions of the Old Testament*, 243–69 (1954); H.J. Polotsky, "Aramaic, Syriac, and Ge'ez," in: *Journal of Semitic Studies* 9 (1964); E. Ullendorff, *Ethiopia and the Bible* (1968); H.F. Fuhs, *Die aethiopische Uebersetzung des Propheten Micha* (1968); O. Loefgren, "The Necessity of a Critical Edition of the Ethiopian Bible," in: *Proceedings of the Third International Conference of Ethiopian Studies* (1970); H.F. Fuhs, *Die aethiopische Uebersetzung des Propheten Hosea* (1971); B. Metzger, *The Early Versions of the New Testament* (1977); H.A. Pilkington, *A Critical Edition of the Book of Proverbs in Ethiopic* (D. Phil. thesis, Oxford, 1978); E. Ullendorff, "Hebrew, Aramaic and Greek: the Versions underlying Ethiopic Translations of the Bible and Intertestamental Literature," in: G. Rendsburg et al. (eds.), *The Biblical World: Essays in Honour of Cyrus H. Gordon* (1980); E. Ullendorff, "Hebrew Elements in the Ethiopic Old Testament," *Jerusalem Studies in Arabic and Islam* 9 (1987); M.A. Knibb, "Hebrew and Syriac Elements in the Ethiopic Version of Ezekiel?" in: *Journal of Semitic Studies* 33 (1988); R. Cowley, *Ethiopian Biblical Interpretation: A Study in Exegetical Tradition and Hermeneutics* (1988); J. VanderKam, *The Book of Jubilees* (1989); P. Marrassini, "Some Considerations on the Problem of the 'Syriac Influences' on Aksumite Ethiopia," in: *Journal of Ethiopian Studies* 23 (1990); R. Zuurmond, "Ethiopic Versions," in: *Anchor Bible Dictionary* (1992); M.A. Knibb, *Translating the Bible: The Ethiopic Version of the Old Testament* (1999); G.W.E. Nickelsburg, *1 Enoch 1* (2001).

[John Huehnergard (2nd ed.)]

Egyptian (Coptic)

Coptic versions of biblical literature – that is, the texts of the Bible translated into a late antique form of the Egyptian language, written in an augmented Greek alphabet which includes seven demotic Egyptian characters – began appearing in the third century C.E. and were well established by the fourth century. Coptic was written, and biblical texts have been preserved, in several dialects and dialect families, the most important for the study of biblical literature being Bohairic (Delta region, to the north) and Sahidic (Upper Egyptian, to the south). Important fragments remain in Fayyumic and Akhmimic.

It is generally agreed that the Coptic versions have as their source Greek witnesses. Of interest is the richness of the extant versions. For example, the Sahidic witnesses vary from each other, bespeaking independent translators and translation families, as well as, perhaps, differing Greek base texts. It should be noted that a host of literatures and genres related to the Bible (among them apocryphal works, hagiography, liturgical texts, and Gnostic literature) were variously written and preserved in Coptic in late antiquity, and that Coptic remains a language in which biblical and liturgical texts are regularly read, spoken, and sung.

BIBLIOGRAPHY: E.A.W. Budge, *The Earliest Known Coptic Psalter: The Text, in the Dialect of Upper Egypt, Edited from the Unique Papyrus Codex Oriental 5000 in the British Museum* (1898); idem, *Coptic Biblical Texts (Deuteronomy, Jonah, Acts, Apocalypse) in the Dialect of Upper Egypt* (1912); G.W. Horner, *The Coptic Version of the New Testament in the Northern Dialect, otherwise Called Memphitic and Bohairic*, 4 vols. (1898–1905); idem, *The Coptic Version of the New Testament in the Southern Dialect, otherwise Called Sahidic and Thebaic*, 7 vols. (1911–24); W. Till, *Die achmîmische Version der zwölf kleinen Propheten (Codex Rainerianus, Wien)* (Coptica 4; 1927); W.H. Worrell, *The Proverbs of Solomon in Sahidic Coptic according to the Chicago Manuscript* (1931); R. Kasser, *Évangile de Jean et Genèse I-IV,2 en bohaïrique ...*, Bibliotheca Bodmeriana series (CSCO 177; 1958); idem, "Les dialectes coptes et les versions coptes bibliques," in: *Biblica*, 46 (1965), 287–310; M.K.H.Peters, *A Critical Edition of the Coptic (Bohairic) Pentateuch* (Septuagint and Cognate Series; Society of Biblical Literature), 1983–86; B.J. Diebner and R. Kasser, *Hamburger Bapurus Bil, 1: Die Alttestamentlichen Texte...* (Cahiers D'Orientalisme 18; 1989), incl. Song of Songs and Lamentations in Fayyumic and Ecclesiastes in both Greek and Fayyumic; F. Feder, *Biblia Sahidica: Ieremias, Lametationes (Threni), Epistula Ieremiae et Baruch* (TU 147) (2002). In addition, the Biblia Coptica project has begun in earnest to collate and codify the extant witnesses: K. Schuessler, *Das sahidische Alte und Neue Testament...* (1995–); vol. 1, parts 1–4 on Old Testament texts was completed in 2000. **WEBSITES:** P.J. Williams, *Coptic Bible Bibliography*, at: www.abdn.ac.uk/divinity/williams/CopticBibleBibliography.htm; Forschungsabteilung fuer Koptologie und Aegyptenkunde, at: www.uni-salzburg.at/fka, incl. information about the Biblia Coptica Project as well as links to the *Journal of Coptic Studies.*

[Frederick W. Weidmann (2nd ed.)]

Armenian

The need for an Armenian Bible arose once the court converted to Christianity early in the fourth century. According to Armenian tradition the Bible was the first book translated into that language. The translation was undertaken directly after the invention of the Armenian alphabet in 406 C.E.; the story of the translation is preserved in the Armenian tradition for which the prime source is the *Vark*ʿ *Maštoc*ʿ*i*, "Life of, Mashtots" (ca. 345–440; after the fifth century the name begins to appear as Mesrop Mashtots) written by Koriwn, his pupil and colleague. Employing the new alphabet, Mashots along with his ecclesiastical patron the Catholicos Sahak Parteʿw and their disciples translated the Bible as well as other Christian religious writings. The initial translation, which according to these sources was made from Syriac, was subsequently revised twice in the light of Greek manuscripts brought from Constantinople and Alexandria. The work was completed by c. 450.

The translation of the Bible as preserved by the Armenian Church is predominantly Hexaplaric in character, equipped with Hexaplaric signs and showing a full text. Further relationships of the versions have been studied only for few books, where it has been demonstrated that it reveals relationships with certain non-Hexaplaric Greek text types and with the Peshitta. There is also evidence for the existence of two recensions in certain books, such as Chronicles and Ben Sira, and Revelation in the New Testament. Khalatianz (Moscow, 1899) published a version of Chronicles apparently reflecting the translation made from Syriac prior to the revision according to Greek manuscripts. The translation has been characterized as "queen of the versions" and its closeness to the Greek original is reflected in sentence structure and word order. It is one of the central works of the golden age of Armenian literature.

The first edition is that of Oskan, published in 1666 in Amsterdam. The best is that published in Venice in 1805 by J. Zabrabian who based his work on eight complete Bible manuscripts and certain additional manuscripts for Isaiah and Psalms. His edition is no longer adequate for scholarly purposes today. There are numerous manuscripts still unstudied. The earliest complete Bible codices date from the 13th century but there are psalters of an earlier date.

The canon is substantially that of the Septuagint. IV Ezra, Testaments of the Twelve Patriarchs, and the Book of Joseph and Asenath are often included in Bible manuscripts. The canon of Zabrabian's version however is that of the Vulgate. The Armenian Bible is of great value in textual criticism of the Septuagint. Critical editions of individual books of the Armenian Bible are underway.

BIBLIOGRAPHY: F.C. Conybeare, in: DB, 1 (1911), 151–3; H. Hyvernat, in: DBI, 1 (1912), 1010–15; H.B. Swete, *An Introduction to the Old Testament in Greek* (1914²), 118–20; H.S. Gehman, in: ZAW, 48 (1930), 82–99; idem, in: JAOS, 54 (1934), 53–59; B. Johnson, *Die armenische Bibeluebersetzung als hexaplarischer Zeuge im 1. Samuelbuch* (1968). **ADD. BIBLIOGRAPHY:** M. Stone, in: C. Rabin (ed.), *Bible Translations* (1984), 143–47; J.R. Russell, in: *Le Muséon* 107 (1994), 317–33; C. Cox, *The Armenian Translation of Deuteronomy* (1981); idem, *Hexaplaric Materials Preserved in the Armenian Version*; A. Zayt'unyan, *Book of Genesis Critical Text* (in Armenian); J. Weitenberg and A. de Leeuw van Wennen, *Lemmatized Index of the Armenian Version of Deuteronomy* (1990); J. Alexanian, in: ABD, VI, 805–8: S. Peter Cowe, *The Armenian Version of Daniel* (1992); M. Jimbachian, *Les techniques de traduction dans la Genèse en arménien classique* (1998); V. Nersessian, *The Bible in the Armenian Tradition* (2001).

[Michael E. Stone / S. David Sperling (2nd ed.)]

Arabic

The need for translation of the Bible into Arabic arose with the expansion of the Islamic empire. During the eighth century the Arabic language spread and replaced Aramaic as the cultural language of Jews and other non-Arabs living under Islamic rule. Around that time, both scholars and lay people started producing translations of the Bible into Judeo-Arabic using the Hebrew alphabet. Evidence for such translations exists in the various collections of the Ben Ezra *Genizah* of Cairo as well as other private and public collections. Other translations were preserved and transmitted within the Jewish communities living in the Islamic milieu. Scholars divide these translations into several main categories – pre-Saadian, Saadian, Karaite, post-Saadian *sharḥ* – and glossaries.

PRE-SAADIAN TRANSLATIONS. Fragments of pre-Saadian translations were identified in the *Genizah* collections by scholars such as Y. Tobi, J. Blau, S. Hopkins, M. Polliack, and Y. Avishur. These fragments are characterized by their typical Judeo-Arabic phonetic orthography common to texts prior to the 10th century (Blau and Hopkins 2000). This early spelling is solely based on Hebrew orthography and is devoid of any influence of classical Arabic (Blau 1992). In addition, these fragments present a strict literal translation. Hence word order and use of prepositions reflect Hebrew syntax and stand in contrast to Arabic. The preposition that marks the Hebrew definite accusative, which does not exists in classical Arabic, is present in these translations in the form of an artificial morpheme (Tobi 1993). These literal translations are often interrupted in the body of the text by strings of alternative translations for a single word. In some instances expansions of an interpretative nature are also added (Polliack 1998). The pre-Saadian fragments found to date include sections from the Books of Proverbs, Genesis, Exodus, Numbers, and Deuteronomy (Blau 1992). It is very likely that additional fragments will surface in the future as the *Genizah* material is researched further. Y. Tobi has shown that these translations were initiated in the Arabian Peninsula by and for Jewish communities prior to the rise of Islam (Tobi 2005). They reflect an oral tradition that was subsequently put into writing.

SAADIAH'S TRANSLATION. By the 10th century the need for a standard translation of the Bible became apparent. The best-known translation of the Bible into Judeo-Arabic was written by *Saadiah (Gaon) b. Joseph al-Fayyumi (882–942), who was born in Fayyum, Egypt, studied in Palestine, and eventually became the *gaon* of Sura, Babylonia. His translation of the Pentateuch soon became the most widespread among the various Jewish communities under Islam and continued to be the most authoritative in some communities until our time, in particular among Yemenite Jewry. In his translation Saadiah standardized Judaeo-Arabic orthography and created a spelling system that reflects classical Arabic. The main principles of this system of spelling include choosing phonemes according to their cognates rather than following audible similarities, and using *matres lectionis* to indicate long vowels in agreement with Arabic orthography. As far as his method is concerned, Saadiah follows Arabic syntax and his translation is anything but literal. He avoids repetitions, and shortens or expands the text for stylistic reasons. To create a coherent text he subordinates originally coordinated clauses. He often changes the legal text by additions and adaptations. At times he alters the text in order to avoid what he deems to be exaggerations. Echoes of the Aramaic translations are detected in his translation as well as an avoidance of anthropomorphism. In fact, Saadiah's translation is one of the most free and individual in the history of Bible translations as it reflects his personal interpretation (Blau, "Saadya …" 1998). Scholars believe that Saadiah completed the translation of the entire Bible; however, so far only the Pentateuch, Isaiah, Job, Proverbs, Psalms, Song of Songs, Ruth, Lamentations, and Esther have been recovered. No autographed manuscripts of Saadiah's translation of the Bible have been found to date. The vast majority of the manuscripts attributed to Saadiah's translation are written in Hebrew characters; however, scholars disagree on the nature of the initial manuscripts. Abraham Ibn Ezra, a medieval Bible commentator, contends that Saadiah wrote his translation "in the language of the Ishmaelites and in their writing (*ketiva-*

tam)" (see Ibn Ezra's commentary to Gen. 2:11). Some scholars understand this statement to mean that the original was written in the Arabic language in Arabic characters. Others interpret it as Arabic language precisely transliterated into Hebrew characters according to Arabic orthography. In fact, in support of the latter opinion, some of the *Genizah* fragments attributed to Saadiah and written in Arabic characters seem to have been transliterated from a text originally written in Hebrew letters (Blau 1981, Tobi 1993, and Polliack 1998). Evidence from the *Genizah* supports the speculation that Saadiah created his interpretative translation first and named it *tafsir*, modeled after similar koranic compositions of his time. He then composed his expanded commentary to the Pentatuech (Polliack 1998). The long *tafsir*, which included both the translation and the commentary for the Pentateuch, fell out of use eventually. However, fragments of the long *tafsir* were found in the *Genizah* and Firkovitch Collections. A compilation of such fragments containing commentary on Genesis were assembled and studied by M. Zucker (Zucker 1984).

Manuscripts and printed editions of Saadiah's translation of the Pentateuch were widespread in Yemenite communities until recent times. The most famous of them is the *Taj*. Two editions of the *Taj* were printed in Jerusalem, one in 1894 and the other in 1982. N.J. Derenbourg published a critical edition of Saadiah's translation to the Pentateuch in 1893 in Paris. His edition is based mainly on the Jewish polyglot of Constantinople (1546) but also on a Yemenite manuscript and on the Christian polyglot of London (1657) (Blau 1998).

Saadiah's translation and commentary to other books of the Bible were less known and of smaller circulation. Some of these manuscripts, which were found in Yemenite collections, were translated into Hebrew and published by Rabbi Y. Kafah. These publications include the Five Scrolls, the Book of Psalms, the Book of Job, the Book of Proverbs, and the Book of Daniel (Kafah 1962, 1965, 1973, 1976, and 1981).

KARAITE TRANSLATIONS. Rejection of rabbinical authority and the Oral Law led the Karaites to reject Saadiah's approach to Bible translation and compelled them to create alternatives. Most Karaite translations of the Bible date back to the 10th and 11th centuries, a time in which scholarly Karaite activity reached its zenith. The Karaites used the same orthography as the one Saadiah standardized. However, they drew upon the pre-Saadian traditions of translation, which they developed further by emphasizing the principles of individualization and pluralism of biblical commentary. Their approach enabled the composition of creative and original translations free from midrashic influence. The Cairo *Genizah* contains numerous Karaite manuscripts from Egypt and Palestine from the 11th and 12th centuries. It is not quite clear how these fragments ended up in the *Genizah* of the Rabbanite synagogue of Palestinian Jews in Fustat. It may partially be attributed to the Crusade of 1099, which caused the destruction of the Karaite centers in Palestine and forced the survivors to join their coreligionists in Cairo.

Karaite translations of the various books of the Hebrew Bible are known, of which the translations of Psalms, Minor Prophets, the Five Scrolls, and the Pentateuch are the most prevalent. Typically the Karaite translation of the Hebrew Bible is sandwiched between a section of the Hebrew source and an Arabic commentary. This structure is also reflected in Rabbanite exegetical works of the time such as Saadiah's. However, Saadiah's *tafsir* of the Pentateuch deviates from this formula and his translation is disconnected from his commentary (Polliack 1997). Often these tripartite manuscripts, which were primarily used for the purpose of study, contain the Hebrew Bible text transliterated into Arabic characters. The Arabic translation may also be found written in Arabic letters, however the Karaite Bibles that were used for religious purposes were written in Hebrew. This bilingual orthography reflects the Karaite ambivalence toward the rabbinical masoretic tradition (Polliack 1997).

Karaite tradition emphasizes accuracy and the implementation of linguistic knowledge in translation and interpretation of scripture. Linguistic studies were regarded as religious duty, and as a consequence the Karaites created literal translations aimed at reflecting accurately the structures of the Hebrew language. Two distinct features characterize Karaite translations. The first is the occasional rendering of two or three synonyms in translating a single word or phrase. The second is the occasional insertions of small clauses of an interpretative nature into the text. In these respects the Karaites' translations resemble pre-Saadian traditions. The Arabic reflected in Karaite translations is Middle Arabic with a great affinity to classical Arabic, albeit spiced with a limited degree of vernacular features. Polliack speculates that the tradition of literality of translations is characteristic of the region of Palestine as reflected in ancient Greek translations (cf. Aquila) as well as Palestinian Aramaic translations. Karaite translations, mostly created in Palestine, may have also been influenced by this literal approach (Polliack 1997).

The single most prolific Karaite translator and commentator who is believed to have translated the entire Bible into Judeo-Arabic is Yefet b. Eli al-Basri (*Japheth ben Ali Ha-Levi) who lived in Jerusalem in the 10th century. The numerous copies of his works found up to date attest to his vast popularity and authority within Karaite circles (Polliack 1997). Yefet's threefold structure, in which his Bible translation was embedded, seems to have been composed in the years 960–990 (Ben Shammai 1976). Furthermore, in the introduction to his work he states his intention to provide a translation of the words of the Book, hence a verbal rendition faithful to the wording of the biblical source. Yefet derives authority from a received tradition of translation, and it is likely that the literal tendencies of his versions do not originate with him. While his literal translation results in often slavish and ungrammatical Arabic it also reflect a conscious interpretative intention and a method intended to demonstrate to the reader the linguistic structure and the basic meaning of the text (Polliack 1997 and Polliack and Schlossberg 2001). Recent publications of his work include his commentary to Genesis (Ben Shammai et al. 2000) and his translation of the Book of Obadiah (Polliack and Schlossberg 2001).

*Jeshua b. Judah, an influential scholar and leader of the Karaite community of Jerusalem in the 11th century, wrote both a short and a long commentary to the Pentateuch. His short commentary includes also a translation of the Pentateuch. Jeshua did not intend to produce a comprehensive translation and commentary on the entire Bible; instead he mostly concentrated on the legal material. Nevertheless his translation of the Pentateuch is the second major source for study of the Karaite tradition of translation. Jeshua's translation seems to rely on an already existing tradition of translation rather than being solely his own product. Presumably, he was influenced by the school of Karaite scholarship that existed in Jerusalem in the 11th century (Polliack 1997).

SHARḤ. Saadiah Gaon's monumental translation of the Pentateuch spread quickly throughout the various Arabic-speaking Jewish communities. It was canonized in no time and accepted as the authoritative translation. About one-third of all translations of the Bible into Arabic found in the *Genizah* are attributed to Saadiah and attest to its great popularity and authority. However, from the 14th century on Saadiah's translation was no longer clear enough to these communities, who had lost their familiarity with the intricate subtleties of classical Arabic. Against this background, popular translations that incorporated features of the local vernaculars began to surface. In a lengthy introduction for his new translation written in the 15th century in Safed, Rabbi Y. ben Susan explains that Saadiah composed his translation in classical Arabic, a dialect no longer understood by Ben Susan's contemporaries, neither by the students nor by the teachers (Doron 1985). Unlike the Yemenite diaspora which adhered to Saadiah's translation until our time, other Jewish communities started creating new translations which are referred to collectively as *sharḥ* (pl. *shurūḥ*). These translations were geared more towards the general public in a synagogue setting than to the scholarly oriented. They often include large sections borrowed from Saadiah's translations, however, simplified both in style and language as well as in their religious content (Maman 2000, Avishur 1998, and Bar Asher 1998). They were composed literally, reflecting the original Hebrew word order and they incorporated local linguistic features. The language of the *sharḥ* stands between middle Arabic and the spoken vernacular. Typically, young school children would recite one verse of the Bible followed by its *sharḥ*, or they might even alternate reciting one Hebrew word followed by its corresponding *sharḥ* (Bar Asher 1998).

Some *sharḥ* are found in printed editions while others are still in manuscripts. Recently scholars have been recording oral recitations creating audible collections of *sharḥ* (Avishur 1988). Fragments of *sharḥ* manuscripts that were found in the *Genizah* collections have been dated between the 14th and the 17th centuries (Polliack 1998). While Ben Susan wrote his *sharḥ* in Palestine there are many other *sharḥ* found in the communities of North Africa, Egypt, Iraq, Syria, and Yemen. Several studies have been conducted recently concerning this corpus. Y. Avishur has studied the Eastern *sharḥ* and B. Hary concentrated on the Egyptian while M. Bar Asher, A. Maman, O. Tirosh-Becker, and D. Doron have studied the Western *sharḥ* of North Africa.

It is worthwhile to mention a few *sharḥ* that have been studied lately by scholars such as the aforementioned Palestinian *sharḥ* by Ben Susan, the 200-year- old *sharḥ* of Rabbi Raphael Birdugo of Morocco (Bar Asher 2001), and an Egyptian *sharḥ* of the Book of Esther probably from the 18th century (Hary 1994). Others include Rabbi Mordecai Hai Dian's of Tunis (Doron 1991) and a more recent one, compiled by Rabbi Joseph David Genasia (1879–1962) of Algeria (Tirosh-Becker 1990).

In general, the *sharḥ* attests to the popular and vibrant culture in which the Bible was translated into Arabic in the pre-modern era (Polliack 1998). While some *sharḥ* seem to have been adapted from Saadiah's translations others bear similarities to the literal pre-Saadian versions. It is reasonable to assume that a tradition of translation that started before Saadiah survived in the shadow of his translation mostly as oral tradition in the private domain, in schools and synagogues, and surfaced again in the post-Saadian era in the form of *sharḥ* (Tobi 1996).

A thorough study of the language of *sharḥ* was undertaken by B. Hary who worked mainly on a collection of Egyptian manuscripts called the Cairo Collection dating to the 18th through the 20th centuries. Hary concludes that the language of the *sharḥ* shows evidence of multiglossia, i.e., that it is composed of several linguistic layers. He further observes that the language of the different *sharḥ* is not constant and can be placed on a continuum from literary to colloquial Judeo-Arabic (Hary 1992 and 1994). Hary suggests that the language of *sharḥ* exhibits a constant tension between the intention of the translator to convey the Hebrew text word-for-word and his desire to be understood and to occasionally interpret the text by substituting words, paraphrasing, and adding elements of the local vernacular. Hary proposes that the compelling desire to adhere to word-for-word translation even when it violates Arabic linguistic structures stems from the motivation to preserve the sacred Hebrew text as literally as possible and to maintain links with a Jewish heritage in a foreign environment. He further suggests that because of their close connection to the Hebrew sacred texts *sharḥ* evolved into sacred texts themselves. Hence they were not updated, and with time they also became unintelligible as the dialects of the old *sharḥ* and the contemporary readers grew apart (Hary 2000).

GLOSSARIES. A special genre, glossaries and word lists, sheds light on the roots of the tradition of Bible translation. Word lists that were found in the *Genizah* are divided into three groups. The first is a list of Hebrew words taken from a continuous biblical segment along with their translation. These lists when read may seem like an uninterrupted translated text. The second is a list of selected words also taken from a continuous segment of text. These words are typically difficult and/or rare. The third group contains a random list of words selected by topics such as botany or zoology or they may be selected according to poetic principles such as alliteration or assonance. In some lists the principle behind their compilation is not apparent, and they may have been created for a one-time didactic situation or a particular sermon in the synagogue. Some of these word lists are spelled phonetically, and often include several alternative translations for a single word. These features are reminiscent of pre-Saadian translations (Polliack 1998). Saadiah himself compiled such a list named *"Pitron shiv'im Millim Bodedot."* Biblical glossography may be viewed as the initiation of Hebrew lexicology and as a phase leading to Hebrew lexicography (see Polliack and Someh 2000, Eldar 2001, and Tobi 1998).

BIBLIOGRAPHY: Y. Avishur, in: M. Bar-Asher (ed.), *Meḥkarim bi-Leshonot ha-Yehudim* (1988), 39–54; idem, in, *Te'udah,* 14 (1998), 1–18; Y. Avrahami, in: T. Alexander et al. (eds.), *Yeẓirah ve-Toladot* (1994), 73–88; M. Bar Asher, *Masorot u-Leshonot…* (1998); idem, *Leshon Limudim* (2001); H. Ben-Shammai, in, *Alei Sefer,* 2 (1976), 17–32; idem, in: *Pe'amim,* 32 (1987), 3–20; H. Ben-Shammai et al., *Yefet ben Eli … Genesis* (2000); J. Blau, *The Emergence and Linguistic Backround of Judaeo-Arabic* (1981); J. Blau, in: H. Ben-Shammai et al. (eds.), *Genizah Research After Ninety Years* (1992), 31–39; H. Ben-Shammai, in *Leshonenu,* 61 (1998), 111–30; idem, in: J. Krasovec (ed.), *The Interpretation of the Bible* (1998), 393–98; idem and S. Hopkins, in: *Pe'amim,* 83 (2000), 4–14; J. Derenbourg, *Oeuvres Completes…* (1893); D. Doron, in: *Sefunot,*18 (1985), 279–98; idem, in: *Sefunot,* 20 (1991), 171–80; I. Eldar, in: *Ha-Ivrit ve-Aḥyoteha,* 1 (2001), 23–37; B. Hary, *Multiglossia in Judeo-Arabic* (1992); idem, in: *WCJS,* 11, D1 (1994), 25–32; idem, in: B. Hary et al (eds.), *Judaism and Islam* (2000), 395–407; idem, in, B.H. Hary et al (eds.), *Judaism and Islam* (2000), 395–407; Y. Kafah, *The Five Scrolls* (1962); idem, *The Book of Psalms* (1965); idem, *The Book of Job* (1973); *The Book of Proverbs* (1976); idem, *The Book of Daniel* (1981); A. Maman, in: *Pe'amim,* 83 (2000), 48–56; M. Polliack, *The Karaite Tradition … Translation* (1997); idem, in: U. Haxen et al. (eds.) *Jewish Studies in a New Europe* (1998), 595–620; idem and S. Someh, in: *Pe'amim,* 83 (2000), 15–47; idem and E. Schlossberg, in: *Pe'amim,* 89 (2001), 61–82; O. Tirosh-Becker, in: *WCJS,* 10 (1990), 197–204; Y. Tobi, in: *Masorot,* 7 (1993), 87–127; idem, in: M. Bar-Asher (ed.), *Studies in Hebrew and Jewish Languages* (1996), 481–501; idem, in: Y. Tobi et al (eds.), *Ben Ever le-Arav,* vol. 1 (1998), 53–74; idem, in: *Ben Ever leArav,* vol. 2 (2001), 17–60; idem, in: *Ha-Ivrit ve-Aḥyoteha,* 4–5 (2005), 115–43; M. Zucker, *Rav Saadya Gaon's Translation of the Torah* (1959); idem, *Saadya's Commentary on Genesis* (1984).

[Ilana Sasson (2nd ed.)]

MODERN VERSIONS

Introduction

Although the translation of the Bible was carried out already in antiquity, in Aramaic, Greek, and Latin, it was the burgeoning Protestant Reformation, some decades after the invention of movable type, which provided the impetus to make the Bible the most translated book in world history. In its desire to bypass the Catholic Church's monopoly on the meaning of the text, the Reformation sought to return "to the source," and the resulting sharpening of focus on the Bible itself, especially for lay people, paved the way for both the modern study of the Bible and its translation into European vernaculars. It is thus the modern period, broadly speaking, that may be described as the energetic, even frenetic, era of Bible translation. Since the 16th century, but especially in the 20th something approaching 3,000 versions of the Bible, including individual books, have appeared, in well over 2,000 of the world's languages, and new ones are continually in preparation. The proliferation of Protestant subgroups, the eventual acceptance of translation by Catholic authorities, and the needs of post-Emancipation (and even traditional) Jews for a fuller understanding of the text in their own tongues, combined with the explosion of knowledge about the biblical world and its languages over the past two centuries, have all played a role in the far-ranging creation and dissemination of multiple Bible translations in modern times. Thus, Franz Rosenzweig's famous phrase, "To translate is to serve two masters," in truth tells only part of the story.

The problems facing modern translators of the Bible, as well as those who worked in antiquity, are twofold, reflecting issues of translation in general. The text to be translated, the "target text," must first be understood on its face. For this, multiple tools are necessary: grasping the place of the Bible's language in context, i.e., amid the linguistic heritage of the ancient Near East; noting the usage of specific words and phrases within a book or even across the Bible as a whole; appreciating historical changes with respect to technical terms; perceiving rhetorical devices utilized in the text, such as alliteration, paronomasia, and the use of theme words; and sensing the innate rhythm of the text. All these activities must be accompanied by the painful awareness that they will sometimes fail to be apprehended, or apprehended correctly, and that there are texts which will stubbornly continue to remain obscure.

Second, the translator must be able to cast his or her creation, the "receptor text," in such a way as to have the desired effect upon the audience. For some, this will mean producing a Bible that reflects traditional Jewish or Christian interpretation; for others, it will lead to one that speaks in contemporary language; many will seek to give the reader a glimpse, however limited, of the qualities of biblical Hebrew, while others will want to provide a text that transfers old ideas and expressions into easily understandable modern form, "as if it had been written in English."

Consequently, translations of the Bible are usually described as occupying one of two poles on a continuum. The first one, variously termed "idiomatic," "dynamic equivalent," or "domesticating," aims to move the text toward the reader, by making it accessible in its language, imagery, and manner of speech. In this mode, the Bible is thus to be read as a text with clear messages, in language that is readily apprehensible. By using contemporary language that tries to produce a reader reaction similar to that imagined in the original, such a translation is willing to sacrifice form in the interests of communication. Most modern translations have tended toward this ideal. The second pole, called "literal," "formal equivalent/correspondent," or "foreignizing," seeks to move the reader back toward the text, as part of a more active process. Here the reader must make the effort to know the text as something from a partially unfamiliar world, with its own distinctive modes of expression, and learn how to read it. In such an approach, stylistic features and modes of speech, such as word order, idioms, and wordplays are particularly important. The result, as in the 20th-century German Buber-Rosenzweig translation, may confound some readers, who are seeking mainly a comfortable way into the text.

Regarding these two directions of translation, E. Greenstein has noted in the former a tinge of Christian missionizing, which is, to be sure, one of the goals of a number of institutions involved in Bible translation, such as the American Bible Society. The latter methodology he views as more essentially Jewish, concerned as it is with the precise wording and nuances of the Hebrew.

Scripture itself seemed to encourage formal correspondence: Deut. 4:2: "You shall not add anything to what I command you or take anything away from it." Consequently, a literal translation alleges exactness. Similarly, for the rabbis, according to Max Margolis, "the multiple sense of the scriptural word was an accepted fact and it is for this very reason that they frowned upon all translation." In a transitional mode, Jerome translated the Vulgate through stages, developing from formal correspondence to a dynamic equivalence. He saw the work of Aquila (a second century C.E. Greek literal translation) as slavish literalism and disparaged "the word for word," seeking instead a "sense for sense" translation. Ultimately, dynamic equivalence was not unappreciated by translators. The 16th-century Martin Luther, who translated the Bible into German, could describe dynamic equivalence:

> Whoever would speak German must not use Hebrew style. Rather, he must see to it – once he understands the Hebrew author – that he concentrates on the sense of the text, asking himself, Pray tell what do the Germans say in such a situation? Once he has the German words to serve the purpose, let him drop the Hebrew words, and express the meaning freely in the best German he knows.... I endeavored to make Moses so German that no one would suspect he was a Jew.

It may be helpful to visualize the broad spectrum of translation by means of a hypothetical illustration. If one imagines a culture in which the description of a heavy rainfall, whether in everyday language or in a recited story, translates out as "the rains fall rhinos and zebras," there are at least four possibilities that present themselves to the translator: (1) "the rains are falling like rhinos and zebras"; (2) "the rain is like stampeding animals"; (3) "it's raining cats and dogs"; and (4) "It's pouring outside!" It will be observed that the first is rather literal, although not totally so ("like" has been inserted for clarity); the second retains the basic concept but is less language-specific; the third uses a parallel image from the target culture, in this case, American; and the fourth is a clear rendering of the action, but without any reference to the original language or mode of cultural expression. In the end, the degree of literalness or idiomatic fluidity in a translation will depend on the translator's goals and on the audience at which the work is aimed. Broadly speaking, 20th century Bible translations tended in the direction of choices 3 and 4, with some more recent movement back toward the earlier numbers.

One specifically biblical illustration of the possible range of translation can be found regarding a common expression, *limẓo ḥen be-einei x*. Available translations render this across the spectrum from literal to idiomatic; hence, in Gen. 19:19, the New International Version has "Your servant has found favor in your eyes," while the New American Standard Bible, 1995 Revision, renders "Your servant has found favor in your sight"; the Revised English Bible for the same phrase reads "You have shown your servant favor," whereas the New Jerusalem Bible proposes "You have already been very good to your servant" (note also the New American Bible's "You have already thought enough of your servant").

Despite the best of intentions, it will not always be possible to realize the translator's goals. For those committed to a "modern," idiomatic rendering, there will be cases where current language sometimes runs afoul of changes in usage. In this regard, the New Revised Standard Version translators note how they had to change the 1952 Revised Standard Version's rendering of Psalm 50:9, "I will take no bull from your house," to "I will not take a bull from your house," for obvious reasons. Similarly, E. Fox's 1972 translation of Gen. 28:17, "How awesome is this place!," gave way to "How awe-inspiring is this place" (1995), to avoid using what had by then become teenage lingo. Such examples demonstrate that changes in usage and taste dictate changes in performance.

At the same time, like any language, biblical Hebrew abounds in idiomatic expressions which pose dilemmas for the literally minded translator. Phrases such as "he lifted up his eyes" or "to fill the hand" (e.g., Ex. 28:41), usually rendered by less literal equivalents such as "he looked up" and "to consecrate," provide one kind of example. Further, *yamim* will often signify "years" instead of "days" in biblical usage, while *leḥem*, nominally "bread," in many contexts denotes the broader "food." Another type of construction is that found in Gen. 44:18, literally "like you is like Pharaoh," which virtually all English translators, albeit some with an explanatory note, render as "you are like Pharaoh."

The Bible translator therefore must decide where he or she fits along the spectrum; yet since a "pure" translation of one extreme or the other is not possible, decisions, often compromises, must be made on every page, in every verse. Tyndale famously coined many words and phrases in his work which have become standard, not only in the English Bible but in the language in general (e.g., scapegoat, Passover) but he also did not hesitate to be less literal in the many cases where he felt that clarity of style was paramount. Thus he felt no compunction to reproduce biblical Hebrew wordplays such as *tohu va-bohu* in Gen. 1:2, or *ve-ha-oniyyah ḥishevah le-hishaver* in Jonah 1:4.

FEMINIST SENSITIVITIES OF TRANSLATION. Contemporary problems for the translator concern inclusive language that does not neglect more than half the human race. The term "inclusive language" primarily refers to gender concerns; the word, however, also includes the concerns of Jews, handicapped, and people of color. In any case, the modern translator is seriously obliged to bring the right word into the right place.

The *Inclusive Lectionary* has brought the problem of inclusive language to worship services. This lectionary is a collection of fixed readings used for services among Anglican, Protestants, and Roman Catholics. The *Inclusive Lectionary* modifies the Revised Standard Version (RSV) of Ps.23:1: "God is my shepherd ... God makes me lie down ..." This avoids the male term "Lord" and the pronoun "he." Other examples are "realm" for "kingdom"; "Abraham and [Sarah]"; "God the [Mother and] Father"; "a person with a disabling condition" for "a cripple"; "the religious authorities" for, when applicable, "Jews," etc. Furthermore, "man" is the celebrated example since the English word is ambiguous, meaning "people," "a human," and "an adult male."

A major example of a translation that attempts to adjust the biblical text to such recent concerns is *New Testament and Psalms: An Inclusive Version* (1995), which is based on New Revised Standard Version. To use its own illustrations, not only is gender-specific language modified – so that, for instance, "son" becomes "child," and in an extreme case, God as "Father" becomes "Father-Mother" – but whenever possible, pejorative references to disability, race, religion, etc., are replaced by more inclusive terms. Thus, in the New Testament, Jews are referred to as "unbelievers," the Pharisees as "the authorities" or "the leaders," and the concept of "darkness" is replaced by "gloom" or "night." In the Psalms, there is a conscious attempt to move away from masculine designations of God (23:2, "God makes me lie down in green pastures," and 8:1, "O God, our Sovereign"). Even the term "right hand," when it denotes power, is designated as the "mighty" or "powerful" hand. This kind of "adjustment" of the text, while jarring to some readers, is but another illustration of the Bible-reading audience's continual need to experience the text on their own terms.

Another recent and more modest attempt at gender-neutral language is a revision of the New International Version, *Today's NIV* (2005); the revised edition of W. Plaut's *The Torah: A Modern Commentary* (2005) also makes gender-related modifications (see below).

Such an approach has, not surprisingly, spawned both acceptance and criticism, often passionately argued. In 1997, a group of evangelical Christian leaders, spearheaded by the group Focus on the Family, issued the "Colorado Springs Guidelines," which sought to mitigate the use of gender-neutral language in English Bible translation, feeling that it distorts the text. The issue will no doubt continue to be debated.

JEWISH SENSITIVITIES OF TRANSLATION (NEW TESTAMENT). The second contemporary problem for the translator also concerns the choice either of dynamic equivalence or formal correspondence. Christian translators of the New Testament have options in how to translate the word, "the Jews," especially in the Gospel of John. There are many examples where "the Jews" in John is the equivalent to "the chief priests and elders" in the other Gospels. There are places in John where "the Jews" are spoken of in a positive context, e.g., "salvation is from the Jews" (John 4:22). There are, however, many places in John that could make the reader think that John is antisemitic. The impression is given that John makes Jesus a non-Jew, rather than a Jew, put to death by Jews, rather than by Gentiles.

Some proposals to solve this problem are to excise passages. Others wish to use dynamic equivalent expressions for "the Jews," as: "my own people"; "in our law"; "some Jews"; "the Jewish leaders"; "the Judeans"; "those opposing him"; "religious leaders." Some demur and prefer a more formal correspondent rendering of "the Jews" since the substitutes do not express John's dualistic thought or his fondness for collective nouns. Yet others think that it is only part of the overall polemical rhetoric of the day.

The Episcopalians have taken a lead on this issue. In their *Guidelines for Jewish-Christian Relations* of 1988, they state: "It is recommended that in the services of the Church and in church school teaching, careful explanations be made of all the New Testament texts which appear to place all Jews in an unfavorable light, particularly the expression 'the Jews' in the English translations of the Gospel of John and in other references."

Other sensitivities are more of an ecumenical nature than a strict translation problem. Some English translations are concerned about the use of the phrase "Old Testament" and have begun to use the phrase the "Hebrew Scriptures." The (NRSV) New Revised Standard Version has on a title page: "The Hebrew Scriptures commonly called The Old Testament." The others have proposed, "First Testament" and "Second Testament" or "Prime Testament" for "Old Testament."

Another ecumenical problem is the ordering of the books in the Bible. The Jewish ordering of the books is not maintained in Christian Bibles so that the Major and Minor Prophets remain as an introduction to the New Testament. The Jewish order ends the Old Testament with the Writings.

TRANSLATING THE NAME OF GOD. A third translation problem is the rendering of the Tetragrammaton. Since the Septuagint and through the Vulgate and the KJV, overwhelmingly the translation has been the equivalent of "the Lord." Even before the closing of the Hebrew biblical canon, the divine name was not pronounced, out of reverence. Later in the New Testament, there is a tendency to avoid saying the name by substituting a surrogate, e.g., "heaven." After World War II, R. Knox, the Jerusalem Bible, the Anchor Bible, and the A.B. Traina *Holy Name Bible* used the Tetragrammaton with supplied vowels, i.e., "Yahweh." E. Fox's *The Five Books of Moses* (1995), a formal correspondent translation, uses just the four consonants without vowels (YHWH), leaving it to the reader to utilize his or her preferred reading ("Lord," "Hashem," etc.). This spelling is fairly standard scholarly practice as well (cf. many volumes of the *Anchor Bible*), and in this vein, one notes the orthography of the Tetragrammaton in Dead Sea Scroll manuscripts, where it alone is written in the older ("Canaanite") Hebrew script. The revised edition of the Plaut *Torah* (2005) has returned to the Mendelssohnian "The Eternal," also popular in French translations. The crucial question here is whether one uses a dynamic equivalent of a proper name and not a title, such as "the LORD," or respects an ancient Masoretic sensitivity.

THE NATURE OF BIBLE TRANSLATION. With all that Bible translation involves detailed philological work, it should not be ignored that it is also, ultimately, about performance in the artistic sense. Many analogies present themselves. One could cite the task of the dramaturg in the theater: establishing a good text, being conversant with historical background and historical performance practice, sensing the proper tone of the work, and monitoring the unfolding of the performance, with the ultimate goal of remaining true to guiding principles and an overall concept of what the work is. Or one could turn to the task of the orchestral conductor, where, once again, it is crucial to establish an accurate working score, to have a sense of past performance history, and to come up with a compelling conception of the piece, marshalling one's forces to present it as clearly as possible. Whether one accepts that the Bible was originally oral or written, it is clear that from antiquity it was recited aloud in some form, whether in public or in private (similar to the Koran), and attention must be paid to this "live" aspect of the text. Many Bible translations have been conceived, as was the King James Version, "to be read in churches," and this fact has had an immeasurable influence on the history of translations.

[Everett Fox (2nd ed.)]

Jewish Languages

JUDEO-PERSIAN. As *Maimonides (*Iggeret Teiman*) attests, a Persian translation of the Pentateuch was in existence centuries before Muhammad. In fact, theological works of the Sassanid period (*Dinkard* and *Shikand Gumanik Vigar*) contain biblical quotations which point to the existence of a Pahlavi version. Nevertheless, this fact and even the reference to the reading of the Book of Esther in the dialects of Media and Elam (Meg. 18a) provide no firm evidence for the existence of a complete or partial translation of the Bible into these languages. The earliest such text is a Pentateuch of 1319 written in *Judeo-Persian, and there are also manuscripts of the Pentateuch, Psalms, and even fragments of the Apocrypha, all predating the 16th century. Their stylistic uniformity suggests that there may possibly have been a school of Judeo-Persian Bible translation in the 14th–15th centuries. The earliest printed text is the Pentateuch of Jacob b. Joseph *Tavus, apparently based on a 13th-century version, which appeared in the Polyglot Pentateuch of Constantinople (1546); here the Judeo-Persian is printed in Hebrew characters. There are also some modern Bible translations in this dialect, notably versions of Psalms, Proverbs, and Job published by a Bokharian Jew, Benjamin Kohen, in 1883, and Simon *Ḥakham's translation of the Pentateuch (5 vols., 1901–02).

See also *Judeo-Persian Literature.

JUDEO-TATAR. The Bible translations into Judeo-Tatar (not to be confused with *Judeo-Tat, spoken by the "Mountain Jews" of Daghestan and the Caucasus) originated among the Karaites of the Crimea, Russia. Authorship of the Tatar translation claimed by the Karaites has been disputed by the Krimchaks (Rabbanite Jews of the Crimea), who also used such texts. There are manuscript copies of this version in the Firkovich collection (Leningrad Library) and elsewhere. Fragments of the Judeo-Tatar Bible are contained in Benjamin *Mussafia's *Zekher Rav* (1831), which includes translations of certain words into Turkish by Joseph Solomon of Eupatoria, a Karaite *ḥakham*. A Hebrew Pentateuch intended for the Karaites of Turkey and the Crimea, containing a translation into Judeo-Tatar (i.e., in Hebrew characters), was published in Constantinople (1836). A complete Judeo-Tatar Bible (ed. Mordecai Tirishkan) followed soon after (4 vols., 1841–42).

[Isaak Dov Ber Markon]

JUDEO-ROMANCE LANGUAGES. During the Middle Ages, there were Jewish translations of the entire Bible in the Romance languages. They appear to have a common source – a traditional version of the Bible in Low Latin, which the Jews of imperial Rome used in the synagogue and for the purposes of study. This translation was probably transmitted orally, and in time the text underwent morphological and phonetic modifications as Low Latin developed into the various Romance languages in various countries. The Judeo-Romance Bible translations are therefore as old as the Romance languages themselves, and much older than the manuscripts containing them or the glosses relating to them. This development may be traced most fully in Italy, where the Jews lived uninterruptedly from Roman times. Traces of the old Latin translation have been discovered in Jewish funerary inscriptions at Rome and in southern Italy dating from early Christian times; a novella of Justinian (553 C.E.) mentions a Jewish Bible translation in the vernacular. Hebrew works from the 11th century onward contain glosses, and in the 13th century the rabbis of Rome decided that for liturgical purposes, Italian versions of the Bible might be considered equivalent to the Targum. From the 15th century onward, Romance dialect versions of the Bible and of the prayer book were preserved in manuscript, as well as handwritten glossaries and a Bible dictionary in Hebrew, Italian, and Arabic (*Makre Dardeke*), which was first printed (at Naples?) in 1488. Their impact has been felt in modern translations.

Several Judeo-Romance versions of biblical books are extant, including a 14th-century *Judeo-Provençal fragment of the Book of Esther by Crescas du Caylar, and manuscript translations of Song of Songs (the oldest dating from the 13th century) and of the entire Bible written in *Judeo-Italian. Although the Old French versions have been lost, their existence is attested by six 13th-century glossaries and two complete biblical dictionaries in *Judeo-French. There may also have been Jewish translations of portions of the Bible in Catalan, since (as in the case of Old French and Judeo-Provençal) biblical glosses (*La'azim) and glossaries in this dialect have inspired scholarly research (see below).

LADINO (JUDEO-SPANISH). Judeo-Spanish translations of the Bible dating from the 13th to 15th centuries were among the earliest Castilian versions of the Bible, and three manuscripts have been preserved in the Escorial Library, Madrid. These early works were invariably written in Latin characters, as was the famous Ferrara Bible (1553), published by Abraham *Usque, of which there were separate editions for Jews and Christians. After the Spanish expulsion, however, Ladino versions of the Bible were mainly printed in Hebrew characters for the use of Jewish refugees in the Sephardi Diaspora. These translations, which were clearly distinguishable from Spanish Christian editions, include Psalms (Constantinople, 1540), the Pentateuch (in the Polyglot Pentateuch, Constantinople, 1546), and Prophets (Salonika, 1572). Judeo-Spanish Bible translations were later produced by Manasseh Ben Israel (1627) and Abraham b. Isaac Assa, whose complete Bible (Constantinople, 1739–45) was long the most popular work of its kind among Sephardi communities of the Orient (see also *Ladino Literature).

[Umberto (Moses David) Cassuto]

YIDDISH. The oldest Yiddish versions of the Bible stem from the scholarly work of German rabbis who produced Yiddish (or Judeo-German = *Juedisch-Deutsch*) glosses of biblical texts from the 13th century. These were subsequently inserted in rabbinical commentaries and specialized glossaries were prepared, five dating to the 13th–14th centuries and four to the 14th–15th centuries. Copies of these have been preserved in various German libraries. Prose translations of various biblical books were written from the 14th century onward, and these were specifically designed for the unlearned and for women, in view of the widespread ignorance of Hebrew. Such "*Teitsch*" versions include a 14th–15th century translation of Proverbs, Job, and Psalms (the oldest extant); one of Psalms (before 1490); and others of Psalms, Proverbs, and the Pentateuch. These are literal and awkward, and appear to derive from a 13th-century source.

Rhymed Yiddish translations of the Bible, which also appeared in medieval times, owe their origin to the influence of the Bibles and chronicles in rhyme produced by German writers from the ninth century onward. There are also rhymed Yiddish paraphrases of the Bible, which flourished in the 14th century, predating the rhymed translations. These paraphrases, unlike the translations, go beyond the original text and show the influence of German epic minstrelsy. The best-known work of this type is the so-called *Shemuel Bukh, a rhymed paraphrase of I and II Samuel, the prototype of which appeared no later than about 1400, although the first printed edition is of a much later date (Augsburg, 1543). The *Shemuel Bukh* served as the model for a host of other biblical paraphrases in rhyme, including: three 14th-century paraphrases of Esther; one of Judges (14th–15th centuries); paraphrases of the five *Megillot*, which were apparently the work of Abraham b. Elijah of Vilna (15th–16th centuries); paraphrases of Judges and Isaiah by Moses b. Mordecai of Mantua (before 1511); and poetic reworkings of the account of the death of Moses and the *Akedah*. The last two display great originality, adorning the biblical stories with legendary motifs drawn from the midrashic *aggadah*, and endowing the biblical personalities and events described with medieval characteristics. By the 15th century there were also prose paraphrases of certain biblical books, most of which have, however, been lost. The existence of such literary works is indicated by the late 15th-century *Ma'asiyyot* ("tales"), stories in prose about the *Akedah*, Jonah, and King Solomon.

From the 16th century onward no new type of Bible translation made its appearance. The only noticeable development was the steady displacement of other genres by the prose paraphrases. Three notable Yiddish glossaries of the Bible, all rooted in medieval scholasticism, were the so-called *Sefer R. Anschel* (Cracow, 1584), Moses Saertels' *Be'er Moshe* (Prague, 1605–05?), and *Lekaḥ Tov* (Prague, 1604). The same scholastic tradition characterizes the oldest printed Yiddish editions of the Pentateuch with *haftarot* and the five *Megillot*, that of the convert Michael Adam (Constance, 1544); another by the convert Paulus Aemilius (Augsburg, 1544); a revision of the Constance edition by Leo Bresch (Cremona, 1560); and a further translation based on the preceding Cremona edition, together with a summary of Rashi's commentary in Yiddish (Basle, 1583). The publishers rarely did more than bring the Yiddish translations up to date, and this was also true of the Yiddish version of Psalms by Elijah *Levita (Venice, 1545), which closely followed earlier editions by Moses b. Mordecai of Brescia (before 1511) and Joseph Yakar (*siddur,* Ichenhausen, 1544). Two further Yiddish translations of the 16th century were Shalom b. Abraham's Judith and Susanna (Cracow, 1571) and an edition of Isaiah with extracts from Kimḥi's commentary (Cracow, 1586). Toward the end of the 17th century, two complete Yiddish Bibles appeared almost simultaneously: one by Jekuthiel b. Isaac Blitz (Amsterdam, 1676–78) and another by Josef Witzenhausen (Amsterdam, 1679), which was more significant than the first.

Rhymed Yiddish translations were rare after the 16th century. They include one of Judges (Mantua, 1564); one of Genesis (Venice, 1551); Moses Stendal's edition of Psalms (Cracow, before 1586); a 17th-century version of Psalms (the *Teitsch-Hallel*), whose author copied the verse form of contemporary German church hymnology; and *Mizmor le-Todah* (Amsterdam, 1644) rhymed translations of stories from the Pentateuch and the *Megillot* by David b. Menahem ha-Kohen. Rhymed paraphrases of various biblical books were still popular in the 16th and 17th centuries, the outstanding example being the *Shemuel Bukh* (see above), of which there were at least seven editions during the years 1543–1612. Another work of this type was a version of the Pentateuch, Joshua, and Judges, written by Jacob b. Isaac ha-Levi of Roethelsee (*Kehillat Ya'akov*, 1692).

Later, Yiddish prose paraphrases of the Bible were much in favor. Some notable examples were the so-called *Lang Megile* on Esther (Cracow, 1589); the *Teutsch-Khumesh* by *Isaac b. Samson ha-Kohen of Prague (Basle, 1590), a paraphrase of the Pentateuch with Midrashim; the *Ze'enah u-Re'enah* (*Tsenerene*; cf. Song 3:11) by Jacob b. Isaac Ashkenazi (Lublin, 1616), a reworking of the Pentateuch filled with edifying and instructive material drawn from the Talmud, the Midrash, and folklore; and the *Sefer ha-Maggid* by the same author (Lublin, 1623), an adaptation of the Prophets and Hagiographa with Rashi's commentary.

The most famous of these was *Ẓe'enah u-Re'enah*, which ran to many editions and continued to serve as a second Bible among East European Jewry during the 19th century. An extract was translated into Latin by Johann Saubert in 1661, and the whole work into French by A. Kraehhaus in 1846. A German version (with an introduction by A. Marmorstein) was serialized in 1911.

With the decline of Yiddish among German Jewry, from the early 19th century onward, these Bible translations and paraphrases were read only by the Jews of Eastern Europe and the U.S. Mendel *Lefin (of Satanow), an early 19th-century Polish apostle of the Enlightenment, produced an excellent Yiddish version of Proverbs (Tarnopol, 1817). Bible translations of outstanding linguistic and artistic merit were later written by two leading Yiddish poets of the 20th century – I.L. *Peretz (the Five Scrolls, 1925) and *Yehoash (pen name of S. Bloomgarden; Yiddish Bible, 1910 ff.). The latter, in particular, was considered a great masterpiece of the Yiddish language. It became a standard work for Yiddish-speaking homes throughout the world. In 1929 Yehuda Leib (Zlotnick) *Avida translated Ecclesiastes into Yiddish. N. Gross published fluid versions of the Five Scrolls (1936) and the Torah (1948). See also *Yiddish Literature.

English

EARLIEST VERSIONS. The Latin Bible, in an essentially Italian form, first reached England in the sixth or seventh century; however, it should be understood that until the late Middle Ages, the "Bible" of the West comprised, for practical purposes, only the Gospels, Catholic (i.e., canonical) Epistles, and Psalms. Codices of the complete Latin Bible were almost unknown before approximately 800 C.E. From the Latin, the Venerable Bede (d. 735) translated the Gospel according to John into Anglo-Saxon, and Aelfric of Eynsham made abridgments of the Old Testament from Genesis to Judges and of some other books. Caedmon wrote an Anglo-Saxon verse paraphrase of Genesis and other portions of the Bible (c. 670) and Alfred the Great attached an Anglo-Saxon version of the Ten Commandments and parts of the Pentateuch to his legal code. The earliest attempts, however, took the form of continuous interlinear glosses to the Latin, e.g., as in the Lindisfarne Gospels (ca. 700; British Museum, coll. Cotton, Ms. Nero D. IV). Psalters with interlinear glosses seem to have been used, particularly in women's convents (coll. Cotton, Ms. Vespasian A.I. from the ninth century, perhaps being the earliest surviving work). Eadwine's Canterbury Psalter (Trinity College, Cambridge, Ms. R. 17. 1) dates from the middle of the 12th century. The Psalter of Richard Rolle of Hampole (c. 1300–49) enjoyed wide popularity and ecclesiastical approbation up to the Reformation.

THE LOLLARD BIBLE. The first comprehensive English translation was produced late in the 14th century; it is connected with the Wycliffite movement, whose adherents were nicknamed Lollards and were treated by the Church as heretics. John Wycliffe (c. 1328–1384) was himself responsible, though not necessarily as a translator, for the earlier version made from the Latin. In his insistence that the Bible, not the Church, was the source of faith, he anticipated the Reformation. The Old Testament part of the translation was done, at least in part, by Nicholas of Hereford, whose translation is characterized by a slavish adherence to the Latin. John Purvey is assumed to have been mainly responsible for the later version (c. 1388), the preface to which acknowledges the use made of *Nicholas de Lyra's commentary on the Old Testament. This version is consequently the first point at which the English Bible was subjected, albeit at one remove, to the influence of Jewish exegesis. Numerous manuscripts of the Lollard Bible are extant, and it was disseminated in part by word of mouth because of ecclesiastical hostility. A measure of the opposition to Wycliffe's work is the fact that in 1425, some four decades after his death, he was denounced at the Council of Constance; three years later, his remains were exhumed and burned.

The Lollard Bible received limited circulation due to its predating the invention of movable type; there was no printed English Bible before the Reformation.

THE 16TH–17TH CENTURIES. Several interacting factors afford the background to the "classical" period of English translations, which may be dated from W. Tyndale (New Testament, 1526) to the King James ("Authorized") Version of 1611. A new theology was to lead, in Protestant churches, to the Authorized Version (1611). The revival of learning meant the provision of chairs for teaching Greek and Hebrew at Oxford and Cambridge, as well as the dawning of a critical approach to the texts of both the Greek New Testament and the Latin Vulgate, printed editions of which were prepared by Erasmus. Estienne (Stephanus) in Paris also published scholarly texts. The polyglot Bible editions made it easier to compare the ancient versions. The new (or rediscovered) methodology of textual criticism demonstrated the importance of basing vernacular versions on original and not on secondary texts; Reuchlin and Luther in Germany were pioneers of the new scholarship. A new theology was to lead, in the reformed churches, to the recognition that ultimate Christian authority lay in Scripture, rather than in the tradition of the Church, and conversely, in the Catholic Church it led to insistence by the Council of Trent in 1546 on the "authentic" quality of the Latin Vulgate, notwithstanding the possibly greater accuracy of contemporary Latin versions of the Bible. Finally, the period – which embraces the age of Shakespeare – witnessed the spectacular advance of the English language as a literary medium.

TYNDALE AND HIS SUCCESSORS. It is primarily to William Tyndale (1494?–1536) that the English-speaking world owes its Bible. He was educated at Oxford, and subsequently at Cambridge, where he learned Greek and was influenced by the writings of Erasmus and, perhaps, by Luther. By the time his revised New Testament appeared in 1535, Tyndale had already learned enough Hebrew on the continent to publish the Pentateuch (1530), followed by Jonah (1531) and further lectionary Old Testament material (1534); the "historical" books of Joshua–II Chronicles, left by Tyndale in manuscript, and somehow preserved after his execution at Antwerp, were printed in 1537 in the *Matthews Bible*, edited by Tyndale's disciple John Rogers but pseudonymously named after two of the New Testament disciples, Thomas and Matthew.

Tyndale's great contribution, along with his impeccable learning, was to create a new and supple English, with a Saxon diction and clarity that encouraged reading aloud. Over two-thirds of the King James Version (properly, of the books he translated), and thus of the English-speaking world's historical experience of much of the Bible, comes from his hand, despite his remove at several generations from the later classic. His ear was unerring, and even those immortal phrases coined by the King James committee, such as "a still small voice" (I Kings 19:12), often owe something to his creativity (in this case, "a small still voice"). It should be noted that, through the medium of the 1917 JPS translation, which is basically the King James-based Revised Version of 1885 in Jewish garb, Tyndale has strongly influenced the ways in which English-speaking Jews have experienced the Torah and Former Prophets, up to the appearance of the NJV ("New JPS Version") in 1962.

An illustration of Tyndale's way with language, in modern spelling, may be seen in his rendering of Ex. 4:10–16:

> And Moses said unto the Lord: Oh my Lord, I am not eloquent, no not in times past and namely since thou hast spoken unto thy servant: but I am slow mouthed and slow tongued. And the Lord said: who hath made man's mouth, or who hath made the dumb or the deaf, the seeing or the blind? Have not I the Lord? Go therefore and I will be with thy mouth and teach thee what thou shalt say. And he said: Oh my Lord, send I pray thee whom thou wilt. And the Lord was angry with Moses and said: I know Aaron thy brother the Levite that he can speak. And moreover behold, he cometh out against thee, and when he seeth thee, he will be glad in his heart. And thou shalt speak to him and put the words in his mouth, and I will be with thy mouth and with his mouth, and will teach you what you shall do. And he shall be thy spokesman unto the people: he shall be thy mouth, and thou shalt be his God....

The King James translators follow the Hebrew structure a bit more closely, in such passages as, "neither heretofore, nor since thou hast spoken" (Tyndale: "no not in times past and namely since thou hast spoken"), "send, I pray thee, by the hand *of him whom* thou wilt send" (Tyndale: "send I pray whom thou wilt"), and "he shall be, *even* he shall be to thee instead of a mouth, and thou shalt be to him instead of a god" (Tyndale: "he shall be thy mouth, and thou shalt be his God"). Yet Tyndale's natural directness of language is winning, and illustrates his stated goal of helping even the "boy that driveth the plow" to understand the Bible, without sacrificing elegance. It is astonishing that the English of 1530 should be clear and readable basically half a millennium later, yet that is precisely the case with this first "modern" English translation of the Bible.

Tyndale's Bible, a factor in promoting the English Reformation, raised hostility less by its content than by its Luther-inspired prefaces and provocative notes, a number of which rail against popes and monks. Ironically, within a year of Tyndale's martyrdom, his famous prayer at the stake – "Lord, open the King of England's eyes" – was answered when Henry VIII broke definitively with the Church of Rome. In 1535 Miles Coverdale, Tyndale's assistant, produced an English Bible under royal auspices, which was actually a private enterprise, and was based not on the original texts but on the Vulgate, together with Pagninus' literal Latin rendering of the Old Testament, and other versions including those of Luther and Erasmus. It was followed by the aforementioned Matthew's Bible of 1537, in which the remaining books were the work of Coverdale himself. This in turn was the basis of the "Great" Bible (so called because of its size, appropriate for public reading) of 1539, known also as Cranmer's from the preface to the 1540 edition, which Henry VIII had ordered to be placed in every parish church. Coverdale was editor, but some of his earlier provocative inclusions were dropped, and although surplus words found in the Vulgate Latin were rendered into English, they were typographically distinguished. Some Latinisms of diction crept in. The translation of the Old Testament was improved by reference to *Muenster's Hebrew-Latin Bible of 1535. This edition's Psalter is the one that has been retained ever since in Anglican church usage.

ANGLICAN, CALVINIST, AND CATHOLIC BIBLES, 1560–1610. In spite of the radicalism of his ecclesiastical politics, Henry VIII was doctrinally a moderate conservative; the successors of his "Great" Bible, produced under Elizabeth I and James I, reflected the "Anglican Compromise." The Scotsman John Knox was the most prominent Briton to take refuge from the Catholic restoration of Mary, in Geneva, where he began to study Hebrew. At the time, not only was *Calvin himself teaching there, but French and Italian Bible-making was also in progress. English versions of Psalms were issued from 1557 on, corrected, and finally superseded by the complete *Geneva* or *"Breeches" Bible* (so-called from its rendering of Gen. 3: 7) of 1560, an elegant and powerful rendering that retains much of Tyndale's accomplishment. It was the first English version in which the poetic sections of the Hebrew Bible – fully half of the text – were translated directly from the original. Typographically, additional words which were idiomatically essential were printed in italic type; the remainder, in roman instead of the black letter of earlier prints. It also contained illustrations and, more importantly, helpful notes which clarify the text at many points. The influence of David Kimhi's commentaries may be observed in the Geneva Bible, which was reprinted until 1644, in well over one hundred editions, reflecting its hold on English hearts until finally overtaken by KJV. It was the Bible of Shakespeare and the Pilgrims.

The next major translation, the *Bishops' Bible* (1568), was fathered by Archbishop Parker, himself responsible for translating Genesis, Exodus, and some of the New Testament. It was intended to offset the pressures of the returned exiles of Mary's reign for an English church settlement on Calvinistic lines and the popularity of their Geneva version from which, however, the Bishops retained some notes and renderings. The contributors were enjoined to avoid polemical exegesis, and were directed to correct the Great Bible, following Pagninus and Muenster for the Hebrew. This Bible was not a great success; its importance lies in its forming the basis of the Authorized Version of 1611, which, in the opinion of many, would have been better served by taking the *Geneva Bible* as its model.

English Catholics who fled to Flanders under Elizabeth I produced their own New Testament at Rheims (1582), followed by the Old Testament printed at Douai (1609–10). This version – characterized by the outspokenly apologetic tone of its editorial matter – was naturally based on the Latin Vulgate.

THE KING JAMES, OR "AUTHORIZED," VERSION, 1611. The incomplete success of the *Bishops' Bible* had made James I sympathetic to pleas from scholars – especially, perhaps, the Hebraist Hugh *Broughton – for a fresh translation; after its publication in 1611, printing of the *Bishops' Bible* was discontinued, and thus the King James version became – without any explicit declaration – the "Authorized" Version, i.e., that "appointed to be read in churches." The work of translation was done by a team of 54, in Westminster, Oxford, and Cambridge; the 47 identified translators including most of the best English Orientalists (although Broughton was himself too cantankerous to be included) and Greek scholars. By now there were much-improved tools of biblical scholarship in the shape of dictionaries and The Antwerp Polyglot Bible (*Biblia Regia*) of 1572, and the team included experts in the cognate Oriental languages, particularly Syriac and Arabic. In addition, the translators paid substantial attention to the Latin version of the Hebrew by the apostate Jew Immanuel *Tremellius (1579), who had settled in England and taught at Cambridge. Then, too, the *Geneva Bible* notes are said to have made James uncomfortable. The *Bishops' Bible* was the basis of the new work; that of Geneva contributed something in precision, and that of Rheims, some Latinizing vocabulary, although standard Anglican ecclesiastical terms were retained. Caution sometimes relegated the correct translation to the status of a marginal variant. Further editorial treatment – other than chapter summaries and headlines – was excluded *a priori*; the loss of the Geneva notes is particularly unfortunate. At the same time, some of the translators' own notes have survived, and the full introduction to the translation is immensely illuminating. As for the language of the work, by 1611, the diction and grammar were slightly archaic, and although the Geneva version was far from being superseded – Lancelot *Andrewes, himself one of King James' translators, continued to use it in his sermons, and it is quoted in the introduction to KJV – the Authorized Version ultimately achieved, and has retained, a preeminent and quasi-sacrosanct position within the English-speaking world. Of other unofficial English ventures in translation prior to the late 19th century none achieved widespread popularity save H. Ainsworth's Psalms (1612), introduced by the Pilgrim Fathers to America, and sundry metrical Psalters such as that of Tate and Brady (1696).

G. Hammond notes that one of the great merits of the KJV, despite its defects of a tone that is sometimes too lofty and a tendency to flatten the style, so that the entire Bible reads as if it were a uniform text, is that in its "care to maintain verbal equivalence" – that is, to in the main keep key words in English as they repeat in the Hebrew – it manages to both echo Hebrew style and create an equivalent in English. It also, following Tyndale, reproduces the Hebrew copula *vav*, usually by "and," a practice dropped by many modern translations.

1611–1945. Subsequent nonofficial translations have been inspired partly by doctrinal and sectarian considerations (for Jewish enterprises), partly by a scholarly desire for improved accuracy, and partly by the motive of either "improving" the literary quality of the English (e.g., E. Harwood, New Testament, 1768) or colloquializing it (e.g., D. Mace, New Testament, 1729). A Revised Version of the Bible was published in Britain in 1881 (New Testament) and 1885 (Old Testament) in order to modernize the 17th-century language of the King James and to revise it in accordance with 19th-century scholarship. The American Standard Version, in cooperation with the Revised, appeared in 1901. Both translations soon proved of great importance to scholarship, but were not widely employed in worship. Subsequent versions created by individuals were those of J. Moffatt (1913–24; revised 1935), E.J. Goodspeed

(New Testament, 1923) and J.W. Powis Smith with others (Old Testament, 1927).

ANGLO-JEWISH VERSIONS. From the early 18th century, progressive anglicization of Jewish settlers in England and America rendered first the Spanish, and ultimately the Yiddish, translations inadequate for educational needs. The King James Version became current in spite of the Christianizing tendency of some of its "headlines" to the Prophets. The Pentateuch with *haftarot* published in London by David Levi (1787) appears to be the King James Version but without offending captions and with Jewish annotations. An earlier Pentateuch was produced by A. Alexander in 1785. In the U.S. Isaac *Leeser published a Pentateuch (5 vols., 1845) and subsequently a complete Old Testament in English (1853), which incorporated matter from the Mendelssohn school's German translation and included the Hebrew text. Leeser used the KJV as a basis, de-Christianizing some renderings (e.g., substituting "this young woman" for *ha-almah* in Is. 7:14) and incorporating rabbinic readings of the Bible into his text via parentheses. Leeser's version stood as pre-eminent in the American Jewish community until the appearance of the "Old JPS" translation of 1917. C.G. *Montefiore's *Bible for Home Reading* was published in 1896. A. *Benisch issued a *Jewish School and Family Bible* (1851–61) and M. *Friedlaender's *Jewish Family Bible* (1881) used the Authorized Version. After the Revised Version of 1885 had appeared, the London Jewish Religious Education Board published (1896) a pamphlet listing essential emendations to make that version acceptable for Jewish use. These modifications were among the material utilized for the version published by the *Jewish Publication Society of America in 1917, which also took into account 19th-century Jewish Bible scholarship and rabbinical commentary (e.g., *Malbim); the edition – issued by a committee representative of both traditional and Reform Judaism – was basically the work of Max L. Margolis. The New Jewish Version, in the course of translation by an American Jewish team presided over by H.M. Orlinsky, while probably being more open than any earlier Jewish version to the findings of non-Jewish biblical scholarship, still remains tied to the Masoretic text, even though it incorporated on its margin emendations based on evidence gathered from ancient versions of Hebrew manuscripts. Its Pentateuch, published in 1962, has consequently met with substantial criticism from Orthodox Jewish circles. Two traditional Pentateuchs are the *Pentateuch and Haftorahs* edited by Chief Rabbi J.H. Hertz (1929–36), which first used the Revised Version and later the 1917 JPS translation – although it was popularly supposed that the translations were Hertz's own – and I. Levi's Hirsch Pentateuch (1958–62), translated from the German [but see Torah Translations by Jews below].

[Raphael Loewe / Everett Fox (2nd ed.)]

SINCE WORLD WAR II. *Introduction.* From 1611 to 1900, some 500 English biblical translations were unable to break the dominance of the King James Version [KJV]. The history of Bible translation since World War II primarily consists of further attempts to break away from the KJV. Many, however, continue to prefer the spiritual nostalgia of the KJV, since it has influenced so much of the English-speaking world. President Harry Truman states it bluntly:

> We were talking about the Bible, and I always read the King James Version, not one of those damn new translations that they've got out lately. I don't know why it is when you've got a good thing, you've got to monkey about changing it. The KJV of the Bible is the best there is or ever has been or will be, and you get a bunch of college professors spending years working on it, and all they do is take the poetry out of it.

Nevertheless, each age has its need for a new translation; textual and philological scholarship make advances, English usage changes, and communities have specific needs. In the case of postwar translations, L. Greenspoon cites the cataclysmic events of the first half of the 20th century, along with the challenge posed by such forces as secularism and Communism, as providing a strong impetus to revisit the Bible, including its retranslation. Thus the last half-century has seen a large number of major renditions of the Bible into English.

Major Versions Since World War II. The fact is that since 1945, as many new translations of all or parts of the Bible have appeared in English as in the three centuries preceding. In the following discussion, major post-World War II versions will each be treated in terms of: (1) the history of the translation; (2) the principles of the translation and representative examples; and (3) the acceptance of the translation. It should be noted that many of these are available for instant comparison on popular Bible software programs, with sophisticated search capabilities.

Knox Bible [= Knox] (1949). History. The Knox Bible is the work of the writer-scholar, Ronald Arbuthnott Knox. His father was the Anglican bishop of Manchester, and both of Knox's grandfathers were Protestant divines. He was a prize-winning student in classics at Oxford and was to become an accomplished author, writing six detective novels. In 1917, at age 29, he joined the Roman Catholic Church.

For nine years he worked an eight-hour-day, six-day-a-week schedule, turning out 24 verses a day on the average. He published the New Testament (1945), the Psalms (1947), and the Old Testament (1948–1949), for which he received the Roman Catholic imprimatur (1955). This authorized version came to surpass the Douay-Rheims-Challoner Version for Catholics.

Principles and Representative Examples. Although Knox translated from the Vulgate, he took cognizance of the original languages in his footnotes. His knowledge of Greek was better than that of Hebrew. His work, however, is a translation of a translation, and the Clementine Vulgate (1592) at that. He stuck closely to the Clementine Vulgate, even where it was evidently in error. Since Jerome relied heavily on the Septuagint and on the Hexapla (which included various Greek versions),

Knox's translation can be said to be a translation of a translation of a translation.

Knox has many deft characteristics in his translation. The poetry of the Bible is not printed as such. Describing parallelism, he said "To our notions of poetic composition, these remorseless repetitions are wholly foreign; when you have read a page or two on end, they begin to cloy." Knox was always looking for "what an Englishman would have said to express this."

His translation of the acrostics in the Hebrew Bible (seven Psalms, Prov. 31, and Lam. 1–4) appealed to him. In 1924, Knox had already published *A Book of Acrostics* and to get a literary taste of the original was his purpose: Ps. 25 (24 in Vulgate) *An Alphabet of Trust*: "All my heart goes out to thee ... Belie not the trust ... Can any that trust in the ... Direct my way, Lord ... Ever let thy truth guide ... Forget not ..."

Knox used "thou" throughout, and Latin spellings of proper names, for example, "Osee" for "Hosea" and "Paralipomena" for "Chronicles."

Many of his translations are idiomatically pleasing. For the Song of Songs 1:1: where RSV has "O that you would kiss me with the kisses of your mouth! For your love is better than wine," Knox reads: "A kiss from the lips. Wine cannot ravish the senses like that embrace."

Acceptance. In 1943, Roman Catholics were given the freedom to translate from the original Hebrew and Greek. Knox's translation has thus been dubbed the "last translation of the Vulgate." Other Catholic translations (Jerusalem Bible [JB] and New American Bible [NAB]) have overshadowed the work of Knox, although not for their prose style. Knox's aspiration was: "To secure, as far as possible, that Englishmen of 2150, if my version is still obtainable then, shall not find it hopelessly 'dated.'" The translation still reads well, but is at present out of print.

Revised Standard Version [= RSV] (1952) and New Revised Standard Version [= NRSV] (1989). History. The RSV is the most scholarly and most modern revision in the tradition of the King James Version. In 1929 the International Council of Religious Education already began to plan a revision of the American Standard Version, which is a 1901 revision of the KJV. In 1937 the council authorized a new version "which embodies the best results of modern scholarship."

The continuing committee of the RSV and NRSV has been working and publishing for half a century: the New Testament (1946), the Old Testament (1952), the books of the Apocrypha (1957), a second edition of the New Testament (1957), an *Oxford Annotated Bible* with a Catholic imprimatur (1966), an ecumenical [for Protestants, Catholics, and Eastern Orthodox] expanded edition with the Apocrypha (1977), a *Reader's Digest Bible*, which abridged the Old Testament to one-half of its original length (1982), and most recently the NRSV (1989). The RSV's formal correspondent translation lends itself to an effective use of a concordance, and one such was published by Richard Whitaker in 1980.

The RSV is a revision in line with the KJV, in contrast to the New English Bible [NEB], which is a completely new translation. In the *Preface to the RSV*: "The RSV is not a new translation in the language of today... It is a revision which seeks to preserve all that is best in the English Bible as it has been known and used through the years." In committee, a ⅔ vote was needed to change the American Standard Version. The RSV, then, aims to be a formal equivalent translation without being wooden.

Principles and Representative Examples. The RSV and NRSV translations are more radical than the slight alterations in the New American Standard Bible [= NASB] or the New King James Bible [=NKJV (1982)], which are both revisions of the KJV. This does not make the RSV a radical translation. Although the RSV is still more often a formal correspondent translation, the guiding maxim seems to be "as literal as possible," and "as free as necessary."

Many examples of modernizing the language of the American Standard Version could be cited. At Gen. 31:36: "Jacob was wroth, and chode with Laban," became in RSV (and NRSV): "Then Jacob became angry, and upbraided Laban."

New forays into modern scholarship show something more than a conservative attitude. Of 13 emendations of Isaiah from the Dead Sea Scrolls, M. Burrows has changed his opinion, "A brief review will show that even in these 13 places the superiority of the manuscript's reading is not always certain. For myself I must confess that in some cases where I probably voted for the emendation I am now convinced that our decision was a mistake, and the Masoretic reading should have been retained."

In the NRSV (1989) there is a new concern for the use of more inclusive language. The NRSV has been even more aggressive than the NEB concerning this point. Ps. 54:3: where the RSV had "insolent men" and "ruthless men" and the word "men" was not actually in the original, the NRSV has rendered "the insolent" and "the ruthless." Ps. 1:1: "Blessed is the man who walks not in the counsel of the wicked," has become in the NRSV: "Happy are those who do not follow the advice of the wicked." The "Fathers" of Israel are now "ancestors." The expression "son of man" in Ezekiel is now rendered in NRSV as "mortal." Yet, masculine metaphors, such as referring to God as "Father," were left intact. There is another type of inclusive language that refers to "people of color" that was also considered in NRSV. RSV had in Cant. 1:5: "I am very dark, but comely," while NRSV has: "I am black and beautiful."

RSV retained "thou" in prayer and praise addressed to the Deity. NRSV drops these remaining occurrences of "thou" and "thy" from the RSV. Another interesting update in language includes Prov. 6:6 in the RSV: "Go to the ant, O sluggard; consider her ways, and be wise." while the NRSV has: "Go to the ant, you lazybones; consider its ways, and be wise."

In NRSV there are many textual changes, especially in Deuteronomy and Jeremiah. The books of Samuel are most affected by text-critical considerations. The sheer number of footnotes in Samuel, for example, went from 174 in the RSV to 268. At 1 Sam. 4:1, the NRSV now follows the Greek and adds to the Hebrew: "In those days the Philistines mustered for war against Israel." In 1 Sam. 10, at the end of the chapter, NRSV adds four sentences from Qumran, which do not appear in the Masoretic Hebrew.

Acceptance. The RSV was burned in fundamentalist pulpits and the RSV committee was accused of being in league with the devil, especially because of their translating Isa. 7:14 as "young woman." The Christian Reformed Church rejected the RSV for pulpit use in 1954. The New International Version [NIV] evangelicals felt that all the messianic prophecies were taken out of the RSV Old Testament.

Despite all the uproar, in the first year, the RSV sold 2 million copies. Until the appearance of the NRSV, it enjoyed wide use on college campuses, especially in study editions such as the *Oxford Annotated Bible*.

Modern Language Bible [= MLB] (1959). History. This Bible is the work of a Dutch-born American, Gerritt Verkuyl, and 20 Hebrew scholars. In 1894, he came to America, not knowing English, and hired himself out as a farm hand in California. He was later educated at Princeton Theological Seminary and the University of Leipzig and did graduate work in Berlin. He served on the Presbyterian Board of Christian Education and became aware that the KJV "was only in part the language of the people." In 1936, in Berkeley, California, Verkuyl began his work of translating. He finished the New Testament in 1945 and completed the work in 1959. This translation was then known as the *Berkeley Version in Modern English*. A revised edition in 1969 took the name, *The Modern Language Bible, The New Berkeley Version in Modern English: Revised Edition, A Completely New Translation From the Original Languages With Informative Notes to Aid the Understanding of the Reader.*

Principles and Representative Examples. The editor in chief had a clear notion of his task of translating. He states: "I aimed at a translation less interpretive than Moffatt's, more cultured in language than Goodspeed's, more American than Weymouth's, and freer from the King James Version than the Revised Standard." The KJV, nevertheless, still so held sway that Verkuyl put in brackets translations that were based on unreliable manuscripts, simply because the KJV had them. Verkuyl also stated that the MLB was not to be a paraphrase, for "that leads so readily to the infusion of human thought with divine revelation, to the confusion of the reader."

For the most part his translation of the Old Testament was concordant or literal ("a translation of every word"). MLB does emend and does accept the Dead Sea Scroll of Isaiah (Isa. 14:4; 45:8; 56:12).

From the conviction of a conservative evangelical, the MLB translates passages using capital letters to point out messianic meanings: Gen. 3:15: "And He will crush your head." Psalm 2 has many capital letters: "The Lord and his Anointed are Supreme…. The Lord said to Me, Thou are My Son."

The footnotes are doctrinal and often moralistic: at Gen. 3:12: "Passing the buck is as old as humanity: it shows lack of repentance." At Ps. 23: "One reason this psalm is so deeply loved is that it comes warm from the heart of a man who knew the meaning of sheep and shepherd and who knew the Lord as thus related to him."

Acceptance. The MLB has been criticized for its wooden, stilted style. In a competitive market, this evangelical Bible has never been popular.

New World Translation [= NWT] (1961). History. This translation is the work of the Watchtower Bible and Tract Society, by a group of scholars who "wish to remain anonymous even after death." They published the New Testament (1950), the Old Testament (1961), and revisions (1970–1971).

Principles and Representative Examples. The most obvious characteristic of this translation is the representation of the divine name as "Jehovah." A feature of this translation is the frequent use of capitals for the plural "YOU," and for the plural imperative. Since the English "you" is ambiguous as to singular and plural, the meaning often suffers. One example from the NWT is Hosea 2:1 [Masoretic Text 2:3]: "say to your brothers, 'My people!' and to your sisters, 'O woman shown mercy!'"

Another venturesome point in the NWT is that the translators use the term "Hebrew-Aramaic Scriptures" (instead of the deprecating "Old Testament"), and for "New Testament" they use "Christian Greek Scriptures." This is not, however, done in response to sensitivities of Jews, but rather because Witness theology denies that these are "covenants."

The translation style is wooden: Ex. 20:3: "You must not have any other gods against my face." Gen. 17:4: "You will certainly become father of a crowd of nations." Another notable feature is the translation's considerable use of the auxiliary verbs "proceeded to," "proved to be," "went on to," and "began" at the beginning of verses, where the Hebrew uses the narrative imperfect with consecutive *vav.*

Acceptance. Being an extremely biased denominational version, this translation is suitable only for the Jehovah's Witnesses, and even they often avoid it. According to the Bible Scholar H.H. Rowley, this version is an example of "how not to translate." Nevertheless, several million copies have been printed.

Anchor Bible [= Anchor] (1964–). History. The Anchor Bible was originally intended to be an ecumenical translation of the whole Bible, to be completed in 1970. Under the general editorship of D. Freedman, however, the series has become a scholarly project in which the individual volumes have come to serve as the standard works for study and reference in the field. Each is accompanied by extensive, often exhaustive, introduction, commentary, notes, and bibliography. *The Anchor Bible* and other sets of commentaries like the *Hermeneia Series* and Word Biblical Commentary have new translations that are not subject to the demands of a denomination which authorizes translations. They are translations by individuals – not by committee – and customarily have a freshness and creativity about them.

Principles and Representative Examples. The principles of translation are as different as the different authors, although the first workers for the Anchor Bible were students of William Foxwell Albright's methodology.

Acceptance. The Anchor Bible volumes are used primarily for study, and thus do not figure in wide public usage such as in congregations. At the same time, they are laboratories for future translations. For the Anchor Bible of the Psalms, E. Speiser's Genesis volume was a fresh approach, strongly influencing the NJV even though it officially appeared after that work. Mitchell Dahood, the author of the Psalms volume, emended extensively, relying on the use of other Semitic languages, especially Ugaritic, for elucidating the Hebrew. W. Propp, in the Exodus 1–18 volume, created a translation that experimentally sought to reflect the stylistic characteristics of the Hebrew text more closely than many of the other contributions to the series.

Jerusalem Koren Edition (1964). History. Koren Publishing published the first Hebrew biblical text edited, typeset, and printed in the State of Israel (1962). The Koren text was published with an English text on facing pages (1964) and called "The Jerusalem Koren Bible." (This should not be confused with the *The Jerusalem Bible* [= JB] (1966) and *The New Jerusalem Bible* [= NJB] (1985).) The presidents of the State of Israel are sworn in on this Bible.

Principles and Representative Examples. The English text is based on the Jewish Family Bible, a translation by Michael Friedlander (1881, 1884, repr. 1953) and edited by Harold Fisch (1964). Salient is its transliteration of Hebrew names such as "Iyyov" for "Job." The Hebrew accents and vowels have been rectified. The Qere is vocalized in the margin, leaving the Ketiv unvocalized in the text. The English text is a formal equivalent translation in line with KJV but follows the paragraphing of the Hebrew text.

Acceptance. With the publication of New Jewish Publication Version [NJV] from the years 1962–1982 and its one volume edition (1985), the Koren edition does not have wide circulation.

Jerusalem Bible [= JB] (1966) and New Jerusalem Bible [= NJB] (1985). History. The JB is the first complete Catholic Bible translated into English from the original languages; previously, Catholic translators had relied on the Vulgate. JB's history begins at the Ecole Biblique in Jerusalem, which in 1949 was entrusted with the Dead Sea Scrolls. Under the leadership of Père Roland de Vaux in the 1940s and 1950s, the Ecole Biblique published 43 individual fascicles of the books of the Bible (1948–1954), commentaries not entirely unlike the *Anchor Bible, World Biblical Commentary*, and *Hermeneia*, mentioned above.

The JB (1966) is a derivative of the one-volume abridgment of these French fascicles, *La Sainte Bible de Jérusalem* (1956). The English JB was translated by Alexander Jones of Christ's College, Liverpool, and 27 principal collaborators. It is a clear departure from the KJV and the Douay-Rheims-Challoner. The JB translation often verges upon a translation of a translation and this French connection is often evident in its choice of words. JB's scholarship benefits from the card catalog of the Ecole Biblique library, which lists every biblical article of the century according to verses treated. The footnotes, marginal notes, introductions, chronological tables, calendar, table of weights and measures, index of biblical themes handled in the notes, and maps, all make this both a study Bible and a translation with commentary. The notes reflect the best Catholic scholarship of its time. The JB weighs in just under five pounds, with some 2,062 pages.

The NJB (1985), edited by H. Wansbrough, corrected shortcomings of the JB. The NJB looked more closely at the original languages, reduced the number of Britishisms, depended on newer scholarship both for translation and footnotes, and generally became more readable.

Principles and Representative Examples. This dynamic equivalent translation is idiosyncratic for its use of Yahweh, the Tetragrammaton. The decision to translate the unpronounced name of the Lord is described in the introduction: "It is not without hesitation that this accurate form has been used, and no doubt those who may care to use this translation of the Psalms can substitute the traditional 'the Lord.'" Scholarship prevailed over Catholic theology. Many renderings were true to scholarship: Job 19:25: "This I know: that my Avenger lives, and he, the Last, will take his stand on earth," for the KJV: "For I know that my redeemer liveth, and that he shall at the latter day upon the earth." (NJB has "I know that I have a living Defender and that he will rise up last, on the dust of the earth.") The scholars often go to the Greek Septuagint while the NJV stays more closely to the Hebrew, often rearranges verses, and proposes conjectures (e.g., Isa. 53).

Acceptance. In 1966 nearly a million copies had been sold by Doubleday. The expense of the NJB, however, has not made it a best seller. Moreover, many comparable scholarly translations, such as NAB, RSV, NJB, REB, and NJV have not become commercial successes. All of these collectively are guessed to be less than 10 percent of the American market.

New American Bible [= NAB] (1970). History. The NAB is the first American Roman Catholic translation from the original languages. Originally, the Confraternity of Christian Doctrine [= CCD] asked the members of the Catholic Biblical Association to translate the Vulgate. This was to be a revision of the Douay-Rheims-Challoner English Version, which itself was a translation of the Latin Vulgate. The New Testament (1941) was translated first.

As a consequence, however, of Pius XII's liberating encyclical, *Divino Afflante Spiritu* (1943), Roman Catholics were permitted to abandon the CCD revision and translate from the original languages. This new Catholic translation appeared piecemeal: *Genesis to Ruth* (1952); *Job to Sirach* (1955); *Isaiah to Malachi* (1961); *Samuel to Macabees* (1969). Non-Catholics were included in the translation committee: Frank Cross did I–II Samuel; David Noel Freedman retranslated Genesis with expanded notes; and James A. Sanders, II Kings. The complete NAB with the deuterocanonicals appeared in 1970. Companion commentaries to the NAB are published under the auspices of the Catholic Biblical Association, *The Jerome Biblical Commentary* (1968) and the updated *The New Jerome Biblical Commentary* (1989).

A revised translation of the New Testament for the liturgical readings appeared in 1987 and was translated with Protestant cooperation. Since the Psalms were actually translated from the *New Latin Psalter* (1944–1945) of the professors of the Pontifical Biblical Institute at Rome, Psalms is in the process of being newly translated (1990) from the Hebrew.

Principles and Representative Examples. There is a strong Catholic bent both to the translation and to the footnotes: the traditional Catholic division of the Ten Commandments is presented (Ex. 20:1–17); Isa. 7:14 is translated as "virgin," and the footnote speaks of a "transcendent fulfillment" of this verse in Matthew; Ps. 51:7 is seen as "foreshadowing the basic Christian doctrine of original sin; the "manna" of Ex. 16:4 is seen as a type of Eucharist; Catholic spelling of proper names ("Isaias," "Osee," "Aggaeus," Paralipomenon," etc., was dropped. The NAB retains "Lord," where the JB/NJB have the Tetragrammaton. The "burnt offering" is rendered infectiously as the "holocaust." The Book of Samuel has been heavily guided by the Cave 4 materials from Qumran and the Greek Septuagint.

Acceptance. The NAB is highly respected and has found its place in the English liturgy of the Roman Catholic church. Theophile Meek of the Chicago Bible noted about the Sapiential books: "It is much more modern in its English and much truer to the original than the highly vaunted RSV." James Barr has said about NAB that it is in advance over NEB for its application of comparative philology and of textual study, keeping in step with the accepted opinion of scholars.

New English Bible [= NEB] (1970) and Revised English Bible [= REB] (1989). History. The NEB is a complete break from the KJV and is authorized by the main Christian churches of the British Isles. British chaplains during World War II complained that they had to translate the KJV for the soldiers into the current language of the day.

The idea of a Bible in contemporary language was proposed by the Church of Scotland (1946). The New Testament (1961) was directed by C.H. Dodd. The Old Testament (1970) was directed first by T.H. Robinson (d. 1957), then by Sir Godfrey Driver, whose use of Arabic for the understanding of difficult Hebrew words was well known in scholarly literature. The Apocrypha was directed by W.D. McHardy and G.D. Kilpatrick. Finally, after 24 years, the Old Testament and the Apocrypha were published (1970), along with a second edition of the New Testament containing 400 minor revisions. A further update of both testaments was published as the REB (1989), a major revision done under the direction of W.D. McHardy.

The NEB is a new translation and has departed from the Tyndale-King James tradition. With modernity of speech, with new meanings for words, with translating "sense for sense" not "word for word," with a boldness for emendation – often the easiest way out of a textual difficulty – and with a strong dependence on the versions, English Christians have truly abandoned the KJV.

Principles and Representative Examples. The NEB has made wide use of the versions and comparative Semitics, especially the use of Arabic for coming up with new meanings for the Hebrew (e.g., 2 Chr. 34:6: "he burnt down" in both NEB and REB; Num. 16:1: "challenged the authority" in both NEB and REB). Often, these new meanings are proposed to scholars for the first time in the NEB. Furthermore, the NEB has about 50 readings in Isaiah derived from the Dead Sea Scrolls. This boldness with the Dead Sea Scrolls is matched with a timidity in the use of Ugaritic.

Some renderings in the NEB engage the reader with its modernity. Ruth 1:1: "Long ago in the time of the Judges;" Ruth 2:1: Boaz is a "well-to-do-man." Some scatological "Driverisms" have made NEB famous or infamous. The most well known concerns Achsah in Judges 1:14: "broke wind," is now changed in REB "she dismounted from her donkey."

Some innovative characteristics of the NEB were not carried through to the REB: the single column page of NEB was replaced in REB with the traditional double column page, thus saving paper; NEB's three levels of indentation, reflecting the number of stressed syllables in Hebrew poetry, were not employed by REB; the marginal verse numbers of the NEB are put back inside the text of REB; the omission in NEB of the traditional superscriptions from the Psalter are restored in REB; the Hebrew *selah* in the Psalms, omitted by NEB, has been restored in the REB; the hybrid word "Jehovah" was used four times for "Lord" (Ex. 3:15; 6:3; 33:19; 34:5–6) in NEB and now in REB all are rendered "Lord"; some of the transpositions of verses in the NEB are returned to their original Masoretic Hebrew order in the REB (e.g., Job 14:21–22; Isa. 5:24–25, etc.); some NEB Britishisms were changed in the REB: "gaoler" in Isa. 10:4 to "prisoners"; "corn" to "grain" in Judg. 15:5.

In response to a period of radical change of language used in the churches, this Bible for the 1990s has abandoned the "thou" form of address for God. In addition, "O" as a form of address is mostly abandoned in REB. Numerous topical subheadings have been added in REB. The REB has also begun to use more inclusive language, especially where "men" applies to both genders. Ps. 8:4 in the NEB: What is man that thou shouldst remember him?" becomes in the REB: "What is a frail mortal, that you should be mindful of him?" Male references to the deity are retained, as are the metaphorical "king" and "son." Other inclusive sensitivity is found in Job 14:22: "His flesh upon him becomes black" becomes in REB "His kinsfolk are grieved for him." In general, REB plays less fast and loose with both Hebrew and English than its predecessor.

Acceptance. The NEB sold two million in its first two years; the newer REB became a Book-of-the-Month Club selection, as was the NEB, assuring high sales. This was buttressed by a 1989 poll of British churchgoers under 45 years old, which found that up to 80% preferred the modernized translations of the Scriptures. T.S. Eliot, however, criticized the style, compared with the KJV, as "vulgar, trivial and pedantic."

New American Standard Bible [= NASB] (1971; rev. 1995). History. The Lockman Foundation, a non-profit Christian organization from La Habra, California, published NASB New Testament (1963) and Old Testament (1971). The translation was carried out by 58 anonymous conservative Protestants, often teachers in seminaries. The purpose of the translation was to "preserve the scholarship and accuracy of the American Standard Version" and to use "a fluent and readable style."

Principles and Representative Examples. This formal equivalent translation is a wooden updating of the American Standard Version of 1901 which has nevertheless been praised for its accuracy. Each verse is printed as a separate paragraph; "Thou" is retained when the Deity is addressed; "Lord" is used for the Tetragrammaton.

Acceptance. With the appearance of the NIV, the popularity of the NASB has dropped off, although in 1990 the text has become accessible on computer. F.F. Bruce has said of the NASB: "If the RSV had never appeared, this revision of the American Standard Version would be a more valuable work than it is. As things are, there are few things done well by the NASB which are not done better by the RSV."

Living Bible [= LB] (1971). History. The LB grew out of Kenneth Taylor's desire to paraphrase the Bible for his 10 children, because they could not understand the American Standard Version of 1901 (a KJV revision) during family devotions. His vision grew from his Wheaton, Illinois, farmhouse until, like Tyndale – "the Father of the English Bible" – he wanted to bring the Bible to "every plowboy." He first paraphrased the Epistle to Romans (1956), and then the *Living Prophecies* (1965). The New Testament was finished in the same year as the *Living Psalms* (1967). Finally, he published the complete *Living Bible Paraphrased* (1971) in his own Tyndale Press.

Principles and Representative Examples. Taylor's work is an evangelical paraphrase – a restatement with the additive of evangelical theology. Some of his renditions that raise eyebrows are the following: Gen. 3:4: "That's a lie!' the serpent hissed"; Ex. 11:8: "Then, red-faced with anger, Moses stomped from the palace"; 1 Kings 4:1: "Here is a list of Solomon's cabinet members"; Judg. 18:25: "Be careful how you talk, mister." Job, Psalms, and the Prophets are entirely in prose format. In the creation story, LB makes an addition to the text that is not internally obvious and for which he offers no explanation: "So he let it shine for awhile, and then there was darkness again."

There is much deserved criticism for the antisemitic character of LB's interpretative paraphrases, John 1:17: "For Moses gave us only the Law with its rigid demands and merciless justice, while Jesus Christ brought us loving forgiveness as well." (NRSV: The law indeed was given through Moses; grace and truth came through Jesus Christ.") The word "Messiah" is switched for "Son of Man," "Son of David," and "Lord," to make a theological point.

Acceptance. The conversational style made it the best seller of 1972 in America. Evangelist Billy Graham, also of Wheaton, Illinois, dispensed some 600,000 free copies for his television crusade. In seven years, 22 million copies of LB were sold.

Scholars have roundly criticized the work for its many errors and rigid evangelical positions. However, Taylor's work has actually licensed every person to make his/her own paraphrase. To this end, in 1974 Tyndale House has published *Eight Translation New Testament* (= KJV, LB, Phillips, RSV, TEV, NIV, JB, NEB). The year 1996 saw a revision of the Living Bible, The New Living Translation.

Today's English Version [= TEV] also called Good News Bible [= GNB] (1976). History. Around 1950, the American Bible Society received requests for a simplified English Version. In 1961 Robert G. Bratcher, an ordained Baptist minister and a research associate on the ABS, was to translate the NT with a team of translators for the Old Testament.

First appeared the Gospel of Mark, *The Right Time* (1964) and then the whole NT *The Good News for Modern Man* (1966). After some publications of individual books, the Old Testament (1976) was published, and with the Apocrypha, *Good News Bible: The Bible in Today's English Version* (1979). Some 600,000 were sold very quickly, and by the end of the first year total sales reached 5 million copies. There are some 500 stick-figure line drawings by Annie Vallotton, a Swiss-born artist living in Paris, which reinforce the relaxed and accessible tone of the work.

Principles and Representative Examples. The principles of the TEV are basically two, and these constitute a radical break from the KJV. First, it is based on the principles of modern linguistics and the ground-breaking work of Eugene A. Nida and his application of the principles of Dynamic Equivalence (cf. Theory and Practice of Translation (1969)). Secondly, the TEV chose simple vocabulary that could even appeal to people to whom English is a second language. Its simplicity, however, should not disguise the gargantuan research and the use of modern knowledge of the world of the Scriptures. The language was to appeal to the educated and the uneducated, new learners of English, and the "unchurched" or "unsynagogued." Given that Hebrew is a language that uses its few words well, the translation accords with this purpose. New Testament Greek was koine Greek as TEV is koine English. [Koine means "common," not the classical Greek].

To this end, the translators took advantage of word-frequency lists, such as that used by the United States Information Agency in its program for editing books into Easy English. Technical terms for the biblical institutions were maintained, such as, unleavened bread, Pentecost, Tabernacles, etc., but "council" was used for "Sanhedrin," and "teachers of the Law" for "scribes." In addition, there is a word list in the back of the TEV with definitions of unfamiliar words, e.g., "Abib," "Abyss," "Acacia," etc.

Acceptance. As people are becoming more aware of the value of dynamic translation, the TEV is becoming more acceptable. J.B. Phillips, the translator of the Phillips New Testament, favorably describes the translation of New Testament as "ordinary workaday English. If the style is rather of the 'plain Jane' variety, well so long as Jane does her work and speaks the truth, what's wrong with her?" Catholics have been encouraged to use an approved (i.e., with an imprimatur) edition of the TEV that includes the deuterocanonical/apocrypha. The sales of the TEV are extremely numerous, usually sold at prices subsidized by the United Bible Society and the American Bible Society. In total, the United Bible Societies in 1981 distributed some 500,000,000 Bibles or parts of Bibles throughout the world.

New International Version [= NIV] (1978). History. The NIV is the Evangelical Christians' answer to their dissatisfaction with the RSV. The 1954 Evangelical Synod advised its consistories that in a number of passages the RSV did not do justice to the unity of Scriptures, the deity of Christ, and messianic prophecy. Therefore, the RSV was unapproved for public worship. After much labor and expense, Zondervan published the NIV New Testament (1973) and completed the Old Testament (1978).

The New International Version was to be an international version – avoiding Britishisms and Americanisms – a language that all understand and no one speaks. The work was sponsored by the New York International Bible Society and done by scholars of 34 different religious groups, working in 20 teams. This was the largest committee ever to work on a translation. The actual work of translation took some 11 years.

Thirteen denominations were represented; 87 of the 97 scholars were Americans; and seven were from Trinity Evangelical Divinity School in Illinois. The whole project took 25 years, 200,000 hours of work, and $2,000,000. It is estimated that 170 man-hours were invested in translating each chapter of the Bible.

To control the total 115 scholars involved an elaborate system of committees was formed: (1) the first draft to be done by two co-translators, two consultants, and an English stylist; (2) an Intermediate Editorial Committee composed of five scholars concerned mainly with exegetical matters; (3) General editorial committees, which included seven scholars to attend to the theology and style; and finally (4) a committee of 15 members, who had the final authority.

Principles and Representative Examples. The principles of the translation are, namely, that the NIV is (1) to be faithful to the original; (2) not to be a paraphrase; (3) to be in the language of the people; (4) to be for both public worship and private study; (5) to be translated by scholars who have a high view of Scripture; (6) and to reflect the unity and harmony of Scripture. "The Bible alone, in its entirety, is the Word of God and is therefore inerrant in the autographs." In effect this means that if a translation is to be reliable, the Old Testament must agree exactly with the New Testament. All efforts are made to "harmonize" the texts of the Old and New Testaments.

There are many translations that reflect the theological interest of the NIV. Is. 7:14: "The virgin will be with child and will give birth to a son, and will call him Immanuel." This harmonizes with Matt. 1:23. Not even a footnote mentions that the term "virgin" might be rendered "a young woman."

Psalm 2 is a parade example of harmonization. Ps. 2:9 rejects the Hebrew MT "you shall break" in favor of the LXX, Vulgate "you shall shepherd," because of the New Testament quotations in Revelations 12:5 and 19:15. At Ps. 2:12 NIV has "kiss the Son" with a marginal note: "son." (RSV has "kiss his feet"; TEV "bow down to him"; NEB "kiss the king.") Through the use of capital letters, Psalm 2 becomes thoroughly messianic: "Anointed One," "King," and "Son," and "Father."

Without comment in the footnotes, the order of creation in Gen. 2 is made to harmonize with Gen. 1 by translating 2:8 and 19 as past perfects: "had planted" and "had formed." Thereby, Adam is not made first in the second account, thus agreeing with Gen. 1.

Another translation avoids a misunderstanding of Jonah 3:3 (RSV), "Now Nineveh was an exceedingly great city, three days' journey in breadth." Such hyperbole is rendered, "Now Nineveh was a very important city – a visit required three days." In Gen. 3:5: polytheism of the KJV is avoided in "you shall be like God," instead of "as Gods" (KJV). In Job 1:6, "Satan" is so rendered despite the definite article that indicates the meaning as "the adversary" or "the accuser."

Theological problems are often relegated to footnotes: Gen. 18:22, "Abraham remained standing before the Lord" instead of the "Lord remained standing before Abraham," which is noted in the footnote. In Job 32:3: "they condemned him (= Job)" with the footnote reading: "condemned God." NIV, at Hos. 4:7, does not follow the *tikkun* [= a Masoretic correction]. "I will exchange." Instead, NIV has "they exchanged their Glory."

Wide scholarship is evident in the NIV. Isa 15:1 translates the Heb. *ki* as an asseverative (i.e., emphatically) from the understanding of an Ugaritic particle. At Gen. 47:21, NIV follows the Samaritan Pentateuch, the Septuagint (and Vulgate) in correcting the Hebrew: "Joseph reduced the people to servitude."

The following sample of interesting translations gives a flavor of the whole: in Isa. 22:5, NIV echoes the Hebrew assonance of "*mehumah, mevusah, mevukhah*," with "a day of tumult and trampling and terror." For "vanity of vanities" NIV renders Ecc. 1:2: "Meaningless! Meaningless!" says the Teacher. "Utterly meaningless! Everything is meaningless."

Acceptance. The NIV has the largest first printing ever for an English Bible. After 4 weeks, 1.2 million copies were sold. These singular sales have continued, and according to the best estimates, they captured some 20–25% of the market in the 1980s, and in the 1990s became the most popular in the U.S. outside of KJV. In spite of its great commercial success, the NIV continues to be criticized for its theological position in translating.

Other Protestant Translations. Two recent works maintain that they have gone to great pains to create a more literal translation of the Bible. The *English Standard Version* (2001) aims at being "essentially faithful" to the text, hewing to "the structure and meaning of the original." In fact it is a finely honed version in the tradition of KJV and RSV, with care taken to consult the original languages, and includes a helpful set of notes. Yet it retains "without form and void" in Gen. 1:2, and "sin offering" in Lev. 4:3, to cite a few instances in which traditional English renderings are retained at the expense of both the form and meaning of the Hebrew. The *Holman Christian Standard Bible* (2004) advertises itself as a cross between dynamic and formal equivalence, coining the term "optimal equivalence" to indicate that it begins with literal understanding and then crafts a readable translation. Produced under Southern Baptist auspices, it does not attempt to introduce modern concepts of gender correctness or to simplify the language (the editors emphasize how the translation retains "rich terms like 'propitiation'...and 'sanctification'"). Its advertising slogan is "Nothing Could Be Closer to the Truth."

Recent examples of freer translation, i.e., paraphrase, have enjoyed widespread circulation. In this regard, the 1990s saw a return to the legacy of *The Living Bible* and *TEV*. Like other similar works, *The New Century Bible* (1993), which stemmed from the 1986 *International Children's Bible*, looked for clarity as its chief goal. Thus its version of Gen. 3:17 reads, "So I will put a curse on the ground, and you will have to work very hard for your food." *The Contemporary English Version* (1995), designed to be comprehensible by both children and non-native speakers of English, also utilizes colloquial ease, as in Gen. 29:5–6: "'Do you know Laban, son of Nahor?' 'Yes,'" they replied. 'How is he?' he asked. 'He's fine,' they replied." A trenchant example of paraphrastic variation can be found in considering I Sam. 20:20, which the *Living Bible* actually renders as "You son of a bitch!" whereas the 1996 *New Living Translation* uses "You stupid son of a whore" – with the note "Heb. You son of a perverse and rebellious woman." Thus in this kind of translation, the variations, and possibilities, are endless. In yet another attempt at a contemporary language Bible, in 1993 retired minister Eugene Peterson published his fourth and final volume of *The Message*, which renders the Bible "not in refined language that appeals to our aspirations after the best but a rough and earthy language that captures God's presence and action when we least expect it." This version, clearly born of pulpit experience, seems best suited for the Prophets and the Psalms; his English rhetoric is vivid and colloquial, often verging on the "hip." As an example, Peterson renders the opening of Psalm 1 as "How well God must like you – / you don't hang out at Sin Saloon, / you don't slink along Dead-End Road, / you don't go to Smart-Mouth College."

New Jewish Version [= NJV] (1985). History. The Jewish Publication Society Bible [= JPS] of 1917 was only a slight modification of the KJV. The JPS kept the vocabulary and Tudor grammar of the Authorized Version [= The Revised Version (of the KJV) of 1885]. Many of the readings of the Authorized version had been made with the help of David Kimḥi's commentary. This Bible, however, was unsatisfactory, and the idea of a new translation was proposed in 1955.

The NJV translation would be completely independent of the KJV and be a rendering in a modern English. In addition, there would be an erudite use of Semitic languages (Akkadian, Aramaic, Syriac, Ugaritic) and of the medieval Jewish scholars (Abraham Ibn Ezra, Kimḥi, Rashbam [Samuel ben Meir], Rashi, and Saadiah). The publication came out in separate volumes over 20 years: *The Torah* (1962 revised in 1967), *The Five Megilloth and Jonah* (1969); The Book of Isaiah (1973); *The Book of Psalms* (1972); *The Book of Jeremiah* (1974); *Nevi'im* [= The Prophets] (1978); Job (1980); and *The Writings* (1982). A one-volume edition was finally published, *Tanakh: The Holy Scriptures* (1985); a dual-language edition, with Hebrew text from BHS, appeared finally in 1999. The three branches of American Judaism, Orthodox, Conservative, and Reform, were all represented on the translation committees. For the *Torah* and *Nevi'im*: Harry M. Orlinsky (Hebrew Union College), editor-in-chief, who had served on the RSV and NRSV Old Testament committees; H.L. Ginsberg (Jewish Theological Seminary); Ephraim A. Speiser (U. of Pennsylvania); Max Arzt (Jewish Theological Seminary); Bernard J. Bamberger (West End Synagogue, N.Y. City); Harry Freedman (Yeshivah University); Solomon Grayzel (editor of the Jewish Publication Society). For the *Kethubim*: Moshe Greenberg (Hebrew University); Jonas C. Greenfield (Hebrew University); Nahum M. Sarna (Brandeis University); Rabbi Saul Leeman (Conservative); Rabbi Martin S. Rozenburg (Reform); Rabbi David Shapiro (Orthodox); Chaim Potok (Editor of the Jewish Publication Society). Over the years the NJV has appeared in a number of formats and settings, eventually coming to occupy a place of prominence in the Jewish community outside of Orthodoxy. It serves as the English text for the Reform Movement's UAHC Commentary of W.G. Plaut (1981, rev. 2005, with additional revisions to Exodus-Deuteronomy; Genesis was newly translated by Chaim Stern), the Conservative Movement's *Etz Ḥayim* Torah/Haftarot volume (2001), the *JPS Commentary* series (1989–), and *The Jewish Study Bible*

(2003). The NJV is also the one most frequently quoted in the works of Jewish Bible scholars in English.

Principles and Representative Examples. There is a plethora of English renderings which are deliberately not literal translations of the Hebrew. The Hebrew word "five" is rendered "several" and "a few"; the Hebrew "ten" is also translated dynamically as "many." Footnotes note the literal Hebrew. The Hebrew torah is translated: "teachings," "instructions," "ritual," "directions," "procedure," "obligation," and "law" (Ex. 12:49). "Ark of the Pact" is used for "ark of the testimony." The Hebrew conjunctive, vav, often slavishly "and" in other English Versions, is rendered "when" or "so" or "then" or "thus" or "although" or "but" or "yet" or "and" or left untranslated. The Hebrew mishpat has a variety of meanings: "norm," "rights," "regulation," "due," "decision," "true way," and "custom." The Hebrew ẓedek is rendered "grace," "victory," "vindication." Ex. 10:19 has "Sea of Reeds." Some Hebrew words are left transliterated: "ephod," and "Ehyeh-Asher-Ehyeh" in Ex. 3:14.

The 54 *parashiyyot* (sections of the Pentateuch) are given with the Hebrew names written in Hebrew. In line with the Vulgate, KJV, RSV, the NJV employs "the LORD" to indicate the personal name of Israel's God. In Ex. 6:3, however, where specific mention is made of the name, the four Hebrew letters, known as the Tetragrammaton, appear in the English text in Hebrew characters. Deut. 6:4: "Hear, O Israel! The Lord is our God, the Lord alone," since monotheism was the issue in a polytheistic society. Isa. 1:8: for the traditional "daughter of Zion," NJV has "fair Zion."

The footnotes present consistent and reliable information and an illustrative example is offered by the first verses of the *Tanakh*: The NJV is the first official (i.e., denominationally approved) translation to read: "When God began to create… and a wind from God…" instead of "In the beginning… the Spirit of God…" The footnotes to this verse are instructive: "When God began to create[a] the heaven and the earth – the earth being unformed and void, with darkness over the surface of the deep and a wind from[b] God sweeping over the water – God said, 'Let there be light'; and there was light."

Footnote (a) Or "In the beginning God created" ["Or" is defined: "Indicates an alternative reading that the committee found almost as acceptable as the one adopted for the text."]

Footnote (b) Others "the spirit of" ["Others" is defined: "Indicates a well-known traditional translation, especially if it was used in the older (1917) JPS version that the committee does not find acceptable even as an alternative reading."]

The footnotes also present renderings from the Dead Sea manuscripts, propose emendations and transpositions in difficult passages (especially in the poetic books), and, unlike most translations, frequently use the intellectually honest term "meaning of Heb. uncertain." In this, the NJV reflects Jewish tradition, with its strong sense of multiple interpretive possibilities and openness to ambiguity. Orlinsky discusses the translation choices in NJV at length in his illuminating *Notes on the New Translation of the Torah.*

Acceptance. NJV's effort to determine the accurate meaning of the Hebrew text has been rewarded with wide acceptance. Theophile Meek, a translator himself, has called the NJV "assuredly the best that has been produced thus far." Most especially, the NIV translators have verified that the Masoretic Text is actually clear in passages where others emend.

The acceptance has a broad base among scholars. The reason for its acceptance is conspicuous from the ecumenical words of H.L. Ginsberg: "Our work does *not* owe all its virtues to our use of sources, mostly Jewish, which others have neglected and to our acumen and ingenuity. Our translation would not be worth the paper it's printed on if we had not drunk deeply at the wells of Gesenius, and Delitzsch, and Driver, and Kittel – aye, and Wellhausen too – and the other Christian scholars who revived biblical and Oriental scholarship while Jewry slept, and are still vigorously cultivating it."

Despite praise for the accuracy of and impressive scholarship behind NJV, it has also occasioned criticism on an artistic level, with some feeling that it does not do justice to the rhetorical force of the Hebrew or to some of its stylistic features.

It should be mentioned that, outside of the aegis of NJV, numerous other translations of single books have been done by Jewish scholars, usually for a wider audience, either as part of a commentary series (e.g., the *Old Testament Library*, which includes J. Levenson's *Esther* (1997) and A. Berlin's *Lamentations* (2002)) or as free-standing volumes. Some examples of the latter, usually accompanied by commentary, are renditions of the Song of Songs by M. Falk (1982, 1990) and C. and A. Bloch (1995); of Samuel by R. Alter (*The David Story,* 1999; includes 1 Kings 1–2) and E. Fox (*Give Us a King!,* 1999); of Job by R. Gordis (*The Book of God and Man*, 1965) and R. Scheindlin (1999); of Ecclesiastes by Gordis (*Koheleth: The Man and His World*, 1968) and M. Fox (*A Time to Tear Down and a Time to Build Up*, 1999); and of Psalms by M. Rozenberg and B. Zlotowitz (1999).

A revised English translation, by Harold Fisch, appeared in 1964. Based on the "Jewish Family Bible" of M. Friedlander, published in 1881, which retained much of the language of the Authorized Version of 1611 but also paid attention to Jewish sentiment and tradition, the language has been modernized where it was felt that the previous linguistic and grammatical forms would cause difficulty to the modern reader. An entirely new system of transcription of proper names has been introduced, providing for the pronunciation of the name to conform exactly to that of the original. A list is given of the new form side by side with that hitherto accepted.

Torah Translations by Jews. The Torah's centrality in Jewish life merits separate discussion when considering Bible translation. In recent decades there has been an upsurge of activity in the translation of the Torah into English among Jews. This may be attributed to a number of factors: the desire of "movements" to produce their own commentaries and accompanying translations, the need to incorporate further discoveries in Semitics and archaeology into translations, and the eagerness of individual scholar-translators with particular approaches to present their own vision of the text. Major translations since NJV (1962) include three traditionalist versions and three more "literary" renderings. Some of these are clearly intended for synagogue use, while others aim at a broader audience.

Aryeh Kaplan, *The Living Torah: A New Translation Based on Traditional Jewish Sources* (1981, no Hebrew), is an example of a translation wrought in line with traditional Jewish teachings. Kaplan was known for his interpretations of Kabbalah and his expositions of traditional Judaism. In his Introduction to *The Living Torah*, he cites the Rabbinic tradition against literal translation (Kid. 49a, Tosef., Meg. 3:21), and promotes an idiomatic approach as the one most likely to avoid misreading. Kaplan approaches narrative texts with an eye to making them readable, as in storytelling; in contrast, he treats legal texts primarily in the light of "the final decision in Jewish law." He summarizes his goal as attempting to create a translation that is "accurate, clear, modern, readable, and above all, in consonance with the living tradition of Judaism." As a rule he supplies a healthy dose of translation alternatives in his notes, drawing mostly on ancient versions (especially Targumim) and a wide selection of medieval commentators.

Example A: Gen. 35:22, "While Jacob was living undisturbed in the area, Reuben went and disturbed the sleeping arrangements of Bilhah, his father's concubine." Kaplan derives this reading from TB Shabbat 55a, b, as distinct from the usual "Reuben went and lay with Bilhah…," but gives other choices in his notes.

Example B: Ex. 33:14, 18, "'My Presence will go and lead you,' replied [God].".... "'Please let me have a vision of Your Glory,' begged Moses." These passages feature a less formal tone, and offer differing renderings for *vayyomar.*

Samson Rafael Hirsch, *The Pentateuch* (English Translation by Gertrude Hirschler) (1990, includes Hebrew), an unusual project in that it incorporates a translation of a translation, reflects the 19th-century German Neo-Orthodox leader's approach of deriving "the meaning of the words from the treasure of linguistic explanations which we possess in our traditional literature" and from his own phonetic-etymological system. His lengthy commentary is largely philosophical, and often makes use of biblical language as a springboard for his thoughts.

Example A: Gen. 1:26, "'Let Us make an Adam (a deputy) in a form worthy of us.'" Here Hirsch understands *adam* as flowing from the "majesty of plurality" suggested in *na'aseh adam* ("Let Us make man"), and notes that "only as a representative of the community as a whole can the sovereign rule over his subjects. In the same spirit, the Creator now wishes to inform the terrestrial world that its [human] master is to be appointed for its own welfare." He also derives *adam* from *adom*, red, which, as "the least-broken ray of the spectrum," is "the closest manifestation of the Divine earth."

Example B: Ex. 17:12, "The hands of Moshe became heavy; and they took a stone and placed it under him, and he sat upon it. Aharon and Hur supported his hands, the one on the one side and the other on the other side; so his hands remained an expression of trust until the sun went down." Hirsch reads *emunah* not as the customary etymology would have it, "firm," but rather theologically, "an expression of trust."

The Chumash (*ArtScroll Series: The Stone Edition; ed. Nosson Scherman*) (1993); incorporated in *Tanach* (*The Stone Edition*) (1996, includes Hebrew), like the previous two works, translates with an eye to rabbinic understandings of the text and incorporates these into the translation when it feels them to be warranted. Strikingly, the English text is printed entirely in italics. The translation is part of ArtScroll's program of presenting classical Jewish texts in English and Hebrew, accompanied by traditionally-based commentaries.

Example A: Deut. 6:5, "You shall love HASHEM, your God, with all your heart, with all your soul, and with all your resources." The choice of "resources" reflects the understanding of *me'od* found in Targum Onkelos, Sifre (Deut. 32), and M. Ber. 9:5.

Example B: Lev. 20:27, "Any man or woman in whom there shall be the sorcery of Ov or of Yid'oni, they shall be put to death." The reader is directed to a note that reads in part, "Ov and Yid'oni were magical means of foretelling the future," differing somewhat from modern scholarly interpretation, which understands them as related to departed spirits.

Everett Fox, *The Five Books of Moses* (*The Schocken Bible*, Vol. 1) (1995; rev. 1997, no Hebrew), following in the footsteps of the German Buber-Rosenzweig translation (q.v.), seeks to echo rhythms and literary devices of the Hebrew text. While not as radical as the German work, given the less malleable nature of English, it is designed, like its predecessor, to be read aloud and to give the English reader an aural feel for the Hebrew text. Thus it is printed in a form resembling free verse, names retain their Hebrew forms, as in Hirsch, and the principle of "leading words" (Buber) – theme words in the text – is reflected in English. Fox's line divisions do not strictly follow the traditional *te'amim*, but they often correspond to them. The text is accompanied by commentary on thematic issues, and notes on specific words. Previous versions of his Genesis appeared in 1972 and 1983; of Exodus, in 1986.

Example A: Ex. 2:10, "She called his name: Moshe/He-Who-Pulls-Out; / she said: For out of the water *meshitihu*/I-pulled-him." The translation, using the Hebrew form of Moses's name and the Hebrew phrase attached to it by Pharaoh's daughter, points to the grammatical significance of the form *Moshe* (in *hiph'il*) as an active foreshadowing of Moses's future role.

Example B: Gen. 6:11, 13, "Now the earth had gone to ruin before God, the earth was filled with wrongdoing. / God saw the earth, and here, it had gone to ruin, / for all flesh had ruined its way upon the earth. / …here, I am about to bring ruin upon them, together with the earth." The repetition of key word "ruin," representing the Hebrew root *sh-h'-t*, appears to be used by the text to express the biblical concept of the punishment corresponding to the crime.

Richard Elliott Friedman, *Commentary on the Torah (with a New English Translation and the Hebrew Text)* (2001), by a prominent advocate of the Documentary Hypothesis, provides along with his commentary a translation that attempts to be clear and to steer a middle course between English and Hebrew. Friedman also published a version of the Torah with documentary sources demarcated, *The Bible with Sources Revealed: A New View of the Five Books of Moses* (2003), and included renditions of passages from the Former Prophets in *The Hidden Book in the Bible* (1998).

Example A: Gen. 1:1–3a, "In the beginning of God's creating the skies and the earth – when the earth had been shapeless and formless, and darkness was on the face of the deep, and God's spirit was hovering on the face of the water – God said, "Let there be light." "Skies" reflects the predominant meaning of *shamayim* in the Biblical world; "shapeless and formless" is meant to echo *tohu va-vohu*.

Example B: Gen. 18:17, "And YHWH had said, 'Shall I conceal what I'm doing from Abraham, since Abraham *will* become a big and powerful nation, and all the nations of the earth will be blessed through him? For I've known him for the purpose that he'll command his children and his house after him, and they'll observe YHWH's way, to do virtue and judgment….'" Friedman uses italics ("*will* become") to express the Hebrew form *hayoh hayah* (lit. "becoming he will become"), utilizes the simple "big" for *gadol*, and in general adopts a relaxed tone.

Robert Alter, *The Five Books of Moses* (2004, no Hebrew), attempts to elicit rhetorical characteristics of the Hebrew text in a readable English style – "an experiment in re-presenting the Bible…in a language that conveys with some precision the semantic nuances and the lively orchestration of literary effects of the Hebrew and at the same time has stylistic and rhythmic integrity in English." His introduction and accompanying commentary discuss these issues in some detail, following in the footsteps of his books on biblical narrative and poetry. Alter previously published a translation of Genesis (1995).

Example A: Gen. 3:6, "And the woman saw that the tree was good for eating and that it was lust to the eyes and the tree was good to look at…." Alter notes, following A. Funkenstein, that *le-haskil* is connected in the Targumim with "looking, regarding," a reading which parallels "a lust to the eyes" and which is also suggested by the usage of *maskil* in Psalm 41:2.

Example B: Ex. 15:1, "Let me sing unto the lord for He surged, O surged…." Alter understands the use of the verb ga'oh as a pun here, reflecting both the customary "triumphed" and the alternate image of the rising tide, appropriate in the context of the divine victory at the Sea of Reeds.

A more direct comparison of the differences between these six works (with the addition of NJV), in approach and tone, might be gleaned from the following table, which presents translations of two passages. The first is Gen. 32:21 (the Hebrew text is:

KAPLAN [Jacob] said [to himself], "I will win him over with the gifts that are being sent ahead, and then I will face him. Hopefully, he will forgive me."

HIRSCH For he thought: "I will first appease his anger with the gift that goes before me and then I will

HIRSCHLER see his countenance; perhaps he will raise my countenance."

ARTSCROLL For he said, "I will appease him with the tribute that precedes me, and afterwards I will face him;

STONE (SCHERMAN) perhaps he will forgive me."

FOX For he said to himself: / I will wipe (the anger from) his face / with the gift that goes ahead of my face; / afterward, when I see his face, / perhaps he will lift up my face!

FRIEDMAN Because he said, "Let me appease his face with the offering that's going in front of me, and after that I'll see his face; maybe he'll raise my face."

ALTER For he thought, "Let me placate him with the tribute that goes before me, and after I shall look on his face, perhaps he will show me a kindly face."

NJV For he reasoned, "If I propitiate him with presents in advance, and then face him, perhaps he will show me favor."

Clearly, all these translators struggle with how to deal with the multiple uses of the sound and concept of Hebrew *panim*, coming up with a variety of solutions that present different English tones. They also are compelled to render *ki amar* in a way that does justice to its semantic range.

A second comparison of translations makes use of a legal passage, Ex. 20:9–10 (the Hebrew reads:

שֵׁשֶׁת יָמִים תַּעֲבֹד וְעָשִׂיתָ כָּל־מְלַאכְתֶּךָ׃ וְיוֹם הַשְּׁבִיעִי שַׁבָּת לַיהוָה אֱלֹהֶיךָ
לֹא־תַעֲשֶׂה כָל־מְלָאכָה אַתָּה | וּבִנְךָ וּבִתֶּךָ עַבְדְּךָ וַאֲמָתְךָ וּבְהֶמְתֶּךָ וְגֵרְךָ
אֲשֶׁר בִּשְׁעָרֶיךָ׃

It yields the following:

KAPLAN Remember the Sabbath day to keep it holy. You can work during the six weekdays and do all your tasks. But Saturday is the Sabbath to God your Lord. Do not do anything that constitutes work.

HIRSCH Remember the Sabbath day to sanctify it. Six days shall you serve and do all your [creating] work, and the seventh day is a Sabbath to *God*, your God. On it you shall not perform any kind of [creating] work….

ARTSCROLL Remember the Sabbath day to sanctify it. Six days shall you work and accomplish all your work; but the seventh day is Sabbath to HASHEM, your God; you shall not do any work….

FOX Remember / the Sabbath day, to hallow it. / For six days, you are to serve, and are to make all your work, / but the seventh day / is Sabbath for YHWH your God: / you are not to make any kind of work….

FRIEDMAN Remember the Sabbath day, to make it holy. Six days you shall labor and do all your work, and the seventh day is a Sabbath to YHWH, your God. You shall not do any work….

ALTER Remember the Sabbath day to hallow it. Six days you shall work and you shall do your tasks, but the seventh day is a Sabbath to the LORD your God. You shall do no task….

NJV Remember the Sabbath day and keep it holy. Six days you shall labor and do all your work, but the seventh day is a Sabbath of the LORD your God: you shall not do any work….

In these illustrations, rhythm, style, diction, and vocabulary point up quite different approaches, all along the spectrum from more literal to more idiomatic translation. Some retain key repeating words, preferring even to stretch English style in the process (Fox's "make work" keeps an important verb of Ex. 25–40 intact), while others focus on clarity in English as a major goal (cf. Kaplan's startling "Saturday" for *yom ha-shevi'i*). Notable also is the varied treatment of the Tetragrammaton, reflecting different forms of both traditional practice and scholarly convention. What the six translations share, despite their considerable differences, is an essentially Jewish approach to the text: they exhibit a reliance on classical sources (Midrash and medieval commentators) to varying degrees, and more significantly, they share a central commitment to the specific wording of the text, with all of its nuances and ambiguities.

A recent entry into Torah translation is the revised edition (2005) of W. Plaut's (UAHC) *The Torah: A Modern Commentary*. Genesis and the *haftarot* were translated anew by C. Stern in a "sense for sense" manner; following his death in 2001, the editors decided to lightly revise the NJV of Exodus-Deuteronomy, incorporating some of JPS's own changes since 1962 and adding some of their own, particularly regarding sacrificial terms. Generally speaking, the new edition pays attention to gender-related issues. For instance, "He said," when God is the subject, is rendered "[God] said," and "His covenant" as "the covenant." The editors characterize their approach as "gender accurate" rather than "gender neutral" – that is, they mitigate the maleness of the text when such an interpretation does not intrude upon the Hebrew. At the same time, they seek, for instance, to tone down a negative view of menstruation, which, they point out, is not a stigma but a state of being. An example of Stern's style in Genesis can be seen in 8:20–21: "Noah then built an altar in honor of the Eternal [a change from the NJV "LORD"]; taking some pure beasts and some pure birds, he offered up whole burnt offerings on the altar. The Eternal, inhaling the soothing fragrance, thought: 'Never again will I bring doom upon the world…'" Similarly idiomatic is his rendering of 48:1: "Look, your father is fading" (for Heb. *hinneh avikha h̦oleh*).

In discussing Torah translation, one additional body of work is relevant. Translation problems, especially as reflected in German versions since Luther and English ones since King James, are frequently discussed by Nehama Leibowitz in her well-known collections of comments to the weekly *parashiyyot* of the Torah, based on the insights of classical commentators, *Iyyunim Be-sefer Bereshit/Shemot/Vayikra/Bemidbar/Devarim*, tr. *Studies in Genesis/Exodus/Leviticus/Numbers/Deuteronomy* (1976–93).

Conclusion. The history of English Bible translation since World War II is a history of Protestants and Jews moving away from the KJV and its English, and of Catholics moving away from the Douay-Rheims-Challoner English translation of the Vulgate. Catholics, after *Divino Afflante Spiritu* (1943), were free to translate from the original languages, and consequently now use the NAB and NJB in worship. For Protestants, the KJV is still entrenched in the hearts of many people and remains one of the top three in sales. Protestants can now choose among a wide variety of translations. Some, particularly in the evangelical community, in which there exists a "King James Only" movement that regards the 1611 classic as the authentic word of God, choose to read the variously cast new editions of the KJV (in modern spelling and/or vocabulary revised in different degrees), which have been published since the 1980s (e.g., *New KJV, KJ2000, KJ21, Revised KJV, Modern KJV, Third Millennium Bible*). For others, the RSV and NIV sufficiently echo the KJV. Others still have gone to the opposite extreme, embracing the LB and its paraphrase, or using the TEV, a clean break from the KJV because of its use of dynamic equivalence as a principle of translation. For Jews, the NJV has been a decisive move away from the KJV, or more precisely, away from the Old JPS, which had taken the latter's place since 1917. In their use of different translations, usually based on personal or congregational preference, Jews echo their tradition, present already in biblical literature itself, of multiple voices and multiple understandings of the text.

The Bible is the chameleon of world literature, changing in the eyes of readers to accommodate each era. The act of translating it typically reflects profound religious, communal, psychological, and aesthetic trends. As such, to paraphrase Ecclesiastes, of the making of English Bible translations there will be no end.

VARIATIONS IN ENGLISH VERSIONS OF PSALM 23. In the following list, nine widely used English translations of this famous poem are cited, verse by verse. They represent a broad swath of denominational and stylistic approaches. Omitted are notes, which occasionally give alternate readings, including those from the KJV. The present layout also flattens the line divisions, which differ slightly from translation to translation.

Verse 1

KJV The LORD is my shepherd; I shall not want.

NAB A psalm of David. The LORD is my shepherd; there is nothing I lack.

NIV A psalm of David. The LORD is my shepherd; I shall not be in want.

NJB Yahweh is my shepherd, I lack nothing.

NRSV The Lord is my shepherd, I shall not want.

REB The LORD is my shepherd; I lack for nothing.

CEV You, LORD, are my shepherd. I will never be in need.

STONE A psalm by David. HASHEM is my shepherd, I shall not lack.

NJV A psalm of David. The LORD is my shepherd; I lack nothing.

Verse 2

KJV He maketh me to lie down in green pastures: he leadeth me beside the still waters.

NAB In green pastures you let me graze; to safe waters you lead me;

NIV He makes me lie down in green pastures, he leads me beside quiet waters,

NJB In grassy meadows he lets me lie. By tranquil streams he leads me

NRSV He makes me lie down in green pastures; he leads me beside still waters;

REB He makes me lie down in green pastures, he leads me to water where I may rest;

CEV You let me rest in fields of green grass. You lead me to streams of peaceful water,

STONE In lush meadows He lays me down, beside tranquil waters He leads me.

NJV He makes me lie down in green pastures; He leads me to water in places of repose.

Verse 3

KJV He restoreth my soul: he leadeth me in the paths of righteousness for his name's sake.

NAB you restore my strength. You guide me along the right path for the sake of your name.

NIV he restores my soul. He guides me in paths of righteousness for his name's sake.

NJB to restore my spirit. He guides me in paths of saving justice as befits his name.

NRSV he restores my soul. He leads me in right paths for his name's sake.

REB he revives my spirit; for his name's sake he guides me in the right paths.

CEV and you refresh my life. You are true to your name, and you lead me along the right paths.

STONE He restores my soul. He leads me on paths of righteousness for His Name' sake.

NJV He renews my life; He guides me in right paths as befits His name.

Verse 4

KJV Yea, though I walk through the valley of the shadow of death, I will fear no evil: for thou art with me; thy rod and thy staff they comfort me.

NAB Even when I walk through a dark valley, I fear no harm for you are at my side; your rod and staff give me comfort.

NIV Even though I walk through the valley of the shadow of death, I will fear no evil, for you are with me; your rod and your staff, they comfort me.

NJB Even were I to walk in a ravine as dark as death I should fear no danger, for you are at my side. Your staff and your crook are there to soothe me.

NRSV Even though I walk through the darkest valley, I fear no evil; for you are with me; your rod and your staff – they comfort me.

REB Even were I to walk through a valley of deepest darkness I should fear no harm, for you are with me; your shepherd's staff and crook afford me comfort.

CEV I may walk through valleys dark as death, but I won't be afraid. You are with me, and your shepherd's rod makes me feel safe.

STONE Though I walk in the valley overshadowed by death, I will fear no evil, for You are with me. Your rod and your staff, they comfort me.

NJV Though I walk through a valley of deepest darkness, I fear no harm, for You are with me; Your rod and Your staff – they comfort me.

Verse 5

KJV Thou preparest a table before me in the presence of mine enemies: thou anointest my head with oil; my cup runneth over.

NAB You set a table before me as my enemies watch; You anoint my head with oil; my cup overflows.

NIV You prepare a table before me in the presence of my enemies. You anoint my head with oil; my cup overflows.

NJB You prepare a table for me under the eyes of my enemies; you anoint my head with oil; my cup brims over.

NRSV You prepare a table before me in the presence of my enemies; you anoint my head with oil; my cup overflows.

REB You spread a table for me in the presence of my enemies; you have richly anointed my head with oil, and my cup brims over.

CEV You treat me to a feast, while my enemies watch. You honor me as your guest, and you fill my cup until it overflows.

STONE You prepare a table before me in view of my tormentors. You anoint my head with oil, my cup overflows.

NJV You spread a table for me in full view of my enemies; You anoint my head with oil; my drink is abundant.

Verse 6

KJV Surely goodness and mercy shall follow me all the days of my life: and I will dwell in the house of the LORD for ever.

NAB Only goodness and love will pursue me all the days of my life; I will dwell in the house of the LORD for years to come.

NIV Surely goodness and love will follow me all the days of my life, and I will dwell in the house of the LORD forever.

NJB Kindness and faithful love pursue me all the days of my life. I make my home in the house of Yahweh for all time to come.

NRSV Surely goodness and mercy shall follow me all the days of my life, and I shall dwell in the house of the Lord my whole life long.

REB Goodness and love unfailing will follow me all the days of my life, and I shall dwell in the house of the LORD throughout the years to come.

CEV Your kindness and love will always be with me each day of my life, and I will live forever in your house, LORD.

STONE May only goodness and kindness pursue m all the days of my life, and I shall dwell in the House of HASHEM for long days.

NJV Only goodness and steadfast love shall pursue me all the days of my life, and I shall dwell in the house of the LORD for many long years.

That the different approaches represented by these translations – and here we are only dealing with English! – cannot be fully bridged by one "definitive" work is a testimony to both the richness of the biblical text and its greatly varied post-canonical life. This must lead to the recognition that many translated versions of the Bible are possible and even desirable, not to mention inevitable. The reality is that for the translator as for the dramatic or musical performer, preconceptions and prejudices, conditioned both by personality and historical/sociological background, always play a role in the final outcome. Thus the success or failure of a translation will be judged differently by scholars, clergy, and audiences of various stripes, and often differently within these categories. Whether the translator's needs and desires, and attempts at solutions, correspond to those of an audience will always be at issue. As an aggregate, however, English translations of he Bible will continue to reflect the powerful hold this text exerts on Western minds and hearts.

[Raphael Loewe / Everett Fox (2nd ed.)]

Arabic

Catholic and Protestant Arabic Bibles were, until the second part of the 19th century, based on the 1671 edition of the (Vatican) Congregation of Propagation of the Faith when three new versions appeared. The American Protestant missionaries in Beirut published in 1864 a translation in modern Arabic, which was started by Eli Smith and finished by C.V.A. van Dyck, with the help of Arab scholars, especially Sheik Nasif el-Yāzijī. This version was reprinted in 1869 and became known as the Oxford Arabic Bible. The Dominicans of Mosul published a four volume Bible based on C.J. David's version (1874–78). About the same time (1876–80) the Jesuits in Beirut published a translation in classical Arabic, in three volumes. The Arabic Bibles in circulation among Christians are based on those versions, although other missionary work has produced more modern renditions (e.g., the *Book of Life* of 1982/1988, in modern Arabic, and a version published in 2003).

Catalan

A Catalan Bible, probably based on a French prototype, was prepared in 1281–91 at the request of Alfonso III of Aragon, but this has not been preserved and perhaps remained unfinished. Various Catalan translations – Psalms (14th–15th centuries), part of Genesis (14th century), a complete Bible by Sabruguera (14th century), and other 15th-century Bibles – were made from the Vulgate using the French and Provençal versions. Sabruguera's Bible was revised by Jaime Borrell and by Bonifacio Ferrer (c. 1400), the printed edition of 1477–78 reproducing the work of the latter, which was destroyed by the Inquisition. During the 16th century, some biblical books were translated from the original Hebrew. In 1832 a complete Catalan Bible was made by the Protestant scholar J.M. Prat (published by the British and Foreign Bible Society). Various Catholic translations appeared in the 20th century, including those by Clascar (1915), the monks of Montserrat (1926), and the Catalan Biblical Foundation (1928–48).

Danish

Although Hans Tausen's Pentateuch (Magdeburg, 1535) is thought to have been only part of a complete Danish translation of the Bible, the earliest surviving complete edition – the so-called Christian III Bible (1550; 1950) – was a reworking by Christiern Pedersen of Luther's German Bible. Like its prototype, the latter was written in an extraordinary pithy style and had a significant impact on the Danish language. It was later revised as the Frederick II Bible (1588–89) and the Christian IV Bible (1632–33). Meanwhile, the need for a translation from the original languages had been recognized, and in 1607 Professor (later Bishop) H.P. Resen published an edition of the Bible that was linguistically distinct from its predecessors. Revised by Professor (later Bishop) Hans Savning in 1647, this remained until modern times the "authorized" Danish version of the Bible. There were also innumerable translations of separate portions of the Bible; and various private biblical projects, two of which were a translation by C.A.H. Kalkar (1847), who was a Jew by birth, and a more significant version by the Orientalist and theologian J.C. Lindberg (1837–54). The first Danish Bible to take cognizance of modern biblical criticism was that produced by Frants Buhl and his associates in 1910; this was in part the basis for a new translation, directed by Bishop Goetzsche, of which the Old Testament appeared in 1931. Another new version of the Old Testament in Danish appeared in 1931, and Catholic Bibles based on the Vulgate were published in 1893 and 1931. The most recent version, produced by the Danish Bible Society, appeared in 1992. Another, ongoing project is a scholarly "secular" translation of the Hebrew Bible, begun in 1998, which treats the text as a product of the ancient Near East and eschews the centuries of interpretation based on Western (mostly Christian) religious traditions. It uses Hebrew names for biblical figures, as well as for books (e.g., "When God Began" for Genesis), and retains the Jewish ordering of biblical books. There have also been some Danish translations under Jewish auspices, notably the Pentateuch of Chief Rabbi A.A. *Wolff (1891), published with the Hebrew text. A new edition, revised by the Jewish education authorities and to which the *haftarot* were added, appeared in 1894. Chief Rabbi Friediger also published Esther with a Danish translation in 1924.

Dutch

There were several medieval Dutch versions of biblical books, but the first Dutch Bible – the complete Bible except for the Psalms – dates from a Flemish work (c. 1300) and was a translation from the Vulgate (published Delft, 1477). A Dutch version of Psalms, produced by another translator, was frequently reprinted from 1480 onward. Later, there was a Dutch translation of Luther's Bible (Antwerp, 1526), and an Old Testament based on Luther and the Delft Bible appeared in 1525. Claes (Nicholas) van Winghe's Dutch Catholic Louvain Bible (1548) underwent many revisions and remained in use well into the 19th century. The Dutch Protestants – Reformed, Lutheran, and Mennonite – all pursued their own adaptations of the Bible, but the first editions based on the original Hebrew appeared only in 1614 and 1623. Early in the 17th century the Dutch States-General commissioned the famous *Statenbijbel* (Leyden, 1636–37), the text of which was later published in the German *Biblia Pentapla*; frequently revised, it remained in use until the mid-20th century. Three early modern Dutch Bibles are the versions of A. van den Schuur and H. van Rhijn (2 vols., 1732); I. van Hamelsveld (1802–03), based on the original languages; and J.H. van den Palm (2 vols., 1818–19). A. *Kuenen's (with I. Hooykaas, W.H. Kosters, and H. Oort) "Leidsche Vertaling," translation and interpretation of the Bible, appeared in Leiden in 1899–1901. A Catholic Bible was published in 1936–37 by the Petrus Canisius Society and a Bible published by the new Katholieke Bijbelstichting St. Willibrord was finished in 1995. An entirely new Protestant Old Testament was published in 1951 by the Dutch Bible Society (NBG). Beginning in 1967, the NBG, together with the Flanders Bible Society, the Flemish Bible Foundation, and the Catholic Bible Society, initiated a new ecumenical translation which was completed in 2004. It has thus far attracted some criticism as being "too modern." In contrast, a group of scholars which had founded the Societas Hebraica Amstelodamensis in 1961 has sought for some years to create a translation which they describe as "concordant" or "idiolectical," grounded in the rhetoric of the Hebrew text after the model of Buber-Rosenzweig. Since 1974, the group has published single books of the Bible under the rubric "A Translation to be Read Aloud," including Ruth, Jonah, Judges, Amos, Obadiah, Micah, the Song of Songs, Genesis, and Ecclesiastes (some of these works have subsequently been revised). Dutch Jews have translated selected Psalms (by M. Levie, 1966) and most of the Old Testament (1826–38, etc.). A new translation of the Pentateuch by I. Dasberg was published in 1970.

See also *Dutch Literature.

Finnish

Because of the linguistic separation of Finland from the rest of Scandinavia, Finnish biblical translation has had an independent history. In 1551 Bishop Michael Agricola published a revised Lutheran version of Psalms, but it was not until 1642 (Stockholm) that a complete Finnish Bible, translated from the original texts, made its appearance. This has since undergone various revisions. A new Finnish Bible translation (*Pyhz Raamatta*) was published in 1938, and another in 1992.

French and Provençal

FRENCH. Although there were two early French (Anglo-Norman) versions of Psalms (c. 1100) and a 12th-century version of Samuel and Kings, the first to possess a complete and accurate translation of the Old Testament in spoken French – and to make regular use of this in teaching and worship – were the Jews. Religious scruples may have prevented the Jews from setting down their whole text in writing, but it did not preclude their compiling explanatory glossaries in the vernacular (*la'azim*). A few of those which have survived, in whole or part, contain fairly long Hebrew commentaries. The glossaries were an aid to teachers instructing children in the Bible according to the traditional word for word method; they also served as an aid to scholarly commentators (*poterim*) working at a higher level, who debated the meaning of a text and, relying upon the glossaries, proposed more subtly phrased translations. Lastly, these glossaries were used by translators officiating in the synagogue.

By contrast, the Church always looked askance at unsupervised reading of the Bible. Herman de Valenciennes' metrical version of the Bible (c. 1190) was followed in 1199 by Pope Innocent III's edict prohibiting any reference to the suspect French Bible. Although the Church declared its opposition to the translation of the Bible into any vernacular at the Council of Toulouse (1229), Louis IX commissioned a French version of the complete Bible (c. 1230), and in the 14th century it was revised by order of John II and Charles V. Nevertheless, the biblical text was submerged, during the later Middle Ages, under a mass of scholastic glosses and amplifications.

The most famous medieval French version was the late 13th-century *Biblehistoriale* of Guiard des Moulins, a paraphrase based on the scholastic compilation of Pierre Comestor. This Bible, much revised and often versified, was one of the earliest French printed books (1478). Only the Psalms inspired fairly accurate translations.

The first Bible translation of the 16th century, which returned to the original Latin – suppressing accumulated glosses and interpolations – was that of Jacques Lefèvre d'Etaples (1528). It was rightly suspected by Rome, Lefèvre's earlier Psalter (1509) having influenced Martin Luther. In its revised form (Louvain, 1550), Lefèvre's Bible ran to more than 200 editions. However, the Louvain Bible, too, contained borrowings from the first Protestant version by Pierre Rovert Olivétan (Neuchâtel, 1535; rev. 1724), which was based on the original Hebrew and Greek texts. Olivétan's version (known from its place of publication as the Serrières Bible) was the outcome of the religious fervor which the Bible had roused among the Waldenses. The Bible of Sebastian Castellio (Châteillon, d. 1555), the tolerant French humanist and theologian who opposed the severity of Calvin, appeared at Basle in 1555. This was written in a style uniquely designed to convey the original meaning of the Hebrew.

In the 17th century the Protestant translation of G. Diodati (Geneva, 1644) is known to have inspired more than one passage in the Jansenist Port-Royal version (Paris, 1672–95), which was mainly the work of Louis Isaac Le Maistre, known as de Sacy. Unfortunately, however, the *Bible de Sacy*, no less than the many versions subsequently based on it, was no more than a paraphrase, overburdened with notes and commentaries. Among the versions of individual biblical books produced at this time was J.B. Bossuet's French edition of Song of Songs (1695).

It was only during the second half of the 19th century that French lay scholars began to devote their attention to the Bible: Ernest Renan published editions of Job (1859), Song of Songs (1862), and Ecclesiastes (1882), and F. Lenormant produced a translation of Genesis (1883). The 19th-century Catholic Bibles of Genoude, J.J.B. Bourassé (illustrated by Doré), Jean Baptiste Glaire, and others possessed little elegance or accuracy and were eventually displaced by better versions: the *Bible de Maredsous* (1949), the J.T. Crampon Bible (1894–1904; 1960), and especially *La Sainte Bible de Jérusalem* (43 vols., 1948–52; in 1 vol., 1956). These modern Catholic translations nevertheless still remained hampered by notes and directions as to "what must be understood from the text."

Despite their wish to preserve textual accuracy, French Protestants were not content with Olivétan's ponderous style and accordingly produced various revisions, the most widely distributed of which were those of D. Martin (Amsterdam, 1707), and J.F. Ostervald (Amsterdam, 1747), and the French *Geneva Bible* (1802–05); perhaps the most successful was the version of Louis Segond and H. Oltramar (2 vols., 1874). The Segond version has been continually revised (1910, with a thorough revision in 1975 and *La nouvelle Bible Segond* in 2000). French Protestants generally use the officially approved *Version synodale* (1910), although the *Bible du Centenaire* (by Société Biblique de Paris, 1916–47; 1950) is considered to be the finest text produced by the Reformed Church. Some Protestants still treasure the Olivétan translation as revised by J.F. Ostervald (1663–1747) (recent revision 1996).

The 19th century also saw the appearance of critical Bible editions, notably that of E. Reuss (11 vols., 1874–81), whose substantial annotations display with unerring, though by now, dated erudition the whole historical and philological background of the biblical text. Two other critical editions are those of P. Giguet (1872), based on the Septuagint, and the more recent, penetrating, and lucid version of E. Dhorme (2 vols., 1956–59).

Modern French Jewish translations only appeared toward the end of the 18th century, and these were followed by the biblical passages and books (Psalms, Job, Five Scrolls) which Mardochée Venture included in his *siddur* (4 vols., Nice, 1772–83). In the 19th century, Samuel Cahen published *La Bible, traduction nouvelle* (7 vols., 1831–51), a remarkable achievement of its kind, in which he secured the collaboration of other modern Jewish commentators. Half a century later this was superseded by the French rabbinate's own clear translations of the Bible, produced under the supervision of Zadoc Kahn (*La Bible du rabbinat français*, 2 vols., 1899–1906; 1966). Though without "claims to great learning," this was faithful to the masoretic tradition and to rabbinic interpretation; combining the letter and the spirit of the Bible in a lucid and stirring style, it succeeded in "satisfying the reader who wishes for religious and moral inspiration from the Bible." Partial translations of the Bible under Jewish auspices include L. Wogue's rather constricted version of the Pentateuch (5 vols., 1860–69), and editions of Psalms by A. Ben-Baruch Créhange (1858), B. Mossé (1878), and André Chouraqui (1956).

There has been a good deal of biblical translation into French in recent years. This activity in many ways mirrors what has transpired in English, with some attempts that present the text in "today's language" (*la Bible en français courant*, 1982, 1997, and *la Bible Parole de vie,* 2000, which uses a 3,500-word vocabulary); renditions under Catholic auspices (*La Bible de Jérusalem*, above, and *La Bible Pastorale de Maredsous* (1977), done by Belgian monks in collaboration with French colleagues); and translations that appeal across denominational lines (*Traduction oecumenique de la Bible*, 1975). A notable and controversial addition is the "Bayard Bible" (*La Bible Nouvelle Traduction*, 2001), cast in modern French usage, in which each book has been prepared by a biblical scholar teamed with a writer of note. As a result, there is no attempt to smooth the overall text into a unified style, and thus, in the view of the editors, the Bible's own diversity is represented. The text is laid out with a minimum of critical apparatus, heightening poetic effect.

In the more literal sphere, one might mention the 1973 translation of E. Osty, and two works by Jews. The first, by Andre Chouraqui (1974–77, including the New Testament!), seeks to bend French toward Hebrew. Thus, for instance, *sefat ha-yam* is rendered as *levre de la mer,* as opposed to a more conventional and idiomatic *bord de mer* or *ricage*. Of more recent vintage are the translations of the literary critic Henri Meschonnic (The Five Scrolls, 1970; Jonah, 1981; Psalms, 2001; Genesis, 2002; and Exodus, 2003). He characterizes his work as an attempt to "rehebraicize the Bible," using Hebrew names (including those of books; his Genesis is not *Genese* but *Au Commencement*) and reflecting Hebrew style (as in such wordplays as *tohu va-vohu* [*vaine et vide*]). Meschonnic is less literal than Chouraqui, who frequently lays bare Hebrew etymology in French (his Genesis begins *En tete*), but both evince an approach and spirit that are akin to Buber-Rosenzweig.

See also *French Literature.

[Everett Fox (2nd ed.)]

PROVENÇAL. In southern France the reformist movements of the Albigenses (Cathars) and Waldenses (Vaudois) promoted the translation of the Bible from the 12th century onward. This partly accounts for the hostile attitude toward vernacular Bibles displayed by the Church of Rome. Provençal versions of Psalms and of a portion of Genesis are known from the 14th century, and a translation of the historical books of the Bible was made from the French during the 15th century. As part of the Félibrige movement for the revival of Provençal culture from the mid-19th century onward, Frédéric Mistral produced an original translation of Genesis (1906). The Waldenses, who survived various persecutions to join French Protestantism, were active from the early 14th century as translators of the Bible. Their dialect versions cover Proverbs, Song of Songs, Ecclesiastes, and parts of Genesis and Job. It has been surmised that there were connections between the translators of the Provençal and Vaudois biblical books, and between them and the scholars who prepared the earliest texts in Italian.

German

BEFORE LUTHER. Only a few verses (from Ezra and Nehemiah) are extant of the Old Testament portion of the Bible translation by the Gothic bishop Ulfilas (Gothic *Wulfila*; 311–383). According to old tradition, Ulfilas (who, according to the Byzantine church historian Socrates (d. c. 450), invented the Gothic alphabet for the purpose of his translation) wrote a complete version of the Bible, excluding only I and II Kings because of the warlike disposition of the Goths.

In fragments of an Old Saxon Genesis in alliterative reverse, a parallel to the Teutonic paraphrase of the New Testament Gospels (the so-called *Heliand*, c. 830) has been found, although it was probably not written by the same author. The surviving fragments cover the biblical narrative from Adam to the destruction of Sodom.

Early in the 11th century, Notker Labeo, a monk of St. Gallen, translated the Psalms and the Song of Songs, as well as the Book of Job, which has been lost. Later in the same century, William of Ebersberg also wrote a commentary on Song of Songs (c. 1065) in Middle High German (critical edition, 1967). Subsequently many other partial translations of the Bible appeared, mainly versions of the Psalter.

Toward the end of the 14th century, a second German Bible (restricted to the Old Testament), renowned for its improved style, made its appearance; the earliest manuscript copy of this translation, written by Martin Rother, was the so-called *Wenzel Bible* (Vienna, after 1389).

The first German Bible to appear in print was Johann Mentel's edition (Strasbourg, 1466), probably written about a century before. This translation, based on the Vulgate, was frequently revised and reprinted, inspiring 13 further pre-Lutheran editions. In 1477 the first Bible in Low German appeared in print. Johann Rellach of Resoem, who may have prepared the original of the 1466 edition, translated Joshua, Judges, and Ruth.

LUTHER AND THE PROTESTANT BIBLES. The classic German Bible is that of Martin *Luther, who transformed it into a German literary work. His translation, which created literary German and consolidated the Reformation, was the basis of all subsequent German versions and also of most other European translations. Luther's Bible, based on the Brescia Hebrew edition of 1495, continued the work of his pioneering New Testament (1522), with the Pentateuch, historical books, Hagiographa (1523–24), Prophets (1532), and Apocrypha (1534). His first complete Bible, *Biblia, das ist: die gantze Heilige Schrifft Deudsch* (6 vols., Wittenberg 1534), underwent 11 successive revisions during his lifetime. The last of these (1544–45) was reproduced at Halle in seven volumes (1845–55) and later reprinted in 1926–28. Over the years, Luther's Bible, which became the canonical version of the German Protestant church, also underwent linguistic revision. The so-called Lutheran Bibles that followed include the Uniform Bible (*Einheitsbibel*) of 1581, the Stader Bible of 1695, the so-called *Probebibel* (1883), and the revised editions of 1892 and 1912. Textual modifications affected not only the German style but also certain concepts that were clarified and explained in the light of later scientific research.

While Luther was engaged in his work, an Anabaptist translation of Prophets, by Ludwig Haetzer and Johann Denck, appeared at Worms in 1527. Until Luther's version reached completion there also appeared several, so-called, "Combined Bibles," in which those portions of the Bible which Luther had not yet completed were supplemented by other translations. The Zurich (Swiss-German) Bible (1527–29) of the Swiss Reformed Church largely preserved a suitable text reworked by Luther; the Prophets were translated by the "Zurich preachers"; and the Apocrypha were translated by Leo Jud, who also headed the project. This edition, repeatedly revised (1755–56, 1772, etc.), increasingly deviated from Luther's version. The so-called (Johannes) Piscator Bible (Herborn, 1602–03) was based on Latin translations and became the Berne Church Bible. Other Protestant editions were J.F. Haug's pietistic Berleburg Bible (8 vols., 1726–42), an adaptation of Luther's with reference to the Zurich text, and three others by J. Saubert (Helmstedt, 1665), Triller (Amsterdam, 1703), and Junckkerot (Offenbach, 1732).

From the 18th century onward, many other German Protestant Bibles made their appearance. Johann Lorenz Schmidt's so-called Wertheim Bible (1735), the first rationalist translation, again referred to the original Hebrew, as did J.D. *Michaelis' scholarly ecclesiastical edition (Goettingen, 7 vols., 1769–85). The translation produced by J.C.W. Augusti and W.M.L. de Wette (1809–14) was the first Bible to proceed from modern biblical investigation, but another translation by Bunsen (9 vols., 1858–70) was a more popular work. Later German Bibles include the edition of P.W. Schmidt and F. von Holtzendorff (1872); the sectarian Eberfeld Bible (1855); scholarly editions by Eduard Reuss (7 vols., 1892–94) and E.F. Kautzsch (1894; 1900; 1922–23[4]); and two popular works, F.E. Schlacter's *Die Heilige Schrift; Miniatur Bibel* (1905, 1952[20]) and Hermann Menge's Bible (1929; 1963). There are also scholarly translations in the exegetical works of W. Nowack, E. Sellin, and H.L. Strack and O. Zoeckler; and poetical versions by other scholars, such as H. Ewald's *Die Dichter des Alten Bundes* (2 vols., 1866–67), J. Wellhausen's *Die kleinen Propheten* (1893[2]), Duhm's *Die poetischen und prophetischen Buecher des Alten Testaments…* (4 vols., 1897–1910), and H. Gunkel's *Ausgewaehlte Psalmen* (1917[4]). Some leading German poets also turned their attention to the Old Testament, Goethe and Herder translating the Song of Songs (1778), and F. Rueckert attempting a metrical version of Isaiah 40–66 and the Minor Prophets (*Hebraeische Propheten*, 1831).

Some current translations are *Die Bibel in heutigen Deutsch* (1982), the 1984 edition of the Luther Bible, the 1995 edition of the evangelical and quite literal *Revidierte Eberfelder Bibel*, and the *Gute Nachricht Bibel* (rev. 1997).

CATHOLIC BIBLES. The earliest complete German Catholic Bible was that of Johann Dietenberger (Mainz, 1534), which was partly modeled on the works of Luther and Leo Jud. The second was by Luther's opponent, Johann Eck (Ingolstadt, 1537), who followed the Vulgate. Caspar Ulenberg's edition (Cologne, 1630), based on Dietenberger and the Vulgate, long remained the standard Catholic text and was often revised, the subsequent translations of T.A. Erhard (1722), G. Cartier (1751), Rosalino (1781), Seibt (1781), I. Weitenauer (1777–81), and Fleischuetz (1778) also referring occasionally to the original Hebrew. Another Catholic Bible appeared anonymously at Vienna in 1794. Heinrich Braun's version (1788–1805) provided the basis for the widely distributed edition of J.F. von Allioli (1830–37), which was revised by Arndt and furnished with notes indicating textual divergences between the Vulgate and the original (1898–99). C.M. Brentano made a translation from the original text (1797), and Jaeck, one from the Vulgate (1847), while Leander van Ess's Bible (1822; 1950–55) and that of V. Loch and W. Reischl (1851) enjoyed the success of Allioli's earlier translation. Modern Catholic editions include those of Nivard Schloegl (1920), which was the first critical edition under Catholic auspices. F. Feldmann and H. Herkenne (1923), J. Nikel (1911–33), P. Riessler (1924), and Pius Parsch (1952).

A work of special interest was the so-called *Biblia Pentapla* of 1710–12 (3 vols.), which compared the texts of Martin Luther, Caspar Ulenberg, and Johannes Piscator, the two remaining columns containing Joseph Witzenhausen's Judeo-German version and the Dutch *Statenbijbel* version. A parallel Bible of 1887–88 contained Luther's text together with a literal translation in modern German.

A translation that has seen widespread use is the *Einheitsuebersetzung* of 1980 (rev. 1994), which combines the work of Catholic and evangelical translators.

JEWISH BIBLES IN GERMAN. The first Jew to translate the Bible into High German was Moses Mendelssohn, whose work was fiercely attacked by the rigidly Orthodox (notably Ezekiel Landau and Phinehas Horowitz of Frankfurt) and repeatedly placed under a ban. Mendelssohn's closest collaborators were Solomon Dubno, Hartwig Wessely, Naphtali Herz Homberg, and Aaron Jaroslaw. The translation, printed in Hebrew characters, appeared under the title *Netivot ha-Shalom*, together with the original Hebrew and a commentary, designated *Be'ur* (*Biur*). Mendelssohn himself translated the Pentateuch (1783), Psalms (1785–91), Ecclesiastes (1770), and Song of Songs (1788; ed. J. Loewe and A. Wolfsohn), and he also prepared a version of the Song of Deborah. The project was completed by his collaborators and successors, the "Biurists." Translations of separate portions of the Bible were supplied by various scholars. A complete edition of the Minor Prophets, prepared by Moses Philippson (Arnswalde), Josef Wolf, Gotthold Salomon (S. Lipman), Israel Neumann, and Joel Loewe, appeared as *Minḥah Ḥadashah* (1805) and reappeared in Moses Israel Landau's edition of the complete Bible (1833–37). Aside from what Mendelssohn had himself prepared, the translation of the remaining biblical books was the work of M.J. Landau, Josef Weisse, Salomon Sachs, Wolf Mayer, Abraham Benisch, and Marcus Goldmann. Mendelssohn's Bible translation also appeared in German orthography (Genesis, 1780; Pentateuch, 1815). In contrast to Luther, who based his rendering of God's name, "der Herr," on the Greek *kyrios* of the Septuagint and the Latin *dominus* of the Vulgate, Mendelssohn used "der Ewige" ("The Eternal"), a term which was accepted by German-speaking Jews. Mendelssohn's work was a landmark for his community, providing a medium through which they could assimilate an elegant German and be weaned away from the Judaeo-German which they had spoken heretofore. It is thus forms a kind of opening to the modern German-Jewish experience, enabling the initial integration of Jews into modern German life and culture.

The next translator of the Bible was Josef Johlson, who furnished his text with scholarly notes (1831–36; only the first half was actually published). Separate biblical books were translated by A.A. Wolf, Phoebus Philippsohn. A. Bernstein (A. Rebenstein), S.H. Auerbach, L. Herzberg, L.H. Loewenstein, and Heymann Arnheim and Michael *Sachs (the combined work of the latter two was later retained in the Bible of Leopold Zunz). With the support of I.N. Mannheimer, Gotthold Salomon published *Deutsche Volksund Schul-Bibel* (1837), the first complete German Bible under Jewish auspices. In his *Die vierundzwanzig Buecher der Heiligen Schrift* (2 vols., 1837; 1935[17]) L. Zunz translated only Chronicles, the remainder being the work of Arnheim, Julius Fuerst, and Sachs. Solomon *Herzheimer's edition (4 vols., 1841–48) was intended for Christians as well as Jews. Jacob Auerbach's *Kleine Schul- und Haus-Bibel* (1858) had a very wide distribution. *Die israelitische Bibel* (3 vols., 1839–54) of Ludwig Philippson was revised by W. Landau and S.I. Kaempf and illustrated with pictures by Doré; this had been preceded in 1865 by an Orthodox edition produced under the auspices of Isaac Dov (Seligman Baer) Bamberger, A. Adler, and M. Lehmann. Orthodox approval was also given to I. Cosman's Pentateuch (1847–52) and, above all, to Samson Raphael *Hirsch's translations of the Pentateuch (5 vols., 1867–78; 3 vols., 1956–58) and Psalms (1882; 1960), to which the latter's son, J. Hirsch, added a version of Isaiah (1911). Other editions were an *Illustrierte Pracht-Bibel* (1874) by J. Fuerst; a Pentateuch (1899, 1939[7]) by J. Wohlgemuth and I. Bleichrode; and a complete Bible (1902; 1929[5]) by Simon Bernfeld and H. Torczyner (4 vols., 1935–37).

Apart from the foregoing, there were also many German Jewish translations of individual books of the Bible, such as L.I. Mandelstamm and M. Kirschstein's edition of Genesis (3 vols., 1862–64). H. Graetz's version of Psalms (1881), and D.Z. Hoffmann's translation and commentary on Leviticus (2 vols., 1905–06) and Deuteronomy (2 vols., 1913–22). An isolated modern attempt to reproduce the Old Testament in German verse was that of M.A. Klausner's *Die Gedichte der Bibel* (1902). Two outstanding modern editions are Lazarus Goldschmidt's *Die heiligen Buecher des Alten Bundes* (the Pentateuch, historical books, and Prophets having appeared by 1923), which referred to rabbinic exegesis, and *Die Schrift* (15 vols., 1926–37?, rev. 4 vols., 1954–1968) by Martin *Buber and Franz *Rosenzweig, which endeavored to do justice to the language and rhythm of the Hebrew text. This last work forms a bracket to the history of modern German Jewry; in its conscious departure from Luther and its attempt to "Germanize the Hebrew" (the translators termed the work a "*Verdeutschung*"), it reversed the usual direction of translation. As mentioned a number of times previously, it has strongly influenced Bible versions in other languages, as well as contemporary (non-Jewish) German readers.

See also *German Literature.

Hungarian

In the 15th century the Hussite movement assailed the Latinity of the Church. Behind the heresy lay, among other social aims, the wish to make the Bible available to the masses, so that people might know the world of the Bible even in the oppressive reality of feudalism, and so become acquainted with the admonitions of the biblical prophets. The oldest Hungarian Hussite Bible translations are preserved in the late 15th-century Vienna codex (Ruth, Esther, Minor Prophets) and the Apor Codex (Psalms). The Codex of Dobrente contains the translations of the Song of Songs and Job (1508). The first Catholic Pentateuch survives in the Jordanszky Codex (1516–19). The Hungarian reformers translated the Bible in the spirit of Erasmus and also emphasized its social message. Unlike the Catholics, who adhered to the Vulgate, Protestant scholars referred to the Hebrew text of the Old Testament. Gáspár Heltai and four Protestant colleagues translated the entire Bible, but several books of the Hagiographa did not appear in this edition (Kolozsvar, 1552–65). The first complete, and most readable, Bible translation was that of Gáspár Károlyi, a Calvinist preacher (Vizsoly, 1590); revised by Albert Szenczi Molnár (1608), it became the official text of the Hungarian Protestant Church and was the basis of a modern (London) Bible Society version.

The Reformation enhanced the ecclesiastical importance of the Psalms, most translations of which were, however, merely paraphrases. Christian terminology and political references were inserted into the text, to the detriment of the original. The first renderings were those of Sztáray (1575), a more poetical version being that of Balint Balassa (1554–94). Accumulated accretions were eliminated by Miklós Bogáti Fazekas, a Unitarian preacher, in his unpublished versified translation of Psalms (1587). Protestant translations of Samuel, Kings, and Job were produced by Peter Melius Juhász in 1565–67.

The Bible translations of the 15th and 16th centuries were stimulated by social motives, while in the 17th century religious concern proved to be the creative force. The greatest accomplishment of Hungarian Protestantism at the time was the *Psalterium Ungaricum* of A. Molnár (Hanau, 1608). This was the first complete Hungarian translation of the Psalms in verse, running to more than 100 editions and it is still extant. It endured because of the beauty of its style and because of its faithfulness to the original text. Simon Péchi, the most renowned member of the Hungarian *Szombatos* (Sabbatarian) sect, who had a good command of the Hebrew language, interpreted the biblical text and his translation adhered strictly to the original (1624–29). The first complete Hungarian Catholic Bible was published by the Jesuit György Káldi (Vienna, 1626). Toward the end of the 17th century a new Protestant Bible translation was prepared by György Csipkés of Komorn (often called György Komáromi, 1675; published Leiden, 1719), who was widely known for his Hebrew sermons.

In time Károlyi's Bible was reworked and his text improved, while Samuel Kámory produced a new version of the Bible for Hungarian Protestants (1870). Poets began to be interested in the Psalms from an aesthetic point of view, the translations of Benedek Virág and Ferenc Versegi having a classical mood in antique verse form. More significant translations of Psalms were those by Károly Kálmán (1883), Sándor Sik (1923), and Béla Teleki (1929). Two versions of the Song of Songs were those of Károly Kerényi, which was based on the Latin text (1941), and István Bernáth (1962).

Although Mór Bloch (Ballagi) produced a Pentateuch in 1840, there was for a long time no demand for a Hungarian Jewish Bible, since the Jews of Hungary used Yiddish and German. The first complete Bible translation under Jewish auspices was that of the Jewish Hungarian Literary Society (IMIT), published in 1898–1907 (in 4 vols.), with Vilmos Becher, József Bánóczi, and Samuel Krauss as editors. Earlier partial translations were József Mannheim's Psalms (1865); H. Deutsch's Pentateuch and *haftarot* (1888); Mór Stern's Psalms (1888); Ignác Füredi's Joshua and Judges (1893); and the Füredi-Stern Pentateuch (1894–95). Bernát Frenkel edited and published the "Holy Scriptures for Family and School" (1924–26) and the IMIT began publishing a Bible for the young, which remained incomplete, only the first and second volumes being printed (1925). During the years 1939–42 the IMIT published a Hungarian version of the Pentateuch edited by Britain's chief rabbi, J.H. Hertz; this was the work of Michael Guttmann, Simon Hevesi, Samuel Loewinger, and others.

Hungarian Jewish prose versions of the Psalms began with Mór Rosenthal's translation (1841); later there were versified translations by József Kiss, Immanuel Loew, Emil Makai, and Arnold Kiss. The translations of Attila Gerö (1894) and Endre Neményi (1917) both displayed an original approach. Other versions of individual biblical books include Immanuel Loew's Song of Songs (1885) and Simon Hevesi's versified Lamentations (1916).

See also *Hungarian Literature.

Icelandic

Although there was no Icelandic translation of the Bible during the Middle Ages, the *Stjórn* ("Guidance") was, as a partial paraphrase of the historical books of the Old Testament, woven together with some later biblical books (republished 1956). Following the Reformation, Gudbrandur Thorláksson, bishop of Hólar, made a complete translation of the Bible (Holum, 1584). Like the Danish Bible of 1550 (Christian II Bible), this had marked literary power and mainly drew from Luther's translation. It was revised by a later bishop of Hólar, Torlak Skulasson, who referred to the Danish Christian IV edition of 1644. Bishop Steinn Jonsson's Icelandic version of H.P. Resen's Danish translation was so unsuccessful that the old edition of Skulasson had to be printed. Headed by the philologist S. Egilsson, an Icelandic commission later undertook a thorough revision of the Icelandic Bible (1841); the work was continued by Haraldur Nielsson in collaboration with other scholars (1912).

Italian

The earliest Italian versions of the Bible, preserved in manuscript, mostly contain only a traditional text, which perhaps originated in northern Italy during the 13th century, but which was also conceivably derived from Waldensian heretical circles. The version gave rise to the two Italian editions of the Bible (based on the Vulgate), which were published in Venice in 1471. Antonio Brucioli's translation (Venice, 1532) labored under the suspicion of heresy (in fact it inspired the Geneva Protestant Bible of 1562). It was followed by the 1607 Geneva version of the Italian Protestant, Giovanni Diodati, based on the original texts; widely distributed, this version has periodically been republished. Archbishop Antonio Martini's authoritative Catholic translation (based on the Vulgate) first appeared in 1776–81. Translations of separate biblical books include editions by G.B. de Rossi and G. Ugdulena in the 19th century, and modern ones by S. Minocchi, di Soragna, G. Ricciotti, and F. Valente as well as new versions of the complete Bible by the Waldensian Protestant, G. Luzzi (4 vols., 1921–30), and by the Pontifical Biblical Institute (1923–58). More recent works include the ecumenical translation of the *Conferenza Episcopale Italiana* (1974, along the lines of the *Bible de Jerusalem*), *Traduzione Interconfessionale in Lingua Corrente* (1985), *La Nuova Diodati* (1991), and *La Sacra Bibbia Nuova Riveduti* (1990 revision of the 1927 *Riveduti*). The CEI has also produced *La Bibbia interattiva* (1995), an ecumenical, modern-language version.

During the 16th and 17th centuries, Jewish Bible translations in Italian were undertaken by David de Pomis, whose Ecclesiastes appeared in 1571 (Job and Psalms were never printed), and C. Rieti (Proverbs, Venice, 1617). Leone Modena also compiled a glossary of the Old Testament entitled *Galut Yehudah* (1612). Jewish translations of the 19th century include those of I. Reggio (Pentateuch, 1821), Lelio della Torre (Psalms, 1854), Samuel David Luzzatto (Job, 1853; Isaiah, 1855–67; Pentateuch, 5 vols., 1858–60), and David Castelli (Ecclesiastes, 1866; Song of Songs, 1892; Job, 1897). A complete Bible was produced by Luzzatto and his disciples in 1866–75 and revised in 1960.

See also *Italian Literature.

Norwegian

The pre-Reformation *Stjórn* of Iceland (see below) was the first biblical work current in Norway. Norway subsequently turned to Denmark for translations of the Bible, even after the political separation of the two countries in 1814. With minor modifications, Hans Savning's revised Danish Bible of 1647 was Norway's standard text during most of the 19th century (rev. 1819, 1830, and 1873). After many tests the Norwegian Bible Society's new *Riksmål* (Danish-Norwegian) translation made its appearance in 1891. The scholars collaborating in this project included the theologian and Orientalist C.P. Caspari, who was of Jewish birth. Linguistically, this Norwegian Bible still remained close to literary Danish. A complete Protestant Bible in *Landsmål* (pure Norwegian) appeared in 1921 (revised in 1938). A Norwegian Catholic *Riksmål* Bible, based on the Vulgate, appeared in 1902 (revised in 1938).

Portuguese

The only notable early Portuguese translations of the Old Testament were the Protestant edition of João Ferreira d'Almeida (Batavia, 2 vols., 1748–53) and a Catholic Bible based on the Vulgate by Antonio Pereira de Figueiredo (Lisbon, 23 vols., 1778–90). A modern edition was published by M. Soares (1927–30), and a new Brazilian Portuguese Bible appeared by the Liga de Estudos Biblicos in 1955.

The upswing in evangelical movements in the 1990s has produced or spurred numerous translations, e.g., *Nova Versão Internacional* (1993/2000), *Almeida Revista e Corrigida* (1997), *and Bíblia na Linguagen de Hoje* (1998).

See also *Spanish and Portuguese Literature and *Ladino Literature.

Romanish (Raeto-Romance)

The neo-Latin dialects known as Romansh, Friulian, Ladin(o), etc., once spoken widely in Austria, northern Italy, and Switzerland, gave rise to Bible translations from the 16th century onward. A complete Romansh Bible was prepared by Vulpi and Dorte (1617) and another by later scholars in 1719.

Romanian

Among the earliest documents preserved in Romanian are two manuscript versions of the Psalms: the *Psaltirea Scheiană* (1482) and the *Psaltirea Voronețeană* (1580). After the invention of printing, various editions of Psalms appeared. The first (1578, 1580) was produced by Coresi, a friar of Brasov; there subsequently appeared a translation in verse by the Moldavian metropolitan Dosoftei Uniev (1673) and a prose version by the metropolitan Antim Ivireanu (1694). Translations of the Psalter multiplied during the 18th century. The Prophets (1673) were soon followed by the first complete Romanian Bible, *Biblia lui Şerban* (Bucharest, 1688; revised, 1795), which was based on the Septuagint. This version of the Bible had a decisive impact on the Romanian language and greatly influenced later translations of the Bible. Other Romanian Bibles include those by Samuil Micu (1795), Ion Eliade Rădulescu (1858), and the outstanding modern Orthodox edition by Gala *Galaction and Vasile Radu (1938). The *Palia (Paloea)*, a Romanian version of Genesis and Exodus containing much legendary material, appeared in 1882. A 20th-century Romanian Protestant Bible, printed in both Cyrillic and Latin characters, was published by the British and Foreign Bible Society. The Cornilescu Version of 1923 remains available, including online. Two modern Romanian editions of the Pentateuch intended for Jewish readers were those of A. Gold (1902) and Moscovic.

See also *Romanian Literature.

Slavonic

BULGARIAN. Translations of the Bible that have been preserved among the Bulgarians are almost exclusively written in Old Church Slavonic. The revival of the old Bulgarian literary and ecclesiastical tradition had its origin in 16th-century Russia. Two modern Bulgarian Bibles are those of P.R. Slaveykov (Constantinople, 1860–64) and of the Orthodox synod (1925). By 1912, a complete Protestant Bible was published (in Constantinople); revisions followed in 1921 and 1924. Despite the strictures of Communist rule, several Bulgarian translations published abroad in the 1950s and 1960s found their way into the country. In 1995, a new Orthodox translation appeared; three new Protestant revisions were published in 2000–1.

CHURCH SLAVONIC. The oldest Slavonic version of the Bible is that of the missionary monks Cyril and Methodius (ninth century C.E.). Cyril, who first acquired a knowledge of Hebrew on a journey to the *Khazar kingdom, borrowed some Hebrew characters for the Slavic alphabet which he invented (see *Bulgarian Literature), and it is thus reasonable to suppose that he was familiar with the original Hebrew text of the Old Testament. It was probably toward the middle of the ninth century that the entire Book of Psalms and liturgical extracts from other biblical books (mainly the Pentateuch, Job, and the Prophets) were translated into Old Moravian, almost certainly with the assistance of Cyril. Presumably these Scriptural portions were first rendered into the Old Moravian tongue and only then into Old Bulgarian (Church Slavonic). According to some accounts, the work of Cyril (d. 869) was completed by his brother, Methodius (d. 885). Although neither the text nor the language of these translations has survived, it may be assumed that they were written in Moravian-Bulgarian. The historical influence and dissemination of the so-called Cyril-Methodius translation among the Slavic peoples passed from the Moravians to the Bulgarians, Serbs, and Poles, and then to the Russians. The Old Bulgarian biblical and liturgical texts reached the Russian Slavs in the second half of the ninth century C.E. – the era of Christianity's spread to the Kiev region. A manuscript Bible in Church Slavonic, dated 1499 and named after Archbishop Gennadi of Novgorod, is extant; revised editions of this translation appeared in 1581, 1663, and 1751.

CZECH AND SLOVAK. The earliest known translations of isolated biblical books into Czech probably date from the 13th century, but it was only in the 15th century, under the impact of the Hussite movement, that the entire Bible was first translated into Czech. John Huss revised and modernized earlier Czech versions at the beginning of the 15th century. The first Czech printed edition (1475) was based on the Vulgate. An impressive Czech version of the Scriptures, based on the original Hebrew and Greek texts, was Jan Blahoslav's *Kralice Bible* (1579–93). Another classic Czech translation was the Catholic Bible edited by Durich and Prochaska at the request of Empress Maria Theresa (1778). Other Czech versions include the Jesuit *Wenceslas Bible* (1677–1715) and that of Sýkora, which was revised by Hejčl and, in 1947, by Col and Josef Heger (1925–48), the latter noted for its stylistic distinction. Recent work continues on the stylistically modern *Nova Bible Kralicka* (NBK), following the trend in many countries that traditionally have used older, "classic" versions. Also in process is a "study edition," with appropriate software, of a translation by the Christian Mission Society. Also to be noted are the *Ekumenická Bible* (1985) and *Slova na cestu* (2000). The first complete Slovak Bible by J. Palkovič (1829–32) was followed by other Catholic versions based on the Vulgate. J. Rohaček's complete Protestant Bible (1926) was also a Slovak translation.

POLISH. Until the 13th century, Polish translations of the Bible were, it is believed, written in Polish Cyrillic rather than Latin orthography. By the end of the 13th century the earliest Polish versions in Latin script made their appearance: the so-called Queen Margaret Psalter and the Bible of Queen Sophia (also known as the Szaros Patak Bible). These texts were written in rather clumsy Polish and based on Czech prototypes. Two early Polish biblical translations were the 14th-century Florian Psalter (published 1834; critical edition by W. Nehring, 1883) and the 15th-century Puławy Psalter (published 1880). With the onset of the Reformation in Poland during the 16th century, various printed editions made their appearance: some Psalters, the first complete Bible in Polish, known as the Cracow Bible (or the Leopolita Bible) of Jan Leopolita (1561), the so-called Radziwill or Brésć Bible of the Polish Calvinists (1563), and S. Budny's Unitarian Nieśwież Bible (1572). Budny's was perhaps the most famous of these. They were followed by the classic Catholic edition of J. Wujek (Cracow, 1599), which was also used by Protestants and has been compared with the King James (Authorized Version) Bible in English. Wujek's edition greatly influenced the development of Polish as a literary language. Another Protestant translation was the Gdansk Bible (Danzig, 1639, reprinted in 1944). The Old Testament had a notable impact on many Polish writers from the 16th century onward. Jan Kochanowski's verse rendering of the Psalms (Cracow, before 1578) inspired a later version by Maciej Rybiński (1605) and paraphrases by Mikołaj Sép-Szarzyński (*Rytmy*, 1601) and other authors. Two 20th-century versions were the Pozńan Bible (1926–32) and the new Cracow Bible (1935; ed. by S. Styś and J. Rostworowski); in 1965 a new edition of the Scriptures was in preparation (to be called the Tyniec Bible). Translation activity since the fall of Communism includes the *Polish Millennium Bible* (1984) "Polish Bible Translation Project," in process under the auspices of the Evangelical Bible Institute in Poznan. Jewish translations of the Old Testament include those of J. Cylkow (1883–1914); F. Aszkenazy (1927–30); J. Mieses (1931); and S. Spitzer (1937). A modern version of Psalms was written by the émigré poet Janusz Artur Ihnatowicz.

See also *Polish Literature.

RUSSIAN AND UKRAINIAN. During the early pre-Mongol period of the Church Slavonic Bible in Russia (before 1240), there was, according to the hypothesis of Golubinski, a whole complex of Old and New Testament writings that were adopted by the Bulgarians. However, only fragments of these have been preserved, mainly the Psalms. On the other hand, a host of biblical texts from the post-Mongol period (15th century onward) has survived. The so-called Judaizing sects of the 15th century gave the strongest impetus to the codifications of the Bible. Adherents of the sects in Novgorod were in possession of a complete Russian Bible, and this moved the archbishop Gennadi to compare the texts of the Greek Orthodox Bible (Septuagint) with those of the Judaizers (see also above on Church Slavonic). With the exception of Esther, all the missing biblical books were translated from the Vulgate. Esther and Psalms were once thought to have been translated from the original Hebrew by the convert Fyodor (Theodore) the Jew, but this has been disputed by Harkavy. Gennadi's great achievement was to produce, for the first time in the annals of Church Slavonic literature, a complete and unified text of the Bible unconnected with the liturgy of the Orthodox church. The 16th-century Bible of the Moscow metropolitan Makari reverted to the former liturgical orientation and order of the biblical books. The first printed Psalter in Russian appeared in 1564–68. The first complete Ukrainian Bible, commissioned by Prince Constantine of Ostrog (1581), followed the text of Gennadi. The first Moscow edition of the Russian Bible (1663) was a more elegant version of the Ostrog text. Soon after this, an attempt was made by Avraami Firsov in his Psalter (1683) to translate the Scriptures into lively Russian. In 1714 Peter the Great commissioned a Church Slavonic Bible, whose text was compared with the Septuagint; this revision (the Czarina Elizabeth Bible) appeared in 1751 and was edited by Valaam Lyaschevski. Here the Old Testament was based on the Septuagint and those biblical books which had earlier appeared only in a translation based on the Vulgate were also translated from the Greek text.

Bible translations of the first half of the 19th century are linked with the activity of the Russian Bible Society. This development was impeded by the political reaction which marked the last years of the reign of Alexander I and the entire reign of Nicholas I. Translations of several biblical books from the original Hebrew, undertaken by the first Russian Hebraist Pavski in the mid-19th century, were placed under a ban. However, the Moscow metropolitan Philaret managed to obtain the Russian Orthodox synod's authorization for a Russian version of the Scriptures in 1860. From 1868 onward a complete translation of the Bible was undertaken by Daniel A. Chwolson; later collaborators in the project included Gulyayev and Bashanov. By virtue of its accuracy and style, this so-called Synodal Bible (1875) is the best available in the Russian language. Canonical books were translated from Hebrew; non-canonical portions, from the Greek and Latin. Ukrainian Bible translations were first attempted in the late Middle Ages, the earliest printed edition being that published at Ostrog in 1581. A Ukrainian version of Psalms appeared at Vilna in 1526, and complete Bibles were printed at Pochayev (1798) and Przemysl (1859), both of these being based on the Russian Czarina Elizabeth Bible of 1751. A 20th-century version was that of P. Kulish, I.S. Levytski, and J. Puluj (1903); another Orthodox Bible was by Metropolitan (John Ohienko) Ilarion (1962); and a third was the Catholic Bible of Ivan Khomenko (1963). All were translated from the original Hebrew and Greek texts. Translation activity has picked up in the 1990s, as in other formerly Communist countries. A Russian Protestant Bible, printed in London in 1875, was first banned in Russia, but a reprint prepared there was later permitted. A new illustrated Russian Old Testament, the first of its kind since the 1917 Revolution, was issued in 100,000 copies by the Soviet State Publishing House in 1967.

The translation of the Bible into modern Russian is clouded by a number of issues: the multiplicity of Russian literary styles, questions of authority and distribution, and above all the relatively small role the Bible has historically played in Eastern Orthodox liturgy and tradition (Batalden, 1990). The periodical *Mir Biblii* (1993–) contains articles, reviews, and translations of portions of Scripture into Russian by different translators.

Among Jewish scholars, various attempts were made from the 1860s onward to produce Russian translations of the Bible. Leon Mandelstamm published a Pentateuch in Berlin (1862), the second edition (1872) being accompanied by his version of Psalms. Pumpyasnski also issued a translation of Psalms (1872), which was followed by Proverbs in 1891. Meanwhile, the Society for the Enlightenment of the Jews in Russia had published a new version of the Pentateuch (1875), which was prepared by J. Herstein with the assistance of the Hebrew poet J.L. Gordon. Another version of the Pentateuch, that of Joshua Steinberg, appeared under the Society's auspices in 1899, and in 1906 Steinberg published translations of Joshua, Judges, and Isaiah.

See also *Russian Literature.

SERBIAN AND CROATIAN; WENDISH. Until 1847 the literary language of the Serbs was Old Slavonic, and Church Slavonic remained dominant in the Serbian Orthodox Church. The earliest complete translation of the Old Testament was produced by the reformer Primož Trubar in Slovenia during the late 16th century; a Croatian Lutheran edition appeared in Tuebingen (1563), and two 19th-century versions were prepared by Matia Petar Katančić in Croatia (1831) and by G. Daničić in Serbia (1865; revised, 1932, 1933). A popular version is the "Zagreb Bible" into modern language (1968). In 2002, the World Bible Translation Center – once again, an evangelical group! – finished a new Bible translation into Croatian; the *Biblija Prijevod KS* had appeared in 1988. A modern Serbian Bible was that of Petar Vlasić (1923–25).

The oldest Protestant translation of part of the Old Testament into the South Lusatian dialect of the Wends (a declining Slav people isolated in eastern Germany) was an edition of Psalms by Pastor Wille (Guben, 1753); a complete Bible was published by Johann Gottlieb Fritz (Cottbus, 1796). There were earlier translations into the North Lusatian Wendish dialect: Psalms by Paul Pretorius, and later Proverbs, Ecclesiastes,

Song of Songs, and Daniel by Christian Leonhardi Georg Dumisch (Loebau, 1719). A complete Bible by Johann Lange, Mattaeus Jockisch, and Johann Boehmer (Bautzen, 1727–28) was prefaced by an introduction in German. The Catholic Wends have no printed versions of the Bible apart from an edition of Psalms translated from the Hebrew by Johann Lara (1872).

See also *Yugoslav Literature.

Spanish

Translations of the bible into Spanish were undertaken in the 13th century, Jews and Christians collaborating in versions antedating 1250. Since the Old Testament translations were based on the original Hebrew rather than on the Vulgate (and perhaps also because of the interreligious scholarly activities), Juan I of Aragon prohibited further Bible translations in 1233, suspecting them of heretical tendencies. However, the more tolerant Alfonso the Wise (Alfonso x of Castile and Leon) encouraged the translation of the Bible into Spanish, but only parts of this version have been preserved. Numerous Bible manuscripts dating from the 14th century onward are extant, and these Spanish versions – some based on the Vulgate, others on the original Hebrew – were the work of Jews or Jewish apostates. The most important of these was the Alba Bible (1422–33), which Moses *Arragel produced at the command of Don Luis de Guzmán, Grand Master of the Order of Calatrava; an edition of this Bible appeared in Madrid in 1920–22. During the 16th–18th centuries, Spanish Catholic scholars only translated the Psalms, the biblical "songs," and the wisdom books, although Fray Luis de León wrote a version of Song of Songs (c. 1561; printed, Madrid, 1798) based on the original Hebrew. Two Protestant translations of the complete Bible (based on the Hebrew text) were Cassiodoro de Reina's (Basle, 1567–69) and an edition by Cipriano de Valera (Amsterdam, 1602). Later Catholic Bibles by Felipe Scio de San Miguel (Valencia, 1790–93) and Felix Torres Amat (1823–25) appeared, as well as translations of separate biblical books by Garcia, Carvajal, and other scholars. The last great Jewish Bible project in Spanish, Abraham Usque's Ferrara edition of 1553, was based on Arragel's 15th-century version and is thought to have inspired translators in Christian Spain. Two modern Spanish Bibles have been produced by E. Nácar Fuster and C.E. Colunga (1944; 1959[9]) and J.M. Bover and F. Cantera Burgos (2 vols., 1947). In 1960 a revision of the classic Reina-Valera version in simple language appeared; it was updated in 1995. The year1985 saw a translation along the lines of TEV, *Dios habla hoy* (*Version Popular*). As elsewhere over the last two decades, evangelical-inspired translations have been published in Spanish, notably *Nueva Versión Internacional* (1999, following the method of NIV, but from the original languages), *La Biblia de las Américas* (1986/1997), and the World Bible Translation Center's *La Palabra de Dios para Todos* (2005).

Swedish

There was no complete Swedish translation of the Bible during the Middle Ages, although individual biblical books were translated during the 14th and 15th centuries. However, after the Reformation, the Gustav Vasa Bible, directed by the archbishop Laurentius Petri, appeared in 1541 and was widely used for some time. A revised version, the Charles XII Bible (1702–03; 1961ff.), which was more closely modeled on Luther's translation, was Sweden's authorized "Church Bible" for a considerable time. A thorough revision of this work, the product of more than a century's research (1773–1878), never received official recognition. A new translation, produced by many scholars, including the philologist Tegnér, enjoyed greater success and, on its completion in 1917, received royal approbation. The outstanding private translation of the Bible was that of HM Melin. A Swedish Catholic translation of the Bible, based on the Vulgate, appeared in 1895. A new Lutheran translation, in preparation for over two decades, is *Bibel 2000*. It is cast in contemporary language.

[David Jacob Simonsen]

Other Languages

Complete Bibles and portions of the Old Testament have also been translated into hundreds of other languages in recent centuries; versions in many of the more remote languages and dialects were the work of Protestant missionary groups, particularly the British and Foreign Bible Society, during the 19th and 20th centuries. Maltese Bible translations include M.A. Camillari's edition of Psalms based on the Hebrew text (1845), R. Taylor's Psalms and Song of Songs (1846), C. Cortis' Ruth (1924), and P.P. Saydon's complete Maltese Bible, *Il-Kotba Mkaddsa bil-Malti* (1929–59). The earliest modern Greek translations of the Old Testament, consisting of the Pentateuch and other biblical books, were probably the work of an unknown Jewish scholar of the 14th century. There were also two early versions of Jonah in *Judeo-Greek. Two early Judeo-Greek works printed at Constantinople were a translation that appeared in the Polyglot Pentateuch (1547) and Job (1576) by Rabbi Moses b. Elias Pobian. A Greek Christian version of Psalms, based on the Septuagint, was published in 1543. The first complete Bible in modern Greek was the Protestant edition of 1840, and an entirely new version was in preparation in Athens during the 1960s, but this was denied general distribution owing to the hostile policy of the Greek government. A Protestant Basque Bible (1859–65), based on the Vulgate was published in London, and Catholic Lithuanian Bibles appeared in 1922 and 1936.

Celtic versions of the Scriptures were first attempted in the Middle Ages, the earliest being a partial translation in Welsh (1346). The English Reformation gave a considerable impetus to Celtic Bible translation. The first complete Welsh Bible was produced by William Morgan and others in 1588 (revised 1620 by R. Parry and J. Davis), and this remained in use with only slight modifications well into the 20th century. An interdenominational Welsh Bible project was begun in 1926 and again after World War II. The first complete Irish (Erse) Bible, based on the English Authorized Version, was produced by Bishop William Bedell and others (1685), and inspired the Scots Gaelic edition of 1783–1801. A new Irish Protestant Bible appeared in 1817. An Irish Catholic Pentateuch, based on the Vulgate, was published in 1861 together with an annotated English text. Two Breton Bibles of the 19th century were Le Gonidec's Catholic edition of 1866 and G. Le Coat's Protestant version of 1889.

The more exotic translations include versions of the Scriptures in Chinese, Japanese, and American Indian dialects. There have been pioneering Bible translations in Sanskrit (1822), Chinese (1823), and Burmese (1834), as well as many translations into the dialects of India. The first Japanese Protestant Bible appeared in the late 19th century (1887), a Catholic version being published only in 1959. A widely distributed Japanese Protestant edition, the work of Japanese scholars, was published in 1955, and the first complete Catholic Bible, in 1964. In North America, John Eliot produced the earliest Amerindian Bible for the Massachusetts Indians in 1663, and by 1830 parts of the Bible had been translated and printed in the Creek and Cherokee languages of the "Five Civilized Tribes," using the alphabet devised by the Cherokee chief Sequoyah. Recent translations along these lines include 2002's Tzotil: Chamula Bible, produced for an indigenous people in Chiapas, Mexico, and a draft of a Bible in Iniktitut, the language of Canadian Inuits, released the same year. Translation work is also burgeoning in Africa: Jerusalem's Home for Bible Translators and Scholars, in conjunction with the Hebrew University's Rothberg International School, has for some years trained participants in biblical Hebrew, with the goal that they may translate the Hebrew Bible for Christians into mostly African languages with a potential readership of 35 million. In the age of the Internet, Bible translations into non-European languages (e.g., Amharic, Creole, Maori, and Vietnamese) may also be found online.

At the turn of the twenty-first century, what is avowedly missionary work continues to produce translations into most of the world's languages and dialects, reaching especially into the Third World. That the Bible remains the gold standard for demonstrating the translator's art can be seen, taken to its logical but absurd conclusion, in the handling of some biblical texts by fans of the late twentieth century television program *Star Trek*. In 1994 a translation of the book of Jonah into Klingon, the language of a fictional planet of aliens, appeared, thus beginning one of several renditions of biblical texts into languages which technically do not exist.

In Cyberspace

Bible translation is well suited for representation on the Internet. A variety of websites explore theoretical aspects of translation as they apply to the Bible as well as provide detailed information about individual translations, even making some of them available online. Further, there are a number of sophisticated software programs (searchable on the Internet under "Bible software programs") which, in addition to providing analytical tools for searching terms and forms in both Hebrew and English, make it possible to toggle between multiple translations of the same passage. They constitute a valuable tool for immediate comparison and for conveying at least a preliminary sense of translation possibilities.

Websites that discuss issues of Bible translation are most easily found under the rubrics "Bible translation," "Bible versions," "modern Bible translation," and "[a particular language] Bible translation." A good deal of information may be found on the websites of the American Bible Society and the International Bible Society; not surprisingly, these organizations, along with the others such as the United Bible Society and the World Bible Translation Center, have as their express purpose the active promotion of Christianity. Thus, many or even most sites on Bible translation are doctrinally driven; a discriminating reader may still, however, glean much useful information from them.

At the turn of this century, one new media-driven development is the NET (New English Translation) Bible, a fresh version which seeks to be simultaneously conservative (i.e., evangelical) and scholarly, and is intended for viewing on and printing off the Web. It contains extensive notes on the text and its translation which are accessible with a mouse click; revisions will be electronically incorporated as time goes on. The avowed purpose of the work is "translating passages consistently and properly within their grammatical, historical, and theological context."

[Everett Fox (2nd ed.)]

BIBLIOGRAPHY: JUDEO-PERSIAN: A. Kohut, *Kritische Beleuchtung der persischen Pentateuch uebersetzung des Jacob ben Joseph Tawus* (1871); E. Nestle, in: *Realencyklopaedie fuer protestantische theologie und Kirche*, 3 (1897), 124–5. JUDEO-ROMANCE LANGUAGES: S. Berger, *La Bible Française au Moyen-Age* (1884); D.S. Blondheim, *Les parlers judéo-romans et la Vetus Latina* (1925); M.L. Margolis, *The Story of Bible Translations* (1917). YIDDISH: W. Staerk and A. Leitzmann, *Die juedisch-deutschen Bibeluebersetzungen von den Anfaengen his zum Ausgang des 18 Jahrhunderts* (1923). ENGLISH UP TO WORLD WAR II: W. Allen, *Translating for King James* (1969); F.F. Bruce, *The English Bible: A History of Translations* (1961); C.C. Butterworth, *The Literary Lineage of the King James Bible, 1340–1611* (1941); W. Chamberlin, *Catalogue of English Bible Translations* (1991); D. Daiches, *The King James Version of the English Bible* (1941); S.L. Greenslade (ed.), *The Cambridge History of the Bible: The West from the Reformation to the Present Day* (1963); D. Daniell, *The Bible in English: Its History and Influence* (2003), and *Tyndale's Old Testament* (1992); P. Gutjahr, *An American Bible* (1999); G. Hammond, "English Translations of the Bible," in: R. Alter and F. Kermode (eds.), *The Literary Guide to the Bible* (1987), *The Making of the English Bible* (1982), and "William Tyndale's Pentateuch: Its Relation to Luther's German Bible and the Hebrew Original," *Renaissance Quarterly*, 33 (1981); A.S. Herbert (ed.), *Historical Catalogue of Printed Editions of the English Bible, 1525–1961* (1968); C. Hill, *The English Bible and the Seventeenth-Century Revolution* (1993); M. Hills, *The English Bible in America: A Bibliography of Editions of the Bible and New Testament Published in America 1777–1957* (1962); A. Hudson, *The Premature Reformation: Wycliffite Texts and Lollard History* (1988); D. Katz, *God's Last Words: Reading the English Bible from the Reformation to Fundamentalism* (2004); P. Levi, *The English Bible from Wycliffe to William Barnes Barnes* (1974); R. Loewe, in: HUCA, 28 (1957), 205–52; J. Long, *The Bible in English: John Wycliffe and William Tyndale* (1998); C. MacKenzie, *The Battle for the Bible in England, 1557–1582* (2002); B. Metzger,

The Bible in Translation: Ancient and English Versions (2001); B. Moynahan, *God's Bestseller* (2002); O. Opfel, *The King James Bible Translators* (1982); J. Pelikan, *The Reformation of the Bible/The Bible of the Reformation* (1996); A.W. Pollard (ed.), *Records of the English* Bible (1911); H. Pope, *English Versions of the Bible* (1952); I. Rashkow, *Upon the Dark Places: Anti-Semitism and Sexism in English Renaissance Biblical Translation* (1990); W. Schwarz, *Principles and Problems of Bible* Translation (1955); P. Theusen, *In Discordance with the Scriptures* (1999); W. Tyndale, *Answer to Sir Thomas More* (1531); B.F. Westcott, *A General View of the History of the English Bible*, 5th ed. (1905); P.J. Wosh, *Spreading the Word: The Bible Business in Nineteenth-Century America* (1994). ENGLISH AFTER WORLD WAR II: *General:* A. Brenner and W. van Henten, eds., *Bible Translation on the Threshold of the Twenty-First Century* (2002); R. Caroll, "As Seeing the Invisible: Ideology in Bible Translation," *Journal of Northwest Semitic Languages*, 19 (1993); J. De Ward and E.A. Nida, *From One Language to Another* (1986); L. Lupas and E. Rhodes (eds.), *Scriptures of the World: A compilation of the 2,018 languages in which at least one book of the Bible has been published since the Bible was first printed by Johann Gutenberg* (1993); M. Margolis, *The Story of Bible Translations* (1917); M. Miller, *Plain Speaking* (1974); E.A. Nida, *Toward a Science of Translation* (1964); idem, "Intelligibility and Acceptability in Bible Translating, *Bible* Translator 39 (1988), 301–308; E.A. Nida and C.R. Taber, *The Theory and Practice of Translation. Helps for Translators*, 8 (1969); S. Porter and R. Hess (eds.), *Translating the Bible: Problems and Prospects* (1999); C.R. Taber, "Translation as Interpretation," in *Interpretation*, 32 (1978), 130–43; R. Worth, *Bible Translations: A History Through Source* Documents (1992); R. Youngblood, M. Strauss, S. Voth, and G. Scorgie, eds., *The Challenge of Bible Translation* (2003). *On the Various Translations in General.* R. Bailey and T. Pippin (eds.), *Race, Class, and the Politics of Bible Translation* (1996). L.R. Bailey (ed.), *The Word of God: A Guide to English Versions of the Bible* (1982), contains articles by Bruce M. Metzger (RSV); Roger A. Bullard (NEB); R. Crim (NJV); Barclay M. Newman, Jr. (NASB); Bruce Vawter (JB); William F. Stinespring (TEV); James D. Smart (LB); Walter Harrelson (NAB); Robert G. Bratcher (NIV); and an annotated bibliography by the editor; J. Barr, "Modern English Bible Versions as a Problem for the Church," *Quarterly Review*, 14:3 (1994); R. Bratcher, "Current Trends in Bible Translation in English," *Bible Translator*, 46:4 (1995); F.F. Bruce, The English Bible: *A History of Translations* (1970); R. Crim, "Versions, English," *Interpreter's Dictionary of the Bible*, Supplementary ON INCLUSIVE LANGUAGE. P.A. Bird, "Translating Sexist Language as a Theological and Cultural Problem," in: *Union Seminary Quarterly Review*, 42 (1988), 89–95; D.M. Bossman, "Insights from Comparative Midrash," in: *Biblical Theology Bulletin*, 14 (1984), 34–35; D. Carson, *The Inclusive Language Debate: A Plea for Realism* (1998); M. Dumais, "Sexist Language and Biblical Translation," *Liturgical Ministry*, 1 (1992); P. Ellingworth, "Translating the Bible Inclusively," in: Meta, 32 (1987), 46–54; *An Inclusive-Language Lectionary* (1984); C. Fontaine, "The NRSV and the REB: A Feminist Critique," *Theology Today*, 47 (1990); W. Harrelson, "Inclusive Language in the New Revised Standard Version," *Princeton Seminary Bulletin*, 11:3 (1990); R. Maggio, *The Nonsexist Word Finder: A Dictionary of Gender-Free Usage* (1987); P. Perkins, "A Biblical Theological Critique," in: *Biblical Theology Bulletin*, 14 (1984), 31–33; M. Strauss, *Distorting Scripture? The Challenge of Bible Translation and Gender Accuracy* (1998); G. Wainwright, Geoffrey, "Systematic Liturgical Observations," in: *Biblical Theology Bulletin*, 14 (1984), 28–30. *On Jewish Sensitivities in Translations of the New Testament.* A. Byatt, "Handling the Tetragrammaton in English Translations," in: *Bible Collectors' World*, 3:4 (1987), 3–8; M.J. Cook, "The New Testament and Judaism: An Historical Perspective on the Theme," in: *Review & Expositor*, 84 (1987), 183–199; idem, "The Gospel of John and the Jews," in: *Review & Expositor*, 84 (1987), 259–271; D. Flusser, "Two Anti-Jewish Montages in Matthew," in: *Judaism and the Origins of Christianity*, (1988); D.J. Harrington, "The Jews in John's Gospel," in: *The Bible Today* (1989), 203–209; L.T. Johnson, "The New Testament's Anti-Jewish Slander and the Conventions of Ancient Polemic," in: *Journal of Biblical Literature*, 108 (1989), 419–441; O.C.M. Kvarme, "From Frantz Delitzsch to David Stern: Translating the New Testament in a Jewish Setting," in: *Text and Theology*, ed. A. Tangberg (1994); D. Rokeah, "The New Testament in Hebrew Garb," *Mishkan*, 20 (1994), 64–72; D.H. Stern, *Jewish New Testament: A Translation of the New Testament that Expresses its Jewishness* (1990). *Knox:* S. Dayras, "The Knox Version, or The Trials of a Translator: Translation or Transgression," in *Translating Religious Texts: Translation, Transgression and Interpretation*, ed. D. Jasper (1993); R.A. Knox, *The Trials of a Translator* (1949), published in England under the title *On Englishing the Bible*; A.R. Whitby, "The Acrostic Psalms," in: *Bible Collectors' World*, 4:2–3 (1988), 3–6. *RSV and NRSV: An Introduction to the Revised Standard Version of the Old Testament* (1952); M. Burrows, "The Revised Standard Version of the Old Testament," in: *Supplements to Vetus Testamentum*, 8 (1960), 206–221; idem, *Dead Sea Scrolls* (1955); C.M. Cooper, "The Revised Standard Version of Psalms," in: *Seventy-Fifth Anniversary* MLB. G. Verkuyl, "The Berkeley Version of the New Testament," in: *Bible Translator*, 2 (1951), 80–85; R.G. Bratcher, "A Review of 'The Berkeley Version of the New Testament' by G. Verkuyl (6th ed.)," in: *Bib. Trans.*, 14 (1963), 140–143. NWT. H.H. Rowley, "How Not to Translate the Bible." *Expository Times*, 65 (Nov. 1953), 41–42. JB AND NJB. H. Cazelles, "A Review of 'The Jerusalem Bible'," in: *The Bible Translator*, 9:4 (1958), 153–155; J. de Savignac, "Observations on the Version of the Bible Called 'The Jerusalem Bible'," in: *The Bible Translator*, 9:4 (1958), 158–161; A. di Lella, "A Review of 'The Jerusalem Bible'," in: *Catholic Biblical Quarterly*, 29 (1967), 148–151; J.A. Fitzmyer, "A Review of 'The Jerusalem Bible'," in: *Theological Studies* 27, (1967), 129–131; F.C. Grant, "A Review of 'The Jerusalem Bible'," in: *Journal of Biblical Literature*, 86 (1967), 91–93; A.S. Herbert, "A Review of 'The Jerusalem Bible'," in: *The Bible Translator*, 18:2 (1967), 153–155; B. Vawter, "A Review of the French Edition 'La Sainte Bible'," in: *Catholic Biblical Quarterly*, 18 (1956), 315–317. NAB. B. Ahern, "Textual Directives of the Encyclical 'Divino Afflante Spiritu'," in: *Catholic Biblical Quarterly*, 7 (1945), 340–347; E.P. Arbez, "The New Catholic Translation of the Old Testament," in: *Catholic Biblical Quarterly*, 14 (1952), 237–254; J. Barr, "After Five Years: A Retrospect on Two Major Translations of the Bible," in: *The Heythrop Journal*, 15 (Oct. 1974), 381–405; K. Crim, "A Review of the 'New American Bible'," in: *The Bible Translator*, 23 (1972), 444–448; M. Dahood, "Northwest Semitic Notes on Genesis," in: *Biblica*, 55 (1974) 76–82; F.W. Danker, "Review of the 'New American Bible'," in: *Catholic Biblical Quarterly*, 33 (1971), 405–409; G.R. Fogarty, "American Catholic Translations of the Bible," in: E. Frerichs (ed.), *The Bible and Bibles in America* (1988), 117–144; G.P. Fogarty, *American Catholic Biblical Scholarship: A History from the Early Republic to Vatican II*; T. Meek, "A Review of 'The Holy Bible, Vol III, The Sapiential Books, Job to Sirach," in: *Catholic Biblical Quarterly*, 18 (1956), 314–315; J. Reumann, "A Review of the 'New American Bible'," in: *Journal of Biblical Literature*, 92 (1973), 275–278; L. Sabourin, "A Review of the 'New American Bible'," in: *Biblical Theology Bulletin*, 2 (1972), 206–208. NEB OR REB. J. Barr, *Comparative Philology and the Text of the Old Testament* (1968); idem, "After Five Years: A Retrospect on Two Major Translations of the Bible," in: *The Heythrop Journal*, 15 (Oct. 1974), 381–405; R. Bratcher, "A Review of 'NEB'," in: *The Bible Translator*, 12 (July, 1961), 97–106; L.H. Brockington, *The*

Hebrew Text of the Old Testament: The Readings Adopted by the Translators of the New English Bible (1973); F.F. Bruce, "The New English Bible," in: *Christianity Today*, 14 (Jan. 30, 1970), 8–11; M. Burrows, "A Review of 'NEB,'" in: *Journal of Biblical Literature*, 89 (1970), 220–222; R. Coleman, "A Contemporary Bible," in: *English Today*, 20 (Oct. 1989), 3–8; K.R. Crim, "The New English Bible," in: *The Bible Translator*, 21 (July 1970) 149–154; M. Dahood, "Hebrew-Ugaritic Lexicography VIII," in: *Biblica*, 51 (1970), 391–404; idem, "A Review of the New English Bible: Old Testament, Apocrypha," in: *Biblica*, 52 (1971), 117–123; D. Daiches, "Translating the Bible," in: *Commentary*, 49 (May, 1970), 59–68; G.R. Driver, "The New English Bible: The Old Testament," in: *Journal of Jewish Studies*, 24 (Spring 1973), 1–7; C.H. Gordon, "The New English Bible: Old Testament," in: *Christianity Today*, 14 (1970), 574–576; G. Hunt, *About the New English Bible* (1970); A.A. MacIntosh, G. Stanton, & D.L. Frost, "The 'New English Bible' Reviewed," in: *Theology*, 74 (April 1971), 154–166; H. Minkoff, "A Review of the REB and NRSV," in: *Bible Review*, 6:3 (1990), 9–10; A. Sauer & F.W. Danker, "A Look at the NEB. – OT," in: *Concordia Theological Monthly*, 41 (Sept. 1970), 491–507; B. Vawter, "A Review of 'New English Bible,'" in: *Catholic Biblical Quarterly*, 32 (1970), 426–428. **ADD. BIBLIOGRAPHY:** M. Hooker, "The Revised English Bible," in: *Epworth Review*, 17 (1990); J. James, "Thoughts on the Revised English Bible," in: *Friends' Quarterly*, 26:3 (1990); W. McKane, "The Revised English Bible (REB): Old Testament," in: *Journal of Northwest Semitic Languages*, 18 (1992). LB. R.G. Bratcher, "A Review of 'The Living New Testament Paraphrased,'" in: *Bible Translator*, 20 (1969), 36–39; K.R. Crim, "A Review of 'The Living Bible Paraphrased,'" in: *Bible Translator*, 22 (1972), 340–344; E.J. Epp, "Jews and Judaism in the Living New Testament," in: G.A. Tuttle (ed.), *Biblical and Near Eastern Studies: Essays in Honor of William Sanford LaSor* (1978); a response by K.N. Taylor, 143–144; idem, "A Review of 'Good News for Modern Man,'" in: *The Bible Translator*, 17:4 (1966), 159–172; idem, "The Nature and Purpose of the New Testament in Today's English Version," in: *The Bible Translator*, 22:3 (1971), 97–107; M. Dahood, "A Review of 'The Psalms for Modern Man,'" in: *Catholic Biblical Quarterly*, 34 (1972), 240–242; J. de Waard, & E.A. Nida, *Functional Equivalence in Bible Translating: From One Language to Another* (1986); Editor, "The Nature and Purpose of the New Testament in Today's English Version," in: *The Bible Translator*, 22:3 (1971), 97–107; D. Lithgow, "Some Notes on the Use of TEV as a Translation Source Text by Translators who speak English as a Second Language," *The Bible Translator*, 28 (1977), 408–412; H.G. May, "A Review of Today's English Version," in: *Interpretation*, 32 (1978), 187–190; H.K. Moulton, "A Review of 'The New Testament in Today's English Version.' Second Edition," in: *The Bible Translator*, 19:4 (1968), 184–187; J.B. Phillips, "A Review of 'Good News for Modern Man: The New Testament in Today's English Version,'" in: *The Bible Translator*, 18:2 (1967), 99–100; W.A. Smalley, "Discourse Analysis and Bible Translation," in: *The Bible Translator*, 31 (1980), 119–125; P.C. Stein, "Biblical Poetry and Translation," in: *Meta*, 32 (1987), 64–75; R.F. Youngblood, "Good News For Modern Man: Becoming a Bible," in: *Christianity Today*, 21 (Oct 8, 1976), 16–19. **ADD. BIBLIOGRAPHY:** J. Wilson, "The Living Bible Reborn: From the Living Bible to the New Living Translation" *Christianity Today*, 40:12 (1996). NIV. K.L. Barker, The NIV: *"The Making of a Contemporary Translation,"* (1986); R.G. Bratcher, "A Review Article: "The Holy Bible – New International Version," in: *Bible Translator*, 30 (1979), 345–350; P.C. Craige, "The New International Version: A Review Article," in: *Journal of Evangelical Theological Society*, 21 (1978), 251–254; B.L. Goddard, *The NIV Story: The Inside Story of the New International Version* (1989); J.C. Jeske, "New International Version Completed," in: *Wisconsin Lutheran Quarterly*, 75 (1978), 292–305; D. Jackson, "The Theology of the NIV," in: *Restoration Quarterly*, 27 (1984), 208–220. W.S. LaSor, "What Kind of Version is the New International?" in: *Christianity Today*, 23 (Oct. 20, 1978), 17–19; B.K. Waltke, "The New International Version and Its Textual Principles in the Book of Psalms," in: *Journal of the Evangelical Theological Society*, 32 (1989), 17–26. **ADD. BIBLIOGRAPHY:** J. Stek, "The New International Version: How It Came to Be," in: Youngblood, Strauss, Voth, and Scorgie, eds., *op. cit.*. NJV. D.M. Beegle, "A New Translation of the Torah:' A Review," *The Bible Translator*, 14:3 (1963), 97–105; M. Brettler, "The Torah, The Prophets and the Writings: A New Jewish Translation," in: *Biblical Archaeology Review*, 7:6 (1982), 63–67; K.R. Crim, "The New Version of the Scriptures," in: *The Bible Translator*, 26:1 (1975), 148–152; M. Dahood, A Review of 'The Torah: The Five Books of Moses," in: *Biblica*, 45 (1964), 281–283; H.L. Ginsberg, "The Story of the Jewish Publications Society's 'New Translation of the Torah,'" in: *The Bible Translator*, 14:3 (1963), 106–113; L. Greenspoon, "Biblical Translators in Antiquity and in the Modern World: A Comparative Study," in: *Hebrew Union College Annual*, 60 (1989), 91–113; M. Margolis, "The New English Translation of the Bible," in: *American Jewish Yearbook* (1917); T.J. Meek "A New Bible Translation," in: *Journal of Biblical Literature*, 82 (1963), 265–271; HM Orlinsky, "The New Jewish Version of the Torah: Toward a New Philosophy of Bible Translation, in: *Journal of Biblical Literature*, 72 (1963), 249–264; idem, *Notes on the New Translation of the Torah* (1969); idem, "Wanted: A New English Translation of the Bible for the Jewish People," in: *Essays in Biblical Culture and Bible Translation* (1974); C. Rabin, "Etymological Miscellanea," in: *Scripta Hierosolymitana*, 8 (1961), 384–400; J.A. Sanders, "Text Criticism and the NJV Torah," in: *Journal of the American Academy of Religion*, 39 (1971), 193–197; J.D. Sarna & N.M. Sarna, "Bible Translation by American Individuals," in: E.S. Frerichs (ed.), op. cit. **ADD. BIBLIOGRAPHY:** M. Greenberg and J. Greenfield, "From the Workshop of the New Jewish Publication Society Ketuvim Translators," in: *Minhah le-Nahum: Biblical and Other Studies Presented to Nahum M. Sarna in Honour of His 70th Birthday*, ed. M. Brettler and M. Fishbane (1993); S. Leeman, "The Old and the New JPS: A Comparative Study," *Jewish Bible Quarterly*, 22:1 (1994); M. Maher, "A Jewish Translation of the Hebrew Bible: The New Jewish Version," *Proceedings of the Irish Bible Association*, 14 (1991); CEV. J. Blenkinsopp, "The Contemporary English Version: Inaccurate Translation Tries to Soften Anti-Judaic Sentiment," *Bible Review*, October (1996); B. Newman, *Creating and Crafting the New English Version: A New Approach to Bible Transalation* (1996). GERMAN: E. Nestle, in: *Realencyklopaedie fuer protestantische Theologie und Kirche*, 3 (1897), 59–84; W. Streitholz, *Die gotische Bibel* (1919); W. Walther, *Die deutschen Bibeluebersetzungen des Mittelalters*, 3 vols. (1889–92); M. Buber and F. Rosenzweig, *Die Schrift und ihre Verdeutschung* (1936; English: *Scripture and Translation*, 1994); S.L. Greenslade (ed.), *The Cambridge History of the Bible* (1963), 94–109, 339–47; E.P. Arbez, in: CBQ, 16 (1954), 343–7; A. Risch, *Die deutsche Bibel in ihrer geschichtlichen Entwickelung* (1907); W. Weintraub, *Targumei ha-Torah la-Lashon ha-Germanit* (1967); A. Gilman, "Between Religion and Culture: Mendelssohn, Buber, Rosenzweig and the Enterprise of Biblical Translation," in: Knobloch, *op. cit.*; Lowenstein, "The Social Dynamics of Jewish Responses to Moses Mendelssohn (with Special Emphasis on the Mendelssohn Bible Translation and on the Berlin Jewish Community)," in: *Moses Mendelssohn und die Kreise Seiner Wirksamkeit*, ed. M. Albrecht (1994); M. Niehoff, "The Buber-Rosenzweig Translation of the Bible Within Jewish-German Tradition," *JJS*, 44:2 (1993); W.G. Plaut, *German-Jewish Bible Translations* (1992); K. Reichert, "It Is Time: The Buber-Rosenzweig Bible Translation in Context," in: S. Budick and W. Iser, eds., *The Translatability of Cul-*

tures: *Figurations of the Space Between* (1996); L. Rosenwald, "On the reception of Buber and Rosenzweig's Bible," in: *Prooftexts*, 14:2 (1994); W. Weinberg, "Moses Mendelssohn's Biblical Translations and Commentaries," in: *Approaches to Ancient Judaism*, New Series, 1, ed. J. Neusner (1990); E. Wendland, "Martin Luther, the Father of Confessional, Functional-Equivalence Bible Translation," in: *Notes on Translation*, 9:1 and 9:2 (1995). (MODERN) ARABIC: T.H. Darlow and H.F. Moule, *Historical Catalogue of the Printed Editions of Holy Scripture*, 2 (1911), 62–84; G. Graf, *Geschichte der christlichen arabischen Literatur*, 1 (1944), 85–297. CATALAN: P. Bohigas, in: *Saggi e ricerche in memoria di Ettore Li Gotti* (1962); L. Arnaldich, *Los estudios bíblicos en España desde el año 1900 al añ 1955* (1957). DUTCH: J. van Kasteren, in: DBI, 4 (1912), 1549–57; S.L. Greenslade (ed.), *The Cambridge History of the Bible: The West from the Reformation to the Present Day* (1963); E.P. Arbez, in: CBQ, 16 (1954), 201–9; E. Nestle, in: *Realencyklopaedie fuer protestantische Theologie und Kirche*, 3 (1897), 119–24. **ADD. BIBLIOGRAPHY:** H. Blok, "Chronicle: A Bible Translation to be Read Aloud," in: *Amsterdamse Cahiers voor Exegese van de Bijbel en zijn Tradities*, Supplement Series 2 (2001). FRENCH: P.M. Bogaert, "La Bible en francais. Reflexions sur l'histoire et l'actualite," in: *RTL*, 7: 337–53. HUNGARIAN: T. Kardos, *A huszita biblia keletkezése* (1952); M. Ballagi, *Tanulmányok a magyar bibliafordítások körül* (1865); A. Boros, *Zsoltárfordítás a kódexek korában* (1908); E. Császár, *A magyar protestáns zsoltárköltészet a XVII és XVIII században* (1902); L. Blau, in: *Magyar Zsidó Szemle* (1910); F. Balogh, in: *Realencyklopaedie fuer protestantische Theologie und Kirche*, 3 (1897), 115–8. ITALIAN: L. Fanin, "Quale traducione della Bibbia preferire?" in: *RivB*, 28: 417–30; S. Minocchi, in: DBI, 3 (1912), 1012–38; A. Vaccari, in: *Enciclopedia Italiana*, 6 (1930–38), 899–903. POLISH: E. Dabrowski (ed.), *Prodreczna encyklopedia biblijna*, 2 (1959); L. Stefaniak, in: *New Testament Studies*, 5 (1958–59), 328–38. PORTUGUESE: A. Ribeiro dos Santos, in: *Memória da Litteratura Portugueza*, 7 (1806), 23–57; J. Pereira, in: DBI, 5 (1912), 562–5; G.L. Santos Ferreira, *A Bíblia em Portugal: Apontamentos para uma monographia, 1495–1850* (1906); H. Wendt, *Die portugiesische Bibeluebersetzung: Ihre Geschichte und ihre Aufgaben mit besonderer Beruecksichtigung des A.T.* (1962). RUSSIAN: M. Spinka, in: JR, 13 (1933), 415–32; A. Osroff, in: *Bible Translator*, 7 (1956), 56–65, 98–101; J. Schweigl, in: *Biblica*, 18 (1937), 51–73; J. Schmid (ed.), *Moderne Bibeluebersetzungen* (1960); **ADD. BIBLIOGRAPHY:** S. Bataladen, "The Politics of Modern Russian Bible Translation," in: P. Stine, ed., *Bible Translation and the Spread of the Church* (1990). SCANDINAVIAN: C.J. Brandt, *Udsigt over vore danske bibeloversaettelsers historie* (1889); H. Nielsson, in: *Festskrift… Buhl* (1925); S.L. Greenslade (ed.), *The Cambridge History of the Bible: The West from the Reformation to the Present Day* (1963), 135–40, 355–8, 541. SPANISH: S. Berger, *Les Bibles castillanes* (1899); F. Pérez, *La Biblia en España*, ed. by B. Orchard (1956), 83–97; J. Llamas (ed.), *Biblia medieval romanceada judío-cristiana* (1950–55); S.L. Greenslade (ed.), *The Cambridge History of the Bible: The West from the Reformation to the Present Day* (1963), 125–9; 540–1. OTHER LANGUAGES: A. Abela, "Two Professional Translations of the Bible in Maltese in the 20th Century," in: *Melita Theologica*, 48 (1996); A. Alexev, "The Song of Songs in the Slavonic Bible Tradition," in: *Bible Translator*, 47:1 (1996); N. Emehgara, "The Concept of God Among the Hebrew of Palestine and the Ibos of Nigeria," in: *Indian Theological Studies*, 30:4 (1993); C. Fiero, "From Hebrew to Algonquian: Problems in Form and Content," in: *International Journal of Translation*, 3:1–2 (1991); R. Fowkes, "The 'Standard' Welsh of the 1588 Bible," in: *Language Sciences* 15/2 (1993), 141–153; M.A.B. Gaiya, "A History of the Hausa Bible: 1980 Edition," in: *Africa Journal of Evangelical Theology*, 12:1 (1993); J. Harris, "Aboriginal Languages, Christian Misionaries, and Bible Translation," in: *Studies in the Humanities*, 22:1–2 (1995); J. Hong, "Revision of the Chinese Union Version Bible," in: *Bible Translator*, 53:2 (April 2002); M. Jinbachian, "Modern Armenian Translations of the Bible," in: *Armenia and the Bible: Papers Presented to the International Symposium Held at Heidelberg, July 16–19, 1990, ed. C. Burchard* (1993); N. Mundhenk, "Linguistic decisions in the Tok Pisn Bible," in: *Melanesian Pidgin and Tok Pisn: Proceedings of the First International Conference of Pidgins and Creoles in Melanesia*, ed. J.W.M. Verhaar (1990); D.D.K. Ruuskanen, "There is No Word for 'Adultery' in Hawaiian: The Translation of Non-Existent Concepts," in: *AFinLan Vuoskirja*, 51 (1993); B. Schneider, Efforts in Japanese Bible Translation Since 1965," in: *Japan Christian Review*, 58 (1992); C. Wai-Boon, "Chinese Translations of the Bible," in: CGST *Journal*, 16 (1994).For additional bibliograpy, see *Bible.

EXEGESIS AND STUDY

TALMUDIC LITERATURE

The voluminous body of talmudic literature – the *Oral Law – is essentially a compilation of hermeneutic, interpretative, and analytic exegesis of the Bible – the Written Law. According to rabbinic tradition, Moses not only received the Oral Law on Mount Sinai, but also the definitive explanation of the meaning buried in the Torah's compact and cryptic literary style. "Moses received the Torah from Sinai and transmitted it to Joshua" (Avot 1:1), providing the material on which generations of exegetes worked, creating the vast store of talmudic literature. According to the talmudic tradition, *Ezra, upon his arrival in Palestine, founded the institution of the *scribe (*sofer*), whose contribution to the teaching and understanding of the Bible has been fundamental. "These early scholars were called *soferim* [which can mean "scribes" or "reckoners"]" the Talmud relates, "because they used to count all the letters in the Torah" (Kid. 30a). In order to certify a biblical text as traditionally correct, the *soferim* first counted the letters to ascertain omissions or additions. The scribal appellation has been associated with certain facets of talmudic interpretative work (see above, The History of the Biblical Text).

The scribes continued their work until the end of the period of the Great Assembly. The *tannaim, who emerged toward the end of the scribal era (second century B.C.E.), together with the *amoraim* (third–sixth centuries C.E.), devoted their efforts to teaching their disciples the true meaning of Scripture. They practiced their exegetical methods on such subjects as theology, ethics, lexicography, homiletics, and religious and civil law. The body of their work is incorporated in the Talmud corpus, comprising the Mishnah, *Gemara*, Tosefta, and *baraita*. An important repository of exegetical work is the midrashic literature, which is made up of a number of collections reflecting different approaches to the task of transmitting the essence of the biblical text; one approach is the halakhic, which produced a collection of Midrashim in order to explain the legalistic (ritual and tort) portions of the Bible and the manner in which the commandments were to be fulfilled. Notable among the collection of halakhic Midrashim are the **Mekhilta*, **Sifrei*, and **Sifra*. Collections exemplifying the aggadic approach, or use of parable and anecdote to explain the text, include, among others, *Genesis Rabbah* and **Ecclesiastes Rabbah*. **Pesikta* and **Tanḥuma* are collections of Midrashim representing the homiletical approach. Based on the Sabbath Torah reading, homilies are arranged according to the text of the weekly portion. Methodologically, a complex system of exegesis was employed. It consisted of a diversified analysis of the text by one or all of the elements of **pardes*, an acronym representing the following: *peshat*, literal translation; *remez*, implied meaning; **derash*, homiletic comprehension; and *sod*, mystical, allegorical meaning. *Peshat* and *derash* are the more popular methods of exegesis, since they are comprehensible to most, while *remez* and *sod* represent the esoteric, mystical, and kabbalistic approaches. These latter exegetical methods were at times considered dangerous for use by the unscholarly man, who might arrive at misinterpretations and risk heresy. *Peshat* is an objective method of obtaining the literal meaning of a passage by analysis of the language, whereas *derash* is a subjective method which attempts to make the text applicable to the time of the exegete. The sages believed that the Oral Law accompanied the receipt of the Written Law, and that it renews itself in each era, i.e., the interpretation of the Oral Law, which is a continuous process, reformulates the Bible's eternal verities, giving them continuing applicability.

*Shemaiah and *Avtalyon were among the earliest expositors of the law. Their disciple, *Hillel, formulated the seven *hermeneutical precepts by which exegesis could be accomplished. These precepts were subsequently expanded by R. *Ishmael into 13 principles, and finally by R. *Eliezer into 32 rules. Two great schools of midrashic interpretation emerged, those of R. Ishmael and R. *Akiva. R. Ishmael's approach was didactic and literal, because he believed that the Torah is written in the language of ordinary usage, and, therefore, holds no hidden meanings. R. Akiva, however, analyzed each word (see above, The History of the Biblical Text). These two schools produced the material collected in *Mekhilta*, *Sifrei*, and *Sifra*. At times, the lines between the respective schools were not clear because disciples were not above enlisting other methods, perhaps more suitable for a particular topic.

BIBLIOGRAPHY: Zunz, Vortraege; M. Soloweitschik and Z. Rubashov, *Toledot Bikkoret ha-Mikra* (1925); H.L. Strack, *Introduction to the Talmud and Midrash* (1945); H. Zernowitsch, *Toledot ha-Halakhah*, 4 (1950); M.Z. Segal, *Parshanut ha-Mikra* (1952^2); Waxman, Literature, 1 (1960^2), 45–138; B.M. Casper, *An Introduction to Jewish Bible Commentary* (1960). **ADD. BIBLIOGRAPHY:** J. Neusner, in: *Shaarei Talmon: Studies in the Bible, Qumran, and the Ancient Near East Presented to Shemaryahu Talmon* (1992), 345–63; D.S. Shapiro, in: *Understanding the Talmud* (1975), 62–64; D. Daube, in: *Understanding the Talmud* (1975), 275–89.

[Abraham Zimels]

MEDIEVAL RABBINIC COMMENTARIES

From the period of the *geonim* until the age of the Haskalah (about 1,000 years), Bible exegesis constituted one of the main themes of Jewish literature, not only in books especially devoted to biblical exegesis, but also in those dealing with philosophy or linguistic research, which often included interpretations of biblical verses. Generally speaking, two broad approaches to biblical exegesis are discernible – the literal and the homiletical. In the former the commentator bases himself on the plain meaning of the text and on the context, and the interpretation is objective. In the homiletic approach the commentator strives to interweave his ideas with the text even if the simple meaning of the language and the context are at variance with his interpretation, and his interpretation is subjective. Homiletic commentary developed because of various cultural requirements and because of the necessity of finding a correspondence between scriptural views and the prevailing opinion in different ages.

A considerable portion of the exegesis of the geonic period consisted of assembling and editing material, much of which had accumulated through traditions handed down over the generations. Included in this material were midrashic collections and the masorah. The task of the masorah scholars, particularly in establishing vocalization and cantillation, was of the utmost importance, providing as they did the most valuable interpretation of the Bible. Vocalization and cantillation insured correct reading of the biblical text and were established, as a rule, in accordance with the *peshat*, the literal meaning. The greatest commentators such as *Rashi, Abraham *Ibn Ezra, and others, based their interpretations on the masorah.

In additon to this work of collation new and original works were created in the geonic period, opening up fresh paths in the field of exegesis and powerfully influencing succeeding generations. Two historic events led to this development: the expansion of Islam and the rise of *Karaism. The efflorescence of learning and science among the Muslims influenced the Jews living among them to participate in philosophic enquiry and linguistic research. Along with the decline of Aramaic as the vernacular came a decline in the use of Aramaic translations of the Bible. The intensification of the Karaite-Rabbanite controversy over readings and interpretations of biblical texts also contributed to this development. The Karaites produced a number of commentators, among them *Anan, the founder of Karaism, who in his interpretations frequently applied the hermeneutic methods of the tannaitic Midrashim, and Benjamin *Nahawāndī, who made use of allegorical explanations. The Rabbanites were thus compelled to intensify their biblical research and to seek new methods of exegesis.

The Work of Saadiah Gaon and Its Influence

The new era was ushered in by *Saadiah Gaon, a considerable portion of whose extensive literary work is connected with Bible commentary. Saadiah endeavored to prove the impossibility of explaining the Scriptures without the masorah and to show that the Midrashim and *halakhot* of the rabbinic sages were based on the literal meaning of scriptural texts. In this context, Saadiah's Arabic translation of the Bible and his commentaries are noteworthy. The translation is actually a paraphrase of the text. His commentaries, particularly those on the Pentateuch, include a wealth of material: explanation of the text, linguistic and philosophic research, and polemics, directed primarily against the Karaites. He even composed a special work against the extreme and heretical views of *Ḥīwī al-Balkhī on biblical subjects.

As a result of Saadiah's biblical studies, Bible commentary emerged from the sphere of homiletics to embark upon the pursuit of direct and close exposition of the biblical text. In his linguistic and philosophic approach Saadiah provided directives for scholars who came after him. That influence is particularly noticeable in *Samuel b. Hophni and his son-in-law *Hai. Samuel b. Hophni, an unusually prolific writer, engaged extensively in Bible commentary. In addition to translating the Scriptures into Arabic, he applied himself to philosophic inquiry. His attempts to explain miracles as natural phenomena were attacked by Hai.

In Spain

A significant flowering of Bible commentary took place in Spain, which had its basis in the researches of *Menahem b. Jacob ibn Saruq, his critic *Dunash b. Labrat, and Menahem's pupil, *Judah b. Ḥayyuj (tenth century). Although their works are mainly concerned with grammatical and linguistic considerations, they are interspersed with numerous elucidations of verses and individual words in Scripture. The novelty of their approach lies in its philological orientation.

Particularly important are the investigations of Jonah *Ibn Janāḥ (Abu al-Walīd) in *Sefer ha-Rikmah* and *Sefer ha-Shorashim*. In illustrating and elucidating his philological and grammatical rules, he cites many biblical passages, explaining them in a profound and original manner. He is unfettered in his inquiry, at times ignoring the masoretic text, and, in some instances, even transposing and emending biblical texts. Though his deviation from the masorah provoked much opposition, his influence on later commentators was very great.

Ongoing progress in Hebrew linguistics produced the philological commentary, two of whose famous exponents were Moses ha-Kohen *Gikatilla and Judah *Ibn Balʿam (11th century). The former is characterized by his freedom and originality, interpreting, for example, the predictions of the prophets as applying strictly to their own times and not to the Messianic era. Judah ibn Balʿam opposed his approach, writing in a far more conservative spirit. In a class by itself stands the Bible research of Moses *Ibn Ezra. Though his book *Shirat Yisrael* was expressly written as a guide to the composition of poetry, his analysis of the various literary forms – "The Twenty Portals of Poetic Embellishment" – is rich in biblical references. Ibn Ezra's investigations bear the strong impress of Arabic poetry and of the scholarship in that area. Belonging to a completely different class of commentary, which was also greatly influenced by Arab culture, is philosophical commentary (see below).

Literal Commentary

Of a quite different nature is the literal commentary, fostered by Rashi and his disciples, which flourished in northern France, and which is relatively free of outside influence. The Jews of France, though occasionally engaging in discussion with Christians on the interpretation of biblical passages, had only limited cultural relations with their neighbors, whose standards in this area in any event were quite low. Thus, their commentaries do not contain such philosophical or philological elements as abound in the commentaries of the Spanish school. The commentary of this school is characterized by the search after the plain meaning, although a certain conflict is discernible between the inclination toward homiletical exegesis and the conscious effort to explain biblical passages according to their plain meaning.

The interpretations of *Menahem b. Ḥelbo contain much homiletics. Rashi, too, introduced many ancient rabbinic Midrashim, but only in addition to the plain meaning, frequently remarking that they were not to be taken as representing the literal meaning of the passage. Rashi often reiterates as his aim the explanation of the text according to its plain meaning or according to the closest aggadic interpretation. This tendency becomes even more marked with Rashi's successors Joseph *Kara, *Samuel b. Meir, *Eliezer of Beaugency and Joseph *Bekhor Shor. It is somewhat surprising that this phenomenon should exist particularly in northern France. Samuel b. Meir and Joseph Bekhor Shor, for example, who are outstanding exponents of literal commentary, are also among the foremost tosafists, and their method with regard to their biblical exegesis is in contrast to that adapted by them in their talmudic exposition. In some instances they even assigned to a biblical text a meaning at variance with the *halakhah*, despite the fact that the *halakhah* was unquestioningly accepted by them, their serene spirit and unswerving faith ruling out any feeling of strain or conflict. A contributing factor to the growth of literal exposition may have been the need felt to counter christological interpretations of certain biblical passages, although these commentators – and particularly Rashi – had a definite influence on some of the Christian biblical exegetes.

Synthetic Commentary

Certain commentators embody all the above methods of interpretation. The main representatives of this synthetic approach are: Abraham ibn Ezra, David *Kimḥi and Naḥmanides. Their commentaries include philological, philosophical, literal, homiletical and, in the case of Naḥmanides, even kabbalistic elements.

While Ibn Ezra bases his commentary principally on the philologic method, contributing much to linguistic research, he also introduces many philosophical explanations. In dealing with halakhic material, he accepts the rabbinic **Midrash Halakhah*, but opposes *Midrash Aggadah* when it is in conflict with the plain meaning of Scripture. He argues that homiletical explanations should not always be taken literally, there being even in *halakhah* instances of derivations which are only formally associated with a biblical verse.

Joseph *Kimḥi was active in Narbonne at the same time and was followed by his sons, Moses and David. The latter's work constitutes a kind of melting pot for the various methods of commentary. From Spain he borrowed the topical, philological, and philosophical commentary, and from Franco-Germany the literal and homiletic methods. He very frequently quotes Midrashim, but gives the literal interpretations with them. He has little recourse to philosophic commentary, resorting to it only when he sees a special need to do so.

An important turning point is reached with the introduction by Naḥmanides of Kabbalah into his Bible commentary. Naḥmanides' approach, too, is eclectic, a blend of the Franco-German school with that of Spain, but the emphasis is less on philological commentary than on a penetrating investigation of the context. Though he discusses the problems raised by philosophers, he does not regard the rational aspect as paramount, and in many places attacks the Aristotelian approach. On occasion, along with other interpretations which he considers acceptable, Naḥmanides quotes from the "Secret Discipline," the Kabbalah, but he employs it sparingly. It is included as an adjunct only, mostly by way of mere allusion and intended solely for those with a knowledge of Kabbalah.

Later Commentary

Philosophic commentary enjoyed a resurgence despite Naḥmanides' opposition, especially in the 14th century. This trend was continued, with certain limitations, by Isaac *Abrabanel in 15th-century Spain. Though he resorts to philosophic explanations, he is at the same time often opposed to the rational approach to Bible commentary. He does not touch on philological questions in his interpretations, confining himself to the conceptual problems arising from Scripture.

In the 16th and 17th centuries occupation with biblical exposition diminished. Two commentators, however, who stand out in this period are David and Hillel *Altschuler, who wrote literal commentaries on the Prophets and the Hagiographa. Their commentaries, *Meẓudat David* and *Meẓudat Ẓiyyon*, attained wide circulation, though they were for the most part gleanings from the works of others (see also *Malbim). Gradually, under the influence of the *pilpul* which characterized Torah study in Poland, there was introduced into biblical commentaries the method of "novellae and ingenious interpretations." A fundamental change in biblical exegesis took place in the Haskalah period. It is characterized by the great influence of Christian Bible commentary on Jewish exposition and, in the wake of this, the expansion of Bible criticism. These are discussed below.

BIBLIOGRAPHY: W. Bacher, *Die Bibelexegese der juedischen Religionsphilosophen des Mittelalters vor Maimuni* (1892); idem, *Die juedische Bibelexegese vom Anfang des zehnten bis zum Ende des fuenfzehnten Jahrhunderts* (1892); S. Poznański, *Mavo al Ḥakhmei Ẓarefat Mefareshei ha-Mikra*, in: *Perush al Yeḥezkel U-Terei-Asar le-Rabbi Eliezer mi-Belganẓi* (1913); D. Yellin, *Toledot Hitpatteḥut ha-Dikduk ha-Ivri* (1945); M.Z. Segal, *Parshanut ha-Mikra* (1952); M. Zucker, *Al Tirgum R. Sa'adyah ha-Ga'on la-Torah* (1959); B. Smalley, *The Study of the Bible in the Middle Ages* (1964), H. Malter, *Saadia Gaon* (Eng., 1921), L. Nemoy (ed.), *Karaite Anthology* (1952), H. Hailperin, *Rashi and the Christian Scholars* (1963). **ADD. BIBLIOGRAPHY:** SAADIAH GAON: R.C. Steiner, in: JQR, 88:3–4 (1998), 213–58; L.E. Goodman, in: *Translation of Scripture* (1990), 47–76; M. Sokolow, in: PAAJR, 51 (1984), 131–74; Y. Tobi, in: HAR, 8 (1985), 241–57; H. Ben-Shammai, in: *Aleph*, 4 (2004), 11–87; J. Blau, in: *The Interpretation of the Bible* (1998), 393–98. RASHI: E.E. Urbach. in: *Meḥkarim be-Mada'ei ha-Yahadut*, 1 (1993), 15–22; S. Cohen, in: *The Idea of Biblical Interpretation* (2004), 449–72; P. Doron, in: *Estudios Bíblicos*, 45:1–2 (1987), 93–104; F. Talmage, in: JAOS, 104, 3 (1984), 576–77; B. Gelles, in: *Rashi et la culture juive en France du Nord au moyen âge* (1997), 97–102; idem, *Peshat and Derash in the Exegesis of Rashi* (1981); N. Sarna, *Studies in Biblical Interpretation* (2000); A.van der Heide, in: *Bibliotheca Orientalis*, 41:3–4 (1984), 292–318; E.L. Greenstein, in: *The Solomon Goldman Lectures*, 6 (1993), 51–71; J.M. Weiser, in: *Tradition*, 29:4 (1995), 30–42. ABRAHAM IBN EZRA: U. Simon, in: *Ha-Mikra be-Re'I Mefarshav* (1994); I. Twersky (ed.), *Rabbi Abraham Ibn Ezra; Studies in the Writings of a Twelfth-Century Jewish Polymath* (1993); M. Ben-Yoseph Linetsky, in: *Jewish Bible Quarterly*, 23:2 (1995), 102–6; S. Leeman, in: *Jewish Bible Quarterly*, 27:2 (1999), 100–3; M. Lockshin, in: *From Ancient Israel to Modern Judaism; Intellect in Quest of Understanding* (1989), 173–86.

[Avraham Grossman]

ALLEGORICAL INTERPRETATIONS

Allegorical interpretation of Scripture is concerned with the "inner" or "spiritual" meaning of the biblical text. Used consistently in the writings of Philo, the Church Fathers, the medieval Jewish philosophers, and the kabbalists down to the ḥasidic teachers, this method does not necessarily discard the literal meaning (*peshat*) but tends to prize the allegorical one more highly. While the Bible itself makes occasional use of allegory, the allegorists claim the right to treat the Bible as a whole or certain of its parts, as a series of allegorical expressions.

(1) Rabbinic *aggadah* and Midrash employed the allegorical method in an uninhibited homiletic rather than in a systematic manner. Their guiding motive was not, as that of the allegorists, a concern for the true, inner meaning of the text, but a pious endeavor to find "everything" (Avot 5:22), in Scripture, to make every biblical passage or word (Sanh. 34a) yield as many "meanings" (*te'amim*) as necessary. Thus while the *aggadah* and Midrash contain many instances of allegorism (*mashal* or *dugma*), these fail to exhibit, as I. Heinemann has shown, any pattern of consistency. The only exceptions are the allegorical interpretations of Proverbs 31:10–31 (the "woman of valor" being understood as the Torah) and of the Song of Songs. But even in the interpretation of the Song of Songs at least three different allegorical themes are apparent: the love between God and Israel; the exodus; interpretations of Jewish laws. Ezekiel's vision of the resurrected dry bones (ch. 37) and the figure of Job are described as allegories (BB 15a; Sanh. 92b), but no detailed allegorical interpretation of these texts is provided. Nor was Proverbs, in spite of its suggestive title

(*mishlei*), expounded allegorically, except for a few passages (including 31:10ff.) and terms (e.g., "father," God; "mother," Israel). Systematic, philosophical allegory was absent in rabbinic literature because no philosophical system presented a real challenge to the literal meaning of Scripture.

(2) The situation, however, differed radically among Hellenistic Jews, many of whom felt the need to prove that the teachings of the Bible are consonant with Greek wisdom. Here the allegorical method, which had been used by the Stoic philosophers to interpret the old Greek myths, provided a means of harmonization. It appears, however, that at first Hellenistic Jewish writers were reluctant to use allegory. The Greek version of the Bible, the Septuagint (see above), shows hardly any traces of it. *Aristobulus of Paneas, who is considered an allegorist (see Eusebius, *Praeparatio Evangelica* 8:10, 2), does distinguish between "mythical" expressions in the Bible and their allegorical sense, i.e., their "physical" or cosmological meaning. However, he only offers metaphorical interpretations of anthropomorphic descriptions of God. The Letter of *Aristeas, on the other hand, emphasizes the symbolic meaning of Jewish law and ritual, and does so for apologetic reasons. Similarly, the Wisdom of *Solomon uses allegorical interpretations: the garments of the high priest, for instance, are said to represent an image of the entire cosmos (18:19). The sect of the *Therapeutae is likewise described by Philo (Cont. 78) as employing the allegorical exposition of Scripture. Nevertheless, it is only in Philo himself that the method comes into its own. According to *Philo, the true significance of Scripture lies in the "underlying meaning" (*hyponoia*, also termed *allegoria*), which is "obscure to the many" and comprehensible only to "the few who study soul characteristics rather than bodily forms." According to H.A. Wolfson, "everything in Scripture, from names, dates, and numbers to the narration of historical events or the prescription of rules for conduct, is to Philo subject to allegorical interpretation" (*Philo*, 1 (1947), 116). Yet this does not mean that the historicity of the Bible or, for that matter, its legal validity is dissolved; its literal meaning is upheld. Thus, the three men who appeared to Abraham (Gen. 18), while representing metaphysical symbols, are still to be regarded as real beings; and, the laws of the Pentateuch, no matter how spiritual in significance, are still to be observed. In fact, Philo denounced those allegorists who regarded practical observances as superfluous (Migr. 93). His main concern, however, was to impress the authority of the Bible upon Jews and Gentiles by showing that its symbolic language concealed profound metaphysical and psychological truths; and that its laws were meant to guide the soul toward the contemplation of God by freeing it from material attachments. His allegorism bears all the marks of a deeply personal spiritual religion.

(3) In the medieval period allegorism in its proper sense, as distinct from the mere employment of metaphorical interpretation, was applied by Jewish neoplatonic and Aristotelian philosophers and kabbalists. By contrast, the Jewish theologians following the methods of Islamic *Kalām, did not engage in allegorism but were content to treat biblical anthropomorphism as metaphors (*ta'wīl*). *Saadiah Gaon laid down the philosophic position on the propriety as well as the limitations of metaphorical interpretation (*ta'wīl*) and it was later acknowledged by Abraham *Ibn Daūd and *Maimonides. According to Saadiah, the literal meaning of a biblical text is to be discarded in favor of *ta'wīl* in four instances only: if it is contradicted by sense perception, by reason, by some other explicit text, or by rabbinic tradition qualifying its apparent meaning. He argued that if license were given for metaphorical interpretation in other than these four instances, all the commandments of the Torah and all the miraculous events narrated in Scripture might be explained as mere metaphors (*Book of Beliefs and Opinions*, 7). Saadiah upholds the literal meaning of passages presumably referring to the resurrection of the dead, but insists on the metaphorical sense of the anthropomorphic descriptions of God. His use of the *ta'wīl* method is sufficiently restricted to prevent allegorism on any significant scale.

(4) Under the impact of neoplatonic and Aristotelian philosophy the situation changed fundamentally. Having expanded the meaning of *ta'wīl* to include the philosophic interpretation of doctrinal matters, the Islamic neoplatonic and Aristotelian philosophers distinguished between the "inner" (*bāṭin*) and "apparent" (*ẓāhir*) meaning of certain words and teachings of the Koran, treating the "apparent" meaning as an allegory replete with philosophic truth. Concurrent with this distinction it was often held that the philosophical truths contained in the allegory should be kept secret from the multitude. Following this tradition Moses *Maimonides insists that the true meaning of certain biblical passages, such as Ezekiel's vision of the Chariot, and chapters in Proverbs, etc., lies in the philosophical truths which they express in allegorical fashion and which should not be revealed to the philosophically untrained. Applying the simile of Proverbs 25:11 ("A word fitly spoken is like apples of gold in settings of silver"), he said that "the inner meaning bears the same relation to the apparent one as gold to silver" (Guide, introd.). Here allegory proper comes into its own. The "inner" meaning is considered superior to the "apparent" one since it alone establishes "the truth in all its reality" (*ibid.*). Philosophic truth, as far as it is demonstrable, is thus made the arbiter of biblical exegesis. Maimonides was less radical when he interpreted anthropomorphic or spatial terms applied to God as either homonyms or metaphors. Maimonides cites the rabbinic phrase, "The Torah speaks in the language of men" (BM 31b), in the sense that Scripture speaks of God in terms appropriate to the mental capacity of the multitude (Guide 1:26). This phrase had already been applied in this sense by earlier exegetes and theologians such as Judah *Ibn Quraysh, *Jacob b. Nissim, *Baḥya ibn Paquda, Judah *Halevi and others. The question of the legitimacy of the allegorical method had been raised by Abraham *Ibn Ezra, who rejected the search for hidden meanings (*sodot; ḥidot*) in passages whose plain meaning did not conflict with reason or sense perception. He also asserted that the apparent and the

inner meanings should be allowed to coexist, like body and soul (Commentary on the Torah, introd., method no. 3).

The issue of the merits or demerits of allegorism became pronounced at the close of the 13th century and was keenly contested in the polemical literature of the second *Maimonidean controversy. While Maimonides declared as allegorical all biblical passages (1) announcing a change in the laws of nature (in the messianic age), (2) dealing with the resurrection of the dead, and (3) foretelling the ultimate destruction of the world, he warned (as reported by Joseph ibn *Aknin) against allegorizing biblical laws.

Maimonides interprets Ezekiel's vision of the Chariot as an allegory of metaphysical doctrines conforming to his neoplatonic brand of Aristotelianism, but he saw no compelling reason to allegorize the biblical account of the createdness of the world, maintaining that Aristotle's view of the eternity of the world had not been demonstrated. Other instances of allegorism in Maimonides are that the ladder in Jacob's dream means the ascent of prophetic knowledge; the adulterous wife in Proverbs 7 is an allegory of matter; the Song of Songs is an allegory of man's love for God. Some of Maimonides' successors went beyond the limitations he had imposed upon himself. Following the more radical allegorism of *Averroes, Isaac *Albalag interpreted the biblical account of the creation in the sense of eternal creation. *Levi b. Gershom, taking his cue from Maimonides' cryptic remarks in the *Guide* 2:30, saw in the story of Paradise an allegory of the human soul, its faculties and its rise to felicity. Jacob *Anatoli and *Levi b. Abraham of Villefranche (author of *Livyat Ḥen*) were frequently denounced as radical allegorists. There is, however, little evidence in their works to justify this accusation. The animosity toward allegorism shown by the traditionalists (e.g., Solomon b. Abraham *Adret) stemmed chiefly from their observation that the philosophical interpretation of Scripture tended to weaken practical religious observance. Jacob b. *Reuben, author of *Milḥamot ha-Shem* (12th century), had already polemicized against those who "twist the verses of Scripture by the allegorical method" (*be-derekh dimyon u-mashal*) and thereby "bring themselves into disrepute" (*le-mashal ve-li-sheninah*; ed. J. Rosenthal (1963), 37). The more orthodox type of Jewish philosophy, aroused by the dangers of Averroism, on the one hand, and the rising power of Kabbalah, on the other, did not discard allegorical interpretation but made it subservient to dogmatic beliefs, strongly emphasizing the validity of the literal meaning side by side with the allegorical. Joseph *Albo (*Sefer ha-Ikkarim*, 3:21) pointed out that the Torah was called "testimony" (*edut*) and as such should be taken as literally as would be a witness in court. Hence, its narratives and laws must not be negated through allegorism, notwithstanding the right to see in them symbols of something higher and more precious than the literal sense. Philosophizing preachers like Joshua *Ibn Shuʿayb, Joseph b. Shem Tov *Ibn Shem Tov and his son Shem Tov, Isaac *Arama and others were eager to plumb the deeper meaning of Scripture and rabbinic *aggadah*, laying particular stress on the themes of creation and providence. Their sermons are an interesting blend of homiletics (*derash*) and allegory (*mashal; sod*). Some of them exhibit strong traces of Kabbalistic influence. *Baḥya b. Asher's commentary on the Torah exemplifies the trend to make use of philosophic and kabbalistic interpretations alike. It offers interpretations: (1) by the literal method; (2) by the homiletical method; (3) by the method of reason (*sekhel*), i.e., the philosophical method; and (4) by the method of Kabbalah. Allegorism, then, in its strict sense is here two-faced, rational and mystical.

BIBLIOGRAPHY: W. Bacher, *Die Bibelexegese der juedischen Religionsphilosophen des Mittelalters vor Maimuni* (1892), 8–14; idem, *Die Bibelexege Moses Maimunis* (1897), 8–22; I. Goldziher, *Die Richtungen der islamischen Koranauslegung* (1920); J. Guttmann, in: MGWJ, 80 (1936), 180–4; I. Heinemann, in: *Bericht des juedisch-theologischen Seminars, Breslau* (1935); idem, in: *Mnemosyne*, 5 (1952), 130–8; idem, in: HUCA, 23 pt. 1 (1950–51), 611–43; W. Jaeger, *Early Christianity and Greek Paideia* (1961), 46–68, 127–36; D. Kaufmann, in: *Jahresbericht der Landes-Rabbinerschule in Budapest* (1899), 63–79; H. Lewy (ed.), *Philosophical Writings of Philo* (1946), 12–16; A. Schmiedl, *Studien ueber juedische, insonders juedisch-arabische Religionsphilosophie* (1869), 215–36; L. Strauss, *Philosophie und Gesetz* (1935), 68–86; G. Vajda, *L'amour de Dieu dans la théologie juive du moyen âge* (1957), index, s.v. *Cantique des Cantiques*, and review by A. Altmann in: KS, 34 (1958/59), 53–54; idem, in: *Sefarad*, 10 (1950), 25–71; H.A. Wolfson, *Philo*, 1 (1947), 115–38; A.S. Halkin, in: PAAJR, 34 (1966), 65–76; idem, in: A. Altmann (ed.), *Jewish Medieval and Renaissance Studies* (1967), 165–84; I. Husik, in: JAOS, 1 (1935), Supplement, 22–40; L. Ginzburg, *On Jewish Law and Lore* (1955), 127–50; B. Smalley, *The Study of the Bible in the Middle Ages* (1952). **ADD. BIBLIOGRAPHY:** W.Z. Harvey, in: *Interpretation and Allegory; Antiquity to the Modern Period* (2000), 181–88

[Alexander Altmann]

EXEGESIS AMONG JEWS IN THE MODERN PERIOD

Jewish biblical exegesis in the period of the Enlightenment must be understood mainly against the background of the period itself. The main concern of the Enlightenment among Western European Jewry was the enlightenment and education of the Jews – and the Bible served as a means for achieving this goal. Moses *Mendelssohn, the "father of the Enlightenment" among the Jews and its earliest spokesman, was also the father and founder of the biblical exegesis of the time, through his bilingual project, the German translation of the Bible and its Hebrew *Biur* (*Be'ur*; "commentary"; see above: Translations, German). Mendelssohn's purpose in undertaking this project was twofold. On the one hand, he wished to open to the Jews a gateway to general culture, since he believed that the Bible could serve as a cultural bridge between European Jews and non-Jews. On the other hand, Mendelssohn wanted to educate the Jews toward good taste and to help them develop an aesthetic outlook, especially toward the Bible.

Mendelssohn's German translation of the Bible introduced nothing new in terms of content, but was novel in terms of form. It is written in a literary, ornate German which is aimed at removing the Jews from Yiddish and at bringing them closer to the Enlightenment through knowledge of the

German language and its literature. The writing of the Hebrew "commentary" to the Torah was actually carried out by various people who were commissioned by Mendelssohn, but Mendelssohn's stamp and his viewpoint are manifest in the commentary (particular mention should be made of Solomon *Dubno, who interpreted Genesis, and Naphtali Hirz Wessely, who interpreted Leviticus). The method and approach of Mendelssohn and his group were influenced by contemporary Christian biblical research and commentary. It should be pointed out that in 1753, approximately 15 years before the beginning of the project, three basic works were published which ushered in a revolution in biblical research, each of which reflected a particular approach: R. *Lowth's book on form criticism (*Praelectiones academicae de sacra poësi Hebraeorum; Lectures on the Sacred Poetry of the Hebrews*, 1829); J. *Astruc's work on source criticism (*Conjectures sur les mémoires originaux dont il paroit que Moyse s'est servi pour composer le livre de la Genèse*); and C.F. Houbigont's work on text criticism (*Biblia hebraica cum notis criticis et versione latina ad notas criticas facta*, 4 vols.). (See below, Bible research and criticism). A short while later J.G. Herder's book on Hebrew poetry (*Vom Geist der hebraeischen Poesie*, 1782) and J.G. Eichhorn's introduction to the Old Testament (*Einleitung in das Alte Testament*, 3 vols., 1780–83) were published.

Mendelssohn's "commentary" was first intended to be an explanation of the reasons for translating the Bible, but it broadened into a comprehensive commentary on the entire Pentateuch. The "commentary" places emphasis on grammatical points, cantillation points, and elements of style, and is based both on traditional Jewish exegesis and biblical research. In matters of style, the commentary relies mainly on Lowth and Herder (see the summary of Mendelssohn's aesthetic views in the preface to Ex. 15). The "commentary" on the Pentateuch was written in simple language and in a scholarly Hebrew style, and despite the fact that five authors collaborated in its composition, the unity of language and style was preserved because of Mendelssohn's editing. In the "commentary" Mendelssohn was attempting to establish a single and homogeneous method for the study of the Bible among the Jews, and for this reason early Jewish commentaries do not appear alongside his commentary (for it is, essentially, an eclectic exegesis). The commentary was very popular and was reprinted about 20 times.

Mendelssohn's followers continued with the method established in the "commentary" in interpreting the Prophets and the Hagiographa, but they made no innovations. These interpretations are only a collection of commentaries, particularly from the medieval commentators, but the introductions to these commentaries were influenced by biblical research, especially by Eichhorn's introduction to the Old Testament.

In the generation after Mendelssohn, young Jews studied in the German universities and adopted the critical method which was prevalent there. Thus they moved to critical interpretation, which was also written in German. In the 19th century, German Jews wrote a number of works on biblical research, but the only one who also dealt with exegesis was H. Graetz in his commentaries to the Song of Songs, Ecclesiastes (1871), and Psalms (1881). The Mendelssohnian Enlightenment's view of the Bible as an independent aesthetic, religious, and moral tract found expression only in Western Europe and Italy (see below), while in Central and Eastern Europe, the Bible was viewed mainly from a talmudic perspective, and the approach to the Bible took on the form of "lower criticism," rather than "higher criticism."

Most noteworthy among the commentaries of Eastern Europe is that of Meir b. Jehiel Michael *Malbim (1809–79). While it was written in the period of the Enlightenment, and reflects, in a number of places, influences of the Enlightenment, this commentary is nonetheless an authentic and typical work of "the culture of the ghetto as it developed among the outstanding and brilliant scholars of Eastern Europe" (Segal). This commentary, which follows the method of *pilpul* (casuistry and harmonization), contains *halakhah* and *aggadah*, philosophy and Kabbalah, philological investigation and moralistic homilies. Despite his declaration that he was interpreting the text in accordance with its literal meaning, Malbim did not recognize the boundaries between literal and homiletical exegesis. He collected investigations of style and language, classifying them into 613 rules, corresponding to the number of the commandments of the Torah. He gathered these rules from the Midrash, and added to them some of his own.

In Western Europe, in contrast to Eastern and Central Europe, the Enlightenment penetrated Italy and influenced Jewish Italian commentators, such as Samuel David *Luzzatto (ShaDaL; 1800–60) and others. Luzzatto combined a comprehensive knowledge of traditional Jewish exegesis in all its forms with a knowledge of non-Hebrew biblical research. He did not, however, tread the beaten path, but was both independent and original, disagreeing with both early and late commentators. He drew on early and late commentaries, ancient translations, and Semitic philology. He had a poetic bent, and understood biblical poetry. Like Mendelssohn's, his work was bilingual and included translation and interpretation. He translated and interpreted the Book of Isaiah (1855). His commentary on the Torah was collected for publication from his lectures in the rabbinical seminary in Padua (1871). His commentaries on Jeremiah, Ezekiel, Proverbs, and Job were published by his son (1876).

Luzzatto introduced many new elements in his interpretations and investigations, but at the same time he relied on his predecessors. He introduced the method of textual emendation (outside of the Pentateuch) into Hebrew biblical analysis, his emendations following his own rules of interpretation. The textual emendations he allowed himself to make were based on the incorrect separation of words in the traditional text, similar letters in the ancient Hebrew script and square (Aramaic) characters, dittography, haplography, incorrect vocalization and cantillations, metathesis, and abbreviations. In these emendations Luzzatto used translations and manuscripts of the Bible. His emendations serve as fundamental touchstones in biblical research.

While non-Hebrew biblical research reached its peak and culmination at the end of the 19th century, its influence on Hebrew interpretation was gradual. At the end of the 19th century and at the beginning of the 20th century there were three Hebrew commentators whose exegesis was novel and original: Meir *Friedmann (Ish-Shalom), Benjamin *Szold, and Arnold *Ehrlich. Friedman and Szold did not rely in their commentaries on non-Hebrew criticism, though they were acquainted with it, but rather on the rabbinic scholars and traditional exegesis, while Ehrlich displayed originality, both in relation to traditional Jewish exegesis and non-Hebrew biblical research.

Arnold Ehrlich's writing was bilingual. His biblical commentary on difficult passages, *Mikra ki-Feshuto* (3 vols, 1899–1901), was written, according to him, "in Hebrew for the sake of my brethren and my people who only know Hebrew." He later published an expanded version of this work in German: *Randglossen zur hebraeischen Bibel* (7 vols., 1908–14). He had a free attitude toward the Bible and his approach was almost secular. He directs sharp criticism against the method of the non-Jewish critics, but emphasizes that in his system "interpretation is primary while criticism is secondary." Rather than referring to the Documentary Hypothesis, Ehrlich prefers to assign "early" and "late" dates to specific passages based on linguistic usage, concepts and institutions. Comments on historicity such as the denial of a factual Egyptian enslavement or exodus are buried in notes to specific passages. Exegesis though, remains the major and decisive basis of his work. With his erudition, his knowledge of Semitic languages, and especially his intuition, his interpretations are often very much to the point. Ehrlich's contribution is described by Orlinsky in the following manner: "The *Randglossen* by A.B. Ehrlich ranks as one of the more important and better-known contributions to biblical studies textual and contextual." While his Hebrew commentary contains some minor emendations, Ehrlich's German commentary is replete with emendations. Haran says of Ehrlich's place in the history of Jewish biblical exegesis: "In his partially secular approach to the Bible he did not lag behind the period of the Enlightenment but rather anticipated the national revival. This moment assures his place at the crossroad of the two periods."

In the period of the Enlightenment, Judaism did not liberate itself from a dogmatic approach to the Bible. The extent of the criticism of Jewish scholars depended on the degree of holiness of the particular section of the Bible with which they were dealing. Thus, they dealt mainly with the Hagiographa, less with the Prophets, and very little with the Pentateuch. As has been stated, this investigation dealt with "lower criticism" and not with "higher criticism," which is concerned with the character of the author, the composition of the work, its editing, and its time. The national revival brought about a change and new evaluation of the Bible. Non-Hebrew biblical criticism made deep and incisive incursions into Hebrew literature. The depth of this penetration is reflected in the thought of *Aḥad Ha-Am, "the father of spiritual Zionism," and it was he who wished for the publication of a Hebrew modern, critical interpretation of the Bible. This desire was actually fulfilled by the exegetical activity of Abraham *Kahana.

Abraham Kahana surrounded himself with the best Jewish scholars of Eastern and Western Europe and divided the labor among them (Samuel by M.Z. Segal; Isaiah by S. Krauss; the Minor Prophets by J.B. Weinkopf, D.S. Loewinger, G. Hirschler, M.L. Margolis, and P. Chajes; Psalms by P. Chajes; Song of Songs by A. Kaminka; Lamentations by F. Perles; Esther by G. Hirschler; Daniel by M. Lambert). He himself interpreted much of the remainder (Genesis, Exodus, Numbers, Jonah, Haggai and Zechariah, Proverbs, Job, Ruth, Ecclesiastes, and Ezra and Nehemiah). Although the commentary was not completed (it was published in 1904–1930), until 1990 it was the only multi-volume critical commentary on the Bible in Hebrew. This series is not uniform and includes interpretations of varying value (the best are those of Chajes on Psalms and Krauss on Isaiah). It gives very clear expression to the conclusions of non-Hebrew analytical investigation in Hebrew and Semitic philology, in comparative literature, based on the great discoveries in the ancient East, and in the Documentary Hypothesis in the study of the Pentateuch.

N.H. *Tur-Sinai (Torczyner), who engaged extensively in the study of the Bible and the Hebrew language, collected his commentaries and summarized his studies in this area in his book *Peshuto shel Mikra* (4 vols. in 6, 1962–68). There is a similarity in name, content, and method, between this work and that of Ehrlich. Tur-Sinai's work also reflects a broad knowledge of Semitic languages together with a familiarity with rabbinic scholarship and the early translations, but numerous textual emendations are suggested in his commentary. Of these suggested emendations, there are some which have been accepted by many scholars. Tur-Sinai wrote a special commentary to the Book of Job, which has been published in various corrected editions (2 vols., 1941, 1954; Eng., 1957). This work, which is the crowning achievement of his exegetical career, is also marked by the same characteristics; and the argument that Job was translated from Aramaic sometimes dictates the interpretation. M.Z. *Segal, who interpreted the Book of Samuel within the framework of Kahana's project (1919, 1922), returned to it later and published a new interpretation (1956), which is very different from the original one. Segal also published many investigations on various books of the Bible. Umberto *Cassuto intended to compose a broad and comprehensive interpretation of the Pentateuch, but did not succeed in completing the work. He did interpret the entire Book of Exodus (1952, Eng., 1967) but only managed to reach chapter 13 of his interpretation of Genesis (2 vols., 1944–49; Eng., 2 vols., 1961–64). Cassuto opposed the Documentary Hypothesis in his comprehensive Italian investigation (*La questione della Genesi*, 1934), and briefly in his Hebrew work (*Torat ha-Te'udot*, 1941; *The Documentary Hypothesis*, 1961). A conception of the unity of the Torah and its form served as a basis for Cassuto's philologic-aesthetic approach. In addition to his monumental work *Toledot ha-Emunah ha-Yisre'elit*, Y. *Kaufmann also engaged, toward the end of his life, in interpreting the books of Joshua (1959, 1963²), and Judges (1962), which actually only served to complete and consolidate the foundations of his theories, both on the history of Israelite religion and on the antiquity of the writing and editing of the books. In these outstanding analytical interpretations Kaufmann inveighs strongly against the German school of biblical analysis of Wellhausen and his circle. In his comprehensive introductions, both to the two commentaries as a whole and to the various chapters, he presents a knowledgeable discussion of the Bible and its research. He attempted to prove that his own method was correct and was the one to be preferred. In his commentaries he demonstrated that the method of omitting a verse or dividing it into various sources and different editions is not always essential. The need for a Hebrew multi-volume critical commentary is finally being met by *Mikra le-Yisrael* (1990–).

BIBLIOGRAPHY: M. Soloveitchik and S. Rubashov, *Toledot Bikkoret ha-Mikra* (1925), 126–61; P. Sendler, *Ha-Be'ur la-Torah shel Moshe Mendelssohn ve-Si'ato* (1941); H. Sheli, *Meḥkar ha-Mikra be-Sifrut ha-Haskalah* (1942); M.Z. Segal, *Parshanut ha-Mikra* (1944), 109–26; M. Diman (Haran), in: *Bitzaron*, 21 (1950), 110–4, 174–8, 256–62; 22 (1951), 189–96; 23 (1952), 38–41, 115–26, 187–93; M. Haran, *Biblical Research in Hebrew* (1970); idem, in: *Molad*, 26 (1970), 97–106; HM Orlinsky, in: JQR, 45 (1954/55), 374–412.

[Isaac Avishur]

BIBLE RESEARCH AND CRITICISM

"Research and criticism" of the Bible is, in one sense, as old as, if not older than, the traditional Bible. Some modern scholars have devoted great efforts to the attempt to trace the details of the process whereby the older semi-canonical materials which went into the final shaping of the canon itself were reapplied and made relevant to their day. After the closing of the canon, quite similar methods continued to be used for centuries (see above, Canon). That is to say, from a purely literary or external (as distinguished from a religious or theological) viewpoint, the distinction between canonical and non-canonical literature is artificial.

Increasing attention has been devoted to the study of the history of the interpretation of the Bible as methods and schools have proliferated. It may be observed that, *mutatis mutandis*, the problem has always been how to be both historically faithful to the text's original significance as well as adequately to convey its meaning and relevance to the contemporary situation. Furthermore, it may be asserted that, in general, the precise methods used in this task at any given time tend, up to a point, to be quite similar in both Judaism and Christianity. Thus a certain common influence exerted by the prevailing philosophy of the time is often noticeable: the strong Platonic influences of the early Common Era: the mystical and Aristotelian influences of the Middle Ages: the philosophical impetus provided by the Renaissance: and the rationalism, historicism, existentialism and most recently, post-modernism. Correspondingly, the precise methods in the two communities also often have much in common: the multiple (and often fourfold) senses ascribed to a text in the Middle Ages as well as the specific types of literary and historical investigation employed in modern times.

Nor is it surprising to note a fair amount of interaction and cross-fertilization: developments within Christianity tended to set the general cultural tone and atmosphere, while there was always much in Judaism's retention of the grammatical text (even when interpreted allegorically) which Christianity, especially with its early preference for the Septuagint, was always in danger of forgetting. Jewish influence on Christian interpretation is especially clear in the case of the dependence of the Antiochene school and of Jerome on the rabbis, and the influence especially of Rashi via Nicholas of Lyra and Reuchlin upon Luther, not to speak of the many contributions by modern Jewish scholars. These generalizations begin to hold true as soon as the two streams diverge. It has long been realized that New Testament principles of interpretation had much in common with that of the mainstream of rabbinism (classically in H.L. Strack and P. Billerbeck, *Kommentar zum Neuen Testament aus Talmud und Midrasch*, 1922–56, and J. Bonsirven, *Exégèse rabbinique et exégèse paulinienne*, 1939). More recently, it has become clear from Qumran that the specific apocalyptic motifs of the Essenic stream of Jewish thought were also very influential in early Christianity (see F.F. Bruce, *Biblical Exegesis in the Qumran Texts*, 1959).

Early Moves Toward Critical Study

Much of the intellectual endeavor of both Judaism and Christianity, until well after the Reformation, was directed to Bible study. In retrospect, various individuals and schools seem to stand out as precursors of modern biblical study. Among these must be noted: the Christian school of Antioch and especially Theodore of Mopsuestia (d. c. 428); the philological emphasis of Saadiah Gaon, especially under the influence of the Aristotelian revival in the Muslim world; its sequel in a sense when Aristotelianism conquered the West in the rationalism of Maimonides and somewhat related manifestations in Rashi, David Kimḥi, and Abraham Ibn Ezra within Judaism, and the 12th-century Victorine School, and Nicholas of Lyra in the 13th century among the Christian expositors.

With the Reformation came a tremendous upsurge of emphasis upon literal, "grammatical" exegesis. "Allegory" and multiple interpretations were indignantly rejected – although, by most modern definitions, sometimes retained under a different title. Simultaneously, the Renaissance and its resurgent humanism were placing great stress upon early sources and plain meanings; in comparison with the ecclesiastical revolution it was sometimes hard to say what was cause and what effect. Most significant, however, in terms of future developments, were the extra-ecclesiastic philosophies which began to appear and slowly gained momentum to usher in the "modern" era. The fundamentally new situation which was gradually developing was that the context of Bible study would no longer exclusively be the synagogue, the church and their related yeshivahs, seminaries, and faculties of theology, but the secular university as well. Among the major names which must be mentioned are René Descartes (d. 1650), who with his *Cogito ergo sum*, "I think therefore I am," virtually provided the creed of the rationalism which dominated the century after his death; Benedict *Spinoza, who applied the new thought more specifically to biblical study, including a portentous questioning of the Mosaic authorship of the Pentateuch; Hugo *Grotius, a Dutch jurist, whose probings have sometimes earned him the title of the "father" of the historical-critical method; Gotthold Ephraim *Lessing, with his famous pronouncement that "accidental truths of history can never become proof of necessary truths of reason"; and Immanuel *Kant, whose emphasis upon "practical reason," i.e., man's conscience and its ethical judgments, was to be of incalculable influence in succeeding years. With Kant's divorce of the "phenomenal" and "noumenal" worlds, the stage was set for that loss of the authority of an inspired Scripture and of a sense of the transcendent in general, which dominated most of the succeeding centuries. Much of the new mood was introduced into Judaism especially through Moses Mendelssohn. In both Judaism and Christianity, there was (and sometimes still is) uncompromising resistance to "higher criticism" (i.e., those aspects of biblical criticism which deal with literary analysis and historical and ideological considerations; as opposed to "lower criticism" which deals with the text, canon, etc.) because of its original connection with rationalistic and other anti-supernaturalistic philosophies. In this climate, precursors of the more technical aspects of the critical study of the Bible also began to appear, especially Isaac la *Peyrere and Richard *Simon, who postulated various authors of the Pentateuch, and particularly the 18th-century Jean *Astruc, who first used criterion of different Hebrew names for the deity in Genesis. These and other preliminary critical investigations were summarized and ordered by Johann *Eichhorn in a three-volume work on the Old Testament. Two 18th-century scholars were especially important in developing further the theoretical foundations of the movement, specifically in breaking away from the restraints of ecclesiastical dogma and tradition. Johann Semler (d. 1791), especially in his *Abhandlung zur freien Untersuchung des Kanons,* campaigned for an approach to the Bible exactly "like another book," free from all dogmatic preassumptions. Similarly Johann Gabler (d. 1787), often known as the father of "biblical theology" because of the distinction he advocated between that discipline and the traditional dogmatic theology, urged that the latter should concentrate on biblical teachings of universal relevance, while "biblical theology" should concern itself with historically and temporally conditioned matters.

Nineteenth-Century Pentateuch Criticism and Wellhausen

Critical investigations into the *Pentateuch in particular continued throughout the 19th century by scholars like Martin de Wette (d. 1843), the first to isolate Deuteronomy as a separate source and associate it with Josiah's reformation (II Kings 22), and Heinrich Ewald (d. 1875), a prolific writer who changed his own position repeatedly, thus typifying the exploratory nature of that period's investigations. By 1850, late datings for Daniel, Second Isaiah (i.e., Isaiah 40–66), the second part of Zechariah, and Psalms had become generally accepted, but no unanimity had been reached on the Pentateuch. W. Vatke's recognition of the lateness of the *Grundschrift* (the later "Priestly Document") eventually provided the needed breakthrough, but his thoroughgoing Hegelianism and Ewald's rejection of his views led to a stalemate which was broken only by Wellhausen and his congeners. When this intermediate period (after Eichhorn) came to an end, a certain "critical orthodoxy" was introduced) in the epoch-making *Prolegomena to the History of Israel* of Julius Wellhausen (1844–1918) in 1878 (Eng. tr. 1965). Others beside Wellhausen were influential in the formulation of the final hypothesis and others worked alongside him in its subsequent elaboration, but Wellhausen's work so successfully presented and popularized the approach that few dispute the appropriateness of epithets like "Wellhausenian," "classical criticism," etc.

The great significance of Wellhausen's achievement lay in the fact that it represented not only the latest in a series of isolated critical investigations, but that these were integrated into an entirely new synthesis and reconstruction of the total course of Israel's religious history, to the stages of which the various literary documents were related. Although L. Perlitt (*Vatke und Wellhausen*, 1965) has attempted to disprove it, it still seems that, however indirect, the ultimate philosophical inspiration of Wellhausen's reconstruction was the idealistic monism of Hegel. (For better or for worse, much of the historicism and immanentalism of this period survived even in the later corrections, and it is doubtful if even the most determinedly conservative today have remained uninfluenced by this "Copernican revolution" which stresses that things can be understood only when their history is known.)

Wellhausen postulated a slow evolutionistic rise from the animism of the earliest, "patriarchal" periods to the "ethical monotheism" of especially the eighth-century prophets. The purest of the pentateuchal sources, from this perspective, was judged to be J or the Yahwist (which used the divine name transliterated as YHWH; JHWH in German), dated to the ninth century, followed by a slow but sure degeneration toward formalism and institutionalism in the subsequent sources, E or the Elohist (using the divine name *Elohim*) perhaps a century later, D or the Deuteronomist (the author of the Book of Deuteronomy) with his incipient "biblicism," writing in connection with Josiah's abortive ventures shortly before the fall of Judah, and P (author of the Priestly document) during or after the Exile, providing the constitution for the small semi-independent hierocracy within the vast Persian empire. All of the sources were understood as providing reliable information primarily only of the period of composition, not of the earlier periods which they described. The Pentateuch was allegedly given its final shape by circles akin to P about the time of Ezra. It was asserted that during the same period, and indeed down to that of the Maccabees, the earlier prophecies of doom were supplemented by more optimistic oracles, and most of the psalms, understood mostly as gems of individualistic piety, were also composed. Vast modifications of Wellhausen's synthesis continue to be made, and the underlying unilinear notion of progress in history has been almost totally repudiated; nevertheless, very little scholarship has turned its back on him completely and his influence is still to be widely detected in biblical research.

In general, it is probably true that much Jewish scholarship, even that which was not totally traditionalistic, was initially and, to a degree, still remains rather cool toward the standard results of German biblical scholarship, well aware of the subtle anti-Judaism, if not antisemitism, which by no means necessarily but very often *de facto* accompanies any depreciation of the Old Testament – and it is undeniable that such implications were often present in much of the "classical" critical literature. Prominent 20th century Israeli scholars including U. *Cassuto attacked the hypothesis frontally, and a coolness is apparent in the works of, M.H. *Segal and others. (Y. Kaufmann opposed Welhausen's evolutionary explanation of monotheism and differed on the dating of P but fully accepted the Documentary Hypothesis.)

The Influence of Archaeology

Probably the major development that led to a modification of the Wellhausenian synthesis was archaeology (and it is perhaps in this area and the subsidiary philological ones that modern Jewish scholars, both in Israel and elsewhere, have made their major contributions). Apart from the various particulars, archaeology's contribution can be summed up by saying that it provided an actual, historical context for interpreting ancient Israel's life and literature instead of the *a priori*, philosophic one on which Wellhausen had largely depended. "Biblical Archaeology" was especially prominent in the United States and Israel in the middle decades of the 20th century. For some of its leading practitioners such as W.F. *Albright and Nelson *Glueck, G.E. Wright and Yigael Yadin the general net effect of archaeological discoveries was seen to enhance the general trustworthiness and substantial historicity of the biblical tradition, although not in the naïve, uncritical sense sometimes expressed by the "prove the Bible true" slogan. Israel's military victory in 1967 facilitated the exploration of the west bank of the Jordan River, the heart of ancient Israel, and the Sinai desert. The newer archaeological evidence has undercut the claims of "substantial historicity," but nowhere to the extent claimed by extreme minimalists.

Gunkel and "Form" Criticism

The first "school" to exploit the new resources provided by archaeology was that of *Religionsgeschichte* ("History of Religion") and, closely allied with it, that of form criticism. In both cases, Hermann *Gunkel (1862–1932) was probably the leading spirit, and his name can be used to epitomize a considerable diversity almost to the extent that Wellhausen's name does for the preceding era. Not only the newer discoveries, but also the tradition of romanticism, as exemplified in the studies of Johann *Herder of ancient Hebrew poetry and to a certain extent the theology of Friedrich Schleiermacher (d. 1834), were highly influential in determining the direction of his work. Various anthropological investigations contributed to the new climate as well. During his lifetime, Gunkel's approach often won only very slow and grudging acceptance from his German colleagues schooled in the more classical approaches, but today it can safely be said that even in Germany, Gunkel generally determined the direction of 20th-century biblical research far more directly than Wellhausen.

In essence, Gunkel's thesis was that in ancient society each *Sitz im Leben* ("life-setting") had its own *Gattung* or "form" (pattern, outline, style, etc.), and the latter could really be understood only in the light of the former. In his *Die Sagen der Genesis* ("Legends of Genesis," 1901) and *Einleitung in die Psalmen* ("Introduction to the Psalms," 1933) and a host of other works, he proposed categories which, in the main, are largely still accepted today. A certain sympathy for the ancient literature on its own terms tended to result, as well as a disposition to date the literature, or at least its roots, much earlier than had previously been the case. Even the cult began to receive more sympathetic treatment as indisputably an important component of pre-secular cultures. Similarly, the recognition of the role of memory in ancient cultures, preceding and continuing alongside written materials, led to consideration of the nature of oral tradition as well as of scribal habits and strictly textual criticism. All these aspects of the new movement were developed, especially by Gunkel's successors, in different ways by various groups and individuals too numerous to detail here.

Perhaps the greatest weakness of the central form-critical effort was its very concentration on individual units, thus, ironically, often leading to an atomism quite similar to the older "scissors-and-paste" literary criticism which it had sought to correct. The subsequent corrective movement of "tradition criticism" (so-called if it dealt with oral materials; often called "redaction-criticism" if the subject was written texts) has attempted to compensate for this weakness by trying to ascertain the "laws" and the process by which the individual units were united. Another weakness was the tendency – in practice at least – to assume the non-historicity of the material unless there was overwhelming evidence to the contrary, or at least to argue that the question itself was irrelevant. The more archaeologically oriented scholars in particular took exception to this tendency, arguing that "external evidence" was required in order to test factuality, something which mere literary techniques could never do, and that Israel's own subjectivity made the question of factual reality something which could not simply be ignored. This division of opinion was for a long time the most serious of all within the ranks of 20th-century biblical scholarship. Many aspects of the division as concerns the early (pre-monarchical) history of Israel may be seen in the two major mid-twentieth century histories of Israel by the American John Bright (1959) and the German Martin *Noth (1950). The disposition of some "biblical theology" writers (especially Gerhard von Rad), to argue that Israel's original theological interpretations stand even if there are no factual traditions behind them may be of help to the theologically minded but to few others.

Certain of the *religionsgeschichtliche* developments stemming from Gunkel's work were at least as problematic. Whereas Wellhausenianism and classical liberalism had solved the problem of distance and relevance by a drastic reductionism to what allegedly had timeless truth and value (mostly ethics!), *Religionsgeschichte* tended to accentuate – and often exaggerate – the distance of the material from modern man and its strangeness to him and evidenced little or no concern for the questions of the relevance and factuality of the material, or for the contemporary philosophical and theological debates in general. Furthermore, the exploitation of the many parallels between Israel and her neighbors easily developed into a "parallelomania" (Sandmel) which judged Israel almost totally in the light of her neighbors. The "pan-Babylonianism" of A. *Jeremias, Friedrich *Delitzsch, and H. *Winckler was one of the major manifestations of this mood, but it continued to some extent in the later "myth and ritual" school of S.H. Hooke, the Uppsala school of I. Engnell, and in the works of Sigmund *Mowinckel. (Not quite so all-encompassing and pretentious were the collections of comparative materials in the many works of J. *Morgenstern and T.H. *Gaster.) Impressive theories about "divine kingship" in Israel and about an alleged autumnal "New Year" festival, strongly patterned along foreign lines are especially associated with Mowinckel. Rival theories, drawing more upon the biblical sources as they now stand, were developed especially by Artur Weiser and Hans-Joachim Kraus. One of the most devastating critiques ever leveled against the cultic "patternism" common to many of these efforts was H. *Frankfort's *Kingship and the Gods* (1948).

Furthermore, in connection with many of the theories of this type, the common assumption was that the cult created its own supporting stories which were later "historified," rather than celebrating historical events to begin with. Similarly, many traditio-historical theories saw the cult as the major factor in not only the production of the stories but in their canonical ordering and interrelationship as well. One of the more curious developments in the attempt to understand biblical antiquity on its own terms was the attempt to isolate "Hebrew thought," especially in contrast to "Greek" (classically perhaps in T. Boman, *Hebrew Thought Compared With Greek*, 1960). While this line of investigation was helpful in excluding certain alien concerns of Western philosophy and rationalism, it easily left the impression that the difference was intrinsically linguistic or ethnic, rather than a matter of pre-secular and pre-philosophic (not "prelogical"!) forms of expression. Sometimes this approach was confused with "biblical theology," and at other times it confused the "mythologic" of paganism with Israel's "empirical logic" (the terms are Albright's) in an indiscriminate "primitivism" (the weakness of J. Pedersen's *Israel* (1926), which, however, is still useful). James Barr leveled especially devastating critiques at this approach. H. Frankfort's *The Intellectual Adventure of Ancient Man* (1946; later reprinted under the title *Before Philosophy*) remains an outstanding study.

"Biblical Theology"

In a way, the last of the supplements to classical Wellhausenianism, although it often overlapped with the movements already noted above, was that of "biblical theology," a movement that initially attracted minimal attention in Judaism. Its roots lay in the post-World War I disillusionment with both the reductionism of the earlier liberalism and the deliberate "irrelevance" of *Religionsgeschichte* (as expressed also in the "neo-orthodoxy" of the Swiss Reformed theologian Karl Barth (1886–1968) in particular). While unwilling to return to the pre-Kantian "orthodoxy" of an objective norm in an inspired Scripture, this movement did strongly affirm the truth of the Bible's "record of revelation" because it allegedly "rang true" to man's existential condition. It revolted especially against the earlier critical tendency to limit criticism to questions of date, authorship, sources, etc., without pressing on seriously to consider the message. No doubt, since Gabler's manifesto, most "biblical theology" had in actuality been little but "history of Israel's religion."

Most work in this field tended to have somewhat of a *Heilsgeschichte* ("salvation history") character. However, no unanimity at all was reached concerning the order or system which was most appropriate, and on this reef the movement itself eventually foundered. Among the major names may be mentioned: Edmond Jacob (1955) who produced a theology using quite traditional categories; Walther Eichrodt (1933) who tried to arrange his material around the internal biblical category of *covenant; and Gerhard von Rad (1957), author of the last and perhaps the greatest of the works of this school, who attempted to return to a more strictly chronological arrangement, thus abandoning all attempts to find any real internal unity in the material. Hence it became plain that this movement too had come full circle, and in subsequent years works on the "religion" of Israel again began to supplant "theologies." Interestingly, Jews showed little interest in biblical theology in its heyday but now seem increasingly open to the enterprise (Brettler in bibliography).

Finally, there is the ecumenical spirit of the age, which has seen Roman Catholicism join most of the rest of Western Christendom and Judaism in the historical-critical enterprise. Jewish and Catholic Bible scholars now participate in collaborative scholarly projects that were once exclusively Protestant. (Oddly, despite Jewish participation in Protestant translations, no Christian scholars have participated in the translations or commentaries sponsored by the Jewish Publication Society.) To the extent that this cooperation has progressed beyond theologically neutral philological matters, probably two traditional blindspots of the previously dominant Protestantism appear to be increasingly corrected: its disregard of cult and ritual, and its tendency to view "Torah" as essentially legalistic, and less worthy an object of study than the more "spiritual" parts of the Bible.

Archaeological Evidence

The contributions of archaeology, beyond those already mentioned, are especially significant in the area of lexicography and textual criticism. In general, the literary finds discovered since 1929 at Ras Shamra (the ancient *Ugarit destroyed in the 12th century B.C.E.) on the northern Phoenician coast are easily the most important for biblical studies. Here in three major epics and much other literature in the *Ugaritic language, there are not only classical versions of the paganism which was Yahwism's major competitor, but also the "language of Canaan" as it was spoken at a time and place not too far removed from "biblical Hebrew" (i.e., mostly, the pre-Exilic dialect of Jerusalem). As a result, all sorts of obscurities in the older biblical text (e.g., Ex. 15, Judg. 5, etc.) can be clarified, as well as many features in even younger texts where tradition apparently transmitted the consonantal text faithfully, but using idioms which the masoretes or other later commentators no longer understood (e.g., an "enclitic *mem*," various meanings of *lamed*, etc.)

H.L. *Ginsberg was among the earliest to recognize and explore the potential of Ugaritic for biblical research and many others have followed suit. It is now clear that ancient Israel was heir to old poetic traditions of Syria-Palestine. The central Syrian city of *Emar, which only began to be unearthed in 1972, has yielded much important comparative material relating to Israelite religion. Biblicists have likewise benefited greatly from having access to the documents published in the ongoing Finnish series State Archives of Assyria (1987ff).

The *Dead Sea Scrolls have been of great importance for an understanding of the complexities of the Judaism of the times as well as of the origins of Christianity. For the Old Testament, however, their significance is largely limited to the field of textual criticism – where their influence has been nearly revolutionary. Above all, since the oldest manuscripts previously known had been nearly a millennium younger, the Qumran scrolls eliminated with one stroke much of the great skepticism which had previously reigned in some quarters concerning the age and reliability of the texts. At the same time, the variation in detail in some of the Hebrew manuscripts showed that no absolutely standardized and uniform text had been fixed at the beginning of the Christian era.

Even more significant, in a way, was the discovery of Hebrew manuscripts in recensions agreeing with the Septuagint and the Samaritan Pentateuch. In the past, the pendulum had swung from one extreme to another in the comparative evaluation of the Hebrew text and the versions; in general, "Wellhausenianism," true to its anti-traditional stance in general, had preferred the versions, while some later correctives discounted them almost entirely. Now it increasingly became plain that all three streams had equally ancient roots, that no *a priori* preferences could be maintained in favor of any of the three, and that, in all likelihood, the original tradition was richer than any one of its three major later derivatives. That is, in contrast to much of the textual criticism of the 19th century which attempted, often on the basis of highly subjective assumptions, to eliminate all the later additions and restore the original "pure" text, it now seems likely that the text has suffered more from losses than from glosses. Apparently, as an official rabbinic or masoretic text gradually came into existence around the beginning of the Christian era, at least three major attempts to revise the Septuagint in conformity with it can be traced. (See F.M. Cross, "The Contribution of the Qumran Discoveries to the Study of the Biblical Text," in IEJ, 16 (1966), 81ff.; E. Tov, *Textual Criticism of the Hebrew Bible* (2001).

[Horace D. Hummel / S. David Sperling (2nd ed.)]

Developments in the 1970s

Bible research and criticism was actively pursued in the 1970s. Yet, despite the intensive discussions and new publications, it is often difficult to discern new major trends, motifs, or "schools."

This situation is partly the result of the passing from the scene of many of the great pacesetters of the previous generation (e.g., Albright, Wright, Mowinckel) without obvious successors; partly the increasing specialization of a burgeoning discipline, and partly, apparently, a reflection of the increasing fragmentation of much Western thought in general. Certainly in the United States, the proliferation of departments of religion at universities has been a major catalyst in the change.

The period witnessed frontal attacks on historical critical method, not only from traditionalist circles, but even from within the ranks themselves. Often it is a matter of semantics, but the challenge nonetheless bears witness to the intensity of the ferment. Thus, W. Wink (The *Bible in Human Transformation*, 1973) decries the objectivism of much biblical study, and proposes paying more attention to the interpreter's subjectivity. With that new approach, "liberation theology," the feminist movement, and other contemporary sociopolitical trends have left their mark. Most, however, do not think so much of abandoning the "method" as of perfecting it somehow.

Although source-critical investigations of a more or less classical type certainly continue, together with it there have appeared massive assaults on the classical results. R. Rendtorff (*Das Überlieferungsgeschichtliche Problem des Pentateuch*, 1977) attacks the traditional documentary hypothesis, and regards the Pentateuch as formed by the linking together of self-contained units which developed independently of each other. Among the less radical, the centrality of the "Deuteronomists" has generally become more axiomatic and pivotal than ever, so much so that some complain of a "pan-Deuteronomism"; cf. E. Nicholson *Preaching to the Exiles* (1970), M. Weinfeld (*Deuteronomy and the Deuteronomic School*, 1972) makes those circles the redactors of the Priestly document, but in other quarters "P" is subject to even more revisionism. Menaḥem *Haran (*Temples and Temple Service in Ancient Israel*, 1978) regards "P" as having reached literary form already before the Exile, while Frank Cross (*Canaanite Myth and Hebrew Epic*, 1973) doubts if it ever was more than a supplement.

Form-critical efforts of the more classical type also continue, but there is evidence of a certain exhaustion, if not abandonment. A plateau may have been reached, and the results to date are conveniently summarized in: John H. Hayes (ed.), *Old Testament Form Criticism* (1974).

In reaction to the "diachronic" or atomistic tendencies of both source-criticism and form-criticism, however, the general trend of the period has clearly been in more holistic or "synchronic" directions. Although of various sorts, they often overlap. Most novel has probably been French-based "structuralism," rooted in the theories of de Saussure, Levi-Strauss, Barthes, and others. It searches for "deep structures" or modalities apart from the author's intentionality. No clear verdict is yet possible, but structuralism's preference for philosophic universals over historical particularities and its dependence upon an esoteric, almost impenetrable, jargon appear to becloud its future. Probably the best general introduction to the approach is R. Polzin, *Biblical Structuralism* (1977).

Also French, but closer to the center of gravity, is the work of Paul Ricoeur (*The Conflict of Interpretations*, (1974), and many other works), who increasingly attracts a following. Ricoeur speaks of a "second naiveté" enabling us to read the ancient texts again with a "hermeneutic of belief," which is "beyond the deserts of criticism."

Less philosophically oriented is the "rhetorical criticism" of Muilenburg and his disciples, which notes overarching unities of stylistic and compositional features in the finished product. A memorial volume to Muilenburg, entitled *Rhetorical Criticism* (J. Jackson and M. Kessler, eds., 1974) explores many of the issues involved. A more extensive example of this type of research is: W. Holladay, *The Architecture of Jeremiah 1–20* (1976). Not immediately aligned, but of the same general type is: D.J.A. Clines, *The Theme of the Pentateuch* (1978).

Mainstream efforts to compensate for the centrifugality of much traditional criticism, however, are best characterized by the label "tradition-history/criticism." In fact, if anything today might be labeled "critical orthodoxy," it would be this approach. Major effort is devoted to attempting to reconstruct the process by which discrete traditions are combined, expanded, supplemented, reinterpreted, and actualized in the course of time, in response to new historical stimuli. The presumably later levels no longer tend to be discounted as "ungenuine" or "epigonic," but an effort is made to listen to the "whole choir of witnesses" – or at least to that one (not necessarily the earliest) which seems most relevant. One can compare two applications of this method in the commentaries on the minor prophets of H.W. Wolff and J. Mays. An excellent, popular introduction is W. Rast, *Tradition History and the Old Testament* (1973). Many issues are thoroughly aired in D. Knight, (ed.), *Tradition and Theology in the Old Testament* (1977), and G. Coats and B. Long (eds.), *Canon and Authority* (1977).

As the last two titles indicate, such literary concerns inevitably overlap with the more theological issues of the nature of biblical authority. The "canonical criticism" of James Sanders (*Torah and Canon*, 1972) attempts to interpret traditional-historical pursuits in relation to the shaping and significance of a *canon*. Brevard Childs goes further. In a series of efforts, beginning especially with *Biblical Theology in Crisis* (1970) and culminating in his *Introduction to the Old Testament as Scripture* (1979), Childs argues that, in the formation of a canon, the literature was deliberately loosened from its original historical particularity in order to expose and release its universal, transhistorical significance. Thus, the normative meaning of a passage is to be found on its canonical level, not at any of the earlier stages (though their existence is not denied, nor the usefulness of the search for them entirely repudiated). Most scholars, however, are not prepared to go that far, and continue to affirm the potential authority of also precanonical stages. Within the same period, J. Blenkinsopp (*Prophecy and Canon*, 1977) has resuscitated an essentially Wellhausenian picture of the canonical process.

In some respects, Childs' unique isagogics is about as close as the period has come to "biblical theology." Although followed by others, he once pronounced that movement as good as dead. Von Rad continues to cast a long shadow, however, and, often following his lead, there have been many investigations of the theologies of individual writers or traditions. But, in spite of much discussion, no agreement could be reached on what "center," if any, could be found in the Bible. Cf. G. Hasel's survey *Old Testament Theology: Basic Issues in the Current Debate* (1972).

Only toward the end of the period have more ambitious "theologies" begun to become frequent again. The noteworthy titles are (in alphabetical order; the first three, 1977): R. Clements, *Old Testament Theology*; W. Kaiser, *Toward an Old Testament Theology*; S. Terrien, *The Elusive Presence*; C. Westermann, *Theologie des Alten Testaments in Grundzüge* (1978); and W. Zimmerli, *Old Testament Theology in Outline* (1972, 1977^2, 1978, ET).

The situation is equally confused in the area of archaeology. There has certainly been no abatement of scientific excavation in biblical lands, especially not in Israel (and it is impossible to note here even the major ones). In fact, so much raw material is accumulating that even specialists are scarcely able to stay abreast of it, and there is great concern here about the "knowledge explosion." Furthermore, there is no consensus on how to deploy the material vis-à-vis biblical studies. The very term "*biblical* archaeology" is increasingly coming under fire. Some of the debate is merely semantic, and some of the objection to the term is well founded (sometimes shoddy workmanship and attempts to "prove" the Bible true). But, on the whole its rejection scarcely conceals a trend away from primary concern with *biblical* history and culture to broader anthropological interest, in which the Bible is often only one concern among many. Parallel to the shift in archaeological goals has been a shift in results, or, at least, in interpretation of the finds (which is cause, and which effect, is debatable). The synthesis hammered out by Albright, Wright, Glueck, etc., ought to defend at least the "substantial historicity" of the biblical traditions about the patriarchs, the exodus, and the conquest. In the past decade, however, that construction has increasingly been assailed from all sides. At the extreme, T. Thompson (*The Historicity of the Patriarchal Narratives*, 1974) and J. van Seters (*Abraham in History and Tradition*, 1975) have championed a return to a sort of prearchaeological *status quo ante*, largely divesting the patriarchs of historicity altogether, and viewing those traditions as mainly postexilic constructs in support of the land claims of that time.

Tradition and Interpretation (G. Anderson, ed., 1979), containing essays by members of the "British Society for Old Testament Study," summarizes developments between Rowley's predecessor's work (1951; see bibliography) and about 1974. To the annual *Book List* of that same society may now be welcomed the American *Old Testament Abstracts* (since February 1978), reviewing also periodical literature. J.W. Rogerson, *Anthropology and the Old Testament* (1978) offers a succinct overview of once popular approaches, which now appear to be in decline. *Encounter with the Text. Form and History in the Hebrew Bible* (M.J. Buss, ed., 1979) contains a helpful review of contemporary methodological competitors. B. Childs' *Introduction to the Old Testament as Scripture* (1979) begins each chapter with a masterful survey of recent research usually highlighting diversity and often mutual incompatibility as a backdrop for his own proposals (see above). *Israelite and Judean History* (J. Hayes and J. Mueller, eds.; 1977) offers an indispensable summary of recent developments in that field. Finally, H. Frei, *The Eclipse of Biblical Narrative* (1974) must be included for its penetrating analysis of the development of modern attitudes toward biblical history. The archaeological evidence itself continues to be indirect, at best, but especially the Ebla finds (see Bible: Related Epigraphic Finds) have raised the possibility that Abraham should be dated some five hundred years earlier than the previous consensus (c. 2300 B.C.E. instead of 1800, i.e., in the "Early Bronze" rather than the "Middle Bronze" period). Excavations in Jordan, at and around Bab-edh-Dhra, near the southeast corner of the Dead Sea, may point in the same direction, conceivably having even located the cities of Sodom and Gomorrah.

Neither has archaeological evidence always been "cooperative," perhaps most notably in Aharoni's various excavations in the Negev. Increasingly ambivalent evidence has been matched by a tendency to think of an "infiltration" rather than a conquest, and to view the process more from a sociological aspect. Some regard "Israel" as entirely a later idealization, it not being a conceptual entity until the monarchy. Mendenhall advanced one version of this thesis in his *Tenth Generation* (1973), as did C.H. de Geus in The *Tribes of Israel* (1976), and, more radically, Gottwald in The *Tribes of Yahweh* (1979). The "nomadic ideal," on which some of the older constructs were based, has been demolished and replaced by a theory of "transhumance" (seasonal migration with flocks) in V.H. Matthews, *Pastoral Nomadism in the Mari Kingdom* (1978).

The hypothesis of an Israelite "amphictyony," which a previous generation regarded as all but established, has been almost completely abandoned. R. de Vaux took strong exception to it in his incomplete *Early History of Israel* (ET, 1978) and A.E. Mayes reached similar conclusions in his *Israel in the Period of the Judges* (1974). With the fall of the amphictyonic hypothesis, the viability of various other once favored hypotheses has been jeopardized, especially that of an early Israelite "covenant renewal festival" and its various spinoffs. A more sociological approach to the phenomenon of prophecy may be noted in this connection: R. Wilson, *Prophecy and Society in Ancient Israel* (1980).

The wisdom corpus has been perhaps the major beneficiary of the newer mood in biblical studies. Not only has there been concern to redress the previous "benign neglect" of that literature, but the surfeit of "*Heilsgeschichte*" and the ascendancy of the more introspective and immantalistic fashions has made "Wisdom" very congenial. Von Rad, developing ideas already set forth in his *Old Testament Theology*, has again set the pace in his *Wisdom in Israel* (1970) (although, it should be noted, his proposal that apocalyptic was an offshoot primarily of wisdom rather than of prophecy, has not been generally accepted). Out of the vast literature, Perdue's important *Wisdom and Cult* (1977) calls for special mention. In it he demonstrates that the ancient wisdom both in Israel and surrounding cultures did not assume the simply anti-cultic posture, which earlier writers had tended to assume.

In general, research into Israel's cultus seems increasingly to be moving toward relative objectivity, at least in contrast to the pejorative dismissal or the bondage to patternistic dogmas, from which it once suffered. A major contribution came in M. Haran's, *Temples and Temple Service in Ancient Israel* (1978), putting together studies of tabernacle-temple ritual theory accumulated over the years. Even sacrifice, long the stepchild of cultic studies in spite of its obvious prominence in the biblical texts, has been accorded attention; particularly to be noted are B.A. Levine, *In the Presence of the Lord* (1974), and J. Milgrom, *Cult and Conscience* (1976).

Apocalyptic literature has also moved toward center stage in recent years, probably partly in resonance with the "apocalyptic" quality of much contemporary history. An increasingly popular construct is that of sharp polarization after the Exile, with the priestly party (Ezekiel, Ezra, etc.) seizing the reins of power, and the more utopian losers (beginning with Deutero-Isaiah) increasingly withdrawing into an otherworldly apocalypticism. O. Plöger (*Theocracy and Eschatology*, 1959; ET 1968) had earlier developed this view, and P. Hanson (The *Dawn of Apocalyptic*, 1975) has given it wide currency in the United States; cf. also D. Petersen, *Late Israelite Prophecy*, 1977). In this scenario, Chronicles is sometimes seen to reflect a mediating, compromise stance (cf., for example, H. Williamson, *Israel in the Books of Chronicles*, 1977). Among the many studies and commentaries on Daniel, worthy of special mention is J. Collins, *The Apocalyptic Vision of the Book* of Daniel (1977).

Recent study of the psalter, in contrast to the above areas, does not appear to describe so marked a contrast to earlier work. The older cultic approach appears to thrive only in England: J.H. Eaton, *Kingship and the Psalms* (1976; cf. his *Festal Drama in Deutero-Isaiah*, 1979); A.R. Johnson, *The Cultic Prophet in Israel's Psalmody* (1979); and J. Gray. The *Biblical Doctrine of the Reign of God* (1979). In contrast to that more corporate accent, there are signs that the pendulum may be swinging back to a more individualistic perspective; a harbinger may be R. Albertz, *Persönliche Frömmigkeit und offizielle Religion* (1979).

Finally, the continuing intense research into the nature of biblical poetry may be noted. The pioneering study of F. Cross and D. Freedman has been reprinted (*Studies in Ancient Yahwistic Poetry* (1975)). Other important investigations include D. Robertson, *Linguistic Evidence for Dating Early Hebrew Poetry* (1972) and M. O'Connor, *Hebrew Verse Structure* (1980). It is apparent, however, that in this area also consensus is far off.

[Horace D. Hummel]

Developments in the Late 20th Century

The last thirty years of the 20th century were momentous in biblical scholarship. The feminist movement brought women scholars into a field that had been almost exclusively male, and in addition, added a feminist dimension to biblical criticism that male scholars had often ignored. In Orthodox Jewish circles in Israel and to a lesser extent in the United States, text-critical and historical study of the Bible became increasingly tolerated, if not whole-heartedly embraced. In the United States, the academic legitimation of ethnic studies, including Jewish studies, the rise of the Christian religious right with its bibliocentrism, and court decisions permitting the teaching of religion in publicly funded schools made for heightened interest in Bible. One result of increased undergraduate instruction in Bible was the "Bible as Literature" movement, now in decline. In contrast to classical "literary criticism" of the Bible, the "literature" approach focused on the final form of the text from a literary-aesthetic point of view, often borrowing methods employed in criticism of world literature after they had passed their prime in their original settings. Ignoring the inconsistencies and inner contradictions of texts resulting from multiple authorship and concentrating on uncovering the "integrated literary whole" (Alter) of the final editor or redactor, the new literary reading made the Bible more accessible to a wider public whose members did not require competence in the increasingly refined text-critical methods or in the ancient literatures that had themselves influenced the Bible. Among the earlier borrowed approaches was structuralism, which asserted the existence of binary oppositions that structure human thought that could be viewed objectively by an observer and could unlock the actual meanings of a text. The weakness of structuralism lay in the simple fact that different readers failed to agree on what constituted an objective understanding. In opposition to structuralism, reader-response theory focused on the role of the reader in progressively producing meaning against the background of the interpretative communities to which the reader belonged. The parameters of meaning would be fixed by the communities. For example, readers of the Old Testament in Christian communities would produce meaning different from communities of rabbinic Jews. A different attack on structuralism was mounted by post-structuralism, or deconstruction, famously associated with the name of the philosopher Jacques *Derrida (1930–2004), which attacked the notion of binary opposition as artificial. Applied to biblical texts (as well as others), deconstruction frankly abandoned the attempt to understand the meaning that an author might have wished to convey in favor of engaging the text and discovering the ways in which it "inscribes" power and privilege. Deconstruction, along with post-Freudian psychoanalytic perspectives, neo-Marxism. M. Foucault's (1926–1984) attention to the complex relations between power and "discourses," and F. Jameson's identification of the contemporary focus on the present and the consequent loss of connection to history, are often grouped under the rubric of post-modernism. As applied to the Bible, post-modernist interpretation resurrected the pre-critical lack of interest in the temporal distance between the biblical text and the contemporary audience. Borrowing the notion of undecidability from physics, post-modernism maintained the impossibility of deciding between two (or more) competing interpretations, harking back to the pluriform approaches of medieval Christianity and Judaism. A useful corrective to modern notions that one could recover the "original meaning" of an ancient text with full confidence, post-modernism tended to reveal more about the interpreter than about the Bible.

The last decade of the twentieth century inaugurated the Minimalist-Maximalist debate. Primarily associated with the names of the Sheffield scholar Philip Davies and the Copenhagen scholars Niels Lemche and Thomas Thompson, the Minimalists (sometimes called "Revisionists") argue for very late datings of the books of the Bible, sometimes characterizing the Bible as a Hellenistic book. They claim, in addition, that the Jewish community of post-exilic times was a mixed population not continuous with the Iron Age people who lived in the central mountain regions of Israel. Accordingly, Minimalists maintain that the biblical narratives covering the period from Abraham to the fall of Jerusalem in 586 lack probative value, and that "Ancient Israel" is a modern scholarly misconstruction. "Maximalists" covers a broader range than the term might imply, including scholars who are skeptical of the biblical accounts of enslavement, exodus and conquest as well as some who continue to maintain the existence of a historical Abraham. Maximalists are united in their belief that the Bible and archaeological evidence clearly establish the existence of an ancient Israel, the contours of whose history are recoverable. The Minimalist critique of earlier overly nthusiastic claims of biblical historicity has proved useful. For their part though the Minimalists have exhibited a tendency to deny archaeological evidence contrary to their position and to accuse archaeologists of outright forgery.

[S. David Sperling (2nd ed.)]

See also *History, *Moses, *Patriarchs, *Pentateuch, *Prophets and Prophecy, *Psalms, *Wisdom Literature.

BIBLIOGRAPHY: Major works have been included in the text. Much further recent bibliography and summary of the last century's developments are found in Herbert Hahn, *The Old Testament in Modern Research*, with a survey of recent literature by H.D. Hummel (1970²). Major essays by specialists on recent developments up to publication date are found in H.H. Rowley (ed.), *The Old Testament in Modern Study* (1951). Many of the pioneering essays themselves are reprinted and interpreted in Samuel Sandmel's handy *Old Testament Issues* (1968). Other major studies include L. Diestel, *Geschichte des Alten Testaments in der christlichen Kirche* (1869); F.W. Farrar, *History of Interpretation* (1886); H.-J. Krauss, *Geschichte der historisch-kritischen Erforschung des Alten Testaments von der Reformation bis zur Gegenwart* (1969²); C. Kraeling, *The Old Testament since the Reformation* (1955); B. Smalley, *The Study of the Bible in the Middle Ages* (Oxford, 1952²); R. Grant, *A Short History of the Interpretation of the Bible* (New York, 1963²), and various articles in the *Interpreter's Dictionary of the Bible* (1962) and vol. 1 of *The Interpreter's Bible* (1952); *Tradition and Interpretation* (G. Anderson, ed., 1979); *Old Testament Abstracts* (1978–),. W. Rogerson, *Anthropology and the Old Testament* (1978); M.J. Buss (ed.), *Encounter with the Text. Form and History in the Hebrew Bible* (1979); B. Childs' *Introduction to the Old Testament as Scripture* (1979); J. Hayes and J. Mueller (eds.);*Israelite and Judean History* (1977); H. Frei, *The Eclipse of Biblical Narrative* (1974). **ADD. BIBLIOGRAPHY:** R. Alter, *The Art of Biblical Narrative* (1981); idem, *The World of Biblical Literature* (1992); A. Berlin and M. Brettler, "The Modern Study of the Bible," in: idem (eds.), *The Jewish Study Bible* (2004), 2084–96; S.D. Sperling, "Modern Jewish Interpretation," ibid, 1908–19; M. Brettler, in, *Journal of Religion*, 77 (1997), 563–83; A. Adam, "Post-Modern Biblical Interpretation," in: DBI, 2:305–08; T. Beal et al, "Literary Theory, Literary Criticism, and the Bible," in: DBI, 2:79–85; E. McKnight, "Reader Response Criticism," in: DBI, 2:370–73; J. Berlinerblau, in, *Hebrew Studies*, 45 (2004), 9–26; W.G. Dever, *What Did the Biblical Writers Know and When Did They Know It?* (2001); P.R. Davies, *In Search of "Ancient Israel"* (1992); N. Lemche, *The Israelites in History and Tradition* (1998); T. Thompson, *The Mythic Past: Biblical Archaeology and the Myth of Israel* (1998); K. Kitchen, *On the Reliability of the Old Testament* (2003); Z. Zevit, in, Biblica, 83 (2002), 1–27.

RELATED EPIGRAPHIC FINDS

Archaeological excavation in Israel and the neighboring Lands of the Bible since the 1970s has added much new inscriptional material to the store of texts which illuminate diverse aspects of life in Ancient Israel and its surroundings. Unfortunately, numerous forgeries have appeared on the antiquities market and all material whose provenance is unknown must be treated with suspicion. The more significant finds are noted here:

(1) Arad ostraca
(2) Khirbet al-Qom
(3) Kuntillet 'Ajrud
(4) Seals and bullae
(5) Deir-'Alla texts
(6) Tel al-Rimah stele
(7) Iran stele
(8) Tel Dan Inscription
(9) Ammonite Inscriptions
(10) Ketef Hinnom
(11) Philistine ostraca
(12) Edomite

Arad Ostraca

In the debris of the Judahite fortress of Arad, over 100 inscribed sherds, seals and vessels were recovered. This singular find doubled the available corpus of Hebrew inscriptions and brought to light details concerning the organization and the functioning of a royal outpost during the 10th–6th centuries B.C.E. The ostraca record the receipt and distribution of food supplies in the eastern Negev, frequently to Kittite (Greek?) mercenaries, under the supervision of Elyashib, perhaps commandant at Arad. (See, e.g., Nos. 1, 2, 4, 7 *et al.*) One text warns of impending Edomite attacks and orders the dispatch of army units to Ramot Negev (see No. 24). A ration list employing Egyptian Hieratic signs for the numerals and an Egyptian measure of volume recovered from a late 7th-century level, testifies to the presence of Egyptians at Arad, under circumstances which remain obscure (No. 25; cf. 34 made up entirely of Hieratic numerals). A number of texts relate to the local sanctuary at Arad, the first such sanctuary to be excavated. The names of many priestly families are recorded, perhaps for purposes of tithing and gifts. (E.g., Korahites, Meremot, Pashhur; see Nos. 49, 50, 54, 103–104). Finally, an intriguing fragment of a letter, seemingly written by a Judahite king, mentions a king of Egypt (No. 88).

Khirbet El-Qom

Located West of Hebron in the hills of ancient Judah, the site whose Arabic name means "ruins of the heap/ tribe" may be ancient Makkedah. An eighth-century tomb inscription for one Uriyahu, difficult to read, refers to YHWH and *<ṭrth*, this last somehow related to *Asherah the goddess or a cultic object of the same name, both of which the biblical writers strongly disapprove. If the reference is to the goddess, the text appears to show that Yahweh was believed by some to have a consort. (Cf. the next paragraph.)

Kuntillet 'Ajrud

Numerous Hebrew and Phoenician inscriptions written on plaster and clay and engraved on stone were recovered at Kuntillet 'Ajrud ("Hill of the water- source"), a site near the main road midway between the southern Mediterranean coast and Eilat. These texts coordinate historically with Judah's renewed activity in the south in the mid-9th century B.C.E. under king Jehoshaphat and his son (cf. I Kings 22:49). At the same time, the script, dialectal features of the texts, and the place name Samaria show Northern Israelite connections perhaps reflecting the good relations between Judah and Israel described in

I Kgs 22. The inscriptions refer to YHWH of Teman, as well as Yahweh of Samaria followed by *<¡rth*. The excavator conjectures that these religious references may indicate the presence of a traveler's chapel at this Negev way-station. Both at this site and at Khirbet El-Qom, whenever a name contains a divine element, it is *yh* or *yhw*, which may, or may not, be significant (Heide in Bibliography). The artistic remains at the site are also of great interest.

Seals and Bullae

Of the numerous stamp seals which have come to light, a few deserve individual mention. The first bears the inscription: [Belonging to Ze]charyau, priest of Dor and may be evidence for priestly activity at a local cult site in the coastal city of Dor. A second seal, preserved only on a bulla, reads: Governor of the City. The paleography and the pronounced Assyrian influence in motif design of the two standing figures suggest that the seal belonged to a senior officer in the Jerusalem administration in the mid-7th century B.C.E. From the same collection as this seal are three others which belonged to personalities who figured in the life of the prophet Jeremiah: Berechiah (Baruch), son of Neriah, his personal scribe (cf. Jer. 36:4); Seriah, son of Neriah (Jer. 51:59), and Jerahmeel (Jer. 36:26), officials at the court of Zedekiah.

A most unusual find of this category is the cache of more than 70 seals and bullae from an unrecorded site in the Jerusalem region dating from the early years of the Judean restoration (end of the 6th century B.C.E.). The stamp of a new governor of the province of Yehud (Judah), Elnathan, and that of his female servant Shelomith, point to the official nature of this collection. Furthermore, the administrative independence of Judah from Samaria prior to the arrival of Nehemiah (c. 445 B.C.E.) is affirmed by the governor's seal.

Deir-'Alla Texts

On the Deir-ʾAlla texts, see *Balaam.

Among the inscriptions in the Akkadian language and in cuneiform script relevant to biblical history are two royal stelae of the New-Assyrian period.

Tel al-Rimah Stele

A stele of Adad-nirari III (810–783 B.C.E.) discovered at Tel al-Rimah, Iraq, commemorates the king's military victories, especially in the west, which were probably accomplished during several campaigns to the area. Among the tributaries is Jehoash, king of Israel (*Iu<asu Samerinâ, Jehoash*, the Samarian). According to biblical records, it was during the reign of King Jehoash (800–784 B.C.E.) that the pressure upon Israel from the Arameans of Damascus eased, this through the aid of a God-sent deliverer (II Kings 13:5). The deliverance ought to be connected with the defeat of Ben-Hadad III of Damascus (Mari' – in the stele) at the hands of Adad-nirari in 796 B.C.E. Upon this occasion, Jehoash recognized the Assyrian monarch as his overlord and delivered the tribute recorded on the stele.

Iran Stele

The Israelite King Menahem (*Minihime Samerinaya* – Menahem: the Samarian) is mentioned among the tribute-paying kings of the west in a stele of Tiglath-Pileser III (744–727 B.C.E.) set up in Iran after the Assyrian campaign in 737. This mention of Menahem clarifies a disputed point in biblical chronology. It is now certain that the Israelite king reigned at least until 738, with Assyrian support and as an Assyrian vassal. (The name of the Tyrian king, Tubail, hitherto unknown, is also recorded in the text).

Ebla

For the significance of *Ebla, see separate entry.

Tel-Dan

A damaged Aramaic insciption discovered in at Tel-Dan in northern Israel dating from the ninth century relates the victories of an Aramaean king. There is mention of a *mlk y∞r<l* "king of Israel, whose name has been variously restored. Much attention and controversy have been directed to the phrase *bytdwd*. (See Schiderski in Bibliography.) Written as a single word, this would appear to be the first extra-biblical reference to the"house of David," which in the Book of Isaiah (7:2,13) refers to a specific king.

Ammonite (see *Ammon, Ammonites)

Ammonite seals have long been known. Larger inscriptions have been available only since the late 1960s. The earliest known Ammonite text, the Citadel inscription, dates from the ninth century. Most of the known texts date from the seventh and sixth centuries. The Tel-Siran bronze bottle (ca. 600 B.C.E.; Ahituv, 223) contains an inscription of King Amminab that enables reconstruction of the Ammonite royal succession. Other inscriptions have been found at Tel Hesban (biblical Heshbon) and as far away as Calah in Iraq. (Ahituv, 228–39; Cross. 70–94). The Ammonite corpus confirms the biblical datum that Milcom was an Ammonite deity, as was El. The Ammonite language is a dialect of Northwest Semitic that would have been intelligible to any reader of Hebew.

Ketef Hinnom

Two Hebrew silver amulets found at this site in Jerusalem date from the mid-seventh century B.C.E. These contain texts very close in wording to the biblical priestly blessing found in Num. 6:24–26.

Philistine Inscriptions

Two ostraca of the early seventh century were found at Tell-Jemmeh, some 10 kilometers south of Gaza. These are administrative lists in a local form of the Hebrew script, apparently demonstrating Judite influence on Philistia (Cross, 165). Of special interest is a seventh century dedicatory temple inscription from Tel Miqne (Ekron). The builder identifies himself as Achish, ruler of Ekron, and provides the name of four ancestral predecessors in that office. Orthographic and dialectal forms identify the language as Phoenician.

Edomite

The Edomite corpus remains small. An ostracon found at Horvat Uzzah, east of Arad, from the beginning of the sixth century is in the form of a letter. The formula "I commend you to (the god) Qaus" is quite similar to Hebrew greeting formulae (Ahituv, 213–14).

BIBLIOGRAPHY: Y. Aharoni, *Arad Inscriptions* (Jerusalem, 1975); A.F. Rainey, in: *Tel Aviv*, 4 (1977), 97–104; Plates 5, 6; Z. Meshel, in: *Qadmoniot*, 36 (1976), 119–24; Plates 3, 4; idem, IEJ, 27 (1977), 52–53; N. Avigad, in: IEJ, 25 (1975) 101–105; Plates 10: C, D; idem, in: IEJ, 26 (1976), 178–82; Plate 33: D, idem, in: IEJ, 28 (1978), 52–56; idem, *Qedem, Monograph* No. 4 (Jerusalem, 1976); J. Hoftijzer, G. van Tijzer, in: BA, 39 (1976), 11–17; S. Page, in: *Iraq*, 30 (1968), 139–153; Plate xxix; H. Tadmor, in: *Iraq*, 35 (1973), 141–50; L.D. Levine, in: BASOR, 206 (1972), 40–42; **ADD. BIBLIOGRAPHY:** J. Naveh, *Early History of the Alphabet* (1982); K. Jackson, *The Ammonite Language of the Iron Age* (1983); M. Cogan and H. Tadmor, *II Kings* (AB; 1988), 335; G.I. Davies, *Ancient Hebrew Inscriptions* (1991); A. Yardeni, in: VT 41 (1991), 176–85; S. Ahituv, *Handbook of Ancient Hebrew Inscriptions* (Hebrew; 1992); J. Holladay, in: ABD, 4:97–9; Z. Meshel, ibid, 103–09; H. Tadmor, *The Inscriptions of Tiglath-Pileser III*... (1994), 106; S. Gitin et al, in, IEJ 47 (1997) 1–16; A. Demsky, in: JANES, 25 (1997), 1–5; idem, in: BAR, 24:5 (1998) 53–57; I. Kottsieper, "Die Inschrift vom Tel Dan...," in: M. Dietrich, I. Kottsieper (eds.), *Und Moses schrieb dieses Lied auf*," (FS O. Loretz; 1998), 475–500; W. Dever, in, ErIsr, 26 (1999), *9–*15; M. Heide, in: WdO, 32 (2002), 110–120; F. Cross, *Leaves from an Epigrapher's Notebook* (2003); D. Schwiderski, *The Old and Imperial Aramaic Inscriptions* (2004), 409; N. Na'aman, in: ErIsr, 26 (1999), 112–18; J. Naveh, in: ibid., 113–22.

[Mordechai Cogan / S. David Sperling (2nd ed.)]

SOCIOLOGY OF THE BIBLE

In the final decades of the 20th century the scholarly study of the Hebrew Bible and ancient Israel was marked by an increasing fondness for interdisciplinary projects. Fin-de-siècle biblicists turned with enthusiasm to fields of inquiry such as feminist analysis, psychology, countless varieties of literary theory, and sociology. Those biblical scholars who embraced the latter would seem to have had a considerable "head start." For they had at their disposal texts written about Scripture by figures who ranked among the architects of sociology itself, if not social-scientific discourse in general. Max Weber (1864–1920), regarded as one of the most influential and brilliant practitioners of his craft, devoted a full-length study to biblical Israel in his *Ancient Judaism* (originally published as essays between 1917 and 1919 and collated in 1921 by Weber's wife, Marianne). William Robertson Smith (1846–1894), whom the anthropologist T.O. Beidelman referred to as "the founder of modern sociology of religion," engaged Scripture in his seminal *The Religions of the Semites* (first series, 1889) and the infamous "Bible" entry in the 1875 *Encyclopaedia Britannica.* That contribution, among others, elicited the transcontinental ructions associated with the advent of higher criticism. It is here, amidst the intellectual turbulence of the late 19th and early 20th centuries, where the sociological study of the Hebrew Bible was born; a birth that coincides with the chrysalis of sociological inquiry.

In spite of such auspicious beginnings, the attempt to bring explicit sociological insights to bear on the Hebrew Bible did not immediately take root in either Europe or the United States. Professional sociologists, for their part, completely ignored the problematic and continue to do so. The reasons for this are complex and rarely discussed, but a few possibilities may be briefly suggested here. As with most social scientists, sociologists tend to view their discipline as distinctly "modern." They thus evince a sort of allergy to the humanistic intellectual traditions and texts of antiquity. Moreover, sociology's well-known secular orientation may conceivably turn its workers' attention away from serious and sustained engagement with issues falling under the purview of religious studies.

In biblical studies as well, the period following Weber's death was not marked by great interest in either his or Robertson Smith's work. Contemporary surveys of Old Testament sociology (McNutt, 16–23; Frick, 20–21) often cite the studies of biblicists such as Johannes Pedersen, Adolphe Lods, A. Causse, Albrecht Alt, Roland de Vaux, and Martin Noth as functioning as a bridge between the "first wave" (i.e., the generation of Robertson Smith and Weber) and the "second wave" which emerged in the 1970s (see below). Yet many of the putatively transitional writers just mentioned used the research of the canonical social theorists sparingly, if they used them at all. The varied questions they posed seemed more in line with what might be called "social studies" than with the types of increasingly specialized initiatives associated with the burgeoning discipline of sociology at mid-century. These biblicists of the post-Weberian era did not confront their subject matter armed with specific sociological theories or methodologies. Rather, they asked general questions about broad social aspects of ancient Israel. As such, Pedersen wrote chapters about "Tribe and City," "The Family, the Father's House and the People," and "The Property of the Family." Lods focused on "Hebrew Nomadism" and the economic and social organization of pre-exilic Israel. Alt submitted influential studies on "The Settlement of the Israelites" and "The Formation of the Israelite State in Palestine." An entire monograph about institutions in ancient Israel was written by Father Roland de Vaux. C. Van Leeuwen studied the poor of ancient Israel. Causse took up the same issue, though here one finds a more strenuous engagement with the writings of Robertson Smith and Émile Durkheim and his school.

Weber's notion of an ancient Israelite confederacy, or a loose, occasionally mutually antagonistic coalition of pre-monarchic tribes who spontaneously coalesced in times of war was taken up, most notably in the work of Noth and Alt and other studies of the "amphictyony" (see Mayes). In the main, however, his insights and those of Roberston Smith were left to languish in obscurity. This is regrettable in so far as *Ancient Judaism* positively teems with hypotheses, insightful asides, and intriguingly refutable hunches. It was Weber who saw ancient Israel as a hodgepodge of competing, even hostile, status groups, each vying to improve their status position. It was Weber who delineated distinct groups of Israelite intellectuals and, using the source-critical insights of his day, correlated them with specific biblical texts and literary/theological genres. It was Weber who argued that the prophets of Israel aspired to de-magicize the world. In this manner they were harbingers of the slow, millennial process of rationalization that culminated in Occidental modernity. It is important to note the trans-civilizational scope of his analysis; the inchoate rationalism of these ancient Israelite intellectuals provides one way in which "Jewish religion has world-historical consequences" that extend into the modern period. It was Weber who audaciously suggested that biblical Decalogues were something of a mnemonic device for the less theologically sophisticated masses. And it was Weber who wondered if the austere ritualistic segregation of ancient Judaism inadvertently triggered the antisemitism of antiquity and beyond.

Yet these theories and their corresponding methodological initiatives were overlooked for nearly half a century. It was only in the 1970s that a sustained effort to think sociologically about ancient Israel garnered widespread interest. Central to the rise of this second wave was Norman Gottwald's *The Tribes of Yahweh: A Sociology of the Religion of Liberated Israel 1250–1050 B.C.E.* This work elicited denunciations of the sociological method as applied to the Bible (Mendenhall) and charges of rank amateurism (Rainey). Whether one agrees with Gottwald's thesis of a peasant rebellion in ancient Palestine, a revolt catalyzed by the enigmatic group known as the *habiru*, his text was crucial in that it consciously attempted to engage in dialogue with the writings of Marx, Weber, Durkheim and Talcott Parsons (Berlinerblau, 2002; Boer). What characterizes Gottwald's project and that of other contemporary biblical sociologists is an attempt to use biblical, epigraphic, and archaeological data as a means of reconstructing ancient Israelite history (Wilson) and society (McNutt). They work closely, if somewhat uncritically, with the biblical text in order to gain insight into ancient Israel as it actually was in the early Iron Age. Gottwald and a few others notwithstanding, biblical sociologists tend to eschew serious engagement with sociological research. Indeed, an astonishingly large number of studies in this field use terms such as "social location," "social world," "social setting," "social-scientific analysis" (a trend initiated by the sociologist Peter Berger's important 1963 article on the social location of prophecy). All of these terms are useful in their own way, but decidedly distinct from the lexicon employed in standard sociology.

What would the third wave of biblical sociology entail? A list of desiderata might be framed as follows. The move from "social studies" to sociology will only take place when biblicists thoroughly and creatively confront the immense canon of sociological literature. Next, a greater degree of sophistication in approaching the Hebrew Bible *qua* historical text is necessary. Philip Davies, in commenting on Gottwald's *Tribes*, aptly notes that there exists a difference between the society represented in the Hebrew Bible and the real society in which the Hebrew Bible was produced. Accordingly, biblical sociology must develop criteria for assessing when scriptural data offers accurate data for sociological reconstruction. Self-reflexivity has always been a staple of the sociological imagination and the study of how knowledge has been produced in biblical studies (across two millennia) and who produces such knowledge, stands as one of the most fertile areas for further exploration. Finally, as a means of moving beyond the rather positivistic project of reconstructing ancient Israelite society, and as a means of remaining loyal to Weber's trans-historical vision, biblical sociologists might look at how the Hebrew Bible itself has functioned across sociological time and space. A sociology of interpretation, or "socio-hermeneutics" (Berlinerblau, 2005) would look at how situated Jewish and Christian interpreters have read the Bible and how such readings came to exert world-altering effects upon the social body in question.

BIBLIOGRAPHY: M. Weber, 1952. *Ancient Judaism*, 194–218, 5, 242, 417; T.O. Beidelman, *W. Robertson Smith and the Sociological Study of Religion* (1974), 68; W.R. Smith, *The Religion of the Semites. Lectures on the Religion of the Semites: Second and Third Series*, J. Day (ed.) (1972); P. McNutt, *Reconstructing the Society of Ancient Israel* (1999); F. Frick, "Norman Gottwald's *The Tribes of Yahweh* in the Context of 'Second-Wave' Social-Scientific Biblical Criticism," in: *Tracking the Tribes of Yahweh: On the Trail of a Classic* (2002); J. Pedersen, *Israel: Its Life and Culture: 1–4* (1926); A. Lods, *Israël. Des origines au milieu du VIIIeme Siècle* (1930); A. Causse, *Du groupe ethnique a la communauté religieuse: Le problem sociologique de la religion d'Israël* (1937); A. Alt, *Essays on Old Testament History and Religion* (1967); R. De Vaux, *Ancient Israel: Its Life and Institutions* (1961); M. Noth, *The History of Israel* (1958); C. Van Leeuwen, *Le développement du sens social en Israël avant lère chrétienne* (1955); C.E.H. Mayes, "Amphictyony," in: *The Anchor Bible Dictionary*, Volume 1:A–C., 212–216 (1992); N. Gottwald, *The Tribes of Yahweh: A Sociology of the Religion of Liberated Israel 1250–1050 B.C.E.* (1980); G. Mendenhall, "Ancient Israel's Hyphenated History," in: *Palestine in Transition: The Emergence of Ancient Israel* (1983); A. Rainey, "Review of *The Tribes of Yahweh: A Sociology of the Religion of Liberated Israel, 1250–1050 B.C.E.*," in: *JAOS*, 107 (1987):540–543; J. Berlinerblau, "The Delicate Flower of Biblical Sociology," in: *Tracking the Tribes of Yahweh: On the Trail of a Classic* (2002), 59-76; R. Wilson, *Sociological Approaches to the Old Testament*, 30-53 (1984); P. Berger, "Charisma and Religious Innovation: The Social Location of Israelite Prophecy," in: *American Sociological Review*, 28 (1963): 940–50; P. Davies,. "The Society of Biblical Israel," in: *Second Temple Studies 2. Temple and Community in the Persian Period* (1991), 23; J. Berlinerblau, *The Secular Bible: Why Nonbelievers Must Take Religion Seriously* (2005); R. Boer (ed.), *Tracking the Tribes of Yahweh: On the Trail of a Classic* (2002).

[Jacques Berlinblau (2nd ed.)]

RELIGIOUS IMPACT

IN JUDAISM

In Hellenistic Judaism

Hellenistic Jewish literature, dating from about 250 B.C.E. to 40 C.E., may be regarded as the fusion of the biblical tradition with the Greek language and culture. The literary activity included paraphrases and analyses of biblical narratives, philosophical commentaries, epic and dramatic poetry. Some of these writings are strictly monotheistic; in others the pagan influence is pronounced; and there are a few remnants whose contents supposedly run counter to the current concepts of monotheism. But, except in one or two instances, the "Jewishness" of these fragments seems assured. The common characteristic that distinguishes these writings from the apocryphal and pseudepigraphal literature is that the names of the authors, though sometimes pseudonymous, are almost invariably known.

The tradition of the translation of the Torah by the Seventy during the reign of Ptolemy Philadelphus presupposes the existence of a professional cadre of translators in Alexandria, who were the first Hellenistic Jewish literati. They coined the term "Holy Bible" (ἡ ἐρά Βίβλος), recorded for the first time during the last two decades of the third century B.C.E. The Bible, or rather what is now known as the Pentateuch, was also called the Law (a translation of Torah), to which epithets were attached such as "the Holy," "God's," "Moses'," or "Israel's."

*Demetrius, who flourished during the reign of Ptolemy IV Philopater (221–204), may be regarded as a representative of the Alexandrian school whose immediate antecedents go back to the Septuagint translators. "Someone asked," he says, "'After having come here unarmed, how did the Israelites have weapons?' (Ex. 13:18)." This suggests that his question had been raised by other biblical commentators. It also shows that the question and answer method, current among Alexandrian pagan exegetes, was adopted by the Jews. Their rendition of the Hebrew word *va-ḥamushim* (Ex. 13:18) differed from that of the known versions of the Septuagint, which translate the term as the fifth generation (of the Israelites in Egypt). In general, in the extant fragments at least, Demetrius devotes most of his comments to chronological and genealogical problems. Chronology was also of great concern for a certain Philo, who may not be identical with *Philo the Elder, mentioned in *Josephus (Apion, 1:218), or Philo the Epicist; *Eupolemus, and Josephus' rival – Justus of *Tiberias.

In contrast to Demetrius and *Aristeas, the author of a history *On the Jews*, who show no direct awareness of the pagan world, writers such as *Pseudo-Eupolemus and *Artapanus reflect syncretistic traditions of biblical Hellenistic historiography. Pseudo-Eupolemus identified Enoch with the Hellenic Atlas, the reputed discoverer of astrology; Noah with Belus, the traditional founder of Babylon; and Melchizedek with the king and priest of the temple on Mount Gerizim. The last identification indicates that syncretistic and Euhemeristic tendencies were prevalent also among the Samaritans. Artapanus, who flourished during the second century B.C.E., represents the most extreme syncretistic school. According to him, Abraham, Joseph, and primarily Moses developed Egypt's science, statecraft, and religion. The story of Moses' war against Ethiopia, found in Artapanus and Josephus (Ant., 2:238–53), may be due to a common source. There is no evidence for the suggestion, maintained by Freudenthal, that Artapanus was a Jew who paraded as an Egyptian priest.

Alexandrian scholars in the middle of the second century B.C.E. also published commentaries that began to interpret Scripture allegorically, somewhat as many Greek exegetes explained Homer. *Aristobulus, "the teacher of Ptolemy" (II Macc. 1:10), argued that anthropomorphic expressions of the Bible such as "God's hand" must be understood as God's power. This may not seem to be quite allegory as the term is now understood, but Aristobulus' censure of the literalists' understanding of Scripture suggests the beginnings of a symbolic exegesis of Scripture (see above Allegorical Interpretations). Interestingly, Aristobulus says that there had existed a Greek translation of the Torah prior to the Septuagint which Homer, Hesiod, Pythagoras, Socrates, Plato, Hecataeus of Abdera and others had allegedly utilized. This indicates that the Jewish forgeries of Greek poets that extolled Jewish religion antedate the middle of the second century B.C.E.

From a literary point of view, the great achievement of the Greco-Jewish writers was in the field of poetry and drama. Philo the Elder composed an epic in Homeric hexameters on Jerusalem; short fragments on Abraham, Joseph, and the fountains and canals of Jerusalem survive. An epic by a Samaritan, *Theodotus, recounts the rape of Dinah (Gen. 34). Without introducing radical changes in the biblical story, there is considerable invention in the remaining 48 lines, attesting to a high degree of poetic inspiration and technical proficiency. Hellenistic Jewish literature attained its zenith in the drama *Exagoge* (*Exodus*) by *Ezekiel the Poet. In a sense this work seems but a paraphrase of the relevant chapters of the Septuagint Book of Exodus. But the dramatist was able to weave into the play interpretations that had been proposed by biblical commentators. Thus Zipporah, Moses' wife, is said to have been identical with the "Ethiopian woman" (Num. 12:1), a view earlier put forward by Demetrius. The heathen environment supplied Ezekiel the Poet with the forms of the play; the Torah, with its content and meaning. The same may be said of most of the Greco-Jewish literature – it was primarily Jewish and secondarily Greek.

See also *Apocrypha, *Josephus, *Pseudo-Philo.

[Ben Zion Wacholder]

Talmud and Medieval Times

With the famous convocation of the people called by Ezra in the fifth century B.C.E., at which the Bible was solemnly and publicly read to the assembled people – "they read in the book, in the law of God, distinctly, and they gave the sense and caused them to understand the reading" (Neh. 8:8) – the Bible became for centuries the main, and for a long time the sole, intellectual preoccupation of the Jewish people. The talmudic interpretations (Meg. 3a) that "they read in the book" refers to the Hebrew text, and "distinctly" (or "with an interpretation") to its translation into the Aramaic vernacular are probably correct, and serve to indicate that for the first time the Bible had become the common cultural and religious possession of the entire Jewish people. This determination to spread knowledge of the Bible among the entire people is probably reflected in the adage of the Men of the Great *Synagogue, who carried on the activity thus initiated: "Set up many disciples" (Avot 1:2).

In discussing the Bible among the Jews it is essential to make a sharp distinction between their preoccupation with the Pentateuch and with the other sections of the Bible. The purpose of the study of the Pentateuch was mainly for the systematic development of the *halakhah*, the "way of life" which the Jew was to follow, and secondarily for homiletical exegesis. The former gave rise to the **Midrash Halakhah* and the latter to the **Midrash Aggadah*. The Pentateuch was regarded as the main authoritative source for the *halakhah*, and verses from the prophets and the Hagiographa were regarded merely as giving secondary support to it. They were called "Kabbalah" (tradition) and it was laid down that "no inference may be drawn concerning statements of the Pentateuch from statements found in the Kabbalah" (Ḥag. 10b). As a result, for the purpose of *halakhah* the entire weight was laid on the Pentateuch, and from the time of Ezra until the compilation of the Mishnah, the Pentateuch was practically the sole textbook for study. Since the purpose of that study was to arrive at the *halakhah*, this became the main subject of study with the compilation of the Mishnah.

A somewhat different situation existed with regard to the study of the Bible by the aggadists. Although their main preoccupation was also with the Pentateuch, they added to it the other portions of the Bible which were publicly read in the *haftarot and the Five Scrolls. In addition to that, however, they deliberately sought to acquaint their listeners with the Bible as a whole, and almost invariably selected as the text of their proem a verse from the Hagiographa, linking it with the scriptural portion. As a result the entire Bible was gradually subjected to intensive study. This process is reflected in the statement of the Midrash: "Ben Azzai was engaged in stringing together verses of the Pentateuch to those of the prophets, and of the prophets to the Hagiographa, and the words of the Torah rejoiced as on the day they were given on Mr. Sinai" (Lev. R. 16:4; cf. Song R. 1:10 where the same is said of "Abba b. Mimi and his colleagues"). As a result of this extensive exegesis, it was possible for later authors to compile Midrashim on individual books of the Prophets and Hagiographa, as well as on the entire Bible, of which the *Yalkut Shimoni is the outstanding example. Their principal sources were the Midrashim to the books which formed part of the synagogue lectionary and exegesis found in the Talmud. Consequently a large proportion of the non-pentateuchal portion of the Bible is commented on in Talmud and Midrash. It should be pointed out, however, that this exegesis was overwhelmingly homiletical and midrashic. Literal exegesis was almost entirely neglected during this period. It is true that R. Kahana stated that "a verse does not lose its interpretation according to the *peshat*" (Shab. 63a), but it is highly doubtful whether *peshat* in this context has the meaning "literal interpretation" given to it in later ages, probably first by Rashi. It seems to mean "the accepted interpretation as given in the schools." Certain interpretations referred to as "*peshat*" in one passage appear as "*derash*" in parallel passages; moreover, in *Ketubbot* 111b, R. Dimi, after giving a homiletical interpretation of Genesis 49:11 in answer to a question as to the "*peshat* of that verse," gives one which is much more midrashic than his previous one. As stated, the importance attached to the study of the Bible was conditioned by its liturgical use. Pride of place was given to the Pentateuch, which was not only read completely from beginning to end (in one year in Babylon and in a triennial cycle in Ereẓ Israel), but also was the basis of the *halakhah*. Next came the Five Scrolls which alone of the Hagiographa are read in their entirety in the synagogue. Of the prophets only the portions selected as the *haftarot* were read. Such portions were chosen from all the books of the Prophets with the exception of Joel, Nahum, Haggai, and Zephaniah. Until recent times it was the traditional and almost invariable practice for the Jewish preacher to select the text of his sermon from the scriptural reading of the week, either expounding its theme or applying his interpretation of the verse to the theme on which he was preaching (see *Preaching).

Insofar as concerns the Bible in the liturgy, one of its interesting aspects is the gradual increase of the number of Psalms included in the liturgy. In talmudic times, apart from the six Psalms of *Hallel and the seven daily Psalms, one of which was recited daily as "the Psalm which the Levites used to say in the Temple," the Psalms did not form part of the daily liturgy, and in fact, the only biblical passages included in the actual prayers were the three paragraphs of the *Shema. As against this, the *Standard Authorized Daily Prayer Book*, current among Ashkenazim in England, gives an index to the 72 Psalms included therein. Of these, 53 belong to statutory services. In addition to the above, the bulk is made up of seven Psalms in the *Pesukei de-Zimra* of weekdays (100 and 145–150) and nine (in the Sephardi rite 11) additional ones for Sabbaths and festivals, six (95–99 and 29) for the Inauguration of the Sabbath, and 16 (104 and 15 Songs of Degrees 120–134) for Sabbath afternoon in winter. The balance comprises Psalm 30 as an introduction to the *Pesukei de-Zimra*; Psalms recited when the Scroll of the Law is returned to the ark (already included in the above); Psalms 6 (in *Taḥanun) and 20 in the concluding part of the daily service; Psalms 144 and 67 for the conclusion of the Sabbath; Psalm 27 during the month of Elul and until Hoshana Rabba; and a number of voluntary additional Psalms. Psalms are also included in every type of non-statutory service, e.g., in the night prayer, the service for the consecration of a house, for sickness, in the house of mourning, at the setting of a tombstone. A number of the above are recited on more than one occasion.

Various other sections of the Bible have also found their way into the prayer book. I Chronicles 16:18–36 is included in the *Pesukei de Zimra* (in the Sephardi rite it precedes them) as are I Chronicles 24:10–13, Nehemiah 9:6–11, and the Song of Moses (Ex. 14:30–15, 18). The last chapter of Proverbs has been instituted for home reading on Friday night. Among other biblical verses, mention should be made of the ten verses each of *Malkhuyyot, Zikhronot* and *Shofarot* – of which four are from the Pentateuch, three from the Prophets, and three from the Hagiographa – and Psalm 47 recited before the sounding of the *shofar* on Rosh ha-Shanah. The individual biblical verses introduced into the liturgy are too numerous to be detailed.

The intensive preoccupation with the aggadic and homiletical interpretation of the Pentateuch brought in its wake a profound familiarity with the Bible, in which, however, the Midrash was paramount. The worthies of the Bible were regarded not as figures from the past but almost as living contemporaries. Abraham's smashing of the idols of his father and his deliverance from the fiery furnace, Esau as the embodiment of wickedness and the prototype of the archenemy of Israel, Aaron as the personification of the love and pursuit of peace, Judah as the mighty warrior, David as the wholly righteous monarch without sin or flaw, all of them the creation of the Midrash, appeared as real, if not more so, than the literal portrayal of them in the biblical narrative. In the Talmud it is laid down (Bet. 8a–b) that one should revise the weekly scriptural reading during the preceding week "twice in the original and once in the Aramaic translation [Targum]." It was later laid down (Tur., OḤ 2:285) that the commentary of Rashi could be substituted for the Targum. This injunction was widely followed throughout the ages, with the natural result that the ordinary Jew acquired an unparalleled and intimate acquaintance with the Pentateuch. Nevertheless, it was emphasized that the study of the Oral Law took precedence over and was regarded as more meritorious than that of the Bible. "Those who occupy themselves with the Written Torah (alone) are of but indifferent merit (lit. "a quality and not a quality"); but they do receive their reward; with Mishnah, are wholly meritorious, with *Gemara – there can be nothing more meritorious" (BM 33a). Tractate *Soferim* expands this with the statement, "the Bible is compared to water, the Mishnah to pepper, the *Gemara* to spices." The world needs all three, and the wealthy man can indulge in all, but "happy is the man whose occupation is with *Gemara*," the only rider being that the study of Bible should be thorough and not a mere springboard ("jumping") to the study of the Oral Law (15:8–9).

The Talmud declares that a person should divide his time into three equal portions, one of which should be devoted to the study of the Bible. Rashi maintains that one should therefore devote two days weekly to the study of Bible, but his grandson R. Tam, while applying the division to each day rather than the week, makes the significant comment that "a person who studies Talmud can ignore that of Bible since Bible is 'intermingled' in it" (Av. Zar. 19b and Rashi and Tos. in loc.). Maimonides, however (Yad. Talmud Torah 1:11), posits the talmudic injunction in its literal sense, which is probably the reason that knowledge of the Bible – indeed its memorization – has been much more widespread among Oriental Jews than among Ashkenazi Jews. The close study of the biblical text, pursued with meticulous care and devotion by the masoretes, who not only set themselves the task of establishing the correct text but provided both punctuation and accents, was of immense service in establishing the accepted and standard text. It became the basis of the independent study of the Bible which was to characterize the Middle Ages.

The other non-Pentateuchal books of the Bible were also studied in the talmudic period. Every child was given a specific verse of the Bible which was, so to speak, regarded as "his own" (Ḥag. 15a–b; Esth. R. 7:13). (It may, however, refer to the verse he had studied that day.) The verses quoted in these two passages alone are from Isaiah (four verses), Jeremiah (two verses), Psalms and Proverbs. The child was introduced to the study of the Bible at an early age. The standard age of five is given in *Avot* (5:21), but a certain amount of flexibility was permitted (BB 21a – see *Education). The Mishnah, however, continues "the age of 10 for the study of Mishnah and of 15 for gemara," evidence that the study of the Bible was regarded as belonging to elementary education, although it was insisted that it be studied thoroughly (Sof. 15:9).

In the Middle Ages and After

The stimulus behind the emergence of the study of the Bible as an independent discipline was largely the result of the challenge provided by biblical exegesis of the *Karaites. Rejecting the entire corpus of talmudic tradition as incorporated in the Oral Law, and calling themselves "Benei Mikra" ("students of the Scripture"), they paid especial attention to the investigation of the biblical text and the derivation of new rules of conduct from it. There is no doubt that it was this challenge which stimulated Saadiah Gaon to branch out into what was to become the new intellectual activity of independent biblical exegesis, which largely took the form of literal exegesis. He was followed, among the Babylonian *geonim*, by Samuel b. Hophni and his son-in-law Hai Gaon, and they may be said to have laid down the foundations for literal exegesis of the Bible. (For the history of subsequent exegesis see above section on Exegesis.) An aspect of this study of the Bible in medieval times as an independent discipline is the fact that from Rashi onward biblical commentary covered the entire Bible. The commentary to the Pentateuch and Early Prophets of Isaac Abrabanel can be regarded as marking the close of this period.

The influence of the close study of the Bible, especially in Spain, is also evident in the neo-Hebrew poetry which developed during this period. Unlike the *paytanim* of Ereẓ Israel and the Franco-German school, the poets of Spain, particularly Solomon ibn *Gabirol, Moses *Ibn Ezra and *Judah Halevi confined themselves to classical biblical Hebrew in their works, paying close attention to the rules of grammar and displaying a perfection and finish which reveals a thorough knowledge of the Bible. Mention must be made of a different approach to the study of the Bible which left a permanent mark. This is the kabbalistic exegesis of the Bible, which reached its full development in the *Zohar, "the Bible of the Mystics." This famous work can be regarded as a midrashic commentary to the Pentateuch, but the interpretation is mystic (*sod*; see *Kabbalah). It is difficult, however, to determine whether the burgeoning of the study of the Bible as a whole, and particularly in France (and Spain) was confined to scholars, or whether it encompassed the entire people. The remarkable explanation given by Rashi, who wrote commentaries on practically the entire Bible, of the deathbed statement of R. Eleazar: "Keep your children from *higgayon*" (meditation) – "Do not accustom them to excessive study of the Bible, because of its attractiveness" (Ber. 28b) – certainly seems to point to a discouragement of the "excessive" study of the Bible as a whole.

The 16th to the 18th centuries are characterized by an almost complete neglect of the study of the Bible as such. Talmud and Kabbalah became almost the sole subjects of study. Only in Italy was the study of the Bible as such pursued, and it produced such epoch-making works as Elijah *Levita's *Masoret ha-Masoret*, Azariah dei *Rossi's *Me'or Einayim*, Abraham *Portaleone's archaeological researches, and the commentaries of Obadiah *Sforno and Moses Ḥefez (*Gentili). Otherwise, biblical commentary consisted largely of novellae, supercommentaries and homiletical disquisition. Various attempts were made, e.g., by *Judah Loew b. Bezalel of Prague, to revive the study of the Bible, but with little effect.

Modern Times

The revival of the study of the Bible among Jews was inaugurated by the pentateuchal commentary of Moses *Mendelssohn, the *Biur*. That commentary heralded the return to the study of the Bible *per se*, with emphasis upon the literal interpretation of the Bible according to its natural meaning. Basing itself largely upon the classic rabbinical commentators of the Bible, Rashi, Samuel b. Meir (Rashbam), Ibn Ezra, and Naḥmanides, it eschewed homiletical interpretation entirely and confined itself solely to establishing the literal meaning of the text. However, this renewed interest in the study of the Bible was confined to scholars. The number engaged in it was small, and it had little effect on renewing interest in the Bible, and hardly penetrated into the consciousness of the Jewish masses. There were theological inhibitions which prevented the introduction of the fruits of modern biblical study, and those scholars who did engage in it had largely to make their contributions in European languages, in which almost all biblical study was developed. The prohibition against women studying Torah enunciated by R. Eliezer (Sotah 3:4) and accepted as *halakhah* (YD 246:6) was regarded as applying only to the Oral Law, and not to the Written. Women were, nevertheless, not encouraged to study the Bible; "she should not be taught in the first instance, but if she was so taught it is not regarded as obscenity" (YD loc. cit. Yad. Talmud Torah 1:13). Thus there was no special study of the Bible by women, yet the *Ẓe'enah U-Re'enah*, a midrashic exposition of the Bible in Yiddish especially written for women, achieved an immense popularity.

An almost dramatic transformation took place with the rise of the national movement after the end of the 19th century. On the one hand, the revival of Hebrew as a spoken language made possible the study and teaching of the Bible in the language in which it was written, and on the other hand, for the first time among the Jewish masses, that study was liberated from the theological confines to which it had been limited. A secular approach to the Bible, which regarded it solely as the greatest cultural and literary monument of Jewish culture, the outstanding achievement of the Jewish people when it lived a full national life in its own homeland, was adopted. It gave impetus to the most striking aspect of study in modern Israel, the restoration of the study of the Bible *per se*. The Bible and its study has come into its own in modern Israel. It is studied with equal interest both in religious and non-religious schools, with the obvious difference, however, that whereas in the former the religious aspect is paramount and there is a complete absence of any reference to biblical criticism, in the latter it is studied from the point of view of literature and history. Its study can be regarded almost as a national pastime. It has become a significant feature of Israel life; it is divided into daily readings so that the entire Bible is read in the course of the year, and those readings (for Prophets and Hagiographa), with a topical commentary, are the subject of a daily broadcast. Biblical "quizzes," whether among youth, in the army, among the general populace, or international have become a popular feature. Criticism has been leveled against this phenomenon in that it tends to emphasize a wide and comprehensive knowledge of the text alone, with no consideration given to its more profound aspects. But for the first time a public exists which employs the language of the Bible as its vernacular and which has a considerable knowledge of the text. As a result, practically for the first time since biblical study became an independent discipline, the possibility has been created for that study to be undertaken and disseminated in Hebrew. It has been suggested that the great enthusiasm for the Bible in Israel is a search for roots. It is witnessed in the popular interest in Bible conferences, in archaeological digs, in the revival of biblical place- and personal-names. Contact with the land of the Bible and its distinctive natural features and tangible conditions has had a distinct influence, for example, in the fields of topography, the history of settlement in Israel, and biblical realia, which have been intensified in recent years.

[Louis Isaac Rabinowitz]

BIBLIOGRAPHY: HELLENISTIC JUDAISM: J. Freudenthal, *Hellenistische Studien*, 2 vols. (1874–75); J. Wieneke, *Ezechielis Judaei poetae Alexandrini fabulae…* (1931); Eusebius, *Praeparatio Evangelica*, ed. by K. Mras, 1 (1954), 419–554; 2 (1956), 165–256; English translation: E.H. Gifford's edition, 3 (1903); F. Jacoby (ed.), *Die Fragmente der griechischen Historiker*, 3C, pt. 2 (1958), 666–713, nos. 722–37; N. Walter, *Der Thoraausleger Aristobulos* (1964); Wacholder, in: HUCA, 34 (1963), 83–113; idem, in: HTR, 61 (1968), 451–81. MODERN TIMES: M. Haran, in: *Ha-Universitah*, 14, no. 3 (1969), 10–12; idem, *Biblical Research in Hebrew* (1970).

IN CHRISTIANITY

Christianity began as a conventicle in Judaism, with a complete and unquestioned acceptance of what had come to be the foundation stone of Judaism's serious view of itself as the one true revealed religion, destined to be the religion of all mankind. Through the years the confidence had matured that in the Bible was the complete and all-embracing record of all that men would ever need to know. Here stood revealed the full and complete will of God: all that men were to do and to be had been revealed to them. Their conduct toward one another and toward Him, the way they were to worship Him and regard Him, even their attitudes of mind and will, all had been revealed and was man's for the knowing. No circumstance could ever arise that had not been anticipated, no question for which the certain answer had not been given. Even before the moment of creation it had stood in the mind of God. Subsequently the blueprint for all time had been revealed by God to men through the agency of Moses and the other specially designated and inspired agents. The Bible was not 24 books, as it might superficially seem to be to Jewish eyes, or 29, to those of the Christians. It was fundamentally one book, with God its one author.

As the movement eventually to be styled Christianity became separate from the parent, it never lost this confidence in the nature of its inherited Scriptures, which, as the true Israel it regularly conceived itself to be, it easily came to believe were actually primarily its own, not the parent's, "for," as Justin *Martyr phrased it in his *Dialogue with Trypho* (ch. 29): "we believe them, but you, though you read them, do not catch the spirit that is in them."

Gradually, in the course of almost exactly 100 years, a large number of additional chapters, so to speak, were produced. As the years passed, many of these later writings became dear to an ever-increasing body of believers, with the result that by the middle of the fourth century 27 more writings had come to be widely regarded and formally accepted as a part of God's Revelation, of which He was the actual author, having seen fit to reveal His mind through the records which evangelists and apostles had written at His dictation.

Through the centuries this view was maintained. It is this which is meant by the statement in the twentieth of the still-authoritative Thirty-Nine Articles that the Bible is "God's word written." In the 18th century Locke was asserting nothing new when he insisted: "It has God for its author, salvation for its end, and truth without any mixture of error for its matter." A century later, an Oxford theologian, Dean Burgon, spelled it out: "The Bible is none other than the voice of Him that sitteth upon the throne. Every book of it, every chapter of it, every word of it, every syllable of it (where are we to stop?), every letter of it, is the direct utterance of the Most High. The Bible is none other than the Word of God, not some part of it more, some part of it less, but all alike the utterance of Him who sitteth upon the throne, faultless, unerring, supreme" (*Inspiration and Interpretation* (1861), 89).

This view of Scripture, despite two centuries of inquiry during which in the eyes of an increasingly large group it has been discredited or drastically qualified, is still with nuances the verdict of Christianity, Orthodox, Roman Catholic, and Protestant alike. The Protestant Reformation did not affect the matter in the slightest. There was and is no real difference between Catholics and Protestants as to the proper attitude toward the Bible or the basis on which they rest their creeds. The sole difference lay – and still lies – in the fact that to the Catholic (and Orthodox) Scripture is not the sole authoritative and infallible source of belief. Scripture (i.e., Old and New Testament including the deuterocanonical books) and tradition are the source of God's revelation. For the Protestants the Scriptures alone can have such a claim. Both, however, accept the Bible as the authoritative and infallible statement of revealed truth. Actually, Protestant scholars at times went to greater extremes in their stress upon biblical interpretation than did Catholics. During the years, ecclesiastical infallibility and scriptural infallibility had grown up together. As a result of the Reformation, ecclesiastical infallibility was thrown overboard by Protestants. The infallibility of the Bible was set up as a bulwark against the rejected infallibility of the Church. It is accordingly not surprising that in consequence a literal view of inspiration, like that enunciated by Dean Burgon, resulted.

Thus the real and distinctive note in the Christian attitude toward the Old Testament has never been whether the Old Testament is or is not Scripture, to be accepted and prized, for this acceptance has been universal. Rather, the problem has always been how the Old Testament is to be interpreted and used.

Beginning, and continuing for many years, as a part of Judaism, sounding the proclamation of Jesus, whom they believed to have been raised from the dead by God and to be with him in heaven soon to return to establish the speedily expected new age, which, like him, they styled the kingdom of God, the Christians' main differences from the rest of orthodox Jewry were their developing views of Jesus himself. So far as fundamentals were concerned, they remained orthodox Jews, in their views of the unity of God, of His relation to Israel, of His complete revelation in Scripture.

With their basic view of the all-inclusive content of the Divine Revelation in Scripture it was not unnatural that Christians saw prophesied therein their movement and their Christ. As the movement came more and more to be separate from Judaism, the conviction deepened that Judaism, which failed to see in the predictions in the Old Testament the Christian Jesus and the success of the movement resulting from his preaching, was blind to the real content of the Scriptures, which Scriptures they were confident were theirs. The Old Testament, according, for example, to the *Epistle of Barnabas*, has meaning only when it is understood in terms of the gospel. It was held that God's covenant has always been made with Christians, and the Old Testament has always been misunderstood by the Jews. This in no wise minimized the Old Testament. "All scripture is inspired by God and helpful for teaching," as the author of II Timothy 3:16 was to insist; but it must be rightly understood.

Much has been written about Paul's rejection of the Mosaic law, but although this is true, it is far from meaning that he rejected the Old Testament. It remains Scripture for Paul and of the profoundest value, as his constant citation to establish or buttress this contention or that indicates, but it is no longer letter but spirit, no longer law but a ministry of grace. By the aid of the Spirit he holds, the Old Testament can be interpreted as a spiritual book – the reason others cannot do so is because they have not received the gift of the spirit. They have been blinded by Satan; true understanding of the Old Testament comes only from God. Paul is adept in finding "spiritual meaning" in the most unlikely texts. He does not view the Old Testament as the Christian's moral guide, for his break with the law, ceremonial and moral alike, was complete. Rather this standard or guide is to be found based on what he calls Jesus' law of love, more exactly, what is worthy of one in Christ. The point often overlooked is that the kind of life which Paul felt worthy of in Christ is precisely the type of life which as a Jew he had been from birth trained to revere, as he had found it revealed in Scripture.

The whole insistence in the *Epistle of Barnabas* is that Christians must avoid a Judaistic conception of the Old Testament. Despite Barnabas' blistering criticism of the literal understanding of passages regarding sacrifices and the food laws, he never thinks of giving up the Old Testament or its divine Creator, as Marcion and most of the Gnostics were subsequently to do. Instead his pages are filled with such words as "Moses received these doctrines concerning food and thus spoke of them in the Spirit; but they [the Jews] received them as merely referring to food, owing to the lust of their flesh" (*Epistle of Barnabas* 10). His reference to gnosis and his anti-Judaism do not mean that he was either a Gnostic or that he rejected the Old Testament. Gnosis, as he uses the term, is simply deeper insight into the truths of Christianity with the aid of allegorical interpretation of the Old Testament which allowed him to find what he sought to discover. His allegorization constantly does violence to the meaning of the text and resolves historical events into exaggerated fantasy. Nor is Barnabas alone. Justin Martyr indicates the same naive and uncritical attitude toward the Old Testament. That he revered it as inspired Scripture is evident in every page; his devotion to allegorical interpretation, which can find Jesus clearly predicted in the most impossible passages and the cross prefigured not alone throughout the Scriptures – the paschal lamb roasted on a spit (*Dialogue with Trypho* 40), the extended hands of Moses (*ibid.* 90), the serpent in the wilderness (*First Apology* 60), the horn of the unicorn (*Dialogue with Trypho* 91) – but also in the nautical rig of masts and yardarms, in the plow and tools of the farmer and mechanic, in the more obscure and misty discourses of Plato, or in the nose which juts from the face which enables the prophet to say, "The breath before our face is the Lord Christ" (*First Apology* 55), reveals vividly, if to a modern age grotesquely, the early Christian confidence that the Old Testament was primarily a Christian book, at least of a sort which must be rightly read to be properly understood. Like Paul, Justin does not deny the historical reality of God's relationship with Israel. What he insists upon is that the earlier covenant looks forward to being superseded. The prophets herald a new covenant with God, and in Christianity with its two predicted advents of Christ – the one already experienced, the other yet to come – their predictions are fully realized.

The Alexandrian school, notably *Origen, deeply indebted to Philo, sets forth most thoroughly the principles or purport of Christian allegorization, and with far less of the bizarre overemphasis of a Barnabas or Justin Martyr. For Origen the fulfillment of prophecy is the proof of its unquestioned inspiration. Thus, in the advent of Jesus the inspiration of the prophetic words and the truly spiritual nature of Moses' law come into full light. The purpose of Scripture is to reveal intellectual truths, not to show God's working in history. Actually history often conceals truth. This, Origen sees clearly evidenced in the pages of both Old and New Testaments. In addition – for, like Philo, Origen was in many ways a very practical and down-to-earth man – much of the legislation in both Testaments cannot be literally observed. Such passages must, accordingly, reveal other important, if less obvious, values. But Origen is far more restrained than were some of his predecessors: the passages which are historically true, he is sure, far outnumber those which are composed with purely spiritual significance – that is, which are not historically true. In sum, all Scripture has a spiritual meaning. It should be observed that Origen is a scholar and thinks and writes as such. His protests against what he terms the literal meaning are directed essentially against the superficial and often absurd misinterpretations put upon Scripture by ignorant people who cannot understand metaphors and parables and who thus regularly read poetry as pedestrian prose.

The allegorical method of interpreting Scripture, which was the outgrowth of the Christian confidence that their movement and their Christ were of course revealed in the all-inclusive Scriptures, and that it was their task to set forth these facts clearly so that when their Lord returned from heaven he would find faith on the earth, encountered much criticism. Marcion, a devoted if misguided Christian – and in no small degree driven to his rejection of the Old Testament as a Christian book by these absurd excesses of allegorization – insisted on a literal understanding of the Hebrew Scriptures, the better to emphasize their crudity. In his eyes the Old Testament was not a Christian book, and no amount of allegorization could make it such. Jesus was not foreseen in any of the prophecies of the Old Testament, nor did his coming in any sense fulfill them; rather, he had come to destroy both the law and the prophets. Marcion stands alone in this rejection, and many interpreters have denied that he was a Christian in any sense of that word.

Others, notably the group of scholars styled the Antiochian school and *Jerome, had a profound respect for the literal meaning of Scripture. Jerome had earlier been an allegorist, as his first biblical commentary clearly shows, but his contacts with Jewish teachers had been influential in his change of front. It is not too much to say that wherever the influence of the Synagogue is to be seen – as in Dorotheus, head of the catechetical school in Antioch, who painstakingly learned Hebrew – there was a tendency toward a literal understanding of the Old Testament. This was not to deny the deeper meaning of Scripture, which was to them unquestioned. Rather, the deeper meaning was built onto the literal, not flatly opposed to it as Barnabas had fulminated.

The most influential of the school of Antioch was Theodore of Mopsuestia. He insisted on the historical reality of biblical revelation. In the prophecies of Christ's coming, allegory is not to be seen, as the Alexandrians had maintained. Rather, the prophets actually foresaw what was to come to pass in Israel and announced it, but in addition they saw – or some of them did – the ultimate coming of Christ. Nor could Alexandria rightly claim Paul's words in Galatians 4 and I Corinthians 10 as its support. Despite Paul's phrase, he was not indulging in allegory. His words were typological. The incident was real, but in addition it typified a deeper truth. The events had taken place; nonetheless they were comparisons and so he could use them as warning examples. Actually Theodore insisted that only four of the Psalms (2, 8, 44, 109) are in any sense to be seen as predictive of Jesus, and that they are not truly messianic but rather give glimpses of the incarnation. Only books containing a prophetic element are to be regarded as canonical; thus Job, Chronicles, Ezra-Nehemiah, and Esther, as well as all the books of the Apocrypha, are to be seen as containing human wisdom alone and are to be rejected from the canon. This exclusion of any of the books of the Hebrew canon was most unusual, and a century later Theodore's writings were burned as heretical – in part because of the views of his pupil Nestorius, for which he was held responsible, and in part because of his exclusion of books universally revered as canonical, quite regardless of the way they were interpreted.

As the Christian movement spread into the gentile world, it was but natural that the current Greek version of their inherited Scripture became their Bible. Because of the confidence that Jesus and the Christian movement were to be found in its pages and because of the Christian conviction that the Jewish understanding of the Scriptures was in error regarding what to them was palpably a Christian book, it is not surprising that the Septuagint speedily lost all authority in Jewish eyes and that the second century saw several new Greek translations (Aquila, Symmachus, Theodotion) stemming from Jewish feelings of outrage that their Scripture was being so crassly misused and turned into a weapon against them. One of the most significant achievements by any early Christian scholar, well indicating the universal Christian acceptance of the Old Testament as a part of their inspired Scripture, was the gigantic Hexapla, with the Old Testament standing in six parallel columns (cf. above, Ancient Versions, Greek). Well aware of the fact, as he was, that frequently the Septuagint and the Hebrew diverge, Origen sought to indicate this. Material in the Septuagint but not in the Hebrew was indicated by warning obeli; material in the Hebrew but not in the Greek was indicated by asterisks. In addition to this monumental work by Origen, other recensions of the Septuagint (Hesychian and Lucianic) were subsequently made. Occasionally Christian scholars in the early days had some knowledge of Hebrew and made use of Hebrew texts, although regularly chided by Jewish scholars for employing inferior and corrupted texts; by and large until the 16th century, when knowledge of Greek and Hebrew became a scholarly must, study of the Old Testament was based upon the Greek texts. Although translations of both Testaments into Latin and Syriac were made early, Greek continued to be the usual medium until the fourth century. Gradually Latin became the common Christian tongue, and a standard authoritative Latin version of both Testaments became necessary to bring order out of the chaos which had arisen and of which Augustine remarked: "Whenever in earlier days a Greek manuscript came into any man's hand, provided he fancied that he had any skill at all in both languages, he did not hesitate to translate it." After completing his revision of the Latin text of the New Testament at Rome at the behest of Pope Damasus, Jerome went to Bethlehem and produced a version of the Old Testament. He claimed that it was a new translation into Latin of the Septuagint on the basis of Origen's hexaplaric text, that is, the fifth column of the Hexapla. Whether this was actually a fresh translation, as Jerome claimed, or simply a revision of the Old Latin text, is uncertain, for Jerome's claims are often unreliable. At any rate, he speedily became convinced of the need of a fresh translation of the Old Testament from the Hebrew text. This he made and, except for the Psalms, it is the present Vulgate (cf. above, Ancient Versions, Latin). His translation of the Hebrew Psalter was never likely to oust in popular regard his earlier translation from the Greek (Gallican Psalter). In consequence of his work, Jerome became convinced that only the books in the Hebrew Bible had warrant to be considered part of the Bible. Despite his arguments and insistence, the Roman Church continued to use the Apocrypha, which had been regularly regarded as canonical by Christians to whom the Septuagint was their Bible; the Apocrypha continued to be, as it is today, an unquestioned part of the Bible of the Roman Catholic Church, not collected at the end, but interspersed, as it was in the Septuagint, among the other Old Testament books. Jerome's objections eventually found acceptance in Protestantism. Luther relegated the Apocrypha to the end of the Old Testament. Subsequently British and American churches came to exclude these books, even as a separate collection, from printed editions of the Bible, although in the 20th century they have regained a measured popularity as valuable reading. They are not, and they have not been since the Reformation, a veritable part of the Bible in Protestant eyes (see also *Luther; *Reformation; *Protestantism). For many centuries the basic contention of both Judaism and Christianity maintained that the Bible is totally different from all other books, and in consequence the rules and procedures for studying and appraising other writings do not apply here. The past three centuries have seen the rise and development of a direct challenge to this contention, in what is commonly styled Higher Criticism. The source analysis of the first six books of the Old Testament, from Astruc and De Wette to Colenso and Wellhausen, has resulted in far more than just a transfer of authorship from Moses to a host of nameless men at a distinctly later date or dates. It has brought these books into clear view as the record of centuries of achievement and of the long pilgrimage of men and women, constantly confronted with the tasks and problems of life, making their mistakes, achieving new and sounder insights. In short, to many Christians the Old Testament now stands as the longest and best record of man's evolution and the growth of his ideas about himself and his God, and the record of the development of morality, politics, and religion, which have, for better or worse, very definitely molded our own culture and patterns of thought.

BIBLIOGRAPHY: A. von Harnack, *Bible Reading in the Early Church* (1912); H.R. Willoughby (ed.), *The Study of the Bible Today and Tomorrow* (1947); R.M. Grant, *The Bible in the Church…* (1948); B. Smalley, *The Study of the Bible in the Middle Ages* (1952^2); E.G. Kraeling, *The Old Testament since the Reformation* (1955); I.M. Price, *The Ancestry of our English Bible* (1956^3); G. Burkhardt (ed.), *Five Essays on the Bible* (1960); S.L. Greenslade (ed.), *The Cambridge History of the Bible* (1963); E.C. Colwell, *The Study of the Bible* (1964^2).

[Morton S. Enslin]

IN ISLAM

The presence of Jewish and Christian communities in the northern and southern Arabian Peninsula during the centuries which preceded the advent of *Muhammad is sufficient explanation that the Arabs already knew of the existence of the Bible in these communities during the period of the *Jāhilīyya* ("ignorance"), i.e., before the "Prophet of Islam" began to herald his religion. The pre-Islamic poets saw the books of the Bible in the possession of the Jewish *ḥakhamim* and the Christian clergymen and monks, and since the overwhelming majority of them could not read or write – Muhammad also prided himself on his ignorance in this field (Sura 7:156; cf. also 4:162; 40:78) – the letters appeared to them as the "faded traces of abandoned campsites" which could only be distinguished with difficulty (but see Brockelmann, Arab Lit, supplement 1 (1937), 32 n. 2). The poets mention the *zabūr* – the definition of which appears to be (the book of) Psalms (of David); Muhammad later pluralized it as *zubūr* in the Koran to denote the whole of the Bible (see Sura 17:57; 26:196). Muhammad knew of the Torah (*tawrāt*; e.g., Sura 3:58, 87), which was given to *ahl al-kitāb* ("the people of the book," i.e., Jews and Christians) and like the Koran it is a revelation of the word of God. The *tawrāt* is held as a way of uprightness and light. According to the book of Allah, the Prophets – who were loyal to Allah – as well as the rabbis and the *aḥbār* (Jewish *ḥakhamim*), judged the Jews (Sura 5:48). Even though it is obvious that Muhammad had heard much of the contents of the Bible, there is no doubt that all of his knowledge was acquired from teachings and tales told to him by Jews and Christians. It appears that he was not the only one in his time who repeated these to his followers. His opponents therefore often mocked him because he told them *asāṭīr al-awwalīn*, stories of the ancients which had been heard more than once (see e.g., Sura 6:25; 8:31; 16:26; et al.). It was natural that such religious sermons – whether their contents were intended for the purpose of teaching or amusement – be delivered in a free style (i.e., not verbatim). Accurate translations of the Bible or enlargements with aggadic paraphrases (similar to Targum Jonathan) were however certainly to be found among the *ahl al-kitāb* – if not in writing, then at least in a fixed oral tradition. Nonetheless, it is doubtful whether Muhammad heard these verbatim – at least not during the first years of his appearance. Even though the Koran relies on the words of the *kitāb* ("the Book") – and in many Suras there is a clear allusion to the Pentateuch and the Prophets – the instances which may be regarded as (rather free) translations of the Bible are very few: in Sura 3:87 "all food was lawful to the children of Israel save what Israel (i.e., Jacob) made unlawful to himself before the law was revealed" (see Gen. 32:33; Sura 5:49; cf. Ex. 21:25–26; both Suras belong to the Medina period). Only in Sura 21:105 (of the Mecca period) can one find a quotation from Psalms (37:29) with the mention of the source: "And already have we written in *zabūr* [Psalms]… 'The earth shall my righteous servants inherit.'" ("The righteous shall possess the land, and dwell upon it forever.")

Muhammad points out that Allah gave The (Holy) Book to Mūsā (= Moses; Sura 25:37; 2:81, 140–1, et al.). However, even before Mūsā, *ṣuḥuf* ("holy scrolls") were given to Ibrāhīm (= Abraham; Sura 53:37–38; 87:19; 19:42) and to Ismāʿīl (= Ishmael; 19:55), and their contents were also revealed to earlier generations (20:13; 87:18). According to Sura 20:133, these scrolls contain clear proofs of the prophecy and the mission of Muhammad; they are identical with the *kitāb*, the original book being in Heaven; it was revealed to the prophets and is the source of all revelations. This book is the *umm al-kitāb* (the "mother of the [Holy] Book," 43:3; 85:21). All the deeds of men from the Creation of the World until the final Day of Judgment are also inscribed in this book. According to Speyer (p. 334) the origin of this expression lies in a Midrash ("Torah… which is called a mother to its students"). The notion of the "Book" preserved in Heaven, in which everything is written and which also serves as a register for the deeds of all creatures, is found in the Bible (Ex. 32:32; Isa. 4:3; et al.); Muhammad received it from Judaism (cf. Hirschberg, *Diwan des as-Samau'al*, 24, 52–58).

When Muhammad met face to face with the *aḥbār*, the Jewish *ḥakhamim*, at *Yathrib-Medina, they began to doubt his prophetic mission, and particularly ridiculed his lack of knowledge of the tales of the Bible. Muhammad then accused the Jews (and also the Christians) of having altered (*ḥarrafa*) the words of the Torah and having substituted (*baddala*) what was written in it (Sura 2:56, 70, 73; 4:48; 5:16; 61:6). At Yathrib-Medina, the sharp turning point in Muhammad's attitude toward the Jews occurred. Indeed, Muhammad's lack of familiarity with the Old and New Testaments was particularly revealed in his Bible tales, because with regard to true monotheistic beliefs there are hardly any conflicts with Jewish views; this is not the case with respect to the divinity of Jesus and the Trinity. In the Bible tales, however, the inexactitudes, changes, lack of consistency, and even errors on almost every subject are conspicuous. However, during the years of Muhammad's activity, many changes also occurred in his approach to the Bible tales, which he sometimes deliberately adapted to the new conditions that had emerged; some of these were political, others were connected with information acquired from others or conclusions which he had reached himself. The commentators of the Koran later attempted to explain some of these faults, but with regard to others they did not conceal the truth. The cause of these errors is sometimes the defective source from which Muhammad drew his information, but one may also assume that Muhammad did not attribute much importance to these details. He employed the narrative material as a creator who sought to form a new structure from it, and therefore often adapted it to his requirements. The function of the tales of the Prophets on the events in antiquity and the attitude toward the emissaries who had preceded him was to explain his mission, his war against the inhabitants of Mecca, his policy, and also his failures. Hence the phenomenon that there is no uniform system in the Koran concerning the tradition of the Bible tales.

(A) Certain figures are mentioned by their names, but with occasional changes in the pronunciation which have been influenced by the Greek or Syrian languages, e.g., Ilyās – Elijah; Ismāʿil – Ishmael; Sulaymān – Solomon; Firʿawn – Pharaoh. Other changes are due to Muhammad's affection for the creation of paronomasian couples, such as Hābīl and Qābīl (Abel and Cain), Hārūn and Qārūn (Aaron and Korah), Jālūt and Ṭālūt (Goliath and Saul), Yājūj and Mājūj (Gog and Magog), etc. Other changes must be attributed to Arabic writing, which as of yet did not have the diacritic marks, e.g., *Qiṭfīr instead of Poti-Phar; Asiya (wife of Pharaoh; see *Firʿawn) instead of Asenath (the daughter of Poti-phera). (In both cases the difference in the reading lies in the placing of the diacritic mark.)

(B) Some figures are alluded to in the Koran in such a way that there is no doubt as to whom Muhammad referred, even though they are not mentioned by their biblical name, e.g., the three (or four!) sons of *Noah (Sura 11:44–49), and Joshua son of Nun (5:23–29). This anonymity at times stems from Muhammad's obvious tendency to use insinuations. In some cases, however, the name was not sufficiently clear to him and he then preferred not to name the person (see: e.g., the Sura on *Balaam son of Beor, in the identification of which the commentators of the Koran also encounter difficulties, 7:174–5).

(C) In contrast to this anonymity, some figures are mentioned in the Koran with different names from those in the Bible; figures from the world of fantasy are cited as well: e.g., *Terah, the father of Abraham, is named Āzar; a figure from the world of folklore is the prophet to whom *Moses went during his journey with his servant. The third Sura of the Koran known as the Sura of ʿAmrān Family, i.e., Amram. It refers to a man whose wife (known as Hannah in post-Koranic legend) gave birth to Mary (Miriam), the mother of Jesus, the messiah, as is apparent from the continuation of the tale (3:31ff.). Miriam, the sister of Aaron and Moses, is not referred to by her name in the Koran. Parenthetically, it should be noted that the space allocated in the Koran to the tales and legends of the New Testament is disproportionately small, a fact which has drawn the attention of all researchers (Hirschberg, *Juedische und christliche Lehren*, 64–66). On the other hand, Christian influence is discernible in the descriptions of some of the biblical characters, such as Lot, Solomon, and Jonah. Many attempts, some of them successful, have been made in the post-Koranic Muslim literature to correct the curiosities in the tales of the Koran, to clarify the intentionally or unintentionally obscure places, to call by their correct names those figures who are mentioned by incorrect names or only by allusion, and to complete that which has been omitted in the continuity of the Bible tales. It is remarkable that in spite of the excessively large number of biblical characters referred to by the title of prophet because God spoke to them, and the figures of the prophets who were sent to the Arab tribes (e.g., *Hud, Ṣāliḥ), the three great prophets, Isaiah, Jeremiah, and Ezekiel, are unknown. Speyer has already noted that Muhammad does not allocate a place of importance to women in the Koran, especially not to unmarried girls. In his opinion this is the reason why the rescue of Moses is attributed to Asiya, the wife of Pharaoh (Sura 28:8), and not his daughter. Similarly, there is no mention in the Koran of the names of Sarah, Hagar, Rebekah, Leah, and Rachel (to whom there is a distinct allusion in Sura 4:27), or to Zipporah, the wife of Moses. He presents the wives of Noah and Lot in dreadful disgrace and describes the wife of Pharaoh as a righteous woman (Sura 66:10–12). In the post-Koranic literature all the above women are mentioned by their names and even Keturah, the wife of Abraham, is not forgotten. This process of exegesis and completion began within the circle of Muhammad's friends and supporters immediately after his death. Similar to the *Hadith collections (traditions dealing with *sunnat al-nabī* – the ways of the Prophet, his practical conduct (*halakhah*) – and based on *isnād*, i.e., an unbroken line of transmission which has been handed down from mouth to mouth beginning from the companions of the Prophet or the Prophet himself) they also began to insert, according to the same system, the explanations, commentaries, and legendary additions of the Koran. The legends which originated in Judaism were called *Isrāʾīliyyāt and are to be found in three literary categories: (1) *The commentaries on the Koran*, the most renowned, detailed, and ancient of which is that of the historian Abu Jaʿfar Muhammad al-Ṭabarī (838/9–992). Al-Ṭabarī published a 30-volume anthology of commentaries in accordance with the Hadith system; he presents the various opinions then prevalent on many subjects (see, e.g., in the entry "Isaac" concerning the question of who was bound by Abraham). Al-Ṭabarī, however, was also familiar with the Bible and knew the details of the story of the conquest of Canaan by Joshua.

(2) *Arabic history books*. Again the first volume of the detailed historical work by al-Ṭabarī is a rich source of Bible tales, as they were current among the Arabs and the Muslims in general.

(3) A third source is the *Qiṣaṣ al-Anbiyaʾ* ("Legends of the Prophets"), in which the tales were also collected in chronological order. The first to gather these tales in writing appears to have been *Wahb ibn Munabbih, the author of the *Isrāʾīliyyāt* which have been lost and are only known from quotations. The detailed work which has been printed many times is that of al-Thaʿlabī (d. 1035), who presents his subjects according to the Hadith system. In addition to the legends, his work contains literal translations and paraphrases from the Bible. A second collection which was published is that of al-Kisaʾī (lived during the 11th century). A third collection is extant in manuscript in the Vatican (Cod. Borgia 165); it is the earliest of the collections and belongs to ʿUmāra ibn Wathīma (eighth century). His work does not attain the completeness of those mentioned above. Much romantic material, which cannot be traced to the Bible or to Jewish literature, has also entered into these tales: e.g., the story of Jarāda, the daughter of the king of Sidon, whom Solomon took for his wife after he had defeated her father and whom he loved more than all his other wives because of her beauty (Ṭabarī, *Taʾrīkh*, 1 (1357 A.H.), 351–352). She continued to worship the idols and Āṣaf ibn Barakhyā, the righteous adviser of Solomon who frequented his palace, rebuked him for this. According to the commentators, there is an allusion to this Āṣaf in Sura 27:40, in the story of Bilqīs, the queen of Sheba.

Abundant and rich biblical material has entered Arabic and Muslim literature by the way of the Koran and tales of *aggadah*. Some of the Bible tales, as well as Muhammad's accusations against the changes (*tabdīl*) and the forgeries (*taḥrīf*) in the Bible in order to refute the prophecy of his coming – found in the Holy Scriptures of the Jews and the Christians – served as the Islamic *polemic against Judaism (and Christianity) in Muslim literature. Ibn Ḥazm used this particular method when he argued with Samuel ha-Nagid (11th century), and also the Jewish apostate al-Samawʾal al-Maghribī (Samuel b. Yaḥya; 12th century). One may see the last echo of this polemic in the words of R. David ibn Abi Zimra, who laments: "The Arabs… regard our prayer as heresy and they say that we have added to, subtracted from, and changed our Torah…" (responsa, vol. 4 (Sudilkov, 1836), 21c).

For biblical tales in Islam see also the following articles: *Aaron (Hārūn); *Abraham (Ibrāhīm); *Adam (Ādam); *Balaam (Balʿam ibn Bāʿurā); *Benjamin (Binyāmīn); *Cain and Abel (Qābīl wa-Hābīl); *Canaan (Kanʿan); *Daniel (Dāniyāl); *David (Daʾūd); *Elijah (Ilyās); *Elisha (Alyasʿa); *Enoch (Idrīs); *Eve (Ḥawwaʾ); *Ezekiel (Ḥizqīl); *Ezra (Uzayr); Gog and *Magog (Yājūj and Mājūj); *Goliath (Jālūt); *Haman (Hāmān); *Isaac (Isḥāq); *Isaiah (Shaʿyā); *Israʾīliyyāt; *Ishmael (Ismāʿil); *Jacob (Yaʿqūb); *Jeremiah (Irmiyā); *Job (Ayyūb); *Jonah (Yūnus); *Joseph (Yūsuf); *Joshua (Yūshʿa); *Korah (Qārūn); *Lot (Lūṭ); *Miriam (Maryam); *Moses (Mūsā); *Nebuchadnezzar (Bukhtanaṣr); *Nimrod (Namrūd); *Noah (Nūḥ); *Pharaoh (Firʿawn); *Potiphar (Qiṭfīr) Queen of *Sheba (Bilqīs); *Samaritans (Sāmirī); *Samuel (Shamwīl); *Saul (Ṭālūt); *Seth (Shīth); *Solomon (Saleiman); *Terah (Āzar).

BIBLIOGRAPHY: A. Geiger, *Was hat Mohammed aus dem Judenthume aufgenommen* (1833); G. Weil, *Biblische Legenden der Muselmaenner* (1845); H. Hirschfeld, *Beitraege zur Erklaerung des Koran* (1886); M. Steinschneider, *Polemische und apologetische Literatur in arabischer Sprache zwischen Muslimen, Christen und Juden* (1877); M. Gruenbaum, *Neue Beitraege zur semitischen Sagenkunde* (1893); W. Rudolph, *Die Abhaengigkeit des Qorans von Judentum und Christentum* (1922); J. Horovitz, in: HUCA, 2 (1925), 145–227; idem, *Koranische Untersuchungen* (1926); T. Andrae, *Der Ursprung des Islams und das Christentum* (1926); R. Bell, *The Origin of Islam in its Christian Environment* (1926); J.W. Hirschberg, *Der Dīwān des as Samauʾal ibn ʿAdijaʾ* (1931); idem, *Juedische und christliche Lehren im vor-und fruehislamischen Arabien* (1939); D. Sidersky, *Les origines des légendes musulmanesdans le Coran et dans les vies des prophètes* (1933); Ch. Cutler Torrey, *The Jewish Foundation of Islam* (1933); A. Jeffery, *The Foreign Vocabulary of the Qurʾān* (1938); H. Speyer, *Die biblischen Erzaehlungen im Qoran* (1961²); E.I.J. Rosenthal, *Judaism and Islam* (1961); A.I. Katsh, *Judaism and the Koran* (1954). **ADD. BIBLIOGRAPHY:** Tawrat, EIS², s.v.

[Haïm Z'ew Hirschberg]

IN THE ARTS

Gabriel Sivan's The *Bible and Civilization* (1973) provides, *inter alia*, the first comprehensive survey of the Hebrew Bible's impact on world literature, art, and music.

LITERATURE

Although the Greek Septuagint translation of the Old Testament inspired a few writers in classical times, the Hebrew Bible's first significant impact on the secular literature of other nations really dates from the Middle Ages with the beginning of drama. Old Testament episodes figured in various cycles of Sacred Mysteries or Miracle Plays sponsored by the Church (mainly in England, France, and Germany), the vernacular eventually replacing Latin dialogue. During the Reformation, writers in many countries produced biblical epics which expressed the national aspirations and religious yearnings of their people. New scope was given to original treatment of Old Testament themes through the appearance of numerous Bible *translations (largely the works of Protestant scholars in Switzerland, Germany, England, Hungary, and other lands); and these not only popularized the Bible stories, but also very often had linguistic repercussions. From the Renaissance era onward, biblical works increasingly contained political and social overtones. Although *Yiddish literature is several centuries old, Yiddish fiction based on biblical themes other than *Purim plays is of recent date. Some notable treatments of Old Testament themes are dramas by Abraham *Goldfaden (*Akeydas Yitskhok*, 1897) and Sholem *Asch's novels *Moses*

(1951) and *The Prophet* (1955). *Judeo-Provençal contains a late 17th-century *Tragediou de la Reine Esther* by Mardochée Astruc, revised and published by Jacob *Lunel (The Hague, 1774); *Ladino literature the early 15th-century *Poema de Yoçef* and Abraham de Toledo's *Coplas de Yoçef* (Constantinople, 1732); and *Judeo-Persian literature four poetic paraphrases of Bible stories by the 14th-century writer Maulana *Shahin of Shiraz, who was emulated by the poet *Imrani in the 16th century and by Yusuf *Yahudi in the 18th century. In other literatures, Jewish writers either followed conventional approaches to Old Testament subjects, or, more frequently, reinterpreted the biblical stories in the light of issues such as Jewish emancipation, religious toleration, and political Zionism.

Allusions as well as explicit references to the Old Testament pervade modern Hebrew literature. The earlier writers based their works on biblical themes and biblical figures (see, for instance, *Mapu's prose or David *Frischmann's *Ba-Midbar*). *Agnon's prose reverberates with biblical allusions and motifs. Saul *Tchernichowsky wrote a number of poems focusing on King Saul, disclosing his empathy for the rather tragic figure of the first Hebrew king. Similarly, some poets identified with biblical figures whose name they bore and expressed it in verse: Legendary poetess *Raḥel (Bluwstein-Sel'a) wrote a number poems about Jacob's beloved wife Rachel, underscoring her inability to give birth to the much-longed for son; Avraham *Shlonsky mentioned his namesake, the biblical patriarch Abraham, while poetess Yocheved *Bat-Miriam chose her family name to underline her identification with Moses' sister, Miriam. Moshe *Shamir depicts the political tensions and military actions of the early state of Israel in the context of the Hasmonean period (*Melekh Basar va-Dam*, 1954), and reverts to an earlier biblical period, to the story of King David and Bath-Sheba in *Kivsat ha-Rash* (1957). Other biblical heroes feature prominently: Samson (for instance in David *Avidan's *Shimshon ha-Gibbor*), Sisra's mother (notably, as a tragic figure!) in a poem by Haim *Gouri), Job (as, for example, in Hanoch *Levin's play *Yisurei Iyov* (*Job's Passion*, 1988). Shulamit *Hareven based many of her prose works on biblical motives (for instance, *Sone ha-Nisim*, *The Miracle Hater*, 1983). Meir *Shalev gave his own original reading of the Bible in *Tanakh Akhshav* (*Bible Now*) and coalesced biblical materials with original fiction in some of his novels, as for example in *Esav* (*Esau*, 1991). Zeruya *Shalev's heroine Yaara in the bestseller *Love Life* (1997) writes a dissertation on legends relating to the destruction of the Temple and even *Kishon's satirical oeuvre is full of references to biblical characters. No doubt the most prominent biblical motive in modern Hebrew literature is that of the *Akedah, the binding of Isaac, which is handled, often with ironic twists and in a most unconventional manner, in poems by Amir *Gilboa, Yehuda *Amichai, David Avidan, Tuvia Ruebner and Chanoch Levin, to name but a few. For some of the poets (Gilboa, for instance) it is not only the son who is sacrificed, but the father. Benjamin Galai, on the other hand, sees (in "Sarah's Lives") the biblical mother Sarah as the real victim of the planned sacrifice of her son, Isaac, while Yehuda Amichai suggests that the real victim of that famous biblical episode is neither Abraham nor Isaac, but – typically for Amichai – the ram that was caught in the thicket by his horns. The Bible has also served as a source of inspiration for various historical novels, such as Shlomit Abrahmson's *Ma'ase Tamar* (2005), which is based on Genesis 38 and the biblical figure of Judah's daughter-in-law.

In *English literature a vast array of biblical figures appear in poetry and prose from the seventh century C.E. onward. Among the Puritans, John *Milton was outstanding (*Paradise Lost*, 1667; *Samson Agonistes*, 1671), biblical motifs also dominating some works by John Dryden (*Absalom and Achitophel*, 1681). After a lull in the 18th century, the impact of the Bible was again evident in Lord *Byron (*Hebrew Melodies*, 1815) and the scholarly Robert *Lowth and Matthew Arnold; while a more mystical vein appeared in the writings of William *Blake. The 19th century saw the emergence of a reckless biblicism in various works by the British *Israelites. With the exception of Isaac *Rosenberg, Jewish writers in England have largely avoided biblical themes. Some later non-Jewish authors who drew inspiration from the Bible were G.B. Shaw (*Back to Methuselah*, 1921); J.M. Barrie (*The Boy David*, 1936); James Bridie (plays including *Tobias and the Angel*, 1930); and Christopher Fry (*A Sleep of Prisoners*, 1941). The Old Testament's first significant impact on *French literature can be traced to the late 16th century, when French Protestants wrote epics of biblical grandeur, notably Salluste *Du Bartas (*La semaine ou création du monde*, 1578; *La seconde semaine*, 1584) and Agrippa d'Aubigné (*Les Tragiques*, 1577–94; published 1616). Biblical dramas of the same era were written by Jean de la Taille (*Saül le furieux*, 1562) and Robert Garnier (*Sédécie ou les Juives*, 1589). An epic poet of the Renaissance whose works were full of biblical and kabbalistic allusions was Guy Le Fèvre de la *Boderie. In the 17th century, Bossuet and *Pascal were profoundly influenced by the Bible, as was the dramatist Jean *Racine (*Esther*, 1689); *Athalie*, 1691). The 18th-century French philosophers were mainly hostile to the Old Testament, but later writers favorably reassessed the Bible, notably Chateaubriand, and the poets Lamartine, de Vigny, and Victor Hugo. Biblical themes also attracted the Catholic writers Léon *Bloy, Paul *Claudel, and Charles *Péguy. In the 20th century, there were plays by André Obey (*Noé*, 1931), and André Gide (*Saül*, 1903), and poems by Pierre Emmanuel and Jean Grosjean. Among Jewish writers, Edmond *Fleg, André *Spire, Gustave *Kahn (*Images bibliques*, 1929), and Benjamin *Fondane were outstanding interpreters of the Bible. The impact of the Old Testament in *Italian literature was rather more limited, although the ex-Marrano poet Solomon *Usque wrote a Purim play about Queen Esther (performed in Venice, 1558), which was both successful and influential. Originally written in Portuguese or Spanish it was reworked in Italian and published by Leone *Modena (1619). Giambattista Andreini's drama *Adamo* (1613) is thought to have inspired the character of Satan in Milton's *Paradise Lost*; and biblical themes dominated some works by Feo Belcari, Pietro Metastasio, and Vittorio Alfieri (*Saul*,

1782; *Abele*, 1797). Two Jewish writers who turned to the Bible for inspiration were David *Levi, the author of an allegorical drama about Jeremiah (*Il profeta*, 1866), and Guido *Bedarida, whose *La bella ridestata* (1927) was a Zionist allegory invoking the figure of Abishag the Shunamite. In *Spanish and Portuguese literature, more than a quarter of the biblical *autos* of the Madrid Codex (1550–75) deal with Old Testament themes. During the Renaissance Luis de *Léon, a humanist of partly New Christian descent, wrote biblical poems and translations, while Usque's Purim play was staged at Venice. Two leading 17th-century dramatists who used biblical motifs were Tirso de Molina (*La venganza de Tamar*, 1634) and Calderón. Marrano and Jewish writers were, however, more prominent as interpreters of Old Testament themes in Spanish during the 17th and 18th centuries. They include the eminent preacher Felipe *Godínez; Francisco (Joseph) de *Caceres; Antonio Enríquez *Gómez (*El Sansón nazareno*, 1651; *La Torre de Babilonia*, 1649); and João (Mose) *Pinto Delgado. Like Pinto Delgado, Isaac Cohen de *Lara was attracted to the story of Esther, publishing a *Comedia famosa de Aman y Mordochay* (Leiden, 1699). Although many Jewish writers made their appearance in Latin America from the late 19th century, few, if any, paid more than cursory attention to biblical motifs.

The Old Testament was a prime cultural influence in *Dutch literature, the Calvinists of Holland seeing themselves as Israelites engaged in a war of liberation against Catholic Spain. The outstanding Dutch biblical writer of the 17th century was, however, a Protestant convert to Catholicism, Joost van den Vondel, whose many biblical dramas include *Joseph in Egypten* (1640), *Salomon* (1648), *Jephta* (1659), *Koning David hersteld* (1660), *Adam in Ballingschap* (1664), and *Noah* (1667). After some decline of interest in the 18th and 19th centuries, biblical writing revived with works such as H. de Bruin's epic drama about Job (1944). Three Jewish writers of the 20th century who dealt with biblical themes were Israël *Querido (*Saul en David*, 1915; *Simson*, 1927), Abel *Herzberg (*Sauls dood*, 1958), and Manuel van *Loggem (*Mozes in Egypte*, 1960). Old Testament themes in *German and Austrian literature have been traced back to the 11th century but, apart from the Miracle plays found also in England and France, the Bible's influence was more important during and after the Reformation. Biblical themes attracted first Sixtus Birck and Hans Sachs, then Christian Weise (*Nebukadnezar*, 1684; *Athalia*, 1687; *Kain und Abel*, 1704) and Johann Bodmer (*Die Synd-Flut*, 1751). Their successors included Solomon Gessner, Friedrich Klopstock, and J.K. Lavater (*Abraham und Isaak*, 1776). Biblical culture exerted varying degrees of influence on *Herder, *Schiller, and *Goethe (whose *Faust* owes much to the book of Job). Old Testament motifs also preoccupied some of the leading 19th-century dramatists, notably Franz Grillparzer (*Esther*, 1877). In the 20th century, Georg Kaiser, Frank Wedekind (*Simson oder Scham und Eifersucht*, 1914), and Thomas *Mann (*Joseph und seine Brueder*, 1933–43) were only three of the many leading writers who turned to the Bible. The Bible also inspired a remarkably large number of Jewish authors from the 19th century onward. Biblical poems were written by *Heine; plays by Karl *Beck (*Saul*, 1841), Arno *Nadel (*Adam*, 1917), Richard *Beer-Hofmann (*Jaakobs Traum*, 1918; *Der junge David*, 1933), Sammy *Gronemann, Max *Brod, Stefan *Zweig (*Jeremias*, 1917), and many others; and biblical novels were published by Joseph *Roth (*Hiob*, 1930), and Lion *Feuchtwanger (*Jefta und seine Tochter*, 1957). The European Holocaust, however, put an end to this vast and creative literary output. In *Hungarian literature, too, biblical influences were at work during the Middle Ages and the Reformation. Biblical themes inspired Protestant epics of the 16th century, and 18th-century dramas, notably *Izsák házassága* ("The Marriage of Isaac", 1704) by Ferenc Pápai Páriz. The Hungarian national revival in the 19th century prompted works by Mihály Tompa (*Samson*, 1863) and Imre Madách (*Mózes*, 1860); and biblical poems were composed by 20th-century writers such as Endre Ady and Attila József. Jewish writers who reinterpreted biblical themes included Emil *Makai, Lajos *Palágyi, Lajos *Szabolcsi and Károly *Pap (*Batséba*, performed 1940; *Mózes*, performed 1944). Several Jewish writers in Hungary also dealt with biblical motifs after World War II. Themes from the Bible have received differing emphases in the Balkan lands. A classic drama of modern *Greek literature was Vikentios Kornaros' *I Thysia tou Abraam* ("The Sacrifice of Abraham, c. 1675), a humanistic interpretation of the *Akedah story. One 20th-century Greek work of biblical inspiration was the drama *Sodhoma kye Ghomorra* (1956) by Nikos Kazantzakis and books by Jewish writers, such as Joseph *Eliyia and Nestoras *Matsas. In *Romanian literature, one of the earliest biblical works was J.A. Vaillant's *Legenda lui Aman şi Mardoheu* (1868). Alexandru Macedonski and Cincinat Pavelescu wrote the tragedy *Saul* (1893); the book of Job inspired poetic works by G. Gârbea (1898) and N. Davidescu (1915); while Eugen Lovinescu wrote the play *Eliezer* (1908). Romania's most prominent biblical writer was the Christian Zionist Gala *Galaction. Among Jewish authors, those who dealt with Old Testament motifs included Enric *Furtuna (*Abişag*, 1963), Camil *Baltazar, and Marcel Breslaşu, who wrote an oratorio based on the Song of Songs. Some of the outstanding figures in *Yugoslav (Serbo-Croatian) literature sought biblical inspiration from the 16th century onward, notably the Ragusan poet Mavro Vetranović. Later Milovan Vidaković composed Serbian epics about Joseph (1805) and Tobias (1825), while Aron Alkalaj, a Jewish banker of Belgrade, wrote a biographical work about Moses (1938). One of the early classics of *Bulgarian literature was Ioan (John) the Exarch's ninth-century *Shestodnev* ("The Six Days"), based on the Creation story. During the later Middle Ages, many biblical works were written by the heretical Bogomils. In the 20th century, Emanuil Pop Dimitrov published *Rut* and *Deshcherite na Yeftaya* ("Jephthah's Daughter"). In *Czechoslovak literature two outstanding biblical works by non-Jews were *Vůdce* (1916; *The Leader*, 1917), a drama about Moses by Stanislav Lom, and *Adam stvořitel* (1927; *Adam the Creator*, 1929), a play by the brothers Josef and Karel čapek. However, Old Testament themes proved more attractive to Jewish authors. Julius

*Zeyer (*Sulamit*, 1883), Jaroslav *Vrchlický, and Eduard *Leda were among the most prominent of these. Biblical works were also written by two later Jewish authors, Ivan *Olbracht and Jiří *Orten. The treatment of Old Testament subjects in early *Polish literature was largely colored by the religious controversies of the Reformation. The Calvinist Mikołaj Rej, who versified the Psalms, wrote a work on Joseph (*Żywot Józefa z pokolenia żydowskiego*, c. 1545) and his contemporary, Jan Kochanowski, who also translated the Psalter, produced epics on the Flood (1558) and Susannah (1562), as well as the biblical *Threny* ("Lamentations", Cracow, 1580). Later Polish writers whose biblical themes symbolized the fate of their homeland were Adam *Mickiewicz, Kornel Ujejski (*Pieśni Salomona*, 1846; *Skargi Jeremiego*, London 1847), *Melodye biblijne*, 1852; and the dramatist Stanisław Wyspiański (*Daniel*, 1908). Since Yiddish was Polish Jewry's cultural language before the Holocaust, Jewish treatments of the Bible in Polish fiction are rare. In *Russian literature, on the other hand, biblical motifs were generally less prominent, although many leading writers were clearly steeped in the language of the Old Testament. The 11th-century *Primary Chronicle* begins with an account of the Tower of Babel, while in the 15th century Bible translations and even some rabbinic motifs appeared in the writings of various Judaizing sects. Modern Russian drama is largely the creation of Semyon Polotski and the German Lutheran pastor Johann Gottfried Grigori, who wrote biblical plays for the Moscow court, where a drama about Esther was staged in 1672. Old Testament themes have been reinterpreted in the 20th century by the writers Alexander Kuprin (*Sulamif*, 1908) and Leonid Andreyev; and by two Jewish authors of the post-Stalin "thaw", Semyon *Kirsanov and Joseph *Brodski.

The Bible and the associated traditions of the Midrash were a major source of Moslem legend. Though in general unspectacular, the Islamic sphere of *Oriental literature also produced a few works on biblical subjects, beginning with poems by the 9th-century Hejaz poet *Samuel b. Adiya (Al-Samw'al Ibn ʿAdiyā). There are also biblical allusions in the poems of a 13th-century Spanish Arabic author, *Ibrāhīm b. Sahl al-Andalūsī (Abu Isḥāq). A 20th-century writer who versified the Old Testament was the Egyptian Karaite Murād *Faraj. The literary use of biblical motifs in *United States literature is very much more recent. Old Testament influence may be seen in the writings of major 19th-century authors such as Emerson, Hawthorne, Whitman, and Whittier. Two best-selling religious romances by Joseph Holt Ingraham were *The Pillar of Fire* (1859) and *The Throne of David* (1860). Some writers of the 20th century who dealt with Old Testament themes were William Vaughn Moody (*The Death of Eve*, 1912), and Archibald MacLeish (*Nobodaddy*, 1926; *J.B.*, 1958). Marc Connelly's play *The Green Pastures* (1930) was a black reinterpretation of the Bible stories. American Jewish writers were prominent among those who sought new ideas in the Old Testament. They include the novelists Robert *Nathan (*Jonah*, 1925), Irving *Fineman (*Jacob*, 1941; *Ruth*, 1949), Howard *Fast (*Moses, Prince of Egypt*, 1958), and Maurice *Samuel; the playwrights Clifford *Odets (whose *The Flowering Peach*, 1954, reinterpreted the story of Noah) and Paddy *Chayefsky (*Gideon*, 1961); and poets such as James *Oppenheim, Charles *Reznikoff, Delmore *Schwartz (*Genesis*, 1943), and Louis *Untermeyer. In *Canadian literature the poets Irving *Layton and Eli Mandel made much of biblical imagery; and Adele Wiseman (in *The Sacrifice*, 1956) retold the story of the *Akedah* in a prairie setting. In more recent years, the women of the Bible have received special attention. Notable works are Anita Diamant's *Red Tent* (1997), telling the story of Dinah, and Marek *Halter's trilogy on Sarah, Zipporah, and Lilah (2004–6).

The Hebrew Bible has been one of the most powerful literary stimuli of the past millennium, inspiring poems, plays, novels, and stories in many languages. The Old Testament's portrayal of the human condition and of man's relation to the Divine remains an inexhaustible source of inspiration for Jews and non-Jews alike, wherever the Bible is freely taught and imbibed.

MUSIC

The musical setting of biblical texts or subjects is a basic element in both the Jewish and the Christian cultures. A biblical text may be attached to a simple melodic pattern and incorporated in the liturgy, or it may be set, with the technical resources of art music, for an ensemble of voices and instruments for performance on the concert stage. The extent of quotation may range from the repetition of a single verse – chosen for its overt or symbolic content – to an exposition of entire chapters or even books, which may vary from the simplest to the most complex. Finally, the "musicalization" of a biblical text or story-subject may serve as a means of carrying both performer and listener away from everyday reality, to the reenactment of a religious or historical experience; or it may be intended to achieve the exact opposite, drawing the traditional words, stories and characters into the contemporary world (as in the *Purimspiel, the Negro Spiritual, or the contemporary Israel "verse-song"). The mere enumeration of the repertoire of "The Bible in Music", even within the limits of printed sources of European art music, is a virtually impossible task, although partial lists have been published. The situation is further complicated by the use of mixed texts, especially in motets and cantatas, where biblical quotations, texts from the New Testament and ecclesiastical literature, and new poetic creations, alternate and complement each other symbolically.

There is no field of Western art music in which the Bible has not been reflected at one time or another; the major forms are the Mass, oratorio, cantata, motet, and opera and operetta. Biblical subjects have also furnished the inspiration for various forms of instrumental music (such as Johann Kuhnau's "Biblical Sonatas" in the 18th century), as well as ballet.

The problem of censorship has left its imprint on the history of the "Bible in Music", as it has on the spoken and visual arts, and especially in those forms intended for actual stage representation. Even when biblical characters were permitted to appear, move and sing, the appearance of God was often forbidden, even as a disembodied voice. The late development of oratorio in France, for instance, is directly connected with such a ban, which was relaxed officially only about the middle of the 18th century. In Russia the prohibition against representing biblical characters in a sung work was in force until the end of the Czarist regime.

See also separate articles on individual characters, subjects and books of the Bible and Apocrypha, and on *Cantillation; *Haggadah; *Hallel; *Hallelujah; *Music; *Priestly Blessing; *Psalms (Music); *Shema.

[Bathja Bayer]

ART

The Hebrew Bible has been a continual source of inspiration to artists from classical antiquity until the present day and was a major source until the 17th century. In early Christian wallpaintings in the Roman catacombs and in the carvings on sarcophagi certain images including "Sacrifice of Isaac", "Moses striking the Rock", the "Three Men in the Fiery Furnace" (Shadrach, Meshach and Abed-Nego), and "Jonah and the Whale" continually recur. These images, which were associated with Christian doctrines concerning the life to come, have their artistic origins in pagan art and also, perhaps, in Jewish visual representations of the Bible, such as those that survive in the wallpaintings of the synagogue at *Dura-Europos. In the East Roman (Byzantine) empire, the visual interpretation of the Bible was dominated by the icon, or "holy image", whose form, credited with a divine origin, was preserved unchanged for hundreds of years. This precluded the development of any narrative interest. The characteristic artform of Byzantium was the mosaic, but the troubled condition of the West after the fall of Rome discouraged ambitious schemes of architectural embellishment and favored instead the more modest illuminated manuscript. This was at first somewhat stylized, but the Carolingian period of the ninth century witnessed a renaissance of creativity. Traditional images were transformed, iconography was developed, and a number of important schools of illumination came into being. Until the close of the Middle Ages, Christian representations of the Bible were governed by certain dogmatic considerations. Scenes from the Old Testament were held to prefigure episodes from the New, and were generally depicted in that light. Thus, the sacrifice of Isaac was taken to be symbolic of the Crucifixion of Jesus; the story of Jonah and the whale as a prefiguration of the Resurrection. In the age of the great Romanesque and Gothic cathedrals, from the 12th century onward, most of the arts tended to be subordinated to a total architectural ensemble. Gradually, however, each art began to regain a life of its own. The static carved figures round the cathedrals began to converse in groups; in Italy they were placed in niches which isolated them in an independent area of space. The same tendency was to be seen in other arts.

The Gothic architecture of the North eliminated wall-space in order to let in the light, so that frescoes were replaced by stained-glass windows. In Italy wallpainting continued to develop but, instead of remaining subordinate to the architectural scheme, it became increasingly of equal importance to its setting. This tendency reached its culmination in Michelangelo's great biblical frescoes in the Sistine Chapel in Rome. In the same way, illuminations which had formerly been integral to the text of a manuscript now developed into miniature paintings, in which an artist's individuality could be expressed. Other changes occurred. Images no longer depended to the same degree on their purely symbolic significance. Artists sought to treat figures naturalistically, placing them in their natural settings. More and more, the biblical subject provided an opportunity for the study of contemporary life. Paintings developed a third dimension, with colors that were naturalistic rather than symbolic. The interest in the natural setting finally developed into landscape-painting. By the 17th century, the landscape in the paintings of Nicholas Poussin was given the same importance as the biblical figures, and in the paintings of his contemporary Claude Lorrain it is given even more. Some of Poussin's biblical scenes are primarily studies of nature; thus his "Ruth and Boaz" (c. 1660–64, Paris, Louvre) is in reality a portrait of summer.

National schools of painting developed, each with its own characteristics. The Italians rendered space according to the laws of perspective and took inspiration for their figures from the art of antiquity. French painters such as Claude Lorrain utilized standardized compositions resembling stage-sets. The Germans sometimes divided up the picture-plane into a number of sections according to the theme. Italian painters favored boldly constructed landscapes and interiors, showing man as the master of space. Italian interiors were clearly visible and well defined, whereas northern interiors could be dark and mysterious, with filtered light such as is found in the works of *Rembrandt. The Italian Renaissance glorified man. In his *Creation of Adam* (1511, Vatican, Sistine Chapel), Michelangelo depicted Adam as the perfect man, the image of God. Michelangelo created several of the most famous interpretations of Old Testament figures. His sculpture of Moses on the tomb of Pope Julius II (c. 1513–16, Rome, S. Pietro in Vincoli) and David (at the Florence Academy) and his painting of Jeremiah (c. 1511) in the Sistine Chapel frescoes are particularly noteworthy. In the 17th century, Rubens treated biblical themes with great dramatic freedom, and Rembrandt restored an element of supernatural mystery to painting, from which it had been banished by the development of naturalistic representation. Rembrandt lived in the heyday of Protestantism, which had brought the Old Testament into favor but at the same time disapproved of paintings of the Bible. Nevertheless, it was a major theme in Rembrandt's work. In his biblical paintings, he abandoned the longstanding tradition of typology and treated each episode on its merits and not as a prefiguration of something else. His tender, emotional treatment often suggested a subject rather than described it. His famous painting of David and Saul, for example, depicts their psychological relationship but not an exact textual passage. He also made many biblical etchings and drawings.

After the late 18th century there was no longer a universally accepted style of painting, and hence no longer a language through which a painter of biblical subjects could easily communicate with the public. Morever, the authority of the Scriptures was no longer unquestioningly accepted. Paintings of the Bible became sporadic, and largely anecdotal or antiquarian. In the 19th century, however, major Jewish artists treated the subject for the first time, and, in the 20th century they accorded it a far more comprehensive treatment. Thus the Old Testament has been the subject of over 40 paintings and numerous etchings by Marc *Chagall and of many works by *Ben-Zion, which bear witness to the fascination the Bible continues to exert on artists up to the present time.

Islamic Art

In Islamic art Bible figures often occur in manuscript illustration, but in less than profoundly religious context, being encountered in histories, scientific works, or the type of book called *Stories of the Prophets*. The important period for this art was from the 14th to the 17th centuries, and the area was that under Persian influence. Various Genesis topics recur – Adam and Eve, Abel, Noah's Ark, and especially Joseph and Potiphar's wife. Moses and Solomon, both part of the Muslim canon, appear, and also Jonah and the whale. Style changes reflect those in the Persian secular miniature, and the manner is equally sensuous and realistic.

ILLUSTRATED BIBLES IN MEDIEVAL ILLUMINATED MANUSCRIPTS

Pictorial biblical cycles in the early Middle Ages probably grew out of early Jewish art. Similarly, iconographical elements of the surviving biblical representations in Jewish monumental art of the third and fourth centuries, and some Christian Greek and Latin illumination, suggest an earlier Jewish prototype. Representations of the midrashic *aggadah* in medieval Christian illumination also point to the same ancient source. It is not known whether the original source for biblical representation was architectural art, such as the third-century fresco cycle in the synagogue of *Dura-Europos, or an illustrated biblical text. No ancient or early medieval Hebrew illuminated Bible has survived, although this does not exclude the possibility that there may have been one in scroll or codex form before the 3rd century. The Cotton Genesis, fragments of a Greek fifth-century Bible probably from Egypt (B.M. Cotton Ms. Otho. B. VI) is the earliest surviving illustrated biblical manuscript. Its framed miniatures, placed within the text pages, may allude to an illustrated scroll as an archetype. The direct iconographic relation of the Cotton Genesis to the mosaics in the church of Sta. Maria Maggiore in Rome further suggests a common prototype. The Cotton Genesis Recension maintained its influence during the Middle Ages in Eastern and Western biblical representations, such as 13th-century mosaics of S. Marco in Venice, and the 12th-century *Hortus Deliciarum*, formerly in Strasbourg. Byzantine biblical representations apparently belonged to another recension related to an important Greek manuscript, the Vienna Genesis (Vienna National Library Ms. Theo. Gr. 31). The incomplete text paraphrases the Book of Genesis, and illustrations appear at the bottom of each page. The position of the illustrations suggests a scroll archetype for the manuscript, since classical scientific scrolls were illustrated in this way. It has been suggested that the manuscript was made for a child's biblical education. This theory accounts for the textual paraphrase, the legendary material, and many everyday scenes. Since the manuscript was painted on purple-tinted vellum, it was probably meant for a child of royal family. The style and motifs date it to the time of Justinian (sixth century). The Cotton and Vienna Genesis manuscripts are but two surviving examples of an important Eastern school of illumination in Alexandria, Antioch and Constantinople. The "Joshua Roll" in the Vatican Library (Palat. Grec. 431), probably of the tenth century, has a very shortened Greek text as captions to the consecutive pictorial episodes from the Book of Joshua, painted on a scroll. The style, iconography and some Classical motifs suggest a prototype which may go back to the second century C.E.

Biblical illustrations of the Western tradition are best exemplified by the full-page illustrations of the Latin Ashburnham Pentateuch (Bib. Nat. Nouv. Acq. Lat. 2334). Dating from the seventh century, but of unknown origin, this manuscript contains iconography different from the Eastern tradition of the Cotton and Vienna Genesis recension, although a complete comparison is not possible because most of the full-page miniatures have been cut out. In the early Middle Ages illustrations existed in the East and West for books of the Bible other than the Pentateuch. There were, for example, the fifth-century "Itala Fragments" illustrating episodes from I Samuel, and the Syrian Book of Kings of 705 C.E. (Paris, Nat. Ms. Syr. 27). The "Itala Fragments" (Berlin Ms. Theo. Lat. fol. 485), which use a Latin translation earlier than that of St. Jerome, were found in a 17th-century binding. Some of the color had disappeared, exposing written instructions by the scribe to the artist regarding what he should illustrate in the miniatures. These instructions suggest the possibility that the illustration of Bible manuscripts may have been a matter of individual choice. By the pre-Iconoclastic period, Byzantine illuminators had developed a system of consecutive biblical illustrations. Such pictures were used, for example, to illustrate the book of Christian Topography by Cosmas Indicopleustes. As soon as the Iconoclastic bans were lifted after 843 C.E., biblical representations returned to Byzantine illumination, fashioned after the surviving Early Christian and Antique representations. One example is the manuscript of the Sermons of St. Gregory of Nazianzus (c. 880 C.E.), which has extensive biblical illustrations. Consecutive cycles also continued in post-Iconoclastic times, mainly in illuminated psalters. Psalters illustrated the life of David, episodes from the Exodus from Egypt, and other passages mentioned in the text. The two main types were the "aristocratic", with full-page miniatures and the "monastic", with marginal illustrations. Among the best known Byzantine biblical manuscripts are the Greek Octateuchs, which contain the Pentateuch and the books of Joshua, Judges, and Ruth. The 11th- to 13th-century Octateuchs have small miniatures within the text.

In the West, the most famous Carolingian center for biblical illustration was the French city of Tours. The Bibles of this school illustrate the life of the first men and Moses with the Israelites in the desert. It is possible that the large Bibles from Tours were inspired by a biblical illuminated manuscript of the Cotton Genesis recension and also by the Ashburnham Pentateuch, which was probably in Tours by the ninth century. Psalters were also illustrated in Carolingian art centers, the most notable being the Utrecht Psalter and the Stuttgart Psalter, which contain illustrations above each psalm. For an unknown reason, no consecutive cycle of biblical episodes existed in Ottonian illumination, and the few biblical representations were usually symbolic. Other regional schools, such as the Anglo-Saxon, Franco-Saxon and Italian, followed the same symbolic method. In Spain, however, a system of biblical text illustrations survived from later antiquity, and formed the Catalan school of illumination of the 10th to 13th centuries. Artists used this system to illustrate the commentaries of Beatus of Liébana on the Apocalypse as well as complete Bibles. It was only through the influence of Byzantine art that biblical cycles were reestablished in the other parts of Western Europe during the 12th century. Most French, German and English Bibles of the 12th century had a few illustrations, probably all derived from Byzantine prototypes. The custom of adding a sequence of full-page biblical illustrations to the psalter was possibly also derived from Byzantine aristocratic psalters. The spread of biblical cycles attached to psalters from England to France during the 13th century is parallel to the development of the Gothic style in illuminated manuscripts. A complete series of biblical illustrations from the Creation to the building of the Second Temple was produced in France, mainly in Paris, during the reign of *Louis IX. The best examples are the Pierpont Morgan Picture Bible and the *Psalter of St. Louis*. This biblical series quickly spread from France to most European countries, and was incorporated into other types of books, such as the German *Weltchroniks* and *Armenbibel*, the French *Histoire Universelle, Bible Moralisée, Biblia Pauperum* and *Speculum Humanae Salvationis*, and the Hebrew Spanish *Haggadot*. During the early part of the Italian Renaissance, it became fashionable to illustrate biblical texts with elaborate miniatures on the first page of each book. Their iconography is mainly based on central and south Italian tradition, which preserved the most classical iconography, both in miniatures and in the monumental art of the period. Examples are the Pantheon Bible of the 12th century, the Padua Bible of the 14th century, and the Bible of Borso d'Este of the 15th century. The early printed bibles mainly used the 15th-century system of Italian illuminated bibles and some of the early printed Gutenberg Bibles were hand decorated as if they were manuscripts. The printed editions of the Poor Men's Bibles mainly followed the hand-produced examples of this type.

[Bezalel Narkiss]

Illuminated Hebrew Manuscripts

The *halakhah* explicitly forbids the decoration of the Scroll of the Law read in the synagogue. (Tradition condemns the Jerusalemites of Alexandria for adorning their scroll with the name of God in gold; Sof. 1:8.) However, Hebrew Bibles in codex form, not used for reading in the synagogue, may have been decorated and illustrated in antiquity, though no such manuscripts have survived. Those illuminated Hebrew Bibles which still exist belong to a later period. They consist of four regional types: Oriental, Spanish, Ashkenazi, and Italian. Their styles differ but they share iconographic and formal elements.

Oriental Bibles may have originated in the first or second century and may have served as a model to the surviving illuminated Bibles. A comparison of ninth- and 13th-century illuminated manuscripts with first- and second-century monuments, such as wall paintings and floor mosaics, suggests that illuminated Bibles consisted of textual illustrations, implements of the Temple, and fully decorated pages which, from their likeness to designs on Oriental carpets, are known as carpet pages. The wall paintings in *Dura-Europos may be an example of a cycle inspired by Bible manuscripts. Later medieval Greek, Latin, and Hebrew illuminated manuscripts contain similar iconography. The Jewish legendary material (*aggadah) depicted in early synagogues and in later manuscripts may allude to an illustrated paraphrase of the Bible, rather than to the canonic text. The early identification of the Temple portal and implements of the Temple with messianic and national aspirations made them an important subject of decoration in minor cult objects as well as in synagogal art. Another element which appears in early synagogal decoration, such as the Aegina and the *Bet Alfa floor mosaic, is the framed carpet-like area decorated with geometrical, repetitive patterns. The reappearance of such decorations in later illuminated Bibles makes it plausible that early Hebrew Bibles might well have been similarly illustrated.

ORIENTAL. Most of the existing Oriental illuminated Hebrew Bibles come from Egypt. The earliest illuminated Bibles, of the ninth and tenth centuries, are of *Karaite rather than *Rabbanite origin. Of these, the earliest existing illuminated manuscript is a ninth-or tenth-century codex of the Latter Prophets, found in the Karaite synagogue in Cairo. This manuscript, together with two Pentateuch fragments of 929 C.E. (Leningrad, Firkovich collection, II, 17) and 951 C.E. (Ms. Firkovich, II, 8), and a tenth-century Karaite Pentateuch written in Arabic characters (British Museum, Ms. Or. 2540) help to establish the system of decorating Oriental Hebrew Bibles from the ninth to the 13th centuries. The style is Oriental and may be either Palestinian or Mesopotamian. Preceding the biblical text, there are fully decorated pages, colored in gold, green, red, and blue, either carpet pages or decorated pages containing patterned masoretic micrography. The carpet pages are composed of repeated geometric designs or a central motif with ornamented frame. In several manuscripts, such as the Cairo Karaite Latter Prophets, there are two geometrical, patterned carpet pages which have an additional palmette motif on the outer border. The origin of such carpet pages is unknown, but similar types can be found in the eighth-century Christian sacred books of Hiberno-Saxon and Northumbrian origin, such as the *Lindisfarne Gospels*. In Hebrew Bibles they are directly related to the traditional opening and closing pages of Koran manuscripts of the same period.

The other type of fully decorated pages in Oriental Bibles incorporates floral and geometric motifs outlined in micrography. The text of the minute script is usually the *masorah magna. Some masoretic pages have a portal-like motif, although most have round, square, or rhomboid shapes. Floral and geometric elements sometimes frame dedicatory and colophon pages. In addition to the carpet pages, the Pentateuch manuscript dated 929 C.E. has two pages with a display or plan of the sacred implements of the tabernacle and Temple. These consist of the seven-branched candelabrum, shovels, the table of shewbread, jars, basins, Aaron's flowering staff, and a highly stylized triple arcade, perhaps symbolizing the facade of the Temple, as well as a stylized Ark of the Covenant. The exposition of the *menorah*, the Ark, the jar of manna, and the triple-gate facade of the Temple probably originated in late Hellenistic tradition. All these elements appear on minor Jewish art objects of the first to the third centuries, such as clay oil lamps, painted gold-leaf glasses, and coins, as well as in monumental wall-painting in synagogues and catacombs and in later synagogal floor motifs.

Within the text of the Oriental Bibles, traditionally written in three columns, divisional motifs demarcate the end of books, portions (*parashot*), and verses. At the end of books, there is usually an ornamental frame containing the number of verses in the book. Sometimes, these frames were extended to decorative panels, like the Sūra headings in the Koran. Decorated roundels or other motifs, occasionally with mnemonic devices, mark the different *parashot* as well as the chapters of the Psalms. The roundels resemble the *ʿashira* (division into verses), and the *sajdah* (pause for prostration) signs in contemporary Korans. Other sections contain similar decorations. Most frequent is a paisley motif, derived from the Arabic letter *ha*, which resembles the *khamise* (five-verse section) notation in Korans. The Songs of Moses (Ex. 15; Deut. 32) are traditionally written in a distinct verse form, sometimes framed by decorative geometric and floral bands. An example is an 11th-century Persian Bible in the British Museum (Or. Ms. 1467, fols. 117v–118v). Of the few existing examples of Oriental Bibles that contain text illustrations, two are 11th-century Persian Pentateuchs. One has pictures of sacred vessels between the text columns of the page, illustrating the text's description of the princes' gifts to the tabernacle in the desert (Num. 7:1; Brit. Mus., Or. Ms. 1467, fols. 43–43v). The other has an illustration of the two tablets of the law inscribed with the opening words of each Commandment, next to the text of the Ten Commandments (Ex. 20:2–17; Brit. Mus., Or. Ms. 2363, fol. 73v). Portions of the Bible, especially the Pentateuch, intended for educational use were also decorated in the same manner. One example is the Jerusalem *Shelaḥ Lekha* portion of 1106 C.E. Oriental Bibles of the 12th and 13th centuries carry on the tradition of carpet pages, decorated micrography, and divisional signs.

SPANISH. The illumination of Spanish Bibles is derived from the Oriental ones. Like them, they contain carpet pages, illustrations of the Temple implements, divisional signs for books, portions, and verses, and patterned masorah. Spanish Bibles also contain innovations, mainly in the comparative masoretic tables. No illuminated Bible from the Islamic "Golden Age" in Spain has survived. The extant Bibles of Christian Spain suggest a link between them and the early Oriental Bibles because of their similar plan and iconography. The carpet pages of 13th- and 14th-century Spanish Bibles are placed mainly at the beginning and in the major divisions of the Bibles. These carpet pages combine painted motifs with figurated masorah and are framed by verses in monumental scripts.

The earliest recognizable Spanish school of Bible illustration developed in Castile during the second half of the 13th century. Examples of illuminated Bibles from this school indicate an Oriental origin in both the type of decoration and the main floral, geometric, and micrographic motifs. The carpet page from the *Damascus Keter*, in the National and University Library in Jerusalem, a Bible copied in Burgos in 1260 by Menahem b. Abraham ibn Malik, is a good example of the Spanish style. The Oriental flavor of the foliage scroll, outlined by micrography, is somewhat subdued by the Western touch of a burnished gold filling and magenta-brown background. Other Bibles from Castile, such as the 14th-century codex from Cervera, near Toledo (Lisbon, National Library, Ms. 72) reveal more Westernized taste, and were probably influenced by the southern French schools of illumination; Provence should be regarded both culturally and socially as part of the northern Spanish schools.

The most common illustrations of the Spanish Bibles are the implements of the Temple. They are usually shown in a double-page spread in front of the manuscript, next to the carpet pages, rather than in the form of a plan of the Temple or tabernacle. A Bible copied in Perpignan in 1299 (Paris, Bibliothèque Nationale, cod. hèb. 7) contains one of the earliest full-page expositions of the implements of the tabernacle. The implements are arranged arbitrarily within frames. The first page (fol. 12v) shows the seven-branched *menorah* and its tongs and fire pans, with two step-like stones on either side of the base, the jar of manna, the staff of Moses and Aaron's flowering rod, the Ark with the tablets of the law deposited in it, the two winged cherubim over the Ark-cover, and the table with the shewbread – two rows of six loaves – above which are two incense ladles. On the second page (fol. 13) are the gold incense altar, silver trumpets, the horn, the sacrificial altar with a leaning ramp, the laver on its stand, vessels, basins, pans, shovels, and forks. An earlier Bible of the same type from Toledo (1277) is in the Biblioteca Palatina, Parma (Ms. 2668).

The *Farḥi Bible* (Sassoon Collection, Ms. 368), one of the richest Bibles of the 14th century, was both copied and decorated by Elisha b. Abraham b. Benveniste b. Elisha, called Crescas (b. 1325). It took him 17 years, from 1366 to 1382, to complete the work which, as his colophon reveals, he undertook for his own use. The manuscript was previously in the possession of the Farḥi family of Damascus and Aleppo. The actual biblical text is preceded by 192 fully decorated pages, 29 of which are carpet pages and nine, full-page miniatures. Among the illustrations are several pages of drawings of the implements. The Bible became a substitute for the Temple and was called *Mikdashiyyah* ("God's Temple"). Thus, in Spanish Bibles the implements symbolize the messianic hope for the rebuilding of the Temple. A tree on a hill representing the *Mount of Olives, where tradition states that the precursor of the Messiah will appear, is included among the implements – a further indication of the messianic intent of the illustration. Plans of the Temple also exist in Spanish illumination. One early example is attached to the *First Ibn Merwas Bible* of Toledo, 1306 (British Museum, Ms. Or. 2201). A large fragment, executed by Joshua b. Abraham ibn Gaon in Soria (1306), is bound together with the *Second Kennicott Bible* (Oxford, Bodleian Library, Ms. Ken. 2). It contains all the implements and vessels of the Second Temple arranged in ground-plan form, unlike the more common random arrangement.

A few Bibles have other illustrations next to the carpet pages. The *Farḥi Bible* has several, among which are the labyrinth of the seven walls of Jericho and the tents of Jacob and his wives. Two novel features appear in the carpet pages of Spanish Bibles. One is the calendar page, according to the Jewish year. Most of the calendars are circular, similar to the zodiac form; some, such as that in the *First Joshua Ibn Gaon Bible* of 1301 (Paris, Bibliothèque Nationale, cod. hèb. 21), consist of movable disks. Contemporary calendars were also added, usually beginning with the year in which the manuscript was written. The second major novelty is the comparative tables of the masorah. The different versions of the masorah of *Ben-Asher and *Ben-Naphtali are written in columns framed by arcades which resemble the early medieval canon tables. In some manuscripts, the tradition of the fully arcaded pages persists even though the text is different. The *First Kennicott Bible*, a masterpiece of Spanish-Jewish art (Oxford, Bodleian Library, Ms. Ken. 1), was copied, punctuated, and edited according to the masorah by Moses Jacob ibn Zabara, and completed, as his colophon shows, on July 24, 1476, in the Spanish town of Corunna, for Isaac son of Don Solomon de Braga. The manuscript was planned and fashioned in scope and decoration on the model of the *Cervera Bible* (1300, Lisbon, Univ. Lib. Ms. 72). The illumination was done by Joseph *Ibn Ḥayyim, who fashioned his colophon in zoo- and anthropomorphic letters, similar to those of *Joseph ha-Ẓarefati, the artist of the *Cervera Bible*. Joseph ibn Ḥayyim however, added many new elements to his work. These additions include 14 fully decorated carpet pages, some illustrating the traditional array of implements of the tabernacle. As in the *Cervera Bible*, a number of pages are decorated with arcades which serve as frames for David *Kimḥi's grammatical compendium. Some of these arcades have pictorial borders, such as an army of hares besieging a wolf in a castle (fol. 443).

The Spanish artists, following the Oriental tradition, used divisional signs for books and *parashot* although in a more elaborate way and with some text illustrations. These can be seen as early as 1260, in some *parashot* signs in the *Damascus Keter*. The *First Kennicott Bible* has several such illustrations (e.g., Phinehas brandishing his spear). Unlike Oriental Bibles, the beginnings of books in some Spanish manuscripts have a text illustration. The *Kennicott Bible* presents Jonah and the whale (fol. 305). The *Cervera Bible* has several text illustrations. The indicator for *Parashat Ki-Tavo* (Deut. 26) displays a basket of fruit, illustrating the offerings of the first fruit in the Temple; above it are an elephant and castle, the royal arms of Castile. At the end of Exodus there is a panel showing the *menorah* (fol. 60). A stag is painted alongside Psalm 42 (fol. 326), and a lamenting grotesque decorates Lamentations (fol. 371v). Zechariah (fol. 316v) is illustrated by his vision of the two olive trees providing oil for the *menorah*. Jonah (fol. 304) opens with a picture of a ship with sailors, under which the prophet is being swallowed head first by a whale – a not uncommon scene in illuminated Spanish Bibles.

A similar picture of a sailing vessel is found at the beginning of Jonah in a Bible written in Soria (1312) by Shem Tov b. Abraham ibn Gaon, probably a brother of Joshua ibn Gaon (Sassoon Collection, Ms. 82). Further resemblances between the *Shem Tov Bible* and the *Cervera Bible*, such as the grammatical and masoretic treatises written within columns and the crouching lions at the bases of arcades, suggest that they are based on a common model. These two manuscripts are also related in artistic style. The numerous text illustrations in the margins and between the columns of the *First Joshua Ibn Gaon Bible* (Paris, Bibliothèque Nationale cod. hèb. 20) include Noah's ark (fol. 13), the dove holding an olive branch (fol. 14), Hagar's water jug (fol. 20), Abraham's sacrificial knife (fol. 20v), the goblet of Pharaoh's butler (fol. 133), David's sling with Goliath's sword, and the bear and lion killed by David (fol. 170). Of all the 15th-century Bibles, the *First Kennicott Bible* has the largest number of text illustrations. At the opening of the Book of Jonah (fol. 305), the traditional picture of the prophet being swallowed head first by a whale, beneath a decorated ship, is depicted in a way similar to that in the *Cervera Bible*. There is also an illustration of King David at the beginning of II Samuel (fol 185) in the *Kennicott Bible*. Floral and geometric shapes composed of micrographic masorah decorate the margins of some text pages. As in the Oriental Bibles, the two songs of Moses are often written in a special form and sometimes have a frame decorated with colors or micrography, which is also used in the ornamentation of carpet pages from the 13th to the 15th centuries.

Hebrew illustrated Bibles must have been so common in Spain that Castilian translations of the Bible may have used their illustrations as early as the 13th century. Jewish iconography is also predominant in the Castilian *Alba Bible.

The 15th-century Yemenite school of illumination, like the Spanish, follows the Oriental school. Many Yemenite Bibles contain carpet pages ornamented with floral and animal motifs in micrography of colors (e.g., Brit. Mus., Or. Ms. 2348 of Sana'a, 1469, and Or. Ms. 2211 of 1475). The micrography in these manuscripts is of biblical verses and Psalms, not the masorah.

ASHKENAZI. Hebrew Bibles of the Ashkenazi school fall into two categories: one consists of complete Bibles, mostly in large, even giant, format, such as the *Ambrosian Bible* (Ulm, 1236–38), written in large script with Aramaic translation incorporated into the text after each verse; the other contains the Pentateuch with its Aramaic translation, the five scrolls, *haftarot, parts of Job, and sometimes the "passages of doom" in Jeremiah (2:29–3:12; 9:24–10:16). Ashkenazi Bibles are illuminated in a different fashion from the Oriental and Spanish ones. Most are decorated by the punctuator-masorete in micrography and pen drawing, either in large initial-word panels or in the margins of the text area. Illuminated Bibles of the Ashkenazi tradition do not contain carpet pages and only occasionally have expositions of the Temple implements. What sometimes appears like a carpet page is in fact an excess of masoretic material copied in decorative shapes, either at the beginning or the end of books of the Bible. Implements of the Temple are very rare. One example occurs in the *Regensburg Pentateuch* of about 1300, now in the Israel Museum, Jerusalem, which has an exposition of the tabernacle implements, including Aaron in his robes extending his arm to light a very large *menorah*, which is depicted on the facing page.

The most common illuminations of French and German Bibles are initial-word panels, which sometimes include text illustrations. The Rashi commentary on the Pentateuch from Wuerzburg, 1233 (Munich, Cod. Heb. 5) has initial-word panels to each *parashah* which includes a text illustration. The *Ambrosian Bible* (Mss. B. 30–32 inf.) has illustrated panels to most of the books. At the end of the third volume, this manuscript has full-page eschatological illustrations, which depict the Feast of the Righteous in Paradise, and a cosmological picture. The *British Museum Miscellany* (Ms. Add. 11.639) of c. 1280 contains three cycles of full-page miniatures of biblical episodes, which were probably intended to illustrate a northern French Bible. Painted initial-word panels also exist and sometimes extend to a full page, as in the *Duke of Sussex Pentateuch* in the British Museum. Sometimes these painted panels illustrate the text, but a few are merely decorative. The 46 medallions of the frontispiece to Genesis in the *Schocken Bible* in Jerusalem depict episodes from the entire Pentateuch, beginning with Adam and Eve by the Tree of Knowledge and ending with Balaam being stopped by an angel while riding his ass.

The other most prominent type of decoration in the Ashkenazi Bible is the elaborate marginal micrography. The masoretic micrography sometimes contains text illustrations. Some opening panels and colophons are also decorated by micrography, and the micrography within the text sometimes forms an illustration of the text. The *Duke of Sussex Pentateuch* (fol. 28) shows the ram caught in a thicket alongside the text of the sacrifice of Isaac. A Bible in the British Museum (Ms. Add. 21160, c. 1300), has some interesting examples of such illustrated micrography; e.g., Joseph riding a horse (fol. 192), Pharaoh's baker carrying a triple basket on his head (fol. 43), the four beasts of Ezekiel's vision (fol. 285), and Jonah being spewed from the mouth of the whale and seated under a tree (fol. 292–292v). However, most of the masoretic variations surrounding the text form grotesques. Ashkenazi Pentateuchs of the second half of the 14th century are smaller and illustrated in a manner differing from that of the earlier period – the *Coburg Pentateuch* of 1369, is an example of this later type.

ITALIAN. Very few illuminated Italian Bibles of the 13th century survive, and most of them are of Roman origin. The *Bishop Bedell Bible* of 1284 (Cambridge, Emmanuel College) is a typical example. It contains two full-page decorated panels, which include some inscriptions. Decorated arches surround the opening pages or text columns of the different books, and the initial word is written in a larger script. *Parashot* signs in the margin follow the Oriental type. A two-volume Bible in the British Museum (Ms. Harl. 5710–11), from about 1300 preserves the two typical techniques of decoration – watercolor pen drawings and painted illuminations. The openings of each book of the Bible are headed by painted initial-word panels and surrounded by foliage scrolls – either around the whole page or one text column. The foliage scrolls are wiry and incorporate animals, birds, fish, and grotesques in a style which was common in the province of Emilia and influenced mainly by the Bolognese school. This Bible contains a few text illustrations. Under the initial-word panel of Genesis (fol. 1), there is a painted panel containing seven medallions, five of which represent the creation of heaven and earth, the sun, moon, and stars, water, trees, and beasts. Each medallion shows the hand of God emerging from segments of the sky. At the end of the Pentateuch (fol. 136), there is a full-page drawing of a delicately formed *menorah* painted in red, green, ocher, and brown. The entire page is framed and filled with painted foliage scrolls combined with grotesques and dragons. Another delicately painted manuscript of Emilian style, from the end of the 13th century, is a psalter in the Biblioteca Palatina in Parma (Ms. 1870). Many of the chapter openings have small initial-word panels with grotesques and animals in the margins. Some illustrate the text: weeping people, with their violins hung upon a willow, illustrate Psalm 137, "By the waters of Babylon there we sat down… We hung our harps upon the willows in the midst thereof"; a man conducting a choir illustrates Psalm 149, "Hallelujah, sing to the Lord a new song." Italian Bibles of the 14th and 15th century are decorated by initial-word and -letter panels, with marginal ornamentation and some illustrations.

The Aberdeen Bible (University of Aberdeen, Ms. 23) was completed probably in Naples in 1493 by Isaac b. David Balansi (i.e., Valensi), presumably a Spaniard who had been expelled from Spain in 1492. While the Spanish influence is evident in the manuscript's masoretic micrography and *parashot* indicators, it does not appear in the fully decorated pages containing the comparative tables of masorah, initial-word panels, and border illumination; these are purely south Italian. The heavy borders, decorated with foliage scrolls, animals, birds, and large pearls framing the table of *haftarot*, are typical of the other illuminated pages in this Bible.

With the Renaissance in Italy, Hebrew illumination reached its artistic peak. It developed through the ready patronage of affluent Jewish loan-bankers who supported such fine illuminators as those who produced the *Rothschild Miscellany* (Ms. 24, Jerusalem, Israel Museum) and the Bibliothèque Nationale's *Portuguese Bible* (Ms. héb. 15). Unique in the richness of their decoration, these manuscripts were in great demand, but only a few families could afford the single productions.

With the invention of the printing press, by the end of the 15th century handwritten Bible illumination practically ceased. The decoration of printed Bibles developed a different form and content, except for the illuminated scrolls of Esther, which evolved a specific tradition.

See also *Illuminated Manuscripts, Illuminated *Haggadot, and illuminated *maḥzorim.

[Bezalel Narkiss]

For more information on individual biblical figures in the arts see also the articles on the following: *Abraham, *Absalom, *Adam, *Akedah, *Athaliah, Babel, Tower *of, *Balaam, *Belshazzar, *Cain (and Abel), *Creation, *Daniel, *David, *Deborah, *Decalogue, *Elijah, *Esther, *Ezekiel, *Gideon, *Habakkuk, *Hezekiah, *Hosea, *Isaac, *Isaiah, *Jacob, *Jephthah, *Jeremiah, *Jerusalem, *Job, *Joel, *Jonah, *Joseph, *Joshua, *Lamentations, *Melchizedek, *Moses, *Nebuchadnezzar, *Noah, *Psalms, *Rachel, *Ruth, *Samson, *Samuel, *Saul, *Sodom (and Gomorrah), *Solomon, *Song of Songs, *Temple.

BIBLIOGRAPHY: IN LITERATURE: N.J.E. Rothschild, Baron de, *Le mistère du Viel Testament…* 6 vols. (1878–91), includes extensive bibliography of biblical plays in French; A. Sakheim, *Das juedische Element in der Weltliteratur* (1924); L. Finkelstein (ed.), *The Jews*, 2 (1960^3), 1452–86; M. Roston, *Biblical Drama in England* (1968); Shunami, Bibliography, 248–58 passim. IN MUSIC: JL, 1 (1927), col. 997–9. IN ART: J. Leveen, *The Hebrew Bible in Art* (1944); R. Wischnitzer, in: L. Finkelstein, *The Jews*, 2 (1960^3), 1322–48; T. Arnold, *The Old and New Testaments in Muslim Religious Art* (1932); JL, 1 (1927), 985–9; *Encyclopedia of World Art*, 2 (1960), 483–516; D.S. Berkowitz, *In Remembrance of Creation: Evolution of Art Scholarship in the Medieval and Renaissance Bible* (1968). ILLUSTRATED BIBLES: Mayer, Art, index; G. Hareloff, in: ZAW, 69 (1957), 103–29; S.C. Cockerell, and M.R. James, *A Book of Old Testament Illustrations of the Middle of the Thirteenth Century* (1927); A. de Laborde, *Etude sur la Bible moralisée illustrée*, 5 vols. (1911–27). ILLUMINATED MANUSCRIPTS: Gutmann, in: *Gesta*, 5 (1966), 39–44; D.S. Sassoon, *Ohel Dawid*, 1 (1932), 6–14, pl. 1; *B. Narkiss, in: Catalogue of the Israel Museum*, 40 (1967), nos. 1, 2, 3, 4, 16, 18, 19; idem, *Hebrew Illuminated Manuscripts* (1969), index; C.O. Nordström, in: *Byzantion*, 25–27 (1955–57), 487–93; idem, *The Duke of Alba's Castilian Bible* (1967); M. Gengaro, F. Leoni and G. Villa, *Codici decorati e Miniati dell'Ambrosiana* (1957), 13–62; Mayer, Art, nos. 53, 523, 670A, 800, 876, 1071, 1190, 1721, 2003, 2074, 2207, 2221, 2223, 2525, 2547, 2775, 2776.

BIBLE CODES, a system of inquiry involving the discovery of pairs of conceptually related terms in the biblical text using Equidistant Letter Sequences (ELS). The system involves choosing or finding a sequence of letters that make up a name or a date, not necessarily in the order in which the name is spelled, that is found in the biblical text at equal distances from one another. Thus, the letters of the Hebrew name, *Rambam*, might appear every 10 letters in a portion of the book of Genesis. Nearby, the letters of the Rambam's date of birth might appear in another sequence of say every 12 letters. The assumption is that the close proximity of these two related letter sequences is not due to chance. The Bible Codes are understood to be the result of a divine hand that planted them in the Bible text. How else can we explain the existence of the names and birth dates of medieval rabbis in a text that is over 3,000 years old – it is asked.

ELS was first applied scientifically to the Bible by Professor Eliyahu Rips, an Israeli mathematician, in 1983. In 1985, Rips, together with Doron Witztum and Yoav Rosenberg, conducted an experiment to find the names of famous rabbis and the dates of their birth or death in the book of Genesis using ELS. The experiment utilized a list of names based on the *Encyclopedia of Great Men in Israel* (Hebrew) compiled by Shlomo Havlin. The experiment, conducted using a computer program, resulted in the discovery of the rabbis' names in close proximity to their dates of birth, a result that could not, it was argued, be the result of chance or coincidence. The Bible text used for the experiment was the Koren Hebrew edition of the Bible. The editor of the professional journal *Statistical Science* requested that the experiment be repeated and it was. Thus, in 1994, Rips, Witztum and Rosenberg published their findings in *Statistical Science* (vol. 9, 1994, no. 3, 429–38).

Since then, the Bible Codes have become the subject of great controversy. The debate can be divided into three areas: (a) statistics; (b) Bible; and (c) education.

Statistics

A number of scholars, especially Brenden McKay, Maya Bar-Hillel, Dror Bar-Natan, Gil Kalai, and Barry Simon have severely criticized the findings of Rips, Witztum, and Rosenberg. They are critical of the way the list of names was compiled because variations on the spelling of names or appellation could have negated the results. In addition, not all of the pairs of rabbis and dates were actually discovered. Barry Simon writes, "…the complexity of the experiment suggests that the result may be sensitive to changes of the method of measuring distances and the statistical method used" (http://www.wopr.com/biblecodes/). Simon, along with others, have used the Bible Codes system to discover rabbis' names and other word sets in both English and Hebrew texts other than the Bible.

Bible

Jewish Bible scholars, such as Menachem Cohen of the Hebrew University (http://cs.anu.edu.au/~bdm/dilugim/cohen_eng.html), and Christian Bible scholars, such as Richard Taylor (*Journal of the Evangelical Theological Society*, December 2000), of the Dallas Theological Seminary, have been very critical of the Bible Codes. Taylor writes, "…most important, I do not believe that the real issues in this discussion actually lie in the discipline of mathematical probability. Bible code advocates have based much of their theory upon arguments from statistical probability. However, the Bible code phenomenon is ultimately an issue of Old Testament textual criticism, and no amount of statistical probability or mathematical speculation can alter that fact. Any Bible code theory that plays loose with known facts concerning the transmission of the Biblical text is working with an inherent flaw that is actually fatal to its claims and conclusions" (ibid.). Put simply, the Koren edition of the Bible is in no way the "authoritative" text of the Bible, for there is none. For instance, there are variant spellings of words throughout the bible that appear in the Aleppo Codex, the Leningrad manuscript, the Sassoon Manuscript, and the original printing of the *Mikra'ot Gedolot* in Venice. These variant spellings, along with other textual phenomena in the Bible, such as *ketiv* and *qeri*, certainly affect the results of a code based on equal distances between letters. Taylor sums it up by saying, "If there are significant textual problems in the Hebrew Bible – whether in the form of pluses, or minuses, or substitutions, etc. – such a problem causes a fatal disaster for any theory of ELS, even if it were theoretically possible to allow for such a phenomenon in the non-extant original text" (ibid.).

Education

The only Jewish organization that is actively using the Bible Codes as part of their educational curriculum is *Aish HaTorah. A lesson about the Bible Codes is included in their Discovery seminars, the purpose of which is to prove the Divine origin of the Torah. An active defense of the Codes and their use is found on their website (http://www.aish.com/seminars/discovery/Codes/codes.htm#prime). Many Jewish educators object to the use of the Codes, especially in teaching those who are relatively uninformed about Judaism (the target population of the Discovery Seminars), given the debate surrounding the validity of the Codes themselves.

In recent times, numerous people have written books purportedly predicting future events on the basis of the Codes, particularly Michael Drosnin (*The Bible Code*, 1997, and *The Bible Code 2*, 2002). Such works have been rejected by both sides of the scholarly debate. It is interesting to note that a Google search of "Bible Codes" reveals 990,000 related websites, the overwhelming majority of which are Christian sites. The Christian community has eagerly accepted the Bible Codes while the broader Jewish community has expressed a greater skepticism. Bible Codes computer programs can be purchased so consumers can run their own Bible Code searches.

BIBLIOGRAPHY: E. Rips, D. Witztum, and Y. Rosenberg, in: *Statistical Science* 9:3 (1994), 429--38; D. Witztum, at: http://www.torahcodes.co.il/; B. McKay et. al., at: http://cs.anu.edu.au/~bdm/dilugim/torah.html; B. Simon, at: http://www.wopr.com/biblecodes/; M. Cohen, at: http://cs.anu.edu.au/~bdm/dilugim/cohen_eng.html; R. Taylor, in: *Journal of the Evangelical Theological Society* (Dec. 2000); http://www.aish.com/seminars/discovery/Codes/codes.htm#prime; http://en.wikipedia.org/wiki/Bible_code; D. Thomas, in: *Skeptical Inquirer* (Mar.–Apr. 1998); idem, in: ibid. (Mar.–Apr. 2003).

[David Derovan (2nd ed.)]

BIBLE SOCIETIES, associations intended to propagate the Christian Bible, i.e., the Old and New Testaments. The first association of this kind was founded in 1719 in Halle an der Saale, and from 1775 was called the Cansteinsche Bibelanstalt. Numerous Bible societies were founded from the beginning of the 19th century in the wake of the missionary societies established between 1792 and 1800 in England, Holland, and Germany. The British and Foreign Bible Society was founded in 1804, the Bible Society of Basle in 1804, that of Berlin in 1805, Holland in 1814, Norway in 1815, the American Bible Society in 1816, and the Société Biblique de Paris in 1818. Other important societies are the American Board of Commissioners for Foreign Missions, the American and Foreign Bible Society, the Baptist Missionary Society, the Bible Translation Society, the Church Missionary Society, the National Bible Society of Scotland, the Society for Promoting Christian Knowledge, and the Trinitarian Bible Society. In general, these societies publish the biblical texts without commentaries, but they have also issued emended texts of existing translations and editions. They have also published the Greek and Latin editions of Nestlé (1879), Kittel's *Biblia Hebraica* (1905; the Bible Society of Wuerttemberg), and the *Bible du Centenaire* (1916–48; Société Biblique de Paris). Photographic reproductions of the British and Foreign Bible Society Hebrew Bible have been issued in various formats by some Jewish publishers. The masoretic Bible of C.D. *Ginsburg was published by the same society in 1926 in London.

Bibles published by these societies are disseminated by the mission societies or by large-scale retailing. Since the beginning of the 19th century, over a thousand million copies of biblical texts in over a thousand languages have been thus published and distributed. The British and Foreign Bible Society alone has published texts in 700 languages and dialects and distributed a total of 550,000,000 copies, 130,000,000 of which were of the Old Testament. In a single year before World War II, this society distributed 11,000,000 copies of the Bible, the National Bible Society of Scotland 4,000,000, and the American Bible Society 7,000,000. In China, before the accession to power of the Communists, 9,000,000 copies of biblical texts were distributed annually. Owing to the low prices they charge, these societies frequently succeed in selling their Hebrew editions of the Bible, with or without translation, to Jews. The issue of equally low-priced Hebrew Bibles by Jewish authorities or institutions, with or without translations, to counteract this disguised missionary activity of the Bible societies is a relatively recent undertaking. The edition of the New Testament in Hebrew translation is more openly designed for missionary work among Jews. The first New Testament in Hebrew was published in 1817 by the London Society for Promoting Christianity among Jews (better known as the London Jews' Society). The translation of the New Testament by F. *Delitzsch appeared between 1877 and 1892 in at least 13 editions. Other translations openly intended for Jews have been published in Yiddish, Judeo-Arabic, Judeo-Persian, and Ladino.

BIBLIOGRAPHY: T.H. Darlow and H.F. Moule (comps.), *Historical Catalogue of the Printed Editions of Holy Scripture in the Library of the British and Foreign Bible Society*, 2 vols. in 4 (1903–11, repr. 1963); S. de Dietrich, *Le Renouveau Biblique* (1949[2]), 89ff.; Bouyer, in: *Bible et Vie Chrétienne*, 13 (1956), 7–21.

[Bernhard Blumenkranz]

°BIBLIANDER (Buchmann), THEODOR (1504–1564), Swiss Hebraist and theologian. In 1531, Bibliander succeeded Zwingli as lecturer in Septuagintal studies, but his denial of absolute predestination cost him his post. His publications include a Hebrew grammar (1535), a commentary on the Hebrew text of Nahum (1534), and a treatise interpreting Ezra with reference to Roman history (1553?). Bibliander left Basle with a projected translation of the Koran (of which he published an interpretation, 1543) when the enterprise encountered local difficulties; he was also a collaborator of Leo Juda in his Latin version of the Bible (1543).

BIBLIOGRAPHY: J.J. Christinger, *Theodor Bibliander* (Ger., 1867); *Dictionnaire historique et biographique de la Suisse* (1921–34); J. Prijs, *Die Basler hebraeischen Drucke*, 1492–1866 (1964), 102, 128.

[Raphael Loewe]

BIBLIOGRAPHY. As in general bibliography, the development of Hebrew bibliography is characterized by the transition from brief listings to more detailed catalogues. The listing of the books of the Bible which appears in the Talmud (BB 14b, 15a) had as its purpose the fixing of an authoritative order for the biblical books as a guide for the copyists. Lists of books for broader purposes, among them those of the Cairo *Genizah*, have come down from the 11th century. Sometimes these listings contain only the name of the book; in other cases, the author's name is also included. In some of the later booklists, short annotations also appear. Bibliographical lists within the biographical listings are found in genealogical works of the 16th century, as in *Sefer Yuḥasin* by Abraham *Zacuto and in *Shalshelet ha-Kabbalah* by Gedaliah *Ibn Yaḥya. In the early part of the 17th century several important ventures in the field of bibliography were undertaken. Johannes *Buxtorf the elder published *De abbreviaturis hebraicis, liber novus et copiosus* (Basle, 1613) in which he included a section on rabbinic literature entitled *Bibliotheca rabbinica ordine alphabetico disposita*. This listing of 324 works, arranged in alphabetical order by titles, is the first bibliographic catalogue of rabbinic literature. *Manasseh Ben Israel, in his listing of sources used by him in the first part of his *Conciliador* (Frankfurt, 1632), distinguished six categories of Hebrew literature: Talmud and Midrash; commentaries on these; commentaries on the Bible; Kabbalah; *posekim* and responsa; sermons, grammar, chronology, and legal literature. The first, however, to compile a true bibliography of Hebrew literature was Giulio *Bartolocci in his *Bibliotheca Magna Rabbinica* (4 vols., Rome, 1675–93; repr. 1969). The Christian scholar Carlo Giuseppe Imbonati added a fifth volume, *Bibliotheca Latina Hebraica* (Rome, 1694). Bartolocci's work is arranged in alphabetical order of authors, supplemented by a list of subjects in Latin and an abridged listing in Hebrew. Leone *Modena assisted the bishop of Lodève, J. Plantavit de la Pause; in his *Bibliotheca Rabbinica* (appended to his *Florilegium Biblicum*, 1645) by supplying him with a list of 500 names of rabbis, which he used for his alphabetic dictionary of 780 Hebrew books. The first Jewish bibliographer was Shabbetai *Bass whose *Siftei Yeshenim* (Amsterdam, 1680) contains a bibliography arranged by title, followed by the name of the author, the date and place of publication, the format, and some indication of content. The approximate number of listings in this bibliography is 2,200, including manuscripts. The third important pioneer bibliographer was another Christian, Johann Christoph *Wolf. He utilized the two previous bibliographies in compiling his own four-volume work, *Bibliotheca Hebraea* (Hamburg, 1715–33; repr. 1969). He corrected some of the material found in the earlier works, using the library of David b. Abraham *Oppenheim. The genealogical reference work of David *Conforte *Kore ha-Dorot* (1746, 1846[2]) contains much valuable bibliographic material. It should be noted, also, that Jehiel *Heilperin included in his *Seder ha-Dorot* (Karlsruhe, 1769) the names of the books which are referred to in Bass' bibliography, though generally he omitted the place and year of publication, even when these were included in the *Siftei Yeshenim*. Especially valuable from a bibliographical standpoint is the H.J.D. *Azulai's *Shem ha-Gedolim* (1774–86, 1853, 1876), which contains an alphabetical listing of Hebrew books and manuscripts. Azulai noted every unusual Hebrew book or manuscript, even those in non-Jewish collections, which came to his notice in the course of his extensive travels without, however, always giving the date and place of publication. The major work of the Christian scholar G.B. *de' Rossi, *Annales Hebraeo-Typographici Seculi XV* (Parma, 1795), dealing with Hebrew incunabula, together with his *Annales Hebraeo-Typographici ab anno 1501 ad 1540* (Parma, 1799), and the *Dizionario storico degli autori Ebrei e delle loro opere* (2 vols., Parma, 1802), as well as assorted lists of Hebrew publications from various Italian cities, serve as a transition to modern bibliography.

With the development of Jewish studies, Hebrew bibliography became a scientific discipline in its own right. L. *Zunz's *Zur Geschichte und Literatur* (1845) contains a complete section on bibliography (pp. 214–303), including material on the dates found in books; on printers and typography in Mantua from 1476 to 1662; and on Hebrew printing in Prague from 1513 to 1657. This work laid the foundation for modern Hebrew bibliography. In 1849 Julius *Fuerst published the first part of his *Bibliotheca Judaica* (3 vols., 1849–63). The book is neither all-inclusive nor completely accurate, but it is important in view of its comprehensiveness. It is arranged according to author, commentator, editor, and publisher, with an alphabetical index to the Hebrew works appended to the end of the third volume. The format of each book is noted, and sometimes the number of pages as well. The preceding bibliographies are overshadowed by the works of Moritz *Steinschneider, in particular by his *Catalogus Librorum Hebraeorum in Bibliotheca Bodleiana* (1852–60) and *Die hebraeischen Uebersetzungen des Mittelalters* (1893). These works set the definitive standard for modern Jewish bibliography. Another important bibliography is Isaac *Benjacob's *Oẓar ha-Sefarim*, (1877–80), listing Jewish books and manuscripts until 1863, and published by the author's son Jacob, together with notes by Steinschneider. By the late 19th century Jewish bibliography, comprising Jewish literature in all languages, had undergone considerable development and today compares favorably with general bibliography. Aaron *Walden, who followed Azulai with the *Shem ha-Gedolim he-Ḥadash* (1864) included a section entitled, "A Catalogue of Books," which includes ḥasidic works absent from earlier listings. However, this listing was not done scientifically. William *Zeitlin, in his *Kiryat Sefer, Bibliotheca Hebraica post-Mendelssohniana* (1891–95), listed the works of the Haskalah movement to that date (more than 3,500 volumes). Ḥayyim David Lippe published a catalogue called *Asaf ha-Mazkir* (1881–89), "a complete listing of all the books, treatises, and Hebrew periodicals which appeared during the period 1880–1887." He also issued a follow-up catalogue, *Asaf ha-Mazkir he-Ḥadash…* (1899), "listing all the books, treatises, and periodicals which appeared during the period 1882–1898." From 1928 to 1931 H.D. *Friedberg published his *Beit Eked Sefarim*, a bibliographical lexicon covering the general field of Hebrew literature, with particular attention to books written in Hebrew and Yiddish; but also including works written in Italian, Latin, Greek, Spanish, Arabic, Persian, and Samaritan, and printed in Hebrew characters from 1475–1900, with their general content, author, date, place of publication, and number of pages. An expanded edition of this work appeared in 1951–54. Though not truly scientific in its approach, it is still very useful. The many, important studies of Abraham Yaari include *Meḥkerei Sefer* (1958), containing among its studies in Hebrew booklore a section on the catalogue of Israel. M. *Kasher and Dov Mandelbaum compiled a bibliography of works covering the years 500–1500 called *Sarei ha-Elef* (1959). Important monographs and articles in the field of Hebrew bibliography have been written by S. *Wiener, I. *Sonne, S. *Seeligmann, D. *Chwolson, A. *Jellinek, A.M. *Habermann, C. *Lieberman, A. *Marx, M. *Roest, G. *Kressel, J. *Zedner, I. *Rivkind, S. Shunami, N. Ben-Menahem, and others. The indispensable handbook today is S. Shunami's *Bibliography of Jewish Bibliographies* (1936, 1965²; repr. 1969, with supplement) which also includes sections on Jewish and Modern Hebrew literature (nos. 1146–1240; 4875–85) as well as on Judeo-German and Yiddish (nos. 1241–1357; 4586–95). In 1960 the Hebrew University, in cooperation with Mosad Bialik and the Ministry of Education and Culture, initiated the Institute for Hebrew Bibliography under the direction of N. Ben-Menahem. Its aim is to compile a definitive bibliographical listing of every Hebrew book which has been published up to 1960 (specimen brochure, 1964).

The first scholar to publish a special periodical devoted to Hebrew and Jewish bibliography was Steinschneider: *Ha-Mazkir, Hebraeische Bibliographie, Blaetter fuer neuere und aeltere Literatur des Judenthums* (HB, 1858–65, 1869–82). Nehemiah *Bruell continued Steinschneider's project in the bimonthly *Centralanzeiger fuer juedische Literatur* (1890) but succeeded in publishing it only during one year (6 issues). At the same time M. *Kayserling published his bibliographical dictionary of Spanish and Portuguese works on Judaism and Jews (the *Biblioteca española-portugueza judaica*, 1890). A few years later the *Zeitschrift fuer Hebraeische Bibliographie* (ZHB; 1896–1921) appeared. The editor of volumes 1–3 was H. Brody; volumes 4–9 were edited jointly by Brody and A. Freimann; and the remaining volumes appeared under the editorship of Freimann alone. The two great authorities on the bibliography of Anglo-Jewish history are C. Roth's *Magna Bibliotheca Anglo-Judaica* (1937), and R.P. *Lehmann's *Nova Bibliotheca Anglo-Judaica* (1961), the latter dealing with the years 1937–60. The most important contemporary bibliographical journal is *Kirjat Sepher* (KS), a quarterly published since 1924 under the auspices of the Jewish National and University Library. Editors during the first two years were S.H. Bergmann and H. Pick, and after that I.B. Joel. Since 1953 a new bibliographical magazine, *Studies in Bibliography and Booklore* (SBB), has been published by the Hebrew Union College Library, Cincinnati. The *Jewish Book Annual* (JBA; founded in 1942) published in New York also contains useful bibliographical material. Of Jewish bibliographic periodicals whose life-span was limited, the following deserve mention: *En Hakore*, edited by D.A. Friedman and Z. *Woyslawski, three issues (Berlin, 1923); *Soncino-Blaetter, Beitraege zur Kunde des juedischen Buches*, edited by H. *Meyer (3 vols., Berlin, 1925–30); and *Journal of Jewish Bibliography*, a quarterly edited by Joshua *Bloch (New York, 1938–43).

The first bookdealers' catalogue of secondhand Hebrew books was published in Amsterdam around 1640 by Manasseh Ben Israel, but no copy is now extant (cf. Roth in *Aresheth*, 2, 413–4). In 1652 his son Samuel published *Catalogo de los Libros que Semuel ben Israel Soeiro vende, estampados todos na sua Typographia, adjuntos os preços, para que cada qual saibo o que valem*. In this catalogue 65 books are noted together with their prices in Dutch currency. The earliest known auction sale catalogues are those of the libraries of two Amsterdam rabbis, Moses Raphael *d'Aguilar (1680) and Isaac *Aboab da Fonseca (1693). The only earlier commercial listings of Hebrew books are in manuscript form, such as some found in the *Genizah*, or the catalogue of Hebrew books printed in Venice prior to 1542, which came into the possession of Konrad Gesner and appeared in his *Pandectarum sive partitionum universalium libri xxi* (20 vols., Zurich 1548–49; cf. ZHB, 10 (1906), 38–42). A catalogue of books compiled for business purposes was printed as an appendix to the collection of responsa by Joseph ibn Lev (vol. 4, Fuerth, 1692). Another commercial book listing, called *Appiryon Shelomo*, was published in 1730 by Solomon Proops, printer and bookdealer of Amsterdam. The advance in the field of Hebrew bibliography resulted in the publication of improved commercial catalogues (see *Booktrade). A number of these newer catalogues are of definite scientific value such as those of M. *Roest, R.N.N. Rabinowitz, L. Schwager and D. Fraenkel, J. Kauffmann, N.W. Bamberger and Wahrmann, Rosenthal (Munich, Oxford), and others. In addition, the detailed catalogues of such libraries as those of Oxford, Amsterdam, Leiden, Leningrad, Frankfurt, the British Museum, and the Bibliothèque Nationale, Paris, have proved extremely useful.

[Abraham Meir Habermann]

In 1975 Shunami published a supplement to the second edition of his *Bibliography of Jewish Bibliographies* (1965). The 500-page supplement contains information on over 2,000 bibliographies published between 1965 and 1975. In his introduction Shunami notes that this number compares with that for the first hundred years of the Wissenschaft des Judentums. He comments on the rapid growth of bibliographies relating to the Holocaust and to the State of Israel. On the other hand, the small number of entries related to Hebrew printing is a reflection of the decline of study of this subject with little extra interest having been aroused by the 500th anniversary of Hebrew printing. There is also a decrease in entries relating to private collections, reflecting a decline in major Jewish book collectors. Shunami also decries the shortage of Jewish bibliographers.

BIBLIOGRAPHY: S. Brisman, *History and Guide to Judaic Bibliography* (1977); C. Roth, in: *Jewish Studies in Memory of Israel Abrahams* (1927), 384–93; Shunami, Bibl, xiv–xv (Eng.), 7ff.; Urbach, in: KS, 15 (1938/39), 237–9; Assaf, *ibid.*, 18 (1941/42), 272–81; Yaari, *ibid.*, 21 (1944/45), 192–203; Zulay, *ibid.*, 25 (1948/49), 203–5; Sonne, in: SBB, 1 (1953–54), 55–76; Aloni, in: *Sefer Assaf* (1953), 33–39; idem, in: *Aresheth*, 1 (1958), 44–60.

BIBLIOPHILES. Little is known about private book collectors in antiquity and in the early Middle Ages. It might be assumed, however, that patrons of learning, such as *Hisdai ibn Shaprut, collected important Hebrew and other books. Historical sources refer to the library of *Samuel ha-Nagid. Judah ibn *Tibbon's advice on how to care for a library is well known. Unfortunately, little is known about the titles of the books making up his collection. Several book lists, some compiled for auctions after the owner's death, were found in the Cairo *Genizah, the best known being that of R. *Abraham b. Samuel he-Ḥasid. His collection consisted of 27 Hebrew books and a number of volumes on medicine, probably in Arabic. The most remarkable of known medieval Jewish book collectors was the world traveler and physician Judah Leon *Mosconi of Majorca. His library included Hebrew and Arabic books in many branches of learning. Two catalogues have been preserved, one of them drawn up for the auction after his death in 1377. The king of Aragon ultimately canceled the sale and seized the library for himself. In Renaissance Italy there were many enthusiastic book collectors, such as *Menahem b. Aaron of Volterra (15th century), whose library is now in the Vatican. The library of Solomon *Finzi, son of the Mantuan scientist Mordecai (Angelo) *Finzi, contained 200 volumes, at that time a number considered worthy of a great humanist. Elijah *Capsali, a Cretan scholar of the 16th century, possessed a famous collection of Hebrew manuscripts, now at the Vatican. The largest Jewish library in the Renaissance period was that built up in successive generations by the family of Da *Pisa. They were outdone in the 17th century by Abraham Joseph Solomon *Graziano, rabbi of Modena, who wrote the initials of his name *ish ger* (איש גר) in vast numbers of books now scattered in Jewish libraries throughout the world. His contemporary Joseph Solomon *Delmedigo, a physician who traveled widely, boasted that he collected no fewer than 4,000 volumes, on which he had expended the vast sum of 10,000 (florins?). Doubtless, many of these were in languages other than Hebrew.

The first printed sale catalogues of private Hebrew libraries emerged in Holland in the 17th century, for example, the one printed for the disposal of the collections of Moses Raphael d'*Aguilar, the earliest such publication known to Jewish booklore, and that of Isaac *Aboab da Fonseca's collection, comprising about 500 volumes, many in Spanish, French, and even Greek and Latin, including some classics and the writings of the Church Fathers. Other book collectors of that period in Amsterdam were *Manasseh Ben Israel and Samuel Abbas. One of the greatest Jewish book collectors of any period was David *Oppenheim, rabbi of Prague, who in 1688 compiled the first catalogue of his collection, comprising the 480 books he owned at the time. Ultimately, he acquired 4,500 printed works in addition to 780 manuscripts, possibly the most important Jewish library in private ownership that has ever been assembled. It was purchased in 1829 by the Bodleian Library in Oxford. The Italian Catholic abbé Giovanni Bernardo de'*Rossi, a Hebrew scholar of repute and a book collector of genius, had opportunities in Italy that were unequaled elsewhere. His great collection of Hebrew manuscripts, catalogued by him and including several superb illuminated codices, is now housed at the Palatine Library in Parma, having been acquired after his death by the ruler of that petty principality. What the printed book collection includes is still barely known, but one example of its treasures is the only known copy of the earliest of dated Hebrew printed books – Rashi's Commentary printed at Reggio di Calabria in 1475. The next century produced a large number of more self-conscious collectors, such as Heimann Joseph *Michael, a Hamburg businessman, not very affluent but a considerable scholar. The learned catalogue he composed, still a standard work of reference, describes 860 manuscripts and 5,400 printed books, which in due course joined the Oppenheim collection in Oxford. At about the same time Solomon *Dubno of Russia and Holland assembled some 2,000 printed books and about 100 manuscripts, which were sold by auction in Amsterdam in 1814. Another scholarly collector was Solomon *Halberstam of Poland. Business reverses compelled him to dispose of his manuscript collection, part going to the Montefiore Library (now in the library of Jews' College, London), and part to the library of the Jewish Theological Seminary, New York. The most valuable part of his collection of printed books was sold to the library of the Vienna Jewish community; the bulk was acquired by Mayer Sulzberger and presented to the Jewish Theological Seminary in New York. Eliakim *Carmoly, rabbi in Brussels, who destroyed the value of everything he owned by embellishing it with ingenious, but sometimes transparent, forgeries possessed some 1,200 printed volumes and 290 manuscripts. His manuscripts can be found in Oxford, the British Museum, and the Guenzburg Library in Moscow.

In Russia David *Guenzburg of St. Petersburg built up a magnificent manuscript collection, which is now in the Lenin State Library, Moscow. In the United States Mayer *Sulzberger, assisted by the dealer Ephraim *Deinard, built up an important collection. In 1903 Sulzberger gave his collection of 3,000 rare books to the Jewish Theological Seminary. Moritz *Steinschneider's library in Berlin, some 4,500 books and manuscripts, was important both for the caliber of its contents and for the copious, scholarly annotations that Steinschneider added to his books. His collection passed into the ownership of the Jewish Theological Seminary, most of it being destroyed by fire in 1966. Judaica was only part of the great library which Salman *Schocken assembled in Germany, but in that field he concentrated on Hebrew poetry and rare printed books. This collection is now housed in the Schocken Library, Jerusalem, in recent years enriched by some remarkable illuminated manuscripts. A specialized library of another sort was that of David *Montezinos of Amsterdam, who created a unique collection of works, largely in Spanish and Portuguese, illustrating the history of that community. He gave it to the Sephardi synagogue, where he then became librarian. This library worked in friendly competition with the Bibliotheca Rosenthaliana in that city for many years. The latter, the library of Leiser *Rosenthal, a rabbi, was given by his son George to the city of Amsterdam; it is now a constituent of the University Library. Another outstanding rabbinical bibliophile was the Hungarian scholar David *Kaufmann whose remarkable collection, largely of Italian provenance, including some splendid illuminated manuscripts, was presented by his widow to the Hungarian Academy of Sciences. Elkan Nathan *Adler, an English lawyer, who traveled around the world in the course of his business affairs, built up a library of incunabula, rare printed works, and manuscripts, which for bulk, if not for quality, was perhaps the greatest collection assembled by a private person. Just after World War I in order to make good the defalcations of a business associate, he was compelled to sell his library to the Jewish Theological Seminary, thus elevating it to a foremost place among the Jewish libraries of the world. Adler's collection also contained some 30,000 fragments from the Cairo *Genizah*, which he had visited even before it achieved fame. Moses *Gaster, *haham* of the English Sephardi community, also built up a great collection of manuscripts reflecting every side of his versatile interests. Toward the end of his life he sold the bulk to the British Museum. Some of the remainder was ruined during the German air raids on London in World War II; what remained, including the Samaritan manuscripts, was acquired by the John Rylands Library in Manchester to add to its already remarkable Hebrew collection. David Solomon *Sassoon of London had the advantage of great wealth, close connections with the Orient, and a family tradition of book collecting. He assembled his collection of manuscripts with scholarly discrimination and described it in an elaborate catalogue, perhaps the most exhaustive work of its type that has appeared in print. This collection went into the possession of his son Solomon David Sassoon in Letchworth, England. The important collection of Berthold Strauss of London (1901–1962), catalogued in part in his *Ohel Barukh* (1959), was acquired after his death for Yeshiva University, New York. The 20th-century scholars whose private collections have become part of established libraries include Israel *Davidson (Jewish Theological Seminary, where it was destroyed by fire), Hyman *Enelow (Jewish Theological Seminary), Lazarus *Goldschmidt (second collection, Royal Library, Copenhagen), Mordecai *Margolioth (Bar-Ilan University), and Alexander *Marx (Jewish Theological Seminary, partly destroyed). Other large private collections were assembled by Saul *Lieberman, Cecil *Roth, and Gershom *Scholem. Significant private collections were also built up by ḥasidic dynasties, e.g., Gerer, Sadagorer, and Lubavitcher. Christian scholars and collectors who owned many important Hebrew books included Johannes *Buxtorf, Bishop Huntington, Bishop Kennicott, Sir Thomas Phillips, Edward Pococke, the Duke of Sussex, and Aldis Wright. Other important private collections belonged to Abraham *Merzbacher (now in Frankfurt City and University Library), Nathan *Porges, Israel *Solomons (Jewish Theological Seminary and Hebrew Union College libraries), Mathias Straschun (part in Heikhal Shelomo, Jerusalem), and Michael Zagayski. Among other collectors, mention should be made of Fritz *Bamberger (New York), Ludwig Jesselson (New York), Jacob Lowy (Montreal), and Israel Mehlman (Jerusalem). A very important collection of early Yiddish literature was that of Judah A. Joffee (Jewish Theological Seminary).

BIBLIOGRAPHY: Zunz, Gesch, 230–48; M. Steinschneider, *Vorlesungen ueber die Kunde hebraeischer Handschriften* (1897), ch. 3; A. Marx, *Studies In Jewish History and Booklore* (1944), 198–237; Shunami, Bibl, 38–76, 788–9; C. Roth, in: JBA, 25 (1967/68), 75–80; S. Simonsohn, *Toledot ha-Yehudim be-Dukkasut Mantovah*; 2 (1964), 495–8; KS, 41 (1967), suppl., index to vols. 1–40; Allony, *ibid.*, 43 (1967/68), 121–39; Szulvas, in: *Talpioth*, 4 (1949), 600–2; Padover, in: J.W. Thompson (ed.), *The Medieval Library* (1939), 338–46; Sonne, in: SBB, 1 (1953–54), 55–76; 2 (1955), 3–19, 156–9.

[Menahem Schmelzer]

BIBLIOTHÈQUE NATIONALE, French national library founded in the 14th century. There was no trace of Hebrew books there before 1544; however, by 1739 there were 516 manuscripts mainly from the collections of Catherine de' Medici, Cardinal Richelieu, and Gilbert Gaulmin. The catalogue of works printed in Hebrew and prepared by Nicolas Rigault remains unedited. The reforms brought about by the French Revolution resulted in several important collections being transferred to the National Library. These consisted of books and manuscripts from convents and from the Sorbonne library. Through the efforts of Solomon *Munk still further acquisitions were added. A description published in 1866 by Herman Zotenberg (*Catalogue des Manuscrits Hébreux et Samaritains de la Bibliothèque Impériale*, based on the preliminary work by Solomon Munk, Joseph *Dernbourg, and Adolphe *Franck), numbers 1,313 works in Hebrew and 11 in Samaritan. In the early 21st century there were a total of 1,481 manuscripts, including some discovered at Qumran, and 61 Samaritan manuscripts. Recent acquisitions were registered in the *Catalogue général des livres imprimés* and in *Ouvrages imprimés en caractères hébraïques*.

BIBLIOGRAPHY: Schwab, in: REJ, 36 (1898), 112–4; 37 (1898), 127–36; 61 (1911), 82–87; 121 (1962), 194–209; M. Schwab (ed.), 64 (1912), 153–6, 280–1; 66 (1913), 290–6; I. Adler, *ibid., Manuscrits hébreux de l'Oratoire* (1911); I. Adler, *Incunables hébraïques de la Bibliothèque Nationale* (1962).

[Georges Vajda]

BICK, JACOB SAMUEL (1772–1831), Hebrew writer and one of the pioneers of *Haskalah in Galicia. Bick, a friend of Solomon Judah *Rapoport, translated French and English poems into Hebrew and published delightful, satirical letters in *Bikkurei ha-Ittim, Kerem Ḥemed*, and in the anthology *Ha-Ẓefirah*, edited by *Letteris. Bick, like other Galician *maskilim* of his day, began by scoffing at the boorish Ḥasidim, but his strong attachment to the common people and his love of tradition led to a change in his views. When Tobias *Feder published his pamphlet *Kol Meḥaẓeẓim* (1816), criticizing Menahem *Lefin (Levin Mendel of Satanov) for having translated the Book of Proverbs into Yiddish, Bick defended Lefin and argued that one should be pleased that the book had been made accessible to the people in a language that they understood. Most of Bick's literary works were destroyed by fire. However, shortly before World War II, Dov Sadan discovered the manuscripts of three anti-ḥasidic Hebrew plays written by Bick in the Joseph Perl library in Tarnopol. These plays probably belong to Bick's early period.

BIBLIOGRAPHY: S. Werses, in: YIVO *Bleter*, 13 (1938), 505–36; G. Bader, *Medinah va-Ḥakhameha* (1934), 36–7; D. Sadan, *Mazkeret Levi* (1953), 96–108.

[Gedalyah Elkoshi]

BICKEL, ALEXANDER M. (1924–1974), U.S. lawyer and a leading authority on the United States Constitution. Son of Solomon *Bickel (1896–1969), Yiddish essayist and literary critic, Bickel was born in Bucharest, Romania, but immigrated to the United States at the age of 14. After graduating from the City College of New York and from Harvard Law School, he became a law officer in the State Department, and subsequently served as clerk to Justice Felix *Frankfurter. He joined the faculty of Yale Law School in 1956, and from 1966 until his death he held distinguished chairs at this institution. He was the author of a number of widely read books on the Supreme Court and on constitutional law: The *Least Dangerous Branch* (1962), *Politics and the Warren Court* (1965), *The Supreme Court and the Idea of Progress* (1970), and *Reform and Continuity* (1971). Bickel became nationally known when he represented the *New York Times* in the famous Pentagon Papers case before the Supreme Court in 1971.

In constitutional and legal philosophy, Bickel was a conservative, not a liberal-activist. In his basic orientation, he was a follower of Justice Frankfurter, who stressed the belief that the ultimate reliance for the vindication of interests and rights must be, not on the courts, but on other agencies of the democratic process. From this point of view, Bickel found many occasions to criticize various decisions of the Supreme Court during the years when Earl Warren was chief justice. His style was often sharply polemical and even strident. But like Frankfurter, Bickel was a liberal in his own political views. Thus, for example, though opposed to any form of racism, he opposed the use of bussing to help achieve school desegregation. His philosophy may perhaps best be associated with that of the Historical School of jurisprudence. In *The Supreme Court and the Idea of Progress* (1970), Bickel wrote that in dealing with problems of great magnitude and with complex roots and unpredictable offshoots, society is best allowed to develop its own strands out of its own traditions; "it moves forward most effectively, perhaps, in empirical fashion, deploying its full tradition, in all its contradictions,… as it retreats and advances, shifts and responds in accordance with experience, and with pressures brought to bear by the political process." In such contexts, he concluded, judicial supremacy is not possible. Bickel's book *The Morality of Consent* (1975) was published posthumously. He also wrote the first part of *History of the Supreme Court of the United States: The Judiciary and Responsible Government: 1910–1921* (vol. IX, 1984).

[Milton Ridvas Konvitz)]

BICKEL, SOLOMON (Shloyme; 1896–1969), Yiddish essayist and literary critic. Born in eastern Galicia, Bickel was an officer in the Austrian army during World War I. As an active Labor Zionist, he was editor of *Di Frayhayt* (1920–22), the Yiddish organ of the Po'alei Zion of Bukovina, and later editor and co-editor of Yiddish literary periodicals in Romania. Immigrating to the United States in 1939, he served, from 1940, as literary critic of the New York Yiddish daily, *Der Tog* and in the 1960s as head of *YIVO's Commission on Research.

Among his ten books, which appeared between 1936 and 1967, the following are the most significant: *A Shtot Mit Yidn* ("A City with Jews," 1943, 1960), a survey of the vanished culture of Kolomyya – written with mild irony, deep sympathy, and tolerant understanding – which highlights acts of moral greatness and poetic, joyous moments in the lives of ordinary Jews; *Dray Brider Zaynen Mir Geven* ("We Were Three Brothers," 1956), further recollections of Kolomyya's Jews; *Remenye* ("Romania," 1961), which chronicled developments of Jewish cultural life in Romania between the two world wars, intimately experienced by the author; *Shrayber fun Mayn Dor* ("Writers of My Generation," 2 vols., 1958–65), essays on Yiddish writers.

Bickel was one of the foremost literary critics and essayists, writing significant works on such writers as Isaac *Bashevis Singer, Itzik *Manger, Avrom *Sutzkever, the *Inzikhist movement, and editing a memorial volume for fellow literary critic Shmuel *Niger. He set each writer in his specific environment, defining his uniqueness at the same time. A jubilee volume, *Shloyme Bikel Yoyvl-Bukh* (1967) summarized and evaluated his role in Yiddish literature, including numerous poetic and prose tributes to him.

BIBLIOGRAPHY: LNYL, 1 (1956), 300–2; J. Glatstein, *In Tokh Genumen* (1956), 473–9; A. Glanz-Leyeles, *Velt un Vort* (1958), 233–40; S.D. Singer, *Dikhter un Prozaiker* (1959), 303–12; D. Sadan, in: *Avnei Miftan* (1962), 279–84; S. Liptzin, *Maturing of Yiddish Literature* (1970), 230–2. **ADD. BIBLIOGRAPHY:** E. Shulman, in: *YIVO Bleter*, 43 (1966), 309–12.

[Sol Liptzin]

BICKELS-SPITZER, ZVI (1887–1917), Yiddish dramatist and literary critic. Born in Lemberg (now Lvov), after finishing school, he studied law there and in Vienna and became a practicing attorney. He sympathized with Zionist ideas but was also an active supporter of and participant in the young Yiddish literary movement in Galicia. In 1910, he co-edited the first modern Yiddish literary collection of the Galician region, *Yung-Galitsisher Almanakh* and in the period 1915–17 edited *Tagblat* (Lemberg). He also wrote dramas, most notably *Der Goyel* ("The Savior"). His selected writings were posthumously published in Hebrew translation, edited by Dov Sadan (1948).

BIBLIOGRAPHY: LNYL, 1 (1956), 302; *Sefer Ẓevi Bickels-Spitzer* (1948); Neugroeschel, in: *Fun Noentn Over*, 1 (1955), 355–62; D. Sadan, in: *Avnei Miftan*, 2 (1970), 278–303.

[Melech Ravitch]

BICKERMAN, ELIAS JOSEPH (1897–1981), historian. Bickerman was born in Kishinev, Russia, and studied at the University of Petrograd (Leningrad). In 1918 he escaped to Germany, studied at the University of Berlin until 1926, and taught there from 1929 until 1932, when he emigrated to France. He was *chargé de cours* in the Ecole Pratique des Hautes Etudes from 1933 to 1940 and in the Centre National de Recherche Scientifique from 1937 on. After the German conquest of France he again escaped, this time to the United States. There he taught at the New School for Social Research and the Ecole Libre in New York (1942–46), was research fellow at the Jewish Theological Seminary (1946–50), taught at the University of Judaism in Los Angeles (1950–52), and was professor of ancient history at Columbia University (1952–67). After his retirement from Columbia he taught at the Jewish Theological Seminary.

Bickerman wrote innumerable articles in scholarly journals in many fields of ancient history, notably law, religion (especially Judaism), epigraphy, chronology, and the political history of the Hellenistic world. Outstanding among his many books are *Der Gott der Makkabaeer* (1937); *The Maccabees* (1947; also as part 2 of his *From Ezra to the Last of the Maccabees*, 1962), which revolutionized the historical understanding of the Maccabean revolt; *Institutions des Séleucides* (1938); and *Chronology of the Ancient World* (1968) – the last two being the fundamental works on their respective subjects. He also wrote *The Ancient History of Western Civilization* (1976); *Studies in Jewish and Christian History*, vol. 3 (published in 1986); and *The Jews in the Greek Age* (published in 1988).

ADD. BIBLIOGRAPHY: A. Momigliano, *Essays on Modern and Ancient Judaism* (1994).

[Morton Smith]

BIDACHE, village in the department of the Basses-Pyrénées, S. France. A Jewish community composed of Marrano refugees from Spain and Portugal was established there from the beginning of the 17th century. The duke of Gramont granted his protection to the Jews of Bidache in statutes of 1665 and 1668. When at the beginning of the 18th century the Auch district authority wished to conduct a general tax assessment on the Portuguese Jews in the area, the duke of Gramont intervened on behalf of the Jews in Bidache, including those not of Portuguese origin, who "enjoyed the privilege of nonassessment." The Jewish community dispersed after the French Revolution and was never reestablished. The former cemetery lies on the Port Road outside Bidache and contains tombstones often with epitaphs in both Hebrew and Portuguese.

BIBLIOGRAPHY: Gross, Gal Jud, 114; J. Labrit, *Les Gramont, souverains de Bidache* (1939), 97–99.

[Bernhard Blumenkranz]

BIDNEY, DAVID (1908–1987), U.S. anthropologist and philosopher. Born in the Ukraine, Bidney was educated in Canada. He taught philosophy at Toronto, Yeshiva, and Yale universities and then gradually shifted the focus of his academic interest to anthropology. Between 1942 and 1950 he was research associate anthropologist with the Wenner-Gren Foundation for Anthropological Research and was then appointed professor of anthropology and philosophy at the University of Indiana. His major interest in philosophy was in interpreting Descartes and Spinoza, as shown in his *Psychology and Ethics of Spinoza* (1962²). In anthropology Bidney was concerned primarily with the philosophical foundations and implications of the discipline, which appeared in his *Theoretical Anthropology* (1967²). He interested himself in the history of anthropological thought, theory of myth, primitive religion, and comparative ethics and law. The symposium he organized, the papers of which he edited in *The Concept of Freedom in Anthropology* (1963), surveyed freedom in the framework of diverse cultures.

[Ephraim Fischoff]

BIE, OSCAR (1864–1938), writer on music and the fine arts. Bie studied music with Philipp Scharwenka in Berlin and devoted himself to musical journalism and the writing of monographs. He was editor of the *Freie Buehne* and the literary review *Die neue Rundschau*; he wrote opera reviews for the *Berliner Boersenkurier*. Bie was appointed lecturer on the history of art at the Berlin Technical High School in 1890 and in 1921 teacher at the Berlin High School of Music. Among his books are *A History of the Pianoforte and Pianoforte Players* (1899), *Intime Musik* (1904), *Tanzmusik* (1905), *Der Tanz* (1906), *Die moderne Musik und Richard Strauss* (1906), *Die Oper* (1913), *Das Ratsel der Musik* (1922), *Franz Schubert* (1925), *Das Deutsche Lied* (1926), and *Richard Wagner und Bayreuth* (1931).

BIBLIOGRAPHY: MGG²; *Baker's Biographical Dictionary of Musicians* (1978⁶).

[Israela Stein (2nd ed.)]

BIEBER, HUGO (1883–1950), German literary historian. Bieber was born in Berlin, where he studied German literature and philosophy. He was for many years editor of the *Volksverband der Buecherfreunde*, Germany's most important book club. Bieber wrote a history of the intellectual and literary movements of the 19th century, *Der Kampf um die Tradition* (1928). *Confessio Judaica* (1925), an anthology of Heinrich *Heine's opinions on Jews and Judaism, demonstrates Heine's unbroken adherence to his Jewish heritage. Bieber wrote another work entitled *Heinrich Heine* which was translated into English and edited by M. Hadas (1956). After the rise of Hitler, Bieber immigrated to New York.

[Rudolf Kayser]

BIEBER, MARGARETE (1879–1979), archaeological scholar and teacher. Born in Schoenau, West Prussia, she studied at Bonn, and then was for some years an assistant at the German Archaeological Institute in Athens. On her return to Germany she worked at the archaeological museum in Cassel until 1919, when she joined the University of Giessen, where she was appointed professor in 1931. She left Germany in 1933, and after a period at Oxford settled in New York, where she first lectured at Barnard College and then became associate professor in the Fine Arts department of Columbia University. After her retirement she was a visiting lecturer at Princeton (1949–51). She was a member of the American Academy of Arts and Sciences. Bieber concentrated on Classical and Hellenistic art, and was distinguished for her profound knowledge of Greco-Roman sculpture and her penetrating insight into archaeological problems. During the first phase of her career her publications included the catalog of the Cassel Museum (1915) and two handbooks, *Die Denkmaeler zum Theaterwesen im Altertum* (1920; *The History of Greek and Roman Theater*, 1939), and *Griechische Kleidung* (1928), on ancient Greek dress. In America, her books include *German Readings in the History and Theory of the Fine Arts* (1946), and the monumental *Sculpture of the Hellenistic Age* (1955).

Bieber's last work, *Copies: a Contribution to the History of Graeco-Roman Sculpture*, was published in 1977 when she was 96 years of age. She was buried as a Christian.

[Penuel P. Kahane (2nd ed.)]

BIEDERMANN (Freistaedtl), MICHAEL LAZAR (1769–1843), Austrian financier, entrepreneur, and communal leader. Born in Pressburg, Biedermann first took up engraving. He settled in Vienna when a youth, and in 1798 was commissioned to engrave the imperial seal. In 1800 he opened a store for jewelry and antiques. He subsequently turned to the wool industry into which he introduced modern production methods. In business with L.A. *Auspitz, Biedermann succeeded in transferring the center of the wool trade in the Hapsburg Empire from Budapest to Vienna. He founded one of the first banks in Austria, and in 1816 gave the emperor an interest-free loan of 300,000 florins to combat famine in Vienna. In 1830 he became court jeweler. Biedermann played a leading role in organizing a congregation in Vienna, of which he became a representative in 1806. He was instrumental in the foundation of a Jewish school in 1812 and of the first synagogue in Vienna (the Seitenstettengassetempel) in 1826. He encouraged welfare activities and built a hospital. I.N. *Mannheimer was invited to Vienna to officiate as rabbi on his recommendation. An advocate of moderate *Reform, Biedermann was one of the leaders in the struggle for Jewish *emancipation.

BIBLIOGRAPHY: S. Husserl, *Gruendungsgeschichte des Stadttempels der Israelitischen Kultusgemeinde Wien* (1906); A.F. Pribram, *Urkunden und Akten zur Geschichte der Juden in Wien*, 2 vols. (1918), index; M. Rosenmann, *Isak Noah Mannheimer* (Ger., 1915²); B. Wachstein, *Die ersten Statuten des Bethauses in der inneren Stadt* (1926), 12; idem, *Inschriften des alten Judenfriedhofes in Wien*, 2 (1917), 514; L. Bato, *Juden im alten Wien* (1928); M. Grunwald, *Vienna* (Eng., 1936); J. Fraenkel (ed.), *Jews in Austria* (1967), 11.

BIEGELEISEN, HENRYK (1855–1934), Polish literary historian and ethnographer. On his mother's side a grandson of Naḥman *Krochmal, Biegeleisen was assimilated and even made his sons convert. He was for many years principal of a girls' school run by the Jewish community at Lvov. Biegeleisen published a number of studies and monographs on Polish romantic literature. These include *Pan Tadeusz Mickiewicza* ("Mickiewicz's Pan Tadeusz," 1884); *Lirnik mazowiecki* ("The Bard of Mazovia," 1913) on the poet Teofil Lenartowicz; and *Ilustrowane dzieje literatury polskiej* ("An Illustrated History of Polish Literature," 5 vols., 1898–1901). He also edited the works of Słowacki, *Mickiewicz, and Fredro, and a Polish translation of Shakespeare. In the field of ethnography Biegeleisen wrote a number of original studies, among them *Matka i dziecko w obrzédach, wierzeniach i zwyczajach ludu polskiego* ("Mother and Child in the Rites, Beliefs, and Customs of the Polish Folk," 1927); *Wesele…* ("Wedding…," 1928); *U Kolebki – przed ołtarzem – nad mogilą* ("At the Cradle – Before the Altar – By the Tomb," 1929); *Lecznictwo ludu polskiego* ("Popular Cures of the Polish Folk," 1930); and *Śmierć w obrzędach, zwyczajach i wierzeniach ludu polskiego* ("Death in the Rites, Customs, and Beliefs of the Polish Folk," 1931). One of his sons, BRONISLAW BIEGELEISEN-ŻELAZOWSKI (b. 1881), was professor of psychology in various Polish universities, and published works in his field.

BIBLIOGRAPHY: *Polski Słownik Biograficzny*, 2 (1936), 30–32; F. Pajączkowski, in: *Pamiętnik Literacki*, 31 (1934), 244–7 (bibl.); *Wielka Encyklopedia Powszeczna*, 1 (1962), 779–80 (on Bronislaw; incl. bibl.).

[Moshe Altbauer]

BIEL, township near Uncastillo, Aragon, Spain. The earliest information on the community of Biel dates from 1294, when a Christian girl disappeared; rumors were spread that the Jews were responsible, and the Jews of Biel were arrested. It was only after the intervention of James II that the charge was withdrawn. In 1305, however, Açac de Çalema, the wealthiest Jew of Biel, was accused of having derided the Christian religion. He was arrested and brought to trial before the Dominicans, and his property was confiscated. In 1294 and in 1305, the Jews of Biel paid an annual sum of 250 *solidi*, amounting to a quarter of the income derived by the king from the locality. In 1361, the king requested Solomon de la *Cavallería to annul an irregular Jewish marriage at Biel. A Jewish community continued to exist until the expulsion of the Jews from Spain in 1492.

BIBLIOGRAPHY: Baer, Studien, 131; Baer, Urkunden, 2 (1936), 184f., 375, 917; Baer, Spain, 2 (1966), 7–8.

[Haim Beinart]

BIEL (Bienne), town in the Swiss canton of Berne. Citizenship (Buergerrecht) was granted to several Jewish families in 1305, although Jews probably settled in Biel earlier. They were allowed to trade freely and engage in moneylending, until their expulsion from the city, the date of which is unknown. Communal life revived after 1848, when several Jewish families from *Alsace-Lorraine settled in Biel. A Moorish-style synagogue was built in 1883. Between 1916 and 1945 the Orthodox Chaim Lauer was its rabbi. For some years there was a separate East European *minyan*. The number of members of the Biel Jewish community dwindled from 1945. This problem was met by a closer cooperation with the community of *Berne and by state recognition for both communities in the 1990s along with the right to levy taxes by the state.

BIBLIOGRAPHY: A. Welder-Steinberg, *Geschichte der Juden in der Schweiz*, 1 (1966), 68; Schweizerischer Israelitischer Gemeindebund, *Festschrift 1904–1954* (1954), 313. **ADD. BIBLIOGRAPHY:** E. Dreifuss, *Juden in Bern. Ein Gang durch die Jahrhunderte* (1983).

[Uri Kaufmann (2nd ed.)]

BIELEFELD, city in North Rhine-Westphalia, Germany. Jews there were massacred during the *Black Death, 1348–49. In 1370 a few Jews again settled in Bielefeld. The prohibition of 1554 on Jewish residence in the duchy of *Juelich also applied to Bielefeld, but Jews resettled there in 1586. Their main occupations were commerce and moneylending. Jews from Bielefeld attended the fairs at *Leipzig at the beginning of the 18th century. The cemetery continued in use from 1665, until a new one was opened in 1891. In 1905 a synagogue to seat 800 was consecrated. The Jewish population numbered 65 in 1783 and 800 in 1933. On Nov. 10, 1938, the synagogue was burned down. At least 500 members of the community perished during the *Holocaust. Only 12 survivors returned to Bielefeld after the war. A few Jews settled there from other places, and there were 66 Jews living in Bielefeld in 1955. A new synagogue was inaugurated in 1951. The Jewish community numbered 23 members in 1989 and 193 in 2003.

BIBLIOGRAPHY: Germ Jud, 2 (1968), 82; MGDJ, 3 (1912), 14–21; U. Niemann (ed.), *Ueberblick ueber die Geschichte der juedischen Gemeinde in Bielefeld* (mimeo 1962); H.A. Maass, in: *Historischer Verein fuer die Grafschaft Ravensburg*, 65 (1966–67), 79–94. **ADD. BIBLIOGRAPHY:** J. Meynert, *Die Juden in der Stadt Bielefeld waehrend der Zeit des Nationalsozialismus* (1983); G. Renda, *Juedisches Leben in Bielefeld* (1997).

[Zvi Avneri]

BIELSKI, TUVIA (1906–1987), **ASAEL** (1908–1944), and **ZUS** (1912–1995), Jewish partisans in World War II. The three brothers grew up in the small village of Stankewicze in western Belorussia. The Bielskis were a poor peasant family and the only Jews in the community. David Bielski, the father, owned a mill and the family farmed its land. They observed the Sabbath and Jewish holidays, but were on good terms and mixed freely with their gentile neighbors.

When the Germans invaded the area in 1941, the widespread murder of its Jewish population began. The brothers' first-hand knowledge of German brutality and intentions regarding the Jews prompted them to take action. At first, they hid separately in the countryside. When their parents, siblings, and other relatives were killed in the Nowogrodek ghetto in 1942, the brothers escaped into the forest. With a few guns and 30 other Jews, they formed a partisan group. Tuvia was the commander, Asael was second in command, and Zus was in charge of reconnaissance. Because they grew up nearby, the Bielski partisans knew the area and its people intimately. This served them well in their efforts to elude the Germans and their collaborators.

The Bielski "Otriad" (partisan unit) was created by and for Jews. From its inception, Tuvia Bielski insisted that saving Jewish lives was as important as acts of sabotage. Some argued that this would compromise the unit's safety, but Tuvia strictly upheld the policy of accepting any Jew into the group regardless of age, gender, or health. Its membership grew to include women, children, and the elderly. As the Final Solution gained momentum, the Bielski partisans' rescue efforts became more aggressive and innovative.

The unit took in Jews who were hiding in the forest and punished those who denounced Jews. Those who left Soviet partisan groups because of antisemitism knew they would find refuge in the Bielski unit. The Otriad even dispatched members to the ghettos to help those inside escape and join their ranks. By cooperating with Soviet partisans in anti-German operations as well as procuring food, the Bielskis earned some protection from them.

From 1942 to 1943, the Bielski group moved from place to place. When, by the end of 1943, the group had grown to 400 people, they established a more permanent base in the Naliboki forest. Within this dense, swampy forest, the camp became a small, organized community with schools, a synagogue, and workshops that enabled economic cooperation with Soviet partisans. By this time the Germans were actively searching for the Bieskis, Tuvia especially, but they evaded the enemy by moving deeper into the forest. While a small number of the unit perished, the Bielski brothers' efforts constituted the largest rescue of Jews by Jews during the Holocaust. When the Russians liberated the area in 1944, 1,200 Jewish men, women, and children emerged alive from the family camp in the forest.

Asael was killed a short time later fighting with the Russians in the battle of Marienbad, Germany. Tuvia and Zus eventually settled with their wives and children in New York.

[Beth Cohen (2nd ed.)]

BIELSKO (Ger. **Bielitz**), town in southwest Poland on the river Biala opposite *Biala, amalgamated with Biała in 1950 to form the city of Biała-Bielsko. A community existed in Bielsko in the first half of the 19th century, which was authorized to open a prayer hall in 1831 and a cemetery in 1849. It became an independent community in 1865. The Jewish population numbered 1,977 in 1890 increasing to 3,955 by 1921, and approximately 5,000 in 1939; most were German speaking. According to the 1921 census, 2,737 declared their nationality as Jewish, of whom 513 declared Yiddish as their mother tongue. The Jews in Bielsko took an important part in the city's commerce and woolen textile industry. Most of the communal institutions were maintained jointly with the Biała community. Michael Berkowicz, Theodor Herzl's Hebrew secretary, taught religious subjects in the secondary school at Bielsko, and attracted many Jews to Zionism. The Hebrew scholar and bibliophile S.Z.H. *Halberstam lived in Bielsko and the scholar Saul *Horovitz officiated as rabbi there from 1888 to 1895.

[Abraham J. Brawer]

Holocaust and Postwar Periods

The approach of the Germans led to mass flight but many had to return to the city when their escape routes were cut off. The German army entered the town on Sept. 3, 1939, and immediately initiated an anti-Jewish reign of terror. On Sept. 4, 1939, the Nazis burned down both synagogues in Bielsko and the Ḥ.N. Bialik Jewish cultural home. A few days later the Germans burned down the two synagogues in nearby Biała, and its Orthodox Jews were forced to throw the holy books into the fire. In the summer of 1940 a ghetto was established in Bielsko. The ghetto was liquidated in June 1942 when the town's remaining Jewish population was deported to the death camp in Auschwitz. Bielsko was amalgamated with *Biała in 1950 to form the city of Bielsko-Biała. After the war a few hundred Jews settled in Bielsko-Biała. A children's home for orphans, survivors of the Holocaust, functioned there for a few years. The Jewish Cultural Society ran a club until June 1967 when the Polish government initiated its antisemitic campaign. After that date almost all the remaining Jews left Poland.

[Stefan Krakowski]

BIBLIOGRAPHY: M. Aronsohn, *Die israelitische Kultusgemeinde in Bielitz 1865–1905* (1905). HOLOCAUST PERIOD: J. Kermisz, *"Akcje" i "wysiedlenia"* (1946), index; *Megillat Polin* (1961), 164; T. Berenstein and A. Rutkowski, in: BŻIH, no. 38 (1961), 3–38, passim; *Yad Vashem Archives*, 0–3/1251. **ADD. BIBLIOGRAPHY:** P. Maser et al., *Juden in Oberschlesie*, 1 (1922), 87–95.

BIELSK PODLASKI, town in N.E. Poland, Bialystok district. Jews are mentioned there in 1487 leasing the local customs house. An organized community existed in Bielsk in the early 16th century and a synagogue was built in 1542. In 1564 a Jewish tax-collector in the town was condemned to death following a blood libel. The Jewish population numbered 94 in 1816 and 298 in 1847. With the coming of the railroad, trade and industry developed and the Jewish population rose to 4,079 in 1897 (54.6% of the total). In 1920 a Jewish school was founded and the Zionist youth organizations began their educational work in the town. Between the world wars the economic condition of the Jews deteriorated as a result of discriminatory government measures and the generally depressed economy

[Shlomo Netzer (2nd ed.)]

In 1921 Bielsk had 2,392 Jews, but under Soviet rule (1939–41) its Jewish population increased to 6,000 when large numbers of refugees arrived from the western parts of Poland occupied by the Germans. In the summer of 1940 a number of refugees were exiled to the Soviet interior. In the spring of 1941 young Jews were drafted into the Soviet Army. When the war broke out between Germany and the U.S.S.R. (June 22, 1941), groups of Jews attempted to flee eastward with the retreating Soviet forces, but few of them succeeded. The Germans entered Bielsk on June 24, 1941. Within ten days they assembled 30 of the Jewish leaders and intellectuals and put them to death. The Germans exacted a fine of four kilograms of gold and 200,000 rubles from the Jewish community. They also imposed a Judenrat, headed by Shlomo Epstein. In August 1941 an "open" ghetto was established. In February 1942 the ghetto was surrounded by barbed wire and closed off from contact with the outside. In Feb. 1943, the Germans rounded up over 5,000 ghetto inhabitants for the Treblinka death camp and murdered 200 old and sick Jews in the local Jewish cemetery. About 40 experts and skilled craftsmen were picked out and sent to the *Bialystok ghetto, where they were eventually liquidated along with the rest of the Jewish inmates. The community was not reconstituted after the war.

[Aharon Weiss]

BIBLIOGRAPHY: I. Schipper (ed.), *Dzieje handlu żydowskiego na ziemiach polskich* (1937), index.

BIEN, JULIUS (1826–1909), U.S. lithographer. Bien was born in Naumburg, Germany, where he studied lithography. After participating in the unsuccessful revolution of 1848, he fled to New York where he established a small lithographic business in 1850. His abilities soon earned him most government contracts for engraving and printing major geographic and geological publications, including a map of the territory west of the Mississippi River, which was standard for 25 years. He produced the maps and atlases accompanying the federal census reports from 1870 to 1900, as well as atlases of New York State (1895) and Pennsylvania (1900). Bien was president of the National Lithographers' Association (1886–96). A director of the Hebrew Technical Institute and Hebrew Orphan Asylum in New York, he was president of the B'nai B'rith order (1854–57, 1868–1900) and instrumental in forming its international structure. Julius' brother HERMAN M. BIEN (1831–1895), U.S. rabbi and author, founded a Hebrew school in San Francisco and served as rabbi of Temple Emanu-El until 1860. He then moved to Virginia City, Nevada, where he organized a school and was elected to the state legislature (1863–65). Moving to New York, he became a merchant in Fort Henry. In 1881 he was appointed rabbi of Congregation Beth Shalom in Chicago, but moved to Vicksburg, Mississippi, in 1885. Among his numerous works are the drama *Samson and Delilah* (1857), and *Ben Beor* (1891), a portrayal of anti-Semites.

[Edward L. Greenstein]

BIENENFELD, FRANZ RUDOLF (1886–1961), lawyer, writer, and Zionist. Born and educated in Vienna, Bienenfeld became an active figure in Zionist and in Jewish communal affairs. He succeeded Robert *Stricker as chairman of the Austrian section of the *World Jewish Congress. Under the nom de plume Anton van Mueller, Bienenfeld published *Deutsche und Juden* (1936; *The Germans and the Jews*, 1939), an analysis of the relationship between Jews and Germans in the period of Hitler, and followed it with *Religion der religionslosen Juden* (1938; *Religion of the Non-Religious Jews*, 1944). In 1939 he fled to England where he worked on the staff of the World Jewish Congress, later becoming a member of the executive, and drafted the claims for German *reparations after World War II. Bienenfeld took part in the juridical preparations for the Nuremberg processes. His book *Rediscovery of Justice* (1947) argued the claim of the Jews to compensation. His writings on Austrian civil law include *Die Haftung ohne Verschulden* (1933).

ADD. BIBLIOGRAPHY: H. Goeppinger, *Juristen juedischer Abstammung im "Dritten Reich"* (1990²), 269–70; R. Heuer (ed.), *Lexikon deutsch-juedischer Autoren* 2, (1993), 428–30 (bibl.).

[Josef J. Lador-Lederer]

BIENENSTOCK, MAX (1881–1923), writer, educator, and Zionist leader of the labor movement. Bienenstock was born in Tarnow, Galicia, and educated at an Austrian high school. He graduated as doctor of philosophy from Cracow University. He taught in government high schools from 1904 until the collapse of the Hapsburg monarchy. From his early youth he was an active Zionist. During the short-lived Jewish autonomy in western Ukraine (1918–19), he was director of the Department of Education and Culture. When the Ukrainian Republic was overthrown by the Polish army, he was arrested for a few months as a political criminal. Afterwards the Polish authorities refused to confirm his appointment as teacher and director of the Hebrew high school in Cracow. From then on, he devoted his efforts to writing and to Zionist education. Attracted by socialist ideology, Bienenstock formed and led the Hitaḥadut party in eastern Galicia. In the Polish parliamentary elections of 1922, his party, in the framework of the Jewish national bloc, elected him to the senate for the Lvov district. Bienenstock was a progressive educator and a gifted writer in Polish, German, and, later, Yiddish. He published two books, *Das juedische Element in Heines Werke* (1910) and *Henrik Ibsens Kunstanschaungen* (1913). He translated Polish classics into German, including *The Ungodly Comedy* by Krasinski. He wrote essays on Zionist socialist topics and, in his last years, on Yiddish literature. He died in Lvov.

BIBLIOGRAPHY: M. Bienenstock, *A Zamelshrift Wegn Zeyn Leben un Shafen* (1924); N.M. Gelber, *Toledot Ha-Tenu'ah ha-Ẓiyyonit be-Galiẓyah*, 2 (1958), 757–8; D. Sadan, *Avnei Zikkaron* (1954), 98–110. **ADD. BIBLIOGRAPHY:** N. Meltzer, *Dr. Max Bienenstock* (1924).

[Aryeh Tartakower]

BIENSTOK, JUDAH LEIB (**Leon**; 1836–1894), Russian writer and community leader. He was born in Volhynia and educated in Zhitomir at the government-sponsored rabbinical seminary. He served as government-appointed rabbi at Zhitomir from 1859 to 1862. Afterward he worked as a specialist for Jewish affairs in the office of the governor of Volhynia. He wrote for the Jewish press in Russian and Yiddish. In 1879 he went to St. Petersburg where for a time he became the secretary of both the Jewish community and the "Society for the

Spreading of Enlightenment." As a friend of *Mendele Mokher Seforim, he translated his *He-Avot Ve-ha-Banim* ("Fathers and Children") into Russian and collaborated with him on a few popular pamphlets in Yiddish, also writing one of the first biographical articles about him (*Voskhod*, 12, 1884). In 1891 he published a study of the Jewish agricultural settlements in the district of Yekaterinoslav (now Dnepropetrovsk). In 1892 when Vladimir *Tiomkin resigned from his post as Ḥovevei Zion representative in Ereẓ Israel, the *Odessa Committee appointed Bienstok in his place. He assisted in the establishment of modern schools in the country and the founding of the Sha'arei Zion library in Jaffa.

BIBLIOGRAPHY: Tidhar, 3 (1958), 1280–81; LNYL, 1 (1956), 297–8.

[Yehuda Slutsky]

BIERER, RUBIN (1835–1931), one of the first active Zionists and members of Ḥovevei Zion in Galicia, Austria, and Bulgaria. Bierer, who was born in Lemberg, completed his studies in medicine in 1863. He was a founder of the Jewish association Shomer Israel in Galicia. From the early 1880s he lived in Vienna, where he was a founder of the Jewish student organization *Kadimah (1882). In the same year, he was one of the founders of the Ahavat Zion society for the settlement of Ereẓ Israel, of which both Pereẓ *Smolenskin and Zalman Spitzer, the leader of the Orthodox Viennese community, were members. He published articles on the idea of Jewish nationhood and settlement of Ereẓ Israel in most of the German Jewish periodicals. Invited to Belgrade to serve as court physician, he transferred his Zionist activities there, and thereafter to Sofia, where he later lived. In Bulgaria he was a devoted assistant to *Herzl, who sent him the first copy of *Der Judenstaat*, inscribed "to the first pioneer of the Zionist idea." He returned to Lemberg in 1905, and continued his Zionist activities almost until his death.

BIBLIOGRAPHY: T. Herzl, *Complete Diaries*, 5 (1960), index; N.M. Gelber, *Toledot ha-Tenuah ha-Ẓiyyonit be-Galizyah*, 2 (1958), index; *Haolam* (Dec. 22, 1931), 1003; EG, 10 (*Bulgariya*) (1967), index.

[Getzel Kressel]

BIGAMY AND POLYGAMY. In Jewish law the concept of bigamy (or polygamy) can involve either (1) a married woman (*eshet ish*) purporting to contract a second marriage to another man (or to other men) during the subsistence of her first marriage; or (2) a married man contracting marriages to other women during the subsistence of his first marriage. These two aspects must be considered separately.

(1) Relating to Women. The general principle is that "a woman cannot be the wife of two [men]" (Kid. 7a and Rashi). In relation to a wife the term *kiddushin* implies her exclusive dedication to her husband. There can therefore be no *kiddushin* between her and another man while the first *kiddushin* subsists, and a purported marriage to another man is thus totally invalid. Such a bigamous "marriage" does incur severe legal consequences – primarily because of the law that sexual intercourse between a married woman and a man other than her husband (i.e., adultery) results in her subsequently being prohibited to both men forever and she then requires a *get* ("divorce") from both of them (see *Divorce, *Adultery). She requires a divorce from her husband, *mi-de-Oraita* ("according to biblical law"), because, although her adultery renders her prohibited to him, her legal marriage to him continues to subsist. To resolve this paradox she needs a *get*. She also requires a divorce from her adulterous "husband," *mi-de-Rabbanan* ("according to rabbinical enactment") – even though her marriage to him is invalid – so that people, ignorant of the true facts and perhaps under the impression that her second "marriage" was a valid one, should not be misled into thinking that she is free of him without a proper divorce (Yev. 88b and Rashi; Maim. Yad, Gerushin 10:5; Sh. Ar., EH 17:56).

Notwithstanding her divorce by both men, on the death of either of them she continues prohibited to the survivor forever (Sot. 27b; Yev. 87b and 88b; Yad, Gerushin, 10:4–5; Sh. Ar., EH 17:56). The aforementioned consequences result whether the bigamous "marriage" was intentional or inadvertent; e.g., if the woman was incorrectly informed by two witnesses of her legal husband's death (Yev. 87b; Yad, Gerushin 10:4 and Sh. Ar., EH 17:56). If, in spite of the said prohibitions, she does subsequently contract a later marriage with either of the two men, such a later marriage is a prohibited one (see Prohibited *Marriages) and must be dissolved (Maim. Yad, Gerushin 10:4). Further legal consequences of a woman's bigamous "marriage" are that her children of the second, adulterous, union are classed as *mamzerim according to biblical law and also that her financial rights are affected (Yev. 87b).

(2) Relating to Men. The law is different in the case of a married man who purports to take a second wife while still married. According to Jewish law this second marriage (and any others) is valid and can therefore only be dissolved by death or divorce (Yev. 65a; *Piskei ha-Rosh, ibid.*, 17; Yad, Ishut, 14:3; Sh. Ar., EH 1:9; 76:7). Permitted according to biblical law, polygamy was practiced throughout the talmudic period and thereafter until the tenth century (*Piskei ha-Rosh* to Yev. 65a; Sh. Ar., EH 1:9). Already in amoraic times, however, the practice was frowned upon by the sages, who prescribed that polygamy was permissible only if the husband was capable of properly fulfilling his marital duties toward each of his wives (see *Marriage). The opinion was also expressed that if a man takes a second wife, he must divorce his first wife, if the latter so demands, and pay her *ketubbah* (Yev. 65a; Alfasi, *Piskei ha-Rosh*, and Sh. Ar., EH 1:9). Similarly, according to talmudic law, a man may not take a second wife if he has specifically undertaken to his first wife, e.g., in the *ketubbah*, not to do so (Sh. Ar., EH 76:8). Taking a second wife is also forbidden wherever *monogamy is the local custom since such custom is deemed an implied condition of the marriage, it being presumed that the wife only wishes to marry in accordance with local custom (Sh. Ar., EH 1:9; *Beit Shemu'el, ibid.*, 20; *Ḥelkat Meḥokek, ibid.*, 15, 76:8). Generally, the husband can only be

released from this restriction with his wife's consent (loc. cit.; *Darkhei Moshe*, EH 1:1, n. 8; Sh. Ar., EH 76).

Ḥerem de-Rabbenu Gershom

SUBSTANCE OF THE BAN. In the course of time and for varying reasons (*Oẓar ha-Posekim*, EH 1:61, 2), it became apparent that there was a need for the enactment of a general prohibition against polygamy, independent of the husband's undertaking to this effect. Accordingly, relying on the principle of endeavoring to prevent matrimonial strife (which principle had already been well developed in talmudic law) Rabbenu *Gershom b. Judah and his court enacted the *takkanah prohibiting a man from marrying an additional wife unless specifically permitted to do so on special grounds by at least 100 rabbis from three "countries" (i.e., districts; see below). This *takkanah*, known as the *Ḥerem de-Rabbenu Gershom*, also prohibited a husband from divorcing his wife against her will. Various versions of the *takkanah* exist (*Oẓar ha-Posekim*, EH 1:61, 1) and, indeed, scholars have even questioned the historical accuracy of ascribing its authorship to Rabbenu Gershom. This, however, does not in any way affect its validity.

Since the prohibition against polygamy is derived from this *takkanah* and not from any undertaking given by the husband to his wife, she is not competent to agree to a waiver of its application, lest she be subjected to undue influence by her husband (Sh. Ar., EH 1:10; *Oẓar ha-Posekim*, EH 1:61, 5). Nevertheless, if the husband does enter into a further marriage it will be considered legally valid (Tur, EH 44; *Darkhei Moshe, ibid.*, n. 1; Sh. Ar., EH 44; *Beit Shemu'el* 11), but as a prohibited marriage, and the first wife can require the court to compel the husband to divorce the other woman. Since the first wife cannot be obliged to live with a *ẓarah* ("rival"), she may also ask that the court order (but not compel) the husband to give her (i.e., the first wife) a divorce (Sh. Ar., EH 154; *Pitḥei Teshuvah*, 5; PDR vol. 7, pp. 65–74, 201–6). The husband continues to be liable to maintain his wife until he complies with the court's order – even though they are living apart –because as long as he refuses to divorce her he is preventing her from remarrying and thus being supported by another husband (*Keneset ha-Gedolah*, EH 1, Tur 16–17; PDR vol. 7 p.74). However, if the first wife and the husband agree on a divorce and this is carried out, he is then released from his obligation to divorce his second wife, although his marriage to her in the first place was in defiance of the prohibition (Sh. Ar., *Pitḥei Teshuvah, 5; Oẓar ha-Posekim*, EH 1:80, 1 and 2).

APPLICABILITY OF THE ḤEREM AS TO TIME AND PLACE. Many authorities were of the opinion that the validity of the *ḥerem* was, from its inception, restricted as to both time and place. Thus, it is stated: "He [Rabbenu Gershom] only imposed the ban until the end of the fifth millennium," i.e., until the year 1240 (Sh. Ar., EH 1:10); others, however, were of the opinion that no time limit was placed on its application. At any rate, even according to the first opinion the *ḥerem* remained in force after 1240, since later generations accepted it as a binding *takkanah*. Accordingly, the *ḥerem*, wherever it was accepted (see below), now has the force of law for all time (Resp. Rosh 43:8; Sh. Ar., EH 1:10; Arukh ha-Shulḥan, EH 1:23; *Oẓar ha-Posekim*, EH 1:76). In modern times it is customary, in some communities, to insert in the *ketubbah* a clause against the husband's taking an additional wife "in accordance with the *takkanah* of Rabbenu Gershom…." However, the prohibition is binding on the husband, even though omitted from the *ketubbah*, as such omission is regarded as a "clerical error" (*Keneset ha-Gedolah*, EH 1, Tur 17; *Arukh ha-Shulḥan*, EH 1:23).

The *ḥerem* did not extend to those countries where it was apparent that the *takkanah* had never been accepted (Sh. Ar., EH 1:10). In a country where the acceptance of the *takkanah* is in doubt, however, its provisions must be observed (*Arukh ha-Shulḥan*, EH 1:23). In general it can be said that the *ḥerem* has been accepted as binding among Ashkenazi communities, but not among the Sephardi and most of the Oriental communities. This is apparently because in those countries where Ashkenazim formed the main part of the Jewish community, as in Europe, America, or Australia where European Jews migrated, polygamy was also forbidden by the dominant religion, Christianity, and therefore by the secular law. This was not the case in Oriental countries, as in Yemen, Iraq, and North Africa, polygamy being permitted in Islam (*Arukh ha-Shulḥan and Oẓar ha-Posekim*, loc. cit.). Thus, Maimonides, who was a Sephardi, makes no reference at all to the *ḥerem*. In practice, therefore, to prohibit polygamy Oriental communities would customarily insert an express provision in the *ketubbah*, whereby the husband was precluded from taking an additional wife except with the consent of his first wife or with the permission of the *bet din*. As this provision was a condition of the marriage, any breach thereof entitled the wife to demand either that her husband complied with the provision, i.e., by divorcing the second wife, or that she be granted a divorce with payment of her *ketubbah* (*Sedei Ḥemed*, Asefat Dinim, Ishut 2; *Keneset ha-Gedolah*, EH 1, *Beit Yosef* 13, 16; *Oẓar ha-Posekim, ibid.*, 1:80, 8; PDR 7:65).

People who move from a country where the *ḥerem* is binding to a country where it is not, or vice versa, are subject to the following rules: (1) the ban adheres to the individual, i.e., it accompanies him from place to place and he always remains subject to it (*Arukh ha-Shulḥan*, loc. cit.; *Oẓar ha-Posekim*, EH 1:75, 1; Sh. Ar., EH 1); (2) local custom is followed, so that if the *ḥerem* applies to a particular country it is binding on everyone, irrespective of their country of origin (*Arukh ha-Shulḥan, ibid.; Oẓar ha-Posekim, ibid.* and 1:75, 3; *Keneset ha-Gedolah*, EH, *Beit Yosef*, 22). Both these rules are strictly applied with the intent of extending the operation of the *ḥerem* as widely as possible. On the other hand, if a man legally married two wives in a country where this was permitted, he is not obliged to divorce either of them on arriving in another country where the *ḥerem* is in force, as the law is only infringed by his taking an additional wife and not when a man already has two (*Arukh ha-Shulḥan, ibid.*).

RELEASE FROM THE PROHIBITION. The object of prohibiting bigamy is to prevent a man from marrying a second wife as long as he is not legally entitled to dissolve his first marriage. Thus, in order to avoid any circumvention of the prohibition, the *ḥerem* also generally prohibits divorce against the will of the wife. This double prohibition may, however, result in the husband being unjustifiably fettered in circumstances where he would not otherwise be required by law to maintain his ties with his wife – and yet may not divorce her against her will. This can, therefore, be obviated by the availability of a *hetter* ("release") from the *ḥerem* against bigamy, which is granted by the *bet din* in the appropriate circumstances. This *hetter* does not mean that the first wife is divorced, but that the husband is granted exceptional permission to contract an additional marriage. Naturally, such a step is only taken if the court, after a full investigation of the relevant facts, is satisfied that a release is legally justified. Thus, for example, a release would be granted in a case where a wife becomes insane. Her husband cannot, therefore, maintain normal married life with her, a fact which would ordinarily entitle him to divorce her; this he cannot do because of her legal incapacity to consent. However, as the first marriage must continue to subsist, the husband remains liable to support his wife – including medical costs – but he is permitted by the court to take an additional wife (Baḥ, EH 119; Sh. Ar., EH 1; *Beit Shemu'el* 1, n. 23; 119, n.6; *Ḥelkat Meḥokek, ibid.*, 10–12; *Oẓar ha-Posekim*, EH 1:72, 19). Should the first wife subsequently recover her sanity she cannot demand that her husband divorce his second wife, as he married her in accordance with the law. On the contrary, the husband would be entitled – and even obliged – to divorce his first wife, so as not to remain with two wives, and if she refuses to accept his *get* he would be free from any further marital obligations towards her, save for the payment of her *ketubbah* (Sh. Ar., EH 1; *Beit Shemu'el, ibid.; Oẓar ha-Posekim*, EH 1:72, 17–18; PDR 3:271). However, the *hetter* would be revoked if the first wife recovered her mental capacity before the second marriage took place (Sh. Ar., EH 1, *Pitḥei Teshuvah*, 16, concl.; *Oẓar ha-Posekim*, EH 1:72, 14).

On the strength of the aforementioned rule, a release from the *ḥerem* may also be obtained by a man whose wife refuses to accept a *get* from him, despite the court's order that she does so, e.g., in the case of her adultery or where the marriage is a prohibited one (Sh. Ar., EH 1:10; *Ḥelkat Meḥokek, ibid.*, 16; *Oẓar ha-Posekim*, EH 1:63, 7). Some authorities are of the opinion that in the event of the wife's adultery the husband only requires a *hetter* from a regular court and not from 100 rabbis, since the *ḥerem* was not meant for such a case (*Oẓar ha-Posekim*, EH 1:73, 2). A *hetter* would be justified where a wife who has had no children during a marriage which has subsisted for at least ten years – a fact which entitles the husband to divorce her – refuses to accept the *get* and thus prevents her husband from remarrying and fulfilling the *mitzvah* to "be fruitful and multiply." In such a case the husband is obliged to take another wife to fulfill the *mitzvah* and so he would be entitled to the *hetter* (Sh. Ar., EH 1:10; *Oẓar ha-Posekim*, EH 1:68; *Arukh ha-Shulḥan*, EH 1:25).

As has already been stated, in Oriental communities for a husband to take a second wife requires either his first wife's consent or the court's permission. The wife is required to give her consent before a regular court (not 100 rabbis) and the court will permit the second marriage only if satisfied, after a thorough investigation of the facts, that the wife has consented wholeheartedly, without anger or under undue influence (*Oẓar ha-Posekim*, EH 1:61, 5, subsec. 3; *Sedei Ḥemed*, Asefat Dinim, Ishut 2). Without her consent, the court will generally only grant a release to the husband in such cases where it would do so were the *ḥerem* to apply (*Sedei Ḥemed; Oẓar ha-Posekim, ibid.*), since it is presumed that the husband's undertaking the *ketubbah* is given on the understanding that no circumstances shall exist which, if the *ḥerem* were to apply, would warrant his release from the prohibition (*Sedei Ḥemed, ibid.; Oẓar ha-Posekim*, EH 1:72, 9).

PROCEDURE FOR GRANTING THE HETTER. After the court has decided that a release from the *ḥerem* should be granted, the matter is referred to 100 rabbis of three "countries" (*Oẓar ha-Posekim*, EH 1:61, 9) for approval and, if so approved, the *hetter* takes effect. As a preliminary, the husband is required to deposit with the court a *get* for his first wife, together with an irrevocable authority for the court to have the *get* delivered to his first wife as soon as she is able and willing to receive it from an agent appointed by the husband at the request of the court. However, in the case where the *hetter* is given because of the first wife's insanity, it is customary to give her a new *get* when she recovers, rather than the one previously deposited with the court, as some doubt could be cast on the latter's validity, since it was the wife's insanity that made it impossible to deliver the *get* to her originally and there may therefore possibly be other legal objections to its validity. The deposited *get* is usually only delivered to her if she is in danger of becoming a deserted wife (see **Agunah; Arukh ha-Shulḥan*, EH 1:26; *Oẓar ha-Posekim*, EH 1:72, 30–31). Furthermore, the husband is also generally required to deposit with the court the amount of the wife's *ketubbah* in cash or provide adequate security (Baḥ, EH 119; Sh. Ar., EH; *Beit Shemu'el* 1, n. 23; *Arukh ha-Shulḥan*, EH 1:25; *Oẓar ha-Posekim*, 1:72, 23–24). Some authorities are of the opinion that the husband must also deposit with the court, or adequately secure in like manner, such sum as the court may determine to cover the wife's maintenance and medical expenses (*Oẓar ha-Posekim*, EH 1:72, 29).

State of Israel

At a national rabbinic conference called in 1950 by the chief rabbis of Israel, an enactment was passed making monogamy (apart from the above-mentioned permissions) binding upon all Jews irrespective of their communal affiliations. This *takkanah*, however, does not render a second marriage invalid according to biblical law, and therefore, if such a marriage does take place, it can be dissolved only by divorce. The criminal law of the state, however, renders it an offense on pain of imprisonment for a married person to contract another marriage (Penal Law Amendment (Bigamy) Law, 5719–1959). Nevertheless, for Jewish citizens no offense is committed if permission to marry a second wife was given by a final judgment of a rabbinical court and approved by the two chief rabbis of Israel. The latter's approval is accepted as conclusive proof that the permission was given according to the law. Special provisions relating to the grant of this permission are laid down in the *Takkanotha-Diyyun be-Vattei ha-Din ha-Rabbaniyyim be-Yisrael*, 5720–1960.

[Ben-Zion (Benno) Schereschewsky]

Following the enactment of the Penal Law, 5737 – 1977, the prohibition on polygamy is now regulated in sections 175–183 of that Law. Polygamy will not be considered an offense if committed pursuant to a permit granted in a final judgment of the rabbinical court, subject to the judgment having been approved by the president of the Rabbinical High Court of Appeals (section 179 of Law).

The Supreme Court was confronted with a question concerning the range of circumstances under which the rabbinical court could give a marriage permit, and thereby decriminalizing the act of bigamy in certain given cases. The specific question considered was whether the rabbinical court was authorized to permit an additional marriage even where the granting of the permit was not the result of the woman's inability to receive a *get* – e.g., due to insanity etc, as stated above – but was a tactic adopted by the rabbinical court to exert pressure on a recalcitrant wife who refuses to accept a *get*. In its ruling in *Street* (HC 301/63, *Street v. Chief Rabbi of Israel* 18 (1) PD 598) the Supreme Court ruled that the goals of the section dealing with the permit that may be given by the rabbinical court must comport with the overall goals of the law prohibiting bigamy. As such, the granting of a permit is only possible when it does not diverge from the purpose of the law, i.e., when the need for a marriage permit stems from an objective inability to give the *get*. In keeping with this determination, the court revoked the permit granted by the rabbinical court in that particular case.

In the judgment in *Boronovsky* (FH 10/69, *Boronovsky v. Chief Rabbis of Israel*, 25 (1) PD 7) the Court changed the *Street* ruling, determining that the statutory recognition of a permit given by the rabbinical court extended to any permit that could be granted *on the basis of any halakhically based grounds*, even when this was done as a means of compelling a recalcitrant wife to accept a *get*.

[Menachem Elon (2nd ed.)]

BIBLIOGRAPHY: L. Loew, in: *Ben Chananja*, 3 (1860), 317–29, 529–39, 657–67; 4 (1861), 111–5, 257–9, 271–3 (reprinted in his *Gesammette Sehriften*, 3 (1893), 33–86); F. Rosenthal, in: *Jubelschrift... Hildesheimer* (1890), 37–53; Finkelstein, Middle Ages, 111–26, 205–15; A.H. Freimann, *Seder Kiddushin ve-Nissu'in* (1945), passim; S. Lowy, in: JJS, 9 (1958), 115–38; I. Glasner, in: *Ha-Peraklit*, 16 (1960), 274–80; Z.W. Falk, *Nissu'in ve-Gerushin...* (1961), passim; P. Tishbi, in: *Tarbiz*, 34 (1964/65), 49–55; S. Eidelberg, *ibid.*, 287f.; I. Schepansky, in: *Hadorom*, 22 (1965), 103–20; I. Ta-Shema, in: *Tarbiz*, 35 (1965/66), 193; E. Berkovitz, *Tenaibe-Nissu'in u-ve-Get* (1966), passim; B.Z. Schereschewsky, *Dinei Mishpahah* (1967), 61–80; M. Elon, in: *Hed ha-Mishpat* (1957), 233–35; idem, *Ḥakikah Datit* (1968), 34–36, 104–16, 122–27. **ADD. BIBLIOGRAPHY:** M. Elon, *Ha-Mishpat Ha-Ivri*, (1988) 1:554–55, 633–34, 653, 675; idem, *Jewish Law* (1994) 2:674–75, 783–86, 807, 833–34; *"Al Averat Ribu'i ha-Nissu'im,"* in: *Hed Hamishpat* 12–13 (1957), 233–35; M.A. Friedman, *Ribu'i Nashim be-Yisrael* (1986); M. Elon and B. Lifshitz, *Mafte'aḥ ha-She'elot ve-ha-Teshuvot shel Ḥakhmei Sefarad u-Ẓefon Afrikah*, vol. 2 (1986), 393–94; B. Lifshitz and E. Shochetman, *Mafte'aḥ ha-She'elot ve-ha-Teshuvot shel Ḥakhmei Ashkenaz, Ẓarfat ve-Italyah* (1997), 290; E. Westreich, *Temurot, be-Ma'amad ha-Isha ba-Mishpat ha-Ivri* (2003).

BIGART, JACQUES (1855–1934), Alsatian rabbi and longtime secretary general of the *Alliance Israélite Universelle. Bigart began his service to the Alliance in 1882 as assistant to the secretary general Isidore Loeb, whom he succeeded in 1892. Single-minded in his devotion to every detail of the policy and administration of the Alliance, Bigart was deeply involved in refugee rescue and immigration management. In 1915, he developed an enduring partnership with Lucien *Wolf of the British Jewish Conjoint, later Joint Foreign Committee, to resist Zionist and Jewish nationalist diplomatic initiatives and uphold acculturationist Judaism. Their joint efforts, which ended only with Wolf's death in 1930, grew and prospered through World War I and into the Paris Peace Conference as they coordinated strategies to protect Jewish minority rights in the succession states and developed programs and relief for refugees and stateless people.

As an Alsatian patriotically committed to France and as a Jew unreservedly committed to regeneration on the French model, Bigart shared the values and objectives of the professional gentlemen who sat on the Alliance's Central Committee. Under his administration, the Alliance prospered and grew, particularly in the area of education, founding schools from Morocco to Teheran, from the Balkans through the Middle East to Cairo. The numbers peaked at the outbreak of World War I when 48,000 students attended 188 schools. Bigart, who knew the minutest detail of every classroom and school building, micro-managed the budgeting and administration of each Alliance-supported institution. Under his leadership, elementary schools for boys and girls grew into secondary schools and vocational and agricultural schools blossomed. Alliance normal schools trained teachers for Romania and ICA schools in South America and Sephardi rabbinical training began in Constantinople. In recognition of his signal services and contributions, the French government awarded Bigart with the Legion of Honor and promoted him to officer.

So many commitments, however, overextended resources just when American and German Jews grew less inclined to support a Franco-centric enterprise and Bigart preserved Gallo-centrism and Jewish heterogeneity at the cost of serious institutional losses and international support. Bigart, who had little interest in the rise of Hebrew studies, was hostile to the Jewish nationalism of Eastern Europe and uncompromisingly rejected Zionism as an overt threat to everything emancipated Jewry had accomplished. Towards the end of his life, the surge of European antisemitism, the coming of Nazism, the threats to Soviet Jewry, and the failure of more liberal options in the succession states, together with consistently closing doors to Jewish emigration, made him slightly more receptive to a broader federation of Jewish organizations to combat these threats

BIBLIOGRAPHY: E. Antébi. "L'Adventurier Immobile: Jacques Bigart (1855–1934)," in: *Les Missionnaires juifs de la France, 1860–1939* (1999); E.C. Black, "Jacques Bigart," in: F. Buisson, ed. *Dictionnaire de pédagogie* (2005); idem, "Lucien Wolf et Jacques Bigart: Partenaires en la politique et la diplomatie," in: *Revue des Études Juives* (2005).

[Eugene C. Black (2nd ed.)]

BIHALJI MERIN, OTO (1904–1990), Yugoslav writer and art historian. He studied painting in Belgrade and Berlin. While his approach to modern art was pan-European, his politics were of the extreme left wing. In Berlin he edited a Communist daily and later he fought in the Spanish Civil War and reported on it. In 1929, he founded the Belgrade progressive publishing house "Nolit," with his brother Pavle Bihalji, who was shot by the Nazis in 1941. Bihalji Merin was taken prisoner by the Germans (1941–45) and became one of the leaders of the Yugoslav resistance in prisoner-of-war camps. In 1945 he returned to Belgrade and with his wife successfully resumed his publishing career. He edited the house magazine and monographs of the publishing firm "Jugoslavija," one of whose notable editions was the **Haggadah* of Sarajevo. An authority on naive art, he helped to keep Yugoslav thinking in touch with new trends. Many of his works have been translated into major languages, the more important being: *Modern German Art* (1938), *Das naive Bild der Welt* (1959; *Modern Primitives: Masters of Naive Painting*, 1961), *Umetnost naivnih u Jugoslaviji* (1963), and *Adventure of Modern Art* (1968). He also wrote two satirical novels on Yugoslavian life.

[Zdenko Lowenthal]

BIHARI, ALEXANDER (1856–1906), Hungarian *genre* painter. The son of a poor housepainter, Bihari studied in Budapest and Vienna. In 1883, a wealthy patron made it possible for him to travel to Paris, where he fully assimilated the style of the French naturalist or realist masters, such as Jules *Adler. Upon his return to Hungary, Bihari settled in Szolnok, an agricultural center in the great Hungarian plains, rather than in a fashionable Budapest studio. He continued to paint *genre* pictures and was soon recognized as Hungary's leading painter in this field. A quality of Parisian wit seemed to guard him against the temptation of overt sentimentality. Using broad brush strokes, Bihari grouped and painted his figures as he saw them in their everyday surroundings. Bihari's masterpiece is perhaps his *Sunday Afternoon* which showed the influence both of Courbet and the impressionists. His work is represented almost exclusively in Hungarian collections.

[Edouard Roditi]

BIJUR, NATHAN (1862–1930), U.S. jurist and communal leader. Bijur achieved prominence in corporation law and participated in the reorganization of many large companies. In 1909 he was elected, with Republican Party endorsement, for a 14-year term as a New York State Supreme Court justice and was reelected in 1923 without opposition. His judicial decisions included important questions of constitutional law involving the extension of legal doctrines to meet modern conditions. Bijur's civic activities included service on the New York State Prison Commission and a special commission that established a municipal ambulance service in New York City. He was among the founders of the National Conference of Jewish Charities and the *American Jewish Committee, and he was a trustee of the Baron de Hirsch Fund and the Hebrew Free Trade School. In 1905 he was elected president of the New York Conference of Charities. Bijur was a supporter of the Hebrew Sheltering and Immigrant Aid Society and was often consulted on legal questions involving Jewish immigration.

[Morton Rosenstock]

BIKAYAM, MEIR BEN ḤALIFA (d. 1769), kabbalist and crypto-Shabbatean. The family name is rare, and the origin of the family is unknown. Bikayam lived in Smyrna. He studied Kabbalah under Jacob *Wilna, belonged to his circle, and was initiated by him into the "mystery of the Godhead" revealed by *Shabbetai Ẓevi (Ms. 2262, Ben-Zvi Institute). Bikayam received from his teacher the kabbalistic works of Solomon ha-Levi which the latter had received from his father, Benjamin ha-Levi. Some of the most learned and pious of the Smyrna community belonged to his circle. Bikayam was a close friend of Ḥayyim *Abulafia and Isaac ha-Kohen Rappaport, the rabbis of the community. One of the wealthy Jews of the town, Solomon *Ardit, supported him and his circle, and even in his old age (c. 1745) the latter studied Kabbalah under him. The wealthy leader of the Constantinople community, Samuel ha-Levi, and Moses b. Joshua Soncino of Smyrna supported and financed the publication of his books. When he went to Salonika in 1747, Abraham Enriques Miranda and Joseph Enriques Miranda, wealthy men of the community, welcomed him with great honor. There he also taught Shabbatean Kabbalah to a group of devotees and published two of his books. He returned to Smyrna about 1747. His books are all concerned with Kabbalah; his Shabbatean leanings are hinted at, but never explicitly revealed. He wrote the following books: (1) *Golel Or*, on the doctrine of **gilgul* ("transmigration"; Smyrna, 1737); (2) *Me'ir la-Areẓ*, on the portions of the Pentateuch, according to the principles of Lurianic Kabbalah (Salonika, 1747); (3) *Magen Avot*, on *Pirkei Avot* (Salonika, 1748); (4) *Me'orei Or*, on the Pentateuch, based on Lurianic Kabbalah (Salonika, 1752); (5) *Kera Mikreh* (Salonika, 1752); (6) *Me'ir Bat Ayin*, on *Ein Ya'akov* (Smyrna, 1755). He composed esoteric as well as nonesoteric prayers. His books contain *piyyutim* on the Redemption which he apparently expected in the year 1740 or before.

BIBLIOGRAPHY: A. Freiman (ed.), *Inyanei Shabbetai Ẓevi* (1912), 145; M. Benayahu, in: *Yerushalayim*, 4 (1952/53), 203–4.

BIKEL, THEODORE MEIR (1924–), actor and folksinger. Born in Vienna, Bikel went to Palestine and joined Kibbutz Massada in 1941. In 1943 he worked at the *Habimah theater in Tel Aviv. In 1944 he became one of the co-founders of the Israeli Chamber Theatre, later called the *Cameri.

Bikel entered the Royal Academy of Dramatic Art in London in 1946, graduating with honors in 1948. Sir Laurence Olivier, impressed with Bikel's performance in several local plays, gave him a small role in his production of *A Streetcar Named Desire* (1949), and in a matter on months Bikel took over the part of Mitch. In London he also performed in *The Love of Four Colonels.* On Broadway, Bikel's stage performances include *Tonight in Samarkand* (1955); *The Rope Dancers* (1957–58); *The Lark* (1956); *The Sound of Music* (1959–63), in which he played Baron von Trapp; *Cafe Crown* (1964); *Pousse-Cafe* (1966); and *The Inspector General* (1978). In American national tours he starred in *Jacques Brel Is Alive and Well and Living in Paris, Zorba, The Rothschilds, The Good Doctor*, and *She Loves Me*. Most widely identified with Tevye in *Fiddler on the Roof*, Bikel played that role more than 2,000 times from 1967 – more than any other actor. In 1997 he co-authored and co-starred with Bruce Adler in the stage show *Greetings ... Sholom Aleichem Lives.*

The films Bikel appeared in include *The African Queen* (1951), *Moulin Rouge* (1952), *The Enemy Below* (1957), *The Defiant Ones* (Oscar nomination for Best Supporting Actor, 1958), *I Want to Live* (1958), *The Blue Angel* (1959), *My Fair Lady* (1964), *The Russians Are Coming* (1966), *Sweet November* (1968), *My Side of the Mountain* (1969), *Prince Jack* (1984), *Dark Tower* (1988), *Crisis in the Kremlin* (1992), *My Family Treasure* (1993), *The Lost Wooden Synagogues of Eastern Europe* (as narrator, 2002), and *Crime and Punishment* (2002).

In addition, Bikel made more than 100 appearances on TV drama series. Fluent in several European and Middle Eastern languages and skilled at accents and dialects, Bikel also sang folksongs in nearly 20 languages, accompanying himself on guitar, mandolin, balalaika, and harmonica, and recordered numerous albums, including many in Yiddish. He traveled widely in the U.S., New Zealand, Australia, and Europe, performing his eclectic repertoire that includes songs from Russia, Eastern Europe, and Israel.

Bikel co-founded the Newport Folk Festival (1960), was a founder of the Arts Chapter of the American Jewish Congress (1961) and served as its national vice president (1963), was president of Actor's Equity (1973–82), and was appointed to the National Council for the Arts (1977–82).

[Ruth Beloff (2nd ed.)]

BIKERMAN, JACOB JOSEPH (1898–1978), U.S. physical chemist. Bikerman was born in Odessa, Russia, and attended the University of St. Petersburg (Leningrad). He held a variety of academic and industrial positions in the U.S.S.R., Germany, and Britain before going to the U.S. in 1946. From 1956 to 1964 he was head of the Adhesives Laboratory of the Massachusetts Institute of Technology. Bikerman contributed many papers to scientific journals, dealing with adhesion, electrokinetics, colloids, rheology, surface tension, contact angles, lubrication, and friction. His works include *Kapillarchemie* (with H. Freundlich, 1932); *Foams: Theory and Industrial Applications* (with J.M. Perri a.o., 1953); *Surface Chemistry* (1958^2); *The Science of Adhesive Joints* (1961); and *Contributions to the Thermodynamics of Surfaces* (1961).

[Samuel Aaron Miller]

BIKERMAN (Bickermann), JOSEPH (1867–1941), journalist active in Jewish political life. Born in Okny, Podolia, Bikerman graduated in philology at Odessa University in 1903. In an article written in 1902 in the monthly *Russkoye Bogatstvo,* he strongly opposed Zionism, and called upon Jews to join with progressive elements in Russia to help in the country's rebirth. His article aroused a controversy in which V. *Jabotinsky and B. *Borochov took part. He contributed to the democratic journal *Yevreyskiy Mir*, and wrote studies in Russian on the Pale of Settlement (*Cherta yevreyskoy oszedlosti*, 1911) and on Jews in the grain trade (*Rol yevreyev v russkoy khlebnoy torgovle*, 1912). After the Bolshevik revolution, Bikerman settled in Berlin. He was one of the founders of the short-lived "Patriotic Union of Russian Jews Abroad," which supported the ideal of the restoration of the Russian monarchy. His views on Jewish political problems are summarized in his Russian pamphlet on the self-knowledge of the Jew (*K samopoznaniyu yevreya*, 1939). He was the father of the historian Elias J. *Bickerman and the scientist Jacob J. *Bikerman.

BIBLIOGRAPHY: B. Dinur, *Bi-Ymei Milḥamah u-Mahpekhah* (1960), 66–68; J. Frumkin (ed.), *Russian Jewry* (1966), index.

BIKKUREI HA-ITTIM (Heb. בִּכּוּרֵי הָעִתִּים; "First Fruits of the Times"), Hebrew literary-scientific annuals, published in Vienna for 12 successive years (1821–32), and a central forum for *Haskalah literature. The editor of the first three volumes, Shalom b. Jacob *Cohen, sought to continue in this publication the tradition of *Ha-Me'assef*, the journal which initiated Hebrew periodical publications in the Haskalah period. (He had previously published and edited the last three volumes of *Ha-Me'assef he-Ḥadash.*) The first volumes also contained a German section (transcribed in Hebrew letters), which was later discontinued. The editors following Cohen were: Moses *Landau (vols. 4–5), Solomon Pergamenter (vol. 6), Issachar Baer Schlesinger (vols. 7–8), Isaac Samuel *Reggio (vols. 9–10), and Judah Loeb *Jeiteles (vols. 11–12). All the various literary genres were represented in these volumes – e.g., fiction, research, as well as translations of world literature (but mainly from German) – and were contributed by writers from Italy, Bohemia, Austria, Galicia, and Hungary. Reprints of a selection of works from *Ha-Me'assef* were also included. The standard improved in the last volumes, especially with S.J. *Rapoport's publication of his biographical monographs on geonic medieval Jewish scholars and authors. Other contributors included S.D. *Luzzatto and Isaac *Erter. With the discontinuation of these annuals, M.E. *Stern attempted in 1844 to publish *Bikkurei ha-Ittim*, and Reggio together with Isidore *Bush, *Bikkurei ha-Ittim ha-Ḥadashim* in 1845. While these attempts were unsuccessful, another annual, *Kokhevei Yiẓḥak*, did succeed. Its publication began in 1845 in Vienna, under the editorship of M.E. Stern, and lasted until 1873.

BIBLIOGRAPHY: B. Wachstein, *Die hebraeische Publizistik in Wien* (1930), xiii–xl (introduction); R. Fahn, *Kitvei Re'uven Fahn*, 2 (1937), 100–41 (*Pirkei Haskalah*).

[Getzel Kressel]

BIKKURIM (Heb. בִּכּוּרִים;"First Fruits"), last and shortest tractate of the Mishnah, Order *Zera'im*, dealing with laws relating to first-fruit offerings (Deut. 26:1–11; cf. also Ex. 23:19; 34:26; Num. 18:13). The Torah commands that the first fruits of the land be brought joyfully to the sanctuary, where they are to be offered in baskets to priests who are entitled to consume them in a state of purity. The offerers must recite a passage expressing their gratitude to God for delivering them from slavery in Egypt and bringing them to a rich land.

The laws set down in the Mishnah are based on an elaborate process of midrashic exegesis of the biblical texts, and the Mishnah (e.g., 1:2–5, 9) cites some of the relevant verses and their interpretations. Thus, the allusions in the recited passage to "fruits of thy land" and "the land which the Lord swore unto our fathers" were understood as excluding from the scope of the obligations people who did not own land or were not of Jewish descent. Similarly, the rabbis limited the precept to the seven fruits enumerated in Deuteronomy 8:8. From these basic premises, the Mishnah (especially in Chapter 1) develops its more detailed discussions of such topics as the relationships between the bringing of the fruits and the scriptural recitation, the appropriate time-frame for performing the precepts, precise identification of which fruits are subject to the obligation, what constitutes land ownership, the status of proselytes, and the extent of the owner's responsibility for the first fruits between the time of their designation and their delivery to the priest.

Most of Chapter 3 is devoted to a vivid narrative description of the ceremonial procession of bringing the first fruits to the Temple in joy, music, and fellowship. As noted by S. Lieberman, the abundance of details that cannot be ascribed to biblical sources or literary convention (e.g., the presence of an ox adorned with a garland on his gold-plated horns, a common feature of pagan *panegyre*) lends credence to the basic historicity of the Mishnah's description of the rustic folk custom. The statement in 3:4 that "even King Agrippa would take the basket and place it on his shoulder" was taken by scholars as an indication that the Mishnah was composed during the reign of one of the kings of that name.

Chapter 2 in the Mishnah is from a separate collection of traditions arranged by the formal pattern "There are features of X that are not in Y, etc." By virtue of the references to first fruits at the beginning of the collection, the entire source was incorporated into the Mishnah.

Some Mishnah editions include a fourth chapter outlining laws related to the status of the *androgynos*. This represents a variant tradition of a passage also found in the Tosefta 2:3–7.

There is a full Palestinian Talmud to the three chapters of the Mishnah, but no Babylonian.

BIBLIOGRAPHY: N. Sacks, *The Mishnah with Variant Readings: Order Zera'im*, vol. 2 (1975); J. Rabbinowitz, *The Jerusalem Talmud (Talmud Yerushalmi): Bikkurim* (1975); S. Lieberman, *Hellenism in Jewish Palestine* (1962²); D. Hoffmann, *The First Mishna and the Controversies of the Tannaim*, trans. P. Forchheimer (1977).

[Eliezer L. Segel (2nd ed.)]

BILBEIS, capital of the "Eastern Province" of Egypt (Sharqīya) during the Middle Ages. It had a well-organized Jewish community, mentioned in a letter written about 1100 by the *dayyan* Abraham b. Shabbetai to all Jews of the area, and also in a letter written by his son and successor Shabbetai later in the 12th century. When Ashkelon was conquered by the Crusaders in 1153, many Jews fled to Bilbeis; 15 years later Bilbeis was itself captured by the Crusaders and the Jewish community undoubtedly suffered. At the end of the 12th century Bilbeis was still considered one of the chief Jewish communities of Egypt. In a community law dated 1187, R. Judah ha-Kohen is mentioned as *dayyan* of Bilbeis (Maimonides, Responsa, ed. by J. Blau, 2 (1960), no. 346). Documents of the early 13th century found in the Cairo **Genizah* contain his signature as head of the rabbinical court. In a letter R. *Abraham b. Moses b. Maimon asked the Bilbeis community for financial assistance for the Jews in Jerusalem. Other documents mention Jews from Jerusalem who were visiting Bilbeis. Throughout the *Fatimid and *Ayyubid caliphates the Jewish community in Bilbeis had its own customs, such as indicating the value of a bride's dowry in the *ketubbah*. According to a late Jewish source, the persecution of Jews in Egypt in 1301 resulted in the conversion of all the Jews in the city to Islam, and of the synagogue into a mosque. However, in the late 15th century, Meshullam da Volterra mentions 50 Jewish families in the city in 1481, while Obadiah di Bertinoro estimated them at 30 a few years later.

BIBLIOGRAPHY: Mann, Egypt, 2 (1922), 25, 327, 329; R. Gottheil and W.H. Worrell, *Fragments from the Cairo Genizah…* (1927), 13ff., 139; S.D. Goitein, in: *Eretz Israel*, 4 (1956), 153ff.; Sambari, in: Neubauer, Chronicles, 1 (1887), 136; A. Yaari, *Iggerot Ereẓ Yisrael* (1943), 60, 124; Ashtor, Toledot, 2 (1951), 423; 3 (1970); idem, in: JJS, 18 (1967), 23–27.

[Eliyahu Ashtor]

BILDERSEE, ADELE (1883–1971), U.S. educator and author. Adele Bildersee was born in New York City. After teaching in New York City's elementary and secondary school system (1903–11), she was appointed instructor of English at Hunter College and remained there for the next 20 years, becoming acting dean in 1926. In 1931 she became dean of women at Brooklyn College, where she was also director of admissions from 1944 until her retirement in 1954. She also served as principal of the Temple Beth-El and Emanuel religious school and wrote several textbooks for Jewish children. Among her published works are *Jewish Post-Biblical History Through Great Personalities* (1918); *Bible Story in Bible Words* (6 vols., 1924–30); *Out of the House of Bondage* (1925); *Imaginative Writing: A Course in College Composition* (1927); and *Hidden Books: Selections from the Apocrypha for the General Reader* (1956).

The Dean Adele Bildersee Scholarship provides full or partial tuition to an outstanding student for graduate study at Brooklyn College.

BILETZKI, ISRAEL ḤAYYIM (1914–1992), Yiddish poet and Hebrew essayist. Born in Kobrin, Biletzki immigrated to Palestine in 1934, and published extensively in Yiddish before and after the founding of the State of Israel. From his first book of Yiddish verse *Umru* ("Anxiety," 1937) to his 15th lyric volume *Shures Tsvantsik* (1982), he displayed impeccable artistry in simple rhymed quatrains as well as in sophisticated free rhythms. While he published books in Yiddish about Itzik *Manger (1976) and Uri Zevi *Greenberg, most of his studies about individual Yiddish writers (e.g., H. *Leivick, *Bashevis Singer (English translation 1995), A. *Sutzkever) and various periods of the Yiddish literature were written in Hebrew.

BIBLIOGRAPHY: LNYL, 1 (1956), 292; M. Ravitch, *Mayn Leksikon* (1958), 85–86; Kressel, Leksikon, 1 (1965), 229. **ADD. BIBLIOGRAPHY:** I. Yanasovitch, in: *Di Goldene Keyt*, 83 (1974), 185–91; B. Kagan, *Leksikon* (1986), 83.

[Sol Liptzin]

BILGORAJ, small town in Lublin province, Poland. A Jewish community had been established there by the second half of the 17th century. Many of the Jews perished during the massacres of 1648–49. In 1765 Jewish poll-tax payers in Bilgoraj and the vicinity numbered 661. The Russian prohibition on Jewish settlement of the western border area (see *Russia) halted the growth of the community until the restriction was rescinded in 1862. The Jewish population numbered 1,637 in 1841; 3,486 in 1897; 3,715 in 1921, and 4,596 in 1931. In interbellum Poland many Jews were employed in the horsehair-weaving industry. The brothers I.J. *Singer and I. Bashevis *Singer, Yiddish writers, were born in Bilgoraj. A Hebrew printing press was established there in 1909 and continued to publish numerous Hebrew and Yiddish books until the Holocaust.

Holocaust Period

It is estimated that over 5,000 Jews lived in Bilgoraj before the outbreak of World War II, constituting more than half the town's population. On Sept. 11, 1939, almost the whole Jewish quarter was set on fire in a heavy bombardment by the German air force. A few days later German troops entered the town and immediately organized anti-Jewish pogroms. On September 29 the German army withdrew, but the occupying Soviet army had to cede the town to the Germans a week later. About 20% of the town's Jewish population left for the Soviet Union together with the retreating Soviet troops. On June 25, 1940, a ghetto was established. In the course of 1941 and 1942 a number of deportations took place; on Nov. 2, 1942 almost all the remaining Jewish population was deported to *Belzec death camp. On Jan. 15, 1943, the last 27 survivors who had remained in hiding were shot. A group of young men organized a small partisan unit which operated in the surrounding forests. The Jewish community was not reestablished after the war.

[Stefan Krakowski]

BIBLIOGRAPHY: T. Brustin-Bernstein, in: *Bleter far Geshikhte*, 3 no. 1–2 (1950), 65–76, table 3; *Khurbn Bilgoraj* (1957).

BILHAH (Heb. בִּלְהָה), servant girl presented to *Rachel by her father (Gen. 29:29). Bilhah was given by Rachel to her husband Jacob as a concubine (see *Nuzi). Bilhah bore two children by him, *Dan and *Naphtali (30:1–8). Reuben cohabited with her while his father was still alive, apparently by way of asserting his right of primogeniture (35:22). This offense is given as the reason for the loss of birthright by Reuben (Gen. 49:3–4; I Chron. 5:1). The meaning of the name is uncertain. It may be derived from the Arabic root *balaha* which means "to be confused" or "lacking in understanding" (cf. Heb. *bhl*), perhaps having some symbolic connotation relative to the status of the tribes descended from this concubine (see also: *Matriarchs, *Patriarchs, The Twelve *Tribes).

[*Encyclopaedia Hebraica*]

In the Aggadah

The *aggadah* indicates Bilhah's righteousness by the statement that, after the death of Rachel and Leah, the *Shekhinah* (which had been continuously present in their households) passed to Bilhah (Zohar 1:175b). After the death of Rachel, Jacob moved Bilhah's bed into his chamber. Bilhah is identified as the "messenger" (Gen. 50:16) sent by the brothers to Joseph, to inform him of his father's will (Tanḥ. B. 3:18).

BIBLIOGRAPHY: C.H. Gordon, in: RB, 44 (1935), 35–36; Noth, Personennamen, 10; S. Yeivin, *Meḥkarim be-Toledot Yisrael ve-Arẓo* (1960), 149–50.

BILL-BELOTSERKOVSKI, VLADIMIR NAUMOVICH (1885–1966), Soviet Russian playwright. Born to a poor, Yiddish-speaking family in Ukraine, Bill-Belotserkovski received little traditional Jewish education. At the age of 16, he ran away to sea and spent the years from 1911 to 1916 in the United States (hence the nickname "Bill," which he eventually adopted as part of his name). After his return to Russia in 1917, Bill-Belotserkovski fought in the Civil War and was one of the founders of the Communist propaganda theater as well as the author of some of the best-known plays in its repertory. These plays, called *agitki*, were primitive one-act dramas designed to rally audiences to the Communist cause; their artistic value was slight. Bill-Belotserkovski's best play, *Shtorm* ("The Storm," 1925), dealt with the Civil War. Its effectiveness was enhanced by its documentary, matter-of-fact style and coarse humor. In later years the playwright tried to tackle social and moral topics, but his tendency to see everything in clearcut terms, his aversion to intellectual subtlety, and his fondness for heroics limited his range. After World War II, Bill-Belotserkovski, who had earned a reputation as an "American expert," was commissioned to produce a number of anti-American works, the best known of which was *Tsvet kozhi* ("The Color of Skin," 1948). In 1937 Bill-Belotserkovski wrote *Pogranichniki* ("The Frontier Guards"). The play's hero, a Soviet army officer, is a Jew named Kogan. Interrogated by anti-Soviet intelligence agents, Kogan proudly emphasizes his Soviet, Communist Jewishness ("My father is the best pig-breeder in Birobidzhan") and, in the end, not unlike the biblical Samson, succeeds in killing himself and his jailers. During the antisemitic, anti-cosmopolitan purges of 1947 through 1953 the play was revived, but the Soviet censorship carefully obliterated all references to Kogan's Jewishness other than his Jewish-sounding name.

BIBLIOGRAPHY: *Teatral'naya entsiklopediya*, 1 (1961), 581–82; M. Friedberg, in: *American Slavic and East European Review*, 13 (Feb. 1954).

[Maurice Friedberg]

BILLIG, LEVI (1897–1936), Arabist. Born in London, he compiled *An Arabic Reader* with Avinoam *Yellin (1931, 1963) which is still one of the best introductions to classical Arabic. In 1926 he was appointed the first lecturer in Arabic language and literature at the Hebrew University. Billig also studied Shiʿa and spent time in Persia for this purpose. During the Palestine riots of 1936 he was shot to death by an Arab terrorist while working in his home. His untimely death prevented him from finalizing a study of the theory of the Imams (the successors of Muhammad).

BIBLIOGRAPHY: *The Times* (London, Aug. 22 and 25, 1936).

[Shelomo Dov Goitein]

BILLIKOPF, JACOB (1883–1950), U.S. social worker. Billikopf, born in Vilna, emigrated to the United States in the late 1890s. He was a son-in-law of Louis *Marshall. An imaginative administrator and fund raiser, receptive to fresh ideas, Billikopf became professionally active in labor relations as well as Jewish social work. He served as superintendent of the Jewish Settlement, Cincinnati (1904–05), of the United Jewish Charities of Milwaukee (1905–07), and of the United Jewish Charities, Kansas City, Missouri (1907). While in Kansas City Billikopf played an important role in the establishment of the pioneering municipal Board of Public Welfare. During World War I Billikopf directed the campaign to raise $25 million for Jewish war relief and in 1918 he directed the National Coordinating Committee for Aid to Refugees and Emigrants. He was appointed executive director of the Federation of Jewish Charities, Philadelphia (1919), which became his base for many services in the labor field. He was the impartial chairman of the Men's Clothing Industry, New York City, and the Ladies' Garment Industry, Philadelphia. In the 1930s he was appointed impartial chairman of the federal Regional Labor Board. Billikopf also served as vice president of the American Association for Old Age Security, chairman of the Committee of One Hundred on Unemployment Relief, Philadelphia (1930–31), and board chairman of the New York Clothing Unemployment Fund.

[Roy Lubove]

°BILLROTH, THEODOR (1829–1894), Viennese surgeon and distinguished representative of the Vienna Medical School. His remarks in a work on the study of medicine in German universities, *Ueber das Lernen der medizinischen Wissenschaften an den Universitaeten der deutscher Nation* (1876; the Eng. translation (1924) tones down the vehemence of the original) gave considerable impetus to antisemitism in the Vienna Medical School. Billroth claimed that Jewish students from Eastern Europe threatened to lower the high standards of the school and recommended the imposition of a numerus clausus against them. Stating that Jews could never be Germans and never make competent physicians he introduced a racial component into early modern feelings against Jewish doctors. The book caused rioting among German nationalist students at Vienna University and a fierce controversy ensued, in which Berthold *Auerbach participated. Billroth's allegations were answered by the German naturalist Matthias Jakob Schleiden in his essay *Die Bedeutung der Juden fuer Erhaltung und Wiederbelebung der Wissenschaften im Mittelalter* (1877; *The Importance of the Jews for the Preservation of Learning in the Middle Ages*, 1911). Although Billroth later acknowledged that he had been wrong, supported the cause of his disadvantaged Jewish colleagues, and became a member of the Verein zur Abwehr des AntiSemitismus, his former agitation had succeeded in unleashing antisemitism at Vienna University.

BIBLIOGRAPHY: J.M. Efron, Medicine and the German Jews (2001), 240–43.

[Mirjam Triendl (2nd ed.)]

BILTMORE PROGRAM, declaration of policy by the World Zionist movement during World War II (May 1942), to the effect that the cause of Zionism could no longer be advanced by the existing British Mandatory regime. It urged, as the next step, that Palestine be established as a Jewish commonwealth and that the Jewish Agency replace the British Mandatory administration's authority for developing the country. The name of the program was derived from the New York Biltmore Hotel where the Extraordinary Zionist Conference was held from May 6 to May 11, 1942. Since no Zionist Congress could be convened because of the war, this conference was practically vested with the authority of a Congress. Its delegates came from every American and Canadian Zionist organization and included all available leaders from Palestine and Europe, among them the president of the World Zionist Organization Chaim *Weizmann. The main speaker was David Ben-Gurion, chairman of the Jewish Agency Executive, who went to New York specifically for the Conference. He explained that the Jews could no longer depend on the British administration to facilitate the establishment of a Jewish National Home in Palestine as promised by the *Balfour Declaration of 1917, and that unless Jewish authority were established over Palestine progress would cease. He stressed the need for immigration and settlement, maintaining that no other regime could accomplish as much in these spheres as the Jews if they were given the required authority. The Biltmore Program was the object of controversy in Zionist and non-Zionist ranks before and after its adoption as official policy by the Zionist General Council (October 1942). The opposing minority included those who objected to the idea of a Jewish state, and others who considered the demand premature and would have preferred to work for the abolition of British restrictions (contained in the White Paper of 1939) and let a Jewish majority gradually develop in the country, or who would have turned over the Mandate to the United Nations. Still others insisted that the whole of Palestine should become an independent "bi-national" Jewish and Arab state, because a Jewish state would include only part of the country. In fact, neither in the resolution itself nor in Ben-Gurion's address was there any mention of the boundaries of the proposed Jewish Commonwealth. However, the Biltmore Program was in time adopted not only by the organized Zionist movement but by nearly all Jewish organizations in America and formed the basis for the political struggle of the Zionist movement from 1943 until the establishment of the State of Israel in 1948.

BIBLIOGRAPHY: J.C. Hurewitz, *Diplomacy in the Near and Middle East*, 2 (1956), 234–5; idem, *Struggle for Palestine* (1950), chs. 10, 12; Weizmann, in: *Foreign Affairs*, 20 (Jan. 1942), 324–38; D. Ben-Gurion, in: *Tav-Shin-Gimmel* (1944), 154–65; B. Halpern, *The Idea of the Jewish State* (1969), ch. 2.

[Moshe Zvi Frank]

BILU (Heb. בִּיל״וּ, Hebrew initials of *Beit Ya'akov Lekhu ve-Nelkhah*; "House of Jacob, come ye and let us go," Isa. 2:5), an organized group of young Russian Jews who pioneered the modern return to Ereẓ Israel. Bilu was a reaction to the 1881 pogroms in southern Russia, when the ideology of Jewish nationalism began to replace that of assimilation, which was prevalent among the youth. At first not linked with any particular country, the Bilu ideology soon came to mean a return to Ereẓ Israel. One of the first Bilu'im, Ḥayyim *Hisin, testified: "The recent pogroms have violently awakened the complacent Jews from their sweet slumbers. Until now, I was uninterested in my origin. I saw myself as a faithful son of Russia, which was to me my raison d'être and the very air I breathed. Each new discovery by a Russian scientist, every classical literary work, every victory of the Russian kingdom would fill my heart with pride. I wanted to devote my whole strength to the good of my homeland, and happily to do my duty, and suddenly they come and show us the door, and openly declare that we are free to leave for the West."

The reawakening of the Jewish spirit coincided with the increasing waves of emigrants and fugitives leaving Russia as a result of the pogroms. Jewish leaders devised various solutions, one of which was settlement of Ereẓ Israel, but most of the emigrants were attracted to the United States. Although a thin stream of settlers flowed to Ereẓ Israel, anticipating the Bilu group by a few months, Bilu was the first organized group of pioneers to go there. Lacking financial resources, they desired only to work, and especially, to work the land.

Founding of Bilu

Bilu was initiated when a fast was held by the Jewish communities in Russia on Jan. 21, 1882, as a result of the pogroms. Israel Belkind, then a student, invited a group of young Kharkov Jews to his home to discuss the state of Russian Jewry. Unlike the *Am Olam Group, which was organized for the purpose of emigration to the U.S., Belkind's group decided to settle in Ereẓ Israel. It first called itself Davio, Hebrew initials for *Dabber el Benei Yisrael Ve-Yissa'u* ("Speak unto the Children of Israel that they go forward," Ex. 14:15), but later changed the name to Bilu for, according to Belkind, "instead of advising the people to go to Ereẓ Israel, we decided to go there ourselves."

Founded with only a handful of members, Bilu rapidly increased its membership to over 500 as a result of effective recruitment campaigns, though only a few were ready to leave for Ereẓ Israel. Kharkov became the Bilu headquarters, and Belkind its leader. Bilu ideology was expressed in different and even contradictory ways. Of the many statutes formulated by the group, one defined the aim as the creation of "a political center for the Jewish people," while another stated that the society pursues "an economic and national-spiritual aim" for the Jewish people "in Syria and Palestine." Ze'ev *Dubnow, a member of Bilu, wrote: "The aim of our journey is rich in plans. We want to conquer Palestine and return to the Jews the political independence stolen from them two thousand years ago. And if it is willed, it is no dream. We must establish agricultural settlements, factories, and industry. We must develop industry and put it into Jewish hands. And above all, we must give young people military training and provide them with weapons. Then will the glorious day come, as prophesied by Isaiah in his promise of the restoration of Israel. With their weapons in their hands, the Jews will declare that they are the masters of their ancient homeland."

Eventually, headquarters were moved to Odessa, from where the pioneers intended to sail. The leaders of the Jewish national movement in Russia were generally opposed to the *aliyah* of the Bilu'im and urged them not to go. Among the Bilu'im themselves two trends emerged. One advocated immediate *aliyah* to Ereẓ Israel in order to work there. The other contended that no practical settlement should be begun so long as Jews had no political guarantees from the Turks. The internal debate between the two trends in Bilu lasted for about two years, diminishing the strength of the group and hindering the first efforts of the group that went to Ereẓ Israel. At first the Bilu'im hoped to receive support from wealthy Russian Jews. Disappointed by their lack of interest, they turned to Laurence *Oliphant, then living in Constantinople and rumored to have close relations with the sultan's court. However, they discovered that Oliphant could give them no practical help, and again split into divergent groups. Some advocated continuing political activity in Constantinople to gain recognition from the Ottoman authorities, while the rest, led by Belkind, decided to go to Ereẓ Israel immediately.

In Ereẓ Israel

The first to arrive in the country was Ya'akov Shertok (father of Moshe *Sharett), who preceded the first group of 14 Bilu'im by a few weeks. The group, led by Belkind, reached Jaffa on July 6, 1882. The day after their arrival they began work at the *Mikveh Israel agricultural school where they lived in a commune, the household being run by the only woman in the group. There they underwent great hardships, as they were unused to physical labor, received meager wages, and were subject to oppression by the director of the school. However, they found a great friend in Charles *Netter, the founder of Mikveh Israel, who adopted a paternal attitude to the Bilu'im, encouraged them, and openly identified himself with their aims. With Netter's death that same year (1882), the Bilu'im were again without a patron, until Yeḥiel *Pines, a writer and public figure, came to their assistance. Elected by the Bilu'im as their leader and guide, he transferred some of them from Mikveh Israel to Jerusalem to become artisans. The Bilu group in Jerusalem called itself "Shehu" (שהו), the initial letters of *Shivat he-Ḥarash ve-ha-Masger* ("Return of the Craftsman and the Smith," cf. II Kings 24:16), and they established a carpentry and woodcraft workshop. However, the scheme eventually failed because of lack of experience, and the Jerusalem members of Bilu dispersed elsewhere in Ereẓ Israel.

In November 1882 some of the members of Bilu, under Belkind's leadership, moved to *Rishon le-Zion, working as hired laborers, sharecroppers, and manual laborers for the village council. Poor yields and difficult relationships between the settlers and hired laborers in the village were greatly disappointing, especially as the Bilu'im hoped to found their own settlement eventually. They continued their search for satisfactory work between Rishon le-Zion and Mikveh Israel. Even the Russian Ḥovevei Zion disappointed them, for they failed to provide them with the means for settlement. After a steady decline in their number abroad, the Bilu association in Russia died out. In June of 1883, about a year after *aliyah*, Bilu numbered 28 members in Ereẓ Israel, of whom 13 were at Rishon le-Zion, seven at Mikveh Israel as hired laborers, and three in Jerusalem. They met on festivals and holidays, organizing a trip on Passover of 1884, together with Eliezer *Ben-Yehuda, speaking Hebrew among themselves and singing Hebrew songs.

When the Bilu members who were in Constantinople realized that their political activities had failed, they also went to Ereẓ Israel (1884). However, their economic situation deteriorated steadily. They worked for a while as laborers at Mikveh Israel but were soon dismissed, and the director of the school even supplied them with means to emigrate to America. At the very last moment, Pines succeeded in saving them by acquiring the land of the Arab village Qaṭra in the Judean foothills, an area of 3,300 dunams (c. 800 acres). Borrowing the money, Pines sent an envoy abroad to sell the land parcels to Zionist associations, on condition that each of them hand over their parcel to the Bilu'im. The Bilu settlement of *Gederah was thus founded, and the Bilu members who had worked at Mikveh Israel and Rishon le-Zion settled there in December of 1884. Although a few Bilu'im settled in Rishon le-Zion and elsewhere, Gederah became known historically as the Bilu settlement.

An estimated total of 53 Bilu members left Russia for Ereẓ Israel during the early 1880s. Some returned to Russia or went on to the U.S., while others remained faithful to the ideal of settling Ereẓ Israel, and some of them later became leaders in the public life of the country.

BIBLIOGRAPHY: N. Sokolow, *Hibbath Zion* (Eng., 1935), ch. 42; idem, *History of Zionism*, 2 vols. (1919), index; B. Halpern, *The Idea of the Jewish State* (1961), 27, 131, 255; M. Meerovitch, *Bi-Ymei Bilu* (1942); idem, *Mi-Zikhronotav shel Aharon ha-Bilu'im* (1946); A. Druyanow (ed.), *Ketavim le-Toledot Ḥibbat Ẓiyyon*, 3 vols. (1919–32), index; I. Klausner, *Be-Hitorer Am* (1962), index; S. Jawnieli (Yavnieli), *Sefer ha-Ẓiyyonut*, 2 vols. (1961²); Z.D. Levontin, *Le-Ereẓ Avoteinu* (1950³), passim. **ADD. BIBLIOGRAPHY:** S. Laskov *Ha-Bilu'im* (1991).

[Getzel Kressel]

BIMAH (Heb. בִּימָה; "elevated place"), platform in the synagogue on which stands the desk from which the Torah is read. Occasionally, the rabbi delivers his sermon from the *bimah*, and on Rosh Ha-Shanah the *shofar* is blown there. In Sephardi synagogues, the *ḥazzan* conducts most of the service from the *bimah*. In some Ashkenazi synagogues, the *ḥazzan* has a separate reading stand immediately in front of and facing the ark from which he conducts the service. Alternative names are *almemar* (from the Arabic *al-minbar*, "platform") or, among Sephardi Jews, *tevah* ("box"). The use of the *bimah* as a pulpit for reading the Torah in public was known as early as the times of Nehemiah (Neh. 8:4). Raised platforms were also known to have existed in the times of the Second Temple (Sot. 7:8). The Talmud mentions a wooden pulpit in the center of the synagogue of Alexandria in Egypt (Suk. 51b). In Orthodox synagogues of the Ashkenazi rite, the *bimah* is often in the center, with some intervening seats between the *bimah* and the ark (based upon the opinion of Maimonides, in Yad, Tefillah, 11: 3; Tur., OḤ 150, and *Rema*, OḤ 150: 5). In Sephardi and Oriental synagogues, the *bimah* is placed in the middle of the room opposite the ark and without intervening seats. The location of the *bimah* close to the western wall in Sephardi synagogues was permitted by Joseph *Caro. In his commentary *Kesef Mishneh* (to Maimonides, *loc. cit.*), he wrote: "It is not essential to place the *bimah* in the center; all depends upon the place and time." A heated dispute, however, resulted from moving the *bimah* from the center toward the ark in Liberal synagogues after the Reform movement started. The most vehement antagonists of this innovation were Moses *Sofer (*Ḥatam Sofer*, OḤ 28), and Ezekiel *Landau (*Noda bi-Yhudah*

Mahadura Tinyana, OḤ 18). Their protest led to a proclamation by 100 rabbis prohibiting worship in a synagogue that does not have the *bimah* in its center (see *Sedei Ḥemed*, Assefat Dinim, Bet ha-Keneset no. 13). Almost all modern Reform and Conservative synagogues combine the *bimah* with the ark.

Forms of the Bimah

Examples of the *bimah* surviving from early times are simple in form and built close to the ground. For instance, the *bimah* at the synagogue at Bet Alfa (sixth century) is one step high. In medieval Spain the *bimah* was a wooden platform raised high above the ground on columns. It was sometimes surmounted by a canopy and reached by an attached stairway. Until the Renaissance the *bimah*, which was placed in the center of the synagogue, had a more dominant position than the ark. In Italy from the 16th century, they were given equal emphasis by being placed at opposite sides in the center of the hall. The ark in the synagogue at Worms, Germany (1175), was placed on the central axis between the two main columns. This became the usual arrangement among Ashkenazi Jews in Central and Eastern Europe. In this area, a new form of *bimah* came into being in the late 17th century. The four central pillars which supported the vaulted ceiling of a synagogue were used as the framework of the *bimah* which thus became a roofed structure. The *bimah* assumed curved, circular, octagonal, and other forms, and was made of many materials such as stone, wood, bronze, marble, and wrought iron. In Eastern Europe from the 16th century it could be found enclosed by a wrought iron cage.

BIBLIOGRAPHY: Elbogen, Gottesdienst, 473ff.; EJ, 2 (1928), 371–84; S. Freehof, *Reform Jewish Practice*, 2 (1952), 16–20; ET, 3 (1951), 112–3.

BIMKO, FISHEL (1890–1965), Yiddish dramatist and novelist. Born in Kielce, Poland, Bimko's first realistic narrative, *Di Aveyre* ("The Transgression"), was published in 1912 and his first play, *Oyfn Breg Vaysel* ("On the Shores of the Vistula"), was staged in Lodz in 1914. Thereafter his plays were produced in the Yiddish theaters of Europe and America. Especially popular were *Ganovim* ("Thieves," 1921), a realistic play depicting the Polish-Jewish underworld, and *East Side* (1938), a naturalistic drama of Jewish life in New York, where Bimko settled in 1921. His selected dramas were published in seven volumes in 1936, and his selected narratives in three volumes in 1941 and 1947.

BIBLIOGRAPHY: Rejzen, Leksikon, 1 (1926), 270–2; LNYL, 1 (1956), 293–5; A. Beckerman, *F. Bimko Dramaturg un Realist* (1944); B. Rivkin, *Undzere Prozaiker* (1951), 297–320. **ADD. BIBLIOGRAPHY:** A. Gordin, *Yiddish Lebn in Amerike* (1957).

[Sol Liptzin]

BIMSTEIN, "WHITEY" (**Morris**; 1897–1969), U.S. boxing trainer. One of the greatest trainers in boxing history, Bimstein worked in the corner of approximately 25 world champions, including Gene Tunney, Max Baer, Jimmy Braddock, Primo Carnera, Harry Greb, Jake LaMotta, and Jewish fighters Barney *Ross, Jackie "Kid" *Berg, Benny *Leonard, Charley Phil Rosenberg, Slapsie Maxie Rosenbloom, Ruby Goldstein, Abe Goldstein, and "Kid" Kaplan. Born on the Lower East Side of Manhattan, Bimstein dropped out of school at the age of 12 and began boxing as a 15-year-old at St. Jerome's Church in the Bronx under the name Johnny White, because he was afraid his father would get angry if he read about his son in the paper. But Bimstein's father allowed him to fight when he found out his son was making more money than he. Bimstein fought as a bantamweight and featherweight until he joined the navy in World War I. After serving in the navy, and a career of 70 professional fights, Bimstein decided to switch to corner work and became an expert cut man. Called Whitey by everyone but his family, Bimstein began a partnership in 1925 with the legendary trainer Ray *Arcel, and the two worked together for nine years, calling themselves the "Siamese Training Twins." After World War II, Bimstein paired with another legendary trainer, Freddie Brown. He worked with Tunney during his two historic fights with Jack Dempsey in 1926 and 1927, and was the corner man for four victorious world champions – Barney Ross, Lou Ambers, Harry Jeffra, and Fred Apostoli – in one night at the Polo Grounds on September 23, 1937. He was also the cut man for Rocky Marciano, closing a split on Marciano's nose during his fight with Ezzard Charles that helped Marciano retain his undefeated record. Bimstein estimated that he worked approximately 35,000 to 40,000 fights during his career, which lasted into the 1960s.

[Elli Wohlgelernter (2nd ed.)]

BI-NATIONALISM, one of the solutions to the Jewish-Arab national conflict in Ereẓ Israel offered by various Jewish individuals and groups in the period before the establishment of the State of Israel. The bi-national idea was based on the principle that since two nations – the Jews and Arabs – laid claim to the same land, which to one was Ereẓ Israel and to the other Palestine, it should not be given to one of them but should become the state of both, and that irrespective of the numerical strength of each, the relations between them should be based on equality. Some supported the idea because they temporarily or permanently lost faith in the ability of the Jewish people to establish an independent Jewish State in Ereẓ Israel, while others supported it for moral or ideological reasons. Some advocated a federal or confederal structure for the bi-national state, while others sought to avoid the partition of the country into states or cantons, and advocated bi-nationalism that was to be based on communities.

The first body to advocate bi-nationalism was *Berit Shalom, which existed from 1925 to 1933. *Ha-Shomer ha-Ẓa'ir started to advocate bi-nationalism as part of its platform in 1929, and some of its members, including Mordekhai *Bentov and Aharon Cohen, continued to support the idea until after the establishment of the State in 1948. Following the outbreak of the 1936 disturbances (or Arab Revolt) a new organization, advocating a rapprochement with the Arab population, was set up, bearing the name Kedmah Mizraḥah ("Forward to the

East"). Towards the end of its existence in 1938, the organization became associated with bi-nationalism, as Haim *Margolis-Kalvaryski became its most active member. Another group that was active in this period, and advocated an agreement with the Arabs which included certain features of bi-nationalism, was known as "the group of five." This group, which included Gad *Frumkin, Moshe *Smilansky, Pinḥas *Rutenberg, Moshe *Novomeysky, and Judah L. *Magnes, and held meetings with both Arab leaders and Zionist leaders, proposed as part of an agreement with the Arabs that would enable continued Zionist development, the establishment of a legislative council based on parity.

On the eve of World War II, all the various groups and individuals that sought a solution of the Jewish-Arab problem on the basis of bi-nationalism got together in an organization that called itself the League for Jewish-Arab Rapprochement and Cooperation. The group included former members of Berit Shalom and Kedmah Mizraḥah, leaders of Ha-Shomer ha-ẓa'ir and Po'alei Zion Semol, members of Aliyah Ḥadashah (a political group made up primarily of new immigrants from Germany), and several members of Mapai and the General Zionists B. The first act of the new group in March 1939 was to publish a pamphlet called *Al Parashat Darkenu* ("At the Crossroads"), which dealt with the Arab problem and ways of resolving it. Among the articles appearing in it were several by Martin *Buber, who had recently immigrated to Ereẓ Israel from Germany and was a supporter of bi-nationalism for moral reasons. In the course of its existence the League published various constitutional proposals for a federal state based on the idea of bi-nationalism. The adoption in May 1942 of the *Biltmore Program, which for the first time singled out the establishment of a Jewish commonwealth in Palestine as the Zionist goal, and news coming out of Europe regarding the Nazi "final solution," strengthened the resolve of the League to struggle for the only plan that it regarded as realistic. Within the League a new group was formed in August 1942, calling itself Iḥud (Unity). Iḥud opposed the idea of establishing an independent Jewish state, which it regarded as ruinous, and advocated a bi-national solution. Among the active members of this group was Judah L. Magnes, Martin Buber, Haim Margolis-Kalvaryski, Moshe Smilansky, Henrietta *Szold, and Justice Joseph Moshe *Valero. Magnes tried to get the Sephardim and Agudat Israel involved in the new organization but failed. Iḥud published a periodical called *Be'ayot* ("Problems"). At the same time Ha-Shomer ha-Ẓa'ir joined the League as an organization.

When the Anglo-American Committee of Inquiry appeared in Ereẓ Israel in March 1946, the League did not appear before it, but Magnes, Buber, and Smilansky did, as representatives of Iḥud. Ha-Shomer ha-Ẓa'ir submitted a memorandum to the Committee, entitled "The Case for a Bi-National State." Both Iḥud and the League appeared before the United Nations Special Committee on Palestine (*UNSCOP). Though the members of both Committees, however, were impressed by the presentations, neither was convinced that a bi-national solution was feasible.

The adoption by the UN General Assembly of the partition plan on November 29, 1947, effectively put an end to the activities of the bi-nationalists, though Iḥud was revived in the early 1950s under the leadership of R. Binyamin, who edited its monthly *Ner* (Candle). After R. Binyamin's death, the monthly was edited by Simon Shereshevsky, until it ceased publication in 1964. Iḥud now devoted its energies to organizing discussions, searching for a solution to the Arab-Israeli conflict on the basis of compromise between Israel and the Arab states, and trying to defend the civil rights of Israel's Arab minority, which until 1966 was subject to a military administration.

BIBLIOGRAPHY: S. Hattis, *The Bi-National Idea in Palestine in Mandatory Times* (1970).

[Susan Hattis Rolef (2nd ed.)]

BINDER, ABRAHAM WOLF (1895–1966), U.S. composer. Born in New York, son and grandson of cantors, Binder became a choir director at the age of 14. In 1916 he formed the Hadassah Choral Union, and in 1917 he organized a music department, the first of its kind, at the 92nd Street YMHA in New York. In 1921 he became instructor in Jewish music at the Jewish Institute of Religion, and in 1922 music director at the Stephen Wise Free Synagogue. Here he was able to reintroduce the traditional chanting of the Bible, while keeping to the spirit of the Reform movement. In his revision of the *Union Hymnal* (1932) he also encouraged contributions by contemporary American Jewish composers. When the Jewish Institute of Religion was combined with the Hebrew Union College in New York, Binder was appointed professor of Jewish liturgical music there and helped to found its School of Sacred Music (1948). A prolific composer, he wrote synagogal services and songs, Hebrew and Yiddish songs, nine cantatas and oratorios (including *Amos on Times Square* and *The Legend of the Ari*), and piano, violin, chamber, and orchestral music. His music library and manuscripts were bequeathed to kibbutz Ein ha-Shofet.

BIBLIOGRAPHY: I. Heskes, *A.W. Binder, his Life and Work* (1965); Sendrey, Music, indexes; L. Appleton (ed.), *The Music of A. W. Binder; a bibliography* (mimeographed, 1964).

[Bathja Bayer]

BING, name of a number of Jewish families from the *Bingen community, which branched out in Germany, Lorraine, England, and the Netherlands. Bingen Jews are mentioned in *Frankfurt in the early and middle 15th century. Expulsions in the 16th and 17th centuries helped to disseminate the name in northeastern France and southwestern Germany; four families from Bingen settled in Frankfurt around 1530 and ten additional families named Bing settled there by the end of the 17th century. *Court Jews named Binge were active in *Hanau and elsewhere. In the late 18th century persons bearing the name were prominent in the community of *Metz. Abbé *Grégoire wrote (February 1789) to Isaiah *Beer-Bing of Nancy encouraging him to avail himself of the opportunity offered by the meeting of the General Estates "to take counsel with other members of your nation, in order to claim the rights and advantages due to citizens…." Prominent also were the physician SOLOMON, born in Bingen (1615), a pupil of Joseph Solomon *Delmedigo; JOSEPH, of Mons, who fought in 1786 for the abolition of the Jewish tax; ABRAHAM, renowned talmudist (b. 1752), Rabbi of Wuerzburg from 1798 to 1839; and ALBERT (1844–1922), Austrian ear specialist. The Danish and English Bing families are not necessarily connected with them.

BIBLIOGRAPHY: A. Dietz, *Stammbuch der Frankfurter Juden* (1907), 31–39; R.Z. Gruenfeld, *Geschichte der Juden in Bingen* (1905); R. Anchel, *Napoléon et les Juifs* (1928), index; AI, 5 (1844), 416–7; REJ, 5 (1882), 148; 8 (1886), 211; C. Roth, *The Great Synagogue London 1690–1940* (1950), 69, 193, 224, 267; P. Levy, *Les noms des Israélites en France* (1960), index; H. Schnee, *Die Hoffinanz und der moderne Staat*, 2 (1954), 279, 355–7; 4 (1960). **ADD. BIBLIOGRAPHY:** S. Loewengart, "Aus der Geschichte der Familie Bing," in: *Buelletin des Leo Baeck Instituts*, 59 (1981), 29–54.

BING, ILSE (1900–1998), photographer. Born into an affluent family in Frankfurt, Germany, Bing was trained in music and art. While she pursued a doctorate in art history and photographed buildings for her dissertation, she developed a passion for photography. In early 1929 she produced picture essays for a Frankfurt newspaper, but she decided to leave for Paris that summer after seeing an exhibition of photographs by Florence Henri, an exponent of New Photography, which was characterized by tight close-ups, unusual angles and the rendering of everyday objects as abstract geometric forms. In the 1930s Bing used the newly marketed 35-millimeter Leica as an extension of her personal vision, and she mastered darkroom techniques to show the subtleties of light and movement against the treacherous streets of Paris at night. She favored overhead shots and tilted angles of German Constructivists, but her photographs were often infused with softer, more lyrical and humanistic qualities.

Like Andre Ketesz and Henri Cartier-Bresson, she caught the spare geometries in ordinary Parisian life. She photographed at night with available light and produced images that were studies of light and deep shadow. She said that as she walked through Paris with her camera, reacting intuitively to what she saw, she was unencumbered by thoughts about "making art." She became a technical innovator, improvising lenses, experimenting with cropping, and discovering the dramatic effects of solarization, which produces a black outline resulting from the controlled use of light during printing. She discovered the process by accident in the darkroom, she said. Her photographs were regularly shown in galleries in Paris in the 1930s alongside the work of other members of the photographic avant-garde. In 1936 she was included in the first modern photography exhibition held at the Louvre, and the next year she was part of the landmark photography show at the Museum of Modern Art in New York. Her best-known work from that period is a self-portrait. She photographed a mirror image of herself, one bent arm leaning against a table, a Leica on a tripod positioned in front of one eye, with a side view of herself reflected in another mirror.

When Bing visited New York in 1936 she was offered a position with the new *Life* magazine but she rejected the offer because her future husband, Konrad Wolff, a pianist and musicologist, lived in Paris. They married in 1937. Three years later, as German Jews, they were interned as enemy aliens by the Vichy government but managed to get themselves free. Later in 1940 they sailed for New York, where they remained for the rest of their lives. Bing continued to photograph, changing to the larger format Rolleiflex in 1950 and working intensively in color from 1957 to 1959. That year, she gave up photography because, she said, "everything moves, nothing stays and I should not hold on." Bing turned to poetry, creating what she called "snapshots without a camera." She also made collages with old photographs and objects, and illustrated whimsical books on etymology and on numbers. Her dealer described her as "very sharp, very funny and very active – she took up the motorcycle when she was in her 70s." For a living, she groomed dogs.

[Stewart Kampel (2nd ed.)]

BING, ISAAC BEN SAMUEL (17th century), scholar. Born in Jerusalem, he went to Europe after his sons had died in a plague, and during 1645–46 wandered from town to town in Poland. In 1646 he arranged for the printing in Lublin of the first part of the *Maggid Meisharim* of Joseph *Caro on the basis of an incomplete manuscript which he had brought with him. In 1654 he was still in Europe and, together with Elisha Ḥayyim b. Jacob Ashkenazi (father of Nathan of Gaza), who had brought the remainder of the manuscript from Jerusalem, published it in Venice (Friedberg, Eked II 546 no. 471; but see Werblowsky, p. 25 and n. 5). Bing should not be confused with the Isaac b. Baruch Bing who lived in Safed during the first quarter of the 17th century.

BIBLIOGRAPHY: I. Bing, in: J. Caro, *Maggid Meisharim* (Lublin, 1646), introd.; Yaari, Sheluḥei, 271; R.J.Z. Werblowsky, *Joseph Karo, Lawyer and Mystic* (1962), 24ff.

[Avraham Yaari]

BINGEN, town in Rhenish Hesse, Germany. *Benjamin of Tudela (mid-12th century) heard of a community there. The Christian burghers attacked the small Jewish quarter on the Jewish New Year's Day of 1198 or 1199, and its inhabitants were then driven from the city. Jews are again found in Bingen as moneylenders in the middle of the 13th century under the jurisdiction of the archbishop of Mainz. In 1343 French Jews settled in Bingen. During the *Black Death (1348–49) the Jews in Bingen, too, suffered severely. They were later placed under the jurisdiction of the Church in order to save them from further excesses (1365). In 1405, however, the archbishop declared a moratorium on one-fifth of the debts owed to Jews by Christians, and subsequently the archbishops repeatedly extorted large sums. Noted rabbis who taught in the small community included Seligmann Oppenheim, who convened the Council of Bingen (1455–56) in an unsuccessful attempt to establish his authority over the whole of Rhineland Jewry. After the proposal was opposed by Moses *Minz, the matter was referred to Isaac *Isserlein, who rejected the project. The Jews were again expelled from Bingen in 1507, and did not return until the second half of the 16th century. There were 21 Jewish families living in Bingen in 1689, and 343 in 1754. The Jewish population numbered 465 in 1933, and 222 in 1939 in the wake of flight and emigration. The 169 Jews who remained in Bingen in 1942 were deported and only four ultimately returned. The synagogue was demolished in 1945, and the community was not reestablished after the war.

BIBLIOGRAPHY: R. Gruenfeld, *Zur Geschichte der Juden in Bingen am Rhein* (1905); Germ Jud, 1 (1963), 26f.; 2 (1968), 82–85; PK.

[Zvi Avneri]

BINSWANGER, ISIDORE (1820–1890), U.S. businessman and communal leader. Binswanger was born in Wallerstein, Bavaria. He immigrated to the United States in 1841, living first in Baltimore, then in Philadelphia, and finally in Richmond, Virginia. In 1869 he became president of the Richmond Granite Company, a position he held until shortly before his death. Binswanger was chairman of the board and later president of the Hebrew Education Society in Philadelphia, and president of the board of trustees of Maimonides College. He was also active in various aid societies and helped organize relief measures in the early 1880s for Jewish immigrants from Russia. His three brothers, Lewis, Samuel, and Harry S., settled in Richmond too, where they also went into business and were active in local Jewish life.

BIBLIOGRAPHY: H.S. Morais, *Jews of Philadelphia* (1894), 250–2; I. Markens, *Hebrews in America* (1888), 200.

BINYAMINAH (Heb. בִּנְיָמִינָה), moshavah in central Israel, at the southern spur of Mt. Carmel, founded in October 1922 by the Palestine Jewish Colonization Association (PICA). The first settlers were immigrants from East Europe. Later, immigrants from Bulgaria, Georgia (U.S.S.R.), and other countries were housed in a new quarter. Naḥalat Jabotinsky, a moshav founded nearby by the *Revisionist movement in 1947, was later incorporated into the village. In 1950 Binyaminah received municipal council status. In 1968 it had 2,570 inhabitants, with its economy based on intensive farming, principally fruit plantations. Prominent among its industrial enterprises was a wine and liquor factory. In the mid-1990s the population was approximately 3,950, increasing to 6,300 by 2002 on 6 sq. mi. (16 sq. km.) of land. The location of a major railroad station in Binyaminah pushed up local housing prices and made it very attractive for people working either in Haifa or Tel Aviv. In 2003 the local municipality of Binyaminah was united with the municipality of nearby *Givat Ada. Binyaminah is named after Baron Binyamin (Edmond) de *Rothschild.

[Efraim Orni / Shaked Gilboa (2nd ed.)]

BIOGRAPHIES AND AUTOBIOGRAPHIES. Apart from the Book of *Nehemiah, which may well be considered an autobiography, *Josephus' apologetic *Vita*, and *hagiographic works, autobiographies and biographies are completely unknown among Jews in ancient times. The first biography known is that of *Saadiah Gaon which was written by his two sons She'erit and *Dosa at the request of *Ḥisdai ibn Shaprut (published by J. Mann, JQR, 11 (1920/21), 423–8, and by A. Scheiber in KS, 40 (1964/65), 571).

In Medieval Hebrew Literature

The biographic genre was also unknown to medieval Hebrew literature and there is almost no writing in the field. The lack of development of this literary vehicle is rooted in two main aspects of medieval Hebrew culture. Historians and chroniclers were mainly concerned with events and not personalities as such; a person was important only insofar as he influenced or participated in a major historical event. The lives of major Jewish personalities are, therefore, outlined only briefly in Jewish historiography, and there is no full biography in the modern sense. Historiographers, who were mainly interested in the process of the transmission of the Torah, tended to list scholars and rabbis in chronological order, briefly describing the achievements of each in the field of learning, and only mentioning by the way such details as birthplace, travels, family, and death. Jewish historiography, focusing primarily on historical events, developed the art of historical description at the expense of biography.

The Influence of Hagiography on Biography

Hagiography, however, influenced the fate of biographic literature probably more than historiography. Hebrew medieval writers who concentrated on an historical figure and gave some biographic facts, usually added legendary or panegyric details and thus turned their accounts into hagiographies. Medieval Judaism viewed the actions of an outstanding personality as model behavior to serve as an exemplum. No full description of his life and personality (his faults and his virtues) was, therefore, needed. The only interest the medieval writer and reader could find in the story of a great personage was in the moral to be drawn from his actions and his character. This ethical and didactic approach, driven to the extreme, rendered almost all Hebrew writings about major personalities into heroic legends and not authentic biographies. The cycle of stories about such figures as Abraham *Ibn Ezra, *Naḥmanides, *Rashi, *Judah b. Samuel he-Ḥasid, Isaac *Luria, *Israel b. Eliezer Ba'al Shem Tov, and many others are legendary hagiographies, having little direct historical data and giving a partial portraiture of the protagonist. Historians like Abraham *Ibn Daud, author of *Sefer ha-Kabbalah*, only briefly mention the sages and scholars who transmitted the Torah. When he dwells on actual personalities, like the scholars in "The Four Captives," his description is purely hagiographic. The same is true of Gedaliah *Ibn Yaḥya and many others, including the first Hebrew medieval chronologist, *Sherira Gaon. Personal accounts sometimes formed polemic material in a religious conflict, e.g., the biography of Anan, the founder of the Karaite sect. Sherira describes him as a frustrated, ambitious, evil man; the Karaites wrote hagiographies to extol his deeds. Biographic elements are scattered throughout Hebrew epistolary, hagiography, and historiography, but as a literary form, biography came into its own only in modern Hebrew literature. An exception to this, however, is the biographical introduction to the *Ma'yenei ha-Yeshu'ah* of Isaac *Abrabanel by Baruch Uzziel b. Baruch Forti (Ḥazketto) in 1551. The author probably gleaned Abrabanel's autobiographical fragments from his introductions to commentaries to Joshua, Kings, and Deuteronomy, and from his responsa to Saul Kohen. *Ahimaaz b. Paltiel wrote his *Megillat Yuḥasin* in the middle of the 11th century on the history of his family.

Historiography Written as Personal Experience

The autobiographic genre was a more apt vehicle of literary expression than the biography in the Middle Ages. This was mainly due to the intrinsic nature of the art itself. The need for self-scrutiny (the characteristic of autobiography) has greater impetus than the biographic sketches of authors. Medieval and Renaissance writings, letters, introductions to books, apologies, and personal diaries contain autobiographic elements and sketches much more than biographic elements. In these works, however, the writer also focused on the historical event and the part he had played in it rather than on his own personal life. Maimonides, describing his life in his letters, gives an account of his daily working schedule and of certain aspects of his life. Azariah dei *Rossi, in the introduction to his *Me'or Einayim* (Mantua, 1574), describes the Ferrara earthquake of 1570 which he witnessed and which in part was the stimulus of the book.

Legendary Autobiography

Since the early Middle Ages, another aspect of autobiography was known in Jewish writings: the legendary autobiography. *Eldad ha-Dani, the first writer of this autobiographic form (appeared in Babylonia in the late ninth century), claimed to be a member of the tribe of Dan. In his work, he describes the life of the Ten Lost Tribes in detail. This, however, forms only part of his whole account, much of which is devoted to his various adventures in faraway lands among strange peoples. This narration is typical of imaginary or legendary autobiography.

The thread of this literary expression was picked up centuries later by a much more accomplished autobiographer, David ha-*Reuveni. In a detailed autobiography he describes his birthplace in the lands of the Ten Lost Tribes, his numerous adventures on his way to Italy and especially in Palestine, and his political and diplomatic efforts to organize an army to conquer Palestine. He even includes in his work a detailed expense account, listing his expenditures at every step of his travels. His autobiography is, in fact, an apology: he blames various treacherous friends for the failure of his venture.

Another autobiography, also an apology, is *Gei Ḥizzayon* by Abraham *Jagel (16th century). It is an imaginative vision of the afterworld containing autobiographical elements. Jagel, in prison, relates his life story and how he came to be imprisoned, to his dead father who appears to him in a dream and takes him on a trip to the various heavenly spheres. This autobiography is probably the first to be written in Hebrew by a minor writer about a comparatively trivial life. The focus is not on any major historical event, nor on the author's participation in a noteworthy adventure. Jagel used the autobiographic form to express his misery and to complain about the injustice done to him. Due to its concentration on the personal. *Gei Ḥizzayon* may be described as the first autobiography to be written in Hebrew. Earlier works belong more to the field of historiography which were written as personal experience.

Modena's Hayyei Yehudah

Probably the most representative work of the genre and literally the best-developed autobiography written in Hebrew during the Middle Ages is *Ḥayyei Yehudah* ("The Life of Judah"), by Leone (Judah Aryeh) *Modena. In short passages and sometimes long stories, Modena describes in detail a 20-year span in his life. The sincere revelation of the inner self in Modena's account has not been equaled by any Hebrew writer until modern times. He candidly describes his addiction to card-playing, which repeatedly threw him into debt and obliged him to use any means and choose any work to earn enough to cover them. He depicts in detail the tragic fate of his three sons: one was killed in an unsuccessful alchemic experiment, the second, in a street fight, and the third left Italy after being condemned to row in the galleys without his father ever learning of his whereabouts. His various illnesses, those of his wife and of his relatives, are discussed in detail, as well as his dreams, his visions, and his astrological beliefs. A profound cynical skepticism can be discerned in his writings. Modena's work may also be seen as an apology: the apology of a man who saw himself as a failure in every way (history today contradicts this judgment). He blamed the stars for the tragedies he had suffered and the misfortunes which befell him. Probably his belief in astrological determinism psychologically allowed him to lay bare unashamedly the different facets of his character (of which he was far from proud).

Other Autobiographic Elements and Sketches

In line with Modena's work, almost full autobiographies can be reconstructed from the letters of R. Moses Ḥayyim *Luzzatto, and from the letters of other writers. Some autobiographic elements and sketches are to be found in ḥasidic literature where various rabbis sincerely describe their own spiritual development, e.g., R. *Naḥman of Bratslav. In kabbalistic literature, another type of autobiography is to be found: kabbalists describing their visions and the development of their mystical insight. The most noteworthy among these are the visions of Solomon *Molcho which, together with some actual autobiographical passages, form a full spiritual autobiography in the modern sense (Abraham b. Joseph Rothenburg, *Ḥayyat Kaneh, Ḥazon Shelomo Molkho*, ed. by A.S. Aescoly, 1938). Such elements are found also in *Maggid Meisharim*, R.

Joseph *Caro's diary on his heavenly revelations, and in other writings of kabbalists.

[Joseph Dan]

Memoirs and Introductions

Memoirs, from those of Glueckel of *Hameln of the 17th century to the diary of Anne *Frank, may be termed "unconscious autobiographies" which were not intended for publication. The valuable autobiographical material, which was sometimes included in the introduction to halakhic works, is the nearest approach to autobiographies of the rabbis. Notable among them are Isaac *Abrabanel's introductions to his biblical commentaries, and those which were produced under the stress of two great catastrophes which overtook European Jewry, the expulsion from Spain in 1492 and the *Chmielnicki massacres of 1648. Prominent among those who described their sufferings in the expulsion from Spain was the author Isaac *Caro (see H.H. Ben-Sasson, in *Zion*, 26 no. 2 (1961), 23–64). Shabbetai b. Meir ha-Kohen and Moses b. Abraham *Mat of Przemysl (in *Matteh Moshe*) are among those who described the period of the Chmielnicki massacres.

Modern Times

With the dawn of emancipation and enlightenment, real biographies began to make their appearance. Among the first of these was Isaac *Euchel's *Toledot Rambaman* on Moses Mendelssohn. Ezekiel *Feivel's *Toledot Adam* on Solomon Zalman b. Isaac of Volozhin (1801), and Moses Kunitz's *Beit Rabbi* on Judah ha-Nasi (1805). Dov Ber *Birkenthal of Bolechow wrote his *Zikhroynes*, an important source for material on Jews of Galicia in the 18th century (Heb., Eng., Yid., 1922). Solomon Maimon's autobiography (1792) was revolutionary in more than one sense and evoked the approval of such literary giants as Goethe and Schiller. The autobiography of L. *Bendavid (1804) also belongs here. The scholarly impulse given by the movement for Wissenschaft des Judentums and the related Haskalah in Eastern Europe prompted men like L. *Zunz and S.J. *Rapoport to write biographical sketches of the great Jewish scholars of the past, whose lives – as distinct from their scholarly work – had remained obscure. Zunz wrote a "Life of Rashi," a task that was later taken up by Maurice Liber and Eliezer Meir Lipschuetz. Rapoport published a series of biographical sketches (*Toledot Gedolim*) covering Eleazar Kallir, Saadiah Gaon, *Hananel b. Ḥushi'el, Nissim b. Jacob, and others. Since then, biographies or lengthy monographs have been written about many of the significant figures in Jewish history and literature. Some, like Louis Finkelstein's *Akiba*, have been major studies, as is the two-volume work in history on *The House of Nasi* by Cecil Roth (*Dona Gracia, The Duke of Naxos*), while Louis *Ginzberg wrote a series of penetrating biographical studies of famous scholars. In recent years some biographies of ḥasidic rabbis, who were previously described in a distinctly hagiographic character, have been written on a rational and scientific basis, an example of which is *The Zaddik* on *Jacob Joseph of Polonnoye, by S.H. Dresner. The list is too numerous to be given, but mention may be made of what may be called biographical anthologies. Israel Kammelhar has written biographies of all the great figures of medieval German Ḥasidim. The *Sarei ha-Me'ah* on the rabbis of the 19th century by Rabbi J.L. *Fishman, though sometimes uncritical, is a treasurehouse of biographical material. Much biographical material from prominent Jewish characters of the 18th–20th centuries is contained in the last three volumes of "The Jewish Library" series, edited by Leo Jung (vol. 6, *Jewish Leaders 1750–1940*, 1953; vol. 7, *Guardians of Our Heritage*, 1958; vol. 8, *Men of Spirit*, 1964). Naturally the general vogue of compiling biographies of contemporary Jewish figures after their decease is as marked among Jews as in general literature, but it contains no specific Jewish aspect. From the end of the last century autobiographies have become more common. Mention may be made of those of Isaac Hirsch Weiss, J.L. Gordon, Ḥ.N. Bialik, Chaim Weizmann, Cyrus Adler, and Nahum Goldmann. H. Ribalow has published an anthology of autobiographies of American Jews (1965). Other collections have included Leo W. *Schwarz's *Memoirs of my People* (1943) and H. Bach's *Juedische Memoiren aus drei Jahrhunderten* (1936).

Yiddish Life-Writing

With the exception of a few pre-modern Yiddish memoirs, most notably the memoirs of Glueckel of Hameln (1689–1719; publ. as *Zikhroynes*, 1896), Yiddish life-writing has developed since the 1860s, beginning with fictional autobiographies Sholem Yankev *Abramovitsh's *Dos Kleyne Mentshele* ("The Little Man," 1864) and Yitskhok Yoel Linetsky's *Dos Poylishe Yingl* ("The Polish Lad," 1867). The first biographical entries on Yiddish writers appeared in Nahum Sokolov's *Sefer Zikkaron le-Sofrei Yisrael ha-Ḥayyim Itanu ka-Yom* ("A Memoir Book of Contemporary Jewish Writers," 1889), and *Sholem Aleichem presented biographical entries on Yiddish writers in his *Di Yidishe Folks-Bibliotek* ("The Yiddish Folk Library," 1888). While the first Yiddish literary autobiography was Sholem Yankev Abramovitsh's *Shloyme Reb Khayims* ("Shloyme, Hayim's Son," 1894–1914, first part in Hebrew, *Petikhta*, later reworked in Yiddish), the two other classical Yiddish writers, Sholem Aleichem (*Funem Yarid*, "From the Fair," 1913–16) and I.L. *Peretz (*Mayne Zikhroynes*, "My Memoirs," 1913–16), also wrote autobiographical novels.

In addition to literary autobiography, other subgenres emerged in the 20th century. Yekhezkel Kotik's *Mayne Zikhroynes* ("My Memoirs," 1913) exemplifies the rich subgenre of Yiddish ethnographic memoir, while the memoirs of Jewish political leaders and party members, cultural leaders, actors, painters, and other artists also appeared. A rich subgenre also developed in the *poeme* or long narrative poem, e.g. Menakhem Boreysho's *Der Geyer. Kapitln fun a Lebn* ("The Walker: Chapters from a Life," 1943). A particularly rich subgenre is the Holocaust memoir, originally crafted as testimony and eyewitness account to the era's unspeakable crimes, exemplified in Mark Turkov's 176-volume series, *Dos Poylishe Yidntum* ("Polish Jewry," Buenos Aires 1946–66), which includes Elie *Wiesel's *Un di Velt hot Geshvign* ("And the World Was Silent," 1955, later reworked in French, *La Nuit*, and English *Night*).

The outstanding examples of Yiddish life-writing are Jacob *Glatstein's autobiographical novels *Ven Yash iz Geforn* ("When Yash Set Out," 1938) and *Ven Yash iz Gekumen* ("When Yash Arrived," 1940); Jonah *Rosenfeld's *Eyner Aleyn* ("All Alone"); Y.Y. *Trunk's seven-volume *Poyln: Zikhroynes un Bilder* ("Poland: Memoirs and Pictures," 1944–53); I.J. *Singer, *Fun a Velt Vos iz Nishto Mer* ("From a World That is No More," 1946): Dovid *Bergelson's *Bam Dnyepr* ("On the Dnieper," 1932, 1940); and I.B. *Singer's rich and diverse œuvre. More recent examples include Joseph Buloff's *Fun Altn Markplats* ("From the Old Marketplace," 1995) and Boris Sandler's *Lamedvovnikes fun Mayn Zikorn* ("Lamedvovniks from My Memory," serialized in *Forverts*, 2005).

While Yiddish women writers have produced few major novels, some, in addition to Glueckel of Hameln, have excelled as autobiographers: e.g., Bella *Chagall's *Brenendike Likht* ("Burning Lights," 1945) and Ester Singer *Kreitman's *Sheydim-Tants* ("Demon's Dance," 1936; published as *Deborah*, 1983). One of the greatest achievements of modern Yiddish literature, Yiddish life-writing differs significantly from the genre in mainstream literatures: the Yiddish writer tends to reject the model of self-revelation that has characterized the genre since Rousseau's *Confessions* (1781) and instead elaborates on his life in entertaining, often humorous ways that depicts "a world that is no more."

[Jan Schwarz (2nd ed.)]

Biographical Lexicons

Although much biographical material about Jews can be found in the medieval Jewish chronicles, the first lexicon of Jewish biographies did not appear till the end of the 18th century. S. Shunami's *Bibliography of Jewish Bibliographies* (1965; supplement 1975) contains sections on biographical dictionaries of Jews in general (nos. 2594–2661), of Jews in Zionism (nos. 1872–76), Jews in America (nos. 2172–83), Jews in the Holocaust (nos. 2539–44), Jews in Palestine and Israel (nos. 2017–27, 2057–66a), as well as on biographical literature (nos. 2662–67). The following is a list of dictionaries of the history of the lives of individual Jews:

GENERAL JEWISH BIOGRAPHICAL LEXICONS

S. Wininger, *Grosse juedische National-Biographie* (7 vols., 1925–36), the most comprehensive work of this kind;

Juedischer Plutarch; oder biographisches Lexikon der markantesten Maenner und Frauen juedischer Abkunft (2 vols., 1848);

Juedisches Athenaeum. Galerie beruehmter Maenner juedischer Abstammung und juedischen Glaubens (1851), limited to the 19th century;

H.S. Morais, *Eminent Israelites of the Nineteenth Century* (1880), 100 biographies, mainly of rabbis and community leaders, but also of some Jews prominent in public life;

A. Kohut, *Beruehmte israelitische Maenner und Frauen in der Kulturgeschichte der Menschheit* (2 vols., 1901), classified by professions, such as writers, composers, etc.

R. Heuer (ed.), *Lexicon deutsch-juedischer Autoren*, 11 vols. (1992–2002).

RABBIS AND TALMUDISTS

J. Heilprin, *Shemot Ba'alei Meḥabberim* (1769);

Ḥ.J.D. Azulai, *Shem ha-Gedolim* (2 vols., 1774–86, reprinted and revised several times, latest edition 1967);

H.J. Michael, *Or ha-Ḥayyim* (1891, reprint 1965). The author, who died in 1846, left incomplete a bio-bibliographical work including over 1,200 entries, covering the same ground as Azulai, but with more modern scientific tools. The work also had the benefit of being edited by the great scholar Leopold Zunz;

A. Hyman, *Toledot Tanna'im ve-Amora'im* (2 vols., 1964^2), sages of the Talmud;

M. *Margaliot, *Enẓiklopedyah le-Ḥakhmei ha-Talmud ve-ha Ge'onim* (2 vols., 1945–46), sages of the Talmud and the *geonim*; idem, *Enẓiklopedyah le-Toledot Gedolei Yisrael* (4 vols., 1945–50), Jewish scholars from the 9th to the 18th centuries;

S.J. Fuenn, *Keneset Yisrael* (1886), scholars from the geonic period up to the present; incomplete, ending with the Hebrew letter *Yod*;

Abraham Stern, *Meliẓei Esh* (3 vols., 1930–38; 1962^2), medieval and modern rabbis and scholars;

A. Walden, *Sefer Shem ha-Gedolim he-Ḥadash* (1865), continuation of Azulai (see above);

B. Eisenstadt, *Dorot ha-Aḥaronim* (vol. 1, 1913–15; vol. 2, 1937–41), rabbis of the recent past;

I. Lewin, *Elleh Ezkerah* (6 vols., 1956–65), rabbis and scholars who perished during World War II;

S. Federbusch, *Ḥokhmat Yisrael be-Ma'arav Eiropah* (3 vols., 1958–65). Vol. 3 also deals with East European scholars.

MEDIEVAL SPAIN

A. Sáenz-Badillos and J. Targarona, *Diccionario de Autores Judíos (Sefarad. Siglos X–XV)* (1988);

M. Orfali, *Biblioteca de Autores Lógicos HispanoJudíos* (Siglos XI–XV) (1997).

ḤASIDIM

Y. Raphael, *Sefer ha-Ḥasidut* (1955^2).

MODERN HEBREW WRITERS

G. Kressel, *Leksikon ha-Sifrut ha-Ivrit be-Dorot ha-Aḥaronim* (2 vols., 1965–67);

W. Zeitlin, *Kirjath Sepher, Bibliotheca hebraica post-Mendelssohniana* (1891–99).

YIDDISH WRITERS

Z. Rejzen, *Leksikon fun der Yidisher Literatur, Prese un Filologye* (4 vols., 1926–30);

Leksikon fun der Nayer Yidisher Literatur (8 vols., 1956–81), ed. by Saul Raskin.

E.E. Lifschutz, *Bibliography of American and Canadian Jewish Memoirs and Autobiographies* (1970);
National Yiddish Book Center list: "BI, Biography, Autobiography, Memoirs" (approx. 850 titles).

YIDDISH THEATER
Z. Zylbercweig, *Leksikon fun Yidishn Teater* (6 vols., 1931–69).

ZIONISTS
S.L. Zitron, *Leksikon Ẓiyyoni* (1924).

AUSTRO-HUNGARY
M. Fruehling, *Biographisches Handbuch der in der k.k. oesterreichisch-ungarischen Armee aktiv gedienten Offiziere juedischen Stammes* (1911), on Jewish officers in Austria-Hungary.

GERMANY
S. Osborne, *Germany and Her Jews* (1939);
E.G. Lowenthal, *Bewaehrung im Untergang* (1966^2), German Jews who perished during World War II;
E. Duckesz, *Ḥakhmei AHW* (1908), religious leaders of Altona, Hamburg, and Wandsbek; with German summary.

ITALY
M. Mortara, *Indice alfabetico dei rabbini e scrittori israeliti in Italia* (1886).

PALESTINE AND ISRAEL
D. Tidhar, *Enẓiklopedyah le-Ḥaluẓei ha-Yishuv u-Vonav* (18 vols., 1947–67, in progress), for 19th and 20th century; a combination of national biography and current Who's Who.

POLAND AND RUSSIA
S. Buber, *Anshei Shem* (1895), lay and rabbinic leaders in Lemberg (Lvov) from 1500–1900;
P. Kaplan, *Byalistoker Leksikon; Biografyes fun Byalistoker Yidishe Perzenlekhkeyten* (1935), for Bialystok.

UNITED STATES
J.R. Rosenbloom, *A Biographical Dictionary of Early American Jews, Colonial Times Through 1800* (1960).

CONTEMPORARIES
Who's Who in World Jewry (1955, 1965, 1972, 1978).
World Jewish Register (1955–56), same material as in *Who's Who in World Jewry* (1955), arranged by professions.

Rabbis and Scholars
B. Eisenstadt, *Dor, Rabbanav ve-Soferav* (6 vols., 1895–1903). Volume 5 is devoted exclusively to the United States;
S.N. Gottlieb, *Oholei Shem* (1912), mainly for Eastern Europe.

Israel
Sefer ha-Ishim (1937) and *Palestine Personalia* (1947);
Who's Who in Israel (1945/46–1967/68), title of first edition: *The Near and Middle East Who's Who*, published almost every year;
Ishim be-Yisrael (1960, 1966), personalities in Israel.

United States
J. Pfeffer, *Distinguished Jews of America* (1917–18). Volume two was also published separately under the titles: *Eminent Jews of America* and *Prominent Jews of America; Who's Who in American Jewry* (1925, 1926, 1928, 1938/39);
Biographical Encyclopedia of American Jews (1935);
American Jews, Their Lives and Achievements (1947, 1958);
Israel Honorarium (5 vols., 1968). Volumes 2–5 contain biographical sketches of American Jews.
M.D. Sherman, *Orthodox Judaism in America: A Biographical Dictionary and Sourcebook* (1996);
P.S. Nadell, *Conservative Judaism in America: A Biographical Dictionary and Sourcebook* (1988);
K.M. Olitzky, L.J. Sussman, and M.H. Stern, *Reform Judaism in America: A Biographical Dictionary and Sourcebook* (1993);
P. Hyman and D.D. Moore, *Jewish Women in America: An Historical Encyclopedia* (1997)

[Theodore Wiener]

BIBLIOGRAPHY: D.S. Zubatsky, *Jewish Autobiographies and Biographies: an Annotated Bibliography of Books and Dissertations in English* (1989); S.W. Baron, *Bibliography of Jewish Social Studies* (1941), 324–48, 214–8; C. Roth, Mag Bibl, 114–56; Waxman, Literature, 2 (1960^2), 506–16; 3 (1960^2), 575; 4 (1960^2), 838–66, 1044–47, and index s.v. *biography, memoirs*; H.U. Ribalow, *Autobiographies of American Jews* (1965), 3–14 (introd.); J. Mazeh, *Zikhronot*, 4 (1936); L.W. Schwarz, *Memoirs of My People* (1943), introduction, 13–26, a popular survey of autobiographies. **ADD. BIBLIOGRAPHY:** M. Moseley, *Being for Myself Alone: Origins of Jewish Autobiography* (2005); J. Schwarz, *Imagining Lives: Autobiographical Fiction of Yiddish Writers* (2005).

BIRAM, ARTHUR (Yiẓḥak; 1878–1967), Hebrew educator. Biram, who was born in Bischofswerda, Germany, attended Berlin University and the *Hochschule fuer die Wissenschaft des Judentums in Berlin. From 1909 to 1913 he taught classics in German high schools. An early member of the Zionist movement, he went to Ereẓ Israel in 1914 and was appointed by the Zionist Executive principal of the Reali High School in Haifa. After serving with the German Army in Palestine during World War I, Biram became in 1918 deputy principal of the Hebrew Teachers' College in Jerusalem. He returned to Haifa in 1920 and again became principal of the Reali High School, where he also taught Bible, until 1948. During his tenure, the school was enlarged and its activities diversified. In 1937 he initiated the paramilitary training program of high school pupils, called *Ḥagam* (abbreviation for *Ḥinnukh Gufani Murḥav*, i.e., "extended physical education"), later renamed *Gadna. In 1943 he established and headed a teachers' seminary at the Reali High School and, in 1953, initiated the establishment of a military academy there. He wrote the three-volume *Divrei Yemei Yisrael bi-Zeman ha-Mikra be-Misgeret Toledot ha-Mizraḥ* ("History of Israel in Biblical Times in the Context of Near Eastern History," 1962–64), based mainly on his own method of teaching the Bible. For Biram the training of pupils toward fulfilling their duties as citizens, and the inculcation of discipline, order, and precision, were educational principles which could determine the fate of the nation. He devoted special attention to physical education, military training, and scouting. Under his direction, the course of studies at the Reali High School consisted of six years of primary and six years of secondary education, the latter being divided into two stages, permitting specialization in the senior grades. Some of Biram's reforms were later incorporated into the educational system of the country. Biram received the Israel Prize for Education in 1954.

BIBLIOGRAPHY: *Sefer Biram* (1956); Tidhar, 4 (1950), 1696f.

[Joseph Bentwich]

BIRAN, AVRAHAM (1909–), archaeologist and diplomat. Born in Petaḥ Tikvah, of a third generation Ereẓ Israel family, Biran received his education at the Reali Secondary School in Haifa and at the David Yellin College in Bet ha-Kerem, Jerusalem. He obtained his M.A. and Ph.D. from Johns Hopkins University in Baltimore, where he studied with William Foxwell *Albright.

From 1935 to 1937 he participated in various archaeological excavations with the University of Pennsylvania in Iraq and with the American Schools of Oriental Research near Irbid in Jordan. He also accompanied Nelson *Glueck on his discoveries along the Gulf of Elath, and in Palestine directed the excavations of the birthplace of the prophet Jeremiah in Anathoth (1935).

In 1937, Biran was appointed District Officer of the Palestine Mandatory Government for the area of the Jezreel Valley. During this period he carried out an archaeological survey of the area. Transferring to Jerusalem in 1945, he became District Officer of the Mandatory Government for Jerusalem. He served as liaison between the United Nations representatives and the Jewish military authorities during the fighting before the 1948 Declaration of Independence.

Biran held a variety of positions with the government of Israel, initially as administrative assistant to Dov *Joseph, the military governor of Jerusalem, becoming governor of Jerusalem for several months. From 1949 to 1958 he was Israel Consul-General in Los Angeles and in 1958 was the director of the Armistice Affairs in the Foreign Ministry.

Returning to archaeology, Biran took up the position of director of antiquities and museums of Israel and in 1974 became director of the Nelson Glueck School of Biblical Archaeology of the Hebrew Union College-Jewish Institute of Religion in Jerusalem. In this capacity he directed the excavation of the Israelite sites of Ira and Aroer in the Negev; the ancient synagogue of Yesud ha-Ma'alah; and the longest ongoing excavations in Israel, at Tel Dan. These last excavations revealed a city founded in the 6th millennium B.C.E.; massive fortifications of the 2nd millennium, including a unique triple-arched gate of the 18th century B.C.E. still standing as originally built; a 14th-century B.C.E. tomb with Mycenean imports; evidence for the first settlement of the tribe of Dan, their installations for metal work; the Israelite sanctuary where *Jeroboam had set the golden calf, the religious center of northern Israel with its high place, chambers, altars; a royal scepter; and a dedicatory inscription in Greek and Aramaic – "To the God who is in Dan." Biran was chairman of the Israel Exploration Society from 1978 (in 1999 he was named its president), the Government Names Committee, and the International Committee of Museums and Sites (Israel) of UNESCO. In 2002 he was awarded the Israel Prize.

[Elaine Hoter]

BIRANIT (Heb. בִּירָנִית; "small fortress"), kibbutz in Israel, on the Lebanese border. Biranit was planned as the large rural center of a group of settlements including Zarit, Netu'ah, Shetulah, and Yakinton, in the framework of the Central Galilee Development Project inaugurated in 1963. Its nucleus was established on Dec. 1, 1964, by a Naḥal group affiliated with Ha-Kibbutz ha-Me'uḥad. The center's initial tasks consisted of land reclamation, afforestation, and restoration of ancient woodlands, planting of fruit orchards, road building, and other development work. In the course of time the settlement was abandoned, the site becoming a military camp.

[Efraim Orni]

BIRIYYAH (Berai) (Heb. בֵּרָי; בִּירִיָּה), in the talmudic period an important Jewish town in Upper Galilee, 1 mi. (1½ km.) N. of Safed. After Safed's importance decreased in the first century C.E. as an outcome of the Jewish war against Rome, Biriyyah took over its role as a regional center and became an important place of learning. Both in the Jerusalem and Babylonian Talmuds (Er. 45a, Git. 34a, TJ Meg. 2:3, 73b et al.) six sages who were residents of Biriyyah are mentioned. The Talmud also relates several episodes from the life of "Benei Berai," i.e., Biriyyah's inhabitants. In Biriyyah, R. Abba Sha'ul, one of the important sages of the Mishnah, is assumedly buried together with his wife, a fact mentioned by a number of travelers as late as 1876. According to kabbalist tradition, the tomb of Benaiah son of Jehoiada, one of the commanders of King David, is also to be found near Biriyyah. The *genizah* literature testifies that Jews lived at Biriyyah also between the 11th and 13th centuries C.E., and it is possible that their descendants continued to be inhabitants of the village until the 16th century, when Biriyyah entered a new phase of ascendancy as many Jews expelled from Spain settled in Safed and its vicinity. It was then that Joseph *Caro completed at Biriyyah the first part of the *Shulḥan Arukh on the 2nd of Elul 5315 (1555 C.E.). The local Jews of that time were farmers and tradesmen, as were the Jewish inhabitants of neighboring villages. At the beginning of the 17th century, there were no longer any Jews living at Biriyyah, but the local synagogue existed until the 18th century, serving the Jewish community of Safed in case of need; its keys were kept by local Arabs who showed great reverence for the synagogue.

After the 1837 earthquake that destroyed Safed, a Hebrew printing press was temporarily brought to Biriyyah before being transferred to Jerusalem. It was the site of an Arab village Bīryā. In January 1945 a group from *Bnei Akiva founded a kibbutz on top of Mt. Biriyyah at an elevation of 3,135 ft. (1950 m.) above sea level, working principally on land reclamation. On March 5, 1946, British Mandatory authorities carried out an arms search and, after discovering weapons, arrested the settlers and occupied the village. Ten days later 3,000 youths went up the mountain, set up a tent camp near the village, and started clearing stones. The British moved up strong military forces and drove the settlers away, but they returned the following night, setting up a new camp. The whole *yishuv* supported the settlers, and the British gave in, first permitting the camp to remain, then releasing the imprisoned settlers, and finally (June 7, 1946) evacuating the village buildings. In September 1948, a new religious kibbutz took over the site and was replaced in 1949 by a moshav founded by immigrants from Tripolitania (Libya). The moshav supported some hill farming, but most of its inhabitants worked in Safed and elsewhere. In the mid-1990s the population was approximately 550, rising to 771 in 2002. A large forest (with nearly 6 million trees in 1968) was planted on Mt. Biriyyah.

[Efraim Orni]

BIRK, YEHUDITH (1926–), Israeli biochemist. Birk was born in Grajewo, Poland, and immigrated to Ereẓ Israel in 1935. She received her M.Sc. in biochemistry and microbiology from the Hebrew University of Jerusalem (1950). Her studies were interrupted by service in the Israel Defense Forces during the War of Independence. In 1954 she received her Ph.D. in nutritional biochemistry at the Hebrew University's Faculty of Agriculture in Reḥovot. After a postdoctoral fellowship at Rutgers University, New Jersey, with Nobel Laureate Selman *Waksman, she returned to the Faculty of Agriculture in 1957, where she became professor and first incumbent of the Karl Bach Chair in Agricultural Biochemistry from 1970.

Birk was the founding director of the School of Nutritional Sciences at the Hebrew University (1972–74) and subsequently professor emeritus. Her world-renowned research concerns the biochemical and nutritional properties of legume seed proteins. With Donald Bowman she identified and characterized a protease inhibitor in legume seeds, the Bowman-Birk Inhibitor (BBI), which protects against contaminating insects and also has anti-cancer properties. Her honors include the Rothschild Prize in agricultural research (1978), election to the Israel Academy of Sciences (1993), and the Israel Prize in agricultural research (1998). She was elected to the European Academy of Sciences and Art in 2004 and was the 2004 awardee of the International Women's Forum (IWF), for "women who make a difference." She made major contributions to developing higher education at all levels in Israel and her academic appointments included dean of the Faculty of Agriculture (1977–80) and pro-rector and acting rector of the Hebrew University of Jerusalem (1990–95). She wrote more than 150 scientific articles and chapters in books and in 2003 published *Plant Protease Inhibitors: Significance in Nutrition, Plant Protection Cancer Prevention and Genetic Engineering.*

[Bracha Rager (2nd ed.)]

BIRKAT HA-MINIM (Heb. בִּרְכַּת הַמִּינִים, "benediction concerning heretics"), the twelfth benediction of the weekday *Amidah* (the *Shmoneh Esreh* prayer). The benediction belongs to the latter part of the *Amidah* petitions, which beseech the redemption of the people of Israel. Worded more like an imprecation (see *Tanḥuma* [Buber ed.], *Vayikra* 3), in its invocation of divine wrath against internal enemies to Jewish integrity and against external enemies of the Jewish people, it differs from the other petitions.

Birkat ha-Minim is also distinguished from the other *Amidah* benedictions by the fact that it was appended after the formulation and fixing of the *Amidah* text. The tradition of its secondary addition at Jabneh is shared by TJ (Ber. 4:3, 8a) and TB, which attributes its formulation to Samuel ha-Katan at the explicit request of the Nasi, Rabban Gamliel (Ber. 28b). Scholarly opinion is divided, however, with regard to the precise understanding of this process. One view holds that the tradition reflected by TB (ibid.) should be accepted literally; accordingly *Birkat ha-Minim* was formulated at Jabneh and added to the already existing eighteen benedictions (see Fleischer), upping the number to nineteen. Accepted in this nineteen-benediction form in the early Babylonian rite, it was subsequently transmitted from this rite to all prayer books up to the present. Others contend (see Heinemann) that Rabban Gamliel's request simply concerned the updating of an already existing benediction among the eighteen – whose content spoke out in general against separatists (see T. Ber. 3:25) – to incorporate explicit mention of the *minim*. This also explains why the versions of the *Amidah* in the Palestinian rite number only eighteen benedictions, inclusive of *Birkat ha-Minim*. The proponents of this view submit that the nineteen-benediction form of the *Amidah* in the Babylonian rite reflects a Babylonian custom of splitting the petition for the building of Jerusalem and for the coming of the Davidic messiah into two separate benedictions. In Palestine, both subjects were combined in a single benediction regarding Jerusalem.

Its exceptional importance in Christian-Jewish relations from the first century C.E. to the present has focused intense scholarly attention on this benediction. The relatively crystallized wording of the benediction in the extant early *siddurim* (ninth to twelfth centuries) makes it likely that the text preserved there closely resembles its original formulation. We find the following wording in a Palestinian siddur from the Cairo Genizah:

> For the apostates let there be no hope. And let the arrogant government be speedily uprooted in our days. Let the *noẓerim* and the *minim* be destroyed in a moment. And let them be blotted out of the Book of Life and not be inscribed together with the righteous. Blessed art thou, O Lord, who humblest the arrogant" (Schechter).

This was also the version commonly used in the Babylonian rite, in which the penultimate sentence, "And let them be blotted out," was replaced by a petition to cut off all enemies, "may all the enemies of your people and their opponents be speedily cut off." Other variants reflect a longer, more elaborated request for obliteration of enemies. The language of the benediction clearly demonstrates that it was directed, not at non-Jews in general, but rather specifically aimed against external persecutors of the Jews and against Jewish separatists who posed a danger to Judaism's internal cohesion. Nonetheless, as early as the first centuries C.E. we find church fathers voicing the claim that the Jews curse the Christians in their prayers. Such contentions, alongside censorship of *siddurim*, wrought significant changes in the wording of the benediction during the Middle Ages. Also contributing to this modificatory process were shifts in the social environment of the Jews and in their worldview. Without exception, the word *noẓerim* was expunged from all Jewish prayer rites, and in many, substitutions were made for *minim* (heretics) and *meshummadim* (apostates), as in the accepted opening in the Ashkenazi rite: "may the slanderers (*malshinim*) have no hope." Some Reform prayer books omit this benediction entirely.

BIBLIOGRAPHY: G. Alon, *The Jews in Their Land in the Talmudic Age (70–640 C.E.)* (1980), 288–307; I. Elbogen, *Jewish Liturgy: A Comprehensive History.* tr. R.P. Scheindlein (1993), 31–34, 45–46; E. Fleischer. *"Le-Kadmoniyyut Tefillot ha-Ḥovah be-Yisrael,"* in: *Tarbiz*, 59 (1990), 435–37; D. Flusser, *"Mikat ma'asei ha-Torah' u-Virkat ha-Minim."* in: *Tarbiz*, 61 (1992), 333–74; J. Heinemann, *Prayer in the Talmud: Forms and Patterns* (1977), 225–26; W. Horbury. "The Benediction of the 'Minim' and Early Jewish-Christian Controversy," in: *Journal of Theological Studies*, 33:1 (1982), 19–61; R. Kimelman. "Birkat Ha-Minim and the Lack of Evidence for an Anti-Christian Prayer in Late Antiquity," in: E.P. Sanders (ed.), *Jewish and Christian Self-Definition*, vol. 2 (1981), 226–44; J.J. Petuchowski, *Prayerbook Reform in Europe* (1968), 223–25; S. Schechter, "Genizah Specimens," in: JQR, 10 (1898), 657.

BIRKAT HA-TORAH (Heb. בִּרְכַּת הַתּוֹרָה), the blessing over the Law. The study of the Law was always regarded as a foremost religious duty and hence had to be preceded by a formula of benediction. This requirement applies both to the liturgical reading of the Torah and to ordinary study. Various formulas are given in the Talmud (Ber. 11a–b) in the name of several rabbis and all have been integrated into the traditional liturgy. These benedictions were instituted in talmudic times based upon Deuteronomy 32:3 (see TJ, Meg. 4:1, 74d) and by *a fortiori* inference from the duty to recite Grace after Meals (TJ, Ber. 7:11a; TJ, Meg. loc. cit.). Three blessings over the Law are pronounced at the beginning of the daily morning prayer. The first praises God for granting Israel the privilege and the duty of studying Torah; the second is a prayer that the study of Torah may be pleasant and that it should be cultivated by one's offspring and the whole house of Israel; the third is identical to the benediction recited before the Reading of the Law in the synagogue service: "Who has chosen us from all nations and hast given us Thy Law." They are followed by selections from Scripture (Num. 6:24–27), the Mishnah (Pe'ah 1:1) and the Talmud (Shab. 127a), recited in symbolic fulfillment of the duty to study Torah. Jacob b. Asher interpreted the words "Torah of truth" to refer to the written Torah, and the words "everlasting life" to refer to the oral tradition. These benedictions contain 40 words, said to symbolize the 40 days Moses spent on Mount Sinai (Tur OH 139). The benedictions over the Law have uniform wording in all modern rituals, including that of Reform Judaism. Only the Reconstructionist trend, which repudiates the notion of the election of Israel, has changed the wording of the middle part of the benediction to read "who hast brought us close to Thy service" instead of "who hast chosen us."

BIBLIOGRAPHY: ET, 4 (1952), 615–31; J. Heinemann, *Ha-Tefillah…* (1964), 105–8; E. Levy, *Yesodot ha-Tefillah* (1952[2]), 130, 315–6; Hertz, Prayer, 12–17, 190–3; E. Munk, *World of Prayer* (1961), 41–49, 174–5.

BIRKENTHAL (Brezhover), DOV BER (Ber of Bolechow; 1723–1805), Hebrew writer and memoirist. Born in Bolechow, Birkenthal adopted a German name in accordance with the decree of Joseph II in 1772, when the city passed from Polish to Austrian rule. He received a traditional Jewish education, but his father, who was a wine dealer and had contact with Polish and Hungarian nobles and priests, agreed to engage a non-Jewish tutor – an unusual step for the time – who taught him Polish, Latin, German, and French. Birkenthal took over his father's business and became the leader of the Bolechow community. In the debate with the followers of Jacob *Frank, which was held in the main church of Lemberg in 1759, Birkenthal served as interpreter and adviser to R. Ḥayyim b. Simḥah ha-Kohen Rapoport, the chief rabbi of Lemberg. His main literary work, *Imrei Binah*, is a study of false-Messiah movements in Jewish history, and the debate with the Frankists occupies a central position in it. The work was discovered in 1910, long after his death, and published by A.J. Brawer in *Ha-Shilo'aḥ* (vols. 33 and 38). A manuscript of his memoirs was discovered in Jews' College, London, in 1912 and was published – with introduction – in 1922 in Berlin by M. Wischnitzer. It was published in Yiddish (*Ber Bolekhovers Zikhroynes*) and in English translation (*The Memoirs of Ber of Bolechow*) in the same year. These two works contain valuable information for the study of Jewish history in Galicia in the 18th century, not only for the Frankist movement but also for the history of the Council of the Lands, the Jewish census in Poland (1764), and for Jewish economic history of that period.

BIBLIOGRAPHY: Zinberg, Sifrut, 5 (1959), 109–11; Wischnitzer, in: JQR, 12 (1921/22), 1–24; Balaban, in: *Festschrift… S. Poznański* (1927), 25 ff.

[Abraham J. Brawer]

BIRMINGHAM, city in Alabama, U.S. The city grew from the intersection of two railroads in 1871, and the discovery of all ingredients necessary to make steel within a short radius. Jews were among the first settlers, but Jewish communal life did not begin to develop until 1882 when Birmingham had a population of 3,086. That year, Temple Emanu-El was formed. The Reform congregation was led in the 1890s by Samuel Ullman, who served on the board of education and pushed for the establishment of the state's first black high school. A poem Ullman wrote later in life, "Youth," was a favorite of General Douglas MacArthur's and has become a cultural mainstay in Japan. Ullman's Birmingham home is now a museum.

Morris *Newfield, who served as rabbi of Temple Emanu-El from 1895 to 1940, was president of the Central Conference of American Rabbis and an acknowledged civic and cultural leader.

An influx of East Europeans arrived from 1900 to 1920. Most of the immigrants had a poor command of English and were impoverished, but quickly found their way in the "Magic City." In 1892, an Orthodox congregation was established, Knesseth Israel, followed by Temple Beth-El in 1906, formed by KI members who wanted mixed seating. In 1926, Beth-El followed Emanu-El as the Jewish population shifted from the Northside to the city's Southside.

Jewish merchants started most of Birmingham's department stores, and Jews entered many other phases of civic life. In the financial panic of 1893, the Steiner brothers of Steiner Bank kept the city from going bankrupt.

After 1920 several important changes took place in the Jewish community. Antisemitism became more pronounced as the Ku Klux Klan gained strength, there was a sharper division between the generations, and there was an increased pace at which Jews moved from their old neighborhoods in the Northside. There was also the beginning of a united, local Jewish community, despite the continuance of a sharp division between the German Jews and the East European Jews. KI and the YMHA were the last to leave the old Northside, in the 1950s. The YMHA had been built in the 1920s with substantial non-Jewish support.

Since Jews were frozen out of local country clubs, they established the Hillcrest in 1883 for German Jews, and the Fairmont in 1920, for East European Jews. They merged in 1969, forming the Pine Tree Country Club, which opened its membership to non-Jews in 1991.

There were many strong Zionists in Birmingham in the 1940s. Rabbi Milton Grafman, who served Emanu-El from 1941 to 1975, broke with much of the Reform movement to support a Jewish state, and for a time anti-Zionist Reform Jews established their own congregation. The aftermath of the Holocaust, the establishment of Israel, and the emerging hostilities of the civil rights struggle began to eliminate the division between Birmingham's Jews.

A bomb with enough dynamite to level a city block was discovered outside Temple Beth-El in 1958. It had malfunctioned just short of detonation. White supremacists also threatened numerous local Jews who spoke out on behalf of civil rights, and much anti-integration material was overtly antisemitic. Many local Jews therefore worked behind the scenes to resolve the crisis, including the effort to change the city's form of government in 1963. The Jewish merchants were caught in the middle, between black customers using their only leverage through boycotts and white city officials who employed boycotts and legal intimidation. Local Jews resented the presence of northern Jews in the civil rights movement, who came down south for what was seen as grandstanding. In the decades that followed, there were numerous ongoing interfaith and interracial dialogues and groups.

The YMHA moved from downtown in 1958 and became the Levite Jewish Community Center. It underwent a major expansion in 1993 and now houses the N.E. Miles Jewish Day School, established in 1973, Collat Jewish Family Services, and the Birmingham Jewish Federation and Foundation. Half of the LJCC's membership is non-Jewish.

In the 1990s, Beth-El and Emanu-El underwent major expansions, a Chabad Center was established, and KI planned to build anew in 2005.

In 2005, the Jewish population of Birmingham was approximately 5,300 in a metro area of 1 million.

[Lawrence Brook (2nd ed.)]

BIRMINGHAM, city in England. The Jewish community there is believed to have come into existence around 1730. The early Jewish settlers included peddlers who used Birmingham as a base. The first known Birmingham glass furnace was set up by Meyer Oppenheim (or Opnaim) in or about 1760. In 1783 a synagogue existed in "The Froggery." A new synagogue, constructed in Severn Street in 1809, was wrecked in the riots of 1813 along with the Nonconformist chapels but was rebuilt and enlarged in 1827. Internecine strife at this period resulted in the formation of a second congregation, but the two groups united to build the Singers Hill Synagogue, consecrated in 1856, and still in use. There were then about 700 Jews in Birmingham. The Jewish community included jewelers, merchants, and manufacturers. In the 20th century Jews were leading figures in property development and in the entertainment world. On the other hand, immigration from Eastern Europe affected Birmingham less than other large cities. Rabbis of the community included M.J. *Raphall (1841–49) and George J. Emanuel (1863–1911), succeeded by Abraham *Cohen (1913–49). To serve the East European Jews who settled in Birmingham a *bet midrash* was opened in 1901, which later became the Central Synagogue. The Hebrew Philanthropic Society, established in 1838, and the Board of Guardians, in 1870, were consolidated in 1926 in the Birmingham United Jewish Benevolent Board. The Birmingham Jewish Representative Council was established in 1937. About 500 German Jewish refugees settled in Birmingham in the late 1930s. Jews have played a prominent part in the civic and business life of Birmingham. Sir David Davis served as lord mayor in 1922 and 1923, as did Louis Glass in 1963–64. Birmingham, whose Jewish population numbered approximately 6,300 in 1967, had the lowest percentage of Jews of any great city in England. By the mid-1990s the Jewish population had dropped to approximately 3,000, while the 2001 British census, which asked an optional question about the religious affiliation of respondents for the first time, found 2,340 declared Jews in Birmingham, although the actual figure was probably still about 3,000. In 2004, Birmingam had two Orthodox synagogues and a Reform temple, a *shehitah board, and other local institutions.

BIBLIOGRAPHY: C. Roth, *Rise of Provincial Jewry* (1950), 32–33; C. Gill and A. Briggs, *History of Birmingham* (1952). **ADD. BIBLIOGRAPHY:** Z. Josephs, *Birmingham Jewry, 1749–1940* (1980); idem., *Birmingham Jewry, Volume 2: More Aspects, 1740–1930* (1984); idem., *Survivors: Jewish Refugees in Birmingham, 1933–45* (1988); JYB, 2004.

[Sefton D. Temkin]

BIRNBAUM, ABRAHAM BAER (1864–1922), cantor and composer. Birnbaum, who was born in Pultusk, Poland, was regarded as an *illui* ("prodigy") in Talmud. He studied the violin in Lodz with Ḥayyim H. Janowski, founder of the Ha-Zamir choral society. At the age 19, he accepted a position as cantor in Hethar, Hungary, but in due course returned to Poland as chief cantor in Czestochowa. His *Hallel ve-Zimrah*, consisting of Sabbath eve melodies arranged for choir and organ, was published in 1897. His main work, which much enriched synagogue music, *Ommanut ha-Ḥazzanut*, was a treatment of liturgical music for cantor and choir, written in two parts (1908, 1912). He composed a "Romance for Violin and Piano" and set to music poems of Bialik, Frischmann, Yaakov Cohen, and Frug. Birnbaum's activities included publishing, and he brought out four numbers of *Yarḥon ha-Ḥazzanim* ("Cantors' Monthly") in 1897, textbooks on music, in Yiddish and Hebrew, written for the cantorial school he opened at Czestochowa (1907) and for the Lodz teachers' seminary. He organized the conference of cantors held in Warsaw for the purpose of founding the Aguddat ha-Ḥazzanim ("Cantorial Association"). His musical collection is in the Hebrew Union College Library, Cincinnati.

BIBLIOGRAPHY: Sendrey, Music, indexes; Friedmann, Lebensbilder, 3 (1927), 58–61; Sherman, in: A.H. Rosen, *Di Geshikhte fun Khazones* (1924), 210–1.

[Joshua Leib Ne'eman]

BIRNBAUM, EDUARD (Asher Anshel; 1855–1920), German cantor and one of the early research workers in Jewish music. Born in Cracow, he spent three years in Vienna studying *ḥazzanut* with Solomon *Sulzer. In 1872 he was appointed assistant cantor of the Magdeburg community. Two years later he became chief cantor of Beuthen, where his duties allowed him to travel to other cities and meet cantors and scholars. He started to collect printed and manuscript music, literature and documents, which became source material for his research and led directly to his critical essay on the *Baal T'fillah* of Abraham *Baer (*Das juedische Literaturblatt*, nos. 24 and 27, 1878). In 1879, Birnbaum succeeded Ẓvi Hirsch Weintraub as chief cantor of Koenigsberg and held this position till his death. Many young cantors came to study with him and some were stimulated to undertake research. He conducted educational work among cantors and teachers by means of lectures and the publication of printed material (*Liturgische Uebungen*, 2 vols., 1900, 1912). He also composed liturgical works, some of which were published after his death (*Aseh le-Ma'an, Ha-Melekh, Kedushah, Lekhah Dodi* in the supplements of *Der juedische Kantor*, 1927–31). Birnbaum's most important achievements were his writings and the "Birnbaum collection", subsequently acquired by the Hebrew Union College, Cincinnati. These contain his thematic catalogue of synagogal melodies, comprising about 7,000 cards, and his collection of references to music in rabbinic texts.

BIBLIOGRAPHY: Sendrey, Music, indexes; A. Friedmann, *Dem Andenken Eduard Birnbaums* (1922); E. Werner, in: HUCA, 18 (1943–44), 397–428.

[Haim Bar-Dayan]

BIRNBAUM, MENACHEM (1893–1944), Austrian portraitist and graphic artist, son of Nathan and Rosa *Birnbaum; brother of philologist Solomon Asher *Birnbaum and the poet Uriel *Birnbaum. Born in Vienna, Birnbaum had limited contact with art teachers and thus trained himself as an autodidact. He moved to Berlin in 1911. In 1912 Menachem Birnbaum was art editor of the Yiddish monthly *Der Ashmeday*, and in 1919 became art editor and contributor to *Der Schlemiel*. In 1920 he published a volume of his drawings, *Chad Gadjo*, which made him famous. He was appointed art director of two important Jewish publishing houses, Juedischer Verlag and Welt-Verlag and designed book covers and illustrations. With the advent of the Nazis (1933) he fled to Holland where he continued to draw portraits. In 1937 he published a small book with caricatures, *Menachem Birnbaum zeigt Karikaturen*, in The Hague. Caught by the Nazis in 1943, he perished in Auschwitz concentration camp. Menachem Birnbaum did not join his father, Nathan, in turning to traditional Judaism but always kept himself aware of his Jewish identity as an individual and as an artist.

BIBLIOGRAPHY: D. Schmauß (ed.), *Menachem Birnbaum: Leben und Werk eines jüdischen Künstlers* (1999); G. Schirmers, "Zum Leben und Werk von Menachem Birnbaum," in: *Exil. Forschung, Erkenntnisse, Ergebnisse. 18,2* (1998), 34–53; K. Zijlmans, "Jüdische Künstler im Exil. Uriel und Menachem Birnbaum," in: *Österreichische Exilliteratur in den Niederlanden 1934–40. Hrsg. v. Hans Wuerzner* (1986), 145–155; M. Birnbaum, *Menachem Birnbaum zeigt Karikaturen* (1937).

[Sonja Beyer (2nd ed.)]

BIRNBAUM, NATHAN (1864–1937), writer (early pen name: **Mathias Acher**), philosopher, one of the originators of Zionist ideology, later a leader of religious Judaism. Born in Vienna of parents of Galician and Hungarian origin, his rabbinical ancestry can be traced back to the Middle Ages. At school he became estranged from observant Judaism. He did not, however, follow the assimilationist path of that period, but conceived the idea that the Jews were an ethnic entity, a people, and propagated his ideas among his schoolmates. In his first year at the Vienna university studying law he founded, together with Reuben *Bierer and Moritz *Schnirer, Kadimah, the first Jewish nationalist students' organization (1882) with the aim of criticizing assimilation and setting up a Jewish nationalist consciousness. In 1884 his first publication appeared, a pamphlet called *Die Assimilationssucht, Ein Wort an die sogenannten Deutschen, Slaven, Magyaren etc. mosaischer Confession von einem Studenten juedischer Nationalitaet*. In 1885 he founded and edited the first Jewish nationalist journal in German, *Selbstemanzipation* (later entitled *Juedische Volkszeitung*), where he coined the terms "Zionist" and "Zionism." The policy and name of the journal came from Leo *Pinsker's pamphlet "*Autoemanzipation*." Birnbaum was, during the decade 1885–1895, "the most distinguished intellectual personality in Jewish national circles in Austria and Germany" (Bein). In 1893 he published *Die nationale Wiedergeburt des juedischen Volkes als Mittel zur Loesung der Judenfrage, Ein Appell an die Guten und Edlen aller Nationen*, a summing up of his first Zionist phase. He now gradually passed to a cultural conception of Zionism, as evidenced by his publication *Die juedische Moderne* (1896) and his official address, *Zionism as a Cultural Movement*, at the First Zionist Congress (1897).

After a short period of service as chief secretary of the central Zionist office run by *Herzl, ideological disagreements broke out between the two. After the Second Zionist Congress (1898) Birnbaum made a fundamental turn in his political thinking: He became a spokesman for "diaspora nationalism," publishing articles in which he severely criticized Herzl's "diplomatism," the "inorganic" nature of the Zionist movement, and the Zionist "negation of the Diaspora," its culture and language (Yiddish). He gradually withdrew from Zionism, affirming that "Israel comes before Zion," i.e., that the striving for Erez Israel must not entail neglect of the Jewish People itself. His concept was now that of an interterritorial nation, comprising and integrating all existing Jewish groups which had a cultural life of their own. The most important group in his eyes was the Yiddish-speaking one in Eastern Europe. The political aspect of these ideas found expression in a demand for the cultural autonomy of the Jews, in conformity with the autonomy principle for the various peoples of the Austro-Hungarian Empire which was then gaining ground. One of its cornerstones was language. In the case of the Jews this was Yiddish. Birnbaum set about working for its recognition as a language in its own right and an important cultural value, mainly through articles in his weekly *Neue Zeitung* (1906–1907). He learned Yiddish himself and used it as a literary medium. In 1907 he ran in Buczacz, Galicia, for the Austrian Reichsrat as a Jewish Nationalist but was fraudulently defeated by the Polish candidate. In 1908, while on a visit to America, he proposed that a world conference on behalf of Yiddish should be called. This took place in Czernowitz in 1908 with the participation of the leading Yiddish writers. A resolution was passed there declaring Yiddish to be a (not the) national language of the Jewish people. From 1908 to 1911 Birnbaum lived in Czernowitz, publishing the newspapers *Dos Folk* and *Vokhen-Blat*.

Birnbaum's acquaintance with East European Jewry was now deepening and he "arrived at the religious core of the nation." His basic attitude underwent another fundamental change. The atheism of his materialist philosophy as well as his secular nationalism were gradually replaced by the conviction that the vocation and destiny of the Jewish People was a religious one. Finally, "God entered into his consciousness." The turning point seems to have been an intimate religious experience in 1908. He later wrote that he had not "sought" God but that God had "sought" him. During the next few years before World War I his writings and lectures dealt with problems of religion. He gradually accepted the Jewish tradition and way of life, and finally joined the ranks of religious Jewry as a practicing Jew. However, he did not feel satisfied with the state of affairs he met with there. He maintained that religious Jewry was not making a serious attempt at fulfilling its world mission as an exemplary people living on the basis of God's Word. He outlined a program toward effecting a change. Those things in the environments, occupations and habits of the Jews which were barring the way to spiritual advancement must be altered. The highest authority of the Jewish nation was to be vested in a body of Guardians of the Faith. The first step would be the founding of a small community of "Those Who (want to) Ascend" (Ḥever Olim), who would act as a nucleus, and for whom he laid down a scheme for disciplined living. These ideas were embodied in *Et La'asot* ("The Time Has Come for Action") and *Divrei ha-Olim* ("The Words of Those Who (want to) Ascend," both in 1917, Heb. and Yid.). He repudiated his own former "pagan-Jewish" life in *Gottes Volk* (1917), with further editions in 1918 and 1921 (translated into English under the title *Confession*, 1946). In *Vom Freigeist zum Glaeubigen* (1919) he described his spiritual development. Upon the refounding of the *Agudat Israel World Organization (1919) he became its first general secretary. At that time, after the war, revolution, and pogroms in Eastern Europe, he devoted much effort to the problem of emigration and endeavored to enlist general Jewish cooperation toward regulating on a big scale what amounted to an unorganized, panic mass flight. His book *Im Dienste der Verheissung* (1927) contains a critical analysis of the "activism" of the Orthodox as a grafting of fashionable ideologies onto an organism that was inherently of a different nature and suggested to the "activists" a more fruitful field – the gigantic task of creating the necessary material preconditions toward effecting a metamorphosis. Nearness to God can only result from a complete inner transformation of the masses through their sociological restratification in favor of a life based mainly on agriculture, and this is to be achieved by the large-scale colonization of sparsely populated or practically uninhabited territories. The anarchy in the life of the Jewish community can be remedied by the establishment not of an interterritorial, state-like organization but of an interterritorial "All Israel Congregation," under authoritative spiritual leadership. The next publication devoted to these ideas was the journal *Der Aufstieg* (1930–1933), many of whose pages were written by himself.

At the advent of Hitler (1933) he left Berlin where he had lived most of the time since 1911, and settled in the Hague-Scheveningen, where he published a journal *Der Ruf* (1934–1937). A series of articles were republished in a booklet, *Rufe* (1936), published in Antwerp, his "testament to the Jewish People." "The great ideal is to create the new Jew, based in the Torah, near to nature and to God, creative, harmonious, happy." There are three books of selections from his writings: from his secular period the important collection, *Ausgewaehlte Schriften zur juedischen Frage* (2 vols, 1910), from his early religious phase, *Um die Ewigkeit* (1920) and from the later one, *Et La'asot* (1938, in Yid.). His son, Solomon *Birnbaum edited a short selection of his religious works, *The Bridge* (1956). His other sons were Menachem *Birnbaum and Uriel *Birnbaum.

BIBLIOGRAPHY: S. Birnbaum, in: L. Jung (ed.), *Men of the Spirit* (1964), 519–49; J. Fraenkel, in: JSOS, 16 (1954), 115–34; A.E. Kaplan and M. Landau (eds.), *Vom Sinn des Judentums* (1925); *Die Freistatt* (May and June 1914); A. Boehm, *Die zionistische Bewegung*, 1 (1935), 135–8; L. Hermann, *Nathan Birnbaum* (1914); *Davar, Literary Supplement* (May 7, 1937); J. Fraenkel, in: *Shivat Ẓiyyon*, 2–3 (1953), 275–99; Kressel, *ibid.*, 4 (1956), 55–99; L.S. Dawidowicz (ed.), *The Golden Tradition* (1967), index. **ADD. BIBLIOGRAPHY:** J.A. Fishman, *Ideology, Society & Language – The Odyssey of Nathan Birnbaum* (1987); "The Metamorphosis of Nathan Birnbaum," in: R. Wistrich, *The Jews of Vienna in the Age of Franz Joseph* (1989); J. Fraenkel, "Mathias Archer's Fight for the Crown of Zion," in: *Jewish Studies*, 16/2 (1954); J.A. Fishman, "Nathan Birnbaum's View of American Jewry," in: *Yiddish, Turning to Life* (1991); Kuehntopf-Gentz, "Nathan Birnbaum" (Diss. Tuebingen, 1990); M. Gelber, *Melancholy Pride* (2000).

BIRNBAUM, PHILIP (1904–1988), U.S. author and translator. Birnbaum was born in Zamowiec, Poland, and immigrated to the United States in 1923. He attended Howard College and completed a Ph.D. degree at Dropsie College. In 1942, he published his dissertation, a critical, scientific edition of the Arabic commentary of the Karaite Yefet Ben Ali, on the Book of Hosea. Birnbaum's edition of Yefet Ben Ali's work was edited from eight manuscripts and included an English language introduction, a translation into Hebrew of the Arabic original, and critical notes on the text.

But Birnbaum's talent and lasting contribution was in popularizing Jewish law and custom, and in translating synagogue liturgy. His popular works included *A Treasury of Judaism* (1957), *A Book of Jewish Concepts* (1975), *The Concise Jewish Bible* (1977), and a selection of the Maimonides Code, the *Mishneh Torah* (1944, 1967), with Hebrew and English translation. Birnbaum was widely known and respected for his fine translation and annotation of synagogue liturgy. His editions of liturgy for daily prayer, Sabbath, festivals, and the High Holidays became immensely popular, selling an estimated 300,000 copies. The Hebrew Publishing Company described him, at his death, as "the most obscure bestselling author."

Birnbaum was a regular columnist and book reviewer for the Hebrew-language weekly, *Hadoar*. He also served on the board of directors of the Histadrut Ivrit b'America, an American association for the promotion of Hebrew language and culture. He also served for many years (1943–63) as principal of a Jewish day school in Wilmington, Delaware, and directed Jewish schools in Birmingham, Alabama, and Camden, New Jersey.

BIBLIOGRAPHY: *New York Times*, B5 (March 22, 1988).

[Moshe Sherman (2nd ed.)]

BIRNBAUM, SOLOMON ASHER (1891–1989), Yiddish philologist and Hebrew paleographer. Birnbaum was born in Vienna, the son of Nathan *Birnbaum, and is the father of Jacob Birnbaum, a key initiator of the U.S. Soviet Jewry Movement. After World War I service, he specialized in Oriental languages. Appointed lecturer in Yiddish at Hamburg University (1922), he was the first in any university to hold a teaching post for Yiddish. He emigrated to England (1933) and then to Toronto (1970). He taught Hebrew paleography at London University's School of Oriental and African studies (1936-57) and Yiddish at the School of Slavonic and East European Studies (1939-58).

Birnbaum wrote over 150 major articles on Yiddish, other Jewish languages, and Hebrew paleography, in German, Yiddish, and later mostly in English. He wrote *Praktische Grammatik der jiddeschen Sprache* (1918, 1966^2, 1979^3, 1984^4), the first fully systematic Yiddish grammar, *Die Yiddische Sprache* (1974, 1986^2), and *Yiddish, A Survey and a Grammar* (1979), as well as *Life and Sayings of the Baal Shem* (1933). His *Hebrew Scripts* (part 2, 1954-57, part 1, 1972), the first comprehensive work on Hebrew paleography with hundreds of illustrations and detailed paleographical examinations, charted the evolution of Hebrew script. He wrote *The Qumran (Dead Sea) Scrolls and Paleography* (1952). Due out in 2007 was S.A. Birnbaum, *A Lifetime of Achievement: 63 Jewish Linguistic and Paleographic Studies*, ed. C. Timm.

BIBLIOGRAPHY: S. Hiley, "S.A. Birnbaum," in: D.B. Kerler (ed.), *History of Yiddish Studies* (1991); Rejzen, Leksikon (1956); J. Spalek and S. Hawrylchak (eds.), *Guide to Archival Materials of German-speaking Emigration to U.S....*, 3/1 (1997).

BIRNBAUM, URIEL (1894–1956), poet and artist; son of Nathan *Birnbaum. Born in Vienna, he began his career as an artist and poet at a very early age as an autodidact. In 1911 the family moved to Berlin, where Uriel volunteered at the "Berliner Sezession." His graphic and literary output continued throughout World War I, even after he was severely wounded when fighting in the Austrian Army. His war experiences found expression in a volume of sonnets, *In Gottes Krieg* (1921). Like his father Nathan, Uriel returned to traditional Judaism in 1913 and his favorite subject in poetry became trust in God as the principle of human life. He chose to deal with biblical history in order to demonstrate God's relationship to man and published several portfolios and volumes of lithographs and paintings: *Welkuntergang* (1921), *Das Buch Jona*

(1921), *Das Kaiser und der Architekt* (1924), *Moses* (1924). In addition, he illustrated the German version of Lewis Carroll's *Through the Looking Glass* (1923). For Birnbaum the breakup of multinational Austria-Hungary was a catastrophe, as he had pushed himself out of contemporary discourse as a result of his pro-monarchical ideas. When Austria was occupied by Nazi Germany he was granted entry to the Netherlands upon the intervention of leading Dutch artists. Here he continued to write but gave up his graphic work for lack of artists' materials. His selection from his poetical output (*Gedichte, eine Auswahl*), appeared in 1957. Because of his uncompromising opposition to fashionable modern ideologies he became an outsider again and died underappreciated in the Netherlands. Since then there has been a revival of interest in him. *Die verschlossene Kassette. Die Legende vom gutherzigen Engel* and *Von der Seltsamkeit der Dinge*, ed. C. Schneider (incl. bibl.) were published in 1978.

BIBLIOGRAPHY: T. Biene, "Uriel Birnbaum – ignoriert, emigriert, vergessen. Stationen im Leben eines prophetischen Dichters, Denkers und Zeichners," in: H. Wuerzner (ed.), *Österreichische Exilliteratur in den Niederlanden 1934–40* (1986), 127–143; G. Schirmers (ed.), *Uriel Birnbaum 1894–1956. Dichter und Maler* (1990); M. Neuwirth: "Die Hoffahrt des Architekten. Künstlerisches Selbstverständnis bei Uriel Birnbaum," in: *Das jüdische Echo*, 48 (1999), 252–260; K. Zijlmans: "Juedische Kuenstler im Exil. Uriel und Menachem Birnbaum," in: H. Wuerzner (ed.), *Oesterreichische Exilliteratur in den Niederlanden 1934–40* (1986), 145–155.

[Sonja Beyer (2nd ed.)]

BIRNBOIM, MOSES JOSEPH (1789–1831), secret agent of the czarist police and blackmailer. He started to work for the Warsaw police in 1820, in charge of about 30 servants recruited to spy on their employers, mostly persons prominent in Polish political and economic life. Later sent to Germany, he mixed in Polish student circles purporting to be an opponent of czarist absolutism to gain the students' confidence. He subsequently returned to Warsaw, using his position to blackmail Jews, exploiting the czarist anti-ḥasidic legislation, and earning the hatred of both Jews and Poles, until he himself was denounced to the police. In an effort to save himself, he apostatized and adopted the name Mateusz Józef, but was arrested in 1824 and in 1830 sentenced to ten years' imprisonment. During the Polish uprising of 1831, Birnboim, along with many traitors and others hated by the Poles, was taken from prison by Jews, brought to Franciszkańska Street in Warsaw, where most of his Jewish victims lived, and hanged from a lantern.

BIBLIOGRAPHY: Warszawski, in: *YIVO Historishe Shriftn*, 2 (1937), 335–54; J. Shatzky, *Geshikhte fun Yidn in Varshe*, 1 (1947), 327–8.

BIRÓ (Blau), LAJOS (1880–1948), Hungarian author and playwright. Biró was born in Vienna. He studied in Hungary, and became a journalist working for the liberal *Budapesti Napló* and the radical *Vil g*. In 1906, for political reasons, he went with his family to Berlin, but returned to Budapest in 1909. During the October Revolution of 1918, Biró was appointed secretary of state at the Foreign Ministry. However, he left Hungary and finally settled in Great Britain, where together with Sir Alexander *Korda he founded the London Film Production Company, of which he remained a director until his death. Biró's Hungarian writing covered short stories and drama. The former included *Huszonegy novella* ("Twenty-one short stories," 1908) and *Kunsz ll si emberek* ("People of Kunszállás," 1912), and among his plays were *Sárga liliom* ("Yellow Lily," 1912) and *Hotel Imperial* (1917). In his later years he turned to writing film scripts, of which the most famous were *The Way of All Flesh* and *The Private Life of Henry VIII*. In 1921, when living in Vienna, he published *A bazini zsidók* ("The Jews of Bazin"), a story about a blood libel in 1529, when the entire Jewish community of a village near Pressburg was tortured and burned to death. In this vivid description, Biró depicts the fate of the Jew in the Diaspora. In his essay, *A zsidók útja* (1921, "The Way of the Jews") he rejected both assimilation and Jewish nationalism, defining the Jewish question as unanswerable, but enthusiastically accepting the existence and continuity of the Jewish people.

BIBLIOGRAPHY: *Magyar Zsidó Lexikon* (1929), 126; *Magyar Irodalmi Lexikon* (1963), 165–6.

[Baruch Yaron]

BIROBIDZHAN, colloquial name of the district (oblast) in Russia, for which the official designation was the "Jewish Autonomous District" (*Avtonomnaya Oblast*). Part of the Khabarovsk territory (*kray*) in the former Soviet Far East, the region is located between 47° 40′–49° 20′ N. and 130° 30′–135° E. To the west, south, and southeast, it is bordered by the Amur River, the boundary between the former U.S.S.R. and Manchuria (China). Its area is 13,900 sq. mi. (36,000 sq. km.). On January 1, 1961, the estimated population of the district numbered 179,000 and that of the capital, the city of Birobidzhan, 49,000. The Jewish population of the region numbered 14,269 (8.8% of the total) in 1959; of these 83.9% lived in cities and urban settlements, while 16.1% lived in villages. The capital is located on the Bolshaya Bira River and on the Trans-Siberian Railroad which cuts through the northern sector of the territory from west to east. Its industries include farm machinery, transformers, textiles, clothing, and furniture. The climate is influenced by the prevailing monsoons and the surrounding mountains to the west and north. It improves progressively southward, the most favorable conditions prevailing in the Amur River strip in the southern part of the region. The winter is cold and dry with little snow, spring is mild, summer is hot and humid, and fall is dry and pleasant. Birobidzhan has numerous rivers and lakes abounding with fish. Most of its area is composed of heavy soils with an excess of moisture. A considerable part consists of swamps and about one-third is covered with forest. Birobidzhan has abundant mineral wealth, for the most part not commercially exploited, except for tin ores which are the basis of a large national metallurgical works, the "Khinganolovo." Grains, pulses, potatoes, vegetables, and other crops are grown. However, at the time when Jewish settlement began here, the region suffered from an almost

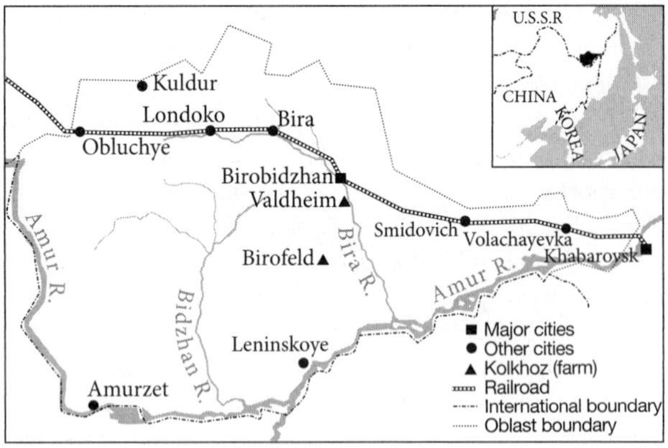

Map of the Birobidzhan region.

complete absence of roads and land suitable for agriculture, insufficient and poor living accommodations, harsh climatic conditions, "*gnus*" (local name for bloodsucking insects), and unsanitary conditions. The Soviet decision to select Birobidzhan for Jewish settlement was influenced by several factors, the decisive one being the desire to strengthen the security of the Soviet Far East, in view of its proximity to Japan and the danger of penetration by the Chinese. The settlement of Birobidzhan became of particular importance to the U.S.S.R. after the Japanese occupation of Manchuria in 1931–32. Since the Soviet government attempted in the late 1920s and early 1930s to improve its relations with the West, the Birobidzhan project could have also played a role in influencing Jewish and pro-Jewish public opinion there. The association of Jews with the settlement of Birobidzhan was also meant to obtain financial support from their conationals abroad, and thus alleviate the allocation of Soviet resources for this purpose. Moreover, such settlement seemed to provide a partial solution to the economic difficulties facing Soviet nationalities. To some of those active in the *Yevsektsiya (the Jewish Section of the Communist Party), Birobidzhan seemed to constitute an ideological alternative to the Zionist idea. The first official step toward implementation of the project was the dispatch of a scientific delegation to Birobidzhan in the summer of 1927, to investigate the feasibility of an agricultural settlement there. Its recommendations led to a resolution by the presidium of the central executive committee of the Soviet Union on March 28, 1928, to entrust Komzet (committee for settling Jews on the land) with the supervision of Jewish settlement in the region. On May 7, 1934, the "Birobidzhan county" (*rayon*), which had been established in 1930, was granted the status of the "Jewish Autonomous District" (JAD), by a decree of the central executive committee.

Jewish immigration to Birobidzhan began in April 1928 and continued at a varying rate. Colonization proceeded under most difficult conditions, especially at the beginning. The first year proved particularly difficult, with heavy rains, floods, and an outbreak of anthrax (horse disease). In the following years a comparatively large number of Jewish settlers arrived in Birobidzhan. However, the inadequate facilities and difficult climatic conditions seriously affected the rate of those who stayed there permanently. Out of prospective settlers who arrived between 1928 and 1933, more than half left. (See the table "Birobidzhan, Jewish Population.") The Birobidzhan project aroused a controversy among those active in Jewish settlement in the U.S.S.R. and among Yevsektsiya leaders. Among its critics were Mikhail (Yuri) *Larin and Abraham Bragin, both active in the Jewish settlement movement. Larin argued that other areas of the Soviet Union, especially the Crimea, were far more suitable for Jewish colonization. The Birobidzhan project found an ardent supporter in Mikhail Kalinin, the titular head of state. In a speech delivered at a congress of the society for Jewish agricultural settlement, Ozet, in 1926, before the Birobidzhan project was born, he had declared: "The Jewish people now faces the great task of preserving its nationality. For this purpose a large segment of the Jewish population must transform itself into a compact farming population, numbering at least several hundred thousand souls." In a reception given to representatives of Moscow workers and the Yiddish press in May 1934, he suggested that the creation of a Jewish territorial center in Birobidzhan would be the only way to normalize the national status of Soviet Jews. He also expressed his hope that "within a decade Birobidzhan will be the most important and probably the only bulwark of national Jewish socialist culture." and that "the transformation of the region into a republic is only a question of time." The visit of Lazar *Kaganovich, a Jew and member of the Politburo, to Birobidzhan in February 1936 greatly encouraged the Jewish leadership of the region. Birobidzhan aroused wide interest in world Jewry, especially among those who believed in Jewish *territorialism. The fact that Jewish settlement in Birobidzhan coincided with the intensification of anti-Jewish repressions in Nazi Germany also contributed to support of the idea by Jews outside the Soviet Union. Almost all sectors of the Zionist movement opposed it. Jewish organizations outside the U.S.S.R. which participated in Jewish colonization projects in the Soviet Union, such as Agro-Joint (American Jewish Joint Agricultural Corporation) and the *Jewish Colonization Association (ICA), generally took a neutral stand. The *Ort-Farband gave limited assistance to the development of industry and workshops. Those Jewish organizations abroad whose membership consisted mostly of Communists and their sympathizers supported the plan without reservation. Among the most active organizations was Icor (the American Association for Jewish Colonization in the Soviet Union), which cooperated closely with Ozet. In 1929 Icor organized a scientific delegation consisting of American specialists in agriculture and settlement to investigate the possibilities for further colonization of Birobidzhan. Ambidjan (American Committee for the Settlement of Foreign Jews in Birobidzhan) supported Jewish settlement in Birobidzhan for a short period in the mid-1930s and after World War II. Jewish organizations supporting Birobidzhan existed in Canada, Western Europe, and South America. Representatives of the Argentinian Jewish organization Procor (Society to Assist the Productivization of the Economically Ruined Jewish Masses in the Soviet Union) visited Birobidzhan in 1929. These organizations, besides holding meetings, issuing publications, and collecting money, also propagandized the colonization of Birobidzhan by Jews from abroad. Thus, about 1,400 Jewish immigrants from countries outside the Soviet Union arrived in Birobidzhan in the early 1930s, emigrating from the United States, South America, Europe, Palestine, and other places.

From the beginning of Jewish colonization in Birobidzhan, and particularly in the mid-1930s, much was done to promote the Jewish character of Birobidzhan. Jewish collective farms were established and Jewish village councils organized. Jews served in key positions of the region. Y. Levin, formerly active in the party apparatus in Belorussia and in the secretariat of Ozet, was appointed as first party secretary of the Birobidzhan district in 1930. After the establishment of the J.A.D. in 1934, another Jew, M. Khavkin, was appointed first secretary of the regional party committee. Joseph Liberberg, head of the Jewish section of the Ukrainian Academy of Sciences, was appointed at the same time chairman of the regional executive committee. He was one of those intellectuals, who, by settling in Birobidzhan, inspired others in their pioneering efforts. A number of resolutions were passed regarding the use of Yiddish as the official language of the region, along with Russian. Schools were established with Yiddish as the language of instruction, and experiments were made to teach Yiddish even in non-Jewish schools. Street signs, rail station signs, and postmarks appeared in both Russian and Yiddish. A Yiddish newspaper and periodicals were published. In 1934 a Jewish state theater was established. A regional library, named after Shalom Aleichem, containing a sizable collection of Judaica and Yiddish works, was founded in the city of Birobidzhan. The mid-1930s was a period of great expectations for Birobidzhan's development as a center of Jewish settlement and culture in the Soviet Union. However, the purges of 1936–38 delivered a severe blow to the developing and rather weak framework of the nascent Jewish statehood in the JAD Leading Jewish personalities of the district, such as Liberberg, were denounced as nationalists and Trotskyites, demoted from their posts, and liquidated. The purges particularly affected the immigrants from abroad. As a result, the late 1930s witnessed a shattering setback in the development of the region. Despite the optimistic plans for continuous settlement of Jews in Birobidzhan, their number was only 13,291 in 1939 (18.57% of the total population), with 10,415 (35.13% of the total) in the capital city. The Soviet annexation of the Baltic states and parts of eastern Poland and Bukovina in 1939–40 resulted in a sudden increase in the Jewish population of the U.S.S.R. During that period plans were initiated to transfer Jewish settlers from the annexed territories to Birobidzhan. However, the outbreak of the Soviet-German war in 1941 put a fast end to these plans. Although the war years did not witness any sizable increase in the Jewish population of the region, the very idea of Birobidzhan as a center for Jewish statehood in the Soviet Union received new meaning.

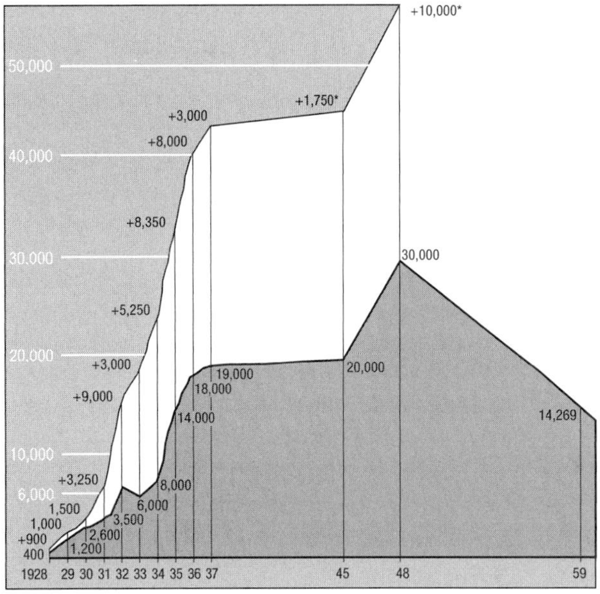

Jewish population of Birobidzhan 1928–59. The lower graph shows the total Jewish population, the upper one the immigration into the region.

The Holocaust and growth of antisemitism in the U.S.S.R. during the war resulted in revived interest in the JAD among Soviet Jews. The growth of national feelings and the difficulties faced by Soviet Jews who had fled to the East, upon their return to their prewar homes in the western parts of the U.S.S.R., caused some to turn to Birobidzhan. Moreover, since the hopes for a planned settlement of Jews in the Crimea did not materialize, Birobidzhan remained the only alternative for a compact Jewish settlement. Numerous requests for immigration to Birobidzhan were received by the JAD authorities in the postwar years, and a flow of new Jewish settlers reached the region between 1946 and 1948. Articles in the *Eynikayt*, organ of the Jewish anti-Fascist Committee, emphasized the idea of Jewish statehood in Birobidzhan. The Soviet Jewish writer *Der Nister, who accompanied a trainload of new settlers, wrote: "There are some travelers whose intentions are only materialistic, and there are others whose intentions are different, of a national character ... and there are also burning enthusiasts, ready to give up everything in order to live there ... and among them a former Palestinian patriot.... Although in his fifties, he hustles about during the day and is sleepless at night, hoping to see his new enterprise come true...." The short postwar migration to Birobidzhan increased the local Jewish population by one-third, and by the end of 1948 it was estimated at about 20,000, the largest ever in the district. The postwar period witnessed an increase in the number of Jews in the local administration and an intensification of Jewish cultural activities. Among local Jewish writers active in the "Soviet Writers' Association of the JAD" were Buzi Miler, Israel *Emiot, Ḥayyim Maltinski, Aaron *Vergelis, and others. Assistance from Jews abroad was permitted once again. The revival of Birobidzhan as a Jewish center came to a halt toward the end of 1948, as a result of Soviet policy to suppress Jewish activities throughout the U.S.S.R., and purge those involved. While the purges of the late 1930s mainly affected individual Jews holding official positions, those of 1948 and thereafter aimed to destroy any sort of Jewish activity in the region. Thus, most of the local Jewish writers were imprisoned, the Birobidzhan Jewish theater was closed, teaching of Yiddish in local schools was discontinued, and a great number of Yiddish books were removed from the Shalom Aleichem Library. Jewish immigration to Birobidzhan ceased, and its Jewish population shrank considerably. The post-Stalin period did not bring any substantial changes to Jewish life in Birobidzhan. Jewish inhabitants comprised less than one-tenth of the general population of the region in 1959, party and administrative positions were not generally held by Jews, and Jewish agriculture was almost nonexistent. In 1970 the Jews numbered 11,452. The sole kolkhoz with a comparatively large Jewish membership is that of Valdheim in the vicinity of the capital, but it is now only a branch of the large kolkhoz "Ilich's Wills" and its Jewish population is diminishing. Such key positions as secretary or chairman of the local party regional and district committees (the district is divided into five administrative counties) were generally not held by Jews, although in 1970 Lev Shapiro was appointed first secretary of the regional Communist Party organization. Of the five deputies to the Council of Nationalities of the U.S.S.R., only a minority was Jewish. The sole expression of Jewish cultural activity in 1970 was a two-page Yiddish newspaper, *Der Birobidzhaner Shtern*, nearly devoid of all Jewish content, which appeared three times weekly and had a circulation of 1,000. There were also a few street signs in Yiddish, and Shalom Aleichem Street remained one of the thoroughfares of the capital. There was one synagogue. All official and public business was conducted exclusively in Russian. N.S. Khrushchev, Soviet premier and first party secretary, stated in an interview for *Le Figaro*, which appeared on April 9, 1958, that "it must be admitted that if we strike a balance we would have to state that the Jewish settlement in Birobidzhan was a failure." He further put the blame for it upon the Soviet Jews, who, according to Khrushchev, never liked collective work and group discipline. It is difficult to ascribe the failure of the Birobidzhan experiment to one single cause. In the history of the Jewish people it belongs to the series of other futile attempts at planned Jewish mass settlement, based on agriculture, whose failure is often attributed to its implicit or explicit negation of the ultimate return to Zion. However, viewed in the context of Soviet Jewish reality, the immediate cause of its failure was undoubtedly the fact that twice, in 1936–37 and in 1948–49, the Stalinist purges put a brutal end to the short periods of developing autonomous Jewish life and culture in Birobidzhan. In the 1990s most remaining Jews immigrated to Israel and the West.

BIBLIOGRAPHY: S. Schwarz, *The Jews in the Soviet Union* (1951), index; idem, in: J. Frumkin (ed.) *Russian Jewry 1917–1967* (1969), 342–95; A.L. Eliav (Benami), *Between Hammer and Sickle* (1969), 176–88; S.W. Baron, *The Russian Jew under Tsars and Soviets* (1964), index; J. Lvavi, *Ha-Hityashevut ha-Yehudit be-Birobidzhan* (1965); A.G. Duker, *Jewish Survival in the World Today* (1939), 47–59; idem, in: *Contemporary Jewish Record* (March–April 1939), 24–26; J. Emiot, *Der Birobidzhaner Inyen* (1960); *Jews in Eastern Europe* (1966ff.), index; Z. Katz, in: *Bulletin on Soviet Jewish Affairs*, 2 (July, 1968); C. Abramsky, in: L. Kochan (ed.), *Jews in Soviet Russia since 1917* (1970), 62–75 (incl. bibl.).

[Jacob Lvavi (Babitzky) / Shimon Redlich]

BIRSTEIN, YOSSEL (1920–2003), Hebrew and Yiddish writer. Born in Poland, Birstein left his hometown at the age of 17 for Australia. During World War II he served in the Australian army and immigrated to Israel in 1950. For several years he was a member of Kibbutz Gevat, where he worked as a shepherd. He then lived in Kiryat Tivon, working in a local bank before settling in Jerusalem, where he held a position at the archives of the Hebrew University. Birstein's early prose was written in Yiddish; Gershon *Shaked in fact considers him to be the definite heir in Israel of Yiddish writer *Shalom Aleikhem. Birstein was introduced to Hebrew readers by Menahem Peri, who translated his stories from Yiddish and published all his works in his series Ha-Sifriah ha-Ḥadashah. Birstein's prose is suffused with melancholy humor, with wisdom and compassion, marked by the author's sensitive observation of people and a fine touch for minute details of everyday life. Birstein is the author of four novels and seven collections of stories. *Ha-Mutavim* ("The Collector," 1982) depicts the world of banks and the stock exchange. *Panim be-Anan* ("A Face in the Cloud," 1991) is the story of old Tishbein, trying to write about his love for a French dancer while being confronted with the fortunes of the dead crook Bitman and his wish to salvage the lost honor of Yiddish literature. The novel is an elegy to European Jewry and to a culture that was brutally destroyed. *Al Tikra Li Iyov* ("Don't Call Me Job," 1996) takes an ironic, gently humorous view of the biblical story. The strains of Job's lament can be heard even in the most mundane and fortunate lives, in that of Shlomo Shapira, who became a millionaire in Australia and later settled in Jerusalem, as well as in that of locksmith Daddon. The comic and the grotesque mark Birstein's realism. His collections of stories include *Midrakhot Ẓarot* ("On Narrow Paths," 1959), *Ketem shel Sheket* ("A Drop of Silence," 1986), *Sippurim mi-Ezor ha-Shalvah* ("Stories from the Realm of Tranquillity," 2004), and others. Several of these collections and novels have been translated into German, Chinese, and Italian. An English translation of the story "Fuchs Was Already Old" is included in M. Gluzman and N. Seidman (eds.), *Israel: A Traveler's Literary Companion* (1996).

BIBLIOGRAPHY: D. Ben-Dor, *Simanim ve-Kolot: Y. Birstein* (1993); M. Peri, "An Interview with Y. Birstein and an Essay," in: *Sippurim mi-Ezor ha-Shalvah* (2004); A. Nowersztern: "The Multi-coloured Patchwork of the Coat of the Prince: On Yossl Birstein's Work," in: *Modern Hebrew Literature* 8-9 (1992), 56-59.

[Anat Feinberg (2nd ed.)]

BIRTH. The injunction to "be fruitful and multiply" (Gen. 1:28) is regarded as the first commandment of the Bible. As a consequence of the disobedience of Eve in the Garden of Eden, the pangs of childbirth were foretold (Gen. 3:16). References to pangs of travail as the most intense of pains are very frequent in the books of the prophets (e.g., Jer. 6:24; 22:23; 49:24; 50:43; and Micah 4:9–10). Midwives assisted in the delivery (Gen. 35:17), and it seems that a birthstool, called *ovnayim*, was often used (Ex. 1:16). The Bible records the deaths of Rachel (Gen. 35:18) and the daughter-in-law of Eli (I Sam. 4:20) in childbirth. The Talmud states that Michal (II Sam. 6:23) also died during childbirth (Sanh. 21a).

Biblical law regarding birth is confined to laying down the period of ritual impurity of the mother (Lev. 12). The mother of a male child is unclean for seven days, followed by a 33-day period of impurity; these periods are doubled in the case of a female child. At the conclusion of these periods a sin-offering and burnt-offering were brought by the mother. According to the Talmud, the sin-offering is incumbent upon her because during the anguish of childbirth, she foreswears any future relations with her husband, which she later regrets (Nid. 31b).

In the Talmud and the Midrash

The sages attributed death during childbirth to neglect of the laws of family purity, failure to separate the dough-offering, and carelessness in kindling the Sabbath lights (Shab. 2:6). Viability began from the time the fetus was six months and one day old, although it was considered as a fact that an eight-month-old fetus was not viable (Tosef., Shah. 15:7; see *Abortion). However, many midrashim and later commentaries report births of a seven-month-old fetus. Thus, according to the commentaries, many of Jacob's sons were born at age seven months. Before birth, it is permissible to perform an embryotomy when the mother's life is in danger, since "her life comes before that of the child." Once the greater part of the child has been born, or his head alone has emerged from the birth canal, he is considered a living being and the mother's life no longer takes precedence (Oho. 7:6). The child is not considered viable until it is 30 days old. No death penalty is therefore incurred for killing a newborn child unless it is certain that he could otherwise have lived for 30 days (Nid. 5:3, Nid. 44b). All work necessary for the delivery of a child may be performed on the Sabbath (Shab. 18:3); if the mother dies during labor, the Sabbath must still be desecrated and all attempts made to save the unborn child (Ar. 7a).

For the purposes of birthdate and setting the time of circumcision, birth is determined by the projection of the fetus' head out of the birth canal (Nid. 42b). Midwives were considered reliable witnesses for accounting for the hour of the birth. The delivery of a child by Caesarean section was not regarded as "an opening of the womb" (Ex. 13:2), and the child had neither the privileges nor the obligations of the firstborn (Bek. 8:2).

Throughout Jewish history, male offspring were desired. However, despite differing opinions, Bet Hillel's position that the birth of a son and a daughter constituted the fulfillment to be fruitful and multiply was eventually accepted (Yev. 62a). In addition, despite contrary opinions in the Talmud, it became accepted that the injunction to be fruitful and multiply was a male and not a female responsibility.

Customs and Folklore Among Ashkenazi Jews

Most of the customs surrounding birth belong to the category of popular folklore, much of which is not specifically Jewish but was adapted from local cultural surroundings (Tosef., Shab. 6:4; Sh. Ar. YD 178). The following biblical selections were recited for a woman in labor: Psalms 20; I Samuel 1; Genesis 21:1–8 or Exodus 8:11. Precious stones and a variety of herbs were used to facilitate delivery, which was usually supervised by an experienced midwife and friends and relatives of the parturient. A magic circle was drawn with chalk or charcoal on the floor of the room to guard against evil spirits. As a good omen for easy and speedy delivery, all the ties and knots in a woman's garments were undone and in some societies all doors in the house were opened wide. If her travail was difficult, the keys of the synagogue were placed in her hand, she was girded with the band of a Torah Scroll, and prayers were recited at the graveside of pious relatives. In extreme danger, prayers were said for the parturient in the synagogue and a Torah scroll was brought to the house and was left in the corner of the birthing chamber. At times the circumference of the cemetery walls was measured and according to their length a number of candles were donated to the synagogue. Mother and child were surrounded by various charms and talismans from the moment of birth until the circumcision (see *Amulet). Most of these charms were to guard them against the female demon *Lilith and her counterparts, such as Frau Holle, and they were known by different names, such as *kimpetsetl* (from *kindbet*, "child bed" and *tsetl*, "a note"), *Shir Hamalos-Tsetl* (from *Shir ha-Ma'alot* – the Song of Degrees), and *Shmir-Tsetl* (from *shemirah*, "guarding"). They were placed above the bed of the woman and above the doorposts of the room. In medieval and early modern Germany, it was customary for the woman to keep an object made out of iron (**BARZEL** – an acronym of Bilhah, Rachel, Zilpah and Leah, Jacob's wives) with her at all times during the weeks following the birth, to protect her from evil spirits. Some of these amulets used kabbalistic names of God, especially the 42-letter name beginning with ABAG YATATZ, which is derived from the abbreviation of the prayer hymn *Anna be-Kho'aḥ*.

A popular custom until modern times, in the case of the birth of a male child, was the vigil ceremony which was performed every night. In Oriental communities it was called *taḥdid*. Friends and relatives nightly gathered at the home of the newborn to recite the *Shema in order to protect the child from demons. Schoolchildren led by their teachers also participated in this ceremony and were rewarded with apples, nuts, and sweets.

Whereas a boy is named at the circumcision, there is no evidence concerning the naming of girls until the 15th century. In early modern sources, we hear of a naming ceremony in the synagogue or at home. In Germany and Western Europe the naming took place in a home ceremony on Sabbath afternoons. Called *Hollekreisch*, the custom originated in German folklore and superstition. This custom, which was observed for boys and girls, included the lifting of the cradle and the giving of a name. For boys, this was a non-Jewish name, a *shem ḥol*, whereas for girls, this was the only naming ceremony. This ritual took place on the afternoon of the Sabbath when the parturient left her home for the first time, about a month after the birth. During the 16th and 17th centuries, in some communities, it became a customary to name girls in the synagogue when the father was called to the reading of the Torah. This custom is still commonly found today. More recently, many families in Israel and the Diaspora have adapted the Sephardi custom of having a special ceremony, often called *Zeved ha-Bat* or *Simḥat Bat*, at which the girl is named.

[Elisheva Baumgarten (2nd ed.)]

Middle Eastern Customs

Among the methods utilized to protect the mother and infant from evil spirits – particularly *Broshah*, the female demon who steals newborn children – was the hanging of a *hamsikah*, an *amulet in the shape of the palm of the hand with fingers, or a seven-branched candelabrum. Amulets containing biblical verses were also used, and it was customary to place sweetmeats under the bed so that the evil spirits would be occupied with eating them. In Salonika it was customary to leave the doors of the house and all its cupboards open during pregnancy to ensure that the mother would not miscarry. It was also customary to measure a string seven times around the grave of a renowned rabbi and then bind it around the stomach of the pregnant woman to ensure an easy pregnancy. The mother and her relatives also prayed at the graves of pious men in the fifth month of her pregnancy. To ensure that the child would be a male, the mother pronounced the intended name of a boy every Friday. She was guarded for 15 days after birth, and blue beads or pieces of ivory and coral were hung above the cradle of the child. Garlic and other plants were hung in the room, and an open hand was painted on the door. An attempt was made to keep the mother awake for the first three days after birth to prevent Lilith from harming her. In Yemen, a festive meal, at which the name was given, was held on the third day. In Kurdistan the mother was not allowed to leave the house after nightfall for 40 days. Since delivery usually takes place now in modern hospitals, most of these traditional customs at childbirth have tended to disappear, particularly since they were primarily based on medieval superstitious folklore. Naming a daughter at the synagogue, however, has been retained in traditional, Conservative, and Reform Jewish practice.

Contemporary Developments in Birth Rituals for Girls

The Jewish feminist movement that began in the 1970s encouraged the development of ceremonies to publicly sanctify the entry of Jewish baby girls into the covenant. By the beginning of the 21st century, public welcomes for baby girls had become normative in American Judaism. Numerous versions of *Brit Bat* (the covenant of a daughter) or *Simḥat Bat* (the joy of a daughter) rituals were available for home and synagogue use by parents and rabbis from all Jewish religious movements. Some of the ceremonies made use of symbols such as candles (*brit ha-nerot*). Although ceremonies for baby girls are most often held in synagogues during services where the Torah is read, many are now conducted at home like those that accompany circumcisions. In Israel the ceremony or party celebrating the birth of a daughter is sometimes called *brita* (a feminization of the word for covenant).

Simḥat bat ceremonies may include a formal welcome by those present as the baby girl is carried in; spelling the child's Hebrew name out with biblical verses; bestowing the priestly benediction and traditional Friday night daughter's blessing; a naming prayer including both father's and mother's names in that of the daughter; explaining the rationale for the name; an expression of thanks for return to good health by the mother (*birkat ha-gomel*); a series of short blessings including the one over wine and sometimes in the format of the seven benedictions (*sheva brakhot*) of the traditional Jewish wedding ceremony; and special added benedictions to the grace after meals after the festive meal (*se'udah shel mitzvah*) which follows the ritual. Often, booklets are printed and distributed which announce the name and provide a "script" for the ceremony so that all present may participate. These manuals serve as vehicles for innovation and as educational tools to enable assimilated Jews and the growing number of non-Jews who attend Jewish life cycle rituals to understand and follow what is going on before them.

Another evolving aspect of contemporary rituals connected with birth is the inclusion of the mother in ceremonies for sons and daughters. Until the last quarter of the 20th century mothers were often absent from the ceremonies for their sons and the naming of their daughters in the synagogue. Today, in some circles the family waits to name the daughter until the mother is able to be present. She may have a Torah honor in the synagogue and recite the prayer for a safe recovery. Both boys and girls may be named as the children of both mother and father. At a circumcision, the mother as well as the father may be in the room and say the prescribed benedictions.

[Rela Mintz Geffen (2nd ed.)]

See also *Circumcision.

BIBLIOGRAPHY: I. Jakobovits, *Jewish Medical Ethics* (1959), 170–91; M. Perlman, *Midrash ha-Refu'ah*, 1 (1926), 18–25; E. Ilinson, in: *Sinai*, 66 (1969/70), 20–49. CUSTOMS AND FOLKLORE: Y. Yehoshua, *Yaldut bi-Y'rushalayim ha-Yeshanah*, 2 (1966), 79–91; Molcho, in: *Saloniki, Ir va-Em be-Yisrael* (1967), 188–93; M. Zadok, *Yehudei Teiman* (1967), 213–4; N.B. Gamlieli, *Telman u-Maḥaneh "Ge'ullah"* (1966). **ADD. BIBLIOGRAPHY:** R. Barkai, *A History of Jewish Gynaecological Texts in the Middle Ages* (1998); E. Baumgarten, *Mothers and Children: Jewish Family Life in Medieval Europe* (2004); R.M. Geffen (ed.), *Celebration & Renewal – Rites of Passage in Judaism* (1993), 12–31; E. Horowitz, "The Eve of Circumcision: A Chapter in the History of Jewish Nightlife," in: *Journal of Social History*, 13 (1989/90), 45–69; M. Klein, *A Time To Be Born: Customs and Folklore of Jewish Birth* (1999); I.G. Marcus, *The Jewish Life Cycle: Rites of Passage From Bib-*

lical To Modern Times (2004); R.L. Millen, *Women, Birth, and Death in Jewish Law and Practice* (2004), 70–108; S. Sabar, "Childbirth and Magic. Jewish Folklore and Material Culture," in: D. Biale (ed.), *Cultures of the Jews: A New History* (2002), 671–722.

BIRTH CONTROL. Jewish tradition ascribed the practice of birth control to the depraved humanity before Noah (Gen. R. 23:2, 4; Rashi to Gen. 4:19, 23). The sole explicit reference in the Bible to what may be considered as some form of birth control occurs in Genesis 38:9–10: the Lord punished Onan by death because he had "spilled his seed on the ground" to prevent the birth of a child from the *levirate marriage to his deceased brother's wife Tamar. On the strength of this passage, and as constituting a deliberate violation of the first commandment to "be fruitful and multiply" (Gen. 1:28), the Talmud sternly inveighs against "bringing forth the seed in vain," considering it a cardinal sin (Nid. 13a). Legislation on contraception proper is to be found in a talmudic passage which permits (or requires, according to another view) the use of a contraceptive tampon by minor, pregnant, or lactating women, to prevent any danger to their own or their offspring's life resulting from a conception under those circumstances (Yev. 12b). A permissive ruling extended to women, but not to men, also allows for the use of a "cup of roots" or "potion of sterility" (Tosef., Yev. 8:4), probably some oral contraceptive known to the ancients, which was to produce temporary or in certain dosages even permanent sterility. While the medieval codes strangely omit any reference to physical birth control devices, they codify the permissive ruling on the oral sterilizing agent (Sh. Ar., EH, 5:12). It is in the rabbinic responsa, especially those of the past 200 years, that the attitude of Jewish law to birth control is defined and discussed in great detail. The many hundreds of rulings recorded in these responsa consider urgent medical reasons as the only valid justification for certain contraceptive precautions. Jewish law regards such decisions as capital judgments and it would, therefore, insist on dealing with each case on its individual merits and on the evidence of competent medical opinion. Where some grave hazard to the mother, however remote, is feared, as a result of pregnancy, the rabbinic attitude is usually quite liberal, all the more readily if the commandment of procreation (which technically requires having a son and a daughter) has already been fulfilled. Under no circumstances, however, does Jewish law sanction any contraceptive acts or safeguards on the part of the male, nor does it ever tolerate the use or distribution of birth control devices outside marriage. While the law proscribes sexual intercourse among spouses in times of famine (Ta'an. 11a; Sh. Ar. OḤ 240:12; 574:4), this is not to be taken as a recognition of the economic argument in favor of birth control. On the contrary, the restriction from which childless couples are in any case excluded is meant simply to curb the pleasures of marital indulgences at a time of great national suffering, just as conjugal relations are among the experiences of pleasure and comfort forbidden on days of national or private mourning. More characteristic of the spirit, if not the letter, of Jewish law is the story related in a famous 13th-century moralistic work: A poor person complained that he could not afford to support any more children and asked a sage for permission to prevent his wife from becoming pregnant again. The sage said: "When a child is born, the Holy One, blessed be He, provides the milk beforehand in the mother's breast; therefore, do not worry!" But the man continued to fret. Then a son was born to him. After a while the child became ill and the father turned to the sage: "Pray for my son that he shall live!" "To you applies the verse," exclaimed the sage, "'Suffer not thy mouth to bring thy flesh into guilt'" (Eccles. 5:5; *Sefer Ḥasidim*, ed. R. Margoliot (1957), no. 520). The sources of Jewish law and morals do not present the problem of "the population explosion" as relevant to birth control. According to some rabbinic authorities, the restrictions on birth control do not necessarily apply to non-Jews as the latter are not held to be bound by the commandment to "be fruitful and multiply" (see *Mishneh le-Melekh*, to Maim., Yad, Melakhim 10:7). The threat of a "population explosion" is less likely to agitate a people that for most of its history has been threatened with virtual annihilation and is now haunted by the specter of "the vanishing Jew," due to the gross imbalance between a low natural increase and a high artificial decrease through drift, assimilation, and intermarriage. In recent times, the practice of birth control has invariably been more prevalent among Jews than other groups living in the same general society, as shown by the disproportionately low Jewish birthrates according to comparative surveys in America, in Europe, and notably in Israel. In Israel, fertility rates for Jewish women in 1995 were down to 2.6 children, as opposed to a high of 4.0 in 1950 and as opposed to 4.7 in 1995 among Israeli Arabs (and 7.4 in Gaza). The Jewish birthrate is appreciably higher only among the Orthodox who, for religious reasons, do not usually resort to birth control. In common with the attitude of most Protestant denominations, Reform Judaism would generally leave the decision on birth control to the individual conscience, recognizing social and economic factors no less than the medical motivation.

BIBLIOGRAPHY: D.M. Feldman, *Birth Control in Jewish Law* (1969); E. Waldenberg, *Ẓiẓ Eli'ezer*, 9 (1967), 208–25 (extensive halakhic treatise); J.Z. Lauterbach, in: CCARY, 37 (1927), 369–84 (early Reform view); I. Jakobovits, *Jewish Medical Ethics* (1959), 167ff., and passim; idem, *Journal of a Rabbi* (19672), 146–7, 163, 213–20; J. Levy, in: *No'am*, 11 (1968), 167–77. **ADD. BIBLIOGRAPHY:** S. DellaPergola, "Demographic Trends in Israel and Palestine: Prospects and Policy Implications," in: AJYB (2003), 25–32.

[Immanuel Jakobovits]

BIRTHDAY. The celebration of birthdays is unknown in traditional Jewish ritual. A comparatively late exception, however, is the *bar mitzvah and the bat mitzvah. The only reference to a birthday in the Bible is that celebrated by Pharaoh (Gen. 40:20). In Reform and Conservative synagogues, special prayers of thanksgiving are recited on the occasion of significant birthdays (e.g., 50th, 70th, 80th, etc.) and at silver and golden wedding anniversaries.

BIBLIOGRAPHY: *Rabbi's Manual* (1928–1962²), 45–49, CCAR (Reform); J. Harlow (ed.), *Likkutei Tefillah, A Rabbi's Manual* (1965), Conservative, 51–55.

BIRZAI (Lith. **Biržai**; Yid. ביריז), district capital in northern Lithuania, near the Latvian border. Jews started to settle there in the beginning of the 17th century. Birzai was one of the three leading communities of the "*medinah* [province] of Zamut" (Zhmud) in the mid-17th to mid-18th century. A small Karaite community also existed there. The Jewish population numbered 1,040 in 1760; 1,685 in 1847; and 2,510 in 1897 (57% of the total). In 1915 the Jews were expelled from Birzai by the Russian military authorities. After the war some of the exiles returned. The Jewish community developed during the period of Lithuanian independence (1918–39). There were approximately 3,000 Jews living in Birzai in 1934 (36% of the total). Three of the 12 city councilors were Jewish. Hebrew and Yiddish schools and a *talmud torah* were in operation. Most Jews earned their livelihoods from trade in wood products and flax; several factories for weaving and spinning were owned by Jews.

Shortly after the occupation of the town by the Germans in June 1941, the Lithuanian nationalists began to murder and maltreat the Jews. A ghetto was established and on August 8, 1941, Lithuanians executed 500 Jewish men. The remaining Jews were similarly murdered shortly thereafter.

BIBLIOGRAPHY: *Yahadut Lita*, 2 (1967), 292–4. **ADD. BIBLIOGRAPHY:** PK Lita, s.v.

[Yehuda Slutsky / Shmuel Spector (2nd ed.)]

BIRZULA (from 1935, Kotovsk), town in Ukraine. Until May 1903 it was a village, and under the "Temporary Regulations" of 1882 (see *May Laws) Jews were prohibited from settling there. The Jewish inhabitants engaged in trade and crafts. They were attacked in a pogrom on October 24, 1905. In 1919, 50 Jews were massacred in Birzula by the followers of Simon *Petlyura. The Jewish population numbered 2,507 in 1926 (25% of the total) and 2,735 in 1939. In the Soviet period they earned their living as blue-collar workers, artisans, and clerks. Birzula was occupied by the Germans on August 6, 1941. In the same month, with the help of the Romanians, they murdered 113 Jews. A ghetto was established, and in November the Jews were marched toward Dubossary, with 650 murdered on the way. Hundreds of Jews from Bessarabia and Bukovina were deported to the area; most were killed or died of starvation or disease. Only 95 were alive on September 1, 1943.

BIBLIOGRAPHY: *Judenpogrome in Russland*, 1 (1909); E.D. Rosenthal, *Megillat ha-Tevaḥ*, 1 (1927); Jewish Colonization Association, *Rapport pour l'année 1925*, (1927), 160–243. **ADD. BIBLIOGRAPHY:** PK Ukrainah, s.v.

[Shmuel Spector (2nd ed.)]

BISCHHEIM, French town in the department of the Bas-Rhin. Jews settled there after their expulsion from *Colmar in 1512. H. *Cerfberr, one of the general syndics of Alsace Jewry in the second half of the 18th century, lived in Bischheim, as did his brother-in-law, David *Sinzheim. Cerfberr set up a foundation on behalf of the community with a capital of 175,000 livres for charitable activities and education. There were 473 Jews living in Bischheim in 1784. The wooden synagogue, built in 1781, was replaced by a new one in 1838. It was sacked during the German occupation in World War II, destroyed in 1944, and rebuilt in 1959. The Jewish community in 1968 had 360 members. It has a *mikveh* which belonged to David Sinzheim.

BIBLIOGRAPHY: M. Ginsburger, *Histoire de la communauté israélite de Bischheim au Saum* (1937); E. Scheid, *Histoire des Juifs d'Alsace* (1887), 102, 175, 249; R. Berg, *La persécution raciale* (1947), 181; Z. Szajkowski, *Analytical Franco-Jewish Gazetteer* (1966), 45, 249.

[Roger Berg]

°**BISCHOFF, ERICH** (c. 1867–1936), German biblical and talmudic scholar. Bischoff repeatedly served as expert on Judaism in court cases, furnishing memoranda on the *blood libel, the ethics of the Talmud and the Shulḥan Arukh, etc. He refused to be termed either anti-or philo-Semitic, but was criticized by Jewish writers and organizations for his views (cf. C. Bloch, *Blut und Eros im Judentum*, 1935). In his *Klarheit in der Ostjudenfrage* (1916) he suggested the introduction of a special *Ostjuden* tax to be raised by Jewish organizations either to improve the conditions of unwanted Eastern European Jews in Germany or to settle them in Palestine. Among Bischoff's published works are also *Kritische Geschichte der Thalmud-Uebersetzungen aller Zeiten und* Zungen… (1889), *Rabbinische Fabeln ueber Talmud, Schulchan Aruch, Kol Nidre…* (1922), *Das Blut im* juedischen Schrifttum und Brauch (1929), and *Das Buch vom Schulchan Aruch* (1942⁴). Bischoff also edited and translated – from an Oxford manuscript – the famous anti-Christian tract *Toledot Yeshu* (*Ein juedisch-deutsches Leben Jesu*, 1895). Though Bischoff pretended to be objective in his judgment on Judaism, his work misinterpreted Jewish sources and was fully exploited by the Nazis.

[Arnold Paucker]

BISCHOFFSHEIM, family of bankers in Belgium, Britain, and France. The family's founder RAPHAEL (NATHAN; 1773–1814) was born in Bischoffsheim on the Tauber and settled as a young man in Mainz, where he became a prominent merchant and president of the Jewish community. His elder son, LOUIS (LUDWIG) RAPHAEL (1800–1873) found work at a banking house in Frankfurt. When he was twenty he moved to Amsterdam where he established a bank. Through his marriage to Amalie Goldschmidt, he became related to Europe's banking aristocracy. His business expanded rapidly and in 1827 he established a branch in Antwerp, in 1836 together with the Goldschmidt family a London branch known as Bischoffsheim and Goldschmidt, and in 1846 another branch in Paris. In 1848 he moved to Paris, where his bank cooperated with great French houses in national and international transactions. At some stages in the development of his banking busi-

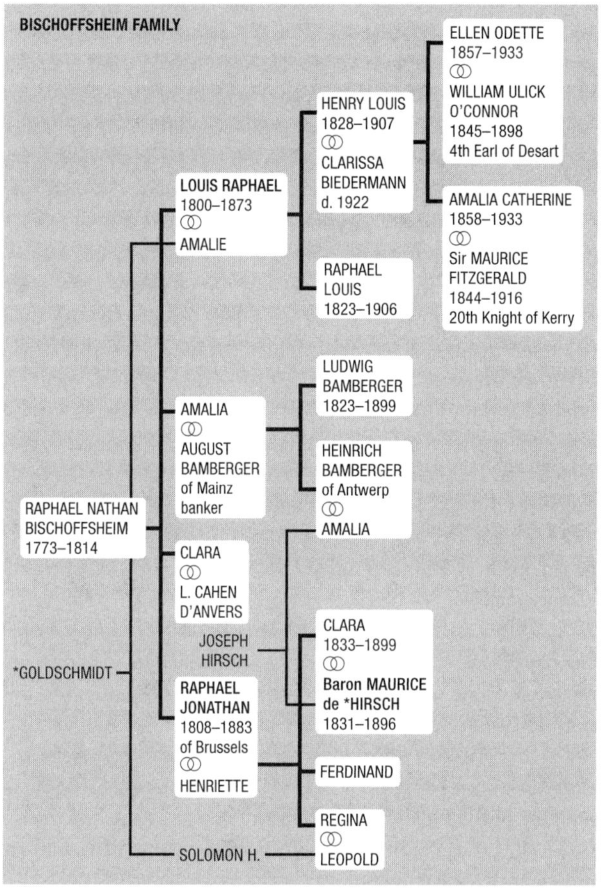

ness, he had the help of his nephew, Ludwig *Bamberger. His many philanthropies were devoted to charitable and educational purposes, including support of the Association Philotechnique, of which he was president, and the Athenée Theater, which he founded.

His brother, RAPHAEL JONATHAN (1808–1883), moved to Brussels in 1830 after Belgium achieved its independence and became one of that country's most influential financial figures. In 1850 he helped found the National Bank of Belgium and served on its board of directors for twenty years. He was adviser to the royal house and in 1862 became a senator, who was regarded by his colleagues as the principal authority in his field. He was an active member of the Jewish consistory and was well known for his benefactions, such as the endowment of a chair for Arabic at the University of Brussels. A street in that city bears his name. His daughter, Clara, married Baron Maurice de *Hirsch in 1855.

Louis Raphael's son RAPHAEL LOUIS (1823–1906), who was born in Amsterdam, succeeded his father as head of the Paris bank. His principal outside interest lay in astronomy, and his generous gifts made possible the building of a number of observatories, the best-known of them at Mont Gras, near Nice. In 1881 he was elected to the Chamber of Deputies.

Louis Raphael's second son, HENRY LOUIS (1828–1907), married Clarissa Biedermann, the sister-in-law of James *Stern of Stern Brothers of London. He headed the London house of Bischoffsheim and Goldschmidt. In conjunction with other financial institutions his bank participated in many international projects, including railway construction in France, Italy, and the Balkans, and the government financing of Turkey, Egypt, and various Latin American countries. In 1881 his eldest daughter, ELLEN ODETTE (1857–1933), married William Ulick O'Connor, the fourth Earl of Desart, and lived at the Desart seat at Kilkenny until her husband's death in 1898. Despite her anti-suffrage agitation, she became the first woman senator of the Irish Free State. This signal honor was the product of her efforts on behalf of Ireland's cultural and economic welfare. Lady Desart remained an active Jew throughout her life, holding office in a number of Jewish philanthropic organizations and supporting them generously. Her sister AMALIA married Sir Maurice Fitzgerald, 20th Knight of Kerry. She also retained her Jewish interests, was active in support of the work of the Jewish National Fund, and organized a project for the rescue of Jewish children from German-controlled territories in the 1930s.

BIBLIOGRAPHY: P.H. Emden, *Jews of Britain* (1943), 536–8; idem, *Money Powers of Europe* (1937). **ADD BIBLIOGRAPHY:** M. Jolles, *Jews and the Carlton Club, with notes on Benjamin Disraeli, Henri Louis Bischoffsheim and Saul Isaac, MP* (2002).

[Joachim O. Ronall]

BISGYER, MAURICE (1897–1973), U.S. social worker and administrator. Bisgyer was born in Brooklyn and graduated from New York University in 1918, beginning his career in Jewish communal service a year later as executive director of the Baltimore Jewish Education Alliance, a post which he held for three years. After a year with YMHA in Trenton, N.J., he became director of the Jewish Community Center in Washington. In the 1930s, his pioneering effort in obtaining sponsors willing to facilitate the entry of Jewish refugees into the United States made it possible to bring 15,000 refugees from Europe to the United States. President Hoover appointed him to the National Advisory Committee on Education in 1929, and President Roosevelt reappointed him in 1933. In 1946, he became a member of Attorney General Tom Clark's Committee on Juvenile Delinquency.

In 1937, Bisgyer became chief administrative officer of the B'nai B'rith, and held the position of executive vice president until his retirement in 1964, when he was named honorary vice president. In addition to his work in the United States, he traveled all over the world and took part in meetings with leaders of governments and with Popes John XXIII and Paul VI. He played an important role in arranging the meeting of President Truman with Chaim *Weizmann in March 1948, to which he accompanied Weizmann. Bisgyer was also a pioneer in Jewish social service. He was co-author (with Henry Monsky) of *Man and his Work* (1947) and wrote *Challenge and Encounter* (1967).

[Frederick R. Lachman]

BISHOP, JOEY (Joseph Gottlieb; 1918–), U.S. actor and comedian. Born in the Bronx, New York, and raised in South Philadelphia, Bishop earned fame as an actor, comedian, talk show host, and member of the "Rat Pack." After dropping out of high school and serving a stint in the U.S. Army during WWII, Bishop began doing stand-up comedy at clubs in New York, Cleveland, Miami, and Philadelphia. He adopted the surname "Bishop" while working with Morris Spector and Sammy Reisman in the comedy troupe "The Bishop Trio," whose members borrowed the name from their chauffeur. During the 1950s, Bishop's relationship with Frank Sinatra led to his inclusion in the "Rat Pack," in which he played the role of the straight-man in their stage performances, and wrote much of the group's comic material. Sinatra considered Bishop such an integral part of the "Rat Pack" and its enormous success that he called Bishop "the hub of the big wheel." Bishop co-starred alongside his fellow "Rat Pack" members in *Ocean's Eleven* (1960). He went on to host two versions of *The Joey Bishop Show* during the 1960s. Bishop also owns the distinction of having co-hosted *The Tonight Show* (starring Johnny Carson) more times than anyone else, 177. His other notable screen credits include *The Deep Six* (1958), *The Naked and the Dead* (1958), *Texas Across the River* (1966), *Valley of the Dolls* (1967), and *The Delta Force* (1986).

[Walter Driver (2nd ed.)]

BISLICHES (Bisseliches), MORDECAI (Marcus) LEIB (1786–1851), bibliophile and rabbinic scholar. Bisliches left his native Brody, Galicia, to lead an unsettled life. In 1816 he went to Paris where he successfully engaged in business. There, in association with his brother Ephraim, he prepared for publication Isaac *Abrabanel's *Yeshu'ot Meshiḥo* from a manuscript in the Bibliothèque Nationale (1828). Bisliches returned home, but soon left again, this time for Holland and England, always searching for rare books and manuscripts. On a third journey he went to Italy where he made many discoveries, and on his return prepared the following works for publication: Shem Tov b. Joseph *Falaquera's *Sefer ha-Nefesh* (1835) and *Moreh ha-Moreh* (1837, 1961²); Samuel ibn *Tibbon's *Yikkavu ha-Mayim* (1837), with a largely autobiographical introduction; *Naḥmanides' novellae to tractate *Shabbat* under the title *Oẓar Neḥmad* (1837); Abba Mari b. Moses (of Lunel)'s *Minḥat Kena'ot* and *Sefer ha-Yare'aḥ* (1838), with a letter concerning Maimonides' Guide; and Abraham *Ibn Ezra's *Sefat Yeter* (1838), with an introduction by M. Letteris. In 1846 Bisliches, in partnership with S.G. Stern, sold 111 manuscripts in 102 volumes to the archduchess Marie Louise of Parma for 8,500 lire; they were added to the *De'Rossi Collection in the Palatine Library. These manuscripts were basically the collection of the 18th-century bibliophile and bookdealer Moses Benjamin *Foà (b. 1729), who was book purveyor to the dukes of Modena. Bisliches also published *Ha-Palit* (1850), a catalog of 80 of his rare Hebrew manuscripts prepared by L. Zunz with annotations by Senior Sachs.

BIBLIOGRAPHY: Loevinson, in: RMI, 7 (1933), 477ff.; Y. Colombo, *ibid.*, 34 (1968), 492.

°BISMARCK, OTTO VON (1815–1898), Prussian statesman and from 1871 first chancellor of the German Empire. His attitude to Jews and Judaism was ambivalent. In 1847, when he was simply a conservative Eastelbian deputy in the Prussian "Vereinigte Landtag," he strongly opposed opening senior governmental positions to Jews. Later he was attacked by antisemites for "being duped by Jewish financiers" (their main target being G. von *Bleichroeder), and for passing the laws of 1869 and 1871 which abolished restrictions based on religious differences, first in the "Norddeutsche Bund," later in the newly founded Deutsche Reich. This legislation, however, was mainly directed by political expediency, while Bismarck's relations with Bleichroeder were financially beneficial to both men. The Jewish Liberal parliamentarians E. *Lasker and L. *Bamberger supported Bismarck in the early years, but when he turned to the Conservatives after 1878 they became his bitter adversaries.

Although Bismarck regarded the rabidly antisemitic court preacher Adolph *Stoecker with disdain, he appreciated Stoecker's services in opposing socialism. In 1878, during the Congress of *Berlin, Bismarck generally supported a policy favorable to the Jews, which resulted in the incorporation of written guarantees in the peace treaties assuring their equality in the Balkan states, in particular in *Romania. A petition (bearing 250,000 signatures) demanding the dismissal of Jews from all government positions (1881) was ignored by Bismarck, who was suspicious of all popular manifestations. However, only apostates were allowed to reach the upper echelons, while the careers of the few Jews employed by the state were severely restricted. In 1885–86, Bismarck supported the expulsion from Prussia of thousands of Russian and Austrian citizens, including around 9,000 Jews. Bismarck, who was contemptuous of all things Polish, despised the East European Jews and adopted the prejudices against *Ostjuden* current even among the Jewish community in Germany. He was also suspicious of the connection between Jewish *Reform in religion and political radicalism, and had a higher opinion of Jewish *Orthodoxy. In the early years of his political career, Bismarck had the support of the vast majority of German Jewry, but he gradually lost it later, as Jews in Germany increasingly turned toward radical liberalism. Concerning his own religious attitudes, Bismarck cultivated strong pietist attitudes, so that he had a vast knowledge of Old Testament.

BIBLIOGRAPHY: O. Joehlinger, *Bismarck und die Juden…* (1921); H. Neubach, *Die Ausweisungen von Polen und Juden aus Preussen, 1885–86…* (1967), index; E. Hamburger, in: YLBI, 9 (1964), 216, 220–2; N.M. Gelber, *ibid.*, 5 (1960), 221–48; D.S. Landes, *ibid.*, 5 (1960), 201–20; **ADD. BIBLIOGRAPHY:** F. Stern, *Gold and Iron* (1978); O. Pflanze, *Bismarck*, 2 (1990), 70–85 and 318–320; Wehler, *Deutsche Gesellschaftsgeschichte*, 3 (1995), 961–964; A. Hopp, *Otto von Bismarck aus der Sicht des juedischen Buergertums* (1999).

[Henry Wasserman / Marcus Pyka (2nd ed.)]

BISTRITA (Rom. **Bistriţa**; Hg. **Beszterce**; Ger. **Bistritz**), town in Northern Transylvania, Romania; within Hungary until 1918 and between 1940 and 1944. The town was established by Saxon immigrants during the 12th century. It was populated over the centuries mostly by German-speaking people, but later Romanians and also Hungarians started to live there. After the prohibition on Jewish settlement there was lifted after 1848, as in general in Transylvania, Jews began to settle in Bistrita, mainly from Bukovina and Galicia. The community in Bistrita was Orthodox with a strong ḥasidic element although there were also Jews who adopted the German and Hungarian culture and language. During the second half of the 19th century the Jewish community there developed and grew strongly. The first Zionist youth organization in Bistrita, in Hungary, Ivriyah, was founded in 1901 by Nissan Kahan, who corresponded with Theodor *Herzl. In World War I, 138 Jews of Bistrita were mobilized in the army. After the war the central office of Orthodox Jewry in Transylvania was established in Bistrita. It represented 80 communities (135,000 persons) and was headed by the rabbi of Bistrita, Solomon Zalman Ullmann, until his death in 1930. Between the two world wars there was an important Zionist movement in the town. There was a large and important yeshivah in Bistrita under the direction of the rabbi.

The Jewish population of the city numbered 718 in 1891 (out of a total of 9,100); 1,316 in 1900 (out of 12,155); 2,198 in 1930 (out of 14,128); and 2,358 in 1941 (out of 16,282). In 1941 the Hungarian authorities deported several dozen Jewish families from Bistrita to *Kamenets-Podolski in the Ukraine, were they were murdered by Hungarian soldiers. In the course of World War II, the Jews were subjected to many restrictions, and Jewish males of military age were drafted into forced labor service. Early in May 1944 the Jews were concentrated in a ghetto set up at the so-called Stamboli Farm, located about two miles from the city. At its peak the ghetto, consisting of a number of barracks and pigsties, held close to 6,000 Jews, including those brought in from the neighboring communities in Beszterce-Naszód County. Among these were the Jews of Borgóbeszterce, Borgóprund, Galacfalva, Kisilva, Marosborgó, Nagyilva, Nagysajó, Naszód, Óradna, and Romoly. The ghetto was liquidated with the deportation of the Jews to Auschwitz in two transports on June 2 and June 6, 1944.

The 1,300 Jews who resettled in Bistrita in 1947 included survivors from the camps, former residents of neighboring villages, and others liberated from camps in *Transnistria and other places. Subsequently, the Jewish population declined steadily as a result of emigration to Israel, the United States, and Canada. By 2002, only 15 mostly elderly Jews lived in the city.

BIBLIOGRAPHY: E. Pistiner, *Bistritz* (Ger., 1953). **ADD. BIBLIOGRAPHY:** R.L. Braham, *Politics of Genocide: The Holocaust in Hungary* (1994^2); PK Romanyah, 101–4.

[Yehouda Marton /
Paul Schveiger and Randolph Braham (2nd ed.)]

BITAN AHARON (Heb. בִּיתַן אַהֲרֹן), moshav in central Israel, in the Ḥefer Plain, affiliated with Tenu'at ha-Moshavim, founded in 1936 by pioneers from East and Central Europe. Its economy was based principally on citrus plantations. It also had a summer vacation center and a rest home for civil servants. In 2002 the population of Bitan Aharon was 505. The village is named after the Canadian Zionist Aharon (Archibald J.) Freiman.

[Efraim Orni]

BITBURG CONTROVERSY. The "Bitburg Controversy" of 1985 constituted one of the most acrimonious confrontations between any U.S. administration and the American Jewish community. At stake was the planned visit by U.S. President Ronald W. Reagan in the company of West German Chancellor Helmut Kohl to the Bitburg Military Cemetery, which contained the graves of 49 members of the Waffen-SS.

Ostensibly, Kohl invited Reagan to accompany him to a German military cemetery during the state visit to celebrate the normalization of relations between their two countries on the 40th anniversary of the end of World War II. In fact, however, ever since coming to power in 1982, the conservative Kohl had endeavored to rehabilitate as many Germans who had served the Third Reich as possible. In 1983, for example, his government had removed the veterans' organizations of the Waffen-SS from a list of extremist right-wing groups on which the West German Ministry of Interior was required to make annual reports to Parliament, and Kohl had repeatedly blocked demands by the opposition Social Democrats to ban the highly controversial reunions of former Waffen-SS members. Kohl's request to have Reagan go to Bitburg was thus part of a strategy to rewrite recent German history and curry favor with the most reactionary elements of the West German electorate.

Reagan's planned trip to Germany first drew fire because it did not include a stop at the site of a Nazi concentration camp. At a press conference on March 21, 1985, Reagan explained that "since the German people have very few alive that remember even the war, and certainly none of them who were adults and participating in any way … they have a feeling and a guilt feeling that's been imposed upon them." Thus, he considered a visit to a concentration camp "unnecessary." Reagan's comments drew a sharp response from Menachem Z. Rosensaft, the founding chairman of the International Network of Children of Jewish Holocaust Survivors. Writing in *The New York Times* on March 30, he pointed out that all Germans who were the same age as the president certainly remembered the war, and that two years earlier he had told a gathering of thousands of Holocaust survivors that the Holocaust must never be forgotten. Rosensaft noted that while it was "politically advantageous for [Reagan] to speak about the Holocaust to Jewish audiences in the United States, he does not want to risk offending anyone – even Nazis – in Germany."

On April 11, the White House announced that the Bitburg cemetery was on Reagan's itinerary, and that Reagan and Kohl would lay a wreath there "in a spirit of reconciliation, in a spirit of forty years of peace, in a spirit of economic and military compatibility." Kenneth J. Bialkin, chairman of the Conference of Presidents of Major Jewish Organizations, called Reagan's decision to visit Bitburg but not Dachau "deeply offensive," and noted author and Holocaust survivor Elie *Wiesel, then chairman of the United States Holocaust Memorial Council, told *The New York Times* that he could not believe that the president "would visit a German military cemetery and refuse to visit Dachau or any other concentration camp."

At a press conference on April 18, Reagan made matters worse by appearing to equate dead German soldiers with the victims of the Holocaust. "They were victims," he said of the soldiers buried at Bitburg, "just as surely as the victims in the concentration camps." Reagan's comments drew angry responses from American Jewish leaders. Rabbi Alexander Schindler, president of the Union of American Hebrew Congregations, described Reagan's remarks as a "distortion of history, a perversion of language, and a callous offense to the Jewish community."

A long-scheduled ceremony in the White House on April 19, awarding, the Congressional Medal of Achievement, provided the charismatic Wiesel with an unprecedented opportunity to publicly confront the White House on national television. Despite fierce pressure to mute the confrontation with Reagan, whose strong support of Israel was valued, Wiesel implored him not to go to Bitburg. "That place," he told the president during a nationally televised White House ceremony, "is not your place. Your place is with the victims of the SS." Other Jewish leaders similarly called on Reagan to reconsider, as did 53 U.S. senators on April 15, and 101 members of the U.S. House of Representatives on April 19 in bipartisan letters to the president.

Immediately after the public castigation by Elie Wiesel, the White House announced that Bergen-Belsen had been added to the president's German itinerary. Two days later, Menachem Rosensaft, addressing thousands of Holocaust survivors gathered in Philadelphia, called on survivors, children of survivors, and American war veterans to confront Reagan at the gates of Bergen-Belsen. If the president insisted "on going to Bitburg," Rosensaft said, "we do not need him and we do not want him in Bergen-Belsen."

Former President Richard M. Nixon, former Secretary of State Henry Kissinger, and conservative columnist William F. Buckley, among others, endorsed the Bitburg visit, and several public opinion polls indicated that only about 52 percent of Americans were opposed to it. West German officials, meanwhile, pressured the Reagan Administration to stand fast. On April 19, Alfred Dregger, the chairman of Kohl's parliamentary group, wrote to U.S. senators who had urged Reagan to change his itinerary that his only brother had died on the Eastern Front in 1944, and that "If you call upon your President to refrain from the noble gesture he plans to make at the military cemetery in Bitburg, I must consider this to be an insult to my brother and my comrades who were killed in action."

Reagan's insistence on going through with the Bitburg visit, and his attempt to combine back-to-back tributes to the Jewish victims of the Holocaust at Bergen-Belsen and to German soldiers at Bitburg, served primarily to offend the Jewish community in general and Holocaust survivors and their families in particular. "President Reagan and Chancellor Kohl have embarked on a macabre tour, an obscene package deal, of Bergen-Belsen and Bitburg," declared Menachem Rosensaft at a protest demonstration at Bergen-Belsen on May 5, minutes after the two leaders had left for Bitburg. "Today we say to them that they can either honor the memory of the victims of Belsen, or they can honor the SS. They cannot do both. And by entering Bitburg, they desecrate the memory of all those who were murdered by the SS, and of all those whom they pretended to commemorate here at Belsen."

In a short speech at the U.S. Air Force base at Bitburg on May 5, Reagan said: "Our duty today is to mourn the human wreckage of totalitarianism, and today, in Bitburg Cemetery, we commemorated the potential good and humanity that was consumed back then, 40 years ago." President Reagan and West German Chancellor Helmut Kohl spoke about the importance of Holocaust remembrance beside the mass-graves of the Nazi concentration camp of Bergen-Belsen, and then proceeded to the Bitburg military cemetery where they participated in a wreath-laying in memory of German soldiers killed during World War II. The visit to Bergen-Belsen was widely seen as a desperate attempt by the White House staff to deflect the controversy over Reagan's agreement to join Kohl at Bitburg during the president's long-planned state visit to Germany.

In fact, however, as a *New York Times* editorial observed on May 6, Reagan's decision to go through with the Bitburg visit was a "blunder," one of the few times that he lost a confrontation in the court of public opinion. Known as the great communicator, Reagan found that Wiesel and others could get their message across to the mass media and the normally sure-footed White House was reeling. From the perspective of two decades, the German chancellor attempt to rehabilitate the reputation of the Waffen-SS has also failed. New research and public exhibitions in German museums further link them to the crimes of the Holocaust. It was, however, regarded by many observers as one of American Jewry's finest moment, when in the words of Wiesel, "truth was spoken to power."

BIBLIOGRAPHY: I. Levkov (ed.), *Bitburg and Beyond: Encounters in American, German and Jewish* (1986); D.E. Lipstadt, "*The Bitburg Controversy,*" in: *American Jewish Year Book*, 1987; E. Wiesel, *And the Sea is Never Full* (1999), 225–50; C.E. Silberman, *A Certain People: American Jews and Their Lives Today* (1985), 360–66.

[Michael Berenbaum (2nd ed.)

BITHIAH, name given by the rabbis to the daughter of Pharaoh who found the infant Moses. Many legends are told of her in the *aggadah*. The name Bithiah ("daughter of God") was given her as a reward for her devotion in treating Moses as her own child (Lev. R. 1:3). Her purpose in bathing in the Nile was to cleanse herself of the impurity of the idolatry rampant in Egypt (Sot. 12b). When her handmaidens refused to disobey the royal decree and save the Israelite child, her arm was lengthened miraculously so that she could reach the casket in which Moses lay; as soon as she reached it she was cured of her leprosy. She called the child Moses, not only because she had "drawn" him out of the water, but because she knew he would "draw" the children of Israel out of Egypt (Mid. Hag. to Ex. 2:10). Although Moses had many names, God called him only by the name Bithiah gave him (Lev. R. 1:3). At Moses' intercession, Bithiah was not afflicted by any of the ten plagues and therefore was the only female firstborn to be spared in Egypt (Ex. R. 18:3). She became a proselyte and married Caleb because, as she had opposed her father, he would oppose the spies (Lev. R. 1:3). Bithiah was one of those who entered Paradise in her lifetime (Mid. Prov. 31:15). She is numbered among the 22 women of valor (Mid. Hag. to Gen. 23:1, s.v. *Takom*).

BIBLIOGRAPHY: Ginzberg, Legends, 2 (1946), 266ff., 369; 5 (1947), 398ff., 435.

BITHYNIA, district of Asia Minor identified in the Talmud with the biblical Tubal (Yoma 10a). There is information, dated from 139 B.C.E., of a Jewish settlement in Amysos which was included in the territory of Bithynia during the period of its expansion (Sampsames in I Macc. 15:23 being identified by Schuerer and others with Amysos in Pontos). Philo, too, testifies to the existence of a Jewish settlement there (*De Legatione ad Gaium*, 281). A Jewish tombstone with a Greek inscription found near the Bosporus marks the burial place of a Jew called Shabbetai who served as elder, scribe, and leader to a Jewish community which is called παλαιοι ("The Ancients," REJ, 23 (1893), 167–71). Talmudic sources (Av. Zar. 2:4; Tosef., Av. Zar. 4:13; Tosef., Shev. 5:9) frequently mention cheeses from Bet-Unyaki which were forbidden "because the majority of calves of that place are offered as sacrifices to idols" (Av. Zar. 34b). This Bet-Unyaki is identified with Bithynia, whose excellent cheeses are also attested to by Pliny (*Natural History* 11:241). The spread of Christianity in Bithynia at the beginning of the second century so alarmed its governor, Pliny the younger (c. 112), that he applied to Trajan for instructions on how to deal with it. The detailed answer given by Trajan exerted a decisive influence for some generations on Rome's policy toward Christianity.

BIBLIOGRAPHY: Epstein, Mishnah, 1104–05; Schuerer, Gesch, 3 (1909[4]), 23; Frey, Corpus, 2 (1952), 50–52; Neubauer, Géogr, 262–3.

[Abraham Schalit]

BITTELMAN, ALEXANDER (1890–1982), U.S. Communist leader and journalist. Bittelman was born and grew up in Odessa, Russia. He joined the socialist *Bund* at an early age, then emigrated to America in 1912 and settled in New York City. Bittelman studied engineering, worked for the People's Relief Committee, and in 1919 became editor of *Der Kampf*, the organ of the Jewish Communist Federation. In the same year he joined the American Communist Party, soon becoming its "Jewish specialist." He was sent to Moscow in 1922 to obtain funds for establishing the party's Yiddish paper, the *Morning Freiheit*. From 1923 to 1928 Bittelman worked in the party's national office in Chicago. He traveled to India on a political mission; then edited the *Communist* upon his return. He devoted himself to writing articles of a historical and ideological nature, several of which were published in 1937 in his *Milestones of the History of the Communist Party*. A member of the Communist Party National Committee after World War II, Bittelman also served as general secretary of the Morning Freiheit Association, which he sought to reorganize as a center for Jewish Communist propaganda and culture. In 1943 his 63-page *Jewish Unity for Victory* was published. Bittelman was indicted under the Smith Act in 1951 for conspiring to overthrow the government and was jailed in 1955 for a three-year term. Released from prison in 1957, he wrote for the *Daily Worker* until his expulsion from the party for revisionism in 1958. In 1960 he published his personal testament, *A Communist Views America's Future*. He also wrote *Jewish People Face the Post-War World* (1945) and *To Secure Jewish Rights: The Communist Position* (1948).

BIBLIOGRAPHY: M. Epstein, *Jews and Communism* (1959), 398–403; T. Draper, *Roots of American Communism* (1957), index.

[Edward L. Greenstein]

BITTERN (Heron; Heb. אֲנָפָה, *anafah*), mentioned among the unclean birds (Lev. 11:19; Deut. 14:18) and referring to birds of the family *Ardeidae* which are aquatic and marsh birds. Various species occur in Israel such as the white heron (*Egretta alba*) whose span can be as much as a yard. On the other hand the buff-backed heron (*Bulbucus ibis*) is much smaller. The latter, as well as many other species of bittern, have greatly increased in recent years in Israel with the spread of fish ponds and irrigation.

BIBLIOGRAPHY: Lewysohn, Zool, 169–70; F.S. Bodenheimer, *Ha-Ḥai be-Arẓot ha-Mikra*, 2 (1956), index; J. Feliks, *Animal World of the Bible* (1962), 84.

[Jehuda Feliks]

BITTUL HA-TAMID (Heb. בִּטּוּל הַתָּמִיד; lit. "abolition of the daily offering"), interruption of prayers and of Torah reading in the synagogue (Heb. עִכּוּב הַקְּרִיאָה, *ikkuv ha-keri'ah* and, therefore, also called *ikkuv ha-keri'ah ikkuv ha-tefillah*, "delay the reading of the Torah," "delay the morning prayers") to seek redress of a wrong, mainly a judicial or moral one. This practice was prevalent mainly in the Middle Ages among Ashkenazi Jewry. The custom of interrupting public religious services was a form of protest and way of arousing public indignation afforded to an individual who felt that an injustice had been perpetrated upon him or her by the constituted authorities or by rich and violent individuals. Ashkenazi *takkanot* of the 12th century set various limits to the exercise of this right to arouse "public scandal for the rights of the individual," while *takkanot* attributed to *Gershom b. Judah sought to regulate it: "If a man summons his neighbor to court and the latter refuses to appear, the plaintiff may not stop the morning prayers and reading of the Torah, unless he has first three times stopped the evening services." A Book of Customs compassionately adds: "However an orphan or a widow may interrupt even the first time until justice is done them." Until 1876 a Jew wishing to protest communal abuses was permitted to rise and say, *"Ich klame."* This privilege was extended to the aggrieved in Eastern Europe also, including cases of complaints against the *kahal* itself. In Russia, after the conscription law of 1827, many a poor mother availed herself of the opportunity to prohibit further prayer until she had stated her protest over the cruel drafting of her male child as a *Cantonist.

BIBLIOGRAPHY: Finkelstein, Middle Ages, index s.v. *Interrupting the prayers*; Baron, Community, index s.v. *Interruptions of Prayers*; I.A. Agus, *Urban Civilization in Pre-Crusade Europe*, 2 (1965), index; S. Assaf, *Battei ha-Din ve-Sidreihem* (1924), 25–29; H.H. Ben-Sasson, *Perakim be-Toledot ha-Yehudim bi-Ymei ha-Beinayim* (1962), 115–6.

[Isaac Levitats]

BITUMEN (Heb. חֵמָר, *ḥemar* and כֹּפֶר, *kofer*; LXX), a black, flammable substance which becomes viscous and absorbent on heating. It occurs in almost every part of the world, including Mesopotamia, Iran, and Israel, and is found in various natural forms: in pure form, as in the Dead Sea, where it floats and collects along the coast; as an ore in sandstone; and in semi-solid and fluid forms. The "pits" in the Valley of Siddim referred to in Genesis 14:10 were probably bitumen quarries. In Mesopotamia bitumen was used in building as a mortar which at the same time soaked into the porous bricks, making them stronger. Bitumen was employed too for waterproofing boats, for constructing model boats for cultic purposes, and for sealing water ducts and irrigation canals. It was used in this way to caulk Noah's ark (Gen. 6:14) and the basket which carried Moses (Ex. 2:3). Whether used for strengthening bricks or for sealing against water, bitumen was mixed with sand, chalk, plaster, or with its own ore, since in its pure form it has a low melting point and will not harden unless amalgamated with another mineral.

BIBLIOGRAPHY: EM, 3 (1965), 187–90 (incl. bibl.); Staples, in: IDB, 1 (1962), 444.

[Ze'ev Yeivin]

BIZTHA (Heb. בִּזְּתָא; Gr. Βαζάν, Μαζάν, Βαζεά), one of the seven eunuchs of *Ahasuerus (Esth. 1:10). On the seventh and last day of his feast for the peoples of Susa, when King Ahasuerus was in high spirits from drinking, he sent his seven attendant eunuchs to summon Queen Vashti so that he might display her beauty before the assembled company. The name Biztha is apparently Persian but no agreement has been reached on its meaning (suggestions include: *besteh*, "bound"; *biz-da*, "double gift"; *Mazdā [dā]na*, "gift of Mazda").

BIBLIOGRAPHY: L.B. Paton, *The Book of Esther* (ICC, 1908), 67; Gehman, in: JBL, 43 (1924), 323; Duchesne-Guillemin, in: *Le Muséon*, 66 (1953), 107.

[Bezalel Porten]

BIẒẒARON (Heb. בִּצָּרוֹן; "stronghold," cf. Zech. 9:12), moshav in the southern Coastal Plain of Israel, affiliated with Tenu'at ha-Moshavim, founded in 1931 by pioneers from the Soviet Union whose training farm "Tel Ḥai" in the Crimea had been closed by the Soviet authorities. They themselves had been imprisoned as Zionists but later permitted to leave. Farming was highly intensive, with citrus plantations as the principal branch. In 2002 the population of Bizzaron was 822.

[Efraim Orni]

BLACK, ALGERNON DAVID (1900–1993), educator, author and Ethical Culture leader. Born to immigrant Russian Jewish parents, Black began a lifelong involvement with the Society for *Ethical Culture after receiving a scholarship to the Ethical Culture School in New York City. After graduating from Harvard in 1923, he returned to teach history, business, and ethics in the Ethical Culture school system. Black combined his teaching responsibilities with voluntary work for a variety of social causes, including efforts to strengthen workers' rights and equalize housing opportunities. This civic engagement reflected the principles and priorities of the Ethical Culture movement, particularly its belief in the importance of the individual, its emphasis on living by ethical standards, and its work on behalf of the poor and disenfranchised. A protégé of Felix *Adler, Black rapidly moved into the leadership cadre of the New York Society for Ethical Culture. He was appointed to the Society's Board of Leaders in 1934, chosen as executive leader in 1943, elected chairman of the Board of Leaders in 1945, and installed as Senior Leader ten years later. He held this office until 1973, but remained active within the Society as its leader emeritus for another decade. "Articulate, energetic, and magnetic in personality," Black was the public face of the movement for over 40 years, speaking regularly on the radio, participating on a plethora of boards, panels, and committees that dealt with social and civil rights issues, and writing five books.

BIBLIOGRAPHY: H. Friess, *Felix Adler and Ethical Culture* (1981); *New York Times* (May 11, 1993).

[Adam Mendelsohn (2nd ed.)]

BLACK, MAX (1909–1988), U.S. philosopher. Black was born in Baku, Russia, and educated in Germany and England. He received his B.A. from Queens College, Cambridge in 1930 and was awarded a fellowship to study at Goettingen. He received his Ph.D. from the University of London in 1939. He lectured on mathematics at the Institution of Education in London from 1936 until 1940, then was appointed to the Philosophy Department at the University of Illinois at Urbana. After six years at Urbana, Black accepted a professorship in philosophy at Cornell University in New York, later becoming Susan Linsage Professor of Philosophy and Humane Letters (1954). Black retired in 1977 but continued lecturing at many universities around the world. He was president of the International Institute of Philosophy from 1981 to 1984, being only the second American at the time to assume that position.

Black's work dealt mainly with problems in contemporary analytical philosophy, ranging from the nature and function of mathematics to the role of ordinary language in the solution of philosophical problems. Though influenced by formalists, his own contributions stress the effectiveness of informalist approaches in the elimination of philosophical perplexity. He edited the influential journal *The Philosophical Review*.

Black's major publications include *The Nature of Mathematics* (1933), *Language and Philosophy* (1949), *Problems of Analysis* (1954), *The Importance of Language* (1962), *Models and Metaphors* (1962), *A Companion to Wittgenstein's Tractatus* (1964), *Philosophy in America* (1965), *The Labyrinth of Language* (1969), *Margins of Precision: Essays in Logic and Language* (1970), *Art, Perception, and Reality* (1972), and *The Prevalence of Humbug and Other Essays* (1983).

[Avrum Stroll / Ruth Beloff (2nd ed.)]

BLACK, SIR MISHA (1910–1977), British architect and industrial designer. Born in Baku, Russia, Black was taken to England as an infant. Before World War II he helped to found the Artists International Association, a radical organization with an anti-Nazi program for assisting refugee artists then attempting to enter Great Britain. In 1933 together with the designer Milner Gray he set up a firm called Industrial Design Partnership in an effort to bring total design methods to Britain. In 1944 they founded the Design Research Unit. Black became a nationally recognized design leader as coordinating architect for a major part of the 1951 Festival of Britain; he later took part in the design of exhibitions in many other countries. Among the most important activities of the Design Research Unit is the redesigning of British Railways, including Black's designs for a diesel locomotive and an electric train, supervision of the Victoria Line opened by the London Underground in 1969, and the Clore Pavilion at the London Zoo.

Black was appointed professor of industrial engineering design at the Royal College of Art in 1959. He served as president of the British Society of Industrial Arts and Design and as a trustee of the British Museum. His publications on exhibition and interior design include *The Practice of Design* (1946) and *Public Interiors* (1959). He was the brother of the philosopher Max *Black (1909–1988), who chiefly taught at Cornell University in the United States.

BIBLIOGRAPHY: *Art and Industry*, 63 (Sept. 1957), 106. **ADD. BIBLIOGRAPHY:** ODNB online; A. Blake, *Misha Black* (1984).

[Charles Samuel Spencer]

BLACK DEATH, epidemic of various contagious diseases, bubonic, septicemic, and pneumonic, all caused by the same bacillus, *pasteurella pestis*, a combination of which raged throughout Europe between 1348 and 1350. (See Map: Black Death). It was the worst plague experienced since the sixth century. Between one-quarter and one-half of the total population perished. In centers with denser populations, such as the monasteries, the proportion of victims was much higher. As the bacteria of this disease live in certain temperatures only, the peak periods of sickness and mortality usually occurred at certain months in the year, according to the local climate.

The impact of this unprecedented catastrophe had a profound effect on the behavior of the population. People reacted by extremes, either seeking recourse to religion through repentance and supplication to God, or reverting to licentiousness, lawbreaking, and savagery. These two types of reaction often combined, in particular where they concerned the attitude of the non-Jewish population to the Jews. Toward the end of 1348 and in early 1349 countless numbers of Jews lost their lives in a wave of massacres which spread throughout Europe as a result of the accusation that the Jews had caused the death of Christians by poisoning the wells and other water sources. According to L.F. Hirst, a leading authority in this field, the Black Death "in all probability… originated somewhere in the central Asiatic hinterland, where a permanent reservoir of infection is maintained among the wild rodents of the steppes. Rumors of a great mortality among Asiatics, especially Chinese, reached Europe in 1346, and by the spring of that year bubonic plague had reached the shores of the Black Sea.… From ports on the shores of the Crimea besieged by Tatars, who perished in vast numbers from the epidemic… the infection was carried on shipboard to Constantinople, Genoa, Venice, and other European ports. The disease spread as rapidly as the transport of those days permitted… to the Mainland." At the time of the Black Death no one was aware of this connection and the existence of contagion was only vaguely perceived. By some persons the catastrophe was ascribed to astrological conjunctions; others regarded it as a divine visitation. Pope *Clement VI, in his bull defending the Jews from these accusations, saw it as "the pestilence with which God is afflicting the Christian people." The vast majority of the population, however, was inclined to view it as a *pestis manufacta* (an artificially induced malady), the simplest explanation to the unsophisticated mind, and therefore sought the human agents thought to be spreading the disease. Initially, the Jews were not the only persons accused; strangers of every type were suspected. An Avignonese physician relates: "Many hesitated, in some countries people believed that the Jews intended to poison the whole world and therefore killed them. In other countries they expelled paupers suffering from deformity; and in yet others, the nobles." Sometimes itinerant monks were suspected of placing the poison and spreading the disease, and they were attacked instead.

Well Poisoning Libel

Soon, however, the feelings of helplessness to stem the plague, and the fierce urge to react against the death and destruction it caused, concentrated the force of the populace on the age-old target of popular Christian hostility, the Jews. Anti-Jewish violence was particularly rabid in *Germany, where it had been preceded by a dark half century of anti-Jewish persecution in conjunction with a succession of *blood libels and accusations of *host desecration. This had added to the sinister traits already attributed to the hateful image of the Jew. In France, also, the way had been paved for this accusation by a similar charge leveled during the *Pastoureaux persecutions of 1321. Amid the general atmosphere of hostility, and the cruelty of the persecutions to which the Jews had been subjected, it was almost logical that Christians could imagine that the Jews might seek revenge. Thus, a Jew who was tortured in *Freiburg im Breisgau in 1349, "was then asked… 'why did they do it…?' Then he answered: 'because you Christians have destroyed so many Jews; because of what king *Armleder did; and also because we too want to be lords; for you have lorded long enough.'" ("*… wan umb das, das ir cristen so menigen juden verdarpten, do kuenig Armleder was, und ouch um das, das wir ouch herren wolten gewesen sin, wan ir genug lang herren gewesen sint;" Urkundenbuch der Stadt Freiburg im Breisgau* (1828), nos. 193, 382).

The first occasion on which Jews were tortured to confess complicity in spreading the Black Death was in September 1348, in the Castle of Chillon on Lake Geneva. The "confessions" thus extracted indicate that their accusers wished to prove that the Jews had set out to poison the wells and food "so as to kill and destroy the whole of Christianity" ("*ad interficiendam et destruendam totam legem Christianam*"). The disease was allegedly spread by a Jew of Savoy on the instructions of a rabbi who told him: "See, I give you a little package, half a span in size, which contains a preparation of poison and venom in a narrow, stitched leathern bag. This you are to dis-

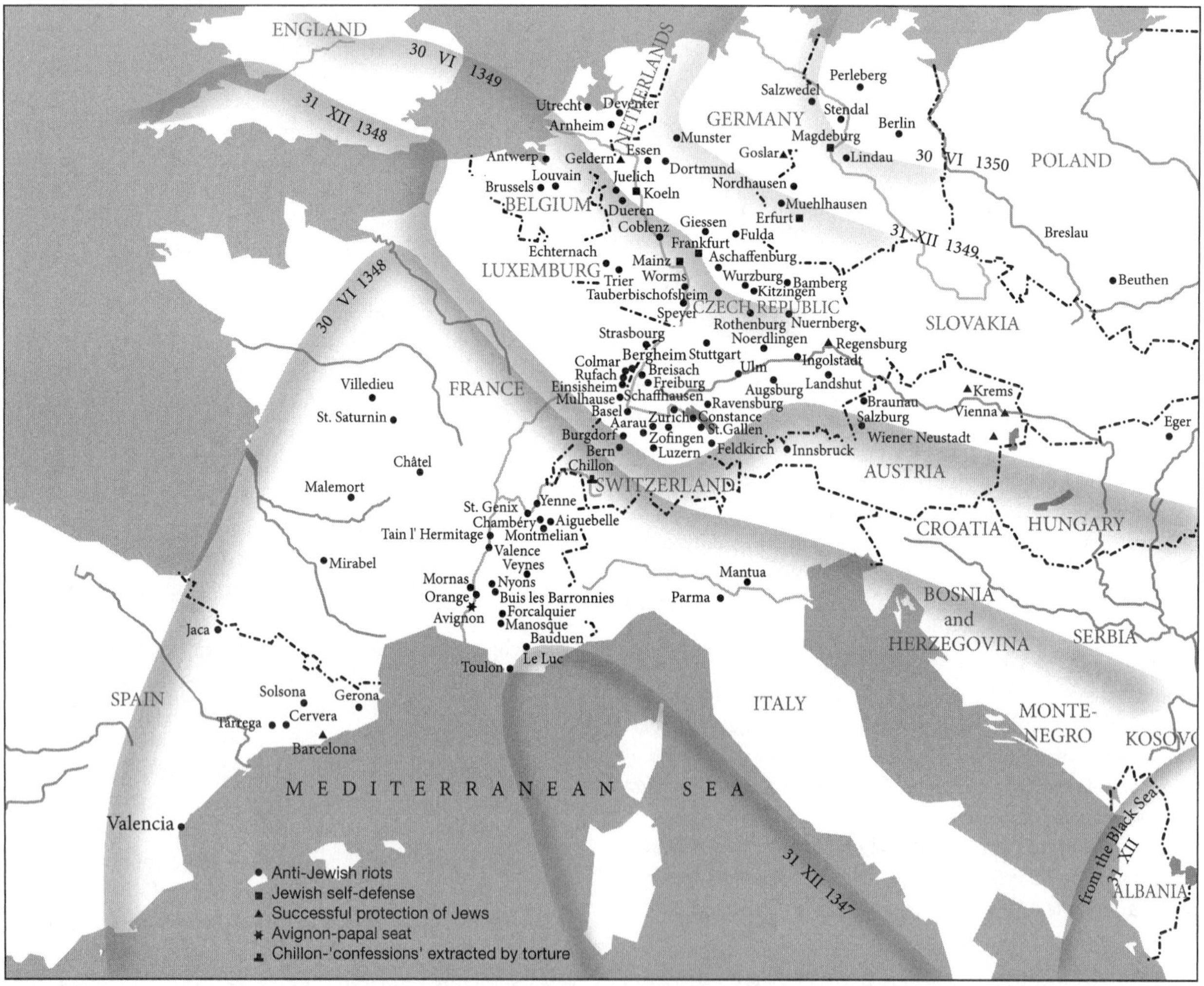

The Black Death. The map shows, in progressive shades of gray, the spread of the plague across Europe in six-month periods from Dec. 31 1347, to June 30, 1350.

tribute among the wells, the cisterns, and the springs about Venice and the other places where you go, in order to poison the people who use the water…." This indictment, therefore, shows that his accusers recognized that the plague had spread from the south northward. As the case dragged on, details were extracted telling of further consultations held among the Jews, about messengers from Toledo, and other wild allegations. On Oct. 3, 1348, during the summing up, an allegation providing a motive for the total destruction of Jewry was made; it was asserted that "before their end they said on their Law that it is true that all Jews, from the age of seven, cannot excuse themselves of this [crime], since all of them in their totality were cognizant and are guilty of the above actions" ("*asseruerunt praefati Judaei ante eorum ultimum supplicium per legem suam esse vera dicentes quod omnes Judaei a septem annis circum non possint super hoc se excusare, quoniam universaliter sciant omnes, et sint culpabiles in dicto facto*").

Outbreak of Persecutions

These "confessions" were sent to various cities in Germany. The accusation that the Jews had poisoned the wells spread there like wildfire, fanned by the general atmosphere of terror. The patricians of *Strasbourg attempted to defend the Jews at a meeting of representatives of the Alsatian towns at Benfeld, but the majority rejected their plea, arguing: "If you are not afraid of poisoning, why have you yourselves covered and guarded your wells?" Correspondence on the subject between the authorities in the various cities has been preserved. In general, it reveals a decision to expel the Jews from the locality concerned for good, and to launch an immediate attack to kill them while they still remained. At *Basle the patricians also unsuccessfully attempted to protect the Jews. In various cities Jews were tortured to confess their part in the conspiracy. The defamation, killings, and expulsions spread through the kingdoms of Christian Spain, France, and Germany, to Poland-Lithuania, affecting about 300 Jewish communities. On Sept. 26, 1348, Pope Clement VI issued a bull in Avignon denouncing this allegation, stating that "certain Christians, seduced by that liar, the devil, are imputing the pestilence to poisoning by Jews." This imputation and the massacre of Jews in consequence were defined by the pope as "a horrible thing." He tried to convince Christians that "since this pestilence is all but universal everywhere, and by a mysterious decree of God has afflicted, and continues to afflict, both Jews and many other nations throughout the diverse regions of the earth to whom a common existence with Jews is unknown [the charge] that the Jews have provided the cause or the occasion for such a crime is without plausibility." Both the emperors Charles IV and Peter IV of Aragon also tried to protect the Jews from the results of the accusation. The arguments generally put forward by the rulers were expressed by the physician Konrad of Megenberg in his *Buch der Natur* arrived at in the light of his own experience: "But I know that there were more Jews in Vienna than in any other German city familiar to me, and so many of them died of the plague that they were obliged to enlarge their cemetery. To have brought this on themselves would have been folly on their part." However, all these appeals to reason were ineffective. The massacres of the Jews continued, and Jewish property was confiscated. Despite his policy of protecting the Jews, in 1350 the emperor Charles IV formally absolved the burghers of *Cheb (Eger) in Bohemia for the killings and robbery they had committed among the Jewish population. In doing so, he stated: "Forgiveness is [granted] for every transgression involving the slaying and destruction of Jews which has been committed without the positive knowledge of the leading citizens, or in their ignorance, or in any other fashion whatsoever." By this time it was well-known that the accusation that Jews had spread the plague was false. In many places Jews were killed even before the plague had visited the locality. Further outbreaks of plague continued later in the 14th century but Jews were no longer accused of being the cause.

The Martyrs

It was recognized by the Jews that the Christians "have opened wide their mouths about me: they have put and spread poison on the water, so they say, in order to libel and attack us," to quote a contemporary dirge. Faced with this overwhelming antagonism, the Jews tried to defend themselves wherever possible and in whatever way they could. In many localities fierce conflicts took place between the Jewish population and their attackers. At *Mainz the Jews set fire to their homes and to the Jewish street: according to some sources, 6,000 Jews perished in the flames. This also occurred at *Frankfurt on the Main. In Strasbourg, 2,000 Jews were burnt on a wooden scaffold in the Jewish cemetery. The manner in which the martyrs met their deaths is described in a contemporary Hebrew source concerning "the holy community of Nordhausen….They asked the burghers to permit them to prepare themselves for martyrdom: permission having been given…they joyfully arrayed themselves in their prayer shawls and shrouds, both men and women. They [the Christians] dug a grave at the cemetery and covered it with wooden scaffolding…The pious ones [among the Jews] asked that a musician be hired to play dancing tunes so that they should enter the presence of God with singing. They took each other by the hand, both men and women, and danced and leapt with their whole strength before God. Their teacher, R. Jacob, went before them; his son, R. Meir, brought up the rear to see that none should lag behind. Singing and dancing they entered the grave, and when all had entered, R. Meir jumped out and walked around to make certain that none had stayed outside. When the burghers saw him they asked him to save his life [by apostasy]. He answered: 'This now is the end of our troubles, you see me only for a while, and then I shall be no more.' He returned to the grave; they set fire to the scaffolding; they died all of them together and not a cry was heard" (*Sefer Minhagim* of Worms). This was the spirit that enabled European Jewry to emerge spiritually unscathed from the avalanche of hatred and cruelty released on the Jews by the Christians in Europe.

The Black Death not only resulted in the immediate destruction of thousands of Jewish lives and the loss of Jewish homes and property in hundreds of communities, but had more far-reaching consequences. Popular imagination invested the already odious image of the Jew with even more horrible characteristics. It was this image that helped to shape the stereotype of the Jew represented by *antisemitism and racism in modern times. After the Black Death the legal status of the Jews deteriorated almost everywhere in Europe. Although Jews were frequently received back into the cities where many had been killed or driven out, sometimes within a year of the decision to expel them for good, they usually only gained permission to resettle on worse terms and in greater isolation than before. The position of the Jews in Aragon and Castile (*Spain) deteriorated sharply after 1348–49. The only countries in Europe where the events of the Black Death did not leave a permanent scar on the Jewish communities were Poland-Lithuania. The reconstruction of the Jewish communities and of Jewish life and cultural activity in the second half of the 14th and the beginning of the 15th century clearly evidence the social and spiritual vitality of the Jewish people in Europe in the period.

BIBLIOGRAPHY: P. Ziegler, *Black Death* (1969); R. Hoeniger, *Der schwarze Tod in Deutschland* (1882); J. Nohl, *Der schwarze Tod* (1924), 239–73; L.F. Hirst, *Conquest of Plague* (1953); E. Carpentier, in: *Annales*, 17 (1962), 1062–92; E. Littmann, in: MGWJ, 72 (1928), 576–600; J. Trachtenberg, *The Devil and the Jews* (1943, repr. paperback 1961), 97–108; S. Guerchberg, in: S.L. Thrupp (ed.), *Change in Medieval Society* (1964), 208–24; Baron, Social 2, 9–12 (1965–67).

[Haim Hillel Ben-Sasson]

BLACK-JEWISH RELATIONS IN THE UNITED STATES. Black-Jewish contacts, and thus black-Jewish relations, date from the earliest years of settlement. Many of the tiny number of Jews who came to America in the colonial period, especially those from Spain and Portugal, engaged in international trade and thus were directly involved in the triangle trade of slavery, sugar, and rum. Others settled in many of the American colonies. In northern cities like Newport, New York, and Boston, Jewish merchants and early industrialists found their livelihoods intertwined with various aspects of slavery and the slave trade; in the South a few Jews owned or traded slaves. By and large, these early Jews reflected the views of their white Gentile neighbors; most Northern Jews opposed slavery, while most Southern Jews supported it. Few were outspoken or active on either side, although there were notable exceptions like abolitionist August Bondi; Rabbi David *Einhorn, who spoke out against slavery in Baltimore and had to leave the city for his own safety; Judah *Benjamin, Jefferson Davis's secretary of war and later state; and Rabbi Morris *Raphall, who used biblical passages to justify slavery. By and large, however, there was very little direct "relationship" at all between them. Most African Americans lived in the rural South, and Jews clustered in the urban North.

In the late 19th and early 20th centuries, however, they began to meet in Northern urban centers as two major migration streams intersected: African Americans moving North and into cities in a decades-long flight from oppression, violence, and discrimination called the Great Migration, and East European Jews fleeing the same forces in a different setting. Both groups often ended up in the same cities, sometimes even in the same neighborhoods. Similarly poor, they had few housing options. And Jews, who were considered not fully white themselves, who had had less exposure to American racism, were less violent than others, and by and large more radicalized by egalitarian ideologies like communism, socialism, and trade unionism, put up less resistance when African Americans moved into their neighborhoods. This is why, over time, many Jewish neighborhoods became black, not without tension but generally without violence.

These migrations enabled both communities to organize politically to address concerns about opportunity and equality. At the same time blacks and Jews met one another face to face, often for the first time, in economic interactions that more often revealed differences between the two communities than any sense of common cause. Both developments were critical in shaping what we call black-Jewish relations.

Migrants from both communities needed help settling in. Both were poor, subject to discrimination and bigotry, and both needed to help others left behind. So both communities established defense and protective organizations. Mutual aid societies, fraternal and trade union groups such as the *Workmen's Circle and the National Association of Colored Women's Clubs encouraged economic development and sustained social and community ties; other agencies like the NAACP and *American Jewish Congress concerned themselves explicitly with political issues affecting their group. Others joined multiracial political organizations like the Communist, Socialist, Democratic and Republican parties, and brought their community's social and cultural values with them. The political Left in particular participated actively in civil rights efforts benefiting blacks and Jews, and stressed interracial action.

Faced with similar challenges, however, there was virtually no cooperation between organizations from the two communities except on the Left. On the individual level, elite or politically well-connected Jews and African Americans often cooperated with one another. Black socialist labor leader A. Philip Randolph considered Jews among his most reliable supporters; Jews were disproportionately represented on the founding boards of the NAACP and National Urban League. The NAACP's first two presidents, Joel and Arthur Spingarn, were Jewish. African American Judge Hubert Delaney defended Jewish interests; Jewish Julius Rosenwald underwrote black educational endeavors; before his appointment to the Supreme Court Louis *Brandeis offered his legal services and his contacts to the NAACP. The black press described East European pogroms and the Jewish press covered lynchings. Beyond these individual or informational contacts, however, formal organizations rarely contacted their counterparts in the other community for cooperative action.

Too poor, too overwhelmed with their own needs, black and Jewish agencies were small and limited in resources. Blacks and Jews stayed apart as well because of black antisemitism and Jewish racism. These attitudes were less potent there than they were among white Christians but they had an impact nonetheless. And there was one more concern, at least from the Jewish side. Jewish organizations struggling for acceptance recognized that racism was the stronger force and feared that any association with such a pariah group as blacks would hurt their own efforts. When Jewish Leo *Frank was convicted of murder in 1913 on the testimony of a black man in an antisemitic trial in Atlanta, and lynched two years later, it prompted the newly formed Anti-Defamation League (ADL) to proclaim its commitment to defending the rights of all. But in practice, Frank's murder convinced many Jews that life in the United States was dangerous enough without taking on black people's problems as well.

While relatively few blacks and Jews interacted politically (outside of the Left), far more encountered each other in economic venues. In virtually every case, Jews had the upper hand. Because Jews were white, they were able to benefit from the American system that apportioned opportunity more by race than by ethnicity or religion. Their white skin and the urban skills they had brought from Europe enabled Jews to succeed more quickly than African Americans; it was the exodus of better-off Jews into better neighborhoods that brought black tenants to Jewish areas in the first place. These Jews, and those that remained, continued to run their original businesses; Jews owned up to 90% of the stores in many black neighborhoods. So the inevitable tensions in poor neighborhoods between landlords and tenants, shopkeepers and customers, social workers and clients came to be seen as black-Jewish conflicts, and they reinforced stereotypes of greedy and unscrupulous Jews, or lazy or irresponsible blacks.

Another point of contact between the two communities was the arts, especially music and the new medium of motion pictures. Meeting first in vaudeville and other performance areas, Jews also rose to positions of greater power and became impresarios and agents for black performers. The same was also true in sports.

Given the limited and hierarchical nature of relations between African Americans and American Jews, and although members of each community recognized the plight of the other, and were sensitive to prejudice, there was little positive mutual interaction in the first third of the 20th century. This changed with the rise of Nazism. With Jews threatened in Europe, and with the rise of fascist and antisemitic groups in the United States, it became clear to Jewish organizations that they desperately needed allies. And for black people, who recognized bigotry when they saw it, anti-Nazi efforts also offered the strongest challenge to American racism. The black press and several black groups therefore launched what they called a Double V campaign: victory against Nazism abroad and racism at home. Outspoken in their protest of Nazi atrocities, black groups also lost no opportunity to draw parallels with lynching and racial bigotry in the United States.

Black-Jewish cooperation in the 1930s was clearly based on mutual self-interest, but one that recognized the shared danger inherent in any form of bigotry. These groups had come to recognize what the Left had been saying all along: that unity among the oppressed was the most effective weapon to bring about change. The Ribbentrop-Molotov, German-Soviet pact, however, discredited the Left in the eyes of many liberals, and the emerging Cold War made suspect all programs espoused by Communists. Stalin's purges alienated still more Jews, who abandoned the Communist Party for liberal and progressive Jewish political organizations. Thus, Nazism and the war brought black and Jewish liberals to a new recognition of the importance of civil rights and racial tolerance. At the same time, anti-Communism also led them to limit their strategies, goals, and coalitions in ways that hobbled the potential for fundamental social change. The stage was set for what many consider the "golden age" of black-Jewish relations.

Political relations between black and Jewish political agencies warmed further as the modern civil rights movement gained real force. The two communities had gotten to know one another through common work. Their organizations had become more desirable allies as their earlier successes brought increased membership, stronger finances, and greater political access. And they shared a set of liberal values, including bringing change within the existing system; employing moderate, non-confrontational tactics in doing so; a commitment to the centrality of individual rights rather than privileges bestowed by membership in a group; and a conviction that it was the obligation of government to foster equal opportunity. They advocated litigation, education, and legislation to bring about equality, evidenced, for example, in the American Jewish Congress's new Commission on Law and Social Action.

By the late 1940s, liberal civil rights organizations rooted in the two communities slowly began to develop a close partnership, launching programs separately and jointly to improve conditions for racial and religious minorities. This can still be viewed as self-interest, but it was now a broader concept. The NAACP, with the help of all the main Jewish organizations, won a Supreme Court case declaring restrictive housing covenants unenforceable, which benefited both groups but particularly economically mobile Jews. The NAACP came to the *Brown v. Board of Education* case, as well as its predecessors, armed with amicus briefs from virtually every other black and Jewish civil rights organization (along with other progressive, union, religious, and civic groups). The creation of New York's state college system was a joint black-Jewish effort to combat religious and racial discrimination in higher education. Together they fought to make permanent the war's Fair

Employment Practices Act, which outlawed employment discrimination based on race, religion, or national origin.

They cooperated on passing anti-Klan and anti-violence legislation, fighting restrictions on employment applications, and challenging racism and antisemitism with educational programs that appealed to American ideals of fairness and democracy. The two leaders of the Leadership Conference on Civil Rights were an African American, Walter White, and a Jew, Arnold *Aronson.

Nor was such collaboration one-sided. Jewish organizations participated in racial segregation cases; black groups advocated expanding immigration to accommodate wartime refugees, endorsed (and lobbied for) the UN resolution on the creation of the state of Israel, and protested Soviet antisemitism.

Because the persistence of economic tensions threatened these partnerships and contradicted their non-discriminatory rhetoric, black and Jewish organizations began to intervene directly. Jewish activists met with (or picketed) Jewish landlords and storeowners, urging them to end segregationist and discriminatory practices. The AJ Congress and ADL organized Jewish merchants in black neighborhoods into associations charged with improving race relations, hiring more African-American clerks, and contributing to community improvement projects. (In many areas, Jews left black neighborhoods completely, diminishing tensions that way.) In both communities leaders worked to educate their own people on the dangers of bigotry against any other group. Such efforts succeeded widely, revealed in the disproportionate number of Jews supporting black civil rights compared with other whites, and a rapid decline in reported antisemitism in the African-American community. In many ways this truly was a golden age for black-Jewish relations.

But these liberal successes brought new challenges. Jews continued to outperform blacks economically and socially. No longer segregated or discriminated against overtly or legally, Jews could make their way in the world far more easily than blacks, who continued to suffer from open discrimination and legal segregation. This divergence produced not only resentment on the part of black people but also Jews' greater satisfaction with the current system. For Jews, educational and reformist methods worked. For African Americans, who continued to face structural barriers, such approaches were inadequate. As black groups turned to increasingly confrontational tactics such as boycotts and mass demonstrations, most Jews moved toward a greater commitment to the status quo.

The 1960s sit-ins and the rhetoric of the more activist civil rights workers heightened these tensions and laid bare the different social positions of Jews and blacks. Southern Jews in particular refused to get involved, save a courageous few very often from the more radical segment of the community. Most Jews, North and South, still supported the goals of, and contributed financially to, black civil rights organizations, but some questioned the tactics of what they feared could become demagogic mob action. For a community invested in law and order to maintain its own security, pickets, civil disobedience, and nationalist rhetoric seemed particularly dangerous. So while younger and more radical – and often more assimilated – Jews continued to be overrepresented among white civil rights workers in groups like the Student Nonviolent Coordinating Committee, their liberal counterparts became skittish at the sound of "Black Power." Two of the three civil rights workers killed in Mississippi in the summer of 1964 were Jews. Abraham Joshua *Heschel marched with Rev. Martin Luther King, Jr., who expressed strong support for Zionism; Rabbi Joachim Prinz, a Berlin-born naturalized American, addressed the 1963 March on Washington. Yet as the civil rights movement moved North and African Americans sought greater social equality, Jewish suburbanites became wary.

Black activists (and white leftists) had become radicalized by the failure of the liberal promise: white resistance, police violence, and the persistence of poverty and segregation suggested that liberal whites could not be trusted. And Jews constituted one of the largest and most visible segments of liberal whites. Nor did it seem that polite, liberal strategies could successfully challenge racism. Might confrontation, even violence, be appropriate? Should primacy be given to individual rights, when black rights were systematically threatened by virtue of their being members of a group? Perhaps race blindness was not as effective as programs that emphasized group rights. To pay for the structural changes required, black manifestos demanded aid and reparations from government, churches, and synagogues. Pan-African nationalism and anti-colonialism shifted black sympathy from Israel to the Palestinians – just at the time of the *Six-Day War. Black antisemitism became visible again. All these developments left Jews feeling threatened and, perhaps more importantly, betrayed.

Meanwhile, riots, violence, nationalism, and confrontational black demands reinforced Jewish racism. Skeptical Jewish leaders backed off from earlier alliances. Many of their constituents, now in suburbs, felt less concerned with urban strife. Others became neoconservatives, arguing that liberalism had lost its way. So African Americans in turn felt betrayed by Jews, whom they believed had abandoned them, and the fight for civil rights.

Dozens of incidents from the late 1960s through the 1990s reveal these stresses, from the struggle over control of schools in Brooklyn, New York's Ocean Hill-Brownsville to the refusal of most Jewish groups to support the NAACP in the 1974 and 1978 affirmative action cases; from Jesse Jackson's "Hymietown" remarks of 1984 to New York City Mayor Ed *Koch's claim that Jews would "have to be crazy" to vote for Jackson. The Nation of Islam and its leader Louis Farrakhan advertised its antisemitism, while academics and students fought their own battles on campuses across the country. At the City University of New York, for example, Professor Leonard Jeffries blamed Jews for the problems facing black people, and

Professor Michael Levin insisted that black people were inferior to whites. And of course there was real violence like that in the Afro-Caribbean and Orthodox Jewish neighborhood of Brooklyn's Crown Heights in 1991. After a member of the Lubavitcher rebbe's entourage accidentally hit and killed a black child, black youths attacked Jewish passers-by. One Jewish youth was stabbed to death. One early dimension of affirmative action particularly troubled Jews: quotas. African Americans intended quotas as a floor, designed to open up and include them, but Jews, for whom quotas were historically used to exclude and limit, balked. Once the legal concept was clarified, most Jews came to support affirmative action.

All this played out against the backdrop of a rightward shift in the larger political scene. Even for those still committed to black-Jewish cooperation, it appeared that few shared issues remained. The black community struggled with problems of poverty, racism, crime, and improving education and opportunity, while Jews became increasingly concerned with issues surrounding Israeli security, Jewish "continuity," and church-state separation. Jewish Studies programs competed with Black or Africana Studies for college curricula funding. It seemed all that was left between the two groups was friction. Pundits proclaimed the death of the black-Jewish relationship.

But that is a distortion. Civil rights coalitions remained active into the 21st century, if less visible. There have been hundreds of local economic and political initiatives around the country: books, articles, and documentaries about blacks and Jews, congregational exchanges, public discussions – from Jews for Racial and Economic Justice and Boston's Black-Jewish Economic Roundtable to *Common Cause*, a journal jointly published by the American Jewish Committee and Howard University; from the Reform Movement Religious Action Center's Common Road to Justice to the Marjory Kovler Institute for Black-Jewish Relations. In Congress, the Black Caucus has established routine and productive cooperation with the more informal "Jewish caucus."

All this sustained, even increasing, mutual engagement suggests that many overlapping concerns do remain, not least of which is the rightward movement of the country itself, opposed by a majority of both communities, who remain staunch Democratic voters. Problems of discrimination, unequal access to opportunity, voting, and education still top both black and Jewish political agendas, as do commitments to civic community, tolerance, and diversity.

BIBLIOGRAPHY: M. Friedman, *What Went Wrong?* (1995); C. Greenberg, *Troubling the Waters: Black Jewish Relations in the American Century* (in press); M. Bauman and B. Kalin (eds.), *The Quiet Voices: Southern Rabbis and Black Civil Rights, 1880s to 1990s* (1997); P. Berman (ed.), *Blacks and Jews* (1994); V.P. Franklin, N. Grant et al. (eds.), *African Americans and Jews in the Twentieth Century* (1998); J. Washington (ed.), *Jews in Black Perspectives* (1984); C. West and J. Salzman (eds.), *Struggles in the Promised Land* (1997); E. Faber, *Jews, Slaves, and the Slave Trade: Setting the Record Straight* (1998).

[Cheryl Greenberg (2nd ed.)]

°**BLACKSTONE, WILLIAM E.** (1841–1935), Chicago businessman who became an evangelist, missionary, and ardent supporter of the return of the Jews to Palestine. His "Zionistic" views sprang from his millennarian theology as expressed in his first book *Jesus is Coming* (1878), which was translated into many languages, including Hebrew. He considered the Jewish restoration to Zion as the fulfillment of biblical prophecies signifying the approach of the second Advent of Jesus. After a visit to Palestine in 1888/89, Blackstone organized meetings of Jews and Christians to promote his Zionist ideas. In 1891 he initiated a memorandum to President Harrison urging the restoration of Palestine to the Jews as a primary solution to the problem of Jewish persecution in Czarist Russia. The petition was signed by 413 outstanding Jewish and Christian personalities in the United States. In 1916 a similar memorandum was sent to President Wilson which may have influenced his positive attitude to the *Balfour Declaration.

[Yona Malachy]

°**BLAKE, WILLIAM** (1757–1827), English poet and engraver. One of the great figures of the English romantic movement, Blake described his poems as prophecies, declaring that his model was the Bible, which he termed "the great code of art." The works of Homer and Ovid were for him, by contrast, perversions of art and imagination. Blake was in touch with various occult circles and shared with them the belief that Britain was the cradle of the Israelite people. This explains his tendency to identify English names and places with those in the Bible. His work is saturated in biblical imagery and allusion. His main biblical poems are "*The Four Zoas*," "*Milton*," and "*Jerusalem*." The last quatrain of his preface to "*Milton*" well illustrates Blake's revolutionary mystique: "I will not cease from mental fight/Nor shall my sword sleep in my hand,/Till we have built Jerusalem/ In England's green and pleasant land." In freeing his verse from the shackles of classical prosody and adopting for his prophetic books something resembling the syntax of the Bible, Blake may have been influenced by the 18th-century Oxford scholar, Robert *Lowth. Although he knew little or no Hebrew, and was not Jewish, Blake was also influenced by ideas which can be traced to the *Kabbalah. His notion of the Giant Albion, whose limbs contain heaven and earth, is derived from the kabbalistic image of **Adam Kadmon* (Primal Man). Equally kabbalistic are his notions of a divine world divided into male and female principles, and his conception of a primordial "Fall" from which all evil flows in both the divine and the human realms. In spite of many Judaistic ideas and currents of feeling, Blake's moral ideas are, paradoxically enough, anti-Judaic, even antisemitic. Like the Gnostics, he viewed the Law and the Commandments as an evil system, and he identified the God of Sinai with some evil demiurge.

BIBLIOGRAPHY: D. Saurat, *Blake and Modern Thought* (1929); J. Bronowski, *Man Without a Mask* (1944); H. Fisch, *Jerusalem and Albion* (1964), 273–80; D. Hirst, *Hidden Riches* (1964); S. Damon, *Blake Dictionary* (1965); M. Roston, *Poet and Prophet* (1965). **ADD. BIBLI-**

OGRAPHY: M. Eaves (ed.), *The Cambridge Companion to William Blake* (2003); N. Frye, *Fearful Symmetry* (1969); ODNB online.

[Harold Harel Fisch]

BLANC, MEL (1908–1989), U.S. voice actor. Born in San Francisco, California, Blanc was one of America's most distinguished and versatile voice actors during his long career with Warner Brothers and Hanna-Barbera cartoons. Blanc was the voice of a number of Warner Brothers' and Hanna-Barbera's most famous cartoon characters, including such favorites as Bugs Bunny, Daffy Duck, Porky Pig, Woody Woodpecker, Tweety Bird, Speedy Gonzalez, and Sylvester the Cat. Blanc's talents first gained recognition when he worked as a regular on the *Jack Benny Program*, on which he served as the voice of Benny's automobile, violin teacher Professor LeBlanc, Polly the Parrot, and Benny's pet polar bear, Carmichael. Blanc appeared on various national radio programs including *Burns and Allen*, *Point Sublime* and *G.I. Journal*, before joining Warner Brothers' renowned cartoon studio, the Leon Schlesinger Studios, in 1936. It was at Warner Brothers that Blanc became the voice of his most celebrated characters. In addition to the aforementioned roles, Blanc was also responsible for the voices of Yosemite Sam, Pepe Lepew, Foghorn Leghorn, Wile E. Coyote, Road Runner, Marvin the Martian, the Tasmanian Devil, and Elmer Fudd, a role inherited from Arthur Q. Bryan. During the early 1960s, Blanc began working at Hanna-Barbera studios, where he worked alongside the prominent vocal actors Daws Butler and Don Messick. Blanc's best-known characters from the Hanna-Barbera era are Barney Rubble, Cosmo G. Spacely, Hardy Harr Harr, and Captain Caveman. His last original character was Heathcliff the Cat, who first appeared in 1981. Blanc's tombstone and autobiography both bear his signature phrase, "That's all, folks!"

[Walter Driver (2nd ed.)]

BLANCHOT, MAURICE (1907–2003), French writer, novelist, essayist, and literary critic, Blanchot began his career as a young monarchist and right-wing journalist in the *Journal des Debats*. While studying German literature and philosophy in Strasbourg, he became a close friend of Emmanuel *Levinas, who introduced him to Heidegger's thought. During the 1930s, despite this friendship, Blanchot wrote in various right-wing newspapers, most of them related to Maurras' *Action Francaise*, which he admired, and his articles were occasionally antisemitic in tone, describing for example Leon Blum in 1937 as "a wog"; but Blanchot was critical of the persecution of the Jews as early as 1933. He also wrote in Thierry Maulnier's *Combat* review, which was anti-Hitlerian but favored a "rational antisemitism." In 1940, he joined the Jeune France movement, a cultural association set up by the Vichy regime. In 1942 he published his novel *Aminadab*, named for a brother of Levinas murdered by the Nazis in Lithuania.

After the war, Blanchot began a journey towards Jewish philosophy and literature, following in the footsteps of Levinas, whose concepts and philosophical language impregnated Blanchot's literary criticism. This turn towards Judaism, clearly perceptible in *L'Entretien infini*, to the point that Philippe Mesnard wrote that Blanchot "tries to think Jewish like Holderlin tried to think Greek," may be seen as an endeavor to cope with the horrors of genocide. Blanchot commented on Kafka, Edmond Jabes, and Martin Buber. In the wake of the May '68 movement, Blanchot joined the extreme left wing, but ultimately left it when French left-wingers became increasingly anti-Israel.

BIBLIOGRAPHY: F. Collins, *Maurice Blanchot et la question de l'écriture* (1986); E. Levinas, *Sur Maurice Blanchot* (1975); A. Toumayan, *Encountering the Other: the Artwork and the Problem of Difference in Blanchot and Levinas* (2004).

[Dror Franck Sullaper (2nd ed.)]

°BLANCKENHORN, MAX (1861–1947), German geologist who became famous principally for his research and publications on the geology of the Near East, Syria, and particularly Ereẓ Israel. Blanckenhorn visited the countries of the Near East many times and worked together with A. *Aaronsohn and the zoologist Israel *Aharoni. He was also a friend of Otto *Warburg, with whom he worked to deepen and spread knowledge of the natural resources of Ereẓ Israel. As the then virtually only expert on the geology of Ereẓ Israel, Blanckenhorn often advised Zionist leaders on matters concerning economic resources of the country. From 1889 to 1940 he published more than 50 pieces of research on the general and structural geology of the Near East, on the stratigraphy, paleontology, prehistory, seismology, and climatology, and on mineral resources such as phosphates, bitumen, and the salts of the Dead Sea. He prepared the first geological maps of the Jerusalem area (1905), of the Near East (in International Map of Europe containing the Mediterranean area, 1902–11), and of Ereẓ Israel on a scale of 1:700,000 (1912). Of great importance are his paleontological monographs on the fossils from Ereẓ Israel and Syria. A detailed list of his publications on the Middle East appeared in *Israel Journal of Earth-Sciences*.

BIBLIOGRAPHY: A. Avnimelech, in: *Israel Journal of Earth-Sciences*, 12 (1963/64), 1–7.

[Moshe A. Avnimelech]

BLANES, JACOB (1877–1943), one of the last cantors of the Portuguese Synagogue of Amsterdam before the Holocaust. He was appointed in 1902. Blanes insisted on full accuracy in recitation, a characteristic feature of Sephardi cantoral singing in Amsterdam. He had a deep knowledge of *Hazande*, including many ancient melodies for the *Kaddish, etc. He had great influence on younger men anxious to preserve the tradition of *ḥazzanut*, and the few pupils of his who survived World War II were afterward to be found in communities in various parts of the world. Blanes himself died after being deported from Holland in 1943.

BIBLIOGRAPHY: ESN, 1 (1949), 70–71.

[Simon Vega]

BLANK, ARTHUR M. (1942–), U.S. entrepreneur, philanthropist. Born in Queens, N.Y., Blank received an accounting degree from Babson College and worked as an accountant before joining a small pharmaceutical company started by his father. When the company was bought by Daylin, Blank became an executive at a Daylin drugstore unit. He then moved to the Handy Dan Improvement Centers, a division of Daylin, where he met Bernard *Marcus. In 1978, Blank and Marcus were fired by Daylin over disagreements about the small chain's future and decided to go into the home-improvement business. After surveying four cities, they settled on Atlanta as the place with the right market and real estate conditions to test their theory that consumers would flock to huge stores offering a broad selection of home improvement products, low prices, and hospitable service. They opened three Home Depot stores in 1979, employing 200 workers, and had $7 million in sales. They lost nearly $1 million. But their fortunes changed and the company went public in 1981. Their goal was to encourage creativity from everyone from sales people to managers, with stock options offered even to the lowest-level employees. Their adversary was the lumberyard down the street, not the boss. This familial structure, plus a ferocious sense of competition, proved a winning combination. Eventually, their muscle helped put Handy Dan out of business. By the end of 1998, Home Depot had grown to almost 800 stores, had 157,000 employees, and recorded more than $30 billion in sales. Home Depot became the do-it-yourself giant, providing everything from screws to electrical wiring for American fixer-uppers. It also opened stores in other countries, in Canada and South America.

Blank served as chief executive from May 1997 until December 2001, when he turned over day-to-day management to an executive from General Electric. During Blank's tenure, Home Depot sales more than doubled and the company's stock price almost tripled. Blank said he planned to devote more time to his family foundation and to his wife, who was expecting twins. In December 2001, Blank also completed a deal to buy the Atlanta Falcons professional football franchise for $545 million. Blank and Marcus became philanthropic leaders in Atlanta and Blank was chairman of the local Chamber of Commerce. When he retired, his stock holdings were estimated at $1.6 billion. His foundation gave away $100 million from 1995 through 2002. His philanthropies ranged from a new venue for the Atlanta Symphony Orchestra to restoring green space in the inner city to helping such nonprofits as Outward Bound and Zoo Atlanta. About 90 percent of the funds the Blank Family Foundation gives away goes to youth projects, but other causes also receive support. The foundation gives to many Jewish organizations. The Home Depot company has spawned as many as 1,000 millionaires. One former executive vice president, Ronald M. Brill, who helped start the company, gave $1 million for an endowment at the Atlanta Jewish Community Center in 1999.

[Stewart Kampel (2nd ed.)]

BLANK, LEON (1867–1934), Yiddish actor. Born in Lithuania, Blank and his family subsequently moved to Romania. He sang in synagogue choirs as a child but was attracted to Yiddish theater. He reached the U.S. in 1886, as a stowaway with Mogulesko's company. He started out as a member of the chorus but soon turned to acting. As a singer and a dramatic reader, Blank made a number of recordings in Yiddish.

His appearance in the play *David's Fidele* ("David's Violin," 1897) brought him recognition and started him on a successful career. Blank was one of the founders of the Hebrew Actor's Union in 1899. In the 1920s he starred in many of Jacob *Gordin's plays at the National Theatre, Liberty Theatre, and Public Theatre in New York. For a short period he was a member of a Yiddish theater company in Philadelphia, but he spent most of his time on the road, performing across the U.S. Despite offers from Broadway and Hollywood, Blank remained attached to the Jewish theater. His memoirs were serialized in *Der Forverts* (Oct. 5, 1928–Jan. 29, 1929).

[Ruth Beloff (2nd ed.)]

BLANK, MAURICE (1848–1921), Romanian banker. Born in Pitesti, Romania, Blank was one of the first Romanian Jews to receive diplomas in economics and finance at the Vienna and Leipzig universities. He went to work in Bucharest in the banking house of Jacob Marmorosh, who later invited him to become a partner. Marmorosh, Blank and Company became Romania's largest bank after the Romanian National Bank. Blank made important connections with East European financial institutions and was instrumental in developing his country's economic relations with the rest of Europe, particularly after Romania became independent in 1878. His bank shared in developing many of the country's industries, helped to introduce steel trains, and made possible the financing of the great tunnel project at Barbosi. Blank was involved in Jewish and general communal affairs, giving generous support to cultural institutions and founding theaters and publishing houses. His son ARISTIDE BLANK (1884–1962) became general director of the bank on his father's death and was also a supporter of many Jewish and general causes. He published a number of studies on finance, and some plays in Romanian and French. Aristide Blank was also a promoter of Romanian culture: he financed the publication of books on history and archaeology, bought the *Adevarul* and *Dimineata* dailies, and supported the Popular Theater of Bucharest and the Romanian school in Paris. He also founded the nonprofit Cultura Nationala publishing house, which published books in the fields of literature, the humanities, and social sciences, with the aim of encouraging writers and promoting good literature. He also financed the translation of the Bible into Romanian by the writer-priest Gala Galaction. In 1950, ruined and persecuted by the Communist regime, Aristide Blank left for Paris, where he lived in poverty and died.

ADD. BIBLIOGRAPHY: S. Bickel, *Yahadut Romanyah* (1978), 47–50, 321; A Mirodan, *Dictionar neconventional*, 1 (1986), 174–79; L. Bathory, in: *Studia Judaica*, 1 (1991), 94–103.

[Joachim O. Ronall / Lucian-Zeev Herscovici (2nd ed.)]

BLANK, SAMUEL LEIB (1893–1962), Hebrew novelist and short-story writer. Blank, who was born in the Ukraine, spent his formative years in Bessarabia and in 1922 settled in the United States. His early stories described the Jewish farmers of Bessarabia, and his tetralogy *Ẓon, Adamah, Naḥalah* (1930–33), and *Moshavah* (1936) focused upon a simple protagonist, significantly and symbolically called "Bo'az." Blank was not a subtle psychologist, but he vividly depicted the Jewish man of the soil in his primitive surroundings. When he attempted to portray the harsher realities of life after World War I, such as the pogroms in the Ukraine in his *Bi-She'at Ḥerum* (1932) or the maladjusted immigrant in America, as in *Mr. Kunis* (1934) or *Iy ha-Dema'ot* (1941), he verged on melodrama. *Al Admat Amerikah* (1958) and *Eẓ ha-Sadeh* (1961) were among his last works.

BIBLIOGRAPHY: Waxman, Literature, 4 (1960^2), 1055–58; 5 (1960^2), 202–4; M. Ribalow, *Im ha-Kad el ha Mabbu'a* (1950), 237–43.

[Eisig Silberschlag]

BLANK, SHELDON HAAS (1896–1989), U.S. rabbi and Bible scholar. Blank was ordained at Hebrew Union College, Cincinnati, Ohio, in 1923. From 1926 he taught Bible at the Hebrew Union College. Blank published numerous studies on many aspects of biblical scholarship, dealing with questions of the text and of social and political history. He made a special contribution by his insights into the religious experience of biblical personalities, especially the prophets, and by his exposition of their religious ideas. These qualities characterize his books *Prophetic Faith in Isaiah* (1958) and *Jeremiah: Man and Prophet* (1961) as well as such essays as "Men against God, the Promethean Element in Biblical Prayer" (in JBL, 72 (1953), 1–13), "Doest Thou Well to Be Angry? A Study in Self-Pity" (in HUCA, 26 (1955), 29–41), and "Of a Truth the Lord Hath Sent Me, an Inquiry into the Source of the Prophet's Authority" (1955). In these studies he strictly followed the canons of critical scholarship. Elsewhere, however, he sought to reinterpret biblical thoughts in terms of the present day: "The Relevance of Prophetic Thought for the Modern Rabbi" (CCARY, 65 (1955), 163–72) and *The Dawn of Our Responsibility* (1961). He was editor of the *Hebrew Union College Annual* for more than 60 years,

BIBLIOGRAPHY: *Dictionary Catalog of the Klau Library*, 4 (1964), 465–70. **ADD. BIBLIOGRAPHY:** *HUC-JIR at 100 Years* (1976).

[Bernard J. Bamberger]

BLANKENSTEIN, MARCUS VAN (1880–1964), Dutch journalist. From 1909 to 1920, Blankenstein reported from Berlin, returned to Rotterdam in 1931, and became chief foreign editor of the *Nieuwe Rotterdamsche Courant*. He left in 1936 when his articles were considered too anti-Nazi. He reached England in 1940 and became chief editor of the Free Dutch weekly *Vrij Nederland* in London. After the war he was a foreign editor and roving correspondent of the daily *Het Parool*.

ADD. BIBLIOGRAPHY: E. van Blankenstein, *Dr. M. van Blankenstein: een Nederlandse dagbladdiplomaat, 1880–1964* (1999).

BLANKFORT, MICHAEL S. (1907–1982), novelist, and screenwriter. After publishing *The Widow-Makers* (1946) and *Big Yankee, the Life of Carlson of the Raiders* (1947), Blankfort, an ardent Zionist, achieved international success with *The Juggler* (1952), which deals with a young refugee's adjustment to normal life in the State of Israel. His other works include *The Strong Hand* (1956), about a young Orthodox rabbi's tragic love affair with a war widow; screenplays, such as his adaptation of Herman Wouk's *The Caine Mutiny* (1954); and *Behold the Fire* (1965), a novel based on the exploits of the *Nili conspirators for which he was awarded the S.Y. Agnon Prize.

ADD. BIBLIOGRAPHY: "Michael Blankfort, 74," in: *New York Times* (July 16, 1982), B4.

BLANKSTEIN, CECIL (1908–1989), Canadian architect. Blankstein was born in Winnipeg, Manitoba, into a building and architectural dynasty. His grandfather Meyer was a contractor and stonemason in Odessa and his father Max was a Russian-trained architect who practiced in Winnipeg from 1905, the first registered Jewish architect in western Canada. Cecil Blankstein graduated with a degree in architecture from the University of Manitoba in 1929. His sister Evelyn and brother Morley were also architects and his son Arthur became an interior designer in Winnipeg and son Max a town planner in Israel.

Heavily influenced by the German Bauhaus tradition, Blankstein's contemporary designs graced residential, commercial, and public building in Winnipeg and elsewhere in Canada, including the Winnipeg Concert Hall, Winnipeg Airport, Winnipeg City Hall, Winnipeg Post Office, the Lorne Building in Ottawa, which until recently housed The National Gallery of Canada, and buildings on several Canadian university campuses. Of special note are Blankstein's contemporary postwar design for Winnipeg's Shaarey Zedek Synagogue and his imaginative conception, in the late 1960s, for a major terraced housing project, Tzameret Habirah, in Jerusalem's French Hill quarter. Blankstein's artful combination of row housing with stacked building techniques set a new standard for hillside residential construction in Israel.

[Harold Troper (2nd ed.)]

BLANTER, MATVEY ISAAKOVICH (1903–1990), songwriter. Born in Pochep, Ukraine, Blanter studied violin, theory, and composition in various institutions in Kiev (1915–17) and Moscow (1917–21). His pieces and music for the Leningrad Satirical Theater attracted early attention. During the period that he worked with the Krokodil miniature theater in Gorky, he developed an individual humorous style. He wrote for musical comedies, and his tune "Katyusha" attained popular success during World War II. His music, which made use of folk melodies, also shows an urban vernacular and jazz influences.

BIBLIOGRAPHY: V. Zak, *Matvey Blanter* (1973); L. Genina, in: *Sovetskaya muzyka*, 4 (1983), 4–7; *Izvestia* (28 Sept. 1990)

BLASER, ISAAC (1837–1907), Russian rabbi and educator. Blaser was one of the foremost disciples of R. Israel *Lipkin (Salanter), whose Musar (ethicist) *movement he helped develop and lead. In the early 1850s, Blaser moved from his native Vilna to Kovno, Lithuania, where he came under the influence of Lipkin. In 1864 he reluctantly accepted the rabbinate of St. Petersburg, hence the name by which he is familiarly known, "Reb Itzelle Peterburger." During this time he wrote halakhic works and responsa, arousing the opposition of the *maskilim*. He left the rabbinate in 1878, returning to Kovno where he headed the *kolel* ("advanced talmudical academy"), and sent emissaries throughout the world to gain support for it. He helped to found the yeshivah of *Slobodka. About 1891, as the result of bitter controversy concerning the Musar movement, he left the *kolel* of Kovno and helped to found other such Musar-oriented schools elsewhere. Increasing opposition to the Musar movement (1896–98) and to Blaser, its chief exponent, forced the yeshivah to leave its premises in Slobodka, and it finally became established in Kelm (1898). In 1904 Blaser, favoring the idea of Jewish colonization of Palestine, immigrated to and settled in Jerusalem, where he died. His main contribution to the Musar movement was his emphasis on acquiring "fear of the Lord" (i.e., piety) by means of emotional meditation in works of *musar*. Unlike other disciples of Salanter, who expounded *musar* intellectually, Blaser held that knowledge and conceptualization were inadequate to the task of curbing man's baser instincts. "Fear of the Lord" could be aroused only by an unsophisticated contemplation of man's physical vulnerability, his moral lowliness, and his punishment for continued disobedience. Since he held that the form of such meditation makes a more lasting impression than the contents, he prescribed the reading aloud of *musar* texts in a melancholy melody, with frequent periods of weeping. Similarly, his preaching was simple, sad, and usually accompanied by tears. Blaser's major literary contribution to the Musar movement, *Or Yisrael* ("Light of Israel," 1900), was often reprinted, and for several decades was the only available exposition of *musar*. Blaser here expounded the fundamentals of the Musar approach and presented excerpts from the letters of Israel Lipkin, along with evaluations of the teachings of the founders of the Musar movement and of some of its leading personalities. His major halakhic work is *Peri Yiẓḥak* ("Fruit of Isaac"); the first volume was published in Vilna in 1881, some 14 years after he had completed writing it. The second volume was published posthumously in 1912. He contributed numerous articles, both on *halakhah* and *musar*, to the various rabbinic journals of the day. Much of his writing remained unpublished.

BIBLIOGRAPHY: D. Katz, *Tenu'at ha-Musar*, 2 (1954), 220–73; S. Bialoblotzki, in: *Yahadut Lita*, 1 (1959), 194–7; Ch. Zaichyk, *Ha-Me'orot ha-Gedolim* (1962), 109–29.

[Norman Lamm]

BLASPHEMY, in the broadest (and least precise) sense any act contrary to the will of God or derogatory to His power. Blasphemy is the term employed to translate the Hebrew verbs *ḥeref, giddef*, and *ni'eẓ* (e.g., Isa. 37:6, *gdf*, where the servants of the king of Assyria denied the Lord's power to save Israel; and Ezek. 20:27, where it refers to Israel's sacrifices on the High Places). In the narrower and more precise sense, the word is used to mean speaking contemptuously of the Deity. The classic instance in the Bible is Leviticus 24:10–23, where the pronouncement (*nakav, naqav*) of the name of God appears in conjunction with the verb *killel* (*qillel*). God (*Elohim*) also appears as the object of the verb *qillel* in Exodus 22:27 (see also I Kings 21:10, 13, where *qillel* is euphemistically displaced by its antonym *berekh*, "to bless" or "to renounce"; see *Euphemism and Dysphemism). The rabbinic interpretation of Leviticus 24:10–23 and Exodus 22:27 as wishing (i.e., wishing harm, Sanh. 7:5) establishes a definition of blasphemy such as to render the actual perpetration (and the application of the penalty, capital punishment) out of the realm of probability. The verb *qallel* rarely means "to curse." Rather it subsumes a wide range of abuse, often nonverbal in nature. "To curse" the Deity meant to repudiate Him, to violate His norms; blasphemy on the part of an Israelite, in the narrow sense, is a concept alien to biblical thought.

[Herbert Chanan Brichto]

In the Talmud

The Mishnah (Sanh. 7:5), rules that the death sentence by stoning should be applied only in the case where the blasphemer had uttered the *Tetragrammaton and two witnesses had warned him prior to the transgression. In the Talmud, however, R. Meir extends this punishment to cases where the blasphemer had used one of the *attributes, i.e., substitute names of God (Sanh. 56a). The accepted *halakhah* is that only the one who has uttered the Tetragrammaton be sentenced to death by stoning; the offender who pronounced the substitute names is only flogged (Maim., Yad, Avodat Kokhavim, 2:7). In the court procedure (Sanh. 5:7 and Sanh. 60a) the witnesses for the prosecution testified to the words of the blasphemer by substituting the expressions "Yose shall strike Yose" (*yakkeh Yose et Yose*). Toward the end of the hearing, however, after the audience had been dismissed, the senior witness was asked to repeat the exact words uttered by the blasphemer. Upon their pronouncement (i.e., of the Tetragrammaton), the judges stood up and rent their garments. The act expressed their profound mourning at hearing the name of God profaned. The custom of tearing one's clothes on hearing blasphemy is attested to in II Kings 18:37, where it is told that Eliakim and his associates tore their garments upon hearing the blasphemous words of the Assyrian warlord *Rab-Shakeh (Sanh. 60a). It is codified in Shulḥan Arukh (YD 340:37) that whoever bears a blasphemy whether with the Tetragrammaton or with attributes, in any language and from a Jew, even from the mouth of a witness, must rend his garment. The second and any successive witnesses only testified: "I have heard the same words" (Sanh. 7:5); according to the opinion of *Abba Saul, whoever utters the Tetragrammaton in public is excluded from the world to come (Av. Zar. 18a). Besides the sacrilege of God, vituperation against the king, God's anointed servant, was also considered blasphemy (cf. Ex. 22:27 and I Kings 21:10). Gentiles, too, are obliged to refrain from blasphemy since this is one of the Seven *Noachide Laws (Sanh. 56a, 60a). Maimonides also classified as blasphemy the erasure of God's name written on paper or engraved on stone, etc., which was to be punished by flogging (Yad, Yesodei ha-Torah 6:1–6). After Jewish courts were deprived of jurisdiction in those cases where capital punishment was applied, excommunication (see *ḥerem) was the usual sanction against a blasphemer (J. Mueller (ed.), *Teshuvot Ge'onei Mizraḥ u-Ma'arav* (1898), 27a, responsum no. 103 by Amram Gaon).

BIBLIOGRAPHY: Eisenstein, Dinim, 68.

BLAU, AMRAM (1894–1974), rabbi, leader of the ultra-Orthodox sect *Neturei Karta. Blau was born in Jerusalem into a noted religious family. He was a leading member of the Agudat Israel youth movement in the early 1930s. Blau and some of his colleagues left the movement in 1935 and founded the extreme anti-Zionist Ḥevrat Ḥayyim, later to become Neturei Karta. His fierce opposition to Zionism and Agudat Israel, sometimes expressed violently, led on several occasions to his prosecution and imprisonment. His anti-Zionist attitude did not change with the establishment of the State of Israel (1948), which he refused to recognize. Blau and his followers rejected the State of Israel on so-called "halakhic" grounds, rejecting a state run by secular Jews. In addition, Blau continually denounced the establishment of a Jewish state before the coming of the Messiah as an act of infamy and blasphemy. In 1965, after the death of his first wife, he married a proselyte, Ruth Ben-David, despite the opposition of the ultra-Orthodox *bet din* and some of his followers.

[Menachem Friedman / David Derovan (2nd ed.)]

BLAU, BRUNO (1881–1954), German lawyer and sociologist. Born in West Prussia, Blau practiced law in Berlin. In 1908 he joined A. *Ruppin as editor, and from 1909 was the sole editor, of the *Zeitschrift fuer Demographie und Statistik der Juden* (1904–19; new series 1924–27), published by the Buero fuer Statistik der Juden, of which Blau became director after Ruppin left for Palestine in 1907. Because of his severe illness, the Nazis did not deport him during World War II but kept him confined in the police section of the Berlin Jewish Hospital. Blau immigrated to the United States after the war, but returned to Germany before his death. Among Blau's many published works are *Kriminalitaet der deutschen Juden* (1906) and *Das Ende der Juden in Deutschland* (1950; *Last Days of German Jewry*, 1953). He also edited the anthology *Statistik der Juden* (1918). Of particular importance is his work on anti-Jewish Nazi legislation and administrative orders, *Ausnahmerecht fuer die Juden in den europaeischen Laendern* (vol. 1, 1952), which is a collection of documents from Germany and was reprinted as *Ausnahmerecht fuer die Juden in Deutschland, 1933–1945* (1954).

BLAU, FRITZ (1865–1929), Austrian chemist. From 1890 he taught at Vienna University. In 1902 he joined the Auregesellschaft in Berlin, and from 1919 was head of research of the Osram Company in Berlin, at that time one of the foremost industrial firms in Germany. He took out 185 patents, some in organic chemistry, but most dealing with tungsten, incandescent electric lamps, gases, and radiation. This work led to other patented developments in wireless telegraphy, electric furnaces, and X-ray machines and techniques. In addition, Blau published many papers in scientific journals on these subjects.

BIBLIOGRAPHY: *Zeitschrift fuer technische Physik*, 6 (1925), 278–359.

[Samuel Aaron Miller]

BLAU, HERBERT (1926–), U.S. theater director and educator. Born in New York, Blau received a bachelor's degree in chemical engineering from New York University (1947), an M.A. in drama from Stanford University (1949), and a Ph.D. in English and American literature from Stanford (1954). He formed the Actor's Workshop in San Francisco with Jules *Irving, in 1952. One of Blau's innovative acts was to present a play to the inmates of San Quentin penitentiary. On November 19, 1957, a group of actors faced an audience of 1,400 convicts. No live play had been performed at San Quentin since Sarah Bernhardt had appeared there in 1913. Now, 45 years later, the play that had been chosen, largely because no women appeared in it, was Samuel Beckett's *Waiting for Godot*. It was an unequivocal success. Overall, this repertory theater was highly successful but failed financially, and closed in 1965. Blau and Irving then directed the Lincoln Center Repertory Theater, New York, but Blau resigned in 1968. His last extended work in the theater was as artistic director of the experimental group KRAKEN (1968–81). Blau served as its first provost as well as dean of the School of Theater. A radical departure from the already innovative theater that Blau had been associated with, the work of KRAKEN included some of the first productions in the U.S. of such controversial dramatists of the modernist period as Brecht, Beckett, *Pinter, Ionesco, Whiting, Arden, Duerrenmatt, Frisch, and Genet.

Blau was distinguished professor of English and Modern Studies at the University of Wisconsin, Milwaukee, where he was also a senior fellow at the Center for 20th Century Studies. Subsequently he was the Byron W. and Alice L. Lockwood Professor in the Humanities at the University of Washington.

Regarded as the reigning theorist of theater and performance in our time, Blau wrote many books on the subject. *Sails of the Herring Fleet: Essays on Beckett* (2000) traces Blau's encounters with the work of Samuel Beckett. He directed Beckett's plays when they were still virtually unknown, and for more than four decades remained one of the leading interpreters of his work. In addition to now-classic essays, the book includes two interviews – one from Blau's experience directing *Waiting for Godot* at San Quentin prison and one from his last visit with Beckett, just before the playwright's death. *Take Up the Bodies: Theater at the Vanishing Point* (1982) and *Blooded Thought: Occasions of Theater* (1982) received the George Jean Nathan Award for Dramatic Criticism. Other books by Blau include *The Impossible Theater. A Manifesto* (1964), *The Eye of Prey: Subversions of the Postmodern* (1987), *The Audience* (1990), *To All Appearances: Ideology and Performance* (1992), *Nothing in Itself: Complexions of Fashion* (1999), and *The Dubious Spectacle: Extremities of Theater, 1976–2000* (2002).

Blau received *The Kenyon Review* award for literary excellence.

[Ruth Beloff (2nd ed.)]

BLAU, JOSEPH LEON (1909–1986), U.S. educator and historian of ideas. Born in Brooklyn, New York, Blau was educated at Columbia University. He taught at Columbia from 1944, where he later became a professor of religion (1962–77). In 1966 he became vice president of the Conference on Jewish Social Studies. Blau followed the philosophic tradition of naturalistic humanism in the line of John Dewey and his school at Columbia. He carried on their interest in the history of philosophy in America in his book *Men and Movements in American Philosophy* (1952) and in monographic studies.

As Blau was a student (and, later, collaborator) of Salo W. *Baron, his approach to Jewish history emphasizes interdisciplinary and cross-cultural influences. He opposes the conventional interpretation that the development of the Jewish religious and philosophical tradition is mainly linear, maintaining that the Jews were not cut off from cross-cultural contact for any significant period of their history. He compiled *The Jews of the United States, 1790–1840* (ed. with S.W. Baron, 1963), and wrote *Judaism in America* (1976). His book *The Story of Jewish Philosophy* (1962) explores the ways in which Jewish thinkers absorbed and modified the ideas current in their cultural environment. In *Modern Varieties of Judaism* (1966), Blau demonstrates the same principle of interplay of tradition and environment in the shaping of Jewish religion since the 18th century. *The Christian Interpretation of the Cabala in the Renaissance* (1944) investigates the flow of ideas in the reverse direction – that is, from Jewish to Christian thinkers.

Blau also edited the book *Essays on Jewish Life and Thought: Presented in Honor of Salo Wittmeyer Baron* (1959).

ADD. BIBLIOGRAPHY: M. Wohlgelernter, *History, Religion, and American Democracy* (1993).

BLAU, JOSHUA (1919–), scholar of biblical Hebrew grammar, Middle Arabic, and **Genizah* manuscripts. Born in Cluj, Transylvania, Blau studied in the Jewish Gymnasium in Budapest and Baden. He had barely spent a year in Jewish studies at the Rabbinical Seminary and Semitic languages at the University of Vienna when he had to flee the country in 1938 after its occupation by the Nazis. He immigrated to Palestine with his parents, where he continued his academic studies in Hebrew, Bible, and Arabic at the Hebrew University of Jerusalem (M.A., 1942). In 1948 he presented his dissertation on *The Grammar of Judeo-Arabic*, but was only awarded a Ph.D. two years later, after the War of Independence, during which he served in the army and took part in battles in Jerusalem.

In 1956 he was appointed senior lecturer at Tel Aviv University and a year later lecturer at the Hebrew University (professor from 1962), where he taught until his retirement in 1986.

Blau was a member of the Academy of Hebrew Language from the 1950s, was its president in 1981–93, and editor of its journal, *Leshonenu*, in 1981–99. Blau was also a member of the Israeli Academy for Sciences and Humanities from 1968 and head of Humanities, 1989–95; honorary fellow of the Royal Asiatic Society; and corresponding fellow of the American Academy for Jewish Research.

Blau's research focused on the fields of biblical Hebrew grammar, Semitic languages, and medieval Arabic. His books *Torat ha-Hegeh ve-ha-Ẓurot* ("Phonology and Morphology of Biblical Hebrew," 1971), *Oẓar Leshon ha-Mikra* ("A Concordance and Dictionary of the Bible," with S.A. Loewenstamm and M.Z. Kaddari, vol. 1 (1957), 2 (1960), 3 (1968)), *Dikduk ha-Aravit ha-Yehudit shel Yemei ha-Beinayim* ("Grammar of Judeo-Arabic of the Middle-Ages," 1962, updated 1980) and others (see below) along with hundreds of articles brought him the fame as the leading authority on Judeo-Arabic and a prominent expert on other branches of Semitic languages. Blau described the rise of Judeo-Arabic in *The Emergence and Linguistic Background of Judaeo-Arabic: A Study of the Origins of Middle Arabic* (1965, 1999³), and also published *A Grammar of Christian Arabic* (3 vols., 1966–67). In these works Blau provided a solid foundation for research into medieval Judeo- and Christian-Arabic. These linguistic types had never been sufficiently studied or assessed before, because they were outside the scope of Muslim culture. In his studies, Blau provided a profound analysis and thorough description of a full-fledged and unique literature. He also showed the importance of this layer of Arabic in the crystallization of general standard Arabic as it has come down to us. Together with Prof. Simon Hopkins, he discovered an early phonetic method of Judeo-Arabic spelling, which enables us to reconstruct the very beginnings of Judeo-Arabic culture. Blau's research project on Middle Arabic will be completed with the publication of his immense *Dictionary of Medieval Judeo-Arabic Texts.*

Another important achievement of Blau's consists in his annotated critical edition of *Teshuvot ha-Rambam* ("Responsa of Maimonides") in three volumes (1958, 1960–61) with a Hebrew translation of the Arabic original, and an additional volume (1986).

Blau was founding president (1983–99) of the Association for Medieval Judeo-Arabic, which holds an international biannual conference.

Blau also contributed to the field of education. Thousands of high school and college students learned Hebrew grammar from his series *Dikduk Ivri Shittati*, *Yesodot ha-Taḥbir*, and *Yesodot Torat ha-Lashon* (2 vols.).

Blau was awarded the Ben-Zvi Prize in 1980; the Wilhelm Bacher Medal (Hungary) in 1999; the Mark Lidzbarski Medal in 2000; the Rothschild Prize in 1992; and the Israel Prize in 1985.

A list of Blau's publications up to 1991 is to be found in *Hebrew and Arabic Studies in Honour of Joshua Blau, Presented by Friends and Students on the Occasion of his Seventieth Birthday* (ed. H. Ben-Shammai; 1993), pp. 1–34. Subsequently he published over 60 articles and three books: *Iyyunim be-Valshanut Ivrit* (1996), *Topics in Hebrew and Semitic Linguistics* (1998), and *A Handbook of Early Middle Arabic* (2003).

Blau's father, Pinchas (Paul), was one of the founders of the Hungarian Zionist daily newspaper **Uj Kelet* at the end of World War I.

BIBLIOGRAPHY: *The Hebrew University of Jerusalem – General Information* (2000), 66; J. Blau, *Mi-Transilvani'ah li-Yerushalayim* (2000); *Perasei Rotshild li-Shenat 1992*, 5; *Perasei Yisrael ha-Tashmah* (1985), 8–9.

[Aharon Maman (2nd ed.)]

BLAU, LUDWIG LAJOS (1861–1936), scholar. Blau studied at yeshivot, the Jewish Theological Seminary of Budapest, and the University of Budapest. As a student he was invited to teach at the Seminary where in 1889 he became a full professor. In 1914 Blau became director of the Seminary. For 40 years he was the editor of the Hungarian Jewish scholarly journal, *Magyar Zsidó Szemle*. In 1911 he founded the Hebrew review *Ha-Ẓofeh le-Ḥokhmat Yisrael be-Ereẓ Hagar*, which he edited until 1931. Blau was a prolific Jewish scholar who contributed to almost every aspect of Jewish learning. He was a regular contributor to most of the Jewish and non-Jewish scholarly periodicals dedicated to theology and philology. His bibliography includes 887 items and in the *Zsidó Szemle* he reviewed 1,383 books. He was among the first to evaluate the talmudic information on the Bible and the masorah (*Masoretische Untersuchungen*, 1891; *Zur Einleitung in die Heilige Schrift*, 1894). He also investigated the information contained in traditional literature on ancient Hebrew booklore (*Studien zum althebraeischen Buchwesen*, 1902). His works subsequently gained added importance in light of interest in old Hebrew scrolls. Blau enriched general folklore by his book *Das altjuedische Zauberwesen* (1898). Equally his *Juedische Ehescheidung und der juedische Scheidebrief* (2 vols., 1911–12) broke new ground; with the discovery of divorce documents among the Bar Kokhba finds, this work takes on new relevance. Blau was among the first to make use of Greek papyri for the evaluation of talmudic law (*Papyri und Talmud in gegenseitiger Beleuchtung*, 1913; "Prosbul im Lichte der griechischen Papyri und der Rechtsgeschichte," in *Festschrift der Landesrabbinerschule*, 1927). He also published the letters of Leone *Modena (*Leo Modenas Briefe und Schriftstuecke*, 2 vols., 1905–06).

BIBLIOGRAPHY: S. Hevesi, in: *Ve-Zot li-Yhudah* (1926), 1–9; D. Friedman, in: *Jubileumi emlékkönyv Blau Lajos… 65. születésnapja… alkalmából* (1926), 14–90 (bibliography); D.S. Loewinger, *Zikhron Yehudah* (1938), 5–45; J. Bakonyi and D. Friedman, *ibid.*, 18–34.

[Alexander Scheiber]

BLAU, MOSHE (1885–1946), *Agudat Israel leader; brother of Amram *Blau. Blau, who was born in Jerusalem, directed the Agudat Israel office there from 1924 until his death. He served as a member of the movement's world executive and edited its weekly *Kol Yisrael* ("Voice of Israel"). From 1933 to 1945 he headed the independent, ultra-Orthodox Edah Ḥaredit (Orthodox community). Despite the community's segregation policy, he cooperated with *yishuv* leaders in representing Jewish interests in dealings with the Mandate government. Blau represented Agudat Israel before various British and international commissions which dealt with the Palestine problem. In 1946, while on a rescue mission to Jewish survivors of the war, Blau fell ill and died in Messina. He was taken to Jerusalem for burial. He wrote *Ammuda di-Nehora* ("Column of Light," 1932), a biography of Rabbi Y.Ḥ. *Sonnenfeld, and *Al Ḥomotayikh Yerushalayim* ("Upon thy Walls, O Jerusalem," 1946), autobiographical notes and memoirs.

BIBLIOGRAPHY: A. Blau, *Shomer ha-Ḥomot* (1957); Tidhar, 1 (1947), 175–6.

[Zvi Kaplan]

BLAU, PETER MICHAEL (1918–2002), sociologist. Born in Vienna, Blau immigrated to the United States. He received his doctorate in sociology from Columbia University in 1952 and held professorial appointments at the University of Chicago. He was a professor of sociology at Columbia University. During the academic year 1966–67, he was Pitt Professor of American History and Institutions at the University of Cambridge. His main interests were the development of group social structure, formal organizations, and occupations. Considered one of the founders of contemporary American sociology, Blau studied macrostructural characteristics of society. His theories sought to explain how such social phenomena as upward mobility, occupational opportunity, heterogeneity, and population structures influence human behavior.

In addition to numerous contributions to professional journals and books, Blau published a large number of his own books, which include *The Dynamics of Bureaucracy: A Study of Interpersonal Relations in Two Government Agencies* (1955), *Bureaucracy in Modern Society* (1956), *Formal Organizations: A Comparative Approach* (1962), *Exchange and Power in Social Life* (1964), *The American Occupational Structure* (1967), *The Structure of Organizations* (1971), *The Organization of Aca-*

demic Work (1973), *On the Nature of Organizations* (1974), *and Crosscutting Social Circles* (1996).

Blau was editor of the *American Journal of Sociology* from 1961 until 1967, a member of the board of the Social Science Research Council in 1967–69, and served as the 65th president of the American Sociological Association in 1974.

From 1979 through 1983 he taught at SUNY-Albany as Distinguished Professor. He taught in Tianjin in China at the Academy of Social Sciences as a Distinguished Honorary Professor (1981 and 1987). In 1988 he retired as a faculty member from Columbia University but taught at UNC at Chapel Hill as the Robert Broughton Distinguished Research Professor until 2001. Blau was professor emeritus at Columbia, a fellow of the National Academy of Sciences, senior fellow at King's College, fellow of the American Philosophical Society, and fellow of the American Academy of Arts and Sciences.

[Jacob Jay Lindenthal / Ruth Beloff (2nd ed.)]

BLAU, TINA (1845–1916), Austrian painter. Blau was born in Vienna. Realizing her early interest in painting her father arranged for lessons with the landscape painter Antal Hanély, with whom she started painting still lifes with fruits and flowers. In the early 1860s August Schaeffer became her tutor. From 1867 her paintings, especially landscapes, were shown in public exhibitions. While visiting Munich and the First International Exhibition in 1869, she discovered the paintings of the School of Barbizon, which influenced her later works, but in the end she adapted French impressionism and became one of the leading Austrian impressionist painters. After her initial success in selling her paintings, she enrolled in the Kunstschule fuer Maedchen in Munich and took an atelier in the house of her teacher Wilhelm Lindenschmitt. Together with her colleague Emil Jakob Schindler she traveled to Hungary and Holland, where she painted *Jew's Street of Amsterdam* (1875/1876, coll. Vera Eisenberger, Vienna). After two sojourns in Italy (1876 and 1879) she opened an atelier in the Vienna Prater, from where her most popular paintings originated, namely luminous views of the Prater such as *Springtime in the Prater* (1882, Vienna, Oesterreichische Galerie Belvedere).

In 1884 Blau returned to Munich, where she converted to Protestantism and married the painter Heinrich Lang. At that time, her own works were presented at international exhibitions such as the World Exhibitions of Antwerp in 1885 and of Paris in 1889. Moreover she started working at the Damenakademie des Muenchner Kuenstlerinnenvereins, an academy of fine arts solely for women, where she taught still life and landscape painting. In the summers she continued traveling, especially to France, Northern Germany, and Denmark. A first solo exhibition in the Munich Kunstverein contributed to the wide appreciation of her work at the end of the 19th century. She continued teaching at the academy until 1915, a year before she died, but was never accepted as a member of the Wiener Kuenstlerhaus.

BIBLIOGRAPHY: G.T. Natter and C. Jesina: *Tina Blau* (1999); *Plenair, die Landschaftsmalerin Tina Blau, 1845–1916* (Catalogue, Jewish Museum, Vienna, 1996).

[Philipp Zschommler (2nd ed.)]

BLAUBAUM, ELIAS (1847–1904), Australian Jewish minister. Born in rural Hesse, Germany, Blaubaum immigrated to Australia in 1873, learning English on the boat en route, and served as minister of Melbourne's St. Kilda Hebrew Congregation until his death. Learned in Jewish law, he defended traditional Orthodoxy and, although never ordained as a rabbi, served on Melbourne's Beth Din. From 1879 he edited the *Jewish Herald* newspaper and was one of the earliest Jewish voices in Australia to assert Jewish identity in an aggressive manner and to combat antisemitism.

BIBLIOGRAPHY: H.L. Rubinstein, "Rev. Elias Blaubaum," in: *Australian Jewish Historical Society Journal,* 9 (Part 8), 1985, 567–81; idem, Australia I, 263–64, index.

[William D. Rubinstein (2nd ed.)]

BLAUSTEIN, U.S. industrialist family. LOUIS (1869–1937) was born in Russia and emigrated to the U.S. in 1888. Starting in business as a kerosene peddler, Blaustein went to work in 1892 for the Standard Oil Company at its Baltimore plant and by 1910 had risen to an executive position. In that year he left Standard Oil and, with a small amount of capital, founded the American Oil Company in Baltimore. The enterprise flourished due in large part to Blaustein's innovations in oil distribution in a period when the automobile was emerging as the major user of petroleum products. He experimented with new forms of gasoline and claimed the first high-test gasoline developed in the country. Blaustein's filling stations spread from Baltimore through Maryland and eventually covered the entire East Coast. In 1924 the giant Pan-American Petroleum and Transport Company (later controlled by Standard Oil Company of Indiana) paid $5,000,000 for a half interest in the American Oil Company and merged with it in 1933. Blaustein remained active in the firm as it continued to expand, building steamship terminals and petroleum refineries. During his later years he gave large sums to charity, usually anonymously. JACOB (1892–1970), son of Louis, was associated with his father in the founding of the American Oil Company in 1910, serving in executive positions and as its president during 1933–37. Later he served as president of the American Trading and Production Corporation as well as director and executive committee member of major national companies in the fields of petroleum, insurance, and banking. He was reportedly one of the richest individuals in America. During World War II Blaustein was vice-chairman of the U.S. Petroleum Administration's marketing committee and served on other wartime committees. His civic activities include support of the American Heritage Foundation, United Negro College Fund, and American Association for the United Nations. Blaustein played an active role in Jewish affairs, with a major commitment to the American Jewish Committee, which he served as executive committee chairman (1944–49) and president (1949–54). As president, Blaustein worked to protect the civil and religious rights of Jews and other minorities and to promote tolerance among races. He served on the boards of the American Friends of the Hebrew University and the Weizmann Institute of Science. His philanthropic activities ranged from local philanthropy in Baltimore, to the American Jewish Joint Distribution Committee, United Service for New Americans, and the Conference on Jewish Claims Against Germany. He was a member of the American delegation to the tenth UN General Assembly and was a leader in the movement to adopt the Convention on Genocide and the Declaration of Human Rights, helping to promote the idea of a UN High Commissioner for Human Rights, a position that was established more than two decades after his death.

Several important institutions have been created and/or funded by the Blaustein family.

The Blaustein Philanthropic Group, located in Baltimore, Maryland, is a constellation of foundations inspired by the legacy of Louis and Henrietta Blaustein. Each foundation represents a different branch of the Blaustein family and has a unique identity, set of priorities, and geographic focus. United by their roots in Jewish tradition, the foundations are dedicated to social justice and equal opportunity. As part of the Blaustein Philanthropic Group, the Jacob and Hilda Blaustein Foundation provides grants to help further the cause of human rights as well as strengthen Jewish life, Israeli democracy, educational opportunity, health, and mental well-being. The Jacob Blaustein Center for Scientific Cooperation, located in Israel, supports a variety of activities related to the promotion of scientific cooperation with scientists and institutions in Israel and around the world. The Institute for Desert Research, established in *Sedeh Boker in 1974 under the auspices of Ben-Gurion University in Beersheba, received a generous contribution from The Jacob and Hilda Blaustein Foundation in 1980 and was named The Jacob Blaustein Institute for Desert Research (BIDR).

BIBLIOGRAPHY: LOUIS BLAUSTEIN: *New York Times* (July 28, 1937), 19. JACOB BLAUSTEIN: H. Frank, in: *Jewish Digest* (March 1962); *Current Biography Yearbook 1949* (1950), 60–61; *Forbes* (Sept. 15, 1968), 26–28.

[Morton Rosenstock / Ruth Beloff (2nd ed.)]

BLAUSTEIN, ABRAHAM (1836–1914), *ḥazzan*. Born in Riga, Blaustein became a cantor in Lomza, later in Vilna, and then settled in Germany. In 1877 he was appointed chief cantor of Bromberg (now Bydgoszcz in Poland), a position he held until his death. He edited a weekly paper for cantors and founded an association for raising professional standards.

BLAUSTEIN, DAVID (1866–1912), educator and communal worker. Born in Lida (province of Vilna), Blaustein fled to Germany in 1883 to evade conscription. There he worked and studied, moving to Schwerin to continue his religious studies, but in 1886 he left for the United States. In Boston he established a modern German-Hebrew school – the first of its kind in the United States – and continued his studies. From 1892 to 1896 he served as rabbi of a Providence Reform congregation and taught at Brown University.

In 1898 Blaustein was appointed superintendent of the Educational Alliance of New York City, then the most important social-educational institution for the Americanization of foreigners. With the untrained social workers of that institution he worked diligently to raise the standards of social work and to turn it into a profession. Respected by Jews and non-Jews alike, he accompanied Robert Watchorn, immigration commissioner at Ellis Island, to Romania in 1900 to study the conditions of the Jews there and the causes of the large-scale emigration from that country.

In 1905 Blaustein became the first president of the Society of Jewish Social Workers of New York. Active in Zionist affairs in New York, he was the first *nasi* (presiding officer) of Order of the Sons of Zion. In 1908 he became director of the Chicago Hebrew Institute, and in 1910 took up a lectureship on Jewish, Italian, and Slavic immigration at the New York School of Philanthropy, where a chair had been established for him.

BIBLIOGRAPHY: DAB, 2 (1929), 360–1; M. Blaustein (ed.), *Memoirs of David Blaustein* (1913).

[Judah Pilch]

BLAU-WEISS ("Blue-White"), first and one of the most influential Jewish youth movement in Germany, founded in 1912. It initiated a Zionist program, basing its organizational format on the German nationalist youth movement Wandervogel (whose increasing antisemitism greatly contributed to the expansion of Blau-Weiss). Before and immediately after World War I Blau-Weiss groups engaged almost exclusively in outings and intimate gatherings, emphasizing nature appreciation and "manliness" in the manner of the German *Jugendbewegung* (youth movement). Instead of the cult of German peasantry and folk traditions, Blau-Weiss introduced new forms of celebrating Jewish holidays outdoors and an interest in the Hebrew language, Hebrew songs, and Yiddish folklore. The main aim of Blau-Weiss was to combine being a Jew with love of the German fatherland. The movement strove to strengthen the body, mind, and spirit of the young with an introduction to Jewish education. Blau-Weiss reached its peak in the early 1920s, with about 3,000 members. At this time a pioneering, Palestine-oriented tendency developed in its ranks and became, under the leadership of Walter Moses, its official program at the Blau-Weiss conference in Prunn (August 1922). The conference decided upon the establishment of a Blau-Weiss settlement in Palestine based not only on agriculture but also on precision workmanship in such fields as tool mechanics. It also decided to streamline the organizational structure of the movement along "hierarchical" lines, and to participate actively in Zionist politics. Subsequent friction with the German Zionist leadership, as well as the economic crisis in Palestine, thwarted this ambitious program. While many members of Blau-Weiss settled in Palestine, some of them prior to the Prunn conference, no specific Blau-Weiss settlement or enterprise materialized. The movement dissolved in Germany in 1929, retaining only the *Praktikantenschaft*, i.e., small *hakhsharah* groups. After the disintegration of the Blau-Weiss most of its remaining members joined the *Kadimah group.

Blau-Weiss also existed in Austria, where it flourished for a time. The Czechoslovak branch of the movement, which from 1919 called itself by the Hebrew equivalent, *Tekhelet-Lavan*, continued as a pioneering organization into the 1930s. The main impact of "the Blau-Weiss experience" was felt in Germany in the early 1920s among Jewish boys and girls of assimilated and semi-assimilated families. Alienated from their affluent parents and excluded from the "Aryanized" youth movements, these young people found their way back to the Jewish people and to Zionism.

BIBLIOGRAPHY: H. Maier-Cronemeyer, in: *Germania Judaica* (Cologne), 8 (1969), 18–40, 59–64, 67–71; H. Tramer, in: BLBI, 5 (1962), 23–43; W. Laqueur, in: YLBI, 6 (1961), 193–205; W. Preuss, *Ha-Ma'agal Nisgar* (1968); M. Calvary, *Das neue Judentum* (1936), 75–87; F. Pollack (ed.), *50 Jahre Blau Weiss* (1962); Bergmann, in: G. Hanokh (ed.), *Darkhei ha-No'ar* (1937), 155–62. **ADD. BIBLIOGRAPHY:** J. Hackeschmidt, *Von Kurt Blumenfeld zu Norbert Elias* (1997), 179–262; G.R. Sharfman, in: *Forging Modern Jewish Identities* (2003), 198–228.

BLAYER, PIETRO (1902–1978), Italian industrialist and Jewish communal leader. Born in Fiume, Blayer graduated in economics at the University of Trieste, and embarked on a banking career. In 1938, however, after the fascist racial laws, he entered his family's printing plant, and toward the end of World War II escaped through the German lines and settled in Rome. Following nationalization of his family properties by the Yugoslavian government, which had annexed his native Istria region, he started a new advanced graphic-printing plant in Rome. In 1961 he was elected to the council of the Unione delle Comunità Israelitiche Italiane, where he directed the Finances and Properties Department for several years, displaying outstanding qualities as administrator. In 1972 he was elected vice president of the U.C.I.I. and in 1976, following the death of S. *Piperno-Beer, was appointed president.

[Sergio Della Pergola (2nd ed.)]

BLAZKO, MARTIN (1920–), Argentine sculptor. Born in Germany, Blazko emigrated to Poland in 1933 and studied under Jankel Adler. Six years later, he settled in the Argentine where he helped to found the Madi group. Blazko's sculptures, intellectually ordered though lacking sensuality, do not require effects of light for vivid presentation. The light values emanate from the planes and the hollows. Blazko consistently based his work on the relationship between plastic form and structure. He received many awards both national and international.

BLECH, LEO (1871–1958), German opera conductor and composer. Born in Aachen, Blech studied with the composer Humperdinck. He was conductor at the Aachen Stadttheater from 1893 to 1898. In 1906 he was appointed choirmaster of the Berlin Royal Opera (State Opera from 1918) and from 1913 to 1923 was its general musical director. In 1924 he became first conductor of the Berlin Folk Opera. Blech returned to the Berlin State Opera in 1926 and remained its conductor until 1937, when the Nazis forced him to resign. He left Germany for Latvia and in 1941 fled to Sweden, where he became conductor of the Stockholm Royal Opera. He returned to Germany in 1949 and once again conducted the Berlin State Opera. Blech composed a number of one-act and three-act operas, the latter including *Aschenbroedel* ("Cinderella", 1905) and *Rappelkopf* (1917).

BIBLIOGRAPHY: MGG; Grove, Dict; Baker, Biog Dict; Riemann-Gurlitt.

BLECHER, MARCEL (1909–1938), Romanian author. Blecher was born in Botoşani, but spent most of his life in the town of Roman. He was something of a phenomenon in Romanian literature. Afflicted with tuberculosis of the bone he was bedridden for the last ten years of his short life. His illness led to a heightened sensitivity and an obsession with death which contributed to the artistry of his writing. Blecher's work appeared in various periodicals before he published his first collection of poems, *Corp transparent*, in 1934. His first novel, *Intîmplări in irealitatea imediată* ("Incidents in the Immediate Unreality," 1935), was one of the first attempts at surrealism in Romanian literature. Despite his remoteness from reality Blecher drew some remarkable portraits of a middle-class Jewish family in a provincial town and some lively scenes of Jewish customs. In his autobiographical novel *Inimi cicatrizate* ("Scarred Souls," 1937) Blecher described life in the sanatorium at Berck-sur-Mer in France where he spent a long time encased in a plaster cast. In his book he examined with deep psychological insight not only his own spiritual experiences but those of his fellow patients. A Yiddish version of "Scarred Souls" appeared in Romania and two editions of the original were published in Israel. At the suggestion of André Gide, Blecher began translating the novel into French, but died before he could complete the task. Among his unpublished works, he left the manuscript of a novel on a Jewish theme entitled *Vizuina luminoasă* ("The Bright Vision").

BIBLIOGRAPHY: G. Cţlinescu, *Istoria Literaturii Romîne dela origini pînă în prezent* (1941), 880, 928; C. Baltazar, *Scriitor şi Om* (1946), 29–34; Crohmălniceanu, in: *Preuves*, no. 202 (Dec. 1967), 36–38; Litani, in: *Al ha-Mishmar* (Sept. 20, 1964); Pană, in: *Revista Cultului Mozaic* (March 1, 1968).

[Dora Litani-Littman]

°**BLEEK, FRIEDRICH** (1793–1859), German Bible critic; professor of theology at Bonn from 1829 to 1859. Bleek maintained that the basic document of the Pentateuch is the Elohist (the E document) which has been supplemented by sections from an unconnected Yahwist strand. He argued for the unity of Daniel, and he wrote on the composition of Isaiah, Ezra, Nehemiah, and the Sibylline Oracles. His most important work was in the area of New Testament exegesis, where he was primarily interested in the defense of Christian tradition against the criticism of the Tuebingen school.

Two of his important works are *Einleitung in das Alte Testament* (1860, 1878^4), and *Einleitung in das Neue Testament* (1866^2).

BIBLIOGRAPHY: Kamphausen, in: ADB, 2 (1875), 701–2.

[Zev Garber]

BLEICH, J. DAVID (1941–), U.S. rabbi and professor; one of the world's leading authorities on Jewish medical ethics. Born in Brooklyn, he studied at Yeshiva Torah Vodaath (1948–53) and was ordained by Mesivta Torah Vodaath (1957). He earned his B.A. at Brooklyn College in Jewish studies (1960); his M.A. from Columbia in philosophy, and a Ph.D. from New York University (1974), writing on *Providence in Late Medieval Jewish Philosophy.*

Bleich was simultaneously the *rosh yeshivah* (professor of Talmud) and *rosh kolel* at the Kollel le-Hora'ah (Postgraduate Institute for Jurisprudence and Family Law) of the Rabbi Isaac Elchanan Theological Seminary; professor of law at the Benjamin N. Cardozo School of Law; and Tenzer Professor of Jewish Law and Ethics, Yeshiva University, while serving as rabbi at the Yorkville Synagogue, New York City. Previously he had taught at the University of Pennsylvania (1991–93), Hunter College, Rutgers University, and Bar-llan University.

His writing centers on problems of *halakhah* and on Jewish medical ethics. His books include *Contemporary Halakhic Problems* (5 vols., 1977–83, 1989, 1995, 2005), *Be-Netivot ha-Halakhah* (3 vols., 1996, 1998, 2000), *Bioethical Dilemmas* (2 vols., 1998), *Judaism and Healing* (1980, 2002), *Time of Death in Jewish Law* (1991), *Providence in the Philosophy of Gersonides* (1973), and *Bircas Ha-Chammah* (1980). He is the editor of *With Perfect Faith: Readings in the Foundations of Jewish Belief* (1983) and, with Fred Rosner, of *Jewish Bioethics* (1979, augmented in 1999); and has written extensively on topics of Jewish law and ethics. His teaching, like his writing, is clear, methodical, and resourceful, and some of his students (e.g., Michael Broyde, Michael Berger) are already, like Bleich himself, among the most learned and analytic students of Jewish law in the next generation of Orthodox scholars. Bleich has also served on numerous boards and committees in all his areas of interest.

[Jeanette Friedman (2nd ed.)]

BLEICHROEDER, German banking family. SAMUEL BLEICHROEDER (1779–1855), German banker, the son of a sexton, opened in his native Berlin a money-changing and lottery store in 1803 which developed into the banking firm of S. Bleichroeder. In 1837 the Rothschild banking house of Frankfurt appointed him their representative in Berlin. The firm became a member of the Rothschild and the Preussen consortiums.

His son GERSON VON BLEICHROEDER (1822–1893), was born in Berlin. He entered the firm at 17, and became its head upon his father's death. Under his direction the bank developed into one of the leading financial houses in Germany, mainly engaged in issuing, underwriting, and financing railroad loans. During the 1860s Bleichroeder became financial adviser and private banker to Bismarck who relied on his advice and assistance to overcome his difficulties with the Prussian parliament concerning the financial preparations for the 1866 war. Bleichroeder also advised Bismarck regarding the indemnities payable by France after the 1870–71 war. In 1872 Bleichroeder was raised to the nobility. During the Congress of Berlin (1878), he cooperated closely with Sir Moses Montefiore and Adolph Crémieux and successfully invoked Bismarck's assistance for the protection and emancipation of the Romanian Jews. But his close connections to Bismarck and Emperor Wilhelm I could not save him from becoming one of the main targets of antisemitic (and anticapitalist) agitation from the mid-1870s until his death; the government did not take any serious measures to oppose the assaults.

After Bleichroeder's death, his cousin, JULIUS LEOPOLD SCHWABACH (d. 1898) and then his son PAUL VON SCHWABACH (d. 1938) continued to run the firm as senior managing directors for Bleichroeder's three sons, HANS, GEORG (d. 1902), and JAMES (d. 1937), who all abandoned the Jewish faith. In 1931 the bank entered into a "community of interest" with the Jewish banking firm of Arnhold Brothers and in 1937 a successor firm was formed in New York under the name of Arnhold and S. Bleichroeder, in anticipation of the "Aryanization" of the Berlin house, which took place in 1938. The New York house does not include any bearers of the Bleichroeder name.

BIBLIOGRAPHY: D.S. Landes, in: YLBI, 5 (1960), 201–21. **ADD. BIBLIOGRAPHY:** F. Stern, *Gold und Eisen* (1978); O. Pflanze, *Bismarck*, 2 (1990), 70–85, 318–20; Reitmeyer, in: A. Gotzmann et al. (eds.), *Juden, Buerger, Deutsche.* (2001), 147–70.

[Joachim O. Ronall / Marcus Pyka (2nd ed.)]

BLEJER, DAVID (1913–1997), Argentine lawyer and politician. Blejer, the son of Jewish colonists in the province of Entre Ríos, was born in Buenos Aires.

He graduated as a lawyer from the University of La Plata and settled in Villaguay in the province of Entre Ríos. He became active in politics and before reaching the age of 30 was elected as councilor of the city.

He was a legal adviser to the Argentine Agrarian Institute and lectured on agrarian economics. He joined the Unión Cívica Radical Party in 1930. In 1956, when the party divided over internal conflicts, Blejer aligned himself with the Unión Cívica Radical Intransigente, which was led by Arturo Frondizi who was elected president of Argentina (1958–62). In 1958 Blejer was appointed undersecretary of the Ministry of the Interior and in 1959 minister of labor and social security.

It was the first time in the history of Argentina that a Jew had become a member of the presidential cabinet. Afterwards he served as ambassador to Mexico. In 1961 he was named chairman of the Instituto Indigenista Interamericano and head of the official delegation of Argentina to the conference of the International Labor Organization. Blejer also published humoristic essays under the pseudonym Julio Mocoroa.

[Efraim Zadoff (2nd ed.)]

BLEJER, MARIO ISRAEL (1948–). Israeli economist. Born in Córdoba, Argentina, to a traditional family, Blejer studied in the local Jewish day school and in 1967 made *aliyah* to study at the Hebrew University of Jerusalem, where he received his B.A. (1970) in economics and Jewish history and his M.A. (1972) in economics. He received his Ph. D. in economics from the University of Chicago in 1975. During his academic career Blejer held the Walther Rathenau Chair in Economics at the Hebrew University of Jerusalem (1996–99) and taught at Boston University, New York University, Johns Hopkins, the University of Geneva, George Washington University, Universidad de San Andrés in Buenos Aires, and the Central European University in Budapest. At the same time (1980–2001) he served at the International Monetary Fund, where he reached the level of senior. In 2001 he returned to Argentina to be appointed deputy governor and in 2002 governor of the Central Bank. He served in that position for one year, dealing with the country's financial crisis. In January 2003, Blejer moved to London, where he became the director of the Centre for Central Banking Studies at the Bank of England and a member of the Financial Stability Board of the Bank. He also served as an advisor to the governor. He published books and numerous articles in specialized journals.

[Efraim Zadoff (2nd ed.)]

BLEMISH (Heb. מוּם), a defect in the body of a man or an animal. Defects of conduct are also metaphorically called blemishes (Deut. 32:5; Prov. 9:7; Job. 11:15). A blemished priest was unfit to serve in the priesthood (Lev. 21:16–23) and was precluded from approaching the altar to offer the fire-offerings. He was permitted to carry out only Temple functions not involving actual service at the altar, since he was not standing before the Lord. The Bible forbade a priest who had been blemished to approach the veil (Lev. 21:23), and as a result he was forbidden during the Second Temple period not only to enter the Temple but even to step between the altar and the sanctuary (Kelim 1:9). He was permitted, however, to go into the other parts of the Temple area and to "eat of the food of his God, of the most holy as well as of the holy" (Lev. 21:22).

Just as the officiating priest had to be unblemished, so no blemished animal was permitted to be offered on the altar (Lev. 22:17–25; Deut. 15:21–23; 17:1; cf. Mal. 1:6ff.). An animal whose blemishes were slight – "with a limb extended or contracted" (Lev. 22:23; see below) – could only be offered as a freewill offering, which was less stringent. A blemished priest was forbidden to approach the veil and approach the altar because "he shall not profane these places sacred to Me" (Lev. 21:23). A blemished sacrifice that was offered would not be acceptable on behalf of the one offering it (Lev. 22:20). Such a sacrifice is called an "abomination" in Deuteronomy 17:1 (cf. the strong words in Mal. 1:8ff. against a prevailing laxness in this regard). The flesh of a blemished animal, however, is permitted as food (Deut. 15:21–22).

The requirement that priests and sacrifices should be without blemish was common to all the ancient civilizations, and there is evidence of this from Egypt, Mesopotamia, Ḥatti (the land of the Hittites), Greece, and Rome. Egyptian documents state that candidates for the priesthood were examined for blemishes, and that the sacrifices were examined in the same way, marking animals fit for sacrifice. Documents from Mesopotamia state that priests and the sacrifices had to be perfect, without any blemish. The Hittites also regarded the presence at the ceremonial ritual of those blemished as an affront to the gods. The requirement that both priests and sacrifices be without blemish is also known from Greece and Rome.

The following blemishes are enumerated as making priests unfit for service in the Temple (Lev. 21:18–20): *ivver* (*iwwer*), a blind man; *pisse'aḥ*, one injured in the thigh, from birth or as the result of an accident (cf. II Sam. 4:4), in contrast to a man who has a broken leg; *ḥarum*, a man whose nose is sunk in between his eyes; *sarua*ʿ, apparently one with hands or feet of unequal length; a man who has a broken leg or broken arm; *gibben* and *dak* (*daq*), whose meanings depend on whether the words are connected with the following (Rashi, Maimonides) or with the previous bone deformities (Ibn Ezra; according to the first explanation *gibben* is one whose eyebrows are long and descend over his eyes and *daq* is one who has a kind of skin (pterygium) over the cornea of his eye; according to the second explanation, *gibben* is a hunchback and *daq* is one whose foot or hand muscles degenerated as a result of corrosion, and are thinner than usual); *tevallul*, a sufferer from cataract; *garav* and *yallefet*, skin diseases, not identified with certainty (*garav* is probably dermatitis and *yallefet* is probably Egyptian herpes, ringworm); *mero'aḥ ashekh*, one with a crushed testicle.

Blemishes that render an animal unifit for sacrifice are (Lev. 22:22, 24) *avveret*, (*awweret*) blindness; *shavur* or *ḥaruẓ*, broken or cracked limbs that cause the animal to be lame; skin diseases (*yabbelet*, a wen, referring to a swelling discernible because of its size; *garav* and *yallefet* (see above)); defects of the testicles due to bruising by hand (*maʿukh*), or cutting with an implement (*katut*), tearing with pincers or a cord (*natuq*), or even complete severence by castration (*karut*); *saruʿa* and *qaluṭ*, very slight blemishes, referring to an animal having one leg longer or shorter than the other (these animals may be sacrificed as a freewill offering (Lev. 22:23)). According to some, only *saruʿa* means "living limbs of unequal length," whereas *qaluṭ* means "club-footed," i.e., in the case of cattle, sheep, and goats, with the hoof uncloven.

In the Talmud

Blemishes in the Talmud can be divided into four categories: those mentioned in the Bible as physical blemishes disqualifying priests for service; physical blemishes disqualifying animals for sacrifice; nonphysical blemishes in both; and moral blemishes.

BLEMISHES IN ANIMALS. Whereas the Bible enumerates only 12 disqualifying blemishes in animals and 12 in the case of a priest, the Mishnah subdivides them in the minutest detail. The whole of chapter 6 of tractate *Bekhorot* is devoted to an enumeration of those blemishes in an animal. They are divided into permanent and transient blemishes, the former referring to those which continue for 80 days. As an example of the detail, where the Bible merely says "blind," the Mishnah 6:2 enumerates a pierced, defective, or slit eyelid, a speck in the eye, a commingling of the iris and the outer part, various growths in the eye, and rheum, or if its lip is pierced. According to the legend of *Kamẓa and Bar Kamẓa in the Talmud, it was the infliction of one of those two blemishes by Bar Kamẓa in the sacrifice offered up by the Roman emperor "which we count as a blemish and Romans do not," and the obstinate refusal of R. Zechariah b. Avkulas to make any exception, which was the immediate cause of the Roman War (Git. 55b, 56a). The list even includes such blemishes as "if the tail of the animal does not reach the knee joint" or if its lower jaw protrudes beyond the upper. Maimonides lists 50 disqualifying blemishes in man and beast (Yad, Bi'at ha-Mikdash, ch. 7).

BLEMISHES IN PRIESTS. All the blemishes enumerated for animals similarly disqualify priests from serving in the Temple, but chapter 7 of *Bekhorot* gives another extensive list of blemishes which disqualify a priest but which are not considered blemishes in an animal, such as baldness, flat nose, bowleggedness, black skin, red skin or albino, and many others. Maimonides numbers 90 blemishes which particularly apply to man (*ibid.*, ch. 8).

NONPHYSICAL BLEMISHES. In addition to bodily defects, the Mishnah enumerates some moral blemishes which disqualify a priest: if he has been guilty of homicide or murder, if he has married a woman forbidden to a kohen (though permitted to a non-kohen), or if he becomes ritually unclean by contact with the dead. In the last two cases he can resume his service if he undertakes to separate himself from the woman or undertakes to adhere in the future to the rules of ritual cleanness applying to a kohen. These blemishes originally applied to actual service in the Temple, and it is explicitly stated that a priest so disqualified could and did participate in reciting the *Priestly Blessing (see Second *Temple, Order of Service). It was, however, stipulated that if a kohen had a disfigurement which caused people to stare at him, he was not to recite the priestly blessing, not because the blemish disqualified him but because it would distract the recipients of the blessing. Thus as far as physical blemishes were concerned, this applied only to the hands, and even included a dyer whose hands were dye-stained (Mishnah Meg. 4:7). The *Gemara* (Meg. 24b) extends this prohibition to the feet, and even to speech impediments. The test was purely pragmatic; thus if the kohen was so well-known that his blemish raised no curiosity, the ban was removed. A complete list of such "non-statutory" blemishes is given in Shulḥan Arukh, Oraḥ Ḥayyim 128:30. Although the prohibition against a blemished priest officiating in the Temple is given in the Bible, the Talmud justifies it by interpreting the word *shalom*, in Numbers 25:12, as *shalem* ("whole") since according to the masorah the *vav* is written with a break (Kid. 66b).

MORAL BLEMISHES. The word *mum* for a blemish in the Bible also refers to moral blemishes (cf. Deut. 32:5) and is used extensively in this sense in the Talmud: "Do not ascribe to your fellow your own blemish" (BM 59b). If a man falsely accused someone of being a slave, it was evident that he himself was a slave, since "a person stigmatizes another with his own blemish" (Kid. 70b).

[Louis Isaac Rabinowitz]

BIBLIOGRAPHY: Pauly Wissowa, 8 (1913), 1417; 18, pt. 1 (1939), 592–4; ERE, 10 (1925), 285; B. Meissner, *Babylonien und Assyrien*, 2 (1925), 54, 83; Jeremias, Alte Test, 423; idem, *Handbuch der altorientalischen Geisteskultur* (1929), 259; E. Dhorme, *Les Religions de Babylonie et d'Assyrie* (1949), 227; H. Bonnet, *Reallexikon der aegyptischen Religionsgeschichte* (1952), 748.

BLESSING AND CURSING. In the Bible these two antonyms have three meanings: (1) the invocation of good or evil; (2) good fortune or misfortune; and (3) the person or thing upon whom or which the fortune or misfortune falls.

Thus the first meaning is best represented in English by the terms benediction and malediction or imprecation. The most common formulas of invocation use the terms *barukh* and *ʾarur*. Despite the frequent assertion that words themselves were regarded as intrinsically power-laden, there is little evidence that biblical Israel was any more prone to such a view than is contemporary man. When, in the Bible, man does the invoking, the source of power is (explicitly or implicitly) the Deity; hence both blessings and curses are basic prayers. When the Deity pronounces either good or evil against anyone, the pronouncement is to be understood as a decree rather than a prayer; when man is the subject of the verb *berekh* and the Deity is the object, the verb denotes praise, for nowhere in the Bible is there any indication that the power of God is itself increased by man's pronouncements. As substantive good, blessing is most frequently represented by the terms *berakhah, shalom*, and *ṭov*; its most common antonyms are *kelalah* (*qelalah*) and *raʿah*. Blessings include health, long life, many and enduring progeny, wealth, honor, and victory. The dependence of Palestinian agronomy on rainfall is reflected in the use of *berakhah* for the rains in their due season. Curses, it follows, bring sickness and death, barrenness in people and cattle, crop failure, poverty, defeat, and disgrace. That the beneficiary of good fortune or the victim of ill fortune is himself sometimes regarded as a blessing or a curse is reflected in such passages as Genesis 12:2, "be a blessing" and Numbers 5:21, "may the Lord make you a curse." This use of the terms reflects the usage of beneficiaries of good or victims of evil as examples of felicity and disaster in benedictions and imprecations (Gen. 48:20; Jer. 24:9).

Terminology

The basic term for imprecation in the Bible is *ʾalah*. In most instances it represents an adjuration, i.e., a conditional curse upon someone in the second or third person. As "imprecation" the *ʾalah* is implicitly present in every oath (*shevuʿah*), for an oath is by definition a conditional self-curse. The close relationship between these two terms accounts for the confusion of the two in many translations; indeed, by the operation of metonymy the term *hishbiʿa*, which normally means "to administer an oath," may have the meaning "to adjure." The root ʾrr (ארר; and the noun derived from it, *meʾerah*) shows traces of the concept of "spell," a malignant state in which the victim is barred from such benefits as a share of the earth's fertility, participation in a fellowship or society, and the like. Thus where *ʾalah* reflects the curse as formulation, *ʾrr* reflects the curse as operational. The third term most frequently associated with the idea of curse is the verb *kallel* (*qallel*; קלל) and the cognate noun *qelalah*. This term has a far broader connotative range. It reflects attitudes, behavior, and actions all the way from contempt, through verbal abuse, to physical violence; just as *berekh* (ברך) and *kibbed* (כבד; and the nouns derived from them) express respect, compliments and good wishes, and material benefit. The failure to recognize the broad range of meanings expressed by *qillel* resulted in the notion (as early as the Septuagint translation) that *qillel ʾElohim* means to "curse God" (cf. Ex. 22:27; Lev. 24:10–23). To avoid this horrendous formulation, the biblical text was altered: in I Samuel 3:13 from *ʾElohim* ("God") to *la-hem* ("to them"); in I Kings 21:13, and Job 1:5, 1:11, 2:9 the original *qillel* is replaced by the *euphemistic antonym *berekh*. The rabbinic tradition in Sanhedrin 7:5 also had recourse to a euphemism in an attempt to understand how imprecation against the Deity is possible in a monotheistic system. In fact, it has been demonstrated that the phrase translated "curse God," *qillel ʾElohim*, usually really means "show disrespect for God" – for the most part by disobeying His moral standards. The antonymous phrase is *yareʾ/yirʾat Elohim*, "to fear God," i.e., show respect for His maxims. Since both blessings and curses are types of prayers, it is not surprising that they are encountered everywhere in the Bible, in everyday contexts, legal and diplomatic proceedings. Salutations of greeting and departure are normally expressions of goodwill, hence the term *b-r-kh* (ברך) for such salutations. Recourse to prayer, i.e., an address to the Deity, is to be expected when human resources are exhausted or, by nature of the situation, unavailing. Hence one notes the employment of oath and adjuration in legal disputes and in treaty formulations.

Ancient Near Eastern treaties exhibit the feature of curses, in that the subjected power invokes its own god or gods to administer punishment in the event of failure to observe the agreed upon (i.e., imposed) terms of the treaty (cf. Ezek. 17:11–19). The formulation of the covenant between Israel and its God follows the pattern of such "vassal treaties." An examination of the curses in Deuteronomy 27:15–26 reveals the essential function of the curse, for all the enumerated breaches of provisions of the covenant are of such a nature that society would be unable to punish them. It follows also that the invocation of God in a curse (be it oath or adjuration) is not only blameless but also praiseworthy, for every such invocation is implicitly an acknowledgment of the Deity's sovereignty. This is made explicit in such passages as Deuteronomy 6:13, 10:20, and Isaiah 45:23. Heinous, by contrast, is swearing or cursing "by the name of" other deities. A frequent formulation of biblical curses is *Ko yaʿaseh* YHWH *ve-kho yosif* ("May the Lord do such-and-such and worse if…"). Another formulation invokes the power of both king and Deity or of one of them only: "by the life (Heb. *ḥai*) of the king/the Lord." This formula is a frozen form, i.e., a relic of a concept no longer in consonance with the thinking of the people who continue to employ it. The earlier belief was that the life of the king or a god could be put in jeopardy by a solemn pronouncement in support of a promise or of the truth of an assertion; thereby involved in the outcome, the king or god (and his punitive power) was brought into an issue which might otherwise have been of no concern to him. (This type of thinking remains in evidence today when a person swears "by" or "on" something more precious than his own life, e.g., the head of his child, or his mother's grave.) Alternatives to ḥai in cursing/swearing by the life of God or king are *nefesh* ("life," "soul") and *shem* ("name"). Thus the Deity Himself is pictured as employing this oath form, swearing "by Myself" (Gen. 22:16, Jer. 22:5; 49:13) or "by My great Name" (Jer. 44:26).

[Herbert Chanan Brichto]

In the Talmud

The rabbis continued to stress the efficacy of blessings and curses. With regard to the former, they ordained that God's name be utilized in the blessing uttered when meeting or greeting people in accordance with the practice of Boaz (Ber. 9:5; Ruth 2:4). Continuing biblical traditions, the rabbis introduced blessings at circumcisions (Targum Uzziel to Gen. 48:20), at marriages (Gen. 24:60), and upon separating from an acquaintance one was advised to say, "Go unto peace" (Ex. 4:18; MK 29a). The sages declared that even "the blessing or the cursing of an ordinary man should not be lightly esteemed" (Meg. 15a). The Jew was also encouraged to respond "Amen" after the blessing of a Gentile (TJ, Ber. 8:9, 12c). Great emphasis was placed upon the blessing of an elder, and people were urged to receive their blessings (Ruth R. 6:2). Likewise, people were encouraged to bless the righteous whenever they mentioned them (Gen. R. 49:1). Abraham blessed everybody, and he was constantly blessed by God (Gen. R. 59:5). The ability to bless others was passed on by Abraham to Isaac (Gen. R. 61:6). All blessings were considered incomplete unless they were also accompanied by peace (Num. R. 11:7).

Cursing

According to the Talmud, even an undeserved curse by a scholar is effective (Mak. 11a), and an undeserved curse will fall back upon him who utters it (Sanh. 49a and Rashi, ad loc.). The biblical prohibitions of cursing were elaborated in rabbinic *halakhah* to comprise (1) The cursing of God (see *Blasphemy). (2) The cursing of parents (Ex. 21:17; Lev. 20:9; cf. Prov. 20:20; 30:11; Sanh. 7:8). This prohibition applies to proselytes toward their unconverted parents (Maim. Yad, Mamrim, 5:11). (3) The cursing of judges and of the chiefs of the people: kings, heads of Sanhedrin, etc. (Ex. 22:27; Eccles. 10:20; Maim. Yad, Sanhedrin, 26:1). (4) The biblical prohibition of cursing the deaf (Lev. 19:14) was interpreted to include any poor, physically handicapped, or even any person in his absence (Sanh. 66a; Yad, loc. cit.). (5) The prohibition of cursing is extended to self-cursing (Shevu. 4:13; Yad, loc. cit.) (6) The cursing by a woman of her husband's parents in his presence is a valid reason for divorcing her without the repayment of her *dowry as stipulated in the **ketubbah* ("marriage contract"; Ket. 72a–b; Sh. Ar., EH 115:4). Cursing is permissible only when prompted by religious motives such as the cursing of those who are guilty of reprehensible actions (Men. 64b), or who mislead the people by calculating the date of the coming of the Messiah (*meḥasehvei kiẓẓin*; Sanh. 97b). While rabbinic ethics does not go to the length of the New Testament demand to "bless them that curse you…" (Luke 6:27), it disapproves of cursing in general and the Talmud quotes a popular proverb, "Be rather of the cursed than of the cursing" (Sanh. 49a). These ideas found their expression in the prayer cited in the Talmud (Ber. 17a) and said thrice daily at the conclusion of the *Amidah: "O my God, guard my tongue from evil and my lips from speaking guile; and to such as curse let my soul be dumb, yea, let my soul be unto all as the dust…."

The popular belief in the magical power of a curse, even if pronounced unintentionally, has led to the custom of reading the verses of the Bible, Leviticus 26:14–43 and Deuteronomy 28:15–68, called *Tokheḥah* ("chastisement"), in a low voice. Out of fear, people were reluctant to be called up to the Torah reading of these particular sections, so it became customary in some congregations to call for a volunteer (*mi she-yirẓeh*), or, when a beadle (*shammash*) was hired, it was agreed that it would be his duty to be called up for the reading of the *Tokheḥah* sections (see Isserles to Sh. Ar., OH 428:6). Some pious rabbis volunteered to read the *Tokheḥah* to prevent embarrassment to other people.

BIBLIOGRAPHY: H. Blank, in: HUCA, 23 (1950–51), 73–95; Speiser, in: JAOS, 80 (1960), 198–200; H.C. Brichto, *The Problem of "Curse" in the Hebrew Bible* (1963); T. Canaan, in: JPOS, 15 (1935), 235–79; J. Scharbert, in: *Biblica*, 39 (1958), 1–26.

BLESSING OF CHILDREN. Belief in the value and efficacy of parental blessing of children is attested to in biblical stories, such as those of Noah's blessing of Shem and Japheth (Gen. 9:26–27); Isaac's blessing of Jacob and Esau (Gen. 27, and 28:1–4); and Jacob's blessing of his sons (Gen. 49) and his grandsons Ephraim and Manasseh (Gen. 48:13–22). The importance of parental blessing is also stressed by Ben Sira (Ecclus. 3:9). The blessing of the children is performed on Sabbath eve either in the synagogue or in the home; on the eves of holy days, of the Day of Atonement, and before leaving for a journey. The blessing is usually given by the father, on special occasions also by the mother, to both small and adult children, by laying the hands upon the head of the child and pronouncing (for a boy) the verse "May God make thee like Ephraim and Manasseh" (Gen. 48:20) or (for a girl) the verse "May God make thee like Sarah, Rebekah, Rachel, and Leah" (cf. Ruth 4:11), followed by the priestly benediction (Num. 6:24–26). From the Middle Ages, the ceremony of blessing children became deeply rooted (see J. Buxtorf, *Synagoga Judaica* (1604), ch. 15, and Jacob *Emden's *Siddur*, 1748). The parental blessing is also recited prior to a child's wedding ceremony and by parents on their deathbed. When grandparents are still alive, it is customary to receive their blessing, too, especially on the eve of the Day of Atonement and before the wedding ceremony (Abraham Danzig, *Ḥayyei Adam* (1810), 143:19). In some communities the parental blessing is also bestowed after the *Havdalah ceremony at the end of the Sabbath (Baer, Seder, 309).

BIBLIOGRAPHY: Eisenstein, Dinim, 56–57; Abrahams, Companion, cxxxiv–cxxxv.

BLEUSTEIN-BLANCHET, MARCEL (1906–1996), French advertising executive and radio pioneer. Born in Enghien, France, Bleustein-Blanchet founded a number of businesses over the years through which he became the foremost individual in advertising in France, a field which he virtually established by introducing advertising into French film, radio, and television. Among his companies were "Publicis" (est. 1927), the largest privately owned advertising agency in France; Radio Cité (1935); Regie Press of which he was chairman (founded 1938); and Cinéma et Publicité (1938). In the early 1920s Bleustein-Blanchet established a private company, "Radio Paris," making him a pioneer of French radio broadcasting. He was sole or part owner of other types of businesses as well, such as the Drugstore restaurants in Paris, and he was the owner of the sixth television network of France, specializing in music. In 1960 he created a foundation named after him that grants scholarships to deserving young writers.

During World War II he was an active member of the Resistance. He served as an adviser for French Foreign Commerce from 1973 to 1975. Bleustein-Blanchet was active in the support of social welfare of the French Jewish community and was president of the Montmartre Israelite Center from

1965. He received France's highest award, Grand Officer of the Legion of Honor.

He wrote *La rage de convaincre* (1970), *La nostalgie du futur* (1978), *Les ondes de la liberté* (1984), *Mémoires d'un lion* (1988), and *Les mots de ma vie* (1990).

ADD. BIBLIOGRAPHY: M. Germon, *Marcel Bleustein-Blanchet: Monsieur Publicité* (1990).

[Gideon Kouts]

BLINDMAN, YERUḤAM (c. 1798–1891), cantor and composer. Blindman, who was called "Yeruḥam ha-Koton" ("little") because of his small stature, served as cantor in Kishinev, Tarnopol, and Berdichev. Though not universally admired, his voice was a remarkable lyric tenor with unlimited falsetto range. The public was attracted by his pious appearance in long, white beard and his great artistry in improvisation. His formal knowledge of music was rudimentary, but his own melodies, composed in the spirit of Jewish folksong against a liturgical background, earned him a reputation as a composer of synagogal music. His singing with choir consistently attracted large crowds, including gentiles. He performed with his choir throughout Russia and Austria.

BIBLIOGRAPHY: H.H. Harris, *Toledot ha-Neginah ve-ha-Ḥazzanut be-Yisrael* (1950), 404–5; Idelsohn, Music, 302–3; A. Rosen (ed.), *Di Geshikhte fun Khazones* (1924), 97.

[Joshua Leib Ne'eman]

BLINDNESS. The standard Hebrew term for a blind person is (Heb. עִוֵּר) (*ʿivver*; Ex. 4:11; et al.), a noun in the form used for bodily defects. The abstract form is עִוָּרוֹן (*ʿivvaron*, "blindness"; Deut. 28:28; Zech. 12:4). The word סַנְוֵרִים (*sanverim*; Gen. 19:11; II Kings 6:18), sometimes incorrectly translated "blindness," means a blinding light causing (possibly temporary) loss of vision (E.A. Speiser). Eyes which cannot see are described by the verbs כהה ("be dim"; Gen. 27:1; et al.), קום ("be fixed," "still", I Sam. 4:15; I Kings 14:4), חשך ("be darkened"; Lam. 5:17; et al.), כבד ("be heavy"; Gen. 48:10), and שעע and טחח ("be smeared over;" Isa. 6:10, 32:3; 44:18; et al.). Genesis 29:17 describes Leah's eyes as *rakkot*, but whether this means "tender" or "weak" is moot.

Incidence and Causes

Blindness was widespread in the ancient Near East. Preventive techniques included the application of hygienic ointments, especially kohl, and surgical operations (cf. *The Code of Hammurapi*, 215–20 in Pritchard, Texts, 175). (There is no evidence that the biblical injunction against eating pork was intended or understood to prevent trichinosis or other diseases which cause blindness.) Biblical cases include Isaac (Gen. 27:1), Jacob (Gen. 48:10), Eli (I Sam. 3:2; 4:15), and Ahijah the Shilonite (I Kings 14:4), all of whose eyesight failed in old age. (Deut. 34:7 makes a point of reporting that Moses' eyesight had not failed in old age.) Both Isaac and Jacob in their blindness reversed the status of a younger and an older descendant in blessing them (Gen. 27 (cf. 29:23–6); 48:8–19).

Aside from old age, natural causes of blindness are not mentioned in the Bible. In a few passages blindness is mentioned as a punishment inflicted by God: it is threatened for Israel's violation of the covenant (Deut. 28:28–29; M. Weinfeld takes this passage metaphorically; see below) and for the "negligent shepherd" of Zechariah 11:15–17; Proverbs (30:17) warns that the eye which is disrespectful to parents will be plucked out by birds of prey (cf. *The Code of Hammurapi*, 193, in Pritchard, Texts, 175). Theologically speaking, all cases of blindness are attributed to God (Ex. 4:11), just as the restoration of sight is credited to Him (Ps. 146:8). However, outside of the specific cases mentioned, blindness in general is nowhere stated to be a punishment for sin. In a few passages God strikes His servants' assailants with blinding flashes (Gen. 19:11; II Kings 6:18–20) or permanent blindness (Zech. 12:4; Ps. 69:24) in order to protect His servants.

As a punishment inflicted by human agency one finds the penalty of "an eye for an eye" in the talion formula (Ex. 21:24; Lev. 24:20; Deut. 19:21), although it is debated whether this was ever carried out literally in Israel (cf. *The Code of Hammurapi*, 196–9, where the relation of the law to actual practice is similarly uncertain). Samson and King Zedekiah were blinded, respectively, by the Philistines and Nebuchadnezzar (Judg. 16:21; II Kings 25:7; Jer. 39:7; 52:11). Nahash the Ammonite demanded the putting out of the right eye of all the people of Jabesh-Gilead as a condition for sparing the city (I Sam. 11:2). Several passages speak of the eyes being "spent" or "pining away" from tears and grief. The verb used is usually כלה ("Be spent"); the context makes it clear that soreness rather than blindness is meant (e.g., Lev. 26:16; Deut. 28:65; Jer. 14:6; Lam. 2:11; 4:17; cf. also עשש, Ps. 6:8, "be spent," "waste away").

Effects

Blind persons are naturally helpless in many ways (cf. II Sam. 5:6; Isa. 35:5–6; Jer. 31:7, which invoke the blind, the lame, and the mute as representative examples of helplessness) and subject to exploitation (Deut. 28:29). Biblical ethics warned against exploiting them (Lev. 19:14; Deut. 27:18; Job 29:15).

As a physical defect blindness disqualified priests from sacrificing or approaching the altar (Lev. 21:17–23) and rendered sacrificial animals unacceptable (Lev. 22:21–22; Deut. 15:21; Mal. 1:8). Some have taken the enigmatic saying "the blind and the lame shall not come into the house" (II Sam. 5:8) to indicate that at one time these were forbidden entrance to temples.

Metaphoric Uses

Blindness is used with several metaphoric meanings in the Bible. Frequently it refers to the lack of intellectual or moral understanding (Isa. 29:9–10, 18). Judges are warned that bribes, or gifts, blind the eyes of the discerning (Ex. 23:8; Deut. 16:19). Isaiah is told that his mission is to besmear the eyes of Israel so that it will not "see" and repent and be healed (6:10). In Isaiah 56:10 blindness refers to negligence, while in Numbers 16:14 putting out the eyes is usually taken to mean deceiving. The

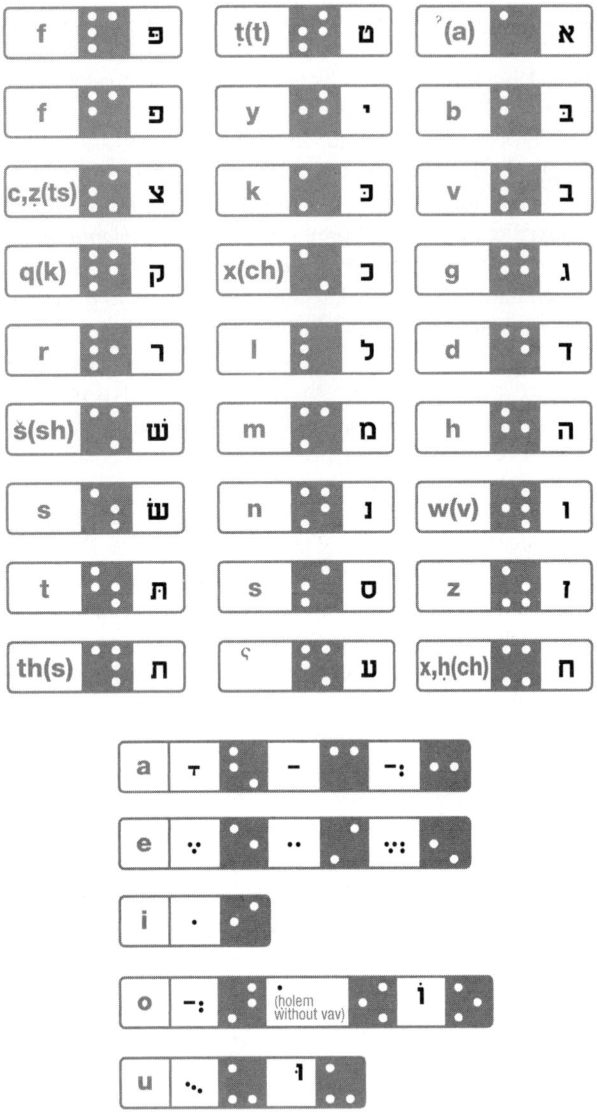

The Hebrew Braille system adopted universally in the 1950s.

helplessness and exploitability of the blind made blindness a natural metaphor for oppression and injustice in Deuteronomy 28:28–29 and Isaiah 59:9–10 (cf. Lam. 4:14; M. Weinfeld has noted that the association of blindness and darkness with oppression in these passages also reflects the Mesopotamian association of the sun-god with justice (cf. a related association in II Sam. 23:3–4; Hos. 6:5b; Zeph. 3:5)). A related metaphor is the use of blindness to describe those who dwell in the darkness of prison or captivity (Isa. 42:7, 16–19; 43:8; 49:9; 61:1; cf. Ps. 146:7–8; this use has roots in Mesopotamian royal inscriptions).

[Jeffrey Howard Tigay]

In Talmud and Jewish Law

The unusually large number of talmudic sages who were blind probably reflects the wide prevalence of this disability in ancient times. In addition to Bava b. Buta, who was blinded by Herod (BB 4a), mention may be made of Nahum of Gimzo (Ta'an. 21a), Dosa b. Harkinas (Yev. 16a), and R. Joseph and R. Sheshet in Babylon (BK 87a), as well as a number of anonymous blind scholars (cf. Ḥag. 5b; tj Pe'ah, end). Matya b. Heresh is said to have deliberately blinded himself to avoid temptation, but his sight was subsequently restored by the angel Raphael (Tanḥ. B., ed. Buber, addition to *Ḥukkat*). The talmudic name for a blind man is *suma* (Ḥag. 1:1; Meg. 4:6), but the euphemism *sagi nahor* ("with excess of light") is often used (Ber. 58a.; TJ Pe'ah end; and especially Lev. R. 34:13 "the *suma* whom we call *sagi nahor*").

Unlike the deaf-mute, who is regarded in Jewish law as subnormal, the blind person is regarded as fully normal, and most of the legal and religious restrictions placed upon him are due to the limitations caused by his physical disability. The statement (Ned. 64b) based on Lamentations 3:6 – "He hath made me to dwell in darkness as those that have been long dead" – that "the blind man is regarded as dead," is of purely homiletic interest and has no practical application. In the second century R. Judah expressed the opinion that a blind man was exempt from all religious obligations, and as late as the time of the blind Babylonian *amora* Joseph (fourth century) the *halakhah* had not yet been determined (see his moving statement in bk 87a), but it was subsequently decided against his view. Even the statement of R. Judah that a person blind from birth cannot recite the *Shema*, since the first of the two introductory blessings is for the daily renewal of light (Meg. 4:6; TB Meg. 24a), was later amended since he enjoys the benefit of light (Rosh, resp. 4:21); the law that a blind man could not be called up to the reading of the Torah, since the passage must be read from the scroll (OḤ 53:14), was abolished with the institution of the *ba'al kore*, who reads the passage for those called up (Taz. to OḤ 141:1). The ruling of Jair Ḥayyim Bacharach (*Ḥavvot Ya'ir* 176) that if there were a person more suitable, a blind person should not conduct the service is an individual opinion and Yehudai Gaon, who himself was blind, gives a contrary opinion (J. Mueller, *Mafte'aḥ li-Teshuvot ha-Ge'onim* (1891), 67).

Similarly, although it was laid down that a totally blind person may not act as a judge, it is stated that when R. Johanan heard of a blind man acting as judge he did not forbid it (Sanh. 34b, cf. ḤM 7:2; for instances in the Middle Ages see *Paḥad Yiẓḥak S.V. Suma*). Even as late as the time of Joseph Caro in the 16th century, it was laid down that a blind person is forbidden to act as a *shoḥet* only "in the first instance"; the total prohibition was enacted later (YD 1:9 and commentaries). A special case was the exemption of a blind person from the duty of going up to Jerusalem on the Pilgrim Festivals. The special nature of this law, which is derived from the homiletical interpretation of a word, is seen in the fact that it applied even to a person blind in only one eye (Ḥag. 1:1, and TB Ḥag. 2a).

During the Middle Ages, blinding was imposed by some *battei din* as a form of extrajudicial punishment and was condoned by contemporary rabbis (Assaf in bibl. nos. 97, 98, 135). Blindness was said to be caused by bloodletting at unfavorable times and by the machinations of demons (see Zimmels in bibl., pp. 88 and 153).

The question has been raised in recent times as to the permissibility of removing the cornea of a deceased person and grafting it on a blind person to restore his sight. Halakhic opinion is almost unanimously in favor, and in a responsum I.J. Unterman added the consideration that the danger to the life of a blind person through accidents is such that it can be regarded as a special case of *pikku'aḥ nefesh* (see *Autopsy).

[Louis Isaac Rabinowitz]

Care of the Blind

The Jewish blind have been traditionally assisted by regular communal and voluntary agencies and associations, as well as special institutions. In the United States the New York Guild for the Jewish Blind, founded around 1908, had a home for aged blind, has offered integrated services to the visually handicapped, and has initiated a nonsegregated living plan for the blind. In the United Kingdom the central agency was the Jewish Blind (now Jewish Blind and Disabled) Society in London, founded in 1819. By 1970 it was caring for the needs of over 1,500 Jewish blind. It maintained a number of residential and holiday facilities, day centers in provincial cities, and the Burr Center for Personal Development which offered various courses for the blind and disabled.

The special conditions in Israel as a country of immigration created the problem that the proportion of blind persons of working age in the state was three times higher than in Anglo-Saxon countries (1956). Much has been done to alleviate this position, while the blind person is as far as possible not treated as a social case. He is, however, exempted from paying income tax. Special placement officers facilitate his employment. In 1956 the proportion of blind to ordinary residents was estimated at approximately 2.5 per 1,000; 87% of them had immigrated after 1948. Over 85% were born in countries of Asia and Africa where in many cases the blind were not cared for or enabled to work. There was a comparatively high proportion of married women or widows due to marriage of blind girls to elderly men. The Jewish Institute for the Blind in Jerusalem, founded in 1902, cared for the majority of blind children in the country. It included a kindergarten, elementary school where subjects were taught in braille, and boarding facilities for 60–90 pupils attending regular secondary school. It also had a vocational school, industrial training shop, a braille printing press, and two houses for mentally or physically handicapped blind adults.

Other agencies and associations for help of the blind in Israel included Migdal Or, the American Israeli Lighthouse Rehabilitation Center for the Blind in Haifa (Kiryat Ḥayyim), which gave casework reorientation, special training and courses, and has developed home industries for blind who are physically incapacitated. The Women's League for Israel of New York assisted joint projects with the Ministry of Social Welfare for rehabilitation of blind girls and women, and maintained a sheltered workshop, Orah, and a bookbindery, Malben, which in 1951 took over Kefar Uriel, a village for the blind established in 1950 by the Jewish Agency for blind immigrants; in 1962 it had 63 families (about 350 persons). Heads of families were employed in four workshops. The Israel Foundation for Guide Dogs for the Blind in Haifa was established around 1950. A Central Library for the Blind, established in 1952 in Netanya, had over 5,000 volumes in braille and a talking book library.

The Association for the Blind and Prevention of Blindness, founded in 1953, had branches in nine centers. The National Council for the Blind, established in 1958 for coordinating, research, and planning, was represented on the World Council for the Blind. Voluntary agencies giving assistance from abroad include Hilfe fuer Blinde in Switzerland and Aide aux Aveugles Israéliens in France. Training for non-Jewish blind has also been given by the Saint Vincent Roman Catholic hostel in Jerusalem, and at handicraft centers established in Nazareth and Shefaram. Isolated Arab villages have been visited by home teachers.

Modern Incidence and Causes

There is no statutory registration of blindness anywhere in the world. All comparative statistics on the incidence and causes of blindness are therefore largely speculative, and this applies in particular to statistics on blindness in Jews, for whom data are usually lacking in whatever national statistics are available. Comparative studies are thus impossible, and little more than some generalizations can be advanced.

The incidence and causes of blindness in most parts of the world are determined essentially by environmental factors. Jews, as a widely dispersed community, therefore suffer from the locally prevailing environmental causes of blindness. In this respect, if the incidence of blindness in a particular Jewish community is different from that in the general population, it will merely reflect the differences found in the various social groupings of the population at large. Thus it occurs in all countries where trachoma is endemic. The disease is more prevalent in rural areas, ill provided with sanitation and health services, than in the more developed urban centers with their populations relatively well housed and well served medically. The high incidence of trachoma in Oriental Jews who immigrated to Israel reflects country of origin and social level, rather than their Jewishness.

In the more highly developed countries, infections and other environmental causes of blindness are steadily declining, and most cases of blindness are now due to affections seen in the elderly (such as "senile" cataract and "senile" macular degeneration) or in the middle-aged (such as glaucoma and, to a lesser extent, myopic atrophy, uveitis, and diabetic retinopathy). These are all "constitutional" diseases, and clinical experience in Western Europe and the United States has brought out a greater incidence of three of these affections in Jews: myopia, diabetic retinopathy, and Tay-Sachs disease, a rare lethal disorder. Although adequate statistics are lacking, this clinical experience is probably well-founded and would be readily explained by the fact that these three affections are all genetically determined, generally by recessive or by polygenic inheritance. Although there is no such thing as a Jewish gene pool, it is true that inbred groups – Quakers no less than Jews and royal families no less than village communities – have many features and genes in common. These are readily perpetuated under the prevailing conditions: a recessive mutant gene is much more likely to spread in a closed community than elsewhere. (The gene for Tay-Sachs disease probably originated as such a mutant in a Jewish family in White Russia during the last century, and by emigration, carriers have spread it into the Jewish communities of Great Britain and the United States.) Contrary to early beliefs, the affection is not exclusively Jewish, for it is seen in other ethnic groups as well. These occasional cases do not add substantially to the instances of hereditary blindness in Jews, and it is a moot point whether the greater incidence of blindness from high myopia and diabetic retinopathy in Western Jews adds to that load. The numbers involved would be relatively slight, and compensating deficiencies in other hereditary causes are theoretically possible; actual data are lacking, however.

See section on Braille in *Alphabet, Hebrew.

[Arnold Sorsby]

BIBLIOGRAPHY: Gordon, in: *Archives of Ophthalmology*, 9 (1933), 751ff.; E.A. Speiser, *Genesis* (1964), 139 (on Gen. 19:11); idem, in: JCS, 6 (1952), 81ff. (esp., 89 n. 52); Harrison, in: IDB, 1 (1962), 448–9; M.Z. Segal, *Sifrei Shemu'el* (1964), 260, 262 (on II Sam. 5:6, 8); Weinfeld, in: *Biblica*, 46 (1965), 420–1; Paul, in: JAOS, 88 (1968), 182; H.J. Zimmels, *Magicians, Theologians and Doctors* (1952), 461 notes; S. Assaf, *Ha-Onshin Aḥarei Ḥatimat ha-Talmud* (1922), 97 98, 135.

BLIOKH (Bloch), IVAN STANISLAVOVICH (1836–1901), Russian financier, writer, and pacifist. Born in Radom, Poland, Bliokh studied in Warsaw and Berlin. In Warsaw, he engaged in banking, a field he developed extensively in St. Petersburg. He also played a leading role in the construction of the Russian railroads and put their operation on a sound management basis. Bliokh won international fame through his dedication to pacifism, which is the theme of his six-volume publication *Budushchaya voyna v tekhnicheskom, ekonomicheskom i politicheskom otnosheniyakh* (1898; last vol. translated as *The Future of War… Is War Now Impossible?*, 1899). He attempted to prove that wars were of no value to a nation because of the massive expenditures involved and the consequent damage to national economies, apart from the human cost. This book, as well as Bliokh's personal endeavors, were among the factors which influenced Czar Nicholas II to convene the 1899 Hague Peace Conference in order to consider the limitation of armaments and the arbitration of international disputes.

Although Bliokh converted to Calvinism, he maintained his interest in the Jewish question and in improving the lot of Russian Jewry. After the pogroms of the 1890s, he fought strenuously in defense of the Jews and pressed the government to end discrimination. In a five-volume work, *Sravneniye materialnago i nravstvennago blagosostayaniya guberniy zapadnykh, velikorossiyskikh i polskikh* ("A Comparison of the Material and Moral Welfare of the Western, Great Russian, and Polish Provinces," 1901), the preparation of which, with the help of many outstanding experts, cost him hundreds of thousands of rubles, he analyzed the economic condition of the Jews in Russia and emphasized their great contribution to the economy. This work constituted a brilliant defense against the government's anti-Jewish arguments, but was confiscated and burned after publication. Fortunately, a number of copies were by chance saved from the censors, and eventually its contents became widely known through a summary by A.P. Subbotin entitled *Yevreyskiy vopros v yego pravilnom osveshchenii* ("The Jewish Question in its Right Light," 1903).

In 1897 Bliokh became involved in the work of the *Jewish Colonization Association (ICA) in Russia and supported it generously. He showed an interest in Zionism and became a friend of Theodor *Herzl, whom he had met in 1899 at the Hague Peace Conference. (Herzl had come to ask the Russian delegates to help him to obtain an audience with the czar. With Bliokh's assistance Herzl met the head of the Russian delegation, de Staal, and other statesmen.) At Herzl's request, in July 1899 Bliokh tried to persuade the Russian authorities to revoke the decree prohibiting the sale of *Jewish Colonial Trust shares. Shortly before his death, Bliokh established the International Museum of War and Peace in Lucerne, Switzerland.

BIBLIOGRAPHY: N. Sokolow, in: JC (Jan. 24, 1902), 11.

[Nathan Feinberg]

BLIS, DAVID (1870–1942), Cuban communal leader. David Blizhnianski-Halpern was born in Grodno and studied in a yeshivah in Volozhin. He continued his studies in the Rabbinical Seminary in Breslau and the Hebrew Union College in Cincinnati. He joined his parents, who settled in *Moisesville (Argentina), but he continued his travels, being more interested in business than in agriculture. He lived in Mexico for a few years and participated in the foundation of the first Jewish organization there, Alianza Monte Sinai (1912). He apprently lent money to President Francisco Madero and fled from Mexico following his assassination, reaching Cuba in 1913. Blis took an active part in the foundation of almost all the early Jewish organizations of Cuba and was later nicknamed "the grandfather of the Jewish community." He founded the Young Men's Hebrew Association (1916), a common social framework for Americans and Sephardim in Cuba. From the early 1920s he took an active part in assisting immigrants from Eastern Europe, and was co-founder (1924) and president of the Centro Hebreo, and the president of the Centro Israelita, which developed from it. From 1933 to 1934 he was president of the Comisión Jurídica, which protected the Jewish community during the political upheavals of that period.

Blis was an ardent Zionist and promoted the early Zionist activities of the Sephardi Jews. As one of the most prominent members of the Unión Sionista he was named honorary president in 1937. On Blis's initiative the Cuban Senate approved unanimously in 1919 a resolution supporting the efforts of the

Jewish people to achieve self- determination and national independence..

BIBLIOGRAPHY: B. Sapir, *Jewish Community of Cuba* (1948), 18–21. **ADD. BIBLIOGRAPHY:** J. Hochstein, "David Blis," in: *Havaner Lebn Almanaque* 1947–48.

[Margalit Bejarano (2nd ed.)]

°**BLISS, FREDERICK JONES** (1859–1937), British archaeologist. The son of a missionary, Bliss taught for a time at the Syrian Protestant College, Beirut. On behalf of the *Palestine Exploration Fund, he excavated at Tell al-Ḥasī (1891), Jerusalem (1894–97), and (in collaboration with R.A.S. *Macalister) at various mounds in the *Shephelah (1899–1900). At Tell al-Ḥasī Bliss continued the work of Sir William Flinders *Petrie and in Jerusalem he discovered the walls of "Mt. Zion" and the wall enclosing the Tyropoeon Valley, in addition to many other minor discoveries. His work in the Shephelah was marked by some important finds but was too hurried to be of lasting value. His publications include *Mound of Many Cities* (1898); *Excavations at Jerusalem 1894–1897* (1898); *Excavations in Palestine 1898–1900* (1902), with R.A.S. Macalister; *Development of Palestine Exploration* (1906); and *Religions of Modern Syria and Palestine* (1912).

[Michael Avi-Yonah]

BLITZER, WOLF (1948–), U.S. journalist. Blitzer earned a bachelor's degree in history from the State University of New York at Buffalo and a master's in international relations from the Johns Hopkins School of Advanced International Studies in Washington. While at SUNY, he spent a year at the Hebrew University of Jerusalem. He started in the news business as a reporter for *Reuters in Tel Aviv in 1972. Three years later he became the Washington correspondent of the *Jerusalem Post* and served for 15 years until 1990. He joined the all-news television network CNN that year as Pentagon correspondent and appeared frequently on screen during the Persian Gulf War. With his work for the *Post* and his coverage of the prosecution of Jonathan *Pollard, an American Jew charged with spying for Israel, Blitzer became an expert on the weapons systems of the Pentagon and on the Iraqi military. He was among a team of CNN reporters who won a Golden Cable Ace award for coverage of the war. In 1992 he became CNN's senior White House correspondent, covering the administration of President Bill Clinton, and served in that capacity until 1999. He became host of *Wolf Blitzer Reports*, a nightly newscast, in December 2000 and took over CNN's *Night Edition,* a Sunday talk show which in 2004 was seen in more than 200 countries. In 1996 Blitzer won an Emmy award for his coverage of the bombing in Oklahoma City. In 1999 he won the Lowell Thomas Broadcast Journalism Award for contributions to broadcast journalism.

Over the years Blitzer covered many key events on the international political scene. In 1973 he was on hand when Willy *Brandt traveled to Israel, marking the first visit of a German chancellor. He also covered the first Israeli-Egyptian peace conference in Egypt in 1977 and in 1979 he traveled with President Jimmy Carter for the final round of negotiations that resulted in the signing of the Israel-Egypt peace treaty.

In addition to receiving several honorary degrees, Blitzer is the author of two books, *Between Washington and Jerusalem: A Reporter's Notebook* (1985) and *Territory of Lies* (1989), which dealt with the Pollard affair. The son of Holocaust survivors, Blitzer has noted an irony in his personal family history. His grandparents were killed on Yom Kippur and two of his parents' grandchildren, Blitzer's nephew and daughter, were born on Yom Kippur.

[Stewart Kampel (2nd ed.)]

BLITZSTEIN, MARC (1905–1964), U.S. composer. Born in Philadelphia, Blitzstein studied with Nadia Boulanger in Paris and Arnold Schoenberg in Berlin. Intensely interested in political problems, he developed a genre of operas of "social significance." His short works, *The Cradle Will Rock* (1937) and *No for an Answer* (1941), were important though transitory landmarks in the American "proletarian opera" movement. Among his other works are *The Airborne* (1946), a cantata resulting from his service with the U.S. army in England during World War II, and a musical drama, *Regina*, based on Lillian *Hellman's play *The Little Foxes* (1949). Blitzstein also made an idiomatic American translation of the libretto of Kurt Weill's *Dreigroschenoper*. His opera on the theme of Sacco and Vanzetti, commissioned by the Ford Foundation for production by the Metropolitan Opera, was left unfinished. He died on the island of Martinique of head injuries suffered in an attack by a group of sailors.

At the time of his death Blitzstein left unfinished two one-act operas based on the short stories of Bernard Malamud. One of them, *Idiots First*, was completed by Leonard Lehrman, assistant chorusmaster of the Metropolitan Opera, and performed on March 1977 in Bloomington, Ind., and received its first New York premiere in January 1978. The story, in 13 short scenes, is of an old Jew, Mendel, spending the last night of his life in seeking means to provide for his retarded son, Yiẓḥak.

BIBLIOGRAPHY: Baker, Biog Dict, and 1965 Supplement; Grove, Dict, s.v; MGG, s.v.

[Nicolas Slonimsky]

BLOC, ANDRÉ (1896–1966), French sculptor and engineer, who was concerned with the relationship of architecture to sculpture. He was the creator of "habitacles" (pieces of sculpture which could be entered) and "constructions," sculptural forms which lie on the borderline between the two arts. Born in Algiers, Bloc studied science in Paris. He then took a degree in engineering, which he practiced from 1930 onward. In 1941 he began to sculpt, and his first important work was executed in 1949. This was a 38-foot "signal" placed outside the Public Works Museum, Paris, on the occasion of the centenary of the invention of reinforced concrete. In 1951 he helped to found the "Espace" group. He was also associated with the foundation of several architectural journals. Bloc died of a fall while visiting a temple in India.

BIBLIOGRAPHY: H. Schaefer-Simmern, *Sculpture in Europe Today* (1955); Gisiger, in: *Werk*, 51 (1964), 271–2.

BLOCH, family of U.S. book publishers. The Bloch Publishing Company was founded by EDWARD BLOCH (1829–1906), who emigrated to the United States from Bohemia. He learned the printing trade in Albany, New York, and in 1854 set up a company in Cincinnati, which published newspapers and books of specific Jewish interest in English and German. His publications included *The American Israelite* and *Die Deborah*. Later the company diversified its activities, and one of its regular clients was a monastery to which he supplied religious books.

In 1885 Edward's son, CHARLES (1861–1940), established a branch of the company in Chicago. He took over the management of *The Chicago Israelite*, an edition of *The American Israelite*, and in 1891 he co-founded the Chicago-based *Reform Advocate*. He succeeded his father as president in 1901 and moved the Bloch Publishing Company to New York City where, in addition to publishing, it was also one of the leading bookstores in the U.S. representing several publishing houses. It concentrated on books of Jewish interest. Charles was also highly active during his years in New York in the Reform movement, taking part in 1907 in the founding of the Free Synagogue of New York, of which he later served as president, and in 1922 of the Jewish Institute of Religion. On his death, Charles was succeeded by his son EDWARD H. (1898–1982), who headed the company for 40 years and under whose management the company's activities continued to expand. Reaching its fifth generation, the company continued to serve the cultural life of American and world Jewry through its publication and distribution of Judaic and Hebraic literature.

BIBLIOGRAPHY: S. Grayzel, in: JBA, 12 (1953–55), 72–76.

[Abraham Meir Habermann]

BLOCH, ANDRÉ (1873–1960), French composer. Born in Wissembourg, Alsace, Bloch studied with Guiraud and Massenet at the Paris Conservatory and received the Prix de Rome in 1895. After World War I he conducted the orchestra of the American Conservatory at Fontainebleau. In 1931–32 he composed the symphonic poems *Béquinage*, *Kaa*, and *Les moissons de l'éternité* with cello as principal instrument. His two operas, the one-act *Brocéliande,* and *Guignol,* were first performed, respectively, at the Opéra Garnier in 1925 and at the Opéra Comique in 1949. In 1948, following the creation of the State of Israel, he composed his most interesting piece, the *Suite Palestinienne,* with cello as principal instrument.

[Amnon Shiloah (2nd ed.)]

BLOCH, CAMILLE (1865–1949), French historian, archivist, and librarian. A professor at the Sorbonne, Bloch was an authority on the French Revolution and its economic and social antecedents; he was secretary-general of the Society for the Study of the French Revolution. He was archivist of the Aude departement (1891–96) and the Loiret departement (1896–1904) and in 1904 became inspector general of libraries and archives. In World War I he became director of the War Library and War Museum in Paris, and historian of the war period. His *Les causes de la guerre mondiale* (1933; *The Causes of the World War*, 1935) is an important work. During the Nazi period, Bloch was hidden in southern France. After 1945 he supervised for the French government the recovery of books looted by the Germans. He left an unfinished study on the Munich Pact of 1938.

BIBLIOGRAPHY: P. Renouvin, in: *Revue Historique*, 202 (1949), 147–9; *Dictionnaire de biographie française*, 6 (1954), 677; *New York Times* (Feb. 16, 1949) 25.

[Herbert A. Strauss]

BLOCH, CHAIM ISAAC (1867–1948), Orthodox rabbi. Bloch was born in Lithuania and studied under Rabbi Simcha Sisel Ziv at the Yeshiva of Grubin (1880–83) and then in Volozhin, Poland (1883–91), under Rabbi Naphtali Ẓevi Judah *Berlin and Rabbi Ḥayyim *Soloveichik. He received his rabbinical ordination from Rabbi Soloveichik and Rabbi Eliezer *Gordon of the Telshe Yeshivah in 1890. He founded a yeshiva in Plunge in 1895, and served at its head until 1899, when he became a pulpit rabbi in Palanga, a nearby town. While he was there, he also earned the equivalent of a high school degree from the local gymnasium.

From 1905 to 1912, after Rabbi Abraham Isaac *Kook left for Palestine, Bloch served as chief rabbi of Bauska in Courland, now Latvia, and became the district rabbi by governmental appointment. In 1914, he was elected chief rabbi of Antwerp but could not accept the position because of the outbreak of World War I. In 1915, he fled to Russia, where he served as an army chaplain, and in 1916 he organized a yeshivah for exiled Jewish children in the Crimea. He then returned to Bauska in 1920. In 1922–23, he left for America and settled in Jersey City, New Jersey, where he was the pulpit rabbi of Congregation Agudath Shalom. He founded *talmud torahs* and societies to encourage people to observe the Shabbat (the Sabbath Alliance) and encouraged a five-day workweek.

For many years, Bloch was dean of Yeshiva of Hudson County, then a fledgling day school and now known as the Rosenbaum Yeshiva of North Jersey with almost 1,000 students from kindergarten through *mesivta*, located in the cities of River Edge and Newark in New Jersey, and also served on the board of Yeshiva University. He was an avid Zionist and member of Mizrachi and the Religious Zionists of America, as well as a member of the Agudat Harabbonim, where he served as treasurer in 1925 and vice president in 1931. He was also treasurer of Ezrat Torah. During World War II, he worked with the Va'ad ha-Hazzalah to help rescue the Jews of Europe.

Bloch's literary career began in 1897, when he edited a column for **Ha-Ẓefirah*, a weekly Hebrew newspaper in Warsaw, and he was a regular contributor to the Slutzk *Yagdil ha-Torah* and *Migdal Torah*. In the U.S. he was a contributor to *Ha-Pardes*, wrote many essays, and published several volumes on the Talmud about material related to the glosses of the medieval rabbi *Yom Tov Ishbili, the Ritba.

BIBLIOGRAPHY: M. Sherman, *Orthodox Judaism in America: A Biographical Dictionary and Sourcebook* (1996), 31–32; A. Rand (ed.), *Toldot Anshei Shem* (1950), 9–10.

[Jeanette Friedman (2nd ed.)]

BLOCH, CHARLES (**Shelomo Yeshayahu**; 1916–), U.S. *ḥazzan*. Bloch was born in New York and studied *ḥazzanut* under Simon Raisen and music at the Brooklyn Conservatory. He also attended the Jewish Theological Seminary and St. Johns University where he graduated in law. After serving as *ḥazzan* for congregations in New York, Maryland, and Pennsylvania, in 1967 he became *ḥazzan* of Temple Anshei Chesed in Manhattan. Bloch made several recordings, including melodies which he composed, and appeared on American radio and television; he gave concerts throughout the United States and Israel.

[Akiva Zimmerman]

BLOCH, CLAUDE (1878–1967), U.S. admiral; commander in chief of the United States Fleet. Born in Woodbury, Kentucky, Bloch entered the U.S. Naval Academy in 1895. He served in the Spanish-American war and was decorated for saving Spaniards from burning ships. In 1900, he fought in the Chinese expedition to suppress the Boxer Rebellion. During World War I Bloch was commander of the USS *Plattsburg* and in 1918 was appointed assistant chief of the Bureau of Ordnance. He was promoted to rear admiral in 1923 and in 1927 he commanded the battleship *California*. After serving as commandant of the Washington Navy Yard, he was promoted to commander of the battle force with the rank of admiral. In 1938, Bloch was made commander in chief of the United States Fleet. Bloch commanded the shore installations of the 14th Naval District, Hawaii, when Pearl Harbor was attacked, but played no significant role in the events of that day. Retired because of age in 1942, he was retained on active duty as a member of the General Board until 1946.

BIBLIOGRAPHY: E. Rubin; *140 Jewish Marshals, Generals and Admirals* (1952).

[Mordechai Kaplan]

BLOCH, ELIJAH MEYER (c. 1894–1955), Lithuanian rabbi and dean of the Telz (Telshe) Yeshivah in the U.S. Bloch, who was born and educated in Telz, Lithuania, was appointed to the faculty of the yeshivah there in 1917. With the Russian occupation of Lithuania, the yeshivah was moved to Cleveland, Ohio, in 1941, under Bloch's leadership. Bloch retained the singular "Telz style" in Talmud study, which stresses precise inductive reasoning. He resisted every attempt at compromise with the Reform elements of the community, yet succeeded in obtaining the support of the Cleveland Jewish Federation for the local Orthodox high school. Active with the Agudat Israel since the Marienbad Conference of 1937, Bloch played a leading role in the American Agudah. He was also a member of Mo'eẓet Gedolei ha-Torah, the international body which guides the World Agudah on questions of Torah principle, where he was known for the universality of his approach. Bloch actively supported Israel.

BIBLIOGRAPHY: *Dos Yidishe Vort* (Feb. 1955).

BLOCH, ERNEST (1880–1959), composer. Bloch, who was born in Geneva, revealed his musical gifts as a child and was only ten when he wrote down a vow that he would become a composer and then, in ritual fashion, burned the inscribed paper over a mound of stones. In the face of parental opposition, he left home at the age of 16 and studied music for eight years in Brussels, Frankfurt, Munich, and Paris. At that time he composed his first big work, the *Symphony in C Sharp Minor*. Returning to Geneva in 1904, Bloch entered the family clockmaking business. During the next three years he composed his opera *Macbeth*. It was first produced in 1910 at the Opéra-Comique in Paris, and was warmly received. Major works produced during the years immediately following include *Trois Poèmes Juifs* for orchestra (1913), *Schelomo*, a "Hebrew rhapsody" for cello and orchestra (1916), and the *Israel Symphony* for orchestra and five solo voices (1912–16). Bloch first went to America in 1916, as conductor for the dancer Maud Allan, and soon won recognition. Early in 1917, Karl Muck invited him to conduct the *Trois Poèmes Juifs* in Boston, and a few months later a concert of his orchestral works was given in New York. In 1920, he founded and organized the Cleveland Institute of Music. He left it in 1925 to become director of the San Francisco Conservatory of Music. During his five years in this post, Bloch composed a number of large-scale works. Best known of these is *America*, an "epic rhapsody" for chorus and orchestra (1926). A counterpart to this work is *Helvetia*, a "symphonic fresco" written in tribute to Bloch's native land.

One of Bloch's most important works is the *Avodath Hakodesh* ("Sacred Service") for Sabbath morning for baritone, mixed chorus, and orchestra which he wrote in seclusion in Switzerland during 1930–33 (commissioned by Gerald Warburg). He spent the years 1934–38 in a remote French village. From this period came the piano sonata, *Voice in the Wilderness* (symphonic poem with cello obbligato), and the violin concerto. Bloch also composed three string quartets (1916, 1945, and 1951–52). In 1938 Bloch returned to America. After a number of tours as conductor, he finally settled in 1941 in Agate Beach, Oregon. There he spent the rest of his life except for annual lecture visits to the University of California. The manuscripts he left when he died are in the university's music library at Berkeley, where an Ernest Bloch Archive was set up.

Many honors came to Bloch in his last years. He continued, however, to go his own way without much regard for musical fashion, and ended his career true to the ideals with which he had begun it. As he once stated: "I do not propose or desire to attempt a reconstruction of the music of the Jews.... It is rather the Hebrew spirit that interests me – the complex, ardent, agitated soul that vibrates for me in the Bible; the vigor and ingenuousness of the Patriarchs, the violence that finds expression in the books of the Prophets, the burning love of justice, the desperation of the preachers of Jerusalem, the sorrow and grandeur of the Book of Job, the sensuality of the Song of Songs. All this is in us, all this is in me, and is the better part of me. This it is which I seek to feel within me and to translate in my music – the sacred race-emotion that lies dormant in our souls."

BIBLIOGRAPHY: M. Tibaldi Chiesa, *Ernest Bloch* (1933), incl. bibl.; D.Z. Kushner, "Ernest Bloch and His Symphonic Works" (unpubl. dissert. 1967); G. Saleski, *Famous Musicians of Jewish Origin* (1949), 18–27; D. Ewen (ed.), *New Book of Modern Composers* (1961), 86–97; G.M. Gatti, in: *Musical Quarterly*, 7 (1921), 20–38; D. Newlin, *ibid.*, 33 (1947), 443–59; California University, *Autograph Manuscripts of Ernest Bloch at the University of California* (1962); Sendrey, Music, index; Grove, Dict; Baker, Biog Dict.

[Dika Newlin]

BLOCH, ERNST (1885–1977), German philosopher. Bloch was born in Ludwigshafen, studied philosophy, musicology, and physics at the universities of Munich and Wuerzburg, and became doctor of philosophy under the direction of O. Kuelpe with a dissertation on "Rickert und das Problem der modernen Erkenntnis." From 1908 to 1912, he studied in Georg Simmel's seminary of philosophy and sociology in Berlin; from 1912 to 1914, he lived in Heidelberg, where he was a permanent guest in Max Weber's seminary. Living in Munich and Garmisch from 1914 to 1917, he was close to the expressionist painters. As a pacifist and opponent of the regime of German Emperor William II, he lived in exile in Switzerland from 1917 to 1919. In his essay "Symbol – die Juden" (1911/12), which begins with the assertion, "The pride in being Jewish is now again awakened," Bloch analyzes the principal characteristics of Jewish identity in the era of modernity. His first book, *Geist der Utopie* (1918, 1923; *Spirit of Utopia*, 2000), which includes "Philosophy of Music," is a metaphysical inquiry into the question of self-recognition and self-identity, marked by the influence of romanticism, mysticism, socialist utopianism, and both Christian and Jewish religiosity. *Thomas Muenzer als Theologe der Revolution* (1921) is marked by a revolutionary romanticism and simultaneously by the effort to bring to the fore the forgotten and repressed history of a radical messianic tendency in German Protestantism (linked to the Peasant's Revolt in the 16th century) opposed to Martin Luther. Three years after the publication of *Spuren* ("Tracks," 1930) – a book which has often been compared to the *Einbahnstrasse* by Walter *Benjamin, he was forced to leave Germany and live as a refugee in Switzerland, Austria, France, and Czechoslovakia. *Erbschaft dieser Zeit,* published in Zurich in 1935, explains the rise of Nazism by the phenomenon of "uncontemporaneousness (*Ungleichzeitigkeit*) in the consciousness of the German middle class. Leaving Prague in 1938, six months before the invasion of the Czech Republic by Nazi Germany, he emigrated via Poland to the United States, where he wrote his major work, *Das Prinzip Hoffnung* (*The Principle of Hope*), whose original title had been *Träume vom besseren Leben* ("Dreams of Better Life") – a great compendium of all the forms of wishful and utopian thinking in culture, religion, architecture, music, etc., based on the theory of the "*antizipierendes Bewusstsein*" ("consciousness in anticipation"). It also outlines a "philosophy of praxis" as "humanity in action, linking messianic hope and the Marxist project of the transformation of world. By the mediation of the category of "possibility," wishes are to be transformed into real human praxis. The second volume, *Freiheit und Ordnung Abriss der Sozialutopien*, is not only a synopsis of all manifestations of utopian thought in the history of philosophy, literature, architecture, music, etc., but also contains a chapter on Zionism ("Altneuland, Programm des Zionismus"), where Bloch's main concern is to criticize Theodor Herzl's "bourgeois Zionism" and to assert that Judaism should not become a territorial nationalism but acknowledge and preserve the best that was in Moses Hess' *Utopia* and transform it into a *messianic international socialism*. During his exile in the United States, Bloch also wrote *Subjekt-Objekt. Erlaeuterungen zu Hegel* (1951, enlarged ed.1962). In 1949, he returned to Europe, accepting a professorship in philosophy in Leipzig and the direction of the Institute of Philosophy. In December 1956, after the bloody repression of the Hungarian uprising by the Russians, he was publicly denounced by the *Neues Deutschland* (the official journal of the East German Communist Party S.E.D.) as a "revisionist," an "idealist," and a "mystical" philosopher, distracted by historical and dialectical materialism. After a political campaign against him, he finally was obliged to accept compulsory retirement in 1957. In August 1961, during a visit to the German Federal Republic, frightened by the news of the construction of the Berlin wall, he resolved not to return to Leipzig but to stay in Tuebingen, where he taught until his death. During the Six-Day War in June 1967 he was the most vocal speaker in an assembly organized at Frankfurt University to proclaim Israel's right to exist ("Frieden im Nahen Osten," 1967). During the 15 years of his last period, Bloch dedicated himself entirely to the publication of his complete writings (*Gesamtausgabe*) in 16 volumes, published by Suhrkamp. These included *Naturrecht und menschliche Wuerde* (1961; *Natural Law and Human Dignity*), *Philosophische Aufsaetze zur objektiven Phantasie* (1969), *Atheismus im Christentum* (1968), *Politische Messungen, Pestzeit, Vormaerz* (1970), and *Experimentum Mundi* (1975). *Tendenz-Latenz-Utopie*, including the *Gedenkbuch fuer Else Bloch-von-Stritzky* (Memorial Book for Else Bloch-von-Stritzky, Bloch's first wife), followed in 1978.

BIBLIOGRAPHY: S. Marcun, *Ernst Bloch in Selbstzeugnissen und Bilddokumenten*, rowohlt (1977); B. Schmidt (ed.), *Materialien zu Ernst Blochs "Das Prinzip Hoffnung"* (1978); R. Traub and H. Wieser (eds.), *Gespraeche mit Ernst Bloch* (1975); *Utopie-marxisme selon Ernst Bloch. Hommages publiés par Gérard Raulet* (1976); A. Muenster (ed.), *Tagtraeume vom aufrechten Gang.Sechs Interviews mit Ernst*

Bloch (1977); idem, *Utopie, Messianismus und Apokalypse im Fruehwerk von Ernst Bloch* (1982); B. Schmidt, *Seminar: Zur Philosophie Ernst Blochs* (1983); V. Caysa et al., *Hoffnung kann enttaeuscht werden. Ernst Bloch in Leipzig* (1992); M. Riedel, *Ernst Bloch und die Tradition* (1993). BIOGRAPHIES: P. Zudeick, *Der Hintern des Teufels. Ernst Blochs Leben und Werk* (1985); A Muenster, *L'utopie concrète d'Ernst Bloch. Une biographie* (2001; (Ger. tr. *Ernst Bloch. Eine politische Biographie* (2004). CORRESPONDENCE: K. Bloch et al. (ed.) *Ernst Bloch. Briefe (1903–1975)*, 2 vols. (1985).

[Arno Muenster (2nd ed.)]

BLOCH, FELIX (1905–1983), U.S. physicist and Nobel Prize laureate. Bloch was born in Zurich. He studied first at the Federal Institute of Technology, where his interest in physics developed and he received his Ph.D. in theoretical physics under Heisenberg's supervision at the University of Leipzig (1928). He worked successively with leading contemporary physicists including Pauli, *Bohr, and Fermi before emigrating to the U.S. in 1933 after the Nazi rise to power. He joined Stanford University (1934), where he was Max Stein Professor of Physics from 1961. He served for one year (1954) as the first director general of CERN. Bloch's research interests started with his doctoral dissertation on the quantum mechanics of electrons in crystals. During World War II he worked on theoretical issues in the early stages of the Manhattan Project and on counteracting radar. He was awarded the Nobel Prize in physics (1952) jointly with E.M. Purcell for his discovery of nuclear induction. This process uses a magnetic field to align nuclear particles on the basis of their intrinsic angular moment (spin) and magnetic moment parallel to this spin. The resulting signals, analogous to radio-frequency spectroscopy, enabled him to measure the moment of the neutron with great accuracy. This discovery forms the basis of nuclear magnetic resonance scanning in medicine and related techniques for analyzing other solid structures. In his later years Bloch worked on the theory of superconductivity at low temperatures.

[Michael Denman (2nd ed.)]

BLOCH, GUSTAVE (1858–1923), French scholar in Roman history. He was deeply influenced by his grandfather, Rabbi Alexandre Aron. Bloch taught at the *lycée* in Besançon until 1873, when he joined the new *Académie Française* in Rome. He was so successful there that he was invited to lecture on Greco-Roman antiquities at Lyons University. While at Lyons he received his doctorate for two brilliant theses: *Les origines du Sénat romain* and *De decretis functorum magistratuum ornamentis* (1883). In 1888 Bloch was named *maître des conférences* at the École Normale in Paris, and established his reputation firmly by a series of articles in learned journals and in the classical encyclopedia of Daremberg and Saglio as well as *la Gaule indépendante et la Gaule romaine* (1900) in the *Histoire de France* edited by Lavisse. In 1904 the post of professor of Roman history was created for him at the Sorbonne. Bloch placed all these honors in jeopardy as an active supporter of *Dreyfus.

BIBLIOGRAPHY: R. Lisbonne, in: *Revue Historique*, 145 (1924), 156; *Gustave Bloch* (a pamphlet published on his death).

[Howard L. Adelson]

BLOCH, ḤAYYIM ISAAC BEN ḤANOKH ZUNDEL HA-KOHEN (1864–1948), rabbi and scholar. Bloch, born in Plunge, Lithuania, studied at Grubin and Volozhin. In 1894 he founded a yeshivah in his native town where he was appointed rabbi in 1898. He became rabbi of Bausk in 1902, succeeding Abraham Isaac ha-Kohen *Kook. Bloch was also appointed the official rabbi by the government. During World War I he wandered in Russia, returning to Bausk in 1920. In 1922 he went to the United States and was appointed rabbi in Jersey City, New Jersey, where he remained until his death. In 1932 Bloch was elected honorary president of the Union of Orthodox Rabbis of the U.S. and Canada. During World War II, he was one of the leaders of the Va'ad ha-Haẓalah, which worked to save the Jews of Europe. He published *Ḥiddushei ha-Ritba* (Yom Tov b. Abraham *Ishbili) on *Mo'ed Katan*, *Megillah*, and *Makkot*, giving the sources, together with an introduction and his own notes and corrections, entitled *Divrei Ḥibah* (**H**ayyim Isaac **B**loch **Ha**-Kohen; 1935–39). Under the same title he published in 1941 a work containing some of the halakhic novellae from discourses that he had delivered at the Plungian yeshivah. Bloch was the author of two works on ethics, published anonymously, *Likkutei ha-Rayiv* (1904) and *Ha-Mavḥin* (1928).

BIBLIOGRAPHY: D. Kamzon (ed.), *Yahadut Lita* (1959), 45, 200ff.; O.Z. Rand and A.M. Gruenblatt, *Toledot Anshei Shem* (1950), 9ff.

[Mordechai Hacohen]

BLOCH, HERBERT (1911–), U.S. classical scholar. Born in Berlin, Bloch achieved prominence in the fields of Latin epigraphy, paleography, archaeology, Greek and Roman historiography, and medieval Latin literature. He participated in excavations at Ostia, Italy, (1938–39) and then went to the United States, where he was appointed instructor in Greek and Latin at Harvard in 1941 and professor in 1953. He taught there until 1982.

While still in Italy, Bloch published the results of his research there on Roman brick stamps, the meager bits of information inscribed on bricks in Roman construction (republished in book form with indices in 1947). He pursued this subject in basic articles in *Harvard Studies in Classical Philology*, vols. 56–59 (1947–48). This work, with its extremely elaborate indices to the portion of the corpus of Latin inscriptions dealing with brick stamps and with many additional inscriptions of the genre never previously published, has proved to be a mine of information for the study of the great senatorial and equestrian families involved in the building industry. It is also important for the study of Roman history, and especially Roman economic history, providing excellent insights into the history of the decline of the Roman Empire, particularly as evinced by the gradual absorption of one of the most important industries into the hands of the emperors. In addition, the stamps have proved extremely valuable in dating buildings. Bloch also wrote important monographs on the historians of the 4th century B.C.E., the manuscript tradition of Sallust's *Histories*, and the pagan revival in the West in the 4th century C.E. He was the editor of Felix Jacoby's collected essays on Greek historiography (1956) and completed a work in three volumes, *Monte Cassino in the Middle Ages* (1986), on one of the most significant intellectual centers of the Middle Ages, which he studied for 30 years. It was awarded the Praemium Urbis in Rome in 1987 and the Haskins Medal of the Medieval Academy in 1988.

While on leave from Harvard, Bloch was professor in charge of the School of Classical Studies of the American Academy in Rome (1957–59), and from 1964 he held the positions of senior fellow of the Society of Fellows at Harvard (1964–79) and trustee of the Loeb Classical Library (1964–73). Bloch was president of the American Philological Association (1968/69) and president of Fellows of the Medieval Academy (1990–93). He was a member of the American Academy of Arts and Sciences, the American Philosophical Society, the Pontificia Accademia Romana di Archeologia (an honorary member since 1990), the German Archaeological Institute, the Zentraldirektion of the *Monumenta Germaniae Historica*. In 1989 he was awarded an L.L.D. by the University of Cassino, and in 1999 he received the Cultori di Roma prize.

BIBLIOGRAPHY: *Who's Who in America* (1972–73), 1, 288

[Louis Harry Feldman / Ruth Beloff (2nd ed.)]

BLOCH, HERMANN (Ḥayyim Ben Ẓevi; 1826–1896), rabbi and author. Born in Breslau, Bloch was a grandson of Abraham *Tiktin, chief rabbi of Breslau, whom he mentions in the introduction to his *Mevo ha-Talmud*. He studied in Breslau under his uncle Solomon Tiktin, and then in Hamburg. At various periods of his life he engaged in business and in his later years was a teacher at a *bet midrash* in Breslau. Bloch did research on the development of the Oral Law, and published *Mevo ha-Talmud* (vol. 1, Berlin, 1853). In his view, "the individual character of a *tanna* or an *amora* was the factor which determined his particular teachings or mode of exegesis in all matters, regardless of whether they were financial, ritual, scientific, or ethical" (p. 11). "Nevertheless, the underlying unity of *tannaim* and *amoraim* forms the foundation of 'the chain of tradition' and of 'the unity of the oral law,' whose source is in the written law" (p. 56). He devotes a detailed study, under the title *Hirhurei Torah* (4 pts., 1887–93), to the rule of the majority (based on Ex. 23:2), discussing its application in the Bible and the Talmud. In *Ẓurat ha-Bayit* (1883) he reconstructs the design of Herod's temple according to talmudic sources. He also published *Omrei Inshei* (1855), a collection of 107 parables found in the Babylonian Talmud, accompanied by a German translation.

BIBLIOGRAPHY: M. Brann, in: MGWJ, 42 (1898), 529 n.3; Kressel, Leksikon, 1 (1965), 246–7.

[Yehoshua Horowitz]

BLOCH, HERMAN SAMUEL (1912–1990), U.S. petroleum chemist. Bloch was born in Chicago and spent most of his career there. After receiving his Ph.D. from the University of Chicago's chemistry department, he joined the Universal Oil Products Company, eventually becoming associate director of its process research department (1959). He won many awards and distinctions for his patents and contributions to the knowledge of petrochemistry and catalysis, as well as for his public service in the fields of education and human relations. These include the North American Catalysis Society's first Eugene J. Houdry Award in Applied Catalysis (1971) and the E.V. Murphree Award in Industrial and Engineering Chemistry (1974). He was a member of the American Chemical Society.

[Ruth Rossing (2nd ed.)]

BLOCH, HYMAN MORRIS (1905–1963), South African Supreme Court judge. Born in the Transvaal, Bloch was admitted to the Cape bar in 1927. He was king's counsel in 1944 and in 1958 was appointed to the bench. He was prominent on the Western Province Zionist Council and the Cape Council of the South African Jewish Board of Deputies. He headed campaigns on behalf of Israel in the Western Province.

BLOCH, ISSACHAR BAER BEN SAMSON (1730–1798), Austrian rabbi. Bloch was born in Hamburg and studied under Jonathan *Eybeschuetz and Ezekiel *Landau. After serving as rabbi in several communities he was rabbi in Boskovice (1793–96), and later in Mattersdorf where he died. He wrote *Binat Yissakhar* (Prague, 1785), a collection of his sermons with a rhymed appendix on the precepts of the priestly benediction and the redemption of the firstborn. He also wrote glosses on the Mishnah (published in the Lemberg edition, 1869) under the title *Benei Yissakhar*. He carried on a halakhic correspondence with some of the renowned contemporary scholars, to which reference is made in Ezekiel Landau's *Noda bi-Yhudah* (1928, pp. 87–89; cf. also Eleazar b. Aryeh Loeb, *Shemen Rokeaḥ*, (1902), 181–2; and Moses *Sofer, *Ḥatam Sofer*, 7 (1912), nos. 17, 18, 21). Bloch, who was childless, adopted Jacob Patraselka, ancestor of the rabbinical family of Duschinsky and the first rabbi in Nádasd (Hungary), who also carried on a correspondence with Moses Sofer (*Ḥatam Sofer*, OḤ, nos. 104, 106, 139; YD, nos. 243, 305; ḤM, no. 206).

BIBLIOGRAPHY: E. Duckesz, *Chachme Ahw* (1908), 24 no. 33 (Heb. section); Eisler, in: *Das juedische Centralblatt*, 11 (1892), 117–8; J.J. Greenwald, *Ha-Yehudim be-Ungarya* (1913), 43 no. 24; idem, *Pe'erei Ḥakhmei Medinatenu* (1910), 94 no. 190; Mandl, in: *Magyar Zsidó Szemle*, 17 (1900), 142; Richtmann, *ibid.*, 22 (1905), 335–6; M. Stein, *Magyar rabbik*, 2 (1905), 103; 3 (1906), 145.

[Samuel Abba Horodezky]

BLOCH, IWAN (1872–1922), German dermatologist and medical historian. After graduating from Wuerzburg University in 1896, Bloch settled in Berlin as a practicing dermatologist. He was one of the first to engage in the scientific study of sex and a leader in the movement for sexual reform. His scientific publications include *Die Praxis der Hautkrankheiten* ("The Practice of Skin Diseases," 1908) and *Ursprung der Syphilis* ("Origin of Syphilis," 1911). In the latter he suggests that the disease was introduced to Europe through the Spaniards after the discovery of South America. Bloch made important contributions to the history of medicine which were published in the monumental *History of Medicine* of Max Neuburger. He also wrote on the history of dermatology and of Indian and Byzantine medicine. Many of his works were written under the pseudonyms of "von Welsenburg" and "Eugen Dühren."

BIBLIOGRAPHY: S.R. Kagan, *Jewish Medicine* (1952), 427.

[Suessmann Muntner]

BLOCH, JEAN-RICHARD (1884–1947), French author and political journalist. Bloch was born into an assimilated family in Paris. His Jewish consciousness was stirred in his boyhood by the antisemitism engendered by the Dreyfus Affair, and Jewish themes came to play a significant part in his writing. He was educated at the Sorbonne and became a teacher of history and literature. One of his earliest books was *Lévy* (1912), in which one of the stories deals with the effects of the Dreyfus case on a Jewish family in a provincial town. His most powerful novel,… *et compagnie*, (1918;… *& Co.*, 1929), is the story of Jewish cloth merchants from Alsace who move their business to a small town in western France. This work portrays the conflicts facing the Jew who wishes to maintain his identity while integrating into French culture. In 1910 Bloch founded a literary review, *L'effort libre*, but his work was interrupted by World War I, in which he was wounded three times. During the 1920s and early 1930s he wrote many novels, short stories, plays, poems, and essays. Two of the novels, *La nuit kurde* (1925; *A Night in Kurdistan*, 1930) and *Sybilla* (1932), reflect his fascination with the East. In 1925 he visited Palestine for the inauguration of the Hebrew University, and thereafter wrote a number of articles on the future role of the Jewish people, notably "Quel service les Juifs peuvent-ils rendre au monde?" (in *Palestine*, 1 (1927), 97–102). An essay entitled "Destin du siècle" (1931) showed that his approach to the Jewish problem had become somewhat ambiguous. From his student days, Bloch had been a socialist, and from the mid-1930s his interests centered mainly in politics. He had joined the Communist Party in 1921 and in 1923 helped to found the communist-oriented literary magazine *Europe* and in 1937, together with the poet Louis Aragon, the Communist daily *Ce Soir*. When the Germans occupied France in 1940 Bloch became an active member of the underground and in 1941 escaped the Gestapo by fleeing to Moscow, where he engaged in resistance broadcasts to the French people. He returned to France in 1945. Jean-Richard Bloch was a brother-in-law of André *Maurois.

BIBLIOGRAPHY: J.R. Bloch and R. Rolland, *Deux hommes se recontrent* (1964); *Europe* (Fr., June 1966).

[Denise R. Goitein]

BLOCH, JOSEPH (1871–1936), German socialist and journalist. Born in Lithuania, he immigrated to Germany where he edited the *Sozialistische Monatshefte*, a monthly publication which attracted a team of outstanding writers. Bloch advocated a union of Continental Europe and when the Bolsheviks came to power in Russia, he proposed a Franco-German Union. After the German revolution of 1918, he advocated a system of German democracy based on workers' councils. The *Monatshefte* gave considerable attention to Jewish questions and supported the Zionist movement. Bloch favored mass immigration to Palestine and was highly critical of British policy there. One of the first victims of Nazi persecution in Germany, he never wavered in his belief in the triumph of socialism and the future of the Zionist enterprise. He died a lonely refugee in Prague.

BIBLIOGRAPHY: K. Blumenfeld, *Erlebte Judenfrage* (1962), 57, 123. **ADD. BIBLIOGRAPHY:** C. Bloch, "Der Kampf Joseph Blochs und der *'Sozialistische Monatshefte'* in der Weimarer Republik," in: *Jahrbuch des Instituts für Deutsche Geschichte*, 3 (1974), 257–88.

BLOCH, JOSEPH LEIB (1860–1930), Lithuanian yeshivah head. He showed exceptional ability from childhood and at the age of 14 he traveled to Chelm where he studied under R. Eliezer *Gordon. He continued his studies with Naphtali Ẓevi Judah *Berlin at Volozhin. After his marriage to the daughter of Eliezer Gordon, he moved to Telz, where he assisted his father-in-law, who had been appointed rabbi and *rosh yeshivah*. In 1902, after resigning from the yeshivah in protest against the resistance of a number of the students to the study of *musar*, he was appointed rabbi of Varna, a small village near Telz. He served later as rabbi of Shadova, where he established his own yeshivah. In 1910 Bloch was appointed rabbi of Telz and *rosh yeshivah*, succeeding his father-in-law. Under his leadership, the yeshivah attracted large numbers of students. In addition to his lectures on *halakhah*, Bloch also gave talks on *musar*. He took the unusual step of founding a teachers' seminary, which produced hundreds of educators, and a preparatory school, in which secular studies were taught. Thanks to these auxiliary institutions, the yeshivah of Telz occupied a central position, with an enrollment, at times, of as many as 500 students. Active in communal affairs, Bloch served as a member of the executive of the Association of Lithuanian Rabbis and as one of the leaders of *Agudat Israel. Prominent among his sons were Abraham Isaac, who succeeded his father in Telz, and Elijah Meir, who was one of the yeshivah principals. His other sons and sons-in-law also taught in Telz. Bloch's ethical essays were published in *Shi'urei Da'at* (pt. 1, 1949; pt. 2, 1953; pt. 3, 1956). His halakhic lectures appeared in *Shi'ur Halakhah* (pt. 1, 1932; pt. 2, 1943; pt. 3, 1958).

BIBLIOGRAPHY: D. Katz, *Tenu'at ha-Musar*, 5 (1962/63), 17–109.

[Itzhak Alfassi]

BLOCH, JOSEPH SAMUEL (1850–1923), rabbi, publicist, and politician in Austria. He acquired distinction for his defense of Judaism against the *blood libel and was praised by Adolf *Jellinek as the "Hercules of the antisemitic Augean stables." Son of a poor baker in Dukla (east Galicia), Bloch attended yeshivot at Lemberg and Eisenstadt and then the universities of Munich and Zurich. After officiating in provincial communities, he became rabbi of the Vienna suburb of Floridsdorf and a teacher at Jellinek's *bet ha-midrash*. During the *Tisza-Eszlár blood libel trial in 1883, when August *Rohling undertook to attest on oath that Jews practiced ritual murder, Bloch attacked him in the press. He challenged Rohling's competence as a scholar, accused him of lying, and offered him 3,000 florins for translating a random page of the Talmud. Rohling was forced to sue Bloch for libel, but after two years' investigations withdrew his action 13 days before the trial was due to open.

Bloch was elected in 1884, 1885, and 1891 to the Austrian Parliament from a preponderantly Jewish constituency of Galicia, and was the first parliamentarian to make Jewish affairs his main political concern, regarding himself as an interpreter and defender of Jewish thought to the non-Jewish public. In 1884 he founded a weekly, *Dr. Blochs Oesterreichische Wochenschrift*, for combating antisemitism, which existed until after World War I, and also established the *Oesterreichisch-Israelitische Union (from 1921: Union deutsch-oesterreichischer Juden). He also lectured in Social Democratic associations on social conditions in the time of Jesus. Bloch was guided in his political activities by Adolf *Fischhof. He developed a previously unknown militancy and Jewish awareness which brought him into conflict with other Jewish leaders in Austria. In *Der nationale Zwist und die Juden in Oesterreich* (1886) he asked Jews to remain neutral in the struggle of the various nationalities within the Hapsburg Empire and to consider themselves "Austrian Jews" and "Jewish Austrians." He thus supplied the ideology for the Hapsburg patriotism with which the majority of Jews in the realm associated themselves around the beginning of the 20th century. Bloch saw the struggle for Jewish rights as part of the fight for the principle of equality for all nationalities in the empire, which the monarchy would have to recognize in order to exist. He also initiated proceedings against further ritual murder accusations by Franz Deckert and Paulus *Meyer and was active during the *Hilsner case.

At first a supporter of Zionism and Theodor *Herzl, Bloch published one of Herzl's articles in 1896 and introduced him to the finance minister, Bilinski. However, Bloch preferred the concept of "colonization-Zionism," regarded Jewish nationality as closely linked with the Jewish religion, and refused to close his paper to non-Zionists. Herzl, on the other hand, failed to appreciate Bloch's fight against antisemitism. By around 1900 Bloch had become alienated from the Zionists. He visited Ereẓ Israel before his death.

For his work in the Jewish cause Bloch was warmly received on visits to the United States in 1912, and again in 1920. During World War I he raised funds on behalf of the Austrian government in neutral countries. He published a compendium of apologetics, *Israel und die Voelker* (1922; *Israel and the Nations*, 1927), based on the evidence of the experts in connection with the Rohling trial, and his memoirs *Erinnerungen aus meinem Leben* (1922; *My Reminiscences*, 1927). He also wrote prolifically on Jewish lore.

BIBLIOGRAPHY: M. Grunwald, in: *Festschrift des juedischtheologischen Seminars Breslau*, 2 (1929), 1–12; L. Kolb, in: *Dr. Blochs Wochenschrift* (Nov. 20, 1920), in honor of his 70th birthday; Ch. Bloch, in: *Herzl Yearbook*, 1 (1958), 154–64; J. Fraenkel (ed.), *Jews of Austria* (1967), index; M. Grunwald, *Vienna* (1936), 433–57; W.J. Cahnman, in: YLBI, 4 (1959), 111–39 and passim.

[Meir Lamed]

BLOCH, JOSHUA (1890–1957), U.S. librarian, bibliographer, and reform rabbi. Born in Dorbian, Lithuania, Bloch went to the U.S. in 1907. He taught at New York University from 1919 to 1928; from 1922 until his death he served as chaplain in several hospitals of the New York State Department of Mental Hygiene. His main work, however, was as head of the Jewish Division of the New York Public Library, a post which he held from 1923 to 1956; under his direction the Library developed as one of the major collections of Judaica in the United States. Bloch arranged many major exhibitions of Judaica there. Many of his bibliographical researches into the history of Hebrew printing were published by the Library, such as *Hebrew Printing in Riva di Trento* (1933; *Bulletin of the New York Public Library*, vol. 37), *Early Hebrew Printing in Spain and Portugal* (1938; *ibid.*, vol. 46). He also founded the quarterly *Journal of Jewish Bibliography* in 1938 and was its editor until 1943. In 1940 he was appointed to the publication committee of the Jewish Publication Society and a year later to the editorial board of the Jewish Apocryphal Literature Series; as a result of these connections he wrote *On the Apocalyptic in Judaism* (1952) and *Of Making Many Books* (1953; an annotated list of the books issued by the Jewish Publication Society, 1890–1952). The following year he published *The People and the Book*, on 300 years of Jewish life in America. His bibliography was collected by Dora Steinglass in *A Bibliography of the Writings of Joshua Bloch (1910–1958)* (1960).

BIBLIOGRAPHY: A. Berger et al. (eds.), *Joshua Bloch Memorial Volume* (1960); idem, in: JBA, 16 (1958/59), 102–4; Shunami, Bibl, index.

[Abraham Berger]

BLOCH, JULES (1880–1953), French philologist, specialist in Indic languages. Bloch taught in Paris at the École Pratique des Hautes Études and the École des Langues Orientales Vivantes. His work covered the entire range of Indic languages, ancient, medieval, and – especially – modern. Bloch's main research was into the Indo-European languages of India, on which he wrote *La formation de la langue marathe* (1915) and *L'Indo-Aryen du Véda aux temps modernes* (1934; *Indo-Aryan from the Vedas to Modern Times*, 1965). He also published an important book on Dravidian languages, *Structure grammaticale des langues dravidiennes* (1946; *The Grammatical Structure of Dravidian Languages*, 1954).

[Herbert H. Paper]

BLOCH, KONRAD (1912–2000), U.S. biochemist and Nobel laureate. Bloch was born in Neisse, Germany (now Poland) and graduated from the Technische Hochschule of Munich in 1934. Forced to leave because he was Jewish, Bloch found a temporary position at the Schweizerische Forschungsinstitut in Davos, Switzerland. In 1936 he immigrated to the United States (becoming an American citizen in 1944) and joined the Department of Biochemistry, College of Physicians and Surgeons, Columbia University. New York. After obtaining his doctorate at Columbia University in 1938, he became a member of the staff there. His collaboration with R. *Schoenheimer stimulated his interest in the biological origin of cholesterol and he began to concentrate on this field in 1941. In 1942 Bloch and David Rittenberg discovered that the two-carbon compound acetic acid was the major building block in the 30 or more steps in the biosynthesis (natural formation) of cholesterol, a waxlike alcohol found in animal cells. In his search to determine how acetic acid molecules combine in this process, Bloch was also joined by Feodor Lynen and his collaborators in Munich and Sir John Warcup Cornforth and George Popják in England. Their discovery facilitated medical research on the relation of blood cholesterol levels to atherosclerosis; research in physiology; and research on the chemistry of terpenes, rubber, and other isoprene derivatives. In 1946 Bloch joined the University of Chicago, becoming professor of biochemistry in 1952. During his years at Chicago Bloch investigated the enzymatic synthesis of the tripeptide glutathione. As a Guggenheim fellow he spent the year 1953 at the Organisch-Chemisches Institut, Eidgenössische Technische Hochschule, in Zurich with L. Ruzicka, V. Prelog, and their colleagues. In 1954 Bloch was appointed Higgins Professor of Biochemistry in the Department of Chemistry, Harvard University, and in 1968 he became chairman of the department. He continued research on various aspects of terpene and sterol biogenesis, going on as well to the enzymatic formation of unsaturated fatty acids and biochemical evolution. He became emeritus professor in 1982. Bloch shared the 1964 Nobel Prize in physiology and medicine with Feodor Lynen for discoveries concerning the synthesis of cholesterol by the body from acetic acid.

He was a member of the American Chemical Society, U.S. National Academy of Sciences, American Academy of Arts and Sciences, and American Society of Biological Chemists, among others. He was associated with the Committee on Growth of the American Cancer Society, the Biochemical Section of the U.S. Public Health Service, and the National Institute of Neurological Diseases and Blindness. He served as an associate editor of the *Journal of Biological Chemistry* and published hundreds of papers. Apart from the topics mentioned, these dealt with creatinine, glutathione, amino acids generally, proteins, and several metabolic processes.

BIBLIOGRAPHY: *Chemical and Engineering News*, 42 (Oct. 26, 1964), 34.

[Samuel Aaron Miller / Ruth Rossing (2nd ed.)]

BLOCH, MARC (1886–1944), French historian. Bloch was professor of medieval history at the University of Strasbourg from 1919 to 1936 and then at the Sorbonne. He fought in both world wars and after the fall of France in 1940 was a leader of the Resistance. He was arrested, tortured, and executed by the Gestapo. One of Bloch's most significant works was in the field of French medieval agrarian history, *Les caractères originaux de l'histoire rurale française* (1931; *French Rural History*, 1966). A further contribution to economic historiography was his founding (together with Lucien Febvre) of the important review, *Annales d'histoire économique et sociale*. Bloch's *La société féodale* (1939–40; *Feudal Society*, 1961) became a standard work on feudalism. He did not accept the identification of feudalism with military service, the view held in England and Germany, still less the Marxist oversimplification of feudalism as exploitation of peasants by landlords. Instead, he analyzed the structure of feudal society and the relationship between history and economics during that period. In a posthumous work, *L'étrange défaite* (1946; *Strange Defeat*, 1949) Bloch affirmed his detachment from the Jewish faith and from all other religious dogmas. Nevertheless, he acknowledged his Jewish descent and his admiration for the tradition of the Hebrew prophets. His other works were *L'Ile-de-France* (1913); *Rois et serfs* (1920); *Apologie pour l'histoire, ou métier d'historien* (1949; *The Historian's Craft*, 1954).

BIBLIOGRAPHY: L. Febvre, in: *Les Cahiers politiques* (March, 1945), 5–11. **ADD. BIBLIOGRAPHY:** C. Fink, *Marc Bloch: A Life in History* (1989); S.W. Friedman, *Marc Bloch, Sociology and Geography* (1996); E. Bloch, *Marc Bloch (1886–1944): Une biographie impossible* (1997); O. Dumoulin, *Marc Bloch* (Fr., 2000).

[Avrom Saltman]

BLOCH, MARCUS (Mordecai) ELIEZER (1723–1799), physician and zoologist. He was born in Bavaria, the son of a poor trader. Bloch received a traditional Jewish education and, at the age of 19, he began to learn German, French, and Latin. He was helped by wealthy relatives to study medicine at Frankfurt on the Oder, and received his doctor's degree in 1747. He became a physician in Berlin, and soon gained a reputation at all levels of society. His friends included Moses *Mendelssohn, who was also his patient. Bloch's main achievement was in his morphological and systematic work on fish. He built himself an aquarium and acquired a marine collection which after his death was incorporated in the Berlin Zoological Museum. He wrote his great ichthyological work, *Allegemeine Naturgeschichte der Fische*, in 12 volumes (1781–1795). The work describes and classifies over 1,500 species of fish. Although Bloch's classification system was primitive and superficial, his book retains its scientific value, with its excellent drawings and diagrams. Bloch also wrote several short works on medical and zoological subjects.

BIBLIOGRAPHY: Hirschberg, in: *Deutsche Medizinische Wochenschrift*, 39 (1913), 900; *Biographisches Lexikon der hervorragenden Aerzte*, 1 (1929^2), 571–2.

BLOCH, MARTIN (1883–1954), German expressionist painter, who became a master of British landscape. Bloch lived in Spain during World War I and subsequently spent many summers painting in Italy. In these years he was influenced by Cézanne, the "fauves," and the German expressionists. When Hitler came to power he fled to England, where he was interned during World War II. During his internment he restricted himself to black and white studies in contM crayons heightened with red chalk. His mature style emerged with a period of painting in Dorset in 1947. He developed a deep love of the British landscape, retaining a German expressionist sense of the dramatic but abandoning the tendency to exaggerate. His developed sense of color became subtle and harmonious. A posthumous exhibition held in 1955 established his reputation.

ADD BIBLIOGRAPHY: D.F. Jenkins (ed.), *Y bryniau tywyll y cymclau trymion* ("The Darks Hills, the Heavy Clouds: An Expression of Landscape Painting," 1981); C. da Costa, *Martin Bloch, 1883–1954: An Exhibition of Paintings and Drawings* (South London Art Gallery, 1984).

[Sonja Beyer (2nd ed.)]

BLOCH, MATTATHIAS BEN BENJAMIN ZE'EV (Wolf) ASHKENAZI (1610/1620–after 1668), preacher and one of the leaders of the Shabbatean movement. Bloch was born in Cracow. His grandfather, Feivel Bloch, was one of the leaders of the community during the first half of the 17th century and its representative at the meetings of the Council of Four Lands in Poland. He studied under the Cracow rabbis Menahem Mendel *Krochmal and Abraham Joshua *Heschel. He suffered during the persecution of the Jews under *Chmielnicki and during the Swedish occupation (1648–57) and was expelled from his town. In 1660 he was in Jassy and in 1665, on his way to Ereẓ Israel, was in Constantinople, where he published *Kelal Katan*, a homily on Deuteronomy 32. He relates that he had two important homiletical books in his possession: *Sefer Kelal Gadol*, written in the *peshat* ("literal"), *remez* ("symbolic"), and *derash* ("homiletic-allegoric") styles; and the second, *Sefer Mattityahu*, a kabbalistic commentary on all sections of the Torah. Apparently Bloch became a Shabbatean in 1665 either while he was still in Constantinople or when he arrived in Jerusalem and met Shabbetai Ẓevi before the latter had left Ereẓ Israel. When, at the end of 1665 in Smyrna, Shabbetai Ẓevi appointed kings in a similar order to that of the ancient kings of Israel and Judah, he appointed Bloch "King Asa." In 1666 Bloch was among the leaders of the Shabbatean movement in Egypt. With the failure of the messianic hopes after Shabbetai Ẓevi's apostasy, he persisted in his belief, but he left Egypt to settle in Mosul (Iraq) where he was accepted as a rabbi or *dayyan*. His influence spread to the communities in Kurdistan, which he encouraged in their Shabbatean belief. His activities as rabbi of the community as well as a Shabbatean leader are recorded in various letters preserved from 1668. After that year nothing is known about him. According to Jacob *Sasportas, Bloch was already elderly at the start of the Shabbatean movement.

BIBLIOGRAPHY: G. Scholem, in: *Zion*, 7 (1942), 175–8, 193–5; Scholem, Shabbetai Ẓevi, index; A. Yaari, in: KS, 36 (1960/61), 525–34.

[Gershom Scholem]

BLOCH, SIR MAURICE (1883–1964), Scottish distiller and philanthropist. Born in Dundee, Bloch settled in Glasgow in 1910. He founded a family distilling business and at the same time played an active role in Jewish communal work. In 1937 he was knighted "for political and social services." In 1954 he gave up his large business to devote himself to civic and Jewish communal affairs. He was president of the Board of Guardians, he represented Scotland on the Chief Rabbinate Council and became chairman of the Queen's Park Synagogue. He was keenly interested in Jewish education and was president of the Glasgow yeshivah, made a generous donation in 1956 to Jews' College, London, and set up a trust fund for the Hebrew University. He also gave sizable gifts to Glasgow University and Royal Faculty of Physicians and Surgeons in Glasgow. In 1948 Bloch was involved in the investigations of the Lynskey Tribunal into the conduct of some ministers of the crown. Throughout Bloch denied corruption though admitting to indiscretions. Nevertheless at the end of the trial his name was removed from the list of magistrates in Glasgow where he had been a justice of the peace for 25 years.

BLOCH, MOSES (1815–1909), rabbi and author. Bloch, who was born in Ronsperg, Bohemia, served as rabbi in several cities of Bohemia and Moravia. In 1877 he was appointed together with David *Kaufmann and Wilhelm *Bacher to the academic staff of the newly founded rabbinical seminary in Budapest. Bloch was professor of Talmud and Codes and also the rector of the seminary, in which capacities he served for 30 years. His main work was *Sha'arei Torat ha-Takkanot* (in 7 volumes, 1879–1906) which traces, on the basis of talmudic sources, the development of **takkanot* from Moses to the end of the talmudic period. In a sequel to this work, *Sha'arei ha-Ma'alot* (1908), Bloch gives a detailed exposition of the various states and degrees of holiness, ritual and family purity as defined in the Mishnah and Talmud. Bloch published important monographs, in German and Hungarian, on biblical and talmudic law, in the yearbooks of the Budapest Seminary. He published the Prague 1608 edition of the responsa of *Meir b. Baruch of Rothenburg, together with notes and indexes (in 1885; 1896^3), and also some hitherto unpublished responsa of R. Meir for the Mekize Nirdamim (1891).

BIBLIOGRAPHY: *Sefer ha-Yovel... Moshe Aryeh Bloch* (1905), ix–xxiv; *Jahresbericht der Landes-Rabbinerschule in Budapest*, 31 (1908), 3–4; 32 (1909), iii–x.

[Moshe Nahum Zobel]

BLOCH, MOSES RUDOLPH (1902–1985), physical chemist. Born in Czechoslovakia, Bloch studied chemistry at the Universities of Prague and Leipzig, and then proceeded to Switzerland and received his doctorate in physical chemistry at Berne in 1926. From 1927 to 1933 he headed the department of metallography and X-ray spectrography at the Higher Technical Institute of Karlsruhe. His researches on silver iodide and refrigeration were interrupted when the Nazis came to power, and he thereafter served as consultant on the technology of refrigeration in Holland, England, and France. Immigrating to Ereẓ Israel in 1936 he worked at the potash works at the Dead Sea, where he introduced a method of increasing evaporation by the sun and was head of the research division of the works. From 1940 to 1968 he was a member of the Scientific Council of Israel and the Advisory Technological Council of the Israel Government. In 1967 he was guest professor for research on water resources at the Hebrew University and at the Institute of Atomic Physics at Heidelberg from 1967 to 1968. Bloch also undertook research on bromine and potash in nature, and climatic and geological research. He was awarded the Israel Prize for Science in 1966.

BLOCH, PHILIPP (1841–1923), German historian and Reform rabbi. He was born at Tworog (Silesia) and studied in Breslau. After a period as teacher with the Munich Jewish communal school (1869–71), he became rabbi of the Liberal congregation Bruedergemeinde of Posen where he remained active for some fifty years. When that city reverted to Poland after World War I, Bloch retired from the rabbinate and moved to Berlin. He took a leading part in the association of Liberal rabbis and in the work of German Jewish scholarly societies; in 1905 he was a co-founder of the General Archives of German Jews. Bloch's contributions to Jewish scholarship were concerned mainly with the philosophy of religion, *aggadah*, and Kabbalah; he also wrote about the history of Jews in Poland and the city and province of Posen. Among his works are a translation of and introduction to the first book of Saadiah's *Emunot ve-De'ot* (1879); a translation of and commentary on the fifth chapter of Book II of Crescas' *Or Adonai* concerning free will (1879); essays on the development of Kabbalah and Jewish religious philosophy for Winter-Wuensche's *Die juedische Literatur* (1894–96); *Die Kabbalah auf ihrem Hoehepunkt…* (1905); *Spuren alter Volksbuecher in der Aggadah* (in *Festschrift … Hermann Cohen, Judaica*, 1912); and *Piskoth fuer die drei Trauersabbathe*, translation and commentary (in *Festschrift … Steinschneider*, 1896).

BIBLIOGRAPHY: M. Brann, *Geschichte des juedisch-theologischen Seminars… in Breslau* (1904), 146–7, bibliography; A. Warschauer, in: MGWJ, 68 (1924), 1–16; idem, in: MGADJ, 6 (1926), 107–9; J. Guttman, in: KAWJ, 5 (1924), 1–7; N.M. Gelber, in: S. Federbusch (ed.), *Ḥokhmat Yisrael be-Ma'arav Eiropah*, 2 (1963), 59–63.

BLOCH, ROLF (1930–), Swiss Jewish community leader. Born into a family of Alsatian origin in Berne, he studied law. His father, Camille Bloch, had built up a chocolate firm in Courtelary, which also produced kosher chocolate.

Rolf Bloch was president of the Berne community between 1975 and 1985. Between 1992 and 2000 he served as president of the Swiss Federation of Jewish Communities. As a moderate figure, he mediated in the clash between American-Jewish organizations and Swiss bankers and politicians in the furor surrounding the assets of Nazi victims. He headed a private foundation endowed by the banks and Swiss industry, distributing 296 million Swiss francs to the victims, 90% of them Jewish. As an able administrator and conciliatory personality he became a popular public figure. The Catholic Faculty of the University of Berne awarded him an honorary Ph.D. for his promotion of Christian-Jewish understanding in Switzerland.

BIBLIOGRAPHY: *Historisches Lexikon der Schweiz*, 2, 496.

[Uri Kaufmann (2nd ed.)]

BLOCH, ROSINE (1844–1891), singer. Bloch made her debut at the Paris Opera as Azucena in Verdi's *Il Trovatore* in 1865 and remained there as one of its most prominent members. Among her most notable parts was that of Fides in Meyerbeer's *Le Prophète*. She sang Amneris in the first French production of *Aida* in 1880, the year she retired.

BLOCH, SAMSON BEN MOSES (d. 1737), *dayyan* and rabbi of Hamburg. Bloch, known also as "Samson the Ḥasid," was one of the first scholars and teachers and later the principal in the *bet midrash* built by Issachar Baer Kohen in 1707. He was known for his erudition and for his close ties with the great halakhic authorities of his generation. Bloch greatly exerted himself for the benefit of his community and it was through his efforts that the Jews were permitted to escape to Altona during a time of danger. The glosses and novellae which he wrote in the margins of the Shulḥan Arukh, *Oraḥ Ḥayyim* were published under the title *Nezirut Shimshon* (Berlin, 1764), and, again, together with the text of the *Oraḥ Ḥayyim* (Prague, 1785). *Tosafot Ḥadashim* (Amsterdam, 1775), his commentary on the Mishnah, was published with the text and later republished in many editions of the Mishnah. Samson also wrote halakhic novellae which have not been published. His sons were Issachar Baer and Moses, *dayyan* of Mezhirech.

BIBLIOGRAPHY: H. Wagenaar, *Toledot Ya'veẓ* (1868), 34, 63; E. Duckesz, *Chachme AHW* (1908), 24–26 (Hebrew section), 9–10 (German section); S.M. Chones, *Toledot ha-Posekim* (1910), 447.

[Abraham David]

BLOCH, SAMSON (Simson) HA-LEVI (1784–1845), one of the early Hebrew authors of the *Haskalah in Galicia. He was, for a number of years, a student of Naḥman *Krochmal and a close friend of Solomon Judah *Rapoport. In the early 1800s he settled in Zamosc, in Russian Poland. In 1809 he published a new edition of *Iggeret ha-Rashba* (Epistle of R. Solomon b. Abraham *Adret) against the study of philosophy, together with *Iggeret ha-Hitnaẓẓelut* (Letter of Defense) by *Jedaiah ha-Penini on behalf of philosophy. In his introduction, Bloch explained that Adret had objected only to philosophical studies at too early an age. In 1813–14, Bloch worked as proofreader of Hebrew books for the Viennese printer Anton Schmid. He published a Hebrew translation (from the German) of *Manasseh Ben Israel's *Vindiciae Iudaeorum* with the title *Teshu'at Yisrael* ("Israel's Salvation," 1814) with an introduction and the author's biography by David Franco-Mendes. Bloch won his place in Hebrew literature with his *Shevilei Olam* ("Paths of the World"), the first general geography in the Hebrew language. The first two parts of this work, on Asia and Africa, appeared during his lifetime (1822–1827); the unfinished third part, on Europe, edited by N.M. Schorr and published posthumously in 1855, under the title *Zehav Shebah. Shevilei Olam*, which ran into four editions, is, in the main, an adaptation of German geography books. However, Bloch was able to give his work a popular Jewish flavor by the inclusion of stories about unusual phenomena in far-off lands, mysterious tales and legendary anecdotes, and by special stress on the importance of each country for Jewish history. Bloch's style is extremely florid and stilted even for his own period, and the book as a whole suffers from numerous irrelevant notes. In 1840 Bloch published a Hebrew translation of Leopold Zunz's biography of Rashi, with important emendations and notes. Bloch spent his last years in solitude and illness in his native town of Kulikow (near Lemberg).

BIBLIOGRAPHY: Klausner, Sifrut, 2 (1952), 350–68.

[Gedalyah Elkoshi]

BLOCH-MICHEL, JEAN (1912–), French novelist and essayist. Bloch-Michel was influenced by his experiences during the Nazi occupation of France and by the moral confusion and crises of conscience affecting his country after World War II. Both his fiction and his essays show him to be a moralist in the French classical tradition with notable psychological insight. Among his best-known works are *Le témoin* (1949; *The Witness*, 1950); a book of war memoirs, *Les grandes circonstances* (1949); *La fuite en Egypte* (1952; *The Flight into Egypt*, 1957), and *Frosinia* (1966). He also wrote a study of French politics, *Journal du désordre* (1955), and an essay on the contemporary novel, *Présent de l'indicatif* (1963). Bloch-Michel was a contributor to a collective work on capital punishment, *Reflexions sur la peine capitale* (1957). Although culturally assimilated, Bloch-Michel expressed his solidarity with Russian Jewry and the State of Israel.

BIBLIOGRAPHY: E.P. Hazard, in: *Saturday Review of Literature* (Feb. 11, 1950); *Évidences*, no. 30 (1953), 8–9.

[Arnold Mandel]

BLOCK, H & R, U.S. tax preparation and financial services firm.

HENRY WOLLMAN BLOCH (1922–) was born in Kansas City, Mo., the second son of a prominent lawyer. He began his college career at the University of Missouri but transferred to the University of Michigan, from which he graduated in 1944. He joined the Army Air Corps and as a navigator on B-17 bombers he flew 31 combat missions over Germany. He was awarded the Air Medal and three Oak Leaf Clusters. The Army Air Corps sent him to the Harvard Business School for training in statistical control. Bloch came under the influence of Sumner Schlicter, a noted economist, who suggested that small business did not have the resources of big business and labor. In 1946 Bloch and his brother Leon founded the United Business Company to offer bookkeeping and other services to small businesses. After a year, Leon left the business to return to law school. But as the company grew, Henry was joined by another brother, Richard, and they offered bookkeeping and tax services to small businesses. Shortly before the 1955 tax season, they placed an ad in *The Kansas City Star* offering tax preparation. The Internal Revenue Service had just discontinued free tax preparation so the Blochs' skills were in demand. The Blochs named the company H&R Block because, they said, the family name had been difficult for people to pronounce and Block could be spelled phonetically. Their success prompted Richard to suggest expanding to New York City, the next city the IRS stopped servicing. H&R Block opened seven offices in 1956 and in its second year the company more than tripled revenues. By 1962 the company had 206 offices and became a public company.

In the 1970s H&R Block built a national brand by offering professional services for a mass market. Beginning in 1972 Henry Bloch appeared in television commercials, which also helped build H&R Block into a national firm. Soon there were 8,600 offices. By 1978 the company offices prepared more than one of every nine tax returns filed in the United States, and by the turn of the century it had over 100,000 associates at more than 12,000 offices around the world.

Widely known as a businessman, civil leader, and avid supporter of the arts in Kansas City, Henry served on the boards of the American Jewish Committee and the Jewish Federation.

RICHARD BLOCH (1926–2004) entered the Wharton School of Finance at the University of Pennsylvania at the age of 16. The youngest member of his class, he received a bachelor of science degree in economics in 1945. Ever the entrepreneur, while in college he purchased and repaired used cars and sold them for a profit to help pay for college expenses. After graduation, he returned to Kansas City and worked in the municipal bond business before joining his brother.

In 1978 Richard was diagnosed with terminal lung cancer and was told he had three months to live. Refusing to accept this diagnosis, he underwent aggressive therapy for two years and was pronounced cured. He promised himself that if he survived he would devote his life to helping others fight cancer. By 1980 he was fulfilling his commitment; in 1982 he sold his interest in H&R Block. Richard and his wife founded the Cancer Hotline in 1980. It educates and provides information to thousands of newly diagnosed cancer patients and their families. They also founded the R.A. Bloch Cancer Management Center and the R.A. Bloch Cancer Support Center at the University of Missouri in Kansas City. Richard Bloch and his wife, Annette, wrote three books about fighting cancer. Their cancer foundation oversees annual rallies each year on the first Sunday in June to raise awareness that death and cancer are not synonymous. At the first rally, in 1990, they dedicated a park to Americans who have been diagnosed with cancer. Since then the Blochs have completed 19 additional cancer survivor parks. Richard Bloch also served a six-year term on the National Cancer Advisory Board.

[Stewart Kampel (2nd ed.)]

BLOCK, HERBERT LAWRENCE (Herblock; 1909–2001), U.S. editorial cartoonist. Born in Chicago, Block started to draw when he was quite young and won a scholarship to the Chicago Art Institute at 12. His critical eye and rapier pen made him one of the leading journalists of his time. In 1929 Block dropped out of Lake Forest College after two years to work for *The Chicago Daily News*. His cartoons were syndicated almost from the start. In 1933 he joined the Newspaper Enterprise Association, where he won his first Pulitzer Prize in 1942. The following year he joined the army, which employed his talent for cartooning in its Information and Education Division. He was mustered out as a sergeant in 1946 and joined *The Washington Post*, where his woodcut-like strokes and pungent, succinct captions chronicled and skewered national and world leaders for decades. Block coined the term "McCarthyism" for the prosecutorial Communist-hunting tactics of Senator Joseph R. McCarthy of Wisconsin, whom he depicted emerging from a sewer with a thug-like heavy beard. It was said that McCarthy shaved twice a day to avoid resembling the caricature. He began drawing Richard M. Nixon the same way in 1948, and Nixon, too, shaved twice a day. Block was unperturbed, saying both men had a "moral 5 o'clock shadow." Sometimes Nixon appeared as a vulture, other times as an undertaker, always as a man ready to benefit from the failure of others. When Nixon was elected president, a Herblock cartoon showed him with a clean shave, but as the administration became mired in Watergate, Nixon's eyebrows grew heavier and his wattles fleshier. Nixon, like Dwight D. Eisenhower before him, canceled the delivery of *The Washington Post* to his home when his children were young, because, he said, "I didn't want the girls to be upset."

Block's second Pulitzer Prize was awarded in 1954 for a drawing of Stalin, who was being accompanied to his grave by the robed figure of death. "You were always a great friend of mine, Joseph," the caption said. In addition to his work as a cartoonist, for which he won another Pulitzer Prize in 1979, Block wrote 12 books in his customary punchy style. "The Soviet state builds bodies," he wrote typically in one of them. "Mounds of them." He continued contributing cartoons to the *Post* until three months before his death when he was 92. In addition to three Pulitzers and a fourth he shared with *The Post* for its coverage of Watergate, Herblock received several honorary degrees and won dozens of journalism prizes. In 1966 he was selected to design the postage stamp commemorating the 175th anniversary of the Bill of Rights. President Bill Clinton, who was often at the end of Herblock's sharp quill, in 1994 awarded him the nation's highest civilian honor, the Presidential Medal of Freedom. In 2000 the Library of Congress mounted a retrospective of Herblock's work. *The Washington Post* so valued Herblock that they referred to his contribution to the editorial page as a signed editorial opinion and not a cartoon.

[Stewart Kampel (2nd ed.)]

BLOCK, PAUL (1877–1941), U.S. publisher of an early newspaper chain. Born in Elmira, N.Y., Block made his first venture into newspaper ownership by purchasing the *Newark Star-Eagle* in 1908. He bought the *Evening Sun* and *Morning Post* (both of Pittsburgh) in 1927 and later was president and publisher of *Pittsburgh Post-Gazette*, the *Toledo Blade*, and *Toledo Times*. He was a contributor to Jewish and other philanthropic causes, and donated $100,000 to Yale University in 1930 for a study of newspapers in the modern world.

BLOEMFONTEIN, capital of the Orange Free State, Republic of South Africa. Jewish families played an important pioneering role in the development of Bloemfontein. Isaac Baumann of Hesse-Cassel (1813–1881), one of the first settlers to buy land in the new township in 1848, established the first trading store. The earliest Day of Atonement services in Bloemfontein were held in his house in 1871. In 1873 marriages by Jewish rites were legalized in the Orange Free State. A Hebrew congregation was formed in 1876, and a synagogue built in 1903. The first president (1902–24) was Wolf Ehrlich. As the East European element increased the communal leadership gradually passed to them, a prominent part being played by Jacob Philips and Henry Bradlow. Jews also took an active part in municipal affairs. Baumann was the second chairman of the Bloemfontein municipal board, the forerunner of the town council. His son Gustav was the first surveyor-general of the Orange Free State. The Baumanns fought on the side of the Boers in the South African War (1899–1902). Moritz Leviseur, who took part in the Basuto War of 1865–66, helped to establish the town's first hospital and founded the National Museum. His wife Sophie wrote *Ouma Looks Back*, an account of the early days, and became known as the "Grand Old Lady of Bloemfontein." Wolf Ehrlich, a friend of the Boer leader General Hertzog (later South African prime minister), sat as a senator in the South African parliament. Jewish mayors of Bloemfontein included Ehrlich (1906–07 and 1911–12), Ivan Haarburger (1912–14), and Sol Harris (1929). The community had a well-developed network of institutions, including a fine communal center for cultural and educational activities. A large new synagogue was built in 1965. In 1956 the Hebrew congregation, *Chevra Kaddisha, talmud torah*, and the charitable institutions combined to form the United Hebrew Institutions of Bloemfontein. Other Jewish institutions included the OFS provincial committee of the South African Board of Deputies and the OFS and Northern Cape Zionist Council. There was also a small Reform group. The Jewish population in 1967 numbered 1,347 out of a total population of 119,000. Thereafter, in common with most other Jewish communities outside the main urban centers of *Johannesburg, *Cape Town, and *Durban, the Bloemfontein Jewish community declined steadily. In 1997, the synagogue was sold and the congregation relocated to the smaller premises of the now defunct Reform congregation. In 2004, the community numbered about 180 Jews.

BIBLIOGRAPHY: G. Saron and L. Hotz (eds.), *Jews in South Africa* (1955), index.

[Lewis Sowden]

BLOGG (also **Bloch**), **SOLOMON BEN EPHRAIM** (c. 1780–1858), Hebrew grammarian and liturgist. He was a teacher at the Jewish community's school at Hanover (Germany), where he founded the Hebrew printing press in 1827, Telgener, which was noted for its neatly and accurately printed books. Blogg published Psalms as well as a Passover Haggadah (1829) with German translation and his own commentaries. He wrote a history of the Hebrew language and literature with a short study on the Targums, *Korot Leshonenu ha-Kedoshah – Geschichte der hebraeischen Sprache und Literatur* (Berlin, 1826^2), included also in his *Binyan Shelomo – Aedificium Salomonis* (Hanover, various ed. starting 1926), dealing with the history of Hebrew and of the Talmud. Blogg also re-edited Solomon London's *Kohelet Shelomo,* a Hebrew work on the liturgy and ceremonial customs according to the Ashkenazi (Polish and German) rite. This work was first published in Amsterdam, in Hebrew (1744), then in Yiddish, in Frankfurt on the Oder (1790 and 1799). Reedited and translated into German by Blogg (1830), it enjoyed great popularity and was several times reprinted (reedited by A. Sulzbach, 1908). Blogg also wrote: a book of devotion for the sick and for the mourners, *Sefer ha-Ḥayyim* (1856, several times reedited, last in 1930); *Seder ha-Piyyutim*, a German translation of the *piyyutim* (1824); *Massekhet Purim*, a parody of a Talmud tractate with a travesty of evening prayers (*ma'aravit*) and *seliḥot* for Purim (1844); and further minor treatises on Moses the elect prophet (1824), on the Jewish Oath (1826), etc.

BIBLIOGRAPHY: Fuerst, Bibliotheca, 1, pt. 1 (1863), 122–3; Steinschneider, Cat Bod, 801, no. 4602; Steinschneider, Handbuch, 23; idem, in: HB, 1 (1858), 16. **ADD. BIBLIOGRAPHY:** S. Weininger, *Grosse juedische National-Biographie mit mehr als 8000 Beschreibungen*, 1 (1925), s.v. "Orient"; M. Roest, *Catalog der Hebraica und Judaica aus der L. Rosenthal'schen Bibliothek*, 80:232f., 322, 703, 709.

[Moshe Nahum Zobel]

BLOIS, capital of the department of Loir-et-Cher, north-central France. The earliest information concerning Jews in Blois dates from 992. The community is known in medieval Jewish annals for the tragic consequences of a *blood libel in 1171, the first ritual murder accusation to be made in France. Thirty-three members of the community including men, women and children, were burned at the stake on May 26, on the orders of Count Theobald. Jacob b. Meir *Tam established the 20th of Sivan, the date of the martyrdom, as a fast day for the Jews in France, England, and the Rhineland. *Ephraim b. Jacob of Bonn, his brother Hillel, and others composed elegies on the martyrs. The tragedy was the subject of a Hebrew drama by S.D. *Goitein, *Pulẓelinah* (1927). Jews possibly settled in Blois again, for in 1345 a quarter known as *la Juiverie* is reported. The present-day rue des Juifs near the cathedral is probably located on the same site. During World War II a few Jews from Alsace settled in Blois. In 1968 there were 60 Jews living in Blois, mainly from North Africa.

BIBLIOGRAPHY: S. Spiegel, in: *Sefer ha-Yovel le-M.M. Kaplan* (1953), 267–87; A.M. Habermann, *Sefer Gezerot Ashkenaz ve-Ẓarefat* (1945); M. Steinschneider, *Die Geschichtsliteratur der Juden* (1905), 34; Zunz, Lit Poesie, 279, 283, 286, 290, 293, 308; Salfeld, Martyrol; Gross, Gal Jud, s.v.; R. Chazan, in: PAAJR, 36 (1968), 13–31.

[Zvi Avneri]

BLOK, ARTHUR (1882–1974), English engineer, first head of the Haifa Technion. Blok studied electrical engineering at University College, London, and became personal assistant to Prof. Ambrose Fleming, the inventor of the radio tube. He personally operated the instrument which flashed radio signals, for the first time in history, from Cornwall to America, in 1901, and became principal examiner in the British Patent Office. Blok became a Zionist during World War I and in 1920 was appointed by the Zionist Executive as a member of the Governing Board of the Haifa Technion. He was the only engineer on that body and was invited to become the first head of the institution. At the request of Sir Herbert Samuel, the British Patent Office granted him extended leave to enable him to take up his position, which he did in August 1924, organizing the first academic staff.

Blok returned to England a year later and did research in nuclear polymers. In 1946 he was awarded the Order of the British Empire for outstanding scientific services during World War II. He continued to take an interest in the Technion and was a member of the Council of Jews' College.

BLONDES, DAVID, victim of a *blood libel in Vilna in 1900. Blondes, a young Jewish barber, was accused by his Polish housemaid of assaulting her and was subsequently imprisoned. Since the charge was made shortly before Passover, rumors began to circulate that the girl had been wounded to obtain blood for ritual purposes. The implications of the accusation deeply stirred Russian Jewry, and the eminent non-Jewish lawyers P.G. Mironov and D.V. Spassovich, led by the noted Jewish lawyer Oscar O. *Grusenberg, were engaged to defend Blondes. The trial jury in Vilna convicted Blondes of injurious intent, but acquitted him of intent to murder; he was sentenced to 16 months imprisonment. The ritual implications of the accusation still remained. Grusenberg appealed to the Russian Senate, and the case was reopened before the same court in 1902. Medical experts from St. Petersburg testified for the defense, showing that the woman's injuries were self-inflicted. The jury subsequently returned a verdict of "not guilty."

BIBLIOGRAPHY: Dubnow, Hist Russ, 3 (1920), 37f.; *Budushchnost'*, 3 (1902), 87–90, 105f.; *Voskhod*, 21 no. 6 (1902), 8f.

[Chasia Turtel]

BLONDHEIM, DAVID SIMON (1884–1934), U.S. Romance scholar. Born in Baltimore, Maryland, Blondheim studied at Johns Hopkins University where he became professor of Romance philology in 1924. During his studies at the École des Hautes Études in Paris he began to work on the notes left by A. *Darmesteter on the Old French glosses, over 1,000 in number, in Rashi's talmudic commentaries. Blondheim, after collating these with early manuscripts, restored their original form, established their exact meaning and published them as the first volume of his *Les glosses françaises dans les commentaires talmudiques de Raschi* (1929). He then proceeded to study each term in all its ramifications, but on his untimely death left only 125 completed studies. They were published posthumously as the second volume of his *Glosses*, with his biography and a very extensive bibliography (1937). The vast amount of historical and philological documentation gathered by Blondheim offers an invaluable source of information.

Examining, at the same time, the biblical translations in Romance languages in medieval Jewish manuscripts, Blondheim was struck by the particular form of the glosses in the different sources and by the close connection between them. He first published 30 such Old French glosses found in Jewish texts (his doctoral dissertation, in *Romania*, 39 (1910), 129ff.), and went on to prove that the specific traits of these Judeo-Romance texts is encountered also in the earliest Latin Bible translation known as the *Vetus Latina*. This was the theme of his major work *Les parlers judéo-romans et la Vetus Latina* (1925). He concluded that the Jews in the Western Roman Empire must have spoken their own *koiné*, which developed into the various Judeo-Romance dialects, and that Jews were responsible for the translation of the Septuagint in the *Vetus Latina*. Blondheim's views, however, did not obtain general approval, being criticized in particular by Cassuto, Banitt (Berenblut), and Fiorentino.

Blondheim's minor writings included many other contributions to the medieval Judeo-Romance dialects, e.g., medieval Judeo-French hymns. His indefatigable scientific endeavors did not hinder him from taking an active part in Jewish affairs, both philanthropic and Zionist. Blondheim prepared the first English translation of L. *Pinsker's *Auto-Emancipation* (1904, 1916^2). His life ended on a tragic note. His manuscripts and papers are now in the National and University Library, Jerusalem.

[Menahem Banitt]

His son, SOLOMON HILLEL BLONDHEIM (1918–), Israeli physician, worked in various New York hospitals and did research into metabolic diseases and bilirubin metabolism before emigrating to Israel in 1951. There he joined the Hadassah-University Hospital in Jerusalem, becoming head of the metabolic unit and laboratory (1957) and associate professor of medicine (1966). He was professor emeritus in the hospital's department of medicine.

BIBLIOGRAPHY: H.H. Shapiro, in: *Modern Language Notes*, 49 (1934), 1199ff.; Cassuto, in: *Studi e materiali di storia delle religioni*, 1 (1926), 145ff.; Fiorentino, in: *Archivio Glottologico*, 29 (1937), 138ff.; idem, in: JQR, 42 (1951/52), 57ff.; M. Berenblut (Banitt), *Judaeo-Italian Translations of the Bible* (1949), 197ff.; idem, in: *Revue de linguistique romane*, 27 (1963), 245ff.

BLOOD. In the Bible there is an absolute prohibition on the consumption of blood. The blood of an animal must be drained before the flesh may be eaten (Lev. 3:17; 7:26; 17:10–14; Deut. 12:15–16, 20–24). This prohibition is not found anywhere else in the ancient Near East. Moreover, within Israelite legislation it is the only prohibition (coupled with murder) enjoined not on Israel alone but on all men (Gen. 9:4). It is thus a more universal law than the Decalogue.

That none of Israel's neighbors possesses this absolute and universally binding prohibition means that it cannot be a vestige of a primitive taboo, but the result of a deliberate, reasoned enactment. This is clear from the rationale appended to the law: blood is life (Lev. 17:11, 14; Deut. 12:23). Men (the sons of Noah) are conceded the right to eat meat, if they drain off the lifeblood, which belongs to the Creator (Gen. 9:3–4, see *Noachide Laws). Israel has an additional obligation to drain the blood of sacrificial animals on the authorized altar, "for it is I who have assigned it to you upon the altar to expiate for your lives; for it is the blood, as life, that can expiate" for your lives when you take the animal's life for its flesh (Lev. 17:11; cf. verse 4; see *Atonement).

An unresolved problem is presented by a second blood prohibition, differently worded: *lo' to'khelu ʿal ha-dam* ("do not eat over the blood"; Lev. 19:26; I Sam. 14:32–33; Ezek. 33:25). Various interpretations of this have been offered: in one, *ʿal* is interpreted as "with" (so LXX, ad loc.; for usage, cf. Ex. 12:8; 23:18; Lev. 23:18, 20; et al.). Thus, the two prohibitions are synonymous: both forbid blood as food. A second interpretation holds that *ʿal* means "over," figuratively. The situation envisaged is that the blood has not been consumed, but has been spilled to the ground instead of being brought to the altar. Such a profane disposition of the blood is forbidden by this law. This accords with the requirement of the priestly code (and of King Saul, I Sam. 14:32–33) that all permitted flesh must be sacrificed (Lev. 17:11, above). However, it is not in agreement with the Deuteronomic Code, which allows profane slaughter and expressly orders that blood be spilled upon the ground (Deut. 12:15, 21–22). *ʿAl* has also been interpreted as "over," literally, in which case the prohibition refers to a pagan rite (see Ibn Ezra and Samuel b. Meir (Rashbam) on Lev. 19:26, and Maimonides, *Guide*, 3:46). According to a recent formulation of this view by Grintz, it harks back to the worship of underground deities, who drank the blood out of a pit in which the animal was slaughtered (e.g., Odyssey, 10:530–40).

Blood plays a pervasive role in the cult. When daubed on the horns of the *altar or sprinkled inside the sanctuary (see *Sacrifices), it purges ritual impurity (see *Atonement; *Day of Atonement). It may also serve this purgative function in the initial rites of purifying the leper (Lev. 14:4–6, 18–29; cf. verses 49–53; see *Leprosy), and in consecrating the priest (Ex. 29:20–21, 33). When dashed upon the side of the altar, as in the case of animals sacrificed for food (see above), its purpose is to expiate sin (see **Kippur*). It also operates as an apotropaic to ward off future harm, e.g., by smearing the paschal blood on doorposts and lintels (Ex. 12:7, 13, 22–23). This usage may also underline the rites of covenanting (*dam berit*; Ex. 24:6–8) and circumcising the Israelites (Ex. 4:24–26; Ezek 16:6).

[Jacob Milgrom]

In Halakhah

The prohibition of blood enjoined in the Bible is defined by the Talmud as referring to the blood of cattle, beasts, and fowl, and prescribes the punishment of **karet* for the consumption of the minimum amount of the volume of an olive (Ker. 5:1). The blood for which one is so liable is "the blood with which the soul emerges," i.e., the lifeblood, but not the blood which oozes out subsequently, or blood in the meat. Blood of all other creatures, fish, locusts, and human blood, is permitted according to the rabbinical interpretations of biblical law, although according to one source (*Tanna de-Vei Eliyahu Rabbah*, 15) human blood is equally forbidden by the Bible. All authorities agree, however, that it is forbidden by rabbinic law (Maim. Yad, Ma'akhalot Asurot, 6:2). The Talmud uses the peculiar phrase "bipeds" (Ker. 20b), and although all the halakhic authorities regard this phrase as a synonym for humans (Sh. Ar., YD 66: 10), J.S. *Bloch, in answer to the *blood accusation whose fomenters quoted this passage in support of their allegation, put forward the intriguing suggestion that it actually refers to simians. Although the content, which enumerates "blood of bipeds, the blood found in eggs, the blood of locusts and of fish" would appear to lend some support to this view, it must be regarded as belonging to the realm of apologetics. Nevertheless, the repugnance felt by Jews for blood caused an extension of the prohibition even of permitted blood "because of appearances" if it were collected in a vessel. Thus it is permitted to swallow the blood from one's bleeding teeth and suck one's bleeding finger, but should a piece of bread, for instance, be stained by blood it must be discarded. Similarly the blood of fish collected in a vessel is forbidden (Ker. 21b).

The prohibition of blood is confined to its consumption; it is, however, permitted for other uses, and the Mishnah (Yoma 5:6) states that the sacrificial blood which flowed into the brook of *Kidron was collected and sold to gardeners as fertilizer. For the most extensive prohibition of blood, the need for its removal from meat before it is fit for Jewish consumption, see *Dietary Laws.

[Louis Isaac Rabinowitz]

Menstrual Blood

The biological reality that women regularly menstruate is central to biblical and rabbinic constructions of the female. Prohibitions against male contact with menstrual blood, deeply rooted in the cultures of the ancient Near East, appear in Leviticus 11–15, where the *niddah*, the menstruating or postpartum woman, is listed among a number of threats to male ritual purity. Leviticus 18:29 specifies sexual contact with a *niddah* as among those sinful acts punished severely by *karet,* or extirpation from the community. In Leviticus 18:9 and 20:18 such contact is part of a list of prohibited sexual unions that has nothing to do with ritual purity. Even when the purity system lapsed after the destruction of the Second Temple in 70 C.E., the prohibition of union with a menstruant endured.

Menstrual blood, an indication of the failure of fertility in women's natural cycle of fruitfulness, is strongly linked with death in rabbinic Judaism. In a religious system which likened ritual impurity to a state of spiritual extinction, periodic female flows of blood were repugnant to men both as a potential source of ritual pollution and as a reminder of women's supposed responsibility for human mortality. Several aggadic passages suggest that women menstruate as punishment or atonement for spilling the blood (*dam*) in perpetuity of Adam (*adam*), who is designated "the blood of the Holy One, blessed be He" or "the blood of the world" (ARNB 9, 42; Gen. R. 17:8, Tanḥ. Noah 1).

[Judith R. Baskin (2nd ed.)]

BIBLIOGRAPHY: J. Milgrom, in: *Interpretation* (July 1963), 288–301; E. Isaac, in: *Anthropos*, 59 (1964), 444–56; J. Grintz, in: *Zion*, 31 (1966), 1–17; D.J. Mc-Carthy, in: JBL, 88 (1969), 166–76; M. Greenberg, *Understanding Exodus*, 2 part 1 (1969), 110–22. IN HALAKHAH: ET, 7 (1956), 422–40ff. **ADD. BIBLIOGRAPHY:** J.R. Baskin, *Midrashic Women* (2002); S.J.D. Cohen, "Menstruants and the Sacred in Judaism and Christianity," in: S.B. Pomeroy (ed.), *Women's History and Ancient History* (1991), 273–99; H. Eilberg-Schwartz. *The Savage in Judaism* (1990).

BLOOD-AVENGER. A person who is authorized by law, or who is duty-bound, to kill a murderer is called *go'el ha-dam* – usually translated as an avenger of blood, but more accurately to be rendered as a redeemer of blood (cf. Lev. 25:25; Ruth 3:12; I Kings 16:11). By putting the murderer to death (Num. 35:19, 21), the avenger expiates the blood shed on the polluted land (Num. 35:33). Originally private revenge was legitimate in Israel, as in other ancient civilizations, not only for homicide but also for mayhem (cf. Gen. 4:23–24) and rape (Gen. 34:25–26); and the restrictions on the avenger's rights and their legal regulation marked the beginnings of a system of criminal law (see B. Cohen in bibl.). It was stipulated that only murder with malice aforethought (Num. 35:20–21; Deut. 19:11–13) or committed with a murderous instrument (Num. 35:16–18; for further examples, see Maim., Yad, Roẓe'aḥ u-Shemirat Nefesh 6:6–9) gave rise to the avenger's right (see Mak. 12a, Sanh. 45b); the unintentional manslayer was entitled to refuge from the avenger (Num. 35:12, 15; Deut. 19:4–6) and was liable to be killed by him only when he prematurely left the city of refuge (Num. 35:26–28). It may be considered a concession to human nature that avenging was not wholly prohibited, but only restricted and regulated: the natural "hot anger" (Deut. 19:6) of the victim's next of kin is left at least some legal outlet.

The avenger's rights were further restricted by being made subject to and dependent on the prior judicial conviction of the murderer – whether the murder was premeditated or not was a question not for the avenger but for the court to decide (Maim. loc. cit. 1:5, following Num. 35:12; "the manslayer may not die unless he has stood trial before the assembly"; but cf. Yad, loc. cit. 5:7–10). Opinions of later jurists were divided as to what the avenger's real function was; some held that he initiated the proceedings, searching for the murderer and bringing him to court for trial (Ramban; Nov.; Sanh. 45b; *Beit ha-Beḥirah* ad loc.); some thought he should appear before the court and participate in the proceedings as a prosecutor (Nissim Gerondi, basing himself on the Targum pseudo-Jonathan who renders *go'el ha-dam* as "claimant of blood"); others relegated the avenger to the role of an executioner, it being his right and privilege to execute the death penalty pronounced by the court (Yad, loc. cit. 1:2; Ritba, Nov., Mak. 10b). That the avenger had a *locus standi* in court appears probable from the scriptural injunction that the court "shall decide between the slayer and the blood-avenger" (Num. 35:24). While the slayer would protest his innocence or, alternatively, his lack of malice, the avenger would plead premeditation (cf. *Malbim* ad loc.); by finding a lack of malice, the court is said to "protect the manslayer from the blood-avenger" (Num. 35:25). When an alleged murderer stood trial but was not convicted (either because of lack of sufficient evidence or because the verdict had not yet been given) and the avenger killed him, most jurists held that while the killing was unlawful, the avenger was not guilty of murder (*Beit ha-Beḥirah*, Sanh. 45b) – the proffered reason being that the avenger had a better right to kill than even the unintentional manslayer (Yad, loc. cit. 6:5), or that Scripture itself recognized the avenger's "hot anger" (Deut. 19:6) as negating premeditation (*Redak* to II Sam. 14:7). However, if the avenger killed the murderer within the walls of the city of refuge, it was murder pure and simple (Tosef., Mak. 3:6).

Any next of kin entitled to inherit the deceased's estate qualified as an avenger (Yad, loc. cit. 1:2). Some later authorities even include maternal relatives although they are not in line for inheritance (*Or Same'aḥ* to Yad, loc. cit., against Maimonides). Women also qualify as avengers (Yad, loc. cit. 1:3). There are biblical instances of a father (II Sam. 13:31–38), a son (II Kings 14:5–6), brothers (Judg. 8:4–21; II Sam. 2:22–23), and also the king (I Kings 2:29–34) as avengers. It was later stipulated that when no next of kin was available or came forward, an avenger was to be appointed by the court (Sanh. 45b).

There is little doubt that legally the rights (and duties) of the blood-avenger became obsolete (*Ḥavvat Ya'ir* 146), though the killing by the avenger of a murderer is even today legally regarded by some scholars as no more than unintentional manslaughter (e.g. *Keẓot ha-Ḥoshen* HM 2). Apart from the law, the right and duty of avenging the blood of one's nearest relatives are still deeply imprinted on the mind and religious conviction of most Oriental (including many Jewish) communities; notwithstanding repeated efforts from various quarters, blood vengeance is not, however, recognized in Israeli law even in mitigating circumstances.

BIBLIOGRAPHY: M. Duschak, *Mosaisch-Talmudisches Strafrecht* (1869), 19f.; S. Mayer, *Rechte der Israeliten, Athener, und Roemer*, 3 (1876), 36–47; E. Goitein, *Vergeltungsprincip im biblischen und talmudischen Strafrecht* (1891); G. Foerster, *Das mosaische Strafrecht…* (1900), 9ff.; J. Weismann, *Talion und oeffentliche Strafe im mosaischen Rechte* (1913); E. Merz, *Blutrache bei den Israeliten* (1916); ET, 5 (1953), 220–33; J.M. Ginzburg, *Mishpatim le-Yisra'el* (1956), 356–74; EM, 2 (1965), 392–4; B. Cohen, *Jewish and Roman Law*, 2 (1966), 624–7; addenda 793f.; I. Warhaftig, *Goel ha-Dam, Tehumim*, 11 (1990), 326-360.

[Haim Hermann Cohn]

BLOODGUILT, liability for punishment for shedding blood. The biblical concept of bloodguilt derives from the belief that deeds generate consequences and that sin, in particular, is a danger to the sinner. The most vivid examples of this belief appear in connection with unlawful homicide, where innocent blood (*dam naki* (*naqi*); Jonah 1:14) cries out for vengeance (Gen. 4:10), is rejected by the earth (Isa. 26:21; Ezek. 24:7), and pollutes it (Num. 35:33–34). Bloodguilt attaches to the slayer and his family (II Sam. 3:28ff.) for generations (II Kings 9:26), and even to his city (Jer. 26:5), nation (Deut. 21:8), and land (Deut. 24:4). The technical term for bearing bloodguilt *damo bo*, or *damo bero'sho,* meant originally "his blood [remains] in him/in his head" (Josh. 2:19; Ezek. 33:5), and the legal formula *mot yumat damav bo* (Lev. 20:9–16) means that in the case of lawful execution, the blood of the guilty victim remains on his own person and does not attach itself to his executioners.

The concept of bloodguilt in the Bible pervades all sources, legal, narrative, and cultic, and entails the following system of graded punishments for homicide.

Deliberate Homicide

The penalty is death by man (Gen. 9:6), or failing that, by God (Gen. 9:5; cf. Lev. 20:4–5). A man can be either the direct cause (Num. 35:16–21) or the indirect cause, e.g., a watchman (II Kings 10:24; Ezek. 33:6), priests (Num. 18:1, 3), homeowner (Deut. 22:8), or subordinate (I Kings 2:31–35). The punishment of the murderer is primarily the responsibility of the *blood-avenger (after court conviction, Num. 35:19; Deut. 19:12), but God is the final guarantor that homicide is ultimately punished. His personal intervention is expressed by the verbs פקד (*pakad* (*paqad*), "attend to," Hos. 1:4); נקם (*nakam* (*naqam*), "avenge," II Kings 9:7); דרש (*darash*, "exact punishment," Ezek. 33:6); and שוב (השיב, *heshiv*, "return") in the idiom *heshiv damim 'al ro'sh* (II Sam. 16:18; I Kings 2:33), which indicates that God will turn back to the head of the slayer the blood of the slain, the punishment the murderer believed he had averted. In the Bible, it should be noted, these idioms have become technical terms: the original phrase remains, but without the crudity of its more primitive implications in other ancient sources. God may postpone punishment to a later generation (II Sam. 12: 13–14; I Kings 21:21). Man, however, does not have this option (Deut. 24:16; II Kings 14:6) unless divinely authorized (II Kings 9:7, 26).

There is no commutation of the death penalty. The notion that deliberate homicide cannot be commuted is the foundation stone of criminal law in the Bible: human life is invaluable, hence incommutable. This concept is not found in any other body of law in the ancient Near East.

Accidental Homicide

Since accidental homicide also results in bloodguilt, the killer may be slain by the *go'el* with impunity (Num. 35:26–27; Deut. 19:4–10). However, as his act was unintentional, the natural death of the high priest is allowed to substitute for his own death (Num. 35:25, 28). In the interim, he is confined to a *city of refuge to protect him from the blood-avenger (Num. 35:9ff; Deut. 4:41–43; 19:1–13; Josh. 20:1ff.) In cases where the slayer is unknown, the community nearest the corpus delicti must disavow complicity and, by means of a ritual, symbolically wash away the blood of the slain (Deut. 21:1–9; see **Eglah Arufah*).

Homicidal Beast

The penalty is death by stoning and the shunning of the carcass. The supreme value of human life in the Bible is best expressed in the law that a homicidal beast is also guilty and that not only must it be killed but its carcass, laden with bloodguilt, must be reviled (Ex. 21:28–29; cf. Gen. 9:5).

Unauthorized Slaughter of an Animal

The reverence for life that informs all biblical legislation reached its summit in the priestly law which sanctions the use of an animal for food on the condition that its blood, containing its life, be drained upon the authorized altar (and thereby be symbolically restored to God; Lev. 17:11). All other slaughter is unlawful bloodshed, punishable by death at the hand of God (Lev. 17:4).

Exceptions

No bloodguilt is incurred by homicide in self-defense (Ex. 22:1), judicial execution (Lev. 20:9–16), and war (I Kings 2:5–6). The priestly legislation may indicate some qualification of the view that war is justifiable homicide. For example, David was disqualified from building the Temple (I Chron. 22:8).

BIBLIOGRAPHY: M. Greenberg, in: *Sefer Yovel Y. Kaufmann* (1960), 5–28; idem, in: IDB, 1 (1962), s.v.; K. Koch, in: VT, 12 (1962), 396–416; J. Milgrom, *Studies in Levitical Terminology*, 1 (1970), 22–33, 56–69.

[Jacob Milgrom]

BLOODLETTING, removal of blood in treating diseases. Bloodletting is frequently mentioned in the Talmud. It was performed not by a physician but by a skilled functionary called *umman* or *gara*, whose status was less than that of a physician. The bloodletter is mentioned in various passages in the Talmud, both favorably and unfavorably (e.g., Ta'an. 21b; Kid. 82a). Some of the directives about bloodletting in the Talmud relate to specific ailments (e.g., Git. 67b; Av. Zar. 29a), but most are in the realm of preventive medicine based on the belief that the regular removal of blood from the body was of hygienic value. Among the ten indispensable requirements of a town, in the absence of which "no scholar should reside there" (Sanh. 17b), is a bloodletter. According to the Talmud, bloodletting is one of the things which should be applied in moderation (Git. 70a), and, in practice, the amount of blood to be let varies with the subject's age. Maimonides (Yad, De'ot 4:18), though in general agreement, suggests, in addition, consideration of the subject's "blood richness" and physical vigor (*Pirkei Moshe*, 12). Many instructions are given in the Talmud with respect to diet and precautions to be taken both before and after bloodletting (e.g., Shab. 129a–b; Git. 70a; Ned. 54b; Av. Zar. 29a; et al.). Maimonides advises moderation in bloodletting: "A man should not accustom himself to let blood regularly, nor should he do so unless he is in great need of it" (Yad, loc. cit.). The views of the Talmud and of Maimonides provide a sharp contrast to those of the ancient and medieval world, where the practice of bloodletting was unrestricted. In late Hebrew literature (e.g., the *Oẓar ha-Ḥayyim* of Jacob *Ẓahalon and the *Ma'aseh Tuviyyah* of Tobias b. Moses *Cohn) directions for bloodletting and cupping are also found.

BIBLIOGRAPHY: J. Preuss, *Biblisch-talmudische Medizin* (1923^3), 36–39, 289–300; M. Perlmann, *Midrash ha-Refu'ah*, 2 (1929), 85–89.

[Joshua O. Leibowitz]

BLOOD LIBEL, the allegation that Jews murder non-Jews, especially Christian children, in order to obtain blood for the Passover or other rituals: most blood libels occurred close to Passover, being basically a another form of the belief that Jews had been and still were responsible for the passion and crucifixion of Jesus Christ, the divine child; a complex of deliberate lies, trumped-up accusations, and popular beliefs about the murder-lust of the Jews and their bloodthirstiness, based on the conception that Jews hate Christianity and mankind in general. It is combined with the delusion that Jews are in some way not human and must have recourse to special remedies and subterfuges to appear, at least outwardly, like other men. The blood libel led to trials and massacres of Jews in the Middle Ages and early modern times; it was revived by the Nazis. Its origin is rooted in ancient, almost primordial, concepts concerning the potency and energies of *blood. In the early 2000s a controversy among scholars surrounded the argument that the blood libel began in the Middle Ages in the wake of the sacrifice of Jewish children by their parents during Crusaders raids on Jewish communities on their way to the Holy Land.

Origins

Blood sacrifices, practiced by many pagan religions, are expressly forbidden by the Torah. The law of meat-salting (*meliḥah*) is designed to prevent the least drop of avoidable blood remaining in food. Yet pagan incomprehension of the Jewish monotheist cult, lacking the customary images and statues, led to charges of ritual killing. At a time of tension between Hellenism and Judaism, it was alleged that the Jews would kidnap a Greek foreigner, fatten him up for a year, and then convey him to a wood, where they slew him, sacrificed his body with the customary ritual, partook of his flesh, and while immolating the Greek swore an oath of hostility to the Greeks. This was told, according to *Apion, to King *Antiochus Epiphanes by an intended Greek victim who had been found in the Jewish Temple being fattened by the Jews for this sacrifice and was saved by the king (Jos., Apion, 2:89–102). Some suspect that stories like this were spread intentionally as propaganda for Antiochus Epiphanes to justify his profanation of the Temple. Whatever the immediate cause, the tale is the outcome of suspicion of the Jews and incomprehension of their religion.

To be victims of this accusation was also the fate of other misunderstood religious minorities. In the second century C.E. the *Church Father Tertullian complained: "We are said to be the most criminal of men, on the score of our sacramental baby-killing, and the baby-eating that goes with it." He complains that judicial torture was applied to the early Christians because of this accusation, for "it ought … to be wrung out of us [whenever that false charge is made] how many murdered babies each of us has tasted.… Oh! the glory of that magistrate who had brought to light some Christian who had eaten up to date a hundred babies!" (*Apologeticus* 7:1 and 1:12, Loeb edition (1931), 10, 36).

Middle Ages

During the Middle Ages some heretical Christian sects were also afflicted by similar accusations. The general attitude of Christians toward the holy bread of the Communion created an emotional atmosphere in which it was felt that the divine child was mysteriously hidden in the partaken bread. The popular preacher Friar Berthold of Regensburg (13th century) felt obliged to explain why communicants do not actually see the holy child by asking the rhetorical question, "Who would like to bite off a baby's head or hand or foot?" Popular beliefs and imaginings of the time, either of classical origin or rooted in Germanic superstitions, held that blood, even the blood of executed malefactors or from corpses, possesses the powers of healing or causing injury. Thus, combined with the general hatred of Jews then prevailing, a charge of clandestine cruel practices and blood-hunting, which had evolved among the pagans and was used against the early Christians, was deflected by Christian society to the most visible and persistent minority in opposition to its tenets.

As Christianity spread in Western Europe and penetrated the popular consciousness, using the emotions and imagination even more than thought and dogma in order to gain influence, various story elements began to evolve around the alleged inhumanity and sadism of the Jews. (See Map: Blood Libels.) In the first distinct case of blood libel against Jews in the Middle Ages, that of *Norwich in 1144, it was alleged that the Jews had "bought a Christian child [the 'boy-martyr' William] before Easter and tortured him with all the tortures wherewith our Lord was tortured, and on Long Friday hanged him on a rood in hatred of our Lord." The motif of torture and murder of Christian children in imitation of Jesus' Passion persisted with slight variations throughout the 12th century (Gloucester, England, 1168; Blois, France, 1171; Saragossa, Spain, 1182), and was repeated in many libels of the 13th century. In the case of Little Saint Hugh of *Lincoln, 1255, it would seem that an element taken directly from Apion's libel (see above) was interwoven into the Passion motif, for the chronicler Matthew Paris relates, "that the Child was first fattened for ten days with white bread and milk and then … almost all the Jews of England were invited to the crucifixion." The crucifixion motif was generalized in the *Siete Partidas* law code of Spain, 1263: "We have heard it said that in certain places on Good Friday the Jews do steal children and set them on the cross in a mocking manner." Even when other motifs eventually predominated in the libel, the crucifixion motif did not disappear altogether. On the eve of the expulsion of the Jews from Spain, there occurred the blood-libel case of "the Holy Child of *La Guardia" (1490–91). There, *Conversos were made to confess under torture that with the knowledge of the chief rabbi of the Jews they had assembled at the time of Passover in a cave, crucified the child, and abused him and cursed him to his face, as was done to Jesus in ancient times. The crucifixion motif explains why the blood libels occurred at the time of Passover.

The Jews were well aware of the implications of sheer sadism involved in the libel. In a dirge lamenting the Jews massacred at Munich because of a blood libel in 1286, the anonymous poet supposedly quotes the words of the Christian killers: "These unhappy Jews are sinning, they kill Christian children, they torture them in all their limbs, they take the blood cruelly to drink" (A.M. Habermann (ed.), *Sefer Gezerot Ashkenaz ve-Ẓarefat* (1946), 199). These words, written in irony, reflect another motif in the libels, the thirst of the Jew for blood, out of his hatred for the good and true. This is combined in 13th-century Germany with the conception that the Jew cannot endure purity: he hates the innocence of the Christian child, its joyous song and appearance. The motif, found in the legendary tales of the monk Caesarius of Heisterbach in Germany, underwent various transmutations. In the source from which Caesarius took his story the child killed by the Jews sings *erubescat judaeus* ("let the Jew be shamed"). In Caesarius' version, the child sings the *Salve Regina*. The Jews cannot endure this pure laudatory song and try to frighten him and stop him from singing it. When he refuses, they cut off his tongue and hack him to pieces. About a century after the expulsion of the Jews from England this motif only became the basis of Geoffrey *Chaucer's "Prioress' Tale." Here the widow's little child sings the *Alma Redemptoris Mater* while "the serpent Sathanas" awakens indignation in the cruel Jewish heart. The Jews obey the promptings of their Satanic master and kill the child; a miracle brings about their deserved punishment. Though the scene of this tale is laid in Asia, at the end of the story Chaucer takes care to connect Asia explicitly with bygone libels in England, and the motif of hatred of the innocent with the motif of mockery of the crucifixion.

In the blood libel of *Fulda (1235) another motif comes to the fore: the Jews taking blood for medicinal remedies (here of five young Christian boys). The strange medley of ideas about the use of blood by the Jews is summed up by the end of the Middle Ages, in 1494, by the citizens of Tyrnau (*Trnava). The Jews need blood because "firstly, they were convinced by the judgment of their ancestors, that the blood of a Christian was a good remedy for the alleviation of the wound of circumcision. Secondly, they were of opinion that this blood, put into food, is very efficacious for the awakening of mutual love. Thirdly, they had discovered, as men and women among them suffered equally from menstruation, that the blood of a Christian is a specific medicine for it, when drunk. Fourthly, they had an ancient but secret ordinance by which they are under obligation to shed Christian blood in honor of God, in daily sacrifices, in some spot or other … the lot for the present year had fallen on the Tyrnau Jews." To the motifs of crucifixion, sadism, hatred of the innocent and of Christianity, and the unnaturalness of the Jews and its cure by the use of good Christian blood, there were added, from time to time, the ingredients of sorcery, perversity, and a kind of "blind obedience to a cruel tradition."

Generation after generation of Jews in Europe was tortured, and Jewish communities were massacred or dispersed and broken up because of this libel. It was spread by various agents. Popular preachers ingrained it in the minds of the common people. It became embedded, through miracle tales, in their imagination and beliefs. This caused in Moravia, for instance, in about 1343, "a woman of ill fame to come with the help of another woman and propose to an old Jew of Brno, named Osel, her child for sale for six marks, because the child was red in hair and in face." Yet the Jew invited Christian officials, who imprisoned the women and punished them horribly (B. Bretholz, *Quellen zur Geschichte der Juden in Maehren* (1935), 27–28). The majority of the heads of state and the church opposed the circulation of the libel. Emperor *Frederick II of Hohenstaufen decided, after the Fulda libel, to clear up the matter definitively, and have all the Jews in the empire killed if the accusation proved to be true, or exonerate them publicly if false, using this as an occasion to arbitrate in a matter affecting the whole of Christendom. The enquiry into the blood libel was thus turned into an all-Christian problem. The emperor, who first consulted the recognized church authorities, later had to turn to a device of his own. In the words of his summing-up of the enquiry (see ZGJD, 1 (1887), 142–4), the usual church authorities "expressed various opinions about the case, and as they have been proved incapable of coming to a conclusive decision … we found it necessary … to turn to such people that were once Jews and have converted to the worship of the Christian faith; for they, as opponents, will not be silent about anything that they may know in this matter against the Jews." The emperor adds that he himself was already convinced, through his knowledge and wisdom, that the Jews were innocent. He sent to the kings of the West, asking them to send him decent and learned converts to Christianity to consult in the matter. The synod of converts took place (in about 1243) and came to the conclusion, which the emperor published: "There is not to be found, either in the Old or the New Testament, that the Jews are desirous of human blood. On the contrary, they avoid contamination with any kind of blood." The document quotes from various Jewish texts in support, adding, "There is also a strong likelihood that those to whom even the blood of permitted animals is forbidden, cannot have a hankering after human blood. Against this accusation stand its cruelty, its unnaturalness, and the sound human emotions which the Jews have also in relation to the Christians. It is also unlikely that they would risk [through such a dangerous action] their life and property." A few years later, in 1247, Pope Innocent IV wrote that "Christians charge falsely … that [the Jews] hold a communion rite … with the heart of a murdered child; and should the cadaver of a dead man happen to be found anywhere they maliciously lay it to their charge." Neither emperor nor pope were heeded.

Jewish scholars in the Middle Ages bitterly rejected this inhuman accusation. They quoted the Law and instanced the Jewish way of life in order to refute it. The general opinion of the Jews is summed up thus: "You are libeling us for you want to find a reason to permit the shedding of our blood" (the 12th–13th centuries *Sefer Nizzaḥon Yashan – Liber Nizzachon Vetus*, p. 159 in *Tela Ignaea Satanae*, ed. J.Ch. Wagenseil, 1681). However, the Jewish denials, like the opinion of enlightened Christian leaders, did not succeed in preventing the blood libels from shaping to a large extent the image of the Jew transmitted from the Middle Ages to modern times. (It was only in 1965 that the church officially repudiated the blood libel of *Trent by canceling the beatification of Simon and the celebrations in his honor.)

Modern Times

From the 17th century, blood-libel cases increasingly spread to Eastern Europe, most notably to Poland and Lithuania). The atmosphere at such trials is conveyed by the protocols of the investigation of two Jews and a Jewess who were put to torture in a blood-libel case at *Lublin in 1636: "Judge: 'For what purpose do Jews need Christian blood?' Fegele: 'Jews use no Christian blood.' Judge: 'And are you a sorceress?' Fegele: 'No. I have nothing to do with this.'" She remained unbroken under torture, even the threat of torture with a red-hot iron, and bravely denied all allegations of sorcery and ritual use of blood, and so did the other accused Jews, who insisted that all Jews are innocent. Hugo *Grotius, the Protestant legal philosopher, when told about the case expressed the opinion that the blood accusation was simply a libel generated by hatred of the Jews and recalled that the early Christians and later Christian sectarians were accused in a similar way (Balaban, in *Festschrift S. Dubnow* (1930), 87–112).

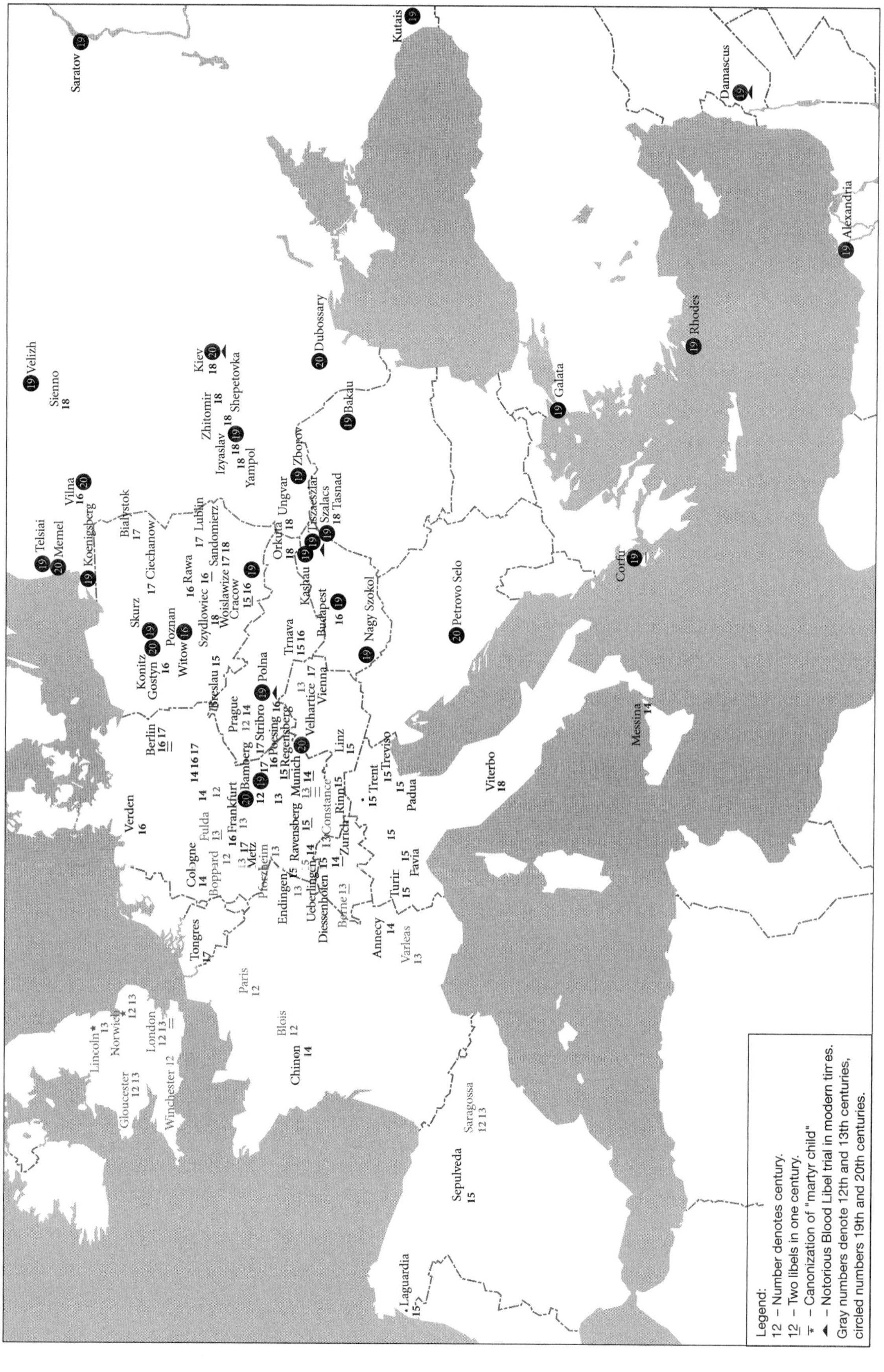

Map showing sites and periods of blood libels.

In Eastern Europe, as late as the 17th century, the blood libel is identified with Jewish sorcery in the minds of the accusers, while the motif of the use of Christian blood for Passover *mazzot* increasingly comes to the fore. As conditions in Poland deteriorated, blood-libel cases multiplied. Through the *Councils of the Lands the Jews sent an emissary to the Holy See who succeeded in having an investigation ordered and carried out by Cardinal Lorenzo Ganganelli, later Pope *Clement XIV. In a detailed report submitted in 1759 Ganganelli examined the veracity of the blood libel in general and of the recent cases in Poland-Lithuania in particular, quoting *in extenso* from former church authorities against the libel. His main conclusion was: "I [...] hope that the Holy See will take some measure to protect the Jews of Poland as Saint Bernard, Gregory IX, and Innocent IV did for the Jews of Germany and France (see bibl., Roth, p. 94).

In the 19th century the ringleaders of Jew-hatred in its modern form of antisemitism made conspicuous use of the blood libel for incitement against Jews in various countries. It was also used as a weapon to arouse the uneducated masses for specific political reasons, as occurred, for instance, in the *Damascus Affair (1840) in the struggle among the western powers for influence in the Near East. Antisemitic self-proclaimed experts wrote treatises which set out to prove the truth of the libel from the records of past accusations and Jewish sources. Two such were Konstantin Cholewa de Pawlikowski (*Talmud in der Theorie und Praxis*, Regensburg, 1866) and H. Desportes (*Le mystère du sang chez les Juifs de tous les temps*, Paris, 1859, with a preface by the French antisemite Edouard-Adolphe *Drumont). In the blood-libel trials held in the second half of the 19th and early 20th century, such as the *Tisza-Eszlar and *Beilis cases, August *Rohling and other known antisemites appeared to testify in court; all were irrefutably answered by Jewish and pro-Jewish scholars (J.S. *Bloch, H.L. *Strack, J. *Mazeh). Another way of implying the truth of the blood-libel charge was to state it as a fact without denying it. For example, in the article *Blut* (in *Handwoerterbuch des deutschen Aberglaubens*, 1 (1927), cols. 1434–42) it is remarked (col. 1436): "Moses in vain prohibited the drinking of blood," and "Trials in modern times show the problem of ritual murder has still not disappeared"; col. 1439).

The Nazis used the blood libel in full force for anti-Jewish propaganda. They revived old allegations and instituted reinvestigations and trials in territories under their rule or influence: at Memel in 1936; at Bamberg in 1937 (a revival); and at Velhartice, Bohemia, in 1940. On May 1, 1934, the Nazi daily, *Der Stuermer*, devoted a special illustrated number to the blood libel, in which German scientists openly served the Nazi aims. The above-mentioned *Handwoerterbuch* (vol. 7 (1935–36), cols. 727–39) printed an article entitled *Ritualmord* written by Peuckert, a man who remained active and respected in German science, which is throughout simply an affirmation and propagation of the blood libel, although using some cautious phrasing. The epitome appears in the remarkable enquiry: "In conclusion to this shocking list, there remains only one question: for what purpose did the Jews use the blood?" (col. 734).

The blood libel, in the various forms it assumed and the tales with which it was associated, is one of the most terrible expressions of the combination of human cruelty and credulity. No psychological or sociological research can convey the depths to which the numerous intentional instigators of such libels, and the more numerous propagators of this phantasmagoria, sank. It resulted in the torture, murder, and expulsion, of countless Jews, and the misery of insults. However, the dark specters it raised were even more harmful in their effects on the minds of Christians. In modern times *Aḥad Ha-Am found "some consolation" in the existence of the blood libel, for it could serve as a spiritual defense against the influence on Jewish self-evaluation of the consensus of hostile opinion. "This accusation is the solitary case in which the general acceptance of an idea about ourselves does not make us doubt whether all the world can be wrong, and we right, because it is based on an absolute lie, and is not even supported by any false inference from particular to universal. Every Jew who has been brought up among Jews knows as an indisputable fact that throughout the length and breadth of Jewry there is not a single individual who drinks human blood for religious purposes.... 'But' – you ask – 'is it possible that everybody can be wrong, and the Jews right?' Yes, it is possible: the blood accusation proves it possible. Here, you see, the Jews are right and perfectly innocent" (*Selected Essays* (1962), 203–4).

[Haim Hillel Ben-Sasson / Dina Porat (2nd ed.)]

IN RUSSIA In modern times Russia has been the principal perpetuator of the blood libel, both medieval and modern factors (see above) combining to enable its deliberate dissemination among the ignorant masses. The first blood-libel case in Russia occurred in the vicinity of Senno, south of Vitebsk, on the eve of Passover 1799, when the body of a woman was found near a Jewish tavern: four Jews were arrested on the ground of the "popular belief that the Jews require Christian blood." *Apostates supplied the court with extracts from a distorted translation of the Shulḥan Arukh and *Shevet Yehudah*. The accused were released through lack of evidence. Nevertheless the poet and administrator G.R. *Derzhavin, in his "Opinion submitted to the czar on the organization of the status of the Jews in Russia," could state that "in these communities persons are to be found who perpetrate the crime, or at least afford protection to those committing the crime, of shedding Christian blood, of which Jews have been suspected at various times and in different countries. If I for my part consider that such crimes, even if sometimes committed in antiquity, were carried out by ignorant fanatics, I thought it right not to overlook them." Thus a semiofficial seal was given to the libel in Russia at the opening of the 19th century. Official Russian circles were divided in their views on the libel. A number of inquiries into the charges were instituted, while the views of the czars themselves fluctuated.

Between 1805 and 1816 various cases of blood libel occurred in places within the *Pale of Settlement, and the investigations always ended by exposing the lie on which they were based. In an attempt to stop their dissemination the minister of ecclesiastic affairs, A. Golitsyn, sent a circular to the heads of the guberniyas (provinces) throughout Russia on March 6, 1817, to this effect. Basing his instruction on the fact that both the Polish monarchs and the popes have invariably invalidated the libels, and that they had been frequently refuted by judicial inquiries, he stated in his circular that the czar directed "that henceforward the Jews shall not be charged with murdering Christian children, without evidence, and through prejudice alone that they allegedly require Christian blood." Nevertheless Alexander I (1801–25) gave instructions to revive the inquiry in the case of the murder of a Christian child in *Velizh (near Vitebsk) where the assassins had not been found and local Jewish notables had been blamed for the crime. The trial lasted for about ten years. Although the Jews were finally exonerated, Nicholas I later refused to endorse the 1817 circular, giving as a reason that he considered that "there are among the Jews savage fanatics or sects requiring Christian blood for their ritual, and especially since to our sorrow such fearful and astonishing groups also exist among us Christians." Other blood libels occurred in Telsiai (Telz) in the guberniya (province) of Kovno, in 1827, and Zaslav (*Izyaslav), in the government of Volhynia, in 1830. The Hebrew writer and scholar I.B. *Levinsohn was stirred by this case to write his book *Efes Damim* (Vilna, 1837), in which he exposed the senselessness of the accusations. A special secret commission was convened by the Russian Ministry of Foreign Affairs to clarify the problem concerning "use by Jews of the blood of Christian children," in which the Russian lexicographer and folklorist V. Dahl took part. The result of the inquiry, which reviewed numerous cases of blood libel in the Middle Ages and modern period, were published in 1844 in a limited edition and presented by Skripitsin, the director of the Department for Alien Religions, to the heads of state. In 1853, a blood libel occurred in *Saratov, when two Jews and an apostate were found guilty of the murder of two Christian children – the only instance in Russia of its kind. The council of state which dealt with the case in its final stages announced that it had confined itself to the purely legal aspect of the case and refrained from "anything bearing on the secret precepts or sects existing within Judaism and their influence on the crime." It thereby *prima facie* deprived the case of its test character as a blood libel. While the case was being considered, between 1853 and 1860, various Jews were accused of "kidnapping" on a number of occasions. The special committee appointed in 1855 had included a number of theologians and orientalists, among them two converts from Judaism, V. Levisohn and D. *Chwolson. The committee reviewed numerous Hebrew publications and manuscripts, and came to the conclusion that there was no hint or evidence to indicate that the Jews made use of Christian blood.

With the growth of an antisemitic movement in Russia in the 1870s, the blood libel became a regular motif in the anti-Jewish propaganda campaign conducted in the press and literature. Leading writers in this sphere were H. *Lutostansky, who wrote a pamphlet "concerning the use of Christian blood by Jewish sects for religious purposes" (1876), which ran into many editions, and J. Pranaitis. Numerous further allegations were made, including a case in Kutais (Georgia) in 1879, in which Jewish villagers were accused of murdering a little Christian girl. The case was tried in the district court and gave the advocates for the defense an opportunity of ventilating the social implications of the affair and the malicious intentions of its instigators. The chief agitators of the blood libels were monks. At the monastery of Suprasl crowds assembled to gaze on the bones of the "child martyr Gabriello," who had been allegedly murdered by Jews in 1690. The wave of blood libels which occurred at the end of the 19th century in central Europe, including the cases in Tiszaeszlar in 1881, *Xanten in 1891, Polna in 1899, etc., also heaped fuel on the flames of the agitation in Russia.

A number of works were published by Jewish writers in Russia to contradict the allegations, such as D. Chwolson's "Concerning Medieval Libels against Jews" (1861); I.B. Levinsohn's *Efes Damim* of 1837 was translated into Russian (1883). Some of the calumniators were also prosecuted (see *Zederbaum v. Lutostansky, 1880). Despite the growing antisemitism and their officially supported anti-Jewish policy, the czarist authorities during the reign of Alexander III (1881–94) did not lend credence to the blood libels. It was only at the beginning of the 20th century that further attempts were renewed. These included the *Blondes Case in Vilna, in 1900, and an attempt in *Dubossary, in the guberniya of Kherson, where a Russian criminal tried to pin the murder of a child on the Jews. However, with the victory of the reactionaries in Russia after the dissolution of the Second *Duma in 1907, and the strengthening of the extreme right wing (*Union of Russian People) in the Third Duma, another attempt at official level was made by the regime to use the blood libel as a weapon in its struggle against the revolutionary movement and to justify its policy toward the Jews. An opportunity for doing so occurred in the *Beilis Case engineered by the minister of justice Shcheglovitov. The trial, which continued from spring 1911 to fall 1913, became a major political issue and the focal point for anti-Jewish agitation in the antisemitic press, in the streets, at public meetings, and in the Duma. The whole of liberal and socialist opinion was ranged behind Beilis' defense, and even a section of the conservative camp. Leading Russian lawyers conducted the defense, and in Russia and throughout Europe hundreds of intellectuals and scholars, headed by V. Korolenko and M. *Gorki, joined in protest against the trial. The exoneration of Beilis was a political defeat for the regime. Despite this, the government continued to assent to the instigation of blood libels and support their dissemination among the masses until the 1917 Revolution. The Soviet government's attitude toward the blood libel was that it had been a weapon of the reaction and a tactic to exploit popular superstition by the czarist regime. The instigators of the Beilis trial were interrogated and tried at an early stage after the revolution. In later years the specter of the blood libel was raised in the Soviet press in remote regions of the U.S.S.R., such as Georgia, Dagestan, and Uzbekistan, in the context of the violent propaganda campaign conducted by the Soviet government against Judaism and the State of Israel. After these attempts had aroused world public opinion, they were dropped.

[Yehuda Slutsky]

IN ARAB COUNTRIES The blood libel was repeated in the Arab countries in modern times in a number of ways in various books, as in Egypt in the 1960s, the titles referring to "talmudic human sacrifices" or "the secrets of Zionism." Mustafa Tlass, a key political figure in Syria for decades, first published his book on the 1860 Damascus blood libel in 1983. The book, called "Matzah of Zion" and reprinted in a number of editions and translated into many languages, became an influential and frequently quoted authority on how Jews and Zionists constantly perpetrate cruel ritual murders. Newspapers as well joined in, with the Egyptian government-sponsored *Al-Ahram* publishing in October 2000 a full-page article called "Jewish Matzah Made from Arab Blood." TV series and discussions also evoke the blood libel, as on the al-Jazeera station and in the Al-Manar (Hizbullah television network) series *The Exile* in 2003. The image of the Zionist in these visual depictions, watched by millions all over the world, is that of the *Der Sturmer* Jew, bloodthirsty and frighteningly ferocious.

[Dina Porat (2nd ed.)]

BIBLIOGRAPHY: M. Samuel, *Blood Accusation* (1966); M. Hacohen (ed.) *Mishpatim ve-Alilot Dam* (1967); H.L. Strack, *The Jew and Human Sacrifice* (1909); C. Roth, *Ritual Murder Libel and the Jew* (1935); K. Hruby, in: W.P. Eckert and E.L. Ehrlich (eds.), *Judenhass-Schuld der Christen?* (1964), 281–358; idem, in: *Der Judenchrist* (1960/62); J. Trachtenberg, *Devil and the Jews* (1943), 124–55; Baer, Spain, 2 (1966), 398–423; *Il Piccolo martire S. Domenichino de Val, Patrono di Chierichetti* (1960); M.I. Seiden, *Paradox of Hate* (1967). IN RUSSIA: Dubnow, Hist, s.v., *Ritual Murder Libel*; C.E. Margolin, *Jews of Eastern Europe* (1926), 155–247; A.M. Tager, *Decay of Czarism, The Beiliss Trial* (1935). **ADD. BIBLIOGRAPHY:** R. Israeli, *Poison, Modern Manifestations of a Blood Libel* (2002); R. Erb (ed.), *Die Legende vom Ritualmord: Zur Geschichte der Blutbeschuldigung gegen Juden* (1993); J. Frankel, *The Damascus Affair: "Ritual Murder," Politics and the Jews in 1840* (1997); H.J. Kieval, "Representation and Knowledge in Medieval and Modern Accounts of Jewish Ritual Murder," in: *Jewish Social Studies* (1994–95); I.J. Yuval, *"Two Nations in Your Womb," Perceptions of Jews and Christians* (in Heb.) (2000); A. Dundes (ed.), *The Blood Libel Legend: A Case-Book in Anti-Semitic Folklore* (1991); Po-Chia R. Hsia, *The Myth of Ritual Murder* (1989).

BLOOM, BENJAMIN SAMUEL (1913–1999), U.S. educator. Bloom studied at Pennsylvania State University and at the University of Chicago, where he taught from 1940 (professor of education, 1953) and worked as a university examiner. He participated in several major educational assessment research efforts, both in America and abroad. His evaluation of school performance among youth of different nationalities was published in *International Study of Achievement in Mathematics; A Comparison of Twelve Countries* (with T. Husen and others, 1966). His other work was in basic studies of measurement and evaluation procedures in education, analyses of stability and change patterns in human behavior, and the classification of educational objectives. At the invitation of the United States Office of Education, Bloom helped set guidelines for federally supported research efforts throughout the United States. He was a member of the Advisory Committee on National Educational Laboratories. In 1965 he was appointed president of the American Educational Research Association and in 1966 was elected a member of the National Academy of Education. His major publications include *Taxonomy of Educational Objectives, Handbook I and II* (1957–64) and *Stability and Change in Human Characteristics* (1964).

Bloom believed that when looking at test scores, a teacher must understand that many factors affect the results: time of learning, resources provided, quality of teaching, and environment. He stressed that environment influences learning and is therefore a significant factor in a student's success. The teacher's role, then, is to give students guidance and support – two ways to help pupils reach their potential. A strong supporter of the theory of mastery learning, Bloom advocated that objectives be written in manageable steps and that they be reached through proper instruction. He believed that learning is a process, so teachers should design lessons and exercises to enable students to meet each objective as well as adjust their methods to achieve that aim. Because students learn at different rates and in different ways, he felt that time was not a relevant factor in the learning process. But feedback and correction, Bloom asserted, should be immediate and students should help one another.

Bloom's taxonomy theory incorporates cognitive, psychomotor, and affective spheres of knowledge into the learning process. During the 1970s and 1980s, his theories were adopted by many public school districts, particularly in Chicago and Boston. But they were subsequently criticized as being ineffective, and many schools no longer implement them.

Other books by Bloom include *Handbook on Formative and Summative Evaluation of Student Learning* (1971), *Human Characteristics and School Learning* (1976), *All Our Children Learning: A Primer for Parents, Teachers, and Other Educators* (1980), and *Developing Talent in Young People* (1985).

[Abraham J. Tannenbaum / Ruth Beloff (2nd ed.)]

BLOOM, CLAIRE (1931–), British actress. Claire Bloom won acclaim in *The Lady's Not for Burning* (1949) and as Juliet in the 1952 Old Vic production of *Romeo and Juliet*. Later plays include *Duel of Angels* (London, 1958) and *Rashomon* (Broadway, 1959). She gained screen fame as the ballerina in Charlie Chaplin's *Limelight* (1951). Other films include *Richard III* (1956), *Alexander the Great* (1956), *The Brothers Karamazov* (1958), *The Pawnbroker* (1965), The *Spy Who Came in From the Cold* (1966), *Charlie* (1968), *A Doll's House* (1973), *Islands* *in the Stream* (1977), *Sammy and Rosie Get Laid* (1987), and *Crimes and Misdemeanors* (1989). She has continued to make films and TV dramas into the 21st century. Claire Bloom has been married three times; her third husband (from 1990 to 1995) was Philip *Roth, the American writer. She is the author of several autobiographical works, including *Limelight and After: Education of an Actress* (1982) and *Leaving a Doll's House: A Memoir* (1998).

[Jonathan Licht and Willian D. Rubinstein (2nd ed)]

BLOOM, HAROLD (1930–), U.S. literary critic. Born to Yiddish-speaking parents in New York City, Bloom taught at Yale from 1955. An authority on Romantic and Victorian poetry, he wrote lengthy studies of Shelley, Blake, and Yeats. Bloom's most significant critical works, including *The Anxiety of Influence: A Theory of Poetry* (1973), *A Map of Misreading* (1975), and *Agon: Towards a Theory of Revisionism* (1982), explore the issue of influence, asserting that poetic creativity involves an Oedipal struggle between a writer and the great poetic figures of the past. All would-be artists, Bloom asserts, experience the anxiety that the great works have already been written; to deal with this anxiety of belatedness, they misread their precursor's work in order to find space at the poetic table. Bloom has applied this model to religious and Jewish texts. In *Ruin the Sacred Truths: Poetry and Belief from the Bible to the Present* (1989), he argues that the Hebrew Bible contains a power and sublimity that permeates all of the best of Western literature. In *The Book of J* (1990), for which he wrote the introduction and commentary, Bloom argues that the J or Yahwist author of earliest elements of the Torah – actually a woman attached to the court of the Israelite successor king to Solomon – was writing an ironic literary critique of the dogmatic, patriarchal religion of her time. Bloom spoke of himself as a "Jewish Gnostic." He delved into Gnosticism and Kabbalah's influences on American spiritual practices in *The American Religion: The Emergence of the Post-Christian Nation* (1992) and *Omens of Millennium: The Gnosis of Angels, Dreams, and Resurrection* (1996), and in *Kabbalah and Criticism* (1975) he uses Kabbalah as a model for contemporary literary criticism.

With *The Western Canon: The Books and School of the Ages* (1994), Bloom aroused widespread interest and controversy, entering into the heart of the American culture wars occurring between those arguing for a multicultural curriculum and those arguing for a return to the Western canon. Many in the press viewed Bloom as the keeper of the canon, asking for his opinions about which contemporary authors did or did not belong in the canon. The more interesting aspect of the work was Bloom's adoption of an organizing principle for literary history based on the 18th-century Neapolitan philosopher Giambattista Vico's cyclical theory of history. Bloom went on to predict the imminent arrival of a new Theocratic Age, possibly Islamic. Mourning the death of reading and attacking what he coined the School of Resentment – the Marxist, feminist, multiculturalist, and historicist schools of criticism, which he characterizes as too focused on a social agenda – for diminishing literature, he argued for the primacy of Shakespeare and Dante, arguing that "the Western Canon *is* Shakespeare and Dante. Beyond them, it is what they absorbed and what absorbed them." Bloom's celebration of Shakespeare, the J author of the Bible, and other canonical writers continued in later works of popular criticism, including *Shakespeare: The Invention of the Human* (1998), in which he argues that our modern sense of the psychologically complex human originated with Shakespeare, *How to Read and Why* (2000), and *Where Shall Wisdom Be Found?* (2004).

[Craig Svonkin (2nd ed.)]

BLOOM, HYMAN (1913–), U.S. painter. Born in Latvia, Bloom and his family moved to Boston in 1920, whereupon they changed their name from Melamed to the more American sounding Bloom. Around the age of 14 Bloom began studying art at a Jewish Community Center with Harold Zimmerman, who was already mentoring Jack *Levine. Bloom and Levine later studied art with Denman Waldo Ross of Harvard University. Some of Bloom's early drawings from this period are part of the permanent collection of Harvard's Fogg Art Museum.

The Federal Art Project of the Works Progress Administration provided Bloom with financial assistance in the late 1930s and early 1940s. At this time, Bloom's Orthodox upbringing influenced his propensity toward religious subjects, which included impressions of Judaic rituals and synagogue interiors rendered in thick pigment in luminescent tones. This style first won him acclaim in 1942 when New York's Museum of Modern Art purchased *The Bride* (1941), a personification of the Sabbath bride, and *The Synagogue* (c. 1940), the latter of which he created in two versions. In the 1940s Bloom painted four canvases of Jews holding torahs. These images employ rich colors that blend the figure with the ritual object.

Bloom based his chandelier paintings of 1945 on the light fixtures in the Boston synagogue he attended as a child. These paintings show enlarged, dazzling chandeliers dominating the canvas. In the same year he painted Christmas trees, indicating that the subject of the work, a glowing object, interested Bloom more than the identity of the light source.

By 1948 Bloom began painting cadavers, influenced in part by his interest in the art of Chaim *Soutine, whose work he had seen at the Museum of Fine Arts in Boston. Even as abstraction rose to prominence, Bloom never let go of representational forms. Indeed, in an artistic climate sometimes hostile to such imagery, Bloom continued to paint traditional subjects, such as landscapes and still lifes, in an expressionistic, painterly fashion.

BIBLIOGRAPHY: F. Wight, *Hyman Bloom* (1954); D.A. Thompson, *Hyman Bloom* (1996)

[Samantha Baskind (2nd ed.)]

BLOOM, SOL (1870–1949), U.S. businessman and politician. Bloom, born in Pekin, Ill., was brought to San Francisco by his parents as a child. He was largely self-educated. At the age of 17 he became a theatrical producer, and began successful financial investments. Moving to Chicago, Bloom managed part of the World's Columbian Exposition of 1893 and prospered as a music publisher. In 1903 he moved to New York where he entered the real estate and construction field. Extremely successful in business, Bloom retired in 1920 and went into politics. He was elected to Congress as a Democrat in 1923, and served continuously until his death. As chairman of the Foreign Affairs Committee he strongly supported and advanced President Roosevelt's internationalist policies. He was a member of the American delegation to the 1943 Bermuda conference on refugees during World War II, and was criticized by those who, unlike Bloom himself, found its results unsatisfactory. He was a delegate to the 1945 San Francisco Conference that wrote the UN Charter; to the UN Relief and Rehabilitation Administration Conference of 1946; and to the 1947 Inter-American Conference at Rio de Janeiro. Bloom, who was favorable to Zionism, opposed President Truman's early Palestine policy and took part in gaining American and UN support for the establishment of the State of Israel. His *Autobiography* was published in 1948.

BIBLIOGRAPHY: *Current Biography Yearbook 1943* (1944), 55–59.

[Stanley L. Falk]

BLOOM, SOLOMON FRANK (1903–1962), U.S. historian of modern Europe. Born in Romania, Bloom went to the U.S. in 1920. In 1931 he was appointed professor of history at Brooklyn College, New York. In 1949 Bloom wrote an article entitled "Dictator of the Lodz Ghetto." Based on sources in Yiddish and French, it was the first English-language account of Mordechai Chaim *Rumkowski, the controversial Nazi-appointed chairman of the *Judenrat of the *Lodz ghetto in Poland (*Commentary* 7 (Feb. 1949): 111–22). In 1950 Bloom wrote an essay on the political role of the heads of the *Judenrate*, entitled "Toward the Ghetto Dictator" (*Jewish Social Studies* 12 (Jan. 1950): 73–78). In *Commentary* magazine, Bloom also wrote his memoirs, entitled "On the Horizon: Memoir of a Rumanian Rope-Climber" (vol. 21, Feb. 1956). Bloom's major works were *The World of Nations* (1941, 1967^2), a study of Karl Marx in the larger context of history; *Europe and America* (1961); and *A Liberal in Two Worlds* (1968).

[Ruth Beloff (2nd ed.)]

BLOOMBERG, MICHAEL R. (1942–), founder of Bloomberg LP, philanthropist, and mayor of New York. Born in Medford, Mass., where his father was the bookkeeper at a local dairy, Bloomberg evinced a thirst for information and technology that led him to Johns Hopkins University, where he parked cars and took out loans to finance his education. After his college graduation, he gained an M.B.A. from Harvard and in 1966 was hired by Salomon Brothers to work on Wall Street. He rose quickly and became a partner in 1972. Soon after he was supervising all of Salomon's stock trading, sales, and its information systems.

When Salomon was acquired by another company in 1981, Bloomberg was ousted. But he used his stake from the Salomon sale to start his own company, an endeavor that would revolutionize the way Wall Street does business. As a young trader, Bloomberg felt that the information-gathering process was archaic, relying on penciled notations in oversize ledgers. On his own, and with the financial backing of Merrill Lynch, he created a financial information computer that would collect and analyze different combinations of past and present securities data and deliver it immediately to the user. In 1982 the company sold 20 subscriptions to its service; 20 years later Bloomberg LP had more than 165,000 subscribers worldwide.

In 1990 the company entered the media business, starting a news service and then radio, television, Internet, and publishing operations. It employed more than 8,000 people, including 2,500 in New York City, in more than 100 offices. As the company grew, Bloomberg dedicated more of his time to philanthropy and civic affairs. He gave to projects to improve education, advance medical research, and increase access to the arts. He donated money to a variety of Jewish causes, including the Anti-Defamation League and the American Jewish World Service, and served on the board of the American Friends of the Israel Museum. He financed programs for victims of domestic violence in New York City, supported construction of new high school athletic fields, and served on the boards of 20 civic, cultural, educational, and medical institutions. He served as chairman of the board of trustees of Johns Hopkins until 2002, and the university named its School of Hygiene and Public Health for him. In 1997 he published his autobiography, *Bloomberg by Bloomberg*.

In 2001, Bloomberg, a long-time Democrat, decided to run for mayor of New York as a Republican, to succeed Rudolph Giuliani, who was barred from seeking re-election. Despite putting $50 million of his own money into the campaign, Bloomberg was a decided underdog, but he received a last-minute endorsement from Giuliani, who became nationally known for his handling of a city in crisis after terrorists struck on Sept. 11, 2001. Bloomberg, who had never run for public office before, won handily against a splintered Democratic Party. Among his first acts as mayor was to ban smoking in bars and clubs, and he also launched a campaign against street vendors.

During the campaign, Bloomberg said that antisemitism had never been a factor in his life. "I don't know whether when I didn't get an opportunity it was because of that or something else," he said. "But if there is anyone who has not been ashamed of their last name, it's me. We do business throughout the world and it has never been an issue, even in the Middle East."

[Stewart Kampel (2nd ed.)]

BLOOMFIELD, LEONARD (1887–1949), American linguist. Bloomfield, chiefly through his book *Language*, became the most influential individual in guiding the development of American descriptive linguistics. He taught at various American universities and from 1940 to 1949 was professor of linguistics at Yale. His interests widened from Indo-European to other language groups and into problems of general linguistics. He published his first inclusive survey of the field *An Introduction to the Study of Language* (1914); later he published *Tagalog Texts with Grammatical Analysis* (1917); and in the early 1920s began his long series of important contributions to the study of the Algonquian languages spoken by many North American Indian tribes. His interest in the practical application of linguistics to the teaching of languages remained strong throughout his life, and he wrote a number of textbooks and a general work, *Outline Guide for the Practical Study of Foreign Languages* (1942). He was one of the founders of the Linguistic Society of America, and served a term as its president. His most important work, *Language* (1933), though outdated in several respects, is still used as a standard textbook in many places. It has provided generations of linguists with a survey of the whole field, an analytical framework, and a basic approach to language as a subject for scientific inquiry.

BIBLIOGRAPHY: B. Bloch, in: *Language*, 25 (1949), 87–98.

[Haim Blanc]

BLOOMFIELD, MAURICE (1855–1928), U.S. expert in Sanskrit. Born in Austria, Bloomfield was taken to the U.S. as a child and received his higher education at the University of Chicago and at Yale, where he studied under the Sanskritist W.D. Whitney. Bloomfield concentrated on research in Vedic language and literature, and after further study at Berlin and Leipzig (1879–81) was appointed professor of Sanskrit and comparative linguistics at Johns Hopkins University. His major works are *A Vedic Concordance* (1906), and *Vedic Variants* (completed after his death by his student and colleague, Franklin Edgerton, and published 1930–34). Bloomfield was president of the American Oriental Society (1910–11).

BIBLIOGRAPHY: *Studies in Honor of Maurice Bloomfield* (1920).

BLOOMFIELD-ZEISLER, FANNY (1863–1927), U.S. virtuoso pianist, known for her recitals in Europe and the U.S. Born in Vienna, Fanny Bloomfield-Zeisler was taken to the U.S. in 1868. She made her debut in Chicago at eleven and then went to Vienna for further study with Theodor Leschetizky (1830–1919). She first toured Europe in 1893 and continued to appear in leading cities until World War I. She gave a special performance in Chicago in 1925, to mark the half-century of her concert career.

BLOOMGARDEN, KERMIT (1904–1976), U.S. theatrical producer. Born in Brooklyn to Zemad and Annie Groden Bloomgarden, he graduated from New York University in 1926 as an accounting major and practiced as a certified public accountant for six years, when he met a Broadway producer at a dinner party who convinced him that "the theater was for me," Bloomgarden recalled. In 1935 Bloomgarden began a ten-year association with Herman Shumlin's production organization, and he was associated with the presentation of several successful plays by Lillian *Hellman, including *The Children's Hour, The Little Foxes*, and *Watch on the Rhine*. Later he produced other Hellman plays on his own. His first venture as a producer was *Heavenly Express*, starring John *Garfield, which gave him experience but no profits before it closed quickly in 1940. Following World War II, Bloomgarden produced *Deep Are the Roots*, a powerful drama about racial conflict, and Hellman's *Another Part of the Forest*. Perhaps the best-known play he produced in that period, in 1949, was Arthur *Miller's *Death of a Salesman,* with a cast headed by Lee J. *Cobb. It is considered one of the greatest American plays of the 20th century, and it won the Tony and New York Drama Critics Circle awards as well as the Pulitzer Prize.

He had failures as well as hits. But between September 1955 and the following May, Bloomgarden, alone or in association with others, presented four major productions: Hellman's adaptation of Jean Anouilh's *The Lark*, the musical *The Most Happy Fella*, Miller's *A View From the Bridge*, and *The Diary of Anne Frank*, based on a diary kept by a doomed Jewish girl in World War II. Directed by Garson *Kanin, it ran for 717 performances, made a star out of Susan *Strasberg, and won the three major drama prizes of 1956: the Pulitzer, the Tony for best play, and the New York Drama Critics Circle award. The play, written by the husband and wife team of Albert *Hackett and Frances Goodrich went through eight drafts over several years before emerging on the stage. The playwrights visited Amsterdam to see the secret hideaway and conferred with Otto Frank, Anne's father. The work was based on *Anne Frank: The Diary of a Young Girl*, the best-selling book about the Dutch girl's wartime experience hiding from the Nazis. The play contains the pivotal line from the diary: "In spite of everything, I still believe that people are really good at heart."

In 1957 Bloomgarden produced *Look Homeward, Angel*, based on the novel by Thomas Wolfe, as well as Meredith Willson's *Music Man*, which won eight Tony awards and ran for 1,375 performances. Over the years his name preceded the credits of Hellman's *Toys in the Attic*, Miller's *The Crucible*, Stephen *Sondheim's *Anyone Can Whistle,* and Lanford Wilson's *The Hot L Baltimore*. He produced more than 30 plays on Broadway, including seven by Hellman and three by Miller. In 1974, after the amputation of his right leg because of arteriosclerosis, he returned to Broadway with Peter Shaffer's *Equus.*

[Stewart Kampel (2nd ed.)]

BLOOMINGDALE, prominent U.S. family. The founder of the family was LYMAN GUSTAVUS (1841–1905), merchant and philanthropist. He was born in New York, son of German Jewish immigrants. After service in the Civil War in the Kansas Volunteers, he returned to New York where he and his brother Joseph opened a hoopskirt and ladies' notion store. In 1886 Bloomingdale Brothers Department Store was established on its present site in midtown New York City. Lyman was a patron of the arts and a noted philanthropist, with his chief interests the Metropolitan Museum of Art and Montefiore Hospital. JOSEPH BERNHARDT (1842–1904), brother of Lyman, was associated with the family's business endeavors in the West and later in New York. Retiring from Bloomingdale Brothers in 1896, he was president of the Hebrew Technical Institute and one of the founders of Barnard College. EMANUEL WATSON (1852–1928), lawyer and merchant, a third brother, received a law degree from Columbia University and was active both as an attorney and in the family business. His major interests included Republican politics, the New York State Bridge and Tunnel Commission, and the Society for Reformation of Juvenile Delinquents. SAMUEL JOSEPH (1873–1968), son of Lyman, was educated at the Columbia University School of Architecture but devoted himself to the management of the family's store, serving as its president during 1905–30. An innovator in retailing techniques, he became a director of Federated Department Stores when it absorbed Bloomingdale Brothers in 1930. Samuel was trustee of the Federation of Jewish Philanthropies and active in the American Jewish Committee, also continuing the family association with the Metropolitan Museum of Art and Montefiore Hospital. HIRAM C. (1876–1953), another son of Lyman, served as vice president of Bloomingdale Brothers and was a leader in the movement to establish standards for accuracy in advertising. Hiram's son ALFRED S. (1916–1982) was founder and chairman of the Diners Club credit organization. In 1970 he left Diners Club, acquiring its International Floatels division. Alfred Bloomingdale and his wife, Betsy, became good friends with Ronald and Nancy *Reagan. In 1981, after Reagan was elected U.S. president, he appointed Bloomingdale to the President's Foreign Intelligence Advisory Board and the following year named him a member of the United States Advisory Commission on Public Diplomacy. When he died at age 66 Alfred Bloomingdale, a practicing Catholic, was buried in the Holy Cross Cemetery in Culver City, California.

But the Bloomingdale legacy lives on. A fixture on New York City's Third Avenue since 1927, in addition to branches nationwide, Bloomingdale's department store is renowned for its flair for fashion and merchandising. Over the years, Bloomingdale's has helped launch the careers of many world-famous designers, such as Ralph *Lauren, Tommy Hilfiger, Calvin *Klein, and Donna *Karan.

[Morton Rosenstock / Ruth Beloff (2nd ed.)]

BLOWITZ, HENRI GEORGES STEPHANE ADOLPHE OPPER DE (1825–1903), French journalist. As chief Paris correspondent of *The Times*, London, in 1875, he originated the technique of interviewing celebrities (among them Bismarck, the sultan of Turkey, and Pope Leo XIII). In 1875 Blowitz, by now influential in European political circles, exposed plans of the military party in Germany for a second invasion of France. Three years later, he obtained the full text of the Berlin Treaty while it was still being negotiated, enabling *The Times* to print it the day it was signed. Blowitz was born Adolf Opper in Bohemia, but in 1860 added the name of his birthplace to his surname. He left home at 15, traveled, learned several languages, and taught for some years at the *lycée* in Tours and then in Marseilles. He wrote for the Paris newspapers and though sometimes in conflict with the French authorities, became naturalized after the Battle of Sedan. At the close of the Franco-Prussian War (1870–71), he helped to suppress the Commune at Marseilles by maintaining a private telegraph line to Versailles. Blowitz showed an excessive desire to remain detached from the Dreyfus Affair. He wrote short stories, comedies and *My Memoirs* (1903).

BIBLIOGRAPHY: F. Giles, *Prince of Journalists* (1962), incl. bibl.

°BLOY, LÉON (1846–1917), French Catholic writer whose work contained many Jewish themes. His prose poem, *Le salut par les Juifs* (1892), described by the author as the "only one of my books I would dare to present to God," opens with a condemnation of antisemitism and its arch-priest, Edouard *Drumont. However, holding a theory of the identity of opposites, Bloy regards the Jews as both glorious and despicable, at one and the same time the elect of God and "une poignée de boue merveilleuse" ("a handful of wonderful mud"). Among Bloy's later writings, *Le Sang du Pauvre* (1909) contains a moving chapter devoted to the Yiddish poet, Morris *Rosenfeld. Those whom he converted to Catholicism included Jacques and Raïssa *Maritain.

BIBLIOGRAPHY: A. Béguin, *Léon Bloy, a Study in Impatience* (1947); J. Petit, *Léon Bloy* (Fr., 1966), incl. bibl.; R. Maritain, *Les grandes amitiés* (1941–44); C. Journet, *Destinées d'Israël à propos du Salut par les Juifs* (1945).

[Denise R. Goitein]

ABBREVIATIONS

GENERAL ABBREVIATIONS

This list contains abbreviations used in the Encyclopaedia (apart from the standard ones, such as geographical abbreviations, points of compass, etc.). For names of organizations, institutions, etc., in abbreviation, see Index. For bibliographical abbreviations of books and authors in Rabbinical literature, see following lists.

*	Cross reference; i.e., an article is to be found under the word(s) immediately following the asterisk (*).
°	Before the title of an entry, indicates a non-Jew (post-biblical times).
‡	Indicates reconstructed forms.
>	The word following this sign is derived from the preceding one.
<	The word preceding this sign is derived from the following one.

ad loc.	*ad locum*, "at the place"; used in quotations of commentaries.
A.H.	*Anno Hegirae*, "in the year of Hegira," i.e., according to the Muslim calendar.
Akk.	Addadian.
A.M.	*anno mundi*, "in the year (from the creation) of the world."
anon.	anonymous.
Ar.	Arabic.
Aram.	Aramaic.
Ass.	Assyrian.
b.	born; *ben, bar.*
Bab.	Babylonian.
B.C.E.	Before Common Era (= B.C.).
bibl.	bibliography.
Bul.	Bulgarian.
c., ca.	Circa.
C.E.	Common Era (= A.D.).
cf.	*confer*, "compare."
ch., chs.	chapter, chapters.
comp.	compiler, compiled by.
Cz.	Czech.
D	according to the documentary theory, the Deuteronomy document.
d.	died.
Dan.	Danish.
diss., dissert,	dissertation, thesis.
Du.	Dutch.
E.	according to the documentary theory, the Elohist document (i.e., using Elohim as the name of God) of the first five (or six) books of the Bible.
ed.	editor, edited, edition.
eds.	editors.
e.g.	*exempli gratia*, "for example."
Eng.	English.
et al.	*et alibi*, "and elsewhere"; or *et alii*, "and others"; "others."
f., ff.	and following page(s).
fig.	figure.
fl.	flourished.
fol., fols	folio(s).
Fr.	French.
Ger.	German.
Gr.	Greek.
Heb.	Hebrew.
Hg., Hung	Hungarian.
ibid	*Ibidem*, "in the same place."
incl. bibl.	includes bibliography.
introd.	introduction.
It.	Italian.
J	according to the documentary theory, the Jahwist document (i.e., using YHWH as the name of God) of the first five (or six) books of the Bible.
Lat.	Latin.
lit.	literally.
Lith.	Lithuanian.
loc. cit.	*loco citato*, "in the [already] cited place."
Ms., Mss.	Manuscript(s).
n.	note.
n.d.	no date (of publication).
no., nos	number(s).
Nov.	Novellae (Heb. *Ḥiddushim*).
n.p.	place of publication unknown.
op. cit.	*opere citato*, "in the previously mentioned work."
P.	according to the documentary theory, the Priestly document of the first five (or six) books of the Bible.
p., pp.	page(s).
Pers.	Persian.
pl., pls.	plate(s).
Pol.	Polish.
Port.	Potuguese.
pt., pts.	part(s).
publ.	published.
R.	Rabbi or Rav (before names); in Midrash (after an abbreviation) – *Rabbah*.
r.	recto, the first side of a manuscript page.
Resp.	Responsa (Latin "answers," Hebrew *She'elot u-Teshuvot* or *Teshuvot),* collections of rabbinic decisions.
rev.	revised.

Rom.	Romanian.
Rus(s).	Russian.
Slov.	Slovak.
Sp.	Spanish.
s.v.	*sub verbo, sub voce*, "under the (key) word."
Sum	Sumerian.
summ.	Summary.
suppl.	supplement.
Swed.	Swedish.
tr., trans(l).	translator, translated, translation.
Turk.	Turkish.
Ukr.	Ukrainian.
v., vv.	*verso*. The second side of a manuscript page; also verse(s).
Yid.	Yiddish.

ABBREVIATIONS USED IN RABBINICAL LITERATURE

Adderet Eliyahu, Karaite treatise by Elijah b. Moses *Bashyazi.
Admat Kodesh, Resp. by Nissim Ḥayyim Moses b. Joseph |Mizraḥi.
Aguddah, Sefer ha-, Nov. by *Alexander Suslin ha-Kohen.
Ahavat Ḥesed, compilation by *Israel Meir ha-Kohen.
Aliyyot de-Rabbenu Yonah, Nov. by *Jonah b. Avraham Gerondi.
Arukh ha-Shulḥan, codification by Jehiel Michel *Epstein.
Asayin (= positive precepts), subdivision of: (1) *Maimonides, *Sefer ha-Mitzvot;* (2) *Moses b. Jacob of Coucy, *Semag.*
Asefat Dinim, subdivision of *Sedei Ḥemed* by Ḥayyim Hezekiah *Medini, an encyclopaedia of precepts and responsa.
Asheri = *Asher b. Jehiel.
Aeret Ḥakhamim, by Baruch *Frankel-Teomim; pt, 1: Resp. to Sh. Ar.; pt2: Nov. to Talmud.
Ateret Zahav, subdivision of the *Levush*, a codification by Mordecai b. Abraham (Levush) *Jaffe; *Ateret Zahav* parallels Tur. YD.
Ateret Ẓevi, Comm. To Sh. Ar. by Ẓevi Hirsch b. Azriel.
Avir Ya'akov, Resp. by Jacob Avigdor.
Avkat Rokhel, Resp. by Joseph b. Ephraim *Caro.
Avnei Millu'im, Comm. to Sh. Ar., EH, by *Aryeh Loeb b. Joseph ha-Kohen.
Avnei Nezer, Resp. on Sh. Ar. by Abraham b. Ze'ev Nahum Bornstein of *Sochaczew.
Avodat Massa, Compilation of Tax Law by Yoasha Abraham Judah.
Azei ha-Levanon, Resp. by Judah Leib *Zirelson.

Ba'al ha-Tanya – *Shneur Zalman of Lyady.
Ba'ei Ḥayyei, Resp. by Ḥayyim b. Israel *Benveniste.
Ba'er Heitev, Comm. To Sh. Ar. The parts on OḤ and EH are by Judah b. Simeon *Ashkenazi, the parts on YD AND ḤM by *Zechariah Mendel b. Aryeh Leib. Printed in most editions of Sh. Ar.
Baḥ = Joel *Sirkes.
Baḥ, usual abbreviation for *Bayit Ḥadash*, a commentary on Tur by Joel *Sirkes; printed in most editions of Tur.
Bayit Ḥadash, see *Baḥ*.
Berab = Jacob Berab, also called Ri Berav.
Bedek ha-Bayit, by Joseph b. Ephraim *Caro, additions to his *Beit Yosef* (a comm. to Tur). Printed sometimes inside *Beit Yosef*, in smaller type. Appears in most editions of Tur.
Be'er ha-Golah, Commentary to Sh. Ar. By Moses b. Naphtali Hirsch *Rivkes; printed in most editions of Sh. Ar.
Be'er Mayim, Resp. by Raphael b. Abraham Manasseh Jacob.
Be'er Mayim Ḥayyim, Resp. by Samuel b. Ḥayyim *Vital.
Be'er Yizḥak, Resp. by Isaac Elhanan *Spector.
Beit ha-Beḥirah, Comm. to Talmud by Menahem b. Solomon *Meiri.
Beit Me'ir, Nov. on Sh. Ar. by Meir b. Judah Leib Posner.
Beit Shelomo, Resp. by Solomon b. Aaron Ḥason (the younger).
Beit Shemu'el, Comm. to Sh. Ar., EH, by *Samuel b. Uri Shraga Phoebus.
Beit Ya'akov, by Jacob b. Jacob Moses *Lorberbaum; pt.1: Nov. to Ket.; pt.2: Comm. to EH.
Beit Yisrael, collective name for the commentaries *Derishah, Perishah,* and *Be'urim* by Joshua b. Alexander ha-Kohen *Falk. See under the names of the commentaries.
Beit Yizḥak, Resp. by Isaac *Schmelkes.
Beit Yosef: (1) Comm. on Tur by Joseph b. Ephraim *Caro; printed in most editions of Tur; (2) Resp. by the same.
Ben Yehudah, Resp. by Abraham b. Judah Litsch (ליטש) Rosenbaum.
Bertinoro, Standard commentary to Mishnah by Obadiah *Bertinoro. Printed in most editions of the Mishnah.
[Be'urei] Ha-Gra, Comm. to Bible, Talmud, and Sh. Ar. By *Elijah b. Solomon Zalmon (Gaon of Vilna); printed in major editions of the mentioned works.
Be'urim, Glosses to Isserles *Darkhei Moshe* (a comm. on Tur) by Joshua b. Alexander ha-Kohen *Falk; printed in many editions of Tur.
Binyamin Ze'ev, Resp. by *Benjamin Ze'ev b. Mattathias of Arta.
Birkei Yosef, Nov. by Ḥayyim Joseph David *Azulai.
Ha-Buẓ ve-ha-Argaman, subdivision of the *Levush* (a codification by Mordecai b. Abraham (Levush) *Jaffe); *Ha-Buẓ ve-ha-Argaman* parallels Tur, EH.

Comm. = Commentary

Da'at Kohen, Resp. by Abraham Isaac ha-Kohen. *Kook.
Darkhei Moshe, Comm. on Tur Moses b. Israel *Isserles; printed in most editions of Tur.
Darkhei No'am, Resp. by *Mordecai b. Judah ha-Levi.
Darkhei Teshuvah, Nov. by Ẓevi *Shapiro; printed in the major editions of Sh. Ar.
De'ah ve-Haskel, Resp. by Obadiah Hadaya (see *Yaskil Avdi).*

Derashot Ran, Sermons by *Nissim b. Reuben Gerondi.
Derekh Ḥayyim, Comm. to *Avot* by *Judah Loew (Lob., Liwa) b. Bezalel (Maharal) of Prague.
Derishah, by Joshua b. Alexander ha-Kohen *Falk; additions to his *Perishah* (comm. on Tur); printed in many editions of Tur.
Derushei ha-Ẓelaḥ, Sermons, by Ezekiel b. Judah Halevi *Landau.
Devar Avraham, Resp. by Abraham *Shapira.
Devar Shemu'el, Resp. by Samuel *Aboab.
Devar Yehoshu'a, Resp. by Joshua Menahem b. Isaac Aryeh Ehrenberg.
Dikdukei Soferim, variae lections of the talmudic text by Raphael Nathan*Rabbinowicz.
Divrei Emet, Resp. by Isaac Bekhor David.
Divrei Ge'onim, Digest of responsa by Ḥayyim Aryeh b. Jeḥiel Ẓevi *Kahana.
Divrei Ḥamudot, Comm. on *Piskei ha-Rosh* by Yom Tov Lipmann b. Nathan ha-Levi *Heller; printed in major editions of the Talmud.
Divrei Ḥayyim several works by Ḥayyim *Halberstamm; if quoted alone refers to his Responsa.
Divrei Malkhi'el, Resp. by Malchiel Tenebaum.
Divrei Rivot, Resp. by Isaac b. Samuel *Adarbi.
Divrei Shemu'el, Resp. by Samuel Raphael Arditi.

Edut be-Ya'akov, Resp. by Jacob b. Abraham *Boton.
Edut bi-Yhosef, Resp. by Joseph b. Isaac *Almosnino.
Ein Ya'akov, Digest of talmudic *aggadot* by Jacob (Ibn) *Habib.
Ein Yiẓḥak, Resp. by Isaac Elhanan *Spector.
Ephraim of Lentshitz = Solomon *Luntschitz.
Erekh Leḥem, Nov. and glosses to Sh. Ar. by Jacob b. Abraham *Castro.
Eshkol, Sefer ha-, Digest of *halakhot* by *Abraham b. Isaac of Narbonne.
Et Sofer, Treatise on Law Court documents by Abraham b. Mordecai *Ankawa, in the 2nd vol. of his Resp. *Kerem Ḥamar.*
Etan ha-Ezraḥi, Resp. by Abraham b. Israel Jehiel (Shrenzl) *Rapaport.
Even ha-Ezel, Nov. to Maimonides' *Yad Ḥazakah* by Isser Zalman *Meltzer.
Even ha-Ezer, also called *Raban* of *Ẓafenat Pa'ne'aḥ,* rabbinical work with varied contents by *Eliezer b. Nathan of Mainz; not identical with the subdivision of Tur, Shulḥan Arukh, etc.
Ezrat Yehudah, Resp. by *Isaar Judah b. Nechemiah of Brisk.

Gan Eden, Karaite treatise by *Aaron b. Elijah of Nicomedia.
Gersonides = *Levi b. Gershom, also called Leo Hebraecus, or Ralbag.
Ginnat Veradim, Resp. by *Abraham b. Mordecai ha-Levi.

Haggahot, another name for *Rema.*
Haggahot Asheri, glosses to *Piskei ha-Rosh* by *Israel of Krems; printed in most Talmud editions.
Haggahot Maimuniyyot, Comm,. to Maimonides' Yad Ḥazakah by *Meir ha-Kohen; printed in most eds. of Yad.
Haggahot Mordekhai, glosses to *Mordekhai* by Samuel *Schlettstadt; printed in most editions of the Talmud after *Mordekhai.*
Haggahot ha-Rashash on Tosafot, annotations of Samuel *Strashun on the Tosafot (printed in major editions of the Talmud).
Ha-Gra = *Elijah b. Solomon Zalman (Gaon of Vilna).
Ha-Gra, Commentaries on Bible, Talmud, and Sh. Ar. respectively, by *Elijah b. Solomon Zalman (Gaon of Vilna); printed in major editions of the mentioned works.
Hai Gaon, Comm. = his comm. on Mishnah.
Ḥakham Ẓevi, Resp. by Ẓevi Hirsch b. Jacob *Ashkenazi.
Halakhot = Rif, *Halakhot.* Compilation and abstract of the Talmud by Isaac b. Jacob ha-Kohen *Alfasi; printed in most editions of the Talmud.
Halakhot Gedolot, compilation of *halakhot* from the Geonic period, arranged acc. to the Talmud. Here cited acc. to ed. Warsaw (1874). Author probably *Simeon Kayyara of Basra.
Halakhot Pesukot le-Rav Yehudai Ga'on compilation of *halakhot.*
Halakhot Pesukot min ha-Ge'onim, compilation of *halakhot* from the geonic period by different authors.
Ḥananel, Comm. to Talmud by *Hananel b. Ḥushi'el; printed in some editions of the Talmud.
Harei Besamim, Resp. by Aryeh Leib b. Isaac *Horowitz.
Ḥassidim, Sefer, Ethical maxims by *Judah b. Samuel he-Ḥasid.
Hassagot Rabad on Rif, Glosses on Rif, *Halakhot,* by *Abraham b. David of Posquières.
Hassagot Rabad [on Yad], Glosses on Maimonides, *Yad Ḥazakah,* by *Abraham b. David of Posquières.
Hassagot Ramban, Glosses by Naḥmanides on Maimonides' *Sefer ha-Mitzvot;* usually printed together with *Sefer ha-Mitzvot.*
Ḥatam Sofer = Moses *Sofer.
Ḥavvot Ya'ir, Resp. and varia by Jair Ḥayyim *Bacharach
Ḥayyim Or Zaru'a = *Ḥayyim (Eliezer) b. Isaac.
Ḥazon Ish = Abraham Isaiah *Karelitz.
Ḥazon Ish, Nov. by Abraham Isaiah *Karelitz
Ḥedvat Ya'akov, Resp. by Aryeh Judah Jacob b. David Dov Meisels (article under his father's name).
Heikhal Yiẓḥak, Resp. by Isaac ha-Levi *Herzog.
Ḥelkat Meḥokek, Comm. to Sh. Ar., by Moses b. Isaac Judah *Lima.
Ḥelkat Ya'akov, Resp. by Mordecai Jacob Breisch.
Ḥemdah Genuzah, , Resp. from the geonic period by different authors.
Ḥemdat Shelomo, Resp. by Solomon Zalman *Lipschitz.
Ḥida = Ḥayyim Joseph David *Azulai.
Ḥiddushei Halakhot ve-Aggadot, Nov. by Samuel Eliezer b. Judah ha-Levi *Edels.
Ḥikekei Lev, Resp. by Ḥayyim *Palaggi.
Ḥikrei Lev, Nov. to Sh. Ar. by Joseph Raphael b. Ḥayyim Joseph Ḥazzan (see article *Ḥazzan Family).
Hil. = Hilkhot … (e.g. *Hilkhot Shabbat).*
Ḥinnukh, Sefer ha-, List and explanation of precepts attributed (probably erroneously) to Aaron ha-Levi of Barcelona (see article *Ha-Ḥinnukh*).
Ḥok Ya'akov, Comm. to Hil. Pesaḥ in Sh. Ar., OḤ, by Jacob b. Joseph *Reicher.
Ḥokhmat Sehlomo (1), Glosses to Talmud, *Rashi* and Tosafot by Solomon b. Jehiel "Maharshal") *Luria; printed in many editions of the Talmud.
Ḥokhmat Sehlomo (2), Glosses and Nov. to Sh. Ar. by Solomon b. Judah Aaron *Kluger printed in many editions of Sh. Ar.
Ḥur, subdivision of the *Levush,* a codification by Mordecai b. Abraham (Levush) *Jaffe; *Hur (*or *Levush ha-Hur)* parallels Tur, OḤ, 242–697.
Ḥut ha-Meshullash, fourth part of the *Tashbeẓ* (Resp.), by Simeon b. Zemaḥ *Duran.

Ibn Ezra, Comm. to the Bible by Abraham *Ibn Ezra; printed in the major editions of the Bible *("Mikra'ot Gedolot").*
Imrei Yosher, Resp. by Meir b. Aaron Judah *Arik.
Ir Shushan, Subdivision of the *Levush,* a codification by Mordecai b. Abraham (Levush) *Jaffe; *Ir Shushan* parallels Tur, ḤM.
Israel of Bruna = Israel b. Ḥayyim *Bruna.
Ittur. Treatise on precepts by *Isaac b. Abba Mari of Marseilles.

Jacob Be Rab = *Be Rab.
Jacob b. Jacob Moses of Lissa = Jacob b. Jacob Moses *Lorberbaum.
Judah B. Simeon = Judah b. Simeon *Ashkenazi.
Judah Minz = Judah b. Eliezer ha-Levi *Minz.

Kappei Aharon, Resp. by Aaron Azriel.
Kehillat Ya'akov, Talmudic methodology, definitions etc. by Israel Jacob b. Yom Tov *Algazi.
Kelei Ḥemdah, Nov. and *pilpulim* by Meir Dan *Plotzki of Ostrova, arranged acc. to the Torah.
Keli Yakar, Annotations to the Torah by Solomon *Luntschitz.
Keneh Ḥokhmah, Sermons by Judah Loeb *Pochwitzer.
Keneset ha-Gedolah, Digest of *halakhot* by Ḥayyim b. Israel *Benveniste; subdivided into annotations to *Beit Yosef* and annotations to Tur.
Keneset Yisrael, Resp. by Ezekiel b. Abraham Katzenellenbogen (see article *Katzenellenbogen Family).
Kerem Ḥamar, Resp. and varia by Abraham b. Mordecai *Ankawa.
Kerem Shelmo. Resp. by Solomon b. Joseph *Amarillo.
Keritut, [Sefer], Methodology of the Talmud by *Samson b. Isaac of Chinon.
Kesef ha-Kedoshim, Comm. to Sh. Ar., ḤM, by Abraham *Wahrmann; printed in major editions of Sh. Ar.
Kesef Mishneh, Comm. to Maimonides, *Yad Ḥazakah,* by Joseph b. Ephraim *Caro; printed in most editions of *Yad Ḥazakah.*
Keẓot ha-Ḥoshen, Comm. to Sh. Ar., ḤM, by *Aryeh Loeb b. Joseph ha-Kohen; printed in major editions of Sh. Ar.
Kol Bo [*Sefer*], Anonymous collection of ritual rules; also called *Sefer ha-Likkutim.*
Kol Mevasser, Resp. by Meshullam *Rath.
Korban Aharon, Comm. to *Sifra* by Aaron b. Abraham *Ibn Ḥayyim; pt. 1 is called: *Middot Aharon.*
Korban Edah, Comm. to Jer. Talmud by David *Fraenkel; with additions: *Shiyyurei Korban;* printed in most editions of Jer. Talmud.
Kunteres ha-Kelalim, subdivision of *Sedei Ḥemed,* an encyclopaedia of precepts and responsa by Ḥayyim Hezekiah *Medini.
Kunteres ha-Semikhah, a treatise by *Levi b. Ḥabib; printed at the end of his responsa.
Kunteres Tikkun Olam, part of *Mispat Shalom* (Nov. by Shalom Mordecai b. Moses *Schwadron).

Lavin (negative precepts), subdivision of: (1) *Maimonides, *Sefer ha-Mitzvot;* (2) *Moses b. Jacob of Coucy, *Semag.*
Leḥem Mishneh, Comm. to Maimonides, *Yad Ḥazakah,* by Abraham [Ḥiyya] b. Moses *Boton; printed in most editions of *Yad Ḥazakah.*
Leḥem Rav, Resp. by Abraham [Ḥiyya] b. Moses *Boton.
Leket Yosher, Resp and varia by Israel b. Pethahiah *Isserlein, collected by *Joseph (Joselein) b. Moses.
Leo Hebraeus = *Levi b. Gershom, also called Ralbag or Gersonides.
Levush = Mordecai b. Abraham *Jaffe.
Levush [Malkhut], Codification by Mordecai b. Abraham (Levush) *Jaffe, with subdivisions: *[Levush ha-] Tekhelet* (parallels Tur OḤ 1–241); *[Levush ha-] Ḥur* (parallels Tur OḤ 242–697); *[Levush] Ateret Zahav* (parallels Tur YD); *[Levush ha-Buẓ ve-ha-Argaman* (parallels Tur EH); *[Levush] Ir Shushan* (parallels Tur ḤM); under the name *Levush* the author wrote also other works.
Li-Leshonot ha-Rambam, fifth part (nos. 1374–1700) of Resp. by *David b. Solomon ibn Abi Zimra (Radbaz).
Likkutim, Sefer ha-, another name for *[Sefer] Kol Bo.*

Ma'adanei Yom Tov, Comm. on *Piskei ha-Rosh* by Yom Tov Lipmann b. Nathan ha-Levi *Heller; printed in many editions of the Talmud.
Mabit = Moses b. Joseph *Trani.
Magen Avot, Comm. to *Avot* by Simeon b. Ẓemaḥ *Duran.
Magen Avraham, Comm. to Sh. Ar., OḤ, by Abraham Abele b. Ḥayyim ha-Levi *Gombiner; printed in many editions of Sh. Ar., OḤ.
Maggid Mishneh, Comm. to Maimonides, *Yad Ḥazakah,* by *Vidal Yom Tov of Tolosa; printed in most editions of the *Yad Ḥazakah.*
Maḥaneh Efrayim, Resp. and Nov., arranged acc. to Maimonides' *Yad Ḥazakah* , by Ephraim b. Aaron *Navon.
Maharai = Israel b. Pethahiah *Isserlein.
Maharal of Prague = *Judah Loew (Lob, Liwa), b. Bezalel.
Maharalbaḥ = *Levi b. Ḥabib.
Maharam Alashkar = Moses b. Isaac *Alashkar.
Maharam Alshekh = Moses b. Ḥayyim *Alashekh.
Maharam Mintz = Moses *Mintz.
Maharam of Lublin = *Meir b. Gedaliah of Lublin.
Maharam of Padua = Meir *Katzenellenbogen.
Maharam of Rothenburg = *Meir b. Baruch of Rothenburg.
Maharam Shik = Moses b. Joseph Schick.
Maharash Engel = Samuel b. Ze'ev Wolf Engel.
Maharashdam = Samuel b. Moses *Medina.
Maharḥash = Ḥayyim (ben) Shabbetai.
Mahari Basan = Jehiel b. Ḥayyim Basan.
Mahari b. Lev = Joseph ibn Lev.
Mahari'az = Jekuthiel Asher Zalman Ensil Zusmir.
Maharibal = *Joseph ibn Lev.
Mahariḥ = Jacob (Israel) *Ḥagiz.
Maharik = Joseph b. Solomon *Colon.
Maharikash = Jacob b. Abraham *Castro.
Maharil = Jacob b. Moses *Moellin.
Maharimat = Joseph b. Moses di Trani (not identical with the Maharit).
Maharit = Joseph b. Moses *Trani.
Maharitaẓ = Yom Tov b. Akiva Ẓahalon. (See article *Ẓahalon Family).
Maharsha = Samuel Eliezer b. Judah ha-Levi *Edels.
Maharshag = Simeon b. Judah Gruenfeld.
Maharshak = Samson b. Isaac of Chinon.
Maharshakh = *Solomon b. Abraham.
Maharshal = Solomon b. Jeḥiel *Luria.
Mahasham = Shalom Mordecai b. Moses *Sschwadron.
Maharyu = Jacob b. Judah *Weil.
Maḥazeh Avraham, Resp. by Abraham Nebagen v. Meir ha-Levi Steinberg.
Maḥazik Berakhah, Nov. by Ḥayyim Joseph David *Azulai.

*Maimonides = Moses b. Maimon, or Rambam.
*Malbim = Meir Loeb b. Jehiel Michael.
Malbim = Malbim's comm. to the Bible; printed in the major editions.
Malbushei Yom Tov, Nov. on *Levush*, OḤ, by Yom Tov Lipmann b. Nathan ha-Levi *Heller.
Mappah, another name for *Rema.*
Mareh ha-Panim, Comm. to Jer. Talmud by Moses b. Simeon *Margolies; printed in most editions of Jer. Talmud.
Margaliyyot ha-Yam, Nov. by Reuben *Margoliot.
Masat Binyamin, Resp. by Benjamin Aaron b. Abraham *Slonik
Mashbir, Ha- = *Joseph Samuel b. Isaac Rodi.
Massa Ḥayyim, Tax *halakhot* by Ḥayyim *Palaggi, with the subdivisions *Missim ve-Arnomiyyot* and *Torat ha-Minhagot.*
Massa Melekh, Compilation of Tax Law by Joseph b. Isaac *Ibn Ezra with concluding part *Ne'ilat She'arim.*
Matteh Asher, Resp. by Asher b. Emanuel Shalem.
Matteh Shimon, Digest of Resp. and Nov. to Tur and *Beit Yosef,* ḤM, by Mordecai Simeon b. Solomon.
Matteh Yosef, Resp. by Joseph b. Moses ha-Levi Nazir (see article under his father's name).
Mayim Amukkim, Resp. by Elijah b. Abraham *Mizraḥi.
Mayim Ḥayyim, Resp. by Ḥayyim b. Dov Beresh Rapaport.
Mayim Rabbim, , Resp. by Raphael *Meldola.
Me-Emek ha-Bakha, , Resp. by Simeon b. Jekuthiel Ephrati.
Me'irat Einayim, usual abbreviation: *Sma* (from: *Sefer Me'irat Einayim*); comm. to Sh. Ar. By Joshua b. Alexander ha-Kohen *Falk; printed in most editions of the Sh. Ar.
Melammed le-Ho'il, Resp. by David Ẓevi *Hoffmann.
Meisharim, [*Sefer*], Rabbinical treatise by *Jeroham b. Meshullam.
Meshiv Davar, Resp. by Naphtali Ẓevi Judah *Berlin.
Mi-Gei ha-Haregah, Resp. by Simeon b. Jekuthiel Ephrati.
Mi-Ma'amakim, Resp. by Ephraim Oshry.
Middot Aharon, first part of *Korban Aharon,* a comm. to *Sifra* by Aaron b. Abraham *Ibn Ḥayyim.
Migdal Oz, Comm. to Maimonides, *Yad Ḥazakah,* by *Ibn Gaon Shem Tov b. Abraham; printed in most editions of the *Yad Ḥazakah.*
Mikhtam le-David, Resp. by David Samuel b. Jacob *Pardo.
Mikkaḥ ve-ha-Mimkar, Sefer ha-, Rabbinical treatise by *Hai Gaon.
Milḥamot ha-Shem, Glosses to Rif, *Halakhot,* by *Naḥmanides.
Minḥat Ḥinnukh, Comm. to *Sefer ha-Ḥinnukh,* by Joseph b. Moses *Babad.
Minḥat Yiẓḥak, Resp. by Isaac Jacob b. Joseph Judah Weiss.
Misgeret ha-Shulḥan, Comm. to Sh. Ar., ḤM, by Benjamin Ze'ev Wolf b. Shabbetai; printed in most editions of Sh. Ar.
Mishkenot ha-Ro'im, Halakhot in alphabetical order by Uzziel Alshekh.
Mishnah Berurah, Comm. to Sh. Ar., OḤ, by *Israel Meir ha-Kohen.
Mishneh le-Melekh, Comm. to Maimonides, *Yad Ḥazakah,* by Judah *Rosanes; printed in most editions of *Yad Ḥazakah.*
Mishpat ha-Kohanim, Nov. to Sh. Ar., ḤM, by Jacob Moses *Lorberbaum, part of his *Netivot ha-Mishpat;* printed in major editions of Sh. Ar.
Mishpat Kohen, Resp. by Abraham Isaac ha-Kohen *Kook.
Mishpat Shalom, Nov. by Shalom Mordecai b. Moses *Schwadron; contains: *Kunteres Tikkun Olam.*
Mishpat u-Ẓedakah be-Ya'akov, Resp. by Jacob b. Reuben *Ibn Ẓur.
Mishpat ha-Urim, Comm. to Sh. Ar., ḤM by Jacob b. Jacob Moses *Lorberbaum, part of his *Netivot ha-Mishpat;* printed in major editons of Sh. Ar.
Mishpat Ẓedek, Resp. by *Melammed Meir b. Shem Tov.
Mishpatim Yesharim, Resp. by Raphael b. Mordecai *Berdugo.
Mishpetei Shemu'el, Resp. by Samuel b. Moses *Kalai (Kal'i).
Mishpetei ha-Tanna'im, Kunteres, Nov on *Levush,* OḤ by Yom Tov Lipmann b. Nathan ha-Levi *Heller.
Mishpetei Uzzi'el (Uziel), Resp. by Ben-Zion Meir Hai *Ouziel.
Missim ve-Arnoniyyot, Tax *halakhot* by Ḥayyim *Palaggi, a subdivision of his work *Massa Ḥayyim* on the same subject.
Mitzvot, Sefer ha-, Elucidation of precepts by *Maimonides; subdivided into *Lavin* (negative precepts) and *Asayin* (positive precepts).
Mitzvot Gadol, Sefer, Elucidation of precepts by *Moses b. Jacob of Coucy, subdivided into *Lavin* (negative precepts) and *Asayin* (positive precepts); the usual abbreviation is *Semag.*
Mitzvot Katan, Sefer, Elucidation of precepts by *Isaac b. Joseph of Corbeil; the usual, abbreviation is *Semak.*
Mo'adim u-Zemannim, Rabbinical treatises by Moses Sternbuch.
Modigliano, Joseph Samuel = *Joseph Samuel b. Isaac, Rodi (Ha-Mashbir).
Mordekhai (Mordecai), halakhic compilation by *Mordecai b. Hillel; printed in most editions of the Talmud after the texts.
Moses b. Maimon = *Maimonides, also called Rambam.
Moses b. Naḥman = Naḥmanides, also called Ramban.
Muram = Isaiah Menahem b. Isaac (from: Morenu R. Mendel).

Naḥal Yiẓḥak, Comm. on Sh. Ar., ḤM, by Isaac Elhanan *Spector.
Naḥalah li-Yhoshu'a, Resp. by Joshua Ẓunẓin.
Naḥalat Shivah, collection of legal forms by *Samuel b. David Moses ha-Levi.
*Naḥmanides = Moses b. Naḥman, also called Ramban.
Naẓiv = Naphtali Ẓevi Judah *Berlin.
Ne'eman Shemu'el, Resp. by Samuel Isaac *Modigilano.
Ne'ilat She'arim, concluding part of *Massa Melekh* (a work on Tax Law) by Joseph b. Isaac *Ibn Ezra, containing an exposition of customary law and subdivided into *Minhagei Issur* and *Minhagei Mamon.*
Ner Ma'aravi, Resp. by Jacob b. Malka.
Netivot ha-Mishpat, by Jacob b. Jacob Moses *Lorberbaum; subdivided into *Mishpat ha-Kohanim,* Nov. to Sh. Ar., ḤM, and *Mishpat ha-Urim,* a comm. on the same; printed in major editions of Sh. Ar.
Netivot Olam, Saying of the Sages by *Judah Loew (Lob, Liwa) b. Bezalel.
Nimmukei Menaḥem of Merseburg, Tax *halakhot* by the same, printed at the end of Resp. Maharyu.
Nimmukei Yosef, Comm. to Rif. *Halakhot,* by Joseph *Ḥabib (Ḥabiba); printed in many editions of the Talmud.
Noda bi-Yhudah, Resp. by Ezekiel b. Judah ha-Levi *Landau; there is a first collection *(Mahadura Kamma)* and a second collection *(Mahadura Tinyana).*
Nov. = Novellae, Ḥiddushim.

Ohel Moshe (1), Notes to Talmud, *Midrash Rabbah,* Yad, *Sifrei* and to several Resp., by Eleazar *Horowitz.

Ohel Moshe (2), Resp. by Moses Jonah Zweig.
Oholei Tam. Resp. by *Tam ibn Yaḥya Jacob b. David; printed in the rabbinical collection *Tummat Yesharim.*
Oholei Ya'akov, Resp. by Jacob de *Castro.
Or ha-Me'ir Resp by Judah Meir b. Jacob Samson Shapiro.
Or Same'aḥ, Comm. to Maimonides, *Yad Ḥazakah,* by *Meir Simḥah ha-Kohen of Dvinsk; printed in many editions of the *Yad Ḥazakah.*
Or Zaru'a [the father] = *Isaac b. Moses of Vienna.
Or Zaru'a [the son] = *Ḥayyim (Eliezer) b. Isaac.
Or Zaru'a, Nov. by *Isaac b. Moses of Vienna.
Orah, Sefer ha-, Compilation of ritual precepts by *Rashi.
Oraḥ la-Ẓaddik, Resp. by Abraham Ḥayyim Rodrigues.
Oẓar ha-Posekim, Digest of Responsa.

Paḥad Yiẓḥak, Rabbinical encyclopaedia by Isaac *Lampronti.
Panim Me'irot, Resp. by Meir b. Isaac *Eisenstadt.
Parashat Mordekhai, Resp. by Mordecai b. Abraham Naphtali *Banet.
Pe'at ha-Sadeh la-Dinim and Pe'at ha-Sadeh la-Kelalim, subdivisions of the *Sedei Ḥemed,* an encyclopaedia of precepts and responsa, by Ḥayyim Hezekaih *Medini.
Penei Moshe (1), Resp. by Moses *Benveniste.
Penei Moshe (2), Comm. to Jer. Talmud by Moses b. Simeon *Margolies; printed in most editions of the Jer. Talmud.
Penei Moshe (3), Comm. on the aggadic passages of 18 treatises of the Bab. and Jer. Talmud, by Moses b. Isaiah Katz.
Penei Yehoshu'a, Nov. by Jacob Joshua b. Ẓevi Hirsch *Falk.
Peri Ḥadash, Comm. on Sh. Ar. By Hezekiah da *Silva.
Perishah, Comm. on Tur by Joshua b. Alexander ha-Kohen *Falk; printed in major edition of Tur; forms together with *Derishah* and *Be'urim* (by the same author) the *Beit Yisrael.*
Pesakim u-Khetavim, 2nd part of the *Terumat ha-Deshen* by Israel b. Pethahiah *Isserlein' also called *Piskei Maharai.*
Pilpula Ḥarifta, Comm. to *Piskei ha-Rosh, Seder Nezikin,* by Yom Tov Lipmann b. Nathan ha-Levi *Heller; printed in major editions of the Talmud.
Piskei Maharai, see *Terumat ha-Deshen,* 2nd part; also called *Pesakim u-Khetavim.*
Piskei ha-Rosh, a compilation of *halakhot,* arranged on the Talmud, by *Asher b. Jehiel (Rosh); printed in major Talmud editions.
Pitḥei Teshuvah, Comm. to Sh. Ar. by Abraham Hirsch b. Jacob *Eisenstadt; printed in major editions of the Sh. Ar.

Rabad = *Abraham b. David of Posquières (Rabad III.).
Raban = *Eliezer b. Nathan of Mainz.
Raban, also called *Ẓafenat Pa'ne'aḥ* or *Even ha-Ezer,* see under the last name.
Rabi Abad = *Abraham b. Isaac of Narbonne.
Radad = David Dov. b. Aryeh Judah Jacob *Meisels.
Radam = Dov Berush b. Isaac Meisels.
Radbaz = *David b Solomon ibn Abi Ziumra.
Radbaz, Comm. to Maimonides, *Yad Ḥazakah,* by *David b. Solomon ibn Abi Zimra.
Ralbag = *Levi b. Gershom, also called Gersonides, or Leo Hebraeus.
Ralbag, Bible comm. by *Levi b. Gershon.
Rama [da Fano] = Menaḥem Azariah *Fano.
Ramah = Meir b. Todros [ha-Levi] *Abulafia.
Ramam = *Menaham of Merseburg.
Rambam = *Maimonides; real name: Moses b. Maimon.
Ramban = *Naḥmanides; real name Moses b. Naḥman.
Ramban, Comm. to Torah by *Naḥmanides; printed in major editions. ("Mikra'ot Gedolot").
Ran = *Nissim b. Reuben Gerondi.
Ran of Rif, Comm. on Rif, *Halakhot,* by Nissim b. Reuben Gerondi.
Ranaḥ = *Elijah b. Ḥayyim.
Rash = *Samson b. Abraham of Sens.
Rash, Comm. to Mishnah, by *Samson b. Abraham of Sens; printed in major Talmud editions.
Rashash = Samuel *Strashun.
Rashba = Solomon b. Abraham *Adret.
Rashba, Resp., see also; *Sefer Teshuvot ha-Rashba ha-Meyuḥasot le-ha-Ramban,* by Solomon b. Abraham *Adret.
Rashbad = Samuel b. David.
Rashbam = *Samuel b. Meir.
Rashbam = Comm. on Bible and Talmud by *Samuel b. Meir; printed in major editions of Bible and most editions of Talmud.
Rashbash = Solomon b. Simeon *Duran.
*Rashi = Solomon b. Isaac of Troyes.
Rashi, Comm. on Bible and Talmud by *Rashi; printed in almost all Bible and Talmud editions.
Raviah = Eliezer b. Joel ha-Levi.
Redak = David *Kimḥi.
Redak, Comm. to Bible by David *Kimḥi.
Redakh = *David b. Ḥayyim ha-Kohen of Corfu.
Re'em = Elijah b. Abraham *Mizraḥi.
Rema = Moses b. Israel *Isserles.
Rema, Glosses to Sh. Ar. by Moses b. Israel *Isserles; printed in almost all editions of the Sh. Ar. inside the text in Rashi type; also called *Mappah* or *Haggahot.*
Remek = Moses Kimḥi.
Remakh = Moses ha-Kohen mi-Lunel.
Reshakh = *Solomon b. Abraham; also called Maharshakh.
Resp. = Responsa, *She'elot u-Teshuvot.*
Ri Berav = *Berab.
Ri Escapa = Joseph b. Saul *Escapa.
Ri Migash = Joseph b. Meir ha-Levi *Ibn Migash.
Riba = Isaac b. Asher ha-Levi; Riba II (Riba ha-Baḥur) = his grandson with the same name.
Ribam = Isaac b. Mordecai (or: Isaac b. Meir).
Ribash = *Isaac b. Sheshet Perfet (or: Barfat).
Rid= *Isaiah b. Mali di Trani the Elder.
Ridbaz = Jacob David b. Ze'ev *Willowski.
Rif = Isaac b. Jacob ha-Kohen *Alfasi.
Rif, *Halakhot,* Compilation and abstract of the Talmud by Isaac b. Jacob ha-Kohen *Alfasi.
Ritba = Yom Tov b. Abraham *Ishbili.
Riẓbam = Isaac b. Mordecai.
Rosh = *Asher b. Jehiel, also called Asheri.
Rosh Mashbir, Resp. by *Joseph Samuel b. Isaac, Rodi.

Sedei Ḥemed, Encyclopaedia of precepts and responsa by Ḥayyim Ḥezekiah *Medini; subdivisions: *Asefat Dinim, Kunteres ha-Kelalim, Pe'at ha-Sadeh la-Dinim, Pe'at ha-Sadeh la-Kelalim.*
Semag, Usual abbreviation of *Sefer Mitzvot Gadol,* elucidation of precepts by *Moses b. Jacob of Coucy; subdivided into *Lavin* (negative precepts) *Asayin* (positive precepts).
Semak, Usual abbreviation of *Sefer Mitzvot Katan,* elucidation of precepts by *Isaac b. Joseph of Corbeil.

Sh. Ar. = *Shulḥan Arukh*, code by Joseph b. Ephraim *Caro.
Sha'ar Mishpat, Comm. to Sh. Ar., ḤM. By Israel Isser b. Ze'ev Wolf.
Sha'arei Shevu'ot, Treatise on the law of oaths by *David b. Saadiah; usually printed together with Rif, *Halakhot;* also called: *She'arim of R. Alfasi.*
Sha'arei Teshuvah, Collection of resp. from Geonic period, by different authors.
Sha'arei Uzzi'el, Rabbinical treatise by Ben-Zion Meir Ha *Ouziel.
Sha'arei Ẓedek, Collection of resp. from Geonic period, by different authors.
Shadal [or Shedal] = Samuel David *Luzzatto.
Shai la-Moreh, Resp. by Shabbetai Jonah.
Shakh, Usual abbreviation of *Siftei Kohen*, a comm. to Sh. Ar., YD and ḤM by *Shabbetai b. Meir ha-Kohen; printed in most editions of Sh. Ar.
Sha'ot-de-Rabbanan, Resp. by *Solomon b. Judah ha-Kohen.
She'arim of R. Alfasi see *Sha'arei Shevu'ot.*
Shedal, see Shadal.
She'elot u-Teshuvot ha-Ge'onim, Collection of resp. by different authors.
She'erit Yisrael, Resp. by Israel Ze'ev Mintzberg.
She'erit Yosef, Resp. by *Joseph b. Mordecai Gershon ha-Kohen.
She'ilat Yaveẓ, Resp. by Jacob *Emden (Yaveẓ).
She'iltot, Compilation arranged acc. to the Torah by *Aḥa (Aḥai) of Shabḥa.
Shem Aryeh, Resp. by Aryeh Leib *Lipschutz.
Shemesh Ẓedakah, Resp. by Samson *Morpurgo.
Shenei ha-Me'orot ha-Gedolim, Resp. by Elijah *Covo.
Shetarot, Sefer ha-, Collection of legal forms by *Judah b. Barzillai al-Bargeloni.
Shevut Ya'akov, Resp. by Jacob b. Joseph Reicher.
Shibbolei ha-Leket Compilation on ritual by Zedekiah b. Avraham *Anav.
Shiltei Gibborim, Comm. to Rif, *Halakhot*, by *Joshua Boaz b. Simeon; printed in major editions of the Talmud.
Shittah Mekubbeẓet, Compilation of talmudical commentaries by Bezalel *Ashkenazi.
Shivat Ẓiyyon, Resp. by Samuel b. Ezekiel *Landau.
Shiyyurei Korban, by David *Fraenkel; additions to his comm. to Jer. Talmud *Korban Edah;* both printed in most editions of Jer. Talmud.
Sho'el u-Meshiv, Resp. by Joseph Saul ha-Levi *Nathanson.
Sh[ulḥan] Ar[ukh] [of Ba'al ha-Tanya], Code by *Shneur Zalman of Lyady; not identical with the code by Joseph Caro.
Siftei Kohen, Comm. to Sh. Ar., YD and ḤM by *Shabbetai b. Meir ha-Kohen; printed in most editions of Sh. Ar.; usual abbreviation: *Shakh.*
Simḥat Yom Tov, Resp. by Tom Tov b. Jacob *Algazi.
Simlah Ḥadashah, Treatise on *Sheḥitah* by Alexander Sender b. Ephraim Zalman *Schor; see also *Tevu'ot Shor.*
Simeon b. Ẓemaḥ = Simeon b. Ẓemaḥ *Duran.
Sma, Comm. to Sh. Ar. by Joshua b. Alexander ha-Kohen *Falk; the full title is: *Sefer Me'irat Einayim;* printed in most editions of Sh. Ar.
Solomon b. Isaac ha-Levi = Solomon b. Isaac *Levy.
Solomon b. Isaac of Troyes = *Rashi.

Tal Orot, Rabbinical work with various contents, by Joseph ibn Gioia.
Tam, Rabbenu = *Tam Jacob b. Meir.
Tashbaẓ = Samson b. Zadok.
Tashbeẓ = Simeon b. Zemaḥ *Duran, sometimes also abbreviation for Samson b. Zadok, usually known as Tashbaẓ.
Tashbeẓ [Sefer ha-], Resp. by Simeon b. Ẓemaḥ *Duran; the fourth part of this work is called: *Ḥut ha-Meshullash.*
Taz, Usual abbreviation of *Turei Zahav*, comm., to Sh. Ar. by *David b. Samnuel ha-Levi; printed in most editions of Sh. Ar.
(Ha)-Tekhelet, subdivision of the *Levush* (a codification by Mordecai b. Abraham (Levush) *Jaffe); *Ha-Tekhelet* parallels Tur, OḤ 1-241.
Terumat ha-Deshen, by Israel b. Pethahiah *Isserlein; subdivided into a part containing responsa, and a second part called *Pesakim u-Khetavim* or *Piskei Maharai.*
Terumot, Sefer ha-, Compilation of *halakhot* by Samuel b. Isaac *Sardi.
Teshuvot Ba'alei ha-Tosafot, Collection of responsa by the Tosafists.
Teshjvot Ge'onei Mizraḥ u-Ma'aav, Collection of responsa.
Teshuvot ha-Geonim, Collection of responsa from Geonic period.
Teshuvot Ḥakhmei Provinẓyah, Collection of responsa by different Provencal authors.
Teshuvot Ḥakhmei Ẓarefat ve-Loter, Collection of responsa by different French authors.
Teshuvot Maimuniyyot, Resp. pertaining to Maimonides' *Yad Ḥazakah;* printed in major editions of this work after the text; authorship uncertain.
Tevu'ot Shor, by Alexander Sender b. Ephraim Zalman *Schor, a comm. to his *Simlah Ḥadashah*, a work on *Sheḥitah.*
Tiferet Ẓevi, Resp. by Ẓevi Hirsch of the "AHW" Communities (Altona, Hamburg, Wandsbeck).
Tiktin, Judah b. Simeon = Judah b. Simeon *Ashkenazi.
Toledot Adam ve-Ḥavvah, Codification by *Jeroham b. Meshullam.
Torat Emet, Resp. by Aaron b. Joseph *Sasson.
Torat Ḥayyim, , Resp. by Ḥayyim (ben) Shabbetai.
Torat ha-Minhagot, subdivision of the *Massa Ḥayyim* (a work on tax law) by Ḥayyim *Palaggi, containing an exposition of customary law.
Tosafot Rid, Explanations to the Talmud and decisions by *Isaiah b. Mali di Trani the Elder.
Tosefot Yom Tov, comm. to Mishnah by Yom Tov Lipmann b. Nathan ha-Levi *Heller; printed in most editions of the Mishnah.
Tummim, subdivision of the comm. to Sh. Ar., ḤM, *Urim ve-Tummim* by Jonathan *Eybeschuetz; printed in the major editions of Sh. Ar.
Tur, usual abbreviation for the *Arba'ah Turim* of *Jacob b. Asher.
Turei Zahav, Comm. to Sh. Ar. by *David b. Samuel ha-Levi; printed in most editions of Sh. Ar.; usual abbreviation: *Taz.*

Urim, subdivision of the following.
Urim ve-Tummim, Comm. to Sh. Ar., ḤM, by Jonathan *Eybeschuetz; printed in the major editions of Sh. Ar.; subdivided in places into *Urim* and *Tummim.*

Vikku'aḥ Mayim Ḥayyim, Polemics against Isserles and Caro by Ḥayyim b. Bezalel.

Yad Malakhi, Methodological treatise by *Malachi b. Jacob ha-Kohen.

Yad Ramah, Nov. by Meir b. Todros [ha-Levi] *Abulafia.
Yakhin u-Vo'az, Resp. by Ẓemaḥ b. Solomon *Duran.
Yam ha-Gadol, Resp. by Jacob Moses *Toledano.
Yam shel Shelomo, Compilation arranged acc. to Talmud by Solomon b. Jehiel (Maharshal) *Luria.
Yashar, Sefer ha-, by *Tam, Jacob b. Meir (Rabbenu Tam); 1st pt.: Resp.; 2nd pt.: Nov.
Yaskil Avdi, Resp. by Obadiah Hadaya (printed together with his Resp. *De'ah ve-Haskel).*
Yaveẓ = Jacob *Emden.
Yehudah Ya'aleh, Resp. by Judah b. Israel *Aszod.
Yekar Tiferet, Comm. to Maimonides' *Yad Ḥazakah,*by David b. Solomon ibn Zimra, printed in most editions of *Yad Ḥazakah.*
Yere'im [*ha-Shalem*], [*Sefer*], Treatise on precepts by *Eliezer b. Samuel of Metz.
Yeshu'ot Ya'akov, Resp. by Jacob Meshullam b. Mordecai Ze'ev *Ornstein.
Yiẓhak Rei'aḥ, Resp. by Isaac b. Samuel Abendanan (see article *Abendanam Family).
Ẓafenat Pa'ne'aḥ (1), also called *Raban* or *Even ha-Ezer*, see under the last name.
Ẓafenat Pa'ne'aḥ (2), Resp. by Joseph *Rozin.
Zayit Ra'anan, Resp. by Moses Judah Leib b. Benjamin Auerbach.
Ẓeidah la-Derekh, Codification by *Menahem b. Aaron ibn Zerah.
Ẓedakah u-Mishpat, Resp. by Ẓedakah b. Saadiah Huẓin.
Zekan Aharon, Resp. by Elijah b. Benjamin ha-Levi.
Zekher Ẓaddik, Sermons by Eliezer *Katzenellenbogen.
Ẓemaḥ Ẓedek (1) Resp. by Menaham Mendel Shneersohn (see under *Shneersohn Family).
Zera Avraham, Resp. by Abraham b. David *Yiẓḥaki.
Zera Emet Resp. by *Ishmael b. Abaham Isaac ha-Kohen.
Ẓevi la-Ẓaddik, Resp. by Ẓevi Elimelech b. David Shapira.
Zikhron Yehudah, Resp. by *Judah b. Asher
Zikhron Yosef, Resp. by Joseph b. Menahem *Steinhardt.
Zikhronot, Sefer ha-, Sermons on several precepts by Samuel *Aboab.
Zikkaron la-Rishonim . . ., by Albert (Abraham Elijah) *Harkavy; contains in vol. 1 pt. 4 (1887) a collection of Geonic responsa.
Ẓiẓ Eliezer, Resp. by Eliezer Judah b. Jacob Gedaliah Waldenberg.

BIBLIOGRAPHICAL ABBREVIATIONS

Bibliographies in English and other languages have been extensively updated, with English translations cited where available. In order to help the reader, the language of books or articles is given where not obvious from titles of books or names of periodicals. Titles of books and periodicals in languages with alphabets other than Latin, are given in transliteration, even where there is a title page in English. Titles of articles in periodicals are not given. Names of Hebrew and Yiddish periodicals well known in English-speaking countries or in Israel under their masthead in Latin characters are given in this form, even when contrary to transliteration rules. Names of authors writing in languages with non-Latin alphabets are given in their Latin alphabet form wherever known; otherwise the names are transliterated. Initials are generally not given for authors of articles in periodicals, except to avoid confusion. Non-abbreviated book titles and names of periodicals are printed in *italics.* Abbreviations are given in the list below.

AASOR	*Annual of the American School of Oriental Research* (1919ff.).
AB	*Analecta Biblica* (1952ff.).
Abel, Géog	F.-M. Abel, *Géographie de la Palestine,* 2 vols. (1933-38).
ABR	*Australian Biblical Review* (1951ff.).
Abr.	Philo, *De Abrahamo.*
Abrahams, Companion	I. Abrahams, *Companion to the Authorised Daily Prayer Book* (rev. ed. 1922).
Abramson, Merkazim	S. Abramson, *Ba-Merkazim u-va-Tefuẓot bi-Tekufat ha-Ge'onim* (1965).
Acts	Acts of the Apostles (New Testament).
ACUM	*Who is who in ACUM* [*Aguddat Kompozitorim u-Meḥabbrim*].
ADAJ	*Annual of the Department of Antiquities, Jordan* (1951ff.).
Adam	Adam and Eve (Pseudepigrapha).
ADB	*Allgemeine Deutsche Biographie,* 56 vols. (1875–1912).
Add. Esth.	The Addition to Esther (Apocrypha).
Adler, Prat Mus	1. Adler, *La pratique musicale savante dans quelques communautés juives en Europe au XVIIe et XVIIIe siècles,* 2 vols. (1966).
Adler-Davis	H.M. Adler and A. Davis (ed. and tr.), *Service of the Synagogue, a New Edition of the Festival Prayers with an English Translation in Prose and Verse,* 6 vols. (1905–06).
Aet.	Philo, *De Aeternitate Mundi.*
AFO	*Archiv fuer Orientforschung* (first two volumes under the name *Archiv fuer Keilschriftforschung)* (1923ff.).
Ag. Ber	*Aggadat Bereshit* (ed. Buber, 1902).
Agr.	Philo, *De Agricultura.*
Ag. Sam.	*Aggadat Samuel.*
Ag. Song	*Aggadat Shir ha-Shirim* (Schechter ed., 1896).
Aharoni, Ereẓ	Y. Aharoni, *Ereẓ Yisrael bi-Tekufat ha-Mikra: Geografyah Historit* (1962).
Aharoni, Land	Y. Aharoni, *Land of the Bible* (1966).

Ahikar	Ahikar (Pseudepigrapha).
AI	*Archives Israélites de France* (1840–1936).
AJA	*American Jewish Archives* (1948ff.).
AJHSP	*American Jewish Historical Society – Publications* (after vol. 50 = AJHSQ).
AJHSQ	*American Jewish Historical (Society) Quarterly* (before vol. 50 =AJHSP).
AJSLL	*American Journal of Semitic Languages and Literature* (1884–95 under the title *Hebraica,* since 1942 JNES).
AJYB	*American Jewish Year Book* (1899ff.).
AKM	Abhandlungen fuer die Kunde des Morgenlandes (series).
Albright, Arch	W.F. Albright, *Archaeology of Palestine* (rev. ed. 1960).
Albright, Arch Bib	W.F. Albright, *Archaeology of Palestine and the Bible* (1935^{3}).
Albright, Arch Rel	W.F. Albright, *Archaeology and the Religion of Israel* (1953^{3}).
Albright, Stone	W.F. Albright, *From the Stone Age to Christianity* (1957^{2}).
Alon, Meḥkarim	G. Alon, *Meḥkarim be-Toledot Yisrael bi-Ymei Bayit Sheni u-vi-Tekufat ha-Mishnah ve-ha Talmud,* 2 vols. (1957–58).
Alon, Toledot	G. Alon, *Toledot ha-Yehudim be-Ereẓ Yisrael bi-Tekufat ha-Mishnah ve-ha-Talmud,* I (1958^{3}), (1961^{2}).
ALOR	Alter Orient (series).
Alt, Kl Schr	A. Alt, *Kleine Schriften zur Geschichte des Volkes Israel,* 3 vols. (1953–59).
Alt, Landnahme	A. Alt, *Landnahme der Israeliten in Palaestina* (1925); also in Alt, Kl Schr, 1 (1953), 89–125.
Ant.	Josephus, *Jewish Antiquities* (Loeb Classics ed.).
AO	*Acta Orientalia* (1922ff.).
AOR	*Analecta Orientalia* (1931ff.).
AOS	American Oriental Series.
Apion	Josephus, *Against Apion* (Loeb Classics ed.).
Aq.	Aquila's Greek translation of the Bible.
Ar.	*Arakhin* (talmudic tractate).
Artist.	Letter of Aristeas (Pseudepigrapha).
ARN^{1}	*Avot de-Rabbi Nathan,* version (1) ed. Schechter, 1887.
ARN^{2}	*Avot de-Rabbi Nathan,* version (2) ed. Schechter, 1945^{2}.
Aronius, Regesten	I. Aronius, *Regesten zur Geschichte der Juden im fraenkischen und deutschen Reiche bis zum Jahre 1273* (1902).
ARW	*Archiv fuer Religionswissenschaft* (1898–1941/42).
AS	*Assyrological Studies* (1931ff.).
Ashtor, Korot	E. Ashtor (Strauss), *Korot ha-Yehudim bi-Sefarad ha-Muslemit,* 1(1966^{2}), 2(1966).
Ashtor, Toledot	E. Ashtor (Strauss), *Toledot ha-Yehudim be-Miẓrayim ve-Suryah Taḥat Shilton ha-Mamlukim,* 3 vols. (1944–70).
Assaf, Ge'onim	S. Assaf, *Tekufat ha-Ge'onim ve-Sifrutah* (1955).

Assaf, Mekorot	S. Assaf, *Mekorot le-Toledot ha-Ḥinnukh be-Yisrael,* 4 vols. (1925–43).
Ass. Mos.	Assumption of Moses (Pseudepigrapha).
ATA	Alttestamentliche Abhandlungen (series).
ATANT	Abhandlungen zur Theologie des Alten und Neuen Testaments (series).
AUJW	*Allgemeine unabhaengige juedische Wochenzeitung* (till 1966 = AWJD).
AV	Authorized Version of the Bible.
Avad.	*Avadim* (post-talmudic tractate).
Avi-Yonah, Geog	M. Avi-Yonah, *Geografyah Historit shel Ereẓ Yisrael* (1962^{3}).
Avi-Yonah, Land	M. Avi-Yonah, *The Holy Land from the Persian to the Arab conquest (536 B.C. to A.D. 640)* (1960).
Avot	*Avot* (talmudic tractate).
Av. Zar.	*Avodah Zarah* (talmudic tractate).
AWJD	*Allgemeine Wochenzeitung der Juden in Deutschland* (since 1967 = AUJW).
AZDJ	*Allgemeine Zeitung des Judentums.*
Azulai	Ḥ.Y.D. Azulai, *Shem ha-Gedolim,* ed. by I.E. Benjacob, 2 pts. (1852) (and other editions).
BA	*Biblical Archaeologist* (1938ff.).
Bacher, Bab Amor	W. Bacher, *Agada der babylonischen Amoraeer* (1913^{2}).
Bacher, Pal Amor	W. Bacher, *Agada der palaestinensischen Amoraeer* (Heb. ed. *Aggadat Amora'ei Ereẓ Yisrael),* 2 vols. (1892–99).
Bacher, Tann	W. Bacher, *Agada der Tannaiten* (Heb. ed. *Aggadot ha-Tanna'im,* vol. 1, pt. 1 and 2 (1903); vol. 2 (1890).
Bacher, Trad	W. Bacher, *Tradition und Tradenten in den Schulen Palaestinas und Babyloniens* (1914).
Baer, Spain	Yitzhak (Fritz) Baer, *History of the Jews in Christian Spain,* 2 vols. (1961–66).
Baer, Studien	Yitzhak (Fritz) Baer, *Studien zur Geschichte der Juden im Koenigreich Aragonien waehrend des 13. und 14. Jahrhunderts* (1913).
Baer, Toledot	Yitzhak (Fritz) Baer, *Toledot ha-Yehudim bi-Sefarad ha-Noẓerit mi-Teḥillatan shel ha-Kehillot ad ha-Gerush,* 2 vols. (1959^{2}).
Baer, Urkunden	Yitzhak (Fritz) Baer, *Die Juden im christlichen Spanien,* 2 vols. (1929–36).
Baer S., Seder	S.I. Baer, *Seder Avodat Yisrael* (1868 and reprints).
BAIU	*Bulletin de l'Alliance Israélite Universelle* (1861–1913).
Baker, Biog Dict	*Baker's Biographical Dictionary of Musicians,* revised by N. Slonimsky (1958^{5}; with Supplement 1965).
I Bar.	I Baruch (Apocrypha).
II Bar.	II Baruch (Pseudepigrapha).
III Bar.	III Baruch (Pseudepigrapha).
BAR	*Biblical Archaeology Review.*
Baron, Community	S.W. Baron, *The Jewish Community, its History and Structure to the American Revolution,* 3 vols. (1942).

Baron, Social	S.W. Baron, *Social and Religious History of the Jews,* 3 vols. (1937); enlarged, 1-2(1952^{2}), 3-14 (1957–69).
Barthélemy-Milik	D. Barthélemy and J.T. Milik, *Dead Sea Scrolls: Discoveries in the Judean Desert,* vol. 1 *Qumram Cave* I (1955).
BASOR	*Bulletin of the American School of Oriental Research.*
Bauer-Leander	H. Bauer and P. Leander, *Grammatik des Biblisch-Aramaeischen* (1927; repr. 1962).
BB	(1) *Bava Batra* (talmudic tractate). (2) *Biblische Beitraege* (1943ff.).
BBB	Bonner biblische Beitraege (series).
BBLA	*Beitraege zur biblischen Landes- und Altertumskunde* (until 1949 ZDPV).
BBSAJ	*Bulletin,* British School of Archaeology, Jerusalem (1922–25; after 1927 included in PEFQS).
BDASI	*Alon* (since 1948) or *Hadashot Arkhe'ologiyyot* (since 1961), bulletin of the Department of Antiquities of the State of Israel.
Begrich, Chronologie	J. Begrich, *Chronologie der Koenige von Israel und Juda* (1929).
Bek.	*Bekhorot* (talmudic tractate).
Bel	Bel and the Dragon (Apocrypha).
Benjacob, Oẓar	I.E. Benjacob, *Oẓar ha-Sefarim* (1880; repr. 1956).
Ben Sira	see Ecclus.
Ben-Yehuda, Millon	E. Ben-Yedhuda, *Millon ha-Lashon ha-Ivrit,* 16 vols (1908–59; repr. in 8 vols., 1959).
Benzinger, Archaeologie	I. Benzinger, *Hebraeische Archaeologie* (1927^{3}).
Ben Zvi, Eretz Israel	I. Ben-Zvi, *Eretz Israel under Ottoman Rule* (1960; offprint from L. Finkelstein (ed.), *The Jews, their History, Culture and Religion* (vol. 1).
Ben Zvi, Ereẓ Israel	I. Ben-Zvi, *Ereẓ Israel bi-Ymei ha-Shilton ha-Ottomani (1955).*
Ber.	*Berakhot* (talmudic tractate).
Beẓah	*Beẓah* (talmudic tractate).
BIES	Bulletin of the Israel Exploration Society, see below BJPES.
Bik.	*Bikkurim* (talmudic tractate).
BJCE	Bibliography of Jewish Communities in Europe, catalog at General Archives for the History of the Jewish People, Jerusalem.
BJPES	Bulletin of the Jewish Palestine Exploration Society – English name of the Hebrew periodical known as: 1. *Yedi'ot ha-Ḥevrah ha-Ivrit la-Ḥakirat Ereẓ Yisrael va-Attikoteha* (1933–1954); 2. *Yedi'ot ha-Ḥevrah la-Ḥakirat Ereẓ Yisrael va-Attikoteha* (1954–1962); 3. *Yedi'ot ba-Ḥakirat Ereẓ Yisrael va-Attikoteha* (1962ff.).
BJRL	*Bulletin of the John Rylands Library* (1914ff.).
BK	*Bava Kamma* (talmudic tractate).
BLBI	*Bulletin of the Leo Baeck Institute* (1957ff.).
BM	(1) *Bava Meẓia* (talmudic tractate). (2) *Beit Mikra* (1955/56ff.). (3) British Museum.
BO	*Bibbia e Oriente* (1959ff.).
Bondy-Dworský	G. Bondy and F. Dworský, *Regesten zur Geschichte der Juden in Boehmen, Maehren und Schlesien von 906 bis 1620,* 2 vols. (1906).
BOR	*Bibliotheca Orientalis* (1943ff.).
Borée, Ortsnamen	W. Borée *Die alten Ortsnamen Palaestinas* (1930).
Bousset, Religion	W. Bousset, *Die Religion des Judentums im neutestamentlichen Zeitalter* (1906^{2}).
Bousset-Gressmann	W. Bousset, *Die Religion des Judentums im spaethellenistischen Zeitalter* (1966^{3}).
BR	*Biblical Review* (1916–25).
BRCI	*Bulletin of the Research Council of Israel* (1951/52–1954/55; then divided).
BRE	*Biblical Research* (1956ff.).
BRF	*Bulletin of the Rabinowitz Fund for the Exploration of Ancient Synagogues* (1949ff.).
Briggs, Psalms	Ch. A. and E.G. Briggs, *Critical and Exegetical Commentary on the Book of Psalms,* 2 vols. (ICC, 1906–07).
Bright, Hist	J. Bright, *A History of Israel* (1959).
Brockelmann, Arab Lit	K. Brockelmann, *Geschichte der arabischen Literatur,* 2 vols. 1898–1902), supplement, 3 vols. (1937–42).
Bruell, Jahrbuecher	*Jahrbuecher fuer juedische Geschichte und Litteratur,* ed. by N. Bruell, Frankfurt (1874–90).
Brugmans-Frank	H. Brugmans and A. Frank (eds.), *Geschiedenis der Joden in Nederland* (1940).
BTS	*Bible et Terre Sainte* (1958ff.).
Bull, Index	S. Bull, *Index to Biographies of Contemporary Composers* (1964).
BW	*Biblical World* (1882–1920).
BWANT	*Beitraege zur Wissenschaft vom Alten und Neuen Testament* (1926ff.).
BZ	*Biblische Zeitschrift* (1903ff.).
BZAW	*Beihefte zur Zeitschrift fuer die alttestamentliche Wissenschaft,* supplement to ZAW (1896ff.).
BŻIH	*Biuletyn Zydowskiego Instytutu Historycznego* (1950ff.).
CAB	*Cahiers d'archéologie biblique* (1953ff.).
CAD	*The* [*Chicago*] *Assyrian Dictionary* (1956ff.).
CAH	*Cambridge Ancient History,* 12 vols. (1923–39)
CAH^{2}	*Cambridge Ancient History,* second edition, 14 vols. (1962–2005).
Calwer, Lexikon	*Calwer, Bibellexikon.*
Cant.	Canticles, usually given as Song (= Song of Songs).

Cantera-Millás, Inscripciones	F. Cantera and J.M. Millás, *Las Inscripciones Hebraicas de España* (1956).
CBQ	*Catholic Biblical Quarterly* (1939ff.).
CCARY	Central Conference of American Rabbis, *Yearbook* (1890/91ff.).
CD	*Damascus Document* from the Cairo *Genizah* (published by S. Schechter, *Fragments of a Zadokite Work*, 1910).
Charles, Apocrypha	R.H. Charles, *Apocrypha and Pseudepigrapha . . .*, 2 vols. (1913; repr. 1963–66).
Cher.	Philo, *De Cherubim.*
I (or II) Chron.	Chronicles, book I and II (Bible).
CIG	*Corpus Inscriptionum Graecarum.*
CIJ	*Corpus Inscriptionum Judaicarum,* 2 vols. (1936–52).
CIL	*Corpus Inscriptionum Latinarum.*
CIS	*Corpus Inscriptionum Semiticarum* (1881ff.).
C.J.	Codex Justinianus.
Clermont-Ganneau, Arch	Ch. Clermont-Ganneau, *Archaeological Researches in Palestine*, 2 vols. (1896–99).
CNFI	*Christian News from Israel* (1949ff.).
Cod. Just.	Codex Justinianus.
Cod. Theod.	Codex Theodosinanus.
Col.	Epistle to the Colosssians (New Testament).
Conder, Survey	Palestine Exploration Fund, *Survey of Eastern Palestine*, vol. 1, pt. I (1889) = C.R. Conder, *Memoirs of the . . . Survey.*
Conder-Kitchener	Palestine Exploration Fund, *Survey of Western Palestine*, vol. 1, pts. 1-3 (1881–83) = C.R. Conder and H.H. Kitchener, *Memoirs.*
Conf.	Philo, *De Confusione Linguarum.*
Conforte, Kore	D. Conforte, *Kore ha-Dorot* (1842²).
Cong.	Philo, *De Congressu Quaerendae Eruditionis Gratia.*
Cont.	Philo, *De Vita Contemplativa.*
I (or II) Cor.	Epistles to the Corinthians (New Testament).
Cowley, Aramic	A. Cowley, *Aramaic Papyri of the Fifth Century B.C.* (1923).
Colwey, Cat	A.E. Cowley, *A Concise Catalogue of the Hebrew Printed Books in the Bodleian Library* (1929).
CRB	*Cahiers de la Revue Biblique* (1964ff.).
Crowfoot-Kenyon	J.W. Crowfoot, K.M. Kenyon and E.L. Sukenik, *Buildings of Samaria* (1942).
C.T.	Codex Theodosianus.
DAB	*Dictionary of American Biography* (1928–58).
Daiches, Jews	S. Daiches, *Jews in Babylonia* (1910).
Dalman, Arbeit	G. Dalman, *Arbeit und Sitte in Palaestina*, 7 vols.in 8 (1928–42 repr. 1964).
Dan	Daniel (Bible).
Davidson, Oẓar	I. Davidson, *Oẓar ha-Shirah ve-ha-Piyyut*, 4 vols. (1924–33); Supplement in: HUCA, 12–13 (1937/38), 715–823.
DB	J. Hastings, *Dictionary of the Bible*, 4 vols. (1963²).
DBI	F.G. Vigoureaux et al. (eds.), *Dictionnaire de la Bible*, 5 vols. in 10 (1912); Supplement, 8 vols. (1928–66)
Decal.	Philo, *De Decalogo.*
Dem.	*Demai* (talmudic tractate).
DER	*Derekh Ereẓ Rabbah* (post-talmudic tractate).
Derenbourg, Hist	J. Derenbourg *Essai sur l'histoire et la géographie de la Palestine* (1867).
Det.	Philo, *Quod deterius potiori insidiari solet.*
Deus	Philo, *Quod Deus immutabilis sit.*
Deut.	Deuteronomy (Bible).
Deut. R.	*Deuteronomy Rabbah.*
DEZ	*Derekh Ereẓ Zuta* (post-talmudic tractate).
DHGE	*Dictionnaire d'histoire et de géographie ecclésiastiques*, ed. by A. Baudrillart et al., 17 vols (1912–68).
Dik. Sof	*Dikdukei Soferim*, variae lections of the talmudic text by Raphael Nathan Rabbinovitz (16 vols., 1867–97).
Dinur, Golah	B. Dinur (Dinaburg), *Yisrael ba-Golah*, 2 vols. in 7 (1959–68) = vols. 5 and 6 of his *Toledot Yisrael*, second series.
Dinur, Haganah	B. Dinur (ed.), *Sefer Toledot ha-Haganah* (1954ff.).
Diringer, Iscr	D. Diringer, *Iscrizioni antico-ebraiche palestinesi* (1934).
Discoveries	*Discoveries in the Judean Desert* (1955ff.).
DNB	*Dictionary of National Biography*, 66 vols. (1921–222) with Supplements.
Dubnow, Divrei	S. Dubnow, *Divrei Yemei Am Olam*, 11 vols (1923–38 and further editions).
Dubnow, Ḥasidut	S. Dubnow, *Toledot ha-Ḥasidut* (1960²).
Dubnow, Hist	S. Dubnow, *History of the Jews* (1967).
Dubnow, Hist Russ	S. Dubnow, *History of the Jews in Russia and Poland*, 3 vols. (1916 20).
Dubnow, Outline	S. Dubnow, *An Outline of Jewish History*, 3 vols. (1925–29).
Dubnow, Weltgesch	S. Dubnow, *Weltgeschichte des juedischen Volkes* 10 vols. (1925–29).
Dukes, Poesie	L. Dukes, *Zur Kenntnis der neuhebraeischen religioesen Poesie* (1842).
Dunlop, Khazars	D. H. Dunlop, *History of the Jewish Khazars* (1954).
EA	El Amarna Letters (edited by J.A. Knudtzon), *Die El-Amarna Tafel*, 2 vols. (1907 14).
EB	*Encyclopaedia Britannica.*
EBI	*Estudios biblicos* (1941ff.).
EBIB	T.K. Cheyne and J.S. Black, *Encyclopaedia Biblica*, 4 vols. (1899–1903).
Ebr.	Philo, *De Ebrietate.*
Eccles.	Ecclesiastes (Bible).
Eccles. R.	*Ecclesiastes Rabbah.*
Ecclus.	Ecclesiasticus or Wisdom of Ben Sira (or Sirach; Apocrypha).
Eduy.	*Eduyyot* (mishanic tractate).

EG	*Enziklopedyah shel Galuyyot* (1953ff.).
EH	*Even ha-Ezer.*
EHA	*Enziklopedyah la-Ḥafirot Arkheologiyyot be-Ereẓ Yisrael,* 2 vols. (1970).
EI	*Enzyklopaedie des Islams,* 4 vols. (1905–14). Supplement vol. (1938).
EIS	*Encyclopaedia of Islam,* 4 vols. (1913–36; repr. 1954–68).
EIS^{2}	*Encyclopaedia of Islam, second edition (1960–2000).*
Eisenstein, Dinim	J.D. Eisenstein, *Oẓar Dinim u-Minhagim* (1917; several reprints).
Eisenstein, Yisrael	J.D. Eisenstein, *Oẓar Yisrael* (10 vols, 1907–13; repr. with several additions 1951).
EIV	*Enziklopedyah Ivrit* (1949ff.).
EJ	*Encyclopaedia Judaica* (German, A-L only), 10 vols. (1928–34).
EJC	*Enciclopedia Judaica Castellana,* 10 vols. (1948–51).
Elbogen, Century	I Elbogen, *A Century of Jewish Life* (1960^{2}).
Elbogen, Gottesdienst	I Elbogen, *Der juedische Gottesdienst ...* (1931^{3}, repr. 1962).
Elon, Mafte'aḥ	M. Elon (ed.), *Mafte'aḥ ha-She'elot ve-ha-Teshuvot ha-Rosh* (1965).
EM	*Enziklopedyah Mikra'it* (1950ff.).
I (or II) En.	I and II Enoch (Pseudepigrapha).
EncRel	*Encyclopedia of Religion,* 15 vols. (1987, 2005^{2}).
Eph.	Epistle to the Ephesians (New Testament).
Ephros, Cant	G. Ephros, *Cantorial Anthology,* 5 vols. (1929–57).
Ep. Jer.	Epistle of Jeremy (Apocrypha).
Epstein, Amora'im	J N. Epstein, *Mevo'ot le-Sifrut ha-Amora'im* (1962).
Epstein, Marriage	L M. Epstein, *Marriage Laws in the Bible and the Talmud* (1942).
Epstein, Mishnah	J. N. Epstein, *Mavo le-Nusaḥ ha-Mishnah,* 2 vols. (1964^{2}).
Epstein, Tanna'im	J. N. Epstein, *Mavo le-Sifruth ha-Tanna'im.* (1947).
ER	*Ecumenical Review.*
Er.	*Eruvin* (talmudic tractate).
ERE	*Encyclopaedia of Religion and Ethics,* 13 vols. (1908–26); reprinted.
ErIsr	*Eretz-Israel,* Israel Exploration Society.
I Esd.	I Esdras (Apocrypha) (= III Ezra).
II Esd.	II Esdras (Apocrypha) (= IV Ezra).
ESE	*Ephemeris fuer semitische Epigraphik,* ed. by M. Lidzbarski.
ESN	*Encyclopaedia Sefaradica Neerlandica,* 2 pts. (1949).
ESS	*Encyclopaedia of the Social Sciences,* 15 vols. (1930–35); reprinted in 8 vols. (1948–49).
Esth.	Esther (Bible).
Est. R.	*Esther Rabbah.*
ET	*Enziklopedyah Talmudit* (1947ff.).
Eusebius, Onom.	E. Klostermann (ed.), *Das Onomastikon* (1904), Greek with Hieronymus' Latin translation.
Ex.	Exodus (Bible).
Ex. R.	*Exodus Rabbah.*
Exs	Philo, *De Exsecrationibus.*
EẒD	*Enziklopeday shel ha-Ẓiyyonut ha-Datit* (1951ff.).
Ezek.	Ezekiel (Bible).
Ezra	Ezra (Bible).
III Ezra	III Ezra (Pseudepigrapha).
IV Ezra	IV Ezra (Pseudepigrapha).
Feliks, Ha-Ẓome'aḥ	*J. Feliks, Ha-Ẓome'aḥ ve-ha-Ḥai ba-Mishnah* (1983).
Finkelstein, Middle Ages	L. Finkelstein, *Jewish Self-Government in the Middle Ages* (1924).
Fischel, Islam	W.J. Fischel, *Jews in the Economic and Political Life of Mediaeval Islam* (1937; reprint with introduction "The Court Jew in the Islamic World," 1969).
FJW	*Fuehrer durch die juedische Gemeindeverwaltung und Wohlfahrtspflege in Deutschland* (1927/28).
Frankel, Mevo	Z. Frankel, *Mevo ha-Yerushalmi* (1870; reprint 1967).
Frankel, Mishnah	Z. Frankel, *Darkhei ha-Mishnah* (1959^{2}; reprint 1959^{2}).
Frazer, Folk-Lore	J.G. Frazer, *Folk-Lore in the Old Testament,* 3 vols. (1918–19).
Frey, Corpus	J.-B. Frey, *Corpus Inscriptionum Iudaicarum,* 2 vols. (1936–52).
Friedmann, Lebensbilder	A. Friedmann, *Lebensbilder beruehmter Kantoren,* 3 vols. (1918–27).
FRLT	*Forschungen zur Religion und Literatur des Alten und Neuen Testaments* (series) (1950ff.).
Frumkin-Rivlin	A.L. Frumkin and E. Rivlin, *Toledot Ḥakhmei Yerushalayim,* 3 vols. (1928–30), Supplement vol. (1930).
Fuenn, Keneset	S.J. Fuenn, *Keneset Yisrael,* 4 vols. (1887–90).
Fuerst, Bibliotheca	J. Fuerst, *Bibliotheca Judaica,* 2 vols. (1863; repr. 1960).
Fuerst, Karaeertum	J. Fuerst, *Geschichte des Karaeertums,* 3 vols. (1862–69).
Fug.	Philo, *De Fuga et Inventione.*
Gal.	Epistle to the Galatians (New Testament).
Galling, Reallexikon	K. Galling, *Biblisches Reallexikon* (1937).
Gardiner, Onomastica	A.H. Gardiner, *Ancient Egyptian Onomastica,* 3 vols. (1947).
Geiger, Mikra	A. Geiger, *Ha-Mikra ve-Targumav,* tr. by J.L. Baruch (1949).
Geiger, Urschrift	A. Geiger, *Urschrift und Uebersetzungen der Bibel* 1928^{2}).
Gen.	Genesis (Bible).
Gen. R.	*Genesis Rabbah.*
Ger.	*Gerim* (post-talmudic tractate).
Germ Jud	M. Brann, I. Elbogen, A. Freimann, and H. Tykocinski (eds.), *Germania Judaica,* vol. 1 (1917; repr. 1934 and 1963); vol. 2, in 2 pts. (1917–68), ed. by Z. Avneri.

GHAT	*Goettinger Handkommentar zum Alten Testament* (1917–22).
Ghirondi-Neppi	M.S. Ghirondi and G.H. Neppi, *Toledot Gedolei Yisrael u-Ge'onei Italyah ... u-Ve'urim al Sefer Zekher Ẓaddikim li-Verakhah . . .*(1853), index in ZHB, 17 (1914), 171–83.
Gig.	Philo, *De Gigantibus.*
Ginzberg, Legends	L. Ginzberg, *Legends of the Jews,* 7 vols. (1909–38; and many reprints).
Git.	*Gittin* (talmudic tractate).
Glueck, Explorations	N. Glueck, *Explorations in Eastern Palestine,* 2 vols. (1951).
Goell, Bibliography	Y. Goell, *Bibliography of Modern Hebrew Literature in English Translation* (1968).
Goodenough, Symbols	E.R. Goodenough, *Jewish Symbols in the Greco-Roman Period,* 13 vols. (1953–68).
Gordon, Textbook	C.H. Gordon, *Ugaritic Textbook* (1965; repr. 1967).
Graetz, Gesch	H. Graetz, *Geschichte der Juden* (last edition 1874–1908).
Graetz, Hist	H. Graetz, *History of the Jews,* 6 vols. (1891–1902).
Graetz, Psalmen	H. Graetz, *Kritischer Commentar zu den Psalmen,* 2 vols. in 1 (1882–83).
Graetz, Rabbinowitz	H. Graetz, *Divrei Yemei Yisrael,* tr. by S.P. Rabbinowitz. (1928 1929^{2}).
Gray, Names	G.B. Gray, *Studies in Hebrew Proper Names* (1896).
Gressmann, Bilder	H. Gressmann, *Altorientalische Bilder zum Alten Testament* (1927^{2}).
Gressmann, Texte	H. Gressmann, *Altorientalische Texte zum Alten Testament* (1926^{2}).
Gross, Gal Jud	H. Gross, *Gallia Judaica* (1897; repr. with add. 1969).
Grove, Dict	*Grove's Dictionary of Music and Musicians,* ed. by E. Blum 9 vols. (1954^{5}) and suppl. (1961^{5}).
Guedemann, Gesch Erz	M. Guedemann, *Geschichte des Erziehungswesens und der Cultur der abendlaendischen Juden,* 3 vols. (1880–88).
Guedemann, Quellenschr	M. Guedemann, *Quellenschriften zur Geschichte des Unterrichts und der Erziehung bei den deutschen Juden* (1873, 1891).
Guide	Maimonides, *Guide of the Perplexed.*
Gulak, Oẓar	A. Gulak, *Oẓar ha-Shetarot ha-Nehugim be-Yisrael* (1926).
Gulak, Yesodei	A. Gulak, *Yesodei ha-Mishpat ha-Ivri, Seder Dinei Mamonot be-Yisrael, al pi Mekorot ha-Talmud ve-ha-Posekim,* 4 vols. (1922; repr. 1967).
Guttmann, Mafte'aḥ	M. Guttmann, *Mafte'aḥ ha-Talmud,* 3 vols. (1906–30).
Guttmann, Philosophies	J. Guttmann, *Philosophies of Judaism* (1964).
Hab.	*Habakkuk* (Bible).
Ḥag.	*Ḥagigah* (talmudic tractate).
Haggai	*Haggai* (Bible).
Ḥal.	*Ḥallah* (talmudic tractate).
Halevy, Dorot	I. Halevy, *Dorot ha-Rishonim,* 6 vols. (1897–1939).
Halpern, Pinkas	I. Halpern (Halperin), *Pinkas Va'ad Arba Araẓot* (1945).
Hananel-Eškenazi	A. Hananel and Eškenazi (eds.), *Fontes Hebraici ad res oeconomicas socialesque terrarum balcanicarum saeculo XVI pertinentes,* 2 vols, (1958–60; in Bulgarian).
HB	*Hebraeische Bibliographie* (1858–82).
Heb.	Epistle to the Hebrews (New Testament).
Heilprin, Dorot	J. Heilprin (Heilperin), *Seder ha-Dorot,* 3 vols. (1882; repr. 1956).
Her.	Philo, *Quis Rerum Divinarum Heres.*
Hertz, Prayer	J.H. Hertz (ed.), *Authorised Daily Prayer Book* (rev. ed. 1948; repr. 1963).
Herzog, Instit	I. Herzog, *The Main Institutions of Jewish Law,* 2 vols. (1936–39; repr. 1967).
Herzog-Hauck	J.J. Herzog and A. Hauch (eds.), *Real-encyklopaedie fuer protestantische Theologie* (1896–1913^{3}).
HḤY	*Ha-Ẓofeh le-Ḥokhmat Yisrael* (first four volumes under the title *Ha-Ẓofeh me-Ereẓ Hagar)* (1910/11–13).
Hirschberg, Afrikah	H.Z. Hirschberg, *Toledot ha-Yehudim be-Afrikah ha-Zofonit,* 2 vols. (1965).
HJ	*Historia Judaica* (1938–61).
HL	*Das Heilige Land* (1857ff.)
ḤM	*Ḥoshen Mishpat.*
Hommel, Ueberliefer.	F. Hommel, *Die altisraelitische Ueberlieferung in inschriftlicher Beleuchtung* (1897).
Hor.	*Horayot* (talmudic tractate).
Horodezky, Ḥasidut	S.A. Horodezky, *Ha-Ḥasidut ve-ha-Ḥasidim,* 4 vols. (1923).
Horowitz, Ereẓ Yis	I.W. Horowitz, *Ereẓ Yisrael u-Shekhenoteha* (1923).
Hos.	Hosea (Bible).
HTR	*Harvard Theological Review* (1908ff.).
HUCA	*Hebrew Union College Annual* (1904; 1924ff.)
Ḥul.	*Ḥullin* (talmudic tractate).
Husik, Philosophy	I. Husik, *History of Medieval Jewish Philosophy* (1932^{2}).
Hyman, Toledot	A. Hyman, *Toledot Tanna'im ve-Amora'im* (1910; repr. 1964).
Ibn Daud, Tradition	Abraham Ibn Daud, *Sefer ha-Qabbalah – The Book of Tradition,* ed. and tr. By G.D. Cohen (1967).
ICC	International Critical Commentary on the Holy Scriptures of the Old and New Testaments (series, 1908ff.).
IDB	*Interpreter's Dictionary of the Bible,* 4 vols. (1962).
Idelsohn, Litugy	A. Z. Idelsohn, *Jewish Liturgy and its Development* (1932; paperback repr. 1967)
Idelsohn, Melodien	A. Z. Idelsohn, *Hebraeisch-orientalischer Melodienschatz,* 10 vols. (1914 32).
Idelsohn, Music	A. Z. Idelsohn, *Jewish Music in its Historical Development* (1929; paperback repr. 1967).

IEJ	*Israel Exploration Journal* (1950ff.).
IESS	*International Encyclopedia of the Social Sciences* (various eds.).
IG	*Inscriptiones Graecae,* ed. by the Prussian Academy.
IGYB	*Israel Government Year Book* (1949/50ff.).
ILR	*Israel Law Review* (1966ff.).
IMIT	*Izraelita Magyar Irodalmi Társulat Évkönyv* (1895 1948).
IMT	International Military Tribunal.
INB	*Israel Numismatic Bulletin* (1962–63).
INJ	*Israel Numismatic Journal* (1963ff.).
Ios	Philo, *De Iosepho.*
Isa.	Isaiah (Bible).
ITHL	Institute for the Translation of Hebrew Literature.
IZBG	*Internationale Zeitschriftenschau fuer Bibelwissenschaft und Grenzgebiete* (1951ff.).
JA	*Journal asiatique* (1822ff.).
James	Epistle of James (New Testament).
JAOS	*Journal of the American Oriental Society* (c. 1850ff.)
Jastrow, Dict	M. Jastrow, *Dictionary of the Targumim, the Talmud Babli and Yerushalmi, and the Midrashic literature,* 2 vols. (1886 1902 and reprints).
JBA	*Jewish Book Annual* (19242ff.).
JBL	*Journal of Biblical Literature* (1881ff.).
JBR	*Journal of Bible and Religion* (1933ff.).
JC	*Jewish Chronicle* (1841ff.).
JCS	*Journal of Cuneiform Studies* (1947ff.).
JE	*Jewish Encyclopedia,* 12 vols. (1901–05 several reprints).
Jer.	Jeremiah (Bible).
Jeremias, Alte Test	A. Jeremias, *Das Alte Testament im Lichte des alten Orients* 1930^{4}).
JGGJČ	*Jahrbuch der Gesellschaft fuer Geschichte der Juden in der Čechoslovakischen Republik* (1929–38).
JHSEM	Jewish Historical Society of England, *Miscellanies* (1925ff.).
JHSET	Jewish Historical Society of England, *Transactions* (1893ff.).
JJGL	*Jahrbuch fuer juedische Geschichte und Literatur* (Berlin) (1898–1938).
JJLG	*Jahrbuch der juedische-literarischen Gesellschaft* (Frankfurt) (1903–32).
JJS	*Journal of Jewish Studies* (1948ff.).
JJSO	*Jewish Journal of Sociology* (1959ff.).
JJV	*Jahrbuch fuer juedische Volkskunde* (1898–1924).
JL	*Juedisches Lexikon,* 5 vols. (1927–30).
JMES	*Journal of the Middle East Society* (1947ff.).
JNES	*Journal of Near Eastern Studies* (continuation of AJSLL) (1942ff.).
J.N.U.L.	Jewish National and University Library.
Job	Job (Bible).
Joel	Joel (Bible).
John	Gospel according to John (New Testament).
I, II and III John	Epistles of John (New Testament).
Jos., Ant	Josephus, *Jewish Antiquities* (Loeb Classics ed.).
Jos. Apion	Josephus, *Against Apion* (Loeb Classics ed.).
Jos., index	*Josephus Works,* Loeb Classics ed., index of names.
Jos., Life	Josephus, *Life* (ed. Loeb Classics).
Jos, Wars	Josephus, *The Jewish Wars* (Loeb Classics ed.).
Josh.	Joshua (Bible).
JPESB	Jewish Palestine Exploration Society Bulletin, see BJPES.
JPESJ	Jewish Palestine Exploration Society Journal – Eng. Title of the Hebrew periodical *Kovez ha-Ḥevrah ha-Ivrit la-Ḥakirat Erez Yisrael va-Attikoteha.*
JPOS	*Journal of the Palestine Oriental Society* (1920–48).
JPS	Jewish Publication Society of America, *The Torah* (1962, 1967^{2}); *The Holy Scriptures* (1917).
JQR	*Jewish Quarterly Review* (1889ff.).
JR	*Journal of Religion* (1921ff.).
JRAS	*Journal of the Royal Asiatic Society* (1838ff.).
JHR	*Journal of Religious History* (1960/61ff.).
JSOS	*Jewish Social Studies* (1939ff.).
JSS	*Journal of Semitic Studies* (1956ff.).
JTS	*Journal of Theological Studies* (1900ff.).
JTSA	Jewish Theological Seminary of America (also abbreviated as JTS).
Jub.	Jubilees (Pseudepigrapha).
Judg.	Judges (Bible).
Judith	Book of Judith (Apocrypha).
Juster, Juifs	J. Juster, *Les Juifs dans l'Empire Romain,* 2 vols. (1914).
JYB	*Jewish Year Book* (1896ff.).
JZWL	*Juedische Zeitschift fuer Wissenschaft und Leben* (1862–75).
Kal.	*Kallah* (post-talmudic tractate).
Kal. R.	*Kallah Rabbati* (post-talmudic tractate).
Katz, England	*The Jews in the History of England, 1485-1850 (1994).*
Kaufmann, Schriften	D. Kaufmann, *Gesammelte Schriften,* 3 vols. (1908 15).
Kaufmann Y., Religion	Y. Kaufmann, *The Religion of Israel* (1960), abridged tr. of his *Toledot.*
Kaufmann Y., Toledot	Y. Kaufmann, *Toledot ha-Emunah ha-Yisre'elit,* 4 vols. (1937 57).
KAWJ	*Korrespondenzblatt des Vereins zur Gruendung und Erhaltung der Akademie fuer die Wissenschaft des Judentums* (1920 30).
Kayserling, Bibl	M. Kayserling, *Biblioteca Española-Portugueza-Judaica* (1880; repr. 1961).
Kelim	*Kelim* (mishnaic tractate).
Ker.	*Keritot* (talmudic tractate).
Ket.	*Ketubbot* (talmudic tractate).

Kid.	*Kiddushim* (talmudic tractate).
Kil.	*Kilayim* (talmudic tractate).
Kin.	*Kinnim* (mishnaic tractate).
Kisch, Germany	G. Kisch, *Jews in Medieval Germany* (1949).
Kittel, Gesch	R. Kittel, *Geschichte des Volkes Israel,* 3 vols. (1922–28).
Klausner, Bayit Sheni	J. Klausner, *Historyah shel ha-Bayit ha-Sheni,* 5 vols. (1950/512).
Klausner, Sifrut	J. Klausner, *Historyah shel haSifrut ha-Ivrit ha-Ḥadashah,* 6 vols. (1952–582).
Klein, corpus	S. Klein (ed.), *Juedisch-palaestinisches Corpus Inscriptionum* (1920).
Koehler-Baumgartner	L. Koehler and W. Baumgartner, *Lexicon in Veteris Testamenti libros* (1953).
Kohut, Arukh	H.J.A. Kohut (ed.), *Sefer he-Arukh ha-Shalem,* by Nathan b. Jehiel of Rome, 8 vols. (1876–92; Supplement by S. Krauss et al., 1936; repr. 1955).
Krauss, Tal Arch	S. Krauss, *Talmudische Archaeologie,* 3 vols. (1910–12; repr. 1966).
Kressel, Leksikon	G. Kressel, *Leksikon ha-Sifrut ha-Ivrit ba-Dorot ha-Aḥaronim,* 2 vols. (1965–67).
KS	*Kirjath Sepher* (1923/4ff.).
Kut.	*Kuttim* (post-talmudic tractate).
LA	Studium Biblicum Franciscanum, *Liber Annuus* (1951ff.).
L.A.	Philo, *Legum allegoriae.*
Lachower, Sifrut	F. Lachower, *Toledot ha-Sifrut ha-Ivrit ha-Ḥadashah,* 4 vols. (1947–48; several reprints).
Lam.	Lamentations (Bible).
Lam. R.	*Lamentations Rabbah.*
Landshuth, Ammudei	L. Landshuth, *Ammudei ha-Avodah* (1857–62; repr. with index, 1965).
Legat.	Philo, *De Legatione ad Caium.*
Lehmann, Nova Bibl	R.P. Lehmann, *Nova Bibliotheca Anglo-Judaica* (1961).
Lev.	Leviticus (Bible).
Lev. R.	*Leviticus Rabbah.*
Levy, Antologia	I. Levy, *Antologia de liturgia judeo-española* (1965ff.).
Levy J., Chald Targ	J. Levy, *Chaldaeisches Woerterbuch ueber die Targumim,* 2 vols. (1967–68; repr. 1959).
Levy J., Nuehebr Tal	J. Levy, *Neuhebraeisches und chaldaeisches Woerterbuch ueber die Talmudim . . .,* 4 vols. (1875–89; repr. 1963).
Lewin, Oẓar	Lewin, *Oẓar ha-Ge'onim,* 12 vols. (1928–43).
Lewysohn, Zool	L. Lewysohn, *Zoologie des Talmuds* (1858).
Lidzbarski, Handbuch	M. Lidzbarski, *Handbuch der nordsemitischen Epigraphik,* 2 vols (1898).
Life	Josephus, *Life* (Loeb Classis ed.).
LNYL	*Leksikon fun der Nayer Yidisher Literatur* (1956ff.).
Loew, Flora	I. Loew, *Die Flora der Juden,* 4 vols. (1924 34; repr. 1967).
LSI	*Laws of the State of Israel* (1948ff.).
Luckenbill, Records	D.D. Luckenbill, *Ancient Records of Assyria and Babylonia,* 2 vols. (1926).
Luke	Gospel according to Luke (New Testament)
LXX	Septuagint (Greek translation of the Bible).
Ma'as.	*Ma'aserot* (talmudic tractate).
Ma'as. Sh.	*Ma'ase Sheni* (talmudic tractate).
I, II, III, and IVMacc.	Maccabees, I, II, III (Apocrypha), IV (Pseudepigrapha).
Maimonides, Guide	Maimonides, *Guide of the Perplexed.*
Maim., Yad	Maimonides, *Mishneh Torah (Yad Ḥazakah).*
Maisler, Untersuchungen	B. Maisler (Mazar), *Untersuchungen zur alten Geschichte und Ethnographie Syriens und Palaestinas,* 1 (1930).
Mak.	*Makkot* (talmudic tractate).
Makhsh.	*Makhshrin* (mishnaic tractate).
Mal.	Malachi (Bible).
Mann, Egypt	J. Mann, *Jews in Egypt in Palestine under the Fatimid Caliphs,* 2 vols. (1920–22).
Mann, Texts	J. Mann, *Texts and Studies,* 2 vols (1931–35).
Mansi	G.D. Mansi, *Sacrorum Conciliorum nova et amplissima collectio,* 53 vols. in 60 (1901–27; repr. 1960).
Margalioth, Gedolei	M. Margalioth, *Enẓiklopedyah le-Toledot Gedolei Yisrael,* 4 vols. (1946–50).
Margalioth, Ḥakhmei	M. Margalioth, *Enẓiklopedyah le-Ḥakhmei ha-Talmud ve-ha-Ge'onim,* 2 vols. (1945).
Margalioth, Cat	G. Margalioth, *Catalogue of the Hebrew and Samaritan Manuscripts in the British Museum,* 4 vols. (1899–1935).
Mark	Gospel according to Mark (New Testament).
Mart. Isa.	Martyrdom of Isaiah (Pseudepigrapha).
Mas.	Masorah.
Matt.	Gospel according to Matthew (New Testament).
Mayer, Art	L.A. Mayer, *Bibliography of Jewish Art* (1967).
MB	*Wochenzeitung* (formerly *Mitteilungsblatt*) *des Irgun Olej Merkas Europa* (1933ff.).
MEAH	*Miscelánea de estudios drabes y hebraicos* (1952ff.).
Meg.	Megillah (talmudic tractate).
Meg. Ta'an.	*Megillat Ta'anit* (in HUCA, 8 9 (1931–32), 318–51).
Me'il	*Me'ilah* (mishnaic tractate).
MEJ	*Middle East Journal* (1947ff.).
Mehk.	*Mekhilta de-R. Ishmael.*
Mekh. SbY	*Mekhilta de-R. Simeon bar Yoḥai.*
Men.	*Menaḥot* (talmudic tractate).
MER	*Middle East Record* (1960ff.).
Meyer, Gesch	E. Meyer, *Geschichte des Alterums,* 5 vols. in 9 (1925–58).
Meyer, Ursp	E. Meyer, *Urspring und Anfaenge des Christentums* (1921).
Mez.	*Mezuzah* (post-talmudic tractate).
MGADJ	*Mitteilungen des Gesamtarchivs der deutschen Juden* (1909–12).
MGG	*Die Musik in Geschichte und Gegenwart,* 14 vols. (1949–68).

MGG²	*Die Musik in Geschichte und Gegenwart, 2nd edition (1994)*
MGH	*Monumenta Germaniae Historica* (1826ff.).
MGJV	*Mitteilungen der Gesellschaft fuer juedische Volkskunde* (1898–1929); title varies, see also JJV.
MGWJ	*Monatsschrift fuer Geschichte und Wissenschaft des Judentums* (1851–1939).
MHJ	*Monumenta Hungariae Judaica,* 11 vols. (1903–67).
Michael, Or	H.Ḥ. Michael, *Or ha-Ḥayyim: Ḥakhmei Yisrael ve-Sifreihem,* ed. by S.Z. Ḥ. Halberstam and N. Ben-Menahem (1965²).
Mid.	*Middot* (mishnaic tractate).
Mid. Ag.	*Midrash Aggadah.*
Mid. Hag.	*Midrash ha-Gadol.*
Mid. Job.	*Midrash Job.*
Mid. Jonah	*Midrash Jonah.*
Mid. Lek. Tov	*Midrash Lekaḥ Tov.*
Mid. Prov.	*Midrash Proverbs.*
Mid. Ps.	*Midrash Tehillim* (Eng tr. *The Midrash on Psalms* (JPS, 1959).
Mid. Sam.	*Midrash Samuel.*
Mid. Song	*Midrash Shir ha-Shirim.*
Mid. Tan.	*Midrash Tanna'im* on Deuteronomy.
Miége, Maroc	J.L. Miège, *Le Maroc et l'Europe,* 3 vols. (1961 62).
Mig.	Philo, *De Migratione Abrahami.*
Mik.	*Mikva'ot* (mishnaic tractate).
Milano, Bibliotheca	A. Milano, *Bibliotheca Historica Italo-Judaica* (1954); supplement for 1954–63 (1964); supplement for 1964–66 in RMI, 32 (1966).
Milano, Italia	A. Milano, *Storia degli Ebrei in Italia* (1963).
MIO	*Mitteilungen des Instituts fuer Orientforschung* 1953ff.).
Mish.	Mishnah.
MJ	*Le Monde Juif* (1946ff.).
MJC	see Neubauer, Chronicles.
MK	*Mo'ed Katan* (talmudic tractate).
MNDPV	*Mitteilungen und Nachrichten des deutschen Palaestinavereins* (1895–1912).
Mortara, Indice	M. Mortara, *Indice Alfabetico dei Rabbini e Scrittori Israeliti ... in Italia ...* (1886).
Mos	Philo, *De Vita Mosis.*
Moscati, Epig	S, Moscati, *Epigrafia ebraica antica* 1935–1950 (1951).
MT	Masoretic Text of the Bible.
Mueller, Musiker	[E.H. Mueller], *Deutisches Musiker-Lexikon* (1929)
Munk, Mélanges	S. Munk, *Mélanges de philosophie juive et arabe* (1859; repr. 1955).
Mut.	Philo, *De Mutatione Nominum.*
MWJ	*Magazin fuer die Wissenshaft des Judentums* (18745 93).
Nah.	Nahum (Bible).
Naz.	*Nazir* (talmudic tractate).
NDB	*Neue Deutsche Biographie* (1953ff.).
Ned.	*Nedarim* (talmudic tractate).
Neg.	*Nega'im* (mishnaic tractate).
Neh.	Nehemiah (Bible).
NG²	*New Grove Dictionary of Music and Musicians* (2001).
Nuebauer, Cat	A. Neubauer, *Catalogue of the Hebrew Manuscripts in the Bodleian Library ...,* 2 vols. (1886–1906).
Neubauer, Chronicles	A. Neubauer, *Mediaeval Jewish Chronicles,* 2 vols. (Heb., 1887–95; repr. 1965), Eng. title of *Seder ha-Ḥakhamim ve-Korot ha-Yamim.*
Neubauer, Géogr	A. Neubauer, *La géographie du Talmud* (1868).
Neuman, Spain	A.A. Neuman, *The Jews in Spain, their Social, Political, and Cultural Life During the Middle Ages,* 2 vols. (1942).
Neusner, Babylonia	J. Neusner, *History of the Jews in Babylonia,* 5 vols. 1965–70), 2nd revised printing 1969ff.).
Nid.	*Niddah* (talmudic tractate).
Noah	Fragment of Book of Noah (Pseudepigrapha).
Noth, Hist Isr	M. Noth, *History of Israel* (1958).
Noth, Personennamen	M. Noth, *Die israelitischen Personennamen. ...* (1928).
Noth, Ueberlief	M. Noth, *Ueberlieferungsgeschichte des Pentateuchs* (1949).
Noth, Welt	M. Noth, *Die Welt des Alten Testaments* (1957³).
Nowack, Lehrbuch	W. Nowack, *Lehrbuch der hebraeischen Archaeologie,* 2 vols (1894).
NT	New Testament.
Num.	Numbers (Bible).
Num R.	*Numbers Rabbah.*
Obad.	Obadiah (Bible).
ODNB online	*Oxford Dictionary of National Biography.*
OḤ	*Oraḥ Ḥayyim.*
Oho.	*Oholot* (mishnaic tractate).
Olmstead	H.T. Olmstead, *History of Palestine and Syria* (1931; repr. 1965).
OLZ	*Orientalistische Literaturzeitung* (1898ff.)
Onom.	Eusebius, *Onomasticon.*
Op.	Philo, *De Opificio Mundi.*
OPD	*Osef Piskei Din shel ha-Rabbanut ha-Rashit le-Ereẓ Yisrael, Bet ha-Din ha-Gadol le-Irurim* (1950).
Or.	*Orlah* (talmudic tractate).
Or. Sibyll.	Sibylline Oracles (Pseudepigrapha).
OS	*L'Orient Syrien* (1956ff.)
OTS	*Oudtestamentische Studien* (1942ff.).
PAAJR	*Proceedings of the American Academy for Jewish Research* (1930ff.)
Pap 4QS^e	A papyrus exemplar of IQS.
Par.	*Parah* (mishnaic tractate).
Pauly-Wissowa	A.F. Pauly, *Realencyklopaedie der klassichen Alertumswissenschaft,* ed. by G. Wissowa et al. (1864ff.)

PD	*Piskei Din shel Bet ha-Mishpat ha-Elyon le-Yisrael* (1948ff.)
PDR	*Piskei Din shel Battei ha-Din ha-Rabbaniyyim be-Yisrael.*
PdRE	*Pirkei de-R. Eliezer* (Eng. tr. 1916. (1965[2]).
PdRK	*Pesikta de-Rav Kahana.*
Pe'ah	*Pe'ah* (talmudic tractate).
Peake, Commentary	A.J. Peake (ed.), *Commentary on the Bible* (1919; rev. 1962).
Pedersen, Israel	J. Pedersen, *Israel, Its Life and Culture,* 4 vols. in 2 (1926–40).
PEFQS	*Palestine Exploration Fund Quarterly Statement* (1869–1937; since 1938–PEQ).
PEQ	*Palestine Exploration Quarterly* (until 1937 PEFQS; after 1927 includes BBSAJ).
Perles, Beitaege	J. Perles, *Beitraege zur rabbinischen Sprach- und Alterthumskunde* (1893).
Pes.	*Pesaḥim* (talmudic tractate).
Pesh.	Peshitta (Syriac translation of the Bible).
Pesher Hab.	Commentary to Habakkuk from Qumran; see 1Qp Hab.
I and II Pet.	Epistles of Peter (New Testament).
Pfeiffer, Introd	R.H. Pfeiffer, *Introduction to the Old Testament* (1948).
PG	J.P. Migne (ed.), *Patrologia Graeca,* 161 vols. (1866–86).
Phil.	Epistle to the Philippians (New Testament).
Philem.	Epistle to the Philemon (New Testament).
PIASH	*Proceedings of the Israel Academy of Sciences and Humanities* (1963/7ff.).
PJB	*Palaestinajahrbuch des deutschen evangelischen Institutes fuer Altertumswissenschaft,* Jerusalem (1905–1933).
PK	*Pinkas ha-Kehillot,* encyclopedia of Jewish communities, published in over 30 volumes by Yad Vashem from 1970 and arranged by countries, regions and localities. For 3-vol. English edition see Spector, *Jewish Life.*
PL	J.P. Migne (ed.), *Patrologia Latina* 221 vols. (1844–64).
Plant	Philo, *De Plantatione.*
PO	R. Graffin and F. Nau (eds.), *Patrologia Orientalis* (1903ff.)
Pool, Prayer	D. de Sola Pool, *Traditional Prayer Book for Sabbath and Festivals* (1960).
Post	Philo, *De Posteritate Caini.*
PR	*Pesikta Rabbati.*
Praem.	Philo, *De Praemiis et Poenis.*
Prawer, Ẓalbanim	J. Prawer, *Toledot Mamlekhet ha-Ẓalbanim be-Ereẓ Yisrael,* 2 vols. (1963).
Press, Ereẓ	I. Press, *Ereẓ-Yisrael, Enẓiklopedyah Topografit-Historit,* 4 vols. (1951–55).
Pritchard, Pictures	J.B. Pritchard (ed.), *Ancient Near East in Pictures* (1954, 1970).
Pritchard, Texts	J.B. Pritchard (ed.), *Ancient Near East Texts* ... (1970[3]).

Pr. Man.	Prayer of Manasses (Apocrypha).
Prob.	Philo, *Quod Omnis Probus Liber Sit.*
Prov.	Proverbs (Bible).
PS	*Palestinsky Sbornik* (Russ. (1881 1916, 1954ff).
Ps.	Psalms (Bible).
PSBA	*Proceedings of the Society of Biblical Archaeology* (1878–1918).
Ps. of Sol	Psalms of Solomon (Pseudepigrapha).
IQ Apoc	The *Genesis Apocryphon* from Qumran, cave one, ed. by N. Avigad and Y. Yadin (1956).
6QD	*Damascus Document* or *Sefer Berit Dammesk* from Qumran, cave six, ed. by M. Baillet, in RB, 63 (1956), 513–23 (see also CD).
QDAP	*Quarterly of the Department of Antiquities in Palestine* (1932ff.).
4QDeut. 32	Manuscript of Deuteronomy 32 from Qumran, cave four (ed. by P.W. Skehan, in BASOR, 136 (1954), 12–15).
4QEx[a]	Exodus manuscript in Jewish script from Qumran, cave four.
4QEx[α]	Exodus manuscript in Paleo-Hebrew script from Qumran, cave four (partially ed. by P.W. Skehan, in JBL, 74 (1955), 182–7).
4QFlor	*Florilegium,* a miscellany from Qumran, cave four (ed. by J.M. Allegro, in JBL, 75 (1956), 176–77 and 77 (1958), 350–54).).
QGJD	*Quellen zur Geschichte der Juden in Deutschland* 1888–98).
IQH	*Thanksgiving Psalms* of *Hodayot* from Qumran, cave one (ed. by E.L. Sukenik and N. Avigad, *Oẓar ha-Megillot ha-Genuzot* (1954).
IQIs[a]	Scroll of Isaiah from Qumran, cave one (ed. by N. Burrows et al., *Dead Sea Scrolls* ..., 1 (1950).
IQIs[b]	Scroll of Isaiah from Qumran, cave one (ed. E.L. Sukenik and N. Avigad, *Oẓar ha-Megillot ha-Genuzot* (1954).
IQM	The *War Scroll* or *Serekh ha-Milḥamah* (ed. by E.L. Sukenik and N. Avigad, *Oẓar ha-Megillot ha-Genuzot* (1954).
4QpNah	Commentary on Nahum from Qumran, cave four (partially ed. by J.M. Allegro, in JBL, 75 (1956), 89–95).
IQphyl	Phylacteries *(tefillin)* from Qumran, cave one (ed. by Y. Yadin, in *Eretz Israel,* 9 (1969), 60–85).
4Q Prayer of Nabonidus	A document from Qumran, cave four, belonging to a lost Daniel literature (ed. by J.T. Milik, in RB, 63 (1956), 407–15).
IQS	*Manual of Discipline* or *Serekh ha-Yaḥad* from Qumran, cave one (ed. by M. Burrows et al., *Dead Sea Scrolls* ..., 2, pt. 2 (1951).

IQS[a] — The *Rule of the Congregation or Serekh ha-Edah* from Qumran, cave one (ed. by Burrows et al., *Dead Sea Scrolls* ..., 1 (1950), under the abbreviation IQ28a).
IQS[b] — *Blessings* or *Divrei Berakhot* from Qumran, cave one (ed. by Burrows et al., *Dead Sea Scrolls* ..., 1 (1950), under the abbreviation IQ28b).
4QSam[a] — Manuscript of I and II Samuel from Qumran, cave four (partially ed. by F.M. Cross, in BASOR, 132 (1953), 15–26).
4QSam[b] — Manuscript of I and II Samuel from Qumran, cave four (partially ed. by F.M. Cross, in JBL, 74 (1955), 147–72).
4QTestimonia — Sheet of Testimony from Qumran, cave four (ed. by J.M. Allegro, in JBL, 75 (1956), 174–87).).
4QT.Levi — *Testament of Levi* from Qumran, cave four (partially ed. by J.T. Milik, in RB, 62 (1955), 398–406).

Rabinovitz, Dik Sof — See Dik Sof.
RB — *Revue biblique* (1892ff.)
RBI — *Recherches bibliques* (1954ff.)
RCB — *Revista de cultura biblica* (São Paulo) (1957ff.)
Régné, Cat — J. Régné, *Catalogue des actes . . . des rois d'Aragon, concernant les Juifs* (1213–1327), in: REJ, vols. 60 70, 73, 75–78 (1910–24).
Reinach, Textes — T. Reinach, *Textes d'auteurs Grecs et Romains relatifs au Judaïsme* (1895; repr. 1963).
REJ — *Revue des études juives* (1880ff.).
Rejzen, Leksikon — Z. Rejzen, *Leksikon fun der Yidisher Literature,* 4 vols. (1927–29).
Renan, Ecrivains — A. Neubauer and E. Renan, *Les écrivains juifs français* ... (1893).
Renan, Rabbins — A. Neubauer and E. Renan, *Les rabbins français* (1877).
RES — *Revue des étude sémitiques et Babyloniaca* (1934–45).
Rev. — Revelation (New Testament).
RGG[3] — *Die Religion in Geschichte und Gegenwart,* 7 vols. (1957–65[3]).
RH — *Rosh Ha-Shanah* (talmudic tractate).
RHJE — *Revue de l'histoire juive en Egypte* (1947ff.).
RHMH — *Revue d'histoire de la médecine hébraïque* (1948ff.).
RHPR — *Revue d'histoire et de philosophie religieuses* (1921ff.).
RHR — *Revue d'histoire des religions* (1880ff.).
RI — *Rivista Israelitica* (1904–12).
Riemann-Einstein — *Hugo Riemanns Musiklexikon,* ed. by A. Einstein (1929[11]).
Riemann-Gurlitt — *Hugo Riemanns Musiklexikon,* ed. by W. Gurlitt (1959–67[12]), Personenteil.
Rigg-Jenkinson, Exchequer — J.M. Rigg, H. Jenkinson and H.G. Richardson (eds.), *Calendar of the Pleas Rolls of the Exchequer of the Jews,* 4 vols. (1905–1970); cf. in each instance also J.M. Rigg (ed.), *Select Pleas* ... (1902).
RMI — *Rassegna Mensile di Israel* (1925ff.).
Rom. — Epistle to the Romans (New Testament).
Rosanes, Togarmah — S.A. Rosanes, *Divrei Yemei Yisrael be-Togarmah,* 6 vols. (1907–45), and in 3 vols. (1930–38[2]).
Rosenbloom, Biogr Dict — J.R. Rosenbloom, *Biographical Dictionary of Early American Jews* (1960).
Roth, Art — C. Roth, *Jewish Art* (1961).
Roth, Dark Ages — C. Roth (ed.), *World History of the Jewish People,* second series, vol. 2, *Dark Ages* (1966).
Roth, England — C. Roth, *History of the Jews in England* (1964[3]).
Roth, Italy — C. Roth, *History of the Jews in Italy* (1946).
Roth, Mag Bibl — C. Roth, *Magna Bibliotheca Anglo-Judaica* (1937).
Roth, Marranos — C. Roth, *History of the Marranos* (2nd rev. ed 1959; reprint 1966).
Rowley, Old Test — H.H. Rowley, *Old Testament and Modern Study* (1951; repr. 1961).
RS — *Revue sémitiques d'épigraphie et d'histoire ancienne* (1893/94ff.).
RSO — *Rivista degli studi orientali* (1907ff.).
RSV — Revised Standard Version of the Bible.
Rubinstein, Australia I — *H.L. Rubinstein, The Jews in Australia, A Thematic History, Vol. I (1991).*
Rubinstein, Australia II — *W.D. Rubinstein, The Jews in Australia, A Thematic History, Vol. II (1991).*
Ruth — Ruth (Bible).
Ruth R. — *Ruth Rabbah.*
RV — Revised Version of the Bible.

Sac. — Philo, *De Sacrificiis Abelis et Caini.*
Salfeld, Martyrol — S. Salfeld, *Martyrologium des Nuernberger Memorbuches* (1898).
I and II Sam. — Samuel, book I and II (Bible).
Sanh. — *Sanhedrin* (talmudic tractate).
SBA — Society of Biblical Archaeology.
SBB — *Studies in Bibliography and Booklore* (1953ff.).
SBE — *Semana Biblica Española.*
SBT — *Studies in Biblical Theology* (1951ff.).
SBU — *Svenkst Bibliskt Uppslogsvesk,* 2 vols. (1962–63[2]).
Schirmann, Italyah — J.Ḥ. Schirmann, *Ha-Shirah ha-Ivrit be-Italyah* (1934).
Schirmann, Sefarad — J.Ḥ. Schirmann, *Ha-Shirah ha-Ivrit bi-Sefarad u-vi-Provence,* 2 vols. (1954–56).
Scholem, Mysticism — G. Scholem, *Major Trends in Jewish Mysticism* (rev. ed. 1946; paperback ed. with additional bibliography 1961).
Scholem, Shabbetai Ẓevi — G. Scholem, *Shabbetai Ẓevi ve-ha-Tenu'ah ha-Shabbeta'it bi-Ymei Ḥayyav,* 2 vols. (1967).
Schrader, Keilinschr — E. Schrader, *Keilinschriften und das Alte Testament* (1903[3]).
Schuerer, Gesch — E. Schuerer, *Geschichte des juedischen Volkes im Zeitalter Jesu Christi,* 3 vols. and index-vol. (1901–11[4]).

Schuerer, Hist	E. Schuerer, *History of the Jewish People in the Time of Jesus,* ed. by N.N. Glatzer, abridged paperback edition (1961).
Set. T.	*Sefer Torah* (post-talmudic tractate).
Sem.	*Semaḥot* (post-talmudic tractate).
Sendrey, Music	A. Sendrey, *Bibliography of Jewish Music* (1951).
SER	*Seder Eliyahu Rabbah.*
SEZ	*Seder Eliyahu Zuta.*
Shab	*Shabbat* (talmudic tractate).
Sh. Ar.	J. Caro Shulḥan Arukh. OḤ – *Oraḥ Ḥayyim* YD – *Yoreh De'ah* EH – *Even ha-Ezer* ḤM – *Ḥoshen Mishpat.*
Shek.	*Shekalim* (talmudic tractate).
Shev.	*Shevi'it* (talmudic tractate).
Shevu.	*Shevu'ot* (talmudic tractate).
Shunami, Bibl	S. Shunami, *Bibliography of Jewish Bibliographies* (1965^{2}).
Sif.	*Sifrei Deuteronomy.*
Sif. Num.	*Sifrei Numbers.*
Sifra	*Sifra* on Leviticus.
Sif. Zut.	*Sifrei Zuta.*
SIHM	Sources inédites de l'histoire du Maroc (series).
Silverman, Prayer	M. Silverman (ed.), *Sabbath and Festival Prayer Book* (1946).
Singer, Prayer	S. Singer *Authorised Daily Prayer Book* (1943^{17}).
Sob.	Philo, *De Sobrietate.*
Sof.	*Soferim* (post-talmudic tractate).
Som.	Philo, *De Somniis.*
Song	Song of Songs (Bible).
Song. Ch.	Song of the Three Children (Apocrypha).
Song R.	*Song of Songs Rabbah.*
SOR	*Seder Olam Rabbah.*
Sot.	*Sotah* (talmudic tractate).
SOZ	*Seder Olam Zuta.*
Spec.	Philo, *De Specialibus Legibus.*
Spector, Jewish Life	*S. Spector (ed.), Encyclopedia of Jewish Life Before and After the Holocaust (2001).*
Steinschneider, Arab lit	M. Steinschneider, *Die arabische Literatur der Juden* (1902).
Steinschneider, Cat Bod	M. Steinschneider, *Catalogus Librorum Hebraeorum in Bibliotheca Bodleiana,* 3 vols. (1852–60; reprints 1931 and 1964).
Steinschneider, Hanbuch	M. Steinschneider, *Bibliographisches Handbuch ueber die . . . Literatur fuer hebraeische Sprachkunde* (1859; repr. with additions 1937).
Steinschneider, Uebersetzungen	M. Steinschneider, *Die hebraeischen Uebersetzungen des Mittelalters* (1893).
Stern, Americans	M.H. Stern, *Americans of Jewish Descent* (1960).
van Straalen, Cat	S. van Straalen, *Catalogue of Hebrew Books in the British Museum Acquired During the Years 1868–1892* (1894).
Suárez Fernández, Docmentos	L. Suárez Fernández, *Documentos acerca de la expulsion de los Judios de España* (1964).
Suk.	*Sukkah* (talmudic tractate).
Sus.	Susanna (Apocrypha).
SY	*Sefer Yeẓirah.*
Sym.	Symmachus' Greek translation of the Bible.
SZNG	*Studien zur neueren Geschichte.*
Ta'an.	*Ta'anit* (talmudic tractate).
Tam.	*Tamid* (mishnaic tractate).
Tanḥ.	*Tanḥuma.*
Tanḥ. B.	*Tanḥuma.* Buber ed (1885).
Targ. Jon	Targum Jonathan (Aramaic version of the Prophets).
Targ. Onk.	Targum Onkelos (Aramaic version of the Pentateuch).
Targ. Yer.	Targum Yerushalmi.
TB	Babylonian Talmud or Talmud Bavli.
Tcherikover, Corpus	V. Tcherikover, A. Fuks, and M. Stern, *Corpus Papyrorum Judaicorum,* 3 vols. (1957–60).
Tef.	*Tefillin* (post-talmudic tractate).
Tem.	*Temurah* (mishnaic tractate).
Ter.	*Terumah* (talmudic tractate).
Test. Patr.	Testament of the Twelve Patriarchs (Pseudepigrapha). Ash. – Asher Ben. – Benjamin Dan – Dan Gad – Gad Iss. – Issachar Joseph – Joseph Judah – Judah Levi – Levi Naph. – Naphtali Reu. – Reuben Sim. – Simeon Zeb. – Zebulun.
I and II	Epistle to the Thessalonians (New Testament).
Thieme-Becker	U. Thieme and F. Becker (eds.), *Allgemeines Lexikon der bildenden Kuenstler von der Antike bis zur Gegenwart,* 37 vols. (1907–50).
Tidhar	D. Tidhar (ed.), *Enẓiklopedyah la-Ḥalutẓei ha-Yishuv u-Vonav* (1947ff.).
I and II Timothy	Epistles to Timothy (New Testament).
Tit.	Epistle to Titus (New Testament).
TJ	Jerusalem Talmud or Talmud Yerushalmi.
Tob.	Tobit (Apocrypha).
Toh.	*Tohorot* (mishnaic tractate).
Torczyner, Bundeslade	H. Torczyner, *Die Bundeslade und die Anfaenge der Religion Israels* (1930^{3}).
Tos.	*Tosafot.*
Tosef.	Tosefta.
Tristram, Nat Hist	H.B. Tristram, *Natural History of the Bible* (1877^{5}).
Tristram, Survey	Palestine Exploration Fund, *Survey of Western Palestine,* vol. 4 (1884) = *Fauna and Flora* by H.B. Tristram.
TS	*Terra Santa* (1943ff.).

TSBA	*Transactions of the Society of Biblical Archaeology* (1872–93).
TY	*Tevul Yom* (mishnaic tractate).
UBSB	United Bible Society, *Bulletin.*
UJE	*Universal Jewish Encyclopedia*, 10 vols. (1939–43).
Uk.	*Ukẓin* (mishnaic tractate).
Urbach, Tosafot	E.E. Urbach, *Ba'alei ha-Tosafot* (1957²).
de Vaux, Anc Isr	R. de Vaux, *Ancient Israel: its Life and Institutions* (1961; paperback 1965).
de Vaux, Instit	R. de Vaux, *Institutions de l'Ancien Testament,* 2 vols. (1958 60).
Virt.	Philo, *De Virtutibus.*
Vogelstein, Chronology	M. Volgelstein, *Biblical Chronology (1944).*
Vogelstein-Rieger	H. Vogelstein and P. Rieger, *Geschichte der Juden in Rom,* 2 vols. (1895–96).
VT	*Vetus Testamentum* (1951ff.).
VTS	*Vetus Testamentum* Supplements (1953ff.).
Vulg.	Vulgate (Latin translation of the Bible).
Wars	Josephus, *The Jewish Wars.*
Watzinger, Denkmaeler	K. Watzinger, *Denkmaeler Palaestinas,* 2 vols. (1933–35).
Waxman, Literature	M. Waxman, *History of Jewish Literature,* 5 vols. (1960²).
Weiss, Dor	I.H. Weiss, *Dor, Dor ve-Doreshav,* 5 vols. (1904⁴).
Wellhausen, Proleg	J. Wellhausen, *Prolegomena zur Geschichte Israels* (1927⁶).
WI	*Die Welt des Islams* (1913ff.).
Winniger, Biog	S. Wininger, *Grosse juedische National-Biographie …,* 7 vols. (1925–36).
Wisd.	Wisdom of Solomon (Apocrypha)
WLB	*Wiener Library Bulletin* (1958ff.).
Wolf, Bibliotheca	J.C. Wolf, *Bibliotheca Hebraea,* 4 vols. (1715–33).
Wright, Bible	G.E. Wright, *Westminster Historical Atlas to the Bible* (1945).
Wright, Atlas	G.E. Wright, *The Bible and the Ancient Near East* (1961).
WWWJ	*Who's Who in the World Jewry* (New York, 1955, 1965²).
WZJT	*Wissenschaftliche Zeitschrift fuer juedische Theologie* (1835–37).
WZKM	*Wiener Zeitschrift fuer die Kunde des Morgenlandes* (1887ff.).
Yaari, Sheluḥei	A. Yaari, *Sheluḥei Ereẓ Yisrael* (1951).
Yad	Maimonides, *Mishneh Torah (Yad Ḥazakah).*
Yad	*Yadayim* (mishnaic tractate).
Yal.	*Yalkut Shimoni.*
Yal. Mak.	*Yalkut Makhiri.*
Yal. Reub.	*Yalkut Reubeni.*
YD	*Yoreh De'ah.*
YE	*Yevreyskaya Entsiklopediya,* 14 vols. (c. 1910).
Yev.	*Yevamot* (talmudic tractate).
YIVOA	*YIVO Annual of Jewish Social Studies* (1946ff.).
YLBI	*Year Book of the Leo Baeck Institute* (1956ff.).
YMḤEY	See BJPES.
YMḤSI	*Yedi'ot ha-Makhon le-Ḥeker ha-Shirah ha-Ivrit* (1935/36ff.).
YMMY	*Yedi'ot ha-Makhon le-Madda'ei ha-Yahadut* (1924/25ff.).
Yoma	*Yoma* (talmudic tractate).
ZA	*Zeitschrift fuer Assyriologie* (1886/87ff.).
Zav.	*Zavim* (mishnaic tractate).
ZAW	*Zeitschrift fuer die alttestamentliche Wissenschaft und die Kunde des nachbiblishchen Judentums* (1881ff.).
ZAWB	*Beihefte* (supplements) to ZAW.
ZDMG	*Zeitschrift der Deutschen Morgenlaendischen Gesellschaft* (1846ff.).
ZDPV	*Zeitschrift des Deutschen Palaestina-Vereins* (1878–1949; from 1949 = BBLA).
Zech.	Zechariah (Bible).
Zedner, Cat	J. Zedner, *Catalogue of Hebrew Books in the Library of the British Museum* (1867; repr. 1964).
Zeitlin, Bibliotheca	W. Zeitlin, *Bibliotheca Hebraica Post-Mendelssohniana* (1891–95).
Zeph.	Zephaniah (Bible).
Zev.	*Zevaḥim* (talmudic tractate).
ZGGJT	*Zeitschrift der Gesellschaft fuer die Geschichte der Juden in der Tschechoslowakei* (1930–38).
ZGJD	*Zeitschrift fuer die Geschichte der Juden in Deutschland* (1887–92).
ZHB	*Zeitschrift fuer hebraeische Bibliographie* (1896–1920).
Zinberg, Sifrut	I. Zinberg, *Toledot Sifrut Yisrael,* 6 vols. (1955–60).
Ẓiẓ.	*Ẓiẓit* (post-talmudic tractate).
ZNW	*Zeitschrift fuer die neutestamentliche Wissenschaft* (1901ff.).
ZS	*Zeitschrift fuer Semitistik und verwandte Gebiete* (1922ff.).
Zunz, Gesch	L. Zunz, *Zur Geschichte und Literatur* (1845).
Zunz, Gesch	L. Zunz, *Literaturgeschichte der synagogalen Poesie* (1865; Supplement, 1867; repr. 1966).
Zunz, Poesie	L. Zunz, *Synogogale Posie des Mittelalters,* ed. by Freimann (1920²; repr. 1967).
Zunz, Ritus	L. Zunz, *Ritus des synagogalen Gottesdienstes* (1859; repr. 1967).
Zunz, Schr	L. Zunz, *Gesammelte Schriften,* 3 vols. (1875–76).
Zunz, Vortraege	L. Zunz, *Gottesdienstliche vortraege der Juden …* 1892²; repr. 1966).
Zunz-Albeck, Derashot	L. Zunz, *Ha-Derashot be-Yisrael,* Heb. Tr. of Zunz Vortraege by H. Albeck (1954²).

TRANSLITERATION RULES

HEBREW AND SEMITIC LANGUAGES:

	General	*Scientific*
א	not transliterated[1]	ʾ
בּ	b	b
ב	v	v, ḇ
גּ	g	g
ג		ḡ
דּ	d	d
ד		ḏ
ה	h	h
ו	v – when not a vowel	w
ז	z	z
ח	ḥ	ḥ
ט	t	ṭ, t
י	y – when vowel and at end of words – i	y
כּ	k	k
כ, ך	kh	kh, ḵ
ל	l	ḻ
מ, ם	m	m
נ, ן	n	n
ס	s	s
ע	not transliterated[1]	ʿ
פּ	p	p
פ, ף	f	p, f, ph
צ, ץ	ẓ	ṣ, ẓ
ק	k	q, k
ר	r	r
שׁ	sh[2]	š
שׂ	s	ś, s
תּ	t	t
ת		ṯ
ג׳	dzh, J	ğ
ז׳	zh, J	ž
צ׳	ch	č
◌ָ		å, o, ȯ (short) â, ā (long)
◌ַ	a	a
◌ֲ		a, ^{a}
◌ֵ		e, ẹ, ē
◌ֶ	e	æ, ä, ę
◌ֱ		œ, ĕ, ^{e}
◌ְ	only *sheva na* is transliterated	ə, ĕ, e; only *sheva na* transliterated
◌ִ ◌ִי	i	i
◌ֹ וֹ	o	o, o, o
◌ֻ וּ	u	u, ŭ û, ū
◌ֵי	ei; biblical e	
‡		reconstructed forms of words

1. The letters א and ע are not transliterated.
   An apostrophe (') between vowels indicates that they do not form a diphthong and are to be pronounced separately.
2. *Dagesh ḥazak* (forte) is indicated by doubling of the letter, except for the letter שׁ.
3. Names. Biblical names and biblical place names are rendered according to the Bible translation of the Jewish Publication Society of America. Post-biblical Hebrew names are transliterated; contemporary names are transliterated or rendered as used by the person. Place names are transliterated or rendered by the accepted spelling. Names and some words with an accepted English form are usually not transliterated.

YIDDISH

א	not transliterated
אַ	a
אָ	o
בּ	b
בֿ	v
ג	g
ד	d
ה	h
ו, וּ	u
וו	v
וי	oy
ז	z
זש	zh
ח	kh
ט	t
טש	tsh, ch
י	(consonant) y (vowel) i
יִ	i
יי	ey
ײַ	ay
כּ	k
כ, ך	kh
ל	l
מ, ם	m
נ, ן	n
ס	s
ע	e
פּ	p
פֿ, ף	f
צ, ץ	ts
ק	k
ר	r
ש	sh
שׂ	s
תּ	t
ת	s

1. Yiddish transliteration rendered according to U. Weinreich's Modern *English-Yiddish Yiddish-English* Dictionary.
2. Hebrew words in Yiddish are usually transliterated according to standard Yiddish pronunciation, e.g., חזנות = *khazones.*

LADINO

Ladino and Judeo-Spanish words written in Hebrew characters are transliterated phonetically, following the General Rules of Hebrew transliteration (see above) whenever the accepted spelling in Latin characters could not be ascertained.

ARABIC

ا ء	a[1]	ض	ḍ
ب	b	ط	ṭ
ت	t	ظ	ẓ
ث	th	ع	c
ج	j	غ	gh
ح	ḥ	ف	f
خ	kh	ق	q
د	d	ك	k
ذ	dh	ل	l
ر	r	م	m
ز	z	ن	n
س	s	ه	h
ش	sh	و	w
ص	ṣ	ي	y
ـَ	a	ـَا ى	ā
ـِ	i	ـِي	ī
ـُ	u	ـُو	ū
ـَو	aw	ـِيّ	iyy[2]
ـَي	ay	ـُوّ	uww[2]

1. not indicated when initial
2. see note (f)

a) The EJ follows the *Columbia Lippincott Gazetteer* and the *Times Atlas* in transliteration of Arabic place names. Sites that appear in neither are transliterated according to the table above, and subject to the following notes.

b) The EJ follows the *Columbia Encyclopedia* in transliteration of Arabic names. Personal names that do not therein appear are transliterated according to the table above and subject to the following notes (e.g., Ali rather than ʿAlī, Suleiman rather than Sulayman).

c) The EJ follows the *Webster's Third International Dictionary, Unabridged* in transliteration of Arabic terms that have been integrated into the English language.

d) The term "Abu" will thus appear, usually in disregard of inflection.

e) Nunnation (end vowels, *tanwīn*) are dropped in transliteration.

f) Gemination (*tashdīd*) is indicated by the doubling of the geminated letter, unless an end letter, in which case the gemination is dropped.

g) The definitive article *al-* will always be thus transliterated, unless subject to one of the modifying notes (e.g., El-Arish rather than al-ʿArīsh; modification according to note (a)).

h) The Arabic transliteration disregards the Sun Letters (the antero-palatals (*al-Ḥurūf al-Shamsiyya*).

i) The *tā-marbūṭa* (o) is omitted in transliteration, unless in construct-stage (e.g., *Khirba* but *Khirbat Mishmish*).

These modifying notes may lead to various inconsistencies in the Arabic transliteration, but this policy has deliberately been adopted to gain smoother reading of Arabic terms and names.

GREEK

Ancient Greek	*Modern Greek*	*Greek Letters*
a	a	*Α; α; ᾳ*
b	v	*Β; β*
g	gh; g	*Γ; γ*
d	dh	*Δ; δ*
e	e	*Ε; ε*
z	z	*Ζ; ζ*
e; e	i	*Η; η; ῃ*
th	th	*Θ; θ*
i	i	*Ι; ι*
k	k; ky	*Κ; κ*
l	l	*Λ; λ*
m	m	*Μ; μ*
n	n	*Ν; ν*
x	x	*Ξ; ξ*
o	o	*Ο; ο*
p	p	*Π; π*
r; rh	r	*Ρ; ρ; ῥ*
s	s	*Σ; σ; ς*
t	t	*Τ; τ*
u; y	i	*Υ; υ*
ph	f	*Φ; φ*
ch	kh	*Χ; χ*
ps	ps	*Ψ; ψ*
o; ō	o	*Ω; ω; ῳ*
ai	e	*αι*
ei	i	*ει*
oi	i	*οι*
ui	i	*υι*
ou	ou	*ου*
eu	ev	*ευ*
eu; ēu	iv	*ηυ*
–	j	*τζ*
nt	d; nd	*ντ*
mp	b; mb	*μπ*
ngk	g	*γκ*
ng	ng	*νγ*
h	–	ʽ
–	–	ʼ
w	–	*ϝ*

RUSSIAN

А	A
Б	B
В	V
Г	G
Д	D
Е	E, Ye[1]
Ё	Yo, O[2]
Ж	Zh
З	Z
И	I
Й	Y[3]
К	K
Л	L
М	M
Н	N
О	O
П	P
Р	R
С	S
Т	T
У	U
Ф	F
Х	Kh
Ц	Ts
Ч	Ch
Ш	Sh
Щ	Shch
Ъ	omitted; see note [1]
Ы	Y
Ь	omitted; see note [1]
Э	E
Ю	Yu
Я	Ya

1. Ye at the beginning of a word; after all vowels except ***Ы***; and after ***Ъ*** and ***Ь***.
2. O after ***Ч***, ***Ш*** and ***Щ***.
3. Omitted after ***Ы***, and in names of people after ***И***.

A. Many first names have an accepted English or quasi-English form which has been preferred to transliteration.
B. Place names have been given according to the *Columbia Lippincott Gazeteer*.
C. Pre-revolutionary spelling has been ignored.
D. Other languages using the Cyrillic alphabet (e.g., Bulgarian, Ukrainian), inasmuch as they appear, have been phonetically transliterated in conformity with the principles of this table.

GLOSSARY

Asterisked terms have separate entries in the Encyclopaedia.

Actions Committee, early name of the Zionist General Council, the supreme institution of the World Zionist Organization in the interim between Congresses. The Zionist Executive's name was then the "Small Actions Committee."

***Adar**, twelfth month of the Jewish religious year, sixth of the civil, approximating to February–March.

***Aggadah**, name given to those sections of Talmud and Midrash containing homiletic expositions of the Bible, stories, legends, folklore, anecdotes, or maxims. In contradistinction to **halakhah.*

***Agunah**, woman unable to remarry according to Jewish law, because of desertion by her husband or inability to accept presumption of death.

***Aharonim**, later rabbinic authorities. In contradistinction to **rishonim* ("early ones").

Ahavah, liturgical poem inserted in the second benediction of the morning prayer *(*Ahavah Rabbah)* of the festivals and/or special Sabbaths.

Aktion (Ger.), operation involving the mass assembly, deportation, and murder of Jews by the Nazis during the *Holocaust.

***Aliyah**, (1) being called to Reading of the Law in synagogue; (2) immigration to Ereẓ Israel; (3) one of the waves of immigration to Ereẓ Israel from the early 1880s.

***Amidah**, main prayer recited at all services; also known as *Shemoneh Esreh* and *Tefillah.*

***Amora** (pl. **amoraim**), title given to the Jewish scholars in Ereẓ Israel and Babylonia in the third to sixth centuries who were responsible for the **Gemara.*

Aravah, the *willow; one of the *Four Species used on *Sukkot ("festival of Tabernacles") together with the **etrog, hadas,* and **lulav.*

***Arvit**, evening prayer.

Asarah be-Tevet, fast on the 10th of Tevet commemorating the commencement of the siege of Jerusalem by Nebuchadnezzar.

Asefat ha-Nivḥarim, representative assembly elected by Jews in Palestine during the period of the British Mandate (1920–48).

***Ashkenaz**, name applied generally in medieval rabbinical literature to Germany.

***Ashkenazi** (pl. **Ashkenazim**), German or West-, Central-, or East-European Jew(s), as contrasted with *Sephardi(m).

***Av**, fifth month of the Jewish religious year, eleventh of the civil, approximating to July–August.

***Av bet din**, vice president of the supreme court (*bet din ha-gadol*) in Jerusalem during the Second Temple period; later, title given to communal rabbis as heads of the religious courts (see **bet din*).

***Badḥan**, jester, particularly at traditional Jewish weddings in Eastern Europe.

***Bakkashah** (Heb. "supplication"), type of petitionary prayer, mainly recited in the Sephardi rite on Rosh Ha-Shanah and the Day of Atonement.

Bar, "son of . . . "; frequently appearing in personal names.

***Baraita** (pl. **beraitot**), statement of **tanna* not found in *Mishnah.

***Bar mitzvah**, ceremony marking the initiation of a boy at the age of 13 into the Jewish religious community.

Ben, "son of . . . ", frequently appearing in personal names.

Berakhah (pl. **berakhot**), *benediction, blessing; formula of praise and thanksgiving.

***Bet din** (pl. **battei din**), rabbinic court of law.

***Bet ha-midrash**, school for higher rabbinic learning; often attached to or serving as a synagogue.

***Bilu**, first modern movement for pioneering and agricultural settlement in Ereẓ Israel, founded in 1882 at Kharkov, Russia.

***Bund**, Jewish socialist party founded in Vilna in 1897, supporting Jewish national rights; Yiddishist, and anti-Zionist.

Cohen (pl. **Cohanim**), see Kohen.

***Conservative Judaism**, trend in Judaism developed in the United States in the 20th century which, while opposing extreme changes in traditional observances, permits certain modifications of *halakhah* in response to the changing needs of the Jewish people.

***Consistory** (Fr. *consistoire*), governing body of a Jewish communal district in France and certain other countries.

***Converso(s)**, term applied in Spain and Portugal to converted Jew(s), and sometimes more loosely to their descendants.

***Crypto-Jew**, term applied to a person who although observing outwardly Christianity (or some other religion) was at heart a Jew and maintained Jewish observances as far as possible (see Converso; Marrano; Neofiti; New Christian; Jadīd al-Islām).

***Dayyan**, member of rabbinic court.

Decisor, equivalent to the Hebrew *posek* (pl. **posekim*), the rabbi who gives the decision (*halakhah*) in Jewish law or practice.

***Devekut**, "devotion"; attachment or adhesion to God; communion with God.

***Diaspora**, Jews living in the "dispersion" outside Ereẓ Israel; area of Jewish settlement outside Ereẓ Israel.

Din, a law (both secular and religious), legal decision, or lawsuit.

Divan, diwan, collection of poems, especially in Hebrew, Arabic, or Persian.

Dunam, unit of land area (1,000 sq. m., c. ¼ acre), used in Israel.

Einsatzgruppen, mobile units of Nazi S.S. and S.D.; in U.S.S.R. and Serbia, mobile killing units.

***Ein-Sof**, "without end"; "the infinite"; hidden, impersonal aspect of God; also used as a Divine Name.

***Elul**, sixth month of the Jewish religious calendar, 12th of the civil, precedes the High Holiday season in the fall.

Endloesung, see *Final Solution.

***Ereẓ Israel**, Land of Israel; Palestine.

***Eruv**, technical term for rabbinical provision permitting the alleviation of certain restrictions.

***Etrog**, citron; one of the *Four Species used on *Sukkot together with the **lulav, hadas,* and *aravah.*

Even ha-Ezer, see Shulḥan Arukh.

***Exilarch**, lay head of Jewish community in Babylonia (see also *resh galuta*), and elsewhere.

***Final Solution** (Ger. *Endloesung*), in Nazi terminology, the Nazi-planned mass murder and total annihilation of the Jews.

***Gabbai**, official of a Jewish congregation; originally a charity collector.

***Galut**, "exile"; the condition of the Jewish people in dispersion.

*Gaon (pl. geonim), head of academy in post-talmudic period, especially in Babylonia.

Gaonate, office of *gaon.

***Gemara**, traditions, discussions, and rulings of the *amoraim*, commenting on and supplementing the *Mishnah, and forming part of the Babylonian and Palestinian Talmuds (see Talmud).

***Gematria**, interpretation of Hebrew word according to the numerical value of its letters.

General Government, territory in Poland administered by a German civilian governor-general with headquarters in Cracow after the German occupation in World War II.

***Genizah**, depository for sacred books. The best known was discovered in the synagogue of Fostat (old Cairo).

Get, bill of *divorce.

***Ge'ullah**, hymn inserted after the *Shema* into the benediction of the morning prayer of the festivals and special Sabbaths.

***Gilgul**, metempsychosis; transmigration of souls.

***Golem**, automaton, especially in human form, created by magical means and endowed with life.

***Ḥabad**, initials of *ḥokhmah, binah, da'at*: "wisdom, understanding, knowledge"; ḥasidic movement founded in Belorussia by *Shneur Zalman of Lyady.

Hadas, *myrtle; one of the *Four Species used on Sukkot together with the *etrog*, *lulav*, and *aravah*.

***Haftarah** (pl. **haftarot**), designation of the portion from the prophetical books of the Bible recited after the synagogue reading from the Pentateuch on Sabbaths and holidays.

***Haganah**, clandestine Jewish organization for armed self-defense in Ereẓ Israel under the British Mandate, which eventually evolved into a people's militia and became the basis for the Israel army.

***Haggadah**, ritual recited in the home on *Passover eve at seder table.

Haham, title of chief rabbi of the Spanish and Portuguese congregations in London, England.

***Hakham**, title of rabbi of *Sephardi congregation.

***Hakham bashi**, title in the 15th century and modern times of the chief rabbi in the Ottoman Empire, residing in Constantinople (Istanbul), also applied to principal rabbis in provincial towns.

Hakhsharah ("preparation"), organized training in the Diaspora of pioneers for agricultural settlement in Ereẓ Israel.

***Halakhah** (pl. **halakhot**), an accepted decision in rabbinic law. Also refers to those parts of the *Talmud concerned with legal matters. In contradistinction to *aggadah*.

Ḥaliẓah, biblically prescribed ceremony (Deut. 25:9–10) performed when a man refuses to marry his brother's childless widow, enabling her to remarry.

***Hallel**, term referring to Psalms 113-18 in liturgical use.

***Ḥalukkah**, system of financing the maintenance of Jewish communities in the holy cities of Ereẓ Israel by collections made abroad, mainly in the pre-Zionist era (see *kolel*).

Ḥalutz (pl. **ḥalutzim**), pioneer, especially in agriculture, in Ereẓ Israel.

Ḥalutziyyut, pioneering.

***Ḥanukkah**, eight-day celebration commemorating the victory of *Judah Maccabee over the Syrian king *Antiochus Epiphanes and the subsequent rededication of the Temple.

Ḥasid, adherent of *Ḥasidism.

***Ḥasidei Ashkenaz**, medieval pietist movement among the Jews of Germany.

***Ḥasidism**, (1) religious revivalist movement of popular mysticism among Jews of Germany in the Middle Ages; (2) religious movement founded by *Israel ben Eliezer Ba'al Shem Tov in the first half of the 18th century.

***Haskalah**, "enlightenment"; movement for spreading modern European culture among Jews c. 1750–1880. See *maskil*.

***Havdalah**, ceremony marking the end of Sabbath or festival.

***Ḥazzan**, precentor who intones the liturgy and leads the prayers in synagogue; in earlier times a synagogue official.

***Ḥeder** (lit. "room"), school for teaching children Jewish religious observance.

Heikhalot, "palaces"; tradition in Jewish mysticism centering on mystical journeys through the heavenly spheres and palaces to the Divine Chariot (see Merkabah).

***Ḥerem**, excommunication, imposed by rabbinical authorities for purposes of religious and/or communal discipline; originally, in biblical times, that which is separated from common use either because it was an abomination or because it was consecrated to God.

Ḥeshvan, see Marḥeshvan.

***Ḥevra kaddisha**, title applied to charitable confraternity (*ḥevrah*), now generally limited to associations for burial of the dead.

***Ḥibbat Zion**, see Ḥovevei Zion.

***Histadrut** (abbr. For Heb. **Ha-Histadrut ha-Kelalit shel ha-Ovedim ha-Ivriyyim be-Ereẓ Israel**). Ereẓ Israel Jewish Labor Federation, founded in 1920; subsequently renamed Histadrut ha-Ovedim be-Ereẓ Israel.

***Holocaust**, the organized mass persecution and annihilation of European Jewry by the Nazis (1933–1945).

***Hoshana Rabba**, the seventh day of *Sukkot on which special observances are held.

Ḥoshen Mishpat, see Shulḥan Arukh.

Ḥovevei Zion, federation of *Ḥibbat Zion, early (pre-*Herzl) Zionist movement in Russia.

Illui, outstanding scholar or genius, especially a young prodigy in talmudic learning.

***Iyyar**, second month of the Jewish religious year, eighth of the civil, approximating to April-May.

I.Ẓ.L. (initials of Heb. ***Irgun Ẓeva'i Le'ummi**; "National Military Organization"), underground Jewish organization in Ereẓ Israel founded in 1931, which engaged from 1937 in retaliatory acts against Arab attacks and later against the British mandatory authorities.

***Jadīd al-Islām** (Ar.), a person practicing the Jewish religion in secret although outwardly observing Islām.

***Jewish Legion**, Jewish units in British army during World War I.

***Jihād** (Ar.), in Muslim religious law, holy war waged against infidels.

***Judenrat** (Ger. "Jewish council"), council set up in Jewish communities and ghettos under the Nazis to execute their instructions.

***Judenrein** (Ger. "clean of Jews"), in Nazi terminology the condition of a locality from which all Jews had been eliminated.

***Kabbalah**, the Jewish mystical tradition:
Kabbala iyyunit, speculative Kabbalah;
Kabbala ma'asit, practical Kabbalah;
Kabbala nevu'it, prophetic Kabbalah.

Kabbalist, student of Kabbalah.

***Kaddish**, liturgical doxology.

Kahal, Jewish congregation; among Ashkenazim, *kehillah*.

*Kalām (Ar.), science of Muslim theology; adherents of the Kalām are called *mutakallimūn*.

*Karaite, member of a Jewish sect originating in the eighth century which rejected rabbinic (*Rabbanite) Judaism and claimed to accept only Scripture as authoritative.

*Kasher, ritually permissible food.

Kashrut, Jewish *dietary laws.

*Kavvanah, "intention"; term denoting the spiritual concentration accompanying prayer and the performance of ritual or of a commandment.

*Kedushah, main addition to the third blessing in the reader's repetition of the *Amidah* in which the public responds to the precentor's introduction.

Kefar, village; first part of name of many settlements in Israel.

Kehillah, congregation; see *kahal*.

Kelippah (pl. **kelippot**), "husk(s)"; mystical term denoting force(s) of evil.

*Keneset Yisrael, comprehensive communal organization of the Jews in Palestine during the British Mandate.

Keri, variants in the masoretic (*masorah) text of the Bible between the spelling (*ketiv*) and its pronunciation (*keri*).

*Kerovah (collective plural (corrupted) from **kerovez̧**), poem(s) incorporated into the **Amidah*.

Ketiv, see *keri*.

*Ketubbah, marriage contract, stipulating husband's obligations to wife.

Kevuz̧ah, small commune of pioneers constituting an agricultural settlement in Erez̧ Israel (evolved later into *kibbutz).

*Kibbutz (pl. **kibbutzim**), larger-size commune constituting a settlement in Erez̧ Israel based mainly on agriculture but engaging also in industry.

*Kiddush, prayer of sanctification, recited over wine or bread on eve of Sabbaths and festivals.

*Kiddush ha-Shem, term connoting martyrdom or act of strict integrity in support of Judaic principles.

*Kinah (pl. **kinot**), lamentation dirge(s) for the Ninth of Av and other fast days.

*Kislev, ninth month of the Jewish religious year, third of the civil, approximating to November-December.

Klaus, name given in Central and Eastern Europe to an institution, usually with synagogue attached, where *Talmud was studied perpetually by adults; applied by Ḥasidim to their synagogue ("*kloyz*").

*Knesset, parliament of the State of Israel.

K(c)ohen (pl. **K(c)ohanim**), Jew(s) of priestly (Aaronide) descent.

*Kolel, (1) community in Erez̧ Israel of persons from a particular country or locality, often supported by their fellow countrymen in the Diaspora; (2) institution for higher Torah study.

Kosher, see *kasher*.

*Kristallnacht (Ger. "crystal night," meaning "night of broken glass"), organized destruction of synagogues, Jewish houses, and shops, accompanied by mass arrests of Jews, which took place in Germany and Austria under the Nazis on the night of Nov. 9–10, 1938.

*Lag ba-Omer, 33rd (Heb. **lag**) day of the **Omer* period falling on the 18th of *Iyyar; a semi-holiday.

Leḥi (abbr. For Heb. ***Loḥamei Ḥerut Israel**, "Fighters for the Freedom of Israel"), radically anti-British armed underground organization in Palestine, founded in 1940 by dissidents from *I.Z.L.

Levir, husband's brother.

*Levirate marriage (Heb. *yibbum*), marriage of childless widow (*yevamah*) by brother (*yavam*) of the deceased husband (in accordance with Deut. 25:5); release from such an obligation is effected through *ḥaliẓah*.

LHY, see Leḥi.

*Lulav, palm branch; one of the *Four Species used on *Sukkot together with the **etrog*, *hadas*, and *aravah*.

*Ma'aravot, hymns inserted into the evening prayer of the three festivals, Passover, Shavuot, and Sukkot.

Ma'ariv, evening prayer; also called **arvit*.

*Ma'barah, transition camp; temporary settlement for newcomers in Israel during the period of mass immigration following 1948.

*Maftir, reader of the concluding portion of the Pentateuchal section on Sabbaths and holidays in synagogue; reader of the portion of the prophetical books of the Bible (**haftarah*).

*Maggid, popular preacher.

*Maḥzor (pl. **maḥzorim**), festival prayer book.

*Mamzer, bastard; according to Jewish law, the offspring of an incestuous relationship.

*Mandate, Palestine, responsibility for the administration of Palestine conferred on Britain by the League of Nations in 1922; mandatory government: the British administration of Palestine.

*Maqāma (Ar. pl. **maqamāt**), poetic form (rhymed prose) which, in its classical arrangement, has rigid rules of form and content.

*Marḥeshvan, popularly called Ḥeshvan; eighth month of the Jewish religious year, second of the civil, approximating to October–November.

*Marrano(s), descendant(s) of Jew(s) in Spain and Portugal whose ancestors had been converted to Christianity under pressure but who secretly observed Jewish rituals.

Maskil (pl. **maskilim**), adherent of *Haskalah ("Enlightenment") movement.

*Masorah, body of traditions regarding the correct spelling, writing, and reading of the Hebrew Bible.

Masorete, scholar of the masoretic tradition.

Masoretic, in accordance with the masorah.

Meliẓah, in Middle Ages, elegant style; modern usage, florid style using biblical or talmudic phraseology.

Mellah, *Jewish quarter in North African towns.

*Menorah, candelabrum; seven-branched oil lamp used in the Tabernacle and Temple; also eight-branched candelabrum used on *Ḥanukkah.

Me'orah, hymn inserted into the first benediction of the morning prayer (*Yoẓer ha-Me'orot*).

*Merkabah, *merkavah*, "chariot"; mystical discipline associated with Ezekiel's vision of the Divine Throne-Chariot (Ezek. 1).

Meshullaḥ, emissary sent to conduct propaganda or raise funds for rabbinical academies or charitable institutions.

*Mezuzah (pl. **mezuzot**), parchment scroll with selected Torah verses placed in container and affixed to gates and doorposts of houses occupied by Jews.

*Midrash, method of interpreting Scripture to elucidate legal points (*Midrash Halakhah*) or to bring out lessons by stories or homiletics (*Midrash Aggadah*). Also the name for a collection of such rabbinic interpretations.

*Mikveh, ritual bath.

*Minhag (pl. **minhagim**), ritual custom(s); synagogal rite(s); especially of a specific sector of Jewry.

*Minḥah, afternoon prayer; originally meal offering in Temple.

***Minyan**, group of ten male adult Jews, the minimum required for communal prayer.

***Mishnah**, earliest codification of Jewish Oral Law.

Mishnah (pl. **mishnayot**), subdivision of tractates of the Mishnah.

Mitnagged (pl. ***Mitnaggedim**), originally, opponents of *Ḥasidism in Eastern Europe.

***Mitzvah**, biblical or rabbinic injunction; applied also to good or charitable deeds.

Mohel, official performing circumcisions.

***Moshav**, smallholders' cooperative agricultural settlement in Israel, see moshav ovedim.

Moshavah, earliest type of Jewish village in modern Ereẓ Israel in which farming is conducted on individual farms mostly on privately owned land.

Moshav ovedim ("workers' moshav"), agricultural village in Israel whose inhabitants possess individual homes and holdings but cooperate in the purchase of equipment, sale of produce, mutual aid, etc.

***Moshav shittufi** ("collective moshav"), agricultural village in Israel whose members possess individual homesteads but where the agriculture and economy are conducted as a collective unit.

Mostegab (Ar.), poem with biblical verse at beginning of each stanza.

***Muqaddam** (Ar., pl. **muqaddamūn**), "leader," "head of the community."

***Musaf**, additional service on Sabbath and festivals; originally the additional sacrifice offered in the Temple.

Musar, traditional ethical literature.

***Musar movement**, ethical movement developing in the latter part of the 19th century among Orthodox Jewish groups in Lithuania; founded by R. Israel *Lipkin (Salanter).

***Nagid** (pl. **negidim**), title applied in Muslim (and some Christian) countries in the Middle Ages to a leader recognized by the state as head of the Jewish community.

Nakdan (pl. **nakdanim**), "punctuator"; scholar of the 9th to 14th centuries who provided biblical manuscripts with masoretic apparatus, vowels, and accents.

***Nasi** (pl. **nesi'im**), talmudic term for president of the Sanhedrin, who was also the spiritual head and later, political representative of the Jewish people; from second century a descendant of Hillel recognized by the Roman authorities as patriarch of the Jews. Now applied to the president of the State of Israel.

***Negev**, the southern, mostly arid, area of Israel.

***Ne'ilah**, concluding service on the *Day of Atonement.

Neofiti, term applied in southern Italy to converts to Christianity from Judaism and their descendants who were suspected of maintaining secret allegiance to Judaism.

***Neology; Neolog; Neologism**, trend of *Reform Judaism in Hungary forming separate congregations after 1868.

***Nevelah** (lit. "carcass"), meat forbidden by the *dietary laws on account of the absence of, or defect in, the act of **sheḥitah* (ritual slaughter).

***New Christians**, term applied especially in Spain and Portugal to converts from Judaism (and from Islam) and their descendants; "Half New Christian" designated a person one of whose parents was of full Jewish blood.

***Niddah** ("menstruous woman"), woman during the period of menstruation.

***Nisan**, first month of the Jewish religious year, seventh of the civil, approximating to March-April.

Niẓoẓot, "sparks"; mystical term for sparks of the holy light imprisoned in all matter.

Nosaḥ (nusaḥ) "version"; (1) textual variant; (2) term applied to distinguish the various prayer rites, e.g., *nosaḥ Ashkenaz*; (3) the accepted tradition of synagogue melody.

***Notarikon**, method of abbreviating Hebrew works or phrases by acronym.

Novella(e) (Heb. **ḥiddush (im)*), commentary on talmudic and later rabbinic subjects that derives new facts or principles from the implications of the text.

***Nuremberg Laws**, Nazi laws excluding Jews from German citizenship, and imposing other restrictions.

Ofan, hymns inserted into a passage of the morning prayer.

***Omer**, first sheaf cut during the barley harvest, offered in the Temple on the second day of Passover.

Omer, Counting of (Heb. *Sefirat ha-Omer*), 49 days counted from the day on which the *omer* was first offered in the Temple (according to the rabbis the 16th of Nisan, i.e., the second day of Passover) until the festival of Shavuot; now a period of semi-mourning.

Oraḥ Ḥayyim, see Shulḥan Arukh.

***Orthodoxy** (Orthodox Judaism), modern term for the strictly traditional sector of Jewry.

***Pale of Settlement**, 25 provinces of czarist Russia where Jews were permitted permanent residence.

***Palmaḥ** (abbr. for Heb. *peluggot maḥaz*; "shock companies"), striking arm of the *Haganah.

***Pardes**, medieval biblical exegesis giving the literal, allegorical, homiletical, and esoteric interpretations.

***Parnas**, chief synagogue functionary, originally vested with both religious and administrative functions; subsequently an elected lay leader.

Partition plan(s), proposals for dividing Ereẓ Israel into autonomous areas.

Paytan, composer of **piyyut* (liturgical poetry).

***Peel Commission**, British Royal Commission appointed by the British government in 1936 to inquire into the Palestine problem and make recommendations for its solution.

Pesaḥ, *Passover.

***Pilpul**, in talmudic and rabbinic literature, a sharp dialectic used particularly by talmudists in Poland from the 16th century.

***Pinkas**, community register or minute-book.

***Piyyut**, (pl. **piyyutim**), Hebrew liturgical poetry.

***Pizmon**, poem with refrain.

Posek (pl. ***posekim**), decisor; codifier or rabbinic scholar who pronounces decisions in disputes and on questions of Jewish law.

***Prosbul**, legal method of overcoming the cancelation of debts with the advent of the *sabbatical year.

***Purim**, festival held on Adar 14 or 15 in commemoration of the delivery of the Jews of Persia in the time of *Esther.

Rabban, honorific title higher than that of rabbi, applied to heads of the *Sanhedrin in mishnaic times.

***Rabbanite**, adherent of rabbinic Judaism. In contradistinction to *Karaite.

Reb, rebbe, Yiddish form for rabbi, applied generally to a teacher or ḥasidic rabbi.

***Reconstructionism**, trend in Jewish thought originating in the United States.

***Reform Judaism**, trend in Judaism advocating modification of *Orthodoxy in conformity with the exigencies of contemporary life and thought.

Resh galuta, lay head of Babylonian Jewry (see exilarch).

Responsum (pl. ***responsa**), written opinion (*teshuvah*) given to question (*she'elah*) on aspects of Jewish law by qualified authorities; pl. collection of such queries and opinions in book form (*she'elot u-teshuvot*).

***Rishonim**, older rabbinical authorities. Distinguished from later authorities (**aharonim*).

***Rishon le-Zion**, title given to Sephardi chief rabbi of Ereẓ Israel.

***Rosh Ha-Shanah**, two-day holiday (one day in biblical and early mishnaic times) at the beginning of the month of *Tishri (September–October), traditionally the New Year.

Rosh Hodesh, *New Moon, marking the beginning of the Hebrew month.

Rosh Yeshivah, see *Yeshivah.

***R.S.H.A.** (initials of Ger. *Reichssicherheitshauptamt*: "Reich Security Main Office"), the central security department of the German Reich, formed in 1939, and combining the security police (Gestapo and Kripo) and the S.D.

***Sanhedrin**, the assembly of ordained scholars which functioned both as a supreme court and as a legislature before 70 C.E. In modern times the name was given to the body of representative Jews convoked by Napoleon in 1807.

***Savora** (pl. **savoraim**), name given to the Babylonian scholars of the period between the **amoraim* and the **geonim*, approximately 500–700 C.E.

S.D. (initials of Ger. *Sicherheitsdienst*: "security service"), security service of the *S.S. formed in 1932 as the sole intelligence organization of the Nazi party.

Seder, ceremony observed in the Jewish home on the first night of Passover (outside Ereẓ Israel first two nights), when the *Haggadah is recited.

***Sefer Torah**, manuscript scroll of the Pentateuch for public reading in synagogue.

***Sefirot, the ten**, the ten "Numbers"; mystical term denoting the ten spheres or emanations through which the Divine manifests itself; elements of the world; dimensions, primordial numbers.

Selektion (Ger.), (1) in ghettos and other Jewish settlements, the drawing up by Nazis of lists of deportees; (2) separation of incoming victims to concentration camps into two categories – those destined for immediate killing and those to be sent for forced labor.

Seliḥah (pl. ***seliḥot**), penitential prayer.

***Semikhah**, ordination conferring the title "rabbi" and permission to give decisions in matters of ritual and law.

Sephardi (pl. ***Sephardim**), Jew(s) of Spain and Portugal and their descendants, wherever resident, as contrasted with *Ashkenazi(m).

Shabbatean, adherent of the pseudo-messiah *Shabbetai Ẓevi (17th century).

Shaddai, name of God found frequently in the Bible and commonly translated "Almighty."

***Shaḥarit**, morning service.

Shali'aḥ (pl. **sheliḥim**), in Jewish law, messenger, agent; in modern times, an emissary from Ereẓ Israel to Jewish communities or organizations abroad for the purpose of fund-raising, organizing pioneer immigrants, education, etc.

Shalmonit, poetic meter introduced by the liturgical poet *Solomon ha-Bavli.

***Shammash**, synagogue beadle.

***Shavuot**, Pentecost; Festival of Weeks; second of the three annual pilgrim festivals, commemorating the receiving of the Torah at Mt. Sinai.

***Sheḥitah**, ritual slaughtering of animals.

***Shekhinah**, Divine Presence.

Shelishit, poem with three-line stanzas.

***Sheluḥei Ereẓ Israel** (or **shadarim**), emissaries from Ereẓ Israel.

***Shema** ([Yisrael]; "hear… [O Israel]," Deut. 6:4), Judaism's confession of faith, proclaiming the absolute unity of God.

Shemini Aẓeret, final festal day (in the Diaspora, final two days) at the conclusion of *Sukkot.

Shemittah, *Sabbatical year.

Sheniyyah, poem with two-line stanzas.

***Shephelah**, southern part of the coastal plain of Ereẓ Israel.

***Shevat**, eleventh month of the Jewish religious year, fifth of the civil, approximating to January–February.

***Shi'ur Komah**, Hebrew mystical work (c. eighth century) containing a physical description of God's dimensions; term denoting enormous spacial measurement used in speculations concerning the body of the **Shekhinah*.

Shivah, the "seven days" of *mourning following burial of a relative.

***Shofar**, horn of the ram (or any other ritually clean animal excepting the cow) sounded for the memorial blowing on *Rosh Ha-Shanah, and other occasions.

Shoḥet, person qualified to perform **sheḥitah*.

Shomer, *Ha-Shomer, organization of Jewish workers in Ereẓ Israel founded in 1909 to defend Jewish settlements.

***Shtadlan**, Jewish representative or negotiator with access to dignitaries of state, active at royal courts, etc.

***Shtetl**, Jewish small-town community in Eastern Europe.

***Shulḥan Arukh**, Joseph *Caro's code of Jewish law in four parts:
Oraḥ Ḥayyim, laws relating to prayers, Sabbath, festivals, and fasts;
Yoreh De'ah, dietary laws, etc;
Even ha-Ezer, laws dealing with women, marriage, etc;
Ḥoshen Mishpat, civil, criminal law, court procedure, etc.

Siddur, among Ashkenazim, the volume containing the daily prayers (in distinction to the **maḥzor* containing those for the festivals).

***Simḥat Torah**, holiday marking the completion in the synagogue of the annual cycle of reading the Pentateuch; in Ereẓ Israel observed on Shemini Aẓeret (outside Ereẓ Israel on the following day).

***Sinai Campaign**, brief campaign in October–November 1956 when Israel army reacted to Egyptian terrorist attacks and blockade by occupying the Sinai peninsula.

Sitra aḥra, "the other side" (of God); left side; the demoniac and satanic powers.

***Sivan**, third month of the Jewish religious year, ninth of the civil, approximating to May–June.

***Six-Day War**, rapid war in June 1967 when Israel reacted to Arab threats and blockade by defeating the Egyptian, Jordanian, and Syrian armies.

***S.S.** (initials of Ger. *Schutzstaffel*: "protection detachment"), Nazi formation established in 1925 which later became the "elite" organization of the Nazi Party and carried out central tasks in the "Final Solution."

***Status quo ante** community, community in Hungary retaining the status it had held before the convention of the General Jewish Congress there in 1868 and the resultant split in Hungarian Jewry.

*Sukkah, booth or tabernacle erected for *Sukkot when, for seven days, religious Jews "dwell" or at least eat in the *sukkah* (Lev. 23:42).

***Sukkot**, festival of Tabernacles; last of the three pilgrim festivals, beginning on the 15th of Tishri.

Sūra (Ar.), chapter of the Koran.

Ta'anit Esther (Fast of *Esther), fast on the 13th of Adar, the day preceding Purim.

Takkanah (pl. ***takkanot**), regulation supplementing the law of the Torah; regulations governing the internal life of communities and congregations.

***Tallit (gadol)**, four-cornered prayer shawl with fringes (*ẓiẓit*) at each corner.

***Tallit katan**, garment with fringes (*ẓiẓit*) appended, worn by observant male Jews under their outer garments.

***Talmud**, "teaching"; compendium of discussion on the Mishnah by generations of scholars and jurists in many academies over a period of several centuries. The Jerusalem (or Palestinian) Talmud mainly contains the discussions of the Palestinian sages. The Babylonian Talmud incorporates the parallel discussion in the Babylonian academies.

Talmud torah, term generally applied to Jewish religious (and ultimately to talmudic) study; also to traditional Jewish religious public schools.

***Tammuz**, fourth month of the Jewish religious year, tenth of the civil, approximating to June-July.

Tanna (pl. ***tannaim**), rabbinic teacher of mishnaic period.

***Targum**, Aramaic translation of the Bible.

***Tefillin**, phylacteries, small leather cases containing passages from Scripture and affixed on the forehead and arm by male Jews during the recital of morning prayers.

Tell (Ar. "mound," "hillock"), ancient mound in the Middle East composed of remains of successive settlements.

***Terefah**, food that is not **kasher*, owing to a defect on the animal.

***Territorialism**, 20th century movement supporting the creation of an autonomous territory for Jewish mass-settlement outside Ereẓ Israel.

***Tevet**, tenth month of the Jewish religious year, fourth of the civil, approximating to December–January.

Tikkun ("restitution," "reintegration"), (1) order of service for certain occasions, mostly recited at night; (2) mystical term denoting restoration of the right order and true unity after the spiritual "catastrophe" which occurred in the cosmos.

Tishah be-Av, Ninth of *Av, fast day commemorating the destruction of the First and Second Temples.

***Tishri**, seventh month of the Jewish religious year, first of the civil, approximating to September–October.

Tokheḥah, reproof sections of the Pentateuch (Lev. 26 and Deut. 28); poem of reproof.

***Torah**, Pentateuch or the Pentateuchal scroll for reading in synagogue; entire body of traditional Jewish teaching and literature.

Tosafist, talmudic glossator, mainly French (12–14th centuries), bringing additions to the commentary by *Rashi.

***Tosafot**, glosses supplied by tosafist.

***Tosefta**, a collection of teachings and traditions of the *tannaim*, closely related to the Mishnah.

Tradent, person who hands down a talmudic statement on the name of his teacher or other earlier authority.

***Tu bi-Shevat**, the 15th day of Shevat, the New Year for Trees; date marking a dividing line for fruit tithing; in modern Israel celebrated as arbor day.

***Uganda Scheme**, plan suggested by the British government in 1903 to establish an autonomous Jewish settlement area in East Africa.

***Va'ad Le'ummi**, national council of the Jewish community in Ereẓ Israel during the period of the British *Mandate.

***Wannsee Conference**, Nazi conference held on Jan. 20, 1942, at which the planned annihilation of European Jewry was endorsed.

Waqf (Ar.), (1) a Muslim charitable pious foundation; (2) state lands and other property passed to the Muslim community for public welfare.

***War of Independence**, war of 1947–49 when the Jews of Israel fought off Arab invading armies and ensured the establishment of the new State.

***White Paper(s)**, report(s) issued by British government, frequently statements of policy, as issued in connection with Palestine during the *Mandate period.

***Wissenschaft des Judentums** (Ger. "Science of Judaism"), movement in Europe beginning in the 19th century for scientific study of Jewish history, religion, and literature.

***Yad Vashem**, Israel official authority for commemorating the *Holocaust in the Nazi era and Jewish resistance and heroism at that time.

Yeshivah (pl. ***yeshivot**), Jewish traditional academy devoted primarily to study of rabbinic literature; *rosh yeshivah*, head of the yeshivah.

YHWH, the letters of the holy name of God, the Tetragrammaton.

Yibbum, see levirate marriage.

Yiḥud, "union"; mystical term for intention which causes the union of God with the **Shekhinah*.

Yishuv, settlement; more specifically, the Jewish community of Ereẓ Israel in the pre-State period. The pre-Zionist community is generally designated the "old yishuv" and the community evolving from 1880, the "new yishuv."

Yom Kippur, Yom ha-Kippurim, *Day of Atonement, solemn fast day observed on the 10th of Tishri.

Yoreh De'ah, see Shulḥan Arukh.

Yoẓer, hymns inserted in the first benediction (*Yoẓer Or*) of the morning **Shema*.

***Ẓaddik**, person outstanding for his faith and piety; especially a ḥasidic rabbi or leader.

Ẓimẓum, "contraction"; mystical term denoting the process whereby God withdraws or contracts within Himself so leaving a primordial vacuum in which creation can take place; primordial exile or self-limitation of God.

***Zionist Commission (1918)**, commission appointed in 1918 by the British government to advise the British military authorities in Palestine on the implementation of the *Balfour Declaration.

Ẓyyonei Zion, the organized opposition to Herzl in connection with the *Uganda Scheme.

***Ẓiẓit**, fringes attached to the **tallit* and **tallit katan*.

***Zohar**, mystical commentary on the Pentateuch; main textbook of *Kabbalah.

Zulat, hymn inserted after the **Shema* in the morning service.

ISBN-13: 978-0-02-865931-2
ISBN-10: 0-02-865931-7